# CLASSICS OF
# POLITICAL AND MORAL
# PHILOSOPHY

# CLASSICS OF POLITICAL AND MORAL PHILOSOPHY

~

Edited by

## Steven M. Cahn

*City University of New York Graduate Center*

New York     Oxford
OXFORD UNIVERSITY PRESS
2002

Oxford University Press

Oxford   New York
Athens   Auckland   Bangkok   Bogotá   Buenos Aires   Cape Town
Dar es Salaam   Delhi   Florence   Hong Kong   Istanbul   Karachi
Kolkata   Kuala Lumpur   Madrid   Melbourne   Mexico City   Mumbai   Nairobi
Paris   São Paulo   Shanghai   Singapore   Taipei   Tokyo   Toronto   Warsaw

and associated companies in
Berlin   Ibadan

Published by Oxford University Press, Inc.
198 Madison Avenue, New York, New York, 10016
http://www.oup-usa.org

Oxford is a registered trademark of Oxford University Press

**Library of Congress Cataloging-in-Publication Data**

Cahn, Steven M.
  Classics of political and moral philosophy / Steven M. Cahn.
    p. cm.
  ISBN 0-19-514091-5 (alk. paper)
  1. Political science—Philosophy.  2. Ethics.  I. Title.

  JA71.C27 2001
  170—dc21
                                                    2001032186

Cover art: Henri Matisse, French, 1869–1954, "Bathers by a River," 1909, 1913,
and 1916, oil on canvas, 259.7 × 389.9 cm, Charles H. and Mary F. S. Worcester
Collection, 1953.158 The Art Institute of Chicago. All Rights Reserved.

Printing (last digit): 9 8 7 6 5 4

Printed in the United States of America
on acid-free paper

*To my wife,*
*Marilyn Ross, M.D.*

# CONTENTS

*\*Complete works.*

# PREFACE

Here in one volume are the major writings from nearly 2,500 years of political philosophy, supplemented by related works of ethical theory. The idea for such a comprehensive collection developed in conversation with my editor, Robert Miller, and I am deeply grateful for his continuing encouragement and advice. I also wish to express my appreciation to Maureen Eckert, my research assistant at The City University Graduate Center, for her untiring efforts in preparing the manuscript for publication; to Ian Gardiner, for his skilled proofreading; to the staff at Oxford University Press, for its generous help at all the stages of production; to Andrea Tschemplik, for granting permission to use her updating of the once celebrated, but now neglected, translation of Plato's *Republic* by John Llewelyn Davies and David James Vaughan; and to David Rosenthal, for calling the Davies and Vaughan translation to my attention.

I owe special thanks to those who kindly provided introductions: Bernard E. Brown (The City University of New York Graduate Center), Thomas Christiano (University of Arizona), Joshua Cohen (Massachusetts Institute of Technology), John Deigh (Northwestern University), Charles L. Griswold, Jr. (Boston University), Paul Guyer (University of Pennsylvania), the late Jean Hampton (University of Arizona), Eva Feder Kittay (State University of New York at Stony Brook), Richard Kraut (Northwestern University), Donald W. Livingston (Emory University), Roger D. Masters (Dartmouth College), Thomas A. McCarthy (Northwestern University), Richard Miller (Cornell University), Richard Schacht (University of Illinois at Urbana), A. John Simmons (University of Virginia), Steven B. Smith (Yale University), Jeremy Waldron (Columbia University), and Paul J. Weithman (University of Notre Dame).

I benefited greatly from advice by Professor Brown regarding the selections from The Federalist, Professor Griswold regarding the selections from Adam Smith, Professor Guyer regarding the selections from Kant, Professor Hampton regarding the selections from Hobbes, Professor Kraut regarding the selections from Aristotle, Professor Livingston regarding the selections from Hume, Professor Masters regarding the selections from Machiavelli, Professor McCarthy regarding the selections from Foucalt and Habermas, Professor Miller regarding the selections from Marx and Engels, Professor Schacht regarding the selections from Nietzsche, and Professor Smith regarding the selections from Hegel. I also receved wise counsel from Professor George Sher of Rice University.

This work is thus a product of the learning and generosity of the community of scholars.

# CLASSICS OF
# POLITICAL AND MORAL
# PHILOSOPHY

# PLATO

~

## Introduction

## Richard Kraut

Plato (427–347 BC) was born into an aristocratic and wealthy Athenian family, and during his early years he experienced the intellectual and political ferment of his time and place. Many of the plays of Sophocles, Euripides, and Aristophanes were written during the last quarter of the fifth century, and the moral and political conflicts they dramatized for their fellow Athenians became his problems as well. His youth also roughly coincided with the Peloponnesian War (431–404), which ended in the defeat of democratic Athens at the hands of Sparta. At the close of the war, Sparta installed in Athens a government of thirty rulers (called "Thirty Tyrants" by later generations), who were selected for their antidemocratic sympathies. One of the most ruthless among them, Critias, was the cousin of Plato's mother; another, Charmides, was her brother. Both appear as interlocutors in some of Plato's dialogues.

Like many young people of his time, Plato fell under the spell of Socrates (469–399), an Athenian philosopher whose way of life is vividly preserved in Plato's *Apology*. Socrates wrote nothing and professed ignorance, but his suspicion that no one possesses moral knowledge, and his conviction that we must spend our lives searching for it, inspired many of his followers, Plato among them, to abandon their worldly ambitions and to live a philosophical life.

The Thirty who had been installed by Sparta were overthrown and democracy was restored in 403; but a few years later, in 399, Socrates was brought to trial and found guilty of not believing in the city's gods, of introducing new gods, and of corrupting the young. Some scholars believe that the prosecution of Socrates was motivated partly by the perception that he was a danger to the restored democracy. It is noteworthy that Plato's account of the speech Socrates gave in his own defense, the *Apology* (*apologia* means "defense") contains both antipopulist elements (31–2) and a reminder that Socrates disobeyed the Thirty (32). Evidently, he could not easily be classified as a democrat or an antidemocrat. Similarly, in the *Crito*, Socrates is described as a man so satisfied with the Athenian legal system that he has hardly left the city's walls (52–3), and yet he insists that one should follow the commands of an expert and pay no attention to the opinions of the many (47). But were not the laws of democratic Athens an expression of the opinion of the many? Socrates does not explain the basis for his high regard for Athenian law.

Still more perplexing is an apparent inconsistency between the willingness Socrates expresses in the *Apology* to engage in various forms of disobedience and the arguments he accepts in the *Crito* for obeying one's city and its laws. He tells the jury that he will obey the god who has commanded him to philosophize rather than any orders they give him (29), and yet in the *Crito* he refuses to escape from jail because he accepts the idea, proposed by the personified Laws of Athens, that he is subordinate to Athens as a child is to a parent or a slave to a master (50–51). If Socrates is willing to disobey his jurors, then why is he not equally willing to disregard its decision that he is to be punished by death?

It is unlikely that Plato means to portray Socrates as a muddled thinker. On the contrary, the impression he means to create is that Socrates is a man of penetrating insight and great argumentative skill. The apparent difficulties in Socrates' ideas are the devices Plato uses to provoke his readers into philosophical reflection. Just as his conversations with Socrates led him to philosophy, so he uses Socrates in his works to produce the same effect in us. Plato's dialogues create a sense of unfinished business: lines of thought are disrupted, and gaps in the argument remain unfilled. It is often difficult to know what Plato intends, because he never speaks in his own voice. He uses dramatic characters and portrays a clash of views because he regards the written word as a stimulus to philosophical insight rather than as the embodiment of wisdom.

We are told by ancient sources that after the death of Socrates in 399, Plato left Athens and spent time in Sicily, North Africa, and Egypt. Several of the thinkers he visited were associated with the Pythagorean school—a group of philosophers (named after the school's sixth-century founder, Pythagoras) who held that the human soul is reborn into other human and animal bodies after death. They were also intensely interested in the mathematical relationships (for example, in musical scales) that underlie many physical phenomena. As Plato moved beyond such early works as the *Apology* and *Crito*, both of these Pythagorean ideas—the transformation of the soul in its many lives and the mathematical nature of reality—came to the fore in his writings. When he returned to Athens in 387, he established a school (called the "Academy," after the grove beyond the city walls that was sacred to the hero Academos) devoted to the study of philosophical and scientific problems. Ancient writers describe two further visits of Plato to Sicily, in 367 and 361, undertaken to influence the course of Syracusan politics, both ending in failure. He remained the head of the Academy until his death in 347.

The works that Plato composed after the founding of his school cover a wider range of subjects than the ones he had explored at the beginning of his philosophical career. The early writings are primarily ethical in purpose, and they contain little more than an outline of positive doctrines. They are investigations of the questions Socrates frequently posed to his interlocutors: "What is courage?," "What is friendship?," "What is piety?" They typically end with the admission that these questions have yet to receive a satisfactory answer. But beginning with such works as the *Meno* and the *Phaedo*, Plato more fully investigates questions that can be called epistemological, metaphysical, and scientific. His writings continue to feature conversations between Socrates and one or more interlocutors, but they are longer than his earliest works, and they offer a series of complex arguments that purport to reach significant positive results. Plato is not a builder of fully articulated systems, but his mature works insist on the interconnectedness of apparently unrelated problems.

Although Socrates insists in the *Apology* that we cannot know what comes after death, in the *Phaedo* (a dialogue in which he holds his final conversation, before drinking a poison and dying) he presents a series of arguments for the immortality of the soul. One of the most striking components of this dialogue and others that were written during this period is their affirmation of the existence of a new kind of objective reality, which Socrates calls a "form" or "idea." (Capital letters—"Form," "Idea"—are sometimes used to name these objects, athough this is not Plato's practice.) For example, the form of equality (Plato is thinking of the mathematical relationship) is not something that can be observed by the senses, but it exists nonetheless. It is an eternal and changeless object that can be known only by means of reason. The equal objects we observe are in some way defective copies of the perfect form; they are called equal because they somehow share in or participate in the form of equality. Plato does not attempt to give a complete list of the forms, but he believes that many of the words we use in mathematics ("triangle," "line," "two") and in evaluative discourse ("justice," "beauty," "good") are really names of these abstract objects. Whenever we speak, we are referring to forms, though most people assume that they are merely talking about a visible and perishable world. They are, Plato thinks, living in a dream world: they fail to realize that what they observe is a mere appearance, and that a greater reality—the world of the forms—stands behind the appearances.

In the *Republic* (composed after the *Apology*, *Crito*, and *Phaedo*), Plato pursues a question that lies at the heart of Socrates' life and death. Although Socrates was a man of the highest moral integrity, he was thought to be so dangerous to his community that the majority of a jury of 501 fellow citizens condemned him to die. Since just action sometimes leads to death, since it can lie hidden from others and even be misinterpreted as injustice, does that not cast the most serious doubt on its value? Plato's guiding assumption, which he inherits from Socrates, is that no progress can be made in answering this question until we come to a fuller understanding of what justice is. (The Greek word is *dikaiosune;* in some contexts, its meaning is broader than that of our "justice" and encompasses any kind of right treatment of others.) Book I of the *Republic* portrays a series of unsuccessful attempts to define justice. Socrates here plays the role of someone who lacks knowledge, and whose mission it is to reveal to others that they are equally ignorant. Although Thrasymachus, the most formidable interlocutor Socrates faces, is eventually defeated in argument, he plays a crucial role in the dialogue: any attempt to vindicate the life of a just person must address itself to the cynicism and immorality that Thrasymachus represents. Plato seems to be saying, in effect, that there is a Thrasymachus in all of us, and that we can exorcise him only by means of a philosophical inquiry as wide ranging as the *Republic*.

Starting with Book II, Socrates sheds his role as an ignorant inquirer who merely poses problems for others. For the remainder of the dialogue, he becomes a systematic philosopher who puts forward a grand theory about the nature of human beings, the ideal state, the soul, mathematics, knowledge, and the highest realities. His main interlocutors (Glaucon and Adeimantus—Plato's brothers) occasionally interact with him, but they play a role far different from the ones assigned to Cephalus, Polemarchus, and Thrasymachus in Book I. The strategy pursued throughout the remainder of the *Republic* is to exploit the fact that it is not merely individuals who can be characterized as just or unjust. We also use these terms to praise or discredit certain forms of government. Perhaps, then, we can grasp the nature of justice by asking what leads to the existence of a political community, and what the justice of such a community consists in. This attempt to construe political and individual justice as the same property eventually leads to the proposal that justice consists in each part of a thing doing its own activity. In a just city or state, each position is filled by a person who is qualified to contribute to the good of the whole community. Similarly, in a just human being, each part of the soul operates in a way that best serves the whole human being.

By the end of Book IV, Socrates seems to be on the verge of completing his demonstration of the great value of justice—but, in a sense, his argument has only begun. The institutions of the ideal city—particularly abolition of the traditional family among rulers and eugenic sharing of sexual partners—have not yet been fully discussed. Plato's aim is to foster the greatest possible unity in the city, and he is willing to go to the greatest lengths to guarantee that his citizens owe their strongest allegiance to each other, rather than to blood relatives. But the topic that looms largest in Books V, VI, and VII is the proposal that the best political community is one that gives complete authority to rigorously trained and morally flawless philosophers. Strictly speaking, the only real philosophers are those whose understanding of value is based on their study of the forms, and in particular the form of the "good." Socrates refrains from saying how good is to be defined, and in this sense the entire project of the *Republic* is radically incomplete. But he seems to be suggesting that goodness has a mathematical nature: that is why it is so important that philosophers first be trained as mathematicians, before they undertake the study of the highest form.

The dialogue reaches its culminating point with its depiction of the philosopher, for he or she is the human being of perfect justice. The search for the value of "justice" has led to the conclusion that this virtue is most fully present in those who understand the nature of the highest realities. Justice is the greatest good because the best sort of life is one in which the structure of one's soul is guided by one's love and understanding of the most valuable and real objects there are—the forms. Books VIII and IX round out Plato's argument by portraying the diseased political structures and fragmented psychologies that arise when worldly values—the love of honor, domination, wealth, and sexual pleasure—take priority over all others. In Book X, the peripheral and external rewards of justice, having been dismissed in Book II, are allowed to return, and provide the finishing touches on Socrates' portrait of justice. Since the soul (or at least the rational part of it) does not perish, the good of justice does not come to an end when the body perishes. By postponing the question of posthumous existence to the end of the *Republic*, Socrates leads us to see that a life of justice would be worth living even if there were no afterlife.

Although the *Republic*, more than any other single dialogue, seeks to integrate the many different components of Plato's thought, it is by no means the final expression of his philosophy. His ideas about ethics, politics, the nature of reality and our ability to know it, continued to evolve. The *Philebus* contains his further thoughts about the structure of goodness; in the *Statesman* and the *Laws* (his longest and latest work), he returns to political theory. In several of these late works, Socrates is assigned a far smaller role than in Plato's earlier dialogues. The principal interlocutors of the *Statesman*, for example, are an unnamed visitor from the city of Elea and a young member of the Academy who happens to be named Socrates. (The more famous Socrates appears only at the beginning of the dialogue.) The dialogue is an elaborate effort to understand the meaning of statesmanship (that is, political expertise). Its principal speaker expresses a higher regard for democracy, and a greater interest in the psychology of ordinary men and women, than Socrates had shown in the *Republic*. One of its most striking ideas is that courage and temperateness are psychological tendencies that push people toward unhealthy extremes, and that a political expert will need to find ways to blend them together so that each serves as a check on the other. We need to study not merely the virtues of those who rule, but the analogues of these qualities among nonphilosophers, because their inculcation has as much to do with the health of the city as does the education of philosophers.

This trend, in which Plato expresses greater interest in the potential that ordinary people have for moral improvement, culminates in the *Laws*, where he describes a well-governed city that is ruled almost entirely by nonphilosophers. It cannot be an accident that in this lengthy work, which describes in great detail the mechanisms of popular self-rule, the figure of Socrates is entirely absent. Socrates serves as a recurrent reminder of the dangers of democracy and popular mistrust of philosophy; he is abandoned as an interlocutor when Plato undertakes to show how large a role nonphilosophers can play in the governance of a healthy city.

For a systematic and detailed discussion of Plato's moral philosophy, see Terence Irwin, *Plato's Ethics* (New York: Oxford University Press, 1995). Essays on many aspects of his thought can be found in Richard Kraut, *The Cambridge Companion to Plato* (Cambridge: Cambridge University Press, 1992); and in Gail Fine's two volumes, *Plato 1* and *Plato 2* (Oxford: Oxford University Press, 1999). For wide-ranging discussions of his early works, see Gerasimos Santas, *Socrates* (London: Routledge & Kegan Paul, 1979); Gregory Vlastos, *Socrates, Ironist and Moral Philosopher* (Cambridge: Cambridge University Press, 1991); and Thomas C. Brickhouse and Nicholas D. Smith, *The Philosophy of Socrates* (Boulder, Colo.: Westview Press, 2000). Full discussions of the *Apology* are provided by Thomas C. Brickhouse and Nicholas D. Smith, *Socrates on Trial* (Princeton, N.J.: Princeton University Press, 1989); and C. D. C. Reeve, *Socrates in the Apology* (Indianapolis: Hackett, 1989). Detailed analysis of the *Crito* is presented by Richard Kraut, *Socrates and the State* (Princeton, N.J.: Princeton University Press, 1989); and Roslyn Weiss, *Socrates Dissatisfied* (New York: Oxford University Press, 1998). For studies of the *Republic*, see Julia Annas, *An Introduction to Plato's Republic* (Oxford: Clarendon Press, 1981); Nicholas P. White, *A Companion to Plato's Republic* (Indianapolis: Hackett, 1979); C. D. C. Reeve, *Philosopher-Kings* (Princeton, N.J.: Princeton University Press, 1988); and Richard Kraut, *Plato's Republic: Critical Essays* (Lanham, Md.: Rowman and Littlefield, 1997). For discussion of the *Statesman*, see Christopher Rowe (ed.), *Reading the Statesman* (Sankt Augustin: Academia Verlag, 1995). *The Cambridge History of Greek and Roman Political Thought* edited by Christopher Rowe and Malcolm Schofield, in association with Simon Harrison and Melissa Lane (Cambridge: Cambridge University Press, 2000), contains seven chapters on Plato's politics.

# Defence of Socrates

17a   I don't know how you, fellow Athenians, have been affected by my accusers, but for my part I felt myself almost transported by them, so persuasively did they speak. And yet hardly a

5     word they have said is true. Among their many falsehoods, one especially astonished me: their warning that you must be careful not to be

b     taken in by me, because I am a clever speaker. It seemed to me the height of impudence on their part not to be embarrassed at being refuted straight away by the facts; once it became apparent that I was not a clever speaker at all—

5     unless indeed they call a 'clever' speaker one who speaks the truth. If that is what they mean, then I would admit to being an orator, although not on a par with them.

      As I said, then, my accusers have said little or nothing true; whereas from me you shall hear the whole truth, though not, I assure you,

c     fellow Athenians, in language adorned with fine words and phrases or dressed up, as theirs was: you shall hear my points made spontaneously in whatever words occur to me—persuaded as I am that my case is just. None of you should expect anything to be put differently, because it would not, of course, be at all

5     fitting at my age, gentlemen, to come before you with artificial speeches, such as might be composed by a young lad.

      One thing, moreover, I would earnestly beg of you, fellow Athenians. If you hear me defending myself with the same arguments I normally use at the bankers' tables in the

10    market-place (where many of you have heard
d     me) and elsewhere, please do not be surprised or protest on that account. You see, here is the

reason: this is the first time I have ever appeared before a court of law, although I am over 70; so I am literally a stranger to the diction of this place. And if I really were a foreigner, you would naturally excuse me, were I      5
to speak in the dialect and style in which I had     18a
been brought up; so in the present case as well I ask you, in all fairness as I think, to disregard my manner of speaking—it may not be as good, or it may be better—but to consider and attend simply to the question whether or not my case is just; because that is the duty of a judge,     5
as it is an orator's duty to speak the truth.

      To begin with, fellow Athenians, it is fair that I should defend myself against the first set of charges falsely brought against me by my first accusers, and then turn to the later charges     b
and the more recent ones. You see, I have been accused before you by many people for a long time now, for many years in fact, by people who spoke not a word of truth. It is those people I fear more than Anytus and his crowd, though they too are dangerous. But those others are more so, gentlemen: they have taken     5
hold of most of you since childhood, and made persuasive accusations against me, yet without an ounce more truth in them. They say that there is one Socrates, a 'wise man', who ponders what is above the earth and investigates everything beneath it, and turns the weaker     c
argument into the stronger.

      Those accusers who have spread such rumour about me, fellow Athenians, are the dangerous ones, because their audience believes that people who inquire into those matters also fail to acknowledge the gods. Moreover, those

5 accusers are numerous, and have been denouncing me for a long time now, and they also
spoke to you at an age at which you would be
most likely to believe them, when some of you
were children or young lads; and their accusations simply went by default for lack of any
defence. But the most absurd thing of all is that
d one cannot even get to know their names or say
who they were—except perhaps one who happens to be a comic playwright. The ones who
have persuaded you by malicious slander, and
also some who persuade others because they
have been persuaded themselves, are all very
5 hard to deal with: one cannot put any of them
on the stand here in court, or cross-examine
anybody, but one must literally engage in a sort
of shadow-boxing to defend oneself, and cross-
examine without anyone to answer. You too,
then, should allow, as I just said, that I have two
e sets of accusers: one set who have accused me
recently, and the other of long standing to
whom I was just referring. And please grant
that I need to defend myself against the latter
first, since you too heard them accusing me earlier, and you heard far more from them than
from these recent critics here.

5 Very well, then. I must defend myself, fellow
19a Athenians, and in so short a time must try to
dispel the slander which you have had so long
to absorb. That is the outcome I would wish
for, should it be of any benefit to you and to
5 me, and I should like to succeed in my
defence—though I believe the task to be a difficult one, and am well aware of its nature. But
let that turn out as God wills: I have to obey the
law and present my defence.

b Let us examine, from the beginning, the
charge that has given rise to the slander against
me—which was just what Meletus relied upon
when he drew up this indictment. Very well
then, what were my slanderers actually saying
when they slandered me? Let me read out their
deposition, as if they were my legal accusers:
'Socrates is guilty of being a busybody, in

that he inquires into what is beneath the earth 5
and in the sky, turns the weaker argument into c
the stronger, and teaches others to do the same.'

The charges would run something like that.
Indeed, you can see them for yourselves,
enacted in Aristophanes' comedy: in that play,
a character called 'Socrates' swings around,
claims to be walking on air, and talks a lot of 5
other nonsense on subjects of which I have no
understanding, great or small.

Not that I mean to belittle knowledge of that
sort, if anyone really is learned in such matters—no matter how many of Meletus' lawsuits I might have to defend myself against—
but the fact is, fellow Athenians, those subjects
are not my concern at all. I call most of you to d
witness yourselves, and I ask you to make that
quite clear to one another, if you have ever
heard me in discussion (as many of you have).
Tell one another, then, whether any of you has
ever heard me discussing such subjects, either 5
briefly or at length; and as a result you will realize that the other things said about me by the
public are equally baseless.

In any event, there is no truth in those
charges. Moreover, if you have heard from
anyone that I undertake to educate people and e
charge fees, there is no truth in that either—
though for that matter I do think it also a fine
thing if anyone *is* able to educate people, as
Gorgias of Leontini, Prodicus of Ceos, and
Hippias of Elis profess to. Each of them can 5
visit any city, gentlemen, and persuade its
young people, who may associate free of
charge with any of their own citizens they 20a
wish, to leave those associations, and to join
with them instead, paying fees and being
grateful into the bargain.

On that topic, there is at present another
expert here, a gentleman from Paros; I heard
of his visit, because I happened to run into a
man who has spent more money on sophists 5
than everyone else put together—Callias, the
son of Hipponicus. So I questioned him, since
he has two sons himself.

'Callias,' I said, 'if your two sons had been born as colts or calves, we could find and
b engage a tutor who could make them both excel superbly in the required qualities—and he'd be some sort of expert in horse-rearing or agriculture. But seeing that they are actually human, whom do you intend to engage as their tutor? Who has knowledge of the required
5 human and civic qualities? I ask, because I assume you've given thought to the matter, having sons yourself. Is there such a person,' I asked, 'or not?'

'Certainly,' he replied.

'Who is he?' I said; 'Where does he come from, and what does he charge for tuition?'

'His name is Evenus, Socrates,' he replied; 'He comes from Paros, and he charges 5 minas.'

I thought Evenus was to be congratulated,
c if he really did possess that skill and imparted it for such a modest charge. I, at any rate, would certainly be giving myself fine airs and graces if I possessed that knowledge. But the fact is, fellow Athenians, I do not.

Now perhaps one of you will interject:
5 'Well then, Socrates, what is the difficulty in your case? What is the source of these slanders against you? If you are not engaged in something out of the ordinary, why ever has so much rumour and talk arisen about you? It would surely never have arisen, unless you
d were up to something different from most people. Tell us what it is, then, so that we don't jump to conclusions about you.'

That speaker makes a fair point, I think; and so I will try to show you just what it is that has earned me my reputation and notoriety. Please
5 hear me out. Some of you will perhaps think I am joking, but I assure you that I shall be telling you the whole truth.

You see, fellow Athenians, I have gained this reputation on account of nothing but a certain sort of wisdom. And what sort of wisdom is that? It is a human kind of wisdom, perhaps,
e since it might just be true that I have wisdom of that sort. Maybe the people I just mentioned

possess wisdom of a superhuman kind; otherwise I cannot explain it. For my part, I certainly do not possess that knowledge; and whoever says I do is lying and speaking with a view to slandering me—

Now please do not protest, fellow Athenians, even if I should sound to you rather boastful: I am not myself the source of the story I 5 am about to tell you, but I shall refer you to a trustworthy authority. As evidence of my wisdom, if such it actually be, and of its nature, I shall call to witness before you the god at Delphi.

You remember Chaerephon, of course. He 21a was a friend of mine from youth, and also a comrade in your party, who shared your recent exile and restoration. You recall too what sort of man Chaerephon was, how impetuous he was in any undertaking. Well, on one occasion he actually went to the Delphic oracle, and had the audacity to put the following question to 5 it—as I said, please do not make a disturbance, gentlemen—he went and asked if there was anyone wiser than myself; to which the Pythia responded that there was no one. His brother here will testify to the court about that story, since Chaerephon himself is deceased.

Now keep in mind why I have been telling b you this: it is because I am going to explain to you the origin of the slander against me. When I heard the story, I thought to myself: 'What ever is the god saying? What can his riddle mean? Since I am all too conscious of not being wise in any matter, great or small, what 5 ever can he mean by pronouncing me to be the wisest? Surely he cannot be lying: for him that would be out of the question.'

So for a long time I was perplexed about what he could possibly mean. But then, with great reluctance, I proceeded to investigate the matter somewhat as follows. I went to one of the people who had a reputation for wisdom, thinking there, if anywhere, to disprove the c oracle's utterance and declare to it: 'Here is someone wiser than I am, and yet you said that I was the wisest.'

So I interviewed this person—I need not mention his name, but he was someone in public life; and when I examined him, my experi-

5  ence went something like this, fellow Athenians: in conversing with him, I formed the opinion that, although the man was thought to be wise by many other people, and especially by himself, yet in reality he was not. So I then

d  tried to show him that he thought himself wise without being so. I thereby earned his dislike, and that of many people present; but still, as I went away, I thought to myself: 'I am wiser than that fellow, anyhow. Because neither of us,

5  I dare say, knows anything of great value; but he thinks he knows a thing when he doesn't; whereas I neither know it in fact, nor think that I do. At any rate, it appears that I am wiser than he in just this one small respect: if I do not know something, I do not think that I do.'

Next, I went to someone else, among people thought to be even wiser than the previous

e  man, and I came to the same conclusion again; and so I was disliked by that man too, as well as by many others.

Well, after that I went on to visit one person after another. I realized, with dismay and alarm, that I was making enemies; but even so, I thought it my duty to attach the highest

5  importance to the god's business; and therefore, in seeking the oracle's meaning, I had to

22a  go on to examine all those with any reputation for knowledge. And upon my word, fellow Athenians—because I am obliged to speak the truth before the court—I truly did experience something like this: as I pursued the god's inquiry, I found those held in the highest esteem were practically the most defective,

5  whereas men who were supposed to be their inferiors were much better off in respect of understanding.

Let me, then, outline my wanderings for you, the various 'labours' I kept undertaking, only to find that the oracle proved completely irrefutable. After I had done with the politicians, I turned to the poets—including tragedi-

b  ans, dithyrambic poets, and the rest—thinking

that in their company I would be shown up as more ignorant than they were. So I picked up the poems over which I thought they had taken

5  the most trouble, and questioned them about their meaning, so that I might also learn something from them in the process.

Now I'm embarrassed to tell you the truth, gentlemen, but it has to be said. Practically everyone else present could speak better than the poets themselves about their very own compositions. And so, once more, I soon realized this truth about them too: it was not from wisdom that they composed their works, but

c  from a certain natural aptitude and inspiration, like that of seers and soothsayers—because those people too utter many fine words, yet know nothing of the matters on which they pronounce. It was obvious to me that the poets were in much the same situation; yet at the

5  same time I realized that because of their compositions they thought themselves the wisest people in other matters as well, when they were not. So I left, believing that I was ahead of them in the same way as I was ahead of the politicians.

Then, finally, I went to the craftsmen, because I was conscious of knowing almost

d  nothing myself, but felt sure that amongst them, at least, I would find much valuable knowledge. And in that expectation I was not disappointed: they did have knowledge in fields where I had none, and in that respect they were wiser than I. And yet, fellow Athe-

5  nians, those able craftsmen seemed to me to suffer from the same failing as the poets: because of their excellence at their own trade, each claimed to be a great expert also on matters of the utmost importance; and this arro- gance of theirs seemed to eclipse their wis-

e  dom. So I began to ask myself, on the oracle's behalf, whether I should prefer to be as I am, neither wise as they are wise, nor ignorant as they are ignorant, or to possess both their attributes; and in reply, I told myself and the

5  oracle that I was better off as I was.

The effect of this questioning, fellow Athe-

23a  nians, was to earn me much hostility of a very vexing and trying sort, which has given rise to numerous slanders, including this reputation I have for being 'wise'—because those present on each occasion imagine me to be wise

5      regarding the matters on which I examine others. But in fact, gentlemen, it would appear that it is only the god who is truly wise; and that he is saying to us, through this oracle, that human wisdom is worth little or nothing. It

b      seems that when he says 'Socrates', he makes use of my name, merely taking me as an example—as if to say, 'The wisest amongst you, human beings, is anyone like Socrates who has recognized that with respect to wisdom he is truly worthless.'

That is why, even to this day, I still go

5      about seeking out and searching into anyone I believe to be wise, citizen or foreigner, in obedience to the god. Then, as soon as I find that someone is not wise, I assist the god by proving that he is not. Because of this occupation, I have had no time at all for any activity to

c      speak of, either in public affairs or in my family life; indeed, because of my service to the god, I live in extreme poverty.

In addition, the young people who follow me around of their own accord, the ones who have plenty of leisure because their parents are wealthiest, enjoy listening to people being cross-examined. Often, too, they copy my

5      example themselves, and so attempt to cross-examine others. And I imagine that they find a great abundance of people who suppose themselves to possess some knowledge, but really know little or nothing. Consequently, the peo-

d      ple they question are angry with me, though not with themselves, and say that there is a nasty pestilence abroad called 'Socrates', who is corrupting the young.

Then, when asked just what he is doing or teaching, they have nothing to say, because they have no idea what he does; yet, rather

5      than seem at a loss, they resort to the stock charges against all who pursue intellectual

inquiry, trotting out 'things in the sky and beneath the earth', 'failing to acknowledge the gods', and 'turning the weaker argument into the stronger'. They would, I imagine, be loath to admit the truth, which is that their pretensions to knowledge have been exposed, and they are totally ignorant. So because these

e      people have reputations to protect, I suppose, and are also both passionate and numerous, and have been speaking about me in a vigorous and persuasive style, they have long been filling your ears with vicious slander. It is on the strength of all this that Meletus, along with Anytus and Lycon, has proceeded against me:

5      Meletus is aggrieved for the poets, Anytus for

24a  the craftsmen and politicians, and Lycon for the orators. And so, as I began by saying, I should be surprised if I could rid your minds of this slander in so short a time, when so much of it has accumulated.

There is the truth for you, fellow Athenians.

5      I have spoken it without concealing anything from you, major or minor, and without glossing over anything. And yet I am virtually certain that it is my very candour that makes enemies for me—which goes to show that I am right: the slander against me is to that effect, and such is its explanation. And whether you look for one

b      now or later, that is what you will find.

So much for my defence before you against the charges brought by my first group of

5      accusers. Next, I shall try to defend myself against Meletus, good patriot that he claims to be, and against my more recent critics. So once again, as if they were a fresh set of accusers, let me in turn review their deposition. It runs something like this:

'Socrates is guilty of corrupting the young, and of failing to acknowledge the gods acknowledged by the city, but introducing new

c      spiritual beings instead.'

Such is the charge: let us examine each item within it.

Meletus says, then, that I am guilty of cor-

5 rupting the young. Well I reply, fellow Athenians, that Meletus is guilty of trifling in a serious matter, in that he brings people to trial on frivolous grounds, and professes grave concern about matters for which he has never cared at all. I shall now try to prove to you too that that is so.

10 Step forward, Meletus, and answer me. It is
d your chief concern, is it not, that our younger people shall be as good as possible?

—It is.

Very well, will you please tell the judges who influences them for the better—because you must obviously know, seeing that you
5 care? Having discovered me, as you allege, to be the one who is corrupting them, you bring me before the judges here and accuse me. So speak up, and tell the court who has an improving influence.

You see, Meletus, you remain silent, and have no answer. Yet doesn't that strike you as shameful, and as proof in itself of exactly what I say—that you have never cared about these matters at all? Come then, good fellow, tell us
10 who influences them for the better.

—The laws.

e Yes, but that is not what I'm asking, excellent fellow. I mean, which *person,* who already knows the laws to begin with?

—These gentlemen, the judges, Socrates.

What are you saying, Meletus? Can these
5 people educate the young, and do they have an improving influence?

—Most certainly.

All of them, or some but not others?

—All of them.

My goodness, what welcome news, and what a generous supply of benefactors you
10 speak of! And how about the audience here in
25a court? Do they too have an improving influence, or not?

—Yes, they do too.

And how about members of the Council?

—Yes, the Councillors too.

5 But in that case, how about people in the

Assembly, its individual members, Meletus? They won't be corrupting their youngers, will they? Won't they all be good influences as well?

—Yes, they will too.

So every person in Athens, it would appear, has an excellent influence on them except for 10 me, whereas I alone am corrupting them. Is that what you're saying?

—That is emphatically what I'm saying.

Then I find myself, if we are to believe you, in a most awkward predicament. Now answer me this. Do you think the same is true of b horses? Is it everybody who improves them, while a single person spoils them? Or isn't the opposite true: a single person, or at least very few people, namely the horse-trainers, can improve them; while lay people spoil them, don't they, if they have to do with horses and 5 make use of them? Isn't that true of horses as of all other animals, Meletus? Of course it is, whether you and Anytus deny it or not. In fact, I dare say our young people are extremely lucky if only one person is corrupting them, c while everyone else is doing them good.

All right, Meletus. Enough has been said to prove that you never were concerned about the young. You betray your irresponsibility plainly, because you have not cared at all about the charges on which you bring me before this court.

Furthermore, Meletus, tell us, in God's 5 name, whether it is better to live among good fellow citizens or bad ones. Come sir, answer: I am not asking a hard question. Bad people have a harmful impact upon their closest companions at any given time, don't they, whereas good people have a good one?

—Yes. 10

Well, is there anyone who wants to be d harmed by his companions rather than benefited?—Be a good fellow and keep on answering, as the law requires you to. Is there anyone who wants to be harmed?

—Of course not. 5

Now tell me this. In bringing me here, do you claim that I am corrupting and depraving the young intentionally or unintentionally?

—Intentionally, so I maintain.

10

e

Really, Meletus? Are you so much smarter at your age than I at mine as to realize that the bad have a harmful impact upon their closest companions at any given time, whereas the good have a beneficial effect? Am I, by contrast, so far gone in my stupidity as not to realize that if I make one of my companions vicious, I risk incurring harm at his hands? And am I, therefore, as you allege, doing so much damage intentionally?

5

That I cannot accept from you, Meletus, and neither could anyone else, I imagine.

26a

Either I am not corrupting them—or if I am, I am doing so unintentionally; so either way your charge is false. But if I am corrupting them unintentionally, the law does not require me to be brought to court for such mistakes, but rather to be taken aside for private instruction and admonition—since I shall obviously stop doing unintentional damage, if I learn bet-

5

ter. But you avoided association with me and were unwilling to instruct me. Instead you bring me to court, where the law requires you to bring people who need punishment rather than enlightenment.

Very well, fellow Athenians. That part of

b

my case is now proven: Meletus never cared about these matters, either a lot or a little. Nevertheless, Meletus, please tell us in what way you claim that I am corrupting our younger people. That is quite obvious, isn't it, from the indictment you drew up? It is by teaching them not to acknowledge the gods acknowledged by

5

the city, but to accept new spiritual beings instead? You mean, don't you, that I am corrupting them by teaching them that?

—I most emphatically do.

Then, Meletus, in the name of those very gods we are now discussing, please clarify the

c

matter further for me, and for the jury here. You see, I cannot make out what you mean. Is

it that I am teaching people to acknowledge that some gods exist—in which case it follows that I do acknowledge their existence myself as well, and am not a complete atheist, hence am not guilty on that count—and yet that those gods are not the ones acknowledged by the city, but different ones? Is that your charge

5

against me—namely, that they are different? Or are you saying that I acknowledge no gods at all myself, and teach the same to others?

—I am saying the latter: you acknowledge no gods at all.

What ever makes you say that, Meletus,

d

you strange fellow? Do I not even acknowledge, then, with the rest of mankind, that the sun and the moon are gods?

—By God, he does not, members of the jury, since he claims that the sun is made of

5

rock, and the moon of earth!

My dear Meletus, do you imagine that it is Anaxagoras you are accusing? Do you have such contempt for the jury, and imagine them so illiterate as not to know that books by Anaxagoras of Clazomenae are crammed with such assertions? What's more, are the young

10

learning those things from me when they can

e

acquire them at the bookstalls, now and then, for a drachma at most, and so ridicule Socrates if he claims those ideas for his own, especially when they are so bizarre? In God's name, do you really think me as crazy as that? Do I acknowledge the existence of no god at all?

—By God no, none whatever.

5

I can't believe you, Meletus—nor, I think, can you believe yourself. To my mind, fellow Athenians, this fellow is an impudent scoundrel who has framed this indictment out of

27a

sheer wanton impudence and insolence. He seems to have devised a sort of riddle in order to try me out: 'Will Socrates the Wise tumble to my nice self-contradiction? Or shall I fool him along with my other listeners?' You see,

5

he seems to me to be contradicting himself in the indictment. It's as if he were saying: 'Socrates is guilty of not acknowledging gods, but of acknowledging gods'; and yet that is sheer tomfoolery.

I ask you to examine with me, gentlemen, just how that appears to be his meaning. Answer for us, Meletus; and the rest of you, please remember my initial request not to protest if I conduct the argument in my usual manner.

Is there anyone in the world, Meletus, who acknowledges that human phenomena exist, yet does not acknowledge human beings?—Require him to answer, gentlemen, and not to raise all kinds of confused objections. Is there anyone who does not acknowledge horses, yet does acknowledge equestrian phenomena? Or who does not acknowledge that musicians exist, yet does acknowledge musical phenomena?

There is no one, excellent fellow: if you don't wish to answer, I must answer for you, and for the jurors here. But at least answer my next question yourself. Is there anyone who acknowledges that spiritual phenomena exist, yet does not acknowledge spirits?

—No.

How good of you to answer—albeit reluctantly and under compulsion from the jury. Well now, you say that I acknowledge spiritual beings and teach others to do so. Whether they actually be new or old is no matter: I do at any rate, by your account, acknowledge spiritual beings, which you have also mentioned in your sworn deposition. But if I acknowledge spiritual beings, then surely it follows quite inevitably that I must acknowledge spirits. Is that not so?—Yes, it is so: I assume your agreement, since you don't answer. But we regard spirits, don't we, as either gods or children of gods? Yes or no?

—Yes.

Then given that I do believe in spirits, as you say, if spirits are gods of some sort, this is precisely what I claim when I say that you are presenting us with a riddle and making fun of us: you are saying that I do not believe in gods, and yet again that I do believe in gods, seeing that I believe in spirits.

On the other hand, if spirits are children of gods, some sort of bastard offspring from nymphs—or from whomever they are traditionally said, in each case, to be born—then who in the world could ever believe that there were children of gods, yet no gods? That would be just as absurd as accepting the existence of children of horses and asses—namely, mules—yet rejecting the existence of horses or asses!

In short, Meletus, you can only have drafted this either by way of trying us out, or because you were at a loss how to charge me with a genuine offence. How could you possibly persuade anyone with even the slightest intelligence that someone who accepts spiritual beings does not also accept divine ones, and again that the same person also accepts neither spirits nor gods nor heroes? There is no conceivable way.

But enough, fellow Athenians. It needs no long defence, I think, to show that I am not guilty of the charges in Meletus' indictment; the foregoing will suffice. You may be sure, though, that what I was saying earlier is true: I have earned great hostility among many people. And that is what will convict me, if I am convicted: not Meletus or Anytus, but the slander and malice of the crowd. They have certainly convicted many other good men as well, and I imagine they will do so again; there is no risk of their stopping with me.

Now someone may perhaps say: 'Well then, are you not ashamed, Socrates, to have pursued a way of life which has now put you at risk of death?'

But it may be fair for me to answer him as follows: 'You are sadly mistaken, fellow, if you suppose that a man with even a grain of self-respect should reckon up the risks of living or dying, rather than simply consider, whenever he does something, whether his c  actions are just or unjust, the deeds of a good man or a bad one. By your principles, presumably, all those demigods who died in the plain of Troy were inferior creatures—yes, even the son of Thetis, who showed so much scorn for danger, when the alternative was to endure

5  dishonour. Thus, when he was eager to slay Hector, his mother, goddess that she was, spoke to him—something like this, I fancy:

> My child, if thou dost avenge the murder of thy
>    friend, Patroclus,
> And dost slay Hector, then straightway [so
>    runs the poem]
> Shalt thou die thyself, since doom is prepared
>    for thee
> Next after Hector's.

10
d  But though he heard that, he made light of death and danger, since he feared far more to live as a base man, and to fail to avenge his dear ones. The poem goes on:

> Then straightway let me die, once I have given
>    the wrongdoer
> His deserts, lest I remain here by the beak-
>    prowed ships,
> An object of derision, and a burden upon the
>    earth.

Can you suppose that he gave any thought to death or danger?

5  You see, here is the truth of the matter, fellow Athenians. Wherever a man has taken up a position because he considers it best, or has been posted there by his commander, that is where I believe he should remain, steadfast in danger, taking no account at all of death or of anything else rather than dishonour. I would

e  therefore have been acting absurdly, fellow Athenians, if when assigned to a post at Potidaea, Amphipolis, or Delium by the superiors you had elected to command me, I remained where I was posted on those occasions at the risk of death, if ever any man did—whereas

5  now that the god assigns me, as I became completely convinced, to the duty of leading the  29a philosophical life by examining myself and others, I desert that post from fear of death or anything else. Yes, that would be unthinkable; and then I truly should deserve to be brought to court for failing to acknowledge the gods' existence, in that I was disobedient to the oracle, was afraid of death, and thought I was wise when I was not.

After all, gentlemen, the fear of death  5 amounts simply to thinking one is wise when one is not: it is thinking one knows something one does not know. No one knows, you see, whether death may not in fact prove the greatest of all blessings for mankind; but people fear it as if they knew it for certain to be the  b greatest of evils. And yet to think that one knows what one does not know must surely be the kind of folly which is reprehensible.

On this matter especially, gentlemen, that may be the nature of my own advantage over most people. If I really were to claim to be wiser than anyone in any respect, it would consist simply in this: just as I do not possess adequate knowledge of life in Hades, so I also  5 realize that I do not possess it; whereas acting unjustly in disobedience to one's betters, whether god or human being, is something I *know* to be evil and shameful. Hence I shall never fear or flee from something which may indeed be a good for all I know, rather than from things I know to be evils.

Suppose, therefore, that you pay no heed to  c Anytus, but are prepared to let me go. He said I need never have been brought to court in the first place, but that once I had been, your only option was to put me to death. He declared before you that, if I got away from you this time, your sons would all be utterly corrupted  5 by practising Socrates' teachings. Suppose, in the face of that, you were to say to me:

'Socrates, we will not listen to Anytus this time. We are prepared to let you go—but only on this condition: you are to pursue that quest of yours and practise philosophy no longer;

and if you are caught doing it any more, you shall be put to death.'

d      Well, as I just said, if you were prepared to let me go on those terms, I should reply to you as follows:

'I have the greatest fondness and affection for you, fellow Athenians, but I will obey my god rather than you; and so long as I draw
5  breath and am able, I shall never give up practising philosophy, or exhorting and showing the way to any of you whom I ever encounter, by giving my usual sort of message. "Excellent friend," I shall say; "You are an Athenian. Your city is the most important and renowned for its wisdom and power; so are you not ashamed that, while you take care to acquire as
e  much wealth as possible, with honour and glory as well, yet you take no care or thought for understanding or truth, or for the best possible state of your soul?"

'And should any of you dispute that, and claim that he does take such care, I will not let
5  him go straight away nor leave him, but I will
30a question and examine and put him to the test; and if I do not think he has acquired goodness, though he says he has, I shall say, "Shame on you, for setting the lowest value upon the most precious things, and for rating inferior ones more highly!" That I shall do for anyone I encounter, young or old, alien or fellow citizen; but all the more for the latter, since your
5  kinship with me is closer.'

Those are my orders from my god, I do assure you. Indeed, I believe that no greater good has ever befallen you in our city than my service to my god; because all I do is to go about, persuading you, young and old alike,
b  not to care for your bodies or for your wealth so intensely as for the greatest possible wellbeing of your souls. 'It is not wealth', I tell you, 'that produces goodness; rather, it is from goodness that wealth, and all other benefits for human beings, accrue to them in their private and public life.'

5  If, in fact, I am corrupting the young by

those assertions, you may call them harmful. But if anyone claims that I say anything different, he is talking nonsense. In the face of that I should like to say: 'Fellow Athenians, you may listen to Anytus or not, as you please; and you may let me go or not, as you please,  c because there is no chance of my acting otherwise, even if I have to die many times over—'

Stop protesting, fellow Athenians! Please abide by my request that you not protest against what I say, but hear me out; in fact, it  5 will be in your interest, so I believe, to do so. You see, I am going to say some further things to you which may make you shout out— although I beg you not to.

You may be assured that if you put to death the sort of man I just said I was, you will not harm me more than you harm yourselves.  10 Meletus or Anytus would not harm me at all;  d nor, in fact, could they do so, since I believe it is out of the question for a better man to be harmed by his inferior. The latter may, of course, inflict death or banishment or disenfranchisement; and my accuser here, along with others no doubt, believes those to be great evils. But I do not. Rather, I believe it a far  5 greater evil to try to kill a man unjustly, as he does now.

At this point, therefore, fellow Athenians, so far from pleading on my own behalf, as might be supposed, I am pleading on yours, in case by condemning me you should mistreat the gift which God has bestowed upon you— because if you put me to death, you will not  e easily find another like me. The fact is, if I may put the point in a somewhat comical way, that I have been literally attached by God to our city, as if to a horse—a large thoroughbred,  5 which is a bit sluggish because of its size, and needs to be aroused by some sort of gadfly. Yes, in me, I believe, God has attached to our city just such a creature—the kind which is  31a constantly alighting everywhere on you, all day long, arousing, cajoling, or reproaching each and every one of you. You will not easily acquire another such gadfly, gentlemen; rather, if you take my advice, you will spare my life. I dare say, though, that you will get angry, like people who are awakened from their doze. Perhaps you will heed Anytus, and give me a swat: you could happily finish me off, and then spend the rest of your life asleep—unless God, in his compassion for you, were to send you someone else.

That I am, in fact, just the sort of gift that God would send to our city, you may recognize from this: it would not seem to be in human nature for me to have neglected all my own affairs, and put up with the neglect of my family for all these years, but constantly minded your interests, by visiting each of you in private like a father or an elder brother, urging you to be concerned about goodness. Of course, if I were gaining anything from that, or were being paid to urge that course upon you, my actions could be explained. But in fact you can see for yourselves that my accusers, who so shamelessly level all those other charges against me, could not muster the impudence to call evidence that I ever once obtained payment, or asked for any. It is I who can call evidence sufficient, I think, to show that I am speaking the truth—namely, my poverty.

Now it may perhaps seem peculiar that, as some say, I give this counsel by going around and dealing with others' concerns in private, yet do not venture to appear before the Assembly, and counsel the city about your business in public. But the reason for that is one you have frequently heard me give in many places: it is a certain divine or spiritual sign which comes to me, the very thing to which Meletus made mocking allusion in his indictment. It has been happening to me ever since childhood: a voice of some sort which comes, and which always—whenever it does come—restrains me from what I am about to do, yet never gives positive direction. That is what opposes my engaging in politics—and its opposition is an excellent thing, to my mind;

because you may be quite sure, fellow Athenians, that if I had tried to engage in politics, I should have perished long since, and should have been of no use either to you or to myself.

And please do not get angry if I tell you the truth. The fact is that there is no person on earth whose life will be spared by you or by any other majority, if he is genuinely opposed to many injustices and unlawful acts, and tries to prevent their occurrence in our city. Rather, anyone who truly fights for what is just, if he is going to survive for even a short time, must act in a private capacity rather than a public one.

I will offer you conclusive evidence of that—not just words, but the sort of evidence that you respect, namely, actions. Just hear me tell my experiences, so that you may know that I would not submit to a single person for fear of death, contrary to what is just; nor would I do so, even if I were to lose my life on the spot. I shall mention things to you which are vulgar commonplaces of the courts; yet they are true.

Although I have never held any other public office in our city, fellow Athenians, I have served on its Council. My own tribe, Antiochis, happened to be the presiding commission on the occasion when you wanted a collective trial for the ten generals who had failed to rescue the survivors from the naval battle. That was illegal, as you all later recognized. At the time I was the only commissioner opposed to your acting illegally, and I voted against the motion. And though its advocates were prepared to lay information against me and have me arrested, while you were urging them on by shouting, I believed that I should face danger in siding with law and justice, rather than take your side for fear of imprisonment or death, when your proposals were contrary to justice.

Those events took place while our city was still under democratic rule. But on a subsequent occasion, after the oligarchy had come to power, the Thirty summoned me and four others to the round chamber, with orders to arrest Leon the Salaminian, and fetch him from Salamis for execution; they were constantly issuing such orders, of course, to many others, in their wish to implicate as many as possible in their crimes. On that occasion, however, I showed, once again not just by words, but by my actions, that I couldn't care less about death—if that would not be putting it rather crudely—but that my one and only care was to avoid doing anything sinful or unjust. Thus, powerful as it was, that regime did not frighten me into unjust action: when we emerged from the round chamber, the other four went off to Salamis and arrested Leon, whereas I left them and went off home. For that I might easily have been put to death, had the regime not collapsed shortly afterwards. There are many witnesses who will testify before you about those events.

Do you imagine, then, that I would have survived all these years if I had been regularly active in public life, and had championed what was right in a manner worthy of a brave man, and valued that above all else, as was my duty? Far from it, fellow Athenians. I would not, and nor would any other man. But in any public undertaking, that is the sort of person that I, for my part, shall prove to have been throughout my life; and likewise in my private life, because I have never been guilty of unjust association with anyone, including those whom my slanderers allege to have been my students.

I never, in fact, was anyone's instructor at any time. But if a person wanted to hear me talking, while I was engaging in my own business, I never grudged that to anyone, young or old; nor do I hold conversation only when I receive payment, and not otherwise. Rather, I offer myself for questioning to wealthy and poor alike, and to anyone who may wish to answer in response to questions from me. Whether any of those people acquires a good character or not, I cannot fairly be held responsible, when I never at any time promised any

of them that they would learn anything from me, nor gave them instruction. And if anyone claims that he ever learnt anything from me, or has heard privately something that everyone else did not hear as well, you may be sure that what he says is untrue.

Why then, you may ask, do some people enjoy spending so much time in my company?—You have already heard, fellow Athenians: I have told you the whole truth—which is that my listeners enjoy the examination of those who think themselves wise but are not, since the process is not unamusing. But for me, I must tell you, it is a mission which I have been bidden to undertake by the god, through oracles and dreams, and through every means whereby a divine injunction to perform any task has ever been laid upon a human being.

That is not only true, fellow Athenians, but is easily verified—because if I do corrupt any of our young people, or have corrupted others in the past, then presumably, when they grew older, should any of them have realized that I had at any time given them bad advice in their youth, they ought now to have appeared here themselves to accuse me and obtain redress. Or else, if they were unwilling to come in person, members of their families—fathers, brothers, or other relations—had their relatives suffered any harm at my hands, ought now to put it on record and obtain redress.

In any case, many of those people are present, whom I can see: first there is Crito, my contemporary and fellow demesman, father of Critobulus here; then Lysanias of Sphettus, father of Aeschines here; next, Epigenes' father, Antiphon from Cephisia, is present; then again, there are others here whose brothers have spent time with me in these studies: Nicostratus, son of Theozotides, brother of Theodotus—Theodotus himself, incidentally, is deceased, so Nicostratus could not have come at his brother's urging; and Paralius here, son of Demodocus, whose brother was Theages; also present is Ariston's son, Adimantus, whose brother is Plato here; and Aeantodorus, whose brother is Apollodorus here.

There are many others I could mention to you, from whom Meletus should surely have called some testimony during his own speech. However, if he forgot to do so then, let him call it now—I yield the floor to him—and if he has any such evidence, let him produce it. But quite the opposite is true, gentlemen: you will find that they are all prepared to support me, their corruptor, the one who is, according to Meletus and Anytus, doing their relatives mischief. Support for me from the actual victims of corruption might perhaps be explained; but what of the uncorrupted—older men by now, and relatives of my victims? What reason would they have to support me, apart from the right and proper one, which is that they know very well that Meletus is lying, whereas I am telling the truth?

There it is, then, gentlemen. That, and perhaps more of the same, is about all I have to say in my defence. But perhaps, among your number, there may be someone who will harbour resentment when he recalls a case of his own: he may have faced a less serious trial than this one, yet begged and implored the jury, weeping copiously, and producing his children here, along with many other relatives and loved ones, to gain as much sympathy as possible. By contrast, I shall do none of those things, even though I am running what might be considered the ultimate risk. Perhaps someone with those thoughts will harden his heart against me; and enraged by those same thoughts, he may cast his vote against me in anger. Well, if any of you are so inclined—not that I expect it of you, but if anyone *should* be—I think it fair to answer him as follows:

'I naturally do have relatives, my excellent friend, because—in Homer's own words—I too was "not born of oak nor of rock", but of human parents; and so I do have relatives— including my sons, fellow Athenians. There

are three of them: one is now a youth, while two are still children. Nevertheless, I shall not produce any of them here, and then entreat you to vote for my acquittal.'

And why, you may ask, will I do no such thing? Not out of contempt or disrespect for you, fellow Athenians—whether or not I am facing death boldly is a different issue. The point is that with our reputations in mind— yours and our whole city's, as well as my own—I believe that any such behaviour would be ignominious, at my age and with the reputation I possess; that reputation may or may not, in fact, be deserved, but at least it is believed that Socrates stands out in some way from the run of human beings. Well, if those of you who are believed to be pre-eminent in wisdom, courage, or any other form of goodness, are going to behave like that, it would be demeaning.

I have frequently seen such men when they face judgment: they have significant reputations, yet they put on astonishing performances, apparently in the belief that by dying they will suffer something unheard of—as if they would be immune from death, so long as you did not kill them! They seem to me to put our city to shame: they could give any foreigner the impression that men preeminent among Athenians in goodness, whom they select from their own number to govern and hold other positions, are no better than women. I say this, fellow Athenians, because none of us who has even the slightest reputation should behave like that; nor should you put up with us if we try to do so. Rather, you should make one thing clear: you will be far more inclined to convict one who stages those pathetic charades and makes our city an object of derision, than one who keeps his composure.

But leaving reputation aside, gentlemen, I do not think it right to entreat the jury, nor to win acquittal in that way, instead of by informing and persuading them. A juror does not sit to dispense justice as a favour, but to determine where it lies. And he has sworn, not that he will favour whomever he pleases, but that he will try the case according to law. We should not, then, accustom you to transgress your oath, nor should you become accustomed to doing so: neither of us would be showing respect towards the gods. And therefore, fellow Athenians, do not require behaviour from me towards you which I consider neither proper nor right nor pious—more especially now, for God's sake, when I stand charged by Meletus here with impiety: because if I tried to persuade and coerce you with entreaties in spite of your oath, I clearly *would* be teaching you not to believe in gods; and I would stand literally self-convicted, by my defence, of failing to acknowledge them. But that is far from the truth: I do acknowledge them, fellow Athenians, as none of my accusers do; and I trust to you, and to God, to judge my case as shall be best for me and for yourselves.

For many reasons fellow Athenians, I am not dismayed by this outcome[1]—your convicting me, I mean—and especially because the outcome has come as no surprise to me. I wonder far more at the number of votes cast on each side, because I did not think the margin would be so narrow. Yet it seems, in fact, that if a mere thirty votes had gone the other way, I should have been acquitted. Or rather, even as things stand, I consider that I have been cleared of Meletus' charges. Not only that, but one thing is obvious to everyone: if Anytus had not come forward with Lycon to accuse me, Meletus would have forfeited 1,000 drachmas, since he would not have gained one-fifth of the votes cast.

But anyhow, this gentleman demands the death penalty for me. Very well, then: what alternative penalty shall I suggest to you, fellow Athenians? Clearly, it must be one I deserve. So what do I deserve to incur or to pay, for having taken it into my head not to lead an inactive life? Instead, I have neglected the things that concern most people—making money, managing an estate, gaining military or civic honours, or other positions of power, or joining political clubs and parties which have formed in our city. I thought myself, in truth, too honest to survive if I engaged in those things. I did not pursue a course, therefore, in which I would be of no use to you or to myself. Instead, by going to each individual privately, I tried to render a service for you which is—so I maintain—the highest service of all. Therefore that was the course I followed: I tried to persuade each of you not to care for any of his possessions rather than care for himself, striving for the utmost excellence and understanding; and not to care for our city's possessions rather than for the city itself; and to care about other things in the same way.

So what treatment do I deserve for being such a benefactor? If I am to make a proposal truly in keeping with my deserts, fellow Athenians, it should be some benefit; and more-over, the sort of benefit that would be fitting for me. Well then, what *is* fitting for a poor man who is a benefactor, and who needs time free for exhorting you? Nothing could be more fitting, fellow Athenians, than to give such a man regular free meals in the Prytaneum; indeed, that is far more fitting for him than for any of you who may have won an Olympic race with a pair or a team of horses: that victor brings you only the appearance of success, whereas I bring you the reality; besides, he is not in want of sustenance, whereas I am. So if, as justice demands, I am to make a proposal in keeping with my deserts, that is what I suggest: free meals in the Prytaneum.

Now, in proposing this, I may seem to you, as when I talked about appeals for sympathy, to be speaking from sheer effrontery. But actually I have no such motive, fellow Athenians. My point is rather this: I am convinced that I do not treat any human being unjustly, at least intentionally—but I cannot make you share that conviction, because we have conversed together so briefly. I say this, because if it were

10  the law here, as in other jurisdictions, that a
capital case must not be tried in a single day,
b   but over several, I think you could have been
convinced; but as things stand, it is not easy to
clear oneself of such grave allegations in a
short time.

Since, therefore, I am persuaded, for my
part, that I have treated no one unjustly, I have
no intention whatever of so treating myself,
5   nor of denouncing myself as deserving ill,
or proposing any such treatment for myself.
Why should I do that? For fear of the penalty
Meletus demands for me, when I say that I
don't know if that is a good thing or a bad
one? In preference to that, am I then to choose
one of the things I know very well to be bad,
and demand that instead? Imprisonment, for
c   instance? Why should I live in prison, in servitude to the annually appointed prison commissioners? Well then, a fine, with imprisonment until I pay? That would amount to what I
just mentioned, since I haven't the means to
pay it.

Well then, should I propose banishment?
5   Perhaps that is what you would propose for
me. Yet I must surely be obsessed with survival, fellow Athenians, if I am so illogical as
that. You, my fellow citizens, were unable to
d   put up with my discourses and arguments, but
they were so irksome and odious to you that
you now seek to be rid of them. Could I not
draw the inference, in that case, that others
will hardly take kindly to them? Far from it,
fellow Athenians. A fine life it would be for a
5   person of my age to go into exile, and spend
his days continually exchanging one city for
another, and being repeatedly expelled—
because I know very well that wherever I go,
the young will come to hear me speaking, as
they do here. And if I repel them, they will
e   expel me themselves, by persuading their elders; while if I do not repel them, their fathers
and relatives will expel me on their account.

Now, perhaps someone may say: 'Socrates,
could you not be so kind as to keep quiet and
5   remain inactive, while living in exile?' This is

the hardest point of all of which to convince
some of you. Why? Because, if I tell you that
that would mean disobeying my god, and that
is why I cannot remain inactive, you will dis-   38a
believe me and think that I am practising a sly
evasion. Again, if I said that it really is the
greatest benefit for a person to converse every
day about goodness, and about the other subjects you have heard me discussing when        5
examining myself and others—and that an
unexamined life is no life for a human being to
live—then you would believe me still less
when I made those assertions. But the facts,
gentlemen, are just as I claim them to be,
though it is not easy to convince you of them.
At the same time, I am not accustomed to think
of myself as deserving anything bad. If I had    b
money, I would have proposed a fine of as
much as I could afford: that would have done
me no harm at all. But the fact is that I have
none—unless you wish to fix the penalty at a
sum I could pay. I could afford to pay you 1    5
mina, I suppose, so I suggest a fine of that
amount—

One moment, fellow Athenians. Plato here,
along with Crito, Critobulus, and Apollodorus, is urging me to propose 30 minas, and
they are saying they will stand surety for that
sum. So I propose a fine of that amount, and
these people shall be your sufficient guaran-    10
tors of its payment.

For the sake of a slight gain in time, fellow    c
Athenians, you will incur infamy and blame
from those who would denigrate our city, for
putting Socrates to death[2]—a 'wise man'—
because those who wish to malign you will say
I am wise, even if I am not; in any case, had
you waited only a short time, you would have    5
obtained that outcome automatically. You can
see, of course, that I am now well advanced in
life, and death is not far off. I address that not   d
to all of you, but to those who condemned me
to death; and to those same people I would add
something further.

Perhaps you imagine, gentlemen, that I

have been convicted for lack of arguments of the sort I could have used to convince you, had I believed that I should do or say anything to gain acquittal. But that is far from true. I have been convicted, not for lack of arguments, but for lack of brazen impudence and willingness to address you in such terms as you would most like to be addressed in—that is to say, by weeping and wailing, and doing and saying much else that I claim to be unworthy of me— the sorts of thing that you are so used to hearing from others. But just as I did not think during my defence that I should do anything unworthy of a free man because I was in danger, so now I have no regrets about defending myself as I did; I should far rather present such a defence and die, than live by defending myself in that other fashion.

In court, as in warfare, neither I nor anyone else should contrive to escape death at any cost. On the battlefield too, it often becomes obvious that one could avoid death by throwing down one's arms and flinging oneself upon the mercy of one's pursuers. And in every sort of danger there are many other means of escaping death, if one is shameless enough to do or to say anything. I suggest that it is not death that is hard to avoid, gentlemen, but wickedness is far harder, since it is fleeter of foot than death. Thus, slow and elderly as I am, I have now been overtaken by the slower runner; while my accusers, adroit and quick-witted as they are, have been overtaken by the faster, which is wickedness. And so I take my leave, condemned to death by your judgment, whereas they stand for ever condemned to depravity and injustice as judged by Truth. And just as I accept my penalty, so must they. Things were bound to turn out this way, I suppose, and I imagine it is for the best.

In the next place, to those of you who voted against me, I wish to utter a prophecy. Indeed, I have now reached a point at which people are most given to prophesying—that is, when they are on the point of death. I warn you, my executioners, that as soon as I am dead retribution

will come upon you—far more severe, I swear, than the sentence you have passed upon me. You have tried to kill me for now, in the belief that you will be relieved from giving an account of your lives. But in fact, I can tell you, you will face just the opposite outcome. There will be more critics to call you to account, people whom I have restrained for the time being though you were unaware of my doing so. They will be all the harder on you since they are younger, and you will rue it all the more— because if you imagine that by putting people to death you will prevent anyone from reviling you for not living rightly, you are badly mistaken. That way of escape is neither feasible nor honourable. Rather, the most honourable and easiest way is not the silencing of others, but striving to make oneself as good a person as possible. So with that prophecy to those of you who voted against me, I take my leave.

As for those who voted for my acquittal, I should like to discuss the outcome of this case while the officials are occupied, and I am not yet on the way to the place where I must die. Please bear with me, gentlemen, just for this short time: there is no reason why we should not have a word with one another while that is still permitted.

Since I regard you as my friends, I am willing to show you the significance of what has just befallen me. You see, gentlemen of the jury—and in applying that term to you, I probably use it correctly—something wonderful has just happened to me. Hitherto, the usual prophetic voice from my spiritual sign was continually active, and frequently opposed me even on trivial matters, if I was about to do anything amiss. But now something has befallen me, as you can see for yourselves, which one certainly might consider—and is generally held—to be the very worst of evils. Yet the sign from God did not oppose me, either when I left home this morning, or when I appeared here in court, or at any point when I was about to say anything during my speech; and yet in other discussions it has very often stopped me in mid-sentence. This time, though, it has not opposed me at any moment in anything I said or did in this whole business.

Now, what do I take to be the explanation for that? I will tell you: I suspect that what has befallen me is a blessing, and that those of us who suppose death to be an evil cannot be making a correct assumption. I have gained every ground for that suspicion, because my usual sign could not have failed to oppose me, unless I were going to incur some good result.

And let us also reflect upon how good a reason there is to hope that death is a good thing. It is, you see, one or other of two things: either to be dead is to be non-existent, as it were, and a dead person has no awareness whatever of anything at all; or else, as we are told, the soul undergoes some sort of transformation, or exchanging of this present world for another. Now if there is, in fact, no awareness in death, but it is like sleep—the kind in which the sleeper does not even dream at all—then death would be a marvellous gain. Why, imagine that someone had to pick the night in which he slept so soundly that he did not even dream, and to compare all the other nights and days of his life with that one; suppose he had to say, upon consideration, how many days or nights in his life he had spent better and more agreeably than that night; in that case, I think he would find them easy to count compared with his other days and nights—even if he were the Great King of Persia, let alone an ordinary person. Well, if death is like that, then for my part I call it a gain; because on that assumption the whole of time would seem no longer than a single night.

On the other hand, if death is like taking a trip from here to another place, and if it is true, as we are told, that all of the dead do indeed exist in that other place, why then, gentlemen of the jury, what could be a greater blessing than that? If upon arriving in Hades, and being rid of these people who profess to be 'jurors',

one is going to find those who are truly judges, and who are also said to sit in judgment there—Minos, Rhadamanthys, Aeacus, Triptolemus, and all other demigods who were righteous in their own lives—would that be a disappointing journey?

Or again, what would any of you not give to share the company of Orpheus and Musaeus, of Hesiod and Homer? I say 'you,' since I personally would be willing to die many times over, if those tales are true. Why? Because my own sojourn there would be wonderful, if I could meet Palamedes, or Ajax, son of Telamon, or anyone else of old who met their death through an unjust verdict. Whenever I met them, I could compare my own experiences with theirs—which would be not unamusing, I fancy—and best of all, I could spend time questioning and probing people there, just as I do here, to find out who among them is truly wise, and who thinks he is without being so.

What would one not give, gentlemen of the jury, to be able to question the leader of the great expedition against Troy, or Odysseus, or Sisyphus, or countless other men and women one could mention? Would it not be unspeakable good fortune to converse with them there, to mingle with them and question them? At least that isn't a reason, presumably, for people in that world to put you to death—because amongst other ways in which people there are more fortunate than those in our world, they have become immune from death for the rest of time, if what we are told is actually true.

Moreover, you too, gentlemen of the jury, should be of good hope in the face of death, and fix your minds upon this single truth: nothing can harm a good man, either in life or in death; nor are his fortunes neglected by the gods. In fact, what has befallen me has come about by no mere accident; rather, it is clear to me that it was better I should die now and be rid of my troubles. That is also the reason why the divine sign at no point turned me back; and for my part, I

bear those who condemned me, and my accusers, no ill will at all—though, to be sure, it was
e not with that intent that they were condemning and accusing me, but with intent to harm me—and they are culpable for that. Still, this much I ask of them. When my sons come of age, gentlemen, punish them: give them the same sort of
5 trouble that I used to give you, if you think they care for money or anything else more than for goodness, and if they think highly of themselves when they are of no value. Reprove them, as I reproved you, for failing to care for
42a the things they should, and for thinking highly of themselves when they are worthless. If you

will do that, then I shall have received my own just deserts from you, as will my sons.

But enough. It is now time to leave—for me to die, and for you to live—though which of us has the better destiny is unclear to everyone, save only to God.                                                      5

## Notes

1. The verdict was 'Guilty'. Socrates here begins his second speech, proposing an alternative to the death penalty demanded by the prosecution.
2. The jury has now voted for the death penalty, and Socrates begins his final speech.

# Crito

43a    *Socrates.* Why have you come at this hour, Crito? It's still very early, isn't it?
    *Crito.* Yes, very.
    *Socrates.* About what time?
    *Crito.* Just before daybreak.
5    *Socrates.* I'm surprised the prison-warder was willing to answer the door.
    *Crito.* He knows me by now, Socrates, because I come and go here so often; and besides, I've done him a small favour.
10    *Socrates.* Have you just arrived, or have
b you been here for a while?
    *Crito.* For quite a while.
    *Socrates.* Then why didn't you wake me up right away instead of sitting by me in silence?
5    *Crito.* Well *of course* I didn't wake you, Socrates! I only wish I weren't so sleepless and wretched myself. I've been marvelling all this time as I saw how peacefully you were sleeping, and I deliberately kept from waking you, so that you could pass the time as peacefully as possible. I've often admired your dis-

position in the past, in fact all your life; but more than ever in your present plight, you bear      10
it so easily and patiently.
    *Socrates.* Well, Crito, it really would be tiresome for a man of my age to get upset if the      c
time has come when he must end his life.
    *Crito.* And yet others of your age, Socrates, are over-taken by similar troubles, but their age brings them no relief from being upset at the fate which faces them.
    *Socrates.* That's true. But tell me, why      5
*have* you come so early?
    *Crito.* I bring painful news, Socrates—not painful for you, I suppose, but painful and hard for me and all your friends—and hardest of all for me to bear, I think.                                      d
    *Socrates.* What news is that? Is it that the ship has come back from Delos, the one on whose return I must die?
    *Crito.* Well no, it hasn't arrived yet, but I think it will get here today, judging from      5
reports of people who've come from Sunium,

where they disembarked. That makes it obvious that it will get here today; and so tomorrow, Socrates, you will have to end your life.

*Socrates.* Well, may that be for the best,
44a  Crito. If it so please the gods, so be it. All the
same, I don't think it will get here today.

*Crito.* What makes you think that?

*Socrates.* I'll tell you. You see, I am to die
on the day after the ship arrives, am I not?

*Crito.* At least that's what the authorities
say.

5     *Socrates.* Then I don't think it will get here
on the day that is just dawning, but on the next
one. I infer that from a certain dream I had in
the night—a short time ago, so it may be just
as well that you didn't wake me.

*Crito.* And what was your dream?

10    *Socrates.* I dreamt that a lovely, handsome
b    woman approached me, robed in white. She
called me and said: 'Socrates,

> *Thou shalt reach fertile Phthia upon the
>     third day.'*

*Crito.* What a curious dream, Socrates.

5     *Socrates.* Yet its meaning is clear, I think,
Crito.

*Crito.* All too clear, it would seem. But
please, Socrates, my dear friend, there is still
time to take my advice, and make your
escape—because if you die, I shall suffer more
than one misfortune: not only shall I lose such a
friend as I'll never find again, but it will look to
10   many people, who hardly know you or me, as if
c    I'd abandoned you—since I could have rescued you if I'd been willing to put up the
money. And yet what could be more shameful
than a reputation for valuing money more
highly than friends? Most people won't believe
that it was you who refused to leave this place
5    yourself, despite our urging you to do so.

*Socrates.* But why should we care so
much, my good Crito, about what most people
believe? All the most capable people, whom
we should take more seriously, will think the
matter has been handled exactly as it has been.

*Crito.* Yet surely, Socrates, you can see       d
that one must heed popular opinion too. Your
present plight shows by itself that the populace
can inflict not the least of evils, but just about
the worst, if someone has been slandered in       5
their presence.

*Socrates.* Ah Crito, if only the populace
*could* inflict the worst of evils! Then they
would also be capable of providing the greatest of goods, and a fine thing that would be.
But the fact is that they can do neither: they are
unable to give anyone understanding or lack of
it, no matter what they do.                        10

*Crito.* Well, if you say so. But tell me this,   e
Socrates: can it be that you are worried for me
and your other friends, in case the blackmailers give us trouble, if you escape, for having
smuggled you out of here? Are you worried
that we might be forced to forfeit all our prop-   5
erty as well, or pay heavy fines, or even incur
some further penalty? If you're afraid of any-    45a
thing like that, put it out of your mind. In rescuing you we are surely justified in taking that
risk, or even worse if need be. Come on, listen
to me and do as I say.

*Socrates.* Yes, those risks do worry me,
Crito—amongst many others.                          5

*Crito.* Then put those fears aside—
because no great sum is needed to pay people
who are willing to rescue you and get you out
of here. Besides, you can surely see that those
blackmailers are cheap, and it wouldn't take      b
much to buy them off. My own means are
available to you and would be ample, I'm sure.
Then again, even if—out of concern on my
behalf—you think you shouldn't be spending
my money, there are visitors here who are
ready to spend theirs. One of them, Simmias
from Thebes, has actually brought enough        5
money for this very purpose, while Cebes and
quite a number of others are also prepared to
contribute. So, as I say, you shouldn't hesitate
to save yourself on account of those fears.

And don't let it trouble you, as you were
saying in court, that you wouldn't know what
to do with yourself if you went into exile. There  c

will be people to welcome you anywhere else you may go: if you want to go to Thessaly, I have friends there who will make much of you and give you safe refuge, so that no one from

5 anywhere in Thessaly will trouble you.

Next, Socrates, I don't think that what you propose—giving yourself up, when you could be rescued—is even just. You are actually hastening to bring upon yourself just the sorts of thing which your enemies would hasten to bring upon you—indeed, they have done so— in their wish to destroy you.

10 What's more, I think you're betraying
d those sons of yours. You will be deserting them, if you go off when you could be raising and educating them: as far as you're concerned, they will fare as best they may. In all likelihood, they'll meet the sort of fate which usually befalls orphans once they've lost their

5 parents. Surely, one should either not have children at all, or else see the toil and trouble of their upbringing and education through to the end; yet you seem to me to prefer the easiest path. One should rather choose the path that a good and resolute man would choose, particularly if one professes to cultivate good-

e ness all one's life. Frankly, I'm ashamed for you and for us, your friends: it may appear that this whole predicament of yours has been handled with a certain feebleness on our part. What with the bringing of your case to court when that could have been avoided, the actual

5 conduct of the trial, and now, to crown it all, this absurd outcome of the business, it may seem that the problem has eluded us through

46a some fault or feebleness on our part—in that we failed to save you, and you failed to save yourself, when that was quite possible and feasible, if we had been any use at all.

Make sure, Socrates, that all this doesn't turn out badly, and a disgrace to you as well as us. Come now, form a plan—or rather, don't

5 even plan, because the time for that is past, and only a single plan remains. Everything needs to be carried out during the coming night; and if we go on waiting around, it won't be possi-

ble or feasible any longer. Come on, Socrates, do all you can to take my advice, and do exactly what I say.

*Socrates.* My dear Crito, your zeal will be b invaluable if it should have right on its side; but otherwise, the greater it is, the harder it makes matters. We must therefore consider whether or not the course you urge should be followed—because it is in my nature, not just now for the first time but always, to follow 5 nothing within me but the principle which appears to me, upon reflection, to be best.

I cannot now reject the very principles that I previously adopted, just because this fate has overtaken me; rather, they appear to me much c the same as ever, and I respect and honour the same ones that I did before. If we cannot find better ones to maintain in the present situation, you can be sure that I won't agree with you— not even if the power of the populace threatens us, like children, with more bogeymen than it 5 does now, by visiting us with imprisonment, execution, or confiscation of property.

What, then, is the most reasonable way to consider the matter? Suppose we first take up the point you make about what people will d think. Was it always an acceptable principle that one should pay heed to some opinions but not to others, or was it not? Or was it acceptable before I had to die, while now it is exposed as an idle assertion made for the sake of talk, when it is really childish nonsense? For 5 my part, Crito, I'm eager to look into this together with you, to see whether the principle is to be viewed any differently, or in the same way, now that I'm in this position, and whether we should disregard or follow it.

As I recall, the following principle always used to be affirmed by people who thought they were talking sense: the principle, as I was e just saying, that one should have a high regard for some opinions held by human beings, but not for others. Come now, Crito: don't you think that was a good principle? I ask because you are not, in all foreseeable likelihood, 47a going to die tomorrow, and my present trouble shouldn't impair your judgment. Consider, then: don't you think it a good principle, that one shouldn't respect all human opinions, but only some and not others; or, again, that one shouldn't respect everyone's opinions, but

5 those of some people, and not those of others? What do you say? Isn't that a good principle?

*Crito.* It is.

*Socrates.* And one should respect the good ones, but not the bad ones?

*Crito.* Yes.

*Socrates.* And good ones are those of people with understanding, whereas bad ones are

10 those of people without it?

*Crito.* Of course.

*Socrates.* Now then, once again, how were

b such points established? When a man is in training, and concentrating upon that, does he pay heed to the praise or censure or opinion of each and every man, or only to those of the individual who happens to be his doctor or trainer?

*Crito.* Only to that individual's.

5 *Socrates.* Then he should fear the censures, and welcome the praises of that individual, but not those of most people.

*Crito.* Obviously.

*Socrates.* So he must base his actions and exercises, his eating and drinking, upon the

10 opinion of the individual, the expert supervisor, rather than upon everyone else's.

*Crito.* True.

c *Socrates.* Very well. If he disobeys that individual and disregards his opinion and his praises, but respects those of most people, who are ignorant, he'll suffer harm, won't he?

*Crito.* Of course.

5 *Socrates.* And what is that harm? What does it affect? What element within the disobedient man?

*Crito.* Obviously, it affects his body, because that's what it spoils.

*Socrates.* A good answer. And in other fields too, Crito—we needn't go through them

10 all, but they surely include matters of just and unjust, honourable and dishonourable, good

and bad, the subjects of our present deliberation—is it the opinion of most people that we    d should follow and fear, or is it that of the individual authority—assuming that some expert exists who should be respected and feared above all others? If we don't follow that person, won't we corrupt and impair the element    5 which (as we agreed) is made better by what is just, but is spoilt by what is unjust? Or is there nothing in all that?

*Crito.* I accept it myself, Socrates.

*Socrates.* Well now, if we spoil the part of us that is improved by what is healthy but cor-    10 rupted by what is unhealthy, because it is not    e expert opinion that we are following, are our lives worth living once it has been corrupted? The part in question is, of course, the body, isn't it?

*Crito.* Yes.

*Socrates.* And are our lives worth living    5 with a poor or corrupted body?

*Crito.* Definitely not.

*Socrates.* Well then, are they worth living if the element which is impaired by what is unjust and benefited by what is just has been    48a corrupted? Or do we consider the element to which justice or injustice belongs, whichever part of us it is, to be of less value than the body?

*Crito.* By no means.

*Socrates.* On the contrary, it is more precious?

*Crito.* Far more.    5

*Socrates.* Then, my good friend, we shouldn't care all that much about what the populace will say of us, but about what the expert on matters of justice and injustice will say, the individual authority, or Truth. In the first place, then, your proposal that we should    10 care about popular opinion regarding just, honourable, or good actions, and their opposites, is mistaken.

'Even so,' someone might say, 'the populace has the power to put us to death.'    b

*Crito. That's* certainly clear enough; one might say that, Socrates.

*Socrates.* You're right. But the principle we've rehearsed, my dear friend, still remains as true as it was before—for me at any rate. And now consider this further one, to see whether or not it still holds good for us. We should attach the highest value, shouldn't we, not to living, but to living well?

*Crito.* Why yes, that still holds.

*Socrates.* And living well is the same as living honourably or justly? Does that still hold or not?

*Crito.* Yes, it does.

*Socrates.* Then in the light of those admissions, we must ask the following question: is it just, or is it not, for me to try to get out of here, when Athenian authorities are unwilling to release me? Then, if it does seem just, let us attempt it; but if it doesn't, let us abandon the idea.

As for the questions you raise about expenses and reputation and bringing up children, I suspect they are the concerns of those who cheerfully put people to death, and would bring them back to life if they could, without any intelligence, namely, the populace. For us, however, because our principle so demands, there is no other question to ask except the one we just raised: shall we be acting justly—we who are rescued as well as the rescuers themselves—if we pay money and do favours to those who would get me out of here? Or shall we in truth be acting unjustly if we do all those things? And if it is clear that we shall be acting unjustly in taking that course, then the question whether we shall have to die through standing firm and holding our peace, or suffer in any other way, ought not to weigh with us in comparison with acting unjustly.

*Crito.* I think that's finely *said,* Socrates; but do please consider what we should *do.*

*Socrates.* Let's examine that question together, dear friend; and if you have objections to anything I say, please raise them, and I'll listen to you—otherwise, good fellow, it's time to stop telling me, again and again, that I should leave here against the will of Athens.

You see, I set great store upon persuading you as to my course of action, and not acting against your will. Come now, just consider whether you find the starting-point of our inquiry acceptable, and try to answer my questions according to your real beliefs.

*Crito.* All right, I'll try.

*Socrates.* Do we maintain that people should on no account whatever do injustice willingly? Or may it be done in some circumstances but not in others? Is acting unjustly in no way good or honourable, as we frequently agreed in the past? Or have all those former agreements been jettisoned during these last few days? Can it be, Crito, that men of our age have long failed to notice, as we earnestly conversed with each other, that we ourselves were no better than children? Or is what we then used to say true above all else? Whether most people say so or not, and whether we must be treated more harshly or more leniently than at present, isn't it a fact, all the same, that acting unjustly is utterly bad and shameful for the agent? Yes or no?

*Crito.* Yes.

*Socrates.* So one must not act unjustly at all.

*Crito.* Absolutely not.

*Socrates.* Then, even if one is unjustly treated, one should not return injustice, as most people believe—given that one should act not unjustly at all.

*Crito.* Apparently not.

*Socrates.* Well now, Crito, should one ever ill-treat anybody or not?

*Crito.* Surely not, Socrates.

*Socrates.* And again, when one suffers ill-treatment, is it just to return it, as most people maintain, or isn't it?

*Crito.* It is not just at all.

*Socrates.* Because there's no difference, I take it, between ill-treating people and treating them unjustly.

*Crito.* Correct.

*Socrates.* Then one shouldn't return injustice or ill-treatment to any human being, no

d matter how one may be treated by that person. And in making those admissions, Crito, watch out that you're not agreeing to anything contrary to your real beliefs. I say that, because I realize that the belief is held by few people, and always will be. Those who hold it share no common counsel with those who don't; but each group is bound to regard the other with
5 contempt when they observe one another's decisions. You too, therefore, should consider very carefully whether you share that belief with me, and whether we may begin our deliberations from the following premiss: neither doing nor returning injustice is ever right, nor should one who is ill-treated defend himself
e by retaliation. Do you agree? Or do you dissent and not share my belief in that premiss? I've long been of that opinion myself, and I still am now; but if you've formed any different view, say so, and explain it. If you stand by our former view, however, then listen to my next point.

*Crito.* Well, I do stand by it and share that view, so go ahead.

5 *Socrates.* All right, I'll make my next point—or rather, ask a question. Should the things one agrees with someone else be done, provided they are just, or should one cheat?

*Crito.* They should be done.

*Socrates.* Then consider what follows. If
50a we leave this place without having persuaded our city, are we or are we not ill-treating certain people, indeed people whom we ought least of all to be ill-treating? And would we be abiding by the things we agreed, those things being just, or not?

*Crito.* I can't answer your question, Soc-
5 rates, because I don't understand it.

*Socrates.* Well, look at it this way. Suppose we were on the point of running away from here, or whatever else one should call it. Then the Laws, or the State of Athens, might come and confront us, and they might speak as follows:

'Please tell us, Socrates, what do you have

in mind? With this action you are attempting, b do you intend anything short of destroying us, the Laws and the city as a whole, to the best of your ability? Do you think that a city can still exist without being overturned, if the legal judgments rendered within it possess no force, but are nullified or invalidated by individuals?' 5

What shall we say, Crito, in answer to that and other such questions? Because somebody, particularly a legal advocate, might say a great deal on behalf of the law that is being invalidated here, the one requiring that judgments, c once rendered, shall have authority. Shall we tell them: 'Yes, that is our intention, because the city was treating us unjustly, by not judging our case correctly'? Is that to be our answer, or what?

*Crito.* Indeed it is, Socrates.

*Socrates.* And what if the Laws say: 'And 5 was that also part of the agreement between you and us, Socrates? Or did you agree to abide by whatever judgments the city rendered?'

Then, if we were surprised by their words, perhaps they might say: 'Don't be surprised at what we are saying, Socrates, but answer us, seeing that you like to use question-and- 10 answer. What complaint, pray, do you have d against the city and ourselves, that you should now attempt to destroy us? In the first place, was it not we who gave you birth? Did your father not marry your mother and beget you under our auspices? So will you inform those of us here who regulate marriages whether you have any criticism of them as poorly framed?'

'No, I have none,' I should say. 5

'Well then, what of the laws dealing with children's upbringing and education, under which you were educated yourself? Did those of us Laws who are in charge of that area not give proper direction, when they required your e father to educate you in the arts and physical training?'

'They did,' I should say.

'Very good. In view of your birth, upbringing, and education, can you deny, first, that

you belong to us as our offspring and slave, as
5    your forebears also did? And if so, do you
imagine that you are on equal terms with us in
regard to what is just, and that whatever treatment we may accord to you, it is just for you
to do the same thing back to us? You weren't
on equal terms with your father, or your master (assuming you had one), making it just for
51a  you to return the treatment you received—
answering back when you were scolded, or
striking back when you were struck, or doing
many other things of the same sort. Will you
then have licence against your fatherland and
5    its Laws, if we try to destroy you, in the belief
that that is just? Will you try to destroy us in
return, to the best of your ability? And will you
claim that in doing so you are acting justly,
you who are genuinely exercised about goodness? Or are you, in your wisdom, unaware
that, in comparison with your mother and
b    father and all your other forebears, your
fatherland is more precious and venerable,
more sacred and held in higher esteem among
gods, as well as among human beings who
have any sense; and that you should revere
your fatherland, deferring to it and appeasing
it when it is angry, more than your own father?
You must either persuade it, or else do whatever it commands; and if it ordains that you
5    must submit to certain treatment, then you
must hold your peace and submit to it: whether
that means being beaten or put in bonds, or
whether it leads you into war to be wounded or
killed, you must act accordingly, and that is
what is just; you must neither give way nor
retreat, nor leave your position; rather, in war-
10   fare, in court, and everywhere else, you must
c    do whatever your city or fatherland commands, or else persuade it as to what is truly
just; and if it is sinful to use violence against
your mother or father, it is far more so to use it
against your fatherland.'
    What shall we say to that, Crito? That the
Laws are right or not?
5    *Crito*. I think they are.

*Socrates*. 'Consider then, Socrates,' the
Laws might go on, 'whether the following is
also true: in your present undertaking you are
not proposing to treat us justly. We gave you
birth, upbringing, and education, and a share in    d
all the benefits we could provide for you along
with all your fellow citizens. Nevertheless, we
proclaim, by the formal granting of permission,
that any Athenian who wishes, once he has
been admitted to adult status, and has observed
the conduct of city business and ourselves, the
Laws, may—if he is dissatisfied with us—go
wherever he pleases and take his property. Not    5
one of us Laws hinders or forbids that: whether
any of you wishes to emigrate to a colony, or to
go and live as an alien elsewhere, he may go     e
wherever he pleases and keep his property, if
we and the city fail to satisfy him.
    'We do say, however, that if any of you
remains here after he has observed the system
by which we dispense justice and otherwise
manage our city, then he has agreed with us by    5
his conduct to obey whatever orders we give
him. And thus we claim that anyone who fails
to obey is guilty on three counts: he disobeys
us as his parents; he disobeys those who nurtured him; and after agreeing to obey us he
neither obeys nor persuades us if we are doing    52a
anything amiss, even though we offer him a
choice, and do not harshly insist that he must
do whatever we command. Instead, we give
him two options: he must either persuade us or
else do as we say; yet he does neither. Those
are the charges, Socrates, to which we say you
too will be liable if you carry out your intention; and among Athenians, you will be not the    5
least liable, but one of the most.'
    And if I were to say, 'How so?' perhaps
they could fairly reproach me, observing that
I am actually among those Athenians who
have made that agreement with them most
emphatically.
    'Socrates,' they would say, 'we have every    b
indication that you were content with us, as
well as with our city, because you would never

have stayed home here, more than is normal
for all other Athenians, unless you were abnor-
mally content. You never left our city for a festival—except once to go to the Isthmus—nor
did you go elsewhere for other purposes, apart
from military service. You never travelled
abroad, as other people do; nor were you eager
for acquaintance with a different city or different laws: we and our city sufficed for you.
Thus, you emphatically opted for us, and
agreed to be a citizen on our terms. In particular, you fathered children in our city, which
would suggest that you were content with it.

'Moreover, during your actual trial it was
open to you, had you wished, to propose exile
as your penalty; thus, what you are now
attempting to do without the city's consent,
you could then have done with it. On that occasion, you kept priding yourself that it would not
trouble you if you had to die: you would choose
death ahead of exile, so you said. Yet now you
dishonour those words, and show no regard for
us, the Laws, in your effort to destroy us. You
are acting as the meanest slave would act, by
trying to run away in spite of those compacts
and agreements you made with us, whereby
you agreed to be a citizen on our terms.

'First, then, answer us this question: are we
right in claiming that you agreed, by your conduct if not verbally, that you would be a citizen on our terms? Or is that untrue?'

What shall we say in reply to that, Crito?
Mustn't we agree?

*Crito.* We must, Socrates.

*Socrates.* 'Then what does your action
amount to,' they would say, 'except breaking
the compacts and agreements you made with
us? By your own admission, you were not
coerced or tricked into making them, or forced
to reach a decision in a short time: you had seventy years in which it was open to you to leave
if you were not happy with us, or if you thought
those agreements unfair. Yet you preferred neither Lacedaemon nor Crete—places you often
say are well governed—nor any other Greek or

foreign city: in fact, you went abroad less often
than the lame and the blind or other cripples.
Obviously, then, amongst Athenians you were
exceptionally content with our city and with us,
its Laws—because who would care for a city
apart from its laws? Won't you, then, abide by
your agreements now? Yes you will, if you listen to us, Socrates; and then at least you won't
make yourself an object of derision by leaving
the city.

'Just consider: if you break those agreements, and commit any of those offences, what
good will you do yourself or those friends of
yours? Your friends, pretty obviously, will risk
being exiled themselves, as well as being disenfranchised or losing their property. As for
you, first of all, if you go to one of the nearest
cities, Thebes or Megara—they are both well
governed—you will arrive as an enemy of their
political systems, Socrates: all who are concerned for their own cities will look askance
at you, regarding you as a subverter of laws.
You will also confirm your jurors in their judgment, making them think they decided your
case correctly: any subverter of laws, presumably, might well be thought to be a corrupter of
young, unthinking people.

'Will you, then, avoid the best-governed
cities and the most respectable of men? And if
so, will your life be worth living? Or will you
associate with those people, and be shameless
enough to converse with them? And what will
you say to them, Socrates? The things you
used to say here, that goodness and justice are
most precious to mankind, along with institutions and laws? Don't you think that the
predicament of Socrates will cut an ugly figure? Surely you must.

'Or will you take leave of those spots, and
go to stay with those friends of Crito's up in
Thessaly? That, of course, is a region of the
utmost disorder and licence; so perhaps they
would enjoy hearing from you about your
comical escape from gaol, when you dressed
up in some outfit, wore a leather jerkin or some

other runaway's garb, and altered your appearance. Will no one observe that you, an old man
e      with probably only a short time left to live, had
the nerve to cling so greedily to life by violating the most important laws? Perhaps not, so
long as you don't trouble anyone. Otherwise,
Socrates, you will hear a great deal to your
own discredit. You will live as every person's
5      toady and lackey; and what will you be
doing—apart from living it up in Thessaly, as
if you had travelled all the way to Thessaly to
54a    have dinner? As for those principles of yours
about justice and goodness in general—tell us,
where will they be then?

'Well then, is it for your children's sake
that you wish to live, in order to bring them up
and give them an education? How so? Will
you bring them up and educate them by taking
5      them off to Thessaly and making foreigners of
them, so that they may gain that advantage
too? Or if, instead of that, they are brought up
here, will they be better brought up and educated just because you are alive, if you are not
with them? Yes, you may say, because those
friends of yours will take care of them. Then
10     will they take care of them if you travel to
Thessaly, but not take care of them if you
travel to Hades? Surely if those professing to
b      be your friends are of any use at all, you must
believe that they will.

'No, Socrates, listen to us, your own nurtur-
ers: do not place a higher value upon children,
upon life, or upon anything else, than upon
5      what is just, so that when you leave for Hades,

this may be your whole defence before the
authorities there: to take that course seems neither better nor more just or holy, for you or for
any of your friends here in this world. Nor will
it be better for you when you reach the next. As
things stand, you will leave this world (if you            c
do) as one who has been treated unjustly not by
us Laws, but by human beings; whereas if you
go into exile, thereby shamefully returning
injustice for injustice and ill-treatment for ill-
treatment, breaking the agreements and compacts you made with us, and inflicting harm
upon the people you should least harm—your-           5
self, your friends, your fatherland, and ourselves—then we shall be angry with you in
your lifetime; and our brother Laws in Hades
will not receive you kindly there, knowing that
you tried, to the best of your ability, to destroy        d
us too. Come then, do not let Crito persuade
you to take his advice rather than ours.'

That, Crito, my dear comrade, is what I
seem to hear them saying, I do assure you. I
am like the Corybantic revellers who think
they are still hearing the music of pipes: the         5
sound of those arguments is ringing loudly in
my head, and makes me unable to hear the others. As far as these present thoughts of mine
go, then, you may be sure that if you object to
them, you will plead in vain. None the less, if
you think you will do any good, speak up.

*Crito*. No, Socrates, I've nothing to say.

*Socrates*. Then let it be, Crito, and let us         e
act accordingly, because that is the direction in
which God is guiding us.

# Republic

## BOOK I

327 I went down yesterday to the Piraeus with Glaucon, the son of Ariston, to offer up prayer to the goddess, and also I wanted to see how the festival, then to be held for the first time, would be celebrated. I was very much pleased with the native Athenian procession; though that of the Thracians appeared to be no less brilliant. We

b had finished our prayers, and satisfied our curiosity, and were returning to the city, when Polemarchus, the son of Cephalus, caught sight of us at a distance, as we were on our way towards home, and told his servant to run and order us to wait for him. The servant came behind me, took hold of my cloak, and said, 'Polemarchus asks you to wait.' I turned round and asked him where his master was. 'There he is,' he replied, 'coming from behind. Wait for him.' 'We will wait,' answered Glaucon. Soon

c afterwards Polemarchus came up, with Adeimantus the brother of Glaucon, and Niceratus the son of Nicias, and a few other persons, apparently coming away from the procession.

Polemarchus then said: Socrates, it looks to me as if you are rushing to leave for town.

You are not wrong in your surmise, I replied.

Well, do you see how many we are?

Certainly I do.

Then either prove yourselves the stronger party, or else stay where you are.

No, I replied, there is still an alternative: suppose we persuade you that you ought to let us go.

Could you possibly persuade us, if we refused to listen?

Certainly not, replied Glaucon.

Get it through your head that we will not listen.

Then Adeimantus interposed and said, Are 328 you not aware that towards evening there will be a torch-race on horseback in honor of the goddess?

On horseback! I exclaimed: that is a novelty. Will they carry torches, and pass them on to one another, while the horses are racing? or how do you mean?

As you say, replied Polemarchus: besides, there will be a night-festival, which will be worth looking at. After dinner we will go out to see this festival, and there we will meet with many of our young men, with whom we can converse. Therefore stay, and do not refuse us. b

Upon this Glaucon said, It seems we shall have to stay.

Well, said I, if you like, let us do so.

We went therefore home with Polemarchus, and found there his brothers Lysias and Euthydemus, and, along with them, Thrasymachus of Chalcedon, and Charmantides the Paeanian, and Cleitophon the son of Aristonymus. Polemarchus's father, Cephalus, was also in the house. He looked much older to me: for it was long since I had seen him. He was sitting on a c cushioned chair, with a garland upon his head, as he happened to have been sacrificing in the court. We found seats placed round him; so we sat down there by his side. The moment Cephalus saw me, he greeted me, and said, It is

Translation based on that of John Llewelyn Davies and David James Vaughan (London: Macmillan & Co., *Golden Treasury Series*, 1950; [originally, *Crown 800*, 1852]). Translation revised by Andrea Tschemplik. © 2000 by Andrea Tschemplik. Used by permission of the translator.

seldom indeed, Socrates, that you pay us a visit at the Piraeus; you ought to come more often. If I were still strong enough to walk with ease to the city, there would be no occasion for your coming here, because we should go to you. But as it is, you ought to come here more frequently. For I assure you that I find the decay of the mere bodily pleasures accompanied by a proportionate growth in my appetite for philosophical conversation and in the pleasure I derive from it. Therefore do not refuse my request, but let these young men have the benefit of your company, and come often to see us as though you were visiting friends and relatives.

To tell you the truth, Cephalus, I replied, I delight in conversing with very old persons. For as they have gone before us on the road over which perhaps we also shall have to travel, I think we ought to try to learn from them what the nature of that road is—whether it be rough and difficult, or smooth and easy. And now that you have arrived at that period of life, which poets call 'the threshold of Age,' there is no one whose opinion I would more gladly ask. Is life painful at that age, or what report do you make of it?

I will certainly tell you, Socrates, what my own experience of it is. I and a few other people of my own age are in the habit of frequently meeting together, true to the old proverb. On these occasions, most of us give way to lamentations, and regret the pleasures of youth, and call up the memory of sex and drinking parties and banquets and similar proceedings. They are grievously discontent at the loss of what they consider great privileges, and describe themselves as living well in those days, whereas now, by their own account, they cannot be said to live at all. Some also complain of the manner in which their relations insult their infirmities, and make this a ground for reproaching old age with the many miseries it brings upon them. But in my opinion, Socrates, these persons miss the true cause of their unhappiness. For if old age were the cause, the same discomforts would

have been also felt by me, as an old man, and by every other person that has reached that period of life. But, as it is, I have before now met with several old men who expressed themselves in a quite different manner; and in particular I may mention Sophocles the poet, who was once asked in my presence, 'How do you feel about love, Sophocles? are you still capable of it?' to which he replied, 'Hush! if you please: to my great delight I have escaped from it, and feel as if I had escaped from a frantic and savage master.' I thought then, as I do now, that he spoke wisely. For unquestionably old age brings us profound repose and freedom from this and other passions. When the appetites have abated, and their force is diminished, the description of Sophocles is perfectly realized. It is like being delivered from a multitude of furious masters. But the complaints on this score, as well as the troubles with relatives, may all be referred to one cause, and that is, not the age, Socrates, but the character of the men. If they possess well-regulated souls and easy tempers, old age itself is no intolerable burden: if they are differently constituted, why in that case, Socrates, they find even youth as irksome to them as old age.

I admired these remarks of Cephalus, and wishing him to go on talking, I endeavored to draw him out by saying: I think, Cephalus, that people do not generally welcome these views of yours, because they think that it is not your character, but your great wealth that enables you to bear with old age. For the rich, it is said, have many consolations.

True, he said, they will not believe me; and they are partly right, though not so right as they suppose. There is great truth in the reply of Themistocles to the Seriphian who tauntingly told him, that his reputation was due not to himself, but to his country: 'I should not have become famous if I had been a native of Seriphus; neither would you, if you had been an Athenian.' And to those who, not being rich, are impatient with old age, it may be said with equal justice, that while on the one hand, a good man cannot be altogether cheerful with old age and poverty combined, so on the other, no wealth can ever make a bad man at peace with himself.

But has your property, Cephalus, been chiefly inherited or acquired?

b    You want to know how I have acquired it, Socrates? Why, in the conduct of money matters, I stand midway between my grandfather and my father. My grandfather, whose name I bear, inherited nearly as much property as I now possess, and increased it until it was many times as large; while my father Lysanias brought it down even below what it now is. For my part, I shall be content to leave it to these my sons not less, but if anything rather larger, than it was when it came into my hands.

I asked the question, I said, because you seemed to me to be not very fond of money—
c    which is generally the case with those who have not made it themselves; whereas those who have made it, are attached to it twice as much as other people. For just as poets love their own works, and fathers their own children, in the same way those who have created a fortune value their money, not merely for its uses, like other persons, but because it is their own production. This makes them moreover disagreeable companions, because they will praise nothing but riches.

It is true, he replied.

d    Indeed it is, said I. But let me ask you one more question. What do you think is the greatest advantage that you have derived from being wealthy?

If I mention it, he replied, I shall perhaps get few persons to agree with me. Be assured, Socrates, that when a man is nearly persuaded that he is going to die, he feels alarmed and concerned about things which never affected him before. Until then he has laughed at the stories concerning those in Hades, which tell us that he
e    who has done wrong here must suffer for it there; but now his mind is tormented with a fear that these stories may possibly be true. And either owing to the infirmity of old age, or be-

cause he is now nearer to what happens there, he has a clearer insight into those mysteries. However that may be, he becomes full of misgiving and apprehension, and sets himself to the task of calculating and reflecting whether he has done any wrong to any one. Hereupon, if he finds his life full of unjust deeds, he is apt to    331
awaken from sleep in terror, as children do, and he lives haunted by gloomy anticipations. But for the man who is conscious of no unjust deeds sweet hope is always present, that 'kind nurse of old age,' as Pindar calls it. For indeed, Socrates, those are beautiful words of his, in which he says of the man who has lived a just and holy life,

'Sweet Hope is his companion, cheering his heart,
  the nurse of age; Hope, which, more than anything else,
  steers the capricious will of mortal men.

There is really a wonderful truth in this description. And it is this consideration, I think, that makes riches chiefly valuable, not    b
for everybody, but for the decent and orderly person. Not to have cheated or lied to anyone against one's will, not to leave for the other world in fear, owing sacrifices to a god or money to a man, to this wealth contributes a great deal. There are many other uses as well. But after weighing them all separately, Socrates, I am inclined to consider this service as anything but the least important which riches can render to a sensible man.

You have spoken admirably, Cephalus. But    c
are we to say that justice is this thing, namely to speak the truth and to give back what one has taken from another? Or is it possible for actions of this very nature to be sometimes just and sometimes unjust? For example, every one, I suppose, would admit, that, if a man, while in the possession of his senses, were to place dangerous weapons in the hands of a friend, and afterwards in a fit of madness to demand them back, such a deposit ought not to be restored, and that his friend would not be a just man if he

either returned the weapons, or consented to tell the whole truth to someone in such a condition.

d      You are right, he replied.

Then it is no true definition of justice to say that it consists in speaking the truth and restoring what one has received.

But it is indeed, Socrates, said Polemarchus, interrupting, at least if we are at all to believe Simonides.

Very well, said Cephalus, I will just leave the discussion to you. It is time for me to attend to the sacrifices.

Then Polemarchus inherits your share in it, does he not? I asked.

Certainly, he replied, with a smile; and immediately withdrew to the sacrifices.

e      Answer me then, I proceeded, you that are the heir to the discussion: What do you maintain to be the correct account of justice, as given by Simonides?

That to restore to each man what is his due, is just. To me it seems that Simonides is right in giving this account of the matter.

Well, certainly it is not an easy matter to disbelieve Simonides: for he is a wise and inspired man. But what he means by his words, you, Polemarchus, may perhaps understand, though I do not. It is clear that he does not mean what we were saying just now, namely, that property given by one person in trust to another, is to be returned to the donor, if he asks for it in a state of insanity. And yet I conclude that property given in trust is due to the truster. Is it not?

332      Yes, it is.

But, when the person who asks for it is not in his senses, it must not be returned on any account, must it?

True, it must not.

Then it would seem that Simonides means something different from this, when he says that it is just to restore what is due.

Most certainly he does, he replied: for he declares that the debt of friend to friend is to do good to one another, and not harm.

I understand: the person who returns money to a depositor does not restore what is due, if the repayment on the one side, and the receipt on the other, prove to be injurious, and if the two parties are friends. Is not this, according to you, the meaning of Simonides?

Certainly it is.

Well, must we restore to our enemies whatever happens to be due to them?

Yes, no doubt, what is due to them; and the debt of an enemy to an enemy is, I suppose, harm—because harm is what is fitting.

So then it would seem that Simonides, after the manner of poets, employed a riddle to describe the nature of justice: for apparently he thought that justice consisted in rendering to each man that which is appropriate to him, which he called his due. What do you think? Suppose that subsequently someone had asked him the following question: 'That being the case, Simonides, what due and appropriate thing is rendered by the art called medicine, and what are the recipients?' What do you think he would have answered us?

Obviously he would have said that bodies are the recipients, and drugs, meats, and drinks, the things rendered.

And what due and appropriate thing is rendered by the art called cookery, and what are the recipients?

Seasoning is the thing rendered; dishes are the recipients.

Good; then what is the thing rendered by the art that we are to call justice, and who are the recipients?

If we are to be at all guided by our previous statements, Socrates, assistance and harm are the things rendered, friends and enemies the recipients.

Then, by justice, Simonides means doing good to our friends and harm to our enemies, does he?

I think so.

Now, in cases of illness, who is best able to do good to friends and harm to enemies, with reference to health and disease?

A physician.

And, on a voyage, who is best able to do good to friends and harm to enemies, with reference to the perils of the sea?

A pilot.

Well, in what transaction, and with reference to what object, is the just man best able to help his friends and injure his enemies?

In the transactions of war, I imagine, as the ally of the former, and the antagonist of the latter.

Good. You will grant, my dear Polemarchus, that a physician is useless to persons in sound health.

Certainly.

And a pilot to persons on shore.

Yes.

Is the just man, also, useless to those who are not at war?

I do not quite think that.

Then justice is useful in time of peace too, is it?

It is.

And so is farming, is it not?

Yes.

That is to say, as a means of acquiring the fruits of the earth.

Yes.

And further, the shoemaker's art is also useful, is it not?

Yes.

As a means of acquiring shoes, I suppose you will say.

Certainly.

Well then, of what does justice, according to you, promote the use or acquisition in time of peace?

Of contracts, Socrates.

And by contracts do you understand partnerships, or something different?

Partnerships, certainly.

Then is it the just man, or the skillful checkers-player, that makes a good and useful partner in playing checkers?

The checkers-player.

Well, in bricklaying and stone masonry is the just man a more useful and a better partner than the regular builder?

By no means.

Well then, in what partnership is the just man superior to the harp-player, in the sense in which the harp-player is a better partner than the just man in playing music?

In a money-partnership, I think.

Excepting perhaps, Polemarchus, when the object is to lay out money—as when a horse is to be bought or sold by the partners—in which case, I imagine, the horse-dealer is better. Is he not?

Apparently he is.

And again, when a ship is to be bought or sold, the ship-builder or pilot is better.

It would seem so.

That being the case, when does the opportunity arrive for that joint use of silver or gold, in which the just man is more useful than any one else?

When you want to place your money in trust and have it safe, Socrates.

That is to say, when it is to be deposited, and not to be put to any use?

Just so.

So that justice can only be usefully applied to money when the money is useless?

It looks like it.

In the same way, when you want to keep a pruning-hook, justice is useful whether you be in partnership or not; but when you want to use it, justice gives place to the art of the vine dresser?

Apparently.

Do you also maintain that, when you want to keep a shield or a lyre without using them, justice is useful; but when you want to use them, you require the art of the soldier or of the musician?

I must.

And so of everything else: justice is useless when a thing is in use, but useful when it is out of use?

So it would seem.

Then, my friend, justice cannot be a very valuable thing if it is only useful as applied to things useless. But let us continue the inquiry thus. Is not the man who is most expert in dealing blows in an encounter, whether in boxing or otherwise, also most expert in parrying blows?

Certainly.

Is it not also true that whoever is expert in repelling a disease, and evading its attack, is also extremely expert in producing it in others?

334     I think so.

And undoubtedly a man is well able to guard an army, when he has also a talent for stealing the enemy's plans and all his other operations.

Certainly.

That is to say, a man can guard expertly whatever he can thieve expertly.

So it would seem.

Hence, if the just man is expert in guarding money, he is also expert in stealing it.

I confess the argument points that way.

Then, to all appearance, it turns out that the
b     just man is a kind of thief—something which you have probably learnt from Homer, with whom Autolycus, the maternal grandfather of Odysseus, is a favorite, because, as the poet says, he outdid all men in thievishness and perjury. Justice therefore, according to you, Homer, and Simonides, appears to be a kind of art of stealing, whose object, however, is to help one's friends and injure one's enemies. Was not this your meaning?

Most certainly it was not, he replied; but I no longer know what I did mean. However, it is still my opinion that it is justice to help one's
c     friends, and hurt one's enemies.

Should you describe a man's friends as those who *seem* to him to be, or those who really are, honest men, though they may not seem so? And do you define a man's enemies on the same principle?

I should certainly expect a man to love all whom he thinks honest, and hate all whom he thinks wicked.

But do not people make mistakes in this matter, and imagine many persons to be honest who are not really honest, and many wicked who are not really wicked?

They do.

Then to such persons the good are enemies, and the bad are friends, are they not?

Certainly they are.                                                          d

And, notwithstanding this, it is just for such persons at such times to help the wicked, and to injure the good.

Apparently it is.

Yet surely the good are just, and injustice is foreign to their nature.

True.

Then, according to your argument, it is just to do harm to those who commit no injustice.

Heaven forbid, Socrates: for that looks like a wicked speech.

Then it is just, said I, to injure the unjust and to assist the just.

That is evidently better than the former.                         e

In that case, Polemarchus, the result will be that, in those numerous instances in which people have thoroughly mistaken their men, it is just for these mistaken persons to injure their friends, because in their eyes they are wicked; and to help their enemies, because they are good. And thus our statement will be in direct opposition to the meaning which we assigned to Simonides.

That consequence certainly follows, he replied. But let us change our positions: for very probably our definition of friend and enemy was incorrect.

What was our definition, Polemarchus?

That a friend is one who seems to be an honest man.

And what is to be our new definition?

That a friend is one who not only seems to  335
be, but really is, an honest man; whereas the man who seems to be, but is not honest, is not really a friend, but only seems one. And I define an enemy on the same principle.

Then, by this way of speaking, the good man will, in all likelihood, be a friend, and the wicked an enemy.

Yes.

Then you would have us attach to the idea of justice more than we at first included in it, when we called it just to do good to our friend and bad to our enemy. We are now, if I understand you, to make an addition to this, and render it thus: It is just to do good to our friend if he is a good man, and to hurt our enemy if he is a bad man. Precisely so, he replied; I think that this would be a right statement.

Now is it the act of a just man, I asked, to hurt anybody?

Certainly it is, he replied; that is to say, it is his duty to hurt those who are both wicked, and enemies of his.

Are horses made better, or worse, by being hurt?

Worse.

Worse with reference to the excellence of dogs, or that of horses?

That of horses.

Are dogs in the same way made worse by being hurt, with reference to the excellence of dogs, and not of horses?

Unquestionably they are.

And must we not, on the same principle, assert, my friend, that men, by being hurt, are lowered in the scale of virtue or human excellence?

Indeed we must.

But is not justice a virtue?

Undoubtedly it is.

And therefore, my friend, those men who are hurt necessarily become more unjust.

So it would seem.

Can musicians, by the art of music, make men unmusical?

They cannot.

Can riding-masters, by the art of riding, make men bad riders?

No.

But if so, can the just by justice make men unjust? In short, can the good by goodness make men bad?

No, it is impossible.

True; for, if I am not mistaken, it is the work, not of warmth, but of its opposite, to make things cold.

Yes.

And it is the work not of drought, but of its opposite, to make things wet.

Certainly.

Then it is the work not of good, but of its opposite, to hurt.

Apparently it is.

Well, is the just man good?

Certainly he is.

Then, Polemarchus, it is the work, not of the just man, but of his opposite, the unjust man, to hurt either friend or any other creature.

You seem to me to be perfectly right, Socrates.

Hence if any one asserts that it is just to render to every man his due, and if he understands by this, that what is due on the part of the just man is injury to his enemies, and assistance to his friends, the assertion is that of an unwise man. For what was said is untrue: because we have discovered that, in no instance, is it just to injure anybody.

I grant you are right.

Then you and I will make common cause against any one who shall attribute this to Simonides, or Bias, or Pittacus, or any other wise and highly favored man.

Very good, said he; I, for one, am quite ready to take my share of the fighting.

Do you know who I think is the author of this saying, that it is just to help our friends, and hurt our enemies?

To whom?

I attribute it to Periander, or Perdiccas, or Xerxes, or Ismenias the Theban, or some other rich man who thought himself very powerful.

You are perfectly right.

Well, but as we have again failed to discover the true definition of justice and the just, what other definition can one propose?

While we were still in the middle of our discussion, Thrasymachus was, more than once, bent on interrupting the conversation with objections; but he was checked on each occasion by those who sat by, who wished to hear the argument out. However, when I had made this last remark and we had come to a pause, he could restrain himself no longer, but, gathering himself up like a wild beast, he sprang upon us,

as if he would tear us in pieces. I and Polemarchus were terrified and startled, while

c   Thrasymachus, raising his voice to the company, said, What nonsense has possessed you
and Polemarchus all this time, Socrates? And
why do you play the fool together, submitting
to one another? No, if you really wish to understand what justice is, do not confine yourself to
asking questions, and making a display of
refuting the answers that are returned—for you
are aware that it is easier to ask questions than
to answer them; but give us an answer also
yourself, and tell us what you assert justice to

d   be, and do not answer me by defining it as the
obligatory, or the advantageous, or the profitable, or the lucrative, or the expedient; but
whatever your definition may be, let it be clear
and precise: for I will not accept your answer, if
you talk such trash as that.

When I heard this speech, I was astounded,
and gazed at the speaker in terror; and I think if
I had not set eyes on him before he eyed me, I
should have been struck dumb. But, as it was,
when he began to be exasperated by the conversation, I had looked him in the face first—so

e   that I was enabled to reply to him, and said with
a slight tremble: Thrasymachus, do not be hard
upon us. If I and Polemarchus are making mistakes in our examination of the subject, be
assured that the error is involuntary. You do not
suppose that, if we were looking for a piece of
gold, we would ever willingly give way to one
another in the search as to spoil the chance of
finding it; and therefore, do not suppose that, in
seeking for justice, which is a thing more precious than many pieces of gold, we should give
way to one another so weakly as you describe,

337  instead of doing our very best to bring it to
light. You, my friend, may think so, if you
choose; but my belief is that the subject is
beyond our powers. Surely then we might very
reasonably expect to be pitied, not harshly
treated, by such clever men as you.

When he had heard my reply, he burst out
laughing very scornfully, and said: O Hercules! here is an instance of that irony which

Socrates affects. I knew how it would be, and
warned the company that you would refuse
to answer, and would be ironic, and do any
thing rather than reply, if any one asked you a
question.

Yes, you are a wise man, Thrasymachus, I
replied; and therefore you were well aware       b
that, if you asked a person what factors make
the number 12, and at the same time warned
him thus: 'Please do not tell me that 12 is twice
6, or 3 times 4, or 6 times 2, or 4 times 3: for I
will not take such nonsense from you;' you
were well aware, I dare say, that no one would
give an answer to such an inquirer. But suppose the person replied to you thus: 'Thrasymachus, explain yourself; am I to be precluded
from all these answers which you have denounced? What, my good sir! even if one of
these is the real answer, am I still to be precluded from giving it, and am I to make a state-    c
ment that is at variance with the truth? or what
is your meaning?' What reply should you
make to this inquiry?

Oh, indeed! he exclaimed; as if the two
cases were alike!

There is nothing to prevent their being so, I
replied. However, suppose they are not alike;
still if one of these answers seems the right one
to the person questioned, do you think that our
forbidding it, or not, will affect his determination to give the answer which he believes to be
the correct one?

Do you not mean that this is what you are
going to do? You will give one of the answers
on which I have put a veto?

It would not surprise me if I did; supposing
I thought right to do so, after examination.       d

Then, what if I produce another answer on
the subject of justice, unlike those I denounced, and superior to them all? What punishment do you think you merit?

Simply the punishment which it is proper
for the non-knower to submit to; and that is, I
suppose, to be instructed by those who know.
This, then, is the punishment which I, among
others, deserve to suffer.

Really you are a pleasant person, he replied. But, besides being instructed, you must make me a payment.

I will, when I have any money, I replied.

But you have, said Glaucon. So, as far as money is a consideration, speak on, Thrasymachus. We will all contribute for Socrates.

e

Oh, to be sure! said he; in order that Socrates, I suppose, may pursue his usual plan of refusing to answer himself, while he criticizes and refutes the answers given by other people.

My excellent friend, said I, how can an answer be given by a person who, in the first place, does not, and confesses he does not, know what to answer; and who, in the next place, if he has any thoughts upon the subject,

338  has been forbidden by a man who is not thoughtless to say what he believes? No, it is more fitting that you should be the speaker; because you profess to know the subject, and to have something to say. Therefore do not decline; but gratify me by answering, and do not grudge to instruct Glaucon and the rest of the company as well.

When I had said this, Glaucon and the others begged him to comply. Now it was evident that Thrasymachus was eager to speak, in order that he might gain glory, because he thought himself in possession of a very fine answer. But he affected to contend for my

b  being the respondent. At last he gave in, and then said: This here then is the wisdom of Socrates! He will not give instruction himself, but he goes about and learns from others, without even showing gratitude for their lessons.

As for my learning from others, Thrasymachus, I replied, there you speak truth; but it is false of you to say that I pay no gratitude in return. I *do* pay all I can; and, as I have no money, I can only give praise. How readily I do this, if in my judgment a person speaks well, you will very soon find, when you make your answer: for I expect *you* to speak well.

c  Then listen, said he. I say that justice is simply the interest of the stronger. Well, why do you not praise me? No, you refuse.

Not so, I replied; I am only waiting to understand your meaning, which at present I do not see. You say that the interest of the stronger is just. What in the world do you mean by this, Thrasymachus? You do not, I presume, mean anything like this, that, if Polydamas, the athlete, is stronger than we are, and it is for his interest to eat beef in order to strengthen his body, such food is for the interest of us weaker men, and therefore is just.

d

You are disgusting, Socrates; you take up my speech in such a way as to damage it most easily.

No, no, my excellent friend; but state your meaning more clearly.

So you are not aware, he continued, that some cities are ruled by a tyrant, and others by a democracy, and others by an aristocracy?

Of course I am.

In every city does not superior strength reside in the ruling body?

Certainly it does.

And further, each regime has its laws framed to suit its own interests: a democracy making democratic laws, a tyrant tyrannical laws, and so on. Now by this procedure these regimes have pronounced that what is for the interest of themselves is just for their subjects; and whoever deviates from this, is chastised by them as guilty of illegality and injustice. Therefore, my good sir, my meaning is, that in all cities the same thing, namely, the interest of the established regime, is just. And superior strength, I presume, is to be found on the side of regime. So that the conclusion of right reasoning is that the same thing, namely, the interest of the stronger, is everywhere just.

e

339

Now I understand your meaning, and I will endeavor to make out whether it is true or not. So then, Thrasymachus, you yourself in your answer have defined justice as interest, though you forbade my giving any such reply. To be sure, you have made an addition, and describe it as the interest of the stronger.

Yes, quite a trifling addition, perhaps.

b

It remains to be seen, whether it is an

important one. We need to examine whether you spoke truly. For we both admit that justice is in harmony with interest; but you lengthen this into the assertion that justice is the interest of the stronger—and I do not know about that. Therefore we must certainly examine it.

Please do so.

It shall be done. Be so good as to answer this question. You no doubt also maintain that it is just to obey the rulers?

I do.

c  Are the rulers infallible in every city, or are they liable to make a few mistakes?

No doubt they are liable to make mistakes.

And therefore, when they undertake to frame laws, is their work sometimes rightly, and sometimes wrongly done?

I should suppose so.

Do 'rightly' and 'wrongly' mean, respectively, legislating for, and against, their own interests? Or how do you state it?

Just as you do.

And do you maintain that whatever has been enacted by the rulers must be obeyed by their subjects, and that this is justice?

d  Unquestionably I do.

Then, according to your argument, it is not only just to do what makes for the interest of the stronger, but also to do what runs counter to his interest, in other words, the opposite of the former.

What are you saying?

What *you* say, I believe. But let us examine the point more thoroughly. Has it not been admitted that, when the rulers enjoin certain acts upon their subjects, they are sometimes thoroughly mistaken as to what is best for themselves; and that, whatever is enjoined by them, it is just for their subjects to obey? Has not this been admitted?

Yes, I think so, he replied.

Then let me tell you, that you have also

e  admitted the justice of doing what runs counter to the interest of the ruling and stronger body on every occasion when this body unintentionally enjoins what is injurious to itself, so long as you maintain that it is just for the subjects to obey, in every instance, the injunctions of their rulers. In that case, O most wise Thrasymachus, must it not follow of course, that it is just to act in direct opposition to what you said? For, obviously, it is enjoined upon the weaker to do what is disadvantageous to the stronger.

Yes, indeed, Socrates, said Polemarchus;  340 that is perfectly clear.

No doubt, retorted Cleitophon, if you appear as a witness in Socrates' behalf.

What do we want witnesses for? said Polemarchus. Thrasymachus himself admits that the rulers sometimes enjoin what is bad for themselves; and that it is just for their subjects to obey such injunctions.

No, Polemarchus; Thrasymachus laid it down that to do what the rulers command is just.

Yes, Cleitophon; and he also laid it down  b that the interest of the stronger is just. And having laid down these two positions, he further admitted that the stronger party sometimes orders its weaker subjects to do what is disadvantageous to its own interests. And the consequence of these admissions is, that what is for the interest of the stronger will be not a bit more just than what is not for his interest.

But, said Cleitophon, by the interest of the stronger he meant, what the stronger conceived to be for his own interest. His position was, that this must be done by the weaker, and that this is the notion of justice.

That was not what he said, replied Polemarchus.

It does not matter, Polemarchus, said I; if  c Thrasymachus chooses to speak this way now, let us make no objection to his doing so.

Tell me then, Thrasymachus, was this the definition you meant to give of justice, that it is what seems to the stronger to be the interest of the stronger, whether it be really for his interest or not? Shall we take that as your account of it?

Certainly not, he replied; do you think I

should call a man who is mistaken, at the time of his mistake, the stronger?

Why I thought that you said as much, when you admitted that rulers are not infallible, but do really commit some mistakes.

d   You are a quibbler, Socrates; do you call, now, that man a physician who is in error about the treatment of the sick, with strict reference to his error? Or do you call another an accountant, who makes a mistake in a calculation, at the time of his mistake, and with reference to that mistake? We say, to be sure, in so many words that the physician was in error, and the accountant or the writer was in error;

e   but in fact each of these, I imagine, in so far as he is what we call him, never falls into error. So that, to speak with precise accuracy, since you require such preciseness of language, no craftsman errs. For it is through a failure of knowledge that a man errs, and to that extent he is no craftsman; so that whether as craftsman, or wise man, or ruler, no one errs while he actually is what he professes to be; although everyone would say that such a physician was in error, or such a ruler was in error. In this

341  sense I would have you to understand my own recent answer. But the statement, if expressed with perfect accuracy, would be that a ruler, in so far as he is a ruler, never errs, and so long as this is the case, he enacts what is best for himself, and that this is what the subject has to do. Therefore, as I began with saying, I call it just to do what is for the interest of the stronger.

Very good, Thrasymachus; you think me a quibbler, do you?

Yes, a thorough quibbler.

Do you think that I put you those questions with a mischievous intent to damage your position in the argument?

I am quite sure of it. However you shall

b   gain nothing by it; for you shall neither injure me by taking me unawares, nor will you be able to overpower me by open argument.

I should not think of attempting it, my excellent friend! But that nothing of this kind

may occur again, tell me whether you employ the words 'ruler' and 'stronger' in the popular sense of them, or with the precise meaning of which you were speaking just now, when you say that it is just for the weaker to do what is for the interest of the ruler as being the stronger.

I mean a ruler in the strictest sense of the word. So now try your powers of quibbling and mischief; I ask for no mercy. But your attempts will be ineffectual.

Why, do you suppose I should be so mad as   c
to attempt to shave a lion, or play off quibbles on a Thrasymachus?

At any rate you tried it just now, though you failed utterly.

Enough of this banter, I replied. Tell me this: is the physician of whom you spoke as being strictly a physician, a maker of money, or a healer of the sick? Take care you speak of the *real* physician.

A healer of the sick.

And what of a pilot? Is the true pilot a sailor or a commander of sailors?

A commander of sailors.

There is no need, I imagine, to take into   d
account his being on board the ship, nor should he be called a sailor: for it is not in virtue of his being on board that he has the name of pilot, but in virtue of his art and of his rule over the sailors.

True.

Has not each of these persons an interest of his own?

Certainly.

And is it not the proper end of their art to seek and procure what is for the interest of each of them?

It is.

Have the arts severally any other interest to pursue than their own highest perfection?

What does your question mean?

Why, if you were to ask me whether it is   e
sufficient for a man's body to be a body, or whether it stands in need of something addi-

tional, I should say, Certainly it does. To this fact the discovery of the healing art is due, because the body is defective, and it is not enough for it to be a body. Therefore the art of medicine has been devised to provide the body with advantageous things. Should I be right, do you think, in so expressing myself, or not?

You would be right.

342    Well then, is the art of medicine itself defective, or does any art whatever require a certain additional virtue: as eyes require sight, and ears hearing, so that these organs need a certain art which shall investigate and provide what is conducive to these ends. Is there, I ask, any defectiveness in an art as such, so that every art should require another art to consider its interests, and this other provisional art a

b    third, with a similar function, and so on, without limit? Or will it investigate its own interest? Or is it unnecessary either for itself, or for any other art, to inquire into the appropriate remedy for its own defects because there are no defects or faults in any art, and because it is not the duty of an art to seek the interests of anything save that to which, as an art, it belongs, being itself free from hurt and blemish as a true art, so long as it continues strictly and in its integrity what it is? View the question according to the strict meaning of terms, as we agreed. Is it so or otherwise?

Apparently it is so, he replied.

c    Then the art of healing does not consider the interest of the art of healing, but the interest of the body.

Yes.

Nor horsemanship what is good for horsemanship, but for horses: nor does any other art seek its own interest—for it has no wants—but the good of that to which as an art it belongs.

Apparently it is so.

Well, but you will grant, Thrasymachus, that an art rules and is stronger than that of which it is the art.

He assented, with great reluctance, to this proposition.

Then no science or knowledge investigates or orders the interest of the stronger, but the interest of the weaker, its subject.

To this also he at last assented, though he attempted to show fight about it. After gaining his admission, I proceeded: Then is it not also true, that no physician, in so far as he is a physician, considers or orders what is for the physician's interest, but that all seek the good of their patients? For we have agreed that a physician strictly so called, is a ruler of bodies, and not a maker of money, have we not?

He allowed that we had.

And that a pilot strictly so called is a commander of sailors, and not a sailor?

We have.                                                                                    e

Then this kind of pilot and commander will not seek and order the pilot's interest, but that of the sailor and the subordinate.

He reluctantly gave his assent.

And thus, Thrasymachus, all who are in any place of ruling, in so far as they are rulers, neither consider nor order their own interest, but that of the subjects for whom they exercise their craft; and in all that they do or say, they act with an exclusive view to *them,* and to what is good and proper for *them.*

When we had arrived at this stage of the    343 discussion, and it had become evident to all that the explanation of justice was completely reversed, Thrasymachus, instead of making any answer, said,

Tell me, Socrates, do you have a wet-nurse?

Why? I rejoined; had you not better answer my questions than make inquiries of that sort?

Why because she leaves you to drivel, and omits to wipe your nose when you require it, so that in consequence of her neglect you cannot even distinguish between sheep and shepherd.

For what particular reason do you think so?

Because you think that shepherds and    b herdsmen regard the good of their sheep and of their oxen, and fatten them and take care of them with other views than to benefit their masters and themselves; and you actually imagine that the rulers in cities, those I mean who are really rulers, are otherwise minded towards their subjects than as one would feel towards sheep, or that they think of anything else by night and by day than how they may secure their own advantage. And you are so far c wrong in your notions respecting justice and injustice, the just and the unjust, that you do not know that the former is really the good of another, that is to say the interest of the stronger and of the ruler, but your own loss, where you are the subordinate and the servant; whereas injustice is the reverse, ruling those that are really simpleminded and just, so that they, as subjects, do what is for the interest of the unjust man who is stronger than they, and promote his happiness by their services, but d not their own in the least degree. You may see by the following considerations, my most simple Socrates, that a just man everywhere has the worst of it, compared with an unjust man.

In the first place, in their mutual dealings, wherever a just man enters into partnership with an unjust man, you will find that at the dissolution of the partnership the just man never has more than the unjust man, but always less. Then again in their dealings with the city, when there is a property-tax to pay, the just man will pay more and the unjust less, on the same amount of property; and when there is anything e to receive, the one gets nothing, while the other makes great gains. And whenever either of them holds any ruling office, if the just man suffers no other loss, at least his private affairs fall into disorder through want of attention to them, while his principles forbid his deriving any benefit from the public money; and besides this, it is his fate to offend his friends and acquaintances every time that he refuses to serve them at the expense of justice. But with the unjust man every thing is reversed. I am speaking of the case I mentioned just now, of

an unjust man who has the power to over-reach.    344 To him you must direct your attention, if you wish to judge how much more profitable it is to a man's own self to be unjust than to be just. And you will learn this truth with the greatest ease, if you turn your attention to the most consummate form of injustice, which, while it makes the wrong-doer most happy, makes those who are wronged, and will not retaliate, most miserable. This form is a tyranny, which proceeds not by small degrees, but by wholesale, in its open or fraudulent appropriation of the property of others, whether it be sacred or profane, public or private; perpetrating offenses, if a person commits a part of the offense    b and is found out, he becomes liable to a penalty and incurs deep disgrace: for partial offenders in this class of crimes are called sacrilegious, kidnappers, burglars, thieves, and robbers. But when a man not only seizes the property of his fellow-citizens but captures and enslaves their persons also, instead of those dishonorable titles he is called happy and highly favored, not    c only by the men of his own city, but also by all others who hear of the comprehensive injustice which he has wrought. For when people abuse injustice, they do so because they are afraid, not of committing it, but of suffering it. Thus it is, Socrates, that injustice, realized on an adequate scale, is a stronger, a freer, and a more lordly thing than justice; and as I said in the beginning, justice is the interest of the stronger; injustice, a thing profitable and advantageous to oneself.

When he had made this speech, Thrasy-    d machus had a mind to take his departure, after deluging our ears like a bath-man with this copious and unbroken flood of words. Our companions however would not let him go, but obliged him to stay and answer for his arguments. I myself also was especially urgent in my entreaties, exclaiming, Really, my good Thrasymachus, after flinging at us such a speech as this, do you have it in mind to take your leave, before you have satisfactorily taught us, or learnt yourself, whether your argument is right or wrong? Do you think you are undertaking to settle some insignificant question, and not the principles on which each of us must conduct his life in order to lead the most profitable existence?

What else am I supposed to think? said Thrasymachus.

So it seems, I said, or else that you are quite indifferent about us, and feel no concern whether we shall live the better or the worse for our ignorance of what you profess to know. But please, my good sir, try to impart your knowledge to us also—any benefit you confer on such a large party as we are will surely be no bad investment. For I tell you plainly for my own part that I am not convinced, and that I do not believe that injustice is more profitable than justice, even if it be let alone and suffered to work its will unchecked. On the contrary, my good sir, let there be an unjust man, and let him have full power to practice injustice, either by evading detection or by overpowering opposition, still I am not convinced that such a course is more profitable than justice. This, perhaps, is the feeling of some others amongst us, as well as mine. Then do convince us satisfactorily, my highly-gifted friend, that we are not well advised in valuing justice above injustice.

But how, said he, can I persuade you? If you are not convinced by my recent statements, what more can I do for you? must I take the speech and thrust it into your soul?

You should not do that; but in the first place, abide by what you say, or if you change your ground, change it openly without deceiving us. As it is, Thrasymachus—for we must not yet take leave of our former investigations—you see that having first defined the meaning of the true physician, you did not think it necessary afterwards to adhere strictly to the true shepherd. On the contrary, you suppose him to feed his sheep, in so far as he is a shepherd, not with

an eye to what is best for the flock, but, like a guest about to be feasted, with an eye to the feasting, or else to their sale, like a money-maker, and not like a shepherd. Whereas the only concern of the shepherd's art is, I presume, how it shall procure what is best for *that,* of which it is the appointed guardian: since as far as concerns its own perfection, sufficient provision is made, I suppose, for that, so long as it is all that is implied in its title; and so I confess I thought we were obliged just now to admit that every regime, in so far as it is a regime, looks solely to the advantage of that which is ruled and tended by it, whether that regime be of a public or a private nature. But what is your opinion? do you think that the rulers in cities, who really rule, do so willingly?

No, I do not *think* it, I am sure of it.

But, Thrasymachus, what about other kinds of regime, do you not observe that no one is willing to rule, if he can help it, but that they all ask to be paid on the assumption that the advantages of their regime will not accrue to themselves, but to the governed? For answer me this question: Do we not say without hesitation, that every art is distinguished from other arts by having a distinctive capacity? Be so good, my dear sir, as not to answer contrary to your opinion, or we shall make no progress.

Yes, that is what distinguishes it.

And does not each of them provide us with some special and peculiar benefit? the art of healing, for example, giving us health, that of piloting safety at sea, and so on?

Certainly.

Then is there not an art of wages which provides us with wages, this being its proper faculty? Or do you call the art of healing and that of piloting identical? Or, if you choose to employ strict definitions as you engaged to do, the fact of a man's regaining his health while acting as a pilot, through the beneficial effects of the sea-voyage, would not make you call the art of the pilot a healing art, would it?

Certainly not.

Nor would you so describe the art of wages, I think, supposing a person to keep his health while in the receipt of wages.

No.

Well then, would you call the physician's art a mercenary art, if fees be taken for medical attendance?

No.

c  Did we not allow that the benefit of each art was peculiar to itself?

Be it so.

Then whatever benefit accrues in common to all craftsmen is clearly derived from a common use of some one and the same thing.

So it would seem.

And we further maintain, that if these craftsmen are benefited by earning wages, they owe it to their use of the wage-earning craft.

He reluctantly assented.

d  Then this advantage, the receipt of pay, does not come to each from his own art, but, strictly considered, the art of healing produces health, and the art of wages produces pay; the art of house-building produces a house, while the art of wages follows it and produces pay; and so of all the rest: each works its own work, and benefits that which is its appointed object. If, however, an art be practiced without pay, does the craftsman derive any benefit from his art?

Apparently not.

e  Does he also confer no benefit, when he works for nothing?

I suppose he does confer benefit.

So far then, Thrasymachus, we see clearly, that an art or a regime never provides that which is profitable for itself, but as we said some time ago, it provides and orders what is profitable for the subject, looking to his interest who is the weaker, and not to the interest of the stronger. It was for these reasons that I said just now, my dear Thrasymachus, that no one will voluntarily take office, or assume the duty

of correcting the disorders of others, but that  347 all ask wages for the work, because one who is to prosper in his art never practices or prescribes what is best for himself, but only what is best for the subject, so long as he acts within the limits of his art; and on these grounds, apparently, wages must be given to make men willing to hold office, in the shape of money or honor, or of punishment, in case of refusal.

What do you mean, Socrates? asked Glaucon. I understand two out of the three kinds of wages; but, what the punishment is, and how you could describe it as playing the part of wages, I do not comprehend.

Then you do not comprehend, I said, the wages of the best men, which induce the most virtuous to hold office, when they consent  b to do so. Do you not know that to be honor-loving and money-loving is considered a disgrace, and really is a disgrace?

I do.

For this reason, then, good men will not consent to rule, either for the sake of money or for that of honor: for they neither wish to get the name of hirelings by openly exacting hire for their duties, nor of thieves by using their power to obtain it secretly; nor yet will they take office for the sake of honor, for they are not honor-  c loving. Therefore compulsion and the fear of a penalty must be brought to bear upon them, to make them consent to hold office—which is probably the reason why it is thought shameful to accept power willingly without waiting to be compelled. Now the heaviest of all penalties is to be ruled by a worse man, in case of one's own refusal to rule; and it is the fear of this, I believe, which induces virtuous men to take the posts of regime and when they do so, they enter upon their rulership, not with any idea of coming into a good thing, but as an unavoidable  d necessity, not expecting to enjoy themselves in it, but because they cannot find any person better or no worse than themselves, to whom they can commit it. For the probability is, that if there were a city composed of none but good men, it would be an object of competition to avoid the possession of power, just as now it is to obtain it; and then it would become clearly evident that it is not the nature of the genuine ruler to look to his own interest, but to that of the subject—so that every judicious man would choose to be the recipient of benefits, rather than to have the trouble of conferring them upon others. Therefore I will on no

e account concede to Thrasymachus that justice is the interest of the stronger. However we will resume this inquiry hereafter, for Thrasymachus now affirms that the life of the unjust man is better than the life of the just man; and this assertion seems to me of much greater importance than the other. Which side do you take, Glaucon? and which do you think the truer statement?

I for my part hold, he replied, that the life of the just man is the more advantageous.

348 Did you hear, I asked, what a long list of attractions Thrasymachus just now attributed to the life of the unjust man?

I did, but I am not convinced.

Should you then like us to convince him, if we can find any means of doing so, that what he says is not true?

Undoubtedly I should.

If then we adopt the plan of matching argument against argument, we enumerating all the advantages of being just, and Thrasymachus replying, and we again putting in a rejoinder:

b it will be necessary to count and measure the advantages which are claimed on both sides. And eventually we shall want a jury to give a verdict between us; but if we proceed in our inquiries, as we lately did, by the method of mutual agreement, we ourselves shall be both judges and advocates.

Precisely so.

Which plan, then, do you prefer?

The latter, he said.

Come then, Thrasymachus, said I, let us start from the beginning, and oblige us by answering: Do you assert that a perfect injus-

tice is more profitable than an equally perfect justice?

Most decidedly I do; and I have said why.  c

Well then, how do you describe them under another aspect? Probably you call one of them a virtue, and the other a vice?

Undoubtedly.

That is, justice a virtue, and injustice a vice?

A likely thing, my facetious friend, when I assert that injustice is profitable, and justice the reverse.

Then what do you say?

Just the contrary.

Do you call justice a vice?

No, but I call it very egregious good nature.

Then do you call injustice ill nature?  d

No, I call it good judgment.

Do you think, Thrasymachus, that the unjust are positively prudent and good?

Yes, those who are able to practice injustice on the complete scale, having the power to reduce whole cities and nations of men to subjection. You, perhaps, imagine that I am speaking of petty criminals, and I certainly allow that even deeds like theirs are profitable if they escape detection; but they are not worthy to be considered in comparison with those I have just mentioned.

I quite understand what you mean; but I did  e wonder at your ranking injustice under the heads of virtue and wisdom, and justice under the opposite.

Well, I do so rank them, without hesitation.

You have now taken up a more stubborn position, my friend, and it is no longer easy to know what to say. If after laying down the position that injustice is profitable, you had still admitted it to be a vice and a baseness, as some others do, we should have had an answer to give, speaking according to generally re-  349 ceived notions; but now it is plain enough that you will maintain it to be beautiful, and strong, and will ascribe to it all the qualities which we have been in the habit of ascribing to justice, seeing that you have actually ventured to rank it as a portion of virtue and of wisdom.

You divine most correctly, he said.

Nevertheless, I must not shrink from pursuing the inquiry and the argument, so long as I suppose that you are saying what you think: for if I am not mistaken, Thrasymachus, you are really not bantering now, but saying what you think to be the truth.

What difference does it make to you whether I think it true or not? Can you not assail the argument?

b    It makes none. But will you endeavor to answer me one more question? Do you think that a just man would wish to outdo another just man in anything?

Certainly not, for then he would not be so charmingly simple as he is.

Would a just man go beyond a just line of conduct?

No, not beyond that either.

But would he go beyond an unjust man without scruple, and think it just to do so, or would he not think it just?

He would think it just, and would not scruple to do it, but he would not be able.

That was not my question, but whether a

c    just man both resolves and desires to outdo an unjust man, but not beyond a just man?

Well, it is so.

But how is it with the unjust man? Would he take upon himself to outdo a just man and a just line of conduct?

Undoubtedly, when he takes upon himself to outdo all and in every thing.

Then will not the unjust man also outdo another unjust man and an unjust action, and smuggle that he may himself obtain more than any one else?

He will.

Then let us put it in this form: The just man goes not beyond his like, but his unlike; the

d    unjust man goes beyond both his like and his unlike?

Very well said.

And further, the unjust man is prudent and good, the just man is neither.

Well spoken again.

Does not the unjust man further resemble the wise and the good, whereas the just man does not resemble them?

Why, of course, a man of a certain character must resemble others of that character; whereas one who is of a different character will not resemble them.

Very good; then the character of each is identical with that of those whom he resembles.

Why, what else would you have?

Very well, Thrasymachus; do you call one man musical, and another unmusical?                    e

I do.

Which of them do you call sensible, and which foolish?

The musical man, of course, I call wise, and the unmusical, foolish.

Do you also say that wherein a man is sensible, in that he is good, and wherein foolish, bad?

Yes.

Do you speak in the same manner of a medical man?

I do.

Do you think then, my excellent friend, that a musician, when he is tuning a lyre, would wish to outdo a musician in the tightening or loosening of the strings, or would claim to get the better of him?

I do not.

Would he wish to get the better of an unmusical person?

Unquestionably he would.

How would a medical man act? would he    350 wish to go beyond a medical man or medical practice in a question of diet?

Certainly not.

But beyond an unprofessional man he would?

Yes.

Consider now, looking at every kind of knowledge and ignorance, whether you think that any knowledgeable man whatever would, by his own consent, choose to do or say more than another knowledgeable man, and not the same that one like himself would do in the same matter.

Well, perhaps the latter view is necessarily the true one.

b But what do you say to the ignorant person? would he not go beyond the knowledgeable and the unknowledgeable alike?

Perhaps.

And the knowledgeable person is wise?

Yes.

And the wise man is good.

Yes.

Then a good and a wise man will not wish to go beyond his like, but his unlike and opposite?

So it would seem.

But a bad and an ignorant man will go beyond both his like and his opposite.

Apparently.

Well then, Thrasymachus, does not our unjust man go beyond both his like and his unlike? was not that your statement?

It was.

c But the just man will not go beyond his like, but only beyond his unlike?

Yes.

Consequently the just man resembles the wise and the good, whereas the unjust man resembles the bad and the ignorant.

So it would seem.

But we agreed, you know, that the character of each of them is identical with the character of those whom he resembles.

We did.

Consequently we have made the discovery, that the just man is wise and good, and the unjust man ignorant and bad.

Thrasymachus had made all these admis-

sions, not in the easy manner in which I now d relate them, but reluctantly and after much resistance, in the course of which he perspired profusely, as it was hot weather to boot: on that occasion also I saw what I had never seen before—Thrasymachus blushing. But when we had thus mutually agreed that justice was a part of virtue and of wisdom, and injustice of vice and ignorance, I proceeded thus: Very good, we will consider this point settled; but we said, you know, that injustice was also strong. Do you not remember it, Thrasymachus?

I do, he replied; but for my part I am not satisfied with your last conclusions, and I know what I could say on the subject. But if I were to express my thoughts, I am sure you would say e that I was haranguing the people like a demagogue. Take your choice then; either allow me to say as much as I please, or if you prefer asking questions, do so; and I will do with you as we do with old women when they tell us stories: I will say 'Good,' and nod my head or shake it, as the occasion requires.

If so, do no violence to your own opinions.

Anything to please you, he said, as you will not allow me to speak. What else do you want?

Nothing, I assure you; but if you will do this, do so; and I will ask questions.

Proceed then.

Well then, I will repeat the question which I put to you just now, that our inquiry may be carried out continuously; namely, what sort of 351 a thing justice is compared with injustice. It was said, I think, that injustice is more powerful and stronger than justice; but now, seeing that justice is both wisdom and virtue, and injustice is ignorance, it may easily be shown, I imagine, that justice is likewise stronger than injustice. No one can now fail to see this. But I do not wish to settle the question in such a simple way, Thrasymachus, but I would investigate it in the following manner: Should you b admit that a city may be unjust, and that it may unjustly attempt to enslave other cities, and so succeed in so doing, and hold many in such slavery to itself?

Undoubtedly I should; and this will be more frequently done by the best city, that is, the one that is most completely unjust, than by any other.

I understand, I said, that this is your position. But the question which I wish to consider is, whether the city that becomes the mistress of another city, will have this power without the aid of justice, or whether justice will be indispensable to it.

c If, as you said just now, justice is wisdom, justice must lend her aid; but if it is as I said, injustice must lend hers.

I am quite delighted to find, Thrasymachus, that you are not content merely to nod and shake your head, but give exceedingly good answers.

I do it to indulge you.

You are very good; but indulge me so far as to say, whether you think that either a city, or an army, or a band of thieves or robbers, or any other body of men, pursuing certain unjust ends in common, could succeed in any enterprise if they were to deal unjustly with one another?

d Certainly not.

If they refrain from such conduct towards one another, will they not be more likely to succeed?

Yes, certainly.

Because, I presume, Thrasymachus, injustice breeds divisions and animosities and broils between man and man, while justice creates unanimity and friendship; does it not?

Be it so, he said, that I may not quarrel with you.

Truly I am very much obliged to you, my excellent friend; but tell me this: if the working of injustice is to implant hatred wherever it exists, will not the presence of it, whether among freemen or slaves, cause them to hate one another, and to form parties, and disable them from doing anything together?

e

Certainly.

Well, and if it exists in two persons, will they not quarrel and hate one another, and be enemies each to the other, and both to the just?

They will.

And supposing, my admirable friend, that injustice has taken up its residence in a single individual, will it lose its proper power, or retain it just the same?

We will say it retains it.

And does not its power appear to be of such a nature, as to make any subject in which it resides, whether it be city, or family, or army, or anything else whatsoever, unable to act unitedly, because of the divisions and quarrels it excites; and moreover hostile both to itself and to everything that opposes it, and to the just? Is it not so?

352

Certainly it is.

Then, if it appears in an individual also, it will produce all these its natural results: in the first place it will make him unable to act because of inward strife and division; in the next place, it will make him an enemy to himself and to the just, will it not?

It will.

And the gods, my friend, are just?

We will suppose they are.

Then to the gods also will the unjust man be an enemy, and the just a friend.

b

Feast on your argument, said he, to your heart's content: I will not oppose you, or I shall give offense to the company.

Be so good, said I, as to make my entertainment complete by continuing to answer as you have now been doing. I am aware, indeed, that the just are shown to be wiser, and better, and more able to act than the unjust, who are indeed, incapable of any combined action. We do not speak with entire accuracy when we say that any party of unjust men ever acted vigorously in concert together: for, had they been thoroughly unjust, they could not have kept their hands off each other. But it is obvious that there was some justice at work in them,

c

which made them refrain at any rate from injuring, at one and the same moment, both their comrades and the objects of their attacks, and which enabled them to achieve what they did achieve; and that their injustice partly disabled them, even in the pursuit of their unjust ends, since those who are complete villains, and thoroughly unjust, are also thoroughly unable to act. I understand that all this is true,

d and that what you at first set down is not true. But whether the just also live a better life, and are happier than the unjust, is a question which we proposed to consider next, and which we now have to investigate. Now, I for my part, think it is already apparent, from what we have said, that they do; nevertheless, we must examine the point still more carefully. For we are debating no trivial question, but the manner in which a man ought to live.

Please consider it.

I will. Tell me, do you think there is such a thing as a horse's work.

e I do.

Would you, then, describe the work of a horse, or of anything else whatever, as that work, for the accomplishment of which it is either the sole or the best instrument?

I do not understand.

Look at it this way. Can you see with anything besides eyes?

Certainly not.

Can you hear with anything besides ears?

No.

Then should we not justly say that seeing and hearing are the functions of these organs?

Yes, certainly.

353 Again, you might cut off a vine-shoot with a carving knife, or chisel, or many other tools?

Undoubtedly.

But with no tool, I imagine, so well as with the pruning knife made for the purpose.

True.

Then shall we not define pruning to be the function of the pruning knife?

By all means.

Now then, I think, you will better understand what I wished to learn from you just now, when I asked whether the function of a thing is not that work for the accomplishment of which it is either the sole or the best instrument?

I do understand, and I believe that this is in b every case the function of a thing.

Very well, do you not also think that everything which has an appointed function has also a proper virtue? Let us go back to the same instances—we say that the eyes have a function?

They have.

Then have the eyes a virtue also?

They have.

And the ears—did we assign them a function?

Yes.

Then have they a virtue also?

They have.

And is it the same with all other things?

The same.

Attend then: Do you suppose that the eyes could accomplish their work well if they had c not their own proper virtue, that virtue being replaced by a vice?

How could they? You mean, probably, if sight is replaced by blindness.

I mean, whatever their virtue be: for I am not come to that question yet. At present I am asking whether it is through their own peculiar virtue that things perform their proper functions well, and through their own peculiar vice that they perform them ill?

You cannot be wrong in that.

Then if the ears lose their own virtue, will they execute their functions ill?

Certainly.

May we include all other things in the same d argument?

I think we may.

Come, then, consider this point next. Has the soul any function which could not be executed by means of anything else whatsoever?

For example, could we in justice assign managing and ruling, deliberation and the like, to anything but the soul, or should we pronounce them to be peculiar to it?

We could ascribe them to nothing else.

Again, shall we declare life to be a function of the soul?

Decidedly.

Do we not also maintain that the soul has a virtue?

We do.

e Then can it ever so happen, Thrasymachus, that the soul will perform its functions well when destitute of its own peculiar virtue, or is that impossible?

Impossible.

Then a bad soul necessarily manages and rules badly, and a good soul must do all these things well.

Unquestionably.

Now did we not grant that justice was a virtue of the soul, and injustice a vice?

We did.

Consequently the just soul and the just man will live well, and the unjust man ill?

354 Apparently, according to your argument.

And you will allow that he who lives well is blessed and happy, and that he who lives otherwise is the reverse.

Unquestionably.

Consequently the just man is happy, and the unjust man miserable.

Let us suppose them to be so.

But surely it is not misery, but happiness, that is advantageous.

Undoubtedly.

Never then, my excellent Thrasymachus, is injustice more advantageous than justice.

Well, Socrates, let this be your entertainment for the feast of Bendis.

I have to thank *you* for it, Thrasymachus, because you recovered your temper, and left

b off being angry with me. Nevertheless, I have not been well entertained; but that was my own fault, and not yours: for as your gluttons seize

upon every new dish as it goes round, and taste its contents before they have had a reasonable enjoyment of its predecessor, so I seem to myself to have left the question which we were at first examining, concerning the real nature of justice, before we had found out the answer to it, in order to rush to the inquiry whether this unknown thing is a vice and an ignorance, or a virtue and a wisdom; and again, when a new theory, that injustice is more profitable than justice, was subsequently started, I could not refrain from passing from the other to this, so that at present the result of our conversation is that I know nothing: for while I do not know c what justice is, I am little likely to know whether it is in fact a virtue or not, or whether its owner is happy or unhappy.

## BOOK II

When I had made these remarks I thought I 357 was to be freed from the discussion; whereas it seems it was only a prelude. For Glaucon, with that eminent courage which he displays on all occasions, would not accept the retreat of Thrasymachus, and began thus: Socrates, do you wish really to convince us that it is on every account better to be just than to be b unjust, or only to seem to have convinced us?

If it were in my power, I replied, I should prefer convincing you really.

Then, he proceeded, you are not doing what you wish. Let me ask you: Is there, in your opinion, a class of good things of such a kind that we are glad to possess them, not because we desire their consequences, but simply welcoming them for their own sake? Take, for example, the feelings of enjoyment and all those pleasures that are harmless, and that are followed by no consequences, beyond simple enjoyment in their possession.

Yes, I certainly think there is a class of this description.

Well, is there another class, do you think, of c

those which we value, both for their own sake and for their results? Such as intelligence, and sight, and health—all of which we surely welcome on both accounts.

Yes.

And do you further recognize a third class of good things, which would include gymnastic training, and submission to medical treatment in illness, as well as the practice of medicine, and all other means of making money? Things like these we should describe as irksome, and yet beneficial to us; and while we should reject them viewed simply in themselves, we accept them for the sake of the rewards, and of the other consequences which result from them.

Yes, undoubtedly there is such a third class also; but what then?

In which of these classes do you place justice?

I should say in the highest—that is, among the good things which will be valued by one who is in the pursuit of true happiness, alike for their own sake and for their consequences.

Then your opinion is not that of the many, by whom justice is ranked in the irksome class, as a thing which in itself, and for its own sake, is disagreeable and repulsive, but which it is well to practice for the advantages to be had from it, with an eye to rewards and to a good name.

I know it is so; and under this idea Thrasymachus has been for a long time disparaging justice and praising injustice. But apparently I am a slow learner.

Listen to my proposal then, and tell me whether you agree to it. Thrasymachus appears to me to have yielded like a snake to your fascination sooner than he need have done; but for my part I am not satisfied as yet with the exposition that has been given of justice and injustice; for I long to be told what they respectively are, and what force they exert, taken simply by themselves, when residing in the soul, dismissing the consideration of their rewards and other consequences. This shall be my plan then, if you do not object: I will revive Thrasymachus's argument, and will first state the common view respecting what kind of thing justice is and how it came to be; in the second place, I will maintain that all who practice it do so against their will, because it is indispensable, not because it is a good thing; and thirdly, that they act reasonably in so doing, because the life of the unjust man is, as men say, far better than that of the just. Not that I think so myself, Socrates; only my ears are ringing so with what I hear from Thrasymachus and a thousand others, that I am puzzled. Now I have never heard the argument for the superiority of justice over injustice maintained to my satisfaction: for I should like to hear it praised, considered simply in itself; and from you if from any one, I should expect such a treatment of the subject. Therefore I will speak as forcibly as I can in praise of an unjust life, and I shall thus give you a specimen of the manner in which I wish to hear you afterwards censure injustice and commend justice. See whether you approve of my plan.

Indeed I do, for on what other subject could a sensible man like better to talk and to hear others talk, again and again?

Admirably spoken! So now listen to me while I speak on my first theme, what kind of thing justice is and how it came to be.

To commit injustice is, they say, in its nature, a good thing, and to suffer it a bad thing; but the bad of the latter exceeds the good of the former; and so, after the two-fold experience of both doing and suffering injustice, those who cannot avoid the latter and choose the former find it expedient to make a contract of mutual abstinence from injustice. Hence arose legislation and contacts between man and man, and hence it became the custom to call that which the law enjoined just, as well as lawful. Such, they tell us, is justice, and so it came into being; and it stands midway between that which is best, to commit injustice with impunity, and that which is worst, to suffer injustice without any power of retaliating. And being a mean between these two extremes, the principle of justice is regarded with satisfaction, not as a positive good, but because the inability to commit injustice has rendered it valuable: for they say that one who had it in his power to be unjust, and who deserved the name of a man, would never be so weak as to contract with any one that both the parties should abstain from injustice. Such is the current account, Socrates, of the nature of justice, and of the circumstances in which it originated.

Even those men who practice justice do so unwillingly, because they lack the power to violate it, will be most readily perceived, if we used the following reasoning. Let us give full liberty to the just man and to the unjust alike, to do whatever they please, and then let us follow them, and see whither the inclination of each will lead him. In that case we shall surprise the just man in the act of traveling in the same direction as the unjust, owing to that desire to gain more, the gratification of which every creature naturally pursues as a good, only that it is forced out of its path by law, and constrained to respect the principle of equality. That full liberty of action would, perhaps, be most effectively realized if they were invested with a power which they say was in old time possessed by the ancestor of Gyges the Lydian. He was a shepherd, so the story runs, in the service of the reigning sovereign of Lydia, when one day a violent storm of rain fell, the ground was rent asunder by an earthquake, and a yawning gulf appeared on the spot where he was feeding his flocks. Seeing what had happened, and wondering at it, he went down into the gulf, and among other marvelous objects he saw, as the legend relates, a hollow brazen horse, with windows in its sides, through which he looked, and beheld in the interior a corpse, apparently of superhuman size; from which he took the only thing remaining, a golden ring on the hand, and therewith made his way out. Now when the usual meeting of the shepherds occurred, for the purpose of sending to the king their monthly report of the state of his flocks, this shepherd came with the rest, wearing the ring. And, as he was seated with the company, he happened to turn the hoop of the ring round towards himself, until it came to the inside of his hand. Whereupon he became invisible to his neighbors, who fell to talking about him as if he were gone away. While he was marveling at this, he again began playing with the ring, and turned the hoop to the outside, upon which he became once more visible. Having noticed this effect, he made experiments with the ring, to see whether it possessed this virtue; and so it was, that when he turned the hoop inwards he became invisible, and when he turned it outwards he was again visible. After this discovery, he immediately contrived to be appointed one of the messengers to carry the report to the king; and upon his arrival he seduced the queen, and conspiring with her, slew the king, and took possession of the throne.

If then there were two such rings in existence, and if the just and the unjust man were each to put on one, it is to be thought that no one would be so steeled against temptation as to abide in the practice of justice, and resolutely to abstain from touching the property of his neighbors, when he had it in his power to help himself without fear to any thing he pleased in the market, or to go into private houses and have intercourse with whom he would, or to kill and release from prison according to his own pleasure, and in every thing else to act among men with the power of a god. And in thus following out his desires the just man will be doing precisely what the unjust man would do; and so they would both be pursuing the same path. Surely this will be allowed to be strong evidence that none are just willingly, but only by compulsion, because to be just is not a good to the individual; for all violate justice whenever they imagine that there is nothing to hinder them. And they do so because every one thinks that, in the individual case, injustice is much more profitable than justice; and they are

d  right in so thinking, as the speaker of this speech will maintain. For if any one having this licence within his grasp were to refuse to do any injustice, or to touch the property of others, all who were aware of it would think him a most pitiful and irrational creature, though they would praise him before each other's faces, deceiving one another, through their fear of suffering injustice. And so much for this topic.

e  But in actually deciding between the lives of the two persons in question, we shall be enabled to arrive at a correct conclusion, by contrasting together the thoroughly just and the thoroughly unjust man, and only by so doing. Well then, how are we to contrast them? In this way. Let us take anything away either from the injustice of the unjust, or from the justice of the just, but let us suppose each to be perfect in his own line of conduct. First of all then, the unjust man must act as skillful craftsmen do. For a first-rate pilot or physician perceives the difference between what is doable and what is

361 undoable in his art; and while he attempts the former, he leaves the latter alone; and moreover, should he happen to make a false step, he is able to recover himself. In the same way, if we are to form a conception of a consummately unjust man, we must suppose that he makes no mistake in the prosecution of his unjust enterprises, and that he escapes detection; but if he be found out, we must look upon him as a bungler: for it is the perfection of injustice to seem just without really being so. We must therefore grant to the perfectly unjust man, without taking anything away, the most perfect injustice; and we must concede to him, that while committing the grossest acts of injustice he has won

b  himself the highest reputation for justice; and that should he make a false step, he is able to recover himself, partly by a talent for speaking with effect in case he be called in question for any of his misdeeds, and partly because his

courage and strength, and his command of friends and money, enable him to employ force with success, whenever force is required. Such being our unjust man, let us, in speech, place the just man by his side, a man of true simplicity and nobleness, resolved, as Aeschylus says, not to seem, but to be, good. We must certainly take away the seeming: for if he be thought to

c  be a just man, he will have honors and gifts on the strength of this reputation, so that it will be uncertain whether it is for justice's sake, or for the sake of the gifts and honors, that he is what he is. Yes, we must strip him bare of everything but justice, and make his whole case the reverse of the former. Without being guilty of one unjust act, let him have the worst reputation for injustice, so that his justice may be thoroughly tested, and shown to be proof against infamy and all its consequences; and let him go on until the day of his death, steadfast in his justice, but

d  with a lifelong reputation for injustice, in order that, having brought both the men to the utmost limits of justice and of injustice respectively, we may then give judgment as to which of the two is the happier.

Good heavens! my dear Glaucon, said I, how vigorously you work, scouring the two characters clean for our judgment, like a pair of statues.

I do it as well as I can, he said. And after describing the men as we have done, there will be no further difficulty, I imagine, in proceed-

e  ing to sketch the kind of life which awaits them respectively. Let me therefore describe it. And if the description be somewhat coarse, do not regard it as mine, Socrates, but as coming from those who commend injustice above justice. They will say that in such a situation 362 the just man will be scourged, racked, fettered, will have his eyes burnt out, and at last, after suffering every kind of torture, will be crucified; and thus learn that it is best to resolve, not to be, but to seem, just. Indeed those words of Aeschylus are far more applicable to the unjust man than to the just. For it is in fact the unjust man, they will maintain, inasmuch as he devotes himself to a course which is allied to reality, and does not live with an eye to appearances, who 'is resolved not to seem, but to be,' unjust,

b
　　'Reaping a harvest of wise purposes,
　　　Sown in the fruitful furrows of his mind';

being enabled first of all to rule in the city through his reputation for justice, and in the next place to choose a wife wherever he will, and marry his children into whatever family he pleases, to enter into contracts and join in partnership with any one he likes, and besides all this, to enrich himself by large profits, because he is not too nice to commit a fraud. Therefore, whenever he engages in a contest, whether public or private, he defeats and over-reaches his enemies, and by so doing grows

c
rich, and is enabled to benefit his friends and injure his enemies, and to offer sacrifices and dedicate gifts to the gods in magnificent abundance; and thus having greatly the advantage of the just man to do service to the gods, as well as to such men as he chooses, he is also more likely than the just man, to be dearer to the gods. And therefore they affirm, Socrates, that a better provision is made both by gods and men for the life of the unjust, than for the life of the just.

d
　　When Glaucon had said this, before I could make the reply I had in mind, his brother Adeimantus exclaimed, You surely do not suppose, Socrates, that the doctrine has been satisfactorily expounded.

Why not? said I.

The very point which it was most important to urge has been omitted.

Well then, according to the proverb, 'May a brother be present to help one,' it is for you to supply his deficiencies, if there are any, by your assistance. But indeed, for my part, what Glaucon has said is enough to prostrate me, and put it out of my power to come up to the rescue of justice.

e
　　You are not in earnest, he said: listen to the

following argument also; for we must now go through those representations which, reversing the declarations of Glaucon, commend justice and disparage injustice, in order to bring out more clearly what I take to be his meaning. Now, surely, fathers tell their sons and those in whom they feel an interest, that one must be just, and impress it upon their children or those in whom they feel an interest, they do not

363
praise justice in itself, but only the respectability which it gives—their object being that a reputation for justice may be gained, and that this reputation may bring the offices, marriages, and the other good things which Glaucon has just told us are secured to the just man by his high character. And these persons carry the advantages of a good name still further; for, by introducing the good opinion of the gods, they are enabled to describe innumerable blessings which the gods, they say, grant to the pious, as the excellent Hesiod tells us, and Homer too—the former saying, that the gods cause the oak-trees of the just

b
　　'On their tops to bear acorns, and swarms
　　　of bees in the middle;
　　Also their wool-laden sheep sink under the
　　　weight of their fleeces'

with many other good things of the same sort; while the latter, in a similar passage, speaks of one,

c
　　'Like to a blameless king, who, godlike
　　　in virtue and wisdom,
　　Justice ever maintains; whose rich land
　　　fruitfully yields him
　　Harvests of barley and wheat, and his
　　　orchards are heavy with fruit;
　　Strong are the young of his flocks; and the sea
　　　gives him fish in abundance.'

But the blessings which Musaeus and his son Eurnolpus represent the gods as bestowing upon the just, are still more delectable than these; for they bring them to the abode of Hades, and describe them as reclining on couches at a banquet of the pious, and with garlands on their heads spending all time in wine-d bibbing, the fairest reward of virtue being, in their estimation, an everlasting carousal. Others, again, do not stop even here in their enumeration of the rewards bestowed by the gods; for they tell us that the man who is pious and true to his oath leaves children's children and a posterity to follow him. Such, among others, are the commendations which they lavish upon justice. The ungodly, on the other hand, and the unjust, they plunge into a swamp in Hades, and condemn them to carry water in a sieve; and while they are still alive, they bring them into

e ill repute, and inflict upon the unjust precisely those punishments which Glaucon enumerated as the lot of the just who are reputed to be unjust; more they cannot. Such is their method of praising the one character and condemning the other.

Once more, Socrates, take into consideration another and a different mode of speaking

364 with regard to justice and injustice, which we meet with both in common life and in the poets. All as with one mouth proclaim, that to be temperate and just is an admirable thing certainly, but at the same time a hard and an irksome one; while intemperance and injustice are pleasant things and of easy acquisition, and only rendered base by law and public opinion. But they say that justice is in general less profitable than injustice, and they do not hesitate to call wicked men happy, and to honor them both in public and in private, when they are rich or possess other sources of power, and on the other hand to treat with dishonor and dis-

b dain those who are in any way feeble or poor, even while they admit that the latter are better men than the former. But of all their statements the most wonderful are those which relate to the gods and to virtue; according to which even the gods allot to many good men a calamitous and bad life, and to men of the opposite character an opposite portion. And there are quacks and soothsayers who flock to the rich man's doors, and try to persuade him that they have a power procured from the gods, which enables them, by sacrifices and

incantations performed amid feasting and indulgence, to make amends for any crime com-

c mitted either by the individual himself or by his ancestors; and that, should he desire to do a mischief to any one, it may be done at a trifling expense, whether the object of his hostility be a just or an unjust man: for they profess that by certain invocations and spells they can prevail upon the gods to do their bidding. And in support of all these assertions they produce the evidence of poets—some, to exhibit the facilities of vice, quoting the words

*'Whoso wickedness seeks, may even in masses* d
*obtain it*
*Easily. Smooth is the way, and short, for nigh*
*is her dwelling.*
*Virtue, Heav'n has ordained, shall be reached*
*by the sweat of the forehead,'*

and by a long and up-hill road; while others, to prove that the gods may be turned from their purpose by men, adduce the testimony of Homer, who has said:

*'Yea, even the gods do yield to entreaty;* e
*Therefore to them men offer both victims and*
*meek supplications,*
*Incense and melting fat, and turn them from*
*anger to mercy;*
*Sending up sorrowful prayers, when trespass*
*and sin is committed.'*

And they produce a host of books written by Musaeus and Orpheus, children, as they say, of Selene and of the Muses, which form their ritual, persuading not individuals merely, but 365 whole cities also, that men may be absolved and purified from crimes, both while they are still alive and even after their death, by means of certain sacrifices and pleasurable amusements which they call Mysteries—which deliver us from the torments of the other world, while the neglect of them is punished by an awful doom.

When views like these, he continued, my dear Socrates, are proclaimed and repeated with so much variety, concerning the honors in which virtue and vice are respectively held by gods and men, what can we suppose is the effect produced on the minds of all those good-natured young men, who are able, after skimming like birds, as it were, over all that they hear, to draw conclusions from it, respecting the character which a man must possess, and

b  the path in which he must walk, in order to live the best possible life? In all probability a young man would say to himself in the words of Pindar, 'Shall I by justice or by crooked wiles climb to a loftier stronghold, and, having thus fenced myself in, live my life?' For common opinion declares that to be just without being also thought just, is no advantage to me, but only entails manifest trouble and loss; whereas if I am unjust and get myself a name for justice, an unspeakably happy life is promised me.

c  Very well then, since the appearance, as the wise inform me, overpowers the truth, and is the sovereign dispenser of felicity, to this I must of course wholly devote myself; I must draw round about me a picture of virtue to serve as an exterior front, but behind me I must keep the fox with its cunning and shiftiness—of which that most clever Archilochus tells us. Yes, but it will be objected, it is not an easy matter always to conceal one's wickedness.

d  No, we shall reply, nor yet is anything else easy that is great; nevertheless, if happiness is to be our goal, this must be our path, as the steps of the argument indicate. To assist in keeping up the deception, we will form secret societies and clubs. There are, moreover, teachers of persuasion, who impart skill in popular and forensic oratory; and so by fair means or by foul, we shall gain our ends, and carry on our dishonest proceedings with impunity. But, it is urged, neither evasion nor violence can succeed with the gods. Well, but if they either do not exist, or do not concern themselves with the affairs of men, why need *we* concern ourselves to evade

e  their observation? But if they do exist, and do pay attention to us, we know nothing and have heard nothing of them from any other quarter

than the current traditions and the genealogies of poets; and these very authorities state that the gods are beings who may be wrought upon and diverted from their purpose by sacrifices and meek supplications and votive offerings. Therefore we must believe them in both statements or in neither. If we are to believe them, we will act unjustly, and offer sacrifices from the proceeds of our crimes. For if we are just,  366 we shall, it is true, escape punishment at the hands of the gods, but we renounce the profits which accrue from injustice; but if we are unjust, we shall not only make these gains, but also by putting up prayers when we overstep and make mistakes, we shall prevail upon the gods to let us go unscathed. But then, it is again objected, in Hades we shall pay the just penalty for the crimes committed here, either in our own persons or in those of our children's children. But my friend, the champion of the argument will continue, the mystic rites, again, are very powerful, and the absolving divinities, as  b we are told by the mightiest cities, and by the sons of the gods who have appeared as poets and inspired prophets, who inform us that these things are so.

What consideration, therefore, remains which should induce us to prefer justice to the greatest injustice? Since if we combine injustice with a spurious decorum, we shall fare to our liking with the gods and with men, in this life and the next, according to the most numerous and the highest authorities. Considering all that has been said, by what device, Socrates, can a man who has any advantages, either  c of high talent, or wealth, or personal appearance, or birth, bring himself to honor justice, instead of smiling when he hears it praised? Indeed, if there is any one who is able to show the falsity of what we have said, and who is fully convinced that justice is best, far from being angry with the unjust, he doubtless makes great allowance for them, knowing that, with the exception of those who may possibly refrain from injustice through the disgust of a

godlike nature or from the acquisition of knowledge, there is certainly no one else who
d is willingly just; but it is from cowardice, or age, or some other infirmity, that men condemn injustice, simply because they lack the power to commit it. And the truth of this is proved by the fact, that the first of these people who comes to power is the first to commit injustice, to the extent of his ability.

And the cause of all this is simply that fact, which my brother and I both stated at the very commencement of this address to you, Soc-
e rates, saying: With all due respect, to you who profess to be admirers of justice—beginning with the heroes of old, of whom accounts have descended to the present generation—have every one of you, without exception, made the praise of justice and condemnation of injustice turn solely upon the reputation and honor and gifts resulting from them; but what each is in itself, by its own peculiar force as it resides in the soul of its possessor, unseen either by gods or men, has never, in poetry or in prose been adequately discussed, so as to show that injustice is the greatest bane that a soul can receive into itself, and justice the greatest blessing. Had this been the language used by all of you
367 from the start, and had you tried to persuade us of this from our childhood, we should not be on the watch to check one another in the commission of injustice, because every one would be his own watchman, fearful lest by committing injustice he might attach to himself the greatest of evils.

All this, Socrates, and perhaps still more than this, would be put forward respecting justice and injustice, by Thrasymachus, and I dare say by others also; thus vulgarly, in my opin-
b ion, turning around the power of each. For my own part, I confess—for I do not want to hide anything from you—that I have a great desire to hear you defend the opposite view, and therefore I have exerted myself to speak as forcefully as I can. So do not limit your argument to the proposition that justice is stronger

than injustice, but show us what is that influence exerted by each of them on its possessor, whereby the one is in itself a blessing, and the other a curse; and take away the estimation in which the two are held, as Glaucon urged you to do. For if you omit to withdraw from each quality its true reputation and to add the false, we shall declare that you are praising, not the reality, but the semblance of justice, and blaming, not the reality, but the semblance of injus- c tice; that your advice, in fact, is to be unjust without being found out, and that you hold with Thrasymachus, that justice is another man's good, being for the interest of the stronger; injustice a man's own interest and advantage, but against the interest of the weaker. Since then you have allowed that justice belongs to the highest class of good things, the possession of which is valuable, both for the sake of their results, and also in a higher degree for their own sake, such as sight, hearing, understanding, health, and everything else which is genuinely good in its own nature and not merely reputed to be good. Select for commendation d this particular feature of justice, I mean the benefit which in itself it confers on its possessor, in contrast with the harm which injustice inflicts. The rewards and reputations leave to others to praise; because in others I can tolerate this mode of praising justice and condemning injustice, which consists in eulogizing or reviling the reputations and the rewards which are connected with them; but in you I cannot, unless you require it, because you have spent your whole life in investigating such questions, e and such only. Therefore do not content yourself with proving to us that justice is better than injustice; but show us what is that influence exerted by each on its possessor, by which, whether gods and men see it or not, the one is in itself a good, and the other a detriment.

Much as I had always admired the nature of both Glaucon and Adeimantus, I confess that on this occasion I was quite charmed with what I had heard; so I said: Aptly indeed did 368

Glaucon's admirer address you, sons of the man there named, in the first line of his elegiac poem, after you had distinguished yourselves in the battle of Megara, saying:

> 'Race of a famous man, ye godlike sons
>     of Ariston.'

There seems to me to be great truth in this epithet, my friends: for there is something truly god-like in the state of your minds, if you are not convinced that injustice is better than justice, when you can plead its cause so well. I b do believe that you really are not convinced of it. But I infer it from your general character; for judging merely from your statements I should have distrusted you: but the more I place confidence in you, the more I am perplexed how to deal with the case; for though I do not know how I am to render assistance, having learnt how unequal I am to the task from your rejection of my answer to Thrasymachus, wherein I imagined that I had demonstrated that justice is better than injustice; yet, on the other hand, I dare not refuse my assistance: because I am afraid that it might be posc itively wrong in me, when I hear justice disparaged in my presence, to lose heart and desert her, so long as breath and utterance are left in me. My best plan, therefore, is to succor her in such fashion as I can.

Thereupon Glaucon, and all the rest with him, requested me by all means to give my assistance, and not to let the conversation drop, but thoroughly to investigate the real nature of justice and injustice, and the truth with regard to their respective advantages. So I said what seemed to me to be the case. The inquiry we are undertaking is no trivial one, but demands a keen sight, according to my notion of it. Thered fore, since I am not a clever person, I think we had better adopt a mode of inquiry which may be thus illustrated. Suppose we had been ordered to read small writing at a distance, not having very good eye-sight, and that one of us

discovered that the same writing was to be found somewhere else in larger letters, and upon a larger space, we should have looked upon it as a piece of luck, I imagine, that we could read the latter first, and then examine the smaller, and observe whether the two were alike.

Undoubtedly we should, said Adeimantus; but what parallel can you see to this, Socrates, e in our inquiry after justice?

I will tell you, I replied. We speak of justice as residing in an individual man, and also as residing in an entire city, do we not?

Certainly we do, he said.

Well, a city is larger than one man.

It is.

Perhaps, then, justice may exist in larger proportions in the greater subject, and thus be  369 easier to discover; so, if you please, let us first investigate its character in cities; afterwards let us apply the same inquiry to the individual, looking for the counterpart of the greater as it exists in the form of the less.

Indeed, he said, I think your plan is a good one.

If then we were to trace in thought the gradual formation of a city, should we also see the growth of its justice or of its injustice?

Perhaps we should.

Then, if this were done, might we not hope to see more easily the object of our search?  b

Yes, much more easily.

Is it your advice, then, that we should attempt to carry out our plan? It is no trifling task, I imagine; therefore consider it well.

We have considered it, said Adeimantus; yes, do so by all means.

Well then, I proceeded, the formation of a city is due, as I imagine, to this fact, that we are not individually independent, but have many wants. Or would you assign any other principle for the founding of cities?

No I agree with you, he replied.

Thus it is, then, that owing to our many  c wants, and because each seeks the aid of others to supply his various requirements, we gather many associates and helpers into one dwelling-place, and give to this joint dwelling the name of city. Is it so?

Undoubtedly.

And every one who gives or takes in exchange, whatever it be that he exchanges, does so from a belief that he is consulting his own interest.

Certainly.

Now then, let us construe our imaginary city from the beginning. It will owe its construction, it appears, to our needs.

Unquestionably.

d    Well, but the first and most pressing of all wants is that of sustenance to enable us to exist as living creatures.

Most decidedly.

Our second want would be that of a house, and our third that of clothing and the like.

True.

Then let us know what will render our city adequate to the supply of so many things. Must we not begin with a farmer for one, and a house-builder, and besides these a weaver? Will these suffice, or shall we add to them a shoemaker, and perhaps one or two more of the class of people who minister to our bodily wants?

By all means.

Then the smallest possible city will consist of four or five men.

So we see.

e    To proceed then: ought each of these to place his own work at the disposal of the community, so that the single farmer, for example, shall provide food for four, spending four times the amount of time and labor upon the preparation of food, and sharing it with others;

370  or must he be regardless of them, and produce for his own consumption alone the fourth part of this quantity of food, in a fourth part of the time, spending the other three parts, one in making his house, another in procuring him-

self clothes, and the third in providing himself with shoes, saving himself the trouble of sharing with others, and doing his own business by himself, and for himself?

To this Adeimantus replied, Well, Socrates, perhaps the former plan is the easier of the two.

Really, I said, it is not improbable; for I recollect myself, after your answer, that, in the first place, no two persons are born exactly alike, but each differs in his nature, one being suited for one occupation, and another for    b another. Do you not think so?

I do.

Well, when is a man likely to succeed best? When he divides his exertions among many trades, or when he devotes himself exclusively to one?

When he devotes himself to one.

Again, it is also clear, I imagine, that if a person lets the right moment for any work go by, it never returns.

It is quite clear.

For the thing to be done does not choose, I imagine, to await the leisure of the doer, but the doer must be at the call of the thing to be    c done, and not treat it as a secondary affair.

He must.

From these considerations it follows that all things will be produced in superior quantity and quality, and with greater ease, when each man works at a single occupation, in accordance with his nature, and at the right moment, without meddling with anything else.

Unquestionably.

More than four citizens, then, Adeimantus, are needed to provide the requisites which we named. For the farmer, it appears, will not make his own plough, if it is to be a good one, nor his hoe, nor any of the other tools employed    d in agriculture. No more will the builder make the numerous tools which he also requires; and so of the weaver and the shoemaker.

True.

Then we shall have carpenters and smiths,

and many other artisans of the kind, who will become members of our little city, and create a population.

Certainly.

Still it will not yet be very large, supposing we add to them cowherds and shepherds, and the rest of that class, in order that the farmers e may have oxen for ploughing, and the house-builders, as well as the farmers, beasts of burden for hauling, and the weavers and shoemakers wool and leather.

It will not be a small city, either, if it contains all these.

Moreover, it is scarcely possible to plant the actual city in a place where it will have no need of imports.

No, it is impossible.

Then it will further require a new class of persons to bring from other cities all that it requires.

It will.

Well, but if the agent goes empty-handed, carrying with him none of the commodities in 371 demand among those people from whom our city is to procure what it requires, he will also come empty-handed away, will he not?

I think so.

Then it must produce at home not only enough for itself, but also articles of the right kind and quantity to accommodate those whose services it needs.

It must.

Then our city requires larger numbers both of farmers and other craftsmen.

Yes, it does.

And among the rest it will need more of those agents also, who are to export and import the several commodities; and these are merchants, are they not?

Yes.

Then we shall require merchants also.

Certainly.

And if the commerce is carried on by sea, there will be a further demand for a consider-able number of other persons, who are skilled b in the practice of navigation.

A considerable number, undoubtedly.

But now tell me: in the city itself how are they to exchange their several productions? For it was to promote this exchange, you know, that we formed the community, and so founded our city.

Clearly, by buying and selling.

Then this will give rise to a market and a currency, for the sake of exchange.

Undoubtedly.

Suppose then that the farmer, or one of the c other craftsmen, should come with some of his produce into the market, at a time when none of those who wish to make an exchange with him are there, is he to leave his occupation and sit idle in the market-place?

By no means, there are persons who, with an eye to this contingency, undertake the service required; and these in well-regulated cities are, generally speaking, persons of excessive physical weakness, who are of no use in other kinds of labor. Their business is to remain on the spot in the market, and give d money for goods to those who want to sell, and goods for money to those who want to buy.

This demand, then, causes a class of tradesmen to spring up in our city. For do we not give the name of retail dealers to those who station themselves in the market, to minister to buying and selling, applying the term merchants to those who go about from city to city?

Exactly so.

In addition to these, I imagine, there is also e another class of servants, consisting of those whose reasoning capacities do not recommend them as associates, but whose bodily strength is equal to hard labor, these, selling the use of their strength and calling the price of it hire, are thus named, I believe, hired laborers. Is it not so?

Precisely.

Then hired laborers also form, as it seems, a complementary portion of a city.

I think so.

Shall we say then, Adeimantus, that our city has at length grown to its full stature?

Perhaps so.

Where then, I wonder, shall we find justice and injustice in it? With which of these elements that we have contemplated, has it simultaneously made its entrance?

372   I have no notion, Socrates, unless perhaps it be discoverable somewhere in the mutual relations of these same persons.

Well, perhaps you are right. We must investigate the matter, and not flinch from the task.

Let us consider then, in the first place, what kind of life will be led by persons thus provided. I presume they will produce bread and wine, and clothes and shoes, and build themselves houses; and in summer, no doubt, they will generally work naked and without shoes, while in winter they will be suitably

b   clothed and shod. And they will live, I suppose, on barley and wheat, baking cakes of the meal, and kneading loaves of the flour. And spreading these excellent cakes and loaves upon mats of straw or on clean leaves, and themselves reclining on rude beds of yew or myrtle-boughs, they will make merry, themselves and their children, drinking their wine, wearing garlands, and singing the praises of the gods, enjoying one another's society, and

c   not begetting children beyond their means, through a prudent fear of poverty or war.

Glaucon here interrupted me, remarking, Apparently you describe your men as feasting without any seasonings.

True, I said, I had forgotten. Of course they will have something to season their food—salt, no doubt, and olives and cheese, together with the country fare of boiled onions and cabbage. We shall also set before them a dessert, I imagine, of figs and chickpeas and beans; and they may roast myrtle-berries and beech-nuts at the

d   fire, taking wine with their fruit in moderation.

And thus passing their days in tranquillity and sound health, they will, in all probability, live to an advanced age, and dying, bequeath to their children a life in which their own will be reproduced.

Upon this Glaucon exclaimed, Why Socrates, if you were founding a community of swine, this is just the style in which you would fatten them up!

How then, said I, would you have them live, Glaucon?

In a civilized manner, he replied. They ought to recline on couches, I should think, if they are not to have a hard life of it, and dine off tables, and have the usual dishes and dessert of a modern dinner.

Very good. I understand. Apparently we     e are considering the growth not of a city merely, but of a luxurious city. I dare say it is not a bad plan: for by this extension of our inquiry we shall perhaps discover how it is that justice and injustice take root in cities. Now it appears to me that the city which we have described is the genuine and, so to speak, healthy city. But if you wish us to contemplate     373 a city that is suffering from inflammation, there is nothing to hinder us. Some people will not be satisfied, it seems, with the fare or the mode of life which we have described, but must have, in addition, couches and tables and every other article of furniture, as well as seasonings and fragrant oils, and perfumes, and courtesans, and confectionery; and all these in plentiful variety. Moreover, we must not limit ourselves now to essentials in those articles which we specified at first, I mean houses and clothes and shoes, but we must set painting and embroidery to work, and acquire gold and ivory, and all similar valuables, must we not?

Yes.                                                                                                                                 b

Then we shall also have to enlarge our city, for our first or healthy city will not now be of sufficient size, but requires to be increased in bulk, and needs to be filled with a multitude of callings, which do not exist in cities to satisfy any natural want: for example, the whole class of hunters, and all who practice the art of imitation, including many who use forms and colors, and many who use music; and poets also—and their helpers, the rhapsodes, actors, dancers, contractors; and lastly, the craftsmen of all sorts of articles, and among others those who make parts of women's dresses. We shall

c similarly require more personal servants, shall we not? that is to say, teachers, wet-nurses, dry-nurses, beauticians, barbers, and cooks moreover, and butchers? Swineherds again are among the additions we shall require, a class of persons not to be found, because not wanted, in our former city, but needed among the rest in this. We shall also need great quantities of all kinds of cattle, for those who may wish to eat them, shall we not?

Of course we shall.

d Then shall we not experience the need of medical men also, to a much greater extent under this than under the former regime?

Yes, indeed.

The country too, I presume, which was formerly adequate to the support of its then inhabitants will be now too small, and adequate no longer. Shall we say so?

Certainly.

Then must we not cut ourselves a slice of our neighbor's territory, if we are to have land enough both for pasture and tillage, while they will do the same to ours, if they, like us, permit themselves to overstep the limit of necessities, and plunge into the unbounded acquisition of wealth?

e It must inevitably be so, Socrates.

Will our next step be to go to war, Glaucon, or how will it be?

As you say.

At this stage of our inquiry let us avoid asserting either that war does good or that it does harm, confining ourselves to this statement, that we have further traced the origin of

war to causes which are the most fruitful sources of whatever ills befall a city, either in its public capacity, or in its individual members.

Exactly so.

Once more then, my friend, our city must be larger and not just by a small extent, I mean that of a whole army, which must go forth and 374 do battle with all invaders in defense of its entire property, and of the persons whom we were just now describing.

How? he asked; are not those persons sufficient of themselves?

They are not, if you and all the rest of us were right in the admissions which we made, when we were modeling our city. We admitted, I think, if you remember, that it was impossible for one man to work well at many professions.

True.

Well then, is not the business of war looked b upon as a profession in itself?

Undoubtedly.

And have we not as much reason to concern ourselves about the trade of war as about the trade of shoemaking?

Quite as much.

But we cautioned the shoemaker, you know, against attempting to be a farmer or a weaver or a builder besides, with a view to our shoemaking work being well done; and to every other artisan we assigned in like manner one occupation, namely, that for which he was naturally fitted, and in which, if he let other things alone, and worked at it all his time without neglecting his opportunities, he was likely c to prove a successful workman. Now is it not of the greatest moment that the work of war should be well done? Or is it so easy, that any one can succeed in it and be at the same time a farmer or a shoemaker or a laborer at any other trade whatever, although there is no one in the world who could become a good checkers-player or dice-player by merely taking up the game at unoccupied moments, instead of pursuing it as his special study from his childhood? And will it be enough for a man merely to handle a shield or the other arms and implements of war? Will that make him competent to play his part well on that very day in an engagement of heavy troops or in any other military service—although the mere handling of any other instrument will never make any one a true craftsman or athlete, nor will such instrument be even useful to one who has neither learnt its capabilities nor exercised himself sufficiently in its practical applications?

If it were so, these implements of war would be very valuable.

In proportion, then, to the importance of the work which these guardians have to do, it will require more leisure than most, as well as extraordinary skill and attention.

I quite think so.

Will it not also require natural endowments suited to this particular occupation?

Undoubtedly.

Then, apparently, it will be up to us to choose, if we can, the kind of nature which qualifies its possessors for the guardianship of a city.

Certainly; it belongs to us.

Then, I assure you, we have taken upon ourselves no trifling task: nevertheless, there must be no flinching, so long as our strength holds out.

No, there must not.

Do you think then, I asked, that there is any difference, in the qualities required for keeping guard, between a well-bred dog and a gallant young man?

I do not quite understand you.

Why, I suppose, for instance, they ought both of them to be quick to discover an enemy, and swift to overtake him when discovered, and strong also, in case they have to fight when they have come up with him.

Certainly, all these qualities are required.

Moreover, they must be brave if they are to fight well.

Undoubtedly.

But will either a horse, or a dog, or any other animal, be likely to be brave if it is not spirited? or have you failed to observe what an irresistible and unconquerable thing the spirit is, so that under its influence every creature will be fearless and unconquerable in the face of any danger?

I have observed it.

We know then what bodily qualities are required in our guardian.

We do.

And also what qualities of the mind, namely, that he must be spirited.

Yes.

How then, Glaucon, if such be their natural disposition, are they to be kept from behaving fiercely to one another, and to the rest of the citizens?

It will not be easy.

Nevertheless, they certainly ought to be gentle to their friends, and dangerous only to their enemies—else they will not wait for others to destroy them, but will be the first to do it for themselves.

True.

What then shall we do? Where shall we find a character at once gentle and high-spirited? For I suppose a gentle nature is the opposite of a spirited one?

Apparently it is.

Nevertheless a man who is devoid of either gentleness or spirit cannot possibly make a good guardian. And as they seem to be incompatible, the result is, that a good guardian is an impossibility.

It looks like it, he said.

Here then I was perplexed, but having reconsidered our conversation, I said, We deserve, my friend, to be puzzled: for we have deserted the illustration which we set before us.

How so?

It never struck us, that after all there are natures, though we fancied there were none, which combine these opposite qualities.

And where is such a combination to be found?

e   You may see it in several animals, but particularly in the one which we ourselves compared to our guardian. For I suppose you know that it is the natural disposition of well-bred dogs to be perfectly gentle to their friends and acquaintance, but the reverse to strangers.

Certainly I do.

Therefore the thing is possible; and we are not contradicting nature in our endeavor to give such a character to our guardian.

So it would seem.

Then is it your opinion, that in one who is to make a good guardian it is further required that his character should be philosophical as well as high-spirited?

376   How so? I do not understand you.

You will notice in dogs this other trait, which is really marvelous in the creature.

What is that?

Whenever they see a stranger they are irritated before they have been provoked by any ill-usage; but when they see an acquaintance they welcome him, though they may never have experienced any kindness at his hands. Has this never excited your wonder?

I never applied my mind to it hitherto; but no doubt they do behave so.

Well, but this affection is a very clever b   thing in the dog, and truly philosophical.

How so?

Why, because the only mark by which he distinguishes between the appearance of a friend and that of an enemy is, that he knows the former and is ignorant of the latter. How, I ask, can the creature be other than fond of learning when it makes knowledge and ignorance the criteria of the familiar and the strange?

Beyond a question, it must be fond of learning.

Well, is not the love of learning identical with a philosophical disposition?

It is.

Shall we not then assert with confidence in the case of a man also, that if he is to show a     c gentle disposition towards his relatives and acquaintances, he must have a turn for learning and philosophy?

Be it so.

Then in our judgment the man who is a fine and good guardian of the city will be in his nature philosophical, high-spirited, swift-footed, and strong.

Undoubtedly he will. . . .

## BOOK III
412

. . . Very good; then what will be the next point for us to settle? is it not this, which of the persons so educated are to be the rulers, and which the ruled?

Unquestionably it is.                                                          c

There can be no doubt that the rulers must be the elderly men, and the subjects would be the younger.

True.

And also that the rulers must be the best men among them.

True again.

Are not the best farmers those who are most farmer-like?

Yes.

In the present case, as we require the best guardians, shall we not find them in those who are most capable of guarding a city?

Yes.

Then for this purpose must they not be intelligent and powerful, and, moreover, careful of the city?

They must.                                                                     d

And a man will be most careful of that which he loves?

Of course.

And assuredly he will love that most whose

interests he regards as identical with his own, and in whose prosperity or adversity he believes his own fortunes to be involved.

Just so.

Then we must select from the whole body of guardians those individuals who appear to us, after due observation, to be remarkable above others for the zeal with which, through their whole life, they have done what they have thought advantageous to the city, and inflexibly refused to do what they thought the reverse.

e

Yes, these are the suitable persons, he said.

Then I think we must watch them at every stage of their life, to see if they are tenacious guardians of this conviction, and never bewitched or forced into a forgetful banishment of the belief that they ought to do what is best for the city.

What is this banishment you speak of?

413 I will tell you. Opinion appears to depart from our reasoning, either by a voluntary or involuntary act; a false opinion by a voluntary act, when the holder learns his error; but a true opinion invariably by an involuntary act.

I understand the notion of a voluntary abandonment, but I have yet to learn the meaning of the involuntary.

Well, then, do you not agree with me, that men are deprived of good things against their will, of bad things with their will? And is it not a bad thing to be the victim of a lie, and a good thing to possess the truth? And do you not think that a man is in possession of the truth when his opinions represent things as they are?

Yes, you are right; and I believe that men are deprived of a true opinion against their will.

b Then, when this happens, must it not be owing either to theft, or witchcraft, or violence?

I still do not understand.

I am afraid I use language as obscure as tragedy. By those who have a theft practiced on them, I mean such as are argued out of, or forget, their opinions, because, argument in the one case and time in the other robs them of their opinion unawares. Now, I suppose you understand?

Yes.

By those who have violence done to them I mean all whose opinions are changed by pain or grief.

That too I understand, and I think you are right.

And those who are bewitched, you would yourself, I believe, assert to be those who change their opinion either through the seductions of pleasure or under the pressure of fear.

c

Yes, everything that deceives may be said to bewitch.

Then, as I said just now, we must inquire who are the best guardians of this inward conviction, that they must always do that which they think best for the city. We must watch them, I say, from their earliest childhood, giving them actions to perform in which people would be most likely to forget, or be beguiled of, such a belief, and then we must select those whose memory is tenacious, and who are proof against deceit, and exclude the rest. Must we not?

d

Yes.

We must also appoint them labors, and vexations, and contests, in which we must watch for the same symptoms of character.

Rightly so.

And, as a third kind of test, we must try them with witchcraft, and observe their behavior; and, just as young horses are taken into the presence of noise and tumult, to see whether they are timid, so must we bring our men, while still young, into the midst of objects of terror, and presently transfer them to scenes of pleasure, trying them much more thoroughly than gold is tried in the fire, to find whether they show themselves under all circumstances inaccessible to witchcraft, and proper in their bearing, good guardians of themselves and of the music which they have been taught, proving themselves on every occasion true to the

e

414 laws of rhythm and harmony, and acting in such a way as would render them most useful to themselves and the city. And whoever, from time to time, after being put to the proof, as a child, as a youth, and as a man, comes forth uninjured from the trial, must be appointed a ruler and guardian of the city, and must receive honors in life and in death, and be admitted to the highest privileges, in the way of funeral rites and other tributes to his memory. And all who are the reverse of this character must be rejected. Such appears to me, Glaucon, to be the true method of selecting and appointing our rulers and guardians, described simply in outline, without accuracy in detail.

I am pretty much of your mind.

b Is it not then entirely correct to give them the name of thorough-going guardians, as being qualified to take care that their friends at home shall not wish, and their enemies abroad not be able, to do any mischief; and to call the young men, whom up to this time we called 'guardians,' 'auxiliaries' and helpers with the decrees of the rulers?

I think so, he said.

This being the case, I continued, can we contrive any ingenious mode of bringing into c play one of those noble lies of which we lately spoke, so that, propounding a single noble lie, we may bring even the rulers themselves, if possible, to believe it, or if not them, the rest of the city?

What kind of a lie?

Nothing new, but a Phoenician story, which has been realized often before now, as the poets tell and mankind believe, but which in our time has not been, nor, so far as I know, is likely to be realized, and for which it would require great powers of persuasion for it to be creditable.

You seem very reluctant to tell it.

You will think my reluctance very natural when I have told it.

Speak out boldly and without fear.

Well I will; and yet I hardly know where I d shall find the courage or where the words to express myself. I shall try, I say, to persuade first the rulers themselves and the military class, and after them the rest of the city, that when we were training and instructing them, they only thought, as in dreams, that all this was happening to them and about them, while in reality they were in course of formation and training in the bowels of the earth, where they themselves, their armor, and the rest of their equipments were manufactured, and whence, e as soon as they were finished, the earth, their real mother, sent them up to its surface; and, consequently, that they ought now to take thought for the land in which they dwell, as their mother and nurse, and repel all attacks upon it, and to feel towards their fellow-citizens as brothers born of the earth.

It was not without reason that you were so long ashamed to tell us your fiction.

I dare say; nevertheless, hear the rest of the 415 story. We shall tell our people, in mythical language: You are doubtless all brethren, as many as inhabit the city, but the god who created you mixed gold in the composition of such of you as are qualified to rule, which gives them the highest value; while in the auxiliaries he made silver an ingredient, assigning iron and bronze to the cultivators of the soil and the other workmen. Therefore, inasmuch as you are all related to one another, although your children will generally resemble their parents, yet sometimes a golden parent will b produce a silver child, and a silver parent a golden child, and so on, each producing any. The rulers therefore have received this in charge first and above all from the gods, to observe nothing more closely, in their character of vigilant guardians, than the children that are born, to see which of these metals enters into the composition of their souls; and if a child be born in their class with an alloy of bronze or iron, they are to have no manner of pity upon it, but giving it the value that

belongs to its nature, they are to thrust it away
c    into the class of artisans or farmers; and if
again among these a child be born with any
admixture of gold or silver, when they have
examined it, they are to raise it either to the
class of guardians, or to that of auxiliaries:
because there is an oracle which declares that
the city shall then perish when it is guarded by
iron or bronze. Can you suggest any device by
which we can make them believe this fiction?

d        None at all by which we could persuade the
men with whom we begin our new city: but I
think their sons, and the next generation, and
all subsequent generations, might be taught to
believe it.

Well, I said, even this might have a good
effect towards making them care more for the
city and for one another; for I think I understand what you mean. However, we will leave
this fiction to posterity; but for our part, when
we have armed these children of the soil, let us
lead them forward under the command of their
officers, until they arrive at the city; then let
them look around them to discover the most
eligible position for their camp, from which
they may best coerce the inhabitants, if there
e    be any disposition to refuse obedience to the
laws, and repel foreigners, if an enemy should
come down like a wolf on the fold. And when
they have pitched their camp, and offered sacrifices to the proper divinities, let them arrange
their sleeping-places. Is all this right?

It is.

And these sleeping-places must be such as
will keep out the weather both in winter and
summer, must they not?

Certainly; you mean dwelling-houses, if I
am not mistaken.

I do; but the dwelling-houses of soldiers,
not of moneyed men.

416      What is the difference which you imply?

I will endeavor to explain it to you, I
replied. I presume it would be a most monstrous and scandalous proceeding in shepherds
to keep for the protection of their flocks such a

breed of dogs, or so to treat them, that owing
to unruly tempers, or hunger, or any bad propensity whatever, the dogs themselves should
begin to worry the sheep, and behave more
like wolves than dogs.

It would be monstrous, undoubtedly.

Then must we not take every precaution        b
that our auxiliary class, being stronger than the
other citizens, may not act towards them in a
similar fashion, and so resemble savage despots rather than friendly allies?

We must.

And will they not be furnished with the best
of safeguards, if they are really well educated?

But they are *that* already, he exclaimed.

To which I replied, It is not worth while
now to insist upon that point, my dear Glaucon; but it is most necessary to maintain what
we said this minute, that they must have the      c
right education, whatever it may be, if they are
to have what will be most effectual in rendering them gentle to one another, and to those
whom they guard.

True.

But besides this education a rational man
would say that their dwellings and property
generally should be arranged on such a scale
as shall neither prevent them from being perfect thorough-going guardians, nor provoke      d
them to do mischief to the other citizens.

He will say so with truth.

Consider then, I continued, whether the following plan is the right one for their lives and
their dwellings, if they are to be of the character I have described. In the first place, no one
should possess any private property, except as
necessary; secondly, no one should have a
dwelling or storehouse into which all who
please may not enter; whatever necessaries are
required by moderate and courageous men,
who are trained to war, they should receive by
regular appointment from their fellow-citizens,    e
as wages for their services, and the amount
should be such as to leave neither a surplus on
the year's consumption nor a deficit; and they

should attend common messes and live together as men do in a camp; as for gold and silver, we must tell them that they are in perpetual possession of a divine species of the precious metals placed in their souls by the gods themselves, and therefore have no need of the 417 earthly ore; that in fact it would be profanation to pollute their spiritual riches by mixing them with the possession of mortal gold, because the world's coinage has been the cause of countless impieties, whereas theirs is undefiled. Therefore to them, as distinguished from the rest of the people, it is forbidden to handle or touch gold and silver, or enter under the same roof with them, or to wear them on their dresses, or to drink out of the precious metals. If they follow these rules, they will be safe themselves and the saviors of the city; but whenever they b come to possess lands, and houses, and money of their own, they will be householders and cultivators instead of guardians, and will become hostile masters of their fellow-citizens rather than their allies; and so they will spend their whole lives, hating and hated, plotting and plotted against, standing in more frequent and intense alarm of their enemies at home than of their enemies abroad; by which time they and the rest of the city will be running on the very brink of ruin. On all these accounts, I asked, shall we say that the foregoing is the right arrangement of the houses and other concerns of our guardians, and shall we legislate accordingly; or not?

Yes, by all means, answered Glaucon.

## BOOK IV

427 . . . Then the organization of our city is now
d complete, son of Ariston; and the next thing for you to do is to examine it, furnishing yourself with the necessary light from any quarter you can, and calling to your aid your brother and Polemarchus and the rest, in order to try if we can see where justice may be found in it, and where injustice, and wherein they differ

the one from the other, and which of the two the man who desires to be happy ought to possess, whether all gods and men know it or not.

That will not do! exclaimed Glaucon; it was you that engaged to make the inquiry, on the                e ground that it would not be holy for you to refuse to give justice.

I recollect that it was as you say, I replied; and I must do so, but you also must assist me.

We will.

I hope, then, that we may find the object of our search thus. I imagine that our city, being rightly organized, is a perfectly good city.

It must be.

Then obviously it is wise and brave and temperate and just.

Obviously.

Then if we can find some of these qualities in the city, there will be a remainder consisting of the undiscovered qualities.

Undoubtedly.                                                  428

Suppose then that there were any other four things, contained in any subject, and that we were in search of one of them. If we discovered this before the other three, we should be satisfied; but if we recognized the other three first, the thing sought for would by this very fact have been found; for it is plain that it could only be the remainder.

You are right.

Ought we not to adopt this mode of inquiry in the case before us, since the qualities in question are also four in number?

Clearly we ought.

To begin then, in the first place wisdom seems to be plainly discernible in our subject;            b and there seems to be something strange about it.

What is that?

The city which we have described is really wise, if I am not mistaken, inasmuch as it is prudent in counsel, is it not?

It is.

And this very quality, prudence in counsel, is evidently a kind of knowledge: for it is not ignorance, I imagine, but knowledge, that makes men deliberate prudently.

Evidently.

But there are many different kinds of knowledge in the city.

Unquestionably there are.

Is it then in virtue of the knowledge of its carpenters that the city is to be described as wise, or prudent in counsel?

c    Certainly not; for in virtue of such knowledge it could only be called a city of good carpentry.

Then it is not the knowledge it employs in considering how vessels of wood may best be made, that will justify us in calling our city wise.

Certainly not.

Well, is it the knowledge which has to do with vessels of bronze, or any other of this kind?

No, none whatever.

Neither will a knowledge of the mode of raising produce from the soil give a city the claim to the title of wise, but only to that of a successful agricultural city.

So I think.

Tell me, then, does our newly organized city contain any kind of knowledge, residing in any section of the citizens, which takes

d    measures, not in behalf of anything in the city, but in behalf of the city as a whole, devising in what manner its internal and foreign relations may best be regulated?

Certainly it does.

What is this knowledge, and in whom does it reside? It is the science of guardianship, and it resides in that ruling part, whom we just now called our perfect guardians.

Then in virtue of this knowledge what do you call the city?

I call it prudent in counsel and truly wise.

Which do you suppose will be the more

e    numerous class in our city, the smiths, or these genuine guardians?

The smiths will far outnumber the others.

Then will the guardians be the smallest of

all the classes possessing this or that branch of knowledge, and bearing this or that name in consequence?

Yes, much the smallest.

Then it is the knowledge residing in its smallest part or section, that is to say, in the predominant and ruling body, which entitles a city, organized agreeably to nature, to be called wise as a whole; and that part whose right and duty it is to partake of the knowledge   429 which alone of all kinds of knowledge is properly called wisdom, is naturally, as it appears, the least numerous body in the city.

Most true.

Here then we have made out—I do not know how—in some way or other, one of the four qualities, and the part of the city in which it is seated.

To my mind, said he, it has been made out satisfactorily.

Again, there can assuredly be no great difficulty in discerning courage itself, and the part in which it resides, and which entitles the city to be called brave.

How so?

In pronouncing a city to be cowardly or    b brave, who would look to any but that portion of it which fights in its defense and takes the field in its behalf?

No one would look to anything else.

No; and for this reason, I imagine, that the cowardice or courage of the city itself is not necessarily implied in that of the other parts.

No, it is not.

Then a city is brave as well as wise, in virtue of a certain portion of itself, because it    c has in that portion a power which can without intermission keep safe the right opinion concerning things to be feared, which teaches that they are such as the legislator has declared in the prescribed education. Is not this what you call courage?

I did not quite understand what you said; be so good as to repeat it.

I say that courage is a kind of safe keeping.

What kind of safe keeping?

The safe keeping of the opinion created by law through education, which teaches what things and what kind of things are to be feared. And when I spoke of keeping it safe without intermission, I meant that it was to be thor-
d   oughly preserved alike in moments of pain and of pleasure, of desire and of fear, and never to be cast away. And if you like, I will illustrate it by a comparison which seems to me an apt one.

I should like it.

Well then, you know that dyers, when they wish to dye wool so as to give it the true sea-purple, first select from the numerous colors one variety, that of white wool, and then subject it to much careful preparatory dressing, that it may take the color as brilliantly as possible; after which they proceed to dye it. And
e   when the wool has been dyed on this system, its color is indelible, and no washing either with or without soap can rob it of its brilliancy. But when this course has not been pursued, you know the results, whether this or any other color be dyed without previous preparation.

I know that the dye washes out in a ridiculous way.

You may understand from this what we
430   were laboring, to the best of our ability, to bring about, when we were selecting our soldiers and training them in music and gymnastic. Imagine that we were only contriving how they might be best persuaded to accept, as it were, the color of the laws, in order that their opinion concerning things to be feared, and on all other subjects, might be indelible, owing to their congenial nature and appropriate training, and that their color might not be washed out by such terribly efficacious detergents as pleasure, which works more powerfully than
b   soda or lye, and pain, and fear, and desire, which are more potent than any other solvent in the world. This power, therefore, to hold fast continually the right and lawful opinion concerning things to be feared and things not to be feared, I define to be courage, and call it by that name, if you do not object.

No, I do not; for when the right opinion on these matters is held without education, as by beasts and slaves, you would not, I think, regard it as altogether legitimate, and you would   c
give it some other name than courage.

Most true.

Then I accept this account of courage.

Do so, at least as an account of the courage of citizens, and you will be right. On a future occasion, if you like, we will go into this question more fully; at present it is beside our inquiry, the object of which is justice: we have done enough therefore, I imagine, for the investigation of courage.

You are right.

Two things, I proceeded, now remain, that we must look for in the city, temperance, and   d
that which is the cause of all these investigations, justice.

Exactly so.

Well, not to trouble ourselves any further about temperance, is there any way by which we can discover justice?

For my part, said he, I do not know, nor do I wish justice to be brought to light first, if we are to make no further inquiry after temperance; so, if you wish to gratify me, examine into the latter, before you proceed to the former.

Indeed, I do wish it, for I am not unjust.   e

Proceed then with the examination.

I will; and from our present point of view, temperance has more the appearance of a concord or harmony, than the former qualities had.

How so?

Temperance is, I imagine, a kind of order and a mastery, as men say, over certain pleasures and desires. Thus we plainly hear people talking of a man's being master of himself, in some sense or other; and other similar expressions are used, in which we may trace a print of the thing. Is it not so?

Most certainly it is.

But is not the expression 'master of himself'
a ridiculous one? For the man who is master of   431
himself will also, I presume, be the slave of

himself, and the slave will be the master. For the subject of all these phrases is the same person.

Undoubtedly.

Well, I continued, it appears to me that the meaning of the expression is, that in the man himself, that is, in his soul, there resides a good principle and a bad, and when the naturally good principle is master of the bad, this state of things is described by the term 'master of himself': certainly it is a term of praise; but when in consequence of poor training, or the influence of associates, the smaller force of the good principle is overpowered by the superior numbers of the bad, the person so situated b is described in terms of reproach and condemnation, as a slave of self, and a dissolute person.

Yes, this seems a likely account of it.

Now turn your eyes towards our new city, and you will find one of these conditions realized in it: for you will allow that it may fairly be called 'master of itself,' if temperance and self-mastery may be predicated of that in which the good principle governs the bad.

I am looking as you direct, and I acknowledge the truth of what you say.

It will further be admitted that those desires, and pleasures, and pains, which are many and c various, will be chiefly found in children, and women, and servants; and those who are called free among the common many.

Precisely so.

On the other hand, those simple and moderate desires, which go hand in hand with mind and right opinion, under the guidance of reasoning, will be found in a small number of men, that is, in those of the best natural endowments, and the best education.

True.

Do you not see that the parallel to this exists d in your city—in other words, that the desires of the vulgar many are there controlled by the desires and the wisdom of the cultivated few?

I do.

If any city then may be described as master of itself, its pleasures and its desires, ours may be so characterized.

Most certainly.

May we not then also call it temperate, on all these accounts?

Surely we may.

And again, if there is any city in which the rulers and the ruled are unanimous on the question who ought to govern, such unanimity e will exist in ours. Do you not think so?

Most assuredly I do.

In which of the two classes of citizens will you say that temperance resides, when they are in this condition? in the rulers or in the ruled?

In both, I suppose.

Do you see, then, that we were not bad prophets when we divined just now that temperance resembled a kind of harmony?

How do you mean?

Because it does not operate like courage and wisdom, which, by residing in particular sections of the city, make it brave and wise 432 respectively; but simply spreads throughout the whole, producing a unison between the weakest and the strongest and the middle part, whether you measure by the standard of prudence, or bodily strength, or numbers, or wealth, or anything else of the kind: so that we shall be fully justified in pronouncing temperance to be that unanimity, which we described as a concord between the naturally better element and the naturally worse, whether in a city or in a single person, as to which of the two has the right to rule.

I fully agree with you.                                          b

Very well, I continued; we have discerned in our city three out of the four principles; at least such is our present impression. Now what will that remaining principle be through which the city will further participate in virtue? for this, we may be sure, is justice.

Evidently it is.

Now then, Glaucon, we must be like hunters surrounding a bush, and must take care that justice nowhere escape us and disappear from our view: for it is manifest that she is    c somewhere here; so look for her, and strive to gain a sight of her, for perhaps you may discover her first, and give the alarm to me.

I wish I might, replied he; but you will use me quite well enough, if, instead of that, you will treat me as one who is following your steps, and is able to see what is pointed out to him.

Follow me then, after joining your prayers with mine.

I will do so; just you lead the way.

Truly, said I, the place seems to be shady and inaccessible, dark and hard to traverse; but still we must go on.

d  Yes, that we must.

Here I caught a glimpse, and exclaimed, Ho! ho! Glaucon, here is something that looks like a track, and I believe the game will not altogether escape us.

That is good news.

Upon my word, said I, we are in a most foolish predicament.

How so?

Why, my good sir, it appears that what we were looking for has been rolling before our feet from the beginning, and we never saw it, but did the most ridiculous thing. Just as people at times go about looking for something e  which they hold in their hands, so we, instead of fixing our eyes upon the thing itself, kept gazing at some point in the distance, and this was probably the reason why it eluded our search.

What do you mean?

This—that I believe we ourselves were just now saying and hearing it, without understanding that we were in a way describing it ourselves.

Your preface seems long to one who is anxious for the explanation.

433  Well then, listen, and judge whether I am right or not. What at the beginning we laid down as a universal rule of action, when we were founding our city, this, if I am not mistaken, or some modification of it, is justice. I think we affirmed, if you recollect, and fre-

quently repeated, that every individual ought to have some one occupation in the city, which should be that to which his natural capacity was best adapted.

We did say so.

And again, we have often heard people say, that to mind one's own business, and not be meddlesome, is justice; and we have often said the same thing ourselves.

We have said so.                                                b

Then it would seem, my friend, that to do one's own business, in some shape or other, is justice. Do you know from what I infer this?

No; be so good as to tell me.

I think that the remainder left in the city, after eliminating the things we have already considered, I mean temperance, and courage, and wisdom, must be that which made their entrance into it possible, and which preserves them there so long as they exist in it. Now we affirmed that the remainder, when three out of    c the four were found, would be justice.

Yes, unquestionably it would.

If, however, it were required to decide which of these qualities will have most influence in perfecting by its presence the virtue of our city, it would be difficult to determine; whether it will be the harmony of opinion between the rulers and the ruled, or the faithful adherence on the part of the soldiers to the lawful belief concerning the things which are, and the things which are not, to be feared; or the existence of wisdom and watchfulness in the     d rulers; or whether the virtue of the city may not be chiefly traced to the presence of that fourth principle in every child and woman, in every slave, freeman, and artisan, in the ruler and in the ruled, requiring each to do his own work, and not meddle with many things.

It would be a difficult point to settle, unquestionably.

Thus it appears that, in promoting the virtue of a city, the power that makes each member of it do his own work, may compete with its wisdom, and its temperance, and its courage.

Decidedly it may.

But if there is a principle which rivals these qualities in promoting the virtue of a city, will you not determine it to be justice?

Most assuredly.

Consider the question in another light, and see whether you will come to the same conclusion. Will you assign to the rulers of the city the judging of law-suits?

Certainly.

Will not their judgments be guided, above everything, by the desire that no one may appropriate what belongs to others, nor be deprived of what is his own?

Yes, that will be their main study.

Because that is just?

Yes.

Thus, according to this view also, it will be granted that to have and do what belongs to us and is our own, is justice.

True.

Now observe whether you hold the same opinion that I do. If a carpenter should undertake to execute the work of a shoemaker, or a shoemaker that of a carpenter, either by interchanging their tools and honors, or by the same person undertaking both trades, with all the changes involved in it, do you think it would greatly damage the city?

Not very greatly.

But when one whom nature has made an artisan, or a producer of any other kind, is so elated by wealth, or a large connection, or bodily strength, or any similar advantages, as to intrude himself into the class of the warriors; or when a warrior intrudes himself into the class of the counselors and guardians, of which he is unworthy, and when these interchange their tools and their distinctions, or when one and the same person attempts to discharge all these duties at once, then, I imagine, you will agree with me, that such change and meddling among these will be ruinous to the city.

Most assuredly they will.

Then any intermeddling in the three parts, or change from one to another, would inflict great damage on the city, and may with perfect propriety be described, in the strongest sense, as doing harm.

Quite so.

And will you not admit that the greatest harm towards one's own city is injustice?

Unquestionably.

This then is injustice. On the other hand, let us state that, conversely, adherence to their own business on the part of the merchants, the military, and the guardians, each of these doing its own work in the city, is justice, and will render the city just.

I fully agree, he said.

Let us not state it yet quite positively; but if we find, on applying this form to the individual man, that there too it is recognized as constituting justice, we will then give our assent—for what more can we say?—but if not, in that case we will begin a new inquiry. At present, however, let us complete the investigation which we undertook in the belief that, if we first endeavored to contemplate justice in some larger subject which contains it, we should find it easier to discern its nature in the individual man. Such a subject we recognized in a city, and accordingly we organized the best we could, being sure that justice must reside in a *good* city. The view, therefore, which presented itself to us there, let us now apply to the individual; and if it be admitted, we shall be satisfied; but if we should find something different in the case of the individual, we will again go back to our city, and put our theory to the test. And perhaps by considering the two cases side by side, and rubbing them together, we may cause justice to flash out from the contact, like fire from dry bits of wood, and when it has become visible to us, may settle it firmly in our own minds.

There is method in your proposal, he replied, and so let us do.

I proceeded therefore to ask: When two things, a greater and a less, are called by a common name, are they, in so far as the common name applies, unlike or like?

Like.

Then a just man will not differ from a just

b  city, so far as the form of justice is involved, but the two will be like.

They will.

Well, but we resolved that a city was just, when the three natural kinds present in it were severally occupied in doing their proper work; and that it was temperate, and brave, and wise, in consequence of certain affections and conditions of these same classes.

True.

Then, my friend, we shall make the same

c  claim in the case of the single individual, and, supposing him to have the same forms in his soul, on account of having the same affections as those in the city, we shall judge that he can be deemed worthy of the same names as the city.

It must inevitably be so.

Once more then, my excellent friend, we have stumbled on an easy question concerning the nature of the soul, namely, whether it contains these three forms or not.

Not so very easy a question, I think; but perhaps, Socrates, the common saying is true, that the beautiful is difficult.

It would appear so; and I tell you plainly,

d  Glaucon, that in my opinion we shall never attain to exact truth on this subject, by such methods as we are employing in our present discussion. However, the path that leads to that goal is too long and toilsome; and I dare say we may arrive at the truth by our present methods, in a manner not unworthy of our former arguments and speculations.

Shall we not be content with that? For my part it would satisfy me for the present.

Well, certainly it will be quite enough for me.

Do not give up, then, but proceed with the inquiry.

e  Then tell me, I continued, can we possibly

refuse to admit that there exist in each of us the same forms and characters as are found in the city? For I presume the city has not received them from any other source. It would be ridiculous to imagine that the presence of the spirited element in cities is not to be traced to individuals, wherever this character is imputed to the people, as it is to the natives of Thrace, and Scythia, and generally speaking, of the northern countries; or the love of study, which would be chiefly attributed to our own   436 country; or the love of riches, which people would especially connect with the Phoenicians and the Egyptians.

Certainly.

This then is a fact so far, and one which it is not difficult to apprehend.

No, it is not.

But here begins a difficulty. Are all our actions alike performed by the one faculty, or are there three faculties operating severally in our different actions? Do we learn with one faculty, and become angry with another, and with a third feel desire for all the pleasures connected with eating and drinking, and the propa-   b gation of the species; or upon every impulse to action, do we perform these several operations with the whole soul? The difficulty will consist in settling these points in a satisfactory manner.

I think so too.

Let us try therefore the following plan, in order to ascertain whether the faculties engaged are distinct or identical.

What is your plan?

It is manifest that the same thing cannot do two opposite things, or be in two opposite states, in the same part of it, and with reference to the same object; so that where we find these   c phenomena occurring, we shall know that the subjects of them are not identical, but more than one.

Very well.

Now consider what I say.

Speak on.

Is it possible for the same thing to be at the

same time, and in the same part of it, at rest and in motion?

Certainly not.

Let us come to a still more exact understanding, lest we should chance to differ as we proceed. If it were said of a man who is standing still, but moving his hands and his head, that the same individual is at the same time at rest and in motion, we should not, I imagine, allow this to be a correct way of speaking, but should say, that part of the man is at rest, and part in motion; should we not?

We should.

And if the objector should indulge in yet further pleasantries, so far refining as to say, that at any rate a top is wholly at rest and in motion at the same time, when it spins with its peg fixed on a given spot, or that anything else revolving in the same place, is an instance of the same thing, we should reject his illustration, because in such cases the things are not both stationary and in motion in respect of the same parts of them; and we should reply, that they contain an axis and a circumference, and that in respect of the axis they are stationary, inasmuch as they do not lean to any side; but in respect of the circumference they are moving round and round; but if, while the rotatory motion continues, the axis at the same time inclines to the right or to the left, forwards or backwards, then they cannot be said in any sense to be at rest.

That is true.

Then no objection of that kind will alarm us, or tend at all to convince us that it is ever possible for one and the same thing, at the same time, in the same part of it, and relatively to the same object to be acted upon in two opposite ways or to be two opposite things, or to produce two opposite effects.

It will not alarm me, at any rate.

However, that we may not be compelled to spend time in discussing all such objections, and convincing ourselves that they are unsound, let us assume this to be the fact, and proceed forwards, with the understanding that, if ever we take a different view of this matter, all the conclusions founded on this assumption will fall to the ground.

Yes, that will be the best way.

Well then, I continued, would you place assent and dissent, the seeking after an object and the refusal of it, attraction and repulsion, and the like, in the class of mutual opposites? Whether they be active or passive processes will not affect the question.

Yes, I should.

Well, would you not, without exception, include hunger and thirst, and the desires generally, and likewise willing and wishing, somewhere under the earlier forms just mentioned? For instance, would you not say that the soul of a man under the influence of desire always either seeks after the object of desire, or attracts to itself that which it wishes to have; or again, so far as it wills the possession of anything, it assents inwardly thereto, as though it were asked a question, longing for the accomplishment of its wish?

I should.

Again, shall we not classify disinclination, unwillingness, and not-desiring with the soul's thrusting and driving away from itself, and alongside the opposites of the previously discussed cases?

Unquestionably.

This being the case, shall we say that desires form a class, the most marked of which are what we call thirst and hunger?

We shall.

The one being a desire of drink, and the other of food?

Yes.

Can thirst then, so far as it is thirst, be a desire of anything more than drink? That is to say, is thirst, as such, a thirst for hot drink or cold, for much or little, or, in one word, for any particular kind of drink? Or, will it not rather be true that, if there be heat combined with the thirst, the desire of cold drink will be superadded to it, and if there be cold, of hot drink;

and if owing to the presence of 'muchness,' the thirst be great, the desire of much will be added, and if little, the desire of little; but that thirst in itself cannot be a desire of anything else than its natural object, which is simple drink, or again, hunger, of anything but food?

You are right, he replied; every desire in itself is of its natural object, while the desire for this or that particular is added on.

438    Let not any one, I proceeded, for want of consideration on our part, disturb us by the objection, that no one desires drink simply, but good drink, nor food simply, but good food; because, since all desire good things, if thirst is a desire, it must be a desire of something good, whether that something, which is its object, be drink or anything else; an argument which applies to all the desires.

True, there might seem to be something in the objection.

Recollect, however, that in the case of all essentially correlative terms, when the first member of the relation is qualified, the second

b    is also qualified, if I am not mistaken; but individually they are both related to something which is unqualifiedly itself.

I do not understand you.

Do you not understand that 'greater' is a relative term, implying another term?

Certainly.

It implies a 'less,' does it not?

Yes.

And a much greater implies a much less, does it not?

Yes.

Does a once greater also imply a once less, and a future greater a future less?

Inevitably.

c    Does not the same reasoning apply to the correlative terms, 'more' and 'fewer,' 'double' and 'half,' and all relations of quantity; also to the terms, 'heavier' and 'lighter,' 'quicker' and 'slower'; and likewise to 'cold' and 'hot,' and all similar terms?

Certainly it does.

But how is it with the various types of knowledge? Does not the same principle hold? That is, knowledge itself is knowledge simply of the knowable, or of whatever that be called which is the object of knowledge; but a particular science, of a particular kind, has a particular object of a particular kind. To explain my meaning: as soon as a knowledge of the con-    d struction of houses arose, was it not distinguished from other kinds of knowledge, and thus called the science of building?

Undoubtedly.

And is it not because it is of a particular character, which no other science possesses?

Yes.

And is not its particular character derived from the particular character of its object? and may we not say the same of all the other arts and sciences?

We may.

This then you are to regard as having been my meaning before—provided, that is, you now understand that in the case of all correlative terms, of whatever sort the first member is, the second is also of that sort; if the second is qualified, the first is also qualified. I do not mean to say that the qualities of the two are    e identical, as for instance, that the science of health is healthy, and the science of disease diseased; or that the science of evil things is evil, and of good things good: but as soon as knowledge, instead of limiting itself to those objects to which knowledge is related, became related to a particular kind of object, namely, in the present case, the conditions of health and disease, the result was that the knowledge also came to be qualified in a certain manner, so that it was no longer called simply science, but, by the addition of a qualifying epithet, medical science.

I understand, and I think what you say is true.

To return to the case of thirst, I continued, do you not consider this to be one of the things whose nature it is to have an object correlative    439 with themselves, assuming that there is such a thing as thirst?

I do, and its object is drink.

Then, for any particular kind of drink there is a particular kind of thirst; but thirst itself is neither for much drink, nor for little, neither for good drink nor for bad, nor, in one word, for any kind of drink, but simply and absolutely thirst for drink, is it not?

Most decidedly so.

b Then the soul of a thirsty man, in so far as he is thirsty, has no other wish than to drink; but this it desires, and towards this it is impelled.

Clearly so.

Therefore, whenever anything pulls back a soul that is under the influence of thirst, it will be something in the soul distinct from the principle which thirsts, and which drives it like a beast to drink: for we hold it to be impossible that the same thing should, at the same time, with the same part of itself, in reference to the same object, be doing two opposite things.

Certainly it is.

Just as, I imagine, it would not be right to say of the bowman, that his hands are at the same time drawing the bow towards him, and pushing it from him—the fact being, that one of his hands pushes it from him, and the other pulls it to him.

Precisely so.

c Now, can we say that people sometimes are thirsty, and yet do not wish to drink?

Yes, certainly; it often happens to many people.

What then can one say of them, except that their soul contains one principle which commands, and another which forbids them to drink, the latter being distinct from and stronger than the former?

That is my opinion.

Whenever the authority which forbids such d indulgences grows up in the soul, is it not engendered there by reasoning; while the powers which lead and draw the soul towards them, owe their presence to passive and morbid states?

It would appear so.

Then we shall have reasonable grounds for assuming that these are two principles distinct one from the other, and for giving to that part of the soul with which it reasons the title of the rational principle, and to that part with which it loves and hungers and thirsts, and experiences the flutter of the other desires, the title of the irrational and appetitive principle, the ally of sundry indulgences and pleasures.

Yes, he replied; it will not be unreasonable e to think so.

Let us consider it settled, then, that these two specific parts exist in the soul. But now, will spirit, or that by which we feel indignant, constitute a third distinct part? If not, with which of the two former has it a natural affinity?

Perhaps with the appetitive principle.

But I was once told a story, which I can quite believe, to the effect, that Leontius, the son of Aglaion, as he was walking up from the Piraeus, and approaching the northern wall from the outside, observed some dead bodies on the ground, and the executioner standing by them. He immediately felt a desire to look at them, but at the same time loathing the thought he tried to divert himself from it. For some 440 time he struggled with himself, and covered his eyes, until at length, over-mastered by the desire, he opened his eyes wide with his fingers, and running up to the bodies, exclaimed, 'There! you wretches! gaze your fill at the beautiful spectacle!'

I have heard this too.

This story, however, indicates that anger sometimes fights against the desires, which implies that they are two distinct principles.

True, it does indicate that.

And do we not often observe in other cases that when a man is overpowered by the desires b against the dictates of his reason, he reviles himself, and resents the violence thus exerted within him, and that, in this struggle of contending parties, the spirit sides with the reason? But that it should make common cause with the desires, when the reason pronounces that they ought not to act against itself, is a thing which I suppose you will not profess to have experienced yourself, nor yet, I imagine, have you ever noticed it in any one else.

No, I am sure I have not.

c      Well, and when any one thinks he is in the wrong, is he not, in proportion to the nobleness of his character, so much the less able to be angry at being made to suffer hunger or cold or any similar pain at the hands of him whom he thinks justified in so treating him; his spirit, as I describe it, refusing to be roused against his punisher?

True.

On the other hand, when any one thinks he is wronged, does he not instantly boil and chafe, and enlist himself on the side of what he thinks to be justice; and whatever extremities of hunger and cold and the like he may have to suffer, does he not endure until he conquers, d      never ceasing from his noble efforts, until he has either gained his point, or perished in the attempt, or been recalled and calmed by the voice of reason within, as a dog is called off by a shepherd?

Yes, he replied, the case answers very closely to your description; and in fact, in our city we made the auxiliaries, like sheep-dogs, subject to the rulers, who are as it were the shepherds of the city.

You rightly understand my meaning. But try whether you also apprehend my next observation.

e      What is it?

That our recent view of the spirited principle is exactly reversed. Then we thought it had something of the appetitive character, but now we say that, far from this being the case, it much more readily takes arms on the side of the rational principle in the party conflict of the soul.

Decidedly it does.

Is it then distinct from this principle also; or is it only a modification of it, thus making two instead of three distinct principles in the soul, namely, the rational and the appetitive? Or ought we to say that, as the city was held to-      441 gether by three great classes, the producing part, the auxiliary, and the deliberative, so also in the soul the spirited principle constitutes a third element, the natural ally of the rational principle, if it be not corrupted by bad training?

It must be a third, he replied.

Yes, I continued; if it shall appear to be distinct, from the rational principle, as we found it different from the appetitive.

That will easily appear. For even in little children any one may see this, that from their very birth they have plenty of spirit, whereas reason is a principle to which most men only      b attain after many years, and some, in my opinion, never.

Upon my word, well said. In brute beasts also one may see what you describe exemplified. And besides, that passage in Homer, which we quoted on a former occasion, will support our view:

*'Smiting his breast, to his heart thus spake
he in accents of chiding.'*

For in this line Homer has distinctly made a      c difference between the two principles, representing that which had considered the good or the bad of the action as rebuking that which was indulging in unreflecting resentment.

You are perfectly right.

Here then, I proceeded, after a hard swim, we have, though with difficulty, reached the land; and we are pretty well satisfied that there are corresponding divisions, equal in number, in a city, and in the soul of every individual.

True.

Then does it not necessarily follow that, as and whereby the city was wise, so and thereby the individual is wise?

Without doubt it does.

And that as and whereby the individual is      d brave, so and thereby is the city brave; and that everything conducing to virtue which is possessed by the one, finds its counterpart in the other?

It must be so.

Then we shall also assert, I imagine, Glaucon, that a man is just, in the same way in which we found the city to be just.

This too is a necessary corollary.

But surely we have not allowed ourselves to forget, that what makes the city just, is the fact of each of the three parts therein doing its own work.

No; I think we have not forgotten this.

e    We must bear in mind, then, that each of us also, if his inward parts do severally their proper work, will, in virtue of that, be a just man, and a doer of his proper work.

Certainly, it must be borne in mind.

Is it not then essentially the domain of the rational principle to command, inasmuch as it is wise, and has to exercise forethought in behalf of the entire soul, and the domain of the spirited principle to be its subject and ally?

Yes, certainly.

442   And will not the combination of music and gymnastic bring them, as we said, into unison—elevating and fostering the one with lofty discourses and scientific teachings, and lowering the tone of the other by soothing address, until its wildness has been tamed by harmony and rhythm?

Yes, precisely so.

And so these two, having been thus trained, and having truly learned their parts and having been educated, will exercise control over the appetitive principle, which in every man forms the largest portion of the soul, and is by nature most insatiable. And they will watch it narrowly, that it may not be filled with what are called the pleasures of the body, as to grow large and strong, and forthwith refuse to do its

b    proper work, and even aspire to subjugate and dominate over that which it has no right to rule by virtue of its class, thus totally upsetting the life of all.

Certainly they will.

And would not these two principles be the best qualified to guard the entire soul and body against enemies from without—the one taking counsel, and the other fighting its battles, in obedience to the ruling power, to whose designs it gives effect by its bravery?

True.

In like manner, I think, we call an individ-   c
ual brave, in virtue of the spirited element of his nature, when this part of him holds fast, through pain and pleasure, the instructions of the reason as to what is to be feared, and what is not.

Yes, and rightly.

And we call him wise, in virtue of that small part which reigns within him, and issues these instructions, and which also in its turn contains within itself a true knowledge of what is advantageous for the whole community composed of these three principles, and for each member of it.

Exactly so.

Again, do we not call a man temperate, in virtue of the friendship and harmony of these same principles, that is to say, when the two that are governed agree with that which governs in regarding the rational principle as the rightful sovereign, and set up no opposition to   d
its authority?

Certainly, he replied; temperance is nothing else than this, whether in city or individual.

Lastly, a man will be just, in the way and by the means which we have repeatedly described.

Unquestionably he will.

Tell me then, I proceeded, do we find anything indistinct in our view of justice, which makes us regard it as something different from what we found it to be in the city?

I do not think so.

Because we might thoroughly confirm our opinion, if we have any lingering doubts in   e
our souls, by applying commonplace examples to it.

What kind of examples do you mean?

For example, if in speaking of this city, and

of an individual who in nature and training resembles it, we were required to declare whether we think that such an individual would
443   despoil a deposit of gold or silver committed to his charge, do you suppose that any one would think him more likely to do such a deed than other men who are not such as he is?

No one would think so.

And will he not also be clear of suspicion of temple robbery, and of theft, and of being either false to his friends, or a traitor to his country?

He will.

Moreover, he will be wholly incapable of bad faith, in the case of an oath or of any other kind of contract.

Clearly he will.

Again, he is the last person in the world to be guilty of adultery, or neglect of parents, or indifference to the worship of the gods.

Certainly he is.

And is not all this attributable to the fact
b   that each of his inward principles keeps to his own work in regard to the relations of ruler and the ruled?

Yes, it may be entirely attributed to this.

Do you still seek then for any other account of justice than that it is the power which creates such men and such cities?

No, he replied, assuredly I do not.

Then our dream is completely realized, or that suspicion which we expressed, that at the
c   very beginning of the work of constructing our city we were led by some divine intervention, as it would seem, to a kind of rudimentary type of justice.

Yes, it certainly is.

And so there really was, Glaucon, an image of justice—and hence of its utility—in the principle that it is right for a man whom nature intended for a shoemaker to confine himself to shoemaking, and for a man who has a turn for carpentering to do carpenter's work, and so on.

It appears so.

The truth being that justice is indeed, to all appearance, something of the kind, only that,

instead of dealing with a man's outward performance of his own work, it has to do with that inward performance of it which truly concerns   d
the man himself, and his own interests: so that the just man will not permit the several principles within him to do any work but their own, nor allow the distinct classes in his soul to interfere with each other, but will really set his house in order; and having gained the mastery over himself, will so regulate his own character as to be on good terms with himself, and to set those three principles in tune together, as if they were verily three chords of a harmony, a higher and a lower and a middle, and whatever may lie between these; and after he has bound all these together, and reduced the many elements of his nature to a real unity, as a temper-   e
ate and duly harmonized man, he will then at length proceed to do whatever he may have to do, whether it involve a business transaction, or the care of his body, a political matter or a private contract; in all which he will believe and profess that the just and honorable course is that which preserves and assists in creating the aforesaid condition, and that the genuine knowledge which presides over such conduct is wisdom; while on the other hand, he will hold that an unjust action is one which tends to   444
destroy this habit, and that the mere opinion which presides over unjust conduct, is folly.

What you say is thoroughly true, Socrates.

Very good; if we were to say we have discovered the just man and the just city, and what justice is as found in them, it would not be thought, I imagine, to be an altogether false statement.

No, indeed, it would not.

Shall we say so then?

We will.

Be it so, I continued. In the next place we have to investigate, I imagine, what injustice is.

Evidently we have.

Must it not then, as the reverse of justice, be   b
a state of strife between the three principles, and the disposition to meddle and interfere, and the insurrection of a part of the soul against the

whole, this part aspiring to the supreme power within the soul, to which it has no right, its proper place and destination being, on the contrary, to do service to any member of the rightfully ruling part? Such doings as these, I imagine, and the confusion and bewilderment of the aforesaid principles, will, in our opinion, constitute injustice, and licentiousness, and cowardice, and folly, and, in one word, all vice.

Yes, precisely so.

c   And is it not now quite clear to us what it is to act unjustly, and to be unjust, and, on the other hand, what it is to act justly, knowing as we do the nature of justice and injustice?

How so?

Because there happens to be no difference with regard to the health and disease of the body and the soul.

In what way?

The conditions of health, I presume, produce health, and those of disease engender disease.

Yes.

d   In the same way, does not the practice of justice beget the habit of justice, and the practice of injustice the habit of injustice?

Inevitably.

Now to produce health is so to constitute the bodily forces as that they shall master and be mastered by one another in accordance with nature; and to produce disease is to make them govern and be governed by one another in a way which violates nature.

True.

Similarly, will it not be true that to beget justice is so to constitute the powers of the soul that they shall master and be mastered by one another in accordance with nature, and that to beget injustice is to make them rule and be ruled by one another in a way which violates nature?

Quite so.

Then virtue, it appears, will be a kind of
e   health and beauty, and good habit of the soul; and vice will be a disease, and deformity, and sickness of it.

True.

And may we not add, that all fair practices tend to the acquisition of virtue, and all foul practices to that of vice?

Undoubtedly they do.

What now remains for us, apparently, is to inquire whether it is also profitable to act justly, and to pursue honorable aims, and to be   445 just, whether a man be known to be such or not, or to act unjustly, and to be unjust, if one suffer no punishment, and be not made a better man by chastisement.

To me, Socrates, I confess that the inquiry begins to assume a ludicrous appearance, now that the real nature of justice and injustice has presented itself to us in the light described above. Do people think that when the constitution of the body is ruined, life is not worth having, though you may command all varieties of food and drink, and possess endless wealth and power; and shall we be told that, when the con-   b stitution of that very principle whereby we live is going to rack and ruin, life is still worth having, let a man do what he will, if that is excepted which will enable him to get rid of vice and injustice, and to acquire virtue and justice?

Yes, it is ludicrous, I replied; still, since we have arrived at this point, we must not lose heart, until we have ascertained, in the clearest possible manner, the correctness of our conclusions.

No, indeed; anything rather than lose heart.

Come with me, then, that you may see how   c many varieties of vice there are, according to my belief, looking only at those which are worth the survey.

I follow you; just tell me.

Well, I can see as it were from a watchtower, now that we have ascended to this lofty stage in the argument, that while there is only one form of virtue, there are infinite varieties of vice, of which four in particular deserve to be noticed.

How do you mean?

It would seem that there are as many char-   d acters of soul, as there are distinctive forms of government.

How many are they?

There are five forms of regime and five characters of soul.

Tell me what they are.

I will: one form of government will be that which we have been describing, and it may be called by two different names—should there arise among the governing body one man excelling the rest, it will be called a kingdom; if there be more than one of equal excellence, it will be entitled an aristocracy.

e     True.

This then I call one form: for whether it belongs to one or many, any law of the city worth mentioning will not change, if their training and education be such as we have described.

So we may justly expect, he replied.

# BOOK V

449     Such then is the city and commonwealth which I call good and right, and such is the good man. And if this one be right, I must call the rest bad and wrong; applying these terms both to the organization of cities, and to the formation of individual character; and the vicious forms are reducible to four varieties.

And what are these? he asked.

b     Hereupon I was proceeding to speak of them in order as they appeared to me to pass severally into one another when Polemarchus, who was seated a little further off than Adeimantus, put out his hand to take hold of his cloak high up near the shoulder, drew him towards himself, and leaning forwards whispered a few words into his ear, of which we only caught the following:

Shall we let him off then, or what shall we do?

Certainly not, said Adeimantus, beginning to speak aloud.

Whereupon I said, And what may that be which you are not going to let off?

You, he replied.

And how so? I further inquired.                          c

We have an idea that you are lagging, and stealing a whole section, and that a very important one, from the subject, in order to avoid handling it; and we suppose you thought that we should not notice your passing it over with the very slight remark, that every one would see that the rule, 'among friends every thing is common property,' would apply to the women and children.

Well, and was I not right, Adeimantus?

Yes; but this word 'right,' like the rest, needs explanation. We must be told on what     d plan, among the many possible ones, this community of property is to be carried out. Do not therefore omit to tell us what plan you propose. For we have been long waiting in the expectation that you would specify the conditions under which children are to be begotten, and the manner of rearing them after they are born, and, in fact, that you would give a complete description of the community of women and children intended by you: for we are of the opinion that the mode of carrying out this idea, according as it is right or wrong, will be a matter of great, indeed of vital importance, to a regime. So, finding that you are taking in hand another form of regime, before you have satisfactorily settled these points, we have come to the resolution which you overheard, not to let     450 you go until you have discussed all these questions as fully as the others.

Add my vote also, said Glaucon, as a supporter of this motion.

In short, Socrates, said Thrasymachus, you may look upon us as unanimous in this resolution.

What a deed you have done! I exclaimed, in thus laying hands upon me. What a large question are you again raising, as if we were beginning anew, on the subject of our regime! I was rejoicing in the idea of having already done with it, and was only too glad that those points should be let alone, and accepted as they were

then delivered. You do not know what a
swarm of questions you are rousing by calling
in these topics; but I saw at the time how the
case stood, and therefore let the subject go by,
lest it should occasion us endless trouble.

How so? exclaimed Thrasymachus; do you
suppose that we came here on a gold-hunting
errand, and not expressly to hear a philosophical discussion?

Yes, one of reasonable length, I replied.

True, Socrates, said Glaucon; and in the
eyes of sensible people their whole life is but a
reasonable time for hearing such discussions.
So never mind us; but do not grow tired yourself of stating your views on the subjects about
which we were asking, I mean, as to the nature
of this community of women and children,
which is to subsist among our guardians; and
as to the training of the young, in the interval
between their birth and education, which is
considered the most troublesome business of
all. Try to explain to us on what principle this
is to be conducted.

It is no easy matter, my gifted friend, to discuss this question: for it is beset with many
doubts, even more than our previous deliberation. In the first place, it will not be believed
that what was said is possible; and in the next
place, supposing them to be most completely
carried out, their desirableness will be questioned. And that is why I feel a reluctance to
grapple with the subject, lest, my dear friend,
our argument be thought to be merely wishful
thinking.

You need feel no reluctance, he replied: for
your auditors are neither stupid, nor incredulous, nor unfriendly.

Upon which I asked, My excellent friend,
did you wish to encourage me by your assurance?

I did.

Then, let me tell you, you have done just the
contrary. If I were confident of my own knowledge of the subject, your encouragement would
have been well and good; for to speak on the
most momentous and interesting topics in the
company of intelligent friends, is a thing that
may be done with courage and safety, if one
really knows the subject; but to broach the
arguments while one is still in the position of a
doubting inquirer, as I am going to do, is a slippery course, and makes me afraid, not of being
laughed at—that would be childish—but lest I
should miss my footing upon the truth, and
falling, drag my friends down with me, and that
upon ground on which a false step is especially
to be dreaded. I bow to Nemesis, Glaucon, for
what I am going to say; for I believe that being
accused of involuntary manslaughter is less of
a fault than being a deceiver concerning what is
lawfully beautiful, good, and just. Such a risk it
were better to run among enemies than among
friends; so that you are happy in your choice of
encouragement.

At this Glaucon laughed, and said, Well,
Socrates, should your speech do us any harm,
our blood shall not be upon your head; we
absolve you from the guilt of deceiving us;
therefore speak boldly.

To be sure, I replied, the law tells us that,
when a man has been absolved from murder,
he is clean even in the next world; and therefore, in all probability, in this world also.

Very well then, let not this fear hinder you
from proceeding.

I must return, then, to a portion of our subject which perhaps I ought to have discussed
before in its proper place. But after all, the
present order may be the best; the male drama
having been played out; we proceed then with
the performance of the women; especially
since this is the order of your challenge.

For men born and educated as we have described, the only right method, in my opinion,
of acquiring and treating children and women
will be found in following out that original
impulse which we communicated to them. The
aim of our argument was, I believe, to make our
men as it were guardians of a flock.

Yes.

d       Let us keep on the same track, and give corresponding rules for the propagation of the species, and for rearing the young; and let us observe whether we find them suitable or not.

How do you mean?

Thus. Do we think that the females of watch-dogs ought to guard the flock along with the males, and hunt with them, and share in all their other duties; or that the females ought to stay at home, because they are disabled by having to breed and rear the cubs, while the males are to labor and be charged with all the care of the flocks?

e       We expect them to share in whatever is to be done; only we treat the females as the weaker, and the males as the stronger.

Is it possible to use animals for the same work, if you do not give them the same training and education?

It is not.

452    If then we are to employ the women in the same duties as the men, we must give them the same instructions.

Yes.

To the men we gave music and gymnastic.

Yes.

Then we must train the women also in the same two arts, giving them besides a military education, and treating them in the same way as the men.

It follows naturally from what you say.

Perhaps many of the details of the question before us might appear unusually ridiculous, if carried out in the manner proposed.

No doubt they would.

Which of them do you find the most ridiculous? Is it not obviously the notion of the

b   women exercising naked in the schools with the men, and not only the young women, but even those of an advanced age, just like those old men in the gymnasia, who, in spite of wrinkles and ugliness, still keep up their fondness for active exercises?

Yes, indeed; at the present day that would appear truly ridiculous.

Well then, as we have started the subject, we must not be afraid of the numerous jests which worthy men may make upon the notion of carrying out such a change in reference to c the gymnasia and music; and above all, in the wearing of armor and riding on horseback.

You are right.

On the contrary, as we have begun the discussion, we must travel on to the rougher ground of our law, entreating these witty men to leave off their usual practice, and try to be serious; and reminding them that not long since it was thought discreditable and ridiculous among the Greeks, as it is now among most barbarians, for men to be seen naked. And when the Cretans first, and after them the Lacedaemonians, began the practice of gymnastic exercises, the wits of the time had it in d their power to make sport of those novelties. Do you not think so?

I do.

But when experience had shown that it was better to strip than to cover up the body, and when the ridiculous effect of this plan on the eye had given way before the arguments establishing its superiority, it was at the same time demonstrated, I imagine, that he is a fool who thinks anything ridiculous but that which is bad, and who attempts to raise a laugh by assuming any object to be ridiculous but that e which is unwise and bad; or who chooses for the aim of his serious admiration any other mark save that which is good.

Most assuredly.

Must we not then first come to an agreement as to whether the regulations proposed are possible or not, and give to any one, 453 whether of a humorous or serious turn, an opportunity of raising the question, whether the nature of the human female is such as to enable her to share in all the employments of the male, or whether she is wholly unequal to any, or equal to some and not to others; and if so, to which class military service belongs? Will not this be the way to make the best beginning, and, in all probability, the best ending also?

Yes, quite so.

Would you like, then, that we should argue against ourselves in behalf of an objector, that the opposition may not be attacked without a defense?

b     There is no reason why we should not.

Then let us say in his behalf: 'Socrates and Glaucon, there is no need for others to advance anything against you; for you yourselves, at the beginning of your scheme for constructing a city, admitted that every individual therein ought, in accordance with nature, to do the one work which belongs to him.' 'We did admit
c     this, I imagine; how could we do otherwise?' 'Can you deny that there is a very marked difference between the nature of woman and that of man?' 'Of course there is a difference.' 'Then is it not fitting to assign to each sex a different work, appropriate to its peculiar nature?' 'Undoubtedly.' 'Then if so, you must be in error now, and be contradicting yourselves when you go on to say, that men and women ought to engage in the same occupations, when their natures are so widely diverse?' Do you have any answer to that objection, my clever friend?

It is not so very easy to find one at a moment's notice; but I shall beg you, and I do so now, to state what the arguments on our side are, and to expound them for us.

These objections, Glaucon, and many oth-
d     ers like them, are what I anticipated all along; and that is why I was afraid and reluctant to meddle with the law that regulates the possession of the women and children, and the rearing of the latter.

To say the truth, it does seem no easy task.

Why no; but the fact is, that whether you fall into a small swimming-bath, or into the middle of the great ocean, you have to swim all the same.

Exactly so.

Then is it not best for us, in the present instance, to strike out and endeavor to emerge in safety from the discussion, in the hope that either a dolphin may take us on his back, or some other unlooked-for deliverance present itself?

It would seem so.                                                    e

Come then, I continued, let us see if we can find the way out. We admitted, you say, that different natures ought to have different occupations, and that the natures of men and women are different; but now we maintain that these different natures ought to engage in the same occupations. Is this your charge against us?

Precisely.

Truly, Glaucon, the power of the art of con-   454
tradiction is very extraordinary.

How so?

Because it seems to me that many fall into it even against their will, and think they are discussing, when they are merely debating, because they cannot distinguish the meanings of a term, in their investigation of any question, but carry on their opposition to what is stated, by attacking the mere words, employing the art of eristical debate, and not that of dialectical discussion.

This is no doubt the case with many; does it apply to us at the present moment?

Most assuredly it does; at any rate there is    b
every appearance of our having fallen unintentionally into a verbal contradiction.

How so?

In hard pursuit of the name, we say, in the most courageous style of eristical debate that different natures ought not to engage in the same pursuits; but we did not in any way consider what form of sameness and difference of nature and what that referred to; and what we had in view in our definition, when we assigned different pursuits to different natures, and the same pursuits to the same natures.

It is true we have not considered that.

That being the case, it is open to us appar-   c
ently to ask ourselves whether bald men and

long-haired men are of the same or of opposite natures, and after admitting the latter to be the case, we may say that if bald men make shoes, long-haired men must not be allowed to make them, or if the long-haired men make them, the others must be forbidden to do so.

No, that would be ridiculous.

Would it be ridiculous, except for the reason that we did not agree on 'the same' and 'different nature' in every respect, being engaged only with that form of likeness and difference which applied directly to the pursuits in question? For example, we said that a male and female physician have the same nature and soul. Or do you not think so?

I do.

And that a man who would make a good physician had a different nature from one who would make a good carpenter.

Of course he has.

If, then, the male and the female sex appear to differ in reference to any art, or other occupation, we shall say that such occupation must be appropriated to the one or the other; but if we find the difference between the sexes to consist simply in the parts they respectively bear in the propagation of the species, we shall assert that it has not yet been by any means demonstrated that the difference between man and woman touches our purpose; on the contrary, we shall still think it proper for our guardians and their wives to engage in the same pursuits.

And rightly.

Shall we not proceed to call upon our opponents to inform us what is that particular art or occupation connected with the organization of a city, in reference to which the nature of a man and a woman are not the same, but diverse?

We certainly are entitled to do so.

Well, perhaps it might be pleaded by others, as it was a little while ago by you, that it is not easy to give a satisfactory answer at a moment's notice; but that, with time for consideration, it would not be difficult to do so.

True, it might.

Would you like us then to beg the author of such objections to accompany us, to see if we can show him that no occupation which belongs to the ordering of a city is peculiar to women?

By all means.

Well then, we will address him thus: Tell us whether, when you say that one man possesses talents for a particular study, and that another is without them, you mean that the former learns it easily, the latter with difficulty; and that the one with little instruction can find out much for himself in the subject he has studied, whereas the other after much teaching and practice cannot even retain what he has learnt; and that the reasoning of the one is duly aided, that of the other thwarted, by the bodily powers? Are not these the only marks by which you define the possession and the want of natural talents for any pursuit?

Every one will say yes.

Well then, do you know of any branch of human industry in which the female sex is not inferior in these respects to the male? or need we go the length of specifying the art of weaving, and the manufacture of pastry and preserves, in which women are thought to excel, and in which their defeat is most laughed at?

You are perfectly right, that in almost every employment the one sex is vastly superior to the other. There are many women, no doubt, who are better in many things than many men; but, speaking generally, it is as you say.

I conclude then, my friend, that none of the occupations concerned with ordering a city belong to woman as woman, nor yet to man as man; but natural gifts are to be found here and there, in both sexes alike; and, so far as her nature is concerned, the woman is admissible to all pursuits as well as the man; though in all of them the woman is weaker than the man.

Precisely so.

Shall we then appropriate all duties to men, and none to women?

How can we?

On the contrary, we shall hold, I imagine, that one woman may have talents for medicine, and another be without them; and that one may be musical, and another unmusical.

Undoubtedly.

456 And shall we not also say, that one woman may have qualifications for gymnastic exercises, and for war, and another be unwarlike, and without a taste for gymnastics?

I think we shall.

Again, may there not be a lover of wisdom in one, and a hatred of it in another? and may not one be spirited, and another spiritless?

True again.

If that be so, there are some women who are fit, and others who are unfit, for the office of guardians. For were not those the qualities that we selected, in the case of the men, as marking their fitness for that office?

Yes, they were.

Then as far as the guardianship of a city is concerned, there is not difference between the natures of the man and of the woman, but only various degrees of weakness and strength.

Apparently there is none.

b  Then we shall have to select duly qualified women also, to share in the life and official labors of the duly qualified men; since we find that they are competent to the work, and of kindred nature with the men.

Just so.

And must we not assign the same pursuit to the same natures?

We must.

Then we have come full circle to our former position, and we admit that it is no violation of nature to assign music and gymnastic to the wives of our guardians.

Precisely so.

c  Then our intended legislation was not impossible, or visionary, since the proposed law was in accordance with nature; but rather it is the contrary way of doing things nowadays, that most likely is what is against nature.

So it appears.

Our inquiry was, whether the proposed arrangement would be possible, and whether it was the most desirable one, was it not?

It was.

Are we quite agreed that it is possible?

Yes.

Then the next point to be settled is, that it is also the most desirable arrangement?

Yes, obviously.

Very well; if the question is how to render a woman fit for the office of guardian, we shall not have one education for men, and another for women, especially as the nature affected is  d the same in both cases.

No, the education will be the same.

Well then, I should like to have your opinion on the following question.

And what is it?

On what principle do you in your own mind estimate one man as better than another? or do you look upon all as equal?

Certainly I do not.

Then in the city we were founding, which of the two classes have, in your opinion, been made the better men, the guardians educated as we have described, or the shoemakers brought up to shoemaking?

It is ridiculous to ask.

I understand you; but tell me, are not these the best of all the citizens?

Yes, by far.  e

And will not these women be better than all the other women?

Yes, by far, again.

Can there be anything better for a city than that it should contain the best possible men and women?

There cannot.

And this result will be brought about by music and gymnastic employed as we described?

Undoubtedly.  457

Then our intended regulation is not only possible, but also one most desirable for the city.

It is.

Then the women of our guardians must strip for their exercises, inasmuch as they will put on virtue instead of robes, and must bear their part in war and the other duties comprised in the guardianship of the city, and must engage in no other occupations; though of these tasks the lighter parts must be given to the women rather than to the men, in consideration of the weakness of their sex. But as for the man who laughs at the idea of undressed

b women going through gymnastic exercises, as a means of realizing what is most perfect, his ridicule is but 'unripe fruit plucked from the tree of wisdom,' and he knows not, to all appearance, what he is laughing at or what he is doing: for it is and ever will be a most excellent maxim, that the useful is noble, and the hurtful base.

Most assuredly it is.

Here then is one wave, as I may call it, which we may perhaps consider ourselves to have surmounted, in our discussion of the law relating to women; so that, instead of our being altogether swamped by our assertion that it is the duty of our male and female guardians to have all their pursuits in common,

c our argument is found to be in a manner at one with itself as to the possibility and advisability of the plan.

Yes indeed, he replied, it is no insignificant wave that you have surmounted.

You will not call it a large one, I continued, when you see the next.

Just go on, and let me see it.

The last law and those which preceded it involve, as I conceive, another to this effect.

What is it?

That these women shall be, without excep-

d tion, the common wives of these men, and that no one shall have a wife of his own: likewise that the children shall be common, and that the parent shall not know his child, nor the child his parent.

This law, he replied, is much more likely than the former to excite distrust both as to its possibility and as to its advisability.

As to the latter, I said, I think no one could deny that it would be an immense advantage

for the women and children to be common to all, if it were possible; but I expect there would be most controversy about the practicability of the scheme.

Both points might very well be disputed.          e

Then there will be a conflict of argument. I thought I should run away and get off from one of them, if you agreed to the utility of the plan, so that I should only have to discuss its feasibility.

But you were found out in your attempt to escape; so please give an account of both.

I must pay the penalty. Grant me however this one favor: permit me to take a holiday,     458 like one of those men of indolent mind, who are used to feasting themselves on their own thoughts, whenever they travel alone. Such persons, you know, before they have found out any means of offering their wishes, pass that by, to avoid the fatigue of thinking whether such wishes are possible or not, and assume that what they desire is already theirs; after which they proceed to arrange the remainder of the business, and please themselves with running over what they mean to do under the assumed circumstances, thus aggravating the     b indolence of an already indolent mind. So at this moment I too am yielding to laziness, and am desirous of putting off for subsequent investigation the question of possibility; and for the present assuming the possibility, I shall inquire, if you will permit me, what arrangements the ruling body will make when our rule is carried out, endeavoring also to show that in practice it would be the most advantageous of all things, both to the city and to its guardians. These points I will first endeavor to examine thoroughly in company with you, and take the others afterwards, if you permit me.

You have my permission, he replied. So proceed with the inquiry.

I think then, I proceeded, that if our rulers shall prove worthy of the name, and their aux-     c iliaries likewise, the latter will be willing to execute the orders they receive, and the former, in issuing those orders, will obey our laws, and in whatever cases we have left the details to them, they will imitate the laws.

So we may expect.

It will be your duty, therefore, as their law-giver, to select the women just as you selected the men, and to place them together, taking care, as far as possible, that they shall be of similar nature. Now inasmuch as the dwellings and mess-tables are all common, and no one d possesses anything in the shape of private property, both sexes will live together, and as a consequence of their mingling in the gymnasium in active exercises, and in the rest of their daily life, they will be led, I imagine, by an inborn necessity, through which they will mix with one another. Do you not think this will be inevitable?

The necessity surely will not be a mathematical necessity, but that of love, which perhaps is more constraining than the other in its power to persuade and draw after it the mass of men.

Quite so. But in the next place, Glaucon, disorderly mixing, or indeed irregularity of e any kind, would not be holy among the members of a happy city, and will not be permitted by the rulers.

And rightly so.

Manifestly then our next care will be to make the marriage-union as sacred a thing as we possibly can: and this sanctity will attach to the marriages which are most beneficial.

Precisely so.

459 Then tell me, Glaucon, how this end is to be attained. For I know you keep in your house both sporting dogs, and a great number of game birds. I ask you in the name of Zeus, therefore, to inform me whether you have paid any attention to the intercourse and the breeding of these animals.

In what respect?

In the first place, though all are well-bred, are there not some which are, or grow to be, superior to the rest?

There are.

Do you then breed from all alike, or are you anxious to breed as much as possible from the best?

From the best.

And at what age? when they are very b young, or very old, or when they are in their prime?

When they are in their prime.

And if you were to pursue a different course, do you think your breed of birds and dogs would degenerate very much?

I do.

Do you think it would be different with horses, or any other animals?

Certainly not; it would be absurd to suppose it.

Good heavens! my dear friend, I exclaimed, what very first-rate men our rulers ought to be, if the analogy hold with regard to the human race.

Well, it certainly does: but why first-rate? c

Because they will be obliged to use medicine to a great extent. Now you know when invalids do not require medicine, but are willing to submit to a regimen, we think an ordinary doctor good enough for them; but when it is necessary to administer medicines, we know that a more able physician must be called in.

True; but how does this apply?

Thus. It is probable that our rulers will be compelled to have recourse to a good deal of falsehood and deceit for the benefit of their d subjects. And, if you recollect, we said that all such practices were useful in the character of medicine.

Yes, and we were right.

Well then, it appears that this right principle applies particularly to the questions of marriage and propagation.

How so?

It follows from what has been already granted, that the best of both sexes ought to be brought together as often as possible, and the worst as seldom as possible, and that the off-e    spring of the former unions ought to be reared, and that of the latter abandoned, if the flock is to attain to first-rate excellence; and these proceedings ought to be kept a secret from all but the rulers themselves, if the herd of guardians is also to be as free as possible from internal strife.

You are perfectly right.

Then we shall have to ordain certain festivals, at which we shall bring together the brides and the bridegrooms, and we must have 460    sacrifices performed, and hymns composed by our poets in strains appropriate to the occasion; but the number of marriages we shall place under the control of the rulers, in order that they may, as far as they can, keep the population at the same point, taking into consideration the effects of war and disease, and all such agents, that our city may, to the best of our power, be prevented from becoming either too great or too small.

You are right.

We must therefore contrive an ingenious system of lots, I fancy, in order that those inferior persons, of whom I spoke, may impute the manner in which couples are united, to chance, and not to the rulers.

Certainly.

b    And those of our young men who distinguish themselves in the field or elsewhere, will receive, along with other privileges and rewards, more plentiful intercourse with the women, in order that, under color of this pretext, the greatest number of children may be the offspring of such parents.

You are right.

And, as fast as the children are born, they will be received by the officers appointed for the purpose, whether men or women, or both: for I presume that the city-offices also will be held in common both by men and women.

They will.

c    Well, these officers, I suppose, will take the children of good parents, and place them in the general nursery under the charge of certain nurses, living apart in a particular quarter of the city; while the issue of inferior parents, and all imperfect children that are born to the others, will be concealed, as is fitting, in some mysterious and unknown hiding-place.

Yes, if the breed of the guardians is to be kept pure.

And will not these same officers have to care for the rearing of the children, bringing the mothers to the nursery when their breasts are full, but taking every precaution that no         d mother shall know her own child, and providing other women that have milk, if the mothers have not enough; and must they not take care to limit the time during which the mothers are to suckle the children, committing the task of sitting up at night, and the other troubles that go with infancy, to nurses and attendants?

You make child-bearing a very easy business for the wives of the guardians.

Yes, and so it ought to be. Now let us proceed to the next object of our interest. We said, you remember, that the children ought to be the offspring of parents who are still in their prime.

True.

And do you agree with me that the prime of      e life may be reasonably reckoned at a period of twenty years for a woman, and thirty for a man?

Which years?

I should make it the rule for a woman to bear children to the city from her twentieth to her fortieth year; and for a man, after getting over the sharpest burst in the race of life, thenceforward to beget children to the city until he is fifty-five years old.

Doubtless, he said, in both sexes, this is the    461 period of their prime, both of body and in terms of prudence.

If then a man who is either above or under this age shall meddle with the business of begetting children for the regime, we shall declare his act to be an offense against religion and justice; inasmuch as he is raising up a child for the city, who, should detection be avoided, instead of having been begotten under the sanction of those sacrifices and prayers, which are to be offered up at every marriage ceremonial, by priests and priestesses, and the whole city, to the effect that the children to be born may ever be more virtuous

b   and more useful than their virtuous and useful parents, will have been conceived under cover of darkness by the aid of dire incontinence.

You are right.

The same law will hold should a man, who is still of an age to be a father, meddle with a woman, who is also of the proper age, without the introduction of the ruler: for we shall accuse him of raising up to the city an illegitimate, unsponsored, and unholy child.

You are perfectly right.

But as soon as the women and the men are past the prescribed age, we shall allow the lat-

c   ter, I imagine, to associate freely with whomsoever they please, except a daughter, or mother, or daughter's child, or grandmother; and in like manner we shall permit the women to associate with any man, except a son or a father, or one of their relations in the direct line, ascending or descending; but only after giving them strict orders to do their best, if possible, to prevent any child, if one should be so conceived, from seeing the light, but if that cannot sometimes be helped, to dispose of the infant on the understanding that the fruit of such a union is not to be reared.

That too is a reasonable plan; but how are

d   they to distinguish fathers, and daughters, and the relations you described just now?

Not at all, I replied; only, all the children that are born between the seventh and tenth month from the day on which one of their number was married, are to be called by him, if male, his sons, if female, his daughters; and they shall call him father, and their children he shall call his grandchildren; these again shall call him and his fellow-bridegrooms and brides, grandfathers and grandmothers; like-

wise all shall regard as brothers and sisters those that were born in the period during which their own fathers and mothers were bringing them into the world; and as we said   e just now, all these shall refrain from touching one another. But the law will allow intercourse between brothers and sisters, if the lot chances to fall that way, and if the Delphic priestess also gives it her sanction.

That is quite right, said he.

Such will be the character, Glaucon, of the community of women and children that is to prevail among the guardians of your city. The argument must now go on to establish that the plan is in keeping with the rest of our polity, and quite the best conceivable arrangement. Or can you propose any other course?

Do as you say, by all means.                      462

Will not the first principle for an agreement on this point between us be, to ask ourselves what we can name as the greatest good in the constitution of a city, at which the legislator ought to aim in making his laws, and what as the greatest harm; and the next, to inquire whether the plan we described just now fits into our outline of the good, but not with the bad?

Most decidedly.

Do we know then of any greater harm to the city, than that which should tear it asunder, and make it into a multitude of cities instead of   b one? Or of any higher good than that which should bind it together, and make it one?

We do not.

Well, then, does not a community of feeling in pleasure and pain bind the citizens together, when they all, so far as is possible, rejoice and grieve alike, at the same births and the same deaths?

Most assuredly it does.

And does not isolation in these feelings produce disunion, when some are much pleased and others equally grieved, at the same events affecting the city and its inmates?

Of course it does.                                   c

And does not this state of things arise when the words 'mine' and 'not mine' are not pronounced by all simultaneously in the city? and when there is the same discrepancy in the use of the word 'another's'?

Precisely so.

That city then is best managed in which the largest proportion of citizens apply the words 'mine' and 'not mine' similarly to the same objects.

Yes, much the best.

Or, in other words, that city which comes nearest to the condition of an individual man. Thus, when one of our fingers is hurt, the whole fellowship that spreads through the body up to the soul, and there forms an organized unity under the ruling principle, is sensible of the hurt, and there is a universal and simultaneous feeling of pain in sympathy with the wounded part; and therefore we say that the *man* has a pain in his finger: and in speaking of any part of our frame whatsoever, the same account may be given of the pain felt when it suffers, and the pleasure felt when it is easy.

The same, no doubt; and to return to your question, there is a very close analogy between such a case and the condition of the best-governed city.

Then I think that, when any good or harm comes to one of the citizens, a city such as we are describing will be more likely than another to regard the affected member as a part of itself, and to sympathize as a whole with his pleasure or his pain.

It must do so, if it be well ordered.

It will now be time, I continued, for us to go back to our city, and to take notice whether it possesses in the highest degree the qualities to which our inquiry has unanimously brought us, or is surpassed therein by some other city.

We had better do so.

463   Well then, other cities, and ours like the rest, contain rulers and people, do they not?

They do.

And they will all address one another as citizens?

Of course.

But besides calling the one 'citizens,' what do the people in other cities call their rulers?

In most cases it calls them masters, but in democracies simply rulers.

But in our city, what name besides that of citizens does the people bestow on the rulers?

It calls them preservers and auxiliaries.      b

And what do *they* call the people?

Paymasters and care-givers.

And in other cities the rulers call the people, what?

Slaves.

And what do the rulers call one another?

Fellow-rulers.

And ours?

Fellow-guardians.

Can you say whether in other cities a ruler, speaking of his fellow-rulers, might describe one of them as a relative, and another as a stranger?

Yes, many might.

And in so doing, does he not regard and speak of the former as belonging to himself,      c and the latter as not belonging to himself?

He does.

Well, could any of your guardians regard or describe one of his fellow-guardians as a stranger?

Certainly not; for they must look upon every one whom they meet as either a brother, or a sister, or a father, or a mother, or a son, or a daughter, or one of the children or parents of these.

Excellently said; but answer me one more question; shall you be satisfied with instituting family names, or shall you further require them to act in every instance in accordance      d with the names, enjoining in the treatment of the fathers, all that it is usual to enjoin towards fathers, as that a child shall honor, aid, and be obedient to his parents, otherwise it will be worse for him both before the gods and before men; inasmuch as his conduct, if he acts differently, will be an outrage upon religion and justice? Will you have these sayings, or any others, sounded from the beginning by all citizens in the ears of the children, with reference to those who are pointed out to them as fathers, and to all other relations?

e     These, certainly; for it would be ridiculous if family names were merely uttered with the lips, without actions to correspond.

This then is the city, above all others, in which, when an individual is doing well or badly, every member will with one accord apply the expressions spoken of just now, saying, 'It is well with my affairs,' or 'It is ill with my affairs.'

Most true.

464   And did we not say that a general sympathy in pleasure and in pain goes hand in hand with this mode of thinking and speaking?

Yes, and we said so rightly.

Then will not our citizens be remarkable for sharing in the same interest, which they will call 'mine,' and, having this common interest, thereby possess in a remarkable degree a community in pleasure and pain?

Yes, in a very remarkable degree.

Well, is not this owing, among the other features of our constitution, to the fact that our guardians hold their women and children in common?

Yes, mainly to this.

b     But, if you remember, we admitted this to be the greatest good in a city, comparing the condition of a well-ordered city to the relation of a body to its members in the matter of pleasure and pain.

Yes; and we were right in our admission.

Then we have discovered that the greatest good in the city is due to the community of women and children, which is to prevail among our auxiliaries.

Exactly so.

And in this arrangement we were moreover consistent with our former conclusions; for

I believe we said that all private property, whether in houses, or lands, or any thing else, must be forbidden to our guardians, who are to receive a maintenance from the rest of the citizens, as the wages of their office, and to use it up in common, if they are destined to be guardians indeed.                                                        c

True.

Well then, will not the regulations laid down before, and still more those we are now describing, make men genuine guardians, and prevent them from tearing the city asunder by applying the term 'mine' each to a different object, instead of all to the same, and by severally dragging to their several distinct abodes whatever they can acquire independently of the rest, and, amongst other things, separate     d
women and children, thus creating exclusive pleasures and pains by their exclusive interests; causing them, on the contrary, to tend unitedly to a common center, by the fact of holding but one opinion concerning what is their own, and thus to be, as far as is possible, simultaneously affected by pleasure and pain?

Precisely so.

Further, will not all lawsuits and prosecutions disappear, so to speak, from among them, seeing that there is nothing which a man can call his own except his body, all other things being common property? And will not this deliver them from all those feuds which are     e
occasioned among men by the separate possession of money and children and kindred?

They cannot fail to be rid of them.

Moreover, there will be, by rights, no actions for forcible seizure, or for assault and battery among them. For we shall probably maintain that to defend oneself against an assailant of one's own age, is consistent both with honor and justice, recognizing the necessity of taking care of the person.

Rightly so.

There is also this advantage, I continued, in     465
such a law—if any one should happen to fall into a passion with another, he would find a

vent for his anger by a personal encounter, and thus the quarrel will be less likely to assume a more serious character.

Certainly.

An older person, however, will be authorized to command and chastise any that are younger than himself.

Clearly.

And surely it is to be expected that no younger man will presume either to strike or otherwise do violence to an elder, unless the rulers commission him to do so. Nor yet, I think, will a young man insult his seniors in any other way; for there are two guards that will sufficiently hinder him, namely, fear and
b    shame; shame restraining him from laying violent hands on one whom he regards as a parent, and fear, lest the person attacked should be assisted by the rest, in the character of sons, brothers, and fathers.

Yes, those will be the results of our regulations.

Then in every way the laws will secure mutual peace among our men.

Yes, in a high degree.

But if the men of this class be free from internal dissensions, there is no danger that the rest of the citizens will quarrel either with them or with one another.

No, there is not.
c    There are, moreover, petty mischiefs, so mean that I hesitate even to mention them, from which they will be exempt: I allude to the flatteries paid by the poor to the rich, and those embarrassments and vexations which beset men in rearing a family, and in the acquisition of the money that is needed for the bare maintenance of domestics, now borrowing and now repudiating, and by indiscriminate means procuring property which they place in the hands of their women and servants, and entrust to their management; all the troubles that these circumstances occasion, my dear friend, are obvious enough, and besides they are ignoble, and do not deserve to be described.
d    True, they are obvious even to the blind.

While they are free from all these ills, they will live a life more blessed than that blissful life which is the lot of conquerors at the Olympic games.

How so?

Why, the happiness ascribed to these Olympic victors includes but a small part of the blessings enjoyed by our men, whose victory is as much more glorious as their public maintenance is more complete. The victory they win is the preservation of the whole city, and while living they receive crowns and privileges from their country in the shape of maintenance and all that life requires, themselves and their children, and when they die they are    e admitted to an honorable burial.

Yes, indeed, these are glorious privileges.

Do you remember then, I continued, that some time back we were accused by some objector of not making our guardians happy,    466 because, with the power to take all that the citizens had, they possessed nothing of their own? To which we replied, I believe, that we would consider that point hereafter, if it should fall in our way; but that our object then was to make our guardians really guardians, and the city itself as happy as we could, without any idea of fixing our attention on any one group, and providing happiness for it?

I remember.

Well, but as we have now found that the life of the auxiliaries is much more glorious and more desirable than that of Olympian victors, can it be thought that the life of the shoemak-    b ers or any other artisans, or that of the farmers, is in any sense comparable to it?

I think not, he replied.

However it is but right to repeat here what I said at the time, that if ever our guardians attempt to make themselves happy in such a way that they cease to be guardians, if, instead of being satisfied with a life merely moderate and stable, such as we think the best, they become possessed with a silly and childish notion of happiness, impelling them to use    c their power to appropriate all the good things in the city, they will discover that Hesiod was truly wise when he said that in a certain sense 'the half is more than the whole.'

If they take my advice they will abide by the life assigned to them.

Then you concede the principle, that the women are to be put upon the same footing as the men, according to our description, in education, in bearing children and in watching over the other citizens, and that, whether they remain at home or are sent into the field, they

d      are to share the duties of guardianship with the men, and join with them in the chase like dogs, and have every thing in common with them so far as is at all possible, and that in so doing they will be following the most desirable course, and not violating the natural relation which ought to govern the communion of the sexes?

I do concede all this, he replied.

Then does it not remain for us, I proceeded, to determine whether this community can possibly subsist among men, as it can among other animals, and what are the conditions of its possibility?

You have anticipated me in a suggestion I was about to make.

e      As for their warlike operations, I suppose it is easy to see how they will be conducted.

How? he asked.

Why, both sexes will take the field together, and they will also carry with them to the wars such of their children as are strong enough, in order that, like the children of all other crafts-men, they may be spectators of those occupa-

467    tions in which, when grown up, they will them-selves be engaged; and they will require them, besides looking on, to act as servants and attendants in all the duties of war, and to wait upon their fathers and mothers. You have doubtless observed in the various trades, how the children of potters, for example, look on and fetch and carry for their parents, long before they put their own hand to the making of pots.

Certainly, I have.

Shall potters then show more carefulness than our guardians in educating their children,

by making them see and practice their proper duties?

No, that would be indeed ridiculous.

Then, again, every creature will fight with peculiar courage in the presence of its off-      b spring.

True; but there is considerable danger, Socrates, in case of one of those reverses which are common in war, that the children may be sacrificed with the parents, and so the rest of the city be weakened beyond the power of recovery.

That is quite true, I replied. But let me ask you, in the first place, whether you think we are bound to take measures to avoid every possible danger?

By no means.

Well, if danger is ever to be encountered, ought it not to be in a case in which success will be a means of improvement?

Manifestly it ought.

And do you regard it as a point too unim-      c portant to justify the risk, whether children who are to become soldiers should see something of war in their childhood, or not?

It is certainly important for the purpose you describe.

Then it must be a fixed rule to make the children spectators of war, and also to contrive some plan for ensuring their safety; and then all will be well, will it not?

It will.

Now, in the first place, will not their fathers be intelligent and sagacious judges, so far as men can be, as to what campaigns are likely to      d prove dangerous and what the reverse?

In all probability they will.

If so, they will carry their children to the latter, while they will be cautious about taking them to the former.

Rightly so.

And I presume they will set officers over them, not chosen for their worthlessness, but men qualified by experience and age to be their guides and tutors.

It is fit they should.

Still we must admit that many people have met with results contrary to their expectations.

Yes, very frequently.

Then, to meet such emergencies, my dear friend, we must provide our children from the first with wings, to enable them, in case of necessity, to fly away and escape.

e      What do you mean?

We must put them on horseback at the earliest possible age, and when we have taught them to ride, we must take them to see the fighting, mounted, not on spirited animals, or good chargers, but on horses selected for speed and docility. For by this plan they will obtain the best view of their future occupation, and at the same time will be most secure of making good their escape in case of need, following in the train of leaders of mature years.

I think your plan is the right one.

468     To come now to the matters concerning war, I proceeded; how must your soldiers behave, both among themselves, and as regards the enemy? Tell me whether I am right in my views or not.

Let me know what they may be.

If one of the soldiers deserts his rank or throws away his arms, or is guilty of any such act of cowardice, must we not degrade him to the rank of an artisan, or a farmer?

Decidedly.

And if a soldier falls alive into the hands of the enemy, ought we not to make a present of him to any one that will have him, to do what he pleases with his booty?

b      Yes, by all means.

But if a soldier highly distinguishes himself and gains himself credit in the first place, while the army is still in the field, do you not think that he ought to be crowned with a garland by each of the youths and children in turn, among his comrades in arms?

Yes, I think so.

And shaken by the hand?

Yes, and shaken by the hand.

But I suppose you will hardly extend your approval to my next proposition.

What is that?

That he should kiss and be kissed by them all.

Most certainly I do; and I would add to the law, that during the continuance of the campaign, no one whom he has a mind to kiss be permitted to refuse him the satisfaction; in order that, if any soldier happens to entertain an admiration for either a male or a female comrade, he may be the more stimulated to carry off the prize for valor.

c

Good, I replied; and we have already said that a brave man will be allowed to enter into marriage-relations more frequently than others will, and to exercise more than the usual liberty of choice in such matters, so that as many children as possible may be obtained from a father of this character.

True, we did say so.

Again there are other honors with which, even according to Homer, it is just to reward those young men that distinguish themselves by good conduct. Homer says that Ajax having won renown in the war, received by way of distinction 'whole sides of beef'; it being considered that an honor which, besides the glory of it, would augment his physical strength, was peculiarly appropriate to a brave man in the prime of his manhood.

d

A very just idea.

Then in this point at least we will follow the suggestion of Homer. We too, at our sacrificial feasts and all similar entertainments, will honor our meritorious soldiers, according to the degree of merit they have displayed, not only with hymns and the privileges we have just stated, but also with 'goblets full to the brim, and meats and places of honor,' intending thereby not only to do honor to our brave men and women, but also to promote their training.

e

An excellent plan, he said.

Very good; and when there are any killed in a campaign, shall we not in the first place give out that those who fell with honor belong to the golden race?

Most assuredly we shall.

And shall we not be persuaded by Hesiod that when any of this race die,

469  'They into spirits are changed, earth-haunting, beneficent, holy,
       Mighty to screen us from harm, and of speech-gifted men the protectors'?

Yes, certainly we shall.

Shall we then inquire of the god how and with what distinctions we ought to bury daimonic and divine beings, and then proceed to bury them, in the manner and with the ceremonies that the god prescribes?

Of course we shall.

b   And for the future, shall we regard their tombs as those of superior beings, and pay them the due respect and worship? and shall we observe these same practices, whenever any citizen, who has been esteemed eminent for his bravery during his lifetime, dies of old age or from any other cause?

Certainly, it is but just to do so.

Again, what will be the conduct of our soldiers in dealing with their enemies?

In what respects?

In the first place, take the custom of making slaves. Does it seem just for Greeks to make slaves of the freemen of Greek cities? Ought they not rather to do what they can to prevent c   the practice, and to introduce the custom of sparing their own race, from a prudent fear of being reduced to bondage by the barbarians?

The latter is the better course beyond all comparison.

Then it is better also not even to have Greek slaves in their possession, and to advise the other Greeks against the practice.

Decidedly so: their thoughts would then be more turned against the barbarians, and they would be less likely to molest one another.

Again, is it well to strip the slain, after a victory, of any thing except their arms? Or does not the practice offer an excuse to cowards for not facing those who are still fighting, d   so long as they can pretend that they are in the way of their duty, when they are stooping to rifle a dead body? and have not many armies before now been destroyed through this habit of pillaging?

No doubt of it.

And does it not seem a piece of ignoble avarice to plunder the dead, and is it not the sign of a womanish and petty mind to regard with hostile feelings the body of a dead man, when the real enemy has flown away, leaving only the instrument with which he fought? Are those who act this way any better, do you think, than dogs which growl at the stones that   e   have been thrown at them, but let the person who threw them alone?

No, not one bit better.

Then must we banish the practices of stripping the dead, and interfering with the removal of the bodies?

Yes, we must indeed.

Neither, I presume, shall we carry the arms of our enemies to the temples, to dedicate them there, especially the arms of Greeks, if   470   we care to cultivate a good understanding with the rest of the Greeks; on the contrary, we shall be fearful of desecrating a temple, if we carry to it such trophies won from our own brethren; that is to say, unless the god of the oracle shall pronounce a different judgment.

You are quite right.

Well, I continued, and how will your soldiers behave towards their enemies in the matter of ravaging the lands and burning the houses of Greeks?

I should like to hear your own opinion on the subject, he replied.

For my part, then, I confess I disapprove of both these practices, and should only allow the   b   annual crop to be carried off. Would you like me to tell you my reasons?

I should.

It appears to me, that as there are two names in use, war and faction, so there are two things representing two distinct kinds of disagreement. In the one case the parties are friends and relations, in the other, aliens and foreigners. Now when hostility exists among the former, it is called faction; when between strangers, it is called war.

There is nothing unreasonable in what you say.

c     Observe whether what I am going to add is equally reasonable; I affirm that all members of the Greek race are brethren and kinsmen to one another, but aliens and foreigners to the barbarian world.

True.

Therefore when Greeks and barbarians fight together, we shall describe them as natural enemies, warring against one another; and to this kind of hostility we shall give the name of 'war'; but when Greeks are on this sort of footing with Greeks, we shall say that they are natural friends, whereas in the case of mutual warfare Greece is in a sick and seditious state of civil conflict; and to this kind of hostility we d     shall give the name of 'faction.'

I quite agree with this view.

Then bear in mind, I said, that in what is now by general agreement called 'sedition,' wherever this state of things arises and a city is divided, if each party ravage the lands and burn the houses of the other, the conflict is thought a wicked one, and both parties are looked upon as unpatriotic; for had they been patriotic, they would never have had the heart to mangle their nurse and mother. But it is thought that the victorious party cannot in fairness do more than carry off the crops of its e     adversaries, and ought to feel that they will one day be reconciled again, and not continue at war for ever.

Yes, he said; this way of thinking is much tamer than the other.

Very good, and is not the city you are founding to be a Greek city?

It certainly should be.

Then will not its citizens be gentle and tame?

Certainly they will.

And will they not be patriotic Greeks, look-

ing upon all Hellas as their own country, and sharing with their fellow-countrymen in the rites of a common religion?

Most certainly they will.

Thus regarding all the Greeks as their 471 brethren, will they not look upon a quarrel with them in the light of a sedition, and refuse it the name of a war?

They will.

And therefore feel, throughout the quarrel, like persons who are presently to be reconciled?

Exactly so.

They will, therefore, correct them in a friendly spirit, and chastise them without any thought of enslaving or destroying them— simply as schoolmasters, not as enemies.

Just so.

Then being Greeks, they will not devastate Greece, nor burn houses, nor admit that all the men, women, and children in a city are their foes; always confining this name to those few who were the authors of the quarrel. And on all     b these accounts they will refrain from laying waste the land, or razing the houses, because the owners are in most cases their friends; and they will push the quarrel only thus far, until the innocent have done justice upon the guilty who plague them.

I readily admit, he said, that our citizens ought to adopt these rules in their conduct towards their adversaries; while I would have them behave to barbarians as the Greeks now behave to one another.

Then are we to add to our enactments a law forbidding our guardians either to ravage lands     c or set houses on fire?

Let us do so, he replied; and let us assume that both this and our former regulations are right.

But I really think, Socrates, he continued, that if you be permitted to go on in this way, you will never recollect what you put aside some time ago before you entered on all these questions, namely, the task of showing that

this regime is possible, and how it might be realized. For in proof of the assertion that, if it were realized, it would ensure all kinds of advantages to a city which was the seat of it, I can myself mention things which you have omitted, as, that such soldiers would fight to
d perfection against their enemies, in consequence of the unwillingness to desert one another which would arise from their knowing one another as brothers, fathers, or sons, and using these endearing names familiarly; and if the female sex were to serve in the army, whether in the same ranks with the men, or posted as a reserve behind, to strike terror into the enemy and render assistance at any point in case of need, I know that this would render them quite invincible: moreover, I see all the
e advantages, omitted by you, which they would enjoy at home. But as I fully admit the presence of all these merits and a thousand others in this regime, if it were brought into existence, you need describe it no further. Rather let us try now to convince ourselves of this, that the thing *is* possible, and *how* it is possible, leaving all other questions to themselves.

472 What a sudden onslaught, I replied, you have made upon my argument! you have no sympathy for me and my loitering. Perhaps you do not know that after I have barely surmounted the first two waves, you are now bringing down upon me the third breaker, which is the most mountainous and formidable of the three; but when you have seen or rather heard it, you will think my conduct quite excusable, and you will allow that I had good reasons for hesitating and trembling to broach such a paradoxical claim, and to undertake the investigation of it.

The more you talk in this strain, he said, the
b less likely shall we be to let you off from explaining how this regime is possible. So proceed with your explanation, and let us have no more delay.

Well, then, I continued, in the first place we ought not to forget that we have been brought to this point by an inquiry into the nature of justice and injustice.

True; but what of that?

Why nothing. But, if we find out what justice is, shall we expect the character of a just man not to differ in any point from that of jus- c tice itself, but to be like justice in every way? Or shall we be content provided he comes as near it as is possible, and partakes more largely of it than the rest of the world?

The latter. We shall be content.

Then the design of our investigations into the nature of justice in itself, and the character of the perfectly just man, as well as the possibility of his existence, and likewise into the nature of injustice, and the character of the perfectly unjust man, was to use them as patterns, so that by looking upon the two men, and observing how they stand in reference to happiness and its opposite, we might be com- d pelled to admit in our own case, that he who resembles them most closely in character, will also have a fate most closely resembling theirs; but it was not our intention to demonstrate the possibility of these things in practice.

That is quite true, he said.

Do you think any the worse of the merits of an artist, who has painted a paradigm of the most beautiful human being, and has left nothing lacking in the picture, because he cannot prove that such a man as he has painted might possibly exist?

No, indeed, I do not.

Well, were not we likewise professing to e construe in speech the pattern of a perfect city?

Yes, certainly.

Then will our argument suffer at all in your good opinion, if we cannot prove that it is possible for a city to be organized in the way we have said?

Certainly not.

This then is the truth of it; but if for your gratification I must also exert myself and demonstrate in what way and under what conditions it is most possible, I must ask you to agree again to the same points for the sake of this demonstration.

Which do you mean?

473   In any case, can anything be accomplished in the city as it is said? Or is it the case that practice by nature attains less to the truth than does speech? Never mind if some think otherwise; tell me whether you admit this fact or not.

I do admit it.

Then do not force me to exhibit the details in every way in deed as we went through them in speech; but if we find out how a city may be organized in very close accordance with our description, you must admit that we have discovered the possibility of realizing the plan which you require me to consider. Shall you not be content if you gain this much? for my own part I shall be.

So shall I.

Then our next step apparently must be, to endeavor to search out and demonstrate what there is now amiss in the working of our cities, preventing their being regulated in the manner described, and what is the smallest change that would enable a city to assume this form of regime, confining ourselves, if possible, to a single change; if not, to two; or else, to such as are fewest in number and least important in their influence.

Let us by all means endeavor so to do.

Well, I proceeded, there is one change by which, as I think we might show, the required revolution would be secured; but it is certainly neither a small nor an easy change, though it is a possible one.

What is it?

I am now on the point of confronting that very statement which we compared to the huge wave. Nevertheless it shall be spoken, even if it is to deluge me, literally like an exploding wave, with laughter and infamy. Pay attention to what I am going to say.

Say on, he replied.

Unless it happen either that philosophers acquire the kingly power in cities, or that those who are now called kings and the powers-that-be, be imbued with a sufficient measure of genuine philosophy, that is to say, unless political power and philosophy be united in the same person, most of those minds which at present pursue one to the exclusion of the other being necessarily excluded from either, there will be no deliverance, my dear Glaucon, for cities, nor yet, I believe, for the human race; neither can the regime, which we have now sketched in speech, ever grow into a possibility until then, and see the light of day. But my awareness how entirely paradoxical this was made me all along so reluctant to give expression to it: for it is difficult to see that there is no other way by which happiness can be attained, by the city or by the individual.

Whereupon Glaucon remarked: The language and sentiments, Socrates, to which you have just given utterance, are of such a nature, that you may expect large numbers of by no means contemptible assailants to rush desperately upon you without a moment's delay, after throwing off their upper garments, as it were, and grasping, in that city, the first offensive weapon that comes in their way, making a determined rush at you to do amazing things; so that if you fail to repel them with the weapons of argument, and make your escape, you will certainly suffer the penalty of being well jeered.

Well, I said, was it not you that brought all this upon me?

Yes, and I did quite right. But I promise not to desert you; on the contrary, I will assist you with the weapons at my disposal, which are, good-will and encouragement; and perhaps in my answers I may show more care than another. Therefore, relying on this assistance, endeavor to show to the incredulous that what you say is true.

I must make the attempt, I said, since you offer me such a valuable alliance. Now, if we are to have a chance of escaping from the assailants you speak of, I think it essential to give them our definition of 'philosophers,' and show whom we mean, when we venture to assert that such persons ought to rule; in order that, their character having been made thoroughly apparent, we may be able to defend

c ourselves by demonstrating that it is the natural domain of these men to embrace philosophy, and take the lead in a city, and the domain of all others to let philosophy alone, and follow the lead of the former.

Yes, it is a fit time, he said, to give this definition.

Come then, follow my steps, and let us try if we can in some way or other satisfactorily expound our notion.

Lead on.

Will it be necessary to remind you, or do you remember without it, that when we state that a man loves some object, we are bound to show, if the statement be correct, that he does not love one part of that object to the exclusion of another, but that he takes delight in the whole?

d I require to be reminded, it seems; for I do not quite understand you.

Such a confession, Glaucon, would have been more appropriate in another person. A man of your amorous nature ought not to forget that a boy-lover is in some way or other attracted and excited by the charms of all who are in their bloom, and thinks they all deserve his attentions and addresses. Is not this the manner in which you behave to your favorites? You will praise a boy with a turned-up nose as having a winning look; the hooked

e nose of another you consider king-like; while a third, whose nose is between the two extremes, has a beautifully proportioned face: the dark, you say, have a manly look, the fair are children of the gods; and who do you suppose coined the phrase 'honey-pale' but a lover who could palliate and easily put up with paleness, when he found it on the cheek of youth? In one word, you invent all kinds of

excuses, and employ every variety of expression, sooner than reject any that are in the flower and prime of life.

475

If you wish, replied Glaucon, to found on my case an assertion that erotic men act in this way, I will allow you to do so for the argument's sake.

To take another illustration; do you not observe that those who are fond of wine behave in a precisely similar manner, finding some excuse or other to admire every sort of wine?

Yes, certainly.

And you doubtless have seen how persons who love honor will command a company, if they cannot lead an army, and in default of being honored by great and important personages, are glad to receive the respect of the little and the insignificant; so desirous are they of honor in any shape.

b

Precisely so.

Then answer me yes or no to this: when we describe a man as having a longing for something, are we to assert that he longs after the whole class that the term includes, or only after one part, to the exclusion of another?

He longs after the whole.

Then shall we not maintain that the philosopher, or the lover of wisdom, is one who longs for wisdom, not partially, but wholly?

True.

So that if a person makes difficulties about his studies, especially while he is young and unable to discriminate between what is profitable and what is not, we shall pronounce him to be no lover of learning or of wisdom; just as when a man is a fussy eater, we deny that he is hungry or desirous of food, and instead of describing him as fond of eating, we call him a bad feeder.

c

Yes, and we shall be right in doing so.

On the other hand, when a man is ready and willing to taste every kind of knowledge, and addresses himself joyfully to his studies with an appetite which never can be satiated, we shall justly call such a person a philosopher, shall we not?

d        To which Glaucon replied, You will find your description includes a great number and a strange company. All the lovers of sights, I conclude, are philosophers, because they take pleasure in acquiring knowledge; and those who delight in hearing are a very singular set to reckon among philosophers, those, I mean, who will never, if they can help it, be present at a philosophical discussion, or any similar entertainment, but are unfailing attendants at every Dionysian festival, whether held in town or country, and run about as if they had let out their ears on hire to listen to all the choruses of the season. Are we then to give the title of philosophers to all these people, as well as to

e        others who have a taste for any similar studies, and to those who learn petty arts?

Certainly not, I replied; we must call them 'counterfeit philosophers.'

And whom, he asked, do you call genuine philosophers?

Those who love to see truth, I answered.

In that, he said, you cannot be wrong; but will you explain what you mean?

That would be not at all easy, with a different questioner: but I imagine you will agree with me about the following.

What is it?

That since beautiful is the opposite of ugly, they are two things.

476      Of course they are.

Then since they are two, each of them taken separately is one thing.

That also is true.

The same thing may be said likewise of justice and injustice, good and bad, and all forms. Each of them in itself is one thing, but by the intermixture with actions and bodies and with one another, through which they are everywhere made visible, each appears to be many things.

You are right.

By the help of this principle, then, I draw a distinction between those whom you described just now as lovers of sights, lovers of arts, and practical persons, on the one hand, and on the other, those about whom we are now inquiring, to whom alone we can rightly        b give the name of philosophers.

Explain what you mean.

Why, I suppose that those who love seeing and hearing admire beautiful sounds, and colors, and shapes, and all artistic products into which these enter; but the nature of beauty in itself their reasoning is unable to behold and embrace.

Yes, it certainly is as you say.

But those who are capable of reaching a contemplation of beauty itself by itself will be rare exceptions, will they not?

They will indeed.        c

Therefore if a man recognizes the existence of beautiful things, but disbelieves in beauty itself, and has not the power to follow should another lead the way to the knowledge of it, do you think that his life is a dreaming or a waking one? Just consider. Is it not dreaming when a person, whether asleep or awake, mistakes the likeness of anything for the real thing of which it is a likeness?

I confess I should say that a person in that predicament was dreaming.

Take again the opposite case, of one who        d acknowledges beauty itself, and has the power to discern both it itself and those things which participate or share in it, and who never mistakes the participants for the thing itself nor vice versa, does such a person live a dreaming or a waking life, do you think?

A waking life, undoubtedly.

If so, shall we not be right in calling the reasoning of the latter 'knowledge,' because he really knows; and that of the former, opinion, because he merely opines?

Yes, perfectly right.

Well then, should this person, whom we describe as opining, but not knowing, grow harsh with us, and contend that what we say is not true, shall we be able to appease his indignation and gently convince him, disguising from him the fact that he is in an unsound state?

That were certainly desirable.

Come then, consider what we are to say to him. Would you like us to make certain inquiries of him, promising that if he really does know anything, we shall not in the least begrudge him his knowledge? On the contrary, we shall be truly glad to find that it is so. But answer us this question, we shall say: When a man knows, does he know something or nothing? Be so good, Glaucon, as to answer on his behalf.

My answer will be, that he knows something.

Something that exists, or does not exist?

477 Something that exists; for how could a thing that does not exist be known?

Are we then quite sure of this fact, in whatever variety of ways we might examine it, that what completely exists may be completely known, whereas that which has no existence at all must be wholly unknown?

We are perfectly sure of it.

Good; now, if there be anything so constituted, as at the same time to be and not to be, must it not lie somewhere between that which is purely and simply that which is and that which is not at all?

Yes, it would be in between.

Well then, as knowledge is correlative to that which is, and ignorance necessarily to that which is not, must we not try to find something intermediate between knowledge and ignorance, if there is anything of the kind, to corre-
b spond to what is intermediate between that which is and that which is not?

Yes, by all means.

Do we speak of opinion as a something?

Undoubtedly we do.

Do we consider it a faculty distinct from knowledge or identical with it?

Distinct from it.

Therefore opinion is assigned to one domain and knowledge to another, each acting according to its own peculiar power.

Just so.

Is it not the nature of knowledge, as correlative to that which is, to know how that which is exists? But first there is a distinction which I think it necessary to establish.

What is that?

We shall hold that faculties, as a certain    c
general class, are the things whereby we, and every other thing, are able to do whatever we can do: for example, I call sight and hearing faculties, if you happen to understand the special conception which I wish to describe.

I do understand it.

Then let me tell you what view I take of them. In a faculty I do not see either color or shape or any of those qualities that I observe in many other things, and by regarding those I can in many cases distinguish to myself between one thing and another. No, in a fac-    d
ulty I look only to its domain and its function, and thus I am led to call it in each case by this name, pronouncing those faculties to be identical whose domains and functions are identical, and those diverse whose domains and functions are diverse; but how do you proceed?

Just in the same way.

Now then, return with me, my excellent friend. Do you say that knowledge is a faculty or in what class do you put it?

Yes I do: it is of all the faculties the most powerful.

Well, what about opinion? Is it a faculty; or    e
are we to refer it to some other form?

Not to any other; for that whereby we are able to opine, can only be opinion.

Well, but a little while ago you admitted that knowledge and opinion are not identical.

Why how could a sensible man identify the fallible with the infallible?

Very good; so we are clearly agreed that    478
opinion is a thing distinct from knowledge?

It is.

If so, each of them has by its nature a different domain, and a different efficacy.

The inference is inevitable.

Knowledge, I believe, has for its domain to know the nature of what is.

Yes.

And the domain of opinion is, we say, to opine.

Yes.

Is opinion acquainted with the very same things that knowledge knows? In other words, is the opinionable the same as the knowable?

b It is impossible, after the admissions we have made; that is, if it be granted that different faculties have different domains, and that both opinion and knowledge are faculties, and that the two are distinct, all of which we affirm. These premises make it impossible to identify the domain of knowledge and that of opinion.

Then, if what is is the knowable, the opinionable must be something other than that which is?

It must.

Well then, does opinion exercise itself upon that which is not, or is it impossible to apprehend even in opinion that which does not exist? Consider: does not the person opining carry his thought towards something? Or is it possible to have an opinion, but an opinion about nothing?

It is impossible.

Then the person who opines has an opinion about some one thing?

Yes.

c Well, but that which is not could not be called some one thing; it might, on the contrary, in the most correct way, be addressed as nothing at all.

Just so.

But to that which is not we were constrained to assign ignorance, and to that which is, knowledge.

And rightly.

Then neither that which is nor that which is not is the object of opinion?

No.

Therefore opinion cannot be either ignorance or knowledge.

Apparently not.

Then does it lie beyond either of these, so as to surpass either knowledge in certainty or ignorance in uncertainty?

It does neither.

Then tell me, do you look upon opinion as something more dusky than knowledge, more luminous than ignorance?

Yes, it is strongly so distinguished from   d either.

And does it lie within these extremes?

Yes.

Then opinion must be something between the two.

Precisely so.

Now a little while back, did we not say, that if anything could be found so constituted as at the same time to be and not to be, it must lie between what purely is and what in no way is, and must be the object neither of knowledge nor yet of ignorance, but of a third faculty, which should be similarly discovered in the interval between knowledge and ignorance?

We did.

But now we have discovered between these two a faculty which we call opinion.

We have.

It will remain then for us, apparently, to   e find what that is which partakes both of being and of not being, and which cannot be rightly said to be either of these purely and simply; in order that, should it discover itself to us, we may justly proclaim it to be the object of opinion; thus assigning extremes to extremes, and means to means.

Am I not right?

You are.

These positions then being laid down, I shall proceed to interrogate that worthy man who   479 denies the existence of beauty itself or any idea of beauty itself, which for ever continues the same and unchangeable, though he acknowledges a variety of beautiful objects—that lover of sights, who cannot endure to be told that beauty is one, and justice one, and so on of the rest: My good sir, I shall say, of all these beautiful things, is there one which may not appear ugly? Of all these just things, is there one which may not appear unjust? Or of these holy things, one which may not appear unholy?

b No, answered Glaucon; they must inevitably appear in a certain sense both fair and foul, both just and unjust, both holy and unholy.

Again, may not the many double things be considered halves just as well as doubles?

Just as well.

In the same way, have the things which we describe as great, small, light, heavy, any better claim to these titles, than to their opposites?

No, they will always be equally entitled to either.

Would it be more correct, then, to predicate of those many objects, that each of them is, or is not, that which it is said to be?

You remind me of the conundrums with a contradiction in them, that are proposed at a
c feast, and of the children's riddle about the eunuch who threw at the bat, hinting darkly with what he hit it, and on what it sat: for the things in question have the same ambiguous character, and one cannot positively conceive of them as either being or not being, as both being and not being, or as neither.

Can you tell then, said I, what to do with them, or where they may be better put than in the in-between area between being and not being? For I presume they will not appear either darker than that which is not, and thus is
d less, or more luminous than that which is, and thus is more.

You are perfectly right.

Hence we have discovered, apparently, that the customary beliefs of the many about beauty and the rest, roam about between the confines of pure being and pure non-being.

We have.

And we before agreed, that if anything of this kind should be brought to light, it ought to

be described as the object of opinion, and not of knowledge—these intermediate rovers being caught by the intermediate faculty.

We did make this admission.

Therefore, when people have an eye for a e multitude of beautiful objects, but can neither see beauty itself, nor follow those who would lead them to it—when they behold a number of just things, but not justice itself, and so in every instance, we shall say they have in every case an opinion, but no real knowledge of the things about which they opine.

It is a necessary inference.

But what, on the other hand, must we say of those who contemplate things as they are in themselves, and as they are always the same and immutable? Shall we not speak of them as knowing, not opining?

That also is a necessary inference.

Then shall we not assert that such persons 480 admire and love the objects of knowledge, the others, the objects of opinion? For we have not forgotten, have we, that we spoke of these latter as loving and looking upon beautiful sounds and colors and the like, while they will not hear of the existence of beauty itself?

We have not forgotten it.

Shall we commit any fault then, if we call these people philodoxical rather than philosophical, that is to say, lovers of opinion rather than lovers of wisdom? And will they be very much offended with us for telling them so?

No, not if they will take my advice; for it is wrong to be offended with the truth.

Those therefore that set their affections on that which in each case really is, we must call not philodoxical, but philosophical?

Yes, by all means.

## BOOK VI

Thus, Glaucon, I said, after pursuing a pro- 484 longed inquiry we have, with difficulty, discovered who the philosophers and nonphilosophers are.

Yes, he replied; probably it was not easy to shorten the inquiry.

Apparently not, I said. However that may be, I think, for my part, that the result would have been brought out still more clearly, if we had to speak of this only, without discussing the many points that still await our notice, if we wish to ascertain wherein the superiority of a just over an unjust life consists.

b    Then what are we to do next?

We have only to take the step next in order. Since those who are able to apprehend the eternal and immutable, are philosophers, while those who are incapable of this and who wander in the region of that which is many and which changes in every kind of way, are not philosophers, which of the two, tell me, ought to be leaders of the city?

What must I reply, if I am to speak in a measured way?

c    Ask yourself which of the two are to be thought capable of guarding the laws and customs of cities, and let these be appointed guardians.

You are right.

Can there be any question as to whether a blind man, or one with keen sight, is the right person to guard and keep any thing?

There can be no question about it.

Then do you think that there is a particle of difference between the condition of blind persons, and the state of those who are absolutely destitute of the knowledge of things as they

d    really are, and who possess in their soul no distinct exemplar, and cannot, like painters, fix their eyes on what is most true as a perpetual standard of reference, to be contemplated with the minutest care, before they proceed to give laws about things beautiful and just and good, laying them down where they are required, and where they already exist watching over their preservation?

No, indeed, there is not much difference.

Shall we then appoint such persons to the office of guardians, rather than those who

know what each thing is and who are second to none when it comes to experience or any other part of virtue?

Why, if these latter are not wanting in the other qualifications, it would be perfectly absurd to choose any others. For just the point in which they are superior may be said to be the most important of all.

Then shall we proceed to explain how the    485 same persons will be enabled to possess both qualifications?

By all means.

If so, we must begin by gaining a thorough insight into their proper character, as we said at the outset of this discussion. And I think, if we agree tolerably on that point, we shall also agree that the two qualifications may be united in the same persons, and that such characters, and no others, are the proper leaders of cities.

How so?

With regard to the philosophic nature, let us take for granted that its possessors love all learning that reveals to them something of that    b essence which is not made to wander about by generation and decay.

Let it be granted.

Again, I said, let us also assume that they love all of it, and willingly resign no part of it, whether small or great, honored or slighted; as we showed previously, when speaking of honor-lovers and erotic lovers.

You are right.

Now then proceed to consider, whether we ought not to find a third feature in the character of those who are to realize our description.    c

What feature do you mean?

A determination never to admit falsehood in any shape, if it can be helped, but to abhor it and love the truth.

Yes, it is probable we shall find it.

It is not only probable, my friend, but inevitable, that one who is by nature a lover of someone should care for everything that is bound by the closest ties to the beloved.

True, he said.

And can you find anything more closely akin to wisdom than truth?

Certainly not.

d  And is it possible for the same nature to love wisdom, and at the same time love falsehood?

Unquestionably it is not.

Consequently, the genuine lover of knowledge must, from his youth up, strive intensely after all truth.

Yes, he must thoroughly.

Well, but we cannot doubt that when a person's desires set strongly in one direction, they run with corresponding feebleness in every other channel, like a stream whose waters have been diverted into another bed.

Undoubtedly they do.

So that when the current has set towards learning and all its branches, a man's desires will, I imagine, hover around pleasures of the soul itself according to itself, abandoning
e  those in which the body is instrumental, provided he is a genuine philosopher.

It cannot be otherwise.

Again, such a person will be temperate and in no way a money-lover, for he is the last person in the world to value those objects, which make men anxious for money at any cost.

True.

Once more, there is another point which
486  you ought to take into consideration, when you are endeavoring to distinguish a philosophical from an unphilosophical character.

What is that?

You must take care not to overlook any taint of stinginess. For surely small-mindedness more than anything thwarts the soul that is always reaching for the whole and everything both divine and human.

That is most true.

And do you think that reasoning to which belongs magnificence and contemplation of all time and all essence, can possibly attach any great importance to this life?

No, it is impossible.

Such a person will not regard death as   b
something formidable, will he?

Certainly not.

So that a mean and cowardly character can have no part, as it seems, in true philosophy.

I think it cannot.

What then? Can the well-regulated man, free from covetousness, stinginess, pretentiousness, and cowardice, possibly be unjust or hard to deal with?

No, it is impossible.

Therefore, when you are noticing the indications of a philosophical or unphilosophical temper, you must also observe in early youth whether the soul is just and gentle, or unsociable and fierce.

Quite so.

There is still another point, which I think   c
you must certainly not omit.

What is that?

Whether he is quick or slow at learning. For you can never expect a person to delight in an occupation which he goes through with pain, and in which he makes small progress with great exertion?

No, it would be impossible.

Again, if he can remember nothing of what he has learned, can he fail, being thus full of forgetfulness, to be void of knowledge?

No, he cannot.

Then, will not his fruitless toil, do you think, compel him at last to hate both himself and such employment?

Doubtless it will.

Let us never, then, admit a forgetful soul   d
into the ranks of those that are counted worthy of philosophy; but let us look out for a good memory as a requirement for such admission.

Yes, by all means.

Again, we should certainly say that the tendency of an unmusical and awkward nature is wholly towards disproportion.

Certainly.

And do you think that truth is akin to disproportion, or to proportion?

To proportion.

In addition, then, to our other requirements, let us search for reasoning which is naturally well-proportioned and graceful, and which naturally grows by itself to the idea of each thing as it is.

By all means.

e     What then? Do you think that the qualities which we have enumerated are in any way unnecessary or inconsistent with one another, provided the soul is to partake sufficiently and perfectly in the things that are?

487     On the contrary, they are most strictly necessary.

Then can you find any fault with an employment which requires of a man who would pursue it satisfactorily, that nature shall have given him a retentive memory, and made him quick at learning, magnificent and graceful, the friend and brother of truth, justice, courage, and temperance?

No, he replied; Momus, the god of ridicule, could find no fault with that.

Well, can you hesitate to entrust such characters with the sole management of public affairs, when time and education have made them ripe for the task?

b     Here Adeimantus interposed and said; It is true, Socrates, that no one can dispute these conclusions; but still, every time such theories are propounded by you, the hearers feel certain misgivings of the following kind. They imagine that, from want of practice in your method of question and answer, they are at each question led a little astray by the reasoning, until, at the close of the discussion, these little divergences are found to amount to a serious false step, which makes them contradict their original statements. And, as unskillful checkers-players are in the end hemmed into a corner by

c     the skillful, until they cannot make a move, just in the same way your hearers conceive themselves to be at last hemmed in and reduced to silence by this novel kind of checkers, played with words instead of counters. For

they are not at all the more convinced that the conclusion to which they are brought is the true one. And, in saying this, I have the present occasion before my eye. For at this moment a person will tell you, that though at each question he cannot oppose you with words, yet in practice he sees that all the students of philosophy, who have devoted themselves to it for any length of time, instead of taking it up for educational purposes and relin-     d quishing it while still young, in most cases become exceedingly eccentric, quite depraved in fact, while even those who appear the most respectable are nonetheless far worse off for the pursuit which you commend, that they become useless to their cities.

When he had said this, I replied: Then do you think that what has been said is deceptive?

I am not sure, he answered; but I should be glad to hear what you think of it.

Let me tell you, that I think we were speaking the truth.

How then can it be right to assert that the     e miseries of our cities will find no relief, until those philosophers who, on our own admission, are useless to them, become their rulers?

You are asking a question, I replied, which I must answer by the help of an image.

And you, I suppose, have not been in the habit of using images.

Ah! you are making fun of me, do you, now that you have got me upon a subject in which demonstration is so difficult?

However, listen to the illustration, that you     488 may see still better how niggardly I am about images. So cruel is the position in which those respectable men are placed, in reference to their cities, that there is no single thing whose position is analogous to theirs. Consequently I have to collect materials from several quarters for the imaginary case which I am to use in their defense, like painters when they paint goat-stags and similar monsters.

Think of a fleet, or a single ship, in which the state of affairs on board is as follows. The b owner, you are to suppose, is taller and stronger than any of the crew, but rather deaf, and rather near-sighted, and correspondingly deficient in nautical skill; and the sailors are quarreling together about piloting, each of them thinking he has a right to steer the vessel, although up to that moment he has never studied the art, and cannot name his instructor, or the time when he served his apprenticeship; more than this, they assert that it is a thing which positively cannot be taught, and are even ready to tear in pieces the person who affirms that it can. Meanwhile they crowd

e incessantly round the person of the shipowner, begging and beseeching him with every importunity to entrust the helm to them; and occasionally, failing to persuade him, while others succeed better, these disappointed candidates kill their successful rivals, or fling them overboard, and, after binding the high-spirited ship-owner hand and foot with drugs or strong drink, or disabling him by some other contrivance, they remain masters of the ship, and apply its contents to their own purposes, and pass their time at sea in drinking and feasting, as you might expect with such a crew; and besides all this, they compliment

d with the title of 'able seaman,' 'excellent pilot,' 'skillful navigator,' any sailor that can second them cleverly in either persuading or forcing the ship-owner into installing them in command of the ship, while they condemn as useless every one whose talents are of a different order, having no notion that the true pilot must devote his attention to the year and its seasons, to the sky, and the stars, and the winds, and all that concerns his art, if he

e intends to be really fit to command a ship; and thinking it impossible to acquire and practice, along with the pilot's art, the art of maintaining the pilot's authority whether some of the crew like it or not. Such being the state of things on board, do you not think that the pilot who is really master of his craft is sure to be

489 called a useless, star-gazing babbler by the mariners who form the crews of ships so circumstanced?

Yes, that he will, replied Adeimantus.

Well, said I, I suppose you do not need to scrutinize my image, to remind you that it is a true picture of our cities in so far as their disposition towards philosophers is concerned; on the contrary, I think you understand my meaning.

Yes, quite.

That being the case, when a person expresses his astonishment that philosophers are not respected in our cities, begin by telling him our illustration, and endeavor to persuade him that it would be far more astonishing if b they were respected.

Well, I will.

And go on to tell him that he is right in saying that those most suitable for philosophy are considered most useless by the many; only recommend him to lay the fault of it not on these good people themselves, but upon those who decline their services. For it is not in the nature of things that a pilot should petition the sailors to submit to his authority, or that the wise should wait at the rich man's door. No, the author of that bit of cleverness was wrong: for the real truth is, that, just as a sick man, whether he be rich or poor, must attend at the physician's door, so all who require to be ruled c must attend at the gate of him who is able to rule, it being against nature that the ruler, supposing him to be really good for anything, should have to entreat his subjects to submit to his rule. In fact, you will not be wrong, if you compare the statesmen of our time to the sailors whom we were just now describing, and the useless visionary talkers, as they are called by our politicians, you can compare to those who are truly pilots.

You are perfectly right.

Under these circumstances, and amongst men like these, it is not easy for that noblest of occupations to be in good repute with those to whose pursuits it is directly opposed. But far d the most grievous and most obstinate slander, under which philosophy labors, is due to her professed followers—who are doubtless the persons meant by the accuser of philosophy, when he declares, as you tell us, that most of those who approach her are utterly depraved, while even her best pupils are useless—to the truth of which remark I assented, did I not?

Yes, you did.

We have explained the reason why the good are useless, have we not?

Certainly we have.

Would you have us proceed next to discuss why the majority are inevitably depraved, and
e  try to show, if we can, that philosophy is also guiltless in this regard?

Yes, by all means.

Let us then speak and listen alternately, recollecting the point where we were describing what ought to be the natural character of one
490  who is to turn out a perfectly accomplished and virtuous man. The first and leading feature in such a person's character was, if you recollect, truth, which he was bound to pursue with the most absolute devotion, at the risk, should he be found an impostor, of being denied all share in true philosophy.

Yes, we said so.

Well, does not this point, for one, run strongly counter to the received opinion upon the subject?

Certainly it does.

Then shall we not be making a reasonably good defense, if we say that the lover of learn-
b  ing naturally strives towards that which is; and, far from resting at the many particulars in the domain of opinion, he presses on, undiscouraged, and desists not from his passion, until he has grasped the nature of each thing as it really is, with that part of his soul whose property it is to lay hold of such things, in virtue of its affinity to them; and that having, by means of this, approached and mingled with that which really is, he begets wisdom and truth, so then, and not until then, he

knows, enjoys true life, and receives true nourishment, and is at length released from his labor-pains?

The defense will be the most sensible, he replied.

Well, will such a person be tinged with any love of falsehood? Will he not, on the contrary, be imbued with a positive hatred of it?

He will.                                                                       c

Now, if truth leads the way, we can never admit that a train of evils follows in her steps.

Certainly not.

On the contrary, we shall assert that she is attended by a sound and just disposition, followed in its turn by temperance.

True.

And surely we need not repeat our demonstrations, and marshal over again from the beginning the remaining retinue of the philosophical character. For we found, as you doubtless remember, that the natural accompaniments of the preceding are manliness, magnificence, a quick apprehension, and a good memory. Upon this you objected, that, though every one will be compelled to assent to our conclusions, still when one comes to   d  drop the argument and turn his eyes simply to the persons who are the subjects of it, he will assert his conviction that a few are merely useless, the majority totally depraved. We therefore inquired into the grounds of this prejudice, and have now arrived at the question, why are the majority depraved? And this was the reason why we took up again the character of the true philosophers and found ourselves compelled to define it.

True.                                                                          e

We must, therefore, study the pernicious influences which destroy this character in many persons, and from which only a few escape, who, you tell me, are called useless, though not depraved. And then we must take into consideration the natures of the souls which imitate the truly philosophical, and set-   491  tle down into the same pursuits, and how they enter upon a profession which is too good and too high for them, and commit such a variety of blunders, that they have everywhere and with all the world attached to philosophy the reputation you describe.

But what, he asked, are the pernicious influences to which you refer?

I will try to describe them to you, if I can. Every one will agree with us in this, I think, that such a character, possessing all those qualities which we assigned to it but now as essential to a full capacity for philosophy, is a rare occur-

b rence among men. Or do you think otherwise?

No, indeed I do not.

Then consider how many fatal dangers beset these rare characters.

And what are they?

The thing which sounds most marvelous is this, that every one of the qualities commended by us has a tendency to vitiate and distract from philosophy the soul which possesses it. I allude to manliness, temperance, and all the characteristics which we have discussed.

It does sound strange.

c And then, in addition to this, all the reputed advantages of beauty, wealth, strength of body, powerful connections in a city, and all their accompaniments, exercise a corrupting and a distracting influence. You get the type of thing I mean?

Yes; and I shall be glad to learn it in more detail.

Correctly grasp it as a whole, and it will present itself to you in a clear light, and my previous remarks will not appear so strange.

What do you tell me to do?

d In the case of all seeds, and of everything that grows, whether vegetable or animal, we know that whatever fails to find its appropriate nourishment, season, and soil, will lack its proper virtues the more, in proportion as it is more vigorous. For the bad is, I presume, more opposed to what is good than to what is not good.

Certainly.

Hence I think we may reasonably conclude that the finest natures get more harm, than those of an inferior sort, when exposed to an unsuitable nourishment.

Yes, we may.

Then may we not assert, Adeimantus, that   e minds, naturally of the highest order, do in like manner, if they happen to be ill-trained, become peculiarly wicked? Or do you think that great crimes and unmixed badness spring, not, as I suppose, from a splendid character ruined by improper treatment, but from a worthless one; and that a feeble nature will ever produce anything great, whether good or bad?

No, I think with you.

Well then, the nature which we appropri-   492 ated to the philosopher, must, I think, provided it meets with proper instruction, grow and attain to all excellence; but if it be sown, planted, and nourished in unsuitable soil, it is sure to run into the very opposite vices, unless some deity should providentially interpose. Or do you hold, with the multitude, that there are certain individuals corrupted by sophists in their youth, and certain individual sophists who corrupt in a private capacity to any considerable extent? Do you not rather think that those who use this language are themselves   b the greatest of sophists, training most elaborately, and educating to their own liking, both young and old, men and women?

When is that?

Whenever they crowd to the popular assembly, the law-courts, the theaters, the army camp, or any other public gathering of large bodies, and there sit in a dense and uproarious mass to censure some of the things said or done, and applaud others, always in excess—shouting and clapping, until, in addition to their   c own noise, the rocks and the place wherein they are echo back redoubled the uproar of their censure and applause. At such a moment, how do you suppose that a young man to is retain his self-possession? Can any private education that he has received hold out against such a torrent of censure and applause, and avoid being swept away down the stream, wherever it may lead, until he is brought to adopt the language of these men as to what is honorable and dishonorable, and to imitate all their practices, and become their very counterpart?

d        It is the sure consequence, Socrates.

However, I proceeded, we have not yet mentioned the surest influence at work.

What is that? he asked.

It is one which these schoolmasters and sophists bring into actual practice, if their words fail of success. For you cannot be ignorant that they chastise the disobedient with disfranchisement, and fines, and death.

They do, most decidedly.

Then what other sophist, do you think, or what individual speeches made in opposition, can prevail over these?

e        None can, I imagine.

No, they cannot, I said; indeed, the very attempt would be mere folly. For there is not, has not been, and indeed there never can be, a character that will regard virtue with different feelings, if he received the same education as that which popular assemblies impart. I am speaking humanly, my friend; for by all means let us except the divine, as the proverb says. For you may be well assured, that you will not
493  be wrong in asserting that whatever has been preserved, and made what it ought to be, while the constitution of cities is what it is, has been preserved through a divine interposition.

I am very much of that opinion.

Then I would further have you add the following to the list of your opinions.

What is it?

That all those mercenary adventurers who, as we know, are called sophists by the multitude, and regarded as rivals, really teach nothing but the opinions of the majority to which expression is given when large masses are assembled, and dignify them with the title of wisdom. A person might as well investigate

the caprices and desires of some huge and          b
powerful monster in his keeping, studying how it is to be approached, and how handled; at what times and under what circumstances it becomes most dangerous, or most gentle; on what occasions it is in the habit of uttering its various cries, and further, what sounds uttered by another person soothe or exasperate it; and when he has mastered all these particulars, by long continued intercourse, as well might he call his results wisdom, systematize them into an art, and open a school, though in reality he is wholly ignorant which of these humors and desires is fair, and which foul, which good and which bad, which just and which unjust;          c
and therefore is content to affix all these names to the opinions of the huge animal, calling what it likes good, and what it dislikes bad, without being able to render any other account of them,—in fact, giving the titles of just and fair to things done under compulsion, because he has not discerned himself, and therefore cannot point out to others, that wide distinction which really holds between the nature of the compulsory and the good. Tell me, in the name of Zeus, do you not think that such a person would make a strange instructor?

Yes, I do think so.

And do you think that there is any difference between such a person and the man who makes wisdom consist in having studied the whims and pleasures of the assembled many-          d
headed multitude, whether in painting, or in music, or finally in politics? For though it be true, that if a man mix with the many, and ask their judgment on some poem, or other work of art, or service rendered to the city, thus putting himself in their power further than he is obliged, he finds himself irresistibly compelled to do whatever they command; yet tell me if you have ever in your life heard any one of them offer an argument which was not ridiculous, to prove that what the multitude commands is really good and fair?

No; and I think I never shall.          e

Then if you have laid all this to heart, let me remind you of another point: will it be possible for the multitude to tolerate or believe that the beautiful itself exists rather than many beautiful things or anything in itself rather than the many particulars?

494

Certainly not.

Then the multitude cannot be philosophical.

It cannot.

And consequently philosophers are sure to be condemned by them.

They are.

And of course by those private adventurers who associate with the mob, and desire to please it.

Clearly.

Such being the case, what salvation do you see for a philosophic character that will enable it to persist in its vocation until it has reached the goal? Take our previous conclusions into your consideration; we agreed, you know, that a quick apprehension, a good memory, a manly and magnificent spirit, are qualities of the philosophic character.

b

Yes, we did.

Then, will not such a person, from his childhood, be first in everything; especially if the body in nature resembles the soul?

To be sure he will.

Then, I suppose, his friends and fellow-citizens will wish, when he grows older, to use him for their own purposes.

Doubtless.

Consequently they will fall down at his feet with prayers and compliments, securing and flattering in anticipation his future power.

c

Yes, it is certainly a common case.

Then how do you expect such a person to behave under these circumstances, above all, if he happen to be a rich and high-born member of a powerful city, and if he is tall and handsome besides? Will he not be full of extravagant hopes, and conceive himself competent to direct the affairs of Greeks and bar-barians, and make that an excuse for giving himself lofty airs, until he is swollen with self-importance and empty mindless conceit?

d

Undoubtedly he will

While he is in this frame of mind, suppose some one approaches him gently, and tells him, what is quite true, that there is no intelligence in him, and that he stands in need of it, and that without slaving for its acquisition it cannot be gained; do you think it an easy matter to gain his attention in the midst of such evil influences?

No, it is very far from easy.

If, however, I continued, thanks to an excellent nature and an inborn taste for such speeches, one such individual shall somehow pay attention to it, and allow himself to be turned and drawn towards philosophy, what do we think will be the behavior of those who count upon losing his services and his companionship? Will they leave a word unsaid, or a deed undone, that can possibly prevent the pupil from yielding, or the master from succeeding in his persuasions—calling in private machinations and public prosecutions?

e

Of course, that is what they will do, he replied.

495

Will it be possible, then, for such a person to philosophize?

Certainly not.

Thus you see, do you not, how right we were in saying, that in fact the very ingredients of the philosophic character, when subjected to an injurious treatment, are in a way the causes of a man's falling away from the pursuit of philosophy; to which result the so-called goods, wealth, and all such provisions, likewise contribute.

Yes, indeed, it was a true observation.

This, then, my excellent friend, is the ruin, such and so grievous the corruption of the finest character with regard to the noblest pursuit, a character which is, in addition, rarely to be met with, as we say. And it is among these

b

men, no doubt, that we find those who inflict the greatest injury on cities and individuals, and also those who labor for their good, when the tide turns that way; whereas a petty nature never influences in any great degree either individuals or cities.

That is very true.

Thus it comes to pass that those, who, as her nearest relatives, are most bound to espouse philosophy, fall away, and leave her desolate and unconsummated; and while for their part they live a life unsuited to them and untrue, philosophy, bereft as it were of relatives, is exposed to the advances of different persons unworthy of her, who bring her to shame, and attach to her those reproaches, with which you tell me she is loaded, to the effect that her associates are either worth nothing, or, as in the majority of cases, deserving of heavy punishment.

Why certainly that is the common remark.

Yes, I said, and a fitting remark. For other puny men, seeing this field open, albeit rich in grand names and showy titles, are only too thankful to desert their trades and rush into philosophy, like criminals who break out of prison and run for refuge to a temple, whenever they happen to be cleverest in their own little trades. For though all this is come upon philosophy, nevertheless the rank and splendor which she still retains far transcend those of any other profession; and these are desired by many whose natural talents were defective from the first, and whose souls have since been so grievously marred and enervated by their life of drudgery, as their bodies have been disfigured by their trades and crafts. Must not that be the case?

Certainly it must.

And does their appearance strike you as much better than that of a little bald-headed tinker, who has made some money, has just had his chains knocked off, has been washed in a bath, dressed out in a new coat, and got up as a bridegroom, thus, owing to his master's

poverty and destitution, he is about to marry his daughter?

I see no difference at all between the two cases. 496

Then what may we expect the offspring of such a match to be like? Will it not be baseborn and ordinary?

It cannot be otherwise.

Well, and when those, who are all unworthy of instruction, draw near and associate with her beyond what they deserve, how must we describe the character of those thoughts and opinions which are the offspring of such a connection? May they not be called, with the utmost propriety, sophisms—a spurious brood, without a trace of genuine prudence?

Yes, precisely so.

Hence, Adeimantus, I continued, those who worthily associate with philosophy form a very small remainder, made up, I conceive, either of noble and well-trained characters, condemned to exile, who, in the absence of all pernicious influences, have been true to their nature, and continued steadfast to philosophy; or of some great-souled men, bred in petty cities, who have looked down with contempt upon the politics of their city. Possibly, too, a small section may have come to her from other professions, which natural gifts have justified them in despising. Moreover, the bridle which curbs our friend Theages may be equally efficacious in other instances. For Theages is kept in check by ill-health, which excludes him from a public life, though in all other respects he has every inducement to desert philosophy. I need not mention the sign, which restrains me; for I suppose it has been granted to few, if any, before my time. Now he who has become a member of this little band, and has tasted how sweet and blessed his treasure is, and has watched the madness of the many, with the full assurance that there is scarcely a person who takes a single judicious step in his public life, and that there is no ally with whom he may safely march to the help of the just;

indeed, should he attempt it, he will be like a man who has fallen among wild beasts, unwilling to join them in doing injustice, and unable singly to resist the fury of all, and therefore destined to perish before he can be of any service to his city or his friends and do no good to himself or any one else. Having weighed all this, such a man keeps quiet and confines himself to his own concerns, like one who takes shelter behind a wall on a stormy day, when the wind is driving before it a hurricane of dust and rain; and when from his retreat he sees the infection of lawlessness spreading over the rest of mankind, he is well content, if he can in any way live his life here untainted in his own person by injustice and

e unholy deeds, and, when the time for his release arrives, take his departure amid bright hopes with cheerfulness and serenity.

Well, said Adeimantus, he will certainly
497 have offered before his departure not the least important things.

Nor yet, I rejoined, the most important, if he fails to find a political constitution suited to him; for under such a regime he will not only himself reach a higher stage of growth, but he will also secure his city's welfare together with his own.

Well then, I continued, the causes of the slander against philosophy, and the injustice of it, have in my opinion been satisfactorily disposed of, unless you have anything to add.

No, I have nothing more to say on this topic. But which of the constitutions of our time is the one that you consider suitable to philosophy?

b There is none that I can say that of; and what I complain of is precisely this, that no city, as now constituted, is a worthy sphere for a philosophic nature. Hence that nature becomes warped and deteriorated. For just as foreign seed when sown in alien soil, is overcome and fades away, and eventually passes into a native plant of the country; so this kind of character at the present day, failing to pre-

serve its peculiar virtues, degenerates into tendencies that are not its own; but if it could only find the most perfect constitution, answering to itself as the most perfect of characters, it will then give proof that it is the true divine type; whereas all other kinds of natures and practices are merely human. Having said this, it is clear that you will ask me what this constitution is.

You are mistaken, he said; what I was going to ask was, whether you were thinking of the one we spoke of when founding the city, or of another.

The same, I replied, in all points but one; and this one point was alluded to during the discussion, when we said that it would be necessary to have constantly present in the city something which would understand the constitution in the very light in which you, the legislator, understood it, when you framed the laws.

True, it was alluded to.

But it was not sufficiently developed, because I was alarmed by your objections, which showed that the demonstration of it would be tedious and difficult: for it is by no means the easiest part of the discussion that is left.

What is that part?

To show in what way a city may handle philosophy without incurring utter destruction. For we know that all great things are hazardous, and, according to the proverb, beautiful things are indeed difficult to attain.

Nevertheless, he said, let this point be cleared up, in order that the demonstration may be complete.

The hindrance, if any, will arise, not from want of will, but from want of ability. Anyway you will see my zeal with your own eyes. Observe at once with what reckless zeal I proceed to assert that a city ought to deal with the pursuit of philosophy on a plan the very reverse of that now in vogue.

How so?

498     At present, those who pursue philosophy at all are mere striplings, just emerged from boyhood, who take it up in the intervals between housekeeping and business; and, after just dipping into the most difficult part of the study—by which I mean that which is concerned with speeches—abandon the pursuit altogether, and these are the most advanced philosophers; and ever afterwards, if, on being invited, they consent to listen to others whose attention is devoted to it, they think it a great condescension, because they imagine that philosophy ought to be made a mere secondary occupation; and on

b the approach of old age, all but a few are far more extinguished than the sun of Heraclitus, since, unlike it, they are not rekindled.

    And what is the right plan? he asked.

    Just the opposite. In youth and boyhood they ought to be put through a course of training in philosophy, suited to their years; and while their bodies are growing up to manhood, special attention should be paid to them, to acquire the habit of service to philosophy. At the approach of that period, during which the soul begins to attain its maturity, the mental exercises ought to be rendered more severe. Finally, when their bodily powers begin to

c fail, and they are released from public duties and military service, from that time forward they graze freely and do nothing else except side-activities, if they are to live happily on earth, and after death to crown the life they have led with a corresponding destiny in that other place.

    Well, indeed, Socrates, I do not doubt your zeal. But I expect most of your hearers, beginning with Thrasymachus, will oppose you with still greater zeal, and will not be at all convinced.

    Do not create a quarrel between me and

d Thrasymachus, when we have just become friends; though I do not mean to say that we were enemies before. I shall leave nothing untried, until I have either persuaded him, along with the rest, or have achieved something for their good in that future life, should they happen to encounter similar discussions.

    You are speaking of just a short time, he exclaimed.

    Rather speak of it as nothing as compared with all time. However, it need not surprise us that most people disbelieve what has been discussed; for they have never yet seen anything that corresponds to what we just now dis-

e cussed. No, what is much more likely is, that they have met with proposals somewhat resembling ours, but forced expressly into appearing of a piece with one another, instead of falling spontaneously into agreement, as in the present case. They have never yet seen, in either one or more instances, a man molded into the most perfect possible conformity and

499 likeness to virtue, both in words and in works, reigning in a city as perfect as himself. Or do you think they have?

    No, indeed I do not.

    And further, my dear friend, they have not listened often enough to discussions beautiful and free, confined to the strenuous investigation of truth by all possible means, simply for the sake of knowing it; and which therefore will, when used both in private discussions and in public trials, keep at a respectful distance from those subtleties and special pleadings, which solely aim at opinion and disputations.

    You are right again.

    It was for these reasons, and in anticipation of these results, that, notwithstanding my fears,

b I was constrained by the force of truth on a former occasion to assert, that no city, or regime, or individual either, can ever become perfect, until these few philosophers, who are at present described as useless though not depraved, find themselves accidentally compelled, whether they like it or not, to accept the care of a city, which in its turn finds itself compelled to be obedient to them; or until the present sover-

c eigns and kings, or their sons, are divinely inspired with a genuine love of genuine philosophy. Now to assert the impossibility of both or

either of these contingencies, I for my part pronounce irrational. If they are impossible, we
may justly be held up to derision for saying
nothing but prayers. Am I not right?

You are.

If, then, persons sharpest in philosophy,
either in the countless ages that are past have
been constrained, or in some barbarian place
far beyond the limits of our horizon at the
present moment are constrained, or hereafter
d    shall by some necessity be constrained to
undertake the charge of a city, I am prepared to
argue to the death in defense of this assertion
that the constitution described has existed,
does exist, and indeed will exist, wherever the
Muse aforesaid has become mistress of a city.
For its realization is no impossibility, nor are
our speculations impossible, though their difficulty is even by us acknowledged.

I am of the same opinion, said he.

But are you prepared to say, that the majority, on the contrary, entertain a different opinion?

Perhaps so.

My excellent friend, beware how you bring
e    so heavy a charge against the multitude. No
doubt they will change their minds, if you
avoid controversy, and endeavor with all gentleness to remove their prejudice against the
love of learning, by showing them whom you
500   understand by philosophers, and defining, as
we have just done, their nature and their practice, that they may not suppose you to mean
such characters as are uppermost in their own
thoughts; or shall you venture to maintain that,
even if they look at them from your point of
view, they will entertain a different opinion
from yours, and return another sort of answer?
In other words, do you think that an unmali-
cious and gentle person can quarrel with one
who is not quarrelsome, or feel malice towards
one who is not malicious? I will anticipate you
with the declaration that, in my opinion, so
harsh a nature may be found in some few
cases, but not in the majority of mankind.

I am myself entirely of your opinion, he
replied.

Then are you not also of my opinion on just    b
this point, that the ill-will which the multitude
bear to philosophy is to be traced to those who
have forced their way in, like tipsy men, where
they had no concern, and who abuse one
another and delight in picking quarrels, and
are always discoursing about persons, conduct
peculiarly unsuitable to philosophy?

Very unsuitable.

For surely, Adeimantus, he who has his
thought truly set on the things that really are,
cannot even spare time to look down upon the    c
occupations of men, and, by disputing with
them, catch the infection of malice and hostility. On the contrary, he devotes all his time to
the contemplation of things that are arranged
and always in the same condition; and beholding how they neither wrong nor are wronged
by each other, but are all obedient to order and
in harmony with reason, he studies to imitate
and resemble them as closely as he can. Or do
you think it possible for a man to avoid imitating that which he admires and with which he
associates?

No, it is impossible.

Hence the philosopher, by associating with
what is god-like and orderly, becomes, as far
as is permitted to man, orderly and god-like    d
himself; though here, as everywhere, there is
room for slander.

Indeed, you are right.

So that, if he ever finds himself compelled
to study how he may introduce into the characters of men, both in public and in private
life, the things that draw his notice in that
higher region, and could to others as well as
himself, do you think that he will prove an
indifferent artist in the production of temperance and justice and all popular virtue?

Certainly not.

Well, but if the multitude are made to perceive that our description is a correct one, will    e
they really be angry with the philosophers, and

will they discredit our assertion, that a city can only attain to true happiness, if it be delineated by painters who copy the divine paradigm?

501    They will not be angry, if they are made sensible of the fact. But how do you mean them to sketch it?

They will take for their canvas, I replied, a city and the characters of mankind, and begin by making a clean surface—which is by no means an easy task. However, you are aware, that at the very outset they will differ from all other artists in this respect, that they will refuse to meddle with man or city, and hesitate to pencil laws, until they have either found a clear canvas, or made it clear by their own exertions.

Yes, and they are right.

In the next place, do you not suppose that they will sketch in outline the form of their constitution?

Doubtless they will.

b      Their next step, I imagine, will be to fill out this outline; and in doing this they will often turn their eyes to this side and to that, first to that which is by nature just, beautiful, temperate, and the like, and then to the notions current among mankind; and thus, by mingling and combining the results, they forge an image of man, guided by those realizations of it among men, which, if you remember, even Homer has described as godly and god-like.

You are right.

And, I imagine, they will go on rubbing out here and repainting there, until they have done c      all in their power to make the disposition of men as pleasing as may be in the eyes of the gods.

Well, certainly their picture will be a very beautiful one.

Do we then, I continued, make any progress in persuading those assailants, who by your account were marching stoutly to attack us, that such a painter of constitutions is to be found in the man whom we praised lately in their hearing, and who occasioned their displeasure, because we proposed to deliver up our cities into his hands? And do they feel

rather less exasperation at being told the same thing now?

Yes, much less, if they are wise.

I think so too; for how will they be able to      d dispute our position? Can they deny that philosophers are enamored of that which is and of the truth?

No, it would indeed be ridiculous to do that.

Well; can they maintain that their nature, such as we have described it, is not akin to the best?

No, they cannot.

Once more; will they tell us that such a character, placed within reach of its appropriate studies, will fail to become as thoroughly good and philosophical as any character can become? Or will they give the preference to those whom we discarded?

Surely not.                                               e

Will they then persist in their anger, when I assert that, until the class of philosophers be invested with the supreme authority in a city, such city and its citizens will find no rest from ills, and the fabled city which we are describing will not be actually realized?

Probably they will grow less angry.

What do you say to our assuming, not merely that they are less angry, but that they are perfectly pacified and convinced, in order   502 that we may shame them into acquiescence, if nothing else will do?

By all means assume it.

Well then, let us regard these persons as convinced so far. But, in the next place, will anybody maintain that kings and sovereigns cannot by any possibility beget sons gifted with a philosophic nature?

No one in the world will maintain that.

And can any one assert, that, if born with such a nature, they must necessarily be corrupted? I grant that their preservation is a difficult matter; but I ask, is there any one who   b will maintain that in the whole course of time not one of all that number can ever be preserved from contamination?

Who could maintain that?

But, I continued, one such person, with a submissive city, has it in his power to realize all that is now discredited.

True, he has.

For, surely, if a ruler establishes the laws and practices which we have detailed, it is, I presume, not impossible for the citizens to consent to carry them out.

Certainly not.

And, would it be so astonishing and impossible, if what we think right were thought right by others also?

c For my part I think not.

But I believe we have quite convinced ourselves, in the foregoing discussion, that our plan, if possible, is the best.

Yes, quite.

So that the conclusion, apparently, to which we are now brought with regard to our legislation, is, that what we propose is best, if it can be realized; and that to realize it is difficult, but certainly not impossible.

True, that is our conclusion, he said.

Well, then, this part of the subject having been laboriously completed, shall we proceed to discuss the questions still remaining, in what way, and by the help of what studies and prac-
d tices, there will develop a group capable of saving the regime, and what must be the age at which these studies are severally undertaken?

Let us do so by all means.

It was not wise for me, I continued, to omit the unpleasantness about the possession of women and the begetting of children, and the appointment of rulers; which I was induced to leave out from knowing what odium the perfectly correct method would incur, and how
e difficult it would be to carry into effect. Notwithstanding all my precautions, the moment has now arrived when these points must be discussed. It is true the question of the women and children has already been settled, but the inquiry concerning the rulers must be pursued
503 afresh from the beginning. In describing them, we said, if you remember, that they must appear to love the city, that they must be tested

by pleasure and by pain, and proved never to have deserted their principles in the midst of toil and danger and every vicissitude of fortune, on pain of forfeiting their position if their powers of endurance fail; and that whoever comes forth from the trial without a flaw, like gold tried in the fire, must be appointed to office, and receive, during life and after death, privileges and rewards. This was pretty nearly the drift of our argument, which, from fear of awakening the question now pending, turned b aside and hid its face.

Your account is quite correct, he said; I remember perfectly.

Yes, my friend, I shrank from making assertions which I have since dared, but now let me venture upon this declaration, that we must make philosophers the most precise guardians.

We hear you, he replied.

Now consider what a small supply of these men you will, in all probability, find. For the parts of that nature, which we described as essential to philosophers, will seldom grow together in the same place: in most cases that nature grows disjointed.

What do you mean? c

You are aware that persons endowed with a quick grasp, a good memory, sagacity, quickness, and their attendant qualities, do not readily grow up to be at the same time so noble and magnificent as to consent to live a regular, calm, and steady life; on the contrary, such persons are carried away by their quickness hither and thither, and all steadiness vanishes from their life.

True.

On the other hand, those steady and invariable characters, whose trustiness makes one anxious to employ them, and who in war are d slow to take alarm, behave in the same way when pursuing their studies—that is to say, they are torpid and stupid, as if they were benumbed, and are constantly dozing and yawning, whenever they have to toil at anything of the kind.

That is true.

But we declare that, unless a person possesses a pretty fair amount of both qualifications, he must not share in the strictest education, in honor, and in ruling.

We are right.

Then do you not anticipate a scanty supply of such characters?

Most assuredly I do.

e     Hence we must not be content with testing their behavior in the toils, dangers, and pleasures, which we mentioned before; but we must go on to try them in ways which we then omitted, exercising them in a variety of studies, and observing whether their character will be able to support the greatest studies, or 504  whether it will flinch from the trial, like those who flinch under other circumstances.

No doubt it is proper to examine them in this way. But which do you mean by the greatest studies?

I presume you remember, that, after separating the soul into three specific parts, we deduced the several natures of justice, temperance, courage, and wisdom?

Why, if I did not remember, I should deserve not to hear the rest of the discussion.

Do you also remember the remark which preceded that one?

What was that?

b     We remarked, I believe, that to obtain the best possible view of the question, we should have to take a different and a longer route, which would bring us to a thorough insight into the subject; still that it would be possible to add proofs on the same level as the previous demonstrations. Thereupon you said that such a demonstration would satisfy you; and then followed those investigations, which, to my own mind, were less than exact; but you can tell me whether they were satisfactory to you?

Well, to speak for myself, I thought them measured; and certainly the rest of the party held the same opinion.

c     But, my friend, no measure of such a sub-

ject, which falls perceptibly short of the truth, can be said to be a measure at all: for nothing imperfect is a measure of anything; though people sometimes suppose that enough has been done, and that there is no call for further investigation.

Yes, he said, that is a very common habit, and it arises from sluggishness.

Yes, but it is a habit remarkably undesirable in the guardian of a city and its laws.

So I should suppose.

That being the case, my friend, such a person must go round by that longer route, and           d must labor as devotedly in his studies as in his bodily exercises. Otherwise, as we were saying just now, he will never reach the goal of that greatest study, which is most peculiarly his own.

What! he exclaimed, are not these the greatest? Is there still something greater than justice and those other things which we have discussed?

Yes indeed, I replied. And here we must not contemplate a rude outline, as we have been doing; on the contrary, we must be satisfied with nothing short of the most complete elaboration. For would it not be ridiculous to exert oneself on other subjects of small value, taking           e all imaginable pains to bring them to the most exact and spotless perfection; and at the same time to ignore the claim of the greatest subjects to a corresponding exactitude of the highest order?

The sentiment is a very just one. But do you suppose that any one would let you go without asking what that study is which you call the greatest, and of what it treats?

Certainly not, I replied; so put the question yourself. Assuredly you have heard the answer many a time; but at this moment either you have forgotten it, or else you intend to cause           505 the trouble in turn. I incline to think this; for you have often been told that the idea of the good is the highest study, and it is by relation to it that just acts and other things become useful and advantageous. And at this moment you can scarcely doubt that I am going to assert this, and to assert, besides, that we are not sufficiently acquainted with this. And if so—if, I say, we know everything else perfectly, without knowing this—you are aware that it will profit us nothing; just as it would be equally b profitless to possess everything without possessing what is good. Or do you imagine it would be a gain to possess all things that can be possessed, with the single exception of things good; or to apprehend all things, without apprehending what is good, while understanding nothing with regard to the beautiful and the good?

Not I, believe me.

Moreover, you doubtless know besides, that the good is supposed by the multitude to be pleasure, and by the more enlightened prudence?

Of course I know that.

And you are aware, my friend, that the advocates of this latter opinion are unable to explain what they mean by prudence, and are compelled at last to explain it as being about the good.

Yes, they are in a ludicrous difficulty.

c They certainly are: since they reproach us with ignorance of that which is good, and then speak to us the next moment as if we knew what it was. For they tell us that the good is prudence about the good, assuming that we understand their meaning, as soon as they have uttered the term 'good.'

It is perfectly true.

Again, are not those, whose definition identifies pleasure with good, just as much infected with error as the preceding? For they are forced to admit the existence of bad pleasures, are they not?

Certainly they are.

From which it follows, I should suppose, that they must admit the same thing to be both good and bad.

Does it not?

Certainly it does.                                                          d

Then is it not evident that this is a subject often and severely disputed?

Doubtless it is.

Well then, is it not evident, that though many persons would be ready to do and seem to do, or to possess and seem to possess, what seems just and beautiful, without really being so; yet, when you come to things good, no one is content to acquire what only seems such; on the contrary, everybody seeks the reality, and semblances are here, if nowhere else, treated with universal contempt?

Yes, that is quite evident.

This good, then, which every soul pursues, as the end of all its actions, divining its exis-      e tence, but perplexed and unable to apprehend satisfactorily its nature, or to enjoy that steady confidence in relation to it, which it does enjoy in relation to other things, and therefore doomed to forfeit any advantage which it might have derived from those same things;      506 are we to maintain that, on a subject of such overwhelming importance, the blindness we have described is a desirable feature in the character of those best members of the city in whose hands everything is to be placed?

Most certainly not.

At any rate, if it be not known in what way just things and beautiful things come to be also good, I imagine that such things will not possess a very valuable guardian in the person of him who is ignorant on this point. And I surmise that none will know the just and the beautiful satisfactorily until he knows the good.

You are right in your surmise.

Then will not the arrangement of our regime be perfect, provided it be overlooked by a guardian who is a knower of these things?      b

Unquestionably. But tell us, Socrates, do *you* assert the good to be knowledge or pleasure or something different from both?

I saw long ago that you are the kind of man who would certainly not put up with the opinions of other people on these subjects.

Why, Socrates, it appears to me to be positively wrong in one who has devoted so much
c   time to these questions, to be able to state the opinions of others, without being able to state his own.

Well, I said, do you think it is just to speak as if one knows when one in fact does not know about these things?

Certainly not as if one knew, but I think it right to be willing to state one's opinion for what it is worth.

Well, but have you not noticed that opinions divorced from knowledge are all ugly? At the best they are blind. Or do you conceive that those who, unaided by the mind, entertain a correct opinion, are at all superior to blind men, who manage to keep the straight path?

Not at all superior, he replied.

Then is it your desire to contemplate
d   objects that are ugly, blind, and crooked, when it is in your power to learn from other people about bright and beautiful things?

I implore you in the name of Zeus, Socrates, cried Glaucon, not to hang back, as if you had come to the end. We shall be content even if you only discuss the subject of the good in the style in which you discussed justice, temperance, and the rest.

Yes, my friend, and I likewise should be thoroughly content. But I distrust my own powers, and I feel afraid that my awkward zeal will subject me to ridicule. No, I will have to
e   put aside, for the present at any rate, all inquiry into the good itself. For, it seems to me, it is beyond the measure of this effort to find the way to what is, after all, only my present opinion on the subject. But I am willing to talk to you about that which appears to be an offshoot of the good, and bears the strongest resemblance to it, provided it is also agreeable to you; but if it is not, I will let it alone.

But please tell us about it, he replied. You shall remain in our debt for an account of the parent.

507      I wish that I could pay, and you receive, the parent sum, instead of having to content ourselves with the interest springing from it. However, here I present you with the interest and the child of the good itself. Only take care that I do not involuntarily impose upon you by handing in a spurious account of this offspring.

We will take all the care we can; only proceed.

I will do so as soon as we have come to a settlement together, and you have been reminded of certain statements made in a previous part of our conversation, and renewed before now again and again.

What statements exactly?                                b

In the course of the discussion we have distinctly maintained the existence of a multiplicity of things that are beautiful, and good, and so on.

True, we have.

And also the existence of beauty itself, and good itself, and so on; reducing all those things which before we regarded as manifold, to a single idea and a single substance in each case, and addressing each as 'that which is.'

Just so.

And we assert that the former address themselves to the eye, and not to the mind, whereas the ideas address themselves to the mind, and not to the eye.

Certainly.

Now with what part of ourselves do we see     c
that which is visible?

With the eye-sight.

In the same way we hear sounds with the hearing, and perceive everything sensible with the other senses, do we not?

Certainly.

Then have you noticed how very lavishly the craftsman of the senses has fashioned the faculty of seeing and being seen?

Not exactly, he replied.

Well then, look at it in this light. Is there any other kind of thing, which the ear and the voice require, to enable the one to hear, and

the other to be heard, in the absence of which
d   third thing the one will not hear, and the other
will not be heard?

No, there is not.

And I believe that very few, if any, of the
other senses require any such third thing. Can
you mention one that does?

No, I cannot.

But do you not perceive that, in the case of
vision and visible objects, there is a demand
for something additional?

How so?

Why, granting that vision is seated in the
eye, and that the owner of it is attempting to
use it, and that color is present in what is to be
e   seen; still, unless there be present a third kind
of thing, devoted to this special purpose, you
are aware that the eyesight will see nothing,
and the colors will be invisible.

And what is the third thing to which you
refer?

Of course I refer to what you call light.

You are right.

Hence it appears, that of all the pairs afore-
508  said, the sense of sight, and the power of being
seen, are coupled by the more honorable link,
whose nature is anything but insignificant,
unless light is not an honorable thing.

No, indeed; it is very far from being dishonorable.

To whom, then, of the gods in heaven can
you refer as the author and dispenser of this
blessing? And whose light is it that enables our
sight to see so excellently well, and makes the
visible appear?

There can be but one opinion on the subject, he replied: your question evidently al-
ludes to the sun.

Then the relation between eyesight and this
deity is of the following nature, is it not?

Describe it.

Neither the sight itself, nor the eye, which
b   is the seat of sight, can be identified with the
sun.

Certainly not.

And yet, of all the organs of sensation, the
eye, I think, bears the closest resemblance to
the sun.

Yes, quite so.

Further, is not the faculty which the eye
possesses dispensed to it from the sun, and
held by it as a kind of overflow?

Certainly it is.

Then is it not also true, that the sun, though
not identical with sight, is nevertheless the
cause of sight, and is moreover seen by its aid?

Yes, quite true.

Well then, I continued, understand that I
meant the sun when I spoke of the offspring of
the good, begotten by it in a certain resem-          c
blance to itself—that is to say, bearing the
same relation in the visible world to sight and
to the visible, which the good bears in the
intelligible world to mind and the knowable.

How so? Be so good as to explain it to me
more at length.

Are you aware that whenever a person
makes an end of looking at things, upon which
the light of day is shedding color, and looks
instead at things colored by the light of the
moon and stars, his eyes grow dim and appear
almost blind, as if they were not the seat of distinct vision?

I am fully aware of it.

But whenever the same person looks at       d
things on which the sun is shining, these very
eyes, I believe, see clearly, and are evidently
the seat of distinct vision?

Unquestionably it is so.

In the same way understand the condition
of the soul as follows. Whenever it has fastened upon those things, over which truth and
that which is are shining, it seizes it by an act
of mind, and knows it, and thus proves itself to
be possessed of reason; but whenever it has
fixed upon objects that are blent with darkness,
the world of becoming and passing away, it
rests in opinion, and its sight grows dim, as its
opinions shift backwards and forwards, and it
has the appearance of being destitute of mind.

True, it has.

e    Now, this power, which supplies the knowable with the truth that is in them, and which renders to him who knows them the faculty of knowing them, you must consider to be the idea of the good and you must regard it as the cause of knowledge and of truth, so far as the latter comes within the range of knowledge; and though knowledge and truth are both very beautiful things, you will be right in
509  looking upon good as something distinct from them, and even more beautiful. And just as, in the analogous case, it is right to regard light and vision as resembling the sun, but wrong to identify them with the sun; so, in the case of knowledge and truth, it is right to regard both of them as resembling good, but wrong to identify either of them with good; because, on the contrary, the having of the good is still more honorable.

That implies an inexpressible beauty, if it not only is the source of knowledge and truth, but also surpasses them in beauty; for, I presume, you do not mean by it pleasure.

Hush! I exclaimed, not a word of that. But you had better examine the illustration further, as follows.

b    Show me how.

I think you will admit that the sun supplies the visible things, not only the faculty of being seen, but also their generation, growth, and nutriment, though it is not itself the same as generation.

Of course it is not.

Then admit that, in like manner, the knowable not only derives from the good the gift of being known, but is further endowed by it with being and essence; so the good, far from being identical with it, is beyond being in dignity and power.

c    Hereupon Glaucon exclaimed with a very amusing air, By Apollo! what amazing hyperbole!

Well, I said, you are the person to blame, because you compel me to state my opinions on the subject.

Let me entreat you not to stop, until you have at all events gone through the likeness of the sun, if you are leaving anything out.

Well, to tell the truth, I am leaving out a great deal.

Then do not omit even a trifle.

I think I shall leave much unsaid; however, if I can help it under the circumstances, I will not intentionally make any omission.

Please do not.

Now understand that, according to us, there    d
are two powers reigning, one over an intelligible and the other over a visible region and class. If I were to use the term firmament you might think I was playing on the word. Well then, are you in possession of these as two kinds, one visible, the other intelligible?

Yes, I am.

Suppose you take a line divided into two unequal parts—one to represent the visible class of objects, the other the intelligible—and divide each part again into two segments in the same proportion. Then, if you make the lengths of the segments represent degrees of distinctness or indistinctness, one of the two    510
segments of the part which stands for the visible world will represent all images—meaning by images, first of all, shadows; and, in the next place, reflections in water, and in close-grained, smooth, bright substances, and everything of the kind, if you understand me.

Yes, I do understand.

Let the other segment stand for that which corresponds to these images—namely, the animals about us, and everything that grows and the whole class of crafted things.

Would you also consent to say that, with reference to this class, there is, in point of truth and untruthfulness, the same distinction between the copy and the original, that there is between what is a matter of opinion and what is a matter of knowledge?

Certainly I should.    b

Then let us proceed to consider how we must divide that part of the whole line which represents the intelligible world.

How must we do it?

Thus one segment of it will represent what the soul is compelled to investigate by the aid of the segments of the other part, which it employs as images, starting from hypotheses, and traveling not to a first principle, but to a conclusion. The other segment will represent the soul, as it makes its way from a hypothesis to a first principle which is not hypothetical, unaided by those images which the former division employs, and shaping its journey by the sole help of the forms themselves.

I have not understood your description so well as I might wish.

c    Then we will try again. You will understand me more easily when I have made some previous observations. I think you know that the students of subjects like geometry and calculation, assume by way of materials, in each investigation, all odd and even numbers, figures, three kinds of angles, and other similar things. These things they assume as known, and having adopted them as hypotheses, they decline to give any account of them, either to themselves or to others, on the assumption that they are self-evident; and, making these their
d    starting point, they proceed to travel through the remainder of the subject, and arrive at last, with perfect unanimity, at that which they have proposed as the object of investigation.

I am perfectly aware of the fact, he replied.

Then you also know that they summon to their aid visible forms, and discourse about them, though their thoughts are busy not with these forms, but with their originals, and though they discourse not with a view to the particular square and diameter which they draw, but with a view to the square itself and the diameter
e    itself, and so on. For while they employ by way of images those figures and diagrams aforesaid, which again have their shadows and images in water, they are really endeavoring to behold things themselves, which a person can only see
511  with the eye of reasoning.

True.

This, then, was the class of things which I called intelligible; but I said that the soul is constrained to employ hypotheses while engaged in the investigation of them, not traveling to a first principle, because it is unable to step out of, and mount above, its hypotheses, but using as images the copies presented by things below, which copies, as compared with the originals, are vulgarly esteemed distinct and valued accordingly.

I understand you to be speaking of the sub-    b
ject matter of the various branches of geometry and the kindred arts.

Again, by the second segment of the intelligible world understand me to mean all that reason itself apprehends by the force of dialectic, when it considers hypotheses not as first principles, but in the truest sense, that is to say, as stepping-stones and impulses, whereby it may force its way up to something that is not hypothetical, and arrive at the first principle of every thing, and seize it in its grasp; which done, it turns round, and takes hold of that which takes hold of this first principle, until at last it comes down to a conclusion, calling in the aid of no sensible object whatever, but    c
simply employing the self-subsisting forms themselves, and terminating in the same.

I do not understand you so well as I could wish, for I believe you to be describing an arduous task; but at any rate I understand that you wish to declare distinctly, that what is and is intelligible, as contemplated by the knowledge of dialectics, is more clear than the field investigated by what are called the arts, in which hypotheses constitute first principles, which the students are compelled, it is true, to contemplate with the mind and not with the senses; but, at the same time, as they do not come back, in the course of inquiry, to a first principle, but    d
push on from hypothetical premises, you think that they do not exercise mind on the questions that engage them, although taken in connection with a first principle these questions come within the domain of reason. And I believe you apply the term reasoning, not understanding, to the habit of such people as geometricians,

regarding reasoning as something intermediate between opinion and understanding.

You have taken in my meaning most satisfactorily; and I beg you will accept these four dispositions in the soul, as corresponding to the four segments, namely understanding corresponding to the highest, reasoning to the sec‑
e   ond, trust to the third, and imagination to the last; and now arrange them in gradation, and believe them to partake of distinctness in a degree corresponding to the truth of their respective domains.

I understand you, said he. I quite agree with you, and will arrange them as you desire.

## BOOK VII

514   Now then, I proceeded to say, go on to compare our natural condition, as far as education and ignorance are concerned, to a state of things like the following. Imagine a number of men living in an underground cave-like chamber, with an entrance open to the light, extending along the entire length of the cave, in which they have been confined, from their childhood, with their legs and necks so shackled, that they are obliged to sit still and look straight forwards, because their chains make it
b   impossible for them to turn their heads round. And imagine a bright fire burning some way off, above and behind them, and a kind of roadway above which passes between the fire and the prisoners, with a low wall built along it, like the screens which puppeteers put up in front of their audience, and above which they exhibit their wonders.
c      I have it, he replied.

Also picture to yourself a number of per‑
515   sons walking behind this wall, and carrying with them statues of men, and images of other animals, fashioned in wood and stone and all kinds of materials, together with various other articles, which are above the wall; and, as you might expect, let some of the passers-by be talking, and others silent.

You are describing a strange scene, and strange prisoners.

They resemble us, I replied. For let me ask you, in the first place, whether persons so confined could have seen anything of themselves or of each other, beyond the shadows thrown by the fire upon the part of the cave facing them?

Certainly not, if you suppose them to have been compelled all their lifetime to keep their   b
heads unmoved.

And what about the things carried past them? Is not the same true with regard to them?

Unquestionably it is.

And if they were able to converse with one another, do you not think that they would be in the habit of giving names to the things which they saw before them?

Doubtless they would.

Again, if their prison-house returned an echo from the part facing them, whenever one of the passers-by opened his lips, to what, let me ask you, could they refer the voice, if not to the shadow which was passing?

Unquestionably they would refer it to that.

Then surely such persons would hold the   c
shadows of those manufactured articles to be the only truth.

Without a doubt they would.

Now consider what would happen if the course of nature brought them a release from their fetters, and a remedy for their foolishness, in the following manner. Let us suppose that one of them has been released, and compelled suddenly to stand up, and turn his neck round and walk with open eyes towards the light—and let us suppose that he goes through all these actions with pain, and that the dazzling splendor renders him incapable of perceiving those things of which he formerly used to see only the shadows. What answer should you expect him to give, if someone were to tell   d
him that in those days he was watching foolery, but that now he is somewhat nearer to reality, and is turned towards things more real,

and sees more correctly? Above all, if he were to point out to him the several objects that are passing by, and question him, and compel him to answer what they are? Should you not expect him to be puzzled, and to regard his old visions as truer than the objects now forced upon his notice?

Yes, much truer.

e    And if he were further compelled to gaze at the light itself, would not his eyes be distressed, do you think, and would he not shrink and turn away to the things which he could see distinctly, and consider them to be really clearer than the things pointed out to him?

Just so.

And if some one were to drag him violently up the rough and steep ascent from the cave, and refuse to let him go until he had drawn him
516  out into the light of the sun, do you not think that he would be vexed and indignant at such treatment, and on reaching the light, would he not find his eyes so dazzled by the glare as to be incapable of making out so much as one of the objects that are now called true?

Yes, he would find it so at first.

Hence, I suppose, it will be necessary for him to become accustomed before he is able to perceive the things above. At first he will be most successful in distinguishing shadows, then he will discern the reflections of men and other things in water, and afterwards the things
b    themselves? and after this he will raise his eyes to encounter the light of the moon and stars, finding it less difficult to study the heavenly bodies and the heaven itself by night, than the sun and the sun's light by day?

Doubtless.

Last of all, I imagine, he will be able to observe and contemplate the nature of the sun, not as it *appears* in water or on alien ground, but as it *is* in itself in its own territory.

Of course.

His next step will be to draw the conclusion, that the sun is the provider of the seasons
c    and the years, and the guardian of all things in the visible world, and in a manner the cause of

all those things which he and his companions used to see.

Obviously, this will be his next step.

What then? When he recalls to mind his first home, and the wisdom of the place, and his old fellow-prisoners, do you not think he will think himself happy on account of the change, and pity them?

Assuredly he will.

And if it was their practice in those days to receive honor and praise one from another, and to give prizes to him who had the keenest eye for the things passing by, and who remembered best all that used to precede and follow and accompany it, and from these divined       d
most ably what was going to come next, do you imagine that he will desire these prizes, and envy those who receive honor and exercise authority among them? Do you not rather imagine that he will feel what Homer describes, to "drudge on the lands of a master, serving a man of no great estate," and be ready to go through anything, rather than entertain       e
those opinions, and live in that fashion?

For my own part, he replied, I am quite of that opinion. I believe he would consent to go through anything rather than live in that way.

And now consider what would happen if such a man were to descend again and seat himself on his old seat? Coming so suddenly out of the sun, would he not find his eyes blinded with the darkness of the place?

Certainly, he would.

And if he were forced to deliver his opinion again, about those previously mentioned shadows, and to compete earnestly against those     517
who had always been prisoners, while his sight continued dim, and his eyes unsteady, and if he needed quite some time to get adjusted— would he not be made a laughingstock, and would it not be said of him, that he had gone up only to come back again with his eyesight destroyed, and that it was not worth while even to attempt the ascent? And if any one endeavored to set them free and carry them to the light, would they not go so far as to put him

to death, if they could only manage to get their hands on him?

Yes, that they would.

Now this imaginary case, my dear Glaucon, you must apply in all its parts to our former statements, by comparing the region which the eye reveals, to the prison-house, and the light of the fire to the power of the sun; and if, by the upward ascent and the contemplation of the things above, you understand the journeying of the soul into the intelligible region, you will not disappoint my hopes, since you desire to be told what they are; though, indeed, god only knows whether they are true. But, be that as it may, the view which I take of the phenomena is to the following effect. In the world of knowledge, the essential idea of the good is the limit of what can be seen, and can barely be perceived; but, when perceived, we cannot help concluding that it is in every case the source of all that is right and beautiful, in the visible world giving birth to light and its master, and in the intelligible world, as master, providing truth and mind—and that whoever would act wisely, either in private or in public, must see it.

To the best of my power, said he, I quite agree with you.

That being the case, I continued, agree with me on another point, and do not be surprised, that those who have climbed so high are unwilling to take part in the affairs of men, because their souls are eager to spend all their time in that upper region. For how could it be otherwise, if in turn it follows from the image we've discussed before?

True, it could scarcely be otherwise.

Well, do you think it amazing that a person, who has turned from the contemplation of the divine to the study of human infirmities, should betray awkwardness, and appear very ridiculous, when with his sight still dazed, and before he has become sufficiently accustomed to the surrounding darkness, he finds himself compelled to contend in courts of law, or elsewhere, about the shadows of justice, or images

which cast the shadows, and to take up in what way the lists are to be grasped by those who have never yet had a glimpse of justice itself?

No, it is anything but amazing.

Right, for a sensible man will recollect that the eyes may be confused in two distinct ways and from two distinct causes, that is to say, by sudden transitions either from light to darkness, or from darkness to light. And, believing the same idea holds for the soul, whenever such a person sees a case in which the soul is perplexed and unable to distinguish objects, he will not laugh irrationally, but will rather examine whether it has just come from a brighter life, and has been blinded by the novelty of darkness, or whether it has come from the depths of ignorance into a more brilliant life, and has been dazzled by the unusual splendor; and not until then will he consider the one happy in its life and condition, or have pity on the other; and if he chooses to laugh, such laughter will be less ridiculous than that which is raised at the expense of the soul that has descended from the light of a higher region.

You are speaking in a sensible manner.

Hence, if this is true, we must consider the following about these matters, that education is not what certain men proclaim. They say, I think, that they can infuse the soul with knowledge, when it was not in there, just as sight might be instilled in blinded eyes.

True, such are their pretensions.

Whereas, our present argument shows us that there is a faculty residing in the soul of each person, and an instrument enabling each of us to learn; and that, just as we might suppose it to be impossible to turn the eye round from darkness to light without turning the whole body, so must this faculty, or this instrument, be wheeled round, in company with the entire soul, from the perishing world, until it be enabled to endure the contemplation of the real world and the brightest part thereof, which, according to us, is the idea of the good. Am I not right?

You are.

Hence, I continued, there should be an art of this turning around, involving the way that the change will most easily and most effectually be brought about. Its object will not be to produce in the person the power of seeing. On the contrary, it assumes that he possesses it, though he is turned in a wrong direction, and does not look towards the right quarter—and its aim is to remedy this defect.

So it would appear.

Hence, while, on the one hand, the other so-called virtues of the soul seem to resemble those of the body, inasmuch as they really do e not pre-exist in the soul, but are formed in it in the course of time by habit and exercise; while the virtue of prudence, on the other hand, does, above everything else, appear to come from a more divine substance, which never loses its energy, but by a turn-around becomes useful 519 and serviceable, or else remains useless and injurious. For you must have noticed how keen-sighted are the puny souls of those who have the reputation of being wise but vicious, and how sharply they see through the things to which they are directed, thus proving that their powers of vision are by no means feeble, though they have been compelled to become the servants of wickedness, so that the more sharply they see, the more numerous are the harms which they work.

Yes, indeed it is the case.

But, I proceeded, if from earliest childhood this part of their nature had been shorn and b stripped of those leaden, earth-born weights, which grow and cling to the pleasures of eating and gluttonous enjoyments of a similar nature, and keep the eye of the soul turned upon the things below—if, I repeat, they had been released from these snares, and turned round to look at true things, then these very same souls of these very same men would have had as keen an eye for such pursuits as they actually have for those in which they are now engaged.

Yes, probably it would be so.

Once more, is it not also probable, or rather does it not follow our previous remarks, that neither those who are uneducated and ignorant of truth, nor those who spend their time continuously on their education all their life, can ever be competent guardians of the city, the former, because they have no single mark in c life, which they are to constitute the end and aim of all their conduct both in private and in public? And the latter, because they will not act without compulsion, believing that, while yet alive, they have emigrated to the islands of the blest?

That is true.

It is, therefore, our task as founders of the city, I continued, to constrain the best natures to arrive at that learning which we formerly pronounced the highest, and to set eyes upon d the good, and to mount that ascent we spoke of; and, when they have mounted and looked long enough, we must take care to refuse to permit them that which is at present allowed.

And what is that?

Staying where they are, and refusing to descend again to those prisoners, or partake of their toils and honors, be they mean or be they exalted.

Then are we to do them a wrong, and make them live a life that is worse than the one within their reach?

You have again forgotten, my friend, that e law does not ask itself how some one part of a city is to live extraordinarily well. On the contrary, it tries to bring about this result in the entire city—for which purpose it links the citizens together by persuasion and by constraint, makes them share with one another the benefit 520 which each individual can contribute to the commonwealth, and does actually create men of this exalted character in the city, not with the intention of letting them go each on his own way, but by using them to make a beginning towards binding the city together.

True, he replied, I had forgotten.

Therefore reflect, Glaucon, that far from wronging the future philosophers of our city, we shall only be treating them with strict justice, if we put them under the additional obligation of guarding and caring for the others. We shall say with good reason that when men of

b   this type come to be in other cities, it is likely that they will not partake in the labor of the city. For they take root in a city spontaneously, against the will of the prevailing regime. And it is but fair that a self-sown plant, which is indebted to no one for support, should have no inclination to pay to anybody wages for attendance. But in your case, it is we that have begotten you for the city as well as for yourselves, to be like leaders and kings of a hive, better and more perfectly educated than the

c   rest, and more capable of playing a part in both modes of life. You must therefore descend by turns, and associate with the rest of the community, and you must accustom yourselves to the contemplation of these dark things. For, when accustomed, you will see ten thousand times better than the residents, and you will recognize what each image is, and what is its original, because you have seen the truth of which beautiful and just and good things are copies. And in this way, for you and for us, the city is ruled in a waking state and not in a dream like so many of our present cities, which are mostly composed of men who fight among themselves for shadows, and are at feud for the administration of affairs, which they regard as a great

d   good. Whereas I conceive the truth stands thus: That city in which those who are going to rule are least eager to rule will inevitably be ruled in the best and least factious manner, and a contrary result will ensue if the rulers are of a contrary disposition.

You are perfectly right.

And do you imagine that our pupils, when addressed in this way, will disobey our commands, and refuse to toil with us in the city by turns, while they spend most of their time together in that pure region?

e   Impossible, he replied, for certainly it is a just command and those who are to obey it are just men. No, doubtless each of them will

undertake ruling as an unavoidable duty—the opposite of what is pursued by the present rulers in each city.

True, my friend, the case stands thus. If you can find a life better than ruling for those who    521 are going to rule, you may possibly realize a well-governed city: for only in such a city will the rulers be those who are really rich, not in gold, but in a good and prudent life, which is the wealth necessary for a happy man. But if beggars, and persons who hunger after private advantages, take the reins of the city, supposing that they are privileged to snatch advantage from their power, all goes wrong. For then ruling is made an object of strife, both civil war and family feuds, and conflicts of this nature, ruin not only the contending parties, but also the rest of the city.

That is most true.

And can you mention any life which    b despises city offices, except the life of true philosophy?

No indeed, I cannot.

Well, but the task of ruling must be undertaken by persons not enamored of it; otherwise, their rivals will fight.

Unquestionably it must.

Then what persons will you compel to become guardians of the city other than the ones who are most prudent about how best to rule the city and who have other honors and a life better than the political life.

None other, he said. . . .

## BOOK VIII

Very well, then we agree on these points,    543 Glaucon, namely that, if a city is to be governed on a high level, it must recognize a community of women, a community of children, and a common education in all its branches; and, in like manner, a community of pursuits in war and in peace; and its kings must be those who have shown the greatest ability in philosophy and the greatest aptitude for war.

Yes, we agree so far.

b     In addition to this, we also admitted, that as soon as the rulers have established their position, they are to take the soldiers, and settle them in dwelling places of a certain description—which are not private in any way, but everything is in common. And, besides determining the nature of their dwellings, we also determined, if you recall, how far they were to be permitted to have anything, which they could call their own.

Yes, he replied, I recollect that we pronounced against their holding any such property as is commonly held at the present day, and

c     decided that, in their capacity of trained soldiers and guardians, they ought to receive in return for their guardianship year by year from the other citizens the maintenance required by their position, and devote their attention to the whole city including themselves.

You are right. But now that we have concluded this subject, let us recall to mind the point from which we diverged, in order that we may resume our old route.

That will not be difficult, he replied. You were talking pretty much as you are now doing, giving us to understand that you had finished the discussion of the city, and saying that you applied the term 'good' to such a city as you had then described, and to the man who resembled it; though, as it would seem, you had it in

d     your power to tell us of a still more excellent

544   city, and of a still more excellent man. At the same time, you declared that, if your city were right, all others must be wrong. Of the remaining regimes, I remember you mentioned four principal varieties, which you said it might be worth while to consider, noticing their faults, and observing in their turn the men who resemble them; in order that, after viewing them all and agreeing as to the best and the worst man, we might examine whether, or not, the best is

happiest, and the worst most wretched. And on my asking you to specify the four regimes, to     b which you alluded, we were interrupted by Polemarchus and Adeimantus; and thereupon you took up the discussion which has brought you to this point.

Your memory is perfectly correct.

Then allow me to grapple with you, like a wrestler, in my old attitude; and, when I repeat my former question, take pains to give me the answer that you were going to give them.

I will do my best, I replied.

Well, it is my particular desire to be told what the four regimes are to which you referred.

I shall find no difficulty in answering your     c question. The regimes to which I allude, and to which in fact special names have been given, are the following. First, we have the constitution of Crete and Sparta, which has popular acclaim in its favor. Second in order, as in estimation, stands oligarchy, as it is called, a regime full of many evils; then comes democracy, which is the adversary and successor of oligarchy; and finally that 'noble tyranny,' which differs from all the preceding, and constitutes the fourth and worst disease of a state. I suppose you do not have any other idea of a regime, which stands conspicuously by itself as a different kind? For I believe we may regard     d as links in the chain just presented all principalities and purchased sovereignties and similar regimes, which are to be found fully as often among the barbarians as among the Greeks.

Yes, we certainly hear of many strange instances of them.

Now are you aware that there must be as many forms of human character as of existing constitutions? Or do you imagine that constitutions grow upon a tree or rock, instead of springing out of the dispositions of the members of each city, according as this or that dis-     e position turns the scale, as it were, and drags everything else in its wake?

I believe the latter to be their sole origin.

Consequently if there are five arrangements for the city, there must be also five for the soul.

Certainly.

545 We have already discussed the man who resembles aristocracy, whom we rightly affirm to be both good and just.

We have.

Then must we proceed to describe those inferior men, the victory-lover and the honor-lover, corresponding to the Spartan constitution; and likewise the oligarchic, the democratic, and the tyrannical man—in order that we may get a view of the most unjust man, and contrast him with the most just, and so may complete our inquiry into the respective merits of pure justice and pure injustice, so far as the happiness or misery of their possessors is concerned. Thus we may either listen to Thrasymachus and pursue injustice, or yield to b the argument which is coming into view, and follow after justice?

We ought by all means do so.

Well then, as our practice from the first has been to examine dispositions in the city prior to doing so in the individual, because that will be much clearer; so, if you please, we will begin on the present occasion by examining the honor-loving constitution—I do not know of any other name in use; we must call it timocracy, or timarchy—and, with this in sight, we will proceed to examine the honor-loving man, and then go on to oligarchy and the oligarchic man; and next, after looking at democc racy, we will contemplate the democratic man; and lastly, we will enter into a city which is governed by a tyrant and observe it, and then look into the soul which is its counterpart, and so endeavor to become competent judges of the question proposed.

It would be reasonable to observe and judge this way.

Come then, I proceeded; let us endeavor to describe how timocracy will grow out of aristocracy. May we not lay down the rule, that changes in any regime originate, without exception, from the side of the ruling part, and only when factions arise within it. So long as it continues unanimous, it cannot be shaken, though it be very insignificant in point of numbers.

Yes, that is true.

Then, Glaucon, how will our city state be shaken, and in what way will divisions arise either between the auxiliaries and the rulers, or in these bodies themselves? Would you have us pray to the muses, like Homer, to tell us, 'How first dissension entered'? And would you have e us describe them as talking in tragic, high-flown style, playing with us as children, and jesting while they pretend to speak seriously?

What will their answer be?

Something to this effect: It is indeed difficult for a city thus constituted, to be shaken. 546 But since everything that has come into being must one day perish, even a construction like ours will not endure for all time, but must suffer dissolution. The dissolution will be as follows: Not only the vegetable, but also the animal kingdom, is liable to alternations of fertility and barrenness, in soul and body. And these alternations are coincident with certain cyclical revolutions, which vary in each case in length according to the length of life of the particular thing. Now, as touching the fruitfulness and barrenness of your own part, though b the persons, whom you have trained to be rulers of the city, are men of wisdom, yet, in spite of all observation and calculation, they will miss the propitious time. It will give them the slip and they will beget children on wrong occasions. Now for the divine there is a cycle of birth comprehended by a perfect number, but for human births is expressed by a geometrical number, on which depends the good or bad quality of the births. . . .

d   And when your guardians, from ignorance of this, arrange unseasonable marriages, the children of such marriages will not be well-endowed or fortunate. The best of them will be established in power by their predecessors; but nevertheless they will be unworthy of it—and having taken over the powers of their fathers, they will first of all begin to slight us, in defiance of their duties as guardians, and underrate music first, and then gymnastic. Thus your e   young men will grow up worse educated—and, in consequence of this, rulers will take office who will fail in their duty of discriminating Hesiod's races and yours, that is to say 547   the golden and silver and bronze and iron. And this mixture of iron with silver and of bronze with gold will breed dissimilar and disproportionate irregularity; and, wherever these take root, their growth always produces enmity and war. So that we may positively assert that the rise of such a generation will invariably be marked by dissension.

Yes, and we shall allow that the answer of the muses is the right one.

How could it be otherwise, when the muses speak?

b   And what do the Muses say next? he asked.

As soon as a division had arisen, the two parties would be likely to diverge rapidly, the races of iron and bronze inclining to money-making and the acquisition of land and houses and silver and gold; while the other two, gold and silver, not being poor but rich by nature, turn their souls to virtue and the ancient constitution of things. But the violence of their mutual contentions would induce the two parties to agree on a middle way, on the understanding c   that they should divide and appropriate the land and houses, and enslave their wards, who were formerly free, their friends, and supporters, to be held from then on as an inferior tribe of servants, and they themselves concentrate on war and on their own protection.

I believe you have described correctly the passage to timocracy.

Then will not this regime be a kind of mean between aristocracy and oligarchy?

Assuredly it will.

Since this is how the transformation will occur, how will the city in question conduct d   itself after the change? Is it not obvious that, being a mean between its former constitution and oligarchy, it will imitate partly the one, and partly the other, besides having some peculiarities of its own?

Precisely so.

Then, in the way that the warrior class will honor the rulers, and in the abstinence of that class from farming, handicrafts, and all other pursuits of gain, and in the establishment of public messes, and devotion to gymnastic and the training which war requires—in all such points it will imitate the former regime, will it not?

It will.

But in its fear of installing the wise in office, e   because the wise men are no longer men who are simple and earnest, but of compound nature, and in its degenerate inclination towards men of spirit and of a narrower character, with a greater turn for war than for peace, and in the value which it set upon the arts and stratagems which 548   war calls out, and in the incessant hostilities which it carries on—in most of these points it will have a character of its own, will it not?

It will.

Again, I continued, such persons will, like the members of oligarchies, be desirous of money, and will have a passionate but concealed regard for gold and silver, from the fact of their owning storehouses and private treasuries, in which they can deposit and hide their riches, and also walled houses, which are much like private nests, in which they may spend with a lavish hand on women and b   whomever else they wish.

Most true, he said.

Hence, while they love to spend other people's money, they will at the same time be stingy with their own, because they value it and have to conceal the possession of it; and they will enjoy their pleasures in secret, shunning the law as boys shun their father, because they have been trained not by persuasion but by force, inasmuch as they have slighted the true muse, that goes hand in hand with pro-
c found philosophical inquiry, and have honored gymnastic above music.

You are certainly describing a regime which is a mixture of good and bad.

Yes, it is a mixture, I replied, but, owing to the preponderance of the spirited element, there is one thing in particular which it exhibits in the clearest colors, and that is its love of victory and its love of honors.

Yes, decidedly it does.

Such, then, will be the origin, and such, or nearly such, the character of this regime, if we are satisfied to outline it in speech, without perfectly elaborating it, which we need not do,
d because we can distinguish sufficiently even from such a sketch the most just and the most unjust man, and because it is a very long task to discuss without any omission every regime and every character.

You are right, he said.

Who then is the man that answers to this regime? What is his origin, and what is his character?

I imagine, said Adeimantus, that, as a lover of victory, he must rather closely resemble our friend Glaucon.
e Perhaps so, I replied; but in the following points I do not think that his nature and Glaucon's correspond.

What are these points?

He must be more self-willed than Glaucon, and rather less fond of music; still he must be
549 studious, and fond of listening, but no speaker. A person of this character will not despise

slaves, like the perfectly educated man, though he will behave harshly to them and at the same time gently to the free-born. He will also be exceedingly obedient to the rulers, with a passion for distinction and command, to which he lays claim not on the ground of oratory or anything of the kind, but on accomplishments in war and everything connected with war, devoted as he is to bodily exercise and hunting.

True, this is the disposition of the corresponding regime.

In addition to this, will not such a person in his younger days despise wealth? But, as he        b grows older, will he not be always paying it more respect, because he has a touch of the nature of the money-lover, and because his virtue is not free from blemish, owing to his having parted from the best guardian?

Who is that guardian? asked Adeimantus.

Argumentation, I replied, blended with music: for this alone by its presence and indwelling can preserve its owner in the possession of life-long virtue.

It is well said.

Such we find to be the character of the timocratic young man, who resembles the timocratic city.

Very true.                                                          c

Again, his origin, I proceeded, may be traced as follows. He is the youthful son of an excellent father, who living, as is not uncommon, in a city where the regime is defective, avoids honors and offices and litigation and all similar marks of a busybody, and is willing to suffer loss rather than get into trouble.

Then please describe the formation of such a character.

It dates from the time when the son listens to his mother's complaint, who is looked down upon by the other women, because her husband is not a part of the ruling class, and who also sees that he does not concern himself        d much about money, and will not fight and rail as a litigant in the law-courts or in the public assemblies, toward all of which he exhibits great indifference—and who further perceives that he is always inwardly reflecting, and that he pays no great respect to herself, though he offers her no disrespect: for all of these reasons she is vexed, and tells her son that his father lacks manliness and is too easy-going, not to mention all the other choice expressions e which women are in the habit of lavishing on such men.

Indeed, said Adeimantus, they have indeed plenty to say that is quite in keeping with their own character.

And no doubt you are aware, I continued, that the servants of such persons also—servants who seem to have their masters' interests at heart—do sometimes privately make similar observations to the sons; and that, if they see a man in debt to the father, or wronging him in any other way, with no proceedings taken against him, they exhort the son, when he is grown up, to take revenge on all such people, 550 and be more of a man than his father. Likewise, when the son goes out, he hears and sees other instances of the same thing. He hears the quiet and unmeddlesome called 'simpletons' in the city, and sees that they are held in small esteem; while the busybodies are honored and commended. Thereupon the young man, hearing and seeing all this, and on the other hand listening to his father's conversation and narrowly examining his pursuits side by side with those of other men, is pulled two ways by two influences. On the one hand his father is b watering and nursing the calculating part of his soul, and on the other hand every one else is watering and nursing the appetitive and the spirited element of his nature; and because, though his disposition is not that of a bad man, he nevertheless has mixed in the bad society of others, he is drawn by these combined influences into a middle ground, where he delivers up the rule of himself to that middle element which is hot-tempered and contentious,

and turns out a high-spirited, victory-loving man.

It appears to me, said he, that you have exactly described the production of such a character.

Then we are in possession of the second c regime and the second man.

We are.

Must we not then, using the words of Aeschylus, proceed to describe

> 'Another man matched with another city'? Or rather, according to our plan, must we not begin with the city?

By all means, he replied.

Well, I think that the regime which comes next in order will be oligarchy.

What kind of regime do you mean by an oligarchy?

A regime grounded upon a property qualification, I replied, in which the wealthy rule, d while the poor have no part in the rule.

I understand.

Should we not describe the first steps in the transition from timarchy to oligarchy?

We should.

Well, no doubt even a blind man could find out how the transition is brought about.

How?

It is the influx of gold into those private treasuries that ruins the regime just described. For the first result of this is that the owners invent ways of spending their money, and pervert the laws with that intent, and disobey them in their own persons, and in the persons of their wives.

It would be strange if they did not.

They then proceed, if I am not mistaken, to e eye one another with jealous looks, and to enter upon a course of rivalry, which stamps the same character on the general body of which they are members.

It is what we might expect.

And thenceforth they press forward on the

path of money-getting, losing their esteem for virtue in proportion as the esteem for wealth grows upon them. For can you deny that there is such a gulf between wealth and virtue, that, when weighed as it were in the two scales of a balance, one of the two always falls, as the other rises?

That is quite true.

551      Consequently when wealth and the wealthy are honored in a city, virtue and the virtuous sink in estimation.

Obviously.

And what is honored at any time is practiced, and what is dishonored is neglected.

True.

Hence, instead of being victory- and honor-loving, such persons end up as profit- and money-lovers; and while they commend and admire and confer office upon the wealthy, they despise the poor.

Assuredly they do.

So that at length they pass a law, defining
b      an oligarchic constitution, by which they agree upon a certain sum, which is larger or smaller according to the strength of the oligarchic principle, and forbid any share in ruling to those who do not have property up to the stipulated amount. And they bring about these measures by violence with arms in their hands, if they have not previously succeeded in establishing the proposed regime by the alarm which they have inspired. Or am I wrong?

No, you are right.

And this, in a word, is the establishment of oligarchy.

True. But what is the character of the
c      regime, and what are the faults which we attributed to it?

Its first fault, I answered, lies in its very definition. For consider what would be the result, if we elected our pilots on this principle of a property qualification, refusing the post to the poor man, though he were a better pilot.

We should make sad work with the voyage, he replied.

Does not this apply to any management of anything else whatever?

Yes, I think so.

Do you except a city? I asked. Or do you include it?

I include it most especially, he replied, in consideration of the superior difficulty and importance of its management.

Then here is one of the faults of oligarchy,      d
and that a grievous one.

Evidently.

Again, is the following fault in any way less grievous than the first?

What is it?

Why, that such a city must necessarily lose its unity and become two cities, one comprising the rich, and the other the poor—who reside together on the same ground, and are always plotting against one another.

Why this fault, I am sure, is quite as bad as the former.

Once again, it is certainly not a commendable thing that they should be incapable, as they probably will be, of waging any war—the fact being that, if they arm and employ the populace, they cannot help dreading them more than the enemy; whereas, if they hesitate      e
to employ them, they must appear veritable oligarchs in the actual battle—to which we must add that their love of money renders them unwilling to pay war-taxes.

You are right.

Again, to return to a previous point about      552
busybodies—do you think it right that the same persons should be engaged at the same time in the various occupations of farming, trade, and war, which is the case under such a regime?

No, there is nothing to be said for it.

Now, consider whether the following ill, which is greater than all the others, is not admitted by this constitution, and by none of the preceding.

What is it?

I refer to the practice of allowing one person to sell all his property, and another to acquire it—the former owner living in the city without belonging to any of its parts, either as trader, artisan, knight, or foot-soldier—but described as a destitute man, and a pauper.

b    None of the preceding constitutions admitted such a practice.

To say the least, this sort of thing is not prohibited in cities whose rule is oligarchic. Otherwise it would be impossible for some persons to be extravagantly rich, while others are utter paupers.

True.

Let me ask you to examine another point. At the time when such a man was spending money in his wealthy days, was he in any way more useful to the city for the purposes which we were just now specifying? Or was it the case, that though he seemed to be one of the rulers, he was really neither ruler nor servant of the city, but only a consumer of its resources?

c    The latter is the true account, he replied. He seemed to be what you say; but he was really only a consumer.

Then would you have us assert that, as the drone grows up in the hive to be the plague of the bees, so also does such a man grow up as a drone in his house, to be the plague of the city?

Undoubtedly, Socrates, he does.

And is it not true, Adeimantus, that, though god has provided none of the flying drones with stings, he has made only some of these walking drones stingless, while to some he has given formidable stings; and that while the stingless ones end in an old age of beggary, the

d    stinging drones, on the contrary, furnish out of their ranks all who are called criminals?

It is most true.

It is quite clear then, that, whenever you see beggars in a city, you may be certain that in the same place lurk thieves, pickpockets, temple-robbers, and the craftsmen of all similar crimes.

True.

Well, and in oligarchic cities do you not see beggars?

Yes, he said, almost all are beggars except the rulers.

Then is it, or is it not, our opinion, that there    e
are also many wrongdoers in such cities, armed with stings, whom the rulers are careful to keep down by force?

Certainly it is our opinion.

Then shall we not assert that the cause which produces such persons is want of education, and bad training, and a bad condition of the regime?

Yes, we shall.

This then, or something like it, will be the character of a city ruled by an oligarchy; and it will contain quite as many evils, if not more.

You are near the mark, he said.

Then let us close our account here of this    553
regime which is called oligarchy, and which takes its rulers by a property qualification; and let us proceed to examine how the man who resembles it grows up, and what he is when he has grown up.

By all means let us do so.

Tell me then, is the transition from the timocratic man, whom we have described, to the oligarchic, effected thus, or nearly thus?

How?

The timocratic man has a son, who at first emulates his father and follows his steps; and    b
then suddenly sees him crashing against the city, as on a sunken rock, and his property and his person thrown overboard, sees him, after commanding his country's armies or holding some other high office, brought to trial, damaged by lying informers, and either put to death, or banished, or disfranchised, and all his property taken from him.

All this might very well happen, he replied.

Well, my friend, the instant the son has seen and felt this, and lost his property, he becomes alarmed, I suppose, and thrusts honor-loving and that high-spirited element head-foremost    c
from the throne of his heart; and being humbled

by poverty he turns to money-getting, makes mean and petty savings, and by working hard accumulates wealth. Do you not think that such a person will put on that throne the desiring element and the love of money, and make of it a Persian 'Great King' within himself, adorning it with diadem and collar, and girding the scimitar by its side?

I do, he answered.

d    But the rational and the high-spirited elements, I think, he sets down on the ground below it, on this side and on that, as subjects and slaves, forbidding the former to investigate or reason about anything, save how to multiply riches, and forbidding the latter to admire or esteem anything save wealth and the wealthy, or to be ambitious after a single object save the acquisition of riches, and whatever else may conduce to this.

There can be no other transformation of an honor-loving into a money-loving young man so speedy and so thorough.

e    Then tell me, is such a person oligarchic?

Well, at any rate the man from whom he is by transformation derived, resembled the regime which came before oligarchy.

Let us examine whether he will resemble oligarchy.

554    Yes, let us.

Well then, first of all, will he not resemble oligarchy in setting the highest value on money?

Assuredly he will.

And also in the fact that he is thrifty and hard-working, satisfying only his necessary appetites, and refusing himself all other expenses, and subjugating his other desires as idle.

Exactly so.

In other words, he is a squalid man, making a profit out of everything, and given to hoarding—one of those persons who are positively commended by the great body of men. Or am I wrong in supposing that such will be the man

b    commended by the great body of men. Or am I wrong in supposing that such will be the man

who resembles the regime we have just described?

If you ask me, I think you are right. At any rate, the oligarchic city, as well as the person under discussion, values money above every thing.

The reason being, I believe, that such a man has taken no pains with his education.

I imagine he has not; else he would not have appointed, nor would he so highly honor, a blind leader of the chorus.

Very true. And now let me ask you to consider whether we must not assert that drone-like appetites, which are either beggarly or criminal, grow up in him owing to his want of    c
education, and that these appetites are forcibly held down by other concerns.

Certainly we must assert it.

And do you know where you must look in order to see their wrongdoings?

Where?

You must look to occasions where they are guardians of orphans, and to any similar accidents which put it completely in their power to act unjustly.

True.

Then is it not clear from this, that in his other contracts, in which his apparent justice secures him a good name, such a person is holding down by a kind of constrained moderation a class of bad desires that are within him,    d
which he does not tame by reason, or convince that it would be wrong to gratify them, but which circumstances and his own apprehensions teach him to suppress, because he trembles for the rest of his substance?

Yes, it is quite clear.

Indeed, my friend, I am quite sure that, when these people have to spend what is not their own, you will find that most of them possess the appetites akin to the drone.

Most decidedly they do.

Hence such a person, far from being at peace within himself, will be a double-e minded, not a single-minded, man; though he will generally find his lower appetites vanquished by his higher ones.

True.

555 And for these reasons, I think, such a person will present a better outside than many; but the genuine virtue of a soul attuned to concord and harmony will fly somewhere far away from him.

So I think.

And no doubt the miserly man makes a low-grade rival as a private citizen, when a prize or any other honorable distinction is contested; for he will not spend money to win himself renown in such matches, from fear of exciting his expensive appetites by inviting them to share in the struggle and the rivalry: so that in fact he follows the practice of an oligarchy in employing only some few parts of himself in his wars, and in most cases spares his purse and submits to defeat.

Exactly so.

Then are we still incredulous, I asked, as to the similarity and correspondence subsisting between the oligarchic city and the miserly money-hunter?

b Not at all, he answered.

And now we must proceed, I should suppose, to examine in what way democracy arises, and what is its character when it has arisen: in order that once again we may discover the character of the corresponding man, and place him by our side for judgment.

Yes, if we would act consistently, we must take that course.

Is not the transition from oligarchy to democracy brought about by an intemperate craving for extravagant wealth, which is publicly acknowledged to be the greatest of blessings, and the attainment of which is considered a duty, the transition itself taking the following form?

Describe it.

c Since the power of the rulers in an oligarchic city is, I believe, wholly due to their great wealth, they are unwilling to put the licentious young men of their time under restraint, to the extent of rendering it illegal for them to spend and waste their property: because they hope, by purchasing the possessions of such persons, and by lending money to them, to make themselves still richer and more honored.

Most unquestionably.

And is it not manifest by this time, that it is impossible for the citizens of a city to honor wealth, and at the same time acquire a proper d amount of temperance: because they cannot avoid neglecting either the one or the other?

It is pretty well manifest, he replied.

Hence the rulers in such cities, by their reckless admission of unrestrained license, not unfrequently compel men of noble birth to become poor.

Yes, that they do.

And the persons thus impoverished lurk, I should suppose, in the city, harnessed and armed with stings—some owing debts, and others disfranchised, and others laboring under both misfortunes—hating and plotting against the new owners of their property, and against all who are better off than themselves, and longing for change.

True. e

These money-makers, on the other hand, keep prying after their own interests, and apparently do not see their enemies; and, whenever one of the remainder yields them opportunity, they wound him by infusing their poisonous money, and then recover interest 556 many times as great as the parent sum, and thus make the drone and the beggar multiply in the city.

Yes, that they do.

And they cannot make up their minds to extinguish this great ill, as it is bursting into flames, either by prohibiting people from disposing of their property at their own pleasure, or by employing another method, which provides by a different law for the removal of such dangers.

What law do you mean?

I mean one which is next best to the former, and which constrains the citizens to apply themselves to virtue. For if it be enacted that voluntary contracts be as a general rule entered into at the proper risk of the contractor, people will be less shameless in their money-dealings in the city, and such ills as we have just now described will be less common.

Yes, much less common.

But as it is, the various inducements I have mentioned encourage the ruling body in the city to handle their subjects in this way. On the other hand, if we look at the rulers themselves and their children, do we not see that the young men are made luxurious and lazy both in body and mind, and so idle and soft that they cannot resist pleasure and encounter pain?

Unquestionably they are.

And that their seniors are indifferent to everything except making money, and as careless about virtue as the poor themselves?

Certainly they are.

In this state of things, when the rulers and their subjects encounter one another either in traveling or in some other common occupation, whether it be a pilgrimage or a military expedition, in which they are fellow-sailors or fellow-soldiers; or when they are witnesses of one another's behavior in moments of danger, in which the poor can by no possibility be despised by the rich, because it often happens that a rich man, reared in the shade and with excess fat, finds himself posted in battle by the side of some lean and sunburnt poor man, to whom by his labored breathing he betrays his sore distress. When, I repeat, all this takes place, do you imagine that these poor men can avoid thinking, that it is through their own cowardice that such incapable people are wealthy, or that they can refrain from repeat-

ing to one another, when they meet in private, 'Our men are nothing'?

I am quite sure that they do so.

Now just as a sickly body requires but a small additional impulse from without to bring on an attack of illness, and sometimes even without any external provocation is divided against itself; so, in the same way, does not this city, whose condition is identical with that of a diseased body, require only the slight excuse of an external alliance introduced by the one party from an oligarchic city, or by the other from a democratic, to bring on an acute disease and an inward battle? And is it not sometimes, even without such external influences, distracted by factions?

Most decidedly it is.

Democracy, then, I think, arises, whenever the poor win the day, killing some of the opposite party, expelling others, and admitting the remainder to an equal participation in civic rights and offices, and most commonly the offices in such a city are given by lot.

Yes, you have correctly described the establishment of democracy, whether it be brought about by resorting to arms, or by the terrified withdrawal of the other party.

And now tell me, I continued, in what style these persons administer the city, and what is the character of this third regime. For obviously we shall find the corresponding man marked, to a certain extent, with the same features.

True, said he.

First of all, are they not free, and does not liberty of act and speech abound in the city, and has not a man license therein to do what he wants?

Yes, so we are told.

And clearly, where such license is permitted, every citizen will arrange his own manner of life as suits his pleasure.

Clearly he will.

Hence I should suppose, that in this regime there will be the greatest diversity of character.

Unquestionably there will.

Possibly, I proceeded, this regime may be the prettiest of all. Embroidered as it is with every kind of character, it may be thought as beautiful as a colored dress embroidered with every kind of flower. And perhaps, I added, as children and women admire dresses of many colors, so many persons will judge to be the most beautiful.

No doubt many will.

d    Yes, my excellent friend, and it would be a good plan to explore it, if we were in search of a regime.

Why so?

Because it contains within it every kind of regime in consequence of that license of which I spoke; and perhaps a person wishing to found a city, as we were just now doing, ought to go into a democratic city, as a bazaar of regimes, and pick out whatever sort pleases him, and then found his regime according to the choice he has made.

e    We may safely say that he is not likely to be at a loss for patterns.

Again, consider that, in this city, you are not obliged to rule, though your talents may be equal to the task; and that you need not submit to being ruled, if you dislike it, or go to war when your fellow-citizens are at war, or keep peace when they are doing so, if you do not want peace; and again, consider that, though a law forbids your holding office or sitting on a
558 jury, you may nevertheless do both the one and the other, should it occur to you to do so. And now tell me, is not such a course of life divinely pleasant for the moment?

Yes perhaps it is, he replied, for the moment.

Once more. Is not the leniency regarding some who have been tried in a court of law exquisite? Or have you failed to notice in such a regime how men, who have been condemned

to death or exile, stay all the same, and walk about the streets, and parade like heroes, as if no one saw or cared?

I have seen many instances of it, he replied.

And is there not something splendid in the  b
sympathy of such a regime, lacking pettiness? It positively scorns what we were saying when we were founding our city, to the effect that no one, who is not endowed with a transcendent nature, can ever become a good man, unless from his earliest childhood he plays among beautiful objects and studies all beautiful things. How magnificently it tramples all this underfoot, without troubling itself in the least about the previous pursuits of those who enter on a political course, whom it raises to honor, if they only assert to the multitude that they  c
wish well.

Yes, he said, it behaves very grandly.

These, then, will be some of the features of democracy, to which we might add others of the same family; and it will be, in all likelihood, an agreeable, anarchic, many-colored regime, dealing with all alike on a footing of equality, whether they be really equal or not.

The facts you mention are notorious.

And now let me ask you to examine the character of the corresponding individual. Or must we begin, as in the case of the regime, by investigating his origin?

Yes, he replied.

Then am I not right in supposing that he will be the son of the miserly and oligarchic  d
man, bred up under his father's eye, and in his father's character?

Doubtless he will.

And this son, like the father, will put a violent constraint upon those pleasures within him that tend to extravagance and not to money-getting—which, you know, are called unnecessary pleasures.

Clearly he will.

Now, that we may not talk in the dark,

would you like us first to define the necessary and unnecessary appetites?

I should.

e   May we not justly apply the term necessary to those appetites which we cannot get rid of, and to those whose satisfaction does us good? For our nature cannot help feeling both these classes of desires, can it?

Certainly it cannot.

559   Then we shall be justified in applying necessity to them.

We shall.

Again, shall we not be right to assert that all those appetites are unnecessary, which we can get rid of from youth—and anyway their presence never does us any good, and in some cases does positive harm?

Yes, we shall be right.

Would it not be as well to select an example of the existing appetites of each kind, in order that we may gain a general type?

Decidedly it would.

b   Will not the appetite for food—that is to say, simple bread and meat—within the bounds of health and good bodily habit, be a necessary appetite?

I think so.

The appetite for bread at least is surely necessary by a double claim, being not only beneficial, but also indispensable to the support of life.

Yes.

On the other hand, the appetite for meat is necessary, so far as it may contribute advantageously to a good habit of body.

Certainly.

Again, the appetite for other meats of a less simple kind, of which most people can rid themselves by early correction and training, and which is hurtful to the body, and hurtful to the soul, in its endeavors after wisdom and temperance, may be rightly styled an unneces-

c   sary appetite, may it not?

Yes, most rightly.

And must we not assert that the appetites of this second class are also expensive, whereas the others contribute to money-making, because they are a help towards production?

Undoubtedly.

Can we say the same of the passion of love and the other appetites?

Yes.

Now did we not describe the man, to whom we lately gave the name of 'drone,' as one burdened with those expensive pleasures and desires, and governed by the unnecessary appetites; while we described the man, who is ruled by the necessary, as miserly and oligarchic?

Undoubtedly we did.

Let us now return, I continued, and explain how the oligarchic man is transformed into the democratic.

How is it?                                                        d

I would have you suppose that a young man's transition from inward oligarchy to democracy begins the moment when, after being brought up as we were saying just now, without education and in a miserly way, he has tasted the honey of the drones, and made acquaintance with fiery and terrible wild beasts, who are able to procure him all kinds of   e pleasures, of a varied and manifold nature.

It cannot be otherwise.

And may we say that, just as the city was transformed by the assistance given by a foreign alliance to one of the two parties, like to like; so, in the same way, the young man is transformed by the analogous assistance from without, afforded by a form of appetites kindred and similar to one of the two parties present with him.

Assuredly we may.

And should the oligarchic element within him be supported by some counter-alliance, derived perhaps from his father, or perhaps   560 from his other relations, who rebuke and reproach him, then, I imagine, there follows discord and resistance and an inward battling with himself.

Undoubtedly.

And occasionally, I imagine, the democratic interest yields to the oligarchic, and certain of the appetites are either cut to pieces or expelled, owing to the presence of a sense of shame in the young man's soul—and order is once more restored.

Yes, this does take place sometimes.

b   But some new appetites, I conclude, akin to those expelled, are secretly nurtured, and, owing to the lack of knowledge in his father's training, become numerous and strong.

Yes, this is generally the case.

And these appetites, of course, draw him to his old associates, and by their secret communications engender in him a multitude of others.

Undoubtedly.

And finally, I imagine, they seize upon the acropolis of the young man's heart, because they perceive it to be destitute of beautiful studies and practices and true speeches, which are the very ones to keep the best watch and ward over the thought of men who are the favorites of the gods.

c   Yes, quite the best.

And to supply their place, I think, false and pretentious speeches and opinions rise up in the man, and seize that place.

That they do.

Does he not, in consequence, return to those Lotus-eaters, and dwell with them without disguise? And if his relatives send any assistance to the miserly element of his soul, do not those pretensions close the gates of the royal fortress within him, and not only refuse an entrance to the actual auxiliary force, but

d   even decline to admit an embassy of individuals in the shape of admonitions from elder persons? And do they not fight in person and gain the day, giving shame a dishonorable discharge in the name of folly, and expelling temperance with insults under the name of cowardice? And do they not prove, by the aid of many useless appetites, that moderation and orderly expenditure are boorish and illiberal, and banish them as such beyond the border?

Most certainly they do.

And no doubt, when, by emptying out these virtues they have purified the soul of him who is now in their power, and is being initiated by   e them into the great mysteries, they proceed at once to restore insolence, anarchy, wastefulness, and shamelessness, in great splendor, accompanied by a numerous chorus, and with crowns on their heads, extolling them, and calling them by soft names, describing inso-   561 lence as a good education, anarchy as freedom, wastefulness as magnificence, and shamelessness as courage. Is not this, I asked, pretty much the way in which the man who is brought up in the gratification only of necessary appetites changes, already in his youth, liberating from servitude and control the unnecessary and injurious pleasures?

Yes, very evidently it is, he replied.

From that day forward a man of this description spends, I should suppose, just as much money and labor and time on unnecessary as upon necessary pleasures. But, should he be so fortunate as to set a limit to his wildness, and, as he grows older, when the tumult of passion has mostly gone by, should he go so far as to readmit to a certain extent portions   b of the banished, and not surrender himself wholly to the invaders, in that case, it is the habit of his life to make no distinction between his pleasures, but hands over the rule to passing pleasures, as if chosen by lot, and to turn to another, when the first is satisfied—scorning none, but fostering equality.

Exactly so.

Yes, I proceeded, and whenever he is told that though some pleasures belong to the appetites which are good and honorable, others belong to the bad appetites; and that the   c former ought to be practiced and respected, but the latter chastised and enslaved, he does not receive this true speech, or admit it into his watchpost. On the contrary, at all these assertions he shakes his head, and maintains that all appetites are alike, and ought to be equally respected.

Yes, this is precisely his condition, and his behavior.

Hence, I continued, he lives from day to day to the end, in the gratification of the casual appetites—now drinking himself drunk while listening to the flute, and presently putting himself on a diet—sometimes idling and neglecting everything, and then living like a student of philosophy. And often he takes a part in public affairs, and starting up, speaks and acts according to the impulse of the moment. Now he follows eagerly in the steps of certain great generals he admires; and soon he takes to trade, because he envies the successful trader. And there is no order or constraining rule in his life; but he calls this life of his pleasant, and liberal, and happy, and follows it out to the end.

Well, said he, you have certainly described the life of a man who believes in legal equality.

Yes, I replied, and I conceive it to be also a manifold life, replete with very many characters. And I imagine that this is the man who, by the beautiful variety of his nature, answers to the city which we described—a man whose life many men and many women would envy, and who contains within him very many exemplars of regimes and characters.

True.

What then? May we place this man opposite democracy, in the belief that he may be rightly addressed as democratic?

Be it so, he replied.

It only remains for us, I continued, to describe the most beautiful of all regimes, and the most beautiful of all men, that is to say, tyranny and the tyrant.

You are quite right.

Come then, my dear friend, tell me in what way tyranny arises. That it is a transformation of democracy, is all but obvious.

It is.

Then does democracy give birth to tyranny, precisely in the way in which oligarchy gave birth to democracy?

Explain this.

The thing which oligarchy professed to regard as supremely good, and which was instrumental in establishing it, was excessive wealth, was it not?

It was.

Well, it was the insatiable craving for wealth, and the disregard of everything else for the sake of money-making, that destroyed oligarchy.

True, it was.

Then may we say that democracy, like oligarchy, is destroyed by its insatiable craving for that which it defines as supremely good?

And what according to you, is that?

Freedom, I replied; for I imagine that in a democratic city you will be told that it has, in freedom, the most beautiful of possessions, and that therefore such a city is the only fit abode for the man who is free by nature.

Why certainly such language is very much in fashion.

To return, then, to the remark which I was trying to make a moment ago: am I right in saying that the insatiable craving for a single object and the disregard of all else transform democracy as well as oligarchy, and pave the way, as a matter of course, for tyranny?

How so?

Whenever a democratic city which is thirsting for freedom has fallen under the leadership of wicked wine-bearers, and has drunk the unmixed wine of liberty far beyond due measure: it proceeds, I should imagine, to arraign its rulers as accursed oligarchs, and punishes them, unless they become very submissive, and supply it with freedom in copious draughts.

Yes, that is what is done.

And likewise it insults those who are obedient to the rulers with the titles of willing slaves and worthless fellows; while it commends and honors, both privately and publicly, the rulers who carry themselves like subjects, and the subjects who carry themselves like rulers. Must it not follow that in such a city freedom goes to all lengths?

Of course it must.

Yes, my friend, and does not the prevailing anarchy steal into private houses, and spread on every side, until at last it takes root even among the beasts?

What are we to understand by this?

I mean, for example, that a father accustoms himself to behave like a child, and stands in awe of his sons, and that a son behaves himself like a father, and ceases to respect or fear his parents, in order to prove his freedom. And I mean that citizens, and resident aliens, and foreigners, are all perfectly equal.

Yes, that is how it happens.

I have told you some of the results; let me tell you a few more trifles of the kind. The schoolmaster, in these circumstances, fears and flatters his pupils, and the pupils despise their masters and also their tutors. And, speaking generally, the young copy their elders, and enter the lists with them both in talking and in acting; and the old men condescend so far as to abound in wit and pleasantry, in imitation of the young, in order, by their own account, to avoid the imputation of being odious or domineering.

Exactly so.

But the extreme limit, my friend, to which the freedom of the populace grows in such a regime is only attained when the purchased slaves of both sexes are just as free as the purchasers. Also I had almost forgotten to mention to what extent this liberty and equality is carried in the mutual relations subsisting between men and women.

Then, in the words of Aeschylus, said he, shall we not give utterance to that which is already on our lips?

By all means, I replied. I, for one, am doing so, when I tell you that no one could be persuaded without having experienced it—how much more free the domestic animals are here than anywhere else. The hound, according to the proverb, is like the mistress of the house; and truly even horses and asses adopt a gait expressive of remarkable freedom and dignity, and run at anybody who meets them in the streets, if he does not get out of their way— and all the other animals become in the same way gorged with freedom.

It is my own dream that you are repeating to me. This often happens to me when I walk into the country.

Now putting all these things together, I proceeded, do you perceive that they amount to this, that the soul of the citizens is rendered so sensitive as to be indignant and impatient at the smallest symptom of slavery? For surely you are aware that they end by making light of the laws themselves, whether written or unwritten, in order that, as they say, they may not have the shadow of a master.

I am very well aware of it.

This then, my friend, if I am not mistaken, is the beginning, so fair and vigorous, out of which tyranny grows.

Vigorous, indeed! But what is the next step?

That very disease, I replied, which broke out in oligarchy and ruined it, appears in democracy, but bigger and stronger, aggravated by the license of the place, and occasions its enslavement. Indeed, to do anything in excess seldom fails to provoke a violent reaction to the opposite extreme, not only in the seasons of the year and in the animal and vegetable kingdoms, but also especially in regimes.

This is only natural.

Thus, excessive freedom is unlikely to pass into anything but excessive slavery, in the case of cities as well as individuals.

It is.

Hence, in all likelihood, democracy, and only democracy, lays the foundation of tyranny—that is to say, the most intense freedom lays the foundation for the heaviest and the fiercest slavery.

Yes, it is a reasonable statement.

However, this, I think, was not your question: you were asking, what is this disease, which fastens upon democracy as well as upon oligarchy, and reduces the former to bondage.

That was my question.

Well then, I referred to that class of idle and extravagant men, in which the bravest lead and the more cowardly follow. We compared them, if you recall, to stinging and stingless drones, respectively.

Yes, and rightly so.

Now the presence of these two classes, like phlegm and bile in the body, breeds in every regime disturbance. Therefore a skillful physician and legislator, just like a cunning beekeeper, must take measures in advance, if possible, to prevent their presence; but, should they make their appearance, he must have them cut out, as quickly as possible, cells and all.

That must be, without a doubt.

Then let us handle the matter thus, in order that we may see more distinctly what we wish to see.

How?

Let us suppose a democratic city to be divided, as is really the case, into three parts. The class of people we have described constitutes, I believe, one of these divisions, and is generated by license in a democratic as abundantly as in an oligarchic city.

True.

But it is much more fierce in the former than in the latter.

How so?

In the latter it is despised, and excluded from office, and therefore proves untrained and feeble. But in democracy it is, I conceive, with a few exceptions, the sole ruling body;

and its fiercest members speak and act, while the rest settle down, swarming around the speaker's platform, humming applause, and brooking no contradiction. So that all the concerns of such a regime are, with some trifling exceptions, in the hands of this body.

Certainly.

In addition to this, a second body is being constantly distinguished from the many.

What is it like?

If all are occupied in amassing riches, I presume that those who are most orderly by nature generally become wealthiest.

It is likely to be so.

Hence I conclude, that out of these persons, the readiest and most copious supply of honey is squeezed out for the drones.

To be sure, how could honey be squeezed out of the poor?

And the wealthy, I suppose, are called the fodder of the drones.

Pretty nearly so.

The third class will consist of those members of the people who work with their own hands, and do not meddle with politics, and are not very well off. And this class is, in a democracy, the most numerous and the most important of all, when assembled.

True, but it will seldom assemble, unless it receives a share of the honey.

And therefore it always does receive a share—with this proviso, that its leaders, while depriving the moneyed class of their substance, and making division of it among the commons, manage, if possible, to keep the largest share for themselves.

Undoubtedly, with that proviso, it does get a share.

Now those who have been robbed are compelled, I imagine, to defend themselves, by speaking before the people, and acting to the best of their ability.

Of course.

And, for this behavior, even if they do not desire a revolution, they are accused by the opposite party of plotting against the people, and of being oligarchs.

Undoubtedly.

Therefore in the end, when they see that from ignorance and in consequence of the artful misrepresentations of their slanderers, the people are unwittingly bent on wronging them,
c from that moment forward, whether they wish it or not, they become, as a matter of course, veritable oligarchs. For this ill, amongst others, is engendered in them by the sting of that drone of which we spoke.

Yes, precisely so.

Hence arise impeachments, prosecutions, and trials, directed by each party against the other.

Certainly.

And is it not always the practice of the people to select a special leader of their cause, whom they maintain and exalt to greatness?

Yes, it is their practice.
d Then, obviously, whenever a tyrant grows up, his origin may be traced wholly to this leadership, which is the stem from which he shoots.

That is quite obvious.

And what are the first steps in the transformation of the leader into a tyrant? Can we doubt that the change dates from the time when the leader has begun to act like the man in that legend which is current in reference to the temple of Lycaean Zeus in Arcadia?

What legend?

According to it, the worshiper who tasted the one human entrail, which was minced up
e with the other entrails of other victims, was inevitably metamorphosed into a wolf. Have you never heard the story?

Yes, I have.

In like manner, should the people's leader find the populace so very compliant that he need make no scruple of shedding kindred blood; should he bring unjust charges against a man, as such persons love to do, prosecute his victim, and murder him, making away with human life, and tasting the blood of his fellows

with unholy tongue and lips; should he banish, 566 and kill, and give the signal for cancelling debts and redistributing the land; is it not thenceforth the inevitable destiny of such a man either to be destroyed by his enemies, or to become a tyrant, and be metamorphosed from a man into a wolf?

There is no escape from the alternative.

Such is the fate of the man who stirs up faction against the propertied class.

It is.

And if he is banished, and afterwards restored in despite of his enemies, does he not return a complete tyrant?

Obviously he does.

And if his enemies find themselves unable b to expel him, or to put him to death, by accusing him before the city, in that case they take measures to remove him secretly by a violent end.

Yes, that is the usual expedient.

In order to prevent this, those who have gone so far always adopt that notorious device of the tyrant, which consists in asking the people for a body-guard, in order that the people's friend may not be lost to them.

Just so. c

And the people, I imagine, grant the request: for they are alarmed on his account, while they are confident on their own.

Just so.

Consequently, when this is observed by a man who has wealth, and with his wealth the character of being a hater of democracy, forthwith, in accordance with the oracle given to Croesus,

'By the pebbly bed of the Hermus,
He flies and stays no more, nor shuns the
reproach for being a coward.'

He would not have the chance of shunning it a second time.

And those that are arrested are given up to death, I imagine.

Of course they are.

But as for that leader himself, it is quite clear that far from being laid 'great in his greatness,' he has overthrown many others, and stands in the chariot of the city, metamorphosed from a leader into a perfected tyrant.

Yes, there is no help for it.

Well, I continued, are we to discuss the happiness both of the man himself, and of the city in which such a mortal resides?

By all means let us do so, he replied.

Well, in his early days, and at the beginning of his tyranny, has he not a smile and a greeting for everybody that he meets, and does he not repudiate the idea of his being a tyrant, and promise largely both in public and in private; and is it not his practice to forgive debts, and make grants of land to the people and to all those around him, while he pretends to be mild and gracious to all?

It cannot be otherwise.

But as soon as he has relieved himself of his exiled enemies, by becoming reconciled to some, and by destroying others, his first measure is, I imagine, to be constantly inciting wars, in order that the people may stand in need of a leader.

It is his natural course.

Is it not further his intention so to impoverish his subjects by war-taxes, as to constrain them to devote themselves to the requirements of the day, and thus render them less likely to plot against himself?

Manifestly it is.

And am I not right in supposing that, should he suspect any persons of harboring a spirit of freedom such as would not allow him to reign in peace, it is his intention to throw them in the way of the enemy, and so get rid of them without suspicion? For all these reasons must not a tyrant be always stirring up war?

He must.

Then is it not the obvious result of such a course, that he gets more and more detested by the citizens?

Of course it is.

And does it not follow that the bravest of those who helped to establish him and who are in power speak their mind fearlessly to him and to one another, and criticize his policies?

So one would expect.

Now, if the tyrant is to keep up his authority, he must put all these people quietly out of the way, until he has left himself not a friend nor an enemy who is worth anything.

Certainly he must.

Then he must keenly notice who is manly, who high-minded, who prudent, who wealthy. And in such a happy condition is he, that, whether he wishes it or not, he is compelled to be the enemy of all these, and to plot against them, until he has purged them out of the city.

What a glorious purification!

Yes, said I, it runs directly counter to the process by which the physician purges the body. For the physician removes what is bad, and leaves what is good; but the tyrant removes the good, and leaves the bad.

Why, apparently, it is his only course, if he wishes to reign.

In fact he is bound in the chains of a delightful necessity, which orders him either to live amongst persons the majority of whom are good for nothing, and to live hated by them, or else to cease to exist.

That is the alternative.

Hence, in proportion as he grows more and more detested by the citizens for such conduct, he will require a more numerous and a more trusty body-guard, will he not?

Of course he will.

And tell me what people he can he trust, and where will he get them from?

Oh, they will come in flocks spontaneously, if he pays them their wages.

By my word, I believe you are thinking of another miscellaneous swarm of foreign drones.

You are not mistaken.

But would he hesitate to enlist recruits on the spot?

By what process?

By taking their slaves from the citizens, emancipating them, and enrolling them in his own body-guard.

Most decidedly he would not hesitate: for indeed such persons are really his most trusty adherents.

568 A tyrant is, indeed, a divinely happy creature, according to your account, if he adopts such men as friends and faithful adherents, after he has destroyed those former ones.

Well, he certainly does take this course.

And do not these comrades of his admire him highly, and do not the young citizens associate with him, while the good hate and shun him?

How can it be otherwise?

It is not without reason, said I, that people regard tragedy on the whole as wise, and Euripides as a master therein.

Why is that?

b Because, among other remarks, he has made the following, which shows a thoughtful mind, 'tyrants are wise through intercourse with the wise.' And he clearly meant by the 'wise,' those with whom the tyrant associates.

Yes, and, as one of its numerous merits, tyranny is extolled as something godlike, by the other poets as well as by Euripides.

This being the case, the writers of tragedy, like the wise men that they are, will excuse us, and those who copy our regime, for refusing them admittance into the city, because they sing hymns to tyranny.

c I imagine that, at any rate, all polite tragedians will excuse us.

At the same time, I believe, they will go around to other cities, gather together the populace, hire fine, loud, persuasive voices; and thus draw regimes toward tyranny and democracy.

To be sure they will.

And for these services they are, moreover, paid and honored, by tyrants chiefly, as we should expect, and to a smaller extent by democracy. But in proportion as they climb the ladder of regimes, their honor flags more

and more, as if it were prevented from mount- d ing by loss of breath.

Exactly so.

However, this is a digression. Let us return to the inquiry, how that army of the tyrant, that goodly, large, diversified, and ever-changing army, is to be supported.

It is clear, he replied, that, if there be sacred money in the city, the tyrant will spend it as long as it lasts, along with the property of those whom he has destroyed, so that the war-taxes, which the people are compelled to pay, will be proportionally diminished.

But what is he to do when this resource e fails?

Evidently he will draw on his father's property for the maintenance of himself and his drinking buddies, his messmates and his mistresses.

I understand you. You mean that the people that begat the tyrant, will maintain him and his companions.

It cannot avoid doing so.

But do explain yourself, I proceeded. Suppose the people are annoyed, and assert, that it is unjust for a father to have to maintain a grown-up son, since, on the contrary, the son 569 ought to maintain the father; and that they had begotten and installed him not with the intent, that, when he was grown big, they should be made the slaves of their own slaves, and maintain him and them with a mob of others, but with the intent that, under his leadership, they should be freed from the rich men of the city, and the gentlemen, as they are called; and suppose they now bid him depart out of the city, together with his friends, like a father expelling a son from home along with some riotous drinking buddies? What then?

The people will then, at length, most certainly discover how feeble they are in comparison with the nursling which they have begot- b ten and cherished and exalted, and that, in ejecting him, they are the weaker expelling the stronger.

What! I exclaimed. Will the tyrant venture

to lay violent hands on his father, and beat him if he refuses to comply with his wishes?

Yes, that he will, once he has taken away his father's weapons.

You call the tyrant a parricide, and a hard-hearted nurse of old age; and, apparently, the regime will henceforth be an open and avowed tyranny; and, according to the proverb, the people, trying to avoid the frying-pan of the service

c of free men, will have fallen into the fire of a tyranny exercised by slaves—in other words, they will have exchanged that vast and unseasonable liberty for the new dress of the harshest and bitterest of all types of slavery.

No doubt that is the course of events.

Well then, will any one be disposed to disagree with us, if we assert that we have discussed satisfactorily the transition from democracy to tyranny, and the character of the latter when established?

We have done so quite satisfactorily, he replied.

# BOOK IX

571 It only remains for us, I proceeded, to inquire how the democratic man is transformed into the tyrannical, and what kind of person he is, and whether his manner of living is happy or the reverse.

True, this case is still remaining, he said.

Then do you know, I asked, what I am still missing?

What is that?

I think that the number and nature of the appetites has not been satisfactorily defined; and while this deficiency continues, the inquiry upon which we are entering will be

b wrapped in obscurity.

It is not too late to make up for that?

Certainly it is not. Observe the peculiarity which I wish to notice in the case before us. It is this. Some of the unnecessary pleasures and appetites, if I am not mistaken, are hazardous to

the law, and come to be in all men; though, in the case of some persons, under the correction of the laws and the higher appetites aided by reason, they either wholly disappear, or only a few weak ones remain; while, in the case of others, they continue strong and numerous.      c

And what are the appetites to which you refer?

I refer to those appetites which wake up in sleep—when, during the slumbers of that other part of the soul, which is rational and tamed and master of the former, the wild animal part, sated with meat or drink, becomes rampant, and pushing sleep away, endeavors to set out after the gratification of its own proper character. You know that in such moments there is nothing that it dares not do, released and delivered as it is from any sense of shame and reflection. It does not shrink from attempting, as it thinks, unholy intercourse with a mother, or with any man or deity      d or animal whatever; and it does not hesitate to commit the foulest murder, or to indulge itself in the most defiling meats. In one word, there is no limit either to its folly or to its audacity.

Your description is perfectly true.

But, I imagine, whenever a man relates to himself in a healthy and temperate way, and, when going to sleep, he has stimulated the rational part of him, and feasted it on beautiful discussions and high inquiries, by means of close and inward reflection; while, on the other hand, he has neither stinted nor gorged the      e appetitive part in order that it may sleep instead of troubling with its joys or its griefs      572 that highest part, which may thus be permitted to pursue its studies in purity and independence, and to strain forward to perceive something until then unknown, either past, present, or future; and when, in like manner, he has calmed the spirited element by avoiding every burst of passion, which would send him to sleep with his spirit stirred—when, I say, he proceeds to rest, with two elements out of the three quieted, and the third, wherein wisdom resides, aroused, you are aware that, at such moments, he is best able to apprehend truth, and that the visions, which present themselves in his dreams, are then anything but unlawful.

I concur with your opinion.

Well, we have been carried too far out of our way, in order to make these remarks. What we wish to recognize is, that apparently a terrible species of wild and lawless appetites resides in every one of us, even when in some cases we have the appearance of being perfectly self-restrained. And this fact, it seems, becomes evident in sleep. Consider whether you think I am right, and whether you agree with me.

Yes, I do agree.

Remember then the character which we ascribed to the man of the people. He grew up from his youth, I believe, reared under the eye of a miserly father, who respected only the money-making appetites, and despised those unnecessary appetites which have for their object amusement and display. Am I not right?

You are.

By intercourse with more fashionable men, replete with those appetites which we just now discussed, he had run, like them, into utter riot, in detestation of his father's miserliness; but, as he possessed a better disposition than his corrupters, he was drawn in two directions, and ended by adopting an intermediate character; and while enjoying every pleasure in perfect moderation, as he imagined, he lived a life which was neither unfree nor unlawful, and was thus transformed from an oligarchical into a democratic man.

Yes, this was and is our opinion about this person.

Well then, I continued, suppose that this man has grown old in his turn, and that a young son is raised again in his habits.

Very good.

Suppose furthermore, that the same things that happened to his father happen to him—that he is seduced into an utter violation of law, or, to use the language of his seducers,

into perfect freedom, and that his father and his other relations bring support to these intermediate appetites, which is met by counter support on the other side; and when these terrible sorcerers and tyrant-makers have despaired of securing the young man by other spells, imagine that they contrive to engender in him some passion, to champion those idle appetites which divide among themselves what comes to hand; and this passion you may describe as a kind of huge, winged drone: for how else can you describe the passion entertained by such men?

I cannot describe it otherwise.

This done, the other appetites, overflowing with incense and perfumes and garlands and wines and the loose pleasures which form part of such get-togethers, begin to buzz around this drone, and exalt and nurse him to the uttermost, until they have engendered in him the sting of desire; and from that moment forward this leader of the soul, with frenzy for his body-guard, is goaded on to madness; and if he deters within himself any opinions or appetites which are regarded as good, and which still feel a sense of shame, he destroys them or thrusts them from his presence, until he has purged out temperance, and filled himself with imported madness.

You exactly describe the generation of a tyrannical man.

Is not this the reason why love has of old been called a tyrant?

Probably it is.

Also, my friend, does not a drunken man possess what may be called a tyrannical spirit?

He does.

And we know that an insane, or deranged person, expects to be able to lord it not only over men, but even over gods, and attempts to do so.

Certainly he does.

So, my excellent friend, a man becomes strictly tyrannical, whenever, by nature, or by habit, or by both together, he has fallen under the dominion of wine, or love, or melancholy.

Yes, precisely so.

d    Such is his origin, apparently, and such his nature; but how does he live?

As they say in the game, he replied, *you* must tell *me* that.

So be it, I said. Well, if I am not mistaken, from henceforth feasts and revels and banquets and mistresses, and every thing of the kind, become the order of the day with persons whose souls are wholly piloted by an indwelling tyrant passion.

It must be so.

And do not many frightful appetites, needy of many things, shoot up by their side every day and every night?

Yes, many indeed.

So that all existing revenues are soon spent.

Of course they are.

e    Then follow schemes for raising money, and consequent loss of property.

Undoubtedly.

And when every resource has failed, must not those violent appetites, which have nestled thickly within, lift up their voices? And goaded on, as these people are, by their appetites, and especially by that ruling passion under which all the rest serve as body-guard, must they not, in a frenzy of rage, look out for anyone who has anything, whom they may rob by fraud or violence?

574

Yes, indeed, they must.

So that if they cannot pillage in every quarter, they are constrained to suffer grievous throes and pangs.

They are.

Now, just as the inward pleasures of later growth bested the original pleasures and took away what belonged to them, in the same way will not the man himself determine to have more than his father and mother, though he is younger than they, and to help himself at their expense out of his father's property, if he has expended his own share?

Undoubtedly he will.

And if his parents oppose his designs, will    b
he not attempt in the first instance to cheat and outwit them?

Assuredly he will.

And whenever that is impossible, will he proceed to robbery and violence?

I think so.

Then if his aged father and mother hold out against him and offer resistance, will he be so scrupulous as to shrink from playing the tyrant?

I am not altogether without my fears for the parents of such a man.

But do you think, Adeimantus, that his attachment to his unnecessary and unconnected mistress is new, while his love for his    c
very own indispensable mother is old, and that his affection for his unnecessary and unconnected friend who is in the bloom of youth, is of recent date compared with that for his very own father, his oldest friend, faded and aged as he is. This being the case, can you believe that he would beat his mother and father for the sake of his mistress and his friend, and that he would make the former the slaves of the latter, if he brought them into the same house?

Upon my word I believe he would, he replied.

Then to all appearance it is a most delightful thing to be the parents of a tyrannical son.

Yes, that it is.

However, when the property of his father    d
and mother begins to fail the son, while at the same time the swarm of pleasures has collected within him, will not his first exploit be to break into a house or strip some traveler of his clothes by night, and will he not afterwards proceed to sweep off the contents of some temple? And in the meantime those old and, in common estimation, just opinions, which he held from childhood on the subject of base and noble actions, will be defeated by those opinions which have been just emancipated from slavery, aided by that ruling passion whose body-

e   guard they form, opinions which, so long as he was subject to the laws and to his father, and while his inward constitution was democratic, used to be emancipated only in the dreams of sleep. But, now that he is tyrannized by Eros, that character, which used to be his only in dreams, and at rare intervals, has become his constant waking state. There is not a dire mur-der, a forbidden meat, or an unholy act, from
575 which he will restrain himself; but this passion that lives and reigns within him, in the midst of utter anarchy and lawlessness, will, by virtue of its being sole king, seduce its possessor, as in the case of a city, into unbounded recklessness, to procure means for the maintenance of itself and its attendant rowdy crowd, which has partly made entrance from without as a result of wicked companionship, and partly been lib-erated and released from within by the same bad habits. Or am I wrong in my description of the life of such a man?

No, you are right, he replied.

And if, I proceeded, a city contains only a few such characters, the rest of the population
b   being sober-minded, these people leave and enlist in the body-guard of some other tyrant, or else serve as mercenaries in any war that may be going on. But if they live in a time of peace and quiet, they commit many small mis-chiefs on the spot in the city.

Such as what?

Such as theft, burglary, purse snatching, stealing clothes, sacrilege, kidnaping—and sometimes they turn sycophant, if they have a talent for speaking, and perjure themselves, and take bribes.
c   True, these are small mischiefs, if the per-petrators are few in number.

Things that are small, I replied, are small comparatively; and assuredly all these mis-chiefs, in their bearings on the corruption and misery of a city, do not, as the proverb says, nearly come up to the mark of a tyrant. For whenever such persons, and others, their fol-lowers, become numerous in a city, and per-ceive their own numbers, then, assisted by the folly of the people, these men generate the tyrant, who is simply that one of their number whose own soul contains the mightiest and   d
hugest tyrant.

So one might expect, because such a person must have most of the tyrant about him.

Consequently if the citizens obey willingly, all goes smoothly. But if the city cannot be relied on, the tyrant will chastise his father-land, if he can, just as in the former case he chastised his mother and father; and to do this, he will summon to his assistance youthful comrades, to whom he enslaves his once-beloved mother-country, as the Cretans call it, or father-land. And this will be the consum-mation of the appetite of such a person.

Assuredly it will.                                           e

And do not these persons display the same character in private, even before they become rulers? In the first place, in their intercourse with others, is it not the case either that all their associates are their flatterers and ready to serve them in everything, or that, if they want anything from anybody, they go down on their knees for it, acting as though they belonged to him, whereas when they have gained their   576
point they become distant and estranged?

Precisely so.

Thus all their life long they live friendless, and they are always either masters or slaves: for a tyrant nature can never taste true freedom and friendship.

Certainly not.

Then shall we not be right if we call such persons faithless?

Undoubtedly we shall.

And not only faithless, but also supremely unjust, if we were right in our former conclu-   b
sions as to the nature of justice.

And certainly we were right.

Then let us describe summarily the most wicked man. He is one whose waking state is the very counterpart of the dreamlike description which we have given.

Exactly so.

Such is the end of the man, who, with a nature most tyrannical, gains sole rule—and the longer his life of tyranny lasts, the more exactly does he answer to our description.

That is unquestionably true, said Glaucon, taking up the reply.

c   That being the case, I continued, will not the man, who shall be proved to be most vicious, be thereby proved to be also most miserable? And will it not be apparent that the man, whose tyranny has lasted longest in the intensest form, has really been for the longest time most intensely vicious and miserable, notwithstanding the variety of opinions entertained by the many?

Yes, that much is certain, he replied.

And can we help regarding the tyrannical man as the counterpart and representative of the city which is under the sway of a tyrant, the democratic man of the democratic city, and so on?

d   Unquestionably we cannot.

Hence, as city is to city in point of virtue and happiness, so also is man to man; is it not so?

Undoubtedly it is.

Then, in point of virtue, how does a city under a tyrant stand as compared with a city under such a kingly government, as we at first described?

They are the very opposite of one another, he replied: one is the most virtuous, and the other the most wicked.

I shall not ask you which is which, because that is obvious. But do you decide the question of happiness and misery in the same way, or not? And here let us not be dazzled by looking only at the tyrant, who is just one man, or at a few of his immediate followers; but, as it is our duty to enter and survey the city as a whole, let

e   us, before giving our opinion, creep into every part of it and look about.

Well, your proposal is a just one; indeed it is clear to everybody, that a city governed by a tyrant is the most miserable of cities; whereas a city under kingly rule is the happiest of cities.

Then shall I not do right, if, in discussing the corresponding men, I make the same proposal,   577 and recognize only *his* verdict, who can in thought penetrate into a man's character, and look through it, and who does not, like a child, scrutinize the exterior, until he is dazzled by the artificial glitter which the tyrannical man carries on the outside, but on the contrary sees through it all thoroughly? Suppose I give it as my opinion, that we are all bound to listen to the judge, who is not only capable of passing sentence, but has also lived in the same place with the person in question, and has been an eye-witness of his goings on at home, and of his bearing towards the several members of his family, wherein he will be most thoroughly   b stripped of the theatrical garb, and also of his behavior in public perils; and suppose we bid him take all these particulars into consideration, and then pronounce, how, on the score of happiness and misery, the tyrant stands as compared with the other men?

This proposal, he replied, would be also a most just one.

Then, in order that we may have some person who will reply to our questions, do you want us to pretend to be among those who, besides being competent to deliver judgment, have before now encountered people of this description?

Yes, I should.

Come then, let me beg you to consider the   c question in the following light. Bearing in mind the similarity that subsists between the city and the man, examine them singly in turn, and tell me the circumstances in which each is placed.

To what circumstances do you refer?

To begin with the city, do you say of one which is under the dominion of a tyrant that it is free or slave?

Consummate slavery.

And yet you see it contains masters and freemen.

True, it does contain a few such persons; but the mass of the inhabitants, I might say, and the best of them are reduced to a dishonorable and miserable servitude.

d    Now, since the man resembles the city, must not the same order of things exist in him also, and must not his soul be filled with much slavery and servility, those parts of it, which were the best, being enslaved, while a small part, and that the most corrupt and insane, is dominant?

It must be so.

If so, will such a soul, by your account, be slave or free?

I should certainly say the former.

To return, is not the city, which is enslaved to a tyrant, utterly precluded from acting as it likes?

Yes, quite so.

e    Then the soul also, which is the seat of a tyranny, considered as a whole will be very far from doing whatever it wishes. On the contrary it will always be goaded by a gadfly, and filled with confusion and remorse.

Beyond a doubt.

And must the city which is the seat of a tyranny be rich or poor?

It must be poor.

578    Then the tyrannical soul also must always be poverty-stricken and craving.

Just so.

Again, must not such a city and such a man be, as a matter of course, full of fear?

Yes, indeed.

Do you expect to find in any other city more weeping and wailing and lamentation and grief?

Certainly not.

And to return to the individual, do you imagine such things to exist in any one so abundantly as in this tyrannical man, who is maddened by appetites and longings?

Why, how could they?

b    Looking then, I suppose, at all these facts, and others like them, you have decided that the city is the most miserable of cities.

And am I not right?

You are very right. But once more, looking at the same facts, what account do you give of the tyrannical man?

I should say that he is quite the most miserable of all men.

There you are no longer right.

How so?

I believe, that this person is still not the most miserable of all.

Then who is?

You will perhaps think the following person even more miserable.

Describe him.

I refer to the man who, being tyrannical, is    c
prevented from living a private life, because he is so unfortunate as to have the post of tyrant, by some bad luck, procured for him.

I infer from the previous remarks that you are right.

Yes, I said, but you must not be content with surmises here; on the contrary, you must examine an argument such as this thoroughly; for surely the point under investigation is of the greatest importance, since it is the choice between a good and a bad life.

That is perfectly true.

Observe, then, whether I am right. It    d
appears to me that, in examining the question, we ought to begin our inquiry with the following considerations.

What are they?

We must begin by considering the individual case of those private members of cities who are wealthy and possess many slaves. For they have this point in common with the tyrant, that they rule over many persons. The difference lies in the greater number of his subjects.

Yes, it does.

And now, are you aware that such persons are confident and do not fear their servants?

Yes. What should make them fear them?

Nothing, but do you understand the reason for it?

Yes. It is because the entire city supports each private person.

e      You are right. But if some deity were to lift out of the city a single individual, who has fifty slaves or more, and were to plant him with his wife and children in some desert along with the rest of his substance and his servants, where none of the freemen would be likely to help him, do you not think he would be seized with an indescribable terror lest he and his wife and children should be murdered by his servants?

Yes, with utter terror, I think.

579    And would he not be compelled from that time forward to fawn on some of his very slaves, and to make many promises and free them without any demand for it? In fact, would he not appear to be an abject flatterer of his servants?

He is doomed to death if he fails to do so.

But what if the god had surrounded him with a multitude of other neighbors, who would not endure that one person should claim the rights of a master over another, but punished with the utmost severity any such person whom they caught?

b      In that case he would be, I imagine, involved still further in a greater evil, because he would be hemmed in by a ring of warders, and all of them would be his enemies.

And is not the tyrant a prisoner in a similar prison? For if his nature is such as we have described, he is filled with a multitude of terrors and longings of every kind; and, though he has a greedy and inquisitive soul, is he not the only citizen that is precluded from traveling or setting eyes upon all those objects which every freeman desires to see? Does he not bury himself in his house, and live for the

c      most part the life of a woman, while he positively envies all other citizens who travel abroad and see anything good?

Yes, assuredly he does.

Such being his sick condition, I continued, a larger harvest of misery is reaped by that person, who, with a sick inward constitution like that of the tyrannical man, whom you just now judged as most wretched, is forced out of private life, and constrained by some accident to assume tyrannical power, thus undertaking to rule others when he cannot govern himself, just like a person who with a diseased and incontinent body is compelled to pass his life,                    d not in retirement, but in wrestling and contending with other persons.

Undoubtedly, Socrates, the cases are very similar, and your account is very true.

Then, my dear Glaucon, is not the condition of the tyrant utterly wretched, and does he not live a life which is even more intolerable than that of the man who, by your verdict, lives most intolerably?

Unquestionably, he replied.

So, whatever may be thought, a real tyrant is in truth a real slave to the greatest flattery and slavery, and a flatterer of the most vicious;                    e and, far from satisfying his cravings in the smallest degree, he stands in utmost need of numberless things, and is in truth a pauper, in the eyes of one who knows how to contemplate the soul as a whole; and all his life long he is loaded with terrors, and full of convulsions and pangs, if he resembles the disposition of the city over which he rules; and he does resemble it, does he not?

Certainly he does.

Then we shall also, in addition to this,                    580 ascribe to the man what we stated before—namely, that he cannot help being, and, in virtue of his power, becoming more and more envious, faithless, unjust, friendless, unhealthy, and the host and nurse of every vice; and, in consequence of all this, he must in the first place be unhappy in himself, and in the next place he must make those who are near him as unhappy as himself.

No sensible man will contradict you.

Then go on, I proceeded, and, like the judge who passes sentence after going through the whole case, declare forthwith who is first, in                    b your opinion, in point of happiness, and who second, and so on, arranging all the five men in order, the kingly, the timocratic, the oligarchic, the democratic, the tyrannical.

Well, he said, the decision is an easy one. I arrange them, like choruses, in the order of their entrance, in point of virtue and vice, happiness and misery.

Shall we, then, hire a herald, or shall I make proclamation in person, that the son of Ariston has given his verdict to the effect that he is the

c happiest man who is best and most just, that is, who is most kingly, and who rules over himself royally; whereas he is the most wretched man who is worst and most unjust, that is, who is most tyrannical, and who plays the tyrant to the greatest perfection both over himself and over a city?

Let such be your proclamation, he replied.

And am I to add to my proclamation, that it makes no difference whether all men and gods notice their characters, or not?

Do so.

Very well, I proceeded, this will make one

d demonstration for us. The following must make a second, if it shall be approved.

What is it?

Since the soul of each individual has been divided into three parts corresponding to the three classes in the city, our position will admit, I think, of a second demonstration.

What is it?

It is the following. As there are three parts, so there appear to me to be three pleasures, one appropriate to each part, and similarly three appetites, and governing principles.

Explain yourself.

According to us, one part was that with which a man learns, and another that whereby he shows spirit. The third was so multiform

e that we were unable to address it by a single appropriate name. So we named it after that which is its most important and strongest characteristic. We called it appetitive, on account of the intensity of the appetites of hunger, thirst, and sex, and all their accompaniments and we called it peculiarly money-loving, be-

cause money is the chief agent in the gratifica-   581
tion of such appetites.

Yes, we were right.

Then if we were to assert that the pleasure and the love of this third part is of gain, would not this be the best summary of the facts upon which we should be likely to settle by force of argument, so that it is clear to us, whenever we spoke of this part of the soul. And shall we not be right in calling it money-loving and gain-loving?

I think so, he replied.

Again, do we not maintain that the spirited part is wholly bent on winning power and victory and celebrity?

Certainly we do.   b

Then would the title of victory-loving and honor-loving be appropriate to it?

Yes, most appropriate.

Well, but with regard to the part by which we learn, it is obvious to every one that its entire and constant aim is to know the truth as it is, and that this one cares the least about wealth and reputation.

Yes, quite the least.

Then shall we not do well to call it learning-loving and wisdom-loving?

Of course we shall.

Does not this last reign in the souls of some persons, while in the souls of other people one   c
or other of the two former, according to circumstances, is dominant?

You are right.

And for these reasons may we assert that men may be primarily classed under the three heads of lovers of wisdom, of victory, and of gain?

Yes, certainly.

And that there are three kinds of pleasures, respectively underlying the three classes?

Exactly so.

Now, are you aware, I continued, that if you choose to ask three such men each in his turn, which of these lives is the most pleasant, each will extol his own beyond the others? Thus the   d money-making man will tell you, that compared with the pleasures of gain, the pleasures of being honored or of becoming learned are worthless, except in so far as they can produce money.

True.

But what of the honor-loving man? Does he not look upon the pleasure derived from money as a vulgar one, while, on the other hand, he regards the pleasure derived from learning as a mere vapor and absurdity, unless honor be the fruit of it?

That is precisely the case.

And must we not suppose that the lover of wisdom regards all the other pleasures as, by comparison, very far inferior to the pleasure of knowing the truth as it is, and of being constantly occupied with this pursuit of learning; and that he calls those other pleasures strictly necessary, because, if they were not necessary, he would feel no desire for them?

We may be certain that it is so, he replied.

Then whenever a dispute is raised as to the pleasures of each kind and the life itself of each class, not with reference to beauty and ugliness, the worse and the better, but with reference merely to their position in the scale of pleasure and painlessness, how can we know which of the three men speaks most truly?

I am not quite prepared to answer.

Well, look at the question in this light. By what do we judge in order for a judgment to be correct? Must it not be experience, prudence and reasoning? Or can one find better means of judging than these?

Of course we cannot.

Then observe. Of the three men, which is the best acquainted by experience with all the pleasures which we have mentioned? Does the lover of gain study the nature of truth itself as it is, in your opinion, and is he acquainted with the pleasure of knowledge better than the lover of wisdom is acquainted with the pleasure of gain?

There is a great difference, he replied. The lover of wisdom is compelled to taste the pleasures of gain from his childhood; whereas the lover of gain is not compelled to study the nature of the things that are, and thus to taste the sweetness of this pleasure, and become acquainted with it; rather I should say, it is not easy for him to do this, even if he has the inclination.

Hence, I proceeded, the lover of wisdom is far superior to the lover of gain in having experienced both pleasures.

He is indeed.

But what of the lover of honor? Is he acquainted with the pleasure of thinking as thoroughly as the lover of wisdom is acquainted with the pleasure of honor?

Honor waits upon them all, he said, if each works out the object of his pursuit. For the rich man is honored by many people, as well as the courageous and the wise—so that all are acquainted with the nature of the pleasure to be derived from the fact of being honored. But the nature of the pleasure to be found in the vision of that which is, none can have tasted, except the lover of wisdom.

Then, as far as experience goes, the lover of wisdom is the best judge of the three.

Quite so.

Also we know that he alone can lay claim to prudence as well as experience.

Undoubtedly.

Once more, the tool by which judgment is passed is an organ belonging, not to the lover of gain or of honor, but to the lover of wisdom.

What is that tool?

We stated, I believe, that judgment must be passed by means of argument. Did we not?

We did.

And argument is to a special degree, the tool of the lover of wisdom.

Certainly.

Consequently, if wealth and gain were the best tools for deciding questions as they arise, the praise and the censure of the lover of gain would necessarily be most true.

Quite so.

And if honor, victory, and courage, were the best tools for the purpose, the sentence of the lover of honor and of victory would be most true, would it not?

Obviously it would.

But since experience, prudence, and argument, are the best instruments, what then?

Why of course, he replied, the praise of the lover of wisdom and of argument is the truest.

583    Then, if the pleasures are three in number, will the pleasure of this part of the soul, by which we learn, be most pleasant? And will the life of that man amongst us, in whom this part is dominant, be also most pleasant?

Unquestionably it will—at any rate, the man of prudence is fully authorized to praise his own life.

And what life, I asked, does the judge pronounce second, and what pleasure second?

Obviously, the pleasure of the warlike and honor-loving man. For it approaches the first more nearly than the pleasure of the money-making man does.

Then the pleasure of the lover of gain is to be placed last, as it appears.

Undoubtedly, he replied.

b    Thus the just man will be victorious over the unjust twice in a row. And now for the third and last time, address yourself, like a contestant in the Olympic games, to Olympian Zeus, the Preserver, and observe that in the pleasure of all but the prudent man there is something which is not entirely true and which is impure, but is rather like shadow-painting as I think I have been told by some wise man. And let me say, that this bout will be the heaviest and most decisive defeat of all.

Quite so, but explain yourself.

c    I shall find what we want, I replied, if you will respond while I look.

Ask your questions by all means.

Tell me then, I proceeded, do we not assert that pain is the opposite of pleasure?

Assuredly we do.

And also that there is such a thing which is neither pleasure nor pain?

Certainly there is.

In other words, you admit that there is a point midway between the two at which the soul reposes from both. Is not that your meaning?

It is.

Have you forgotten the speeches of sick people when they are ill?

Give me an example of that.

They tell us that nothing is more pleasant than health, but that, before they were ill, they   d had not found out its supreme pleasantness.

I remember.

Do you not also hear persons who are in excessive pain say, that nothing is so pleasant as relief from pain?

I do.

And I think you find that, on many other similar occasions, persons, when they are uneasy, extol as supremely pleasant, not positive joy, but the absence of, and repose from, uneasiness.

True, he replied; and perhaps the reason is, that at such times this relief does become positively pleasant and delightful.

In the same way we might expect, that   e when a person's joy has ceased, the repose from pleasure will be painful.

Perhaps so.

Thus the repose, which we described just now as midway between pleasure and pain, must be now one, now the other.

So it would seem.

Can that, which is neither pleasure nor pain, become both?

I think not.

Again, pleasure and pain, when present in the soul are both of them emotions, are they not?

They are.

But was not the simultaneous absence of   584 pleasure and of pain shown just now to indicate a state of undoubted repose, midway between the two?

It was.

Then how can it be right to regard the absence of pain as pleasant, or the absence of pleasure as painful?

It cannot be right.

Hence, the repose felt at the times we speak of is not really, but only appears to be, pleasant by the side of what is painful, and painful by the side of what is pleasant; and these appearances will in no instance stand the test of comparison with true pleasure, because they are only some kind of bewilderment.

I confess that the argument points to that conclusion.

b     In the next place turn your eyes to pleasures which do not grow out of pains, to prevent your supposing, as perhaps at the present moment you might do, that it should naturally come to be that pleasure should be a cessation of pain, and pain a cessation of pleasure.

Where am I to look, and what pleasures do you mean?

Among many others, I replied, you may, if you will, take as the best example for your consideration the pleasures of smell—which, without the existence of any previous uneasiness, spring up suddenly in extraordinary intensity, and when they are over, leave no pain behind.

That is quite true.

c     Then do not let us be persuaded that pure pleasure consists in the release from pain, or that pure pain consists in the release from pleasure.

No.

But it is certain that, speaking roughly, most of the so-called pleasures which reach the soul through the body, and the keenest of them, belong to this species—that is to say, they are a kind of release from pain.

They are.

Does not the same remark apply to those pleasures and pains of anticipation which precede them?

It does.

Now, are you aware what the character     d of these pleasures is, and what they most resemble?

What?

Do you believe that there is by nature an above, and below, and an intermediate?

Yes, I do.

And do you imagine that a person, carried from below to that intermediate position, could help supposing that he is being carried above? And when he is stationary in that situation, and looks to the place from where he has been carried, do you imagine that he can help supposing his position to be above, if he has not seen the real above?

For my own part, he replied, I assure you I cannot imagine how such a person is to think differently.

Well, supposing him to be carried to his old     e place, would he think that he is being carried below, and would he be right in so thinking?

Of course he would.

And will not all this happen to him, because he has not experienced what is truly above, and between, and below?

Obviously it will.

Then can you wonder, that persons inexperienced in the truth, besides holding a multitude of other unsound opinions, stand to pleasure and pain and their intermediate, in such a position, that though when they are carried to what is painful, they form a correct opinion of     585 their condition, and are really in pain; yet, when they are carried from pain to the middle point between pain and pleasure, they obstinately imagine that they have arrived at fulfillment and pleasure, which they have never experienced, and consequently are deceived by contrasting pain with the absence of pain, like persons who, not knowing white, contrast gray with black, and take it for white?

No, indeed, I cannot wonder at it; in fact, I should wonder much more if it were not so.

Well, consider the question in another light. Are not hunger and thirst, and similar sensa-     b tions, a kind of emptiness of the bodily condition?

Undoubtedly.

Similarly, are not ignorance and folly an emptiness of the condition of the soul?

Yes, certainly.

Will not the man who eats, and the man who gets understanding, be filled?

Of course.

And is fulness more true if it is in relation to that which is more or that which is less?

Obviously, that which is more.

c Then do you think that pure essence participates more in the classes of things like bread and meat and drink, and food generally, than that species of things which includes true opinion and science and mind, and in a word, all virtue? In forming your judgment look at the matter thus. In your opinion, which one is more—that which is attached to what is always similar to itself, deathless, and true, and that which is itself and comes to be in such a sort of thing, or its opposite, that is, something which is never like itself, which is mortal, and which is itself the sort of thing that it becomes?

It is that which is connected with what is always like itself.

And as to the essence of that which is always similar to itself, does it participate more in essence than in knowledge?

Certainly not.

Well, what about truth?

No.

That is to say, if truth participates less, essence participates less also?

Necessarily so.

d Speaking universally, does not the cultivation of the body in all its branches participate in truth and essence less than the cultivation of the soul in all its branches?

Yes, in a much less degree.

And does not the same hold for the body itself as for the soul?

It does.

So, that which is filled with more being and is more real is more truly filled than that which is filled with less.

Undoubtedly it is.

Hence, as it is pleasant to a subject to be filled with the things that are naturally appropriate to it, that subject which is really more filled, and filled with real essences, will in a more real and true sense be productive of true pleasure; whereas that subject which partici- e pates in things less real, will be less really and less securely filled, and will participate in a less true and less trustworthy pleasure.

The conclusion is absolutely inevitable, he replied.

Those, therefore, who are inexperienced 586 with prudence and virtue, and who spend their time in perpetual banqueting and similar indulgences, are carried down, as it appears, and back again only as far as the midway point on the upward road; and between these limits they roam their life long, without ever overstepping them so as to look up towards, or be carried to, the true above—and they have never been really filled with what is real, or tasted sure and unmingled pleasure; but, like cattle, they are always looking downwards, and hanging their heads to the ground, and poking them into their dining-tables, while they graze and get fat and propagate their species; and, to satiate their b greedy desire for these enjoyments, they kick and butt with hoofs and horns of iron, till they kill one another under the influence of ravenous appetites—trying to fill their leaky part with things that are not.

Socrates, said Glaucon, you certainly describe like an oracle the life of the majority of people.

And does it not follow that they consort with pleasures mingled with pain which are mere images and shadow-paintings of the true pleasure, and which are so colored by being c positioned next to pain, that they appear in each case to be extravagantly great, and beget a frantic passion for themselves in the breasts of the foolish people, and are made subjects of contention, like that image of Helen, for which, according to Stesichorus, the combatants at Troy fought, in ignorance of the true Helen?

Such a state of things, he replied, follows as a matter of course.

And now to come to the spirited element. Must not the consequences be the same sort of thing, whenever a man labors for the gratification of this part of his nature, either in the shape of jealousy from motives of honor-loving, or in the shape of violence from victory-loving, or in the shape of anger out of discontent, while he pursues after honor and victory and anger to his own satisfaction, without calculation and mindfulness?

The consequences in this case also must necessarily be similar.

And what is the inference? May we assert confidently, that of all the appetites with which the gain-loving and honor-loving elements are conversant, those which follow the lead of knowledge and reason, and along with them pursue the pleasures which the prudent part directs, until they find them, will find not only the truest pleasures that they can possibly find, in consequence of their devotion to truth, but also the pleasures appropriate to them, since what is best for each is also most appropriate?

Yes, no doubt it is most appropriate.

Hence, so long as the whole soul follows the guidance of the wisdom-loving element without any dissension, each part can not only do its own proper work in all respects, or in other words, be just; but, moreover, it can enjoy its own proper pleasures, in the best and to the greatest extent possible.

Yes, precisely so.

On the other hand, whenever either of the two other elements has gained the mastery, it is fated not only to miss the discovery of its own pleasure, but also to constrain the other principles to pursue an alien and untrue pleasure.

Just so.

Well, the further a thing is removed from philosophy and reason, the more likely will it be to produce such bad effects, will it not?

Yes, much more likely.

And that is furthest removed from reason which is furthest removed from law and order, is it not?

Obviously so.

And have not the passionate or tyrannical appetites been proved to be furthest removed from law and order?

Yes, quite the furthest.

Whereas the kingly and regular appetites stand nearest to law and order, do they not?

They do.

Hence, if I am not mistaken, the tyrant will be furthest from, and the king nearest to, true and specially appropriate pleasure.

It is undeniable.

And therefore the tyrant will live most unpleasantly, and the king most pleasantly.

It is quite undeniable.

And are you aware of the extent to which the discomfort of the tyrant's life exceeds that of the king's?

I wait for you to tell me.

There are three pleasures, it appears,—one genuine, and two spurious. Now the tyrant has trespassed beyond these last, has fled from law and reason, and lives with a body-guard of slavish pleasures; and the extent of his inferiority is hard indeed to state, unless perhaps it may be stated thus.

How?

Reckoning from the oligarchical man, the tyrant stands third, I believe, in the descending line; for the democratic man stood between them.

Yes.

Then, if our former remarks were true, must not the pleasure with which he consorts, be, so far as truth is concerned, a copy of a copy, the original of which is in the possession of the oligarchic man?

Just so.

Again, reckoning from the kingly man, the
d    oligarchic in his turn stands third in the descending line, supposing us to identify the
aristocratic and the kingly?

True, he does.

Therefore the tyrant is thrice three times
removed from true pleasure.

Apparently so.

Then it seems that tyrannical pleasure may
be represented geometrically by a square number, 9.

Exactly so.

And by squaring and cubing, it is made
quite clear to what a great distance the tyrant is
removed.

Yes, to an arithmetician it is.

Conversely, if you wish to state the distance at which the king stands from the tyrant
e    in point of true pleasure, by working out the
multiplication you will find that the former
lives 729 times more pleasantly than the latter,
or that the latter lives more painfully than the
former in the same proportion.

You have brought out an extraordinary
588  result in calculating the difference between the
just man and the unjust, on the score of pleasure and pain.

b    Well, I replied, I am sure that the number is
correct, and applicable to human life, if days
and nights and months and years are applicable thereto.

And no doubt they are.

Then if the good and just man so far surpasses the wicked and unjust in point of pleasure, will he not surpass him incalculably more
in gracefulness of life, in beauty, and in virtue?

Yes, indeed he will, incalculably.

Well, then, I continued, now that we have
arrived at this stage of the argument, let us
resume that first discussion which brought us
here. It was stated, I believe, that injustice is
profitable to the man who is perfectly unjust,
while he is reputed to be just. Or am I wrong
about the statement?

No, you are right.

This is the moment for arguing with the
speaker of this remark, now that we have come
to an agreement as to the respective effects of
a course of injustice, and of a course of justice.

How must we proceed?

We must fashion in speech an image of the
soul, in order that the speaker may perceive
what his remark amounts to.

What kind of image is it to be?                              c

We must imagine, I replied, a creature like
one of those which, according to the legend,
existed in old times, such as Chimera, and
Scylla, and Cerberus, not to mention a host of
other monsters, in the case of which we are
told that several generic forms have grown
together and coalesced into one.

True, we do hear such stories.

Well, mold in the first place the form of a
motley many-headed monster, furnished with a
ring of heads of tame and wild animals, which
he can produce by turns in every instance out of
himself.

It requires a cunning modeler to do so; nev-        d
ertheless, since speech is more pliable than
wax, consider it done.

Now proceed, secondly, to mold the form
of a lion, and, thirdly, the form of a man. But
let the first be much the greatest of the three,
and the second next to it.

That is easier. It is done.

Now combine the three into one, so as to
make them grow together to a certain extent.

I have done so.

Lastly, invest them externally with the
form of one, namely, the man, so that the person who cannot see inside, and only notices
the outside skin, may think that it is one single        e
animal, to wit, a human being.

I have molded the form.

And now to the person who asserts that it is
profitable for this creature man to be unrighteous, and that it is not for his interest to do justice, let us reply that his assertion amounts to
this, that it is profitable for him to feast and
strengthen the multifarious monster and the

589 lion and its members, and to starve and enfeeble the man to such an extent as to leave him at the mercy of the guidance of either of the other two, without making any attempt to habituate or reconcile them to one another, but leaving them together to bite and struggle and devour each other.

True, he replied, the person who praises injustice will certainly in effect say this.

On the other hand, will not the advocate of the profitableness of justice assert that actions and words ought to be such as will enable the
b inward man to have the firmest control over the entire man, and, with the lion for his ally, to cultivate, like a farmer, the many-headed beast, nursing and rearing the tame parts of it, and checking the growth of the wild; and thus to pursue his training on the principle of concerning himself for all jointly, and reconciling them to one another and to himself?

Yes, these again are precisely the assertions of the person who praises justice.

Then in every way the one who praises jus-
c tice will speak the truth, while the one who praises injustice will lie. For whether you look at pleasure, at reputation, or at advantage, the one who praises the righteous man speaks truth, whereas all the criticisms of his enemy are unsound and ignorant.

I am entirely of that opinion, said he.

Let us therefore persuade him mildly—for his mistake is involuntary—and let us put this question to him: My good friend, may we not assert that the practices which are held by law to be beautiful or ugly are beautiful or ugly according as they either subjugate the brutal
d parts of our nature to the man—perhaps I should rather say, to the divine part—or make the tame part the servant and slave of the wild? Will he say, yes? Or how will he reply?

He will say yes, if he will take my advice.

Then according to this argument, I proceeded, can it be profitable for any one to take gold unjustly, since the consequence is, that, in

the moment of taking the gold, he is enslaving
e the best part of him to the most vile? Or, it being admitted that, had he taken gold to sell a son or a daughter into slavery, and a slavery among wild and wicked masters, it could have done him no good to receive even an immense sum for such a purpose, will it be argued that, if he ruthlessly enslaves the most divine part of himself to the most ungodly and accursed, he is not a miserable man, and is *not* being bribed
590 to a far more awful destruction than Eriphyle, when she took the necklace as the price of her husband's life?

I will reply in his behalf, said Glaucon: it is indeed much more awful.

And do you not think that intemperance, again, has been blamed for a long time for reasons of that kind, that, during its outbreaks, that great and multiform beast, which is so terrible, receives more liberty than it ought to have?

Obviously, you are right.

And are not the terms, self-will and discontent, used to convey a reproof, whenever the
b lion-like and serpentine creature is exalted and strengthened unharmoniously?

Exactly so.

Again, are not luxury and softness censured because they relax and unnerve this same creature, by begetting cowardice in him?

Undoubtedly they are.

And are not the reproachful names of flattery and servility bestowed, whenever a person subjugates this same spirited animal to the turbulent monster, and, to gratify the latter's insatiable craving for money, trains the former from the first, by a long course of insult, to become an ape instead of a lion?

Certainly you are right.
c
And why, let me ask you, are the mechanical and manual arts discredited? May we not assert that these terms imply that the most excellent element in the person, to whom they are attributed, is naturally weak, so that instead of being able to govern the creatures

within him, he pays them court, and can only learn how to flatter them?

Apparently so, he replied.

Then, in order that such a person may be governed by an authority similar to that by which the best man is governed, do we not maintain that he ought to be made the servant of that best man, in whom the divine element d is supreme? We do not indeed imagine that the servant ought to be governed to his own detriment, which Thrasymachus held to be the lot of the subject; on the contrary, we believe it to be better for every one to be governed by a wise and divine power, which ought, if possible, to be seated in the man's own heart, the only alternative being to impose it from without; in order that we may be all alike, as far as possible, and all mutual friends, due to the fact that we are steered by the same pilot.

Yes, that is quite right.

e         And this, I continued, is plainly the intention of law, that common friend of all the members of a city, and also of the supervising of children, which consists in withholding their freedom, until the time when we have formed a constitution in them, as we should in a city, and until, by cultivating the noblest principle of their nature, we have established 591 in their hearts a guardian and a sovereign, the very counterpart of our own—from which time forward we let them go free.

Yes that is plain.

On what principle then, Glaucon, and by what line of argument, can we maintain that it is profitable for a man to be unjust, or intemperate, or to commit any disgraceful act, which will sink him deeper in vice, though he may increase his wealth thereby, or acquire additional power?

We cannot maintain this in any way.

And by what argument can we uphold the advantages of disguising the doing of injustice, and escaping the penalties of it? Am I not b right in supposing that the man, who thus

escapes detection, grows still more vicious than before; whereas if he is found out and punished, the brute part of him is put to sleep and tamed, and the tame part is liberated, and the whole soul is molded to its best nature, and thus, through the acquisition of temperance and justice combined with wisdom, attains to a condition which is more precious than that attained by a body endowed with strength and beauty and health, in the exact proportion in which the soul is more precious than the body?

Yes, indeed, you are right.

Hence I conclude, the man who has a mind      c will direct all his energies through life to this one object—his plan being, in the first place, to honor those studies which will fashion this high character upon his soul, while at the same time he dishonors all others.

Obviously.

And as for his bodily habit and bodily support, in the second place, far from living devoted to the indulgence of brute irrational pleasure, he will show that even health is no object with him, and that he does not attach pre-eminent importance to the acquisition of strength or health or beauty, unless they are      d likely to make him temperate; because, in keeping the harmony of the body in tune, his constant aim is to preserve the harmonic symphony which resides in the soul.

Yes, no doubt it is, if he in truth cares for music.

Will he not also show how strictly he upholds that syntax and concord which ought to be maintained in the acquisition of wealth? And will he not avoid being dazzled by the congratulations of the crowd into multiplying infinitely the bulk of his wealth, which would bring him endless trouble?

I think he will.

On the contrary, an anxious look to his inward constitution, and guarding that none of      e its parts be pushed about by having too much or too little—these will be the principles by which, to the best of his ability, he will steer his course in increasing or spending his property.

Precisely so.

592    And, once more, in reference to honors, with the same standard constantly before his eyes, he will be glad to taste and participate in those which he thinks will make him a better man; whereas he will shun, in private and in public, those which he thinks likely to break up his existing condition.

If that is his chief concern, I suppose he will not consent to interfere with politics.

But surely you are wrong, I replied, for he certainly will—at least in his own city, though perhaps not in his fatherland, unless some divine chance should occur.

I understand, he replied. He will do so, you mean, in the city whose organization we have now completed, and which is confined to the region of speech; for I do not believe it is to be found anywhere on earth.                                    b

Well, said I, perhaps in heaven there is laid up a pattern of it for him who wishes to behold it, and, beholding, to organize himself accordingly. And the question of its present or future existence on earth is quite unimportant. For in any case he will adopt the practices of such a city, to the exclusion of those of every other.

Probably he will, he replied.

# Statesman

*Stranger.* Now it has been argued already and we have agreed that no large group of men is capable of acquiring any art, be it what you will.

*Young Socrates.* That stands as our agreed conclusion.

*Stranger.* Granted then that an art of kingly rule exists, the wealthy group or the whole citizen body would never be able to acquire this scientific art of statesmanship.

*Young Socrates.* How could they?

*Stranger.* It seems to follow that there is an invariable rule which these imitative con-
301    stitutions must obey if they mean to reproduce as far as they can that one real constitution, which is government by a real statesman using real statecraft. They must all keep strictly to the laws once they have been laid down and never transgress written enactments or established national customs.

*Young Socrates.* Quite right.

*Stranger.* When the wealthy seek to copy the ideal constitution we call the constitution which results 'aristocracy,' but when they disregard the laws, the constitution produced is 'oligarchy.'

*Young Socrates.* I suppose so.

*Stranger.* But when one individual governs according to laws, imitating the truly wise   b
ruler, we call him 'king.' We make no difference in name between the individual ruler guided by political science and the individual ruler guided by a right opinion and acting according to the laws.

*Young Socrates.* That seems to be so.

*Stranger.* And so if there really were an example of a truly wise ruler in power his name would undoubtedly be the same—'the king'—it could not be anything else. So the total of the names of the constitutions now under consideration comes to five only.

*Young Socrates.* So it seems.

From *Plato's Statesman*, translated by J. B. Skemp (New Haven, Conn., and London: Yale University Press, 1952). Reprinted by permission of the publisher.

*Stranger.* But stay, what of the case where one man rules but does not govern his actions

c  either by laws or by ancient customs, but claims falsely what only the truly wise ruler has a right to claim, and says that the 'best' course must be taken in defiance of written codes? If in fact it is only his passion and his ignorance that lead him to attempt to copy the true statesman in this defiance of law, must we not call him and all like him by the name of tyrant?

*Young Socrates.* Unquestionably.

*Stranger.* So then we have the tyrant and the king, then oligarchy and aristocracy, then democracy, all of which arise when men turn down the idea of the one true and scientific ruler. Men doubt whether any man will ever be found fit to bear such perfect rules. They despair of finding any one man willing and

d  able to rule with moral and intellectual insight and to render every man his due with strictest fairness. They feel sure that a man with such absolute power will be bound to employ it to the hurt and injury of his personal enemies and to put them out of the way. But it remains true that if the ideal ruler we have described were to appear on earth he would be acclaimed, and he would spend his days guiding in strictest justice and perfect felicity that one and only true commonwealth worthy of the name.

*Young Socrates.* That is so of course.

*Stranger.* We must take things as they are, however, and kings do not arise in cities in the

e  natural course of things in the way the royal bee is born in a beehive—one individual obviously outstanding in body and mind and capable of taking charge of things at once. And therefore it seems men gather together and work out written codes, chasing as fast as they can the fading vision of the true constitution.

*Young Socrates.* So it would seem.

*Stranger.* Is it any wonder that under these makeshift constitutions of ours hosts of ills have arisen and more must be expected in the future? They all rest on the sandy foundation of action according to law and custom without real scientific insight. Another art that worked

302  on such a foundation would obviously ruin all that it sought to build up. But something even more remarkable than these besetting ills is the sheer native strength a city possesses nevertheless. For all our cities, as we know, have been subject to such ills for many generations now, and yet some of them have not come to ruin but still stand firm. However, we see many instances of cities going down like sinking ships to their destruction. There have been such wrecks in the past and there surely will be others in the future, caused by the wickedness of captains and crews alike. For these are guilty men, whose sin is supreme ignorance of what matters most. They are men who know little or

b  nothing of real political truth and yet they consider themselves to know it from end to end and suppose that they are better instructed in this art than in any other.

*Young Socrates.* Very true.

*Stranger.* All these imperfect constitutions are difficult to live under, but we might ask ourselves which of them is hardest to bear and which is most tolerable. Ought we perhaps to examine this matter, though it is not directly relevant to our appointed theme? After all one must remember that, speaking quite generally, the aim of all the actions of men everywhere is to secure for themselves the most tolerable life they can.

*Young Socrates.* Then we can hardly help considering the question.

*Stranger.* There is one of three constitu-

c  tions which you must regard as being at once the hardest to live under and the easiest.

*Young Socrates.* How do you mean?

*Stranger.* I just want to remind you that at the beginning of this supplementary discussion we enumerated three constitutions—the rule of one, the rule of the few, and the rule of the many.

*Young Socrates.* We did.

*Stranger.* Dividing each of three into two let us make six, having first separated the true constitution from all, calling it the seventh.

*Young Socrates.* How shall we divide the three others?

d  *Stranger.* Under the rule of one we get kingly rule and tyranny; under the rule of the few, as we said, come the auspicious form of it, aristocracy, and also oligarchy. As for the subdividing of democracy, though we gave both forms of it one name previously, we must now treat it as twofold.

*Young Socrates.* How is this? How can it be divided?

e  *Stranger.* By the same division as the others, even though the word 'democracy' proves to be doing double duty. Rule according to law is as possible under democracy as under the other constitutions.

*Young Socrates.* Yes, it is.

*Stranger.* This division of democracy into two kinds was not serviceable previously as we indicated at the time, for we were seeking then to define a perfect constitution. Now, however, we have excluded the perfect constitution from our reckoning and have before us those that have to serve us as constitutions in default of it. In this group we find the principle of obedience to law or contravention of law dividing each type of ruler into two types.

*Young Socrates.* So it seems from the argument that was put forward just now.

*Stranger.* The rule of one man, if it has been kept within the traces, so to speak, by the written rules we call laws, is the best of all the six. But when it is lawless it is hard, and the most grievous to have to endure.

*Young Socrates.* So it would seem.

303  *Stranger.* As for the rule of a few, just as the few constitute a middle term between the one and the many, so we must regard the rule of the few as of middle potency for good or ill. The rule of the many is weakest in every way;

it is not capable of any real good or of any serious evil as compared with the other two. This is because in a democracy sovereignty has been divided out in small portions among a large number of rulers. If therefore all three constitutions are law-abiding, democracy is the worst of the three, but if all three flout the laws, democracy is the best of them. Thus if all constitutions are unprincipled the best thing to do is to live in a democracy. But when constitutions are lawful and ordered, democracy is the least desirable, and monarchy, the first of the six, is by far the best to live under—unless of course the seventh is possible, for that must always be exalted, like a god among mortals, above all other constitutions.

*Young Socrates.* Things do seem to work out in this way, and so we must take your advice and act as you say.

*Stranger.* Therefore all who take part in one of these governments—apart from the one based on real knowledge—are to be distinguished from the true statesman. They are not statesmen; they are party leaders, leaders of bogus governments and themselves as bogus as their systems. The supreme imitators and tricksters, they are of all Sophists the arch-Sophists.

*Young Socrates.* It seems to me that the wheel has come full circle, now that the title of Sophist goes to those who most deserve it, to the men who get themselves called political leaders.

*Stranger.* So this fantastic pageant that seemed like some strange masque of centaurs or some band of satyrs stands revealed for what it is. At much pains we have succeeded at last in distinguishing them and setting them apart, as we must, from all true practice of statesmanship.

*Young Socrates.* So we see.

*Stranger.* There remains another task, and it is even more difficult because the class to be set apart is closer akin to the kingly ruler and also in itself harder to discern clearly. It seems to me that we have reached a point where we have to act like gold refiners.

*Young Socrates.* How so?

*Stranger.* We are told that at the first stage of their work they separate off earth and stones and much else from the ore. When these are gone there still remain those precious substances akin to gold which are so combined with it as to be separable only in the furnace; I mean bronze and silver and sometimes adamant as well. These are removed only with difficulty as the metal is tried in the refining fire until at last the process yields the sight of unalloyed gold separated off by itself.

*Young Socrates.* Yes, they do say that refining is done like that.

*Stranger.* It looks as though we are in a like situation. We have separated off the elements which are quite different from statesmanship, the elements which are quite foreign and repugnant to it, but there still remain the precious elements which are akin to it. These include the art of generalship, the art of administering justice, and that department of the art of public speaking which is closely allied to the kingly art. This last persuades men to do what is right and therefore takes its share in controlling what goes on in a true community. How can we best separate these arts also from statesmanship and so bring out the nature of the statesman as such, in his essential character? That, after all, is our present object.

*Young Socrates.* Clearly we must make the attempt by one means or another.

*Stranger.* If trying will do it, he shall be shown in his true character. Music will provide us with an example which will help us in our task. I will begin by putting a question to you.

*Young Socrates.* What is it?

*Stranger.* There is such a thing as learning the principles of music or the principles of any of the crafts, is there not?

*Young Socrates.* Yes.

*Stranger.* But are we willing to admit that there exists an art of a higher order also concerned with this process of acquiring special skills? This second art is the one whose province is to decide whether or not we *ought* to learn any particular art.

*Young Socrates.* Yes, we will attest the existence of an art of this higher order.

*Stranger.* We must also agree then, that it is to be distinguished from all arts of the lower order.

*Young Socrates.* Yes.

*Stranger.* Ought there to be no priority at all as between these two orders of art? On the other hand, if there is to be priority, must the lower order control the higher or the higher guide and control the lower?

*Young Socrates.* The higher order should control the lower.

*Stranger.* Your decision is then, that the art which decides whether we learn a skill or not ought to have control of the art which actually teaches us that skill.

*Young Socrates.* Yes, certainly.

*Stranger.* Then in the same way the art which decides whether persuasion should or should not be used ought to control the operation of the art of persuasion itself.

*Young Socrates.* Undoubtedly.

*Stranger.* Which is the art to which we must assign the task of persuading the general mass of the population by telling them suitable stories rather than by giving them formal instruction?

*Young Socrates.* I should say that it is obvious that this is the province to be assigned to rhetoric.

*Stranger.* But to which art must we assign the function of deciding whether in any particular situation we must proceed by persuasion, or by coercive measures against a group of men, or whether it is right to take no action at all?

*Young Socrates.* The art which can teach us how to decide that will be the art which controls rhetoric and the art of public speaking.

*Stranger.* This activity can be none other than the work of the statesman, I suggest.

*Young Socrates.* Excellent! That is exactly what it is.

e *Stranger.* Oratory, it seems, has been quickly set apart from statesmanship. It is distinct from statesmanship, and yet its auxiliary.

*Young Socrates.* Yes.

*Stranger.* Now we must consider the working of another art.

*Young Socrates.* Which is that?

*Stranger.* Consider the taking of decisions on military strategy once war has been declared by the state on an enemy state. What shall we say about this? Is such decision governed by no art at all, or shall we say that there is most certainly an art involved here?

*Young Socrates.* How could we dream of saying that no art is concerned? Surely generalship and the whole art of warfare operates precisely in this field.

*Stranger.* But which is the art which possesses the knowledge and capacity to form a reasoned decision whether to fight or settle a dispute on friendly terms? Is this the work of generalship or does it belong to another art?

*Young Socrates.* Consistency to our earlier argument requires us to say that it is a different one which is involved.

305 *Stranger.* So if our views here are to be consistent with our earlier views on the place of rhetoric, we must decide that this second art controls generalship.

*Young Socrates.* I agree.

*Stranger.* What art can we attempt to enthrone as queen over that mighty and dreadful art, the art of war in all its range, except the art of truly royal rule?

*Young Socrates.* None other.

*Stranger.* Then we must not describe the art that generals practice as statesmanship, for it proves to be but a servant of statesmanship.

*Young Socrates.* Apparently that is so.

b *Stranger.* Now turn to another art and let us consider the activity of judges who make straight judgments.

*Young Socrates.* By all means.

*Stranger.* Does its province extend beyond the sphere of the mutual contractual obligations of the citizens? It has to act in this sphere by judging what is just or unjust according to the standards set up for it and embodied in the legal rules which it has received from the kingly lawgiver. It shows its peculiar virtue by coming to an impartial decision on the conflicting claims it examines, by refusing to pervert the lawgiver's ordinance through yielding to bribery or threats or sentimental appeals, and by rising above all considerations of personal friendship or enmity.

*Young Socrates.* Yes, that is so. You have given us, sir, a succinct account of the juryman's function and of his duty.

*Stranger.* We find, then, that the power of the judges is a lesser thing than the power of the king. The judge guards the law and serves the king.

*Young Socrates.* So it would seem.

*Stranger.* If you will view the three arts we have spoken of as a group with a common character you will be bound to see that none of them has turned out to be itself the art of statesmanship. This is because it is not the province of the real kingly art to act for itself but rather to control the work of the arts which instruct us in the methods of action. The kingly art controls them according to its power to perceive the right occasions for undertaking and setting in motion the great enterprises of state. The other arts must do what they are told to do by the kingly art.

*Young Socrates.* Precisely so.

*Stranger.* The three arts we have just treated in detail may not control one another. They may not even control themselves, in fact. Each has its special field of action and each is entitled to the name which designates its proper sphere.

*Young Socrates.* So it would seem.

*Stranger.* There is an art which controls all these arts. It is concerned with the laws and with all that belongs to the life of the community. It weaves all into its unified fabric with perfect skill. It is a universal art and so we call it by a name of universal scope. That name is one which I believe to belong to this art and to this alone, the name of 'statesmanship.'

*Young Socrates.* Yes, I agree absolutely.

*Stranger.* Now that all the classes of arts active in the government of the state have been distinguished, shall we go on to scrutinize statesmanship and base our scrutiny of it on the art of weaving which provides our example for it?

*Young Socrates.* Most certainly.

*Stranger.* Then we must describe the kingly weaving process. What is it like? How is it done? What is the fabric that results from its labors?

306 *Young Socrates.* These are just the questions we must answer.

*Stranger.* The task of finding the answers is hard, but we cannot shirk it.

*Young Socrates.* No, we must find them at all costs.

*Stranger.* To say that 'one kind of goodness clashes with another kind of goodness' is to preach a doctrine which is an easy target for the disputatious who appeal to commonly accepted ideas.

b *Young Socrates.* I do not follow you.

*Stranger.* Then let me put the matter in this way. You regard courage as one part of virtue I suppose.

*Young Socrates.* Surely.

*Stranger.* Moderation differs from courage but is a specific kind of goodness just as courage is.

*Young Socrates.* Yes.

*Stranger.* We have now to be daring and make a startling statement about these two virtues.

*Young Socrates.* What is it?

*Stranger.* This pair of virtues are in a cer-
c tain sense enemies from of old, ranged in opposition to each other in many realms of life.

*Young Socrates.* What do you mean?

*Stranger.* The doctrine is not a familiar one by any means. I suppose that the usual statement is that all the several parts of goodness are in mutual accord.

*Young Socrates.* Yes.

*Stranger.* Then we must give our very special attention to the matter. Is the position quite so simple as that? Is there not, on the contrary, something inherent in them which keeps alive a family quarrel among them?

*Young Socrates.* Certainly we must consider this. Please tell us how we are to do so.

*Stranger.* We must consider instances drawn from all levels of existence of things which we regard as excellent and yet classify as mutually opposed.

*Young Socrates.* Please explain still more clearly.

*Stranger.* Take swiftness and speed as an instance—swiftness of mind and body and d rapid vibration of sound in a voice. Such swiftness may be seen in an actual living person or it may be represented in music or painting. Have you ever praised examples of such swiftness or listened with approval when one of your friends praised them?

*Young Socrates.* Yes.

*Stranger.* Do you happen to remember the way in which the approval is expressed in all these instances?

*Young Socrates.* No, I can't say that I remember that in the least.

*Stranger.* I wonder if I could really manage to put my thoughts on the subject into words and make them clear to you.

*Young Socrates.* I am sure you could.       e

*Stranger.* You seem to think it a light task! However, let us see the principle at work wherever those mutually opposite qualities are manifested. We admire speed and intensity and vivacity in many forms of action and under all kinds of circumstances. But whether the swiftness of mind or body or the vibrant power of the voice is being praised, we always find ourselves using one word to praise it—the word 'vigorous.'

*Young Socrates.* How so?

*Stranger.* 'That is alert and vigorous,' we say in the first instance, in another case, 'That is speedy and vigorous,' or, in yet another case, 'That is intense and vigorous.' In all the instances we use this epithet 'vigorous,' as applying in common to the people or things concerned, in order to express our approval of this quality in them.

307  *Young Socrates.* True.

*Stranger.* On the other hand, do we not quite often find ourselves approving gentleness and quietness when it is shown in many kinds of human behavior?

*Young Socrates.* Yes, very decidedly.

*Stranger.* Do we not describe this behavior by using an epithet which is the exact opposite of 'vigorous,' which was the term we applied to the other group of things?

*Young Socrates.* How do you mean?

*Stranger.* We constantly admire quietness and moderation, in processes of restrained thinking, in gentle deeds, in a smooth deep
b  voice, in steady balance in movement, or in suitable restraint in artistic representation. Whenever we express such approval do we not use the expression 'controlled' to describe all these excellences rather than the word 'vigorous'?

*Young Socrates.* Very true.

*Stranger.* But when we find either of these kinds of behavior appearing out of its due time, we have different names for each of them and in that case we express our censure by attributing quite contrary qualities when we mention them.

*Young Socrates.* How so?

*Stranger.* If speed and swiftness are excessive and unseasonable and if the voice is harsh to the point of being violent we speak of all these as 'excessive' and even 'maniacal.'
c  Unseasonable heaviness, slowness, or softness we call 'cowardly' or 'indolent.' One can generalize further. The very classes 'energy' and 'moderation' are ranged in mutual exclusive-

ness and in opposition to each other; it is not simply a case of conflict between these particular manifestations of them. They never meet in the activities of life without causing conflicts, and if we pursue the matter further, by studying people whose characters come to be dominated by either of them, we shall find inevitable conflict between them and people of the opposite type.

*Young Socrates.* In what sphere do these conflicts occur?

*Stranger.* In all the things we have just considered, of course, but in many others too,   d
I think. Men react to situations in one way or another according to the affinities of their own dispositions. They favor some forms of action as being akin to their own character, and they recoil from acts arising from opposite tendencies as being foreign to themselves. Thus men come into violent conflict with one another on many issues.

*Young Socrates.* Yes, they seem to do so.

*Stranger.* Considered as a conflict of temperaments, this is a mere trifle, but when the conflict arises over matters of high public importance it becomes the most inimical of all the plagues which can threaten the life of a community.

*Young Socrates.* What kind of evils do you mean?

*Stranger.* Of course I mean all which con-   e
cern the organization of the community as a whole. Men who are notable for moderation are always ready to support 'peace and tranquillity.' They want to keep themselves to themselves and to mind their own business. They conduct all their dealings with their fellow citizens on this principle and are prone to take the same line in foreign policy and preserve peace at any price with foreign states. Because of their indulgence of this passion for peace at the wrong times, whenever they are able to carry their policy into effect they become unwarlike themselves without being aware of it and render their young men unwar-

like as well. Thus they are at the mercy of the chance aggressor. He swoops down on them and the result is that within a very few years they and their children and all the community to which they belong wake up to find that their freedom is gone and that they are reduced to slavery.

308 *Young Socrates.* You have described a hard and bitter experience.

*Stranger.* What then is the history of the party whose bent is rather toward strong action? Do we not find them forever dragging their cities into war and bringing them up against powerful foes on all sides just because they love a military existence too fiercely? And what is the result? Either they destroy their country altogether, or else they bring it into subjection to its enemies just as surely as the peace party did.

b *Young Socrates.* Yes, that is true too.

*Stranger.* Can we deny, then, that in these high matters the two types of character concerned are bound to become hostile to one another and so take up opposing party lines?

*Young Socrates.* We are bound to admit it.

*Stranger.* We have discovered, then, the answer to the question into which we set out to inquire when we began this conversation. We find that important parts of goodness are at variance with one another and that they set at variance the men in whom they predominate.

*Young Socrates.* So it seems.

*Stranger.* There is a further point to consider.

*Young Socrates.* What is it?

c *Stranger.* Does any art which works by combining materials deliberately choose to make any of its products, even the least important of them, out of a combination of good material with bad? Does not every art, whatever material it works in, reject bad material as far as possible and use what is good and serviceable? The materials may be alike or dissimilar, but surely it is desirable that they should

be sound, so that the art may combine them to form one product and fashion them to a structure proper to their specific function.

*Young Socrates.* Yes.

*Stranger.* Surely then the true and genuine d statesmanship we are concerned with could never choose deliberately to construct the life of any community out of a combination of good characters with bad characters? Obviously it will first put the young children to the test in games. After this first test it will go on to entrust the young to competent educators trained to render this particular service, but it will retain direction and oversight of them all the time. This is exactly like weaving. The art of weaving hands over the materials it intends to use for the fabric to the carders and others concerned with preparatory processes, and yet it watches their work at every stage, retaining the direction and oversight itself and indicating to each auxiliary art such duties as it deems that e each can usefully perform to make ready the threads for its own task of fashioning the web.

*Young Socrates.* Precisely.

*Stranger.* This is the way I see the true statesman dealing with those who rear and educate children according to the educational laws. He keeps the power of direction to himself. The only form of training he will permit is the one by which the educator produces the type of character fitted for his own task of weaving the web of state. He bids the educator encourage the young in these activities and in no others. Some pupils cannot be taught to be courageous and moderate and to acquire the other virtuous tendencies, but are impelled to godlessness and to vaunting pride and injustice by the drive of an evil nature. These the king expels from the community. He puts them to death or banishes them or else he chastises them by the severest public disgrace.

*Young Socrates.* So one usually hears it stated.

*Stranger.* Furthermore, he makes those who prove incapable of rising above ignorance 309 and groveling subservience slaves to the rest of the community.

*Young Socrates.* Quite rightly.

*Stranger.* The statesman will then take over all the rest—all those who, under the training process, do in fact achieve sufficient nobility of character to stand up to the royal weaving process and yet to submit to it while it combines them all scientifically into a unity. Those in whom courage predominates will be treated by the statesman as having the firm warplike character as one might call it. The others will be used by him for what we may likewise call the supple, soft, wooflike strands of the web. He then sets about his task of combining and weaving together these two groups exhibiting their mutually opposed characters.

*Young Socrates.* How does he do it?

*Stranger.* He first unites that element in their souls which is supernatural by a divine bond, since this element in them is akin to the divine. After this supernatural link will come the natural bond, human ties to supplement the divine ones.

*Young Socrates.* What do you mean by this? Once more I do not follow.

*Stranger.* When there arises in the soul of men a right opinion concerning what is good, just, and profitable, and what is the opposite of these—an opinion based on absolute truth and settled as an unshakable conviction—I declare that such a conviction is a manifestation of the divine occurring in a race which is in truth of supernatural lineage.

*Young Socrates.* It could not be more suitably described.

*Stranger.* Do we realize that it is the true statesman, in that he is the good and true lawgiver, who alone is able—for who else should possess the power—to forge by the wondrous inspiration of the kingly art this bond of true conviction uniting the hearts of the young folk of whom we were speaking just now—the young folk who have profited as they should from their education?

*Young Socrates.* That is certainly as one would expect.

*Stranger.* The ruler who cannot weld that bond we will never honor with those glorious titles, 'statesman' and 'king.'

*Young Socrates.* Most rightly not.

*Stranger.* Well then, will it not work out like this? The soul full of vigor and courage will be made gentle by its grasp of this truth and there is nothing as well calculated as this to make it a willing member of a community based on justice. If such a soul refused this gift, it will sink in the scale and become savage like a beast.

*Young Socrates.* True.

*Stranger.* What of the moderate soul? Sharing this firm conviction of truth, will it not be truly moderate and prudent, or at any rate prudent enough, to meet its public duties? But if it refuses to share this conviction, it deserves to be called foolish and our reproach of it is entirely proper.

*Young Socrates.* It is indeed.

*Stranger.* Do we agree then that this interweaving, this linking together, can never be lasting and permanent if vicious men are joined with other vicious men or good men with vicious? Surely no art would seriously try to forge such links where these faults of character exist?

*Young Socrates.* How could it?

*Stranger.* But in those of noble nature from their earliest days whose nurture too has been all it should be, the laws can foster the growth of this common bond of conviction and only in these. This is the talisman appointed for them by the design of pure intelligence. This most godlike bond alone can unite the elements of goodness which are diverse in nature and would else be opposing in tendency.

*Young Socrates.* Most true.

*Stranger.* There remain the other bonds, the human ones. When one sets to work with the divine link already forged it is not very difficult to see what these are and then to set about the forging of them.

*Young Socrates.* But what are these links and how can they be forged?

*Stranger.* They are forged by establishing intermarriage between the two types so that the children of the mixed marriages are so to speak shared between them and by restricting private arrangements for marrying off daughters. Most men make unsuitable matches from the point of view of the begetting of children of the best type of character.

*Young Socrates.* What can you mean?

*Stranger.* Would anyone think it worth while to censure in any respect the prevalent practice of pursuing wealth or influence when making such matches?

*Young Socrates.* No, there is nothing very wrong in it.

*Stranger.* But when we are specially concerned with the very people who make much of being 'well connected,' justice requires that we should be all the more outspoken if we find them acting unsuitably.

*Young Socrates.* That is reasonable.

*Stranger.* They do not act on any sound or self-consistent principle. See how they pursue the immediate satisfaction of their desire by hailing with delight those who are like themselves and by disliking those who are different. Thus they assign far too great an importance to their own likes and dislikes.

*Young Socrates.* In what way?

*Stranger.* The moderate natures look for a partner like themselves, and so far as they can, they choose their wives from women of this quiet type. When they have daughters to bestow in marriage, once again they look for this type of character in the prospective husband. The courageous class does just the same thing and looks for others of the same type. All this goes on, though both types should be doing exactly the opposite.

*Young Socrates.* How can they, and why should they?

*Stranger.* Because if a courageous character is reproduced for many generations without any admixture of the moderate type, the natural course of development is that at first it becomes superlatively powerful but in the end it breaks out into sheer fury and madness.

*Young Socrates.* That is to be expected.

*Stranger.* But the character which is too full of modest reticence and untinged by valor and audacity, if reproduced after its kind for many generations, becomes too dull to respond to the challenges of life and in the end becomes quite incapable of acting at all.

*Young Socrates.* Yes, this is also the result one would expect.

*Stranger.* I repeat what I was saying. There is no difficulty in forging these human bonds if the divine bond has been forged first. That bond is a conviction about values and standards shared by both types of character. There is one absorbing preoccupation for the kingly weaver as he makes the web of state. He must never permit the gentle characters to be separated from the brave ones; to avoid this he must make the fabric close and firm by working common convictions in the hearts of each type of citizen and making public honors and triumphs subserve this end, and finally, each must be involved with the other in the solemn pledges of matrimony. When he has woven his web smooth and 'close-woven,' as the phrase goes, out of men of these differing types, he must entrust the various offices of state to them to be shared in all cases between them.

*Young Socrates.* How can he do this?

*Stranger.* When a single magistrate happens to be needed, the statesman must choose a man possessing both characteristics and set him in authority. Where several magistrates are wanted he must bring together some representatives of each type to share the duties. Magistrates of the moderate type are exceedingly cautious, fair, and tenacious of precedent, but they lack pungency and the drive which makes for efficiency.

*Young Socrates.* Yes, that certainly seems to be a fair summing up of the case.

*Stranger.* The courageous type for their part have far less of the gifts of fairness and caution than their moderate brethren, but they have in a marked degree the drive that gets things done. A community can never function well either in the personal intercourse of its citizens or in its public activities unless both of these elements of character are present and active.

*Young Socrates.* Of course that is so.

*Stranger.* Now we have reached the appointed end of the weaving of the web of state. It is fashioned by the statesman's weaving; the strands run true, and these strands are the gentle and the brave. Here these strands are woven together into a unified character. For this unity is won where the kingly art draws the life of both types into a true fellowship by mutual concord and by ties of friendship. It is the finest and best of all fabrics. It infolds all who dwell in the city, bond or free, in its firm contexture. Its kingly weaver maintains his control and oversight over it, and it lacks nothing that makes for happiness so far as happiness is obtainable in a human community.

*Young Socrates.* You have done what we requested of you, sir, and you have set beside your definition of the Sophist a picture drawn to perfection of the true king and statesman.

# ARISTOTLE

~

## INTRODUCTION

## RICHARD KRAUT

Aristotle (384–322 bc) was born in Stagira, a town near the Aegean Sea in the north of Greece, and was raised in the royal residence of Macedon, where his father, Nicomachus, was a doctor attached to the court of King Amyntas III. In 367, at the age of 17, he was sent to Athens to study at the Academy, a school established by Plato for inquiry into philosophical, scientific, and political questions. He remained as one of its members for twenty years, and departed at Plato's death in 347. He subsequently took up residence in several locations where he could pursue his research—Assos (in Asia Minor) and Lesbos (in the eastern Aegean)—and then in 343 returned to Macedon, where he remained until 336. Ancient sources tell us that during this time he was a tutor to the son of Philip II, Alexander (familiar to us as Alexander the Great), who was 13 when Aristotle arrived. Philip had taken over the throne of Macedon in 359, at the end of a power struggle caused by the death of Amyntas some ten years earlier. During his reign Macedonia's military power increased greatly, and in 338, having defeated Athens and Corinth in the battle of Chaeronea, it held sway over the Greek world. Philip was assassinated in 336 (a fact noted without comment by Aristotle at *Politics* V.10 1311b1–2). The following year Aristotle returned to Athens and established his own center of research and teaching in the Lyceum. During that period his wife, Pythias, whom he had married during his stay in Assos, died, and he formed a relationship with Herpyllis, who bore him a son, named Nicomachus (after his grandfather). Aristotle departed once again in 323 when Alexander died and several cities, including

Athens, unsuccessfully tried to escape from the control of Macedon. There is little doubt that this second departure (one year before his death in 322) was motivated by the Athenian revolt against Macedon. Although Aristotle spent a considerable part of his adult life in Athens, he was never an Athenian citizen, and his relationship with the city was, at times, evidently strained.

Ancient testimony about Aristotle's works indicates that many of them were lost during the centuries that followed his death. Some were written in dialogue form—the genre favored by Plato—and were intended for a broad audience. The works that survive, some in an unfinished and roughly organized form, are highly concentrated in expression and are intended for a more specialized group of students. Some of them formed the basis for lectures that Aristotle gave at the Lyceum. They occupy almost 2,500 pages of small print in modern editions, and cover nearly all of the branches of knowledge that existed in Aristotle's time or that he helped invent.

Aristotle was the founder of the formal study of inferential relationships (logic), and he developed a conception of knowledge and reality that gives a larger role to perception, material composition, and empirical research than had been allowed by Plato. A large proportion of his writings are devoted to the exploration of scientific matters (particularly biology), and to questions about the concepts (for example: cause, essence, change) that must be employed in our understanding of nature. He champions the idea that we must pursue knowledge by different methods, each appropriate to the subject matter under investigation. Practical questions, for example, must be explored in order to improve human life, and not simply for the sake of knowledge. By contrast, the celestial world and biological species (both of which Aristotle took to be eternal and unchanging) are to be studied because theoretical understanding is by itself a precious thing. Aristotle holds that the proper pursuit of scientific understanding will lead to the realization that there must be a single divine cause of the universe. His god is a perfect being that causes all change without itself being changed; this god should inspire our love and admiration, but does not have moral qualities or a concern for human life.

Although Aristotle believes that one aspect of the human soul survives the destruction of the body, he does not follow Plato in regarding our mortal existence as a time of preparation for a future life, or as a punishment for mistakes we made in a previous life—for he holds that we have no such past or future lives. To talk about the soul (and Aristotle believes that all living things have souls, even plants and animals) is not to refer to a self-standing entity that can inhabit different bodies, but rather to the various powers that an embodied thing has: such processes as growth, reproduction, perception, and locomotion. Since humans are a kind of animal, we of course have the powers of the soul that all animals have, but we differ from the rest of nature in that we also have the capacity to make choices, experience emotions that are susceptible to rational control, learn a language, and look for and find reasons for what we believe. All of these capacities are comprehended by Aristotle's word for reason (*logos*). We are unique in that the matter of which we are composed is arranged in a way that makes us capable of all of these activities of reason.

Because Aristotle takes human beings to be essentially enmattered, he assumes that death is an event that brings our well-being to a close, and the whole of his practical philosophy is therefore devoted to the question of what it is for mortal beings like ourselves to fare well. His principal work devoted to this question is the *Nicomachean Ethics*. The word "Nicomachean" is not used by Aristotle himself; presumably it was added by a later editor, and is a reference to Aristotle's son or father. (An earlier treatise, similar in content and structure to the *Nicomachean Ethics,* is called the *Eudemian Ethics.* Eudemus was a student and friend of Aristotle's and shared many of his research interests.) But the word *ethos,* from which our "ethics" is derived, is ubiquitous in Aristotle's practical writings, and he refers to some of these as ethical discourses. *Ethos* means "character," and the *Nicomachean Ethics* therefore announces in its title that it is a study of character and the many forms it takes.

But the starting point of Aristotle's practical thought is not character but *eudaimonia* (often translated "happiness"). He points out that our desires and actions are not all at the same level: some goals and activities are pursued for the sake of something else, and those further goals are in turn subordinate to others. What lies at the top of this hierarchy is of the utmost importance, and it is therefore the foremost task of ethical theory to arrive at a better understanding of what it is. Aristotle holds that the best conception of our highest end will identify it not with some distant goal that we achieve only at the end of our lives, or with some extrinsic reward that can easily be lost, but with the day-by-day excellent use we can make of our powers as rational beings. Happiness, in other words, consists in the excellent or virtuous activity of the rational soul, and all lower goods (honors, pleasures, power, wealth) are to be pursued because they in some way accompany excellent activity or provide us with the resources we need to engage in virtuous activity over the course of our lives. Character is of central importance to human life because in order to excel in all of its many important spheres, we must learn how to become a certain sort of person. We must train our judgment and emotions so that we know which pleasures to pursue, how to control our fear and make effective decisions in the face of great danger, how to spend money wisely and avoid both excessive disdain for or attraction to it, how to make fair allocations of goods to others, and so on. In each of these areas of life, success involves skill at finding the act that best avoids excess or deficiency, and therefore each of the ethical virtues is a state that lies between a vice of excess and a vice of deficiency.

Aristotle holds that the life that most fully develops the practical virtues is one of active engagement in the most important deliberative matters that face one's city—a political life, in other words. Although he believes that political activity should not be valued as highly as philosophy (which includes the study of science and culminates in reverence for the divine), he realizes that a life of theoretical study will be of interest only to a small number of his contemporaries. Most members of his audience, he assumes, plan to lead a political life, and so he takes his principal task as a practical philosopher to be the examination of the various ways in which civic life can be improved. He conceives of the *Nicomachean Ethics* as a political treatise, because the political leaders he is training must be guided by a full understanding of the proper goal of all legislation: human well-being.

The treatise he refers to as *Politics* was written during his final period of residence in Athens, as were his ethical works. Book I provides a preliminary discussion of the origin of the *polis* (often translated "city," or "state," or "city-state"), and the elements out of which it is made (households). The growth of the city out of smaller social units provides evidence that it is the sort of thing that exists by nature rather than convention. There is nothing arbitrary about leading a life devoted to the well-being of the political community, because the *polis* is the inevitable outgrowth of our natural psychological dispositions. Just as a seed naturally tends to develop in ways that serve its good, so human beings, over many generations, will come to participate in complex social organizations governed by collective deliberation. That is what Aristotle means when he says that human beings are political animals. But he also holds that some human beings (most women, and most inhabitants of lands to the north or east of Greece) do not possess the capacity to engage in political deliberation, and must play subordinate roles in civic life—marriage partners (in the case of Greek women), and slaves (in the case of non-Greek men and women).

The rest of the *Politics* serves a double purpose: it investigates the question, "What is the best constitution we can achieve, when we are at our best?," and it also examines the various ways in which any regime—even a tyranny—can be improved. (The project of constitutional amelioration was pursued in the Lyceum through empirical research: it produced studies of the constitutions of 158 cities. Only one—that of Athens—survives; it was discovered in the late nineteenth century.) Aristotle's ideal city is one in which all citizens are educated to be virtuous. Unlike the utopian scheme Plato depicts in the *Republic,* it is a community in which all citizens participate as equals, each having received from the city the same education, and all sharing a single conception of well-being. Although Aristotle claims in Book I that the city is naturally prior to each of its citizens, he does not take this to mean that the city is the only community to which we should form an allegiance. Against the *Republic,* which proposes the abolition of the family and private property within the ruling class, Aristotle holds, in Book II of the *Politics,* that young children are best cared for by their own parents and that property will best serve the common good if each citizen has control over the allocation of his resources.

Books III through VI examine a wide variety of political systems, ranging from such correct forms as kingship, aristocracy, and *politeia* (often translated "polity," or "republic"), to the defective regimes that correspond to them—tyranny, oligarchy, and democracy. Aristotle has a deep awareness of the ways in which the mutual hatred of rich and poor corrodes public life. His assumption that democracy is inherently corrupt rests on his allegation that in cities like Athens the poor develop a class consciousness that undermines their capacity to treat the wealthy in a fair way. But he believes that the rich are no less prone to class bias than the poor, and argues that the poor can achieve a wisdom of sorts when they meet collectively—provided that they have a minimal degree of decency. The best sort of political system that requires only an ordinary level of character development is one in which most citizens have a middling level of wealth and thereby avoid the corrupting effects that are likely when resources are excessive or deficient. That middling kind of constitution, Aristotle thinks, would not be as desirable as a kingship or aristocracy, because the latter are regimes governed by individuals so outstanding that the collective wisdom of the many is no match for theirs. But he is pessimistic about the chances of achieving any of the three correct political systems. For the most part, political leaders must make the best of bad materials. They must learn how to make oligarchies and democracies—the rule of the rich or of the poor—less uniformly oligarchical or democratic. Elites and masses must learn how to work with each other, each party using its mistrust of the other to ensure that the injustices so common in political life do not get out of hand. Evidently, Aristotle is fully aware that politics must usually settle for modest accomplishments, but that does not undermine his conviction that, for most of us, a life devoted to the public good is the best we can achieve.

Brief and accessible accounts of Aristotle's approach to philosophy are presented by J. L. Ackrill, *Aristotle the Philosopher* (New York: Oxford University Press, 1981); Jonathan

Lear, *Aristotle: The Desire to Understand* (Cambridge: Cambridge University Press, 1988); and Jonathan Barnes (ed.), *The Cambridge Companion to Aristotle* (Cambridge: Cambridge University Press, 1995). A comprehensive discussion of his epistemology, metaphysics, ethics, and politics can be found in Terence Irwin, *Aristotle's First Principles* (Oxford: Clarendon Press, 1988). Full analyses of nearly all of the topics in the *Nicomachean Ethics* are available in W. F. R. Hardie, *Aristotle's Ethical Theory,* 2d ed. (Oxford: Clarendon Press, 1980); and Sarah Broadie, *Ethics with Aristotle* (New York: Oxford University Press, 1991). Aristotle's moral psychology is discussed by John M. Cooper in *Reason and Emotion* (Princeton, N.J.: Princeton University Press, 1998), chs. 8–19. The relation between contemplative and practical activity is examined in Richard Kraut, *Aristotle on the Human Good* (Princeton, N.J.: Princeton University Press, 1989); and C. D. C. Reeve, *Practices of Reason* (Oxford: Clarendon Press, 1992). Helpful collections of essays are: Amelie Rorty, *Essays on Aristotle's Ethics* (Berkeley: University of California Press, 1980); Nancy Sherman, *Aristotle's Ethics: Critical Essays* (Lanham, Md.: Rowman & Littlefield, 1999); and David Keyt and Fred Miller, Jr., *A Companion to Aristotle's Politics* (Oxford: Blackwell, 1991). Wide-ranging studies of Aristotle as a political philosopher are: Steven Salkever, *Finding the Mean* (Princeton, N.J.: Princeton University Press, 1990); Bernard Yack, *The Problems of a Political Animal* (Berkeley: University of California Press, 1993); and Fred Miller, Jr., *Nature, Justice and Rights in Aristotle's Politics* (Oxford: Clarendon Press, 1995). Aristotle's conception of value is contrasted with that of Plato by Martha C. Nussbaum, *The Fragility of Goodness* (Cambridge: Cambridge University Press, 1986). *The Cambridge History of Greek and Roman Political Thought,* edited by Christopher Rowe and Malcolm Schofield, in association with Simon Harrison and Melissa Lane (Cambridge: Cambridge University Press, 2000), contains five chapters on Aristotle's politics.

# Nicomachean Ethics

## BOOK I • THE GOOD FOR MAN

### Subject of Our Inquiry

*All human activities aim at some good: some goods subordinate to others*

1. Every art and every inquiry, and similarly every action and pursuit, is thought to aim at some good; and for this reason the good has rightly been declared to be that at which all things aim. But a cer-

tain difference is found among ends; some are activities, others are products apart from the activities that produce them. Where there are ends apart from the actions, it is the nature of the products to be better than the activities. Now, as there are many actions, arts, and sciences, their ends also are many; the end of the medical art is health, that of shipbuilding a vessel, that of strategy victory, that of economics wealth. But where such arts fall under a single capacity—as bridle-making and the other arts concerned with the equipment of horses fall under the

From *Aristotle's Nicomachean Ethics*, translated by W. D. Ross, revised by J. L. Ackrill and J. O. Urmson (1925; 1980). Reprinted by permission of Oxford University Press.

art of riding, and this and every military action under strategy, in the same way other arts fall under yet others—in all of these the ends of the master arts are to be preferred to all the subordinate ends; for it is for the sake of the former that the latter are pursued. It makes no difference whether the activities themselves are the ends of the actions, or something else apart from the activities, as in the case of the sciences just mentioned.

### The science of the good for man is politics

2. If, then, there is some end of the things we do, which we desire for its own sake (everything else being desired for the sake of this), and if we do not choose everything for the sake of something else (for at that rate the process would go on to infinity, so that our desire would be empty and vain), clearly this must be the good and the chief good. Will not the knowledge of it, then, have a great influence on life? Shall we not, like archers who have a mark to aim at, be more likely to hit upon what is right? If so, we must try, in outline at least, to determine what it is, and of which of the sciences or capacities it is the object. It would seem to belong to the most authoritative art and that which is most truly the master art. And politics appears to be of this nature; for it is this that ordains which of the sciences should be studied in a state, and which each class of citizens should learn and up to what point they should learn them; and we see even the most highly esteemed of capacities to fall under this, e.g. strategy, economics, rhetoric; now, since politics uses the rest of the sciences, and since, again, it legislates as to what we are to do and what we are to abstain from, the end of this science must include those of the others, so that this end must be the good for man. For even if the end is the same for a single man and for a state, that of the state seems at all events something greater and more complete whether to attain or to preserve; though it is worth while to attain the end merely for one man, it is finer and more godlike to attain it for a nation or for city-states. These, then, are the ends at which our inquiry aims, since it is political science, in one sense of that term.

### Nature of the Science

*We must not expect more precision than the subject-matter admits of. The student should have reached years of discretion*

3. Our discussion will be adequate if it has as much clearness as the subject-matter admits of, for precision is not to be sought for alike in all discussions, any more than in all the products of the crafts. Now fine and just actions, which political science investigates, exhibit much variety and fluctuation, so that they may be thought to exist only by convention, and not by nature. And goods exhibit a similar fluctuation because they bring harm to many people; for before now men have been undone by reason of their wealth, and others by reason of their courage. We must be content, then, in speaking of such subjects and with such premises to indicate the truth roughly and in outline, and in speaking about things which are only for the most part true, and with premises of the same kind, to reach conclusions that are no better. In the same spirit, therefore, should each type of statement be *received;* for it is the mark of an educated man to look for precision in each class of things just so far as the nature of the subject admits; it is evidently equally foolish to accept probable reasoning from a mathematician and to demand from a rhetorician demonstrative proofs.

Now each man judges well the things he knows, and of these he is a good judge. And so the man who has been educated in a subject is a good judge of that subject, and the man who has received an all-round education is a good judge in general. Hence a young man is not a proper hearer of lectures on political science; for he is inexperienced in the actions that occur in life, but its discussions start from these and are about these; and, further, since he tends to follow his passions, his study will be vain and unprofitable, because the end aimed at is not knowledge but action. And it makes no difference whether he is young in years or youthful in character; the defect does not depend on time, but on his living, and pursuing each successive object, as passion directs. For to such persons, as to the incontinent, knowledge brings no profit; but to those who desire and act in accordance with a rational principle knowledge about such matters will be of great benefit.

These remarks about the student, the sort of treatment to be expected, and the purpose of the inquiry, may be taken as our preface.

## What Is the Good for Man?

*It is generally agreed to be happiness, but there are various views as to what happiness is. What is required at the start is an unreasoned conviction about the facts, such as is produced by a good upbringing*

4.  Let us resume our inquiry and state, in view of the fact that all knowledge and every pursuit aims at some good, what it is that we say political science aims at and what is the highest of all goods achievable by action. Verbally there is very general agreement; for both the general run of men and people of superior refinement say that it is happiness, and identify living well and faring well with being happy; but with regard to what happiness is they differ, and the many do not give the same account as the wise. For the former think it is some plain and obvious thing, like pleasure, wealth, or honour; they differ, however, from one another—and often even the same man identifies it with different things, with health when he is ill, with wealth when he is poor; but, conscious of their ignorance, they admire those who proclaim some great thing that is above their comprehension. Now some thought that apart from these many goods there is another which is good in itself and causes the goodness of all these as well. To examine all the opinions that have been held were perhaps somewhat fruitless; enough to examine those that are most prevalent or that seem to be arguable.

Let us not fail to notice, however, that there is a difference between arguments from and those to the first principles. For Plato, too, was right in raising this question and asking, as he used to do, 'Are we on the way from or to the first principles?' There is a difference, as there is in a race-course between the

course from the judges to the turning-point and the way back. For, while we must begin with what is evident, things are evident in two ways—some to us, some without qualification. Presumably, then, *we* must begin with things evident to *us*. Hence any one who is to listen intelligently to lectures about what is noble and just and, generally, about the subjects of political science must have been brought up in good habits. For the fact is a starting-point, and if this is sufficiently plain to him, he will not need the reason as well; and the man who has been well brought up has or can easily get starting-points. And as for him who neither has nor can get them, let him hear the words of Hesiod:

*Far best is he who knows all things himself;*
*Good, he that hearkens when men counsel right;*
*But he who neither knows, nor lays to heart*
*Another's wisdom, is a useless wight.*

*Discussion of the popular views that the good is pleasure, honour, wealth; a fourth kind of life, that of contemplation, deferred for future discussion*

5.  Let us, however, resume our discussion from the point at which we digressed. To judge from the lives that men lead, most men, and the men of the most vulgar type, seem (not without some ground) to identify the good, or happiness, with pleasure; which is the reason why they love the life of enjoyment. For there are, we may say, three prominent types of life—that just mentioned, the political, and thirdly the contemplative life. Now the mass of mankind are evidently quite slavish in their tastes, preferring a life suitable to beasts, but they get some ground for their view from the fact that many of those in high places share the tastes of Sardanapallus. A consideration of the prominent types of life shows that people of superior refinement and of active disposition identify happiness with honour; for this is, roughly speaking, the end of the political life. But it seems too superficial to be what we are looking for, since it is thought to depend on those who bestow honour rather than on him who receives it, but the good we divine to be something of one's own and not easily taken from

one. Further, men seem to pursue honour in order that they may be assured of their merit; at least it is by men of practical wisdom that they seek to be honoured, and among those who know them, and on the ground of their virtue; clearly, then, according to them, at any rate, virtue is better. And perhaps one might even suppose this to be, rather than honour, the end of the political life. But even this appears somewhat incomplete; for possession of virtue seems actually compatible with being asleep, or with lifelong inactivity, and, further, with the greatest sufferings and misfortunes; but a man who was living so no one would call happy, unless he were maintaining a thesis at all costs. But enough of this; for the subject has been sufficiently treated even in the popular discussions. Third comes the contemplative life, which we shall consider later.

The life of money-making is one undertaken under compulsion, and wealth is evidently not the good we are seeking; for it is merely useful and for the sake of something else. And so one might rather take the aforenamed objects to be ends; for they are loved for themselves. But it is evident that not even these are ends; yet many arguments have been wasted on the support of them. Let us leave this subject, then. . . .

*The good must be something final and self-sufficient. Definition of happiness reached by considering the characteristic function of man*

7. Let us again return to the good we are seeking, and ask what it can be. It seems different in different actions and arts; it is different in medicine, in strategy, and in the other arts likewise. What then is the good of each? Surely that for whose sake everything else is done. In medicine this is health, in strategy victory, in architecture a house, in any other sphere something else, and in every action and pursuit the end; for it is for the sake of this that all men do whatever else they do. Therefore, if there is an end for all that we do, this will be the good achievable by action, and if there are more than one, these will be the goods achievable by action.

So the argument has by a different course reached the same point; but we must try to state this even more clearly. Since there are evidently more than one end, and we choose some of these (e.g. wealth, flutes, and in general instruments) for the sake of something else, clearly not all ends are final ends; but the chief good is evidently something final. Therefore, if there is only one final end, this will be what we are seeking, and if there are more than one, the most final of these will be what we are seeking. Now we call that which is in itself worthy of pursuit more final than that which is worthy of pursuit for the sake of something else, and that which is never desirable for the sake of something else more final than the things that are desirable both in themselves and for the sake of that other thing, and therefore we call final without qualification that which is always desirable in itself and never for the sake of something else.

Now such a thing happiness, above all else, is held to be; for this we choose always for itself and never for the sake of something else, but honour, pleasure, reason, and every virtue we choose indeed for themselves (for if nothing resulted from them we should still choose each of them), but we choose them also for the sake of happiness, judging that through them we shall be happy. Happiness, on the other hand, no one chooses for the sake of these, nor, in general, for anything other than itself.

From the point of view of self-sufficiency the same result seems to follow; for the final good is thought to be self-sufficient. Now by self-sufficient we do not mean that which is sufficient for a man by himself, for one who lives a solitary life, but also for parents, children, wife, and in general for his friends and fellow citizens, since man is born for citizenship. But some limit must be set to this; for if we extend our requirement to ancestors and descendants and friends' friends we are in for an infinite series. Let us examine this question, however, on another occasion; the self-sufficient we now define as that which when isolated makes life desirable and lacking in nothing; and such we think happiness to be; and further we think it most desirable of all things, not a thing counted as one good thing among others—if it were so counted it would clearly be made more desirable by the addition of even the least of goods; for that which is added becomes an excess of goods, and of goods the greater is always more desirable. Happiness, then, is something final and self-sufficient, and is the end of action.

Presumably, however, to say that happiness is the chief good seems a platitude, and a clearer account of what is is still desired. This might perhaps be given, if we could first ascertain the function of man. For just as for a flute-player, a sculptor, or any artist, and, in general, for all things that have a function or activity, the good and the 'well' is thought to reside in the function, so would it seem to be for man, if he has a function. Have the carpenter, then, and the tanner certain functions or activities, and has man none? Is he born without a function? Or as eye, hand, foot, and in general each of the parts evidently has a function, may one lay it down that man similarly has a function apart from all these? What then can this be? Life seems to belong even to plants, but we are seeking what is peculiar to man. Let us exclude, therefore, the life of nutrition and growth. Next there would be a life of perception, but *it* also seems to be shared even by the horse, the ox, and every animal. There remains then, an active life of the element that has a rational principle; of this, one part has such a principle in the sense of being obedient to one, the other in the sense of possessing one and exercising thought. And, as 'life of the rational element' also has two meanings, we must state that life in the sense of activity is what we mean; for this seems to be the more proper sense of the term. Now if the function of man is an activity of soul which follows or implies a rational principle, and if we say 'a so-and-so' and 'a good so-and-so' have a function which is the same in kind, e.g. a lyre-player and a good lyre-player, and so without qualification in all cases, eminence in respect of goodness being added to the name of the function (for the function of a lyre-player is to play the lyre, and that of a good lyre-player is to do so well): if this is the case [and we state the function of man to be a certain kind of life, and this to be an activity or actions of the soul implying a rational principle, and the function of a good man to be the good and noble performance of these, and if any action is well performed when it is performed in

accordance with the appropriate excellence: if this is the case], human good turns out to be activity of soul exhibiting excellence, and if there are more than one excellence, in accordance with the best and most complete.

But we must add 'in a complete life'. For one swallow does not make a summer, nor does one day; and so too one day, or a short time, does not make a man blessed and happy.

Let this serve as an outline of the good; for we must presumably first sketch it roughly, and then later fill in the details. But it would seem that any one is capable of carrying on and articulating what has once been well outlined, and that time is a good discoverer or partner in such a work; to which facts the advances of the arts are due; for any one can add what is lacking. And we must also remember what has been said before, and not look for precision in all things alike, but in each class of things such precision as accords with the subject-matter, and so much as is appropriate to the inquiry. For a carpenter and a geometer investigate the right angle in different ways; the former does so in so far as the right angle is useful for his work, while the latter inquires what it is or what sort of thing it is; for he is a spectator of the truth. We must act in the same way, then, in all other matters as well, that our main task may not be subordinated to minor questions. Nor must we demand the cause in all matters alike; it is enough in some cases that the *fact* be well established, as in the case of the first principles; the fact is a primary thing and first principle. Now of first principles we see some by induction, some by perception, some by a certain habituation, and others too in other ways. But each set of principles we must try to investigate in the natural way, and we must take pains to determine them correctly, since they have a great influence on what follows. For the beginning is thought to be more than half of the whole, and many of the questions we ask are cleared up by it.

*Our definition is confirmed by current beliefs about happiness*

8. But we must consider happiness in the light not only of our conclusion and our premises, but also of

what is commonly said about it; for with a true view all the data harmonize, but with a false one the facts soon clash. Now goods have been divided into three classes, and some are described as external, others as relating to soul or to body; we call those that relate to soul most properly and truly goods, and psychical actions and activities we class as relating to soul. Therefore our account must be sound, at least according to this view, which is an old one and agreed on by philosophers. It is correct also in that we identify the end with certain actions and activities; for thus it falls among goods of the soul and not among external goods. Another belief which harmonizes with our account is that the happy man lives well and fares well; for we have practically defined happiness as a sort of living and faring well. The characteristics that are looked for in happiness seem also, all of them, to belong to what we have defined happiness as being. For some identify happiness with virtue, some with practical wisdom, others with a kind of philosophic wisdom, others with these, or one of these, accompanied by pleasure or not without pleasure; while others include also external prosperity. Now some of these views have been held by many men and men of old, others by a few eminent persons; and it is not probable that either of these should be entirely mistaken, but rather that they should be right in at least some one respect, or even in most respects.

With those who identify happiness with virtue or some one virtue our account is in harmony; for to virtue belongs virtuous activity. But it makes, perhaps, no small difference whether we place the chief good in possession or in use, in state of mind or in activity. For the state of mind may exist without producing any good result, as in a man who is asleep or in some other way quite inactive, but the activity cannot; for one who has the activity will of necessity be acting, and acting well. And as in the Olympic Games it is not the most beautiful and the strongest that are crowned but those who compete (for it is some of these that are victorious), so those who act win, and rightly win, the noble and good things in life.

Their life is also in itself pleasant. For pleasure is a state of *soul*, and to each man that which he is said to be a lover of is pleasant; e.g. not only is a horse pleasant to the lover of horses, and a spectacle to the lover of sights, but also in the same way just acts are pleasant to the lover of justice and in general virtuous acts to the lover of virtue. Now for most men their pleasures are in conflict with one another because these are not by nature pleasant, but the lovers of what is noble find pleasant the things that are by nature pleasant; and virtuous actions are such, so that these are pleasant for such men as well as in their own nature. Their life, therefore, has no further need of pleasure as a sort of adventitious charm, but has its pleasure in itself. For, besides what we have said, the man who does not rejoice in noble actions is not even good; since no one would call a man just who did not enjoy acting justly, nor any man liberal who did not enjoy liberal actions; and similarly in all other cases. If this is so, virtuous actions must be in themselves pleasant. But they are also good and noble, and have each of these attributes in the highest degree, since the good man judges well about these attributes; his judgment is such as we have described. Happiness then is the best, noblest, and most pleasant thing in the world, and these attributes are not severed as in the inscription at Delos—

*Most noble is that which is justest, and best is health;*
*But most pleasant it is to win what we love.*

For all these properties belong to the best activities; and these, or one—the best—of these, we identify with happiness.

Yet evidently, as we said, it needs the external goods as well; for it is impossible, or not easy, to do noble acts without the proper equipment. In many actions we use friends and riches and political power as instruments; and there are some things the lack of which takes the lustre from happiness— good birth, goodly children, beauty; for the man who is very ugly in appearance or ill-born or solitary and childless is not very likely to be happy, and perhaps a man would be still less likely if he had thoroughly bad children or friends or had lost good children or friends by death. As we said, then, happiness seems to need this sort of prosperity in addition; for which reason some identify happiness with good fortune, though others identify it with virtue.

*Is happiness acquired by learning or habituation, or sent by God or by chance?*

9. For this reason also the question is asked, whether happiness is to be acquired by learning or by habituation or some other sort of training, or comes in virtue of some divine providence or again by chance. Now if there is *any* gift of the gods to men, it is reasonable that happiness should be god-given, and most surely god-given of all human things inasmuch as it is the best. But this question would perhaps be more appropriate to another inquiry; happiness seems, however, even if it is not god-sent but comes as a result of virtue and some process of learning or training, to be among the most godlike things; for that which is the prize and end of virtue seems to be the best thing in the world, and something godlike and blessed.

It will also on this view be very generally shared; for all who are not maimed as regards their potentiality for virtue may win it by a certain kind of study and care. But if it is better to be happy thus than by chance, it is reasonable that the facts should be so, since everything that depends on the action of nature is by nature as good as it can be, and similarly everything that depends on art or any rational cause, and especially if it depends on the best of all causes. To entrust to chance what is greatest and most noble would be a very defective arrangement.

The answer to the question we are asking is plain also from the definition of happiness; for it has been said to be a virtuous activity of soul, of a certain kind. Of the remaining goods, some must necessarily preexist as conditions of happiness, and others are naturally co-operative and useful as instruments. And this will be found to agree with what we said at the outset; for we stated the end of political science to be the best end, and political science spends most of its pains on making the citizens to be of a certain character, viz. good and capable of noble acts.

It is natural, then, that we call neither ox nor horse nor any other of the animals happy; for none of them is capable of sharing in such activity. For this reason also a boy is not happy; for he is not yet capable of such acts, owing to his age; and boys who are called happy are being congratulated by reason of the hopes we have for them. For there is required, as we said, not only complete virtue but also a complete life, since many changes occur in life, and all manner of chances, and the most prosperous may fall into great misfortunes in old age, as is told of Priam in the Trojan Cycle; and one who has experienced such chances and has ended wretchedly no one calls happy. . . .

## Kinds of Virtue

*Division of the faculties, and resultant division of virtue into intellectual and moral*

13. Since happiness is an activity of soul in accordance with perfect virtue, we must consider the nature of virtue; for perhaps we shall thus see better the nature of happiness. The true student of politics, too, is thought to have studied virtue above all things; for he wishes to make his fellow citizens good and obedient to the laws. As an example of this we have the lawgivers of the Cretans and the Spartans, and any others of the kind that there may have been. And if this inquiry belongs to political science, clearly the pursuit of it will be in accordance with our original plan. But clearly the virtue we must study is human virtue; for the good we were seeking was human good and the happiness human happiness. By human virtue we mean not that of the body but that of the soul; and happiness also we call an activity of soul. But if this is so, clearly the student of politics must know somehow the facts about the soul, as the man who is to heal the eyes must know about the whole body also; and all the more since political science is more prized and better than medical; but even among doctors the best educated spend much labour on acquiring knowledge of the body. The student of politics, then, must study the soul, and must study it with these objects in view, and do so just to the extent which is sufficient for the questions we are discussing; for further precision would perhaps involve more labour than our purposes require.

Some things are said about it, adequately enough, even in the discussions outside our school, and we must use these; e.g. that one element in the soul is irrational and one has a rational principle. Whether these are separated as the parts of the body or of anything divisible are, or are distinct by definition but by nature inseparable, like convex and concave in the circumference of a circle, does not affect the present question.

Of the irrational element one division seems to be widely distributed, and vegetative in its nature, I mean that which causes nutrition and growth; for it is this kind of power of the soul that one must assign to all nurslings and to embryos, and this same power to full-grown creatures; this is more reasonable than to assign some different power to them. Now the excellence of this seems to be common to all species and not specifically human; for this part or faculty seems to function most in sleep, while goodness and badness are least manifest in sleep (whence comes the saying that the happy are no better off than the wretched for half their lives; and this happens naturally enough, since sleep is an inactivity of the soul in that respect in which it is called good or bad), unless perhaps to a small extent some of the movements actually penetrate to the soul, and in this respect the dreams of good men are better than those of ordinary people. Enough of this subject, however; let us leave the nutritive faculty alone, since it has by its nature no share in human excellence.

There seems to be also another irrational element in the soul—one which in a sense, however, shares in a rational principle. For we praise the rational principle of the continent man and of the incontinent, and the part of their soul that has such a principle, since it urges them aright and towards the best objects; but there is found in them also another natural element beside the rational principle, which fights against and resists that principle. For exactly as paralysed limbs, when we intend to move them to the right, turn on the contrary to the left, so is it with the soul; the impulses of incontinent people move in contrary directions. But while in the body we see that which moves astray, in the soul we do not. No doubt, however, we must none the less suppose that in the soul too there is something beside the rational

principle, resisting and opposing it. In what sense it is distinct from the other elements does not concern us. Now even this seems to have a share in a rational principle, as we said; at any rate in the continent man it obeys the rational principle—and presumably in the temperate and brave man it is still more obedient; for in him it speaks, on all matters, with the same voice as the rational principle.

Therefore the irrational element also appears to be twofold. For the vegetative element in no way shares in a rational principle, but the appetitive and in general the desiring element in a sense shares in it, in so far as it listens to and obeys it; this is the sense in which we speak of 'taking account' of one's father or one's friends, not that in which we speak of 'accounting' for a mathematical property. That the irrational element is in some sense persuaded by a rational principle is indicated also by the giving of advice and by all reproof and exhortation. And if this element also must be said to have a rational principle, that which has a rational principle (as well as that which has not) will be twofold, one subdivision having it in the strict sense and in itself, and the other having a tendency to obey as one does one's father.

Virtue too is distinguished into kinds in accordance with this difference; for we say that some of the virtues are intellectual and others moral, philosophic wisdom and understanding and practical wisdom being intellectual, liberality and temperance moral. For in speaking about a man's character we do not say that he is wise or has understanding, but that he is good-tempered or temperate; yet we praise the wise man also with respect to his state of mind; and of states of mind we call those which merit praise virtues.

## BOOK II • MORAL VIRTUE

### Moral Virtue, How Produced, in What Medium and in What Manner Exhibited

#### Moral virtue, like the arts, is acquired by repetition of the corresponding acts

1. Virtue, then, being of two kinds, intellectual and moral, intellectual virtue in the main owes both its

birth, and its growth to teaching (for which reason it requires experience and time), while moral virtue comes about as a result of habit, whence also its name (ἠθική) is one that is formed by a slight variation from the word ἔθος (habit). From this it is also plain that none of the moral virtues arises in us by nature; for nothing that exists by nature can form a habit contrary to its nature. For instance the stone which by nature moves downwards cannot be habituated to move upwards, not even if one tries to train it by throwing it up ten thousand times; nor can fire be habituated to move downwards, nor can anything else that by nature behaves in one way be trained to behave in another. Neither by nature, then, nor contrary to nature do the virtues arise in us; rather we are adapted by nature to receive them, and are made perfect by habit.

Again, of all the things that come to us by nature we first acquire the potentiality and later exhibit the activity (this is plain in the case of the senses; for it was not by often seeing or often hearing that we got these senses, but on the contrary we had them before we used them, and did not come to have them by using them); but the virtues we get by first exercising them, as also happens in the case of the arts as well. For the things we have to learn before we can do them, we learn by doing them, e.g. men become builders by building and lyre-players by playing the lyre; so too we become just by doing just acts, temperate by doing temperate acts, brave by doing brave acts.

This is confirmed by what happens in states; for legislators make the citizens good by forming habits in them, and this is the wish of every legislator, and those who do not effect it miss their mark, and it is in this that a good constitution differs from a bad one.

Again, it is from the same causes and by the same means that every virtue is both produced and destroyed, and similarly every art; for it is from playing the lyre that both good and bad lyre-players are produced. And the corresponding statement is true of builders and of all the rest; men will be good or bad builders as a result of building well or badly. For if this were not so, there would have been no need of a teacher, but all men would have been born good or bad at their craft. This, then, is the case with the virtues also; by doing the acts that we do in our trans-

actions with other men we become just or unjust, and by doing the acts that we do in the presence of danger, and by being habituated to feel fear or confidence, we become brave or cowardly. The same is true of appetites and feelings of anger; some men become temperate and good-tempered, others self-indulgent and irascible, by behaving in one way or the other in the appropriate circumstances. Thus, in one word, states of character arise out of like activities. This is why the activities we exhibit must be of a certain kind; it is because the states of character correspond to the differences between these. It makes no small difference, then, whether we form habits of one kind or of another from our very youth; it makes a very great difference, or rather *all* the difference.

*These acts cannot be prescribed exactly, but must avoid excess and defect*

2. Since, then, the present inquiry does not aim at theoretical knowledge like the others (for we are inquiring not in order to know what virtue is, but in order to become good, since otherwise our inquiry would have been of no use), we must examine the nature of actions, namely how we ought to do them; for these determine also the nature of the states of character that are produced, as we have said. Now, that we must act according to the right rule is a common principle and must be assumed—it will be discussed later, i.e. both what the right rule is, and how it is related to the other virtues. But this must be agreed upon beforehand, that the whole account of matters of conduct must be given in outline and not precisely, as we said at the very beginning that the accounts we demand must be in accordance with the subject-matter; matters concerned with conduct and questions of what is good for us have no fixity, any more than matters of health. The general account being of this nature, the account of particular cases is yet more lacking in exactness; for they do not fall under any art or precept, but the agents themselves must in each case consider what is appropriate to the occasion, as happens also in the art of medicine or of navigation.

But though our present account is of this nature we must give what help we can. First, then, let us consider this, that it is the nature of such things to be destroyed by defect and excess, as we see in the case of strength and of health (for to gain light on things imperceptible we must use the evidence of sensible things); exercise either excessive or defective destroys the strength, and similarly drink or food which is above or below a certain amount destroys the health, while that which is proportionate both produces and increases and preserves it. So too is it, then, in the case of temperance and courage and the other virtues. For the man who flies from and fears everything and does not stand his ground against anything becomes a coward, and the man who fears nothing at all but goes to meet every danger becomes rash; and similarly the man who indulges in every pleasure and abstains from none becomes self-indulgent, while the man who shuns every pleasure, as boors do, becomes in a way insensible; temperance and courage, then, are destroyed by excess and defect, and preserved by the mean.

But not only are the sources and causes of their origination and growth the same as those of their destruction, but also the sphere of their actualization will be the same; for this is also true of the things which are more evident to sense, e.g. of strength; it is produced by taking much food and undergoing much exertion, and it is the strong man that will be most able to do these things. So too is it with the virtues; by abstaining from pleasures we become temperate, and it is when we have become so that we are most able to abstain from them; and similarly too in the case of courage; for by being habituated to despise things that are fearful and to stand our ground against them we become brave, and it is when we have become so that we shall be most able to stand our ground against them.

*Pleasure in doing virtuous acts is a sign that the virtuous disposition has been acquired: a variety of considerations show the essential connexion of moral virtue with pleasure and pain*

3. We must take as a sign of states of character the pleasure or pain that supervenes upon acts; for the man who abstains from bodily pleasures and delights in this very fact is temperate, while the man who is annoyed at it is self-indulgent, and he who stands his ground against things that are terrible and delights in this or at least is not pained is brave, while the man who is pained is a coward. For moral excellence is concerned with pleasures and pains; it is on account of the pleasure that we do bad things, and on account of the pain that we abstain from noble ones. Hence we ought to have been brought up in a particular way from our very youth, as Plato says, so as both to delight and to be pained by the things that we ought; this is the right education.

Again, if the virtues are concerned with actions and passions, and every passion and every action is accompanied by pleasure and pain, for this reason also virtue will be concerned with pleasures and pains. This is indicated also by the fact that punishment is inflicted by these means; for it is a kind of cure, and it is the nature of cures to be effected by contraries.

Again, as we said but lately, every state of soul has a nature relative to and concerned with the kind of things by which it tends to be made worse or better; but it is by reason of pleasures and pains that men become bad, by pursuing and avoiding these—either the pleasures and pains they ought not or when they ought not or as they ought not, or by going wrong in one of the other similar ways that may be distinguished. Hence men even define the virtues as certain states of impassivity and rest; not well, however, because they speak absolutely, and do not say 'as one ought' and 'as one ought not' and 'when one ought or ought not', and the other things that may be added. We assume, then, that this kind of excellence tends to do what is best with regard to pleasures and pains, and vice does the contrary.

The following facts also may show us that virtue and vice are concerned with these same things. There being three objects of choice and three of avoidance, the noble, the advantageous, the pleasant, and their contraries, the base, the injurious, the painful, about all of these the good man tends to go right and the bad man to go wrong, and especially about pleasure; for this is common to the animals, and also it accompanies all objects of choice; for even the noble and the advantageous appear pleasant.

Again, it has grown up with us all from our

infancy; this is why it is difficult to rub off this passion, engrained as it is in our life. And we measure even our actions, some of us more and others less, by the rule of pleasure and pain. For this reason, then, our whole inquiry must be about these; for to feel delight and pain rightly or wrongly has no small effect on our actions.

Again, it is harder to fight with pleasure than with anger, to use Heraclitus' phrase, but both art and virtue are always concerned with what is harder; for even the good is better when it is harder. Therefore for this reason also the whole concern both of virtue and of political science is with pleasures and pains, for the man who uses these well will be good, he who uses them badly bad.

That virtue, then, is concerned with pleasures and pains, and that by the acts from which it arises it is both increased and, if they are done differently, destroyed, and that the acts from which it arose are those in which it actualizes itself—let this be taken as said.

*The actions that produce moral virtue are not good in the same sense as those that flow from it: the latter must fulfil certain conditions not necessary in the case of the arts*

4. The question might be asked, what we mean by saying that we must become just by doing just acts, and temperate by doing temperate acts; for if men do just and temperate acts, they are already just and temperate, exactly as, if they do what is in accordance with the laws of grammar and of music, they are grammarians and musicians.

Or is this not true even of the arts? It is possible to do something that is in accordance with the laws of grammar, either by chance or under the guidance of another. A man will be a grammarian, then, only when he has both said something grammatical and said it grammatically; and this means doing it in accordance with the grammatical knowledge in himself.

Again, the case of the arts and that of the virtues are not similar; for the products of the arts have their goodness in themselves, so that it is enough that they should have a certain character, but if the arts that are in accordance with the virtues have themselves a certain character it does not follow that they are done justly or temperately. The agent also must be in a certain condition when he does them; in the first place he must have knowledge, secondly he must choose the acts, and choose them for their own sakes, and thirdly his action must proceed from a firm and unchangeable character. These are not reckoned in as conditions of the possession of the arts, except the bare knowledge; but as a condition of the possession of the virtues knowledge has little or no weight, while the other conditions count not for a little but for everything, i.e. the very conditions which result from often doing just and temperate acts.

Actions, then, are called just and temperate when they are such as the just or the temperate man would do; but it is not the man who does those that is just and temperate, but the man who also does them as just and temperate men do them. It is well said, then, that it is by doing just acts that the just man is produced, and by doing temperate acts the temperate man; without doing these no one would have even a prospect of becoming good.

But most people do not do these, but take refuge in theory and think they are being philosophers and will become good in this way, behaving somewhat like patients who listen attentively to their doctors, but do none of the things they are ordered to do. As the latter will not be made well in body by such a course of treatment, the former will not be made well in soul by such a course of philosophy.

## Definition of Moral Virtue

*The genus of moral virtue: it is a state of character, not a passion, nor a faculty*

5. Next we must consider what virtue is. Since things that are found in the soul are of three kinds—passions, faculties, states of character—virtue must be one of these. By passions I mean appetite, anger, fear, confidence, envy, joy, friendly feeling, hatred, longing, emulation, pity, and in general the feelings that are accompanied by pleasure or pain; by facul-

ties the things in virtue of which we are said to be capable of feeling these, e.g. of becoming angry or being pained or feeling pity; by states of character the things in virtue of which we stand well or badly with reference to the passions, e.g. with reference to anger we stand badly if we feel it violently or too weakly, and well if we feel it moderately; and similarly with reference to the other passions.

Now neither the virtues nor the vices are *passions,* because we are not called good or bad on the ground of our passions, but are so called on the ground of our virtues and our vices, and because we are neither praised nor blamed for our passions (for the man who feels fear or anger is not praised, nor is the man who simply feels anger blamed, but the man who feels it in a certain way), but for our virtues and our vices we *are* praised or blamed.

Again, we feel anger and fear without choice, but the virtues are modes of choice or involve choice. Further, in respect of the passions we are said to be moved, but in respect of the virtues and the vices we are said not to be moved but to be disposed in a particular way.

For these reasons also they are not *faculties;* for we are neither called good or bad, nor praised or blamed, for the simple capacity of feeling the passions; again, we have the faculties by nature, but we are not made good or bad by nature; we have spoken of this before.

If, then, the virtues are neither passions nor faculties, all that remains is that they should be *states of character.*

Thus we have stated what virtue is in respect of its genus.

### The differentia of moral virtue: it is a disposition to choose the mean

6. We must, however, not only describe virtue as a state of character, but also say what sort of state it is. We may remark, then, that every virtue or excellence both brings into good condition the thing of which it is the excellence and makes the work of that thing be done well; e.g. the excellence of the eye makes both the eye and its work good; for it is by the excellence of the eye that we see well. Similarly the excellence of the horse makes a horse both good in itself and good at running and at carrying its rider and at awaiting the attack of the enemy. Therefore, if this is true in every case, the virtue of man also will be the state of character which makes a man good and which makes him do his own work well.

How this is to happen we have stated already, but it will be made plain also by the following consideration of the specific nature of virtue. In everything that is continuous and divisible it is possible to take more, less, or an equal amount, and that either in terms of the thing itself or relatively to us; and the equal is an intermediate between excess and defect. By the intermediate in the object I mean that which is equidistant from each of the extremes, which is one and the same for all men; by the intermediate relatively to us that which is neither too much nor too little—and this is not one, nor the same for all. For instance, if ten is many and two is few, six is the intermediate, taken in terms of the object; for it exceeds and is exceeded by an equal amount; this is intermediate according to arithmetical proportion. But the intermediate relatively to us is not to be taken so; if ten pounds are too much for a particular person to eat and two too little, it does not follow that the trainer will order six pounds; for this also is perhaps too much for the person who is to take it, or too little—too little for Milo, too much for the beginner in athletic exercises. The same is true of running and wrestling. Thus a master of any art avoids excess and defect, but seeks the intermediate and chooses this—the intermediate not in the object but relatively to us.

If it is thus, then, that every art does its work well—by looking to the intermediate and judging its works by this standard (so that we often say of good works of art that it is not possible either to take away or to add anything, implying that excess and defect destroy the goodness of works of art, while the mean preserves it; and good artists, as we say, look to this in their work), and if, further, virtue is more exact and better than any art, as nature also is, then virtue must have the quality of aiming at the intermediate. I mean moral virtue; for it is this that is concerned with passions and actions, and in these there is excess, defect, and the intermediate. For instance, both fear and confidence and appetite and anger and pity and in general pleasure and pain may be felt both too much and too little, and in both cases not well; but to feel them at the right times, with reference to the right objects, towards the right people, with the right motive, and in the right way, is what is both intermediate and best, and this is characteristic of virtue. Similarly with regard to actions also there is excess, defect, and the intermediate. Now virtue is concerned with passions and actions, in which excess is a form of failure, and so is defect, while the intermediate is praised and is a form of success; and being praised and being successful are both characteristics of virtue. Therefore virtue is a kind of mean, since, as we have seen, it aims at what is intermediate.

Again, it is possible to fail in many ways (for evil belongs to the class of the unlimited, as the Pythagoreans conjectured, and good to that of the limited), while to succeed is possible only in one way (for which reason also one is easy and the other difficult—to miss the mark easy, to hit it difficult); for these reasons also, then, excess and defect are characteristic of vice, and the mean of virtue;

For men are good in but one way, but bad in many.

Virtue, then, is a state of character concerned with choice, lying in a mean, i.e., the mean relative to us, this being determined by a rational principle, and by that principle by which the man of practical wisdom would determine it. Now it is a mean between two vices, that which depends on excess and that which depends on defect; and again it is a mean because the vices respectively fall short of or exceed what is right in both passions and actions, while virtue both finds and chooses that which is intermediate. Hence in respect of what it is, i.e. the definition which states its essence, virtue is a mean, with regard to what is best and right it is an extreme.

But not every action nor every passion admits of a mean; for some have names that already imply badness, e.g. spite, shamelessness, envy, and in the case of actions adultery, theft, murder; for all of these and suchlike things imply by their names that

they are themselves bad, and not the excesses or deficiencies of them. It is not possible, then, ever to be right with regard to them; one must always be wrong. Nor does goodness or badness with regard to such things depend on committing adultery with the right woman, at the right time, and in the right way, but simply to do any of them is to go wrong. It would be equally absurd, then, to expect that in unjust, cowardly, and voluptuous action there should be a mean, an excess, and a deficiency; for at that rate there would be a mean of excess and of deficiency, an excess of excess, and a deficiency of deficiency. But as there is no excess and deficiency of temperance and courage because what is intermediate is in a sense an extreme, so too of the actions we have mentioned there is no mean nor any excess and deficiency, but however they are done they are wrong; for in general there is neither a mean of excess and deficiency, nor excess and deficiency of a mean.

### The above proposition illustrated by reference to particular virtues

7. We must, however, not only make this general statement, but also apply it to the individual facts. For among statements about conduct those which are general apply more widely, but those which are particular are more true, since conduct has to do with individual cases, and our statements must harmonize with the facts in these cases. We may take these cases from our table. With regard to feelings of fear and confidence courage is the mean; of the people who exceed, he who exceeds in fearlessness has no name (many of the states have no name), while the man who exceeds in confidence is rash, and he who exceeds in fear and falls short in confidence is a coward. With regard to pleasures and pains—not all of them, and not so much with regard to the pains—the mean is temperance, the excess self-indulgence. Persons deficient with regard to the pleasures are not often found; hence such persons also have received no name. But let us call them 'insensible'.

With regard to giving and taking of money the mean is liberality, the excess and the defect prodigality and meanness. In these actions people exceed and fall short in contrary ways; the prodigal exceeds in spending and falls short in taking, while the mean man exceeds in taking and falls short in spending. (At present we are giving a mere outline or summary, and are satisfied with this; later these states will be more exactly determined.) With regard to money there are also other dispositions—a mean, magnificence (for the magnificent man differs from the liberal man; the former deals with large sums, the latter with small ones), an excess, tastelessness and vulgarity, and a deficiency, niggardliness; these differ from the states opposed to liberality, and the mode of their difference will be stated later.

With regard to honour and dishonour the mean is proper pride, the excess is known as a sort of 'empty vanity', and the deficiency is undue humility; and as we said liberality was related to magnificence, differing from it by dealing with small sums, so there is a state similarly related to proper pride, being concerned with small honours while that is concerned with great. For it is possible to desire honour as one ought, and more than one ought, and less, and the man who exceeds in his desires is called ambitious, the man who falls short unambitious, while the intermediate person has no name. The dispositions also are nameless, except that that of the ambitious man is called ambition. Hence the people who are at the extremes lay claim to the middle place; and we ourselves sometimes call the intermediate person ambitious and sometimes unambitious, and sometimes praise the ambitious man and sometimes the unambitious. The reason of our doing this will be stated in what follows; but now let us speak of the remaining states according to the method which has been indicated.

With regard to anger also there is an excess, a deficiency, and a mean. Although they can scarcely be said to have names, yet since we call the intermediate person good-tempered let us call the mean good temper; of the persons at the extremes let the one who exceeds be called irascible, and his vice irascibility, and the man who falls short an unirascible sort of person, and the deficiency unirascibility.

There are also three other means, which have a certain likeness to one another, but differ from one another: for they are all concerned with intercourse in words and actions, but differ in that one is concerned with truth in this sphere, the other two with pleasantness; and of this one kind is exhibited in giving amusement, the other in all the circumstances of life. We must therefore speak of these too, that we may the better see that in all things the mean is praiseworthy, and the extremes neither praiseworthy nor right, but worthy of blame. Now most of these states also have no names, but we must try, as in the other cases, to invent names ourselves so that we may be clear and easy to follow. With regard to truth, then, the intermediate is a truthful sort of person and the mean may be called truthfulness, while the pretence which exaggerates is boastfulness and the person characterized by it a boaster, and that which understates is mock modesty and the person characterized by it mock-modest. With regard to pleasantness in the giving of amusement the intermediate person is ready-witted and the disposition ready wit, the excess is buffoonery and the person characterized by it a buffoon, while the man who falls short is a sort of boor and his state is boorishness. With regard to the remaining kind of pleasantness, that which is exhibited in life in general, the man who is pleasant in the right way is friendly and the mean is friendliness, while the man who exceeds is an obsequious person if he has no end in view, a flatterer if he is aiming at his own advantage, and the man who falls short and is unpleasant in all circumstances is a quarrel-some and surly sort of person.

There are also means in the passions and concerned with the passions; since shame is not a virtue, and yet praise is extended to the modest man. For even in these matters one man is said to be intermediate, and another to exceed, as for instance the bashful man who is ashamed of everything; while he who falls short or is not ashamed of anything at all is shameless, and the intermediate person is modest. Righteous indignation is a mean between envy and spite, and these states are concerned with the pain and pleasure that are felt at the fortunes of our neighbours; the man who is characterized by righteous indignation is pained at undeserved good fortune, the envious man, going beyond him, is pained at all good fortune, and the spiteful man falls so far short of being pained that he even rejoices. But these states there will be an opportunity of describing elsewhere; with regard to justice, since it has not one simple meaning, we shall, after describing the other states, distinguish its two kinds and say how each of them is a mean; and similarly we shall treat also of the rational virtues. . . .

## BOOK III • MORAL VIRTUE (*cont.*)

### *Inner Side of Moral Virtue: Conditions of Responsibility for Action*

*Praise and blame attach to voluntary actions, i.e., actions done (1) not under compulsion, and (2) with knowledge of the circumstances*

1. Since virtue is concerned with passions and actions, and on voluntary passions and actions praise and blame are bestowed, on those that are involuntary pardon, and sometimes also pity, to distinguish the voluntary and the involuntary is presumably necessary for those who are studying the nature of virtue, and useful also for legislators with a view to the assigning both of honours and of punishments.

Those things, then, are thought involuntary, which take place by force or owing to ignorance; and that is compulsory of which the moving principle is outside, being a principle in which nothing is contributed by the person who acts—or, rather, is acted upon, e.g. if he were to be carried somewhere by a wind, or by men who had him in their power.

But with regard to the things that are done from fear of greater evils or for some noble object (e.g. if a tyrant were to order one to do something base, having one's parents and children in his power, and if one did the action they were to be saved, but otherwise would be put to death), it may be debated whether such actions are involuntary or voluntary. Something of the sort happens also with regard to the throwing of goods overboard in a storm; for in the abstract no one throws goods away voluntarily, but on condition of its securing the safety of himself and his crew any

sensible man does so. Such actions, then, are mixed, but are more like voluntary actions; for they are worthy of choice at the time when they are done, and the end of an action is relative to the occasion. Both the terms, then, 'voluntary' and 'involuntary', must be used with reference to the moment of action. Now the man acts voluntarily; for the principle that moves the instrumental parts of the body in such actions is in him, and the things of which the moving principle is in a man himself are in his power to do or not to do. Such actions, therefore, are voluntary, but in the abstract perhaps involuntary; for no one would choose any such act in itself.

For such actions men are sometimes even praised, when they endure something base or painful in return for great and noble objects gained; in the opposite case they are blamed, since to endure the greatest indignities for no noble end or for a trifling end is the mark of an inferior person. On some actions praise indeed is not bestowed, but pardon is, when one does a wrongful act under pressure which overstrains human nature and which no one could withstand. But some acts, perhaps, we cannot be forced to do, but ought rather to face death after the most fearful sufferings; for the things that 'forced' Euripides' Alcmaeon to slay his mother seem absurd. It is difficult sometimes to determine what should be chosen at what cost, and what should be endured in return for what gain, and yet more difficult to abide by our decisions; for as a rule what is expected is painful, and what we are forced to do is base, whence praise and blame are bestowed on those who have been forced or have not.

What sort of acts, then, should be called forced? We answer that without qualification actions are so when the cause is in the external circumstances and the agent contributes nothing. But the things that in themselves are involuntary, but now and in return for these gains are worthy of choice, and whose moving principle is in the agent, are in themselves involuntary, but now and in return for these gains voluntary. They are more like voluntary acts; for actions are in the class of particulars, and the particular acts here are voluntary. What sort of things are to be chosen, and in return for what, it is not easy to state; for there are many differences in the particular cases.

But if someone were to say that pleasant and noble objects have a forcing power, forcing us from without, all acts would be for him forced; for it is for these objects that all men do everything they do. And those who act by force and unwillingly act with pain, but those who do acts for their pleasantness or nobility do them with pleasure; it is absurd to make external circumstances responsible, and not oneself, as being easily caught by such attractions, and to make oneself responsible for noble acts but the pleasant objects responsible for base acts. The forced, then, seems to be that whose moving principle is outside, the person forced contributing nothing.

Everything that is done by reason of ignorance is *not* voluntary; it is only what produces pain and regret that is *in*voluntary. For the man who has done something owing to ignorance, and feels not the least vexation at his action, has not acted voluntarily, since he did not know what he was doing, nor yet involuntarily, since he is not pained. Of people, then, who act by reason of ignorance he who regrets is thought an involuntary agent, and the man who does not regret may, since he is different, be called a not voluntary agent; for, since he differs from the other, it is better that he should have a name of his own.

Acting by reason of ignorance seems also to be different from acting *in* ignorance; for the man who is drunk or in a rage is thought to act as a result not of ignorance but of one of the causes mentioned, yet not knowingly but in ignorance.

Now every wicked man is ignorant of what he ought to do and what he ought to abstain from, and error of this kind makes men unjust and in general bad; but the term 'involuntary' tends to be used not if a man is ignorant of what is to his advantage—for it is not mistaken purpose that makes an action involuntary (*it* makes men *wicked*), nor ignorance of the universal (for *that* men are *blamed*), but ignorance of particulars, i.e. of the circumstances of the action and the objects with which it is concerned. For it is on these that both pity and pardon depend, since the person who is ignorant of any of these acts involuntarily.

Perhaps it is just as well, therefore, to determine their nature and number. A man may be ignorant, then, of who he is, what he is doing, what or whom he is acting on, and sometimes also what (e.g. what

instrument) he is doing it with, and to what end (e.g. he may think his act will conduce to someone's safety), and how he is doing it (e.g. whether gently or violently). Now of all of these no one could be ignorant unless he were mad, and evidently also he could not be ignorant of the agent; for how could he not know himself? But of what he is doing a man might be ignorant, as for instance people say 'it slipped out of their mouths as they were speaking', or 'they did not know it was a secret', as Aeschylus said of the mysteries, or a man might say he 'let it go off when he merely wanted to show its working', as the man did with the catapult. Again, one might think one's son was an enemy, as Merope did, or that a pointed spear had a button on it, or that a stone was pumice-stone; or one might give a man a draught to save him, and really kill him; or one might want to touch a man, as people do in sparring, and really wound him. The ignorance may relate, then, to any of these things, and the man who was ignorant of any of these is thought to have acted involuntarily, and especially if he was ignorant on the most important points; and these are thought to be the circumstances of the action and its end. Further, the doing of an act that is called involuntary in virtue of ignorance of this sort must be painful and involve regret.

Since that which is done by force or by reason of ignorance is involuntary, the voluntary would seem to be that of which the moving principle is in the agent himself, he being aware of the particular circumstances of the action. Presumably acts done by reason of anger or appetite are not rightly called involuntary. For in the first place, on that showing none of the other animals will act voluntarily, nor will children; and secondly, is it meant that we do not do voluntarily *any* of the acts that are due to appetite or anger, or that we do the noble acts voluntarily and the base acts involuntarily? Is not this absurd, when one and the same thing is the cause? But it would surely be odd to describe as involuntary the things one ought to desire; and we ought both to be angry at certain things and to have an appetite for certain things, e.g. for health and for learning. Also what is involuntary is thought to be painful, but what is in accordance with appetite is thought to be pleasant. Again, what is the difference in respect of involuntariness between errors committed upon calculation and those committed in anger? Both are to be avoided, but the irrational passions are thought not less human than reason is, and therefore also the actions which proceed from anger or appetite are the man's actions. It would be odd, then, to treat them as involuntary.

*Moral virtue implies that the action is done (3) by choice: the object of choice is the result of previous deliberation*

2. Both the voluntary and the involuntary having been delimited, we must next discuss choice; for it is thought to be most closely bound up with virtue, and to discriminate characters better than actions do.

Choice, then, seems to be voluntary, but not the same thing as the voluntary; the latter extends more widely. For both children and the lower animals share in voluntary action, but not in choice, and acts done on the spur of the moment we describe as voluntary, but not as chosen.

Those who say it is appetite or anger or wish or a kind of opinion do not seem to be right. For choice is not common to irrational creatures as well, but appetite and anger are. Again, the incontinent man acts with appetite, but not with choice; while the continent man on the contrary acts with choice, but not with appetite. Again, appetite is contrary to choice, but not appetite to appetite. Again, appetite relates to the pleasant and the painful, choice neither to the painful nor to the pleasant.

Still less is it anger; for acts due to anger are thought to be less than any other objects of choice.

But neither is it wish, though it seems near to it; for choice cannot relate to impossibles, and if any one said he chose them he would be thought silly; but there may be a wish even for impossibles, e.g. for immortality. And wish may relate to things that could in no way be brought about by one's own efforts, e.g. that a particular actor or athlete should win in a competition; but no one chooses such things, but only the things that he thinks could be brought about by his own efforts. Again, wish relates rather to the end, choice to the means; for instance,

we wish to be healthy, but we choose the acts which will make us healthy, and we wish to be happy and say we do, but we cannot well say we choose to be so; for, in general, choice seems to relate to the things that are in our own power.

For this reason, too, it cannot be opinion; for opinion is thought to relate to all kinds of things, no less to eternal things and impossible things than to things in our own power; and it is distinguished by its falsity or truth, not by its badness or goodness, while choice is distinguished rather by these.

Now with opinion in general perhaps no one even says it is identical. But it is not identical even with any kind of opinion; for by choosing what is good or bad we are men of a certain character, which we are not by holding certain opinions. And we choose to get or avoid something good or bad, but we have opinions about what a thing is or whom it is good for or how it is good for him; we can hardly be said to opine to get or avoid anything. And choice is praised for being related to the right object or for being *right,* opinion for being true. And we choose what we best know to be good, but we opine what we do not in the least know to be good; and it is not the same people that are thought to make the best choices and to have the best opinions, but some are thought to have fairly good opinions, but by reason of vice to choose what they should not. If opinion precedes choice or accompanies it, that makes no difference; for it is not this that we are considering, but whether choice is *identical* with some kind of opinion.

What, then, or what kind of thing is it, since it is none of the things we have mentioned? It seems to be voluntary, but not all that is voluntary to be an object of choice. Is it, then, what has been deliberated about before? At any rate choice involves a rational principle and thought. Even the name seems to suggest that it is what is chosen before other things.

*The nature of deliberation and its objects: choice is deliberate desire of things in our own power*

3. Do we deliberate about everything, and is everything a possible subject of deliberation, or is deliber-

ation impossible about some things? We ought presumably to call not what a fool or a madman would deliberate about, but what a sensible man would deliberate about, a subject of deliberation. Now about eternal things no one deliberates, e.g. about the material universe or the incommensurability of the diagonal and the side of a square. But no more do we deliberate about the things that involve movement but always happen in the same way, whether of necessity or by nature or from any other cause, e.g. the solstices and the risings of the stars; nor about things that happen now in one way, now in another, e.g. droughts and rains; nor about chance events, like the finding of treasure. But we do not deliberate even about all human affairs; for instance, no Spartan deliberates about the best constitution for the Scythians. For none of these things can be brought about by our own efforts.

We deliberate about things that are in our power and can be done; and these are in fact what is left. For nature, necessity, and chance are thought to be causes, and also reason and everything that depends on man. Now every class of men deliberates about the things that can be done by their own efforts. And in the case of exact and self-contained sciences there is no deliberation, e.g. about the letters of the alphabet (for we have no doubt how they should be written); but the things that are brought about by our own efforts, but not always in the same way, are the things about which we deliberate, e.g. questions of medical treatment or of money-making. And we do so more in the case of the art of navigation than in that of gymnastics, inasmuch as it has been less exactly worked out, and again about other things in the same ratio, and more also in the case of the arts than in that of the sciences; for we have more doubt about the former. Deliberation is concerned with things that happen in a certain way for the most part, but in which the event is obscure, and with things in which it is indeterminate. We call in others to aid us in deliberation on important questions, distrusting ourselves as not being equal to deciding.

We deliberate not about ends but about means. For a doctor does not deliberate whether he shall heal, nor an orator whether he shall convince, nor a statesman whether he shall produce law and order, nor does any

one else deliberate about his end. Having set the end, they consider how and by what means it is to be attained; and if it seems to be produced by several means they consider by which it is most easily and best produced, while if it is achieved by one only they consider how it will be achieved by this and by what means *this* will be achieved, till they come to the first cause, which in the order of discovery is last. For the person who deliberates seems to inquire and analyse in the way described as though he were analysing a geometrical construction (not all inquiry appears to be deliberation—for instance mathematical inquiries—but all deliberation is inquiry), and what is last in the order of analysis seems to be first in the order of becoming. And if we come on an impossibility, we give up the search, e.g. if we need money and this cannot be got; but if a thing appears possible we try to do it. By 'possible' things I mean things that might be brought about by our own efforts; and these in a sense include things that can be brought about by the efforts of our friends, since the moving principle is in ourselves. The subject of investigation is sometimes the instruments, sometimes the use of them; and similarly in the other cases—sometimes the means, sometimes the mode of using it or the means of bringing it about. It seems, then, as has been said, that man is a moving principle of actions; now deliberation is about the things to be done by the agent himself, and actions are for the sake of things other than themselves. For the end cannot be a subject of deliberation, but only the means; nor indeed can the particular facts be a subject of it, e.g. whether this is bread or has been baked as it should; for these are matters of perception. If we are to be always deliberating, we shall have to go on to infinity.

The same thing is deliberated upon and is chosen, except that the object of choice is already determinate, since it is that which has been decided upon as a result of deliberation that is the object of choice. For everyone ceases to inquire how he is to act when he has brought the moving principle back to himself and to the ruling part of himself; for this is what chooses. This is plain also from the ancient constitutions, which Homer represented; for the kings announced their choices to the people. The object of choice being one of the things in our own power which is desired after deliberation, choice will be deliberate desire of things in our own power; for when we have reached a judgement as a result of deliberation, we desire in accordance with our deliberation.

We may take it, then, that we have described choice in outline; we have stated the nature of its objects and the fact that it is concerned with means.

### The object of rational wish is the end, i.e. the good or apparent good

4. That *wish* is for the end has already been stated; some think it is for the good, others for the apparent good. Now those who say that the good is the object of wish must admit in consequence that that which the man who does not choose aright wishes for is not an object of wish (for if it is to be so, it must also be good; but it may well have been bad); while those who say that apparent good is the object of wish must admit that there is no natural object of wish, but only what seems good to each man. Now different things appear good to different people, and, if it so happens, even contrary things.

If these consequences are unpleasing, are we to say that absolutely and in truth the good is the object of wish, but for each person the apparent good; that that which is in truth an object of wish is an object of wish to the good man, while any chance thing may be so to the bad man, as in the case of bodies also the things that are in truth wholesome are wholesome for bodies which are in good condition, while for those that are diseased other things are wholesome—or bitter or sweet or hot or heavy, and so on; since the good man judges each class of things rightly, and in each the truth appears to him? For each state of character has its own ideas of the noble and the pleasant, and perhaps the good man differs from others most by seeing the truth in each class of things, being as it were the norm and measure of them. In most things the error seems to be due to pleasure; for this appears a good when it is not. We therefore choose the pleasant as a good and avoid pain as an evil.

### We are responsible for bad as well as for good actions

5. The end, then, being what we wish for, the means what we deliberate about and choose, actions concerning means must be according to choice and voluntary. Now the exercise of the virtues is concerned with means. Therefore virtue also is in our own power, and so too vice. For where it is in our power to act it is also in our power not to act, and *vice versa;* so that, if to act, where this is noble, is in our power, not to act, which will be base, will also be in our power, and if not to act, where this is noble, is in our power, to act, which will be base, will also be in our power. Now if it is in our power to do noble or base acts, and likewise in our power not to do them, and this was what being good or bad meant, then it is in our power to be virtuous or vicious.

The saying that 'no one is voluntarily wicked nor involuntarily happy' seems to be partly false and partly true; for no one is involuntarily happy, but wickedness *is* voluntary. Or else we shall have to dispute what has just been said, at any rate, and deny that man is a moving principle or begetter of his actions, as of children. But if these facts are evident and we cannot refer actions to moving principles other than those in ourselves, the acts whose moving principles are in us must themselves also be in our power and voluntary.

Witness seems to be borne to this both by individuals in their private capacity and by legislators themselves; for these punish and take vengeance on those who do wicked acts (unless they have acted under compulsion or as a result of ignorance for which they are not themselves responsible), while they honour those who do noble acts, as though they meant to encourage the latter and deter the former. But no one is encouraged to do the things that are neither in our power nor voluntary; it is assumed that there is no gain in being persuaded not to be hot or in pain or hungry or the like, since we shall experience these feelings none the less. Indeed, we punish a man for his very ignorance, if he is thought responsible for the ignorance, as when penalties are doubled in the case of drunkenness; for the moving principle is in the man himself, since he had the power of not getting drunk and his getting drunk was the cause of his ignorance. And we punish those who are ignorant of anything in the laws that they ought to know and that is not difficult, and so too in the case of anything else that they are thought to be ignorant of through carelessness; we assume that it is in their power not to be ignorant, since they have the power of taking care.

But perhaps a man is the kind of man not to take care. Still they are themselves by their slack lives responsible for becoming men of that kind, and men are themselves responsible for being unjust or self-indulgent, in that they cheat or spend their time in drinking-bouts and the like; for it is activities exercised on particular objects that make the corresponding character. This is plain from the case of people training for any contest or action; they practise the activity the whole time. Now not to know that it is from the exercise of activities on particular objects that states of character are produced is the mark of a thoroughly senseless person. Again, it is irrational to suppose that a man who acts unjustly does not wish to be unjust or a man who acts self-indulgently to be self-indulgent. But if *without* being ignorant a man does the things which will make him unjust, he will be unjust voluntarily. Yet it does not follow that if he wishes he will cease to be unjust and will be just. For neither does the man who is ill become well on those terms. We may suppose a case in which he is ill voluntarily, through living incontinently and disobeying his doctors. In that case it was *then* open to him not to be ill, but not now, when he has thrown away his chance, just as when you have let a stone go it is too late to recover it; but yet it was in your power to throw it, since the moving principle was in you. So, too, to the unjust and to the self-indulgent man it was open at the beginning not to become men of this kind; and so they are unjust and self-indulgent voluntarily; but now that they have become so it is not possible for them not to be so.

But not only are the vices of the soul voluntary, but those of the body also for some men, whom we accordingly blame; while no one blames those who are ugly by nature, we blame those who are so owing to want of exercise and care. So it is, too, with respect to weakness and infirmity; no one would reproach a man blind from birth or by disease or from a blow, but rather pity him, while every one would blame a man who was blind from drunkenness or some other form of self-indulgence. Of vices of the body, then, those in our own power are blamed, those not in our power are not. And if this be so, in the other cases also the vices that are blamed must be in our own power.

Now someone may say that all men aim at the apparent good, but have no control over the appearance, but the end appears to each man in a form answering to his character. We reply that if each man is somehow responsible for his state of character, he will also be himself somehow responsible for the appearance; but if not, no one is responsible for his own evildoing, but everyone does evil acts through ignorance of the end, thinking that by these he will get what is best, and the aiming at the end is not self-chosen but one must be born with an eye, as it were, by which to judge rightly and choose what is truly good, and he is well endowed by nature who is well endowed with this. For it is what is greatest and most noble, and what we cannot get or learn from another, but must have just such as it was when given us at birth, and to be well and nobly endowed with this will be perfect and true excellence of natural endowment. If this is true, then, how will virtue be more voluntary than vice? To both men alike, the good and the bad, the end appears and is fixed by nature or however it may be, and it is by referring everything else to this that men do whatever they do.

Whether, then, it is not by nature that the end appears to each man such as it does appear, but something also depends on him, or the end is natural but because the good man adopts the means voluntarily virtue is voluntary, vice also will be none the less voluntary; for in the case of the bad man there is equally present that which depends on himself in his actions even if not in his end. If, then, as is asserted, the virtues are voluntary (for we are ourselves somehow part-causes of our states of character, and it is by being persons of a certain kind that we set the end to be so and so), the vices also will be voluntary; for the same is true of them.

With regard to the virtues *in general* we have stated their genus in outline, viz. that they are means and that they are states of character, and that they tend, and by their own nature, to the doing of the acts by which they are produced, and that they are in our power and voluntary, and act as the right rule prescribes. But actions and states of character are not voluntary in the same way; for we are masters of our actions from the beginning right to the end, if we know the particular facts, but though we control the beginning of our states of character the gradual progress is not obvious, any more than it is in illnesses; because it was in our power, however, to act in this way or not in this way, therefore the states are voluntary. . . .

## BOOK V • MORAL VIRTUE (*cont.*)

### *Justice: Its Sphere and Outer Nature: In What Sense It Is a Mean*

*The just as the lawful (universal justice) and the just as the fair and equal (particular justice): the former considered*

1. With regard to justice and injustice we must consider (1) what kind of actions they are concerned with, (2) what sort of mean justice is, and (3) between what extremes the just act is intermediate. Our investigation shall follow the same course as the preceding discussions.

We see that all men mean by justice that kind of state of character which makes people disposed to do what is just and makes them act justly and wish for what is just; and similarly by injustice that state which makes them act unjustly and wish for what is unjust. Let us too, then, lay this down as a general basis. For the same is not true of the sciences and the faculties as of states of character. A faculty or a science which is one and the same is held to relate to contrary objects, but a state of character which is one of two contraries does *not* produce the contrary results; e.g. as a result of health we do not do what is the opposite of healthy, but only what is healthy; for we say a man walks healthily, when he walks as a healthy man would.

Now often one contrary state is recognized from its contrary, and often states are recognized from the subjects that exhibit them; for (A) if good condition is known, bad condition also becomes known, and (B) good condition is known from the things that are in good condition, and they from it. If good condition is firmness of flesh, it is necessary both that bad condition should be flabbiness of flesh and that the wholesome should be that which causes firmness in flesh. And it follows for the most part that if one contrary is ambiguous the other also will be ambiguous; e.g. that if 'just' is so, 'unjust' will be so too.

Now 'justice' and 'injustice' seem to be ambiguous, but because their different meanings approach near to one another the ambiguity escapes notice and is not obvious as it is, comparatively, when the meanings are far apart, e.g. (for here the difference in outward form is great) as the ambiguity in the use of *kleis* for the collar-bone of an animal and for that with which we lock a door. Let us take as a starting-point, then, the various meanings of 'an unjust man'. Both the lawless man and the grasping and unfair man are thought to be unjust, so that evidently both the law-abiding and the fair man will be just. The just, then, is the lawful and the fair, the unjust the unlawful and the unfair.

Since the unjust man is grasping, he must be concerned with goods—not all goods, but those with which prosperity and adversity have to do, which taken absolutely are always good, but for a particular person are not always good. Now men pray for and pursue these things; but they should not, but should pray that the things that are good absolutely may also be good for them, and should choose the things that *are* good for them. The unjust man does not always choose the greater, but also the less—in the case of things bad absolutely; but because the lesser evil is itself thought to be in a sense good, and graspingness is directed at the good, therefore he is thought to be grasping. And he is unfair; for this contains and is common to both.

Since the lawless man was seen to be unjust and the law-abiding man just, evidently all lawful acts are in a sense just acts; for the acts laid down by the legislative art are lawful, and each of these, we say, is just. Now the laws in their enactments on all subjects aim at the common advantage either of all or of the best or of those who hold power, or something of the sort; so that in one sense we call those acts just that tend to produce and preserve happiness and its components for the political society. And the law bids us do both the acts of a brave man (e.g. not to desert our post nor take to flight nor throw away our arms), and those of a temperate man (e.g. not to commit adultery nor to gratify one's lust), and those of a good-tempered man (e.g. not to strike another nor to speak evil), and similarly with regard to the other virtues and forms of wickedness, commanding some acts and forbidding others; and the rightly-framed law does this rightly, and the hastily conceived one less well.

This form of justice, then, is complete virtue, although not without qualification, but in relation to our neighbour. And therefore justice is often thought to be the greatest of virtues, and 'neither evening nor morning star' is so wonderful; and proverbially 'in justice is every virtue comprehended'. And it is complete virtue in its fullest sense because it is the actual exercise of complete virtue. It is complete because he who possesses it can exercise his virtue not only in himself but towards his neighbour also; for many men can exercise virtue in their own affairs, but not in their relations to their neighbour. This is why the saying of Bias is thought to be true, that 'rule will show the man'; for a ruler is necessarily in relation to other men, and a member of a society. For this same reason justice, alone of the virtues, is thought to be 'another's good', because it is related to our neighbour; for it does what is advantageous to another, either a ruler or a co-partner. Now the worst man is he who exercises his wickedness both towards himself and towards his friends, and the best man is not he who exercises his virtue towards himself but he who exercises it towards another; for this is a difficult task. Justice in this sense, then, is not part of virtue but virtue entire, nor is the contrary injustice a part of vice but vice entire. What the difference is between virtue and justice in this sense is plain from what we have said; they are the same but their essence is not the same; what, as a relation to

one's neighbour, is justice is, as a certain kind of state without qualification, virtue.

### The just as the fair and equal: divided into distribution and rectificatory justice

2. But at all events what we are investigating is the justice which is a *part* of virtue; for there is a justice of this kind, as we maintain. Similarly it is with injustice in the particular sense that we are concerned.

That there is such a thing is indicated by the fact that while the man who exhibits in action the other forms of wickedness acts wrongly indeed, but not graspingly (e.g. the man who throws away his shield through cowardice or speaks harshly through bad temper or fails to help a friend with money through meanness), when a man acts graspingly he often exhibits none of these vices—no, nor all together, but certainly wickedness of some kind (for we blame him) and injustice. There is, then, another kind of injustice which is a part of injustice in the wide sense, and a use of the word 'unjust' which answers to a part of what is unjust in the wide sense of 'contrary to the law'. Again, if one man commits adultery for the sake of gain and makes money by it, while another does so at the bidding of appetite though he loses money and is penalized for it, the latter would be held to be self-indulgent rather than grasping, but the former is unjust, but not self-indulgent; evidently, therefore, he is unjust by reason of his making gain by his act. Again, all other unjust acts are ascribed invariably to some particular kind of wickedness, e.g. adultery to self-indulgence, the desertion of a comrade in battle to cowardice, physical violence to anger; but if a man makes gain, his action is ascribed to no form of wickedness but injustice. Evidently, therefore, there is apart from injustice in the wide sense another, 'particular', injustice which shares the name and nature of the first, because its definition falls within the same genus; for the significance of both consists in a relation to one's neighbour, but the one is concerned with honour or money or safety—or that which includes all these, if we had a single name for it—and its motive is the pleasure that arises from gain; while the other is concerned with all the objects with which the good man is concerned.

It is clear, then, that there is more than one kind of justice, and that there is one which is distinct from virtue entire; we must try to grasp its genus and differentia.

The unjust has been divided into the unlawful and the unfair, and the just into the lawful and the fair. To the unlawful answers the aforementioned sense of injustice. But since the unfair and the unlawful are not the same, but are different as a part is from its whole (for all that is unfair is unlawful, but not all that is unlawful is unfair), the unjust and injustice in the sense of the unfair are not the same as but different from the former kind, as part from whole; for injustice in this sense is a part of injustice in the wide sense, and similarly justice in the one sense of justice in the other. Therefore we must speak also about particular justice and particular injustice, and similarly about the just and the unjust. The justice, then, which answers to the whole of virtue, and the corresponding injustice, one being the exercise of virtue as a whole, and the other that of vice as a whole, towards one's neighbour, we may leave on one side. And how the meanings of 'just' and 'unjust' which answer to these are to be distinguished is evident; for practically the majority of the acts commanded by the law are those which are prescribed from the point of view of virtue taken as a whole; for the law bids us practise every virtue and forbids us to practise any vice. And the things that tend to produce virtue taken as a whole are those of the acts prescribed by the law which have been prescribed with a view to education for the common good. But with regard to the education of the individual as such, which makes him without qualification a good *man,* we must determine later whether this is the function of the political art or of another; for perhaps it is not the same to be a good man and a good citizen of any state taken at random.

Of particular justice and that which is just in the corresponding sense, (A) one kind is that which is manifested in distributions of honour or money or the other things that fall to be divided among those who have a share in the constitution (for in these it is possible for one man to have a share either unequal or equal to that of another), and (B) one is that which

plays a rectifying part in transactions between man and man. Of this there are two divisions; of transactions (1) some are voluntary and (2) others involuntary—voluntary such transactions as sale, purchase, loan for consumption, pledging, loan for use, depositing, letting (they are called voluntary because the *origin* of these transactions is voluntary), while of the involuntary (*a*) some are clandestine, such as theft, adultery, poisoning, procuring, enticement of slaves, assassination, false witness, and (*b*) others are violent, such as assault, imprisonment, murder, robbery with violence, mutilation, abuse, insult. . . .

### *Natural and legal justice*

7. Of political justice part is natural, part legal,—natural, that which everywhere has the same force and does not exist by people's thinking this or that; legal, that which is originally indifferent, but when it has been laid down is not indifferent, e.g. that a prisoner's ransom shall be a mina, or that a goat and not two sheep shall be sacrificed, and again all the laws that are passed for particular cases, e.g. that sacrifice shall be made in honour of Brasidas, and the provisions of decrees. Now some think that all justice is of this sort, because that which is by nature is unchangeable and has everywhere the same force (as fire burns both here and in Persia), while they see change in the things recognized as just. This, however, is not true in this unqualified way, but is true in a sense; or rather, with the gods it is perhaps not true at all, while with us there is something that is just even by nature, yet all of it is changeable; but still some is by nature, some not by nature. It is evident which sort of thing, among things capable of being otherwise, is by nature; and which is not but is legal and conventional, assuming that both are equally changeable. And in all other things the same distinction will apply; by nature the right hand is stronger, yet it is possible that all men should come to be ambidextrous. The things which are just by virtue of convention and expediency are like measures; for wine and corn measures are not everywhere equal, but larger in wholesale and smaller in retail markets. Similarly, the things which are just not by nature but by human enactment are not everywhere the same, since constitutions also are not

the same, though there is but one which is everywhere by nature the best.

Of things just and lawful each is related as the universal to its particulars; for the things that are done are many, but of *them* each is one, since it is universal.

There is a difference between the act of injustice and what is unjust, and between the act of justice and what is just; for a thing is unjust by nature or by enactment; and this very thing, when it has been done, is an act of injustice, but before it is done is not yet that but is unjust. So, too, with an act of justice (though the general term is rather 'just action', and 'act of justice' is applied to the correction of the act of injustice).

Each of these must later be examined separately with regard to the nature and number of its species and the nature of the things with which it is concerned. . . .

### Equity, a corrective of legal justice

10. Our next subject is equity and the equitable, and their respective relations to justice and the just. For on examination they appear to be neither absolutely the same nor generically different; and while we sometimes praise what is equitable and the equitable man (so that we apply the name by way of praise even to instances of the other virtues, instead of 'good', meaning by 'more equitable' that a thing is better), at other times, when we reason it out, it seems strange if the equitable, being something different from the just, is yet praiseworthy; for either the just or the equitable is not good, if they are different; or, if both are good, they are the same.

These, then, are pretty much the considerations that give rise to the problem about the equitable; they are all in a sense correct and not opposed to one another; for the equitable, though it is better than one kind of justice, yet is just, and it is not as being a different class of thing that it is better than the just. The same thing, then, is just and equitable, and while both are good the equitable is superior. What creates the problem is that the equitable is just, but not the legally just but a correction of legal justice. The reason is that all law is universal but about some things it is not possible to make a universal statement which shall be cor-

rect. In those cases, then, in which it is necessary to speak universally, but not possible to do so correctly, the law takes the usual case, though it is not ignorant of the possibility of error. And it is none the less correct; for the error is not in the law nor in the legislator but in the nature of the thing, since the matter of practical affairs is of this kind from the start. When the law speaks universally, then, and a case arises on it which is not covered by the universal statement, then it is right, where the legislator fails us and has erred by over-simplicity, to correct the omission—to say what the legislator himself would have said had be been present, and would have put into his law if he had known. Hence the equitable is just, and better than one kind of justice—not better than absolute justice, but better than the error that arises from the absoluteness of the statement. And this is the nature of the equitable, a correction of law where it is defective owing to its universality. In fact this is the reason why all things are not determined by law, viz. that about some things it is impossible to lay down a law, so that a decree is needed. For when the thing is indefinite the rule also is indefinite, like the leaden rule used in making the Lesbian moulding; the rule adapts itself to the shape of the stone and is not rigid, and so too the decree is adapted to the facts.

It is plain, then, what the equitable is, and that it is just and is better than one kind of justice. It is evident also from this who the equitable man is; the man who chooses and does such acts, and is no stickler for his rights in a bad sense but tends to take less than his share though he has the law on his side, is equitable, and this state of character is equity, which is a sort of justice and not a different state of character. . . .

## BOOK VI • INTELLECTUAL VIRTUE

### *Introduction*

*Reasons for studying intellectual virtue: intellect divided into the contemplative and the calculative*

1. Since we have previously said that one ought to choose that which is intermediate, not the excess nor the defect, and that the intermediate is determined

by the dictates of the right rule, let us discuss the nature of these dictates. In all the states of character we have mentioned, as in all other matters, there is a mark to which the man who has the rule looks, and heightens or relaxes his activity accordingly, and there is a standard which determines the mean states which we say are intermediate between excess and defect, being in accordance with the right rule. But such a statement, though true, is by no means clear; for not only here but in all other pursuits which are objects of knowledge it is indeed true to say that we must not exert ourselves nor relax our efforts too much or too little, but to an intermediate extent and as the right rule dictates; but if a man had only this knowledge he would be none the wiser—e.g. we should not know what sort of medicines to apply to our body if someone were to say 'all those which the medical art prescribes, and which agree with the practice of one who possesses the art'. Hence it is necessary with regard to the states of the soul also, not only that this true statement should be made, but also that it should be determined what is the right rule and what is the standard that fixes it.

We divided the virtues of the soul and said that some are virtues of character and others of intellect. Now we have discussed in detail the moral virtues; with regard to the others let us express our view as follows, beginning with some remarks about the soul. We said before that there are two parts of the soul—that which grasps a rule or rational principle, and the irrational; let us now draw a similar distinction within the part which grasps a rational principle. And let it be assumed that there are two parts which grasp a rational principle—one by which we contemplate the kind of things whose originative causes are invariable, and one by which we contemplate variable things; for where objects differ in kind the part of the soul answering to each of the two is different in kind, since it is in virtue of a certain likeness and kinship with their objects that they have the knowledge they have. Let one of these parts be called the scientific and the other the calculative; for to deliberate and to calculate are the same thing, but no one deliberates about the invariable. Therefore the calculative is one part of the faculty which

grasps a rational principle. We must, then, learn what is the best state of each of these two parts; for this is the virtue of each.

*The proper object of contemplation is truth; that of calculation is truth corresponding with right desire*

2. The virtue of a thing is relative to its proper work. Now there are three things in the soul which control action and truth—sensation, reason, desire.

Of these sensation originates no action; this is plain from the fact that the lower animals have sensation but no share in action.

What affirmation and negation are in thinking, pursuit and avoidance are in desire; so that since moral virtue is a state of character concerned with choice, and choice is deliberate desire, therefore both the reasoning must be true and the desire right, if the choice is to be good, and the latter must pursue just what the former asserts. Now this kind of intellect and of truth is practical; of the intellect which is contemplative, not practical nor productive, the good and the bad state are truth and falsity respectively (for this is the work of everything intellectual); while of the part which is practical and intellectual the good state is truth in agreement with right desire.

The origin of action—its efficient, not its final cause—is choice, and that of choice is desire and reasoning with a view to an end. This is why choice cannot exist either without reason and intellect or without a moral state; for good action and its opposite cannot exist without a combination of intellect and character. Intellect itself, however, moves nothing, but only the intellect which aims at an end and is practical; for this rules the productive intellect as well, since everyone who makes makes for an end, and that which is made is not an end in the unqualified sense (but only an end in a particular relation, and the end of a particular operation)—only that which is *done* is that; for good action is an end, and desire aims at this. Hence choice is either desiderative reason or ratiocinative desire, and such an origin of action is a man. (It is to be noted that nothing that is past is an object of choice, e.g. no one chooses to have sacked Troy; for no one *deliberates* about the past, but about what is future and capable of being otherwise, while what is past is not capable of not having taken place; hence Agathon is right in saying:

*For this alone is lacking even to God,*
*To make undone things that have once been done.)*

The work of both the intellectual parts, then, is truth. Therefore the states that are most strictly those in respect of which each of these parts will reach truth are the virtues of the two parts.

## The Chief Intellectual Virtues

### Science—demonstrative knowledge of the necessary and eternal

3. Let us begin, then, from the beginning, and discuss these states once more. Let it be assumed that the states by virtue of which the soul possesses truth by way of affirmation or denial are five in number, i.e. art, scientific knowledge, practical wisdom, philosophic wisdom, intuitive reason; we do not include judgement and opinion because in these we may be mistaken.

Now what *scientific knowledge* is, if we are to speak exactly and not follow mere similarities, is plain from what follows. We all suppose that what we know is not even capable of being otherwise; of things capable of being otherwise we do not know, when they have passed outside our observation, whether they exist or not. Therefore the object of scientific knowledge is of necessity. Therefore it is eternal; for things that are of necessity in the unqualified sense are all eternal; and things that are eternal are ungenerated and imperishable. Again, every science is thought to be capable of being taught, and its object of being learnt. And all teaching starts from what is already known, as we maintain in the *Analytics* also; for it proceeds sometimes through induction and sometimes by syllogism. Now induction is the starting-point which knowledge even of the universal presupposes, while syllogism proceeds *from* universals. There are therefore starting-points from which syllogism proceeds, which are not reached by syllogism; it is therefore by induction that they are acquired. Scientific knowledge is, then, a state of capacity to demonstrate, and has the other limiting characteristics which we specify in the *Analytics;* for it is when a man believes in a certain way and the starting-points are known to him that he has scientific knowledge, since if they are not better known to him than the conclusion, he will have his knowledge only incidentally.

Let this, then, be taken as our account of scientific knowledge. . . .

### Practical wisdom—knowledge of how to secure the ends of human life

5. Regarding *practical wisdom* we shall get at the truth by considering who are the persons we credit with it. Now it is thought to be a mark of a man of practical wisdom to be able to deliberate well about what is good and expedient for himself, not in some particular respect, e.g. about what sorts of thing conduce to health or to strength, but about what sorts of thing conduce to the good life in general. This is shown by the fact that we credit men with practical wisdom in some particular respect when they have calculated well with a view to some good end which is one of those that are not the object of any art. It follows that in the general sense also the man who is capable of deliberating has practical wisdom. Now no one deliberates about things that are invariable, or about things that it is impossible for him to do. Therefore, since scientific knowledge involves demonstration, but there is no demonstration of things whose first principles are variable (for all such things might actually be otherwise), and since it is impossible to deliberate about things that are of necessity, practical wisdom cannot be scientific knowledge or art; not science because that which can be done is capable of being otherwise, not art because action and making are different kinds of thing. The remaining alternative, then, is that it is a true and reasoned state of capacity to act with regard to the things that are good or bad for man. For while making has an end other than itself, action cannot; for

good action itself is its end. It is for this reason that we think Pericles and men like him have practical wisdom, viz. because they can see what is good for themselves and what is good for men in general; we consider that those can do this who are good at managing households or states. (This is why we call temperance (*sōphrosunē*) by this name; we imply that it preserves one's practical wisdom (*sōzousa tēn phronēsin*). Now what it preserves is a judgement of the kind we have described. For it is not any and every judgement that pleasant and painful objects destroy and pervert, e.g. the judgement that the triangle has or has not its angles equal to two right angles, but only judgements about what is to be done. For the originating causes of the things that are done consist in the end at which they are aimed; but the man who has been ruined by pleasure or pain forthwith fails to see any such originating cause—to see that for the sake of this or because of this he ought to choose and do whatever he chooses and does; for vice is destructive of the originating cause of action.)

Practical wisdom, then, must be a reasoned and true state of capacity to act with regard to human goods. But further, while there is such a thing as excellence in art, there is no such thing as excellence in practical wisdom; and in art he who errs willingly is preferable, but in practical wisdom, as in the virtues, he is the reverse. Plainly, then, practical wisdom is a virtue and not an art. There being two parts of the soul that can follow a course of reasoning, it must be a virtue of one of the two, i.e. of that part which forms opinions; for opinion is about the variable and so is practical wisdom. But yet it is not only a reasoned state; this is shown by the fact that a state of that sort may be forgotten but practical wisdom cannot.

## Intuitive reason—knowledge of the principles from which science proceeds

6. Scientific knowledge is judgement about things that are universal and necessary; and the conclusions of demonstration, and all scientific knowledge, follow from first principles (for scientific knowledge involves proof). This being so, the first principle from which what is scientifically known follows cannot be an object of scientific knowledge, of art, or of practi-

cal wisdom; for that which can be scientifically known can be demonstrated, and art and practical wisdom deal with things that are variable. Nor are these first principles the objects of philosophic wisdom, for it is a mark of the philosopher to have *demonstration* about some things. If, then, the states of mind by which we have truth and are never deceived about things invariable or even variable are scientific knowledge, practical wisdom, philosophic wisdom, and intuitive reason, and it cannot be any of the three (i.e. practical wisdom, scientific knowledge, or philosophic wisdom), the remaining alternative is that it is *intuitive reason* that grasps the first principles.

## Philosophic wisdom—the union of intuitive reason and science

7. *Wisdom* (1) in the arts we ascribe to their most finished exponents, e.g. to Phidias as a sculptor and to Polyclitus as a maker of portrait-statues, and here we mean nothing by wisdom except excellence in art; but (2) we think that some people are wise in general, not in some particular field or in any other limited respect, as Homer says in the *Margites*,

> Him did the gods make neither a digger nor yet
>   a ploughman
> Nor wise in anything else.

Therefore wisdom must plainly be the most finished of the forms of knowledge. It follows that the wise man must not only know what follows from the first principles, but must also possess truth about the first principles. Therefore wisdom must be intuitive reason combined with scientific knowledge—scientific knowledge of the highest objects which has received as it were its proper completion.

Of the highest objects, we say; for it would be strange to think that the art of politics, or practical wisdom, is the best knowledge, since man is not the best thing in the world. Now if what is healthy or good is different for men and for fishes, but what is white or straight is always the same, anyone would say that what is wise is the same but what is practically wise is different; for it is to that which considers well the various matters concerning itself that one ascribes practical wisdom, and it is to this that one will entrust such matters. This is why we say that some even of the lower animals have practical wisdom, viz. those which are found to have a power of foresight with regard to their own life. It is evident also that philosophic wisdom and the art of politics cannot be the same; for if the state of mind concerned with a man's own interests is to be called philosophic wisdom, there will be many philosophic wisdoms; there will not be one concerned with the good of all animals (any more than there is one art of medicine for all existing things), but a different philosophic wisdom about the good of each species.

But if the argument be that man is the best of the animals, this makes no difference; for there are other things much more divine in their nature even than man, e.g., most conspicuously, the bodies of which the heavens are framed. From what has been said it is plain, then, that philosophic wisdom is scientific knowledge, combined with intuitive reason, of the things that are highest by nature. This is why we say Anaxagoras, Thales, and men like them have philosophic but not practical wisdom, when we see them ignorant of what is to their own advantage, and why we say that they know things that are remarkable, admirable, difficult, and divine, but useless; viz. because it is not human goods that they seek.

Practical wisdom on the other hand is concerned with things human and things about which it is possible to deliberate; for we say this is above all the work of the man of practical wisdom, to deliberate well, but no one deliberates about things invariable, or about things which have not an end which is a good that can be brought about by action. The man who is without qualification good at deliberating is the man who is capable of aiming in accordance with calculation at the best for man of things attainable by action. Nor is practical wisdom concerned with universals only—it must also recognize the particulars; for it is practical, and practice is concerned with particulars. This is why some who do not know, and especially those who have experience, are more practical than others who know; for if a man knew that light meats are digestible and wholesome, but did not know which sorts of meat are light, he would not produce health, but the man who knows that chicken is wholesome is more likely to produce health.

Now practical wisdom is concerned with action;

therefore one should have both forms of it, or the latter in preference to the former. But here, too, there must be a controlling kind.

*Relations between practical wisdom and political science*

8. Political wisdom and practical wisdom are the same state of mind, but their essence is not the same. Of the wisdom concerned with the city, the practical wisdom which plays a controlling part is legislative wisdom, while that which is related to this as particulars to their universal is known by the general name 'political wisdom'; this has to do with action and deliberation, for a decree is a thing to be carried out in the form of an individual act. This is why the exponents of this art are alone said to 'take part in politics'; for these alone 'do things' as manual labourers 'do things'.

Practical wisdom also is identified especially with that form of it which is concerned with a man himself—with the individual; and this is known by the general name 'practical wisdom'; of the other kinds one is called household management, another legislation, the third politics, and of the latter one part is called deliberative and the other judicial. Now knowing what is good for oneself will be one kind of knowledge, but it is very different from the other kinds; and the man who knows and concerns himself with his own interests is thought to have practical wisdom, while politicians are thought to be busybodies; hence the words of Euripides:

> *But how could I be wise, who might at ease,*
> *Numbered among the army's multitude,*
> *Have had an equal share? . . .*
> *For those who aim too high and do too much. . . .*

Those who think thus seek their own good, and consider that one ought to do so. From this opinion, then, has come the view that such men have practical wisdom; yet perhaps one's own good cannot exist without household management, nor without a form of government. Further, how one should order one's own affairs is not clear and needs inquiry.

What has been said is confirmed by the fact that while young men become geometricians and mathematicians and wise in matters like these, it is thought that a young man of practical wisdom cannot be found. The cause is that such wisdom is concerned not only with universals but with particulars, which become familiar from experience, but a young man has no experience, for it is length of time that gives experience; indeed one might ask this question too, why a boy may become a mathematician, but not a philosopher or a physicist. Is it because the objects of mathematics exist by abstraction, while the first principles of these other subjects come from experience, and because young men have no conviction about the latter but merely use the proper language, while the essence of mathematical objects is plain enough to them?

Further, error in deliberation may be either about the universal or about the particular; we may fail to know either that all water that weighs heavy is bad, or that this particular water weighs heavy.

That practical wisdom is not scientific knowledge is evident; for it is, as has been said, concerned with the ultimate particular fact, since the thing to be done is of this nature. It is opposed, then, to intuitive reason; for intuitive reason is of the limiting premisses, for which no reason can be given, while practical wisdom is concerned with the ultimate particular, which is the object not of scientific knowledge but of perception—not the perception of qualities peculiar to one sense but a perception akin to that by which we perceive that the particular figure before us is a triangle; for in that direction as well there will be a limit. But this is rather perception than practical wisdom, though it is another kind of perception than that of the qualities peculiar to each sense. . . .

### Relation of Philosophic to Practical Wisdom

*What is the use of philosophic and of practical wisdom? Philosophic wisdom is the formal cause of happiness; practical wisdom is what ensures the taking of proper means to the proper ends desired by moral virtue*

12. Difficulties might be raised as to the utility of these qualities of mind. For (1) philosophic wisdom will contemplate none of the things that will make a man happy (for it is not concerned with any coming into being), and though practical wisdom has *this* merit, for what purpose do we need it? Practical wisdom is the quality of mind concerned with things just and noble and good for man, but these are the things which it is the mark of a *good* man to do, and we are none the more able to act for *knowing* them if the virtues are states of *character,* just as we are none the better able to act for knowing the things that are healthy and sound, in the sense not of producing but of issuing from the state of health; for we are none the more able to act for having the art of medicine or of gymnastics. But (2) if we are to say that a man should have practical wisdom not for the sake of knowing moral truths but for the sake of becoming good, practical wisdom will be of no use to those who *are* good; but again it is of no use to those who have *not* virtue; for it will make no difference whether they have practical wisdom themselves or obey others who have it, and it would be enough for us to do what we do in the case of health; though we wish to become healthy, yet we do not learn the art of medicine. (3) Besides this, it would be thought strange if practical wisdom, being inferior to philosophic wisdom, is to be put in authority over it, as seems to be implied by the fact that the art which produces anything rules and issues commands about that thing.

These, then, are the questions we must discuss; so far we have only stated the difficulties.

(1) Now first let us say that in themselves these states must be worthy of choice because they are the virtues of the two parts of the soul respectively, even if neither of them produces anything.

(2) Secondly, they do produce something, not as the art of medicine produces health, however, but as health produces health; so does philosophic wisdom produce happiness; for, being a part of virtue entire, by being possessed and by actualizing itself it makes a man happy.

(3) Again, the work of man is achieved only in accordance with practical wisdom as well as with moral virtue; for virtue makes us aim at the right mark, and practical wisdom makes us take the right means. (Of the fourth part of the soul—the nutritive—there is no such virtue; for there is nothing which it is in its power to do or nor to do.)

(4) With regard to our being none the more able to do because of our practical wisdom what is noble and just, let us begin a little further back, starting with the following principle. As we say that some people who do just acts are not necessarily just, i.e. those who do the acts ordained by the laws either unwillingly or owing to ignorance or for some other reason and not for the sake of the acts themselves (though, to be sure, they do what they should and all the things that the good man ought), so is it, it seems, that in order to be good one must be in a certain state when one does the several acts, i.e. one must do them as a result of choice and for the sake of the acts themselves. Now virtue makes the choice right, but the question of the things which should naturally be done to carry out our choice belongs not to virtue but to another faculty. We must devote our attention to these matters and give a clearer statement about them. There is a faculty which is called cleverness; and this is such as to be able to do the things that tend towards the mark we have set before ourselves, and to hit it. Now if the mark be noble, the cleverness is laudable, but if the mark be bad, the cleverness is mere smartness; hence we call even men of practical wisdom clever or smart. Practical wisdom is not the faculty, but it does not exist without this faculty. And this eye of the soul acquires its formed state not without the aid of virtue, as has been said and is plain; for the syllogisms which deal with acts to be done are things which involve a starting-point, viz. 'since the end, i.e. what is best, is of such and such a nature', whatever it may be (let it for the sake of argument be what we please); and this is not evident except to the good man; for wickedness perverts us and causes us to be deceived about the starting-points of action. Therefore it is evident that it is impossible to be practically wise without being good.

*Relation of practical wisdom to natural virtue, moral virtue, and the right rule*

13. We must therefore consider virtue also once more; for virtue too is similarly related; as practical wisdom is to cleverness—not the same, but like it— so is natural virtue to virtue in the strict sense. For all men think that each type of character belongs to its possessors in some sense by nature; for from the very moment of birth we are just or fitted for self-control or brave or have the other moral qualities; but yet we seek something else as that which is good in the strict sense—we seek for the presence of such qualities in another way. For both children and brutes have the natural dispositions to these qualities, but without reason these are evidently hurtful. Only we seem to see this much, that, while one may be led astray by them, as a strong body which moves without sight may stumble badly because of its lack of sight, still, if a man once acquires reason, that makes a difference in action; and his state, while still like what it was, will then be virtue in the strict sense. Therefore, as in the part of us which forms opinions there are two types, cleverness and practical wisdom, so too in the moral part there are two types, natural virtue and virtue in the strict sense, and of these the latter involves practical wisdom. This is why some say that all the virtues are forms of practical wisdom, and why Socrates in one respect was on the right track while in another he went astray; in thinking that all the virtues were forms of practical wisdom he was wrong, but in saying they implied practical wisdom he was right. This is confirmed by the fact that even now all men, when they define virtue, after naming the state of character and its objects add 'that (state) which is in accordance with the right rule'; now the right rule is that which is in accordance with practical wisdom. All men, then, seem somehow to divine that this kind of state is virtue, viz. that which is in accordance with practical wisdom. But we must go a little further. For it is not merely the state in accordance with the right rule, but the state that implies the *presence* of the right rule, that is virtue; and practical wisdom is a right rule about such matters. Socrates, then, thought the virtues were rules or rational principles (for he thought they were, all of them, forms of scientific knowledge), while we think they *involve* a rational principle.

It is clear, then, from what has been said, that it is not possible to be good in the strict sense without practical wisdom, or practically wise without moral virtue. But in this way we may also refute the dialectical argument whereby it might be contended that the virtues exist in separation from each other; the same man, it might be said, is not best equipped by nature for all the virtues, so that he will have already acquired one when he has not yet acquired another. This is possible in respect of the natural virtues, but not in respect of those in respect of which a man is called without qualification good; for with the presence of the one quality, practical wisdom, will be given all the virtues. And it is plain that, even if it were of no practical virtue, we should have needed it because it is the virtue of the part of us in question; plain too that the choice will not be right without practical wisdom any more than without virtue; for the one determines the end and the other makes us do the things that lead to the end.

But again it is not *supreme* over philosophic wisdom, i.e. over the superior part of us, any more than the art of medicine is over health; for it does not use it but provides for its coming into being; it issues orders, then, for its sake, but not to it. Further, to maintain its supremacy would be like saying that the art of politics rules the gods because it issues orders about all the affairs of the state.

## BOOK VII • CONTINENCE AND INCONTINENCE: PLEASURE

### *Continence and Incontinence*

*Six varieties of character: method of treatment: current opinions*

1. Let us now make a fresh beginning and point out that of moral states to be avoided there are three kinds—vice, incontinence, brutishness. The contraries of two of these are evident—one we call virtue, the other continence; to brutishness it would be most fitting to oppose superhuman virtue, a heroic and divine kind of virtue, as Homer has represented Priam saying of Hector that he was very good,

> *For he seemed not, he,*
> *The child of a mortal man, but as one that of God's*
> *seed came.*

Therefore if, as they say, men become gods by excess of virtue, of this kind must evidently be the state opposed to the brutish state: for as a brute has no vice or virtue, so neither has a god; his state is higher than virtue, and that of a brute is a different kind of state from vice.

Now, since it is rarely that a godlike man is found—to use the epithet of the Spartans, who when they admire anyone highly call him a 'godlike man'—so too the brutish type is rarely found among men; it is found chiefly among barbarians, but some brutish qualities are also produced by disease or deformity; and we also call by this evil name those who surpass ordinary men in vice. Of this kind of disposition, however, we must later make some mention, while we have discussed vice before; we must now discuss incontinence and softness (or effeminacy), and continence and endurance; for we must treat each of the two neither as identical with virtue or wickedness, nor as a different genus. We must, as in all other cases, set the apparent facts before us and, after first discussing the difficulties, go on to prove, if possible, the truth of all the common opinions about these affections of the mind, or, failing this, of the greater number and the most authoritative; for if we both resolve the difficulties and leave the common opinions undisturbed, we shall have proved the case sufficiently.

Now (1) both continence and endurance are thought to be included among things good and praiseworthy, and both incontinence and softness among things bad and blameworthy; and the same man is thought to be continent and ready to abide by the result of his calculations, or incontinent and ready to abandon them. And (2) the incontinent man, knowing that what he does is bad, does it as a result of passion, while the continent man, knowing that his appetites are bad, refuses on account of his rational principle to follow them. (3) The temperate man all men call continent and disposed to endurance, while the continent man some maintain to be always temperate but others do not; and some call the self-indulgent man incontinent and the incontinent man self-indulgent indiscriminately, while others distinguish them. (4) The man of practical wisdom, they sometimes say, cannot be incontinent, while sometimes they say that some who are practically wise and clever *are* incontinent. Again, (5) men are said to be incontinent even with respect to anger, honour, and gain.—These, then, are the things that are said.

*Contradictions involved in the current opinions*

2.  Now we may ask (1) what kind of right judgement has the man who behaves incontinently. That he should behave so when he has knowledge, some say is impossible; for it would be strange—so Socrates thought—if when knowledge was in a man something else could master it and drag it about like a slave. For *Socrates* was entirely opposed to the view in question, holding that there is no such thing as incontinence; no one, he said, when he judges acts against what he judges best—people act so only by reason of ignorance. Now this view plainly contradicts the apparent facts, and we must inquire about what happens to such a man; if he acts by reason of ignorance, what is the manner of his ignorance? For that the man who behaves incontinently does not, before he gets into this state, *think* he ought to act so, is evident. But there are *some* who concede certain of Socrates' contentions but not others; that nothing is stronger than knowledge they admit, but not that no one acts contrary to what has seemed to him the better course, and therefore they say that the incontinent man has not knowledge when he is mastered by his pleasures, but opinion. But *if* it is opinion and not knowledge, if it is not a strong conviction that resists but a weak one, as in men who hesitate, we sympathize with their failure to stand by such convictions against strong appetites; but we do not sympathize with wickedness, nor with any of the other blameworthy states. Is it then *practical wisdom* whose resistance is mastered? That is the strongest of all states. But this is absurd; the same man will be at once practically wise and incontinent, but *no one* would say that it is the part of a practically wise man to do willingly the basest acts. Besides, it has been shown before that the man of practical wisdom is one who will *act* (for he is a man concerned with the individual facts) and who has the other virtues.

(2)  Further, if continence involves having strong and bad appetites, the temperate man will not be continent nor the continent man temperate; for a temperate man will have neither excessive nor bad appetites. But the continent man *must;* for if the appetites are good, the state of character that restrains us from following them is bad, so that not all continence will be good; while if they are weak and not bad, there is nothing admirable in resisting them, and if they are weak and bad, there is nothing great in resisting these either.

(3)  Further, if continence makes a man ready to stand by any and every opinion, it is bad, i.e. if it makes him stand even by a false opinion; and if incontinence makes a man apt to abandon any and every opinion, there will be a good incontinence, of which Sophocles, Neoptolemus in the *Philoctetes* will be an instance; for he is to be praised for not standing by what Odysseus persuaded him to do, because he is pained at telling a lie.

(4)  Further, the sophistic argument presents a difficulty; the syllogism arising from men's wish to expose paradoxical results arising from an opponent's view, in order that they may be admired when they succeed, is one that puts us in a difficulty (for thought is bound fast when it will not rest because the conclusion does not satisfy it, and cannot advance because it cannot refute the argument). There is an argument from which it follows that folly coupled with incontinence is virtue; a man does the opposite of what he thinks right, owing to incontinence, but thinks what is good to be evil and something that he should not do, and in consequence he will do what is good and not what is evil.

(5)  Further, he who on conviction does and pursues and chooses what is pleasant would be thought to be better than one who does so as a result not of calculation but of incontinence; for he is easier to cure since he may be persuaded to change his mind. But to the incontinent man may be applied the proverb 'When water chokes, what is one to wash it down with?' If he had been persuaded of the rightness of what he does, he would have desisted when he was persuaded to change his mind; but now he acts in spite of his being persuaded of something quite different.

(6)  Further, if incontinence and continence are concerned with any and every kind of object, who is

it that is incontinent in the unqualified sense? No one has all the forms of incontinence, but we say some people are incontinent without qualification.

*Solution of the problem, how the incontinent man's knowledge is impaired*

3. Of some such kind are the difficulties that arise; some of these points must be refuted and the others left in possession of the field; for the solution of the difficulty is the discovery of the truth. (1) We must consider first, then, whether incontinent people act knowingly or not, and with what sort of knowledge; then (2) with what sorts of object the incontinent and the continent man may be said to be concerned (i.e. whether with any and every pleasure and pain or with certain determinate kinds), and whether the continent man and the man of endurance are the same or different; and similarly with regard to the other matters germane to this inquiry. The starting-point of our investigation is (*a*) the question whether the continent man and the incontinent are differentiated by their objects or by their attitude, i.e. whether the incontinent man is incontinent simply by being concerned with such-and-such objects, or, instead, by his attitude, or, instead of that, by both these things; (*b*) the second question is whether incontinence and continence are concerned with any and every object or not. The man who is incontinent in the unqualified sense neither is concerned with any and every ob-ject, but with precisely those with which the self-indulgent man is concerned, nor is he characterized by being simply related to these (for then his state would be the same as self-indulgence), but by being related to them in a certain way. For the one is led on in accordance with his own choice, thinking that he ought always to pursue the present pleasure; while the other does not think so, but yet pursues it.

(1) As for the suggestion that it is true opinion and not knowledge against which we act incontinently, that makes no difference to the argument; for some people when in a state of opinion do not hesitate, but think they know exactly. If, then, the notion is that owing to their weak conviction those who have opinion are more likely to act against their judgement than those who know, we answer that there need be no difference between knowledge and opinion in this respect; for some men are no less convinced of what they think than others of what they know; as is shown by the case of Heraclitus. But (*a*), since we use the word 'know' in two senses (for both the man who has knowledge but is not using it and he who is using it are said to know), it *will* make a difference whether, when a man does what he should not, he has the knowledge but is not exercising it, or is exercising it; for the latter seems strange, but not the former.

(*b*) Further, since there are two kinds of premisses, there is nothing to prevent a man's having both premisses and acting against his knowledge, provided that he is using only the universal premiss and not the particular; for it is particular acts that have to be done. And there are also two kinds of universal term; one is predictable of the agent, the other of the object; e.g. 'dry food is good for every man', and 'I am a man', or 'such-and-such food is dry'; but whether 'this food is such-and-such', of this the incontinent man either has not or is not exercising the knowledge. There will, then, be, firstly, an enormous difference between these manners of knowing, so that to know in one way when we act incontinently would not seem anything strange, while to know in the other way would be extraordinary.

And further (*c*) the possession of knowledge in another sense than those just named is something that happens to men; for within the case of having knowledge but not using it we see a difference of state, admitting of the possibility of having knowledge in a sense and yet not having it, as in the instance of a man asleep, mad, or drunk. But now this is just the condition of men under the influence of passions; for outbursts of anger and sexual appetites and some other such passions, it is evident, actually alter our bodily condition, and in some men even produce fits of madness. It is plain, then, that incontinent people must be said to be in a similar condition to men asleep, mad, or drunk. The fact that men use the language that flows from knowledge proves nothing; for even men under the influence of these passions utter scientific proofs and verses of Empedocles, and those who have just begun to learn a science can string together its phrases, but do not yet know it; for it has to become part of themselves, and that takes time; so that we must suppose that the use of language by men in an incontinent state means no more than its utterance by actors on the stage.

(*d*) Again, we may also view the cause as follows in the way a student of nature would. The one opinion is universal, the other is concerned with the particular facts, and here we come to something within the sphere of perception; when a single opinion results from the two, the soul must in one type of case affirm the conclusion, while in the case of opinions concerned with production it must immediately act (e.g. if 'everything sweet ought to be tasted', and 'this is sweet', in the sense of being one of the particular sweet things, the man who can act and is not restrained must at the same time actually act accordingly). When, then, the universal opinion is present in us restraining us from tasting, and there is also the opinion that 'everything sweet is pleasant', and that 'this is sweet' (now this is the opinion that is active), and when appetite happens to be present in us, the one opinion bids us avoid the object, but appetite leads us towards it (for it can move each of our bodily parts); so that it turns out that a man behaves incontinently under the influence (in a sense) of a rule and an opinion, and of one not contrary in itself, but only incidentally—for the appetite is contrary, not the opinion—to the right rule. It also follows that this is the reason why the lower animals are not incontinent, viz. because they have no universal judgement but only imagination and memory of particulars.

The explanation of how the ignorance is dissolved and the incontinent man regains his knowledge, is the same as in the case of the man drunk or asleep and is not peculiar to this condition; we must go to the students of natural science for it. Now, the last premiss being an opinion about a perceptible object, and being also what determines our actions, this a man either has not when he is in the state of passion, or has it in the sense in which having knowledge did not mean knowing but only talking, as a drunken man may mutter the verses of Empedocles. And because the last term is not universal nor equally an object of scientific knowledge with the

universal term, the position that Socrates sought to establish actually seems to result; for it is not in the presence of what is thought to be knowledge proper that the passion occurs (nor is it this that is 'dragged about' as a result of the passion), but in that of perceptual knowledge.

This must suffice as our answer to the question of whether an incontinent man acts knowingly or not, and with what sort of knowledge it is possible to be incontinent. . . .

## Book 10
### *Happiness is good activity, not amusement*

6. Now that we have spoken of the virtues, the forms of friendship, and the varieties of pleasure, what remains is to discuss in outline the nature of happiness, since this is what we state the end of human affairs to be. Our discussion will be the more concise if we first sum up what we have said already. We said, then, that it is not a state; for if it were it might belong to someone who was asleep throughout his life, living the life of a plant, or, again, to someone who was suffering the greatest misfortunes. If these implications are unacceptable, and we must rather class happiness as an activity, as we have said before, and if some activities are necessary, and desirable for the sake of something else, while others are so in themselves, evidently happiness must be placed among those desirable in themselves, not among those desirable for the sake of something else; for happiness does not lack anything, but is self-sufficient. Now those activities are desirable in themselves from which nothing is sought beyond the activity. And of this nature virtuous actions are thought to be; for to do noble and good deeds is a thing desirable for its own sake.

Pleasant amusements also are thought to be of this nature: we choose them not for the sake of other things; for we are injured rather than benefited by them, since we are led to neglect our bodies and our property. But most of the people who are deemed happy take refuge in such pastimes, which is the reason why those who are ready-witted at them are highly esteemed at the courts of tyrants; they make themselves pleasant companions in the tyrants' favourite pursuits, and that is the sort of man they want. Now these things are thought to be of the nature of happiness because people in despotic positions spend their leisure in them, but perhaps such people prove nothing; for virtue and reason, from which good activities flow, do not depend on despotic position; nor, if these people, who have never tasted pure and generous pleasure, take refuge in the bodily pleasures, should these for that reason be thought more desirable; for boys, too, think the things that are valued among themselves are the best. It is to be expected, then, that, as different things seem valuable to boys and to men, so they should to bad men and to good. Now, as we have often maintained, those things are both valuable and pleasant which are such to the good man; and to each man the activity in accordance with his own state is most desirable, and therefore to the good man that which is in accordance with virtue. Happiness, therefore, does not lie in amusement; it would, indeed, be strange if the end were amusement, and one were to take trouble and suffer hardship all one's life in order to amuse oneself. For, in a word, everything that we choose we choose for the sake of something else—except happiness, which is an end. Now to exert oneself and work for the sake of amusement seems silly and utterly childish. But to amuse oneself in order that one may exert oneself, as Anacharsis puts it, seems right; for amusement is a sort of relaxation, and we need relaxation because we cannot work continuously. Relaxation, then, is not an end; for it is taken for the sake of activity.

The happy life is thought to be virtuous; now a virtuous life requires exertion, and does not consist in amusement. And we say that serious things are better than laughable things and those connected with amusement, and that the activity of the better of any two things—whether it be two elements of our being or two men—is the more serious; but the activity of the better is *ipso facto* superior and more of the nature of happiness. And any chance person—even a slave—can enjoy the bodily pleasures no less than the best man; but no one assigns to a slave a share in happiness—unless he assigns to him also a share in human life. For happiness does not lie in such occu-

pations, but, as we have said before, in virtuous activities.

### *Happiness in the highest sense is the contemplative life*

7. If happiness is activity in accordance with virtue, it is reasonable that it should be in accordance with the highest virtue; and this will be that of the best thing in us. Whether it be reason or something else that is this element which is thought to be our natural ruler and guide and to take thought of things noble and divine, whether it be itself also divine or only the most divine element in us, the activity of this in accordance with its proper virtue will be perfect happiness. That this activity is contemplative we have already said.

Now this would seem to be in agreement both with what we said before and with the truth. For, firstly, this activity is the best (since not only is reason the best thing in us, but the objects of reason are the best of knowable objects); and, secondly, it is the most continuous, since we can contemplate truth more continuously than we can *do* anything. And we think happiness ought to have pleasure mingled with it, but the activity of philosophic wisdom is admittedly the pleasantest of virtuous activities; at all events the pursuit of it is thought to offer pleasures marvellous for their purity and their enduringness, and it is to be expected that those who know will pass their time more pleasantly than those who inquire. And the self-sufficiency that is spoken of must belong most to the contemplative activity. For while a philosopher, as well as a just man or one possessing any other virtue, needs the necessaries of life, when they are sufficiently equipped with things of that sort the just man needs people towards whom and with whom he shall act justly, and the temperate man, the brave man, and each of the others is in the same case, but the philosopher, even when by himself, can contemplate truth, and the better the wiser he is; he can perhaps do so better if he has fellow workers, but still he is the most self-sufficient. And this activity alone would seem to be loved for its own sake; for nothing arises from it apart from the contemplating, while from practical activities we gain more or less apart from the action. And happiness is thought to depend on leisure; for we are busy that we may have leisure, and make war that we may live in peace. Now the activity of the practical virtues is exhibited in political or military affairs, but the actions concerned with these seem to be unleisurely. Warlike actions are completely so (for no one chooses to be at war, or provokes war, for the sake of being at war; anyone would seem absolutely murderous if he were to make enemies of his friends in order to bring about battle and slaughter); but the action of the statesman also is unleisurely, and aims—beyond the political action itself—at despotic power and honours, or at all events happiness, for him and his fellow citizens—a happiness different from political action, and evidently sought as being different. So if among virtuous actions political and military actions are distinguished by nobility and greatness, and these are unleisurely and aim at an end and are not desirable for their own sake, but the activity of reason, which is contemplative, seems both to be superior in serious worth and to aim at no end beyond itself, and to have its pleasure proper to itself (and this augments the activity), and the self-sufficiency, leisureliness, unweariedness (so far as this is possible for man), and all the other attributes ascribed to the supremely happy man are evidently those connected with this activity, it follows that this will be the complete happiness of man, if it be allowed a complete term of life (for none of the attributes of happiness is *in*complete).

But such a life would be too high for man; for it is not in so far as he is man that he will live so, but in so far as something divine is present in him; and by so much as this is superior to our composite nature is its activity superior to that which is the exercise of the other kind of virtue. If reason is divine, then, in comparison with man, the life according to it is divine in comparison with human life. But we must not follow those who advise us, being men, to think of human things, and, being mortal, of mortal things, but must, so far as we can, make ourselves immortal, and strain every nerve to live in accordance with the best thing in us; for even if it be small in bulk, much more does it in power and worth surpass every-

thing. And this would seem actually to *be* each man, since it is the authoritative and better part of him. It would be strange, then, if he were to choose not the life of himself but that of something else. And what we said before will apply now: that which is proper to each thing is by nature best and most pleasant for each thing; for man, therefore, the life according to reason is best and pleasantest, since reason more than anything else *is* man. This life therefore is also the happiest.

### Superiority of the contemplative life further considered

8. But in a secondary degree the life in accordance with the other kind of virtue is happy; for the activities in accordance with this befit our human estate. Just and brave acts, and other virtuous acts, we do in relation to each other, observing our respective duties with regard to contracts and services and all manner of actions and with regard to passions; and all of these seem to be typically human. Some of them seem even to arise from the body, and virtue of character to be in many ways bound up with the passions. Practical wisdom, too, is linked to virtue of character, and this to practical wisdom, since the principles of practical wisdom are in accordance with the moral virtues and rightness in morals is in accordance with practical wisdom. Being connected with the passions also, the moral virtues must belong to our composite nature; and the virtues of our composite nature are human; so, therefore, are the life and the happiness which correspond to these. The excellence of the reason is a thing apart: we must be content to say this much about it, for to describe it precisely is a task greater than our purpose requires. It would seem, however, also to need external equipment but little, or less than moral virtue does. Grant that both need the necessaries, and do so equally, even if the statesman's work is the more concerned with the body and things of that sort; for there will be little difference there; but in what they need for the exercise of their activities there will be much difference. The liberal man will need money for the doing of his liberal deeds, and the just man too will need it for the returning of services (for wishes

are hard to discern, and even people who are not just *pretend* to wish to act justly); and the brave man will need power if he is to accomplish any of the acts that correspond to his virtue, and the temperate man will need opportunity; for how else is either he or any of the others to be recognized? It is debated, too, whether the will or the deed is more essential to virtue, which is assumed to involve both; it is surely clear that its perfection involves both; but for deeds many things are needed, and more, the greater and nobler the deeds are. But the man who is contemplating the truth needs no such thing, at least with a view to the exercise of his activity; indeed they are, one may say, even hindrances, at all events to his contemplation; but in so far as he is a man and lives with a number of people, he chooses to do virtuous acts; he will therefore need such aids to living a human life.

But that perfect happiness is a contemplative activity will appear from the following consideration as well. We assume the gods to be above all other beings blessed and happy; but what sort of actions must we assign to them? Acts of justice? Will not the gods seem absurd if they make contracts and return deposits, and so on? Acts of a brave man, then, confronting dangers and running risks because it is noble to do so? Or liberal acts? To whom will they give? It will be strange if they are really to have money or anything of the kind. And what would their temperate acts be? Is not such praise tasteless, since they have no bad appetites? If we were to run through them all, the circumstances of action would be found trivial and unworthy of gods. Still, everyone supposes that they *live* and therefore that they are active; we cannot suppose them to sleep like Endymion. Now if you take away from a living being action, and still more production, what is left but contemplation? Therefore the activity of God, which surpasses all others in blessedness, must be contemplative; and of human activities, therefore, that which is most akin to this must be most of the nature of happiness.

This is indicated, too, by the fact that the other animals have no share in happiness, being completely deprived of such activity. For while the whole life of the gods is blessed, and that of men too in so far as some likeness of such activity belongs to them, none of the other animals is happy, since they in no way share in contemplation. Happiness extends, then, just so far as contemplation does, and those to whom contemplation more fully belongs are more truly happy, not as a mere concomitant but in virtue of the contemplation; for this is in itself precious. Happiness, therefore, must be some form of contemplation.

But, being a man, one will also need external prosperity; for our nature is not self-sufficient for the purpose of contemplation, but our body also must be healthy and must have food and other attention. Still, we must not think that the man who is to be happy will need many things or great things, merely because he cannot be supremely happy without external goods; for self-sufficiency and action do not involve excess, and we can do noble acts without ruling earth and sea; for even with moderate advantages one can act virtuously (this is manifest enough; for private persons are thought to do worthy acts no less than despots—indeed even more); and it is enough that we should have so much as that; for the life of the man who is active in accordance with virtue will be happy. Solon, too, was perhaps sketching well the happy man when he described him as moderately furnished with externals but as having done (as Solon thought) the noblest acts, and lived temperately; for one can with but moderate possessions do what one ought. Anaxagoras also seems to have supposed the happy man not to be rich nor a despot, when he said that he would not be surprised if the happy man were to seem to most people a strange person; for they judge by externals, since these are all they perceive. The opinions of the wise seem, then, to harmonize with our arguments. But while even such things carry some conviction, the truth in practical matters is discerned from the facts of life; for these are the decisive factor. We must therefore survey what we have already said, bringing it to the test of the facts of life, and if it harmonizes with the facts we must accept it, but if it clashes with them we must suppose it to be mere theory. Now he who exercises his reason and cultivates it seems to be both in the best state of mind and most dear to the gods. For if the gods have any care for human affairs, as they are thought to have, it would be reasonable both that they should delight in that which was best and most akin to them (i.e. reason) and that they should reward those who love and honour this most, as caring for the things that are dear to them and acting both rightly and nobly. And that all these attributes belong most of all to the philosopher is manifest. He, therefore, is the dearest to the gods. And he who is that will presumably be also the happiest; so that in this way too the philosopher will more than any other be happy.

### Legislation is needed if the end is to be attained: transition to the Politics

9. If these matters and the virtues, and also friendship and pleasure, have been dealt with sufficiently in outline, are we to suppose that our programme has reached its end? Surely, as the saying goes, where there are things to be done the end is not to survey and recognize the various things, but rather to do them; with regard to virtue, then, it is not enough to know, but we must try to have and use it, or try any other way there may be of becoming good. Now if arguments were in themselves enough to make men good, they would justly, as Theognis says, have won very great rewards, and such rewards should have been provided; but as things are, while they seem to have power to encourage and stimulate the generous-minded among our youth, and to make a character which is gently born, and a true lover of what is noble, ready to be possessed by virtue, they are not able to encourage the *many* to nobility and goodness. For these do not by nature obey the sense of shame, but only fear, and do not abstain from bad acts because of their baseness but through fear of punishment; living by passion they pursue their own pleasures and the means to them, and avoid the opposite pains, and have not even a conception of what is noble and truly pleasant, since they have never tasted it. What argument would remould such people? It is hard, if not impossible, to remove by argument the traits that have long since been incorporated in the character; and perhaps we must be content if, when all the influences by which we are thought to become good are present, we get some tincture of virtue.

Now some think that we are good by nature, others by habituation, others by teaching. Nature's part

evidently does not depend on us, but as a result of some divine causes is present in those who are truly fortunate; while argument and teaching, we may suspect, are not powerful with all men, but the soul of the student must first have been cultivated by means of habits for noble joy and noble hatred, like earth which is to nourish the seed. For he who lives as passion directs will not hear argument that dissuades him, nor understand it if he does; and how can we persuade one in such a state to change his ways? And in general passion seems to yield not to argument but to force. The character, then, must somehow be there already with a kinship to virtue, loving what is noble and hating what is base.

But it is difficult to get from youth up a right training for virtue if one has not been brought up under right laws; for to live temperately and hardily is not pleasant to most people, especially when they are young. For this reason their nurture and occupations should be fixed by law; for they will not be painful when they have become customary. But it is surely not enough that when they are young they should get the right nurture and attention: since they must, even when they are grown up, practise and be habituated to them, we shall need laws for this as well, and generally speaking to cover the whole of life; for most people obey necessity rather than argument, and punishments rather than the sense of what is noble.

This is why some think that legislators ought to stimulate men to virtue and urge them forward by the motive of the noble, on the assumption that those who have been well advanced by the formation of habits will attend to such influences; and that punishments and penalties should be imposed on those who disobey and are of inferior nature, while the incurably bad should be completely banished. A good man (they think), since he lives with his mind fixed on what is noble, will submit to argument, while a bad man, whose desire is for pleasure, is corrected by pain like a beast of burden. This is, too, why they say the pains inflicted should be those that are most opposed to the pleasures such men love.

However that may be, if (as we have said) the man who is to be good must be well trained and habituated, and go on to spend his time in worthy occupations and neither willingly nor unwillingly do bad actions, and if this can be brought about if men live in accordance with a sort of reason and right order, provided this has force—if this be so, the paternal command indeed has not the required force or compulsive power (nor in general has the command of one man, unless he be a king or something similar), but the law *has* compulsive power, while it is at the same time a rule proceeding from a sort of practical wisdom and reason. And while people hate *men* who oppose their impulses, even if they oppose them rightly, the law in its ordaining of what is good is not burdensome.

In the Spartan state alone, or almost alone, the legislator seems to have paid attention to questions of nurture and occupation; in most states such matters have been neglected, and each man lives as he pleases, Cyclops-fashion, 'to his own wife and children dealing law'. Now it is best that there should be a public and proper care for such matters; but if they are neglected by the community it would seem right for each man to help his children and friends towards virtue, and that they should have the power, or at least the will, to do this.

It would seem from what has been said that he can do this better if he makes himself capable of legislating. For public control is plainly effected by laws, and good control by good laws; whether written or unwritten would seem to make no difference, nor whether they are laws providing for the education of individuals or of groups—any more than it does in the case of music or gymnastics and other such pursuits. For as in cities laws and prevailing types of character have force, so in households do the injunctions and the habits of the father, and these have even more because of the tie of blood and the benefits he confers; for the children start with a natural affection and disposition to obey. Further, private education has an advantage over public, as private medical treatment has; for while in general rest and abstinence from food are good for a man in a fever, for a particular man they may not be; and a boxer presumably does not prescribe the same style of fighting to all his pupils. It would seem, then, that the detail is worked out with more precision if the control is private; for each person is more likely to get what suits his case.

But the details can be best looked after, one by one, by a doctor or gymnastic instructor or anyone else who has the general knowledge of what is good for everyone or for people of a certain kind (for the sciences both are said to be, and are, concerned with what is universal); not but what some particular detail may perhaps be well looked after by an unscientific person, if he has studied accurately in the light of experience what happens in each case, just as some people seem to be their own best doctors, though they could give no help to anyone else. None the less, it will perhaps be agreed that if a man does wish to become master of an art or science he must go to the universal, and come to know it as well as possible; for, as we have said, it is with this that the sciences are concerned.

And surely he who wants to make men, whether many or few, better by his care must try to become capable of legislating, if it is through laws that we can become good. For to get anyone whatever—anyone who is put before us—into the right condition is not for the first chance comer; if anyone can do it, it is the man who knows, just as in medicine and all other matters which give scope for care and prudence.

Must we not, then, next examine whence or how one can learn how to legislate? Is it, as in all other cases, from statesmen? Certainly it was thought to be a part of statesmanship. Or is a difference apparent between statesmanship and the other sciences and arts? In the others the same people are found offering to teach the arts and practising them, e.g. doctors or painters; but while the sophists profess to teach politics, it is practised not by any of them but by the politicians, who would seem to do so by dint of a certain skill and experience rather than of thought; for they are not found either writing or speaking about such matters (though it were a nobler occupation perhaps than composing speeches for the law-courts and the assembly), nor again are they found to have made statesmen of their own sons or any other of their friends. But it was to be expected that they should if they could; for there is nothing better than such a skill that they could have left to their cities, or could prefer to have for themselves, or, therefore, for those dearest to them. Still, experience seems to contribute not a little; else they could not have become politicians by familiarity with politics; and so it seems that those who aim at knowing about the art of politics need experience as well.

But those of the sophists who profess the art seem to be very far from teaching it. For, to put the matter generally, they do not even know what kind of things it is nor what kinds of things it is about; otherwise they would not have classed it as identical with rhetoric or even inferior to it, nor have thought it easy to legislate by collecting the laws that are thought well of; they say it is possible to select the best laws, as though even the selection did not demand intelligence and as though right judgement were not the greatest thing, as in matters of music. For while people experienced in any department judge rightly the works produced in it, and understand by what means or how they are achieved, and what harmonizes with what, the inexperienced must be content if they do not fail to see whether the work has been well or ill made—as in the case of painting. Now laws are as it were the 'works' of the political art; how then can one learn from them to be a legislator, or judge which are best? Even medical men do not seem to be made by a study of textbooks. Yet people try, at any rate, to state not only the treatments, but also how particular classes of people can be cured and should be treated—distinguishing the various habits of body; but while this seems useful to experienced people, to the inexperienced it is valueless. Surely, then, while collection of laws, and of constitutions also, may be serviceable to those who can study them and judge what is good or bad and what enactments suit what circumstances, those who go through such collections without a practised faculty will not have right judgement (unless it be as a spontaneous gift of nature), though they may perhaps become more intelligent in such matters.

Now our predecessors have left the subject of legislation to us unexamined; it is perhaps best, therefore, that we should ourselves study it, and in general study the question of the constitution, in order to complete to the best of our ability the philosophy of human nature. First, then, if anything has been said well in detail by earlier thinkers, let us try to review it; then in the light of the constitutions we have collected let us study what sorts of influence preserve and destroy states, and what sorts preserve or destroy the particular kinds of constitution, and to what causes it is due that some are well and others ill administered. When these matters have been studied we shall perhaps be more likely to see with a comprehensive view which constitution is best, and how each must be ordered, and what laws and customs it must use, if it is to be at its best. Let us make a beginning of our discussion.

# Politics

## BOOK I

### *The Household and the City*

*A: The Political Association and Its Relation
to Other Associations*

#### CHAPTER I

*All associations have ends: the political
association has the highest; but the principle of
association expresses itself in different forms,
and through different modes of government.*

**1252ª1** Observation shows us, first, that every
city [*polis*] is a species of association, and, secondly, that all associations come into being for the
sake of some good—for all men do all their acts with
a view to achieving something which is, in their
view, a good. It is clear therefore that all associations
aim at some good, and that the particular association
which is the most sovereign of all, and includes all
the rest, will pursue this aim most, and will thus be
directed to the most sovereign of all goods. This
most sovereign and inclusive association is the city
[or *polis*], as it is called, or the political association.

**1252ª7** It is a mistake to believe that the statesman
is the same as the monarch of a kingdom, or the manager of a household, or the master of a number of
slaves. Those who hold this view consider that each
one of these differs from the others not with a difference of kind, but according to the number, large or
small, of those with whom he deals. On this view
someone who is concerned with few people is a master, someone who is concerned with more is the manager of a household, and someone who is concerned
with still more is a statesman, or a monarch. This
view abolishes any real difference between a large

household and a small city; and it also reduces the difference between the 'statesman' and the monarch to
the one fact that the latter has an uncontrolled and
sole authority, while the former exercises his authority in conformity with the rules imposed by the art of
statesmanship and as one who rules and is ruled in
turn. But this is a view which cannot be accepted as
correct.

**1252ª18** Our point will be made clear if we proceed to consider the matter according to our normal
method of analysis. Just as, in all other fields, a compound should be analysed until we reach its simple
elements (or, in other words, the smallest parts of the
whole which it constitutes), so we must also consider
analytically the elements of which a city is composed. We shall then gain a better insight into the
way in which these differ from one another; and we
shall also be in a position to discover whether there
is any kind of expertise to be acquired in connection
with the matters under discussion.

#### CHAPTER 2

*To distinguish the different forms of association
we must trace the development successively of
the association of the household, that of the
village, and that of the city or* polis. *The* polis,
*or political association, is the crown: it
completes and fulfils the nature of man: it is thus
natural to him, and he is himself 'naturally a
polis-animal'; it is also prior to him, in the
sense that it is the presupposition of his true and
full life.*

**1252ª24** In this, as in other fields, we shall be able to
study our subject best if we begin at the beginning
and consider things in the process of their growth.

From *Politics,* translated by Ernest Barker, revised by R. F. Stalley. Reprinted by permission of Oxford University Press.

First of all, there must necessarily be a union or pairing of those who cannot exist without one another. Male and female must unite for the reproduction of the species—not from deliberate intention, but from the natural impulse, which exists in animals generally as it also exists in plants, to leave behind them something of the same nature as themselves. Next, there must necessarily be a union of the naturally ruling element with the element which is naturally ruled, for the preservation of both. The element which is able, by virtue of its intelligence, to exercise forethought, is naturally a ruling and master element; the element which is able, by virtue of its bodily power, to do the physical work, is a ruled element, which is naturally in a state of slavery; and master and slave have accordingly a common interest.

**1252<sup>b</sup>2** The female and the slave are naturally distinguished from one another. Nature makes nothing in a miserly spirit, as smiths do when they make the Delphic knife to serve a number of purposes: she makes each separate thing for a separate end; and she does so because the instrument is most perfectly made when it serves a single purpose and not a variety of purposes. Among barbarians, however, the female and the slave occupy the same position—the reason being that no naturally ruling element exists among them, and conjugal union thus comes to be a union of a female who is a slave with a male who is also a slave. This is why our poets have said,

*Meet it is that barbarous peoples should be governed by the Greeks*

the assumption being that barbarian and slave are by nature one and the same.

The first result of these two elementary associations is the household or family. Hesiod spoke truly in the verse,

*First house, and wife, and ox to draw the plough,*

for oxen serve the poor in lieu of household slaves. The first form of association naturally instituted for the satisfaction of daily recurrent needs is thus the family; and the members of the family are accordingly termed by Charondas 'associates of the bread-

chest', as they are also termed by Epimenides the Cretan 'associates of the manager'.

**1252<sup>b</sup>17** The next form of association—which is also the first to be formed from more households than one, and for the satisfaction of something more than daily recurrent needs—is the village. The most natural form of the village appears to be that of a colony [or offshoot] from a family; and some have thus called the members of the village by the name of 'sucklings of the same milk', or, again, of 'sons and the sons of sons'. This, it may be noted, is the reason why cities were originally ruled, as the peoples of the barbarian world still are, by kings. They were formed of people who were already monarchically governed, for every household is monarchically governed by the eldest of the kin, just as villages, when they are offshoots from the household, are similarly governed in virtue of the kinship between their members. This is what Homer describes:

*Each of them ruleth*
*Over his children and wives,*

a passage which shows that they lived in scattered groups, as indeed men generally did in ancient times. The fact that men generally were governed by kings in ancient times, and that some still continue to be governed in that way, is the reason that leads everyone to say that the gods are also governed by a king. People make the lives of the gods in the likeness of their own—as they also make their shapes.

**1252<sup>b</sup>27** When we come to the final and perfect association, formed from a number of villages, we have already reached the city [or *polis*]. This may be said to have reached the height of full self-sufficiency; or rather we may say that while it comes into existence for the sake of mere life, it exists for the sake of a good life. For this reason every city exists by nature, just as did the earlier associations [from which it grew]. It is the end or consummation to which those associations move, and the 'nature' of things consists in their end or consummation; for what each thing is when its growth is completed we call the nature of that thing, whether it be a man or a horse or a family. Again the end, or final cause, is the best and self-sufficiency is both the end, and the best.

**1253ª2** From these considerations it is evident that the city belongs to the class of things that exist by nature, and that man is by nature a political animal. He who is without a city, by reason of his own nature and not of some accident, is either a poor sort of being, or a being higher than man: he is like the man of whom Homer wrote in denunciation:

*Clanless and lawless and hearthless is he.*

The man who is such by nature at once plunges into a passion of war; he is in the position of a solitary advanced piece in a game of draughts.

**1253ª7** It is thus clear that man is a political animal, in a higher degree than bees or other gregarious animals. Nature, according to our theory, makes nothing in vain; and man alone of the animals is furnished with the faculty of language. The mere making of sounds serves to indicate pleasure and pain, and is thus a faculty that belongs to animals in general: their nature enables them to attain the point at which they have perceptions of pleasure and pain, and can signify those perceptions to one another. But language serves to declare what is advantageous and what is the reverse, and it is the peculiarity of man, in comparison with other animals, that he alone possesses a perception of good and evil, of the just and the unjust, and other similar qualities; and it is association in these things which makes a family and a city.

**1253ª18** We may now proceed to add that the city is prior in the order of nature to the family and the individual. The reason for this is that the whole is necessarily prior to the part. If the whole body is destroyed, there will not be a foot or a hand, except in that ambiguous sense in which one uses the same word to indicate a different thing, as when one speaks of a 'hand' made of stone; for a hand, when destroyed [by the destruction of the whole body], will be no better than a stone 'hand'. All things derive their essential character from their function and their capacity; and it follows that if they are no longer fit to discharge their function, we ought not to say that they are still the same things, but only that, by an ambiguity, they still have the same names.

**1253ª25** We thus see that the city exists by nature and that it is prior to the individual. For if the individual is not self-sufficient when he is isolated he will stand in the same relation to the whole as other parts do to their wholes. The man who is isolated, who is unable to share in the benefits of political association, or has no need to share because he is already self-sufficient, is no part of the city, and must therefore be either a beast or a god. There is therefore a natural impulse in all men towards an association of this sort. But the man who first constructed such an association was none the less the greatest of benefactors. Man, when perfected, is the best of animals; but if he be isolated from law and justice he is the worst of all. Injustice is all the graver when it is armed injustice; and man is furnished from birth with weapons which are intended to serve the purposes of wisdom and goodness, but which may be used in preference for opposite ends. That is why, if he be without goodness [of mind and character], he is a most unholy and savage being, and worse than all others in the indulgence of lust and gluttony. The virtue of justice belongs to the city; for justice is an ordering of the political association, and the virtue of justice consists in the determination of what is just.

### B: The Association of the Household and its Different Factors

#### CHAPTER 3

*1. The constituent elements of the household. The three relations of master and slave, husband and wife, parent and child. The fourth element of 'acquisition'.*

**1253ᵇ1** Having ascertained, from the previous analysis, what are the elements of which the city is constituted, we must first consider the management of the household; for every city is composed of households. The parts of household management will correspond to the parts of which the household itself is constituted. A complete household consists of slaves and freemen. But every subject of inquiry should first be examined in its simplest elements; and the primary and simplest elements of the household are the connection of master and slave, that of the husband and wife, and that of parents and children. We must accordingly consider each of these connections, examining the nature of each and the qualities it ought to possess. The factors to be examined are therefore three: first, the relationship of master and slave; next, what may be called the marital relationship (for there is no word in our language which exactly describes the union of husband and wife); and lastly, what may be called the parental relationship, which again has no single word in our language peculiar to itself. But besides the three factors which thus present themselves for examination there is also a fourth, which some regard as identical with the whole of household management, and others as its principal part. This is the element called 'the art of acquisition'; and we shall have to consider its nature.

**1253<sup>b</sup>14** We may first speak of master and slave, partly in order to gather lessons bearing on the necessities of practical life, and partly in order to discover whether we can attain any view, superior to those now generally held, which is likely to promote an understanding of the subject. There are some who hold that the exercise of authority over slaves is a kind of knowledge. They believe (as we said in the beginning) that household management, slave ownership, statesmanship, and kingship are all the same. There are others, however, who regard the control of slaves by a master as contrary to nature. In their view the distinction of master and slave is due to law or convention; there is no natural difference between them: the relation of master and slave is based on force, and so has no warrant in justice.

CHAPTER 4

*2. Slavery. The instruments of the household form its stock of property: they are animate and inanimate: the slave is an animate instrument, intended (like all the instruments of the household) for action, and not for production.*

**1253<sup>b</sup>23** Property is part of the household and the art of acquiring property is part of household management, for it is impossible to live well, or indeed at all, unless the necessary conditions are present. Thus the same holds true in the sphere of household man-

agement as in the specialized arts: each must be furnished with its appropriate instruments if its function is to be fulfilled. Instruments are partly inanimate and partly animate: the steersman of a ship, for instance, has an inanimate instrument in the rudder, and an animate instrument in the look-out man (for in the arts a subordinate is of the nature of an instrument). Each article of property is thus an instrument for the purpose of life, property in general is a quantity of such instruments, the slave is an animate article of property, and subordinates, or servants, in general may be described as instruments which are prior to other instruments. We can imagine a situation in which each instrument could do its own work, at the word of command or by intelligent anticipation, like the statues of Daedalus or the tripods made by Hephaestus, of which the poet relates that

*Of their own motion they entered the conclave of Gods on Olympus.*

A shuttle would then weave of itself, and a plectrum would do its own harp-playing. In this situation managers would not need subordinates and masters would not need slaves.

**1254<sup>a</sup>1** The instruments of which we have just been speaking are instruments of production; but property is an instrument of action. From the shuttle there issues something which is different, and exists apart, from the immediate act of its use, but from garments or beds there comes only the one fact of their use. We may add that, since production and action are different in kind, and both of them need instruments, those instruments must also show a corresponding difference. Life is action and not production; and therefore the slave is a servant in the sphere of action.

**1254<sup>a</sup>8** The term 'article of property' is used in the same way in which the term 'part' is also used. A part is not only a part of something other than itself: it also belongs entirely to that other thing. It is the same with an article of property. Accordingly, while the master is merely the master of the slave, and does not belong to him, the slave is not only the slave of his master; he also belongs entirely to him.

**1254<sup>a</sup>13** From these considerations we can see

clearly what is the nature of the slave and what is his capacity: anybody who by his nature is not his own man, but another's, is by his nature a slave; anybody who, being a man, is an article of property is another's man; an article of property is an instrument intended for the purpose of action and separable from its possessor.

## CHAPTER 5

*There is a principle of rule and subordination in nature at large: it appears especially in the realm of animate creation. By virtue of that principle, the soul rules the body; and by virtue of it the master, who possesses the rational faculty of the soul, rules the slave, who possesses only bodily powers and the faculty of understanding the directions given by another's reason. But nature, though she intends, does not always succeed in achieving a clear distinction between men born to be masters and men born to be slaves.*

**1254ᵃ17** We have next to consider whether there are, or are not, some people who are by nature such as are here defined; whether, in other words, there are some people for whom slavery is the better and just condition, or whether the reverse is the case and all slavery is contrary to nature. The issue is not difficult, whether we study it philosophically in the light of reason, or consider it empirically on the basis of the actual facts. The relation of ruler and ruled is one of those things which are not only necessary, but also beneficial; and there are species in which a distinction is already marked, immediately at birth, between those of its members who are intended for being ruled and those who are intended to rule. There are also many kinds both of ruling and ruled elements. (Moreover the rule which is exercised over the better sort of subjects is a better sort of rule—as, for example, rule exercised over a man is better than rule over an animal. The reason is that the value of something which is produced increases with the value of those contributing to it; and where one element rules and the other is ruled, there is something which they jointly produce.) In all cases where there is a compound, constituted of more than one part but forming one common entity, whether the parts be continuous or discrete, a ruling element and a ruled can always be traced. This characteristic is present in animate beings by virtue of the whole constitution of nature; for even in things which are inanimate there is a sort of ruling principle, such as is to be found, for example, in a musical harmony. But such considerations perhaps belong to a more popular method of inquiry; and we may content ourselves here with saying that animate beings are composed, in the first place, of soul and body, with the former naturally ruling and the latter naturally ruled. When investigating the natural state of things, we must fix our attention, not on those which are in a corrupt, but on those which are in a natural condition. It follows that we must consider the man who is in the best state both of body and soul, and in whom the rule of soul over body is accordingly evident; for with vicious people or those in a vicious condition, the reverse would often appear to be true—the body ruling the soul as the result of their evil and unnatural condition.

**1254ᵇ2** It is possible, as we have said, to observe first in animate beings the presence of a ruling authority, both of the sort exercised by a master over slaves and of the sort exercised by a statesman over fellow citizens. The soul rules the body with the authority of a master: reason rules the appetite with the authority of a statesman or a monarch. In this sphere it is clearly natural and beneficial to the body that it should be ruled by the soul, and again it is natural and beneficial to the affective part of the soul that it should be ruled by the reason and the rational part; whereas the equality of the two elements, or their reverse relation, is always detrimental. The same principle is true of the relation of man to other animals. Tame animals have a better nature than wild, and it is better for all such animals that they should be ruled by man because they then get the benefit of preservation. Again, the relation of male to female is naturally that of the superior to the inferior, of the ruling to the ruled. This general principle must similarly hold good of all human beings generally.

**1254ᵇ16** We may thus conclude that all men who differ from others as much as the body differs from the soul, or an animal from a man (and this is the case with all whose function is bodily service, and who produce their best when they supply such service)—all such are by nature slaves. In their case, as in the other cases just mentioned, it is better to be ruled by a master. Someone is thus a slave by nature if he is capable of becoming the property of another (and for this reason does actually become another's property) and if he participates in reason to the extent of apprehending it in another, though destitute of it himself. Other animals do not apprehend reason but obey their instincts. Even so there is little divergence in the way they are used; both of them (slaves and tame animals) provide bodily assistance in satisfying essential needs.

**1254<sup>b</sup>27** It is nature's intention also to erect a physical difference between the bodies of freemen and those of the slaves, giving the latter strength for the menial duties of life, but making the former upright in carriage and (though useless for physical labour) useful for the various purposes of civic life—a life which tends, as it develops, to be divided into military service and the occupations of peace. The contrary of nature's intention, however, often happens: there are some slaves who have the bodies of freemen, as there are others who have a freeman's soul. But, if there were men who were as distinguished in their bodies alone as are the statues of the gods, all would agree that the others should be their slaves. And if this is true when the difference is one of the body, it may be affirmed with still greater justice when the difference is one of the soul; though it is not as easy to see the beauty of the soul as it is to see that of the body.

**1254<sup>b</sup>39** It is thus clear that, just as some are by nature free, so others are by nature slaves, and for these latter the condition of slavery is both beneficial and just.

CHAPTER 6

*Legal or conventional slavery: the divergence of views about its justice, and the reason for this divergence. In spite of the divergence, there is a general consensus—though it is not clearly formulated—that superiority in goodness justifies the owning and controlling of slaves. Granted such superiority in the master, slavery is a beneficial and just system.*

**1255<sup>a</sup>3** But it is easy to see that those who hold an opposite view are also in a way correct. 'Slavery' and 'slave' are terms which are used in two different senses; for there is also a kind of slave, and of slavery, which owes its existence to law. (The law in question is a kind of understanding that those vanquished in war are held to belong to the victors.) That slavery can be justified by such a convention is a principle against which a number of jurists bring an 'indictment of illegality', as one might against an orator. They regard it as a detestable notion that someone who is subjugated by force should become the slave and subject of one who has the capacity to subjugate him, and is his superior in power. Even among men of judgement there are some who accept this and some who do not. The cause of this divergence of view, and the reason why the opposing contentions overlap one another, is to be found in the following consideration. There is a sense in which good qualities, when they are furnished with the right resources, have the greatest power to subjugate; and a victor is always pre-eminent in respect of some sort of good. It thus appears that 'power never goes without good qualities'; and the dispute between the two sides thus comes to turn exclusively on the point of justice. (In this matter some think that being just consists in goodwill while others hold that the rule of the stronger is in itself justice.) If these different positions are distinguished from one another, no other argument has any cogency, or even plausibility, against the view that one who is superior in goodness ought to rule over, and be the master of, his inferiors.

**1255<sup>b</sup>21** There are some who, clinging, as they think, to a sort of justice (for law is a sort of justice), assume that slavery in war is just. Simultaneously, however, they contradict that assumption; for in the first place it is possible that the original cause of a war may not be just, and in the second place no one would ever say that someone who does not deserve to be in a condition of slavery is really a slave. If such a view were accepted, the result would be that men reputed to be of the highest rank would be turned into slaves or the children of slaves, if they [or their parents] happened to be captured and sold into slavery. This is the reason why they do not like to call such people slaves, but prefer to confine the term to barbarians. But by this use of terms they are, in reality, only seeking to express that same idea of the natural slave which we began by mentioning. They are driven, in effect, to admit that there are some who are everywhere slaves, and others who are everywhere free. The same line of thought is followed in regard to good birth. Greeks regard themselves as well born not only in their own country, but absolutely and in all places; but they regard barbarians as well born only in their own country—thus assuming that there is one sort of good birth and freedom which is absolute, and another which is only relative. We are reminded of what Helen says in the play of Theodectes:

> Scion of Gods, by both descent alike,
> Who would presume to call me serving-maid?

When they use such terms as these, men are using the one criterion of the presence, or absence, of goodness for the purpose of distinguishing between slave and freeman, or again, between the well-born and the low-born. They are claiming that just as man is born of man, and animal of animal, so a good man is born of good men. It is often the case, however, that nature wishes but fails to achieve this result.

**1255ᵇ4** It is thus clear that there is some reason for the divergence of view which has been discussed—it is not true that the one group are natural slaves and the other natural freemen. It is also clear that there are cases where such a distinction exists, and that here it is beneficial and just that the former should actually be a slave and the latter a master— the one being ruled, and the other exercising the kind of rule for which he is naturally intended and therefore acting as master. But a wrong exercise of his rule by a master is a thing which is disadvantageous for both master and slave. The part and the whole, like the body and the soul, have an identical interest; and the slave is a part of the master, in the sense of being a living but separate part of his body. There is thus a community of interest, and a relation of friendship, between master and slave, when both of them naturally merit the position in which they stand. But the reverse is true, when matters are otherwise and slavery rests merely on legal sanction and superior power.

# BOOK II

## *Review of Constitutions*

### A: Constitutions in Theory

#### CHAPTER I

*1. Plato's Republic. Before describing our own conception of the best constitution we must consider both those constitutions that are in force in cities considered to be well governed and those constitutions that have been proposed by our predecessors. In doing so we should note that political association is a sharing: so we may ask 'How much should be shared?' In Plato's* Republic *it is proposed that women, children, and property should be held in common.*

**1260ᵇ27** Our purpose is to consider what form of political association is best for people able so far as possible to live as they would wish. We must therefore consider not only constitutions actually in force in cities that are said to be well governed, but also other forms of constitution which people have proposed if these are thought to have merit. In this way we will be able to see in what respects these constitutions are properly designed and useful. What is more, when we proceed to look for something different from them, we shall not seem to be the sort of people who desire at all costs to show their own ingenuity, but rather to have adopted our method in consequence of the defects we have found in existing forms.

**1260ᵇ36** Our starting-point must be the one that is natural for such a discussion. It is necessary either that the citizens have all things in common, or that they have nothing in common, or that they have some things in common, and others not. It is clearly impossible that they should have nothing in common: the constitution of a city involves in itself some sort of association, and its members must in the first place share a common locality. Just as a single city [*polis*] must have a single locality, so citizens are those who share in a single city. But is it better that a city which is to be well conducted should share in all the things in which it is possible for it to share, or that it should share in some things and not in others? It is certainly possible that the citizens should share children and women and property with one another. This is the plan proposed in the *Republic* of Plato, where 'Socrates' argues that children and women and property should be held in common. We are thus faced by the question whether it is better to remain in our present condition or to follow the rule of life laid down in the *Republic*.

## CHAPTER 2

*Community of women and children. Criticisms of the end or object (unity) which Plato proposes to attain by it: (a) carried to its logical extreme, that object would produce a one-man city; (b) it neglects the social differentiation necessary in a city (a differentiation which, even in a city of 'equals and likes', produces the distinction of rulers and ruled); (c) it thus makes self-sufficiency impossible, because self-sufficiency involves different elements making different contributions.*

**1261ª10** A system in which women are common to all involves, among many others, the following difficulties. The *object* for which Socrates states that it ought to be instituted is evidently not established by the arguments which he uses. Moreover, the end which he states as necessary for the city [ *polis*] is impracticable; and yet he gives no account of the lines on which it ought to be interpreted. I have in mind here the idea, which Socrates takes as his premiss, that the greatest possible unity of the whole city is the supreme good. Yet it is obvious that a city which goes on becoming more and more of a unit, will eventually cease to be a city at all. A city, by its nature, is some sort of plurality. If it becomes more of a unit, it will first become a household instead of a city, and then an individual instead of a household; for we should all call the household more of a unit than the city, and the individual more of a unit than the household. It follows that, even if we could, we ought not to achieve this object: it would be the destruction of the city.

**1261ª22** Not only is the city composed of a *number* of people: it is also composed of different *kinds* of people, for a city cannot be composed of those who are like one another. There is a difference between a city and a military alliance. An alliance, formed by its very nature for the sake of the mutual help which its members can render to one another, possesses utility purely in virtue of its quantity, even if there is no difference of kind among its members. It is like a weight which depresses the scales more heavily in the balance. In this respect a *city* will also differ from a tribe, assuming that the members of the tribe are not scattered in separate villages, but [are united in a confederacy] like the Arcadians. A real unity must be made up of elements which differ in kind. It follows that the stability of every city depends on each of its elements rendering to the others an amount equivalent to what it receives from them—a principle already laid down in the *Ethics*. This has to be the case even among free and equal citizens. They cannot all rule simultaneously; they must therefore each hold office for a year, unless they adopt some other arrangement or some other period of time. In this way it comes about that all are rulers, just as it would if shoemakers and carpenters changed their occupations so that the same people were not always following these professions. Since the arrangement [followed in the arts and crafts] is also better when applied to the affairs of the political association, it would clearly be better for the same people always to be rulers wherever possible. But where this is impossible, through the natural equality of all the citizens—and also because justice requires the participation of all in office (whether office be a good thing or a bad)—there is an imitation of it, if equals retire from office in turn and are all, apart from their period of office, in the same position. This means that some rule, and others are ruled, in turn, as if they had become, for the time being, different people. We may add that even those who are rulers differ from one another, some holding one kind of office and some another.

**1261ᵇ6** These considerations are sufficient to show, first, that it is not the nature of the city to be a unit in the sense in which some thinkers say that it is, and secondly, that what is said to be the supreme good of a city is really its ruin. But surely the 'good' of each thing is what preserves it in being.

**1261ᵇ10** There is still another consideration which may be used to prove that the policy of attempting an extreme unification of the city is not a good policy. A household is something which attains a greater degree of self-sufficiency than an individual; and a city, in turn, is something which attains self-sufficiency to a greater degree than a household. But it becomes fully a city, only when the association which forms it is large enough to be self-sufficing. On the assumption, therefore, that the higher degree of self-sufficiency is the more desirable thing, the lesser degree of unity is more desirable than the greater.

CHAPTER 3

*Community of women and children (continued). Criticisms of such community considered as a means for producing the end of unity:* (a) *as all collectively, and not each individually, are parents, there will be no real feeling, but rather a general apathy;* (b) *kinship will be fractional kinship (when 1,000 are father to the same child, each father is only 1/1,000 father);* (c) *nature will 'recur', and spoil the scheme.*

**1261ᵇ16** Even if it were the supreme good of a political association that it should have the greatest possible unity, this unity does not appear to follow from the formula of 'All men saying "Mine" and "Not mine" at the same time', which, in the view of 'Socrates', is the index of the perfect unity of a city. The word 'all' has a double sense: if it means 'each separately', the object which 'Socrates' desires to realize may perhaps be realized in a greater degree: each and all separately will then say 'My wife' (or 'My son') of one and the same person; and each and all separately will speak in the same way of property, and of every other concern. But it is not in the sense of 'each separately' that all who have children and women in common will actually speak of them. They will all call them 'Mine'; but they will do so collectively, and not individually. The same is true of property also; [all will call it 'Mine'] but they will do so in the sense of 'all collectively', and not in the sense of 'each separately'. It is therefore clear that there is a

certain fallacy in the use of the term 'all'. 'All' and 'both' and 'odd' and 'even' are liable by their ambiguity to produce captious arguments even in reasoned discussions. We may therefore conclude that the formula of 'all men saying "Mine" of the same object' is in one sense something fine but impracticable, and in another sense does nothing to promote harmony.

**1261ᵇ32** In addition to these problems the formula also involves another disadvantage. What is common to the greatest number gets the least amount of care. People pay most attention to what is their own: they care less for what is common; or, at any rate, they care for it only to the extent to which each is individually concerned. Even where there is no other cause for inattention, people are more prone to neglect their duty when they think that another is attending to it: this is what happens in domestic service, where many attendants are sometimes of less assistance than a few. [The scheme proposed in the *Republic* means that] each citizen will have a thousand sons: they will not be the sons of each citizen individually: any son whatever will be equally the son of any father whatever. The result will be that all will equally neglect them.

**1262ᵃ1** Furthermore each person, when he says 'Mine' of any citizen who is prosperous or the reverse, is speaking fractionally. He means only that he is 'Mine' to the extent of a fraction determined by the total number of citizens. When he says 'He is mine' or 'He is so-and-so's', the term 'Mine' or 'So-and-so's' is used with reference to the whole body concerned—the whole thousand, or whatever may be the total number of citizens. Even so he cannot be sure; for there is no evidence who had a child born to him, or whether, if one was born, it managed to survive. Which is the better system—that each of two thousand, or ten thousand, people should say 'Mine' of a child in this fractional sense, or that each should say 'Mine' in the sense in which the word is now used in ordinary cities? As things are, one man calls by the name of '*My* son' the same person whom a second man calls by the name of '*My* brother': a third calls him '*My* cousin' or '*My* relative', because he is somehow related to him, either by blood or by connection through marriage; while besides these different modes of address someone else may use still another, and call him '*My* clansman' or '*My* tribesman'. It is better to be someone's own cousin than to be his son after this fashion. Even on Plato's system it is impossible to avoid the chance that some of the citizens might guess who are their brothers, or children, or fathers, or mothers. The resemblances between children and parents must inevitably lead to their drawing conclusions about one another. That this actually happens in real life is stated as fact by some of the writers on descriptive geography. They tell us that some of the inhabitants of upper Libya have their women in common; but the children born of such unions can still be distinguished by their resemblance to their fathers. Indeed there are some women, and some females in the animal world (mares, for instance, and cows), that show a strong natural tendency to produce offspring resembling the male parent: the Pharsalian mare which was called the 'Just Return' is a good example.

### CHAPTER 4

*Community of women and children (continued). Problems arise when parents do not know their children, or children their parents. At best such a community produces a watery sort of friendship. The addition to it of a scheme of transposition of ranks raises further difficulties.*

**1262ª25** There are also other difficulties which those who construct such a community will not find it easy to avoid. We may take as examples cases of assault, homicide, whether unintentional or intentional, fighting, and slander. All these offences, when they are committed against father or mother or a near relative, differ from offences against people who are not so related, in being breaches of natural piety. Such offences must happen more frequently when men are ignorant of their relatives than when they know who they are; and when they do happen, the customary penance can be made if people know their relatives, but none can be made if they are ignorant of them. It is also surprising that, after having

made sons common to all, he should simply forbid lovers from engaging in carnal intercourse. Nor does he forbid other familiarities which, if practised between son and father, or brother and brother, are the very height of indecency, all the more as this form of love [even if it is not expressed] is in itself indecent. It is surprising, too, that he should debar male lovers from carnal intercourse on the one ground of the excessive violence of the pleasure, and that he should think it a matter of indifference that the lovers may be father and son, or again that they may be brothers.

**1262ª40** Community of women and children would seem to be more useful if it were practised among the farmers rather than among the guardians. The spirit of friendship is likely to exist to a lesser degree where women and children are common; and the governed class ought to have little of that spirit if it is to obey and not to attempt revolution. Generally, such a system must produce results directly opposed to those which a system of properly constituted laws should produce, and equally opposed to the very object for which, in the view of 'Socrates', this community of women and children ought to be instituted. Friendship, we believe, is the chief good of cities, because it is the best safeguard against the danger of factional disputes. 'Socrates' himself particularly commends the ideal of the unity of the city; and that unity is commonly held, and expressly stated by him, to be the result of friendship. We may cite the argument of the discourses on love, where 'Aristophanes', as we know, speaks of lovers desiring out of friendship to grow together into a unity, and to be one instead of two. Now in that case it would be inevitable that both or at least one of them should cease to exist. But in the case of the political association there would be merely a watery sort of friendship: a father would be very little disposed to say 'Mine' of a son, and a son would be as little disposed to say 'Mine' of a father. Just as a little sweet wine, mixed with a great deal of water, produces a tasteless mixture, so family feeling is diluted and tasteless when family names have as little meaning as they have in a constitution of this sort, and when there is so little reason for a father treating his sons as sons, or a son treating his father as a father, or brothers one another as brothers. There are two things which particularly move people to care for and love an object. One of these is that the object should belong to yourself: the other is that you should like it. Neither of these motives can exist among those who live under a constitution such as this.

**1262<sup>b</sup>24** There is still a further difficulty. It concerns the way in which children born among the farmers and craftsmen are to be transferred to the guardian class, and vice versa. How such transposition is actually to be effected is a matter of great perplexity; and in any case those who transfer such children, and assign them their new place, will be bound to know who are the children so placed and with whom they are being placed. In addition, those problems of assault, unnatural affection, and homicide, which have already been mentioned, will occur even more in the case of these people. Those transferred from the guardian class to that of the other citizens will cease for the future to address the guardians as brothers, or children, or fathers, or mothers, as the case may be; and it will have the same effect for those who have been transferred from among the other citizens to the guardians. Such people will no longer avoid committing these offences on account of their kinship.

**1262<sup>b</sup>35** This may serve as a determination of the issues raised by the idea of community of women and children.

### CHAPTER 5

*Community of property. Three possible systems of property. The difficulties of a system under which ownership and use are both common: the merits of a system under which ownership is private and use is common—it gives more pleasure, and it encourages goodness more. Communism cannot remedy evils which really spring from the defects of human nature: it is also based on a false conception of unity, and neglects the true unity which comes from education; finally, it is contradicted by experience. Plato's particular scheme of community of property leaves the position of the farming class obscure. The system of government which he connects with his scheme is too absolute, and is likely to cause discontent: it also deprives the ruling class of any happiness.*

**1262<sup>b</sup>39** The next subject for consideration is property. What is the proper system of property for citizens who are to live under the best form of constitution? Should property be held in common or not? This is an issue which may be considered in itself, and apart from any proposals for community of women and children. Even if women and children are held separately, as is now universally the case, questions relating to property still remain for discussion. Should use and ownership both be common? For example, there may be a system under which plots of land are owned separately, but the crops (as actually happens among some tribal peoples) are brought into a common stock for the purpose of consumption. Secondly, and conversely, the land may be held in common ownership, and may also be cultivated in common, but the crops may be divided among individuals for their private use: some of the barbarian peoples are also said to practise this second method of sharing. Thirdly, the plots and the crops may both be common.

**1263<sup>a</sup>8** When the cultivators of the soil are a different body from the citizens who own it, the position will be different and easier to handle; but when the citizens who own the soil do the work themselves, the problems of property will cause a good deal of trouble. If they do not share equally in the work and in the enjoyment of the produce, those who do more work and get less of the produce will be bound to raise complaints against those who get a large reward and do little work. In general it is a difficult business to live together and to share in any form of human activity, but it is specially difficult in such matters. Fellow-travellers who merely share in a journey furnish an illustration: they generally quarrel about ordinary matters and take offence on petty occasions. So, again, the servants with whom we are most prone to take offence are those who are particularly employed in ordinary everyday services.

**1263<sup>a</sup>21** Difficulties such as these, and many others, are involved in a system of community of property. The present system would be far preferable, if it were embellished with social customs and the enactment of proper laws. It would possess the advantages of both systems, and would combine the merits of a system of community of property with those of the system of private property. For, although there is a sense in which property *ought* to be common, it should in general be private. When everyone has his own separate sphere of interest, there will not be the same ground for quarrels; and they will make more effort, because each man will feel that he is applying himself to what is his own.

**1263ᵃ30** On such a scheme, too, moral goodness will ensure that the property of each is made to serve the use of all, in the spirit of the proverb which says 'Friends' goods are goods in common'. Even now there are some cities in which the outlines of such a scheme are so far apparent, as to suggest that it is not impossible; in well-ordered cities, more particularly, there are some elements of it already existing, and others which might be added. [In these cities] each citizen has his own property; part of which he makes available to his friends, and part of which he uses as though it was common property. In Sparta, for example, men use one another's slaves, and one another's horses and dogs, as if they were their own; and they take provisions on a journey, if they happen to be in need, from the farms in the countryside. It is clear from what has been said that the better system is that under which property is privately owned but is put to common use; and the function proper to the legislator is to make men so disposed that they will treat property in this way.

**1263ᵃ40** In addition, to think of a thing as your own makes an inexpressible difference, so far as pleasure is concerned. It may well be that regard for oneself is a feeling implanted by nature, and not a mere random impulse. Self-love is rightly censured, but that is not so much loving oneself as loving oneself in excess. It is the same with one who loves money; after all, virtually everyone loves things of this kind. We may add that a very great pleasure is to be found in doing a kindness and giving some help to friends, or guests, or comrades; and such kindness and help become possible only when property is privately owned. But not

only are these pleasures impossible under a system in which the city is excessively unified; the activities of two forms of goodness are also obviously destroyed. The first of these is temperance in the matter of sexual relations (it is an act of moral value to keep away from the wife of another through temperance): the second is generosity in the use of property. In a city which is excessively unified no man can show himself generous, or indeed do a generous act; for the function of generosity consists in the proper use which is made of property.

**1263ᵇ15** This kind of legislation may appear to wear an attractive face and to demonstrate benevolence. The hearer receives it gladly, thinking that everybody will feel towards everybody else some marvellous sense of friendship—all the more as the evils now existing under ordinary forms of government (lawsuits about contracts, convictions for perjury, and obsequious flatteries of the rich) are denounced as due to the absence of a system of common property. None of these, however, is due to property not being held in common. They all arise from wickedness. Indeed it is a fact of observation that those who own common property, and share in its management, are far more often at variance with one another than those who have property separately—though those who are at variance in consequence of sharing in property look to us few in number when we compare them with the mass of those who own their property privately.

**1263ᵇ27** What is more, justice demands that we should take into account not only the evils which people will be spared when they have begun to hold their property in common, but also the benefits of which they will be deprived. Their life can be seen to be utterly impossible.

**1263ᵇ29** The cause of the fallacy into which 'Socrates' falls must be held to be his incorrect premiss. It is true that unity in some respects is necessary both for the household and for the city, but unity in all respects is not. There is a point at which a city, by advancing in unity, will cease to be a city: there is another point at which it will still be a city, but a worse one because it has come close to ceasing altogether to be a city. It is as if you were to turn harmony into mere unison, or to reduce a theme to a single beat. The truth is that the city, as has already been said, is a plurality; and education is therefore *the* means of making it a community and giving it unity. It is therefore surprising that one who intends to introduce a system of education, and who believes that the city can achieve goodness by means of this system, should none the less think that he is setting it on the right track by such methods as he actually proposes, rather than by the method of social customs, of mental culture, and of legislation. An example of such legislation may be found in Sparta and Crete, where the legislator has made the institution of property serve a common use by the system of common meals.

**1264ª1** There is another matter which must not be ignored: we are bound to pay some regard to the long past and the passage of the years, in which these things would not have gone unnoticed if they had been really good. Almost everything has been discovered already; though some things have not been combined with one another, and others are not put into practice. It would shed a great deal of light on these matters, if we could watch the actual construction of such a constitution. The foundation of any city will always involve the division and distribution of its members into classes, partly in the form of associations for common meals, and partly in that of clans and tribes. It follows that the only peculiar feature of the legislation is the rule that the guardians are not to farm the land; and even that is a rule which the Spartans are already attempting to follow.

**1264ª11** 'Socrates' does not explain the character of the whole constitution so far as concerns those who share in it, nor indeed is it easy to explain. The mass of the citizens who are not guardians will be, in effect, nearly the whole of the citizen body. But their position is left undefined. We are not told whether the farmers are also to have property in common, or to own it individually; nor do we learn whether their women and children are to be common to them all, or to belong to each separately.

**1264ª17** The first alternative is that all things should belong to them all in common. In that case, what will be the difference between them and the guardians? What advantage will they gain by accepting the government of the guardians? What con-

vinces them actually to accept it?—unless it be some device such as is used in Crete, where the serfs are allowed to enjoy the same general privileges as their masters, and are excluded only from athletic exercises and the possession of arms.

**1264ª22** The second alternative is that these institutions should be the same for the farmers as they are in most cities today. In that case, we may inquire, what the character of their association will be? There will inevitably be two cities in one, and those cities will be opposed to one another—the guardians being made into something of the nature of an army of occupation, and the farmers, artisans, and others being given the position of ordinary civilians. Again, legal complaints, and actions at law, and all the other evils which he describes as existing in cities as they are, will equally exist among them. Certainly 'Socrates' says that, in virtue of their education, they will not need a number of regulations (such as city ordinances, market by-laws, and the like); but it is also true that he provides education only for the guardians. A further difficulty is that he has the farmers control their holdings on condition that they pay a quota of their produce to the guardians. This is likely to make them far more difficult to handle, and much more filled with high ideas of their own importance, than other people's helots, penestae, or serfs.

**1264ª36** In any case there is no indication whether it is necessary for these arrangements to be the same [for the farmers as for the guardians] or not, nor are other matters connected with this made clear—matters such as the position of the farmers in the political system, the nature of their education, and the character of the law they are to observe. We thus find it difficult to discover what the farming class will be like, and yet this is a matter of the highest importance if the common life of the guardians is to be preserved. The third and last alternative is that the farmers should have a system of community of women, combined with a system of private property. In that case, who will see to the house while the men are seeing to the business of the fields? And, for that matter, who will see to the house, when the farmers have property as well as women in common? It is strange, too, that Plato should draw an analogy from the animal world in order to prove that women should follow the same pursuits as men. Animals do not have households to manage.

**1264ᵇ6** There is also an element of danger in the method of government which 'Socrates' proposes to institute. He makes the same people be rulers all the time. This is a system which must cause factional conflict even among the elements which have no particular standing, and all the more, therefore, among the high-spirited and martial elements. It is obviously necessary for him to make the same people rulers all the time. The 'divine gold' cannot be sometimes mixed in the souls of one group and sometimes in those of another, but must always be in the same people. This is why he says that when they were first created 'the god mixed gold in the composition' of some, silver in that of others, and brass and iron in that of the rest, who were to be craftsmen and farmers. It is a further objection that he deprives his guardians even of happiness, maintaining that the object of the legislator should be for the whole city to be happy. It is impossible for the whole city to be happy unless all, or most, or at least some of its parts are happy. The quality of being happy is not of the same order as the quality of being even. That may exist in a whole without existing in either of its parts: the quality of being happy cannot. Furthermore, if the guardians are not happy, who else is? Certainly not the craftsmen, or the mass of the common people.

**1264ᵇ24** We may thus conclude that the constitution which 'Socrates' describes raises all the difficulties we have mentioned, and others which are no less serious.

# BOOK III

## *The Theory of Citizenship and Constitutions*

### *A: Citizenship*

#### CHAPTER I

*To understand what a constitution (politeia) is, we must inquire into the nature of the city (polis); and to understand that—since the city is a body of citizens (politai)—we must examine the nature of citizenship. Citizenship is not determined by residence, or by merely having access to the courts of law. Rather 'a citizen is one who permanently shares in the administration of justice and the holding of office'. This definition is more especially true in a democracy: to make it generally applicable, we must modify it to run, 'a citizen is one who shares for any period of time in judicial and deliberative office'.*

**1274ᵇ32** When we are dealing with constitutions, and seeking to discover the essence and the attributes of each form, our first investigation may well be directed to the city [the *polis*] itself; and we may begin by asking, 'What is the city?' This is at present a disputed question—while some say, 'It was the city that did such and such an act', others say, 'It was not the city, but the oligarchy or the tyrant.' All the activity of the statesman and the lawgiver is obviously concerned with the city, and a constitution is a way of organizing the inhabitants of a city.

**1274ᵇ38** A city belongs to the order of 'compounds', just like any other thing which forms a single 'whole', while being composed, none the less, of a number of different parts. This being the case, it clearly follows that we must inquire first about the citizen. In other words, a city is a certain number of citizens; and so we must consider who should properly be called a citizen and what a citizen really is. The definition of a citizen is a question which is often disputed: there is no general agreement on who is a citizen. It may be that someone who is a citizen in a democracy is not one in an oligarchy. We may leave out of consideration those who enjoy the title of 'citizen' in some special sense, for example, naturalized citizens. A citizen proper is not one by virtue of residence in a given place: for even aliens and slaves may share the common place of residence. Nor [can the title of 'citizen' be given to] those who share in legal processes only to the extent of being entitled to sue and be sued in the courts. This is something which belongs also to aliens who share it by virtue of a treaty; though it is to be noted that there are many places where resident aliens are obliged to choose a legal protector, so that they only share to a limited extent in this form of association. They are like children who are still too young to be entered on the roll of citizens, or men who are old enough to have been excused from civic duties. There is a sense in which these may be called citizens, but it is not altogether an unqualified sense: we must add the reservation that the young are undeveloped, and the old superannuated citizens, or we must use some other qualification; the exact term we apply does not matter, for the meaning is clear.

**1275ᵃ19** We are seeking to discover the citizen in the strict sense, who has no such defect to be made good. Similar questions may also be raised and answered about those who are exiled or disenfranchised. The citizen in this strict sense is best defined by the one criterion that he shares in the administration of justice and in the holding of office. Offices may be divided into two kinds. Some are discontinuous in point of time: in other words, they are of the sort that either cannot be held at all for more than a single term or can only be held for a second term after some definite interval. Others, however, have no limit of time, for example, the office of jurymen, or the office of a member of the popular assembly. It may possibly be contended that such people are not holders of 'office', and do not share in 'office' by virtue of their position. But it would be ridiculous to exclude from the category of holders of office those who actually hold the most sovereign position in the city; and, since the argument turns on a word, we should not let it make a difference. The point is that we have no word to denote what is common to the juryman and the member of the assembly, or to describe the position held by both. Let us, in the interest of a clear analysis, call it 'indeterminate office'. On that basis we may lay it down that citizens are those who share in the holding of office as so defined.

**1275ᵃ33** The definition of citizen which will most satisfactorily cover the position of all who bear the name is of this general kind. We must also notice that there are certain kinds of thing which may be based on different kinds of principle, one of them standing first, another second, and so on down the series. Things belonging to this class, when considered purely as such, have no common denominator what-

ever, or, if they have one, they have it only to a meagre extent. Constitutions obviously differ from one another in kind, with some of them coming later in the order and others earlier; for constitutions which are defective and perverted (we shall explain later in what sense we are using the term 'perverted') are necessarily secondary to those which are free from defects. It follows that the citizen under each different kind of constitution must also necessarily be different. We may thus conclude that the citizen of our definition is particularly and especially the citizen of a democracy. Citizens living under other kinds of constitution may possibly, but do not necessarily, correspond to the definition. There are some cities, for example, in which there is no popular element: such cities have no regular meetings of the assembly, but only meetings specially summoned; and they decide different kinds of legal case by different means. In Sparta, for example, the Ephors take cases of contracts (not as a body, but each sitting separately); the Council of Elders take cases of homicide; and some other authority may take other cases. Much the same is also true of Carthage, where a number of official bodies are entitled to decide cases of all kinds.

**1275ᵇ13** But our definition of citizenship can be amended. In other kinds of constitution members of the assembly and the courts do not hold that office for an indeterminate period. They hold it for a limited term; and it is to some or all of these that the citizen's function of deliberating and judging (whether on all issues or only a few) is assigned: From these considerations it emerges clearly who a citizen is. We say that one who is entitled to share in deliberative or judicial office is thereby a citizen of that city, and a city, in its simplest terms, is a body of such people adequate in number for achieving a self-sufficient existence.

## CHAPTER 2

*A popular and pragmatic view of citizenship makes it depend on birth, i.e. descent from a citizen parent or two citizen parents. This does not carry us far, and in any case it only relates to old established citizens. A more serious question is raised when we consider new citizens, who have been allowed to participate in the constitution as the result of a revolution. Are they actually citizens? On the criterion of sharing in judicial and deliberative office (which is a functional criterion), they are actually citizens when once they possess that function.*

**1275<sup>b</sup>22** For practical purposes, it is usual to define a citizen as 'one born of citizen parents on both sides', and not on the father's or mother's side only; but sometimes this requirement is carried still farther back, to the length of two, three, or more stages of ancestry. This popular and facile definition has induced some thinkers to raise the question, 'How did the citizen of the third or fourth stage of ancestry himself come to be a citizen?' Gorgias of Leontini—perhaps partly from a sense of this difficulty and partly in irony—said, 'As mortars are things which are made by the craftsmen who are mortar-makers, so Larissaeans are made by the craftsmen who are Larissaean-makers'. But the matter is really simple. If, in their day, they had a share in the constitution in the sense of our own definition, they were certainly citizens. It is obviously impossible to apply the requirement of descent from a citizen father or a citizen mother to those who were the first inhabitants or original founders of a city.

**1275<sup>b</sup>34** A more serious difficulty is perhaps raised by the case of those who have acquired a share as the result of a change in the constitution. We may take as an example the action of Cleisthenes at Athens, when after the expulsion of the tyrants he enrolled in the tribes a number of resident aliens both foreigners and slaves. The question raised by such an addition to the civic body is not 'Who is actually a citizen?' but, 'Are they rightly or wrongly such?' It must be admitted, however, that someone might also raise the further question whether a man who is not justly a citizen is really a citizen, on the grounds that the unjust comes to the same as the false. Obviously there are office-holders who have no just title to their office; but we still say that they hold office, though we do not say it is just for them to do so. The citizen also is defined by the fact of holding a sort of office (for the definition we have given to the citizen involves his sharing in office of the deliberative and judicial kind); and it follows, therefore, that these people must be called citizens.

CHAPTER 3

*The question, 'Are they justly citizens?' leads to the further question 'When can a given act be considered an act of the city or polis?' This in turn raises the general question of the identity of the city. Is the city identical with the government for the time being? Generally, what are the factors which constitute its identity? The identity of a city does not depend on its being surrounded by one set of walls, or on its consisting of one stock of inhabitants. The city is a compound; and its identity, like that of all compounds, is determined by the scheme of its composition, i.e. by its constitution.*

**1276<sup>a</sup>6** The question whether these people are, in justice, citizens or not is a different matter, which is closely connected with a larger question already mentioned. Some people have wondered when a given act can, and when it cannot, be considered to be the act of the city. We may take as an example the case of an oligarchy or tyranny which changes into a democracy. In such a case some people are reluctant to fulfil public contracts, on the grounds that these were made, not by the city, but by the governing tyrant, and they are unwilling to meet other obligations of a similar nature because they hold that some constitutions exist by virtue of force, and not for the sake of the common good. It would follow that if a democracy exists in this fashion [i.e. by force] we have to admit that acts done under the government of such a democracy are no more acts of the city concerned than were acts done under the oligarchy or tyranny.

**1276<sup>a</sup>17** Our discussion would seem to be closely connected with the following problem: 'On what principles ought we to say that a city has retained its identity, or conversely, that it has lost its identity and become a different city?' The most obvious mode of dealing with this question is to consider simply territory and population. On this basis we may note that the territory and population of a city may be divided into sections, with some of the population residing in one block of territory, and some of it in another. This question need not be regarded as particularly difficult: the issue which it raises can easily be met if we remember that the word 'city' is used in different senses.

**1276ᵃ24** In the case of a population which inhabits a single territory, we may likewise ask 'When should we consider that there is a single city?' For, of course, the identity of a city is not constituted by its walls—it would be possible to surround the whole of the Peloponnese by a single wall. Babylon (which, it is said, had been captured for three whole days before some of its inhabitants knew of the fact) may perhaps be counted a city of this dubious nature: so, too, might any city which had the dimensions of a people [*ethnos*] rather than those of a city [or *polis*]. But it will be better to reserve the consideration of this question for some other occasion. (To determine the size of a city—to settle how large it can properly be, and whether it ought to consist of the members of several races—is a duty incumbent on the statesman.)

**1276ᵃ34** Assuming a single population inhabiting a single territory, shall we say that the city retains its identity as long as the stock of its inhabitants continues to be the same (although the old members are always dying and new members are always being born), and shall we thus apply to the city the analogy of rivers and fountains, to which we ascribe a constant identity in spite of the fact that part of their water is always flowing in and part always flowing out? Or must we take a different view, and say that even though the population remains the same, the city, for the reason already mentioned, may none the less change?

**1276ᵇ1** If a city is a form of association, and if this form of association is an association of citizens in a constitution, it would seem to follow inevitably that when the constitution undergoes a change in form, and becomes a different constitution, the city will likewise cease to be the same city. We say that a chorus which appears at one time as a comic and at another as a tragic chorus is not the same—and this in spite of the fact that the members often remain the

same. What is true of the chorus is also true of every other kind of association, and of all other compounds generally. If the form of its composition is different, the compound becomes a different compound. A scale composed of the same notes will be a different scale depending on whether it is in the Dorian or the Phrygian mode. If this is the case, it is obvious that in determining the identity of the city we must look to the constitution. Whether the same group of people inhabits a city, or a totally different group, we are free to call it the same city, or a different city. It is a different question whether it is right to pay debts or to repudiate them when a city changes its constitution into another form.

### CHAPTER 4

*Aristotle now raises the question, 'What is the relation of the excellence of the good citizen to the excellence of the good man?' If we look at constitutions generally, we must note that different constitutions require different types of good citizen, while the good man is always the same. If we look at the best constitution, we may argue that even here there must be different types of good citizen, because there are different sorts of civic function; and thus here too the good citizen cannot be identified with the good man. On the whole, therefore, the good citizen and the good man cannot be identified. But there is one case in which they can be. This is the case of the good ruler who possesses the quality of moral wisdom required for being a good subject. The quality of moral wisdom which he possesses is the essential quality of the good man; and in his case the excellence of the good citizen is identical with that of the good man.*

**1276ᵇ16** A question connected with those which have just been discussed is the question whether the excellence of a good man and that of a good citizen are identical or different. If this question is to be investigated, we must first describe the excellence of the citizen in some sort of outline. Just as a sailor is a member of an association, so too is a citizen.

Sailors differ from one another in virtue of the different capacities in which they act: one is a rower, another a steersman, another a look-out man; and others will have still other such titles. It is, nevertheless, clear that, while the most accurate definition of the excellence of each sailor will be special to the man concerned, a common definition of excellence will apply to all, inasmuch as safety in navigation is the common task of all and the object at which each of the sailors aims. The same is also true of citizens. Though they differ, the end which they all serve is the safety of their association; and this association consists in the constitution. The conclusion to which we are thus led is that the excellence of the citizen must be an excellence relative to the constitution. It follows that if there are several different kinds of constitution there cannot be a single absolute excellence of the good citizen. But the good man is a man so called in virtue of a single absolute excellence.

**1276ᵇ34** It is thus clear that it is possible to be a good citizen without possessing the excellence by which one is a good man. But we may reach the same conclusion in another way, by discussing the question with particular reference to the best constitution. Although it is impossible for a city to be composed entirely of good men, each citizen must, none the less, perform well his particular function and this requires [the appropriate kind of] excellence. But, since it is impossible for all the citizens to be alike, the excellence of a citizen cannot be identical with that of a good man. The excellence of a good citizen must belong to all citizens, because that is the condition necessary for the city being the best city; but the excellence of a good man cannot possibly belong to all—unless, indeed, we hold that every citizen of a good city must also be a good man. Furthermore, the city is composed of unlike elements. Just as a living being is composed of soul and body, or the soul of the different elements of reason and appetite, or the household of man and wife, or property of master and slave, so the city too is composed of different and unlike elements, among them not only the various elements already mentioned, but also others in addition. It follows that there cannot be a single excellence common to all the citizens, any more than

there can be a single excellence common to the leader of a dramatic chorus and his assistants.

**1277ᵃ12** Although it is clear from these considerations why they are not in all cases identical, the question may still be raised whether there are not some cases in which the excellence of the good man and that of the good citizen are the same. We say that a good ruler is a good man and possesses practical wisdom, while the citizen does not need to have practical wisdom. Indeed there are some who hold that the very training of the ruler should be, from the first, of a different kind; and it is a matter of observation that the sons of kings are specially trained in riding and the art of war. Thus Euripides says

*No subtleties for me,*
*But what the city most needs,*

which implies a special training for the ruler. We may thus assume that the excellence of the good ruler is identical with that of the good man. But subjects too are citizens. It follows that the excellence of the good citizen cannot be identical with that of the good man in all cases, though it may be so in a particular case. The excellence of the ordinary citizen is different from that of the ruler; and this may well be the reason why Jason [the tyrant of Pherae] said that he was 'a hungry man except when he was tyrant', meaning that he did not know how to live as an ordinary person.

**1277ᵃ25** On the other hand, people hold in esteem the capacity both to rule and to obey, and they regard the excellence of a good citizen as being a matter of ruling and obeying well. Now if the excellence of the good man is in ruling, while that of the good citizen is in both ruling and obeying, these two excellences cannot be held in the same esteem.

**1277ᵃ29** Since it thus seems that ruler and ruled should acquire different kinds of knowledge, rather than the same kind, while the citizen should have both sorts of knowledge, and share in both, we can now see the next step which our argument has to take. There is rule of the sort which is exercised by a master; and by this we mean the sort of rule connected with the necessary functions of life. Here it is not necessary for the ruler to know how to do the task himself, but only to know how to use those who do: indeed the former kind of knowledge (by which we mean an ability to do menial services personally) has a servile character. There are a number of kinds of servant, because there are a number of kinds of menial service which have to be rendered. One of these forms of service is that which is rendered by manual labourers. These, as their very name signifies, are those who live by the work of their hands; and the menial craftsman [or mechanic] belongs to this class. This is the reason why in some cities the manual workers were once upon a time excluded from office, in the days before the institution of the extreme form of democracy. The occupations pursued by those who are subject to rule of the sort just mentioned need never be studied by the good man, or by the statesman, or by the good citizen—except occasionally and in order to satisfy some personal need, in which case there ceases to be any question of the relation of master and slave.

**1277ᵇ7** But there is also rule of the sort which is exercised over those who are similar in birth to the ruler, and are similarly free. Rule of this sort is what we call political rule; and this is the sort of rule which the ruler must begin to learn by being ruled— just as one learns to be a commander of cavalry by serving under another commander, or to be a general of infantry by serving under another general and by acting first as colonel and, even before that, as captain. This is why it is a good saying that 'you cannot be ruler unless you have first been ruled'. Ruler and ruled have indeed different excellences; but the fact remains that the good citizen must possess the knowledge and the capacity requisite for ruling as well as for being ruled, and the excellence of a citizen may be defined as consisting in 'a knowledge of rule over free men from both points of view'.

**1277ᵇ16** A good man, also, will need both, even though the temperance and justice required for ruling have a different character. Equally, the excellence (justice, for example) of a good man who is a subject in a free city will not be of a single kind. It will include different sorts: one sort which fits him to act

as a ruler, and one which fits him to act as a subject. The temperance and the courage of a man differ from those of a woman in much the same sort of way. A man would be thought cowardly if his courage were only the same as that of a courageous woman; and conversely a woman would be thought a gossip if she showed no more decorum than that which befits a good man. The function of the man in the household is different from that of the woman: it is the function of the one to acquire, and of the other to keep.

**1277ᵇ25** Practical wisdom is the only form of excellence which is peculiar to the ruler. The other forms must, it would seem, belong equally to rulers and subjects. The excellence of subjects cannot be practical wisdom, and may be defined as 'right opinion'. The ruled may be compared to a flute-maker: the ruler is like a flute-player who uses what the flute-maker makes.

**1277ᵇ30** These considerations will show whether the excellence of the good man and that of the good citizen are identical or different—or in what sense they are identical and in what sense they are different.

### B: Constitutions and Their Classification

#### CHAPTER 6

*The definition of a constitution. The classification of constitutions depends on (1) the ends pursued by cities, and (2) the kind of rule exercised by their governments. The true end of a city is a good life, and it is the common interest to achieve this: the right kind of rule is authority exercised in the common interest. We may thus distinguish 'right' constitutions, which are directed to the common interest, and 'wrong' or 'perverted' constitutions directed to the selfish interest of the ruling body.*

**1278ᵇ6** Having determined these matters we have next to consider whether there is a single type of constitution, or whether there are a number of types. If there are a number of types, what are these types; how many of them are there; and how do they differ? A constitution [or *politeia*] may be defined as 'the organization of a city [or *polis*], in respect of its offices generally, but especially in respect of that particular office which is sovereign in all issues'. The civic body is everywhere the sovereign of the city; in fact the civic body is the constitution itself. In democratic cities, for example, the people [*dēmos*] is sovereign: in oligarchies, on the other hand, the few [or *oligoi*] have that position; and this difference in the sovereign bodies is the reason why we say that the two types of constitution differ—as we may equally apply the same reasoning to other types besides these.

**1278ᵇ15** We must first ascertain two things: the nature of the end for which a city exists, and the various kinds of rule to which mankind and its associations are subject. It has already been stated, in our first book (where we were concerned with the management of the household and the control of slaves), that 'man is a political animal'. For this reason people desire to live a social life even when they stand in no need of mutual succour; but they are also drawn together by a common interest, in proportion as each attains a share in the good life. The good life is the chief end, both for the community as a whole and for each of us individually. But people also come together, and form and maintain political associations, merely for the sake of life; for perhaps there is some element of the good even in the simple fact of living, so long as the evils of existence do not preponderate too heavily. It is an evident fact that most people cling hard enough to life to be willing to endure a good deal of suffering, which implies that life has in it a sort of healthy happiness and a natural quality of pleasure.

**1278ᵇ30** It is easy enough to distinguish the various kinds of rule of which people commonly speak; and indeed we have often had occasion to define them ourselves in works intended for the general public. The rule of a master is one kind; and here, though there is really a common interest which unites the natural master and the natural slave, the fact remains that the rule is primarily exercised with a view to the master's interest, and only incidentally with a view to that of the slave, who must be preserved in existence if the rule is to remain. Rule over wife and children, and over the household generally, is a second kind of rule, which we have called by the name of household management. Here the rule is either exercised in the interest of the ruled or for the attainment of some advantage common to both ruler and ruled. Essentially it is exercised in the interest of the ruled, as is also plainly the case with other arts besides that of ruling, such as medicine and gymnastics—though an art may incidentally be exercised for the benefit of its practitioner, and there is nothing to prevent (say) a trainer from becoming occasionally a member of the class he instructs, in the same sort of way as a steersman is always one of the crew. Thus a trainer or steersman primarily considers the good of those who are subject to his authority; but when he becomes one of them personally, he incidentally shares in the benefit of that good—the steersman thus being also a member of the crew, and the trainer (though still a trainer) becoming also a member of the class which he instructs.

**1279ᵃ8** For this reason, when the constitution of a city is constructed on the principle that its members are equals and peers, the citizens think it proper that they should hold office by turns. At any rate this is the natural system, and the system which used to be followed in the days when people believed that they ought to serve by turns, and each assumed that others would take over the duty of considering his benefit, just as he himself, during his term of office, had considered their interest. Today because of the profits to be derived from office and the handling of public property, people want to hold office continuously. It is as if they were invalids, who got the benefit of being healthy by being permanently in office: at any rate their ardour for office is just what it would be if that were the case. The conclusion which follows is clear: those constitutions which consider the common interest are right constitutions, judged by the standard of absolute justice. Those constitutions which consider only the personal interest of the rulers are all wrong constitutions, or perversions of the right forms. Such perverted forms are despotic; whereas the city is an association of freemen.

## CHAPTER 7

*These two types of constitution each fall into three subdivisions on the basis of number, i.e. according as the One, or the Few, or the Many are the ruling authority in each type. We have thus, as the three subdivisions of the 'right' type, Kingship, Aristocracy, and 'Constitutional Government' or 'Polity': as the three subdivisions of the 'wrong' type, Tyranny, Oligarchy, and Democracy.*

**1279ᵃ22** Now that these matters have been determined, the next subject for consideration is the number and nature of the different constitutions. We may first examine those constitutions that are rightly formed, since, when these have been determined, the different perversions will at once be apparent.

**1279ᵃ25** The term 'constitution' [*politeia*] signifies the same thing as the term 'civic body' [*politeuma*]. The civic body in every city [*polis*] is the sovereign [*to kurion*]; and the sovereign must necessarily be either One, or Few, or Many. On this basis we may say that when the One, or the Few, or the Many rule with a view to the common interest, the constitutions under which they do so must necessarily be right constitutions. On the other hand, the constitutions directed to the personal interest of the One, or the Few, or the Masses, must necessarily be perversions. Either we should say that those who do not share in the constitution are not citizens, or they ought to have their share of the benefits. According to customary usage, among monarchical forms of government the type which looks to the common interest is called Kingship; among forms of government by a few people (but more than one) it is called Aristocracy—that name being given to this species either because the best [*aristoi*] are the rulers, or because its object is what is best [*ariston*] for the city and its members. Finally, when the masses govern the city with a view to the common interest, the form of government is called by the generic name common to all constitutions (or polities)—the name of 'Constitutional Government'. There is a good reason for this usage: it is possible for one man, or a few, to

be of outstanding excellence; but when it comes to a large number, we can hardly expect precision in all the varieties of excellence. What we can expect particularly is the military kind of excellence, which is the kind that shows itself in a mass. This is the reason why the defence forces are the most sovereign body under this constitution, and those who possess arms are the ones who participate in it.

**1279ᵇ4** The perversions that correspond to the constitutions just mentioned are: Tyranny, [the perversion of] Kingship; Oligarchy [the perversion of] Aristocracy; and Democracy [the perversion of] 'Constitutional Government' [or polity]. Tyranny is a government by a single person directed to the interest of that person; Oligarchy is directed to the interest of the well-to-do; Democracy is directed to the interest of the poor. None of these benefits the common interest.

## CHAPTER 8

*The basis of number is not, however, adequate. The real basis, at any rate so far as oligarchy and democracy are concerned, is social class: what makes an oligarchy is the rule of the rich (rather than the few), and what makes a democracy is the rule of the poor (rather than the many). Number is an accidental, and not an essential, attribute; but the accidental generally accompanies the essential.*

**1279ᵇ11** We must consider at somewhat greater length what each of these constitutions is. There are certain difficulties involved; and when one is pursuing a philosophical method of inquiry in any branch of study, and not merely looking to practical considerations, the proper course is to set out the truth about every particular with no neglect or omission.

**1279ᵇ16** Tyranny, as has just been said, is single-person government of the political association on the lines of despotism; oligarchy exists where those who have property are the sovereign authority of the constitution; and, conversely, democracy exists where the sovereign authority is composed of the poorer classes, who are without much property.

**1279ᵇ20** The first difficulty which arises is a matter of definition. It could be that the majority are well-to-do and that these hold the sovereignty in a city; but when the majority is sovereign there is [said to be] democracy. Similarly it could happen that the poorer classes were fewer in number than the well-to-do, and yet were stronger and had sovereign authority in the constitution; but where a small number has sovereignty there is said to be oligarchy. Thus it may seem that the definitions we have given of these constitutions cannot be correct.

**1279ᵇ26** We might attempt to overcome the difficulty by combining both of the factors: wealth with paucity of numbers, and poverty with mass. On this basis oligarchy might be defined as the constitution under which the rich, being also few in number, hold the public offices; and similarly democracy might be defined as the constitution under which the poor, being also many in number, are in control. But this involves us in another difficulty. If there are no forms of oligarchy and democracy other than those enumerated, what names are we to give to the constitutions just suggested as conceivable—those where the wealthy form a majority and the poor a minority, and where the wealthy majority in the one case, and the poor minority in the other, are the sovereign authority of the constitution? The course of the argument thus appears to show that whether the sovereign body is small or large in number (as it is respectively in oligarchies or in democracies) is an accidental attribute, due to the simple fact that the wealthy are generally few and the poor are generally numerous. Therefore the causes originally mentioned are not in fact the real causes of the difference between oligarchies and democracies. The real ground of the difference between oligarchy and democracy is poverty and riches. It is inevitable that there should be an oligarchy where the rulers, whether they are few or many, owe their position to riches; and it is equally inevitable that there should be democracy where the poor rule.

**1280ᵃ2** It happens, however, as we have just remarked, that the former [i.e. the wealthy] are few and the latter [i.e. the poor] are numerous. It is only a few who have riches, but all alike share in free status; and it is on these grounds that the two parties dispute the control of the constitution.

### C: The Principles of Oligarchy and Democracy and the Nature of Distributive Justice

### CHAPTER 9

*The principle of a constitution is its conception of justice; and this is the fundamental ground of difference between oligarchy and democracy. Democrats hold that if men are equal by birth, they should in justice have an equal share in office and honours: oligarchs hold that if they are unequal in wealth, they should in justice have unequal shares in these things. True justice means that those who have contributed to the end of the city should have privileges in proportion to their contribution to that end. The end of the city is not mere life, nor an alliance for mutual defence, it is the common promotion of a good quality of life. Thus although the citizens of a city must always inhabit a single territory, engage in intermarriage, and co-operate with each other in economic matters, the operative aim is always the promotion of a good quality of life. Those who contribute most to the realization of that aim should in justice have the largest share of office and honour.*

**1280ᵃ7** We must next ascertain what are said to be the distinctive principles of oligarchy and democracy, and what are the oligarchical and the democratic conceptions of justice. All parties have a hold on a sort of conception of justice; but they both fail to carry it far enough, and do not express the true conception of justice in the whole of its range. For example, justice is considered to mean equality. It does mean equality—but equality for those who are equal, and not for all. Again, inequality is considered to be just; and indeed it is—but only for those who are unequal, and not for all. These people fail to consider for whom there should be equality or inequality and thus make erroneous judgements. The reason is that they are judging in their own case; and most people, as a rule, are bad judges where their own interests are involved. Justice is concerned with people; and a just distribution is one in which there is proportion between the things distributed and those to whom they are distributed, a point which has already been made in the *Ethics*. There is general agreement about what constitutes equality in the thing, but disagreement about what constitutes it in people. The main reason for this is the reason just stated, they are judging, and judging erroneously, in their own case; but there is also another reason, they are misled by the fact that they are professing a sort of conception of justice, and professing it up to a point, into thinking that they profess one which is absolute and complete. Some think that if they are superior in one point, for example in wealth, they are superior in all: others believe that if they are equal in one respect, for instance in free birth, they are equal all round.

**1280ᵃ25** Both sides, however, fail to mention the really cardinal factor. If property is the end for which people come together and form an association, one's share of the city would be proportionate to one's share of the property; and in that case the argument of the oligarchical side would appear to be strong: they say that is not just for someone who has contributed one mina to share in a sum of a hundred minae on equal terms with one who has contributed all the rest and that this applies both to the original sum and to the interest accruing upon it. But the end of the city is not mere life; it is, rather, a good quality of life. Otherwise, there might be a city of slaves, or even a city of animals; but in the world as we know it any such city is impossible, because slaves and animals do not share in happiness nor in living according to their own choice. Similarly, it is not the end of the city to provide an alliance for mutual defence against all injury, nor does it exist for the purpose of exchange or [commercial] dealing. If that had been the end, the Etruscans and the Carthaginians would be in the position of belonging to a single city; and the same would be true to all peoples who have commercial treaties with one another. It is true that such peoples have agreements about imports; treaties to ensure just con-

duct; and written terms of alliance for mutual defence. On the other hand, they have no common offices to deal with these matters: each, on the contrary, has its own offices, confined to itself. Neither party concerns itself to ensure a proper quality of character among the members of the other; neither of them seeks to ensure that all who are included in the scope of the treaties are just and free from any form of vice; and they do not go beyond the aim of preventing their own members from committing injustice against one another. But it is the goodness or badness in the life of the city which engages the attention of those who are concerned to secure good government.

**1280ᵇ6** The conclusion which clearly follows is that any city which is truly so called, and is not merely one in name, must devote itself to the end of encouraging goodness. Otherwise, a political association sinks into a mere alliance, which only differs in space [i.e. in the contiguity of its members] from other forms of alliance where the members live at a distance from one another. Otherwise, too, law becomes a mere covenant—or (in the phrase of the sophist Lycophron) 'a guarantor of just claims'—but lacks the capacity to make the citizens good and just.

**1280ᵇ12** That this is the case may be readily proved. If two different sites could be united in one, so that the city [i.e. the *polis*] of Megara and that of Corinth were embraced by a single wall, that would not make a single city. If the citizens of two cities intermarried with one another, that would not make a single city, even though intermarriage is one of the forms of social life which are characteristic of a city. Nor would it make a city if a number of people, living at a distance from one another, but not at so great a distance but they could still associate, had a common system of laws to prevent their injuring one another in the course of exchange. We can imagine, for instance, one being a carpenter, another a farmer, a third a shoemaker, and others producing other goods; and we can imagine a total number of as many as 10,000. But if these people were associated in nothing further than matters such as exchange and alliance, they would still have failed to reach the stage of a city. Why should this be the case? It cannot

be ascribed to any lack of contiguity in such an association. The members of a group so constituted might
come together on a single site; but if that were all—if
each still treated his private house as if it were a city,
and all of them still confined their mutual assistance
to action against aggressors (as if it were only a question of a defensive alliance)—if, in a word, they associated with each other in the same fashion after coming together as they did when they were living
apart—their association, even on its new basis, could
not be deemed by any accurate thinker to be a city.

**1280ᵇ29** It is clear, therefore, that a city is not an
association for residence on a common site, or for the
sake of preventing mutual injustice and easing
exchange. These are indeed conditions which must
be present before a city can exist; but the presence of
all these conditions is not enough, in itself, to constitute a city. What constitutes a city is an association of
households and clans in a good life, for the sake of
attaining a perfect and self-sufficing existence. This,
however, will not come about unless the members
inhabit one and the self-same place and practise intermarriage. It was for this reason that the various institutions of a common social life—marriage-connec-
tions, kin-groups, religious gatherings, and social
pastimes generally—arose in cities. This sort of thing
is the business of friendship, for the pursuit of a common social life is friendship. Thus the purpose of a
city is the good life, and these institutions are means
to that end. A city is constituted by the association of
families and villages in a perfect and self-sufficing
existence; and such an existence, on our definition,
consists in living a happy and truly valuable life.

**1281ᵃ2** It is therefore for the sake of actions valuable in themselves, and not for the sake of social life,
that political associations must be considered to
exist. Those who contribute most to this association
have a greater share in the city than those who are
equal to them (or even greater) in free birth and
descent, but unequal in civic excellence, or than
those who surpass them in wealth but are surpassed
by them in excellence. From what has been said it is
plain that all sides in the dispute about constitutions
profess only a partial conception of justice.

CHAPTER 10

*What person or body of people should be
sovereign in a city: the people, the rich, the
better sort of citizens, the one best, or the
tyrant? All these alternatives present
difficulties; and there is a difficulty even in a
further alternative, that no person or body of
people, but law, should be sovereign.*

**1281ᵃ11** A difficulty arises when we turn to consider what body should be sovereign in the city. The
people at large, the wealthy, the better sort, the one
who is best of all, the tyrant. But all these alternatives
appear to involve unpleasant results: indeed, how
can it be otherwise? What if the poor, on the ground
of their being a majority, proceed to divide among
themselves the possessions of the wealthy—will not
this be unjust? 'No, by heaven' (someone may
reply); 'it has been justly decreed so by the sovereign
body.' But if this is not the extreme of injustice, what
is? Whenever a majority takes everything and
divides among its members the possessions of a
minority, that majority is obviously ruining the city.
But goodness does not ruin whatever possesses it,
nor can justice be such as to ruin a city. It is therefore
clear that a law of this kind cannot possibly be just.
The tyrant's acts too would necessarily be just; for he
too uses coercion by virtue of superior power in just
the same sort of way as the people coerce the
wealthy. Is it just that a minority composed of the
wealthy should rule? Then if they too behave like
the others—if they plunder and confiscate the property of the people—their action is just. If it is, then
this behaviour would also be just in the former case.
It is clear that all these acts of oppression are mean
and unjust. But should the better sort have authority
and be sovereign in all matters? In that case, the rest
of the citizens will necessarily be deprived of honour, since they will not enjoy the honour of holding
civic office. We speak of offices as honours; and
when the same people hold office all the time, the rest
of the community must necessarily be deprived
of honour. Is it better that the one best man should
rule? This is still more oligarchical because the num-

ber of those deprived of honour is even greater. It may perhaps be urged that it is a poor sort of policy to vest sovereignty in a human being, rather than in law; for human beings are subject to the passions that beset their souls. But the law itself may incline either towards oligarchy or towards democracy; and what difference will the sovereignty of law then make in the problems which have just been raised? The consequences already stated will follow just the same.

### CHAPTER II

*It is possible, however, to defend the alternative, that the people should be sovereign. The people, when they are assembled, have a combination of qualities which enables them to deliberate wisely and to judge soundly. This suggests that they have a claim to be the sovereign body; it also suggests the scope of affairs in which they should be sovereign, or the powers which they should exercise. They should exercise deliberative and judicial functions; in particular, they should elect the magistrates and examine their conduct at the end of their tenure. Two objections may be raised. (1) It may be argued that experts are better judges than the non-expert; but this objection may be met by reference to (a) the combination of qualities in the assembled people (which makes them collectively better judges than the expert), and (b) the fact that in some cases laymen are in as good a position to judge as experts (which enables them to pass judgement on the behaviour of magistrates). (2) It may be urged that the people, if they have such powers, have more authority than the better sort of citizens who hold office as magistrates, though they are not of so good a quality; but we may answer to this that the people as a whole may well be of a high quality. We have always, however, to remember that rightly constituted laws should be the final sovereign, and that personal authority of any sort should only act in the particular cases which cannot be covered by a general law.*

**1281ᵃ39** The other alternatives may be reserved for later inquiry; but the suggestion that the people at large should be sovereign rather than the few best men would [seem to present problems which] need resolution, and while it presents some difficulty it perhaps also contains some truth. There is this to be said for the many: each of them by himself may not be of a good quality; but when they all come together it is possible that they may surpass—collectively and as a body, although not individually—the quality of the few best, in much the same way that feasts to which many contribute may excel those provided at one person's expense. For when there are many, each has his share of goodness and practical wisdom; and, when all meet together, the people may thus become something like a single person, who, as he has many feet, many hands, and many senses, may also have many qualities of character and intelligence. This is the reason why the many are also better judges of music and the writings of poets: some appreciate one part, some another, and all together appreciate all. The thing which makes a good man differ from a unit in the crowd—as it is also the thing which is generally said to make a beautiful person differ from one who is not beautiful, or an artistic representation differ from ordinary reality—is that elements which are elsewhere scattered and separate are here combined in a unity. If the elements are taken separately, one may say of an artistic representation that it is surpassed by the eye of this person and by some other feature of that.

**1281ᵇ15** It is not clear, however, that this contrast between the many, on the one hand, and the few good men, on the other, can apply to every people and to every large group. Perhaps, by heaven, there are some of which it clearly cannot be true; for otherwise the same argument would apply to the beasts. Yet what difference, one may ask, is there between some men and the beasts? All the same, there is nothing to prevent the view we have stated from being true of a particular group.

**1281ᵇ21** It would thus seem possible to solve, by the considerations we have advanced, both the problem raised in the previous chapter ['Which people should be sovereign?'] and the further problem which follows upon it, 'What are the matters over which freemen, or the general body of citizens—the sort of people who neither have wealth nor can make any claim on the ground of goodness—should properly exercise sovereignty?' Of course there is a danger in people of this sort sharing in the highest offices, as injustice may lead them into wrongdoing, and thoughtlessness into error. But there is also a serious risk in not letting them have some share of power; for a city with a body of disfranchised citizens who are numerous and poor must necessarily be a city which is full of enemies. The alternative left is to let them share in the deliberative and judicial functions. This is why Solon, and some of the other legislators, allow the people to elect officials and to call them to account at the end of their tenure of office, but not to hold office themselves in their individual capacity. When they all meet together, the people display a good enough gift of perception, and combined with the better class they are of service to the city (just as impure food, when it is mixed with pure, makes the whole concoction more nutritious than a small amount of the pure would be); but each of them is imperfect in the judgements he forms by himself.

**1281ᵇ38** But this arrangement of the constitution presents some difficulties. The first difficulty is that it may well be held that the function of judging when medical attendance has been properly given should belong to those whose profession it is to attend patients and cure the complaints from which they suffer—in a word, to members of the medical profession. The same may be held to be true of all other professions and arts; and just as medical men should have their conduct examined before a body of medics, so, too, should those who follow other professions have theirs examined before a body of members of their own profession. But the term 'medic' is applied to the ordinary practitioner, to the specialist who directs the course of treatment, and to someone who has some general knowledge of the art of medicine. (There are people of this last type to be found in connection with nearly all the arts.) We credit those who have a general knowledge with the power of judging as much as we do the experts. When we turn to consider the matter of election, the same principles would appear to apply. To make a proper election is equally the work of

experts. It is the work of those who are versed in geometry to choose a geometrician, or again, of those who are acquainted with steering to choose a steersman; and even if, in some occupations and arts, there are some non-experts who also share in the ability to choose, they do not share in a higher degree than the experts. It would thus appear, on this line of argument, that the people should not be made sovereign, either in the matter of election of magistrates or in that of their examination.

**1282ᵃ14** It may be, however, that these arguments are not altogether well founded for the reason given above—provided, that is to say, that the people is not too debased in character. Each individual may indeed be a worse judge than the experts; but all, when they meet together, are either better than experts or at any rate no worse. In the second place, there are a number of arts in which the craftsman is not the only, or even the best, judge. These are the arts whose products can be understood even by those who do not possess any skill in the art. A house, for instance, is something which can be understood by others besides the builder: indeed the user of a house, or in other words the householder, will judge it even better than he does. In the same way a steersman will judge a rudder better than a shipwright does; and the diner, not the cook, will be the best judge of a feast.

**1282ᵃ23** The first difficulty would appear to be answered sufficiently by these considerations. But there is a second difficulty still to be faced, which is connected with the first. It would seem to be absurd that people of poor character should be sovereign on issues which are more important than those assigned to the better sort of citizens. The election of officials, and their examination at the end of their tenure, are the most important of issues; and yet there are constitutions, as we have seen, under which these issues are assigned to the people, since the assembly is sovereign in all such matters. To add to the difficulty, membership of the assembly, which carries deliberative and judicial functions, is vested in people of little property and of any age; but a high property qualification is demanded from those who serve as treasurers or generals, or hold any of the highest offices.

**1282ª32** This difficulty too may, however, be met in the same way as the first; and the practice followed in these constitutions is perhaps, after all, correct. It is not the individual juryman, councillor, or assemblyman, who is vested with office, but the court, the council, or the popular assembly; and in these bodies each member, whether he be a councillor, an assemblyman, or a juryman, is simply a part of the whole. It is therefore just that the people should be sovereign on the more important issues, since the assembly, the council, and the court consist of many people. Moreover, the property owned by all these people is greater than that of those who either as individuals or as members of small bodies hold the highest offices.

**1282ª41** This may serve as a settlement of the difficulties which have been discussed. But the discussion of the first of these difficulties leads to one conclusion above all others. Rightly constituted laws should be [the final] sovereign; but rulers, whether one or many, should be sovereign in those matters on which law is unable, owing to the difficulty of framing general rules for all contingencies, to make an exact pronouncement. But what rightly constituted laws ought to be is a matter that is not yet clear; and here we are still confronted by the difficulty stated at the end of the previous chapter. Laws must be good or bad, just or unjust in the same way as the constitutions to which they belong. The one clear fact is that laws must be laid down in accordance with constitutions; and if this is the case, it follows that laws which are in accordance with right constitutions must necessarily be just, and laws which are in accordance with perverted constitutions must be unjust.

### CHAPTER 12

*Justice is the political good. It involves equality, or the distribution of equal amounts to those who are equal. But who are equals, and by what criterion are they to be reckoned as equals? Many criteria can be applied; but the only proper criterion, in a political society, is that of contribution to the function of that society. Those who are equal in that respect should*

*receive equal amounts: those who are superior or inferior should receive superior or inferior amounts, in proportion to the degree of their superiority or inferiority. If all are thus treated proportionately to the contribution they make, all are really receiving equal treatment; for the proportion between contribution and reward is the same in every case. The sort of equality which justice involves is thus proportionate equality; and this is the essence of distributive justice.*

**1282ᵇ14** In all branches of knowledge and in every kind of craft the end in view is some good. In the most sovereign of these, the capacity for [leadership in] political matters, the end in view is the greatest good and the good which is most to be pursued. The good in the sphere of politics is justice; and justice consists in what tends to promote the common interest. General opinion makes it consist in some sort of equality. Up to a point this agrees with the philosophical inquiries which contain our conclusions on ethics. In other words, it holds, that justice involves two factors—things, and those to whom things are assigned—and it considers that those who are equal should have assigned to them equal things. But here there arises a question which must not be overlooked. Equals and unequals—yes; but equals and unequals in what? This is a question which raises difficulties, and involves us in philosophical speculation on politics. It is possible to argue that offices and honours ought to be distributed unequally on the basis of superiority in any kind of goodness whatsoever—even if those concerned are similar, and do not differ, in any other respect. The reason is that where people differ from one another there must be a difference in what is just and proportionate to their merits. If this argument were right, the mere fact of a better complexion, or greater height, or any other such advantage, would establish a claim for a greater share of political rights to be given to its possessor. But is not the argument obviously wrong? To be clear that it is, we have only to consider other kinds of knowledge and ability. In dealing with a number of equally skilled flute-players, you should not assign a better supply of flutes to those who are better born. Rather those who are better at the job should be given the better supply of tools. If our point is not yet plain, it can be made so if we push it still further. Let us suppose someone who is superior to others in flute-playing, but far inferior in birth and beauty. Even if birth and beauty are greater goods than ability to play the flute, and even if those who possess them may surpass the flute-player proportionately more in these qualities than he surpasses them in his flute-playing, the fact remains that he is the one who ought to get the superior flutes. Superiority, whether in birth or in wealth, ought to contribute something to the performance of that function; and here these qualities contribute nothing to such performance.

**1283ª3** There is a further objection. If we accept this argument, every quality will have to be commensurable with every other. You will begin by reckoning a given degree of (say) height as superior to a given degree of some other quality, and you will thus be driven to pit height in general against (say) wealth and birth in general. But on this basis—i.e. that, *in a given case,* A is counted as excelling in height to a greater degree than B does in goodness, and that, *in general,* height is counted as excelling to a greater degree than goodness does—qualities are made commensurable. [We are involved in mere arithmetic]; for if amount X of some quality is 'better' than amount Y of some other, some amount which is other than X must clearly be equal to it [i.e. must be *equally* good]. This is impossible. It is therefore clear that in matters political there is no good reason for basing a claim to the exercise of authority on any and every kind of superiority. (Some may be swift and others slow, but this is no reason why the one should have more, and the other less—it is in athletic contests that the superiority of the swift receives its reward.) Claims must be based on the elements which constitute the being of the city. There are thus good grounds for the claims to honour which are made by people of good descent, free birth, or wealth, since those who hold office must necessarily be free men and pay the property assessment. (A city could not be composed entirely of those without means, any more than it could be composed entirely of slaves.) But we must add that if wealth and free birth are necessary elements, the qualities of being just and being a good soldier are also necessary. These too are elements which must be present if people are to live together in a city. The one difference is that the first two elements are necessary for the simple existence of a city, and the last two for its good life.

# BOOK IV

## *Actual Constitutions and Their Varieties*

### A: Introductory

#### CHAPTER I

*Politics, like other branches of knowledge, must consider not only the ideal; but also the various problems of the actual—e.g. which is the best constitution practicable in the given circumstances; what are the best means of preserving actual constitutions; which is the best average constitution for the majority of cities; what are the different varieties of the main types of constitution, and especially of democracy and oligarchy. Politics, too, must consider not only constitutions, but also laws, and the proper relation of laws to constitutions.*

**1288ᵇ10** It is true of all those practical arts and those branches of knowledge which are complete in the sense that they cover the whole of a subject rather than dealing with it in a piecemeal fashion, that each of them has to consider the different methods appropriate to the different categories of its subject. For instance, the art of physical training has to consider (1) which type of training is appropriate to which type of physique; (2) which is the best type of training (for the best type of training must be one which is suitable for the best endowed and best equipped physique); and (3) which is the type of training that can be generally applied to the majority of physiques—for that too is one of the problems to be solved by the art of physical training. Nor is this all. (4) If someone wants to have physical training, but does not want to attain the standard of skill and condition which is needed for competitions, it is the task of the trainer and the gymnastic master to impart the level of ability he requires. The same is obviously true of medicine, of shipbuilding, tailoring, and of all the other arts.

**1288<sup>b</sup>21** It follows that it is the task of the same branch of knowledge [i.e. politics] to consider first which is the best constitution, and what qualities a constitution must have to come closest to the ideal when there are no external factors to hinder its doing so, and secondly which sort of constitution suits which sort of civic body. The attainment of the best constitution is likely to be impossible for many cities; and the good lawgiver and the true statesman must therefore have their eyes open not only to what is the absolute best, but also to what is the best in relation to actual conditions. A third task is to consider the sort of constitution which depends upon an assumption—in other words, to study a given constitution with a view to explaining how it may have arisen and how it may be made to enjoy the longest possible life. The sort of case which we have in mind is one where a city has neither the [ideally] best constitution (nor even the elementary conditions needed for it) nor the best constitution possible under the actual conditions, but has only a constitution of an inferior type. In addition to all these tasks, it is important also to know the type of constitution which is best suited to cities in general. For this reason most of the writers who treat of politics, even if they deal well with other matters, fail when they come to matters of practical utility. We have to study not only the best constitution, but also the one which is practicable, and likewise the one which is easiest to work and most suitable to cities generally.

**1288<sup>b</sup>39** As things are, some confine their investigations to the extreme of perfection, which requires large resources. Others, addressing themselves to what is more generally attainable, still do away with the constitutions that now exist, and simply extol the Spartan constitution or some other type. The sort of constitutional system which ought to be proposed is one such that people will have little difficulty in accepting it or taking part in it, given the system they already have. It is as difficult a matter to reform an old constitution as it is to construct a new one; as hard to unlearn a lesson as it was to learn it initially. The statesman [*politikos*], therefore, must not confine himself to the matters we have just mentioned: he must also be able, as we said previously, to help any existing constitution. He cannot do so unless he knows how many different kinds of constitutions there are. As things are people believe that there is only one sort of democracy and one sort of oligarchy. This is an error. To avoid that error, we must keep in mind the different varieties of each constitution; we must be aware of their number, and of the number of different ways in which they are constituted.

**1289<sup>a</sup>11** The same kind of understanding is needed to see which laws are [absolutely] best and which are appropriate to each constitution. Laws ought to be made to suit constitutions (as indeed in practice they always are), and not constitutions made to suit laws. The reason is this. A constitution is an organization of offices in a city, by which the method of their distribution is fixed, the sovereign authority is determined, and the nature of the end to be pursued by the association and all its members is prescribed. Laws, apart from those that frame the constitution, are the rules by which the magistrates should exercise their powers, and should watch and check transgressors. It follows that one must always bear in mind both the varieties and the definition of each constitution, with a view to enacting appropriate laws. If there are several forms of democracy, and several forms of oligarchy, rather than a single form of each, the same laws cannot possibly be beneficial to all oligarchies or to all democracies.

*B: The Varieties of the Main Types*
*of Constitution Especially Democracy,*
*Oligarchy, and 'Constitutional Government'*
*or Polity*

### CHAPTER 3

*The reason for the variety of constitutions is the*
*varieties to be found in the 'parts' or social*

*elements of the city—especially among the populace and the notables. A constitution is an arrangement of offices; and there will be as many constitutions as there are methods of distributing offices among the different parts of the city. There is a general opinion that there are only two sorts of constitutions, just as there are only two sorts of winds and two sorts of musical modes; but this is a simplification which cannot be accepted.*

**1289ᵇ27** The reason why there are many different constitutions is to be found in the fact that every city has many different parts. In the first place, every city is obviously composed of households. Secondly, in this number there are bound to be some rich, some poor, and some in the middle, with the rich possessing and the poor being without the equipment of the heavy-armed soldier. Thirdly, the common people [or *dēmos*] are engaged partly in agriculture, partly in trade, and partly in menial jobs. Fourthly, there are also differences among the notables—differences based on their wealth and the amount of their property; and these differences appear, for example, in the matter of keeping horses. This can only be done by the very wealthy, which is the reason why cities whose strength lay in cavalry were in former times the homes of oligarchies. These oligarchies used their cavalry in wars with adjoining cities: we may cite the examples of Eretria and Chalcis [in the island of Euboea] and of Magnesia on the Maeander and many other cities in Asia Minor. Besides differences of wealth, there is also difference of birth, and difference of merit; and there are differences based on other factors of the same order—factors already described as being parts of a city in our discussion of aristocracy, where we distinguished and enumerated the essential parts from which every city is composed.

**1290ᵃ3** Sometimes all these parts share in the control of the constitution; sometimes only a few of them share; sometimes a number of them share. It thus follows clearly that there must be a number of constitutions, which differ from one another in kind. This is because the parts differ in kind from one

another. A constitution is an arrangement in regard to the offices of the city. By this arrangement the citizen body distributes office, either on the basis of the power of those who participate in it, or on the basis of some sort of general equality (i.e. the equality of the poor, or of the rich, or an equality existing among both rich and poor). There must therefore be as many constitutions as there are modes of arranging the distribution of office according to the superiorities and the differences of the parts of the city.

**1290ᵃ13** There is indeed a prevalent opinion that there are only two constitutions. Just as winds, in ordinary speech, are simply described as north or south, and all other winds are treated as deviations from these, so constitutions are also described as democratic or oligarchical. On this basis aristocracy is classified as being a sort of oligarchy, under the heading of oligarchical, and similarly the so-called 'constitutional government' [polity] is classified under the heading of democracy—just as westerly winds are classified under the head of northerly, and easterly winds under that of southerly. The situation is much the same, so some people think, with the modes in music. In their case also two modes (the Dorian and the Phrygian) are treated as basic and other arrangements are called by one or other of these two names. But though this is the prevalent view about constitutions in current opinion, we shall do better, and we shall come nearer the truth, if we classify them on a different basis, as has already been suggested. On that basis we shall have one or two constitutions which are properly formed; all the others will be perversions of the best constitution (just as in music we may have perversions of the properly tempered modes); and these perversions will be oligarchical when they are too severe and dominant, and democratic when they are soft and relaxed.

### C: The Type of Constitution Which Is Most Generally Practicable

#### CHAPTER II

*We are here concerned with the best constitution and way of life for the majority of people and cities. Goodness itself consists in a mean; and in any city the middle class is a mean between the rich and the poor. The middle class is free from the ambition of the rich and the pettiness of the poor: it is a natural link which helps to ensure political cohesion. We may thus conclude that a constitution based on this class, i.e. a 'constitutional government' or polity, is most likely to be generally beneficial. It will be free from faction, and will be likely to be stable. But 'constitutional governments' have been historically rare, partly for internal reasons, and partly because the policy of the Athenian and the Spartan empires has encouraged extremes in preference to a middle way. Still, the 'constitutional government' may serve as a standard in judging the merits of actual constitutions.*

**1295ª25** We have now to consider what is the best constitution and the best way of life for the majority of cities and the majority of mankind. In doing so, we shall not employ a standard of excellence above the reach of ordinary people, or a standard of education requiring exceptional natural endowments and equipment, or the standard of a constitution which attains an ideal level. We shall be concerned only with the sort of life which most people are able to share and the sort of constitution which it is possible for most cities to enjoy. The 'aristocracies', so called, of which we have just been treating, either lie at one extreme, beyond the reach of most cities, or they approach so closely to what is called 'constitutional government' [polity] that the two can be considered as a single form.

**1295ª34** The issues we have just raised can all be decided in the light of one body of fundamental principles. If we were right when, in the *Ethics*, we stated that the truly happy life is one of goodness lived in freedom from impediments and that goodness consists in a mean, it follows that the best way of life is one which consists in a mean, and a mean of the kind attainable by each individual. Further, the same criteria should determine the goodness or badness of the city and that of the constitution; for a constitution is

the way in which a city lives. In all cities there are three parts: the very rich, the very poor, and the third class which forms the mean between these two. Now, since it is admitted that moderation and the mean are always best it is clear that in the ownership of all gifts of fortune a middle condition will be the best. Those who are in this condition are the most ready to listen to reason. Those who are over-handsome, over-strong, over-noble, or over-wealthy, and, at the opposite extreme, those who are over-poor, over-weak, or utterly ignoble, find it hard to follow the lead of reason. Those in the first class tend more to arrogance and serious offences: those in the second tend too much to criminality and petty offences; and most wrong-doing arises either from arrogance or criminality. [It is a further characteristic of those in the middle that] they are least prone either to refuse office or to seek it, both of which tendencies are dangerous to cities.

**1295ᵇ13** It must also be added that those who enjoy too many advantages—strength, wealth, friends, and so forth—are both unwilling to obey and ignorant how to obey. This [defect] appears in them from the first, during childhood and in home-life: nurtured in luxury, they never acquire a habit of obedience, even in school. But those who suffer from a lack of such things are far too mean and poor-spirited. Thus there are those who are ignorant how to rule and only know how to obey, as if they were slaves, and, on the other hand, there are those who are ignorant how to obey any sort of authority and only know how to rule as if they were masters [of slaves]. The result is a city, not of freemen, but only of slaves and masters: a state of envy on the one side and of contempt on the other. Nothing could be further removed from the spirit of friendship or of a political association. An association depends on friendship—after all, people will not even take a journey in common with their enemies. A city aims at being, as far as possible, composed of equals and peers, which is the condition of those in the middle, more than any group. It follows that this kind of city is bound to have the best constitution since it is composed of the elements which, on our view, naturally go to make up a city. The middle classes enjoy a greater security themselves than any other class. They do not, like the poor, desire the goods of others; nor do others desire their possessions, as the poor desire those of the rich, and since they neither plot against others, nor are plotted against themselves, they live free from danger. Phocylides was therefore right when he prayed:

*Many things are best for those in the middle;*
*I want to be at the middle of the city.*

**1295ᵇ34** It is clear from our argument, first, that the best form of political association is one where power is vested in the middle class, and, secondly, that good government is attainable in those cities where there is a large middle class—large enough, if possible, to be stronger than both of the other classes, but at any rate large enough to be stronger than either of them singly; for in that case its addition to either will suffice to turn the scale, and will prevent either of the opposing extremes from becoming dominant. It is therefore the greatest of blessings for a city that its members should possess a moderate and adequate property. Where some have great possessions, and others have nothing at all, the result is either an extreme democracy or an unmixed oligarchy; or it may even be, as a result of the excesses of both sides, a tyranny. Tyranny grows out of the most immature type of democracy, or out of oligarchy, but much less frequently out of constitutions of the middle order, or those which approximate to them. We shall explain the reason for this later, when we come to treat of the ways in which constitutions change.

**1296ᵃ7** Meanwhile, it is clear that the middle type of constitution is best. It is the one type free from faction; where the middle class is large, there is less likelihood of faction and dissension than in any other constitution. Large cities are generally more free from faction just because they have a large middle class. In small cities, on the other hand, it is easy for the whole population to be divided into only two classes; nothing is left in the middle, and all, or almost all, are either poor or rich. Democracies are generally more secure and more permanent than oligarchies because of their middle class. This is more

numerous, and has a larger share of [offices and] honours, than it does in oligarchies. Where democracies have no middle class, and the poor are greatly superior in number, trouble ensues, and they are speedily ruined. It must also be considered a proof of its value that the best legislators have come from the middle class. Solon was one, as he makes clear in his poems: Lycurgus was another (after all he was not a king); and the same is true of Charondas and most of the other legislators.

**1296ᵃ22** What has just been said also serves to explain why most constitutions are either democratic or oligarchical. The middle class in these cities is often small; and the result is that as happens whenever one class—be it the owners of property or the masses—gains the advantage, it oversteps the mean, and draws the constitution in its own direction so that either a democracy or an oligarchy comes into being. In addition, factious disputes and struggles readily arise between the masses and the rich; and the side, whichever it is, that wins the day, instead of establishing a constitution based on the common interest and the principle of equality, exacts as the prize of victory a greater share in the constitution. It then institutes either a democracy or an oligarchy. Furthermore, those who have gained ascendancy in Greece have paid an exclusive regard to their own types of constitution; one has instituted democracies in the cities [under its control], while the other has set up oligarchies: each has looked to its own advantage, and neither to that of the cities it controlled. These reasons explain why a middle or mixed type of constitution has never been established—or, at the most, has only been established on a few occasions and in a few cities. One man, and one only, of all who have hitherto been in a position of ascendancy, has allowed himself to be persuaded to allow this sort of system to be established. And now it has also become the habit for cities not even to want a system of equality. Instead they seek to dominate or, if beaten, to submit.

**1296ᵇ2** It is clear, from these arguments, which is the best constitution, and what are the reasons why it is so and it is easy to see which of the others (given that we distinguish several varieties of democracy and several varieties of oligarchy) should be placed first, which second, and so on in turn, according as their quality is better or worse. The nearest to the best must always be better, and the one farthest removed from the mean must always be worse, unless we are judging on the basis of a particular assumption. I use the words 'on the basis of a particular assumption' because it often turns out that, although one sort of constitution may be preferable, there is nothing to prevent another sort from being better suited to certain peoples.

# BOOK V

## *Causes of Factional Conflict and Constitutional Change*

### *A: The General Causes of Factional Conflict and Change in All Types of Constitution*

#### CHAPTER I

*Different interpretations of justice and equality lead to the making of different claims by different parties; and the conflict of these claims causes political struggles and changes. The different forms which programmes of political change may take either imply the overthrow of the existing constitution, or involve some sort of modification. Whatever the difference of form may be, the general motive is always a passion for some conception of equality, which is held to be involved in the very idea of justice. There are two main conceptions of equality, the numerical and the proportionate: democracy is based on the one, and oligarchy on the other. Neither conception should be exclusively followed; but, of the two, the democratic is the safer, and the less likely to provoke factional conflict.*

**1301ª19** We have now discussed practically all the topics stated in our programme apart from the following. What are the general causes which produce changes in constitutions, and what is the num-

ber and nature of these causes? In what particular ways is each constitution liable to degenerate—i.e. what forms of constitution are most likely to change to what? In addition we must ask which policies are likely to ensure the stability of constitutions, collectively and individually, and what means may best be employed to secure each particular constitution. We must now consider these questions.

**1301ª25** We must first assume, as a basis of our argument, that the reason why there is a variety of different constitutions is the fact, already mentioned, that while everybody is agreed about justice, and the principle of proportionate equality, people fail to achieve it in practice. Democracy arose out of an opinion that those who were equal in any one respect were equal absolutely, and in all respects. (People are prone to think that the fact of their all being equally free-born means that they are all absolutely equal.) Oligarchy similarly arose from an opinion that those who were unequal in some one respect were altogether unequal. (Those who are superior in point of wealth readily regard themselves as absolutely superior.) Thus those on one side claim an equal share in everything, on the ground of their equality, while those on the other press for a greater share, on the ground that they are unequal, since to be greater is to be unequal. Both sides are based on a sort of justice; but they both fall short of absolute justice. For this reason each side engages in factional conflict if it does not enjoy a share in the constitution in keeping with the conception of justice it happens to entertain. Those who are pre-eminent in merit would be the most justified in forming factions (though they are the last to make the attempt); for they, and they only, can reasonably be regarded as enjoying an absolute superiority. There are also those who possess an advantage of birth and regard themselves as entitled to more than an equal share on the ground of this advantage, for those whose ancestors had merit and wealth are commonly regarded as 'well-born'.

**1301ᵇ4** These, in a general sense, are the sources and springs of faction, and the reasons why people engage in faction-fighting. These considerations will also explain the two different ways in which constitutional changes may happen. (1) Sometimes factions are directed against the existing constitution, and are intended to change it from its established form—to turn democracy into oligarchy, or oligarchy into democracy; or, again, to turn democracy and oligarchy into 'constitutional government' [polity] and aristocracy, or, conversely, these latter [constitutions] into the former. (2) Sometimes, however, they are not directed against the existing constitution. Those forming a faction may choose to maintain the system of government—an oligarchy, for example, or a monarchy—as it stands; but they desire to get the administration into their own hands. Or they may wish to make the constitution more pronounced or more moderate. They may wish, for example, to make an oligarchy more, or less, oligarchical. They may wish to make a democracy more, or less, democratic. They may similarly seek to tighten, or loosen, any of the other forms of constitution. They may also direct their efforts towards changing only one part of the constitution. They may wish, for example, to erect, or to abolish, some particular office. Some writers state that Lysander attempted to abolish the kingship at Sparta, and King Pausanias the 'ephoralty'. At Epidamnus, again, there was a partial change of the constitution; and a council was substituted for the tribal leaders. But even at the present time those holding office are the only members of the civic body who are obliged to attend the public assembly, when the appointment to an office is being put to the vote; and the existence of a supreme official [called an *archōn*] was another oligarchical feature.

**1301**b**26** Factional conflict is always the result of inequality except, that is, where unequals are treated in proportion to the inequality existing between them. An hereditary monarchy only involves inequality when it exists among equals. It is the passion for equality which is thus at the root of faction. But equality is of two sorts. One sort is numerical equality: the other sort is equality proportionate to desert. 'Numerical equality' means being treated equally, or identically, in the number and volume of things which you get; 'equality proportionate to desert' means being treated on the basis of equality of ratios. To give an example—numerically, the excess of 3 over 2 is equal to the excess of 2 over 1; but proportionally the excess

of 4 over 2 is equal to the excess of 2 over 1, 2 being the same fraction of 4 as 1 is of 2. Now people are ready to agree to the principle that absolute justice consists in proportion to desert; but, as we noted above, they differ [in practice]. Some consider that if they are equal in one respect, they are equal in all: others consider that if they are superior in one respect, they may claim superiority in everything.

**1301**b**39** For this reason two types of constitution—democracy and oligarchy—are particularly prevalent. Good birth and merit are found in few people; but the qualities on which democracy and oligarchy are based are found in a much larger number. In no city would you find as many as a hundred people of good birth and merit: there are many in which you would find that number of wealthy people. But a system based absolutely, and at all points, on either kind of equality is a poor sort of thing. The facts are evidence enough: no constitution of this sort ever endures. The reason is simple. When one begins with an initial error, it is inevitable that one should end badly. The right course is to use the principle of numerical equality in some cases, and that of equality proportionate to desert in others. Yet it must be admitted that democracy is a form of government which is safer, and less vexed by faction, than oligarchy. Oligarchies are prone to two sorts of faction-fighting—among themselves, and between themselves and the populace. In democracies there is only faction-fighting against the oligarchs; and there are no internal dissensions—at any rate none worth mentioning—which divide the populace against itself. Furthermore, the form of constitution based on the middle [group of citizens], which is the most stable of all the forms with which we are here concerned, is nearer to democracy than to oligarchy.

*C: Methods of Ensuring Constitutional Stability in the Three Previous Types of Constitution and More Generally*

CHAPTER 8

*Precautions should be taken against lawlessness, and especially against its petty forms. No reliance should be placed on devices intended to hoodwink the masses. A spirit of fairness should be cultivated; and something of the temper, and even some of the institutions, of democracy may therefore be advisable in oligarchies and aristocracies. To maintain a feeling of emergency may help to maintain the government. Promotions, and the award or withdrawal of honours, should be carefully handled. Watch should be kept both on private extravagance and the sudden rise of a whole social class to a new degree of prosperity. In particular, steps should be taken to prevent office from being made a source of profit. Finally, democracies will do well to spare the rich, and oligarchies to encourage and help the poor.*

**1307ᵇ26** It remains to treat of the methods for preserving constitutions in general, and for each particular type. It is clear, to begin with, that to know the causes which destroy constitutions is also to know the causes which ensure their preservation. Opposite effects are brought about by opposite causes; and destruction and preservation are opposite effects.

**1307ᵇ30** On this basis we may draw a number of conclusions. The first is that in constitutions where the elements are well mixed there is one thing as vitally important as any: to keep a look-out against all lawlessness, and, more particularly, to be on guard against any of its petty forms. Lawlessness may creep in unperceived, just as petty expenditures, constantly repeated, will gradually destroy the whole of a fortune. Because it is not all incurred at once, such expenditure goes unperceived; and our minds are misled by it in the same way as they are misled by the logical fallacy, 'When each is small, all are small too'. This is true in one sense, but it is not true in another. The whole or total is not small, even though the elements of which it is composed are small.

**1307ᵇ39** This is one precaution which ought to be taken—to prevent the trouble beginning in this way. Secondly, we may lay down the rule that confidence should never be placed in devices intended to hoodwink the masses. They are always under-

mined by events. (We have already explained the nature of the constitutional devices to which we are here referring.)

**1308ᵃ3** Thirdly, we have to observe that some aristocracies (and also some oligarchies) survive, not because they have stable constitutions, but because those who hold office give good treatment to those outside the constitution as well as to the members of the civic body: they do not treat those without a share in the constitution unjustly; on the contrary, they bring their leading members within the constitution; they do not wrong the ambitious among them on points of honour, or the mass of the people in matters of [money and] profit; they behave towards one another and to those who are members of the constitution in a democratic spirit.

**1308ᵃ11** The principle of equality which democrats apply to the masses is not only just but expedient when applied to those who really are 'peers'. When, therefore, the members of the governing class are numerous, a number of democratic institutions will be expedient. It will be expedient, for instance, to restrict the tenure of office to a period of six months, and thus to enable all who belong to the class of 'peers' to enjoy their turn. A numerous class of 'peers' is already, by its nature, a sort of democracy; and that is why, as has already been noticed, we often find demagogues emerging in such a class. When such a policy is adopted, oligarchies and aristocracies are less prone to fall into the hands of family cliques. Those who hold office with a short tenure can hardly do as much harm as those who have a long tenure; and it is long possession of office which leads to the rise of tyrannies in oligarchies and democracies. Those who make a bid for tyranny, in both types of constitution, are either the most powerful people (who in democracies are the demagogues, and in oligarchies the heads of great families), or else the holders of the main offices who have held them for a long period.

**1308ᵃ24** The preservation of a constitution may not only be due to the fact that those who would destroy it are far away; it may also, on occasion, be due to the fact that they are close at hand. When danger is imminent, people are anxious, and they therefore keep a firmer grip on their constitution. All who are concerned for the constitution should therefore create anxieties, which will put people on their guard, and will make them keep watch without relaxing, like sentinels on night-duty. They must, in a word, make the remote come near.

**1308ª31** An endeavour should also be made, by legislation as well as by personal action, to guard against quarrels and factions among the notables; and watch should also be kept in advance on those who are not yet involved, before they too have caught the spirit of rivalry. Ordinary people cannot see the beginning of troubles ahead; that requires the genuine statesman.

**1308ª35** Change may arise, in oligarchies and 'constitutional governments' [polities], as a result of the assessment required for the property qualification. It will tend to arise, for example, when the monetary amount of the property qualification is left unchanged but the amount of money in circulation shows a large increase. To meet this danger a comparison should regularly be made between the present sum-total of all the assessments and their sum-total in a previous year. Where the assessment is annual, the comparison should be made annually; where—as in the larger cities—the assessment is made at intervals of three or four years, the comparison should be made at those intervals. If the sum-total is then found to be many times greater (or many times less) than it was on the previous occasion when the assessments obligatory under the constitution were fixed, a law should be passed to provide for the raising (or lowering) of the qualification required. Where the total is greater than it was the assessment should be tightened by means of a proportionate increase; where it is less it should be relaxed by making it smaller. In oligarchies and 'constitutional governments' [polities] where this policy is not adopted change will be inevitable. In one case the change will be from 'constitutional government' to oligarchy, and from oligarchy to a family clique; in the other change will move in the reverse direction—from a 'constitutional government' to a democracy, and from an oligarchy either to a 'constitutional government' or a democracy.

**1308ᵇ10** A rule which applies both to democracies and oligarchies—indeed it applies to all constitutions—is that no one should be advanced disproportionately. It is a better policy to award small honours over a period of time than to give honours rapidly. (People are easily spoiled; and it is not all who can stand prosperity.) If this rule is not followed, and if many honours are bestowed at the same time, the least that can be done is not to revoke them all at the same time, but to do so by degrees. It is also good policy to aim so to shape things, by appropriate legislation, that no one gains a position of superiority by the strength of his friends or of his wealth. Failing that, those who gain such a position should be removed from it by being sent out of the country.

**1308ᵇ20** Since people tend to become revolutionaries from circumstances connected with their private lives an office should be instituted to supervise those who live in a way that is out of harmony with the constitution—who in a democracy do not live democratically; in an oligarchy, do not live oligarchically; and so in each other type of constitution. For similar reasons watch should be kept over whatever section in the city is particularly flourishing at any moment. The remedy is either (*a*) always to give the conduct of affairs and the enjoyment of office to the opposite section (I mean by this that the respectable people are opposite to the masses, and the poor to the wealthy), and thus to attempt a balance or fusion between the poor and the wealthy section, or (*b*) to seek to increase the strength of the middle or intervening element. Such a policy will prevent the factional disputes which arise from inequality.

**1308ᵇ31** The most important rule of all, in all types of constitution, is that provision should be made—not only by law, but also by the general system of economy—to prevent the officials from being able to use their office for their own gain. This is a matter which demands attention in oligarchical constitutions, above all others. The masses are not so greatly offended at being excluded from office (they may even be glad to be given the leisure for attending to their own business); what really annoys them is to think that those who have the enjoyment of office are embezzling public funds. That makes them feel a double annoyance at a double loss—the loss of profit as well as office. If an arrangement could be made to stop people from using office as a means of private gain, it would provide a way—the only possible way—for combining democracy with aristocracy. Both the notables and the masses could then get what they desire. All would be able to hold office, as befits a democracy: the notables would actually be in office, as befits an aristocracy. Both results could be achieved simultaneously if the use of office as a means of profit were made impossible. The poor would no longer desire to hold office (because they would derive no advantage from doing so), and they would prefer to attend to their own affairs. The rich would be able to afford to take office, as they would need no subvention from public funds to meet its expenses. The poor would thus have the advantage of becoming wealthy by diligent attention to work; the notables would enjoy the consolation of not being governed by any chance comer.

**1309ᵃ10** To prevent the embezzling of public money, the outgoing officers should hand over the funds [under their charge] in the presence of the whole civic body; and inventories of them should be deposited with each clan, ward, and tribe. To ensure that no profit should be made by any official in other ways, the law should provide for the award of honours to those who earn a good reputation.

**1309ᵃ14** In democracies, the rich should be spared. Not only should their estates be safe from the threat of redistribution: the produce of the estates should be equally secure; and the practice of sharing it out, which has insensibly developed under some constitutions, should not be allowed. It is good policy, too, to prevent the rich, even if they are willing, from undertaking expensive, and yet useless, public services, such as the equipping of choruses for dramatic festivals, or the provision of the expenses of torch-races, or other services of that sort. In oligarchies, on the other hand, a good deal of attention should be paid to the poor. They should be assigned those offices from which profits can be made; and if a rich man does violence against them the penalties

should be heavier than if he had been guilty of violence against members of his own class. Nor should inheritances pass by title of bequest; they should go by descent, and not more than one inheritance should ever go to one person. On this system estates would be more evenly distributed, and more of the poor might rise to a position of affluence.

**1309ᵃ27** In matters other than property it is beneficial both for oligarchies and for democracies to give a position of equality, or even of precedence, to those who have a smaller share in the constitution—in a democracy to the rich; in an oligarchy to the poor. An exception must, however, be made for the sovereign offices of the constitution. These should be entrusted only, or at any rate entrusted mainly, to those who have [full] membership in the constitution.

CHAPTER 9

*Further consideration of the methods of ensuring constitutional stability in the three first types of constitution. In the interest of constitutional stability, three qualities are required in the holders of high office; their relative importance. It is always wise to ensure that a majority of the citizen body is in favour of the constitution. The value of the mean, and of refusing to push political issues to an extreme: not all democratic or oligarchic measures are calculated to ensure the permanence of democracy or oligarchy. The cardinal importance of educating citizens to live and act in the spirit of the constitution: this is too often neglected, especially in extreme democracies, which encourage the idea of 'living as one likes'.*

**1309ᵃ33** Three qualifications are necessary in those who have to fill the sovereign offices. The first is loyalty to the established constitution. The second is a high degree of capacity for the duties of the office. The third is goodness of character and justice, in the particular form which suits the nature of each constitution. (If what is just varies from constitution to constitution, the quality of justice must also have its corresponding varieties.) Where these three qualifications are not united in a single person, a problem obviously arises: [how is the choice to be made?] For instance, A may possess military capacity, but be neither good in character nor loyal to the constitution. B may be just in character and loyal to the constitution, [but deficient in capacity]. How are we to choose? It would seem that we ought to consider two points—which quality do people on the whole have more of and which less. Thus, for a military office, we must have regard to military experience rather than character: people in general have less military capacity and more honesty. For the post of custodian of property, or that of treasurer, we must follow the opposite rule: such posts require a standard of character above the average, but the knowledge which they demand is such as we all possess. A further problem may also be raised: if someone possesses the two qualifications of capacity and loyalty to the constitution, is there any need for him to have the third qualification (a good character), and will not the first two, by themselves, secure the public interest? We may answer that those who possess these two first qualifications may lack self-control, and just as such people fail to serve their own interests—even though they possess self-knowledge and self-loyalty—so nothing prevents some people from being in the same position with regard to the public interest.

**1309ᵇ14** Generally, we may add, a constitution will tend to be preserved by the observance of all the legal rules already suggested, in the course of our argument, as making for constitutional stability. Here we may note, as of paramount importance, the elementary principle which has been again and again suggested—the principle of ensuring that the number of those who wish a constitution to continue shall be greater than the number of those who do not.

**1309ᵇ18** In addition to all these things, there is another which ought to be remembered, but which, in fact, is forgotten in perverted forms of government. This is the value of the mean. Many of the measures which are reckoned democratic really undermine democracies: many which are reckoned oligarchical actually undermine oligarchies. Those who think that theirs is the only form of goodness, push matters to an extreme. They fail to see that proportion is as necessary to a constitution as it is (let us say) to a nose. A nose may deviate in some degree from the ideal of straightness, and incline towards the hooked or the snub, without ceasing to be well shaped and agreeable to the eye. But push the deviation still further towards either of these extremes, and the nose will begin to be out of proportion with the rest of the face: carry it further still, and it will cease to look like a nose at all, because it will go too far towards one, and too far away from the other, of these two opposite extremes. What is true of the nose, and of other parts of the body, is true also of constitutions. Both oligarchy and democracy may be tolerable forms of government, even though they deviate from the ideal. But if you push either of them further still [in the direction to which it tends], you will begin by making it a worse constitution, and you may end by turning it into something which is not a constitution at all.

**1309ᵇ35** It is thus the duty of legislators and statesmen to know which democratic measures preserve, and which destroy, a democracy; similarly, it is their duty to know which oligarchical measures will save, and which will ruin, an oligarchy. Neither of these constitutions can exist, or continue in existence, unless it includes both the rich and the poor. If, therefore, a system of equal ownership is introduced into either, the result will inevitably be a new and different form of constitution; and the radical legislation which abolishes riches and poverty will thus abolish along with them the constitutions [based on their presence]. Errors are made alike in democracies and oligarchies. They are made, for instance, by demagogues, in those democracies where the will of the people is superior to the law. Demagogues are always dividing the city into two, and waging war against the rich. Their proper policy is the very reverse: they should always profess to be speaking in defence of the rich. A similar policy should be followed in oligarchies: the oligarchs should profess to speak on behalf of the poor; and the oaths they take should be the opposite of those which they now take. There are cities in which their oath runs, 'I will bear ill will to the people, and I will plan against them all the evil I can.' The opinion which they ought to hold and exhibit is the very opposite; and their oaths should contain the declaration, 'I will not do wrong to the people.'

**1310ᵃ12** The greatest, however, of all the means we have mentioned for ensuring the stability of constitutions—but one which is nowadays generally neglected—is the education of citizens in the spirit of their constitution. There is no advantage in the best of laws, even when they are sanctioned by general civic consent, if the citizens themselves have not been attuned, by the force of habit and the influence of teaching, to the right constitutional temper—which will be the temper of democracy where the laws are democratic, and where they are oligarchical will be that of oligarchy. If an individual can lack self-control, so can a city. The education of a citizen in the spirit of his constitution does not consist in his doing the actions in which the partisans of oligarchy, or the adherents of democracy, delight. It consists in his doing the actions which make it possible to have an oligarchy, or a democracy. Actual practice, today, is on very different lines. In oligarchies the sons of those in office live lives of luxury, and this at a time when the sons of the poor are being hardened by exercise, and by their daily work, and are thus acquiring the will and the power to create a revolution. In democracies of the type which is regarded as being peculiarly democratic the policy followed is the very reverse of their real interest. The reason for this is a false conception of liberty. There are two features which are generally held to define democracy. One of them is the sovereignty of the majority; the other is the liberty of individuals. Justice is assumed to consist in equality and equality in regarding the will of the masses as sovereign; liberty is assumed to consist in 'doing what one likes'. The result of such a view is that, in these extreme democracies, each individual lives as he likes—or, as Euripides says,

*For any end he chances to desire.*

This is a mean conception [of liberty]. To live by the rule of the constitution ought not to be regarded as slavery, but rather as salvation.

Such, in general, are the causes which lead to the change and destruction of constitutions, and such are the means of ensuring their preservation and stability.

# BOOK VII

## *Political Ideals and Educational Principles*

### *A: Political Ideals: The Nature of the Highest Good and of the Best and Happiest Life*

#### CHAPTER I

*The three 'goods'—external goods; goods of the body; and goods of the soul. The primacy of the goods of the soul is attested by experience and evinced by philosophy: the possession of such goods—courage, wisdom, and the other virtues—depends not on fortune but on ourselves; and it is, for cities as well as for individuals, the condition and the cause of the best and happiest life. We thus come to the conclusion that 'the best way of life, both for cities and for individuals, is the life of goodness, duly equipped with such a store of requisites— i.e. external goods and goods of the body—as makes it possible to share in the activities of goodness'.*

**1323ᵃ14** Anyone who is going to make a proper inquiry about the best form of constitution must first determine what mode of life is most to be desired. As long as that is obscure, the best constitution must also remain obscure. It is to be expected that, provided that nothing extraordinary happens, those who live under the constitution that is best for those in their circumstances will have the best way of life. We must therefore, first of all, find some agreed conception of the way of life which is most desirable for all men and in all cases; and we must then discover whether or not the same way of life is desirable in the case of the community as in that of the individual.

**1323ᵃ21** Assuming that our extensive discussions of the best way of life in works intended for the general public are adequate, we should make use of them here. There is one classification of goods which it is certain that no one would challenge. This is the classification of these elements into three groups: external goods; goods of the body; and goods of the soul. These all belong to the happy man. No one would call a man happy who had no particle of courage, temperance, justice, or wisdom; who feared the flies buzzing about his head; who abstained from none of the extremest forms of extravagance whenever he felt hungry or thirsty; who would ruin his dearest friends for the sake of a quarter of an obol; whose mind was as senseless, and as much deceived, as that of a child or a madman. These are all propositions which would be accepted by nearly everybody as soon as they are stated, but people differ about the amount [of each different kind of good that is required] and about their relative superiority. So far as goodness [of mind and character] is concerned any amount is regarded as adequate; but wealth and property, power, reputation, and all such things, are coveted without limit. In answer to these people we shall say: 'The facts themselves make it easy for you to assure yourselves on these issues. You can see for yourselves that the goods of the soul are not gained or maintained by external goods. It is the other way round. You can see for yourselves that the happy life—no matter whether it consists in pleasure, or goodness, or both—belongs more to those who have cultivated their character and mind to the uttermost, and kept acquisition of external goods within moderate limits, than it does to those who have managed to acquire more external goods than they can use, and are lacking in the goods of the soul.' But the problem can also be easily solved if we consider it theoretically.

**1323ᵇ7** External goods, like all other instruments, have a necessary limit of size. Indeed everything which is useful is useful for some purpose; and any excessive amount of such things must either cause its possessor some injury, or, at any rate, bring him no benefit. But with goods of the soul, the greater the amount of each, the greater is its usefulness—if indeed it is proper to predicate 'usefulness' at all here, and we ought not simply to predicate 'value'. In general terms, we are clearly entitled to lay down

that the best state of one thing is superior to the best state of another, to the same degree that the things of which they are states differ. If, therefore, the soul is a thing more precious—intrinsically as well as in relation to us—than either our property or our body, the best state of the soul must necessarily bear the same relation to the best state of either our property or our body. Let us add that it is for the sake of the soul that these other things are desirable, and should accordingly be desired by everyone of good sense—not the soul for the sake of them.

**1323ᵇ21** We may therefore join in agreeing that the amount of happiness which falls to each individual man is equal to the amount of his goodness and his wisdom, and of the good and wise acts that he does. God himself bears witness to this conclusion. He is happy and blessed; but he is so in and by himself, by reason of the nature of his being, and not by virtue of any external good. This will explain why there must always be a difference between being happy and being fortunate. Accident and chance are causes of the goods external to the soul; but no man can be just and temperate merely from chance or by chance.

**1323ᵇ29** The next point, which is based on the same general train of reasoning, is that the best city is the one which is happy and 'does well'. To do well is impossible unless you also do fine deeds; and there can be no doing fine deeds for a city, any more than there can be for an individual, in the absence of goodness and wisdom. The courage of a city, and the justice and wisdom of a city, have the same force, and the same character, as the qualities which cause individuals who have them to be called just, wise, and temperate.

**1323ᵇ36** These observations may serve, at any rate so far as they go, as a preface to our argument. They deal with matters on which it is impossible not to touch; but it is equally impossible to develop here the whole of the argument which is involved. That is a matter for another and different branch of study. Here it may be sufficient to take this much as established: the best way of life, for individuals separately as well as for cities collectively, is the life of goodness duly equipped with such a store of requisites as makes it possible to share in the activities of goodness. This may conceivably be challenged; but we must leave the matter there—so far as our present inquiry is concerned—and defer to a later occasion any attempt to answer the arguments of those who refuse to accept our views.

## CHAPTER 2

*Assuming that the best way of life, alike for the city and for the individual, is the life of goodness, we may go on to raise the question whether the life of goodness consists more in external action, or more in internal development. So far as cities are concerned, we are presented with a choice between (a) the life of politics and action, which issues in the assumption of authority over other cities, and (b) the life of the self-contained city, engaged in developing its own resources and culture. The former ideal is illustrated by Sparta, and by other military and imperialist cities; but it raises doubts in the mind when one reflects on the ethics of conquest and the claims of liberty. The conclusion which suggests itself is that while a city should put itself in a position to maintain its own independence, military activity is only a means to the highest good, which is to share in a good life and the happiness of that life.*

**1324ª5** It remains to discuss whether the happiness of the city is the same as that of the individual, or different. The answer is clear: all are agreed that they are the same. Those who believe that the well-being of the individual consists in his wealth, will also believe that the city as a whole is happy when it is wealthy. Those who rank the life of a tyrant higher than any other, will also rank the city which possesses the largest empire as being the happiest city. Anyone who grades individuals by their goodness, will also regard the happiness of cities as proportionate to their goodness.

**1324ª13** Two questions arise at this point which both need consideration. The first is, 'Which way of life is the more desirable: to join with other citizens and share in the city's activity, or to live in it like an alien, released from the ties of the political association?' The second is, 'Which is the best constitution and the best way of organizing a city—no matter whether we assume that it is desirable for all to have a share in the city, or regard it as desirable for the majority only?'

**1324ª19** This second question—unlike the first, which raises the issue of what is good for the individual—is a matter for political thought and political speculation; and as we are now engaged on a discussion which belongs to that field, we may regard it as falling within the scope of our present inquiry—as the other question can hardly be said to do. There is one thing clear about the best constitution: it must be a political organization which will enable anyone to be at his best and live happily. But if that is clear, there is another point on which opinions diverge. Even those who agree in holding that the good life is most desirable are divided upon the issue, 'Which way of life is the more desirable? The way of politics and action? Or the way of detachment from all external things—the way, let us say, of contemplation, which some regard as the only way that is worthy of a philosopher?' Here, we may say, are the two ways of life—the political and the philosophic—that are evidently chosen by those who have been most eager to win a reputation for goodness, in our own and in previous ages. It is a matter of no small moment on which of the two sides truth lies: for whether individuals or cities are in question, wisdom must aim at the higher mark.

**1324ª25** There are some who regard it as the height of injustice to exercise despotic rule over one's neighbours. Ruling over them constitutionally does not, they believe, involve this injustice but it does interfere with one's own well-being. Others again take an opposite view: they hold that the practical and political life is the only life for a man: they believe that a private life gives no more scope for action in any of the fields of goodness than the life of public affairs and political interests. This is the position adopted by some of them, but others argue that the despotic and tyrannical form of constitution is the only one which gives happiness; and indeed there are cities where the exercise of despotic authority over neighbouring cities is made the standard to which both constitution and laws must conform.

**1324ᵇ5** It is for this reason that, although in most cities, most of the laws are only a miscellaneous heap of legislation, where they are directed, in any degree, to a single object, that object is always conquest. In Sparta, for instance, and in Crete the system of education and most of the laws are framed with a general view to war. Similarly all the barbarian peoples which are strong enough to conquer others pay the highest honours to military prowess; as witness the Scythians, the Persians, the Thracians, and the Celts. Some of these nations even have laws for the definite encouragement of military qualities: Carthage, for instance, is said to decorate its soldiers with an armlet for every campaign they go on. Macedonia, again, had once a law condemning those who had never killed an enemy to wear a halter instead of a belt. It was a custom among the Scythians that a man who had never killed an enemy was not entitled to drink from the loving-cup passed round at a certain festival. The Iberians, who are a warlike people, have a similar custom: they place a circle of pointed stones round the tombs of the dead, one for each enemy they have killed.

**1324ᵇ20** There are many institutions of this kind, which vary from people to people—some of them sanctioned by laws, and some of them matters of custom. Yet it cannot, perhaps, but appear very strange, to anyone ready to reflect on the matter, that it should be the function of a statesman to be able to lay plans for ruling and dominating neighbouring cities whether or not they give their consent. How can something which is not even lawful be proper for a statesman or lawmaker? (It is unlawful to rule without regard to the justice or injustice of what you are doing—one may be a conqueror without acting justly.) There is no profession in which we can find a parallel for statesmanship of this type. Doctors and pilots are never expected to use coercion or cajolery in handling their patients or crews. But when it comes to politics most people appear to believe that mastery is the true statesmanship; and they are not ashamed of behaving to others in ways which they

would refuse to acknowledge as just, or even expedient, among themselves. For their own affairs, and among themselves, they want an authority based on justice; but when other people are in question, their interest in justice stops. It would be curious if there were not some elements which are meant by nature to be subject to control as well as some which are not. If that is the case any attempt to establish control should be confined to the elements meant for control, and not extended to all. One does not hunt men to furnish a banquet or a festival: one hunts what is meant to be hunted for that purpose; and what is meant to be hunted for that purpose is any wild animal meant to be eaten. It is possible to imagine a solitary city which is happy in itself and in isolation. Assume such a city, living somewhere or other all by itself, and living under a good system of law. It will obviously have a good constitution; but the scheme of its constitution will have no regard to war, or to the conquest of enemies, who, upon our hypothesis, will not exist.

**1325ᵃ5** It is clear, then, from the course of the argument, that if military pursuits are one and all to be counted good [they are good in a qualified sense]. They are not the chief end of man, transcending all other ends: they are means to his chief end. The task of a good lawgiver is to see how any city or race of men or society with which he is concerned, may share in a good life and in whatever form of happiness is available to them. Some of the laws enacted will vary according to circumstances. If a city has neighbours, it will be the duty of its legislator to see what modes of [military] training should be adopted to match their different characters, and, how appropriate measures may be taken to deal with each of them. But the problem here raised—which is that of the end at which the best constitution should aim—may well be reserved for consideration at a later stage.

### CHAPTER 3

*From discussing the relative claims of external action and internal development in their bearing on cities, we may now turn to discuss them in their bearing on the individual. Is it better for him to follow the way of political action, with his life wrapped up in that of the city, or to follow the more solitary way of thought and contemplation? It may be argued that the activity of political management of equals, in a free society, is something higher and finer than the activity of managing slaves; and it may also be argued that true happiness, by its nature, connotes activity. On the other hand, the permanent management of others, whatever its basis may be, is not a desirable object; and even if happiness means activity, thought is an activity as much as action itself, and it may even be more of an activity than action is. The self-contained individual—like the self-contained city—may be busily active: the activity of God and the universe is that of a self-contained life.*

**1325ª16** We must now consider the views of those who are agreed in accepting the general principle that a life of goodness is most desirable, but divided in their opinion about the right way of living that life. Two different schools of opinion have thus to be discussed. One is the school which eschews political office, distinguishing the life of the individual freeman from that of the politician, and preferring it to all others. The other is the school which regards the life of the politician as best; they argue that those who do nothing cannot be said to 'do well', and they identify happiness with active 'well-doing'. Both of these schools are right on some points and wrong on others. The first school is right in holding that the life of a free individual is better than that of the master of any number of slaves. There is nothing very dignified in managing slaves, when they are acting in that capacity; and giving orders about menial duties has nothing fine about it. On the other hand, it is wrong to regard every form of authority as so much 'mastery'. Ruling over freemen differs as much from ruling over slaves as that which is by nature free differs from that which is by nature servile. But enough has already been said on that theme in the first book. It is also a mistake to praise inaction in preference to action. Happiness is a

state of activity; and the actions of just and temperate men bring many fine things to fulfilment.

**1325ª34** The conclusion to which we have just come may possibly be interpreted to mean that sovereign power is the highest of all goods, because it is also the power of practising the greatest number of the highest and best activities. It would follow on this that a man who is able to wield authority should never surrender it to his neighbour; on the contrary, he should wrest it from him. A father should pay no regard to his children, children none to their father, and friends of any kind none to their friends: no man should think of another when it comes to this cardinal point: all should act on the principle, 'The best is the most desirable': and 'to do well is the best'. There might be truth in such a view if it were really the case that those who practised plunder and violence did attain a supremely desirable object. But it is perhaps impossible that they should; they are rather making a false assumption, for it is not possible [for a ruler] to do fine deeds unless he has a degree of pre-eminence over [those he rules] as great as a husband has over his wife, or a parent over his children, or a master over his slaves. It follows that the transgressor can never achieve any subsequent gain which will equal the loss of goodness already involved in his transgression.

**1325ᵇ7** Among those who are like one another it is a just and fine thing that office should go on the principle of rotation, for that is to treat people equally and alike. But that equals should be given unequal shares, and those who are alike treated in ways that are not alike, is contrary to nature; and what is contrary to nature is not a fine thing. If, of course, someone emerges who is superior to others in goodness and in capacity for actually doing the best, it is a fine thing to follow him, and just to obey him. Goodness by itself is not enough: there must also be a capacity for being active in doing good.

**1325ᵇ14** If we are right in our view, and happiness should be held to consist in 'well-doing', it follows that the life of action is best, alike for every city as a whole and for each individual in his own conduct. But the life of action need not be, as is sometimes thought, a life which involves relations to others. Nor should our thoughts be held to be active only when they are directed to objects which have to be achieved by action. Thoughts with no object beyond themselves, and speculations and trains of reflection followed purely for their own sake, are far more deserving of the name of active. 'Well-doing' is the end we seek: action of some sort or other is therefore our end and aim; but, even in the sphere of outward acts, action can also be predicated—and that in the fullest measure and the true sense of the word—of those who, by their thoughts, are the prime authors of such acts. Cities situated by themselves, and resolved to live in isolation, need not be therefore inactive. They can achieve activity by sections: the different sections of such a city will have many mutual connections. This is also, and equally, true of the individual human being. If it were not so, there would be something wrong with God himself and the whole of the universe, who have no activities other than those of their own internal life.

It is therefore clear that the same way of life which is best for the individual must also be best for the city as a whole and for all its members.

CHAPTER 8

*4. The social structure. We must begin by making a distinction between 'integral parts' and 'necessary conditions'. The integral parts of a city are the full citizens who share actively in the full good life of the city: the necessary conditions are the ancillary members who make it possible for the full citizens to share in that life. Including together both 'parts' and 'conditions', we may enumerate six services which must be supplied by the social structure of the city: the service of agriculture; the service of arts and crafts; the service of defence; the service of landownership; the service of public worship; and the service of political deliberation and civil jurisdiction.*

**1328ª21** In the city, as in other natural compounds, the conditions which are necessary for the existence of the whole are not parts of the whole sys-

tem which they serve. The conclusion which clearly follows is that we cannot regard the elements which are necessary for the existence of the city, or of any other association forming a single whole, as being 'parts' of the city or of any other such association.

**1328ª26** There must be some one thing which is common to all the members, and identical for them all, though their shares in it may be equal, or unequal. The thing itself may be various—food, for instance, or a stretch of territory, or anything else of the kind. Now there is nothing joint or common to the means which serve an end and the end which is served by those means—except that the means produce and the end takes over the product. Take, for example, the relation in which building tools, and the workmen who use them, stand to the result produced by their action. There is nothing in common between the builder and the house he builds: the builder's skill is simply a means, and the house is the end. Thus, while cities need property, property is not a part of the city. It is true that property includes a number of animate beings, as well as inanimate objects. But the city is an association of equals; and its object is the best and highest life possible. The highest good is happiness; and that consists in the actualization and perfect practice of goodness. But, as things happen, some may share in it fully, but others can only share in it partially or cannot even share at all. Obviously this is the reason why there are different kinds and varieties of cities, and a number of different constitutions. Pursuing this goal in various ways and by various means, different peoples create for themselves different ways of life and different constitutions.

**1328ᵇ2** We must inquire how many elements are necessary for the existence of the city. These will, of course, include what we have called the 'parts' of the city as well as what we have termed its 'conditions'. We must first determine how many services a city performs; and then we shall easily see how many elements it must contain. The first thing to be provided is food. The next is crafts; for life requires many tools. The third is arms: the members of a city must bear arms in person, partly in order to maintain their rule over those who disobey, and partly in order to meet any threat of external aggression. The fourth thing which has to be provided is a certain supply of property, alike for domestic use and for military purposes. The fifth (but really first) is an establishment for the service of the gods, or, as it is called, public worship. The sixth thing, and the most vitally necessary, is a method of deciding what is demanded by the public interest and what is just in men's private dealings. These are the services which every city may be said to need. A city is not a mere casual group. It is a group which, as we have said, must be self-sufficient for the purposes of life; and if any of these services is missing it cannot be totally self-sufficient. A city should accordingly be so constituted as to be competent for all these services. It must therefore contain a body of farmers to produce the necessary food; craftsmen; a military force; a propertied class; priests; and those who decide necessary issues and determine what is the public interest.

### CHAPTER 9

*The question arises whether each of the necessary services should be performed by a separate social class, or whether some of them may be combined—and, if so, which. We may answer that (1) the first two services— agriculture, and the arts and crafts—cannot be rendered by the full citizens, because their life needs leisure, and (2) three of the other services—defence, public worship, and the service of deliberation and jurisdiction—should, from one point of view, be combined in the hands of the same people, but, from another, be discharged by different people. This last result can be achieved if (a) all full citizens are concerned with all these three services at some time or other of their lives, but (b) the younger citizens are set to render the service of defence, the middle-aged to render the service of deliberation and jurisdiction, and the aged to render the service of public worship. The effect will be that each citizen will be concerned with each of these three services, but will be*

*concerned with each at a different period of his life. The remaining service—that of landownership—should be assigned to the whole body of full citizens (which is the contrary of Plato's view in the* Republic, *where the full citizens are debarred from the ownership of land).*

**1328^b24** Now that these points have been determined, it remains to consider whether everyone should share in the performance of all these services? (That is a possibility: the same people may all be engaged simultaneously in farm work, the practice of arts and crafts, and the work of deliberation and jurisdiction.) Or should we assume different people for each of the different services? Or, again, should some of the services be assigned to different sets of people, and others be shared by all? The system is not the same in every constitution, for, as we have noted, it is possible for all to share in all functions, and also for all not to share in all but for [only] some people to share in some of them. These alternatives lead to the different constitutions: in democracies everyone shares in all functions, while the opposite practice is followed in oligarchies. Here we are concerned only with the best constitution. Now the best constitution is that under which the city can attain the greatest happiness; and that, as we have already stated, cannot exist without goodness. Upon these principles it clearly follows that in a city with the best possible constitution—a city which has for its members people who are absolutely just, rather than ones who are merely just in relation to some particular standard— the citizens must not live the life of mechanics or shopkeepers, which is ignoble and inimical to goodness. Nor can those who are to be citizens engage in farming: leisure is a necessity, both for growth in goodness and for the pursuit of political activities.

**1329^a2** On the other hand, a military force and a body to deliberate on matters of public interest and to give decisions in matters of justice are both essential, and are evidently 'parts' of the city in a special sense. Should they be kept separate? or should both functions be given to one and the same set of people?

The obvious answer is that from one point of view they should be given to the same people, but from another point of view they ought to be given to different ones. Either function requires a different prime of life: one needs wisdom while the other needs strength; from this point of view they ought to go to different people. But those who are strong enough to use force (or to prevent it from being used) cannot possibly be expected to remain in subjection; and from this point of view the two functions should go to the same people. After all those who have military power also have the power to determine whether or not the constitution will survive. The only course thus left to us is to vest these constitutional powers in one set of the people—that is, in both age-groups—but not at the same time. The order of nature gives strength to youth and wisdom to years; and it is prudent to follow that order in distributing powers among both age-groups. It is just, as well as prudent; for distribution on such a basis is in proportion to desert.

**1329ª17** Property must also belong to these people, for the citizens must have a supply of property and these are citizens. The class of mechanics has no share in the city; nor has any other class which is not a 'producer' of goodness. This conclusion clearly follows from the principle [of the best city]. That principle requires that happiness should go hand in hand with goodness, and in calling a city happy we should have regard, not just to a part of it, but to all the citizens. A further argument is provided for the view that property ought to belong to citizens, if we consider that the farm-workers ought to be slaves or barbarian serfs.

**1329ª27** Of the elements which we enumerated, only the priesthood is left. The plan on which it ought to be based is clear. Nobody belonging to the farming or the mechanic class should be made a priest. The cult of the gods should be undertaken by citizens. Now the citizen body has been divided into two sections, the military and the deliberative. Moreover, it is appropriate for the service of the gods and the relaxation which it brings to be assigned to those who have given up [these tasks]

through age. It is to these people, therefore, that the priestly offices should be assigned.

**1329ª34** This completes our survey of the factors without which a city cannot exist, and those which constitute 'parts' of the city. Farm-workers, craftsmen, and the general body of day-labourers, must necessarily be present in cities, while the military force and the deliberative body are parts of the city. Each of these is a separate element—the separation being permanent in some cases, and by turns in others.

### C: The General Principles of Education

#### CHAPTER 13

*1. The end and the means. For the attainment of well-being, or happiness, it is necessary to know the right end as well as to choose the right means. (a) So far as the end is concerned, happiness has been defined in the* Ethics, *as 'the complete actualization and practice of goodness, in an absolute rather than a conditional sense'. The point of the words 'in an absolute sense' is that goodness must not be handicapped (in which case the manner of its energy will only be 'conditional'), but must go into action furnished with the proper advantages of health, wealth, and general equipment. In order, therefore, to be in a position to attain the end of happiness, a city must start with the proper advantages—which is a matter of good fortune rather than of man's art; in order actually to attain it, a city (i.e. its members) must achieve 'the actualization and practice of goodness'—and this belongs to the realm of human knowledge and purpose, where the art of the legislator can operate. We thus turn to consider means. (b) There are three means by which the members of a city may achieve goodness—nature; habit; and reason. Nature has already been considered in Chapter 7: we have now to discuss habit and reason; and here we enter the domain of education and legislative art.*

**1331ᵇ24** We have now to speak of the constitution itself; and here we have to explain the nature and character of the elements required if a city is to enjoy a happy life and possess a good constitution. There are two things in which well-being always and everywhere consists. The first is to determine aright the aim and end of your actions. The second is to find out the actions which will best conduce to that end. These two things—ends and means—may be concordant or discordant. Sometimes the aim is determined aright, but there is a failure to attain it in action. Sometimes the means to the end are all successfully attained, but the end originally fixed is only a poor sort of end. Sometimes there is failure in both respects: in medicine, for example, one may fail both to judge correctly what a healthy body should be like and to discover the means that produce the object which one actually has in view. When using any kind of skill or practical knowledge one ought to be in control of both these things, that is, of the end itself and also of the actions which conduce to the end.

**1331ᵇ39** Obviously everyone aims at the good life, or happiness, but some have the capacity to attain it, whereas others, as a result of some chance or something in their own natural endowment, do not. A certain amount of equipment is necessary for the good life, and while this amount need not be so great for those whose endowment is good, more is required for those whose endowment is poor. Others, again, start wrong from the outset; and though they have the power of attaining happiness they seek it along the wrong lines. Here, and for the purposes of our inquiry, it is obviously necessary to be clear about the nature of happiness. The object we have in view is to discover the best constitution. The best constitution is that under which the city is best constituted. The best constituted city is the city which possesses the greatest possibility of achieving happiness.

**1332ᵃ7** It has been argued in the *Ethics* (if the argument there used is of any value) that happiness is 'the complete actualization and practice of goodness, in an absolute rather than a conditional sense'. By 'conditional' I mean 'unavoidable' and by 'absolute' I mean 'possessing [intrinsic] value'. Consider, for example, the case of just actions. To inflict a just penalty or punishment is indeed an act of goodness; but it is also an act which is necessary, and it has value only as being necessary. (It would be better if neither individuals nor cities ever needed recourse to any such action.) Acts done with a view to bestowing honours and wealth on others are acts of the highest value in the absolute sense. Acts of the first kind undo evils: acts of the second kind have an opposite character—they are the foundations and origins of good things. Similarly, while a good man would handle well the evils of poverty, sickness, and the other mishaps of life, the fact remains that happiness consists in the opposites [of these evils]. The truly good and happy man, as we have stated elsewhere in our arguments on ethics, is one for whom, because of his goodness of character, the things which are absolutely good are good [in practice]. It is plain that his use of such goods must be good and valuable in the absolute sense. But this leads people to think that external advantages are the causes of happiness. One might as well say that a well-executed piece of fine harp-playing was due to the instrument, and not to the skill of the artist.

**1332ᵃ28** It follows from what has been said that some elements of the city should be 'given', or ready to hand, and the rest should be provided by the art of the legislator. Thus we pray that the establishment of the city be blessed with fortune, in matters where fortune is sovereign (for we hold that she is sovereign). But the goodness of the city is not the work of fortune; it requires knowledge and purpose. A city is good in virtue of the goodness of the citizens who have a share in its constitution. In our city all the citizens have a share in the constitution. We have therefore to consider how a man can become good. Even if it is possible for all to be good [collectively], without each being good individually, the latter is preferable, for if each individual is good it will follow that all [collectively] are good.

**1332ᵃ38** There are three means by which individuals become good and virtuous. These three are nature, habit, and reason. So far as nature is concerned, we must start by being men—and not some other species of animal—and men too who have certain qualities both of body and soul. There are, indeed, some qualities which it is no help to have had at the start. Habits cause them to change: implanted by nature in a neutral form, they can be modified by the force of habit either for better or worse.

**1332ᵇ2** Animate beings other than men live mostly by natural impulse, though some are also guided to a slight extent by habit. Man lives by reason too; and he is unique in having this. It follows that these [three powers of man] must be tuned to agree: men are often led by reason not to follow habit and natural impulse, once they have been persuaded that some other course is better. We have already determined, in an earlier chapter, the character of the natural endowment which is needed for our citizens, if they are to be easily moulded by the art of the legislator. The rest is entirely a matter of education; they will learn some things by habituation and others by listening [to instruction].

CHAPTER I4

*2. Education and citizenship; education for leisure, and education of character. The system of education which is appropriate to a city depends on the way in which rulers and ruled are distinguished from one another. In our city the young must learn to obey a free government of which they will eventually be members; and in doing so they will also be learning to govern when their turn comes. In thus learning generally 'the virtue of the good citizen', they will also be learning 'the virtue of the good man'; for the two virtues, as has been argued before (in Book III, ch. 9), are here fundamentally the same. In planning the system of education which will produce the good man and citizen, we must distinguish the different parts of the soul—the part which has reason (in its turn divided into a practical and speculative part), and the part which has simply the capacity for obeying reason. We must also distinguish the different parts or aspects of life— action and leisure; war and peace. Education must regard all the different parts of the soul and the different parts or aspects of life. The*

*laws of Sparta have been much praised but they are fundamentally defective because they are directed towards victory in war and the subjugation of other peoples. In reality cities, like individuals, should devote themselves chiefly to that aspect of life which is concerned with peace and leisure.*

**1332ᵇ12** As all political associations are composed of rulers and ruled, we have to consider whether different people should be rulers and the ruled or whether the same people [should occupy these roles] throughout their lives. The system of education will necessarily vary according to the answer we give. We may imagine one set of circumstances in which it would be obviously better that the one group should once and for all be rulers and one group should be ruled. This would be if there were one class in the city surpassing all others as much as gods and heroes are supposed to surpass mankind— a class so outstanding, physically as well as mentally, that the superiority of the rulers was indisputably clear to those over whom they ruled. But that is a difficult assumption to make; and we have nothing in actual life like the gulf between kings and subjects which the writer Scylax describes as existing in India. We may therefore draw the conclusion, which can be defended on many grounds, that all should share alike in a system of government under which they rule and are ruled by turns. In a society of peers equality means that all should have the same [privileges]: and a constitution can hardly survive if it is founded on injustice. Along with those who are ruled there will be all those [serfs] from the countryside who want a revolution; those who belong to the citizen body cannot possibly be sufficient in number to overcome all these. On the other hand, it cannot be denied that there should be a difference between governors and governed. How they can differ, and yet, share alike, is a dilemma which legislators have to solve. This is a matter we have already discussed.

**1332ᵇ35** Nature, we have suggested, has provided us with the distinction we need. She has divided a body identical in species into two different age-groups, a younger and an older, one of them meant to be ruled and the other to rule. No one in his youth resents being ruled, or thinks himself better [than his rulers]; especially if he knows that he will redeem his contribution on reaching the proper age. In one sense, therefore, it has to be said that rulers and ruled are the same; in another, that they are different. The same will be true of their education: from one point of view it must be the same; from another it has to be different, and, as the saying goes, one who would learn to rule well, must first learn to be ruled. Ruling, as has already been said in our first part, takes two forms, one for the benefit of the rulers, the other for the benefit of the ruled. The former is what we call 'despotic'; the latter involves ruling over freemen.

**1333ª6** Some of the duties imposed [on the free] differ [from those of slaves] not in the work they involve, but in the object for which they are to be done. This means that a good deal of the work which is generally accounted menial may none the less be the sort of work which young freemen can honourably do. It is not the inherent nature of actions, but the end or object for which they are done, which makes one action differ from another in the way of honour or dishonour.

**1333ª11** We have said that the excellence of the citizen who is a ruler is the same as that of the good man and that the same person who begins by being ruled must later be a ruler. It follows on this that the legislator must labour to ensure that his citizens become good men. He must therefore know what institutions will produce this result, and what is the end or aim to which a good life is directed.

**1333ª16** There are two different parts of the soul. One of these parts has reason intrinsically and in its own nature. The other has not; but it has the capacity for obeying such a principle. When we speak of a man as being 'good', we mean that he has the goodnesses of these two parts of the soul. But in which of the parts is the end of man's life more particularly to be found? The answer is one which admits of no doubt to those who accept the division just made. In the world of nature as well as of art that which is worse always exists for the sake of that which is better. The part which has reason is the better part. But

this part is in turn divided, on the scheme which we generally follow, into two parts of its own. Reason, according to that scheme, is partly practical, partly speculative. It is obvious, therefore, that the part of the soul which has this principle must fall into two corresponding parts. We may add that the same goes for the activities [of those parts]. It follows that those who can attain all the activities possible, or two of those activities, will be bound to prefer the activity of the part which is in its nature better. All of us always prefer the highest we can attain.

**1333ª30** Life as a whole is also divided into action and leisure, war and peace; and actions are divided into those which are [merely] necessary, or useful, and those which have value [in themselves]. The same [pattern of] choice applies to these as applies to the parts of the soul and their different activities—war for the sake of peace; work for the sake of leisure; and acts which are merely necessary or useful for the sake of those which are valuable in themselves. The legislation of the true statesman must be framed with a view to all of these factors: it must cover the different parts of the soul and their different activities and should be directed more to the higher than the lower, and rather to ends than means. The same goes for the different parts or ways of life and for the choice of different activities. It is true that one must be able to engage in work and in war; but one must be even more able to lead a life of leisure and peace. It is true, again, that one must be able to do necessary or useful acts; but one must be even more able to do deeds of value. These are the general aims which ought to be followed in the education of childhood and of the stages of life which still require education.

**1333ᵇ5** The Greek cities of our day which are counted as having the best constitutions, and the legislators who framed their constitutions, have plainly not drawn up their constitutional arrangements with a view to the highest goal, nor have they directed their laws and systems of education to all the virtues. On the contrary, there has been a vulgar decline into the cultivation of qualities supposed to be useful and of a more profitable character. A similar spirit appears in some of our recent writers who have adopted this point of view. They praise the constitution of Sparta, and they admire the aim of the Spartan legislator in directing the whole of this legislation to the goal of conquest and war. This is a view which can be easily refuted by argument, and it has now been also refuted by the evidence of fact. Most people are believers in the cause of empire, on the ground that empire leads to a large accession of material prosperity. It is evidently in this spirit that Thibron, like all the other writers on the constitution of Sparta, lauds its legislator for having trained men to meet danger and so created an empire. Today the Spartans have lost their empire; and we can all see for ourselves that they are not a happy community and that their legislator was not a good one. It is indeed a strange result of his labours: here is a people which has stuck to his laws and never been hindered in carrying them out, and yet it has lost the ability to live in a way that has real value. In any case the partisans of Sparta are in error about the type of government for which the legislator should show a preference. Ruling over freemen is a finer thing and one more connected with goodness, than ruling despotically.

**1333ᵇ29** There is another reason why a city should not be considered happy, or its legislator praised, when its citizens are trained for victory in war and the subjugation of neighbouring cities. Such a policy involves a great risk of injury. It obviously implies that any citizen who can do so should make it his object to rule his own city. This is exactly what the Spartans accuse their King Pausanias of having attempted to do—and this although he already held an office of such great dignity. We may justly conclude that none of these arguments and none of these systems of law is statesmanlike, or useful, or right.

**1333ᵇ37** The same things are best both for individuals and for communities; and it is these which the legislator ought to instil into the minds of his citizens. Training for war should not be pursued with a view to enslaving people who do not deserve such a fate. Its objects should be these—first, to prevent us from ever becoming enslaved ourselves; secondly, to put us in a position to exercise leadership—but leadership directed to the interest of those who are ruled, and not to the establishment of a general system of slavery; and thirdly, to enable us to make ourselves masters of those who naturally deserve to be slaves. In support of the view that the legislator should make leisure and peace the cardinal aims of all legislation bearing on war—or indeed, for that matter, on anything else—we may cite the evidence of actual fact. Most of the cities which make war their aim are safe only while they are fighting. They collapse as soon as they have established an empire, and lose their edge like iron, in time of peace. The legislator is to blame for having provided no training for the proper use of leisure.

CHAPTER 15

*If leisure is thus of major importance, we may go on to notice that its enjoyment demands certain conditions, or, in other words, requires certain virtues—especially the virtues of wisdom and temperance. This will explain why a training such as the Spartan, which encourages only the virtue of courage, is defective and breaks down in practice . . . Reverting now to the means of education— training in habits and the training of reason— we must inquire, 'Which of them should first be employed?' The answer is that the training of reason should, from the very first, be kept in view as the ultimate aim; but the training which ought to be given first is that of the part of the soul which has the capacity for obeying reason, and we must therefore begin by providing for the training of this part in habits. But even prior to the training of this part of the soul, there is a physical problem to be considered—the problem of ensuring a good physique which will be a good servant of the soul.*

**1334ᵃ11** The final end of human beings is the same whether they are acting individually or acting collectively; and the standard followed by the best man is thus the same as the standard followed by the best constitution. It is therefore evident that the qualities required for the use of leisure must belong [to the city as well as the individual]; for, as we have repeatedly argued, peace is the final end of war, and leisure the final end of work. The good qualities required for the use of leisure and the cultivation of the mind are twofold. Some of them are operative during leisure itself: some are operative while we are at work. A number of necessary conditions must be present, before leisure is possible. This is why a city must possess the quality of temperance, and why, again, it must possess the quality of courage and endurance. 'There's no leisure for slaves', as the proverb goes, and those who cannot face danger courageously become the slaves of those who attack them. The quality of courage and endurance is required for work: wisdom is required for leisure: temperance and justice are qualities required for both times—though they are particularly required by those who enjoy peace and leisure. War automatically enforces temperance and justice: the enjoyment of prosperity, and leisure accompanied by peace, is more apt to make people overbearing. A great deal of justice and a great deal of temperance is therefore required in those who appear to be faring exceptionally well and enjoying all that is generally accounted to be happiness, like those, if there are any, who dwell in 'the happy isles' of which poets sing; and the greater the leisure which these people enjoy, when they are set among an abundance of blessings, the greater too will be their need of wisdom, as well as of temperance and justice.

**1334ª35** We can now understand why a city which seeks to achieve happiness, and to be good, must share in these virtues. If some shame must always attach to anyone who cannot use properly the goods of life, a special measure of shame must attach to those who cannot use them properly in times of leisure—to those who show themselves good in work and war, but sink to the level of slaves in times of peace and leisure.

**1334ª40** Excellence must not be sought by a training such as the Spartan. The Spartans are like the rest of the world in their view of the nature of life's highest goods: they only differ from others in thinking that the right way of getting them is to cul-

tivate a particular kind of excellence. Regarding external goods as higher than any others, and the enjoyment they give as greater than that derived from the general cultivation of excellence, [they cultivate only the single excellence which they consider useful as a means to securing those goods. But it is the whole of excellence which ought to be cultivated, and cultivated] for its own sake, as our argument has already shown. That still leaves us, however, with the problem, 'How, and by what means, is a general excellence to be achieved?'

**1334ᵇ6** We have already explained that there is need for natural endowment, habit, and reason. So far as the first of these is concerned, we have already determined the character of the endowment which our citizens should have. It remains to consider whether training in habit or training in reason ought to come first. The two modes of training must harmonize with one another to the highest degree; reason may fail to arrive at the best principle and one may likewise be led astray by habit. The following points, at any rate, are evident. First, in human life (as in all life generally), birth has a first beginning, but the end attained from such a beginning is only a step to some further end. Reason and thought is the ultimate end of our nature. It is therefore with a view to these that we should regulate, from the first, the birth and the training in habits [of our citizens]. Secondly, as soul and body are two, so there are also two parts of the soul, the irrational and the rational; and there are also two corresponding states of these parts—appetite and thought. By birth, the body is prior to the soul, and the irrational part of the soul to the rational. This is proved by the fact that anger, will, and desire are visible in children from their very birth; while reasoning and thought naturally appear, as they grow older. The conclusion which follows is obvious. Children's bodies should be given attention before their souls; and their appetites should be the next part of them to be regulated. But the regulation of their appetites should be intended for the benefit of their minds—just as the attention given to their bodies should be intended for the benefit of their souls.

# EPICURUS

~

## INTRODUCTION

## RICHARD KRAUT

Epicurus (341–270 BC) was born in Samos, a colony of Athens on an island (also named Samos) just off the coast of Asia Minor. He did military service in Athens and then rejoined his family, who had moved to Colophon, on the Asian mainland. He studied philosophy and, during his 30s, resided first in Mytilene (on the Aegean island, Lesbos) and then in Lampsacus (a city at the exit of the Black Sea). He began to acquire devoted followers. In 306 he bought a house in Athens, where he remained until his death. There he established a community of philosophers (called "The Garden," because of the enclosed garden attached to his house) who lived together and devoted themselves to the way of life he prescribed. His sect (which admitted women and slaves as members) became one of the principal schools of Athens, and his philosophy continued to win adherents into the fifth century AD. The other major schools of Athens during the time of Epicurus's residency there were the Academy (founded in 387 by Plato), the Lyceum (founded by Aristotle in 335), and the Stoa (founded by Zeno of Citium around 301). The Stoa (literally "porch" or "colonnade") around which Zeno's associates gathered gave the name "Stoicism" to his school. Stoicism, Epicureanism, and Skepticism (Plato's Academy came to be dominated by Skeptics around the time of Epicurus's death) vied with each other for pupils, each offering a different conception of how life should be lived. (The Lyceum declined in importance after the death of Aristotle's successor, Theophrastus, in about 286; the principal venue for Aristotelian research became the museum and library at Alexandria.)

Epicurus wrote voluminously, but most of his works are lost. Fortunately, Diogenes Laertius, who wrote a popular *Lives of the Philosophers* around 200 AD, included in his book three letters of Epicurus and a collection of *Principal Doctrines*. The "*Letter to Herodotus*" (not the historian) summarizes Epicurus's philosophy of nature, the "*Letter to Pythocles*" offers a theory of astronomy and meteorology, and the "*Letter to Menoeceus*" is a popular exposition of his ethics. Fragments of his lengthy work *On Nature* are being recovered from the volcanic ash at Herculaneum (a Roman town near Naples). The fullest exposition of the Epicurean philosophy is found in the great Latin poem of Lucretius, *On the Nature of Things,* which was composed during the first century BC.

Epicurus's philosophy of nature is a form of materialism: everything that exists—including souls and gods—is made of matter. The division of matter into parts is not a process that can be carried out ad infinitum, and so there must be pieces of matter that do not admit of further division. These are atoms (*atomos* means "indivisible"): their existence had been proclaimed by Leucippus and Democritus several generations before Epicurus established his school in Athens, and he was guided by their writings. Atoms are in constant motion, and differ from each other only in shape, weight, and size. They move in a void (for motion could not occur without empty space), and because they are indivisible, they cannot be destroyed. They collide with each other, because their downward paths are sometimes deflected by random swerves. (These swerves also allow human beings to choose freely.) Occasionally atoms are so shaped that their collisions cause them to adhere to each other and to form longlasting compounds. But whatever is united can also be dissolved, and the passage of time will eventually lead to the dissolution of all compounds into their component parts. The cosmos we observe around us came to have its order simply because some chance combinations are more enduring than others; but it too will come to an end, and will be succeeded by another such cosmos. There is an infinity of world orders, just as the spatial extent of the universe is unlimited. There is therefore no need to invoke the existence of divine purpose and power to explain the harmonious structure of the universe or the adaptability of the parts of the body to the purposes they serve. Epicureanism does not deny the existence of gods; rather, it holds that the gods are not world-creators and take no interest in human life. They are blessedly happy, and it would in fact detract from their lives if they had to concern themselves with the maintenance of the cosmos or the prayers and sufferings of human beings.

The soul is also made out of atoms, but it too is a compound that begins to dissolve when the rest of the body perishes. Since we do not exist after death, there is no reason (as many Greeks supposed) to fear what may happen to us in an afterlife, and no reason to prepare for the judgment of the gods. The sole standard one should use in living one's life is the happiness of this life, and happiness consists entirely in pleasure, for that is what all animals seek, and we can experience its goodness by feeling it. Physical pleasures are certainly one component of a well-lived life, but Epicurus holds that one of the greatest mistakes we can make in the conduct of our lives is to underestimate the value of mental pleasures, particularly those of tranquility and friendship. As Plato had already emphasized, many physical pleasures, especially those that are intense, are mixed with pain or the discomforts of longing and unsatisfied appetite. By contrast, Epicurus insists there is great pleasure and no pain attached to the confident assurance that one has within oneself the resources one needs to live one's life in a way that is free from internal disturbance. If one sees that death cannot be a bad thing, if one is without fear of the gods, if one has desires that are easily satisfied, if one is at peace with one's neighbors and enjoys their comradeship, and one is confident that these conditions will persist, then one is living a life that is close to that of the gods. And all of these conditions are easily within our reach, when we train ourselves not to have desires that become insatiable or difficult to fulfill—such desires as those for fame, riches, and domination. Of course, there is no way to ensure that our lives will be devoid of physical suffering, but an Epicurean will not live in fear of future distress, because he holds that the sharpest pains are necessarily short in duration, and that enduring pains are bearable. The very realization that whatever is bad in one's life pales in comparison with the quiet pleasures of friendship gives the Epicurean the tranquility that is the greatest pleasure of all.

One striking feature of this ethical theory is its thesis that such virtues as justice are merely the best means for acquiring happiness and are not in themselves worth possessing. An Epicurean might argue that one should be just toward one's friends, because there are pleasures to be had in doing so. But why should one be just to distant members of one's community, or to strangers? The Epicurean reply is that it is impossible for anyone who violates the norms of his community to live in perfect tranquility. Whether or not one will in fact be detected, there is no way to relieve oneself of the anxiety that one might be; and it is pointless to take on this burden, when a simple and law-abiding life can provide a godlike happiness.

Epicurus and his followers counseled against a life of active political engagement, and one can easily see why. Our social nature impels us to live in the company of others, but we need go no further than a small circle of intimate friends to meet this need. To pursue glory and honor is a violation of the Epicurean principle that one should train oneself to want only those things that are easy to acquire and retain. To be devoted to the good of the whole community is to undertake a task that is incompatible with tranquility, as such advocates of the political life as Aristotle and Cicero would certainly concede. If the Epicurean is right that one's own pleasure is the proper goal of life, then little can be said in favor of active citizenship or a career in politics.

Helpful overviews of Epicureanism and the other Hellenistic schools are provided by A. A. Long, *Hellenistic Philosophy* (London: Duckworth, 1974); and R. W. Sharples, *Stoics, Epicureans and Sceptics* (London: Routledge, 1996). A translation of the principal sources, with brief commentary, is provided by A. A. Long and D. N. Sedley, *The Hellenistic Philosophers,* vol. 1, (Cambridge: Cambridge University Press, 1987). A critical assessment of Epicureanism is presented by Martha C. Nussbaum, *The Therapy of Desire* (Princeton, N.J.: Princeton University Press, 1994, ch. 4). More detailed discussions of Epicurus are provided by J. M. Rist, *Epicurus: An Introduction* (Cambridge: Cambridge University Press, 1972); and Philip Mitsis, *Epicurus's Ethical Theory* (Ithaca, N.Y.: Cornell University Press, 1988). For analysis of the Epicurean conception of pleasure, see J. Gosling and C. C. W. Taylor, *The Greeks on Pleasure* (Oxford: Clarendon Press, 1982, ch. 18–20). On Lucretius, see Charles Segal, *Lucretius on Death and Anxiety* (Princeton, N.J.: Princeton University Press, 1990); and D. N. Sedley, *Lucretius and the Transformation of Greek Wisdom* (Cambridge: Cambridge University Press, 1998). For a brief discussion of the Epicurean attitude toward politics, see Malcolm Schofield's contribution to *The Cambridge History of Greek and Roman Political Thought,* edited by Christopher Rowe and Malcolm Schofield, in association with Simon Harrison and Melissa Lane (Cambridge: Cambridge University Press, 2000), pp. 437–443.

# Letter to Menoeceus

Let no one when young delay to study philosophy, nor when he is old grow weary of his study. For no one can come too early or too late to secure the health of his soul. And the man who says that the age for philosophy has either not yet come or has gone by is like the man who says that the age for happiness is not yet come to him, or has passed away. Wherefore both when young and old a man must study philosophy, that as he grows old he may be young in blessings through the grateful recollection of what has been, and that in youth he may be old as well, since he will know no fear of what is to come. We must then meditate on the things that make our happiness, seeing that when that is with us we have all, but when it is absent we do all to win it.

The things which I used unceasingly to commend to you, these do and practice, considering them to be the first principles of the good life. First of all believe that god is a being immortal and blessed, even as the common idea of a god is engraved on men's minds, and do not assign to him anything alien to his immortality or ill-suited to his blessedness: but believe

From *Epicurus: The Extant Remains,* translated by Cyril Bailey (1926). Reprinted by permission of Oxford University Press.

about him everything that can uphold his blessedness and immortality. For gods there are, since the knowledge of them is by clear vision. But they are not such as the many believe them to be: for indeed they do not consistently represent them as they believe them to be. And the impious man is not he who denies the gods of the many, but he who attaches to the gods the beliefs of the many. For the statements of the many about the gods are not conceptions derived from sensation, but false suppositions, according to which the greatest misfortunes befall the wicked and the greatest blessings the good by the gift of the gods. For men being accustomed always to their own virtues welcome those like themselves, but regard all that is not of their nature as alien.

Become accustomed to the belief that death is nothing to us. For all good and evil consists in sensation, but death is deprivation of sensation. And therefore a right understanding that death is nothing to us makes the mortality of life enjoyable, not because it adds to it an infinite span of time, but because it takes away the craving for immortality. For there is nothing terrible in life for the man who has truly comprehended that there is nothing terrible in not living. So that the man speaks but idly who says that he fears death not because it will be painful when it comes, but because it is painful in anticipation. For that which gives no trouble when it comes, is but an empty pain in anticipation. So death, the most terrifying of ills, is nothing to us, since so long as we exist, death is not with us; but when death comes, then we do not exist. It does not then concern either the living or the dead, since for the former it is not, and the latter are no more.

But the many at one moment shun death as the greatest of evils, at another yearn for it as a respite from the evils in life. But the wise man neither seeks to escape life nor fears the cessation of life, for neither does life offend him nor does the absence of life seem to be any evil. And just as with food he does not seek simply the larger share and nothing else, but rather the most pleasant, so he seeks to enjoy not the longest period of time, but the most pleasant.

And he who counsels the young man to live well, but the old man to make a good end, is foolish, not merely because of the desirability of life, but also because it is the same training which teaches to live well and to die well. Yet much worse still is the man who says it is good not to be born, but

*'once born make haste to pass the gates of Death'.*
[THEOGNIS, 427]

For if he says this from conviction why does he not pass away out of life? For it is open to him to do so, if he had firmly made up his mind to this. But if he speaks in jest, his words are idle among men who cannot receive them.

We must then bear in mind that the future is neither ours, nor yet wholly not ours, so that we may not altogether expect it as sure to come, nor abandon hope of it, as if it will certainly not come.

We must consider that of desires some are natural, others vain, and of the natural some are necessary and others merely natural; and of the necessary some are necessary for happiness, others for the repose of the body, and others for very life. The right understanding of these facts enables us to refer all choice and avoidance to the health of the body and the soul's freedom from disturbance, since this is the aim of the life of blessedness. For it is to obtain this end that we always act, namely, to avoid pain and fear. And when this is once secured for us, all the tempest of the soul is dispersed, since the living creature has not to wander as though in search of something that is missing, and to look for some other thing by which he can fulfil the good of the soul and the good of the body. For it is then that we have need of pleasure, when we feel pain owing to the absence of pleasure; but when we do not feel pain, we no longer need pleasure. And for this cause we call pleasure the beginning and end of the blessed life. For we recognize pleasure as the first good innate in us, and from pleasure we begin every act of choice and avoidance, and to pleasure we return again, using the feeling as the standard by which we judge every good.

And since pleasure is the first good and natural to us, for this very reason we do not choose every pleasure, but sometimes we pass over many pleasures, when greater discomfort accrues to us as the result of them: and similarly we think many pains better than pleasures, since a greater pleasure comes to us when we have endured pains for a long time. Every pleasure then because of its natural kinship to us is good, yet not every pleasure is to be chosen: even as every pain also is an evil, yet not all are always of a nature to be avoided. Yet by a scale of comparison and by the consideration of advantages and disadvantages we must form our judgement on all these matters. For the good on certain occasions we treat as bad, and conversely the bad as good.

And again independence of desire we think a great good—not that we may at all times enjoy but a few things, but that, if we do not possess many, we may enjoy the few in the genuine persuasion that those have the sweetest pleasure in luxury who least need it, and that all that is natural is easy to be obtained, but that which is superfluous is hard. And so plain savours bring us a pleasure equal to a luxurious diet, when all the pain due to want is removed; and bread and water produce the highest pleasure, when one who needs them puts them to his lips. To grow accustomed therefore to simple and not luxurious diet gives us health to the full, and makes a man alert for the needful employments of life, and when after long intervals we approach luxuries disposes us better towards them, and fits us to be fearless of fortune.

When, therefore, we maintain that pleasure is the end, we do not mean the pleasures of profligates and those that consist in sensuality, as is supposed by some who are either ignorant or disagree with us or do not understand, but freedom from pain in the body and from trouble in the mind. For it is not continuous drinkings and revellings, nor the satisfaction of lusts, nor the enjoyment of fish and other luxuries of the wealthy table, which produce a pleasant life, but sober reasoning, searching out the motives for all choice and avoidance, and banishing mere opinions, to which are due the greatest disturbance of the spirit.

Of all this the beginning and the greatest good is prudence. Wherefore prudence is a more precious thing even than philosophy: for from prudence are sprung all the other virtues, and it teaches us that it is not possible to live pleasantly without living prudently and honourably and justly, nor, again, to live a life of prudence, honour, and justice without living pleasantly. For the virtues are by nature bound up with the pleasant life, and the pleasant life is inseparable from them. For indeed who, think you, is a better man than he who holds reverent opinions concerning the gods, and is at all times free from fear of death, and has reasoned out the end ordained by nature? He understands that the limit of good things is easy to fulfil and easy to attain, whereas the course of ills is either short in time or slight in pain: he laughs at destiny, whom some have introduced as the mistress of all things. He thinks that with us lies the chief power in determining events, some of which happen by necessity and some by chance, and some are within our control; for while necessity cannot be called to account, he sees that chance is inconstant, but that which is in our control is subject to no master, and to it are naturally attached praise and blame. For, indeed, it were better to follow the myths about the gods than to become a slave to the destiny of the natural philosophers: for the former suggests a hope of placating the gods by worship, whereas the latter involves a necessity which knows no placation. As to chance, he does not regard it as a god as most men do (for in a god's acts there is no disorder), nor as an uncertain cause of all things: for he does not believe that good and evil are given by chance to man for the framing of a blessed life, but that opportunities for great good and great evil are afforded by it. He therefore thinks it better to be unfortunate in reasonable action than to prosper in unreason. For it is better in a man's actions that what is well chosen should fail, rather than that what is ill chosen should be successful owing to chance.

Meditate therefore on these things and things akin to them night and day by yourself, and with a companion like to yourself, and never shall you be disturbed waking or asleep, but you shall live like a god among men. For a man who lives among immortal blessings is not like to a mortal being.

# Principle Doctrines

I. The blessed and immortal nature knows no trouble itself nor causes trouble to any other, so that it is never constrained by anger or favour. For all such things exist only in the weak.

II. Death is nothing to us: for that which is dissolved is without sensation; and that which lacks sensation is nothing to us.

III. The limit of quantity in pleasures is the removal of all that is painful. Wherever pleasure is present, as long as it is there, there is neither pain of body nor of mind, nor of both at once.

IV. Pain does not last continuously in the flesh, but the acutest pain is there for a very short time, and even that which just exceeds the pleasure in the flesh does not continue for many days at once. But chronic illnesses permit a predominance of pleasure over pain in the flesh.

V. It is not possible to live pleasantly without living prudently and honourably and justly, [nor again to live a life of prudence, honour, and justice] without living pleasantly. And the man who does not possess the pleasant life, is not living prudently and honourably and justly, and the man who does not possess the virtuous life, cannot possibly live pleasantly.

VI. To secure protection from men anything is a natural good, by which you may be able to attain this end.

VII. Some men wished to become famous and conspicuous, thinking that they would thus win for themselves safety from other men. Wherefore if the life of such men is safe, they have obtained the good which nature craves; but if it is not safe, they do not possess that for which they strove at first by the instinct of nature.

VIII. No pleasure is a bad thing in itself: but the means which produce some pleasures bring with them disturbances many times greater than the pleasures.

IX. If every pleasure could be intensified so that it lasted and influenced the whole organism or the most essential parts of our nature, pleasures would never differ from one another.

X. If the things that produce the pleasures of profligates could dispel the fears of the mind about the phenomena of the sky and death and its pains, and also teach the limits of desires and of pains, we should never have cause to blame them: for they would be filling themselves full with pleasures from every source and never have pain of body or mind, which is the evil of life.

XI. If we were not troubled by our suspicions of the phenomena of the sky and about death, fearing that it concerns us, and also by our failure to grasp the limits of pains and desires, we should have no need of natural science.

XII. A man cannot dispel his fear about the most important matters if he does not know what is the nature of the universe but suspects the truth of some mythical story. So that without natural science it is not possible to attain our pleasures unalloyed.

XIII. There is no profit in securing protection in relation to men, if things above and things beneath the earth and indeed all in the boundless universe remain matters of suspicion.

XIV. The most unalloyed source of protection from men, which is secured to some extent by a certain force of expulsion, is in fact the immunity which results from a quiet life and the retirement from the world.

From *Epicurus: The Extant Remains,* translated by Cyril Bailey (1926). Reprinted by permission of Oxford University Press.

XV. The wealth demanded by nature is both limited and easily procured; that demanded by idle imaginings stretches on to infinity.

XVI. In but few things chance hinders a wise man, but the greatest and most important matters reason has ordained and throughout the whole period of life does and will ordain.

XVII. The just man is most free from trouble, the unjust most full of trouble.

XVIII. The pleasure in the flesh is not increased, when once the pain due to want is removed, but is only varied: and the limit as regards pleasure in the mind is begotten by the reasoned understanding of these very pleasures and of the emotions akin to them, which used to cause the greatest fear to the mind.

XIX. Infinite time contains no greater pleasure than limited time, if one measures by reason the limits of pleasure.

XX. The flesh perceives the limits of pleasure as unlimited and unlimited time is required to supply it. But the mind, having attained a reasoned understanding of the ultimate good of the flesh and its limits and having dissipated the fears concerning the time to come, supplies us with the complete life, and we have no further need of infinite time: but neither does the mind shun pleasure, nor, when circumstances begin to bring about the departure from life, does it approach its end as though it fell short in any way of the best life.

XXI. He who has learned the limits of life knows that that which removes the pain due to want and makes the whole of life complete is easy to obtain; so that there is no need of actions which involve competition.

XXII. We must consider both the real purpose and all the evidence of direct perception, to which we always refer the conclusions of opinion; otherwise, all will be full of doubt and confusion.

XXIII. If you fight against all sensations, you will have no standard by which to judge even those of them which you say are false.

XXIV. If you reject any single sensation and fail to distinguish between the conclusion of opinion as to the appearance awaiting confirmation and that which is actually given by the sensation or feeling, or each intuitive apprehension of the mind, you will confound all other sensations as well with the same groundless opinion, so that you will reject every standard of judgement. And if among the mental images created by your opinion you affirm both that which awaits confirmation and that which does not, you will not escape error, since you will have preserved the whole cause of doubt in every judgement between what is right and what is wrong.

XXV. If on each occasion instead of referring your actions to the end of nature, you turn to some other nearer standard when you are making a choice or an avoidance, your actions will not be consistent with your principles.

XXVI. Of desires, all that do not lead to a sense of pain, if they are not satisfied, are not necessary, but involve a craving which is easily dispelled, when the object is hard to procure or they seem likely to produce harm.

XXVII. Of all the things which wisdom acquires to produce the blessedness of the complete life, far the greatest is the possession of friendship.

XXVIII. The same conviction which has given us confidence that there is nothing terrible that lasts for ever or even for long, has also seen the protection of friendship most fully completed in the limited evils of this life.

XXIX. Among desires some are natural and necessary, some natural but not necessary, and others neither natural nor necessary, but due to idle imagination.

XXX. Wherever in the case of desires which are physical, but do not lead to a sense of pain, if they are not fulfilled, the effort is intense, such pleasures are due to idle imagination, and it is not owing to their own nature that they fail to be dispelled, but owing to the empty imaginings of the man.

XXXI. The justice which arises from nature is a pledge of mutual advantage to restrain men from harming one another and save them from being harmed.

XXXII. For all living things which have not been able to make compacts not to harm one another or be harmed, nothing ever is either just or unjust; and likewise too for all tribes of men which have been unable or unwilling to make compacts not to harm or be harmed.

XXXIII. Justice never is anything in itself, but in the dealings of men with one another in any place whatever and at any time it is a kind of compact not to harm or be harmed.

XXXIV. Injustice is not an evil in itself, but only in consequence of the fear which attaches to the apprehension of being unable to escape those appointed to punish such actions.

XXXV. It is not possible for one who acts in secret contravention of the terms of the compact not to harm or be harmed, to be confident that he will escape detection, even if at present he escapes a thousand times. For up to the time of death it cannot be certain that he will indeed escape.

XXXVI. In its general aspect justice is the same for all, for it is a kind of mutual advantage in the dealings of men with one another: but with reference to the individual peculiarities of a country or any other circumstances the same thing does not turn out to be just for all.

XXXVII. Among actions which are sanctioned as just by law, that which is proved on examination to be of advantage in the requirements of men's dealings with one another, has the guarantee of justice, whether it is the same for all or not. But if a man makes a law and it does not turn out to lead to advantage in men's dealings with each other, then it no longer has the essential nature of justice. And even if the advantage in the matter of justice shifts from one side to the other, but for a while accords with the general concept, it is none the less just for that period in the eyes of those who do not confound themselves with empty sounds but look to the actual facts.

XXXVIII. Where, provided the circumstances have not been altered, actions which were considered just, have been shown not to accord with the general concept in actual practice, then they are not just. But where, when circumstances have changed, the same actions which were sanctioned as just no longer lead to advantage, there they were just at the time when they were of advantage for the dealings of fellow-citizens with one another; but subsequently they are no longer just, when no longer of advantage.

XXXIX. The man who has best ordered the element of disquiet arising from external circumstances has made those things that he could akin to himself and the rest at least not alien: but with all to which he could not do even this, he has refrained from mixing, and has expelled from his life all which it was of advantage to treat thus.

XL. As many as possess the power to procure complete immunity from their neighbours, these also live most pleasantly with one another, since they have the most certain pledge of security, and after they have enjoyed the fullest intimacy, they do not lament the previous departure of a dead friend, as though he were to be pitied.

# CICERO

## Introduction

## Richard Kraut

Marcus Tullius Cicero (106–43 BC) was born in Arpinum, about 70 miles southeast of Rome, to a family that had powerful connections and was active in local politics. After several years of military service, he studied law and oratory in Rome, and became acquainted with the ideas of Stoicism and Academic Skepticism. He came under the influence of Philo of Larissa, the head of Plato's Academy in Athens, who had fled to Rome in 88 to escape the invasion of hostile forces. Philo advocated a mild form of Skepticism: although certainty is never achievable, the best strategy for forming one's beliefs is to examine both sides of every question and accept whichever seems, at the time, more persuasive. That principle was to form the basis of Cicero's approach to philosophy.

He began his legal career while in his 20s, but interrupted it for several years to travel and to continue his studies in Athens. During this period he became more fully acquainted with the wide range of philosophical options being debated by rival schools of thought: Stoicism, Epicureanism, and updated versions of Platonism and Aristotelianism. He returned to Rome in the mid-70s and resumed his career in law and politics, which culminated in his election to the office of consul, the supreme Roman magistracy, at the age of 43 (the minimal age required for this office). He exposed and thwarted a revolutionary conspiracy (headed by Cataline), and championed the execution of the conspirators without trial—an action that won him powerful enemies. His influence began to decline when, in the year 60, Caesar, Pompey, and Crassus formed a triumvirate.

Cicero turned increasingly to a career as a writer in the 50s, and composed *On the Republic* and *On the Laws* during this period. Civil war between Caesar and Pompey broke out in 49. As the war continued, Cicero withdrew entirely from public life for the first time. His output during this period was remarkable: over a dozen substantial works between 46 and 44. It was also during this time that he divorced his wife, remarried and divorced again, and suffered the loss of his daughter. Caesar, whom Cicero regarded as a villain, was named perpetual dictator in 44, and was killed by conspirators on March 15 of the same year—an event that forms the center of Shakespeare's *Julius Caesar.* The following year, Antony (also the subject of one of Shakespeare's plays), Lepidus, and Octavian formed a second triumvirate—an event that led to Cicero's assassination on December 7.

Cicero's principal contributions to moral and political philosophy are contained in four works: *On the Republic, On the Laws, On Ends,* and *On Duties. On Ends* examines the conflict between Epicureans and Stoics regarding the final end of human life: should it be pleasure (the Epicurean view) or virtue (as Stoics think)? *On Duties* contains an examination of the principal virtues: wisdom, social virtue (subdivided into justice and liberality), greatness of spirit, and seemliness (*decorum*); followed by an examination of two questions inspired by Plato's *Republic:* What is beneficial? Is it possible for the paths of virtue and benefits to diverge? In both of these treatises, Cicero writes as a defender of Stoic ideas—an option that the Skepticism he learned from Philo left open to him. On balance, he finds unpersuasive the Epicurean argument that makes pleasure the end of life. And although he rejects the view, widely accepted among Stoics, that virtue is the sole good, he finds no cases in which there is a genuine conflict between virtue and other goods.

It is not merely in the field of ethics that Cicero finds the Stoics have better arguments than do the Epicureans. He is repelled by the Epicurean thesis that a wise person will refrain from a life of active political participation. The Stoic principle that virtue is the sole good is one that has considerable appeal to him, because it provides a grounding for one of his strongest convictions: that the highest calling for a human being is to devote himself to the political community of which he is a part. Another work of Cicero's, *On the Nature of the Gods,* also features a debate between the Epicureans and the Stoics. The former portray the gods as beings so self-sufficient and happy that they take no interest in creating worlds or guiding human life. By contrast, the Stoics regard the cosmos as a single connected substance permeated by divine and rational guidance. At the end of the dialogue, Cicero indicates his preference for the Stoic conception of the world, which provides a far better basis for a moral order among human beings.

Cicero's earlier political works—*On the Republic* and *On the Laws*—take their inspiration from the Platonic dialogues after which they are named. They are linked works: *On the Republic* proposes a conception of the ideal constitution, and *On the Laws* fills out the details by proposing a system of laws for such a state. (By contrast, the two Platonic dialogues that Cicero took as his models portray quite different cities: the first is ruled exclusively by philosophers, the second almost exclusively by nonphilosophers.) We possess only about one-quarter of the text of *On the Republic* (a work divided into six books); even that much was lost between 600 and 1819, and its contents were known only through the references and citations of authors (particularly Augustine) who had read Cicero before 600. (Its final section, "Scipio's Dream," discusses the immortality of the soul and the final rewards of the statesman. It was well known in the medieval period.) *On the Laws* was left incomplete; we have much of Books I and II, and less of III, but there are indications that Cicero planned and perhaps wrote portions of at least two more books. Despite the fragmentary availability of these texts, their influence on moral and political thought from the medieval through the modern periods was enormous. Cicero's stature as a judicious thinker and prose stylist, a philosopher whose balanced judgments took on added credibility because they were informed by years of political experience, reached its height in the eighteenth century, when he won the admiration of Charles de Secondat Montesquieu, David Hume, Adam Smith, Edmund Burke, John Adams, and Thomas Jefferson.

Cicero opens *On the Republic* with an introduction in praise of the political life, but the rest of the work contains a conversation, which he says had been reported to him, between Scipio (more fully: Publius Cornelius Scipio Aemilianus Africanus), a great general and orator of the second century, and several of his associates. The conversation takes place during a political crisis in 129; Cicero's contemporary readers would have known that Scipio was overtaken by events and murdered several days later. Scipio therefore plays for Cicero a role similar to the one Socrates had played for Plato: he was a hero whose ideas did not prevail, and whose country suffered his loss. *On the Republic* holds up Roman institutions as precisely the ones that an ideal state must have—but Cicero places a discussion of those institutions in the past, because he thinks that, since the time of Scipio, they have been corrupted by such men as Caesar. There is a striking contrast here between Cicero's work and Plato's: the Greek philosopher is eager to show how radically different an ideal city would be from the one in which he is a citizen, whereas the Roman thinker believes that the Rome that had existed only a few generations ago had already reached an ideal form.

The starting point the interlocutors use for their discussion of the best form of government is the division of forms of rule into three kinds: rule by one (monarchy), by few (aristocracy), or by many (popular rule). This typology dates back to the Greeks: it can be found in Herodotus and was more fully developed by Plato in the *Statesman* and Aristotle in the *Politics*. Scipio says that any of these three systems can, under the right conditions, be tolerable; and he rehearses the arguments that can be given for and against each. He concludes, however, that although monarchy is the best of the three simple forms, a still better arrangement—in fact, the best possible—is not to give exclusive power to one, or few, or many, but rather to balance each of these three factors, giving each its appropriate weight. In effect,

Cicero using Scipio as his mouthpiece, is arguing that the structure of the Roman Republic, which gives to its two elected consuls regal power and to the senate aristocratic power, with the tribunes and popular assemblies wielding democratic power, has achieved the ideal political balance. In designating a mixed government as ideal, Scipio is following the lead of Polybius, the Greek historian of the second century BC, who, in Book 6 of his *Histories,* attributed the remarkable rise and military success of Rome to the fact that it had a mixed constitution. Scipio does not claim that each of the three elements that need to be mixed should have equal power. But it is significant that he regards popular participation as one necessary element in an ideal constitution. That popular element is present in his theory from the start, for the opening move he makes in his conversation is to define the *res publica* as a *res populi:* "a commonwealth is the property of a people."

Like Plato's *Laws,* Cicero's *On the Laws* consists of a dialogue among three people on a long summer day. The principal speaker is Cicero himself, and his interlocutors are his younger brother, Quintus, and his close friend, Atticus. Most of the work is devoted to a detailed description of an ideal law code, but as a preliminary step Cicero puts forward a conception of law as "the highest reason implanted in nature." Here Cicero is relying, once again, on Stoic ideas, for the Stoics see the whole cosmos as infused with divine and rational planning. Although the written laws devised by imperfect human beings may vary from one place to another, and may be abolished, the true laws upon which our human laws should be modeled exist at all times and are to be obeyed by all human beings. Their basis lies in the nature of human beings, who exhibit the same sociability and tendencies toward good and bad ends alike. Once we acknowledge that tyrants must be resisted, and that the popularity of a decree does not make it just, we must recognize the validity of eternal and universal law. Cicero's ideas on this subject played an important role in Aquinas's analysis of law in the *Summa Theologiae.*

For an overview of Cicero's political thought, see E. M. Atkins's contribution to *The Cambridge History of Greek and Roman Political Thought,* edited by Christopher Rowe and Malcolm Schofield, in association with Simon Harrison and Melissa Lane (Cambridge: Cambridge University Press, 2000), pp. 477–516. A recent translation of *On the Republic* and *On the Laws,* together with helpful notes, is provided by James G. Zetzel (Cambridge: Cambridge University Press, 1999). For the background to Cicero's writings, see Elizabeth Rawson, *Intellectual Life in the Late Roman Republic* (Baltimore: Johns Hopkins University Press, 1985). See too her brief biography, *Cicero: A Portrait* (London: Allen Lane, 1975). Various aspects of Cicero's thought are explored in J. G. F. Powell (ed.), *Cicero the Philosopher* (Oxford: Clarendon Press, 1995). A brief introduction to the Hellenistic schools is provided by R. W. Sharples, *Stoics, Epicureans, and Skeptics* (London: Routledge, 1996). For a comprehensive study that stresses Cicero's conservatism, see Neal Wood, *Cicero's Social and Political Thought* (Berkeley: University of California Press, 1988).

# On the Republic

## BOOK I

[IV. Few may have imagined, in view of all I had suffered, that when,] as I retired from the consulship, I took my oath before an assembly of the people, and the Roman people took the same oath, that the republic was safe [as a result of my efforts alone,] I was amply repaid thereby for all the anxiety and vexation that resulted from the injustice done to me. And yet my sufferings brought me more honour than trouble, more glory than vexation, and the joy I found in the affectionate longing felt for me by good citizens was greater than my grief at the exultation of the wicked. But, as I said before, if it had happened otherwise, how could I complain? For none of the misfortunes that fell to my lot in consequence of my great services was unexpected by me or more serious than I had foreseen. For such was my nature that, although, on account of the manifold pleasures I found in the studies which had engaged me from boyhood, it would have been possible for me, on the one hand, to reap greater profit from a quiet life than other men, or, on the other hand, if any disaster should happen to us all, to suffer no more than my fair share of the common misfortune, yet I could not hesitate to expose myself to the severest storms, and, I might almost say, even to thunderbolts, for the sake of the safety of my fellow-citizens, and to secure, at the cost of my own personal danger, a quiet life for all the rest. For, in truth, our country has not given us birth and education without expecting to receive some sustenance, as it were, from us in return; nor has it been merely to serve our convenience that she has granted to our leisure a safe refuge and for our moments of repose a calm retreat; on the contrary, she has given us these advantages so that she may appropriate to her own use the greater and more important part of our courage, our talents, and our wisdom, leaving to us for our own private uses only so much as may be left after her needs have been satisfied.

V. Moreover we ought certainly not to listen to the other excuses to which these men resort, that they may be more free to enjoy the quiet life. They say, for example, that it is mostly worthless men who take part in politics, men with whom it is degrading to be compared, while to have conflict with them, especially when the mob is aroused, is a wretched and dangerous task. Therefore, they maintain, a wise man should not attempt to take the reins, as he cannot restrain the insane and untamed fury of the common herd; nor is it proper for a freeman, by contending with vile and wicked opponents, to submit to the scourgings of abuse or expose himself to wrongs which are intolerable to the wise—as if, in the view of good, brave, and high-minded men, there could be any nobler motive for entering public life than the resolution not to be ruled by wicked men and not to allow the republic to be destroyed by them, seeing that the philosophers themselves, even if they should desire to help, would be impotent.

VI. And who in the world can approve of the single exception they make, when they say that no wise man will take any part in public affairs unless some emergency compels him to do so? As if any greater emergency could come upon anyone than that with which I was confronted; and what could I have done in that crisis unless I had been consul at the time? And how could I have been consul unless I had held to a manner of life from my boyhood which led me to the highest office of State in spite of my equestrian birth?

Hence it is clear that the opportunity of serving the State, however great be the dangers with which it is threatened, does not come suddenly, or when we wish it, unless we are in such a position that it is possible for us to take action. It has always seemed to me that the most amazing of the teachings of learned men is that they deny their own ability to steer when the sea is calm, having never learned the art nor cared to know it, while at the same time they assure us that, when the waves dash highest, they will take the helm. For it is their habit to proclaim openly, and even to make it their great boast, that they have neither learned nor do they teach anything about the principles of the State, either to establish it or to safeguard it, and that they consider the knowledge of such things unsuited to learned or wise men, but better to be left to those who have trained themselves in that business. How can it be reasonable, therefore, for them to promise to aid the State in case they are compelled by an emergency to do so, when they do not know how to rule the State when no emergency threatens it, though this is a much easier task than the other? Indeed, if it be true that the wise man does not, as a general thing, willingly descend from his lofty eights to statecraft, but does not decline the duty if conditions force him to assume it, yet I should think he ought by no means to neglect this science of politics, because it is his duty to acquire in advance all the knowledge that, for aught he knows, it may be necessary for him to use at some future time.

VII. I have treated these matters at considerable length because I have planned and undertaken in this work a discussion of the State; hence, in order that this discussion might not be valueless, I had, in the first place, to remove all grounds for hesitation about taking part in public affairs. Yet if there be any who are influenced by the authority of philosophers, let them for a few moments listen and attend to those whose authority and reputation stand highest among learned men; for even if these have not governed the State themselves, nevertheless, since they have dealt with the State in many investigations and treatises, I consider that they have performed a certain function of their own in the State. And in fact I note that nearly every one of those Seven whom the Greeks

called "wise" took an important part in the affairs of government. For there is really no other occupation in which human virtue approaches more closely the august function of the gods than that of founding new States or preserving those already in existence.

VIII. Wherefore, since it is my good fortune to have accomplished, in the actual government of the republic, something worthy to live in men's memories, and also to have acquired some skill in setting forth political principles through practice and also by reason of my enthusiasm for learning and teaching, [I consider myself not unsuited to the task I have now undertaken; for, as a matter of fact, this combination of accomplishments is rare among those who are considered] authorities [on statecraft], since while certain men in former times have shown great skill in theoretical discussion, they are discovered to have accomplished nothing practical, and there have been others who have been efficient in action, but clumsy in exposition. Indeed the principles I am about to state are not at all new or original to myself, but it is my intention to recall a discussion carried on by men who were at a certain period the most eminent and wisest in our republic. This discussion was once reported to you, in your youth, and to me by Publius Rutilius Rufus, when we were spending several days together at Smyrna; in it, I believe, very little is omitted that would contribute greatly to a logical exposition of the whole subject.

XXIV. *Scipio.* I will . . . at once begin my discussion, following the rule which, I think, ought always to be observed in the exposition of a subject if one wishes to avoid confusion; that is, that if the name of a subject is agreed upon, the meaning of this name should first be explained. Not until this meaning is agreed upon should the actual discussion be begun; for the qualities of the thing to be discussed can never be understood unless one understands first exactly what the thing itself is. Therefore, since the commonwealth is the subject of our investigation, let us first consider exactly what it is that we are investigating. . . .

XXV. *Scipio.* Well, then, a commonwealth is the property of a people. But a people is not any collection of human beings brought together in any sort of way, but an assemblage of people in large numbers associated in an agreement with respect to justice and a partnership for the common good. The first cause of such an association is not so much the weakness of the individual as a certain social spirit which nature has implanted in man. . . .

XXVI. Such an assemblage of men . . . established itself in a definite place, at first in order to provide dwellings; and this place being fortified by its natural situation and by their labours, they called such a collection of dwellings a town or city, and provided it with shrines and gathering places which were common property. Therefore every people, which is such a gathering of large numbers as I have described, every city, which is an orderly settlement of a people, every commonwealth, which, as I said, is "the property of a people," must be governed by some deliberative body if it is to be permanent. And this deliberative body must, in the first place, always owe its beginning to the same cause as that which produced the State itself. In the second place, this function must either be granted to one man, or to certain selected citizens, or must be assumed by the whole body of citizens. And so when the supreme authority is in the hands of one man, we call him a king, and the form of this State a kingship. When selected citizens hold this power, we say that the State is ruled by an aristocracy. But a popular government (for so it is called) exists when all the power is in the hands of the people. And any one of these three forms of government (if only the bond which originally joined the citizens together in the partnership of the State holds fast), though not perfect or in my opinion the best, is tolerable, though one of them may be superior to another. For either a just and wise king, or a select number of leading citizens, or even the people itself, though this is the least commendable type, can nevertheless, as it seems, form a government that is not unstable, provided that no elements of injustice or greed are mingled with it.

XXVII. But in kingships the subjects have too small a share in the administration of justice and in deliberation; and in aristocracies the masses can hardly have their share of liberty, since they are entirely excluded from deliberation for the common

weal and from power; and when all the power is in the people's hands, even though they exercise it with justice and moderation, yet the resulting equality itself is inequitable, since it allows no distinctions in rank. Therefore, even though the Persian Cyrus was the most just and wisest of kings, that form of government does not seem to me the most desirable, since "the property of the people" (for that is what a commonwealth is, as I have said) is administered at the nod and caprice of one man; even though the Massilians, now under our protection, are ruled with the greatest justice by a select number of their leading citizens, such a situation is nevertheless to some extent like slavery for a people; and even though the Athenians at certain periods, after they had deprived the Areopagus of its power, succeeded in carrying on all their public business by the resolutions and decrees of the people, their State, because it had no definite distinctions in rank, could not maintain its fair renown.

XXVIII. I am now speaking of these three forms of government, not when they are confused and mingled with one another, but when they retain their appropriate character. All of them are, in the first place, subject each to the faults I have mentioned, and they suffer from other dangerous faults in addition: for before every one of them lies a slippery and precipitous path leading to a certain depraved form that is a close neighbour to it. For underneath the tolerable, or, if you like, the lovable King Cyrus (to cite him as a pre-eminent example) lies the utterly cruel Phalaris, impelling him to an arbitrary change of character; for the absolute rule of one man will easily and quickly degenerate into a tyranny like his. And a close neighbour to the excellent Massilian government, conducted by a few leading citizens, is such a partisan combination of thirty men as once ruled Athens. And as for the absolute power of the Athenian people—not to seek other examples of popular government— . . . it changed into the fury and licence of a mob . . .

XXIX. . . . A wise man should be acquainted with these changes, but it calls for great citizens and for a man of almost divine powers to foresee them when they threaten, and, while holding the reins of government, to direct their courses and keep them under his control. Therefore I consider a fourth form of government the most commendable—that form which is a well-regulated mixture of the three which I mentioned at first.

XXX. *Laelius.* I know that is your opinion, Africanus, for I have often heard you say so. Nevertheless, if it will not give you too much trouble, I should like to know which you consider the best of the three forms of government of which you have been speaking . . .

XXXI. *Scipio.* Every State is such as its ruler's character and will make it. Hence liberty has no dwelling-place in any State except that in which the people's power is the greatest, and surely nothing can be sweeter than liberty; but if it is not the same for all, it does not deserve the name of liberty. And how can it be the same for all, I will not say in a kingdom, where there is no obscurity or doubt about the slavery of the subject, but even in States where everyone is ostensibly free? I mean States in which the people vote, elect commanders and officials, are canvassed for their votes, and have bills proposed to them, but really grant only what they would have to grant even if they were unwilling to do so, and are asked to give to others what they do not possess themselves. For they have no share in the governing power, in the deliberative function, or in the courts, over which selected judges preside, for those privileges are granted on the basis of birth or wealth. But in a free nation, such as the Rhodians or the Athenians, there is not one of the citizens who [may not hold the offices of State and take an active part in the government.] . . .

XXXII. [Our authorities] say [that] when one person or a few stand out from the crowd as richer and more prosperous, then, as a result of the haughty and arrogant behaviour of these, there arises [a government of one or a few], the cowardly and weak giving way and bowing down to the pride of wealth. But if the people would maintain their rights, they say that no form of government would be superior, either in liberty or happiness, for they themselves would be masters of the laws and the courts, of war and peace, of international agreements, and of every citizen's

life and property; this government alone, they believe, can rightly be called a commonwealth, that is, "the property of the people." And it is for that reason, they say, that "the property of the people" is often liberated from the domination of kings or senators, while free peoples do not seek kings or the power and wealth of aristocracies. And indeed they claim that this free popular government ought not to be entirely rejected on account of the excesses of an unbridled mob, for, according to them, when a sovereign people is pervaded by a spirit of harmony and tests every measure by the standard of their own safety and liberty, no form of government is less subject to change or more stable. And they insist that harmony is very easily obtainable in a State where the interests of all are the same, for discord arises from conflicting interests, where different measures are advantageous to different citizens. Therefore they maintain that when a senate has been supreme, the State has never had a stable government, and that such stability is less attainable by far in kingdoms, in which, as Ennius says,

*No sacred partnership or honour is.*

Therefore, since law is the bond which unites the civic association, and the justice enforced by law is the same for all, by what justice can an association of citizens be held together when there is no equality among the citizens? For if we cannot agree to equalize men's wealth, and equality of innate ability is impossible, the legal rights at least of those who are citizens of the same commonwealth ought to be equal. For what is a State except an association or partnership in justice? . . .

XXXIII. Indeed they think that States of the other kinds have no right at all to the names which they arrogate to themselves. For why should I give the name of king the title of Jupiter the Best, to a man who is greedy for personal power and absolute authority, a man who lords it over an oppressed people? Should I not rather call him tyrant? For tyrants may be merciful as well as oppressive; so that the only difference between the nations governed by these rulers is that between the slaves of a kind and those of a cruel master; for in any case the subjects must be slaves. And how could Sparta, at the time when the mode of life inculcated by her constitution was considered so excellent, be assured of always having good and just kings, when a person of any sort, if he was born of the royal family, had to be accepted as king? As to aristocrats, who could tolerate men that have claimed the title without the people's acquiescence, but merely by their own will? For how is a man adjudged to be "the best"? On the basis of knowledge, skill, learning, [and similar qualities surely, not because of his own desire to possess the title!] . . .

XXXIV. If [the State] leaves [the selection of its rulers] to chance, it will be as quickly overturned as a ship whose pilot should be chosen by lot from among the passengers. But if a free people chooses the men to whom it is to entrust its fortunes, and, since it desires its own safety, chooses the best men, then certainly the safety of the State depends upon the wisdom of its best men, especially since Nature has provided not only that those men who are superior in virtue and in spirit should rule the weaker, but also that the weaker should be willing to obey the stronger.

But they claim that this ideal form of State has been rejected on account of the false notions of men, who, through their ignorance of virtue—for just as virtue is possessed by only a few, so it can be distinguished and perceived by only a few—think that the best men are those who are rich, prosperous, or born of famous families. For when, on account of this mistaken notion of the common people, the State begins to be ruled by the riches, instead of the virtue, of a few men, these rulers tenaciously retain the title, though they do not possess the character, of the "best." For riches, names, and power, when they lack wisdom and the knowledge of how to live and to rule over others, are full of dishonour and insolent pride, nor is there any more depraved type of State than that in which the richest are accounted the best. But what can be nobler than the government of the State by virtue? For then the man who rules others is not himself a slave to any passion, but has already acquired for himself all those qualities to which he is training

and summoning his fellows. Such a man imposes no laws upon the people that he does not obey himself, but puts his own life before his fellow-citizens as their law. If a single individual of this character could order all things properly in a State, there would be no need of more than one ruler; or if the citizens as a body could see what was best and agree upon it, no one would desire a selected group of rulers. It has been the difficulty of formulating policies that has transferred the power from a king to a larger number; and the perversity and rashness of popular assemblies that have transferred it from the many to the few. Thus, between the weakness of a single ruler and the rashness of the many, aristocracies have occupied that intermediate position which represents the utmost moderation; and in a State ruled by its best men, the citizens must necessarily enjoy the greatest happiness, being freed from all cares and worries, when once they have entrusted the preservation of their tranquillity to others, whose duty it is to guard it vigilantly and never to allow the people to think that their interests are being neglected by their rulers. For that equality of legal rights of which free peoples are so fond cannot be maintained (for the people themselves, though free and un-restrained, give very many special powers to many individuals, and create great distinctions among men and the honours granted to them), and what is called equality is really most inequitable. For when equal honour is given to the highest and the lowest—for men of both types must exist in every nation—then this very "fairness" is most unfair; but this cannot happen in States ruled by their best citizens. These arguments and others like them, Laelius, are approximately those which are advanced by men who consider this form of government the best.

XXXV. *Laelius.* But what about yourself, Scipio? Which of these three forms do you consider the best?

*Scipio.* You are right to ask which I consider the best of the three, for I do not approve of any of them when employed by itself, and consider the form which is a combination of all them superior to any single one of them. But if I were compelled to approve one single unmixed form, [I might choose] the kingship . . . the name of king seems like that of father to us, since the king provides for the citizens as if they were his own children, and is more eager to protect them than . . . to be sustained by the care of one man who is the most virtuous and most eminent. But here are the aristocrats, with the claim that they can do this more effectively, and that there will be more wisdom in the counsels of several than in those of one man, and an equal amount of fairness and scrupulousness. And here also are the people, shouting with a loud voice that they are willing to obey neither one nor a few, that nothing is sweeter than liberty even to wild beasts, and that all who are slaves, whether to a king or to an aristocracy, are deprived of liberty. Thus kings attract us by our affection for them, aristocracies by their wisdom, and popular governments by their freedom, so that in comparing them it is difficult to say which one prefers. . . .

XLII. *Scipio.* When I have set forth my ideas in regard to the form of State which I consider the best, I shall have to take up in greater detail those changes to which States are liable, though I think it will not be at all easy for any such changes to take place in the State which I have in mind. But the first and most certain of these changes is the one that takes place in kingships: when the king begins to be unjust, that form of government is immediately at an end, and the king has become a tyrant. This is the worst sort of government, though closely related to the best. If the best men overthrow it, as usually happens, then the State is in the second of its three stages; for this form is similar to a kingship, being one in which a paternal council of leading men makes good provision for the people's welfare. But if the people themselves have killed or driven out the tyrant, they govern rather moderately, as long as they are wise and prudent, and, delighting in their exploit, they endeavour to maintain the government they have themselves set up. But if the people ever rebel against a just king and deprive him of his kingdom, or, as happens more frequently, taste the blood of the aristocracy and subject the whole State to their own caprices (and do not dream, Laelius, that any sea or any conflagration is so powerful that it cannot be more easily subdued than an unbridled multitude enjoying unwonted power), then we have a condition which is splendidly described by Plato, if only I can reproduce his description in Latin; it is difficult, but I will attempt it.

XLIII. He says: "When the insatiable throats of the people have become dry with the thirst for liberty, and, served by evil ministers, they have drained in their thirst a draught of liberty which, instead of being moderately tempered, is too strong for them, then, unless the magistrates and men of high rank are very mild and indulgent, serving them with liberty in generous quantities, the people persecute them, charge them with crime and impeach them, calling them despots, kings, and tyrants." I think you are acquainted with this passage.

*Laelius.* It is very familiar to me.

*Scipio.* He continues thus: "Those who follow the lead of prominent citizens are persecuted by such a people and called willing slaves; but those who, though in office, try to act like private citizens, and those private citizens who try to destroy all distinction between a private citizen and a magistrate are praised to the skies and loaded with honours. It necessarily follows in such a State that liberty prevails everywhere, to such an extent that not only are homes one and all without a master, but the vice of anarchy extends even to the domestic animals, until finally the father fears his son, the son flouts his father, all sense of shame disappears, and all is so absolutely free that there is no distinction between citizen and alien; the schoolmaster fears and flatters his pupils, and pupils despise their masters; youths take on the gravity of age, and old men stoop to the games of youth, for fear they may be disliked by their juniors and seem to them too serious. Under such conditions even the slaves come to behave with unseemly freedom, wives have the same rights as their husbands, and in the abundance of liberty even the dogs, the horses, and the asses are so free in their running about that men must make way for them in the streets. Therefore," he concludes, "the final result of this boundless licence is that the minds of the citizens become so squeamish and sensitive that, if the authority of government is exercised in the smallest degree, they become angry and cannot bear it. On this account they begin to neglect the laws as well, and so finally are utterly without a master of any kind."

XLIV. *Laelius.* You have given us his description with great exactness.

*Scipio.* Well, to return now to my own style of discourse, he also says that from this exaggerated licence, which is the only thing such people call liberty, tyrants spring up as from a root, and are, as it were, engendered. For just as an excess of power in the hands of the aristocrats results in the overthrow of an aristocracy, so liberty itself reduces a people who possess it in too great degree to servitude. Thus everything which is in excess—when, for instance, either in the weather, or in the fields, or in men's bodies, conditions have been too favourable—is usually changed into its opposite; and this is especially true in States, where such excess of liberty either in nations or in individuals turns into an excess of servitude. This extreme liberty gives birth to a tyrant and the utterly unjust and cruel servitude of the tyranny. For out of such an ungoverned, or rather, untamed, populace someone is usually chosen as leader against those leading citizens who have already been subjected to persecution and cast down from their leadership—some bold and depraved man, who shamelessly harasses oftentimes even those who have deserved well of the State, and curries favour with the people by bestowing upon them the property of others as well as his own. To such a man, because he has much reason to be afraid if he remains a private citizen, official power is given and continually renewed; he is also surrounded by armed guards, as was Pisistratus at Athens; and finally he emerges as a tyrant over the very people who have raised him to power. If the better citizens overthrow such a tyrant, as often happens, then the State is re-established; but if it is the bolder sort who do so, then we have that oligarchy which is only a tyranny of another kind. This same form of government also arises from the excellent rule of an aristocracy, when some bad influence turns the leading citizens themselves from the right path. Thus the ruling power of the State, like a ball, is snatched from kings by tyrants, from tyrants by aristocrats or the people, and from them again by an oligarchical faction or a tyrant, so that no single form of government ever maintains itself very long.

XLV. Since this is true, the kingship, in my opinion, is by far the best of the three primary forms, but a moderate and balanced form of government which is a combination of the three good simple forms is preferable even to the kingship. For there should be a supreme and royal element in the State, some power also ought to be granted to the leading citizens, and certain matters should be left to the judgment and desires of the masses. Such a constitution, in the first place, offers in a high degree a sort of equality, which is a thing free men can hardly do without for any considerable length of time, and, secondly, it has stability. For the primary forms already mentioned degenerate easily into the corresponding perverted forms, the king being replaced by a despot, the aristocracy by an oligarchical faction, and the people by a mob and anarchy; but whereas these forms are frequently changed into new ones, this does not usually happen in the case of the mixed and evenly balanced constitution, except through great faults in the governing class. For there is no reason for a change when every citizen is firmly established in his own station, and there underlies it no perverted form into which it can plunge and sink.

# On the Laws

## BOOK I

V. *Atticus.* I consider it a logical thing that, since you have already written a treatise on the constitution of the ideal State, you should also write one on its laws. For I note that this was done by your beloved Plato, whom you admire, revere above all others, and love above all others.

*Marcus.* Is it your wish, then, that, as he discussed the institutions of States and the ideal laws with Clinias and the Spartan Megillus in Crete on a summer day amid the cypress groves and forest paths of Cnossus, sometimes walking about, sometimes resting— you recall his description—we, in like manner, strolling or taking our ease among these stately poplars on the green and shady river bank, shall discuss the same subjects along somewhat broader lines than the practice of the courts calls for?

*A.* I should certainly like to hear such a conversation.

*M.* What does Quintus say?

*Q.* No other subject would suit me better.

*M.* And you are wise, for you must understand that in no other kind of discussion can one bring out so clearly what Nature's gifts to man are, what a wealth of most excellent possessions the human mind enjoys, what the purpose is, to strive after and accomplish which we have been born and placed in this world, what it is that unites men, and what natural fellowship there is among them. For it is only after all these things have been made clear that the origin of Law and Justice can be discovered.

*A.* Then you do not think that the science of law is to be derived from the praetor's edict, as the majority do now, or from the Twelve Tables, as people used to think, but from the deepest mysteries of philosophy?

*M.* Quite right; for in our present conversation, Pomponius, we are not trying to learn how to protect ourselves legally, or how to answer clients' questions. Such problems may be important, and in fact they are; for in former times many eminent men made a specialty of their solution, and at present one person performs this duty with the greatest authority and skill. But in our present investigation we intend to cover the whole range of universal Justice and Law in such a way that our own civil law, as it is called, will be confined to a small and narrow corner. For we must explain the nature of Justice, and this must be sought for in the nature of man; we must also consider the laws by which States ought to be governed; then we must deal with the enactments and decrees of nations which are already formulated and put in writing; and among these the civil law, as it is called, of the Roman people will not fail to find a place.

VI. *Q.* You probe deep, and seek, as you should, the very fountain-head, to find what we are after, brother. And those who teach the civil law in any other way are teaching not so much the path of justice as of litigation.

*M.* There you are mistaken, Quintus, for it is rather ignorance of the law than knowledge of it that leads to litigation. But that will come later; now let us investigate the origins of Justice.

Well then, the most learned men have determined to begin with Law, and it would seem that they are right, if, according to their definition, Law is the highest reason, implanted in Nature, which commands what ought to be done and forbids the opposite. This reason, when firmly fixed and fully developed in the human mind, is Law. And so they believe that Law is intelligence, whose natural function it is to command right conduct and forbid wrongdoing. They think that this quality has derived its name in Greek from the idea of granting to every man his own, and in our language I believe it has been named from the idea of choosing. For as they have attributed the idea of fairness to the word law, so we have given it that of selection, though both ideas properly belong to Law. Now if this is correct, as I think it to be in general, then the origin of Justice is to be found in Law, for Law is a natural force; it is the mind and reason of the intelligent man, the standard by which Justice and Injustice are measured. But since our whole discussion has to do with the reasoning of the populace, it will sometimes be necessary to speak in the popular manner, and give the name of law to that which in written form decrees whatever it wishes, either by command or prohibition. For such is the crowd's definition of law. But in determining what Justice is, let us begin with that supreme Law which had its origin ages before any written law existed or any State had been established.

*Q.* Indeed that will be preferable and more suitable to the character of the conversation we have begun.

*M.* Well, then, shall we seek the origin of Justice itself at its fountain-head? For when that is discovered we shall undoubtedly have a standard by which the things we are seeking may be tested.

*Q.* I think that is certainly what we must do.

*A.* Put me down also as agreeing with your brother's opinion.

*M.* Since, then, we must retain and preserve that constitution of the State which Scipio proved to be the best in the six books devoted to the subject, and all our laws must be fitted to that type of State, and since we must also inculcate good morals, and not prescribe everything in writing, I shall seek the root of Justice in Nature, under whose guidance our whole discussion must be conducted.

*A.* Quite right. Surely with her as our guide, it will be impossible for us to go astray.

VII. *M.* Do you grant us, then, Pomponius (for I am aware of what Quintus thinks), that it is by the might of the immortal gods, or by their nature, reason, power, mind, will, or any other term which may make my meaning clearer, that all Nature is governed? For if you do not admit it, we must begin our argument with this problem before taking up anything else.

*A.* Surely I will grant it, if you insist upon it, for the singing of the birds about us and the babbling of the streams relieve me from all fear that I may be overheard by any of my comrades in the School.

*M.* Yet you must be careful; for it is their way to become very angry at times, as virtuous men will; and they will not tolerate your treason, if they hear of it, to the opening passage of that excellent book, in which the author has written, "God troubles himself about nothing, neither his own concerns nor those of others."

*A.* Continue, if you please, for I am eager to learn what my admission will lead to.

*M.* I will not make the argument long. Your admission leads us to this: that animal which we call man, endowed with foresight and quick intelligence, complex, keen, possessing memory, full of reason and prudence, has been given a certain distinguished status by the supreme God who created him; for he is the only one among so many different kinds and varieties of living beings who has a share in reason and thought, while all the rest are deprived of it. But what is more divine, I will not say in man only, but in all heaven and earth, than reason? And reason, when it is full grown and perfected, is rightly called wisdom. Therefore, since there is nothing better than reason, and since it exists both in man and God, the first common possession of man and God is reason. But those who have reason in common must also have right reason in common. And since right reason is Law, we must believe that men have Law also in common with the gods. Further, those who share Law must also share Justice; and those who share these are to be regarded as members of the same commonwealth. If indeed they obey the same authorities and powers, this is true in a far greater degree; but as a matter of fact they do obey this celestial system, the divine mind, and the God of transcendent power. Hence we must now conceive of this whole universe as one commonwealth of which both gods and men are members. . . .

X. *A.* Ye immortal gods, how far back you go to find the origins of Justice! And you discourse so eloquently that I not only have no desire to hasten on to the consideration of the civil law, concerning which I was expecting you to speak, but I should have no objection to your spending even the entire day on your present topic; for the matters which you have taken up, no doubt, merely as preparatory to another subject, are of greater import than the subject itself to which they form an introduction.

*M.* The points which are now being briefly touched upon are certainly important; but out of all the material of the philosophers' discussions, surely there comes nothing more valuable than the full realization that we are born for Justice, and that right is based, not upon men's opinions, but upon Nature. This fact will immediately be plain if you once get a clear conception of man's fellowship and union with his fellow-men. For no single thing is so like another, so exactly its counterpart, as all of us are to one another. Nay, if bad habits and false beliefs did not twist the weaker minds and turn them in whatever direction they are inclined, no one would be so like his own self as all men would be like all others. And so, however we may define man, a single definition will apply to all. This is a sufficient proof that there is no difference in kind between man and man; for if there were, one definition could not be applicable to all men; and indeed reason, which alone raises us above the level of the beasts and enables us to draw inferences, to prove and disprove, to discuss and solve problems, and to come to conclusions, is certainly common to us all, and, though varying in what it learns, at least in the capacity to learn it is invariable. For the same things are invariably perceived by the senses, and those things which stimulate the senses, stimulate them in the same way in all

men; and those rudimentary beginnings of intelligence to which I have referred, which are imprinted on our minds, are imprinted on all minds alike; and speech, the mind's interpreter, though differing in the choice of words, agrees in the sentiments expressed. In fact, there is no human being of any race who, if he finds a guide, cannot attain to virtue.

XI. The similarity of the human race is clearly marked in its evil tendencies as well as in its goodness. For pleasure also attracts all men; and even though it is an enticement to vice, yet it has some likeness to what is naturally good. For it delights us by its lightness and agreeableness; and for this reason, by an error of thought, it is embraced as something wholesome. It is through a similar misconception that we shun death as though it were a dissolution of nature, and cling to life because it keeps us in the sphere in which we were born; and that we look upon pain as one of the greatest of evils, not only because of its cruelty, but also because it seems to lead to the destruction of nature. In the same way, on account of the similarity between moral worth and renown, those who are publicly honoured are considered happy, while those who do not attain fame are thought miserable. Troubles, joys, desires, and fears haunt the minds of all men without distinction, and even if different men have different beliefs, that does not prove, for example, that it is not the same quality of superstition that besets those races which worship dogs and cats as gods, as that which torments other races. But what nation does not love courtesy, kindliness, gratitude, and remembrance of favours bestowed? What people does not hate and despise the haughty, the wicked, the cruel, and the ungrateful? Inasmuch as these considerations prove to us that the whole human race is bound together in unity, it follows, finally, that knowledge of the principles of right living is what makes men better. . . .

XV. But the most foolish notion of all is the belief that everything is just which is found in the customs or laws of nations. Would that be true, even if these laws had been enacted by tyrants? If the well-known Thirty had desired to enact a set of laws at Athens, or if the Athenians without exception were delighted by the tyrants' laws, that would not entitle such laws to be regarded as just, would it? No more, in my opinion, should that law be considered just which a Roman interrex proposed, to the effect that a dictator might put to death with impunity any citizen he wished, even without a trial. For Justice is one; it binds all human society, and is based on one Law, which is right reason applied to command and prohibition. Whoever knows not this Law, whether it has been recorded in writing anywhere or not, is without Justice.

But if Justice is conformity to written laws and national customs, and if, as the same persons claim, everything is to be tested by the standard of utility, then anyone who thinks it will be profitable to him will, if he is able, disregard and violate the laws. It follows that Justice does not exist at all, if it does not exist in Nature, and if that form of it which is based on utility can be overthrown by that very utility itself. And if Nature is not to be considered the foundation of Justice, that will mean the destruction [of the virtues on which human society depends]. For where then will there be a place for generosity, or love of country, or loyalty, or the inclination to be of service to others or to show gratitude for favours received? For these virtues originate in our natural inclination to love our fellow-men, and this is the foundation of Justice. Otherwise not merely consideration for men but also rites and pious observances in honour of the gods are done away with; for I think that these ought to be maintained, not through fear, but on account of the close relationship which exists between man and God.

XVI. But if the principles of Justice were founded on the decrees of peoples, the edicts of princes, or the decisions of judges, then Justice would sanction robbery and adultery and forgery of wills, in case these acts were approved by the votes or decrees of the populace. But if so great a power belongs to the decisions and decrees of fools that the laws of Nature can be changed by their votes, then why do they not ordain that what is bad and baneful shall be considered good and salutary? Or, if a law can make Justice out of Injustice, can it not also

make good out of bad? But in fact we can perceive the difference between good laws and bad by referring them to no other standard than Nature; indeed, it is not merely Justice and Injustice which are distinguished by Nature, but also and without exception things which are honourable and dishonourable. For since an intelligence common to us all makes things known to us and formulates them in our minds, honourable actions are ascribed by us to virtue, and dishonourable actions to vice; and only a madman would conclude that these judgments are matters of opinion, and not fixed by Nature. For even what we, by a misuse of the term, call the virtue of a tree or of a horse, is not a matter of opinion, but is based on Nature. And if that is true, honourable and dishonourable actions must also be distinguished by Nature. For if virtue in general is to be tested by opinion, then its several parts must also be so tested; who, therefore, would judge a man of prudence and, if I may say so, hard common sense, not by his own character but by some external circumstance? For virtue is reason completely developed; and this certainly is natural; therefore everything honourable is likewise natural.

XVII. For just as truth and falsehood, the logical and illogical, are judged by themselves and not by anything else, so the steadfast and continuous use of reason in the conduct of life, which is virtue, and also inconstancy, which is vice, [are judged] by their own nature.

[Or, when a farmer judges the quality of a tree by nature,] shall we not use the same standard in regard to the characters of young men? Then shall we judge character by Nature, and judge virtue and vice, which result from character, by some other standard? But if we adopt the same standard for them, must we not refer the honourable and the base to Nature also? Whatever good thing is praiseworthy must have within itself something which deserves praise, for goodness itself is good by reason not of opinion but of Nature. For, if this were not true, men would also be happy by reason of opinion; and what statement could be more absurd than that? Wherefore since both good and evil are judged by Nature and are natural principles, surely honourable and base actions must also be distinguished in a similar way and referred to the standard of Nature. But we are confused by the variety of men's beliefs and by their disagreements, and because this same variation is not found in the senses, we think that Nature has made these accurate, and say that those things about which different people have different opinions and the same people not always identical opinions are unreal. However, this is far from being the case. For our senses are not perverted by parent, nurse, teacher, poet, or the stage, nor led astray by popular feeling; but against our minds all sorts of plots are constantly being laid, either by those whom I have just mentioned, who, taking possession of them while still tender and unformed, colour and bend them as they wish, or else by that enemy which lurks deep within us, entwined in our every sense—that counterfeit of good, which is, however, the mother of all evils—pleasure. Corrupted by her allurements, we fail to discern clearly what things are by Nature good, because the same seductiveness and itching does not attend them.

XVIII. To close now our discussion of this whole subject, the conclusion, which stands clearly before our eyes from what has already been said, is this: Justice and all things honourable are to be sought for their own sake. And indeed all good men love fairness in itself and Justice in itself, and it is unnatural for a good man to make such a mistake as to love what does not deserve love for itself alone. Therefore Justice must be sought and cultivated for her own sake; and if this is true of Justice, it is also true of equity; and if this is the case with equity, then all the other virtues are also to be cherished for their own sake.

What of generosity? Is it disinterested or does it look to a recompense? If a man is kind without any reward, then it is disinterested; but if he receives payment, then it is hired. It cannot be doubted that he who is called generous or kind answers the call of duty, not of gain. Therefore equity also demands no reward or price; consequently it is sought for its own sake. And the same motive and purpose characterize all the virtues.

In addition, if it be true that virtue is sought for the sake of other benefits and not for its own sake, there will be only one virtue, which will most properly be called a vice. For in proportion as anyone makes his own advantage absolutely the sole standard of all his actions, to that extent he is absolutely not a good man; therefore those who measure virtue by the reward it brings believe in the existence of no virtue except vice. For where shall we find a kindly man, if no one does a kindness for the sake of anyone else than himself? Who can be considered grateful, if even those who repay favours have no real consideration for those to whom they repay them? What becomes of that sacred thing, friendship, if even the friend himself is not loved for his own sake, "with the whole heart," as people say? Why, according to this theory, a friend should even be deserted and cast aside as soon as there is no longer hope of benefit and profit from his friendship! But what could be more inhuman than that? If, on the other hand, friendship is to be sought for its own sake, then the society of our fellow-men, fairness, and Justice, are also to be sought for their own sake. If this is not the case then there is no such thing as Justice at all, for the very height of injustice is to seek pay for Justice.

# AUGUSTINE

~

## INTRODUCTION

## PAUL J. WEITHMAN

Augustine (354–430) was born in Thagaste in a part of northern Africa that is included in present-day Algeria but was then one of the backwaters of the Roman Empire. He was a promising young man who received the education typical of a well-schooled provincial. His education first in Thagaste and then in Carthage emphasized the Latin classics. A gifted writer and speaker, he became a teacher of rhetoric in Thagaste. Augustine's early successes sparked his aspirations for achievement in the larger world. In 383 he left north Africa for Italy and in 384 settled in Milan to teach rhetoric. He soon became disillusioned with his early careerism and retired to study philosophy in 386. In 387, after a dramatic conversion, Augustine was baptized a Christian. He returned to north Africa in 388 and was ordained a priest in 391. Intending to lead a quiet life, he was instead consecrated bishop of Hippo in 395.

Augustine was to live and serve in Hippo for the remaining thirty-five years of his life. He produced a vast literary corpus of sermons, commentaries, treatises, and letters while attending to the daily administrative duties of an important church official. But the events of Augustine's professional life are merely visible peaks pushed upward by great subterranean movements. The real drama of Augustine's life was interior. His was a riveting spiritual and intellectual journey that led him from the ambitions of a young rhetorician to the monastic life, from there to the episcopacy of Hippo, and thence to accomplishments that make him one of the greatest theologians of Latin Christianity. Augustine chronicles the first thirty-three years of this journey in his *Confessions,* a classic of Western literature.

Augustine's interior drama was played out against the backdrop of the late Roman Empire. It is hard to overstate Rome's importance for his life and thought. He was educated in Latin, the lingua franca of the empire and a language he spoke and wrote with consummate skill. For a time he aspired to prominence within it and gravitated toward its center. He imbibed Rome's literature and its history. He absorbed and then reacted against its culture and mores. It was the most powerful empire the world had ever known. He thought its evident decline in his own adulthood signaled what he called the "old age of the world." The invasion of Rome by the Goths provided the occasion for his greatest work, *The City of God,* a work in which Rome's accomplishments typify the glories sought and achieved by human societies. In his old age Augustine saw Rome's grip on north Africa being broken. When he died in 430, the Vandals were besieging Hippo. Augustine's political thought was profoundly conditioned by his reflections on the moral and political rise and decay of Rome.

Claims about Augustine's political philosophy must be made with care. Augustine never wrote a book or a treatise devoted to such philosophy. Discussions of politics and political philosophy crop up often in his work, but Augustine is primarily a theologian rather than a philosopher. It is questionable whether he thought political philosophy has a subject matter that can be cleanly marked off from that of theology. His own discussions of politics draw heavily on theology, as well as on psychology, history, and social theory. Even so, it is possible to assemble a coherent body of political thought from remarks and discussions scattered throughout Augustine's many writings, especially from his monumental *The City of God.*

Augustine began writing *The City of God* after Rome was sacked in 410. The sack caused many wealthy and cultured Romans to flee the city. In due course some found their way to Augustine's part of north Africa. Trying to comprehend what had happened, many of them blamed the sack on Rome's abandonment of the traditional deities who had long protected it in favor of a Christian god whose impotence left them vulnerable. Thus the tragedy that befell Rome was, they alleged, the consequence of the conversion of the empire under Constantine nearly a century before. Augustine took up his pen to answer the charge and defend Christianity. When he finally put it down fourteen years later, he had completed a massive work of theology, polemical history, philosophy of culture, and social psychology.

In *The City of God* Augustine argued that despite the surface diversity of language, nations, and ways of life, human beings are most fundamentally divided by a single cleavage: that between those who belong to the City of God and those who belong to the Earthly City. This is not a divide between citizens of two different political entities, like Rome and Carthage, nor is it a divide between the institutional church and the world. Augustine is emphatic that members of both the City of God and the Earthly City can be found in any political society. Members of both cities can also be found both inside and outside the church. Rather the difference between the members of the two cities is a difference in their most fundamental orientations to what is good. It is a difference, Augustine would say, in their most fundamental loves.

Augustine distinguishes two ways of loving that are especially important. One is what he calls "use"; the other is what he calls "enjoyment." We enjoy things when we love them for their own sake. We use them when we love them for the sake of something else. Only God is worthy of being loved entirely for His own sake, Augustine thinks, and only the enjoyment of God can quiet all our desires. Other things and persons, including ourselves, ought to be loved in relation to God. Human sinfulness is a turn away from God. It is a tendency to love oneself and to love other things in relation to self. This elevation of the self and the self's desires Augustine associates with the sin of pride. Augustine thinks that all human beings are sinful to some extent. All, he thinks, are at least somewhat tainted by the sin of pride. At the same time, Augustine thinks all human beings retain a desire for God. This shows itself in a desire for true peace, for the quiescence of desire that only love of God can bring. Because all human beings are prone to love of self while they retain at least a confused love of God, all human beings, Augustine thinks, have divided wills. This tension within each person is responsible for the tensions that mar even the most intimate of human relationships and are a salient feature of political life.

Despite the fact that all human beings have divided wills, Augustine thinks some are fundamentally oriented toward God while others love themselves. Those whose fundamental orientation is toward God constitute the City of God. This is a city dispersed in time and space, and includes the angels and the saints as well as some of those in earthly life. Those whose fundamental orientation is toward the self constitute the Earthly City. The latter enjoy the world and are at home in it. Those of the former who are in this world are, Augustine says, merely "on pilgrimage" in it. Citizens of both cities live side by side in every political society and in the church, to be sorted out only at the last judgment.

In Book XIX of *The City of God,* Augustine says that earthly peace—peace within an earthly society and peace between societies—is a compromise between members of the two cities. This suggests that politics is driven by conflicts among members of the two groups. In fact, Augustine's analysis of politics is considerably more subtle. Augustine does think that those who most fundamentally love themselves also love glory, fame, and domination. In *The City of God* Augustine seizes on the love of domination as one of the driving forces of political history. It accounts for why human beings build empires. It accounts for the pride that citizens of an empire take in its power and for the patriotism that makes them willing to die for it. The Romans' love of domination helps to account for the hegemony of the Roman Empire over Augustine's world. It also accounts for the conflict, tension, and disorder that erupt within groups. But Augustine would be quick to point out that because all human beings are divided, even those who love God can be moved by pride, love of domination, and undue attachment to material goods. They too need to be humbled and disciplined.

Humility and discipline are exactly what Augustine thinks political authority exists to provide. Augustine thinks of political power as the power to control adults through coercion and the threat of coercion. If human beings had remained sinless, this form of authority would not be needed. Human groups could have been directed by forms of authority more like paternal authority than political. That is why Augustine says at the beginning of Book XIX, chapter 15, that according to the order of nature, human beings have dominion over animals but not over other human beings. Political authority is the divinely ordained response to human sinfulness and the disordered loves that result from sinfulness.

The proper aims of political authority must be limited because the means at its disposal are of limited efficacy. One of Augustine's constant themes is the opacity of the human heart. Human beings cannot fully know their own or others' motives. It follows that those in political authority cannot know the hearts and minds of their subjects, still less restore their hearts and minds to order by the use of force. Since perfect peace, Augustine says, is perfect tranquility and order within and among human beings, political authority can hope only to bring about a partial and imperfect peace. The most it can hope to do is restrain people so that they are not too harmful to one another. By doing so, it establishes the limited peace that all need in order to live. Members of the Earthly City enjoy this peace and try to establish it on their own terms. Members of the City of God use it in the course of their pilgrimage but they do not enjoy it.

By claiming that political authority cannot make human beings good but can only restrain their wickedness, Augustine takes a firm stand against a tradition of republican political thought known to him through the writings of Cicero. One of the best known of Cicero's works is *De Re Publica,* a dialogue that Augustine knew well. The main character in the dialogue is Scipio Africanus the younger, the Roman general who defeated Carthage in 136 BC. In a passage to which Augustine refers in Book XIX of *The City of God,* Cicero attributes to Scipio the view that political societies like Rome are partnerships of justice and that their strength depends upon the virtue of their citizens. Augustine notes that justice requires giving to each his due. He continues that it therefore requires worshipping the true God. Since the true God was not worshipped in Rome at the time of Cicero, Augustine thinks it follows that Rome was unjust. If Scipio's definition is correct, then Rome was not a society. Furthermore, since Augustine insists that human beings can be truly virtuous only when they worship the true God, it follows that the Romans whose virtue Scipio credits with preserving their city were not really virtuous at all.

This conclusion is one Augustine repeats throughout his writings, but most forcefully in *The City of God.* Some of the most rhetorically powerful passages in that work are those in which he recalls episodes of injustice and brutality from Roman history that apologist historians of the empire prefer to overlook. Again and again he insists that those who built and sustained Rome were moved by an idolatrous pride in their city, and by desires for its fame and domination. Because these vices required some self-restraint, they were able to masquerade as the virtues for which Augustine thinks Scipio mistook them. The republican view of politics, according to which political life develops the virtues that are needed to sustain political society, is one Augustine thinks he has undercut by the time he arrives at Book XIX.

But if a society like Rome does not depend upon or develop the virtues of citizens, what does sustain it? In Book XIX of *The City of God,* Augustine famously offers an alternative definition of society. According to his definition, a society is a group united by a common object of love. To assess the moral quality of a society, it is necessary to look at what it loves. Because earthly societies contain both those who love God and those who exalt themselves, both members of the City of God and members of the Earthly City, Augustine thinks that what holds societies together is simply their citizens' common desire for peace. The peace the Romans tried to establish was a peace on their own terms, one that gave them dominion over others. The peace of this most powerful of empires, and the peace of all other earthly societies as well, therefore pales beside the true peace of the City of God. Thus in Book XIX Augustine realizes the aim of *The City of God,* which he says in Book I is to glorify the City of God by comparing it with "cities of other allegiance."

The best biography of Augustine in any language is Peter Brown's *Augustine of Hippo* (Berkeley: University of California Press, 1967). Relatively few works on Augustine's political thought are available in English. Herbert Deane's *The Political and Social Ideas of St. Augustine* (New York: Columbia University Press, 1963) is the most useful; J. N. Figgis's *The Political Aspects of St. Augustine's "City of God"* (London: Longman's, 1921) is dated but should not be overlooked. R. A. Markus's *Saeculum* (Cambridge: Cambridge University Press, 1970) is a classic work that bears on Augustine's political thought.

# The City of God

## BOOK XIX

### Chapter 12

Whoever joins me in an examination, however cursory, of human affairs and our common human nature will acknowledge that, just as there is no one who does not wish to be joyful, so there is no one who does not wish to have peace. Indeed, even when men choose to wage war, they desire nothing but victory. By means of war, therefore, they desire to achieve peace with glory; for what else is victory but the subjugation of those who oppose us? And when this is achieved, there will be peace. Wars themselves, then, are conducted with the intention of peace, even when they are conducted by those who are concerned to exercise their martial prowess in command and battle. Hence it is clear that peace is the desired end of war. For every man seeks peace, even in making war; but no one seeks war by making peace. Indeed, even those who wish to disrupt an existing state of peace do so not because they hate peace, but because they desire the present peace to be exchanged for one of their own choosing. Their desire, therefore, is not that there should be no peace, but that it should be the kind of peace that they wish for. And even when they have separated themselves from others by sedition, they cannot bring about what they intend unless they maintain at least some kind of peace with their co-conspirators or confederates. Indeed, even robbers wish to have peace with their fellows, if only in order to invade the peace of others with greater force and safety. One robber may, of course, be so unsurpassed in strength, and so suspicious of others, that he does not trust any accomplice, but plots his crimes and commits his robberies and murders on his own. Even he, however, maintains some shadow of peace, at least with those whom he cannot kill, and from whom he wishes to conceal his deeds. Also, he is at pains to ensure peace in his own household, with his wife and children and whomever else he has there. Without doubt he takes delight in their obedience to his nod, and, if this does not happen, he is angry. He rebukes and punishes; and, if necessary, he employs harsh measures to impose upon his household a peace which, he believes, cannot exist unless all the other members of the same domestic society are subject to one head; and this head, in his own house, is himself. Thus, if he were offered the servitude of a larger number—of a city, or of a nation—who would serve him in just the same way as he had required his household to serve him, then he would no longer lurk like a robber in his lair; he would raise himself up as a king for all to see. But the same greed and malice would remain in him. All men, then, desire to have peace with their own people, whom they wish to see living according to their will. For they wish to make even those against whom they wage wars their own if they can, and to subdue them by imposing upon them the laws of their own peace.

Let us, however, consider a creature depicted in poetry and fable: a creature so unsociable and wild that people have preferred to call him a semi-man rather than a man. His kingdom was the solitude of an awful cavern, and he was so singular in his wickedness that a name was found for him reflecting that fact—for he was called Cacus, and *kakos* is the Greek word for 'wicked'. He had no wife with whom to give and receive caresses; no children to play with when little or to instruct when a little bigger; and no friends with whom to enjoy converse, not even his father Vulcan. He was happier than his father only in not having begotten another such monster as himself. He gave nothing to anyone; rather, he took what he wanted from anyone he could and whenever he could. Despite all this, however, in the solitude of his own cave, the floor of which, as Virgil describes it, ever reeked with the blood of recent butchery, he wished for nothing other than a peace in which no one should molest him, and a rest which no man's violence, or the fear of it, should disturb. Also, he desired to be at peace with his own body; and in so far as he had such peace, all was well with him. For he governed his members, and they obeyed him. His mortal nature rebelled against him when it needed anything, and stirred up the sedition of hunger, which threatened to banish and exclude the soul from the body; and so he made haste to pacify that nature as far as possible: he hunted, slew and devoured. Thus, for all his monstrous and wild savagery, his aim was peace; for he sought, by these monstrous and ferocious means, only to preserve the peace of his own life. Thus, had he been willing to make with other men the peace which he was ready enough to make in his own cave and with himself, he would not have been called wicked, nor a monster, nor a semi-man. Or if it was the appearance of his body and his vomiting of smoke and flames that frightened away human companions, perhaps it was not the desire to do harm that made him so ferocious, but the necessity of preserving his own life. Or perhaps he never existed after all, or, more probably, was not as the poets have in their vanity described him as being. For if Cacus had not been excessively blamed, Hercules would have been less fulsomely praised for slaying him. As in the case of many such poetic fictions, therefore, the existence of such a man—or rather, as I have said, semi-man—is not to be believed in.

Even the most savage beasts, then, from whom Cacus derived the ferocious part of his nature (for he is also called a semi-beast) protect their own kind by a kind of peace. They mate, they beget and bear young, and they rear and nourish them. They do this even when, as in most cases, they are unsocial and solitary: when they are not, that is, like sheep, deer, doves, starlings, and bees, but like lions, wolves, foxes, eagles and owls. What tigress does not purr softly over her cubs and lay her fierceness aside while she caresses them? What kite, solitary as he is while he hovers over his prey, does not take a mate, make a nest, help to hatch the eggs, rear the chicks, and preserve with the mother of his family, as it were, a domestic society which is as peaceful as he can make it? How much more strongly, then, is a man drawn by the laws of his nature, so to speak, to enter into a similarly peaceful association with his fellow men, so far as it lies within his power to do so? For even the wicked wage war only to maintain the peace of their own people. They wish to make all men their own people, if they can, so that all men and all things might serve one master; but how could that happen, unless they should consent to be at peace with him, either through love or fear?

Thus, pride is a perverted imitation of God. For pride hates a fellowship of equality under God, and wishes to impose its own dominion upon its equals, in place of God's rule. Therefore, it hates the just peace of God, and it loves its own unjust peace; but it cannot help loving peace of some kind or other. For no vice is so entirely contrary to nature as to destroy even the last vestiges of nature.

Thus, he who has learnt to prefer right to wrong and the rightly ordered to the perverse, sees that, in comparison with the peace of the just, the peace of the unjust is not worthy to be called peace at all. Even that which is perverse, however, must of necessity be in, or derived from, or associated with, and to that extent at peace with, some part of the order of things among which it has its being or of which it consists. Otherwise, it would not exist at all. For example, if someone were to hang upside-down, this position of the body and disposition of the limbs would certainly be a perverted one. For what nature places above would be beneath, and what nature intends to be beneath would be above. This perversity disturbs the peace of the flesh, and therefore causes distress. Nonetheless, the spirit is at peace with its body and strives to secure its health: it is precisely for that reason that there is pain. And even if the spirit is driven out of the body by the latter's distresses, still, as long as the disposition of the body's members remains intact, what is left is not without a kind of peace: which is why there is still something to hang there. And if the earthly body presses down towards the ground, and strains against the bond by which it is suspended, it tends towards the position of its own peace, and by the voice of its own weight, so to speak, entreats a place where it may rest. And so even when lifeless and without any sensation, it does not depart from the peace of its natural position, either while occupying that position or tending towards it. Again, if remedies and preservatives are applied to prevent the dissolution and decomposition of the corpse in its present form, a kind of peace still joins one part to another and maintains the whole mass in an earthly condition which is suitable, and in that sense peaceable. If, on the other hand, no such treatment is applied, and the body is abandoned to the usual course of nature, there is for a while a kind of tumult of exhalations which are disagreeable and offensive to our senses (that is, the stench of decay of which we are aware). This persists until the body unites with the elements of the world and, little by little, particle by particle, passes away into their peace.

In all this, however, nothing is in any way removed from the sway of the laws made by the supreme Creator and Ordainer Who directs the peace of the universe. For although minute animals are produced in the carcase of a larger animal, all those little bodies, by the same law of their Creator, serve their little spirits in the peace that preserves their lives. Even when the flesh of dead animals is devoured by other animals, it still finds itself subject to the same laws: to the laws which are distributed throughout the universe for the preservation of every kind of mortal creature, and which give peace by bringing suitable things suitably together. This is true no matter where it is taken, no matter with what substances it is joined, and no matter what substances it is converted and changed into.

## *Chapter 13*

The peace of the body, therefore, lies in the balanced ordering of its parts; the peace of the irrational soul

lies in the rightly ordered disposition of the appetites; the peace of the rational soul lies in the rightly ordered relationship of cognition and action; the peace of body and soul lies in the rightly ordered life and health of a living creature; peace between mortal man and God is an ordered obedience, in faith, under an eternal law; and peace between men is an ordered agreement of mind with mind. The peace of a household is an ordered concord, with respect to command and obedience, of those who dwell together; the peace of a city is an ordered concord, with respect to command and obedience, of the citizens; and the peace of the Heavenly City is a perfectly ordered and perfectly harmonious fellowship in the enjoyment of God, and of one another in God. The peace of all things lies in the tranquillity of order; and order is the disposition of equal and unequal things in such a way as to give to each its proper place.

The wretched, however, insofar as they are wretched, are clearly not in a condition of peace. Therefore, they lack that tranquillity of order in which there is no disturbance. Precisely because of their misery, however, even they cannot be said to lie beyond the sphere of order; for they are miserable deservedly and justly. They are not, indeed, united with the blessed; yet it is by the law of order that they are severed from them. And when they become accustomed to the condition in which they are, with at any rate some degree of harmony, they are then without disturbance of mind. Thus, they have among them some tranquillity of order, and therefore some peace. But they are still wretched, simply because, although they are to some extent serene and free from pain, they are not in that place where they would be wholly serene and free from pain. They would, however, be all the more wretched if they were not at peace with that law according to which the natural order is organised. For when they suffer, their peace is disturbed in the part where they suffer; yet there is still peace in that part which does not feel the pain of burning, and in so far as their nature is not dissolved. Just as there can be life without pain, therefore, but no pain without life, so there can be peace without any war, but no war without some degree of peace. This is not because of the nature of war itself, but because war can only be waged by or within persons who are in some sense natural beings: beings who could not exist at all if peace of some kind did not exist within them.

There exists, then, a nature in which there is no evil, and in which evil cannot exist at all. But there cannot exist a nature in which there is no good. Hence, in so far as it is a nature, not even the nature of the devil himself is evil. It is perversion that makes it evil. Thus, the devil did not abide in the truth, but he did not escape the judgment of the Truth. He did not remain in the tranquillity of order, but he did not thereby avoid the power of the Ordainer. The good imparted by God, which the devil has in his nature, does not remove him from God's justice, by which his punishment is ordained; nor does God punish the good which He has created, but the evil which the devil has committed. Moreover, God does not take away everything that He gave to that nature. He removes something, yet He leaves something also, so that there may be something left to feel pain at what has been taken away. And this pain itself testifies to both the good that was taken away and the good that is left; for, if there had been no good left, there could be no grief for the good which was taken away. He who sins is in a worse condition still if he rejoices in the loss of righteousness; but the sinner who suffers grief, even though he acquires no good thereby, is at least grieving at the loss of salvation. For righteousness and salvation are both goods, and the loss of any good is a matter for grief rather than rejoicing: if, that is, the loss is not counteracted by the gain of a greater good; for instance, righteousness of soul is a greater good than health of body. It is more fitting, therefore, for an unrighteous man to grieve over his punishment than to rejoice in his fault. Hence, just as the delight in forsaking good which a man takes when he sins is evidence of a bad will, so the grief which he feels at the loss of good when he is punished is evidence of a good nature. For when a man grieves over the loss of his nature's peace, his grief arises from some remnants of that peace, whereby his nature befriends itself. Moreover, it is right that, in the final punishment, the wicked and ungodly should in their torments lament the loss of their natural goods, knowing that they have been most justly deprived of those

goods by the God Whom they despised when He most graciously bestowed them.

God, therefore, is the most wise Creator and just Ordainer of all natures, Who has established the mortal human race as the greatest adornment of things earthly, and Who has given to men certain good things appropriate to this life. These are: temporal peace, in proportion to the short span of a mortal life, consisting in bodily health and soundness, and the society of one's own kind; and all things necessary for the preservation and recovery of this peace. These latter include those things which are appropriate and accessible to our senses, such as light, speech, breathable air, drinkable water, and whatever the body requires to feed, clothe, shelter, heal or adorn it. And these things are given under a most fair condition: that every mortal who makes right use of these goods suited to the peace of mortal men shall receive ampler and better goods, namely, the peace of immortality and the glory and honour appropriate to it, in an eternal life made fit for the enjoyment of God and of one's neighbour in God. He who uses temporal goods ill, however, shall lose them, and shall not receive eternal goods either.

## Chapter 15

This is prescribed by the order of nature: it is thus that God created man; for He said, 'Let them have dominion over the fish of the sea, and over the fowl of the air, and over every creeping thing which creepeth on the earth.' He did not intend that His rational creature, made in His own image, should have lordship over any but irrational creatures: not man over man, but man over the beasts. Hence, the first just men were established as shepherds of flocks, rather than as kings of men. This was done so that in this way also God might indicate what the order of nature requires, and what the desert of sinners demands. For we believe that it is with justice that a condition of servitude is imposed on the sinner. That is why we do not read the word 'slave' anywhere in the Scriptures until Noah, the just man, punished his son's sin with this name. That son deserved this name, then, not because of his nature, but because of his fault. The Latin word for slave [*servus*] is believed to have derived its origin from the fact that those who might have been slain under the laws of war were sometimes spared [*servabantur*] by the victors, and so were called *servi* because they had been preserved. But even this preservation could not have come about other than through the deserts of sin. For even when a just war is waged, it is in defence of his sin that he against whom it is waged is fighting; and every victory, even when it goes to the wicked, is a humiliation inflicted upon the conquered by divine judgment, either to correct their sins or to punish them. Daniel, a man of God, bears witness to this when, in captivity, he confesses to God his own sins and the sins of his people, and in pious grief testifies that they are the cause of that captivity.

The first cause of servitude, therefore, is sin, by which man was placed under man in a condition of bondage: a condition which can come about only by the judgment of God, in Whom there is no injustice, and Who knows how to distribute different punishments according to the merits of the offenders. As the Lord on high says, 'Every one who doeth sin is the servant of sin.' Thus, while many godly persons are the slaves of unrighteous masters, the masters whom they serve are themselves not free men; 'for of whom a man is overcome, of the same is he brought in bondage'. Clearly, it is a happier lot to be the slave of a man than of a lust: indeed, the lust for mastery, to say nothing of any other, is itself the harshest kind of mastery, which lays waste the hearts of mortal men. However, in that order of peace which prevails among men when some are placed under others, humility is as profitable to those who serve as pride is harmful to those who rule.

By nature, then, in the condition in which God first created man, no man is the slave either of another man or of sin. But it is also true that servitude itself is ordained as a punishment by that law which enjoins the preservation of the order of nature, and forbids its disruption. For if nothing had been done in violation of that law, there would have been no need for the discipline of servitude as a punishment. The apostle therefore admonishes servants to be obedient to their masters, and to serve them loyally and with a good will, so that, if they cannot be freed by their masters, they can at least make their own slavery to some extent free. They can do this by serving not with cunning fear, but in faithful love, until all unrighteousness shall cease, and all authority and power be put down, that God may be all in all.

## *Chapter 16*

. . . [T]hose who are truly 'fathers of their families' are as much concerned for the welfare of all in their households, in respect of the worship and service of God, as if they were all their children. They desire and pray that they may all come to that heavenly home, where the duty of commanding mortal men will no longer be necessary because there will no longer be a necessary duty of caring for the welfare of those who now enjoy the happiness of immortality. Until that home is reached, however, fathers have a duty to exercise their mastery which is greater than that of slaves to endure their servitude. If anyone in the household is an enemy to domestic peace because of his disobedience, he is corrected by a word, or by a blow, or by whatever other kind of punishment is just and lawful, to the extent permitted by human society; but this is for the benefit of the person corrected, so that he may be readmitted to the peace from which he has sundered himself. For just as it is not an act of kindness to help someone if he thereby loses a greater good, so it is not a blameless act to spare someone if he thereby falls into a graver sin. If we are to be blameless, therefore, our duty includes not only doing no harm to anyone, but also restraining him from sin or punishing his sin, so that either he who is chastised may be corrected by his experience, or others may be warned by his example.

A man's household, then, ought to be the beginning, or a little part, of the city; and every beginning has reference to some end proper to itself, and every part has reference to the integrity of the whole of which it is a part. From this, it appears clearly enough that domestic peace has reference to civic peace: that is, that the ordered concord of domestic rule and obedience has reference to the ordered concord of civic rule and obedience. Thus, it is fitting that the father of a family should draw his own precepts from the law of the city, and rule his household in such a way that it is brought into harmony with the city's peace.

## *Chapter 17*

But a household of men who do not live by faith strives to find an earthly peace in the goods and advantages which belong to this temporal life. By contrast, a household of men who live by faith looks forward to the blessings which are promised as eternal in the life to come; and such men make use of earthly and temporal things like pilgrims: they are not captivated by them, nor are they deflected by them from their progress towards God. They are, of course, sustained by them, so that they may more easily bear the burdens of the corruptible body which presses down the soul; but they do not in the least allow these things to increase such burdens.

Thus both kinds of men and both kinds of household make common use of those things which are necessary to this mortal life; but each has its own very different end in using them. So also, the earthly city, which does not live by faith, desires an earthly peace, and it establishes an ordered concord of civic obedience and rule in order to secure a kind of co-operation of men's wills for the sake of attaining the things which belong to this mortal life. But the Heavenly City—or, rather, that part of it which is a pilgrim in this condition of mortality, and which lives by faith—must of necessity make use of this peace also, until this mortal state, for which such peace is necessary, shall have passed away. Thus, it lives like a captive and a pilgrim, even though it has already received the promise of redemption, and the gift of the Spirit as a kind of pledge of it. But, for as long as it does so, it does not hesitate to obey the laws of the earthly city, whereby the things necessary for the support of this mortal life are administered. In this way, then, since this mortal condition is common to both cities, a harmony is preserved between them with respect to the things which belong to this condition.

But the earthly city has had among its members certain wise men whose doctrines are rejected by the divine teaching. Deceived either by their own speculations or by demons, these philosophers believed that there are many gods who must be induced to take an interest in human affairs. They believed also that these gods have, as it were, different spheres of influence with different offices attached to them. Thus the body is the responsibility of one god, the mind that of another; and, within the body, one god has charge of the head, another of the neck, and so on with each of the parts in turn. Similarly, within the mind, one god is responsible for intelligence, another for learning, another for anger, another for desire. And so too with all the things which touch our lives: there is a god who has charge of cattle, of corn, of wine, of oil, of woodlands, of money, of navigation, of war and victory, of marriage, of birth, of fertility, and so on. But the Heavenly City knows only one God Who is to be worshipped, and it decrees, with faithful piety, that to Him alone is to be given that service which the Greeks call *latreia,* and which is due only to God. Because of this difference, it has not been possible for the Heavenly City to have laws of religion in common with the earthly city. It has been necessary for her to dissent from the earthly city in this regard, and to become a burden to those who think differently. Thus, she has had to bear the brunt of the anger and hatred and persecutions of her adversaries, except insofar as their minds have sometimes been struck by the multitude of the Christians and by the divine aid always extended to them.

Therefore, for as long as this Heavenly City is a pilgrim on earth, she summons citizens of all nations and every tongue, and brings together a society of pilgrims in which no attention is paid to any differences in the customs, laws, and institutions by which earthly peace is achieved or maintained. She does not rescind or destroy these things, however. For whatever differences there are among the various nations, these all tend towards the same end of earthly peace. Thus, she preserves and follows them, provided only that they do not impede the religion by which we are taught that the one supreme and true God is to be worshipped. And so even the Heavenly City makes use of earthly peace during her pilgrimage, and desires and maintains the co-operation of men's wills in attaining those things which belong to the mortal nature of man, in so far, as this may be allowed without prejudice to true godliness and religion. Indeed, she directs that earthly peace towards heavenly peace: towards the peace which is so truly such that—at least so far as rational creatures are concerned—only it can really be held to be peace and called such. For this peace is a perfectly ordered and perfectly harmonious fellowship in the enjoyment of God, and of one another in God. When we have reached that peace, our life will no longer be a mortal one; rather, we shall then be fully and certainly alive. There will be no animal body to press down the soul by its corruption, but a spiritual body standing in need of nothing: a body subject in every part to the will. This peace the Heavenly City possesses in faith while on its pilgrimage, and by this faith it lives righteously, directing towards the attainment of that peace every good act which it performs either for God, or—since the city's life is inevitably a social one—for neighbour.

### *Chapter 21*

I come now, then, to the place where, as I promised in the second book of this work, I shall demonstrate that, according to the definitions proposed by Scipio in Cicero's book *De republica,* there never was a Roman commonwealth. I shall do this as briefly and as clearly as I can.

Scipio briefly defines a commonwealth as 'the property of a people.' If this is a true definition, however, there never was a Roman commonwealth, for the Roman state was never 'the property of a people' which the definition requires a commonwealth to be. Scipio defined a 'people' as a multitude 'united in fellowship by common agreement as to what is right and by a community of interest'. In the course of the discussion, he explains what he means by 'common agreement as to what is right', showing that a commonwealth cannot be maintained without justice. Where, therefore, there is no true justice there can be no right. For that which is done according to right is inevitably a just act, whereas nothing that is done

unjustly can be done according to right. But the unjust institutions of men are neither to be called right nor supposed to be such; for even men themselves say that 'right' [*ius*] is that which flows from the fount of justice [*iustitia*]. As for the definition of justice commonly offered by certain persons who do not understand the matter rightly, that it is 'the interest of the stronger': this is false.

Where there is no true justice, then, there can be no association of men 'united in fellowship by common agreement as to what is right', and therefore no people according to the definition of Scipio or Cicero. And if there is no people then there is no 'property of a people', but only a multitude of some kind, not worthy of the name of a people. If, therefore, a commonwealth is 'the property of a people', and if there is no 'people' where there is no 'common agreement as to what is right', and if there is no right where there is no justice, then it follows beyond doubt that where there is no justice there is no commonwealth. Moreover, justice is that virtue which gives to each his due. What kind of justice is it, then, that takes a man away from the true God and subjects him to impure demons? Is this giving to each his due? Or are we to call a man unjust if he takes a piece of property away from one who has bought it and hands it over to someone who has no right to it, yet just if he takes himself away from the lordship of the God who made him, and serves evil spirits?

In this same book, *De republica,* a most vigorous and forceful argument is developed on behalf of justice against injustice. Earlier in the discussion a case was made out in favour of injustice and against justice, and it was stated that a commonwealth cannot stand or be governed except by injustice. For it was proposed as a quite incontrovertible point here that it is unjust for some men to rule and others to serve; yet an imperial city to which a great commonwealth belongs cannot govern her provinces other than by means of such injustice. On the side of justice, it was urged in reply that this state of affairs is, in fact, just, because servitude may be to the advantage of such men as the provincials are, and is indeed so when rightly established: that is, when dishonest men are deprived of their freedom to do wrong. It was also urged that subjugated peoples will in any case be better off, because they were worse off when they were not subjugated. To strengthen this reasoning, there is added a notable example taken from nature. 'Why', it is asked, 'does God rule man, the soul the body, and the reason the desires and other vicious parts of the soul?' By this example it is shown plainly enough that servitude is beneficial for some men, and that servitude to God is indeed beneficial for all. For, when it serves God, the soul rules the body rightly; and, in the soul itself, when the reason is subject to God as its Lord, it rightly governs the desires and other such things. That being so, however, what justice can we suppose there to be in a man who does not serve God? For if the soul does not serve God it cannot by any means govern the body justly, nor can human reason govern the vices. And if there is no justice in such a man, then it is beyond doubt that there is no justice in a collection of men consisting of persons of this kind. Here, then, there is not that 'common agreement as to what is right' by which a multitude is made into a 'people' whose 'property' a commonwealth is said to be. And why need I say anything of that 'community of interest' which, according to our definition, makes a gathering of men into a 'people'? For if you attend diligently to the matter, you will see for yourself that nothing is 'in the interest' of those who live godlessly—of those, that is, who serve not God, but demons: demons whose impiety is all the greater in that they desire to have sacrifices offered to them as if they were gods rather than most unclean spirits. For my part, I consider that what I have already said concerning a 'common agreement as to what is right' is enough to make it apparent that, by this definition, there can be no 'people', and therefore no 'property' called a commonwealth, where there is no justice.

But perhaps our adversaries will say that the Romans did not serve unclean spirits in their commonwealth, but good and holy gods. Must we, then, repeat yet again those things which we have already said often enough, and more than often enough? Must not anyone who has perused the earlier books of this work down to this point be either exceedingly stupid or shamelessly contentious if he still doubts that the Romans served evil and impure demons? But, to say no more of the kind of gods whom the Romans worshipped with sacrifice, it is written in the Law of the true God, 'He that sacrificeth unto any god save unto the Lord only, shall be utterly destroyed.' He Who uttered so great a threat does not desire that we should sacrifice either to good or bad gods.

## *Chapter 23*

. . . Yet it is we ourselves, His own City, who are His most wonderful and best sacrifice. And, as the faithful know, and as we have explained in previous books, we celebrate the mystery of this sacrifice in our offerings. For it was proclaimed by divine oracles through the holy prophets that the sacrificial victims which the Jews offered as a foreshadowing of what was to come should cease, and that all nations, from the rising of the sun even unto the going down of the same, were to offer one sacrifice; and now we see that these things have come to pass. I have, however, already selected as many of these oracles as seemed sufficient, and distributed them throughout this work.

Thus, justice is found where the one supreme God rules an obedient City according to His grace, so that it sacrifices to none but Him; and where, in consequence, the soul rules the body in all men who belong to that City and obey God, and the reason faithfully rules the vices in lawful order. In that City, both the individual just man and the community and people of the just live by faith, which works by love: by that love with which a man loves God as God ought to be loved, and his neighbour as himself. But where there is not this justice, there certainly is no association of men united by a common agreement as to what is right and by a community of interest. And so there is no commonwealth; for where there is no 'people', there is no 'property of a people'.

## *Chapter 24*

But let us disregard this definition of a people and adopt another: let us say that a 'people' is an assembled multitude of rational creatures bound together by a common agreement as to the objects of their love. In this case, if we are to discover the character of any people, we have only to examine what it loves. If it is an assembled multitude, not of animals but of rational creatures, and is united by a common agreement as to what it loves, then it is not absurd to call it a 'people', no matter what the objects of its love may be. Clearly, however, the better the objects of this agreement, the better the people; and the worse the objects, the worse the people.

According to this definition of ours, the Roman people is indeed a people, and its 'property' is without doubt a commonwealth. As to the objects of that people's love—both in the earliest days and in the times which followed—and the morals of that people as it fell into bloody seditions and thence into social and civil wars, and so ruptured or corrupted that bond of concord which is, as it were, the health of a people: we have the testimony of history for all this, and I have presented many illustrations in the preceding books. I do not, however, on this account say that the Roman people was not really a people, or that Rome was not a commonwealth, so long as there remains an association of some kind between a multitude of rational creatures bound together by a common agreement as to the objects of their love. . . .

# THOMAS AQUINAS

~

## INTRODUCTION

## PAUL J. WEITHMAN

Thomas Aquinas (1224–1274) was born to a family of minor nobility in southern Italy. The part of Italy in which he was born was then part of the Kingdom of Sicily, which was itself part of the Holy Roman Empire. His family estate was close to the frontier between Sicily and the papal states. Because of the ongoing struggle between the emperor and the pope for control of Italy, the estate's location required Aquinas's family to shift their political allegiances with the changing fortunes of the two sides. Despite the facts that Thomas's father and brother were active participants in the struggle and that his brother apparently tried to attract him to the emperor's court, Thomas took no part. Aquinas was attached to the papal court for some time during his adulthood, but in an academic rather than a political capacity. Though he made important contributions to political philosophy, his work does not bear the imprint of his own or his family's political experiences.

Aquinas spent most of his life as a member of the Order of Friars Preachers, also known as the "Dominicans" after their founder St. Dominic. In Aquinas's time the Dominicans lived in the cities of Europe rather than in rural monasteries. They were poor corporately as well as individually and their communities were supported by alms begged by some of their members.

Aquinas began his higher education by studying the liberal arts in Paris. There he first encountered the texts of Aristotle, which were to exercise a powerful hold on his philosophical work. He continued his study of philosophy under Albertus Magnus (1206–1280) in Cologne and began the advanced study of theology under him. Aquinas returned to Paris in 1252 and became a professor of theology at the university there in 1256. He held the chair of theology for a three-year term, then spent two years in both Paris and Italy. From 1268 until 1272 he held a chair in Paris for a second time, after which he went to Naples for the last two years of his teaching career.

A few weeks before Christmas of 1273 Aquinas had what he subsequently described as a profoundly moving mystical experience, one that led him to believe that the works on which he had spent his life were intellectually worthless. Overcome by the memory of this experience, weakened by chronic obesity and habitual overwork, he produced virtually nothing more. While on a journey early in February of 1274 he suffered a seizure, quite probably brought on by a subdural hematoma resulting from an accidental blow to the head. Aquinas died on March 7, 1274.

Throughout his life and after his death Aquinas had a reputation for great piety and personal sanctity. He was declared a saint in 1323.

Aquinas achieved a staggering literary output during his seventeen years as a teacher and scholar. He commented on all four gospels, on many of the Pauline epistles, and on several books of the Hebrew bible. He wrote commentaries on much of Aristotle. He left behind homilies, a few letters, a number of short treatises on philosophical subjects and lengthy treatises on a variety of topics in philosophy and theology. He also left a number of "Quodlibetal Questions," long answers to theological and philosophical questions posed during open debates held at the University of Paris. Aquinas's two most substantial and best known works are the *Summa Contra Gentiles* and the much longer *Summa Theologiae*. In them Aquinas attempted to present and defend the teachings of Catholicism in a systematic way that provided them a rigorous philosophical basis. In doing so he confronted his views, not only with counterarguments that were in the air during his own time, but also with arguments drawn from Maimonides, from Arabic philosophers, and from classical and patristic sources. The most important influence on this work, however, was the philosophy of Aristotle.

The works of Aristotle had been lost to the West and largely unknown to it for centuries before Aquinas, though they were known to and commented on in the Islamic world. Aristotle's texts made their way into Europe in the early part of the thirteenth century through contacts between Christian and Arab scholars. His philosophical works seemed to present a systematic view of the world, of human inquiry, and of the good human life that was at odds with the central tenets of European Christianity. The god of Aristotle's *Metaphysics,* for example, was detached and self-absorbed, and took no active part in human history. The good life as Aristotle envisioned it seemed that of a cultured Athenian gentleman rather than that of the Christian saint. The study and teaching of Aristotle was therefore not only novel but also highly controversial in Aquinas's time. It was Aquinas's great achievement to show Aristotle's thought to be consistent with Christianity by building his own vast philosophical and theological system upon it. Much of the difficult technical vocabulary that permeates Aquinas's work is drawn from Aristotle. The influence of Aristotle is evident in virtually every element of his thought.

Aquinas's views on the central questions of political philosophy are not easy to discern. Despite his huge output, he never completed a free-standing work of political philosophy. His commentary on Aristotle's *Politics* was unfinished at his death. He began a work called *On Kingship* for a king of Cyprus who was also a Dominican benefactor. When the king died before its completion, Aquinas stopped work on the treatise and it was later finished by his student Ptolemy of Lucca. Aquinas paid very little attention to questions about political institutions. There are places where he suggests a preference for a mixed constitution if the people are sufficiently virtuous to participate in governing themselves either directly or through representatives. Like Aristotle, he is also attracted to unmixed monarchy if someone worthy of the office can be found. The political situation of his day should have interested him in the relationship between the papacy and secular rulers. His remarks on the subject are cautious rather than groundbreaking. He considers the authority of non-Christian rulers and the permissibility of non-Christian religious practices: on both subjects he is cautiously tolerant.

The substance of Aquinas's political thought must and can be culled from passages scattered throughout his work, especially from the *Summa Theologiae*. There he wrote much that has implications for politics and political philosophy, but he almost always did so in the course of discussing something else. His treatment of peace occurs in a long discussion of charity, where it is followed closely by a discussion of mercy and more distantly by treatments of war and schism. His discussion of property comes early in a long treatment of justice, a discussion in which he gives a good deal more attention to various forms of verbal injustice like slander than he does to theft.

While Aristotle explicitly treats political questions at much greater length than does Aquinas, Aquinas's location of political questions in his discussion of moral ones is Aristotelian in spirit. This is because Aristotle's treatment of political questions was highly moralized. Aristotle thought of political life as an arena in which the good human life is lived. In it, he thought, citizens develop and exercise the virtues. It is natural that a follower of Aristotle like Aquinas should take up political questions in the course of discussing virtues like charity and justice and vices like injustice, quarrelsomeness, and avarice.

The central notion in Aquinas's political thought is one that he found in Aristotle: the common good of political society, sometimes called the "political common good." This is a good shared in by, and hence common to, the members of a given political society. It consists, Aquinas says, in a society's justice and peace. These are goods of which all members partake. The prevalence of justice and peace makes it possible for members of society to enjoy other goods Aquinas thinks part of a good life, like family life and religion. Family life and religious life, in turn, reach their fullest expression or are "perfected" when enjoyed in a just and peaceful society. The fact that these ingredients of the good life are perfected in a well-ordered political community explains why Aquinas, like Aristotle, thinks of such a community as the self-sufficient arena in which the good life can be lived.

The most influential part of Aquinas's political thought, interestingly, is also the part of it that is least Aristotelian. That is his discussion of law. His treatment of law, like his treatment of other political questions, is located in a much larger discussion of other moral issues. Thus he takes up human and natural law, as well as divine and eternal law, in the course of a very long discussion of the various causes of human action; in this discussion law takes its place alongside a general discussion of passions, habits, virtues, vices, and grace.

The eternal law, Aquinas says, is the divine plan by which God created and rules the universe. God intended all created things to flourish. The eternal law or divine plan indicates the activities in which they do so. Given the complexity of the created world, Aquinas thinks that much of the eternal law is known only to God. The natural law is that part of the divine law which is accessible to human reason and which indicates how human beings flourish. It includes the basic provisions of morality that must be observed if human beings are to live well. These, Aquinas thinks, are invariant across time and place. Human law, sometimes called "positive law," is the law made or posited by human legislators; to be authoritative, that law must be consistent with the natural law. It cannot enjoin things that the fundamental principles of morality forbid. If it does, Aquinas insists that no one is bound to obey it. Latter-day advocates of civil disobedience have often turned to Aquinas's discussion of unjust laws to defend their actions. Aquinas thinks that human law must also foster religion. It cannot justly enjoin heretical practices; if circumstances permit, it should encourage orthodox ones. Finally, it must promote the common good rather than the legislator's own benefit.

Aquinas's discussion of law is drawn from the *Summa Theologiae,* each article of which has a complicated internal structure. After posing the subquestion with which a given article is concerned, Aquinas will raise several objections to the position he is about to defend. Sometimes these will be cited without attribution. Since scholastic writers never cite living authors by name, these may have been objections propounded by his contemporaries. Other objections will be drawn from scripture or from patristic or classical sources. Aquinas will then adduce an authoritative statement, prefaced by, "On the contrary," which supports his own position. Only then does he proceed to defend his own view, beginning with, "I answer that." Finally, he will answer the objections with which he began, thus showing how his own position can be reconciled with arguments to the contrary that have some authority behind them.

Aquinas's style, which seems unusual to us, would have been quite familiar to the university students for whom Aquinas wrote the *Summa.* "Disputations" were common events in medieval universities. In them a professor posed a question or was asked one from the audience. Graduate students would be assigned one or the other side of the question, and would have to produce arguments and authorities in support of the thesis they were assigned. After the arguments for both sides had been heard, the master would "determine" the question by giving arguments supporting his own position and showing where those on the contrary had gone wrong. Many of Aquinas's students would have participated in these ego-bruising events, and all would have seen them. They would have thought the *Summa* was organized in a natural way, though Aquinas seems to be the first actually to have organized his writings in the disputational format. Modern readers find it easiest to begin with Aquinas's own answer to a question, and only then to work through his objections and replies.

The best biographies of Aquinas in English are James A. Weisheipl, OP, *Friar Thomas D'Aquino* (Washington, D.C.: Catholic University of America Press, 1983) and J.-P. Torrell, OP, *Saint Thomas Aquinas: The Man and His Work* (Washington, D.C.: Catholic University of America Press, 1996) (trans. Robert Royal). The best discussion of Aquinas's political thought is John Finnis, *Aquinas: Moral, Political and Legal Theory* (Oxford: Oxford University Press, 1998). A useful introduction to Aquinas's natural law ethics is Ralph McInery, *Ethica Thomistica* (Washington, D.C.: Catholic University of America Press, 1997).

# Summa Theologiae

## QUESTION 90: OF THE ESSENCE OF LAW

### [In Four Articles]

We have now to consider the extrinsic principles of acts. Now the extrinsic principle inclining to evil is the devil, of whose temptations we have spoken in the First Part. But the extrinsic principle moving to good is God, Who both instructs us by means of His law and assists us by His grace; wherefore, in the first place, we must speak of law; in the second place, of grace.

Concerning law, we must consider (1) law itself in general; (2) its parts. Concerning law in general, three points offer themselves for our consideration: (1) its essence; (2) the different kinds of law; (3) the effects of law.

Under the first head, there are four points of inquiry: (1) Whether law is something pertaining to reason? (2) concerning the end of law; (3) its cause; (4) the promulgation of law.

### First Article: Is Law Something Pertaining to Reason?

*We proceed thus to the First Article:*

*Objection 1.* It would seem that law is not something pertaining to reason. For the Apostle says: "I see another law in my members," etc. But nothing pertaining to reason is in the members, since the reason does not make use of a bodily organ. Therefore, law is not something pertaining to reason.

*Obj. 2.* Further, in the reason there is nothing else but power, habit, and act. But law is not the power itself of reason. In like manner, neither is it a habit of reason, because the habits of reason are the intellectual virtues of which we have spoken above. Nor, again, is it an act of reason because then law would cease when the act of reason ceases, for instance, while we are asleep. Therefore, law is nothing pertaining to reason.

*Obj. 3.* Further, the law moves those who are subject to it to act aright. But it belongs properly to the will to move to act, as is evident from what has been said above. Therefore, law pertains not to the reason but to the will, according to the words of the Jurist: "Whatever pleases the ruler has the force of law."

*On the contrary,* It belongs to the law to command and to forbid. But it belongs to reason to command, as stated above. Therefore, law is something pertaining to reason.

*I answer that* Law is a certain rule and measure of acts whereby man is induced to act or is restrained from acting; for *lex* (law) is derived from *ligare* (to bind) because it binds one to act. Now the rule and measure of human acts is reason, which is the first principle of human acts, as is evident from what has been stated above, since it belongs to reason to direct to the end, which is the first principle in all matters of action, according to the Philosopher. Now, that which is the principle in any genus is the rule and measure of that genus, for instance, unity in the genus of numbers, and the first movement in the genus of movements. Consequently, it follows that law is something pertaining to reason.

*Reply Obj. 1.* Since law is a kind of rule and measure, it may be in something in two ways. First, as in that which measures and rules; and since this is

Reprinted from Aquinas, *On Law, Morality, and Politics,* edited, with introduction, by William P. Baumgarth and Richard J. Regan, S.J. (Cambridge, Mass.: Avatar Books of Cambridge, 1988) by permission of the publisher.

proper to reason, it follows that, in this way, law is in reason alone. Second, as in that which is measured and ruled. In this way, law is in all those things that are inclined to something by reason of some law, so that any inclination arising from a law may be called a law, not essentially but by participation as it were. And thus the inclination of the members to concupiscence is called "the law of the members."

*Reply Obj. 2.* Just as, in external action, we may consider the work and the work done—for instance, the work of building and the house built, so in the acts of reason we may consider the act itself of reason, i.e., to understand and to reason, and something produced by this act. With regard to the speculative reason, this is first of all the definition; secondly, the proposition; thirdly, the syllogism or argument. And since also the practical reason makes use of a kind of syllogism in respect to the work to be done, as stated above and as the Philosopher teaches, hence we find in the practical reason something that holds the same position in regard to operations as, in the speculative intellect, the proposition holds in regard to conclusions. Suchlike universal propositions of the practical intellect that are directed to actions have the nature of law. And these propositions are sometimes under our actual consideration, while sometimes they are retained in the reason by means of a habit.

*Reply Obj. 3.* Reason has its power of moving from the will, as stated above, for it is due to the fact that one wills the end that the reason issues its commands as regards things ordained to the end. But in order that the volition of what is commanded may have the nature of law, it needs to be in accord with some rule of reason. And in this sense is to be understood the saying that the will of the ruler has the force of law; otherwise, the ruler's will would savor of lawlessness rather than of law.

### Second Article: Is the Law Always Directed to the Common Good?

*We proceed thus to the Second Article:*

*Obj. 1.* It would seem that the law is not always directed to the common good as to its end. For it belongs to law to command and to forbid. But commands are directed to certain individual goods. Therefore, the end of the law is not always the common good.

*Obj. 2.* Further, the law directs man in his actions. But human actions are concerned with particular matters. Therefore, the law is directed to some particular good.

*Obj. 3.* Further, Isidore says, "If the law is based on reason, whatever is based on reason will be a law." But reason is the foundation not only of what is ordained to the common good but also of that which is directed to private good. Therefore, the law is not only directed to the common good but also to the private good of an individual.

*On the contrary,* Isidore says that "Laws are enacted for no private profit but for the common benefit of the citizens."

*I answer that,* As stated above, the law belongs to that which is a principle of human acts because it is their rule and measure. Now, as reason is a principle of human acts, so in reason itself there is something which is the principle in respect of all the rest; wherefore to this principle chiefly and mainly law must needs be referred. Now the first principle in practical matters, which are the object of the practical reason, is the last end, and the last end of human life is bliss or happiness, as stated above. Consequently, the law must needs regard principally the relationship to happiness. Moreover, since every part is ordained to the whole as imperfect to perfect, and since a single man is a part of the perfect community, the law must needs regard properly the relationship to universal happiness. Wherefore the Philosopher, in the above definition of legal matters, mentions both happiness and the body politic, for he says that we call those legal matters just "which are adapted to produce and preserve happiness and its parts for the body politic" since the political community is a perfect community, as he says in *Politics* I, 1.

Now, in every genus, that which belongs to it most of all is the principle of the others, and the others belong to that genus in subordination to that thing; thus fire, which is chief among hot things, is the cause of heat in mixed bodies, and these are said to be hot insofar as they have a share of fire. Consequently, since the law is chiefly ordained to the common good, any other precept in regard to some individual work must needs be devoid of the nature of a law, save insofar as it is ordered to the common good. Therefore, every law is ordained to the common good.

*Reply Obj. 1.* A command denotes an application of a law to matters regulated by the law. Now the order to the common good, at which the law aims, is applicable to particular ends. And in this way, commands are given even concerning particular matters.

*Reply Obj. 2.* Actions are indeed concerned with particular matters, but those particular matters are referable to the common good, not as to a common genus or species, but as to a common final cause, according as the common good is said to be the common end.

*Reply Obj. 3.* Just as nothing stands firm with regard to the speculative reason except that which is traced back to the first indemonstrable principles, so nothing stands firm with regard to the practical reason unless it be directed to the last end which is the common good, and whatever stands to reason in this sense has the nature of a law.

### Third Article: Is the Reason of Any Person Competent to Make Laws?

*We proceed thus to the Third Article:*

*Obj. 1.* It would seem that the reason of any person is competent to make laws. For the Apostle says that "when the Gentiles, who have not the law, do by nature those things that are of the law, . . . they are a law to themselves." Now he says this of all in general. Therefore, anyone can make a law for himself.

*Obj. 2.* Further, as the Philosopher says, "The intention of the lawgiver is to lead men to virtue." But every man can lead another to virtue. Therefore, the reason of any man is competent to make laws.

*Obj. 3.* Further, just as the ruler of a political community governs the political community, so every father of a family governs his household. But the ruler of a political community can make laws for the political community. Therefore, every father of a family can make laws for his household.

*On the contrary,* Isidore says, "A law is an ordi-

nance of the people, whereby something is sanctioned by nobles together with commoners." Not everyone, therefore, is competent to make law.

*I answer that* Law, properly speaking, regards first and chiefly an ordering to the common good. Now to order anything to the common good belongs either to the whole people or to someone who is the vicegerent of the whole people. And, therefore, the making of law belongs either to the whole people or to a public personage who has care of the whole people, since, in all other matters, the directing of anything to the end concerns him to whom the end belongs.

*Reply Obj. 1.* As stated above, law is in a person not only as in one that rules but also by participation as in one that is ruled. In the latter way, each one is a law to himself, insofar as he shares the direction that he receives from one who rules him. Hence the same text goes on, "who show the work of the law written in their hearts."

*Reply Obj. 2.* A private person cannot lead another to virtue efficaciously, for he can only advise, and if his advice be not taken, it has no coercive power, such as the law should have in order to prove an efficacious inducement to virtue, as the Philosopher says. But this coercive power is vested in the whole people or in some public personage to whom it belongs to inflict penalties, as we shall state further on. Wherefore, the framing of laws belongs to him alone.

*Reply Obj. 3.* As one man is a part of the household, so a household is a part of the political community, and the political community is a perfect community, according to *Politics* I, 1. And, therefore, as the good of one man is not the last end but is ordained to the common good, so too the good of one household is ordained to the good of a single political community, which is a perfect community. Consequently, he that governs a family can indeed make certain commands or ordinances but not such as to have properly the nature of law.

### Fourth Article: Is Promulgation Essential to a Law?

*We proceed thus to the Fourth Article:*

*Obj. 1.* It would seem that promulgation is not

essential to a law. For the natural law above all has the nature of law. But the natural law needs no promulgation. Therefore, it is not essential to a law that it be promulgated.

*Obj. 2.* Further, it belongs properly to a law to bind one to do or not to do something. But the obligation of fulfilling a law touches not only those in whose presence it is promulgated but also others. Therefore, promulgation is not essential to a law.

*Obj. 3.* Further, the obligation of a law extends even to the future since "laws are binding in matters of the future," as the jurists say. But promulgation is made to those who are present. Therefore, it is not essential to a law.

*On the contrary,* It is laid down in the *Decretum,* dist. 4, that "Laws are established when they are promulgated."

*I answer that,* As stated above, a law is imposed on others by way of a rule and measure. Now a rule or measure is imposed by being applied to those who are to be ruled and measured by it. Wherefore, in order that a law obtain the binding force which is proper to a law, it must needs be applied to the men who have to be ruled by it. Such application is made by its being notified to them by promulgation. Wherefore promulgation is necessary for the law to obtain its force.

Thus, from the four preceding articles, the definition of law may be gathered, and it is nothing else than a certain ordinance of reason for the common good, made by him who has care of the community, and promulgated.

*Reply Obj. 1.* The natural law is promulgated by the very fact that God instilled it into men's minds so as to be known by them naturally.

*Reply Obj. 2.* Those who are not present when a law is promulgated are bound to observe the law, insofar as it is notified or can be notified to them by others after it has been promulgated.

*Reply Obj. 3.* The promulgation that takes place now extends to future time by reason of the durability of written characters, by which means it is continually promulgated. Hence Isidore says that "*lex* (law) is derived from *legere* (to read) because it is written."

# QUESTION 91: OF THE VARIOUS KINDS OF LAW

## [In Six Articles]

We must now consider the various kinds of law, under which head there are six points of inquiry: (1) Whether there is an eternal law? (2) Whether there is a natural law? (3) Whether there is a human law? (4) Whether there is a divine law? (5) Whether there is one divine law or several? (6) Whether there is a law of sin?

### First Article: Is There an Eternal Law?

*We proceed thus to the First Article:*

*Obj. 1.* It would seem that there is no eternal law because every law is imposed on someone. But there was not someone from eternity on whom a law could be imposed since God alone was from eternity. Therefore, no law is eternal.

*Obj. 2.* Further, promulgation is essential to law. But promulgation could not be from eternity because there was no one to whom it could be promulgated from eternity. Therefore, no law can be eternal.

*Obj. 3.* Further, a law implies order to an end. But nothing ordained to an end is eternal, for the last end alone is eternal. Therefore, no law is eternal.

*On the contrary,* Augustine says, "That law which is the supreme reason cannot be understood to be otherwise than unchangeable and eternal."

*I answer that,* As stated above, a law is nothing else but a dictate of practical reason in the ruler who governs a perfect community. Now it is evident, granted that the world is ruled by divine providence, as was stated in the First Part, that the whole community of the universe is governed by divine reason. Wherefore, the very idea of the government of things in God the Ruler of the universe has the nature of a law. And since the divine reason's conception of things is not subject to time but is eternal, according to Pr. 8:23, therefore it is that this kind of law must be called eternal.

*Reply Obj. 1.* Those things that are not in themselves exist with God inasmuch as they are foreknown and preordained by Him, according to Rom.

4:17, "Who calls those things that are not, as those that are." Accordingly, the eternal concept of the divine law bears the nature of an eternal law insofar as it is ordained by God to the government of things foreknown by Him.

*Reply Obj. 2.* Promulgation is made by word of mouth or in writing, and in both ways the eternal law is promulgated, because both the divine word and the writing of the Book of Life are eternal. But the promulgation cannot be from eternity on the part of the creature that hears or reads.

*Reply Obj. 3.* The law implies order to an end actively, insofar as it directs certain things to an end, but not passively—that is to say, the law itself is not ordained to an end—except accidentally, in a governor whose end is extrinsic to him, and to which end his law must needs be ordained. But the end of the divine government is God Himself, and His law is not distinct from Himself. Wherefore the eternal law is not ordained to another end.

### Second Article: Is There a Natural Law in Us?

*We proceed thus to the Second Article:*

*Obj. 1.* It would seem that there is no natural law in us because man is governed sufficiently by the eternal law; for Augustine says that "the eternal law is that by which it is right that all things should be most orderly." But nature does not abound in superfluities, as neither does it fail in necessaries. Therefore, there is no natural law in man.

*Obj. 2.* Further, by the law man is directed in his acts to the end, as stated above. But the directing of human acts to their end is not by nature, as is the case in irrational creatures, which act for an end solely by their natural appetite, whereas man acts for an end by his reason and will. Therefore, there is no natural law for man.

*Obj. 3.* Further, the more a man is free, the less is he under the law. But man is freer than all other animals on account of his free will, with which he is endowed above all other animals. Since, therefore, other animals are not subject to a natural law, neither is man subject to a natural law.

*On the contrary,* A gloss on Rom. 2:14 ("When the Gentiles, who have not the law, do by nature those things that are of the law") comments as follows: "Although they have no written law, yet they have the natural law, whereby each one knows, and is conscious of, what is good and what is evil."

*I answer that,* As stated above, law, being a rule and measure, can be in a person in two ways: in one way, as in him that rules and measures; in another way, as in that which is ruled and measured, since a thing is ruled and measured insofar as it partakes of the rule or measure. Wherefore, since all things subject to divine providence are ruled and measured by the eternal law, as was stated above, it is evident that all things partake somewhat of the eternal law insofar as, namely, from its being imprinted on them, they derive their respective inclinations to their proper acts and ends. Now among all others, the rational creature is subject to divine providence in a more excellent way, insofar as it partakes of a share of providence, by being provident both for itself and for others. Wherefore it has a share of the eternal reason, whereby it has a natural inclination to its proper act and end, and this participation of the eternal law in the rational creature is called the natural law. Hence the Psalmist, after saying "offer up the sacrifice of justice," as though someone asked what the works of justice are, adds: "Many say, 'Who shows us good things?'," in answer to which question he says: "The light of Your countenance, O lord, is signed upon us"; thus implying that the light of natural reason, whereby we discern what is good and what is evil, which pertains to the natural law, is nothing else than an imprint on us of the divine light. It is therefore evident that the natural law is nothing else than the rational creature's participation of the eternal law.

*Reply Obj. 1.* This argument would hold if the natural law were something different from the eternal law, whereas it is nothing but a participation thereof, as stated above.

*Reply Obj. 2.* Every act of reason and will in us is derived from that which is according to nature, as stated above; for every act of reasoning is based on principles that are known naturally, and every act of appetite in respect of the means is derived from the natural appetite in respect of the last end. Accordingly, the first direction of our acts to their end must needs be in virtue of the natural law.

*Reply Obj. 3.* Even irrational animals partake in their own way of the eternal reason, just as the rational creature does. But because the rational creature partakes thereof in an intellectual and rational manner, therefore the participation of the eternal law in the rational creature is properly called a law, since a law is something pertaining to reason, as stated above. Irrational creatures, however, do not partake thereof in a rational manner, wherefore, there is no participation of the eternal law in them, except by way of similitude.

### Third Article: Is There a Human Law?

*We proceed thus to the Third Article:*

*Obj. 1.* It would seem that there is not a human law. For the natural law is a participation of the eternal law, as stated above. Now, through the eternal law, "all things are most orderly," as Augustine states. Therefore, the natural law suffices for the ordering of all human affairs. Consequently, there is no need for a human law.

*Obj. 2.* Further, a law has the nature of a measure, as stated above. But human reason is not a measure of things, but vice versa, as stated in *Metaphysics* IX, 1. Therefore, no law can emanate from human reason.

*Obj. 3.* Further, a measure should be most certain, as stated in *Metaphysics* 10. But the dictates of human reason in matters of conduct are uncertain, according to Wisdom 9:14: "The thoughts of mortal men are fearful, and our counsels uncertain." Therefore, no law can emanate from human reason.

*On the contrary,* Augustine distinguishes two kinds of law: the one eternal; the other temporal, which he calls human.

*I answer that,* As stated above, a law is a certain dictate of practical reason. Now it is to be observed that the same procedure takes place in the practical and in the speculative reason, for each proceeds from principles to conclusions, as stated above (ibid.). Accordingly, we conclude that just as, in the specu-

lative reason, from naturally known indemonstrable principles we draw the conclusions of the various sciences, the knowledge of which is not imparted to us by nature but acquired by the efforts of reason, so too it is from the precepts of the natural law, as from general and indemonstrable principles, that the human reason needs to proceed to certain particular determinations of the laws. These particular determinations, devised by human reason, are called human laws, provided the other essential conditions of law be observed as stated above. Wherefore, Tully says in his *Rhetoric* that "justice has its source in nature; thence certain things came into custom by reason of their utility; afterward these things which emanated from nature and were approved by custom were sanctioned by fear and reverence for the law."

*Reply Obj. 1.* The human reason cannot have a full participation of the dictate of the divine reason but according to its own mode and imperfectly. Consequently, as on the part of the speculative reason, by a natural participation of divine wisdom, there is in us the knowledge of certain general principles but not proper knowledge of each single truth, such as that contained in the divine wisdom, so too on the part of the practical reason, man has a natural participation of the eternal law according to certain general principles but not as regards the particular determinations of individual cases, which are, however, contained in the eternal law. Hence the need for human reason to proceed further to particular legal sanctions.

*Reply Obj. 2.* Human reason is not of itself the rule of things, but the principles impressed on it by nature are general rules and measures of all things relating to human conduct, whereof the natural reason is the rule and measure, although it is not the measure of things that are from nature.

*Reply Obj. 3.* The practical reason is concerned with practical matters, which are singular and contingent, but not with necessary things, with which the speculative reason is concerned. Wherefore human laws cannot have that inerrancy that belongs to the demonstrated conclusions of sciences. Nor is it necessary for every measure to be altogether unerring and certain but according as it is possible in its own particular genus.

# QUESTION 94:
# OF THE NATURAL LAW

## *[In Six Articles]*

We must now consider the natural law, concerning which there are six points of inquiry: (1) What is the natural law? (2) What are the precepts of the natural law? (3) Whether all acts of virtue are prescribed by the natural law? (4) Whether the natural law is the same in all? (5) Whether it is changeable? (6) Whether it can be abolished from the heart of man?

### First Article: Is the Natural Law a Habit?

*We proceed thus to the First Article:*

*Obj. 1.* It would seem that the natural law is a habit because, as the Philosopher says, "there are three things in the soul: power, habit, and passion." But the natural law is not one of the soul's powers, nor is it one of the passions, as we may see by going through them one by one. Therefore, the natural law is a habit.

*Obj. 2.* Further, Basil says that the conscience or "*synderesis* is the law of our mind," which can only apply to the natural law. But *synderesis* is a habit, as was shown in the First Part. Therefore, the natural law is a habit.

*Obj. 3.* Further, the natural law abides in man always, as will be shown further on. But man's reason, to which the law pertains, does not always think about the natural law. Therefore, the natural law is not an act but a habit.

*On the contrary,* Augustine says that "a habit is that whereby something is done when necessary." But such is not the natural law since it is in infants and in the damned who cannot act by it. Therefore, the natural law is not a habit.

*I answer that,* A thing may be called a habit in two ways. First, properly and essentially, and thus the natural law is not a habit. For it has been stated above that the natural law is something appointed by reason, just as a proposition is a work of reason. Now, that which a man does is not the same as that whereby he does it, for he makes a becoming speech by the habit of grammar. Since, then, a habit is that by which we act, a law cannot be a habit properly and essentially.

Secondly, the term "habit" may be applied to that which we hold by a habit; thus faith may mean that which we hold by faith. And accordingly, since the precepts of the natural law are sometimes considered by reason actually, while sometimes they are in the reason only habitually, in this way the natural law may be called a habit. Thus, in speculative matters, the indemonstrable principles are not the habit itself whereby we hold those principles but are the principles the habit of which we possess.

*Reply Obj. 1.* The Philosopher proposes there to discover the genus of virtue, and since it is evident that virtue is a principle of action, he mentions only those things which are principles of human acts, viz., powers, habits, and passions. But there are other things in the soul besides these three: there are acts; thus to will is in the one that wills; again, things known are in the knower. Moreover, its own natural properties are in the soul, such as immortality and the like.

*Reply Obj. 2. Synderesis* is said to be the law of our mind because it is a habit containing the precepts of the natural law, which are the first principles of human actions.

*Reply Obj. 3.* This argument proves that the natural law is held habitually, and this is granted.

To the argument advanced in the contrary sense we reply that sometimes a man is unable to make use of that which is in him habitually on account of some impediment; thus, on account of sleep, a man is unable to use the habit of reasoning. In like manner, through the deficiency of his age, a child cannot use the habit of understanding principles, or the natural law, which is in him habitually.

### Second Article: Does the Natural Law Contain Several Precepts or One Only?

*We proceed thus to the Second Article:*

*Obj. 1.* It would seem that the natural law contains, not several precepts, but one only. For law is a kind of precept, as stated above. If, therefore, there were many precepts of the natural law, it would follow that there are also many natural laws.

*Obj. 2.* Further, the natural law is consequent to human nature. But human nature as a whole is one, though, as to its parts, it is manifold. Therefore, either there is but one precept of the law of nature, on account of the unity of nature as a whole, or there are many by reason of the number of parts of human nature. The result would be that even things relating to the inclination of the concupiscible faculty belong to the natural law.

*Obj. 3.* Further, law is something pertaining to reason, as stated above. Now, reason is but one in man. Therefore, there is only one precept of the natural law.

*On the contrary,* The precepts of the natural law in man stand in relation to practical matters as the first principles to matters of demonstration. But there are several first indemonstrable principles. Therefore, there are also several precepts of the natural law.

*I answer that,* As stated above, the precepts of the natural law are to the practical reason what the first principles of demonstrations are to the speculative reason because both are self-evident principles. Now a thing is said to be self-evident in two ways: first, in itself; secondly, in relation to us. Any proposition is said to be self-evident in itself if its predicate is contained in the notion of the subject, although, to one who knows not the definition of the subject, it happens that such a proposition is not self-evident. For instance, this proposition, "Man is a rational being," is in its very nature self-evident, since who says "man" says "a rational being," and yet to one who knows not what a man is, this proposition is not self-evident. Hence it is that, as Boethius says, certain axioms or propositions are universally self-evident to all, and such are those propositions whose terms are known to all, as "Every whole is greater than its part," and, "Things equal to one and the same are equal to one another." But some propositions are self-evident only to the wise who understand the meaning of the terms of such propositions; thus to one who understands that an angel is not a body, it is self-evident that an angel is not circumspectively in

a place, but this is not evident to the unlearned, for they cannot grasp it.

Now, a certain order is to be found in those things that are apprehended universally. For that which, before aught else, falls under apprehension, is "being," the notion of which is included in all things whatsoever a man apprehends. Wherefore the first indemonstrable principle is that the same thing cannot be affirmed and denied at the same time, which is based on the nature of "being" and "not-being," and on this principle all others are based, as it is stated in *Metaphysics* IV. Now, as "being" is the first thing that falls under the apprehension simply, so "good" is the first thing that falls under the apprehension of the practical reason, which is directed to action, since every agent acts for an end under the aspect of good. Consequently, the first principle in the practical reason is one founded on the notion of good, viz., that good is that which all things seek after. Hence this is the first precept of law, that good is to be done and pursued, and evil is to be avoided. All other precepts of the natural law are based upon this, so that whatever the practical reason naturally apprehends as man's good (or evil) belongs to the precepts of the natural law as something to be done or avoided.

Since, however, good has the nature of an end, and evil the nature of a contrary, hence it is that all those things to which man has a natural inclination are naturally apprehended by reason as being good and, consequently, as objects of pursuit, and their contraries as evil and objects of avoidance. Wherefore the order of the precepts of the natural law is according to the order of natural inclinations. Because in man there is first of all an inclination to good in accordance with the nature which he has in common with all substances, inasmuch as every substance seeks the preservation of its own being according to its nature, and by reason of this inclination, whatever is a means of preserving human life and of warding off its obstacles to the natural law. Secondly, there is in man an inclination to things that pertain to him more specially according to that nature which he has in common with other animals, and in virtue of this inclination, those things are said to belong to the natural law "which nature has taught to all animals," such as sexual intercourse, education of offspring, and so forth. Thirdly, there is in man an inclination to good according to the nature of his reason, which nature is proper to him; thus man has a natural inclination to know the truth about God and to live in society, and in this respect, whatever pertains to this inclination belongs to the natural law, for instance, to shun ignorance, to avoid offending those among whom one has to live, and other such things regarding the above inclination.

*Reply Obj. 1.* All these precepts of the law of nature have the character of one natural law inasmuch as they flow from one first precept.

*Reply Obj. 2.* All the inclinations of any parts whatsoever of human nature, e.g., of the concupiscible and irascible parts, insofar as they are ruled by reason, belong to the natural law and are reduced to one first precept, as stated above, so that the precepts of the natural law are many in themselves but are based on one common foundation.

*Reply Obj. 3.* Although reason is one in itself, yet it directs all things regarding man, so that whatever can be ruled by reason is contained under the law of reason.

### Third Article: Are All Acts of Virtue Prescribed by the Natural Law?

*We proceed thus to the Third Article:*

*Obj. 1.* It would seem that not all acts of virtue are prescribed by the natural law because, as stated above, it is essential to a law that it be ordained to the common good. But some acts of virtue are ordained to the private good of the individual, as is evident especially in regard to acts of temperance. Therefore, not all acts of virtue are the subject of natural law.

*Obj. 2.* Further, every sin is opposed to some virtuous act. If, therefore, all acts of virtue are prescribed by the natural law, it seems to follow that all sins are against nature, whereas this applies to certain special sins.

*Obj. 3.* Further, those things which are according to nature are common to all. But acts of virtue are not common to all, since a thing is virtuous in one and vicious in another. Therefore, not all acts of virtue are prescribed by the natural law.

*On the contrary,* Damascene says that "virtues are natural." Therefore, virtuous acts also are a subject of the natural law.

*I answer that* We may speak of virtuous acts in two ways: first, under the aspect of virtuous; secondly, as such and such acts considered in their proper species. If, then, we speak of acts of virtue considered as virtuous, thus all virtuous acts belong to the natural law. For it has been stated that to the natural law belongs everything to which a man is inclined according to his nature. Now each thing is inclined naturally to an operation that is suitable to it according to its form; thus fire is inclined to give heat. Wherefore, since the rational soul is the proper form of man, there is in every man a natural inclination to act according to reason, and this is to act according to virtue. Consequently, considered thus, all acts of virtue are prescribed by the natural law, since each one's reason naturally dictates to him to act virtuously. But if we speak of virtuous acts considered in themselves, i.e., in their proper species, thus not all virtuous acts are prescribed by the natural law; the many things are done virtuously to which nature does not incline at first, but which, through the inquiry of reason, have been found by men to be conducive to well-living.

*Reply Obj. 1.* Temperance is about the natural concupiscences of food, drink, and sexual matters, which are indeed ordained to the natural common good, just as other matters of law are ordained to the moral common good.

*Reply Obj. 2.* By human nature we may mean either that which is proper to man—and in this sense all sins, as being against reason, are also against nature, as Damascene states—or we may mean that nature which is common to man and other animals, and in this sense certain special sins are said to be against nature; thus, contrary to heterosexual intercourse, which is natural to all animals, is male homosexual union, which has received the special name of the unnatural vice.

*Reply Obj. 3.* This argument considers acts in themselves. For it is owing to the various conditions of men that certain acts are virtuous for some as being proportionate and becoming to them, while they are vicious for others as being out of proportion to them.

### Fourth Article: Is the Natural Law the Same in All Men?

*We proceed thus to the Fourth Article:*

*Obj. 1.* It would seem that the natural law is not the same in all. For it is stated in the *Decretum* that "the natural law is that which is contained in the Law and the Gospel." But this is not common to all men because, as it is written, "all do not obey the gospel." Therefore, the natural law is not the same in all men.

*Obj. 2.* Further, "Things which are according to the law are said to be just," as stated in *Ethics* V. But it is stated in the same book that nothing is so universally just as not to be subject to change in regard to some men. Therefore, even the natural law is not the same in all men.

*Obj. 3.* Further, as stated above, to the natural law belongs everything to which a man is inclined according to his nature. Now, different men are naturally inclined to different things, some to the desire of pleasures, others to the desire of honors, and other men to other things. Therefore, there is not one natural law for all.

*On the contrary,* Isidore says, "The natural law is common to all nations."

*I answer that,* As stated above, to the natural law belong those things to which a man is inclined naturally, and among these, it is proper to man to be inclined to act according to reason. Now the process of reason is from the common to the proper, as stated in *Phys.* I. The speculative reason, however, is differently situated in this matter from the practical reason. For, since the speculative reason is concerned chiefly with necessary things, which cannot be otherwise than they are, its proper conclusions, like the universal principles, contain the truth without fail. The practical reason, on the other hand, is concerned with contingent matters, about which human actions are concerned, and consequently, although there is necessity in the general principles, the more we descend to matters of detail, the more frequently we encounter deviations. Accordingly, then, in speculative matters, truth is the same for all men both as to principles and as to conclusions, although the truth is not known to all as regards the conclusions but only as regards the principles which are called common notions. But in matters of action, truth or practical rectitude is not the same for all as to matters of detail but only as to the general principles, and where there is the same rectitude in matters of detail, it is not equally known to all.

It is, therefore, evident that, as regards the general principles, whether of speculative or practical reason, truth or rectitude is the same for all and is equally known by all. As to the proper conclusions of the speculative reason, the truth is the same for all but is not equally known to all; thus it is true for all that the three angles of a triangle are together equal to two right angles, although it is not known to all. But as to the proper conclusions of the practical reason, neither is the truth or rectitude the same for all, nor, where it is the same, is it equally known by all. Thus it is right and true for all to act according to reason, and from this principle, it follows as a proper conclusion that goods entrusted to another should be restored to their owner. Now this is true for the majority of cases, but it may happen in a particular case that it would be injurious, and therefore unreasonable, to restore goods held in trust, for instance, if they are claimed for the purpose of fighting against one's country. And this principle will be found to fail the more according as we descend further into detail, e.g., if one were to say that goods held in trust should be restored with such and such a guarantee or in such and such a way, because the greater the number of conditions added, the greater the number of ways in which the principle may fail, so that it be not right to restore or not to restore.

Consequently, we must say that the natural law as to general principles is the same for all both as to rectitude and as to knowledge. But as to certain matters of detail, which are conclusions, as it were, of those general principles, it is the same for all in the majority of cases both as to rectitude and as to knowledge, and yet, in some few cases, it may fail both as to rectitude by reason of certain obstacles (just as natures subject to generation and corruption fail in some few cases on account of some obstacle) and as to knowledge, since, in some, the reason is perverted by passion or evil habit or an evil disposition of nature; thus, formerly, theft, although it is expressly contrary to the natural law, was not considered wrong among the Germans, as Julius Caesar relates.

*Reply Obj. 1.* The meaning of the sentence quoted is not that whatever is contained in the Law and the Gospel belongs to the natural law, since they contain many things that are above nature, but that whatever belongs to the natural law is fully contained in them. Wherefore Gratian, after saying that "the natural law is what is contained in the Law and the Gospel," adds at once, by way of example, "by which everyone is commanded to do to others as he would be done by."

*Reply Obj. 2.* The saying of the Philosopher is to be understood of things that are naturally just, not as general principles but as conclusions drawn from them, having rectitude in the majority of cases but failing in a few.

*Reply Obj. 3.* As, in man, reason rules and commands the other powers, so all the natural inclinations belonging to the other powers must needs be directed according to reason. Wherefore it is universally right for all men that all their inclinations should be directed according to reason.

### Fifth Article: Can the Natural Law Be Changed?

*We proceed thus to the Fifth Article:*

*Obj. 1.* It would seem that the natural law can be changed because, on Sir. 17:9, "He gave them instructions, and the law of life," a gloss says: "He wished the law of the letter to be written in order to correct the law of nature." But that which is corrected is changed. Therefore, the natural law can be changed.

*Obj. 2.* Further, the slaying of the innocent, adultery, and theft are against the natural law. But we find these things changed by God, as when God commanded Abraham to slay his innocent son, and when He ordered the Jews to borrow and purloin the

vessels of the Egyptians, and when He commanded Hosea to take to himself "a wife of fornications." Therefore, the natural law can be changed.

*Obj. 3.* Further, Isidore says that "the possession of all things in common and universal freedom are matters of natural law." But these things are seen to be changed by human laws. Therefore, it seems that the natural law is subject to change.

*On the contrary,* It is said in the *Decretum:* "The natural law dates from the creation of the rational creature. It does not vary according to time but remains unchangeable."

*I answer that* A change in the natural law may be understood in two ways. First, by way of addition. In this sense, nothing hinders the natural law from being changed, since many things, for the benefit of human life, have been added over and above the natural law both by the divine law and by human laws.

Secondly, a change in the natural law may be understood by way of subtraction, so that what previously was according to the natural law ceases to be so. In this sense, the natural law is altogether unchangeable in its first principles, but in its secondary principles, which, as we have said, are like certain proper conclusions closely related to the first principles, the natural law is not changed so that what it prescribes be not right in most cases. But it may be changed in some particular cases of rare occurrence through some special causes hindering the observance of such precepts, as stated above.

*Reply Obj. 1.* The written law is said to be given for the correction of the natural law, either because it supplies what was wanting to the natural law or because the natural law was perverted in the hearts of some men as to certain matters, so that they esteemed those things good which are naturally evil, which perversion stood in need of correction.

*Reply Obj. 2.* All men alike, both guilty and innocent, die the death of nature, which death of nature is inflicted by the power of God on account of original sin, according to 1 Kings: "The Lord kills and makes alive." Consequently, by the command of God, death can be inflicted on any man, guilty or innocent, without any injustice whatever. In like manner, adultery is intercourse with another's wife, who is allotted to him by the law handed down by God. Consequently, intercourse with any woman, by the command of God, is neither adultery nor fornication. The same applies to theft, which is the taking of another's property. For whatever is taken by the command of God, to Whom all things belong, is not taken against the will of its owner, whereas it is in this that theft consists. Nor is it only in human things that whatever is commanded by God is right but also in natural things—whatever is done by God is, in some way, natural, as stated in the First Part.

*Reply Obj. 3.* A thing is said to belong to the natural law in two ways. First, because nature inclines thereto, e.g., that one should not do harm to another. Secondly, because nature did not bring in the contrary; thus we might say that for man to be naked is of the natural law because nature did not give him clothes, but art invented them. In this sense, "the possession of all things in common and universal freedom" are said to be of the natural law because, to wit, the distinction of possessions and slavery were not brought in by nature but devised by human reason for the benefit of human life. Accordingly, the law of nature was not changed in this respect except by addition.

### Sixth Article: Can the Law of Nature Be Abolished from the Heart of Man?

*We proceed thus to the Sixth Article:*

*Obj. 1.* It would seem that the natural law can be abolished from the heart of man because, on Rom. 2:14, "When the Gentiles who have not the law," etc., a gloss says that "the law of righteousness, which sin had blotted out, is graven on the heart of man when he is restored by grace." But the law of righteousness is the law of nature. Therefore, the law of nature can be blotted out.

*Obj. 2.* Further, the law of grace is more efficacious than the law of nature. But the law of grace is blotted out by sin. Much more, therefore, can the law of nature be blotted out.

*Obj. 3.* Further, that which is established by law is made just. But many things are legally established which are contrary to the law of nature. Therefore, the law of nature can be abolished from the heart of man.

*On the contrary,* Augustine says, "Thy law is written in the hearts of men, which iniquity itself effaces not." But the law which is written in men's hearts is the natural law. Therefore, the natural law cannot be blotted out.

*I answer that,* As stated above, there belong to the natural law, first, certain most general precepts that are known to all; and secondly, certain secondary and more detailed precepts which are, as it were, conclusions following closely from first principles. As to those general principles, the natural law, in the abstract, can nowise be blotted out from men's hearts. But it is blotted out in the case of particular action insofar as reason is hindered from applying the general principles to a particular point of practice on account of concupiscence or some other passion, as stated above. But as to the other, i.e., the secondary precepts, the natural law can be blotted out from the human heart either by evil persuasions, just as in speculative matters errors occur in respect of necessary conclusions, or by vicious customs and corrupt habits, as among some men theft and even unnatural vices, as the Apostle states, were not esteemed sinful.

*Reply Obj. 1.* Sin blots out the law of nature in particular cases, not universally, except perchance in regard to the secondary precepts of the natural law, in the way stated above.

*Reply Obj. 2.* Although grace is more efficacious than nature, yet nature is more essential to man and therefore more enduring.

*Reply Obj. 3.* The argument is true of the secondary precepts of the natural law, against which some legislators have framed certain enactments which are unjust.

## QUESTION 95: OF HUMAN LAW

### [In Four Articles]

We must now consider human law, and (1) this law considered in itself; (2) its power; (3) its mutability.

Under the first head, there are four points of inquiry: (1) its utility; (2) its origin; (3) its quality; (4) its divisions.

### First Article: Was It Useful for Laws to Be Framed by Men?

*We proceed thus to the First Article:*

*Obj. 1.* It would seem that it was not useful for laws to be framed by men because the purpose of every law is that man be made good thereby, as stated above. But men are more to be induced to be good willingly by means of admonitions than against their will by means of laws. Therefore, there was no need to frame laws.

*Obj. 2.* Further, as the Philosopher says, "men have recourse to a judge as to justice in the flesh." But justice in the flesh is better than inanimate justice, which is contained in laws. Therefore, it would have been better for the execution of justice to be entrusted to the decision of judges than to frame laws in addition.

*Obj. 3.* Further, every law is framed for the direction of human actions, as is evident from what has been stated above. But since human actions are about singulars, which are infinite in number, matters pertaining to the direction of human actions cannot be taken into sufficient consideration except by a wise man who looks into each one of them. Therefore, it would have been better for human acts to be directed by the judgment of wise men than by the framing of laws. Therefore, there was no need of human laws.

*On the contrary,* Isidore says, "Laws were made that, in fear thereof, human audacity might be held in check, that innocence might be safeguarded in the midst of wickedness, and that the dread of punishment might prevent the wicked from doing harm." But these things are most necessary to mankind. Therefore, it was necessary that human laws should be made.

*I answer that,* As stated above, man has a natural aptitude for virtue, but the perfection of virtue must be acquired by man by means of some kind of training. Thus we observe that man is helped by industry in his necessities, for instance, in food and clothing. Certain beginnings of these he has from nature, viz.,

his reason and his hands, but he has not the full complement, as other animals have to whom nature has given sufficiency of clothing and food. Now, it is difficult to see how man could suffice for himself in the matter of this training, since the perfection of virtue consists chiefly in withdrawing man from undue pleasures, to which, above all, man is inclined, and especially the young, who are more capable of being trained. Consequently, a man needs to receive this training from another whereby to arrive at the perfection of virtue. And as to those young people who are inclined to acts of virtue by their good natural disposition or by custom, or rather by the gift of God, paternal training suffices, which is by admonitions. But since some are found to be depraved and prone to vice and not easily amenable to words, it was necessary for such to be restrained from evil by force and fear in order that they might at least desist from evil-doing and leave others in peace, and that they themselves, by being habituated in this way, might be brought to do willingly what hitherto they did from fear and thus become virtuous. Now this kind of training which compels through fear of punishment is the discipline of laws. Therefore, in order that man might have peace and virtue, it was necessary for laws to be framed, for, as the Philosopher says, "a man is the most noble of animals if he be perfect in virtue, so is he the lowest of all if he be severed from law and justice." Because man can use his reason to devise means of satisfying his lusts and evil passions, which other animals are unable to do.

*Reply Obj. 1.* Men who are well disposed are led willingly to virtue by being admonished better than by coercion, but men who are evilly disposed are not led to virtue unless they are compelled.

*Reply Obj. 2.* As the Philosopher says, "It is better that all things be regulated by law than left to be decided by judges," and this for three reasons. First, because it is easier to find a few wise men competent to frame right laws than to find the many who would be necessary to judge aright of each single case. Secondly, because those who make laws consider long beforehand what laws to make, whereas judgment on each single case has to be pronounced as soon as it arises, and it is easier for man to see what is right by taking many instances into consideration than by considering one solitary fact. Thirdly, because lawgivers judge in the abstract and of future events, whereas those who sit in judgment judge of things present, toward which they are affected by love, hatred, or some kind of cupidity; wherefore their judgment is perverted.

Since, then, the embodied justice of the judge is not found in every man, and since it can be deflected, therefore it was necessary, whenever possible, for the law to determine how to judge, and for very few matters to be left to the decision of men.

*Reply Obj. 3.* Certain individual facts which cannot be covered by the law "have necessarily to be committed to judges," as the Philosopher says in the same passage, for instance, "concerning something that has happened or not happened" and the like.

## Second Article: Is Every Human Law Derived from the Natural Law?

*We proceed thus to the Second Article:*

*Obj. 1.* It would seem that not every human law is derived from the natural law. For the Philosopher says that "the legal just is that which originally was a matter of indifference." But those things which arise from the natural law are not matters of indifference. Therefore, the enactments of human laws are not all derived from the natural law.

*Obj. 2.* Further, positive law is contrasted with natural law, as stated by Isidore and the Philosopher. But those things which flow as conclusions from the general principles of the natural law belong to the natural law, as stated above. Therefore, that which is established by human law does not belong to the natural law.

*Obj. 3.* Further, the law of nature is the same for all, since the Philosopher says that "the natural just is that which is equally valid everywhere." If, therefore, human laws were derived from the natural law, it would follow that they too are the same for all, which is clearly false.

*Obj. 4.* Further, it is possible to give a reason for things which are derived from the natural law. But "it is not possible to give the reason for all the legal enactments of the lawgivers," as the Jurist says.

Therefore, not all human laws are derived from the natural law.

*On the contrary,* Tully says, "Things which emanated from nature and were approved by custom were sanctioned by fear and reverence for the laws."

*I answer that,* As Augustine says, "that which is not just seems to be no law at all"; wherefore the force of a law depends on the extent of its justice. Now, in human affairs a thing is said to be just from being right according to the rule of reason. But the first rule of reason is the law of nature, as is clear from what has been stated above. Consequently, every human law has just so much of the nature of law as it is derived from the law of nature. But if, in any point, it deflects from the law of nature, it is no longer a law but a perversion of law.

But it must be noted that something may be derived from the natural law in two ways: first, as a conclusion from premises; secondly, by way of determination of certain generalities. The first way is like to that by which, in the sciences, demonstrated conclusions are drawn from the principles, while the second mode is likened to that whereby, in the arts, general forms are particularized as to details; thus the craftsman needs to determine the general form of a house to some particular shape. Some things are, therefore, derived from the general principles of the natural law by way of conclusion, e.g., that "one must not kill" may be derived as a conclusion from the principle that "one should do harm to no man"; while some are derived therefrom by way of determination, e.g., the law of nature has it that the evildoer should be punished; but that he be punished in this or that way is not directly by natural law but is a certain determination of it.

Accordingly, both modes of derivation are found in the human law. But those things which are derived in the first way are contained in human law, not as emanating therefrom exclusively but having some force from the natural law also. But those things which are derived in the second way have no other force than that of human law.

*Reply Obj. 1.* The Philosopher is speaking of those enactments which are by way of determination or specification of the precepts of the natural law.

*Reply Obj. 2.* This argument avails for those things that are derived from the natural law by way of conclusions.

*Reply Obj. 3.* The general principles of the natural law cannot be applied to all men in the same way on account of the great variety of human affairs, and hence arises the diversity of positive laws among various people.

*Reply Obj. 4.* These words of the Jurist are to be understood as referring to decisions of rulers in determining particular points of the natural law, on which determinations the judgment of expert and prudent men is based as on its principle, insofar, to wit, as they see at once what is the best thing to decide.

Hence the Philosopher says that, in such matters, "we ought to pay as much attention to the undemonstrated sayings and opinions of persons who surpass us in experience, age, and prudence as to their demonstrations."

## QUESTION 96: OF THE POWER OF HUMAN LAW

### *[In Six Articles]*

We must now consider the power of human law. Under this head, there are six points of inquiry: (1) Whether human law should be framed for the community? (2) Whether human law should repress all vices? (3) Whether human law is competent to direct all acts of virtue? (4) Whether it binds man in conscience? (5) Whether all men are subject to human law? (6) Whether those who are under the law may act beside the letter of the law?

### *First Article: Should Human Law Be Framed for the Community Rather Than for the Individual?*

*We proceed thus to the First Article:*

*Obj. 1.* It would seem that human law should be framed, not for the community, but rather for the individual. For the Philosopher says that "the legal just . . . includes all particular acts of legislation . . .

and all those matters which are the subject of decrees," which are also individual matters, since decrees are framed about individual actions. Therefore, law is framed not only for the community but also for the individual.

*Obj. 2.* Further, law is the director of human acts, as stated above. But human acts are about individual matters. Therefore, human laws should be framed, not for the community, but rather for the individual.

*Obj. 3.* Further, law is a rule and measure of human acts, as stated above. But a measure should be most certain, as stated in *Metaphysics* X. Since, therefore, in human acts no general proposition can be so certain as not to fail in some individual cases, it seems that laws should be framed not in general but for individual cases.

*On the contrary,* The Jurist says that "laws should be made to suit the majority of instances, and they are not framed according to what may possibly happen in an individual case."

*I answer that* Whatever is for an end should be proportionate to that end. Now the end of law is the common good, because, as Isidore says, "Law should be framed, not for any private benefit, but for the common good of all the citizens." Hence human laws should be proportionate to the common good. Now the common good comprises many things. Wherefore law should take account of many things, as to persons, as to occupations, and as to times, because the political community is composed of many citizens and its good is procured by many actions; nor is it established to endure for only a short time but to last for all time, by the citizens succeeding one another, as Augustine says.

*Reply Obj. 1.* The Philosopher divides the "legal just," i.e., positive law, into three parts. For some things are laid down simply in a general way, and these are the general laws. Of these, he says that "the legal is that which originally was a matter of indifference, but which, when enacted is so no longer," as the fixing of the ransom of a captive. Some things affect the community in one respect and individuals in another. These are called "privileges," i.e., "private laws," as it were, because they regard private persons, although their power extends to many matters, and in regard to these, he adds: "and further all prescriptions in particular cases." Other matters are legal, not through being laws but through being applications of general laws to particular cases; such are decrees which have the force of law, and in regard to these, he adds: "all matters subject to decrees."

*Reply Obj. 2.* A principle of direction should be applicable to many; wherefore the Philosopher says that all things belonging to one genus are measured by one which is the first in that genus. For if there were as many rules or measures as there are things measured or ruled, they would cease to be of use, since their use consists in being applicable to many things. Hence law would be of no use if it did not extend further than to one single act because the decrees of prudent men are made for the purpose of directing individual actions, whereas law is a general precept, as stated above.

*Reply Obj. 3.* "We must not seek the same degree of certainty in all things." Consequently, in contingent matters such as natural and human things, it is enough for a thing to be certain as being true in the greater number of instances, though at times and less frequently it fail.

### Second Article: Does It Belong to Human Law to Repress All Vices?

*We proceed thus to the Second Article:*

*Obj. 1.* It would seem that it belongs to human law to repress all vices. For Isidore says that "laws were made in order that, in fear thereof, man's audacity might be held in check." But it would not be held in check sufficiently unless all evils were repressed by law. Therefore, human law should repress all evils.

*Obj. 2.* Further, the intention of the lawgiver is to make the citizens virtuous. But a man cannot be virtuous unless he forbear from all kinds of vice. Therefore, it belongs to human law to repress all vices.

*Obj. 3.* Further, human law is derived from the natural law, as stated above. But all vices are contrary to the law of nature. Therefore, human law should repress all vices.

*On the contrary,* We read in *De libero arbitrio:* "It seems to me that the law which is written for the gov-

erning of the people rightly permits these things, and that divine providence punishes them." But divine providence punishes nothing but vices. Therefore, human law rightly allows some vices by not repressing them.

*I answer that,* As stated above, law is imposed as a certain rule or measure of human actions. Now, a measure should be homogeneous with that which it measures, as stated in *Metaphysics* X, since different things are measured by different measures. Wherefore laws imposed on men should also be in keeping with their condition, for, as Isidore says, law should be "possible both according to nature and according to the customs of the country." Now, possibility or faculty of action is due to an interior habit or disposition, since the same thing is not possible to one who has not a virtuous habit as is possible to one who has. Thus, the same is not possible to a child as to a full-grown man, for which reason, the law for children is not the same as for adults, since many things are permitted to children which in an adult are punished by law or at any rate are open to blame. In like manner, many things are permissible to men not perfect in virtue which would be intolerable in a virtuous man.

Now, human law is framed for a number of human beings, the majority of whom are not perfect in virtue. Wherefore, human laws do not forbid all vices from which the virtuous abstain but only the more grievous vices from which it is possible for the majority to abstain and chiefly those that are to the hurt of others, without the prohibition of which human society could not be maintained; thus human law prohibits murder, theft, and suchlike.

*Reply Obj. 1.* Audacity seems to refer to the assailing of others. Consequently, it belongs to those sins chiefly whereby one's neighbor is injured, and these sins are forbidden by human law, as stated.

*Reply Obj. 2.* The purpose of human law is to lead men to virtue, not suddenly but gradually. Wherefore it does not lay upon the multitude of imperfect men the burdens of those who are already virtuous, viz., that they should abstain from all evil. Otherwise, these imperfect ones, being unable to bear such precepts, would break out into yet greater evils; thus it is written: "He that violently blows his nose, brings out blood," and that if "new wine," i.e., precepts of a perfect life, is "put into old bottles," i.e., into imperfect men, "the bottles break, and the wine runs out," i.e., the precepts are despised, and those men, from contempt, break out into evils worse still.

*Reply Obj. 3.* The natural law is a participation in us of the eternal law, while human law falls short of the eternal law. Now Augustine says: "The law which is framed for the government of political communities allows and leaves unpunished many things that are punished by divine providence. Nor, if this law does not attempt to do everything, is this a reason why it should be blamed for what it does." Wherefore, too, human law does not prohibit everything that is forbidden by the natural law.

### Third Article: Does Human Law Prescribe Acts of All the Virtues?

*We proceed thus to the Third Article:*

*Obj. 1.* It would seem that human law does not prescribe acts of all the virtues. For vicious acts are contrary to acts of virtue. But human law does not prohibit all vices, as stated above. Therefore, neither does it prescribe all acts of virtue.

*Obj. 2.* Further, a virtuous act proceeds from a virtue. But virtue is the end of law, so that whatever is from a virtue cannot come under a precept of law. Therefore, human law does not prescribe all acts of virtue.

*Obj. 3.* Further, law is ordained to the common good, as stated above. But some acts of virtue are ordained not to the common good but to private good. Therefore, the law does not prescribe all acts of virtue.

*On the contrary,* The Philosopher says that the law "prescribes the performance of the acts of a brave man . . . and the acts of the temperate man . . . and the acts of the meek man and in like manner as regards the other virtues and vices prescribing the former, forbidding the latter."

*I answer that* The species of virtues are distinguished by their objects, as explained above. Now all the objects of virtues can be referred either to the private good of an individual or to the common good

of the multitude; thus matters of fortitude may be achieved either for the safety of the political community or for upholding the rights of a friend, and in like manner with the other virtues. But law, as stated above, is ordained to the common good. Wherefore, there is no virtue whose acts cannot be prescribed by the law. Nevertheless, human law does not prescribe concerning all the acts of every virtue but only in regard to those that are ordained to the common good—either immediately, as when certain things are done directly for the common good, or mediately, as when a lawgiver prescribes certain things pertaining to good training whereby the citizens are disciplined in the upholding of the common good of justice and peace.

*Reply Obj. 1.* Human law does not forbid all vicious acts by the obligation of a precept, as neither does it prescribe all acts of virtue. But it forbids certain acts of each vice, just as it prescribes some acts of each virtue.

*Reply Obj. 2.* An act is said to be an act of virtue in two ways. First, from the fact that a man does something virtuous; thus the act of justice is to do what is right, and an act of fortitude is to do brave things—and in this way law prescribes certain acts of virtue. Secondly, an act of virtue is when a man does a virtuous thing in a way in which a virtuous man does it. Such an act always proceeds from virtue, and it does not come under a precept of law but is the end at which every lawgiver aims.

*Reply Obj. 3.* There is no virtue whose act is not ordainable to the common good, as stated above, either mediately or immediately.

### Fourth Article: Does Human Law Bind a Man in Conscience?

*We proceed thus to the Fourth Article:*

*Obj. 1.* It would seem that human law does not bind a man in conscience. For an inferior power has no jurisdiction in a court of higher power. But the power of man which frames human law is beneath the divine power. Therefore, human law cannot impose its precept in a divine court, such as is the court of conscience.

*Obj. 2.* Further, the judgment of conscience depends chiefly on the commandments of God. But sometimes God's commandments are made void by human laws, according to Mt. 15:6: "You have made void the commandment of God for your tradition." Therefore, human law does not bind a man in conscience.

*Obj. 3.* Further, human laws often bring loss of character and injury on man, according to Is. 10:1: "Woe to them that make wicked laws, and when they write, write injustice; to oppress the poor in judgment and do violence to the cause of the humble of My people." But it is lawful for anyone to avoid oppression and violence. Therefore, human laws do not bind man in conscience.

*On the contrary,* It is written: "This is thanksworthy, if for conscience . . . a man endure sorrows, suffering wrongfully."

*I answer that* Laws framed by man are either just or unjust. If they be just, they have the power of binding in conscience from the eternal law whence they are derived, according to Pr. 8:15: "By Me kings reign, and lawgivers decree just things." Now laws are said to be just from the end, when, to wit, they are ordained to the common good, and from their author, that is to say, when the law that is made does not exceed the power of the lawgiver, and from their form, when, to wit, burdens are laid on the subjects according to an equality of proportion and with a view to the common good. For, since one man is a part of the community, each man, in all that he is and has, belongs to the community, just as a part, in all that it is, belongs to the whole; wherefore nature inflicts a loss on the part in order to save the whole, so that, on this account, such laws as these which impose proportionate burdens are just and binding in conscience and are legal laws.

On the other hand, laws may be unjust in two ways: first, by being contrary to human good, through being opposed to the things mentioned above—either in respect of the end, as when an authority imposes on his subjects burdensome laws conducive, not to the common good, but rather to his own cupidity or vainglory; or in respect of the author, as when a man makes a law that goes beyond the power committed to him; or in respect of the

form, as when burdens are imposed unequally on the community, although with a view to the common good. The like are acts of violence rather than laws, because, as Augustine says, "A law that is not just, seems to be no law at all." Wherefore such laws do not bind in conscience, except perhaps in order to avoid scandal or disturbance, for which cause a man should even yield his right, according to Mt. 5:40, 41: "If a man . . . take away your coat, let go your cloak also unto him, and whosoever will force you one mile, go with him other two."

Secondly, laws may be unjust through being opposed to the divine good; such are the laws of tyrants inducing to idolatry or to anything else contrary to the divine law, and laws of this kind must nowise be observed because, as stated in Acts 5:29, "we ought to obey God rather than men."

*Reply Obj. 1.* As the Apostle says, all human power is from God . . . ; "therefore, he that resists the power" in matters that are within its scope "resists the ordinance of God," so that he becomes guilty according to his conscience.

*Reply Obj. 2.* This argument is true of laws that are contrary to the commandments of God, which is beyond the scope of (human) power. Wherefore in such matters human law should not be obeyed.

*Reply Obj. 3.* This argument is true of a law that inflicts unjust hurt on its subjects. The power that man holds from God does not extend to this; wherefore neither in such matters is man bound to obey the law, provided he avoid giving scandal or inflicting a more grievous hurt.

### Fifth Article: Are All Subject to the Law?

*We proceed thus to the Fifth Article:*

*Obj. 1.* It would seem that not all are subject to the law. For those alone are subject to a law for whom a law is made. But the Apostle says: "The law is not made for the just man." Therefore, the just are not subject to the law.

*Obj. 2.* Further, Pope Urban says: "He that is guided by a private law need not for any reason be bound by the public law." Now all spiritual men are led by the private law of the Holy Spirit, for they are the sons of God, of whom it is said: "Whosoever are led by the Spirit of God, they are the sons of God." Therefore, not all men are subject to human law.

*Obj. 3.* Further, the Jurist says that "the ruler is exempt from the laws." But he that is exempt from the law is not bound thereby. Therefore, not all are subject to the law.

*On the contrary,* The Apostle says, "Let every soul be subject to the higher powers." But subjection to a power seems to imply subjection to the laws framed by that power. Therefore, all men should be subject to human law.

*I answer that,* As stated above, the notion of law contains two things: first, that it is a rule of human acts; secondly, that it has coercive power. Wherefore a man may be subject to law in two ways. First, as the regulated is subject to the regulator, and, in this way, whoever is subject to a power is subject to the law framed by that power. But it may happen in two ways that one is not subject to a power. In one way, by being altogether free from its authority; hence the subjects of one city of kingdom are not bound by the laws of the sovereign of another city or kingdom, since they are not subject to his authority. In another way, by being under a yet higher law; thus the subject of a proconsul should be ruled by his command but not in those matters in which the subject receives his orders from the emperor, for in these matters he is not bound by the mandate of the lower authority since he is directed by that of a higher. In this way, one who is simply subject to a law may not be subject thereto in certain matters in respect of which he is ruled by a higher law.

Secondly, a man is said to be subject to a law as the coerced is subject to the coercer. In this way, the virtuous and righteous are not subject to the law but only the wicked. Because coercion and violence are contrary to the will, but the will of the good is in harmony with the law, whereas the will of the wicked is discordant from it. Wherefore, in this sense, the good are not subject to the law but only the wicked.

*Reply Obj. 1.* This argument is true of subjection by way of coercion, for, in this way, "the law is not made for the just men," because "they are a law to themselves" since they "show the work of the law written in their hearts," as the Apostle says. Conse-

quently, the law does not enforce itself upon them as it does on the wicked.

*Reply Obj. 2.* The law of the Holy Spirit is above all law framed by man, and, therefore, spiritual men, insofar as they are led by the law of the Holy Spirit, are not subject to the law in those matters that are inconsistent with the guidance of the Holy Spirit. Nevertheless, the very fact that spiritual men are subject to law is due to the leading of the Holy Spirit, according to 1 Pet.: "Be you subject . . . to every human creature for God's sake."

*Reply Obj. 3.* The ruler is said to be "exempt from the law" as to its coercive power, since, properly speaking, no man is coerced by himself, and law has no coercive power save from the power of the ruler. Thus, then, is the ruler said to be exempt from the law because none is competent to pass sentence on him if he acts against the law. Wherefore on Ps. 50:6: "To You only have I sinned," a gloss says that "there is no man who can judge the deeds of a king." But as to the directive force of law, the ruler is subject to the law by his own will, according to the statement that "whatever law a man makes for another, he should keep himself." And a wise authority says: "Obey the law that you make yourself." Moreover, the Lord reproaches those who "say and do not," and who "bind heavy burdens and lay them on men's shoulders, but with a finger of their own, they will not move them." Hence, in the judgment of God, the ruler is not exempt from the law as to its directive force, but he should fulfill it of his own free will and not of constraint. Again, the ruler is above the law insofar as, when it is expedient, he can change the law and dispense from it according to time and place.

### Sixth Article: May He Who Is Under a Law Act Beside the Letter of the Law?

*We proceed thus to the Sixth Article:*

*Obj. 1.* It seems that he who is subject to a law may not act beside the letter of the law. For Augustine says: "Although men judge about temporal laws when they make them, yet, when once they are made and confirmed, they must pass judgment, not on them but according to them." But if anyone disregard the letter of the law, saying that he observes the intention of the lawgiver, he seems to pass judgment on the law. Therefore, it is not right for one who is under a law to disregard the letter of the law in order to observe the intention of the lawgiver.

*Obj. 2.* Further, he alone is competent to interpret the law who can make the law. But those who are subject to the law cannot make the law. Therefore, they have no right to interpret the intention of the lawgiver but should always act according to the letter of the law.

*Obj. 3.* Further, every wise man knows how to explain his intention by words. But those who framed the laws should be reckoned wise, for Wisdom says: "By Me kings reign, and lawgivers decree just things." Therefore, we should not judge of the intention of the lawgiver otherwise than by the words of the law.

*On the contrary,* Hilary says, "The meaning of what is said is according to the motive for saying it, because things are not subject to speech, but speech to things." Therefore, we should take more account of the motive of the lawgiver than to his very words.

*I answer that,* As stated above, every law is directed to the common weal of men and derives the force and nature of law accordingly, but it has no power to oblige morally if it fails to be so directed. Hence the Jurist says: "By no reason of law or favor of equity is it allowable for us to interpret harshly and render burdensome those useful measures which have been enacted for the welfare of man." Now, it happens often that the observance of some point of law conduces to the common weal in the majority of instances, and yet in some cases is very hurtful. Since, then, the lawgiver cannot have in view every single case, he shapes the law according to what happens most frequently, by directing his attention to the common good. Wherefore, if a case arise wherein the observance of that law would be hurtful to the general welfare, it should not be observed. For instance, suppose that, in a besieged city, it be an established law that the gates of the city are to be kept closed, this is good for public welfare as a general rule, but if it were to happen that the enemy are in pursuit of certain citizens who are defenders of the city, it would be a great loss to the city if the gates

were not opened to them, and so, in that case, the gates ought to be opened, contrary to the letter of the law, in order to maintain the common weal, which the lawgiver had in view.

Nevertheless, it must be noted that if the observance of the law according to the letter does not involve any sudden risk needing instant remedy, it is not competent for everyone to expound what is useful and what is not useful to the political community; those alone can do this who are in authority, and who, on account of suchlike cases, have the power to dispense from the laws. If, however, the peril be so sudden as not to allow of the delay involved by referring the matter to authority, the mere necessity brings with it a dispensation, since necessity knows no law.

*Reply Obj. 1.* He who in a case of necessity acts beside the letter of the law does not judge of the law but of a particular case in which he sees that the letter of the law is not to be observed.

*Reply Obj. 2.* He who follows the intention of the lawgiver does not interpret the law indiscriminately but in a case in which it is evident, by reason of the manifest harm, that the lawgiver intended otherwise. For if it be a matter of doubt, he must either act according to the letter of the law or consult those in power.

*Reply Obj. 3.* No man is so wise as to be able to take account of every single case; wherefore he is not able sufficiently to express in words all those things that are suitable for the end he has in view. And even if a lawgiver were able to take all the cases into consideration, he ought not to mention them all, in order to avoid confusion, but should frame the law according to that which is of most common occurrence.

## QUESTION 97: OF CHANGE IN LAWS

### *[In Four Articles]*

We must now consider change in laws, under which head there are four points of inquiry: (1) Whether human law is changeable? (2) Whether it should always be changed whenever something better occurs? (3) Whether it is abolished by custom, and whether custom obtains the force of law? (4) Whether the application of human law should be changed by dispensation of those in authority?

### First Article: Should Human Law Be Changed in Any Way?

*We proceed thus to the First Article:*

*Obj. 1.* It would seem that human law should not be changed in any way at all because human law is derived from the natural law, as stated above. But the natural law endures unchangeably. Therefore, human law should also remain without any change.

*Obj. 2.* Further, as the Philosopher says, a measure should be absolutely stable. But human law is the measure of human acts, as stated above. Therefore, it should remain without change.

*Obj. 3.* Further, it is of the essence of law to be just and right, as stated above. But that which is right once is right always. Therefore, that which is law once should be always law.

*On the contrary,* Augustine says, "A temporal law, however just, may be justly changed in course of time."

*I answer that,* As stated above, human law is a dictate of reason whereby human acts are directed. Thus there may be two causes for the just change of human law: one on the part of reason; the other on the part of man, whose acts are regulated by law. The cause on the part of reason is that it seems natural to human reason to advance gradually from the imperfect to the perfect. Hence, in speculative sciences, we see that the teaching of the early philosophers was imperfect, and that it was afterward perfected by those who succeeded them. So also in practical matters; for those who first endeavored to discover something useful for the human community, not being able by themselves to take everything into consideration, set up certain institutions which were deficient in many ways, and these were changed by subsequent lawgivers who made institutions that might prove less frequently deficient in respect of the common weal.

On the part of man, whose acts are regulated by law, the law can be rightly changed on account of the changed condition of man, to whom different things are expedient according to the difference of his condition. An example is proposed by Augustine:

> If the people have a sense of moderation and responsibility and are most careful guardians of the common weal, it is right to enact a law allowing such a people to choose their own magistrates for the government of the commonwealth. But if, as time goes on, the same people become so corrupt as to sell their votes and entrust the government to scoundrels and criminals, then the right of appointing their public officials is rightly forfeit to such a people, and the choice devolves to a few good men.

*Reply Obj. 1.* The natural law is a participation of the eternal law, as stated above, and, therefore, endures without change, owing to the unchangeableness and perfection of the divine reason, the Author of nature. But the reason of man is changeable and imperfect; wherefore his law is subject to change. Moreover, the natural law contains certain universal precepts which are everlasting, whereas human law contains certain particular precepts according to various emergencies.

*Reply Obj. 2.* A measure should be as enduring as possible. But nothing can be absolutely unchangeable in things that are subject to change. And, therefore, human law cannot be altogether unchangeable.

*Reply Obj. 3.* Of corporeal objects, "right" ["straight"] is predicated absolutely and, therefore, as far as itself is concerned, always remains "right." But "right" is predicated of law with reference to the common weal, to which one and the same thing is not always adapted, as stated above; wherefore, rectitude of this kind is subject to change.

### Second Article: Should Human Law Always Be Changed Whenever Something Better Occurs?

*We proceed thus to the Second Article:*

*Obj. 1.* It would seem that human law should be changed whenever something better occurs because human laws are devised by human reason, like other arts. But in the other arts, the tenets of former times give place to others if something better occurs. Therefore, the same should apply to human laws.

*Obj. 2.* Further, by taking note of the past, we can provide for the future. Now unless human laws had been changed when it was found possible to improve them, considerable inconvenience would have ensued because the laws of old were crude in many points. Therefore, it seems that laws should be changed whenever anything better occurs to be enacted.

*Obj. 3.* Further, human laws are enacted about single acts of man. But we cannot acquire perfect knowledge in singular matters except by experience, which "requires time," as stated in *Ethics* II, 1. Therefore, it seems that, as time goes on, it is possible for something better to occur for legislation.

*On the contrary,* It is stated in the *Decretum:* "It is absurd and a detestable shame that we should suffer those traditions to be changed which we have received from the fathers of old."

*I answer that,* As stated above, human law is rightly changed insofar as such change is conducive to the common weal. But, to a certain extent, the mere change of law is of itself prejudicial to the common good because custom avails much for the observance of laws, seeing that what is done contrary to general custom, even in slight matters, is looked upon as grave. Consequently, when a law is changed, the binding power of the law is diminished insofar as custom is abolished. Wherefore, human law should never be changed unless, in some way or other, the common weal be compensated according to the extent of the harm done in this respect. Such compensation may arise either from some very great and very evident benefit conferred by the new enactment or from the extreme urgency of the case, due to the fact that either the existing law is clearly unjust or its observance extremely harmful. Wherefore the Jurist says that "in establishing new laws, there should be evidence of the benefit to be derived before departing from a law which has long been considered just."

*Reply Obj. 1.* Rules of art derive their force from reason alone, and, therefore, whenever something better occurs, the rule followed hitherto should be changed. But "laws derive very great force from custom," as the Philosopher states; consequently, they should not be quickly changed.

*Reply Obj. 2.* This argument proves that laws ought to be changed, not in view of any improvement but for the sake of a great benefit or in a case of great urgency, as stated above. This answer applies also to the *Third Objection.*

### Third Article: Can Custom Obtain Force of Law?

*We proceed thus to the Third Article:*

*Obj. 1.* It would seem that custom cannot obtain force of law nor abolish a law because human law is derived from the natural law and from the divine law, as stated above. But human custom cannot change either the law of nature or the divine law. Therefore, neither can it change human law.

*Obj. 2.* Further, many evils cannot make one good. But he who first acted against the law did evil. Therefore, by multiplying such acts, nothing good is the result. Now a law is something good, since it is a rule of human acts. Therefore, law is not abolished by custom so that the mere custom should obtain force of law.

*Obj. 3.* Further, the framing of laws belongs to those public men whose business it is to govern the community; wherefore private individuals cannot make laws. But custom grows by the acts of private individuals. Therefore, custom cannot obtain force of law so as to abolish the law.

*On the contrary,* Augustine says, "The customs of God's people and the institutions of our ancestors are to be considered as laws. And those who throw contempt on the customs of the Church ought to be punished as those who disobey the law of God."

*I answer that* All law proceeds from the reason and will of the lawgiver: the divine and natural laws from the reasonable will of God, the human law from the will of man regulated by reason. Now just as human reason and will, in practical matters, may be made manifest by speech, so may they be made known by deeds, since, seemingly, a man chooses as good that which he carries into execution. But it is evident that, by human speech, law can be both changed and expounded insofar as it manifests the interior movement and thought of human reason. Wherefore, by actions also, especially if they be repeated so as to make a custom, law can be changed and expounded, and also something can be established which obtains force of law insofar as, by repeated external actions, the inward movement of the will and concepts of reason are most effectually declared; for when a thing is done again and again, it seems to proceed from a deliberate judgment of reason. Accordingly, custom has the force of labor, abolishes law, and is the interpreter of law.

*Reply Obj. 1.* The natural and divine laws proceed from the divine will, as stated above. Wherefore, they cannot be changed by a custom proceeding from the will of man but only by divine authority. Hence it is that no custom can prevail over the divine or natural laws, for Isidore says: "Let custom yield to authority; evil customs should be eradicated by law and reason."

*Reply Obj. 2.* As stated above, human laws fail in some cases; wherefore, it is possible sometimes to act beside the law, namely, in a case where the law fails, yet the act will not be evil. And when such cases are multiplied, by reason of some change in man, then custom shows that the law is no longer useful, just as it might be declared by the verbal promulgation of a law to the contrary. If, however, the same reason remains for which the law was useful hitherto, then it is not the custom that prevails against the law but the law that overcomes the custom, unless perhaps the sole reason for the law seeming useless be that it is not "possible according to the custom of the country," which has been stated to be one of the conditions of law. For it is not easy to set aside the custom of a whole people.

*Reply Obj. 3.* The people among whom a custom is introduced may be of two conditions. For if they are free and able to make their own laws, the consent of the whole people expressed by a custom counts far more in favor of a particular observance than does the authority of the ruler, who has not the power to frame laws except as representing the people. Wherefore, although single individuals cannot make laws, yet the whole people can. If, however, the people have not the free power to make their own laws or to abolish a law made by a higher authority, nevertheless, with such a people, a prevailing custom obtains force of law insofar as it is tolerated by those to whom it belongs to make laws for that people, because, by the very fact that they tolerate it, they seem to approve of that which is introduced by custom.

## Fourth Article: Can the Rulers of the People Dispense from Human Laws?

*We proceed thus to the Fourth Article:*

*Obj. 1.* It would seem that the rulers of the people cannot dispense from human laws. For the law is established for the "common weal," as Isidore says. But the common good should not be set aside for the private convenience of an individual, because, as the Philosopher says, "the good of the nation is more godlike than the good of one man." Therefore, it seems that a man should not be dispensed from acting in compliance with the general rule.

*Obj. 2.* Further, those who are placed over others are commanded as follows: "You shall hear the little as well as the great; neither shall you respect any man's person, because it is the judgment of God." But to allow one man to do that which is equally forbidden to all seems to be respect of persons. Therefore, the rulers of a community cannot grant such dispensations, since this is against a precept of the divine law.

*Obj. 3.* Further, human law, in order to be just, should accord with the natural and divine laws, else it would not "foster religion nor be helpful to discipline," which is a requisite of law as laid down by Isidore. But no man can dispense from the divine and natural laws. Neither, therefore, can he dispense from the human law.

*On the contrary,* The Apostle says, "A dispensation is committed to me."

*I answer that* Dispensation, properly speaking, denotes a measuring out to individuals of some common goods; thus the head of a household is called a dispenser because, to each member of the household, he distributes work and necessaries of life in due weight and measure. Accordingly, in every community, a man is said to dispense from the very fact that he directs how some general precept is to be fulfilled by each individual. Now it happens at times that a precept which is conducive to the common weal as a general rule is not good for a particular individual or in some particular case, either because it would hinder some greater good or because it would be the occasion of some evil, as explained above. But it would be dangerous to leave this to the discretion of each individual, except perhaps by reason of an evident and sudden emergency, as stated above (ibid.). Consequently, he who is placed over a community is empowered to dispense in a human law that rests upon his authority, so that, when the law fails in its application to persons or circumstances, he may allow the precept of the law not to be observed. If, however, he grant this permission without any such reason and of his mere will, he will be an unfaithful or an imprudent dispenser: unfaithful if he has not the common good in view; imprudent if he ignores the reasons for granting dispensations. Hence our Lord says: "Who, think you, is the faithful and wise dispenser, whom his lord sets over his family?"

*Reply Obj. 1.* When a person is dispensed from observing the general law, this should not be done to the prejudice of, but with the intention of benefiting, the common good.

*Reply Obj. 2.* It is not "respect of persons" if unequal measures are served out to those who are themselves unequal. Wherefore, when the condition of any person requires that he should reasonably receive special treatment, it is not "respect of persons" if he be the object of a special favor.

*Reply Obj. 3.* Natural law, so far as it contains general precepts, which never fail, does not allow of dispensation. In the other precepts, however, which are as conclusions of the general precepts, man sometimes grants a dispensation: for instance, that a loan should not be paid back to the betrayer of his country, or something similar. But to the divine law, each man stands as a private person to the public law to which he is subject. Wherefore, just as none can dispense from public human law except the man from whom the law derives its authority or his delegate, so, in the precepts of the divine law, which are from God, none can dispense but God or the man to whom He may give special power for that purpose.

# NICCOLÒ MACHIAVELLI
~

## INTRODUCTION

## ROGER D. MASTERS

Niccolò Machiavelli (1469–1527) was born in Florence during the most brilliant epoch of the Italian Renaissance. A member of an old Florentine family, Machiavelli was trained as a classical humanist. With the fall of Savanorola's puritanical regime in 1498, Machiavelli entered the service of his native city as second chancellor of the Signoria and secretary to the Committee of Ten, the body responsible for foreign and military affairs. Closely connected with Piero Soderini, the *Gonfaloniere* or "head of state," Machiavelli was entrusted with a number of delicate diplomatic missions. During the autumn of 1502, he was at the court of Cesare Borgia. While there, he apparently met Leonardo da Vinci, who was to work with Machiavelli on several projects between 1503 and 1507. Among these was an attempt in 1503 to 1504 to divert the Arno River during the siege of Pisa—a strategy that failed for technical reasons. Machiavelli was also directly active in raising a citizen militia to end Florence's reliance on mercenary troops, only to have the newly formed army defeated by the Spanish at Prato (1512).

As a consequence of this defeat, the Medici overthrew the Florentine republic in 1512. Machiavelli was deprived of his governmental positions and, when his name was found on a list of conspirators, was imprisoned and tortured. Released from jail on condition that for one year he neither leave the territory of Florence nor enter the government offices, Machiavelli retired to his home in San Casciano, where he began writing *The Prince* and the *Discourses on Titus Livy*. In subsequent years, Machiavelli wrote in a variety of genres, including *Mandragola* (1518)—sometimes called the greatest comedy in the Italian language; *The Art of War* (1521)—a dialogue on military strategy incorporating ancient practices and his own experience; and *Florentine Histories* (1525)—an account of the history of his native city commissioned by the Medici pope Leo X. Despite attempts to secure political employment from the Medici, Machiavelli never regained office. He died in 1527, shortly after the Medici were overthrown and a republic restored.

Although Machiavelli is often described as the founder of modern political theory, there is much controversy about his intentions and theories. *The Prince*, Machiavelli's best known work, circulated in manuscript before his death and was published posthumously in 1532. It is dedicated to Lorenzo de Medici, ruler of Florence from 1516 to 1519, and seems to espouse the unscrupulous methods of ambitious leaders like Cesare Borgia. His *Discourses on Titus Livy*, also published posthumously (1531), uses Roman political history as the basis for republican political principles. The apparent contradictions between these two works have led many to treat Machiavelli as a teacher of political expediency and immorality, with little concern for fundamental principles. For some, however, he was the proponent of classical or pagan republicanism, opposed to Christianity and feudal monarchy. Others see him as the first to adopt an objective or "scientific" perspective on politics.

Understanding Machiavelli is difficult. One key may be Machiavelli's assertion, in both *The Prince* and *Discourses*, that his understanding of politics is based on a combination of "long experience" of modern things (his responsibilities for the Florentine republic) and a "continuous study of antiquity" (especially such pagan writers as Xenophon and Polybius, as well as Livy). As those who consult Machiavelli's diplomatic dispatches and private correspondence discover, Machiavelli often wrote in code and used obscurity to ensure that his messages were understood only by his addressee. More important, Machiavelli's diplomatic papers prove that the apparent praise of Cesare Borgia in *The Prince* is not to be taken at face value. Rousseau concluded that

> *The Prince* of Machiavelli is the book of republicans [because] the mere choice of his execrable hero sufficiently manifests his secret intention; and the opposition of the maxims of his book *The Prince* and those of his *Discourses on Titus Livy* and his *History of Florence* shows that this profound political theorist has had until now only superficial or corrupt readers.
>
> (Rousseau, *Of The Social Contract*, Book 3, ch. 6)

Even those who dispute Rousseau's republican interpretation often agree that Machiavelli does much to introduce a secular, materialistic orientation at odds with traditional Christianity. Aware of Leonardo's use of scientific inquiry to invent weapons and imagine a technologically founded regime, Machiavelli seeks to show how ambitious leaders can "channel" fortune through the "dikes and dams" of good laws and good arms. But perhaps chastened by the failure of his technical and military projects, Machiavelli remained skeptical of the notion, later developed by Bacon, that humans can definitively or permanently "conquer nature" for the "relief of man's estate." As Machiavelli puts it in chapter 25 of *The Prince*, humans can control "about half" of fortune or chance through a combination of force, intelligence, and impulsiveness.

It is possible to reconcile the diverse interpretations of Machiavelli's works by viewing the ambitious leader of *The Prince* as the legislator or founder of the republican regime favored in the *Discourses*. Such a reading suggests that Machiavelli sought the creation of "new modes and orders" capable of establishing lasting states. To this end, laws must channel the selfish desires and conflicts inherent in political life, while fear ensures obedience to law and those in power. Rejecting "imagined principalities," whether in the form of Plato's *Republic* or Augustine's *City of God*, Machiavelli thus tries to direct the ambitious leader to the task of founding and maintaining "good arms and good laws" (*The Prince*, ch. 12). In this interpretation, Machiavelli combines views of human nature and prudence derived from pagan antiquity with a conception of secular power and technology that has come to characterize modernity.

There is thus good reason for the widespread opinion that Machiavelli initiated "modern" political thought. In the preface to Book I of the *Discourses*, Machiavelli says he seeks to open a "new route" and compares this goal to Columbus's discovery of America. In chapter 15 of *The Prince*, Machiavelli explicitly asserts that he differs from "others"—presumably *all* prior writers on political theory—with regard to the relationship between rulers and ruled. Even his play *Mandragola* opens with a novelty: The personage of the author comes on stage to address the audience directly, and tells them they will see a "new case."

What, however, did Machiavelli mean by the novelty of his teaching? Many commentators focus on his worldly emphasis on the "actual truth" rather than on the "imagined principalities" of the Platonic and Christian tradition, citing chapter 15 of *The Prince*. But that chapter states Machiavelli's intention quite explicitly as theoretical rather than practical: "[M]y intention is to write something useful for *whoever understands it*." Readers who think that Machiavelli was merely concerned with practical advice to rulers ignore his explicit assertion that the ancients used "covert" images in the education of rulers (*The Prince*, ch. 18), and therefore fail to see how that work relates to Machiavelli's stated goal of working "for the common benefit of all" (*Discourses*, preface to Book I).

When read very carefully, Machiavelli's works present a coherent political philosophy. Nurtured by his study of ancient philosophy (there exists a copy of Lucretius' *De Rerum Natura* copied in Machiavelli's own hand), Machiavelli intentionally challenges the Western philosophic tradition. He does not, however, claim there is any novelty in his skeptical view of human nature (men are "ungrateful, fickle pretenders and dissemblers, evaders of danger, eager for gain"; *The Prince*, ch. 17). On the contrary, Machiavelli explicitly states that "all writers on politics have pointed out . . . [that] it must needs be taken for granted that all men are wicked" (*Discourses*, I, 3). Far from being a novelty, Machiavelli's theory of human nature simply endorses a traditional view, such as the teachings of Xenophon (the classical author suggested as required reading in both *The Prince* and *Discourses*).

The novelty of the Machiavellian teaching is, rather, the use of science and technology to control nature and achieve, by design, consequences hitherto only achieved by good luck (fortune). In pagan antiquity, science or philosophy was limited to understanding nature rather than designing technologies that control it. Modernity, in contrast, is characterized by the continuous development of scientific and technological developments devoted to the Baconian "conquest of nature." Machiavelli marks the transition with his suggestion that humans could control about half of history or fortune.

The famous allegory of fortune as a river (*The Prince*, ch. 25), which symbolizes this view, echoes Machiavelli's experience in the attempt to channel the Arno as a means of defeating Pisa in 1503–1504. Leonardo da Vinci, who had gained great expertise in hydraulic engineering during sixteen years as advisor to Ludovico Sforza, Duke of Milan, was the technical advisor who approved the project; Machiavelli supervised it. Along with other evidence of Leonardo's influence, this experience suggests that Machiavelli was the first major thinker to consider the political implications of the integration of theoretical science and technology that became the hallmark of the modern epoch.

The full development of modernity can be associated with Hobbes, who extends the constructive view of science and politics by combining Galileo's new view of physics (inertia as the principle of continuous motion) with Euclidean geometry (mathematics as the model of certain knowledge). For moderns following Hobbes, all humans are equal in the essential respect. As Locke later put it, the human brain is a tabula rasa, or blank slate, on which experience or nurture engraves all thought. Machiavelli does not go this far, retaining the ancient view that individual natures (intelligence, boldness, caution, and the like) differ in ways that cannot be totally controlled by human will. Because findings in contemporary biology call into question the premises of Hobbes, Locke, and other moderns, Machiavelli's works take on renewed importance as a complex and powerful political philosophy with continued relevance for understanding human life.

The secondary literature on Machiavelli is immense. For biographies, see Roberto Ridolfi, *The Life of Niccolò Machiavelli*, translated by Cecil Grayson (Chicago: University of Chicago Press, 1963); and Alfred de Grazia, *Machiavelli in Hell* (Princeton, N.J.: Princeton University Press, 1989). On the premodern elements in Machiavelli's thought, see J. G. A. Pocock, *The Machiavellian Moment: Florentine Thought and the Atlantic Republican Tradition* (Princeton, N.J.: Princeton University Press, 1975); and Anthony J. Parel, *The Machiavellian Cosmos* (New Haven, Conn.: Yale University Press, 1992). On Machiavelli's political career, see Denis Fachard's biography of Machiavelli's assistant, *Biagio Buonaccorsi* (Bologna: Massimiliano Boni, 1976); Felix Gilbert, *Machiavelli and Guiccardini; Politics and History in Sixteenth Century Florence* (Princeton, N.J.: Princeton University Press, 1965); and John H. Najemy, *Between Friends: Discourses of Power and Desire in the Machiavelli-Vettori Letters of 1513–1515* (Princeton, N.J.: Princeton University Press, 1993). For the interpretation of Machiavelli as the founder of modernity, see Leonardo Olschlei, *Machiavelli the Scientist* (Berkeley: University of California Press, 1945); Leo Strauss, *Natural Right and History* (Chicago: University of Chicago Press, 1957); as well as *Thoughts on Machiavelli* (Glencoe, Ill: Free Press, 1964); and—with special emphasis on the relationship with Leonardo da Vinci—Roger D. Masters, *Machiavelli, Leonardo, and the Science of Power* (Notre Dame, Ind.: University of Notre Dame Press, 1996).

# The Prince

## CHAPTER I

### *How Many Kinds of Principalities There Are and the Way They Are Acquired*

All states, all dominions that have had and continue to have power over men were and still are either republics or principalities. Principalities are either hereditary, in which instance the family of the prince has ruled for generations, or they are new. The new ones are either completely new, as was Milan for Francesco Sforza, or they are like members added to the hereditary state of the prince who acquires them, as is the Kingdom of Naples for the King of Spain. Dominions taken in this way are either used to living under a prince or are accustomed to being free; and they are gained either by the arms of others or by one's own, either through fortune or through ingenuity.

## CHAPTER II

### *On Hereditary Principalities*

I shall set aside any discussion of republics, because I treated them elsewhere at length. I shall consider solely the principality, developing as I go the topics mentioned above; and I shall discuss how these principalities can be governed and maintained.

I say, then, that in hereditary states accustomed to the rule of their prince's family there are far fewer difficulties in maintaining them than in new states; for it suffices simply not to break ancient customs, and then to suit one's actions to unexpected events; in this manner, if such a prince is of ordinary ability,

he will always maintain his state, unless some extraordinary and inordinate force deprive him of it; and although it may be taken away from him, he will regain it with the slightest mistake of the usurper.

As an example, we have in Italy the Duke of Ferrara, who withstood the assaults of the Venetians in 1484 and those of Pope Julius in 1510 for no other reason than the tradition of his rule in that dominion. Because a prince by birth has fewer reasons and less need to harm his subjects, it is natural that he should be more loved; and if no unusual vices make him hated, it is reasonable and natural that he be well liked by them. And in the antiquity and continuity of his rule, the records and causes of innovations die out, because one change always leaves space for the construction of another.

## CHAPTER III

### *On Mixed Principalities*

But it is the new principality that causes difficulties. In the first place, if it is not completely new but is instead an acquisition (so that the two parts together may be called mixed), its difficulties derive from one natural problem inherent in all new principalities: men gladly change their masters, thinking to better themselves; and this belief causes them to take arms against their ruler; but they fool themselves in this, since with experience they see that things have become worse. This stems from another natural and ordinary necessity, which is that a new prince must always offend his new subjects both through his soldiers and other countless injuries that are involved in his new conquest; thus, you have made enemies of all those you injured in occupying the principality and you are unable to maintain as friends those who helped you to rise to power, since you cannot satisfy them in the way that they had supposed, nor can you use strong measures against them, for you are in their debt; because, although one may have the most powerful of armies, he always needs the support of the inhabitants to seize a province. For these reasons, Louis XII, King of France, quickly occupied Milan and just as quickly lost it; and the first time, the troops of Ludovico alone were needed to retake it from him, because those citizens who had opened the gates of the city to the king, finding themselves deceived in their beliefs and in that future improvement they had anticipated, could not support the offences of the new prince.

It is indeed true that when lands which have rebelled once are taken a second time, it is more difficult to lose them; for the lord, taking advantage of the revolt, is less reticent about punishing offenders, ferreting out suspects, and shoring up weak positions. So that, if only a Duke Ludovico threatening the borders was sufficient for France to lose Milan the first time, the whole world had to oppose her and destroy her armies or chase them from Italy to cause her to lose it the second time; and this happened for the reasons mentioned above. Nevertheless, it was taken from her both the first and the second time.

The general explanations for the first loss have been discussed; now there remains to specify those for the second, and to see what remedies the King of France had, and those that one in the same situation might have, so that he might be able to maintain a stronger grip on his conquest than did France. Therefore, I say that those dominions which, upon being conquered, are added to the long-established state of him who acquires them are either of the same province and language or they are not. When they are, it is easier to hold them, especially when they are unaccustomed to freedom; and to possess them securely, it is only necessary to have extinguished the family line of the prince who ruled them, because in so far as other things are concerned, men live peacefully as long as their old way of life is maintained and there is no change in customs: thus, we have seen what happened in the case of Burgundy, Brittany, Gascony, and Normandy, which have been part of France for such a long time; and although there are some linguistic differences, nevertheless the customs are similar and they have been able to get along together easily. And anyone who acquires these lands and wishes to maintain them must bear two things in mind: first, that the family line of the old prince must be extinguished; second, that neither their laws nor their taxes be altered; as a result they will become in a very brief time one body with the old principality.

But when dominions are acquired in a province that is not similar in language, customs, and laws, it is here that difficulties arise; and it is here that one needs much good fortune and much diligence to hold on to them. And one of the best and most efficacious remedies would be for the person who has taken possession of them to go and live there. This would make that possession more secure and durable, as the Turks did with Greece; for despite all the other precautions they took to retain that dominion, if they had not gone there to live, it would have been impossible for them to hold on to it. Because, by being on the spot, one sees trouble at its birth and one can quickly remedy it; not being there, one hears about it after it has grown and there is no longer any remedy. Moreover, the province would not be plundered by one's own officers; the subjects would be pleased to have direct recourse to their prince; thus, wishing to be good subjects, they have more reason to love him and, wanting to be otherwise, more reason to fear him. Anyone who might wish to invade that dominion from abroad would be more hesitant; so that, living right there, the prince can only with the greatest of difficulties lose it.

The other and better solution is to send colonies into one or two places that will act as supports for your own state; for it is necessary that the prince either do this or maintain a large number of infantry and cavalry. Colonies do not cost much, and with little or no expense a prince can send and maintain them; and in so doing he hurts only those whose fields and houses have been taken and given to the new inhabitants, who are only a small part of that state; and those that he hurts, being dispersed and poor, can never be a threat to him, and all others remain on the one hand unharmed (and because of this, they should remain silent), and on the other afraid of making a mistake, for fear that what happened to those who were dispossessed might happen to them. I conclude that these colonies are not expensive, they are more faithful, and they create fewer difficulties; and those who are hurt cannot pose a threat, since they are poor and scattered, as I have already said. Concerning this, it should be noted that one must either pamper or do away with men, because they will avenge themselves for minor offences while for more serious ones they cannot; so that any harm done to a man must be the kind that removes any fear of revenge. But by maintaining soldiers there instead of colonies, one spends much more, being obliged to consume all the revenues of the state in guarding its borders, so that the profit becomes a loss; and far greater injury is committed, since the entire state is harmed by the army changing quarters from one place to another; everybody resents this inconvenience, and everyone becomes an enemy; and these are enemies that can be harmful, since they remain, although conquered, in their own home. And so, in every respect, this kind of defence is as useless as the other kind, colonization, is useful.

## CHAPTER V

### *How Cities or Principalities Should Be Governed That Lived by Their Own Laws Before They Were Occupied*

As I have said, when those states that are acquired are used to living by their own laws and in freedom, there are three methods of holding on to them: the first is to destroy them; the second is to go there in person to live; the third is to allow them to live with their own laws, forcing them to pay a tribute and creating

therein a government made up of a few people who will keep the state friendly toward you. For such a government, having been created by that prince, knows it cannot last without his friendship and his power, and it must do everything possible to maintain them; and a city used to living in freedom is more easily maintained through the means of its own citizens than in any other way, if you decide to preserve it.

As examples, there are the Spartans and the Romans. The Spartans held Athens and Thebes by building therein a government consisting of a few people; eventually they lost them both. The Romans, in order to hold Capua, Carthage, and Numantia, destroyed them and did not lose them; they wished to hold Greece in almost the same manner as the Spartans held it, making it free and leaving it under its own laws, and they did not succeed; thus, they were obliged to destroy many of the cities in that province in order to retain it. For, in fact, there is no secure means of holding on to them except by destroying them. And anyone who becomes lord of a city used to living in liberty and does not destroy it may expect to be destroyed by it, because such a city always has as a refuge, in any rebellion, the spirit of liberty and its ancient institutions, neither of which is ever forgotten either because of the passing of time or because of the bestowal of benefits. And it matters little what one does or foresees, since if one does not separate or scatter the inhabitants, they will not forget that spirit or those institutions; and immediately, in every case, they will return to them just as Pisa did after one hundred years of being held in servitude by the Florentines. But when cities or provinces are accustomed to living under a prince and the family of that prince has been extinguished, they, being on the one hand used to obedience and, on the other, not having their old prince and not being able to agree on choosing another from amongst themselves, yet not knowing how to live as free men, are as a result hesitant in taking up arms, and a prince can win them over and assure himself of their support with greater ease. But in republics there is greater vitality, greater hatred, greater desire for revenge; the memory of ancient liberty does not and cannot allow them to submit, so that the most secure course is either to destroy them or to go there to live.

## CHAPTER VI

### *On New Principalities Acquired by One's Own Arms and Skill*

No one should marvel if, in speaking of principalities that are totally new as to their prince and organization, I use the most illustrious examples; since men almost always tread the paths made by others and proceed in their affairs by imitation, although they are not completely able to stay on the path of others nor attain the skill of those they imitate, a prudent man should always enter those paths taken by great men and imitate those who have been most excellent, so that if one's own skill does not match theirs, at least it will have the smell of it; and he should proceed like those prudent archers who, aware of the strength of their bow when the target they are aiming at seems too distant, set their sights much higher than the designated target, not in order to reach to such a height with their arrow but rather to be able, with the aid of such a high aim, to strike the target.

I say, therefore, that in completely new principalities, where there is a new prince, one finds in maintaining them more or less difficulty according to the greater or lesser skill of the one who acquires them. And because this act of transition from private citizen to prince presupposes either ingenuity or fortune, it appears that either the one or the other of these two things should, in part, mitigate many of the problems; nevertheless, he who relies upon fortune less maintains his position best. Things are also facilitated when the prince, having no other dominions to govern, is constrained to come to live there in person. But to come to those who, by means of their own skill and not because of fortune, have become princes, I say that the most admirable are Moses, Cyrus, Romulus, Theseus, and the like. And although we should not discuss Moses, since he was a mere executor of things ordered by God, nevertheless he must be admired, if for nothing but that grace which made

him worthy of talking with God. But let us consider Cyrus and the others who have acquired or founded kingdoms; you will find them all admirable; and if their deeds and their particular institutions are considered, they will not appear different from those of Moses, who had so great a guide. And examining their deeds and their lives, one can see that they received nothing from fortune except the opportunity, which gave them the material they could mould into whatever form they desired; and without that opportunity the strength of their spirit would have been extinguished, and without that strength the opportunity would have come in vain.

It was therefore necessary for Moses to find the people of Israel in Egypt slaves and oppressed by the Egyptians in order that they might be disposed to follow him to escape this servitude. It was necessary for Romulus not to stay in Alba and to be exposed at birth so that he might become King of Rome and founder of that nation. It was necessary for Cyrus to find the Persians discontented with the empire of the Medes, and the Medes soft and effeminate after a lengthy peace. Theseus could not have shown his skill if he had not found the Athenians scattered. These opportunities, therefore, made these men successful, and their outstanding ingenuity made that opportunity known to them, whereby their nations were ennobled and became prosperous.

Like these men, those who become princes through their skill acquire the principality with difficulty, but they hold on to it easily; and the difficulties they encounter in acquiring the principality grow, in part, out of the new institutions and methods they are obliged to introduce in order to found their state and their security. And one should bear in mind that there is nothing more difficult to execute, nor more dubious of success, nor more dangerous to administer than to introduce a new order of things; for he who introduces it has all those who profit from the old order as his enemies, and he has only lukewarm allies in all those who might profit from the new. This lukewarmness partly stems from fear of their adversaries, who have the law on their side, and partly from the scepticism of men, who do not truly believe in new things unless they have actually had personal experience of them. Therefore, it happens that whenever those who are enemies have the chance to attack, they do so enthusiastically, whereas those others defend hesitantly, so that they, together with the prince, are in danger.

It is necessary, however, if we desire to examine this subject thoroughly, to observe whether these innovators act on their own or are dependent on others: that is, if they are forced to beg or are able to use power in conducting their affairs. In the first case, they always come to a bad end and never accomplish anything; but when they depend on their own resources and can use power, then only seldom do they find themselves in peril. From this comes the fact that all armed prophets were victorious and the unarmed came to ruin. Besides what has been said, people are fickle by nature; and it is simple to convince them of something but difficult to hold them in that conviction; and, therefore, affairs should be managed in such a way that when they no longer believe, they can be made to believe by force. Moses, Cyrus, Theseus, and Romulus could not have made their institutions long respected if they had been unarmed; as in our times happened to Brother Girolamo Savonarola, who was ruined by his new institutions when the populace began no longer to believe in them, since he had no way of holding steady those who had believed nor of making the disbelievers believe. Therefore, such men have great problems in getting ahead, and they meet all their dangers as they proceed, and they must overcome them with their skill; but once they have overcome them and have begun to be respected, having removed those who were envious of their merits, they remain powerful, secure, honoured, and happy.

To such noble examples I should like to add a minor one; but it will have some relation to the others, and I should like it to suffice for all similar cases: and this is Hiero of Syracuse. From a private citizen, this man became the prince of Syracuse; he did not receive anything from fortune except the opportunity, for since the citizens of Syracuse were oppressed, they elected him as their leader; and from that rank he proved himself worthy of becoming their prince. And he was so skillful while still a private citizen that someone who wrote about him said 'that he lacked nothing to reign save a kingdom.' He did away with the old militia and established a new one; he put aside old friendships and made new ones; and since he had allies and soldiers that depended on him, he was able to construct whatever building he wished on such a foundation; so that it cost him great effort to acquire and little to maintain.

## CHAPTER VII

### On New Principalities Acquired with the Arms of Others and by Fortune

Those private citizens who become princes through fortune alone do so with little effort, but they maintain their position only with a great deal; they meet no obstacles along their way since they fly to success, but all their problems arise when they have arrived. And these are the men who are granted a state either because they have money or because they enjoy the favour of him who grants it: this occurred to many in Greece in the cities of Ionia and the Hellespont, where Darius created princes in order that he might hold these cities for his security and glory; in like manner were set up those emperors who from private citizens came to power by bribing the soldiers. Such men depend solely upon two very uncertain and unstable things; the will and the fortune of him who granted them the state; they do not know how and are not able to maintain their position. They do not know how, since if men are not of great intelligence and ingenuity, it is not reasonable that they know how to rule, having always lived as private citizens; they are not able to, since they do not have forces that are friendly and faithful. Besides, states that rise quickly, just as all the other things of nature that are born and grow rapidly, cannot have roots and ramifications; the first bad weather kills them, unless these men who have suddenly become princes, as I have noted, are of such ability that they know how to prepare themselves quickly and to preserve what fortune has put in their laps, and to construct afterwards those foundations that others have built before becoming princes. . . .

# CHAPTER VIII

## On Those Who Have Become Princes Through Wickedness

But because there are yet two more ways one can from an ordinary citizen become prince, which cannot completely be attributed to either fortune or skill, I believe they should not be left unmentioned, although one of them will be discussed at greater length in a treatise on republics. These two are: when one becomes prince through some wicked and nefarious means or when a private citizen becomes prince of his native city through the favour of his fellow citizens. And in discussing the first way, I shall cite two examples, one from classical times and the other from recent days, without otherwise entering into the merits of this method, since I consider them sufficient for anyone forced to imitate them.

Agathocles the Sicilian, not only from being an ordinary citizen but from being of low and abject status, became King of Syracuse. This man, a potter's son, lived a wicked life at every stage of his career; yet he joined to his wickedness such strength of mind and of body that, when he entered upon a military career, he rose through the ranks to become commander of Syracuse. Once placed in such a position, having decided to become prince and to hold with violence and without any obligations to others what had been granted to him by universal consent, and having made an agreement with Hamilcar the Carthaginian, who was waging war with his armies in Sicily, he called together one morning the people and the senate of Syracuse as if he were going to discuss things concerning the state; and with a prearranged signal, he had his troops kill all the senators and the richest citizens; and when they were dead, he seized and held the rule of the city without any opposition from the citizenry. And although he was twice defeated by the Carthaginians and eventually besieged, not only was he able to defend his city but, leaving part of his troops for the defence of the siege, with his other men he attacked Africa, and in a short time he freed Syracuse from the siege and forced the Carthagini-

ans into dire straits: they were obliged to make peace with him and to be content with possession of Africa and to leave Sicily to Agathocles.

Anyone, therefore, who examines the deeds and the life of this man will observe nothing or very little that can be attributed to fortune; since, as was said earlier, not with the aid of others but by rising through the ranks, which involved a thousand hardships and dangers, did he come to rule the principality which he then maintained by many brave and dangerous actions. Still, it cannot be called ingenuity to kill one's fellow citizens, to betray friends, to be without faith, without mercy, without religion; by these means one can acquire power but not glory. For if one were to consider Agathocles's ability in getting into and out of dangers, and his greatness of spirit in supporting and in overcoming adversaries, one can see no reason why he should be judged inferior to any most excellent commander; nevertheless, his vicious cruelty and inhumanity, along with numerous wicked deeds, do not permit us to honour him among the most excellent of men. One cannot, therefore, attribute to either fortune or skill what he accomplished without either the one or the other. . . .

One might wonder how Agathocles and others like him, after so many betrayals and cruelties, could live for such a long time secure in their cities and defend themselves from outside enemies without being plotted against by their own citizens; many others, using cruel means, were unable even in peaceful times to hold on to their state, not to speak of the uncertain times of war. I believe that this depends on whether cruelty be well or badly used. Well used are those cruelties (if it is permitted to speak well of evil) that are carried out in a single stroke, done out of necessity to protect oneself, and are not continued but are instead converted into the greatest possible benefits for the subjects. Badly used are those cruelties which, although being few at the outset, grow with the passing of time instead of disappearing. Those who follow the first method can remedy their condition with God and with men as Agathocles did; the others cannot possibly survive.

Wherefore it is to be noted that in taking a state its conqueror should weigh all the harmful things he must do and do them all at once so as not to have to repeat them every day, and in not repeating them to be able to make men feel secure and win them over with the benefits he bestows upon them. Anyone who does otherwise, either out of timidity or because of poor advice, is always obliged to keep his knife in his hand; nor can he ever count upon his subjects, who, because of their fresh and continual injuries, cannot feel secure with him. Injuries, therefore, should be inflicted all at the same time, for the less they are tasted, the less they offend; and benefits should be distributed a bit at a time in order that they may be savoured fully. And a prince should, above all, live with his subjects in such a way that no unforeseen event, either good or bad, may make him alter his course; for when emergencies arise in adverse conditions, you are not in time to resort to cruelty, and the good you do will help you little, since it will be judged a forced measure and you will earn from it no thanks whatsoever.

## CHAPTER IX

### *On the Civil Principality*

But coming to the second instance, when a private citizen, not through wickedness or any other intolerable violence, but with the favour of his fellow citizens, becomes prince of his native city (this can be called a civil principality, the acquisition of which neither depends completely upon skill nor upon fortune, but instead upon a mixture of shrewdness and luck), I maintain that one reaches this princedom either with the favour of the common people or with that of the nobility. For these two different humours are found in every body politic; and they arise from the fact that the people do not wish to be commanded or oppressed by the nobles, and the nobles desire to command and to oppress the people; and from these two opposed appetites there arises one of three effects: either a principality or liberty or anarchy.

A principality is brought about either by the common people or by the nobility, depending on which of the two parties has the opportunity. For when the

nobles see that they cannot resist the populace, they begin to support one among them and make him prince in order to be able, under his protection, to satisfy their appetites. The common people as well, seeing that they cannot resist the nobility, give their support to one man and make him prince in order to have the protection of his authority. He who attains the principality with the aid of the nobility maintains it with more difficulty than he who becomes prince with the assistance of the common people, for he finds himself a prince amidst many who feel themselves to be his equals, and because of this he can neither govern nor manage them as he wishes. But he who attains the principality through popular favour finds himself alone and has around him either no one or very few who are not ready to obey him. Moreover, one cannot honestly satisfy the nobles without harming others, but the common people can certainly be satisfied: their desire is more just than that of the nobles—the former want not to be oppressed and the latter want to oppress. Moreover, a prince can never make himself secure when the people are his enemy because they are so many; he can make himself secure against the nobles because they are so few. The worst that a prince can expect from a hostile people is to be abandoned by them; but with a hostile nobility not only does he have to fear being abandoned but also that they will unite against him; for, being more perceptive and shrewder, they always have time to save themselves, to seek the favours of the side they believe will win. Furthermore, a prince must always live with the same common people; but he can easily do without the same nobles, having the power to create them and to destroy them from day to day and to take away and give back their prestige as he sees fit.

And in order to clarify this point better, I say that the nobles should be considered chiefly in two ways: either they conduct themselves in such a way that they commit themselves completely to your cause or they do not. Those who commit themselves and are not greedy should be honoured and loved; those who do not commit themselves can be analysed in two ways. They act in this manner out of fear and a natural lack of courage, in which case you should make use of them, especially those who are wise advisers, since in prosperous times they will gain you honour and in adverse times you need not fear them. But when, cunningly and influenced by ambition, they refrain from committing themselves to you, this is a sign that they think more of themselves than of you; and the prince should be wary of such men and fear them as if they were open enemies, because they will always, in adverse times, help to bring about his downfall.

However, one who becomes prince with the support of the common people must keep them as his friends; this is easy for him, since the only thing they ask of him is not to be oppressed. But one who, against the will of the common people, becomes prince with the assistance of the nobility should, before all else, seek to win the people's support, which should be easy if he takes them under his protection. And because men, when they are well treated by those from whom they expected harm, are more obliged to their benefactor, the common people quickly become better disposed toward him than if he had become prince with their support. And a prince can gain their favour in various ways, but because they vary according to the situation no fixed rules can be given for them, and therefore I shall not talk about them. I shall conclude by saying only that a prince must have the friendship of the common people; otherwise he will have no support in times of adversity.

Nabis, prince of the Spartans, withstood the attacks of all of Greece and of one of Rome's most victorious armies, and he defended his city and his own rule against them, and when danger was near he needed only to protect himself from a few of his subjects; but if he had had the common people against him, this would not have been sufficient. And let no one dispute my opinion by citing that trite proverb, 'He who builds upon the people builds upon the mud', because that is true when a private citizen lays his foundations and allows himself to believe that the common people will free him if he is oppressed by enemies or by the public officials (in this case a man might often find himself deceived, like the Gracchi of Rome or like Messer Giorgio Scali of Florence); but when the prince who builds his foundations on the people is one who is able to command and is a man of spirit, not

bewildered by adversities, and does not lack other necessities, and through his courage and his institutions keeps up the spirits of the populace, he will never find himself deceived by the common people, and he will discover that he has laid sound foundations.

Principalities of this type are usually endangered when they are about to change from a proper civil society to an absolute form of government. For these princes either rule by themselves or by means of public officials; in the latter case their position is weaker and more dangerous since they depend entirely upon the will of those citizens who are appointed to hold the offices; these men, especially in adverse times, can very easily seize the state either by open opposition or by disobedience. And in such times of danger the prince has no time for taking absolute control, for the citizens and subjects who are used to receiving their orders from public officials are, in these crises, not willing to obey his orders; and in doubtful times he will always find a scarcity of men he can trust. Such a prince cannot rely upon what he sees during periods of calm, when the citizens need his rule, because then everyone comes running, makes promises, and each one is willing to die for him—since death is unlikely; but in times of adversity, when the state needs its citizens, then few are to be found. And this experiment is all the more dangerous in that it can be made but once. And, therefore, a wise prince should think of a method by which his citizens, at all times and in every circumstance, will need the assistance of the state and of himself; and then they will always be loyal to him.

## CHAPTER X

### *How the Strength of All Principalities Should Be Measured*

In analysing the qualities of these principalities, another consideration must be discussed; that is, whether the prince has so much power that he can, if necessary, stand on his own, or whether he always needs the protection of others. And in order to clarify this section, I say that I judge those princes self-sufficient who, either through abundance of troops or of money, are able to gather together a suitable army and fight a good battle against whoever should attack them; and I consider those who always need the protection of others to be those who cannot meet their enemy in the field, but must seek refuge behind their city walls and defend them. The first case has already been treated, and later on I shall say whatever else is necessary on the subject. Nothing more can be added to the second case than to encourage such princes to fortify and provision their cities and not to concern themselves with the surrounding countryside. And anyone who has well fortified his city and has well managed his affairs with his subjects in the manner I detailed above (and discuss below) will be besieged only with great caution; for men are always enemies of undertakings in which they foresee difficulties, and it cannot seem easy to attack someone whose city is well fortified and who is not hated by his people.

The cities of Germany are completely free, they have little surrounding territory, they obey the emperor when they wish, and they fear neither him nor any other nearby power, as they are fortified in such a manner that everyone thinks their capture would be a tedious and difficult affair. For they all have sufficient moats and walls; they have adequate artillery; they always store in their public warehouses enough to drink and to eat and to burn for a year; and besides all this, in order to be able to keep the lower classes fed without exhausting public funds, they always have in reserve a year's supply of raw materials sufficient to give these people work at those trades which are the nerves and the lifeblood of that city and of the industries from which the people earn their living. Moreover, they hold the military arts in high regard, and they have many regulations for maintaining them.

Therefore, a prince who has a strong city and who does not make himself hated cannot be attacked; and even if he were to be attacked, the enemy would have to depart in shame, for human affairs are so changeable that it is almost impossible that one maintain a siege for a year with his troops idle. And if it is objected that if the people have their possessions outside the city and see them destroyed, they will lose patience, and the long siege and self-interest will cause them to forget their prince, I reply that a power-

ful and spirited prince will always overcome all such difficulties, inspiring his subjects now with the hope that the evil will not last long, now with the fear of the enemy's cruelty, now by protecting himself with clever manoeuvres against those who seem too outspoken. Besides this, the enemy will naturally burn and waste the surrounding country on arrival, just when the spirits of the defenders are still ardent and determined on the city's defence; and thus the prince needs to fear so much the less, because after a few days, when their spirits have cooled down a bit, the damage has already been inflicted and the evils suffered, and there is no means of correcting the matter; and now the people will rally around their prince even more, for it would appear that he is bound to them by obligations, since their homes were burned and their possessions wasted in his defence. And the nature of men is such that they find themselves obligated as much for the benefits they confer as for those they receive. Thus, if everything is taken into consideration, it will not be difficult for a prudent prince to keep high the spirits of his citizens from the beginning to the conclusion of the siege, so long as he does not lack enough food and the means for his defence. . . .

## CHAPTER XII

### *On the Various Kinds of Troops and Mercenary Soldiers*

Having treated in detail all the characteristics of those principalities which I proposed to discuss at the beginning, and having considered, to some extent, the reasons for their success or shortcomings, and having demonstrated the ways by which many have tried to acquire them and to maintain them, it remains for me now to speak in general terms of the kinds of offence and defence that can be adopted by each of the previously mentioned principalities. We have said above that a prince must have laid firm foundations; otherwise he will of necessity come to grief. And the principal foundations of all states, the new as well as the old or mixed, are good laws and good armies. And since there cannot exist good laws where there are no good armies, and where there are good armies there must be good laws, I shall leave aside the treatment of laws and discuss the armed forces.

Let me say, therefore, that the armies with which a prince defends his state are made up of his own people, or of mercenaries, or auxiliaries, or of mixed troops. Mercenaries and auxiliaries are useless and dangerous. And if a prince holds on to his state by means of mercenary armies, he will never be stable or secure; for they are disunited, ambitious, without discipline, disloyal; they are brave among friends; among enemies they are cowards; they have no fear of God, they keep no faith with men; and your downfall is deferred only so long as the attack is deferred; and in peace you are plundered by them, in war by your enemies. The reason for this is that they have no other love nor other motive to keep them in the field than a meagre wage, which is not enough to make them want to die for you. They love being your soldiers when you are not making war, but when war comes they either flee or desert. This would require little effort to demonstrate, since the present ruin of Italy is caused by nothing other than her dependence for a long period of time on mercenary forces. These forces did, at times, help some get ahead, and they appeared courageous in combat with other mercenaries; but when the invasion of the foreigner came they showed themselves for what they were; and thus, Charles, King of France, was permitted to take Italy with a piece of chalk. And the man who said that our sins were the cause of this disaster spoke the truth, but they were not at all those that he had in mind, but rather these that I have described; and because they were the sins of princes, the princes in turn have suffered the penalty for them.

I wish to demonstrate more fully the sorry nature of such armies. Mercenary captains are either excellent soldiers or they are not; if they are, you cannot trust them, since they will always aspire to their own greatness either by oppressing you, who are their masters, or by oppressing others against your intent; but if the captain is without skill, he usually ruins you. And if someone were to reply that anyone who bears arms will act in this manner, mercenary or not, I would answer that armies have to be commanded either by a prince or by a republic: the prince must go in person and perform the duties of a captain himself; the republic must send its own citizens; and when they send one who does not turn out to be an able man, they must replace him; if he is capable, they ought to restrain him with laws so that he does not go beyond his authority. And we see from experience that only princes and armed republics make very great advances, and that mercenaries do nothing but harm; and a republic armed with its own citizens is less likely to come under the rule of one of its citizens than a city armed with foreign soldiers.

## CHAPTER XV

### *On Those Things for Which Men, and Particularly Princes, Are Praised or Blamed*

Now there remains to be examined what should be the methods and procedures of a prince in dealing with his subjects and friends. And because I know that many have written about this, I am afraid that by writing about it again I shall be thought of as presumptuous, since in discussing this material I depart radically from the procedures of others. But since my intention is to write something useful for anyone who understands it, it seemed more suitable to me to search after the effectual truth of the matter rather than its imagined one. And many writers have imagined for themselves republics and principalities that have never been seen nor known to exist in reality; for there is such a gap between how one lives and how one ought to live that anyone who abandons what is done for what ought to be done learns his ruin rather than his preservation: for a man who wishes to profess goodness at all times will come to ruin among so many who are not good. Hence it is necessary for a prince who wishes to maintain his position to learn how not to be good, and to use this knowledge or not to use it according to necessity.

Leaving aside, therefore, the imagined things concerning a prince, and taking into account those that are true, I say that all men, when they are spoken of, and particularly princes, since they are placed on a higher level, are judged by some of these qualities which bring them either blame or praise. And this is why one is considered generous, another miserly (to use a Tuscan word, since 'avaricious' in our language is still used to mean one who wishes to acquire by means of theft; we call 'miserly' one who excessively avoids using what he has); one is considered a giver, the other rapacious; one cruel, another merciful; one treacherous, another faithful; one effeminate and cowardly, another bold and courageous; one humane, another haughty; one lascivious, another chaste; one trustworthy, another frivolous; one religious, another unbelieving; and the like. And I know that everyone will admit that it would be a very praiseworthy thing to find in a prince, of the qualities mentioned above, those that are held to be good; but since it is neither possible to have them nor to observe them all completely, because the human condition does not permit it, a prince must be prudent enough to know how to escape the bad reputation of those vices that would lose the state for him, and must protect himself from those that will not lose it for him, if this is possible; but if he cannot, he need not concern himself unduly if he ignores these less serious vices. And, moreover, he need not worry about incurring the bad reputation of those vices without which it would be difficult to hold his state; since, carefully taking everything into account, he will discover that something which appears to be a virtue, if pursued, will end in his destruction; while some other thing which seems to be a vice, if pursued, will result in his safety and his well-being.

## CHAPTER XVI

### *On Generosity and Miserliness*

Beginning, therefore, with the first of the above-mentioned qualities, I say that it would be good to be considered generous; nevertheless, generosity used in such a manner as to give you a reputation for it will harm you; because if it is employed virtuously and as one should employ it, it will not be recognized and you will not avoid the reproach of its opposite. And so, if a prince wants to maintain his reputation for generosity among men, it is necessary for him not to neglect any possible means of lavish display; in so doing such a prince will always use up all his resources and he will be obliged, eventually, if he wishes to maintain his reputation for generosity, to burden the people with excessive taxes and to do everything possible to raise funds. This will begin to make him hateful to his subjects, and, becoming impoverished, he will not be much esteemed by anyone; so that, as a consequence of his generosity, having offended many and rewarded few, he will feel the effects of any slight unrest and will be ruined at the first sign of danger; recognizing this and wishing to alter his policies, he immediately runs the risk of being reproached as a miser.

A prince, therefore, being unable to use this virtue of generosity in a manner which will not harm himself, if he is known for it, should, if he is wise, not worry about being called a miser; for with time he will come to be considered more generous once it is evident that, as a result of his parsimony, his income is sufficient, he can defend himself from anyone who makes war against him, and he can undertake enterprises without overburdening his people, so that he comes to be generous with all those from whom he takes nothing, who are countless, and miserly with all those to whom he gives nothing, who are few. In our times we have not seen great deeds accomplished except by those who were considered miserly; the others were failures. Pope Julius II, although he made use of his reputation for generosity in order to gain the papacy, then decided not to maintain it in order to be able to wage war; the present King of France has waged many wars without imposing extra taxes on his subjects, only because his habitual parsimony has provided for the additional expenditures; the present King of Spain, if he had been considered generous, would not have engaged in or won so many campaigns.

Therefore, in order not to have to rob his subjects, to be able to defend himself, not to become poor and contemptible, and not to be forced to become rapacious, a prince must consider it of little importance if he incurs the reputation of being a miser, for this is one of those vices that permits him to rule. And if someone were to say: Caesar with his generosity achieved imperial power, and many others, because they were generous and known to be so, achieved very high positions; I would reply: you are either already a prince or you are on the way to becoming one; in the first instance such generosity is damaging; in the second it is very necessary to be thought generous. And Caesar was one of those who wanted to gain the principality of Rome; but if, after obtaining this, he had lived and had not moderated his expenditures, he would have destroyed his rule. And if someone were to reply: there have existed many princes who have accomplished great deeds with their armies who have been reputed to be generous; I would answer you: a prince either spends his own money and that of his subjects or that of others; in the first case he must be economical; in the second he must not restrain any part of his generosity. And for that prince who goes out with his soldiers and lives by looting, sacking, and ransoms, who controls the property of others, such generosity is necessary; otherwise he would not be followed by his troops. And with what does not belong to you or to your subjects you can be a more liberal giver, as were Cyrus, Caesar, and Alexander; for spending the wealth of others does not lessen your reputation but adds to it; only the spending of your own is what harms you. And there is nothing that uses itself up faster than generosity, for as you employ it you lose the means of employing it, and you become either poor and despised or else, in order to escape poverty, you become rapacious and hated. And above all other things a prince must guard himself against being despised and hated; and generosity leads you to both one and the other. So it is wiser to live with the reputation of a miser, which produces reproach without hatred, than to be forced to incur the reputation of rapacity, which produces reproach along with hatred, because you want to be considered generous.

## CHAPTER XVII

### On Cruelty and Mercy, and Whether It Is Better to Be Loved Than to Be Feared or the Contrary

Proceeding to the other qualities mentioned above, I say that every prince must desire to be considered merciful and not cruel; nevertheless, he must take care not to misuse this mercy. Cesare Borgia was considered cruel; none the less, his cruelty had brought order to Romagna, united it, restored it to peace and obedience. If we examine this carefully, we shall see that he was more merciful than the Florentine people, who, in order to avoid being considered cruel, allowed the destruction of Pistoia. Therefore, a prince must not worry about the reproach of cruelty when it is a matter of keeping his subjects united and loyal; for with a very few examples of cruelty he will be more compassionate than those who, out of excessive mercy, permit disorders to continue, from which arise murders and plundering; for these usually harm the community at large, while the executions that come from the prince harm particular individuals. And the new prince, above all other princes, cannot escape the reputation of being called cruel, since new states are full of dangers. And Virgil, through Dido, states: 'My difficult condition and the newness of my rule make me act in such a manner, and to set guards over my land on all sides.'

Nevertheless, a prince must be cautious in believing and in acting; nor should he be afraid of his own shadow; and he should proceed in such a manner, tempered by prudence and humanity, so that too much trust may not render him imprudent nor too much distrust render him intolerable.

From this arises an argument: whether it is better to be loved than to be feared, or the contrary. I reply that one should like to be both one and the other; but since it is difficult to join them together, it is much safer to be feared than to be loved when one of the two must be lacking. For one can generally say this about men: that they are ungrateful, fickle, simulators and deceivers, avoiders of danger, greedy for gain; and while you work for their good they are completely yours, offering you their blood, their property, their lives, and their sons, as I said earlier, when danger is far away; but when it comes nearer to you they turn away. And that prince who bases his power entirely on their words, finding himself completely without other preparations, comes to ruin; for friendships that are acquired by a price and not by greatness and nobility of character are purchased but are not owned, and at the proper moment they cannot be spent. And men are less hesitant about harming someone who makes himself loved than one who makes himself feared because love is held together by a chain of obligation which, since men are wretched creatures, is broken on every occasion in which their own interests are concerned; but fear is sustained by a dread of punishment which will never abandon you.

A prince must nevertheless make himself feared in such a manner that he will avoid hatred, even if he does not acquire love; since to be feared and not be hated can very well be combined; and this will always be so when he keeps his hands off the property and the women of his citizens and his subjects. And if he must take someone's life, he should do so when there is proper justification and manifest cause; but, above all, he should avoid seizing the property of others; for men forget more quickly the death of their father than the loss of their patrimony. Moreover, reasons for seizing their property are never lacking; and he who begins to live by stealing always finds a reason for taking what belongs to others; on the contrary, reasons for taking a life are rarer and disappear sooner.

But when the prince is with his armies and has under his command a multitude of troops, then it is absolutely necessary that he not worry about being considered cruel; for without that reputation he will never keep an army united or prepared for any combat. Among the praiseworthy deeds of Hannibal is counted this: that, having a very large army, made up of all kinds of men, which he commanded in foreign lands, there never arose the slightest dissension, neither among themselves nor against their leader, both during his good and his bad fortune. This could not have arisen from anything other than his inhuman cruelty, which along with his many other qualities, made him always respected and terrifying in the eyes of his soldiers; and without that, to attain the same effect, his other qualities would not have sufficed. And the writers of history, having considered this matter very little, on the one hand admire these deeds of his and on the other condemn the main cause of them.

And that it is true that his other qualities would not have been sufficient can be seen from the example of Scipio, a most extraordinary man not only in his time but in all recorded history, whose armies in Spain rebelled against him; this came about from nothing other than his excessive compassion, which gave to his soldiers more liberty than military discipline allowed. For this he was censured in the senate by Fabius Maximus, who called him the corruptor of the Roman militia. The Locrians, having been ruined by one of Scipio's officers, were not avenged by him, nor was the arrogance of that officer corrected, all because of his tolerant nature; so that someone in the senate who tried to apologize for him said that there were many men who knew how not to err better than they knew how to correct errors. Such a nature would have, in time, damaged Scipio's fame and glory if he had continued to command armies; but, living under the control of the senate, this harmful characteristic of his not only was concealed but brought him glory.

I conclude, therefore, returning to the problem of being feared and loved, that since men love at their own pleasure and fear at the pleasure of the prince, a wise prince should build his foundation upon that which belongs to him, not upon that which belongs to others: he must strive only to avoid hatred, as has been said.

## CHAPTER XVIII

### How a Prince Should Keep His Word

How praiseworthy it is for a prince to keep his word and to live by integrity and not by deceit everyone knows; nevertheless, one sees from the experience of our times that the princes who have accomplished great deeds are those who have known how to manipulate the minds of men by shrewdness; and in the end they have surpassed those who laid their foundations upon loyalty.

You must, therefore, know that there are two means of fighting: one according to the laws, the other with force; the first way is proper to man, the second to beasts; but because the first, in many cases

is not sufficient, it becomes necessary to have recourse to the second. Therefore, a prince must know
how to use wisely the natures of the beast and the
man. This policy was taught to princes allegorically
by the ancient writers, who described how Achilles
and many other ancient princes were given to Chiron
the Centaur to be raised and taught under his discipline. This can only mean that, having a half-beast
and half-man as a teacher, a prince must know how to
employ the nature of the one and the other; and the
one without the other cannot endure.

Since, then, a prince must know how to make
good use of the nature of the beast, he should choose
from among the beasts the fox and the lion; for the
lion cannot defend itself from traps and the fox cannot protect itself from wolves. It is therefore necessary to be a fox in order to recognize the traps and a
lion in order to frighten the wolves. Those who play
only the part of the lion do not understand matters.
A wise ruler, therefore, cannot and should not keep
his word when such an observance of faith would be
to his disadvantage and when the reasons which
made him promise are removed. And if men were
all good, this rule would not be good; but since men
are a contemptible lot and will not keep their promises to you, you likewise need not keep yours to
them. A prince never lacks legitimate reasons to
break his promise. Of this one could cite an endless
number of modern examples to show how many
pacts, how many promises have been made null and
void because of the infidelity of princes; and he who
has known best how to use the fox has come to a
better end. But it is necessary to know how to disguise this nature well and to be a great hypocrite and
a liar: and men are so simple-minded and so controlled by their present needs that one who deceives
will always find another who will allow himself to
be deceived.

I do not wish to remain silent about one of these
recent instances. Alexander VI did nothing else, he
thought about nothing else, except to deceive men,
and he always found the occasion to do this. And
there never was a man who had more forcefulness in
his oaths, who affirmed a thing with more promises,
and who honoured his word less; nevertheless, his

tricks always succeeded perfectly since he was well
acquainted with this aspect of the world.

Therefore, it is not necessary for a prince to have
all of the above-mentioned qualities, but it is very
necessary for him to appear to have them. Furthermore, I shall be so bold as to assert this: that having
them and practising them at all times is harmful; and
appearing to have them is useful; for instance, to
seem merciful, faithful, humane, trustworthy, religious, and to be so; but his mind should be disposed
in such a way that should it become necessary not to
be so, he will be able and know how to change to the
contrary. And it is essential to understand this: that a
prince, and especially a new prince, cannot observe
all those things for which men are considered good,
for in order to maintain the state he is often obliged
to act against his promise, against charity, against
humanity, and against religion. And therefore, it is
necessary that he have a mind ready to turn itself
according to the way the winds of fortune and the
changeability of affairs require him; and, as I said
above, as long as it is possible, he should not stray
from the good, but he should know how to enter into
evil when necessity commands.

A prince, therefore, must be very careful never to
let anything slip from his lips which is not full of the
five qualities mentioned above: he should appear,
upon seeing and hearing him, to be all mercy, all
faithfulness, all integrity, all kindness, all religion.
And there is nothing more necessary than to seem to
possess this last quality. And men in general judge
more by the eyes than their hands; for everyone can
see but few can feel. Everyone sees what you seem
to be, few touch upon what you are, and those few
who do not dare to contradict the opinion of the
many who have the majesty of the state to defend
them; and in the actions of all men, and especially of
princes, where there is no impartial arbiter, one must
consider the final result. Let a prince therefore act to
conquer and to maintain the state; his methods will
always be judged honourable and will be praised by
all; for ordinary people are always deceived by
appearances and by the outcome of a thing; and in
the world there is nothing but ordinary people; and
there is no room for the few, while the many have a

place to lean on. A certain prince of the present day, whom I shall refrain from naming, preaches nothing but peace and faith, and to both one and the other he is entirely opposed; and both, if he had put them into practice, would have cost him many times over either his reputation or his state.

# CHAPTER XIX

## *On Avoiding Being Despised and Hated*

But now that I have talked about the most important of the qualities mentioned above, I would like to discuss the others briefly in this general manner: that the prince, as was noted above, should concentrate upon avoiding those things which make him hated and despised; and when he has avoided this, he will have carried out his duties and will find no danger whatsoever in other vices. As I have said, what makes him hated above all else is being rapacious and a usurper of the property and the women of his subjects; he must refrain from this; and in most cases, so long as you do not deprive them of either their property or their honour, the majority of men live happily; and you have only to deal with the ambition of a few, who can be restrained without difficulty and by many means. What makes him despised is being considered changeable, frivolous, effeminate, cowardly, irresolute; from these qualities a prince must guard himself as if from a reef, and he must strive to make everyone recognize in his actions greatness, spirit, dignity, and strength; and concerning the private affairs of his subjects, he must insist that his decision be irrevocable; and he should maintain himself in such a way that no man could imagine that he can deceive or cheat him.

That prince who projects such an opinion of himself is greatly esteemed; and it is difficult to conspire against a man with such a reputation and difficult to attack him, provided that he is understood to be of great merit and revered by his subjects. For a prince should have two fears: one, internal, concerning his subjects; the other, external, concerning foreign powers. From the latter he can defend himself by his good

troops and friends; and he will always have good friends if he has good troops; and internal affairs will always be stable when external affairs are stable, provided that they are not already disturbed by a conspiracy; and even if external conditions change, if he is properly organized and lives as I have said and does not lose control of himself, he will always be able to withstand every attack, just as I said that Nabis the Spartan did. But concerning his subjects, when external affairs do not change, he has to fear that they may conspire secretly: the prince secures himself from this by avoiding being hated or despised and by keeping the people satisfied with him; this is a necessary accomplishment, as was treated above at length. And one of the most powerful remedies a prince has against conspiracies is not to be hated by the masses; for a man who plans a conspiracy always believes that he will satisfy the people by killing the prince; but when he thinks he might anger them, he cannot work up the courage to undertake such a deed; for the problems on the side of the conspirators are countless. And experience demonstrates that there have been many conspiracies but few have been concluded successfully; for anyone who conspires cannot be alone, nor can he find companions except from amongst those whom he believes to be dissatisfied; and as soon as you have revealed your intention to one malcontent, you give him the means to make himself content, since he can have everything he desires by uncovering the plot; so much is this so that, seeing a sure gain on the one hand and one doubtful and full of danger on the other, if he is to maintain faith with you he has to be either an unusually good friend or a completely determined enemy of the prince. And to repeat the matter briefly, I say that on the part of the conspirator there is nothing but fear, jealousy, and the thought of punishment that terrifies him; but on the part of the prince there is the majesty of the principality, the laws, the defences of friends and the state to protect him; so that, with the good will of the people added to these things, it is impossible for anyone to be so rash as to plot against him. For, where usually a conspirator has to be afraid before he executes his evil deed, in this case he must be afraid even after the crime is performed, having the people as an enemy, nor can he hope to find any refuge because of this.

One could cite countless examples on this subject; but I shall be satisfied with only the one which occurred during the time of our fathers. Messer Annibale Bentivogli, prince of Bologna and grandfather of the present Messer Annibale, was murdered by the Canneschi family, who conspired against him; he left behind no heir except Messer Giovanni, then only a baby. As soon as this murder occurred, the people rose up and killed all the Canneschi. This came about because of the good will that the house of the Bentivogli enjoyed in those days; this good will was so great that with Annibale dead, there being no one of that family left in the city who could rule Bologna, the Bolognese people, having heard that in Florence there was one of the Bentivogli blood who was believed until that time to be the son of a blacksmith, went to Florence to find him, and they gave him the control of that city; it was ruled by him until Messer Giovanni became of age to rule.

I conclude, therefore, that a prince should not be too concerned with conspiracies when the people are well disposed toward him; but when the populace is hostile and regards him with hatred, he must fear everything and everyone. And well-organized states and wise princes have, with great diligence, taken care not to anger the nobles and to satisfy the common people and keep them contented; for this is one of the most important concerns that a prince has.

## CHAPTER XXI

### How a Prince Should Act to Acquire Esteem

Nothing makes a prince more esteemed than great undertakings and examples of his unusual talents. In our own times we have Ferdinand of Aragon, the present King of Spain. This man can be called almost a new prince, since from being a weak ruler he became, through fame and glory, the first king of Christendom; and if you consider his accomplishments, you will find them all very grand and some even extraordinary. In the beginning of his reign he attacked Granada, and that enterprise was the basis of his state. First, he acted while things were peaceful and when he had no fear of opposition: he kept the minds of the barons of Castile busy with this, and they, concentrating on that war, did not consider changes at home. And he acquired, through that means, reputation and power over them without their noticing it; he was able to maintain armies with money from the Church and the people, and with that long war he laid a basis for his own army, which has since brought him honour. Besides this, in order to be able to undertake greater enterprises, always using religion for his own purposes, he turned to a pious cruelty, hunting down and clearing out the Moors from his kingdom: no example could be more pathetic or more unusual than this. He attacked Africa, under the same cloak of religion; he undertook the invasion of Italy; he finally attacked France. And in such a manner, he has always done and planned great deeds which have always kept the minds of his subjects in suspense and amazed and occupied with their outcome. And one action of his would spring from another in such a way that between one and the other he would never give men enough time to be able to work calmly against him.

It also helps a prince a great deal to display rare examples of his skills in dealing with internal affairs, such as those which are reported about Messer Bernabò Visconti of Milan. When the occasion arises that a person in public life performs some extraordinary act, be it good or evil, he should find a way of rewarding or punishing him that will provoke a great deal of discussion. And above all, a prince should strive in all of his deeds to give the impression of a great man of superior intelligence.

A prince is also respected when he is a true friend and a true enemy; that is, when he declares himself on the side of one prince against another without any reservation. Such a policy will always be more useful than that of neutrality; for if two powerful neighbours of yours come to blows, they will be of the type that, when one has emerged victorious, you will either have cause to fear the victor or you will not. In either of these two cases, it will always be more useful for you to declare yourself and to fight an open war; for, in the first case, if you do not declare your intentions, you will always be the prey of the victor to the delight and satisfaction of the vanquished, and you will have no reason why anyone would come to your assistance; because whoever wins does not want reluctant allies who would not assist him in times of adversity; and whoever loses will not give you refuge since you were unwilling to run the risk of coming to his aid.

Antiochus came into Greece, sent there by the Aeolians to drive out the Romans. Antiochus sent envoys to the Achaeans, who were friends of the Romans, to encourage them to adopt a neutral policy; and, on the other hand, the Romans were urging them to take up arms on their behalf. This matter came up for debate in the council of the Achaeans, where the legate of Antiochus persuaded them to remain neutral; to this the Roman legate replied: 'The counsel these men give you about not entering the war is indeed contrary to your interests; without respect, without dignity, you will be the prey of the victors.'

And it will always happen that he who is not your friend will request your neutrality and he who is your friend will ask you to declare yourself by taking up your arms. And irresolute princes, in order to avoid present dangers, follow the neutral road most of the time, and most of the time they are ruined. But when the prince declares himself vigorously in favour of one side, if the one with whom you have joined wins, although he may be powerful and you may be left to his discretion, he has an obligation to you and there does exist a bond of friendship; and men are never so dishonest that they will crush you with such a show of ingratitude; and then, victories are never so clear-cut that the victor need be completely free of caution, especially when justice is concerned. But if the one with whom you join loses, you will be taken in by him; and while he is able, he will help you, and you will become the comrade of a fortune which can rise up again.

In the second case, when those who fight together are of such a kind that you need not fear the one who wins, it is even more prudent to join his side, since you go to the downfall of a prince with the aid of another prince who should have saved him if he had been wise; and in winning he is at your discretion, and it is impossible for him not to win with your aid.

And here it is to be noted that a prince should avoid ever joining forces with one more powerful than himself against others unless necessity compels it, as was said above; for you remain his prisoner if you win, and princes should avoid, as much as possible, being left at the mercy of others. The Venetians allied themselves with France against the Duke of Milan; and they could have avoided that alliance, which resulted in their ruin. But when such an alliance cannot be avoided (as happened to the Florentines when the Pope and Spain led their armies to attack Lombardy), then a prince should join in, for the reasons given above. Nor should any state ever believe that it can always choose safe courses of action; on the contrary, it should think that they will all be doubtful; for we find this to be in the order of things: that we never try to avoid one disadvantage without running into another; but prudence consists in knowing how to recognize the nature of disadvantages and how to choose the least bad as good.

A prince also should demonstrate that he is a lover of talent by giving recognition to men of ability and by honouring those who excel in a particular field. Furthermore, he should encourage his subjects to be free to pursue their trades in tranquillity, whether in commerce, agriculture, or in any other trade a man may have. And he should act in such a way that a man is not afraid to increase his goods for fear that they will be taken away from him, while another will not be afraid to engage in commerce for fear of taxes; instead, he must set up rewards for those who wish to do these things, and for anyone who seeks in any way to aggrandize his city or state. He should, besides this, at the appropriate times of the year, keep the populace occupied with festivals and spectacles. And because each city is divided into guilds or clans, he should take account of these groups, meet with them on occasion, offer himself as an example of humanity and munificence, always, nevertheless, maintaining firmly the dignity of his position, for this should never be lacking in any way.

## CHAPTER XXII

### *On the Prince's Private Advisers*

The choice of advisers is of no little import to a prince; and they are good or not, according to the wisdom of the prince. The first thing one does to evaluate the wisdom of a ruler is to examine the men that he has around him; and when they are capable and faithful one can always consider him wise, for he has known how to recognize their ability and to keep them loyal; but when they are otherwise one can always form a low impression of him; for the first error he makes is made in this choice of advisers.

There was no one who knew Messer Antonio da Venafro, adviser of Pandolfo Petrucci, Prince of Siena, who did not judge Pandolfo to be a very worthy man for having him as his minister. For there are three types of intelligence: one understands on its own, the second discerns what others understand, the third neither understands by itself nor through the intelligence of others; that first kind is most excellent, the second excellent, the third useless; therefore, it was necessary that if Pandolfo's intelligence were not of the first sort it must have been of the second: for, whenever a man has the intelligence to recognize the good or the evil that a man does or says, although he may not have original ideas of his own, he recognizes the bad deeds and the good deeds of the adviser, and he is able to praise the latter and to correct the others; and the adviser cannot hope to deceive him and thus he maintains his good behaviour.

But as to how a prince may know the adviser, there is this way which never fails. When you see that the adviser thinks more about himself than about you, and that in all his deeds he seeks his own interests, such a man as this will never be a good adviser

and you will never be able to trust him; for a man who has the state of another in his hand must never think about himself but always about his prince, and he must never be concerned with anything that does not concern his prince. And on the other hand, the prince should think of the adviser in order to keep him good—honouring him, making him wealthy, putting him in his debt, giving him a share of the honours and the responsibilities—so that the adviser sees that he cannot exist without the prince and so his abundant wealth will not make him desire more riches, or his many duties make him fear changes. When, therefore, advisers and princes are of such a nature in their dealings with each other, they can have faith in each other; and when they are otherwise, the outcome will always be harmful either to the one or to the other.

## CHAPTER XXIII

### *On How to Avoid Flatterers*

I do not wish to omit an important matter and an error from which princes protect themselves with difficulty if they are not very clever or if they do not have good judgement. And these are the flatterers which fill the courts; for men delight so much in their own concerns, deceiving themselves in this manner, that they protect themselves from this plague with difficulty; and wishing to defend oneself from them brings with it the danger of becoming despised. For there is no other way to guard yourself against flattery than by making men understand that telling you the truth will not offend you; but when each man is able to tell you the truth you lose their respect. Therefore, a wise prince should take a third course, choosing wise men for his state and giving only those free rein to speak the truth to him, and only on such matters as he inquires about and not on others. But he should ask them about everything and should hear their opinions, and afterwards he should deliberate by himself in his own way; and with these counsels and with each of his advisers he should conduct himself in such a manner that all will realize that the more freely they speak the more they will be acceptable to him; besides these things, he should not want to hear any others, he should follow through on the policy decided upon, and he should be firm in his decisions. Anyone who does otherwise is either prey for flatterers or changes his mind often with the variance of opinions: because of this he is not respected.

I wish, in this regard, to cite a modern example. Father Luca, the representative of the present Emperor Maximilian, explained, speaking about His Majesty, how the emperor never sought advice from anyone, nor did he ever do anything in his own way; this came about because of the emperor's secretive nature, a policy contrary to the one discussed above. He communicates his plans to no one, he accepts no advice about them; but as they begin to be recognized and discovered as they are put into effect, they begin to be criticized by those around him; and he, being easily influenced, is drawn away from his plans. From this results the fact that those things he achieves in one day he destroys during the next, and no one ever understands what he wishes or plans to do, and one cannot rely upon his decisions.

A prince, therefore, should always seek counsel, but when he wishes and not when others wish it; on the contrary, he should discourage anyone from giving him counsel unless it is requested. But he should be a great inquisitor and then, concerning the matters inquired about, a patient listener to the truth; furthermore, if he learns that anyone, for any reason, does not tell him the truth, he should become angry. And although many feel that any prince who is considered clever is so reputed not because of his own character but because of the good advisers he has around him, without a doubt they are deceived. For this is a general rule which never fails: that a prince who is not wise in his own right cannot be well advised, unless by chance he has submitted himself to a single person who governs him in everything and who is a very prudent individual. In this case he could well receive good advice, but it would not last long because that adviser would in a brief time take

the state away from him. But if he seeks advice from more than one, a prince who is not wise will never have consistent advice, nor will he know how to make it consistent on his own; each of his advisers will think about his own interests; he will not know either how to correct or to understand them. And one cannot find advisers who are otherwise, for men always turn out badly for you unless some necessity makes them good. Therefore, it is to be concluded that good advice, from whomever it may come, must arise from the prudence of the prince and not the prince's prudence from the good advice.

## CHAPTER XXV

### *On Fortune's Role in Human Affairs and How She Can Be Dealt With*

It is now unknown to me that many have held, and still hold, the opinion that the things of this world are, in a manner, controlled by fortune and by God, that men with their wisdom cannot control them, and, on the contrary, that men can have no remedy whatsoever for them; and for this reason they might judge that they need not sweat much over such matters but let them be governed by fate. This opinion has been more strongly held in our own times because of the great variation of affairs that has been observed and that is being observed every day which is beyond human conjecture. Sometimes, as I think about these things, I am inclined to their opinion to a certain extent. Nevertheless, in order that our free will be not extinguished, I judge it to be true that fortune is the arbiter of one half of our actions, but that she still leaves the control of the other half, or almost that, to us. And I compare her to one of those ruinous rivers that, when they become enraged, flood the plains, tear down the trees and buildings, taking up earth from one spot and placing it upon another; everyone flees from them, everyone yields to their onslaught, unable to oppose them in any way. But although they are of such a nature, it does not follow that when the weather is calm we cannot take precautions with embankments and dikes, so that when they rise up again either the waters will be channelled off or their impetus will not be either so unchecked or so damaging. The same things happen where fortune is concerned: she shows her force where there is no organized strength to resist her; and she directs her impact there where she knows that dikes and embankments are not constructed to hold her. And if you consider Italy, the seat of these changes and the nation which has set them in motion, you will see a country without embankments and without a single bastion: for if she were defended by the necessary forces, like Germany, Spain, and France, either this flood would not have produced the great changes that it has or it would not have come upon us at all. And this I consider enough to say about fortune in general terms.

But, limiting myself more to particulars, I say that one sees a prince prosper today and come to ruin tomorrow without having seen him change his character or any of the reasons that have been discussed at length earlier; that is, that a prince who relies completely upon fortune will come to ruin as soon as she changes; I also believe that the man who adapts his course of action to the nature of the times will succeed and, likewise, that the man who sets his course of action out of tune with the times will come to grief. For one can observe that men, in the affairs which lead them to the end that they seek—that is, glory and wealth—proceed in different ways; one by caution, another with impetuousness; one through violence, another with guile; one with patience, another with its opposite; and each one by these various means can attain his goals. And we also see, in the case of two cautious men, that one reaches his goal while the other does not; and, likewise, two men equally succeed using two different means, one being cautious and the other impetuous: this arises from nothing else than the nature of the times that either suit or do not suit their course of action. From this results that which I have said, that two men, working in opposite ways, can produce the same outcome; and of two men working in the same fashion one achieves his goal and the other does not. On this also depends the variation of what is good; for, if a man governs himself with caution and patience, and the times and conditions are turning in

such a way that his policy is a good one, he will prosper; but if the times and conditions change, he will be ruined because he does not change his method of procedure. Nor is there to be found a man so prudent that he knows how to adapt himself to this, both because he cannot deviate from that to which he is by nature inclined and also because he cannot be persuaded to depart from a path, having always prospered by following it. And therefore the cautious man, when it is time to act impetuously, does not know how to do so, and he is ruined; but if he had changed his conduct with the times, fortune would not have changed.

Pope Julius II acted impetuously in all his affairs, and he found the times and conditions so apt to this course of action that he always achieved successful results. Consider the first campaign he waged against Bologna while Messer Giovanni Bentivogli was still alive. The Venetians were unhappy about it; so was the King of Spain; Julius still had negotiations going on about it with France; and nevertheless, he started personally on this expedition with his usual ferocity and lack of caution. Such a move kept Spain and the Venetians at bay, the latter out of fear and the former out of a desire to regain the entire Kingdom of Naples; and at the same time it drew the King of France into the affair, for when the King saw that the Pope had already made this move, he judged that he could not deny him the use of his troops without obviously harming him, since he wanted his friendship in order to defeat the Venetians. And therefore Julius achieved with his impetuous action what no other pontiff would ever have achieved with the greatest of human wisdom; for, if he had waited to leave Rome with agreements settled and things in order, as any other pontiff might have done, he would never have succeeded, because the King of France would have found a thousand excuses and the others would have aroused in him a thousand fears. I wish to leave unmentioned his other deeds, which were all similar and which were all successful. And the brevity of his life did not let him experience the opposite, since if times which necessitated caution had come his ruin would have followed from it: for never would he have deviated from those methods to which his nature inclined him.

I conclude, therefore, that since fortune changes

and men remain set in their ways, men will succeed when the two are in harmony and fail when they are not in accord. I am certainly convinced of this: that it is better to be impetuous than cautious, because fortune is a woman, and it is necessary, in order to keep her down, to beat her and to struggle with her. And it is seen that she more often allows herself to be taken over by men who are impetuous than by those who make cold advances; and then, being a woman, she is always the friend of young men, for they are less cautious, more aggressive, and they command her with more audacity.

# Discourses

## BOOK ONE

### *The Preface*

Although owing to the envy inherent in man's nature it has always been no less dangerous to discover new ways and methods than to set off in search of new seas and unknown lands because most men are much more ready to belittle than to praise another's actions, none the less, impelled by the natural desire I have always had to labour, regardless of anything, on that which I believe to be for the common benefit of all, I have decided to enter upon a new way, as yet untrodden by anyone else. And, even if it entails a tiresome and difficult task, it may yet reward me in that there are those who will look kindly on the purpose of these my labours. And if my poor ability, my limited experience of current affairs, my feeble knowledge of antiquity, should render my efforts imperfect and of little worth, they may none the less point the way for another of greater ability, capacity for analysis, and judgement, who will achieve my ambition; which, if it does not earn me praise, should not earn me reproaches.

When, therefore, I consider in what honour antiquity is held, and how—to cite but one instance—a bit of an old statue has fetched a high price that someone may have it by him to give honour to his house and that it may be possible for it to be copied by those who are keen on this art; and how the latter then with great industry take pains to reproduce it in all their works; and when, on the other hand, I notice that what history has to say about the highly virtuous actions performed by ancient kingdoms and republics, by their kings, their generals, their citizens, their legislators, and by others who have gone to the trouble of serving their country, is rather admired than imitated; nay, is so shunned by everybody in each little thing they do, that of the virtue of bygone days there remains no trace, it cannot but fill me at once with astonishment and grief. The more so when I see that in the civic disputes which arise between citizens and in the diseases men get, they always have recourse to decisions laid down by the ancients and to the prescriptions they drew up. For the civil law is nothing but a collection of decisions, made by jurists of old, which the jurists of today have tabulated in orderly fashion for our instruction. Nor, again, is medicine anything but a record of experiments, performed by doctors of old, upon which the doctors of our day base their prescriptions. In spite of which in constituting republics, in maintaining states, in governing kingdoms, in forming an army or conducting a war, in dealing with subjects, in extending the empire, one finds neither prince nor republic who repairs to antiquity for examples.

This is due in my opinion not so much to the weak state to which the religion of today has brought the world, or to the evil wrought in many provinces and cities of Christendom by ambition conjoined with idleness, as to the lack of a proper appreciation of history, owing to people failing to realize the significance of what they read, and to their having no taste for the delicacies it comprises. Hence it comes about

Translated by Leslie J. Walker, S.J., revised by Brian Richardson.

that the great bulk of those who read it take pleasure in hearing of the various incidents which are contained in it, but never think of imitating them, since they hold them to be not merely difficult but impossible of imitation, as if the heaven, the sun, the elements and man had in their motion, their order, and their potency, become different from what they used to be.

Since I want to get men out of this wrong way of thinking, I have thought fit to write a commentary on all those books of Titus Livy which have not by the malignity of time had their continuity broken. It will comprise what I have arrived at by comparing ancient with modern events, and think necessary for the better understanding of them, so that those who read what I have to say may the more easily draw those practical lessons which one should seek to obtain from the study of history. Though the enterprise is difficult, yet, with the help of those who have encouraged me to undertake the task, I think I can carry it out in such a way that there shall remain to another but a short road to traverse in order to reach the place assigned.

## 1. Concerning the Origin of Cities in General and of Rome in Particular

Those who read of the origin of the city of Rome, of its legislators and of its constitution, will not be surprised that in this city such great virtue was maintained for so many centuries, and that later on there came into being the empire into which that republic developed.

Since this first discourse will deal with its origin, I would point out that all cities are built either by natives of the place in which they are built, or by people from elsewhere. The first case comes about when inhabitants, dispersed in many small communities, find that they cannot enjoy security since no one community of itself, owing to its position and to the smallness of its numbers, is strong enough to resist the onslaught of an invader, and, when the enemy arrives, there is no time for them to unite for their defence; or, if there be time, they have to abandon many of their strongholds, and thus at once fall as prey to their enemies. Hence, to escape these dan-

gers, either of their own accord or at the suggestion of someone of greater authority among them, such communities undertake to live together in some place they have chosen in order to live more conveniently and the more easily to defend themselves.

This was the case with Athens and Venice, among many others. Athens was built under the authority of Theseus for reasons such as these by inhabitants who were dispersed; Venice by numerous peoples who had sought refuge in certain islets at the top of the Adriatic Sea that they might escape the wars which daily arose in Italy after the decline of the Roman empire owing to the arrival of a new lot of barbarians. There, without any particular person or prince to give them a constitution, they began to live as a community under laws which seemed to them appropriate for their maintenance. And this happened because of the long repose the situation afforded them in that the sea at their end had no exit and the peoples who were ravaging Italy had no ships in which to infest them. This being so, a beginning, however small, sufficed to bring them to their present greatness.

The second case occurs when a city is built by men of a foreign race. They may either be free men, or men dependent on others, as are the colonies sent out either by a republic or a prince to relieve their towns of some of the population or for the defence of newly acquired territory which they desire to hold securely and without expense. The Romans built a number of such cities, and this throughout the whole of their empire. Others have been built by a prince, not that he may dwell there, but to enhance his reputation, as the city of Alexandria was built by Alexander. And since such cities are not at the outset free, it very seldom happens that they make great progress or that of their own doing they come to be reckoned among the capitals of kingdoms.

It was thus that Florence came to be built; for—whether it was built by the soldiers of Sulla, or was built by chance by inhabitants from the hills of Fiesole who, relying on the long peace which the world enjoyed under Octavian, came to dwell in the plains above the Arno—it was built under the Roman empire, and could at the outset make no addition to its territory save such as was allowed by the courtesy of the emperor.

Free cities are those which are built by peoples who, either under a prince or of their own accord, are driven by pestilence or famine or war to abandon the land of their birth and to look for new habitations. These may be either cities they find in countries they have occupied and in which they go to dwell, as Moses did; or new cities which they build, as Aeneas did. In this case the virtue of the builder is discernible in the fortune of what was built, for the city is more or less remarkable according as he is more or less virtuous who is responsible for the start. This virtue shows itself in two ways: first in the choice of a site, and secondly in the drawing up of laws.

Since men work either of necessity or by choice, and since there is found to be greater virtue where choice has less to say to it, the question arises whether it would not be better to choose a barren place in which to build cities so that men would have to be industrious and less given to idleness, and so would be more united because, owing to the poor situation, there would be less occasion for discord; as happened in Ragusa and in many other cities built in such-like places.

Such a choice would undoubtedly be wiser and more advantageous were men content to earn their own living and not anxious to lord it over others. Since, however, security for man is impossible unless it be conjoined with power, it is necessary to avoid sterile places and for cities to be put in very fertile places where, when expansion has taken place owing to the fruitfulness of the land, it may be possible for them both to defend themselves against attack and to overcome any who stand in the way of the city's greatness. As to the idleness which such a situation may encourage, it must be provided for by laws imposing that need to work which the situation does not impose. It is advisable here to follow the example of those wise folk who have dwelt in most beautiful and fertile lands, i.e. in such lands as tend to produce idleness and ineptitude for training in virtue of any kind, and who, in order to obviate the disasters which the idleness induced by the amenities of the land might cause, have imposed the need

for training on those who were to become soldiers, and have made this training such that men there have become better soldiers than those in countries which were rough and sterile by nature.

A case in point is the kingdom of the Egyptians which, not withstanding the amenities of the land, imposed the need to work so successfully by means of laws that it produced most excellent men, whose names, if they had not been lost in antiquity, would be even more celebrated than that of Alexander the Great, and than those of many others whose memory is still fresh. So, too, anyone who has reflected on the kingdom of the Sultan, on the discipline of the Mamelukes, and on that of their troops, before they were wiped out by Selim, the Great Turk, might have noted there the many exercises the troops underwent and might have inferred from this how greatly they feared the idleness to which the beneficence of the country might have led if they had not obviated it by very strict laws.

I maintain, then, that it is more prudent to place a city in a fertile situation, provided its fertility is kept in due bounds by laws. When Alexander the Great was proposing to build a city that should redound to his credit, Deinocrates, the architect, came to him and suggested that he should build it on Mount Athos, for, besides being a strong place, it could be so fashioned as to give the city a human form, which would be a remarkable thing, a rare thing, and worthy of his greatness. And on what, Alexander asked, would the inhabitants live? Deinocrates replied that he had not thought of this. Whereupon Alexander laughed, and, leaving the mountain alone, built Alexandria where inhabitants would be glad to live owing to the richness of the land and to the conveniences afforded by the sea and by the Nile.

For those, then, who, having examined the question how Rome came to be built, hold that Aeneas was its first founder, it will be a city built by foreigners, but for those who prefer Romulus, it will be a city built by natives of the place. But, whichever be the case, both will recognize that it began as a free city, dependent upon no one. They will also recognize, as we shall presently point out, under what strict discipline it was placed by the laws made by Romulus, Numa, and others, and that, in consequence, neither its fertile situation, the convenience afforded by the sea, its frequent victories, nor the greatness of its empire, were for many centuries able to corrupt it, but that these laws kept it so rich in virtue that there has never been any other city or any other republic so well adorned.

Wherefore since what was done by this city, as Titus Livy records it, was done sometimes in accordance with public enactments, sometimes on the initiative of private individuals, and sometimes within the city, sometimes abroad, I shall begin by discussing such of the events due to public decrees as I shall judge to be more worthy of comment, and with the events shall conjoin their consequences to which the discourses of this first book or first part will be restricted.

## 2. How Many Kinds of State There Are and of What Kind Was That of Rome

I propose to dispense with a discussion of cities which from the outset have been subject to another power, and shall speak only of those which have from the outset been far removed from any kind of external servitude, but, instead, have from the start been governed in accordance with their wishes, whether as republics or principalities. As such cities have had diverse origins, so too they have had diverse laws and institutions. For either at the outset, or before very long, to some of them laws have been given by some one person at some one time, as laws were given to the Spartans by Lycurgus; whereas others have acquired them by chance and at different times as occasion arose. This was the case in Rome.

Happy indeed should we call that state which produces a man so prudent that men can live securely under the laws which he prescribes without having to emend them. Sparta, for instance, observed its laws for more than eight hundred years without corrupting them and without any dangerous disturbance. Unhappy, on the other hand, in some degree is that city to be deemed which, not having chanced to meet with a prudent organizer, has to reorganize itself. And, of such, that is the more unhappy which

is the more remote from order; and that is the more remote from order whose institutions have missed altogether the straight road which leads it to its perfect and true destiny. For it is almost impossible that states of this type should by any eventuality be set on the right road again; whereas those which, if their order is not perfect, have made a good beginning and are capable of improvement, may become perfect should something happen which provides the opportunity. It should, however, be noted that they will never introduce order without incurring danger, because few men ever welcome new laws setting up a new order in the state unless necessity makes it clear to them that there is need for such laws; and since such a necessity cannot arise without danger, the state may easily be ruined before the new order has been brought to completion. The republic of Florence bears this out, for owing to what happened at Arezzo in '02 it was reconstituted, and owing to what happened at Prato in '12 its constitution was destroyed.

It being now my intention to discuss what were the institutions of the city of Rome and what events conduced to its perfection, I would remark that those who have written about states say that there are to be found in them one of three forms of government, called by them *Principality*, *Aristocracy* and *Democracy*, and that those who set up a government in any particular state must adopt one of them, as best suits their purpose.

Others—and with better judgement many think—say that there are six types of government, of which three are very bad, and three are good in themselves but easily become corrupt, so that they too must be classed as pernicious. Those that are good are the three above mentioned. Those that are bad are the other three, which depend on them, and each of them is so like the one associated with it that it easily passes from one form to the other. For *Principality* easily becomes *Tyranny*. From *Aristocracy* the transition to *Oligarchy* is an easy one. *Democracy* is without difficulty converted into *Anarchy*. So that if anyone who is organizing a commonwealth sets up one of the three first forms of government, he sets up what will last but for a while, since there are no means whereby to prevent it passing into its contrary, on account of the likeness which in such a case virtue has to vice.

These variations of government among men are due to chance. For in the beginning of the world, when its inhabitants were few, they lived for a time scattered like the beasts. Then, with the multiplication of their offspring, they drew together and, in order the better to be able to defend themselves, began to look about for a man stronger and more courageous than the rest, made him their head, and obeyed him.

It was thus that men learned how to distinguish what is honest and good from what is pernicious and wicked, for the sight of someone injuring his benefactor evoked in them hatred and sympathy and they blamed the ungrateful and respected those who showed gratitude, well aware that the same injuries might have been done to themselves. Hence to prevent evil of this kind they took to making laws and to assigning punishments to those who contravened them. The notion of justice thus came into being.

In this way it came about that, when later on they had to choose a prince, they did not have recourse to the boldest as formerly, but to one who excelled in prudence and justice.

But when at a yet later stage they began to make the prince hereditary instead of electing him, his heirs soon began to degenerate as compared with their ancestors, and, forsaking virtuous deeds, considered that princes have nought else to do but to surpass other men in extravagance, lasciviousness, and every other form of licentiousness. With the result that the prince came to be hated, and, since he was hated, came to be afraid, and from fear soon passed to offensive action, which quickly brought about a tyranny.

From which, before long, was begotten the source of their downhill; for tyranny gave rise to conspiracies and plots against princes, organized not by timid and weak men, but by men conspicuous for their liberality, magnanimity, wealth and ability, for such men could not stand the dishonourable life the prince was leading. The masses, therefore, at the instigation of these powerful leaders, took up arms against the prince, and, when he had been liquidated, submitted to the authority of those whom they looked upon as their liberators. Hence the latter, to whom the very term 'sole head' had become odious, formed themselves into a government. Moreover, in the beginning, mindful of what they had suffered under a tyranny, they ruled in accordance with the laws which they had made, subordinated their own convenience to the common advantage, and, both in private matters and public affairs, governed and preserved order with the utmost diligence.

But when the administration passed to their descendants who had no experience of the changeability of fortune, had not been through bad times, and instead of remaining content with the civic equality then prevailing, reverted to avarice, ambition and to seizing other men's womenfolk, they caused government by an aristocracy to become government by an oligarchy in which civic rights were entirely disregarded; so that in a short time there came to pass in their case the same thing as happened to the tyrant, for the masses, sick of their government, were ready to help anyone who had any sort of plan for attacking their rulers; and so there soon arose someone who with the aid of the masses liquidated them.

Then, since the memory of the prince and of the injuries inflicted by him was still fresh, and since, having got rid of government by the few, they had no desire to return to that of a prince, they turned to a democratic form of government, which they organized in such a way that no sort of authority was vested either in a few powerful men or in a prince.

And, since all forms of government are to some extent respected at the outset, this democratic form of government maintained itself for a while but not for long, especially when the generation that had organized it had passed away. For anarchy quickly supervened, in which no respect was shown either for the individual or for the official, and which was such that, as everyone did what he liked, all sorts of outrages were constantly committed. The outcome was inevitable. Either at the suggestion of some good man or because this anarchy had to be got rid of somehow, principality was once again restored. And from this there was, stage by stage, a return to anarchy, by way of the transitions and for the reasons assigned.

This, then, is the cycle through which all commonwealths pass, whether they govern themselves or are governed. But rarely do they return to the same form of government, for there can scarce be a state of such vitality that it can undergo often such changes and yet remain in being. What usually happens is that, while in a state of commotion in which it lacks both counsel and strength, a state becomes subject to a neighbouring and better organized state. Were it not so, a commonwealth might go on for ever passing through these governmental transitions.

I maintain then, that all the forms of government mentioned above are far from satisfactory, the three good ones because their life is so short, the three bad ones because of their inherent malignity. Hence prudent legislators, aware of their defects, refrained from adopting as such any one of these forms, and chose instead one that shared in them all, since they thought such a government would be stronger and more stable, for if in one and the same state there was principality, aristocracy and democracy each would keep watch over the other.

Lycurgus is one of those who have earned no small measure of praise for constitutions of this kind. For in the laws which he gave to Sparta, he assigned to the kings, to the aristocracy and to the populace each its own function, and thus introduced a form of government which lasted for more than eight hundred years to his every great credit and to the tranquillity of that city.

It was not so in the case of Solon, who drew up laws for Athens, for he set up merely a democratic form of government, which was so short-lived that he saw before his death the birth of a tyranny under Pisistratus; and though, forty years later, Pisistratus' heirs were expelled, and Athens returned to liberty because it again adopted a democratic form of government in accordance with Solon's laws, it did not retain its liberty for more than a hundred years. For, in spite of the fact that many constitutions were made whereby to restrain the arrogance of the upper class and the licentiousness of the general public, for which Solon had

made no provision, none the less Athens had a very short life as compared with that of Sparta because with democracy Solon had not blended either princely power or that of the aristocracy.

But let us come to Rome. In spite of the fact that Rome had no Lycurgus to give it at the outset such a constitution as would ensure to it a long life of freedom, yet, owing to friction between the plebs and the senate, so many things happened that chance effected what had not been provided by a law giver. So that, if Rome did not get fortune's first gift, it got its second. For her early institutions, though defective, were not on wrong lines and so might pave the way to perfection. For Romulus and the rest of the kings made many good laws quite compatible with freedom; but, because their aim was to found a kingdom, not a republic, when the city became free, it lacked many institutions essential to the preservation of liberty, which had to be provided, since they had not been provided by the kings. So, when it came to pass that its kings lost their sovereignty, for reasons and in the manner described earlier in this discourse, those who had expelled them at once appointed two consuls to take the place of the king, so that what they expelled was the title of king, not the royal power. In the republic, then, at this stage there were the consuls and the senate, so that as yet it comprised but two of the aforesaid estates, namely, Principality and Aristocracy. It remained to find a place for Democracy. This came about when the Roman nobility became so overbearing for reasons which will be given later— that the populace rose against them, and they were constrained by the fear that they might lose all, to grant the populace a share in the government; the senate and the consuls retaining, however, sufficient authority for them to be able to maintain their position in the republic.

It was in this way that tribunes of the plebs came to be appointed, and their appointment did much to stabilize the form of government in this republic, for in its government all three estates now had a share. And so favoured was it by fortune that, though the transition from Monarchy to Aristocracy and thence to Democracy, took place by the very stages and for the very reasons laid down earlier in this discourse, none the less the granting of authority to the aristocracy did not abolish altogether the royal estate, nor was the authority of the aristocracy wholly removed when the populace was granted a share in it. On the contrary, the blending of these estates made a perfect commonwealth; and since it was friction between the plebs and the senate that brought this perfection about, in the next two chapters we shall show more fully how this came to be.

## 9. That It Is Necessary to Be the Sole Authority if One Would Constitute a Republic Afresh or Would Reform It Thoroughly Regardless of Its Ancient Institutions

To some it will appear strange that I have got so far in my discussion of Roman history without having made any mention of the founders of that republic or of either its religious or its military institutions. Hence, that I may not keep the minds of those who are anxious to hear about such things any longer in suspense, let me say that many perchance will think it a bad precedent that the founder of a civic state, such as Romulus, should first have killed his brother, and then have acquiesced in the death of Titus Tatius, the Sabine, whom he had chosen as his colleague in the kingdom. They will urge that, if such actions be justifiable, ambitious citizens who are eager to govern, will follow the example of their prince and use violence against those who are opposed to *their* authority. A view that will hold good provided we leave out of consideration the end which Romulus had in committing these murders.

One should take it as a general rule that rarely, if ever, does it happen that a state, whether it be a republic or a kingdom, is either well-ordered at the outset or radically transformed *vis-à-vis* its old institutions unless this be done by one person. It is likewise essential that there should be but one person upon whose mind and method depends any similar process of organization. Wherefore the prudent organizer of a state whose intention it is to govern

not in his own interests but for the common good, and not in the interest of his successors but for the sake of that fatherland which is common to all, should contrive to be alone in his authority. Nor will any reasonable man blame him for taking any action, however extraordinary, which may be of service in the organizing of a kingdom or the constituting of a republic It is a sound maxim that reprehensible actions may be justified by their effects, and that when the effect is good, as it was in the case of Romulus, it always justifies the action. For it is the man who uses violence to spoil things, not the man who uses it to mend them, that is blameworthy.

The organizer of a state ought further to have sufficient prudence and virtue not to bequeath the authority he has assumed to any other person, for, seeing that men are more prone to evil than to good, his successor might well make ambitious use of that which he had used virtuously. Furthermore, though but one person suffices for the purpose of organization, what he has organized will not last long if it continues to rest on the shoulders of one man, but may well last if many remain in charge and many look to its maintenance. Because, though the many are incompetent to draw up a constitution since diversity of opinion will prevent them from discovering how best to do it, yet when they realize it has been done, they will not agree to abandon it.

That Romulus was a man of this character, that for the death of his brother and of his colleague he deserves to be excused, and that what he did was done for the common good and not to satisfy his personal ambition, is shown by his having at once instituted a senate with which he consulted and with whose views his decisions were in accord. Also, a careful consideration of the authority which Romulus reserved to himself will show that all he reserved to himself was the command of the army in time of war and the convoking of the senate. It is clear, too, that when the Tarquins were expelled and Rome became free, none of its ancient institutions were changed, save that in lieu of a permanent king there were appointed each year two consuls. This shows that the original institutions of this city as a whole were more in conformity with a political and self-governing state than with absolutism or tyranny.

I might adduce in support of what I have just said numberless examples, for example Moses, Lycurgus, Solon and other founders of kingdoms and republics who assumed authority that they might formulate laws to the common good; but this I propose to omit since it is well known. I shall adduce but one further example, not so celebrated but worth considering by those who are contemplating the drawing up of good laws. It is this. Agis, King of Sparta, was considering how to confine the activities of the Spartans to the limits originally set for them by the laws of Lycurgus, because it seemed to him that it was owing to their having deviated from them in part that this city had lost a good deal of its ancient virtue, and, in consequence, a good deal of its power and of its empire. He was, however, while his project was still in the initial stage, killed by the Spartan ephors, who took him to be a man who was out to set up a tyranny. But Cleomenes, his successor in that kingdom, having learned from some records and writings of Agis which he had discovered, what was the latter's true mind and intention, determined to pursue the same plan. He realized, however, that he could not do this for the good of his country unless he became the sole authority there, and, since it seemed to him impossible owing to man's ambition to help the many against the will of the few, he took a suitable opportunity and had all the ephors killed and anybody else who might obstruct him. He then renewed in their entirety the laws of Lycurgus. By so doing he gave fresh life to Sparta, and his reputation might thereby have become as great as that of Lycurgus if it had not been for the power of the Macedonians and the weakness of other Greek republics. For, after Sparta had thus been reorganized, it was attacked by the Macedonians, and, since its forces proved to be inferior and it could get no outside help, it was defeated, with the result that Cleomenes' plans, however just and praiseworthy, were never brought to completion.

All things considered, therefore, I conclude that it is necessary to be the sole authority if one is to organize a state, and that Romulus' action in regard to the death of Remus and Titus Tatius is excusable, not blameworthy.

## 10. Those Who Set Up a Tyranny Are No Less Blameworthy Than Are the Founders of a Republic or a Kingdom Praiseworthy

Of all men that are praised, those are praised most who have played the chief part in founding a religion. Next come those who have founded either republics or kingdoms. After them in the order of celebratees are ranked army commanders who have added to the extent of their own dominions or to that of their country's. With whom may be conjoined men of letters of many different kinds who are each celebrated according to their status. Some modicum of praise is also ascribed to any man who excels in some art and in the practice of it, and of these the number is legion. On the other hand, those are held to be infamous and detestable who extirpate religion, subvert kingdoms and republics, make war on virtue, on letters, and on any art that brings advantage and honour to the human race, i.e. the profane, the violent, the ignorant, the worthless, the idle, the coward. Nor will there ever be anyone, be he foolish or wise, wicked or good, who, if called upon to choose between these two classes of men, will not praise the one that calls for praise and blame the one that calls for blame.

And yet, notwithstanding this, almost all men, deceived by the false semblance of good and the false semblance of renown, allow themselves either wilfully or ignorantly to slip into the ranks of those who deserve blame rather than praise; and, when they might have founded a republic or a kingdom to their immortal honour, turn their thoughts to tyranny, and fail to see what fame, what glory, security, tranquillity, conjoined with peace of mind, they are missing by adopting this course, and what infamy, scorn, abhorrence, danger and disquiet they are incurring.

Nor is it possible for anybody, whether he be but a private citizen living in some republic, or has been fortunate enough or virtuous enough to have become a prince, to read history and to make use of the records of ancient deeds, without preferring, if he be a private citizen, to conduct himself in his fatherland rather as Scipio did than as Caesar did, or, if he be a prince, as did Agesilaus, Timoleon and Dion, rather than as did Nabis, Phalaris and Dionysius, for he could not but see how strongly the latter are dismissed with scorn, and how highly the former are praised. He would also notice that Timoleon and the like had no less authority in their respective countries than had Dionysius or Phalaris in theirs, and would observe that they enjoyed far greater security.

Nor should anyone be deceived by Caesar's renown when he finds writers extolling him before others, for those who praise him have either been corrupted by his fortune or overawed by the long continuance of the empire which, since it was ruled under that name, did not permit writers to speak freely of him. If, however, anyone desires to know what writers would have said, had they been free, he has but to look at what they say of Catiline. For Caesar is the more blameworthy of the two, in that he who has done wrong is more blameworthy than he who has but desired to do wrong. Or, again, let him look at the praise bestowed on Brutus: Caesar they could not find fault with on account of his power, so they cry up his enemy.

Let he who has become a prince in a republic consider, after Rome became an Empire, how much more praise is due to those emperors who acted, like good princes, in accordance with the laws, than to those who acted otherwise. It will be found that Titus, Nerva, Trajan, Hadrian, Antoninus and Marcus, had no need of soldiers to form a praetorian guard, nor of a multitude of legions to protect them, for their defence lay in their habits, the goodwill of the people, and the affection of the senate. It will be seen, too, in the case of Caligula, Nero, Vitellius and other bad emperors, how it availed them little to have armies from the East and from the West to save them from the enemies they had made by their bad habits and their evil life.

If the history of these emperors be pondered well, it should serve as a striking lesson to any prince, and should teach him to distinguish between the ways of renown and of infamy, the ways of security and of

fear. For of the twenty-six emperors from Caesar to Maximinus, sixteen were assassinated and only ten died a natural death. And, if some of those who were killed were good men, as Galba and Pertinax were, their death was due to the corruption which their predecessors had introduced among the troops. While, if among those who died ordinary death, there was a wicked man, like Severus, it must be put down to his great good luck and to his 'virtue', two things of which few men enjoy both. It will be seen, too, from a perusal of their history on what principle a good kingdom should rest; for all the emperors who acquired imperial power by inheritance were bad men, with the exception of Titus; those who acquired it through adoption, were all good, like the five counting from Nerva to Marcus; and when it fell to their heirs a period of decadence again ensued.

Let a prince put before himself the period from Nerva to Marcus, and let him compare it with the preceding period and with that which came after, and then let him decide in which he would rather have been born, and during which he would have chosen to be emperor. What he will find when good princes were ruling, is a prince securely reigning among subjects no less secure, a world replete with peace and justice. He will see the senate's authority respected, the magistrates honoured, rich citizens enjoying their wealth, nobility and virtue held in the highest esteem, and everything working smoothly and going well. He will notice, on the other hand, the absence of any rancour, any licentiousness, corruption or ambition, and that in this golden age everyone is free to hold and to defend his own opinion. He will behold, in short, the world triumphant, its prince glorious and respected by all, the people fond of him and secure under his rule.

If he then looks attentively at the times of the other emperors, he will find them distraught with wars, torn by seditions, brutal alike in peace and in war, princes frequently killed by assassins, civil wars and foreign wars constantly occurring, Italy in travail and ever a prey to fresh misfortunes, its cities demolished and pillaged. He will see Rome burnt, its Capitol demolished by its own citizens, ancient temples lying desolate, religious rites grown corrupt, adultery rampant throughout the city. He will find the sea covered with exiles and the rocks stained with blood. In Rome he will see countless atrocities perpetrated; rank, riches, the honours men have won, and, above all, virtue, looked upon as a capital crime. He will find calumniators rewarded, servants suborned to turn against their masters, freed men to turn against their patrons, and those who lack enemies attacked by their friends. He will thus happily learn how much Rome, Italy, and the world owed to Caesar.

There can be no question but that every human being will be afraid to imitate the bad times, and will be imbued with an ardent desire to emulate the good. And, should a good prince seek worldly renown, he should most certainly covet possession of a city that has become corrupt, not, with Caesar, to complete its spoliation, but, with Romulus, to reform it. Nor in very truth can the heavens afford men a better opportunity of acquiring renown; nor can men desire anything better than this. And if in order to reform a city one were obliged to give up the principate, someone who did not reform it in order not to fall from that rank would have some excuse. There is, however, no excuse if one can both keep the principate and reform the city.

In conclusion, then, let those to whom the heavens grant such opportunities reflect that two courses are open to them: either so to behave that in life they rest secure and in death become renowned, or so to behave that in life they are in continual straits, and in death leave behind all imperishable record of their infamy.

## BOOK TWO

### The Preface

Men always, but not always with good reason, praise bygone days and criticize the present, and so partial are they to the past that they not only admire past ages the knowledge of which has come down to them in written records, but also, when they grow old, what they remember having seen in their youth.

And, when this view is wrong, as it usually is, there are, I am convinced, various causes to which the mistake may be due.

The first of them is, I think, this. The whole truth about olden times is not grasped, since what redounds to their discredit is often passed over in silence, whereas what is likely to make them appear glorious is pompously recounted in all its details. For so obsequious are most writers to the fortune of conquerors that, in order to make their victories seem glorious, they not only exaggerate their own valorous deeds, but also magnify the exploits of the enemy, so that anyone born afterwards either in the conquering or in the conquered province may find cause to marvel at such men and such times, and is bound, in short, to admire them and to feel affection for them.

Another reason is that, since it is either through fear or through envy that men come to hate things, in the case of the past the two most powerful incentives for hating it are lacking, since the past cannot hurt you nor give you cause for envy. Whereas it is otherwise with events in which you play a part and which you see with your own eyes, for of these you have an intimate knowledge, are in touch with every detail, and in them find, mingled with the good, also much which displeases you; so that you cannot help thinking them far inferior to the remote past, even though in fact the present may be much more deserving of praise and renown. I am not here referring to what pertains to the arts, for in themselves they have so much lustre that time can scarce take away or add much to the glory which they themselves deserve. I am speaking of things appertaining to human life and human customs, the evidence for whose merit is not so clear to one's eyes.

My answer is, then, that it is true there exists this habit of praising the past and criticizing the present, and not always true that to do so is a mistake, for it must be admitted that sometimes such a judgment is valid because, since human affairs are ever in a state of flux, they move either upwards or downwards. Thus one sees a city or a province that has been endowed with a sound political constitution by some eminent man, thanks to its founder's virtue for a time go on steadily improving. Anyone born in such a state at such a time, is wrong if he gives more praise to the past than to the present, and his mistake will be due to the causes we have mentioned above. But those who are born in this city or province later on, when there has come a time in which it is on the decline and is deteriorating, will not then be in error.

When I reflect that it is in this way that events pursue their course it seems to me that the world has always been in the same condition, and that in it there has been just as much good as there is evil, but that this evil and this good has varied from province to province. This may be seen from the knowledge we have on ancient kingdoms, in which the balance of good and evil changed from one to the other owing to changes in their customs, whereas the world as a whole remained the same. The only difference was that the world's virtue first found a home in Assyria, then flourished in Media and later in Persia, and at length arrived in Italy and Rome. And, if since the Roman empire there has been no other which has lasted, and in which the world's virtue has been centered, one none the less finds it distributed among many nations where men lead virtuous lives. There was, for instance, the kingdom of the Franks; the kingdom of the Turks, [i.e.] that of the Sultan; and today all the peoples of Germany. Earlier still there were the Saracens, who performed such great exploits and occupied so much of the world, since they broke up the Roman empire in the East. Hence, after ruin had overtaken the Romans, there continued to exist in all these provinces and in all these separate units, and still exists in some of them, that virtue which is desired and quite rightly praised. If, then, anyone born there praises the past over and above the present, he may well be mistaken; but anyone born in Italy who has not become at heart an ultramontane, or anyone born in Greece who has not become at heart a Turk, has good reason to criticize his own times and to praise others, since in the latter there are plenty of things to evoke his admiration, whereas in the former he comes across nothing but extreme misery, infamy and contempt, for there is no observance either of religion or of the laws, or of military traditions, but all is besmirched with filth of every kind. And so much the more are these vices detestable when they are more prevalent among those who sit on the judgement seat, prescribe rules for others, and expect from them adoration.

But to return to our main point, I maintain that if man's judgement is biased when he tries to decide which is the better, the present age, or some past age of which he cannot have so perfect a knowledge as he has of his own times precisely because it is long since past, this ought not to bias the judgment of old men when they compare the days of their youth with those of their old age, for of both they have had the same knowledge and experience. Nor would it in point of fact, if during the various phases of their lives men judged always in the same way and had the same appetites. But, as men's appetites change, even though their circumstances remain the same, it is impossible that things should look the same to them seeing that they have other appetites, other interests, other standpoints, from what they had in their youth. For, since, when men grow old, they lack energy but increase in judgement and prudence, it is inevitable that what in their youth appeared to be tolerable and good, in their old age should become intolerable and bad; so that, instead of blaming the times, they should lay the blame on their own judgement.

Furthermore, human appetites are insatiable, for by nature we are so constituted that there is nothing we cannot long for, but by fortune we are such that of these things we can attain but few. The result is that the human mind is perpetually discontented, and of its possessions is apt to grow weary. This makes it find fault with the present, praise the past, and long for the future; though for its doing so no rational cause can be assigned. Hence I am not sure but that I deserve to be reckoned among those who thus deceive themselves if in these my discourses I have praised too much the days of the ancient Romans and have found fault with our own. Indeed, if the virtue which then prevailed and the vices which are prevalent today were not as clear as the sun, I should be more reserved in my statements lest I should fall into the very fault for which I am blaming others. But as the facts are there for any one to see, I shall make so bold as to declare plainly what I think of those days and of our own, so that the minds of young men who read what I have written may turn from the one and prepare to imitate the other whenever fortune provides them with occasion for so doing. For it is the duty of a good man to point out to others what is well done, even though the malignity of the times or of fortune has not permitted you to do it for yourself, to the end that, of the many who have the capacity, some one, more beloved of heaven, may be able to do it.

Having, therefore, in the discourses of the last book spoken of the decisions the Romans came to in regard to the internal affairs of the city, in this we shall speak of the measures the Roman people took to increase their empire.

### 1. Whether Virtue or Fortune Was the Principal Cause of the Empire Which Rome Acquired

Many are of opinion, and among them Plutarch, a writer of great weight, that the Roman people was indebted for the empire it acquired rather to fortune than to virtue. Among other reasons he adduces he says that the Roman people by their own confession admit this since they ascribed all their victories to fortune, and erected more temples to Fortune than to any other god. It would seem that with this view Livy also agrees, for rarely does he put into the mouth of any Roman a speech in which he tells of virtue without conjoining fortune with it.

With this view I cannot by any means agree, nor do I think it can be upheld. For if there is nowhere to be found a republic so successful as was Rome, this is because there is nowhere to be found a republic so constituted as to be able to make the conquests Rome made. For it was the virtue of her armies that caused Rome to acquire an empire, and it was her constitutional procedure and the peculiar customs which she owed to her first legislator that enabled her to maintain what she had acquired, as will be explained at length in many of the discourses which follow.

The aforesaid writers claim that Rome's never having been engaged in two very big wars at one and the same time was due to the fortune, not to the virtue, of the Roman people; for there was no war with the Latins until Rome had so thoroughly beaten the Sam-

nites that she had to go to war in their defence. Nor did the Romans fight the Tuscans until the Latins had been subjugated and the Samnites were almost entirely exhausted by frequent defeats; yet had two of these powers, while yet intact and vigorous, united together, it is easy to conjecture, nor can one doubt, that it would have meant ruin for the Roman republic. Anyhow, however it came about, it is a fact that the Romans never had two very big wars going on at the same time; on the contrary, one finds that either when one began the other faded out, or that when one faded out the other began. This can easily be seen from the order in which their wars took place. For, setting aside those waged before Rome was taken by the Gauls, we see that, while they were fighting with the Aequi and the Volsci, no other people attacked them so long as the Aequi and Volsci were strong. It was only after they were beaten that the war with the Samnites arose; and although before this war was over the Latin peoples rebelled against the Romans, yet, when this rebellion occurred, the Samnites were already in alliance with Rome and with their armies helped the Romans to subjugate Latin insolence. When they had been subjugated, the war with Samnium flared up again. And when the forces of the Samnites were beaten owing to the many routes inflicted on them, war with the Tuscans broke out; and, when this was settled, the Samnites started a fresh one, owing to the arrival of Pyrrhus in Italy. On Pyrrhus being repulsed and sent back to Greece, they started on their first war with the Carthaginians; and, scarce was this war over, when all the Gauls, both from this and from the other side of the Alps, conspired against the Romans, with the result that they were defeated with immense slaughter between Popolonia and Pisa, where the tower of St. Vincent now stands. When this war ended, they had no war of any importance for the space of twenty years, for they fought with no one except the Ligurians and what remained of the Gauls in Lombardy. Matters stood thus until the second Punic war, which led to Italy's being occupied for sixteen years. When this came to an end amid great glory, the Macedonian war broke out, and, when this was over, there came the war with Antiochus and with Asia. After which victories there remained in the whole world neither princes nor republics which, either alone or all together, could successfully oppose the forces of Rome.

If, before the final victory, we consider well the order in which these wars took place and the Roman method of procedure, it will be seen that in them, mingled with fortune, was virtue and prudence of a very high order. Hence, if one looks for the cause of this fortune, it should be easy to find. For it is quite certain that, when a prince and a people has acquired such repute that each of the neighbouring princes and peoples is afraid to attack it and fears it, no one will ever assault it unless driven thereunto by necessity; so that it will be open, so to speak, to that power to choose the neighbour on which it seems best to make war, and industriously to foster tranquillity among the rest. In this, owing in part to the respect they have for its power, and in part to their being deceived by the means it takes to lull them to sleep, they readily acquiesce. For other powers, which are farther away and have no intercourse with it, look on the affair as remote from their interests and as no concern of theirs; and in this error they remain until the conflagration is at their door. Nor, when it arrives, have they any means of stopping it except by their own forces, which will then be inadequate since the state in question has become very powerful.

I do not propose to deal with the Samnites, who stood by, watching the Roman people overcome the Volsci and the Aequi; and lest I should be too prolix, only the Carthaginians, who were already a great power and in great esteem when the Romans were fighting the Samnites and the Tuscans, for they held the whole of Africa, held Sardinia and Sicily, and had dominion over part of Spain. This their power, conjoined with the fact that they were remote from the confines of the Roman people, accounts for their never having thought of attacking the Romans, or of helping the Samnites and Tuscans. On the contrary, they acted as men do when things seem to be moving rapidly in another's favour, namely, came to terms with her, and sought her friendship. Nor was the mistake thus made at the outset realized until the Romans had conquered all the peoples that lay between them

and the Carthaginians and they began to contend with each other for the dominion of Sicily and Spain. The same thing happened to the Gauls, to Philip, king of Macedon, and to Antiochus as happened to the Carthaginians. Whilst Rome was engaged with some other state, each of them thought the other state would beat Rome, and that they had time enough to protect themselves against her either by peaceful or by warlike methods. I am of opinion, therefore, that the fortune which Rome had in these matters, all rulers would have who should emulate Roman methods and should be imbued with the same virtue.

I should point out in this connection how the Romans behaved on entering foreign provinces, had I not spoken of it at length in my treatise on principalities, for I have there discussed the question fully. Here I shall make but this remark in passing. The Romans always took care to have in new provinces some friend to act as a ladder up which to climb or a door by which to enter, or as a means whereby to hold it. Thus we see that with the help of the Capuans they got into Samnium, of the Camertini into Tuscany, of the Mamertini into Sicily, of the Saguntines into Spain, of Masinissa into Africa, of the Aetolians into Greece, of Eumenes and other princes into Asia, of the Massilians and the Aedui into Gaul. Hence they never lacked supporters of this kind to facilitate their enterprise alike in acquiring the province and in holding it. Peoples who observe such customs will be found to have less need of fortune than those who do not observe them well.

That everyone may the better know how much more virtue helped the Romans to acquire their empire than did fortune, we shall in the next chapter discuss the character of the peoples with whom they had to fight, and show how obstinate they were in defending their liberty.

## 2. Concerning the Kind of People the Romans Had to Fight, and How Obstinately They Defended Their Freedom

Nothing made it harder for the Romans to conquer the peoples of the central and outlying parts of Italy than the love which in those times many peoples had for liberty. So obstinately did they defend it that only by outstanding virtue could they ever have been subjugated. For numerous instances show to what dangers they exposed themselves in order to maintain or to recover it, and what vendettas they kept up against those who had taken it away. The study of history reveals, too, the harm that servitude has done to peoples and to cities. There is, indeed, in our own times only one country which can be said to have in it free cities, whereas in ancient times quite a number of genuinely free peoples were to be found in all countries. One sees how in the times of which we are speaking at present the peoples of Italy from the Apennines which now divide Tuscany from Lombardy, right down to its toe, were all of them free. The Tuscans, the Romans, the Samnites were, for instance, and so were many other peoples who dwelt in other parts of Italy. One never hears of there being any kings, apart from those who reigned in Rome, and Porsenna, the king of Tuscany, whose stock became extinct, though history does not tell us how. It is quite clear, however, that at the time when the Romans laid siege to Veii, Tuscany was free. Moreover, it enjoyed its freedom so much, and so hated the title of prince, that, when the people of Veii appointed a king in that city for the purpose of defence, and asked the Tuscans to help them against the Romans, the Tuscans after many consultations had been held, decided not to give help to the people of Veii so long as they lived under a king, since they held that they could not well defend a country whose people had already placed themselves in subjection to someone else.

It is easy to see how this affection of peoples for self-government comes about, for experience shows that cities have never increased either in dominion or wealth, unless they have been independent. It is truly remarkable to observe the greatness which Athens attained in the space of a hundred years after it had been liberated from the tyranny of Pisistratus. But most marvellous of all is it to observe the greatness which Rome attained after freeing itself from its kings. The reason is easy to understand; for it is not the well-being of individuals that makes cities great, but the well-being of the community; and it is beyond question that it is only in republics that the common good is looked to properly in that all that promotes it is carried out; and, however much this or that private person may be the loser on this account, there are so many who benefit thereby that the common good can be realized in spite of those few who suffer in consequence.

The opposite happens where there is a prince; for what he does in his own interests usually harms the city, and what is done in the interests of the city harms him. Consequently, as soon as tyranny replaces self-government the least of the evils which this tyranny brings about are that it ceases to make progress and to grow in power and wealth: more often than not, nay always, what happens is that it declines. And should fate decree the rise of an efficient tyrant, so energetic and so proficient in warfare that he enlarges his dominions, no advantage will accrue to the commonwealth, but only to himself, for he cannot bestow honours on the valiant and good citizens over whom he tyrannizes, since he does not want to have any cause to suspect them. Nor yet can he allow the cities he acquires to make their submission to, or to become the tributaries of, the city of which he is the tyrant, for to make it powerful is not to his interest. It is to his interest to keep the state divided so that each town and each district may recognize only him as its ruler. In this way he alone profits by his acquisitions, not his country. Should anyone desire to confirm this view by a host of further arguments, let him read Xenophon's treatise *On Tyrannicide*.

It is no wonder, then, that peoples of old detested tyrants and gave them no peace, or that they were so fond of liberty and held the word itself in such esteem, as happened when Hieronymus, the grandson of Hiero, the Syracusan, was killed in Syracuse, and the news of his death came to his army which was then not very far from Syracuse. At first there was a tumult, and men took up arms against those who had killed him, but when they perceived that in Syracuse the cry was for liberty, they were so delighted to hear the word, that all became quiet, and setting aside their anger against the tyrannicides, they began to consider how self-government could be organized in that city.

Nor is it surprising that peoples are so extraordinarily revengeful towards those who have destroyed their liberty. Of this there are numerous examples, but I propose to give but one, which happened in Corcyra, a city of Greece, during the Peloponnesian war. Greece was then divided into two parties, of which one supported the Athenians, the other the Spartans. The result was that in many cities internal dissensions arose, some advocating an alliance with Sparta, others an alliance with Athens. This happened in Corcyra, where the nobles got the upper hand, and deprived the populace of its liberty. But with the help of the Athenians the populace regained their strength, laid hands on all the nobles, and shut them up in one prison which held them all. Then they took them, eight or ten at a time, on the plea of banishing them to various parts, and then to set an example put them to death with much cruelty. When those who were left heard of this, they considered whether there was any possible way in which they could escape this ignominious death. So, having armed themselves with anything at hand, they defended the entrance to the prison, and fought with those who tried to get in. The result was that, when rumors of this reached the populace, they came in a crowd, removed the upper storey and roof from the building, and smothered the inmates beneath the ruins. Many well-known instances of a like horrible nature happened later in this country. We thus see how true it is that a liberty which you have actually had taken away is avenged with much greater ferocity than is a liberty which someone has only tried to take away.

If one asks oneself how it comes about that peoples of old were more fond of liberty than they are today, I think the answer is that it is due to the same cause that makes men today less bold than they used to be; and this is due, I think, to the difference between our education and that of bygone times, which is based on the difference between our religion and the religion of those days. For our religion, having taught us the truth and the true way of life, leads us to ascribe less esteem to worldly honour. Hence the gentiles, who held it in high esteem and looked upon it as their highest good, displayed in their actions more ferocity than we do. This is evidenced by many of their institutions. To begin with, compare the magnificence of their sacrifices with the humility that characterizes ours. The ceremonial in ours is delicate rather than imposing, and there is no display of ferocity or courage. Their ceremonies lacked neither pomp nor magnificence, but, conjoined with this, were sacrificial acts in which there was much shedding of blood and much ferocity; and in them great numbers of animals were killed. Such spectacles, because terrible, caused men to become like them. Besides, the old religion did not beatify men unless they were replete with worldly glory: army commanders, for instance, and rulers of republics. Our religion has glorified humble and contemplative men, rather than men of action. It has assigned as man's highest good humility, abnegation, and contempt for mundane things, whereas the other identified it with magnanimity, bodily strength, and everything else that conduces to make men very bold. And, if our religion demands that in you there be strength, what it asks for is strength to suffer rather than strength to do bold things.

This pattern of life, therefore, appears to have made the world weak, and to have handed it over as a prey to the wicked, who run it successfully and securely since they are well aware that the generality of men, with paradise for their goal, consider how best to bear, rather than how best to avenge, their injuries. But, though it looks as if the world were become effeminate and as if heaven were powerless, this undoubtedly is due rather to the pusillanimity of those who have interpreted our religion in terms of *laissez faire*, not in terms of *virtù*. For, had they borne in mind that religion permits us to exalt and defend the fatherland, they would have seen that it also wishes us to love and honour it, and to train ourselves to be such that we may defend it.

This kind of education, then, and these grave misinterpretations account for the fact that we see in the world fewer republics than there used to be of old, and that, consequently, in peoples we do not find the same love of liberty as there then was. Yet I can well believe that it was rather the Roman empire, which, with its armed forces and its grandiose ideas, wiped out all republics and all their civic institutions, that was the cause of this. And though, later on, Rome's empire disintegrated, its cities have never been able to pull themselves together nor to set up again a constitutional regime, save in one or two parts of that empire.

Anyhow, however this may be, the Romans encountered in all parts of the world, however small, a combination of well-armed republics, extremely obstinate in the defence of their liberty; which shows that, if the virtue of the Roman people had not been of a rare and very high order, they would never have been able to overcome them. Of instances which bear this out, I shall cite but one case, that of the Samnites. It is a remarkable thing, as Livy admits, that they should have been so powerful and their arms so strong that they were able to withstand the Romans right up to the time of Papirius Cursor, the consul, son of the first Papirius; i.e. to withstand them for the space of forty-six years in spite of many disastrous defeats, the destruction of towns and the slaughter of the inhabitants of their country, a slaughter so great that this country, in which there were formerly seen so many cities and so many inhabitants, was now almost deserted, whereas at one time, it was so well ordered and so strong that it would have been insuperable if it had not been confronted with a virtue such as Rome's.

It is easy, moreover, to see whence arose that order and how this disorder came about. For it is all due to the independence which then was and to the servitude which now is. Because, as has been said before, all towns and all countries that are in all respects free, profit by this enormously. For, wherever increasing populations are found, it is due to the freedom with which marriage is contracted and to its being more desired by men. And this comes about where every man is ready to have children, since he believes that he can rear them and feels sure that his patrimony will not be taken away, and since he knows that not only will they be born free, instead of into slavery, but that, if they have virtue,

they will have a chance of becoming rulers. One observes, too, how riches multiply and abound there, alike those that come from agriculture and those that are produced by the trades. For everybody is eager to acquire such things and to obtain property, provided he be convinced that he will enjoy it when it has been acquired. It thus comes about that, in competitions one with the other, men look both to their own advantage and to that of the public; so that in both respects wonderful progress is made. The contrary of this happens in countries which live in servitude; and the harder the servitude the more does the well-being to which they are accustomed dwindle.

Of all forms of servitude, too, that is the hardest which subjects you to a republic. First because it is more lasting, and there is no hope of escape; secondly because the aim of a republic is to deprive all other corporations of their vitality and to weaken them, to the end that its own body corporate may increase. A prince who makes you his subject, does not do this unless he be a barbarian who devastates the country and destroys all that man has done for civilization, as oriental princes do. On the contrary, if his institutions be humane and he behave constitutionally, he will more often than not be equally fond of all the cities that are subject to him, and will leave them in possession of all their trades and all their ancient institutions. So that, if they are unable to increase, as free cities do, they will not be ruined like those that are enslaved. I refer here to the servitude that befalls cities which are subject to a foreigner, for of those that are subject to one of their own citizens I have already spoken.

He who reflects, therefore, on all that has been said, will not wonder at the power the Samnites had when free, or at the weakness that befell them later, when they became a subject state. This Titus Livy attests in several places, particularly in his account of the war with Hannibal, where he shows how the Samnites, when they had been maltreated by a legion which lay at Nola, sent messengers to Hannibal to ask him to come to their aid. In their address they told him that for a hundred years they had been fighting the Romans with their own troops and their own officers, and that often they had held up two consular armies and two consuls, but that now they had come to such a pass that they could scarce hold their own against the small Roman legion that was at Nola. . . .

## 5. Changes of Religion and of Language, Together with Such Misfortunes as Floods or Pestilences, Obliterate the Records of the Past

To those philosophers who want to make out that the world is eternal, I think the answer might be that, if it really were as old as all this, it would be reasonable to expect there would be records going back further than five thousand years, did we not see how the records of times gone by are obliterated by diverse causes, of which some are due to men and some to heaven. Those which are due to men are changes in religious institutions and in language. For, when a new religious institution comes into being, i.e. a new religion, its first care is, for the sake of its own reputation, to wipe out the old one; and, when the founders of a new religion happen to speak a different tongue, the old one is easily abolished. This becomes clear if we consider the measures which Christianity adopted *vis-à-vis* Paganism; how it abolished all pagan institutions, all pagan rites, and destroyed the records of the theology of the ancients. It is true that Christianity did not succeed in wiping out altogether the record of what outstanding men of the old religion had done; which was due to the retention of the Latin language, for this they had to retain so that they might use it in writing down their new laws. Had they been able to write them in a new tongue, there would, if we bear in mind the way they persecuted in other matters, have been no record of the past left at all.

Whoever reads of the measures taken by Saint Gregory and other heads of the Christian religion, will see what a fuss they made about getting rid of all records of the past, how they burnt the works of poets and historians, destroyed images and spoiled everything else that betokened in any way antiquity. So much so that, if to this persecution there had been conjoined a new language, in a short time one would

have found all traces of the past wiped out. One can well believe, therefore, that what Christianity did with regard to Paganism, Paganism did to the religion that preceded it; and, as there have been two or three changes of religion in five or six thousand years, the record of what happened before that has been lost; or, if of it there remains a trace, it is regarded as a fable and no credence is given to it; as has happened with regard to the *History of Diodorus Siculus*, which covers a period of some forty or fifty thousand years, but is looked upon as untrustworthy, as I believe it to be.

The causes due to heaven are those which wipe out a whole generation and reduce the inhabitants in certain parts of the world to but a few. This is brought about by pestilence or by famine or by a flood and of these the most important is the last alike because it is more widespread and because those who survive are all of them rude mountain-dwellers who have no knowledge of antiquity and so cannot hand it down to posterity; and should there be among the survivors anyone who has such knowledge he will conceal it or distort it in his own fashion so as to establish his own reputation and that of his family, with the result that there will remain to this successors just so much as he has chosen to record and nothing more.

That these floods, pestilences and famines happen, I do not think anyone can doubt, for plenty of them are recorded everywhere in history, their effect in obliterating the past is plain to see, and it seems reasonable that it should be so. For, as in the case of simple bodies, when nature has accumulated too much superfluous material, it frequently acts in the same way and by means of a purge restores health to the body. Similarly in the case of that body which comprises a mixture of human races, when every province is replete with inhabitants who can neither obtain a livelihood nor move elsewhere since all other places are occupied and full up, and when the craftiness and malignity of man has gone as far as it can go, the world must needs be purged in one of these three ways so that mankind, being reduced to comparatively few and humbled by adversity, may adopt a more appropriate form of life and grow better.

There was, then, as we have said before, a time when Tuscany was a powerful country, full of religion and of virtue, with its own customs and its own language, all of which we know was wiped out by the power of Rome, so that of it, as has been said, there remains nought but the remembrance of its name. . . .

### 29. Fortune Blinds Men's Minds When She Does Not Wish Them to Obstruct Her Designs

If one ponders well the course of human affairs, it will be seen that many events happen and many misfortunes come about, against which the heavens have not been willing that any provision at all should be made. Since this statement holds good in the case of Rome, which was conspicuous alike for virtue, religion and orderly conduct, it is no wonder that the same thing happens yet more often in cities and provinces which are lacking in these respects. There is a well-known passage in which Titus Livy shows at length and with great force the power that heaven exercises over human affairs. He says that, with a view to making the Romans recognize its power, heaven first caused the Fabii to act wrongly when sent as ambassadors to the Gauls, and by means of what they did excited the Gauls to make war on Rome; then ordained that in Rome nothing worthy of the Roman people should be done to meet their attack; for first it brought about that Camillus, who was the only hope they had in those evil days, should be sent as an exile to Ardea; then that, when the Gauls were marching on Rome, they did not appoint a dictator, as they had done many times to meet the attack of the Volsci and other enemies in the neighborhood. It also caused them to be weak and to take no particular care in calling up troops, who were so slow in taking up arms that they scarce had time to confront the Gauls on the banks of the Allia, which was but ten miles from Rome. There the tribunes set up their camp without their accustomed diligence, since they did not inspect the site beforehand, nor surround it with trenches and stockades, nor take any other precautions, either human or divine; while in preparing for battle they made their ranks thin and weak, and neither troops nor of-

ficers behaved as Roman discipline required. No blood was shed during the battle because at the first onslaught the Romans ran away, the greater number going to Veii, and the rest retiring to Rome, where they sought refuge in the Capitol without first going home; whereupon the senate took so little thought for Rome's defence that, for one thing, they omitted to close the gates; and some of its members fled, while others went with the rest into the Capitol. Granted, in their defence of the Capitol they used some sort of discipline, for they did not pack all the useless people inside, and they got in all the corn they could, so as to be able to stand the siege; while of the useless crowd of old men, women and children, most fled to the country round about, and the rest stayed in Rome at the mercy of the Gauls. So that no one who had read of what was done so often in years gone by and were to read what was now being done, would think they were one and the same people.

Having described all the disorders mentioned above, Titus Livy concludes with the remark: 'To such an extent does fortune blind the minds of men when she does not want them to oppose the force she is using.'

Nor can anything be more true than the conclusion Livy draws. Hence men who in this life normally either suffer great adversity or enjoy great prosperity, deserve neither praise nor blame; for one usually finds that they have been driven either to ruin or to greatness by the prospect of some great advantage which the heavens have held out, whereby they have been given the chance, or have been deprived of the chance, of being able to act virtuously. Fortune arranges this quite nicely. For, when it wants a man to take the lead in doing great things, it chooses a man of high spirits and great virtue who will seize the occasion it offers him. And in like manner, when it wants a man to bring about a great disaster, it gives precedence to men who will help to promote it; and, if anyone gets in the way, it either kills him off or deprives him of all power of doing good.

It plainly appears from Livy's evidence that, in order to make Rome greater and to lead it on to its future greatness, fortune decided it was necessary first to chastize it in a way that will be described at length in the beginning of the next book, but did not want to ruin it altogether. Hence we see that it made an exile of Camillus, but did not cause him to die; that it caused Rome to be taken, but not the Capitol; that it arranged matters so that nothing useful was thought of to help Rome, nor anything overlooked that could help in the defence of the Capitol. It brought it about that, since Rome was to be taken, the greater part of the troops which were routed at Allia, should go on to Veii, thus leaving the city without any men to defend it. But in arranging things thus, it also prepared the way for Rome's recovery; for since there was a Roman army at Veii, and Camillus was at Ardea, it became possible to make a more vigorous attempt to deliver the fatherland under a general whose career was free from the stain of defeat and whose reputation was untarnished.

In confirmation of this one might adduce further examples from modern times, but I do not think this necessary, so pass them over, since that I have given should be enough to satisfy anybody. I assert once again as a truth to which history as a whole bears witness that men may second their fortune, but cannot oppose it; that they may weave its warp, but cannot break it. Yet they should never give up, because there is always hope, though they know not the end and move towards it along roads which cross one another and as yet are unexplored; and since there is hope, they should not despair, no matter what fortune brings or in what travail they find themselves.

## BOOK THREE

### 1. In Order That a Religious Institution or a State Should Long Survive It Is Essential That It Should Frequently Be Restored to Its Original Principles

It is a well-established fact that the life of all mundane things is of finite duration. But things which complete the whole of the course appointed them by heaven are in general those whose bodies do not disintegrate, but maintain themselves in orderly fashion so that if there is no change; or, if there be change, it tends rather to their conservation than to their destruction. Here I am concerned with composite bodies, such as are states and religious institutions, and in their regard I affirm that those changes make for their conservation which lead them back to their origins. Hence those are better constituted and have a longer life whose institutions make frequent renovations possible, or which are brought to such a renovation by some event which has nothing to do with their constitution. For it is clearer than daylight that, without renovation, these bodies do not last.

The way to renovate them, as has been said, is to reduce them to their starting-points. For at the start religious institutions, republics and kingdoms have in all cases some good in them, to which their early reputation and progress is due. But since in process of time this goodness is corrupted, such a body must of necessity die unless something happens which brings it up to the mark. Thus, our medical men, speaking of the human body, say that 'every day it absorbs something which from time to time requires treatment'.

This return to its original principles in the case of a republic, is brought about either by some external event or by its own intrinsic good sense. Thus, as an example of the former, we see how it was necessary that Rome should be taken by the Gauls in order that it should be re-born and in its re-birth take on alike a new vitality and a new virtue, and also take up again the observance of religion and justice, both of which had begun to show blemishes. This plainly appears from Livy's account where he shows how, when the Romans led out their army against the Gauls and created tribunes with consular power, they observed no religious ceremony. And, in like manner, not only did they not punish the three Fabii who had attacked the Gauls 'in contravention of the Law of Nations', but they made them tribunes. Whence it is easy to infer that of the good constitutions established by Romulus and by those other wise princes they had begun to take less account than was reasonable and necessary for the maintenance of a free state. This defeat in a war with outsiders, therefore, came about so that the institutions of this city should be renovated and to show this people that not only is it essential to uphold religion and justice, but also to hold in high esteem good citizens and to look upon their virtue as of greater value than those comforts of which there appeared to them to be a lack owing to what these men had done. This actually came about. For as soon as Rome had been recovered they renewed all the ordinances of their ancient religion and punished the Fabii who had fought 'in contravention of the Law of Nations'. They also set such esteem on the virtue and goodness of Camillus that the senate and the rest, putting envy aside, laid on his shoulders the whole burden of this republic.

It is, therefore, as I have said, essential that men who live together under any constitution should frequently have their attention called to themselves either by some external or by some internal occurrence. When internal, such occurrences are usually due to some law which from time to time causes the members of this body to review their position; or again to some good man who arises in their midst and by his example and his virtuous deeds produces the same effect as does the constitution.

Such benefits, therefore, are conferred on a republic either by the virtue of some individual or by the virtue of an institution. In regard to the latter, the institutions which caused the Roman republic to return to its start were the introduction of plebeian tribunes, of the censorship, and of all the other laws which put a check on human ambition and arrogance; to which institutions life must needs be given by some virtuous citizen who cooperates strenuously in giving them effect despite the power of those who contravene them. Notable among such drastic actions, before the taking of Rome by the Gauls, were the death of Brutus' sons, the death of the ten citizens, and that of Maelius, the corn-dealer. After the taking of Rome there was the death of Manlius Capitolinus, the death of Manlius Torquatus' son, the action taken by Papirius Cursor against Fabius, his master of horse, and the charge brought against the Scipios. Such events, because of their unwonted severity and their notoriety, brought men back to the mark every time one of them happened; and when they began to

occur less frequently, they also began to provide occasion for men to practise corruption, and were attended with more danger and more commotion. For between one case of disciplinary action of this type and the next there ought to elapse at most ten years, because by this time men begin to change their habits and to break the laws; and, unless something happens which recalls to their minds the penalty involved and reawakens fear in them, there will soon be so many delinquents that it will be impossible to punish them without danger.

In regard to this, those who governed the state of Florence from 1434 to 1494 used to say that it was necessary to reconstitute the government every five years; otherwise it was difficult to maintain it; where by 'reconstituting the government' they meant instilling men with that terror and that fear with which they had instilled them when instituting it—in that at this time they had chastised those who, looked at from the established way of life, had misbehaved. As, however, the remembrance of this chastisement disappears, men are emboldened to try something fresh and to talk sedition. Hence provision has of necessity to be made against this by restoring that government to what it was at its origins.

Such a return to their original principles in republics is sometimes due to the simple virtue of one man alone, independently of any laws spurring you to action. For of such effect is a good reputation and good example that men seek to imitate it, and the bad are ashamed to lead lives which go contrary to it. Those who in Rome are outstanding examples of this good influence, are Horatius Cocles, Scaevola, Fabricius, the two Decii, Regulus Attilius, and several others, whose rare and virtuous examples wrought the same effects in Rome as laws and institutions would have done. If then effective action of the kind described above, together with this setting of good example, had occurred in that city at least every ten years, it necessarily follows that it would never have become corrupt. But when both the one and the other began to occur more rarely, corruption began to spread. For, after the time of Marcus Regulus, there appeared no examples of this kind, and, though in Rome there arose the two Catos, between them and any prior instance there was so great an interval, and again between the Catos themselves, and they stood so alone that their good example could have no good effect; especially in the case of the younger Cato who found the greater part of the city so corrupt that he could not by his example effect any improvement among the citizens. So much then for republics.

As to religious institutions one sees here again how necessary these renovations are from the example of our own religion, which, if it had not been restored to its starting-point by St Francis and St Dominic, would have become quite extinct. For these men by their poverty and by their exemplification of the life of Christ revived religion in the minds of men in whom it was already dead, and so powerful were these new religious orders that they prevented the depravity of prelates and of religious heads from bringing ruin on religion. They also lived so frugally and had such prestige with the populace as confessors and preachers that they convinced them it is an evil thing to talk evilly of evil doing, and a good thing to live under obedience to such prelates, and that, if they did wrong, it must be left to God to chastise them. And, this being so, the latter behave as badly as they can, because they are not afraid of punishments which they do not see and in which they do not believe. It is, then, this revival which has maintained and continues to maintain this religion.

Kingdoms also need to be renovated and to have their laws brought back to their starting-points. The salutary effect this produces is seen in the kingdom of France, for the conduct of affairs in this kingdom is controlled by more laws and more institutions than it is in any other. These laws and these institutions are maintained by *parlements,* notably by that of Paris, and by it they are renovated whenever it takes action against a prince of this realm or in its judgements condemns the king. Up to now it has maintained its position by the pertinacity with which it has withstood the nobility of this realm. But should it at any time let an offence remain unpunished and should offences begin to multiply, the result would unquestionably be either that they would have to be corrected to the accompaniment of grievous disorders or that the kingdom would disintegrate.

The conclusion we reach, then, is that there is nothing more necessary to a community, whether it be a religious establishment, a kingdom or a republic, than to restore to it the prestige it had at the outset, and to take care that either good institutions or good men shall bring this about rather than that external force should give rise to it. For though this on occasion may be the best remedy, as it was in Rome's case, it is so dangerous that in no case is it what one should desire.

In order to make it clear to all how much the action of particular men contributed to the greatness of Rome and produced in that city so many beneficial results, I shall proceed to narrate and to discuss their doings, and shall confine myself to this topic in this third and last book on this first Decad [of Livy's history]. And, though the actions of the kings were great and noteworthy, since history deals with them at length I shall not mention them here, except where they may have done things with a view to their personal advantage. I begin, then, with Brutus, the father of Rome's liberties.

## 7. *How It Comes About That Changes from Liberty to Servitude and from Servitude to Liberty Sometimes Occur Without Bloodshed and Sometimes Abound in It*

Some perchance may wonder how it comes about that of many revolutions involving a change from freedom to tyranny or the other way about, some are accompanied by bloodshed and others not. For it is plain from history that in such revolutions sometimes vast numbers of men get killed, and that in others nobody at all gets hurt, as happened in the change which Rome made from kingship to rule by consult, for in it no one was banished except the Tarquins, and nobody else at all got hurt.

The answer is that it all depends upon whether the change in form of government is or is not brought about by violence; for when it is accompanied by violence it is inevitable that many should get hurt, and then of necessity those who in their downfall have been injured seek revenge, and this desire for vengeance gives rise to bloodshed and loss of life;

but when that form of government has been brought into being by the common consent of a whole people which has made it great, there is no reason why, when the said people as a whole meets its downfall, they should harm anyone except its head. This was the case with Rome's government and with the expulsion of the Tarquins. It was also the case with the government of the Medici in Florence, which, when it fell in 1494, harmed nobody but the Medici themselves.

Revolutions of this kind, therefore, are not attended with much danger. Those, on the other hand, are extremely dangerous which are brought about by men who are out for vengeance, and have invariably been of such a kind as to appal those who read of them, to say the least. Since of such revolutions there are plenty of instances in history, I propose to leave it at that.

## 8. *He Who Would Transform a Republic Should Take Due Note of the Governed*

That a bad citizen cannot do much harm in a republic that is not corrupt has been shown in a previous discourse, and, in addition to the reasons there adduced, this conclusion is confirmed by the case of Spurius Cassius and that of Manlius Capitolinus. The former, an ambitious man, desirous of acquiring extraordinary authority in Rome, ingratiated himself with the plebs by conferring on them many benefits, such as dividing among them the lands which the Romans had taken from the Hernici. When the city fathers discovered his ambitious projects and made them known, he became so suspect that, on his addressing the populace and offering to give them the money accruing from the sale of the corn which the public had caused to be brought from Sicily, they refused it outright, since it seemed to them that Spurius was offering it them as the price of their liberty. Whereas, had the populace been corrupt, they would have accepted the money, and would have laid open the way to tyranny instead of closing it.

The example of Manlius Capitolinus is even more remarkable; for from his case it may be seen how the inordinate desire to rule afterwards cancels out virtues of mind and body and services rendered to one's country, however great they may be. This desire, it is clear, was in his case aroused by the envy he felt for Camillus on whom great honours had been bestowed, and in him it begat so great a mental blindness that without pausing to reflect on the mode of life prevailing in the city, or to inquire with what kind of subjects he had to deal and whether they were yet averse to accept a bad form of government, he set about raising tumults in Rome alike against the senate and against his country's laws. This incident shows how perfect the city then was and how good the material of which it was composed; for in his case none of the nobles, who were usually very keen to defend one another, rose to support him, nor did any of his relations make a move on his behalf; nor yet, though it was customary in the case of an accused person for his relations to appear in mourning, clad in black, and all of them sorrowing, so as to evoke sympathy in favour of the accused, did anyone at all appear in Manlius's case. The tribunes of the plebs, who were wont always to look favourably on causes which appeared likely to benefit the populace, and to promote them the more vigorously the more inimical they were to the nobles, in this case joined with the nobles in suppressing a common pest. The Roman populace, looking eagerly to its own interests and sympathetic to projects which might thwart the nobility, in spite of its having been so favourable to Manlius, none the less when the tribunes cited him to appear, and referred his case to the judgement of the populace, this same populace, become now the judge of its defender, paid no attention to this, but condemned him to death.

Hence I do not think that there is any example in the history we are considering, capable of showing more clearly than this, how sound were all the institutions of that republic, in view of the fact that not a soul in that city was disposed to defend a citizen who was replete with virtue of every kind and alike in public and in private had done very many things worthy of commendation. For with all of them love of country weighed more than any other consideration, and they looked upon the present dangers for which he was responsible as of much greater importance than his former merits; with the result that they chose he should die in order that they might remain free. 'Such,' says Titus Livy, 'was the fate of a man who would have been illustrious if he had not been born in a free city.'

There are two things here which should be borne in mind. One is that, in order to obtain glory, a man must use different methods in a city that is corrupt from what he would use in one in which political life is still vigorous. The other, which is almost the same as the first, is that in the way they behave, and especially where deeds of moment are concerned, men should take account of the times, and act accordingly.

Those who owing to bad judgement or to their natural inclinations are out of touch with the times are in most cases unfortunate in their life and unsuccessful in their undertakings. But it is otherwise with those who are in accord with the times. From the words of the historian cited above, it may without hesitation be inferred that, had Manlius been born in the days of Marius or Sulla, when the material was corrupt and it would have been possible to impress on it the form to which his ambition looked, he would have met with the same success that attended the actions of Marius and Sulla and others who, after them, aspired to tyranny. And in the same way, had Sulla and Marius lived in the time of Manlius, they would have been crushed at the very outset of their careers. For a man can easily by his behaviour and his evil devices begin to corrupt the populace in a city, but it is impossible for him to live long enough to corrupt it to such an extent that he himself shall reap the fruits. And, even if it were possible for him to live long enough to do this, it would still be impossible for him to succeed, for men are so impatient in the way they carry on that they cannot restrain their passions for very long. Consequently they make mistakes in handling their affairs, especially when they are too eager; with the result that, either through impatience or through mistakes, they are likely to take premature action and to meet with disaster.

If anyone, then, wants to seize supreme power in a republic and to impose on it a bad form of government, it is essential that he should find there a material which has in course of time become disordered, and that this disorder shall have been introduced lit-

tle by little and in one generation after another. And this, as we have remarked in a previous discourse, must of necessity come about unless that republic be given fresh life by the example of good men or by fresh legislation be brought back to what it was at the start.

Manlius, therefore, would have been an exceptional and a remarkable man, had he been born in a corrupt city. Hence citizens who in republics take up any enterprise, whether in favour of liberty or with a view to tyranny, should take account of the subjects with which they have to deal and on this should base their estimate of the difficulties their undertaking involves; for it is just as difficult and dangerous to try to free a people that wants to remain servile as it is to enslave a people that wants to remain free.

Since I have remarked above that in human affairs men should study the nature of the times and act accordingly, of this we shall speak at length in the next chapter.

### 9. That It Behoves One to Adapt Oneself to the Times if One Wants to Enjoy Continued Good Fortune

I have often thought that the reason why men are sometimes unfortunate, sometimes fortunate, depends upon whether their behaviour is in conformity with the times. For one sees that in what they do some men are impetuous, others look about them and are cautious; and that, since in both cases they go to extremes and are unable to go about things in the right way, in both cases they make mistakes. On the other hand, he is likely to make fewer mistakes and to prosper in his fortune when circumstances accord with his conduct, as I have said, and one always proceeds as the force of nature compels one.

Everybody knows how Fabius Maximus, when in command of the army, proceeded circumspectly and with a caution far removed from the impetuosity and boldness characteristic of the Roman; and by good luck this sort of thing just fitted the circumstances. For Hannibal had arrived in Italy, a young man flushed with success, and had twice routed the

Roman people, so that this republic had lost almost all its best troops and was alarmed. Hence it could not have been more fortunate than to have had a general who by his slowness and his caution held the enemy at bay. Nor could Fabius have met with circumstances more suited to his ways; and it is to this that his fame was due.

That in so doing Fabius behaved naturally and not by choice is shown by the fact that, when Scipio wanted to go to Africa with his armies to bring the war to an end, Fabius was much against this, since he could not get out of his ways and habits; so that, if it had been left to him, Hannibal would still be in Italy, for he did not see that times had changed, and that new methods of warfare were called for. So that, if Fabius had been king of Rome, he might easily have lost this war, since he was incapable of altering his methods according as circumstances changed. Since, however, he was born in a republic where there were diverse citizens with diverse dispositions, it came about that, just as it had a Fabius, who was the best man to keep the war going when circumstances required this, so later it had a Scipio at a time suited to its victorious consummation.

For this reason a republic has a fuller life and enjoys good fortune for a longer time than a principality, since it is better able to adapt itself to diverse circumstances owing to the diversity found among its citizens than a prince can do. For a man who is accustomed to act in one particular way, never changes, as we have said. Hence, when times change and no longer suit his ways, he is inevitably ruined.

Piero Soderini, whom we have mentioned several times, conducted all his affairs in his good-natured and patient way. So long as circumstances suited the way in which he carried on, both he and his country prospered. But when afterwards there came a time which required him to drop his patience and his humility, he could not bring himself to it; so that both he and his country were ruined. Pope Julius II during the whole course of his pontificate acted with impetuosity and dash, and, since the times suited him well, he succeeded in all his undertakings; but had other times come which called for other counsels, he would of necessity have been undone, for he could not have changed his ways or his method of handling affairs.

There are two reasons why we cannot change our ways. First, it is impossible to go against what nature inclines us to. Secondly, having got on well by adopting a certain line of conduct, it is impossible to persuade men that they can get on well by acting otherwise. It thus comes about that a man's fortune changes, for she changes his circumstances but he does not change his ways. The downfall of cities also comes about because institutions in republics do not change with the times, as we have shown at length already, but change very slowly because it is more painful to change them since it is necessary to wait until the whole republic is in a state of upheaval; and for this it is not enough that one man alone should change his own procedure.

Since we have mentioned Fabius Maximus who held Hannibal at bay, it seems to me appropriate in the next chapter to discuss whether a general who is determined at all costs to force the enemy to fight, can be prevented by the enemy from doing this.

# THOMAS HOBBES

~

## INTRODUCTION

## JEAN HAMPTON

Thomas Hobbes (1588–1679) was born in Malmesbury, England, arriving prematurely because, he claimed, rumors that the Spanish armada was off the coast of England ready to invade scared his mother: "She brought twins to birth, myself and fear at the same time." Ironically, fear of death was the central psychological assumption of his moral and political theorizing as an adult. Hobbes's father was a clergyman, whom some reports describe as prone to drink and violence, and who eventually deserted his family to avoid a charge of assault. Educated at the expense of his uncle, Hobbes attended Oxford from 1603 to 1608. Because he was not from a wealthy family, on graduation he got a job as the tutor and companion of William Cavendish, who eventually became the Earl of Devonshire. Thus began Hobbes's long association with that family; except for a few brief periods, he remained in service to them for nearly seventy years. He also worked briefly for Sir Francis Bacon, serving as his amanuensis and translator.

According to his friend and biographer John Aubrey, Hobbes's philosophical interests owed much to the geometer Euclid, whose proofs he loved because of the way they relied on logical reasoning to derive surprising and sometimes seemingly implausible conclusions from highly plausible and seemingly innocuous premises. However, his first full-scale philosophical manuscript was not circulated until 1640. This work, called *The Elements of Laws, Natural and Politic,* advocated the creation of an absolute sovereign in order to secure the peace and stability of the community. Because of the antiroyalist sentiment at this time (which eventually resulted in full-scale civil war and the beheading of King Charles I), many people, including members of Parliament, were outraged by the manuscript, and Hobbes believed he had to flee for his life to Europe (he used to boast that he was one of the "first to flee" from England). Like many prominent royalist sympathizers he spent the rest of the civil war in Paris, where he enjoyed philosophical conversations with French intellectuals (such as Gassendi and Mersenne) and exiled British thinkers. During that time he wrote *De Cive (The Citizen)* (1642), a reworked version of his argument in *The Elements of Laws* (written in Latin but later published in English in 1651 under the title *The Philosophical Rudiments of Government*). In 1651 he published his masterpiece *Leviathan,* which contains his mature argument for absolute sovereignty.

Oliver Cromwell was in power when *Leviathan* was completed, and Cromwell supposedly welcomed the book because of the way its arguments could be used to justify any de facto political authority even if it was installed through rebellion. Accordingly, Hobbes was allowed to come home, unlike other royalist exiles (who resented Hobbes's return and considered him to have sold out to the new Puritan regime). On his return, he continued philosophizing in areas other than political philosophy, producing works in philosophy of law, history, metaphysics, and epistemology (including ontology, scientific method, and free will), and topics in science and mathematics (including optics, geometry, and human physiology). After the restoration of King Charles II, Hobbes enjoyed access to the king because of his wit and intelligence. However, he remained a highly controversial figure throughout the country, both because of his political absolutism and because of his materialistic metaphysics and his views on free will and religion, which were viewed by many of the larger population as "atheistic" and heretical. Hobbes died at the ripe old age of 91.

Hobbes's argument for absolute sovereignty in all his political writings makes use of the idea of a "social contract," an idea also used by other political thinkers of his day but which Hobbes revolutionized in ways that powerfully influenced the political thinking of subsequent philosophers such as Locke, Rousseau, and Kant. Imagine, says Hobbes, a "state of nature" prior to the creation of all governments. In this state human behavior would be unchecked by law, and since Hobbes believed that human beings are predominantly self-interested (concerned above all else with their own preservation), he argues that they would inevitably come into conflict with one another, while having little or no other-regarding sentiments or psychological resources to resolve those conflicts. So before long, he says, there would be a "war of every one against every one," so that every person's life in this natural state would be "solitary, poor, nasty, brutish and short" (*Leviathan,* ch. 13). To remedy such war and satisfy their desire for self-preservation, people, Hobbes argues, would be rational to contract with one another to create a government run by a sovereign holding absolute power, because only absolute power is sufficient to resolve disputes that otherwise would precipitate conflict dissolving the commonwealth and threatening the lives of all. Such an argument is meant to show the kind of government we contemporary human beings would be rational to create and sustain, lest we descend into a state of war analogous to the one that would exist in the state of nature. Note that Hobbes doesn't require that sovereignty be held only by an absolute monarchy; he also recognizes that sovereignty can be invested in a small number of people, constituting an oligarchy, or in all the people, constituting a democracy. Hobbes explicitly prefers the absolute monarchy, but believes the other two forms of government are also viable. What is not viable, in his view, is some form of "mixed" government with different branches of government holding different components of political authority, or governments in which power is supposed to be limited by a constitution or by a contract made between the government and the people. Such limits or divisions, says Hobbes, will only lead to conflicts that cannot be resolved by self-interested people, who require for peace a unified sovereignty with the power to decide any issue that might lead to conflict in the regime.

Hobbes's use of this social contract argument was occasioned in large part by his rejection of the scholastic philosophizing of many of his contemporaries and his forebears, whom he thought were too inclined to appeal to authority rather than reason, and too inclined to use nonsensical or empty terms (such as "immaterial substance" or "consubstantiation"). Accordingly, Hobbes turned to science, and particularly to geometry, as a guide to constructing a theory of our moral and political life. Starting with what he took to be sound premises, Hobbes sought to construct a social contract argument so as to derive, in geometric fashion, valid conclusions about morals and politics in a way that would command assent even from those reluctant to endorse such conclusions. Hobbes's faith in the power of reason to provide truth in moral and political matters makes him an Enlightenment thinker, although, ironically, it is partly because he thinks there will be persistent failures of rationality in any human community that peace must be secured by giving the ruler absolute power.

Does Hobbes's argument work? To create an absolute sovereign, Hobbes says that each person must agree with every other person to "give up" his or her "right to all things" to the sovereign, thereby "authorizing" the sovereign to rule in this community. But can people who are committed to securing their self-preservation above all else rationally risk giving up *all* their rights to another? Hobbes explicitly compares subjects to servants and sovereigns to masters. But is such voluntary political "enslavement" even psychologically possible for people as Hobbes describes them? Observant readers will note qualifications to the alienation of all power to the sovereign in chapter 21. For example, Hobbes writes: "The obligation of subjects to the sovereign is understood to last as long as, and no longer than, the power lasteth, by which he is able to protect them. For the right men have by nature to protect themselves when none else can protect them can by no covenant be relinquished."

But is such a qualification consistent with the idea that the sovereign has absolute power over his subjects? The ultimate validity of Hobbes's argument has been questioned by generations of readers, who have tended to be both intrigued by its power and alarmed by its conclusions.

For an overview of Hobbes's work, see Tom Sorell, *Hobbes* (London: Routledge & Kegan Paul, 1986). For a view of Hobbes's life by one of his contemporaries, see the discussion of Hobbes in John Aubrey's *Brief Lives,* edited by Oliver Lawson Dick. (Ann Arbor: University of Michigan Press, 1975). For three detailed examinations of the validity of Hobbes's social contract argument, see David Gauthier, *The Logic of Leviathan* (Oxford: Oxford University Press, 1969); Jean Hampton, *Hobbes and the Social Contract Tradition* (Cambridge: Cambridge University Press, 1986); and Gregory Kavka, *Hobbesian Moral and Political Theory* (Princeton, N.J.: Princeton University Press, 1986). Many of the nonpolitical aspects of Hobbes's thinking are discussed in J. W. N. Watkins, *Hobbes's System of Ideas* (London: Hutchison, 1965). For a discussion of Hobbes's religious arguments in *Leviathan,* see A. P. Martinich, *The Two Gods of Leviathan* (Cambridge: Cambridge University Press, 1992); and S. A. Lloyd, *Ideals as Interest in Hobbes's Leviathan* (Cambridge: Cambridge University Press, 1992). Finally, for a collection of classic interpretive essays on Hobbes's work, see K. C. Brown, *Hobbes Studies* (Oxford: Blackwell, 1965).

# Leviathan

## THE INTRODUCTION

Nature (the art whereby God hath made and governs the world) is by the *art* of man, as in many other things, so in this also imitated, that it can make an artificial animal. For seeing life is but a motion of limbs, the beginning whereof is in some principal part within; why may we not say that all *automata* (engines that move themselves by springs and wheels as doth a watch) have an artificial life? For what is the *heart,* but a *spring;* and the *nerves,* but so many *strings;* and the *joints,* but so many *wheels,* giving motion to the whole body, such as was intended by the artificer? *Art* goes yet further, imitating that rational and most excellent work of nature, *man.* For by art is created that great LEVIATHAN called a COMMONWEALTH, or STATE, (in Latin CIVITAS) which is but an artificial man; though of greater stature and strength than the natural, for whose protection and defence it was intended; and in which, the *sovereignty* is an artificial *soul,* as giving life and motion to the whole body; the *magistrates,* and other *officers* of judicature and execution, artificial *joints; reward* and *punishment* (by which fastened to the seat of the sovereignty every joint and member is moved to perform his duty) are the *nerves,* that do the same in the body natural; the *wealth* and *riches* of all the particular members, are the *strength; salus populi* (the *people's safety*) its *business; counsellors,* by whom all things needful for it to know are suggested unto it, are the *memory; equity,* and *laws,* an artificial *reason* and *will; concord, health; sedition, sickness;* and *civil war, death.* Lastly, the *pacts* and *covenants,* by which the parts of this body politic were at first made, set together, and united, resemble that *fiat,* or the *let us make man,* pronounced by God in the creation.

> *To describe the nature of this artificial man, I will consider*
> *First, the* matter *thereof, and the* artificer; *both which is* man.
> *Secondly,* how, *and by what* covenants *it is made; what are the* rights *and just* power *or* authority *of a sovereign; and what it is that* preserveth *and* dissolveth *it.*
> *Thirdly, what is a* Christian commonwealth.
> *Lastly, what is the* kingdom of darkness.

Concerning the first, there is a saying much usurped of late, that *wisdom* is acquired, not by reading of *books,* but of *men.* Consequently whereunto, those persons, that for the most part can give no other proof of being wise, take great delight to show what they think they have read in men, by uncharitable censures of one another behind their backs. But there is another saying not of late understood, by which they might learn truly to read one another, if they would take the pains; and that is, *nosce teipsum, read thyself:* which was not meant, as it is now used, to countenance, either the barbarous state of men in power, towards their inferiors; or to encourage men of low degree, to a saucy behaviour towards their betters; but to teach us, that for the similitude of the thoughts and passions of one man, to the thoughts and passions of another, whosoever looketh into himself, and considereth what he doth, when he does *think, opine, reason, hope, fear,* &c. and upon what grounds; he shall thereby read and know, what are the thoughts and passions of all other men upon the like occasions. I say the similitude of passions, which are the same in all men, *desire, fear, hope,* &c.; not the similitude of the objects of the passions, which are the things *desired, feared, hoped,* &c.; for these the constitution individual, and particular education, do so vary and they are so easy to be kept from our knowledge, that the characters of man's heart, blotted and confounded as they are with dissembling, lying, counterfeiting, and erroneous doctrines, are legible only to him that searcheth hearts. And though by men's actions we do discover their design sometimes; yet to do it without comparing them with our own, and distinguishing all circumstances, by which the case may come to be altered, is to decypher without a key, and be for the most part deceived, by too much trust, or by too much diffidence; as he that reads, is himself a good or evil man.

But let one man read another by his actions never so perfectly, it serves him only with his acquaintance, which are but few. He that is to govern a whole nation, must read in himself, not this or that particular man; but mankind: which though it be hard to do, harder than to learn any language or science; yet when I shall have set down my own reading orderly, and perspicuously, the pains left another, will be only to consider, if he also find not the same in himself. For this kind of doctrine admitteth no other demonstration.

# PART 1

## *Of Man*

### *Chapter 1*

#### OF SENSE

Concerning the thoughts of man, I will consider them first *singly,* and afterwards in *train,* or dependence upon one another. *Singly,* they are every one a *representation* or *appearance,* of some quality, or other accident of a body without us; which is commonly called an *object.* Which object worketh on the eyes, ears, and other parts of a man's body; and by diversity of working, produceth diversity of appearances.

The original of them all, is that which we call SENSE; (For there is no conception in a man's mind,

which hath not at first, totally, or by parts, been begotten upon the organs of sense.) The rest are derived from that original.

To know the natural cause of sense, is not very necessary to the business now in hand; and I have elsewhere written of the same at large. Nevertheless, to fill each part of my present method, I will briefly deliver the same in this place.

The cause of sense, is the external body, or object, which presseth the organ proper to each sense, either immediately, as in the taste and touch; or mediately, as in seeing, hearing, and smelling; which pressure, by the mediation of nerves, and other strings and membranes of the body, continued inwards to the brain and heart, causeth there a resistance, or counter-pressure, or endeavour of the heart, to deliver it self: which endeavour, because *outward,* seemeth to be some matter without. And this *seeming,* or, *fancy,* is that which men call *sense;* and consisteth, as to the eye, in a *light,* or *colour figured;* to the ear, in a *sound;* to the nostril, in an *odour;* to the tongue and palate, in a *savour;* and to the rest of the body, in *heat, cold, hardness, softness,* and such other qualities as we discern by *feeling.* All which qualities called *sensible,* are in the object, that causeth them, but so many several motions of the matter, by which it presseth our organs diversely. Neither in us that are pressed, are they any thing else, but divers motions; (for motion produceth nothing but motion.) But their appearance to us is fancy, the same waking, that dreaming. And as pressing, rubbing, or striking the eye, makes us fancy a light; and pressing the ear, produceth a din; so do the bodies also we see, or hear, produce the same by their strong, though unobserved action. For if those colours and sounds were in the bodies, or objects that cause them, they could not be severed from them, as by glasses, and in echoes by reflection, we see they are; where we know the thing we see, is in one place; the appearance in another. And though at some certain distance, the real and very object seem invested with the fancy it begets in us; yet still the object is one thing, the image or fancy is another. So that sense in all cases, is nothing else but original fancy, caused (as I have said) by the pressure, that is, by the motion, of external things upon our eyes, ears, and other organs thereunto ordained.

But the philosophy-schools, through all the universities of Christendom, grounded upon certain texts of *Aristotle,* teach another doctrine; and say, for the cause of *vision,* that the thing seen, sendeth forth on every side a *visible species* (in English) a *visible show, apparition,* or *aspect,* or *a being seen;* the receiving whereof into the eye, is *seeing.* And for the cause of *hearing,* that the thing heard, sendeth forth an *audible species,* that is, an *audible aspect,* or *audible being seen;* which entering at the ear, maketh *hearing.* Nay for the cause of *understanding* also, they say the thing understood, sendeth forth *intelligible species,* that is, an *intelligible being seen;* which coming into the understanding, makes us understand. I say not this, as disapproving the use of universities; but because I am to speak hereafter of their office in a commonwealth. I must let you see on all occasions by the way, what things would be amended in them; amongst which the frequency of insignificant speech is one.

## *Chapter 2*

### OF IMAGINATION

That when a thing lies still, unless somewhat else stir it, it will lie still for ever, is a truth that no man doubts of. But that when a thing is in motion, it will eternally be in motion, unless somewhat else stay it, though the reason be the same, (namely, that nothing can change it self,) is not so easily assented to. For men measure, not only other men, but all other things, by themselves: and because they find themselves subject after motion to pain, and lassitude, think every thing else grows weary of motion, and seeks repose of its own accord; little considering, whether it be not some other motion, wherein that desire of rest they find in themselves, consisteth. From hence it is, that the schools say, heavy bodies fall downwards, out of an appetite to rest, and to conserve their nature in that place which is most proper for them; ascribing appetite and knowledge of what is good for their conservation, (which is more than man has) to things inanimate, absurdly.

When a body is once in motion, it moveth (unless something else hinder it) eternally; and whatsoever hindreth it, cannot in an instant, but in time, and by degrees quite extinguish it: And as we see in the water, though the wind cease, the waves give not over rolling for a long time after; so also it happeneth in that motion, which is made in the internal parts of a man, then, when he sees, dreams, &c. For after the object is removed, or the eye shut, we still retain an image of the thing seen, though more obscure than when we see it. And this is it, the Latins call *imagination,* from the image made in seeing; and apply the same, though improperly, to all the other senses. But the Greeks call it *fancy;* which signifies *appearance,* and is as proper to one sense, as to another. IMAGINATION therefore is nothing but *decaying sense;* and is found in men, and many other living creatures, as well sleeping, as waking.

The decay of sense in men waking, is not the decay of the motion made in sense; but an obscuring of it, in such manner as the light of the sun obscureth the light of the stars; which stars do no less exercise their virtue, by which they are visible, in the day, than in the night. But because amongst many strokes, which our eyes, ears, and other organs receive from external bodies, the predominant only is sensible; therefore the light of the sun being predominant, we are not affected with the action of the stars. And any object being removed from our eyes, though the impression it made in us remain; yet other objects more present succeeding, and working on us, the imagination of the past is obscured, and made weak, as the voice of a man is in the noise of the day. From whence it followeth, that the longer the time is, after the sight or sense of any object, the weaker is the imagination. For the continual change of man's body destroys in time the parts which in sense were moved: so that distance of time, and of place, hath one and the same effect in us. For as at a great distance of place, that which we look at appears dim, and without distinction of the smaller parts; and as voices grow weak, and inarticulate: so also, after great distance of time, our imagination for the past is weak; and we lose (for example) of cities we have seen, many particular streets, and of actions, many particular circumstances. This *decaying sense,* when we would express the thing it self, (I mean *fancy* it self,) we call *imagination,* as I said before: but when we would express the *decay,* and signify that the sense is fading, old and past, it is called *memory.* So that *imagination* and *memory* are but one thing, which for divers considerations hath divers names.

Much memory, or memory of many things, is called *experience.* Again, imagination being only of those things which have been formerly perceived by sense, either all at once, or by parts at several times; the former, (which is the imagining the whole object, as it was presented to the sense) is *simple imagination;* as when one imagineth a man, or horse, which he hath seen before. The other is *compounded;* as when from the sight of a man at one time, and of a horse at another, we conceive in our mind a Centaur. So when a man compoundeth the image of his own person with the image of the actions of another man; as when a man imagines himself a *Hercules* or an *Alexander,* (which happeneth often to them that are much taken with reading of romances) it is a compound imagination, and properly but a fiction of the mind. There be also other imaginations that rise in men, (though waking) from the great impression made in sense: as from gazing upon the sun, the impression leaves an image of the sun before our eyes a long time after; and from being long and vehemently attent upon geometrical figures, a man shall in the dark, (though awake) have the images of lines and angles before his eyes: which kind of fancy hath no particular name; as being a thing that doth not commonly fall into men's discourse.

The imaginations of them that sleep are those we call *dreams.* And these also (as all other imaginations) have been before, either totally or by parcels in the sense. And because in sense, the brain and nerves, which are the necessary organs of sense, are so benumbed in sleep, as not easily to be moved by the action of external objects, there can happen in sleep no imagination; and therefore no dream, but what proceeds from the agitation of the inward parts of man's body; which inward parts, for the connexion they have with the brain, and other organs, when they be distempered, do keep the same in motion; whereby the imaginations there formerly made, appear as if a man were waking: saving that the organs of sense being now benumbed, so as there is no new object,

which can master and obscure them with a more vigorous impression, a dream must needs be more clear, in this silence of sense, than are our waking thoughts. And hence it cometh to pass, that it is a hard matter, and by many thought impossible to distinguish exactly between sense and dreaming. For my part, when I consider that in dreams, I do not often, nor constantly think of the same persons, places, objects, and actions that I do waking; nor remember so long a train of coherent thoughts, dreaming, as at other times; and because waking I often observe the absurdity of dreams, but never dream of the absurdities of my waking thoughts; I am well satisfied, that being awake, I know I dream not; though when I dream I think myself awake.

And seeing dreams are caused by the distemper of some of the inward parts of the body; divers distempers must needs cause different dreams. And hence it is, that lying cold breedeth dreams of fear, and raiseth the thought and image of some fearful object (the motion from the brain to the inner parts, and from the inner parts to the brain being reciprocal;) and that as anger causeth heat in some parts of the body, when we are awake; so when we sleep the over heating of the same parts causeth anger, and raiseth up in the brain the imagination of an enemy. In the same manner, as natural kindness, when we are awake, causeth desire; and desire makes heat in certain other parts of the body; so also, too much heat in those parts, while we sleep, raiseth in the brain an imagination of some kindness shown. In sum, our dreams are the reverse of our waking imaginations; the motion when we are awake, beginning at one end; and when we dream, at another.

The most difficult discerning of a man's dream, from his waking thoughts, is then, when by some accident we observe not that we have slept: which is easy to happen to a man full of fearful thoughts; and whose conscience is much troubled; and that sleepeth, without the circumstances, of going to bed, or putting off his clothes, as one that noddeth in a chair. For he that taketh pains, and industriously lays himself to sleep, in case any uncouth and exorbitant fancy come unto him, cannot easily think it other than a dream. We read of *Marcus Brutus,* (one that had his life given him by *Julius Caesar,* and was also his favourite, and notwithstanding murdered him), how at *Philippi,* the night before he gave battle to *Augustus Caesar,* he saw a fearful apparition, which is commonly related by historians as a vision; but considering the circumstances, one may easily judge to have been but a short dream. For sitting in his tent, pensive and troubled with the horror of his rash act, it was not hard for him, slumbering in the cold, to dream of that which most affrighted him; which fear, as by degrees it made him wake; so also it must needs make the apparition by degrees to vanish; and having no assurance that he slept, he could have no cause to think it a dream, or any thing but a vision. And this is no very rare accident; for even they that be perfectly awake, if they be timorous, and superstitious, possessed with fearful tales, and alone in the dark, are subject to the like fancies; and believe they see spirits and dead men's ghosts walking in churchyards; whereas it is either their fancy only, or else the knavery of such persons, as make use of such superstitious fear, to pass disguised in the night, to places they would not be known to haunt.

From this ignorance of how to distinguish dreams, and other strong fancies, from vision and sense, did arise the greatest part of the religion of the Gentiles in time past, that worshipped satyrs, fawns, nymphs, and the like; and now-a-days the opinion that rude people have of fairies, ghosts, and goblins, and of the power of witches. For as for witches, I think not that their witchcraft is any real power; but yet that they are justly punished, for the false belief they have, that they can do such mischief, joined with their purpose to do it if they can: their trade being nearer to a new religion than to a craft or science. And for fairies, and walking ghosts, the opinion of them has I think been on purpose, either taught, or not confuted, to keep in credit the use of exorcism, of crosses, of holy water, and other such inventions of ghostly men. Nevertheless, there is no doubt, but God can make unnatural apparitions: But that he does it so often, as men need to fear such things, more than they fear the stay, or change, of the course of nature, which he also can stay, and change, is no point of Christian faith. But evil men under pre-

text that God can do any thing, are so bold as to say any thing when it serves their turn, though they think it untrue; it is the part of a wise man, to believe them no further, than right reason makes that which they say, appear credible. If this superstitious fear of spirits were taken away, and with it, prognostics from dreams, false prophecies, and many other things depending thereon, by which, crafty ambitious persons abuse the simple people, men would be much more fitted than they are for civil obedience.

And this ought to be the work of the schools: but they rather nourish such doctrine. For (not knowing what imagination, or the senses are), what they receive, they teach: some saying, that imaginations rise of themselves, and have no cause; others, that they rise most commonly from the will; and that good thoughts are blown (inspired) into a man by God, and evil thoughts by the Devil; or that good thoughts are poured (infused) into a man by God, and evil ones by the Devil. Some say the senses receive the species of things, and deliver them to the common sense; and the common sense delivers them over to the fancy, and the fancy to the memory, and the memory to the judgement, like handing of things from one to another, with many words making nothing understood.

The imagination that is raised in man (or any other creature indued with the faculty of imagining) by words, or other voluntary signs, is that we generally call *understanding;* and is common to man and beast. For a dog by custom will understand the call, or the rating of his master; and so will many other beasts. That understanding which is peculiar to man, is the understanding not only his will, but his conceptions and thoughts, by the sequel and contexture of the names of things into affirmations, negations, and other forms of speech; and of this kind of understanding I shall speak hereafter.

## *Chapter 3*

### OF THE CONSEQUENCE OR TRAIN OF IMAGINATIONS

By *Consequence,* or TRAIN of thoughts, I understand that succession of one thought to another, which is called (to distinguish it from discourse in words) *mental discourse.*

When a man thinketh on any thing whatsoever, his next thought after, is not altogether so casual as it seems to be. Not every thought to every thought succeeds indifferently. But as we have no imagination, whereof we have not formerly had sense, in whole, or in parts; so we have no transition from one imagination to another, whereof we never had the like before in our senses. The reason whereof is this. All fancies are motions within us, relics of those made in the sense: and those motions that immediately succeeded one another in the sense, continue also together after sense: insomuch as the former coming again to take place, and be predominant, the latter followeth, by coherence of the matter moved, in such manner, as water upon a plain table is drawn which way any one part of it is guided by the finger. But because in sense, to one and the same thing perceived, sometimes one thing, sometimes another succeedeth, it comes to pass in time, that in the imagining of any thing, there is no certainty what we shall imagine next; only this is certain, it shall be something that succeeded the same before, at one time or another.

This train of thoughts, or mental discourse, is of two sorts. The first is *unguided, without design,* and inconstant; wherein there is no passionate thought, to govern and direct those that follow, to it self, as the end and scope of some desire, or other passion: in which case the thoughts are said to wander, and seem impertinent one to another, as in a dream. Such are commonly the thoughts of men, that are not only without company, but also without care of any thing; though even then their thoughts are as busy as at other times, but without harmony; as the sound which a lute out of tune would yield to any man; or in tune, to one that could not play. And yet in this wild ranging of the mind, a man may oft-times perceive the way of it, and the dependance of one thought upon another. For in a discourse of our present civil war, what could seem more impertinent, than to ask (as one did) what was the value of a Roman penny? Yet the coherence to me was manifest enough. For the thought of the war, introduced the thought of the delivering up the king to his enemies; the thought of that, brought in the thought of the delivering up of Christ; and that again the thought of the 30 pence, which was the price of that treason; and thence easily followed that malicious question, and all this in a moment of time; for thought is quick.

The second is more constant; as being *regulated* by some desire, and design. For the impression made by such things as we desire, or fear, is strong, and permanent, or, (if it cease for a time,) of quick return; so strong it is sometimes, as to hinder and break our sleep. From desire, ariseth the thought of some means we have seen produce the like of that which we aim at; and from the thought of that, the thought of means of that mean; and so continually, till we come to some beginning within our own power. And because the end, by the greatness of the impression, comes often to mind, in case our thoughts begin to wander, they are quickly again reduced into the way; which observed by one of the seven wise men, made him give men this precept, which is now worn out, *Respice finem;* that is to say, in all your actions, look often upon what you would have, as the thing that directs all your thoughts in the way to attain it.

The train of regulated thoughts is of two kinds; one, when of an effect imagined, we seek the causes, or means that produce it: and this is common to man and beast. The other is, when imagining any thing whatsoever, we seek all the possible effects, that can by it be produced; that is to say, we imagine what we can do with it, when we have it. Of which I have not at any time seen any sign, but in man only; for this is a curiosity hardly incident to the nature of any living creature that has no other passion but sensual, such as are hunger, thirst, lust, and anger. In sum, the discourse of the mind, when it is governed by design, is nothing but *seeking,* or the faculty of invention, which the Latins called *sagacitas,* and *solertia;* a hunting out of the causes, of some effect, present or past; or of the effects, of some present or past cause. Sometimes a man seeks what he hath lost; and from that place, and time, wherein he misses it, his mind runs back, from place to place, and time to time, to find where, and when he had it; that is to say, to find some certain, and limited time and place, in which to begin a method of seeking.

Again, from thence, his thoughts run over the same places and times, to find what action, or other occasion might make him lose it. This we call *remembrance,* or calling to mind: the Latins call it *reminiscentia,* as it were a *re-conning* of our former actions.

Sometimes a man knows a place determinate, within the compass whereof he is to seek; and then his thoughts run over all the parts thereof, in the same manner as one would sweep a room, to find a jewel; or as a spaniel ranges the field, till he find a scent; or as a man should run over the alphabet, to start a rhyme.

Sometime a man desires to know the event of an action; and then he thinketh of some like action past, and the events thereof one after another; supposing like events will follow like actions. As he that foresees what will become of a criminal, recons what he has seen follow on the like crime before; having this order of thoughts, the crime, the officer, the prison, the judge, and the gallows. Which kind of thoughts, is called *foresight,* and *prudence,* or *providence;* and sometimes *wisdom;* though such conjecture, through the difficulty of observing all circumstances, be very fallacious. But this is certain; by how much one man has more experience of things past, than another; by so much also he is more prudent, and his expectations the seldomer fail him. The *present* only has a being in nature; things *past* have a being in the memory only, but things *to come* have no being at all; the *future* being but a fiction of the mind, applying the sequels of actions past, to the actions that are present; which with most certainty is done by him that has most experience; but not with certainty enough. And though it be called prudence, when the event answereth our expectation; yet in its own nature, it is but presumption. For the foresight of things to come, which is providence, belongs only to him by whose will they are to come. From him only, and supernaturally, proceeds prophecy. The best prophet naturally is the best guesser; and the best guesser, he that is most versed and studied in the matters he guesses at: for he hath most *signs* to guess by.

A *sign* is the event antecedent of the consequent; and contrarily, the consequent of the antecedent, when the like consequences have been observed, before: and the oftener they have been observed, the

less uncertain is the sign. And therefore he that has most experience in any kind of business, has most signs, whereby to guess at the future time: and consequently is the most prudent: and so much more prudent than he that is new in that kind of business, as not to be equalled by any advantage of natural and extemporary wit: though perhaps many young men think the contrary.

Nevertheless it is not prudence that distinguisheth man from beast. There be beasts, that at a year old observe more, and pursue that which is for their good, more prudently, than a child can do at ten.

As prudence is a *presumption* of the *future,* contracted from the *experience* of time *past;* so there is a presumption of things past taken from other things (not future but) past also. For he that hath seen by what courses and degrees, a flourishing state hath first come into civil war, and then to ruin; upon the sight of the ruins of any other state, will guess, the like war, and the like courses have been there also. But this conjecture, has the same uncertainty almost with the conjecture of the future; both being grounded only upon experience.

There is no other act of man's mind, that I can remember, naturally planted in him, so as to need no other thing, to the exercise of it, but to be born a man, and live with the use of his five senses. Those other faculties, of which I shall speak by and by, and which seem proper to man only, are acquired, and increased by study and industry; and of most men learned by instruction, and discipline; and proceed all from the invention of words, and speech. For besides sense, and thoughts, and the train of thoughts, the mind of man has no other motion: though by the help of speech, and method, the same faculties may be improved to such a height, as to distinguish men from all other living creatures.

Whatsoever we imagine is *finite.* Therefore there is no idea, or conception of any thing we call *infinite.* No man can have in his mind an image of infinite magnitude; nor conceive infinite swiftness, infinite time, or infinite force, or infinite power. When we say any thing is infinite, we signify only, that we are not able to conceive the ends, and bounds of the things named; having no conception of the thing, but of our own inability. And therefore the name of God is used, not to make us conceive him; (for he is *incomprehensible;* and his greatness, and power are unconceivable;) but that we may honour him. Also because whatsoever (as I said before,) we conceive, has been perceived first by sense, either all at once, or by parts; a man can have no thought, representing any thing, not subject to sense. No man therefore can conceive any thing, but he must conceive it in some place; and indued with some determinate magnitude; and which may be divided into parts; nor that any thing is all in this place, and all in another place at the same time; nor that two, or more things can be in one, and the same place at once; for none of these things ever have, or can be incident to sense; but are absurd speeches, taken upon credit (without any signification at all,) from deceived philosophers, and deceived, or deceiving schoolmen.

## *Chapter 6*

### OF THE INTERIOR BEGINNINGS OF VOLUNTARY MOTIONS: COMMONLY CALLED THE PASSIONS; AND THE SPEECHES BY WHICH THEY ARE EXPRESSED

There be in animals, two sorts of *motions* peculiar to them: one called *vital;* begun in generation, and continued without interruption through their whole life; such as are the *course* of the *blood,* the *pulse,* the *breathing,* the *concoction, nutrition, excretion,* &c.; to which motions there needs no help of imagination: the other is *animal motion,* otherwise called *voluntary motion;* as to *go,* to *speak,* to *move* any of our limbs, in such manner as is first fancied in our minds. That sense is motion in the organs and interior parts of man's body, caused by the action of the things we see, hear, &c.; and that fancy is but the relics of the same motion, remaining after sense, has been already said in the first and second chapters. And because *going, speaking,* and the like voluntary motions, depend always upon a precedent thought of *whither, which way,* and *what;* it is evident, that the imagination is the first internal beginning of all voluntary motion. And although unstudied men do not conceive any motion at all to be there, where the

thing moved is invisible; or the space it is moved in, is (for the shortness of it) insensible; yet that doth not hinder, but that such motions are. For let a space be never so little, that which is moved over a greater space, whereof that little one is part, must first be moved over that. These small beginnings of motion, within the body of man, before they appear in walking, speaking, striking, and other visible actions, are commonly called ENDEAVOUR.

This endeavour, when it is toward something which causes it, is called APPETITE, or DESIRE; the latter, being the general name; and the other, oftentimes restrained to signify the desire of food, namely *hunger* and *thirst.* And when the endeavour is fromward something, it is generally called AVERSION. These words, *appetite* and *aversion,* we have from the *Latins;* and they both of them signify the motions, one of approaching, the other of retiring. So also do the Greek words for the same, which are ὁρμὴ and ἀφορμὴ. For nature itself does often press upon men those truths, which afterwards, when they look for somewhat beyond nature, they stumble at. For the Schools find in mere appetite to go, or move, no actual motion at all: but because some motion they must acknowledge, they call it metaphorical motion; which is but an absurd speech: for though words may be called metaphorical; bodies and motions cannot.

That which men desire, they are also said to LOVE: and to HATE those things for which they have aversion. So that desire and love are the same thing; save that by desire, we always signify the absence of the object; by love, most commonly the presence of the same. So also by aversion, we signify the absence; and by hate, the presence of the object.

Of appetites and aversions, some are born with men; as appetite of food, appetite of excretion and exoneration, (which may also and more properly be called aversions, from somewhat they feel in their bodies;) and some other appetites, not many. The rest, which are appetites of particular things, proceed from experience, and trial of their effects upon themselves or other men. For of things we know not at all, or believe not to be, we can have no further desire, than to taste and try. But aversion we have for things, not only which we know have hurt us, but also that we do not know whether they will hurt us, or not.

Those things which we neither desire, nor hate, we are said to *contemn;* CONTEMPT being nothing else but an immobility, or contumacy of the heart, in resisting the action of certain things; and proceeding from that the heart is already moved otherwise, by other more potent objects; or from want of experience of them.

And because the constitution of a man's body is in continual mutation, it is impossible that all the same things should always cause in him the same appetites, and aversions: much less can all men consent, in the desire of almost any one and the same object.

But whatsoever is the object of any man's appetite or desire, that is it which he for his part calleth *good:* and the object of his hate and aversion, *evil;* and of his contempt, *vile* and *inconsiderable.* For these words of good, evil, and contemptible, are ever used with relation to the person that useth them: there being nothing simply and absolutely so; nor any common rule of good and evil, to be taken from the nature of the objects themselves; but from the person of the man (where there is no commonwealth;) or, (in a commonwealth,) from the person that representeth it; or from an arbitrator or judge, whom men disagreeing shall by consent set up, and make his sentence the rule thereof.

The Latin tongue has two words, whose significations approach to those of good and evil; but are not precisely the same; and those are *pulchrum* and *turpe.* Whereof the former signifies that, which by some apparent signs promiseth good; and the latter, that which promiseth evil. But in our tongue we have not so general names to express them by. But for *pulchrum* we say in some things, *fair;* in others, *beautiful,* or *handsome,* or *gallant,* or *honourable,* or *comely,* or *amiable;* and for *turpe, foul, deformed, ugly, base, nauseous,* and the like, as the subject shall require; all which words, in their proper places, signify nothing else but the *mine,* or countenance, that promiseth good and evil. So that of good there be three kinds; good in the promise, that is *pulchrum;* good in effect, as the end desired, which is called *jucundum, delightful;* and good as the means, which

is called *utile, profitable;* and as many of evil: for *evil* in promise, is that they call *turpe;* evil in effect, and end, is *molestum, unpleasant, troublesome;* and evil in the means, *inutile, unprofitable, hurtful.*

As, in sense, that which is really within us, is, (as I have said before,) only motion, caused by the action of external objects, but in apparence; to the sight, light and colour; to the ear, sound; to the nostril, odour, &c.: so, when the action of the same object is continued from the eyes, ears, and other organs to the heart, the real effect there is nothing but motion, or endeavour; which consisteth in appetite, or aversion, to or from the object moving. But the apparence, or sense of that motion is that we either call *delight,* or *trouble of mind.*

This motion, which is called appetite, and for the apparence of it *delight,* and *pleasure,* seemeth to be a corroboration of vital motion, and a help thereunto; and therefore such things as caused delight, were not improperly called *jucunda, (a juvando,)* from healing or fortifying; and the contrary, *molesta, offensive,* from hindering, and troubling the motion vital.

*Pleasure* therefore, (or *delight,*) is the apparence, or sense of good; and *molestation* or *displeasure,* the apparence, or sense of evil. And consequently all appetite, desire, and love, is accompanied with some delight more or less; and all hatred and aversion, with more or less displeasure and offence.

Of pleasures or delights, some arise from the sense of an object present; and those may be called *pleasures of sense,* (the word *sensual,* as it is used by those only that condemn them, having no place till there be laws.) Of this kind are all onerations and exonerations of the body; as also all that is pleasant, in the *sight, hearing, smell, taste, or touch.* Others arise from the expectation, that proceeds from foresight of the end, or consequence of things; whether those things in the sense please or displease. And these are *pleasures of the mind* of him that draweth those consequence, and are generally called JOY. In the like manner, displeasures are some in the sense, and called PAIN; others in the expectation of consequences, and are called GRIEF.

These simple passions called *appetite, desire, love, aversion, hate, joy,* and *grief,* have their names for divers considerations diversified. As first, when they one succeed another, they are diversely called from the opinion men have of the likelihood of attaining what they desire. Secondly, from the object loved or hated. Thirdly, from the consideration of many of them together. Fourthly, from the alteration or succession it self.

- For *appetite,* with an opinion of attaining, is called HOPE.
- The same, without such opinion, DESPAIR.
- *Aversion,* with opinion of *hurt* from the object, FEAR.
- The same, with hope of avoiding that hurt by resistance, COURAGE.
- Sudden *courage,* ANGER.
- Constant *hope,* CONFIDENCE of ourselves.
- Constant *despair,* DIFFIDENCE of ourselves.
- *Anger* for great hurt done to another, when we conceive the same to be done by injury, INDIGNATION.
- *Desire* of good to another, BENEVOLENCE, GOOD WILL, CHARITY. If to man generally, GOOD NATURE.
- *Desire* of riches, COVETOUSNESS: a name used always in signification of blame; because men contending for them, are displeased with one another's attaining them; though the desire in itself, be to be blamed, or allowed, according to the means by which those riches are sought.
- *Desire* of office, or precedence, AMBITION: a name used also in the worse sense, for the reason before mentioned.
- *Desire* of things that conduce but a little to our ends, and fear of things that are but of little hindrance, PUSILLANIMITY.
- *Contempt* of little helps and hindrances, MAGNANIMITY.
- *Magnanimity,* in danger of death or wounds, VALOUR, FORTITUDE.
- *Magnanimity,* in the use of riches, LIBERALITY.
- *Pusillanimity,* in the same, WRETCHEDNESS, MISERABLENESS, or PARSIMONY; as it is liked or disliked.

- *Love* of persons for society, KINDNESS.
- *Love* of persons for pleasing the sense only, NATURAL LUST.
- *Love* of the same, acquired from rumination, that is, imagination of pleasure past, LUXURY.
- *Love* of one singularly, with desire to be singularly beloved, THE PASSION OF LOVE. The same, with fear that the love is not mutual, JEALOUSY.
- *Desire,* by doing hurt to another, to make him condemn some fact of his own, REVENGEFULNESS.
- *Desire* to know why and how, CURIOSITY; such as is in no living creature but *man;* so that man is distinguished, not only by his reason, but also by this singular passion from other *animals;* in whom the appetite of food, and other pleasures of sense, by predominance, take away the care of knowing causes; which is a lust of the mind, that by a perseverance of delight in the continual and indefatigable generation of knowledge, exceedeth the short vehemence of any carnal pleasure.
- *Fear* of power invisible, feigned by the mind, or imagined from tales publicly allowed, RELIGION; not allowed, SUPERSTITION. And when the power imagined, is truly such as we imagine, TRUE RELIGION.
- *Fear,* without the apprehension of why, or what, PANIC TERROR, called so from the fables, that make *Pan* the author of them; whereas in truth, there is always in him that so feareth, first, some apprehension of the cause, though the rest run away by example, every one supposing his fellow to know why. And therefore this passion happens to none but in a throng, or multitude of people.
- *Joy,* from apprehension of novelty, ADMIRATION; proper to man, because it excites the appetite of knowing the cause.
- *Joy,* arising from imagination of a man's own power and ability, is that exultation of the mind which is called GLORYING: which if

grounded upon the experience of his own former actions, is the same with *confidence:* but if grounded on the flattery of others; or only supposed by himself, for delight in the consequences of it, is called VAINGLORY: which name is properly given; because a well grounded *confidence* begetteth attempt; whereas the supposing of power does not, and is therefore rightly called *vain.*

• *Grief,* from opinion of want of power, is called DEJECTION of mind.

• The *vain-glory* which consisteth in the feigning or supposing of abilities in ourselves, which we know are not, is most incident to young men, and nourished by the histories, or fictions of gallant persons; and is corrected oftentimes by age, and employment.

• *Sudden glory,* is the passion which maketh those *grimaces* called LAUGHTER; and is caused either by some sudden act of their own, that pleaseth them; or by the apprehension of some deformed thing in another, by comparison whereof they suddenly applaud themselves. And it is incident most to them, that are conscious of the fewest abilities in themselves; who are forced to keep themselves in their own favour, by observing the imperfections of other men. And therefore much laughter at the defects of others, is a sign of pusillanimity. For of great minds, one of the proper works is, to help and free others from scorn; and compare themselves only with the most able.

• On the contrary, *sudden dejection,* is the passion that causeth WEEPING; and is caused by such accidents, as suddenly take away some vehement hope, or some prop of their power: and they are most subject to it, that rely principally on helps external, such as are women, and children. Therefore some weep for the loss of friends; others for their unkindness; others for the sudden stop made to their thoughts of revenge, by reconciliation. But in all cases, both laughter, and weeping, are sudden motions; custom taking them both away. For no man laughs at old jests; or weeps for an old calamity.

• *Grief,* for the discovery of some defect of ability, is SHAME, or the passion that discovereth itself in BLUSHING; and consisteth in the apprehension of some thing dishonourable; and in young men, is a sign of the love of good reputation, and commendable; in old men it is a sign of the same; but because it comes too late, not commendable.

• The *contempt* of good reputation is called IMPUDENCE.

• *Grief,* of the calamity of another, is PITY; and ariseth from the imagination that the like calamity may befall himself; and therefore is called also COMPASSION, and in the phrase of this present time a FELLOW-FEELING: and therefore for calamity arriving from great wickedness, the best men have the least pity; and for the same calamity, those have least pity, that think themselves least obnoxious to the same.

• *Contempt,* or little sense of the calamity of others, is that which men call CRUELTY; proceeding from security of their own fortune. For, that any man should take pleasure in other men's great harms, without other end of his own, I do not conceive it possible.

• *Grief,* for the success of a competitor in wealth, honour, or other good, if it be joined with endeavour to enforce our own abilities to equal or exceed him, is called EMULATION: but joined with endeavour to supplant, or hinder a competitor, ENVY.

When in the mind of man, appetites, and aversions, hopes, and fears, concerning one and the same thing, arise alternately; and divers good and evil consequences of the doing, or omitting the thing propounded, come successively into our thoughts; so that sometimes we have an appetite to it; sometimes an aversion from it; sometimes hope to be able to do it; sometimes despair, or fear to attempt it; the whole sum of desires, aversions, hopes and fears continued till the thing be either done, or thought impossible, is that we call DELIBERATION.

Therefore of things past, there is no *deliberation;*

because manifestly impossible to be changed: nor of things known to be impossible, or thought so; because men know, or think such deliberation vain. But of things impossible, which we think possible, we may deliberate; not knowing it is in vain. And it is called *deliberation;* because it is a putting an end to the *liberty* we had of doing, or omitting, according to our own appetite, or aversion.

This alternate succcession of appetites, aversions, hopes and fears, is no less in other living creatures than in man: and therefore beasts also deliberate.

Every *deliberation* is then said to *end,* when that whereof they deliberate is either done, or thought impossible; because till then we retain the liberty of doing, or omitting, according to our appetite, or aversion.

In *deliberation,* the last appetite, or aversion, immediately adhering to the action, or to the omission thereof, is that we call the WILL; the act, (not the faculty,) of *willing.* And beasts that have *deliberation,* must necessarily also have *will.* The definition of the *will,* given commonly by the Schools, that it is a *rational appetite,* is not good. For if it were, then could there be no voluntary act against reason. For a *voluntary act* is that, which proceedeth from the *will,* and no other. But if instead of a rational appetite, we shall say an appetite resulting from a precedent deliberation, then the definition is the same that I have given here. *Will* therefore is *the last appetite in deliberating.* And though we say in common discourse, a man had a will once to do a thing, that nevertheless he forbore to do; yet that is properly but an inclination, which makes no action voluntary; because the action depends not of it, but of the last inclination, or appetite. For if the intervenient appetites, make any action voluntary; then by the same reason all intervenient aversions, should make the same action involuntary; and so one and the same action, should be both voluntary and involuntary.

By this it is manifest, that not only actions that have their beginning from covetousness, ambition, lust, or other appetites to the thing propounded; but also those that have their beginning from aversion, or fear of those consequences that follow the omission, are *voluntary actions.*

The forms of speech by which the passions are expressed, are partly the same, and partly different from those, by which we express our thoughts. And first, generally all passions may be expressed *indicatively;* as *I love, I fear, I joy, I deliberate, I will, I command:* but some of them have particular expressions by themselves, which nevertheless are not affirmations, unless it be when they serve to make other inferences, besides that of the passion they proceed from. Deliberation is expressed *subjunctively;* which is a speech proper to signify suppositions, with their consequences; as, *if this be done, then this will follow;* and differs not from the language of reasoning, save that reasoning is in general words; but deliberation for the most part is of particulars. The language of desire, and aversion, is *imperative;* as *do this, forbear that;* which when the party is obliged to do, or forbear, is *command;* otherwise *prayer;* or else *counsel.* The language of vain-glory, of indignation, pity and revengefulness, *optative:* but of the desire to know, there is a peculiar expression, called *interrogative;* as, *what is it, when shall it, how is it done,* and *why so?* other language of the passions I find none: of cursing, swearing, reviling, and the like, do not signify as speech; but as the actions of a tongue accustomed.

These forms of speech, I say, are expressions, or voluntary significations of our passions: but certain signs they be not; because they may be used arbitrarily, whether they that use them, have such passions or not. The best signs of passions present, are either in the countenance, motions of the body, actions, and ends, or aims, which we otherwise know the man to have.

And because in deliberation, the appetites, and aversions, are raised by foresight of the good and evil consequences, and sequels of the action whereof we deliberate; the good or evil effect thereof dependeth on the foresight of a long chain of consequences, of which very seldom any man is able to see to the end. But for so far as a man seeth, if the good in those consequences be greater than the evil, the whole chain is that which writers call *apparent,* or *seeming good.* And contrarily, when the evil exceedeth the good, the whole is *apparent,* or *seeming evil:* so that he who hath by experience, or reason, the greatest and surest prospect of consequences, deliberates best himself; and is able when he will, to give the best counsel unto others.

*Continual success* in obtaining those things which a man from time to time desireth, that is to say, continual prospering, is that men call FELICITY; I mean the felicity of this life. For there is no such thing as perpetual tranquillity of mind, while we live here; because life itself is but motion, and can never be without desire, nor without fear, no more than without sense. What kind of felicity God hath ordained to them that devoutly honour Him, a man shall no sooner know, than enjoy; being joys, that now are as incomprehensible, as the word of school-men *beatifical vision* is unintelligible.

The form of speech whereby men signify their opinion of the goodness of any thing, is PRAISE. That whereby they signify the power and greatness of any thing, is MAGNIFYING. And that whereby they signify the opinion they have of a man's felicity, is by the Greeks called μακαρισμός for which we have no name in our tongue. And thus much is sufficient for the present purpose, to have been said of the PASSIONS. . . .

## *Chapter 10*

### OF POWER, WORTH, DIGNITY, HONOUR, AND WORTHINESS

The power *of a man,* (to take it universally), is his present means, to obtain some future apparent good; and is either *original* or *instrumental.*

*Natural power,* is the eminence of the faculties of body, or mind: as extraordinary strength, form, prudence, arts, eloquence, liberality, nobility. *Instrumental* are those powers, which acquired by these, or by fortune, are means and instruments to acquire more: as riches, reputation, friends, and the secret working of God, which men call good luck. For the nature of power, is in this point, like to fame, increasing as it proceeds; or like the motion of heavy bodies, which the further they go, make still the more haste.

The greatest of human powers, is that which is compounded of the powers of most men, united by consent, in one person, natural, or civil, that has the use of all their powers depending on his will; such as is the power of a common-wealth: or depending on the wills of each particular; such as is the power of a faction or of divers factions leagued. Therefore to have servants, is power; to have friends, is power: for they are strengths united.

Also riches joined with liberality, is power; because it procureth friends, and servants: without liberality, not so; because in this case they defend not; but expose men to envy, as a prey.

Reputation of power, is power; because it draweth with it the adherence of those that need protection.

So is reputation of love of a man's country, (called popularity,) for the same reason.

Also, what quality soever maketh a man beloved, or feared of many; of the reputation of such quality, is power; because it is a means to have the assistance, and service of many.

Good success is power; because it maketh reputation of wisdom, or good fortune; which makes men either fear him, or rely on him.

Affability of men already in power, is increase of power; because it gaineth love.

Reputation of prudence in the conduct of peace or war, is power; because to prudent men, we commit the government of ourselves, more willingly than to others.

Nobility is power, not in all places, but only in those commonwealths, where it has privileges: for in such privileges consisteth their power.

Eloquence is power, because it is seeming prudence.

Form is power; because being a promise of good, it recommendeth men to the favour of women and strangers.

The sciences, are small power; because not eminent; and therefore, not acknowledged in any man; nor are at all, but in a few, and in them, but of a few things. For science is of that nature, as none can understand it to be, but such as in a good measure have attained it.

Arts of public use, as fortification, making of engines, and other instruments of war; because they confer to defence, and victory, are power: and though the true mother of them, be science, namely the mathematics; yet, because they are brought into the light, by the hand of the artificer, they be esteemed (the midwife passing with the vulgar for the mother,) as his issue.

The *value,* or WORTH of a man, is as of all other things, his price; that is to say, so much as would be given for the use of his power: and therefore is not absolute; but a thing dependant on the need and judgment of another. An able conductor of soldiers, is of great price in time of war present, or imminent; but in peace not so. A learned and uncorrupt judge, is much worth in time of peace; but not so much in war. And as in other things, so in men, not the seller, but the buyer determines the price. For let a man (as most men do,) rate themselves at the highest value they can; yet their true value is no more than it is esteemed by others. . . . .

## *Chapter 11*

### OF THE DIFFERENCE OF MANNERS

By manners, I mean not here, decency of behaviour; as how one man should salute another, or how a man should wash his mouth, or pick his teeth before company, and such other points of the *small morals;* but those qualities of mankind, that concern their living together in peace, and unity. To which end we are to consider, that the felicity of this life, consisteth not in the repose of a mind satisfied. For there is no such *finus ultimus,* (utmost aim,) nor *summum bonum,* (greatest good,) as is spoken of in the books of the old moral philosophers. Nor can a man any more live, whose desires are at an end, than he, whose senses and imaginations are at a stand. Felicity is a continual progress of the desire, from one object to another; the attaining of the former, being still but the way to the latter. The cause whereof is, that the object of man's desire, is not to enjoy once only, and for one instant of time; but to assure for ever, the way of his future desire. And therefore the voluntary actions, and inclinations of all men, tend, not only to the procuring, but also to the assuring of a contented life; and differ only in the way: which ariseth partly from the diversity of passions, in divers men; and partly from the difference of the knowledge, or opin-

ion each one has of the causes, which produce the effect desired.

So that in the first place, I put for a general inclination of all mankind, a perpetual and restless desire of power after power, that ceaseth only in death. And the cause of this, is not always that a man hopes for a more intensive delight, than he has already attained to; or that he cannot be content with a moderate power: but because he cannot assure the power and means to live well, which he hath present, without the acquisition of more. And from hence it is, that kings, whose power is greatest, turn their endeavors to the assuring it at home by laws, or abroad by wars: and when that is done, there succeedeth a new desire; in some, of fame from new conquest; in others, of ease and sensual pleasure; in others, of admiration, or being flattered for excellence in some art, or other ability of the mind.

Competition of riches, honour, command, or other power, inclineth to contention, enmity, and war: because the way of one competitor, to the attaining of his desire, is to kill, subdue, supplant, or repel the other. Particularly, competition of praise, inclineth to a reverence of antiquity. For men contend with the living, not with the dead; to these ascribing more than due, that they may obscure the glory of the other.

Desire of ease, and sensual delight, disposeth men to obey a common power: because by such desires, a man doth abandon the protection might be hoped for from his own industry, and labour. Fear of death, and wounds, disposeth to the same: and for the same reason. On the contrary, needy men, and hardy, not contented with their present condition; as also, all men that are ambitious of military command, are inclined to continue the causes of war; and to stir up trouble and sedition: for there is no honour military but by war; not any such hope to mend an ill game, as by causing a new shuffle.

Desire of knowledge, and arts of peace, inclineth men to obey a common power: For such desire, containeth a desire of leisure; and consequently protection from some other power than their own.

Desire of praise, disposeth to laudable actions, such as please them whose judgment they value; for of those men whom we contemn, we contemn also the praises. Desire of fame after death does the same. And though after death, there be no sense of the praise given us on earth, as being joys, that are either swallowed up in the unspeakeable joys of Heaven, or extinguished in the extreme torments of hell: yet is not such fame vain; because men have a present delight therein, from the foresight of it, and of the benefit that may redound thereby to their posterity: which though they now see not, yet they imagine; and any thing that is pleasure in the sense, the same also is pleasure in the imagination. . . .

## Chapter 12

### OF RELIGION

Seeing there are no signs, nor fruit of *religion,* but in man only; there is no cause to doubt, but that the seed of *religion,* is also only in man; and consisteth in some peculiar quality, or at least in some eminent degree thereof, not to be found in other living creatures.

And first, it is peculiar to the nature of man, to be inquisitive into the causes of the events they see, some more, some less; but all men so much, as to be curious in the search of the causes of their own good and evil fortune.

Secondly, upon the sight of any thing that hath a beginning, to think also it had a cause, which determined the same to begin, then when it did, rather than sooner or later.

Thirdly, whereas there is no other felicity of beasts, but the enjoying of their quotidian food, ease, and lusts; as having little or no foresight of the time to come, for want of observation, and memory of the order, consequence, and dependence of the things they see; man observeth how one event hath been produced by another; and remembereth in them antecedence and consequence; and when he cannot assure himself of the true causes of things, (for the causes of good and evil fortune for the most part are invisible,) he supposes causes of them, either such as his own fancy suggesteth; or trusteth to the authority of other men, such as he thinks to be his friends, and wiser than himself.

The two first, make anxiety. For being assured that there be causes of all things that have arrived hitherto, or shall arrive hereafter; it is impossible for a man, who continually endeavoureth to secure himself against the evil he fears, and procure the good he desireth, not to be in a perpetual solicitude of the time to come; so that every man, especially those that are over provident, are in an estate like to that of *Prometheus.* For as *Prometheus,* (which interpreted, is, *the prudent man,*) was bound to the hill *Caucasus,* a place of large prospect, where, an eagle feeding on his liver, devoured in the day, as much as was repaired in the night: so that man, which looks too far before him, in the care of future time, hath his heart all the day long, gnawed on by fear of death, poverty, or other calamity; and has no repose, nor pause of his anxiety, but in sleep.

This perpetual fear, always accompanying mankind in the ignorance of causes, as it were in the dark, must needs have for object something. And therefore when there is nothing to be seen, there is nothing to accuse, either of their good, or evil fortune, but some *power,* or agent *invisible:* in which sense perhaps it was, that some of the old poets said, that the gods were at first created by human fear: which spoken of the gods, (that is to say, of the many gods of the Gentiles) is very true. But the acknowledging of one God, eternal, infinite, and omnipotent, may more easily be derived, from the desire men have to know the causes of natural bodies, and their several virtues, and operations; than from the fear of what was to befall them in time to come. For he that from any effect he seeth come to pass, should reason to the next and immediate cause thereof, and from thence to the cause of that cause, and plunge himself profoundly in the pursuit of causes; shall at last come to this, that there must be (as even the heathen philosophers confessed) one first mover; that is, a first, and an eternal cause of all things; which is that which men mean by the name of God: and all this without thought of their fortune; the solicitude whereof, both inclines to fear, and hinders them from the search of the causes of other things; and thereby gives occasion of feigning of as many gods, as there be men that feign them.

And for the matter, or substance of the invisible agents, so fancied; they could not by natural cogitation, fall upon any other conceit, but that it was the same with that of the soul of man; and that the soul of man, was of the same substance, with that which appeareth in a dream, to one that sleepeth; or in a looking-glass, to one that is awake; which, men not knowing that such apparitions are nothing else but creatures of the fancy, think to be real, and external substances; and therefore call them ghosts; as the Latins called them *imagines,* and *umbrae,* and thought them spirits, that is, thin aerial bodies; and those invisible agents, which they feared, to be like them; save that they appear, and vanish when they please. But the opinion that such spirits were incorporeal, or immaterial, could never enter into the mind of any man by nature; because, though men may put together words of contradictory signification, as *spirit,* and *incorporeal;* yet they can never have the imagination of any thing answering to them: and therefore, men that by their own meditation, arrive to the acknowledgment of one infinite, omnipotent, and eternal God, choose rather to confess he is incomprehensible, and above their understanding, than to define his nature by *spirit incorporeal,* and then confess their definition to be unintelligible: or if they give him such a title, it is not *dogmatically,* with intention to make the divine nature understood; but *piously,* to honour him with attributes, of significations, as remote as they can from the grossness of bodies visible.

Then, for the way by which they think these invisible agents wrought their effects; that is to say, what immediate causes they used, in bringing things to pass, men that know not what it is that we call *causing,* (that is, almost all men) have no other rule to guess by, but by observing, and remembering what they have seen to precede the like effect at some other time, or times before, without seeing between the antecedent and subsequent event, any dependence or connexion at all: and therefore from the like things past, they expect the like things to come; and hope for good or evil luck, superstitiously, from things that have no part at all in the causing of it: as the Athenians did for their war at *Lepanto,* demand

another *Phormio;* the Pompeian faction for their war in *Africa,* another *Scipio;* and others have done in divers other occasions since. In like manner they attribute their fortune to a stander by, to a lucky or unlucky place, to words spoken, especially if the name of God be amongst them; as charming and conjuring (the liturgy of witches;) insomuch as to believe, they have power to turn a stone into bread, bread into a man, or any thing into any thing.

Thirdly, for the worship which naturally men exhibit to powers invisible, it can be no other, but such expression of their reverence, as they would use towards men; gifts, petitions, thanks, submission of body, considerate addresses, sober behavior, premeditated words, swearing (that is, assuring one another of their promises,) by invoking them. Beyond that reason suggesteth nothing; but leaves them either to rest there; or for further ceremonies, to rely on those they believe to be wiser than themselves.

Lastly, concerning how these invisible powers declare to men the things which shall hereafter come to pass, especially concerning their good or evil fortune in general, or good or ill success in any particular undertaking, men are naturally at a stand; save that using to conjecture of the time to come, by the time past, they are very apt, not only to take casual things, after one or two encounters, for prognostics of the like encounter ever after, but also to believe the like prognostics from other men, of whom they have once conceived a good opinion.

And in these four things, opinion of ghosts, ignorance of second causes, devotion towards what men fear, and taking of things casual for prognostics, consisteth the natural seed of *religion;* which by reason of the different fancies, judgments, and passions of several men, hath grown up into ceremonies so different, that those which are used by one man, are for the most part ridiculous to another.

For these seeds have received culture from two sorts of men. One sort have been they, that have nourished, and ordered them, according to their own invention. The other have done it, by God's commandment, and direction: but both sorts have done it, with a purpose to make those men that relied on them, the more apt to obedience, laws, peace, charity, and civil society. So that the religion of the former sort, is a part of human politics; and teacheth part of the duty which earthly kings require of their subjects. And the religion of the latter sort is divine politics; and containeth precepts to those that have yielded themselves subjects in the kingdom of God. Of the former sort, were all the founders of commonwealths, and the lawgivers of the Gentiles: of the latter sort, were *Abraham, Moses* and our *blessed Saviour;* by whom have been derived unto us the laws of the kingdom of God. . . .

## *Chapter 13*

### OF THE NATURAL CONDITION OF MANKIND AS CONCERNING THEIR FELICITY, AND MISERY

Nature hath made men so equal, in the faculties of body, and mind; as that though there be found one man sometimes manifestly stronger in body, or of quicker mind than another; yet when all is reckoned together, the difference between man, and man, is not so considerable, as that one man can thereupon claim to himself any benefit, to which another may not pretend, as well as he. For as to the strength of body, the weakest has strength enough to kill the strongest, either by secret machination, or by confederacy with others, that are in the same danger as himself.

And as to the faculties of the mind, (setting aside the arts grounded upon words, and especially that skill of proceeding upon general, and infallible rules, called science; which very few have, and but in few things; as being not a native faculty, born with us; nor attained, (as prudence,) while we look after someone else,) I find yet a greater equality amongst men, than that of strength. For prudence, is but experience; which equal time, equally bestows on all men, in those things they equally apply themselves unto. That which may perhaps make such equality incredible, is but a vain conceit of one's own wisdom, which almost all men think they have in a greater degree, than the vulgar; that is, than all men but themselves, and a few others, whom by fame, or for concurring with themselves, they approve. For such is the nature of men, that howsoever they may

acknowledge many others to be more witty, or more eloquent, or more learned; yet they will hardly believe there be many so wise as themselves: For they see their own wit at hand, and other men's at a distance. But this proveth rather that men are in that point equal, than unequal. For there is not ordinarily a greater sign of the equal distribution of any thing, than that every man is contented with his share.

From this equality of ability, ariseth equality of hope in the attaining of our ends. And therefore if any two men desire the same thing, which nevertheless they cannot both enjoy, they become enemies; and in the way to their end, (which is principally their own conservation, and sometimes their delectation only,) endeavour to destroy, or subdue one another. And from hence it comes to pass, that where an invader hath no more to fear, than another man's single power; if one plant, sow, build, or possess a convenient seat, others may probably be expected to come prepared with forces united, to dispossess, and deprive him, not only of the fruit of his labour, but also of his life, or liberty. And the invader again is in the like danger of another.

And from this diffidence of one another, there is no way for any man to secure himself, so reasonable, as anticipation; that is, by force, or wiles, to master the persons of all men he can, so long, till he see no other power great enough to endanger him: and this is no more than his own conservation requireth, and is generally allowed. Also because there be some, that taking pleasure in contemplating their own power in the acts of conquest, which they pursue farther than their security requires; if others, that otherwise would be glad to be at ease within modest bounds, should not by invasion increase their power, they would not be able, long time, by standing only on their defence, to subsist. And by consequence, such augmentation of dominion over men, being necessary to a man's conservation, it ought to be allowed him.

Again, men have no pleasure, (but on the contrary a great deal of grief) in keeping company, where there is no power able to over-awe them all. For every man looketh that his companion should value him, at the same rate he sets upon himself: and upon all signs of contempt, or undervaluing, naturally endeavours, as far as he dares (which amongst them that have no common power to keep them in quiet, is far enough to make them destroy each other,) to extort a greater value from his contemners, by damage; and from others, by the example.

So that in the nature of man, we find three principal causes of quarrel. First, competition; secondly, diffidence; thirdly, glory.

The first, maketh man invade for gain; the second, for safety; and the third, for reputation. The first use violence, to make themselves masters of other men's persons, wives, children, and cattle; the second, to defend them; the third, for trifles, as a word, a smile, a different opinion, and any other sign of undervalue, either direct in their persons, or by reflection in their kindred, their friends, their nation, their profession, or their name.

Hereby it is manifest, that during the time men live without a common power to keep them all in awe, they are in that condition which is called war; and such a war, as is of every man, against every man. For WAR, consisteth not in battle only, or the act of fighting; but in a tract of time, wherein the will to contend by battle is sufficiently known: and therefore the notion of *time,* is to be considered in the nature of war; as it is in the nature of weather. For as the nature of foul weather, lieth not in a shower or two of rain; but in an inclination thereto of many days together: so the nature of war, consisteth not in actual fighting; but in the known disposition thereto, during all the time there is no assurance to the contrary. All other time is PEACE.

Whatsoever therefore is consequent to a time of war, where every man is enemy to every man; the same is consequent to the time, wherein men live without other security, than what their own strength, and their own invention shall furnish them withal. In such condition, there is no place for industry; because the fruit thereof is uncertain: and consequently no culture of the earth; no navigation, nor use of the commodities that may be imported by sea; no commodious building; no instruments of moving, and removing such things as require much force; no knowledge of the face of the earth; no account of time; no arts; no letters; no society; and which is worst of all, continual fear, and danger of violent death; and the life of man, solitary, poor, nasty, brutish, and short.

It may seem strange to some man, that has not well weighed these things; that nature should thus dissociate, and render men apt to invade, and destroy one another: and he may therefore, not trusting to this inference, made from the passions, desire perhaps to have the same confirmed by experience. Let him therefore consider with himself, when taking a journey, he arms himself, and seeks to go well accompanied; when going to sleep, he locks his doors; when even in his house he locks his chests; and this when he knows there be laws, and public officers, armed, to revenge all injuries shall be done him; what opinion he has of his fellow subjects, when he rides armed; of his fellow citizens, when he locks his doors; and of his children, and servants, when he locks his chests. Does he not there as much accuse mankind by his actions, as I do by my words? But neither of us accuse man's nature in it. The desires, and other passions of man, are in themselves no sin. No more are the actions, that proceed from those passions, till they know a law that forbids them: which till laws be made they cannot know: nor can any law be made, till they have agreed upon the person that shall make it.

It may peradventure be thought, there was never such a time, nor condition of war as this; and I believe it was never generally so, over all the world: but there are many places, where they live so now. For the savage people in many places of *America,* except the government of small families, the concord whereof dependeth on natural lust, have no government at all; and live at this day in that brutish manner, as I said before. Howsoever, it may be perceived what manner of life there would be, where there were no common power to fear; by the manner of life, which men that have formerly lived under a peacefull government, use to degenerate into, in a civil war.

But though there had never been any time, wherein particular men were in a condition of war one against another; yet in all times, kings, and persons of sovereign authority, because of their independency, are in continual jealousies, and in the state and posture of gladiators; having their weapons pointing, and their eyes fixed on one another; that is, their forts, garrisons, and guns upon the frontiers of their kingdoms; and continual spies upon their neighbours; which is a posture of war. But because they uphold thereby, the industry of their subjects; there does not follow from it, that misery, which accompanies the liberty of particular men.

To this war of every man against every man, this also is consequent; that nothing can be unjust. The notions of right and wrong, justice and injustice have there no place. Where there is no common power, there is no law: where no law, no injustice. Force, and fraud, are in war the two cardinal virtues. Justice, and injustice are none of the faculties neither of the body, nor mind. If they were, they might be in a man that were alone in the world, as well as his senses, and passions. They are qualities, that relate to men in society, not in solitude. It is consequent also to the same condition, that there be no propriety, no dominion, no *mine* and *thine* distinct; but only that to be every man's, that he can get; and for so long, as he can keep it. And thus much for the ill condition, which many by mere nature is actually placed in; though with a possibility to come out of it, consisting partly in the passions, partly in his reason.

The passions that incline men to peace, are fear of death; desire of such things as are necessary to commodious living; and a hope by their industry to obtain them. And reason suggesteth convenient articles of peace, upon which men may be drawn to agreement. These articles, are they, which otherwise are called the Laws of Nature; whereof I shall speak more particularly, in the two following chapters.

## *Chapter 14*

### OF THE FIRST AND SECOND NATURAL LAWS, AND OF CONTRACTS

The RIGHT OF NATURE, which writers commonly call *jus naturale,* is the liberty each man hath, to use his own power, as he will himself, for the preservation of his own nature; that is to say, of his own life; and consequently, of doing any thing, which in his own judgment, and reason, he shall conceive to be the aptest means thereunto.

By LIBERTY, is understood, according to the proper signification of the word, the absence of external impediments: which impediments, may oft take away part of a man's power to do what he would; but cannot hinder him from using the power left him, according as his judgment, and reason shall dictate to him.

A LAW OF NATURE, (*lex naturalis,*) is a precept, or general rule, found out by reason, by which a man is forbidden to do that, which is destructive of his life, or taketh away the means of preserving the same; and to omit that, by which he thinketh it may be best preserved. For though they that speak of this subject, use to confound *jus*, and *lex, right* and *law;* yet they ought to be distinguished; because RIGHT, consisteth in liberty to do, or to forbear; whereas LAW, determineth, and bindeth to one of them: so that law, and right, differ as much, as obligation, and liberty; which in one and the same matter are inconsistent.

And because the condition of man, (as hath been declared in the precedent chapter) is a condition of war of every one against every one; in which case every one is governed by his own reason; and there is nothing he can make use of, that may not be a help unto him, in preserving his life against his enemies; it followeth, that in such a condition, every man has a right to every thing: even to one another's body. And therefore, as long as this natural right of every man to every thing endureth, there can be no security to any man, (how strong or wise soever he be,) of living out the time, which nature ordinarily alloweth men to live. And consequently it is a precept, or general rule of reason, *that every man, ought to endeavour peace, as far as he has hope of obtaining it; and when he cannot obtain it, that he may seek, and use, all helps, and advantages of war.* The first branch of which rule, containeth the first, and fundamental law of nature; which is, *to seek peace, and follow it.* The second, the sum of the right of nature; which is, *by all means we can, to defend ourselves.*

From this fundamental law of nature, by which men are commanded to endeavor peace, is derived this second law; *that a man be willing, when others are so too, as farforth, as for peace, and defence of himself he shall think it necessary, to lay down this right to all things; and be contented with so much liberty against other men, as he would allow other men against himself.* For as long as every man holdeth this right, of doing any thing he liketh; so long are all men in the condition of war. But if other men will not lay down their right, as well as he; then there is no reason for any one, to divest himself of his: for that were to expose himself to prey, (which no man is bound to) rather than to dispose himself to peace. This is that law of the Gospel; *whatsoever you require that others should do for you, that do ye to them.* And that law of all men, *quod tibi fieri non vis, alteri ne feceris.*

To *lay down* a man's *right* to any thing, is to *divest* himself of the *liberty,* of hindering another of the benefit of his own right to the same. For he that renounceth, or passeth away his right, giveth not to any other man a right which he had not before; because there is nothing to which every man had not right by nature: but only standeth out of his way, that he may enjoy his own original right, without hindrance from him; not without hindrance from another. So that the effect which redoundeth to one man, by another man's defect of right, is but so much diminution of impediments to the use of his own right original.

Right is laid aside, either by simply renouncing it; or by transferring it to another. By *simply* RENOUNCING; when he cares not to whom the benefit thereof redoundeth. By TRANSFERRING; when he intendeth the benefit thereof to some certain person, or persons. And when a man hath in either manner abandoned, or granted away his right; then is he said to be OBLIGED, or BOUND, not to hinder those, to whom such right is granted, or abandoned, from the benefit of it: and that he *ought,* and it is his DUTY, not to make void that voluntary act of his own: and that such hindrance is INJUSTICE, and INJURY, as being *sine jure;* the right being before renounced, or transferred. So that *injury,* or *injustice,* in the controversies of the world, is somewhat like to that, which in the disputations of scholars is called *absurdity.* For as it is there called an absurdity, to contradict what one maintained in the beginning: so in the world, it is called injustice, and injury, voluntarily to undo that, which from the beginning he had voluntarily done. The way by which a man either simply renounceth, or transferreth his right, is a declaration, or signification, by some voluntary and sufficient sign, or signs, that he doth so renounce, or transfer; or hath so renounced, or transferred the same, to him that accepteth it. And these signs are either words only, or actions only; or (as it happeneth most often) both words, and actions. And the same are the BONDS, by which men are bound, and obliged: bonds, that have their strength, not from their own nature, (for nothing is more easily broken than a man's word,) but from fear of some evil consequence upon the rupture.

Whensoever a man transferreth his right, or renounceth it; it is either in consideration of some right reciprocally transferred to himself; or for some other good he hopeth for thereby. For it is a voluntary act: and of the voluntary acts of every man, the object is some *good to himself.* And therefore there be some rights, which no man can be understood by any words, or other signs, to have abandoned, or transferred. As first a man cannot lay down the right of resisting them, that assault him by force, to take away his life; because he cannot be understood to aim thereby, at any good to himself. The same may be said of wounds, and chains, and imprisonment; both because there is no benefit consequent to such patience; as there is to the patience of suffering another to be wounded, or imprisoned: as also because a man cannot tell, when he seeth men proceed against him by violence, whether they intend his death or not. And lastly the motive, and end for which this renouncing, and transferring of right is introduced, is nothing else but the security of a man's person, in his life, and in the means of so preserving life, as not to be weary of it. And therefore if a man by words, or other signs, seem to despoil himself of the end, for which those signs were intended; he is not to be understood as if he meant it, or that it was his will; but that he was ignorant of how such words and actions were to be interpreted.

The mutual transferring of right, is that which men call CONTRACT.

There is difference between transferring of right to the thing; and transferring, or tradition, that is, delivery of the thing it self. For the thing may be delivered together with the translation of the right; as in buying and selling with ready money; or exchange of goods, or lands: and it may be delivered some time after.

Again, one of the contractors, may deliver the thing contracted for on his part, and leave the other to perform his part at some determinate time after, and in the mean time be trusted; and then the contract on his part, is called PACT, or COVENANT: or both parts may contract now, to perform hereafter: in which cases, he that is to perform in time to come, being trusted, his performance is called *keeping of promise,* or faith; and the failing of performance (if it be voluntary) *violation of faith.*

When the transferring of right, is not mutual; but one of the parties transferreth, in hope to gain thereby friendship, or service from another, or from his friends; or in hope to gain the reputation of charity, or magnanimity; or to deliver his mind from the pain of compassion; or in hope of reward in heaven; this is not contract, but GIFT, FREE-GIFT, GRACE: which words signify one and the same thing.

Signs of contract, are either *express,* or *by inference.* Express, are words spoken with understanding of what they signify: and such words are either of the time *present,* or *past;* as, *I give, I grant, I have given, I have granted, I will that this be yours:* or of the future; as, *I will give, I will grant:* which words of the future are called PROMISE.

Signs by inference, are sometimes the consequence of words; sometimes the consequence of silence; sometimes the consequence of actions; sometimes the consequence of forbearing an action: and generally a sign by inference, of any contract, in whatsoever sufficiently argues the will of the contractor.

Words alone, if they be of the time to come, and contain a bare promise, are an insufficient sign of a free-gift and therefore not obligatory. For if they be of the time to come, as, *tomorrow I will give,* they are a sign I have not given yet, and consequently that my right is not transferred, but remaineth till I trans-

fer it by some other act. But if the words be of the time present, or past, as, *I have given, or do give to be delivered tomorrow,* then is my tomorrow's right given away to day; and that by the virtue of the words, though there were no other argument of my will. And there is a great difference in the signification of these words, *volo hoc tuum esse cras,* and *cras dabo;* that is, between *I will that this be thine tomorrow,* and, *I will give it thee tomorrow:* for the word *I will,* in the former manner of speech, signifies an act of the will present; but in the latter, it signifies a promise of an act of the will to come: and therefore the former words, being of the present, transfer a future right; the latter, that be of the future, transfer nothing. But if there be other signs of the will to transfer a right, besides words; then, though the gift be free, yet may the right be understood to pass by words of the future: as if a man propound a prize to him that comes first to the end of a race; the gift is free; and though the words be of the future, yet the right passeth: for if he would not have his words so be understood, he should not have let them run.

In contracts, the right passeth, not only where the words are of the time present, or past, but also where they are of the future: because all contract is mutual translation, or change of right; and therefore he that promiseth only, because he hath already received the benefit for which he promiseth, is to be understood as if he intended the right should pass: for unless he had been content to have his words so understood, the other would not have performed his part first. And for that cause, in buying, and selling, and other acts of contract, a promise is equivalent to a covenant; and therefore obligatory.

He that performeth first in the case of a contract, is said to MERIT that which he is to receive by the performance of the other; and he hath it as *due.* Also when a prize is propounded to many, which is to be given to him only that winneth; or money is thrown amongst many, to be enjoyed by them that catch it; though this be a free gift; yet so to win, or so to catch, is to *merit,* and to have it as DUE. For the right is transferred in the propounding of the prize, and in throwing down the money; though it be not determined to whom, but by the event of the contention.

But there is between these two sorts of merit, this difference, that in contract, I merit by virtue of my own power, and the contractor's need; but in this case of free gift, I am enabled to merit only by the benignity of the giver: in contract, I merit at the contractor's hand that he should depart with his right; in this case of gift, I merit not that the giver should part with his right; but that when he has parted with it, it should be mine, rather than another's. And this I think to be the meaning of that distinction of the Schools, between *meritum congrui,* and *meritum condigni.* For God Almighty, having promised Paradise to those men (hoodwinked with carnal desires,) that can walk through this world according to the precepts, and limits prescribed by him; they say, he that shall so walk, shall merit Paradise *ex congruo.* But because no man can demand a right to it, by his own righteousness, or any other power in himself, but by the free grace of God only; they say, no man can merit Paradise *ex condigno.* This I say, I think is the meaning of that distinction; but because disputers do not agree upon the signification of their own terms of art, longer than it serves their turn; I will not affirm any thing of their meaning: only this I say; when a gift is given indefinitely, as a prize to be contended for, he that winneth meriteth, and may claim the prize as due.

If a covenant be made, wherein neither of the parties perform presently, but trust one another; in the condition of mere nature, (which is a condition of war of every man against every man,) upon any reasonable suspicion, it is void: but if there be a common power set over them both, with right and force sufficient to compel performance, it is not void. For he that performeth first, has no assurance the other will perform after; because the bonds of words are too weak to bridle men's ambition, avarice, anger, and other passions, without the fear of some coercive power; which in the condition of mere nature, where all men are equal, and judges of the justness of their own fears, cannot possibly be supposed. And therefore he which performeth first, does but betray himself to his enemy; contrary to the right (he can never abandon) of defending his life, and means of living.

But in a civil estate, where there is a power set up to constrain those that would otherwise violate their faith, that fear is no more reasonable; and for that cause, he which by the covenant is to perform first, is obliged so to do.

The cause of fear, which maketh such a covenant invalid, must be always something arising after the covenant made; as some new fact, or other sign of the will not to perform: else it cannot make the covenant void. For that which could not hinder a man from promising, ought not to be admitted as a hindrance of performing.

He that transferreth any right, transferreth the means of enjoying it, as far as lieth in his power. As he that selleth land, is understood to transfer the herbage, and whatsoever grows upon it; nor can he that sells a mill turn away the stream that drives it. And they that give to a man the right of government in sovereignty, are understood to give him the right of levying money to maintain soldiers; and of appointing magistrates for the administration of justice.

To make covenants with brute beasts, is impossible; because not understanding our speech, they understand not, nor accept of any translation of right; not can translate any right to another: and without mutual acceptation, there is no covenant.

To make covenant with God, is impossible, but by mediation of such as God speaketh to, either by revelation supernatural, or by his lieutenants that govern under him, and in his name: for otherwise we know not whether our covenants be accepted, or not. And therefore they that vow any thing contrary to any law of nature, vow in vain; as being a thing unjust to pay such vow. And if it be a thing commanded by the law of nature, it is not the vow, but the law that binds them.

The matter, or subject of a covenant, is always something that falleth under deliberation; (for to covenant, is an act of the will; that is to say an act, and the last act, of deliberation;) and is therefore always understood to be something to come; and which is judged possible for him that covenanteth, to perform.

And therefore, to promise that which is known to be impossible, is no covenant. But if that prove impossible afterwards, which before was thought possible, the covenant is valid, and bindeth, (though not to the thing it self,) yet to the value, or if that also be impossible, to the unfeigned endeavour of performing as much as is possible: for to more no man can be obliged.

Men are freed of their covenants two ways; by performing; or by being forgiven. For performance, is the natural end of obligation; and forgiveness, the restitution of liberty; as being a retransferring of that right, in which the obligation consisted.

Covenants entered into by fear, in the condition of mere nature, are obligatory. For example, if I covenant to pay a ransom, or service for my life, to an enemy; I am bound by it. For it is a contract, wherein one receiveth the benefit of life; the other is to receive money, or service for it; and consequently, where no other law (as in the condition, of mere nature) forbiddeth the performance, the covenant is valid. There are prisoners of war, if trusted with the payment of their ransom, are obliged to pay it, and if a weaker prince, make a disadvantageous peace with a stronger, for fear; he is bound to keep it; unless (as hath been said before) there ariseth some new, and just cause of fear, to renew the war. And even in commonwealths, if I be forced to redeem myself from a thief by promising him money, I am bound to pay it, till the civil law discharge me. For whatsoever I may lawfully do without obligation, the same I may lawfully covenant to do through fear: and what I lawfully covenant, I cannot lawfully break.

A former covenant, makes void a later. For a man that hath passed away his right to one may today, hath it not to pass tomorrow to another: and therefore the later promise passeth no right, but is null.

A covenant not to defend myself from force, by force, is always void. For (as I have showed before) no man can transfer, or lay down his right to save himself from death, wounds, and imprisonment, (the avoiding whereof is the only end of laying down any right, and therefore the promise of not resisting force, in no covenant transferreth any right; nor is obliging. For though a man may covenant thus, *unless I do so, or so, kill me;* he cannot covenant thus, *unless I do so, or so, I will not resist you, when you come to kill me.* For man by nature chooseth the lesser evil, which is danger of death in resisting;

rather than the greater, which is certain and present death in not resisting. And this is granted to be true by all men, in that they lead criminals to execution, and prison, with armed men, notwithstanding that such criminals have consented to the law, by which they are condemned.

A covenant to accuse one self, without assurance of pardon, is likewise invalid. For in the condition of nature, where every man is judge, there is no place for accusation: and in the civil state, the accusation is followed with punishment; which being force, a man is not obliged not to resist. The same is also true, of the accusation of those, by whose condemnation a man falls into misery; as of a father, wife, or benefactor. For the testimony of such an accuser, if it be not willingly given, is presumed to be corrupted by nature; and therefore not to be received: and where a man's testimony is not to be credited, he is not bound to give it. Also accusations upon torture, are not to be reputed as testimonies. For torture is to be used but as means of conjecture, and light, in the further examination, and search of truth: and what is in that case confessed, tendeth to the ease of him that is tortured, not to the informing of the torturers: and therefore ought not to have the credit of a sufficient testimony: for whether he deliver himself by true, or false accusation, he does it by the right of preserving his own life.

The force of words, being (as I have formerly noted) too weak to hold men to the performance of their covenants; there are in man's nature, but two imaginable helps to strengthen it. And those are either a fear of the consequence of breaking their word; or a glory, or pride in appearing not to need to break it. This latter is a generosity too rarely found to be presumed on, especially in the pursuers of wealth, command, or sensual pleasure; which are the greatest part of mankind. The passion to be reckoned upon, is fear; whereof there be two very general objects: one, the power of spirits invisible; the other, the power of those men they shall therein offend. Of these two, though the former be the greater power, yet the fear of the latter is commonly the greater fear. The fear of the former is in every man, his own religion: which hath place in the nature of man before civil society. The latter hath not so; at least not place enough, to keep men to their promises; because in the condition of mere nature, the inequality of power is not discerned, but by the event of battle. So that before the time of civil society, or in the interruption thereof by war, there is nothing can strengthen a covenant of peace agreed on, against the temptations of avarice, ambition, lust, or other strong desire, but the fear of that invisible power, which they every one worship as God; and fear as a revenger of their perfidy. All therefore that can be done between two men not subject to civil power, is to put one another to swear by the God he feareth: which *swearing,* or OATH, is a *form of speech, added to a promise; by which he that promiseth, signifieth, that unless he perform, he renounceth the mercy of his God, or calleth to him for vengeance on himself.* Such was the heathen form, *Let* Jupiter *kill me else, as I kill this beast.* So is our form, *I shall do thus, and thus, so help me God.* And this, with the rites and ceremonies, which every one useth in his own religion, that the fear of breaking faith might be the greater.

By this it appears, that an oath taken according to any other form, or rite, than his, that sweareth, is in vain; and no oath: and that there is no swearing by any thing which the swearer thinks not God. For though men have sometimes used to swear by their kings, for fear, or flattery; yet they would have it thereby understood, they attributed to them divine honour. And that swearing unnecessarily by God, is but prophaning of his name: and swearing by other things, as men do in common discourse, is not swearing, but an impious custom, gotten by too much vehemence of talking.

It appears also, that the oath adds nothing to the obligation. For a covenant, if lawful, binds in the sight of God, without the oath, as much as with it: if unlawful, bindeth not at all; though it be confirmed with an oath.

## *Chapter 15*

### OF OTHER LAWS OF NATURE

From that law of nature, by which we are obliged to transfer to another, such rights, as being retained, hinder the peace of mankind, there followeth a third;

which is this, *that men perform their covenants made:* without which, covenants are in vain, and but empty words, and the right of all men to all things remaining, we are still in the condition of war.

And in this law of nature, consisteth the fountain and original of JUSTICE. For where no covenant hath preceded, there hath no right been transferred, and every man has right to every thing; and consequently, no action can be unjust. But when a covenant is made, then to break it is *unjust;* and the definition of INJUSTICE, is no other than *the not performance of covenant.* And whatsoever is not unjust, is *just.*

But because covenants of mutual trust, where there is fear of not performance on either part, (as hath been said in the former chapter,) are invalid; though the original of justice be the making of covenants; yet injustice actually there can be none, till the cause of such fear be taken away; which while men are in the natural condition of war, cannot be done. Therefore before the names of just, and unjust can have place, there must be some coercive power, to compel men equally to the performance of their covenants, by the terror of some punishment, greater than the benefit they expect by the breach of their covenant; and to make good that propriety, which by mutual contract men acquire, in recompense of the universal right they abandon: and such power there is none before the erection of a commonwealth. And this is also to be gathered out of the ordinary definition of justice in the Schools: for they say, that *justice is the constant will of giving to every man his own.* And therefore where there is no *own,* that is, no propriety, there is no injustice; and where there is no coercive power erected, that is, where there is no comonwealth, there is no propriety; all men having right to all things: therefore where there is no commonwealth, there nothing is unjust. So that the nature of justice, consisteth in keeping of valid covenants: but the validity of covenants begins not but with the constitution of a civil power, sufficient to compel men to keep them: and then it is also that propriety begins.

The fool hath said in his heart, there is no such thing as justice; and sometimes also with his tongue;

seriously alleging, that every man's conservation, and contentment, being committed to his own care, there could be no reason, why every man might not do what he thought conduced thereunto: and therefore also to make, or not make; keep, or not keep covenants, was not against reason, when it conduced to one's benefit. He does not therein deny, that there be covenants; and that they are sometimes broken, sometimes kept; and that such breach of them may be called injustice, and the observance of them justice: but he questioneth, whether injustice, taking away the fear of God, (for the same fool hath said in his heart there is no God,) may not sometimes stand with that reason, which dictateth to every man his own good; and particularly then, when it conduceth to such a benefit, as shall put a man in a condition, to neglect not only the dispraise, and revilings, but also the power of other men. The kingdom of God is gotten by violence: but what if it could be gotten by unjust violence? were it against reason so to get it, when it is impossible to receive hurt by it? and if it be not against reason, it is not against justice; or else justice is not to be approved for good. From such reasoning as this, successful wickedness hath obtained the name of virtue: and some that in all other things have disallowed the violation of faith; yet have allowed it, when it is for the getting of a kingdom. And the heathen that believed, that *Saturn* was deposed by his son *Jupiter,* believed nevertheless the same *Jupiter* to be the avenger of injustice: somewhat like to a piece of law in *Coke's Commentaries on Littleton;* where he says, if the right heir of the crown be attainted of treason; yet the crown shall descend to him, and *eo instante* the attainder be void: from which instances a man will be very prone to infer; that when the heir apparent of a kingdom, shall kill him that is in possession, though his father; you may call it injustice, or by what other name you will; yet it can never be against reason, seeing all the voluntary actions of men tend to the benefit of themselves; and those actions are most reasonable, that conduce most to their ends. This specious reasoning is nevertheless false.

For the question is not of promises mutual, where there is no security of performance on either side; as when there is no civil power erected over the parties promising; for such promises are no covenants: but either where one of the parties has performed already; or where there is a power to make him perform; there is the question whether it be against reason, that is, against the benefit of the other to perform, or not. And I say it is not against reason. For the manifestation whereof, we are to consider; first, that when a man doth a thing, which notwithstanding any thing can be foreseen, and reckoned on, tendeth to his own destruction, howsoever some accident which he could not expect, arriving may turn it to his benefit; yet such events do not make it reasonably or wisely done. Secondly, that in a condition of war, wherein every man to every man, for want of a common power to keep them all in awe, is an enemy, there is no man can hope by his own strength, or wit, to defend himself from destruction, without the help of confederates; where every one expects the same defence by the confederation, that any one else does: and therefore he which declares he thinks it reason to deceive those that help him, can in reason expect no other means of safety, than what can be had from his own single power. He therefore that breaketh his covenant, and consequently declareth that he thinks he may with reason do so, cannot be received into any society, that unite themselves for peace and defence, but by the error of them that receive him; nor when he is received, be retained in it, without seeing the danger of their error; which errors a man cannot reasonably reckon upon as the means of his security: and therefore if he be left, or cast out of society, he perisheth; and if he live in society, it is by the errors of other men, which he could not foresee, nor reckon upon; and consequently against the reason of his preservation; and so, as all men that contribute not to his destruction, forbear him only out of ignorance of what is good for themselves.

As for the instance of gaining the secure and perpetual felicity of heaven, by any way; it is frivolous: there being but one way imaginable; and that is not breaking, but keeping of covenant.

And for the other instances of attaining sovereignty by rebellion; it is manifest, that though the event follow, yet because it cannot reasonably be expected, but rather the contrary; and because by gaining it so, others are taught to gain the same in like manner, the attempt thereof is against reason. Justice therefore, that is to say, keeping of covenant, is a rule of reason, by which we are forbidden to do any thing destructive to our life; and consequently a law of nature.

There be some that proceed further; and will not have the law of nature, to be those rules which conduce to the preservation of man's life on earth; but to the attaining of an eternal felicity after death; to which they think the breach of covenant may conduce; and consequently be just and reasonable; (such are they that think it a work of merit to kill, or depose, or rebel against, the sovereign power constituted over them by their own consent.) But because there is no natural knowledge of man's estate after death; much less of the reward that is then to be given to breach of faith; but only a belief grounded upon other men's saying, that they know it supernaturally, or that they know those, that knew them, that knew others, that knew it supernaturally; breach of faith cannot be called a precept of reason, or nature.

Others, that allow for a law of nature, the keeping of faith, do nevertheless make exception of certain persons; as heretics, and such as use not to perform their covenant to others: and this also is against reason. For if any fault of a man, be sufficient to discharge our covenant made; the same ought in reason to have been sufficient to have hindered the making of it.

The names of just, and unjust, when they are attributed to men, signify one thing; and when they are attributed to actions, another. When they are attributed to men, they signify conformity, or inconformity of manners, to reason. But when they are attributed to actions, they signify the conformity, or inconformity to reason, not of manners, or manner of life, but of particular actions. A just man therefore, is he that taketh all the care he can, that his actions may all be just: and an unjust man, is he that neglecteth it. And such men are more often in our language styled by the names of righteous, and unrighteous; than just, and unjust; though the meaning be the same. Therefore a righteous man, does not lose that title, by one, or a few unjust actions, that proceed from sudden passion, or mistake of things, or persons: nor does an unrighteous man, lose his character, for such actions, as he does, or forbears to do, for fear: because his will is not framed by the justice, but by the apparent benefit of what he is to do. That which gives to human actions the relish of justice, is a certain nobleness or gallantness of courage, (rarely found,) by which a man scorns to be beholding for the contentment of his life, to fraud, or breach of promise. This justice of the manners, is that which is meant, where justice is called a virtue; and injustice a vice.

But the justice of actions denominates men, not just, but *guiltless:* and the injustice of the same, (which is also called injury,) gives them but the name of *guilty.*

Again, the injustice of manners, is the disposition, or aptitude to do injury; and is injustice before it proceed to act; and without supposing any individual person injured. But the injustice of an action, (that is to say injury,) supposeth an individual person injured; namely him, to whom the covenant was made: and therefore many times the injury is received by one man, when the damage redoundeth to another. As when the master commandeth his servant to give money to a stranger; if it be not done, the injury is done to the master, whom he had before covenanted to obey; but the damage redoundeth to the stranger, to whom he had no obligation; and therefore could not injure him. And so also in commonwealths, private men may remit to one another their debts; but not robberies or other violences, whereby they are endamaged; because the detaining of debt, is an injury to themselves; but robbery and violence, are injuries to the person of the commonwealth.

Whatsoever is done to a man, conformable to his own will signified to the doer, is no injury to him. For if he that doeth it, hath not passed away his original right to do what he please, by some antecedent covenant, there is no breach of covenant; and therefore no injury done him. And if he have; then his will to have it done being signified, is a release of that covenant: and so again there is no injury done him.

Justice of actions, is by writers divided into *commutative,* and *distributive:* and the former they say consisteth in proportion arithmetical; the latter in proportion geometrical. Commutative therefore, they place in the equality of value of the things contracted for; and distributive, in the distribution of equal benefit, to men of equal merit. As if it were injustice to sell dearer than we buy; or to give more to a man than he merits. The value of all things contracted for, is measured by the appetite of the contractors: and therefore the just value, is that which they be contented to give. And merit, (besides that which is by covenant, where the performance on one part, meriteth the performance of the other part, and falls under justice commutative, not distributive,) is not due by justice; but is rewarded of grace only. And therefore this distinction, in the sense wherein it useth to be expounded, is not right. To speak properly, commutative justice, is the justice of a contractor; that is, a performance of covenant, in buying, and selling; hiring, and letting to hire; lending, and borrowing; exchanging, bartering, and other acts of contract.

And distributive justice, the justice of an arbitrator; that is to say, the act of defining what is just. Wherein, (being trusted by them that make him arbitrator,) if he perform his trust, he is said to distribute to every man his own: and this is indeed just distribution, and may be called, (though improperly,) distributive justice; but more properly equity; which also is a law of nature, as shall be shown in due place.

As justice dependeth on antecedent covenant; so does GRATITUDE depend on antecedent grace; that is to say, antecedent free-gift: and is the fourth law of nature: which may be conceived in this form, *that a man which receiveth benefit from another of mere grace, endeavour that he which giveth it, have no reasonable cause to repent him of his good will.* For no man giveth, but with intention of good to himself; because gift is voluntary; and of all voluntary acts, the object is to every man his own good; of which if men see they shall be frustrated, there will be no beginning of benevolence, or trust; nor consequently of mutual help; nor of reconciliation of one man to another; and therefore they are to remain still in the condition of *war;* which is contrary to the first and fundamental law of nature, which commandeth men

to *seek peace.* The breach of this law, is called *ingratitude;* and hath the same relation to grace, that injustice hath to obligation by covenant.

A fifth law of nature, is COMPLAISANCE; that is to say, *that every man strive to accommodate himself to the rest.* For the understanding whereof, we may consider, that there is in men's aptness to society, a diversity of nature, rising from their diversity of affections; not unlike to that we see in stones brought together for the building of an edifice. For as that stone which by the asperity, and irregularity of figure, takes more room from others, than itself fills; and for the hardness, cannot be easily made plain, and thereby hindereth the building, is by the builders cast away as unprofitable, and troublesome: so also, a man that by asperity of nature, will strive to retain those things which to himself are superfluous, and to others necessary; and for the stubbornness of his passions, cannot be corrected, is to be left, or cast out of society, as cumbersome thereunto. For seeing every man, not only by right, but also by necessity of nature, is supposed to endeavour all he can, to obtain that which is necessary for his conservation; he that shall oppose himself against it, for things superfluous, is guilty of the war that thereupon is to follow; and therefore doth that, which is contrary to the fundamental law of nature, which commandeth *to seek peace.* The observers of this law, may be called SOCIABLE, (the Latins call them *commodi;*) the contrary, *stubborn, insociable, froward, intractable.*

A sixth law of nature, is that, *that upon caution of the future time, a man ought to pardon the offences past of them that repenting, desire it.* For PARDON, is nothing but granting of peace; which though granted to them that persevere in their hostility, be not peace, but fear; yet not granted to them that give caution of the future time, is sign of an aversion to peace; and therefore contrary to the law of nature.

A seventh is, *that in revenges,* (that is retribution of evil for evil,) *men look not at the greatness of the evil past, but the greatness of the good to follow.* Whereby we are forbidden to inflict punishment with any other design, than for correction of the offender, or direction to others. For this law is consequent to the next before it, that commandeth pardon, upon secu-

rity of the future time. Besides, revenge without respect to the example, and profit to come, is a triumph,
or glorying in the hurt of another, tending to no end;
(for the end is always somewhat to come;) and glorying to no end, is vain-glory, and contrary to reason;
and to hurt without reason, tendeth to the introduction
of war; which is against the law of nature; and is commonly styled by the name of *cruelty.*

And because all signs of hatred, or contempt, provoke to fight, insomuch as most men choose rather to
hazard their life, than not to be revenged; we may in
the eighth place, for a law of nature, set down this
precept, *that no man by deed, word, countenance, or
gesture, declare hatred, or contempt of another.* The
breach of which law, is commonly called *contumely.*

The question who is the better man, has no place
in the condition of mere nature; where, (as has been
shewn before,) all men are equal. The inequality that
now is, has been introduced by the laws civil. I know
that *Aristotle* in the first book of his *Politics,* for a
foundation of his doctrine, maketh men by nature,
some more worthy to command, meaning the wiser
sort, (such as he thought himself to be for his philosophy;) others to serve, (meaning those that had
strong bodies, but were not philosophers as he;) as if
master and servant were not introduced by consent
of men, but by difference of wit: which is not only
against reason; but also against experience. For there
are very few so foolish, that had not rather govern
themselves, than be governed by others; nor when
the wise in their own conceit, contend by force, with
them who distrust their own wisdom, do they
always, or often, or almost at any time, get the victory. If nature therefore have made men equal, that
equality is to be acknowledged: or if nature have
made men unequal; yet because men that think
themselves equal, will not enter into conditions of
peace, but upon equal terms, such equality must be
admitted. And therefore for the ninth law of nature,
I put this, *that every man acknowledge other for his
equal by nature.* The breach of this precept is *pride.*

On this law, dependeth another, *that at the
entrance into conditions of peace, no man require to
reserve to himself any right, which he is not content
should be reserved to every one of the rest.* As it is

necessary for all men that seek peace, to lay down
certain rights of nature; that is to say, not to have liberty to do all they list: so is it necessary for man's
life, to retain some; as right to govern their own bodies; enjoy air, water, motion, ways to go from place
to place; and all things else without which a man
cannot live, or not live well. If in this case, at the
making of peace, men require for themselves, that
which they would not have to be granted to others,
they do contrary to the precedent law, that commandeth the acknowledgment of natural equality, and
therefore also against the law of nature. The
observers of this law, are those we call *modest,* and
the breakers *arrogant* men. The Greeks call the violation of this law πλεονξια; that is, a desire of more
than their share.

Also if *a man be trusted to judge between man
and man,* it is a precept of the law of nature, *that he
deal equally between them.* For without that, the
controversies of men cannot be determined but by
war. He therefore that is partial in judgment, doth
what in him lies, to deter men from the use of
judges, and arbitrators; and consequently, (against
the fundamental law of nature,) is the cause of war.

The observance of this law, from the equal distribution to each man, of that which in reason
belongeth to him, is called EQUITY, and (as I have
said before) distributive justice: the violation,
*acception of persons,* προσωποληψία.

And from this followeth another law, *that such
things as cannot be divided, be enjoyed in common,
if it can be; and if the quantity of the thing permit,
without stint; otherwise proportionably to the number of them that have right.* For otherwise the distribution is unequal, and contrary to equity.

But some things there be, that can neither be
divided, nor enjoyed in common. Then, the law of
nature, which prescribeth equity, requireth, *that the
entire right; or else, (making the use alternate,) the
first possession, be determined by lot.* For equal distribution, is of the law of nature; and other means of
equal distribution cannot be imagined.

Of *lots* there be two sorts, *arbitrary,* and *natural.*
Arbitrary, is that which is agreed on by the competitors: natural, is either *primogeniture,* (which the

Greek calls κληρονονία, which signifies, *given by lot;* or *first seizure.*

And therefore those things which cannot be enjoyed in common, nor divided, ought to be adjudged to the first possessor; and in some cases to the first-born, as acquired by lot.

It is also a law of nature, *that all men that mediate peace, be allowed safe conduct.* For the law that commandeth peace, as the *end,* commandeth intercession, as the *means;* and to intercession the means is safe conduct.

And because, though men be never so willing to observe these laws, there may nevertheless arise questions concerning a man's action; first, whether it were done, or not done; secondly, (if done,) whether against the law, or not against the law; the former whereof, is called a question *of fact;* the latter a question *of right;* therefore unless the parties to the question, covenant mutually to stand to the sentence of another, they are as far from peace as ever. This other, to whose sentence they submit, is called an ARBITRATOR. And therefore it is of the law of nature, *that they that are at controversy, submit their right to the judgment of an arbitrator.*

And seeing every man is presumed to do all things in order to his own benefit, no man is a fit arbitrator in his cause: and if he were never so fit; yet equity allowing to each party equal benefit, if one be admitted to be judge, the other is to be admitted also; and so the controversy, that is, the cause of war, remains, against the law of nature.

For the same reason no man in any cause ought to be received for arbitrator, to whom greater profit, or honour, or pleasure apparently ariseth out of the victory of one party, than of the other: for he hath taken (though an unavoidable bribe, yet) a bribe; and no man can be obliged to trust him. And thus also the controversy, and the condition of war remaineth, contrary to the law of nature.

And in a controversy of *fact,* the judge being to give no more credit to one, than to the other, (if there be no other arguments,) must give credit to a third; or to a third and fourth; or more: for else the question is undecided, and left to force, contrary to the law of nature.

These are the laws of nature, dictating peace, for a means of the conservation of men in multitudes; and which only concern the doctrine of civil society. There be other things tending to the destruction of particular men; as drunkenness, and all other parts of intemperance; which may therefore also be reckoned amongst those things which the law of nature hath forbidden; but are not necessary to be mentioned, nor are pertinent enough to this place.

And though this may seem too subtle a deduction of the laws of nature, to be taken notice of by all men; whereof the most part are too busy in getting food, and the rest too negligent to understand; yet to leave all men inexcusable, they have been contracted into one easy sum, intelligible, even to the meanest capacity; and that is, *Do not that to another, which thou wouldest not have done to thyself;* which sheweth him, that he has no more to do in learning the laws of nature, but, when weighing the actions of other men with his own, they seem too heavy, to put them into the other part of the balance, and his own into their place, that his own passions, and self-love, may add nothing to the weight; and then there is none of these laws of nature that will not appear unto him very reasonable.

The laws of nature oblige in *foro interno;* that is to say, they bind to a desire they should take place: but *in foro externo;* that is, to the putting them in act, not always. For he that should be modest, and tractable, and perform all he promises, in such time, and place, where no man else should do so, should but make himself a prey to others, and procure his own certain ruin, contrary to the ground of all laws of nature, which tend to nature's preservation. And again, he that having sufficient security, that others shall observe the same laws towards him, observes them not himself, seeketh not peace, but war; and consequently the destruction of his nature by violence.

And whatsoever laws bind *in foro interno,* may be broken, not only by a fact contrary to the law, but also by a fact according to it, in case a man think it contrary. For though his action in this case, be according to the law; yet his purpose was against the law; which, where the obligation is *in foro interno,* is a breach.

The laws of nature are immutable and eternal; for injustice, ingratitude, arrogance, pride, iniquity, acception of persons, and the rest, can never be made lawful. For it can never be that war shall preserve life, and peace destroy it.

The same laws, because they oblige only to a desire, and endeavour, I mean an unfeigned and constant endeavour, are easy to be observed. For in that they require nothing but endeavour; he that endeavoureth their performance, fulfilleth them; and he that fulfilleth the law, is just.

And the science of them, is the true and only moral philosophy. For moral philosophy is nothing else but the science of what is *good,* and *evil,* in the conversation, and society of mankind. *Good,* and *evil,* are names that signify our appetites, and aversions; which in different tempers, customs, and doctrines of man, are different: and divers men, differ not only in their judgment, on the senses of what is pleasant, and unpleasant to the taste, smell, hearing, touch, and sight; but also of what is comfortable, or disagreeable to reason, in the actions of common life. Nay, the same man, in divers times, differs from himself; and one time praiseth, that is, calleth good, what another time he dispraiseth, and calleth evil: from whence arise disputes, controversies, and at last war. And therefore so long a man is in the condition of mere nature, (which is a condition of war,) as private appetite is the measure of good, and evil: and consequently all men agree on this, that peace is good, and therefore also the way, or means of peace, which, (as I have shewed before) are *justice, gratitude, modesty, equity, mercy,* and the rest of the laws of nature, are good; that is to say, *moral virtues;* and their contrary *vices;* evil. Now the science of virtue and vice, is moral philosophy; and therefore the true doctrine of the laws of nature, is the true moral philosophy. But the writers of moral philosopy, though they acknowledge the same virtues and vices; yet not seeing wherein consisted their goodness; nor that they come to be praised, as the means of peaceable, sociable, and comfortable living; place them in a mediocrity of passions: as if not the cause, but the degree of daring, made fortitude; or not the cause, but the quantity of a gift, made liberality.

These dictates of reason, men use to call by the name of laws; but improperly: for they are but conclusions, or theorems concerning what conduceth to the conservation and defence of themselves; whereas law, properly, is the word of him, that by right hath command over others. But yet if we consider the same theorems, as delivered in the word of God, that by right commandeth all things; then are they properly called laws.

## PART 2

## *Of Commonwealth*

### *Chapter 17*

#### OF THE CAUSES, GENERATION, AND DEFINITION OF A COMMONWEALTH

The final cause, end, or design of men, (who naturally love liberty, and dominion over others,) in the introduction of that restraint upon themselves, (in which we see them live in commonwealths,) is the foresight of their own preservation, and of a more contented life thereby; that is to say, of getting themselves out from that miserable condition of war, which is necessarily consequent (as hath been shown), to, the natural passions of men, when there is no visible power to keep them in awe, and tie them by fear of punishment to the performance of their covenants, and observation of those laws of nature set down in the fourteenth and fifteenth chapters.

For the laws of nature (as *justice, equity, modesty, mercy,* and (in sum) *doing to others, as we would be done to,*) of themselves, without the terror of some power, to cause them to be observed, are contrary to our natural passions, that carry us to partiality, pride, revenge, and the like. And covenants, without the sword, are but words, and of no strength to secure a man at all. Therefore notwithstanding the laws of nature, (which every one hath then kept, when he has the will to keep them, when he can do it safely,) if there be no power erected, or not great enough for our security; every man will, and may lawfully rely on his own strength and art, for caution against all other men. And in all places, where men have lived by small families, to rob and spoil one another, has been a trade, and so far from being reputed against the law of nature, that the greater spoils they gained, the greater was their honour; and men observed no other laws therein, but the laws of honour; that is, to abstain from cruelty, leaving to men their lives, and instruments of husbandry. And as small families did then; so now do cities and kingdoms which are but greater families (for their own security) enlarge their dominions, upon all pretences of danger, and fear of invasion, or assistance that may be given to invaders, endeavour as much as they can, to subdue, or weaken their neighbours, by open force, and secret arts, for want of other caution, justly; and are remembered for it in after ages with honour.

Nor is it the joining together of a small number of men, that gives them this security; because in small numbers, small additions on the one side or the other, make the advantage of strength so great, as is sufficient to carry the victory; and therefore gives encouragement to an invasion. The multitude sufficient to confide in for our security, is not determined by any certain number, but by comparison with the enemy we fear; and is then sufficient, when the odds of the enemy is not of so visible and conspicuous moment, to determine the event of war, as to move him to attempt.

And be there never so great a multitude; yet if their actions be directed according to their particular judgments, and particular appetites, they can expect thereby no defence, nor protection, neither against a common enemy, nor against the injuries of one another. For being distracted in opinions concerning the best use and application of their strength, they do not help, but hinder one another; and reduce their strength by mutual opposition to nothing: whereby they are easily, not only subdued by a very few that agree together; but also when there is no common enemy, they make war upon each other, for their particular interests. For if we could suppose a great multitude of men to consent in the observation of justice, and other laws of nature, without a common power to keep them all in awe; we might as well suppose all

mankind to do the same; and then there neither would be, nor need to be any civil government, or commonwealth at all; because there would be peace without subjection.

Nor is it enough for the security, which men desire should last all the time of their life, that they be governed, and directed by one judgment, for a limited time; as in one battle, or one war. For though they obtain a victory by their unanimous endeavour against a foreign enemy; yet afterwards, when either they have no common enemy, or he that by one part is held for an enemy, is by another part held for a friend, they must needs by the difference of their interests dissolve, and fall again into a war amongst themselves.

It is true, that certain living creatures, as bees, and ants, live sociably one with another, (which are therefore by *Aristotle* numbered amongst political creatures;) and yet have no other direction, than their particular judgments and appetites; nor speech, whereby one of them can signify to another, what he thinks expedient for the common benefit: and therefore some man may perhaps desire to know, why mankind cannot do the same. To which I answer,

First, that men are continually in competition for honour and dignity, which these creatures are not; and consequently amongst men there ariseth on that ground, envy and hatred, and finally war; but amongst these not so.

Secondly, that amongst these creatures, the common good differeth not from the private; and being by nature inclined to their private, they procure thereby the common benefit. But man, whose joy consisteth in comparing himself with other men, can relish nothing but what is eminent.

Thirdly, that these creatures, having not, (as man) the use of reason, do not see, nor think they see any fault, in the administration of their common business; whereas amongst men, there are very many, that think themselves wiser, and abler to govern the public, better than the rest; and these strive to reform and innovate, one this way, another that way; and thereby bring it into distraction and civil war.

Fourthly, that these creatures, though they have

some use of voice, in making known to one another their desires, and other affections; yet they want that art of words, by which some men can represent to others, that which is good, in the likeness of evil; and evil, in the likeness of good; and augment, or diminish the apparent greatness of good and evil; discontenting men, and troubling their peace at their pleasure.

Fifthly, irrational creatures cannot distinguish between *injury,* and *damage;* and therefore as long as they be at ease, they are not offended with their fellows: whereas man is then most troublesome, when he is most at ease: for then it is that he loves to shew his wisdom, and control the actions of them that govern the commonwealth.

Lastly, the agreement of these creatures is natural; that of men, is by covenant only, which is artificial: and therefore it is no wonder if there be somewhat else required (besides covenant) to make their agreement constant and lasting; which is a common power, to keep them in awe, and to direct their actions to the common benefit.

The only way to erect such a common power, as may be able to defend them from the invasion of foreigners, and the injuries of one another, and thereby to secure them in such sort, as that by their own industry, and by the fruits of the earth, they may nourish themselves and live contentedly; is, to confer all their power and strength upon one man, or upon one assembly of men, that may reduce all their wills, by plurality of voices, unto one will: which is as much as to say, to appoint one man, or assembly of men, to bear their person; and even one to own, and acknowledge himself to be author of whatsoever he that so beareth their person, shall act, or cause to be acted, in those things which concern the common peace and safety; and therein to submit their wills, every one to his will, and their judgments, to his judgment. This is more than consent, or concord; it is a real unity of them all, in one and the same person, made by covenant of every man with every man, in such manner, as if every man should say to every man, *I authorise and give up my right of governing myself, to this man, or to this assembly of*

*men, on this condition, that thou give up thy right to him, and authorize all his actions in like manner.* This done, the multitude so united in one person, is called a COMMONWEALTH, in Latin CIVITAS. This is the generation of that great LEVIATHAN, or rather (to speak more reverently) of that *mortal god,* to which we owe under the *immortal God,* our peace and defence. For by this authority, given him by every particular man in the commonwealth, he hath the use of so much power and strength conferred on him, that by terror thereof, he is enabled to form the wills of them all, to peace at home, and mutual aid against their enemies abroad. And in him consisteth the essence of the commonwealth; which (to define it,) *is one person, of whose acts a great multitude, by mutual covenants one with another, have made themselves every one the author, to the end he may use the strength and means of them all, as he shall think expedient, for their peace and common defence.*

And he that carrieth this person, is called SOVEREIGN, and said to have sovereign power; and every one besides, his SUBJECT.

The attaining to this sovereign power, is by two ways. One, by natural force; as when a man maketh his children, to submit themselves, and their children to his government, as being able to destroy them if they refuse; or by war subdueth his enemies to his will, giving them their lives on that condition. The other, is when men agree amongst themselves, to submit to some man, or assembly of men, voluntarily, on confidence to be protected by him against all others. This latter, may be called a political commonwealth, or commonwealth by *institution;* and the former, a commonwealth by *acquisition.* And first, I shall speak of a commonwealth by institution.

## Chapter 18

### OF THE RIGHTS OF SOVEREIGNS BY INSTITUTION

A *commonwealth* is said to be *instituted,* when a *multitude* of men do agree, and *covenant, every one, with every one,* that to whatsoever *man,* or *assembly of men,* shall be given by the major part, the *right to present* the person of them all, (that is to say, to be their *representative;*) every one, as well he that *voted for it,* as he that *voted against it,* shall *authorize* all the actions and judgments, of that man, or assembly of men, in the same manner, as if they were his own, to the end, to live peaceably amongst themselves, and be protected against other men.

From this institution of a commonwealth are derived all the *rights,* and *faculties* of him, or them, on whom the sovereign power is conferred by the consent of the people assembled.

First, because they covenant, it is to be understood, they are not obliged by former covenant to any thing repugnant hereunto. And consequently they that have already instituted a commonwealth, being thereby bound by covenant, to own the actions, and judgments of one, cannot lawfully make a new covenant, amongst themselves, to be obedient to any other, in any thing whatsoever, without his permission. And therefore, they that are subjects to a monarch, cannot without his leave cast off monarchy, and return to the confusion of a disunited multitude; nor transfer their person from him that beareth it, to another man, or other assembly of men: for they are bound, every man to every man, to own, and be reputed author of all, that he that already is their sovereign, shall do, and judge fit to be done: so that any one man dissenting, all the rest should break their covenant made to that man, which is injustice: and they have also every man given the sovereignty to him that beareth their person; and therefore if they depose him, they take from him that which is his own, and so again it is injustice. Besides, if he that attempteth to depose his sovereign, be killed, or punished by him for such attempt, he is author of his own punishment, as being by the institution, author of all his sovereign shall do: and because it is injustice for a man to do any thing, for which he may be punished by his own authority, he is also upon that title, unjust. And whereas some men have pretended for their disobedience to their sovereign, a new covenant, made, not with men, but with God; this also is unjust: for there is no covenant with God, but by mediation of somebody that representeth God's person; which

none doth but God's lieutenant, who hath the sovereignty under God. But this pretence of covenant with God, is so evident a lie, even in the pretender's own consciences, that it is not only an act of an unjust, but also of a vile, and unmanly disposition.

Secondly, because the right of bearing the person of them all, is given to him they make sovereign, by covenant only of one to another, and not of him to any of them; there can happen no breach of covenant on the part of the sovereign; and consequently none of his subjects, by any pretence of forfeiture, can be freed from his subjection. That he which is made sovereign maketh no covenant with his subjects beforehand, is manifest; because either he must make it with the whole multitude, as one party to the covenant; or he must make a several covenant with every man. With the whole, as one party, it is impossible; because as yet they are not one person: and if he make so many several covenants as there be men, those covenants after he hath the sovereignty are void, because what act soever can be pretended by any one of them for breach thereof, is the act both of himself, and of all the rest, because done in the person, and by the right of every one of them in particular. Besides, if any one, or more of them, pretend a breach of the covenant made by the sovereign at his institution; and others, or one other of his subjects, or himself alone, pretend there was no such breach, there is in this case, no judge to decide the controversy; it returns therefore to the sword again; and every man recovereth the right of protecting himself by his own strength, contrary to the design they had in the institution. It is therefore in vain to grant sovereignty by way of precedent covenant. The opinion that any monarch receiveth his power by covenant, that is to say, on condition, proceedeth from want of understanding this easy truth, that covenants being but words and breath, have no force to oblige, contain, constrain, or protect any man, but what it has from the public sword; that is, from the untied hands of that man, or assembly of men that hath the sovereignty, and whose actions are avouched by them all, and performed by the strength of them all, in him united. But when an assembly of men is made sovereign; then no man imagineth any such covenant to have passed in the institution; for no man is so dull as to say, for example, the people of Rome made a covenant with the Romans, to hold the sovereignty on such or such conditions; which not performed, the Romans might lawfully depose the Roman people. That men see not the reason to be alike in a monarchy, and in a popular government, proceedeth from the ambition of some, that are kinder to the government of an assembly, whereof they may hope to participate, than of monarchy, which they despair to enjoy.

Thirdly, because the major part hath by consenting voices declared a sovereign; he that dissented must now consent with the rest; that is, be contented to avow all the actions he shall do, or else justly be destroyed by the rest. For if he voluntarily entered into the congregation of them that were assembled, he sufficiently declared thereby his will, (and therefore tacitly covenanted) to stand to what the major part should ordain: and therefore if he refuse to stand thereto, or make protestation against any of their decrees, he does contrary to his covenant, and therefore unjustly. And whether he be of the congregation, or not; and whether his consent be asked, or not, he must either submit to their decrees, or be left in the condition of war he was in before; wherein he might without injustice be destroyed by any man whatsoever.

Fourthly, because every subject is by this institution author of all the actions, and judgments of the sovereign instituted; it follows, that whatsoever he doth, it can be no injury to any of his subjects; nor ought he to be by any of them accused of injustice. For he that doth any thing by authority from another, doth therein no injury to him by whose authority he acteth; but by this institution of a commonwealth, every particular man is author of all the sovereign doth; and consequently he that complaineth of injury from his sovereign, complaineth of that whereof he himself is author; and therefore ought not to accuse any man but himself; no nor himself of injury; because to do injury to one's self, is impossible. It is true that they that have sovereign power, may commit iniquity; but not injustice, or injury in the proper signification.

Fifthly, and consequently to that which was said

last, no man that hath sovereign power can justly be put to death, or otherwise in any manner by his subjects punished. For seeing every subject is author of the actions of his sovereign; he punisheth another, for the actions committed by himself.

And because the end of this institution, is the peace and defence of them all; and whosoever has right to the end, has right to the means; it belongeth of right, to whatsoever man, or assembly that hath the sovereignty, to be judge both of the means of peace and defence; and also of the hindrances, and disturbances of the same; and to do whatsoever he shall think necessary to be done, both beforehand, for the preserving of peace and security, by prevention of discord at home, and hostility from abroad; and, when peace and security are lost, for the recovery of the same. And therefore,

Sixthly, it is annexed to the sovereignty, to be judge of what opinions and doctrines are averse, and what conducting to peace; and consequently, on what occasions, how far, and what, men are to be trusted withal, in speaking to multitudes of people; and who shall examine the doctrines of all books before they be published. For the actions of men proceed from their opinions; and in the well-governing of opinions, consisteth the well-governing of men's actions, in order to their peace, and concord. And though in matter of doctrine, nothing ought to be regarded but the truth; yet this is not repugnant to regulating of the same by peace. For doctrine repugnant to peace, can no more be true, than peace and concord can be against the law of nature. It is true, that in a commonwealth, where by the negligence, or unskillfulness of governors, and teachers, false doctrines are by time generally received; the contrary truths may be generally offensive: Yet the most sudden, and rough busling in of a new truth, that can be, does never break the peace, but only sometimes awake the war. For those men that are so remissly governed, that they dare take up arms, to defend, or introduce an opinion, are still in war; and their condition not peace, but only a cessation of arms for fear of one another; and they live as it were, in the precincts of battle continually. It belongeth therefore to him that hath the sovereign power, to be judge, or constitute all judges of opinions and doctrines, as a thing necessary to peace; thereby to prevent discord and civil war.

Seventhly, is annexed to the sovereignty, the whole power of prescribing the rules, whereby every man may know, what goods he may enjoy, and what actions he may do, without being molested by any of his fellow-subjects; and this is it men call *propriety.* For before constitution of sovereign power (as hath already been shown) all men had right to all things; which necessarily causeth war: and therefore this propriety, being necessary to peace, and depending on sovereign power, is the act of that power, in order to the public peace. These rules of propriety (or *meum* and *tuum*) and of *good, evil, lawful,* and *unlawful* in the actions of subjects, are the civil laws; that is to say, the laws of each commonwealth in particular; though the name of civil law be now restrained to the ancient civil laws of the city of *Rome;* which being the head of a great part of the world, her laws at that time were in these parts the civil law.

Eighthly, is annexed to the sovereignty, the right of judicature; that is to say, of hearing and deciding all controversies, which may arise concerning law, either civil, or natural; or concerning fact. For without the decision of controversies, there is no protection of one subject, against the injuries of another; the laws concerning *meum* and *tuum* are in vain; and to every man remaineth, from the natural and necessary appetite of his own conservation, the right of protecting himself by his private strength, which is the condition of war; and contrary to the end for which every commonwealth is instituted.

Ninthly, is annexed to the sovereignty, the right of making war and peace with other nations, and commonwealths; that is to say, of judging when it is for the public good, and how great forces are to be assembled, armed, and paid for that end; and to levy money upon the subjects, to defray the expenses thereof. For the power by which the people are to be defended, consisteth in their armies; and the strength of an army, in the union of their strength under one command; which command the sovereign instituted, therefore hath; because the command of the *militia,* without other institution, maketh him that hath it

sovereign. And therefore whosoever is made general of an army, he that hath the sovereign power is always generalissimo.

Tenthly, is annexed to the sovereignty, the choosing of all counsellors, ministers, magistrates, and officers, both in peace, and war. For seeing the sovereign is charged with the end, which is the common peace and defence, he is understood to have power to use such means, as he shall think most fit for his discharge.

Eleventhly, to the sovereign is committed the power of rewarding with riches, or honour; and of punishing with corporal, or pecuniary punishment, or with ignominy every subject according to the law he hath formerly made; or if there be no law made, according as he shall judge most to conduce to the encouraging of men to serve the commonwealth, or deterring of them from doing disservice to the same.

Lastly, considering what values men are naturally apt to set upon themselves; what respect they look for from others; and how little they value other men; from whence continually arise amongst them, emulation, quarrels, factions, and at last war, to the destroying of one another, and diminution of their strength against a common enemy; it is necessary that there be laws of honour, and a public rate of the worth of such men as have deserved, or are able to deserve well of the commonwealth; and that there be force in the hands of some or other, to put those laws in execution. But it hath already been shown, that not only the whole *militia,* or forces of the commonwealth; but also the judicature of all controversies, is annexed to the sovereignty. To the sovereign therefore it belongeth also to give titles of honour; and to appoint what order of place, and dignity, each man shall hold; and what signs of respect, in public or private meetings, they shall give to one another.

These are the rights, which make the essence of sovereignty; and which are the marks, whereby a man may discern in what man, or assembly of men, the sovereign power is placed, and resideth. For these are incommunicable, and inseparable. The power to coin money; to dispose of the estate and persons of infant heirs; to have praeemption in markets; and all other statute prerogatives, may be transferred by the sovereign; and yet the power to protect his subjects be retained. But if he transfer the *militia,* he retains the judicature in vain, for want of execution of the laws: or if he grant away the power of raising money; the *militia* is in vain: or if he give away the government of doctrines, men will be frighted into rebellion with the fear of spirits. And so if we consider any one of the said rights, we shall presently see, that the holding of all the rest will produce no effect, in the conservation of peace and justice, the end for which all commonwealths are instituted. And this division is it, whereof it is said, *a kingdom divided in itself cannot stand;* for unless this division precede, division into opposite armies can never happen. If there had not first been an opinion received of the greatest part of England, that these powers were divided between the King, and the Lords, and the House of Commons, the people had never been divided and fallen into this civil war; first between those that disagreed in politics; and after between the dissenters about the liberty of religion; which have so instructed men in this point of sovereign right, that there be few now (in *England,*) that do not see, that these rights are inseparable, and will be so generally acknowledged at the next return of peace; and so continue, till their miseries are forgotten; and no longer, except the vulgar be better taught than they have hitherto been.

And because they are essential and inseparable rights, it follows necessarily, that in whatsoever words any of them seem to be granted away, yet if the sovereign power itself be not in direct terms renounced, and the name of sovereign no more given by the grantees to him that grants them, the grant is void: for when he has granted all he can, if we grant back the sovereignty, all is restored, as inseparably annexed thereunto.

This great authority being indivisible, and inseparably annexed to the sovereignty, there is little ground for the opinion of them, that say of sovereign kings, though they be *singulis majores,* of greater power than every one of their subjects, yet they be *universis minores,* of less power than them all together. For if by *all together,* they mean not the collective body as one person, then *all together,* and *every one,* signify the same; and the speech is absurd. But if by *all together,* they understand them as one person, (which person the sovereign bears,) then the power of all together, is the same with the sovereign's power; and so again the speech is absurd: which absurdity they see well enough, when the sovereignty is in an assembly of the people; but in a monarch they see it not; and yet the power of sovereignty is the same in whomsoever it be placed.

And as the power, so also the honour of the sovereign, ought to be greater, than that of any, or all the subjects. For in the sovereignty is the fountain of honour. The dignities of lord, earl, duke, and prince are his creatures. As in the presence of the master, the servants are equal, and without any honour at all; so are the subjects, in the presence of the sovereign. And though they shine some more, some less, when they are out of his sight; yet in his presence, they shine no more than the stars in presence of the sun.

But a man may here object, that the condition of subjects is very miserable; as being obnoxious to the lusts, and other irregular passions of him, or them that have so unlimited a power in their hands. And commonly that they live under a monarch, think it the fault of monarchy; and they that live under the government of democracy, or other sovereign assembly, attribute all the inconvenience to that form of commonwealth; whereas the power in all forms, if they be perfect enough to protect them, is the same; not considering that the estate of man can never be without some incommodity or other; and that the greatest, that in any form of government can possibly happen to the people in general, is scarce sensible, in respect to the miseries, and horrible calamities, that accompany a civil war, or that dissolute condition of masterless men, without subjection to laws, and a coercive power to tie their hands from rapine and revenge: nor considering that the greatest pressure of sovereign governors, proceedeth not from any delight, or profit they can expect in the damage or weakening of their subjects, in whose vigour, consisteth their own strength and glory; but in the restiveness of themselves, that unwillingly contributing to their own defence, make it necessary for their governors to draw from them what they can in time of peace, that they may have means on any emergent occasion, or sudden need, to resist, or take advantage on their enemies. For all men are by nature provided of notable multiplying glasses, (that is their passions and self-love,) through which, every little payment appeareth a great grievance; but are destitute of those prospective glasses, (namely moral and civil science,) to see afar off the miseries that hang over them, and cannot without such payments be avoided.

## Chapter 19

OF THE SEVERAL KINDS
OF COMMONWEALTH BY INSTITUTION,
AND OF SUCCESSION
TO THE SOVEREIGN POWER

The difference of commonwealths, consisteth in the difference of the sovereign, or the person representative of all and every one of the multitude. And because the sovereignty is either in one man, or in an assembly of more than one; and into that assembly either every man hath right to enter, or not every one, but certain men distinguished from the rest; it is manifest, there can be but three kinds of commonwealth. For the representative must needs be one man, or more: and if more, then it is the assembly of all, or but of a part. When the representative is one man, then is the commonwealth a MONARCHY: when an assembly of all that will come together, then it is a DEMOCRACY, or popular commonwealth: when an assembly of a part only, then it is called an ARISTOCRACY. Other kind of commonwealth there can be none: for either one, or more, or all, must have the sovereign power (which I have shown to be indivisible) entire.

There be other names of government, in the histories, and books of policy; as *tyranny,* and *oligarchy:* But they are not the names of other forms of government, but of the same forms misliked. For they that are discontented under *monarchy,* call it *tyranny;* and they that are displeased with *aristocracy,* call it *oligarchy:* so also, they which find themselves grieved under a *democracy,* call it *anarchy,* (which signifies want of government;) and yet I think no man believes, that want of government, is any new kind of government: nor by the same reason ought they to believe, that the government is of one kind, when they like it, and another, when they mislike it, or are oppressed by the governors.

It is manifest, that men who are in absolute liberty, may, if they please, give authority to one man, to represent them every one; as well as give such authority to any assembly of men whatsoever; and consequently may subject themselves, if they think good, to a monarch, as absolutely, as to any other representative. Therefore, where there is already erected a sovereign power, there can be no other representative of the same people, but only to certain particular ends, by the sovereign limited. For that were to erect two sovereigns; and every man to have his person represented by two actors, that by opposing one another, must needs divide that power, which (if men will live in peace) is indivisible; and thereby reduce the multitude into the condition of war, contrary to the end for which all sovereignty is instituted. And therefore as it is absurd, to think that a sovereign assembly, inviting the people of their dominion, to send up their deputies, with power to make known their advice, or desires, should therefore hold such deputies, rather than themselves, for the absolute representative of the people: so it is absurd also, to think the same in a monarchy. And I know not how this so manifest a truth, should of late be so little observed; that in a monarchy, he that had the sovereignty from a descent of 600 years, was alone called sovereign, had the title of Majesty from every one of his subjects, and was unquestionably taken by them for their king, was notwithstanding never considered as their representative; that name without contradiction passing for the title of those men, which at his command were sent up by the people to carry their petitions, and give him (if he permitted it) their advice. Which may serve as an admonition, for those that are the true, and absolute representative of a people, to instruct men in the nature of that office, and to take heed how they admit of any other general representation upon any occasion whatsoever, if they mean to discharge the trust committed to them.

The difference between these three kinds of commonwealth, consisteth not in the difference of power; but in the difference of convenience, or aptitude to produce the peace, and security of the people; for which end they were instituted. And to compare monarchy with the other two, we may observe; first, that whosoever beareth the person of the people, or is one of that assembly that bears it, beareth also his own natural person. And though he be careful in his politic person to procure the common interest; yet he is more, or no less careful to procure the private good of himself, his family, kindred and friends; and for the most part, if the public interest chance to cross the private, he prefers the private: for the passions of men, are commonly more potent than their reason. From whence it follows, that where the public and private interest are most closely united, there is the public most advanced. Now in monarchy, the private interest is the same with the public. The riches, power, and honour of a monarch arise only from the riches, strength and reputation of his subjects. For no king can be rich, nor glorious, nor secure, whose subjects are either poor, or contemptible, or too weak through want, or dissention, to maintain a war against their enemies: whereas in a democracy, or aristocracy, the public prosperity confers not so much to the private fortune of one that is corrupt, or ambitious, as doth many times a perfidious advice, a treacherous action, or a civil war.

Secondly, that a monarch receiveth counsel of whom, when, and where he pleaseth; and consequently may hear the opinion of men versed in the matter about which he deliberates, of what rank or quality soever, and as long before the time of action, and with as much secrecy, as he will. But when a sovereign assembly has need of counsel, none are admitted but such as have a right thereto from the beginning; which for the most part are of those who have been versed more in the acquisition of wealth than of knowledge; and are to give their advice in long discourses, which may, and do commonly excite men to action, but not govern them in it. For the *understanding* is by the flame of the passions, never enlightened, but dazzled: Nor is there any place, or time, wherein an assembly can receive counsel with secrecy, because of their own multitude.

Thirdly, that the resolutions of a monarch, are subject to no other inconstancy, than that of human nature; but in assemblies, besides that of nature, there ariseth an inconstancy from the number. For the absence of a few, that would have the resolution once taken, continue firm, (which may happen by security, negligence, or private impediments,) or the diligent appearance of a few of the contrary opinion, undoes to day, all that was concluded yesterday.

Fourthly, that a monarch cannot disagree with himself, out of envy, or interest; but an assembly may; and that to such a height, as may produce a civil war.

Fifthly, that in monarchy there is this inconvenience; that any subject, by the power of one man, for the enriching of a favourite or flatterer, may be deprived of all he possesseth; which I confess is a great and inevitable inconvenience. But the same may as well happen, where the sovereign power is in an assembly: for their power is the same; and they are as subject to evil counsel, and to be seduced by orators, as a monarch by flatterers; and becoming one another's flatterers, serve one another's covetousness and ambition by turns. And whereas the favourites of monarchs, are few, and they have none else to advance but their own kindred; the favourites of an assembly, are many; and the kindred much more numerous, than of any monarch. Besides, there is no favourite of a monarch, which cannot as well succour his friends, as hurt his enemies: but orators, that is to say, favourites of sovereign assemblies, though they have great power to hurt, have little to save. For to accuse, requires less eloquence (such is man's nature) than to excuse; and condemnation, than absolution more resembles justice.

Sixthly, that it is an inconvenience in monarchy, that the sovereignty may descend upon an infant, or one that cannot discern between good and evil: and consisteth in this, that the use of his power, must be in the hand of another man, or of some assembly of men, which are to govern by his right, and in his name; as curators, and protectors of his person, and authority. But to say there is inconvenience, in putting the use of the sovereign power, into the hand of a man, or an assembly of men; is to say that all government is more inconvenient, than confusion, and civil war. And therefore all the danger that can be pretended, must arise from the contention of those, that for an office of so great honour, and profit, may become competitors. To make it appear, that this inconvenience, proceedeth not from that form of government we call monarchy, we are to consider, that the precedent monarch, hath appointed who shall have the tuition of his infant successor, either expressly by testament, or tacitly, by not controlling the custom in that case received: and then such inconvenience, (if it happen) is to be attributed, not to the monarchy, but to the ambition, and injustice of the subjects; which in all kinds of government, where the people are not well instructed in their duty, and the rights of sovereignty, is the same. Or else the precedent monarch hath not at all taken order for such tuition; and then the law of nature hath provided this sufficient rule, that the tuition shall be in him, that hath by nature most interest in the preservation of the authority of the infant, and to whom least benefit can accrue by his death, or diminution. For seeing every man by nature seeketh his own benefit, and promotion; to put an infant into the power of those, that can promote themselves by his destruction, or damage, is not tuition, but treachery. So that sufficient provision being taken, against all just quarrel, about the government under a child, if any contention arise to the disturbance of the public peace, it is not to be attributed to the form of monarchy, but to the ambition of subjects, and ignorance of their duty. On the other side, there is no great commonwealth, the sovereignty whereof is in a great assembly, which is not, as to consultations of peace, and war, and making of laws, in the same condition, as if the government were in a child. For as a child wants the judgment to dissent from counsel given him, and is thereby necessitated to take the advice of them, or him, to whom he is committed: so an assembly wanteth the liberty, to dissent from the counsel of the major part, be it good, or bad. And as a child has need of a tutor, or protector, to preserve his person and authority: so also (in great commonwealths,) the sovereign assembly, in all great dangers and troubles, have need of *custodes libertatis;*

that is of dictators, or protectors of their authority; which are as much as temporary monarchs; to whom for a time, they may commit the entire exercise of their power; and have (at the end of that time) been oftener deprived thereof, than infant kings, by their protectors, regents, or any other tutors.

Though the kinds of sovereignty be, as I have now shown, but three; that is to say, monarchy, where one man has it; or democracy, where the general assembly of subjects hath it; or aristocracy, where it is in an assembly of certain persons nominated, or otherwise distinguished from the rest: yet he that shall consider the particular commonwealths that have been, and are in the world, will not perhaps easily reduce them to three, and may thereby be inclined to think there be other forms, arising from these mingled together. As for example, elective kingdoms; where kings have the sovereign power put into their hands for a time; or kingdoms, wherein the king hath a power limited: which governments, are nevertheless by most writers called monarchy. Likewise if a popular, or aristocratical commonwealth, subdue an enemy's country, and govern the same, by a president, procurator, or other magistrate; this may seem perhaps at first sight, to be a democratical, or aristocratical government. But it is not so. For elective kings, are not sovereigns, but ministers of the sovereign; nor limited kings sovereigns, but ministers of them that have the sovereign power; nor are those provinces which are in subjection to a democracy, or aristocracy of another commonwealth, democratically, or aristocratically governed, but monarchically.

And first, concerning an elective king, whose power is limited to his life, as it is in many places of Christendom at this day; or to certain years or months, as the dictator's power amongst the Romans; if he have right to appoint his successor, he is no more elective but hereditary. But if he have no power to elect his successor, then there is some other man, or assembly known, which after his decrease may elect anew, or else the commonwealth dieth, and dissolveth with him, and returneth to the condition of war. If it be known who have the power to give the sovereignty after his death, it is known also that the sovereignty was in them before: for none have right to give that which they have not right to possess, and keep to themselves, if they think good. But if there be none that can give the sovereignty, after the decease of him that was first elected; then has he power, nay he is obliged by the law of nature, to provide, by establishing his successor, to keep those that had trusted him with the government, from relapsing into the miserable condition of civil war. And consequently he was, when elected, a sovereign absolute.

Secondly, that king whose power is limited, is not superior to him, or them that have the power to limit it; and he that is not superior, is not supreme; that is to say not sovereign. The sovereignty therefore was always in that assembly which had the right to limit him; and by consequence the government not monarchy, but either democracy, or aristocracy; as of old time in *Sparta;* where the kings had a privilege to lead their armies; but the sovereignty was in the *Ephori.*

Thirdly, whereas heretofore the Roman people governed the land of *Judea* (for example) by a president; yet was not *Judea* therefore a democracy; because they were not governed by any assembly, into which, any of them, had right to enter; nor by an aristocracy; because they were not governed by any assembly, into which, any man could enter by their election: but they were governed by one person, which though as to the people of *Rome* was an assembly of the people, or democracy; yet as to people of *Judea,* which had no right at all of participating in the government, was a monarch. For though where the people are governed by an assembly, chosen by themselves out of their own number, the government is called a democracy, or aristocracy; yet when they are governed by an assembly, not of their own choosing, it is a monarchy; not of *one* man, over another man; but of one people, over another people.

Of all these forms of government, the matter being mortal, so that not only monarchs, but also whole assemblies die, it is necessary for the conservation of the peace of men, that as there was order taken for an artificial man, so there be order also taken for an artificial eternity of life; without which, men that are governed by an assembly, should return into the condition of war in every age; and they that

are governed by one man, as soon as their governor dieth. This artificial eternity, is that which men call the right of *succession.*

There is no perfect form of government, where the disposing of the succession is not in the present sovereign. For if it be in any other particular man, or private assembly, it is in a person subject, and may be assumed by the sovereign at his pleasure; and consequently the right is in himself. And if it be in no particular man, but left to a new choice; then is the commonwealth dissolved; and the right is in him that can get it; contrary to the intention of them that did institute the commonwealth, for their perpetual, and not temporary security.

In a democracy, the whole assembly cannot fail, unless the multitude that are to be governed fail. And therefore questions of the right of succession, have in that form of government no place at all.

In an aristocracy, when any of the assembly dieth, the election of another into his room belongeth to the assembly, as the sovereign, to whom belongeth the choosing of all counsellors and officers. For that which the representative doth, as actor, every one of the subjects doth, as author. And though the sovereign assembly may give power to others, to elect new men, for supply of their court; yet it is still by their authority, that the election is made; and by the same it may (when the public shall require it) be recalled.

The greatest difficulty about the right of succession, is in monarchy: and the difficulty ariseth from this, that at first sight, it is not manifest who is to appoint the successor; nor many times, who it is whom he hath appointed. For in both these cases, there is required a more exact ratiocination, than every man is accustomed to use. As to the question, who shall appoint the successor, of a monarch that hath the sovereign authority; that is to say, who shall determine of the right of inheritance, (for elective kings and princes have not the sovereign power in propriety, but in use only,) we are to consider, that either he that is in possession, has right to dispose of the succession, or else that right is again in the dissolved multitude. For the death of him that hath the sovereign power in propriety, leaves the multitude without any sovereign at all; that is, without any representative in whom they should be united, and be capable of doing any one action at all: and therefore they are incapable of election of any new monarch; every man having equal right to submit himself to such as he thinks best able to protect him; or if he can, protect himself by his own sword, which is a return to confusion, and to the condition of a war of every man against every man, contrary to the end for which monarchy had its first institution. Therefore it is manifest, that by the institution of monarchy, the disposing of the successor, is always left to the judgment and will of the present possessor.

And for the question (which may arise sometimes) who it is that the monarch in possession, hath designed to the succession and inheritance of his power; it is determined by his express words, and testament; or by other tacit signs sufficient.

By express words, or testament, when it is declared by him in his lifetime, *viva voce,* or by writing; as the first emperors of *Rome* declared who should be their heirs. For the word heir does not of itself imply the children, or nearest kindred of a man; but whomsoever a man shall any way declare, he would have to succeed him in his estate. If therefore a monarch declare expressly, that such a man shall be his heir, either by word or writing, then is that man immediately after the decease of his predecessor, invested in the right of being monarch.

But where testament, and express words are wanting, other natural signs of the will are to be followed: whereof the one is custom. And therefore where the custom is that the next of kindred absolutely succeedeth, there also the next of kindred hath right to the succession; for that, if the will of him that was in possession had been otherwise, he might easily have declared the same in his life time. And likewise where the custom is, that the next of the male kindred succeedeth, there also the right of succession is in the next of the kindred male, for the same reason. And so it is if the custom were to advance the female. For whatsoever custom a man may by a word control, and does not, it is a natural sign he would have that custom stand.

But where neither custom, nor testament hath pre-

ceded, there it is to be understood, first, that a monarch's will is, that the government remain monarchical; because he hath approved that government in himself. Secondly, that a child of his own, male, or female, be preferred before any other; because men are presumed to be more inclined by nature, to advance their own children, than the children of other men; and of their own, rather a male than a female; because men, are naturally fitter than women, for actions of labour and danger. Thirdly, where his own issue faileth, rather a brother than a stranger; and so still the nearer in blood, rather than the more remote; because it is always presumed that the nearer of kin, is the nearer in affection; and it is evident that a man receives always, by reflection, the most honour from the greatness of his nearest kindred.

But if it be lawful for a monarch to dispose of the succession by words of contract, or testament, men may perhaps object a great inconvenience: for he may sell, or give his right of governing to a stranger; which, because strangers (that is, men not used to live under the same government, nor speaking the same language) do commonly undervalue one another, many turn to the oppression of his subjects; which is indeed a great inconvenience: but it proceedeth not necessarily from the subjection to a stranger's government, but from the unskilfulness of the governors, ignorant of the true rules of politics. And therefore the Romans when they had subdued many nations, to make their government digestible, were wont to take away that grievance, as much as they thought necessary, by giving sometimes to whole nations, and sometimes to principal men of every nation they conquered, not only the privileges, but also the name of Romans; and took many of them into the senate, and offices of charge, even in the Roman city. And this was it our most wise king, king *James,* aimed at, in endeavouring the union of his two realms of *England* and *Scotland.* Which if he could have obtained, had in all likelihood prevented the civil wars, which make both those kingdoms, at this present, miserable. It is not therefore any injury to the people, for a monarch to dispose of the succession by will; though by the fault of many princes, it hath been sometimes found inconvenient. Of the lawfulness of it, this also is an argument, that what-soever inconvenience can arrive by giving a king-dom to a stranger, may arrive also by so marrying with strangers, as the right of succession may descend upon them: yet this by all men is accounted lawful.

## *Chapter 20*

### OF DOMINION PATERNAL, AND DESPOTICAL

A *commonwealth by acquisition,* is that, where the sovereign power is acquired by force; and it is acquired by force, when men singly, or many together by plurality of voices, for fear of death, or bonds, do authorize all the actions of that man, or assembly, that hath their lives and liberty in his power.

And this kind of dominion, or sovereignty, differ-eth from sovereignty by institution, only in this, that men who choose their sovereign, do it for fear of one another, and not of him whom they institute: but in this case, they subject themselves, to him they are afraid of. In both cases they do it for fear: which is to be noted by them, that hold all such covenants, as pro-ceed from fear of death, or violence, void: which if it were true, no man, in any kind of commonwealth, could be obliged to obedience. It is true, that in a com-monwealth once instituted, or acquired, promises proceeding from fear of death or violence, are no covenants, nor obliging, when the thing promised is contrary to the laws; but the reason is not, because it was made upon fear, but because he that promiseth, hath no right in the thing promised. Also, when he may lawfully perform, and doth not, it is not the inva-lidity of the covenant, that absolveth him, but the sen-tence of the sovereign. Otherwise, whensoever a man lawfully promiseth, he unlawfully breaketh: but when the sovereign, who is the actor, acquitteth him, then he is acquitted by him that extorted the promise, as by the author of such absolution.

But the rights, and consequences of sovereignty, are the same in both. His power cannot, without his consent, be transferred to another: he cannot forfeit it: he cannot be accused by any of his subjects, of injury: he cannot be punished by them: he is judge of what is necessary for peace; and judge of doctrines: he is sole legislator; and supreme judge of contro-versies; and of the times, and occasions of war, and peace: to him it belongeth to choose magistrates, counsellors, commanders, and all other officers, and ministers; and to determine of rewards, and punish-ments, honour, and order. The reasons whereof, are the same which are alleged in the precedent chapter, for the same rights, and consequences of sover-eignty by institution.

Dominion is acquired two ways; by generation, and by conquest. The right of dominion by genera-tion, is that, which the parent hath over his children; and is called PATERNAL. And is not so derived from the generation, as if therefore the parent had dominion over his child because be begat him; but from the child's consent, either express, or by other sufficient arguments declared. For as to the genera-tion, God hath ordained to man a helper; and there be always two that are equally parents: the domin-ion therefore over the child, should belong equally to both; and he be equally subject to both, which is impossible; for no man can obey two masters. And whereas some have attributed the dominion to the man only, as being of the more excellent sex; they misreckon in it. For there is not always that differ-ence of strength, or prudence between the man and the woman, as that the right can be determined with-out war. In commonwealths, this controversy is decided by the civil law: and for the most part, (but not always) the sentence is in favour of the father; because for the most part commonwealths have been erected by the fathers, not by the mothers of families. But the question lieth now in the state of mere nature; where there are supposed no laws of matrimony; no laws for the education of children; but the law of nature, and the natural inclination of the sexes, one to another, and to their children. In this condition of mere nature, either the parents between themselves dispose of the dominion over the child by contract; or do not dispose thereof at all. If they dispose thereof, the right passeth according to the contract. We find in history that the *Amazons* contracted with the men of the neighbouring coun-tries, to whom they had recourse for issue, that the issue male should be sent back, but the female remain with themselves: so that the dominion of the females was in the mother.

If there be no contract, the dominion is in the mother. For in the condition of mere nature, where there are no matrimonial laws, it cannot be known who is the father, unless it be declared by the mother: and therefore the right of dominion over the child dependeth on her will, and is consequently hers. Again, seeing the infant is first in the power of the mother, so as she may either nourish, or expose it; if she nourish it, it oweth its life to the mother; and is therefore obliged to obey her, rather than any other; and by consequence the dominion over it is hers. But if she expose it, and another find and nourish it, the dominion is in him that nourisheth it. For it ought to obey him by whom it is preserved; because preservation of life being the end, for which one man becomes subject to another, every man is supposed to promise obedience, to him, in whose power it is to save, or destroy him.

If the mother be the father's subject, the child, is in the father's power: and if the father be the mother's subject, (as when a sovereign queen marrieth one of her subjects,) the child is subject to the mother; because the father also is her subject.

If a man and woman, monarchs of two several kingdoms, have a child, and contract concerning who shall have the dominion of him, the right of the dominion passeth by the contract. If they contract not, the dominion followeth the dominion of the place of his residence. For the sovereign of each country hath dominion over all that reside therein.

He that hath the dominion over the child, hath dominion also over the children of the child; and over their children's children. For he that hath dominion over the person of a man, hath dominion over all that is his; without which, dominion were but a title, without the effect.

The right of succession to paternal dominion, proceedeth in the same manner, as doth the right of succession to monarchy; of which I have already sufficiently spoken in the precedent chapter.

Dominion acquired by conquest, or victory in war, is that which some writers call DESPOTICAL, from Δεσπότης, which signifieth a *lord,* or *master;* and is the dominion of the master over his servant. And this dominion is then acquired to the victor, when the vanquished, to avoid the present stroke of death, convenanteth either in express words, or by other sufficient signs of the will, that so long as his life, and the liberty of his body is allowed him, the victor shall have the use thereof, at his pleasure. And after such covenant made, the vanquished is a SERVANT, and not before: for by the word *servant,* (whether it be derived from *servire,* to serve, or from *servare,* to save, which I leave to grammarians to dispute) is not meant a captive, which is kept in prison, or bonds, till the owner of him that took him, or bought him of one that did, shall consider what to do with him: (for such men, (commonly called slaves,) have no obligation at all; but may break their bonds, or the prison; and kill, or carry away captive their master, justly:) but one, that being taken, hath corporal liberty allowed him; and upon promise not to run away, nor to do violence to his master, is trusted by him.

It is not therefore the victory, that giveth the right of dominion over the vanquished, but his own covenant. Nor is he obliged because he is conquered; that is to say, beaten, and taken, or put to flight; but because he cometh in, and submitteth to the victor; nor is the victor obliged by an enemy's rendering himself, (without promise of life,) to spare him for this his yielding to discretion; which obliges not the victor longer, than in his own discretion he shall think fit.

And that which men do, when they demand (as it is now called) *quarter,* (which the Greeks called Ζωγρία, *taking alive,*) is to evade the present fury of the victor, by submission, and to compound for their life, with ransom, or service: and therefore he that hath quarter, hath not his life given, but deferred till farther deliberation; for it is not an yielding on condition of life, but to discretion. And then only is his life in security, and his service due, when the victor hath trusted him with his corporal liberty. For slaves that work in prisons, or fetters, do it not of duty, but to avoid the cruelty of their task-masters.

The master of the servant, is master also of all he

hath; and may exact the use thereof; that is to say, of his goods, of his labour, of his servants, and of his children, as often as he shall think fit. For he holdeth his life of his master, by the covenant of obedience; that is, of owning, and authorizing whatsoever the master shall do. And in case the master, if he refuse, kill him, or cast him into bonds, or otherwise punish him for his disobedience, he is himself the author of the same; and cannot accuse him of injury.

In sum, the rights and consequences of both *paternal* and *despotical* dominion, are the very same with those of a sovereign by institution; and for the same reasons: which reasons are set down in the precedent chapter. So that for a man that is monarch of divers nations, whereof he hath, in one the sovereignty by institution of the people assembled, and in another by conquest, that is by the submission of each particular, to avoid death or bonds; to demand of one nation more than of the other, from the title of conquest, as being a conquered nation, is an act of ignorance of the rights of sovereignty. For the sovereign is absolute over both alike; or else there is no sovereignty at all; and so every man may lawfully protect himself, if he can, with his own sword, which is the condition of war.

By this it appears; that a great family if it be not part of some commonwealth, is of itself, as to the rights of sovereignty, a little monarchy; whether that family consist of a man and his children; or of a man and his servants; or of a man, and his children, and servants together: wherein the father or master is the sovereign. But yet a family is not properly a commonwealth; unless it be of that power by its own number, or by other opportunities, as not to be subdued without the hazard of war. For where a number of men are manifestly too weak to defend themselves united, every one may use his own reason in time of danger, to save his own life, either by flight, or by submission to the enemy, as he shall think best; in the same manner as a very small company of soldiers, surprised by an army, may cast down their arms, and demand quarter, or run away, rather than be put to the sword. And thus much shall suffice; concerning what I find by speculation, and deduction, of sovereign rights, from the nature, need, and

designs of men, in erecting of commonwealths, and putting themselves under monarchs, or assemblies, entrusted with power enough for their protection.

Let us now consider what the Scripture teacheth in the same point. To Moses, the children of *Israel* say thus: *Speak thou to us, and we will hear thee; but let not God speak to us, lest we die. (Exod. 20. 19.)* This is absolute obedience to Moses. Concerning the right of kings, God himself by the mouth of Samuel, saith, (1 *Sam.* 8. 11, 12, &c.) *This shall be the right of the king you will have to reign over you. He shall take your sons, and set them to drive his chariots, and to be his horsemen, and to run before his chariots; and gather in his harvest; and to make his engines of war, and instruments of his chariots; and shall take your daughters to make perfumes, to be his cooks, and bakers. He shall take your fields, your vine-yards, and your olive-yards, and give them to his servants. He shall take the tithe of your corn and wine, and give it to the men of his chamber, and to his other servants. He shall take your man-servants, and your maid-servants, and the choice of your youth, and employ them in his business. He shall take the tithe of your flocks; and you shall be his servants.* This is absolute power, and summed up in the last words, *you shall be his servants.* Again, when the people heard what power their king was to have, yet they consented thereto, and say thus, (*verse* 19) *we will be as all other nations, and our king shall judge our causes, and go before us, to conduct our wars.* Here is confirmed the right that sovereigns have, both to the *militia,* and to all *judicature;* in which is contained as absolute power, as one man can possibly transfer to another. Again, the prayer of king Solomon to God, was this (1 *Kings,* 3. 9): *Give to thy servant understanding, to judge thy people, and to discern between good and evil.* It belongeth therefore to the sovereign to be judge, and to prescribe the rules of *discerning good* and *evil:* which rules are laws; and therefore in him is the legislative power. Saul sought the life of *David;* yet when it was in his power to slay *Saul,* and his servants would have done it, *David* forbad them, saying, (1 *Sam.* 24. 9) *God forbid I should do such an act against my Lord, the anointed of God.* For obedience of servants St. *Paul* saith; (*Col. 3. 20*) *Servants obey your masters in all things;* and, (*Verse* 22) *children obey your parents in all things.* There is simple obedience in those that are subject to paternal, or despotical dominion. Again, *Matt.* 23. 2, 3) *The Scribes and Pharisees sit in Moses' chair, and therefore all that they shall bid you observe, that observe and do.* There again is simple obedience. And St. *Paul,* (*Titus* 3. 2) *Warn them that they subject themselves to princes, and to those that are in authority, and obey them.* This obedience is also simple. Lastly, our Saviour himself acknowledges, that men ought to pay such taxes as are by kings imposed, where he says, *Give to Caesar that which is Caesar's;* and paid such taxes himself. And that the king's word, is sufficient to take any thing from any subject, when there is need; and that the king is judge of that need: for he himself, as king of the Jews, commanded his disciples to take the ass, and ass's colt to carry him into Jerusalem, saying, (*Matth.* 21. 2, 3) *Go into the village over against you, and you shall find a she ass tied, and her colt with her, untie them, and bring them to me. And if any man ask you, what you mean by it, say the Lord hath need of them: and they will let them go.* They will not ask whether his necessity be a sufficient title; nor whether he be judge of that necessity; but acquiesce in the will of the Lord.

To these places may be added also that of *Genesis,* (*Genesis* 3. 5) *Ye shall be as gods, knowing good and evil.* And *verse* 11. *Who told thee that thou wast naked? hast thou eaten of the tree, of which I commanded thee thou shouldest not eat?* For the cognizance or judicature of good and evil, being forbidden by the name of the fruit of the tree of knowledge, as a trial of *Adam's* obedience; the devil to inflame the ambition of the woman, to whom that fruit already seemed beautiful, told her that by tasting it, they should be as gods, knowing *good* and *evil.* Whereupon having both eaten, they did indeed take upon them God's office, which is judicature of good and evil; but acquired no new ability to distinguish between them aright. And whereas it is said, that having eaten, they saw they were naked; no man hath so interpreted that place, as if they had been for-

merly blind, and saw not their own skins: the meaning is plain, that it was then they first judged their nakedness (wherein it was God's will to create them) to be uncomely; and by being ashamed, did tacitly censure God himself. And thereupon God saith, *Hast thou eaten, &c.* as if he should say, doest thou that owest me obedience, take upon thee to judge of my commandments? Whereby it is clearly, (though allegorically,) signified, that the commands of them that have the right to command, are not by their subjects to be censured, nor disputed.

So that it appeareth plainly, to my understanding, both from reason, and Scripture, that the sovereign power, whether placed in one man, as in monarchy, or in one assembly of men, as in popular, and aristocratical commonwealths, is as great, as possibly men can be imagined to make it. And though of so unlimited a power, men may fancy many evil consequences, yet the consequences of the want of it, which is perpetual war of every man against his neighbour, are much worse. The condition of man in this life shall never be without inconveniences; but there happeneth in no commonwealth any great inconvenience, but what proceeds from the subject's disobedience, and breach of those covenants, from which the commonwealth hath its being. And whosoever thinking sovereign power too great, will seek to make it less, must subject himself, to the power, that can limit it; that is to say, to a greater.

The greatest objection is, that of the practice; when men ask, where, and when, such power has by subjects been acknowledged. But one may ask them again, when or where has there been a kingdom long free from sedition and civil war. In those nations, whose commonwealths have been long-lived, and not been destroyed but by foreign war, the subjects never did dispute of the sovereign power. But howsoever, an argument from the practice of men, that have not sifted to the bottom, and with exact reason weighed the causes, and nature of commonwealths, and suffer daily those miseries, that proceed from the ignorance thereof, is invalid. For though in all places of the world, men should lay the foundation of their houses on the sand, it could not thence be inferred, that so it ought to be. The skill of making, and maintaining commonwealths, consisteth in certain rules, as doth arithmetic and geometry; not (as tennis-play) on practice only: which rules, neither poor men have the leisure, nor men that have had the leisure, have hitherto had the curiosity, or the method to find out.

## Chapter 21

### OF THE LIBERTY OF SUBJECTS

LIBERTY, or FREEDOM, signifieth (properly) the absence of opposition; (by opposition, I mean external impediments of motion;) and may be applied no less to irrational, and inanimate creatures, than to rational. For whatsoever is so tied, or environed, as it cannot move, but within a certain space, which space is determined by the opposition of some external body, we say it hath not liberty to go further. And so of all living creatures, whilst they are imprisoned, or restrained, with walls, or chains; and of the water whilst it is kept in by banks, or vessels, that otherwise would spread itself into a larger space, we use to say, they are not at liberty, to move in such manner, as without those external impediments they would. But when the impediment of motion, is in the constitution of the thing itself, we use not to say, it wants the liberty; but the power to move; as when a stone lieth still, or a man is fastened to his bed by sickness.

And according to this proper, and generally received meaning of the word, *a* FREEMAN, *is he, that in those things, which by his strength and wit he is able to do, is not hindered to do what he has a will to.* But when the words *free,* and *liberty,* are applied to any thing but *bodies,* they are abused; for that which is not subject to motion, is not subject to impediment: and therefore, when it is said (for example) the way is free, no liberty of the way is signified, but of those that walk in it without stop. And when we say a gift is free, there is not meant any liberty of the gift, but of the giver, that was not bound by any law, or covenant to give it. So when we *speak freely,* it is not the liberty of voice, or pronunciation, but of the man, whom no law hath obliged to speak otherwise than he did. Lastly, from the use of the word *freewill,* no liberty can be inferred of the will,

desire, or inclination, but the liberty of the man; which consisteth in this, that he finds no stop, in doing what he has the will, desire, or inclination to do.

Fear, and liberty are consistent; as when a man throweth his goods into the sea for *fear* the ship should sink, he doth it nevertheless very willingly, and may refuse to do it if he will: it is therefore the action of one that was *free:* so a man sometimes pays his debt, only for *fear* of imprisonment, which because nobody hindered him from detaining, was the action of a man at *liberty.* And generally all actions which men do in commonwealths, for *fear* of the law, are actions, which the doers had *liberty* to omit.

*Liberty,* and *necessity* are consistent: as in the water, that hath not only *liberty,* but a *necessity* of descending by the channel; so likewise in the actions which men voluntarily do: which, because they proceed from their will, proceed from *liberty;* and yet, because every act of man's will, and every desire, and inclination proceedeth from some cause, and that from another cause, in a continual chain, (whose first link is in the hand of God the first of all causes,) they proceed from *necessity.* So that to him that could see the connexion of those causes, the *necessity* of all men's voluntary actions, would appear manifest. And therefore God, that seeth, and disposeth all things, seeth also that the *liberty* of man in doing what he will, is accompanied with the *necessity* of doing that which God will, and no more, nor less. For though men may do many things, which God does not command, nor is therefore author of them; yet they can have no passion, nor appetite to any thing, of which appetite God's will is not the cause. And did not his will assure the *necessity* of man's will, and consequently of all that on man's will dependeth, the *liberty* of men would be a contradiction, and impediment to the omnipotence and *liberty* of God. And this shall suffice, (as to the matter in hand) of that natural *liberty,* which only is properly called *liberty.*

But as men, for the attaining of peace, and conservation of themselves thereby, have made an artificial man, which we call a commonwealth; so also have they made artificial chains, called *civil laws,* which they themselves, by mutual covenants, have fastened at one end, to the lips of that man, or assembly, to whom they have given the sovereign power; and at the other end to their own ears. These bonds in their own nature but weak, may nevertheless be made to hold, by the danger, though not by the difficulty of breaking them.

In relation to these bonds only it is, that I am to speak now, of the *liberty* of *subjects.* For seeing there is no commonwealth in the world, wherein there be rules enough set down, for the regulating of all the actions, and words of men, (as being a thing impossible:) it followeth necessarily, that in all kinds of actions, by the laws praetermitted, men have the liberty, of doing what their own reasons shall suggest, for the most profitable to themselves. For if we take liberty in the proper sense, for corporal liberty; that is to say, freedom from chains, and prison, it were very absurd for men to clamour as they do, for the liberty they so manifestly enjoy. Again, if we take liberty, for an exemption from laws, it is no less absurd, for men to demand as they do, that liberty, by which all other men may be masters of their lives. And yet as absurd as it is, this is it they demand; not knowing that the laws are of no power to protect them, without a sword in the hands of a man, or men, to cause those laws to be put in execution. The liberty of a subject, lieth therefore only in those things, which in regulating their actions, the sovereign hath praetermitted: such as is the liberty to buy, and sell, and otherwise contract with one another; to choose their own abode, their own diet, their own trade of life, and institute their children as they themselves think fit; and the like.

Nevertheless we are not to understand, that by such liberty, the sovereign power of life and death, is either abolished, or limited. For it has been already shown, that nothing the sovereign representative can do to a subject, on what pretence soever, can properly be called injustice, or injury; because every subject is author of every act the sovereign doth; so that he never wanteth right to any thing, otherwise, than as he himself is the subject of God, and bound thereby to observe the laws of nature. As therefore it

may, and doth often happen in commonwealths, that a subject may be put to death, by the command of the sovereign power; and yet neither do the other wrong: as when *Jephtha* caused his daughter to be sacrificed: in which, and the like cases, he that so dieth, had liberty to do the action, for which he is nevertheless, without injury put to death. And the same holdeth also in a sovereign prince, that putteth to death an innocent subject. For though the action be against the law of nature, as being contrary to equity, (as was the killing of *Uriah,* by *David;*) yet it was not an injury to *Uriah;* but to *God.* Not to *Uriah,* because the right to do what he pleased, was given him by *Uriah* himself: and yet to *God,* because *David* was *God's* subject; and prohibited all iniquity of the law of nature. Which distinction, *David* himself, when he repented the fact, evidently confirmed, saying, *To thee only have I sinned.* In the same manner, the people of *Athens,* when they banished the most potent of their commonwealth for ten years, thought they committed no injustice; and yet they never questioned what crime he had done; but what hurt he would do: nay they commanded the banishment of they know not whom; and every citizen bringing his oystershell into the market place, written with the name of him he desired should be banished, without actual accusing him, sometimes banished an *Aristides,* for his reputation of justice; and sometimes a scurrilous jester, as *Hyperbolus,* to make a jest of it. And yet a man cannot say, the sovereign people of *Athens* wanted right to banish them; or an *Athenian* the liberty to jest, or to be just.

The liberty, whereof there is so frequent and honourable mention, in the histories, and philosophy of the ancient Greeks, and Romans, and in the writings, and discourse of those that from them have received all their learning in the politics, is not the liberty of particular men; but the liberty of the commonwealth: which is the same with that, which every man then should have, if there were no civil laws, nor commonwealth at all. And the effects of it also be the same. For as amongst masterless men, there is perpetual war, of every man against his neighbour; no inheritance, to transmit to the son, nor to expect from the father; no propriety of goods, or lands; no security; but a full and absolute liberty in every particular man: so in states, and commonwealths not dependent on one another, every commonwealth, (not every man) has an absolute liberty, to do what it shall judge (that is to say, what that man, or assembly that representeth it, shall judge) most conducing to their benefit. But withal, they live in the condition of a perpetual war, and upon the confines of battle, with their frontiers armed, and cannons planted against their neighbours round about. The *Athenians,* and *Romans* were free; that is, free commonwealths: not that any particular men had the liberty to resist their own representative; but that their representative had the liberty to resist, or invade other people. There is written on the turrets of the city of *Lucca* in great characters at this day, the word *LIBERTAS:* yet no man can thence infer, that a particular man has more liberty, or immunity from the service of the commonwealth there, than in *Constantinople.* Whether a commonwealth be monarchical, or popular, the freedom is still the same.

But it is an easy thing, for men to be deceived, by the specious name of *liberty,* and for want of judgment to distinguish, mistake that for their private inheritance, and birth right, which is the right of the public only. And when the same error is confirmed by the authority of men in reputation for their writings in this subject, it is no wonder if it produce sedition, and change of government. In these western parts of the world, we are made to receive our opinions concerning the institution, and rights of commonwealths, from *Aristotle, Cicero,* and other men, Greeks and Romans, that living under popular states, derived those rights, not from the principles of nature, but transcribed them into their books, out of the practice of their own commonwealths, which were popular; as the grammarians describe the rules of language, out of the practice of the time; or the rules of poetry, out of the poems of *Homer* and *Virgil.* And because the Athenians were taught, (to keep them from desire of changing their government,) that they were freemen, and all that lived under monarchy were slaves; therefore Aristotle puts it down in his *Politics, (lib. 6. cap. 2.) In democracy,* Liberty *is to be supposed: for it is commonly held, that no man is* Free *in any other government.* And as Aristotle; so Cicero, and other writers have grounded their civil doctrine, on the opinions of the Romans, who were taught to hate monarchy, at first, by them that having deposed their sovereign, shared amongst them the sovereignty of *Rome;* and afterwards by their successors. And by reading of these Greek, and Latin authors, men from their childhood have gotten a habit (under a false show of liberty,) of favouring tumults, and of licentious controlling the actions of their sovereigns; and again of controlling those controllers, with the effusion of so much blood; as I think I may truly say, there was never any thing so dearly bought, as these western parts have bought the learning of the Greek and Latin tongues.

To come now to the particulars of the true liberty of a subject; that is to say, what are the things, which though commanded by the sovereign, he may nevertheless, without injustice, refuse to do; we are to consider, what rights we pass away, when we make a commonwealth; or (which is all one,) what liberty we deny ourselves, by owning all the actions (without exception) of the man, or assembly we make our sovereign. For in the act of our *submission,* consisteth both our *obligation,* and our *liberty;* which must therefore be inferred by arguments taken from thence; there being no obligation on any man, which ariseth not from some act of his own; for all men equally, are by nature free. And because such arguments, must either be drawn from the express words, *I authorise all his actions,* or from the intention of him that submitteth himself to his power, (which intention is to be understood by the end for which he so submitteth;) the obligation, and liberty of the subject, is to be derived, either from those words, (or others equivalent;) or else from the end of the institution of sovereignty, namely, the peace of the subjects within themselves, and their defence against a common enemy.

First therefore, seeing sovereignty by institution, is by covenant of every one to every one; and sovereignty by acquisition, by covenants of the vanquished to the victor, or child to the parent; it is manifest, that every subject has liberty in all those things, the right whereof cannot by covenant be transferred. I have shewn before in the 14th chapter, that covenants, not to defend a man's own body, are void. Therefore,

If the sovereign command a man (though justly condemned,) to kill, wound, or maim himself; or not to resist those that assault him; or to abstain from the use of food, air, medicine, or any other thing, without which he cannot live; yet hath that man the liberty to disobey.

If a man be interrogated by the sovereign, or his authority, concerning a crime done by himself, he is not bound (without assurance of pardon) to confess it; because no man (as I have shown in the same chapter) can be obliged by covenant to accuse himself.

Again, the consent of a subject to sovereign power, is contained in these words, *I authorize, or take upon me, all his actions;* in which there is no restriction at all, of his own former natural liberty: for by allowing him to *kill me,* I am not bound to kill myself when he commands me. It is one thing to say, *kill me, or my fellow, if you please;* another thing to say, *I will kill myself, or my fellow.* It followeth therefore, that

No man is bound by the words themselves, either to kill himself, or any other man; and consequently, that the obligation a man may sometimes have, upon the command of the sovereign to execute any dangerous, or dishonourable office, dependeth not on the words of our submission; but on the intention, which is to be understood by the end thereof. When therefore our refusal to obey, frustrates the end for which the sovereignty was ordained; then there is no liberty to refuse: otherwise there is.

Upon this ground, a man that is commanded as a soldier to fight against the enemy, though his sovereign have right enough to punish his refusal with death, may nevertheless in many cases refuse, without injustice; as when he substituteth a sufficient soldier in his place: for in this case he deserteth not the service of the commonwealth. And there is allowance to be made for natural timorousness; not only to women, (of whom no such dangerous duty is expected,) but also to men of feminine courage. When armies fight, there is on one side, or both, a running away; yet when they do it not out of treach-

ery, but fear, they are not esteemed to do it unjustly, but dishonourably. For the same reason, to avoid battle, is not injustice, but cowardice. But he that inrolleth himself a soldier, or taketh imprest money, taketh away the excuse of a timorous nature; and is obliged, not only to go to the battle, but also not to run from it, without his captain's leave. And when the defence of the commonwealth, requireth at once the help of all that are able to bear arms, every one is obliged; because otherwise the institution of the commonwealth, which they have not the purpose, or courage to preserve, was in vain.

To resist the sword of the commonwealth, in defence of another man, guilty, or innocent, no man hath liberty; because such liberty, takes away from the sovereign, the means of protecting us; and is therefore destructive of the very essence of government. But in case a great many men together, have already resisted the sovereign power unjustly, or committed some capital crime, for which every one of them expecteth death, whether have they not the liberty then to join together, and assist, and defend one another? Certainly they have: for they but defend their lives, which the guilty man may as well do, as the innocent. There was indeed injustice in the first breach of their duty; their bearing of arms subsequent to it, though it be to maintain what they have done, is no new unjust act. And if it be only to defend their persons, it is not unjust at all. But the offer of pardon taketh from them, to whom it is offered, the plea of self-defence, and maketh their perserverance in assisting, or defending the rest, unlawful.

As for other liberties, they depend on the silence of the law. In cases where the sovereign has prescribed no rule, there the subject hath the liberty to do, or forbear, according to his own discretion. And therefore such liberty is in some places more, and in some less; and in some times more, in other times less, according as they that have the sovereignty shall think most convenient. As for example, there was a time, when in *England* a man might enter into his own land, (and dispossess such as wrongfully possessed it,) by force. But in aftertimes, that liberty of forcible entry, was taken away by a statute made (by the king,) in parliament. And in some places of the world, men have the liberty of many wives: in other places, such liberty is not allowed.

If a subject have a controversy with his sovereign, of debt, or of right of possession of lands or goods, or concerning any service required at his hands, or concerning any penalty, corporal, or pecuniary, grounded on a precedent law; he hath the same liberty to sue for his right, as if it were against a subject; and before such judges, as are appointed by the sovereign. For seeing the sovereign demandeth by force of a former law, and not by virtue of his power; he declareth thereby, that he requireth no more, than shall appear to be due by that law. The suit therefore is not contrary to the will of the sovereign; and consequently the subject hath the liberty to demand the hearing of his cause; and sentence, according to that law. But if he demand, or take any thing by pretence of his power; there lieth, in that case, no action of law: for all that is done by him in virtue of his power, is done by the authority of every subject, and consequently, he that brings an action against the sovereign, brings it against himself.

If a monarch, or sovereign assembly, grant a liberty to all, or any of his subjects, which grant standing, he is disabled to provide for their safety, the grant is void; unless he directly renounce, or transfer the sovereignty to another. For in that he might openly, (if it had been his will,) and in plain terms, have renounced, or transferred it, and did not; it is to be understood it was not his will; but that the grant proceeded from ignorance of the repugnancy between such a liberty and the sovereign power: and therefore the sovereignty is still retained; and consequently all those powers, which are necessary to the exercising thereof; such as are the power of war, and peace, of judicature, of appointing officers, and councillors, of levying money, and the rest named in the 18th chapter.

The obligation of subjects to the sovereign, is understood to last as long, and no longer, than the power lasteth, by which he is able to protect them. For the right men have by nature to protect themselves, when none else can protect them, can by no covenant be relinquished. The sovereignty is the soul of the commonwealth; which once departed from the body, the members do no more receive their motion from it. The end of obedience is protection; which, wheresoever a man seeth it, either in his own, or in another's sword, nature applieth his obedience to it, and his endeavour to maintain it. And though sovereignty, in the intention of them that make it, be immortal; yet is it in its own nature, not only subject to violent death, by foreign war; but also through the ignorance, and passions of men, it hath in it, from the very institution, many seeds of a natural mortality, by intestine discord.

If a subject be taken prisoner in war; or his person, or his means of life be within the guards of the enemy, and hath his life and corporal liberty given him, on condition to be subject to the victor, he hath liberty to accept the condition; and having accepted it, is the subject of him that took him; because he had no other way to preserve himself. The case is the same, if he be detained on the same terms, in a foreign country. But if a man be held in prison, or bonds, or is not trusted with the liberty of his body; he cannot be understood to be bound by convenant to subjection; and therefore may, if he can, make his escape by any means whatsoever.

If a monarch shall relinquish the sovereignty, both for himself, and his heirs; his subjects return to the absolute liberty of nature; because, though nature may declare who are his sons, and who are the nearest of his kin; yet it dependeth on his own will, (as hath been said in the precedent chapter,) who shall be his heir. If therefore he will have no heir, there is no sovereignty, nor subjection. The case is the same, if he die without known kindred, and without declaration of his heir. For then there can no heir be known, and consequently no subjection be due.

If the sovereign banish his subject; during the banishment, he is not subject. But he that is sent on a message, or hath leave to travel, is still subject; but it is, by contract between sovereigns, not by virtue of the covenant of subjection. For whosoever entereth into another's dominion, is subject to all the laws thereof; unless he have a privilege by the amity of the sovereigns, or by special licence.

If a monarch subdued by war, render himself

subject to the victor; his subjects are delivered from their former obligation, and become obliged to the victor. But if he be held prisoner, or have not the liberty of his own body; he is not understood to have given away the right of sovereignty; and therefore his subjects are obliged to yield obedience to the magistrates formerly placed, governing not in their own name, but in his. For, his right remaining, the question is only of the administration; that is to say, of the magistrates and officers; which, if he have not means to name, he is supposed to approve those, which he himself had formerly appointed.

## Chapter 29

### OF THOSE THINGS THAT WEAKEN,
### OR TEND TO THE DISSOLUTION
### OF A COMMONWEALTH

Though nothing can be immortal, which mortals make; yet, if men had the use of reason they pretend to, their commonwealths might be secured, at least, from perishing by internal diseases. For by the nature of their institution, they are designed to live, as long as mankind, or as the laws of nature, or as justice itself, which gives them life. Therefore when they come to be dissolved, not by external violence, but intestine disorder, the fault is not in men, as they are the *matter;* but as they are the *makers,* and orderers of them. For men, as they become at last weary of irregular jostling, and hewing one another, and desire with all their hearts, to conform themselves into one firm and lasting edifice; so for want, both of the art of making fit laws, to square their actions by, and also of humility, and patience, to suffer the rude and cumbersome points of their present greatness to be taken off, they cannot without the help of a very able architect, be compiled, into any other than a crazy building, such as hardly lasting out their own time, must assuredly fall upon the heads of their posterity.

Amongst the *infirmities* therefore of a commonwealth, I will reckon in the first place, those that arise from an imperfect institution, and resemble the diseases of a natural body, which proceed from a defectuous procreation.

Of which, this is one, *that a man to obtain a king-*

*dom, is sometimes content with less power, than to the peace, and defence of the commonwealth is necessarily required.* From whence it cometh to pass, that when the exercise of the power laid by, is for the public safety to be resumed, it hath the resemblance of an unjust act; which disposeth great numbers of men (when occasion is presented) to rebel; in the same manner as the bodies of children, gotten by diseased parents, are subject either to untimely death, or to purge the ill quality, derived from their vicious conception, by breaking out into biles and scabs. And when kings deny themselves some such necessary power, it is not always (though sometimes), out of ignorance of what is necessary to the office they undertake; but many times out of a hope to recover the same again at their pleasure: Wherein they reason not well; because such as will hold them to their promises, shall be maintained against them by foreign commonwealths; who in order to the good of their own subjects let slip few occasions to *weaken* the estate of their neighbours. So was *Thomas Becket,* archbishop of *Canterbury,* supported against *Henry* the Second, by the Pope; the subjection of ecclesiastics to the commonwealth, having been dispensed with by *William the Conqueror* at his reception, when he took an oath, not to infringe the liberty of the church. And so were the *barons,* whose power was by *William Rufus* (to have their help in transferring the succession from his elder brother, to himself,) increased to a degree, inconsistent with the sovereign power, maintained in their rebellion against *King John,* by the French.

Nor does this happen in monarchy only. For whereas the style of the ancient Roman commonwealth, was, *the senate, and people of Rome;* neither senate, nor people pretended to the whole power; which first caused the seditions, of *Tiberius Gracchus, Caius Gracchus, Lucius Saturninus,* and others; and afterwards the wars between the senate and the people, under *Marius* and *Sylla;* and again under *Pompey* and *Caesar,* to the extinction of their democracy, and the setting up of monarchy.

The people of *Athens* bound themselves but from one only action; which was, that no man on pain of death should propound the renewing of the war for the island of *Salamis;* and yet thereby, if *Solon* had not caused to be given out he was mad, and afterwards in gesture and habit of a madman, and in verse, propounded it to the people that flocked about him, they had had an enemy perpetually in readiness, even at the gates of their city; such damage, or shifts, are all commonwealths forced to, that have their power never so little limited.

In the second place, I observe the *diseases* of a commonwealth, that proceed from the poison of seditious doctrines, whereof one is, *That every private man is judge of good and evil actions.* This is true in the condition of mere nature, where there are no civil laws; and also under civil government, in such cases as are not determined by the law. But otherwise it is manifest, that the measure of good and evil actions, is the civil law; and the judge the legislator, who is always representative of the commonwealth. From this false doctrine, men are disposed to debate with themselves, and dispute the commands of the commonwealth; and afterwards to obey, or disobey them, as in their private judgments they shall think fit. Whereby the commonwealth is distracted and *weakened.*

Another doctrine repugnant to civil society, is, that *whatsoever a man does against his conscience, is sin;* and it dependeth on the presumption of making himself judge of good and evil. For a man's conscience, and his judgment is the same thing; and as the judgment, so also the conscience may be erroneous. Therefore, though he that is subject to no civil law, sinneth in all he does against his conscience, because he has no other rule to follow but his own reason; yet it is not so with him that lives in a commonwealth; because the law is the public conscience, by which he hath already undertaken to be guided. Otherwise in such diversity, as there is of private consciences, which are but private opinions, the commonwealth must needs be distracted, and no man dare to obey the sovereign power, farther than it shall seem good in his own eyes.

It hath been also commonly taught, *that faith and sanctity, are not to be attained by study and reason, but by supernatural inspiration, or infusion,* which granted, I see not why any man should render a rea-

son of his faith; or why every Christian should not be also a prophet; or why any man should take the law of his country, rather than his own inspiration, for the rule of his action. And thus we fall again into the fault of taking upon us to judge of good and evil; or to make judges of it, such private men as pretend to be supernaturally inspired, to the dissolution of all civil government. Faith comes by hearing, and hearing by those accidents, which guide us into the presence of them that speak to us; which accidents are all contrived by God Almighty; and yet are not supernatural, but only, for the great number of them that concur to every effect, unobservable. Faith and sanctity, are indeed not very frequent; but yet they are not miracles, but brought to pass by education, discipline, correction, and other natural ways, by which God worketh them in his elect, at such time as he thinketh fit. And these three opinions, pernicious to peace and government, have in this part of the world, proceeded chiefly from the tongues, and pens of unlearned divines; who joining the words of Holy Scripture together, otherwise than is agreeable to reason, do what they can, to make men think, that sanctity and natural reason, cannot stand together.

A fourth opinion, repugnant to the nature of a commonwealth, is this, *that he that hath the sovereign power, is subject to the civil laws.* It is true, that sovereigns are all subject to the laws of nature; because such laws be divine, and cannot by any man, or commonwealth be abrogated. But to those laws which the sovereign himself, that is, which the commonwealth maketh, he is not subject. For to be subject to laws, is to be subject to the commonwealth, that is to the sovereign representative, that is to himself; which is not subjection, but freedom from the laws. Which error, because it setteth the laws above the sovereign, setteth also a judge above him, and a power to punish him; which is to make a new sovereign; and again for the same reason a third, to punish the second; and so continually without end, to the confusion, and dissolution of the commonwealth.

A fifth doctrine, that tendeth to the dissolution of a commonwealth, is, *that every private man has an absolute propriety in his goods; such, as excludeth the right of the sovereign.* Every man has indeed a propriety that excludes the right of every other subject: and he has it only from the sovereign power; without the protection whereof, every other man should have equal right to the same. But if the right of the sovereign also be excluded, he cannot perform the office they have put him into; which is, to defend them both from foreign enemies, and from the injuries of one another; and consequently there is no longer a commonwealth.

And if the propriety of subjects, exclude not the right of the sovereign representative to their goods; much less to their offices of judicature, or execution, in which they represent the sovereign himself.

There is a sixth doctrine, plainly, and directly against the essence of a commonwealth; and it is this, *that the sovereign power may be divided.* For what is it to divide the power of a commonwealth, but to dissolve it; for powers divided mutually destroy each other. And for these doctrines, men are chiefly beholding to some of those, that making profession of the laws, endeavour to make them depend upon their own learning, and not upon the legislative power.

And as false doctrine, so also oftentimes the example of different government in a neighbouring nation, disposeth men to alteration of the form already settled. So the people of the Jews were stirred up to reject God, and to call upon the prophet *Samuel,* for a king after the manner of the nations: so also the lesser cities of *Greece,* were continually disturbed, with seditions of the aristocratical, and democratical factions; one part of almost every commonwealth, desiring to imitate the Lacedemonians; the other, the Athenians. And I doubt not, but many men, have been contented to see the late troubles in *England,* out of an imitation of the Low Countries; supposing there needed no more to grow rich, than to change, as they had done, the form of their government. For the constitution of man's nature, is of itself subject to desire novelty: When therefore they are provoked to the same, by the neighbourhood also of those that have been enriched by it, it is almost impossible for them, not to be content with those that solicit them to change; and love the first beginnings,

though they be grieved with the continuance of disorder; like hot bloods, that having gotten the itch, tear themselves with their own nails, till they can endure the smart no longer.

And as to rebellion in particular against monarchy; one of the most frequent causes of it, is the reading of the books of policy, and histories of the ancient Greeks, and Romans; from which, young men, and all others that are unprovided of the antidote of solid reason, receiving a strong, and delightful impression, of the great exploits of war, achieved by the conductors of their armies, receive withal a pleasing idea, of all they have done besides; and imagine their great prosperity, not to have proceeded from the emulation of particular men, but from the virtue of their popular form of government: not considering the frequent seditions, and civil wars, produced by the imperfection of their policy. From the reading, I say, of such books, men have undertaken to kill their kings, because the Greek and Latin writers, in their books and discourses of policy, make it lawful, and laudable, for any man so to do; provided, before he do it, he call him tyrant. For they say not *regicide,* that is, killing of a king, but *tyrannicide,* that is, killing of a tyrant is lawful. From the same books, they that live under a monarch conceive an opinion, that the subjects in a popular commonwealth enjoy liberty; but that in a monarchy they are all slaves. I say, they that live under a monarchy conceive such an opinion; not they that live under a popular government: for they find no such matter. In sum, I cannot imagine, how any thing can be more prejudicial to a monarchy, than the allowing of such books to be publicly read, without present applying such correctives of discreet masters, as are fit to take away their venom: which venom I will not doubt to compare to the biting of a mad dog, which is a disease the physicians call *hydrophobia,* or *fear of water.* For as he that is so bitten, has a continual torment of thirst, and yet abhorreth water; and is in such an estate, as if the poison endeavoured to convert him into a dog: so when a monarchy is once bitten to the quick, by those democratical writers, that continually snarl at that estate; it wanteth nothing more than a strong monarch, which nevertheless out of a certain *tyrannophobia,* or fear of being strongly governed, when they have him, they abhor.

As there have been doctors, that hold there be three souls in a man; so there be also that think there may be more souls, (that is, more sovereigns,) than one, in a commonwealth; and set up a *supremacy* against the *sovereignty; canons* against *laws;* and a *ghostly authority* against the *civil;* working on men's minds, with words and distinctions, that of themselves signify nothing, but bewray (by their obscurity) that there walketh (as some think invisibly) another kingdom, as it were a kingdom of fairies, in the dark. Now seeing it is manifest, that the civil power, and the power of the commonwealth is the same thing; and that supremacy, and the power of making canons, and granting faculties, implieth a commonwealth; it followeth, that where one is sovereign, another supreme; where one can make laws, and another make canons; there must needs be two commonwealths, of one and the same subjects; which is a kingdom divided in itself, and cannot stand. For notwithstanding the insignificant distinction of *temporal,* and *ghostly,* they are still two kingdoms, and every subject is subject to two masters. For seeing the *ghostly* power challengeth the right to declare what is sin it challengeth by consequence to declare what is law, (sin being nothing but the transgression of the law;) and again, the civil power challenging to declare what is law, every subject must obey two masters, who both will have their commands be observed as law; which is impossible. Or, if it be but one kingdom, either the *civil,* which is the *power* of the commonwealth, must be subordinate to the *ghostly,* and then there is no sovereignty but the *ghostly;* or the *ghostly,* must be subordinate to the *temporal,* and then there is no *supremacy,* but the *temporal.* When therefore these two powers oppose one another, the commonwealth cannot but be in great danger of civil war, and dissolution. For the *civil* authority being more visible, and standing in the clearer light of natural reason, cannot choose but draw to it in all times a very considerable part of the people: and the *spiritual,* though it stand in the darkness of School distinctions, and hard words; yet because the fear of darkness, and ghosts, is greater than other fears, cannot want a party sufficient to trouble, and sometimes to destroy a commonwealth, and this is a disease which not unfitly may be compared to the epilepsy, or falling sickness (which the Jews took to be one kind of possession by spirits) in the body natural. For as in this disease, there is an unnatural spirit, or wind in the head that obstructeth the roots of the nerves, and moving them violently, taketh away the motion which naturally they should have from the power of the soul in the brain, and thereby causeth violent, and irregular motions (which men call convulsions) in the parts; insomuch as he that is seized therewith, falleth down sometimes into the water, and sometimes into the fire, as a man deprived of his senses; so also in the body politic, when the spiritual power, moveth the members of a commonwealth, by the terror of punishments, and hope of rewards (which are the nerves of it,) otherwise than by the civil power (which is the soul of the commonwealth), they ought to be moved; and by strange, and hard words suffocates their understanding, it must needs thereby distract the people, and either overwhelm the commonwealth with oppression, or cast it into the fire of a civil war.

Sometimes also in the merely civil government, there be more than one soul: as when the power of levying money, (which is the nutritive faculty,) has depended on a general assembly; the power of conduct and command, (which is the motive faculty,) on one man; and the power of making laws, (which is the rational faculty,) on the accidental consent, not only of those two, but also of a third; this endangereth the commonwealth, sometimes for want of consent to good laws; but most often for want of such nourishment, as is necessary to life, and motion. For although few perceive, that such government, is not government, but division of the commonwealth into three factions, and call it mixed monarchy; yet the truth is, that it is not one independent commonwealth, but three independent factions; nor one representative person, but three. In the kingdom of God, there may be three persons independent, without breach of unity in God that reigneth; but where men reign, that be subject to diversity of opinions, it cannot be so. And therefore if the king bear the person of the people, and the general assembly bear also the person of the people, and another assembly bear the person of a part of the people, they are not one person, nor one sovereign, but three persons, and three sovereigns.

To what disease in the natural body of man I may exactly compare this irregularity of a commonwealth, I know not. But I have seen a man, that had another man growing out of his side, with an head, arms, breast, and stomach, of his own: if he had had another man growing out of his other side, the comparison might then have been exact.

Hitherto I have named such diseases of a commonwealth, as are of the greatest, and most present danger. There be other, not so great; which nevertheless are not unfit to be observed. As first, the difficulty of raising money, for the necessary uses of the commonwealth; especially in the approach of war. This difficulty ariseth from the opinion, that every subject hath of a propriety in his lands and goods, exclusive of the sovereign's right to the use of the same. From whence it cometh to pass, that the sovereign power, which foreseeth the necessities and dangers of the commonwealth, (finding the passage of money to the public treasure obstructed, by the tenacity to the people,) whereas it ought to extend itself, to encounter, and prevent such dangers in their beginnings, contracteth itself as long as it can, and when it cannot longer, struggles with the people by stratagems of law, to obtain little sums, which not sufficing, he is fain at last violently to open the way for present supply, or perish: and being put often to these extremities, at last reduceth the people to their due temper; or else the commonwealth must perish. Insomuch as we may compare this distemper very aptly to an ague; wherein, the fleshy parts being congealed, or by venomous matter obstructed; the veins which by their natural course empty themselves into the heart, are not (as they ought to be) supplied from the arteries, whereby there succeedeth at first a cold contraction, and trembling of the limbs: and afterwards a hot, and strong

endeavour of the heart, to force a passage for the blood; and before it can do that, contenteth itself with the small refreshments of such things as cool for a time, till (if nature be strong enough), it break at last the contumacy of the parts obstructed, and dissipateth the venom into sweat; or (if nature be too weak) the patient dieth.

Again, there is sometimes in a commonwealth, a disease, which resembleth the pleurisy; and that is, when the treasure of the commonwealth, flowing out of its due course, is gathered together in too much abundance in one, or a few private men, by monopolies, or by farms of the public revenues; in the same manner as the blood in a pleurisy, getting into the membrane of the breast, breedeth there an inflammation, accompanied with a fever, and painful stitches.

Also the popularity of a potent subject, (unless the commonwealth have very good caution of his fidelity,) is a dangerous disease; because the people (which should receive their motion from the authority of the sovereign,) by the flattery, and by the reputation of an ambitious man, are drawn away from their obedience to the laws, to follow a man, of whose virtues, and designs they have no knowledge. And this is commonly of more danger in a popular government, than in a monarchy; because an army is of so great force, and multitude, as it may easily be made believe, they are the people. By this means it was, that *Julius Caesar,* who was set up by the people against the senate, having won to himself the affections of his army, made himself master, both of senate and people. And this proceeding of popular, and ambitious men, is plain rebellion; and may be resembled to the effects of witchcraft.

Another infirmity of a commonwealth, is the immoderate greatness of a town, when it is able to furnish out of its own circuit, the number, and expense of a great army: as also the great number of corporations; which are as it were many lesser commonwealths in the bowels of a greater, like worms in the entrails of a natural man. To which may be added, the liberty of disputing against absolute power, by pretenders to political prudence; which though bred for the most part in the lees of the people; yet animated by false doctrines, are perpetually meddling with the fundamental laws, to the molestation of the commonwealth; like the little worms, which physicians call *ascarides.*

We may further add, the insatiable appetite, or Bulimia, of enlarging dominion; with the incurable *wounds* thereby many times received from the enemy; and the *wens,* of ununited conquests, which are many times a burthen, and with less danger lost, than kept; as also the *lethargy* of ease, and *consumption* of riot and vain expense.

Lastly, when in a war (foreign or intestine,) the enemies get a final victory; so as (the forces of the commonwealth keeping the field no longer), there is no farther protection of subjects in their loyalty; then is the commonwealth DISSOLVED, and every man at liberty to protect himself by such courses as his own discretion shall suggest unto him. For the sovereign, is the public soul, giving life and motion to the commonwealth; which expiring, the members are governed by it no more, than the carcase of a man, by his departed (though immortal) soul. For though the right of a sovereign monarch cannot be extinguished by the act of another; yet the obligation of the members may. For he that wants protection, may seek it any where; and when he hath it, is obliged (without fraudulent pretence of having submitted himself out of fear,) to protect his protection as long as he is able. But when the power of an assembly is once suppressed, the right of the same perisheth utterly; because the assembly itself is extinct; and consequently, there is no possibility for the sovereignty to re-enter.

# BARUCH SPINOZA

## INTRODUCTION

## STEVEN B. SMITH

Baruch (Benedict) Spinoza (1632–1677) was born in Amsterdam, a descendent of Portuguese Marranos, that is, Jews who had fled the Inquisition for the relative safety of Holland. Virtually nothing is known of Spinoza's early life. He was educated at a traditional Jewish yeshiva where he studied Hebrew and Talmud. Spinoza was a polymath who spoke Spanish, Portuguese, and Dutch and wrote his major philosophical works in Latin. At the age of 24, he was put under the *herem,* or "edict of excommunication," expelling him from the synagogue. The reasons for the ban on Spinoza are not fully known, although they are almost certainly connected to the increasingly heterodox opinions on religion that he had come to espouse.

Spinoza left Amsterdam in 1660, settling first in Rijnsburg, a suburb of Leiden, and later moving to Voorsburg outside The Hague. He earned his living as a lens grinder, and famously turned down an offer of a professorship at Heidelberg on the grounds that it would interfere with his independence of mind. Spinoza lived a life of uncommon detachment and isolation. He was befriended by members of some of the more liberal Protestant sects of the time, but Spinoza was not an apostate and refused to convert to Christianity. Although he lived alone and aloof, he was sought out by the leading scientists and philosophers of the day, including Leibniz and Henry Oldenburg, the secretary of the Royal Academy in London. Spinoza died of consumption in The Hague at the age of 44.

Spinoza was a writer who combined an unusual degree of boldness and secrecy. As an excommunicated Jew living on the margins of Dutch society, he knew at first hand the sting of religious persecution and the dangers of speaking one's mind openly. His signet ring bore the Latin inscription *caute*, or "caution." He took pains to conceal his opinions even from those most intimate with him. With the exception of an early commentary on the philosophy of Descartes (1663), none of the other works published by Spinoza bore his name. His major work of political philosophy, the *Theologico-Political Treatise* (TPT) was published anonymously in 1670 and carried the imprimatur of a fictitious Hamburg publishing house. The work for which he is best known, the *Ethics*, was published posthumously for reasons of prudence and safety. A shorter work, *The Political Treatise*, was left unfinished at the time of his death.

At the same time that he expressed a prudent fear of the power of the multitude, Spinoza took an active stand on the major political struggles of his time. Like Machiavelli's *Prince*, which Spinoza greatly admired, the *TPT* was a passionate and partisan tract written to advance the fortunes of a political cause. This cause was the republican faction in Dutch politics championed by Jan de Witt against the monarchist faction led by the House of Orange and supported by the Calvinist clergy. Like the Collegiants and Mennonites with whom he associated, Spinoza was a republican in politics and an advocate of toleration in theology. The best state, he declared, is one where "everyone's judgment is free and unshackled" and where "each may worship God as his conscience dictates." Two years after the publication of the *TPT*, De Witt and his brother were savagely murdered by an angry mob, an action that signaled Spinoza's withdrawal from political involvement. *Ultimi barbarorum* was his final judgment on the De Witt affair.

As the title of the *TPT* implies, it is a work divided into two distinguishable, yet hardly equal, parts. The first fifteen chapters are devoted to a lengthy and painstaking critique of biblical theology. Taking up the traditional themes of prophecy, law, and miracles, Spinoza submits each in turn to withering criticism. The Bible is on his account an imaginative, but ultimately primitive, record of the mentality of an ancient culture. Its teachings were intended to instill habits of obedience and justice in superstitious and fear-driven people. The aim of the first part of the *TPT* was to liberate human reason (or philosophy) from the authority of Scripture.

Having completed the critique of theology in the first fifteen chapters of the *TPT*, Spinoza devotes the remainder of the book to the critique of politics. The *TPT* is notable as the first work of modern political philosophy to endorse democracy as the best regime (*optima Republica*). Spinoza derives the legitimacy of democratic government at least in part from premises borrowed from his most important contemporary, Thomas Hobbes. Like Hobbes, Spinoza begins with a perfectly realistic, hard-boiled picture of human nature. There is in every living being an impulse (*conatus*) toward self-preservation. It follows that in the state of nature every being has the natural right to preserve itself by whatever means are at its disposal. Like Hobbes also, Spinoza invokes the metaphor of a social contract as the means by which individuals agree with one another to reduce the state of war to a condition of peace.

Spinoza departs from Hobbes, however, in two interesting and important ways. First, because the natural right of every being is identical to its power, Spinoza draws the conclusion that the majority in any community has by definition the preponderance of right on its side. Unlike Hobbes's contract that displays a marked preference for monarchy, for Spinoza only a democratic sovereign can ensure against the dangers of arbitrary rule stemming from the investiture of power in the hands of one person. Second, unlike Hobbes, who maintained that the avoidance of war is the greatest political good, Spinoza endorses democracy for its enhancement of human freedom. Democracy is desirable because it fosters the conditions for reason and the expression of our individual faculties. To a degree developed later by Rousseau and Kant, not peace and security but freedom becomes the true end of political life. Democracy is the form of government most consistent with the modern treatment of natural right and in agreement with human liberty.

The kind of democracy advocated by Spinoza is what today would be called a "liberal democracy". A central feature of this democracy is its incorporation of the widest possible freedom of thought and opinion. The *TPT* provides several, not necessarily consistent, justifications for toleration. In the first place, toleration is said to follow from the doctrine of natural right strictly understood. If the right of nature means the liberty to do whatever our power permits, then by nature the sovereign's power must be limited to the control of external behavior. Because "no man's mind can possibly lie wholly at the disposition of another," the sovereign must leave the contents of the mind entirely to the individual's private discretion.

The *TPT* also argues historically and pragmatically that attempts to control the content of thought have invariably backfired. Rather than producing consensus and harmony, policies of intolerance and persecution have unwittingly bred conflict and opposition. The effort to criminalize opinions has led even honorable men to don the mantle of revolution. Note that unlike later defenders of toleration, Spinoza does not say that the effort to control thought violates some sacred or privileged sphere of individual privacy. Persecution is wrong, not because it is immoral, but because it is inherently self-defeating.

Most importantly, Spinoza defends freedom of speech because it fosters a certain kind of human being with certain distinctive traits of character and mind. Like John Stuart Mill in the mid-nineteenth century, Spinoza defends toleration, not as an end in itself but because it encourages the development of individual judgment and personal autonomy. The kind of human being envisaged by Spinoza is one who prizes individual liberty "before all things dear and precious." In the *Ethics*, Spinoza provides a particularly vivid portrait of the autonomous individual as one who strives to be independent of tradition and external sources of authority, who acts rather than being acted upon, and whose thoughts and actions stem not from envy and fear but from feelings of love and friendship. Above all, this person thinks of nothing so much as life itself and the means necessary to its enhancement. While Spinoza's idea of freedom has certain classical precedents in the works of Plato and the Stoics, it remains to a considerable degree a modern creation. To a greater extent than in the past, freedom is based on notions of individual autonomy, self-mastery, and courage.

Spinoza is one of the first thinkers to argue that the fruits of toleration are beneficial, not merely for the individual, but for society as a whole. The *TPT* draws an explicit connection between freedom of speech and the progress of the liberal arts. Like Descartes, Spinoza saw the tremendous potential locked inside the emergent sciences of nature, especially medicine, as a tool for increasing the ease and comfort of life. But Spinoza also recognized that intellectual and material progress does not take place in a vacuum. The progress of the arts and sciences is linked by him to issues of trade and commerce. Intellectual freedom is only possible in an environment that encourages commercial freedom. Spinoza's democracy is, then, necessarily a commercial republic where one finds a combination of economic, political, and religious liberty.

Spinoza's preference for the modern commercial republic is based on an emphatic rejection of the older classical republic theorized in the writings of Plato and Aristotle. For the ancients, the republic was a small, polis-like body characterized by a high degree of moral and religious homogeneity. Spinoza's defense of commercial and intellectual freedom indicates a preference for large, cosmopolitan, or "open" societies marked by a diversity of opinions and lifestyles. Furthermore, the classical republics displayed a severity and moral austerity demanding from its citizens a self-sacrificing devotion to the common good. Conversely, Spinoza's commercial republic is characterized less by virtue than by liberty in its many dimensions. Liberty is said to bring not only the progress of the arts and sciences but also the refinement and improvement of behavior. The *TPT* concludes with a ringing praise of the commercial republic of Amsterdam, where the effects of liberty are on display for all to see.

Only in the following century would Spinoza's arguments in favor of the commercial republic bear fruit in the works of Montesquieu, Hume, and Adam Smith. Everywhere the commercial republic was proposed as a more humane alternative to the theologico-political regimes that had previously dominated European thought and practice. Such a regime would favor commercial over rural interests, the city over the country, and the rule of interest and utility over the devotion to lofty but intangible goals. The enjoyment of life rather than its mortification, a disposition to cultivate freedom rather than regret it, the celebration of the urbane pleasures of good food, companionship, the appreciation of beauty and music—such were the goals of Spinoza's *optima Republica*.

The number of studies of Spinoza's political thought available in English is limited. Among the better works are Leo Strauss, *Spinoza's Critique of Religion*, translated by E. M. Sinclair (New York: Schocken, 1965), which puts Spinoza's political theory within the context of his critique of theology; Yirmiyahu Yovel, *Spinoza and Other Heretics,* two vols. (Princeton, N.J.: Princeton University Press, 1991), which examines Spinoza's excommunication against the background of the Marrano community of Amsterdam; Antonio Negri, *The Savage Anomaly*, translated by Michael Hardt (Minneapolis: University of Minnesota Press, 1991), a Marxist reading focusing on Spinoza's conception of power as the key to his politics and metaphysics; Steven B. Smith, *Spinoza, Liberalism, and the Question of Jewish Identity* (New Haven, Conn.: Yale University Press, 1997), which interprets Spinoza as an architect of modern Jewish identity; Etienne Balibar, *Spinoza and Politics*, translated by Peter Snowdon (London: Verso, 1998), which provides a useful account of Spinoza's relation to radical currents within Dutch politics of his time; and Steven Nadler, *Spinoza: A Life* (Cambridge: Cambridge University Press, 1999), an excellent biographical introduction.

# Theologico-Political Treatise

## CHAPTER XVI

### Of the Foundations of a State; Of the Natural and Civil Rights of Individuals; and Of the Rights of the Sovereign Power

Hitherto our care has been to separate philosophy from theology, and to show the freedom of thought which such separation insures to both. It is now time to determine the limits to which such freedom of thought and discussion may extend itself in the ideal state. For the due consideration of this question we must examine the foundations of a state, first turning our attention to the natural rights of individuals, and afterwards to religion and the state as a whole.

By the right and ordinance of nature, I merely mean those natural laws wherewith we conceive every individual to be conditioned by nature, so as to live and act in a given way. For instance, fishes are naturally conditioned for swimming, and the greater for devouring the less; therefore fishes enjoy the water, and the greater devour the less by sovereign natural right. For it is certain that nature, taken in the abstract, has sovereign right to do anything she can; in other words, her right is co-extensive with her power. The power of nature is the power of God, which has sovereign right over all things; and, inasmuch as the power of nature is simply the aggregate of the powers of all her individual components, it follows that every individual has sovereign right to do all that he can; in other words, the rights of an individual extend to the utmost limits of his power as it has been conditioned. Now it is the sovereign law and right of nature that each individual should endeavour to preserve itself as it is, without regard to anything but itself; therefore this sovereign law and right

belongs to every individual, namely, to exist and act according to its natural conditions. We do not here acknowledge any difference between mankind and other individual natural entities, nor between men endowed with reason and those to whom reason is unknown; nor between fools, madmen, and sane men. Whatsoever an individual does by the laws of its nature it has a sovereign right to do, inasmuch as it acts as it was conditioned by nature, and cannot act otherwise. Wherefore among men, so long as they are considered as living under the sway of nature, he who does not yet know reason, or who has not yet acquired the habit of virtue, acts solely according to the laws of his desire with as sovereign a right as he who orders his life entirely by the laws of reason.

That is, as the wise man has sovereign right to do all that reason dictates, or to live according to the Laws of reason, as also the ignorant and foolish man has sovereign right to do all that desire dictates, or to live according to the laws of desire. This is identical with the teaching of Paul, who acknowledges that previous to the law—that is, as long as men are considered of as living under the sway of nature, there is no sin.

The natural right of the individual man is thus determined, not by sound reason, but by desire and power. All are not naturally conditioned so as to act according to the laws and rules of reason; nay, on the contrary, all men are born ignorant, and before they can learn the right way of life and acquire the habit of virtue, the greater part of their life, even if they have been well brought up, has passed away. Nevertheless, they are in the meanwhile bound to live and preserve themselves as far as they can by the unaided impulses of desire. Nature has given them no other guide, and has denied them the present

Translated by R. H. M. Elwes.

power of living according to sound reason; so that they are no more bound to live by the dictates of an enlightened mind, than a cat is bound to live by the laws of the nature of a lion.

Whatsoever, therefore, an individual (considered as under the sway of nature) thinks useful for himself, whether led by sound reason or impelled by the passions, that he has a sovereign right to seek and to take for himself as he best can, whether by force, cunning, entreaty, or any other means; consequently he may regard as an enemy anyone who hinders the accomplishment of his purpose.

It follows from what we have said that the right and ordinance of nature, under which all men are born, and under which they mostly live, only prohibits such things as no one desires, and no one can attain: it does not forbid strife, nor hatred, nor anger, nor deceit, nor, indeed, any of the means suggested by desire.

This we need not wonder at, for nature is not bounded by the laws of human reason, which aims only at man's true benefit and preservation; her limits are infinitely wider, and have reference to the eternal order of nature, wherein man is but a speck; it is by the necessity of this alone that all individuals are conditioned for living and acting in a particular way. If anything, therefore, in nature seems to us ridiculous, absurd, or evil, it is because we only know in part, and are almost entirely ignorant of the order and interdependence of nature as a whole, and also because we want everything to be arranged according to the dictates of our human reason; in reality that which reason considers evil, is not evil in respect to the order and laws of nature as a whole, but only in respect to the laws of our reason.

Nevertheless, no one can doubt that it is much better for us to live according to the laws and assured dictates of reason, for, as we said, they have men's true good for their object. Moreover, everyone wishes to live as far as possible securely beyond the reach of fear, and this would be quite impossible so long as everyone did everything he liked, and reason's claim was lowered to a par with those of hatred and anger; there is no one who is not ill at ease in the midst of enmity, co-extensive with my power) that if I can free myself from this robber by stratagem, by assenting to his demands, I have the natural right to do so, and to pretend to accept his conditions. Or again, suppose I have genuinely promised someone that for the space of twenty days I will not taste food or any nourishment; and suppose I afterwards find that my promise was foolish, and cannot be kept without very great injury to myself; as I am bound by natural law and right to choose the least of two evils, I have complete right to break my compact, and act as if my promise had never been uttered. I say that I should have perfect natural right to do so, whether I was actuated by true and evident reason, or whether I was actuated by mere opinion in thinking I had promised rashly; whether my reasons were true or false, I should be in fear of a greater evil, which, by the ordinance of nature, I should strive to avoid by every means in my power.

We may, therefore, conclude that a compact is only made valid by its utility, without which it becomes null and void. It is, therefore, foolish to ask a man to keep his faith with us for ever, unless we also endeavour that the violation of the compact we enter into shall involve for the violator more harm than good. This consideration should have very great weight in forming a state. However, if all men could be easily led by reason alone, and could recognize what is best and most useful for a state, there would be no one who would not forswear deceit, for every one would keep most religiously to their compact in their desire for the chief good, namely, the preservation of the state, and would cherish good faith above all things as the shield and buckler of the commonwealth. However, it is far from being the case that all men can always be easily led by reason alone; everyone is drawn away by his pleasure, while avarice, ambition, envy, hatred, and the like so engross the mind that reason has no place therein. Hence, though men make promises with all the appearances of good faith, and agree that they will keep to their engagement, no one can absolutely rely on another man's promise unless there is something behind it. Everyone has by nature a right to act deceitfully, and to

break his compacts, unless he be restrained by the hope of some greater good, or the fear of some greater evil.

However, as we have shown that the natural right of the individual is only limited by his power, it is clear that by transferring, either willingly or under compulsion, this power into the hands of another, he in so doing necessarily cedes also a part of his right; and further, that the sovereign right over all men belongs to him who has sovereign power, wherewith he can compel men by force, or restrain them by threats of the universally feared punishment of death; such sovereign right he will retain only so long as he can maintain his power of enforcing his will; otherwise he will totter on his throne, and no one who is stronger than he will be bound unwillingly to obey him.

In this manner a society can be formed without any violation of natural right, and the covenant can always be strictly kept—that is, if each individual hands over the whole of his power to the body politic, the latter will then possess sovereign natural right over all things; that is, it will have sole and unquestioned dominion, and everyone will be bound to obey, under pain of the severest punishment. A body politic of this kind is called a Democracy, which may be defined as a society which wields all its power as a whole. The sovereign power is not restrained by any laws, but everyone is bound to obey it in all things; such is the state of things implied when men either tacitly or expressly handed over to it all their power of self-defence, or in other words, all their right. For if they had wished to retain any right for themselves, they ought to have taken precautions for its defence and preservation; as they have not done so, and indeed could not have done so without dividing and consequently ruining the state, they placed themselves absolutely at the mercy of the sovereign power; and, therefore, having acted (as we have shown) as reason and necessity demanded, they are obliged to fulfil the commands of the sovereign power, however absurd these may be, else they will be public enemies, and will act against reason, which urges the preservation of the state as a primary duty. For reason bids us choose the least of two evils.

Furthermore, this danger of submitting absolutely to the dominion and will of another, is one which may be incurred with a light heart: for we have shown that sovereigns only possess this right of imposing their will, so long as they have the full power to enforce it: if such power be lost their right to command is lost also, or lapses to those who have assumed it and can keep it. Thus it is very rare for sovereigns to impose thoroughly irrational commands, for they are bound to consult their own interests, and retain their power by consulting the public good and acting according to the dictates of reason, as Seneca says, "violenta imperia nemo continuit diu." No one can long retain a tyrant's sway.

In a democracy, irrational commands are still less to be feared: for it is almost impossible that the majority of a people, especially if it be a large one, should agree in an irrational design: and, moreover, the basis and aim of a democracy is to avoid the desires as irrational, and to bring men as far as possible under the control of reason, so that they may live in peace and harmony: if this basis be removed the whole fabric falls to ruin.

Such being the ends in view for the sovereign power, the duty of subjects is, as I have said, to obey its commands, and to recognize no right save that which it sanctions.

It will, perhaps, be thought that we are turning subjects into slaves: for slaves obey commands and free men live as they like; but this idea is based on a misconception, for the true slave is he who is led away by his pleasures and can neither see what is good for him nor act accordingly: he alone is free who lives with free consent under the entire guidance of reason.

Action in obedience to orders does take away freedom in a certain sense, but it does not, therefore, make a man a slave, all depends on the object of the action. If the object of the action be the good of the state, and not the good of the agent, the latter is a slave and does himself no good. But in a state or kingdom where the weal of the whole people, and not that of

the ruler, is the supreme law, obedience to the sovereign power does not make a man a slave, of no use to himself, but a subject. Therefore, that state is the freest whose laws are founded on sound reason, so that every member of it may, if he will, be free; that is, live with full consent under the entire guidance of reason.

Children, though they are bound to obey all the commands of their parents, are yet not slaves: for the commands of parents look generally to the children's benefit.

We must, therefore, acknowledge a great difference between a slave, a son, and a subject; their positions may be thus defined. A slave is one who is bound to obey his master's orders, though they are given solely in the master's interest: a son is one who obeys his father's orders, given in his own interest; a subject obeys the orders of the sovereign power, given for the common interest, wherein he is included.

I think I have now shown sufficiently clearly the basis of a democracy: I have especially desired to do so, for I believe it to be of all forms of government the most natural, and the most consonant with individual liberty. In it no one transfers his natural right so absolutely that he has no further voice in affairs, he only hands it over to the majority of a society, whereof he is a unit. Thus all men remain, as they were in the state of nature, equals.

This is the only form of government which I have treated of at length, for it is the one most akin to my purpose of showing the benefits of freedom in a state.

I may pass over the fundamental principles of other forms of government, for we may gather from what has been said whence their right arises without going into its origin. The possessor of sovereign power, whether he be one, or many, or the whole body politic, has the sovereign right of imposing any commands he pleases: and he who has either voluntarily, or under compulsion, transferred the right to defend him to another, has, in so doing, renounced his natural right and is therefore bound to obey, in all things, the commands of the sovereign power; and will be bound so to do so long as the king, or nobles, or the people preserve the sovereign power which formed the basis of the original transfer. I need add no more.

The bases and rights of dominion being thus displayed, we shall readily be able to define private civil right, wrong, justice, and injustice, with their relations to the state; and also to determine what constitutes an ally, or an enemy, or the crime of treason.

By private civil right we can only mean the liberty every man possesses to preserve his existence, a liberty limited by the edicts of the sovereign power, and preserved only by its authority: for when a man has transferred to another his right of living as he likes, which was only limited by his power, that is, has transferred his liberty and power of self-defence, he is bound to live as that other dictates, and to trust to him entirely for his defence. Wrong takes place when a citizen, or subject, is forced by another to undergo some loss or pain in contradiction to the authority of the law, or the edict of the sovereign power.

Wrong is conceivable only in an organized community: nor can it ever accrue to subjects from any act of the sovereign, who has the right to do what he likes. It can only arise, therefore, between private persons, who are bound by law and right not to injure one another. Justice consists in the habitual rendering to every man his lawful due: injustice consists in depriving a man, under the pretence of legality, of what the laws, rightly interpreted, would allow him. These last are also called equity and iniquity, because those who administer the laws are bound to show no respect of persons, but to account all men equal, and to defend every man's right equally, neither envying the rich nor despising the poor.

The men of two states become allies, when for the sake of avoiding war, or for some other advantage, they covenant to do each other no hurt, but on the contrary, to assist each other if necessity arises, each retaining his independence. Such a covenant is valid so long as its basis of danger or advantage is in force: no one enters into an engagement, or is bound to stand by his compacts unless there be a hope of some accruing good, or the fear of some evil: if this basis be removed the compact thereby becomes void: this has been abundantly shown by experience. For although

different states make treaties not to harm one another, they always take every possible precaution against such treaties being broken by the stronger party, and do not rely on the compact, unless there is a sufficiently obvious object and advantage to both parties in observing it. Otherwise they would fear a breach of faith, nor would there be any wrong done thereby: for who in his proper senses, and aware of the right of the sovereign power, would trust in the promises of one who has the will and the power to do what he likes, and who aims solely at the safety and advantage of his dominion? Moreover, if we consult loyalty and religion, we shall see that no one in possession of power ought to abide by his promises to the injury of his dominion; for he cannot keep such promises without breaking the engagement he made with his subjects, by which both he and they are most solemnly bound.

An enemy is one who lives apart from the state, and does not recognize its authority either as a subject or as an ally. It is not hatred which makes a man an enemy, but the rights of the state. The rights of the state are the same in regard to him who does not recognize by any compact the state authority, as they are against him who has done the state an injury: it has the right to force him as best it can, either to submit, or to contract an alliance.

Lastly, treason can only be committed by subjects, who by compact, either tacit or expressed, have transferred all their rights to the state: a subject is said to have committed this crime when he has attempted, for whatever reason, to seize the sovereign power, or to place it in different hands. I say, *has attempted*, for if punishment were not to overtake him till he had succeeded, it would often come too late, the sovereign rights would have been acquired or transferred already.

I also say, *has attempted, for whatever reason, to seize the sovereign power*, and I recognize no difference whether such an attempt should be followed by public loss or public gain. Whatever be his reason for acting, the crime is treason, and he is rightly condemned: in war, everyone would admit the justice of his sentence. If a man does not keep to his post, but approaches the enemy without the knowledge of his commander, whatever may be his motive, so long as he acts on his own motion, even if he advances with the design of defeating the enemy, he is rightly put to death, because he has violated his oath, and infringed the rights of his commander. That all citizens are equally bound by these rights in time of peace, is not so generally recognized, but the reasons for obedience are in both cases, identical. The state must be preserved and directed by the sole authority of the sovereign, and such authority and right have been accorded by universal consent to him alone: if, therefore, anyone else attempts, without his consent, to execute any public enterprise, even though the state might (as we said) reap benefit therefrom, such person has none the less infringed the sovereign's right, and would be rightly punished for treason.

In order that every scruple may be removed, we may now answer the inquiry, whether our former assertion that everyone who has not the practice of reason, may, in the state of nature, live by sovereign natural right, according to the laws of his desires, is not in direct opposition to the law and right of God as revealed. For as all men absolutely (whether they be less endowed with reason or more) are equally bound by the Divine command to love their neighbour as themselves, it may be said that they cannot, without wrong, do injury to anyone, or live according to their desires.

This objection, so far as the state of nature is concerned, can be easily answered, for the state of nature is, both in nature and in time, prior to religion. No one knows by nature that he owes any obedience to God, nor can he attain thereto by any exercise of his reason, but solely by revelation confirmed by signs. Therefore, previous to revelation, no one is bound by a Divine law and right of which he is necessarily in ignorance. The state of nature must by no means be confounded with a state of religion, but must be conceived as without either religion or law, and consequently without sin or wrong: this is how we have described it, and we are confirmed by the authority of Paul. It is not only in respect of ignorance that we conceive the state of nature as prior to,

and lacking the Divine revealed law and right; but in respect of freedom also, wherewith all men are born endowed.

If men were naturally bound by the Divine law and right, or if the Divine law and right were a natural necessity, there would have been no need for God to make a covenant with mankind, and to bind them thereto with an oath and agreement.

We must, then, fully grant that the Divine law and right originated at the time when men by express covenant agreed to obey God in all things, and ceded, as it were, their natural freedom, transferring their rights to God in the manner described in speaking of the formation of a state.

However, I will treat of these matters more at length presently.

It may be insisted that sovereigns are as much bound by the Divine law as subjects: whereas we have asserted that they retain their natural rights, and may do whatever they like.

In order to clear up the whole difficulty, which arises rather concerning the natural right than the natural state, I maintain that everyone is bound, in the state of nature, to live according to Divine law, in the same way as he is bound to fire according to the dictates of sound reason; namely, inasmuch as it is to his advantage, and necessary for his salvation; but, if he will not so live, he may do otherwise at his own risk. He is thus bound to live according to his own laws, not according to anyone else's, and to recognize no man as a judge, or as a superior in religion. Such, in my opinion, is the position of a sovereign, for he may take advice from his fellow-men, but he is not bound to recognize any as a judge, nor anyone besides himself as an arbitrator on any question of right, unless it be a prophet sent expressly by God and attesting his mission by indisputable signs. Even then he does not recognize a man, but God Himself as His judge.

If a sovereign refuses to obey God as revealed in His law, he does so at his own risk and loss, but without violating any civil or natural right. For the civil right is dependent on his own decree; and natural right is dependent on the laws of nature, which latter are not adapted to religion, whose sole aim is the good of humanity, but to the order of nature—that is, to God's eternal decree unknown to us.

This truth seems to be adumbrated in a somewhat obscurer form by those who maintain that men can sin against God's revelation, but not against the eternal decree by which He has ordained all things.

We may be asked, what should we do if the sovereign commands anything contrary to religion, and the obedience which we have expressly vowed to God? should we obey the Divine law or the human law? I shall treat of this question at length hereafter, and will therefore merely say now, that God should be obeyed before all else, when we have a certain and indisputable revelation of His will: but men are very prone to error on religious subjects, and, according to the diversity of their dispositions, are wont with considerable stir to put forward their own inventions, as experience more than sufficiently attests, so that if no one were bound to obey the state in matters which, in his own opinion concern religion, the rights of the state would be dependent on every man's judgment and passions. No one would consider himself bound to obey laws framed against his faith or superstition; and on this pretext he might assume unbounded license. In this way, the rights of the civil authorities would be utterly set at nought, so that we must conclude that the sovereign power, which alone is bound both by Divine and natural right to preserve and guard the laws of the state, should have supreme authority for making any laws about religion which it thinks fit; all are bound to obey its behests on the subject in accordance with their promise which God bids them to keep.

However, if the sovereign power be heathen, we should either enter into no engagements therewith, and yield up our lives sooner than transfer to it any of our rights; or, if the engagement be made, and our rights transferred, we should (inasmuch as we should have ourselves transferred the right of defending ourselves and our religion) be bound to obey them, and to keep our word: we might even rightly be bound so to do, except in those cases where God, by indisputable revelation, has promised His special aid against tyranny, or given us special exemption from obedience. Thus we see that, of all the Jews in Babylon,

there were only three youths who were certain of the help of God, and, therefore, refused to obey Nebuchadnezzar. All the rest, with the sole exception of Daniel, who was beloved by the king, were doubtless compelled by right to obey, perhaps thinking that they had been delivered up by God into the hands of the king, and that the king had obtained and preserved his dominion by God's design. On the other hand, Eleazar, before his country had utterly fallen, wished to give a proof of his constancy to his compatriots, in order that they might follow in his footsteps, and go to any lengths, rather than allow their right and power to be transferred to the Greeks, or brave any torture rather than swear allegiance to the heathen. Instances are occurring every day in confirmation of what I here advance. The rulers of Christian kingdoms do not hesitate, with a view to strengthening their dominion, to make treaties with Turks and heathen, and to give orders to their subjects who settle among such peoples not to assume more freedom, either in things secular or religious, than is set down in the treaty, or allowed by the foreign government. We may see this exemplified in the Dutch treaty with the Japanese, which I have already mentioned.

## CHAPTER XX

### *That in a Free State Every Man May Think What He Likes, and Say What He Thinks*

If men's minds were as easily controlled as their tongues, every king would sit safely on his throne, and government by compulsion would cease; for every subject would shape his life according to the intentions of his rulers, and would esteem a thing true or false, good or evil, just or unjust, in obedience to their dictates. However, we have shown already (Chapter XVII) that no man's mind can possibly lie wholly at the disposition of another, for no one can willingly transfer his natural right of free reason and judgment, or be compelled so to do. For this reason government which attempts to control minds is accounted tyrannical, and it is considered an abuse of sovereignty and a usurpation of the rights of subjects, to seek to prescribe what shall be accepted as true, or rejected as false, or what opinions should actuate men in their worship of God. All these questions fall within a man's natural right, which he cannot abdicate even with his own consent.

I admit that the judgment can be biased in many ways, and to an almost incredible degree, so that while exempt from direct external control it may be so dependent on another man's words, that it may fitly be said to be ruled by him; but although this influence is carried to great lengths, it has never gone so far as to invalidate the statement, that every man's understanding is his own, and that brains are as diverse as palates.

Moses, not by fraud, but by Divine virtue, gained such a hold over the popular judgment that he was accounted superhuman, and believed to speak and act through the inspiration of the Deity; nevertheless, even he could not escape murmurs and evil interpretations. How much less then can other monarchs avoid them! Yet such unlimited power, if it exists at all, must belong to a monarch, and least of all to a democracy, where the whole or a great part of the people wield authority collectively. This is a fact which I think everyone can explain for himself.

However unlimited, therefore, the power of a sovereign may be, however implicitly it is trusted as the exponent of law and religion, it can never prevent men from forming judgments according to their intellect, or being influenced by any given emotion. It is true that it has the right to treat as enemies all men whose opinions do not, on all subjects, entirely coincide with its own; but we are not discussing its strict rights, but its proper course of action. I grant that it has the right to rule in the most violent manner, and to put citizens to death for very trivial causes, but no one supposes it can do this with the approval of sound judgment. Nay, inasmuch as such things cannot be done without extreme peril to itself, we may even deny that it has the absolute power to do them, or, consequently, the absolute right; for the rights of the sovereign are limited by his power.

Since, therefore, no one can abdicate his freedom of judgment and feeling; since every man is by inde-

feasible natural right the master of his own thoughts, it follows that men thinking in diverse and contradictory fashions, cannot, without disastrous results, be compelled to speak only according to the dictates of the supreme power. Not even the most experienced, to say nothing of the multitude, know how to keep silence. Men's common failing is to confide their plans to others, though there be need for secrecy, so that a government would be most harsh which deprived the individual of his freedom of saying and teaching what he thought; and would be moderate if such freedom were granted. Still we cannot deny that authority may be as much injured by words as by actions; hence, although the freedom we are discussing cannot be entirely denied to subjects, its unlimited concession would be most baneful; we must, therefore, now inquire, how far such freedom can and ought to be conceded without danger to the peace of the state, or the power of the rulers; and this, as I said at the beginning of Chapter XVI, is my principal object.

It follows, plainly, from the explanation given above, of the foundations of a state, that the ultimate aim of government is not to rule, or restrain, by fear, nor to exact obedience, but contrariwise, to free every man from fear, that he may live in all possible security; in other words, to strengthen his natural right to exist and work without injury to himself or others.

No, the object of government is not to change men from rational beings into beasts or puppets, but to enable them to develop their minds and bodies in security, and to employ their reason unshackled; neither showing hatred, anger, or deceit, nor watched with the eyes of jealousy and injustice. In fact, the true aim of government is liberty.

Now we have seen that in forming a state the power of making laws must either be vested in the body of the citizens, or in a portion of them, or in one man. For, although men's free judgments are very diverse, each one thinking that he alone knows everything, and although complete unanimity of feeling and speech is out of the question, it is impossible to preserve peace, unless individuals abdicate their right of acting entirely on their own judgment. Therefore, the individual justly cedes the right of free action, though not of free reason and judgment; no one can act against the authorities without danger to the state, though his feelings and judgment may be at varience therewith; he may even speak against them, provided that he does so from rational conviction, not from fraud, anger, or hatred, and provided that he does not attempt to introduce any change on his private authority.

For instance, supposing a man shows that a law is repugnant to sound reason, and should therefore be repealed; if he submits his opinion to the judgment of the authorities (who, alone, have the right of making and repealing laws), and meanwhile acts in nowise contrary to that law, he has deserved well of the state, and has behaved as a good citizen should; but if he accuses the authorities of injustice, and stirs up the people against them, or if he seditiously strives to abrogate the law without their consent, he is a mere agitator and rebel.

Thus we see how an individual may declare and teach what he believes, without injury to the authority of his rulers, or to the public peace; namely, by leaving in their hands the entire power of legislation as it affects action, and by doing nothing against their laws, though he be compelled often to act in contradiction to what he believes, and openly feels, to be best.

Such a course can be taken without detriment to justice and dutifulness, nay, it is the one which a just and dutiful man would adopt. We have shown that justice is dependent on the laws of the authorities, so that no one who contravenes their accepted decrees can be just, while the highest regard for duty, as we have pointed out in the preceding chapter, is exercised in maintaining public peace and tranquillity; these could not be preserved if every man were to live as he pleased; therefore it is no less than undutiful for a man to act contrary to his country's laws, for if the practice became universal the ruin of states would necessarily follow.

Hence, so long as a man acts in obedience to the laws of his rulers, he in nowise contravenes his reason, for in obedience to reason he transferred the right of controlling his actions from his own hands to theirs. This doctrine we can confirm from actual custom, for in a conference of great and small powers, schemes are seldom carried unanimously, yet all unite in carrying out what is decided on, whether they voted for or against. But I return to my proposition.

From the fundamental notions of a state, we have discovered how a man may exercise free judgment without detriment to the supreme power: from the same premises we can no less easily determine what opinions would be seditious. Evidently those which by their very nature nullify the compact by which the right of free action was ceded. For instance, a man who holds that the supreme power has no rights over him, or that promises ought not to be kept, or that everyone should live as he pleases, or other doctrines of this nature in direct opposition to the above-mentioned contract, is seditious, not so much from his actual opinions and judgment, as from the deeds which they involve; for he who maintains such theories abrogates the contract which tacitly, or openly, he made with his rulers. Other opinions which do not involve acts violating the contract, such as revenge, anger, and the like, are not seditious, unless it be in some corrupt state, where superstitious and ambitious persons, unable to endure men of learning, are so popular with the multitude that their word is more valued than the law.

However, I do not deny that there are some doctrines which, while they are apparently only concerned with abstract truths and falsehoods, are yet propounded and published with unworthy motives. This question we have discussed in Chapter XV, and shown that reason should nevertheless remain unshackled. If we hold to the principle that a man's loyalty to the state should be judged, like his loyalty to God, from his actions only—namely, from his charity towards his neighbours; we cannot doubt that the best government will allow freedom of philosophical speculation no less than of religious belief. I confess that from such freedom inconveniences may sometimes arise, but what question was ever settled so wisely that no abuses could possibly spring therefrom? He who seeks to regulate everything by law, is more likely to arouse vices than to reform them. It is best to grant what cannot be abolished, even though it be in itself harmful. How many evils spring from luxury, envy, avarice, drunkenness, and the like, yet these are tolerated—vices as they are—because they cannot be prevented by legal enactments. How much more then should free thought be granted, seeing that it is in itself a virtue and that it cannot be crushed! Besides, the evil results can easily be checked, as I will show, by the secular authorities, not to mention that such freedom is absolutely necessary for progress in science and the liberal arts: for no man follows such pursuits to advantage unless his judgment be entirely free and unhampered.

But let it be granted that freedom may be crushed, and men be so bound down, that they do not dare to utter a whisper, save at the bidding of their rulers; nevertheless this can never be carried to the pitch of making them think according to authority, so that the necessary consequences would be that men would daily be thinking one thing and saying another, to the corruption of good faith, that mainstay of government, and to the fostering of hateful flattery and perfidy, whence spring stratagems, and the corruption of every good art.

It is far from possible to impose uniformity of speech, for the more rulers strive to curtail freedom of speech, the more obstinately are they resisted; not indeed by the avaricious, the flatterers, and other numskulls, who think supreme salvation consists in filling their stomachs and gloating over their money-bags, but by those whom good education, sound morality, and virtue have rendered more free. Men, as generally constituted, are most prone to resent the branding as criminal of opinions which they believe to be true, and the prescription as wicked of that which inspires them with piety towards God and man; hence they are ready to forswear the laws and conspire against the authorities, thinking it not shameful but honourable to stir up seditions and perpetuate any sort of crime with this end in view. Such being the constitution of human nature, we see that laws directed against opinions affect the generous-minded rather than the wicked, and are adapted less for coercing criminals than for irritating the upright; so that they cannot be maintained without great peril to the state.

Moreover, such laws are almost always useless, for those who hold that the opinions proscribed are sound, cannot possibly obey the law; whereas those who already reject them as false, accept the law as a kind of privilege, and make such boast of it, that authority is powerless to repeal it, even if such a course be subsequently desired.

To these considerations may be added what we said in Chapter XVIII in treating of the history of the Hebrews. And, lastly, how many schisms have arisen in the Church from the attempt of the authorities to decide by law the intricacies of theological controversy! If men were not allured by the hope of getting the law and the authorities on their side, of triumphing over their adversaries in the sight of an applauding multitude, and of acquiring honourable distinctions, they would not strive so maliciously, nor would such fury sway their minds. This is taught not only by reason but by daily examples, for laws of this kind prescribing what every man shall believe and forbidding anyone to speak or write to the contrary, have often been passed, as sops or concessions to the anger of those who cannot tolerate men of enlightenment, and who, by such harsh and crooked enactments, can easily turn the devotion of the masses into fury and direct it against whom they will.

How much better would it be to restrain popular anger and fury, instead of passing useless laws, which can only be broken by those who love virtue and the liberal arts, thus paring down the state till it is too small to harbour men of talent. What greater misfortune for a state can be conceived than that honourable men should be sent like criminals into exile, because they hold diverse opinions which they cannot disguise? What, I say, can be more hurtful than that men who have committed no crime or wickedness should, simply because they are enlightened, be treated as enemies and put to death, and that the scaffold, the terror of evil-doers, should become the arena where the highest examples of tolerance and virtue are displayed to the people with all the marks of ignominy that authority can devise?

He that knows himself to be upright does not fear the death of a criminal, and shrinks from no punishment; his mind is not wrung with remorse for any disgraceful deed: he holds that death in a good cause is no punishment, but an honour, and that death for freedom is glory.

What purpose then is served by the death of such men, what example is proclaimed? The cause for which they die is unknown to the idle and the foolish, hateful to the turbulent, loved by the upright. The only lesson we can draw from such scenes is to flatter the persecutor, or else to imitate the victim.

If formal assent is not to be esteemed above conviction, and if governments are to retain a firm hold of authority and not be compelled to yield to agitators, it is imperative that freedom of judgment should be granted, so that men may live together in harmony, however diverse, or even openly contradictory their opinions may be. We cannot doubt that such is the best system of government and open to the fewest objections, since it is the one most in harmony with human nature. In a democracy (the most natural form of government, as we have shown in Chapter XVI) everyone submits to the control of authority over his actions, but not over his judgment and reason; that is, seeing that all cannot think alike, the voice of the majority has the force of law, subject to repeal if circumstances bring about a change of opinion. In proportion as the power of free judgment is withheld we depart from the natural condition of mankind, and consequently the government becomes more tyrannical.

In order to prove that from such freedom no inconvenience arises, which cannot easily be checked by the exercise of the sovereign power, and that men's actions can easily be kept in bounds, though their opinions be at open varience, it will be well to cite an example. Such an one is not very far to seek. The city of Amsterdam reaps the fruit of this freedom in its own great prosperity and in the admiration of all other people. For in this most flourishing state, and most splendid city, men of every nation and religion live together in the greatest harmony, and ask no questions before trusting their goods to a fellow-citizen, save whether he be rich or poor, and whether he generally acts honestly, or the reverse. His religion and sect is considered of no importance: for it has no effect before the judges in gaining or losing a cause,

and there is no sect so despised that its followers, provided that they harm no one, pay every man his due, and live uprightly, are deprived of the protection of the magisterial authority.

On the other hand, when the religious controversy between Remonstrants and Counter-Remonstrants began to be taken up by politicians and the States, it grew into a schism, and abundantly showed that laws dealing with religion and seeking to settle its controversies are much more calculated to irritate than to reform, and that they give rise to extreme licence: further, it was seen that schisms do not originate in a love of truth, which is a source of courtesy and gentleness, but rather in an inordinate desire for supremacy. From all these considerations it is clearer than the sun at noonday, that the true schismatics are those who condemn other men's writings, and seditiously stir up the quarrelsome masses against their authors, rather than those authors themselves, who generally write only for the learned, and appeal solely to reason. In fact, the real disturbers of the peace are those who, in a free state, seek to curtail the liberty of judgment which they are unable to tyrannize over.

I have thus shown:—I. That it is impossible to deprive men of the liberty of saying what they think. II. That such liberty can be conceded to every man without injury to the rights and authority of the sovereign power, and that every man may retain it without injury to such rights, provided that he does not presume upon it to the extent of introducing any new rights into the state, or acting in any way contrary to the existing laws. III. That every man may enjoy this liberty without detriment to the public peace, and that no inconveniences arise therefrom which cannot easily be checked. IV. That everyman may enjoy it without injury to his allegiance. V. That laws dealing with speculative problems are entirely useless. VI. Lastly, that not only may such liberty be granted without prejudice to the public peace, to loyalty, and to the rights of rulers, but that it is even necessary for their preservation. For when people try to take it away, and bring to trial not only the acts which alone are capable of offending, but also the opinions of mankind, they only succeed in surrounding their victims with an appearance of martyrdom, and raise feelings of pity and revenge rather than of terror. Uprightness and good faith are thus corrupted, flatterers and traitors are encouraged, and sectarians triumph, inasmuch as concessions have been made to their animosity, and they have gained the state sanction for the doctrines of which they are the interpreters. Hence they arrogate to themselves the state authority and rights, and do not scruple to assert that they have been directly chosen by God, and that their laws are Divine, whereas the laws of the state are human, and should therefore yield obedience to the laws of God—in other words, to their own laws. Everyone must see that this is not a state of affairs conducive to public welfare. Wherefore, as we have shown in Chapter XVIII, the safest way for a state is to lay down the rule that religion is comprised solely in the exercise of charity and justice, and that the rights of rulers in sacred, no less than in secular matters, should merely have to do with actions, but that every man should think what he likes and say what he thinks.

I have thus fulfilled the task I set myself in this treatise. It remains only to call attention to the fact that I have written nothing which I do not most willingly submit to the examination and approval of my country's rulers; and that I am willing to retract anything which they shall decide to be repugnant to the laws, or prejudicial to the public good. I know that I am a man, and as a man liable to error, but against error I have taken scrupulous care, and have striven to keep in entire accordance with the laws of my country, with loyalty, and with morality.

# JOHN LOCKE

~

## INTRODUCTION

### A. JOHN SIMMONS

John Locke was born in Somerset, England, in 1632, the son of an attorney and small landowner. Locke's family had Puritan leanings, and his father served during Locke's youth in one of the parliamentary armies fighting the forces of Charles I during the civil war. Thanks to his father's connections, Locke received an excellent education of the sort generally reserved for the more privileged, concluding at Christ Church, Oxford, with which Locke remained associated in various capacities until 1684. Locke's (unpublished) writings from his time at Christ Church (in the early 1660s) were surprisingly illiberal, arguing against many of the positions we would today identify as paradigmatically Lockean (such as religious toleration and popular consent as the basis of political authority). Locke's turn toward more liberal views seems to have been a product of his close association with Lord Ashley, later the first Earl of Shaftesbury, for whom Locke served in various positions beginning in 1667. Shaftesbury was a leading Whig politician of the period, and through him Locke gained both intimate knowledge of English political life and an appreciation of the Whig principles that are given philosophical expression and defense in Locke's mature writings.

It was also through Shaftesbury that Locke became involved in the revolutionary political plotting of the early 1680s, in which the opposition Whigs attempted to prevent the Catholic Duke of York (later James II) from succeeding his brother Charles II on the English throne. The full extent of Locke's involvement in the radical Whig plans for assassination and insurrection is not known, but the clear danger of arrest forced Locke to follow Shaftesbury into exile in Holland in 1683. Locke did not return to England until 1689, after the Glorious Revolution and Settlement had removed James and initiated the reign of William and Mary. It was 1689 as well that saw Locke's first publications (at the age of 57), which included all of Locke's best known philosophical works—*An Essay Concerning Human Understanding, Two Treatises of Government,* and *A Letter Concerning Toleration* (though all of these were largely completed considerably earlier and the latter two were published anonymously). Locke spent his remaining years actively, enjoying his new role as a revered intellectual, holding a number of minor political offices, and writing extensively on religion, education, and finance. Locke lived during this period, and eventually died in 1704, at the home of his longtime friend Lady Masham, daughter of the philosopher Ralph Cudworth. Locke's influence on both political philosophy and political practice was considerable; his work inspired later socialists (like the young Marx), liberals, and conservatives alike, and many revolutionaries of the eighteenth century knew and were guided by Locke's work.

Locke is generally characterized as one of the first great liberal political philosophers. While he was certainly not as much of an egalitarian as are most contemporary liberals, this characterization still seems fair; for Locke's entire philosophy (including his epistemology and philosophy of language) sides with individual freedom against the forces of authoritarian repression and inculcation, and Locke was one of the first noteworthy philosophers of whom this was true. Locke straightforwardly embraces the moral and political individualism of liberalism, according to which individual persons are the proper primary subjects of moral judgments and polities must be viewed as artificial constructions for the purpose of serving individuals' interests. Similarly, the hard distinction between the private and public realms, so central to liberal thought, is prominently displayed in Locke's philosophy. According to Locke, my religion is my own business, like my finances, my health, and my family life. What I labor to produce is private to me, an extension of my person. Provided only that I observe the requirements of natural law, these private matters are beyond society's rightful reach.

The public realm, by contrast, is to be thought of as simply a just framework of institutions, designed solely to secure our basic rights and provide what is necessary for a stable, peaceful society, within the limited constraints of which each person may freely choose his or her private lifestyle. The proper end of society, Locke claims, is what people aim at in entering it, which is no more than peace and security for their private endeavors. From this view flows naturally the liberal emphases on limited government and toleration of diverse views and lifestyles. Society should refuse to tolerate only that which endangers others or society (though Locke, notoriously, believed that Catholicism and atheism could be rightly suppressed on these grounds).

The general structure of Locke's moral and political philosophy can be helpfully characterized if we view it as attempting to reveal the nature and limits of the political relationship—that is, of the relationship between persons that makes them members of the same political society (what Locke calls a civil society or commonwealth). This relationship, as Locke understands it, is a moral relationship that can hold only between free persons and that can be based only on freely given consent. The argument of the *Second Treatise* can then be seen as having the following structure: the first six chapters concern *non*political relations; chapters 7 through 9 concern the source or ground of the political relationship; and chapters 10 through 19 concern the forms and limits of the political relationship.

Chapters 1 through 6 are devoted to explaining those relations that are conceptually pre-political, in the sense that they are relations whose moral bases can hold independent of civil society; this is Locke's way of attempting to define the boundaries of the political. Thus, we are offered in these chapters accounts of the state of nature (that relation in which stand any two persons who are not members of the same civil society), the state of war (into which people can enter without civil societies), the right to freedom from subjection (that all who are under the law of nature naturally enjoy), and the natural duties (also imposed by natural law) that stand as moral constraints even in the absence of legal and political institutions. Just punishment, private property, and marital and family rights and responsibilities are all explained in nonlegal, nonpolitical terms; all are possible in the state of nature, without civil laws or states.

This understanding of the natural moral condition of persons then sets the terms for understanding the political relationship, as requiring certain kinds of departures from the natural condition. The right to punish (according to our own conception of what natural law permits), which each possesses naturally, must be surrendered by each to society; a genuine civil society enjoys a moral monopoly on the use of force (except for rightful self-defense) within its territories. Similarly, private property (and particularly property in land) must be subjected to society's jurisdiction; civil societies have the right to enforce their laws throughout (and control the boundaries of) their incorporated territories. The political relationship, then, is defined in terms of transitions from our natural condition, with the rights of civil societies being understood as simply composed from those surrendered by individuals in their transitions from natural to political conditions.

Chapters 7 through 9 of the *Second Treatise* argue for this understanding of the political, maintaining as well that the sole possible source of the transition from natural to political is the voluntary consent of each individual who becomes a member of a civil society. This consent can be either tacit or express, but it is not binding if given under duress. Civil societies originate, Locke maintains, in a contract between all of their members, which transfers rights to the society and which binds the members together into one society committed to mutual security. That society may then entrust the rights it holds to a government, which must exercise those entrusted rights for the common good. Societies or governments that obtain their power in other ways are simply illegitimate (i.e., not genuine civil societies at all).

The remainder of the *Second Treatise* is devoted to elaboration of the limits on and possible forms of the political relationship (and, consequently, of the moral limits on governments), as well as the consequences of societies or governments exceeding those limits. We can only give binding consent, Locke argues, to participate in arrangements that satisfy the demands of natural law and that improve our condition over that which we would enjoy in a state of nature. These limits on our power to bind ourselves set as well the limits on societal and governmental authority famously elaborated by Locke in Chapter 11 of the *Second Treatise;* societies or governments that exceed those limits count as attempting to make war upon or to enslave their subjects, and binding consent to such efforts cannot be given.

Thus, governments that obtain their power by force, rather than by trust from their subjects, or those once-legitimate governments that exceed the limits of authority to which we can give binding consent (as Locke supposed the government of the Stuart monarchs had done), simply fail to possess any de jure authority at all. Such illegitimate powers can be rightfully resisted (by any wronged individual), removed from power, and forced to make reparations for harms done in their wrongful uses of coercion, just as a highwayman or a pirate can rightfully be treated. Locke's language even suggests his approval of tyrannicide (a quite radical position for Locke's day), since those who make unjust war upon (or attempt to enslave) others can, according to the argument of chapters 3 and 4, be justifiably killed at will by those they have wronged.

The most central and most influential theses of the *Second Treatise* seem to be these: (a) that all persons are naturally free, born to (and enjoying fully on achieving mature rationality) a set of natural rights to freely govern their own lives within the bounds of natural law; (b) that labor is the sole source of original property, grounding for the laborer private property rights in the products of that labor (provided that enough and as good of what nature provides is left for others to claim through their labor); (c) that free consent is the sole source of legitimate political authority and of the correlative political obligations of citizens in a civil society; (d) that political authority is limited in its legitimate scope to securing by legal coercion persons' natural rights to life, liberty, health, and estate; and (e) that popular resistance to government, including resistance by force, is justified wherever governments cause serious harm to persons by operating beyond these limits on political authority.

The relations between the arguments of the *Second Treatise* and those of *A Letter Concerning Toleration* are not entirely clear, for nowhere in the *Treatises* does Locke discuss (or even mention) religious toleration (nor does he directly mention or closely reproduce any of the arguments of the *Treatises* in the *Letter*). The explanation for this is certainly not that Locke regarded questions of religious toleration as of secondary importance in his political philosophy, for he had written extensively on them throughout his adult life (and he added three more letters on the subject after the first, the last of which he was writing at the time of his death). Perhaps their omission from the *Treatises* was due to Locke's fear that his views on toleration would lack wide appeal, thus diluting the influence of a text (the *Treatises*) that was designed to encourage popular resistance to the government.

Nonetheless, it is easy to read the *Letter* as simply an unincorporated part of the argument of the *Second Treatise*. For Locke uses in the *Letter* the same kinds of arguments used in the *Second Treatise* to establish the limits on the authority of societies and governments. Here, however, they are used to establish the conclusion that toleration of diverse (harmless) religious practices is required within a legitimate civil society. The argument from the limits on binding consent again appears, though in a different form: the people cannot consent to (hence, render legitimate) policies of religious intolerance, Locke argues, because they cannot conform their wills in matters of religious belief to an authority's commands. And Locke again argues that the civil magistrate's (or government's) authority is limited to that which is necessary to the end of civil society, which is again characterized in terms of securing individuals' possession and pursuit of their civil interests (in life, liberty, health, and property). Since control over people's (harmless) religious practices is not necessary to this end, religious toleration is required, as part of respecting the rights the people must be understood to retain in any consensual creation of civil society.

The magistrate's monopoly on the use of force, essential for securing the people's property (i.e., their rights), can have no role in securing for them salvation. Our political authorities are no more likely than we to know, are far less interested in our progress on than are we, and can in any event do with coercion nothing to advance us down, the road to knowledge and sincere practice of the true religion. Locke's views on these issues changed considerably during the course of his writings on toleration. In his (unpublished) 1660 *First Tract on Government,* Locke argued that because the magistrate requires the power to legislate on "indifferent" matters (i.e., concerning behavior neither commanded nor forbidden by God), he must have the right to legislate on indifferent religious matters (and so to control his subjects' religious practices). By the time of his 1689 *Letter,* however, Locke had distinguished between those indifferent matters that are and those that are not the magistrate's proper business; and religious indifferent matters (such as the details of religious observances), having no real impact on the process of securing our rights, are no longer thought by Locke to fall within the proper scope of governmental authority.

The *Second Treatise* and the *Letter* were not, of course, Locke's only works in political and moral philosophy. Locke's *Essay Concerning Human Understanding* includes discussions of the nature of moral knowledge, as well as hints of the justifications Locke intends for the natural law morality he employs in the *Treatises.* Further, in addition to Locke's subsequent letters on toleration and his *First Treatise of Government* (which is principally a polemic against, and a duel of scriptural interpretation with, the works of Robert Filmer), Locke produced many unpublished essays on these subjects, including his early, substantial *Two Tracts on Government* and *Essays on the Law of Nature.*

All of the most important of Locke's unpublished essays are included in M. Goldie (ed.), *Locke: Political Essays* (Cambridge: Cambridge University Press, 1997). A few of the many noteworthy secondary works on Locke's moral and political philosophy are: J. Dunn, *The Political Thought of John Locke* (Cambridge: Cambridge University Press, 1969); J. Tully, *A Discourse on Property* (Cambridge: Cambridge University Press, 1980); J. Colman, *John Locke's Moral Philosophy* (Edinburgh: Edinburgh University Press, 1983); R. Ashcraft, *Locke's Two Treatises of Government* (Boston: Allen & Unwin 1987); A. J. Simmons, *The Lockean Theory of Rights* (Princeton, N.J.: Princeton University Press, 1992) and *On the Edge of Anarchy* (Princeton, N.J.: Princeton University Press, 1993); J. Marshall, *John Locke* (Cambridge: Cambridge University Press, 1994); and D. A. Lloyd Thomas, *Locke on Government* (London: Routledge, 1995).

# Second Treatise of Government

## CHAPTER I

1. It having been shown in the foregoing discourse,

1. That Adam had not, either by natural right of fatherhood, or by positive donation from God, any such authority over his children, or dominion over the world, as is pretended:
2. That if he had, his heirs, yet, had no right to it:
3. That if his heirs had, there being no law of nature, nor positive law of God, that determines, which is the right heir in all cases that may arise, the right of succession, and consequently of bearing rule, could not have been certainly determined:
4. That if even that had been determined, yet the knowledge of which is the eldest line of Adam's posterity, being so long since utterly lost, that in the races of mankind and families of the world, there remains not to one above another the least presence to be the eldest house, and to have the right of inheritance:

All these premises having, as I think, been clearly made out, it is impossible that the rulers now on earth, should make any benefit, or derive any the least shadow of authority from that, which is held to be the fountain of all power, *Adam's private dominion and paternal jurisdiction;* so that he that will not give just occasion to think that all government in the world is the product only of force and violence, and that men live together by no other rules but that of beasts, where the strongest carries it, and so lay a foundation for perpetual disorder and mischief, tumult, sedition, and rebellion (things that the followers of that hypothesis so loudly cry out against) must of necessity find out another rise of government, another original of political power, and another way of designing and knowing the persons that have it, than what Sir Robert Filmer hath taught us.

2. To this purpose, I think it may not be amiss, to set down what I take to be political power; that the power of a *magistrate* over a subject may be distinguished from that of a *father* over his children, a *master* over his servant, a *husband* over his wife, and a *lord* over his slave. All which distinct powers happening sometimes together in the same man, if he be considered under these different relations, it may help us to distinguish these powers one from another, and shew the difference betwixt a ruler of a commonwealth, a father of a family, and a captain of a galley.

3. *Political power,* then, I take to be a *right* of making laws and penalties of death, and consequently all less penalties for the regulating and preserving of property, and of employing the force of the community, in the execution of such laws, and in the defence of the commonwealth from foreign injury; and all this only for the public good.

## CHAPTER II

### *Of the State of Nature*

4. To understand political power, right, and derive it from its original, we must consider what state all men are naturally in, and that is, *a state of perfect freedom* to order their actions, and dispose of their possessions and persons, as they think fit, within the bounds of the law of nature; without asking leave, or depending upon the will of any other man.

A *state also of equality,* wherein all the power and jurisdiction is reciprocal, no one having more than another; there being nothing more evident, than that creatures of the same species and rank, promiscuously born to all the same advantages of nature, and the use of the same faculties, should also be equal one amongst another without subordination or subjection; unless the lord and master of them all should, by any manifest declaration of his will, set one above another, and confer on him, by an evident and clear appointment, an undoubted right to dominion and sovereignty.

5. This *equality* of men by nature, the judicious Hooker looks upon as so evident in itself, and beyond all question, that he makes it the foundation of that obligation to mutual love amongst men, on which he builds the duties we owe one another, and from whence he derives the great maxims of *justice* and *charity*. His words are,

> The like natural inducement hath brought men to know, that it is no less their duty to love others than themselves; for seeing those things which are equal, must needs all have one measure; if I cannot but wish to receive good, even as much at every man's hands, as any man can wish unto his own soul, how should I look to have any part of my desire herein satisfied, unless myself be careful to satisfy the like desire, which is undoubtedly in other men, being of one and the same nature? To have any thing offered them repugnant to this desire, must needs in all respects grieve them as much as me; so that if I do harm, I must look to suffer, there being no reason that others should shew greater measure of love to me, than they have by me shewed unto them: my desire therefore to be loved of my equals in nature, as much as possibly may be, imposeth upon me a natural duty of bearing to them-ward fully the like affection: From which relation of equality between ourselves and them that are as ourselves, what several rules and canons natural reason hath drawn, for direction of life, no man is ignorant.
>
> Eccl. Pol. L. I.

6. But though this be *a state of liberty,* yet *it is not a state of licence:* though man in that state have an uncontrollable liberty to dispose of his person or possessions, yet he has not liberty to destroy himself, or so much as any creature in his possession, but where some nobler use than its bare preservation calls for it. The *state of nature* has a law of nature to govern it, which obliges every one: And reason, which is that

law, teaches all mankind, who will but consult it, that being all *equal and independent,* no one ought to harm another in his life, health, liberty, or possessions. For men being all the workmanship of one omnipotent and infinitely wise Maker; all the servants of one sovereign master, sent into the world by his order, and about his business; they are his property, whose workmanship they are, made to last during his, not another's pleasure. And being furnished with like faculties, sharing all in one community of nature, there cannot be supposed any such subordination among us, that may authorize us to destroy another, as if we were made for one another's uses, as the inferior ranks of creatures are for ours. Every one, as he is *bound to preserve himself,* and not to quit his station willfully, so by the like reason, when his own preservation comes not in competition, ought he, as much as he can, *to preserve the rest of mankind,* and may not, unless it be to do justice to an offender, take away or impair the life, or what tends to the preservation of life, the liberty, health, limb, or goods of another.

7. And that all men may be restrained from invading others rights, and from doing hurt to one another, and the law of nature be observed, which willeth the peace and *preservation of all mankind,* the *execution* of the law of nature is, in that state, put into every man's hands, whereby every one has a right to punish the transgressors of that law to such a degree as may hinder its violation. For the *law of nature* would, as all other laws that concern men in this world, be in vain, if there were no body that in the state of nature had a *power to execute* that law, and thereby preserve the innocent and restrain offenders. And if any one in the state of nature may punish another for any evil he has done, every one may do so. For in that *state of perfect equality,* where naturally there is no superiority or jurisdiction of one over another, what any may do in prosecution of that law, every one must needs have a right to do.

8. And thus, in the state of nature, *one man comes by a power over another;* but yet no absolute or arbitrary power, to use a criminal, when he has got him in his hands, according to the passionate heats, or boundless extravagancy of his own will; but only to

retribute to him, so far as calm reason and conscience dictate, what is proportionate to his *transgression;* which is so much as may serve for reparation and *restraint.* For these two are the only reasons, why one man may lawfully do harm to another, which is that we call *punishment.* In transgressing the law of nature, the offender declares himself to live by another rule than that of reason and common equity, which is that measure God has set to the actions of men, for their mutual security; and so he becomes dangerous to mankind, the tye, which is to secure them from injury and violence, being slighted and broken by him. Which being a trespass against the whole species, and the peace and safety of it, provided for by the law of nature; every man upon this score, by the right he hath to preserve mankind in general, may restrain, or, where it is necessary, destroy things noxious to them, and so may bring such evil on any one, who hath transgressed that law, as may make him repent the doing of it, and thereby deter him, and by his example others, from doing the like mischief. And in this case, and upon this ground, *every man hath a right to punish the offender, and be executioner of the law of nature.*

9. I doubt not but this will seem a very strange doctrine to some men: but before they condemn it, I desire them to resolve me, by what right any prince or state can put to death, or *punish an alien,* for any crime he commits in their country. It is certain their laws, by virtue of any sanction they receive from the promulgated will of the legislative, reach not a stranger. They speak not to him, nor, if they did, is he bound to hearken to them. The legislative authority, by which they are in force over the subjects of that commonwealth, hath no power over him. Those who have the supreme power of making laws in England, France, or Holland, are to an Indian but like the rest of the world, men without authority: And therefore, if by the law of nature every man hath not a power to punish offences against it, as he soberly judges the case to require, I see not how the magistrates of any community can *punish an alien* of another country; since in reference to him, they can have no more power, than what every man naturally may have over another.

10. Besides the crime which consists in violating the law, and varying from the right rule of reason, whereby a man so far becomes degenerate, and declares himself to quit the principles of human nature, and to be a noxious creature, there is commonly injury done to some person or other, and some other man receives damage by his transgression, in which case he who hath received any damage, has besides the right of punishment common to him with other men, a particular right to seek *reparation* from him that has done it. And any other person who finds it just, may also join with him that is injured, and assist him in recovering from the offender so much as may make satisfaction for the harm he has suffered.

11. From these *two distinct rights,* the one of *punishing* the *crime for restraint,* and preventing the like offence, which right of punishing is in every body; the other of taking reparation, which belongs only to the injured party; comes it to pass that the magistrate, who by being magistrate, hath the common right of punishing put into his hands, can often, where the public good demands not the execution of the law, *remit* the punishment of criminal offences by his own authority, but yet cannot *remit* the satisfaction due to any private man, for the damage he has received. That, he who has suffered the damage has a right to demand in his own name, and he alone can remit: The damnified person has this power of appropriating to himself the goods or service of the offender, *by right of self-preservation,* as every man has a power to punish the crime, to prevent its being committed again, *by the right he has of preserving all mankind;* and doing all reasonable things he can in order to that end: And thus it is, that every man, in the state of nature, has a power to kill a murderer, both to deter others from doing the like injury, which no reparation can compensate, by the example of the punishment that attends it from every body, and also *to secure* men from the attempts of a criminal, who having renounced reason, the common rule and measure, God hath given to mankind, hath by the unjust violence and slaughter he hath committed upon one, declared war against all mankind; and therefore may be destroyed as a *lion* or a *tiger,* one of those wild savage beasts, with

whom men can have no society nor security: And upon this is grounded the great law of nature, "Whoso sheddeth man's blood, by man shall his blood be shed." And Cain was so fully convinced, that every one had a right to destroy such a criminal, that after the murder of his brother, he cries out, "Every one that findeth me, shall slay me;" so plain was it writ in the hearts of all mankind.

12. By the same reason may a man in the state of nature *punish the lesser breaches* of that law. It will perhaps be demanded, with death? I answer, each transgression may be *punished* to that *degree,* and with so much *severity,* as will suffice to make it an ill bargain to the offender, give him cause to repent, and terrify others from doing the like. Every offence that can be committed in the state of nature, may in the state of nature be also punished equally, and as far forth as it may, in a commonwealth: for though it would be besides my present purpose, to enter here into the particulars of the law of nature, or its *measures of punishment;* yet it is certain there is such a law, and that too, as intelligible and plain to a rational creature, and a studier of that law, as the positive laws of commonwealths, nay possibly plainer; as much as reason is easier to be understood, than the fancies and intricate contrivances of men, following contrary and hidden interests put into words; for so truly are a great part of the *municipal laws* of countries, which are only so far right, as they are founded on the law of nature, by which they are to be regulated and interpreted.

13. To this strange doctrine, viz. That *in the state of nature every one has the executive power* of the law of nature, I doubt not but it will be objected, that it is unreasonable for men to be judges in their own cases, that self-love will make men partial to themselves and their friends: And on the other side, that ill nature, passion and revenge will carry them too far in punishing others; and hence nothing but confusion and disorder will follow, and that therefore God hath certainly appointed government to restrain the partiality and violence of men. I easily grant, that civil government is the proper remedy for the inconveniencies of the state of nature, which must certainly be great, where men may be judges in their

own case, since it is easy to be imagined, that he who was so unjust as to do his brother an injury, will scarce be so just as to condemn himself for it: But I shall desire those who make this objection to remember, that *absolute monarchs* are but men, and if government is to be the remedy of those evils, which necessarily follow from men's being judges in their own cases, and the state of nature is therefore not to be endured, I desire to know what kind of government that is, and how much better it is than the state of nature, where one man commanding a multitude, has the liberty to be judge in his own case, and may do to all his subjects whatever he pleases, without the least liberty to any one to question or control those who execute his pleasure? and in whatsoever he doth, whether led by reason, mistake or passion, must be submitted to? Much better it is in the state of nature, wherein men are not bound to submit to the unjust will of another: And if he that judges, judges amiss in his own, or any other case, he is answerable for it to the rest of mankind.

14. It is often asked as a mighty objection, *where are,* or ever were, there any *men in such a state of nature*? To which it may suffice as an answer at present: That since all princes and rulers of independent governments, all through the world, are in a state of nature, it is plain the world never was, nor ever will be, without numbers of men in that state. I have named all governors of independent communities, whether they are, or are not, in league with others. For it is not every compact that puts an end to the state of nature between men, but only this one of agreeing together mutually to enter into one community, and make one body politic; other promises and compacts men may make one with another, and yet still be in the state of nature. The promises and bargains for truck, &c. between the two men in the desert island, mentioned by Garcilasso de la Vega, in his history of Peru; or between a Swiss and an Indian, in the woods of America, are binding to them, though they are perfectly in a state of nature, in reference to one another. For truth and keeping of faith belongs to men as men, and not as members of society.

15. To those that say, there were never any men in the state of nature, I will not only oppose the

authority of the judicious Hooker, *Eccl. Pol. lib. I. sect. 10,* where he says, "The laws which have been hitherto mentioned," i.e. the laws of nature,

> do bind men absolutely, even as they are men, although they have never any settled fellowship, never any solemn agreement amongst themselves what to do or not to do, but for as much as we are not by our selves sufficient to furnish ourselves with competent store of things, needful for such a life, as our nature doth desire, a life fit for the dignity of man; therefore to supply those defects and imperfections which are in us, as living singly and solely by ourselves, we are naturally induced to seek communion and fellowship with others. This was the cause of men's uniting themselves at first in politic societies.

But I moreover affirm, that all men are naturally in that state, and remain so, till by their own consents they make themselves members of some politic society; and I doubt not in the sequel of this discourse to make it very clear.

# CHAPTER III

## *Of the State of War*

16. The *state of war* is a state of *enmity* and *destruction:* And therefore declaring by word or action, not a passionate and hasty, but a sedate settled design upon another man's life, *puts him in a state of war* with him against whom he has declared such an intention, and so has exposed his life to the other's power to be taken away by him, or any one that joins with him in his defence, and espouses his quarrel: it being reasonable and just I should have a right to destroy that which threatens me with destruction. For *by the fundamental law of nature, man being to be preserved* as much as possible, when all cannot be preserved, the safety of the innocent is to be preferred: And one may destroy a man who makes war upon him, or has discovered an enmity to his being, for the same reason that he may kill a *wolf* or a *lion;* because such men are not under the ties of the common law of reason, have no other rule, but that of force and violence, and so may be treated as beasts of prey, those dangerous and noxious creatures, that will be sure to destroy him whenever he falls into their power.

17. And hence it is, that he who attempts to get another man into his absolute power, does thereby *put himself into a state of war* with him; it being to be understood as a declaration of a design upon his life. For I have reason to conclude, that he who would get me into his power without my consent, would use me as he pleased when he got me there, and destroy me too when he had a fancy to it; for no body can desire to *have me in his absolute power* unless it be to compel me by force to that which is against the right of my freedom, i.e. make me a slave. To be free from such force is the only security of my preservation; and reason bids me look on him, as an enemy to my preservation, who would take away that freedom which is the fence to it; so that he who makes an *attempt to enslave* me, thereby puts himself into a state of war with me. He that, in the state of nature, *would take away the freedom* that belongs to any one in that state, must necessarily be supposed to have a design to take away every thing else, that *freedom* being the foundation of all the rest: As he that, in the state of society, would take away the freedom belonging to those of that society or commonwealth, must be supposed to design to take away from them every thing else, and so be looked on as *in a state of war.*

18. This makes it lawful for a man to *kill a thief,* who has not in the least hurt him, nor declared any design upon his life, any farther, than by the use of force, so to get him in his power, as to take away his money, or what he pleases, from him; because using force, where he has no right, to get me into his power, let his pretence be what it will, I have no reason to suppose, that he, who would *take away my liberty,* would not, when he had me in his power, take away every thing else. And therefore it is lawful for me to treat him as one who has put *himself into a state of war* with me, i.e. kill him if I can; for to that hazard does he justly expose himself, whoever introduces a state of war, and is aggressor in it.

19. And here we have the plain *difference between the state of nature and the state of war;* which however some men have confounded, are as far distant, as a state of peace, good will, mutual assistance and preservation, and a state of enmity, malice, violence and mutual destruction, are one from another. Men living together according to reason, without a common superior on earth, with authority to judge between them, is *properly the state of nature.* But force, or a declared design of force, upon the person of another, where there is no common superior on earth to appeal to for relief, *is the state of war:* And it is the want of such an appeal gives a man the right of war even against an aggressor, though he be in society and a fellow subject. Thus a *thief,* whom I cannot harm, but by appeal to the law, for having stolen all that I am worth, I may kill, when he sets on me to rob me but of my horse or coat; because the law, which was made for my preservation, where it cannot interpose to secure my life from present force, which, if lost, is capable of no reparation, permits me my own defence, and the right of war, a liberty to kill the aggressor, because the aggressor allows not time to appeal to our common judge, nor the decision of the law, for remedy in a case where the mischief may be irreparable. *Want of a common judge with authority, puts all men in a state of nature: Force without right, upon a man's person, makes a state of war,* both where there is, and is not, a common judge.

20. But when the actual force is over, the *state of war ceases* between those that are in society, and are equally on both sides subjected to the fair determination of the law; because then there lies open the remedy of appeal for the past injury, and to prevent future harm: but where no such appeal is, as in the state of nature, for want of positive laws, and judges with authority to appeal to, *the state of war once begun, continues* with a right to the innocent party to destroy the other whenever he can, until the aggressor offers peace, and desires reconciliation on such terms as may repair any wrongs he has already done, and secure the innocent for the future: nay, where an appeal to the law, and constituted judges, lies open, but the remedy is denied by a manifest perverting of justice, and a barefaced wresting of the laws to protect or indemnify the violence or injuries of some men, or party of men, *there* it is hard to imagine any thing but *a state of war.* For wherever violence is used, and injury done, though by hands appointed to administer justice, it is still violence and injury, however coloured with the name, pretences, or forms of law, the end whereof being to protect and redress the innocent, by an unbiassed application of it, to all who are under it; wherever that is not *bona fide* done, *war is made* upon the sufferers, who having no appeal on earth to right them, they are left to the only remedy in such cases, an appeal to heaven.

21. To avoid this *state of war* (wherein there is no appeal but to heaven, and wherein every the least difference is apt to end, where there is no authority to decide between the contenders) is one *great reason of men's putting themselves into society,* and quitting the state of nature. For where there is an authority, a power on earth, from which relief can be had by *appeal,* there the continuance of the *state of war* is excluded, and the controversy is decided by that power. Had there been any such court, any superior jurisdiction on earth, to determine the right between Jephthah and the Ammonites, they had never come to *a state of war:* But we see he was forced to appeal to heaven. "The Lord the Judge," says he, "be judge this day, between the children of Israel and the children of Ammon," *Judg.* xi. 27, and then prosecuting, and relying on his appeal, he leads out his army to battle: and therefore in such controversies, where the question is put, *who shall be judge?* it cannot be meant, who shall decide the controversy; every one knows what Jephthah here tells us, that "the Lord the Judge" shall judge. Where there is no judge on earth, the appeal lies to God in heaven. That question then cannot mean, who shall judge? whether another hath put himself in a *state of war* with me, and whether I may, as Jephthah did, *appeal to heaven* in it? of that I myself can only be judge in my own conscience, as I will answer it, at the great day, to the supreme judge of all men.

## CHAPTER IV

### *Of Slavery*

22. The *natural liberty* of man is to be free from any superior power on earth, and not to be under the will or legislative authority of man, but to have only the law of nature for his rule. The *liberty of man,* in society, is to be under no other legislative power; but that established, by consent, in the commonwealth; nor under the dominion of any will, or restraint of any law, but what that legislative shall enact, according to the trust put in it. Freedom then is not what Sir Robert Filmer tells us, O, A. 55. "a liberty for every one to do what he lists, to live as he pleases, and not to be tied by any laws:" But *freedom of men under government,* is, to have a standing rule to live by, common to every one of that society, and made by the legislative power erected in it; a liberty to follow my own will in all things, where the rule prescribes not; and not to be subject to the inconstant, uncertain, unknown, arbitrary will of another man: As *freedom of nature* is, to be under no other restraint but the law of nature.

23. This freedom from absolute, arbitrary power, is so necessary to, and closely joined with a man's preservation, that he cannot part with it, but by what forfeits his preservation and life together. For a man, not having the power of his own life, cannot, by compact, or his own consent, enslave himself to any one, nor put himself under the absolute, arbitrary power of another, to take away his life, when he pleases. No body can give more power than he has himself; and he that cannot take away his own life, cannot give another power over it. Indeed, having by his fault forfeited his own life, by some act that deserves death; he, to whom he has forfeited it, may (when he has him in his power) delay to take it, and make use of him to his own service, and he does him no injury by it. For, whenever he finds the hardship of his slavery outweigh the value of his life, it is in his power, by resisting the will of his master, to draw on himself the death he desires.

24. This is the perfect condition of *slavery,* which

is nothing else, but *the state of war continued, between a lawful conqueror and a captive.* For, if once compact enter between them, and make an agreement for a limited power on the one side, and obedience on the other, the state of war and slavery ceases, as long as the compact endures. For, as has been said, no man can, by agreement, pass over to another that which he hath not in himself, a power over his own life.

I confess, we find among the Jews, as well as other nations, that men did sell themselves; but, it is plain, this was only to *drudgery, not to slavery.* For it is evident, the person sold was not under an absolute, arbitrary, despotical power. For the master could not have power to kill him, at any time, whom, at a certain time, he was obliged to let go free out of his service: and the master of such a servant was so far from having an arbitrary power over his life, that he could not, at pleasure, so much as maim him, but the loss of an eye, or tooth, set him free, *Exod.* xxi.

## CHAPTER V

### *Of Property*

25. Whether we consider natural *reason,* which tells us, that men, being once born, have a right to their preservation, and consequently to meat and drink, and such other things as nature affords for their subsistence: or *revelation,* which gives us an account of those grants God made of the world to Adam, and to Noah, and his sons, it is very clear, that God, as King David says, *Psal.* cxv. 16, "has given the earth to the children of men," given it to mankind in common. But this being supposed, it seems to some a very great difficulty how any one should ever come to have a *property* in any thing: I will not content myself to answer, that if it be difficult to make out *property,* upon a supposition, that God gave the world to Adam, and his posterity in common; it is impossible that any man, but one universal monarch, should have any property upon a

supposition, that God gave the world to Adam, and his heirs in succession, exclusive of all the rest of his posterity. But I shall endeavour to shew, how men might come to have a *property* in several parts of that which God gave to mankind in common, and that without any express compact of all the commoners.

26. God, who hath given the world to men in common, hath also given them reason to make use of it to the best advantage of life, and convenience. The earth, and all that is therein, is given to men for the support and comfort of their being. And though all the fruits it naturally produces, and beasts it feeds, belong to mankind in common, as they are produced by the spontaneous hand of nature; and no body has originally a private dominion, exclusive of the rest of mankind, in any of them, as they are thus in their natural state: yet being given for the use of men, there must of necessity be *a means to appropriate* them some way or other, before they can be of any use, or at all beneficial to any particular man. The fruit, or venison, which nourishes the wild Indian, who knows no enclosure, and is still a tenant in common, must be his, and so his, i.e. a part of him, that another can no longer have any right to it, before it can do him any good for the support of his life.

27. Though the earth, and all inferior creatures, be common to all men, yet every man has a property in his own person: this no body has any right to but himself. The labour of his body, and the work of his hands, we may say, are properly his. Whatsoever then he removes out of the state that nature hath provided, and left it in, he hath mixed his labour with, and joined to it something that is his own, and thereby makes it his property. It being by him removed from the common state nature hath placed it in, it hath by this labour something annexed to it, that excludes the common right of other men. For this labour being the unquestionable property of the labourer, no man but he can have a right to what that is once joined to, at least where there is enough, and as good, left in common for others.

28. He that is nourished by the acorns he picked up under an oak, or the apples he gathered from the trees in the wood, has certainly appropriated them to himself. No body can deny but the nourishment is his. I ask then, when did they begin to be his? When he digested? Or when he eat? Or when he boiled? Or when he brought them home? Or when he picked them up? And it is plain, if the first gathering made them not his, nothing else could. That *labour* put a distinction between them and common: that added something to them more than nature, the common mother of all, had done; and so they became his private right. And will any one say he had no right to those acorns or apples he thus appropriated, because he had not the consent of all mankind to make them his? Was it a robbery thus to assume to himself what belonged to all in common? If such a consent as that was necessary, man had starved, notwithstanding the plenty God had given him. We see in *commons*, which remain so by compact, that it is the taking any part of what is common, and removing it out of the state nature leaves it in, which *begins the property;* without which the common is of no use. And the taking of this or that part does not depend on the express consent of all the commoners. Thus the grass my horse has bit; the turfs my servant has cut; and the ore I have digged in any place, where I have a right to them in common with others, become my *property,* without the assignation or consent of any body. The *labour* that was mine, removing them out of that common state they were in, hath *fixed* my *property* in them.

29. By making an explicit consent of every commoner necessary to any one's appropriating to himself any part of what is given in common, children or servants could not cut the meat, which their father or master had provided for them in common, without assigning to every one his peculiar part. Though the water running in the fountain be every one's, yet who can doubt, but that in the pitcher is his only who drew it out? His *labour* hath taken it out of the hands of nature, where it was common, and belonged equally to all her children, and *hath* thereby *appropriated* it to himself.

30. Thus this law of reason makes the deer that Indian's who hath killed it; it is allowed to be his goods, who hath bestowed his labour upon it, though before it was the common right of every one. And

amongst those who are counted the civilized part of mankind, who have made and multiplied positive laws to determine *property,* this original law of nature, for the *beginning of property,* in what was before common, still takes place; and by virtue thereof, what fish any one catches in the ocean, that great and still remaining common of mankind; or what ambergreise any one takes up here, is *by the labour* that removes it out of that common state nature left it in, *made* his *property,* who takes that pains about it. And even amongst us, the hare that any one is hunting, is thought his who pursues her during the chase. For being a beast that is still looked upon as common, and no man's private possession; whoever has employed so much *labour* about any of that kind, as to find and pursue her, has thereby removed her from the state of nature, wherein she was common, and hath *begun a property*.

31. It will perhaps be objected to this, that "*if gathering the acorns, or other fruits of the earth, &c.* makes a right to them, then any one may engross as much as he will." To which I answer, Not so. The same law of nature, that does by this means give us property, does also *bound* that *property* too. "God has given us all things richly," 1 *Tim;* vi. 17, is the voice of reason confirmed by inspiration. But how far has he given it us? To *enjoy.* As much as any one can make use of to any advantage of life before it spoils, so much he may by his labour fix a property in: whatever is beyond this, is more than his share, and belongs to others. Nothing was made by God for man to spoil or destroy. And thus, considering the plenty of natural provisions there was a long time in the world, and the few spenders; and to how small a part of that provision the industry of one man could extend itself, and engross it to the prejudice of others; especially keeping within the *bounds,* set by reason, *of* what might serve for his *use;* there could be then little room for quarrels or contentions about property so established.

32. But the *chief matter of property* being now not the fruits of the earth, and the beasts that subsist on it, but the *earth it self;* as that which takes in, and carries with it all the rest: I think it is plain, that *property* in that too is acquired as the former. *As much land* as a man tills, plants, improves, cultivates, and can use the product of, so much is his *property.* He by his labour does, as it were, enclose it from the common. Nor will it invalidate his right, to say every body else has an equal title to it; and therefore he cannot appropriate, he cannot enclose, without the consent of all his fellow commoners, all mankind. God, when he gave the world in common to all mankind, commanded man also to labour, and the penury of his condition required it of him. God and his reason commanded him to subdue the earth, i.e. improve it for the benefit of life, and therein lay out something upon it that was his own, his labour. He that, in obedience to this command of God, subdued, tilled, and sowed any part of it, thereby annexed to it something that was his *property*, which another had no title to, nor could without injury take from him.

33. Nor was this *appropriation* of any parcel of *land,* by improving it, any prejudice to any other man, since there was still enough, and as good left; and more than the yet unprovided could use. So that, in effect, there was never the less left for others because of his enclosure for himself. For he that leaves as much as another can make use of, does as good as take nothing at all. No body could think himself injured by the drinking of another man, though he took a good draught, who had a whole river of the same water left him to quench his thirst: And the case of land and water, where there is enough of both, is perfectly the same.

34. God gave the world to men in common; but since he gave it them for their benefit, and the greatest conveniences of life they were capable to draw from it, it cannot be supposed he meant it should always remain common and uncultivated. He gave it to the use of the industrious and rational, (and *labour* was to be *his title* to it) not to the fancy or covetousness of the quarrelsome and contentious. He that had as good left for his improvement, as was already taken up, needed not complain, ought not to meddle with what was already improved by another's labour: If he did, it is plain he desired the benefit of another's pains, which he had no right to, and not the ground which God had given him in

common with others to labour on, and whereof there was as good left, as that already possessed, and more than he knew what to do with, or his industry could reach to.

35. It is true, in *land* that is *common* in England, or any other country, where there is plenty of people under government, who have money and commerce, no one can enclose or appropriate any part, without the consent of all his fellow-commoners: Because this is left common by compact, i.e. by the law of the land, which is not to be violated. And though it be common, in respect of some men, it is not so to all mankind, but is the joint property of this country, or this parish. Besides, the remainder, after such enclosure, would not be as good to the rest of the commoners, as the whole was when they could all make use of the whole: whereas in the beginning and first peopling of the great common of the world, it was quite otherwise. The law man was under, was rather for appropriating. God commanded, and his wants forced him to *labour*. That was his *property* which could not be taken from him wherever he had fixed it. And hence subduing or cultivating the earth, and having dominion, we see are joined together. The one gave title to the other. So that God, by commanding to subdue, gave authority so far to *appropriate:* And the condition of human life, which requires labour and materials to work on, necessarily introduces private possessions.

36. The *measure of property* nature has well set by the extent of men's *labour, and the conveniences of life:* No man's labour could subdue or appropriate all; nor could his enjoyment consume more than a small part; so that it was impossible for any man, this way, to intrench upon the right of another, or acquire to himself a property, to the prejudice of his neighbour, who would still have room for as good, and as large a possession (after the other had taken out his) as before it was appropriated. This *measure* did confine every man's *possession* to a very moderate proportion, and such as he might appropriate to himself, without injury to any body, in the first ages of the world, when men were more in danger to be lost, by wandering from their company, in the then vast wilderness of the earth, than to be straitened for want

of room to plant in. And the same measure may be allowed still without prejudice to any body, as full as the world seems. For supposing a man, or family, in the state they were at first peopling of the world by the children of Adam, or Noah; let him plant in some inland, vacant places of America, we shall find that the *possessions* he could make himself, upon the *measures* we have given, would not be very large, nor, even to this day, prejudice the rest of mankind, or give them reason to complain, or think themselves injured by this man's encroachment, though the race of men have now spread themselves to all the corners of the world, and do infinitely exceed the small number was at the beginning. Nay, the extent of *ground* is of so little value, *without labour,* that I have heard it affirmed, that in Spain itself a man may be permitted to plough, sow, and reap, without being disturbed, upon land he has no other title to, but only his making use of it. But, on the contrary, the inhabitants think themselves beholden to him, who by his industry on neglected and consequently waste land, has increased the stock of corn, which they wanted. But be this as it will, which I lay no stress on; this I dare boldly affirm, that the same *rule of propriety,* (*viz.*) that every man should have as much as he could make use of, would hold still in the world, without straitening any body, since there is land enough in the world to suffice double the inhabitants, had not the *invention of money,* and the tacit agreement of men to put a value on it, introduced (by consent) larger possessions, and a right to them; which, how it has done, I shall by and by shew more at large.

37. This is certain, that in the beginning, before the desire of having more than man needed had altered the intrinsic value of things, which depends only on their usefulness to the life of man; or had *agreed, that a little piece of yellow metal,* which would keep without wasting or decay, should be worth a great piece of flesh, or a whole heap of corn; though men had a right to appropriate, by their labour, each one to himself as much of the things of nature as he could use: yet this could not be much, nor to the prejudice of others, where the same plenty was still left to those who would use the same industry. To which let me add,

that he who appropriates land to himself by his labour, does not lessen, but increase the common stock of mankind. For the provisions serving to the support of human life, produced by one acre of enclosed and cultivated land, are (to speak much within compass) ten times more than those which are yielded by an acre of land of an equal richness lying waste in common. And therefore he that encloses land, and has a greater plenty of the conveniencies of life from ten acres, than he could have from an hundred left to nature, may truly be said to give ninety acres to mankind. For his labour now supplies him with provisions out of ten acres, which were by the product of an hundred lying in common. I have here rated the improved land very low, in making its product but as ten to one, when it is much nearer an hundred to one. For I ask, whether in the wild woods and uncultivated waste of America, left to nature, without any improvement, tillage, or husbandry, a thousand acres yield the needy and wretched inhabitants as many conveniencies of life, as ten acres equally fertile land do in Devonshire, where they are well cultivated?

Before the appropriation of land, he who gathered as much of the wild fruit, killed, caught, or tamed, as many of the beasts as he could; he that so employed his pains about any of the spontaneous products of nature, as any way to alter them from the state which nature put them in, *by* placing any of his *labour* on them, did thereby *acquire a propriety in them:* but if they perished, in his possession, without their due use; if the fruits rotted, or the venison putrified, before he could spend it, he offended against the common law of nature, and was liable to be punished; he invaded his neighbour's share, for he had *no right, farther than his use* called for any of them, and they might serve to afford him conveniencies of life.

38. The same *measures* governed the *possession of land* too: whatsoever he tilled and reaped, laid up and made use of, before it spoiled, that was his peculiar right; whatsoever he enclosed, and could feed, and make use of, the cattle and product was also his. But if either the grass of his inclosure rotted on the ground, or the fruit of his planting perished without gathering, and laying up, this part of the earth, notwithstanding his inclosure, was still to be looked on as waste, and might be the possession of any other. Thus at the beginning, Cain might take as much ground as he could till, and make it his own land, and yet leave enough to Abel's sheep to feed on; a few acres would serve for both their possessions. But as families increased, and industry enlarged their stocks, their *possessions enlarged* with the need of them; but yet it was commonly *without any fixed property in the ground* they made use of, till they incorporated, settled themselves together, and built cities, and then, by consent, they came in time to set out the *bounds of their distinct territories,* and agree on limits between them and their neighbours; and by laws within themselves settled the *properties* of those of the same society. For we see, that in that part of the world which was first inhabited, and therefore like to be best peopled, even as low down as Abraham's time, they wandered with their flocks, and their herds, which was their substance, freely up and down; and this Abraham did, in a country where he was a stranger. Whence it is plain, that at least a great part of the *land lay in common;* that the inhabitants valued it not, nor claimed property in any more than they made use of. But when there was not room enough in the same place, for their herds to feed together, they by consent, as Abraham and Lot did, *Gen.* xiii. 5. separated and enlarged their pasture, where it best liked them. And for the same reason Esau went from his father, and his brother, and planted in Mount Seir, *Gen.* xxxvi. 6.

39. And thus, without supposing any private dominion, and property in Adam, over all the *world,* exclusive of all other men, which can no way be proved, nor any one's property be made out from it; but supposing the *world* given, as it was, to the children of men in *common,* we see how *labour* could make men distinct titles to several parcels of it, for their private uses; wherein there could be no doubt of right, no room for quarrel.

40. Nor is it so strange, as perhaps before consideration it may appear, that the *property of labour* should be able to over-balance the community of land. For it is *labour* indeed that *puts the difference of value* on every thing; and let any one consider what the difference is between an acre of land

planted with tobacco or sugar, sown with wheat or barley, and an acre of the same land lying in common, without any husbandry upon it, and he will find, that the improvement of *labour makes* the far greater part of the value. I think it will be but a very modest computation to say, that of the *products* of the earth useful to the life of man, nine tenths are the *effects of labour:* nay, if we will rightly estimate things as they come to our use, and cast up the several expences about them, what in them is purely owing to *nature,* and what to *labour,* we shall find, that in most of them ninety-nine hundredths are wholly to be put on the account of *labour.*

41. There cannot be a clearer demonstration of any thing, than several nations of the Americans are of this, who are rich in land, and poor in all the comforts of life; whom nature having furnished as liberally as any other people, with the materials of plenty, i.e. a fruitful soil, apt to produce in abundance what might serve for food, raiment, and delight; yet *for want of improving it by labour,* have not one hundredth part of the conveniencies we enjoy: and a king of a large and fruitful territory there feeds, lodges, and is clad worse than a day labourer in England.

42. To make this a little clearer, let us but trace some of the ordinary provisions of life, through their several progresses, before they come to our use, and see how much they receive of their *value from human industry.* Bread, wine, and cloth, are things of daily use, and great plenty, yet notwithstanding, acorns, water, and leaves, or skins, must be our bread, drink, and cloathing, did not labour furnish us with these more useful commodities. For whatever bread is more worth than acorns, wine than water, and *cloth* or *silk,* than leaves, skins, or moss, that is *wholly owing to labour* and *industry.* The one of these being the food and raiment which unassisted nature furnishes us with; the other, provisions which our industry and pains prepare for us, which how much they exceed the other in value, when any one hath computed, he will then see how much *labour makes the far greatest part of the value* of things we enjoy in this world: and the ground which produces the materials, is scarce to be reckoned in, as any, or, at most, but a very small part of it: so little, that even

amongst us, land that is left wholly to nature, that hath no improvement of pasturage, tillage, or planting, is called, as indeed it is, *waste;* and we shall find the benefit of it amount to little more than nothing.

This shews how much numbers of men are to be preferred to largeness of dominions; and that the increase of lands, and the right of employing of them, is the great art of government: and that prince, who shall be so wise and godlike, as by established laws of liberty to secure protection and encouragement to the honest industry of mankind, against the oppression of power and narrowness of party, will quickly be too hard for his neighbours; but this by the by. To return to the argument in hand.

43. An acre of land, that bears here twenty bushels of wheat, and another in America, which, with the same husbandry, would do the like, are, without doubt, of the same natural intrinsic value: but yet the benefit mankind receives from the one in a year, is worth £5, and from the other possibly not worth a penny, if all the profit an Indian received from it were to be valued, and sold here; at least, I may truly say, not one thousandth. It is *labour* then which *puts the greatest part of the value upon land,* without which it would scarcely be worth any thing: it is to that we owe the greatest part of all its useful products; for all that the straw, bran, bread, of that acre of wheat, is more worth than the product of an acre of as good land, which lies waste, is all the effect of labour. For it is not barely the ploughman's pains, the reaper's and thresher's toil, and the baker's sweat is to be counted into the *bread* we eat; the labour of those who broke the oxen, who digged and wrought the iron and stones, who felled and framed the timber employed about the plough, mill, oven, or any other utensils, which are a vast number requisite to this corn, from its being seed to be sown, to its being made bread, must all be *charged on* the account of *labour,* and received as an effect of that: nature and the earth furnished only the almost worthless materials, as in themselves. It would be a strange *catalogue of things, that industry provided and made use of, about every loaf of bread,* before it came to our use, if we could trace them; iron, wood, leather, bark, timber, stone, bricks, coals, lime,

cloth, dying drugs, pitch, tar, masts, ropes, and all the materials made use of in the ship, that brought any of the commodities made use of by any of the workmen, to any part of the work, all which it would be almost impossible, at least too long, to reckon up.

44. From all which it is evident, that though the things of nature are given in common, yet man, by being master of himself, and *proprietor of his own person, and the actions or labour of it, had still in himself the great foundation of property;* and that, which made up the great part of what he applied to the support or comfort of his being, when invention and arts had improved the conveniences of life, was perfectly his own, and did not belong in common to others.

45. Thus *labour,* in the beginning, *gave a right of property,* wherever any one was pleased to employ it upon what was common, which remained a long while the far greater part, and is yet more than mankind makes use of. Men, at first, for the most part, contented themselves with what unassisted nature offered to their necessities: and though afterwards, in some parts of the world, (where the increase of people and stock, with the *use of money,* had made land scarce, and so of some value) the several *communities* settled the bounds of their distinct territories, and by laws within themselves regulated the properties of the private men of their society, and so, by *compact* and agreement, *settled the property* which labour and industry began; and the leagues that have been made between several states and kingdoms, either expressly or tacitly disowning all claim and right to the land in the others possession, have, by common consent, given up their pretences to their natural common right, which originally they had to those countries, and so have, by *positive agreement, settled a property* amongst themselves, in distinct parts and parcels of the earth; yet there are still *great tracts of ground* to be found, which (the inhabitants thereof not having joined with the rest of mankind, in the consent of the use of their common money) *lie waste,* and are more than the people who dwell on it do, or can make use of, and so still lie in common. Though this can scarce happen amongst that part of mankind that have consented to the use of money.

46. The greatest part of *things really useful* to the life of man, and such as the necessity of subsisting made the first commoners of the world look after, as it doth the Americans now, *are* generally things of *short duration;* such as, if they are not consumed by use, will decay and perish of themselves: gold, silver, and diamonds, are things that fancy or agreement hath put the value on, more than real use, and the necessary support of life. Now of those good things which nature hath provided in common, every one had a right, (as hath been said) to as much as he could use, and property in all that he could affect with his labour; all that his industry could extend to, to alter from the state nature had put it in, was his. He that *gathered* a hundred bushels of acorns or apples, had thereby a *property* in them, they were his goods as soon as gathered. He was only to look, that he used them before they spoiled, else he took more than his share, and robbed others. And indeed it was a foolish thing, as well as dishonest, to hoard up more than he could make use of. If he gave away a part to any body else, so that it perished not uselessly in his possession, these he also made use of. And if he also bartered away plums, that would have rotted in a week, for nuts that would last good for his eating a whole year, he did no injury; he wasted not the common stock; destroyed no part of the portion of goods that belonged to others, so long as nothing perished uselessly in his hands. Again, if he would give his nuts for a piece of metal, pleased with its colour; or exchange his sheep for shells, or wool for a sparkling pebble or a diamond, and keep those by him all his life, he invaded not the right of others, he might heap up as much of these durable things as he pleased; the *exceeding of the bounds of* his *just property* not lying in the largeness of his possession, but the perishing of any thing uselessly in it.

47. And thus *came in the use of money,* some lasting thing that men might keep without spoiling, and that by mutual consent men would take in exchange for the truly useful, but perishable supports of life.

48. And as different degrees of industry were apt to give men possessions in different proportions, so

this *invention of money* gave them the opportunity to continue and enlarge them. For supposing an island, separate from all possible commerce with the rest of the world, wherein there were but an hundred families, but there were sheep, horses, and cows, with other useful animals, wholesome fruits, and land enough for corn for a hundred thousand times as many, but nothing in the island, either because of its commonness, or perishableness, fit to supply the place of *money:* What reason could any one have there to enlarge his possessions beyond the use of his family and a plentiful supply to its *consumption,* either in what their own industry produced, or they could barter for like perishable, useful commodities with others? Where there is not something, both lasting and scarce, and so valuable to be hoarded up, there men will not be apt to enlarge their *possessions of land,* were it never so rich, never so free for them to take. For I ask, what would a man value ten thousand, or an hundred thousand acres of excellent *land,* ready cultivated and well stocked too with cattle, in the middle of the inland parts of America, where he had no hopes of commerce with other parts of the world, to draw *money* to him by the sale of the product? It would not be worth the enclosing, and we should see him give up again to the wild common of nature, whatever was more than would supply the conveniences of life to be had there for him and his family.

49. Thus in the beginning all the world was America, and more so than that is now; for no such thing as *money* was any where known. Find out something that hath the *use and value of money* amongst his neighbours, you shall see the same man will begin presently to *enlarge* his possessions.

50. But since gold and silver, being little useful to the life of man in proportion to food, raiment, and carriage, has its *value* only from the consent of men, whereof *labour* yet *makes* in great part, the *measure,* it is plain, that men have agreed to a disproportionate and unequal *possession of the earth,* they having, by a tacit and voluntary consent, found out a way how a man may fairly possess more land than he himself can use the product of, by receiving in exchange for the overplus, gold and silver, which may be hoarded up without injury to any one; these metals not spoiling or

decaying in the hands of the possessor. This partage of things in an inequality of private possessions, men have made practicable out of the bounds of society, and without compact, only by putting a value on gold and silver, and tacitly agreeing in the use of money. For in governments, the laws regulate the right of property, and the possession of land is determined by positive constitutions.

51. And thus, I think, it is very easy to conceive, without any difficulty *how labour could at first begin a title of property* in the common things of nature, and how the spending it upon our uses bounded it. So that there could then be no reason of quarrelling about title, nor any doubt about the largeness of possession it gave. Right and conveniency went together; for as a man had a right to all he could employ his labour upon, so he had no temptation to labour for more than he could make use of. This left no room for controversy about the title, nor for encroachment on the right of others; what portion a man carved to himself, was easily seen; and it was useless, as well as dishonest, to carve himself too much, or take more than he needed.

## CHAPTER VI

### *Of Paternal Power*

52. It may perhaps be censured as an impertinent criticism, in a discourse of this nature, to find fault with words and names, that have obtained in the world: and yet possibly it may not be amiss to offer new ones, when the old are apt to lead men into mistakes, as this of *paternal power* probably has done, which seems so to place the power of parents over their children wholly in the *father,* as if the *mother* had no share in it, whereas, if we consult reason or revelation, we shall find she hath an equal title. This may give one reason to ask, whether this might not be more properly called *parental power.* For whatever obligation nature and the right of generation lays on children, it must certainly bind them equally to both concurrent causes of it. And accordingly we see the positive law of God every where joins them together

without distinction, when it commands the obedience of children: "Honour thy father and thy mother," *Exod.* xx. 12. "Whosoever curseth his father or his mother," *Lev.* xx. 9. "Ye shall fear every man his mother and his father," *Lev.* xix. 5. "Children, obey your parents," &c. *Eph.* vi. 1, is the style of the Old and New Testament.

53. Had but this one thing been well considered, without looking any deeper into the matter, it might perhaps have kept men from running into those gross mistakes they have made, about this power of parents; which, however it might, without any great harshness, bear the name of absolute dominion, and regal authority, when under the title of *paternal power* it seemed appropriated to the father, would yet have sounded but oddly, and in the very name strewn the absurdity, if this supposed absolute power over children had been called *parental;* and thereby have discovered, that it belonged to the *mother* too. For it will but very ill serve the turn of those men, who contend so much for the absolute power and authority of the fatherhood, as they call it, that the mother should have any share in it. And it would have but ill supported the monarchy they contend for, when by the very name it appeared that that fundamental authority, from whence they would derive their government of a single person only, was not placed in one, but two persons jointly. But to let this of names pass.

54. Though I have said above, chap. ii. "That all men by nature are equal," I cannot be supposed to understand all sorts of *equality: age* or *virtue* may give men a just precedency: *excellency of parts* and *merit* may place others above the common level: *birth* may subject some, and *alliance* or *benefits* others, to pay an observance to those whom nature, gratitude, or other respects, may have made it due; and yet all this consists with the *equality,* which all men are in, in respect of jurisdiction or dominion one over another; which was the *equality* I there spoke of, as proper to the business in hand, being that *equal right,* that every man hath, *to his natural freedom,* without being subjected to the will or authority of any other man.

55. *Children,* I confess, are not born in this state of *equality,* though they are born to it. Their parents have a sort of rule and jurisdiction over them, when they come into the world, and for some time after, but it is but a temporary one. The bonds of this subjection are like the swaddling clothes they are wrapt up in, and supported by, in the weakness of their infancy: Age and reason, as they grow up, loosen them, till at length they drop quite off, and leave a man at his own free disposal.

56. Adam was created a perfect man, his body and mind in full possession of their strength and reason, and so was capable from the first instant of his being to provide for his own support and preservation; and govern his actions according to the dictates of the law of reason which God had implanted in him. From him the world is peopled with his descendants, who are all born infants, weak and helpless, without knowledge or understanding: But to supply the defects of this imperfect state, till the improvement of growth and age hath removed them, Adam and Eve, and after them all parents were, by the law of nature, *under an obligation to preserve, nourish, and educate the children,* they had begotten; not as their own workmanship, but the workmanship of their own maker, the Almighty, to whom they were to be accountable for them.

57. The law, that was to govern Adam, was the same that was to govern all his posterity, the *law of reason.* But his offspring having another way of entrance into the world, different from him, by a natural birth, that produced them ignorant and without the use of *reason,* they were not presently *under that law;* for no body can be under a law, which is not promulgated to him: and this law being promulgated or made known by *reason* only, he that is not come to the use of his *reason,* cannot be said to be *under this law;* and Adam's children, being not presently as soon as born, *under this law of reason,* were not presently free. For law, in its true notion, *is* not so much the limitation, *as the direction of a free and intelligent agent* to his proper interest, and prescribes no farther than is for the general good of those under that law. Could they be happier without it, the law, as an useless thing, would of it self vanish: and that ill deserves the name of confinement which hedges us

in only from bogs and precipices. So that, however it may be mistaken, *the end of law* is not to abolish or restrain, but *to preserve and enlarge freedom*. For in all the states of created beings capable of laws, *where there is no law, there is no freedom*. For liberty is to be free from restraint and violence from others which cannot be where there is no law: but freedom is not, as we are told, "a liberty for every man to do what he lists:" (for who could be free, when every other man's humour might domineer over him?) but a liberty to dispose, and order as he lists, his person, actions, possessions, and his whole property, within the allowance of those laws under which he is, and therein not to be subject to the arbitrary will of another, but freely follow his own.

58. The *power,* then, *that parents have* over their children, arises from that duty which is incumbent on them, to take care of their offspring during the imperfect state of childhood. To inform the mind, and govern the actions of their yet ignorant nonage, till reason shall take its place, and ease them of that trouble, is what the children want, and the parents are bound to. For God having given man an understanding to direct his actions, has allowed him a freedom of will, and liberty of acting, as properly belonging thereunto, within the bounds of that law he is under. But whilst he is in an estate, wherein he has not understanding of his own to direct his will, he is not to have any will of his own to follow: he that understands for him, must will for him too; he must prescribe to his will, and regulate his actions: but when he comes to the estate that made his *father a freeman,* the *son is a freeman* too.

59. This holds in all the laws a man is under, whether natural or civil. Is a man under the law of nature? *What made him free* of that law? What gave him a free disposing of his property according to his own will, within the compass of that law? I answer, a state of maturity, wherein he might be supposed capable to know that law, that so he might keep his actions within the bounds of it. When he has acquired that state, he is presumed to know how far that law is to be his guide, and how far he may make use of his *freedom,* and so comes to have it; till then, some body else must guide him, who is presumed to

know how far the law allows a liberty. If such a state of reason, such an age of discretion *made him free,* the same shall make his son free too. Is a man under the law of England? *What made him free* of that law? That is, to have the liberty to dispose of his actions and possessions according to his own will within the permission of that law? A capacity of knowing that law. Which is supposed by that law, at the age of one and twenty years, and in some cases sooner. If this made the father free, it shall make the son free too. Till then we see the law allows the son to have no will, but he is to be guided by the will of his father or guardian, who is to understand for him. And if the father die, and fail to substitute a deputy in his trust; if he hath not provided a tutor to govern his son, during his minority, during his want of understanding; the law takes care to do it; some other must govern him, and be a will to him, till he hath *attained to a state of freedom,* and his understanding be fit to take the government of his will. But after that, the father and son are equally free as much as tutor and pupil after nonage: equally subjects of the same law together, without any dominion left in the father over the life, liberty, or estate of his son, whether they be only in the state and under the law of nature, or under the positive laws of an established government.

60. But if, through defects that may happen out of the ordinary course of nature, any one comes not to such a degree of reason, wherein he might be supposed capable of knowing the law, and so living within the rules of it; he is *never capable of being a free man,* he is never let loose to the disposure of his own will (because he knows no bounds to it, has not understanding, its proper guide) but is continued under the tuition and government of others, all the time his own understanding is incapable of that charge. And so *lunatics* and *idiots* are never set free from the government of their parents. "Children, who are not as yet come into those years whereat they may have; and innocents which are excluded by a natural defect from ever having; thirdly, madmen, which for the present cannot possibly have the use of right reason to guide themselves; have for their guide the reason that guideth other men, which are tutors over them, to seek and procure their good for

them," says Hooker, Eccl. Pol. Lib. I. Sect. 7. All which seems no more than that duty which God and nature has laid on man, as well as other creatures, to preserve their offspring, till they can be able to shift for themselves, and will scarce amount to an instance or proof of parents regal authority.

61. Thus we are *born free,* as we are born rational; not that we have actually the exercise of either: age, that brings one, brings with it the other too. And thus we see how *natural freedom and subjection to parents* may consist together, and are both founded on the same principle. A *child* is *free* by his father's title, by his father's understanding, which is to govern him till he hath it of his own. The *freedom of a man at years of discretion,* and the *subjection* of a child *to* his parents, whilst yet short of that age, are so consistent, and so distinguishable, that the most blinded contenders for monarchy, *by right of fatherhood,* cannot miss this difference; the most obstinate cannot but allow their consistency. For were their doctrine all true, were the right heir of Adam now known, and by that title settled a monarch in his throne, invested with all the absolute unlimited power, Sir Robert Filmer talks of; if he should die as soon as his heir were born, must not the child, notwithstanding he were never so free, never so much sovereign, be in subjection to his mother and nurse, to tutors and governors, till age and education brought him reason and ability to govern himself and others? The necessities of his life, the health of his body, and the information of his mind, would require him to be directed by the will of others, and not his own; and yet will any one think, that this restraint and subjection were inconsistent with, or spoiled him of, that liberty or sovereignty he had a right to, or gave away his empire to those who had the government of his nonage? This government over him only prepared him the better and sooner for it. If any body should ask me when my son is of *age to be free?* I shall answer, just when his monarch is of age to govern. "But at what time," says the judicious Hooker, Eccl. Pol. Lib. I. Sect. 6 "a man may be said to have attained so far forth the use of reason, as sufficeth to make him capable of those laws whereby he is then bound to guide his actions: this is a great deal

more easy for sense to discern, than for any one by skill and learning to determine."

62. Commonwealths themselves take notice of, and allow, that there *is a time when men* are to *begin to act like free men,* and therefore till that time require not oaths of fealty, or allegiance, or other public owning of, or submission to, the government of their countries.

63. The *freedom* then of man, and liberty of acting according to his own will, is *grounded* on his having *reason,* which is able to instruct him in that law he is to govern himself by, and make him know how far he is left to the freedom of his own will. To turn him loose to an unrestrained liberty, before he has reason to guide him, is not allowing him the privilege of his nature to be free; but to thrust him out amongst brutes, and abandon him to a state as wretched, and as much beneath that of a man, as theirs. This is that which puts the *authority* into the *parents* hands to govern the *minority* of their children. God hath made it their business to employ this care on their offspring, and hath placed in them suitable inclinations of tenderness and concern to temper this power, to apply it, as his wisdom designed it, to the children's good as long as they should need to be under it. . . .

## CHAPTER VII

### *Of Political or Civil Society*

77. God having made man such a creature, that in his own judgment, it was not good for him to be alone, put him under strong obligations of necessity, convenience, and inclination, to drive him into society, as well as fitted him with understanding and language to continue and enjoy it. The first society was between man and wife, which gave beginning to that between parents and children; to which, in time, that between master and servant came to be added; and though all these might, and commonly did meet together, and make up but one family, wherein the master or mistress of it had some sort of rule proper to a family; each of these, or all together, came short

of *political society,* as we shall see, if we consider the different ends, ties, and bounds of each of these.

78. *Conjugal society* is made by a voluntary compact between man and woman; and though it consist chiefly in such a communion and right in one another's bodies as is necessary to its chief end, procreation; yet it draws with it mutual support and assistance, and a communion of interests too, as necessary not only to unite their care and affection, but also necessary to their common offspring, who have a right to be nourished and maintained by them, till they are able to provide for themselves.

79. For the end of *conjunction between male and female* being not barely procreation, but the continuation of the species; this conjunction betwixt male and female ought to last, even after procreation, so long as is necessary to the nourishment and support of the young ones, who are to be sustained by those that got them, till they are able to shift and provide for themselves. This rule, which the infinite wise Maker hath set to the works of his hands, we find the inferior creatures steadily obey. In those viviparous animals which feed on grass, the *conjunction between male and female* lasts no longer than the very act of copulation; because the teat of the dam being sufficient to nourish the young, till it be able to feed on grass, the male only begets, but concerns not himself for the female or young, to whose sustenance he can contribute nothing. But in beasts of prey the conjunction lasts longer: because the dam not being able well to subsist herself, and nourish her numerous offspring by her own prey alone, a more laborious, as well as more dangerous way of living, than by feeding on grass; the assistance of the male is necessary to the maintenance of their common family, which cannot subsist till they are able to prey for themselves, but by the joint care of male and female. The same is to be observed in all birds (except some domestic ones, where plenty of food excuses the cock from feeding, and taking care of the young brood), whose young needing food in the nest, the cock and hen continue mates, till the young are able to use their wing, and provide for themselves.

80. And herein I think lies the chief, if not the only reason, *why the male and female in mankind are tied to a longer conjunction* than other creatures, viz. because the female is capable of conceiving, and *de facto* is commonly with child again, and brings forth too a new birth, long before the former is out of a dependency for support on his parents help, and able to shift for himself, and has all the assistance that is due to him from his parents: whereby the father, who is bound to take care for those he hath begot, is under an obligation to continue in conjugal society with the same woman longer than other creatures, whose young being able to subsist of themselves before the time of procreation returns again, the conjugal bond dissolves of itself, and they are at liberty, till Hymen at his usual anniversary season summons them again to choose new mates. Wherein one cannot but admire the wisdom of the great Creator, who having given to man foresight, and an ability to lay up for the future, as well as to supply the present necessity, hath made it necessary, that *society of man and wife should be more lasting,* than of male and female amongst other creatures; that so their industry might be encouraged, and their interest better united, to make provision and lay up goods for their common issue, which uncertain mixture, or easy and frequent solutions of conjugal society, would mightily disturb.

81. But though these are ties upon *mankind,* which make the *conjugal bonds* more firm and lasting in man, than the other species of animals; yet it would give one reason to inquire, why this compact, where procreation and education are secured, and inheritance taken care for, may not be made determinable, either by consent, or at a certain time, or upon certain conditions, as well as any other voluntary compacts, there being no necessity in the nature of the thing, nor to the ends of it, that it should always be for life; I mean, to such as are under no restraint of any positive law, which ordains all such contracts to be perpetual.

82. But the husband and wife, though they have but one common concern, yet having different understandings, will unavoidably sometimes have different wills too; it therefore being necessary that the last determination, i.e. the rule, should be placed somewhere; it naturally falls to the man's share, as the

abler and the stronger. But this reaching but to the things of their common interest and property, leaves the wife in the full and free possession of what by contract is her peculiar right, and gives the husband no more power over her life than she has over his. The *power of the husband* being so far from that of an absolute monarch, that the *wife* has in many cases a liberty to separate from him, where natural right or their contract allows it; whether that contract be made by themselves in the state of nature, or by the customs or laws of the country they live in; and the children upon such separation fall to the father's or mother's lot, as such contract does determine.

83. For all the ends of *marriage* being to be obtained under politic government, as well as in the state of nature, the civil magistrate doth not abridge the right or power of either naturally necessary to those ends, viz. procreation and mutual support and assistance whilst they are together; but only decides any controversy that may arise between man and wife about them. If it were otherwise, and that absolute sovereignty and power of life and death naturally belonged to the husband, and were *necessary to the society between man and wife,* there could be no matrimony in any of those countries where the husband is allowed no such absolute authority. But the ends of matrimony requiring no such power in the husband, the condition of conjugal society put it not in him, it being not at all necessary to that state. Conjugal society could subsist and attain its ends without it; nay, community of goods, and the power over them, mutual assistance and maintenance, and other things belonging to conjugal society, might be varied and regulated by that contract which unites man and wife in that society, as far as may consist with procreation and the bringing up of children till they could shift for themselves; nothing being necessary to any society, that is not necessary to the ends for which it is made.

84. The *society betwixt parents and children,* and the distinct rights and powers belonging respectively to them, I have treated of so largely, in the foregoing chapter, that I shall not here need to say anything of it. And I think it is plain, that it is far different from a politic society.

85. *Master* and *servant* are names as old as history, but given to those of far different condition; for a free man makes himself a servant to another, by selling him, for a certain time, the service he undertakes to do, in exchange for wages he is to receive: and though this commonly puts him into the family of his master, and under the ordinary discipline thereof: yet it gives the master but a temporary power over him, and no greater than what is contained in the *contract* between them. But there is another sort of servants, which by a peculiar name we call *slaves,* who being captives taken in a just war, are by the right of nature subjected to the absolute dominion and arbitrary power of their masters. These men having, as I say, forfeited their lives, and with it their liberties, and lost their estates; and being in the *state of slavery,* not capable of any property, cannot in that state be considered as any part of *civil society;* the chief end whereof is the preservation of property,

86. Let us therefore consider a *master of a family* with all these subordinate relations of *wife, children, servants,* and *slaves,* united under the domestic rule of a family; which, what resemblance soever it may have in its order, offices, and number too, with a little commonwealth, yet is very far from it, both in its constitution, power, and end: or if it must be thought a monarchy, and the *paterfamilias* the absolute monarch in it, absolute monarchy will have but a very shattered and short power, when it is plain by what has been said before, that the *master of the family* has a very distinct and differently limited power, both as to time and extent, over those several persons that are in it. For excepting the slave (and the family is as much a family, and his power as *paterfamilias* as great, whether there be any slaves in his family or no) he has no legislative power of life and death over any of them, and none too but what a *mistress of a family* may have as well as he. And he certainly can have no absolute power over the whole family, who has but a very limited one over every individual in it. But how a family, or any other society of men, differ from that which is properly political society, we shall best see by considering wherein political society itself consists.

87. Man being born, as has been proved, with a title to perfect freedom, and an uncontrolled enjoyment of all the rights and privileges of the law of nature, equally with any other man, or number of men in the world, hath by nature a power, not only to preserve his property, that is, his life, liberty, and estate, against the injuries and attempts of other men; but to judge of and punish the breaches of that law in others, as he is persuaded the offence deserves, even with death itself, in crimes where the heinousness of the fact, in his opinion, requires it. But because no *political* society can be, nor subsist, without having in itself the power to preserve the property, and, in order thereunto, punish the offences of all those of that society; there and there only is *political society,* where every one of the members hath quitted his natural power, resigned it up into the hands of the community in all cases that excludes him not from appealing for protection to the law established by it. And thus all private judgment of every particular member being excluded, the community comes to be umpire by settled standing rules, indifferent, and the same to all parties; and by men having authority from the community, for the execution of those rules, decides all the differences that may happen between any members of that society concerning any matter of right; and punishes those offences which any member hath committed against the society, with such penalties as the law has established, whereby it is easy to discern, who are, and who are not, in *political society* together. Those who are united into one body, and have a common established law and judicature to appeal to, with authority to decide controversies between them, and punish offenders, *are in civil society* one with another: but those who have no such common appeal, I mean on earth, are still in the state of nature, each being, where there is no other, judge for himself, and executioner: which is, as I have before shewed, the perfect *state of nature*.

88. And thus the commonwealth comes by a power to set down what punishment shall belong to the several transgressions which they think worthy of it, committed amongst the members of that society, (which is the *power of making laws*) as well as it

has the power to punish any injury done unto any of its members, by any one that is not of it, (which is the power of war and peace,) and all this for the preservation of the property of all the members of that society, as far as is possible. But though every man who has entered into civil society, and is become a member of any commonwealth, has thereby quitted his power to punish offences against the law of nature, in prosecution of his own private judgment; yet with the judgment of offences, which he has given up to the legislative in all cases, where he can appeal to the magistrate, he has given a right to the commonwealth to employ his force, for the execution of the judgments of the commonwealth whenever he shall be called to it; which indeed are his own judgments, they being made by himself, or his representative. And herein we have the original of the legislative and executive power of civil society, which is to judge by standing laws, how far offences are to be punished, when committed within the commonwealth; and also to determine, by occasional judgments founded on the present circumstances of the fact, how far injuries from without are to be vindicated; and in both these to employ all the force of all the members, when there shall be need.

89. Whenever therefore any number of men are so united into one society, as to quit every one his executive power of the law of nature, and to resign it to the public, there and there only is a political, or civil society. And this is done, wherever any number of men, in the state of nature, enter into society to make one people, one body politic, under one supreme government; or else when any one joins himself to, and incorporates with any government already made. For hereby he authorizes the society, or, which is all one, the legislative thereof, to make laws for him, as the public good of the society shall require; to the execution whereof, his own assistance (as to his own degrees) is due. And this puts men out of a state of nature into that of a commonwealth, by setting up a judge on earth, with authority to determine all the controversies, and redress the injuries that may happen to any member of the commonwealth: which judge is the legislative, or magistrate appointed by it. And wherever there are any number

of men, however associated, that have no such decisive power to appeal to, there they are still in the state of nature.

90. Hence it is evident, that absolute monarchy, which by some men is counted the only government in the world, is indeed inconsistent with civil society, and so can be no form of civil government at all; for the end of civil society being to avoid and remedy these inconveniencies of the state of nature, which necessarily follow from every man's being judge in his own case, by setting up a known authority, to which every one of that society may appeal upon any injury received, or controversy that may arise, and which every one of the society ought to obey; wherever any persons are, who have not such an authority to appeal to for the decision of any difference between them, there those persons are still *in the state of nature*. And so is every *absolute prince*, in respect of those who are under his dominion.

91. For he being supposed to have all, both legislative and executive power in himself alone, there is no judge to be found, no appeal lies open to any one, who may fairly, and indifferently, and with authority decide, and from whose decision relief and redress may be expected of any injury or inconveniency that may be suffered from the prince, or by his order: so that such a man, however intitled, *czar*, or *grand seignior*, or how you please, is as much in *the state of nature*, with all under his dominion, as he is with the rest of mankind. For wherever any two men are, who have no standing rule, and common judge to appeal to on earth, for the determination of controversies of right betwixt them, there they are still *in the state of nature*, and under all the inconveniencies of it, with only this woful difference to the subject, or rather slave of an absolute prince; that whereas in the ordinary state of nature he has a liberty to judge of his right, and, according to the best of his power, to maintain it; now, whenever his property is invaded by the will and order of his monarch, he has not only no appeal, as those in society ought to have, but, as if he were degraded from the common state of rational creatures, is denied a liberty to judge of, or to defend his right; and so is exposed to all the misery and inconveniencies that a

man can fear from one, who being in the unrestrained state of nature, is yet corrupted with flattery, and armed with power

# CHAPTER VIII

## *Of the Beginning of Political Societies*

95. Men being, as has been said, by nature, all free, equal, and independent, no one can be put out of this estate, and subjected to the political power of another, without his own consent. The only way, whereby any one divests himself of his natural liberty, and puts on the *bonds of civil society*, is by agreeing with other men to join and unite into a community, for their comfortable, safe, and peaceable living one amongst another, in a secure enjoyment of their properties, and a greater security against any, that are not of it. This any number of men may do, because it injures not the freedom of the rest; they are left as they were in the liberty of the state of nature. When any number of men have so *consented to make one community or government*, they are thereby presently incorporated, and make *one body politic*, wherein the *majority* have a right to act and conclude the rest.

96. For when any number of men have, by the consent of every individual, made a *community*, they have thereby made that *community* one body, with a power to act as one body, which is only by the will and determination of the majority. For that which acts any community, being only the *consent* of the individuals of it, and it being necessary to that which greater force carries it, which is the *consent of the majority:* or else it is impossible it should act or continue one body, one community, which the consent of every individual that united into it, agreed that it should; and so every one is bound by that consent to be concluded by the majority. And therefore we see, that in assemblies, impowered to act by positive laws, where no number is set by that positive law which impowers them, the *act of the majority* passes for the act of the whole, and of course determines, as having, by the law of nature and reason, the power of the whole.

97. And thus every man, by consenting with others to make one body politic under one government, puts himself under an obligation, to every one of that society, to submit to the determination of the majority, and to be concluded by it; or else this *original compact,* whereby he with others incorporate into one society, would signify nothing, and be no compact, if he be left free, and under no other ties than he was in before in the state of nature. For what appearance would there be of any compact? What new engagement if he were no farther tied by any decrees of the society, than he himself thought fit, and did actually consent to? This would be still as great a liberty, as he himself had before his compact, or any one else in the state of nature hath, who may submit himself, and consent to any acts of it if he thinks fit.

98. For if *the consent of the majority* shall not, in reason, be received as *the act of the whole,* and conclude every individual; nothing but the consent of every individual can make any thing to be the act of the whole: But such a consent is next to impossible ever to be had, if we consider the infirmities of health, and avocations of business, which in a number, though much less than that of a commonwealth, will necessarily keep many away from the public assembly. To which if we add the variety of opinions, and contrariety of interests, which unavoidably happen in all collections of men, the coming into society upon such terms would be only like Cato's coming into the theatre, only to go out again. Such a constitution as this would make the mighty *leviathan* of a shorter duration than the feeblest creatures, and not let it outlast the day it was born in: which cannot be supposed, till we can think, that rational creatures should desire and constitute societies only to be dissolved. For where the majority cannot conclude the rest, there they cannot act as one body, and consequently will be immediately dissolved again.

99. Whosoever therefore out of a state of nature unite into a community, must be understood to give up all the power, necessary to the ends for which they unite into society, to the majority of the community, unless they expressly agreed in any number greater than the majority. And this is done by barely agreeing to *unite into one political society,* which is

all the compact that is, or needs be, between the individuals, that enter into, or make up a commonwealth. And thus, that which begins and actually *constitutes any political society,* is nothing, but the consent of any number of freemen capable of a majority, to unite and incorporate into such a society. And this is that, and that only, which did, or could give beginning to any lawful government in the world. . . .

119. Every man being, as has been shewed, naturally free, and nothing being able to put him into subjection to any earthly power, but only his own consent; it is to be considered, what shall be understood to be a *sufficient declaration of* a man's *consent, to make him subject* to the laws of any government. There is a common distinction of an express and a tacit consent, which will concern our present case. No body doubts but an express consent, of any man entering into any society, makes him a perfect member of that society, a subject of that government. The difficulty is, what ought to be looked upon as a *tacit consent,* and how far it binds, i.e. how far any one shall be looked on to have consented, and thereby submitted to any government, where he has made no expressions of it at all. And to this I say, that every man, that hath any possessions, or enjoyment of any part of the dominions of any government, doth thereby give his *tacit consent*, and is as far forth obliged to obedience to the laws of that government, during such enjoyment, as any one under it; whether this his possession be of land, to him and his heirs for ever, or a lodging only for a week; or whether it be barely travelling freely on the highway: and, in effect, it reaches as far as the very being of any one within the territories of that government.

120. To understand this the better, it is fit to consider, that every man, when he at first incorporates himself into any commonwealth, he, by his uniting himself thereunto, annexed also, and submits to the community, those possessions which he has, or shall acquire, that do not already belong to any other government. For it would be a direct contradiction, for any one to enter into society with others for the securing and regulating of property, and yet to suppose, his land, whose property is to be regulated by the laws of the society, should be exempt from the

jurisdiction of that government, to which he himself, the proprietor of the land, is a subject. By the same act therefore, whereby any one unites his person, which was before free, to any commonwealth; by the same he unites his possessions, which were before free, to it also: and they become, both of them, person and possession, subject to the government and dominion of that commonwealth, as long as it hath a being. Whoever therefore, from thenceforth, by inheritance, purchase, permission, or otherways, *enjoys any part of the land* so annexed to, and under the government *of that commonwealth, must take it with the condition* it is under; that is, *of submitting to the government of the commonwealth,* under whose jurisdiction it is, as far forth as any subject of it.

121. But since the government has a direct jurisdiction only over the land, and reaches the possessor of it, (before he has actually incorporated himself in the society) only as he dwells upon, and enjoys that; the obligation any one is under, by virtue of such enjoyment, to *submit to the government, begins and ends with the enjoyment:* so that whenever the owner, who has given nothing but such a tacit consent to the government, will, by donation, sale, or otherwise, quit the said possession, he is at liberty to go and incorporate himself into any other commonwealth; or to agree with others to begin a new one, *in vacuis locis,* in any part of the world they can find free and unpossessed: whereas he, that has once, by actual agreement, and any express declaration, given his *consent* to be of any commonwealth, is perpetually and indispensably obliged to be, and remain unalterably a subject to it, and can never be again in the liberty of the state of nature; unless, by any calamity, the government he was under comes to be dissolved, or else by some public act cuts him off from being any longer a member of it.

122. But submitting to the laws of any country, living quietly, and enjoying privileges and protection under them, *makes not a man a member of that society:* this is only a local protection and homage due to and from all those, who, not being in a state of war, come within the territories belonging to any government, to all parts whereof the force of its laws extends. But this no more *makes a man a member of*

*that society,* a perpetual subject of that commonwealth, than it would make a man a subject to another, in whose family he found it convenient to abide for some time, though, whilst he continued in it, he were obliged to comply with the laws, and submit to the government he found there. And thus we see, that foreigners, by living all their lives under another government, and enjoying the privileges and protection of it, though they are bound, even in conscience, to submit to its administration, as far forth as any denison; yet do not thereby come to be *subjects or members of that commonwealth*. Nothing can make any man so, but his actually entering into it by positive engagement, and express promise and compact. This is that, which I think, concerning the beginning of political societies, and that *consent which makes any one a member of any commonwealth.*

## CHAPTER IX

### *Of the Ends of Political Society and Government*

123. If man in the state of nature be so free, as has been said; if he be absolute lord of his own person and possessions, equal to the greatest, and subject to no body, why will he part with his freedom? why will he give up his empire, and subject himself to the dominion and control of any other power? To which it is obvious to answer, that though in the state of nature he hath such a right, yet the enjoyment of it is very uncertain, and constantly exposed to the invasion of others. For all being kings as much as he, every man his equal, and the greater part no strict observers of equity and justice, the enjoyment of the property he has in this state is very unsafe, very unsecure. This makes him willing to quit this condition, which, however free, is full of fears and continual dangers: and it is not without reason, that he seeks out, and is willing to join in society with others, who are already united, or have a mind to unite, for the mutual preservation of their lives, liberties, and estates, which I call by the general name, property.

124. The great and *chief end,* therefore, of men's uniting into commonwealths, and putting themselves under government, is *the preservation of their property*. To which in the state of nature there are many things wanting.

*First,* There wants an established, settled, known law, received and allowed by common consent to be the standard of right and wrong, and the common measure to decide all controversies between them. For though the law of nature be plain and intelligible to all rational creatures; yet men being biassed by their interest, as well as ignorant for want of studying it, are not apt to allow of it as a law binding to them in the application of it to their particular cases.

125. *Secondly,* In the state of nature there wants *a known and indifferent judge,* with authority to determine all differences according to the established law. For every one in that state being both judge and executioner of the law of nature, men being partial to themselves, passion and revenge is very apt to carry them too far, and with too much heat, in their own cases; as well as negligence, and unconcernedness, to make them too remiss in other men's.

126. *Thirdly,* In the state of nature, there often wants power to back and support the sentence when right, and to give it due execution. They who by any injustice offended, will seldom fail, where they are able, by force to make good their injustice; such resistance many times makes the punishment dangerous, and frequently destructive, to those who attempt it.

127. Thus mankind, notwithstanding all the privileges of the state of nature, being but in an ill condition, while they remain in it, are quickly driven into society. Hence it comes to pass that we seldom find any number of men live any time together in this state. The inconveniencies that they are therein exposed to, by the irregular and uncertain exercise of the power every man has of punishing the transgressions of others, make them take sanctuary under the established laws of government, and therein seek *the preservation of their property*. It is this makes them so willingly give up every one his single power of punishing, to be exercised by such alone, as shall be appointed to it amongst them; and by such rules as the community, or those authorized by them to that

purpose, shall agree on. And in this we have the original *right and rise of both the legislative and executive power,* as well as of the governments and societies themselves.

128. For in the state of nature, to omit the liberty he has of innocent delights, a man has two powers.

The first is to do whatsoever he thinks fit for the preservation of himself and others within the permission of the *law of nature:* by which law, common to them all, he and all the rest of *mankind are one community*, make up one society, distinct from all other creatures. And, were it not for the corruption and viciousness of degenerate men, there would be no need of any other; no necessity that men should separate from this great and natural community, and by positive agreements combine into smaller and divided associations.

The other power a man has in the state of nature, is the *power to punish the crimes* committed against that law. Both these he gives up, when he joins in a private, if I may so call it, or particular politic society, and incorporates into any commonwealth, separate from the rest of mankind.

129. The first *power,* viz. *of doing whatsoever he thought fit for the preservation of himself,* and the rest of mankind, *he gives up* to be regulated by laws made by the society, so far forth as the preservation of himself and the rest of that society shall require; which laws of the society in many things confine the liberty he had by the law of nature.

130. *Secondly,* The *power of punishing he wholly gives up,* and engages his natural force, (which he might before employ in the execution of the law of nature, by his own single authority, as he thought fit) to assist the executive power of the society, as the law thereof shall require. For being now in a new state, wherein he is to enjoy many conveniencies, from the labour, assistance, and society of others in the same community, as well as protection from its whole strength; he is to part also, with as much of his natural liberty, in providing for himself, as the good, prosperity, and safety of the society shall require; which is not only necessary, but just, since the other members of the society do the like.

131. But though men, when they enter into society, give up the equality, liberty, and executive power they had in the state of nature, into the hands of the society, to be so far disposed of by the legislative, as the good of the society shall require; yet it being only with an intention in every one the better to preserve himself, his liberty and property; (for no rational creature can be supposed to change his condition with an intention to be worse) the power of the society, or legislative constituted by them, *can never be supposed to extend farther, than the common good;* but is obliged to secure every one's property, by providing against those three defects above mentioned, that made the state of nature so unsafe and uneasy. And so whoever has the legislative or supreme power of any commonwealth, is bound to govern by established standing laws, promulgated and known to the people, and not by extemporary decrees; by indifferent and upright judges, who are to decide controversies by those laws; and to employ the force of the community at home, *only in the execution of such laws;* or abroad to prevent or redress foreign injuries, and secure the community from inroads and invasion. And all this to be directed to no other *end,* but the *peace, safety,* and *public good* of the people.

## CHAPTER X

### *Of the Forms of a Commonwealth*

132. The majority having, as has been shewed, upon men's first uniting into society, the whole power of the community naturally in them, may employ all that power in making laws for the community from time to time, and executing those laws by officers of their own appointing; and then the *form* of the government is a perfect *democracy:* or else may put the power of making laws into the hands of a few select men, and their heirs or successors; and then it is an *oligarchy:* or else into the hands of one man, and then it is a *monarchy:* if to him and his heirs, it is an *hereditary monarchy:* if to him only for life, but upon his death the power only of nominating a suc-

cessor to return to them; an *elective monarchy.* And so accordingly of these the community may make compounded and mixed forms of government, as they think good. And if the legislative power be at first given by the majority to one or more persons only for their lives, or any limited time, and then the supreme power to revert to them again; when it is so reverted, the community may dispose of it again anew into what hands they please, and so constitute a new form of government. For the *form of government depending upon the placing* the supreme power, which is the legislative (it being impossible to conceive that an inferiour power should prescribe to a superiour, or any but the supreme make laws), according as the power of making laws is placed, such is the *form of the commonwealth.*

133. By commonwealth, I must be understood all along to mean, not a democracy, or any form of government, but *any independent community,* which the Latines signified by the word *civitas;* to which the word which best answers in our language, is *commonwealth,* and most properly expresses such a society of men, which community or city in English does not. For there may be subordinate communities in government; and city amongst us has quite a different notion from commonwealth: and therefore, to avoid ambiguity, I crave leave to use the word *commonwealth* in that sense, in which I find it used by King *James the first:* and I take it to be its genuine signification; which if any body dislike, I consent with him to change it for a better.

## CHAPTER XI

### *Of the Extent of the Legislative Power*

134. The great end of men's entering into society being the enjoyment of their properties in peace and safety, and the great instrument and means of that being the laws established in that society; *the first and fundamental positive law* of all commonwealths *is the establishing of the legislative* power; as the *first and fundamental natural law,* which is to govern even the legislative itself, *is the preservation of the*

*society,* and (as far as will consist with the public good) of every person in it. This *legislative* is not only *the supreme power* of the commonwealth, but sacred and unalterable in the hands where the community have once placed it; nor can any edict of any body else, in what form soever conceived, or by what power soever backed, have the force and obligation of a law, which has not its *sanction from* that *legislative* which the public has chosen and appointed; for without this the law could not have that, which is absolutely necessary to its being a *law, the consent of the society;* over whom no body can have a power to make laws, but by their own consent, and by authority received from them; and therefore all the obedience, which by the most solemn ties any one can be obliged to pay, ultimately terminates in this supreme power, and is directed by those laws which it enacts; nor can any oaths to any foreign power whatsoever, or any domestic subordinate power, discharge any member of the society from his *obedience to the legislative,* acting pursuant to their trust; nor oblige him to any obedience contrary to the laws so enacted, or farther than they do allow; it being ridiculous to imagine one can be tied ultimately to obey any power in the society, which is not the supreme.

135. Though the legislative, whether placed in one or more, whether it be always in being, or only by intervals, though it be the supreme power in every commonwealth; yet,

*First,* It is *not,* nor can possibly be absolutely *arbitrary* over the lives and fortunes of the people. For it being but the joint power of every member of the society given up to that person, or assembly, which is legislator, it can be no more than those persons had in a state of nature before they entered into society, and gave up to the community. For no body can transfer to another more power than he has in himself; and no body has an absolute arbitrary power over himself, or over any other, to destroy his own life, or take away the life or property of another. A man, as has been proved, cannot subject himself to the arbitrary power of another; and having in the state of nature no arbitrary power over the life, liberty, or possession of another, but only so much as the law of nature gave him for the preservation of

himself and the rest of mankind; this is all he doth, or can give up to the commonwealth, and by it to the legislative power, so that the legislative can have no more than this. Their power, in the utmost bounds of it, is *limited to the public good* of the society. It is a power, that hath no other end but preservation, and therefore can never have a right to destroy, enslave, or designedly to impoverish the subjects. The obligations of the law of nature cease not in society, but only in many cases are drawn closer, and have by human laws known penalties annexed to them, to enforce their observation. Thus the law of nature stands as an eternal rule to all men, legislators as well as others. The rules that they make for other men's actions, must, as well as their own and other men's actions, be conformable to the law of nature, i.e. to the will of God, of which that is a declaration; and the *fundamental law of nature being the preservation of mankind,* no human sanction can be good or valid against it.

136. *Secondly,* The legislative or supreme authority cannot assume to itself a power to rule, by extemporary, arbitrary decrees, but *is bound to dispense justice,* and decide the rights of the subject, *by promulgated, standing laws, and known authorised judges.* For the law of nature being unwritten, and so no-where to be found, but in the minds of men; they who through passion, or interest, shall miscite, or misapply it, cannot so easily be convinced of their mistake, where there is no established judge: and so it serves not, as it ought, to determine the rights, and fence the properties of those that live under it; especially where every one is judge, interpreter, and executioner of it too, and that in his own case: and he that has right on his side having ordinarily but his own single strength, hath not force enough to defend himself from injuries, or to punish delinquents. To avoid these inconveniencies, which disorder men's properties in the state of nature, men unite into societies, that they may have the united strength of the whole society to secure and defend their properties, and may have standing rules to bound it, by which every one may know what is his. To this end it is that men give up all their natural power to the society which they enter into, and the community put the

legislative power into such hands as they think fit: with this trust, that they shall be governed by *declared laws,* or else their peace, quiet, and property will still be at the same uncertainty, as it was in the state of nature.

137. Absolute arbitrary power, or governing without *settled standing laws,* can neither of them consist with the ends of society and government, which men would not quit the freedom of the state of nature for, and tie themselves up under, were it not to preserve their lives, liberties, and fortunes, and by *stated rules* of right and property to secure their peace and quiet. It cannot be supposed that they should intend, had they a power so to do, to give to any one, or more, an *absolute arbitrary power* over their persons and estates, and put a force into the magistrate's hand to execute his unlimited will arbitrarily upon them. This were to put themselves into a worse condition than the state of nature, wherein they had a liberty to defend their right against the injuries of others, and were upon equal terms of force to maintain it, whether invaded by a single man, or many in combination. Whereas by supposing they have given up themselves to the absolute arbitrary power and will of a legislator, they have disarmed themselves, and armed him, to make a prey of them when he pleases. He being in a much worse condition, who is exposed to the arbitrary power of one man, who has the command of 100,000, than he that is exposed to the arbitrary power of 100,000 single men; no body being secure, that his will, who has such a command, is better than that of other men, though his force be 100,000 times stronger. And therefore, whatever form the commonwealth is under, the ruling power ought to govern by declared and received laws, and not by extemporary dictates and undetermined resolutions. For then mankind will be in a far worse condition than in the state of nature, if they shall have armed one or a few men with the joint power of a multitude, to force them to obey at pleasure the exorbitant and unlimited decrees of their sudden thoughts, or unrestrained, and till that moment unknown wills, without having any measures set down which may guide and justify their actions; for all the power the government has, being

only for the good of the society, as it ought not to be arbitrary and at pleasure, so it ought to be exercised by *established and promulgated laws;* that both the people may know their duty, and be safe and secure within the limits of the law, and the rulers too kept within their bounds, and not to be tempted, by the power they have in their hands, to employ it to such purposes, and by such measures, as they would not have known, and own not willingly.

138. *Thirdly,* The *supreme power cannot take* from any man part of his property without his own consent. For the preservation of property being the end of government, and that for which men enter into society, it necessarily supposes and requires, that the people should *have property,* without which they must be supposed to lose that, by entering into society, which was the end for which they entered into it; too gross an absurdity for any man to own. *Men* therefore *in society having property,* they have such right to the goods, which by the law of the community are theirs, that no body hath a right to take their substance or any part of it from them, without their own consent; without this they have no property at all. For I have truly no property in that, which another can by right take from me, when he pleases, against my consent. Hence it is a mistake to think, that the *supreme or legislative power* of any commonwealth can do what it will, and dispose of the estates of the subject arbitrarily, or take any part of them at pleasure. This is not much to be feared in governments where the legislative consists, wholly or in part, in assemblies which are variable, whose members, upon the dissolution of the assembly, are subjects under the common laws of their country, equally with the rest. But in governments, where the legislative is in one lasting assembly always in being, or in one man, as in absolute monarchies, there is danger still, that they will think themselves to have a distinct interest from the rest of the community; and so will be apt to increase their own riches and power by taking what they think fit from the people. For a man's property is not at all secure, though there be good and equitable laws to set the bounds of it between him and his fellow subjects, if he who

commands those subjects, have power to take from any private man, what part he pleases of his property, and use and dispose of it as he thinks good.

139. But government, into whatsoever hands it is put, being, as I have before shewed, intrusted with this condition, and *for this end,* that men might have and secure their properties; the prince, or senate, however it may have power to make laws, for the regulating of property between the subjects one amongst another, yet can never have a power to take to themselves the whole, or any part of the subject's property, without their own consent. For this would be in effect to leave them no property at all. And to let us see, that even absolute power where it is necessary, is not arbitrary by being absolute, but is still limited by that reason, and confined to those ends, which required it in some cases to be absolute, we need look no farther than the common practice of martial discipline. For the preservation of the army, and in it of the whole commonwealth, requires an absolute obedience to the command of every superiour officer, and it is justly death to disobey or dispute the most dangerous or unreasonable of them; but yet we see, that neither the serjeant, that could command a soldier to march up to the mouth of a cannon, or stand in a breach, where he is almost sure to perish, can command that soldier to give him one penny of his money; nor the general, that can condemn him to death for deserting his post, or for not obeying the most desperate orders, can yet, with all his absolute power of life and death, dispose of one farthing of that soldier's estate, or seize one jot of his goods; whom yet he can command any thing, and hang for the least disobedience: because such a blind obedience is necessary to that end, for which the commander has his power, viz. the preservation of the rest; but the disposing of his goods has nothing to do with it.

140. It is true, governments cannot be supported without great charge, and it is fit every one who enjoys his share of the protection, should pay out of his estate his proportion for the maintenance of it. But still it must be with his own consent, i.e. the consent of the majority, giving it either by themselves, or their representatives chosen by them. For if any one shall claim a *power to lay* and levy *taxes* on the people, by

his own authority, and without such consent of the people, he thereby invades the *fundamental law of property*, and subverts the end of government. For what property have I in that, which another may by right take when he pleases, to himself?

141. *Fourthly,* The *legislative cannot transfer the power of making laws* to any other hands. For it being but a delegated power from the people, they who have it cannot pass it over to others. The people alone can appoint the form of the commonwealth, which is by constituting the legislative, and appointing in whose hands that shall be. And when the people have said, we will submit to rules, and be governed by laws made by such men, and in such forms, no body else can say other men shall make laws for them; nor can the people be bound by any laws, but such as are enacted by those whom they have chosen, and authorized to make laws for them. The power of the legislative being derived from the people by a positive voluntary grant and institution, can be no other than what that positive grant conveyed, which being only to make laws, and not to make legislators, the legislative can have no power to transfer their authority of making laws and place it in other hands.

142. These are the bounds which the trust, that is put in them by the society and the law of God and nature, have *set to the legislative* power of every commonwealth, in all forms of government.

*First,* They are to govern by *promulgated established laws,* not to be varied in particular cases, but to have one rule for rich and poor, for the favourite at court, and the countryman at plough.

*Secondly,* These laws also ought to be designed for no other end ultimately, but *the good of the people.*

*Thirdly,* They must *not raise taxes* on the *property of the people, without the consent of the people,* given by themselves or their deputies. And this properly concerns only such governments where the legislative is always in being, or at least where the people have not reserved any part of the legislative to deputies, to be from time to time chosen by themselves.

*Fourthly,* The legislative neither must *nor can transfer the power of making laws* to any body else, or place it any where, but where the people have.

## CHAPTER XII

### *Of the Legislative, Executive, and Federative Power of the Commonwealth*

143. The legislative power is that, which has a right *to direct how the force of the commonwealth* shall be employed for preserving the community and the members of it. But because those laws which are constantly to be executed, and whose force is always to continue, may be made in a little time; therefore there is no need, that the legislative should be always in being, not having always business to do. And because it may be too great a temptation to human frailty, apt to grasp at power, for the same persons, who have the power of making laws, to have also in their hands the power to execute them, whereby they may exempt themselves from obedience to the laws they make, and suit the law, both in its making and execution, to their own private advantage, and thereby come to have a distinct interest from the rest of the community, contrary to the end of society and government: therefore in well ordered commonwealths, where the good of the whole is so considered, as it ought, the legislative power is put into the hands of divers persons, who, duly assembled, have by themselves, or jointly with others, a power to make laws; which when they have done, being separated again, they are themselves subject to the laws they have made; which is a new and near tie upon them, to take care that they make them for the public good.

144. But because the laws, that are at once, and in a short time made, have a constant and lasting force, and need a *perpetual execution,* or an attendance thereunto: therefore it is necessary there should be a *power always in being,* which should see to the execution of the laws that are made, and remain in force. And thus the legislative and executive power come often to be separated.

145. There is another power in every commonwealth, which one may call *natural,* because it is that which answers to the power every man naturally had before he entered into society. For though in a commonwealth, the members of it are distinct persons still in reference to one another, and as such are governed by the laws of the society; yet in reference to the rest of mankind, they make one body, which is, as every member of it before was, still in the state of nature with the rest of mankind. Hence it is, that the controversies that happen between any man of the society with those that are out of it, are managed by the public; and an injury done to a member of their body engages the whole in the reparation of it. So that, under this consideration, the whole community is one body in the state of nature, in respect of all other states or persons out of its community.

146. This therefore contains the power of war and peace, leagues and alliances, and all the transactions, with all persons and communities without the commonwealth; and may be called federative, if any one pleases. So the thing be understood, I am indifferent as to the name.

147. These two powers, executive and federative, though they be really distinct in themselves, yet one comprehending the execution of the municipal laws of the society within itself, upon all that are parts of it; the other the management of the *security and interest of the public without,* with all those that it may receive benefit or damage from; yet they are always almost united. And though this *federative power* in the well or ill management of it be of great moment to the commonwealth, yet it is much less capable to be directed by antecedent, standing, positive laws, than the executive; and so must necessarily be left to the prudence and wisdom of those whose hands it is in, to be managed for the public good. For the laws that concern subjects one amongst another, being to direct their actions, may well enough precede them. But what is to be done in reference to foreigners, depending much upon their actions, and the variation of designs, and interests, must be left in great part to the prudence of those who have this power committed to them, to be managed by the best of their skill, for the advantage of the commonwealth.

148. Though, as I said, the executive and federative power of every community be really distinct in themselves, yet they are hardly to be separated, and placed at the same time in the hands of distinct persons. For both of them requiring the force of the

society for their exercise, it is almost impracticable to place the force of the commonwealth in distinct, and not subordinate hands; or that the executive and federative power should be placed in persons that might act separately, whereby the force of the public would be under different commands: which would be apt some time or other to cause disorder and ruin.

## CHAPTER XIII

### *Of the Subordination of the Powers of the Commonwealth*

149. Though in a constituted commonwealth, standing upon its own basis, and acting according to its own nature, that is, acting for the preservation of the community, there can be but *one supreme power,* which is the *legislative,* to which all the rest are and must be subordinate; yet the legislative being only a fiduciary power to act for certain ends, there remains still *in the people a supreme power to remove or alter the legislative,* when they find the legislative act contrary to the trust reposed in them. For all *power given with trust* for the attaining an end, being limited by that end; whenever that end is manifestly neglected or opposed, the trust must necessarily be forfeited, and the power devolve into the hands of those that gave it, who may place it anew where they shall think best for their safety and security. And thus the *community* perpetually *retains a supreme power* of saving themselves from the attempts and designs of any body, even of their legislators, whenever they shall be so foolish, or so wicked, as to lay and carry on designs against the liberties and properties of the subject. For no man, or society of men, having a power to deliver up their preservation, or consequently the means of it, to the absolute will and arbitrary dominion of another; whenever any one shall go about to bring them into such a slavish condition, they will always have a right to preserve what they have not a power to part with; and to rid themselves of those who invade this fundamental, sacred, and unalterable law of self-preservation, for which they

entered into society. And thus the community may be said in this respect to be *always the supreme power,* but not as considered under any form of government, because this power of the people can never take place till the government be dissolved.

150. In all cases, whilst the government subsists, the *legislative is the supreme power.* For what can give laws to another, must needs be superiour to him; and since the legislative is no otherwise legislative of the society, but by the right it has to make laws for all the parts, and for every member of the society, prescribing rules to their actions, and giving power of execution, where they are transgressed; the legislative must needs be the supreme, and all other powers, in any members or parts of the society, derived from and subordinate to it.

151. In some commonwealths, where the legislative is not always in being, and the executive is vested in a single person, who has also a share in the legislative; there that single person in a very tolerable sense may also be called supreme; not that he has in himself all the supreme power, which is that of law-making; but because he has in him the supreme execution, from whom all inferiour magistrates derive all their several subordinate powers, or at least the greatest part of them: having also no legislative superiour to him, there being no law to be made without his consent, which cannot be expected should ever subject him to the other part of the legislative, he is properly enough in this sense *supreme.* But yet it is to be observed, that though *oaths of allegiance* and fealty are taken to him, it is not to him as supreme legislator, but as *supreme executor* of the law, made by a joint power of him with others: allegiance being nothing but an *obedience according to law,* which when he violates, he has no right to obedience, nor can claim it otherwise, than as the public person invested with the power of the law; and so is to be considered as the image, phantom, or representative of the commonwealth, acted by the will of the society, declared in its laws; and thus he has no will, no power, but that of the law. But when he quits this representation, this public will, and acts by his own private will, he degrades himself, and is but a single private person without power, and without will, that

has no right to obedience; the members owing no obedience but to the public will of the society.

152. The *executive power,* placed any where but in a person that has also a share in the legislative, is visibly subordinate and accountable to it, and may be at pleasure changed and displaced; so that it is not the *supreme executive power* that is exempt from subordination, but the *supreme executive power* vested in one, who having a share in the legislative, has no distinct superiour legislative to be subordinate and accountable to, farther than he himself shall join and consent; so that he is no more subordinate than he himself shall think fit, which one may certainly conclude will be but very little. Of other ministerial and subordinate powers in a commonwealth, we need not speak, they being so multiplied with infinite variety in the different customs and constitutions of distinct commonwealths, that it is impossible to give a particular account of them all. Only thus much, which is necessary to our present purpose, we may take notice of concerning them, that they have no manner of authority, any of them, beyond what is by positive grant and commission delegated to them, and are all of them accountable to some other power in the commonwealth.

153. It is not necessary, no, nor so much as convenient, that the *legislative* should be *always in being.* But absolutely necessary that the executive power should; because there is not always need of new laws to be made, but always need of execution of the laws that are made. When the legislative hath put the execution of the laws they make into other hands, they have a power still to resume it out of those hands, when they find cause, and to punish for any mall-administration against the laws. The same holds also in regard of the federative power, that and the executive being both *ministerial and subordinate to the legislative,* which, as has been shewed, in a constituted commonwealth is the supreme. The legislative also in this case being supposed to consist of several persons, (for if it be a single person, it cannot but be always in being, and so will, as supreme, naturally have the supreme executive power, together with the legislative) may *assemble, and exercise their legislature,* at the times that either their original

constitution, or their own adjournment, appoints, or when they please; if neither of these hath appointed any time, or there be no other way prescribed to convoke them. For the supreme power being placed in them by the people, it is always in them, and they may exercise it when they please, unless by their original constitution they are limited to certain seasons, or by an act of their supreme power they have adjourned to a certain time; and when that time comes, they have a right to assemble and act again.

154. If the legislative, or any part of it, be made up of representatives chosen for that time by the people, which afterwards return into the ordinary state of subjects, and have no share in the legislature but upon a new choice, this power of choosing must also be exercised by the people, either at certain appointed seasons, or else when they are summoned to it; and in this latter case the power of convoking the legislative is ordinarily placed in the executive, and has one of these two limitations in respect of time: that either the original constitution requires their assembling and acting at certain intervals, and then the executive power does nothing but ministerially issue directions for their electing and assembling according to due forms; or else it is left to his prudence to call them by new elections, when the occasions, or exigencies of the public require the amendment of old, or making of new laws, or the redress or prevention of any inconveniencies, that lie on, or threaten the people.

155. It may be demanded here, What if the executive power, being possessed of the force of the commonwealth, shall make use of that force to hinder the *meeting* and *acting of the legislative;* when the original constitution, or the public exigencies require it? I say, using force upon the people without authority, and contrary to the trust put in him that does so, is a state of war with the people, who have a right to *reinstate* their *legislative in the exercise* of their power. For having erected a legislative, with an intent they should exercise the power of making laws, either at certain set times, or when there is need of it; when they are hindered by any force from what is so necessary to the society, and wherein the safety and preservation of the people

consists, the people have a right to remove it by force. In all states and conditions, the true remedy of force without authority, is to oppose force to it. The use of force without authority, always puts him that uses it into a *state of war*, as the aggressor; and renders him liable to be treated accordingly.

## CHAPTER XVI

### *Of Conquest*

175. Though governments can originally have no other rise than that before-mentioned, nor *polities* be *founded* on any thing but *the consent of the people;* yet such have been the disorders ambition has filled the world with, that in the noise of war, which makes so great a part of the history of mankind, *this consent* is little taken notice of: and therefore many have mistaken the force of arms for the consent of the people, and reckon conquest as one of the originals of government. But conquest is as far from setting up any government, as demolishing an house is from building a new one in the place. Indeed, it often makes way for a new frame of a commonwealth, by destroying the former; but, without the consent of the people, can never erect a new one.

176. That the *aggressor,* who puts himself into the state of war with another, and *unjustly invades* another man's right, can, by such an unjust war, *never* come to *have a right over the conquered,* will be easily agreed by all men, who will not think, that robbers and pirates have a right of empire over whomsoever they have force enough to master; or that men are bound by promises, which unlawful force extorts from them. Should a robber break into my house, and with a dagger at my throat, make me seal deeds to convey my estate to him, would this give him any title? Just such a title, by his sword, has an *unjust conqueror*, who forces me into submission. The injury and the crime are equal, whether committed by the wearer of the crown, or some petty villain. The title of the offender, and the number of his followers, make no difference in the offence, unless it be to aggravate it. The only difference is, great robbers punish little ones, to keep them in their obedience; but the great ones are rewarded with laurels and triumphs; because they are too big for the weak hands of justice in this world, and have the power in their own possession, which should punish offenders. What is my remedy against a robber, that so broke into my house? Appeal to the law for justice. But perhaps justice is denied, or I am crippled and cannot stir, robbed and have not the means to do it. If God has taken away all means of seeking remedy, there is nothing left but patience. But my son, when able, may seek the relief of the law, which I am denied: he or his son may renew his appeal, till he recover his right. But the conquered, or their children, have no court, no arbitrator on earth to appeal to. Then they may appeal, as Jephthah did, to heaven, and repeat their appeal till they have recovered the native right of their ancestors, which was, to have such a legislative over them, as the majority should approve, and freely acquiesce in. If it be objected, this would cause endless trouble; I answer, no more than justice does, where she lies open to all that appeal to her. He that troubles his neighbour without a cause, is punished for it by the justice of the court he appeals to. And he that *appeals to heaven* must be sure he has right on his side; and a right too that is worth the trouble and cost of the appeal, as he will answer at a tribunal that cannot be deceived, and will be sure to retribute to every one according to the mischiefs he hath created to his fellow-subjects; that is, any part of mankind: from whence it is plain, that he that *conquers in an unjust war, can thereby have no title to the subjection and obedience of the conquered.*

177. But supposing victory favours the right side, let us consider *a conqueror in a lawful war,* and see what power he gets, and over *whom.*

*First,* it is plain, *he gets no power by his conquest over those that conquered with him.* They that fought on his side cannot suffer by the conquest, but must at least be as much freemen as they were before. And most commonly they serve upon terms, and on conditions to share with their leader, and enjoy a part of the spoil, and other advantages that attended the conquering sword; or at least have a part of the subdued country bestowed upon them. And *the conquering people are not, I hope, to be slaves by conquest,* and wear their laurels only to shew they are sacrifices to their leader's triumph. They that found absolute monarchy upon the title of the sword, make their heroes, who are the founders of such monarchies, arrant Drawcansirs, and forget they had any officers and soldiers that fought on their side in the battles they won, or assisted them in the subduing, or shared in possessing, the countries they mastered. We are told by some, that the English monarchy is founded in the Norman conquest, and that our princes have thereby a title to absolute dominion: which if it were true, (as by the history it appears otherwise) and that William had a right to make war on this island; yet his dominion by conquest could reach no farther than to the Saxons and Britons, that were then inhabitants of this country. The Normans that came with him, and helped to conquer, and all descended from them, are freemen, and no subjects by conquest, let that give what dominion it will. And if I, or any body else, shall claim freedom, as derived from them, it will be very hard to prove the contrary; and it is plain, the law, that has made no distinction between the one and the other, intends not there should be any difference in their freedom or privileges.

178. But supposing, which seldom happens, that the conquerors and conquered never incorporate into one people, under the same laws and freedom. Let us see next *what power a lawful conqueror has over the subdued;* and that I say is purely despotical. He has an absolute power over the lives of those who by an unjust war have forfeited them; but not over the lives or fortunes of those who engaged not in the war, nor over the possessions even of those who were actually engaged in it.

179. *Secondly,* I say then the conqueror gets no power but only over those who have actually assisted, concurred, or consented to that unjust force that is used against him. For the people having given to their governors no power to do an unjust thing, such as is to make an unjust war, (for they never had such a power in themselves) they ought not to be charged as guilty of the violence and injustice that is committed in an unjust war, any farther than they actually abet it; no more than they are to be thought guilty of any violence or oppression their governors should use upon the people themselves, or any part of their fellow subjects, they having impowered them no more to the one than to the other. Conquerors, it is true, seldom trouble themselves to make the distinction, but they willingly permit the confusion of war to sweep all together: but yet this alters not the right; for the conqueror's power over the lives of the conquered being only because they have used force to do, or maintain an injustice, he can have that power only over those who have concurred in that force; all the rest are innocent; and he has no more title over the people of that country, who have done him no injury, and so have made no forfeiture of their lives, than he has over any other, who without any injuries or provocations, have lived upon fair terms with him.

180. *Thirdly,* The *power a conqueror gets* over those he overcomes *in a just war, is perfectly despotical:* he has an absolute power over the lives of those, who, by putting themselves in a state of war, have forfeited them; but he has not thereby a right and title to their possessions. This I doubt not but at first sight will seem a strange doctrine, it being so quite contrary to the practice of the world; there being nothing more familiar in speaking of the dominion of countries, than to say such an one conquered it. As if conquest, without any more ado, conveyed a right of possession. But when we consider, that the practice of the strong and powerful, how universal soever it may be, is seldom the rule of right, however it be one part of the subjection of the conquered, not to argue against the conditions cut out to them by the conquering sword.

181. Though in all war there be usually a complication of force and damage, and the aggressor seldom fails to harm the estate, when he uses force against the persons of those he makes war upon; yet it is the use of force only that puts a man into the state of war. For whether by force he begins the injury, or else, having quietly, and by fraud, done the injury, he refuses to make reparation, and by force maintains it, (which is the same thing, as at first to have done it by force) it is the unjust use of force that makes the war.

For he that breaks open my house, and violently turns me out of doors; or, having peaceably got in, by force keeps me out; does in effect the same thing; supposing we are in such a state, that we have no common judge on earth, whom I may appeal to, and to whom we are both obliged to submit. For of such I am now speaking. It is the *unjust use of force then, that puts a man into the state of war* with another; and thereby he that is guilty of it makes a forfeiture of his life. For quitting reason, which is the rule given between man and man, and using force, the way of beasts, he becomes liable to be destroyed by him he uses force against as any savage ravenous beast, that is dangerous to his being. . . .

190. Every man is born with a double right: *first, a right of freedom to his person,* which no other man has a power over, but the free disposal of it lies in himself. *Secondly, a right,* before any other man, *to inherit with* his brethren his *father's goods.*

191. By the first of these, a man is *naturally free* from subjection to any government, though he be born in a place under its jurisdiction. But if he disclaim the lawful government of the country he was born in, he must also quit the right that belonged to him by the laws of it, and the possessions there descending to him from his ancestors, if it were a government made by their consent.

192. By the second, the inhabitants of any country, who are descended, and derive a title to their estates from those who are subdued, and had a government forced upon them against their free consents, *retain a right to the possession of their ancestors,* though they consent not freely to the government, whose hard conditions were by force imposed on the possessors of that country. For, the first *conqueror never having had a title to the land* of that country, the people who are the descendants of, or claim under those who were forced to submit to the yoke of a government by constraint, have always a right to shake it off, and free themselves from the usurpation or tyranny which the sword hath brought in upon them, till their rulers put them under such a frame of government as they willingly and of choice consent to. Who doubts but the Grecian Christians, descendants of the ancient possessors of that country, may justly cast off the Turk-ish yoke, which they have so long groaned under, whenever they have an opportunity to do it? For no government can have a right to obedience from a people who have not freely consented to it; which they can never be supposed to do, till either they are put in a full state of liberty to choose their government and governors, or at least till they have such standing laws, to which they have by themselves or their representatives given their free consent; and also till they are allowed their due property, which is, so to be proprietors of what they have, that no body can take away any part of it without their own consent, without which, men under any government are not in the state of freemen, but are direct slaves under the force of war.

193. But granting that the *conqueror* in a just war has a right to the estates, as well as power over the persons of the conquered; which, it is plain, he *hath* not: nothing of absolute power will follow from hence, in the continuance of the government. Because the descendants of these being all freemen, if he grants them estates and possessions to inhabit his country (without which it would be worth nothing) whatsoever he grants them, they have, so far as it is granted, property in. The nature whereof is, that *without a man's own consent, it cannot be taken from him.*

194. Their *persons* are *free* by a native right, and their properties, be they more or less, are *their own, and at their own dispose,* and not at his; or else it is no property. Supposing the conqueror gives to one man a thousand acres, to him and his heirs for ever; to another he lets a thousand acres for his life, under the rent of £50 or £500 per annum, has not the one of these a right to his thousand acres for ever, and the other during his life, paying the said rent? and hath not the tenant for life a property in all that he gets over and above his rent, by his labour and industry during the said term, supposing it to be double the rent? Can any one say, the king, or conqueror, after his grant, may, by his power of conqueror, take away all, or part of the land from the heirs of one, or from the other during his life, he paying the rent? Or can he take away from either the goods or money they have got upon the said land, at his pleasure? If he can, then

all free and voluntary contracts cease, and are void in the world; there needs nothing to dissolve them at any time but power enough: and all the grants and *promises* of *men in power* are but mockery and collusion. For can there be any thing more ridiculous than to say, I give you and yours this for ever, and that in the surest and most solemn way of conveyance can be devised; and yet it is to be understood, that I have a right, if I please, to take it away from you again tomorrow?

195. I will not dispute now, whether princes are exempt from the laws of their country; but this I am sure, they owe subjection to the laws of God and nature. No body, no power, can exempt them from the obligations of that eternal law. Those are so great, and so strong, in the case of *promises*, that omnipotency itself can be tied by them. *Grants, promises, and oaths,* are *bonds* that *hold the Almighty:* whatever some flatterers say to princes of the world, who all together, with all their people joined to them, are in comparison of the great God, but as a drop of the bucket, or a dust on the balance, inconsiderable, nothing!

196. The short of the *case in conquest* is this. The conqueror, if he have a just cause, has a despotical right over the persons of all that actually aided, and concurred in the war against him, and a right to make up his damage and cost out of their labour and estates, so he injure not the right of any other. Over the rest of the people, if there were any that consented not to the war, and over the children of the captives themselves, or the possessions of either, he has no power and so can have, *by virtue of conquest, no lawful title* himself *to dominion* over them, or derive it to his posterity; but is an aggressor, if he attempts upon their properties, and thereby puts himself in a state of war against them: and has no better a right of principality, he, nor any of his successors, than Hingar, or Hubba, the Danes, had here in England; or Spartacus had he conquered Italy, would have had; which is to have their yoke cast off, as soon as God shall give those under their subjection courage and opportunity to do it. Thus, notwithstanding whatever title the kings of Assyria had over Judah, by the sword, God assisted Hezekiah to throw off the dominion of that conquering empire. "And the Lord was with Hezekiah, and he prospered; wherefore he went forth, and he rebelled against the king of Assyria, and served him not," *2 Kings*, xviii. 7. Whence it is plain, that shaking off a power, which force, and not right, hath set over any one, though it hath the name of *rebellion*, yet is no offence before God, but is that which he allows and countenances, though even promises and covenants, when obtained by force, have intervened. For it is very probable, to any one that reads the story of Ahaz and Hezekiah attentively, that the Assyrians subdued Ahaz, and deposed him, and made Hezekiah king in his father's life-time; and that Hezekiah by agreement had done him homage, and paid him tribute all this time.

# CHAPTER XVII

## *Of Usurpation*

197. As conquest may be called a foreign usurpation, so usurpation is a kind of domestic conquest; with this difference, that an usurper can never have right on his side, it being no *usurpation* but where one is got into the *possession of what another has right to*. This, so far as it is *usurpation,* is a change only of persons, but not of the forms and rules of the government; for if the usurper extend his power beyond what of right belonged to the lawful princes, or governors of the commonwealth, it is *tyranny* added to *usurpation.*

198. In all lawful governments, the designation of the persons, who are to bear rule, is as natural and necessary a part, as the form of the government itself, and is that which had its establishment originally from the people; the anarchy being much alike to have no form of government at all, or to agree, that it shall be monarchical, but to appoint no way to design the person that shall have the power, and be the monarch. Hence all commonwealths, with the form of government established, have rules also of appointing those who are to have any share in the public authority, and settled methods of conveying

the right to them. For the anarchy is much alike to have no form of government at all, or to agree that it shall be monarchical, but to appoint no way to know or design the person that shall have the power and be the monarch. Whoever gets into the exercise of any part of the power, by other ways than what the laws of the community have prescribed, hath no right to be obeyed, though the form of the commonwealth be still preserved; since he is not the person the laws have appointed, and consequently not the person the people have consented to. Nor can such an *usurper*, or any deriving from him, ever have a title, till the people are both at liberty to consent, and have actually consented to allow, and confirm in him the power he hath till then usurped.

## CHAPTER XVIII

### Of Tyranny

199. As usurpation is the exercise of power, which another hath a right to, so *tyranny is the exercise of power beyond right,* which no body can have a right to. And this is making use of the power any one has in his hands, not for the good of those who are under it, but for his own private separate advantage. When the governor, however intitled, makes not the law, but his will, the rule; and his commands and actions are not directed to the preservation of the properties of his people, but the satisfaction of his own ambition, revenge, covetousness, or any other irregular passion.

200. If one can doubt this to be truth, or reason, because it comes from the obscure hand of a subject, I hope the authority of a king will make it pass with him. King James the first, in his speech to the parliament, 1603, tells them thus:

I will ever prefer the weal of the public, and of the whole commonwealth, in making of good laws and constitutions, to any particular and private ends of mine. Thinking ever the wealth and weal of the commonwealth to be my greatest weal and worldly felicity; a point wherein a lawful king doth directly differ from a tyrant. For I do acknowledge, that the

special and greatest point of difference that is between a rightful king and an usurping tyrant, is this, that whereas the proud and ambitious tyrant doth think his kingdom and people are only ordained for satisfaction of his desires and unreasonable appetites, the righteous and just king doth by the contrary acknowledge himself to be ordained for the procuring of the wealth and property of his people.

And again, in his speech to the parliament, 1609, he hath these words:

The king binds himself by a double oath to the observation of the fundamental laws of his kingdom; tacitly, as by being a king, and so bound to protect as well the people, as the laws of his kingdom; and expressly, by his oath at his coronation; so as every just king, in a settled kingdom, is bound to observe that paction made to his people by his laws, in framing his government agreeable thereunto, according to that paction which God made with Noah after the deluge: Hereafter, seed-time and harvest, and cold and heat, and summer and winter, and day and night, shall not cease while the earth remaineth. And therefore a king governing in a settled kingdom, leaves to be a king, and degenerates into a tyrant, as soon as he leaves off to rule according to his laws.

And a little after, therefore all kings that are not tyrants, or perjured, will be glad to bound themselves within the limits of their laws; and they that persuade them the contrary, are vipers, and pests, both against them and the commonwealth. Thus that learned king, who well understood the notions of things, makes the difference betwixt a *king* and a *tyrant* to consist only in this, that one makes the laws the bounds of his power, and the good of the public the end of his government; the other makes all give way to his own will and appetite.

201. It is a mistake to think this fault is proper only to monarchies; other forms of government are liable to it, as well as that. For wherever the power, that is put in any hands for the government of the people, and the preservation of their properties, is applied to other ends, and made use of to impoverish, harass, or sub-

due them to the arbitrary and irregular commands of those that have it; there it presently becomes tyranny, whether those that thus use it are one or many. Thus we read of the thirty tyrants at Athens, as well as one at Syracuse; and the intolerable dominion of the decemviri at Rome was nothing better.

202. *Wherever law ends, tyranny begins*, if the law be transgressed to another's harm; and whosoever in authority exceeds the power given him by the law, and makes use of the force he has under his command, to compass that upon the subject, which the law allows not, ceases in that to be a magistrate; and, acting without authority, may be opposed as any other man, who by force invades the right of another. This is acknowledged in subordinate magistrates. He that hath authority to seize my person in the street, may be opposed as a thief and a robber if he endeavours to break into my house to execute a writ, notwithstanding that I know he has such a warrant, and such a legal authority, as will impower him to arrest me abroad. And why this should not hold in the highest, as well as in the most inferiour magistrate, I would gladly be informed. Is it reasonable that the eldest brother, because he has the greatest part of his father's estate, should thereby have a right to take away any of his younger brother's portions? Or, that a rich man, who possessed a whole country, should from thence have a right to seize, when he pleased, the cottage and garden of his poor neighbour? The being rightfully possessed of great power and riches, exceedingly beyond the greatest part of the sons of Adam, is so far from being an excuse, much less a reason for rapine and oppression, which the endamaging another without authority is, that it is a great aggravation of it. For the exceeding the bounds of authority is no more a right in a great, than in a petty officer; no more justifiable in a king than a constable; but is so much the worse in him, in that he has more trust put in him, has already a much greater share than the rest of his brethren, and is supposed, from the advantages of his education, employment, and counsellors, to be more knowing in the measures of right or wrong.

203. May the *commands* then *of a prince be opposed*? may he be resisted as often as any one shall find himself aggrieved, and but imagine he has not right done him? This will unhinge and overturn all polities, and, instead of government and order, leave nothing but anarchy and confusion.

204. To this I answer, that *force* is to be *opposed* to nothing but to unjust and unlawful *force;* whoever makes any opposition in any other case, draws on himself a just condemnation both from God and man; and so no such danger or confusion will follow, as is often suggested. For,

205. *First,* As, in some countries, the person of the prince by the law is sacred; and so, whatever he commands or does, his person is still free from all question or violence, not liable to force, or any judicial censure or condemnation. But yet opposition may be made to the illegal acts of any inferiour officer, or other commissioned by him; unless he will, by actually putting himself into a state of war with his people, dissolve the government, and leave them to that defence which belongs to every one in the state of nature. For of such things who can tell what the end will be? And a neighbour kingdom has shewed the world an odd example. In all other cases the *sacredness* of the *person exempts him from all inconveniencies,* whereby he is secure, whilst the government stands, from all violence and harm whatsoever; than which there cannot be a wiser constitution. For the harm he can do in his own person not being likely to happen often, nor to extend itself far; nor being able by his single strength to subvert the laws, nor oppress the body of the people, should any prince have so much weakness and ill-nature as to be willing to do it, the inconveniency of some particular mischiefs that may happen sometimes, when a heady prince comes to the throne, are well recompensed by the peace of the public, and security of the government, in the person of the chief magistrate, thus set out of the reach of danger: it being safer for the body that some few private men should be sometimes in danger to suffer, than that the head of the republic should be easily, and upon slight occasions, exposed.

206. *Secondly,* But this privilege belonging only to the king's person, hinders not, but they may be questioned, opposed, and resisted, who use unjust

force, though they pretend a commission from him, which the law authorizes not. As is plain in the case of him that has the king's writ to arrest a man, which is a full commission from the king; and yet he that has it cannot break open a man's house to do it, nor execute this command of the king upon certain days, nor in certain places, though this commission have no such exception in it, but they are the limitations of the law, which if any one transgress, the king's commission excuses him not. For the king's authority being given him only by the law, he cannot impower any one to act against the law, or justify him, by his commission, in so doing. The *commission or command of any magistrate, where he has no authority,* being as void and insignificant, as that of any private man. The difference between the one and the other being that the magistrate has some authority so far, and to such ends, and the private man has none at all. For it is not the commission, but the authority, that gives the right of acting; and *against the laws there can be no authority.* But notwithstanding such resistance, the king's person and authority are still both secured, and so *no danger to governor or government.*

207. *Thirdly,* Supposing a government wherein the person of the chief magistrate is not thus sacred; yet this *doctrine* of the lawfulness of *resisting* all unlawful exercises of his power, *will not* upon every slight occasion endanger him, or *embroil the government.* For where the injured party may be relieved, and his damages repaired by appeal to the law, there can be no pretence for force, which is only to be used where a man is intercepted from appealing to the law. For nothing is to be accounted hostile force, but where it leaves not the remedy of such an appeal. And it is such force alone, that puts him that uses it *into a state of war,* and makes it lawful to resist him. A man with a sword in his hand, demands my purse in the highway, when perhaps I have not twelve-pence in my pocket: this man I may lawfully kill. To another I deliver £100 to hold only whilst I alight, which he refuses to restore me, when I am got up again, but draws his sword to defend the possession of it by force, if I endeavour to retake it. The mischief this man does me is an hundred, or possibly a thousand times more than the other perhaps intended me (whom I killed before he really did me any;) and yet I might lawfully kill the one, and cannot so much as hurt the other lawfully. The reason whereof is plain; because the one using force, which threatened my life, I could not have *time to appeal* to the law to secure it: and when it was gone, it was too late to appeal. The law could not restore life to my dead carcass, the loss was irreparable: which to prevent, the law of nature gave me a right to destroy him, who had put himself into a state of war with me, and threatened my destruction. But in the other case, my life not being in danger, I may have the *benefit of appealing* to the law, and have reparation for my £100 that way.

208. *Fourthly,* But if the unlawful acts done by the magistrate be maintained (by the power he has got) and the remedy which is due by law, be by the same power obstructed: yet the *right of resisting,* even in such manifest acts of tyranny, will not suddenly, or on slight occasions, disturb the government. For if it reach no farther than some private men's cases, though they have a right to defend themselves, and to recover by force what by unlawful force is taken from them: yet the right to do so will not easily engage them in a contest, wherein they are sure to perish; it being as impossible for one, or a few oppressed men to *disturb the government,* where the body of the people do not think themselves concerned in it, as for a raving madman, or heady malecontent, to overturn a well-settled state, the people being as little apt to follow the one, as the other.

209. But if either these illegal acts have extended to the majority of the people; or if the mischief and oppression has lighted only on some few, but in such cases, as the precedent and consequences seem to threaten all; and they are persuaded in their consciences, that their laws, and with them their estates, liberties, and lives are in danger, and perhaps their religion too: how they will be hindered from resisting illegal force, used against them, I cannot tell. This is an *inconvenience,* I confess, that *attends all governments* whatsoever, when the governors have brought it to this pass, to be generally suspected of their people; the most dangerous state which they can possibly put themselves in; wherein they are the less to be

pitied, because it is so easy to be avoided; it being as impossible for a governor, if he really means the good of his people, and the preservation of them, and their laws together, not to make them see and feel it, as it is for the father of a family, not to let his children see he loves and takes care of them.

210. But if all the world shall observe pretences of one kind, and actions of another; arts used to elude the law, and the trust of prerogative, (which is an arbitrary power in some things left in the prince's hand to do good, not harm, to the people) employed contrary to the end for which it was given: if the people shall find the ministers and subordinate magistrates chosen suitable to such ends, and favoured, or laid by, proportionately as they promote or oppose them: if they see several experiments made of arbitrary power, and that religion underhand favoured (though publicly proclaimed against) which is readiest to introduce it; and the operators in it supported, as much as may be; and when that cannot be done, yet approved still, and liked the better: if a *long train of actions shew the councils* all tending that way; how can a man any more hinder himself from being persuaded in his own mind, which way things are going; or from casting about how to save himself, than he could from believing the captain of the ship he was in, was carrying him, and the rest of the company, to Algiers, when he found him always steering that course, though cross winds, leaks in his ship, and want of men and provisions did often force him to turn his course another way for some time, which he steadily returned to again, as soon as the wind, weather, and other circumstances would let him?

# CHAPTER XIX

## *Of the Dissolution of Government*

211. He that will with any clearness speak of the *dissolution of government*, ought in the first place to distinguish between the *dissolution of the society* and the *dissolution of the government*. That which makes the community, and brings men out of the loose state of nature into *one politic society*, is the agreement which every one has with the rest to incorporate, and act as one body, and so be one distinct commonwealth. The usual, and almost only way whereby *this union is dissolved*, is the inroad of foreign force making a conquest upon them. For in that case, (not being able to maintain and support themselves, as *one entire* and *independent body*) the union belonging to that body which consisted therein, must necessarily cease, and so every one return to the state he was in before, with a liberty to shift for himself, and provide for his own safety, as he thinks fit, in some other society. Whenever the *society is dissolved*, it is certain the government of that society cannot remain. Thus conquerors' swords often cut up governments by the roots, and mangle societies to pieces, separating the subdued or scattered multitude from the protection of, and dependence on, that society which ought to have preserved them from violence. The world is too well instructed in, and too forward to allow of, this way of dissolving of governments, to need any more to be said of it; and there wants not much argument to prove, that where the *society is dissolved*, the government cannot remain; that being as impossible, as for the frame of a house to subsist when the materials of it are scattered and dissipated by a whirlwind, or jumbled into a confused heap by an earthquake.

212. Besides this overturning from without, *governments are dissolved from within*.

*First*, When the *legislative is altered*. Civil society being a state of peace, amongst those who are of it, from whom the state of war is excluded by the umpirage, which they have provided in their legislative, for the ending all differences that may arise amongst any of them; it is in their legislative, that the members of a commonwealth are united, and combined together into one coherent living body. This *is the soul that gives form, life, and unity* to the commonwealth: from hence the several members have their mutual influence, sympathy, and connexion; and therefore, when the legislative is broken, or dissolved, dissolution and death follows. For, *the essence and union of the society* consisting in having one will, the legislative, when once established by the majority, has the declaring, and as it were keeping of that will. The *constitution of the legislative* is the first and fundamental act of society, whereby provision is made for the *continuation of their union,* under the direction of persons, and bonds of laws, made by persons authorized thereunto, by the consent and appointment of the people; without which no one man, or number of men, amongst them, can have authority of making laws that shall be binding to the rest. When any one, or more, shall take upon them to make laws, whom the people have not appointed so to do, they make laws without authority, which the people are not therefore bound to obey; by which means they come again to be out of subjection, and may constitute to themselves a new legislative, as they think best, being in full liberty to resist the force of those, who without authority would impose any thing upon them. Every one is at the disposure of his own will, when those who had, by the delegation of the society, the declaring of the public will, are excluded from it, and others usurp the place, who have no such authority or delegation.

213. This being usually brought about by such in the commonwealth who misuse the power they have, it is hard to consider it aright, and know at whose door to lay it, without knowing the form of government in which it happens. Let us suppose then the legislative placed in the concurrence of three distinct persons.

1. A single hereditary person, having the constant, supreme, executive power, and with it the power of convoking and dissolving the other two, within certain periods of time.
2. An assembly of hereditary nobility.
3. An assembly of representatives chosen *pro tempore,* by the people. Such a form of government supposed, it is evident.

214. *First,* That when such a single person, or prince, sets up his own arbitrary will in place of the laws, which are the will of the society, declared by the legislative, then the *legislative is changed.* For that being in effect the legislative, whose rules and laws are put in execution, and required to be obeyed; when other laws are set up, and other rules pretended, and enforced, than what the legislative, constituted by the society, have enacted, it is plain that the *legislative is changed.* Whoever introduces new

laws, not being thereunto authorized, by the fundamental appointment of the society, or subverts the old, disowns and overturns the power by which they were made, and so sets up a *new legislative.*

215. *Secondly,* When the prince hinders the legislative from assembling in its due time, or from acting freely, pursuant to those ends for which it was constituted, the *legislative is altered:* for it is not a certain number of men, no, nor their meeting, unless they have also freedom of debating, and leisure of perfecting, what is for the good of the society, wherein the legislative consists: when these are taken away or altered, so as to deprive the society of the due exercise of their power, the legislative is truly altered. For it is not names that constitute governments, but the use and exercise of those powers that were intended to accompany them; so that he, who takes away the freedom, or hinders the acting of the legislative in its due seasons, in effect *takes away the legislative,* and *puts an end to the government.*

216. *Thirdly,* When, by the arbitrary power of the prince, the electors, or ways of election, are altered, without the consent, and contrary to the common interest of the people, there also the *legislative is altered.* For, if others than those whom the society hath authorized thereunto, do choose, or in another way than what the society hath prescribed, those chosen are not the legislative appointed by the people.

217. *Fourthly,* The delivery also of the people into the subjection of a foreign power, either by the prince, or by the legislative, is certainly a *change of the legislative,* and so a *dissolution of the government.* For the end why people entered into society being to be preserved one intire, free, independent society, to be governed by its own laws; this is lost, whenever they are given up into the power of another.

218. Why, in such a constitution as this, the *dissolution of the government* in these cases is to be imputed to the prince, is evident; because he, having the force, treasure, and offices of the state to employ, and often persuading himself, or being flattered by others, that as supreme magistrate, he is uncapable of control; he alone is in a condition to make great

advances toward such changes, under pretence of lawful authority, and has it in his hands to terrify or suppress opposers, as factious, seditious, and enemies to the government: whereas no other part of the legislative, or people, is capable by themselves to attempt any alteration of the legislative, without open and visible rebellion, apt enough to be taken notice of; which, when, it prevails, produces effects very little different from foreign conquest. Besides, the prince in such a form of government having the power of dissolving the other parts of the legislative, and thereby rendering them private persons, they can never in opposition to him, or without his concurrence, alter the legislative by a law, his consent being necessary to give any of their decrees that sanction. But yet, so far as the other parts of the legislative any way contribute to any attempt upon the government, and do either promote, or not, what lies in them, hinder such designs; they are guilty, and partake in this, which is certainly the greatest crime men can be guilty of one towards another.

219. There is one way more whereby such a government may be dissolved, and that is, when he who has the supreme executive power neglects and abandons that charge, so that the laws already made can no longer be put in execution. This is demonstratively to reduce all to anarchy, and so effectually to *dissolve the government*. For laws not being made for themselves, but to be, by their execution, the bonds of the society, to keep every part of the body politic in its due place and function; when that totally ceases, the *government* visibly *ceases*, and the people become a confused multitude, without order or connexion. Where there is no longer the administration of justice, for the securing of men's rights, nor any remaining power within the community to direct the force, or provide for the necessities of the public; there certainly is *no government left*. Where the laws cannot be executed, it is all one as if there were no laws; and a government without laws is, I suppose, a mystery in politics, inconceivable to human capacity, and inconsistent with human society.

220. In these and the like cases, *when the government is dissolved,* the people are at liberty to provide for themselves, by erecting a new legislative, differing from the other, by the change of persons, or form, or both, as they shall find it most for their safety and good. For the *society* can never, by the fault of another, lose the native and original right it has to preserve itself; which can only be done by a settled legislative, and a fair and impartial execution of the laws made by it. But the state of mankind is not so miserable that they are not capable of using this remedy, till it be too late to look for any. To tell *people* they *may provide for themselves,* by erecting a new legislative, when by oppression, artifice, or being delivered over to a foreign power, their old one is gone, is only to tell them, they may expect relief when it is too late, and the evil is past cure. This is in effect no more, than to bid them first be slaves, and then to take care of their liberty; and when their chains are on, tell them, they may act like freemen. This, if barely so, is rather mockery than relief; and men can never be secure from tyranny, if there be no means to escape it, till they are perfectly under it: And therefore it is, that they have not only a right to get out of it, but to prevent it.

221. There is, therefore, secondly, another way whereby *governments are dissolved,* and that is, when the legislative, or the prince either of them, act contrary to their trust.

*First,* The *legislative acts against the trust* reposed in them, when they endeavour to invade the property of the subject, and to make themselves, or any part of the community, masters, or arbitrary disposers of the lives, liberties, or fortunes of the people.

222. The reason why men enter into society, is the preservation of their property; and the end why they choose and authorize a legislative, is, that there may be laws made, and rules set, as guards and fences to the properties of all the members of the society: to limit the power, and moderate the dominion, of every part and member of the society. For since it can never be supposed to be the will of the society, that the legislative should have a power to destroy that, which every one designs to secure, by entering into society, and for which the people submitted themselves to legislators of their own making, whenever the *legislators endeavour to take away and destroy the property of the people,* or to reduce them to slavery under arbi-

trary power, they put themselves into a state of war with the people, who are thereupon absolved from any farther obedience, and are left to the common refuge, which God hath provided for all men, against force and violence. Whensoever therefore the *legislative* shall transgress this fundamental rule of society; and either by ambition, fear, folly or corruption, *endeavour to grasp* themselves, *or put into the hands of any other an absolute power* over the lives, liberties, and estates of the people; by this breach of trust they *forfeit the power,* the people had put into their hands, for quite contrary ends, and it devolves to the people, who have a right to resume their original liberty, and, by the establishment of a new legislative, (such as they shall think fit) provide for their own safety and security, which is the end for which they are in society. What I have said here, concerning the legislative in general, holds true also concerning the supreme executor, who having a double trust put in him, both to have a part in the legislative, and the supreme execution of the law, acts against both, when he goes about to set up his own arbitrary will, as the law of the society. He *acts* also *contrary to his trust,* when he either employs the force, treasure, and offices of the society to corrupt the *representatives,* and gain them to his purposes; or openly pre-engages the *electors,* and prescribes to their choice, such, whom he has by solicitations, threats, promises, or otherwise, won to his designs: and employs them to bring in such, who have promised before-hand, what to vote, and what to enact. Thus to regulate candidates and electors, and new model the ways of election, what is it but to cut up the government by the roots, and poison the very fountain of public security? for the people having reserved to themselves the choice of their *representatives,* as the fence to their properties, could do it for no other end, but that they might always be freely chosen, and so chosen, freely act, and advise, as the necessity of the commonwealth, and the public good should, upon examination and mature debate, be judged to require. This, those who give their votes before they hear the debate, and have weighed the reasons on all sides, are not capable of doing. To prepare such an assembly as this, and endeavour to set up the declared abettors of his own will, for the true representatives of the people, and the law-makers of the society, is certainly as great a *breach of trust,* and as perfect a declaration of a design to subvert the government, as is possible to be met with. To which if one shall add rewards and punishments visibly employed to the same end, and all the arts of perverted law made use of, to take off and destroy all that stand in the way of such a design, and will not comply and consent to betray the liberties of their country, it will be past doubt what is doing. What power they ought to have in the society, who thus employ it contrary to the trust that went along with it in its first institution, is easy to determine; and one cannot but see, that he, who has once attempted any such thing as this, cannot any longer be trusted.

223. To this perhaps it will be said, that the people being ignorant, and always discontented, to lay the foundation of government in the unsteady opinion and uncertain humour of the people, is to expose it to certain ruin; and *no government will be able long to subsist,* if the people may set up a new legislative, whenever they take offence at the old one. To this I answer, quite the contrary. People are not so easily got out of their old forms as some are apt to suggest. They are hardly to be prevailed with to amend the acknowledged faults in the frame they have been accustomed to. And if there be any original defects, or adventitious ones introduced by time, or corruption: it is not an easy thing to get them changed, even when all the world sees there is an opportunity for it. This slowness and aversion in the people to quit their old constitutions, has in the many revolutions which have been seen in this kingdom, in this and former ages, still kept us to, or, after some interval of fruitless attempts, still brought us back again to, our old legislative of king, lords, and commons: and whatever provocations have made the crown be taken from some of our princes heads, they never carried the people so far as to place it in another line.

224. But it will be said, this *hypothesis* lays a *ferment* for frequent *rebellion.* To which I *answer,*

*First,* No more than any other *hypothesis:* for when the people are made miserable, and find themselves *exposed to the ill usage of arbitrary power,* cry up their governors as much as you will, for *sons of*

*Jupiter;* let them be sacred or divine, descended, or authorized from heaven; give them out for whom or what you please, the same will happen. *The people generally ill treated,* and contrary to right, will be ready upon any occasion to ease themselves of a burden that sits heavy upon them. They will wish, and seek for the opportunity, which in the change, weakness, and accidents of human affairs, seldom delays long to offer itself. He must have lived but a little while in the world, who has not seen examples of this in his time; and he must have read very little, who cannot produce examples of it in all sorts of governments in the world.

225. *Secondly,* I answer, such *revolutions happen* not upon every little mismanagement in public affairs. *Great mistakes* in the ruling part, many wrong and inconvenient laws, and all the slips of human frailty, will be *borne by the people* without mutiny or murmur. But if a long train of abuses, prevarications and artifices, all tending the same way, make the design visible to the people, and they cannot but feel what they lie under, and see whither they are going; it is not to be wondered, that they should then rouse themselves, and endeavour to put the rule into such hands which may secure to them the ends for which government was at first erected; and without which, ancient names, and specious forms, are so far from being better, that they are much worse, than the state of nature, or pure anarchy; the inconveniencies being all as great and as near, but the remedy farther off and more difficult.

226. *Thirdly,* I answer, that *this doctrine* of a power in the people of providing for their safety anew, by a new legislative, when their legislators have acted contrary to their trust, by invading their property, is the *best fence against rebellion,* and the probablest means to hinder it. For *rebellion* being an opposition, not to persons, but authority, which is founded only in the constitutions and laws of the government; those, whoever they be, who by force break through, and by force justify their violation of them, are truly and properly *rebels.* For when men, by entering into society and civil government, have excluded force, and introduced laws for the preservation of property, peace, and unity amongst themselves; those who set up force again in opposition to the laws, do *rebellare,* that is, bring back again the state of war, and are properly rebels: Which they who are in power, (by the pretence they have to authority, the temptation of force they have in their hands, and the flattery of those about them) being likeliest to do; the properest way to prevent the evil, is to shew them the danger and injustice of it, who are under the greatest temptation to run into it.

227. In both the forementioned cases, when either the legislative is changed, or the legislators act contrary to the end for which they were constituted, those who are guilty are *guilty of rebellion;* for if any one by force takes away the established legislative of any society, and the laws by them made pursuant to their trust, he thereby takes away the umpirage, which every one had consented to, for a peaceable decision of all their controversies, and a bar to the state of war amongst them. They who remove, or change the legislative, take away this decisive power, which no body can have but by the appointment and consent of the people; and so destroying the authority which the people did, and no body else can set up, and introducing a power which the people hath not authorized, they actually *introduce a state of war,* which is that of force without authority; and thus by removing the legislative established by the society, (in whose decisions the people acquiesced and united, as to that of their own will) they untie the knot, and *expose the people anew to the state of war.* And if those, who by force take away the legislative, are *rebels,* the *legislators* themselves, as has been shewn, can be no less esteemed so; when they, who were set up for the protection and preservation of the people, their liberties and properties, shall by force invade and endeavour to take them away; and so they putting themselves into a state of war with those who made them the protectors and guardians of their peace, are properly, and with the greatest aggravation, *rebellantes,* rebels.

228. But if they, who say, "it lays a foundation for rebellion," mean that it may occasion civil wars, or intestine broils, to tell the people they are absolved from obedience when, illegal attempts are made upon their liberties or properties, and may

oppose the unlawful violence of those who were their magistrates, when they invade their properties contrary to the trust put in them; and that therefore this doctrine is not to be allowed, being so destructive to the peace of the world: they may as well say, upon the same ground, that honest men may not oppose robbers or pirates, because this may occasion disorder or bloodshed. If any *mischief* come in such cases, it is not to be charged upon him who defends his own right, but *on him that invades* his neighbour's. If the innocent honest man must quietly quit all he has, for peace sake, to him who will lay violent hands upon it, I desire it may be considered, what a kind of peace there will be in the world, which consists only in violence and rapine; and which is to be maintained only for the benefit of robbers and oppressors. Who would not think it an admirable peace betwixt the mighty and the mean, when the lamb, without resistance, yielded his throat to be torn by the imperious wolf? Polyphemus's den gives us a perfect pattern of such a peace, and such a government, wherein Ulysses and his companions had nothing to do, but quietly to suffer themselves to be devoured. And no doubt Ulysses, who was a prudent man, preached up *passive obedience,* and exhorted them to a quiet submission, by representing to them of what concernment peace was to mankind; and by strewing the inconveniencies might happen, if they should offer to resist Polyphemus, who had now the power over them.

229. The end of government is the good of mankind: and which is *best for mankind,* that the people should be always exposed to the boundless will of tyranny; or that the rulers should be sometimes liable to be opposed, when they grow exorbitant in the use of their power, and employ it for the destruction, and not the preservation of the properties of their people?

230. Nor let any one say, that mischief can arise from hence, as often as it shall please a busy head, or turbulent spirit, to desire the alteration of the government. It is true, such men may stir, whenever they please; but it will be only to their own just ruin and perdition. For till the mischief be grown general, and the ill designs of the rulers become visible, or their attempts sensible to the greater part, the people, who are more disposed to suffer than right themselves by resistance, are not apt to stir. The examples of particular injustice or oppression, of here and there an unfortunate man, moves them not. But if they universally have a persuasion, grounded upon manifest evidence, that designs are carrying on against their liberties, and the general course and tendency of things cannot but give them strong suspicions of the evil intention of their governors, who is to be blamed for it? Who can help it, if they, who might avoid it, bring themselves into this suspicion? Are the people to be blamed, if they have the sense of rational creatures, and can think of things no otherwise than as they find and feel them? And is it not rather *their fault,* who put things into such a posture, that they would not have them thought to be as they are? I grant, that the pride, ambition, and turbulency of private men, have sometimes caused great disorders in commonwealths, and factions have been fatal to states and kingdoms. But whether *the mischief* hath *oftener* begun *in the peoples wantonness,* and a desire to cast off the lawful authority of their rulers, or in *the rulers insolence,* and endeavours to get and exercise an arbitrary power over their people; whether oppression, or disobedience, gave the first rise to the disorder; I leave it to impartial history to determine. This I am sure, whoever, either ruler or subject, by force goes about to invade the rights of either prince or people, and lays the foundation for *overturning* the constitution and frame of *any just government;* is highly guilty of the greatest crime, I think, a man is capable of; being to answer for all those mischiefs of blood, rapine, and desolation, which the breaking to pieces of governments bring on a country. And he who does it, is justly to be esteemed the common enemy and pest of mankind, and is to be treated accordingly.

231. That *subjects* or *foreigners,* attempting by force on the properties of any people, may be resisted with force, is agreed on all hands. But that *magistrates,* doing the same thing, may be *resisted,* hath of late been denied: as if those who had the greatest privileges and advantages by the law, had thereby a power to break those laws, by which alone they were

set in a better place than their brethren: whereas their offence is thereby the greater, both as being ungrateful for the greater share they have by the law, and breaking also that trust which is put into their hands by their brethren.

232. Whosoever uses *force without right,* as every one does in society, who does it without law, puts himself into a *state of war* with those against whom he so uses it; and in that state all former ties are cancelled, all other rights cease, and every one has a right to defend himself, and to *resist the aggressor.* This is so evident, that Barclay himself, that great assertor of the power and sacredness of kings, is forced to confess, that it is lawful for the people, in some cases, to resist their king; and that too in a chapter, wherein he pretends to shew, that the divine law shuts up the people from all manner of rebellion. Whereby it is evident, even by his own doctrine, that, since they may in some cases resist, all resisting of *princes* is not rebellion. . . .

240. Here, it is like, the common question will be made, *Who shall be judge,* whether the prince or legislative act contrary to their trust? This, perhaps, ill-affected and factious men may spread amongst the people, when the prince only makes use of his due prerogative. To this I reply, "The people shall be judge;" for who shall be *judge* whether his trustee or deputy acts well, and according to the trust reposed in him, but he who deputes him, and must by having deputed him, have still a power to discard him, when he fails in his trust? If this be reasonable in particular cases of private men, why should it be otherwise in that of the greatest moment, where the welfare of millions is concerned, and also where the evil, if not prevented, is greater, and the redress very difficult, dear, and dangerous?

241. But farther, this question, ("Who shall be judge?") cannot mean that there is no judge at all. For where there is no judicature on earth, to decide controversies amongst men, God in heaven is judge. He alone, it is true, is judge of the right. But *every man is judge* for himself, as in all other cases, so in this, whether another hath put himself into a state of war with him, and whether he should appeal to the supreme judge, as Jephthah did.

242. If a controversy arise betwixt a prince and some of the people, in a matter where the law is silent, or doubtful, and the thing be of great consequence, I should think the proper *umpire,* in such a case, should be the body of the *people:* for in cases where the prince hath a trust reposed in him, and is dispensed from the common ordinary rules of the law; there, if any men find themselves aggrieved, and think the prince acts contrary to, or beyond that trust, who so proper to *judge* as the body of the *people,* (who, at first, lodged that trust in him) how far they meant it should extend? But if the prince, or whoever they be in the administration, decline that way of determination, the appeal then lies no where but to heaven; force between either persons, who have no known superior on earth, or which permits no appeal to a judge on earth, being properly a state of war, wherein the appeal lies only to heaven; and in that state the *injured party must judge* for himself, when he will think fit to make use of that appeal, and put himself upon it.

243. To conclude, The *power that every individual gave the society,* when he entered into it, can never revert to the individuals again, as long as the society lasts, but will always remain in the community; because without this there can be no community, no commonwealth, which is contrary to the original agreement: so also when the society hath placed the legislative in any assembly of men, to continue in them and their successors, with direction and authority for providing such successors, the *legislative can never revert to the people* whilst that government lasts: Because, having provided a legislative with power to continue for ever, they have given up their political power to the legislative, and cannot resume it. But if they have set limits to the duration of their legislative, and made this supreme power in any person, or assembly, only temporary; or else, when by the miscarriages of those in authority, it is forfeited; upon the forfeiture, or at the determination of the time set, *it reverts to the society,* and the people have a right to act as supreme, and continue the legislative in themselves; or erect a new form, or under the old form place it in new hands, as they think good.

# Letter Concerning Toleration

HONORED SIR,

Since you are pleased to inquire what are my thoughts about the mutual toleration of Christians in their different professions of religion, I must needs answer you freely that I esteem that toleration to be the chief characteristic mark of the true church. For whatsoever some people boast of the antiquity of places and names, or of the pomp of their outward worship; others, of the reformation of their discipline; all, of the orthodoxy of their faith—for everyone is orthodox to himself—these things, and all others of this nature, are much rather marks of men striving for power and empire over one another than of the church of Christ. Let anyone have never so true a claim to all these things, yet if he be destitute of charity, meekness, and goodwill in general toward all mankind, even to those that are not Christians, he is certainly yet short of being a true Christian himself. "The kings of the Gentiles exercise lordship over them," said our Saviour to His disciples, "but ye shall not be so" [Luke 22:25]. The business of true religion is quite another thing. It is not instituted in order to the erecting of an external pomp, nor to the obtaining of ecclesiastical dominion, nor to the exercising of compulsive force, but to the regulating of men's lives, according to the rules of virtue and piety. Whosoever will list himself under the banner of Christ must in the first place, and above all things, make war upon his own lusts and vices. It is in vain for any man to usurp the name of Christian without holiness of life, purity of manners, benignity and meekness of spirit. "Let everyone that nameth the name of Christ, depart from iniquity" [2 Tim. 2:19]. "Thou, when thou art converted, strengthen thy brethren," said our Lord to Peter [Luke 22:32]. It would, indeed, be very hard for one that appears careless about his salvation to persuade me that he were extremely concerned for mine. For it is impossible that those should sincerely and heartily apply themselves to make other people Christians who have not really embraced the Christian religion in their own hearts. If the Gospel and the apostles may be credited, no man can be a Christian without charity, and without that faith which works, not by force, but by love. Now I appeal to the consciences of those that persecute, torment, destroy, and kill other men upon pretense of religion, whether they do it out of friendship and kindness toward them or no? And I shall then indeed, and not until then, believe they do so, when I shall see those fiery zealots correcting, in the same manner, their friends and familiar acquaintance for the manifest sins they commit against the precepts of the Gospel; when I shall see them persecute with fire and sword the members of their own communion that are tainted with enormous vices, and without amendment are in danger of eternal perdition; and when I shall see them thus express their love and desire of the salvation of their souls by the infliction of torments and exercise of all manner of cruelties. For if it be out of a principle of charity, as they pretend, and love to men's souls, that they deprive them of their estates, maim them with corporal punishments, starve and torment them in noisome prisons, and in the end even take away their lives—I say, if all this be done merely to make men Christians and procure their salvation, why then do they suffer whoredom, fraud, malice, and suchlike enormities, which (according to the apostle [Rom. 1]) manifestly relish of heathenish corruption, to predominate so much and abound amongst their flocks and people? These, and suchlike things, are certainly more contrary to the glory of God, to the purity of the church, and to the salvation of souls, than any conscientious dissent from ecclesiastical decisions, or separation from public worship, whilst accompanied with innocence of life. Why then does this burning zeal for God, for the church, and for the salvation of souls—burning I say, literally, with fire and faggot—pass by those moral vices and wickednesses, without any chastisement, which are acknowledged by all men to be diametrically opposite to the profession of Christianity, and bend all its nerves either to the introducing of ceremonies, or to the establishment of opinions, which for the most part are about nice and intricate matters that exceed the capacity of ordinary understandings? Which of the parties contending about these things is in the right, which of them is guilty of schism or heresy, whether those that domineer or those that suffer, will then at last be manifest when the causes of their separation comes to be judged of. He, certainly, that follows Christ embraces His doctrine and bears His yoke, though he forsake both father and mother, separate from the public assemblies and ceremonies of his country, or whomsoever or whatsoever else he relinquishes, will not then be judged a heretic.

Now, though the divisions that are amongst sects should be allowed to be never so obstructive of the salvation of souls; yet, nevertheless, adultery, fornication, uncleanliness, lasciviousness, idolatry, and suchlike things, cannot be denied to be works of the flesh, concerning which the apostle has expressly declared [Gal. 5] that "they who do them shall not inherit the kingdom of God." Whosoever, therefore, is sincerely solicitous about the kingdom of God, and thinks it his duty to endeavor the enlargement of it amongst men, ought to apply himself with no less care and industry to the rooting out of these immoralities than to the extirpation of sects. But if anyone do otherwise, and whilst he is cruel and implacable toward those that differ from him in opinion, he be indulgent to such iniquities and immoralities as are unbecoming the name of a Christian, let such a one talk never so much of the church, he plainly demonstrates by his actions that it is another kingdom he aims at, and not the advancement of the kingdom of God.

That any man should think fit to cause another man—whose salvation he heartily desires—to expire in torments, and that even in an unconverted state, would, I confess, seem very strange to me and I think to any other also. But nobody, surely, will ever believe that such a carriage can proceed from charity, love, or goodwill. If anyone maintain that men ought to be compelled by fire and sword to profess certain doctrines, and conform to this or that exterior worship, without any regard had unto their morals; if anyone endeavor to convert those that are erroneous unto the faith, by forcing them to profess things that they do not believe and allowing them to practice things that the Gospel does not permit, it cannot be doubted indeed but such a one is desirous to have a numerous assembly joined in the same profession with himself; but that he principally intends by those means to compose a truly Christian church is altogether incredible. It is not, therefore, to be wondered at if those who do not really contend for the advancement of the true religion, and of the church of Christ, make use of arms that do not belong to the Christian warfare. If, like the Captain of our salvation, they sincerely desired the good of souls, they would tread in the steps and follow the perfect example of that Prince of Peace, who sent out His soldiers to the subduing of nations, and gathering them into His church, not armed with the sword or other instruments of force, but prepared with the Gospel of peace and with the exemplary holiness of their conversation. This was His method. Though if infidels were to be converted by force, if those that are either blind or obstinate were to be drawn off from their errors by armed soldiers, we know very well that it was much more easy for Him to do it with armies of heavenly legions than for any son of the church, how potent soever, with all his dragoons.

The toleration of those that differ from others in matters of religion is so agreeable to the Gospel of Jesus Christ, and to the genuine reason of mankind, that it seems monstrous for men to be so blind as not to perceive the necessity and advantage of it in so clear a light. I will not here tax the pride and ambition of some, the passion and uncharitable zeal of others. These are faults from which human affairs can perhaps scarce ever be perfectly freed; but yet such as nobody will bear the plain imputation of, without covering them with some specious color; and so pretend to commendation, whilst they are carried away by their own irregular passions. But, however, that some may not color their spirit of persecution and un-Christian cruelty with a pretense of care of the public weal and observation of the laws; and that others, under pretense of religion, may not seek impunity for their libertinism and licentiousness—in a word, that none may impose either upon himself or others by the pretenses of loyalty and obedience to the prince, or of tenderness and sincerity in the worship of God; I esteem it above all things necessary to distinguish exactly the business of civil government from that of religion, and to settle the just bounds that lie between the one and the other. If this be not done, there can be no end put to the controversies that will be always arising between those that have, or at least pretend to have, on the one side, a concernment for the interest of men's souls, and, on the other side, a care of the commonwealth.

The commonwealth seems to me to be a society of men constituted only for the procuring, preserving, and advancing their own civil interests.

Civil interests I call life, liberty, health, and indolency of body; and the possession of outward things, such as money, lands, houses, furniture, and the like.

It is the duty of the civil magistrate, by the impartial execution of equal laws, to secure unto all the people in general, and to every one of his subjects in particular, the just possession of these things belonging to this life. If anyone presume to violate the laws of public justice and equity, established for the preservation of those things, his presumption is to be checked by the fear of punishment consisting of the deprivation or diminution of those civil interests or goods which otherwise he might and ought to enjoy. But seeing no man does willingly suffer himself to be punished by the deprivation of any part of his goods, and much less of his liberty or life, therefore is the magistrate armed with the force and strength of all his subjects, in order to the punishment of those that violate any other man's rights.

Now that the whole jurisdiction of the magistrate reaches only to these civil concernments; and that all civil power, right and dominion is bounded and confined to the only care of promoting these things; and that it neither can nor ought in any manner to be extended to the salvation of souls, these following considerations seem unto me abundantly to demonstrate.

First, because the care of souls is not committed to the civil magistrate any more than to other men. It is not committed unto him, I say, by God; because it appears not that God has ever given any such authority to one man over another, as to compel anyone to his religion. Nor can any such power be vested in the magistrate by the consent of the people, because no man can so far abandon the care of his own salvation as blindly to leave to the choice of any other, whether prince or subject, to prescribe to him what faith or worship he shall embrace. For no man can, if he would, conform his faith to the dictates of another. All the life and power of true religion consist in the inward and full persuasion of the mind; and faith is not faith without believing. Whatever profession we make, to whatever outward worship we conform, if we are not fully satisfied in our own mind that the one is true, and the other well pleasing unto God, such profession and such practice, far from being any furtherance, are indeed great obstacles to our salvation. For in this manner, instead of expiating other sins by the exercise of religion, I say, in offering thus unto God Almighty such a worship as we esteem to be displeasing unto Him, we add unto the number of our other sins those also of hypocrisy and contempt of His Divine Majesty.

In the second place, the care of souls cannot belong to the civil magistrate because his power consists only in outward force; but true and saving religion consists in the inward persuasion of the mind, without which nothing can be acceptable to God. And such is the nature of the understanding that it cannot be compelled to the belief of anything by outward force. Confiscation of estate, imprisonment, torments, nothing of that nature can have any such efficacy as to make men change the inward judgment that they have framed of things.

It may indeed be alleged that the magistrate may make use of arguments, and thereby draw the heterodox into the way of truth and procure their salvation. I grant it; but this is common to him with other men. In teaching, instructing, and redressing the erroneous by reason, he may certainly do what becomes any good man to do. Magistracy does not oblige him to put off either humanity or Christianity; but it is one thing to persuade, another to command; one thing to press with arguments, another with penalties. This civil power alone has a right to do; to the other, good-will is authority enough. Every man has commission to admonish, exhort, convince another of error, and, by reasoning, to draw him into truth; but to give laws, receive obedience, and compel with the sword, belongs to none but the magistrate. And upon this ground I affirm that the magistrate's power extends not to the establishing of any articles of faith or forms of worship by the force of his laws. For laws are of no force at all without penalties, and penalties in this case are absolutely impertinent, because they are not proper to convince the mind. Neither the profession of any articles of faith, nor the conformity to any outward form of worship (as has been already said), can be available to the salvation of souls unless the truth of the one, and the acceptableness of the other unto God, be thoroughly believed by those that so profess and practice. But penalties are no way capable to produce such belief. It is only light and evidence that can work a change in men's opinions; which light can in no manner proceed from corporal sufferings or any other outward penalties.

In the third place, the care of the salvation of men's souls cannot belong to the magistrate; because, though the rigor of laws and the force of penalties were capable to convince and change men's minds, yet would not that help at all to the salvation of their souls. For there being but one truth, one way to heaven, what hope is there that more men would be led into it if they had no rule but the religion of the court, and were put under the necessity to quit the light of their own reason, and oppose the dictates of their own consciences, and blindly to resign themselves up to the will of their governors and to the religion which either ignorance, ambition, or superstition had chanced to establish in the countries where they were born? In the variety and contradiction of opinions in religion, wherein the princes of the world are as much divided as in their secular interests, the narrow way would be much straitened; one country alone would be in the right, and all the rest of the world put under an obligation of following their princes in the ways that lead to destruction; and that

which heightens the absurdity, and very ill suits the notion of a Deity, men would owe their eternal happiness or misery to the places of their nativity.

These considerations, to omit many others that might have been urged to the same purpose, seem unto me sufficient to conclude that all the power of civil government relates only to men's civil interests, is confined to the care of the things of this world, and hath nothing to do with the world to come.

Let us now consider what a church is. A church, then, I take to be a voluntary society of men, joining themselves together of their own accord in order to the public worshiping of God in such manner as they judge acceptable to Him, and effectual to the salvation of their souls.

I say it is a free and voluntary society. Nobody is born a member of any church; otherwise the religion of parents would descend unto children by the same right of inheritance as their temporal estates, and everyone would hold his faith by the same tenure he does his lands, than which nothing can be imagined more absurd. Thus, therefore, that matter stands. No man by nature is bound unto any particular church or sect, but everyone joins himself voluntarily to that society in which he believes he has found that profession and worship which is truly acceptable to God. The hope of salvation, as it was the only cause of his entrance into that communion, so it can be the only reason of his stay there. For if afterwards he discover anything either erroneous in the doctrine or incongruous in the worship of that society to which he has joined himself, why should it not be as free for him to go out as it was to enter? No member of a religious society can be tied with any other bonds but what proceed from the certain expectation of eternal life. A church, then, is a society of members voluntarily uniting to that end.

It follows now that we consider what is the power of this church, and unto what laws it is subject.

Forasmuch as no society, how free soever, or upon whatsoever slight occasion instituted, whether of philosophers for learning, of merchants for commerce, or of men of leisure for mutual conversation and discourse, no church or company, I say, can in the least subsist and hold together, but will presently dissolve and break in pieces, unless it be regulated by some laws, and the members all consent to observe some order. Place and time of meeting must be agreed on; rules for admitting and excluding members must be established; distinction of officers, and putting things into a regular course, and suchlike, cannot be omitted. But since the joining together of several members into this church society, as has already been demonstrated, is absolutely free and spontaneous, it necessarily follows that the right of making its laws can belong to none but the society itself; or, at least (which is the same thing), to those whom the society by common consent has authorized thereunto.

Some, perhaps, may object that no such society can be said to be a true church unless it have in it a bishop or presbyter, with ruling authority derived from the very apostles, and continued down to the present times by an uninterrupted succession.

To these I answer: In the first place, let them show me the edict by which Christ has imposed that law upon His church. And let not any man think me impertinent if in a thing of this consequence I require that the terms of that edict be very express and positive; for the promise He has made us [Matt. 18:20], that wheresoever two or three are gathered together in His name He will be in the midst of them, seems to imply the contrary. Whether such an assembly want anything necessary to a true church, pray do you consider. Certain I am that nothing can be there wanting unto the salvation of souls, which is sufficient to our purpose.

Next, pray observe how great have always been the divisions amongst even those who lay so much stress upon the divine institution and continued succession of a certain order of rulers in the church. Now their very dissension unavoidably puts us upon a necessity of deliberating and, consequently, allows a liberty of choosing that which upon consideration we prefer.

And, in the last place, I consent that these men have a ruler in their church, established by such a long series of succession as they judge necessary, provided I may have liberty at the same time to join myself to that society in which I am persuaded those things are to be found which are necessary to the salvation of my soul. In this manner ecclesiastical liberty will be preserved on all sides, and no man will have a legislator imposed upon him but whom himself has chosen.

But since men are so solicitous about the true church, I would only ask them here, by the way, if it be not more agreeable to the church of Christ to make the conditions of her communion consist in such things, and such things only, as the Holy Spirit has in the Holy Scriptures declared, in express words, to be necessary to salvation; I ask, I say, whether this be not more agreeable to the church of Christ than for men to impose their own inventions and interpretations upon others as if they were of Divine authority, and to establish by ecclesiastical laws, as absolutely necessary to the profession of Christianity, such things as the Holy Scriptures do either not mention or at least not expressly command? Whosoever requires those things in order to ecclesiastical communion, which Christ does not require in order to life eternal, he may, perhaps, indeed constitute a society accommodated to his own opinion and his own advantage; but how that can be called the church of Christ which is established upon laws that are not His, and which excludes such persons from its communion as He will one day receive into the Kingdom of Heaven, I understand not. But this being not a proper place to inquire into the marks of the true church, I will only mind those that contend so earnestly for the decrees of their own society and that cry out continually, The Church! the Church! with as much noise, and perhaps upon the same principle, as the Ephesian silversmiths did for their Diana; this, I say, I desire to mind them of, that the Gospel frequently declares that the true disciples of Christ must suffer persecution; but that the church of Christ should persecute others, and force others by fire and sword to embrace her faith and doctrine, I could never yet find in any of the books of the New Testament.

The end of a religious society (as has already been said) is the public worship of God and, by means thereof, the acquisition of eternal life. All discipline ought therefore to tend to that end, and all ecclesiastical laws to be thereunto confined. Nothing ought nor can be transacted in this society relating to the possession of civil and worldly goods. No force is here to be made use of upon any occasion whatsoever. For force belongs wholly to the civil magistrate, and the possession of all outward goods is subject to his jurisdiction.

But, it may be asked, by what means then shall ecclesiastical laws be established if they must be thus destitute of all compulsive power? I answer: They must be established by means suitable to the nature of such things, whereof the external profession and observation—if not proceeding from a thorough conviction and approbation of the mind—is altogether useless and unprofitable. The arms by which the members of this society are to be kept within their duty are exhortations, admonitions, and advices. If by these means the offenders will not be reclaimed and the erroneous convinced, there remains nothing further to be done but that such stubborn and obstinate persons who give no ground to hope for their reformation, should be cast out and separated from the society. This is the last and utmost force of ecclesiastical authority. No other punishment can thereby be inflicted than that, the relation ceasing between the body and the member which is cut off. The person so condemned ceases to be a part of that church.

These things being thus determined, let us inquire, in the next place, how far the duty of toleration extends, and what is required from everyone by it?

And, first, I hold that no church is bound, by the duty of toleration, to retain any such person in her bosom as, after admonition, continues obstinately to offend against the laws of the society. For these being the condition of communion and the bond of the society, if the breach of them were permitted without any animadversion the society would immediately be thereby dissolved. But, nevertheless, in all such cases care is to be taken that the sentence of excommunication, and the execution thereof, carry with it no rough usage of word or action whereby the ejected person may any wise be damnified in body or estate. For all force (as has often been said) belongs only to the magistrate, nor ought any private persons at any time to use force unless it be in self-defense against unjust violence. Excommunication neither does nor can, deprive the excommunicated person of any of those civil goods that he formerly possessed. All those things belong to the civil government and

are under the magistrate's protection. The whole force of excommunication consists only in this: that the resolution of the society in that respect being declared, the union that was between the body and some member comes thereby to be dissolved; and that relation ceasing, the participation of some certain things which the society communicated to its members, and unto which no man has any civil right, comes also to cease. For there is no civil injury done unto the excommunicated person by the church minister's refusing him that bread and wine, in the celebration of the Lord's Supper, which was not bought with his but other men's money.

Secondly, no private person has any right in any manner to prejudice another person in his civil enjoyments because he is of another church or religion. All the rights and franchises that belong to him as a man or as a denizen are inviolably to be preserved to him. These are not the business of religion. No violence nor injury is to be offered him, whether he be Christian or pagan. Nay, we must not content ourselves with the narrow measures of bare justice; charity, bounty, and liberality must be added to it. This the Gospel enjoins, this reason directs, and this that natural fellowship we are born into requires of us. If any man err from the right way, it is his own misfortune, no injury to thee; nor therefore art thou to punish him in the things of this life because thou supposest he will be miserable in that which is to come.

What I say concerning the mutual toleration of private persons differing from one another in religion, I understand also of particular churches which stand, as it were, in the same relation to each other as private persons among themselves: nor has any one of them any manner of jurisdiction over any other; no, not even when the civil magistrate (as it sometimes happens) comes to be of this or the other communion. For the civil government can give no new right to the church, nor the church to the civil government. So that whether the magistrate join himself to any church, or separate from it, the church remains always as it was before—a free and voluntary society. It neither requires the power of the sword by the magistrate's coming to it, nor does it lose the right of instruction and excommunication by his going from it. This is the fundamental and immutable right of a spontaneous society—that it has power to remove any of its members who transgress the rules of its institution; but it cannot, by the accession of any new members, acquire any right of jurisdiction over those that are not joined with it. And therefore peace, equity, and friendship are always mutually to be observed by particular churches, in the same manner as by private persons, without any pretense of superiority or jurisdiction over one another.

That the thing may be made clearer by an example, let us suppose two churches—the one of Arminians, the other of Calvinists—residing in the city of Constantinople. Will anyone say that either of these churches has right to deprive the members of the other of their estates and liberty (as we see practiced elsewhere), because of their differing from it in some doctrines and ceremonies, whilst the Turks in the meanwhile silently stand by and laugh to see with what inhuman cruelty Christians thus rage against Christians? But if one of these churches hath this power of treating the other ill, I ask which of them it is to whom that power belongs, and by what right? It will be answered, undoubtedly, that it is the orthodox church which has the right of authority over the erroneous or heretical. This is, in great and specious words, to say just nothing at all. For every church is orthodox to itself; to others, erroneous or heretical. For whatsoever any church believes it believes to be true; and the contrary unto those things it pronounces to be error. So that the controversy between these churches about the truth of their doctrines and the purity of their worship is on both sides equal; nor is there any judge, either at Constantinople or elsewhere upon earth, by whose sentence it can be determined. The decision of that question belongs only to the Supreme Judge of all men, to whom also alone belongs the punishment of the erroneous. In the meanwhile, let those men consider how heinously they sin, who, adding injustice, if not to their error, yet certainly to their pride, do rashly and arrogantly take upon them to misuse the servants of another master, who are not at all accountable to them.

Nay, further: if it could be manifest which of these two dissenting churches were in the right, there would not accrue thereby unto the orthodox any right of destroying the other. For churches have neither any jurisdiction in worldly matters, nor are fire and sword any proper instruments wherewith to convince men's minds of error, and inform them of the truth. Let us suppose, nevertheless, that the civil magistrate inclined to favor one of them and to put his sword into their hands, that (by his consent) they might chastise the dissenters as they pleased. Will any man say that any right can be derived unto a Christian church over its brethren from a Turkish emperor? An infidel, who has himself no authority to punish Christians for the articles of their faith, cannot confer such an authority upon any society of Christians, nor give unto them a right which he has not himself. This would be the case at Constantinople; and the reason of the thing is the same in any Christian kingdom. The civil power is the same in every place. Nor can that power, in the hands of a Christian prince, confer any greater authority upon the church than in the hands of a heathen; which is to say, just none at all.

Nevertheless, it is worthy to be observed and lamented that the most violent of these defenders of the truth, the opposers of errors, the exclaimers against schism, do hardly ever let loose this their zeal for God, with which they are so warmed and inflamed, unless where they have the civil magistrate on their side. But so soon as ever court favor has given them the better end of the staff, and they begin to feel themselves the stronger, then presently peace and charity are to be laid aside. Otherwise they are religiously to be observed. Where they have not the power to carry on persecution and to become masters, there they desire to live upon fair terms and preach up toleration. When they are not strengthened with the civil power, then they can bear most patiently and unmovedly the contagion of idolatry, superstition, and heresy in their neighborhood; of which on other occasions the interest of religion makes them to be extremely apprehensive. They do not forwardly attack those errors which are in fashion at court or are countenanced by the government. Here they can be content to spare their arguments; which yet (with their leave) is the only right method of propagating truth, which has no such way of prevailing as when strong arguments and good reason are joined with the softness of civility and good usage.

Nobody, therefore, in fine, neither single persons nor churches, nay, nor even commonwealths, have any just title to invade the civil rights and worldly goods of each other upon pretense of religion. Those that are of another opinion would do well to consider with themselves how pernicious a seed of discord and war, how powerful a provocation to endless hatreds, rapines, and slaughters they thereby furnish unto mankind. No peace and security, no, not so much as common friendship, can ever be established or preserved amongst men so long as this opinion prevails that dominion is founded in grace and that religion is to be propagated by force of arms.

# JEAN-JACQUES ROUSSEAU
~

## INTRODUCTION

## JOSHUA COHEN

Jean-Jacques Rousseau (1712–1778) was born in Geneva. His mother died two days after his birth, and his father—a watchmaker—fled when Rousseau was 10. Raised by his uncle, Rousseau left Geneva at age 16 and eventually settled in Paris in the early 1740s. Despite the geographic separation, Rousseau maintained a strong public identification with Geneva throughout much of his life. He came to intellectual maturity in absolutist France, in debate with the leading thinkers of the French Enlightenment, but the image of Geneva as a small, self-governing republic, in which the people are sovereign and all citizens are subject to law, continued to provide political bearings.

Whereas Rousseau's early experience in Geneva inspired his political thought, his theory of human nature came to him later, and in a flash, as he walked from Paris to Vincennes in 1749 (he was on his way to visit Diderot, then imprisoned in the château of Vincennes). Reflecting on a question set by the Academy of Dijon—"Has the restoration of the sciences and the arts contributed to the purification of morals?"—Rousseau was overtaken, he says, by a flood of ideas, "a thousand lights." Lying at the heart of this "sudden inspiration" was the thought that dominated his subsequent writing: "that man is naturally good, and that it is solely by [our] institutions that men become wicked." This conception of natural goodness—an alternative to the Augustinian doctrine of original sin and the Hobbesian theory of human nature—is, as Rousseau explained to Archbishop Beaumont of Paris, the "fundamental principle of all morals," and the basis of "all my writings."

Unified by this fundamental idea, Rousseau's principal writings on human nature and politics fall into three groups. In his early, "critical" essays—the *Discourse on the Arts and Sciences* (1750), *Discourse on the Origins of Inequality* (1755), and *Letter to M. d'Alembert on the Theater* (1758)—he challenges the Enlightenment view that the advance of science and understanding has improved the human condition, making human life freer, happier, and more virtuous. Rousseau rejects this complacent view, and reveals a darker side to intellectual progress. Connecting enlightenment with the evolution of constraint, unhappiness, and vice, he explains how human beings, though naturally good, have been corrupted. His more positive writings—*Of the Social Contract, Emile*, the best-selling novel *New Heloise* (1761), *Letters from the Mountain* (1764), and constitutional proposals for Corsica (1765) and Poland (1772)—present a scheme of political institutions and a program of education that would cure our corrupt condition, restoring freedom through virtue and providing us with a life suited to our nature. In his autobiographical, confessional writings—including his *Confessions, Reveries of the Solitary Walker*, and *Rousseau, Judge of Jean-Jacques*, all published after Rousseau's death—Rousseau testifies to his own authenticity, insisting that he has not been caught up in the web of deception, hypocrisy, and manipulation that defines conventional society. These writings, though intensely personal and self-revealing, also present a universal message: Rousseau's own uncorrupted sincerity is evidence of humanity's natural goodness, and illustrates the possibility of extricating ourselves from self-imposed misery and vice.

Rousseau's political philosophy describes the terms of that extrication. The fundamental political problem, he says, is "to find a form of association that defends and protects the person and goods of each associate with all the common force, and by means of which each one uniting with all, nevertheless obeys only himself and remains as free as before." The importance of this problem reflects the central role in our nature of self-love and freedom. Because we love ourselves, we cannot be indifferent to the security of our person and goods. But not just any form of protection will do. We are "born free," with a capacity to choose and to regulate our own conduct. This capacity is the source of humanity's special worth, of our standing as moral agents who can make claims on others and take responsibility for our conduct. Freedom is so fundamental that "renouncing one's liberty is renouncing one's dignity as a man, the rights of humanity and even its duties." So we must find a form of security that does not demand such renunciation.

*Of the Social Contract* presents Rousseau's solution: a political society that achieves a "harmony of obedience and freedom." In this society, obedience to authority does not require a subordination of will that denies our freedom and corrupts our sensibilities. The proposed harmony is puzzling. How *could* each person accept political authority, thus uniting with all for common security, while obeying only himself or herself, achieving the "moral freedom" that consists in giving the law to oneself, and so remaining "as free as before?"

Rousseau's explanation has two components, corresponding to two kinds of doubt about the possibility of such a political society—doubts about *content* and *motivation*.

The problem of content arises because accepting authority, which is required for security, appears to involve letting oneself be ruled by the decisions of others (perhaps the majority). To show that self-government can be reconciled with the chains of social connection and bonds of political authority, we need some way to dispel this appearance—to show that the idea of such reconciliation is even coherent.

Rousseau's conception of a society guided by a *general will* addresses this problem. In such a society, the political obligations of citizens are fixed by laws; those laws reflect a shared understanding of the common good; and that understanding expresses an equal concern for the good of each citizen. Because the content of the conception of the common good reflects an equal concern with the well-being of each citizen, the society provides security for the person and goods of each. Because citizens share the conception, and it is embodied in law, each citizen remains free in fulfilling legal obligations. Those obligations are acceptable to citizens as free agents because each can regard the obligations to the common good as self-imposed.

Rousseau's solution to the fundamental problem requires, then, that the parties to the social compact treat each other as equals, both in the institution of equal citizenship and in regulating conduct by reference to reasons of the common good. To institutionalize and sustain the supremacy of the general will, Rousseau proposes a system of nonrepresentative, direct democracy. Citizens themselves are to assemble regularly to reaffirm their social bonds, evaluate the performance of the executive, and choose the fundamental laws that will best advance their common good.

Even if we grant, however, that the society of the general will solves the content problem, we may still wonder whether such an ideal society is a human possibility. It requires, after all, a shared conception of, and allegiance to, the common good. But widespread vice—selfishness, pride, jealousy, envy—naturally prompts the thought that this ideal is inconsistent with human motivations.

Hobbes would certainly have rejected Rousseau's view for this reason. Surveying what he called the "known natural inclinations of mankind," Hobbes found desires for individual preservation and happiness; he noted the strength of human fears about violent death; he observed (in at least some people) passions of pride, jealousy, and envy rooted in a sense of natural differences of worth and a concern that relative social standing mirror those presumptively natural differences. And he found that people are often blinded by passion into acting for near-term advantages and against their own longer term interests. Departing from these observations, he concluded that we need a sovereign with unconditional authority, whose power is sufficient to overawe subjects, tame their pride with fear, and ensure the social peace required to protect human life and happiness.

Hobbes's defense of political submission is driven, in short, by his general pessimism about human capacities for self-regulation. More particularly, he was skeptical about the motivational power of reason of the common good because he did not see human beings as moved by a concern to treat others as equals. Concerned with preservation and happiness, we have at most an instrumental concern with equality; and insofar as we are prone to pride, we will reject equality as inconsistent with our naturally superior worth and an insult to our dignity.

Rousseau's case for the motivational possibility of a general will and the political autonomy it makes possible would have been simpler had he rejected Hobbes's psychological observations. But Rousseau found little basis for disagreeing with Hobbes's dismal description: "Men are wicked," he says in the *Discourse on the Origins of Inequality*, adding that "a sad and constant experience makes proof unnecessary." We observe widespread vice, and underlying that vice can discern a "frenzy to distinguish ourselves," an "ardent desire to raise one's relative fortune less out of genuine need than in order to place oneself above others." This frenzy and desire, in turn, have roots in an inflated, false sense of self-worth; struck by differences of social station, we fail to see that "man is the same in all stations."

This description naturally prompts the pessimistic thought that the society of the general will is incompatible with human motivations, that human nature has no place for the commitment to equality and the common good required for political autonomy. And if we could directly infer intrinsic properties of human nature from observed motivations—if, for example, the "ardent desire" for advantage over others were an original predisposition, or the inflated sense of self-worth an original sentiment—that pessimistic thought would be true, and we would be compelled to reject the possibility of a political society in which citizens give the law to themselves. But we are not required to accept that direct inference, and therefore not required to draw the pessimistic implications. That is the point of Rousseau's *Second Discourse*. It presents, as Rousseau describes it, a "genealogy of vice." The point of that genealogy is to turn back an argument that begins with the "sad and constant experience" of human vice, that attributes such vice to a natural desire for advantage, or a naturally exaggerated sense of our own worth, and that ends by rejecting as unrealistic an ideal of free association among equals. Rousseau's strategy is to explain all human vice in terms of social circumstance, without postulating any original predisposition to it: Although human beings are *naturally good*, the experience of social inequality encourages the desire for advantage and inflamed sense of self-worth that produce constraint, vice, and misery.

Rousseau's explanation, then, constitutes a defense of human nature. And that defense permits us to hope, with reason, for a society whose members respect one another as equals, and in so doing respond to the demands of self-love and freedom.

On the unity of Rousseau's writings, see Ernst Cassirer, *The Question of Jean-Jacques Rousseau*, translated and edited by Peter Gay (Bloomington: University of Indiana Press, 1963). Jean Starobinski provides a psychological interpretation of Rousseau's work, underscoring Rousseau's concern for transparency in human relations, in *Jean-Jacques Rousseau: Transparency and Obstruction*, translated by Arthur Goldhammer (Chicago: University of Chicago Press, 1988). On the theory of natural goodness, see Arthur Melzer, *The Natural Goodness of Man: The System of Rousseau's Thought* (Chicago: University of Chicago Press, 1990), and Joshua Cohen, "The Natural Goodness of Humanity," in *Reclaiming the History of Ethics: Essays for John Rawls*, Barbara Herman, Christine Korsgaard, and Andrews Reath, eds. (Cambridge: Cambridge University Press, 1996). For a discussion of Rousseau's political thought against the background of early modern political theory, see Robert Derathe, *Jean-Jacques Rousseau et la Science Politique de son Temps* (Paris: Presses Universitaire de France, 1950). For a discussion of Rousseau's views in connection with Genevan culture and politics, see John Stephenson Spink, *Jean-Jacques Rousseau et Gèneve: essai sur les idées politiques et religieuses dé Rousseau dans leur relation avec la penseé genevoise au XVIII^e* (Paris: Boívín, 1934). On Rousseau's conception of democracy, in relation to traditional debate about democracy and political conflict in eighteenth-century Geneva, see James Miller, *Rousseau: Dreamer of Democracy* (New Haven, Conn.: Yale University Press, 1984). On Rousseau's critique of representative government, see Richard Fralin, *Rousseau and Representation* (New York: Columbia University Press, 1978). The best discussion of Rousseau's psychological views is N. J. Dent's *Rousseau* (Oxford: Blackwell, 1988). For Rousseau's views on women, see Susan Moller Okin, *Women and Political Thought* (Princeton, N.J.: Princeton University Press, 1979), Part 3, and Joel Schwartz, *The Sexual Politics of Jean-Jacques Rousseau* (Chicago: University of Chicago Press, 1984). Patrick Riley provides an illuminating account of the theological background to Rosseau's conception of the general will in *The General Will Before Rousseau: The Transformation of the Divine into the Civic* (Princeton, N.J.: Princeton University Press, 1986).

# Discourse on the Origin of Inequality

## THE FIRST PART

Important as it may be, in order to judge rightly of the natural state of man, to consider him from his origin, and to examine him, as it were, in the embryo of his species, I shall not follow his organization through its successive developments, nor shall I stay to inquire what his animal system must have been at the beginning, in order to become at length what it actually is. . . . I shall suppose his conformation to have been at all times what it appears to us at this day; that he always walked on two legs, made use of his hands as we do, directed his looks over all nature, and measured with his eyes the vast expanse of the heavens.

If we strip this being, thus constituted, of all the supernatural gifts he may have received, and all the artificial faculties he can have acquired only by a long process; if we consider him, in a word, just as he must have come from the hands of nature, we behold in him an animal weaker than some, and less agile than others; but, taking him all round, the most advantageously organized of any. I see him satisfying his hunger at the first oak, and slaking his thirst at the first brook: finding his bed at the foot of the tree which afforded him a repast; and, with that, all his wants supplied.

While the earth was left to its natural fertility and covered with immense forests, whose trees were never mutilated by the axe, it would present on every side both sustenance and shelter for every species of animal. Men, dispersed up and down among the rest, would observe and imitate their industry, and thus attain even to the instinct of the beasts, with the advantage that, whereas every species of brutes was confined to one particular instinct, man, who perhaps has not any one peculiar to himself, would appropriate them all, and live upon most of those different foods, which other animals shared among themselves; and thus would find his subsistence much more easily than any of the rest.

Accustomed from their infancy to the inclemencies of the weather and the rigour of the seasons, inured to fatigue, and forced, naked and unarmed, to defend themselves and their prey from other ferocious animals, or to escape them by flight, men would acquire a robust and almost unalterable constitution. The children, bringing with them into the world the excellent constitution of their parents, and fortifying it by the very exercises which first produced it, would thus acquire all the vigour of which the human frame is capable. Nature in this case treats them exactly as Sparta treated the children of her citizens: those who come well formed into the world she renders strong and robust, and all the rest she destroys . . . .

We should beware, therefore, of confounding the savage man with the men we have daily before our eyes. Nature treats all the animals left to her care with a predilection that seems to show how jealous she is of that right. The horse, the cat, the bull, and even the ass are generally of greater stature, and always more robust, and have more vigour, strength, and courage, when they run wild in the forests than when bred in the stall. By becoming domesticated, they lose half these advantages; and it seems as if all our care to feed and treat them well serves only to deprave them. It is thus with man also: as he becomes sociable and

Translated by G. D. H. Cole, revised by J. H. Brumfitt and John C. Hall, updated by P. D. Jimack. Everyman's Library, David Campbell Publishers Ltd. Reprinted by permission of the publisher.

a slave, he grows weak, timid, and servile; his effeminate way of life totally enervates his strength and courage. To this it may be added that there is still a greater difference between savage and civilized man than between wild and tame beasts; for men and brutes having been treated alike by nature, the several conveniences in which men indulge themselves still more than they do their beasts, are so many additional causes of their deeper degeneracy. . . .

But be the origins of language and society what they may, it may be at least inferred, from the little care which nature has taken to unite mankind by mutual wants, and to facilitate the use of speech, that she has contributed little to make them sociable, and has put little of her own into all they have done to create such bonds of union. It is in fact impossible to conceive why, in a state of nature, one man should stand more in need of the assistance of another, than a monkey or a wolf of the assistance of another of its kind: or, granting that he did, what motives could induce that other to assist him; or, even then, by what means they could agree about the conditions. I know it is incessantly repeated that man would in such a state have been the most miserable of creatures; and indeed, if it be true, as I think I have proved, that he must have lived many ages, before he could have either desire or an opportunity of emerging from it, this would only be an accusation against nature, and not against the being which she had thus unhappily constituted. But as I understand the word 'miserable', it either has no meaning at all, or else signifies only a painful privation of something, or a state of suffering either in body or soul. I should be glad to have explained to me, what kind of misery a free being, whose heart is at ease and whose body is in health, can possibly suffer. I would like to know which is the more likely to become insupportable to those who take part in it: the life of society or the life of nature. We hardly see anyone around us except people who are complaining of their existence; many even deprive themselves of it if they can and all divine and human laws put together can hardly put a stop to this disorder. I would like to know if anyone has heard of a savage who took it into his head, when he was free, to complain of life and to kill himself. Let us be less

arrogant, then, when we judge on which side real misery is found. Nothing, on the other hand, could be more miserable than a savage exposed to the dazzling light of our 'civilization', tormented by our passions and reasoning about a state different from his own. It appears that providence most wisely determined that the faculties, which he potentially possessed, should develop themselves only as occasion offered to exercise them, in order that they might not be superfluous or perplexing to him, by appearing before their time, nor slow and useless when the need for them arose. In instinct alone, he had all he required for living in the state of nature; and with a developed understanding he has only just enough to support life in society.

It appears, at first view, that men in a state of nature, having no moral relations or determinate obligations one with another, could not be either good or bad, virtuous or vicious; unless we take these terms in a physical sense, and call, in an individual, those qualities vices which may be injurious to his preservation, and those virtues which contribute to it; in which case, he would have to be accounted most virtuous, who put least check on the pure impulses of nature. But without deviating from the ordinary sense of the words, it will be proper to suspend the judgment we might be led to form on such a state, and be on our guard against our prejudices, till we have weighed the matter in the scales of impartiality, and seen whether virtues or vices preponderate among civilized men: and whether their virtues do them more good than their vices do harm; till we have discovered whether the progress of the sciences sufficiently indemnifies them for the mischiefs they do one another, in proportion as they are better informed of the good they ought to do; or whether they would not be, on the whole, in a much happier condition if they had nothing to fear or to hope from any one, than as they are, subjected to universal dependence, and obliged to take everything from those who engage to give them nothing in return.

Above all, let us not conclude, with Hobbes, that because man has no idea of goodness, he must be naturally wicked; that he is vicious because he does not know virtue; that he always refuses to do his fellow-creatures services which he does not think they have a right to demand; or that by virtue of the right he justly claims to all he needs, he foolishly imagines himself the sole proprietor of the whole universe. Hobbes had seen clearly the defects of all the modern definitions of natural right: but the consequences which he deduces from his own show that he understands it in an equally false sense. In reasoning on the principles he lays down, he ought to have said that the state of nature, being that in which the care for our own preservation is the least prejudicial to that of others, was consequently the best calculated to promote peace, and the most suitable for mankind. He does say the exact opposite, in consequence of having improperly admitted, as a part of savage man's care for self-preservation, the gratification of a multitude of passions which are the work of society, and have made laws necessary. A bad man, he says, is a robust child. But it remains to be proved whether man in a state of nature is this robust child: and, should we grant that he is, what would he infer? Why truly, that if this man, when robust and strong, were dependent on others as he is when feeble, there is no extravagance he would not be guilty of; that he would beat his mother when she was too slow in giving him her breast; that he would strangle one of his younger brothers, if he should be troublesome to him, or bite the leg of another, if he put him to any inconvenience. But that man in the state of nature is both strong and dependent involves two contrary suppositions. Man is weak when he is dependent, and is his own master before he comes to be strong. Hobbes did not reflect that the same cause, which prevents a savage from making use of his reason, as our jurists hold, prevents him also from abusing his faculties, as Hobbes himself allows: so that it may be justly said that savages are not bad merely because they do not know what it is to be good: for it is neither the development of the understanding nor the restraint of law that hinders them from doing ill; but the peacefulness of their passions, and their ignorance of vice: *tanto plus in illis proficit vitiorum ignoratio, quam in his cognitio virtutis.*[1] There is another principle which has escaped Hobbes; which, having been bestowed on mankind, to moderate, on certain occasions, the impetuosity of *amour-propre,*

or, before its birth, the desire of self-preservation, tempers the ardour with which he pursues his own welfare, by an innate repugnance at seeing a fellow-creature suffer.[2] I think I need not fear contradiction in holding man to be possessed of the only natural virtue, which could not be denied him by the most violent detractor of human virtue. I am speaking of compassion, which is a disposition suitable to creatures so weak and subject to so many evils as we certainly are: by so much the more universal and useful to mankind, as it comes before any kind of reflection; and at the same time so natural, that the very brutes themselves sometimes give evident proofs of it. Not to mention the tenderness of mothers for their offspring and the perils they encounter to save them from danger, it is well known that horses show a reluctance to trample on living bodies. One animal never passes by the dead body of another of its species without disquiet: some even give their fellows a sort of burial; while the mournful lowings of the cattle when they enter the slaughter-house show the impressions made on them by the horrible spectacle which meets them. We find, with pleasure, the author of *The Fable of the Bees* obliged to own that man is a compassionate and sensible being, and laying aside his cold subtlety of style, in the example he gives, to present us with the pathetic description of a man who, from a place of confinement, is compelled to behold a wild beast tear a child from the arms of its mother, grinding its tender limbs with its murderous teeth, and tearing its palpitating entrails with its claws. What horrid agitation must not the eye-witness of such a scene experience, although he would not be personally concerned! What anguish would he not suffer at not being able to give any assistance to the fainting mother and the dying infant!

Such is the pure emotion of nature, prior to all kinds of reflection! Such is the force of natural compassion, which the greatest depravity of morals has as yet hardly been able to destroy! for we daily find at our theatres men affected, nay, shedding tears at the sufferings of a wretch who, were he in the tyrant's place, would probably even add to the torments of his enemies; like the bloodthirsty Sulla, who was so sensitive to ills he had not caused, or that Alexander of Pheros who did not dare to go and see any tragedy acted, for fear of being seen weeping with Andromache and Priam, though he could listen without emotion to the cries of all the citizens who were daily strangled at his command. . . .

Mandeville well knew that, in spite of all their morality, men would have never been better than monsters, had not nature bestowed on them a sense of compassion, to aid their reason: but he did not see that from this quality alone flow all those social virtues, of which he denied man the possession. But what is generosity, clemency, or humanity but compassion applied to the weak, to the guilty, or to mankind in general? Even benevolence and friendship are, if we judge rightly, only the effects of compassion, constantly set upon a particular object: for how is it different to wish that another person may not suffer pain and uneasiness and to wish him happy? Were it even true that pity is no more than a feeling which puts us in the place of the sufferer, a feeling obscure yet lively in a savage, developed yet feeble in civilized man; this truth would have no other consequence than to confirm my argument. Compassion must, in fact, be the stronger, the more the animal beholding any kind of distress identifies himself with the animal that suffers. Now, it is plain that such identification must have been much more perfect in a state of nature than it is in a state of reason. It is reason that engenders *amour-propre*, and reflection that confirms it: it is reason which turns man's mind back upon itself, and divides him from everything that could disturb or afflict him. It is philosophy that isolates him, and bids him say, at sight of the misfortunes of others: 'Perish if you will, I am secure.' Nothing but such general evils as threaten the whole community can disturb the tranquil sleep of the philosopher, or tear him from his bed. A murder may with impunity be committed under his window; he has only to put his hands to his ears and argue a little with himself, to prevent nature, which is shocked within him, from identifying itself with the unfortunate sufferer. Uncivilized man has not this admirable talent; and for want of reason and wisdom, is always foolishly ready to obey the first

promptings of humanity. It is the populace that flocks together at riots and street brawls, while the wise man prudently makes off. It is the mob and the market-women, who part the combatants, and stop decent people from cutting one another's throats.

It is then certain that compassion is a natural feeling, which, by moderating the activity of love of self in each individual, contributes to the preservation of the whole species. It is this compassion that hurries us without reflection to the relief of those who are in distress: it is this which in a state of nature supplies the place of laws, morals, and virtues, with the advantage that none are tempted to disobey its gentle voice: it is this which will always prevent a sturdy savage from robbing a weak child or a feeble old man of the sustenance they may have with pain and difficulty acquired, if he sees a possibility of providing for himself by other means: it is this which, instead of inculcating that sublime maxim of rational justice, *Do to others as you would have them do unto you,* inspires all men with that other maxim of natural goodness, much less perfect indeed, but perhaps more useful; *Do good to yourself with as little evil as possible to others*. In a word, it is rather in this natural feeling than in any subtle arguments that we must look for the cause of that repugnance, which every man would experience in doing evil, even independently of the maxims of education. Although it might belong to Socrates and other minds of the like craft to acquire virtue by reason, the human race would long since have ceased to be, had its preservation depended only on the reasonings of the individuals composing it.

With passions so little active, and so good a curb, men, being rather wild than wicked, and more intent to guard themselves against the mischief that might be done them, than to do mischief to others, were by no means subject to very perilous dissensions. They maintained no kind of intercourse with one another, and were consequently strangers to vanity, deference, esteem, and contempt; they had not the least idea of 'mine' and 'thine', and no true conception of justice; they looked upon every violence to which they were subjected, rather as an injury that might easily be repaired than as a crime that ought to be punished; and they never thought of taking revenge, unless perhaps mechanically and on the spot, as a dog will sometimes bite the stone which is thrown at him. Their quarrels therefore would seldom have very bloody consequences; for the subject of them would be merely the question of subsistence. But I am aware of one greater danger, which remains to be noticed.

Of the passions that stir the heart of man, there is one which makes the sexes necessary to each other, and is extremely ardent and impetuous; a terrible passion that braves danger, surmounts all obstacles, and in its transports seems calculated to bring destruction on the human race which it is really destined to preserve. What must become of men who are left to this brutal and boundless rage, without modesty, without shame, and daily upholding their amours at the price of their blood?

It must, in the first place, be allowed that, the more violent the passions are, the more are laws necessary to keep them under restraint. But, setting aside the inadequacy of laws to effect this purpose, which is evident from the crimes and disorders to which these passions daily give rise among us, we should do well to inquire if these evils did not spring up with the laws themselves; for in this case, even if the laws were capable of repressing such evils, it is the least that could be expected from them, that they should check a mischief which would not have arisen without them.

Let us begin by distinguishing between the physical and moral ingredients in the feeling of love. The physical part of love is that general desire which urges the sexes to union with each other. The moral part is that which determines and fixes this desire exclusively upon one particular object; or at least gives it a greater degree of energy toward the object thus preferred. It is easy to see that the moral part of love is a factitious feeling, born of social usage, and enhanced by the women with much care and cleverness, to establish their empire, and put in power the sex which ought to obey. This feeling, being founded on certain ideas of beauty and merit which a savage is not in a position to acquire, and on comparisons which he is incapable of making, must be for him almost non-existent; for, as his mind cannot form abstract ideas of proportion and regularity, so his heart

is not susceptible to the feelings of love and admiration, which are even insensibly produced by the application of these ideas. He follows solely the character nature has implanted in him, and not tastes which he could never have acquired; so that every woman equally answers his purpose.

Men in a state of nature being confined merely to what is physical in love, and fortunate enough to be ignorant of those excellences, which whet the appetite while they increase the difficulty of gratifying it, must be subject to fewer and less violent fits of passion, and consequently fall into fewer and less violent disputes. The imagination, which causes such ravages among us, never speaks to the heart of savages, who quietly await the impulses of nature, yield to them involuntarily, with more pleasure than ardour, and, their wants once satisfied, lose the desire. It is therefore incontestable that love, as well as all other passions, must have acquired in society that glowing impetuosity, which makes it so often fatal to mankind. And it is the more absurd to represent savages as continually cutting one another's throats to indulge their brutality, because this opinion is directly contrary to experience; the Caribbeans, who have as yet least of all deviated from the state of nature, being in fact the most peaceable of people in their amours, and the least subject to jealousy, though they live in a hot climate which seems always to inflame the passions.

With regard to the inferences that might be drawn, in the case of several species of animals, the males of which fill our poultry yards with blood and slaughter, or in spring make the forests resound with their quarrels over their females; we must begin by excluding all those species, in which nature has plainly established, in the comparative power of the sexes, relations different from those which exist among us: thus we can base no conclusion about men on the habits of fighting cocks. In those species where the proportion is better observed, these battles must be entirely due to the scarcity of females in comparison with males; or, what amounts to the same thing, to the intervals during which the female constantly refuses the advances of the male: for if each female admits the male but during two months in the year, it is the same as if the number of females were five-sixths less. Now, neither of these two cases is applicable to the human species, in which the number of females usually exceeds that of males, and among whom it has never been observed, even among savages, that the females have, like those of other animals, their stated times of passion and indifference. Moreover, in several of these species, the individuals all take fire at once, and there comes a fearful moment of universal passion, tumult, and disorder among them; a scene which is never beheld in the human species, whose love is not thus seasonal. We must not then conclude from the combats of such animals for the enjoyment of the females, that the case would be the same with mankind in a state of nature: and, even if we drew such a conclusion, we see that such contests do not exterminate other kinds of animals, and we have no reason to think they would be more fatal to ours. It is indeed clear that they would do still less mischief than is the case in a state of society; especially in those countries in which, morals being still held in some repute, the jealousy of lovers and the vengeance of husbands are the daily cause of duels, murders, and even worse crimes; where the obligation of eternal fidelity only occasions adultery, and the very laws of honour and continence necessarily increase debauchery and lead to the multiplication of abortions.

Let us conclude then that man in a state of nature, wandering up and down the forests, without industry, without speech, and without home, an equal stranger to war and to all ties, neither standing in need of his fellow-creatures nor having any desire to hurt them, and perhaps even not distinguishing them one from another; let us conclude that, being self-sufficient and subject to so few passions, he could have no feelings or knowledge but such as befitted his situation; that he felt only his actual necessities, and disregarded everything he did not think himself immediately concerned to notice, and that his understanding made no greater progress than his vanity. If by accident he made any discovery, he was the less able to communicate it to others, as he did not know even his own children. Every art would necessarily perish with its inventor, where there was no kind of

education among men, and generations succeeded generations without the least advance; when, all setting out from the same point, centuries must have elapsed in the barbarism of the first ages; when the race was already old, and man remained a child.

If I have expatiated at such length on this supposed primitive state, it is because I had so many ancient errors and inveterate prejudices to eradicate, and therefore thought it incumbent on me to dig down to their very root, and show, by means of a true picture of the state of nature, how far even the natural inequalities of mankind are from having that reality and influence which modern writers suppose.

It is in fact easy to see that many of the differences between men which are ascribed to nature stem rather from habit and the diverse modes of life of men in society. Thus a robust or delicate constitution, and the strength or weakness attaching to it, are more frequently the effects of a hardy or effeminate method of education than of the original endowment of the body. It is the same with the powers of the mind; for education not only makes a difference between such as are cultured and such as are not, but even increases the differences which exist among the former, in proportion to their respective degrees of culture: as the distance between a giant and a dwarf on the same road increases with every step they take. If we compare the prodigious diversity, which obtains in the education and manner of life of the various orders of men in the state of society, with the uniformity and simplicity of animal and savage life, in which every one lives on the same kind of food and in exactly the same manner, and does exactly the same things, it is easy to conceive how much less the difference between man and man must be in a state of nature than in a state of society, and how greatly the natural inequality of mankind must be increased by the inequalities of social institutions.

But even if nature really affected, in the distribution of her gifts, that partiality which is imputed to her, what advantage would the greatest of her favourites derive from it, to the detriment of others, in a state that admits of hardly any kind of relation between them? Where there is no love, of what advantage is beauty? Of what use is wit to those who do not converse, or cunning to those who have no business with others? I hear it constantly repeated that, in such a state, the strong would oppress the weak; but what is here meant by oppression? Some, it is said, would violently domineer over others, who would groan under a servile submission to their caprices. This indeed is exactly what I observe to be the case among us; but I do not see how it can be inferred of men in a state of nature, who could not easily be brought to conceive what we mean by dominion and servitude. One man, it is true, might seize the fruits which another had gathered, the game he had killed, or the cave he had chosen for shelter; but how would he ever be able to exact obedience, and what ties of dependence could there be among men without possessions? If, for instance, I am driven from one tree, I can go to the next; if I am disturbed in one place, what hinders me from going to another? Again, should I happen to meet with a man so much stronger than myself, and at the same time so depraved, so indolent, and so barbarous, as to compel me to provide for his sustenance while he himself remains idle; he must take care not to have his eyes off me for a single moment; he must bind me fast before he goes to sleep, or I shall certainly either knock him on the head or make my escape. That is to say, he must in such a case voluntarily expose himself to much greater trouble than he seeks to avoid, or can give me. After all this, let him be off his guard ever so little; let him but turn his head aside at any sudden noise, and I shall be instantly twenty paces off, lost in the forest, and, my fetters burst asunder, he would never see me again.

Without my expatiating thus uselessly on these details, every one must see that as the bonds of servitude are formed merely by the mutual dependence of men on one another and the reciprocal needs that unite them, it is impossible to make any man a slave, unless he be first reduced to a situation in which he cannot do without the help of others: and, since such a situation does not exist in a state of nature, every one is there his own master, and the law of the strongest is of no effect.

Having proved that the inequality of mankind is hardly felt, and that its influence is next to nothing in a state of nature, I must next show its origin and trace its progress in the successive developments of the human mind. Having shown that human *perfectibility,* the social virtues, and the other faculties which natural man potentially possessed, could never develop of themselves, but must require the fortuitous concurrence of many foreign causes that might never arise, and without which he would have remained for ever in his primitive conditions, I must now collect and consider the different accidents which may have improved the human understanding while depraving the species, and made man wicked while making him sociable; so as to bring him and the world from that distant period to the point at which we now behold them.

I confess that, as the events I am going to describe might have happened in various ways, I have nothing to determine my choice but conjectures: but such conjectures become reasons when they are the most probable that can be drawn from the nature of things, and the only means of discovering the truth. The consequences, however, which I mean to deduce will not be barely conjectural; as, on the principles just laid down, it would be impossible to form any other theory that would not furnish the same results, and from which I could not draw the same conclusions.

This will be a sufficient apology for my not dwelling on the manner in which the lapse of time compensates for the little probability in the events; on the surprising power of trivial causes, when their action is constant; on the impossibility, on the one hand, of destroying certain hypotheses, though on the other we cannot give them the certainty of known matters of fact, on its being within the province of history, when two facts are given as real, and have to be connected by a series of intermediate facts, which are unknown or supposed to be so, to supply such facts as may connect them; and on its being in the province of philosophy when history is silent, to determine similar facts to serve the same end; and lastly, on the influence of similarity, which, in the case of events, reduces the facts to a much smaller number of different classes than is commonly imagined. It is enough for me to offer these hints to the consideration of my judges, and to have so arranged that the general reader has no need to consider them at all.

## THE SECOND PART

The first man who, having enclosed a piece of ground, bethought himself of saying 'this is mine', and found people simple enough to believe him, was the real founder of civil society. From how many crimes, wars, and murders, from how many horrors and misfortunes might not any one have saved mankind, by pulling up the stakes, or filling up the ditch, and crying to his fellows: 'Beware of listening to this impostor; you are undone if you once forget that the fruits of the earth belong to us all, and the earth itself to nobody.' But there is great probability that things had then already come to such a pitch, that they could no longer continue as they were; for the idea of property depends on many prior ideas, which could only be acquired successively, and cannot have been formed all at once in the human mind. Mankind must have made very considerable progress, and acquired considerable knowledge and industry which they must also have transmitted and increased from age to age, before they arrived at this last point of the state of nature. Let us then go farther back, and endeavour to unify under a single point of view that slow succession of events and discoveries in the most natural order.

Man's first feeling was that of his own existence, and his first care that of self-preservation. The produce of the earth furnished him with all he needed, and instinct told him how to use it. Hunger and other appetites made him at various times experience various modes of existence; and among these was one which urged him to propagate his species—a blind propensity that, having nothing to do with the heart, produced a merely animal act. The want once gratified, the two sexes knew each other no more; and even the offspring was nothing to its mother, as soon as it could do without her.

Such was the condition of infant man; the life of an animal limited at first to mere sensations, and hardly profiting by the gifts nature bestowed on him, much less capable of entertaining a thought of forcing anything from her. But difficulties soon presented themselves, and it became necessary to learn how to surmount them: the height of the trees, which prevented him from gathering their fruits, the competition of other animals desirous of the same fruits, and the ferocity of those who sought to deprive man himself of life, all obliged him to apply himself to bodily exercises. He had to be active, swift of foot, and vigorous in fight. Natural weapons, stones, and sticks, were easily found: he learnt to surmount the obstacles of nature, to contend in case of necessity with other animals, and to dispute for the means of subsistence even with other men, or to indemnify himself for what he was forced to give up to a stronger.

In proportion as the human race grew more numerous, men's cares increased. The difference of soils, climates, and seasons, must have introduced some differences into their manner of living. Barren years, long and sharp winters, scorching summers which parched the fruits of the earth, must have demanded a new industry. On the seashore and the banks of rivers, they invented the hook and line, and became fishermen and eaters of fish. In the forests they made bows and arrows, and became huntsmen and warriors. In cold countries they clothed themselves with the skins of the beasts they had slain. The lightning, a volcano, or some lucky chance acquainted them with fire, a new resource against the rigours of winter: they next learned how to preserve this element, then how to reproduce it, and finally how to prepare with it the flesh of animals which before they had eaten raw.

The way these different beings and phenomena impinged on him and on each other must naturally have engendered in man's mind the awareness of certain relationships. Thus the relationships which we denote by the terms great, small, strong, weak, swift, slow, fearful, bold, and the like, almost insensibly compared at need, must have at length produced in him a kind of reflection, or rather a mechanical prudence, which would indicate to him the precautions most necessary to his security.

The new intelligence which resulted from this development increased his superiority over other animals, by making him sensible of it. He would now endeavour, therefore, to ensnare them, would play them a thousand tricks, and though many of them might surpass him in swiftness or in strength, would in time become the master of some and the scourge of others. Thus, the first time he looked into himself, he felt the first emotion of pride; and, at a time when he scarce knew how to distinguish the different orders of beings, by looking upon his species as of the highest order, he prepared the way for assuming pre-eminence as an individual.

Other men, it is true, were not then to him what they now are to us, and he had no greater intercourse with them than with other animals; yet they were not neglected in his observations. The conformities, which he would in time discover between them, and between himself and his female, led him to judge of others which were not then perceptible; and finding that they all behaved as he himself would have done in like circumstances, he naturally inferred that their manner of thinking and acting was altogether in conformity with his own. This important truth, once deeply impressed on his mind, must have induced him, from an intuitive feeling more certain and much more rapid than any kind of reasoning, to pursue the rules of conduct, which he had best observe towards them, for his own security and advantage.

Taught by experience that the love of well-being is the sole motive of human actions, he found himself in a position to distinguish the few cases, in which mutual interest might justify him in relying upon the assistance of his fellows; and also the still fewer cases in which a conflict of interests might give cause to suspect them. In the former case, he joined in the same herd with them, or at most in some kind of loose association, that laid no restraint on its members, and lasted no longer than the transitory occasion that formed it. In the latter case, every one sought his own private advantage, either by open force, if he thought himself strong enough, or by address and cunning, if he felt himself the weaker.

In this manner, men may have insensibly acquired some gross ideas of mutual undertakings, and of the advantages of fulfilling them: that is, just so far as their present and apparent interest was concerned; for they were perfect strangers to foresight, and were so far from troubling themselves about the distant future, that they hardly thought of the morrow. If a deer was to be taken, every one saw that, in order to succeed, he must abide faithfully by his post: but if a hare happened to come within the reach of any one of them, it is not to be doubted that he pursued it without scruple, and, having seized his prey, cared very little, if by so doing he caused his companions to miss theirs.

It is easy to understand that such intercourse would not require a language much more refined than that of rooks or monkeys, who associate together for much the same purpose. Inarticulate cries, plenty of gestures, and some imitative sounds, must have been for a long time the universal language; and by the addition, in every country, of some conventional articulate sounds (of which, as I have already intimated, the first institution is not too easy to explain) particular languages were produced; but these were rude and imperfect, and nearly such as are now to be found among some savage nations.

Hurried on by the rapidity of time, by the abundance of things I have to say, and by the almost insensible progress of things in their beginnings, I pass over in an instant a multitude of ages; for the slower the events were in their succession, the more rapidly may they be described.

These first advances enabled men to make others with greater rapidity. In proportion as they grew enlightened, they grew industrious. They ceased to fall asleep under the first tree, or in the first cave that afforded them shelter; they invented several kinds of implements of hard and sharp stones, which they used to dig up the earth, and to cut wood; then they made huts out of branches, and afterwards learnt to plaster them over with mud and clay. This was the epoch of a first revolution, which established and distinguished families, and introduced a kind of property, in itself the source of a thousand quarrels and conflicts. As, however, the strongest were probably the first to build themselves huts which they felt themselves able to defend, it may be concluded that the weak found it much easier and safer to imitate, than to attempt to dislodge them: and of those who were once provided with huts, none could have any inducement to appropriate that of his neighbour;

not indeed so much because it did not belong to him, as because it could be of no use, and he could not make himself master of it without exposing himself to a desperate battle with the family which occupied it.

The first expansions of the human heart were the effects of a novel situation, which united husbands and wives, fathers and children, under one roof. The habit of living together soon gave rise to the finest feelings known to humanity, conjugal love and paternal affection. Every family became a little society, the more united because liberty and reciprocal attachment were the only bonds of its union. The sexes, whose manner of life had been hitherto the same, began now to adopt different ways of living. The women became more sedentary, and accustomed themselves to mind the hut and their children, while the men went abroad in search of their common subsistence. From living a softer life, both sexes also began to lose something of their strength and ferocity: but, if individuals became to some extent less able to encounter wild beasts separately, they found it, on the other hand, easier to assemble and resist in common.

The simplicity and solitude of man's life in this new condition, the paucity of his wants, and the implements he had invented to satisfy them, left him a great deal of leisure, which he employed to furnish himself with many conveniences unknown to his fathers: and this was the first yoke he inadvertently imposed on himself, and the first source of the evils he prepared for his descendants. For, besides continuing thus to enervate both body and mind, these conveniences lost with use almost all their power to please, and even degenerated into real needs, till the want of them became far more disagreeable than the possession of them had been pleasant. Men would have been unhappy at the loss of them, though the possession did not make them happy.

We can here see a little better how the use of speech became established, and insensibly improved in each family, and we may form a conjecture also concerning the manner in which various causes may have extended and accelerated the progress of language, by making it more and more necessary. Floods or earth-

quakes surrounded inhabited districts with precipices or waters: revolutions of the globe tore off portions from the continent, and made them islands. It is readily seen that among men thus collected and compelled to live together, a common idiom must have arisen much more easily than among those who still wandered through the forests of the continent. Thus it is very possible that after their first essays in navigation the islanders brought over the use of speech to the continent: and it is at least very probable that communities and languages were first established in islands, and even came to perfection there before they were known on the mainland.

Everything now begins to change its aspect. Men, who have up to now been roving in the woods, by taking to a more settled manner of life, come gradually together, form separate bodies, and at length in every country arises a distinct nation, united in character and manners, not by regulations or laws, but by uniformity of life and food, and the common influence of climate. Permanent neighbourhood could not fail to produce, in time, some connection between different families. Young people of opposite sexes lived in neighbouring huts and the casual unions between them which resulted from the call of nature soon led, as they came to know each other better, to another kind which was no less pleasant and more permanent. They became accustomed to looking more closely at the different objects of their desires and to making comparisons; imperceptibly they acquired ideas of beauty and merit which led to feelings of preference. In consequence of seeing each other often, they could not do without seeing each other constantly. A tender and pleasant feeling insinuated itself into their souls, and the least opposition turned it into an impetuous fury: with love arose jealousy; discord triumphed, and human blood was sacrificed to the gentlest of all passions.

As ideas and feelings succeeded one another, and heart and head were brought into play, men continued to lay aside their original wildness; their private connections became every day more intimate as their limits extended. They accustomed themselves to assemble before their huts round a large tree; singing and dancing, the true offspring of love and leisure, became the amusement, or rather the occupation, of men and women thus assembled together with nothing else to do. Each one began to consider the rest, and to wish to be considered in turn; and thus a value came to be attached to public esteem. Whoever sang or danced best, whoever was the handsomest, the strongest, the most dexterous, or the most eloquent, came to be of most consideration; and this was the first step towards inequality, and at the same time towards vice. From these first distinctions arose on the one side vanity and contempt and on the other shame and envy: and the fermentation caused by these new leavens ended by producing combinations fatal to innocence and happiness.

As soon as men began to value one another, and the idea of consideration had got a footing in the mind, every one put in his claim to it, and it became impossible to refuse it to any with impunity. Hence arose the first obligations of civility even among savages; and every intended injury became an affront; because, besides the hurt which might result from it, the party injured was certain to find in it a contempt for his person, which was often more insupportable than the hurt itself.

Thus, as every man punished the contempt shown him by others, in proportion to his opinion of himself, revenge became terrible, and men bloody and cruel. This is precisely the state reached by most of the savage nations known to us: and it is for want of having made a proper distinction in our ideas, and seen how very far they already are from the state of nature, that so many writers have hastily concluded that man is naturally cruel, and requires civil institutions to make him more mild; whereas nothing is more gentle than man in his primitive state, as he is placed by nature at an equal distance from the stupidity of brutes, and the fatal ingenuity of civilized man. Equally confined by instinct and reason to the sole care of guarding himself against the mischiefs which threaten him, he is restrained by natural compassion from doing any injury to others, and is not led to do such a thing even in return for injuries received. For, according to the axiom of the wise Locke, 'There can be no injury, where there is no property.'

But it must be remarked that the society thus formed, and the relations thus established among men, required of them qualities different from those which they possessed from their primitive constitution. Morality began to appear in human actions, and every one, before the institution of law, was the only judge and avenger of the injuries done him, so that the goodness which was suitable in the pure state of nature was no longer proper in the new-born state of society. Punishments had to be made more severe, as opportunities of offending became more frequent, and the dread of vengeance had to take the place of the rigour of the law. Thus, though men had become less patient, and their natural compassion had already suffered some diminution, this period of expansion of the human faculties, keeping a just mean between the indolence of the primitive state and the petulant activity of our *amour-propre,* must have been the happiest and most stable of epochs. The more we reflect on it, the more we shall find that this state was the least subject to revolutions, and altogether the very best man could experience; so that he can have departed from it only through some fatal accident, which, for the public good, should never have happened. The example of savages, most of whom have been found in this state, seems to prove that men were meant to remain in it, that it is the real youth of the world, and that all subsequent advances have been apparently so many steps towards the perfection of the individual, but in reality towards the decrepitude of the species.

So long as men remained content with their rustic huts, so long as they were satisfied with clothes made of the skins of animals and sewn together with thorns and fish-bones, adorned themselves only with feathers and shells, and continued to paint their bodies different colours, to improve and beautify their bows and arrows, and to make with sharp-edged stones fishing boats or clumsy musical instruments; in a word, so long as they undertook only what a single person could accomplish, and confined themselves to such arts as did not require the joint labour of several hands, they lived free, healthy, honest, and happy lives, in so far as their nature allowed, and they continued to enjoy the pleasures of mutual and independent intercourse. But from the moment one man began to stand in need of the help of another; from the moment it appeared advantageous to any one man to have enough provisions for two, equality disappeared, property was introduced, work became indispensable, and vast forests became smiling fields, which man had to water with the sweat of his brow, and where slavery and misery were soon seen to germinate and grow up with the crops.

Metallurgy and agriculture were the two arts which produced this great revolution. The poets tell us it was gold and silver, but, for the philosophers, it was iron and corn, which first civilized men, and ruined humanity. Thus both were unknown to the savages of America, who for that reason are still savage: the other nations also seem to have continued in a state of barbarism while they praised only one of these arts. One of the best reasons, perhaps, why Europe has been, if not longer, at least more constantly and highly civilized than the rest of the world, is that it is at once the most abundant in iron and the most fertile in corn.

It is difficult to conjecture how men first came to know and use iron; for it is impossible to suppose they would of themselves think of digging the ore out of the mine, and preparing it for smelting, before they knew what would be the result. On the other hand, we have the less reason to suppose this discovery the effect of any accidental fire, as mines are only formed in barren places, bare of trees and plants; so that it looks as if nature had taken pains to keep the fatal secret from us. There remains, therefore, only the extraordinary accident of some volcano which, by ejecting metallic substances already in fusion, suggested to the spectators the idea of imitating the natural operation. And we must further conceive them as possessed of uncommon courage and foresight, to undertake so laborious a work, with so distant a prospect of drawing advantage from it; yet these qualities are united only in minds more advanced than we can suppose those of these first discoverers to have been.

With regard to agriculture, the principles of it were known long before they were put in practice; and it is indeed hardly possible that men, constantly employed in drawing their subsistence from plants and trees, should not readily acquire a knowledge of the means made use of by nature for the propagation of plant life. It was in all probability very long, however, before their industry took that turn, either because trees, which together with hunting and fishing afforded them food, did not require their attention; or because they were ignorant of the use of corn, or without instruments to cultivate it; or because they lacked foresight to future needs; or lastly, because they were without means of preventing others from robbing them of the fruit of their labour.

When they grew more industrious, it is natural to believe that they began, with the help of sharp stones and pointed sticks, to cultivate a few vegetables or roots around their huts; though it was long before they knew how to prepare corn, or were provided with the implements necessary for raising it in any large quantity; not to mention how essential it is, for husbandry, to consent to immediate loss, in order to reap a future gain—a precaution very foreign to the turn of a savage's mind; for, as I have said, he hardly foresees in the morning what he will need at night.

The invention of the other arts must therefore have been necessary to compel mankind to apply themselves to agriculture. No sooner were artificers wanted to smelt and forge iron, than others were required to maintain them; the more hands that were employed in manufactures, the fewer were left to provide for the common subsistence, though the number of mouths to be furnished with food remained the same: and as some required commodities in exchange for their iron, the rest at length discovered the method of making iron serve for the multiplication of commodities. By this means the arts of husbandry and agriculture were established on the one hand, and the art of working metals and multiplying their uses on the other.

The cultivation of the earth necessarily brought about its distribution; and property, once recognized, gave rise to the first rules of justice; for, to secure each man his own, it had to be possible for each to have something. Besides, as men began to look forward to the future, and all had something to lose, every one had reason to apprehend that reprisals would follow any injury he might do to another. This origin is so much the more natural, as it is impossible to conceive how property can come from anything but manual labour: for what else can a man add to things which he does not originally create, so as to make them his own property? It is the husbandman's labour alone that, giving him a title to the produce of the ground he has tilled, gives him a claim also to the land itself, at least till harvest; and so, from year to year, a constant possession which is easily transformed into property. When the ancients, says Grotius, gave to Ceres the title of Legislatrix, and to a festival celebrated in her honour the name of Thesmophoria, they meant by that that the distribution of lands had produced a new kind of right: that is to say, the right of property, which is different from the right deducible from the law of nature.

In this state of affairs, equality might have been sustained, had the talents of individuals been equal, and had, for example, the use of iron and the consumption of commodities always exactly balanced each other; but, as there was nothing to preserve this balance, it was soon distributed; the strongest did most work; the most skilful turned his labour to best account; the most ingenious devised methods of diminishing his labour: the husbandman wanted more iron, or the smith more corn, and, while both laboured equally, the one gained a great deal by his work, while the other could hardly support himself. Thus natural inequality unfolds itself insensibly with that of combination, and the difference between men, developed by their different circumstances, becomes more sensible and permanent in its effects, and begins to have an influence, in the same proportion, over the lot of individuals.

Matters once at this pitch, it is easy to imagine the rest. I shall not detain the reader with a description of the successive invention of other arts, the development of language, the trial and utilization of talents, the inequality of fortunes, the use and abuse of riches, and all the details connected with them which the reader can easily supply for himself. I shall confine myself to a glance at mankind in this new situation.

Behold then all human faculties developed, memory and imagination in full play, *amour-propre*

interested, reason active, and the mind almost at the highest point of its perfection. Behold all the natural qualities in action, the rank and condition of every man assigned him; not merely his share of property and his power to serve or injure others, but also his wit, beauty, strength or skill, merit or talents: and these being the only qualities capable of commanding respect, it soon became necessary to possess or to affect them.

It now became the interest of men to appear what they really were not. To be and to seem became two totally different things; and from this distinction sprang insolent pomp and cheating trickery, with all the numerous vices that go in their train. On the other hand, free and independent as men were before, they were now, in consequence of a multiplicity of new wants, brought into subjection, as it were, to all nature, and particularly to one another; and each became in some degree a slave even in becoming the master of other men: if rich, they stood in need of the services of others; if poor, of their assistance; and even a middle condition did not enable them to do without one another. Man must now, therefore, have been perpetually employed in getting others to interest themselves in his lot, and in making them, apparently at least, if not really, find their advantage in promoting his own. Thus he must have been sly and artful in his behaviour to some, and imperious and cruel to others; being under a kind of necessity to ill-use all the persons of whom he stood in need, when he could not frighten them into compliance, and did not judge it his interest to be useful to them. Insatiable ambition, the thirst of raising their respective fortunes, not so much from real want as from the desire to surpass others, inspired all men with a vile propensity to injure one another, and with a secret jealousy, which is the more dangerous, as it puts on the mask of benevolence, to carry its point with greater security. In a word, there arose rivalry and competition on the one hand, and conflicting interests on the other, together with a secret desire on both of profiting at the expense of others. All these evils were the first effects of property, and the inseparable attendants of growing inequality.

Before the invention of signs to represent riches, wealth could hardly consist in anything but lands and cattle, the only real possessions men can have. But, when inheritances so increased in number and extent as to occupy the whole of the land, and to border on one another, one man could aggrandize himself only at the expense of another; at the same time the supernumeraries, who had been too weak or too indolent to make such acquisitions, and had grown poor without sustaining any loss, because, while they saw everything change around them, they remained still the same, were obliged to receive their subsistence, or steal it, from the rich; and this soon bred, according to their different characters, dominion and slavery, or violence and rapine. The wealthy, on their part, had no sooner begun to taste the pleasure of command, than they disdained all others, and, using their old slaves to acquire new, thought of nothing but subduing and enslaving their neighbours; like ravenous wolves, which, having once tasted human flesh, despise every other food and thenceforth seek only men to devour.

Thus, as the most powerful or the most miserable considered their might or misery as a kind of right to the possessions of others, equivalent, in their opinion, to that of property, the destruction of equality was attended by the most terrible disorders. Usurpations by the rich, robbery by the poor, and the unbridled passions of both, suppressed the cries of natural compassion and the still feeble voice of justice, and filled men with avarice, ambition, and vice. Between the tide of the strongest and that of the first occupier, there arose perpetual conflicts, which never ended but in battles and bloodshed. The new-born state of society thus gave rise to a horrible state of war; men thus harassed and depraved were no longer capable of retracing their steps or renouncing the fatal acquisitions they had made, but, labouring by the abuse of the faculties which do them honour, merely to their own confusion, brought themselves to the brink of ruin.

*Attonitus novitate mali, divesque miserque,*
*Effugere optat opes; et quae modo voverat odit.*[3]

It is impossible that men should not at length have reflected on so wretched a situation, and on the calamities that overwhelmed them. The rich, in par-

ticular, must have felt how much they suffered by a constant state of war, of which they bore all the expense; and in which, though all risked their lives, they alone risked their property. Besides, however speciously they might disguise their usurpations, they knew that they were founded on precarious and false titles; so that, if others took from them by force what they themselves had gained by force, they would have no reason to complain. Even those who had been enriched by their own industry, could hardly base their proprietorship on better claims. It was in vain to repeat: 'I built this well; I gained this spot by my industry.' Who gave you your standing, it might be answered, and what right have you to demand payment of us for doing what we never asked you to do? Do you not know that numbers of your fellow-creatures are starving, for want of what you have too much of? You ought to have had the express and universal consent of mankind, before appropriating more of the common subsistence than you needed for your own maintenance. Destitute of valid reasons to justify and sufficient strength to defend himself, able to crush individuals with ease, but easily crushed himself by a troop of bandits, one against all, and incapable, on account of mutual jealousy, of joining with his equals against numerous enemies united by the common hope of plunder, the rich man, thus urged by necessity, conceived at length the profoundest plan that ever entered the mind of man: this was to employ in his favour the forces of those who attacked him, to make allies of his adversaries, to inspire them with different maxims, and to give them other institutions as favourable to himself as the law of nature was unfavourable.

With this view, after having represented to his neighbours the horror of a situation which armed every man against the rest, and made their possessions as burdensome to them as their wants, and in which no safety could be expected either in riches or in poverty, he readily devised plausible arguments to make them close with his design. 'Let us join,' said he, 'to guard the weak from oppression, to restrain the ambitious, and secure to every man the possession of what belongs to him: let us institute rules of justice and peace, to which all without exception may be obliged to conform; rules that may in some measure make amends for the caprices of fortune, by subjecting equally the powerful and the weak to the observance of reciprocal obligations. Let us, in a word, instead of turning our forces against ourselves, collect them in a supreme power which may govern us by wise laws, protect and defend all the members of the association, repulse their common enemies, and maintain eternal harmony among us.'

Far fewer words to this purpose would have been enough to impose on men so barbarous and easily seduced; especially as they had too many disputes among themselves to do without arbitrators, and too much ambition and avarice to go long without masters. All ran headlong to their chains, in hopes of securing their liberty; for they had just wit enough to perceive the advantages of political institutions, without experience enough to enable them to foresee the dangers. The most capable of foreseeing the dangers were the very persons who expected to benefit by them; and even the most prudent judged it not inexpedient to sacrifice one part of their freedom to ensure the rest; as a wounded man has his arm cut off to save the rest of his body.

Such was, or may well have been, the origin of society and law, which bound new fetters on the poor, and gave new powers to the rich; which irretrievably destroyed natural liberty, eternally fixed the law of property and inequality, converted clever usurpation into unalterable right, and, for the advantage of a few ambitious individuals, subjected all mankind to perpetual labour, slavery, and wretchedness. It is easy to see how the establishment of one community made that of all the rest necessary, and how, in order to make head against united forces, the rest of mankind had to unite in turn. Societies soon multiplied and spread over the face of the earth, till hardly a corner of the world was left in which a man could escape the yoke, and withdraw his head from beneath the sword which he saw perpetually hanging over him by a thread. Civil right having thus become the common rule among the members of each community, the law of nature maintained its place only between different communities, where, under the name of the right of nations, it was qualified by certain tacit conventions, in order to make commerce practicable, and serve as a substitute for natural compassion, which lost, when applied to societies, almost all the influence it had over individuals, and survived no longer except in some great cosmopolitan spirits, who, breaking down the imaginary barriers that separate different peoples, follow the example of our Sovereign Creator, and include the whole human race in their benevolence.

But bodies politic, remaining thus in a state of nature among themselves, presently experienced the inconveniences which had obliged individuals to forsake it; for this state became still more fatal to these great bodies than it had been to the individuals of whom they were composed. Hence arose national wars, battles, murders, and reprisals, which shock nature and outrage reason; together with all those horrible prejudices which class among the virtues the honour of shedding human blood. The most distinguished men hence learned to consider cutting each other's throats a duty; at length men massacred their fellow-creatures by thousands without so much as knowing why, and committed more murders in a single day's fighting, and more violent outrages in the sack of a single town, than were committed in the state of nature during whole ages over the whole earth. Such were the first effects which we can see to have followed the division of mankind into different communities. . . .

## Notes

1. [Justin, *Hist*. ii, 2. So much more does the ignorance of vice profit the one sort than the knowledge of virtue the other.]

2. *Amour-propre* must not be confused with love of self: for they differ both in themselves and in their effects. Love of self is a natural feeling which leads every animal to look to its own preservation, and which, guided in man by reason and modified by compassion, creates humanity and virtue. *Amour-propre* is a purely relative and factitious feeling, which arises in the state of society, leads each individual to make more of himself than of any other, causes all the mutual damage men inflict one on another, and is the real source of the 'sense of honour'. This being understood, I maintain that, in our primitive condition, in the true state of nature, *amour-propre* did not exist; for as each man regarded himself as the only observer of his

actions, the only being in the universe who took any interest in him, and the sole judge of his deserts, no feeling arising from comparisons he could not be led to make could take root in his soul; and for the same reason, he could know neither hatred nor the desire for revenge, since these passions can spring only from a sense of injury: and as it is the contempt or the intention to hurt, and not the harm done, which constitutes the injury, men who neither valued nor compared themselves could do one another much violence, when it suited them, without feeling any sense of injury. In a word, each man, regarding his fellows almost as he regarded animals of different species, might seize the prey of a weaker or yield up his own to a stronger, and yet consider these acts of violence as mere natural occurrences, without the slightest emotion of insolence or despite, or nay other feeling than the joy or grief of success or failure.

3. Ovid, *Metamorphoses*, xi. 127, "Both rich and poor, shocked at their new found ills, / Would fly from wealth, and lose what they had sought."

# Of the Social Contract

## BOOK ONE

I want to inquire whether, taking men as they are and laws as they can be, it is possible to have some legitimate and certain rule of administration in civil affairs. In this investigation I shall always strive to ally what right permits with what interest prescribes, so that justice and utility may not be divided.

I enter upon this inquiry without proving the importance of my subject. I shall be asked whether I am a prince or a legislator that I write on Politics. I reply that I am not, and that it is for this reason that I write on Politics. If I were a prince or a legislator, I should not waste my time in saying what ought to be done; I should do it or remain silent.

Having been born a citizen of a free State, and a member of the sovereign, however feeble an influence my voice may have in public affairs, the right to vote upon them is sufficient to impose on me the duty of informing myself about them. I feel happy, whenever I meditate on governments, always to find in my researches new reasons for loving that of my own country!

## I. Subject of This First Book

Man is born free, and everywhere he is in chains. One believes himself the master of others, and yet he is a greater slave than they. How has this change come about? I do not know. What can render it legitimate? I believe that I can settle this question.

If I considered only force and the results that proceed from it, I should say that so long as a People is compelled to obey and does obey, it does well; but that, so soon as it can shake off the yoke and does shake it off, it does better; for, recovering its liberty by the same right by which it was taken away, either it is justified in resuming it, or there was no justification for depriving them of it. But the social order is a sacred right which serves as a basis for all others. Yet this right does not come from nature; it is therefore based on conventions. The question is to know what these conventions are. Before coming to that, I must establish what I have just laid down.

## II. Of the First Societies

The most ancient of all societies, and the only natural one, is the family. Nevertheless children remain bound to their father only as long as they have need of him for their own preservation. As soon as this need ceases, the natural bond is dissolved. The children freed from the obedience which they owe to their father, and the father from the cares which he owes to his children, become equally independent. If they remain united, it is no longer naturally but voluntarily, and the family itself is kept together only by convention.

Translated by Charles M. Sherover; reprinted with his permission.

This common liberty is a consequence of man's nature. His first law is to attend to his own preservation, his first cares are those which he owes to himself, and as soon as he comes to years of discretion, being sole judge of the means adapted for his own preservation, he becomes thereby his own master.

## III. Of the Right of the Strongest

The strongest man is never strong enough to be always master, unless he transforms his force into right, and obedience into duty. Hence the right of the strongest—a right assumed ironically in appearance, and really established in principle. But will this word never be explained to us? Force is a physical power; I do not see what morality can result from its effects. To yield to force is an act of necessity, not of will; it is at most an act of prudence. In what sense could it be a duty?

Let us suppose for a moment this pretended right. I say that nothing results from it but an inexplicable muddle. For as soon as force constitutes right, the effect changes with the cause; every force which overcomes the first succeeds to its right (privilege). As soon as one can disobey with impunity, he may do so legitimately; and since the strongest is always in the right, it remains merely to act in such a way that one may be the strongest. But what sort of a right perishes when force ceases? If it is necessary to obey by compulsion, there is no need to obey by duty; and if men are no longer forced to obey, obligation is at an end. Obviously, then, this word "right" adds nothing to force; it means nothing here at all.

Obey the powers that be. If that means yield to force, the precept is good but superfluous; I warrant that it will never be violated. All power comes from God, I admit; but every disease does also. Does it follow that we are prohibited from calling in a physician? If a brigand should surprise me in the recesses of a wood: not only am I bound to give up my purse when forced, but am I also in conscience bound to do so when I might conceal it? For after all, the pistol which he holds is also a power.

Let us agree, then, that might does not make right, and that we are obligated to obey only legitimate powers. Thus my original questions ever recur.

## IV. Of Slavery

Since no man has a natural authority over his fellow men, and since force is not the source of right, conventions remain as the basis of all legitimate authority among men.

If an individual, says Grotius, can alienate his liberty and become the slave of a master, why should a whole people not be able to alienate theirs, and subject themselves to a king? In this there are a good many equivocal words that require explanation; but let us confine ourselves to the word *alienate*. To alienate is to give or sell. Now a man who becomes another's slave does not give himself; he sells himself at the very least for his subsistence; but why does a people sell itself? Far from a king supplying to his subjects their subsistence, he draws his from them; and according to Rabelais, a king does not live on little. Do subjects, then, give up their persons on condition that their goods also shall be taken? I do not see what is left for them to keep.

It will be said that the despot secures to his subjects civil peace. Just so; but what do they gain by that, if the wars which his ambition brings upon them, together with his insatiable greed and the vexations of his administration, dishearten them more than their own dissensions would? What do they gain if this peace itself is one of their miseries? One lives peacefully also in dungeons; is this enough to find them good? The Greeks confined in the cave of the Cyclops lived peacefully until their turn came to be devoured.

To say that a man gives himself for nothing is to say something absurd and inconceivable; such an act is illegitimate and worthless, for the simple reason that he who performs it is not in his right mind. To say the same thing of a whole people is to suppose a people of madmen; and madness does not make right.

Even if each person could alienate himself, he could not alienate his children; they are born men and free; their liberty belongs to them, and no one has a right to dispose of it except themselves. Before they have come to an age of discretion, the father can, in their name, stipulate conditions for their preservation and welfare, but not surrender them irrevocably and unconditionally; for such a bequest is contrary to the ends of nature, and exceeds the rights of paternity. It would be necessary, therefore, to ensure that an arbitrary government might be legitimate, that with each generation the people have the option of accepting it or rejecting it; but in that case this government would no longer be arbitrary.

To renounce one's liberty is to renounce one's quality as a man, the rights of humanity and even its duties. For whoever renounces everything there is no possible compensation. Such renunciation is incompatible with man's nature; and to deprive his actions of all morality is tantamount to depriving his will of all freedom. Finally, a convention which stipulates absolute authority on the one side and unlimited obedience on the other is vain and contradictory. Is it not clear that one is under no obligations whatsoever toward a man from whom one has a right to demand everything? And does not this single condition, without equivalent, without exchange, entail the nullity of the act? For what right would my slave have against me, since all that he has belongs to me? His right being mine, this right of me against myself is a meaningless phrase.

## V. That It Is Always Necessary to Go Back to a First Convention

Even if I were in accord with all that I have so far refuted, those who favor despotism would be no farther advanced. There will always be a great difference between subduing a multitude and ruling a society. If scattered men, however numerous they may be, are subjected successively to a single person, this seems to me only a case of master and slaves, not of a people and its chief: they form, if you will, an aggregation, but not an association, for they have neither public property nor a body politic. Such a man, had he enslaved half the world, is always only one individual; his interest, separated from that of the rest, is always only a private interest. If he dies, his empire after him is left scattered and disunited, as an oak dissolves and becomes a heap of ashes after the fire has consumed it.

A people, says Grotius, can give itself to a king. According to Grotius, a people, then, is a people before it gives itself to a king. This gift itself is a civil act, and presupposes a public deliberation. Hence, before examining the act by which a people elects a king, it would be good to examine the act by which a people is a people. For this act being necessarily anterior to the other, is the real foundation of the society.

In fact, if there were no anterior convention, where, unless the election were unanimous, would be the obligation upon the minority to submit to the decision of the majority? And whence do the hundred who desire a master derive the right to vote on behalf of ten who do not desire one? The law of the plurality of votes is itself established by convention, and presupposes unanimity at least once.

## VI. Of the Social Pact

I suppose that men have reached a point at which the obstacles that endanger their preservation in the state of nature prevail by their resistance over the forces which each individual can exert in order to maintain himself in that state. Then this primitive condition can no longer subsist, and the human race would perish unless it changed its manner of being.

Now as men cannot create any new forces, but only unite and direct those that exist, they have no other means of self-preservation than to form by aggregation a sum of forces which may overcome the resistance, to put them in action by a single motive power, and to make them work in concert.

This sum of forces can be produced only by the combination of many; but the strength and freedom of each man being the primary instruments of his preservation, how can he pledge them without injuring himself, and without neglecting the care which he owes to himself? This difficulty, applied to my subject, may be stated in these terms:

"To find a form of association which defends and protects with the whole force of the community the person and goods of every associate, and by means of which each, uniting with all, nevertheless obeys only himself, and remains as free as before." Such is the fundamental problem to which the social contract gives the solution.

The clauses of this contract are so determined by the nature of the act that the slightest modification would render them vain and ineffectual; so that, although perhaps they have never been formally enunciated, they are everywhere the same, everywhere tacitly admitted and recognized; until, the social pact being violated, each man regains his initial rights and recovers his natural liberty, while losing the conventional liberty for which he renounced it.

These clauses, rightly understood, are all reducible to one only, namely the total alienation of each associate, with all of his rights, to the whole community: For, in the first place, as each gives himself up entirely, the condition is equal for all, and, the condition being equal for all, no one has any interest in making it burdensome to others.

Further, the alienation being made without reserve, the union is as perfect as it can be, and no associate has anything more to claim. For if some rights were left to individuals, since there would be no common superior who could judge between them and the public, each, being on some point his own judge, would soon claim to be so on all; the state of nature would still subsist, and the association would necessarily become tyrannical or useless.

Finally, each, in giving himself to all, gives himself to nobody; and as there is not one associate over whom we do not acquire the same rights which we concede to him over ourselves, we gain the equivalent of all that we lose, and more power to preserve what we have.

If, then, everything which is not of the essence of the social pact is set aside, one finds that it reduces itself to the following terms: *Each of us puts in common his person and his whole power under the supreme direction of the general will; and in return we receive in a body every member as an indivisible part of the whole.*

Forthwith, instead of the particular person of each contracting part, this act of association produces a moral and collective body, which is composed of as many members as the assembly has voices, and which receives from this same act its unity, its common *self* [*moi*], its life, and its will. This public person, which is thus formed by the union of all the individual members, formerly took the name of *City* and now takes that of *Republic* or *body politic*, which is called by its members *State* when it is pas-sive, *Sovereign* when it is active, *Power* when it is compared to similar bodies. With regard to the associates, they take collectively the name of *people*, and are called individually *Citizens*, as participating in the sovereign authority, and *Subjects*, as subjected to the laws of the State. But these terms are often confused and are mistaken one for another; it is sufficient to know how to distinguish them when they are used with complete precision.

## VII. Of the Sovereign

One sees by this formula that the act of association includes a reciprocal engagement between the public and the individual, and that each individual, contracting so to speak with himself, is engaged in a double relation: namely, as a member of the Sovereign toward individuals, and as a member of the State toward the Sovereign. But we cannot apply here the maxim of civil right that no one is bound by engagements made with himself; for there is a great difference between being obligated to oneself and to a whole of which one forms a part.

It is necessary to note further that the public deliberation which can obligate all subjects to the Sovereign in consequence of the two different relations under which each of them is regarded cannot, for a contrary reason, bind the Sovereign to itself; and that accordingly it is contrary to the nature of the body politic for the Sovereign to impose on itself a law which it cannot transgress. As it can only be considered under one and the same relation, it is in the position of an individual contracting with himself; thus we see that there is not, nor can there be, any kind of fundamental law obligatory for the body of the people, not even the social contract. This does not imply that such a body cannot perfectly well enter into engagements with others in what does not derogate from this contract; for, with regard to foreigners, it becomes a simple being, an individual.

But the body politic or Sovereign, deriving its existence only from the sanctity of the contract, can never bind itself, even to others, in anything that derogates from the original act, such as to alienate some portion of itself, or submission to another Sovereign. To violate the act by which it exists would be to annihilate itself; and what is nothing produces nothing.

As soon as this multitude is thus united into one body, it is impossible to injure one of the members without attacking the body; still less to injure the body without the members feeling the effects. Thus duty and interest equally obligate the two contracting parties to give mutual assistance; and the same men should seek to combine in this twofold relationship all the advantages which are attendant on it.

Now the Sovereign, being formed only of the individuals who compose it, neither has nor can have any interest contrary to theirs; consequently the Sovereign power needs no guarantee toward its subjects, because it is impossible that the body should wish to injure all its members; and we shall see hereafter that it can injure no one in particular. The Sovereign, for the simple reason that it is, is always everything that it ought to be.

But this is not the case with respect to the relation of subjects to the Sovereign, which, notwithstanding the common interest, would have no security for the performance of their engagements, unless it found means to ensure their fidelity.

Indeed, each individual may, as a man, have a particular will contrary to, or divergent from, the general will which he has as a Citizen. His private interest may speak to him quite differently from the common interest; his absolute and naturally independent existence may make him regard what he owes to the common cause as a gratuitous contribution, the loss of which will be less harmful to others than will the payment of it be onerous to him; and viewing the moral person that constitutes the State as a being of reason because it is not a man, he would be willing to enjoy the rights of a citizen without being willing to fulfill the duties of a subject: an injustice, the progress of which would bring about the ruin of the body politic.

In order, then, that the social pact may not be a vain formula, it tacitly includes this engagement, which can alone give force to the others—that whoever refuses to obey the general will shall be constrained to do so by the whole body; which means nothing else than that he shall be forced to be free;

for such is the condition which, giving each Citizen to his Fatherland, guarantees him from all personal dependence, a condition that makes up the spark and interplay of the political mechanism, and alone renders legitimate civil engagements, which, without it, would be absurd and tyrannical, and subject to the most enormous abuse.

## VIII. Of the Civil State

This passage from the state of nature to the civil state produces in man a very remarkable change, by substituting in his conduct injustice for instinct, and by giving his actions the morality that they previously lacked. It is only when the voice of duty succeeds physical impulsion, and right succeeds appetite, that man, who till then had only looked after himself, sees that he is forced to act on other principles, and to consult his reason before listening to his inclinations. Although, in this state, he is deprived of many advantages he holds from nature, he gains such great ones in return, that his faculties are exercised and developed; his ideas are expanded; his feelings are ennobled; his whole soul is exalted to such a degree that, if the abuses of this new condition did not often degrade him below that from which he has emerged, he should ceaselessly bless the happy moment that removed him from it forever, and transformed him from a stupid and ignorant animal into an intelligent being and a man.

Let us reduce this whole balance to terms easy to compare. What man loses by the social contract is his natural liberty and an unlimited right to anything which tempts him and which he is able to attain; what he gains is civil liberty and the ownership of all that he possesses. In order not to be mistaken about these compensations, we must clearly distinguish natural liberty, which is limited only by the force of the individual, from civil liberty, which is limited by the general will; and possession, which is only the result of force or the right of the first occupant, from ownership, which can only be based on a positive title.

Besides the preceding, one can add to the acquisitions of the civil state the moral freedom which alone renders man truly master of himself; for the impulsion of mere appetite is slavery, and obedience to the law one prescribes to oneself is freedom. But I have already said too much on this subject, and the philosophical meaning of the term *liberty* does not belong to my subject here.

## IX. Of Real Property

Each member of the community gives himself up to it at the moment of its formation, just as he actually is, himself and all his force, of which the goods he possesses form a part. It is not that by this act possession changes its nature in changing hands and becomes property in those of the Sovereign; but, as the powers of the City are incomparably greater than those of an individual, public possession is also, in fact, more secure and more irrevocable, without being more legitimate, at least for foreigners. For the State, with regard to its members, is master of all their property by the social contract, which in the State serves as the basis of all rights; but with regard to other powers it is master only by right of first occupant which it holds from private individuals.

The right of first occupant, although more real than that of the strongest, becomes a true right only after the establishment of property [ownership]. Every man has by nature a right to all that is necessary to him; but the positive act which makes him owner of certain goods excludes him from the rest. His portion having been allotted, he ought to confine himself to it, and he has no further right against the community. That is why the right of first occupant, so weak in the state of nature, is respected by every member of a civil society. In this right one respects not so much what belongs to others as what does not belong to oneself.

Generally, in order to authorize the right of first occupant over any land whatsoever, the following conditions are needed. First, the land must not yet be inhabited by anyone; second, a man must occupy only the area required for his subsistence; third, he must take possession of it not by an empty ceremony but by labor and cultivation, the only mark of ownership which, in the absence of legal title, ought to be respected by others.

Indeed, to grant the right of first occupant according to necessity and labor, is it not to extend this right as far as it can go? Can one assign limits to this right? Will the mere setting foot on common ground be sufficient to presume an immediate claim to the ownership of it? Will the power of driving away other men from it for a moment suffice to deprive them of the right of ever returning to it? How can a man or a people take possession of an immense territory and rob the whole human race of it except by a punishable usurpation, since henceforth other men are deprived of the place of residence and sustenance which nature gives to them in common? When Núñez de Balboa on the seashore took possession of the Pacific Ocean and of the whole of South America in the name of the crown of Castile, was this sufficient to dispossess all the inhabitants, and exclude from it all the Princes in the world? On this stand, such ceremonies might have been multiplied vainly enough; and the Catholic King in his cabinet might, by a single stroke, have taken possession of the whole universe; only cutting off afterward from his empire what was previously occupied by other Princes.

It can be understood how the lands of individuals, united and contiguous, become public territory, and how the right of sovereignty, extending itself from the subjects to the land which they occupy, becomes at once real and personal; this places the possessors in greater dependence, and makes their own powers a guarantee for their fidelity. An advantage which ancient monarchs do not appear to have clearly sensed, for, calling themselves only Kings of the Persians or Scythians or Macedonians, they seem to have viewed themselves as chiefs of men rather than as owners of countries. Those of today call themselves more cleverly Kings of France, Spain, England, etc. In thus holding the land they are quite sure of holding its inhabitants.

What is remarkable about this alienation is that the community, in receiving the property of individuals, far from robbing them of it, only assures them lawful possession, and changes usurpation into true right, enjoyment into ownership. Then the possessors, being considered as depositaries of the public property, and their rights being respected by all members of the State, and maintained with all its power against the foreign intruder, have, as it were, by a transfer advantageous to the public and still more to themselves, acquired all that they have given up. This is a paradox which is easily explained by distinguishing between the rights which the Sovereign and the owner have over the same property, as shall be seen later.

It may also happen that men begin to unite before they possess anything, and that afterward taking over territory sufficient for all, they enjoy it in common, or share it among themselves, either equally or in proportions fixed by the Sovereign. In whatever manner this acquisition is made, the right which every individual has over his own property is always subordinate to the right which the community has over all; otherwise there would be neither solidity in the social union, nor real force in the exercise of Sovereignty.

I shall close this chapter and this book with a remark which ought to serve as a basis for the whole social system; it is that instead of destroying natural equality, the fundamental pact, on the contrary, substitutes a moral and legitimate equality for the physical inequality which nature imposed upon men, so that, although unequal in strength or talent, they all become equal by convention and legal right.[1]

## BOOK TWO

### I. That Sovereignty Is Inalienable

The first and most important consequence of the principles established above is that the general will can only direct the forces of the State in keeping with the end for which it was instituted, which is the common good; for if the opposition of private interests has made the establishment of societies necessary, the harmony of these same interests has made it possible. That which is common to these different interests forms the social bond; and if there were not some point in which all interests agree, no society could exist. Now it is only on this common interest that the society should be governed.

I say, then, that sovereignty, being only the exercise of the general will, can never be alienated, and that the Sovereign, which is only a collective being, can be represented only by itself; power can well be transmitted, but will cannot.

In fact, if it is not impossible that a private will agree on some point with the general will, it is at least impossible that this agreement should be lasting and constant, for the private will naturally tends to preferences, and the general will to equality. It is still more impossible to have a guarantee for this agreement; even though it should always exist, it would be an effect not of art but of chance. The Sovereign may indeed say: I now will what a certain man wills, or at least what he says that he wills; but it cannot say: what that man wills tomorrow, I shall also will; since it is absurd that the will should bind itself for the future and since it is not incumbent on any will to consent to anything contrary to the good of the being that wills. If, then, the people promises simply to obey, it dissolves itself by that act, it loses its quality as a people; at the instant that there is a master, there is no longer a Sovereign, and forthwith the body politic is destroyed.

This is not to say that the orders of the chiefs cannot pass for expressions of the general will, so long as the Sovereign, free to oppose them, does not do so. In such case, from the universal silence one should presume the consent of the people. This will be explained at greater length.

### II. That Sovereignty Is Indivisible

For the same reason that sovereignty is inalienable, it is indivisible. For either the will is general[2] or it is not; it is the will either of the body of the people, or only of a part. In the first case, this declared will is an act of sovereignty and constitutes law. In the second case, it is only a private will, or an act of magistracy; it is at most a decree.

But our political men, not being able to divide sovereignty in its principles, divide it in its object: they divide it into force and will, into legislative power and executive power; into rights of taxation, of justice, and of war; into internal administration and power of treating with foreigners: sometimes they confound all these parts and sometimes separate them. They make the Sovereign to be a fantastic being formed of borrowed pieces; it is as if they composed a man from several bodies, one having eyes, another having arms, another having feet, and nothing more. Charlatans of Japan, it is said, cut up a child before the eyes of the spectators; then, throwing all its limbs, one after another, into the air, they make the child come back down alive and whole. Such almost are the juggler's tricks of our politicians; after dismembering the social body by a deception worthy of a carnival, they recombine the parts, one knows not how.

This error comes from not having formed exact notions of sovereign authority, and from having taken as parts of this authority what are only emanations from it. Thus, for example, the act of declaring war and that of making peace have been looked at as acts of sovereignty; but this is not the case, since each of these acts is not a law, but only an application of the law, a particular act which determines the case of the law, as will be clearly seen when the idea attached to the word *law* will be fixed.

In following out the other divisions in the same way, one would find that whenever sovereignty appears divided, a mistake has been made; that the rights which are taken as parts of that sovereignty are all subordinate to it, and always suppose supreme wills of which these rights are merely the execution.

### III. Whether the General Will Can Err

It follows from what precedes that the general will is always upright and always tends toward the public utility; but it does not follow that the deliberations of the people always have the same rectitude. One wishes always his own good, but does not always discern it. The people is never corrupted, though often deceived, and then only does it seem to will that which is bad.

There is often a great difference between the will

of all and the general will; the latter regards only the common interest, the other regards private interests and is only the sum of particular wills: but remove from these wills the pluses and minuses which cancel each other out[3] and the general will remains as the sum of the differences.

If, when an adequately informed people deliberates, the Citizens having no communication among themselves, from the large number of small differences the general will would always result, and the deliberation would always be good. But when factions are formed, partial associations at the expense of the whole, the will of each of these associations becomes general with regard to its members, and particular with regard to the State: one is then able to say that there are no longer as many voters as there are men, but only as many as there are associations. The differences become less numerous and yield a less general result. Finally, when one of these associations is so large that it overcomes the rest, you no longer have a sum of small differences as the result, but a unique difference; then there no longer is a general will, and the opinion which dominates is only a private opinion.

It matters, then, in order to have the general will expressed well, that there be no partial societies in the State, and that each Citizen speak only his own opinions.[4] Such was the unique and sublime institution of the great Lycurgus. But if there are partial associations, it is necessary to multiply their number and so prevent inequality, as was done by Solon, Numa, and Servius. These precautions are the only valid ones, in order that the general will always be enlightened and that the people are not deceived.

### IV. Of the Limits of the Sovereign Power

If the State or the City is only a moral person whose life consists in the union of its members, and if the most important of its cares is that of its own conservation, it needs a universal and compulsive force to move and dispose every part in the manner most appropriate for the whole. As nature gives each man an absolute power over all his limbs, the social pact gives the body politic an absolute power over all its members, and it is the same power which, directed by the general will, bears, as I have said, the name of sovereignty.

But beyond the public person, we have to consider the private persons who compose it, and whose life and liberty are naturally independent of it. It is then necessary to distinguish clearly the respective rights of the Citizens and of the Sovereign[5] as well as between the duties which the former have to fulfill as subjects and the natural right which they ought to enjoy in their quality as men.

Granted that whatever part of his power, his goods, and his liberty each alienates by the social pact is only that part whose use is important to the community; we must also agree that the Sovereign alone is judge of that importance.

All the services that a citizen can render to the State, he owes to it as soon as the Sovereign demands them; but the Sovereign, on its side, cannot impose any burden on its subjects that is useless to the community; it cannot even wish to do so; because under the law of reason nothing happens without cause, just as under the law of nature.

The engagements which bind us to the social body are obligatory only because they are mutual, and their nature is such that in fulfilling them one cannot work for others without also working for oneself. Why is the general will always upright, and why do all constantly desire the well-being of each, if not because no one appropriates this word *each* to himself without thinking of himself as voting on behalf of all? This proves that equality of right and the notion of justice it produces derive from the preference which each gives to himself, and consequently from the nature of man; that the general will, to be truly such, must be just in its object as in its essence; that it ought to proceed from all in order to be applicable to all; and that it loses its natural rectitude when it is directed to some individual and determinate object, because in that case, judging from what is foreign to us, we have no true principle of equity to guide us.

In effect, so soon as a matter of fact or particular right is in question on a point which has not been regulated by a previous general convention, the affair becomes contentious. It is a lawsuit in which the interested individuals are one of the parties and the public the other, but in which I perceive neither the law which must be followed, nor the judge who should decide. It would be ridiculous to wish to refer the matter for an express decision of the general will, which can only be the decision of one of the parties, and which, consequently, is for the other party only a will that is foreign, partial, and inclined on such an occasion to injustice as well as it is subject to error. Thus, just as a particular will cannot represent the general will, the general will in turn changes its nature when it has a particular object and cannot, as general, decide about either a man or a fact. When the people of Athens, for example, named or deposed their chiefs, decreed honor to one, imposed penalties on another, and by multitudes of particular decrees exercised indiscriminately all the functions of government, the people no longer had any general will properly so called; it no longer acted as Sovereign but as Magistrate. This will appear contrary to common ideas, but I must be allowed time to set forth my own.

What generalizes the will, one must see from this, is not so much the number of voices as the common interest that unites them; for, in this institution, each necessarily submits to the conditions that he imposes on others: an admirable accord of interest and justice which gives to common deliberations a spirit of equity that seems to disappear in the discussion of any particular affair, for want of a common interest to unite and identify the ruling principle of the judge with that of the party.

By whatever path we return to our principle, we always arrive at the same conclusion: the social pact establishes among citizens such an equality that they all engage themselves under the same conditions and ought to enjoy the same rights. Thus, by the nature of the pact, every act of sovereignty, that is to say every authentic act of the general will, obligates or favors all the citizens equally; so that the Sovereign knows only the body of the nation, and distinguishes none of those who compose it. What then is properly an act of sovereignty? It is not a convention of the superior with an inferior, but a convention of the body with each of its members. A legitimate convention, because it has the social contract for its base; equitable, because it is common to all; useful, because it can have no object other than the general welfare; and firm, because it has for its guarantee the public force and supreme power. So long as the subjects submit only to such conventions, they obey no one, but only their own will; and to ask how far the respective rights of the Sovereign and the Citizens extend is to ask up to which point the latter can engage themselves, each toward all and all toward each.

One sees thereby that the Sovereign power, wholly absolute, wholly sacred, wholly inviolable as it is, neither passes nor can pass the limits of general conventions, and that every man can fully dispose of what is left to him of his goods and his liberty by these conventions; so that the Sovereign never has a right to burden one subject more than another, because then the matter becomes individual, and its power is no longer competent.

These distinctions once admitted, it is so false that in the social contract there is, on the part of individuals, any real renunciation, that their situation, as a result of this contract, is in reality preferable to what it was before: instead of an alienation they have only made an advantageous exchange of an uncertain and precarious mode of existence for a better and more assured one, of natural independence for liberty, of the power to injure others for their own safety, and of their strength, which others might overcome, for a right which the social union renders invincible. Their life itself, which they have dedicated to the State, is continually protected by it; and when they expose their lives for its defense, what do they do but restore what they have received from it? What do they do but what they would do more frequently and with more risk in the state of nature, when, engaging in inevitable struggles, they would defend at the peril of their lives their means of preserving it? All have to fight, if need be, for the fatherland, it is true; but then no one ever has to fight for himself. Do we not gain, still, to run this risk for that which assures our safety,

a part of the risks we would have to run for ourselves as soon as our security was taken away?

## VI. Of the Law

By the social pact we have given existence and life to the body politic; it is now a matter of giving it movement and will through legislation. For the original act by which this body is formed and united still determines nothing with respect to what it should do to preserve itself.

What is good and conforming to order is such by the nature of things and independent of human conventions. All justice comes from God, he alone is the source; but if we knew how to receive it from so high, we would need neither government nor laws. Without doubt there is a universal justice emanating from reason alone; but this justice, in order to be admitted among us, must be reciprocal. Considering things from a human viewpoint, the laws of justice, lacking a natural sanction, are ineffectual among men; they only bring good to the wicked and evil to the just man when he observes them with everyone else and no one observes them with him. Conventions and laws are then needed in order to unite rights with duties and to bring justice to its object. In the state of nature, where everything is common, I owe nothing to those to whom I have promised nothing, and I recognize as belonging to others only what is useless to me. It is not so in the civil state, where all the rights are fixed by the law.

But what then is a law? As long as one continues to attach to this word only metaphysical ideas, one will continue to reason without understanding, and when one will have said what a law of nature is, one will not have a better idea of what is a law of the State.

I have already said that there is no general will concerning a particular object. In effect, this particular object is either in the State or outside the State. If it is outside the State, a will that is foreign to it is not general in relation to it; and if within the State, that object is part of it; then there is formed between the whole and its part a relation which makes the whole two separate entities, of which the part is one, and the whole less this same part is the other. But the whole less one part is not the whole, and so long as the relation subsists, there is no longer any whole but two unequal parts: from which it follows that the will of one of them is no longer general in relation to the other.

But when the whole people decrees for the whole people, it considers only itself; and if a relation is then formed, it is between the entire object from one point of view and the whole object from another point of view, without any division of the whole. It is this act that I call a law.

When I say that the object of the laws is always general, I mean that the law considers the subjects in a body and the actions as abstract, never a man as an individual nor a particular action. Thus the law can very well decree that there will be privileges, but it cannot confer them on anyone by name; the law can create several Classes of Citizens, even assign the characteristics that confer a right to membership in these Classes, but it cannot name specific persons to be admitted to them; it can establish a royal Government and a hereditary succession, but it cannot elect a king or appoint a royal family; in a word, no function that relates to an individual object belongs to the legislative power.

On this idea one sees instantly that it is no longer necessary to ask who is responsible for making the laws, since they are acts of the general will; nor whether the Prince is above the laws, since he is a member of the State; nor if the law can be unjust, since no one is unjust to himself; nor how one is free and subject to the laws, since they are only registers of our wills.

One sees further that the law uniting the universality of the will with that of the object, what any man, whoever he may be, orders on his own, is not a law; what is ordered even by the Sovereign regarding a particular object is not a law, but a decree, not an act of sovereignty, but of magistracy.

I therefore call every State ruled by laws a Republic, under whatever form of administration it could have; for then only the public interest governs and the public entity [Latin: *res publica*] is real. Every legitimate Government is republican;[6] I will explain later what Government is.

Laws are properly only the conditions of the civil association. The People, submitting to the laws, ought to be their author; it concerns only those who are associating together to regulate the conditions of the society. But how will they regulate them? Will it be in a common accord by sudden inspiration? Does the body politic have an organ to announce its will? Who will give it the foresight necessary to frame its acts and publish them in advance, or how will it pronounce them at the moment of need? How will a blind multitude, which often does not know what it wants because it rarely knows what is good for it, carry out an enterprise so great and also difficult as a system of legislation? By itself the people always wants the good, but by itself does not always discern it. The general will is always upright, but the judgment which guides it is not always enlightened. It is necessary to make it see objects as they are, sometimes as they ought to appear, to point out the good road it seeks, to guard it from the seduction of private wills, to bring before its eyes considerations of places and times, to balance the attraction of present and tangible advantages against the danger of distant and hidden evils. Private individuals see the good they reject; the public wants the good it does not see. All have equal need of guides. It is necessary to obligate the former to conform their wishes to their reason; it is necessary to teach the latter to know what it wants. Then from public enlightenment results the union of the understanding and the will in the social body, hence the precise concourse of the parts, and finally the maximum force of the whole. From this arises the necessity of a Legislator.

## VII. *Of the Legislator*

In order to discover the best rules of society which are suitable to nations, there would be needed a superior intelligence who saw all the passions of men and who had not experienced any of them; who would have no relation to our nature and yet knew it thoroughly; whose happiness would not depend on us and who would be quite willing to occupy himself with ours; finally, one who, preparing for himself a distant glory in the progress of time, could work in one age and find satisfaction in another.[7] Gods would be needed to give laws to men.

The same reasoning that Caligula used as to fact, Plato used with regard to right in order to define the civil or royal person whom he seeks in his book on ruling [i.e., the *Statesman*]. But if it is true that a great Prince is a rare man, what will a great Legislator be? The first has only to follow the model which the other has to propose. The latter is the engineer who invents the machine, the former is only the workman who puts it in readiness and makes it work. In the birth of societies, says Montesquieu, it is the chiefs of republics who make the institutions, and afterward it is the institutions which form the chiefs of republics.

He who dares to undertake the instituting of a people ought to feel himself capable, as it were, of changing human nature; of transforming each individual, who in himself is a perfect and solitary whole, into part of a greater whole from which this individual receives in some way his life and his being; of altering the constitution of man so as to reinforce it; of substituting a partial and moral existence for the physical and independent existence we have all received from nature. It is necessary, in a word, to remove man's own forces in order to give him some that are strange and which he is not able to use without the help of others. The more these natural forces are dead and annihilated, the greater and more durable are those acquired, the more too is the institution solid and perfect: so that if each Citizen is nothing, and can be nothing, except in combination with all others, and if the force acquired by the whole be equal or superior to the sum of the natural forces of all individuals, one can say that legislation has attained the highest possible point of perfection.

The Legislator is in all respects an extraordinary man in the State. If he ought to be so by his genius, he is not less so by his function. It is not magistracy, it is not sovereignty. This office, which constitutes the republic, does not enter into its constitution; it is a particular and superior function which has nothing

in common with human dominion; for if he who controls men should not have control over the laws, he who has control over the laws should not control men; otherwise, the laws, as ministers of his passions, would often serve only to perpetuate his acts of injustice; he would never be able to prevent his private views from corrupting the sacredness of his work. . . .

He who drafts the laws, then, does not have or should not have any legislative right, and even the people cannot, if it wishes, divest itself of this incommunicable right, because according to the fundamental pact, only the general will obligates individuals and one cannot be assured that a particular will has conformed to the general will until after it has been submitted to the free votes of the people; I have already said that, but it is not useless to repeat it.

Thus one finds at the same time in the work of legislation two things which seem incompatible: an enterprise above human force, and to execute it an authority that is nothing.

Another difficulty merits attention. Wise men who wish to speak their own language to the people instead of using the common speech will not be understood. Besides, there are a thousand kinds of ideas that it is impossible to translate into the language of the people. Very general views and very remote objects are equally beyond their grasp: each individual, appreciating no other plan of government than that which relates to his private interest, appreciates with difficulty the advantages he should receive from the continual privations which good laws impose. For a newly formed people to be able to appreciate the sane maxims of politics and to follow the fundamental rules of statecraft, it would be necessary that the effect could become the cause; that the social spirit, which ought to be the accomplishment of the institution, would preside over the institution itself; and that men be already, prior to the laws, that which they should become by means of them. Since the Legislator is able to employ neither force nor reasoning, he must have recourse to an authority of a different order, which can win without violence and persuade with convincing.

This is what in all times has forced the fathers of

nations to have recourse to the intervention of heaven, and to give the Gods credit for their own wisdom, to the end that the peoples, brought under the laws of the State as to those of nature, and recognizing the same power in the formation of man and in that of the city, obey with liberty and bear with docility the yoke of public felicity.

This sublime reason which rises above the reach of common men the Legislator places in the mouth of the immortals in order to win over by divine authority those unable to be moved by human prudence.[8] But not every man can make the Gods speak or be believed when he announces himself as their interpreter. The great soul of the Legislator is the true miracle which should prove his mission. Any man can engrave stone tablets, or buy an oracle, or feign a secret relationship with some divinity, or train a bird to speak in his ear, or find some other crude means of imposing on the people. He who knows only this could even assemble by chance a crowd of madmen, but he will never found an empire and his extravagant work will soon perish with him. Vain delusions form a transient bond; only wisdom renders it durable. The Judaic law which still subsists, and that of the child of Ishmael, which has ruled half the world for ten centuries, still proclaim today the great men who enunciated them; and while proud philosophy or blind party spirit sees in them only lucky impostors, the true student of politics admires in their institutions this great and powerful genius who presides over durable institutions.

It is not necessary to conclude from this with Warburton that politics and religions have among us a common object, but rather that in the origin of nations, one serves as instrument of the other.

### XI. Of the Diverse Systems of Legislation

If one seeks to find precisely what constitutes the greatest good of all, which ought to be the goal of every system of legislation, one will find that it reduces itself to two principal objects, *liberty* and *equality*. Liberty, because all self-dependence is so much force taken away from the body of the State; equality because liberty cannot subsist without it.

I have already said what civil liberty is; with regard to equality, it is necessary not to understand by this word that every degree of power and of wealth should be absolutely the same, but that, as to power, it should be above all violence and never exercised except in virtue of position and the laws; and as to wealth, no citizen should be so opulent as to be able to buy another, and none so poor as to be constrained to sell himself.[9] This presumes on the side of the mighty moderation, of goods and influence, and on the side of the lowly, moderation of avarice and of covetousness.

This equality is said to be a chimerical fantasy which cannot exist in practice. But if abuse is inevitable, does it follow that abuse should not be at least regulated? It is precisely because the force of things always tends to destroy equality that the force of legislation should always tend to maintain it. . . .

Among these diverse Classes, the political laws, which constitute the form of Government, are alone relevant to my subject.

### BOOK THREE

Before speaking of the diverse forms of Government, let us try to fix the precise meaning of that word, which has not yet been very well explained.

### I. Of Government in General

I warn the reader that this chapter should be read with care, and that I do not know the art of being clear to those who do not wish to be attentive.

Every free action has two causes which concur to produce it, the one moral, namely the will that determines the act; the other physical, namely the power that executes it. When I walk toward an object, it is first necessary that I want to go there; in the second place, that my feet carry me there. Should a paralytic wish to run, should an agile man not wish to do so, both will remain where they are. The body politic has the same motive power: in it one likewise distinguishes force and will. The latter is under the name of *legislative power*, the former under the name of *exec-*

*utive power.* Nothing is or should be done there [in the body politic] without their concurrence.

We have seen that the legislative power belongs to the people, and can belong to it alone. It is easy to see, on the contrary, by the principles already established, that the executive power cannot belong to the general public as Legislative or Sovereign; because this power consists only in particular acts which are not the province of the law, nor consequently of the Sovereign, all of whose acts can only be laws.

It is then necessary for the public force to have an appropriate agent that unifies it and puts it to work according to the directions of the general will, which serves as the means of communication between the State and the Sovereign, which in some way accomplishes in the public person what the union of soul and body does in man. This is in the State the reason for Government, improperly confused with the Sovereign, of which it is only the Minister.

What then is the Government? An intermediate body established between the subjects and the Sovereign for their mutual correspondence, charged with the execution of the laws, and to the maintenance of liberty, both civil and political.

The members of this body are called Magistrates or *Kings,* that is to say *Governors;* and the body as a whole bears the name of *Prince.* Thus those who claim that the act by which a people submits to its chiefs is not a contract are quite correct. It is absolutely only a commission, an employment in which simple officers of the Sovereign exercise in its name the power which it has entrusted to them, and which it can limit, modify, and take back when it pleases to do so, since the alienation of such a right is incompatible with the nature of the social body, and contrary to the goal of the association.

I then call *Government* or supreme administration the legitimate exercise of the executive power, and Prince or Magistrate, the man or the body charged with that administration.

In the Government are found the intermediary forces, whose relationship composes the relation of the whole to the whole or of the Sovereign to the State. One can represent this last relation by that of the extremes of a continuous proportion, of which the proportional mean is the Government. The Government receives from the Sovereign the orders it gives to the people, and so that the State may be in good equilibrium it is necessary, all things considered that there be equality between the product or power of the Government taken in itself and the product or power of the citizens, who are sovereigns on one side and subjects on the other.

Further, one could not alter any of these three terms without instantly destroying the proportion. If the Sovereign wishes to govern, or if the Magistrate wishes to provide laws, or if the subjects refuse to obey, disorder takes the place of regularity, force and will no longer act in concert, and the State falls into despotism or anarchy. Finally, as there is only one proportional mean in each relationship, only one good government is possible in a State. But, as a thousand events can change the relationships of a people, different Governments are able to be good not only for diverse peoples, but for the same people at different times.

To try to give an idea of the diverse relations which reign between the two extremes, I will take as an example the number of people, as an easy relationship to express.

Suppose the State is composed of ten thousand citizens. The Sovereign can only be considered collectively and as a body. But each private person in his quality as subject is considered as an individual. Thus the Sovereign is to the subject as ten thousand to one; this is to say that each member of the State is only one ten thousandth of the sovereign authority, even he is entirely subjected to it. Should the people be composed of one hundred thousand men, the condition of the subjects does not change, and each bears equally the entire dominion of the laws, while his vote, reduced to one hundred thousandth, has ten times less influence in their forming. The subject, then, always remains one, the ratio of the Sovereign to the subject always increases in proportion to the number of Citizens. Whence it follows that the larger the State grows, the more liberty diminishes.

When I say that the ratio increases, I understand that it is farther removed from equality. Thus the larger the ratio in the geometric sense, the lesser the relation in the everyday sense; in the first, the relation is considered according to the quantity measured by the quotient, and in the latter, considered according to identity, estimated by similarity.

Now the less the individual wills relate to the general will, that is to say customary conduct to the laws, the more repressive force has to be increased. The Government, then, in order to be good, should be relatively stronger as the people becomes more numerous.

On the other hand, the growth of the State giving the trustees of public authority more temptations and means to abuse their power, the more the Government has to have force to contain the people, the more force the Sovereign should have in turn in order to contain the Government. I speak here not of an absolute force, but of the relative force of the diverse parts of the State.

It follows from this double ratio that the continued proportion between the Sovereign, the Prince, and the people is hardly an arbitrary idea, but a necessary consequence of the nature of the political body. It follows further that one of the extremes, namely the people as subject, being fixed and represented by unity, whenever the double ratio increases or diminishes, the single ratio increases or diminishes similarly, and consequently the middle term is changed. This serves to show that there is no one constitution of Government unique and absolute, but that it is possible to have as many Governments of different natures as there are States of different sizes.

If, in reducing this system to ridicule, one would say that in order to find this proportional mean, and form the body of Government, it is only necessary, according to me, to take the square root of the number of the people, I would respond that I take that number here only as an example, that the relations of which I speak are measured not solely by the number of men, but in general by the amount of action, which results from combining a multitude of causes; that, moreover, if to express myself in fewer words I borrow geometric terms for a moment, I am aware of the fact that geometric precision has no place in moral quantities.

The Government is on a small scale what the body politic which contains it is on the large scale. It is a moral person endowed with certain faculties, active as the Sovereign, passive as the State, and one can break it down into other, similar relations, from which consequently arise a new proportion, and still another within this, similar to the order of tribunals, until one arrives at an indivisible middle term, that is to say one sole chief or supreme magistrate, who is able to be represented, in the middle of this progression, much as the unifying element between the series of fractions and that of whole numbers.

Without embarrassing ourselves with this multiplication of terms, let us be content to consider the Government as a new body within the State, distinct from the people and the Sovereign, and intermediate between the two.

The essential difference between these two bodies is that the State exists by itself, and the Government exists only through the Sovereign. Thus only the dominant will of the Prince is or ought to be the general will or the law; its force is only the public force concentrated in itself: as soon as it wishes to derive from itself some absolute and independent act, the bond tying the whole together begins to loosen. Finally, if it should happen that the Prince have a particular will more active than that of the Sovereign, and if, in order to obey this private will, he use some of the public force which is in its hands, so that there would be, so to speak, two Sovereigns, one of right and the other of fact: at that instant the social union would vanish and the body politic be dissolved.

However, for the body of the Government to have an existence, a real life that distinguishes it from the body of the State, for all its members to be able to act in concert and fulfill the purpose for which it has been instituted, it needs a particular *self*, a sensibility common to its members, a force, a will of its own that tends toward its own conservation. This particular existence presumes assemblies, councils, a power to deliberate, to resolve, rights, titles, privileges which belong exclusively to the Prince, and which render the condition of the magistrate more honorable, in proportion to which it is more arduous. The difficulties lie in the method of disposing, within the whole, this subordinate whole, in such a way that it may not weaken the general constitution while strengthening its own; that it always distinguish its particular force directed to its own conservation from the public force directed to the conservation of the State, and that, in a word, it always be ready to sacrifice the Government to the people and not the people to the Government.

Besides, although the artificial body of the Government is the product of another artificial body, and has in some respects only a borrowed and subordinate life, that does not prevent it from being able to act with more or less vigor or speed, to enjoy, so to speak, more or less robust health. Finally, without directly departing from the goal for which it was instituted, it can deviate more or less from it according to the manner in which it is constituted.

From all these differences arise the diverse relations that the Government ought to have with the body of the State, according to the accidental and particular relationships by which that same State is modified. For often the Government that is best in itself will become the most vicious, if its relations are not altered according to the defects of the body politic to which it belongs.

## II. Of the Principle Which Constitutes the Diverse Forms of Government

In order to expose the general cause of these differences, it is necessary to distinguish here the Prince and the Government, as I have already distinguished the State from the Sovereign.

The body of the magistracy can be composed of a greater or lesser number of members. We have said that the relation of the Sovereign to the subjects was greater as the number of people was greater, and by an evident analogy we can say the same of the Government with regard to the Magistrates.

Now the total force of the Government, being always that of the State, does not vary: from which it follows that the more of that force it uses on its own members, the less remains for it to act on the whole people.

Thus the more numerous are the Magistrates, the weaker the Government. As that maxim is fundamental, let us apply it to clarify it better.

We can distinguish in the person of the magistrate three essentially different wills. First, the individual's own will, which tends only to his private advantage; second, the common will of the magistrates, which relates itself uniquely to the advantage of the Prince, and which can be called the corporate will, being general in relation to the Government, and particular in relation to the State, of which the Government is a part; third, the will of the people, or the sovereign will, which is general as much in relation to the State considered as the whole, as in relation to the Government considered as part of the whole.

In a perfect system of legislation, the particular or individual will ought to be null, the corporate will proper to the Government very subordinate, and consequently the general or sovereign will always dominant and the sole rule of all the others.

According to the natural order, on the contrary, these different wills become more active as they become more concentrated. Thus the general will is always the weakest, the corporate will has the second rank, and the private will is first of all; so that in the Government each member is first himself, then Magistrate, and then citizen, a gradation directly opposed to what the social order requires.

Granting this, suppose that the whole Government is in the hands of one man. The particular will and the corporate will are then perfectly united, and consequently the latter is in the highest possible degree of intensity. Further, as it is the degree of will on which the use of force depends, and the absolute force of the Government does not vary, it follows that the most active of Governments is that of one man.

On the contrary, suppose we unite the Government with the legislative authority; let us make the Sovereign into the Prince and all of the Citizens into as many Magistrates. Then the corporate will, confounded with the general will, will be no more active than it and will leave to the particular will its full force. Thus the Government, always with the same absolute force, will have attained its *minimum* relative force or activity.

These relations are incontestable, and other considerations also serve to confirm them. One sees, for example, that each magistrate is more active in his group than each citizen is in his, and consequently the particular will has much more influence in the acts of the Government than in those of the Sovereign; for each magistrate is nearly always charged with some function of Government, while each citizen, taken separately, exercises no function of sovereignty. Besides, the more a State is extended, the more its real force is increased even though not by reason of its size: but if the State remains the same, the magistrates may well be multiplied without the Government acquiring any more real force, because that force is the force of the State, whose measure remains unchanged. Thus the relative force or activity of the Government diminishes, without its absolute or real force being able to increase.

It is also certain that public matters are expedited more slowly as more people are charged with them, that in giving too much importance to prudence one does not give enough to fortune, that one lets opportunity escape, and that owing to excessive deliberation the fruits of deliberation are often lost.

I have just proved that the Government is weakened as the magistrates are multiplied, and I have already proved that the larger the population, the more the repressive force should be increased. From this it follows that the ratio of the magistrates to the Government ought to be the inverse ratio of subjects to Sovereign; this is to say that the more the State grows, the more the Government should shrink; so that the number of chiefs diminishes as the number of people is increased.

But I speak here only of the relative force of Government, not of its rectitude: for, on the contrary, the more numerous the magistracy, the more the corporate will approaches the general will; whereas under a single magistrate, this same corporate will is, I have said, only a particular will. Thus one loses on one side what one gains on the other, and the art of the Legislator is to know how to fix the point where the force and the will of the Government are always combined in the reciprocal proportion most advantageous to the State.

### III. Division of Governments

We have seen in the preceding chapter why one distinguishes the diverse species or forms of Governments by the number of members who compose them; it remains to see here how this division is made.

The Sovereign can, in the first place, commit the charge of Government to all the people or the majority of the people, in such a way that more citizens are magistrates than simply individual citizens. One gives to this form of government the name of *Democracy*.

Or it can confine the Government to the hands of a small number, so that there are more simple Citizens than magistrates; this form bears the name of *Aristocracy*.

Finally, it can concentrate the whole Government in the hands of one sole magistrate from whom all the others derive their power. This third form is the most common and is called *Monarchy* or royal Government.

One should note that all these forms or at least the first two are more or less variable and may indeed have a considerable range; for Democracy can embrace all the people or be restricted to half. Aristocracy, in its turn, can confine itself to half the number down to the smallest, indeterminately. Royalty itself is susceptible to some division. Sparta always had two Kings by its constitution; and one has seen in the Roman Empire as many as eight Emperors at one time without being able to say that the Empire was divided. Thus there is a point where each form of Government blends with the next, and one sees that, under three sole types, Government can really be divided into as many diverse forms as the State has Citizens.

There is more: this same Government being in some respects able to subdivide itself into other parts, one part administered in one manner and the other part in another, from these three combined forms there can emerge a multitude of mixed forms, each of which is multipliable by all the simple forms.

In all times, there has been much dispute about the best form of Government, without considering that each of them is the best in certain cases, and the worst in others.

If in different States the number of supreme magistrates should be in an inverse ratio to that of the Citizens, it follows that generally Democratic Government suits small states, Aristocratic medium-sized, and Monarchical large ones. This rule is immediately derived from the principle, but how count the multitude of circumstances which can furnish exceptions?

## IV. Of Democracy

He who makes the law knows better than anyone how it ought to be executed and interpreted. It seems then that there could be no better constitution than the one in which the executive power is joined to the legislative. But it is just that which renders this Government insufficient in certain regards, because things that ought to be distinguished are not, and the prince and the Sovereign, being the same person, only form as it were a Government without a Government.

It is not good that he who makes the laws execute them, nor that the body of the people turn their attention away from general considerations in order to give it to particular objects. Nothing is more dangerous than the influence of private interests in public affairs, and the abuse of laws by the Government is a lesser evil than the corruption of the Legislator, the inevitable result of private considerations. Then, the State having been corrupted in its substance, all reform becomes impossible. A people who would never abuse the Government would not abuse independence either; a people who would always govern well would have no need of being governed.

To take the term in a rigorous sense, there has never existed a true Democracy, and it will never exist. It is contrary to the natural order that the greater number should govern and that the lesser number should be governed. One cannot imagine the people remaining constantly assembled in order to attend to public affairs, and one readily sees that it would not know how to establish commissions for this purpose without the form of the administration changing.

In fact, I think it possible to lay down as a principle that when the functions of the government are divided among several tribunals, sooner or later those with the fewest members acquire the greatest authority, if only because of the facility in expediting the public business which naturally brings this about.

Besides, how many things difficult to unite does this Government presume! First, a very small State where the people are easily assembled and where each citizen can easily know all the others; second, a great simplicity of moral customs, which prevents a multitude of public matters and thorny discussions; next, a great equality of rank and fortune, without which equality in rights and authority would not long subsist; finally, little or no luxury because luxury either is the result of wealth or renders it necessary; it corrupts both the rich and the poor, the one by possession, the other by covetousness; it sells the fatherland to indolence and vanity; it deprives the State of all its citizens in order to enslave some to others, and all to opinion.

That is why a celebrated author has named virtue as the principle of the Republic, for all these conditions could not subsist without virtue; but failing to make the necessary distinctions, this great genius often lacked accuracy and sometimes clarity, and did not see that the Sovereign authority being everywhere the same, the same principle ought to function in every well-constituted State, more or less, it is true, according to the form of Government.

Let us add that there is no Government so subject to civil wars and internal agitations as the Democratic or popular, because there is none which tends so strongly and continually to change its form, nor demands more vigilance and courage in order to be maintained in its own form. It is especially in this constitution that the Citizen ought to arm himself with force and steadfastness and to say each day of his life from his heart what a virtuous Palatine said in the Diet of Poland: "Malo periculosam libertatem quam quietum servitium." [I prefer liberty with danger to peace with slavery.]

If there were a people of Gods, it would govern

itself democratically. A Government so perfect is not suited to men.

### V. Of Aristocracy

We have here two very distinct moral persons, namely the Government and the Sovereign, and consequently two general wills, the one in relation to all the citizens, the other solely for the members of the administration. Thus, although the Government is able to regulate its internal policy as it pleases, it is never able to speak to the people in the name of the Sovereign, that is to say in the name of the people itself; this must never be forgotten.

The first societies governed themselves aristocratically. The family heads deliberated among themselves about public affairs. The young people deferred without distress to the authority of experience. Hence the names of *Priests, Ancients, Senate, Elders*. The savages of North America still govern themselves this way in our day, and are very well governed.

But, as the inequality due to institutions prevailed over natural inequality, wealth or power[10] was preferred to age, and Aristocracy became elective. Finally, the power transmitted with the father's goods to the children created patrician families, rendering the Government hereditary, and one witnessed Senators twenty years of age.

There are then three kinds of Aristocracy: natural, elective, hereditary. The first is suited only for simple peoples; the third is the worst of all governments. The second is the best: it is Aristocracy properly named.

Beyond the advantage of the distinction between the two powers, aristocracy has that of the choice of its members; for in popular Government all the Citizens are born magistrates; but this one limits them to a small number, and they only become so by election:[11] a means by which probity, insight, experience, and all the other reasons for public preference and esteem are so many new guarantees of being wisely governed.

Additionally, assemblies are more conveniently held, public affairs are better discussed, expedited with more order and diligence, the repute of the State is better sustained abroad by venerable Senators than by an unknown or scorned multitude.

In a word, it is the best and most natural order that the wisest should govern the multitude, when it is certain that they will govern it for its profit and not for their own; there being no need to uselessly multiply devices, nor to do with twenty thousand men what one hundred well-chosen men can do still better. But it need be remarked that the corporate interest begins here to direct the public force less under the rule of the general will, and that another inevitable propensity removes from the laws a part of the executive power.

With regard to particular proprieties, a State should not be so small, nor a people so simple and righteous, that the execution of the laws immediately ensues from the public will, as in a good Democracy. Nor again must a nation be so large that the chiefs, dispersed in order to govern, are able to determine the Sovereign each in his own department, and begin by making themselves independent in order to finally become the masters.

But if Aristocracy requires some fewer virtues than popular Government, it requires others which are properly its own; as moderation among the wealthy and contentment among the poor; for it seems that a rigorous equality would be out of place there; it was not even observed in Sparta.

Further, if this form permits a certain inequality of fortune, it is indeed so that generally the administration of public affairs should be entrusted to those who are better able to give their time to it, but not, as Aristotle claims, so that the wealthy always be preferred. On the contrary, it is important that an opposite choice should sometimes inform the people that there are more important reasons for preference in the merits of men than in their wealth.

### VI. Of Monarchy

Up to this point we have considered the Prince as a moral and collective person, united by the force of the laws, and entrusted with the executive power in the State. We now have to consider this power united in the hands of one natural person, a real man, who alone has the right to dispose of it according to the laws. He is what one calls a Monarch or a King.

Completely contrary to other administrations where a collective entity represents an individual, in this one an individual represents a collective entity; so that the moral unity which constitutes the Prince is at the same time a physical unity, in which all the faculties which the law combines in the other with such effort are found naturally combined.

Thus the will of the people, and the will of the Prince, and the public force of the State, and the private force of the Government, all respond to the same motive, all the mechanisms of the machine are in the same hand, everything works to the same end; there are no opposing movements that cancel each other, and one can imagine no kind of constitution in which a lesser effort produces more notable an action. Archimedes tranquilly seated on the shore and effortlessly pulling along a large Vessel represents to me a skillful monarch governing his vast States from his private study, and making everything move while appearing to be motionless.

But if there is no Government that has more vigor, there is none where the private will has greater sway and more easily dominates others; everything works to the same end, it is true, but this end is not the goal of public happiness, and the very force of the Administration ceaselessly operates to the detriment of the State.

Kings want to be absolute, and from afar one calls out to them that the best means for being so is to make themselves loved by their peoples. This maxim is very fine and even very true in some respects. Unfortunately, it will always be jeered at in the Courts. Power which comes from the love of the peoples is without doubt the greater; but it is precarious and conditional, and never will satisfy Princes. The best Kings wish to be able to be wicked if it pleases them, without ceasing to be the masters. A political sermonizer will tell them in vain that the power of the people being their own, their greatest interest is that the people should be flourishing, numerous, formidable. They know very well that is not true. Their personal interest is first that the People be weak, miserable, and never able to resist them. I admit that, supposing the subjects always perfectly submissive, the interest of the Prince should then be that the people are powerful, to the end that this power, being his own, would make him formidable to his neighbors; but this interest is only secondary and subordinate, and as the two suppositions are incompatible, it is natural that Princes always give preference to the maxim which is most immediately useful to them. It is this that Samuel strongly represented to the Hebrews; it is this that Machiavelli made evident. While feigning to give lessons to the Kings he has given great ones to the peoples. *The Prince* of Machiavelli is the book of republicans.[12]

We have found, by general relationships, that monarchy is suitable only to large States, and we find this again by examining it itself. The more numerous the public administration, the more the ratio of the Prince to the subjects diminishes and approaches equality, so that this relation is one of equality even as in Democracy. This same ratio increases as the Government shrinks, and it is at its *maximum* when the Government is in the hands of a single man. Then there is found too great a distance between the Prince and the People, and the State lacks cohesiveness. In order to create this, intermediary orders are needed. Princes, Grandees, and the nobility are necessary to fill them. Now none of this is suited to a small State, which is ruined by all these distinctions.

But if it is difficult that a large State be well governed, it is much more difficult that it be well governed by one man alone, and everyone knows what happens when the King appoints deputies.

An essential and inevitable defect which will always place monarchical government beneath the republican is that in the latter the public voice hardly ever raises to the highest positions any but enlightened and capable men, who fill them with honor; whereas those who attain rank in monarchies are most often merely petty bunglers, petty rascals, petty intriguers, whose petty talents, which enable them to attain high posts in the Courts, only serve to show the public their ineptitude as soon as they have attained these posts. The people is mistaken in its choice much less than the Prince, and a man of true merit is almost as rare in the ministry as a fool at the head of a republican government. Also, when by some lucky chance one of those men born to govern takes control of public business in a monarchy almost wrecked by this crowd of fine managers, one is totally surprised by the resources that he finds, and it is an epoch-making event in a country.

For a monarchical State to be well governed, it would be necessary that its size or extent be proportionate to the capabilities of he who governs. It is easier to conquer than to rule. With a sufficient lever, the world can be moved by a finger, but to sustain it requires the shoulders of Hercules. Should the State be the least bit large, the Prince is nearly always too small for it. When on the contrary it happens that the State is too small for its chief, which is very rare, it is still badly governed, because the chief, always following the grandeur of his views, forgets the people's interest, and makes them no less discontent by the abuse of his overabundant talents than does a chief limited by those which he lacks. It would require, so to speak, that a kingdom enlarge or contract itself in every reign according to the capacity of the Prince; rather, as the talents of a Senate are more stable, the State is able to have permanent boundaries and the administration would not go on any less well.

The most perceptible inconvenience of the Government of a single person is the lack of that continual succession which forms in the other two an uninterrupted bond. One King dies, another is needed; elections leave dangerous intervals, they are stormy, and unless the Citizens have a disinterestedness and integrity which this Government hardly manages to permit, intrigue and corruption intermingle throughout. It is difficult for one to whom the State has been sold not to sell it in turn, and recoup for himself from the helpless the money that the powerful have extorted from him. Sooner or later everything becomes venal under such an administration, and the peace which is enjoyed under kings is worse than the disorder of these interregnums.

What has been done to prevent these ills? Crowns have been made hereditary in certain families, and an order of succession has been established which prevents any dispute at the death of Kings. That is to say, substituting the inconvenience of regencies for that of elections, an apparent tranquillity has been preferred to a wise administration, and it is preferred to risk having infants, monsters, or imbeciles for chiefs than having to argue over the choice of good Kings; it has not been considered that in thus exposing oneself to the risk of this alternative, one sets nearly all the odds against himself. It was a very sensible reply that Dionysius the Younger gave to his father, who, reproaching him for a dishonorable action, said: "Have I given you such an example?" "Ah," replied the son, "your father was not king."

Everything conspires to deprive a man elevated to command others of justice and reason. Much trouble is taken, it is said, to teach young Princes the art of ruling: it does not seem that this education profits them. One would do better to begin by teaching them the art of obeying. The greatest kings celebrated by history were not brought up to rule; it is a science that one has never mastered less than after having studied it too much, and that one acquires better by obeying than by commanding. *Nam ultissimus idem ac brevissimus bonarum malarumque rerum delectus, cogitare quid aut nolueris sub alio principe, aut volueris.* [Because the best and shortest way to discover what is good and what is bad is to ask what you would have wished to happen or not to happen, if another than you had been king.][13]

One consequence of this lack of coherence is the instability of royal government, which, being regulated alternatively on one level and then on another, according to the character of the ruling Prince or of the people ruling for him, cannot long maintain a fixed aim or a consistent course of conduct: this variation, which always makes the state drift from maxim to maxim, from project to project, does not take place in other Governments, where the prince is always the same. Thus one sees that in general if there is more cunning in a Court, there is more wisdom in a Senate, and that Republics go to their goals by more constant and better-followed policies; whereas each revolution in the [royal] Ministry produces one in the State; the maxim common to all

Ministers, and nearly all Kings, being to take up the reverse of their predecessors in everything.

From this same incoherence is found the solution of a sophism very familiar to all defenders of royalty; not only is civil Government compared to the Government of the household and the prince to the father of the family, an error already refuted, but all the virtues of which he will have need are liberally ascribed to this magistrate, while always supposing that the Prince is what he ought to be; with the aid of this supposition royal Government is evidently preferable to any other, because it is incontestably the strongest, and in order to also be the best, it lacks only a corporate will more conformable to the general will.

But if, according to Plato[14] the king by nature is such a rare person, how many times will nature and fortune converge to crown him? And if royal education necessarily corrupts those who receive it, what should one hope from a succession of men trained to rule? It is surely deliberate self-deception to confound royal Government with that of a good King. To see what this Government is in itself, it is necessary to consider it under stupid or wicked Princes; for they will come to the Throne as such, or the Throne will make them such.

These difficulties have not escaped our Authors, but they are not embarrassed by them. The remedy is, they say, to obey without a murmur. God gives bad Kings in his anger, and one must endure them as chastisements from Heaven. This discourse is edifying, without doubt; but I do not know if it is not more appropriate to the pulpit than in a book about politics. What is to be said of a doctor who promises miracles and whose entire art is to exhort his sick charge to have patience? One knows well that it is necessary to suffer a bad Government when one has one: the question should be how to find a good one.

### VII. Of Mixed Governments

Properly speaking, there is no simple Government. A single Chief must have subordinate magistrates; a popular Government must have a Chief. Thus, in the partition of the executive power, there is always a gradation from the greater number to the less, with this difference, that sometimes the greater number depends on the lesser number, and sometimes the lesser number on the greater number.

Sometimes there is an equal division, either when the constituent parts are in mutual dependence, as in the Government of England; or when the authority of each part is independent but imperfect, as in Poland. This latter form is bad, because there is no unity in the government, and the State lacks cohesion.

Which is better, a simple Government or a mixed Government? This question is much debated among political thinkers, and it requires the same response I have already given concerning every form of Government.

Simple Government is best in itself, solely because it is simple. But when the executive power does not depend enough on the legislative, that is to say when there is a greater ratio between the Prince and the Sovereign than between the people and the Prince, this defect of proportion must be remedied by dividing the Government; for then all its parts have no less authority over the subjects, and their division renders all of them together less strong against the Sovereign.

The same disadvantage is also prevented by establishing intermediate magistrates who, leaving the Government in its entirety, only serve to balance the two powers and to maintain their respective rights. Then the Government is not mixed, it is tempered.

One can remedy the opposite disadvantage by similar means, and when the Government is too loose, Tribunals can be established to concentrate it: this is practiced in all Democracies. In the first case one divides the Government to weaken it, and in the second, in order to reinforce it; for the *maximum* force and weakness are found equally in simple Governments, whereas the mixed forms provide a medium force.

### IX. Of the Signs of a Good Government

When one then asks what is absolutely the best Government, one poses a question as insoluble as indeterminate; or, if you wish, it has as many correct solutions as there are possible combinations in the absolute and relative positions of peoples.

But if one asked by what sign one can know that a given people is well or badly governed, this would be another thing, and the question of fact could be resolved.

However, it is not resolved, because each wants to do so in his own way. The subjects extol public tranquillity, the Citizens the liberty of private individuals; the one prefers the security of possessions, the other that of persons; one holds that the best Government is the most severe, the other maintains that it is the mildest; one believes that crimes should be punished, and the other that they should be prevented; one finds it good to be feared by neighbors, the other prefers to be ignored by them; one is satisfied when money circulates, the other demands that the people have bread. Even though agreement should be had on these and similar points, would we have advanced? Moral quantities lacking any precise measure, if there were agreement on the sign, how could there be about its evaluation?

For my part, I am always astounded that such a simple sign is overlooked, or that one has the bad faith not to admit it. What is the end of political association? It is the preservation and the prosperity of its members. And what is the surest sign that they are preserved and prospering? It is their number and population. Do not go then to look elsewhere for this much-disputed sign. All other things being equal, the Government under which, without external aids, without naturalizations, without colonies, the Citizens become populous and multiply most is infallibly the best; that under which a people diminish and wither away is the worst. Calculators, it is now your concern; count, measure, compare.

### X. Of the Abuse of the Government, and of Its Tendency to Degenerate

As the private will incessantly acts against the general will, so the Government makes a continual effort against the Sovereignty. The more this effort increases, the more the constitution deteriorates, and as there is here no other corporate will which, by resisting that of the Prince, would balance it, sooner or later there must come a time when the Prince finally oppresses the Sovereign and breaks the social treaty. It is this inherent and inevitable vice that, from the birth of the body politic, tends without respite to destroy it, just as old age and death finally destroy the body of a man.

There are two general ways by which a Government degenerates: namely, when it shrinks, or when the State dissolves.

The government shrinks when it passes from a large to a small number, that is from Democracy to Aristocracy, and from Aristocracy to Royalty. That is its natural inclination. If it were to go backward from a small number to a large one, it could be said that it slackens, but this inverse progress is impossible.

In effect, the government only changes its form when its exhausted mainspring leaves it too weakened to be able to preserve itself. Now if it would slacken more as it extends itself, its force would become completely null, and it would subsist still less. It is then necessary to wind and adjust the spring as it unravels; otherwise the State which it sustains will fall into ruin.

The dissolution of the State can occur in two ways.

First, when the Prince no longer administers the State in accordance with laws and usurps the sovereign power. Then a remarkable change occurs; it is not the Government but the State that shrinks: I mean to say that the large State dissolves and another is formed within it, composed solely of the members of the Government, and it is for the rest of the People only its master and tyrant. So that at the instant that the Government usurps sovereignty, the social pact is broken; and all ordinary Citizens, returning by right to their natural liberty, are forced but no longer obligated to obey.

The same situation also occurs when the members of the Government separately usurp the power which they only ought to exercise as a body; this is no less a violation of the laws, and produces a still greater disorder. Then one has, so to say, as many Princes as Magistrates; and the State, no less divided than the Government, perishes or changes its form.

When the State dissolves, the abuse of Government, whatever it might be, takes the common name of *anarchy*. To distinguish, Democracy degenerates into *Ochlocracy*, Aristocracy into *Oligarchy*; I should add that Royalty degenerates into *Tyranny*, but this last word is equivocal and requires explanation.

In the ordinary sense, a Tyrant is a King who governs with violence and without regard to justice and to the laws. In the precise sense, a Tyrant is a private individual who arrogates royal authority to himself without having a right to it. It is thus that the Greeks understood this word Tyrant: they gave it indifferently to good and bad Princes whose authority was not legitimate. Hence *Tyrant* and *usurper* are two perfectly synonymous words.

To give different names to different things, I call the usurper of royal authority a *Tyrant*, and the usurper of the Sovereign power a *Despot*. The Tyrant is he who intrudes himself contrary to the laws in order to govern according to the law; the Despot is he who places himself above the laws themselves. Thus the Tyrant may not be a Despot but the Despot is always a Tyrant.

## XI. Of the Death of the Body Politic

Such is the natural and inevitable inclination of the best-constituted Governments. If Sparta and Rome have perished, what State can hope to last forever? If we wish to form a durable establishment, let us then not seek to make it eternal. In order to succeed, one should neither attempt the impossible, nor flatter oneself with giving to the work of men a solidity that human things do not admit of.

The body politic, just as the human body, begins to die at its moment of birth and carries within itself the causes of its destruction. But each can have a constitution more or less robust and suited to preserve it for a longer or shorter time. The constitution of man is the work of nature; that of the State is the work of art. It does not rest with men to prolong their lives; it is the responsibility of men to prolong that of the State as far as possible, by giving it the best constitution that it can have. The best-constituted will come to an end, but later than another, if no unforeseen accident brings about its premature destruction.

The principle of political life is in the Sovereign authority. The legislative power is the heart of the Sovereign authority. The legislative power is the heart of the State, the executive power is its brain, which gives movement to all the parts. The brain can fall into paralysis and the individual still lives. A man remains an imbecile and lives, but as soon as the heart has ceased its functions, the animal is dead.

It is not by the laws that the State subsists, but by the legislative power. The law of yesterday does not obligate today, but tacit consent is presumed from silence, and the sovereign is deemed to confirm continually the laws which it does not abrogate while being able to do so. Whatever it has once declared it wills it wills always, until the declaration is revoked.

Why then is so much respect paid to ancient laws? It is for that very reason. One must believe that it is only the excellence of ancient wills which has enabled them to be so long preserved: if the Sovereign had not constantly recognized them as salutary, it would have revoked them a thousand times. That is why, far from being weakened, the laws unceasingly acquire new strength in every well-constituted State; the prejudice in favor of antiquity renders them more venerable each day; in contrast, wherever the laws weaken as they grow older, it is proof that there is no longer legislative power, and that the State no longer lives.

## XV. Of Deputies or Representatives

As soon as public service ceases to be the principal concern of the Citizens, and they prefer to serve with their purses instead of their persons, the State is already nearly in ruin. Is it necessary to march to combat? they pay for troops and remain at home; is it necessary to go to the Council? they name deputies and remain at home. By dint of laziness and money, they finally have soldiers to enslave the fatherland and representatives to sell it.

It is the worry over commerce and the arts, the greedy pursuit of gain, indolence, and the love of comforts, which exchange personal services for money. One gives part of his profit in order to augment it at his convenience. Give money and soon enough you will have chains. This word *finance* is a slave's word; it is unknown in the City. In a truly free State the citizens do everything with their arms and nothing with money. Far from paying to exempt themselves from their duties, they will pay to perform them Themselves. I am certainly far from commonly held ideas; I believe that forced labor is less contrary to liberty than taxes.

The better the State is constituted, the more do public affairs outweigh private ones in the minds of the Citizens. There is even a much smaller number of private affairs, because as the sum of general well-being provides considerably more to that of each individual, less remains to be sought by individual exertions. In a well-conducted city each hastens to the assemblies; under a bad Government nobody wants to take a step to attend them, because no one takes an interest in what is done there, as it is foreseen that the general will does not prevail; and so in the end domestic concerns absorb everything. Good laws lead to better laws; bad laws bring on worse ones. As soon as someone says of the affairs of the State *Why is it important to me?* one should count the State as lost.

The cooling of the love of the fatherland, the activity of private interest, the immensity of States, conquests, the abuse of Government, have suggested the procedure of using Deputies or Representatives of the people in the assemblies of the Nation. This is what in certain countries one dares to call the Third Estate. Thus the particular interest of two orders is placed at first and second rank; the public interest is only at the third.

Sovereignty cannot be represented for the same reason that it cannot be alienated; it consists essentially in the general will, and the will cannot be represented: it is itself, or it is something other; there is no middle ground. The deputies of the people then are not and cannot be its representatives, they are only its commissioners; they can conclude nothing definitively. Every law that the People in person has not ratified is null; it is not a law. The English people thinks itself free, but is greatly mistaken; it is only free during the election of the members of Parliament: as soon as they are elected, it is enslaved, it is nothing. In the short moments of its liberty, the use made of it well merits its loss.

The idea of Representatives is modern: it comes to us from feudal Government, from that iniquitous and absurd Government in which the human species is degraded, and where the name of man is dishonored. In the ancient Republics and even in the Monarchies, the people never had representatives; they did not know this word. It is yet noteworthy that in Rome, where the Tribunes were so sacred, one could not even imagine that they might usurp the functions of the people, and in the midst of such a large multitude, they never tried to pass a single Plebiscite on their own authority. One can, however, imagine the embarrassment sometimes caused by the crowd by what occurred in the times of the Gracchi, when a part of the Citizens gave their vote from the rooftops.

Where right and liberty are everything, inconveniences are nothing. Among this wise people, everything was estimated in its just measure; it allowed the Lictors to do what the Tribunes would not have dared to do; it did not fear that the Lictors would wish to represent it.

To explain, however, how the Tribunes sometimes represented it, it suffices to understand how the Government represents the Sovereign. The Law being only the declaration of the general will, it is clear that, in the legislative power, the people cannot be represented; but it can and ought to be in the executive power, which is only force applied to the Law. This shows on close examination that very few Nations have laws. Be that as it may, it is certain that the Tribunes, not having any part of the executive power, were never able to represent the Roman people by right of their office, but only by usurping those of the Senate.

Among the Greeks, everything the people had to do it did by itself: it was unceasingly assembled in the public square. It lived in a mild climate; it was not avaricious; slaves did its work; its prime business was its liberty. Not having the same advantages, how conserve the same rights? Your more rigorous climate gives you more needs, six months of the year the public square is not usable, your indistinct tongues cannot be understood in the open air; you give more for your own gain than for your liberty, and you fear slavery far less than misery.

What! is liberty only maintained with the support of servitude? Perhaps. The two extremes meet. Everything not in nature has its inconveniences, and civil society more than all the rest. There are such unfortunate circumstances where one can save his liberty only at the expense of another, and where the citizen can only be perfectly free when the slave is completely enslaved. Such was the position of Sparta. As for you modern peoples, you have no slaves, but you are slaves; you pay for their liberty with your own. You boast of your preference in vain; I find in it more of cowardice than of humanity.

I do mean by all this neither that slaves are necessary nor that the right of slavery is legitimate, since I have proved the contrary: I only state the reasons why modern peoples who believe themselves free have Representatives, and why ancient peoples did not. Be that as it may, the instant that a People gives itself Representatives, it is no longer free; it is no more.

All things considered, I do not see that it should henceforth be possible for the Sovereign to preserve among us the exercise of its rights unless the City is very small. But if it is very small, will it be subjugated? No. I will show later[15] how the external power of a great People can be united with the convenient polity and good order of a small State.

## XVI. That the Institution of the Government Is Not a Contract

The Legislative power once well established, it is a matter of establishing the executive power as well; for this latter, only operating by particular acts, not being of the essence of the other, is naturally separate from it. If it were possible for the Sovereign, considered as such, to have executive power, right and fact would be so confounded that one would no longer know what is law and what is not, and the body politic thus denatured would soon fall prey to the violence against which it was instituted.

The Citizens being all equal by the social contract, all can prescribe what all ought to do, whereas no one has a right to make another do what he does not do himself. Now it is properly this right, that the Sovereign gives to the Prince in instituting the Government.

Several have held that the act of this establishment was a contract between the People and the chiefs it gives itself; a contract by which is stipulated between the two parties the conditions under which the latter obligates itself to command and the former to obey. One will agree, I am sure, that this is a strange manner of contracting. But let us see if this opinion is tenable.

First, the supreme authority can no more be modified than alienated; to limit it is to destroy it. It is absurd and contradictory that the Sovereign give itself a superior; to obligate oneself to obey a master is to go back to one's full liberty.

Further, it is evident that this contract of the people with such or such persons would be a particular act. Whence it follows that this contract would be neither a law nor an act of sovereignty, and consequently it would be illegitimate.

One sees also that the contracting parties would be under the law of nature alone and without any guarantee of their reciprocal engagements, which is repugnant in every way to the civil state. He who has force in hand being always the master of its use, we might as well give the name of contract to the act of a man who would say to another: "I give you all my goods, on the condition that you will return to me whatever pleases you."

There is only one contract in the State; it is that of association, and that alone excludes all others. No public Contract can be imagined which would not be a violation of the first.

## XVII. Of the Institution of the Government

Under what idea, then, must we conceive the act by which the Government is instituted? I will first note that this act is complex or composed of two others: namely, the establishment of the law and the execution of the law.

By the first the Sovereign resolves that there will be a body of Government established under such form; and it is clear that this act is a law.

By the second, the People name the chiefs who will be entrusted with the established Government. Now this naming, being a particular act, is not a second law, but only a consequence of the first and a function of Government.

The difficulty is to understand how one can have an act of Government before the Government exists, and how the People, who is only Sovereign or subject, can become Prince or Magistrate in certain circumstances.

It is here that is uncovered one of those astounding properties of the body politic, by which it reconciles seemingly contradictory operations. For here occurs a sudden conversion of Sovereignty into Democracy; so that, without any perceivable change, and solely by a new relation of all to all, the Citizens having become Magistrates pass from general acts to particular acts, and from the law to its execution.

This changing of relation is not a subtlety of speculation without example in practice: it occurs every day in the Parliament of England, where the lower Chamber on certain occasions turns itself into a Committee of the Whole, in order to better discuss its business, and thus becomes a simple commission, from the Sovereign Court that it was the preceding moment; as such it then reports to itself, as the House of Commons, what it decided in the Committee of the Whole, and deliberates again under one title about what it has already resolved under another.

Such is the advantage proper to Democratic Government, that it can be established in fact by a simple act of the general will. After this, that provisional Government remains in office, if such form is adopted, or establishes in the name of the Sovereign the Government prescribed by the law, and thus all is according to rule. It is not possible to institute the Government in any other legitimate manner without renouncing the principles heretofore established.

## XVIII. Means of Preventing Usurpation of the Government

From these clarifications it follows, in confirmation of Chapter XVI, that the act which institutes the Government is not a contract but a Law, that those entrusted with the executive power are not the masters of the people but its officers, whom it can establish and depose when it pleases, that there is no question for them of contracting but of obeying, and that in undertaking the functions which the State imposes on them, they are only fulfilling their duty as Citizens, without having any sort of right to dispute about the conditions.

When it happens that the People institutes a hereditary Government, be it monarchical in one family, or aristocratic in an order of Citizens, it is not an engagement that it undertakes: it is a provisional form which it gives to the administration, until it pleases it to put in order another.

It is true that these changes are always dangerous, and that the established Government must only be touched if it becomes incompatible with the public good; but this circumspection is a maxim of politics and not a rule of right, and the State is no more bound to leave civil authority to its chiefs than military authority to its Generals.

It is also true that in such a case one should observe with greatest care all the requisite formalities in order to distinguish a regular and legitimate act from a seditious tumult, and the will of a whole people from the clamors of a faction. Especially in this odious case one should only concede in full rigor of what is right what cannot be refused, and it is also from this obligation that the Prince draws a great advantage in preserving its power despite the people, without anyone being able to say that it has usurped the power. For in seeming to exercise only its rights, it could very easily extend them, and under the pretext of maintaining the public peace obstruct the assemblies destined to reestablish good order; so that it takes advantage of a silence it prevents from being broken, or of irregularities it has had committed, in order to suppose in its favor the consent of those whom fear silences and to punish those who dare to speak. It is thus that the Decemvirs, having first been elected for one year, then continued for another, tried to retain their power perpetually by not permitting the *comitia* to assemble; and it is by this easy means that all governments in the world, when once invested with public force, sooner or later usurp the Sovereign authority.

The periodical assemblies of which I have already spoken are suited to prevent or defer this evil, especially when they have no need of formal convocation; for then the Prince would not be able to prevent them without openly declaring himself violator of the laws and enemy of the State.

The opening of these assemblies, which have for their only object the maintenance of the social treaty, should always be done with two propositions that cannot be suppressed, and which pass separately by vote.

The first: "Whether it pleases the Sovereign to preserve the present form of Government."

The second: "Whether it please the People to leave the administration to those presently charged with it."

I presume here what I believe I have demonstrated: namely, that there is in the State no fundamental law which cannot be revoked, not even the social pact; for if all the Citizens assemble in order to break this pact by common accord, one cannot doubt that it would be very legitimately broken. Grotius even thinks that each person can renounce the State of which he is a member, and regain his natural liberty and his goods on leaving the country.[16] Now it would be absurd that all the Citizens together cannot do what each of them can do separately.

# BOOK FOUR

## *I. That the General Will Is Indestructible*

As long as several men together consider themselves as a single body, they have only one will which relates to the common preservation and to the general well-being. Then all the activities of the State

are vigorous and simple, its maxims are clear and luminous, it has no entangled and conflicting interests, the common good is clearly apparent everywhere and only good sense is needed to perceive it. Peace, union, equality, are enemies of political subtleties. Upright and simple men are hard to deceive because of their simplicity; snares and refined pretexts do not impose upon them; they are not even clever enough to be duped. When one sees among the happiest people in the world groups of peasants regulating the affairs of State under an oak tree and always conducting themselves wisely, can one keep from scorning the refinement of other nations, who render themselves illustrious and miserable with so much art and mystery?

A State thus governed has need of very few Laws, and to the extent that it becomes necessary to promulgate new ones, this necessity is universally seen. The first man who proposes them does no more than say what all have already felt, and there is no question of intrigues or eloquence in order to pass into law what each has already resolved to do, as soon as he is sure that the others will do likewise.

What deceives those who reason is that seeing only States badly constituted from their origin, they are impressed by the impossibility of maintaining a similar polity in such States. They laugh on imagining all the follies to which a cunning knave, an insinuating speaker, could persuade the people of Paris or London. They do not know that Cromwell would have been put to hard labor by the people of Berne, and the Duke of Beaufort imprisoned by the Genevans.

But when the social bond begins to loosen and the State to weaken; when private interests begin to make themselves felt and the small societies to influence the great one, the common interest degenerates and finds opponents: unanimity reigns no more in the votes, the general will is no longer the will of all, contradictions, debates arise, and the best advice does not pass without disputes.

Finally, when the State, near its ruin, subsists only as a vain and illusory form, when the social bond is broken in all hearts, when the vilest interest impudently takes on the sacred name of the public good, then the general will becomes mute; all, guided by secret motives, no longer express their opinions as Citizens, as if the State had never existed; and they falsely pass under the name of Laws iniquitous decrees which have only private interest as their goal.

Does it follow from this that the general will is annihilated or corrupted? No, it is always constant, unalterable, and pure; but it is subordinated to others that prevail over it. Each, detaching his own interest from the common interest, sees clearly that he cannot completely separate himself from it, but his part in the public evil does not seem anything to him compared with the exclusive good he intends to appropriate. This private good excepted, he wishes the general good for his own interest as strongly as anyone else. Even in selling his vote for money he does not extinguish the general will in himself; he eludes it. The fault he commits is to change the status of the question and to answer another than what he has been asked; so that instead of saying by his vote, "It is advantageous to the State," he says, "It is advantageous to a certain man or a certain party that such or such a motion passes." Thus the law of public order in the assemblies is not so much to maintain the general will as to make sure that it always is questioned and that it always responds.

I could here present many reflections on the simple right of voting in every act of sovereignty; a right which nothing is able to take away from the Citizens; and on the right to state opinions, to propose, divide, to discuss, that the Government has always great care to leave only to its members; but this important matter would require a separate treatise, and I cannot say everything in this one.

## II. Of Voting

From the preceding chapter one sees that the manner in which general affairs are managed gives a sufficiently accurate indication of the actual state of the habitual conduct, and the health of the body politic. The more harmony reigns in the assemblies, that is to say the closer opinions approach unanimity, the more dominant is the general will; but long debates,

dissensions, tumult, indicate the ascendancy of private interests and the decline of the State.

This seems less evident when two or more orders enter into its constitution, as in Rome the Patricians and the Plebeians, whose quarrels often troubled the *comitia*, even in the finest times of the republic; but this exception is more apparent than real, for then, by the vice inherent in the body politic, there are, so to speak, two States in one: what is not true of the two together is true of each separately. And in fact, even in the stormiest times the plebiscites of the people, when the Senate did not interfere with them, always passed tranquilly and by a large majority of votes: the Citizens having only one interest, the people only one will.

At the other extremity of the circle unanimity returns. It is when the citizens, having fallen into slavery, no longer have either liberty or will. Then fright and flattery change votes into acclamations; one no longer deliberates, but adores or curses. Such was the vile manner of expressing opinions in the Senate under the Emperors. Sometimes it was done with ridiculous precautions. Tacitus observed that under Otho, the Senators, in overwhelming Vitellius with execrations, arranged to make a frightening noise at the same time so that if, by chance, he became the master, he would not know what each of them had said.

From these diverse considerations arise the maxims by which one ought to regulate the manner of counting the votes and comparing opinions, according to whether the general will is more or less easy to know, and the State more or less declining.

There is only one single law which by its nature requires unanimous consent. It is the social pact: for civil association is the most voluntary act in the world; every man being born free and master of himself, no one can, under any pretext whatever, subjugate him without his assent. To decide that the son of a slave is born a slave is to decide that he is not born a man.

If, then, at the time of the social pact, there are found some opponents of it, their opposition does not invalidate the contract, it only prevents them from being included in it: they are foreigners among citizens. When the State is instituted, consent is in residence; to live in a territory is to submit oneself to sovereignty.[17]

Outside of this basic contract, the voice of the greater number always obliges all the others; it is a consequence of the contract itself. But one asks how a man can be free and forced to conform to wills that are not his own. How are opponents free and yet subject to laws to which they have not consented?

I respond that the question is poorly posed. The citizen consents to all the laws, even those which are passed despite him, and even to those that punish him when he dares to violate any of them. The constant will of all the members of the State is the general will: by it they are citizens and free.[18] When a law is proposed in the assembly of the People, what is asked of them is not precisely whether they approve the proposition or reject it, but whether or not it conforms to the general will which is their own: each in giving his vote states his opinion on that question, and from the counting of the votes is taken the declaration of the general will. When the opinion contrary to mine prevails, that only proves that I was mistaken, and that what I had considered to be the general will was not. If my private opinion had prevailed, I would have done something other than I had wanted to do, and then I would not have been free.

This supposes, it is true, that all the characteristics of the general will are still in the majority; when they cease to be there, whichever side one takes, there is no longer any liberty.

In showing earlier how private wills have been substituted for the general will in public deliberations, I have sufficiently indicated the practicable means for preventing this abuse; I will speak of it again later on. With regard to the proportional number of the votes required to declare this will, I have also stated the principles by which one can determine it. The difference of a single vote breaks a tie, only one opposed breaks unanimity; but between unanimity and a tie vote there are many unequal divisions, at each of which one can fix this number according to the condition and needs of the body politic.

Two general maxims can serve to regulate these ratios: the one, that the more important and serious the deliberations, the closer the prevailing opinion should approach unanimity; the other, that the more the matter requires speed of decision, the more one can reduce the prescribed difference in the division of opinions: in deliberations that must be resolved immediately, a majority by one vote should suffice. The first of these maxims seems more suitable to laws, and the second to business matters. Be that as it may, it is by their combination that the best ratios are established by which a majority can decide.

## VI. Of the Dictatorship

The inflexibility of laws, which prevents them from adapting to events, can in certain cases render them pernicious and cause the ruin of the State in a crisis. The order and slowness of formalities demand a space of time which circumstances sometimes refuse. A thousand cases can present themselves for which the legislator has not provided, and it is a very necessary foresight to sense that everything cannot be foreseen.

It is then not necessary to want to strengthen political institutions so much that the power to suspend their effect is removed. Even Sparta let her laws lie dormant.

But only the greatest dangers can outweigh the danger of altering the public order, and the sacred power of the laws should never be arrested unless it is a matter of the safety of the fatherland. In these rare and obvious cases, public security is provided for by a special act which entrusts its responsibility to the most worthy. This commission can be conferred in two ways, according to the kind of danger.

If, in order to remedy it, it suffices to augment the activity of the government, one may concentrate this activity in one or two of its members. Thus it is not the authority of the laws that is changed but only the form of their administration. But if the danger is such that the formal process of the law is an obstacle to guaranteeing them, then a supreme chief is named who silences all the laws and suspends for a moment the Sovereign authority; in such case, the general is not doubted, and it is evident that the first intention of the people is that the State should not perish. In this way the suspension of the legislative authority does not abolish it: the magistrate who silences it cannot make it speak; he dominates it without power to represent it; he can do everything except make laws. . . .

## VIII. Of Civil Religion

. . . Among us, the kings of England have established themselves chiefs of the Church, as have the Czars: but, by this title, they have rendered themselves less its masters than its Ministers; they have acquired less the right to change it than the power to maintain it; they are not its legislators, they are only its Princes. Wherever the clergy forms a body,[19] it is master and legislator in its fatherland. There are then two powers, two Sovereigns, in England and in Russia, as everywhere else.

Of all the Christian authors, the philosopher Hobbes is the only one who has clearly seen the evil and the remedy, who has dared to propose uniting the two heads of the eagle, and bring everything back to political unity, without which no State or Government will ever be well constituted. But he should have seen that the dominating spirit of Christianity was incompatible with his system, and that the interest of the priest would always be stronger than that of the State. It is not so much what is horrible and false in his political theory as what it has that is just and true that has rendered it odious.

I believe that in developing the historical facts under this viewpoint, one would easily refute the opposed sentiments of Bayle and Warburton, one of whom claims that no Religion is useful to the body politic, and the other that to the contrary, Christianity is its strongest support. To the first, one could prove that no State was ever founded without Religion serving as its base, and to the second, that Christian law is more injurious than useful to a firm constitution of the State. In order to make myself understood, it is only needed to give a little more precision to the overly vague ideas of Religion relative to my subject.

Religion considered by its relation to the society, which is either general or particular, can also be divided into two kinds: namely, the Religion of man and that of the Citizen. The first, without temples, without altars, without rites, limited to the purely internal worship of the Supreme God and to the eternal duties of morality, is the pure and simple Religion of the Gospel, the true Theism, and what one can call the divine natural right. The other, inscribed in a single country, gives it its Gods, its proper and tutelary patrons; its has its dogmas, its rites, it external worship prescribed by the laws: outside of the single Nation that follows it, all is for it infidel, foreign, barbarous; it extends the duties and rights of man only as far as its altars. Such were all the Religions of the early peoples, to which one can give the name of divine, civil, or positive right.

There is a third, more bizarre kind of Religion which, giving to men two legislations, two chiefs, two fatherlands, subjects them to contradictory duties and prevents them from being able to be at one time devout and Citizens. Such is the religion of the Lamas, such is that of the Japanese, such is Roman Christianity. One can call this the religion of the Priest. There results from it a kind of mixed unsociable right which has no name.

Considered politically, these three kinds of religions all have their defects. The third is so evidently bad that it is a waste of time to amuse oneself demonstrating it. Whatever destroys social unity is worthless. All institutions which place man in contradiction with himself are worthless.

The second is good insofar as it unites divine worship with the love of the laws, and by making the fatherland the object of the adoration of the Citizens it teaches them that to serve the State is to serve the tutelary God. It is one kind of theocracy, in which there should be no other pontiff but the Prince, nor other priests than the magistrates. Then to die for one's country is to go to martyrdom, to violate the laws is to be impious, and to subject a guilty man to public execration is to deliver him to the anger of the gods: *sacer esto.*

But it is bad in that being founded on error and on falsehood it deceives men, renders them credulous, superstitious, and drowns the true worship of the Divinity in a vain ceremonial. It is again bad when, becoming exclusive and tyrannical, it renders a people sanguinary and intolerant, so that it breathes only murder and massacre, and believes it is performing a holy action by killing whoever does not admit its gods. This places such a people in a natural state of war with all others, very detrimental to its own security.

There remains then the Religion of man or Christianity, not that of today, but that of the Gospel, which is altogether different. By this holy, sublime, and true Religion, men, children of the same God, all recognize themselves as brothers, and the society which unites them is not even dissolved at death.

But this Religion, having no particular relation with the body politic, leaves to the laws only the force that they derive from themselves without adding any other to them, and thus one of the great bonds of a particular society remains ineffective. What is more, far from attaching the hearts of the Citizens to the State, it detaches them as from all things of the earth; I know nothing more contrary to the social spirit.

We are told that a people of true Christians would form the most perfect society that one can imagine. I see only one great difficulty in this supposition; it is that a society of true Christians would no longer be a society of men.

I even say that this supposed society with all its perfection would be neither the strongest nor the most durable. By dint of being perfect, it would lack cohesion; its destructive vice would be in its very perfection.

Each would fulfill his duty; the people would be subject to the laws, the chiefs would be just and moderate, the magistrates honest and incorruptible; the soldiers would despise death; there would be neither vanity nor luxury: all this is very good, but let us look further.

Christianity is an entirely spiritual religion, only occupied by things of Heaven; the fatherland of the Christian is not of this world. He does his duty, it is true, but he does it with a profound indifference to the good or bad outcome of his cares. Provided he has nothing for which to reproach himself, it is of little import to him whether all fares well or poorly

here below. If the State is flourishing, he hardly dares to enjoy the public felicity, for he fears to take selfish pride in the glory of his country; if the State declines, he blesses the hand of God that weighs down heavily on his people.

In order that the society be peaceable and harmony be maintained, all Citizens without exception would have to be equally good Christians. But if unfortunately there is found in it a single ambitious man, a single hypocrite, a Catiline, for example, a Cromwell, such a man very certainly would have an advantage over his pious compatriots. The Christian charity does not easily permit one to think ill of one's neighbor. As soon as he will have found by some ruse the art of imposing on them and securing to himself a part of the public authority, behold a man invested with dignity. God wills that he should be respected; soon he is a power; God wills that one obeys him; does the depositary of this power abuse it? He is the rod with which God punishes his children. It would violate conscience to chase out the usurper: it would be necessary to trouble the public peace, to use violence, to shed blood; all this is not accordant with the meekness of the Christian; and after all, does it matter whether one is free or serf in this vale of misery? The essential thing is to go to paradise, and resignation is only one more means toward that.

Does some foreign war occur? The Citizens march to combat without distress; none among them thinks of flight; they do their duty, but without passion for victory; they know better how to die than how to conquer. Whether they are victors or vanquished, does it matter? Doesn't Providence know better than they what they need? Imagine what advantage a proud, impetuous, passionate enemy can wrest from their stoicism. Place them against those courageous people consumed with an ardent love of glory and the fatherland; suppose your Christian Republic facing Sparta or Rome: the pious Christians will be beaten, crushed, destroyed, before they have had time to know where they are, or they will owe their safety only to the scorn their enemies have for them. To my mind it was a fine oath that the soldiers of Fabius took; they did not swear to die or conquer, they swore to return as conquerors, and kept their oath. Never would Christians have done such a thing; they would have believed they were tempting God.

But I am mistaken in speaking of a Christian Republic; each of these two words excludes the other. Christianity only preaches servitude and dependence. Its spirit is too favorable to tyranny for it not to always profit by it. True Christians are made to be slaves; they know it and are hardly moved by it; this short life has too little value in their eyes.

We are told Christian troops are excellent. I deny it. Let me be shown such. As for me, I do not know of any Christian Troops. I am told of the Crusades. Without disputing the valor of the Crusaders, I will note that, far from being Christians, they were soldiers of the priest, they were Citizens of the Church: they battled for its Spiritual country, which the Church had rendered temporal, one knows not how. Properly regarded, this returns us to paganism: as the Gospel does not establish a national Religion, any holy war is impossible among Christians.

Under the pagan emperors Christian soldiers were brave; all the Christian authors affirm this, and I believe it: there was a competition for honor against the pagan Troops. As soon as the Emperors became Christians this competition no longer subsisted; and when the cross had driven out the eagle, all Roman valor disappeared.

But setting aside political considerations, let us return to right, and settle the principles on this important point. The right which the social pact gives to the Sovereign over the subjects does not pass, as I have said, the limits of public utility.[20] The subjects then owe no account of their opinions to the Sovereign except as these opinions are important to the community. Now it matters greatly to the State that each Citizen have a Religion which makes him love his duties; but the dogmas of this Religion concern neither the State nor its members except as these dogmas relate to morality and to the duties that anyone who professes it is bound to fulfill toward others. Each may have in addition whatever opinions please him, without it being the Sovereign's business to know what they are. For as the Sovereign has no

competence in the other world, whatever may be the destiny of the subjects in the life to come is not its affair, provided that they are good citizens in this life.

There is then a purely civil profession of faith, the articles of which it is the business of the Sovereign to settle, not precisely as dogmas of religion, but as sentiments of sociability, without which it is impossible to be a good Citizen or faithful subject.[21] Without being able to obligate anyone to believe them, it can banish from the State anyone who does not believe them; it can banish him, not as impious, but as unsociable, as incapable of sincerely loving the laws, and justice, and of sacrificing at need his life to his duty. If anyone, after publicly acknowledging these dogmas, behaves as though he does not believe them, he should be punished by death; he has committed the greatest of crimes, he has lied before the laws.

The dogmas of this civil religion ought to be simple, few in number, stated with precision, without explanations or commentaries. The existence of the Deity, powerful, intelligent, beneficent, prescient, and provident; the life to come, the happiness of the just, the punishment of the wicked, the sanctity of the social Contract and the Laws: these are the positive dogmas. As for the negative dogmas, I limit them to only one, intolerance: it belongs in the creeds we have excluded.

Those who distinguish civil intolerance from theological intolerance are, in my opinion, mistaken. These two kinds of intolerance are inseparable. It is impossible to live in peace with people whom one believes to be damned; to love them would be to hate God who punishes them: it is absolutely necessary that they be reclaimed or tormented. Wherever theological intolerance is admitted, it is impossible that it not have some civil effect,[22] and as soon as it has any, the Sovereign is no longer Sovereign, even in temporal matters; from then on the Priests are the true masters; the Kings are only their officers.

Now that there is no longer and can never be an exclusive national Religion, one should tolerate all those which tolerate the others, so far as their dogmas have nothing contrary to the duties of the Citizen. But whoever dares to say: *outside of the Church there is no salvation,* ought to be chased from the State, unless the State be the Church, and the Prince be the Pontiff. Such a dogma is good only in a Theocratic Government; in any other it is pernicious. The reason for which Henry IV embraced the Roman Religion ought to make any honest man, and especially any Prince who would know how to reason, leave it.

## IX. Conclusion

After having set forth the true principles of political right and attempted to found the State on its base, it would remain to support it by its external relations; this would comprise the law of the peoples, commerce, the right of war and conquest, the public right, alliances, negotiations, treaties, etc. But all that forms a new object which is too vast for my limited scope; I should always have confined myself to what is nearer to me.

## Notes

1. Under bad governments, this equality is only apparent and illusory; it serves only to keep the poor man in his misery and the rich in his usurpations. In fact, laws are always useful to those who possess and injurious to those who have nothing; whence it follows that the social state is advantageous to men only so far as they all have something, and none of them has too much.

2. For a will to be general, it is not always necessary that it be unanimous, but it is necessary for all the voices to be counted; any formal exclusion destroys the generality.

3. "Every interest," says the Marquis d'Argenson, "has different principles. The accord of two private interests is formed by opposition to that of a third." He might have added that the accord of all interests is formed by opposition of it to each. Unless there were different interests, the common interest would scarcely be felt and would never meet with any obstacles; everything would go of itself, and politics would cease to be an art.

4. "It is true," says Machiavelli, "that some divisions harm the republic while others are beneficial to it; those that are injurious are accompanied by cabals and factions; those that assist it are maintained without cabals and factions. No founder of a republic can provide against enmi-

ties within it, and so he therefore ought to provide at least that there shall be cabals" (*History of Florence,* Book VII).

5. Attentive readers, I beg you, do not hasten to accuse me here of contradiction. I have not been able to avoid it in these terms, owing to the poverty of the language; but wait.

6. I do not understand by this word only an Aristocracy or a Democracy, but in general any government directed by the general will, which is the law. In order to be legitimate, the Government must not confound itself with the Sovereign, but should be its minister; then monarchy itself is a republic. This will be clarified in the next book.

7. A people only become famous when its legislation begins to decline. One does not know for how many centuries the institutions of Lycurgus conferred happiness on the Spartans before they came to be known by the rest of Greece.

8. "And truly," says Machiavelli, "there never was any lawgiver among any people who did not have recourse to God, for otherwise his laws would not have been accepted, for many benefits are known to a prudent man who does not have reasons evident enough to enable him to persuade others" (*Discourses on Titus Livy,* I, 11).

9. Do you wish, then, to give stability to the State? Bring the two extremes together as much as possible: allow neither excess opulence nor beggars. These two conditions, naturally inseparable, are equally fatal to the common good; from one springs the fomenters of tyranny, from the other the tyrants: it is always between them that the trading of public liberty transpires: one buys it, the other sells it.

10. It is clear that the word *optimates,* among the ancients, meant not the best, but the most powerful.

11. It is very important to regulate by laws the form of the election of the magistrates, because leaving it to the will of the prince, one could not escape falling into hereditary Aristocracy, as happened in the Republics of *Venice* and *Berne.* Also, the first has long been a dissolved State; but the second maintains itself by the extreme wisdom of its Senate: it is a very honorable and very dangerous exception.

12. Machiavelli was an honest man and a good citizen; but, attached to the house of Medici, he was forced, during the oppression of his fatherland, to disguise his love for liberty. The mere choice of his execrable hero sufficiently manifests his secret intention; and the opposition of the maxims of his book *The Prince* and those of his

*Discourses on Titus Livy* and his *History of Florence* shows that this profound political thinker has had until now only superficial or corrupt readers. The court of Rome has sternly prohibited his book; I certainly believe it: it is that court which he most clearly depicts.

13. Tacitus, *Histories* I, 16.

14. The *Statesman*.

15. It is this which I intended to do in a sequel to this work, when in considering foreign relations I would come to confederations. This is a wholly new matter and one where the principles have still to be established.

16. It being well understood that one does not leave in order to evade his duty and avoid serving the fatherland at the moment it has need of us. Flight then would be criminal and punishable; it would no longer be withdrawal, but desertion.

17. This should always be understood for a free State; for otherwise family, goods, need for asylum, necessity, or violence can detain an inhabitant in the country despite himself; and then his residence alone no longer supposes his consent to the contract or to the violations of the contract.

18. In Genoa, one reads in front of the prisons and on the chains of those condemned to the galleys the word *Libertas*. This application of the motto is fine and just. It is only the malefactors in all states who prevent the Citizen from being free. In a country where all such people would be in the Galleys, one would enjoy the most perfect liberty.

19. It is well to note that it is not so much formal assemblies, as those in France, which tie the clergy into a body, but the communion of the Churches. Communion and excommunication are the social pact of the clergy, a pact by which they will always be the master of peoples and of kings. All the priests who communicate together are fellow citizens, be they from the two ends of the world. This invention is a masterpiece of politics. There is nothing similar among pagan priests, thus they have never constituted a body of clergy.

20. "In the republic," says M. d'A., "each is perfectly free in that which does not injure others." That is the invariable limit; it cannot be more exactly stated. I have not been able to refuse myself the pleasure of sometimes citing this manuscript, although it is not known to the public, in order to render honor to the memory of an illustrious and respectable man, who had preserved even in the ministry the heart of a true citizen, and upright and sound views on the government of his country.

21. Caesar, pleading for Catiline, tried to establish the dogma of the mortality of the soul; Cato and Cicero, in order to refute him, did not amuse themselves philosophizing: they contented themselves with showing that Caesar spoke as a bad citizen and advanced a doctrine pernicious to the state. Indeed, it was that which the Roman Senate had to judge, and not a question of theology.

22. Marriage, for example, being a civil contract has civil effects, without which it is impossible that society subsist. Let us suppose then that a clergy ascribe to itself alone the right of performing this act, a right it must necessarily usurp in every intolerant religion; then is it not clear that in asserting the authority of the Church it renders empty that of the prince, who will have no other subjects than those the clergy is willing to give him? Master of which people can or cannot marry, according to whether they hold or do not hold such or such doctrine, according to whether they admit or reject such or such a formula, according to whether they are more or less devoted to it, is it not clear that by behaving prudently and keeping firm, the Church alone will dispose of inheritances, offices, citizens, and the State itself, which cannot subsist when composed only of bastards? But, it will be said, men will appeal against such abuses; they will adjourn, decree, seize temporal holdings. What a pity! The clergy, however little it may have, I do not say of courage but of good sense, will let this be done and go its way; it will quietly permit appealing, adjourning, decreeing, seizing, and will end by being the master. It is not, it seems to me, a great sacrifice to abandon a part when one is sure of taking possession of the whole.

# DAVID HUME

## INTRODUCTION

## DONALD W. LIVINGSTON

David Hume (1711–1776) was born in the border country of Scotland into an old and moderately wealthy family of gentry lawyers. He spent two to three years at the University of Edinburgh and left without a degree. By his late teens he had framed the idea of a science of human nature. A decade of intense research and writing produced his masterpiece, *A Treatise of Human Nature* (1739–1740). Though it was reviewed in journals as far away as Germany, the *Treatise* did not sell well, and Hume immediately began to expand its ideas and to recast them into the more engaging form of essays. A four-volume set was published in 1753 under the title *Essays and Treatises on Several Subjects.* These were immensely popular and established Hume's reputation as a writer.

Having failed to win a teaching post at Edinburgh or Glasgow University, Hume secured, in 1752, the position of keeper of the Advocates Library in Edinburgh. With this extensive library at his disposal, he began writing *The History of England,* a project he had conceived while working on the *Treatise.* The first and most important volume (1754) covered the reigns of James I and Charles I and the English Civil War. By 1762 Hume had traced the history of England back to the invasion of Julius Caesar.

The *History* became a classic in Hume's lifetime. It passed through more than 160 posthumous editions and was continually in print to the end of the nineteenth century. The young Winston Churchill learned English history from an abridged edition for students. Hume is unique in the history of philosophy in being both a great historian and a great philosopher. He is usually ranked (along with Robertson, Voltaire, and Gibbon) as one of the four most important eighteenth-century historians. Nor is this an accident, for Hume is one of the first of those modern philosophers—along with Vico, Hegel, Marx, and Collingwood—whose conception of philosophy requires a rapprochement with history. Consequently, the *History* should be viewed as an integral part of Hume's political philosophy.

To understand why such a rapprochement is necessary, something must be said about Hume's conception of philosophy. The ancient Greeks viewed philosophy as the rational pursuit of human happiness, or wisdom. Each sect had a theory of the source of human misery: the Epicureans, pain; the Platonists, ignorance; the Stoics, a lawless will; the Cynics, the tyranny of convention; the Aristoteleans, immoderation. The Pyrrhonian Skeptics, however, taught that *philosophical reason* itself is the source of misery. They resolved to find happiness in the prereflective order of custom, inclination, and tradition out of which philosophical reflection had emerged and over which it claimed dominion. Hume identified with much of this skeptical tradition, but he rejected the Pyrrhonian attempt to do away with philoso-

phy on the grounds that man is a reasoning creature as well as a natural one and that the
attempt to suppress the inclination to know reality would lead to frustration and misery, not
happiness. Instead of eliminating philosophy, Hume forged a distinction between what he
calls true and false philosophy. The latter is a source of misery, the former is not.

Hume argued that the hubristic attempt of philosophy to emancipate itself entirely from the
prereflective domain of custom and tradition, if consistently carried out, leads to a paralyzing
skepticism. Philosophers are typically *not* led to skepticism, but arrive there only because they
unwittingly and inconsistently smuggle in some favorite prejudice from the prereflective
domain and pass it off as the work of autonomous reason untainted by prejudice. Such philosophy is false in that it is self-deceived. It both denies the authority of the prereflective *and* presupposes it. If philosophy is to be coherent, it must reform itself. Whereas false philosophy presumes the prereflective order as a whole to lack authority, Hume's reform presumes the
prereflective order to have authority. Criticism within the order is possible, but only by presupposing the authority of the whole. And so Hume says of the judgements of true philosophy that
they are "nothing but reflections on common life, methodized and corrected." The standards of
criticism are themselves immanent in the inherited practices of common life. The task of true
philosophy is to make these explicit and to render them as coherent as possible. Because the
standards of critical thought are immanent in common life and are viewed as *inherited,* the true
philosopher, as such, must pass through an act of historical understanding.

In stark opposition to this conception of true philosophy were the many forms of philosophical rationalism that dominated in Hume's time. His entire philosophical project may be
viewed as an attack on philosophical rationalism in all its forms: epistemological, moral,
political, and religious. The selections from *A Treatise of Human Nature* printed here present the basic structure of Hume's critique of rationalism in morals and politics. Hume begins
by arguing that reason properly so-called is not the source of conduct. The source of conduct is a sentiment of desire or aversion. Reason reveals truth regarding either relations of
ideas (as in mathematics and logic) or matters of empirical fact. Beliefs about these truths
may give rise to a passion or may destroy one, but the passion itself is not a judgement of
truth. Hume concludes that reason is not the master and guide of passion but its servant. As
the servant, reason has a critical task to perform in "methodizing and correcting" the judgments that make up the moral life, but it is not the source of that life. Hume's critique of
moral rationalism applies not only to his contemporaries Wollastan and Clarke but also to
later philosophers such as Kant.

Turning to political rationalism, Hume rejects the doctrine that justice is a natural virtue.
Justice is an "artificial virtue" internal to a historically developed convention. But one must
be careful. By a "convention" Hume does not mean something that is the result of conscious
planning and choice. A good example of a Humean convention would be the English language. English is an artifice in that it is not a natural feature of all human societies. Yet it is
not the result of any conscious design. It evolved spontaneously over many generations to
satisfy human needs. English is structured by a systematic and intricate set of rules, but again
these rules are not the result of rational planning. We may abstract the rules and cultivate
them, but they are only abstractions. The rules cannot be said to preexist the successful practice of the convention. Indeed, it is only by successfully engaging in the practice, without
knowing what the rules are, that we can later know that we have abstracted and codified the
correct rules. The error of rationalism is to think that human thought and conduct are mat-

ters of applying rules that reason has self-consciously determined to be the correct ones, independent of custom and tradition.

The rich display of human culture is for Hume an order of historically evolved conventions: science, language, money, art, war, peace, morals, politics, religion, and so on. Just as reason is not the guide of correct conduct, but an abstraction from correct conduct, so reason is not the source of civilization; rather it is civilization that is the source of reason. The convention of justice developed to resolve conflicts over possessions due to a universal scarcity of goods and to a universal limit in human benevolence. What we call property is determined by rules internal to a particular convention of justice; and although Hume shows that these will differ as natural languages do, he argues that there is a set of rules that all conventions of justice share: the stability of possessions, their transfer by consent, and the enforcement of promises.

The convention of government spontaneously evolved to enforce the rules of justice. For Hume this means that the convention of property is inseparable from the convention of government. This inverts the teaching of the most famous form of political rationalism, namely the contract theory, especially as put forth by John Locke. Hume called it "our fashionable system of politics," and it has many adherents today. Locke held that there is an inalienable natural right to property antecedent to the formation of government. Governments are instituted by a social contract to protect this right, and are legitimated only by consent of the governed. Hume admired the sentiment expressed in the theory and acknowledged that consent is a noble ideal of government. He denied, however, that it is the source of political obligation. Hume found it odd that human beings, throughout history, have displayed no knowledge of a natural right to property supposedly self-evidently available to all rational beings. And he further wondered how the authority of government could be grounded in a contract when the idea of a contract presupposes the authority of government to enforce it. Here we have a good example of what Hume calls false philosophy. The thinker becomes obsessed with an aspect of experience—in this case contractual relations—that is then transmuted by the alchemy of a corrupt philosophical reflection into the whole of political experience. In this way the ordinary notion of "contract" is transformed into a philosophical absolute, thereby becoming a source of endless and implacable dispute.

What Hume calls false philosophy is not merely a matter of adhering to propositions that do not correspond to fact. False philosophy is a profound disorder of the soul, and a political philosophy of this corrupt form can generate a profound disorder in society. Hume's neo-Pyrrhonian conception of false philosophy as a source of misery enabled him to work out the first systematic critique of modern political ideologies. In the essay "Of Parties in General," reprinted here, he observes that political ideologies "are known only to modern times, and are, perhaps, the most extraordinary and unaccountable *phenomenon,* that has yet appeared in human affairs."

Hume treats the Puritan revolution, in the volumes of the *History* covering the Stuart kings, as the first manifestation of this modern disposition to philosophically pathological forms of social disorder. Though ostensibly a religion, Puritanism, he argues, resembles more a system of abstract metaphysics than a religion and so can be exhibited as a clinical case of a philosophical-religious pathology. During the last decade of Hume's life—in connection with the spectacular "Wilkes and Liberty" riots that lasted for years, and the American crisis—he thought he saw a similar form of disorder emerging from purely secular philosophical theories of liberty such as the contract theory of Locke.

But Hume's political philosophy is more than a study of philosophical pathologies in politics. Its positive teachings range over many topics. Many of these are explored more fully in the *Essay* than in the *Treatise*. But the central one is the topic that dominated his age: liberty, and its complement, authority. Unlike most theorists in the liberal tradition, Hume never presents an abstract timeless theory of liberty of the sort given, for instance, by Mill in *On Liberty*. For Hume liberty is an inherited convention of practice. To theorize the practice of liberty is to "methodize and correct" it, and this presupposes historical understanding of the practice. Hume's *History* is largely the story of how the practice of liberty evolved in England; consequently, no understanding of Hume's political philosophy is complete without a careful study of that account. In other writings—especially the *Essay*—Hume distinguishes between ancient and modern practices of liberty and argues for the superiority of the modern. And he praises modern governments, whether republican or monarchical, for being more stable and humane than their ancient counterparts.

Hume teaches that there is no liberty without authority, and paradoxically, that the source of authority is typically illiberal. He observes that the practice of liberty is as secure in some absolute monarchies as in republics. But Locke taught that the source of authority for liberty must itself be liberal, that is, consent of the governed. Hume considers Locke's contract theory to be dangerous, because, as he argues in the essay "of the Social Contract," if taken seriously and consistently pursued, the theory must declare illegitimate all regimes not based on consent. In Hume's view that would include most regimes that have ever existed, including liberal ones. It was these anti-Whig strains in Hume's thought that caused Thomas Jefferson to ban the *History* from the University of Virginia.

To theorize about a practice is not merely to understand its structure as inherited; it is also to explore how it can be extended into the future. Any practice suggests a number of ways it can be extended. From these intimations, choices are made and ideals formed to guide participants in the practice. Hume defended an ethic of individualism, private property, the rule of law, and free trade. In the essay "Idea of a Perfect Commonwealth," not printed here, he rejected the traditional view that republics have to be small. Large modern states—the size of Britain and France—could be republics if properly decentralized into "county republics" in a federal system. And he imagined a future Europe of such large-scale republics ordered by free trade, cultural competition, and a policy of the balance of power. This argument for a large-scale republic, as well as other aspects of Hume's political thought, influenced the American Founders, especially James Madison and Alexander Hamilton.

Hume also saw dispositions in the practice of liberty that threatened to undermine the practice. Modern states are disposed to concentrate power in the capital at the expense of the provinces, a disposition that the invention of public credit makes almost impossible to restrain. Hume's attack on public credit, in the essay "Of Public Credit," sounds quite Jeffersonian: public credit leads to needless wars, debts, taxes, centralization, and eventually to a revolution in which a new monied class of men, without virtue, comes to dominate government. It was public credit that made possible the British Empire that was emerging. Hume was an early opponent of the empire, and argued that the English should leave both the East and West Indies. As part of this anti-imperialist stance, he urged complete independence for the colonies as early as 1768, before the idea had occurred to most Americans, and he consistently held to that position, to the dismay of his friends, until his death on August 25, 1776, five days after the Declaration of Independence was published in Edinburgh's *Caledonian Mercury*.

Hume enjoyed a European reputation in his lifetime. He was personally acquainted with many of the luminaries of the age such as Franklin, Rousseau, Turgot, Diderot, and d'Holbach. His *History* was especially popular in France. The parallel between the French Revolution and Hume's account of the Puritan revolution and the execution of Charles I was widely used by both left and right as an authority with which to justify policy or to understand the meaning of the events they were living through. In this way the *History* was not only a remarkable account of events, but became an instrument in the shaping of future events.

Two general studies of Hume's thought are Fredrick G. Whelan, *Order and Artifice in Hume's Political Thought* (Princeton, N.J.: Princeton University Press, 1985); and David Miller, *Philosophy and Ideology in Hume's Political Thought* (Oxford: Clarendon Press, 1981). For a comprehensive study of Hume's conception of philosophy and its relation to political thought, see Donald W. Livingston, *Philosophical Melancholy and Delirium* (Chicago: University of Chicago Press, 1998). The following works consider Hume's *History* as an integral part of his political thought: Duncan Forbes, *Hume's Philosophical Politics* (Cambridge: Cambridge University Press, 1975); Donald W. Livingston, *Hume's Philosophy of Common Life* (Chicago: University of Chicago, 1985); and Laurence Bongie, *David Hume, Prophet of the Counter-Revolution* (Indianapolis: Liberty Press, 2000). John B. Stewart, *Opinion and Reform in Hume's Political Philosophy* (Princeton, N.J.: Princeton University Press, 1992), views Hume as a liberal reformer.

# A Treatise of Human Nature

## BOOK II—OF THE PASSIONS

### Part III—Of the Will and Direct Passions

#### Section III

##### OF THE INFLUENCING MOTIVES OF THE WILL

Nothing is more usual in philosophy, and even in common life, than to talk of the combat of passion and reason, to give the preference to reason, and assert that men are only so far virtuous as they conform themselves to its dictates. Every rational creature, it is said, is obliged to regulate his actions by reason; and if any other motive or principle challenge the direction of his conduct, he ought to oppose it, till it be entirely subdued, or at least brought to a conformity with that superior principle. On this method of thinking the greatest part of moral philosophy, ancient and modern, seems to be founded; nor is there an ampler field, as well for metaphysical arguments, as popular declamations, than this supposed preëminence of reason above passion. The eternity, invariableness and divine origin of the former, have been displayed to the best advantage: the blindness, inconstancy, and deceitfulness of the latter, have been as strongly insisted on. In order to show the fallacy of all this philosophy, I shall endeavour to prove *first,* that reason alone can never be a motive to any action of the will; and *secondly,* that it can never oppose passion in the direction of the will.

The understanding exerts itself after two different ways, as it judges from demonstration or probability; as it regards the abstract relations of our ideas, or those relations of objects of which experience only gives us information. I believe it scarce will be asserted, that the first species of reasoning alone is ever the cause of any action. As its proper province is the world of ideas, and as the will always places us in that of realities, demonstration and volition seem upon that account to be totally removed from each other. Mathematics, indeed, are useful in all mechanical operations, and arithmetic in almost every art and profession: but it is not of themselves they have any influence. Mechanics are the art of regulating the motions of bodies *to some designed end or purpose;* and the reason why we employ arithmetic in fixing the proportions of numbers, is only that we may discover the proportions of their influence and operation. A merchant is desirous of knowing the sum total of his accounts with any person: why? but that he may learn what sum will have the same *effects* in paying his debt, and going to market, as all the particular articles taken together. Abstract or demonstrative reasoning, therefore, never influences any of our actions, but only as it directs our judgment concerning causes and effects; which leads us to the second operation of the understanding.

It is obvious, that when we have the prospect of pain or pleasure from any object, we feel a consequent emotion of aversion or propensity, and are carried to avoid or embrace what will give us this uneasiness or satisfaction. It is also obvious, that this emotion rests not here, but, making us cast our view on every side, comprehends whatever objects are connected with its original one by the relation of cause and effect. Here then reasoning takes place to discover this relation; and according as our reasoning varies, our actions receive a subsequent variation. But it is evident, in this case, that the impulse arises not from reason, but is only directed by it. It is from the prospect of pain or pleasure that the aversion or propensity arises towards any object: and these emotions extend themselves to the causes and effects of that object, as they are pointed out to us by reason and experience. It can never in the least concern us to know, that such objects are causes, and such others effects, if both the causes and effects be indifferent to us. Where the objects themselves do not affect us, their connection can never give them any influence; and it is plain that, as reason is nothing but the discovery of this connection, it cannot be by its means that the objects are able to affect us.

Since reason alone can never produce any action, or give rise to volition, I infer, that the same faculty is as incapable of preventing volition, or of disputing the preference with any passion or emotion. This consequence is necessary. It is impossible reason could have the latter effect of preventing volition, but by giving an impulse in a contrary direction to our passions; and that impulse, had it operated alone, would have been ample to produce volition. Nothing

can oppose or retard the impulse of passion, but a contrary impulse; and if this contrary impulse ever arises from reason, that latter faculty must have an original influence on the will, and must be able to cause, as well as hinder, any act of volition. But if reason has no original influence, it is impossible it can withstand any principle which has such an efficacy, or ever keep the mind in suspense a moment. Thus, it appears, that the principle which opposes our passion cannot be the same with reason, and is only called so in an improper sense. We speak not strictly and philosophically, when we talk of the combat of passion and of reason. Reason is, and ought only to be, the slave of the passions, and can never pretend to any other office than to serve and obey them. As this opinion may appear somewhat extraordinary, it may not be improper to confirm it by some other considerations.

A passion is an original existence, or, if you will, modification of existence, and contains not any representative quality, which renders it a copy of any other existence or modification. When I am angry, I am actually possessed with the passion, and in that emotion have no more a reference to any other object, than when I am thirsty, or sick, or more than five feet high. It is impossible, therefore, that this passion can be opposed by, or be contradictory to truth and reason; since this contradiction consists in the disagreement of ideas, considered as copies, with those objects which they represent.

What may at first occur on this head is, that as nothing can be contrary to truth or reason, except what has a reference to it, and as the judgments of our understanding only have this reference, it must follow that passions can be contrary to reason only, so far as they are *accompanied* with some judgment or opinion. According to this principle, which is so obvious and natural, it is only in two senses that any affection can be called unreasonable. First, When a passion, such as hope or fear, grief or joy, despair or security, is founded on the supposition of the existence of objects, which really do not exist. Secondly, When in exerting any passion in action, we choose means sufficient for the designed end, and deceive ourselves in our judgment of causes and effects.

Where a passion is neither founded on false suppositions, nor chooses means insufficient for the end, the
understanding can neither justify nor condemn it. It
is not contrary to reason to prefer the destruction of
the whole world to the scratching of my finger. It is
not contrary to reason for me to choose my total ruin,
to prevent the least uneasiness of an Indian, or person wholly unknown to me. It is as little contrary to
reason to prefer even my own acknowledged lesser
good to my greater, and have a more ardent affection
for the former than the latter. A trivial good may,
from certain circumstances, produce a desire superior to what arises from the greatest and most valuable enjoyment; nor is there anything more extraordinary in this, than in mechanics to see one pound
weight raise up a hundred by the advantage of its situation. In short, a passion must be accompanied with
some false judgment, in order to its being unreasonable; and even then it is not the passion, properly
speaking, which is unreasonable, but the judgment.

The consequences are evident. Since a passion
can never, in any sense, be called unreasonable, but
when founded on a false supposition, or when it
chooses means insufficient for the designed end, it is
impossible that reason and passion can ever oppose
each other, or dispute for the government of the will
and actions. The moment we perceive the falsehood
of any supposition, or the insufficiency of any
means, our passions yield to our reason without any
opposition. I may desire any fruit as of an excellent
relish; but whenever you convince me of my mistake, my longing ceases. I may will the performance
of certain actions as means of obtaining any desired
good; but as my willing of these actions is only secondary, and founded on the supposition that they are
causes of the proposed effect; as soon as I discover
the falsehood of that supposition, they must become
indifferent to me.

It is natural for one, that does not examine objects
with a strict philosophic eye, to imagine, that those
actions of the mind are entirely the same, which produce not a different sensation, and are not immediately distinguishable to the feeling and perception.
Reason, for instance, exerts itself without producing
any sensible emotions; and except in the more sublime disquisitions of philosophy, or in the frivolous
subtilties of the schools, scarce ever conveys any
pleasure or uneasiness. Hence it proceeds, that
every action of the mind which operates with the
same calmness and tranquillity, is confounded with
reason by all those who judge of things from the first
view and appearance. Now it is certain there are certain calm desires and tendencies, which, though
they be real passions, produce little emotion in the
mind, and are more known by their effects than by
the immediate feeling or sensation. These desires
are of two kinds; either certain instincts originally
implanted in our natures, such as benevolence and
resentment, the love of life, and kindness to children; or the general appetite to good, and aversion to
evil, considered merely as such. When any of these
passions are calm, and cause no disorder in the soul,
they are very readily taken for the determinations of
reason, and are supposed to proceed from the same
faculty with that which judges of truth and falsehood. Their nature and principles have been supposed the same, because their sensations are not evidently different.

Besides these calm passions, which often determine the will, there are certain violent emotions of
the same kind, which have likewise a great influence
on that faculty. When I receive any injury from
another, I often feel a violent passion of resentment,
which makes me desire his evil and punishment,
independent of all considerations of pleasure and
advantage to myself. When I am immediately
threatened with any grievous ill, my fears, apprehensions, and aversions rise to a great height, and
produce a sensible emotion.

The common error of metaphysicians has lain in
ascribing the direction of the will entirely to one of
these principles, and supposing the other to have no
influence. Men often act knowingly against their
interest; for which reason, the view of the greatest
possible good does not always influence them. Men
often counteract a violent passion in prosecution of
their interests and designs; it is not, therefore, the
present uneasiness alone which determines them. In
general we may observe that both these principles
operate on the will; and where they are contrary, that

either of them prevails, according to the *general* character or *present* disposition of the person. What we call strength of mind, implies the prevalence of the calm passions above the violent; though we may easily observe, there is no man so constantly possessed of this virtue as never on any occasion to yield to the solicitations of passion and desire. From these variations of temper proceeds the great difficulty of deciding concerning the actions and resolutions of men, where there is any contrariety of motives and passions.

## BOOK III—OF MORALS

### Part I—*Of Virtue and Vice in General*

#### Section I

##### MORAL DISTINCTIONS
##### NOT DERIVED FROM REASON

There is an inconvenience which attends all abstruse reasoning, that it may silence, without convincing an antagonist, and requires the same intense study to make us sensible of its force, that was at first requisite for its invention. When we leave our closet, and engage in the common affairs of life, its conclusions seem to vanish like the phantoms of the night on the appearance of the morning; and it is difficult for us to retain even that conviction which we had attained with difficulty. This is still more conspicuous in a long chain of reasoning, where we must preserve to the end the evidence of the first propositions, and where we often lose sight of all the most received maxims, either of philosophy or common life. I am not, however, without hopes, that the present system of philosophy will acquire new force as it advances; and that our reasonings concerning *morals* will corroborate whatever has been said concerning the *understanding* and the *passions*. Morality is a subject that interests us above all others; we fancy the peace of society to be at stake in every decision concerning it; and it is evident that this concern must make our speculations appear more real and solid, than where the subject is in a great measure indifferent to us. What affects us, we conclude, can never be

a chimera; and, as our passion is engaged on the one side or the other, we naturally think that the question lies within human comprehension; which, in other cases of this nature, we are apt to entertain some doubt of. Without this advantage, I never should have ventured upon a third volume of such abstruse philosophy, in an age wherein the greatest part of men seem agreed to convert reading into an amusement, and to reject everything that requires any considerable degree of attention to be comprehended.

It has been observed, that nothing is ever present to the mind but its perceptions; and that all the actions of seeing, hearing, judging, loving, hating, and thinking, fall under this denomination. The mind can never exert itself in any action which we may not comprehend under the term of *perception;* and consequently that term is no less applicable to those judgments by which we distinguish moral good and evil, than to every other operation of the mind. To approve of one character, to condemn another, are only so many different perceptions.

Now, as perceptions resolve themselves into two kinds, viz. *impressions* and *ideas,* this distinction gives rise to a question, with which we shall open up our present inquiry concerning morals, *whether it is by means of our* ideas *or* impressions *we distinguish betwixt vice and virtue, and pronounce an action blamable or praiseworthy?* This will immediately cut off all loose discourses and declamations, and reduce us to something precise and exact on the present subject.

Those who affirm that virtue is nothing but a conformity to reason; that there are eternal fitnesses and unfitnesses of things, which are the same to every rational being that considers them; that the immutable measure of right and wrong impose an obligation, not only on human creatures, but also on the Deity himself: all these systems concur in the opinion, that morality, like truth, is discerned merely by ideas, and by their juxtaposition and comparison. In order, therefore, to judge of these systems, we need only consider whether it be possible from reason alone, to distinguish betwixt moral good and evil, or whether there must concur some other principles to enable us to make that distinction.

If morality had naturally no influence on human passions and actions, it were in vain to take such pains to inculcate it; and nothing would be more fruitless than that multitude of rules and precepts with which all moralists abound. Philosophy is commonly divided into *speculative* and *practical;* and as morality is always comprehended under the latter division, it is supposed to influence our passions and actions, and to go beyond the calm and indolent judgments of the understanding. And this is confirmed by common experience, which informs us that men are often governed by their duties, and are deterred from some actions by the opinion of injustice, and impelled to others by that of obligation.

Since morals, therefore, have an influence on the actions and affections, it follows that they cannot be derived from reason; and that because reason alone, as we have already proved, can never have any such influence. Morals excite passions, and produce or prevent actions. Reason of itself is utterly impotent in this particular. The rules of morality, therefore, are not conclusions of our reason.

No one, I believe, will deny the justness of this inference; nor is there any other means of evading it, than by denying that principle on which it is founded. As long as it is allowed, that reason has no influence on our passions and actions, it is in vain to pretend that morality is discovered only by a deduction of reason. An active principle can never be founded on an inactive; and if reason be inactive in itself, it must remain so in all its shapes and appearances, whether it exerts itself in natural or moral subjects, whether it considers the powers of external bodies, or the actions of rational beings.

It would be tedious to repeat all the arguments by which I have proved that reason is perfectly inert, and can never either prevent or produce any action or affection. It will be easy to recollect what has been said upon that subject. I shall only recall on this occasion one of these arguments, which I shall endeavour to render still more conclusive, and more applicable to the present subject.

Reason is the discovery of truth or falsehood. Truth or falsehood consists in an agreement or disagreement either to the *real* relations of ideas, or to *real* existence and matter of fact. Whatever therefore is not susceptible of this agreement or disagreement, is incapable of being true or false, and can never be an object of our reason. Now, it is evident our passions, volitions, and actions, are not susceptible of any such agreement or disagreement; being original facts and realities, complete in themselves, and implying no reference to other passions, volitions, and actions. It is impossible, therefore, they can be pronounced either true or false, and be either contrary or conformable to reason.

This argument is of double advantage to our present purpose. For it proves *directly,* that actions do not derive their merit from a conformity to reason, nor their blame from a contrariety to it; and it proves the same truth more *indirectly,* by showing us, that as reason can never immediately prevent or produce any action by contradicting or approving of it, it cannot be the source of moral good and evil, which are found to have that influence. Actions may be laudable or blamable; but they cannot be reasonable or unreasonable: laudable or blamable, therefore, are not the same with reasonable or unreasonable. The merit and demerit of actions frequently contradict, and sometimes control our natural propensities. But reason has no such influence. Moral distinctions, therefore, are not the offspring of reason. Reason is wholly inactive, and can never be the source of so active a principle as conscience, or a sense of morals.

But perhaps it may be said, that though no will or action can be immediately contradictory to reason, yet we may find such a contradiction in some of the attendants of the actions, that is, in its causes or effects. The action may cause a judgment, or may be *obliquely* caused by one, when the judgment concurs with a passion; and by an abusive way of speaking, which philosophy will scarce allow of, the same contrariety may, upon that account, be ascribed to the action. How far this truth or falsehood may be the source of morals, it will now be proper to consider.

It has been observed that reason, in a strict and philosophical sense, can have an influence on our conduct only after two ways: either when it excites

*Reason doesn't create action, it only leads to truth or falsehood.*

a passion, by informing us of the existence of something which is a proper object of it; or when it discovers the connection of causes and effects, so as to afford us means of exerting any passion. These are the only kinds of judgment which can accompany our actions, or can be said to produce them in any manner; and it must be allowed, that these judgments may often be false and erroneous. A person may be affected with passion, by supposing a pain or pleasure to lie in an object which has no tendency to produce either of these sensations, or which produces the contrary to what is imagined. A person may also take false measures for the attaining of his end, and may retard, by his foolish conduct, instead of forwarding the execution of any object. These false judgments may be thought to affect the passions and actions, which are connected with them, and may be said to render them unreasonable, in a figurative and improper way of speaking. But though this be acknowledged, it is easy to observe, that these errors are so far from being the source of all immorality, that they are commonly very innocent, and draw no manner of guilt upon the person who is so unfortunate as to fall into them. They extend not beyond a mistake of *fact,* which moralists have not generally supposed criminal, as being perfectly involuntary. I am more to be lamented than blamed, if I am mistaken with regard to the influence of objects in producing pain or pleasure, or if I know not the proper means of satisfying my desires. No one can ever regard such errors as a defect in my moral character. A fruit, for instance, that is really disagreeable, appears to me at a distance, and, through mistake, I fancy it to be pleasant and delicious. Here is one error. I choose certain means of reaching this fruit, which are not proper for my end. Here is a second error; nor is there any third one, which can ever possibly enter into our reasonings concerning actions. I ask, therefore, if a man in this situation, and guilty of these two errors, is to be regarded as vicious and criminal, however unavoidable they might have been? Or if it be possible to imagine that such errors are the sources of all immorality?

And here it may be proper to observe, that if moral distinctions be derived from the truth or false-

hood of those judgments, they must take place wherever we form the judgments; nor will there be any difference, whether the question be concerning an apple or a kingdom, or whether the error be avoidable or unavoidable.

For as the very essence of morality is supposed to consist in an agreement or disagreement to reason, the other circumstances are entirely arbitrary, and can never either bestow on any action the character of virtuous or vicious, or deprive it of that character. To which we may add, that this agreement or disagreement, not admitting of degrees, all virtues and vices would of course be equal.

Should it be pretended, that though a mistake of *fact* be not criminal, yet a mistake of *right* often is; and that this may be the source of immorality: I would answer, that it is impossible such a mistake can ever be the original source of immorality, since it supposes a real right and wrong; that is, a real distinction in morals, independent of these judgments. A mistake, therefore, of right, may become a species of immorality; but it is only a secondary one, and is founded on some other antecedent to it.

As to those judgments which are the *effects* of our actions, and which, when false, give occasion to pronounce the actions contrary to truth and reason; we may observe, that our actions never cause any judgment, either true or false, in ourselves, and that it is only on others they have such an influence. It is certain that an action, on many occasions, may give rise to false conclusions in others; and that a person, who, through a window, sees any lewd behaviour of mine with my neighbour's wife, may be so simple as to imagine she is certainly my own. In this respect my action resembles somewhat a lie or falsehood; only with this difference, which is material, that I perform not the action with any intention of giving rise to a false judgment in another, but merely to satisfy my lust and passion. It causes, however, a mistake and false judgment by accident; and the falsehood of its effects may be ascribed, by some odd figurative way of speaking, to the action itself. But still I can see no pretext of reason for asserting, that the tendency to cause such an error is the first spring or original source of all immorality.

vice certainty   demonstration vice
virtue certainty        "        virtue

Thus, upon the whole, it is impossible that the distinction betwixt moral good and evil can be made by reason; since that distinction has an influence upon our actions, of which reason alone is incapable. Reason and judgment may, indeed, be the mediate cause of an action, by prompting or by directing a passion; but it is not pretended that a judgment of this kind, either in its truth or falsehood, is attended with virtue or vice. And as to the judgments, which are caused by our judgments, they can still less bestow those moral qualities on the actions which are their causes.

But, to be more particular, and to show that those eternal immutable fitness and unfitnesses of things cannot be defended by sound philosophy, we may weigh the following considerations.

If the thought and understanding were alone capable of fixing the boundaries of right and wrong, the character of virtuous and vicious either must lie in some relations of objects, or must be a matter of fact which is discovered by our reasoning. This consequence is evident. As the operations of human understanding divide themselves into two kinds, the comparing of ideas, and the inferring of matter of fact, were virtue discovered by the understanding, it must be an object of one of these operations; nor is there any third operation of the understanding which can discover it. There has been an opinion very industriously propagated by certain philosophers, that morality is susceptible of demonstration; and though no one has ever been able to advance a single step in those demonstrations, yet it is taken for granted that this science may be brought to an equal certainty with geometry or algebra. Upon this supposition, vice and virtue must consist in some relations; since it is allowed on all hands, that no matter of fact is capable of being demonstrated. Let us therefore begin with examining this hypothesis, and endeavour, if possible, to fix those moral qualities which have been so long the objects of our fruitless researches; point out distinctly the relations which constitute morality or obligation, that we may know wherein they consist, and after what manner we must judge of them.

If you assert that vice and virtue consist in relations susceptible of certainty and demonstration, you must confine yourself to those *four* relations which alone admit of that degree of evidence; and in that case you run into absurdities from which you will never be able to extricate yourself. For as you make the very essence of morality to lie in the relations, and as there is no one of these relations but what is applicable, not only to an irrational but also to an inanimate object, it follows that even such objects must be susceptible of merit or demerit. *Resemblance, contrariety, degrees in quality,* and *proportions in quantity and number;* all these relations belong as properly to matter as to our actions, passions, and volitions. It is unquestionable, therefore, that morality lies not in any of these relations, nor the sense of it in their discovery.

Should it be asserted, that the sense of morality consists in the discovery of some relations distinct from these, and that our enumeration was not complete when we comprehended all demonstrable relations under four general heads; to this I know not what to reply, till some one be so good as to point out to me this new relation. It is impossible to refute a system which has never yet been explained. In such a manner of fighting in the dark, a man loses his blows in the air, and often places them where the enemy is not present.

I must therefore, on this occasion, rest contented with requiring the two following conditions of any one that would undertake to clear up this system. *First,* as moral good and evil belong only to the actions of the mind, and are derived from our situation with regard to external objects, the relations from which these moral distinctions arise must lie only betwixt internal actions and external objects, and must not be applicable either to internal actions, compared among themselves, or to external objects, when placed in opposition to other external objects. For as morality is supposed to attend certain relations, if these relations could belong to internal actions considered singly, it would follow, that we might be guilty of crimes in ourselves, and independent of our situation with respect to the universe; and in like manner, if these moral relations could be applied to external objects, it would follow that even inanimate beings would be susceptible of moral beauty and deformity. Now, it seems difficult to imagine that any relation can be discovered betwixt our passions, volitions, and actions, compared to external objects, which relation might not belong either to these passions and volitions, or to these external objects, compared among *themselves.*

But it will be still more difficult to fulfil the *second* condition, requisite to justify this system. According to the principles of those who maintain an abstract rational difference betwixt moral good and evil, and a natural fitness and unfitness of things, it is not only supposed, that these relations, being eternal and immutable, are the same, when considered by every rational creature, but their *effects* are also supposed to be necessarily the same; and it is concluded they have no less, or rather a greater, influence in directing the will of the Deity, than in governing the rational and virtuous of our own species. These two particulars are evidently distinct. It is one thing to know virtue, and another to conform the will to it. In order, therefore, to prove that the measures of right and wrong are eternal laws, *obligatory* on every rational mind, it is not sufficient to show the relations upon which they are founded: we must also point out the connection betwixt the relation and the will, and must prove that this connection is so necessary, that in every well-disposed mind, it must take place and have its influence; though the difference betwixt these minds be in other respects immense and infinite. Now, besides what I have already proved, that even in human nature no relation can ever alone produce any action; besides this, I say, it has been shown, in treating of the understanding, that there is no connection of cause and effect, such as this is supposed to be, which is discoverable otherwise than by experience, and of which we can pretend to have any security by the simple consideration of the objects. All beings in the universe, considered in themselves, appear entirely loose and independent of each other. It is only by experience we learn their influence and connection; and this influence we ought never to extend beyond experience.

Thus it will be impossible to fulfil the *first* condition required to the system of eternal rational measures of right and wrong; because it is impossible to show those relations, upon which such a distinction may be founded: and it is as impossible to fulfil the *second* condition; because we cannot prove *a priori,* that these relations, if they really existed and were perceived, would be universally forcible and obligatory.

But to make these general reflections more clear and convincing, we may illustrate them by some particular instances, wherein this character of moral good or evil is the most universally acknowledged. Of all crimes that human creatures are capable of committing, the most horrid and unnatural is ingratitude, especially when it is committed against parents, and appears in the more flagrant instances of wounds and death. This is acknowledged by all mankind, philosophers as well as the people: the question only arises among philosophers, whether the guilt or moral deformity of this action be discovered by demonstrative reasoning, or be felt by an internal sense, and by means of some sentiment, which the reflecting on such an action naturally occasions. This question will soon be decided against the former opinion, if we can show the same relations in other objects, without the notion of any guilt or iniquity attending them. Reason or science is nothing but the comparing of ideas, and the discovery of their relations; and if the same relations have different characters, it must evidently follow, that those characters are not discovered merely by reason. To put the affair, therefore, to this trial, let us choose any inanimate object, such as an oak or elm; and let us suppose, that, by the dropping of its seed, it produces a sapling below it, which, springing up by degrees, at last overtops and destroys the parent tree: I ask, if, in this instance, there be wanting any relation which is discoverable in parricide or ingratitude? Is not the one tree the cause of the other's existence; and the latter the cause of the destruction of the former, in the same manner as when a child murders his parent? It is not sufficient to reply, that a choice or will is wanting. For in the case of parricide, a will does not give rise to any *different* relations, but is only the cause from which the action is derived; and consequently produces the *same* rela-

*will or choice  vs.  laws of matter motion.*

tions, that in the oak or elm arise from some other principles. It is a will or choice that determines a man to kill his parent: and they are the laws of matter and motion that determine a sapling to destroy the oak from which it sprung. Here then the same relations have different causes; but still the relations are the same: and as their discovery is not in both cases attended with a notion of immorality, it follows, that that notion does not arise from such a discovery.

But to choose an instance still more resembling; I would fain ask any one, why incest in the human species is criminal, and why the very same action, and the same relations in animals, have not the smallest moral turpitude and deformity? If it be answered, that this action is innocent in animals, because they have not reason sufficient to discover its turpitude; but that man, being endowed with that faculty, which *ought* to restrain him to his duty, the same action instantly becomes criminal to him. Should this be said, I would reply, that this is evidently arguing in a circle. For, before reason can perceive this turpitude, the turpitude must exist; and consequently is independent of the decisions of our reason, and is their object more properly than their effect. According to this system, then, every animal that has sense and appetite and will, that is, every animal must be susceptible of all the same virtues and vices, for which we ascribe praise and blame to human creatures. All the difference is, that our superior reason may serve to discover the vice or virtue, and by that means may augment the blame or praise: but still this discovery supposes a separate being in these moral distinctions, and a being which depends only on the will and appetite, and which, both in thought and reality, may be distinguished from reason. Animals are susceptible of the same relations with respect to each other as the human species, and therefore would also be susceptible of the same morality, if the essence of morality consisted in these relations. Their want of a sufficient degree of reason may hinder them from perceiving the duties and obligations of morality, but can never hinder these duties from existing; since they must antecedently exist, in order to their being perceived. Reason must find them, and can never produce them. This argu-

ment deserves to be weighed, as being, in my opinion, entirely decisive.

Nor does this reasoning only prove, that morality consists not in any relations that are the objects of science; but if examined, will prove with equal certainty, that it consists not in any *matter of fact,* which can be discovered by the understanding. This is the *second* part of our argument; and if it can be made evident, we may conclude that morality is not an object of reason. But can there be any difficulty in proving that vice and virtue are not matters of fact, whose existence we can infer by reason? Take any action allowed to be vicious; wilful murder, for instance. Examine it in all lights, and see if you can find that matter of fact, or real existence, which you call *vice.* In whichever way you take it, you find only certain passions, motives, volitions, and thoughts. There is no other matter of fact in the case. The vice entirely escapes you, as long as you consider the object. You never can find it, till you turn your reflection into your own breast, and find a sentiment of disapprobation, which arises in you, towards this action. Here is a matter of fact; but it is the object of feeling, not of reason. It lies in yourself, not in the object. So that when you pronounce any action or character to be vicious, you mean nothing, but that from the constitution of your nature you have a feeling or sentiment of blame from the contemplation of it. Vice and virtue, therefore, may be compared to sounds, colours, heat, and cold, which, according to modern philosophy, are not qualities in objects, but perceptions in the mind: and this discovery in morals, like that other in physics, is to be regarded as a considerable advancement of the speculative sciences; though, like that too, it has little or no influence on practice. Nothing can be more real, or concern us more, than our own sentiments of pleasure and uneasiness; and if these be favourable to virtue, and unfavourable to vice, no more can be requisite to the regulation of our conduct and behaviour.

I cannot forbear adding to these reasonings an observation, which may, perhaps, be found of some importance. In every system of morality which I have hitherto met with, I have always remarked, that the author proceeds for some time in the ordinary way of reasoning, and establishes the being of a God, or makes observations concerning human affairs; when of a sudden I am surprised to find, that instead of the usual copulations of propositions, *is,* and *is not,* I meet with no proposition that is not connected with an *ought,* or an *ought not.* This change is imperceptible; but is, however, of the last consequence. For as this *ought,* or *ought not,* expresses some new relation or affirmation, it is necessary that it should be observed and explained; and at the same time that a reason should be given, for what seems altogether inconceivable, how this new relation can be a deduction from others, which are entirely different from it. But as authors do not commonly use this precaution, I shall presume to recommend it to the readers; and am persuaded, that this small attention would subvert all the vulgar systems of morality, and let us see that the distinction of vice and virtue is not founded merely on the relations of objects, nor is perceived by reason.

## Section II

### MORAL DISTINCTIONS DERIVED FROM A MORAL SENSE

Thus the course of the argument leads us to conclude, that since vice and virtue are not discoverable merely by reason, or the comparison of ideas, it must be by means of some impression or sentiment they occasion, that we are able to mark the difference betwixt them. Our decisions concerning moral rectitude and depravity are evidently perceptions; and as all perceptions are either impressions or ideas, the exclusion of the one is a convincing argument for the other. Morality, therefore, is more properly felt than judged of; though this feeling or sentiment is commonly so soft and gentle that we are apt to confound it with an idea, according to our common custom of taking all things for the same which have any near resemblance to each other.

The next question is, of what nature are these impressions, and after what manner do they operate upon us? Here we cannot remain long in suspense, but must pronounce the impression arising from

virtue to be agreeable, and that proceeding from vice to be uneasy. Every moment's experience must convince us of this. There is no spectacle so fair and beautiful as a noble and generous action; nor any which gives us more abhorrence than one that is cruel and treacherous. No enjoyment equals the satisfaction we receive from the company of those we love and esteem; as the greatest of all punishments is to be obliged to pass our lives with those we hate or contemn. A very play or romance may afford us instances of this pleasure which virtue conveys to us; and pain, which arises from vice.

Now, since the distinguishing impressions by which moral good or evil is known, are nothing but *particular* pains or pleasures, it follows, that in all inquiries concerning these moral distinctions, it will be sufficient to show the principles which make us feel a satisfaction or uneasiness from the survey of any character, in order to satisfy us why the character is laudable or blamable. An action, or sentiment, or character, is virtuous or vicious; why? because its view causes a pleasure or uneasiness of a particular kind. In giving a reason, therefore, for the pleasure or uneasiness, we sufficiently explain the vice or virtue. To have the sense of virtue, is nothing but to *feel* a satisfaction of a particular kind from the contemplation of a character. The very *feeling* constitutes our praise or admiration. We go no further; nor do we inquire into the cause of the satisfaction. We do not infer a character to be virtuous, because it pleases; but in feeling that it pleases after such a particular manner, we in effect feel that it is virtuous. The case is the same as in our judgments concerning all kinds of beauty, and tastes, and sensations. Our approbation is implied in the immediate pleasure they convey to us.

I have objected to the system which establishes eternal rational measures of right and wrong, that it is impossible to show, in the actions of reasonable creatures, any relations which are not found in external objects; and therefore, if morality always attended these relations, it were possible for inanimate matter to become virtuous or vicious. Now it may, in like manner, be objected to the present system, that if virtue and vice be determined by pleasure and pain, these qualities must, in every case, arise from the sensations; and consequently any object, whether animate or inanimate, rational or irrational, might become morally good or evil, provided it can excite a satisfaction or uneasiness. But though this objection seems to be the very same, it has by no means the same force in the one case as in the other. For, *first,* it is evident that, under the term *pleasure,* we comprehend sensations, which are very different from each other, and which have only such a distant resemblance as is requisite to make them be expressed by the same abstract term. A good composition of music and a bottle of good wine equally produce pleasure; and, what is more, their goodness is determined merely by the pleasure. But shall we say, upon that account, that the wine is harmonious, or the music of a good flavour? In like manner, an inanimate object, and the character or sentiments of any person, may, both of them, give satisfaction; but, as the satisfaction is different, this keeps our sentiments concerning them from being confounded, and makes us ascribe virtue to the one and not to the other. Nor is every sentiment of pleasure or pain, which arises from characters and actions, of that *peculiar* kind which makes us praise or condemn. The good qualities of an enemy are hurtful to us, but may still command our esteem and respect. It is only when a character is considered in general, without reference to our particular interest, that it causes such a feeling or sentiment as denominates it morally good or evil. It is true, those sentiments from interest and morals are apt to be confounded, and naturally run into one another. It seldom happens that we do not think an enemy vicious, and can distinguish betwixt his opposition to our interest and real villainy or baseness. But this hinders not but that the sentiments are in themselves distinct; and a man of temper and judgment may preserve himself from these illusions. In like manner, though it is certain a musical voice is nothing but one that naturally gives a *particular* kind of pleasure; yet it is difficult for a man to be sensible that the voice of an enemy is agreeable, or to allow it to be musical. But a person of a fine ear, who has the command of himself, can separate these feelings, and give praise to what deserves it.

*Secondly,* we may call to remembrance the preceding system of the passions, in order to remark a still more considerable difference among our pains and pleasures. Pride and humility, love and hatred, are excited, when there is anything presented to us that both bears a relation to the object of the passion, and produces a separate sensation, related to the sensation of the passion. Now, virtue and vice are attended with these circumstances. They must necessarily be placed either in ourselves or others, and excite either pleasure or uneasiness; and therefore must give rise to one of these four passions, which clearly distinguishes them from the pleasure and pain arising from inanimate objects, that often bear no relation to us; and this is, perhaps, the most considerable effect that virtue and vice have upon the human mind.

It may now be asked, *in general,* concerning this pain or pleasure that distinguishes moral good and evil, *From what principle is it derived, and whence does it arise in the human mind?* To this I reply, *first,* that it is absurd to imagine that, in every particular instance, these sentiments are produced by an *original* quality and *primary* constitution. For as the number of our duties is in a manner infinite, it is impossible that our original instincts should extend to each of them, and from our very first infancy impress on the human mind all that multitude of precepts which are contained in the completest system of ethics. Such a method of proceeding is not conformable to the usual maxims by which nature is conducted, where a few principles produce all that variety we observe in the universe, and everything is carried on in the easiest and most simple manner. It is necessary, therefore, to abridge these primary impulses, and find some more general principles upon which all our notions of morals are founded.

But, in the *second* place, should it be asked, whether we ought to search for these principles in *nature,* or whether we must look for them in some other origin? I would reply, that our answer to this question depends upon the definition of the word Nature, than which there is none more ambiguous and equivocal. If *nature* be opposed to miracles, not only the distinction betwixt vice and virtue is natural, but also every event which has ever happened in the world, *excepting those miracles on which our religion is founded.* In saying, then, that the sentiments of vice and virtue are natural in this sense, we make no very extraordinary discovery.

But *nature* may also be opposed to rare and unusual; and in this sense of the word, which is the common one, there may often arise disputes concerning what is natural or unnatural; and one may in general affirm, that we are not possessed of any very precise standard by which these disputes can be decided. Frequent and rare depend upon the number of examples we have observed; and as this number may gradually increase or diminish, it will be impossible to fix any exact boundaries betwixt them. We may only affirm on this head, that if ever there was anything which could be called natural in this sense, the sentiments of morality certainly may; since there never was any nation of the world, nor any single person in any nation, who was utterly deprived of them, and who never, in any instance, showed the least approbation or dislike of manners. These sentiments are so rooted in our constitution and temper, that, without entirely confounding the human mind by disease or madness, it is impossible to extirpate and destroy them.

But *nature* may also be opposed to artifice, as well as to what is rare and unusual; and in this sense it may be disputed, whether the notions of virtue be natural or not. We readily forget that the designs, and projects, and views of men are principles as necessary in their operation as heat and cold, moist and dry; but, taking them to be free and entirely our own, it is usual for us to set them in opposition to the other principles of nature. Should it therefore be demanded, whether the sense of virtue be natural or artificial, I am of opinion that it is impossible for me at present to give any precise answer to this question. Perhaps it will appear afterwards that our sense of some virtues is artificial, and that of others natural. The discussion of this question will be more proper, when we enter upon an exact detail of each particular vice and virtue.

Meanwhile, it may not be amiss to observe, from these definitions of *natural* and *unnatural,* that nothing can be more unphilosophical than those systems which assert that virtue is the same with what is natural, and vice with what is unnatural. For, in the first sense of the word, nature, as opposed to miracles, both vice and virtue are equally natural; and, in the second sense, as opposed to what is unusual, perhaps virtue will be found to be the most unnatural. At least it must be owned, that heroic virtue, being as unusual, is as little natural as the most brutal barbarity. As to the third sense of the word, it is certain that both vice and virtue are equally artificial and out of nature. For, however it may be disputed, whether the notion of a merit or demerit in certain actions, be natural or artificial, it is evident that the actions themselves are artificial, and performed with a certain design and intention; otherwise they could never be ranked under any of these denominations. It is impossible, therefore, that the character of natural and unnatural can ever, in any sense, mark the boundaries of vice and virtue.

Thus we are still brought back to our first position, that virtue is distinguished by the pleasure, and vice by the pain, that any action, sentiment, or character, gives us by the mere view and contemplation. This decision is very commodious; because it reduces us to this simple question, *Why any action or sentiment, upon the general view or survey, gives a certain satisfaction or uneasiness,* in order to show the origin of its moral rectitude or depravity, without looking for any incomprehensible relations and qualities, which never did exist in nature, nor even in our imagination, by any clear and distinct conception? I flatter myself I have executed a great part of my present design by a state of the question, which appears to me so free from ambiguity and obscurity.

## Part II—Of Justice and Injustice

### Section I

#### JUSTICE, WHETHER A NATURAL OR ARTIFICIAL VIRTUE?

I have already hinted, that our sense of every kind of virtue is not natural; but that there are some virtues that produce pleasure and approbation by means of an artifice or contrivance, which arises from the circumstances and necessity of mankind. Of this kind I assert *justice* to be; and shall endeavour to defend this opinion by a short, and, I hope, convincing argument, before I examine the nature of the artifice, from which the sense of that virtue is derived.

It is evident that, when we praise any actions, we regard only the motives that produced them, and consider the actions as signs or indications of certain principles in the mind and temper. The external performance has no merit. We must look within to find the moral quality. This we cannot do directly; and therefore fix our attention on actions, as on external signs. But these actions are still considered as signs; and the ultimate object of our praise and approbation is the motive that produced them.

After the same manner, when we require any action, or blame a person for not performing it, we always suppose that one in that situation should be influenced by the proper motive of that action, and we esteem it vicious in him to be regardless of it. If we find, upon inquiry, that the virtuous motive was still powerful over his breast, though checked in its operation by some circumstances unknown to us, we retract our blame, and have the same esteem for him, as if he had actually performed the action which we require of him.

It appears, therefore, that all virtuous actions derive their merit only from virtuous motives, and are considered merely as signs of those motives. From this principle I conclude, that the first virtuous motive which bestows a merit on any action, can never be a regard to the virtue of that action, but must be some other natural motive or principle. To suppose that the mere regard to the virtue of the action, may be the first motive which produced the action, and rendered it virtuous, is to reason in a circle. Before we can have such a regard, the action must be really virtuous; and this virtue must be derived from some virtuous motive: and, consequently, the virtuous motive must be different from the regard to the virtue of the action. A virtuous motive is requisite to render an action virtuous. An action must be virtuous before we can have a regard to its virtue. Some virtuous motive, therefore, must be antecedent to that regard.

Nor is this merely a metaphysical subtilty; but enters into all our reasoning in common life, though perhaps we may not be able to place it in such distinct philosophical terms. We blame a father for neglecting his child. Why? because it shows a want of natural affection, which is the duty of every parent. Were not natural affection a duty, the care of children could not be a duty; and it were impossible we could have the duty in our eye in the attention we give to our offspring. In this case, therefore, all men suppose a motive to the action distinct from a sense of duty.

Here is a man that does many benevolent actions; relieves the distressed, comforts the afflicted, and extends his bounty even to the greatest strangers. No character can be more amiable and virtuous. We regard these actions as proofs of the greatest humanity. This humanity bestows a merit on the actions. A regard to this merit is, therefore, a secondary consideration, and derived from the antecedent principles of humanity, which is meritorious and laudable.

In short, it may be established as an undoubted maxim, *that no action can be virtuous, or morally good, unless there be in human nature some motive to produce it distinct from the sense of its morality.*

But may not the sense of morality or duty produce an action, without any other motive? I answer, it may: but this is no objection to the present doctrine. When any virtuous motive or principle is common in human nature, a person who feels his heart devoid of that motive, may hate himself upon that account, and may perform the action without the motive, from a certain sense of duty, in order to acquire, by practice, that virtuous principle, or at least to disguise to himself, as much as possible, his want of it. A man that really feels no gratitude in his temper, is still pleased to perform grateful actions, and thinks he has, by that means, fulfilled his duty. Actions are at first only considered as signs of motives: but it is usual, in this case, as in all others, to fix our attention on the signs, and neglect, in some measure, the thing signified. But though, on some occasions, a person may perform an action merely out of regard to its moral obligation, yet still this supposes in human nature some distinct principles, which are capable of producing the action, and whose moral beauty renders the action meritorious.

Now, to apply all this to the present case; I suppose a person to have lent me a sum of money, on condition that it be restored in a few days; and also suppose, that after the expiration of the term agreed on, he demands the sum: I ask, *What reason or motive have I to restore the money?* It will perhaps be said, that my regard to justice, and abhorrence of villainy and knavery, are sufficient reasons for me, if I have the least grain of honesty, or sense of duty and obligation. And this answer, no doubt, is just and satisfactory to man in his civilised state, and when trained up according to a certain discipline and education. But in his rude and more *natural* condition, if you are pleased to call such a condition natural, this answer would be rejected as perfectly unintelligible and sophistical. For one in that situation would immediately ask you, *Wherein consists this honesty and justice, which you find in restoring a loan, and abstaining from the property of others?* It does not surely lie in the external action. It must, therefore, be placed in the motive from which the external action is derived. This motive can never be a regard to the honesty of the action. For it is a plain fallacy to say, that a virtuous motive is requisite to render an action honest, and, at the same time, that a regard to the honesty is the motive of the action. We can never have a regard to the virtue of an action, unless the action be antecedently virtuous. No action can be virtuous, but so far as it proceeds from a virtuous motive. A virtuous motive, therefore, must precede the regard to the virtue; and it is impossible that the virtuous motive and the regard to the virtue can be the same.

It is requisite, then, to find some motive to acts of justice and honesty, distinct from our regard to the honesty; and in this lies the great difficulty. For should we say, that a concern for our private interest or reputation, is the legitimate motive to all honest actions: it would follow that wherever that concern ceases, honesty can no longer have place. But it is certain that self-love, when it acts at its liberty, instead of engaging us to honest actions, is the source of all injustice and violence; nor can a man ever correct those vices, without correcting and restraining the *natural* movements of that appetite.

But should it be affirmed that the reason or motive of such actions is the *regard to public interest,* to which nothing is more contrary than examples of injustice and dishonesty; should this be said, I would propose the three following considerations as worthy of our attention. *First,* Public interest is not naturally attached to the observation of the rules of justice; but is only connected with it, after an artificial convention for the establishment of these rules, as shall be shown more at large hereafter. *Secondly,* If we suppose that the loan was secret, and that it is necessary for the interest of the person, that the money be restored in the same manner (as when the lender would conceal his riches), in that case the example ceases, and the public is no longer interested in the actions of the borrower; though I suppose there is no moralist who will affirm that the duty and obligation ceases. *Thirdly,* Experience sufficiently proves that men, in the ordinary conduct of life, look not so far as the public interest, when they pay their creditors, perform their promises, and abstain from theft, and robbery, and injustice of every kind. That is a motive too remote and too sublime to affect the generality of mankind, and operate with any force in actions so contrary to private interest as are frequently those of justice and common honesty.

In general, it may be affirmed, that there is no such passion in human minds as the love of mankind, merely as such, independent of personal qualities, of services, or of relation to ourself. It is true, there is no human, and indeed no sensible creature, whose happiness or misery does not, in some measure, affect us, when brought near us, and represented in lively colours: but this proceeds merely from sympathy, and is no proof of such an universal affection to mankind, since this concern extends itself beyond our own species. An affection betwixt the sexes is a passion evidently implanted in human nature; and this passion not only appears in its peculiar symptoms, but also in inflaming every other principle of affection, and raising a stronger love from beauty, wit, kindness, than what would otherwise flow from them. Were there an universal love among all human creatures, it would appear after the same manner. Any degree of a good quality would cause a stronger affection than the same degree of a bad quality would cause hatred; contrary to what we find by experience. Men's tempers are different, and some have a propensity to the tender, and others to the rougher affections: but in the main, we may affirm, that man in general, or human nature, is nothing but the object both of love and hatred, and requires some other cause, which, by a double relation of impressions and ideas, may excite these passions. In vain would we endeavour to elude this hypothesis. There are no phenomena that point out any such kind affection to men, independent of their merit, and every other circumstance. We love company in general; but it is as we love any other amusement. An Englishman in Italy is a friend; an European in China; and perhaps a man would be beloved as such, were we to meet him in the moon. But this proceeds only from the relation to ourselves; which in these cases gathers force by being confined to a few persons.

If public benevolence, therefore, or a regard to the interests of mankind, cannot be the original motive to justice, much less can *private benevolence,* or a *regard to the interests of the party concerned,* be this motive. For what if he be my enemy, and has given me just cause to hate him? What if he be a vicious man, and deserves the hatred of all mankind? What if he be a miser, and can make no use of what I would deprive him of? What if he be a profligate debauchee, and would rather receive harm than benefit from large possessions? What if I be in necessity, and have urgent motives to acquire something to my family? In all these cases, the original motive to justice would fail; and consequently the justice itself, and along with it all property, right and obligation.

A rich man lies under a moral obligation to communicate to those in necessity a share of his superfluities. Were private benevolence the original motive to justice a man would not be obliged to leave others in the possession of more than he is obliged to give them. At least, the difference would be very inconsiderable. Men generally fix their affections more on what they are possessed of, than on what they never enjoyed: for this reason, it would be greater cruelty to dispossess a man of anything, than not to give it him. But who will assert that this is the only foundation of justice?

Besides, we must consider, that the chief reason why men attach themselves so much to their possessions, is, that they consider them as their property, and as secured to them inviolably by the laws of society. But this is a secondary consideration, and dependent on the preceding notions of justice and property.

A man's property is supposed to be fenced against every mortal, in every possible case. But private benevolence is, and ought to be, weaker in some persons than in others: and in many, or indeed in most persons, must absolutely fail. Private benevolence, therefore, is not the original motive of justice.

From all this it follows, that we have no real or universal motive for observing the laws of equity, but the very equity and merit of that observance; and as no action can be equitable or meritorious, where it cannot arise from some separate motive, there is here an evident sophistry and reasoning in a circle. Unless, therefore, we will allow that nature has established a sophistry, and rendered it necessary and unavoidable, we must allow, that the sense of justice and injustice is not derived from nature, but arises artificially, though necessarily, from education and human conventions.

I shall add, as a corollary to this reasoning, that since no action can be laudable or blamable, without some motives or impelling passions, distinct from the sense of morals, these distinct passions must have a great influence on that sense. It is according to their general force in human nature that we blame or praise. In judging of the beauty of animal bodies, we always carry in our eye the economy of a certain species; and where the limbs and features observe that proportion which is common to the species, we pronounce them handsome and beautiful. In like manner, we always consider the *natural* and *usual* force of the passions, when we determine concerning vice and virtue; and if the passions depart very much from the common measures on either side, they are always disapproved as vicious. A man naturally loves his children better than his nephews, his nephews better than his cousins, his cousins better than strangers, where everything else is equal. Hence arise our common measures of duty, in preferring the one to the other. Our sense of duty always follows the common and natural course of our passions.

To avoid giving offence, I must here observe, that when I deny justice to be a natural virtue, I make use of the word *natural,* only as opposed to *artificial.* In another sense of the word, as no principle of the human mind is more natural than a sense of virtue, so no virtue is more natural than justice. Mankind is an inventive species; and where an invention is obvious and absolutely necessary, it may as properly be said to be natural as anything that proceeds immediately from original principles, without the intervention of thought or reflection. Though the rules of justice be *artificial,* they are not *arbitrary.* Nor is the expression improper to call them *Laws of Nature;* if by natural we understand what is common to any species, or even if we confine it to mean what is inseparable from the species.

## *Section II*

### OF THE ORIGIN OF JUSTICE AND PROPERTY

We now proceed to examine two questions, viz. *concerning the manner in which the rules of justice are established by the artifice of men;* and *concerning the reasons which determine us to attribute to the observance or neglect of these rules a moral beauty and deformity.* These questions will appear afterwards to be distinct. We shall begin with the former.

Of all the animals with which this globe is peopled, there is none towards whom nature seems, at first sight, to have exercised more cruelty than towards man, in the numberless wants and necessities with which she has loaded him, and in the slender means which she affords to the relieving these necessities. In other creatures, these two particulars generally compensate each other. If we consider the lion as a voracious and carnivorous animal, we shall easily discover him to be very necessitous; but if we turn our eye to his make and temper, his agility, his courage, his arms, and his force, we shall find that his advantages hold proportion with his wants. The sheep and ox are deprived of all these advantages; but their appetites are moderate, and their food is of easy purchase. In man alone this unnatural conjunc-

tion of infirmity and of necessity may be observed in its greatest perfection. Not only the food which is required for his sustenance flies his search and approach, or at least requires his labour to be produced, but he must be possessed of clothes and lodging to defend him against the injuries of the weather; though, to consider him only in himself, he is provided neither with arms, nor force, nor other natural abilities which are in any degree answerable to so many necessities.

It is by society alone he is able to supply his defects, and raise himself up to an equality with his fellow-creatures, and even acquire a superiority above them. By society all his infirmities are compensated; and though in that situation his wants multiply every moment upon him, yet his abilities are still more augmented, and leave him in every respect more satisfied and happy than it is possible for him, in his savage and solitary condition, ever to become. When every individual labours apart, and only for himself, his force is too small to execute any considerable work; his labour being employed in supplying all his different necessities, he never attains a perfection in any particular art; and as his force and success are not at all times equal, the least failure in either of these particulars must be attended with inevitable ruin and misery. Society provides a remedy for these *three* inconveniences. By the conjunction of forces, our power is augmented; by the partition of employments, our ability increases; and by mutual succour, we are less exposed to fortune and accidents. It is by this additional *force, ability,* and *security,* that society becomes advantageous.

But, in order to form society, it is requisite not only that it be advantageous, but also that men be sensible of these advantages; and it is impossible, in their wild uncultivated state, that by study and reflection alone they should ever be able to attain this knowledge. Most fortunately, therefore, there is conjoined to those necessities, whose remedies are remote and obscure, another necessity, which, having a present and more obvious remedy, may justly be regarded as the first and original principle of human society. This necessity is no other than that natural appetite betwixt the sexes, which unites them together, and preserves their union, till a new tie takes place in their concern for their common offspring. This new concern becomes also a principle of union betwixt the parents and offspring, and forms a more numerous society, where the parents govern by the advantage of their superior strength and wisdom, and at the same time are restrained in the exercise of their authority by that natural affection which they bear their children. In a little time, custom and habit, operating on the tender minds of the children, makes them sensible of the advantages which they may reap from society, as well as fashions them by degrees for it, by rubbing off those rough corners and untoward affections which prevent their coalition.

For it must be confessed, that however the circumstances of human nature may render a union necessary, and however those passions of lust and natural affection may seem to render it unavoidable, yet there are other particulars in our *natural temper,* and in our *outward circumstances,* which are very incommodious, and are even contrary to the requisite conjunction. Among the former we may justly esteem our *selfishness* to be the most considerable. I am sensible that, generally speaking, the representations of this quality have been carried much too far; and that the descriptions which certain philosophers delight so much to form of mankind in this particular, are as wide of nature as any accounts of monsters which we meet with in fables and romances. So far from thinking that men have no affection for anything beyond themselves, I am of opinion that, though it be rare to meet with one who loves any single person better than himself, yet it is as rare to meet with one in whom all the kind affections, taken together, do not overbalance all the selfish. Consult common experience; do you not see, that though the whole expense of the family be generally under the direction of the master of it, yet there are few that do not bestow the largest part of their fortunes on the pleasures of their wives and the education of their children, reserving the smallest portion for their own proper use and entertainment? This is what we may observe concerning such as have those endearing ties; and may presume, that the case would be the same with others, were they placed in a like situation.

But though this generosity must be acknowledged to the honour of human nature, we may at the same time remark, that so noble an affection, instead of fitting men for large societies, is almost as contrary to them as the most narrow selfishness. For while each person loves himself better than any other single person, and in his love to others bears the greatest affection to his relations and acquaintance, this must necessarily produce an opposition of passions, and a consequent opposition of actions, which cannot but be dangerous to the new-established union.

It is, however, worth while to remark, that this contrariety of passions would be attended with but small danger, did it not concur with a peculiarity in our *outward circumstances,* which affords it an opportunity of exerting itself. There are three different species of goods which we are possessed of; the internal satisfaction of our minds; the external advantages of our body; and the enjoyment of such possessions as we have acquired by our industry and good fortune. We are perfectly secure in the enjoyment of the first. The second may be ravished from us, but can be of no advantage to him who deprives us of them. The last only are both exposed to the violence of others, and may be transferred without suffering any loss or alteration; while at the same time there is not a sufficient quantity of them to supply every one's desires and necessities. As the improvement, therefore, of these goods is the chief advantage of society, so the *instability* of their possession, along with their *scarcity,* is the chief impediment.

In vain should we expect to find, in *uncultivated nature,* a remedy to this inconvenience; or hope for any inartificial principle of the human mind which might control those partial affections, and make us overcome the temptations arising from our circumstances. The idea of justice can never serve to this purpose, or be taken for a natural principle, capable of inspiring men with an equitable conduct towards each other. That virtue, as it is now understood, would never have been dreamed of among rude and savage men. For the notion of injury or injustice implies an immorality or vice committed against some other person: And as every immorality is derived from some defect or unsoundness of the passions, and as this defect must be judged of, in a great measure, from the ordinary course of nature in the constitution of the mind, it will be easy to know whether we be guilty of any immorality with regard to others, by considering the natural and usual force of those several affections which are directed towards them. Now, it appears that, in the original frame of our mind, our strongest attention is confined to ourselves; our next is extended to our relations and acquaintance; and it is only the weakest which reaches to strangers and indifferent persons. This partiality, then, and unequal affection, must not only have an influence on our behaviour and conduct in society, but even on our ideas of vice and virtue; so as to make us regard any remarkable transgression of such a degree of partiality, either by too great an enlargement or contraction of the affections, as vicious and immoral. This we may observe in our common judgments concerning actions, where we blame a person who either centres all his affections in his family, or is so regardless of them as, in any opposition of interest, to give the preference to a stranger or mere chance acquaintance. From all which it follows, that our natural uncultivated ideas of morality, instead of providing a remedy for the partiality of our affections, do rather conform themselves to that partiality, and give it an additional force and influence.

The remedy, then, is not derived from nature, but from *artifice;* or, more properly speaking, nature provides a remedy, in the judgment and understanding, for what is irregular and incommodious in the affections. For when men, from their early education in society, have become sensible of the infinite advantages that result from it, and have besides acquired a new affection to company and conversation, and when they have observed that the principal disturbance in society arises from those goods, which we call external, and from their looseness and easy transition from one person to another, they must seek for a remedy, by putting these goods, as far as possible, on the same footing with the fixed and constant advantages of the mind and body. This can be done after no other manner, than by a convention entered into by all the members of the society to bestow stability on the possession of those external goods, and leave every one in the peaceable enjoyment of what he may acquire by his fortune and industry. By this means every one knows what he may safely possess; and the passions are restrained in their partial and contradictory motions. Nor is such a restraint contrary to these passions; for, if so, it could never be entered into nor maintained; but it is only contrary to their heedless and impetuous movement. Instead of departing from our own interest, or from that of our nearest friends, by abstaining from the possessions of others, we cannot better consult both these interests than by such a convention; because it is by that means we maintain society, which is so necessary to their well-being and subsistence, as well as to our own.

This convention is not of the nature of a *promise;* for even promises themselves, as we shall see afterwards, arise from human conventions. It is only a general sense of common interest; which sense all the members of the society express to one another, and which induces them to regulate their conduct by certain rules. I observe, that it will be for my interest to leave another in the possession of his goods, *provided* he will act in the same manner with regard to me. He is sensible of a like interest in the regulation of his conduct. When this common sense of interest is mutually expressed, and is known to both, it produces a suitable resolution and behaviour. And this may properly enough be called a convention or agreement betwixt us, though without the interposition of a promise; since the actions of each of us have a reference to those of the other, and are performed upon the supposition that something is to be performed on the other part. Two men who pull the oars of a boat, do it by an agreement or convention, though they have never given promises to each other. Nor is the rule concerning the stability of possessions the less derived from human conventions, that it arises gradually, and acquires force by a slow progression, and by our repeated experience of the inconveniences of transgressing it. On the contrary, this experience assures us still more, that the sense of interest has become common to all our fellows, and gives us a confidence of the future regularity of their conduct;

and it is only on the expectation of this that our moderation and abstinence are founded. In like manner are languages gradually established by human conventions, without any promise. In like manner do gold and silver become the common measures of exchange, and are esteemed sufficient payment for what is of a hundred times their value.

After this convention, concerning abstinence from the possessions of others, is entered into, and every one has acquired a stability in his possessions, there immediately arise the ideas of justice and injustice; as also those of *property, right,* and *obligation.* The latter are altogether unintelligible, without first understanding the former. Our property is nothing but those goods, whose constant possession is established by the laws of society; that is, by the laws of justice. Those, therefore, who make use of the words *property,* or *right,* or *obligation,* before they have explained the origin of justice, or even make use of them in that explication, are guilty of a very gross fallacy, and can never reason upon any solid foundation. A man's property is some object related to him. This relation is not natural, but moral, and founded on justice. It is very preposterous, therefore, to imagine that we can have any idea of property, without fully comprehending the nature of justice, and showing its origin in the artifice and contrivance of men. The origin of justice explains that of property. The same artifice gives rise to both. As our first and most natural sentiment of morals is founded on the nature of our passions, and gives the preference to ourselves and friends above strangers, it is impossible there can be naturally any such thing as a fixed right or property, while the opposite passions of men impel them in contrary directions, and are not restrained by any convention or agreement.

No one can doubt that the convention for the distinction of property, and for the stability of possession, is of all circumstances the most necessary to the establishment of human society, and that, after the agreement for the fixing and observing of this rule, there remains little or nothing to be done towards settling a perfect harmony and concord. All the other passions, beside this of interest, are either easily restrained, or are not of such pernicious consequence when indulged. *Vanity* is rather to be esteemed a social passion, and a bond of union among men. *Pity* and *love* are to be considered in the same light. And as to *envy* and *revenge,* though pernicious, they operate only by intervals, and are directed against particular persons, whom we consider as our superiors or enemies. This avidity alone, of acquiring goods and possessions for ourselves and our nearest friends, is insatiable, perpetual, universal, and directly destructive of society. There scarce is any one who is not actuated by it; and there is no one who has not reason to fear from it, when it acts without any restraint, and gives way to its first and most natural movements. So that, upon the whole, we are to esteem the difficulties in the establishment of society to be greater or less, according to those we encounter in regulating and restraining this passion.

It is certain, that no affection of the human mind has both a sufficient force and a proper direction to counterbalance the love of gain, and render men fit members of society, by making them abstain from the possessions of others. Benevolence to strangers is too weak for this purpose; and as to the other passions, they rather inflame this avidity, when we observe, that the larger our possessions are, the more ability we have of gratifying all our appetites. There is no passion, therefore, capable of controlling the interested affection, but the very affection itself, by an alteration of its direction. Now, this alteration must necessarily take place upon the least reflection; since it is evident that the passion is much better satisfied by its restraint than by its liberty, and that, in preserving society, we make much greater advances in the acquiring possessions, than in the solitary and forlorn condition which must follow upon violence and an universal licence. The question, therefore, concerning the wickedness or goodness of human nature, enters not in the least into that other question concerning the origin of society; nor is there anything to be considered but the degrees of men's sagacity or folly. For whether the passion of self-interest be esteemed vicious or virtuous, it is all a case, since itself alone restrains it; so that if it be virtuous, men become social by their virtue; if vicious, their vice has the same effect.

Now, as it is by establishing the rule for the stability of possession that this passion restrains itself, if that rule be very abstruse and of difficult invention, society must be esteemed in a manner accidental, and the effect of many ages. But if it be found that nothing can be more simple and obvious than that rule; that every parent, in order to preserve peace among his children, must establish it; and that these first rudiments of justice must every day be improved, as the society enlarges: if all this appear evident, as it certainly must, we may conclude that it is utterly impossible for men to remain any considerable time in that savage condition which precedes society, but that his very first state and situation may justly be esteemed social. This, however, hinders not but that philosophers may, if they please, extend their reasoning to the supposed *state of nature;* provided they allow it to be a mere philosophical fiction, which never had, and never could have, any reality. Human nature being composed of two principal parts, which are requisite in all its actions, the affections and understanding, it is certain that the blind motions of the former, without the direction of the latter, incapacitate men for society; and it may be allowed us to consider separately the effects that result from the separate operations of these two component parts of the mind. The same liberty may be permitted to moral, which is allowed to natural philosophers; and it is very usual with the latter to consider any motion as compounded and consisting of two parts separate from each other, though at the same time they acknowledge it to be in itself uncompounded and inseparable.

This *state of nature,* therefore, is to be regarded as a mere fiction, not unlike that of the *golden age* which poets have invented; only with this difference, that the former is described as full of war, violence, and injustice; whereas the latter is painted out to us as the most charming and most peaceable condition that can possibly be imagined. The seasons, in that first age of nature, were so temperate, if we may believe the poets, that there was no necessity for men to provide themselves with clothes and houses as a security against the violence of heat and cold. The rivers flowed with wine and milk; the oaks yielded honey;

and nature spontaneously produced her greatest delicacies. Nor were these the chief advantages of that happy age. The storms and tempests were not alone removed from nature; but those more furious tempests were unknown to human breasts, which now cause such uproar, and engender such confusion. Avarice, ambition, cruelty, selfishness, were never heard of: cordial affection, compassion, sympathy, were the only movements with which the human mind was yet acquainted. Even the distinction of *mine* and *thine* was banished from that happy race of mortals, and carried with them the very notions of property, and obligation, justice and injustice.

This, no doubt, is to be regarded as an idle fiction; but yet deserves our attention, because nothing can more evidently show the origin of those virtues, which are the subjects of our present inquiry. I have already observed, that justice takes it rise from human conventions; and that these are intended as a remedy to some inconveniences, which proceed from the concurrence of certain *qualities* of the human mind with the *situation* of external objects. The qualities of the mind are *selfishness* and *limited generosity:* and the situation of external objects is their *easy change,* joined to their *scarcity* in comparison of the wants and desires of men. But however philosophers may have been bewildered in those speculations, poets have been guided more infallibly, by a certain taste or common instinct, which, in most kinds of reasoning, goes further than any of that art and philosophy with which we have been yet acquainted. They easily perceived, if every man had a tender regard for another, or if nature supplied abundantly all our wants and desires, that the jealousy of interest, which justice supposes, could no longer have place; nor would there be any occasion for those distinctions and limits of property and possession, which at present are in use among mankind. Increase to a sufficient degree the benevolence of men, or the bounty of nature, and you render justice useless, by supplying its place with much nobler virtues, and more valuable blessings. The selfishness of men is animated by the few possessions we have, in proportion to our wants; and it is to restrain this selfishness, that men have been obliged to separate themselves from the community, and to distinguish betwixt their own goods and those of others.

Nor need we have recourse to the fictions of poets to learn this; but, beside the reason of the thing, may discover the same truth by common experience and observation. It is easy to remark, that a cordial affection renders all things common among friends; and that married people, in particular, mutually lose their property, and are unacquainted with the *mine* and *thine*, which are so necessary, and yet cause such disturbance in human society. The same effect arises from any alteration in the circumstances of mankind; as when there is such a plenty of anything as satisfies all the desires of men: in which case the distinction of property is entirely lost, and everything remains in common. This we may observe with regard to air and water, though the most valuable of all external objects; and may easily conclude, that if men were supplied with everything in the same abundance, or if *every one* had the same affection and tender regard for *every one* as for himself, justice and injustice would be equally unknown among mankind.

Here then is a proposition, which, I think, may be regarded as certain, *that it is only from the selfishness and confined generosity of man, along with the scanty provision nature has made for his wants, that justice derives its origin.* If we look backward we shall find, that this proposition bestows an additional force on some of those observations which we have already made on this subject.

*First,* We may conclude from it, that a regard to public interest, or a strong extensive benevolence, is not our first and original motive for the observation of the rules of justice; since it is allowed, that if men were endowed with such a benevolence, these rules would never have been dreamed of.

*Secondly,* We may conclude from the same principle, that the sense of justice is not founded on reason, or on the discovery of certain connections and relations of ideas, which are eternal, immutable, and universally obligatory. For since it is confessed, that such an alteration as that above mentioned, in the temper and circumstances of mankind, would entirely alter our duties and obligations, it is necessary upon the common system, *that the sense of virtue is derived from reason,* to show the change which this must produce in the relations and ideas. But it is evident, that the only cause why the extensive generosity of man, and the perfect abundance of everything, would destroy the very idea of justice, is, because they render it useless; and that, on the other hand, his confined benevolence, and his necessitous condition, give rise to that virtue, only by making it requisite to the public interest, and to that of every individual. It was therefore a concern for our own and the public interest which made us establish the laws of justice; and nothing can be more certain, than that it is not any relation of ideas which gives us this concern, but our impressions and sentiments, without which everything in nature is perfectly indifferent to us, and can never in the least affect us. The sense of justice, therefore, is not founded on our ideas, but on our impressions.

*Thirdly,* We may further confirm the foregoing proposition, *that those impressions, which give rise to this sense of justice, are not natural to the mind of man, but arise from artifice and human conventions.* For, since any considerable alteration of temper and circumstances destroys equally justice and injustice; and since such an alteration has an effect only by changing our own and the public interest, it follows that the first establishment of the rules of justice depends on these different interests. But if men pursued the public interest naturally, and with a hearty affection, they would have never dreamed of restraining each other by these rules; and if they pursued their own interest, without any precaution, they would run headlong into every kind of injustice and violence. These rules, therefore, are artificial, and seek their end in an oblique and indirect manner; nor is the interest which gives rise to them of a kind that could be pursued by the natural and inartificial passions of men.

To make this more evident, consider, that, though the rules of justice are established merely by interest, their connection with interest is somewhat singular, and is different from what may be observed on other occasions. A single act of justice is frequently contrary to *public interest;* and were it to stand alone, without being followed by other acts, may, in itself, be very prejudicial to society. When a man of merit, of a beneficent disposition, restores a great fortune to a miser, or a seditious bigot, he has acted justly and laudably; but the public is a real sufferer. Nor is every single act of justice, considered apart, more conducive to private interest than to public; and it is easily conceived how a man may impoverish himself by a single instance of integrity, and have reason to wish, that, with regard to that single act, the laws of justice were for a moment suspended in the universe. But, however single acts of justice may be contrary, either to public or private interest, it is certain that the whole plan or scheme is highly conducive, or indeed absolutely requisite, both to the support of society, and the well-being of every individual. It is impossible to separate the good from the ill. Property must be stable, and must be fixed by general rules. Though in one instance the public be a sufferer, this momentary ill is amply compensated by the steady prosecution of the rule, and by the peace and order which it establishes in society. And even every individual person must find himself a gainer on balancing the account; since, without justice, society must immediately dissolve, and every one must fall into that savage and solitary condition, which is infinitely worse than the worst situation that can possibly be supposed in society. When, therefore, men have had experience enough to observe, that, whatever may be the consequence of any single act of justice, performed by a single person, yet the whole system of actions concurred in by the whole society, is infinitely advantageous to the whole, and to every part, it is not long before justice and property take place. Every member of society is sensible of this interest: every one expresses this sense to his fellows, along with the resolution he has taken of squaring his actions by it, on condition that others will do the same. No more is requisite to induce any one of them to perform an act of justice, who has the first opportunity. This becomes an example to others; and thus justice establishes itself by a kind of convention or agreement, that is, by a sense of interest, supposed to be common to all, and where every single act is performed in expectation that others are

to perform the like. Without such a convention, no one would ever have dreamed that there was such a virtue as justice, or have been induced to conform his actions to it. Taking any single act, my justice may be pernicious in every respect; and it is only upon the supposition that others are to imitate my example, that I can be induced to embrace that virtue; since nothing but this combination can render justice advantageous, or afford me any motives to conform myself to its rules.

We come now to the *second* question we proposed, viz. *Why we annex the idea of virtue to justice, and of vice to injustice.* This question will not detain us long after the principles which we have already established. All we can say of it at present will be despatched in a few words: and for further satisfaction, the reader must wait till we come to the *third* part of this book. The *natural* obligation to justice, viz. interest, has been fully explained; but as to the *moral* obligation, or the sentiment of right and wrong, it will first be requisite to examine the natural virtues, before we can give a full and satisfactory account of it.

After men have found by experience, that their selfishness and confined generosity, acting at their liberty, totally incapacitate them for society; and at the same time have observed that society is necessary to the satisfaction of those very passions, they are naturally induced to lay themselves under the restraint of such rules, as may render their commerce more safe and commodious. To the imposition, then, and observance of these rules, both in general, and in every particular instance, they are at first induced only by a regard to interest; and this motive, on the first formation of society, is sufficiently strong and forcible. But when society has become numerous, and has increased to a tribe or nation, this interest is more remote; nor do men so readily perceive that disorder and confusion follow upon every breach of these rules, as in a more narrow and contracted society. But though, in our own actions, we may frequently lose sight of that interest which we have in maintaining order, and may follow a lesser and more present interest, we never fail to observe the prejudice we receive, either mediately or immediately, from the injustice of others; as not being in that case either blinded by passion, or biassed by any contrary temptation. Nay, when the injustice is so distant from us as no way to affect our interest, it still displeases us; because we consider it as prejudicial to human society, and pernicious to every one that approaches the person guilty of it. We partake of their uneasiness by *sympathy;* and as everything which gives uneasiness in human actions, upon the general survey, is called Vice, and whatever produces satisfaction, in the same manner, is denominated Virtue, this is the reason why the sense of moral good and evil follows upon justice and injustice. And though this sense, in the present case, be derived only from contemplating the actions of others, yet we fail not to extend it even to our own actions. The *general rule* reaches beyond those instances from which it arose; while, at the same time, we naturally *sympathise* with others in the sentiments they entertain of us.

Though this progress of the sentiments be *natural,* and even necessary, it is certain that it is here forwarded by the artifice of politicians, who, in order to govern men more easily, and preserve peace in human society, have endeavoured to produce an esteem for justice, and an abhorrence of injustice. This, no doubt, must have its effect; but nothing can be more evident than that the matter has been carried too far by certain writers on morals, who seem to have employed their utmost efforts to extirpate all sense of virtue from among mankind. Any artifice of politicians may assist nature in the producing of those sentiments, which she suggests to us, and may even, on some occasions, produce alone an approbation or esteem for any particular action; but it is impossible it should be the sole cause of the distinction we make betwixt vice and virtue. For if nature did not aid us in this particular, it would be in vain for politicians to talk of *honourable* or *dishonourable, praiseworthy* or *blamable.* These words would be perfectly unintelligible, and would no more have any idea annexed to them, than if they were of a tongue perfectly unknown to us. The

utmost politicians can perform, is to extend the natural sentiments beyond their original bounds; but still nature must furnish the materials, and give us some notion of moral distinctions.

As public praise and blame increase our esteem for justice, so private education and instruction contribute to the same effect. For as parents easily observe, that a man is the more useful, both to himself and others, the greater degree of probity and honour he is endowed with, and that those principles have greater force when custom and education assist interest and reflection: for these reasons they are induced to inculcate on their children, from their earliest infancy, the principles of probity, and teach them to regard the observance of those rules by which society is maintained, as worthy and honourable, and their violation as base and infamous. By this means the sentiments of honour may take root in their tender minds, and acquire such firmness and solidity, that they may fall little short of those principles which are the most essential to our natures, and the most deeply radicated in our internal constitution.

What further contributes to increase their solidity, is the interest of our reputation, after the opinion, *that a merit or demerit attends justice or injustice,* is once firmly established among mankind. There is nothing which touches us more nearly than our reputation, and nothing on which our reputation more depends than our conduct with relation to the property of others. For this reason, every one who has any regard to his character, or who intends to live on good terms with mankind, must fix an inviolable law to himself, never, by any temptation, to be induced to violate those principles which are essential to a man of probity and honour.

I shall make only one observation before I leave this subject, viz. that, though I assert that, in the *state of nature,* or that imaginary state which preceded society, there be neither justice nor injustice, yet I assert not that it was allowable, in such a state, to violate the property of others. I only maintain, that there was no such thing as property; and consequently could be no such thing as justice or injustice. I shall have occasion to make a similar reflection with regard to *promises,* when I come to treat of them; and I hope this reflection, when duly weighed, will suffice to remove all odium from the foregoing opinions, with regard to justice and injustice.

### *Section III*

#### OF THE RULES WHICH DETERMINE PROPERTY

Though the establishment of the rule, concerning the stability of possession, be not only useful, but even absolutely necessary to human society, it can never serve to any purpose, while it remains in such general terms. Some method must be shown, by which we may distinguish what particular goods are to be assigned to each particular person, while the rest of mankind are excluded from their possession and enjoyment. Our next business, then, must be to discover the reasons which modify this general rule, and fit it to the common use and practice of the world.

It is obvious that those reasons are not derived from any utility or advantage, which either the *particular* person or the public may reap from his enjoyment of any *particular* goods, beyond what would result from the possession of them by any other person. It were better, no doubt, that every one were possessed of what is most suitable to him, and proper for his use: But besides, that this relation of fitness may be common to several at once, it is liable to so many controversies, and men are so partial and passionate in judging of these controversies, that such a loose and uncertain rule would be absolutely incompatible with the peace of human society. The convention concerning the stability of possession is entered into, in order to cut off all occasions of discord and contention; and this end would never be attained were we allowed to apply this rule differently in every particular case, according to every particular utility which might be discovered in such an application. Justice, in her decisions, never regards the fitness or unfitness of objects to particular persons, but conducts herself by more extensive views. Whether a man be generous, or a miser, he is equally well received by her, and obtains, with the same facility, a decision in his favour, even for what is entirely useless to him.

It follows, therefore, that the general rule, *that possession must be stable,* is not applied by particular judgments, but by other general rules, which must extend to the whole society, and be inflexible either by spite or favour. To illustrate this, I propose the following instance. I first consider men in their savage and solitary condition; and suppose that, being sensible of the misery of that state, and foreseeing the advantages that would result from society, they seek each other's company, and make an offer of mutual protection and assistance. I also suppose that they are endowed with such sagacity as immediately to perceive that the chief impediment to this project of society and partnership lies in the avidity and selfishness of their natural temper; to remedy which, they enter into a convention for the stability of possession, and for mutual restraint and forbearance. I am sensible that this method of proceeding is not altogether natural; but, besides that, I here only suppose those reflections to be formed at once, which, in fact, arise insensibly and by degrees; besides this, I say, it is very possible that several persons, being by different accidents separated from the societies to which they formerly belonged, may be obliged to form a new society among themselves; in which case they are entirely in the situation above mentioned.

It is evident, then, that their first difficulty in this situation, after the general convention for the establishment of society, and for the constancy of possession, is, how to separate their possessions, and assign to each his particular portion, which he must for the future unalterably enjoy. This difficulty will not detain them long; but it must immediately occur to them, as the most natural expedient, that every one continue to enjoy what he is at present master of, and that property or constant possession be conjoined to the immediate possession. Such is the effect of custom, that it not only reconciles us to anything we have long enjoyed, but even gives us an affection for it, and makes us prefer it to other objects, which may be more valuable, but are less known to us. What has long lain under our eye, and has often been employed to our advantage, *that* we are always the most unwilling to part with; but can easily live without possessions which we never have enjoyed, and are not accustomed to. It is evident, therefore, that men would easily acquiesce in this expedient, *that every one continue to enjoy what he is at present possessed of:* and this is the reason why they would so naturally agree in preferring it.

But we may observe, that, though the rule of the assignment of property to the present possessor be natural, and by that means useful, yet its utility extends not beyond the first formation of society; nor would anything be more pernicious than the constant observance of it; by which restitution would be excluded, and every injustice would be authorised and rewarded. We must, therefore, seek for some other circumstance, that may give rise to property after society is once established; and of this kind I find four most considerable, viz. Occupation, Prescription, Accession, and Succession. We shall briefly examine each of these, beginning with *occupation.*

The possession of all external goods is changeable and uncertain; which is one of the most considerable impediments to the establishment of society, and is the reason why, by universal agreement, express or tacit, men restrain themselves by what we now call the rules of justice and equity. The misery of the condition which precedes this restraint is the cause why we submit to that remedy as quickly as possible; and this affords us an easy reason why we annex the idea of property to the first possession, or to *occupation.* Men are unwilling to leave property in suspense, even for the shortest time, or open the least door to violence and disorder. To which we may add, that the first possession always engages the attention most; and did we neglect it, there would be no colour of reason for assigning property to any succeeding possession.

There remains nothing but to determine exactly what is meant by possession; and this is not so easy as may at first sight be imagined. We are said to be in possession of anything, not only when we immediately touch it, but also when we are so situated with respect to it, as to have it in our power to use it; and may move, alter, or destroy it, according to our present pleasure or advantage. This relation, then, is a species of cause and effect; and as property is nothing but a stable possession, derived from the rules of justice, or the conventions of men, it is to be considered as the same species of relation. But here we may observe, that, as the power of using any object becomes more or less certain, according as the interruptions we may meet with are more or less probable; and as this probability may increase by insensible degrees, it is in many cases impossible to determine when possession begins or ends; nor is there any certain standard by which we can decide such controversies. A wild boar that falls into our snares, is deemed to be in our possession if it be impossible for him to escape. But what do we mean by impossible? How do we separate this impossibility from an improbability? And how distinguish that exactly from a probability? Mark the precise limits of the one and the other, and show the standard, by which we may decide all disputes that may arise, and, as we find by experience, frequently do arise upon this subject.

But such disputes may not only arise concerning the real existence of property and possession, but also concerning their extent; and these disputes are often susceptible of no decision, or can be decided by no other faculty than the imagination. A person who lands on the shore of a small island that is desert and uncultivated, is deemed its possessor from the very first moment, and acquires the property of the whole; because the object is there bounded and circumscribed in the fancy, and at the same time is proportioned to the new possessor. The same person landing on a desert island as large as Great Britain, extends his property no further than his immediate possession; though a numerous colony are esteemed the proprietors of the whole from the instant of their debarkment.

But if it often happens that the title of first possession becomes obscure through time, and that it is impossible to determine many controversies which may arise concerning it; in that case, long possession or *prescription* naturally takes place, and gives a person a sufficient property in anything he enjoys. The nature of human society admits not of any great accuracy; nor can we always remount to the first origin of things, in order to determine their present condition. Any considerable space of time sets objects at such a distance that they seem in a manner to lose their reality, and have as little influence on the mind as if they never had been in being. A man's title that is clear and certain at present, will seem obscure and doubtful fifty years hence, even though the facts on which it is founded should be proved with the greatest evidence and certainty. The same facts have not the same influence after so long an interval of time. And this may be received as a convincing argument for our preceding doctrine with regard to property and justice. Possession during a long tract of time conveys a title to any object. But as it is certain that, however everything be produced in time, there is nothing real that is produced by time, it follows, that property being produced by time, is not anything real in the objects, but is the offspring of the sentiments, on which alone time is found to have any influence.

We acquire the property of objects by *accession,* when they are connected in an intimate manner with objects that are already our property, and at the same time are inferior to them. Thus, the fruits of our garden, the offspring of our cattle, and the work of our slaves, are all of them esteemed our property, even before possession. Where objects are connected together in the imagination, they are apt to be put on the same footing, and are commonly supposed to be endowed with the same qualities. We readily pass from one to the other, and make no difference in our judgments concerning them, especially if the latter be inferior to the former.

The right of *succession* is a very natural one, from the presumed consent of the parent or near relation, and from the general interest of mankind, which requires that men's possessions should pass to those who are dearest to them, in order to render them more industrious and frugal. Perhaps these causes are seconded by the influence of *relation,* or the association of ideas, by which we are naturally directed to con-

sider the son after the parent's decease, and ascribe to him a title to his father's possessions. Those goods must become the property of somebody: but *of whom* is the question. Here it is evident the person's children naturally present themselves to the mind; and being already connected to those possessions by means of their deceased parent, we are apt to connect them still further by the relation of property. Of this there are many parallel instances.

## Section IV

### OF THE TRANSFERENCE OF PROPERTY BY CONSENT

However useful, or even necessary, the stability of possession may be to human society, it is attended with very considerable inconveniences. The relation of fitness or suitableness ought never to enter into consideration, in distributing the properties of mankind; but we must govern ourselves by rules which are more general in their application, and more free from doubt and uncertainty. Of this kind is *present* possession upon the first establishment of society; and afterwards *occupation, prescription, accession, and succession.* As these depend very much on chance, they must frequently prove contradictory both to men's wants and desires; and persons and possessions must often be very ill adjusted. This is a grand inconvenience, which calls for a remedy. To apply one directly, and allow every man to seize by violence what he judges to be fit for him, would destroy society; and therefore the rules of justice seek some medium betwixt a rigid stability and this changeable and uncertain adjustment. But there is no medium better than that obvious one, that possession and property should always be stable, except when the proprietor consents to bestow them on some other person. This rule can have no ill consequence in occasioning wars and dissensions, since the proprietor's consent, who alone is concerned, is taken along in the alienation; and it may serve to many good purposes in adjusting property to persons. Different parts of the earth produce different commodities; and not only so, but different men both are by nature fitted for different employments, and attain to greater perfection in any one, when they confine themselves to it alone. All this requires a mutual exchange and commerce; for which reason the translation of property by consent is founded on a law of nature, as well as its stability without such a consent.

So far is determined by a plain utility and interest. But perhaps it is from more trivial reasons, that *delivery,* or a sensible transference of the object is commonly required by civil laws, and also by the laws of nature, according to most authors, as a requisite circumstance in the translation of property. The property of an object, when taken for something real, without any reference to morality, or the sentiments of the mind, is a quality perfectly insensible, and even inconceivable; nor can we form any distinct notion, either of its stability or translation. This imperfection of our ideas is less sensibly felt with regard to its stability, as it engages less our attention, and is easily passed over by the mind, without any scrupulous examination. But as the translation of property from one person to another is a more remarkable event, the defect of our ideas becomes more sensible on that occasion and obliges us to turn ourselves on every side in search of some remedy. Now, as nothing more enlivens any idea than a present impression, and a relation betwixt that impression and the idea; it is natural for us to seek some false light from this quarter. In order to aid the imagination in conceiving the transference of property, we take the sensible object, and actually transfer its possession to the person on whom we would bestow the property. The supposed resemblance of the actions, and the presence of this sensible delivery, deceive the mind, and make it fancy that it conceives the mysterious transition of the property. And that this explication of the matter is just, appears hence, that men have invented a *symbolical* delivery, to satisfy the fancy where the real one is impracticable. Thus the giving the keys of a granary is understood to be the delivery of the corn contained in it; the giving of stone and earth represents the delivery of a manor. This is a kind of superstitious practice in civil laws, and in the laws of nature, resembling the *Roman Catholic* superstition in religion. As the *Roman Catholics* represent the inconceivable mysteries of the *Christian* religion, and render them more present to the mind, by a taper, or habit, or grimace, which is supposed to resemble them; so lawyers and moralists have run into like inventions for the some reason, and have endeavoured by those means to satisfy themselves concerning the transference of property by consent.

## *Section V*

### OF THE OBLIGATION OF PROMISES

That the rule of morality, which enjoins the performance of promises, is not *natural,* will sufficiently appear from these two propositions, which I proceed to prove, viz. *that a promise would not be intelligible before human conventions had established it;* and *that even if it were intelligible, it would not be attended with any moral obligation.*

I say, *first,* that a promise is not intelligible naturally, nor antecedent to human conventions; and that a man, unacquainted with society, could never enter into any engagements with another, even though they could perceive each other's thoughts by intuition. If promises be natural and intelligible, there must be some act of the mind attending these words, *I promise;* and on this act of the mind must the obligation depend. Let us therefore run over all the faculties of the soul, and see which of them is exerted in our promises.

The act of the mind, expressed by a promise, is not a *resolution* to perform anything; for that alone never imposes any obligation. Nor is it a *desire* of such a performance; for we may bind ourselves without such a desire, or even with an aversion, declared and avowed. Neither is it the *willing* of that action which we promise to perform; for a promise always regards some future time, and the will has an influence only on present actions. It follows, therefore, that since the act of the mind, which enters into a promise, and produces its obligation, is neither the resolving, desiring, nor willing any particular performance, it must necessarily be the *willing* of that *obligation* which arises from the promise. Nor is this only a conclusion of philosophy, but is entirely conformable to our common ways of thinking and of expressing ourselves, when we say that we are bound by our own consent, and that the obligation arises from our mere will and pleasure. The only question then is, whether there be not a manifest absurdity in supposing this act of the mind, and such an absurdity as no man could fall into, whose ideas are not confounded with prejudice and the fallacious use of language.

All morality depends upon our sentiments; and when any action or quality of the mind pleases us *after a certain manner,* we say it is virtuous; and when the neglect or non-performance of it displeases us *after a like manner,* we say that we lie under an obligation to perform it. A change of the obligation supposes a change of the sentiment; and a creation of a new obligation supposes some new sentiment to arise. But it is certain we can naturally no more change our own sentiments than the motions of the heavens; nor by a single act of our will, that is, by a promise, render any action agreeable or disagreeable, moral or immoral, which, without that act, would have produced contrary impressions, or have been endowed with different qualities. It would be absurd, therefore, to will any new obligation, that is, any new sentiment of pain or pleasure; nor is it possible that men could naturally fall into so gross an absurdity. A promise, therefore, is *naturally* something altogether unintelligible, nor is there any act of the mind belonging to it.

But, *secondly,* if there was any act of the mind belonging to it, it could not *naturally* produce any obligation. This appears evidently from the foregoing reasoning. A promise creates a new obligation. A new obligation supposes new sentiments to arise. The will never creates new sentiments. There could not naturally, therefore, arise any obligation from a promise, even supposing the mind could fall into the absurdity of willing that obligation.

The same truth may be proved still more evidently by that reasoning which proved justice in general to be an artificial virtue. No action can be required of us as our duty, unless there be implanted in human nature some actuating passion or motive capable of producing the action. This motive cannot be the sense of duty. A sense of duty supposes an antecedent obligation; and where an action is not required by any natural passion, it cannot be required by any natural obligation; since it may be omitted without proving any defect or imperfection in the mind and temper, and consequently without any vice. Now, it is evident we have no motive leading us to the performance of promises, distinct from a sense of duty. If we thought that promises had no moral obligation, we never should feel any inclination to observe them. This is not the case with the natural virtues. Though there was no obligation to relieve the miserable, our humanity would lead us to it; and when we omit that duty, the immorality of the omission arises from its being a proof that we want the natural sentiments of humanity. A father knows it to be his duty to take care of his children, but he has also a natural inclination to it. And if no human creature had that inclination, no one could lie under any such obligation. But as there is naturally no inclination to observe promises distinct from a sense of their obligation, it follows that fidelity is no natural virtue, and that promises have no force antecedent to human conventions.

If any one dissent from this, he must give a regular proof of these two propositions, viz. *that there is a peculiar act of the mind annexed to promises; and that consequent to this act of the mind, there arises an inclination to perform, distinct from a sense of duty.* I presume that it is impossible to prove either of these two points; and therefore I venture to conclude, that promises are human inventions, founded on the necessities and interests of society.

In order to discover these necessities and interests, we must consider the same qualities of human nature which we have already found to give rise to the preceding laws of society. Men being naturally selfish, or endowed only with a confined generosity, they are not easily induced to perform any action for the interest of strangers, except with a view to some reciprocal advantage, which they had no hope of obtaining but by such a performance. Now, as it frequently happens that these mutual performances cannot be finished at the same instant, it is necessary that one party be contented to remain in uncertainty, and depend upon the gratitude of the other for a return of kindness. But so much corruption is there among men, that, generally speaking, this becomes but a slender security; and as the benefactor is here supposed to bestow his favours with a view to self-interest, this both takes off from the obligation, and sets an example of selfishness, which is the true mother of ingratitude. Were we, therefore, to follow the natural course of our passions and inclinations, we should perform but few actions for the advantage of others from disinterested views, because we are naturally very limited in our kindness and affection; and we should perform as few of that kind out of regard to interest, because we cannot depend upon their gratitude. Here, then, is the mutual commerce of good offices in a manner lost among mankind, and every one reduced to his own skill and industry for his well-being and subsistence. The invention of the law of nature, concerning the *stability* of possession, has already rendered men tolerable to each other; that of the *transference* of property and possession by consent has begun to render them mutually advantageous; but still these laws of nature, however strictly observed, are not sufficient to render them so serviceable to each other as by nature they are fitted to become. Though possession be *stable,* men may often reap but small advantage from it, while they are possessed of a greater quantity of any species of goods than they have occasion for, and at the same time suffer by the want of others. The *transference* of property, which is the proper remedy for this inconvenience, cannot remedy it entirely; because it can only take place with regard to such objects as are *present* and *individual,* but not to such as are *absent* or *general.* One cannot transfer the property of a particular house, twenty leagues distant, because the consent cannot be attended with delivery, which is a requisite circumstance. Neither can one transfer the property of ten bushels of corn, or five hogsheads of wine, by the mere expression and consent, because these are only general terms, and have no distinct relation to any particular heap of corn or barrels of wine. Besides, the commerce of mankind is not confined to the barter of commodities, but may extend to services and actions, which we may exchange to our mutual interest and advantage. Your corn is ripe to-day; mine will

be so to-morrow. It is profitable for us both that I should labour with you to-day, and that you should aid me to-morrow. I have no kindness for you, and you know you have as little for me. I will not, therefore, take any pains upon your account; and should I labour with you upon my own account, in expectation of a return, I know I should be disappointed, and that I should in vain depend upon your gratitude. Here, then, I leave you to labour alone: you treat me in the same manner. The seasons change; and both of us lose our harvests for want of mutual confidence and security.

All this is the effect of the natural and inherent principles and passions of human nature; and as these passions and principles are unalterable, it may be thought that our conduct, which depends on them, must be so too, and that it would be in vain, either for moralists or politicians, to tamper with us, or attempt to change the usual course of our actions, with a view to public interest. And, indeed, did the success of their designs depend upon their success in correcting the selfishness and ingratitude of men, they would never make any progress, unless aided by Omnipotence, which is alone able to new-mould the human mind, and change its character in such fundamental articles. All they can pretend to is, to give a new direction to those natural passions, and teach us that we can better satisfy our appetites in an oblique and artificial manner, than by their headlong and impetuous motion. Hence I learn to do a service to another, without bearing him any real kindness; because I foresee that he will return my service, in expectation of another of the same kind, and in order to maintain the same correspondence of good offices with me or with others. And accordingly, after I have served him, and he is in possession of the advantage arising from my action, he is induced to perform his part, as foreseeing the consequences of his refusal.

But though this self-interested commerce of men begins to take place, and to predominate in society, it does not entirely abolish the more generous and noble intercourse of friendship and good offices. I may still do services to such persons as I love, and am more particularly acquainted with, without any prospect of advantage; and they may make me a return in the same manner, without any view but that of recompensing my past services. In order, therefore, to distinguish those two different sorts of commerce, the interested and the disinterested, there is a *certain form of word* invented for the former, by which we bind ourselves to the performance of any action. This form of words constitutes what we call a *promise,* which is the sanction of the interested commerce of mankind. When a man says *he promises anything,* he in effect expresses a *resolution* of performing it; and along with that, by making use of this *form of words,* subjects himself to the penalty of never being trusted again in case of failure. A resolution is the natural act of the mind, which promises express; but were there no more than a resolution in the case, promises would only declare our former motives, and would not create any new motive or obligation. They are the conventions of men, which create a new motive, when experience has taught us that human affairs would be conducted much more for mutual advantage, were there certain *symbols* or *signs* instituted, by which we might give each other security of our conduct in any particular incident. After these signs are instituted, whoever uses them is immediately bound by his interest to execute his engagements, and must never expect to be trusted any more if he refuse to perform what he promised.

Nor is that knowledge, which is requisite to make mankind sensible of this interest in the *institution* and *observance* of promises, to be esteemed superior to the capacity of human nature, however savage and uncultivated. There needs but a very little practice of the world to make us perceive all these consequences and advantages. The shortest experience of society discovers them to every mortal; and when each individual perceives the same sense of interest in all his fellows, he immediately performs his part of any contract, as being assured that they will not be wanting in theirs. All of them, by concert, enter into a scheme of actions, calculated for common benefit, and agree to be true to their word; nor is there anything requisite to form this concert or convention, but that every one have a sense of interest in the faithful fulfilling of engagements, and express that

sense to other members of the society. This immediately causes that interest to operate upon them; and interest is the *first* obligation to the performance of promises.

Afterwards a sentiment of morals concurs with interest, and becomes a new obligation upon mankind. This sentiment of morality, in the performance of promises, arises from the same principles as that in the abstinence from the property of others. *Public interest, education,* and *the artifices of politicians,* have the same effect in both cases. The difficulties that occur to us in supposing a moral obligation to attend promises, we either surmount or elude. For instance, the expression of a resolution is not commonly supposed to be obligatory; and we cannot readily conceive how the making use of a certain form of words should be able to cause any material difference. Here, therefore, we *feign* a new act of the mind, which we call the *willing* an obligation; and on this we suppose the morality to depend. But we have proved already that there is no such act of the mind, and consequently, that promises impose no natural obligation.

To confirm this, we may subjoin some other reflections concerning that will, which is supposed to enter into a promise, and to cause its obligation. It is evident that the will alone is never supposed to cause the obligation, but must be expressed by words or signs, in order to impose a tie upon any man. The expression being once brought in as subservient to the will, soon becomes the principal part of the promise; nor will a man be less bound by his word, though he secretly give a different direction to his intention, and withhold himself both from a resolution, and from willing an obligation. But though the expression makes on most occasions the whole of the promise, yet it does not always so; and one who should make use of any expression of which he knows not the meaning, and which he uses without any intention of binding himself, would not certainly be bound by it. Nay, though he knows its meaning, yet if he uses it in jest only, and with such signs as show evidently he has no serious intention of binding himself, he would not lie under any obligation of performance; but it is necessary that the words be a perfect expression of the will, without any contrary signs. Nay, even this we must not carry so far as to imagine, that one, whom, by our quickness of understanding, we conjecture, from certain signs, to have an intention of deceiving us, is not bound by his expression or verbal promise, if we accept of it; but must limit this conclusion to those cases where the signs are of a different kind from those of deceit. All these contradictions are easily accounted for, if the obligation of promises be merely a human invention for the convenience of society; but will never be explained, if it be something *real* and *natural,* arising from any action of the mind or body.

I shall further observe, that, since every new promise imposes a new obligation of morality on the person who promises, and since this new obligation arises from his will; it is one of the most mysterious and incomprehensible operations that can possibly be imagined, and may even be compared to *transubstantiation* or *holy orders,* where a certain form of words, along with a certain intention, changes entirely the nature of an external object, and even of a human creature. But though these mysteries be so far alike, it is very remarkable that they differ widely in other particulars, and that this difference may be regarded as a strong proof of the difference of their origins. As the obligation of promises is an invention for the interest of society, it is warped into as many different forms as that interest requires, and even runs into direct contradictions, rather than lose sight of its object. But as those other monstrous doctrines are mere priestly inventions, and have no public interest in view, they are less disturbed in their progress by new obtacles; and it must be owned, that, after the first absurdity, they follow more directly the current of reason and good sense. Theologians clearly perceived that the external form of words, being mere sound, require an intention to make them have any efficacy; and that this intention being once considered as a requisite circumstance, its absence must equally prevent the effect, whether avowed or concealed, whether sincere or deceitful. Accordingly, they have commonly determined, that the intention of the priest makes the sacrament, and that when he secretly withdraws his intention, he is highly criminal in himself; but still destroys the baptism, or communion, or holy orders. The terrible consequences of this doctrine were not able to hinder its taking place; as the inconvenience of a similar doctrine, with regard to promises, have prevented that doctrine from establishing itself. Men are always more concerned about the present life than the future; and are apt to think the smallest evil which regards the former more important than the greatest which regards the latter.

We may draw the same conclusion concerning the origin of promises, from the *force* which is supposed to invalidate all contracts, and to free us from their obligation. Such a principle is a proof that promises have no natural obligation, and are mere artificial contrivances for the convenience and advantage of society. If we consider aright of the matter, force is not essentially different from any other motive of hope or fear, which may induce us to engage our word, and lay ourselves under any obligation. A man, dangerously wounded, who promises a competent sum to a surgeon to cure him, would certainly be bound to performance; though the case be not so much different from that of one who promises a sum to a robber, as to produce so great a difference in our sentiments of morality, if these sentiments were not built entirely on public interest and convenience.

## *Section VI*

### SOME FURTHER REFLECTIONS CONCERNING JUSTICE AND INJUSTICE

We have now run over the three fundamental laws of nature, *that of the stability of possession, of its transference by consent,* and *of the performance of promises.* It is on the strict observance of those three laws that the peace and security of human society entirely depend; nor is there any possibility of establishing a good correspondence among men, where these are neglected. Society is absolutely necessary for the well-being of men; and these are as necessary to the support of society. Whatever restraint they may impose on the passions of men, they are the real offspring of those passions, and are only a more artful and more refined way of satisfying them. Nothing is more vigilant and inventive than our passions; and nothing is more obvious than the convention for the observance of these rules. Nature has, therefore, trusted this affair entirely to the conduct of men, and has not placed in the mind any peculiar original principles, to determine us to a set of actions, into which the other principles of our frame and constitution were sufficient to lead us. And to convince us the more fully of this truth, we may here stop a moment, and, from a review of the preceding reasonings, may draw some new arguments, to prove that those laws, however necessary, are entirely artificial, and of human invention; and consequently, that justice is an artificial, and not a natural virtue.

I. The first argument I shall make use of is derived from the vulgar definition of justice. Justice is commonly defined to be *a constant and perpetual will of giving every one his due.* In this definition it is supposed that there are such things as right and property, independent of justice, and antecedent to it; and that they would have subsisted, though men had never dreamt of practising such a virtue. I have already observed, in a cursory manner, the fallacy of this opinion, and shall here continue to open up, a little more distinctly, my sentiments on that subject.

I shall begin with observing that this quality, which we call *property,* is like many of the imaginary qualities of the *Peripatetic* philosophy, and vanishes upon a more accurate inspection into the subject, when considered apart from our moral sentiments. It is evident property does not consist in any of the sensible qualities of the object. For these may continue invariably the same, while the property changes. Property, therefore, must consist in some relation of the object. But it is not in its relation with regard to other external and inanimate objects. For these may also continue invariably the same, while the property changes. This quality, therefore, consists in the relations of objects to intelligent and rational beings. But it is not the external and corporeal relation which forms the essence of property. For that relation may be the same betwixt inanimate objects, or with regard to brute creatures; though in those cases it forms no property. It is therefore in some internal relation that the property consists; that is, in some influence which the external relations of the object have on the mind and actions. Thus the external relation which we call *occupation* or first possession, is not of itself imagined to be the property of the object, but only to cause its property. Now, it is evident this external relation causes nothing in external objects, and has only an influence on the mind, by giving us a sense of duty in abstaining from that object, and in restoring it to the first possessor. These actions are properly what we call *justice;* and consequently it is on that virtue that the nature of property depends, and not the virtue on the property.

If any one, therefore, would assert that justice is a natural virtue, and injustice a natural vice, he must assert that abstracting from the notions of *property* and *right* and *obligation* a certain conduct and train of actions, in certain external relations of objects, has naturally a moral beauty or deformity, and causes an original pleasure or uneasiness. Thus the restoring a man's goods to him is considered as virtuous, not because nature has annexed a certain sentiment of pleasure to such a conduct with regard to the property of others, but because she has annexed that sentiment to such a conduct, with regard to those external objects of which others have had the first or long possession, or which they have received by the consent of those who have had first or long possession. If nature has given us no such sentiment, there is not naturally, nor antecedent to human conventions, any such thing as property. Now, though it seems sufficiently evident, in this dry and accurate consideration of the present subject, that nature has annexed no pleasure or sentiment of approbation to such a conduct, yet, that I may leave as little room for doubt as possible, I shall subjoin a few more arguments to confirm my opinion.

*First,* If nature had given us a pleasure of this kind, it would have been as evident and discernible as on every other occasion; nor should we have found any difficulty to perceive that the consideration of such actions, in such a situation, gives a certain pleasure and sentiment of approbation. We should not have been obliged to have recourse to notions of property in the definition of justice, and at the same time make use of the notions of justice in the definition of property. This deceitful method of reasoning is a plain proof that there are contained in the subject some obscurities and difficulties which we are not able to surmount, and which we desire to evade by this artifice.

*Secondly,* Those rules by which properties, rights, and obligations are determined, have in them no marks of a natural origin, but many of artifice and contrivance. They are too numerous to have proceeded from nature; they are changeable by human laws; and have all of them a direct and evident tendency to public good, and the support of civil society. This last circumstance is remarkable upon two accounts. *First,* Because, though the cause of the establishment of these laws had been a *regard* for the public good, as much as the public good is their natural tendency, they would still have been artificial, as being purposely contrived and directed to a certain end. *Secondly,* Because, if men had been endowed with such a strong regard for public good, they would never have restrained themselves by these rules; so that the laws of justice arise from natural principles, in a manner still more oblique and artificial. It is self-love which is their real origin; and as the self-love of one person is naturally contrary to that of another, these several interested passions are obliged to adjust themselves after such a manner as to concur in some system of conduct and behaviour. This system, therefore, comprehending the interest of each individual, is of course advantageous to the public, though it be not intended for that purpose by the inventors.

II. In the *second* place, we may observe that all kinds of vice and virtue run insensibly into each other, and may approach by such imperceptible degrees as will make it very difficult, if not absolutely impossible, to determine when the one ends, and the other begins; and from this observation we may derive a new argument for the foregoing principle. For, whatever may be the case with regard to all kinds of vice and virtue, it is certain that rights, and obligations, and property, admit of no such insensible gradation, but that a man either has a full and perfect property, or none at all; and is either entirely obliged to perform any action, or lies under no manner of obligation. However civil laws may talk of a perfect *dominion,* and of an imperfect, it is easy to observe, that this arises from a fiction, which has no foundation in reason, and can never enter into our notions of natural justice and equity. A man that hires a horse, though but for a day, has as full a right to make use of it for that time, as he whom we call its proprietor has to make use of it any other day; and it is evident that, however the use may be bounded in time or degree, the right itself is not susceptible of any such gradation, but is absolute and entire, so far as it extends. Accordingly, we may observe that this right both arises and perishes in an instant; and that a man entirely acquires the property of any object by occupation, or the consent of the proprietor; and loses it by his own consent, without any of that insensible gradation which is remarkable in other qualities and relations. Since, therefore, this is the case with regard to property, and rights, and obligations, I ask, how it stands with regard to justice and injustice? After whatever manner you answer this question, you run into inextricable difficulties. If you reply, that justice and injustice admit of degree, and run insensibly into each other, you expressly contradict the foregoing position, that obligation and property are not susceptible of such a gradation. These depend entirely upon justice and injustice, and follow them in all their variations. Where the justice is entire, the property is also entire: where the justice is imperfect, the property must also be imperfect. And *vice versa,* if the property admit of no such variations, they must also be incompatible with justice. If you assent, therefore, to this last proposition, and assert that justice and injustice are not susceptible of degrees, you in effect assert that they are not *naturally* either vicious or virtuous; since vice and virtue, moral good and evil, and indeed all *natural* qualities, run insensibly into each other, and are on many occasions undistinguishable.

And here it may be worth while to observe, that though abstract reasoning and the general maxims of philosophy and law establish this position, *that property, and right, and obligation, admit not of degrees,* yet, in our common and negligent way of thinking, we find great difficulty to entertain that opinion, and do even *secretly* embrace the contrary principle. An object must either be in the possession of one person or another. An action must either be performed or not. The necessity there is of choosing one side in these dilemmas, and the impossibility there often is of finding any just medium, oblige us, when we reflect on the matter, to acknowledge that all property and obligations are entire. But, on the other hand, when we consider the origin of property and obligation, and find that they depend on public utility, and sometimes on the propensity of the imagination, which are seldom entire on any side, we are naturally inclined to imagine that these moral relations admit of an insensible gradation. Hence it is that in references, where the consent of the parties leave the referees entire masters of the subject, they commonly discover so much equity and justice on both sides as induces them to strike a medium, and divide the difference betwixt the parties. Civil judges, who have not this liberty, but are obliged to give a decisive sentence on some one side, are often at a loss how to determine, and are necessitated to proceed on the most frivolous reasons in the world. Half rights and obligations, which seem so natural in common life, are perfect absurdities in their tribunal; for which reason they are often obliged to take half arguments for whole ones, in order to terminate the affair one way or the other.

III. The *third* argument of this kind I shall make use of may be explained thus. If we consider the ordinary course of human actions, we shall find that the mind restrains not itself by any general and universal rules, but acts on most occasions as it is determined by its present motives and inclination. As each action is a particular individual event, it must proceed from particular principles, and from our immediate situation within ourselves, and with respect to the rest of the universe. If on some occasions we extend our motives beyond those very circumstances which gave rise to them, and form something like *general rules* for our conduct, it is easy to observe that these rules are not perfectly inflexible, but allow of many exceptions. Since, therefore, this is the ordinary course of human actions, we may conclude that the laws of justice, being universal and perfectly inflexi-

ble, can never be derived from nature, nor be the immediate offspring of any natural motive or inclination. No action can be either morally good or evil, unless there be some natural passion or motive to impel us to it, or deter us from it; and it is evident that the morality must be susceptible of all the same variations which are natural to the passion. Here are two persons who dispute for an estate; of whom one is rich, a fool, and a bachelor; the other poor, a man of sense, and has a numerous family: the first is my enemy; the second my friend. Whether I be actuated in this affair by a view to public or private interest, by friendship or enmity, I must be induced to do my utmost to procure the estate to the latter. Nor would any consideration of the right and property of the persons be able to restrain me, were I actuated only by natural motives, without any combination or convention with others. For as all property depends on morality, and as all morality depends on the ordinary course of our passions and actions, and as these again are only directed by particular motives, it is evident such a partial conduct must be suitable to the strictest morality, and could never be a violation of property. Were men, therefore, to take the liberty of acting with regard to the laws of society, as they do in every other affair, they would conduct themselves, on most occasions, by particular judgments, and would take into consideration the characters and circumstances of the persons, as well as the general nature of the question. But it is easy to observe, that this would produce an infinite confusion in human society, and that the avidity and partiality of men would quickly bring disorder into the world, if not restrained by some general and inflexible principles. It was therefore with a view to this inconvenience that men have established those principles, and have agreed to restrain themselves by general rules, which are unchangeable by spite and favour, and by particular views of private or public interest. These rules, then, are artificially invented for a certain purpose, and are contrary to the common principles of human nature, which accommodate themselves to circumstances, and have no stated invariable method of operation.

Nor do I perceive how I can easily be mistaken in this matter. I see, evidently, that when any man imposes on himself general inflexible rules in his conduct with others, he considers certain objects as their property, which he supposes to be sacred and inviolable. But no proposition can be more evident, than that property is perfectly unintelligible without first supposing justice and injustice; and that these virtues and vices are as unintelligible, unless we have motives, independent of the morality, to impel us to just actions, and deter us from unjust ones. Let those motives, therefore, be what they will, they must accommodate themselves to circumstances, and must admit of all the variations which human affairs, in their incessant revolutions, are susceptible of. They are, consequently, a very improper foundation for such rigid inflexible rules as the laws of nature; and it is evident these laws can only be derived from human conventions, when men have perceived the disorders that result from following their natural and variable principles.

Upon the whole, then, we are to consider this distinction betwixt justice and injustice, as having two different foundations, viz. that of *interest,* when men observe that it is impossible to live in society without restraining themselves by certain rules; and that of *morality,* when this interest is once observed, and men receive a pleasure from the view of such actions as tend to the peace of society, and an uneasiness from such as are contrary to it. It is the voluntary convention and artifice of men which makes the first interest take place; and therefore those laws of justice are so far to be considered as *artificial.* After that interest is once established and acknowledged, the sense of morality in the observance of these rules follows *naturally,* and of itself; though it is certain that it is also augmented by a new *artifice,* and that the public instructions of politicians, and the private education of parents, contribute to the giving us a sense of honour and duty, in the strict regulation of our actions with regard to the properties of others.

## Section VII

### OF THE ORIGIN OF GOVERNMENT

Nothing is more certain than that men are in a great measure governed by interest, and that, even when they extend their concern beyond themselves, it is not to any great distance; nor is it usual for them, in common life, to look further than their nearest friends and acquaintance. It is no less certain, that it is impossible for men to consult their interest in so effectual a manner, as by an universal and inflexible observance of the rules of justice, by which alone they can preserve society, and keep themselves from falling into that wretched and savage condition which is commonly represented as the *state of nature.* And as this interest which all men have in the upholding of society, and the observation of the rules of justice, is great, so is it palpable and evident, even to the most rude and uncultivated of the human race; and it is almost impossible for any one who has had experience of society, to be mistaken in this particular. Since, therefore, men are so sincerely attached to their interest, and their interest is so much concerned in the observance of justice, and this interest is so certain and avowed, it may be asked, how any disorder can ever arise in society, and what principle there is in human nature so *powerful* as to overcome so strong a passion, or so *violent* as to obscure so clear a knowledge?

It has been observed, in treating of the Passions, that men are mightily governed by the imagination, and proportion their affections more to the light under which any object appears to them, than to its real and intrinsic value. What strikes upon them with a strong and lively idea commonly prevails above what lies in a more obscure light; and it must be a great superiority of value that is able to compensate this advantage. Now, as everything that is contiguous to us, either in space or time, strikes upon us with such an idea, it has a proportional effect on the will and passions, and commonly operates with more force than any object that lies in a more distant and obscure light. Though we may be fully convinced that the latter object excels the former, we are not able to regulate our actions by this judgment, but yield to the solicitations of our passions, which always plead in favour of whatever is near and contiguous.

This is the reason why men so often act in contradiction to their known interest; and, in particular, why they prefer any trivial advantage that is present, to the maintenance of order in society, which so much depends on the observance of justice. The consequences of every breach of equity seem to lie very remote, and are not liable to counterbalance any immediate advantage that may be reaped from it. They are, however, never the less real for being remote; and as all men are, in some degree, subject to the same weakness, it necessarily happens, that the violations of equity must become very frequent in society, and the commerce of men, by that means, be rendered very dangerous and uncertain. You have the same propension that I have in favour of what is contiguous above what is remote. You are, therefore, naturally carried to commit acts of injustice as well as me. Your example both pushes me forward in this way by imitation, and also affords me a new reason for any breach of equity, by showing me that I should be the cully of my integrity, if I alone should impose on myself a severe restraint amidst the licentiousness of others.

This quality, therefore, of human nature, not only is very dangerous to society, but also seems, on a cursory view, to be incapable of any remedy. The remedy can only come from the consent of men; and if men be incapable of themselves to prefer remote to contiguous, they will never consent to anything which would oblige them to such a choice, and contradict, in so sensible a manner, their natural principles and propensities. Whoever chooses the means, chooses also the end; and if it be impossible for us to prefer what is remote, it is equally impossible for us to submit to any necessity which would oblige us to such a method of acting.

But here it is observable, that this infirmity of human nature becomes a remedy to itself, and that we provide against our negligence about remote objects, merely because we are naturally inclined to that negligence. When we consider any objects at a distance, all their minute distinctions vanish, and we always give the preference to whatever is in itself preferable, without considering its situation and circumstances. This gives rise to what, in an improper sense, we call *reason,* which is a principle that is often contradictory to those propensities that display themselves upon the approach of the object. In reflecting on any action which I am to perform a twelvemonth hence, I always resolve to prefer the greater good, whether at that time it will be more contiguous or remote; nor does any difference in that particular make a difference in my present intentions and resolutions. My distance from the final determination makes all those minute differences vanish, nor am I affected by anything but the general and more discernible qualities of good and evil. But on my nearer approach, those circumstances which I at first overlooked begin to appear, and have an influence on my conduct and affections. A new inclination to the present good springs up, and makes it difficult for me to adhere inflexibly to my first purpose and resolution. This natural infirmity I may very much regret, and I may endeavour, by all possible means, to free myself from it. I may have recourse to study and reflection within myself; to the advice of friends; to frequent meditation, and repeated resolution: And having experienced how ineffectual all these are, I may embrace with pleasure any other expedient by which I may impose a restraint upon myself, and guard against this weakness.

The only difficulty, therefore, is to find out this expedient, by which men cure their natural weakness, and lay themselves under the necessity of observing the laws of justice and equity, notwithstanding their violent propension to prefer contiguous to remote. It is evident such a remedy can never be effectual without correcting this propensity; and as it is impossible to change or correct anything material in our nature, the utmost we can do is to change our circumstances and situation, and render the observance of the laws of justice our nearest interest, and their violation our most remote. But this being impracticable with respect to all mankind, it can only take place with respect to a few, whom we thus immediately interest in the execution of justice. These are the persons whom we call civil magistrates, kings and their ministers, our governors and rulers, who, being indifferent persons to the greatest part of the state, have no interest, or but a remote one, in any act of injustice; and, being satisfied with their present condition, and with their part in society, have an immediate interest in every execution of justice, which is so necessary to the upholding of society. Here, then, is the origin of civil government and society. Men are not able radically to cure, either in themselves or others, that narrowness of soul which makes them prefer the present to the remote. They cannot change their natures. All they can do is to change their situation, and render the observance of justice the immediate interest of some particular persons, and its violation their more remote. These persons, then, are not only induced to observe those rules in their own conduct, but also to constrain others to a like regularity, and enforce the dictates of equity through the whole society. And if it be necessary, they may also interest others more immediately in the execution of justice, and create a number of officers, civil and military, to assist them in their government.

But this execution of justice, though the principal, is not the only advantage of government. As violent passion hinders men from seeing distinctly the interest they have in an equitable behaviour towards others, so it hinders them from seeing that equity itself, and gives them a remarkable partiality in their own favours. This inconvenience is corrected in the same manner as that above mentioned. The same persons who execute the laws of justice, will also decide all controversies concerning them; and, being indifferent to the greatest part of the society, will decide them more equitably than every one would in his own case.

By means of these two advantages in the *execution* and *decision* of justice, men acquire a security against each other's weakness and passion, as well as against their own, and, under the shelter of their governors, being to taste at ease the sweets of society and mutual assistance. But government extends further its beneficial influence; and, not contented to protect men in those conventions they make for their mutual interest, it often obliges them to make such conventions, and forces them to seek their own advantage, by a concurrence in some common end or purpose. There is no quality in human nature which causes more fatal errors in our conduct, than that which leads us to prefer whatever is present to the distant and remote, and makes us desire objects more according to their situation than their intrinsic value. Two neighbours may agree to drain a meadow, which they possess in common: because it is easy for them to know each other's mind; and each must perceive, that the immediate consequence of his failing in his part, is the abandoning the whole project. But it is very difficult, and indeed impossible, that a thousand persons should agree in any such action; it being difficult for them to concert so complicated a design, and still more difficult for them to execute it; while each seeks a pretext to free himself of the trouble and expense, and would lay the whole burden on others. Political society easily remedies both these inconveniences. Magistrates find an immediate interest in the interest of any considerable part of their subjects. They need consult nobody but themselves to form any scheme for the promoting of that interest. And as the failure of any one piece in the execution is connected, though not immediately, with the failure of the whole, they prevent that failure, because they find no interest in it, either immediate or remote. Thus, bridges are built, harbours opened, ramparts raised, canals formed, fleets equipped, and armies disciplined, everywhere, by the care of government, which, though composed of men subject to all human infirmities, becomes, by one of the finest and most subtle inventions imaginable, a composition which is in some measure exempted from all these infirmities.

# Of Parties in General

Of all men, that distinguish themselves by memorable *atchievements*, the first place of honour seems due to Legislators and founders of states, who transmit a system of laws and institutions to secure the peace, happiness, and liberty of future generations. The influence of useful inventions in the arts and sciences may, perhaps, extend farther than that of wise laws, whose effects are limited both in time and place; but the benefit arising from the former, is not so sensible as that which results from the latter. Speculative sciences do, indeed, improve the mind; but this advantage reaches only to a few persons, who have leisure to apply themselves to them. And as to practical arts, which encrease the commodities and enjoyments of life, it is well known, that men's happiness consists not so much in an abundance of these, as in the peace and security with which they possess them; and those blessings can only be derived from good government. Not to mention, that general virtue and good morals in a state, which are so requisite to happiness, can never arise from the most refined precepts of philosophy, or even the severest injunctions of religion; but must proceed entirely from the virtuous education of youth, the effect of wise laws and institutions. I must, therefore, presume to differ from Lord Bacon in this particular, and must regard antiquity as somewhat unjust in its distribution of honours, when it made gods of all the inventors of useful arts, such as Ceres Bacchus Aesculapius; and dignify legislators, such as Romulus and Theseus, only with the appellation of demigods and heroes.

As much as legislators and founders of states ought to be honoured and respected among men, as much ought the founders of sects and factions to be detested and hated; because the influence of faction is directly contrary to that of laws. Factions subvert government, render laws impotent, and beget the fiercest animosities among men of the same nation, who ought to give mutual assistance and protection to each other. And what should render the founders of parties more odious is, the difficulty of extirpating these weeds, when once they have taken root in any state. They naturally propagate themselves for many centuries, and seldom end but by the total dissolution of that government, in which they are sown. They are, besides, plants which grow most plentifully in the richest soil; and though absolute governments be not wholly free from them, it must be confessed, that they rise more easily, and propagate themselves faster in free governments, where they always infect the legislature itself, which alone could be able, by the steady application of rewards and punishments, to eradicate them.

Factions may be divided into Personal and Real that is, into factions, founded on personal friendship or animosity among such as compose the contending parties, and into those founded on some real difference of sentiment or interest. The reason of this distinction is obvious; though I must acknowledge, that parties are seldom found pure and unmixed, either of the one kind or the other. It is not often seen, that a government divides into factions, where there is no difference in the views of the constituent members, either real or apparent, trivial or material: And in those factions, which are founded on the most real and most material difference, there is always observed a great deal of personal animosity or affection. But notwithstanding this mixture, a party may be denominated either personal or real, according to that principle which is predominant, and is found to have the greatest influence.

Personal factions arise most easily in small republics. Every domestic quarrel, there, becomes an affair of state. Love, vanity, emulation, any passion, as well as ambition and resentment, begets public division. The Neri and Bianchi of Florence the Fregosi and Adorni of Genoa, the Colonesi and Orsini of modern Rome, were parties of this kind.

Men have such a propensity to divide into personal factions, that the smallest appearance of real difference will produce them. What can be imagined more trivial than the difference between one colour of livery and another in horse races? Yet this difference begat two most inveterate factions in the Greek empire, the Prasini and Veneti who never suspended their animosities, till they ruined that unhappy government.

We find in the Roman history a remarkable dissension between two tribes, the Pollia and Papiria, which continued for the space of near three hundred years, and discovered itself in their suffrages at every election of magistrates.

This faction was the more remarkable, as it could continue for so long a tract of time; even though it did not spread itself, nor draw any of the other tribes into a share of the quarrel. If mankind had not a strong propensity to such divisions, the indifference of the rest of the community must have suppressed this foolish animosity, that had not any aliment of new benefits and injuries, of general sympathy and antipathy, which never fail to take place, when the whole state is rent into two equal factions.

Nothing is more usual than to see parties, which have begun upon a real difference, continue even after that difference is lost. When men are once inlisted on opposite sides, they contract an affection to the persons with whom they are united, and an animosity against their antagonists: And these passions they often transmit to their posterity. The real difference between Guelf and Ghibbelline was long lost in Italy, before these factions were extinguished. The Guelfs adhered to the pope, the Ghibbellines to the emperor; yet the family of Sforza, who were in alliance with the emperor, though they were Guelfs, being expelled from Milan by the king of France assisted by Jacomo Trivulzio and the Ghibbellines, the pope concurred with the latter, and they formed leagues with the pope against the emperor.

The civil wars which arose some few years ago in Morocco, between the *blacks* and *whites*, merely on account of their complexion, are founded on a pleasant difference. We laugh at them; but I believe, were things rightly examined, we afford much more occa-

sion of ridicule to the Moors. For, what are all the wars of religion, which have prevailed in this polite and knowing part of the world? They are certainly more absurd than the Moorish civil wars. The difference of complexion is a sensible and a real difference: But the controversy about an article of faith, which is utterly absurd and unintelligible, is not a difference in sentiment, but in a few phrases and expressions, which one party accepts of, without understanding them; and the other refuses in the same manner.

*Real* factions may be divided into those from *interest*, from *principle* and from *affection*. Of all factions, the first are the most reasonable, and the most excusable. Where two orders of men, such as the nobles and people, have a distinct authority in a government, not very accurately balanced and modelled, they naturally follow a distinct interest; nor can we reasonably expect a different conduct, considering that degree of selfishness implanted in human nature. It requires great skill in a legislator to prevent such parties; and many philosophers are of opinion, that this secret, like the *grand elixir*, or *perpetual motion*, may amuse men in theory, but can never possibly be reduced to practice. In despotic governments, indeed, factions often do not appear; but they are not the less real; or rather, they are more real and more pernicious, upon that very account. The distinct orders of men, nobles and people, soldiers and merchants, have all a distinct interest; but the more powerful oppresses the weaker with impunity, and without resistance; which begets a seeming tranquillity in such governments.

There has been an attempt in England to divide the *landed* and *trading* part of the nation; but without success. The interests of these two bodies are not really distinct, and never will be so, till our public debts encrease to such a degree, as to become altogether oppressive and intolerable.

Parties from *principle*, especially abstract speculative principle, are known only to modern times, and are, perhaps, the most extraordinary and unaccountable *phoenomenon*, that has yet appeared in human affairs. Where different principles beget a contrariety of conduct, which is the case with all different political principles, the matter may be more easily explained. A man, who esteems the true right of government to lie in one man, or one family, cannot easily agree with his fellow-citizen, who thinks that another man or family is possessed of this right. Each naturally wishes that right may take place, according to his own notions of it. But where the difference of principle is attended with no contrariety of action, but every one may follow his own way, without interfering with his neighbour, as happens in all religious controversies; what madness, what fury can beget such unhappy and such fatal divisions?

Two men travelling on the highway, the one east, the other west, can easily pass each other, if the way be broad enough: But two men, reasoning upon opposite principles of religion, cannot so easily pass, without shocking; though one should think, that the way were also, in that case, sufficiently broad, and that each might proceed, without interruption, in his own course. But such is the nature of the human mind, that it always lays hold on every mind that approaches it; and as it is wonderfully fortified by an unanimity of sentiments, so is it shocked and disturbed by any contrariety. Hence the eagerness, which most people discover in a dispute; and hence their impatience of opposition, even in the most speculative and indifferent opinions.

This principle, however frivolous it may appear, seems to have been the origin of all religious wars and divisions. But as this principle is universal in human nature, its effects would not have been confined to one age, and to one sect of religion, did it not there concur with other more accidental causes, which raise it to such a height, as to produce the greatest misery and devastation. Most religions of the ancient world arose in the unknown ages of government, when men were as yet barbarous and uninstructed, and the prince, as well as peasant, was disposed to receive, with implicit faith, every pious tale or fiction, which was offered him. The magistrate embraced the religion of the people, and entering cordially into the care of sacred matters, naturally acquired an authority in them, and united the ecclesiastical with the civil power. But the *Christian* religion arising, while principles directly opposite to it were firmly established

in the polite part of the world, who despised the nation that first broached this novelty; no wonder, that, in such circumstances, it was but little countenanced by the civil magistrate, and that the priesthood was allowed to engross all the authority in the new sect. So bad a use did they make of this power, even in those early times, that the primitive persecutions may, perhaps, *in part*, be ascribed to the violence instilled by them into their followers. And the same principles of priestly government continuing, after Christianity became the established religion, they have engendered a spirit of persecution, which has ever since been the poison of human society, and the source of the most inveterate factions in every government. Such divisions, therefore, on the part of the people, may justly be esteemed factions of *principle;* but, on the part of the priests, who are the prime movers, they are really factions of *interest*.

There is another cause (beside the authority of the priests, and the separation of the ecclesiastical and civil powers) which has contributed to render Christendom the scene of religious wars and divisions. Religions, that arise in ages totally ignorant and barbarous, consist mostly of traditional tales and fictions, which may be different in every sect, without being contrary to each other; and even when they are contrary, every one adheres to the tradition of his own sect, without much reasoning or disputation. But as philosophy was widely spread over the world, at the time when Christianity arose, the teachers of the new sect were obliged to form a system of speculative opinions; to divide, with some accuracy, their articles of faith; and to explain, comment, confute, and defend with all the subtilty of argument and science. Hence naturally arose keenness in dispute, when the Christian religion came to be split into new divisions and heresies: And this keenness assisted the priests in their policy, of begetting a mutual hatred and antipathy among their deluded followers. Sects of philosophy, in the ancient world, were more zealous than parties of religion; but in modern times, parties of religion are more furious and enraged than the most cruel factions that ever arose from interest and ambition.

I have mentioned parties from *affection* as a kind

of *real* parties, beside those from *interest* and *principle*. By parties from affection, I understand those which are founded on the different attachments of men towards particular families and persons, whom they desire to rule over them. These factions are often very violent; though, I must own, it may seem unaccountable, that men should attach themselves so strongly to persons, with whom they are no wise acquainted, whom perhaps they never saw, and from whom they never received, nor can ever hope for any favour. Yet this we often find to be the case, and even with men, who, on other occasions, discover no great generosity of spirit, nor are found to be easily transported by friendship beyond their own interest. We are apt to think the relation between us and our sovereign very close and intimate. The splendour of majesty and power bestows an importance on the fortunes even of a single person. And when a man's good-nature does not give him this imaginary interest, his ill-nature will, from spite and opposition to persons whose sentiments are different from his own.

# Of the Original Contract

As no party, in the present age, can well support itself, without a philosophical or speculative system of principles, annexed to its political or practical one; we accordingly find, that each of the factions, into which this nation is divided, has reared up a fabric of the former kind, in order to protect and cover that scheme of actions, which it pursues.

The people being commonly very rude builders, especially in this speculative way, and more especially still, when actuated by party-zeal; it is natural to imagine, that their workmanship must be a little unshapely, and discover evident marks of that violence and hurry, in which it was raised. The one party, by tracing up government to the Deity, endeavour to render it so sacred and inviolate, that it must be little less than sacrilege, however tyrannical it may become, to touch or invade it, in the smallest article. The other party, by founding government altogether on the consent of the People, suppose that there is a kind of *original contract,* by which the subjects have tacitly reserved the power of resisting their sovereign, whenever they find themselves aggrieved by that authority, with which they have, for certain purposes, voluntarily entrusted him. These are the speculative principles of the two parties; and these too are the practical consequences deduced from them.

I shall venture to affirm, *That both these* systems *of speculative principles are just; though not in the sense intended by the parties*: and, *That both the* schemes *of practical consequences are prudent; though not in the extremes, to wh ich each party, in opposition to the other, has commonly endeavoured to carry them.*

That the Deity is the ultimate author of all government will never be denied by any, who admit a general providence, and allow, that all events in the universe are conducted by an uniform plan, and directed to wise purposes. As it is impossible for the human race to subsist, at least in any comfortable or secure state, without the protection of government; this institution must certainly have been intended by that beneficent Being, who means the good of all his creatures: And as it has universally, in fact, taken place, in all countries, and all ages; we may conclude, with still greater certainty, that it was intended by that omniscient Being, who can never be deceived by any event or operation. But since he gave rise to it, not by any particular or miraculous interposition, but by his concealed and universal efficacy; a sovereign cannot, properly speaking, be called his vicegerent, in any other sense than every power or force, being derived from him, may be said to act by his commission. Whatever actually happens is comprehended in the general plan or intention of providence; nor has the greatest and most lawful prince any more reason, upon that account, to plead a peculiar sacredness or inviolable authority, than an inferior magistrate, or even an usurper, or even a robber and a pyrate. The same divine superintendent, who, for wise purposes, invested a Titus or a Trajan with authority, did also, for purposes, no doubt, equally wise, though unknown, bestow power on a Borgia or an Angria. The same causes, which gave rise to the sovereign power in every state, established likewise every petty jurisdiction in it, and every limited authority. A constable, therefore, no less than a king, acts by a divine commission, and possesses an indefeasible right.

When we consider how nearly equal all men are in their bodily force, and even in their mental powers and faculties, till cultivated by education; we must necessarily allow, that nothing but their own consent could, at first, associate them together, and subject them to any authority. The people, if we trace government to its first origin in the woods and deserts, are the source of all power and jurisdiction, and voluntarily, for the sake of peace and order, abandoned their native liberty, and received laws from their equal and companion. The conditions, upon which they were willing to submit, were either expressed, or were so clear and obvious, that it might well be esteemed superfluous to express them. If this, then, be meant by the *original contract,* it cannot be denied, that all government is, at first, founded on a contract, and that the most ancient rude combinations of mankind were formed chiefly by that principle. In vain, are we asked in what records this charter of our liberties is registered. It was not written on parchment, nor yet on leaves or barks of trees. It preceded the use of writing and all the other civilized arts of life. But we trace it plainly in the nature of man, and in the equality, or something approaching equality, which we find in all the individuals of that species. The force, which now prevails, and which is founded on fleets and armies, is plainly political, and derived from authority, the effect of established government. A man's natural force consists only in the vigour of his limbs, and the firmness of his courage; which could never subject multitudes to the command of one. Nothing but their own consent, and their sense of the advantages resulting from peace and order, could have had that influence.

Yet even this consent was long very imperfect,

and could not be the basis of a regular administration. The chieftain, who had probably acquired his influence during the continuance of war, ruled more by persuasion than command; and till he could employ force to reduce the refractory and disobedient, the society could scarcely be said to have attained a state of civil government. No compact or agreement, it is evident, was expressly formed for general submission; an idea far beyond the comprehension of savages: Each exertion of authority in the chieftain must have been particular, and called forth by the present exigencies of the case: The sensible utility, resulting from his interposition, made these exertions become daily more frequent; and their frequency gradually produced an habitual, and, if you please to call it so, a voluntary, and therefore precarious, acquiescence in the people.

But philosophers, who have embraced a party (if that be not a contradiction in terms) are not contented with these concessions. They assert, not only that government in its earliest infancy arose from consent or rather the voluntary acquiescence of the people; but also, that, even at present, when it has attained full maturity, it rests on no other foundation. They affirm, that all men are still born equal, and owe allegiance to no prince or government, unless bound by the obligation and sanction of a *promise.* And as no man, without some equivalent, would forego the advantages of his native liberty, and subject himself to the will of another; this promise is always understood to be conditional, and imposes on him no obligation, unless he meet with justice and protection from his sovereign. These advantages the sovereign promises him in return; and if he fail in the execution, he has broken, on his part, the articles of engagement, and has thereby freed his subject from all obligations to allegiance. Such, according to these philosophers, is the foundation of authority in every government; and such the right of resistance, possessed by every subject.

But would these reasoners look abroad into the world, they would meet with nothing that, in the least, corresponds to their ideas, or can warrant so refined and philosophical a system. On the contrary, we find, every where, princes, who claim their subjects as their property, and assert their independent right of sovereignty, from conquest or succession. We find also, every where, subjects, who acknowledge this right in their prince, and suppose themselves born under obligations of obedience to a certain sovereign, as much as under the ties of reverence and duty to certain parents. These connexions are always conceived to be equally independent of our consent, in Persia and China; in France and Spain; and even in Holland and England, wherever the doctrines abovementioned have not been carefully inculcated. Obedience or subjection becomes so familiar, that most men never make any enquiry about its origin or cause, more than about the principle of gravity, resistance, or the most universal laws of nature. Or if curiosity ever move them; as soon as they learn, that they themselves and their ancestors have, for several ages, or from time immemorial, been subject to such a form of government or such a family; they immediately acquiesce, and acknowledge their obligation to allegiance. Were you to preach, in most parts of the world, that political connexions are founded altogether on voluntary consent or a mutual promise, the magistrate would soon imprison you, as seditious, for loosening the ties of obedience; if your friends did not before shut you up as delirious, for advancing such absurdities. It is strange, that an act of the mind, which every individual is supposed to have formed, and after he came to the use of reason too, otherwise it could have no authority; that this act, I say, should be so much unknown to all of them, that, over the face of the whole earth, there scarcely remain any traces or memory of it.

But the contract, on which government is founded, is said to be the *original contract*; and consequently may be supposed too old to fall under the knowledge of the present generation. If the agreement, by which savage men first associated and conjoined their force, be here meant, this is acknowledged to be real; but being so ancient, and being obliterated by a thousand changes of government and princes, it cannot now be supposed to retain any authority. If we would say any thing to the purpose, we must assert, that every particular government, which is lawful, and which imposes any duty of alle-

giance on the subject, was, at first, founded on consent and a voluntary compact. But besides that this supposes the consent of the fathers to bind the children, even to the most remote generations, (which republican writers will never allow) besides this, I say, it is not justified by history or experience, in any age or country of the world.

Almost all the governments, which exist at present, or of which there remains any record in story, have been founded originally, either on usurpation or conquest, or both, without any presence of a fair consent, or voluntary subjection of the people. When an artful and bold man is placed at the head of an army or faction, it is often easy for him, by employing, sometimes violence, sometimes false pretences, to establish his dominion over a people a hundred times more numerous than his partizans. He allows no such open communication, that his enemies can know, with certainty, their number or force. He gives them no leisure to assemble together in a body to oppose him. Even all those, who are the instruments of his usurpation, may wish his fall; but their ignorance of each other's intention keeps them in awe, and is the sole cause of his security. By such arts as these, many governments have been established; and this is all the *original contract*, which they have to boast of.

The face of the earth is continually changing, by the encrease of small kingdoms into great empires, by the dissolution of great empires into smaller kingdoms, by the planting of colonies, by the migration of tribes. Is there any thing discoverable in all these events, but force and violence? Where is the mutual agreement or voluntary association so much talked of?

Even the smoothest way, by which a nation may receive a foreign master, by marriage or a will, is not extremely honourable for the people; but supposes them to be disposed of, like a dowry or a legacy, according to the pleasure or interest of their rulers.

But where no force interposes, and election takes place; what is this election so highly vaunted? It is either the combination of a few great men, who decide for the whole, and will allow of no opposition: Or it is the fury of a multitude, that follow a seditious ringleader, who is not known, perhaps, to a dozen among them, and who owes his advancement merely to his own impudence, or to the momentary caprice of his fellows.

Are these disorderly elections, which are rare too, of such mighty authority, as to be the only lawful foundation of all government and allegiance?

In reality, there is not a more terrible event, than a total dissolution of government, which gives liberty to the multitude, and makes the determination or choice of a new establishment depend upon a number, which nearly approaches to that of the body of the people: For it never comes entirely to the whole body of them. Every wise man, then, wishes to see, at the head of a powerful and obedient army, a general, who may speedily seize the prize, and give to the people a master, which they are so unfit to chuse for themselves. So little correspondent is fact and reality to those philosophical notions.

Let not the establishment at the *Revolution* deceive us, or make us so much in love with a philosophical origin to government, as to imagine all others monstrous and irregular. Even that event was far from corresponding to these refined ideas. It was only the succession, and that only in the regal part of the government, which was then changed: And it was only the majority of seven hundred, who determined that change for near ten millions. I doubt not, indeed, but the bulk of those ten millions acquiesced willingly in the determination: But was the matter left, in the least, to their choice? Was it not justly supposed to be, from that moment, decided, and every man punished, who refused to submit to the new sovereign? How otherwise could the matter have ever been brought to any issue or conclusion?

The republic of Athens was, I believe, the most extensive democracy, that we read of in history: Yet if we make the requisite allowances for the women, the slaves, and the strangers, we shall find, that that establishment was not, at first, made, not any law ever voted, by a tenth part of those who were bound to pay obedience to it: Not to mention the islands and foreign dominions, which the Athenians claimed as theirs by right of conquest. And as it is well known, that popular assemblies in that city were always full of licence and disorder, notwithstanding the institutions and laws by which they were checked: How

much more disorderly must they prove, where they form not the established constitution, but meet tumultuously on the dissolution of the ancient government, in order to give rise to a new one? How chimerical must it be to talk of a choice in such circumstances?

The Acheans enjoyed the freest and most perfect democracy of all antiquity; yet they employed force to oblige some cities to enter into their league, as we learn from Polybius.

Harry the IVth and Harry the VIIth of England, had really no title to the throne but a parliamentary election; yet they never would acknowledge it, lest they should thereby weaken their authority. Strange, if the only real foundation of all authority be consent and promise!

It is in vain to say, that all governments are or should be, at first, founded on popular consent, as much as the necessity of human affairs will admit. This favours entirely my pretension. I maintain, that human affairs will never admit of this consent; seldom of the appearance of it. But that conquest or usurpation, that is, in plain terms, force, by dissolving the ancient governments, is the origin of almost all the new ones, which were ever established in the world. And that in the few cases, where consent may seem to have taken place, it was commonly so irregular, so confined, or so much intermixed either with fraud or violence, that it cannot have any great authority.

My intention here is not to exclude the consent of the people from being one just foundation of government where it has place. It is surely the best and most sacred of any. I only pretend, that it has very seldom had place in any degree, and never almost in its full extent. And that therefore some other foundation of government must also be admitted.

Were all men possessed of so inflexible a regard to justice, that, of themselves, they would totally abstain from the properties of others; they had for ever remained in a state of absolute liberty, without subjection to any magistrate or political society: But this is a state of perfection, of which human nature is justly deemed incapable. Again; were all men possessed of so perfect an understanding, as always to know their own interests, no form of government had ever been submitted to, but what was established on consent, and was fully canvassed by every member of the society: But this state of perfection is likewise much superior to human nature. Reason, history, and experience shew us, that all political societies have had an origin much less accurate and regular; and were one to choose a period of time, when the people's consent was the least regarded in public transactions, it would be precisely on the establishment of a new government. In a settled constitution, their inclinations are often consulted; but during the fury of revolutions, conquests, and public convulsions, military force or political craft usually decides the controversy.

When a new government is established, by whatever means, the people are commonly dissatisfied with it, and pay obedience more from fear and necessity, than from any idea of allegiance or of moral obligation. The prince is watchful and jealous, and must carefully guard against every beginning or appearance of insurrection. Time, by degrees, removes all these difficulties, and accustoms the nation to regard, as their lawful or native princes, that family, which, at first, they considered as usurpers or foreign conquerors. In order to found this opinion, they have no recourse to any notion of voluntary consent or promise, which, they know, never was, in this case, either expected or demanded. The original establishment was formed by violence, and submitted to from necessity. The subsequent administration is also supported by power, and acquiesced in by the people, not as a matter of choice, but of obligation. They imagine not, that their consent gives their prince a title: But they willingly consent, because they think, that, from long possession, he has acquired a title, independent of their choice or inclination.

Should it be said, that, by living under the dominion of a prince, which one might leave, every individual has given a *tacit* consent to his authority, and promised him obedience; it may be answered, that such an implied consent can only have place, where a man imagines, that the matter depends on his choice. But where he thinks (as all mankind do who are born under established governments) that by his birth he owes allegiance to a certain prince or certain form of government; it would be absurd to infer a consent or choice, which he expressly, in this case, renounces and disclaims.

Can we seriously say, that a poor peasant or arti-

zan has a free choice to leave his country, when he knows no foreign language or manners, and lives from day to day, by the small wages which he acquires? We may as well assert, that a man, by remaining in a vessel, freely consents to the dominion of the master; though he was carried on board while asleep, and must leap into the ocean, and perish, the moment he leaves her.

What if the prince forbid his subjects to quit his dominions; as in Tiberius's time, it was regarded as a crime in a Roman knight that he had attempted to fly to the Parthians, in order to escape the tyranny of that emperor? Or as the ancient Muscovites prohibited all travelling under pain of death? And did a prince observe, that many of his subjects were seized with the frenzy of migrating to foreign countries, he would doubtless, with great reason and justice, restrain them, in order to prevent the depopulation of his own kingdom. Would he forfeit the allegiance of all his subjects, by so wise and reasonable a law? Yet the freedom of their choice is surely, in that case, ravished from them.

A company of men, who should leave their native country, in order to people some uninhabited region, might dream of recovering their native freedom; but they would soon find, that their prince still laid claim to them, and called them his subjects, even in their new settlement. And in this he would but act conformably to the common ideas of mankind.

The truest *tacit* consent of this kind, that is ever observed, is when a foreigner settles in any country, and is beforehand acquainted with the prince, and government, and laws, to which he must submit: Yet is his allegiance, though more voluntary, much less expected or depended on, than that of a natural born subject. On the contrary, his native prince still asserts a claim to him. And if he punish not the renegade, when he seizes him in war with his new prince's commission; this clemency is not founded on the municipal law, which in all countries condemns the prisoner; but on the consent of princes, who have agreed to this indulgence, in order to prevent reprisals.

Did one generation of men go off the stage at once, and another succeed, as is the case with silkworms and butterflies, the new race, if they had sense enough to choose their government, which surely is never the case with men, might voluntarily, and by general consent, establish their own form of civil polity, without any regard to the laws or precedents, which prevailed among their ancestors. But as human society is in perpetual flux, one man every hour going out of the world, another coming into it, it is necessary, in order to preserve stability in government, that the new brood should conform themselves to the established constitution, and nearly follow the path which their fathers, treading in the footsteps of theirs, had marked out to them. Some innovations must necessarily have place in every human institution, and it is happy where the enlightened genius of the age give these a direction to the side of reason, liberty, and justice: but violent innovations no individual is entitled to make: they are even dangerous to be attempted by the legislature: more ill than good is ever to be expected from them: and if history affords examples to the contrary, they are not to be drawn into precedent, and are only to be regarded as proofs, that the science of politics affords few rules, which will not admit of some exception, and which may not sometimes be controlled by fortune and accident. The violent innovations in the reign of Henry VIII proceeded from an imperious monarch, seconded by the appearance of legislative authority: Those in the reign of Charles I were derived from faction and fanaticism; and both of them have proved happy in the issue: But even the former were long the source of many disorders, and still more dangers; and if the measures of allegiance were to be taken from the latter, a total anarchy must have place in human society, and a final period at once be put to every government.

Suppose, that an usurper, after having banished his lawful prince and royal family, should establish his dominion for ten or a dozen years in any country, and should preserve so exact a discipline in his troops, and so regular a disposition in his garrisons, that no insurrection had ever been raised, or even murmur heard, against his administration: Can it be asserted, that the people, who in their hearts abhor his treason, have tacitly consented to his authority, and promised him allegiance, merely because, from necessity, they live under his dominion? Suppose again their native prince restored, by means of an army, which he levies in foreign countries: They receive him with joy and exultation, and shew plainly with what reluctance they had submitted to any other yoke. I may now ask, upon what foundation the prince's title stands? Not on popular consent surely: For though the people willingly acquiesce in his authority, they never imagine, that their consent made him sovereign. They consent; because they apprehend him to be already, by birth, their lawful sovereign. And as to that tacit consent, which may now be inferred from their living under his dominion, this is no more than what they formerly gave to the tyrant and usurper.

When we assert, that all lawful government arises from the consent of the people, we certainly do them a great deal more honour than they deserve, or even expect and desire from us. After the Roman dominions became too unwieldly for the republic to govern them, the people, over the whole known world, were extremely grateful to Augustus for that authority, which, by violence, he had established over them; and they shewed an equal disposition to submit to the successor, whom he left them, by his last will and testament. It was afterwards their misfortune, that there never was, in one family, any long regular succession; but that their line of princes was continually broken, either by private assassinations or public rebellions. The *praetorian* bands, on the failure of every family, set up one emperor; the legions in the East a second; those in Germany, perhaps, a third: And the sword alone could decide the controversy. The condition of the people, in that mighty monarchy, was to be lamented, not because the choice of the emperor was never left to them; for that was impracticable: But because they never fell under any succession of masters, who might regularly follow each other. As to the violence and wars and bloodshed, occasioned by every new settlement; these were not blameable, because they were inevitable.

The house of Lancaster ruled in this island about sixty years; yet the partizans of the white rose seemed daily to multiply in England. The present establishment has taken place during a still longer period. Have all views of right in another family been utterly extinguished; even though scarce any man now alive had arrived at years of discretion, when it was expelled, or could have consented to its dominion, or have promised it allegiance? A sufficient indication surely of the general sentiment of mankind on this head. For we blame not the partizans of the abdicated family, merely on account of the long time, during which they have preserved their imaginary loyalty. We blame them for adhering to a family, which, we affirm, has been justly expelled, and which, from the moment the new settlement took place, had forfeited all title to authority.

But would we have a more regular, at least a more philosophical, refutation of this principle of an original contract or popular consent; perhaps, the following observations may suffice.

All *moral* duties may be divided into two kinds. The *first* are those, to which men are impelled by a natural instinct or immediate propensity, which operates on them, independent of all ideas of obligation, and of all views, either to public or private utility. Of this nature are, love of children, gratitude to benefactors, pity to the unfortunate. When we reflect on the advantage, which results to society from such humane instincts, we pay them the just tribute of moral approbation and esteem: But the person, actuated by them, feels their power and influence, antecedent to any such reflection.

The *second* kind of moral duties are such as are not supported by any original instinct of nature, but are performed entirely from a sense of obligation, when we consider the necessities of human society, and the impossibility of supporting it, if these duties were neglected. It is thus *justice* or a regard to the property of others, *fidelity* or the observance of promises, become obligatory, and acquire an authority over mankind. For as it is evident, that every man loves himself better than any other person, he is naturally impelled to extend his acquisitions as much as possible; and nothing can restrain him in this propensity, but reflection and experience, by which he learns the pernicious effects of that licence, and the total dissolution of society which must ensue from it. His original inclination, therefore, or instinct, is here checked and restrained by a subsequent judgment or observation.

The case is precisely the same with the political or civil duty of *allegiance* as with the natural duties of justice and fidelity. Our primary instincts lead us, either to indulge ourselves in unlimited freedom, or to seek dominion over others: And it is reflection only which engages us to sacrifice such strong passions to the interests of peace and public order. A small degree of experience and observation suffices to teach us, that society cannot possibly be maintained without the authority of magistrates, and that this authority must soon fall into contempt, where exact obedience is not payed to it. The observation of these general and obvious interests is the source of all allegiance, and of that moral obligation, which we attribute to it.

What necessity, therefore, is there to found the duty of *allegiance* or obedience to magistrates on that of *fidelity* or a regard to promises, and to suppose, that it is the consent of each individual, which subjects him to government; when it appears, that both allegiance and fidelity stand precisely on the same foundation, and are both submitted to by mankind, on account of the apparent interests and necessities of human society? We are bound to obey our sovereign, it is said; because we have given a tacit promise to that purpose. But why are we bound to observe our promise? It must here be asserted, that the commerce and intercourse of mankind, which are of such mighty advantage, can have no security where men pay no regard to their engagements. In like manner, may it be said, that men could not live at all in society, at least in a civilized society, without laws and magistrates and judges, to prevent the encroachments of the strong upon the weak, of the violent upon the just and equitable. The obligation to allegiance being of like force and authority with the obligation to fidelity, we gain nothing by resolving the one into the other. The general interests or necessities of society are sufficient to establish both.

If the reason be asked of that obedience, which we are bound to pay to government, I readily answer, *because society could not otherwise subsist*: And this answer is clear and intelligible to all mankind. Your answer is, *because we should keep our word*. But besides, that no body, till trained in a philosophical system, can either comprehend or relish this answer: Besides this, I say, you find yourself embarrassed, when it is asked, *why we are bound to keep our word?* Nor can you give any answer, but what would, immediately, without any circuit, have accounted for our obligation to allegiance.

But *to whom is allegiance due? And who is our lawful sovereign?* This question is often the most difficult of any, and liable to infinite discussions. When people are so happy, that they can answer, *Our present sovereign, who inherits, in a direct line, from ancestors, that have governed us for many ages;* this answer admits of no reply; even though historians, in tracing up to the remotest antiquity, the origin of that royal family, may find, as commonly happens, that its first authority was derived from usurpation and violence. It is confessed, that private justice, or the abstinence from the properties of others, is a most cardinal virtue: Yet reason tells us, that there is no property in durable objects, such as lands or houses, when carefully examined in passing from hand to hand, but must, in some period, have been founded on fraud and injustice. The necessities of human society, neither in private nor public life, will allow of such an accurate enquiry: And there is no virtue or moral duty, but what may, with facility, be refined away, if we indulge a false philosophy, in sifting and scrutinizing it, by every captious rule of logic, in every light or position, in which it may be placed.

The questions with regard to private property have filled infinite volumes of law and philosophy, if in both we add the commentators to the original text; and in the end, we may safely pronounce, that many of the rules, there established, are uncertain, ambiguous, and arbitrary. The like opinion may be formed with regard to the succession and rights of princes and forms of government. Several cases, no doubt, occur, especially in the infancy of any constitution, which admit of no determination from the laws of justice and equity: And our historian Rapin pretends, that the controversy between Edward the Third and Philip de Valois was of this nature, and could be decided only by an appeal to heaven, that is, by war and violence.

Who shall tell me, whether Germanicus or Drusus ought to have succeeded to Tiberius, had he died, while they were both alive, without naming any of them for his successor? Ought the right of adoption to be received as equivalent to that of blood, in a nation, where it had the same effect in private families, and had already, in two instances, taken place in the public? Ought Germanicus to be esteemed the elder son because he was born before Drusus; or the younger, because he was adopted after the birth of his brother? Ought the right of the elder to be regarded in a nation, where he had no advantage in the succession of private families? Ought the Roman empire at that time to be deemed hereditary, because of two examples; or ought it, even so early, to be regarded as belonging to the stronger or to the present possessor, as being founded on so recent an usurpation?

Commodus mounted the throne after a pretty long succession of excellent emperors, who had acquired their title, not by birth, or public election, but by the fictitious rite of adoption. That bloody debauchee being murdered by a conspiracy suddenly formed between his wench and her gallant, who happened at that time to be *Praetorian Praefect;* these immediately deliberated about choosing a master to human kind, to speak in the style of those ages; and they cast their eyes on Pertinax. Before the tyrant's death was known, the *Praefect* went secretly to that senator, who, on the appearance of the soldiers, imagined that his execution had been ordered by Commodus. He was immediately saluted emperor by the officer and his attendants; cheerfully proclaimed by the populace; unwillingly submitted to by the guards; formally recognized by the senate; and passively received by the provinces and armies of the empire.

The discontent of the *Praetorian* bands broke out in a sudden sedition, which occasioned the murder of that excellent prince: And the world being now without a master and without government, the guards thought proper to set the empire formally to sale. Julian, the purchaser, was proclaimed by the soldiers, recognized by the senate, and submitted to by the people; and must also have been submitted to by the provinces, had not the envy of the legions begotten opposition and resistance. Pescennius Niger in Syria elected himself emperor, gained the tumultuary consent of his army, and was attended with the secret good-will of the senate and people of Rome. Albinus in Britain found an equal right to set up his claim; but Severus, who governed Pannonia, prevailed in the end above both of them. That able politician and warrior, finding his own birth and dignity too much inferior to the imperial crown, professed, at first, an intention only of revenging the death of Pertinax. He marched as general into Italy; defeated Julian; and without our being able to fix any precise commencement even of the soldiers' consent, he was from necessity acknowledged emperor by the senate and people; and fully established in his violent authority by subduing Niger and Albinus.

*Inter haec Gordianus Caesar* (says Capitolinus, speaking of another period) *sublatus a militibus. Imperator est appellatus, quia non erat alius in proesenti*. It is to be remarked, that Gordian was a boy of fourteen years of age.

Frequent instances of a like nature occur in the history of the emperors; in that of Alexander's successors; and of many other countries: Nor can any thing be more unhappy than a despotic government of this kind; where the succession is disjointed and irregular, and must be determined, on every vacancy, by force or election. In a free government, the matter is often unavoidable, and is also much less dangerous. The interests of liberty may there frequently lead the people, in their own defence, to alter the succession of the crown. And the constitution, being compounded of parts, may still maintain a sufficient stability, by resting on the aristocratical or democratical members, though the monarchical be altered, from time to time, in order to accommodate it to the former.

In an absolute government, when there is no legal prince, who has a title to the throne, it may safely be determined to belong to the first occupant. Instances of this kind are but too frequent, especially in the eastern monarchies. When any race of princes expires, the will or destination of the last sovereign will be regarded as a title. Thus the edict of Lewis the XIVth, who called the bastard princes to the succession in case of the failure of all the legitimate princes, would, in such an event, have some authority. Thus the will of Charles the Second disposed of the whole Spanish monarchy. The cession of the ancient proprietor, especially when joined to conquest, is likewise deemed a good title. The general obligation, which binds us to government, is the interest and necessities of society; and this obligation is very strong. The determination of it to this or that particular prince or form of government is frequently more uncertain and dubious. Present possession has considerable authority in these cases, and greater than in private property; because of the disorders which attend all revolutions and changes of government.

We shall only observe, before we conclude, that, though an appeal to general opinion may justly, in the speculative sciences of metaphysics, natural philosophy, or astronomy, be deemed unfair and inconclusive, yet in all questions with regard to morals, as well as criticism, there is really no other standard, by which any controversy can ever be decided. And nothing is a clearer proof, that a theory of this kind is erroneous, than to find, that it leads to paradoxes, repugnant to the common sentiments of mankind, and to the practice and opinion of all nations and all ages. The doctrine, which founds all lawful government on an *original contract*, or consent of the people, is plainly of this kind; nor has the most noted of its partizans, in prosecution of it, scrupled to affirm, *that absolute monarchy is inconsistent with civil society, and so can be no form of civil government at all; and that the supreme power in a state cannot take from any man, by taxes and impositions, any part of his property, without his own consent or that of his representatives*. What authority any moral reasoning can have, which leads into opinions so wide of the general practice of mankind, in every place but this single kingdom, it is easy to determine.

The only passage I meet with in antiquity, where the obligation of obedience to government is ascribed to a promise, is in Plato's *Crito*: where Socrates refuses to escape from prison, because he had tacitly promised to obey the laws. Thus he builds a *tory* consequence of passive obedience, on a *whig* foundation of the original contract.

New discoveries are not to be expected in these matters. If scarce any man, till very lately, ever imagined that government was founded on compact, it is certain, that it cannot, in general, have any such foundation.

The crime of rebellion among the ancients was commonly expressed by the terms νεωτερίζειν, *novas res moliri*.

# ADAM SMITH

~

## INTRODUCTION

## CHARLES L. GRISWOLD, JR.

Adam Smith (1723–1790) was a luminary in what is now called "the Scottish Enlightenment." Relatively little is known about his private life; he did not write an autobiography, and in spite of his fame as well as his friendship with leading figures of the day (such as Hume and Voltaire), his correspondence reveals surprisingly little about him as a man. He was clearly of stern character, strict discipline, skeptical disposition (and thus much opposed to extravagant religious or political claims), and complete trustworthiness. In many ways he appears to have been the perfect Stoic, needing little, independent, self-directed, and with emotions under watchful supervision. He did not live a monastic life, however; he had a wide circle of friends from many walks of life and regularly participated in meetings of literary, scientific, and business circles.

Smith attended Glasgow University, where he studied with Francis Hutcheson, and then Oxford, on the educational quality of which he subsequently commented caustically in the *Wealth of Nations*. Between 1748 and 1751, Smith lectured at Edinburgh under the patronage of Lord Kames; his topics were rhetoric, belles lettres, and jurisprudence. Student notes of Smith's lectures have survived, and while imperfect as such notes must be, the notes show that Smith possessed an impressive knowledge of the history of rhetoric and literature, backed up by a command of the relevant languages, ancient and modern. From the start, Smith also evinced a deep interest in the uses and development of language (as is shown by his first publications) and put his command of rhetoric to work in his own writings.

In 1751, Smith was named professor of logic at Glasgow University; he taught logic (which he rapidly transformed into a course on rhetoric), jurisprudence, and political theory. The next year, he became professor of moral philosophy at Glasgow, and his subject expanded to include ethics. After rising to the position of vice-rector of the university, Smith resigned his chair in 1764 to serve as traveling tutor to the third Duke of Buccleuch. Smith spent the next several years in France, where he met many of the leading *philosophes*, as well as French political economists. By 1767, he had returned to his native Kirkcaldy, where he lived with his mother (Smith never married) and worked on further revision of his books, as well as on drafts of others. In 1778, he was named commissioner of customs for Scotland and of salt duties, and he relocated to Edinburgh. A decade later, he also served as rector of Glasgow University. As appropriate to his international reputation and position, Smith was consulted about various issues of the day, including about relations with the American colonies.

Smith published just two books, *The Theory of Moral Sentiments* (first edition 1759) and *An Inquiry into the Nature and Causes of the Wealth of Nations* (first edition 1776), each in a series of emended and expanded editions. From the first editions on, these two books were remarkably successful, and with impressive speed elevated Smith to the stature of an international celebrity. His work was rapidly translated into several languages and taken seriously by thinkers of the order of Burke, Hume, Bentham, Kant, and Hegel. Smith conceived of these books as parts of a much more extended corpus that was to have included a "Philosophical History of the Liberal and Elegant Arts"; a treatment of "natural jurisprudence" (an analysis of the "natural rules of justice" or "general principles of law and government"); and a detailed account of the evolution of these rules of natural justice. Unfortunately, Smith instructed that almost all of his unpublished manuscripts were to be destroyed on his death. Two sets of student notes of his lectures on jurisprudence were discovered long after, and they help us understand what part of the missing system might have looked like. A number of posthumously published essays (now available in a volume entitled *Essays on Philosophical Subjects*), along with the student notes of his lectures on rhetoric, give us a reasonable picture of his "philosophical history" of rhetoric, the imitative arts, and both philosophy and science. These essays demonstrate Smith's vast and imaginative grasp of those areas and outline a philosophy of science that seeks to account for theory acceptance in broadly "aesthetic" terms. The "psychology" of inquiry, and the connection between knowledge, rhetoric, and aesthetics, clearly fascinated Smith, as is evident in the *Theory of Moral Sentiments* as well.

In the *Theory of Moral Sentiments*, Smith sought to answer two questions. The first is "wherein does virtue consist? Or what is the tone of temper and tenour of conduct, which constitutes the excellent and praise-worthy character, the character which is the natural object of esteem, honour, and approbation?" The second treats of what we might call the "psychology of ethics" or "moral psychology." As Smith put it, "by what power or faculty in the mind is it, that this [excellent and praise-worthy] character, whatever it be, is recommended to us?" His answer to the first question—viz., that virtue is to be understood as the "mean" or the appropriate pitch of a passion or emotion in the given case—revives parts of the Aristotelian view of virtue. His answer to the second question built on Hume's theory of "sympathy", a term denoting our ability to put ourselves imaginatively in the situation of another, as well as on the notion of the "impartial spectator." Sympathy is possible thanks to the imagination; for Smith the moral imagination is the glue that holds society together. As we judge others, so they judge us; we learn early on to view ourselves through the eyes of others, to imagine what they are imagining about us. For Smith, society is a spectatorial, theatrical affair. As we naturally seek the approval of others and they of us—thanks to *sympathy*—we feel bound to each other's praise and blame. Smith's view of the "self" is thoroughly social, and is ultimately at odds with perfectionist doctrines such as those of Plato, Aristotle, and Aquinas. However, we are also capable of viewing ourselves through the eyes of an imagined, impartial spectator; the judgments of a given society are not necessarily final.

Smith throughout exhibits skepticism about metaphysical and theological views of virtue and of the psychology of morals. The self-understanding of reasonable moral actors ought to serve as the moral philosopher's guide. Smith's discussion in the *Theory of Moral Sentiments* ranges from the motivation for wealth-getting to the psychological causes of dangerous religious and political fanaticism. The threat of fanaticism concerned Smith deeply, as it did so many other thinkers of the period (including Thomas Jefferson and James Madison): "Of all the corrupters of moral sentiments . . . faction and fanaticism have always been by far the greatest." Smith's criticisms of wealth-getting are as merciless as those of many traditional moralists; yet he also reconciles us to our desire to "better our own condition" by observing the ways in which it is both natural and productive. Here as elsewhere, Smith shows himself capable of both critical detachment from the phenomena he analyzes and moderation in his hopes for amelioration.

The *Wealth of Nations* attempts to explain why free economic, political, and religious markets are not only more efficient (when properly regulated) in increasing the wealth of nations but also more in keeping with nature, more likely to win the approval of an impartial spectator than would monopolistic alternatives, and of course praiseworthy because supportive of liberty. The book thus makes a broad-gauged case for a modern commercial society. Taken together, Smith's two books attempt to show how virtue, liberty, and material welfare can complement each other. He shows full awareness of the potentially dehumanizing force of what was later called "capitalism", and sought remedies for it in schemes for liberal education and properly organized religion. He harshly criticized colonialism, slavery, and racism. Book V of the *Wealth of Nations* offers an ingenious "free market" solution to the problem of religious faction, one that depends on the assumptions in the *Theory of Moral Sentiments* about the psychology of moderation and fanaticism, a solution that strikingly foreshadows James Madison's famous proposals in the tenth and fifty-first *Federalist Papers* for controlling civil strife. Smith hopes that the result of fair competition among religions will be to "reduce the doctrine of the greater part of them to that pure and rational religion, free from every mixture of absurdity, imposture, or fanaticism, such as wise men have in all ages of the world wished to see established." Unlike Marx, Smith did not take religion to be the opium of the people, nor did he think that the religious impulse can, or should, be extirpated. He thought that it can have a constructive role, but under conditions of liberty of religious belief. The argument in the *Wealth of Nations* in favor of liberty is not only based on its utility in the service of wealth but also on its connection with justice and the flourishing of virtues such as moderation and prudence. The relationship between liberal institutional arrangements (such as the separation between church and state) and virtue is a circular one for Smith. The wrong arrangements elicit fanaticism and corruption, which in turn further illiberal institutions.

In the "obvious and simple system of natural liberty," Smith writes, "every man, as long as he does not violate the laws of justice, is left perfectly free to pursue his own interest his own way, and to bring both his industry and capital into competition with those of any other man, or order of men." The government is left with the duties of promoting public works, protecting society from invasion, and protecting its citizens from one other. These are areas in which the efforts of individuals are insufficient. In Smith's hands, these supply a wide entrance for government intervention in society, and he is never dogmatic in defining precisely what government may or may not do. Smith does not advocate mere laissez-faire, and he sees a role for the state in regulating, or encouraging, or even supporting the arts, education, commerce, and many other areas.

In complex ways, Smith's work self-consciously synthesizes ancient and modern thought; it is both of the Enlightenment and the counter-Enlightenment, as is clear in Smith's subtle discussions of the relationship between commerce and virtue. Smith provides a fascinating window on the old "quarrel between ancients and moderns." He does so with marked self-consciousness about his approach, showing a sophisticated awareness of his own methodology and rhetoric.

The combination of the incompleteness of Smith's corpus, his decision in the two published books not to comment on the unity of the moral philosophy and political economy, the dialectical quality of his writing, the intrinsic difficulty of the issues, and the eclecticism of his thinking, have made it a challenge to articulate the unity of his project. The problem of the unity of Smith's books became a cause célèbre in nineteenth-century German scholarship, where it gained the impressive technical designation of "das Adam-Smith Problem." The alleged problem consisted in part in the unity of the doctrine of sympathy and benevolence of the one work, with that of selfishness and acquisitiveness of the other. While stated thus, the problem is based on a misunderstanding of the terms "sympathy" and "self-interest." At a deeper level, the questions of the relationship between self-interest and duty toward others, between socially derived morals and independent moral norms, remains. But these are general philosophical problems, and to Smith's credit he thought them through with integrity and an open mind. His general argument in favor of a modern commercial republic is nuanced and qualified as appropriate, and is all the more powerful for it.

The secondary literature on Smith is vast. A small sample of the widely divergent but fine work on Smith would include V. Brown's *Adam Smith's Discourse: Canonicity, Commerce and Conscience* (London: Routledge, 1994), a book that deploys recent literary theory in a novel interpretation of Smith; J. Cropsey's classic *Polity and Economy: An Interpretation of the Principles of Adam Smith* (Westport, Conn.: Greenwood Press, 1977), in which Smith is placed in the decisively "modern" tradition of political philosophy stemming from Machiavelli and Hobbes; and K. Haakonssen's *The Science of a Legislator: The Natural Jurisprudence of David Hume & Adam Smith* (Cambridge: Cambridge University Press, 1981), a work exploring Smith's theory of justice and arguing for the centrality of "natural jurisprudence" to Smith's philosophy. *Wealth and Virtue* (Cambridge: Cambridge University Press, 1983), edited by I. Hont and M. Ignatieff, contains useful essays about Smith's seemingly paradoxical arguments on this classical theme. D. D. Raphael's *Adam Smith* (Oxford: Oxford University Press, 1985) supplies a useful and precise overview of Smith and his thought. A. S. Skinner's *A System of Social Science: Paper Relating to Adam Smith* (Oxford: Clarendon Press, 1979) brings together a number of Skinner's seminal papers on Smith, while D. Winch's *Adam Smith's Politics: An Essay in Historiographic Revision* (Cambridge: Cambridge University Press, 1978) counters the view that Smith assimilated "politics" to "economics," and with attention to the historical context reconstructs the substance of Smith's political theory. For an overview of the secondary literature, see M. B. Lightwood's *A Selected Bibliography of Significant Works About Adam Smith* (Philadelphia: University of Pennsylvania Press, 1984); and F. Cordasco's and B. Franklin's *Adam Smith: A Bibliographical Checklist* (New York: B. Franklin, 1950).

For a recent comprehensive discussion of Smith's philosophy (one that places particular emphasis on connections between Smith and contemporary moral and political philosophy, as well as on Smith's contribution to and criticisms of the Enlightenment), see C. L. Griswold, *Adam Smith and the Virtues of Enlightenment* (Cambridge: Cambridge University Press, 1999). Another recent philosophical work of relevance is S. Fleischacker's *A Third Concept of Liberty: Judgment and Freedom in Kant and Adam Smith* (Princeton, N.J.: Princeton University Press, 1999).

# The Theory of Moral Sentiments

## PART IV

### *Of the Effect of Utility upon the Sentiment of Approbation*

#### *Chapter 1*

OF THE BEAUTY WHICH THE APPEARANCE
OF UTILITY BESTOWS UPON ALL THE
PRODUCTIONS OF ART,
AND OF THE EXTENSIVE INFLUENCE
OF THIS SPECIES OF BEAUTY

That utility is one of the principal sources of beauty has been observed by every body, who has considered with any attention what constitutes the nature of beauty. The conveniency of a house gives pleasure to the spectator as well as its regularity, and he is as much hurt when he observes the contrary defect, as when he sees the correspondent windows of different forms, or the door not placed exactly in the middle of the building. That the fitness of any system or machine to produce the end for which it was intended, bestows a certain propriety and beauty upon the whole, and renders the very thought and contemplation of it agreeable, is so very obvious that nobody has overlooked it.

The cause too, why utility pleases, has of late been assigned by an ingenious and agreeable philosopher, who joins the greatest depth of thought to the greatest elegance of expression, and possesses the singular and happy talent of treating the abstrusest subjects not only with the most perfect perspicuity, but with the most lively eloquence. The utility of any object, according to him, pleases the master by perpetually suggesting to him the pleasure or conveniency which it is fitted to promote. Every time he looks at it, he is put in mind of this pleasure; and the object in this manner becomes a source of perpetual satisfaction and enjoyment. The spectator enters by sympathy into the sentiments of the master, and necessarily views the object under the same agreeable aspect. When we visit the palaces of the great, we cannot help conceiving the satisfaction we should enjoy if we ourselves were the masters, and were possessed of so much artful and ingeniously contrived accommodation. A similar account is given why the appearance of inconveniency should render any object disagreeable both to the owner and to the spectator.

But that this fitness, this happy contrivance of any production of art, should often be more valued, than the very end for which it was intended; and that the exact adjustment of the means for attaining any conveniency or pleasure, should frequently be more regarded, than that very conveniency or pleasure, in the attainment of which their whole merit would seem to consist, has not, so far as I know, been yet taken notice of by any body. That this however is very frequently the case, may be observed in a thousand instances, both in the most frivolous and in the most important concerns of human life.

When a person comes into his chamber, and finds the chairs all standing in the middle of the room, he is angry with his servant, and rather than see them continue in that disorder, perhaps takes the trouble himself to set them all in their places with their backs to the wall. The whole propriety of this new situation arises from its superior conveniency in leaving the floor free and disengaged. To attain this conveniency he voluntarily puts himself to more trouble than all he could have suffered from the want of it; since nothing was more easy, than to have set himself down upon one of them, which is probably what he does when his labour is over. What he wanted therefore, it seems, was not so much this conveniency, as that arrangement of things which promotes it. Yet it is this conveniency which ultimately recommends that arrangement, and bestows upon it the whole of its propriety and beauty.

A watch, in the same manner, that falls behind above two minutes in a day, is despised by one curious in watches. He sells it perhaps for a couple of guineas, and purchases another at fifty, which will not lose above a minute in a fortnight. The sole use of watches however, is to tell us what o'clock it is, and to hinder us from breaking any engagement, or suffering any other inconveniency by our ignorance in that particular point. But the person so nice with regard to this machine, will not always be found either more scrupulously punctual than other men, or more anxiously concerned upon any other account, to know precisely what time of day it is. What interests him is not so much the attainment of this piece of knowledge, as the perfection of the machine which serves to attain it.

How many people ruin themselves by laying out money on trinkets of frivolous utility? What pleases these lovers of toys is not so much the utility, as the aptness of the machines which are fitted to promote it. All their pockets are stuffed with little conveniencies. They contrive new pockets, unknown in the clothes of other people, in order to carry a greater number. They walk about loaded with a multitude of baubles, in weight and sometimes in value not inferior to an ordinary Jew's-box, some of which may sometimes be of some little use, but all of which might at all times be very well spared, and of which the whole utility is certainly not worth the fatigue of bearing the burden.

Nor is it only with regard to such frivolous objects that our conduct is influenced by this principle; it is often the secret motive of the most serious and important pursuits of both private and public life.

The poor man's son, whom heaven in its anger has visited with ambition, when he begins to look around him, admires the condition of the rich. He finds the cottage of his father too small for his accommodation, and fancies he should be lodged more at his ease in a palace. He is displeased with being obliged to walk a-foot, or to endure the fatigue of riding on horseback. He sees his superiors carried about in machines, and imagines that in one of these he could travel with less inconveniency. He feels himself naturally indolent, and willing to serve himself with his own hands as lit-

tle as possible; and judges, that a numerous retinue of servants would save him from a great deal of trouble. He thinks if he had attained all these, he would sit still contentedly, and be quiet, enjoying himself in the thought of the happiness and tranquillity of his situation. He is enchanted with the distant idea of this felicity. It appears in his fancy like the life of some superior rank of beings, and, in order to arrive at it, he devotes himself for ever to the pursuit of wealth and greatness. To obtain the conveniencies which these afford, he submits in the first year, nay in the first month of his application, to more fatigue of body and more uneasiness of mind than he could have suffered through the whole of his life from the want of them. He studies to distinguish himself in some laborious profession. With the most unrelenting industry he labours night and day to acquire talents superior to all his competitors. He endeavours next to bring those talents into public view, and with equal assiduity solicits every opportunity of employment. For this purpose he makes his court to all mankind; he serves those whom he hates, and is obsequious to those whom he despises. Through the whole of his life he pursues the idea of a certain artificial and elegant repose which he may never arrive at, for which he sacrifices a real tranquillity that is at all times in his power, and which, if in the extremity of old age he should at last attain to it, he will find to be in no respect preferable to that humble security and contentment which he had abandoned for it. It is then, in the in last dregs of life, his body wasted with toil and diseases, his mind galled and ruffled by the memory of a thousand injuries and disappointments which he imagines he has met with from the injustice of his enemies, or from the perfidy and ingratitude of his friends, that he begins at last to find that wealth and greatness are mere trinkets of frivolous utility, no more adapted for procuring ease of body or tranquillity of mind than the tweezer-cases of the lover of toys; and like them too, more troublesome to the person who carries them about with him than all the advantages they can afford him are commodious. There is no other real difference between them, except that the conveniencies of the one are somewhat more observable than those of the other. The palaces, the gardens, the equipage, the retinue of the great, are objects of which the obvious conveniency strikes every body. They do not require that their masters should point out to us wherein consists their utility. Of our own accord we readily enter into it, and by sympathy enjoy and thereby applaud the satisfaction which they are fitted to afford him. But the curiosity of a tooth-pick, of an ear-picker, of a machine for cutting the nails, or of any other trinket of the same kind, is not so obvious. Their conveniency may perhaps be equally great, but it is not so striking, and we do not so readily enter into the satisfaction of the man who possesses them. They are therefore less reasonable subjects of vanity than the magnificence of wealth and greatness; and in this consists the sole advantage of these last. They more effectually gratify that love of distinction so natural to man. To one who was to live alone in a desolate island it might be a matter of doubt, perhaps, whether a palace, or a collection of such small conveniencies as are commonly contained in a tweezer-case, would contribute most to his happiness and enjoyment. If he is to live in society, indeed, there can be no comparison, because in this, as in all other cases, we constantly pay more regard to the sentiments of the spectator, than to those of the person principally concerned, and consider rather how his situation will appear to other people, than how it will appear to himself. If we examine, however, why the spectator distinguishes with such admiration the condition of the rich and the great, we shall find that it is not so much upon account of the superior ease or pleasure which they are supposed to enjoy, as of the numberless artificial and elegant contrivances for promoting this ease or pleasure. He does not even imagine that they are really happier than other people: but he imagines that they possess more means of happiness. And it is the ingenious and artful adjustment of those means to the end for which they were intended, that is the principal source of his admiration. But in the languor of disease and the weariness of old age, the pleasures of the vain and empty distinctions of greatness disappear. To one, in this situation, they are no longer capable of recommending those toilsome pursuits in which they had formerly engaged him. In his

heart he curses ambition, and vainly regrets the ease and the indolence of youth, pleasures which are fled for ever, and which he has foolishly sacrificed for what, when he has got it, can afford him no real satisfaction. In this miserable aspect does greatness appear to every man when reduced either by spleen or disease to observe with attention his own situation, and to consider what it is that is really wanting to his happiness. Power and riches appear then to be, what they are, enormous and operose machines contrived to produce a few trifling conveniencies to the body, consisting of springs the most nice and delicate, which must be kept in order with the most anxious attention, and which in spite of all our care are ready every moment to burst into pieces, and to crush in their ruins their unfortunate possessor. They are immense fabrics, which it requires the labour of a life to raise, which threaten every moment to overwhelm the person that dwells in them, and which while they stand, though they may save him from some smaller inconveniencies, can protect him from none of the severer inclemencies of the season. They keep off the summer shower, not the winter storm, but leave him always as much, and sometimes more exposed than before, to anxiety, to fear, and to sorrow; to diseases, to danger, and to death.

But though this splenetic philosophy, which in time of sickness or low spirits is familiar to every man, thus entirely depreciates those great objects of human desire, when in better health and in better humour, we never fail to regard them under a more agreeable aspect. Our imagination, which in pain and sorrow seems to be confined and cooped up within our own persons, in times of ease and prosperity expands itself to every thing around us. We are then charmed with the beauty of that accommodation which reigns in the palaces and oeconomy of the great; and admire how every thing is adapted to promote their ease, to prevent their wants, to gratify their wishes, and to amuse and entertain their most frivolous desires. If we consider the real satisfaction which all these things are capable of affording, by itself and separated from the beauty of that arrangement which is fitted to promote it, it will always appear in the highest degree contemptible and trifling. But we rarely view it in this abstract and philosophical light. We naturally confound it in our imagination with the order, the regular and harmonious movement of the system, the machine or economy by means of which it is produced. The pleasures of wealth and greatness, when considered in this complex view, strike the imagination as something grand and beautiful and noble, of which the attainment is well worth all the toil and anxiety which we are so apt to bestow upon it.

And it is well that nature imposes upon us in this manner. It is this deception which rouses and keeps in continual motion the industry of mankind. It is this which first prompted them to cultivate the ground, to build houses, to found cities and commonwealths, and to invent and improve all the sciences and arts, which ennoble and embellish human life; which have entirely changed the whole face of the globe, have turned the rude forests of nature into agreeable and fertile plains, and made the track less and barren ocean a new fund of subsistence, and the great high road of communication to the different nations of the earth. The earth by these labours of mankind has been obliged to redouble her natural fertility, and to maintain a greater multitude of inhabitants. It is to no purpose, that the proud and unfeeling landlord views his extensive fields, and without a thought for the wants of his brethren, in imagination consumes himself the whole harvest that grows upon them. The homely and vulgar proverb, that the eye is larger than the belly, never was more fully verified than with regard to him. The capacity of his stomach bears no proportion to the immensity of his desires, and will receive no more than that of the meanest peasant. The rest he is obliged to distribute among those, who prepare, in the nicest manner, that little which he himself makes use of, among those who fit up the palace in which this little is to be consumed, among those who provide and keep in order all the different baubles and trinkets, which are employed in the oeconomy of greatness; all of whom thus derive from his luxury and caprice, that share of the necessaries of life,

which they would in vain have expected from his humanity or his justice. The produce of the soil maintains at all times nearly that number of inhabitants which it is capable of maintaining. The rich only select from the heap what is most precious and agreeable. They consume little more than the poor, and in spite of their natural selfishness and rapacity, though they mean only their own conveniency, though the sole end which they propose from the labours of all the thousands whom they employ, be the gratification of their own vain and insatiable desires, they divide with the poor the produce of all their improvements. They are led by an invisible hand to make nearly the same distribution of the necessaries of life, which would have been made, had the earth been divided into equal portions among all its inhabitants, and thus without intending it, without knowing it, advance the interest of the society, and afford means to the multiplication of the species. When Providence divided the earth among a few lordly masters, it neither forgot nor abandoned those who seemed to have been left out in the partition. These last too enjoy their share of all that it produces. In what constitutes the real happiness of human life, they are in no respect inferior to those who would seem so much above them. In ease of body and peace of mind, all the different ranks of life are nearly upon a level, and the beggar, who suns himself by the side of the highway, possesses that security which kings are fighting for.

The same principle, the same love of system, the same regard to the beauty of order, of art and contrivance, frequently serves to recommend those institutions which tend to promote the public welfare. When a patriot exerts himself for the improvement of any part of the public police, his conduct does not always arise from pure sympathy with the happiness of those who are to reap the benefit of it. It is not commonly from a fellow-feeling with carriers and waggoners that a public-spirited man encourages the mending of high roads. When the legislature establishes premiums and other encouragements to advance the linen or woollen manufactures, its conduct seldom proceeds from pure sympathy with the wearer of cheap or fine cloth, and much less from that with the manufacturer or merchant. The perfection of police, the extension of trade and manufactures, are noble and magnificent objects. The contemplation of them pleases us, and we are interested in whatever can tend to advance them. They make part of the great system of government, and the wheels of the political machine seem to move with more harmony and ease by means of them. We take pleasure in beholding the perfection of so beautiful and grand a system, and we are uneasy till we remove any obstruction that can in the least disturb or encumber the regularity of its motions. All constitutions of government, however, are valued only in proportion as they tend to promote the happiness of those who live under them. This is their sole use and end. From a certain spirit of system, however, from a certain love of art and contrivance, we sometimes seem to value the means more than the end, and to be eager to promote the happiness of our fellow-creatures, rather from a view to perfect and improve a certain beautiful and orderly system, than from any immediate sense or feeling of what they either suffer or enjoy. There have been men of the greatest public spirit, who have shown themselves in other respects not very sensible to the feelings of humanity. And on the contrary, there have been men of the greatest humanity, who seem to have been entirely devoid of public spirit. Every man may find in the circle of his acquaintance instances both of the one kind and the other. Who had ever less humanity, or more public spirit, than the celebrated legislator of Muscovy? The social and well-natured James the First of Great Britain seems, on the contrary, to have had scarce any passion, either for the glory or the interest of his country. Would you awaken the industry of the man who seems almost dead to ambition, it will often be to no purpose to describe to him the happiness of the rich and the great; to tell him that they are generally sheltered from the sun and the rain, that they are seldom hungry, that they are seldom cold, and that they are rarely exposed to weariness, or to want of any kind. The most eloquent exhortation of this kind will have little effect upon him. If you would hope to succeed, you must describe to him the conveniency and arrangement of the different apartments in their palaces; you must explain to him the propriety of their equipages, and point out to him the number, the order, and the different offices of all their attendants. If any thing is capable of making impression upon him, this will. Yet all these things tend only to keep off the sun and the rain, to save them from hunger and cold, from want and weariness. In the same manner, if you would implant public virtue in the breast of him who seems heedless of the interest of his country, it will often be to no purpose to tell him, what superior advantages the subjects of a well-governed state enjoy; that they are better lodged, that they are better clothed, that they are better fed. These considerations will commonly make no great impression. You will be more likely to persuade, if you describe the great system of public police which procures these advantages, if you explain the connexions and dependencies of its several parts, their mutual subordination to one another, and their general subserviency to the happiness of the society; if you show how this system might be introduced into his own country, what it is that hinders it from taking place there at present, how those obstructions might be removed, and all the several wheels of the machine of government be made to move with more harmony and smoothness, without grating upon one another, or mutually retarding one another's motions. It is scarce possible that a man should listen to a discourse of this kind, and not feel himself animated to some degree of public spirit. He will, at least for the moment, feel some desire to remove those obstructions, and to put into motion so beautiful and so orderly a machine. Nothing tends so much to promote public spirit as the study of politics, of the several systems of civil government, their advantages and disadvantages, of the constitution of our own country, its situation, and interest with regard to foreign nations, its commerce, its defence, the disadvantages it labours under, the dangers to which it may be exposed, how to remove the one, and how to guard against the other. Upon this account political disquisitions, if just, and reasonable, and practicable, are of all the works of speculation the most useful. Even the weakest and the worst of them are not altogether without their utility. They serve at least to animate the public passions of men, and rouse them to seek out the means of promoting the happiness of the society.

### *Chapter II*

#### OF THE BEAUTY WHICH THE APPEARANCE OF UTILITY BESTOWS UPON THE CHARACTERS AND ACTIONS OF MEN; AND HOW FAR THE PERCEPTION OF THIS BEAUTY MAY BE REGARDED AS ONE OF THE ORIGINAL PRINCIPLES OF APPROBATION

The characters of men, as well as the contrivances of art, or the institutions of civil government, may be fitted either to promote or to disturb the happiness both of the individual and of the society. The prudent, the equitable, the active, resolute, and sober character promises prosperity and satisfaction, both to the person himself and to every one connected with him. The rash, the insolent, the slothful, effeminate, and voluptuous, on the contrary, forebodes ruin to the individual, and misfortune to all who have any thing to do with him. The first turn of mind has at least all the beauty which can belong to the most perfect machine that was ever invented for promoting the most agreeable purpose: and the second, all the deformity of the most awkward and clumsy contrivance. What institution of government could tend so much to promote the happiness of mankind as the general prevalence of wisdom and virtue? All government is but an imperfect remedy for the deficiency of these. Whatever beauty, therefore, can belong to civil government upon account of its utility, must in a far superior degree belong to these. On the contrary, what civil policy can be so ruinous and destructive as the vices of men? The fatal effects of bad government arise from nothing, but that it does not sufficiently guard against the mischiefs which human wickedness gives occasion to.

This beauty and deformity which characters appear to derive from their usefulness or inconveniency, are apt to strike, in a peculiar manner, those who consider, in an abstract and philosophical light, the actions and conduct of mankind. When a philosopher goes to examine why humanity is approved of,

or cruelty condemned, he does not always form to himself, in a very clear and distinct manner, the conception of any one particular action either of cruelty or of humanity, but is commonly contented with the vague and indeterminate idea which the general names of those qualities suggest to him. But it is in particular instances only that the propriety or impropriety, the merit or demerit of actions is very obvious and discernible. It is only when particular examples are given that we perceive distinctly either the concord or disagreement between our own affections and those of the agent, or feel a social gratitude arise towards him in the one case, or a sympathetic resentment in the other. When we consider virtue and vice in an abstract and general manner, the qualities by which they excite these several sentiments seem in a great measure to disappear, and the sentiments themselves become less obvious and discernible. On the contrary, the happy effects of the one and the fatal consequences of the other seem then to rise up to the view, and as it were to stand out and distinguish themselves from all the other qualities of either.

The same ingenious and agreeable author who first explained why utility pleases, has been so struck with this view of things, as to resolve our whole approbation of virtue into a perception of this species of beauty which results from the appearance of utility. No qualities of the mind, he observes, are approved of as virtuous, but such as are useful or agreeable either to the person himself or to others; and no qualities are disapproved of as vicious but such as have a contrary tendency. And Nature, indeed, seems to have so happily adjusted our sentiments of approbation and disapprobation, to the conveniency both of the individual and of the society, that after the strictest examination it will be found, I believe, that this is universally the case. But still I affirm, that it is not the view of this utility or hurtfulness which is either the first or principal source of our approbation and disapprobation. These sentiments are no doubt enhanced and enlivened by the perception of the beauty or deformity which results from this utility or hurtfulness. But still, I say, they are originally and essentially different from this perception.

For first of all, it seems impossible that the approbation of virtue should be a sentiment of the same kind with that by which we approve of a convenient and well-contrived building; or that we should have no other reason for praising a man than that for which we commend a chest of drawers.

And secondly, it will be found, upon examination, that the usefulness of any disposition of mind is seldom the first ground of our approbation; and that the sentiment of approbation always involves in it a sense of propriety quite distinct from the perception of utility. We may observe this with regard to all the qualities which are approved of as virtuous, both those which, according to this system, are originally valued as useful to ourselves, as well as those which are esteemed on account of their usefulness to others.

The qualities most useful to ourselves are, first of all, superior reason and understanding, by which we are capable of discerning the remote consequences of all our actions, and of foreseeing the advantage or detriment which is likely to result from them: and secondly, self-command, by which we are enabled to abstain from present pleasure or to endure present pain, in order to obtain a greater pleasure or to avoid a greater pain in some future time. In the union of those two qualities consists the virtue of prudence, of all the virtues that which is most useful to the individual.

With regard to the first of those qualities, it has been observed on a former occasion, that superior reason and understanding are originally approved of as just and right and accurate, and not merely as useful or advantageous. It is in the abstruser sciences, particularly in the higher parts of mathematics, that the greatest and most admired exertions of human reason have been displayed. But the utility of those sciences, either to the individual or to the public, is not very obvious, and to prove it, requires a discussion which is not always very easily comprehended. It was not, therefore, their utility which first recommended them to the public admiration. This quality was but little insisted upon, till it became necessary to make some reply to the reproaches of those, who, having themselves no taste for such sublime discoveries, endeavoured to depreciate them as useless.

That self-command, in the same manner, by which we restrain our present appetites, in order to gratify them more fully upon another occasion, is approved of, as much under the aspect of propriety, as under that of utility. When we act in this manner, the sentiments which influence our conduct seem exactly to coincide with those of the spectator. The spectator does not feel the solicitations of our present appetites. To him the pleasure which we are to enjoy a week hence, or a year hence, is just as interesting as that which we are to enjoy this moment. When for the sake of the present, therefore, we sacrifice the future, our conduct appears to him absurd and extravagant in the highest degree, and he cannot enter into the principles which influence it. On the contrary, when we abstain from present pleasure, in order to secure greater pleasure to come, when we act as if the remote object interested us as much as that which immediately presses upon the senses, as our affections exactly correspond with his own, he cannot fail to approve of our behaviour: and as he knows from experience, how few are capable of this self-command, he looks upon our conduct with a considerable degree of wonder and admiration. Hence arises that eminent esteem with which all men naturally regard a steady perseverance in the practice of frugality, industry, and application, though directed to no other purpose than the acquisition of fortune. The resolute firmness of the person who acts in this manner, and in order to obtain a great though remote advantage, not only gives up all present pleasures, but endures the greatest labour both of mind and body, necessarily commands our approbation. That view of his interest and happiness which appears to regulate his conduct, exactly tallies with the idea which we naturally form of it. There is the most perfect correspondence between his sentiments and our own, and at the same time, from our experience of the common weakness of human nature, it is a correspondence which we could not reasonably have expected. We not only approve, therefore, but in some measure admire his conduct, and think it worthy of a considerable degree of applause. It is the consciousness of this merited approbation and esteem which is alone capable of supporting the agent in this tenour of conduct. The pleasure which we are to enjoy ten years hence interests us so little in comparison with that which we may enjoy to-day, the passion which the first excites, is naturally so weak in comparison with that violent emotion which the second is apt to give occasion to, that the one could never be any balance to the other, unless it was supported by the sense of propriety, by the consciousness that we merited the esteem and approbation of every body, by acting in the one way, and that we became the proper objects of their contempt and derision by behaving in the other.

Humanity, justice, generosity, and public spirit, are the qualities most useful to others. Wherein consists the propriety of humanity and justice has been explained upon a former occasion, where it was shewn how much our esteem and approbation of those qualities depended upon the concord between the affections of the agent and those of the spectators.

The propriety of generosity and public spirit is founded upon the same principle with that of justice. Generosity is different from humanity. Those two qualities, which at first sight seem so nearly allied, do not always belong to the same person. Humanity is the virtue of a woman, generosity of a man. The fair-sex, who have commonly much more tenderness than ours, have seldom so much generosity. That women rarely make considerable donations, is an observation of the civil law. Humanity consists merely in the exquisite fellow-feeling which the spectator entertains with the sentiments of the persons principally concerned, so as to grieve for their sufferings, to resent their injuries, and to rejoice at their good fortune. The most humane actions require no self-denial, no self-command, no great exertion of the sense of propriety. They consist only in doing what this exquisite sympathy would of its own accord prompt us to do. But it is otherwise with generosity. We never are generous except when in some respect we prefer some other person to ourselves, and sacrifice some great and important interest of our own to an equal interest of a friend or of a superior. The man who gives up his pretensions to an office that was the great object of his ambition, because he imagines that the services of another are better entitled to it; the man who exposes his life to defend that of his friend, which he judges to be of

more importance; neither of them act from humanity, or because they feel more exquisitely what concerns that other person than what concerns themselves. They both consider those opposite interests, not in the light in which they naturally appear to themselves, but in that in which they appear to others. To every bystander, the success or preservation of this other person may justly be more interesting than their own; but it cannot be so to themselves. When to the interest of this other person, therefore, they sacrifice their own, they accommodate themselves to the sentiments of the spectator, and by an effort of magnanimity act according to those views of things which, they feel, must naturally occur to any third person. The soldier who throws away his life in order to defend that of his officer, would perhaps be but little affected by the death of that officer, if it should happen without any fault of his own; and a very small disaster which had befallen himself might excite a much more lively sorrow. But when he endeavours to act so as to deserve applause, and to make the impartial spectator enter into the principles of his conduct, he feels, that to every body but himself, his own life is a trifle compared with that of his officer, and that when he sacrifices the one to the other, he acts quite properly and agreeably to what would be the natural apprehensions of every impartial bystander.

It is the same case with the greater exertions of public spirit. When a young officer exposes his life to acquire some inconsiderable addition to the dominions of his sovereign, it is not because the acquisition of the new territory is, to himself, an object more desireable than the preservation of his own life. To him his own life is of infinitely more value than the conquest of a whole kingdom for the state which he serves. But when he compares those two objects with one another, he does not view them in the light in which they naturally appear to himself, but in that in which they appear to the nation he fights for. To them the success of the war is of the highest importance; the life of a private person of scarce any consequence. When he puts himself in their situation, he immediately feels that he cannot be too prodigal of his blood, if, by shedding it, he can promote so valuable a purpose. In thus thwarting, from a sense of duty and propriety, the strongest of all natural propensities, consists the heroism of his conduct. There is many an honest Englishman, who, in his private station, would be more seriously disturbed by the loss of a guinea, than by the national loss of Minorca, who yet, had it been in his power to defend that fortress, would have sacrificed his life a thousand times rather than, through his fault, have let it fall into the hands of the enemy. When the first Brutus led forth his own sons to a capital punishment, because they had conspired against the rising liberty of Rome, he sacrificed what, if he had consulted his own breast only, would appear to be the stronger to the weaker affection. Brutus ought naturally to have felt much more for the death of his own sons, than for all that probably Rome could have suffered from the want of so great an example. But he viewed them, not with the eyes of a father, but with those of a Roman citizen. He entered so thoroughly into the sentiments of this last character, that he paid no regard to that tie, by which he himself was connected with them; and to a Roman citizen, the sons even of Brutus seemed contemptible, when put into the balance with the smallest interest of Rome. In these and in all other cases of this kind, our admiration is not so much founded upon the utility, as upon the unexpected, and on that account the great, the noble, and exalted propriety of such actions. This utility, when we come to view it, bestows upon them, undoubtedly, a new beauty, and upon that account still further recommends them to our approbation. This beauty, however, is chiefly perceived by men of reflection and speculation, and is by no means the quality which first recommends such actions to the natural sentiments of the bulk of mankind.

It is to be observed, that so far as the sentiment of approbation arises from the perception of this beauty of utility, it has no reference of any kind to the sentiments of others. If it was possible, therefore, that a person should grow up to manhood without any communication with society, his own actions might, notwithstanding, be agreeable or disagreeable to him on account of their tendency to his happiness or disadvantage. He might perceive a beauty of this kind in prudence, temperance, and good conduct, and a deformity in the opposite behaviour: he might view his own temper and character with that sort of satisfaction with which we consider a well-contrived machine, in the one case; or with that sort of distaste and dissatisfaction with which we regard a very awkward and clumsy contrivance, in the other. As these perceptions, however, are merely a matter of taste, and have all the feebleness and delicacy of that species of perceptions, upon the justness of which what is properly called taste is founded, they probably would not be much attended to by one in this solitary and miserable condition. Even though they should occur to him, they would by no means have the same effect upon him, antecedent to his connexion with society, which they would have in consequence of that connexion. He would not be cast down with inward shame at the thought of this deformity; nor would he be elevated with secret triumph of mind from the consciousness of the contrary beauty. He would not exult from the notion of deserving reward in the one case, nor tremble from the suspicion of meriting punishment in the other. All such sentiments suppose the idea of some other being, who is the natural judge of the person that feels them; and it is only by sympathy with the decisions of this arbiter of his conduct, that he can conceive, either the triumph of self-applause, or the shame of self-condemnation.

# The Wealth of Nations

## INTRODUCTION AND PLAN OF THE WORK

The annual labour of every nation is the fund which originally supplies it with all the necessaries and conveniencies of life which it annually consumes, and which consist always, either in the immediate produce of that labour, or in what is purchased with that produce from other nations.

According therefore, as this produce, or what is purchased with it, bears a greater or smaller proportion to the number of those who are to consume it, the nation will be better or worse supplied with all the necessaries and conveniencies for which it has occasion.

But this proportion must in every nation be regulated by two different circumstances; first, by the skill, dexterity, and judgment with which its labour is generally applied; and, secondly, by the proportion between the number of those who are employed in useful labour, and that of those who are not so employed. Whatever be the soil, climate, or extent of territory of any particular nation, the abundance or scantiness of its annual supply must, in that particular situation, depend upon those two circumstances.

The abundance or scantiness of this supply too seems to depend more upon the former of those two circumstances than upon the latter. Among the savage nations of hunters and fishers, every individual who is able to work, is more or less employed in useful labour, and endeavours to provide, as well as he can, the necessaries and conveniencies of life, for himself, or such of his family or tribe as are either too old, or too young, or too infirm to go a hunting and fishing. Such nations, however, are so miserably poor, that, from mere want, they are frequently reduced, or, at least, think themselves reduced, to the necessity sometimes of directly destroying, and sometimes of abandoning their infants, their old people, and those afflicted with lingering diseases, to perish with hunger, or to be devoured by wild beasts. Among civilized and thriving nations, on the contrary, though a great number of people do not labour at all, many of whom consume the produce of ten times, frequently of a hundred times more labour than the greater part of those who work; yet the produce of the whole labour of the society is so great, that all are often abundantly supplied, and a workman, even of the lowest and poorest order, if he is frugal and industrious, may enjoy a greater share of the necessaries and conveniencies of life than it is possible for any savage to acquire.

The causes of this improvement, in the productive powers of labour, and the order, according to which its produce is naturally distributed among the different ranks and conditions of men in the society, make the subject of the First Book of this Inquiry.

Whatever be the actual state of the skill, dexterity, and judgment with which labour is applied in any nation, the abundance or scantiness of its annual supply must depend, during the continuance of that state, upon the proportion between the number of those who are annually employed in useful labour, and that of those who are not so employed. The number of useful and productive labourers, it will hereafter appear, is every where in proportion to the quantity of capital stock which is employed in setting them to work, and to the particular way in which it is so employed. The Second Book, therefore, treats of the nature of capital stock, of the manner in which it is gradually accumulated, and of the different quantities of labour which it puts into motion, according to the different ways in which it is employed.

Nations tolerably well advanced as to skill, dexterity, and judgment, in the application of labour, have followed very different plans in the general conduct or direction of it; and those plans have not all been equally favourable to the greatness of its produce. The policy of some nations has given extraordinary encouragement to the industry of the country; that of others to the industry of towns. Scarce any nation has dealt equally and impartially with every sort of industry. Since the downfall of the Roman empire, the policy of Europe has been more favourable to arts, manufactures, and commerce, the industry of towns; than to agriculture, the industry of the country. The circumstances which seem to have introduced and established this policy are explained in the Third Book.

Though those different plans were, perhaps, first introduced by the private interests and prejudices of particular orders of men, without any regard to, or foresight of, their consequences upon the general welfare of the society; yet they have given occasion to very different theories of political economy; of which some magnify the importance of that industry which is carried on in towns, others of that which is carried on in the country. Those theories have had a considerable influence, not only upon the opinions of men of learning, but upon the public conduct of princes and sovereign states. I have endeavoured, in the Fourth Book, to explain, as fully and distinctly as I can, those different theories, and the principal effects which they have produced in different ages and nations.

To explain in what has consisted the revenue of the great body of the people, or what has been the nature of those funds which, in different ages and nations, have supplied their annual consumption, is the object of these Four first Books. The Fifth and last Book treats of the revenue of the sovereign, or commonwealth. In this Book I have endeavoured to show; first, what are the necessary expences of the sovereign, or commonwealth; which of those expences ought to be defrayed by the general contribution of the whole society; and which of them, by that of some particular part only, or of some particular members of it; secondly, what are the different methods in which the whole society may be made to contribute towards defraying the expences incumbent on the whole society, and what are the principal advantages and inconveniencies of each of those methods: and, thirdly and

lastly, what are the reasons and causes which have induced almost all modern governments to mortgage some part of this revenue, or to contract debts, and what have been the effects of those debts upon the real wealth, the annual produce of the land and labour of the society.

# BOOK I

## *Of the Causes of Improvement in the Productive Powers of Labour, and of the Order According to Which Its Produce Is Naturally Distributed Among the Different Ranks of the People*

### *Chapter 1*

#### OF THE DIVISION OF LABOUR

The greatest improvement in the productive powers of labour, and the greater part of the skill, dexterity, and judgment with which it is any where directed, or applied, seem to have been the effects of the division of labour.

The effects of the division of labour, in the general business of society, will be more easily understood, by considering in what manner it operates in some particular manufactures. It is commonly supposed to be carried further in some very trifling ones; not perhaps that it really is carried further in them than in others of more importance: but in those trifling manufactures which are destined to supply the small wants of but a small number of people, the whole number of workmen must necessarily be small; and those employed in every different branch of the work can often be collected into the same workhouse, and placed at once under the view of the spectator. In those great manufactures, on the contrary, which are destined to supply the great wants of the great body of the people, every different branch of the work employs so great a number of workmen, that it is impossible to collect them all into the same workhouse. We can seldom see more, at one time, than those employed in one single branch. Though in such manufactures, therefore, the work may really be divided into a much greater number of parts, than in those of a more trifling nature, the division is not near so obvious, and has accordingly been much less observed.

To take an example, therefore, from a very trifling manufacture; but one in which the division of labour has been very often taken notice of, the trade of the pin-maker; a workman not educated to this business (which the division of labour has rendered a distinct trade), nor acquainted with the use of the machinery employed in it (to the invention of which the same division of labour has probably given occasion), could scarce, perhaps, with his utmost industry, make one pin in a day, and certainly could not make twenty. But in the way in which this business is now carried on, not only the whole work is a peculiar trade, but it is divided into a number of branches, of which the greater part are likewise peculiar trades. One man draws out the wire, another straights it, a third cuts it, a fourth points it, a fifth grinds it at the top for receiving the head; to make the head requires two or three distinct operations; to put it on, is a peculiar business, to whiten the pins is another; it is even a trade by itself to put them into the paper; and the important business of making a pin is, in this manner, divided into about eighteen distinct operations, which, in some manufactories, are all performed by distinct hands, though in others the same man will sometimes perform two or three of them. I have seen a small manufactory of this kind where ten men only were employed, and where some of them consequently performed two or three distinct operations. But though they were very poor, and therefore but indifferently accommodated with the necessary machinery, they could, when they exerted themselves, make among them about twelve pounds of pins in a day. There are in a pound upwards of four thousand pins of a middling size. Those ten persons, therefore, could make among them upwards of forty-eight thousand pins in a day. Each person, therefore, making a tenth part of forty-eight thousand pins, might be considered as making four thousand eight hundred pins in a day. But if they had all wrought separately and independently, and without any of them having been educated to this peculiar business, they certainly could not each of them have made

twenty, perhaps not one pin in a day; that is, certainly, not the two hundred and fortieth, perhaps not the four thousand eight hundredth part of what they are at present capable of performing, in consequence of a proper division and combination of their different operations. . . .

This great increase of the quantity of work, which, in consequence of the division of labour, the same number of people are capable of performing, is owing to three different circumstances; first, to the increase of dexterity in every particular workman; secondly, to the saving of the time which is commonly lost in passing from one species of work to another; and lastly, to the invention of a great number of machines which facilitate and abridge labour, and enable one man to do the work of many.

First, the improvement of the dexterity of the workman necessarily increases the quantity of the work he can perform, and the division of labour, by reducing every man's business to some one simple operation, and by making this operation the sole employment of his life, necessarily increases very much the dexterity of the workman. A common smith, who, though accustomed to handle the hammer, has never been used to make nails, if upon some particular occasion he is obliged to attempt it, will scarce, I am assured, be able to make above two or three hundred nails in a day, and those too very bad ones. A smith who has been accustomed to make nails, but whose sole or principal business has not been that of a nailer, can seldom with his utmost diligence make more than eight hundred or a thousand nails in a day. I have seen several boys under twenty years of age who had never exercised any other trade but that of making nails, and who, when they exerted themselves, could make, each of them, upwards of two thousand three hundred nails in a day. The making of a nail, however, is by no means one of the simplest operations. The same person blows the bellows, stirs or mends the fire as there is occasion, heats the iron, and forges every part of the nail: In forging the head too he is obliged to change his tools. The different operations into which the making of a pin, or of a metal button, is subdivided, are all of them much more simple, and the dexterity of the person, of whose life it has been the sole business to perform them, is usually much greater. The rapidity with which some of the operations of those manufactures are performed, exceeds what the human hand could, by those who had never seen them, be supposed capable of acquiring.

Secondly, the advantage which is gained by saving the time commonly lost in passing from one sort of work to another, is much greater than we should at first view be apt to imagine it. It is impossible to pass very quickly from one kind of work to another, that is carried on in a different place, and with quite different tools. A country weaver, who cultivates a small farm, must lose a good deal of time in passing from his loom to the field, and from the field to his loom. When the two trades can be carried on in the same workhouse, the loss of time is no doubt much less. It is even in this case, however, very considerable. A man commonly saunters a little in turning his hand from one sort of employment to another. When he first begins the new work he is seldom very keen and hearty; his mind, as they say, does not go to it, and for some time he rather trifles than applies to good purpose. The habit of sauntering and of indolent careless application, which is naturally, or rather necessarily acquired by every country workman who is obliged to change his work and his tools every half hour, and to apply his hand in twenty different ways almost every day of his life; renders him almost always slothful and lazy, and incapable of any vigorous application even on the most pressing occasions. Independent, therefore, of his deficiency in point of dexterity, this cause alone must always reduce considerably the quantity of work which he is capable of performing.

Thirdly, and lastly, every body must be sensible how much labour is facilitated and abridged by the application of proper machinery. It is unnecessary to give any example. I shall only observe, therefore, that the invention of all those machines by which labour is so much facilitated and abridged, seems to have been originally owing to the division of labour. Men are much more likely to discover easier and readier methods of attaining any object, when the whole attention of their minds is directed towards that single object, than when it is dissipated among a great variety of things. But in consequence of the division of labour, the whole of every man's attention comes naturally to be directed towards some one very simple object. It is naturally to be expected, therefore, that some one or other of those who are employed in each particular branch of labour should soon find out easier and readier methods of performing their own particular work, wherever the nature of it admits of such improvement. A great part of the machines made use of in those manufactures in which labour is most subdivided, were originally the inventions of common workmen, who, being each of them employed in some very simple operation, naturally turned their thoughts towards finding out easier and readier methods of performing it. Whoever has been much accustomed to visit such manufactures, must frequently have been shewn very pretty machines, which were the inventions of such workmen, in order to facilitate and quicken their own particular part of the work. In the first fire-engines, a boy was constantly employed to open and shut alternately the communication between the boiler and the cylinder, according as the piston either ascended or descended. One of those boys, who loved to play with his companions, observed that, by tying a string from the handle of the valve, which opened this communication, to another part of the machine, the valve would open and shut without his assistance, and leave him at liberty to divert himself with his play-fellows. One of the greatest improvements that has been made upon this machine, since it was first invented, was in this manner the discovery of a boy who wanted to save his own labour.

All the improvements in machinery, however, have by no means been the inventions of those who had occasion to use the machines. Many improvements have been made by the ingenuity of the makers of the machines, when to make them became the business of a peculiar trade; and some by that of those who are called philosophers or men of speculation, whose trade it is, not to do any thing, but to observe every thing; and who, upon that account, are often capable of combining together the powers of the most distant and dissimilar objects. In the progress of society, philosophy or speculation becomes, like every other employment, the principal or sole trade and occupation of a particular class of citizens. Like every other employment too, it is sub-divided into a great number of different branches, each of which affords occupation to a peculiar tribe or class of philosophers; and this subdivision of employment in philosophy, as well as in every other business, improves dexterity, and saves time. Each individual becomes more expert in his own peculiar branch, more work is done upon the whole, and the quantity of science is considerably increased by it.

It is the great multiplication of the productions of all the different arts, in consequence of the division of labour, which occasions, in a well-governed society, that universal opulence which extends itself to the lowest ranks of the people. Every workman has a great quantity of his own work to dispose of beyond what he himself has occasion for; and every other workman being exactly in the same situation, he is enabled to exchange a great quantity of his own goods for a great quantity, or, what comes to the same thing, for the price of a great quantity of theirs. He supplies them abundantly with what they have occasion for, and they accommodate him as amply with what he has occasion for, and a general plenty diffuses itself through all the different ranks of the society.

Observe the accommodation of the most common artificer or day-labourer in a civilized and thriving country, and you will perceive that the number of people of whose industry a part, though but a small part, has been employed in procuring him this accommodation, exceeds all computation. The woollen coat, for example, which covers the day-labourer, as coarse and rough as it may appear, is the produce of the joint labour of a great multitude of workmen. The shepherd, the sorter of the wool, the wool-comber or carder, the dyer, the scribbler, the spinner, the weaver, the fuller, the dresser, with many others, must all join their different arts in order to complete even this homely production. How many merchants and carriers, besides, must have been employed in transporting the materials from some of those workmen to others who often live in a very distant part of the country! How much commerce and navigation in particular, how many ship-builders, sailors, sail-makers, rope-makers, must have been employed in order to bring together the different drugs made use of by the dyer, which often come from the remotest corners of the world! What a variety of labour too is necessary in order to produce the tools of the meanest of those workmen! To say nothing of such complicated machines as the ship of the sailor, the mill of the fuller, or even the loom of the weaver, let us consider only what a variety of labour is requisite in order to form that very simple machine, the shears with which the shepherd clips the wool. The miner, the builder of the furnace for smelting the ore, the feller of the timber, the burner of the charcoal to be made use of in the smelting-house, the brick-maker, the bricklayer, the workmen who attend the furnace, the mill-wright, the forger, the smith, must all of them join their different arts in order to produce them. Were we to examine, in the same manner, all the different parts of his dress and household furniture, the coarse linen shirt which he wears next his skin, the shoes which cover his feet, the bed which he lies on, and all the different parts which compose it, the kitchen-grate at which he prepares his victuals, the coals which he makes use of for that purpose, dug from the bowels of the earth, and brought to him perhaps by a long sea and a long land carriage, all the other utensils of his kitchen, all the furniture of his table, the knives and forks, the earthen or pewter plates upon which he serves up and divides his victuals, the different hands employed in preparing his bread and his beer, the glass window which lets in the heat and the light, and keeps out the wind and the rain, with all the knowledge and art requisite for preparing that beautiful and happy invention, without which these northern parts of the world could scarce have afforded a very comfortable habitation, to-gether with the tools of all the different workmen employed in producing those different conveniencies; if we examine, I say, all these things, and consider what a variety of labour is employed about each of them, we shall be sensible that without the assistance and co-operation of many thousands, the very meanest person in a civilized country could not be provided, even according to, what we very falsely imagine, the easy and simple manner in which he is commonly accommodated. Compared, indeed, with the more extravagant luxury of the great, his accommodation must no doubt appear extremely simple and easy; and yet it may be true, perhaps, that the accommodation of an European prince does not always so much exceed that of an industrious and frugal peasant, as the accommodation of the latter exceeds that of many an African king, the absolute master of the lives and liberties of ten thousand naked savages.

## Chapter II

### OF THE PRINCIPLE WHICH GIVES OCCASION TO THE DIVISION OF LABOUR

This division of labour, from which so many advantages are derived, is not originally the effect of any human wisdom, which foresees and intends that general opulence to which it gives occasion. It is the necessary, though very slow and gradual consequence of a certain propensity in human nature which has in view no such extensive utility; the propensity to truck, barter, and exchange one thing for another.

Whether this propensity be one of those original principles in human nature, of which no further account can be given; or whether, as seems more probable, it be the necessary consequence of the faculties of reason and speech, it belongs not to our present subject to enquire. It is common to all men, and to be found in no other race of animals, which seem to know neither this nor any other species of contracts. Two greyhounds, in running down the same hare, have sometimes the appearance of acting in some sort of concert. Each turns her towards his companion, or endeavours to intercept her when his companion turns her towards himself. This, however, is not the effect of any contract, but of the accidental concurrence of their passions in the same object at that particular time. Nobody ever saw a dog make a fair and deliberate exchange of one bone for another with another dog. Nobody ever saw one ani-

mal by its gestures, and natural cries signify to another, this is mine, that yours; I am willing to give this for that. When an animal wants to obtain something either of a man or of another animal, it has no other means of persuasion but to gain the favour of those whose service it requires. A puppy fawns upon its dam, and a spaniel endeavours by a thousand attractions to engage the attention of its master who is at dinner, when it wants to be fed by him. Man sometimes uses the same arts with his brethren, and when he has no other means of engaging them to act according to his inclinations, endeavours by every servile and fawning attention to obtain their good will. He has not time, however, to do this upon every occasion. In civilized society he stands at all times in need of the co-operation and assistance of great multitudes, while his whole life is scarce sufficient to gain the friendship of a few persons. In almost every other race of animals each individual, when it is grown up to maturity, is intirely independent, and in its natural state has occasion for the assistance of no other living creature. But man has almost constant occasion for the help of his brethren, and it is in vain for him to expect it from their benevolence only. He will be more likely to prevail if he can interest their self-love in his favour, and shew them that it is for their own advantage to do for him what he requires of them. Whoever offers to another a bargain of any kind, proposes to do this. Give me that which I want, and you shall have this which you want, is the meaning of every such offer; and it is in this manner that we obtain from one another the far greater part of those good offices which we stand in need of. It is not from the benevolence of the butcher, the brewer, or the baker, that we expect our dinner, but from their regard to their own interest. We address ourselves, not to their humanity but to their self-love, and never talk to them of our own necessities but of their advantages. Nobody but a beggar chuses to depend chiefly upon the benevolence of his fellow-citizens. Even a beggar does not depend upon it entirely. The charity of well-disposed people, indeed, supplies him with the whole fund of his subsistence. But though this principle ultimately provides him with all the necessaries of life which he has occasion for, it neither does nor can provide him with them as he has occasion for them. The greater part of his occasional wants are supplied in the same manner as those of other people, by treaty, by barter, and by purchase. With the money which one man gives him he purchases food. The old cloaths which another bestows upon him he exchanges for other old cloaths which suit him better, or for lodging, or for food, or for money, with which he can buy either food, cloaths, or lodging, as he has occasion.

As it is by treaty, by barter, and by purchase, that we obtain from one another the greater part of those mutual good offices which we stand in need of, so it is this same trucking disposition which originally gives occasion to the division of labour. In a tribe of hunters or shepherds a particular person makes bows and arrows, for example, with more readiness and dexterity than any other. He frequently exchanges them for cattle or for venison with his companions; and he finds at last that he can in this manner get more cattle and venison, than if he himself went to the field to catch them. From a regard to his own interest, therefore, the making of bows and arrows grows to be his chief business, and he becomes a sort of armourer. Another excels in making the frames and covers of their little huts or moveable houses. He is accustomed to be of use in this way to his neighbours, who reward him in the same manner with cattle and with venison, till at last he finds it his interest to dedicate himself entirely to this employment, and to become a sort of house-carpenter. In the same manner a third becomes a smith or a brazier, a fourth a tanner or dresser of hides or skins, the principal part of the clothing of savages. And thus the certainty of being able to exchange all that surplus part of the produce of his own labour, which is over and above his own consumption, for such parts of the produce of other men's labour as he may have occasion for, encourages every man to apply himself to a particular occupation, and to cultivate and bring to perfection whatever talent or genius he may possess for that particular species of business.

The difference of natural talents in different men is, in reality, much less than we are aware of; and the very different genius which appears to distinguish men of different professions, when grown up to maturity, is not upon many occasions so much the cause, as the effect of the division of labour. The difference between the most dissimilar characters, between a philosopher and a common street porter, for example, seems to arise not so much from nature, as from habit, custom, and education. When they came into the world, and for the first six or eight years of their existence, they were, perhaps, very much alike, and neither their parents nor play-fellows could perceive any remarkable difference. About that age, or soon after, they come to be employed in very different occupations. The difference of talents comes then to be taken notice of, and widens by degrees, till at last the vanity of the philosopher is willing to acknowledge scarce any resemblance. But without the disposition to truck, barter, and exchange, every man must have procured to himself every necessary and conveniency of life which he wanted. All must have had the same duties to perform, and the same work to do, and there could have been no such difference of employment as could alone give occasion to any great difference of talents.

As it is this disposition which forms that difference of talents, so remarkable among men of different professions, so it is this same disposition which renders that difference useful. Many tribes of animals acknowledged to be all of the same species, derive from nature a much more remarkable distinction of genius, than what, antecedent to custom and education, appears to take place among men. By nature a philosopher is not in genius and disposition half so different from a street porter, as a mastiff is from a greyhound, or a greyhound from a spaniel, or this last from a shepherd's dog. Those different tribes of animals, however, though all of the same species, are of scarce any use to one another. The strength of the mastiff is not, in the least, supported either by the swiftness of the greyhound, or by the sagacity of the spaniel, or by the docility of the shepherd's dog. The effects of those different geniuses and talents, for want of the power or disposition to barter and exchange, cannot be brought into a common stock, and do not in the least contribute to the better accommodation and conveniency of the species. Each animal is still obliged to support and defend itself, separately and independently, and derives no sort of advantage from that variety of talents with which nature has distinguished its fellows. Among men, on the contrary, the most dissimilar geniuses are of use to one another; the different produces of their respective talents, by the general disposition to truck, barter, and exchange, being brought, as it were, into common stock, where every man may purchase whatever part of the produce of other men's talents he has occasion for.

## *Chapter IV*

### OF THE ORIGIN AND USE OF MONEY

When the division of labour has been once thoroughly established, it is but a very small part of a man's wants which the produce of his own labour can supply. He supplies the far greater part of them by exchanging that surplus part of the produce of his own labour, which is over and above his own consumption, for such parts of the produce of other men's labour as he has occasion for. Every man thus lives by exchanging, or becomes in some measure a merchant, and the society itself grows to be what is properly a commercial society.

But when the division of labour first began to take place, this power of exchanging must frequently have been very much clogged and embarrassed in its operations. One man, we shall suppose, has more of a certain commodity than he himself has occasion for, while another has less. The former consequently would be glad to dispose of, and the latter to purchase, a part of this superfluity. But if this latter should chance to have nothing that the former stands in need of, no exchange can be made between them. The butcher has more meat in his shop than he himself can consume, and the brewer and the baker would each of them be willing to purchase a part of it. But they have nothing to offer in exchange, except the different productions of their respective trades, and the butcher is already provided with all the bread and beer which he has immediate occasion for. No exchange can, in this case, be made between them.

He cannot be their merchant, nor they his customers; and they are all of them thus mutually less serviceable to one another. In order to avoid the inconveniency of such situations, every prudent man in every period of society, after the first establishment of the division of labour, must naturally have endeavoured to manage his affairs in such a manner, as to have at all times by him, besides the peculiar produce of his own industry, a certain quantity of some one commodity or other, such as he imagined few people would be likely to refuse in exchange for the produce of their industry.

Many different commodities, it is probable, were successively both thought of and employed for this purpose. In the rude ages of society, cattle are said to have been the common instrument of commerce; and, though they must have been a most inconvenient one, yet in old times we find things were frequently valued according to the number of cattle which had been given in exchange for them. The armour of Diomede, says Homer, cost only nine oxen; but that of Glaucus cost an hundred oxen. Salt is said to be the common instrument of commerce and exchanges in Abyssinia; a species of shells in some parts of the coast of India; dried cod at Newfoundland; tobacco in Virginia; sugar in some of our West India colonies; hides or dressed leather in some other countries; and there is at this day a village in Scotland where it is not uncommon, I am told, for a workman to carry nails instead of money to the baker's shop or the ale-house.

In all countries, however, men seem at last to have been determined by irresistible reasons to give the preference, for this employment, to metals above every other commodity. Metals can not only be kept with as little loss as any other commodity, scarce any thing being less perishable than they are, but they can likewise, without any loss, be divided into any number of parts, as by fusion those parts can easily be re-united again; a quality which no other equally durable commodities possess, and which more than any other quality renders them fit to be the instruments of commerce and circulation. The man who wanted to buy salt, for example, and had nothing but cattle to give in exchange for it, must have been obliged to buy salt to the value of a whole ox, or a whole sheep at a time. He could seldom buy less than this, because what he was to give for it could seldom be divided without loss; and if he had a mind to buy more, he must, for the same reasons, have been obliged to buy double or triple the quantity, the value, to wit, of two or three oxen, or of two or three sheep. If, on the contrary, instead of sheep or oxen, he had metals to give in exchange for it, he could easily proportion the quantity of the metal to the precise quantity of the commodity which he had immediate occasion for. . . .

It is in this manner that money has become in all civilized nations the universal instrument of commerce, by the intervention of which goods of all kinds are bought and sold, or exchanged for one another.

What are the rules which men naturally observe in exchanging them either for money or for one another, I shall now proceed to examine. These rules determine what may be called the relative or exchangeable value of goods.

The word Value, it is to be observed, has two different meanings, and sometimes expresses the utility of some particular object, and sometimes the power of purchasing other goods which the possession of that object conveys. The one may be called 'value in use;' the other, 'value in exchange.' The things which have the greatest value in use have frequently little or no value in exchange; and, on the contrary, those which have the greatest value in exchange have frequently little or no value in use. Nothing is more useful than water: but it will purchase scarce any thing; scarce any thing can be had in exchange for it. A diamond, on the contrary, has scarce any value in use; but a very great quantity of other goods may frequently be had in exchange for it.

In order to investigate the principles which regulate the exchangeable value of commodities, I shall endeavour to shew,

First, what is the real measure of this exchangeable value; or, wherein consists the real price of all commodities,

Secondly, what are the different parts of which this real price is composed or made up.

And, lastly, what are the different circumstances which sometimes raise some or all of these different parts of price above, and sometimes sink them below their natural or ordinary rate; or, what are the causes which sometimes hinder the market price, that is, the actual price of commodities, from coinciding exactly with what may be called their natural price.

I shall endeavour to explain, as fully and distinctly as I can, those three subjects in the three following chapters, for which I must very earnestly entreat both the patience and attention of the reader: his patience in order to examine a detail which may perhaps in some places appear unnecessarily tedious; and his attention in order to understand what may, perhaps, after the fullest explication which I am capable of giving of it, appear still in some degree obscure. I am always willing to run some hazard of being tedious in order to be sure that I am perspicuous; and after taking the utmost pains that I can to be perspicuous, some obscurity may still appear to remain upon a subject in its own nature extremely abstracted.

## Chapter V

### OF THE REAL AND NOMINAL PRICE OF COMMODITIES, OR OF THEIR PRICE IN LABOUR, AND THEIR PRICE IN MONEY

Every man is rich or poor according to the degree in which he can afford to enjoy the necessaries, conveniencies, and amusements of human life. But after the division of labour has once thoroughly taken place, it is but a very small part of these with which a man's own labour can supply him. The far greater part of them he must derive from the labour of other people, and he must be rich or poor according to the quantity of that labour which he can command, or which he can afford to purchase. The value of any commodity, therefore, to the person who possesses it, and who means not to use or consume it himself, but to exchange it for other commodities, is equal to the quantity of labour which it enables him to purchase or command. Labour, therefore, is the real measure of the exchangeable value of all commodities.

The real price of every thing, what every thing really costs to the man who wants to acquire it, is the toil and trouble of acquiring it. What every thing is really worth to the man who has acquired it, and who wants to dispose of it or exchange it for something else, is the toil and trouble which it can save to himself, and which it can impose upon other people. What is bought with money or with goods is purchased by labour as much as what we acquire by the toil of our own body. That money or those goods indeed save us this toil. They contain the value of a certain quantity of labour which we exchange for what is supposed at the time to contain the value of an equal quantity. Labour was the first price, the original purchase money that was paid for all things. It was not by gold or by silver, but by labour, that all the wealth of the world was originally purchased; and its value, to those who possess it and who want to exchange it for some new productions, is precisely equal to the quantity of labour which it can enable them to purchase or command.

Wealth, as Mr. Hobbes says, is power. But the person who either acquires, or succeeds to a great fortune, does not necessarily acquire or succeed to any political power, either civil or military. His fortune may, perhaps, afford him the means of acquiring both, but the mere possession of that fortune does not necessarily convey to him either. The power which that possession immediately and directly conveys to him, is the power of purchasing; a certain command over all the labour, or over all the produce of labour which is then in the market. His fortune is greater or less, precisely in proportion to the extent of this power; or to the quantity either of other men's labour, or, what is the same thing, of the produce of other men's labour, which it enables him to purchase or command. The exchangeable value of every thing must always be precisely equal to the extent of this power which it conveys to its owner.

But though labour be the real measure of the exchangeable value of all commodities, it is not that by which their value is commonly estimated. It is often difficult to ascertain the proportion between two different quantities of labour. The time spent in two different sorts of work will not always alone determine this proportion. The different degrees of

hardship endured, and of ingenuity exercised, must likewise be taken into account. There may be more labour in an hour's hard work than in two hours easy business; or in an hour's application to a trade which it cost ten years labour to learn, than in a month's industry at an ordinary and obvious employment. But it is not easy to find any accurate measure either of hardship or ingenuity. In exchanging indeed the different productions of different sorts of labour for one another, some allowance is commonly made for both. It is adjusted, however, not by any accurate measure, but by the higgling and bargaining of the market, according to that sort of rough equality which, though not exact, is sufficient for carrying on the business of common life.

Every commodity besides, is more frequently exchanged for, and thereby compared with, other commodities than with labour. It is more natural, therefore, to estimate its exchangeable value by the quantity of some other commodity than by that of the labour which it can purchase. The greater part of people too understand better what is meant by a quantity of a particular commodity, than by a quantity of labour. The one is a plain palpable object; the other an abstract notion, which, though it can be made sufficiently intelligible, is not altogether so natural and obvious.

But when barter ceases, and money has become the common instrument of commerce, every particular commodity is more frequently exchanged for money than for any other commodity. The butcher seldom carries his beef or his mutton to the baker, or the brewer, in order to exchange them for bread or for beer, but he carries them to the market, where he exchanges them for money, and afterwards exchanges that money for bread and for beer. The quantity of money which he gets for them regulates too the quantity of bread and beer which he can afterwards purchase. It is more natural and obvious to him, therefore, to estimate their value by the quantity of money, the commodity for which he immediately exchanges them, than by that of bread and beer, the commodities for which he can exchange them only by the intervention of another commodity; and rather to say that his butcher's meat is worth threepence or fourpence a pound, than that it is worth three or four pounds of bread, or three or four quarts of small beer. Hence it comes to pass, that the exchangeable value of every commodity is more frequently estimated by the quantity of money, than by the quantity either of labour or of any other commodity which can be had in exchange for it.

Gold and silver, however, like every other commodity, vary in their value, are sometimes cheaper and sometimes dearer, sometimes of easier and sometimes of more difficult purchase. The quantity of labour which any particular quantity of them can purchase or command, or the quantity of other goods which it will exchange for, depends always upon the fertility or barrenness of the mines which happen to be known about the time when such exchanges are made. The discovery of the abundant mines of America reduced, in the sixteenth century, the value of gold and silver in Europe to about a third of what it had been before. As it cost less labour to bring those metals from the mine to the market, so when they were brought thither they could purchase or command less labour; and this revolution in their value, though perhaps the greatest, is by no means the only one of which history gives some account. But as a measure of quantity, such as the natural foot, fathom, or handful, which is continually varying in its own quantity, can never be an accurate measure of the quantity of other things; so a commodity which is itself continually varying in its own value, can never be an accurate measure of the value of other commodities. Equal quantities of labour, at all times and places, may be said to be of equal value to the labourer. In his ordinary state of health, strength and spirits; in the ordinary degree of his skill and dexterity, he must always lay down the same portion of his ease, his liberty, and his happiness. The price which he pays must always be the same, whatever may be the quantity of goods which he receives in return for it. Of these, indeed, it may sometimes purchase a greater and sometimes a smaller quantity; but it is their value which varies, not that of the labour which purchases them. At all times and places that is dear which it is difficult to come at, or which it costs much labour to acquire;

and that cheap which is to be had easily, or with very little labour. Labour alone, therefore, never varying in its own value, is alone the ultimate arid real standard by which the value of all commodities can at all times and places be estimated and compared. It is their real price; money is their nominal price only.

But though equal quantities of labour are always of equal value to the labourer, yet to the person who employs him they appear sometimes to be of greater and sometimes of smaller value. He purchases them sometimes with a greater and sometimes with a smaller quantity of goods, and to him the price of labour seems to vary like that of all other things. It appears to him dear in the one case, and cheap in the other. In reality, however, it is the goods which are cheap in the one case, and dear in the other.

In this popular sense, therefore, labour, like commodities, may be said to have a real and a nominal price. Its real price may be said to consist in the quantity of the necessaries and conveniencies of life which are given for it; its nominal price, in the quantity of money. The labourer is rich or poor, is well or ill rewarded, in proportion to the real, not to the nominal price of his labour. . . .

## Chapter VI

### OF THE COMPONENT PARTS
### OF THE PRICE OF COMMODITIES

In that early and rude state of society which precedes both the accumulation of stock and the appropriation of land, the proportion between the quantities of labour necessary for acquiring different objects seems to be the only circumstance which can afford any rule for exchanging them for one another. If among a nation of hunters, for example, it usually costs twice the labour to kill a beaver which it does to kill a deer, one beaver should naturally exchange for or be worth two deer. It is natural that what is usually the produce of two days or two hours labour, should be worth double of what is usually the produce of one day's or one hour's labour.

If the one species of labour should be more severe than the other, some allowance will naturally be made for this superior hardship; and the produce of one hour's labour in the one way may frequently exchange for that of two hours labour in the other.

Or if the one species of labour requires an uncommon degree of dexterity and ingenuity, the esteem which men have for such talents, will naturally give a value to their produce, superior to what would be due to the time employed about it. Such talents can seldom be acquired but in consequence of long application, and the superior value of their produce may frequently be no more than a reasonable compensation for the time and labour which must be spent in acquiring them. In the advanced state of society, allowances of this kind, for superior hardship and superior still, are commonly made in the wages of labour; and something of the same kind must probably have taken place in its earliest and rudest period.

In this state of things, the whole produce of labour belongs to the labourer; and the quantity of labour commonly employed in acquiring or producing any commodity, is the only circumstance which can regulate the quantity of labour which it ought commonly to purchase, command, or exchange for.

As soon as stock has accumulated in the hands of particular persons, some of them will naturally employ it in setting to work industrious people, whom they will supply with materials and subsistence, in order to make a profit by the sale of their work, or by what their labour adds to the value of the materials. In exchanging the complete manufacture either for money, for labour, or for other goods, over and above what may be sufficient to pay the price of the materials, and the wages of the workmen, something must be given for the profits of the undertaker of the work who hazards his stock in this adventure. The value which the workmen add to the materials, therefore, resolves itself in this case into two parts, of which the one pays their wages, the other the profits of their employer upon the whole stock of materials and wages which he advanced. He could have no interest to employ them, unless he expected from the sale of their work something more than what was sufficient to replace his stock to him; and he could have no interest to employ a great stock rather than a small one, unless his profits were to bear some proportion to the extent of his stock.

The profits of stock, it may perhaps be thought, are only a different name for the wages of a particular sort of labour, the labour of inspection and direction. They are, however, altogether different, are regulated by quite different principles, and bear no proportion to the quantity, the hardship, or the ingenuity of this supposed labour of inspection and direction. They are regulated altogether by the value of the stock employed, and are greater or smaller in proportion to the extent of this stock. Let us suppose, for example, that in some particular place, where the common annual profits of manufacturing stock are ten per cent, there are two different manufactures, in each of which twenty workmen are employed at the rate of fifteen pounds a year each, or at the expence of three hundred a year in each manufactory. Let us suppose too, that the coarse materials annually wrought up in the one cost only seven hundred pounds, while the finer materials in the other cost seven thousand. The capital annually employed in the one will in this case amount only to one thousand pounds; whereas that employed in the other will amount to seven thousand three hundred pounds. At the rate of ten per cent, therefore, the undertaker of the one will expect an yearly profit of about one hundred pounds only; while that of the other will expect about seven hundred and thirty pounds. But though their profits are so very different, their labour of inspection and direction may be either altogether or very nearly the same. In many great works, almost the whole labour of this kind is committed to some principal clerk. His wages properly express the value of this labour of inspection and direction. Though in settling them some regard is had commonly, not only to his labour and skill, but to the trust which is reposed in him, yet they never bear any regular proportion to the capital of which he oversees the management; and the owner of this capital, though he is thus discharged of almost all labour, still expects that his profits should bear a regular proportion to his capital. In the price of commodities, therefore, the profits of stock constitute a component part altogether different from the wages of labour, and regulated by quite different principles.

In this state of things, the whole produce of labour does not always belong to the labourer. He must in most cases share it with the owner of the stock which employs him. Neither is the quantity of labour commonly employed in acquiring or producing any commodity, the only circumstance which can regulate the quantity which it ought commonly to purchase, command, or exchange for. An additional quantity, it is evident, must be due for the profits of the stock which advanced the wages and furnished the materials of that labour.

As soon as the land of any country has all become private property, the landlords, like all other men, love to reap where they never sowed, and demand a rent even for its natural produce. The wood of the forest, the grass of the field, and all the natural fruits of the earth, which, when land was in common, cost the labourer only the trouble of gathering them, come, even to him, to have an additional price fixed upon them. He must then pay for the licence to gather them; and must give up to the landlord a portion of what his labour either collects or produces. This portion, or, what comes to the same thing, the price of this portion, constitutes the rent of land, and in the price of the greater part of commodities makes a third component part.

The real value of all the different component parts of price, it must be observed, is measured by the quantity of labour which they can, each of them, purchase or command. Labour measures the value not only of that part of price which resolves itself into labour, but of that which resolves itself into rent, and of that which resolves itself into profit. . . .

# BOOK IV

## *Of Systems of Political Economy*

### *Introduction*

Political economy, considered as a branch of the science of a statesman or legislator, proposes two distinct objects; first, to provide a plentiful revenue or subsistence for the people, or more properly to enable them to provide such a revenue or subsistence for themselves; and secondly, to supply the state or commonwealth with a revenue sufficient for the publick services. It proposes to enrich both the people and the sovereign.

The different progress of opulence in different ages and nations, has given occasion to two different systems of political economy, with regard to enriching the people. The one may be called the system of commerce, the other that of agriculture. I shall endeavour to explain both as fully and distinctly as I can, and shall begin with the system of commerce. It is the modern system, and is best understood in our own country and in our own times.

## *Chapter II*

### OF RESTRAINTS UPON THE IMPORTATION FROM FOREIGN COUNTRIES OF SUCH GOODS AS CAN BE PRODUCED AT HOME

. . . Every individual is continually exerting himself to find out the most advantageous employment for whatever capital he can command. It is his own advantage, indeed, and not that of the society, which he has in view. But the study of his own advantage naturally, or rather necessarily leads him to prefer that employment which is most advantageous to the society.

First, every individual endeavours to employ his capital as near home as he can, and consequently as much as he can in the support of domestick industry; provided always that he can thereby obtain the ordinary, or not a great deal less than the ordinary profits of stock.

Thus upon equal or nearly equal profits, every wholesale merchant naturally prefers the home-trade to the foreign trade of consumption, and the foreign trade of consumption to the carrying trade. In the home-trade his capital is never so long out of his sight as it frequently is in the foreign trade of consumption. He can know better the character and situation of the persons whom he trusts, and if he should happen to be deceived, he knows better the laws of the country from which he must seek redress. In the carrying trade, the capital of the merchant is, as it were, divided between two foreign countries, and no part of it is ever necessarily brought home, or placed under his own immediate view and command. The capital which an Amsterdam merchant employs in carrying corn from Konnigsberg to Lisbon, and fruit and wine from Lisbon to Konnigsberg, must generally be the one-half of it at Konnigsberg and the other half at Lisbon. No part of it need ever come to Amsterdam. The natural residence of such a merchant should either be at Konnigsberg or Lisbon, and it can only be some very particular circumstances which can make him prefer the residence of Amsterdam. The uneasiness, however, which he feels at being separated so far from his capital, generally determines him to bring part both of the Konnigsberg goods which he destines for the market of Lisbon, and of the Lisbon goods which he destines for that of Konnigsberg, to Amsterdam: and though this necessarily subjects him to a double charge of loading and unloading, as well as to the payment of some duties and customs, yet for the sale of having some part of his capital always under his own view and command, he willingly submits to this extraordinary charge; and it is in this manner that every country which has any considerable share of the carrying trade, becomes always the emporium, or general market, for the goods of all the different countries whose trade it carries on. The merchant, in order to save a second loading and unloading, endeavours always to sell in the home-market as much of the goods of all those different countries as he can, and thus, so far as he can, to convert his carrying trade into a foreign trade of consumption. A merchant, in the same manner, who is engaged in the foreign trade of consumption, when he collects goods for foreign markets, will always be glad, upon equal or nearly equal profits, to sell as great a part of them at home as he can. He saves himself the risk and trouble of exportation, when, so far as he can, he thus converts his foreign trade of consumption into a home-trade. Home is in this manner the center, if I may say so, round which the capitals of the inhabitants of every country are continually circulating, and towards which they are always tending, though by particular causes they may sometimes be driven off and repelled from it towards more distant employments. But a capital employed in the home-trade, it has already been shown, necessarily puts into motion a greater quantity of domestic industry, and gives revenue and employment to a greater number of the inhabitants of the country, than an equal capital employed in the foreign trade of consumption: and one employed in the foreign trade of consumption has the same advantage over an equal capital employed in the carrying trade. Upon equal, or only nearly equal profits, therefore, every individual naturally inclines to employ his capital in the manner in which it is likely to afford the greatest support to domestick industry, and to give revenue and employment to the greatest number of people of his own country.

Secondly, every individual who employs his capital in the support of domestick industry, necessarily endeavours so to direct that industry, that its produce may be of the greatest possible value.

The produce of industry is what it adds to the subject or materials upon which it is employed. In proportion as the value of this produce is great or small, so will likewise be the profits of the employer. But it is only for the sake of profit that any man employs a capital in the support of industry; and he will always, therefore, endeavour to employ it in the support of that industry of which the produce is likely to be of the greatest value or to exchange for the greatest quantity either of money or of other goods.

But the annual revenue of every society is always precisely equal to the exchangeable value of the whole annual produce of its industry, or rather is precisely the same thing with that exchangeable value. As every individual, therefore, endeavours as much as he can both to employ his capital in the support of domestick industry, and so to direct that industry that its produce may be of the greatest value; every individual necessarily labours to render the annual revenue of the society as great as he can. He generally, indeed, neither intends to promote the publick interest, nor knows how much he is promoting it. By preferring the support of domestick to that of foreign industry, he intends only his own security; and by directing that industry in such a manner as its produce may be of the greatest value, he intends only his own gain, and he is in this, as in many other cases, led by an invisible hand to promote an end which was no part of his intention. Nor is it always the worse for the society that it was no part of it. By pursuing his own interest he frequently promotes that of the society more effectually than when he really intends to promote it. I have never known much good done by those who affected to trade for the publick good. It is an affectation, indeed, not very common among merchants, and very few words need be employed in dissuading them from it.

What is the species of domestick industry which his capital can employ, and of which the produce is likely to be of the greatest value, every individual, it is evident, can, in his local situation, judge much better than any statesman or lawgiver can do for him. The stateman, who should attempt to direct private people in what manner they ought to employ their capitals, would not only load himself with a most unnecessary attention, but assume an authority which could safely be trusted, not only to no single person, but to no council or senate whatever, and which would nowhere be so dangerous as in the hands of a man who had folly and presumption enough to fancy himself fit to exercise it. . . .

## Chapter IX

### OF THE AGRICULTURAL SYSTEMS . . .

. . . All systems either of preference or of restraint, therefore, being thus completely taken away, the obvious and simple system of natural liberty establishes itself of its own accord. Every man, as long as he does not violate the laws of justice, is left perfectly free to pursue his own interest his own way, and to bring both his industry and capital into competition with those of any other man, or order of men. The sovereign is completely discharged from a duty, in the attempting to perform which he must always be exposed to innumerable delusions, and for the proper performance of which no human wisdom or knowledge could ever be sufficient; the duty of superintending the industry of private people, and of directing it towards the employments most suitable to the interest of the society. According to the system of natural liberty, the sovereign has only three duties to attend to; three duties of great importance, indeed, but plain and intelligible to common understandings: first, the duty of protecting the society from the violence and invasion of other independent societies; secondly, the duty of protecting, as far as possible,

every member of the society from the injustice or oppression of every other member of it, or the duty of establishing an exact administration of justice; and, thirdly, the duty of erecting and maintaining certain publick works and certain publick institutions, which it can never be for the interest of any individual, or small number of individuals, to erect and maintain; because the profit could never repay the expence to any individual or small number of individuals, though it may frequently do much more than repay it to a great society. . . .

The proper performance of those several duties of the sovereign necessarily supposes a certain expence; and this expence again necessarily requires a certain revenue to support it. In the following book, therefore, I shall endeavour to explain; first, what are the necessary expences of the sovereign or commonwealth; and which of those expences ought to be defrayed by the general contribution of the whole society; and which of them, by that of some particular part only, or of some particular members of the society: secondly, what are the different methods in which the whole society may be made to contribute towards defraying the expences incumbent on the whole society, and what are the principal advantages and inconveniencies of each of those methods: and, thirdly, what are the reasons and causes which have induced almost all modern governments to mortgage some part of this revenue, or to contract debts, and what have been the effects of those debts upon the real wealth, the annual produce of the land and labour of the society. The following book, therefore, will naturally be divided into three chapters.

# BOOK V

## Of the Revenue of the Sovereign or Commonwealth

### Chapter I

### OF THE EXPENCES OF THE SOVEREIGN OR COMMONWEALTH

. . . The expence of defending the society, and that of supporting the dignity of the chief magistrate, are both laid out for the general benefit of the whole society. It is reasonable, therefore, that they should be defrayed by the general contribution of the whole society, all the different members contributing, as nearly as possible, in proportion to their respective abilities.

The expence of the administration of justice too, may, no doubt, be considered as laid out for the benefit of the whole society. There is no impropriety, therefore, in its being defrayed by the general contribution of the whole society. The persons, however, who give occasion to this expence are those who, by their injustice in one way or another, make it necessary to seek redress or protection from the courts of justice. The persons again most immediately benefited by this expence, are those whom the courts of justice either restore to their rights, or maintain in their rights. The expence of the administration of justice, therefore, may very properly be defrayed by the particular contribution of one or other, or both of those two different sets of persons, according as different occasions may require, that is, by the fees of court. It cannot be necessary to have recourse to the general contribution of the whole society, except for the conviction of those criminals who have not themselves any estate or fund sufficient for paying those fees.

Those local or provincial expences of which the benefit is local or provincial (what is laid out, for example, upon the police of a particular town or district) ought to be defrayed by a local or provincial revenue, and ought to be no burden upon the general revenue of the society. It is unjust that the whole society should contribute towards an expence of which the benefit is confined to a part of the society.

The expence of maintaining good roads and communications is, no doubt, beneficial to the whole society, and may, therefore, without any injustice, be defrayed by the general contribution of the whole society. This expence, however, is most immediately and directly beneficial to those who travel or carry goods from one place to another, and to those who consume such goods. . . .

The expence of the institutions for education and religious instruction, is likewise, no doubt, benefi-

cial to the whole society, and may, therefore, without injustice, be defrayed by the general contribution of the whole society. This expence, however, might perhaps with equal propriety, and even with some advantage, be defrayed altogether by those who receive the immediate benefit of such education and instruction, or by the voluntary contribution of those who think they have occasion for either the one or the other.

When the institutions or publick works which are beneficial to the whole society, either cannot be maintained altogether, or are not maintained altogether by the contribution of such particular members of the society as are most immediately benefited by them, the deficiency must in most cases be made up by the general contribution of the whole society. The general revenue of the society, over and above defraying the expence of defending the society, and of supporting the dignity of the chief magistrate, must make up for the deficiency of many particular branches of revenue. The sources of this general or publick revenue, I shall endeavour to explain in the following chapter.

## Chapter II

### OF THE SOURCES OF THE GENERAL OR PUBLICK REVENUE OF THE SOCIETY

The revenue which must defray, not only the expence of defending the society and of supporting the dignity of the chief magistrate, but all the other necessary expences of government, for which the constitution of the state has not provided any particular revenue, may be drawn, either, first, from some fund which peculiarly belongs to the sovereign or commonwealth, and which is independent of the revenue of the people; or, secondly, from the revenue of the people.

Part II. *Of Taxes* . . . Before I enter upon the examination of particular taxes, it is necessary to premise the four following maxims with regard to taxes in general.

I. The subjects of every state ought to contribute towards the support of the government, as nearly as possible, in proportion to their respective abilities; that is, in proportion to the revenue which they respectively enjoy under the protection of the state. The expence of government to the individuals of a great nation, is like the expence of management to the joint tenants of a great estate who are all obliged to contribute in proportion to their respective interests in the estate. In the observation or neglect of this maxim consists, what is called the equality or inequality of taxation. Every tax, it must be observed once for all, which falls finally upon one only of the three sorts of revenue above-mentioned, is necessarily unequal, in so far as it does not affect the other two. In the following examination of different taxes I shall seldom take much further notice of this sort of inequality, but shall, in most cases, confine my observations to that inequality which is occasioned by a particular tax falling unequally even upon that particular sort of private revenue which is affected by it.

II. The tax which each individual is bound to pay ought to be certain, and not arbitrary. The time of payment, the manner of payment, the quantity to be paid, ought all to be clear and plain to the contributor, and to every other person. Where it is otherwise, every person subject to the tax is put more or less in the power of the tax-gatherer, who can either aggravate the tax upon any obnoxious contributor, or extort, by the terror of such aggravation, some present or perquisite to himself. The uncertainty of taxation encourages the insolence and favours the corruption of an order of men who are naturally unpopular, even where they are neither insolent nor corrupt. The certainty of what each individual ought to pay is, in taxation, a matter of so great importance, that a very considerable degree of inequality, it appears, I believe, from the experience of all nations, is not near so great an evil as a very small degree of uncertainty.

III. Every tax ought to be levied at the time, or in the manner in which it is most likely to be convenient for the contributor to pay it. A tax upon the rent of land or of houses, payable at the same term at which such rents are usually paid, is levied at the time when it is most likely to be convenient for the contributor to pay; or, when he is most likely to have

wherewithal to pay. Taxes upon such consumable goods as are articles of luxury, are all finally paid by the consumer, and generally in a manner that is very convenient for him. He pays them by, little and little, as he has occasion to buy the goods. As he is at liberty too, either to buy, or not to buy as he pleases, it must be his own fault if he ever suffers any considerable inconveniency from such taxes.

IV. Every tax ought to be so contrived as both to take out and to keep out of the pockets of the people as little as possible, over and above what it brings into the publick treasury of the state. A tax may either take out or keep out of the pockets of the people a great deal more than it brings into the publick treasury, in the four following ways. First, the levying of it may require a great number of officers, whose salaries may eat up the greater part of the produce of the tax, and whose perquisites may impose another additional tax upon the people. Secondly, it may obstruct the industry of the people, and discourage them from applying to certain branches of business which might give maintenance and employment to great multitudes. While it obliges the people to pay, it may thus diminish, or perhaps destroy some of the funds, which might enable them more easily to do so. Thirdly, by the forfeitures and other penalties which those unfortunate individuals incur who attempt unsuccessfully to evade the tax, it may frequently ruin them, and thereby put an end to the benefit which the community might have received from the employment of their capitals. An injudicious tax offers a great temptation to smuggling. But the penalties of smuggling must rise in proportion to the temptation. The law, contrary to all the ordinary principles of justice, first creates the temptation, and then punishes those who yield to it; and it commonly enhances the punishment too in proportion to the very circumstance which ought certainly to alleviate it, the temptation to commit the crime. Fourthly, by subjecting the people to the frequent visits, and the odious examination of the tax-gatherers, it may expose them to much unnecessary trouble, vexation, and oppression; and though vexation is not, strictly speaking, expence, it is certainly equivalent to the expence at which every man would be willing to redeem himself from it. It is in some one or other of these four different ways that taxes are frequently so much more burdensome to the people than they are beneficial to the sovereign.

## Chapter III

### OF PUBLICK DEBTS

. . . A country abounding with merchants and manufacturers, necessarily abounds with a set of people through whose hands not only their own capitals, but the capitals of all those who either lend them money, or trust them with goods, pass as frequently, or more frequently, than the revenue of a private man, who, without trade or business, lives upon his income, passes through his hands. The revenue of such a man can regularly pass through his hands only once in a year. But the whole amount of the capital and credit of a merchant, who deals in a trade of which the returns are very quick, may sometimes pass through his hands two, three, or four times in a year. A country abounding with merchants and manufacturers, therefore, necessarily abounds with a set of people who have it at all times in their power to advance, if they chuse to do so, a very large sum of money to government. Hence the ability in the subjects of a commercial state to lend.

Commerce and manufactures can seldom flourish long in any state which does not enjoy a regular administration of justice, in which the people do not feel themselves secure in the possession of their property, in which the faith of contracts is not supported by law, and in which the authority of the state is not supposed to be regularly employed in enforcing the payment of debts from all those who are able to pay. Commerce and manufactures, in short, can seldom flourish in any state in which there is not a certain degree of confidence in the justice of government. The same confidence which disposes great merchants and manufacturers, upon ordinary occasions, to trust their property to the protection of a particular government; disposes them, upon extraordinary occasions, to trust that government with the use of their property. By lending money to government, they do not even for a moment diminish their ability to carry on their trade and manufactures. On the contrary, they commonly augment it. The necessities of the state render government upon most occasions willing to borrow upon terms extremely advantageous to the lender. The security which it grants to the original creditor, is made transferable to any other creditor, and, from the universal confidence in the justice of the state, generally sells in the market for more than was originally paid for it. The merchant or monied man makes money by lending money to government, and instead of diminishing, increases his trading capital. He generally considers it as a favor, therefore, when the administration admits him to share in the first subscription for a new loan. Hence the inclination or willingness in the subjects of a commercial state to lend.

The government of such a state is very apt to repose itself upon this ability and willingness of its subjects to lend it their money on extraordinary occasions. It foresees the facility of borrowing, and therefore dispenses itself from the duty of saving.

In a rude state of society there are no great mercantile or manufacturing capitals. The individuals who hoard whatever money they can save, and who conceal their hoard, do so from a distrust of the justice of government, from a fear that if it was known that they had a hoard, and where that hoard was to be found, they would quickly be plundered. In such a state of things few people would be able, and nobody would be willing, to lend their money to government on extraordinary exigencies. The sovereign feels that he must provide for such exigencies by saving, because he foresees the absolute impossibility of borrowing. This foresight increases still further his natural disposition to save.

The progress of the enormous debts which at present oppress, and will in the long-run probably ruin, all the great nations of Europe, has been pretty uniform. Nations, like private men, have generally begun to borrow upon what may be called personal credit, without assigning or mortgaging any particular fund for the payment of the debt; and when this resource has failed them, they have gone on to borrow upon assignments or mortgages of particular funds. . . .

It is not contrary to justice that . . . America should contribute towards the discharge of the publick debt of Great Britain.

The expence of the peace establishment of the colonies was, before the commencement of the present disturbances, very considerable, and is an expence which may, and if no revenue can be drawn from them, ought certainly to be saved altogether. This constant expence in time of peace, though very great, is insignificant in comparison with what the defence of the colonies has cost us in time of war. The last war, which was undertaken altogether on account of the colonies, cost Great Britain, it has already been observed, upwards of ninety millions. The Spanish war of 1739 was principally undertaken on their account; in which, and in the French war that was the consequence of it, Great Britain spent upwards of forty millions, a great part of which ought justly to be charged to the colonies. In those two wars the colonies cost Great Britain much more than double the sum which the national debt amounted to before the commencement of the first of them. Had it not been for those wars that debt might, and probably would by this time, have been completely paid; and had it not been for the colonies, the former of those wars might not, and the latter certainly would not have been undertaken. It was because the colonies were supposed to be provinces of the British empire, that this expence was laid out upon them. But countries which contribute neither revenue nor military force towards the support of the empire, cannot be considered as provinces. They may perhaps be considered as appendages, as a sort of splendid and showy equipage, of the empire. But if the empire can no longer support the expence of keeping up this equipage, it ought certainly to lay it down; and if it cannot raise its revenue in proportion to its expence, it ought, at least, to accommodate its expence to its revenue. If the colonies, notwithstanding their refusal to submit to British taxes, are still to be considered as provinces of the British empire, their defence in some future war may cost Great Britain as great an expence as it ever has done in any former war. The rulers of Great Britain have, for more than a century past, amused the people with the imagination that they possessed a great empire on the west side of the Atlantic. This empire, however, has hitherto existed in imagination only. It has hitherto been, not an empire, but the project of an empire; not a gold mine, but the project of a gold mine; a project which has cost, which continues to cost, and which, if pursued in the same way as it has been hitherto, is likely to cost immense expence, without being likely to bring any profit; for the effects of the monopoly of the colony trade, it has been shewn; are, to the great body of the people, mere loss instead of profit. It is surely now time that our rulers should either realize this golden dream, in which they have been indulging themselves, perhaps, as well as the people; or, that they should awake from it themselves, and endeavour to awaken the people. If the project cannot be compleated, it ought to be given up. If any of the provinces of the British empire cannot be made to contribute towards the support of the whole empire, it is surely time that Great Britain should free herself from the expence of defending those provinces in time of war, and of supporting any part of their civil or military establishments in time of peace, and endeavour to accommodate her future views and designs to the real mediocrity of her circumstances.

# ALEXANDER HAMILTON
# AND JAMES MADISON

~

## INTRODUCTION

## BERNARD E. BROWN

*The Federalist Papers*, also referred to as *The Federalist*, were a series of eighty-five papers written by Alexander Hamilton, James Madison, and John Jay (under the pseudonym Publius, or the Public Man) to persuade the citizens of New York State to vote in favor of ratification of the proposed Constitution. The papers appeared in various New York journals from October 1787 through May 1788. They were an answer to attacks by opponents of the Constitution, particularly a series of articles under the signature of Cato (assumed at the time to be the governor, George Clinton, but he may have been an associate). The Antifederalists or opponents of the new Constitution won by a 2-to-1 margin. Through skillful maneuvering in the ratification convention, the Federalists were able to secure a vote in favor of ratification by the narrow margin of 31 to 29.

The authors of *The Federalist Papers* kept their anonymity for several years. It is now generally agreed that Hamilton wrote fifty-one numbers, Madison twenty-six, Jay five, and Hamilton and Madison together three. The papers were published immediately as a book, then republished in 1799 and 1802, and continually since then. They won immediate acclaim as an authoritative expression of the theory behind the Constitution. Charles A. Beard called *The Federalist Papers* the greatest work of political theory ever written by Americans, and the greatest work of political science in any language.

The main organizer of the enterprise, Alexander Hamilton (1755–1804) was born in the West Indies' island of Nevis, the illegitimate son of a Scottish merchant and an Englishwoman, herself a native of the West Indies. Abandoned by his father, Alexander worked as a clerk in an import-export firm in Saint-Croix. With the help of his employer, and also of a clergyman who recognized his intellectual ability, he arrived in New York in 1772. He met and became friendly with John Jay, and entered King's College (later Columbia) the following year. Winning a commission as an artillery officer, he participated in several battles, and was chosen by George Washington as an aide-de-camp. In 1780 Hamilton married Elizabeth Schuyler, the daughter of a wealthy landowner, which assured him social position. After the war he became one of New York's leading lawyers, participated actively in politics, and was a delegate to Congress. Under the new government, Hamilton served as secretary of the treasury (1789–1795), then returned to the practice of law, continuing to play an active role in politics. He was killed in a duel with Aaron Burr.

James Madison (1751–1836) was descended from early English immigrants to Virginia. His family maintained a large plantation and estate in Orange County, not far from Jefferson's Monticello. Madison attended the College of New Jersey (later Princeton), a stronghold of revolutionary sentiment, graduating in 1771. He entered politics in 1774, first in his native Orange County, then as a member of the Virginia Convention. He and Thomas Jefferson became close friends and political associates. Madison was chosen to be a member of the Virginia Council of State, which advised and shared responsibility with the governor. In this capacity he served with governors Patrick Henry and Thomas Jefferson. Both Madison and Jefferson condemned the lack of an independent executive in wartime Virginia. Madison was chosen as a delegate to the Continental Congress in 1780; he played a major role in the Philadelphia Convention in 1787. After adoption of the new Constitution, Madison was elected to the House of Representatives, and worked closely with Jefferson in opposing the emerging Federalist party. He left Congress in 1797, served a term in the Virginia legislature, and became secretary of state (1801–1809) under President Jefferson. He succeeded Jefferson as president (1809–1817).

John Jay (1745–1829) was the oldest and at the time best known of the authors. Jay was descended from French Huguenot merchants of La Rochelle who fled to America after the revocation of the Edict of Nantes. He married Sarah Livingston, thus gaining entry into one of the wealthiest Whig families of New Jersey. After attending King's College he became a successful lawyer, and was elected a delegate to the Continental Congress in 1774. An active political career began: He drafted a constitution for the state of New York, served as chief justice of the New York Supreme Court, was elected president of the Continental Congress in 1778, then was named ambassador to Spain, later joining Benjamin Franklin in Paris to negotiate peace with Britain. On his return to New York in 1784, Jay was named secretary for foreign affairs under the Articles of Confederation, in which post he was still serving when he contributed to the *Federalist Papers*. Subsequently he became the first chief justice of the United States (1789). As special envoy he negotiated a treaty with Britain (1794), then resigned as chief justice to serve as governor of New York (1795–1801).

The very first of the *Federalist* papers, written by Hamilton (according to legend, overnight in the cabin of the sloop taking him back to New York from legal business in Albany), posed the question: "whether societies of men are really capable or not of establishing good government from reflection and choice, or whether they are forever destined to depend for their political constitutions on accident and force." The immediate and most obvious meaning was whether the citizens of New York, after hearing arguments on both sides, would vote in favor of ratification of the new Constitution. A "wrong" choice, said Hamilton, should be considered the "general misfortune of mankind." Hamilton also sought to highlight the significance of the ratification process itself. The Americans thought they were in the forefront of the struggle against feudalism, a system they condemned as degrading to humanity, based on accident of birth and force of tradition. But in an age of enlightenment, people were active agents of their own destiny. The first *Federalist* paper was the opening salvo of a global democratic revolution.

Hamilton and Jay then analyzed the defects of the government under the Articles of Confederation. Most obvious was its inability to defend the nation in dealing with foreign powers, to resolve conflicts among the states (who were creating barriers to the flow of commerce and laying rival claims to the western territories), and to levy taxes directly instead of depending on the states for contributions. In addition, Madison stressed the tendency to disregard minority rights by local majorities in the states. He challenged Montesquieu's advocacy of small republics linked together by compact, which was popular among Antifederalists.

For Publius, the defects of the Confederation would be remedied by a strong general government, levying its own taxes, able to deal on terms of equality with foreign powers, capable of defending a larger public interest and of avoiding internecine strife, and protecting rights of individuals and minorities. It would have the power to enforce its decisions directly on individuals, through courts.

For Madison, popular government did not mean direct participation by the people in government (called, in Number 10, "pure democracy"). Direct popular rule was not feasible in governing a large territory; it was not desirable even when feasible. The very form of government itself is defective in that skilled orators could sway the populace by appealing to their passions. In a republic, the people elect representatives who can "refine and enlarge upon the public views." Representation also makes it possible to create checks and balances in order to avoid abuse of power and allow time for reflection and reconsideration.

The major cause of instability in popular government, argued Madison in Number 10, is "faction" and the spirit of party. So long as men have different "faculties," and the liberty to develop them, they will have different opinions and hold different types of property, which is the most durable source of faction. Madison's conception of property makes a break with the feudal emphasis on land ownership; he rather grants equal validity to commercial and manufacturing interests, describing an interaction characteristic of modern economies. One role of government is to protect the faculties of men; but Madison and Hamilton believed that government should regulate property and reduce the disparity between wealth and poverty. The new Constitution helps control the effects of faction principally by extending the republic in order to take in a greater variety of interests, thus making it difficult for any one faction to dominate. But this was only a tendency. An extended republic might also be paralyzed by the conflict among factions and parties. Hence, the need for an "energetic government" with a "proper structure."

Government must be able to defend a public good over and beyond the clash of factions. The public good is characterized by a long-term view, as opposed to immediate interests. In Rhode Island, cited several times by Publius, a majority in the state legislature, representing debtors, authorized the issuance of paper money that rapidly became worthless. To secure a short-term advantage, the dominant majority thus sacrificed its own long-term interest in commercial exchange based on mutual confidence and economic growth. Government protects the "permanent and aggregate interests of the community" by creating the infrastructure of an expanding economy ("new improvements" like roads and canals, observed Madison in Number 14, along with a sound currency, a system of justice, schools).

Interests must be represented in government, but not be able to dominate. Government must be capable of action, but with provision for deliberation. Separation of the branches of government permits each branch to specialize in different functions, thereby becoming more effective in their totality. An executive was to embody the principle of "energy," Hamilton explained in Number 70, while the legislature was best suited to perform the indispensable functions of representation and conciliation of interests, reflection, and judgment. The role of the judicial power was to uphold clearly stated limits set down in the fundamental law; it was not anticipated that the judicial branch would be able to interpret the "spirit" of the Constitution. Hamilton's argument in Numbers 78 to 84 remains a source of inspiration for both defenders and opponents of judicial activism. Each branch would be given sufficient power to defend itself, noted Madison in Numbers 47 and 51, thus maintaining the system of specialized functions. It is particularly important in a republic, he emphasized in Number 48, to prevent the legislature from encroaching upon the executive, for that would lead to instability, chaos, and ultimately a call for a dictator. The alternative to Union, warned Hamilton in Number 85, was anarchy, civil war, and "perhaps the military despotism of a victorious demagogue."

The reputation of *The Federalist* has reflected the evolution of the Constitution it explained and justified. The victory of the North in the Civil War seemed to vindicate the supremacy of the general government over the states, and its role in promoting the growth of a modern society. But the social and economic tensions of industrialization led some progressives and socialists to view the Constitution as a mechanism, and *The Federalist* as a theory, serving the interests of a dominant capitalist class by making property rights inviolable and preventing the formation of a popular and anticapitalist majority. The rise of fascism and communism, and the growing crisis of communism after World War II, led to a new appreciation of *The Federalist* and of the success of the American revolutionaries in establishing a stable republic that averted dictatorship, preserved individual liberties, and promoted the growth of an increasingly prosperous society. There is renewed interest in *The Federalist* today by Europeans seeking to create unity out of diversity through the European Union, and by the peoples of former Communist systems striving to establish viable representative institutions. The theory of legislative-executive relations in *The Federalist* seems to have been vindicated. In stable democracies an executive power is able to initiate policy and guide the legislature. Autonomy of the executive may be assured through party controls enabling a prime minister and cabinet, once invested by the legislature, to lead; or it may be achieved by giving the executive a measure of independence from the legislature (as in presidential systems). Legislative dominance, as in the cases of the Articles of Confederation, revolutionary assemblies in France, the Third and Fourth French Republics, and the Weimar Republic, led to instability, collapse, and sometimes the rise of a dictator.

Hamilton has been the subject of many biographies. Forrest McDonald, *Alexander Hamilton, A Biography* (New York: W. W. Norton, 1979), is good on intellectual influences; Richard Brookhiser, *Alexander Hamilton, American* (New York: The Free Press, 1999), is an engaging account of his life. John C. Miller, *Alexander Hamilton and the Growth of the New Nation* (New York: Harper and Row, 1959), emphasizes political factors; Clinton Rossiter, *Alexander Hamilton and the Constitution* (New York: Harcourt, Brace & World, 1964), is valuable for Hamilton's political and constitutional thought; Jacob Cooke, *Alexander Hamilton* (New York: Scribner, 1982), draws upon Freudian theory in appraising his personality. On Madison: Irving Brant, *The Fourth President: A Life of James Madison* (Indianapolis: Bobbs-Merrill, 1970), is a one-volume abridgment of the author's monumental six-volume biography; Ralph Ketcham, *James Madison* (New York: Macmillan, 1971), pays special attention to politics; Drew R. McCoy, *The Last of the Fathers: James Madison and the Republican Legacy* (New York: Cambridge University Press, 1989), deals with the evolution of Madison's views on the crises of the early years of the Republic, notably nullification and slavery. Lance Banning, *The Sacred Fire of Liberty: James Madison and the Founding of the American Republic* (Ithaca, N.Y.: Cornell University Press, 1995), argues that Madison consistently sought to protect and perfect a democratic revolution; Gary Rosen, *American Compact: James Madison and the Problem of Founding* (Lawrence: University of Kansas Press, 1999), presents the social compact as central to Madison's thought; Robert A. Goldwin, *From Parchment to Power: How James Madison Used the Bill of Rights to Save the Constitution* (Washington, D.C.: American Enterprise Institute Press, 1997), examines the evolution of Madison's views on a bill of rights in a republic. For a lively account of the role played by the three Publii in the making of the Constitution and the ratification debate, see Richard B. Morris, *Witnesses at the Creation: Hamilton, Madison, Jay, and the Constitution* (New York: Henry Holt, 1985).

Among the critical works: Douglas Adair, *Fame and the Founding Fathers* (New York: W. W. Norton, 1974), argues that David Hume was a major source; and Garry Wills, *Explaining America: The Federalist* (New York: Doubleday & Co., 1981), explicates the text of *The Federalist*, and follows Adair in attributing decisive influence to Hume and the Scottish Enlightenment. More diverse influences are identified by contributors to Allan Bloom (ed.), *Confronting the Constitution* (Washington, D.C.: American Enterprise Institute, 1990). Analytic themes (separation of powers, justice, rule of law, constitutionalism) are treated by contributors to Charles R. Kesler (ed.), *Saving the Revolution: The Federalist Papers and the American Founding* (New York: Free Press, 1987).

Scholarly and balanced treatments include: David F. Epstein, *The Political Theory of The Federalist* (Chicago: University of Chicago Press, 1984); and George W. Carey, *The Federalist: Design for a Constitutional Republic* (Urbana: University of Illinois Press, 1989). Samuel H. Beer, *To Make a Nation: The Rediscovery of American Federalism* (Cambridge, Mass.: Harvard University Press, 1993), deals with the theory of federalism expounded in *The Federalist*, and assesses the evolution of the system. On *The Federalist* as a model of political science, see the essay by Harvey C. Mansfield, Jr., in Allan Bloom (ed.), *Confronting the Constitution*, cited above.

# The Federalist Papers

## NUMBER 1

After an unequivocal experience of the inefficiency of the subsisting federal government, you are called upon to deliberate on a new Constitution for the United States of America. The subject speaks its own importance; comprehending in its consequences nothing less than the existence of the Union, the safety and welfare of the parts of which it is composed, the fate of an empire in many respects the most interesting in the world. It has been frequently remarked that it seems to have been reserved to the people of this country, by their conduct and example, to decide the important question, whether societies of men are really capable or not of establishing good government from reflection and choice, or whether they are forever destined to depend for their political constitutions on accident and force. If there be any truth in the remark, the crisis at which we are arrived may with propriety be regarded as the era in which that decision is to be made; and a wrong election of the part we shall act may, in this view, deserve to be considered as the general misfortune of mankind.

This idea will add the inducements of philanthropy to those of patriotism, to heighten the solicitude which all considerate and good men must feel for the event. Happy will it be if our choice should be directed by a judicious estimate of our true interests, unperplexed and unbiased by considerations not connected with the public good. But this is a thing more ardently to be wished than seriously to be expected.

The plan offered to our deliberations affects too many particular interests, innovates upon too many local institutions, not to involve in its discussion a variety of objects foreign to its merits, and of views, passions and prejudices little favorable to the discovery of truth.

Among the most formidable of the obstacles which the new Constitution will have to encounter may readily be distinguished the obvious interest of a certain class of men in every State to resist all changes which may hazard a diminution of the power, emolument, and consequence of the offices they hold under the State establishments; and the perverted ambition of another class of men, who will either hope to aggrandize themselves by the confusions of their country, or will flatter themselves with fairer prospects of elevation from the subdivision of the empire into several partial confederacies than from its union under one government.

It is not, however, my design to dwell upon observations of this nature. I am well aware that it would be disingenuous to resolve indiscriminately the opposition of any set of men (merely because their situations might subject them to suspicion) into interested or ambitious views. Candor will oblige us to admit that even such men may be actuated by upright intentions; and it cannot be doubted that much of the opposition which has made its appearance, or may hereafter make its appearance, will spring from sources, blameless at least, if not respectable—the honest errors of minds led astray by preconceived jealousies and fears. So numerous indeed and so powerful are the causes which serve to give a false bias to the judgment, that we, upon many occasions, see wise and good men on the wrong as well as on the right side of questions of the first magnitude to society. This circumstance, if duly attended to, would furnish a lesson of moderation to those who are ever so much persuaded of their being in the right in any controversy. And a further reason for caution, in this respect, might be drawn from the reflection that we are not always sure that those who advocate the truth are influenced by purer principles than their antagonists. Ambition, avarice, personal animosity, party opposition, and many other motives not more laudable than these, are apt to operate as well upon those who support as those who oppose the right side of a question. Were there not even inducements to moderation, nothing could be more ill-judged than that intolerant spirit which has, at all times, characterized political parties. For in politics, as in religion, it is equally absurd to aim at making proselytes by fire and sword. Heresies in either can rarely be cured by persecution.

And yet, however just these sentiments will be allowed to be, we have already sufficient indications that it will happen in this as in all former cases of great national discussion. A torrent of angry and malignant passions will be let loose. To judge from the conduct of the opposite parties, we shall be led to conclude that they will mutually hope to evince the justness of their opinions, and to increase the number of their converts by the loudness of their declamations and the bitterness of their invectives. An enlightened zeal for the energy and efficiency of government will be stigmatized as the offspring of a temper fond of despotic power and hostile to the principles of liberty. An over-scrupulous jealousy of danger to the rights of the people, which is more commonly the fault of the head than of the heart, will be represented as mere presence and artifice, the stale bait for popularity at the expense of the public good. It will be forgotten, on the one hand, that jealousy is the usual concomitant of love, and that the noble enthusiasm of liberty is apt to be infected with a spirit of narrow and illiberal distrust. On the other hand, it will be equally forgotten that the vigor of government is essential to the security of liberty; that, in the contemplation of a sound and well-informed judgment, their interest can never be separated; and that a dangerous ambition more often lurks behind the specious mask of zeal for the rights of the people than under the forbidding appearance of zeal for the firmness and efficiency of government. History will teach us that the former has been found a much more certain road to the introduction of despotism than the latter, and that of those men who have overturned the liberties of republics, the greatest number have begun their career by paying an obsequious court to the people; commencing demagogues, and ending tyrants.

In the course of the preceding observations, I have had an eye, my fellow-citizens, to putting you upon your guard against all attempts, from whatever quarter, to influence your decision in a matter of the utmost moment to your welfare, by any impressions other than those which may result from the evidence of truth. You will, no doubt, at the same time, have collected from the general scope of them, that they proceed from a source not unfriendly to the new Constitution. Yes, my countrymen, I own to you that, after having given it an attentive consideration, I am clearly of opinion it is your interest to adopt it. I am convinced that this is the safest course for your liberty, your dignity, and your happiness. I affect not reserves which I do not feel. I will not amuse you with an appearance of deliberation when I have decided. I frankly acknowledge to you my convictions, and I will freely lay before you the reasons on which they are founded. The consciousness of good intentions disdains ambiguity. I shall not, however, multiply professions on this head. My motives must remain in the depository of my own breast. My arguments will be open to all, and may be judged of by all. They shall at least be offered in a spirit which will not disgrace the cause of truth.

I propose, in a series of papers, to discuss the following interesting particulars:—*The utility of the Union to your political prosperity—The insufficiency of the present Confederation to preserve that Union—The necessity of a government at least equally energetic with the one proposed, to the attainment of this object—The conformity of the proposed Constitution to the true principles of republican government—Its analogy to your own State constitution*—and lastly, *The additional security which its adoption will afford to the preservation of that species of government, to liberty, and to property.*

In the progress of this discussion I shall endeavor to give a satisfactory answer to all the objections which shall have made their appearance, that may seem to have any claim to your attention.

It may perhaps be thought superfluous to offer arguments to prove the utility of the Union, a point, no doubt, deeply engraved on the hearts of the great body of the people in every State, and one, which it

may be imagined, has no adversaries. But the fact is, that we already hear it whispered in the private circles of those who oppose the new Constitution, that the thirteen States are of too great extent for any general system, and that we must of necessity resort to separate confederacies of distinct portions of the whole.[1] This doctrine will, in all probability, be gradually propagated, till it has votaries enough to countenance an open avowal of it. For nothing can be more evident, to those who are able to take an enlarged view of the subject, than the alternative of an adoption of the new Constitution or a dismemberment of the Union. It will therefore be of use to begin by examining the advantages of that Union, the certain evils, and the probable dangers, to which every State will be exposed from its dissolution. This shall accordingly constitute the subject of my next address.

Publius [Hamilton]

## NUMBER 9

A firm Union will be of the utmost moment to the peace and liberty of the States as a barrier against domestic faction and insurrection. It is impossible to read the history of the petty republics of Greece and Italy without feeling sensations of horror and disgust at the distractions with which they were continually agitated, and at the rapid succession of revolutions by which they were kept in a state of perpetual vibration between the extremes of tyranny and anarchy. If they exhibit occasional calms, these only serve as short-lived contrasts to the furious storms that are to succeed. If now and then intervals of felicity open themselves to view, we behold them with a mixture of regret, arising from the reflection that the pleasing scenes before us are soon to be overwhelmed by the tempestuous waves of sedition and party rage. If momentary rays of glory break forth from the gloom, while they dazzle us with a transient and fleeting brilliancy, they at the same time admonish us to lament that the vices of government should pervert the direction and tarnish the luster of those bright talents and exalted endowments for which the favored soils that produced them have been so justly celebrated.

From the disorders that disfigure the annals of those rebuplics the advocates of despotism have drawn arguments, not only against the forms of republican government, but against the very principles of civil liberty. They have decried all free government as inconsistent with the order of society, and have indulged themselves in malicious exultation over its friends and partisans. Happily for mankind, stupendous fabrics reared on the basis of liberty, which have flourished for ages, have, in a few glorious instances, refuted their gloomy sophisms. And, I trust, America will be the broad and solid foundation of other edifices, not less magnificent, which will be equally permanent monuments of their errors.

But it is not to be denied that the portraits they have sketched of republican government were too just copies of the originals from which they were taken. If it had been found impracticable to have devised models of a more perfect structure, the enlightened friends to liberty would have been obliged to abandon the cause of that species of government as indefensible. The science of politics, however, like most other sciences, has received great improvement. The efficacy of various principles is now well understood, which were either not known at all, or imperfectly known to the ancients. The regular distribution of power into distinct departments; the introduction of legislative balances and checks; the institution of courts composed of judges holding their offices during good behaviour; the representation of the people in the legislature by deputies of their own election: these are wholly new discoveries, or have made their principal progress towards perfection in modern times. They are means, and powerful means, by which the excellencies of republican government may be retained and its imperfections lessened or avoided. To this catalogue of circumstances that tend to the amelioration of popular systems of civil government, I shall venture, however novel it may appear to some, to add one more, on a principle which has been made the foundation of an objection to the new Constitution; I mean the ENLARGEMENT of the ORBIT within such systems are to revolve, either in respect to the dimensions of a single State, or to the consolidation of several smaller States into one great Confederacy. The latter is that which immediately concerns the object under consideration. It will, however, be of use to examine the principle in its application to a single State, which shall be attended to in another place.

The utility of a Confederacy, as well as to supress faction and to guard the internal tranquillity of States as to increase their external force and security, is in reality not a new idea. It has been practiced upon in different countries and ages, and has received the sanction of the most applauded writers on the subjects of politics. The opponents of the PLAN proposed have, with great assiduity, cited and circulated the observations of Montesquieu on the necessity of a contracted territory for a republican government. But they seem not to have been apprised of the sentiments of that great man expressed in another part of his work, not to have adverted to the consequences of the principle to which they subscribe with such ready acquiescence.

When Montesquieu recommends a small extent for republics, the standards he had in view were of dimensions far short of the limits of almost every one of these States. Neither Virginia, Massachusetts, Pennsylvania, New York, North Carolina, nor Georgia can by any means be compared with the models from which he reasoned and to which the terms of his description apply. If we therefore take his ideas on this point as the criterion of truth, we shall be driven to the alternative either of taking refuge at once in the arms of monarchy, or of splitting ourselves into an infinity of little, jealous, clashing, tumultuous commonwealths, the wretched nurseries of unceasing discord and the miserable objects of universal pity or contempt. Some of the writers who have come forward on the other side of the question seem to have been aware of the dilemma; and have even been bold enough to hint at the division of the larger States as a desirable thing. Such an infatuated policy, such a desperate expedient, might, by the multiplication of petty offices, answer the views of men who possess not qualifications to extend their influence beyond the narrow circles of personal intrigue, but it could never promote the greatness or happiness of the people of America.

Referring the examination of the principle itself

to another place, as has been already mentioned, it will be sufficient to remark here that, in the sense of the author who has been most emphatically quoted upon the occasion, it would only dictate a reduction of the SIZE of the more considerable MEMBERS of the Union, but would not militate against their being all comprehended in one confederate government. And this is the true question, in the discussion of which we are at present interested.

So far are the suggestions of Montesquieu from standing in opposition to a general Union of the States that he explicitly treats of a CONFEDERATE REPUBLIC as the expedient for extending the sphere of popular government and reconciling the advantages of monarchy with those of republicanism.

"It is very probable" (says he[2]) "that mankind would have been obliged at length to live constantly under the government of a SINGLE PERSON, had they not contrived a kind of constitution that has all the internal advantages of a republican, together with the external force of a monarchical, government. I mean a CONFEDERATE REPUBLIC.

"This form of government is a convention by which several smaller *states* agree to become a larger *one*, which they intend to form. It is a kind of assemblage of societies that constitute a new one, capable of increasing, by means of new associations, till they arrive to such a degree of power as to be able to provide for the security of the united body.

"A republic of this kind, able to withstand an external force, may support itself without any internal corruptions. The form of this society prevents all manner of inconveniences.

"If a single member should attempt to usurp the supreme authority, he could not be supposed to have an equal authority and credit in all the confederate states. Were he to have too great influence over one, this would alarm the rest. Were he to subdue a part, that which would still remain free might oppose him with forces independent of those which he had usurped, and overpower him before he could be settled in his usurpation."

"Should a popular insurrection happen in one of the confederate states, the others are able to quell it. Should abuses creep into one part, they are reformed by those that remain sound. The state may be destroyed on one side, and not on the other; the con-

federacy may be dissolved, and the confederates preserve their sovereignty.

"As this government is composed of small republics, it enjoys the internal happiness of each; and with respect to its external situation, it is possessed, by means of the association, of all the advantages of large monarchies."

I have thought it proper to quote at length these interesting passages, because they contain a luminous abridgment of the principal arguments in favor of the Union, and must effectually remove the false impressions which a misapplication of other parts of the world was calculated to produce. They have, at the same time, an intimate connection with the more immediate design of this paper, which is to illustrate the tendency of the Union to repress domestic faction and insurrection.

A distinction, more subtle than accurate, has been raised between a *confederacy* and a *consolidation* of the States. The essential characteristic of the first is said to be the restriction of its authority to the members in their collective capacities, without reaching to the individuals of whom they are composed. It is contended that the national council ought to have no concern with any object of internal administration. An exact equality of suffrage between the members has also been insisted upon as a leading feature of a confederate government. These positions are, in the main, arbitrary; they are supported neither by principle nor precedent. It has indeed happened that governments of this kind have generally operated in the manner which the distinction, taken notice of, supposes to be inherent in their nature; but there have been in most of them extensive exceptions to the practice, which serve to prove, as far as example will go, that there is no absolute rule on the subject. And it will be clearly shown, in the course of this investigation, that as far as the principle contended for has prevailed, it has been the cause of incurable disorder and imbecility in the government.

The definition of a *confederate republic* seems simply to be "an assemblage of societies," or an association of two or more states into one state. The extent, modifications, and objects of the federal authority are mere matters of discretion. So long as the separate organization of the members be not abolished; so long as it exists, by a constitutional necessity, for local purposes; though it should be in perfect subordination to the general authority of the union, it would still be, in fact and in theory, an association of states, or a confederacy. The proposed Constitution, so far from implying an abolition of the State governments, makes them constituent parts of the national sovereignty, by allowing them a direct representation in the Senate, and leaves in their possession certain exclusive and very important portions of sovereign power. This fully corresponds, in every rational import of the terms, with the idea of a federal government.

In the Lycian confederacy, which consisted of twenty-three CITIES, or republics, the largest were entitled to *three* votes in the COMMON COUNCIL, those of the middle class to *two*, and the smallest to *one*. The COMMON COUNCIL had the appointment of all the judges and magistrates of the respective CITIES. This was certainly the most delicate species of interference in their internal administration; for if there be any thing that seems exclusively appropriated to the local jurisdiction, it is the appointment of their own officers. Yet Montesquieu, speaking of this association, says: "Were I to give a model of an excellent Confederate Republic, it would be that of Lycia." Thus we perceive that the distinctions insisted upon were not within the contemplation of this enlightened civilian; and we shall be led to conclude that they are the novel refinements of an erroneous theory.

Publius [Hamilton]

## NUMBER 10

Among the numerous advantages promised by a well-constructed Union, none deserves to be more accurately developed than its tendency to break and control the violence of faction. The friend of popular governments never finds himself so much alarmed for their character and fate, as when he contemplates their propensity to this dangerous vice. He will not fail, therefore, to set a due value on any plan which, without violating the principles to which he is attached, provides a proper cure for it. The instability,

injustice, and confusion introduced into the public councils, have, in truth, been the mortal diseases under which popular governments have everywhere perished; as they continue to be the favorite and fruitful topics from which the adversaries to liberty derive their most specious declamations. The valuable improvements made by the American constitutions on the popular models, both ancient and modern, cannot certainly be too much admired; but it would be an unwarrantable partiality, to contend that they have as effectually obviated the danger on this side, as was wished and expected. Complaints are everywhere heard from our most considerate and virtuous citizens, equally the friends of public and private faith, and of public and personal liberty, that our governments are too unstable, that the public good is disregarded in the conflicts of rival parties, and that measures are too often decided, not according to the rules of justice and the rights of the minor party, but by the superior force of an interested and overbearing majority. However anxiously we may wish that these complaints had no foundation, the evidence of known facts will not permit us to deny that they are in some degree true. It will be found, indeed, on a candid review of our situation, that some of the distresses under which we labor have been erroneously charged on the operation of our governments; but it will be found, at the same time, that other causes will not alone account for many of our heaviest misfortunes; and, particularly, for that prevailing and increasing distrust of public engagements, and alarm for private rights, which are echoed from one end of the continent to the other. These must be chiefly, if not wholly, effects of the unsteadiness and injustice with which a factious spirit has tainted our public administrations.

By a faction, I understand a number of citizens, whether amounting to a majority or minority of the whole, who are united and actuated by some common impulse of passion, or of interest, adverse to the rights of other citizens, or to the permanent and aggregate interests of the community.

There are two methods of curing the mischiefs of faction: the one, by removing its causes; the other, by controlling its effects.

There are again two methods of removing the causes of faction: the one, by destroying the liberty which is essential to its existence; the other, by giving to every citizen the same opinions, the same passions, and the same interests.

It could never be more truly said than of the first remedy, that it was worse than the disease. Liberty is to faction what air is to fire, an aliment without which it instantly expires. But it could not be less folly to abolish liberty, which is essential to political life, because it nourishes faction, than it would be to wish the annihilation of air, which is essential to animal life, because it imparts to fire its destructive agency.

The second expedient is as impracticable as the first would be unwise. As long as the reason of man continues fallible, and he is at liberty to exercise it, different opinions will be formed. As long as the connection subsists between his reason and his self-love, his opinions and his passions will have a reciprocal influence on each other; and the former will be objects to which the latter will attach themselves. The diversity in the faculties of men, from which the rights of property originate, is not less an insuperable obstacle to a uniformity of interests. The protection of these faculties is the first object of government. From the protection of different and unequal faculties of acquiring property, the possession of different degrees and kinds of property immediately results; and from the influence of these on the sentiments and views of the respective proprietors, ensues a division of the society into different interests and parties.

The latent causes of faction are thus sown in the nature of man; and we see them everywhere brought into different degrees of activity, according to the different circumstances of civil society. A zeal for different opinions concerning religion, concerning government, and many other points, as well of speculation as of practice; an attachment to different leaders ambitiously contending for pre-eminence and power; or to persons of other descriptions whose fortunes have been interesting to the human passions, have, in turn, divided mankind into parties, inflamed them with mutual animosity, and rendered them much more disposed to vex and oppress each other than to co-operate for their common good. So strong is this propensity of mankind to fall into mutual animosities, that where no substantial occasion presents itself, the most frivolous and fanciful distinctions have been sufficient to kindle their unfriendly passions and excite their most violent conflicts. But the most common and durable source of factions has been the various and unequal distribution of property. Those who hold and those who are without property have ever formed distinct interests in society. Those who are creditors, and those who are debtors, fall under a like discrimination. A landed interest, a manufacturing interest, a mercantile interest, a moneyed interest, with many lesser interests, grow up of necessity in civilized nations, and divide them into different classes, actuated by different sentiments and views. The regulation of these various and interfering interests forms the principal task of modern legislation, and involves the spirit of party and faction in the necessary and ordinary operations of the government.

No man is allowed to be a judge in his own cause, because his interest would certainly bias his judgment, and, not improbably, corrupt his integrity. With equal, nay with greater reason, a body of men are unfit to be both judges and parties at the same time; yet what are many of the most important acts of legislation, but so many judicial determinations, not indeed concerning the rights of single persons, but concerning the rights of large bodies of citizens? And what are the different classes of legislators but advocates and parties to the causes which they determine? Is a law proposed concerning private debts? It is a question to which the creditors are parties on one side and the debtors on the other. Justice ought to hold the balance between them. Yet the parties are, and must be, themselves the judges; and the most numerous party, or, in other words, the most powerful faction must be expected to prevail. Shall domestic manufactures be encouraged, and in what degree, by restrictions on foreign manufactures? are questions which would be differently decided by the landed and the manufacturing classes, and probably by neither with a sole regard to justice and the public good. The apportionment of taxes on the various descriptions of property is an act which seems to require the most exact impartiality; yet there is, perhaps, no legislative act in which greater opportunity and temptation are given to a predominant party to trample on the rules of justice. Every shilling with which they overburden the inferior number, is a shilling saved to their own pockets.

It is in vain to say that enlightened statesmen will be able to adjust these clashing interests, and render them all subservient to the public good. Enlightened statesmen will not always be at the helm. Nor, in many cases, can such an adjustment be made at all without taking into view indirect and remote considerations, which will rarely prevail over the immediate interest which one party may find in disregarding the rights of another or the good of the whole.

The inference to which we are brought is, that the *causes* of faction cannot be removed, and that relief is only to be sought in the means of controlling its *effects*.

If a faction consists of less than a majority, relief is supplied by the republican principle, which enables the majority to defeat its sinister views by regular vote. It may clog the administration, it may convulse the society; but it will be unable to execute and mask its violence under the forms of the Constitution. When a majority is included in a faction, the form of popular government, on the other hand, enables it to sacrifice to its ruling passion or interest both the public good and the rights of other citizens. To secure the public good and private rights against the danger of such a faction, and at the same time to preserve the spirit and the form of popular government, is then the great object to which our inquiries are directed. Let me add that it is the great desideratum by which this form of government can be rescued from the opprobrium under which it has so long labored, and be recommended to the esteem and adoption of mankind.

By what means is this object attainable? Evidently by one of two only. Either the existence of the same passion or interest in a majority at the same time must be prevented, or the majority, having such coexistent passion or interest, must be rendered, by their number and local situation, unable to concert and carry into effect schemes of oppression. If the impulse and the opportunity be suffered to coincide, we well know that neither moral nor religious motives can be relied on as an adequate control. They are not found to be such on the injustice and violence of individuals, and lose their efficacy in proportion to the number combined together, that is, in proportion as their efficacy becomes needful.

From this view of the subject it may be concluded that a pure democracy, by which I mean a society consisting of a small number of citizens, who assemble and administer the government in person, can admit of no cure for the mischiefs of faction. A common passion or interest will, in almost every case, be felt by a majority of the whole: a communication and concert result from the form of government itself; and there is nothing to check the inducements to sacrifice the weaker party or an obnoxious individual. Hence it is that such democracies have ever been spectacles of turbulence and contention; have ever been found incompatible with personal security or the rights of property; and have in general been as short in their lives as they have been violent in their deaths. Theoretic politicians, who have patronized this species of government, have erroneously supposed that by reducing mankind to a perfect equality in their political rights, they would, at the same time, be perfectly equalized and assimilated in their possessions, their opinions, and their passions.

A republic, by which I mean a government in which the scheme of representation takes place, opens a different prospect, and promises the cure for which we are seeking. Let us examine the points in which it varies from pure democracy, and we shall comprehend both the nature of the cure and the efficacy which it must derive from the Union.

The two great points of difference between a democracy and a republic are: first, the delegation of the government, in the latter, to a small number of citizens elected by the rest; secondly, the greater number of citizens, and greater sphere of country, over which the latter may be extended.

The effect of the first difference is, on the one hand, to refine and enlarge the public views, by passing them through the medium of a chosen body of citizens, whose wisdom may best discern the true interest of their country, and whose patriotism and love of justice will be least likely to sacrifice it to temporary or partial considerations. Under such a regulation, it may well happen that the public voice, pronounced by the representatives of the people, will be more consonant to the public good than if pronounced by the people themselves, convened for the purpose. On the other hand, the effect may be inverted. Men of factious tempers, of local prejudices, or of sinister designs, may, by intrigue, by corruption, or by other means, first obtain the suffrages, and then betray the interests, of the people. The question resulting is, whether small or extensive republics are more favorable to the election of proper guardians of the public weal; and it is clearly decided in favor of the latter by two obvious considerations:

In the first place, it is to be remarked that, however small the republic may be, the representatives must be raised to a certain number, in order to guard against the cabals of a few; and that, however large it may be, they must be limited to a certain number, in order to guard against the confusion of a multitude. Hence, the number of representatives in the two cases not being in proportion to that of the two constituents, and being proportionally greater in the small republic, it follows that, if the proportion of fit characters be not less in the large than in the small republic, the former will present a greater option, and consequently a greater probability of a fit choice.

In the next place, as each representative will be chosen by a greater number of citizens in the large than in the small republic, it will be more difficult for unworthy candidates to practice with success the vicious arts by which elections are too often carried; and the suffrages of the people being more free, will be more likely to centre in men who possess the most attractive merit and the most diffusive and established characters.

It must be confessed that in this, as in most other cases, there is a mean, on both sides of which inconveniences will be found to lie. By enlarging too much the number of electors, you render the representative too little acquainted with all their local circumstances and lesser interests; as by reducing it too much, you render him unduly attached to these, and

too little fit to comprehend and pursue great and national objects. The federal Constitution forms a happy combination in this respect; the great and aggregate interests being referred to the national, the local and particular to the State legislatures.

The other point of difference is, the greater number of citizens and extent of territory which may be brought within the compass of republican than of democratic government; and it is this circumstance principally which renders factious combinations less to be dreaded in the former than in the latter. The smaller the society, the fewer probably will be the distinct parties and interests composing it; the fewer the distinct parties and interests, the more frequently will a majority be found of the same party; and the smaller the number of individuals composing a majority, and the smaller the compass within which they are placed, the more easily will they concert and execute their plans of oppression. Extend the sphere and you take in a greater variety of parties and interests; you make it less probable that a majority of the whole will have a common motive to invade the rights of other citizens; or if such a common motive exists, it will be more difficult for all who feel it to discover their own strength, and to act in unison with each other. Besides other impediments, it may be remarked that, where there is a consciousness of unjust or dishonorable purposes, communication is always checked by distrust in proportion to the number whose concurrence is necessary.

Hence, it clearly appears, that the same advantage which a republic has over a democracy, in controlling the effects of faction, is enjoyed by a large over a small republic,—is enjoyed by the Union over the States composing it. Does the advantage consist in the substitution of representatives whose enlightened views and virtuous sentiments render them superior to local prejudices and to schemes of injustice? It will not be denied that the representation of the Union will be most likely to possess these requisite endowments. Does it consist in the greater security afforded by a greater variety of parties, against the event of any one party being able to outnumber and oppress the rest? In an equal degree does the increased variety of parties comprised within the

Union, increase this security. Does it, in fine, consist in the greater obstacles opposed to the concert and accomplishment of the secret wishes of an unjust and interested majority? Here, again, the extent of the Union gives it the most palpable advantage.

The influence of factious leaders may kindle a flame within their particular States, but will be unable to spread a general conflagration through the other States. A religious sect may degenerate into a political faction in a part of the Confederacy; but the variety of sects dispersed over the entire face of it must secure the national councils against any danger from that source. A rage for paper money, for an abolition of debts, for an equal division of property, or for any other improper or wicked project, will be less apt to pervade the whole body of the Union than a particular member of it; in the same proportion as such a malady is more likely to taint a particular county or district, than an entire State.

In the extent and proper structure of the Union, therefore, we behold a republican remedy for the diseases most incident to republican government. And according to the degree of pleasure and pride we feel in being republicans, ought to be our zeal in cherishing the spirit and supporting the character of Federalists.

Publius [Madison]

## NUMBER 15

In the course of the preceding papers, I have endeavored, my fellow-citizens, to place before you in a clear and convincing light the importance of Union to your political safety and happiness. I have unfolded to you a complication of dangers to which you would be exposed, should you permit that sacred knot which binds the people of America together to be severed or dissolved by ambition or by avarice, by jealousy or by misrepresentation. In the sequel of the inquiry through which I propose to accompany you, the truths intended to be inculcated will receive further confirmation from facts and arguments hitherto unnoticed. If the road over which you will still have to pass should in some places appear to you tedious or irksome, you will recollect that you are in quest of information on a subject the most momentous which can engage the attention of a free people, that the field through which you have to travel is in itself spacious, and that the difficulties of the journey have been unnecessarily increased by the mazes with which sophistry has beset the way. It will be my aim to remove the obstacles to your progress in as compendious a manner as it can be done, without sacrificing utility to dispatch.

In pursuance of the plan which I have laid down for the discussion of the subject, the point next in order to be examined is the "insufficiency of the present Confederation to the preservation of the Union." It may perhaps be asked what need there is of reasoning or proof to illustrate a position which is not either controverted or doubted, to which the understandings and feelings of all classes of men assent, and which in substance is admitted by the opponents as well as by the friends of the new Constitution. It must in truth be acknowledged that, however these may differ in other respects, they in general appear to harmonize in this sentiment, at least, that there are material imperfections in our national system, and that something is necessary to be done to rescue us from impending anarchy. The facts that support this opinion are no longer objects of speculation. They have forced themselves upon the sensibility of the people at large, and have at length extorted from those, whose mistaken policy has had the principal share in precipitating the extremity at which we are arrived, a reluctant confession of the reality of those defects in the scheme of our federal government, which have been long pointed out and regretted by the intelligent friends of the Union.

We may indeed with propriety be said to have reached almost the last stage of national humiliation. There is scarcely any thing that can wound the pride or degrade the character of an independent nation which we do not experience. Are there engagements to the performance of which we are held by every tie respectable among men? These are the subjects of constant and unblushing violation. Do we owe debts to foreigners and to our own citizens contracted in a time of imminent peril for the preservation of our political existence? These remain without any proper or satisfactory provision for their discharge. Have we valuable territories and important posts in the possession of a foreign power which, by express stipulations, ought long since to have been surrendered? These are still retained, to the prejudice of our interests, not less than of our rights. Are we in a condition to resent or to repel the aggression? We have neither troops, nor treasury, nor government.[3] Are we even in a condition to remonstrate with dignity? The just imputations on our own faith, in respect to the same treaty, ought first to be removed. Are we entitled by nature and compact to a free participation in the navigation of the Mississippi? Spain excludes us from it. Is public credit an indispensable resource in time of public danger? We seem to have abandoned its cause as desperate and irretrievable. Is commerce of importance to national wealth? Ours is at the lowest point of declension. Is respectability in the eyes of foreign powers a safeguard against foreign encroachments? The imbecility of our government even forbids them to treat with us. Our ambassadors abroad are the mere pageants of mimic sovereignty. Is a violent and unnatural decrease in the value of land a symptom of national distress? The price of improved land in most parts of the country is much lower than can be accounted for by the quantity of waste land at market, and can only be fully explained by that want of private and public confidence, which are so alarmingly prevalent among all ranks, and which have a direct tendency to depreciate property of every kind. Is private credit the friend and patron of industry? That most useful kind which relates to borrowing and lending is reduced within the narrowest limits, and this still more from an opinion of insecurity than from the scarcity of money. To shorten an enumeration of particulars which can afford neither pleasure nor instruction, it may in general be demanded, what indication is there of national disorder, poverty, and insignificance that could befall a community so peculiarly blessed with natural advantages as we are, which does not form a part of the dark catalogue of our public misfortunes.

This is the melancholy situation to which we have been brought by those very maxims and councils which would now deter us from adopting the proposed Constitution; and which, not content with having conducted us to the brink of a precipice, seem resolved to plunge us into the abyss that awaits us below. Here, my countrymen, impelled by every motive that ought to influence an enlightened people, let us make a firm stand for our safety, our tranquillity, our dignity, our reputation. Let us at last break the fatal charm which has too long seduced us from the paths of felicity and prosperity.

It is true, as has been before observed, that facts, too stubborn to be resisted, have produced a species of general assent to the abstract proposition that there exist material defects in our national system; but the usefulness of the concession, on the part of the old adversaries of federal measures, is destroyed by a strenuous opposition to a remedy, upon the only principles that can give it a chance of success. While they admit that the government of the United States is destitute of energy, they contend against conferring upon it those powers which are requisite to supply that energy. They seem still to aim at things repugnant and irreconcilable; at an augmentation of federal authority, without a diminution of State authority; at sovereignty in the Union, and complete independence in the members. They still, in fine, seem to cherish with blind devotion the political monster of an *imperium in imperio*. This renders a full display of the principal defects of the Confederation necessary, in order to show that the evils we experience do not proceed from minute or partial imperfections, but from fundamental errors in the structure of the building, which cannot be amended otherwise than by an alteration in the first principles and main pillars of the fabric.

The great and radical vice in the construction of the existing Confederation is in the principle of LEGISLATION for STATES OR GOVERNMENTS, in their CORPORATE or COLLECTIVE CAPACITIES, and as contradistinguished from the INDIVIDUALS of which they consist. Though this principle does not run through all the powers delegated to the Union, yet it pervades and governs those on which the efficacy of the rest depends. Except as to the rule of apportionment, the United States has an indefinite discretion to make requisitions for men and money; but they have no authority to raise either, by regulations extending to the individual citizens of America. The consequence of this is, that though in theory their resolutions concerning those objects are laws, constitutionally binding on the members of the Union, yet in practice they are mere recommendations which the States observe or disregard at their option.

It is a singular instance of the capriciousness of the human mind, that after all the admonitions we have had from experience on this head, there should still be found men who object to the new Constitution, for deviating from a principle which has been found the bane of the old, and which is in itself evidently incompatible with the idea of GOVERNMENT; a principle, in short, which, if it is to be executed at all, must substitute the violent and sanguinary agency of the sword to the mild influence of the magistracy.

There is nothing absurd or impracticable in the idea of a league or alliance between independent nations for certain defined purposes precisely stated in a treaty regulating all the details of time, place, circumstance, and quantity; leaving nothing to future discretion; and depending for its execution on the good faith of the parties. Compacts of this kind exist among all civilized nations, subject to the usual vicissitudes of peace and war, of observance and non-observance, as the interests or passions of the contracting powers dictate. In the early part of the present century there was an epidemical rage in Europe for this species of compacts, from which the politicians of the times fondly hoped for benefits which were never realized. With a view to establishing the equilibrium of power and the peace of that part of the world, all the resources of negotiations were exhausted, and triple and quadruple alliances were formed; but they were scarcely formed before they were broken, giving an instructive but afflicting lesson to mankind, how little dependence is to be placed on treaties which have no other sanction than the obligations of good faith, and which oppose general considerations of peace and justice to the impulse of any immediate interest or passion.

If the particular States in this country are disposed to stand in a similar relation to each other, and to drop the project of a general DISCRETIONARY SUPERINTENDENCE, the scheme would indeed be pernicious, and would entail upon us all the mischiefs which have been enumerated under the first head; but it would have the merit of being, at least, consistent and practicable. Abandoning all views towards a confederate government, this would bring us to a simple alliance offensive and defensive; and would place us in a situation to be alternate friends and enemies of each other, as our mutual jealousies and rivalships, nourished by the intrigues of foreign nations, should prescribe to us.

But if we are unwilling to be placed in this perilous situation; if we still will adhere to the design of a national government, or, which is the same thing, of a superintending power, under the direction of a common council, we must resolve to incorporate into our plan those ingredients which may be considered as forming the characteristic difference between a league and a government; we must extend the authority of the Union to the persons of the citizens—the only proper objects of government.

Government implies the power of making laws. It is essential to the idea of a law, that it be attended with a sanction; or, in other words, a penalty or punishment for disobedience. If there be no penalty annexed to disobedience, the resolutions or commands which pretend to be laws will, in fact, amount to nothing more than advice or recommendation. This penalty, whatever it may be, can only be inflicted in two ways: by the agency of the courts and ministers of justice, or by military force; by the COERCION of the magistracy, or by the COERCION of arms. The first kind can evidently apply only to men; the last kind must of necessity, be employed against bodies politic, or communities, or States. It is evident that there is no process of a court by which the observance of the laws can, in the last resort, be enforced. Sentences may be denounced against them for violations of their duty; but these sentences can only be carried into execution by the sword. In an association where the general authority is confined to the collective bodies of the communities that compose it, every breach of the laws must involve a state of war; and military execution must become the only instrument of civil obedience.

Such a state of things can certainly not deserve the name of government, nor would any prudent man choose to commit his happiness to it.

There was a time when we were told that breaches, by the States, of the regulations of the federal authority were not to be expected; that a sense of common interest would preside over the conduct of the respective members, and would beget a full compliance with all the constitutional requisitions of the Union. This language, at the present day, would appear as wild as a great part of what we now hear from the same quarter will be thought, when we shall have received further lessons from that best oracle of wisdom, experience. It at all times betrayed an ignorance of the true springs by which human conduct is actuated, and belied the original inducements to the establishment of civil power. Why has government been instituted at all? Because the passions of men will not conform to the dictates of reason and justice, without constraint. Has it been found that bodies of men act with more rectitude or greater disinterestedness than individuals? The contrary of this has been inferred by all accurate observers of the conduct of mankind; and the inference is founded upon obvious reasons. Regard to reputation has a less active influence, when the infamy of a bad action is to be divided among a number, than when it is to fall singly upon one. A spirit of faction, which is apt to mingle its poison in the deliberations of all bodies of men, will often hurry the persons of whom they are composed into improprieties and excesses, for which they would blush in a private capacity.

In addition to all this, there is, in the nature of sovereign power, an impatience of control, that disposes those who are invested with the exercise of it, to look with an evil eye upon all external attempts to restrain or direct its operations. From this spirit it happens, that in every political association which is formed upon the principle of uniting in a common interest a number of lesser sovereignties, there will be found a kind of eccentric tendency in the subordinate or inferior orbs, by the operation of which there will be a perpetual effort in each to fly off from the common centre. This tendency is not difficult to be accounted for. It has its origin in the love of

power. Power controlled or abridged is almost always the rival and enemy of that power by which it is controlled or abridged. This simple proposition will teach us, how little reason there is to expect, that the persons intrusted with the administration of the affairs of the particular members of a confederacy will at all times be ready, with perfect good-humor, and an unbiased regard to the public weal, to execute the resolutions or decrees of the general authority. The reverse of this results from the constitution of human nature.

If, therefore, the measures of the Confederacy cannot be executed without the intervention of the particular administrations, there will be little prospect of their being executed at all. The rulers of the respective members, whether they have a constitutional right to do it or not, will undertake to judge of the propriety of the measures themselves. They will consider the conformity of the thing proposed or required to their immediate interests or aims; the momentary conveniences or inconveniences that would attend its adoption. All this will be done; and in a spirit of interested and suspicious scrutiny, without that knowledge of national circumstances and reasons of state, which is essential to a right judgment, and with that strong predilection in favor of local objects, which can hardly fail to mislead the decision. The same process must be repeated in every member of which the body is constituted; and the execution of the plans, framed by the councils of the whole, will always fluctuate on the discretion of the ill-informed and prejudiced opinion of every part. Those who have been conversant in the proceedings of popular assemblies; who have seen how difficult it often is, where there is no exterior pressure of circumstances, to bring them to harmonious resolutions on important points, will readily conceive how impossible it must be to induce a number of such assemblies, deliberating at a distance from each other, at different times, and under different impressions, long to cooperate in the same views and pursuits.

In our case, the concurrence of thirteen distinct sovereign wills is requisite, under the Confederation, to the complete execution of every important measure that proceeds from the Union. It has happened as was to have been foreseen. The measures of the Union have not been executed; the delinquencies of the States have, step by step, matured themselves to an extreme, which has, at length, arrested all the wheels of the national government, and brought them to an awful stand. Congress at this time scarcely possess the means of keeping up the forms of administration, till the States can have time to agree upon a more substantial substitute for the present shadow of a federal government. Things did not come to this desperate extremity at once. The causes which have been specified produced at first only unequal and disproportionate degrees of compliance with the requisitions of the Union. The greater deficiencies of some States furnished the pretext of example and the temptation of interest to the complying, or to the least delinquent States. Why should we do more in proportion than those who are embarked with us in the same political voyage? Why should we consent to bear more than our proper share of the common burden? These were suggestions which human selfishness could not withstand, and which even speculative men, who looked forward to remote consequences, could not, without hesitation, combat. Each State, yielding to the persuasive voice of immediate interest or convenience, has successively withdrawn its support, till the frail and tottering edifice seems ready to fall upon our heads, and to crush us beneath its ruins.

Publius [Hamilton]

## NUMBER 39

The last paper having concluded the observations which were meant to introduce a candid survey of the plan of government reported by the convention, we now proceed to the execution of that part of our undertaking.

The first question that offers itself is, whether the general form and aspect of the government be strictly republican. It is evident that no other form would be reconcilable with the genius of the people of America; with the fundamental principles of the Revolution; or with that honorable determination which animates every votary of freedom, to rest all our political experiments on the capacity of mankind for self-government. If the plan of the convention, therefore, be found to depart from the republican character, its advocates must abandon it as no longer defensible.

What, then, are the distinctive characters of the republican form? Were an answer to this question to be sought, not by recurring to principles, but in the application of the term by political writers, to the constitutions of different States, no satisfactory one would ever be found. Holland, in which no particle of the supreme authority is derived from the people, has passed almost universally under the denomination of a republic. The same title has been bestowed on Venice, where absolute power over the great body of the people is exercised, in the most absolute manner, by a small body of hereditary nobles. Poland, which is a mixture of aristocracy and of monarchy in their worst forms, has been dignified with the same appellation. The government of England, which has one republican branch only, combined with an hereditary aristocracy and monarchy, has, with equal impropriety, been frequently placed on the list of republics. These examples, which are nearly as dissimilar to each other as to a genuine republic, show the extreme inaccuracy with which the term has been used in political disquisitions.

If we resort for a criterion to the different principles on which different forms of government are established, we may define a republic to be, or at least may bestow that name on, a government which derives all its powers directly or indirectly from the great body of the people, and is administered by persons holding their offices during pleasure, for a limited period, or during good behavior. It is *essential* to such a government that it be derived from the great body of the society, not from an inconsiderable proportion, or a favored class of it; otherwise a handful of tyrannical nobles, exercising their oppressions by a delegation of their powers, might aspire to the rank of republicans, and claim for their government the honorable title of republic. It is *sufficient* for such a government that the persons administering it be appointed, either directly or indirectly, by the people; and that they hold their appointments by either of the tenures just specified; otherwise every government in the United States, as well as every other popular government that has been or can be well organized or well executed, would be degraded from the republican character. According to the constitution of every State in the Union, some or other of the officers of government are appointed indirectly only by the people. According to most of them, the chief magistrate himself is so appointed. And according to one, this mode of appointment is extended to one of the coordinate branches of the legislature. According to all the constitutions, also, the tenure of the highest offices is extended to a definite period, and in many instances, both within the legislative and executive departments, to a period of years. According to the provisions of most of the constitutions, again, as well as according to the most respectable and received opinions on the subject, the members of the judiciary department are to retain their offices by the firm tenure of good behavior.

On comparing the Constitution planned by the convention with the standard here fixed, we perceive at once that it is, in the most rigid sense, conformable to it. The House of Representatives, like that of one branch at least of all the State legislatures, is elected immediately by the great body of the people. The Senate, like the present Congress, and the Senate of Maryland, derives its appointment indirectly from the people. The President is indirectly derived from the choice of the people, according to the example in most of the States. Even the judges with all other officers of the Union, will, as in the several States, be the choice, though a remote choice, of the people themselves. The duration of the appointments is equally conformable to the republican standard, and to the model of State constitutions. The House of Representatives is periodically elective, as in all the States; and for the period of two years, as in the State of South Carolina. The Senate is elective, for the period of six years; which is but one year more than the period of the Senate of Maryland, and but two more than that of the Senates of New York and Virginia. The President is to continue in office for the period of

four years; as in New York and Delaware the chief magistrate is elected for three years, and in South Carolina for two years. In the other States the election is annual. In several of the States, however, no constitutional provision is made for the impeachment of the chief magistrate. And in Delaware and Virginia he is not impeachable till out of office. The President of the United States is impeachable at any time during his continuance in office. The tenure by which the judges are to hold their places, is, as it unquestionably ought to be, that of good behavior. The tenure of the ministerial offices generally, will be a subject of legal regulation, conformably to the reason of the case and the example of the State constitutions.

Could any further proof be required of the republican complexion of this system, the most decisive one might be found in its absolute prohibition of titles of nobility, both under the federal and the State governments; and in its express guaranty of the republican form to each of the latter.

"But it was not sufficient," say the adversaries of the proposed Constitution, "for the convention to adhere to the republican form. They ought, with equal care, to have preserved the *federal* form, which regards the Union as a *Confederacy* of sovereign states; instead of which, they have framed a *national* government, which regards the Union as a *consolidation* of the States." And it is asked by what authority this bold and radical innovation was undertaken? The handle which has been made of this objection requires that it should be examined with some precision.

Without inquiring into the accuracy of the distinction on which the objection is founded, it will be necessary to a just estimate of its force, first, to ascertain the real character of the government in question; secondly, to inquire how far the convention were authorized to propose such a government; and thirdly, how far the duty they owed to their country could supply any defect of regular authority.

*First.*—In order to ascertain the real character of the government, it may be considered in relation to the foundation on which it is to be established; to the sources from which its ordinary powers are to be drawn; to the operation of those powers; to the extent of them; and to the authority by which future changes in the government are to be introduced.

On examining the first relation, it appears, on one hand, that the Constitution is to be founded on the assent and ratification of the people of America, given by deputies elected for the special purpose; but, on the other, that this assent and ratification is to be given by the people, not as individuals composing one entire nation, but as composing the distinct and independent States to which they respectively belong. It is to be the assent and ratification of the several States, derived from the supreme authority in each State—the authority of the people themselves. The act, therefore, establishing the Constitution, will not be a *national*, but a *federal* act.

That it will be a federal and not a national act, as these terms are understood by the objectors; the act of the people, as forming so many independent States, not as forming one aggregate nation, is obvious from this single consideration, that it is to result neither from the decision of a *majority* of the people of the Union, nor from that of a *majority* of the States. It must result from the *unanimous* assent of the several States that are parties to it, differing no otherwise from their ordinary assent than in its being expressed, not by the legislative authority, but by that of the people themselves. Were the people regarded in this transaction as forming one nation, the will of the majority of the whole people of the United States would bind the minority, in the same manner as the majority in each State must bind the minority; and the will of the majority must be determined either by a comparison of the individual votes, or by considering the will of the majority of the States as evidence of the will of a majority of the people of the United States. Neither of these rules has been adopted. Each State, in ratifying the Constitution, is considered as a sovereign body, independent of all others, and only to be bound by its own voluntary act. In this relation, then, the new Constitution will, if established, be a *federal*, and not a *national* constitution.

The next relation is, to the sources from which the ordinary powers of government are to be derived. The House of Representatives will derive its powers from the people of America; and the people will be represented in the same proportion, and on the same principle, as they are in the legislature of a particular State. So far the government is *national*, not *federal*. The Senate, on the other hand, will derive its powers from the States, as political and coequal societies; and these will be represented on the principle of equality in the Senate, as they now are in the existing Congress. So far the government is *federal,* not *national*. The executive power will be derived from a very compound source. The immediate election of the President is to be made by the States in their political characters. The votes allotted to them are in a compound ratio, which considers them partly as distinct and coequal societies, partly as unequal members of the same society. The eventual election, again, is to be made by that branch of the legislature which consists of the national representatives; but in this particular act they are to be thrown into the form of individual delegations, from so many distinct and coequal bodies politic. From this aspect of the government, it appears to be of a mixed character, presenting at least as many *federal* as *national* features.

The difference between a federal and national government, as it relates to the *operation of the government*, is supposed to consist in this, that in the former the powers operate on the political bodies composing the Confederacy, in their political capacities; in the latter, on the individual citizens composing the nation, in their individual capacities. On trying the Constitution by this criterion, it falls under the *national*, not the *federal* character; though perhaps not so completely as has been understood. In several cases, and particularly in the trial of controversies to which States may be parties, they must be viewed and proceeded against in their collective and political capacities only. So far the national countenance of the government on this side seems to be disfigured by a few federal features. But this blemish is perhaps unavoidable in any plan; and the operation of the government on the people, in their individual capacities, in its ordinary and most essential proceedings, may, on the whole, designate it, in this relation, a *national* government.

But if the government be national with regard to the *operation* of its powers, it changes its aspect again when we contemplate it in relation to the extent of its powers. The idea of a national government involves in it, not only an authority over the individual citizens, but an indefinite supremacy over all persons and things, so far as they are objects of lawful government. Among a people consolidated into one nation, this supremacy is completely vested in the national legislature. Among communities united for particular purposes, it is vested partly in the general and partly in the municipal legislatures. In the former case, all local authorities are subordinate to the supreme; and may be controlled, directed, or abolished by it at pleasure. In the latter, the local or municipal authorities form distinct and independent portions of the supremacy, no more subject, within their respective spheres, to the general authority, than the general authority is subject to them, within its own sphere. In this relation, then, the proposed government cannot be deemed a *national* one; since its jurisdiction extends to certain enumerated objects only, and leaves to the several States a residuary and inviolable sovereignty over all other objects. It is true that in controversies relating to the boundary between the two jurisdictions, the tribunal which is ultimately to decide, is to be established under the general government. But this does not change the principle of the case. The decision is to be impartially made, according to the rules of the Constitution; and all the usual and most effectual precautions are taken to secure this impartiality. Some such tribunal is clearly essential to prevent an appeal to the sword and a dissolution of the compact; and that it ought to be established under the general rather than under the local governments, or, to speak more properly, that it could be safely established under the first alone, is a position not likely to be combated.

If we try the Constitution by its last relation to the authority by which amendments are to be made, we find it neither wholly *national* nor wholly *federal*. Were it wholly national, the supreme and ultimate authority would reside in the *majority* of the people of the Union; and this authority would be competent at all times, like that of a majority of every national society, to alter or abolish its established government. Were it wholly federal, on the other hand, the concurrence of each State in the Union would be essential to every alteration that would be binding on all. The mode provided by the plan of the convention is not founded on either of these principles. In requiring more than a majority, and particularly in computing the proportion by *States*, not by citizens, it departs from the *national* and advances towards the *federal* character; in rendering the concurrence of less than the whole number of States sufficient, it loses again the *federal* and partakes of the *national* character.

The proposed Constitution, therefore, is, in strictness, neither a national nor a federal Constitution, but a composition of both. In its foundation it is federal, not national; in the sources from which the ordinary powers of the government are drawn, it is partly federal and partly national; in the operation of these powers, it is national, not federal; in the extent of them, again, it is federal, not national; and, finally, in the authoritative mode of introducing amendments, it is neither wholly federal nor wholly national.

Publius [Madison]

## NUMBER 47

Having reviewed the general form of the proposed government and the general mass of power allotted to it, I proceed to examine the particular structure of this government, and the distribution of this mass of power among its constituent parts.

One of the principal objections inculcated by the more respectable adversaries to the Constitution, is its supposed violation of the political maxim, that the legislative, executive, and judiciary departments ought to be separate and distinct. In the structure of the federal government, no regard, it is said, seems to have been paid to this essential precaution in favor of liberty. The several departments of power are distributed and blended in such a manner as at once to destroy all symmetry and beauty of form, and to expose some of the essential parts of the edifice to the danger of being crushed by the disproportionate weight of other parts.

No political truth is certainly of greater intrinsic value, or is stamped with the authority of more enlightened patrons of liberty, than that on which the objection is founded. The accumulation of all powers, legislative, executive, and judiciary, in the same hands, whether of one, a few, or many, and whether hereditary, self-appointed, or elective, may justly be pronounced the very definition of tyranny. Were the federal Constitution, therefore, really chargeable with the accumulation of power, or with a mixture of powers, having a dangerous tendency to such an accumulation, no further arguments would be necessary to inspire a universal reprobation of the system. I persuade myself, however, that it will be made apparent to every one, that the charge cannot be supported, and that the maxim on which it relies has been totally misconceived and misapplied. In order to form correct ideas on this important subject, it will be proper to investigate the sense in which the preservation of liberty requires that the three great departments of power should be separate and distinct.

The oracle who is always consulted and cited on this subject is the celebrated Montesquieu. If he be not the author of this invaluable precept in the science of politics, he has the merit at least of displaying and recommending it most effectually to the attention of mankind. Let us endeavor, in the first place, to ascertain his meaning on this point.

The British Constitution was to Montesquieu what Homer has been to the didactic writers on epic poetry. As the latter have considered the work of the immortal bard as the perfect model from which the principles and rules of the epic art were to be drawn, and by which all similar works were to be judged, so this great political critic appears to have viewed the Constitution of England as the standard, or to use his own expression, as the mirror of political liberty; and to have delivered, in the form of elementary truths, the several characteristic principles of that particular system. That we may be sure, then, not to mistake his meaning in this case, let us recur to the source from which the maxim was drawn.

On the slightest view of the British Constitution, we must perceive that the legislative, executive, and judiciary departments are by no means totally separate and distinct from each other. The executive magistrate forms an integral part of the legislative authority. He alone has the prerogative of making treaties with foreign sovereigns, which, when made, have, under certain limitations, the force of legislative acts. All the members of the judiciary department are appointed by him, can be removed by him on the address of the two Houses of Parliament, and form, when he pleases to consult them, one of his constitutional councils. One branch of the legislative department forms also a great constitutional council to the executive chief, as, on another hand, it is the sole depositary of judicial power in cases of impeachment, and is invested with the supreme appellate jurisdiction in all other cases. The judges, again, are so far connected with the legislative department as often to attend and participate in its deliberations, though not admitted to a legislative vote.

From these facts, by which Montesquieu was guided, it may clearly be inferred that, in saying "There can be no liberty where the legislative and executive powers are united in the same person, or body of magistrates," or, "if the power of judging be not separated from the legislative and executive powers," he did not mean that these departments ought to have no *partial agency* in, or no *control* over, the acts of each other. His meaning, as his own words import, and still more conclusively as illustrated by the example in his eye, can amount to no more than this, that where the *whole* power of one department is exercised by the same hands which possess the *whole* power of another department, the fundamental principles of a free constitution are subverted. This would have been the case in the constitution examined by him, if the king, who is the sole executive magistrate, had possessed also the complete legislative power, or the supreme administration of justice; or if the entire legislative body had possessed the supreme judiciary, or the supreme executive authority. This, however is not among the vices of that constitution. The magistrate in whom the whole executive power resides cannot of himself make a law, though he can put a negative on every law; nor administer justice in person, though he has the appointment of those who do administer it. The judges can exercise no executive prerogative, though they are shoots from the executive stock; nor any legislative function, though they may be advised with by the legislative councils. The entire legislature can perform no judiciary act, though by the joint act of two of its branches the judges may be removed from their offices, and though one of its branches is possessed of the judicial power in the last resort. The entire legislature, again, can exercise no executive prerogative, though one of its branches constitutes the supreme executive magistracy, and another, on the impeachment of a third, can try and condemn all the subordinate officers in the executive department.

The reasons on which Montesquieu grounds his maxim are a further demonstration of his meaning. "When the legislative and executive powers are united in the same person or body," says he, "there can be no liberty, because apprehensions may arise lest *the same* monarch or senate should *enact* tyrannical laws to *execute* them in a tyrannical manner." Again: "Were the power of judging joined with the legislative, the life and liberty of the subject would be exposed to arbitrary control, for *the judge* would then be *the legislator*. Were it joined to the executive power, *the judge* might behave with all the violence of *an oppressor*." Some of these reasons are more fully explained in other passages; but briefly stated as they are here, they sufficiently establish the meaning which we have put on this celebrated maxim of this celebrated author.

If we look into the constitutions of the several States, we find that, notwithstanding the emphatical and, in some instances, the unqualified terms in which this axiom has been laid down, there is not a single instance in which the several departments of power have been kept absolutely separate and distinct. New Hampshire, whose constitution was the last formed, seems to have been fully aware of the impossibility and inexpediency of avoiding any mixture whatever of these departments, and has qualified the doctrine by declaring "that the legislative, executive, and judiciary powers ought to be kept as separate from, and independent of, each other *as the nature of a free government will admit; or as is consistent with that chain of connection that binds the whole fabric of the constitution in one indissoluble bond of unity and amity.*" Her constitution accordingly mixes these departments in several respects. The Senate, which is a branch of the legislative department, is also a judicial tribunal for the trial of impeachments. The President, who is the head of the executive department, is the presiding member also of the Senate; and, besides an equal vote in all cases, has a casting vote in case of a tie. The executive head is himself eventually elective every year by the legislative department, and his council is every year chosen by and from the members of the same department. Several of the officers of state are also appointed by the legislature. And the members of the judiciary department are appointed by the executive department.

The constitution of Massachusetts has observed a sufficient though less pointed caution, in expressing this fundamental article of liberty. It declares "that the legislative departments shall never exercise the executive and judicial powers, or either of them; the executive shall never exercise the legislative and judicial powers, or either of them; the judicial shall never exercise the legislative and executive powers, or either of them." This declaration corresponds precisely with the doctrine of Montesquieu, as it has been explained, and is not in a single point violated by the plan of the convention. It goes no farther than to prohibit any one of the entire departments from exercising the powers of another department. In the very constitution to which it is prefixed, a partial mixture of powers has been admitted. The executive magistrate has a qualified negative on the legislative body, and the Senate, which is a part of the legislature, is a court of impeachment for members both of the executive and judiciary departments. The members of the judiciary department, again, are appointable by the executive department, and removable by the same authority on the address of the two legislative branches. Lastly, a number of the officers of government are annually appointed by the legislative department. As the appointment to offices, particularly executive offices, is in its nature an executive function, the compilers of the constitution have, in this last point at least, violated the rule established by themselves.

I pass over the constitutions of Rhode Island and Connecticut, because they were formed prior to the Revolution, and even before the principle under examination had become an object of political attention.

The constitution of New York contains no declaration on this subject; but appears very clearly to have been framed with an eye to the danger of improperly blending the different departments. It gives, nevertheless, to the executive magistrate, a partial control over the legislative department; and, what is more, gives a like control to the judiciary department; and even blends the executive and judiciary departments in the exercise of this control. In its council of appointment members of the legislative are associated with the executive authority, in the appointment of officers, both executive and judiciary. And its court for the trial of impeachments and correction of errors is to consist of one branch of the legislature and the principal members of the judiciary department.

The constitution of New Jersey has blended the different powers of government more than any of the preceding. The governor, who is the executive magistrate, is appointed by the legislature; is chancellor and ordinary, or surrogate of the State; is a member of the Supreme Court of Appeals, and president, with a casting vote, of one of the legislative branches. The same legislative branch acts again as executive council of the governor, and with him constitutes the Court of Appeals. The members of the judiciary department are appointed by the legislative department, and removable by one branch of it, on the impeachment of the other.

According to the constitution of Pennsylvania, the president, who is the head of the executive department, is annually elected by a vote in which the legislative department predominates. In conjunction with an executive council, he appoints the members of the judiciary department, and forms a court of impeachment for trial of all officers, judiciary as well as executive. The judges of the Supreme Court

and justices of the peace seem also to be removable by the legislature; and the executive power of pardoning in certain cases, to be referred to the same department. The members of the executive council are made EX-OFFICIO justices of peace throughout the State.

In Delaware, the chief executive magistrate is annually elected by the legislative department. The speakers of the two legislative branches are vice-presidents in the executive department. The executive chief, with six others, appointed, three by each of the legislative branches, constitutes the Supreme Court of Appeals; he is joined with the legislative department in the appointment of the other judges. Throughout the States, it appears that the members of the legislature may at the same time be justices of the peace; in this State, the members of one branch of it are EX-OFFICIO justices of the peace; as are also the members of the executive council. The principal officers of the executive department are appointed by the legislative; and one branch of the latter forms a court of impeachments. All officers may be removed on address of the legislature.

Maryland has adopted the maxim in the most unqualified terms; declaring that the legislative, executive, and judicial powers of government ought to be forever separate and distinct from each other. Her constitution, notwithstanding, makes the executive magistrate appointable by the legislative department; and the members of the judiciary by the executive department.

The language of Virginia is still more pointed on this subject. Her constitution declares, "that the legislative, executive, and judiciary departments shall be separate and distinct; so that neither exercise the powers properly belonging to the other; nor shall any person exercise the powers of more than one of them at the same time, except that the justices of county courts shall be eligible to either House of Assembly." Yet we find not only this express exception, with respect to the members of the inferior courts, but that the chief magistrate, with his executive council, are appointable by the legislature; that two members of the latter are triennially displaced at the pleasure of the legislature; and that all the principal offices, both executive and judiciary, are filled by the same department. The executive prerogative of pardon, also, is in one case vested in the legislative department.

The constitution of North Carolina, which declares "that the legislative, executive, and supreme judicial powers of government ought to be forever separate and distinct from each other," refers, at the same time, to the legislative department, the appointment not only of the executive chief, but all the principal officers within both that and the judiciary department.

In South Carolina, the constitution makes the executive magistracy eligible by the legislative department. It gives to the latter, also, the appointment of the members of the judiciary department, including even justices of the peace and sheriffs; and the appointment of officers in the executive department, down to captains in the army and navy of the State.

In the constitution of Georgia, where it is declared "that the legislative, executive, and judiciary departments shall be separate and distinct, so that neither exercise the powers properly belonging to the other," we find that the executive department is to be filled by appointments of the legislature; and the executive prerogative of pardon to be finally exercised by the same authority. Even justices of the peace are to be appointed by the legislature.

In citing these cases, in which the legislative, executive, and judiciary departments have not been kept totally separate and distinct, I wish not to be regarded as an advocate for the particular organizations of the several State governments. I am fully aware that among the many excellent principles which they exemplify, they carry strong marks of the haste, and still stronger of the inexperience, under which they were framed. It is but too obvious that in some instances the fundamental principle under consideration has been violated by too great a mixture, and even an actual consolidation, of the different powers; and that in no instance has a competent provision been made for maintaining in practice the separation delineated on paper. What I have wished to evince is, that the charge brought against the pro-

posed Constitution, of violating the sacred maxim of free government, is warranted neither by the real meaning annexed to that maxim by its author, nor by the sense in which it has hitherto been understood in America. This interesting subject will be resumed in the ensuing paper.                    Publius [Madison]

## NUMBER 48

It was shown in the last paper that the political apothegm there examined does not require that the legislative, executive, and judiciary departments should be wholly unconnected with each other. I shall undertake, in the next place, to show that unless these departments be so far connected and blended as to give to each a constitutional control over the others, the degree of separation which the maxim requires, as essential to a free government, can never in practice be duly maintained.

It is agreed on all sides, that the powers properly belonging to one of the departments ought not to be directly and completely administered by either of the other departments. It is equally evident, that none of them ought to possess, directly or indirectly, an overruling influence over the others, in the administration of their respective powers. It will not be denied, that power is of an encroaching nature, and that it ought to be effectually restrained from passing the limits assigned to it. After discriminating, therefore, in theory, the several classes of power, as they may in their nature be legislative, executive, or judiciary, the next and most difficult task is to provide some practical security for each, against the invasion of the others. What this security ought to be, is the great problem to be solved.

Will it be sufficient to mark, with precision, the boundaries of these departments, in the constitution of the government, and to trust to these parchment barriers against the encroaching spirit of power? This is the security which appears to have been principally relied on by the compilers of most of the American constitutions. But experience assures us, that the efficacy of the provision has been greatly overrated; and that some more adequate defence is indispensably necessary for the more feeble, against the more powerful, members of the government. The legislative department is everywhere extending the sphere of its activity, and drawing all power into its impetuous vortex.

The founders of our republics have so much merit for the wisdom which they have displayed, that no task can be less pleasing than that of pointing out the errors into which they have fallen. A respect for truth, however, obliges us to remark, that they seem never for a moment to have turned their eyes from the danger to liberty from the overgrown and all-grasping prerogative of an hereditary magistrate, supported and fortified by an hereditary branch of the legislative authority. They seem never to have recollected the danger from legislative usurpations, which, by assembling all power in the same hands, must lead to the same tyranny as is threatened by executive usurpations.

In a government where numerous and extensive prerogatives are placed in the hands of an hereditary monarch, the executive department is very justly regarded as the source of danger, and watched with all the jealousy which a zeal for liberty ought to inspire. In a democracy, where a multitude of people exercise in person the legislative functions, and are continually exposed, by their incapacity for regular deliberation and concerted measures, to the ambitious intrigues of their executive magistrates, tyranny may well be apprehended, on some favorable emergency, to start up in the same quarter. But in a representative republic, where the executive magistracy is carefully limited, both in the extent and the duration of its power; and where the legislative power is exercised by an assembly, which is inspired, by a supposed influence over the people, with an intrepid confidence in its own strength; which is sufficiently numerous to feel all the passions which actuate a multitude, yet not so numerous as to be incapable of pursuing the objects of its passions, by means which reason prescribes; it is against the enterprising ambition of this department that the people ought to indulge all their jealousy and exhaust all their precautions.

The legislative department derives a superiority in our governments from other circumstances. Its con-

stitutional powers being at once more extensive, and less susceptible of precise limits, it can, with the greater facility, mask, under complicated and indirect measures, the encroachments which it makes on the coordinate departments. It is not unfrequently a question of real nicety in legislative bodies, whether the operation of a particular measure will, or will not, extend beyond the legislative sphere. On the other side, the executive power being restrained within a narrower compass, and being more simple in its nature, and the judiciary being described by landmarks still less uncertain, projects of usurpation by either of these departments would immediately betray and defeat themselves. Nor is this all: as the legislative department alone has access to the pockets of the people, and has in some constitutions full discretion, and in all a prevailing influence, over the pecuniary rewards of those who fill the other departments, a dependence is thus created in the latter, which gives still greater facility to encroachments of the former.

I have appealed to our own experience for the truth of what I advance on this subject. Were it necessary to verify this experience by particular proofs, they might be multiplied without end. I might find a witness in every citizen who has shared in, or been attentive to, the course of public administrations. I might collect vouchers in abundance from the records and archives of every State in the Union. But as a more concise, and at the same time equally satisfactory, evidence, I will refer to the example of two States, attested by two unexceptionable authorities.

The first example is that of Virginia, a State which, as we have seen, has expressly declared in its constitution, that the three great departments ought not to be intermixed. The authority in support of it is Mr. Jefferson, who, besides his other advantages for remarking the operation of the government, was himself the chief magistrate of it. In order to convey fully the ideas with which his experience had impressed him on this subject, it will be necessary to quote a passage of some length from his very interesting *Notes on the State of Virginia,* p. 195. "All the powers of government, legislative, executive, and judiciary, result to the legislative body. The concentrating these in the same hands, is precisely the definition of despotic government. It will be no alleviation, that these powers will be exercised by a plurality of hands, and not by a single one. One hundred and seventy-three despots would surely be as oppressive as one. Let those who doubt it, turn their eyes on the republic of Venice. As little will it avail us, that they are chosen by ourselves. An *elective despotism* was not the government we fought for; but one which should not only be founded on free principles, but in which the powers of government should be so divided and balanced among several bodies of magistracy, as that no one could transcend their legal limits, without being effectually checked and restrained by the others. For this reason, that convention which passed the ordinance of government, laid its foundation on this basis, that the legislative, executive, and judiciary departments should be separate and distinct, so that no person should exercise the powers of more than one of them at the same time. *But no barrier was provided between these several powers.* The judiciary and the executive members were left dependent on the legislative for their subsistence in office, and some of them for their continuance in it. If, therefore, the legislature assumes executive and judiciary powers, no opposition is likely to be made; nor, if made, can be effectual; because in that case they may put their proceedings into the form of acts of Assembly, which will render them obligatory on the other branches. They have accordingly, *in many* instances, *decided rights* which should have been left to *judiciary controversy*, and *the direction of the executive, during the whole time of their session, is becoming habitual and familiar."*

The other State which I shall take for an example is Pennsylvania; and the other authority, the Council of Censors, which assembled in the years 1783 and 1784. A part of the duty of this body, as marked out by the constitution, was "to inquire whether the constitution had been preserved inviolate in every part; and whether the legislative and executive branches of government had performed their duty as guardians of the people, or assumed to themselves, or exercised, other or greater powers than they are entitled to by the constitution." In the execution of this trust, the council were necessarily led to a comparison of both the legislative and executive proceedings, with the constitutional powers of these departments; and from the facts enumerated, and to the truth of most of which both sides in the council subscribed, it appears that the constitution had been flagrantly violated by the legislature in a variety of important instances.

A great number of laws had been passed, violating, without any apparent necessity, the rule requiring that all bills of a public nature shall be previously printed for the consideration of the people; although this is one of the precautions chiefly relied on by the constitution against improper acts of the legislature.

The constitutional trial by jury had been violated, and powers assumed which had not been delegated by the constitution.

Executive powers had been usurped.

The salaries of the judges, which the constitution expressly requires to be fixed, had been occasionally varied; and cases belonging to the judiciary department frequently drawn within legislative cognizance and determination.

Those who wish to see the several particulars falling under each of these heads, may consult the journals of the council, which are in print. Some of them, it will be found, may be imputable to peculiar circumstances connected with the war; but the greater part of them may be considered as the spontaneous shoots of an ill-constituted government.

It appears, also, that the executive department had not been innocent of frequent breaches of the constitution. There are three observations, however, which ought to be made on this head: *first,* a great proportion of the instances were either immediately produced by the necessities of the war, or recommended by Congress or the commander-in-chief; *secondly,* in most of the other instances, they conformed either to the declared or the known sentiments of the legislative department; *thirdly,* the executive department of Pennsylvania is distinguished from that of the other States by the number of members composing it. In this respect, it has as much affinity to a legislative assembly as to an executive council. And being at once exempt from the restraint of an individual responsibility for the acts of the body, and deriving confidence from mutual example and joint influence, unauthorized measures would, of course, be more freely hazarded, than where the executive department is administered by a single hand, or by a few hands.

The conclusion which I am warranted in drawing from these observations is, that a mere demarcation on parchment of the constitutional limits of the several departments, is not a sufficient guard against those encroachments which lead to a tyrannical concentration of all the powers of government in the same hands.                                   Publius [Madison]

## NUMBER 51

To what expedient, then, shall we finally resort, for maintaining in practice the necessary partition of power among the several departments, as laid down in the Constitution? The only answer that can be given is, that as all these exterior provisions are found to be inadequate the defect must be supplied, by so contriving the interior structure of the government as that its several constituent parts may, by their mutual relations, be the means of keeping each other in their proper places. Without presuming to undertake a full development of this important idea, I will hazard a few general observations, which may perhaps place it in a clearer light, and enable us to form a more correct judgment of the principles and structure of the government planned by the convention.

In order to lay a due foundation for that separate and distinct exercise of the different powers of government, which to a certain extent is admitted on all hands to be essential to the preservation of liberty, it is evident that each department should have a will of its own; and consequently should be so constituted that the members of each should have as little agency as possible in the appointment of the members of the others. Were this principle rigorously adhered to, it would require that all the appointments for the supreme executive, legislative, and judiciary magistracies should be drawn from the same fountain of authority, the people, through channels having no

communication whatever with one another. Perhaps such a plan of constructing the several departments would be less difficult in practice than it may in contemplation appear. Some difficulties, however, and some additional expense would attend the execution of it. Some deviations, therefore, from the principle must be admitted. In the constitution of the judiciary department in particular, it might be inexpedient to insist rigorously on the principle: first, because peculiar qualifications being essential in the members, the primary consideration ought to be to select that mode of choice which best secures these qualifications; secondly, because the permanent tenure by which the appointments are held in that department, must soon destroy all sense of dependence on the authority conferring them.

It is equally evident, that the members of each department should be as little dependent as possible on those of the others, for the emoluments annexed to their offices. Were the executive magistrate, or the judges, not independent of the legislature in this particular, their independence in every other would be merely nominal.

But the great security against a gradual concentration of the several powers in the same department, consists in giving to those who administer each department the necessary constitutional means and personal motives to resist encroachments of the others. The provision for defence must in this, as in all other cases, be made commensurate to the danger of attack. Ambition must be made to counteract ambition. The interest of the man must be connected with the constitutional rights of the place. It may be a reflection on human nature, that such devices should be necessary to control the abuses of government. But what is government itself, but the greatest of all reflections on human nature? If men were angels, no government would be necessary. If angels were to govern men, neither external nor internal controls on government would be necessary. In framing a government which is to be administered by men over men, the great difficulty lies in this: you must first enable the government to control the governed; and in the next place oblige it to control itself. A dependence on the people is, no doubt, the primary control on the government; but experience has taught mankind the necessity of auxiliary precautions.

This policy of supplying, by opposite and rival interests, the defect of better motives, might be traced through the whole system of human affairs, private as well as public. We see it particularly displayed in all the subordinate distributions of power, where the constant aim is to divide and arrange the several offices in such a manner as that each may be a check on the other—that the private interest of every individual may be a sentinel over the public rights. These inventions of prudence cannot be less requisite in the distribution of the supreme powers of the State.

But it is not possible to give to each department an equal power of self-defence. In republican government, the legislative authority necessarily predominates. The remedy for this inconveniency is to divide the legislature into different branches; and to render them, by different modes of election and different principles of action, as little connected with each other as the nature of their common functions and their common dependence on the society will admit. It may even be necessary to guard against dangerous encroachments by still further precautions. As the weight of the legislative authority requires that it should be thus divided, the weakness of the executive may require, on the other hand, that it should be fortified. An absolute negative on the legislature appears, at first view, to be the natural defence with which the executive magistrate should be armed. But perhaps it would be neither altogether safe nor alone sufficient. On ordinary occasions it might not be exerted with the requisite firmness, and on extraordinary occasions it might be perfidiously abused. May not this defect of an absolute negative be supplied by some qualified connection between this weaker department and the weaker branch of the stronger department, by which the latter may be led to support the constitutional rights of the former, without being too much detached from the rights of its own department?

If the principles on which these observations are founded be just, as I persuade myself they are, and they be applied as a criterion to the several State constitutions, and to the federal Constitution, it will be found that if the latter does not perfectly correspond with them, the former are infinitely less able to bear such a test.

There are, moreover, two considerations particularly applicable to the federal system of America, which place that system in a very interesting point of view.

*First.* In a single republic, all the power surrendered by the people is submitted to the administration of a single government; and the usurpations are guarded against by a division of the government into distinct and separate departments. In the compound republic of America, the power surrendered by the people is first divided between two distinct governments, and then the portion allotted to each subdivided among distinct and separate departments. Hence a double security arises to the rights of the people. The different governments will control each other, at the same time that each will be controlled by itself.

*Second.* It is of great importance in a republic not only to guard the society against the oppression of its rulers, but to guard one part of the society against the injustice of the other part. Different interests necessarily exist in different classes of citizens. If a majority be united by a common interest, the rights of the minority will be insecure. There are but two methods of providing against this evil: the one by creating a will in the community independent of the majority—that is, of the society itself; the other, by comprehending in the society so many separate descriptions of citizens as will render an unjust combination of a majority of the whole very improbable, if not impracticable. The first method prevails in all governments possessing an hereditary or self-appointed authority. This, at best, is but a precarious security; because a power independent of the society may as well espouse the unjust views of the major, as the rightful interests of the minor party, and may possibly be turned against both parties. The second method will be exemplified in the federal republic of the United States. Whilst all authority in it will be derived from and dependent on the society, the society itself will be broken into so many parts, interests and classes of citizens, that the rights of individuals, or of the minority, will be in little danger from interested combinations of the majority. In a free government the security for civil rights must be the same as that for religious rights. It consists in the one case in the multiplicity of interests, and in the other in the multiplicity of sects. The degree of security in both cases will depend on the number of interests and sects; and this may be presumed to depend on the extent of country and number of people comprehended under the same government. This view of the subject must particularly recommend a proper federal system to all the sincere and considerate friends of republican government, since it shows that in exact proportion as the territory of the Union may be formed into more circumscribed Confederacies, or States, oppressive combinations of a majority will be facilitated; the best security, under the republican forms, for the rights of every class of citizens, will be diminished; and consequently the stability and independence of some member of the government, the only other security, must be proportionally increased. Justice is the end of government. It is the end of civil society. It ever has been and ever will be pursued until it be obtained, or until liberty be lost in the pursuit. In a society under the forms of which the stronger faction can readily unite and oppress the weaker, anarchy may as truly be said to reign as in a state of nature, where the weaker individual is not secured against the violence of the stronger; and as, in the latter state, even the stronger individuals are prompted, by the uncertainty of their condition, to submit to a government which may protect the weak as well as themselves; so, in the former state, will the more powerful factions or parties be gradually induced, by a like motive, to wish for a government which will protect all parties, the weaker as well as the more powerful. It can be little doubted that if the State of Rhode Island was separated from the Confederacy and left to itself, the insecurity of rights under the popular form of government within such narrow limits would be displayed by such reiterated oppressions of factious majorities that some power altogether independent of the people would soon be called for by the voice of the very factions whose misrule had proved the necessity of it. In the extended republic of the United States, and among the great variety of interests, par-

ties, and sects which it embraces, a coalition of a majority of the whole society could seldom take place on any other principles than those of justice and the general good; whilst there being thus less danger to a minor from the will of a major party, there must be less pretext, also, to provide for the security of the former, by introducing into the government a will not dependent on the latter, or, in other words, a will independent of the society itself. It is no less certain than it is important, notwithstanding the contrary opinions which have been entertained, that the larger the society, provided it lie within a practical sphere, the more duly capable it will be of self-government. And happily for the *republican cause,* the practicable sphere may be carried to a very great extent, by a judicious modification and mixture of the *federal principle.*                    Publius [Madison]

## NUMBER 55

The number of which the House of Representatives is to consist forms another and a very interesting point of view under which this branch of the federal legislature may be contemplated. Scarce any article, indeed, in the whole Constitution seems to be rendered more worthy of attention by the weight of character and the apparent force of argument with which it has been assailed. The charges exhibited against it are, first, that so small a number of representatives will be an unsafe depository of the public interests; second, that they will not possess a proper knowledge of the local circumstances of their numerous constituents; third, that they will be taken from that class of citizens which will sympathize least with the feelings of the mass of the people and be most likely to aim at a permanent elevation of the few on the depression of the many; fourth, that defective as the number will be in the first instance, it will be more and more disproportionate, by the increase of the people and the obstacles which will prevent a correspondent increase of the representatives.

In general it may be remarked on this subject that no political problem is less susceptible of a precise solution than that which relates to the number most convenient for a representative legislature; nor is there any point on which the policy of the several States is more at variance, whether we compare their legislative assemblies directly with each other, or consider the proportions which they respectively bear to the number of their constituents. Passing over the difference between the smallest and largest States, as Delaware, whose most numerous branch consists of twenty-one representatives; and Massachusetts, where it amounts to between three and four hundred, a very considerable difference is observable among States nearly equal in population. The number of representatives in Pennsylvania is not more than one fifth of that in the State last mentioned. New York, whose population is to that of South Carolina as six to five, has little more than one third of the number of representatives. As great a disparity prevails between the States of Georgia and Delaware or Rhode Island. In Pennsylvania, the representatives do not bear a greater proportion to their constituents than of one for every four or five thousand. In Rhode Island, they bear a proportion of at least one for every thousand. And according to the constitution of Georgia, the proportion may be carried to one to every ten electors; and most unavoidably far exceed the proportion in any of the other States.

Another general remark to be made is that the ratio between the representatives and the people ought not to be the same where the latter are very numerous as where they are very few. Were the representatives in Virginia to be regulated by the standard in Rhode Island, they would, at this time, amount to between four and five hundred; and twenty or thirty years hence, to a thousand. On the other hand, the ratio of Pennsylvania, if applied to the State of Delaware, would reduce the representative assembly of the latter to seven or eight members. Nothing can be more fallacious than to found our political calculations on arithmetical principles. Sixty or seventy men may be more properly trusted with a given degree of power than six or seven. But it does not follow that six or seven hundred would be proportionably a better depositary. And if we carry on the supposition to six or seven thousand, the whole reasoning ought to be reversed. The truth is that in all cases a certain number

at least seems to be necessary to secure the benefits of free consultation and discussion, and to guard against too easy a combination for improper purposes; as, on the other hand, the number ought at most to be kept within a certain limit, in order to avoid the confusion and intemperance of a multitude. In all very numerous assemblies, of whatever characters composed, passion never fails to wrest the scepter from reason. Had every Athenian citizen been a Socrates, every Athenian assembly would still have been a mob.

It is necessary also to recollect here the observations which were applied to the case of biennial elections. For the same reason that the limited powers of the Congress, and the control of the State legislatures, justify less frequent election than the public safety might otherwise require, the members of the Congress need be less numerous than if they possessed the whole power of legislation, and were under no other than the ordinary restraints of other legislative bodies.

With these general ideas in our minds, let us weigh the objections which have been stated against the number of members proposed for the House of Representatives. It is said, in the first place, that so small a number cannot be safely trusted with so much power.

The number of which this branch of the legislature is to consist, at the outset of the government, will be sixty-five. Within three years a census is to be taken, when the number may be augmented to one for every thirty thousand inhabitants; and within every successive period of ten years the census is to be renewed, and augmentations may continue to be made under the above limitation. It will not be thought an extravagant conjecture that the first census will, at the rate of one for every thirty thousand, raise the number of representatives to at least one hundred. Estimating the Negroes in the proportion of three fifths, it can scarcely be doubted that the population of the United States will by that time, if it does not already, amount to three millions. At the expiration of twenty-five years, according to the computed rate of increase, the number of representatives will amount to two hundred; and of fifty years, to four hundred. This is a number which, I presume, will put an end to all fears arising from the smallness of the body. I take for granted here what I shall, in answering the fourth objection, hereafter show, that the number of representatives will be augmented from time to time in the manner provided by the Constitution. On a contrary supposition, I should admit the objection to have very great weight indeed.

The true question to be decided, then, is whether the smallness of the number, as a temporary regulation, be dangerous to the public liberty? Whether sixty-five members for a few years, and a hundred or two hundred for a few more, be a safe depositary for a limited and well-guarded power of legislating for the United States? I must own that I could not give a negative answer to this question, without first obliterating every impression which I have received with regard to the present genius of the people of America, the spirit which actuates the State legislatures, and the principles which are incorporated with the political character of every class of citizens. I am unable to conceive that the people of America, in their present temper, or under any circumstances which can speedily happen, will choose, and every second year repeat the choice of, sixty-five or a hundred men who would be disposed to form and pursue a scheme of tyranny or treachery. I am unable to conceive that the State legislatures, which must feel so many motives to watch and which possess so many means of counteracting the federal legislature, would fail either to detect or to defeat a conspiracy of the latter against the liberties of their common constituents. I am equally unable to conceive that there are at this time, or can be in any short time, in the United States, any sixty-five or a hundred men capable of recommending themselves to the choice of the people at large, who would either desire or dare, within the short space of two years, to betray the solemn trust committed to them. What change of circumstances time, and a fuller population of our country may produce requires a prophetic spirit to declare, which makes no part of my pretensions. But judging from the circumstances now before us, and from the probable state of them within a moderate period of time, I must pronounce that the liberties of America cannot be unsafe in the number of hands proposed by the federal Constitution.

From what quarter can the danger proceed? Are we afraid of foreign gold? If foreign gold could so easily corrupt our federal rulers and enable them to ensnare and betray their constituents, how has it happened that we are at this time a free and independent nation? The Congress which conducted us through the Revolution was a less numerous body than their successors will be; they were not chosen by, nor responsible to, their fellow-citizens at large; though appointed from year to year, and recallable at pleasure, they were generally continued for three years, and, prior to the ratification of the federal articles, for a still longer term. They held their consultations always under the veil of secrecy; they had the sole transaction of our affairs with foreign nations, through the whole course of the war they had the fate of their country more in their hands than it is to be hoped will ever be the case with our future representatives; and from the greatness of the prize at stake, and the eagerness of the party which lost it, it may well be supposed that the use of other means than force would not have been scrupled. Yet we know by happy experience that the public trust was not betrayed; nor has the purity of our public councils in this particular ever suffered, even from the whispers of calumny.

Is the danger apprehended from the other branches of the federal government? But where are the means to be found by the President, or the Senate, or both? Their emoluments of office, it is to be presumed, will not, and without a previous corruption of the House of Representatives cannot, more than suffice for very different purposes; their private fortunes, as they must all be American citizens, cannot possibly be sources of danger. The only means, then, which they can possess, will be in the dispensation of appointments. Is it here that suspicion rests her charge? Sometimes we are told that this fund of corruption is to be exhausted by the President in subduing the virtue of the Senate. Now, the fidelity of the other House is to be the victim. The improbability of such a mercenary and perfidious combination of the several members of government, standing on as different foundations as republican principles will well admit, and at the same time accountable to the society over which they are placed, ought alone to quiet this apprehension. But, fortunately, the Constitution has provided a still further safeguard. The members of the Congress are rendered ineligible to any civil offices that may be created, or of which the emoluments may be increased, during the term of their election. No offices therefore can be dealt out to the existing members but such as may become vacant by ordinary casualties: and to suppose that these would be sufficient to purchase the guardians of the people, selected by the people themselves, is to renounce every rule by which events ought to be calculated, and to substitute an indiscriminate and unbounded jealousy, with which all reasoning must be vain. The sincere friends of liberty who give themselves up to the extravagancies of this passion are not aware of the injury they do their own cause. As there is a degree of depravity in mankind which requires a certain degree of circumspection and distrust, so there are other qualities in human nature which justify a certain portion of esteem and confidence. Republican government presupposes the existence of these qualities in a higher degree than any other form. Were the pictures which have been drawn by the political jealousy of some among us faithful likenesses of the human character, the inference would be that there is not sufficient virtue among men for self-government, and that nothing less than the chains of despotism can restrain them from destroying and devouring one another.

Publius [Madison]

## NUMBER 58

The remaining charge against the House of Representatives, which I am to examine, is grounded on a supposition that the number of members will not be augmented from time to time; as the progess of population may demand.

It has been admitted that this objection, if well supported, would have great weight. The following observations will show that, like most other objections against the Constitution, it can only proceed from a partial view of the subject, or from a jealousy which discolors and disfigures every object which is beheld.

1. Those who urge the objection seem not to have recollected that the federal Constitution will not suffer by a comparison with the State constitu-

ions, in the security provided for a gradual augmentation of the number of representatives. The number which is to prevail in the first instance is declared to be temporary. Its duration is limited to the short term of three years.

Within every successive term of ten years a census of inhabitants is to be repeated. The unequivocal objects of these regulations are, first, to readjust, from time to time, the apportionment of representatives to the number of inhabitants, under the single exception that each State shall have one representative at least; secondly, to augment the number of representatives at the same periods, under the single exception that each State shall have one representative at least; secondly, to augment the number of representatives at the same periods, under the sole limitation that the whole number shall not exceed one for every thirty thousand inhabitants. If we review the constitutions of the several States we shall find that some of them contain no determinate regulations on this subject, that others correspond pretty much on this point with the federal Constitution, and that the most effectual security in any of them is resolvable into a mere directory provision.

2. As far as experience has taken place on this subject, a gradual increase of representatives under the State constitution has at least kept pace with that of the constituents, and it appears that the former have been as ready to concur in such measures as the latter have to call for them.

3. There is a peculiarity in the federal Constitution, which insures a watchful attention in a majority both of the people and of their representatives to a constitutional augmentation of the latter. The peculiarity lies in this, that one branch of the legislature is a representation of citizens, the other of the States: in the former, consequently, the larger States will have most weight; in the latter, the advantage will be in favor of the smaller States. From this circumstance it may with certainty be inferred that the larger States will be strenuous advocates for increasing the number and weight of that part of the legislature in which their influence predominates. And it so happens that four only of the largest will have a majority of the whole votes in the House of Representatives. Should

the representatives or people, therefore, of the smaller States oppose at any time a reasonable addition of members, a coalition of a very few States will be sufficient to overrule the opposition; a coalition which, notwithstanding the rivalship and local prejudices which might prevent it on ordinary occasions, would not fail to take place when not merely prompted by common interest, but justified by equity and the principles of the Constitution.

It may be alleged, perhaps, that the Senate would be prompted by like motives to an adverse coalition; and as their concurrence would be indispensable, the just and constitutional views of the other branch might be defeated. This is the difficulty which has probably created the most serious apprehensions in the jealous friends of a numerous representation. Fortunately it is among the difficulties which, existing only in appearance, vanish on a close and accurate inspection. The following reflections will, if I mistake not, be admitted to be conclusive and satisfactory on this point.

Notwithstanding, the equal authority which will subsist between the two houses on all legislative subjects, except the originating of money bills, it cannot be doubted that the House, composed of the greater number of members, when supported by the more powerful States, and speaking the known and determined sense of a majority of the people, will have no small advantage in a question depending on the comparative firmness of the two houses.

This advantage must be increased by the consciousness, felt by the same side of being supported in its demands by right, by reason, and by the Constitution; and the consciousness, on the opposite side, of contending against the force of all these solemn considerations.

It is farther to be considered that in the gradation between the smallest and largest States there are several which, though most likely in general to arrange themselves among the former, are too little removed in extent and population from the latter to second an opposition to their just and legitimate pretensions. Hence it is by no means certain that a majority of votes, even in the Senate, would be unfriendly to proper augmentations in the number of representatives.

It will not be looking too far to add that the senators from all the new States may be gained over to the just view of the House of Representatives by an expedient too obvious to be overlooked. As these States will, for a great length of time, advance in population with peculiar rapidity, they will be interested in frequent reapportionments of the representatives to the number of inhabitants. The large States, therefore, who will prevail in the House of Representatives, will have nothing to do but to make reapportionments and augmentations mutually conditions of each other; and the senators from all the most growing States will be bound to contend for the latter, by the interest which their States will feel in the former.

These considerations seem to afford ample security on this subject, and ought alone to satisfy all the doubts and fears which have been indulged with regard to it. Admitting, however, that they should all be insufficient to subdue the unjust policy of the smaller States, or their predominant influence in the councils of the Senate, a constitutional and infallible resource still remains with the larger States by which they will be able at all times to accomplish their just purposes. The House of Representatives cannot only refuse, but they alone can propose the supplies requisite for the support of government. They, in a word, hold the purse—that powerful instrument by which we behold, in the history of the British Constitution, an infant and humble representation of the people gradually enlarging the sphere of its activity and importance, and finally reducing, as far as it seems to have wished, all the overgrown perogatives of the other branches of the government. This power over the purse may, in fact, be regarded as the most complete and effectual weapon with which any constitution can arm the immediate representatives of the people, for obtaining a redress of grievance, and for carrying into effect every just and salutary measure.

But will not the House of Representatives be as much interested as the Senate in maintaining the government in its proper functions, and will they not therefore be unwilling to stake its existence or its reputation on the pliancy of the Senate? For, if such a trial of firmness between the two branches were hazarded, would not the one be as likely first to yield as the other? These questions will create no difficulty with those who reflect that in all cases the smaller the number, and the more permanent and conspicuous the station of men in power, the stronger must be the interest which they will individually feel in whatever concerns the governenment. Those who represent the dignity of their country in the eyes of other nations will be particularly sensible to every prospect of public danger, or of a dishonorable stagnation in public affairs. To those causes we are to ascribe the continual triumph of the British House of Commons over the other branches of the government, whenever the engine of a money bill has been employed. An absolute inflexibility on the side of the latter, although it could not have failed to involve every department of the state in the general confusion, has neither been apprehended nor experienced. The utmost degree of firmness that can be displayed by the federal Senate or President will not be more than equal to a resistance in which they will be supported by constitutional and patriotic principles.

In this review of the Constitution of the House of Representatives, I have passsed over the circumstances of economy which, in the present state of affairs, might have had some effect in lessening the temporary number of representatives, and a disregard of which would probably have been as rich a theme of declamation against the Constitution as has been furnished by the smallness of the number proposed. I omit also any remarks on the difficulty which might be found, under present circumstances, in engaging in the federal service a large number of such characters as the people will probably elect. One observation, however, I must be permitted to add on this subject as claiming, in my judgment, a very serious attention. It is that in all legislative assemblies the greater the number composing them may be, the fewer will be the men who will in fact direct their proceedings. In the first place, the more numerous any assembly may be, of whatever characters composed, the greater is known to be the ascendancy of passion over reason. In the next place, the larger the number, the greater will be the proportion of members of lim-

ited information and of weak capacities. Now, it is precisely on characters of this description that the eloquence and address of the few are known to act with all their force. In the ancient republics, where the whole body of the people assembled in person, a single orator, or an artful statesman, was generally seen to rule with as complete a sway as if a scepter had been placed in his single hand. On the same principle, the more multitudinous a representative assembly may be rendered, the more it will partake of the infirmities incident to collective meetings of the people. Ignorance will be the dupe of cunning, and passion the slave of sophistry and declamation. The people can never err more than in supposing that by multiplying their representatives beyond a certain limit they strengthen the barrier against the government of a few. Experience will forever admonish them that, on the contrary, *after securing a sufficient number for the purposes of safety, of local information, and of diffusive sympathy with the whole society,* they will counteract their own views by every addition to their representatives. The countenance of the government may become more democratic, but the soul that animates it will be more oligarchic. The machine will be enlarged, but the fewer, and often the more secret, will be the springs by which its motions are direct.

As connected with the objection against the number of representatives may properly be here noticed that which has been suggested against the number made competent for legislative business. It has been said that more than a majority ought to have been required for a quorum for a decision. That some advantages might have resulted from such a precaution cannot be denied. It might have been an additional shield to some particular interests, and another obstacle generally to hasty and partial measures. But these considerations are outweighed by the inconveniences in the opposite scale. In all cases where justice or the general good might require new laws to be passed, or active measures to be pursued, the fundamental principle of free government would be reversed. It would be no longer the majority that would rule: the power would be transferred to the minority. Were the defensive privilege limited to particular cases, an interested minority might take advantage of it to screen themselves from equitable sacrifices to the general weal, or, in particular emergencies, to extort unreasonable indulgences. Lastly, it would facilitate and foster the baneful practice of secessions, a practice which has shown itself even in States where a majority only is required; a practice subversive of all the principles of order and regular government; a practice which leads more directly to public convulsions and the ruin of popular governments than any other which has yet been displayed among us.                    Publius [Madison]

## NUMBER 62

Having examined the constitution of the House of Representatives, and answered such of the objections against it as seemed to merit notice, I enter next on the examination of the Senate. The heads into which this member of the government may be considered are: I. The qualifications of senators; II. The appointment of them by the State legislatures; III. The equality of representation in the Senate; IV. The number of senators, and the term for which they are to be elected; V. The powers vested in the Senate.

I. The qualifications proposed for senators, as distinguished from those of representatives, consist in a more advanced age and a longer period of citizenship. A senator must be thirty years of age at least; as a representative must be twenty-five. And the former must have been a citizen nine years; as seven years are required for the latter. The propriety of these distinctions is explained by the nature of the senatorial trust, which, requiring greater extent of information and stability of character, requires at the same time that the senator should have reached a period of life most likely to supply these advantages; and which, participating immediately in transactions with foreign nations, ought to be exercised by none who are not thoroughly weaned from the prepossessions and habits incident to foreign birth and education. The term of nine years appears to be a prudent mediocrity between a total exclusion of adopted citizens, whose merits and talents may claim a share in the public confidence, and an indiscriminate and hasty admis-

sion of them, which might create a channel for foreign influence on the national councils.

II. It is equally unnecessary to dilate on the appointment of senators by the State legislatures. Among the various modes which might have been devised for constituting this branch of the government, that which has been proposed by the convention is probably the most congenial with the public opinion. It is recommended by the double advantage of favoring a select appointment, and of giving to the State governments such an agency in the formation of the federal government as must secure the authority of the former, and may form a convenient link between the two systems.

III. The equality of representation in the Senate is another point which, being evidently the result of compromise between the opposite pretensions of the large and the small States, does not call for much discussion. If indeed it be right that among a people thoroughly incorporated into one nation every district ought to have a *proportional* share in the government and that among independent and sovereign States, bound together by a simple league, the parties, however unequal in size, ought to have an *equal* share in the common councils, it does not appear to be without some reason that in a compound republic, partaking both of the national and federal character, the government ought to be founded on a mixture of the principles of proportional and equal representation. But it is superfluous to try, by the standard of theory, a part of the Constitution which is allowed on all hands to be the result, not of theory, but "of a spirit of amity, and that mutual deference and concession which the peculiarity of our political situation rendered indispensable." A common government, with powers equal to its objects, is called for by the voice, and still more loudly by the political situation, of America. A government founded on principles more consonant to the wishes of the larger States is not likely to be obtained from the smaller States. The only option, then, for the former lies between the proposed government and a government still more objectionable. Under this alternative, the advice of prudence must be to embrace the lesser evil; and instead of indulging a fruitless anticipation of the possible mischiefs which may ensue, to contemplate rather the advantageous consequences which may qualify the sacrifice.

In this spirit it may be remarked that the equal vote allowed to each State is at once a constitutional recognition of the portion of sovereignty remaining in the individual States and an instrument for preserving that residuary sovereignty. So far the equality ought to be no less acceptable to the large than to the small States; since they are not less solicitous to guard, by every possible expedient, against an improper consolidation of the States into one simple republic.

Another advantage accruing from this ingredient in the constitution of the Senate is the additional impediment it must prove against improper acts of legislation. No law or resolution can now be passed without the concurrence, first, of a majority of the people, and then of a majority of the States. It must be acknowledged that this complicated check on legislation may in some instances be injurious as well as beneficial; and that the peculiar defense which it involves in favor of the smaller States would be more rational if any interests common to them and distinct from those of the other States would otherwise be exposed to peculiar danger. But as the larger States will always be able, by their power over the supplies, to defeat unreasonable exertions of this prerogative of the lesser States, and as the facility and excess of lawmaking seem to be the diseases to which our governments are most liable, it is not impossible that this part of the Constitution may be more convenient in practice than it appears to many in contemplation.

IV. The number of senators and the duration of their appointment come next to be considered. In order to form an accurate judgment on both these points it will be proper to inquire into the purposes which are to be answered by a senate; and in order to ascertain these it will be necessary to review the inconveniences which a republic must suffer from the want of such an institution.

*First*. It is a misfortune incident to republican government, though in a less degree than to other governments, that those who administer it may forget their obligations to their constituents and prove un-

faithful to their important trust. In this point of view a senate, as a second branch of the legislative assembly distinct from and dividing the power with a first, must be in all cases a salutary check on the government. It doubles the security to the people by requiring the concurrence of two distinct bodies in schemes of usurpation of perfidy, where the ambition or corruption of one would otherwise be sufficient. This is a precaution founded on such clear principles, and now so well understood in the United States, that it would be more than superfluous to enlarge on it. I will barely remark that as the improbability of sinister combinations will be in proportion to the dissimilarity in the genius of the two bodies, it must be politic to distinguish them from each other by every circumstance which will consist with a due harmony in all proper measures, and with the genuine principles of republican government.

*Second*. The necessity of a senate is not less indicated by the propensity of all single and numerous assemblies to yield to the impulse of sudden and violent passions, and to be seduced by factious leaders into intemperate and pernicious resolutions. Examples on this subject might be cited without number; and from proceedings within the United States, as well as from the history of other nations. But a position that will not be contradicted need not be proved. All that need be remarked is that a body which is to correct this infirmity ought itself to be free from it, and consequently ought to be less numerous. It ought, moreover, to possess great firmness, and consequently ought to hold its authority by a tenure of considerable duration.

*Third*. Another defect to be supplied by a senate lies in a want of due acquaintance with the objects and principles of legislation. It is not possible that an assembly of men called for the most part from pursuits of a private nature; continued in appointments for a short time and led by no permanent motive to devote the intervals of public occupation to a study of the laws, the affairs, and the comprehensive interests of their country, should, if left wholly to themselves, escape a variety of important errors in the exercise of their legislative trust. It may be affirmed, on the best grounds, that no small share of the present embarrassments of America is to be charged on the blunders of our governments; and that these have proceeded from the heads rather than the hearts of most of the authors of them. What indeed are all the repealing, explaining, and amending laws, which fill and disgrace our voluminous codes, but so many monuments of deficient wisdom; so many impeachments exhibited by each succeeding against each preceding session; so many admonitions to the people of the value of those aids which may be expected from a well-constituted senate?

A good government implies two things: first, fidelity to the object of government, which is the happiness of the people; secondly, a knowledge of the means by which that object can be best attained. Some governments are deficient in both these qualities; most governments are deficient in the first. I scruple not to assert that in American governments too little attention has been paid to the last. The federal Constitution avoids this error; and what merits particular notice, it provides for the last in a mode which increases the security for the first.

*Fourth.* The mutability in the public councils arising from a rapid succession of new members, however qualified they may be, points out, in the strongest manner, the necessity of some stable institution in the government. Every new election in the States is found to change one half of the representatives. From this change of men must proceed a change of opinions; and from a change of opinions, a change of measures. But a continual change even of good measures is inconsistent with every rule of prudence and every prospect of success. The remark is verified in private life, and becomes more just, as well as more important, in national transactions.

To trace the mischievous effects of a mutable government would fill a volume. I will hint a few only, each of which will be perceived to be a source of innumerable others.

In the first place, it forfeits the respect and confidence of other nations, and all the advantages connected with national character. An individual who is observed to be inconstant to his plans, or perhaps to carry on his affairs without any plan at all, is marked at once by all prudent people as a speedy victim to his own unsteadiness and folly. His more friendly neighbors may pity him, but all will decline to connect their fortunes out of his; and not a few will seize the opportunity of making their fortunes out of his. One nation is to another what one individual is to another; with this melancholy distinction, perhaps, that the former, with fewer of the benevolent emotions than the latter, are under fewer restraints also from taking undue advantage of the indiscretions of each other. Every nation, consequently, whose affairs betray a want of wisdom and stability, may calculate on every loss which can be sustained from the more systematic policy of its wiser neighbors. But the best instruction on this subject is unhappily conveyed to America by the example of her own situation. She finds that she is held in no respect by her friends; that she is the derision of her enemies; and that she is a prey to every nation which has an interest in speculating on her fluctuating councils and embarrassed affairs.

The internal effects of a mutable policy are still more calamitous. It poisons the blessings of liberty itself. It will be of little avail to the people that the laws are made by men of their own choice if the laws be so voluminous that they cannot be read, or so incoherent that they cannot be understood; if they be repealed or revised before they are promulgated, or undergo such incessant changes that no man, who knows what the law is today, can guess what it will be tomorrow. Law is defined to be a rule of action; but how can that be a rule, which is little known, and less fixed?

Another effect of public instability is the unreasonable advantage it gives to the sagacious, the enterprising, and the moneyed few over the industrious and uninformed mass of the people. Every new regulation concerning commerce or revenue, or in any manner affecting the value of the different species of property, presents a new harvest to those who watch the change, and can trace its consequences; a harvest, reared not by themselves, but by the toils and cares of the great body of their fellow-citizens. This is a state of things in which it may be said with some truth that laws are made for the *few*, not for the *many*.

In another point of view, great injury results from

an unstable government. The want of confidence in the public councils damps every useful undertaking, the success and profit of which may depend on a continuance of existing arrangements. What prudent merchant will hazard his fortunes in any branch of commerce when he knows not but that his plans may be rendered unlawful before they can be executed? What farmer or manufacturer will lay himself out for the encouragement given to any particular cultivation or establishment, when he can have no assurance that his preparatory labors and advances will not render him a victim to an inconstant government? In a word, no great improvement or laudable enterprise can go forward which requires the auspices of a steady system of national policy.

But the most deplorable effect of all is that diminution of attachment and reverence which steals into the hearts of the people towards a political system which betrays so many marks of infirmity, and disappoints so many of their flattering hopes. No government, any more than an individual, will long be respected without being truly respectable; nor be truly respectable without possessing a certain portion of order and stability.                    Publius [Madison]

# NUMBER 63

A *fifth* desideratum, illustrating the utility of a senate, is the want of a due sense of national character. Without a select and stable member of the government, the esteem of foreign powers will not only be forfeited by an unenlightened and variable policy, proceeding from the causes already mentioned, but the national councils will not possess that sensibility to the opinion of the world, which is perhaps not less necessary in order to merit, than it is to obtain, its respect and confidence.

An attention to the judgment of other nations is important to every government for two reasons: the one is, that, independently of the merits of any particular plan or measure, it is desirable, on various accounts, that it should appear to other nations as the offspring of a wise and honorable policy; the second is, that in doubtful cases, particularly where the national councils may be warped by some strong pas-

sion or momentary interest, the presumed or known opinion of the impartial world may be the best guide that can be followed. What has not America lost by her want of character with foreign nations; and how many errors and follies would she not have avoided, if the justice and propriety of her measures had, in every instance, been previously tried by the light in which they would probably appear to the unbiased part of mankind?

Yet however requisite a sense of national character may be, it is evident that it can never be sufficiently possessed by a numerous and changeable body. It can only be found in a number so small that a sensible degree of the praise and blame of public measures may be the portion of each individual; or in an assembly so durably invested with public trust, that the pride and consequence of its members may be sensibly incorporated with the reputation and prosperity of the community. The half-yearly representatives of Rhode Island would probably have been little affected in their deliberations on the iniquitous measures of that State, by arguments drawn from that light in which such measures would be viewed by foreign nations, or even by the sister States; whilst it can scarcely be doubted that if the concurrence of a select and stable body had been necessary, a regard to national character alone would have prevented the calamities under which that misguided people is now laboring.

I add, as a *sixth* defect, the want, in some important cases, of a due responsibility in the government to the people, arising from that frequency of elections which in other cases produces this responsibility. This remark will, perhaps, appear not only new, but paradoxical. It must nevertheless be acknowledged, when explained, to be as undeniable as it is important.

Responsibility, in order to be reasonable, must be limited to objects within the power of the responsible party, and in order to be effectual, must relate to operations of that power, of which a ready and proper judgment can be formed by the constituents. The objects of government may be divided into two general classes: the one depending on measures which have singly an immediate and sensible operation; the other depending on a succession of well-chosen and well-connected measures, which have a gradual and perhaps unobserved operation. The importance of the latter description to the collective and permanent welfare of every country, needs no explanation. And yet it is evident that an assembly elected for so short a term as to be unable to provide more than one or two links in a chain of measures, on which the general welfare may essentially depend, ought not to be answerable for the final result, any more than a steward or tenant, engaged for one year, could be justly made to answer for places or improvements which could not be accomplished in less than half a dozen years. Nor is it possible for the people to estimate the *share* of influence which their annual assemblies may respectively have on events resulting from the mixed transactions of several years. It is sufficiently difficult to preserve a personal responsibility in the members of a *numerous* body, for such acts of the body as have an immediate, detached, and palpable operation on its constituents.

The proper remedy for this defect must be an additional body in the legislative department, which, having sufficient permanency to provide for such objects as require a continued attention, and a train of measures, may be justly and effectually answerable for the attainment of those objects.

Thus far I have considered the circumstances which point out the necessity of a well-constructed Senate only as they relate to the representatives of the people. To a people as little blinded by prejudice or corrupted by flattery as those whom I address, I shall not scruple to add, that such an institution may be sometimes necessary as a defence to the people against their own temporary errors and delusions. As the cool and deliberate sense of the community ought, in all governments, and actually will, in all free governments, ultimately prevail over the views of its rulers; so there are particular moments in public affairs when the people, stimulated by some irregular passion, or some illicit advantage, or misled by the artful misrepresentations of interested men, may call for measures which they themselves will afterwards be the most ready to lament and condemn. In these critical moments, how salutary will be the interference of some temperate and respectable body of citizens, in order to check the misguided career, and to suspend the blow meditated by the people against

themselves, until reason, justice, and truth can regain their authority over the public mind? What bitter anguish would not the people of Athens have often escaped if their government had contained so provident a safeguard against the tyranny of their own passions? Popular liberty might then have escaped the indelible reproach of decreeing to the same citizens the hemlock on one day and statues on the next.

It may be suggested, that a people spread over an extensive region cannot, like the crowded inhabitants of a small district, be subject to the infection of violent passions, or to the danger of combining in pursuit of unjust measures. I am far from denying that this is a distinction of peculiar importance. I have, on the contrary, endeavored in a former paper to show, that it is one of the principal recommendations of a confederated republic. At the same time, this advantage ought not to be considered as superseding the use of auxiliary precautions. It may even be remarked, that the same extended situation, which will exempt the people of America from some of the dangers incident to lesser republics, will expose them to the inconveniency of remaining for a longer time under the influence of those misrepresentations which the combined industry of interested men may succeed in distributing among them.

It adds no small weight to all these considerations, to recollect that history informs us of no long-lived republic which had not a senate. Sparta, Rome, and Carthage are, in fact, the only states to whom that character can be applied. In each of the two first there was a senate for life. The constitution of the senate in the last is less known. Circumstantial evidence makes it probable that it was not different in this particular from the two others. It is at least certain, that it had some quality or other which rendered it an anchor against popular fluctuations; and that a smaller council, drawn out of the senate, was appointed not only for life, but filled up vacancies itself. These examples, though as unfit for the imitation, as they are repugnant to the genius, of America, are, notwithstanding, when compared with the fugitive and turbulent existence of other ancient republics, very instructive proofs of the necessity of some institution that will blend stability with liberty. I am not unaware of the circumstances which distinguish the American from other popular governments, as well ancient as modern; and which render extreme circumspection necessary, in reasoning from one case to the other. But after allowing due weight to this consideration, it may still be maintained, that there are many points of similitude which render these examples not unworthy of our attention. Many of the defects, as we have seen, which can only be supplied by a senatorial institution, are common to a numerous assembly frequently elected by the people, and to the people themselves. There are others peculiar to the former, which require the control of such an institution. The people can never wilfully betray their own interests; but they may possibly be betrayed by the representatives of the people; and the danger will be evidently greater where the whole legislative trust is lodged in the hands of one body of men, than where the concurrence of separate and dissimilar bodies is required in every public act.

The difference most relied on, between the American and other republics, consists in the principle of representation; which is the pivot on which the former move, and which is supposed to have been unknown to the latter, or at least to the ancient part of them. The use which has been made of this difference, in reasonings contained in former papers, will have shown that I am disposed neither to deny its existence nor to undervalue its importance. I feel the less restraint, therefore, in observing, that the position concerning the ignorance of the ancient governments on the subject of representation, is by no means precisely true in the latitude commonly given to it. Without entering into a disquisition which here would be misplaced, I will refer to a few known facts, in support of what I advance.

In the most pure democracies of Greece, many of the executive functions were performed, not by the people themselves, but by officers elected by the people, and *representing* the people in their *executive* capacity.

Prior to the reform of Solon, Athens was governed by nine Archons, annually *elected by the people at large*. The degree of power delegated to them seems to be left in great obscurity. Subsequent to that period, we find an assembly, first of four, and after-

wards of six hundred members, annually *elected by the people;* and *partially* representing them in their *legislative* capacity, since they were not only associated with the people in the function of making laws, but had the exclusive right of originating legislative propositions to the people. The senate of Carthage, also, whatever might be its power, or the duration of its appointment, appears to have been elective by the suffrages of the people. Similar instances might be traced in most, if not all the popular governments of antiquity.

Lastly, in Sparta we meet with the Ephori, and in Rome with the Tribunes; two bodies, small indeed in numbers, but annually *elected by the whole body of the people,* and considered as the *representatives* of the people, almost in their *plenipotentiary* capacity. The Cosmi of Crete were also annually *elected by the people,* and have been considered by some authors as an institution analogous to those of Sparta and Rome, with this difference only, that in the election of that representative body the right of suffrage was communicated to a part only of the people.

From these facts, to which many others might be added, it is clear that the principle of representation was neither unknown to the ancients nor wholly overlooked in their political constitutions. The true distinction between these and the American governments, lies in *the total exclusion of the people, in their collective capacity,* from any share in the *latter,* and not in the *total exclusion of the representatives of the people* from the administration of the *former*. The distinction, however, thus qualified, must be admitted to leave a most advantageous superiority in favor of the United States. But to insure to this advantage its full effect, we must be careful not to separate it from the other advantage, of an extensive territory. For it cannot be believed, that any form of representative government could have succeeded within the narrow limits occupied by the democracies of Greece.

In answer to all these arguments, suggested by reason, illustrated by examples, and enforced by our own experience, the jealous adversary of the Constitution will probably content himself with repeating, that a senate appointed not immediately by the people, and for the term of six years, must gradually acquire a dangerous preeminence in the government, and finally transform it into a tyrannical aristocracy.

To this general answer, the general reply ought to be sufficient, that liberty may be endangered by the abuses of liberty as well as by the abuses of power; that there are numerous instances of the former as well as of the latter; and that the former, rather than the latter, are apparently most to be apprehended by the United States. But a more particular reply may be given.

Before such a revolution can be effected, the Senate, it is to be observed, must in the first place corrupt itself; must next corrupt the State legislatures; must then corrupt the House of Representatives; and must finally corrupt the people at large. It is evident that the Senate must be first corrupted before it can attempt an establishment of tyranny. Without corrupting the State legislatures, it cannot prosecute the attempt, because the periodical change of members would otherwise regenerate the whole body. Without exerting the means of corruption with equal success on the House of Representatives, the opposition of that co-equal branch of the government would inevitably defeat the attempt; and without corrupting the people themselves, a succession of new representatives would speedily restore all things to their pristine order. Is there any man who can seriously persuade himself that the proposed Senate can, by any possible means within the compass of human address, arrive at the object of a lawless ambition, through all these obstructions?

If reason condemns the suspicion, the same sentence is pronounced by experience. The constitution of Maryland furnishes the most apposite example. The Senate of that State is elected, as the federal Senate will be, indirectly by the people, and for a term less by one year only than the federal Senate. It is distinguished, also, by the remarkable prerogative of filling up its own vacancies within the term of its appointment, and, at the same time, is not under the control of any such rotation as is provided for the federal Senate. There are some other lesser distinctions, which would expose the former to colorable objections, that do not lie against the latter. If the federal Senate, therefore, really contained the danger

which has been so loudly proclaimed, some symptoms at least of a like danger ought by this time to have been betrayed by the Senate of Maryland, but no such symptoms have appeared. On the contrary, the jealousies at first entertained by men of the same description with those who view with terror the correspondent part of the federal Constitution, have been gradually extinguished by the progress of the experiment; and the Maryland constitution is daily deriving, from the salutary operation of this part of it, a reputation in which it will probably not be rivaled by that of any State in the Union.

But if any thing could silence the jealousies on this subject, it ought to be the British example. The Senate there, instead of being elected for a term of six years, and of being unconfined to particular families or fortunes, is an hereditary assembly of opulent nobles. The House of Representatives, instead of being elected for two years, and by the whole body of the people, is elected for seven years, and, in very great proportion, by a very small proportion of the people. Here, unquestionably, ought to be seen in full display the aristocratic usurpations and tyranny which are at some future period to be exemplified in the United States. Unfortunately, however, for the anti-federal argument, the British history informs us that this hereditary assembly has not been able to defend itself against the continual encroachments of the House of Representatives; and that it no sooner lost the support of the monarch, than it was actually crushed by the weight of the popular branch.

As far as antiquity can instruct us on this subject, its examples support the reasoning which we have employed. In Sparta, the Ephori, the annual representatives of the people, were found an overmatch for the senate for life, continually gained on its authority and finally drew all power into their own hands. The Tribunes of Rome, who were the representatives of the people, prevailed, it is well known, in almost every contest with the senate for life, and in the end gained the most complete triumph over it. The fact is the more remarkable, as unanimity was required in every act of the Tribunes, even after their number was augmented to ten. It proves the irresistible force possessed by that branch of a free government, which has the people on its side. To these examples might be added that of Carthage, whose senate, according to the testimony of Polybius, instead of drawing all power into its vortex, had, at the commencement of the second Punic War, lost almost the whole of its original portion.

Besides the conclusive evidence resulting from this assemblage of facts, that the federal Senate will never be able to transform itself, by gradual usurpations, into an independent and aristocratic body, we are warranted in believing, that if such a revolution should ever happen from causes which the foresight of man cannot guard against, the House of Representatives, with the people on their side, will at all times be able to bring back the Constitution to its primitive form and principles. Against the force of the immediate representatives of the people, nothing will be able to maintain even the constitutional authority of the Senate, but such a display of enlightened policy, and attachment to the public good, as will divide with that branch of the legislature the affections and support of the entire body of the people themselves.                    Publius [Madison]

# NUMBER 70

There is an idea, which is not without its advocates, that a vigorous Executive is inconsistent with the genius of republican government. The enlightened well-wishers to this species of government must at least hope that the supposition is destitute of foundation; since they can never admit its truth, without at the same time admitting the condemnation of their own principles. Energy in the Executive is a leading character in the definition of good government. It is essential to the protection of the community against foreign attacks; it is not less essential to the steady administration of the laws; to the protection of property against those irregular and high-handed combinations which sometimes interrupt the ordinary course of justice; to the security of liberty against the enterprises and assault of ambition, of faction, and of anarchy. Every man the least conversant in Roman history, knows

how often that republic was obliged to take refuge in the absolute power of a single man, under the formidable title of Dictator, as well against the intrigues of ambitious individuals who aspired to the tyranny, and the seditions, of whole classes of the community whose conduct threatened the existence of all government, as against the invasions of external enemies who menaced the conquest and destruction of Rome.

There can be no need, however, to multiply arguments or examples on this head. A feeble Executive implies a feeble execution of the government. A feeble execution is but another phrase for a bad execution; and a government ill executed, whatever it may be in theory, must be, in practice, a bad government.

Taking it for granted, therefore, that all men of sense will agree in the necessity of an energetic Executive, it will only remain to inquire, what are the ingredients which constitute this energy? How far can they be combined with those other ingredients which constitute safety in the republican sense? And how far does this combination characterize the plan which has been reported by the convention?

The ingredients which constitute energy in the Executive are, first, unity; secondly, duration; thirdly, an adequate provision for its support; fourthly, competent powers.

The ingredients which constitute safety in the republican sense are, first, a due dependence on the people; secondly, a due responsibility.

Those politicians and statesmen who have been the most celebrated for the soundness of their principles and for the justice of their views, have declared in favor of a single Executive and a numerous legislature. They have, with great propriety, considered energy as the most necessary qualification of the former, and have regarded this as most applicable to power in a single hand; while they have, with equal propriety, considered the latter as best adapted to deliberation and wisdom, and best calculated to conciliate the confidence of the people and to secure their privileges and interests.

That unity is conducive to energy will not be disputed. Decision, activity, secrecy, and despatch will generally characterize the proceedings of one man in a much more eminent degree than the proceedings of any greater number; and in proportion as the number is increased, these qualities will be diminished.

This unity may be destroyed in two ways: either by vesting the power in two or more magistrates of equal dignity and authority; or by vesting it ostensibly in one man, subject, in whole or in part, to the control and co-operation of others, in the capacity of counsellors to him. Of the first, the two Consuls of Rome may serve as an example; of the last, we shall find examples in the constitutions of several of the States. New York and New Jersey if I recollect right, are the only States which have intrusted the executive authority wholly to single men.[4] Both these methods of destroying the unity of the Executive have their partisans; but the votaries of an executive council are the most numerous. They are both liable, if not to equal, to similar objections, and may in most lights be examined in conjunction.

The experience of other nations will afford little instruction on this head. As far, however, as it teaches anything, it teaches us not to be enamoured of plurality in the Executive. We have seen that the Achaeans, on an experiment of two Praetors, were induced to abolish one. The Roman history records many instances of mischiefs to the republic from the dissensions between the Consuls, and between the military Tribunes, who were at times substituted for the Consuls. But it gives us no specimens of any peculiar advantages derived to the state from the circumstance of the plurality of those magistrates. That the dissensions between them were not more frequent or more fatal, is matter of astonishment, until we advert to the singular position in which the republic was almost continually placed, and to the prudent policy pointed out by the circumstances of the state, and pursued by the Consuls, of making a division of the government between them. The patricians engaged in a perpetual struggle with the plebeians for the preservation of their ancient authorities and dignities; the Consuls, who were generally chosen out of the former body, were commonly united by the personal interest they had in the defence of the privileges of their order. In addition to this motive of union, after the arms of the republic had considerably expanded the bounds of its empire, it became an established custom with the Consuls to divide the administration between themselves by lot—one of them remaining at Rome to govern the city and its environs, the other taking command in the more distant provinces. This expedient must, no doubt, have had great influence in preventing those collisions and rivalships which might otherwise have embroiled the peace of the republic.

But quitting the dim light of historical research, attaching ourselves purely to the dictates of reason and good sense, we shall discover much greater cause to reject than to approve the idea of plurality in the Executive, under any modification whatever.

Wherever two or more persons are engaged in any common enterprise or pursuit, there is always danger of difference of opinion. If it be a public trust or office, in which they are clothed with equal dignity and authority, there is peculiar danger of personal emulation and even animosity. From either, and especially from all these causes, the most bitter dissensions are apt to spring. Whenever these happen, they lessen the respectability, weaken the authority, and distract the plans and operations of those whom they divide. If they should unfortunately assail the supreme executive magistracy of a country, consisting of a plurality of persons, they might impede or frustrate the most important measures of the government, in the most critical emergencies of the state. And what is still worse, they might split the community into the most violent and irreconcilable factions, adhering differently to the different individuals who composed the magistracy.

Men often oppose a thing, merely because they have had no agency in planning it, or because it may have been planned by those whom they dislike. But if they have been consulted, and have happened to disapprove, opposition then becomes, in their estimation, an indispensable duty of self-love. They seem to think themselves bound in honor, and by all the motives of personal infallibility, to defeat the success of what has been resolved upon contrary to their sentiments. Men of upright, benevolent tempers have too many opportunities of remarking, with horror, to what desperate lengths this disposition is sometimes carried, and how often the great interests of society are sacrificed to the vanity, to the conceit, and to the obstinacy of individuals, who have credit enough to make their passions and their caprices interesting to mankind. Perhaps the question now before the public may, in its consequences, afford melancholy proofs of the effects of this despicable frailty, or rather detestable vice, in the human character.

Upon the principles of a free government, inconveniences from the source just mentioned must necessarily be submitted to in the formation of the legislature; but it is unnecessary, and therefore unwise, to introduce them into the constitution of the Executive. It is here too that they may be most pernicious. In the legislature, promptitude of decision is oftener an evil than a benefit. The differences of opinion, and the jarrings of parties in that department of the government, though they may sometimes obstruct salutary plans, yet often promote deliberation and circumspection, and serve to check excesses in the majority. When a resolution too is once taken, the opposition must be at an end. That resolution is a law, and resistance to it punishable. But no favorable circumstances palliate or atone for the disadvantages of dissension in the executive department. Here, they are pure and unmixed. There is no point at which they cease to operate. They serve to embarrass and weaken the execution of the plan or measure to which they relate, from the first step to the final conclusion of it. They constantly counteract those qualities in the Executive which are the most necessary ingredients in its composition,—vigor and expedition, and this without any counterbalancing good. In the conduct of war, in which the energy of the Executive is the bulwark of the national security, every thing would be to be apprehended from its plurality.

It must be confessed that these observations apply with principal weight to the first case supposed— that is, to a plurality of magistrates of equal dignity and authority, a scheme, the advocates for which are not likely to form a numerous sect; but they apply, though not with equal, yet with considerable weight to the project of a council, whose concurrence is made constitutionally necessary to the operations of the ostensible Executive. An artful cabal in that council would be able to distract and to enervate the whole system of administration. If no such cabal should exist, the mere diversity of views and opin-

ions would alone be sufficient to tincture the exercise of the executive authority with a spirit of habitual feebleness and dilatoriness.

But one of the weightiest objections to a plurality in the Executive, and which lies as much against the last as the first plan, is, that it tends to conceal faults and destroy responsibility. Responsibility is of two kinds—to censure and to punishment. The first is the more important of the two, especially in an elective office. Man, in public trust, will much oftener act in such a manner as to render him unworthy of being any longer trusted, than in such a manner as to make him obnoxious to legal punishment. But the multiplication of the Executive adds to the difficulty of detection in either case. It often becomes impossible, amidst mutual accusations, to determine on whom the blame or the punishment of a pernicious measure, or series of pernicious measures, ought really to fall. It is shifted from one to another with so much dexterity, and under such plausible appearances, that the public opinion is left in suspense about the real author. The circumstances which may have led to any national miscarriage of misfortune are sometimes so complicated that, where there are a number of actors who may have had different degrees and kinds of agency, though we may clearly see upon the whole that there has been mismanagement, yet it may be impracticable to pronounce to whose account the evil which may have been incurred is truly chargeable.

"I was overruled by my council. The council were so divided in their opinions that it was impossible to obtain any better resolution on the point." These and similar pretexts are constantly at hand, whether true or false. And who is there that will either take the trouble or incur the odium of a strict scrutiny into the secret springs of the transaction? Should there be found a citizen zealous enough to undertake the unpromising task, if there happen to be collusion between the parties concerned, how easy it is to clothe the circumstances with so much ambiguity, as to render it uncertain what was the precise conduct of any of those parties.

In the single instance in which the governor of this State is coupled with a council—that is, in the appointment to offices, we have seen the mischiefs of it in the view now under consideration. Scandalous appointments to important offices have been made. Some cases, indeed, have been so flagrant that ALL PARTIES have agreed in the impropriety of the thing. When inquiry has been made, the blame has been laid by the governor on the members of the council, who, on their part, have charged it upon his nomination; while the people remain altogether at a loss to determine, by whose influence their interests have been committed to hands so unqualified and so manifestly improper. In tenderness to individuals, I forbear to descend to particulars.

It is evident from these considerations, that the plurality of the Executive tends to deprive the people of the two greatest securities they can have for the faithful exercise of any delegated power, *first,* the restraints of public opinion, which lose their efficacy, as well on account of the division of the censure attendant on bad measures among a number, as on account of the uncertainty on whom it ought to fall; and, *secondly,* the opportunity of discovering with facility and clearness the misconduct of the persons they trust, in order either to their removal from office, or to their actual punishment in cases which admit of it.

In England, the king is a perpetual magistrate; and it is a maxim which has obtained for the sake of the public peace, that he is unaccountable for his administration, and his person sacred. Nothing, therefore, can be wiser in that kingdom, than to annex to the king a constitutional council, who may be responsible to the nation for the advice they give. Without this, there would be no responsibility whatever in the executive department—an idea inadmissible in a free government. But even there the king is not bound by the resolutions of his council, though they are answerable for the advice they give. He is the absolute master of his own conduct in the exercise of his office, and may observe or disregard the counsel given to him at his sole discretion.

But in a republic, where every magistrate ought to be personally responsible for his behavior in office, the reason which in the British Constitution dictates the propriety of a council, not only ceases to apply, but turns against the institution. In the monarchy of Great Britain, it furnishes a substitute for the prohibited responsibility of the chief magistrate, which

serves in some degree as a hostage to the national justice for his good behavior. In the American republic, it would serve to destroy, or would greatly diminish, the intended and necessary responsibility of the Chief Magistrate himself.

The idea of a council to the Executive, which has so generally obtained in the State constitutions, has been derived from that maxim of republican jealousy which considers power as safer in the hands of a number of men than of a single man. If the maxim should be admitted to be applicable to the case, I should contend that the advantage on that side would not counterbalance the numerous disadvantages on the opposite side. But I do not think the rule at all applicable to the executive power. I clearly concur in opinion, in this particular, with a writer whom the celebrated Junius pronounces to be "deep, solid, and ingenious," that "the executive power is more easily confined when it is ONE"[5]; that it is far more safe there should be a single object for the jealousy and watchfulness of the people; and, in a word that all multiplication of the Executive is rather dangerous than friendly to liberty.

A little consideration will satisfy us, that the species of security sought for in the multiplication of the Executive, is unattainable. Numbers must be so great as to render combination difficult, or they are rather a source of danger than of security. The united credit and influence of several individuals must be more formidable to liberty, than the credit and influence of either of them separately. When power, therefore, is placed in the hands of so small a number of men, as to admit of their interests and views being easily combined in a common enterprise, by an artful leader, it becomes more liable to abuse, and more dangerous when abused, than if it be lodged in the hands of one man; who, from the very circumstance of his being alone, will be more narrowly watched and more readily suspected, and who cannot unite so great a mass of influence as when he is associated with others. The Decemvirs of Rome, whose name denotes their number,[6] were more to be dreaded in their usurpation than any ONE of them would have been. No person would think of proposing an Executive much more numerous than that body; from six to a dozen have been suggested for the number of the council. The extreme of these numbers, is not too great for an easy combination; and from such a combination America would have more to fear, than from the ambition of any single individual. A council to a magistrate who is himself responsible for what he does, are generally nothing better than a clog upon his good intentions, are often the instruments and accomplices of his bad, and are almost always a cloak to his faults.

I forbear to dwell upon the subject of expense; though it be evident that if the council should be numerous enough to answer the principal end aimed at by the institution, the salaries of the members, who must be drawn from their homes to reside at the seat of government, would form an item in the catalogue of public expenditures too serious to be incurred for an object of equivocal utility. I will only add that, prior to the appearance of the Constitution, I rarely met with an intelligent man from any of the States, who did not admit, as the result of experience, that the UNITY of the executive of this State was one of the best of the distinguishing features of our constitution.                        Publius [Hamilton]

## NUMBER 71

Duration in office has been mentioned as the second requisite to the energy of the executive authority. This has relation to two objects: to the personal firmness of the executive magistrate in the employment of his constitutional powers, and to the stability of the system of administration which may have been adopted under his auspices. With regard to the first, it must be evident that the longer the duration in office, the greater will be the probability of obtaining so important an advantage. It is a general principle of human nature that a man will be interested in whatever he possesses, in proportion to the firmness or precariousness of the tenure by which he holds it; will be less attached to what he holds by a momentary or uncertain title, than to what he enjoys by a durable or certain title; and, of course, will be willing to risk more for the sake of the one than for the sake of the other. This remark is not less applicable to a political privilege, or honor, or trust, than to any

article of ordinary property. The inference from it is that a man acting in the capacity of chief magistrate, under a consciousness that in a very short time he *must* lay down his office, will be apt to feel himself too little interested in it to hazard any material censure or perplexity from the independent exertion of his powers, or from encountering the ill humors, however transient, which may happen to prevail, either in a considerable part of the society itself, or even in a predominant faction in the legislative body. If the case should only be that he *might* lay it down, unless continued by a new choice and if he should be desirous of being continued, his wishes, conspiring with his fears, would tend still more powerfully to corrupt his integrity, or debase his fortitude. In either case, feebleness and irresolution must be the characteristics of the station.

There are some who would be inclined to regard the servile pliancy of the executive to a prevailing current, either in the community or in the legislature, as its best recommendation. But such men entertain very crude notions, as well of the purposes for which government was instituted, as of the true means by which the public happiness may be promoted. The republican principle demands that the deliberate sense of the community should govern the conduct of those to whom they intrust the management of their affairs; but it does not require an unqualified complaisance to every sudden breeze of passion, or to every transient impulse which the people may receive from the arts of men, who flatter their prejudices to betray their interests. It is a just observation that the people commonly *intend* the PUBLIC GOOD. This often applies to their very errors. But their good sense would despise the adulator who should pretend that they always *reason right* about the *means* of promoting it. They know from experience that they sometimes err; and the wonder is that they so seldom err as they do, beset as they continually are by the wiles of parasites and sycophants, by the snares of the ambitious, the avaricious, the desperate, by the artifices of men who possess their confidence more than they deserve it, and of those who seek to possess rather than to deserve it. When occasions present themselves in which the interests of the people are at variance with their inclinations, it is the duty of the persons whom they have appointed to be the guardians of those interests to withstand the temporary delusion in order to give them time and opportunity for more cool and sedate reflection. Instances might be cited in which a conduct of this kind has saved the people from very fatal consequences of their own mistakes, and has procured lasting monuments of their gratitude to the men who had courage and magnanimity enough to serve them at the peril of their displeasure.

But however inclined we might be to insist upon an unbounded complaisance in the executive to the inclinations of the people, we can with no propriety contend for a like complaisance to the humors of the legislature. The latter may sometimes stand in opposition to the former, and at other times the people may be entirely neutral. In either supposition, it is certainly desirable that the executive should be in a situation to dare to act his own opinion with vigor and decision.

The same rule which teaches the propriety of a partition between the various branches of power teaches likewise that this partition ought to be so contrived as to render the one independent of the other. To what purpose separate the executive or the judiciary from the legislative, if both the executive and the judiciary are so constituted as to be at the absolute devotion of the legislative? Such a separation must be merely nominal, and incapable of producing the ends for which it was established. It is one thing to be subordinate to the laws, and another to be dependent on the legislative body. The first comports with, the last violates, the fundamental principles of good government; and, whatever may be the forms of the Constitution, unites all power in the same hands. The tendency of the legislative authority to absorb every other has been fully displayed and illustrated by examples in some preceding numbers. In governments purely republican, this tendency is almost irresistible. The representatives of the people, in a popular assembly, seem sometimes to fancy that they are the people themselves, and betray strong symptoms of impatience and disgust at the least sign of opposition from any other quarter; as if the exercise of its rights, by either the executive or judiciary, were a breach of their privilege and an outrage to their dignity. They often appear disposed to exert an imperious control over the other departments; and as they commonly have the people on their side, they always act with such momentum as to make it very difficult for the other members of the government to maintain the balance of the Constitution.

It may perhaps be asked how the shortness of the duration in office can affect the independence of the executive on the legislature, unless the one were possessed of the power of appointing or displacing the other. One answer to this inquiry may be drawn from the principle already remarked—that is, from the slender interest a man is apt to take in a short-lived advantage, and the little inducement it affords him to expose himself, on account of it, to any considerable inconvenience or hazard. Another answer, perhaps more obvious, though not more conclusive, will result from the consideration of the influence of the legislative body over the people, which might be employed to prevent the re-election of a man who, by an upright resistance to any sinister project of that body, should have made himself obnoxious to its resentment.

It may be asked also whether a duration of four years would answer the end proposed; and if it would not, whether a less period, which would at least be recommended by greater security against ambitious designs, would not, for that reason, be preferable to a longer period which was, at the same time, too short for the purpose of inspiring the desired firmness and independence of the magistrate.

It cannot be affirmed that a duration of four years, or any other limited duration, would completely answer the end proposed; but it would contribute towards it in a degree which would have a material influence upon the spirit and character of the government. Between the commencement and termination of such a period there would always be a considerable interval in which the prospect of annihilation would be sufficiently remote not to have an improper effect upon the conduct of a man endowed with a tolerable portion of fortitude; and in which he might reasonably promise himself that there would be time enough before it arrived to make the community sensible of the propriety of the measures he might incline to pursue. Though it be probable that, as he approached the moment when the public were, by a new election, to signify their sense of his conduct, his confidence, and with it his firmness, would decline; yet both the one and the other would derive support from the opportunities which his previous continuance in the station had afforded him, of establishing himself in the esteem and good will of his constituents. He might, then, hazard with safety, in proportion to the proofs he had given of his wisdom and integrity, and to the title he had acquired to the respect and attachment of his fellow-citizens. As on the one hand, a duration of four years will contribute to the firmness of the executive in a sufficient degree to render it a very valuable ingredient in the composition, so, on the other, it is not long enough to justify any alarm for the public liberty. If a British House of Commons, from the most feeble beginnings, *from the mere power of assenting or disagreeing to the imposition of a new tax*, have, by rapid strides, reduced the prerogatives of the crown and the privileges of the nobility within the limits they conceived to be compatible with the principles of a free government, while they raised themselves to the rank and consequence of a co-equal branch of the legislature; if they have been able, in one instance, to abolish both the royalty and the aristocracy, and to overturn all the ancient establishments, as well in the Church as State; if they have been able, on a recent occasion, to make the monarch tremble at the prospect of an innovation[7] attempted by them, what would be to be feared from an elective magistrate of four years' duration with the confined authorities of a President of the United States? What, but that he might be unequal to the task which the Constitution assigns him? I shall only add that if his duration be such as to leave a doubt of his firmness, that doubt is inconsistent with a jealousy of his encroachments.          Publius [Hamilton]

## NUMBER 78

We proceed now to an examination of the judiciary department of the proposed government.

In unfolding the defects of the existing Confederation, the utility and necessity of a federal judicature have been clearly pointed out. It is the less necessary to recapitulate the considerations there urged, as the propriety of the institution in the abstract is not disputed; the only questions which have been raised being relative to the manner of constituting it, and to its extent. To these points, therefore, our observations shall be confined.

The manner of constituting it seems to embrace these several objects: 1st. The mode of appointing the judges. 2d. The tenure by which they are to hold their places. 3d. The partition of the judiciary authority between different courts, and their relations to each other.

*First*. As to the mode of appointing the judges; this is the same with that of appointing the officers of the Union in general, and has been so fully discussed in the two last numbers, that nothing can be said here which would not be useless repetition.

*Second*. As to the tenure by which the judges are to hold their places: this chiefly concerns their duration in office; the provisions for their support; the precautions for their responsibility.

According to the plan of the convention, all judges who may be appointed by the United States are to hold their offices *during good behavior;* which is comfortable to the most approved of the State constitutions, and among the rest, to that of this State. Its propriety having been drawn into question by the adversaries of that plan, is no light symptom of the rage for objection, which disorders their imaginations and judgments. The standard of good behavior for the continuance in office of the judicial magistracy, is certainly one of the most valuable of the modern improvements in the practice of government. In a monarchy it is an excellent barrier to the despotism of the prince; in a republic it is a no less excellent barrier to the encroachments and oppressions of the representative body. And it is the best expedient which can be devised in any government, to secure a steady, upright, and impartial administration of the laws.

Whoever attentively considers the different departments of power must perceive, that, in a government in which they are separated from each other, the judiciary, from the nature of its functions, will always be the least dangerous to the political rights of the Constitution; because it will be least in a capacity to annoy or injure them. The Executive not only dispenses the honors, but holds the sword of the community. The legislature not only commands the purse, but prescribes the rules by which the duties and rights of every citizen are to be regulated. The judiciary, on the contrary, has no influence over either the sword or the purse; no direction either of the strength or of the wealth of the society; and can take no active resolution whatever. It may truly be said to have neither FORCE nor WILL but merely judgment; and must ultimately depend upon the aid of the executive arm even for the efficacy of its judgments.

This simple view of the matter suggests several important consequences. It proves incontestably, that the judiciary is beyond comparison the weakest of the three departments of power[8]; that it can never attack with success either of the other two; and that all possible care is requisite to enable it to defend itself against their attacks. It equally proves, that though individual oppression may now and then proceed from the courts of justice, the general liberty of the people can never be endangered from that quarter; I mean so long as the judiciary remains truly distinct from both the legislature and the Executive. For I agree, that "there is no liberty, if the power of judging be not separated from the legislative and executive powers."[9] And it proves, in the last place, that as liberty can have nothing to fear from the judiciary alone, but would have every thing to fear from its union with either of the other departments; that as all the effects of such a union must ensue from a dependence of the former on the latter, notwithstanding a nominal and apparent separation; that as, from the natural feebleness of the judiciary, it is in continual jeopardy of being overpowered, awed, or influenced by its coordinate branches; and that as nothing can contribute so much to its firmness and independence as permanency in office, this quality may therefore be justly regarded as an indispensable ingredient in its constitution, and, in a great measure, as the citadel of the public justice and the public security.

The complete independence of the courts of justice is peculiarly essential in a limited Constitution. By a limited Constitution, I understand one which contains certain specified exceptions to the legislative authority; such, for instance, as that it shall pass no bills of attainder, no *ex-post-facto* laws, and the like. Limitations of this kind can be preserved in practice no other way than through the medium of courts of justice, whose duty it must be to declare all acts contrary to the manifest tenor of the Constitution void. Without this, all the reservations of particular rights or privileges would amount to nothing.

Some perplexity respecting the rights of the courts to pronounce legislative acts void, because contrary to the Constitution, has arisen from an imagination that the doctrine would imply a superiority of the judiciary to the legislative power. It is urged that the authority which can declare the acts of another void, must necessarily be superior to the one whose acts may be declared void. As this doctrine is of great importance in all the American constitutions, a brief discussion of the ground on which it rests cannot be unacceptable.

There is no position which depends on clearer principles, than that every act of a delegated authority, contrary to the tenor of the commission under which it is exercised, is void. No legislative act, therefore, contrary to the Constitution, can be valid. To deny this, would be to affirm, that the deputy is greater than his principal; that the servant is above his master; that the representatives of the people are superior to the people themselves; that men acting by virtue of powers, may do not only what their powers do not authorize, but what they forbid.

If it be said that the legislative body are themselves the constitutional judges of their own powers, and that the construction they put upon them is conclusive upon the other department, it may be answered, that this cannot be the natural presumption, where it is not to be collected from any particular provisions in the Constitution. It is not otherwise to be supposed, that the Constitution could intend to enable the representatives of the people to substitute their *will* to that of their constituents. It is far more rational to suppose, that the courts were designed to be an intermediate body between the people and the legislature, in order, among other things, to keep the latter within the limits assigned to their authority. The interpretation of the laws is the proper and peculiar province of the courts. A constitution is, in fact, and must be regarded by the judges, as a fundamental law. It therefore belongs to them to ascertain its meaning, as well as the meaning of any particular act proceeding from the legislative body. If there should happen to be an irreconcilable variance between the two, that which has the superior obligation and validity ought, of course, to be preferred; or, in other words, the Constitution ought to be preferred to the statute, the intention of the people to the intention of their agents.

Nor does this conclusion by any means suppose a superiority of the judicial to the legislative power. It only supposes that the power of the people is superior to both; and that where the will of the legislature, declared in its statutes, stands in opposition to that of the people, declared in the Constitution, the judges ought to be governed by the latter rather than the former. They ought to regulate their decisions by the fundamental laws, rather then by those which are not fundamental.

This exercise of judicial discretion, in determining between two contradictory laws, is exemplified in a familiar instance. It not uncommonly happens, that there are two statutes existing at one time, clashing in whole or in part with each other, and neither of them containing any repealing clause or expression. In such a case, it is the province of the courts to liquidate and fix their meaning and operation. So far as they can, by any fair construction, be reconciled to each other, reason and law conspire to dictate that this should be done; where this is impracticable, it becomes a matter of necessity to give effect to one, in exclusion of the other. The rule which has obtained in the courts for determining their relative validity is, that the last in order of time shall be preferred to the first. But this is a mere rule of construction, not derived from any positive law, but from the nature and reason of the thing. It is a rule not enjoined upon the courts by legislative provision, but adopted by themselves, as consonant to truth and propriety, for the direction of their conduct as interpreters of the law. They thought it reasonable, that between the interfering acts of an *equal* authority, that which was the last indication of its will should have the preference.

But in regard to the interfering acts of a superior and subordinate authority, of an original and derivative power, the nature and reason of the thing indicate the converse of that rule as proper to be followed. They teach us that the prior act of a superior ought to be preferred to the subsequent act of an inferior and subordinate authority; and that accordingly, whenever a particular statute contravenes the Constitution, it will be the duty of the judicial tribunals to adhere to the latter and disregard the former.

It can be of no weight to say that the courts, on the pretence of a repugnancy, may substitute their own pleasure to the constitutional intentions of the legislature. This might as well happen in the case of two contradictory statutes; or it might as well happen in every adjudication upon any single statute. The courts must declare the sense of the law; and if they should be disposed to exercise WILL instead of JUDGMENT, the consequence would equally be the substitution of their pleasure to that of the legislative body. The observation, if it prove any thing, would prove that there ought to be no judges distinct from that body.

If, then, the courts of justice are to be considered as the bulwarks of a limited Constitution against legislative encroachments, this consideration will afford a strong argument for the permanent tenure of judicial offices, since nothing will contribute so much as this to that independent spirit in the judges which must be essential to the faithful performance of so arduous a duty.

This independence of the judges is equally requisite to guard the Constitution and the rights of individuals from the effects of those ill humors, which the arts of designing men, or the influence of particular conjunctures, sometimes disseminate among the people themselves, and which, though they speedily give place to better information, and more deliberate reflection, have a tendency, in the meantime, to occasion dangerous innovations in the government, and serious oppressions of the minor party in the community. Though I trust the friends of the proposed Constitution will never concur with its enemies,[10] in questioning that fundamental principle of republican government, which admits the right of the people to alter or abolish the established Constitution, whenever they find it inconsistent with their happiness, yet it is not to be inferred from this principle, that the representatives of the people, whenever a momentary inclination happens to lay hold of a majority of their constituents, incompatible with the provisions in the existing Constitution, would, on that account, be justifiable in a violation of those provisions; or that the courts would be under a greater obligation to connive at infractions in this shape, than when they had proceeded wholly from the cabals of the representative body. Until the people have, by some solemn and authoritative act, annulled or changed the established form, it is binding upon themselves collectively, as well as individually; and no presumption, or even knowledge, of their sentiments, can warrant their representatives in a departure from it, prior to such an act. But it is easy to see, that it would require an uncommon portion of fortitude in the judges to do their duty as faithful guardians of the Constitution, where legislative invasions of it had been instigated by the major voice of the community.

But it is not with a view to infractions of the Constitution only, that the independence of the judges may be an essential safeguard against the effects of occasional ill humors in the society. These sometimes extend no farther than to the injury of the private rights of particular classes of citizens, by unjust and partial laws. Here also the firmness of the judicial magistracy is of vast importance in mitigating the severity and confining the operation of such laws. It not only serves to moderate the immediate mischiefs of those which may have been passed, but it operates as a check upon the legislative body in passing them; who, perceiving that obstacles to the success of iniquitous intention are to be expected from the scruples of the courts, are in a manner compelled, by the very motives of the injustice they meditate, to qualify their attempts. This is a circumstance calculated to have more influence upon the character of our governments, than but few may be aware of. The benefits of the integrity and moderation of the judiciary have already been felt in more States than one; and though they may have displeased those whose sinister expectations they may have disappointed, they must have commanded the esteem and applause of all the virtuous and disinterested. Considerate men, of every description, ought to prize whatever will tend to beget or fortify that temper in the courts; as no man can be sure that he may not be tomorrow the victim of a spirit of injustice, by which he may be a gainer today. And every man must now feel, that

the inevitable tendency of such a spirit is to sap the foundations of public and private confidence, and to introduce in its stead universal distrust and distress.

That inflexible and uniform adherence to the rights of the Constitution, and of individuals, which we perceive to be indispensable in the courts of justice, can certainly not be expected from judges who hold their offices by a temporary commission. Periodical appointments, however regulated, or by whomsoever made, would, in some way or other, be fatal to their necessary independence. If the power of making them was committed either to the Executive or legislature, there would be danger of an improper complaisance to the branch which possessed it; if to both, there would be an unwillingness to hazard the displeasure of either; if to the people, or to persons chosen by them for the special purpose, there would be too great a disposition to consult popularity, to justify a reliance that nothing would be consulted but the Constitution and the laws.

There is yet a further and a weightier reason for the permanency of the judicial offices, which is deducible from the nature of the qualifications they require. It has been frequently remarked, with great propriety, that a voluminous code of laws is one of the inconveniences necessarily connected with the advantages of a free government. To avoid an arbitrary discretion in the courts, it is indispensable that they should be bound down by strict rules and precedents, which serve to define and point out their duty in every particular case that comes before them; and it will readily be conceived from the variety of controversies which grow out of the folly and wickedness of mankind, that the records of those precedents must unavoidably swell to a very considerable bulk, and must demand long and laborious study to acquire a competent knowledge of them. Hence it is, that there can be but few men in the society who will have sufficient skill in the laws to qualify them for the stations of judges. And making the proper deductions for the ordinary depravity of human nature, the number must be still smaller of those who unite the requisite integrity with the requisite knowledge. These considerations apprise us, that the government can have no great option between fit character; and that a temporary duration in office, which would naturally discourage such characters from quitting a lucrative line of practice to accept a seat on the bench, would have a tendency to throw the administration of justice into hands less able, and less well qualified, to conduct it with utility and dignity. In the present circumstances of this country, and in those in which it is likely to be for a long time to come, the disadvantages on this score would be greater than they may at first sight appear; but it must be confessed, that they are far inferior to those which present themselves under the other aspects of the subject.

Upon the whole, there can be no room to doubt that the convention acted wisely in copying from the models of those constitutions which have established *good behavior* as the tenure of their judicial offices, in point of duration; and that so far from being blamable on this account, their plan would have been inexcusably defective, if it had wanted this important feature of good government. The experience of Great Britain affords an illustrious comment on the excellence of the institution.

Publius [Hamilton]

## NUMBER 85

According to the formal division of the subject of these papers announced in my first number, there would appear still to remain for discussion two points: "the analogy of the proposed government to your own State constitution," and "the additional security which its adoption will afford to republican government, to liberty, and to property." But these heads have been so fully anticipated and exhausted in the progress of the work that it would now scarcely be possible to do anything more than repeat, in a more dilated form, what has been heretofore said, which the advanced stage of the question and the time already spent upon it conspire to forbid.

It is remarkable that the resemblance of the plan of the convention to the act which organizes the government of this State holds, not less with regard to many of the supposed defects than to the real excel-

lences of the former. Among the pretended defects are the re-eligibility of the executive, the want of a council, the omission of a formal bill of rights, the omission of a provision respecting the liberty of the press. These and several others which have been noted in the course of our inquiries are as much chargeable on the existing constitution of this State as on the one proposed for the Union; and a man must have slender pretensions to consistency who can rail at the latter for imperfections which he finds no difficulty in excusing in the former. Nor indeed can there be a better proof of the insincerity and affectation of some of the zealous adversaries of the plan of the convention among us who profess to be the devoted admirers of the government under which they live than the fury with which they have attacked that plan, for matters in regard to which our own constitution is equally or perhaps more vulnerable.

The additional securities to republican government, to liberty, and to property, to be derived from the adoption of the plan under consideration, consist chiefly in the restraints which the preservation of the Union will impose on local factions and insurrections, and on the ambition of powerful individuals in single States who might acquire credit and influence enough from leaders and favorites to become the despots of the people; in the diminution of the opportunities to foreign intrigue, which the dissolution of the Confederacy would invite and facilitate; in the prevention of extensive military establishments, which could not fail to grow out of wars between the States in a disunited situation; in the express guaranty of a republican form of government to each; in the absolute and universal exclusion of titles of nobility; and in the precautions against the repetition of those practices on the part of the State governments which have undermined the foundations of property and credit, have planted mutual distrust in the breasts of all classes of citizens, and have occasioned an almost universal prostration of morals.

Thus have I, fellow-citizens, executed the task I had assigned to myself; with what success your conduct must determine. I trust at least you will admit that I have not failed in the assurance I gave you respecting the spirit with which my endeavors should be conducted. I have addressed myself purely to your judgments, and have studiously avoided those asperities which are too apt to disgrace political disputants of all parties and which have been not a little provoked by the language and conduct of the opponents of the Constitution. The charge of a conspiracy against the liberties of the people which has been indiscriminately brought against the advocates of the plan has something in it too wanton and too malignant not to excite the indignation of every man who feels in his own bosom a refutation of the calumny. The perpetual changes which have been rung upon the wealthy, the well-born, and the great have been such as to inspire the disgust of all sensible men. And the unwarrantable concealments and misrepresentations which have been in various ways practiced to keep the truth from the public eye have been of a nature to demand the reprobation of all honest men. It is not impossible that these circumstances may have occasionally betrayed me into intemperances of expression which I did not intend; it is certain that I have frequently felt a struggle between sensibility and moderation; and if the former has in some instances prevailed, it must be my excuse that it has been neither often nor much.

Let us now pause and ask ourselves whether, in the course of these papers, the proposed Constitution has not been satisfactorily vindicated from the aspersions thrown upon it; and whether it has not been shown to be worthy of the public approbation and necessary to the public safety and prosperity. Every man is bound to answer these questions to himself, according to the best of his conscience and understanding, and to act agreeably to the genuine and sober dictates of his judgment. This is a duty from which nothing can give him a dispensation. 'Tis one that he is called upon, nay, constrained by all the obligations that form the bonds of society, to discharge sincerely and honestly. No partial motive, no particular interest, no pride of opinion, no temporary passion or prejudice, will justify to himself, to his country, or to his posterity, an improper election of the part he is to act. Let him beware of an obstinate adherence to party; let him reflect that the object upon which he is to decide is not a particular interest of the community, but the very existence of the nation; and let him remember that a majority of America has already given its sanction to the plan which he is to approve or reject.

I shall not dissemble that I feel an entire confidence in the arguments which recommend the proposed system to your adoption, and that I am unable to discern any real force in those by which it has been opposed. I am persuaded that it is the best which our political situation, habits, and opinions will admit, and superior to any the revolution has produced.

Concessions on the part of the friends of the plan that it has not a claim to absolute perfection have afforded matter of no small triumph to its enemies. "Why," say they, "should we adopt an imperfect thing? Why not amend it and make it perfect before it is irrevocably established?" This may be plausible enough, but it is only plausible. In the first place I remark that the extent of these concessions has been greatly exaggerated. They have been stated as amounting to an admission that the plan is radically defective and that without material alterations the rights and the interests of the community cannot be safely confided to it. This, as far as I have understood the meaning of those who make the concessions, is an entire perversion of their sense. No advocate of the measure can be found who will not declare as his sentiment that the system, though it may not be perfect in every part, is, upon the whole, a good one; is the best that the present views and circumstances of the country will permit; and is such a one as promises every species of security which a reasonable people can desire.

I answer in the next place that I should esteem it the extreme of imprudence to prolong the precarious state of our national affairs and to expose the Union to the jeopardy of successive experiments in the chimerical pursuit of a perfect plan. I never expect to see a perfect work from imperfect man. The result of the deliberations of all collective bodies must necessarily be a compound, as well of the errors and prejudices as of the good sense and wisdom of the individuals of whom they are composed. The compacts which are to embrace thirteen distinct States in a common bond of amity and union must as necessarily be a compromise of as many dissimilar interests and inclinations. How can perfection spring from such materials?

The reasons assigned in an excellent little pamphlet lately published in this city[11] are unanswerable to show the utter improbability of assembling a new convention under circumstances in any degree so favorable to a happy issue as those in which the late convention met, deliberated, and concluded. I will not repeat the arguments there used, as I presume the production itself has had an extensive circulation. It is certainly well worth the perusal of every friend to his country. There is, however, one point of light in which the subject of amendments still remains to be considered, and in which it has not yet been exhibited to public view. I cannot resolve to conclude without first taking a survey of it in this aspect.

It appears to me susceptible of absolute demonstration that it will be far more easy to obtain subsequent than previous amendments to the Constitution. The moment an alteration is made in the present plan it becomes, to the purpose of adoption, a new one, and must undergo a new decision of each State. To its complete establishment throughout the Union it will therefore require the concurrence of thirteen States. If, on the contrary, the Constitution proposed should once be ratified by all the States as it stands, alterations in it may at any time be effected by nine States. Here, then, the chances are as thirteen to nine[12] in favor of subsequent amendment, rather than of the original adoption of an entire system.

This is not all. Every Constitution for the United States must inevitably consist of a great variety of particulars in which thirteen independent States are to be accommodated in their interests or opinions of interest. We may of course expect to see, in any body of men charged with its original formation, very different combinations of the parts upon different points. Many of those who form a majority on one question may become the minority on a second, and an association dissimilar to either may constitute the majority on a third. Hence the necessity of moulding and arranging all the particulars which are to compose the whole in such a manner as to satisfy all the parties to the compact; and hence, also, an immense

multiplication of difficulties and casualties in obtaining the collective assent to a final act. The degree of that multiplication must evidently be in a ratio to the number of particulars and the number of parties.

But every amendment to the Constitution, if once established, would be a single proposition, and might be brought forward singly. There would then be no necessity for management or compromise in relation to any other point—no giving nor taking. The will of the requisite number would at once bring the matter to a decisive issue. And consequently, whenever nine, or rather ten States, were united in the desire of a particular amendment, that amendment must infallibly take place. There can, therefore, be no comparison between the facility of effecting an amendment and that of establishing, in the first instance, a complete Constitution.

In opposition to the probability of subsequent amendments, it has been urged that the persons delegated to the administration of the national government will always be disinclined to yield up any portion of the authority of which they were once possessed. For my own part, I acknowledge a thorough conviction that any amendments which may, upon mature consideration, be thought useful, will be applicable to the organization of the government, not to the mass of its powers; and on this account alone I think there is no weight in the observation just stated. I also think there is little weight in it on another account. The intrinsic difficulty of governing THIRTEEN STATES at any rate, independent of calculations upon an ordinary degree of public spirit and integrity will, in my opinion, constantly *impose* on the national rulers the *necessity* of a spirit of accommodation to the reasonable expectations of their constituents. But there is yet a further consideration, which proves beyond the possibility of doubt that the observation is futile. It is this: that the national rulers, whenever nine States concur, will have no option upon the subject. By the fifth article of the plan, the Congress will be *obliged* "on the application of the legislatures of two thirds of the States [which at present amount to nine], to call a convention for proposing amendments which *shall be valid,* to all intents and purposes, as part of the Constitution, when ratified by the legislatures of three fourths of the states, or by conventions in three fourths thereof." The words of this article are peremptory. The Congress "*shall* call a convention." Nothing in this particular is left to the discretion of that body. And of consequence all the declamation about the disinclination to a change vanishes in air. Nor however difficult it may be supposed to unite two thirds or three fourths of the State legislatures in amendments which may affect local interests can there be any room to apprehend any such difficulty in a union on points which are merely relative to the general liberty or security of the people. We may safely rely on the disposition of the State legislatures to erect barriers against the encroachments of the national authority.

If the foregoing argument is a fallacy, certain it is that I am myself deceived by it for it is, in my conception, one of those rare instances in which a political truth can be brought to the test of mathematical demonstration. Those who see the matter in the same light with me, however zealous they may be for amendments, must agree in the propriety of a previous adoption as the most direct road to their own object.

The zeal for attempts to amend, prior to the establishment of the Constitution, must abate in every man who is ready to accede to the truth of the following observations of a writer equally solid and ingenious: "To balance a large state or society [says he], whether monarchical or republican, on general laws, is a work of so great difficulty that no human genius, however comprehensive, is able, by the mere dint of reason and reflection, to effect it. The judgments of many must unite in the work; EXPERIENCE must guide their labor; TIME must bring it to perfection, and the FEELING of inconveniences must correct the mistakes which they *inevitably* fall into in their first trials and experiments."[13] These judicious reflections contain a lesson of moderation to all the sincere lovers of the Union, and ought to put them upon their guard against hazarding anarchy, civil war, a perpetual alienation of the States from each other, and perhaps the military despotism of a victorious demagogue, in the pursuit of what they are not likely to obtain, but from TIME and EXPERIENCE. It may be in me a defect of political fortitude but I acknowledge that I cannot entertain an equal tranquillity with those who affect to treat the dangers of a longer continuance in our present situation as imaginary. A NATION without a NATIONAL GOVERNMENT is, in my view, an awful spectacle. The establishment of a Constitution, in time of profound peace, by the voluntary consent of a whole people, is a PRODIGY, to the completion of which I look forward with trembling anxiety. I can reconcile it to no rules of prudence to let go the hold we now have, in so arduous an enterprise, upon seven out of the thirteen States, and after having passed over so considerable a part of the ground, to recommence the course. I dread the more the consequences of new attempts because I know that POWERFUL INDIVIDUALS, in this and other States, are enemies to a general national government in every possible shape.

Publius [Hamilton]

## Notes

1. The same idea, tracing the arguments to their consequences is held out in several of the late publications against the new Constitution.

2. *Spirit of Laws,* vol. I. Book IX. cp. I.

3. "I mean for the Union."

4. New York has no council except for the single purpose of appointing to offices; New Jersey has a council whom the governor may consult. But I think, from the terms of the constitution, their resolutions do not bind him.

5. De Lolme.

6. Ten.

7. This was the case with respect to Mr. Fox's India bill, which was carried in the House of Commons and rejected in the House of Lords, to the entire satisfaction, as it is said, of the people.

8. The celebrated Montesquieu, speaking of them, says: "Of the three powers above mentioned, the judiciary is next to nothing."—"Spirit of Laws," vol. I, p. 186.

9. *Idem,* p. 181.

10. *Vide* "Protest of the Minority of the Convention of Pennsylvania," Martin's Speech, etc.

11. Entitled "An Address to the People of the State of New York."

12. It may rather be said TEN, for though two thirds may set on foot the measure, three fourths must ratify.

13. Hume's *Essays.* vol. I. p. 128: "The Rise of Arts and Sciences."

# JEREMY BENTHAM

~

## INTRODUCTION

## JEREMY WALDRON

Jeremy Bentham is the best known of the English utilitarians, a group of philosophical radicals working at the end of the eighteenth and beginning of the nineteenth centuries to formulate and apply utilitarian principles as criteria for the detailed criticism and reform of law, politics, and social institutions.

Bentham was born in 1748; he was educated at Westminster School and Queen's College, Oxford. He was admitted to the English bar in 1769, but soon forswore the practice of law as it is for the more solitary, less remunerative, but temperamentally more congenial study of the law as it ought to be. In his earliest writings—*A Fragment on Government*, published in 1776, and *A Comment upon the Commentaries* (unpublished until 1928)—Bentham attacked the characterization of the common law and the English Constitution in William Blackstone's *Commentaries on the Laws of England* (1767), an attack that continues in the later chapters of the extract presented here.

Throughout his life, Bentham insisted that law could be understood only in terms of the determinate commands of an identifiable sovereign backed up by sanctions of some sort. He was a legal positivist, not in the sense that he thought law was or should be morally neutral or value-free, but in the sense that he rejected the idea of natural law, regarding laws instead as social facts, though of course *mutable* social facts that the community was entitled to take charge of and change and improve for the sake of the general welfare. Since law sprang from the human will, law making was to be evaluated in the same way as all other conduct concerning other people—by its tendency to promote the happiness of those affected. On this account, the student of law and politics had a twofold function: first to find out what the existing state of the law was and the effects of its operation on society, and second, to work out what the greatest-happiness principle demanded in the particular circumstances of a given society, to propose rules and institutions for putting those demands into effect, and to persuade powerful sovereigns to include those proposals in the content of their sanctioned commands.

This utilitarian approach to law, politics, and ethics was a product of the intellectual optimism that dominated continental philosophy in the eighteenth century. Under the influence of Enlightenment figures like Cesare Beccaria and Claude Helvetius, Bentham developed a precisely formulated version of utilitarianism, which he set out in perhaps his best-known work, *An Introduction to the Principles of Morals and Legislation* (1789). (The extract that follows is from an adaptation of the *Introduction* published originally in French by Bentham's disciple Etienne Dumont.)

Bentham's utilitarianism is at once a psychological theory and a normative principle: "Nature has placed mankind under the governance of two sovereign masters, *pain* and *plea-*

*sure*. It is for them alone to determine what we ought to do, as well as to determine what we shall do." The "ought" side of this equation is pretty clear. The utilitarian principle approves or disapproves of actions, including legislative actions, by their effects on the happiness of the members of the community ("the greatest happiness of the greatest number"), and Bentham provided an elaborate account of the various dimensions on which pleasure and pain would have to be measured in the "moral arithmetic" that legislative calculations ought ideally to involve.

What is less clear is how this comports with the "is" side of his theory, the view about psychological motivation. If sovereigns are motivated in fact by pleasure and pain, they are likely to pass laws that promote their own interests rather than those of their subjects. Bentham never really came to terms with this difficulty in his earlier work, but by the beginning of the nineteenth century he had become convinced that the promotion of the greatest happiness of the greatest number could be secured only by giving the greatest number some degree of influence over the careers (and thus the happiness) of their legislators, making the latter effectively accountable to them. In this way the tension between the normative and the psychological sides of Benthamism generated a pretty powerful argument for democracy.

The paradigm of utilitarian moral calculation—adding costs and benefits to members of the community, multiplying each one by its intensity and discounting it by its uncertainty—dominated Bentham's thought throughout his life. He did not believe it could be applied meticulously "to every moral judgment or to every legislative operation." And he did believe it should be supplemented by what he called "axioms of mental pathology," that is, empirical generalizations "expressive of the connexion between such occurrences as are continually taking place, or liable to take place, and the pleasures and pains representing the result of them." (The law of the diminishing marginal utility of money is a good example.) But the calculus of utility was "always to be kept in view," if only as a way of discrediting other less consequentialist—and on Bentham's account less rational—approaches to politics, such as appeals to tradition, religion, or natural law.

In particular, it is Bentham's consequentialism that explains his antipathy to that other great reforming creed of his day, the doctrine of natural rights expounded by the American and French revolutionaries. Though Bentham supported both revolutions, he regarded the invocation of rights as a dangerous argument stopper in politics: "When I hear of natural rights . . . I always see in the background a cluster of daggers and pikes introduced into the National Assembly." The problem with rights was conceptual as well as political. Bentham's polemic *Anarchical Fallacies* (written in the 1790s as a response to the French Declaration of the Rights of Man and the Citizen) is famous for the quip, "Natural rights is simple nonsense: natural and imprescriptible rights, rhetorical nonsense—nonsense upon stilts," and the word "nonsense" here is not just a term of abuse but the mark of another of Bentham's convictions: the need for analytical clarity and linguistic precision. This concern is apt to seem pedantic to us, or even cranky in the context of Bentham's obsession with elaborate taxonomies and coining of new terms such as "demosio-tameutic" to settle problems of definition. We forget, though, how riddled with confusion political and legal discourse was in Bentham's day and how often verbal equivocation was put to the service of reaction. Macaulay was not exaggerating when he described Bentham as "the man who found jurisprudence a gibberish and left it a science."

Much the same can be said about Bentham's more practical schemes for legal and social reform. In his later years, Bentham sent out a steady stream of legislative and constitutional proposals touching almost every aspect of public affairs, from the codification of civil law to the detailed design of prisons. The recipients included not only the government of his own country but also those of Russia, France, Spain, and particularly the new republics of North and South America. During this period, the previously solitary Bentham accumulated a number of acolytes who took on the task of making his often illegible and chaotic manuscripts available in orderly form to the general public. (This process continues, with no end in sight, to this day.) He died in 1832, surrounded by these acolytes and by well over seventy thousand pages of manuscript material.

That few of Bentham's proposals were ever taken up directly by those who received them might lead us to regard this body of work as the cranky production of a utilitarian Mad Hatter, closeted in his study and beguiled by the intricacies of his own crabbed system. In fact, his lasting legacy was the spirit of rational reform that came to dominate English politics through the work of those whose intelligence and political instincts were molded by Bentham's example. We tend to underestimate this legacy now, because we take for granted many of the reforms that were animated by the rational, radical, and calculating spirit of Benthamism. It is easy to forget how savage and chaotic the English criminal law was until the utilitarians set about campaigning for its reform and rationalization in the nineteenth century. It was not just the criminal law. One commentator offered this list in the London *Times,* a century after Bentham's death:

> The reform of the representative system in Parliament; the removal of defects in the jury system, the abolition of imprisonment for debt, the sweeping away of usury laws, reform of the law of evidence, reform of the Poor Law, the establishment of a national system of education, an extension of the idea of savings banks, cheap postage, a complete and uniform Register of Births, Deaths and Marriages, a Code for Merchant Shipping, protection of inventors, uniform and scientific methods of drafting Acts of Parliament, the passing of public health legislation. . . .

To us, the commentator remarked, the list makes quite dull reading. But in 1800 it was an heroic adventure, "for when Bentham set forth his polity all these things were impossible, absurd, ridiculous. Great intellects waved them away. . . ."

Thus we should read the extract that follows not just as a practical manifesto, but as an earnest, if rather labored, attempt to found a new political culture, not forgetting how hard it was at the beginning of the nineteenth century to sustain thinking in these or any similar terms in public life, against the baying of prejudice, terror, superstition, equivocation, and humbug that for time immemorial had greeted any attempt to rehabilitate the fabric of English society and its law.

There are excellent discussions of Bentham's political philosophy in Ross Harrison, *Bentham* (London: Routledge, 1983); in "The Arguments of the Philosophers" series, in Douglas Long, *Bentham on Liberty* (Toronto: University of Toronto Press, 1977); and in Nancy Rosenblum, *Bentham's Theory of the State* (Cambridge, Mass.: Harvard University Press, 1978). For his legal theory, see Gerald Postema, *Bentham and the Common Law Tradition* (Oxford: Clarendon Press, 1986), and *Essays on Bentham* (Oxford: Clarendon Press, 1983) by one of this century's most distinguished Bentham editors, H. L. A. Hart.

# Principles of Legislation

## CHAPTER I

### *The Principle of Utility*

The Public Good ought to be the object of the legislator; General Utility ought to be the foundation of his reasonings. To know the true good of the community is what constitutes the science of legislation; the art consists in finding the means to realize that good.

The principle of *utility,* vaguely announced, is seldom contradicted; it is even looked upon as a sort of commonplace in politics and morals. But this almost universal assent is only apparent. The same ideas are not attached to this principle; the same value is not given to it; no uniform and logical manner of reasoning results from it.

To give it all the efficacy which it ought to have, that is, to make it the foundation of a system of reasonings, three conditions are necessary.

First,—To attach clear and precise ideas to the word *utility,* exactly the same with all who employ it.

Second,—To establish the unity and the sovereignty of this principle, by rigorously excluding every other. It is nothing to subscribe to it in general; it must be admitted without any exception.

Third,—To find the processes of a moral arithmetic by which uniform results may be arrived at.

The causes of dissent from the doctrine of utility may all be referred to two false principles, which exercise an influence, sometimes open and sometimes secret, upon the judgments of men. If these can be pointed out and excluded, the true principle will remain in purity and strength.

These three principles are like three roads which often cross each other, but of which only one leads to the wished-for destination. The traveller turns often from one into another, and loses in these wanderings more than half his time and strength. The true route is however the easiest; it has mile-stones which cannot be shifted, it has inscriptions, in a universal language, which cannot be effaced; while the two false routes have only contradictory direction in enigmatical characters. But without abusing the language of allegory, let us seek to give a clear idea of the true principle, and of its two adversaries.

Nature has placed man under the empire of *pleasure* and of *pain.* We owe to them all our ideas; we refer to them all our judgments and all the determinations of our life. He who pretends to withdraw himself from this subjection knows not what he says. His only object is to seek pleasure and to shun pain, even at the very instant that he rejects the greatest pleasures or embraces pains the most acute. These eternal and irresistible sentiments ought to be the great study of the moralist and the legislator. The *principle of utility* subjects everything to these two motives.

*Utility* is an abstract term. It expresses the property or tendency of a thing to prevent some evil or to procure some good. *Evil* is pain, or the cause of pain. *Good* is pleasure, or the cause of pleasure. That which is comfortable to the utility, or the interest of an individual, is what tends to augment the total sum of his happiness. That which is conformable to the utility, or the interest of a community, is what tends to augment the total sum of happiness of the individuals that compose it.

A *principle* is a first idea, which is made the beginning or basis of a system of reasonings. To illustrate it by a sensible image, it is a fixed point to which the first link of a chain is attached. Such a

Translated by Richard Hildreth.

711

principle must be clearly evident—to illustrate and to explain it must secure its acknowledgment. Such are the axioms of mathematics; they are not proved directly; it is enough to show that they cannot be rejected without falling into absurdity.

The *logic of utility* consists in setting out, in all the operations of the judgment, from the calculation or comparison of pains and pleasures, and in not allowing the interference of any other idea.

I am a partisan of the *principle of utility* when I measure my approbation or disapprobation of a public or private act by its tendency to produce pleasure or pain; when I employ the words *just, unjust, moral, immoral, good, bad,* simply as collective terms including the ideas of certain pains or pleasures; it always being understood that I use the words *pain* and *pleasure* in their ordinary signification, without inventing any arbitrary definition for the sake of excluding certain pleasures or denying the existence of certain pains. In this matter we want no refinement, no metaphysics. It is not necessary to consult Plato, nor Aristotle. *Pain* and *pleasure* are what everybody feels to be such—the peasant and the prince, the unlearned as well as the philosopher.

He who adopts the *principle of utility,* esteems virtue to be a good only on account of the pleasures which result from it; he regards vice as an evil only because of the pains which it produces. Moral good is *good* only by its tendency to produce physical good. Moral evil is *evil* only by its tendency to produce physical evil; but when I say *physical,* I mean the pains and pleasures of the soul as well as the pains and pleasures of sense. I have in view man, such as he is, in his actual constitution.

## Programs for Reform

If the partisan of the *principle of utility* finds in the common list of virtues an action from which there results more pain than pleasure, he does not hesitate to regard that pretended virtue as a vice; he will not suffer himself to be imposed upon by the general error; he will not lightly believe in the policy of employing false virtues to maintain the true.

If he finds in the common list of offenses some indifferent action, some innocent pleasure, he will not hesitate to transport this pretended offence into the class of lawful actions; he will pity the pretended criminals, and will reserve his indignation for their persecutors.

## CHAPTER II

### *The Ascetic Principle*[1]

This principle is exactly the rival, the antagonist of that which we have just been examining. Those who follow it have a horror of pleasures. Everything which gratifies the senses, in their view, is odious and criminal. They found morality upon privations, and virtue upon the renouncement of one's self. In one word, the reverse of the partisans of utility, they approve everything which tends to diminish enjoyment, they blame everything, which tends to augment it.

This principle has been more or less followed by two classes of men, who in other respects have scarce any resemblance, and who even affect a mutual contempt. The one class are philosophers, the other, devotees. The ascetic philosophers, animated by the hope of applause, have flattered themselves with the idea of seeming to rise above humanity, by despising vulgar pleasures. They expect to be paid in reputation and in glory, for all the sacrifices which they seem to make to the severity of their maxims. The ascetic devotees are foolish people, tormented by vain terrors. Man, in their eyes, is but a degenerate being, who ought to punish himself without ceasing for the crime of being born, and never to turn off his thoughts from that gulf of eternal misery which is ready to open beneath his feet. Still, the martyrs to these absurd opinions have, like all others, a fund of hope. Independent of the worldly pleasures attached to the reputation of sanctity, these atrabilious pietists flatter themselves that every instant of voluntary pain here below will procure them an age of happiness in another life. Thus, even the ascetic principle reposes upon some false idea of utility. It acquired its ascendancy only through mistake.[2]

The devotees have carried the ascetic principle much further than the philosophers. The philosophical party has confined itself to censuring pleasures; the religious sects have turned the infliction of pain into a duty. The stoics said that pain was not an evil; the Jansenists maintained that it was actually a good. The philosophical party never reproved pleasures in the mass, but only those which it called gross and sensual, while it exalted the pleasures of sentiment and understanding. It was rather a preference for the one class, than a total exclusion of the other. Always despised, or disparaged under its true name, pleasure was received and applauded when it took the titles of *honour, glory, reputation, decorum,* or *self-esteem.*

Not to be accused of exaggerating the absurdity of the ascetics, I shall mention the least unreasonable origin which can be assigned to their system.

It was early perceived that the attraction of pleasure might seduce into pernicious acts; that is, acts of which the good was not equivalent to the evil. To forbid these pleasures, in consideration of their bad effects, is the object of sound morals and good laws. But the ascetics have made a mistake, for they have attacked pleasure itself; they have condemned it in general; they have made it the object of a universal prohibition, the sign of a reprobate nature; and it is only out of regard for human weakness that they have had the indulgence to grant some particular exemptions.

## CHAPTER III

### *The Arbitrary Principle; or the Principle of Sympathy and Antipathy*

This principle consists in approving or blaming by sentiment, without giving any other reason for the decision except the decision itself. *I love; I hate;* such is the pivot on which this principle turns. An action is judged to be good or bad, not because it is conformable, or on the contrary, to the interest of those whom it affects, but because it pleases or displeases him who judges. He pronounces sovereignly; he admits no appeal; he does not think himself obliged to justify his opinion by any consideration relative to the good of society. "It is my interior persuasion; it is my intimate conviction; I feel it; sentiment consults nobody; the worse for him who does not agree with me—he is not a man, he is a monster in human shape." Such is the despotic tone of these decisions.

But, it may be asked, are there men so unreasonable as to dictate their particular sentiments as laws, and to arrogate to themselves the privilege of infallibility? What you call the *principle of sympathy and antipathy* is not a principle of reasoning; it is rather the negation, the annihilation of all principle. A true anarchy of ideas results from it; since every man having an equal right to give *his* sentiments as a universal rule, there will no longer be any common measure, no ultimate tribunal to which we can appeal.

Without doubt the absurdity of this principle is sufficiently manifest. No man, therefore, is bold enough to say openly, "I wish you to think as I do, without giving me the trouble to reason with you." Every one would revolt against a pretension so absurd. Therefore, recourse is had to diverse inventions of disguise. Despotism is veiled under some ingenious phrase. Of this the greater part of philosophical systems are a proof.

One man tells you that he has in himself something which has been given him to teach what is good and what is evil; and this he calls either his *conscience* or his *moral sense.* Then, working at his case, he decides such a thing to be good, such another to be bad. Why? Because my moral sense tells me so; because my conscience approves or disapproves it.

Another comes and the phrase changes. It is no longer the moral sense,—it is *common sense* which tells him what is good and what is bad. This common sense is a sense, he says, which belongs to everybody; but then he takes good care in speaking of everybody to make no account of those who do not think as he does.

Another tells you that this moral sense and this common sense are but dreams; that the *understanding* determines what is good and what is bad. His understanding tells him so and so; all good and wise men have just such an understanding as he has. As to those who do not think in the same way, it is a clear proof that their understandings are defective or corrupt.

Another tells you that he has an *eternal and immutable rule of right,* which rule commands this and forbids that; then he details to you his own particular sentiments, which you are obliged to receive as so many branches of the eternal rule of right.

You hear a multitude of professors, of jurists, of magistrates, of philosophers, who make the *law of nature* echo in your ears. They all dispute, it is true, upon every point of their system; but no matter— each one proceeds with the same confident intrepidity, and utters his opinions as so many chapters of the *law of nature*. The phrase is sometimes modified, and we find in its place, *natural right, natural equity, the rights of man,* etc.

One philosopher undertakes to build a moral system upon what he calls *truth;* according to him, the only evil in the world is lying. If you kill your father, you commit a crime, because it is a particular fashion of saying that he is not your father. Everything which this philosopher does not like, he disapproves under the pretext that it is a sort of falsehood—since it amounts to asserting that we ought to do what ought not to be done. . . .

To sum up—the *ascetic principle* attacks utility in front. The *principle of sympathy* neither rejects it nor admits it; it pays no attention to it; it floats at hazard between good and evil. The ascetic principle is so unreasonable, that its most senseless followers have never attempted to carry it out. The principle of sympathy and antipathy does not prevent its partisans from having recourse to the principle of utility. This last alone neither asks nor admits any exceptions. *Qui non sub me contra me;* that which is not under me is against me; such is its motto. According to this principle, to legislate is an affair of observation and calculation; according to the ascetics, it is an affair of fanaticism; according to the principle of sympathy and antipathy, it is a matter of humour, of imagination, of taste. The first method is adapted to philosophers; the second to monks; the third is the favourite of wits, of ordinary moralists, of men of the world, of the multitude.

## CHAPTER IV

### *Operation of These Principles Upon Legislation*

. . . The principle which has exercised the greatest influence upon governments, is that of sympathy and antipathy. In fact, we must refer to that principle all those specious objects which governments pursue, without having the general good for a single and independent aim; such as good morals, equality, liberty, justice, power, commerce, religion; objects respectable in themselves, and which ought to enter into the views of the legislator; but which too often lead him astray, because he regards them as ends, not as means. He substitutes them for public happiness, instead of making them subordinate to it.

Thus, a government, entirely occupied with wealth and commerce, looks upon society as a workshop, regards men only as productive machines, and cares little how much it torments them, provided it makes them rich. The customs, the exchanges, the stocks, absorb all its thoughts. It looks with indifference upon a multitude of evils which it might easily cure. It wishes only for a great production of the means of enjoyment, while it is constantly putting new obstacles in the way of enjoying.

Other governments esteem power and glory as the sole means of public good. Full of disdain for those states which are able to be happy in a peaceful security, they must have intrigues, negotiations, wars and conquests. They do not consider of what misfortunes this glory is composed, and how many victims these bloody triumphs require. The *éclat* of victory, the acquisition of a province, conceal from them the desolation of their country, and make them mistake the true end of government.

Many persons do not inquire if a state be well administered; if the laws protect property and persons; if the people are happy. What they require, without giving attention to anything else, is political liberty—that is, the most equal distribution which can be imagined of political power. Wherever they do not see the form of government to which they are attached, they see nothing but slaves; and if these pretended slaves are well satisfied with their condition, if they do not desire to change it, they despise and insult them. In their fanaticism they are always ready to stake all the happiness of a nation upon a civil war, for the sake of transporting power into the hands of those whom an invincible ignorance will not permit to use it, except for their own destruction. . . .

# CHAPTER VII

## *Pains and Pleasures Considered as Sanctions*

The will cannot be influenced except by motives; but when we speak of *motives* we speak of *pleasures* or *pain.* A being whom we could not effect either by painful or pleasurable emotions would be completely independent of us.

The pain or pleasure which is attached to a law form what is called its sanction. The laws of one state are not laws in another because they have no sanction there, no obligatory force.

Pleasures and pains may be distinguished into four classes:

1st. Physical.

2nd. Moral.

3rd. Political.

4th. Religious.

Consequently, when we come to consider pains and pleasures under the character of punishments and rewards, attached to certain rules of conduct, we may distinguish four sanctions.

1st. Those pleasures and pains which may be expected from the ordinary course of nature, acting by itself, without human intervention, compose the *natural* or *physical sanction.*

2nd. The pleasures or pains which may be expected from the action of our fellow-men, in virtue of their friendship or hatred, of their esteem or their contempt—in one word, of their spontaneous disposition towards us, compose the *moral sanction;* or it may be called the *popular sanction, sanction of public opinion, sanction of honour, sanction of the pains and pleasures of sympathy.*

3rd. The pleasures or pains which may be expected from the action of the magistrate, in virtue of the laws, compose the *political sanction;* it may also be called the *legal sanction.*

4th. The pleasures or pains which may be expected in virtue of the threats or promises of religion, compose the *religious sanction.*

A man's house is destroyed by fire. Is it in consequence of his imprudence?—It is a pain of the natural sanction. Is it by the sentence of a judge?—It is a pain of the political sanction. Is it by the malice of his neighbours?—It is a pain of the popular sanction. Is it supposed to be the immediate act of an offended Divinity?—In such a case it would be a pain of the religious sanction, or vulgarly speaking, a judgement of God.

It is evident from this example that the same sort of pains belong to all the sanctions. The only difference is in the circumstances which produce them.

This classification will be very useful in the course of this work. It is an easy and uniform nomenclature, absolutely necessary to distinguish and describe the different kinds of moral powers, those intellectual levers which constitute the machinery of the human heart.

These four sanctions do not act upon all men in the same manner, nor with the same degree of force. They are sometimes rivals, sometimes allies, and sometimes enemies. When they agree, they operate with an irresistible power; when they are in opposition, they mutually enfeeble each other; when they are rivals, they produce uncertainties and contradictions in the conduct of men.

Four bodies of laws may be imagined, corresponding to these four sanctions. The highest point of perfection would be reached if these four codes constituted but one. This perfection, however, is as yet far distant, though it may not be impossible to attain it. But the legislator ought always to recollect that he can operate directly only by means of the political sanction. The three others must necessarily be its rivals or its allies, its antagonists or its ministers. If he neglects them in his calculations, he will be deceived in his results; but if he makes them subservient to his views, he will gain an immense power. There is no chance of uniting them, except under the standard of utility.

The natural sanction is the only one which always acts; the only one which works of itself; the only one which is unchangeable in its principal characteristics. It insensibly draws all the others to it, corrects their deviations, and produces whatever uniformity there is in the sentiments and the judgments of men.

The popular sanction and the religious sanction are more variable, more dependant upon human caprices. Of the two, the popular sanction is more equal, more steady, and more constantly in accordance with the principle of utility. The force of the religious sanction is more unequal, more apt to change with times and individuals, more subject to dangerous deviations. It grows weak by repose, but revives by opposition.

In some respects the political sanction has the advantage of both. It acts upon all men with a more equal force; it is clearer and more precise in is precepts; it is surer and more exemplary in its operations; finally, it is more susceptible of being carried to perfection. Its progress has an immediate influence upon the progress of the other two; but it embraces only actions of a certain kind; it has not a sufficient hold upon the private conduct of individuals; it cannot proceed except upon proofs which it is often impossible to obtain; and secrecy, force, or stratagem are able to escape it. It thus appears, from considering what each of these sanctions can effect, and what they cannot, that neither ought to be rejected, but that all should be employed and directed towards the same end. They are like magnets, of which the virtue is destroyed when they are presented to each other by their contrary poles, while their power is doubled when they are united by the poles which correspond.

It may be observed, in passing, that the systems which have most divided men have been founded upon an exclusive preference given to one or the other of these sanctions. Each has had its partisans, who have wished to exalt it above the others. Each has had its enemies, who have sought to degrade it by showing its weak side, exposing its errors, and developing all the evils which have resulted from it, without making any mention of its good effects. Such is the true theory of all those paradoxes which elevate nature against society, politics against religion, religion against nature and government, and so on.

Each of these sanctions is susceptible of error, that is to say, of some applications contrary to the principle of utility. But by applying the nomenclature above explained, it is easy to indicate by a single word the seat of the evil. Thus, for example, the reproach which after the punishment of a criminal falls upon an innocent family is an error of the popular sanction. The offence of usury, that is, of receiving interest above the legal interest, is an error of the political sanction. Heresy and magic are errors of the religious sanction. Certain sympathies and antipathies are errors of the natural sanction. The first germ of mistake exists in some single sanction, whence it commonly spreads into the others. It is necessary, in all these cases, to discover the origin of the evil before we can select or apply the remedy.

## CHAPTER VIII

### *The Measure of Pleasures and Pains*

The sole object of the legislator is to increase pleasures and to prevent pains; and for this purpose he ought to be well acquainted with their respective values. As pleasures and pains are the only instruments which he employs, he ought carefully to study their power.

If we examine the *value* of a pleasure, considered in itself, and in relation to a single individual, we shall find that it depends upon four circumstances,—

1st. *Its intensity.*

2nd. *Its duration.*

3rd. *Its certainty.*

4th. *Its proximity.*

The value of a pain depends upon the same circumstances.

But it is not enough to examine the value of pleasures and pains as if they were isolated and independent. Pains and pleasures may have other pains and pleasures as their consequences. Therefore, if we wish to calculate the *tendency* of an act from which there results an immediate pain or pleasure, we must take two additional circumstances into the account, viz.—

5th. *Its productiveness.*

6th. *Its purity.*

A *productive pleasure* is one which is likely to be followed by other pleasures of the same kind.

A *productive pain* is one which is likely to be followed by other pains of the same kind.

A *pure pleasure* is one which is not likely to produce pains.

A *pure pain* is one which is not likely to produce pleasures.

When the calculation is to be made in relation to a collection of individuals, yet another element is necessary,—

7th. *Its extent.*

That is, the number of persons who are likely to find themselves affected by this pain or pleasure.

When we wish to value an action, we must follow in detail all the operations above indicated. These are the elements of moral calculation; and legislation thus becomes a matter of arithmetic. The *evil* produced is the outgo, the *good* which results is the income. The rules of this calculation are like those of any other. This is a slow method, but a sure one; while what is called sentiment is a prompt estimate, but apt to be deceptive. It is not necessary to recommence this calculation upon every occasion. When one has become familiar with the process; when he has acquired the justness of estimate which results from it; he can compare the sum of good and evil with so much promptitude as scarcely to be conscious of the steps of the calculation. It is thus that we perform many arithmetical calculations, almost without knowing it. The analytical method, in all its details, becomes essential, only when some new or complicated matter arises; when it is necessary to clear up some disputed point, or to demonstrate a truth to those who are yet unacquainted with it.

This theory of moral calculation, though never clearly explained, has always been followed in practice; at least, in every case where men have had clear ideas of their interest. What is it, for example, that makes up the value of a landed estate? Is it not the amount of pleasure to be derived from it? and does not this value vary according to the length of time for which the estate is to be enjoyed; according to the nearness or the distance of the moment when the

possession is to begin; according to the certainty or uncertainty of its being retained?

Errors, whether in legislation or the moral conduct of men, may be always accounted for by a mistake, a forgetfulness, or a false estimate of some one of these elements, in the calculation of good and evil.

# CHAPTER IX

## *Circumstances Which Affect Sensibility*

All causes of pleasure do not give the same pleasure to all; all causes of pain do not always produce the same pain. It is in this that *difference of sensibility* consists. This difference is in degree, or in kind: in degree, when the impression of a given cause upon many individuals is uniform, but unequal; in kind, when the same cause produces opposite sensations in different individuals.

This difference of sensibility depends upon certain circumstances which influence the physical or moral condition of individuals, and which, being changed, produce a corresponding change in their feelings. This is an experimental fact. Things do not affect us in the same manner in sickness and ill health, in plenty and in poverty, in infancy and old age. But a view so general is not sufficient; it is necessary to go deeper into the human heart. Lyonet wrote a quarto volume upon the anatomy of the caterpillar; morals are in need of an investigator as patient and philosophical. I have not courage to imitate Lyonet. I shall think it sufficient if I open a new point of view—if I suggest a surer method to those who wish to pursue this subject.

The foundation of the whole is *temperament,* or the original constitution. By this word I understand that radical and primitive disposition which attends us from our birth, and which depends upon physical organization, and the nature of the soul.

But although this radical constitution is the basis of all the rest, this basis lies so concealed that it is very difficult to get at it, so as to distinguish those varieties of sensibility which it produces from those which belong to other causes.

It is the business of the physiologist to distinguish these temperaments; to follow out their mixtures; and to trace their effects. But these grounds are as yet too little known to justify the moralist or legislator in founding anything upon them. . . .

## CHAPTER X

### Analysis of Political Good and Evil—How They Are Diffused Through Society

It is with government as with medicine; its only business is the choice of evils. Every law is an evil, for every law is an infraction of liberty. Government, I repeat it, has but the choice of evils. In making that choice, what ought to be the object of the legislator? He ought to be certain of two things: 1st, that in every case, the acts which he undertakes to prevent are really evils; and, 2nd, that these evils are greater than those which he employs to prevent them.

He has then two things to note—the evil of the offence, and the evil of the law; the evil of the malady, and the evil of the remedy.

An evil seldom comes alone. A portion of evil can hardly fall upon an individual, without spreading on every side, as from a centre. As it spreads, it takes different forms. We see an evil of one kind coming out of an evil of another kind; We even see evil coming out of good, and good out of evil. . . .

The propagation of good is less rapid and less sensible than that of evil. The seed of good is not so productive in hopes as the seed of evil is fruitful in alarms. But this difference is abundantly made up, for good is a necessary result of natural causes which operate always; while evil is produced only by accident, and at intervals.

Society is so constituted that, in labouring for our particular good, we labour also for the good of the whole. We cannot augment our own means of enjoyment without augmenting also the means of others. Two nations, like two individuals, grow rich by a mutual commerce; and all exchange is founded upon reciprocal advantages.

It is fortunate also that the effects of evil are not always evil. They often assume the contrary quality.

Thus, juridical punishments applied to offenses, although they produce an evil of the first order, are not generally regarded as evils, because they produce a good of the second order. They produce alarm and danger,—but for whom? Only for a class of evildoers, who are voluntary sufferers. Let them obey the laws, and they will be exposed neither to danger nor alarm.

We should never be able to subjugate, however imperfectly, the vast empire of evil, had we not learned the method of combatting one evil by another. It has been necessary to enlist auxiliaries among pains, to oppose other pains which attack us on every side. So, in the art of curing pains of another sort, poisons well applied have proved to be remedies.

## CHAPTER XII

### The Limits Which Separate Morals from Legislation

Morality in general is the art of directing the actions of men in such a way as to produce the greatest possible sum of good.

Legislation ought to have precisely the same object.

But although these two arts, or rather sciences, have the same end they differ greatly in extent. All actions, whether public or private, fall under the jurisdiction of morals. It is a guide which leads the individual, as it were, by the hand through all the details of his life, all his relations with his fellows. Legislation cannot do this; and, if it could, it ought not to exercise a continual interference and dictation over the conduct of men.

Morality commands each individual to do all that is advantageous to the community, his own personal advantages included. But there are many acts useful to the community which legislation ought not to command. There are also many injurious actions which it ought not to forbid, although morality does so. In a word, legislation has the same centre with morals, but it has not the same circumference.

There are two reasons for this difference: 1st. Legislation can have no direct influence upon the conduct of men, except by punishments. Now these punishments are so many evils, which are not justifiable, except so far as there results from them a greater sum of good. But, in many cases in which we might desire to strengthen a moral precept by a punishment, the evil of the punishment would be greater than the evil of the offence. The means necessary to carry the law into execution would be of a nature to spread through society a degree of alarm more injurious than the evil intended to be prevented.

2nd. Legislation is often arrested by the danger of overwhelming the innocent in seeking to punish the guilty. Whence comes this danger? From the difficulty of defining an offence, and giving a clear and precise idea of it. For example, hardheartedness, ingratitude, perfidy, and other vices which the popular sanction punishes, cannot come under the power of the laws, unless they are defined as exactly as theft, homicide, or perjury.

But, the better to distinguish the true limits of morals and legislation, it will be well to refer to the common classification of moral duties.

Private morality regulates the actions of men, either in that part of their conduct in which they alone are interested, or in that which may affect the interests of others. The actions which affect a man's individual interest compose a class called, perhaps improperly, *duties to ourselves;* and the quality or disposition manifested in the accomplishment of those duties receives the name of *prudence.* That part of conduct which relates to others composes a class of actions called *duties to others.* Now there are two ways of consulting the happiness of others: the one negative, abstaining from diminishing it; the other positive, labouring to augment it. The first constitutes *probity;* the second is *beneficence.*

Morality upon these three points needs the aid of the law; but not in the same degree, nor in the same manner.

I. The rules of prudence are almost always sufficient of themselves. If a man fails in what regards his particular private interest, it is not his will which is in fault, it is his understanding. If he does wrong, it can only be through mistake. The fear of hurting himself is a motive of repression sufficiently strong;

it would be useless to add to it the fear of an artificial pain.

Does any one object, that facts show the contrary? That excesses of play, those of intemperance, the illicit intercourse between the sexes, attended so often by the greatest dangers, are enough to prove that individuals have not always sufficient prudence to abstain from what hurts them?

Confining myself to a general reply, I answer, in the first place, that, in the greater part of these cases, punishment would be so easily eluded, that it would be inefficacious; secondly, that the evil produced by the penal law would be much beyond the evil of the offence.

Suppose, for example, that a legislator should feel himself authorized to undertake the extirpation of drunkenness and fornication by direct laws. He would have to begin by a multitude of regulations. The first inconvenience would therefore be a complexity of laws. The easier it is to conceal these vices, the more necessary it would be to resort to severity of punishment, in order to destroy by the terror of examples the constantly recurring hope of impunity. This excessive rigour of laws forms a second inconvenience not less grave than the first. The difficulty of procuring proofs would be such that it would be necessary to encourage informers, and to entertain an army of spies. This necessity forms a third inconvenience, greater than either of the others. Let us compare the results of good and evil. Offenses of this nature, if that name can be properly given to imprudences, produce no alarm; but the pretended remedy would spread a universal terror; innocent or guilty, every one would fear for himself or his connexions; suspicions and accusations would render society dangerous; we should fly from it; we should involve ourselves in mystery and concealment; we should shun all the disclosures of confidence. Instead of suppressing one vice, the laws would produce other vices, new and more dangerous.

It is true that example may render certain excesses contagious; and that an evil which would be almost imperceptible, if it acted only upon a small number of individuals, may become important by its extent. All that the legislator can do in reference to offenses of this kind is, to submit them to some slight punishment in cases of scandalous notoriety. This will be sufficient to give them a taint of illegality, which will excite the popular sanction against them.

It is in cases of this kind that legislators have governed too much. Instead of trusting to the prudence of individuals, they have treated them like children, or slaves. They have suffered themselves to be carried away by the same passion which has influenced the founders of religious orders, who, to signalize their authority, and through a littleness of spirit, have held their subjects in the most abject dependence, and have traced for them, day by day, and moment by moment, their occupations, their food, their rising up, their lying down, and all the petty details of their life. There are celebrated codes, in which are found a multitude of clogs of this sort; there are useless restraints upon marriage; punishments decreed against celibacy; sumptuary laws regulating the fashion of dress, the expense of festivals, the furniture of houses, and the ornaments of women; there are numberless details about ailments, permitted or forbidden; about ablutions of such or such a kind; about the purifications which health or cleanliness require; and a thousand similar puerilities, which add, to all the inconveniences of useless restraint, that of besotting the people, by covering these absurdities with a veil of mystery, to disguise their folly.

Yet more unhappy are the States in which it is attempted to maintain by penal laws a uniformity of religious opinions. The choice of their religion ought to be referred entirely to the prudence of individuals. If they are persuaded that their eternal happiness depends upon a certain form of worship or a certain belief, what can a legislator oppose to an interest so great? It is not necessary to insist upon this truth—it is generally acknowledged; but, in tracing the boundaries of legislation, I cannot forget those which it is the most important not to overstep.

As a general rule, the greatest possible latitude should be left to individuals, in all cases in which they can injure none but themselves, for they are the best judges of their own interests. If they deceive themselves, it is to be supposed that the moment they

discover their error they will alter their conduct. The power of the law need interfere only to prevent them from injuring each other. It is there that restraint is necessary; it is there that the application of punishments is truly useful, because the rigour exercised upon an individual becomes in such a case the security of all.

II. It is true that there is a natural connection between prudence and probity; for our own interest, well understood, will never leave us without motives to abstain from injuring our fellows. . . .

A man enlightened as to his own interest will not indulge himself in a secret offence through fear of contracting a shameful habit, which sooner or later will betray him; and because the having secrets to conceal from the prying curiosity of mankind leaves in the heart a sediment of disquiet, which corrupts every pleasure. All he can acquire at the expense of security cannot make up for the loss of that; and, if he desires a good reputation, the best guarantee he can have for it is his own esteem.

But, in order that an individual should perceive this connection between the interests of others and his own, he needs an enlightened spirit and a heart free from seductive passions. The greater part of men have neither sufficient light, sufficient strength of mind, nor sufficient moral sensibility to place their honesty above the aid of the laws. The legislator must supply the feebleness of this natural interest by adding to it an artificial interest, more steady and more easily perceived.

More yet. In many cases morality derives its existence from the law; that is, to decide whether the action is morally good or bad, it is necessary to know whether the laws permit or forbid it. It is so of what concerns property. A manner of selling or acquiring, esteemed dishonest in one country, would be irreproachable in another. It is the same with offenses against the state. The state exists only by law, and it is impossible to say what conduct in this behalf morality requires of us before knowing what the legislator has decreed. There are countries where it is an offence to enlist into the service of a foreign power, and others in which such a service is lawful and honourable.[3]

III. As to beneficence some distinctions are necessary. The law may be extended to general objects, such as the care of the poor; but, for details, it is necessary to depend upon private morality. Beneficence has its mysteries, and loves best to employ itself upon evils so unforeseen or so secret that the law cannot reach them. Besides, it is to individual free will that benevolence owes its energy. If the same acts were commanded, they would no longer be benefits, they would lose their attractions and their essence. It is morality and especially religion, which here form the necessary complement to legislation, and the sweetest tie of humanity.

However, instead of having done too much in this respect, legislators have not done enough. They ought to erect into an offence the refusal or the omission of a service to humanity when it would be easy to render it, and when some distinct ill clearly results from the refusal; such, for example, as abandoning a wounded man in a solitary road without seeking any assistance for him; not giving information to a man who is ignorantly meddling with poisons; not reaching out the hand to one who has fallen into a ditch from which he cannot extricate himself; in these, and other similar cases, could any fault be found with a punishment, exposing the delinquent to a certain degree of shame, or subjecting him to a pecuniary responsibility for the evil which he might have prevented?

I will add, that legislation might be extended further than it is in relation to the interests of the inferior animals. I do not approve the laws of the Hindus on this subject. There are good reasons why animals should serve for the nourishment of man, and for destroying those which incommode us. We are the better for it, and they are not the worse; for they have not, as we have, long and cruel anticipations of the future; and the death which they receive at our hands may always be rendered less painful than that which awaits them in the inevitable course of nature. But what can be said to justify the useless torments they are made to suffer; the cruel caprices which are exercised upon them? Among the many reasons which might be given for making criminal such gratuitous cruelties, I confine myself to that which relates to my subject. It is a means of cultivating a general senti-

ment of benevolence, and of rendering men more mild; or at least of preventing that brutal depravity, which, after fleshing itself upon animals, presently demands human suffering to satiate its appetite.[4]

# CHAPTER XIII

## *False Methods of Reasoning on the Subject of Legislation*

It has been the object of this introduction to give a clear idea of the principle of utility, and of the method of reasoning conformable to that principle. There results from it a legislative logic, which can be summed up in a few words. What is it to offer a *good reason* with respect to a law? It is to allege the good or evil which the law tends to produce: so much good, so many arguments in its favour; so much evil, so many arguments against it; remembering all the time that good and evil are nothing else than pleasure and pain.

What is it to offer a *false reason?* It is the alleging for or against a law something else than its good or evil effects.

Nothing can be more simple, yet nothing is more new. It is not the principle of utility which is new; on the contrary, that principle is necessarily as old as the human race. All the truth there is in morality, all the good there is in the laws, emanate from it; but utility has often been followed by instinct, while it has been combatted by argument. If in books of legislation it throws out some sparks here and there, they are quickly extinguished in the surrounding smoke. BECCARIA is the only writer who deserves to be noted as an exception; yet even in his work there is some reasoning drawn from false sources.

It is upwards of two thousand years since Aristotle undertook to form, under the title of *Sophisms,* a complete catalogue of the different kinds of false reasoning. This catalogue, improved by the information which so long an interval might furnish, would here have its place and its uses. But such an undertaking would carry me too far. I shall be content with presenting some heads of error on the subject of legislation. By means of such a contrast, the principle of utility will be put into a clearer light.

I. *Antiquity Is Not a Reason.* The antiquity of a law may create a prejudice in its favour; but in itself, it is not a reason. If the law in question has contributed to the public good, the older it is, the easier it will be to enumerate its good effects, and to prove its utility by a direct process.

2. *The Authority of Religion Is Not a Reason.* Of late, this method of reasoning has gone much out of fashion, but till recently its use was very extensive. The work of Algernon Sidney is full of citation from the Old Testament, and he finds there the foundation of a system of Democracy, as Bossuet had found the principle of absolute power. Sidney wished to combat the partisans of divine right and passive obedience with their own weapons.

If we suppose that a law emanates from the Deity, we suppose that it emanates from supreme wisdom, and supreme bounty. Such a law, then, can only have for its object the most eminent utility; and this utility, put into a clear light, will always be an ample justification of the law.

3. *Reproach of Innovation Is Not a Reason.* To reject innovation is to reject progress; in what condition should we be, if that principle had been always followed? All which exists had had a beginning; all which is established has been innovation. Those very persons who approve a law today because it is ancient, would have opposed it as new when it was first introduced.

4. *An Arbitrary Definition Is Not a Reason.* Nothing is more common, among jurists and political writers, than to base their reasonings, and even to write long works, upon a foundation of purely arbitrary definitions. This artifice consists in taking a work in a particular sense, foreign from its common usage; in employing that word as no one ever employed it before; and in puzzling the reader by an appearance of profoundness and of mystery.

Montesquieu himself has fallen into this fault in the very beginning of his work. Wishing to give a definition of law, he proceeds from metaphor to metaphor; he brings together the most discordant objects—the Divinity, the material world, superior intelligence, beasts and men. We learn, at last, that *laws are relations; and eternal relations.* Thus the definition is more obscure than the thing to be defined. The word *law*, in its proper sense, excites in every mind a tolerably clear idea, the word *relation* excites no idea at all. The word *law*, in its figurative sense, produces nothing, but equivocations; and Montesquieu, who ought to have dissipated the darkness has only increased it.

It is the character of a false definition, that it can only be employed in a particular way. That author, a little further on (ch. iii.), gives another definition. *Law in general,* he says, *is human reason, in so far as it governs all the people of the earth.* These terms are more familiar; but no clear idea results from them. Is it the fact, that so many laws, contradictory, ferocious, or absurd, and in a perpetual state of change, are always *human reason*? It would seem that reason, so far from being the law, is often in opposition to it.

This first chapter of Montesquieu has given occasion to an abundance of nonsense. The brain has been racked in search of metaphysical mysteries, where none in fact exist. Even Beccaria has suffered himself to be carried away by this obscure notion of *relations.* To interrogate a man in order to know whether he is innocent or guilty, is to force him, he tells us, to accuse himself. To this procedure he objects; and why? because, as he says, it is to *confound all relations.*[5] But what does that mean? To enjoy, to suffer, to cause enjoyment, to cause suffering: those are expressions which I understand; but to follow relations and to confound relations, is what I do not understand at all. These abstract terms do not excite any idea in my mind; they do not awaken any sentiment. I am absolutely indifferent about *relations*:—*pleasures* and *pains* are what interest me.

Rousseau has not been satisfied with the definition of Montesquieu. He has given his own, which he announces as a great discovery. *Law*, he says, *is the expression of the general will.* There are, then, no laws except where the people have spoken in a body. There is no law except in an absolute democracy. Rousseau has suppressed, by this supreme decree, all existing laws; and at the same time he has deprived of the possibility of existence all those which are likely to be made hereafter,—the legislation of the republic of San Marino alone excepted.

5. *Metaphors Are Not Reasons.* I mean either metaphor properly so called, or allegory, used at first for illustration or ornament, but afterwards made the basis of an argument.

Blackstone, so great an enemy of all reform, that he has gone so far as to find fault with the introduction of the English language into the reports of cases decided by the courts, has rejected no means of inspiring his readers with the same prejudice. He represents the law as a castle, as a fortress, which cannot be altered without being weakened. I allow that he does not advance this metaphor as an argument; but why does he employ it? To gain possession of the imagination; to prejudice his readers against every idea of reform; to excite in them an artificial fear of all innovation in the laws. There remains in the mind a false image, which produces the same effect with false reasoning. He ought to have recollected that this allegory might be employed against himself. When they see the law turned into a castle, is it not natural for ruined suitors to represent it as a castle inhabited by robbers?

A man's house, say the English, is his castle. This poetical expression is certainly no reason; for if a man's house be his castle by night, why not by day? If it is an inviolable asylum for the owner, why is it not so for every person whom he chooses to receive there? The course of justice is sometimes interrupted in England by this puerile notion of liberty. Criminals seem to be looked upon like foxes; they are suffered to have their burrows, in order to increase the sports of the chase.

A church in Catholic countries is the *House of God.* This metaphor has served to establish asylums for criminals. It would be a mark of disrespect for the Divinity to seize by force those who had taken refuge in his house.

The *balance of trade* has produced a multitude of reasonings founded upon metaphor. It has been imagined that in the course of mutual commerce nations rose and sank like the scales of a balance loaded with unequal weights; people have been terribly alarmed at what appeared to them a want of equilibrium; for it has been supposed that what one nation gained the other must lose, as if a weight had been transferred from one scale to another.

The word *mother-country* has produced a great number of prejudices and false reasonings in all questions concerning colonies and the parent state. Duties have been imposed upon colonies, and they have been accused of offenses, founded solely upon the metaphor of their filial dependence.

6. *A Fiction Is Not a Reason.* I understand by fiction an assumed fact notoriously false, upon which one reasons as if it were true. . . .

Blackstone, in the seventh chapter of his first book, in speaking of the royal authority, has given himself up to all the puerility of fiction. The king, he tells us, is everywhere present; he can do no wrong; he is immortal.

These ridiculous paradoxes, the fruits of servility, so far from furnishing just ideas of the prerogatives of royalty, only serve to dazzle, to mislead, and to give to reality itself an air of fable and of prodigy. But these fictions are not mere sparkles of imagination. He makes them the foundation of many reasonings. He employs them to explain certain royal prerogatives, which might be justified by very good arguments, without perceiving how much the best cause is injured by attempting to prop it up by falsehoods. *The judges,* he tells us, *are mirrors, in which the image of the king is reflected.* What puerility! Is it not exposing to ridicule the very objects which he designs to render the most respectable?

But there are fictions more bold and more important, which have played a great part in politics, and which have produced celebrated works; these are *contracts.*

The *Leviathan* of Hobbes, a work now-a-days but little known, and detested through prejudice and at second-hand as a defence of despotism, is an attempt to base all political society upon a pretended contract between the people and the sovereign. The people by this contract have renounced their natural liberty, which produced nothing but evil; and have deposited all power in the hands of the prince. All opposing wills have been united in his, or rather annihilated by it. That which he wills is taken to be the will of all his subjects. When David brought about the destruction of Uriah, he acted in that matter with Uriah's consent, for Uriah had consented to all that David might command. The prince, according to this system, might sin against God, but he could not sin against man, because all his actions proceeded from the general consent. It was impossible to entertain the idea of resisting him, because such an idea implied the contradiction of resisting one's self.

Locke, whose name is as dear to the friends of liberty as that of Hobbes is odious, has also fixed the basis of government upon a contract. He agrees that there is a contract between the prince and the people; but according to him the prince takes an engagement to govern according to the laws, and for the public good; while the people, on their side, take an engagement of obedience so long, as the prince remains faithful to the conditions in virtue of which he receives the crown.

Rousseau rejects with indignation the idea of this bilateral contract between the prince and the people. He has imagined a *social contract,* by which all are bound to all, and which is the only legitimate basis of government. Society exists only by virtue of this free convention of associates.

These three systems—so directly opposed—agree, however, in beginning the theory of politics with a fiction, for these three contracts are equally fictitious. They exist only in the imagination of their authors. Not only we find no trace of them in history, but everywhere we discover proofs to the contrary. . . .

It is not necessary to make the happiness of the human race dependent on a fiction. It is not necessary to erect the social pyramid upon a foundation of sand, or upon a clay which slips from beneath it. Let us leave such trifling to children; men ought to speak the language of truth and reason.

The true political tie is the immense interest which men have in maintaining a government. Without a government there can be no security, no domestic enjoyments, no property, no industry. It is in this fact

that we ought to seek the basis and the reason of all governments, whatever may be their origin and their form; it is by comparing them with their object that we can reason with solidity upon their rights and their obligations, without having recourse to pretended contracts which can only serve to produce interminable disputes.

7. *Fancy Is Not a Reason.* Nothing is more common than to say, reason decides, eternal reason orders, etc. But what is this reason? If it is not a distinct view of good or evil, it is mere fancy; it is a despotism, which announces nothing but the interior persuasion of him who speaks. Let us see upon what foundation a distinguished jurist has sought to establish the paternal authority. A man of ordinary good sense would not see much difficulty in that question; but your learned men find a mystery everywhere.

"The right of a father over his children," says Cocceiji, "is founded in reason;—for, 1st, Children are born in a house, of which the father is the master; 2nd, They are born in a family of which he is the chief; 3rd, They are of his seed, and a part of his body." These are the reasons from which he concludes, among other things, that a man of forty ought not to marry without the consent of a father, who in the course of nature must by that time be in his dotage. What there is common to these three reasons is, that none of them has any relation to the interests of the parties. The author consults neither the welfare of the father nor that of the children.

*The right of a father* is an improper phrase. The question is not of an unlimited, nor of an indivisible right. There are many kinds of rights which may be granted or refused to a father, each for particular reasons. . . .

And here we may remark an essential difference between false principles and the true one. The principle of utility, applying itself only to the interests of the parties, bends to circumstances, and accommodates itself to every case. False principles, being founded upon things which have nothing to do with individual interests, would be inflexible if they were consistent. Such is the character of this pretended right founded upon birth. The son naturally belongs to the father, because the matter of which the son is formed once circulated in the father's veins. No matter how unhappy he renders his son;—it is impossible to annihilate his right, because we cannot make his son cease to be his son. The corn of which your body is made formerly grew in my field; how is it that you are not my slave?

8. *Antipathy and Sympathy Are Not Reasons.* Reasoning by antipathy is most common upon subjects connected with penal law; for we have antipathies against actions reputed to be crimes; antipathies against individuals reputed to be criminals; antipathies against the ministers of justice; antipathies against such and such punishments. This false principle has reigned like a tyrant throughout this vast province of law. Beccaria first dared openly to attack it. His arms were of celestial temper; but if he did much towards destroying the usurper, he did very little towards the establishment of a new and more equitable rule.

It is the principle of antipathy which leads us to speak of offenses as *deserving* punishment. It is the corresponding principle of sympathy which leads us to speak of certain action as *meriting* reward. This word *merit* can only lead to passion and to error. It is *effects,* good or bad, which we ought alone to consider.

But when I say that *antipathies and sympathies are no reason,* I mean those of legislator; for the antipathies and sympathies of the people may be reasons, and very powerful ones. However odd or pernicious a religion, a law, a custom may be, it is of no consequence, so long as the people are attached to it. To take away an enjoyment or a hope, chimerical though it may be, is to do the same injury as if we took away a real hope, a real enjoyment. In such a case the pain of a single individual becomes, by sympathy, the pain of all. Thence results a crowd of evils; antipathy against a law which wounds the general prejudice; antipathy against the whole code of that law is a part; antipathy against the government which carries the laws into execution; a disposition not to aid in their execution; a disposition secretly to oppose it; a disposition to oppose it openly and by

force; a disposition to destroy a government which sets itself in opposition to the popular will—all the evils produced by those offences, which, in a collective shape, form that sad compound called *rebellion* or *civil war*—all the evils produced by the punishments which are resorted to as a means of putting a stop to those offences. Such is the succession of fatal consequences which are always ready to arise from fancies and prejudices violently opposed. The legislator ought to yield to the violence of a current which carries away everything that obstructs it. But let us observe, that in such a case, the fancies themselves are not the reason that determines the legislator; his reason is the evils which threaten to grow out of an opposition to those fancies.

But ought the legislator to be a slave to the fancies of those whom he governs? No. Between an imprudent opposition and a servile compliance there is a middle path, honourable and safe. It is to combat these fancies with the only arms that can conquer them—example and instruction. He must enlighten the people, he must address himself to the public reason; he must give time for error to be unmasked. Sound reasons, clearly set forth, are of necessity stronger than false ones. But the legislator ought not to show himself too openly in these instructions, for fear of compromising himself with the public ignorance. Indirect means will better answer his end.

It is to be observed, however, that too much deference for prejudices is a more common fault than the contrary excess. The best projects of laws are for ever stumbling against this common objection— "Prejudice is opposed to it; the people will be offended!" But how is that known? How has public opinion been consulted? What is its organ? Have the whole people but one uniform notion on this subject? Have all the individuals of the community the same sentiment, including perhaps nine out of ten, who never heard the subject spoken of? Besides, if the people are in error, are they compelled always to remain so? Will not an influx of light dissipate the darkness which produces error? Can we expect the people to possess sound knowledge, while it is yet unattained by their legislators, by those who are regarded as the wise men of the land? Have there not been examples of other nations who have come out of similar ignorance, and where triumphs have been achieved over the same obstacles?

After all, popular prejudice serves oftener as a pretext than as a motive. It is a convenient cover for the weakness of statesmen. The ignorance of the people is the favourite argument of pusillanimity and of indolence; while the real motives are prejudices from which the legislators themselves have not been able to get free. The name of the people is falsely used to justify their leaders.

9. *Begging the Question Is Not a Reason.* The petito principii, or begging the question, is one of the sophisms which is noted by Aristotle; but it is a Proteus which conceals itself artfully, and is reproduced under a thousand forms.

Begging the question, or rather assuming the question, consists in making use of the very proposition in dispute, as though it were already proved.

This false procedure insinuates itself into morals and legislation, under the disguise of *sentimental* or *impassioned* terms; that is, terms which, beside their principle sense, carry with them an accessory idea of praise or blame. Neuter terms are those which simply express the thing in question, without any attending presumption of good or evil; without introducing any foreign idea of blame or approbation.

Now it is to be observed that an impassioned term envelops a proposition not expressed, but understood, which always accompanies its employment, though in general unperceived by those who employ it. This concealed proposition implies either blame or praise; but the implication is always vague and undetermined.

Do I desire to connect an idea of utility with a term which commonly conveys an accessory idea of blame? I shall seem to advance a paradox, and to contradict myself. For example, should I say that such a piece of luxury is a good thing? The proposition astonishes those who are accustomed to attach to this word luxury a sentiment of disapprobation.

How shall I be able to examine this particular point without awakening a dangerous association? I must have recourse to a neuter word; I must say, for example, *such a manner of spending one's revenue* is good. This turn of expression runs counter to no prejudice, and permits an impartial examination of the object in question. When Helvetius advanced the idea that all actions have interest for their motive, the public cried out against his doctrine without stopping to understand it. Why? Because the word *interest* has an odious sense; a common acceptation, in which it seems to exclude every motive of pure attachment and of benevolence.

How many reasonings upon political subjects are founded upon nothing but impassioned terms! People suppose they are giving a reason for a law, when they say that it is conformable to the principles of monarchy or of democracy. But that meant nothing. If there are persons in whose minds these words are associated with an idea of approbation, there are others who attach contrary ideas to them. Let these two parties begin to quarrel, the dispute will never come to an end, except through the weariness of the combatants. For, before beginning a true examination, we must renounce these impassioned terms, and calculate the effects of the proposed law in good and evil.

Blackstone admires in the British constitution the combination of the three forms of government; and he hence concludes that it must possess the collected good qualities of monarchy, aristocracy, and democracy. How happened it that he did not perceive, that without changing his premises, a conclusion might be drawn from them, diametrically opposite, yet equally just; to wit, that the British constitution must unite all the particular *faults* of democracy, aristocracy, and monarchy?

To the word *independence,* there are attached certain accessory ideas of dignity and virtue; to the word *dependence,* accessory ideas of inferiority and corruption. Hence it is that the panegyrists of the British constitution admire the *independence* of the three powers of which the legislature is composed. This, in their eyes, is the masterpiece of politics; the happiest trait in that whole scheme of government. On the other side, those who would detract from the merits of that constitution, are always insisting upon the actual *dependence* of one or the other of its branches. Neither the praise nor the censure contain any reasons.

As to the fact, the pretended independence does not exist. The king and the greater part of the lords have a direct influence upon the election of the House of Commons. The king has the power of dissolving that House at any moment; a power of no little efficacy. The king exercises a direct influence by honourable and lucrative employments, which he gives or takes away at pleasure. On the other side, the king is dependent upon the two Houses, and particularly upon the Commons, since he cannot maintain himself without money and troops,—two principal and essential matters which are wholly under the control of the representatives of the people. What pretence has the House of Lords to be called independent, while the king can augment its number at pleasure, and change the vote in his favour by the creation of new lords; exercising too, as he does, an additional influence on the temporal peers, by the prospect of advancement in the ranks of the peerage; and on the bishops, by the bait of ecclesiastical promotion?

Instead of reasoning upon a deceptive word, let us consider effects. It is the reciprocal dependence of these three powers which produces their agreement; which subjects them to fixed rules, which gives them a steady and systematic operation. Hence the necessity of mutual respect, attention, concession, and moderation. If they were absolutely independent, there would be continual shocks between them. It would often be necessary to appeal to force; and the result would be a state of anarchy.

I cannot refrain from giving two other examples of this error of reasoning, founded upon the misuse of terms.

If we attempt a theory upon the subject of *national presentation,* in following out all that appears to be a natural consequence of that abstract idea, we come at last to the conclusion that *universal suffrage* ought to be established; and to the additional conclusion that the representatives ought to be re-chosen as frequently as possible, in order that the national representation may deserve to be esteemed such.

In deciding these same questions according to the principle of utility, it will not do to reason upon

words; we must look only at effects. In the election of a legislative assembly, the right of suffrage should not be allowed except to those who are esteemed by the nation fit to exercise it; for a choice made by men who do not possess the national confidence will weaken the confidence of the nation in the assembly so chosen.

Men who would be thought fit to be electors, are those who cannot be presumed to possess political integrity, and a sufficient degree of knowledge. Now we cannot presume upon the political integrity of those whom want exposes to the temptation of selling themselves; nor of those who have no fixed abode; nor of those who have been found guilty in the courts of justice of certain offenses forbidden by the law. We cannot presume a sufficient degree of knowledge in women, whom their domestic condition withdraws from the conduct of public affairs; in children and adults beneath a certain age; in those who are deprived by their proverty of the first elements of education, etc. etc.

It is according to these principles, and others like them, that we ought to fix the conditions necessary for becoming an elector; and it is in like manner, upon the advantages and disadvantages of frequent elections, without paying any attention to arguments drawn from abstract terms, that we ought to reason in establishing the duration of a legislative assembly.

The last example I shall give will be taken from *contracts:* I mean those political fictions to which this name has been applied by their authors.

When Locke and Rousseau reason upon these pretended contracts; when they affirm that the social or political contract includes such and such a clause, can they prove it otherwise than by the general utility which is supposed to result from it? Grant that this contract which has never been reduced to writing is, however, in full existence. On what depends all its force? It is not upon its utility? Why ought we to fulfil our engagements? Because the faith of promises is the basis of society. It is for the advantage of all that the promises of every individiual should be faithfully observed. There would no longer be any security among men, no commerce, no confidence;—it would be necessary to go back to the woods, if engagements did not possess an obligatory force. It is the same with these political contracts. It is their utility which makes them binding. When they become injurious, they lose their force. If a king had taken an oath to render his subjects unhappy, would such an engagement be valid? If the people were sworn to obey him at all events, would they be bound to suffer themselves to be exterminated by a Nero or a Caligula, rather than violate their promise? If there resulted from the contract effects universally injurious, could there be any sufficient reason for maintaining it? It cannot be denied, then, that the validity of a contract is at bottom only a question of utility—a little wrapped up, a little disguised, and, in consequence, more susceptible of false interpretations.

10. *An Imaginary Law Is Not a Reason.* Natural law, natural rights are two kinds of fictions or metaphors, which play so great a part in books of legislation that they deserve to be examined by themselves.

The primitive sense of the word *law,* and the ordinary meaning of the word, is—the will or command of a legislator. The *law of nature* is a figurative expression, in which nature is represented as a being; and such and such a disposition is attributed to her, which is figuratively called a law. In this sense, all the general inclinations of men, all those which appear to exist independently of human societies, and from which must proceed the establishment of political and civil law, are called *laws of nature.* This is the true sense of the phrase.

But this is not the way in which it is understood. Authors have taken it in a direct sense; as if there had been a real code of natural laws. They appeal to these laws; they cite them, and they oppose them, clause by clause, to the enactments of legislators. They do not see that these natural laws are laws of their own invention; that they are all at odds among themselves as to the contents of this pretended code; that they affirm without proof; that systems are as numerous as authors; and that, in reasoning in this manner, it is necessary to be always beginning anew, because every one can advance what he pleases touching laws which are only imaginary, and so keep on disputing for ever.

What is natural to man is sentiments of pleasure or pain, what are called inclinations. But to call these sentiments and these inclinations laws, is to introduce a false and dangerous idea. It is to set language in opposition to itself; for it is necessary to make *laws* precisely for the purpose of restraining these inclinations. Instead of regarding them as laws, they must be submitted to laws. It is against the strongest natural inclinations that it is necessary to have laws the most repressive. If there were a law of nature which directed all men towards their common good, laws would be useless; it would be employing a creeper to uphold an oak; it would be kindling a torch to add light to the sun.

Blackstone, in speaking of the obligation of parents to provide for the support of their children, says, "that it is a principle of natural law, a duty imposed by nature itself, and by the proper act of the parents in bringing the children into the world." Montesquieu, he adds, "observes with reason, that the natural obligation of the father to support his children, is what has caused the establishment of marriage, which points out the person who ought to fulfill this obligation" (Book i, Chap. 16).

Parents *are inclined* to support their children; parents *ought* to support their children; these are two distinct propositions. The first does not suppose the second; the second does not suppose the first. There are, without doubt, the strongest reasons for imposing upon parents the obligation to bring up their children. Why have not Blackstone and Montesquieu mentioned those reasons? Why do they refer us to what they call the law of nature? What is this law of nature, which needs to be propped up by a secondary law from another legislator? If this natural obligation exists, as Montesquieu says it does, far from serving as the foundation of marriage, it proves its inutility,—at least for the end which he assigns. One of the objects of marriage is, precisely to supply the insufficiency of natural affection. It is designed to convert into obligation that inclination of parents, which would not always be sufficiently strong to surmount the pains and embarrassments of education.

Men are very well disposed to provide for their own support. It has not been necessary to make laws to oblige them to that. If the disposition of parents to provide for the support of their children had been constantly and universally as strong, legislators never would have thought of turning it into an obligation.

The exposure of infants, so common in ancient Greece, is still practised in China, and to a greater extent. To abolish this practice, would it not be necessary to allege other reasons besides this pretended law of nature, which here is evidently at fault?

The word *rights,* the same as the word *law,* has two senses; the one a proper sense, the other a metaphorical sense. *Rights,* properly so called, are the creatures of *law* properly so called, real laws give birth to real rights. *Natural rights* are the creatures of natural law; they are a metaphor which derives its origin from another metaphor.

What there is natural in men is means,—faculties. But to call these means, these faculties, *natural rights,* is again to put language in opposition to itself. For *rights* are established to insure the exercise of means and faculties. The right is the *guarantee;* the faculty is the thing guaranteed. How can we understand each other with a language which confounds under the same term things so different? Where would be the nomenclature of the arts, if we gave to the *mechanic* who makes an article the same name as to the article itself?

Real rights are always spoken of in a legal sense; natural rights are often spoken of in a sense that may be called anti-legal. When it is said, for example, that *law cannot avail against natural rights,* the word *rights* is employed in a sense above the law; for, in this use of it, we acknowledge rights which attack the law; which overturn it, which annul it. In this anti-legal sense, the word *right* is the greatest enemy of reason, and the most terrible destroyer of governments.

There is no reasoning with fanatics, armed with *natural rights,* which each one understands as he pleases, and applies as he sees fit; of which nothing can be yielded, nor retrenched; which are inflexible, at the same time that they are unintelligible; which are consecrated as dogmas, from which it is a crime to vary. Instead of examining laws by their effects, instead of judging them as good or bad, they consider

them in relation to these pretended natural rights; that is to say, they substitute for the reasoning of experience the chimeras of their own imaginations.

This is not a harmless error; it passes from speculation into practice. "Those laws must be obeyed, which are accordant with nature; the others are null in fact; and instead of obeying them, they ought to be resisted. The moment natural rights are attacked, every good citizen ought to rouse up in their defence. These rights, evidence in themselves, do not need to be proved; it is sufficient to declare them. How prove what is evident already? To doubt implies a want of sense, or a fault of intellect," &c.

But not to be accused of gratuitously ascribing such seditious maxims to these inspired politicians of nature, I shall cite a passage from Blackstone, directly to the point; and I choose Blackstone, because he is, of all writers, the one who has shown the most profound respect for the authority of governments. In speaking of these pretended laws of nature, and of the laws of revelation, he says: "Human laws must not be permitted to contradict these; if a human law commands a thing forbidden by the natural or divine law, we are bound to transgress that human law," &c. (1 Comm. p. 43).

Is not this arming every fanatic against all governments? In the immense variety of ideas respecting natural and Divine law, cannot some reason be found for resisting all human laws? Is there a single state which can maintain itself a day, if each individual holds himself bound in conscience to resist the laws, whenever they are not conformed to his particular ideas of natural or Divine law? What a cut-throat scene of it we should have between all the interpreters of the code of nature, and all the interpreters of the law of God!

"The pursuit of happiness is a natural right." The pursuit of happiness is certainly a natural inclination; but can it be declared to be a right?—That depends on the way in which it is pursued. The assassin pursues his happiness, or what he esteems such, by committing an assassination. Has he a right to do so? If not, why declare that he has? What tendency is there in such a declaration to render men more happy or more wise?

Turgot was a great man; but he had adopted the general opinion without examining it. Inalienable and natural rights were the despotism or the dogmatism which he wished to exercise, without himself perceiving it. If he saw no reason to doubt a proposition; if he judged it evidently true; he referred it, without going further, to natural right, to eternal justice. Henceforward he made use of it as an article of faith, which he was no longer permitted to examine.

Utility having been often badly applied, understood in a narrow sense, and having lent its name to crimes, has appeared contrary to eternal justice. It thus became degraded, and acquired a mercenary reputation. It needs courage to restore it to honour, and to re-establish reasoning upon its true basis.

I propose a treaty of conciliation with the partisans of natural rights. If *nature* has made such or such a law, those who cite it with so much confidence, those who have modestly taken upon themselves to be its interpreters, must suppose that nature had some reasons for her law. Would it not be surer, shorter and more persuasive, to give us those reasons directly, instead of urging upon us the will of this unknown legislator, as itself an authority?

All these false methods of reasoning can always be reduced to one or the other of the two false principles. This fundamental distinction is very useful in getting rid of words, and rendering ideas more clear. To refer such or such an argument to one or another of the false principles, is like tying weeds into bundles, to be thrown into the fire.

I conclude with a general observation. The language of error is always obscure and indefinite. An abundance of words serves to cover a paucity and a falsity of ideas. The oftener terms are changed, the easier it is to delude the reader. The language of truth is uniform and simple. The same ideas are always expressed by the same terms. Everything is referred to pleasures or to pains. Every expression is avoided which tends to disguise or intercept the familiar idea, that from such and such actions result such and such pleasures and pains. Trust not to me, but to experience, and especially your own. Of two opposite methods of action, do you desire to know which should have the preference? Calculate their effects in good and evil, and prefer that which promises the greater sum of good.

## Notes

1. *Ascetic,* by its etymology, signifies *one who exercises.* It was applied to the monks, to indicate their favorite practices of devotion and penitence.

2. This mistake consists in representing the Deity in words, as a being of infinite benevolence, yet ascribing to him prohibitions and threats which are the attributes of an implacable being, who uses his power only to satisfy his malevolence.

We might ask these ascetic theologians what life is good for, if not for the pleasures it procures us?—and what pledge we have for the goodness of God in another life, if he has forbidden the enjoyment of this?

3. Here we touch upon one of the most difficult of questions. If the law is not what it ought to be; if it openly combats the principle of utility; ought we to obey it? Ought we to violate it? Ought we to remain neuter between the law which commands an evil, and morality which forbids it? The solution of this question involves considerations both of prudence and benevolence. We ought to examine if it is more dangerous to violate the law than to obey it; we ought to consider whether the probable evils of disobedience are less or greater than the probable evils of obedience.

4. See *Barrow's Voyage to the Cape of Good Hope,* for the cruelties of the Dutch settlers toward their cattle and their slaves.

5. Beccaria. Chap. xii

# IMMANUEL KANT

## INTRODUCTION

## PAUL GUYER

Immanuel Kant (1724–1804) was born and spent his whole life in the remote East Prussian capital of Königsberg. Nevertheless he became the most important philosopher of the European Enlightenment. Kant spent early his early years trying to combine the competing scientific visions of Leibniz and Newton into a coherent mechanics and cosmology. He also began his lifelong project of reconciling modern science with human freedom, as the necessary condition for the possibility of morality. The metaphysical and epistemological basis for this project, which Kant called "transcendental idealism," was outlined in the *Critique of Pure Reason* of 1781. After that work Kant devoted much of his effort to working out his moral and political philosophy, based on the assumption of the unconditional value of human freedom. He expounded this philosophy in three great works: *Groundwork for the Metaphysics of Morals,* 1785; *Critique of Practical Reason,* 1788; and *Metaphysics of Morals,* 1797, which includes his most detailed statement of his political philosophy. But he also presented aspects of his political philosophy in more accessible essays, including "What Is Enlightenment?" (1784) and the essay presented here, "On the Common Saying: This May Be True in Theory, but It Does Not Apply in Practice" (1793). Another work published in 1793, *Religion Within the Boundaries of Mere Reason,* presents Kant's famous argument that religious faith can be grounded only in moral reasoning, rather than the opposite, and also clarifies his theory of the freedom of the will, a central topic in all his major works. The last of Kant's three great critiques, the *Critique of the Power of Judgment* (1790), which deals with aesthetic and teleological judgments, that is, judgments about beauty and sublimity in both nature and art and purposiveness in nature, shows how we can combine our scientific knowledge and our moral principles into a coherent view of our place in the world.

Kant maintained that "the inner worth of the world, the *summum bonum,* is freedom according to a choice that is not necessitated to act." At the same time, he asserted that "if freedom is not restricted by objective rules, the result is much savage disorder." Kant's challenge in moral theory was to establish the unconditional value of human freedom and to explain how human beings can regulate their freedom without sacrificing anything essential to it. The challenge for Kant's political philosophy was to reconcile the essence of the state, namely the possibility of the use of coercion against any of its citizens by those authorized to act in behalf of the whole, with the maintenance of that freedom which is supposed to be advanced by the state, thus both justifying and limiting the organized use of coercion.

The role of freedom itself as our most fundamental value in both moral conduct and political organization is not immediately apparent in Kant's most widely read work in moral philosophy, *Groundwork for the Metaphysics of Morals.* Kant starts by asserting that the most noteworthy feature of morally praiseworthy conduct is the purity of its motivation, that it be motivated not by any consideration of the desirability of the ends that might be obtained by the action in question but only by the thought of duty, or "the necessity of an action from respect for law." Having excluded the desirability of satisfying any inclinations from morally praiseworthy motivation and thus having also excluded any possibility that the fundamental principle of morality could be understood as any sort of principle of instrumental reasoning, prescribing the best means for realizing some suitable set of inclinations, Kant then argues that the fundamental principle of morality can be nothing other than the conformity of the intentions or maxims of a moral agent to the form of rationality itself, its requirement of universality in its principles. Kant writes, "Since I have deprived the will of every impulse that could arise for it from obeying some law, nothing is left but the conformity of actions as such with universal law, which alone is to serve the will as its principle, that is, *I ought never to act except in such a way that I could also will that my maxim should become a universal law.*"

In the second section of the *Groundwork,* Kant reveals that the requirement that moral conduct be guided by the conformity of our maxims for action with the idea of universal law is itself only the means by which the real goal of moral conduct, the preservation and promotion of freedom of choice and action, can be obtained. Contrary to his initial suggestion that moral conduct must disregard any end at all that might be obtained through it, Kant explains that moral conduct is that which aims at an *objective* and *necessary* rather than any merely *subjective* and *contingent* end. And this is where the fundamental value of freedom finally appears in the argument of the *Groundwork:* for Kant argues that the objective end, the absolute value of which imposes the categorical imperative upon us, is the free and rational agency of human beings themselves—and this agency consists in nothing other than the power of human beings freely to set their own particular ends of action. Kant famously requires of us, in the second main formulation of the categorical imperative, that we "so act that [we] use humanity, whether in [our] own person or the person of any other, always at the same time as an end, never merely as a means." What this principle requires of us is that we always treat both ourselves and others as agents who are valuable because they are free. Kant gives four examples of duties, and what these reveal is that our fundamental obligations are duties to preserve the existence of free agents, to preserve the possibility of their exercise of free choice, to promote the conditions under which the particular ends that have been freely chosen can successfully be pursued, and, finally, in appropriate circumstances actually to assist in the successful pursuit of particular freely chosen ends. To treat all persons, ourselves as well as others, as ends and never merely as means, requires both that we treat persons as intrinsically valuable because of their freedom and that we promote the ends that they adopt in the exercise of their freedom.

Kant's second formulation of the categorial imperative not only makes sense of his first formulation, but also gives rise to a third formulation, the requirement to act so that "all maxims from one's own lawgiving are to harmonize with a possible kingdom of ends." A kingdom of ends is precisely what would arise if everyone were treated as an end and never merely as a means. That is, in a kingdom of ends, each person would be treated as an unconditionally valuable free agent, whose existence and capacity for free choice must be preserved, and whose particular objectives are valuable precisely because they have been freely chosen.

Now it is obvious that in a community of free agents people cannot always act upon every one of their inclinations, because the satisfaction of one person's desire can often be incompatible with the satisfaction of someone else's. So the kind of freedom that Kant has in mind as most valuable can only be what he sometimes calls "self-mastery," that is, the ability to free ourselves from domination by our own inclinations by regulating them, that is, by choosing which ones to act upon by the use of our reason. And the principle that reason has available to it for such regulation is nothing other than the principle to act in accordance with universalizable maxims or in a way that treats everyone as an end and never merely as a means. In other words, it is precisely through the acceptance of the categorical imperative that we can achieve mastery over our own inclinations and thus realize the only form of freedom possible for human beings.

The essay "On the Common Saying" is devoted to Kant's political philosophy. Here he tries to show that the fundamental value of human freedom can be reconciled with the coercive nature of the state, and he seeks to determine the limits for the exercise of coercion by the state within which it will be compatible with freedom.

Many readers find it difficult to see how the principles of Kant's political philosophy can be derived from the fundamental principle of morality at all, for morality seems to require that the virtuous agent be motivated entirely internally, merely by respect for the moral law, while the essence of the state as a political institution seems to be the possibility of the authorized use of external disincentives, such as the threat of fines or incarceration, to enforce compliance with its laws. But if we properly understand both Kant's use of the idea of the purity of morally estimable motivation and his conditions for the legitimation of coercion, we will see that he can without paradox derive the principles of politics from those of morality. On the one hand, Kant requires purity of moral motivation as a condition of moral praiseworthiness, and so it follows that the fundamental principle of morality must be one that *can* motivate any agent to act independently of particular inclinations. But that fundamental principle imposes a variety of duties on us that we have to fulfill regardless of our motivation for so doing: For example, we must fulfill our duty to refrain from making deceitful promises however we motivate ourselves to do so, although we only earn special moral praise if we fulfill this duty out of the purely internal motivation of respect for the moral law. On the other hand, since our moral duties constitute the rules we need to follow to preserve and promote the existence and exercise of freedom by all, Kant argues that juridical coercion—the enforcement of duties by the state apparatus of courts and penal institutions—can be justified if and only if coercion is necessary to preserve freedom itself. These conditions are by no means satisfied for all of our duties, so for Kant the sphere of "justice" or "right"—that is, coercively enforceable duties—is derived from the fundamental principle of morality but is considerably more restricted than the whole sphere of morality.

Kant recognizes that reconciling freedom with the possibility of coercion is the key to political philosophy. But isn't any use of coercion a violation of freedom? To reply to this objection, we need a more detailed analysis of the juridical use of coercion than Kant actually offered. What we must realize is that although one person who attacks or deceives another deprives the latter of her freedom by depriving her of any choice in how she is treated, the perpetrator who is threatened or punished with a coercive sanction under the rule of law is not deprived of his freedom of choice in the same way as his victim is. Where the laws and the consequences of violating them are publicly known, a wrongdoer can be considered to have freely chosen to break the law and suffer the consequences. Thus, coercion is indeed consistent with freedom. And given that we cannot always expect people to be motivated by respect for the moral law alone, coercion is sometimes necessary to preserve freedom.

On this basis, Kant erects a theory of the limited scope of government that is one of the classical statements of liberalism, although in terms some of which are unfamiliar to the Anglo-American tradition. In the essay on theory and practice, Kant stresses that a legitimate government must be nonpaternalistic. Like John Stuart Mill in *On Liberty* half a century later, Kant argues that political and juridical intervention in the exercise of personal liberty is permissible only when it is necessary to prevent injury to the liberty of others, not whenever the state thinks it knows better than its subjects what would be good for them. However, in Kant's hands this does not lead to the view that the state exists only to protect individual claims to life, liberty, and property. Rather, within the framework of a continental rather than Anglo-American distinction between "private" and "public" law, Kant defends a complex theory that balances a considerable public right to intervene in the distribution of property with an absolute private right to freedom of conscience and expression that anticipates contemporary liberalism.

The key to this position is Kant's recognition that property rights, although the subject of "private law," are acquired rather than innate, and thus can be reasonably maintained only when they are publicly acceptable. Every person has an "innate right" to freedom of the person, Kant argues, an innate right that is simply the complement of everyone's moral obligation to treat others as ends, that is, beings capable of choosing their own ends, rather than as means. Given Kant's argument about coercion, this innate right to personal freedom can legitimately be defended and enforced by the state. Property rights, however, are not innate rights; rather, they are what Kant calls "acquired rights." In Kant's view a property right is not created by some kind of direct relationship between a person and an object—in contrast to John Locke, for example, who thought such a right was created simply by a person mixing labor with an object—but instead consist only in the consent of all who *could* control and use an object. Thus for Kant there are no natural individual rights to property, only rights acquired by common consent, and the state has an inevitable role in maintaining a fair system for the distribution of property rights. But this condition does not apply in matters of conscience and the expression of belief. One person's expression of beliefs, no matter how outrageous they may be to others, is not an imposition on those others, for they do not have to believe what another tells them unless they choose to do so. Thus the state has neither a need nor a right to control belief.

So Kant defends two of the pillars of modern liberalism, namely, the right of the state to limit the claims of private property in behalf of the public good and the virtually absolute right of freedom of conscience and expression. However, Kant's political philosophy does not include what might be considered the third fundamental principle of modern liberalism—the universal right of political participation. While Kant certainly expects that a republican government will be representative and thus elected, he is willing to place considerable restrictions on the people's right to participate in the electorate. Although quite offensive to later liberals, Kant argues against the right of women and servants to vote, because he is afraid that their economic dependence upon their husbands and masters will make them instruments of the latter rather than free voters—a not altogether unreasonable assumption in the circumstances of Kant's day. Kant's insistence that the state be an expression of the "general will" is meant as a rational ideal and test for the justness of its laws, but it is not an ideal of universal participation in the political process.

Another issue on which Kant seems to differ with modern liberalism, or even to be more conservative than some predecessors such as John Lock, is the controversial issue of a right to rebellion. Once again, Kant's position seems paradoxical: he insists that a just state must fulfill the rational ideal expressed by his universal principle of right, but denies that there can actually be any right to rebel against even an unjust state. Kant has a number of reasons for this claim. He believes that we have a duty to be members of a state, and also that a constitution that included a right to its own overthrow would be incoherent. Kant also argues that because of the importance of having a government, it is wrong to scrutinize the origins of any government too closely, because in fact all governments originate in violence. Kant may seem to be offering an apology for any government currently in power, but he leaves the door open to revolution, implying that while there can be no legally recognized right to revolution, after a successful revolt there can be no critique of the new government because its creation was not rightful. Ultimately, the test for the legitimacy of any government is how well it lives up to the ideal of justice, not how it came into power.

In one last point, Kant's political philosophy goes well beyond many standard conceptions of liberalism, for in the third part of the essay on theory and practice he argues that justice can only be realized in a worldwide federation of republican governments. Kant's argument for this conclusion rests on two premises: first, property rights within any individual state need to be secured from external attacks from other states as well as from internal theft and corruption, and thus no property is secure until the entire world is subject to the rule of law; and second, only republican states, which serve the interests of their citizens rather than the proprietary interests of hereditary dynasties, can be expected to refrain from making war upon each other, an insight that has been confirmed even in the grim history of the twentieth century, for no democracy has ever warred upon another. At the same time, Kant refrains from arguing for a single worldwide government, because in his realism he believes that such a vast government would inevitably degenerate from republic to despotism. This view is representative of the complex mix of realism and idealism present throughout Kant's moral and political philosophy.

The literature on Kant's moral and political philosophy is vast. An older commentary on the *Groundwork* that remains valuable is Herbert James Paton, *The Categorical Imperative: A Study in Kant's Moral Philosophy* (London: Hutchinson, 1947). Among recent books focusing primarily on Kant's moral philosophy, some of the most useful are Marcia W. Baron, *Kantian Ethics Almost Without Apology* (Ithaca, N.Y.: Cornell University Press, 1995); Bruce Aune, *Kant's Theory of Morals* (Princeton, N.J.: Princeton University Press, 1979); Barbara Herman, *The Practice of Moral Judgment* (Cambridge, Mass.: Harvard University, Press, 1993); Thomas E. Hill, Jr., *Dignity and Practical Reason in Kant's Moral Theory* (Ithaca, N.Y.: Cornell University Press, 1992); Christine M. Korsgaard, *Creating the Kingdom of Ends* (Cambridge: Cambridge University Press, 1996); Onora Nell, *Acting on Principle: An Essay on Kantian Ethics* (New York: Columbia University Press, 1975), and, by the same author, now Onora O'Neill, *Constructions of Reason: Explorations of Kant's Practical Philosophy* (Cambridge: Cambridge University Press, 1989); and Allen W. Wood, *Kant's Ethical Thought* (Cambridge: Cambridge University Press, 1999). John Rawls has been the most important contemporary writer to have been influenced by Kant's moral philosophy, and his interpretation of Kant is now available in his *Lectures on the History of Moral Philosophy,* edited by Barbara Herman (Cambridge, Mass.: Harvard University Press, 2000). A collection of important recent articles on Kant's moral philosophy is Paul Guyer (ed.), *Kant's Groundwork of the Metaphysics of Morals: Critical Essays* (Lanham, Md: Rowman & Littlefield, 1998).

Among recent books on Kant's political philosophy, some of the most useful are Howard Williams, *Kant's Political Philosophy* (New York: St. Martin's Press, 1983); Leslie A. Mulholland, *Kant's System of Rights,* (New York: Columbia University Press, 1990); Allen D. Rosen, *Kant's Theory of Justice* (Ithaca, N.Y.: Cornell University Press, 1993); and most recently, Katrin Flikschuh, *Kant and Modern Political Philosophy* (Cambridge: Cambridge University Press, 2000), which disputes Rawls's reconstruction of Kant's political philosophy. An interesting collection of essays on Kant's political philosophy by diverse authors is Jane Kneller and Sidney Axinn (eds.), *Autonomy and Community: Readings in Contemporary Kantian Social Philosophy* (Albany: State University of New York Press, 1998). A collection of essays on Kant's program for world peace is James Bohman and Matthias Lutz-Bachmann (eds.), *Perpetual Peace: Essays on Kant's Cosmopolitan Ideal* (Cambridge, Mass.: MIT Press, 1997).

Finally, three collections of their authors' essays covering both Kant's moral and his political philosophy are Paul Guyer, *Kant on Freedom, Law, and Happiness* (Cambridge: Cambridge University Press, 2000); Thomas E. Hill, Jr., *Respect, Pluralism, and Justice: Kantian Perspectives* (Oxford: Oxford University Press, 2000); and Onora O'Neill, *Bounds of Justice* (Cambridge: Cambridge University Press, 2000).

# Groundwork for the Metaphysics of Morals

Ancient Greek philosophy was divided into three sciences: Physics, Ethics, and Logic. This division is perfectly suitable to the nature of the thing; and the only improvement that can be made in it is to add the principle on which it is based, so that we may both satisfy ourselves of its completeness, and also be able to determine correctly the necessary subdivisions.

All rational knowledge is either *material* or *formal:* the former considers some object, the latter is concerned only with the form of the understanding and of the reason itself, and with the universal laws of thought in general without distinction of its objects. Formal philosophy is called logic. Material philosophy, however, which has to do with determinate objects and the laws to which they are subject, is again twofold; for these laws are either laws of *nature* or of *freedom*. The science of the former is physics, that of the latter, ethics; they are also called *natural philosophy* and *moral philosophy* respectively.

Logic cannot have any empirical part—that is, a part in which the universal and necessary laws of thought should rest on grounds taken from experience; otherwise it would not be logic, that is, a canon for the understanding of the reason, valid for all thought, and capable of demonstration. Natural and moral philosophy, on the contrary, can each have their empirical part, since the former has to determine the laws of nature as an object of experience, the latter of the laws of the human will, so far as it is affected by nature; the former, however, being laws according to which everything does happen, the latter, laws according to which everything ought to happen. Ethics, however, must also consider the conditions under which what ought to happen frequently does not.

We may call all philosophy *empirical,* so far as it is based on grounds of experience; on the other hand, that which delivers its doctrines from *a priori* principles alone we may call *pure* philosophy. When the latter is merely formal, it is *logic;* if it is restricted to definite objects of the understanding, it is *metaphysic.*

In this way there arises the idea of a twofold metaphysic—a *metaphysic of nature* and a *metaphysic of morals.* Physics will thus have an empirical and also a rational part. It is the same with ethics; but here the empirical part might have the special name of *practical anthropology,* the name *morality* being appropriated to the rational part.

All trades, arts, and handiworks have gained by division of labor, namely, when, instead of one man doing everything, each confines himself to a certain kind of work distinct from others in the treatment it requires, so as to be able to perform it with greater facility and in the greatest perfection. Where the different kinds of work are not so distinguished and divided, where everyone is a jack-of-all-trades, there manufactures remain still in the greatest barbarism. It might deserve to be considered whether pure philosophy in all its parts does not require a man specially devoted to it, and whether it would not be better for the whole business of science if those who, to please the tastes of the public, are wont to blend the rational and empirical elements together, mixed in all sorts of proportions unknown to themselves, and who call themselves independent thinkers, giving the name of minute philosophers to those who apply

This translation is by Thomas K. Abbott (1873). The bracketed words in the text are amplifications by the translator. Title has been altered.

themselves to the rational part only—if these, I say, are warned not to carry on two employments together which differ widely in the treatment they demand, for each of which perhaps a special talent is required, and the combination of which in one person only produces bunglers. But I only ask here whether the nature of science does not require that we should always carefully separate the empirical from the rational part, and prefix to physics proper (or empirical physics) a metaphysic of nature, and to practical anthropol-ogy a metaphysic of morals, which must be carefully cleared of everything empirical so that we may know how much can be accomplished by pure reason in both cases, and from what sources it draws this its *a priori* teaching, and that whether the latter inquiry is conducted by all moralists (whose name is legion), or only by some who feel a calling thereto.

As my concern here is with moral philosophy, I limit the question suggested to this: whether it is not of the utmost necessity to construct a pure moral philosophy, perfectly cleared of everything which is only empirical, and which belongs to anthropology? For that such a philosophy must be possible is evident from the common idea of duty and of the moral laws. Everyone must admit that if a law is to have moral force, that is, to be the basis of an obligation, it must carry with it absolute necessity; that, for example, the precept, "Thou shalt not lie," is not valid for men alone, as if other rational beings had no need to observe it; and so with all the other moral laws properly so called; that, therefore, the basis of obligation must not be sought in the nature of man, or in the circumstances in the world in which he is placed, but *a priori* simply in the conceptions of pure reason; and although any other precept which is founded on principles of mere experience may be in certain respects universal, yet in as far as it rests even in the least degree on an empirical basis, perhaps only as to a motive, such a precept, while it may be a practical rule, can never be called a moral law.

Thus not only are moral laws with their principles essentially distinguished from every other kind of practical knowledge in which there is anything empirical, but all moral philosophy rests wholly on

its pure part. When applied to man, it does not borrow the least thing from the knowledge of man himself (anthropology), but gives laws *a priori* to him as a rational being. No doubt these laws require a judgment sharpened by experience, in order, on the one hand, to distinguish in what cases they are applicable, and, on the other, to procure for them access to the will of the man, and effectual influence on conduct; since man is acted on by so many inclinations that, though capable of the idea of a practical pure reason, he is not so easily able to make it effective *in concreto* in his life.

A metaphysic of morals is therefore indispensably necessary, not merely for speculative reasons, in order to investigate the sources of the practical principles which are to be found *a priori* in our reason, but also because morals themselves are liable to all sorts of corruption as long as we are without that clue and supreme canon by which to estimate them correctly. For in order that an action should be morally good, it is not enough that it *conform* to the moral law, but it must also be done *for the sake of the law,* otherwise that conformity is only very contingent and uncertain; since a principle which is not moral, although it may now and then produce actions conformable to the law, will also often produce actions which contradict it. Now it is only in a pure philosophy that we can look for the moral law in its purity and genuineness (and, in a practical matter, this is of the utmost consequence): we must, therefore, begin with pure philosophy (metaphysics), and without it there cannot be any moral philosophy at all. That which mingles these pure principles with the empirical does not deserve the name of philosophy (for what distinguishes philosophy from common rational knowledge is that it treats in separate sciences what the latter only comprehends confusedly); much less does it deserve that of moral philosophy, since by this confusion it even spoils the purity of morals themselves and counteracts its own end.

Let it not be thought, however, that what is here demanded is already extant in the propaedeutic prefixed by the celebrated Wolff to his moral philosophy, namely, his so-called *general practical philosophy,* and that, therefore, we have not to strike into an entirely new field. Just because it was to be a general practical philosophy, it has not taken into consideration a will of any particular kind—say, one which should be determined solely from *a priori* principles without any empirical motives, and which we might call a pure will—but volition in general, with all the actions and conditions which belong to it in this general signification. By this it is distinguished from a metaphysic of morals, just as general logic, which treats of the acts and canons of thought *in general,* is distinguished from transcendental philosophy, which treats of the particular acts and canons of *pure* thought, that is, that whose cognitions are altogether *a priori.* For the metaphysic of morals has to examine the idea and the principles of a possible *pure* will, and not the acts and conditions of human volition generally, which for the most part are drawn from psychology. It is true that moral laws and duty are spoken of in the general practical philosophy (contrary indeed to all fitness). But this is no objection, for in this respect also the authors of that science remain true to their idea of it; they do not distinguish the motives which are prescribed as such by reason alone altogether *a priori,* and which are properly moral, from the empirical motives which the understanding raises to general conceptions merely by comparison of experiences; but without noticing the difference of their sources, and looking on them all as homogeneous, they consider only their greater or less amount. It is in this way they frame their notion of *obligation,* which, though anything but moral, is all that can be asked for in a philosophy which passes no judgment at all on the origin of all possible practical concepts, whether they are *a priori* or only *a posteriori.*

Intending to publish hereafter a metaphysic of morals, I issue in the first instance these fundamental principles. Indeed there is properly no other foundation for it than the *critical examination of a pure practical reason;* just as that of metaphysics is the critical examination of the pure speculative reason, already published. But in the first place the former is not so absolutely necessary as the latter, because in moral concerns human reason can easily be brought to a high degree of correctness and completeness, even in the commonest understanding, while on the contrary in its theoretic but pure use it is wholly dialectical; and in the second place, if the critique of a pure practical reason is to be complete, it must be possible at the same time to show its identity with the speculative reason in a common principle, for it can ultimately be only one and the same reason which has to be distinguished merely in its application. I could not, however, bring it to such completeness here without introducing considerations of a wholly different kind, which would be perplexing to the reader. On this account I have adopted the title of *Fundamental Principles of the Metaphysics of Morals* [*Grundlegung zur Metaphysiks der Sitten*] instead of that of a *critical examination of the pure practical reason.*

But in the third place, since a metaphysic of morals, in spite of the discouraging title, is yet capable of being presented in a popular form, and one adapted to the common understanding, I find it useful to separate from it this preliminary treatise on its fundamental principles, in order that I may not hereafter have need to introduce these necessarily subtle discussions into a book of a more simple character.

The present treatise is, however, nothing more than the investigation and establishment of *the supreme principle of morality,* and this alone constitutes a study complete in itself, and one which ought to be kept apart from every other moral investigation. No doubt, my conclusions on this weighty question, which has hitherto been very unsatisfactorily examined, would receive much light from the application of the same principle to the whole system, and would be greatly confirmed by the adequacy which it exhibits throughout; but I must forego this advantage, which indeed would be after all more gratifying than useful, since the easy applicability of a principle and its apparent adequacy give no very certain proof of its soundness, but rather inspire a certain partiality, which prevents us from examining and estimating it strictly in itself, and without regard to consequences.

I have adopted in this work the method which I think most suitable, proceeding analytically from common knowledge to the determination of its ultimate principle, and again descending synthetically from the examination of this principle and its sources to the common knowledge in which we find it employed. The division will, therefore, be as follows:

1. *First section:* Transition from the common rational knowledge of morality to the philosophical.
2. *Second section:* Transition from popular moral philosophy to the metaphysics of morals.
3. *Third section:* Final step from the metaphysics of morals to the critique of the pure practical reason.

## FIRST SECTION

### *Transition from the Common Rational Knowledge of Morality to the Philosophical*

Nothing can possibly be conceived in the world, or even out of it, which can be called good without qualification, except a *good will.* Intelligence, wit, judgment, and the other *talents* of the mind, however they may be named, or courage, resolution, perseverance, as qualities of temperament, are undoubtedly good and desirable in many respects; but these gifts of nature may also become extremely bad and mischievous if the will which is to make use of them, and which, therefore, constitutes what is called *character,* is not good. It is the same with the *gifts of fortune.* Power, riches, honor, even health, and the general well-being and contentment with one's condition which is called *happiness,* inspire pride, and often presumption, if there is not a good will to correct the influence of these on the mind, and with this also to rectify the whole principle of acting, and adapt it to its end. The sight of a being who is not adorned with a single feature of a pure and good will, enjoying unbroken prosperity, can never give pleasure to an impartial rational spectator. Thus a good will appears to constitute the indispensable condition even of being worthy of happiness.

There are even some qualities which are of service to this good will itself, and may facilitate its actions, yet which have no intrinsic unconditional value, but always presuppose a good will, and this qualifies the esteem that we justly have for them, and does not per-

mit us to regard them as absolutely good. Moderation in the affections and passions, self-control, and calm deliberation are not only good in many respects, but even seem to constitute part of the intrinsic worth of the person; but they are far deserving to be called good without qualification, although they have been so unconditionally praised by the ancients. For without the principles of a good will, they may become extremely bad; and the coolness of a villain not only makes him far more dangerous, but also directly makes him more abominable in our eyes than he would have been without it.

A good will is good not because of what it performs or effects, not by its aptness for the attainment of some proposed end, but simply by virtue of the volition— that is, it is good in itself, and considered by itself is to be esteemed much higher than all that can be brought about by it in favor of any inclination, nay, even of the sum-total of all inclinations. Even if it should happen that, owing to special disfavor of fortune, or the niggardly provision of a stepmotherly nature, this will should wholly lack power to accomplish its purpose, if with its greatest efforts it should yet achieve nothing, and there should remain only the good will (not, to be sure, a mere wish, but the summoning of all means in our power), then, like a jewel, it would still shine by its own light, as a thing which has its whole value in itself. Its usefulness or fruitlessness can neither add to nor take away anything from this value. It would be, as it were, only the setting to enable us to handle it the more conveniently in common commerce, or to attract to it the attention of those who are not yet connoisseurs, but not to recommend it to true connoisseurs, or to determine its value.

There is, however, something so strange in this idea of the absolute value of the mere will, in which no account is taken of its utility, that notwithstanding the thorough assent of even common reason to the idea, yet a suspicion must arise that it may perhaps really be the product of mere high-flown fancy, and that we may have misunderstood the purpose of nature in assigning reason as the governor of our will. Therefore we will examine this idea from this point of view.

In the physical constitution of an organized being, that is, a being adapted suitably to the purposes of life, we assume it as a fundamental principle that no organ for any purpose will be found but what is also the fittest and best adapted for that purpose. Now in a being which has reason and a will, if the proper object of nature were its *conservation,* its *welfare,* in a word, its *happiness,* then nature would have hit upon a very bad arrangement in selecting the reason of the creature to carry out this purpose. For all the actions which the creature has to perform with a view to this purpose, and the whole rule of its conduct, would be far more surely prescribed to it by instinct, and that end would have been attained thereby much more certainly than it ever can be by reason. Should reason have been communicated to this favored creature over and above, it must only have served it to contemplate the happy constitution of its nature, to admire it, to congratulate itself thereon, and to feel thankful for it to the beneficent cause, but not that it should subject its desires to that weak and delusive guidance, and meddle bunglingly with the purpose of nature. In a word, nature would have taken care that reason should not break forth into *practical exercise,* nor have the presumption, with its weak insight, to think out for itself the plan of happiness and of the means of attaining it. Nature would not only have taken on herself the choice of the ends but also of the means, and with wise foresight would have entrusted both to instinct.

And, in fact, we find that the more a cultivated reason applies itself with deliberate purpose to the enjoyment of life and happiness, so much the more does the man fail of true satisfaction. And from this circumstance there arises in many, if they are candid enough to confess it, a certain degree of *misology,* that is, hatred of reason, especially in the case of those who are most experienced in the use of it, because after calculating all the advantages they derive—I do not say from the invention of all the arts of common luxury, but even from the sciences (which seem to them to be after all only a luxury of the understanding)—they find that they have, in fact, only brought more trouble on their shoulders rather than gained in happiness; and they end by envying rather than despising the more common stamp of men who keep closer to the guidance of mere instinct, and do not allow their reason much influence on their conduct. And this we must admit, that the judgment of those who would

very much lower the lofty eulogies of the advantages which reason gives us in regard to the happiness and satisfaction of life, or who would even reduce them below zero, is by no means morose or ungrateful to the goodness with which the world is governed, but that there lies at the root of these judgments the idea that our existence has a different and far nobler end, for which, and not for happiness, reason is properly intended, and which must, therefore, be regarded as the supreme condition to which the private ends of man must, for the most part, be postponed.

For as reason is not competent to guide the will with certainty in regard to its objects and the satisfaction of all our wants (which it to some extent even multiplies), this being an end to which an implanted instinct would have led with much greater certainty); and since, nevertheless, reason is imparted to us as a practical faculty, that is, as one which is to have influence on the *will,* therefore, admitting that nature generally in the distribution of her capacities has adapted the means to the end, its true destination must be to produce a *will,* not merely good as a *means* to something else, but *good in itself,* for which reason was absolutely necessary. This will then, though not indeed the sole and complete good, must be the supreme good and the condition of every other, even of the desire of happiness. Under these circumstances, there is nothing inconsistent with the wisdom of nature in the fact that the cultivation of the reason, which is requisite for the first and unconditional purpose, does in many ways interfere, at least in this life, with the attainment of the second, which is always conditional—namely, happiness. Nay, it may even reduce it to nothing, without nature thereby failing of her purpose. For reason recognizes the establishment of a good will as its highest practical destination, and in attaining this purpose is capable only of a satisfaction of its own proper kind, namely, that from the attainment of an end, which end again is determined by reason only, notwithstanding that this may involve many a disappointment to the ends of inclination.

We have then to develop the notion of a will which deserves to be highly esteemed for itself, and is good without a view to anything further, a notion which exists already in the sound natural understanding, requiring rather to be cleared up than to be taught, and which in estimating the value of our actions always takes the first place and constitutes the condition of all the rest. In order to do this, we will take the notion of duty, which includes that of a good will, although implying certain subjective restrictions and hindrances. These, however, far from concealing it or rendering it unrecognizable, rather bring it out by contrast and make it shine forth so much the brighter.

I omit here all actions which are already recognized as inconsistent with duty, although they may be useful for this or that purpose, for with these the question whether they are done *from duty* cannot arise at all, since they even conflict with it. I also set aside those actions which really conform to duty, but to which men have *no* direct *inclination,* performing them because they are impelled thereto by some other inclination. For in this case we can readily distinguish whether the action which agrees with duty is done *from duty* or from a selfish view. It is much harder to make this distinction when the action accords with duty, and the subject has besides a *direct* inclination to it. For example, it is always a matter of duty that a dealer should not overcharge an inexperienced purchaser; and wherever there is much commerce the prudent tradesman does not overcharge, but keeps a fixed price for everyone, so that a child buys of him as well as any other. Men are thus *honestly* served; but this is not enough to make us believe that the tradesman has so acted from duty and from principles of honesty; his own advantage required it; it is out of the question in this case to suppose that he might besides have a direct inclination in favor of the buyers, so that, as it were, from love he should give no advantage to one over another. Accordingly the action was done neither from duty nor from direct inclination, but merely with a selfish view.

On the other hand, it is a duty to maintain one's life; and, in addition, everyone has also a direct inclination to do so. But on this account the often anxious care which most men take for it has no intrinsic worth, and their maxim has no moral import. They preserve their life *as duty requires,* no doubt, but not *because duty requires.* On the other hand, if adversity and hopeless sorrow have completely taken away the relish for life, if the unfortunate one, strong in mind, indignant at his fate rather than desponding or dejected, wishes for death, and yet preserves his life without loving it—not from inclination or fear, but from duty—then his maxim has a moral worth.

To be beneficent when we can is a duty; and besides this, there are many minds so sympathetically constituted that, without any other motive of vanity or self-interest, they find a pleasure in spreading joy around them, and can take delight in the satisfaction of others so far as it is their own work. But I maintain that in such a case an action of this kind, however proper, however amiable it may be, has nevertheless no true moral worth, but is on a level with other inclinations, for example, the inclination to honor, which, if it is happily directed to that which is in fact of public utility and accordant with duty, and consequently honorable, deserves praise and encouragement, but not esteem. For the maxim lacks the moral import, namely, that such actions be done *from duty,* not from inclination. Put the case that the mind of that philanthropist was clouded by sorrow of his own, extinguishing all sympathy with the lot of others, and that while he still has the power to benefit others in distress, he is not touched by their trouble because he is absorbed with his own; and now suppose that he tears himself out of this dead insensibility and performs the action without any inclination to it, but simply from duty, then first has his action its genuine moral worth. Further still, if nature has put little sympathy in the heart of this or that man, if he, supposed to be an upright man, is by temperament cold and indifferent to the sufferings of others, perhaps because in respect of his own he is provided with the special gift of patience and fortitude, and supposes, or even requires, that others should have the same—and such a man would certainly not be the meanest product of nature—but if nature had not specially framed him for a philanthropist, would he not still find in himself a source from whence to give himself a far higher worth than that of a goodnatured temperament could be? Unquestionably. It is just in this that the moral worth of the character is brought out which is incomparably the highest of all, namely, that he is benefi-cent, not from inclination, but from duty.

To secure one's own happiness is a duty, at least indirectly; for discontent with one's condition, under a pressure of many anxieties and amidst unsatisfied wants, might easily become a great *temptation to transgression of duty.* But here again, without look-ing to duty, all men have already the strongest and most intimate inclination to happiness, because it is just in this idea that all inclinations are combined in one total. But the precept of happiness is often of such a sort that it greatly interferes with some inclinations, and yet a man cannot form any definite and certain conception of the sum of satisfaction of all of them which is called happiness. It is not then to be won-dered at that a single inclination, definite both as to what it promises and as to the time within which it can be gratified, is often able to overcome such a fluctuat-ing idea, and that a gouty patient, for instance, can choose to enjoy what he likes, and to suffer what he may, since, according to his calculation, on this occa-sion at least, he has [only] not sacrificed the enjoy-ment of the present moment to a possibly mistaken expectation of a happiness which is supposed to be found in health. But even in this case, if the general desire for happiness did not influence his will, and supposing that in his particular case health was not a necessary element in this calculation, there yet re-mains in this, as in all other cases, this law—namely, that he should promote his happiness not from incli-nation but from duty, and by this would his conduct first acquire true moral worth.

It is in this manner, undoubtedly, that we are to understand those passages of Scripture also in which we are commanded to love our neighbor, even our enemy. For love, as an affection, cannot be com-manded, but beneficence for duty's sake may, even though we are not impelled to it by any inclination—nay, are even repelled by a natural and unconquer-able aversion. This is *practical* love, and not *patho-logical*—a love which is seated in the will, and not in the propensions of sense—in principles of action and not of tender sympathy; and it is this love alone which can be commanded.

The second proposition is: That an action done from duty derives its moral worth, *not from the pur-pose* which is to be attained by it, but from the maxim by which it is determined, and therefore does not depend on the realization of the object of the action, but merely on the *principle of volition* by which the action has taken place, without regard to any object of desire. It is clear from what precedes that the pur-poses which we may have in view in our actions, or their effects regarded as ends and springs of the will, cannot give to actions any unconditional or moral worth. In what, then, can their worth lie if it is not to consist in the will and in reference to its expected effect? It cannot lie anywhere but in the *principle of the will* without regard to the ends which can be attained by the action. For the will stands between its *a priori* principle, which is formal, and its *a posteri-ori* spring, which is material, as between two roads, and as it must be determined by something, it follows that it must be determined by the formal principle of volition when an action is done from duty, in which case every material principle has been withdrawn from it.

The third proposition, which is a consequence of the two preceding, I would express thus: *Duty is the necessity of acting from respect for the law.* I may have *inclination* for an object as the effect of my pro-posed action, but I cannot have *respect* for it just for this reason that it is an effect and not an energy of will. Similarly, I cannot have respect for inclination, whether my own or another's; I can at most, if my own, approve it; if another's, sometimes even love it, that is, look on it as favorable to my own interest. It is only what is connected with my will as a principle, by no means as an effect—what does not subserve my inclination, but overpowers it, or at least in case of choice excludes it from its calculation—in other words, simply the law of itself, which can be an ob-ject of respect, and hence a command. Now an action done from duty must wholly exclude the influence of inclination, and with it every object of the will, so that nothing remains which can determine the will except objectively the *law,* and subjectively *pure respect* for this practical law, and consequently the maxim[1] that I should follow this law even to the thwarting of all my inclinations.

Thus the moral worth of an action does not lie in the effect expected from it, nor in any principle of action which requires to borrow its motive from this expected effect. For all these effects—agreeableness of one's condition, and even the promotion of the happiness of others—could have been also brought about by other causes, so that for this there would have been no need of the will of a rational being; whereas it is in this alone that the supreme and unconditional good can be found. The pre-eminent good which we call moral can therefore consist in nothing else than *the conception of law* in itself, *which certainly is only possible in a rational being,* in so far as this conception, and not the expected effect, determines the will. This is a good which is already present in the person who acts accordingly, and we have not to wait for it to appear first in the result.[2]

But what sort of law can that be the conception of which must determine the will, even without paying any regard to the effect expected from it, in order that this will may be called good absolutely and without qualification? As I have deprived the will of every impulse which could arise to it from obedience to any law, there remains nothing but the universal conformity of its actions to law in general, which alone is to serve the will as a principle, that is, I am never to act otherwise than so *that I could also will that my maxim should become a universal law.* Here, now, it is the simple conformity to law in general, without assuming any particular law applicable to certain actions, that serves the will as its principle, and must so serve it if duty is not to be a vain delusion and a chimerical notion. The common reason of men in its practical judgments perfectly coincides with this, and always has in view the principle here suggested. Let the question be, for example: May I when in distress make a promise with the intention not to keep it? I readily distinguish here between the two significations which the question may have: whether it is prudent or whether it is right to make a false promise? The former may undoubtedly often be the case. I see clearly indeed that it is not enough to extricate myself from a present difficulty by means of this subterfuge, but it must be well considered whether there may not hereafter spring from this lie much greater inconvenience

than that from which I now free myself, and as, with all my supposed *cunning,* the consequences cannot be so easily foreseen but that credit once lost may be much more injurious to me than any mischief which I seek to avoid at present, it should be considered whether it would not be more *prudent* to act herein according to a universal maxim, and to make it a habit to promise nothing except with the intention of keeping it. But it is soon clear to me that such a maxim will still only be based on the fear of consequences. Now it is a wholly different thing to be truthful from duty, and to be so from apprehension of injurious consequences. In the first case, the very notion of the action already implies a law for me; in the second case, I must first look about elsewhere to see what results may be combined with it which would affect myself. For to deviate from the principle of duty is beyond all doubt wicked; but to be unfaithful to my maxim of prudence may often be very advantageous to me, although to abide by it is certainly safer. The shortest way, however, and an unerring one, to discover the answer to this question whether a lying promise is consistent with duty, is to ask myself, Should I be content that my maxim (to extricate myself from difficulty by a false promise) should hold good as a universal law, for myself as well as for others; and should I be able to say to myself, "Every one may make a deceitful promise when he finds himself in a difficulty from which he cannot otherwise extricate himself"? Then I presently become aware that, while I can will the lie, I can by no means will that lying should be a universal law. For which such a law there would be no promises at all, since it would be in vain to allege my intention in regard to my future actions to those who would not believe this allegation, or if they overhastily did so, would pay me back in my own coin. Hence my maxim, as soon as it should be made a universal law, would necessarily destroy itself.

I do not, therefore, need any far-reaching penetration to discern what I have to do in order that my will may be morally good. Inexperienced in the course of the world, incapable of being prepared for all its contingencies, I only ask myself: Canst thou also will that thy maxim should be a universal law? If not, then it must be rejected, and that not because of a disadvantage accruing from it to myself or even to others, but because it cannot enter as a principle into a possible universal legislation, and reason extorts from me immediate respect for such legislation. I do not indeed as yet *discern* on what this respect is based (this the philosopher may inquire), but at least I understand this—that it is an estimation of the worth which far outweighs all worth of what is recommended by inclination, and that the necessity of acting from pure respect for the practical law is what constitutes duty, to which every other motive must give place because it is the condition of a will being good *in itself,* and the worth of such a will is above everything.

Thus, then, without quitting the moral knowledge of common human reason, we have arrived at its principle. And although, no doubt, common men do not conceive it in such an abstract and universal form, yet they always have it really before their eyes and use it as the standard of their decision. Here it would be easy to show how, with this compass in hand, men are well able to distinguish, in every case that occurs, what is good, what bad, conformably to duty or inconsistent with it, if, without in the least teaching them anything new, we only, like Socrates, direct their attention to the principle they themselves employ; and that, therefore, we do not need science and philosophy to know what we should do to be honest and good, yea, even wise and virtuous. Indeed we might well have conjectured beforehand that the knowledge of what every man is bound to do, and therefore also to know, would be within the reach of every man, even the commonest. Here we cannot forbear admiration when we see how great an advantage the practical judgment has over the theoretical in the common understanding of men. In the latter, if common reason ventures to depart from the laws of experience and from the perceptions of the senses, it falls into mere inconceivabilities and self-contradictions, at least into a chaos of uncertainty, obscurity, and instability. But in the practical sphere it is just when the common understanding excludes all sensible springs from practical laws that its power of judgment begins to show itself to advantage. It then becomes even subtle, whether it be that it chicanes with its own con-

science or with other claims respecting what is to be called right, or whether it desires for its own instruction to determine honestly the worth of actions; and, in the latter case, it may even have as good a hope of hitting the mark as any philosopher whatever can promise himself. Nay, it is almost more sure of doing so, because the philosopher cannot have any other principle, while he may easily perplex his judgment by a multitude of considerations foreign to the matter, and so turn aside from the right way. Would it not therefore be wiser in moral concerns to acquiesce in the judgment of common reason, or at most only to call in philosophy for the purpose of rendering the system of morals more complete and intelligible, and its rules more convenient for use (especially for disputation), but not so as to draw off the common understanding from its happy simplicity, or to bring it by means of philosophy into a new path of inquiry and instruction?

Innocence is indeed a glorious thing; only, on the other hand, it is very sad that it cannot well maintain itself, and is easily seduced. On this account even wisdom—which otherwise consists more in conduct than in knowledge—yet has need of science, not in order to learn from it, but to secure for its precepts admission and permanence. Against all the commands of duty which reason represents to man as so deserving of respect, he feels in himself a powerful counterpoise in his wants and inclinations, the entire satisfaction of which he sums up under the name of happiness. Now reason issues its commands unyieldingly, without promising anything to the inclinations, and, as it were, with disregard and contempt for these claims, which are so impetuous and at the same time so plausible, and which will not allow themselves to be suppressed by any command. Hence there arises a natural *dialectic,* that is, a disposition to argue against these strict laws of duty and to question their validity, or at least their purity and strictness; and, if possible, to make them more accordant with our wishes and inclinations, that is to say, to corrupt them at their very source and entirely to destroy their worth—a thing which even common practical reason cannot ultimately call good.

Thus is the *common reason of man* compelled to

go out of its sphere and to take a step into the field of a *practical philosophy,* not to satisfy any speculative want (which never occurs to it as long as it is content to be mere sound reason), but even on practical grounds, in order to attain in it information and clear instruction respecting the source of its principle, and the correct determination of it in opposition to the maxims which are based on wants and inclinations, so that it may escape from the perplexity of opposite claims, and not run the risk of losing all genuine moral principles through the equivocation into which it easily falls. Thus, when practical reason cultivates itself, there insensibly arises in it a dialectic which forces it to seek aid in philosophy, just as happens to it in its theoretic use; and in this case, therefore, as well as in the other, it will find rest nowhere but in a thorough critical examination of our reason.

## SECOND SECTION

### *Transition from Popular Moral Philosophy to the Metaphysics of Morals*

If we have hitherto drawn our notion of duty from the common use of our practical reason, it is by no means to be inferred that we have treated it as an empirical notion. On the contrary, if we attend to the experience of men's conduct, we meet frequent and, as we ourselves allow, just complaints that one cannot find a single certain example of the disposition to act from pure duty. Although many things are done in *conformity* with what *duty* prescribes, it is nevertheless always doubtful whether they are done strictly *from duty,* so as to have a moral worth. Hence there have at all times been philosophers who have altogether denied that this disposition actually exists at all in human actions, and have ascribed everything to a more or less refined self-love. Not that they have on that account questioned the soundness of the conception of morality; on the contrary, they spoke with sincere regret of the frailty and corruption of human nature, which, though noble enough to take as its rule an idea so worthy of respect, is yet too weak to follow it; and employs reason which ought to give it the law only for the purpose of providing for the interest of the inclinations, whether singly or at the best in the greatest possible harmony with one another.

In fact, it is absolutely impossible to make out by experience with complete certainty a single case in which the maxim of an action, however right in itself, rested simply on moral grounds and on the conception of duty. Sometimes it happens that with the sharpest self-examination we can find nothing beside the moral principle of duty which could have been powerful enough to move us to this or that action and to so great a sacrifice; yet we cannot from this infer with certainty that it was not really some secret impulse of self-love, under the false appearance of duty, that was the actual determining cause of the will. We like then to flatter ourselves by falsely taking credit for a more noble motive; whereas in fact we can never, even by the strictest examination, get completely behind the secret springs of action, since, when the question is of moral worth, it is not with the actions which we see that we are concerned, but with those inward principles of them which we do not see.

Moreover, we cannot better serve the wishes of those who ridicule all morality as a mere chimera of human imagination overstepping itself from vanity, than by conceding to them that notions of duty must be drawn only from experience (as from indolence, people are ready to think is also the case with all other notions); for this is to prepare for them a certain triumph. I am willing to admit out of love of humanity that even most of our actions are correct, but if we look closer at them we everywhere come upon the dear self which is always prominent, and it is this they have in view, and not the strict command of duty, which would often require self-denial. Without being an enemy of virtue, a cool observer, one that does not mistake the wish for good, however lively, for its reality, may sometimes doubt whether true virtue is actually found anywhere in the world, and this especially as years increase and the judgment is partly made wiser by experience, and partly also more acute in observation. This being so, nothing can secure us from falling away altogether from our ideas of duty, or maintain in the soul a well-grounded respect for its law, but the clear conviction that although there should never have been actions which really sprang from such pure sources, yet whether this or that takes place is not at all the question; but that reason of itself, independent on all experience, ordains what ought to take place, that accordingly actions of which perhaps the world has hitherto never given an example, the feasibility even of which might be very much doubted by one who founds everything on experience, are nevertheless inflexibly commanded by reason; that, for example, even though there might never yet have been a sincere friend, yet not a whit the less is pure sincerity in friendship required of every man, because, prior to all experience, this duty is involved as duty in the idea of a reason determining the will by *a priori* principles.

When we add further that, unless we deny that the notion of morality has any truth or reference to any possible object, we must admit that its law must be valid, not merely for men, but for all *rational creatures generally,* not merely under certain contingent conditions or with exceptions, but *with absolute necessity,* then it is clear that no experience could enable us to infer even the possibility of such apodictic laws. For with what right could we bring into unbounded respect as a universal precept for every rational nature that which perhaps holds only under the contingent conditions of humanity? Or how could laws of the determination of *our* will be regarded as laws of the determination of the will of rational beings generally, and for us only as such, if they were merely empirical and did not take their origin wholly *a priori* from pure but practical reason?

Nor could anything be more fatal to morality than that we should wish to derive it from examples. For every example of it that is set before me must be first itself tested by principles of morality, whether it is worthy to serve as an original example, that is, as a pattern, but by no means can it authoritatively furnish the conception of morality. Even the Holy One of the Gospels must first be compared with our ideal of moral perfection before we can recognize Him as such; and so He says of Himself, "Why call ye Me [whom you see] good; none is good [the model of good] but God only [whom ye do not see]?" But whence have we the conception of God as the supreme good? Simply from the *idea* of moral perfec-

tion, which reason frames *a priori* and connects inseparably with the notion of a free will. Imitation finds no place at all in morality, and examples serve only for encouragement, that is, they put beyond doubt the feasibility of what the law commands, they make visible that which the practical rule expresses more generally, but they can never authorize us to set aside the true original which lies in reason, and to guide ourselves by examples.

If then there is no genuine supreme principle of morality but what must rest simply on pure reason, independent of all experience, I think it is not necessary even to put the question whether it is good to exhibit these concepts in their generality (*in abstracto*) as they are established *a priori* along with the principles belonging to them, if our knowledge is to be distinguished from the *vulgar* and to be called philosophical. In our times indeed this might perhaps be necessary; for it we collected votes, whether pure rational knowledge separated from everything empirical, that is to say, metaphysic of morals, or whether popular practical philosophy is to be preferred, it is easy to guess which side would preponderate.

This descending to popular notions is certainly very commendable if the ascent to the principles of pure reason has first taken place and been satisfactorily accomplished. This implies that we first *found* Ethics on Metaphysics, and then, when it is firmly established, procure a *hearing* for it by giving it a popular character. But it is quite absurd to try to be popular in the first inquiry, on which the soundness of the principles depends. It is not only that this proceeding can never lay claim to the very rare merit of a true *philosophical popularity,* since there is no art in being intelligible if one renounces all thoroughness of insight; but also it produces a disgusting medley of compiled observations and half-reasoned principles. Shallow pates enjoy this because it can be used for everyday chat, but the sagacious find in it only confusion, and being unsatisfied and unable to help themselves, they turn away their eyes, while philosophers, who see quite well through this delusion, are little listened to when they call men off for a time from this pretended popularity in order that they might be rightfully popular after they have attained a definite insight.

We need only look at the attempts of moralists in that favorite fashion, and we shall find at one time the special constitution of human nature (including, however, the idea of a rational nature generally), at one time perfection, at another happiness, here moral sense, there fear of God, a little of this and a little of that, in marvelous mixture, without its occurring to them to ask whether the principles of morality are to be sought in the knowledge of human nature at all (which we can have only from experience); and, if this is not so—if these principles are to be found altogether *a priori* free from everything empirical, in pure rational concepts only, and nowhere else, not even in the smallest degree—then rather to adopt the method of making this a separate inquiry, as pure practical philosophy, or (if one may use a name so decried) as metaphysic of morals,[3] to bring it by itself to completeness, and to require the public, which wishes for popular treatment, to await the issue of this undertaking.

Such a metaphysic of morals, completely isolated, not mixed with any anthropology, theology, physics, or hyperphysics, and still less with occult qualities (which we might call hypophysical), is not only an indispensable substratum of all sound theoretical knowledge of duties, but is at the same time a desideratum of the highest importance to the actual fulfilment of their precepts. For the pure conception of duty, unmixed with any foreign addition of empirical attractions, and, in a word, the conception of the moral law, exercises on the human heart, by way of reason alone (which first becomes aware with this that it can of itself be practical), an influence so much more powerful than all other springs[4] which may be derived from the field of experience that in the consciousness of its worth it despises the latter, and can by degrees become their master; whereas a mixed ethics, compounded partly of motives drawn from feelings and inclinations, and partly also of conceptions of reason, must make the mind waver between motives which cannot be brought under any principle, which lead to good only by mere accident, and very often also to evil.

From what has been said, it is clear that all moral conceptions have their seat and origin completely *a priori* in the reason, and that, moreover, in the commonest reason just as truly as in that which is in the highest degree speculative; that they cannot be obtained by abstraction from any empirical, and therefore merely contingent, knowledge; that it is just this purity of their origin that makes them worthy to serve as our supreme practical principle, and that just in proportion as we add anything empirical, we detract from their genuine influence and from the absolute value of actions; that it is not only of the greatest necessity, in a purely speculative point of view, but is also of the greatest practical importance, to derive these notions and laws from pure reason, to present them pure and unmixed, and even to determine the compass of this practical or pure rational knowledge, that is, to determine the whole faculty of pure practical reason; and, in doing so, we must not make its principles dependent on the particular nature of human reason, though in speculative philosophy this may be permitted, or may even at times be necessary; but since moral laws ought to hold good for every rational creature, we must derive them from the general concept of a rational being. In this way, although for its *application* to man morality has need of anthropology, yet, in the first instance, we must treat it independently as pure philosophy, that is, as metaphysic, complete in itself (a thing which in such distinct branches of science is easily done); knowing well that, unless we are in possession of this, it would not only be vain to determine the moral element of duty in right actions for purposes of speculative criticism, but it would be impossible to base morals on their genuine principles, even for common practical purposes, especially of moral instruction, so as to produce pure moral dispositions, and to engraft them on men's minds to the promotion of the greatest possible good in the world.

But in order that in this study we may not merely advance by the natural steps from the common moral judgment (in this case very worthy of respect) to the philosophical, as has been already done, but also from a popular philosophy, which goes no further than it can reach by groping with the help of examples, to metaphysic (which does not allow itself to be checked by anything empirical and, as it must measure the whole extent of this kind of rational knowledge, goes as far as ideal conceptions, where even examples fail us), we must follow and clearly describe the practical faculty of reason, from the general rules of its determination to the point where the notion of duty springs from it.

Everything in nature works according to laws. Rational beings alone have the faculty of acting according to *the conception* of laws—that is, according to principles, that is, have a *will*. Since the deduction of actions from principles requires *reason,* the will is nothing but practical reason. If reason infallibly determines the will, then the actions of such a being which are recognized as objectively necessary are subjectively necessary also, that is, the will is a faculty to choose *that only* which reason independent on inclination recognizes as practically necessary, that is, as good. But if reason of itself does not sufficiently determine the will, if the latter is subject also to subjective conditions (particular impulses) which do not always coincide with the objective conditions, in a word, if the will does not *in itself* completely accord with reason (which is actually the case with men), then the actions which objectively are recognized as necessary are subjectively contingent, and the determination of such a will according to objective laws is *obligation,* that is to say, the relation of the objective laws to a will that is not thoroughly good is conceived as the determination of the will of a rational being by principles of reason, but which the will from its nature does not of necessity follow.

The conception of an objective principle, in so far as it is obligatory for a will, is called a command (of reason), and the formula of the command is called an Imperative.

All imperatives are expressed by the word *ought* [or *shall*], and thereby indicate the relation of an objective law of reason to a will which from its subjective constitution is not necessarily determined by it (an obligation). They say that something would be good to do or to forbear, but they say it to a will which does not always do a thing because it is conceived to be good to do it. That is practically *good,*

however, which determines the will by means of the conceptions of reason, and consequently not from subjective causes, but objectively, that is, on principles which are valid for every rational being as such. It is distinguished from the *pleasant* as that which influences the will only be means of sensation from merely subjective causes, valid only for the sense of this or that one, and not as a principle of reason which holds for every one.[5]

A perfectly good will would therefore be equally subject to objective laws (viz., laws of good), but could not be conceived as *obliged* thereby to act lawfully, because of itself from its subjective constitution it can only be determined by the conception of good. Therefore no imperatives hold for the Divine will, or in general for a *holy* will; *ought* is here out of place because the volition is already of itself necessarily in unison with the law. Therefore imperatives are only formulae to express the relation of objective laws of all volition to the subjective imperfection of the will of this or that rational being, for example, the human will.

Now all *imperatives* command either *hypothetically* or *categorically.* The former represent the practical necessity of a possible action as means to something else that is willed (or at least which one might possibly will). The categorical imperative would be that which represented an action as necessary of itself without reference to another end, that is, as objectively necessary.

Since every practical law represents a possible action as good, and on this account, for a subject who is practically determinable by reason as necessary, all imperatives are formulae determining an action which is necessary according to the principle of a will good in some respects. If now the action is good only as a means *to something else,* then the imperative is *hypothetical;* if it is conceived as good *in itself* and consequently as being necessarily the principle of a will which of itself conforms to reason, then it is *categorical.*

Thus the imperative declares what action possible by me would be good, and presents the practical rule in relation to a will which does not forthwith perform an action simply because it is good, whether because the subject does not always know that it is good, or because, even if it knows this, yet its maxims might be opposed to the objective principles of practical reason.

Accordingly the hypothetical imperative only says that the action is good for some purpose, *possible* or *actual.* In the first case it is a *problematical,* in the second an *assertorial* practical principle. The categorical imperative which declares an action to be objectively necessary in itself without reference to any purpose, that is, without any other end, is valid as an *apodictic* (practical) principle.

Whatever is possible only by the power of some rational being may also be conceived as a possible purpose of some will; and therefore the principles of action as regards the means necessary to attain some possible purpose are in fact infinitely numerous. All sciences have a practical part consisting of problems expressing that some end is possible for us, and of imperatives directing how it may be attained. These may, therefore, be called in general imperatives of *skill.* Here there is no question whether the end is rational and good, but only what one must do in order to attain it. The precepts for the physician to make his patient thoroughly healthy, and for a poisoner to ensure certain death, are of equal value in this respect, that each serves to effect its purpose perfectly. Since in early youth it cannot be known what ends are likely to occur to us in the course of life, parents seek to have their children taught a *great many things,* and provide for their *skill* in the use of means for all sorts of arbitrary ends, of none of which can they determine whether it may not perhaps hereafter be an object to their pupil, but which it is at all events *possible* that he might aim at; and this anxiety is so great that they commonly neglect to form and correct their judgment on the value of the things which may be chosen as ends.

There is *one* end, however, which may be assumed to be actually such to all rational beings (so far as imperatives apply to them, viz., as dependent beings), and, therefore, one purpose which they not merely *may* have, but which we may with certainty assume that they all actually *have* by a natural necessity, and this is *happiness.* The hypothetical impera-

tive which expresses the practical necessity of an action as means to the advancement of happiness is *assertorial.* We are not to present it as necessary for an uncertain and merely possible purpose, but for a purpose which we may presuppose with certainty and *a priori* in every man, because it belongs to his being. Now skill in the choice of means to his own greatest well-being may be called *prudence,*[6] in the narrowest sense. And thus the imperative which refers to the choice of means to one's own happiness, that is, the precept of prudence, is still always *hypothetical;* the action is not commanded absolutely, but only as means to another purpose.

Finally, there is an imperative which commands a certain conduct immediately, without having as its condition any other purpose to be attained by it. This imperative is *categorical.* It concerns not the matter of the action, or its intended result, but its form and the principle of which it is itself a result; and what is essentially good in it consists in the mental disposition, let the consequence be what it may. This imperative may be called that of *morality.*

There is a marked distinction also between the volitions on these three sorts of principles in the *dissimilarity* of the obligation of the will. In order to mark this difference more clearly, I think they would be most suitably named in their order if we said they are either *rules* of skill, or *counsels* of prudence, or *commands (laws)* of morality. For it is *law* only that involves the conception of an *unconditional* and objective necessity, which is consequently universally valid; and commands are laws which must be obeyed, that is, must be followed, even in opposition to inclination. *Counsels,* indeed, involve necessity, but one which can only hold under a contingent subjective condition, viz., they depend on whether this or that man reckons this or that as part of his happiness; the categorical imperative, on the contrary, is not limited by any condition, and as being absolutely, although practically, necessary may be quite properly called a command. We might also call the first kind of imperatives *technical* (belonging to art), the second *pragmatic*[7] (belonging to welfare), the third *moral* (belonging to free conduct generally, that is to morals).

Now arises the question, how are all these imperatives possible? This question does not seek to know how we can conceive the accomplishment of the action which the imperative ordains, but merely how we can conceive the obligation of the will which the imperative expresses. No special explanation is needed to show how an imperative of skill is possible. Whoever wills the end wills also (so far as reason decides his conduct) the means in his power which are indispensably necessary thereto. This proposition is, as regards the volition, analytical; for in willing an object as my effect there is already thought the causality of myself as an acting cause, that is to say, the use of the means; and the imperative deduces from the conception of volition of an end the conception of actions necessary to this end. Synthetical propositions must no doubt be employed in defining the means to a proposed end; but they do not concern the principle, the act of the will, but the object and its realization. For example, that in order to bisect a line on an unerring principle I must draw from its extremities two intersecting arcs; this no doubt is taught by mathematics only in synthetical propositions; but if I know that it is only by this process that the intended operation can be performed, then to say that if I fully will the operation, I also will the action required for it, is an analytical proposition; for it is one and the same thing to conceive something as an effect which I can produce in a certain way, and to conceive myself as acting in this way.

If it were only equally easy to give a definite conception of happiness, the imperatives of prudence would correspond exactly with those of skill, and would likewise be analytical. For in this case as in that, it could be said whoever wills the end wills also (according to the dictate of reason necessarily) the indispensable means thereto which are in his power. But, unfortunately, the notion of happiness is so indefinite that although every man wishes to attain it, yet he never can say definitely and consistently what it is that he really wishes and wills. The reason of this is that all the elements which belong to the notion of happiness are altogether empirical, that is, they must be borrowed from experience, and nevertheless the idea of happiness requires an absolute

whole, a maximum of welfare in my present and all future circumstances. Now it is impossible that the most clear-sighted and at the same time most powerful being (supposed finite) should frame to himself a definite conception of what he really wills in this. Does he will riches, how much anxiety, envy, and snares might he not thereby draw upon his shoulders? Does he will knowledge and discernment, perhaps it might prove to be only an eye so much the sharper to show him so much the more fearfully the evils that are now concealed from him and that cannot be avoided, or to impose more wants on his desires, which already give him concern enough. Would he have long life? Who guarantees to him that it would not be a long misery? Would he at least have health? How often has uneasiness of the body restrained from excesses into which perfect health would have allowed one to fall, and so on? In short, he is unable, on any principle, to determine with certainty what would make him truly happy; because to do so he would need to be omniscient. We cannot therefore act on any definite principles to secure happiness, but only on empirical counsels, for example, of regimen, frugality, courtesy, reserve, etc., which experience teaches do, on the average, most promote well-being. Hence it follows that the imperatives of prudence do not, strictly speaking, command at all, that is, they cannot present actions objectively as practically *necessary;* that they are rather to be regarded as counsels (*consilia*) than precepts (*praecepta*) of reason, that the problem to determine certainly and universally what action would promote the happiness of a rational being is completely insoluble, and consequently no imperative respecting it is possible which should, in the strict sense, command to do what makes happy; because happiness is not an ideal of reason but of imagination, resting solely on empirical grounds, and it is vain to expect that these should define an action by which one could attain the totality of a series of consequences which is really endless. This imperative of prudence would, however, be an analytical proposition if we assume that the means to happiness could be certainly assigned; for it is distinguished from the imperative of skill only by this that in the latter the end is merely *possible,* in the former it is *given;* as, however, both only ordain the means to that which we suppose to be willed as an end, it follows that the imperative which ordains the willing of the means of him who wills the end is in both cases analytical. Thus there is no difficulty in regard to the possibility of an imperative of this kind either.

On the other hand, the question, how the imperative of *morality* is possible, is undoubtedly one, the only one, demanding a solution, as this is not at all hypothetical, and the objective necessity which it presents cannot rest on any hypothesis, as is the case with the hypothetical imperatives. Only here we must never leave out of consideration that we *cannot* make out *by any example,* in other words, empirically, whether there is such an imperative at all; but it is rather to be feared that all those which seem to be categorical may yet be at bottom hypothetical. For instance, when the precept is: Thou shalt not promise deceitfully; and it is assumed that the necessity of this is not a mere counsel to avoid some other evil, so that it should mean: Thou shalt not make a lying promise, lest if it become known thou shouldst destroy thy credit, but that an action of this kind must be regarded as evil in itself, so that the imperative of the prohibition is categorical; then we cannot show with certainty in any example that the will was determined merely by the law, without any other spring of action, although it may appear to be so. For it is always possible that fear of disgrace, perhaps also obscure dread of other dangers, may have a secret influence on the will. Who can prove by experience the non-existence of a cause when all that experience tells us is that we do not perceive it? But in such a case the so-called moral imperative, which as such appears to be categorical and unconditional, would in reality be only a pragmatic precept, drawing our attention to our own interests, and merely teaching us to take these into consideration.

We shall therefore have to investigate *a priori* the possibility of a categorical imperative, as we have not in this case the advantage of its reality being given in experience, so that [the elucidation of] its possibility should be requisite only for its explana-

tion, not for its establishment. In the meantime it may be discerned beforehand that the categorical imperative alone has the purport of a practical law; all the rest may indeed be called *principles* of the will but not laws, since whatever is only necessary for the attainment of some arbitrary purpose may be considered as in itself contingent, and we can at any time be free from the precept if we give up the purpose; on the contrary, the unconditional command leaves the will no liberty to choose the opposite, consequently it alone carries with it that necessity which we require in a law.

Secondly, in the case of this categorical imperative or law of morality, the difficulty (of discerning its possibility) is a very profound one. It is an *a priori* synthetical practical proposition;[8] and as there is so much difficulty in discerning the possibility of speculative propositions of this kind, it may readily be supposed that the difficulty will be no less with the practical.

In this problem we will first inquire whether the mere conception of a categorical imperative may not perhaps supply us also with the formula of it, containing the proposition which alone can be a categorical imperative; for even if we know the tenor of such an absolute command, yet how it is possible will require further special and laborious study, which we postpone to the last section.

When I conceive a hypothetical imperative, in general I do not know beforehand what it will contain until I am given the condition. But when I conceive a categorical imperative, I know at once what it contains. For as the imperative contains besides the law only the necessity that the maxims[9] shall conform to this law, while the law contains no conditions restricting it, there remains nothing but the general statement that the maxim of the action should conform to a universal law, and it is this conformity alone that the imperative properly represents as necessary.

There is therefore but one categorical imperative, namely, this: *Act only on that maxim whereby thou canst at the same time will that it should become a universal law.*

Now if all imperatives of duty can be deduced

from this one imperative as from their principle, then, although it should remain undecided whether what is called duty is not merely a vain notion, yet at least we shall be able to show what we understand by it and what this notion means.

Since the universality of the law according to which effects are produced constitutes what is properly called *nature* in the most general sense (as to form)—that is, the existence of things so far as it is determined by general laws—the imperative of duty may be expressed thus: *Act as if the maxim of thy action were to become by thy will a universal law of nature.*

We will now enumerate a few duties, adopting the usual division of them into duties to ourselves and to others, and into perfect and imperfect duties.[10]

1. A man reduced to despair by a series of misfortunes feels wearied of life, but is still so far in possession of his reason that he can ask himself whether it would not be contrary to his duty to himself to take his own life. Now he inquires whether the maxim of his action could become a universal law of nature. His maxim is: From self-love I adopt it as a principle to shorten my life when its longer duration is likely to bring more evil than satisfaction. It is asked then simply whether this principle founded on self-love can become a universal law of nature. Now we see at once that a system of nature of which it should be a law to destroy life by means of the very feeling whose special nature it is to impel to the improvement of life would contradict itself, and therefore could not exist as a system of nature; hence that maxim cannot possibly exist as a universal law of nature, and consequently would be wholly inconsistent with the supreme principle of all duty.

2. Another finds himself forced by necessity to borrow money. He knows that he will not be able to repay it, but sees also that nothing will be lent to him unless he promises stoutly to repay it in a definite time. He desires to make this promise, but he has still so much conscience as to ask himself: Is it not unlawful and inconsistent with duty to get out of a difficulty in this way? Suppose, however, that he resolves to do so, then the maxim of his action would be expressed thus: When I think myself in want of money, I will borrow money and promise to repay it, although I know that I never can do so. Now this principle of self-love or of one's own advantage may perhaps be consistent with my whole future welfare; but the question now is, Is it right? I change then the suggestion of self-love into a universal law, and state the question thus: How would it be if my maxim were a universal law? Then I see at once that it could never hold as a universal law of nature, but would necessarily contradict itself. For supposing it to be a universal law that everyone when he thinks himself in a difficulty should be able to promise whatever he pleases, with the purpose of not keeping his promise, the promise itself would become impossible, as well as the end that one might have in view in it, since no one would consider that anything was promised to him, but would ridicule all such statements as vain pretenses.

3. A third finds in himself a talent which with the help of some culture might make him a useful man in many respects. But he finds himself in comfortable circumstances and prefers to indulge in pleasure rather than to take pains in enlarging and improving his happy natural capacities. He asks, however, whether his maxim of neglect of his natural gifts, besides agreeing with his inclination to indulgence, agrees also with what is called duty. He sees then that a system of nature could indeed subsist with such a universal law, although men (like the South Sea islanders) should let their talents rest and resolve to devote their lives merely to idleness, amusement, and propagation of their species—in a word, to enjoyment; but he cannot possibly *will* that this should be a universal law of nature, or be implanted in us as such by a natural instinct. For, as a rational being, he necessarily wills that his faculties be developed, since they serve him, and have been given him, for all sorts of possible purposes.

4. A fourth, who is in prosperity, while he sees that others have to contend with great wretchedness and that he could help them, thinks: What concern is it of mine? Let everyone be as happy as Heaven pleases, or as he can make himself; I will take nothing from him nor even envy him, only I do not wish

to contribute anything to his welfare or to his assistance in distress! Now no doubt, if such a mode of thinking were a universal law, the human race might very well subsist, and doubtless even better than in a state in which everyone talks of sympathy and goodwill, or even takes care occasionally to put it into practice, but, on the other side, also cheats when he can, betrays the rights of men, or otherwise violates them. But although it is possible that a universal law of nature might exist in accordance with that maxim, it is impossible to *will* that such a principle should have the universal validity of a law of nature. For a will which resolved this would contradict itself, inasmuch as many cases might occur in which one would have the need of the love and sympathy of others, and in which, by such a law of nature, sprung from his own will, he would deprive himself of all hope of the aid he desires.

These are a few of the many actual duties, or at least what we regard as such, which obviously fall into two classes on the one principle that we have laid down. We must be *able to will* that a maxim of our action should be a universal law. This is the canon of the moral appreciation of the action generally. Some actions are of such a character that their maxim cannot without contradiction be even *conceived* as a universal law of nature, far from it being possible that we should *will* that it *should* be so. In others, this intrinsic impossibility is not found, but still it is impossible to *will* that their maxim should be raised to the universality of a law of nature, since such a will would contradict itself. It is easily seen that the former violate strict or rigorous (inflexible) duty; the latter only laxer (meritorious) duty. Thus it has been completely shown by these examples how all duties depend as regards the nature of the obligation (not the object of the action) on the same principle.

If now we attend to ourselves on occasion of any transgression of duty, we shall find that we in fact do not will that our maxim should be a universal law, for that is impossible for us; on the contrary, we will that the opposite should remain a universal law, only we assume the liberty of making an *exception* in our own favor or (just for this time only) in favor of our inclination. Consequently, if we considered all cases from one and the same point of view, namely, that of reason, we should find a contradiction in our own will, namely, that a certain principle should be objectively necessary as a universal law, and yet subjectively should not be universal, but admit of exceptions. As, however, we at one moment regard our action from the point of view of a will wholly conformed to reason, and then again look at the same action from the point of view of a will affected by inclination, there is not really any contradiction, but an antagonism of inclination to the precept of reason, whereby the universality of the principle is changed into a mere generality, so that the practical principle of reason shall meet the maxim half way. Now, although this cannot be justified in our own impartial judgment, yet it proves that we do really recognize the validity of the categorical imperative and (with all respect for it) only allow ourselves a few exceptions which we think unimportant and forced from us.

We have thus established at least this much—that if duty is a conception which is to have any import and real legislative authority for our actions, it can only be expressed in categorical, and not at all in hypothetical, imperatives. We have also, which is of great importance, exhibited clearly and definitely for every practical application the content of the categorical imperative, which must contain the principle of all duty if there is such a thing at all. We have not yet, however, advanced so far as to prove *a priori* that there actually is such an imperative, that there is a practical law which commands absolutely of itself and without any other impulse, and that the following of this law is duty.

With the view of attaining to this it is of extreme importance to remember that we must not allow ourselves to think of deducing the reality of this principle from the *particular attributes of human nature.* For duty is to be a practical, unconditional necessity of action; it must therefore hold for all rational beings (to whom an imperative can apply at all), and *for this reason only* be also a law for all human wills. On the contrary, whatever is deduced from the particular natural characteristics of humanity, from certain feelings and propensions, nay, even, if possible, from any particular tendency proper to human reason, and which need not necessarily hold for the will of every rational being—this may indeed supply us with a maxim but not with a law; with a subjective principle on which we may have a propension and inclination to act, but not with an objective principle on which we should be *enjoined* to act, even though all our propensions, inclinations, and natural dispositions were opposed to it. In fact, the sublimity and intrinsic dignity of the command in duty are so much the more evident, the less the subjective impulses favor it and the more they oppose it, without being able in the slightest degree to weaken the obligation of the law or to diminish its validity.

Here then we see philosophy brought to a critical position, since it has to be firmly fixed, notwithstanding that it has nothing to support it in heaven or earth. Here it must show its purity as absolute director of its own laws, not the herald of those which are whispered to it by an implanted sense or who knows what tutelary nature. Although these may be better than nothing, yet they can never afford principles dictated by reason, which must have their source wholly *a priori* and thence their commanding authority, expecting everything from the supremacy of the law and the due respect for it, nothing from inclination, or else condemning the man to self-contempt and inward abhorrence.

Thus every empirical element is not only quite incapable of being an aid to the principle of morality, but is even highly prejudicial to the purity of morals; for the proper and inestimable worth of an absolutely good will consists just in this that the principle of action is free from all influence of contingent grounds, which alone experience can furnish. We cannot too much or too often repeat our warning against this lax and even mean habit of thought which seeks for its principle among empirical motives and laws; for human reason in its weariness is glad to rest on this pillow, and in a dream of sweet illusions (in which, instead of Juno, it embraces a cloud) it substitutes for morality a bastard patched up from limbs of various derivation, which looks like anything one chooses to see in it; only not like virtue to one who has once beheld her in her true form.[11]

The question then is this: Is it a necessary law *for all rational beings* that they should always judge of their actions by maxims of which they can themselves will that they should serve as universal laws? If it is so, then it must be connected (altogether *a priori*) with the very conception of the will of a rational being generally. But in order to discover this connection we must, however reluctantly, take a step into metaphysic, although into a domain of it which is distinct from speculative philosophy—namely, the metaphysic of morals. In a practical philosophy, where it is not the reasons of what *happens* that we have to ascertain, but the laws of what *ought to happen,* even although it never does, that is, objective practical laws, there it is not necessary to inquire into the reasons why anything pleases or displeases, how the pleasure of mere sensation differs from taste, and whether the latter is distinct from a general satisfaction of reason; on what the feeling of pleasure or pain rests, and how from it desires and inclinations arise, and from these again maxims by the cooperation of reason; for all this belongs to an empirical psychology, which would constitute the second part of physics, if we regard physics as the *philosophy* of nature, so far as it is based on *empirical laws.* But here we are concerned with objective practical laws, and consequently with the relation of the will to itself so far as it is determined by reason alone, in which case whatever has reference to anything empirical is necessarily excluded; since if *reason of itself alone* determines the conduct (and it is the possibility of this that we are now investigating), it must necessarily do so *a priori.*

The will is conceived as a faculty of determining oneself to action *in accordance with the conception of certain laws.* And such a faculty can be found only in rational beings. Now that which serves the will as the objective ground of its self-determination is the *end,* and if this is assigned by reason alone, it must hold for all rational beings. On the other hand, that which merely contains the ground of possibility of the action of which the effect is the end, this is called the *means.* The subjective ground of the desire is the *spring,* the objective ground of the volition is the *motive;* hence the distinction between subjective ends which rest on springs, and objective ends which depend on motives valid for every rational being. Practical principles are *formal* when they abstract from all subjective ends; they are *material* when they assume these, and therefore particular, springs of action. The ends which a rational being proposes to himself at pleasure as *effects* of his actions (material ends are all only relative, for it is only their relation to the particular desires of the subject that gives them their worth, which therefore cannot furnish principles universal and necessary for all rational beings and for every volition, that is to say, practical laws. Hence all these relative ends can give rise only to hypothetical imperatives.

Supposing, however, that there were something *whose existence* has *in itself* an absolute worth, something which, being *an end in itself,* could be a source of definite laws, then in this and this alone would lie the source of a possible categorical imperative, that is, a practical law.

Now I say: man and generally any rational being *exists* as an end in himself, *not merely as a means* to be arbitrarily used by this or that will, but in all his actions, whether they concern himself or other rational beings, must be always regarded at the same time as an end. All objects of the inclinations have only a conditional worth; for if the inclinations and the wants founded on them did not exist, then their object would be without value. But the inclinations themselves, being sources of want, are so far from having an absolute worth for which they should be desired that, on the contrary, it must be the universal wish of every rational being to be wholly free from them. Thus the worth of any object which is *to be acquired* by our action is always conditional. Beings whose existence depends not on our will but on nature's, have nevertheless, if they are nonrational beings, only a relative value as means, and are therefore called *things;* rational beings, on the contrary, are called *persons,* because their very nature points them out as ends in themselves, that is, as something which must not be used merely as means, and so far therefore restricts freedom of action (and is an object of respect). These, therefore, are not merely subjective ends whose existence has a worth *for us* as an effect of our action, but *objective ends,* that is, things

whose existence is an end in itself—an end, moreover, for which no other can be substituted, which they should subserve *merely* as means, for otherwise nothing whatever would possess *absolute worth;* but if all worth were conditioned and therefore contingent, then there would be no supreme practical principle of reason whatever.

If then there is a supreme practical principle or, in respect of the human will, a categorical imperative, it must be one which, being drawn from the conception of that which is necessarily an end for everyone because it is *an end in itself,* constitutes an *objective* principle of will, and can therefore serve as a universal practical law. The foundation of this principle is: *rational nature exists as an end in itself.* Man necessarily conceives his own existence as being so; so far then this is a *subjective* principle of human actions. But every other rational being regards its existence similarly, just on the same rational principle that holds for me;[12] so that it is at the same time an objective principle from which as a supreme practical law all laws of the will must be capable of being deduced. Accordingly the practical imperative will be as follows: *So act as to treat humanity, whether in thine own person or in that of any other, in every case as an end withal, never as means only.* We will now inquire whether this can be practically carried out.

To abide by the previous examples:

*First,* under the head of necessary duty to oneself: He who contemplates suicide should ask himself whether his action can be consistent with the idea of humanity *as an end in itself.* If he destroys himself in order to escape from painful circumstances, he uses a person merely as *a mean* to maintain a tolerable condition up to the end of life. But a man is not a thing, that is to say, something which can be used merely as means, but must in all his actions be always considered as an end in himself. I cannot, therefore, dispose in any way of a man in my own person so as to mutilate him, to damage or kill him. (It belongs to ethics proper to define this principle more precisely, so as to avoid all misunderstanding, for example, as to the amputation of the limbs in order to preserve myself; as to exposing my life to danger with a view to preserve it, etc. This question is therefore omitted here.)

*Secondly,* as regards necessary duties, or those of

strict obligation, towards others: He who is thinking of making a lying promise to others will see at once that he would be using another man *merely as a mean,* without the latter containing at the same time the end in himself. For he whom I propose by such a promise to use for my own purposes cannot possibly assent to my mode of acting towards him, and therefore cannot himself contain the end of this action. This violation of the principle of humanity in other men is more obvious if we take in examples of attacks on the freedom and property of others. For then it is clear that he who transgresses the rights of men intends to use the person of others merely as means, without considering that as rational beings they ought always to be esteemed also as ends, that is, as beings who must be capable of containing in themselves the end of the very same action.[13]

*Thirdly,* as regards contingent (meritorious) duties to oneself: It is not enough that the action does not violate humanity in our own person as an end in itself, it must also *harmonize with* it. Now there are in humanity capacities of greater perfection which belong to the end that nature has in view in regard to humanity in ourselves as the subject; to neglect these might perhaps be consistent with the *maintenance* of humanity as an end in itself, but not with the *advancement* of this end.

*Fourthly,* as regards meritorious duties towards others: The natural end which all men have is their own happiness. Now humanity might indeed subsist although no one should contribute anything to the happiness of others, provided he did not intentionally withdraw anything from it; but after all, this would only harmonize negatively, not positively, with *humanity as an end in itself,* if everyone does not also endeavor, as far as in him lies, to forward the ends of others. For the ends of any subject which is an end in himself ought as far as possible to be *my* ends also, if that conception is to have its *full* effect with me.

This principle that humanity and generally every rational nature is *an end in itself* (which is the supreme limiting condition of every man's freedom of action), is not borrowed from experience, *first,* because it is universal, applying as it does to all rational beings whatever, and experience is not capable of determining anything about them; *secondly,* because

it does not present humanity as an end to men (subjectively), that is, as an object which men do of themselves actually adopt as an end; but as an objective end which must as a law constitute the supreme limiting condition of all our subjective ends, let them be what we will; it must therefore spring from pure reason. In fact the objective principle of all practical legislation lies (according to the first principle) in *the rule* and its form of universality which makes it capable of being a law (say, for example, a law of nature); but the *subjective* principle is in the *end;* now by the second principle, the subject of all ends is each rational being inasmuch as it is an end in itself. Hence follows the third practical principle of the will, which is the ultimate condition of its harmony with the universal practical reason, viz., the idea of *the will of every rational being as a universally legislative will.*

On this principle all maxims are rejected which are inconsistent with the will being itself universal legislator. Thus the will is not subject to the law, but so subject that it must be regarded *as itself giving the law,* and on this ground only subject to the law (of which it can regard itself as the author).

In the previous imperatives, namely, that based on the conception of the conformity of actions to general laws, as in a *physical system of nature,* and that based on the universal *prerogative* of rational beings as *ends* in themselves—these imperatives just because they were conceived as categorical excluded from any share in their authority all admixture of any interest as a spring of action; they were, however, only *assumed* to be categorical, because such an assumption was necessary to explain the conception of duty. But we could not prove independently that there are practical propositions which command categorically, nor can it be proved in this section; one thing, however, could be done, namely, to indicate in the imperative itself, by some determinate expression, that in the case of volition from duty all interest is renounced, which is the specific criterion of categorical as distinguished from hypothetical imperatives. This is done in the present (third) formula of the principle, namely, in the idea of the will of every rational being as a *universally legislating will.*

For although a will *which is subject to laws* may be attached to this law by means of an interest, yet a will which is itself a supreme lawgiver, so far as it is such, cannot possibly depend on any interest, since a will so dependent would itself still need another law restricting the interest of its self-love by the condition that it should be valid as universal law.

Thus the *principle* that every human will is *a will which in all its maxims gives universal laws,*[14] provided it be otherwise justified, would be very *well adapted* to be the categorical imperative, in this respect, namely, that just because of the idea of universal legislation it is *not based on any interest,* and therefore it alone among all possible imperatives can be *unconditional.* Or still better, converting the proposition, if there is a categorical imperative (that is, a law for the will of every rational being), it can only command that everything be done from maxims of one's will regarded as a will which could at the same time will that it should itself give universal laws, for in that case only the practical principle and the imperative which it obeys are unconditional, since they cannot be based on any interest.

Looking back now on all previous attempts to discover the principle of morality, we need not wonder why they all failed. It was seen that man was bound to laws by duty, but it was not observed that the laws to which he is subject are *only those of his own giving,* though at the same time they are *universal,* and that he is only bound to act in conformity with his own will—a will, however, which is designed by nature to give universal laws. For when one has conceived man only as a subject to a law (no matter what), then this law required some interest, either by way of attraction or constraint, since it did not originate as a law from *his own* will, but this will was according to a law obliged by *something else* to act in a certain manner. Now by this necessary consequence all the labor spent in finding a supreme principle of *duty* was irrevocably lost. For men never elicited duty, but only a necessity of acting from a certain interest. Whether this interest was private or otherwise, in any case the imperative must be conditional, and could not by any means be capable of being a moral command. I will therefore call this the principle of *Autonomy* of the will, in contrast with every other which I accordingly reckon as *Heteronomy.*

The conception of every rational being as one which must consider itself as giving in all the maxims of its will universal laws, so as to judge itself and its actions from this point of view—this conception leads to another which depends on it and is very fruitful, namely, that of a *kingdom of ends.*

By a "kingdom" I understand the union of different rational beings in a system by common laws. Now since it is by laws that ends are determined as regards their universal validity, hence, if we abstract from the personal differences of rational beings, and likewise from all the content of their private ends, we shall be able to conceive all ends combined in a systematic whole (including both rational beings as ends in themselves, and also the special ends which each may propose to himself), that is to say, we can conceive a kingdom of ends, which on the preceding principles is possible.

For all rational beings come under the *law* that each of them must treat itself and all others *never merely as means,* but in every case *at the same time as ends in themselves.* Hence results a systematic union of rational beings by common objective laws, that is, a kingdom which may be called a kingdom of ends, since what these laws have in view is just the relation of these beings to one another as ends and means. It is certainly only an ideal.

A rational being belongs as a *member* to the kingdom of ends when, although giving universal laws in it, he is also himself subject to these laws. He belongs to it *as sovereign* when, while giving laws, he is not subject to the will of any other.

A rational being must always regard himself as giving laws either as member or as sovereign in a kingdom of ends which is rendered possible by the freedom of will. He cannot, however, maintain the latter position merely by the maxims of his will, but only in case he is a completely independent being without wants and with unrestricted power adequate to his will.

Morality consists then in the reference of all action to the legislation which alone can render a kingdom of ends possible. This legislation must be capable of existing in every rational being, and of emanating from his will, so that the principle of this will is never to act on any maxim which could not without contradiction be also a universal law, and accordingly *always* so to act *that the will could at the same time regard itself as giving in its maxims universal laws.* If now the maxims of rational beings are not by their own nature coincident with this objective principle, then the necessity of acting on it is called practical necessitation, that is, *duty.* Duty does not apply to the sovereign in the kingdom of ends, but it does to every member of it and to all in the same degree.

The practical necessity of acting on this principle, that is, duty, does not rest at all on feelings, impulses, or inclinations, but solely on the relation of rational beings to one another, a relation in which the will of a rational being must always be regarded as *legislative,* since otherwise it could not be conceived as *an end in itself.* Reason then refers every maxim of the will, regarding it as legislating universally, to every other will and also to every action towards oneself; and this not on account of any other practical motive or any future advantage, but from the idea of the *dignity* of a rational being, obeying no law but that which he himself also gives.

In the kingdom of ends everything has either *value* or *dignity.* Whatever has a value can be replaced by something else which is *equivalent;* whatever, on the other hand, is above all value, and therefore admits of no equivalent, has a dignity.

Whatever has reference to the general inclinations and wants of mankind has a *market value;* whatever, without presupposing a want, corresponds to a certain taste, that is, to a satisfaction in the mere purposeless play of our faculties, has a *fancy value;* but that which constitutes the condition under which alone anything can be an end in itself, that has not merely a relative worth, that is, value, but an intrinsic worth, that is, *dignity.*

Now morality is the condition under which alone a rational being can be an end in himself, since by this alone it is possible that he should be a legislating member in the kingdom of ends. Thus morality, and humanity as capable of it, is that which alone has dignity. Skill and diligence in labor have a market value;

wit, lively imagination, and humor have fancy value; on the other hand, fidelity to promises, benevolence from principle (not from instinct), have an intrinsic worth. Neither nature nor art contains anything which in default of these it could put in their place, for their worth consists not in the effects which spring from them, not in the use and advantage which they secure, but in the disposition of the mind, that is, the maxims of the will which are ready to manifest themselves in such actions, even though they should not have the desired effect. These actions also need no recommendation from any subjective taste or sentiment, that they may be looked on with immediate favor and satisfaction; they need no immediate propension or feeling for them; they exhibit the will that performs them as an object of an immediate respect, and nothing but reason is required to *impose* them on the will; not to *flatter* it into them, which, in the case of duties, would be a contradiction. This estimation therefore shows that the worth of such a disposition is dignity, and places it infinitely above all value, with which it cannot for a moment be brought into comparison or competition without as it were violating its sanctity.

What then is it which justifies virtue or the morally good disposition, in making such lofty claims? It is nothing less than the privilege it secures to the rational being of participating in the giving of universal laws, by which it qualifies him to be a member of a possible kingdom of ends, a privilege to which he was already destined by his own nature as being an end in himself, and on that account legislating in the kingdom of ends; free as regards all laws of physical nature, and obeying those only which he himself gives, and by which his maxims can belong to a system of universal law to which at the same time he submits himself. For nothing has any worth except what the law assigns it. Now the legislation itself which assigns the worth of everything must for that very reason possess dignity, that is, an unconditional incomparable worth; and the word *respect* alone supplies a becoming expression for the esteem which a rational being must have for it. *Autonomy* then is the basis of the dignity of human and of every rational nature.

The three modes of presenting the principle of morality that have been adduced are at bottom only so many formulae of the very same law, and each of itself involves the other two. There is, however, a difference in them, but it is rather subjectively than objectively practical, intended, namely, to bring an idea of the reason nearer to intuition (by means of a certain analogy), and thereby nearer to feeling. All maxims, in fact, have—

1. A *form,* consisting in universality; and in this view the formula of the moral imperative is expressed thus, that the maxims must be so chosen as if they were to serve as universal laws of nature.

2. A *matter,* namely, an end, and here the formula says that the rational being, as it is an end by its own nature and therefore an end in itself, must in every maxim serve as the condition limiting all merely relative and arbitrary ends.

3. A *complete characterization* of all maxims by means of that formula, namely, that all maxims ought, by their own legislation, to harmonize with a possible kingdom of ends as with a kingdom of nature.[15] There is a progress here in the order of the categories of *unity* of the form of the will (its universality), *plurality* of the matter (the objects, that is, the ends), and *totality* of the system of these. In forming our moral *judgment* of actions it is better to proceed always on the strict method, and start from the general formula of the categorical imperative: *Act according to a maxim which can at the same time make itself a universal law.* If, however, we wish to gain an *entrance* for the moral law, it is very useful to bring one and the same action under the three specified conceptions, and thereby as far as possible to bring it nearer to intuition.

We can now end where we started at the beginning, namely, with the conception of a will unconditionally good. *That will* is *absolutely good* which cannot be evil—in other words, whose maxim, if made a universal law, could never contradict itself. This principle, then, is its supreme law: *Act always on such a maxim as thou canst at the same time will to be a universal law;* this is the sole condition under which a will can never contradict itself; and such an imperative is categorical. Since the validity of the will as a universal law for possible actions is analogous to the universal connection of the existence of things by general laws, which is the formal notion of nature in general, the categorical imperative can also be expressed thus: *Act on maxims which can at the same time have for their object themselves as universal laws of nature.* Such then is the formula of an absolutely good will.

Rational nature is distinguished from the rest of nature by this that it sets before itself an end. This end would be the matter of every good will. But since in the idea of a will that is absolutely good without being limited by any condition (of attaining this or that end) we must abstract wholly from every end *to be effected* (since this would make every will only relatively good), it follows that in this case the end must be conceived, not as an end to be effected, but as an *independently* existing end. Consequently it is conceived only negatively, that is, as that which we must never act against, and which, therefore, must never be regarded as means, but must in every volition be esteemed as an end likewise. Now this end can be nothing but the subject of all possible ends, since this is also the subject of a possible absolutely good will; for such a will cannot without contradiction be postponed to any other object. This principle: So act in regard to every rational being (thyself and others) that he may always have place in thy maxim as an end in himself, is accordingly essentially identical with this other: Act upon a maxim which, at the same time, involves its own universal validity for every rational being. For that in using means for every end I should limit my maxim by the condition of its holding good as a law for every subject, this comes to the same thing as that the fundamental principle of all maxims of action must be that the subject of all ends, that is, the rational being himself, be never employed merely as means, but as the supreme condition restricting the use of all means—that is, in every case as an end likewise.

It follows incontestably that, to whatever laws any rational being may be subject, he being an end in himself must be able to regard himself as also legislating universally in respect of these same laws, since it is just this fitness of his maxims for universal legislation that distinguishes him as an end in himself; also it follows that this implies his dignity (prerogative) above all mere physical beings, that he must always take his maxims from the point of view which regards himself, and likewise every other rational being, as lawgiving beings (on which account they are called persons). In this way a world of rational beings (*mundus intelligibilis*) is possible as a kingdom of ends, and this by virtue of the legislation proper to all persons as members. Therefore, every rational being must so act as if he were by his maxims in every case a legislating member in the universal kingdom of ends. The formal principle of these maxims is: So act as if thy maxim were to serve likewise as the universal law (of all rational beings). A kingdom of ends is thus only possible on the analogy of a kingdom of nature, the former, however, only by maxims—that is, self-imposed rules—the latter only by the laws of efficient causes acting under necessitation from without. Nevertheless, although the system of nature is looked upon as a machine, yet so far as it has reference to rational beings as its ends, it is given on this account the name of a kingdom of nature. Now such a kingdom of ends would be actually realized by means of maxims conforming to the canon which the categorical imperative prescribes to all rational beings, *if they were universally followed.* But although a rational being, even if he punctually follows this maxim himself, cannot reckon upon all others being therefore true to the same, nor expect that the kingdom of nature and its orderly arrangements shall be in harmony with him as a fitting member, so as to form a kingdom of ends to which he himself contributes, that is to say, that it shall favor his expectation of happiness, still that law: Act according to the maxims of a member of a merely possible kingdom of ends legislating in it universally, remains in its full force inasmuch as it commands categorically. And it is just in this that the paradox lies; that the mere dignity of man as a rational creature, without any other end or advantage to be attained thereby, in other words, respect for a mere idea, should yet serve as an inflexible precept of the will, and that it is precisely in this indepen-

dence of the maxim on all such springs of action that its sublimity consists; and it is this that makes every rational subject worthy to be a legislative member in the kingdom of ends, for otherwise he would have to be conceived only as subject to the physical law of his wants. And although we should suppose the kingdom of nature and the kingdom of ends to be united under one sovereign, so that the latter kingdom thereby ceased to be a mere idea and acquired true reality, then it would no doubt gain the accession of a strong spring, but by no means any increase of its intrinsic worth. For this sole absolute lawgiver must, notwithstanding this, be always conceived as estimating the worth of rational beings only by their disinterested behavior, as prescribed to themselves from that idea [the dignity of man] alone. The essence of things is not altered by their external relations, and that which, abstracting from these, alone constitutes the absolute worth of man is also that by which he must be judged, whoever the judge may be, and even by the Supreme Being. *Morality,* then, is the relation of actions to the autonomy of the will, that is, to the potential universal legislation by its maxims. An action that is consistent with the autonomy of the will is *permitted;* one that does not agree therewith is *forbidden.* A will whose maxims necessarily coincide with the laws of autonomy is a *holy* will, good absolutely. The dependence of a will not absolutely good on the principle of autonomy (moral necessitation) is obligation. This, then, cannot be applied to a holy being. The objective necessity of actions from obligation is called *duty.*

From what has just been said, it is easy to see how it happens that, although the conception of duty implies subjection to the law, we yet ascribe a certain *dignity* and sublimity to the person who fulfills all his duties. There is not, indeed, any sublimity in him, so far as he is *subject* to the moral law; but inasmuch as in regard to that very law he is likewise a *legislator,* and on that account alone subject to it, he has sublimity. We have also shown above that neither fear nor inclination, but simply respect for the law, is the spring which can give actions a moral worth. Our own will, so far as we suppose it to act only under the condition that its maxims are potentially universal laws, this ideal will which is possible to us is the proper object of respect; and the dignity of humanity consists just in this capacity of being universally legislative, though with the condition that it is itself subject to this same legislation.

### The Autonomy of the Will as the Supreme Principle of Morality

Autonomy of the will is that property of it by which it is a law to itself (independently on any property of the objects of volition). The principle of autonomy then is: Always so to choose that the same volition shall comprehend the maxims of our choice as a universal law. We cannot prove that this practical rule is an imperative, that is, that the will of every rational being is necessarily bound to it as a condition, by a mere analysis of the conceptions which occur in it, since it is a synthetical proposition; we must advance beyond the cognition of the objects to a critical examination of the subject, that is, of the pure practical reason, for this synthetic proposition which commands apodictically must be capable of being cognized wholly *a priori*. This matter, however, does not belong to the present section. But that the principle of autonomy in question is the sole principle of morals can be readily shown by mere analysis of the conceptions of morality. For by this analysis we find that its principle must be a categorical imperative, and that what this commands is neither more nor less than this very autonomy.

### Heteronomy of the Will as the Source of All Spurious Principles of Morality

If the will seeks the law which is to determine it *anywhere else* than in the fitness of its maxims to be universal laws of its own dictation, consequently if it goes out of itself and seeks this law in the character of any of its objects, there always results *heteronomy*. The will in that case does not give itself the law, but it is given by the object through its relation to the will. This relation, whether it rests on inclination or on conceptions of reason, only admits of hypothetical imperatives: I ought to do something *because I wish for something else*. On the contrary, the moral, and therefore categorical, imperative says: I ought to do

so and so, even though I should not wish for anything else. For example, the former says: I ought not to lie if I would retain my reputation; the latter says: I ought not to lie although it should not bring me the least discredit. The latter therefore must so far abstract from all objects that they shall have no *influence* on the will, in order that practical reason (will) may not be restricted to administering an interest not belonging to it, but may simply show its own commanding authority as the supreme legislation. Thus, for example, I ought to endeavor to promote the happiness of others, not as if its realization involved any concern of mine (whether by immediate inclination or by any satisfaction indirectly gained through reason), but simply because a maxim which excludes it cannot be comprehended as a universal law in one and the same volition.

### Classification

### Of All Principles of Morality Which Can Be Founded on the Conception of Heteronomy

Here as elsewhere human reason in its pure use, so long as it was not critically examined, has first tried all possible wrong ways before it succeeded in finding the one true way.

All principles which can be taken from this point of view are either *empirical* or *rational*. The *former,* drawn from the principle of *happiness,* are built on physical or moral feelings; the *latter,* drawn from the principle of *perfection,* are built either on the rational conception of perfection as a possible effect, or on that of an independent perfection (the will of God) as the determining cause of our will.

*Empirical principles* are wholly incapable of serving as a foundation for moral laws. For the universality with which these should hold for all rational beings without distinction, the unconditional practical necessity which is thereby imposed on them is lost when their foundation is taken from the *particular constitution of human nature* or the accidental circumstances in which it is placed. The principle of *private happiness,* however, is the most objectionable, not merely because it is false, and experience contradicts the supposition that prosperity is always proportioned to good conduct, nor yet merely because it contributes nothing to the establishment of morality—since it is quite a different thing to make a prosperous man and a good man, or to make one prudent and sharp-sighted for his own interests, and to make him virtuous—but because the springs it provides for morality are such as rather undermine it and destroy its sublimity, since they put the motives to virtue and to vice in the same class, and only teach us to make a better calculation, the specific difference between virtue and vice being entirely extinguished. On the other hand, as to moral feeling, this supposed special sense,[16] the appeal to it is indeed superficial when those who cannot *think* believe that *feeling* will help them out, even in what concerns general laws; and besides, feelings which naturally differ infinitely in degree cannot furnish a uniform standard of good and evil, nor has anyone a right to form judgments for others by his own feelings; nevertheless this moral feeling is nearer to morality and its dignity in this respect that it pays virtue the honor of ascribing to her *immediately* the satisfaction and esteem we have for her, and does not, as it were, tell her to her face that we are not attached to her by her beauty but by profit.

Among the *rational* principles of morality, the ontological conception of *perfection,* notwithstanding its defects, is better than the theological conception which derives morality from a Divine absolutely perfect will. The former is, no doubt, empty and indefinite, and consequently useless for finding in the boundless field of possible reality the greatest amount suitable for us; moreover, in attempting to distinguish specifically the reality of which we are now speaking from every other, it inevitably tends to turn in a circle and cannot avoid tacitly presupposing the morality which it is to explain; it is nevertheless preferable to the theological view, first, because we have no intuition of the Divine perfection, and can only deduce it from our own conceptions the most important of which is that of morality, and our explanation would thus be involved in a gross circle; and, in the next place, if we avoid this, the only notion of the Divine will remaining to us is a conception made up of the attributes of desire of glory and dominion,

combined with the awful conceptions of might and vengeance, and any system of morals erected on this foundation would be directly opposed to morality.

However, if I had to choose between the notion of the moral sense and that of perfection in general (two systems which at least do not weaken morality, although they are totally incapable of serving as its foundation), then I should decide for the latter, because it at least withdraws the decision of the question from the sensibility and brings it to the court of pure reason; and although even here it decides nothing, it at all events preserves the indefinite idea (of a will good in itself) free from corruption, until it shall be more precisely defined.

For the rest I think I may be excused here from a detailed refutation of all these doctrines; that would only be superfluous labor, since it is so easy, and is probably so well seen even by those whose office requires them to decide for one of those theories (because their hearers would not tolerate suspension of judgment). But what interests us more here is to know that the prime foundation of morality laid down by all these principles is nothing but heteronomy of the will, and for this reason they must necessarily miss their aim.

In every case where an object of the will has to be supposed, in order that the rule may be prescribed which is to determine the will, there the rule is simply heteronomy; the imperative is conditional, namely, *if* or *because* one wishes for this object, one should act so and so; hence it can never command morally, that is, categorically. Whether the object determines the will by means of inclination, as in the principle of private happiness, or by means of reason directed to objects of our possible volition generally, as in the principle of perfection, in either case the will never determines itself *immediately* by the conception of the action, but only by the influence which the foreseen effect of the action has on the will; *I ought to do something, on this account, because I wish for something else;* and here there must be yet another law assumed in me as its subject, by which I necessarily will this other thing, and this law again requires an imperative to restrict this maxim. For the influence which the conception of an object within the reach of our faculties can exercise on the will of the subject in consequence of its natural properties, depends on the nature of the subject, either the sensibility (inclination and taste) or the understanding and reason, the employment of which is by the peculiar constitution of their nature attended with satisfaction. It follows that the law would be, properly speaking, given by nature, and as such it must be known and proved by experience, and would consequently be contingent, and therefore incapable of being an apodictic practical rule, such as the moral rule must be. Not only so, but it is *inevitably only heteronomy;* the will does not give itself the law, but it is given by a foreign impulse by means of a particular natural constitution of the subject adapted to receive it. An absolutely good will, then, the principle of which must be a categorical imperative, will be indeterminate as regards all objects, and will contain merely the *form of volition* generally, and that as autonomy, that is to say, the capability of the maxims of every good will to make themselves a universal law, is itself the only law which the will of every rational being imposes on itself, without needing to assume any spring or interest as a foundation.

*How such a synthetical practical* a priori *proposition is possible,* and why it is necessary, is a problem whose solution does not lie within the bounds of the metaphysic of morals; and we have not here affirmed its truth, much less professed to have a proof of it in our power. We simply showed by the development of the universally received notion of morality that an autonomy of the will is inevitably connected with it, or rather is its foundation. Whoever then holds morality to be anything real, and not a chimerical idea without any truth, must likewise admit the principle of it that is here assigned. This section, then, like the first, was merely analytical. Now to prove that morality is no creation of the brain, which it cannot be if the categorical imperative and with it the autonomy of the will is true, and as an *a priori* principle absolutely necessary, this supposes the *possibility of a synthetic use of pure practical reason,* which, however, we cannot venture on without first giving a critical examination of this faculty of reason. In the concluding section we

shall give the principal outlines of this critical examination as far as is sufficient for our purpose.

## THIRD SECTION

### *Transition from the Metaphysics of Morals to the Critique of Pure Practical Reason*

#### *The Concept of Freedom Is the Key That Explains the Autonomy of the Will*

The *will* is a kind of causality belonging to living beings in so far as they are rational, and *freedom* would be this property of such causality that it can be efficient, independently of foreign causes *determining* it; just as *physical necessity* is the property that the causality of all irrational beings has of being determined to activity by the influence of foreign causes.

The preceding definition of freedom is *negative,* and therefore unfruitful for the discovery of its essence; but it leads to a *positive* conception which is so much the more full and fruitful. Since the conception of causality involves that of laws, according to which, by something that we call cause, something else, namely, the effect, must be produced; hence, although freedom is not a property of the will depending on physical laws, yet it is not for that reason lawless; on the contrary, it must be a causality acting according to immutable laws, but of a peculiar kind; otherwise a free will would be an absurdity. Physical necessity is a heteronomy of the efficient causes, for every effect is possible only according to this law—that something else determines the efficient cause to exert its causality. What else then can freedom of the will be but autonomy, that is, the property of the will to be a law to itself? But the proposition: The will is in every action a law to itself, only expresses the principle to act on no other maxim than that which can also have as an object itself as a universal law. Now this is precisely the formula of the categorical imperative and is the principle of morality, so that a free will and a will subject to moral laws are one and the same.

On the hypothesis, then, of freedom of the will, morality together with its principle follows from it by mere analysis of the conception. However, the latter is a synthetic proposition, viz., an absolutely good will is that whose maxim can always include itself regarded as a universal law; for this property of its maxim can never be discovered by analyzing the conception of an absolutely good will. Now such synthetic propositions are only possible in this way—that the two cognitions are connected together by their union with a third in which they are both to be found. The *positive* concept of freedom furnishes this third cognition, which cannot, as with physical causes, be the nature of the sensible world (in the concept of which we find conjoined the concept of something in relation as cause to *something else* as effect). We cannot now at once show what this third is to which freedom points us, and of which we have an idea *a priori,* nor can we make intelligible how the concept of freedom is shown to be legitimate from principles of pure practical reason, and with it the possibility of a categorical imperative; but some further preparation is required.

### Freedom

#### Must Be Presupposed as a Property of the Will of All Rational Beings

It is not enough to predicate freedom of our own will, from whatever reason, if we have not sufficient grounds for predicating the same of all rational beings. For as morality serves as a law for us only because we are *rational beings,* it must also hold for all rational beings; and as it must be deduced simply from the property of freedom, it must be shown that freedom also is a property of all rational beings. It is not enough, then, to prove it from certain supposed experiences of human nature (which indeed is quite impossible, and it can only be shown *a priori*), but we must show that it belongs to the activity of all rational beings endowed with a will. Now I say every being that cannot act except *under the idea of freedom* is just for that reason in a practical point of view really free, that is to say, all laws which are inseparably connected with freedom have the same force for him as if his will had been shown to be free in itself by a proof theoretically conclusive.[17] Now I affirm that

we must attribute to every rational being which has a will that it has also the idea of freedom and acts entirely under this idea. For in such a being we conceive a reason that is practical, that is, has causality in reference to its objects. Now we cannot possibly conceive a reason consciously receiving a bias from any other quarter with respect to its judgments, for then the subject would ascribe the determination of its judgment not to its own reason, but to an impulse. It must regard itself as the author of its principles independent on foreign influences. Consequently, as practical reason or as the will of a rational being it must regard itself as free, that is to say, the will of such a being cannot be a will of its own except under the idea of this manner of acting—a worth so great that there cannot be any higher interest—and if we were asked further how it happens that it is by this alone a man believes he feels his own personal worth, in comparison with which that of an agreeable or disagreeable condition is to be regarded as nothing, to these questions we could give no satisfactory answer.

#### Of the Interest Attaching to the Ideas of Morality

We have finally reduced the definite conception of morality to the idea of freedom. This latter, however, we could not prove to be actually a property of ourselves or of human nature; only we saw that it must be presupposed if we would conceive a being as rational and conscious of its causality in respect of its actions, that is, as endowed with a will; and so we find that on just the same grounds we must ascribe to every being endowed with reason and will this attribute of determining itself to action under the idea of its freedom.

Now it resulted also from the presupposition of this idea that we became aware of a law that the subjective principles of action, that is, maxims, must also be so assumed that they can also hold as objective, that is, universal principles, and so serve as universal laws of our own dictation. But why, then, should I subject myself to this principle and that simply as a rational being, thus also subjecting to it all other beings endowed with reason? I will allow that no interest *urges* me to this, for that would not give a categorical imperative, but I must *take* an interest in it and discern how this comes to pass; for this "I ought" is properly an "I would," valid for every rational being, provided only that reason determined his actions without any hindrance. But for beings that are in addition affected as we are by springs of a different kind, namely, sensibility, and in whose case that is not always done which reason alone would do, for these that necessity is expressed only as an "ought," and the subjective necessity is different from the objective.

It seems, then, as if the moral law, that is, the principle of autonomy of the will, were properly speaking only presupposed in the idea of freedom, and as if we could not prove its reality and objective necessity independently. In that case we should still have gained something considerable by at least determining the true principle more exactly than had previously been done; but as regards its validity and the practical necessity of subjecting oneself to it, we should not have advanced a step. For if we were asked why the universal validity of our maxim as a law must be the condition restricting our actions, and on what we ground the worth which we assign to this manner of acting—a worth so great that there cannot be any higher interest—and if we were asked further how it happens that it is by this alone a man believes he feels his own personal worth, in comparison with which that of an agreeable or disagreeable condition is to be regarded as nothing, to these questions we could give no satisfactory answer.

We find indeed sometimes that we can take an interest in a personal quality which does not involve any interest of external condition, provided this quality makes us capable of participating in the condition in case reason were to effect the allotment; that is to say, the mere being worthy of happiness can interest of itself even without the motive of participating in this happiness. This judgment, however, is in fact only the effect of the importance of the moral law which we before presupposed (when by the idea of freedom we detach ourselves from every empirical interest); but that we ought to detach ourselves from these interests, that is, to consider ourselves as free in

action and yet as subject to certain laws, so as to find a worth simply in our own person which can compensate us for the loss of everything that gives worth to our condition, this we are not yet able to discern in this way, nor do we see how it is possible so to act— in other words, *whence the moral law derives its obligation.*

It must be freely admitted that there is a sort of circle here from which it seems impossible to escape. In the order of efficient causes we assume ourselves free, in order that in the order of ends we may conceive ourselves as subject to moral laws; and we afterwards conceive ourselves as subject to these laws because we have attributed to ourselves freedom of will; for freedom and self-legislation of will are both autonomy, and therefore are reciprocal conceptions, and for this very reason one must not be used to explain the other or give the reason of it, but at most only for logical purposes to reduce apparently different notions of the same object to one single concept (as we reduce different fractions of the same value to the lowest terms).

One resource remains to us, namely, to inquire whether we do not occupy different points of view when by means of freedom we think ourselves as causes efficient *a priori,* and when we form our conception of ourselves from our actions as effects which we see before our eyes.

It is a remark which needs no subtle reflection to make, but which we may assume that even the commonest understanding can make, although it be after its fashion by an obscure discernment of judgment which it calls feeling, that all the "ideas" that come to us involuntarily (as those of the senses) do not enable us to know objects otherwise than as they affect us; so that what they may be in themselves remains unknown to us, and consequently that as regards "ideas" of this kind even with the closest attention and clearness that the understanding can apply to them, we can by them only attain to the knowledge of *appearances,* never to that of *things in themselves.* As soon as this distinction has once been made (perhaps merely in consequence of the difference observed between the ideas given us from without, and in which we are passive, and those that we produce simply from ourselves, and in which we show our own activity), then it follows of itself that we must admit and assume behind the appearance something else that is not an appearance, namely, the things in themselves; although we must admit that, as they can never be known to us except as they affect us, we can come no nearer to them, nor can we ever know what they are in themselves. This must furnish a distinction, however crude, between a *world of sense* and the *world of understanding,* of which the former may be different according to the difference of the sensuous impressions in various observers, while the second which is its basis always remains the same. Even as to himself, a man cannot pretend to know what he is in himself from the knowledge he has by internal sensation. For as he does not as it were create himself, and does not come by the conception of himself *a priori* but empirically, it naturally follows that he can obtain his knowledge even of himself only by the inner sense, and consequently only through the appearances of his nature and the way in which his consciousness is affected. At the same time, beyond these characteristics of his own subject, made up of mere appearances, he must necessarily suppose something else as their basis, namely, his *ego,* whatever its characteristics in itself may be. Thus in respect to mere perception and receptivity of sensations he must reckon himself as belonging to the *world of sense;* but in respect of whatever there may be of pure activity in him (that which reaches consciousness immediately and not through affecting the senses), he must reckon himself as belonging to the *intellectual world,* of which, however, he has no further knowledge. To such a conclusion the reflecting man must come with respect to all the things which can be presented to him; it is probably to be met with even in persons of the commonest understanding, who, as is well known, are very much inclined to suppose behind the objects of the senses something else invisible and acting of itself. They spoil it, however, by presently sensualizing this invisible again, that is to say, wanting to make it an object of intuition, so that they do not become a whit the wiser.

Now man really finds in himself a faculty by which he distinguishes himself from everything else, even from himself as affected by objects, and that is *reason.* This being pure spontaneity is even elevated above the *understanding.* For although the latter is a spontaneity and does not, like sense, merely contain intuitions that arise when we are affected by things (and are therefore passive), yet it cannot produce from its activity any other conceptions than those which merely serve *to bring the intuitions of sense under rules,* and thereby to unite them in one consciousness, and without this use of the sensibility it could not think at all; whereas, on the contrary, reason shows so pure a spontaneity in the case of what I call "ideas" [Ideal Conceptions] that it thereby far transcends everything that the sensibility can give it, and exhibits its most important function in distinguishing the world of sense from that of understanding, and thereby prescribing the limits of the understanding itself.

For this reason a rational being must regard himself *qua* intelligence (not from the side of his lower faculties) as belonging not to the world of sense, but to that of understanding; hence he has two points of view from which he can regard himself, and recognize laws of the exercise of his faculties, and consequently of all his actions; *first,* so far as he belongs to the world of sense, he finds himself subject to laws of nature (heteronomy); *secondly,* as belonging to the intelligible world, under laws which, being independent on nature, have their foundation not in experience but in reason alone.

As a reasonable being, and consequently belonging to the intelligible world, man can never conceive the causality of his own will otherwise than on condition of the idea of freedom, for independence on the determining causes of the sensible world (an independence which reason must always ascribe to itself) is freedom. Now the idea of freedom is inseparably connected with the conception of *autonomy,* and this again with the universal principle of morality which is ideally the foundation of all actions of *rational* beings, just as the law of nature is of all phenomena.

Now the suspicion is removed which we raised above, that there was a latent circle involved in our reasoning from freedom to autonomy, and from this to the moral law, viz., that we laid down the idea of freedom because of the moral law only that we might afterwards in turn infer the latter from freedom, and that consequently we could assign no reason at all for this law, but could only [present] it as a *petitio principii* which well-disposed minds would gladly concede to us, but which we could never put forward as a provable proposition. For now we see that when we conceive ourselves as free we transfer ourselves into the world of understanding as members of it, and recognize the autonomy of the will with its consequence, morality; whereas, if we conceive ourselves as under obligation, we consider ourselves as belonging to the world of sense, and at the same time to the world of understanding.

### How Is a Categorical Imperative Possible?

Every rational being reckons himself *qua* intelligence as belonging to the world of understanding, and it is simply as an efficient cause belonging to that world that he calls his causality a *will*. On the other side, he is also conscious of himself as a part of the world of sense in which his actions, which are mere appearances [phenomena] of that causality, are displayed; we cannot, however, discern how they are possible from this causality which we do not know; but instead of that, these actions as belonging to the sensible world must be viewed as determined by other phenomena, namely, desires and inclinations. If therefore I were only a member of the world of understanding, then all my actions would perfectly conform to the principle of autonomy of the pure will; if I were only a part of the world of sense, they would necessarily be assumed to conform wholly to the natural law of desires and inclinations, in other words, to the heteronomy of nature. (The former would rest on morality as the supreme principle, the latter on happiness). Since, however, *the world of understanding contains the foundation of the world of sense, and consequently of its laws also,* and accordingly gives the law to my will (which belongs wholly to the world of understanding) directly, and must be conceived as doing so, it follows that, although on the one side I must regard myself as a being belonging to the world of sense, yet, on the other side, I must recognize

myself, as an intelligence, as subject to the law of the world of understanding, that is, to reason, which contains this law in the idea of freedom, and therefore as subject to the autonomy of the will; consequently I must regard the laws of the world of understanding as imperatives for me, and the actions which conform to them as duties.

And thus what makes categorical imperatives possible is this—that the idea of freedom makes me a member of an intelligible world, in consequence of which, if I were nothing else, all my actions *would* always conform to the autonomy of the will; but as I at the same time intuit myself as a member of the world of sense, they *ought* so to conform, and this *categorical* "ought" implies a synthetic *a priori* proposition, inasmuch as besides my will as affected by sensible desires there is added further the idea of the same will, but as belonging to the world of understanding, pure and practical of itself, which contains the supreme condition according to reason of the former will; precisely as to the intuitions of sense there are added concepts of the understanding which of themselves signify nothing but regular form in general, and in this way synthetic *a priori* propositions become possible, on which all knowledge of physical nature rests.

The practical use of common human reason confirms this reasoning. There is no one, not even the most consummate villain, provided only that he is otherwise accustomed to the use of reason, who, when we set before him examples of honesty of purpose, of steadfastness in following good maxims, of sympathy and general benevolence (even combined with great sacrifices of advantages and comfort), does not wish that he might also possess these qualities. Only on account of his inclinations and impulses he cannot attain this in himself, but at the same time he wishes to be free from such inclinations which are burdensome to himself. He proves by this that he transfers himself in thought with a will free from the impulses of the sensibility into an order of things wholly different from that of his desires in the field of the sensibility; since he cannot expect to obtain by that wish any gratification of his desires, nor any position which would satisfy any of his actual or supposable inclinations (for this would destroy the pre-eminence of the very idea on which rests that wish from him), he can only expect a greater intrinsic worth of his own person. This better person, however, he imagines himself to be when he transfers himself to the point of view of a member of the world of the understanding, to which he is involuntarily forced by the idea of freedom, that is, of independence on *determining* causes of the world of sense; and from this point of view he is conscious of a good will, which by his own confession constitutes the law for the bad will that he possesses as a member of the world of sense—a law whose authority he recognizes while transgressing it. What he morally "ought" is then what he necessarily "would" as a member of the world of the understanding, and is conceived by him as an "ought" only inasmuch as he likewise considers himself as a member of the world of sense.

## On the Extreme Limits
## of All Practical Philosophy

All men attribute to themselves freedom of will. Hence come all judgments upon actions as being such as *ought to have been done,* although they *have not been* done. However, this freedom is not a conception of experience, nor can it be so, since it still remains, even though experience shows the contrary of what on supposition of freedom are conceived as its necessary consequences. On the other side, it is equally necessary that everything that takes place should be fixedly determined according to laws of nature. This necessity of nature is likewise not an empirical conception, just for this reason that it involves the notion of necessity and consequently of *a priori* cognition. But this conception of a system of nature is confirmed by experience; and it must even be inevitably presupposed if experience itself is to be possible, that is, a connected knowledge of the objects of sense resting on general laws. Therefore freedom is only an *idea* [Ideal Conception] of *reason,* and its objective reality in itself is doubtful; while nature is a *concept* of the *understanding* which proves, and must necessarily prove, its reality in examples of experience.

There arises from this a dialectic of reason, since the freedom attributed to the will appears to contradict the necessity of nature, and, placed between these two ways, reason for *speculative purposes* finds the road of physical necessity much more beaten and more appropriate than that of freedom; yet for *practical purposes* the narrow footpath of freedom is the only one on which it is possible to make use of reason in our conduct; hence it is just as impossible for the subtlest philosophy as for the commonest reason of men to argue away freedom. Philosophy must then assume that no real contradiction will be found between freedom and physical necessity of the same human actions, for it cannot give up the conception of nature any more than that of freedom.

Nevertheless, even though we should never be able to comprehend how freedom is possible, we must at least remove this apparent contradiction in a convincing manner. For if the thought of freedom contradicts either itself or nature, which is equally necessary, it must in competition with physical necessity be entirely given up.

It would, however, be impossible to escape this contradiction if the thinking subject, which seems to itself free, conceived itself *in the same sense* or in *the very same relation* when it calls itself free as when in respect of the same action it assumes itself to be subject to the law of nature. Hence it is an indispensable problem of speculative philosophy to show that its illusion respecting the contradiction rests on this that we think of man in a different sense and relation when we call him free, and when we regard him as subject to the laws of nature as being part and parcel of nature. It must therefore show that not only *can* both these very well coexist, but that both must be thought *as necessarily united* in the same subject, since otherwise no reason could be given why we should burden reason with an idea which, though it may possibly *without contradiction* be reconciled with another that is sufficiently established, yet entangles us in a perplexity which sorely embarrasses reason in its theoretic employment. This duty, however, belongs only to speculative philosophy, in order that it may clear the way for practical philosophy. The philosopher, then, has no option whether he will remove the apparent contradiction or leave it untouched; for in the latter case the theory respecting this would be *bonum vacans* into the possession of which the fatalist would have a right to enter, and chase all morality out of its supposed domain as occupying it without title.

We cannot, however, as yet say that we are touching the bounds of practical philosophy. For the settlement of that controversy does not belong to it; it only demands from speculative reason that it should put an end to the discord in which it entangles itself in theoretical questions, so that practical reason may have rest and security from external attacks which might make the ground debatable on which it desires to build.

The claims to freedom of will made even by common reason are founded on the consciousness and the admitted supposition that reason is independent on merely subjectively determined causes which together constitute what belongs to sensation only, and which consequently come under the general designation of sensibility. Man considering himself in this way as an intelligence places himself thereby in a different order of things and in a relation to determining grounds of a wholly different kind when on the one hand he thinks of himself as an intelligence endowed with a will, and consequently with causality, and when on the other he perceives himself as a phenomenon in the world of sense (as he really is also), and affirms that his causality is subject to external determination according to laws of nature. Now he soon becomes aware that both can hold good, nay, must hold good at the same time. For there is not the smallest contradiction in saying that a *thing in appearance* (belonging to the world of sense) is subject to certain laws on which the very same *as a thing* or being *in itself* is independent; and that he must conceive and think of himself in this two-fold way, rests as to the first on the consciousness of himself as an object affected through the senses, and as to the second on the consciousness of himself as an intelligence, that is, as independent on sensible impressions in the employment of his reason (in other words as belonging to the world of understanding).

Hence it comes to pass that man claims the pos-session of a will which takes no account of anything that comes under the head of desires and inclinations, and on the contrary conceives actions as possible to him, nay, even as necessary, which can only be done by disregarding all desires and sensible inclinations. The causality of such actions lies in him as an intelligence and in the law of effects and actions [which depend] on the principles of an intelligible world, of which indeed he knows nothing more than that in it pure reason alone independent of sensibility gives the law; moreover, since it is only in that world, as an intelligence, that he is his proper self (being as man only the appearance of himself), those laws apply to him directly and categorically, so that the incitements of inclinations and appetites (in other words, the whole nature of the world of sense) cannot impair the laws of his volition as an intelligence. Nay, he does not even hold himself responsible for the former or ascribe them to his proper self, that is, his will; he only ascribes to his will any indulgence which he might yield them if he allowed them to influence his maxims to the prejudice of the rational laws of the will.

When practical reason *thinks* itself into a world of understanding, it does not thereby transcend its own limits, as it would if it tried to enter it by *intuition* or *sensation.* The former is only a negative thought in respect of the world of sense, which does not give any laws to reason in determining the will, and is positive only in this single point that this freedom as a negative characteristic is at the same time conjoined with a (positive) faculty and even with a causality of reason, which we designate a will, namely, a faculty of so acting that the principle of the actions shall conform to the essential character of a rational motive, that is, the condition that the maxim have universal validity as a law. But were it to borrow an *object of will,* that is, a motive, from the world of understanding, then it would overstep its bounds and pretend to be acquainted with something of which it knows nothing. The conception of a world of the understanding is then only a *point of view* which reason finds itself compelled to take outside the appearances in order to *conceive itself as practical,* which would not be possible if the influences of the sensibility had a determining power on man, but which is necessary unless he is to be denied the consciousness of himself as an intelligence and consequently as a rational cause, energizing by reason, that is, operating freely. This thought certainly involves the idea of an order and a system of laws different from that of the mechanism of nature which belongs to the sensible world; and it makes the conception of an intelligible world necessary (that is to say, the whole system of rational beings as things in themselves). But it does not in the least authorize us to think of it further than as to its *formal* condition only, that is, the universality of the maxims of the will as laws, and consequently the autonomy of the latter, which alone is consistent with its freedom; whereas, on the contrary, all laws that refer to a definite object give heteronomy, which only belongs to laws of nature, and can only apply to the sensible world.

But reason would overstep all its bounds if it undertook to *explain how* pure reason can be practical, which would be exactly the same problem as to explain *how freedom is possible.*

For we can explain nothing but that which we can reduce to laws the object of which can be given in some possible experience. But freedom is a mere *idea* [ideal conception], the objective reality of which can in no wise be shown according to laws of nature, and consequently not in any possible experience; and for this reason it can never be comprehended or understood because we cannot support it by any sort of example or analogy. It holds good only as a necessary hypothesis of reason in a being that believes itself conscious of a will, that is, of a faculty distinct from mere desire (namely, a faculty of determining itself to action as an intelligence, in other words, by laws of reason independently on natural instincts). Now where determination according to laws of nature ceases, there all *explanation* ceases also, and nothing remains but *defense,* that is, the removal of the objections of those who pretend to have seen deeper into the nature of things, and thereupon boldly declare freedom impossible. We can only point out to them that the supposed contradiction that they have discovered in it arises only from this that in order to be able to apply the law of nature to human actions, they

must necessarily consider man as an appearance; then when we demand of them that they should also think of him *qua* intelligence as a thing in itself, they still persist in considering him in this respect also as an appearance. In this view it would no doubt be a contradiction to suppose the causality of the same subject (that is, his will) to be withdrawn from all the natural laws of the sensible world. But this contradiction disappears if they would only bethink themselves and admit, as is reasonable, that behind the appearances there must also lie at their root (although hidden) the things in themselves, and that we cannot expect the laws of these to be the same as those that govern their appearances.

The subjective impossibility of explaining the freedom of the will is identical with the impossibility of discovering and explaining an interest[18] which man can take in the moral law. Nevertheless he does actually take an interest in it, the basis of which in us we call the moral feeling, which some have falsely assigned as the standard of our moral judgment, whereas it must rather be viewed as the *subjective* effect that the law exercises on the will, the objective principle of which is furnished by reason alone.

In order, indeed, that a rational being who is also affected through the senses should will what reason alone directs such beings that they ought to will, it is no doubt requisite that reason should have a power *to infuse a feeling of pleasure* or satisfaction in the fulfilment of duty, that is to say, that it should have a causality by which it determines the sensibility according to its own principles. But it is quite impossible to discern, that is, to make it intelligible *a priori,* how a mere thought, which itself contains nothing sensible, can itself produce a sensation of pleasure or pain; for this is a particular kind of causality of which, as of every other causality, we can determine nothing whatever *a priori;* we must only consult experience about it. But as this cannot supply us with any relation of cause and effect except between two objects of experience, whereas in this case, although indeed the effect produced lies within experience, yet the cause is supposed to be pure reason acting through mere ideas which offer no object to experience, it follows that for us men it is quite impossible to explain how and why the *universality of the maxim as a law,* that is, morality, interests. This only is certain, that it is not *because it interests* us that it has validity for us (for that would be heteronomy and dependence of practical reason on sensibility, namely, on a feeling as its principle, in which case it could never give moral laws), but that it interests us because it is valid for us as men, inasmuch as it had its source in our will as intelligences, in other words in our proper self, *and what belongs to mere appearance is necessarily subordinated by reason to the nature of the thing in itself.*

The question, then, How a categorical imperative is possible, can be answered to this extent that we can assign the only hypothesis on which it is possible, namely, the idea of freedom; and we can also discern the necessity of this hypothesis, and this is sufficient for the *practical exercise* of reason, that is, for the conviction of the *validity of this imperative,* and hence of the moral law; but how this hypothesis itself is possible can never be discerned by any human reason. On the hypothesis, however, that the will of an intelligence is free, its *autonomy,* as the essential formal condition of its determination, is a necessary consequence. Moreover, this freedom of will is not merely quite *possible* as a hypothesis (not involving any contradiction to the principle of physical necessity in the connection of the phenomena of the sensible world) as speculative philosophy can show; but further, a rational being who is conscious of a causality through reason, that is to say, of a will (distinct from desires), must *of necessity* make it practically, that is, in idea, the condition of all his voluntary actions. But to explain how pure reason can be of itself practical without the aid of any spring of action that could be derived from any other source, that is, how the mere principle of the *universal validity of all its maxims as laws* (which would certainly be the form of a pure practical reason) can of itself supply a spring, without any matter (object) of the will in which one could antecedently take any interest; and how it can produce an interest which would be called purely *moral;* or in other words, *how pure reason can*

*be practical*—to explain this is beyond the power of human reason, and all the labor and pains of seeking an explanation of it are lost.

It is just the same as if I sought to find out how freedom itself is possible as the causality of a will. For then I quit the ground of philosophical explanation, and I have no other to go upon. I might indeed revel in the world of intelligences which still remains to me, but although I have an *idea* of it which is well founded, yet I have not the least *knowledge* of it, nor can I ever attain to such knowledge with all the efforts of my natural faculty of reason. It signifies only a something that remains over when I have eliminated everything belonging to the world of sense from the actuating principles of my will, serving merely to keep in bounds the principle of motives taken from the field of sensibility; fixing its limits and showing that it does not contain all in all within itself, but that there is more beyond it; but this something more I know no further. Of pure reason which frames this ideal, there remains after the abstraction of all matter, that is, knowledge of objects, nothing but the form, namely, the practical law of the universality of the maxims, and in conformity with this the conception of reason in reference to a pure world of understanding as a possible efficient cause, that is, a cause determining the will. There must here be a total absence of springs unless this idea of an intelligible world is itself the spring, or that in which reason primarily takes an interest; but to make this intelligible is precisely the problem that we cannot solve.

Here now is the extreme limit of all moral inquiry, and it is of great importance to determine it even on this account in order that reason may not, on the one hand, to the prejudice of morals, seek about in the world of sense for the supreme motive and an interest comprehensible but empirical; and on the other hand, that it may not impotently flap its wings without being able to move in the (for it) empty space of transcendent concepts which we call the intelligible world, and so lose itself amidst chimeras. For the rest, the idea of a pure world of understanding as a system of all intelligences, and to which we ourselves as rational beings belong (although we are likewise on the other side members of the sensible world), this remains always a useful and legitimate idea for the purposes of rational belief, although all knowledge stops at its threshold, useful, namely, to produce in us a lively interest in the moral law by means of the noble ideal of a universal kingdom of *ends in themselves* (rational beings), to which we can belong as members then only when we carefully conduct ourselves according to the maxims of freedom as if they were laws of nature.

## Concluding Remark

The speculative employment of reason *with respect to nature* leads to the absolute necessity of some supreme cause of *the world;* the practical employment of reason *with a view to freedom* leads also to absolute necessity, but only *of the laws of the actions* of a rational being as such. Now it is an essential *principle* of reason, however employed, to push its knowledge to a consciousness of its *necessity* (without which it would not be rational knowledge). It is, however, an equally essential *restriction* of the same reason that it can neither discern the *necessity* of what is or what happens, nor of what ought to happen, unless a condition is supposed on which it is or happens or ought to happen. In this way, however, by the constant inquiry for the condition, the satisfaction of reason is only further and further postponed. Hence it unceasingly seeks the unconditionally necessary, and finds itself forced to assume it, although without any means of making it comprehensible to itself, happy enough if only it can discover a conception which agrees with this assumption. It is therefore no fault in our deduction of the supreme principle of morality, but an objection that should be made to human reason in general, that it cannot enable us to conceive the absolute necessity of an unconditional practical law (such as the categorical imperative must be). It cannot be blamed for refusing to explain this necessity by a condition, that is to say, by means of some interest assumed as a basis, since the law would then cease to be a moral law, that is, a supreme law of freedom. And thus while we do not comprehend the practical unconditional necessity of the moral imperative, we

yet comprehend its *incomprehensibility,* and this is all that can be fairly demanded of a philosophy which strives to carry its principles up to the very limit of human reason.

## Notes

1. A *maxim* is the subjective principle of volition. The objective principle (i.e., that which would also serve subjectively as a practical principle to all rational beings if reason had full power over the faculty of desire) is the practical *law.*

2. It might be here objected to me that I take refuge behind the word *respect* in an obscure feeling, instead of giving a distinct solution of the question by a concept of the reason. But although respect is a feeling, it is not a feeling *received* through influence, but is *self-wrought* by a rational concept, and, therefore, is specifically distinct from all feelings of the former kind, which may be referred either to inclination or fear. What I recognize immediately as a law for me, I recognize with respect. This merely signifies the consciousness that my will is *subordinate to a law,* without the intervention of other influences on my sense. The immediate determination of the will by the law, and the consciousness of this, is called *respect,* so that this is regarded as an *effect* of the law on the subject, and not as the *cause* of it. Respect is properly the conception of a worth which thwarts my self-love. Accordingly it is something which is considered neither as an object of inclination nor of fear, although it has something analogous to both. The *object* of respect is the *law* only, that is, the law which we impose on *ourselves,* and yet recognize as necessary in itself. As a law, we are subjected to it without consulting self-love; as imposed by us on ourselves, it is a result of our will. In the former aspect it has an analogy to fear, in the latter to inclination. Respect for a person is properly only respect for the law (of honesty, etc.) of which he gives us an example. Since we also look on the improvement of our talents as a duty, we consider that we see in a person of talents, as it were, the *example of a law* (viz., to become like him in this by exercise), and this constitutes our respect. All so-called moral *interest* consists simply in *respect* for the law.

3. Just as pure mathematics are distinguished from applied, pure logic from applied, so if we choose we may also distinguish pure philosophy of morals (metaphysic)

from applied (viz., applied to human nature). By this designation we are also at once reminded that moral principles are not based on properties of human nature, but must subsist *a priori* of themselves, while from such principles practical rules must be capable of being deduced for every rational nature, and accordingly for that of man.

4. I have a letter from the late excellent Sulzer, in which he asks me what can be the reason that moral instruction, although containing much that is convincing for the reason, yet accomplishes so little? My answer was postponed in order that I might make it complete. But it is simply this, that the teachers themselves have not got their own notions clear, and when they endeavor to make up for this by raking up motives of moral goodness from every quarter, trying to make their physic right strong, they spoil it. For the commonest understanding shows that if we imagine, on the one hand, an act of honesty done with steadfast mind, apart from every view to advantage of any kind in this world or another, and even under the greatest temptations of necessity or allurement, and, on the other hand, a similar act which was affected, in however low a degree, by foreign motive, the former leaves far behind and eclipses the second; it elevates the soul, and inspires the wish to be able to act in like manner oneself. Even moderately young children feel this impression, and one should never represent duties to them in any other light.

5. The dependence of the desires on sensations is called inclination, and this accordingly always indicates a *want*. The dependence of a contingently determinable will on principles of reason is called an *interest*. This, therefore, is found only in the case of a dependent will which does not always of itself conform to reason; in the Divine will we cannot conceive any interest. But the human will can also *take an interest* in a thing without therefore acting *from interest*. The former signifies the *practical* interest in the action, the latter the *pathological* in the object of the action. The former indicates only dependence of the will on principles of reason in themselves; the second, dependence on principles of reason for the sake of inclination, reason supplying only the practical rules how the requirement of the inclination may be satisfied. In the first case the action interests me; in the second the object of the action (because it is pleasant to me). We have seen in the first section that in an action done from duty we must look not to the interest in the object, but only to that in the action itself, and in its rational principle (viz., the law).

6. The word *prudence* is taken in two senses: in the one it may bear the name of knowledge of the world, in the other that of private prudence. The former is a man's ability to influence others so as to use them for his own purposes. The latter is the sagacity to combine all these purposes for his own lasting benefit. This latter is properly that to which the value even of the former is reduced, and when a man is prudent in the former sense, but not in the latter, we might say of him that he is clever and cunning, but, on the whole, imprudent.

7. It seems to me that the proper signification of the word *pragmatic* may be most accurately defined in this way. For *sanctions* are called pragmatic which flow properly, not from the law of the states as necessary enactments, but from *precaution* for the general welfare. A history is composed pragmatically when it teaches *prudence,* that is, instructs the world how it can provide for its interests better, or at least as well as the men of former time.

8. I connect the act with the will without presupposing any condition resulting from any inclination, but *a priori,* and therefore necessarily (though only objectively, that is, assuming the idea of a reason possessing full power over all subjective motives). This is accordingly a practical proposition which does not deduce the willing of an action by mere analysis from another already presupposed (for we have not such a perfect will), but connects it immediately with the conception of the will of a rational being, as something not contained in it.

9. A "maxim" is a subjective principle of action, and must be distinguished from the *objective principle,* namely, practical law. The former contains the practical rule set by reason according to the conditions of the subject (often its ignorance or its inclinations), so that it is the principle on which the subject *acts;* but the law is the objective principle valid for every rational being, and is the principle on which it *ought to act*—that is an imperative.

10. It must be noted here that I reserve the division of duties for a future *metaphysic of morals;* so that I give it here only as an arbitrary one (in order to arrange my examples). For the rest, I understand by a perfect duty one that admits no exception in favor of inclination, and then I have not merely external but also internal perfect duties. This is contrary to the use of the word adopted in the schools; but I do not intend to justify it here, as it is all one for my purpose whether it is admitted or not.

11. To behold virtue in her proper form is nothing else but to contemplate morality stripped of all admixture of sensible things and of every spurious ornament of reward or self-love. How much she then eclipses everything else that appears charming to the affections, every one may readily perceive with the least exertion of his reason, if it be not wholly spoiled for abstraction.

12. This proposition is here stated as a postulate. The ground of it will be found in the concluding section.

13. Let it not be thought that the common: *quod tibi non vis fieri, etc.,* could serve here as the rule or principle. For it is only a deduction from the former, though with several limitations; it cannot be a universal law, for it does not contain the principle of duties to oneself, nor of the duties of benevolence to others (for many a one would gladly consent that others should not benefit him, provided only that he might be excused from showing benevolence to them), nor finally that of duties of strict obligation to one another, for on this principle the criminal might argue against the judge who punishes him, and so on.

14. I may be excused from adducing examples to elucidate this principle as those which have already been used to elucidate the categorical imperative and its formula would all serve for the like purpose here.

15. Teleology considers nature as a kingdom of ends; ethics regards a possible kingdom of ends as a kingdom of nature. In the first case, the kingdom of ends is a theoretical idea, adopted to explain what actually is. In the latter it is a practical idea, adopted to bring about that which is not yet, but which can be realized by our conduct, namely, if it conforms to this idea.

16. I class the principle of moral feeling under that of happiness, because every empirical interest promises to contribute to our well-being by the agreeableness that a thing affords, whether it be immediately and without a view to profit, or whether profit be regarded. We must likewise, with Hutcheson, class the principle of sympathy with the happiness of others under his assumed moral sense.

17. I adopt this method of assuming freedom merely *as an idea* which rational beings suppose in their actions, in order to avoid the necessity of proving it in its theoretical aspect also. The form is sufficient for my purpose; for even though the speculative proof should not be made out, yet a being that cannot act except with the idea of freedom is bound by the same laws that would oblige a being who was actually free. Thus we can escape here from the onus which presses on the theory.

18. Interest is that by which reason becomes practical, that is, a cause determining the will. Hence we say of rational beings only that they take an interest in a thing; irrational beings only feel sensual appetites. Reason takes a direct interest in action, then, only when the universal validity of its maxims is alone sufficient to determine the will. Such an interest alone is pure. But if it can determine the will only by means of another object of desire or on the suggestion of a particular feeling of the subject, then Reason takes only an indirect interest in the action; and as Reason by itself without experience cannot discover either objects of the will or a special feeling actuating it, this latter interest would only be empirical, and not a pure rational interest. The logical interest of Reason (namely, to extend its insight) is never direct, but presupposes purposes for which reason is employed.

# On the Common Saying: "This May Be True in Theory, but It Does Not Apply in Practice"

A collection of rules, even of practical rules, is termed a *theory* if the rules concerned are envisaged as principles of a fairly general nature, and if they are abstracted from numerous conditions which, nonetheless, necessarily influence their practical application. Conversely, not all activities are called *practice,* but only those realisations of a particular purpose which are considered to comply with certain generally conceived principles of procedure.

It is obvious that no matter how complete the theory may be, a middle term is required between theory and practice, providing a link and a transition from one to the other. For a concept of the understanding, which contains the general rule, must be supplemented by an act of judgement whereby the practitioner distinguishes instances where the rule applies from those where it does not. And since rules cannot in turn be provided on every occasion to direct the judgement in subsuming each instance under the previous rule (for this would involve an infinite regress),

Reprinted from *Kant: Political Writings* translated by H. B. Nisbet, Cambridge University Press, 1970. Reprinted by permission of Cambridge University Press.

theoreticians will be found who can never in all their lives become practical, since they lack judgement. There are, for example, doctors or lawyers who did well during their schooling but who do not know how to act when asked to give advice. But even where a natural talent for judgement is present, there may still be a lack of premises. In other words, the theory may be incomplete, and can perhaps be perfected only by future experiments and experiences from which the newly qualified doctor, agriculturalist or economist can and ought to abstract new rules for himself to complete his theory. It is therefore not the fault of the theory if it is of little practical use in such cases. The fault is that there is *not enough* theory; the person concerned ought to have learnt from experience. What he learnt from experience might well be true theory, even if he were unable to impart it to others and to expound it as a teacher in systematic general propositions, and were consequently unable to claim the title of a theoretical physician, agriculturalist or the like. Thus no-one can pretend to be practically versed in a branch of knowledge and yet treat theory with scorn, without exposing the fact that he is an ignoramus in his subject. He no doubt imagines that he can get further than he could through theory if he gropes around in experiments and experiences, without collecting certain principles (which in fact amount to what we term theory) and without relating his activities to an integral whole (which, if treated methodically, is what we call a system).

Yet it is easier to excuse an ignoramus who claims that theory is unnecessary and superfluous in his supposed practice than a would-be expert who admits the value of theory for teaching purposes, for example as a mental exercise, but at the same time maintains that it is quite different in practice, and that anyone leaving his studies to go out into the world will realise he has been pursuing empty ideals and philosopher's dreams—in short, that whatever sounds good in theory has no practical validity. (This doctrine is often expressed as: 'this or that proposition is valid *in thesi,* but not *in hypothesi.*') Now all of us would merely ridicule the empirical engineer who criticised general mechanics or the artilleryman who criticised the mathematical theory of ballistics by declaring that,

while the theory is ingeniously conceived, it is not valid in practice, since experience in applying it gives results quite different from those predicted theoretically. For if mechanics were supplemented by the theory of friction and ballistics by the theory of air resistance, in other words if only more theory were added, these theoretical disciplines would harmonise very well with practice. But a theory which concerns objects of perception is quite different from one in which such objects are represented only through concepts, as with objects of mathematics and of philosophy. The latter objects can perhaps quite legitimately be *thought* of by reason, yet it may be impossible for them to be *given.* They may merely exist as empty ideas which either cannot be used at all in practice or only with some practical disadvantages. This would mean that the aforesaid common saying might well be correct in such cases.

But in a theory founded on the *concept of duty,* any worries about the empty ideality of the concept completely disappear. For it would not be a duty to strive after a certain effect of our will if this effect were impossible in experience (whether we envisage the experience as complete or as progressively approximating to completion). And it is with theory of this kind that the present essay is exclusively concerned. For to the shame of philosophy, it is not uncommonly alleged of such theory that whatever may be correct in it is in fact invalid in practice. We usually hear this said in an arrogant, disdainful tone, which comes of presuming to use experience to reform reason itself in the very attributes which do it most credit. Such illusory wisdom imagines it can see further and more clearly with its mole-like gaze fixed on experience than with the eyes which were bestowed on a being designed to stand upright and to scan the heavens.

This maxim, so very common in our sententious, inactive times, does very great harm if applied to matters of morality, i.e. to moral or legal duty. For in such cases, the canon of reason is related to practice in such a way that the value of the practice depends entirely upon its appropriateness to the theory it is based on; all is lost if the empirical (hence contingent) conditions governing the execution of the law are made into conditions of the law itself, so that a practice calculated to produce a result which *previous* experience makes probable is given the right to dominate a theory which is in fact self-sufficient.

I shall divide up this essay in terms of three points of view which the worthy gentleman who so boldly criticises theories and systems adopts in judging his objects. The three attitudes are those of the private individual or *man of affairs,* the *statesman,* and the *man of the world* or cosmopolitan. These three individuals are united in attacking the *academic,* who works for them all, for their own good, on matters of theory. Since they fancy that they understand this better than he does, they seek to relegate him to his classroom as a pedant who, unfitted for practical affairs, merely stands in the way of their experienced wisdom.

We shall therefore deal with the relationship of theory to practice in three separate areas: firstly in *morality* in general, with regard to the welfare of each *individual man,* secondly in *politics,* with regard to the welfare of *states,* and thirdly in the *cosmopolitical* sphere, with regard to the welfare of the *human race* as a whole, in so far as the welfare of mankind is increasing within a series of developments extending into all future ages. The titles of the sections, for reasons arising out of the essay itself, will express the relationship of theory to practice in *morality,* in *political right,* and in *international right.*

# I

## *On The Relationship of Theory to Practice in Morality in General*

### *(In Reply to Some Objections by Professor Garve[1])*

Before I proceed to the actual controversy over what is valid in theory and practice in the application of one and the same concept, I must compare my theory, as I have myself presented it elsewhere, with the picture which Professor Garve presents of it. We may thus see in advance whether we have understood one another.

A. I had provisionally designated the study of morals as the introduction to a discipline which would teach us not how to be happy, but how we should become worthy of happiness.[2] Nor had I omitted to point out at the same time that man is not thereby expected to *renounce* his natural aim of attaining happiness as soon as the question of following his duty arises; for like any finite rational being, he simply cannot do so. Instead, he must completely *abstract* from such considerations as soon as the imperative of duty supervenes, and must on no account make them a *condition* of his obeying the law prescribed to him by reason. He must indeed make every possible conscious effort to ensure that no *motive* derived from the desire for happiness imperceptibly infiltrates his conceptions of duty. To do this, he should think rather of the sacrifices which obedience to duty (i.e. virtue) entails than of the benefits he might reap from it, so that he will comprehend the imperative of duty in its full authority as a self-sufficient law, independent of all other influences, which requires unconditional obedience.

*a.* This proposition of mine is expressed by Garve as follows: I had asserted 'that adherence to the moral law, regardless of happiness, is *the one and only ultimate end* for man, and that it must be considered as the creator's unique intention'. (My theory is that the creator's unique intention is neither human morality in itself nor happiness in itself, but the highest good possible on earth, the union and harmony of them both.)

B. I had further noted that this concept of duty does not need to be based on any particular end, but rather itself *occasions* a new end for the human will, that of striving with all one's power towards the highest good possible on earth, towards the universal happiness of the whole world, combined with and in keeping with the purest morality. Since the attainment of this good lies within our power in one of its two aspects, but not in both taken together, it elicits from our reason a faith, *for practical purposes,* in a moral being who governs the world, and in a future existence. This does not mean that faith in both of these is a necessary condition lending 'support and stability' (i.e. a solid foundation and enough strength to constitute a *motive*) to the general concept of duty. It merely ensures that this concept acquires an *object* in the shape of an ideal of pure reason.[3] For in itself, duty is nothing more than a *limitation* of the will within a universal legislation which was made possible by an initially accepted maxim. The object or aim of the will can be of any kind whatsoever (even including happiness). But in this case, we completely abstract from whatever particular end is adopted. Thus so far as the *principle* of morality is concerned, the doctrine of the *highest good* as the ultimate end of a will which is determined by this doctrine and which conforms to its laws can be by-passed and set aside as incidental. And it will emerge from what follows that the actual controversy is not in fact concerned with this at all, but only with morality in general.

*b.* Garve expresses the above propositions as follows: 'The virtuous man cannot and may not ever lose sight of this consideration (i.e. that of his own happiness), since he would otherwise be completely without access to the invisible world and to belief in the existence of God and of immortality. Such belief, according to this theory, is absolutely necessary *to lend support and stability to the moral system.*' He concludes by briefly summing up as follows the statements he ascribes to me: 'The virtuous man, according to these principles, constantly strives to be worthy of happiness, but never, *in so far as* he is truly virtuous, to be actually happy.' (The words *in so far as* create an ambiguity which must be eliminated before we go any further. They can signify *in the act* of submitting, as a virtuous man, to one's duty—in which case the sentence is perfectly compatible with my theory—or they could imply that if he is never anything but virtuous, the virtuous man should not take happiness into consideration at all, even where the question of duty does not arise and where there is no conflict with duty—in which case the sentence is totally at variance with my statements.)

These objections are therefore nothing but misunderstandings (for I have no wish to see them as misrepresentations). Their very possibility would astonish us, if it were not that such phenomena can be adequately explained by the human tendency to follow a habitual train of thought, even in judging the thoughts of others, and thus to carry the former over into the latter.

Garve follows up this polemical account of the above moral principle with a dogmatic exposition of its direct opposite. By analytical methods, he comes to the following conclusion: 'In the ordering of *concepts,* the states which entitle us to give *preference* to one rather than others must first be recognised and distinguished before we choose any one of them and thus decide in advance what aim we shall pursue. But a state which a being who is aware of himself and of his own state would *prefer* to other ways of existence as soon as he saw it before him, is a *good* state; and a series of good states is the most general notion expressed by the word *happiness.*' He continues: 'A law presupposes motives, but motives presuppose that a difference has already been recognised between a worse state and a better one. This recognised difference is the element of the concept of happiness', and so on. And again: '*Happiness,* in the most general sense of the word, *is the source of the motives behind every effort,* including obedience to the moral law. I must first of all know whether something is good before I can ask whether the fulfilment of moral duties belongs to the category of good things. Man must have an *incentive* to set him in motion *before* he can be given a *goal*[4] towards which this motion should be directed.'

This argument is nothing more than a play upon the ambiguity of the word *good.* For it can be taken to mean something absolutely good in itself, as opposed to that which is evil in itself, or something only relatively good, as opposed to something more or less good than itself. In the latter case, the preferred state may be only comparatively better, yet nonetheless evil in itself. The maxim of absolute obedience to a categorically binding law of the free will (i.e. of duty), without reference to any ulterior end, is essentially different (i.e. different *in kind*) from the maxim of pursuing, as a motive for a certain way of acting, the end which nature itself has imposed upon us and which is generally known as happiness. For the first maxim is good in itself, but the second is not. The second may, if it conflicts with duty, be thoroughly evil. But if a certain end is made basic, so that no law is absolutely binding but always relative to the end adopted, two opposing actions might both be relatively good, with one better than the other, which would then count as comparatively evil. For they would differ only in *degree,* not in *kind.* And it is the same with all actions whose motive is not the absolute law of reason (duty), but an end which we have arbitrarily taken as a basis. For this end will be a part of the total of ends whose attainment we call happiness, and one action may contribute more, and another less to my happiness, so that one will be better or worse than the other. But to *give preference* to one state rather than another as a determinant of the will is merely an act of freedom (*res merae facultatis,* as the lawyers say) which takes no account of whether the particular determinant is good or evil in itself, and is thus neutral in both respects.

A state of being bound by a certain *given end* which I have preferred to all others *of the same kind,* is a comparatively better state in terms of happiness (which *reason* never recognises as more than *relatively good,* according to the extent to which a person is worthy of it). But that state of consciously preferring the moral law of duty in cases where it conflicts with certain of my ends is not just a better state, but the only state which is good in itself. It is good in a completely different sense, in that it takes no account whatsoever of any ends that may present themselves (including their sum total, which is happiness). The determinant in this case is not the content of the will (i.e. a particular basic object) but the pure form of universal lawfulness embodied in its maxim.—Thus it can by no means be said that I class as happiness every state which I *prefer* to all other modes of existence. For I must first be certain that I am not acting against my duty. Only then am I entitled to look round for happiness, in so far as I can reconcile it with the state I know to be morally (not physically) good.[5]

The will, however, must have *motives.* But these are not objects of *physical feeling* as predetermined ends in themselves. They are none other than the absolute *law* itself, and the will's receptivity to it as an absolute compulsion is known as *moral feeling.* This feeling is therefore not the cause but the effect of the will's determinant, and we should not have the least awareness of it within ourselves if such compulsion were not already present in us. Thus the old

refrain that this feeling, i.e. a desire which we take as our end, is the first cause determining the will, so that happiness (of which that desire is an element) is the basis of all objective necessity of action and thus of all moral obligations, is a piece of *trivial sophistry.* For if we go on asking even after we know the cause of a given event, we end up by making an effect the cause of itself.

I have now reached the point which really concerns us here, the task of testing and illustrating with examples the supposedly conflicting interest of theory and practice in philosophy. Garve's above-quoted essay furnishes the best possible illustration. He first says (with reference to the distinction I make between a doctrine of how to be *happy* and one of how to be *worthy* of happiness): 'For my own part, I admit that while I well understand this distinction among ideas in my *mind,* I do not find any such distinction among the desires and aspirations in my *heart,* so that I fail even to comprehend how anyone can be aware of having neatly set apart his actual desire for happiness and thus of having fulfilled his duty completely unselfishly.'

I shall answer the last point first. I willingly concede that no-one can have certain awareness of *having fulfilled* his duty completely unselfishly. For this is part of inward experience, and such awareness of one's psychological state would involve an absolutely clear conception of all the secondary notions and considerations which, through imagination, habit and inclination, accompany the concept of duty. And this is too much to ask for. Besides, the non-existence of something (including that of an unconsciously intended advantage) can never be an object of experience. But man is aware with the utmost clarity that he *ought to fulfil* his duty completely unselfishly, and *must* totally separate his desire for happiness from the concept of duty, in order to preserve the latter's purity. For if anyone thought he did not have this clear awareness, he could reasonably be asked to acquire it, so far as his powers might permit. And he must be able to do so, for the true value of morality consists precisely in the purity of its concept. Perhaps no recognised and respected duty has ever been carried out by anyone without some selfishness or interference from other motives;

perhaps no-one will ever succeed in doing so, however hard he tries. But by careful self-examination, we can perceive a certain amount. We can be aware not so much of any accompanying motives, but rather of our own self-denial with respect to many motives which conflict with the idea of duty. In other words, we can be aware of the maxim of striving towards moral purity. And this is sufficient for us to observe our duty. On the other hand, it is the death of all morality if we make it our maxim to foster such motives, on the pretext that human nature does not permit moral purity (which no-one can say with certainty in any case).

As for Garve's above confession that he cannot find such a distinction (more correctly a separation) in his *heart,* I have no hesitation in contradicting his self-accusation outright and in championing his heart against his mind. For as an honest man, he has in fact always found this separation in his heart, i.e. in the determinants of his will. But even for the purposes of speculative thinking and of comprehending that which is incomprehensible or inexplicable (i.e. the possibility of categorical imperatives such as those of duty), he was unable in his own mind to reconcile this separation with the usual principles of psychological explanation, which are all based on the mechanism of natural necessity.[6]

But I must loudly and resolutely disagree with Garve when he concludes by saying: 'Such subtle distinctions between ideas become *obscure* even when we *think* about particular objects; but they *vanish completely* when it comes to *action,* when they are supposed to apply to desires and intentions. The more simple, rapid and *devoid of clear ideas* the step from consideration of motives to actual action is, the less possible it is to determine exactly and unerringly the precise momentum which each motive has contributed in guiding the step in this and in no other direction.'

The concept of duty in its complete purity is incomparably simpler, clearer and more natural and easily comprehensible to everyone than any motive derived from, combined with, or influenced by happiness, for motives involving happiness always require a great deal of resourcefulness and deliberation. Besides, the concept of duty, if it is presented to the exclusive judgement of even the most ordinary

human reason, and confronts the human will separately and in actual opposition to other motives, is far *more powerful,* incisive and likely to promote success than all incentives borrowed from the latter selfish principle. Let us take, for example, the case of someone who has under his trust an endowment (*depositum*), the owner of which is deceased, while the heirs are ignorant of and could never discover its existence. Let us also suppose that the trustee of this deposit, through no fault of his own, has at this very time suffered a complete collapse in his financial circumstances, and has around him a miserable family of wife and children, oppressed by want, and knows that he could at once relieve this distress if he appropriated the pledge entrusted to him. He is also benevolent and philanthropic, while the heirs are rich, uncharitable, thoroughly extravagant and luxurious, so that it would make little difference if the aforesaid addition to their property were thrown into the sea. Now if this case is explained even to a child of around eight or nine years old, and it is asked whether it might be permissible under the circumstances to devote the deposit to one's own use, the reply will undoubtedly be negative. Whoever we ask will merely answer, without further ado, that *it is wrong,* i.e. that it conflicts with duty. Nothing can be clearer than this, while it is genuinely not the case that the trustee would be furthering his own *happiness* if he surrendered the deposit. For if he expected his decision to be dictated by such considerations, he might for instance reason as follows: 'If I give up unasked to the real owners the property I have here, they will presumably reward me for my honesty. Or if they do not, I will still acquire a good reputation at large, and this could prove very remunerative. But all this is most uncertain. Yet various doubts can also be raised in support of this argument. For if I were to embezzle the deposit to relieve my depressed circumstances at one stroke, I should incur suspicion, if I made quick use of it, as to how and by what means I had so soon bettered my circumstances. But if I used it slowly, my poverty would meanwhile increase so greatly that it would become impossible to alleviate it at all.' Thus a will which follows the maxim of happiness vacillates between various motives in trying to reach a decision. For it considers the possible results of its decision, and these are highly uncertain; and it takes a good head to find a way out of the host of arguments and counter-arguments without miscalculating the total effect. On the other hand, if we ask what duty requires, there is no confusion whatsoever about the answer, and we are at once certain what action to take. We even feel, if the concept of duty means anything to us, a revulsion at the very idea of calculating the advantages we might gain through violating our duty, just as if the choice were still a real one.

When Garve says that these distinctions (which, as we have shown, are not so subtle as he thinks, but are inscribed in the soul of man in the plainest and most legible characters) *vanish completely when it comes to action,* this contradicts even his own experience. Admittedly, it does not contradict the experience which the *history* of maxims derived from various principles provides. Such experience, alas, proves that most of them are based on selfishness. But it does contradict our (necessarily inward) experience that no idea can so greatly elevate the human mind and inspire it with such enthusiasm as that of a pure moral conviction, respecting duty above all else, struggling with countless evils of existence and even with their most seductive temptations, and yet overcoming them—for we may rightly assume that man can do so. The fact that man is aware that he can do this just because he ought to discloses within him an ample store of divine capabilities and inspires him, so to speak, with a holy awe at the greatness and sublimity of his true vocation. And if man were frequently enough reminded so that it became a habit for him to purge virtue of all the superfluous wealth of advantages which could be amassed through obeying his duty, and if he always conceived of virtue in its complete purity and made it a principle of private and public instruction always to use this insight (a method of inculcating duties which has almost invariably been neglected), human morality would soon be improved. Historical experience has not proved the success of our ethical doctrines. The fault lies in the erroneous assumption that a motive derived from the idea of duty in itself is far too subtle for the common understanding, whereas a cruder motive based on advantages which can be expected either in this or in a future

world from obedience to duty (without consideration of the latter itself as a motive) would act more forcibly upon the mind. Another fault is that it has hitherto been a principle of education and homiletics to place more stress on the quest for happiness than on worthiness of happiness, which is the highest postulate of reason. For *precepts* on how to be happy or at least how to avoid one's own disadvantage are not the same as *commandments.* They are never absolutely binding, for having first warned us, they leave us free to choose what we think best, provided that we are prepared to face the consequences. And any evils which might result from our failure to follow the advice we were given could not justifiably be regarded as penalties. For penalties apply only to a free will which violates the law. But nature and inclination cannot give laws to the free will. It is quite different with the idea of duty, for if we violate it, even without considering the disadvantages which might result, we feel the consequences directly, and appear despicable and culpable in our own eyes.

Here, then, is a clear proof that everything in morals which is true in theory must also be valid in practice. As a human being, a being subjected by his own reason to certain duties, each of us is therefore a *man of affairs* and since, as human beings, we never grow out of the school of wisdom, we cannot arrogantly and scornfully relegate the adherent of theory to the classroom and set ourselves up as better trained by experience in all that a man is and all that can be required of him. For all this experience will not in any way help us to escape the precepts of theory, but at most to learn how to apply it in better and more universal ways after we have assimilated it into our principles. But we are here concerned only with the latter, and not with any pragmatic abilities.

# II

## *On the Relationship of Theory to Practice in Political Right*

### *(Against Hobbes)*

Among all the contracts by which a large group of men unites to form a society, the contract establishing a *civil constitution* is of an exceptional nature. For while, so far as its execution is concerned, it has much in common with all others that are likewise directed towards a chosen end to be pursued by joint effort, it is essentially different from all others in the principle of its constitution. In all social contracts, we find a union of many individuals for some common end which they all *share.* But a union as an end in itself which they all *ought to share* and which is thus an absolute and primary duty in all external relationships whatsoever among human beings (who cannot avoid mutually influencing one another), is only found in a society in so far as it constitutes a civil state, i.e. a commonwealth. And the end which is a duty in itself in such external relationships, and which is indeed the highest formal condition of all other external duties, is the *right* of men *under coercive public laws* by which each can be given what is due to him and secured against attack from any others. But the whole concept of an external right is derived entirely from the concept of *freedom* in the mutual external relationships of human beings, and has nothing to do with the end which all men have by nature (i.e. the aim of achieving happiness) or with the recognised means of attaining this end. And thus the latter end must on no account interfere as a determinant with the laws governing external right. *Right* is the restriction of each individual's freedom so that it harmonises with the freedom of everyone else (in so far as this is possible within the terms of a general law). And *public right* is the distinctive quality of the *external laws* which make this constant harmony possible. Since every restriction of freedom through the arbitrary will of another party is termed *coercion,* it follows that a civil constitution is a relationship among *free* men who are subject to coercive laws, while they retain their freedom within the general union with their fellows. Such is the requirement of pure reason, which legislates *a priori,* regardless of all empirical ends (which can all be summed up under the general heading of happiness). Men have different views on the empirical end of happiness and what it consists of, so that as far as happiness is concerned, their will cannot be brought under any common principle nor thus under any external law harmonising with the freedom of everyone.

The civil state, regarded purely as a lawful state, is based on the following *a priori* principles:

1. The *freedom* of every member of society as a *human being.*
2. The *equality* of each with all the others as a *subject.*
3. The *independence* of each member of a commonwealth as a *citizen.*

These principles are not so much laws given by an already established state, as laws by which a state can alone be established in accordance with pure rational principles of external human right. Thus:

1. Man's *freedom* as a human being, as a principle for the constitution of a commonwealth, can be expressed in the following formula. No-one can compel me to be happy in accordance with his conception of the welfare of others, for each may seek his happiness in whatever way he sees fit, so long as he does not infringe upon the freedom of others to pursue a similar end which can be reconciled with the freedom of everyone else within a workable general law—i.e. he must accord to others the same right as he enjoys himself. A government might be established on the principle of benevolence towards the people, like that of a father towards his children. Under such a *paternal government (imperium paternale),* the subjects, as immature children who cannot distinguish what is truly useful or harmful to themselves, would be obliged to behave purely passively and to rely upon the judgement of the head of state as to how they *ought* to be happy, and upon his kindness in willing their happiness at all. Such a government is the greatest conceivable *despotism,* i.e. a constitution which suspends the entire freedom of its subjects, who thenceforth have no rights whatsoever. The only conceivable government for men who are capable of possessing rights, even if the ruler is benevolent, is not a *paternal* but a *patriotic* government. A *patriotic* attitude is one where everyone in the state, not excepting its head, regards the commonwealth as a maternal womb, or the land as the paternal ground from which he himself sprang and which he must leave to his descendants as a treasured pledge. Each regards himself as authorised to

protect the rights of the commonwealth by laws of the general will, but not to submit it to his personal use at his own absolute pleasure. This right of freedom belongs to each member of the commonwealth as a human being, in so far as each is a being capable of possessing rights.

2. Man's *equality* as a subject might be formulated as follows. Each member of the commonwealth has rights of coercion in relation to all the others, except in relation to the head of state. For he alone is not a member of the commonwealth, but its creator or preserver, and he alone is authorised to coerce others without being subject to any coercive law himself. But all who are subject to laws are the subjects of a state, and are thus subject to the right of coercion along with all other members of the commonwealth; the only exception is a single person (in either the physical or the moral sense of the word), the head of state, through whom alone the rightful coercion of all others can be exercised. For if he too could be coerced, he would not be the head of state, and the hierarchy of subordination would ascend infinitely. But if there were two persons exempt from coercion, neither would be subject to coercive laws, and neither could do to the other anything contrary to right, which is impossible.

This uniform equality of human beings as subjects of a state is, however, perfectly consistent with the utmost inequality of the mass in the degree of its possessions, whether these take the form of physical or mental superiority over others, or of fortuitous external property and of particular rights (of which there may be many) with respect to others. Thus the welfare of the one depends very much on the will of the other (the poor depending on the rich), the one must obey the other (as the child its parents or the wife her husband), the one serves (the labourer) while the other pays, etc. Nevertheless, they are all equal as subjects *before the law,* which, as the pronouncement of the general will, can only be single in form, and which concerns the form of right and not the material or object in relation to which I possess rights. For no-one can coerce anyone else other than through the public law and its executor, the head of state, while everyone else can resist the others in the same way and to the same degree. No-one, however,

can lose this authority to coerce others and to have rights towards them except through committing a crime. And no-one can voluntarily renounce his rights by a contract or legal transaction to the effect that he has no rights but only duties, for such a contract would deprive him of the right to make a contract, and would thus invalidate the one he had already made.

From this idea of the equality of men as subjects in a commonwealth, there emerges this further formula: every member of the commonwealth must be entitled to reach any degree of rank which a subject can earn through his talent, his industry and his good fortune. And his fellow-subjects may not stand in his way by *hereditary* prerogatives or privileges of rank and thereby hold him and his descendants back indefinitely.

All right consists solely in the restriction of the freedom of others, with the qualification that their freedom can co-exist with my freedom within the terms of a general law; and public right in a commonwealth is simply a state of affairs regulated by a real legislation which conforms to this principle and is backed up by power, and under which a whole people live as subjects in a lawful state. This is what we call a civil state, and it is characterised by equality in the effects and counter-effects of freely willed actions which limit one another in accordance with the general law of freedom. Thus the *birthright* of each individual in such a state (i.e. before he has performed any acts which can be judged in relation to right) is absolutely *equal* as regards his authority to coerce others to use their freedom in a way which harmonises with his freedom. Since birth is not an act on the part of the one who is born, it cannot create any inequality in his legal position and cannot make him submit to any coercive laws except in so far as he is a subject, along with all the others, of the one supreme legislative power. Thus no member of the commonwealth can have a hereditary privilege as against his fellow-subjects; and no-one can hand down to his descendants the privileges attached to the rank he occupies in the commonwealth, nor act as if he were qualified as a ruler by birth and forcibly prevent others from reaching the higher levels of the hierarchy (which are *superior* and *inferior,* but never *imperans* and *subiectus*) through their own merit. He may hand down everything else, so long as it is material and not pertaining to his person, for it may be acquired and disposed of as property and may over a series of generations create considerable inequalities in wealth among the members of the commonwealth (the employee and the employer, the landowner and the agricultural servants, etc.). But he may not prevent his subordinates from raising themselves to his own level if they are able and entitled to do so by their talent, industry and good fortune. If this were not so, he would be allowed to practise coercion without himself being subject to coercive counter-measures from others, and would thus be more than their fellow-subject. No-one who lives within the lawful state of a commonwealth can forfeit this equality other than through some crime of his own, but never by contract or through military force. For no legal transaction on his part or on that of anyone else can make him cease to be his own master. He cannot become like a domestic animal to be employed in any chosen capacity and retained therein without consent for any desired period, even with the reservation (which is at times sanctioned by religion, as among the Indians) that he may not be maimed or killed. He can be considered happy in any condition so long as he is aware that, if he does not reach the same level as others, the fault lies either with himself (i.e. lack of ability or serious endeavour) or with circumstances for which he cannot blame others, and not with the irresistible will of any outside party. For as far as right is concerned, his fellow-subjects have no advantage over him.[7]

3. The *independence* (*sibisufficientia*) of a member of the commonwealth as a *citizen,* i.e. as a co-legislator, may be defined as follows. In the question of actual legislation, all who are free and equal under existing public laws may be considered equal, but not as regards the right to make these laws. Those who are not entitled to this right are nonetheless obliged, as members of the commonwealth, to comply with these laws, and they thus likewise enjoy their protection (not as *citizens* but as co-beneficiaries of this protection). For all right depends on laws. But a public law which defines for everyone that which is permit-

ted and prohibited by right, is the act of a public will, from which all right proceeds and which must not therefore itself be able to do an injustice to any one. And this requires no less than the will of the entire people (since all men decide for all men and each decides for himself). For only towards oneself can one never act unjustly. But on the other hand, the will of another person cannot decide anything for someone without injustice, so that the law made by this other person would require a further law to limit his legislation. Thus an individual will cannot legislate for a commonwealth. For this requires freedom, equality and *unity* of the will of *all* the members. And the prerequisite for unity, since it necessitates a general vote (if freedom and equality are both present), is independence. The basic law, which can come only from the general, united will of the people, is called the *original contract.*

Anyone who has the right to vote on this legislation is a *citizen* (*citoyen,* i.e. citizen of a state, not *bourgeois* or citizen of a town). The only qualification required by a citizen (apart, of course, from being an adult male) is that he must be his *own master* (*sui uris*), and must have some *property* (which can include any skill, trade, fine art or science) to support himself. In cases where he must earn his living from others, he must earn it only by *selling* that which is his,[8] and not by allowing others to make use of him; for he must in the true sense of the word *serve* no-one but the commonwealth. In this respect, artisans and large or small landowners are all equal, and each is entitled to one vote only. As for landowners, we leave aside the question of how anyone can have rightfully acquired more land than he can cultivate with his own hands (for acquisition by military seizure is not primary acquisition), and how it came about that numerous people who might otherwise have acquired permanent property were thereby reduced to serving someone else in order to live at all. It would certainly conflict with the above principle of equality if a law were to grant them a privileged status so that their descendants would always remain feudal landowners, without their land being sold or divided by inheritance and thus made useful to more people; it would also be unjust if only those belonging to an arbitrarily selected class were allowed to acquire land, should the estates in fact be divided. The owner of a large estate keeps out as many smaller property owners (and their votes) as could otherwise occupy his territories. He does not vote on their behalf, and himself has only *one* vote. It should be left exclusively to the ability, industry and good fortune of each member of the commonwealth to enable each to acquire a part and all to acquire the whole, although this distinction cannot be observed within the general legislation itself. The number of those entitled to vote on matters of legislation must be calculated purely from the number of property owners, not from the size of their properties.

Those who possess this right to vote must agree *unanimously* to the law of public justice, or else a legal contention would arise between those who agree and those who disagree, and it would require yet another higher legal principle to resolve it. An entire people cannot, however, be expected to reach unanimity, but only to show a majority of votes (and not even of direct votes, but simply of the votes of those delegated in a large nation to represent the people). Thus the actual principle of being content with majority decisions must be accepted unanimously and embodied in a contract; and this itself must be the ultimate basis on which a civil constitution is established.

## Conclusion

This, then, is an *original contract* by means of which a civil and thus completely lawful constitution and commonwealth can alone be established. But we need by no means assume that this contract (*contractus originarius* or *pactum sociale*), based on a coalition of the wills of all private individuals in a nation to form a common, public will for the purposes of rightful legislation, actually exists as a *fact,* for it cannot possibly be so. Such an assumption would mean that we would first have to prove from history that some nation, whose rights and obligations have been passed down to us, did in fact perform such an act, and handed down some authentic record or legal instrument, orally or in writing, before we could regard ourselves as bound by a pre-

existing civil constitution. It is in fact merely an *idea* of reason, which nonetheless has undoubted practical reality; for it can oblige every legislator to frame his laws in such a way that they could have been produced by the united will of a whole nation, and to regard each subject, in so far as he can claim citizenship, as if he had consented within the general will. This is the test of the rightfulness of every public law. For if the law is such that a whole people could not *possibly* agree to it (for example, if it stated that a certain class of *subjects* must be privileged as a hereditary *ruling class*), it is unjust; but if it is at least *possible* that a people could agree to it, it is our duty to consider the law as just, even if the people is at present in such a position or attitude of mind that it would probably refuse its consent if it were consulted.[9] But this restriction obviously applies only to the judgement of the legislator, not to that of the subject. Thus if a people, under some existing legislation, were asked to make a judgement which in all probability would prejudice its happiness, what should it do? Should the people not oppose the measure? The only possible answer is that they can do nothing but obey. For we are not concerned here with any happiness which the subject might expect to derive from the institutions or administration of the commonwealth, but primarily with the rights which would thereby be secured for everyone. And this is the highest principle from which all maxims relating to the commonwealth must begin, and which cannot be qualified by any other principles. No generally valid principle of legislation can be based on happiness. For both the current circumstances and the highly conflicting and variable illusions as to what happiness is (and no-one can prescribe to others how they should attain it) make all fixed principles impossible, so that happiness alone can never be a suitable principle of legislation. The doctrine that *salus publica suprema civitatis lex est* retains its value and authority undiminished; but the public welfare which demands *first* consideration lies precisely in that legal constitution which guarantees everyone his freedom within the law, so that each remains free to seek his happiness in whatever way he thinks best, so long as he does not violate the lawful freedom and rights of his fellow subjects at large. If the supreme power makes laws which are primarily directed towards happiness (the affluence of the citizens, increased population etc.), this cannot be regarded as the end for which a civil constitution was established, but only as a means of *securing the rightful state,* especially against external enemies of the people. The head of state must be authorised to judge for himself whether such measures are necessary for the commonwealth's prosperity, which is required to maintain its strength and stability both internally and against external enemies. The aim is not, as it were, to make the people happy against its will, but only to ensure its continued existence as a commonwealth.[10] The legislator may indeed err in judging whether or not the measures he adopts are *prudent,* but not in deciding whether or not the law harmonises with the principle of right. For he has ready to hand as an infallible *a priori* standard the idea of an original contract, and he need not wait for experience to show whether the means are suitable, as would be necessary if they were based on the principle of happiness. For so long as it is not self-contradictory to say that an entire people could agree to such a law, however painful it might seem, then the law is in harmony with right. But if a public law is beyond reproach (i.e. *irreprehensible*) with respect to right, it carries with it the authority to coerce those to whom it applies, and conversely, it forbids them to resist the will of the legislator by violent means. In other words, the power of the state to put the law into effect is also *irresistible,* and no rightfully established commonwealth can exist without a force of this kind to suppress all internal resistance. For such resistance would be dictated by a maxim which, if it became general, would destroy the whole civil constitution and put an end to the only state in which men can possess rights.

It thus follows that all resistance against the supreme legislative power, all incitement of the subjects to violent expressions of discontent, all defiance which breaks out into rebellion, is the greatest and most punishable crime in a commonwealth, for it destroys its very foundations. This prohibition is *absolute.* And even if the power of the state or its agent, the head of state, has violated the original contract by authorising the government to act tyrannically, and has thereby, in the eyes of the subject, forfeited the right to legislate, the subject is still not entitled to offer counter-resistance. The reason for this is that the people, under an existing civil constitution, has no longer any right to judge how the constitution should be administered. For if we suppose that it does have this right to judge and that it disagrees with the judgement of the actual head of state, who is to decide which side is right? Neither can act as judge of his own cause. Thus there would have to be another head above the head of state to mediate between the latter and the people, which is self-contradictory.—Nor can a right of necessity be invoked here as a means of removing the barriers which restrict the power of the people; for it is monstrous to suppose that we can have a right to do wrong in the direst (physical) distress.[11] For the head of state can just as readily claim that his severe treatment of his subjects is justified by their insubordination as the subjects can justify their rebellion by complaints about their unmerited suffering, and who is to decide? The decision must rest with whoever controls the ultimate enforcement of the public law, i.e. the head of state himself. Thus no-one in the commonwealth can have a right to contest his authority.

Nonetheless, estimable men have declared that the subject is justified, under certain circumstances, in using force against his superiors. I need name only Achenwall, who is extremely cautious, precise and restrained in his theories of natural right. He says: 'If the danger which threatens the commonwealth as a result of long endurance of injustices from the head of state is greater than the danger to be feared from taking up arms against him, the people may then resist him. It may use this right to abrogate its contract of subjection and to dethrone him as a tyrant.' And he concludes: 'The people, in dethroning its ruler, thus returns to the state of nature.'

I well believe that neither Achenwall nor any others of the worthy men who have speculated along the same lines as he would ever have given their advice or agreement to such hazardous projects if the case had arisen. And it can scarcely be doubted that if the revolutions whereby Switzerland, the United Netherlands or even Great Britain won their much admired constitutions had failed, the readers of their history would regard the execution of their celebrated founders as no more than the deserved punishment of great political criminals. For the result usually affects our judgement of the rightfulness of an action, although the result is uncertain, whereas the principles of right are constant. But it is clear that these peoples have done the greatest degree of wrong in seeking their rights in this way, even if we admit that such a revolution did no injustice to a ruler who had violated a specific basic agreement with the people, such as the *Joyeuse Entrée*. For such procedures, if made into a maxim, make all lawful constitutions insecure and produce a state of complete lawlessness where all rights cease at least to be effectual. In view of this tendency of so many right-thinking authors to plead on behalf of the people (and to its own detriment), I will only remark that such errors arise in part from the usual fallacy of allowing the principle of happiness to influence the judgement, wherever the principle of right is involved; and partly because these writers have assumed that the idea of an original contract (a basic postulate of reason) is something which must have taken place *in reality,* even where there is no document to show that any contract was actually submitted to the commonwealth, accepted by the head of state, and sanctioned by both parties. Such writers thus believe that the people retains the right to abrogate the original contract at its own discretion, if, in the opinion of the people, the contract has been severely violated.[12]

It is obvious from this that the principle of happiness (which is not in fact a definite principle at all) has ill effects in political right just as in morality, however good the intentions of those who teach it. The sovereign wants to make the people happy as he thinks best, and thus becomes a despot, while the people are unwilling to give up their universal human desire to seek happiness in their own way, and thus become rebels. If they had first of all asked what is lawful (in terms of *a priori* certainty, which no empiricist can upset), the idea of a social contract would retain its authority undiminished. But it would not exist as a fact (as Danton would have it,

declaring that since it does not actually exist, all property and all rights under the existing civil constitution are null and void), but only as a rational principle for judging any lawful public constitution whatsoever. And it would then be seen that, until the general will is there, the people has no coercive right against its ruler, since it can apply coercion legally only through him. But if the will is there, no force can be applied to the ruler by the people, otherwise the people would be the supreme ruler. Thus the people can never possess a right of coercion against the head of state, or be entitled to oppose him in word or deed.

We can see, furthermore, that this theory is adequately confirmed in practice. In the British constitution, of which the people are so proud that they hold it up as a model for the whole world, we find no mention of what the people are entitled to do if the monarch were to violate the contract of 1688. Since there is no law to cover such a case, the people tacitly reserve the right to rebel against him if he should violate the contract. And it would be an obvious contradiction if the constitution included a law for such eventualities, entitling the people to overthrow the existing constitution, from which all particular laws are derived, if the contract were violated. For there would then have to be a *publicly constituted*[13] opposing power, hence a second head of state to protect the rights of the people against the first ruler, and then yet a third to decide which of the other two had right on his side. In fact, the leaders (or guardians—call them what you will) of the British people, fearing some such accusation if their plans did not succeed, *invented* the notion of a voluntary abdication by the monarch they forced out, rather than claim a right to depose him (which would have made the constitution self-contradictory).

While I trust that no-one will accuse me of flattering monarchs too much by declaring them inviolable, I likewise hope that I shall be spared the reproach of claiming too much for the people if I maintain that the people too have inalienable rights against the head of state, even if these cannot be rights of coercion.

Hobbes is of the opposite opinion. According to him (*De Cive,* Chap. 7, § 14), the head of state has no contractual obligations towards the people; he can do no injustice to a citizen, but may act towards him as he pleases. This proposition would be perfectly correct if injustice were taken to mean any injury which gave the injured party a *coercive right* against the one who has done him injustice. But in its general form, the proposition is quite terrifying.

The non-resisting subject must be able to assume that his ruler has no *wish* to do him injustice. And everyone has his inalienable rights, which he cannot give up even if he wishes to, and about which he is entitled to make his own judgements. But if he assumes that the ruler's attitude is one of good will, any injustice which he believes he has suffered can only have resulted through error, or through ignorance of certain possible consequences of the laws which the supreme authority has made. Thus the citizen must, with the approval of the ruler, be entitled to make public his opinion on whatever of the ruler's measures seem to him to constitute an injustice against the commonwealth. For to assume that the head of state can neither make mistakes nor be ignorant of anything would be to imply that he receives divine inspiration and is more than a human being. Thus *freedom of the pen* is the only safeguard of the rights of the people, although it must not transcend the bounds of respect and devotion towards the existing constitution, which should itself create a liberal attitude of mind among the subjects. To try to deny the citizen this freedom does not only mean, as Hobbes maintains, that the subject can claim no rights against the supreme ruler. It also means withholding from the ruler all knowledge of those matters which, if he knew about them, he would himself rectify, so that he is thereby put into a self-stultifying position. For his will issues commands to his subjects (as citizens) only in so far as he represents the general will of the people. But to encourage the head of state to fear that independent and public thought might cause political unrest is tantamount to making him distrust his own power and feel hatred towards his people.

The general principle, however, according to which a people may judge negatively whatever it believes was *not decreed* in good will by the supreme legislation, can be summed up as follows: *Whatever a people cannot impose upon itself cannot be imposed upon it by the legislator either.*

For example, if we wish to discover whether a law which declares permanently valid an ecclesiastical constitution (itself formulated at some time in the past) can be regarded as emanating from the actual will or intention of the legislator, we must first ask whether a people is *authorised* to make a law for itself whereby certain accepted doctrines and outward forms of religion are declared permanent, and whether the people may thus prevent its own descendants from making further progress in religious understanding or from correcting any past mistakes. It is clear that any original contract of the people which established such a law would in itself be null and void, for it would conflict with the appointed aim and purpose of mankind. Thus a law of this kind cannot be regarded as the actual will of the monarch, to whom counter-representations may accordingly be made. In all cases, however, where the supreme legislation did nevertheless adopt such measures, it would be permissible to pass general and public judgements upon them, but never to offer any verbal or active resistance.

In every commonwealth, there must be *obedience* to generally valid coercive laws within the mechanism of the political constitution. There must also be a *spirit of freedom,* for in all matters concerning universal human duties, each individual requires to be convinced by reason that the coercion which prevails is lawful, otherwise he would be in contradiction with himself. Obedience without the spirit of freedom is the effective cause of all *secret societies.* For it is a natural vocation of man to communicate with his fellows, especially in matters affecting mankind as a whole. Thus secret societies would disappear if freedom of this kind were encouraged. And how else can the government itself acquire the knowledge it needs to further its own basic intention, if not by allowing the spirit of freedom, so admirable in its origins and effects, to make itself heard?

Nowhere does practice so readily bypass all pure principles of reason and treat theory so presumptuously as in the question of what is needed for a good political constitution. The reason for this is that a legal constitution of long standing gradually makes the people accustomed to judging both their happiness and their rights in terms of the peaceful *status quo.* Conversely, it does not encourage them to value the existing state of affairs in the light of those concepts of happiness and right which reason provides. It rather makes them prefer this passive state to the dangerous task of looking for a better one, thus bearing out the saying which Hippocrates told physicians to remember: *iudicium anceps, experimentum periculosum.* Thus all constitutions which have lasted for a sufficiently long time, whatever their inadequacies and variations, produce the same result: the people remain content with what they have. If we therefore consider the *welfare of the people,* theory is not in fact valid, for everything depends upon practice derived from experience.

But reason provides a concept which we express by the words *political right.* And this concept has binding force for human beings who coexist in a state of antagonism produced by their natural freedom, so that it has an objective, practical reality, irrespective of the good or ill it may produce (for these can only be known by experience). Thus it is based on *a priori* principles, for experience cannot provide knowledge of what is right, and there is a *theory* of political right to which practice must conform before it can be valid.

The only objection which can be raised against this is that, although men have in their minds the idea of the rights to which they are entitled, their intractability is such that they are incapable and unworthy of being treated as their rights demand, so that they can and ought to be kept under control by a supreme power acting purely from expediency. But this counsel of desperation means that, since there is no appeal to right but only to force, the people may themselves resort to force and thus make every legal constitution insecure. If there is nothing which commands immediate respect through reason, such as the basic rights of man, no influence can prevail upon man's arbitrary will and restrain his freedom. But if both benevolence and right speak out in loud

tones, human nature will not prove too debased to listen to their voice with respect. *Tum pietate gravem meritisque si forte virum quem Conspexere, silent arrectisque auribus adstant* (Virgil).

## III

### *On the Relationship of Theory to Practice in International Right*

#### *Considered from a Universally Philanthropic, i.e. Cosmopolitan Point of View* [14]

##### (AGAINST MOSES MENDELSSOHN)

Is the human race as a whole likeable, or is it an object to be regarded with distaste? Must we simply wish it well (to avoid becoming misanthropists) without really expecting its efforts to succeed, and then take no further interest in it? In order to answer such questions, we must first answer the following one: Does man possess natural capacities which would indicate that the race will always progress and improve, so that the evils of the past and present will vanish in the future good? If this were the case, we could at least admire the human species for its constant advance towards the good; otherwise, we should have to hate or despise it, whatever objections might be raised by pretended philanthropists (whose feelings for mankind might at most amount to good will, but not to genuine pleasure).

For however hard we may try to awaken feelings of love in ourselves, we cannot avoid hating that which is and always will be evil, especially if it involves deliberate and general violation of the most sacred rights of man. Perhaps we may not wish to harm men, but shall not want to have any more to do with them than we can help.

Moses Mendelssohn was of the latter opinion (*Jerusalem* § II, pp. 44–47), which he put forward in opposition to his friend Lessing's hypothesis of a divine education of mankind. He regards it as sheer fantasy to say 'that the whole of mankind here on earth must continually progress and become more perfect through the ages'. He continues: 'We see the human race as a whole moving slowly back and forth, and whenever it takes a few steps forward, it soon relapses twice as quickly into its former state.' (This is truly the stone of Sisyphus; if we adopt an attitude of this kind, as the Indians do, the earth must strike us as a place of atonement for old and forgotten sins.) 'Man as an individual progresses; but mankind constantly fluctuates between fixed limits. Regarded as a whole, however, mankind maintains roughly the same level of morality, the same degree of religion and irreligion, of virtue and vice, of happiness (?) and misery.' He introduces these assertions with the words (p. 46): 'Do you presume to guess the plan of providence for mankind? Do not invent hypotheses' (he had earlier called these theories); 'just look around at what actually happens, and if you can briefly survey the history of all past ages, look at what has happened from time immemorial. All this is fact; it must have been intended and approved within the plan of higher wisdom, or at least adopted along with it.'

I beg to differ. It is a sight fit for a god to watch a virtuous man grappling with adversity and evil temptations and yet managing to hold out against them. But it is a sight quite unfit not so much for a god, but even for the most ordinary, though right-thinking man, to see the human race advancing over a period of time towards virtue, and then quickly relapsing the whole way back into vice and misery. It may perhaps be moving and instructive to watch such a drama for a while; but the curtain must eventually descend. For in the long run, it becomes a farce. And even if the actors do not tire of it—for they are fools—the spectator does, for any single act will be enough for him if he can reasonably conclude from it that the never-ending play will go on in the same way for ever. If it is only a play, the retribution at the end can make up for the unpleasant sensations the spectator has felt. But in my opinion at least, it cannot be reconciled with the morality of a wise creator and ruler of the world if countless vices, even with intermingled virtues, are in actual fact allowed to go on accumulating.

I may thus be permitted to assume that, since the human race is constantly progressing in cultural matters (in keeping with its natural purpose), it is also engaged in progressive improvement in relation to the moral end of its existence. This progress may at times be *interrupted* but never *broken off*. I do not need to prove this assumption; it is up to the adversary to prove his case. I am a member of a series of human generations, and as such, I am not as good as I ought to be or could be according to the moral requirements of my nature. I base my argument upon my inborn duty of influencing posterity in such a way that it will make constant progress (and I must thus assume that progress is possible), and that this duty may be rightfully handed down from one member of the series to the next. History may well give rise to endless doubts about my hopes, and if these doubts could be proved, they might persuade me to desist from an apparently futile task. But so long as they do not have the force of certainty, I cannot exchange my duty (as a *liquidum*) for a rule of expediency which says that I ought not to attempt the impracticable (i.e. an *illiquidum,*) since it is purely hypothetical). And however uncertain I may be and may remain as to whether we can hope for anything better for mankind, this uncertainty cannot detract from the maxim I have adopted, or from the necessity of assuming for practical purposes that human progress is possible.

This hope for better times to come, without which an earnest desire to do something useful for the common good would never have inspired the human heart, has always influenced the activities of right-thinking men. And the worthy Mendelssohn must himself have reckoned on this, since he zealously endeavoured to promote the enlightenment and welfare of the nation to which he belonged. For he could not himself reasonably hope to do this unless others after him continued upon the same path. Confronted by the sorry spectacle not only of those evils which befall mankind from natural causes, but also of those which men inflict upon one another, our spirits can be raised by the prospect of future improvements. This, however, calls for unselfish goodwill on our part, since we shall have been long dead and buried when the fruits we helped to sow are harvested. It is quite irrelevant whether any empirical evidence suggests that these plans, which are founded only on hope, may be unsuccessful. For the idea that something which has hitherto been unsuccessful will therefore never be successful does not justify anyone in abandoning even a pragmatic or technical aim (for example, that of flights with aerostatic balloons). This applies even more to moral aims, which, so long as it is not demonstrably impossible to fulfil them, amount to duties. Besides, various evidence suggests that in our age, as compared with all previous ages, the human race has made considerable moral progress, and short-term hindrances prove nothing to the contrary. Moreover, it can be shown that the outcry about man's continually increasing decadence arises for the very reason that we can see further ahead, because we have reached a higher level of morality. We thus pass more severe judgements on what we are, comparing it with what we ought to be, so that our self-reproach increases in proportion to the number of stages of morality we have advanced through during the whole of known history.

If we now ask what means there are of maintaining and indeed accelerating this constant progress towards a better state, we soon realise that the success of this immeasurably long undertaking will depend not so much upon what *we* do (e.g. the education we impart to younger generations) and upon what methods *we* use to further it; it will rather depend upon what human *nature* may do in and through us, to *compel* us to follow a course which we would not readily adopt by choice. We must look to nature alone, or rather to *providence* (since it requires the highest wisdom to fulfil this purpose), for a successful outcome which will first affect the whole and then the individual parts. The schemes of men, on the other hand, begin with the parts, and frequently get no further than them. For the whole is too great for men to encompass; while they can reach it with their ideas, they cannot actively influence it, especially since their schemes conflict with one another to such an extent that they could hardly reach agreement of their own free volition.

On the one hand, universal violence and the distress it produces must eventually make a people decide to submit to the coercion which reason itself prescribes (i.e. the coercion of public law), and to enter into a *civil* constitution. And on the other hand, the distress produced by the constant wars in which the states try to subjugate or engulf each other must finally lead them, even against their will, to enter into a *cosmopolitan* constitution. Or if such a state of universal peace is in turn even more dangerous to freedom, for it may lead to the most fearful despotism (as has indeed occurred more than once with states which have grown too large), distress must force men to form a state which is not a cosmopolitan common-wealth under a single ruler, but a lawful *federation* under a commonly accepted *international right*.

The increasing culture of the states, along with their growing tendency to aggrandise themselves by cunning or violence at the expense of the others, must make wars more frequent. It must likewise cause increasingly high expenditure on standing armies, which must be kept in constant training and equipped with ever more numerous instruments of warfare. Meanwhile, the price of all necessities will steadily rise, while no-one can hope for any proportionate increase in the corresponding metal currencies. No peace will last long enough for the resources saved during it to meet the expenditure of the next war, while the invention of a national debt, though ingenious, is an ultimately self-defeating expedient. Thus sheer exhaustion must eventually perform what goodwill ought to have done but failed to do: each state must be organised internally in such a way that the head of state, for whom the war actually costs nothing (for he wages it at the expense of others, i.e. the people), must no longer have the deciding vote on whether war is to be declared or not, for the people who pay for it must decide. (This, of course, necessarily presupposes that the idea of an original contract has already been realised.) For the people will not readily place itself in danger of personal want (which would not affect the head of state) out of a mere desire for aggrandisement, or because of some supposed and purely verbal offence. And thus posterity will not be oppressed by any burdens which it has not brought upon itself, and it will be able to make perpetual progress towards a morally superior state. This is not produced by any love on the part of earlier ages for later ones, but only by the love of

IMMANUEL KANT

each age for itself. Each commonwealth, unable to harm the others by force, must observe the laws on its own account, and it may reasonably hope that other similarly constituted bodies will help it to do so.

But this is no more than a personal opinion and hypothesis; it is uncertain, like all judgements which profess to define the appropriate natural cause of an intended effect which is not wholly within our control. And even as such, it does not offer the subject of an existing state any principle by which he could attain the desired effect by force (as has already been demonstrated); only the head of state, who is above coercion, can do so. In the normal order of things, it cannot be expected of human nature to desist voluntarily from using force, although it is not impossible where the circumstances are sufficiently pressing. Thus it is not inappropriate to say of man's moral hopes and desires that, since he is powerless to fulfil them himself, he may look to *providence* to create the circumstances in which they can be fulfilled. The end of *man* as an entire species, i.e. that of fulfilling his ultimate appointed purpose by freely exercising his own powers, will be brought by providence to a successful issue, even although the ends of *men* as individuals run in a diametrically opposite direction. For the very conflict of individual inclinations, which is the source of all evil, gives reason a free hand to master them all; it thus gives predominance not to evil, which destroys itself, but to good, which continues to maintain itself once it has been established.

Nowhere does human nature appear less admirable than in the relationships which exist between peoples. No state is for a moment secure from the others in its independence and its possessions. The will to subjugate the others or to grow at their expense is always present, and the production of armaments for defence, which often makes peace more oppressive and more destructive of internal welfare than war itself, can never be relaxed. And there is no possible way of counteracting this except a state of international right, based upon enforceable public laws to which each state must submit (by analogy with a state of civil or political right among individual men). For a permanent universal peace by means of a so-called

*European balance of power* is a pure illusion, like Swift's story of the house which the builder had constructed in such perfect harmony with all the laws of equilibrium that it collapsed as soon as a sparrow alighted on it. But it might be objected that no states will ever submit to coercive laws of this kind, and that a proposal for a universal federation, to whose power all the individual states would voluntarily submit and whose laws they would all obey, may be all very well in the theory of the Abbé St Pierre or of Rousseau, but that it does not apply in practice. For such proposals have always been ridiculed by great statesmen, and even more by heads of state, as pedantic, childish and academic ideas.

For my own part, I put my trust in the theory of what the relationships between men and states *ought to be* according to the principle of right. It recommends to us earthly gods the maxim that we should proceed in our disputes in such a way that a universal federal state may be inaugurated, so that we should therefore assume that it *is possible*. I likewise rely upon the very nature of things to force men to do what they do not willingly choose. This involves human nature, which is still animated by respect for right and duty. I therefore cannot and will not see it as so deeply immersed in evil that practical moral reason will not triumph in the end, after many unsuccessful attempts, thereby showing that it is worthy of admiration after all. On the cosmopolitan level too, it thus remains true to say that whatever reason shows to be valid in theory, is also valid in practice.

## Notes

1. Cf. *Versuche über verschiedne Gegenstände aus der Moral und Literatur (Essays on Various Topics from Morality and Literature),* by C. Garve, Pt. 1, pp. 111–16. I call this estimable writer's disagreements with my propositions *objections,* for they concern matters in which (as I hope) he wishes to reach agreement with me. They are not attacks, which are disparaging statements designed to provoke defence, for which I here find neither the space nor the inclination. [Christian Garve (1742–1798), was a well-known German philosopher of the Enlightenment.—S.M.C.]

2. Being worthy of happiness is that quality of a person which depends upon the subject's own individual free will and in accordance with which a universal reason, legislating both to nature and to the free will, would agree with all the aims of that person. It is thus entirely different from any aptitude for attaining happiness itself. For if a person's will does not harmonise with the only form of will which is fit to legislate universally to the reason, and thus cannot be contained within the latter (in other words, if his will conflicts with morality), he is not worthy of happiness and of that gift of attaining happiness with which nature endowed him.

3. The necessity of assuming as the ultimate end of all things a *highest good* on earth, which it is possible to achieve with our collaboration, is not a necessity created by a lack of moral incentives, but by a lack of external circumstances within which an object appropriate to these incentives can alone be produced as an end in itself, as an *ultimate moral end.* For there can be no *will* without an end in view, although we must abstract from this end whenever the question of straightforward legal compulsion of our deeds arises, in which case the law alone becomes its determinant. But not every end is moral (that of personal happiness, for example, is not); the end must be an unselfish one. And the necessity of an ultimate end posited by pure reason and comprehending the totality of all ends within a single principle (i.e. a world in which the highest possible good can be realised with our collaboration) is a necessity experienced by the unselfish will as it *rises beyond* mere obedience to formal laws and creates as its own object the highest good. This idea of the totality of all ends is a peculiar kind of determinant for the will. For it basically implies that *if* we stand in a moral relationship to things in the world around us, we must everywhere obey the moral law; and to this is added the further duty of working with all our power to *ensure* that the state of affairs described (i.e. a world conforming to the highest moral ends) will actually exist. In all this, man may see himself as analogous to the divinity. For while the divinity has no subjective need of any external object, it cannot be conceived of as closed up within itself, but only as compelled by the very awareness of its own all-sufficiency to produce the highest good outside itself. In the case of the supreme being, this necessity (which corresponds to duty in man) can be envisaged *by us* only as a moral need. With man likewise, the motive provided by the idea of the highest possible earthly good, attainable through his collaboration, is therefore not that of his own intended happiness, but only that of the idea as an end in itself and of obedience to it as a duty. For it does not hold out any prospect of happiness in the absolute sense, but only of a constant ratio between happiness and the worthiness of the subject, whatever the latter may be. But a determinant of the will which imposes this restriction both on itself and on its intention of becoming part of a whole such as we have described is *not selfish.*

4. This is exactly what I myself insist upon. The incentive which men can have before they are given a specific goal (or end) can obviously be none other than the law itself, through the esteem which it inspires (irrespective of what ends one may have and seek to attain through obedience to the law). For the law, as the formal aspect of will, is all that remains if we discount the will's particular content (i.e. the goal, as Garve calls it).

5. Happiness embodies everything that nature has given us and nothing else. But virtue embodies that which no-one but man can give or take away from himself. If it were replied that by deviating from the latter, man could at least incur blame and moral self-reproach, hence dissatisfaction and unhappiness, we might by all means agree. But only the virtuous man or one who is on the way to virtue is capable of this pure moral dissatisfaction, which comes not from any disadvantage resulting from his actions, but from their unlawfulness itself. His dissatisfaction is consequently not the cause but the effect of his being virtuous; and this unhappiness (if we choose to describe regrets over a crime as such) could not furnish a motive for being virtuous.

6. Garve, in his notes to Cicero's *De Officiis,* 1783 edition, p. 69, makes the following admission, which does credit to his own acuteness: 'It is my innermost conviction that freedom will always remain unresolved and will never be explained.' It is absolutely impossible to find a proof of its reality either in direct or indirect experience, and it cannot be accepted without any proof. Such a proof cannot be derived from purely theoretical considerations (for these would have to be sought in experience), nor therefore from purely practical propositions of reason, nor alternatively from practical propositions in the technical sense (for these too would have to be based on experience), but accordingly only from moral-practical ones. One must therefore wonder why Garve did not take refuge in the concept of freedom, at least in order to salvage the possibility of such imperatives.

7. If we try to find a definite meaning for the word *gracious,* as distinct from kind, beneficent, protective etc., we see that it can be attributed only to a person to whom no *coercive rights* apply. Thus only the head of the *state's*

*government,* who enacts and distributes all benefits that are possible within the public laws (for the *sovereign* who provides them is, as it were, invisible, and is not an agent but the personified law itself), can be given the title of *gracious lord,* for he is the only individual to whom coercive rights do not apply. And even in an aristocratic government, as for example in Venice, the *senate* is the only 'gracious lord'. The nobles who belong to it, even including the *Doge* (for only the *plenary council* is the sovereign), are all subjects and equal to the others so far as the exercise of rights is concerned, for each subject has coercive rights towards every one of them. Princes (i.e. persons with a hereditary right to become rulers) are themselves called gracious lords only with future reference, an account of their claims to become rulers (i.e. by courtly etiquette, *par courtoisie*). But as owners of property, they are nonetheless fellow-subjects of the others, and even the humblest of their servants must possess a right of coercion against them through the head of state. Thus there can be no more than one gracious lord in a state. And as for gracious (more correctly *distinguished*) ladies, they can be considered entitled to this appellation by their *rank* and their *sex* (thus only as opposed to the *male sex*), and this only by virtue of a refinement of manners (known as gallantry) whereby the male sex imagines that it does itself greater honour by giving the fair sex precedence over itself.

8. He who does a piece of work (*opus*) can sell it to someone else, just as if it were his own property. But guaranteeing one's labour (*praestatio operae*) is not the same as selling a commodity. The domestic servant, the shop assistant, the labourer, or even the barber, are merely labourers (*operarii*), not *artists* (*artifices,* in the wider sense) or members of the state, and are thus unqualified to be citizens. And although the man to whom I give my firewood to chop and the tailor to whom I give material to make into clothes both appear to have a similar relationship towards me, the former differs from the latter in the same way as the barber from the wig-maker (to whom I may in fact have given the requisite hair) or the labourer from the artist or tradesman, who does a piece of work which belongs to him until he is paid for it. For the latter, in pursuing his trade, exchanges his property with someone else (*opus*), while the former allows someone else to make use of him.—But I do admit that it is somewhat difficult to define the qualifications which entitle anyone to claim the status of being his own master.

9. If, for example, a war tax were proportionately imposed on all subjects, they could not claim, simply because it is oppressive, that it is unjust because the war is in their opinion unnecessary. For they are not entitled to judge this issue, since it is at least *possible* that the war is inevitable and the tax indispensable, so that the tax must be deemed rightful in the judgement of the subjects. But if certain estate owners were oppressed with levies for such a war, while others of the same class were exempted, it is easily seen that a whole people could never agree to a law of this kind, and it is entitled at least to make representations against it, since an unequal distribution of burdens can never be considered just.

10. Measures of this kind might include certain restrictions on imports, so that the means of livelihood may be developed for the benefit of the subjects themselves and not as an advantage to foreigners or an encouragement for their industry. For without the prosperity of the people, the state would not have enough strength to resist external enemies or to preserve itself as a commonwealth.

11. There is no *casus necessitatis* except where duties, i.e. an *absolute* duty and another which, however pressing, is nevertheless *relative,* come into conflict. For instance, it might be necessary for someone to betray someone else, even if their relationship were that of father and son, in order to preserve the state from catastrophe. This preservation of the state from evil is an absolute duty, while the preservation of the individual is merely a relative duty (i.e. it applies only if he is not guilty of a crime against the state). The first person might denounce the second to the authorities with the utmost unwillingness, compelled only by (moral) necessity. But if a person, in order to preserve his own life, pushes a shipwrecked fellow away from the plank he grasps, it would be quite false to say that (physical) necessity gives him a right to do so. For it is only a relative duty for me to preserve my own life (i.e. it applies only if I can do so without committing a crime). But it is an absolute duty not to take the life of another person who has not offended me and does not even make me risk my own life. Yet the teachers of general civil law are perfectly consistent in authorising such measures in cases of distress. For the authorities cannot combine a *penalty* with this prohibition, since this penalty would have to be death. But it would be a nonsensical law which threatened anyone with death if he did not voluntarily deliver himself up to death when in dangerous circumstances.

12. Even if an actual contract of the people with the head of state has been violated, the people cannot reply immediately as a *commonwealth,* but only by forming factions. For the hitherto existing constitution has been destroyed by the people, but a new commonwealth has still

to be organised. At this point, the state of anarchy super-venes, with all the terrors it may bring with it. And the wrong which is thereby done is done by each faction of the people to the others, as is clear from the case where the rebellious subjects ended up by trying to thrust upon each other a constitution which would have been far more op-pressive than the one they abandoned. For they would have been devoured by ecclesiastics and aristocrats, instead of enjoying greater equality in the distribution of political bur-dens under a single head of state who ruled them all.

13. No right in a state can be tacitly and treacherously included by a secret reservation, and least of all a right

which the people claim to be part of the constitution, for all laws within it must be thought of as arising out of a public will. Thus if the constitution allowed rebellion, it would have to declare this right publicly and make clear how it might be implemented.

14. It is not immediately obvious how a universally *philanthropic* attitude can point the way to a cosmopoli-tan constitution, and this in turn to the establishment of *international justice* as the only state in which those capacities which make our species worthy of respect can be properly developed. But the conclusion of this essay will make this relationship clear.

# G. W. F. HEGEL

~

## INTRODUCTION

## STEVEN B. SMITH

G. W. F. Hegel was born into a middle-class family in Stuttgart in 1770. He attended uni-versity at Tübingen where he was a classmate of the philosopher Schelling and the poet Holderlin. As legend has it, they celebrated together news of the outbreak of the French Rev-olution. Hegel held the post of lecturer at the University of Jena where he finished his first major book, *The Phenomenology of Spirit* in 1807. It was here that he saw Napoleon ("this world soul on horse back") ride through the town. Due to the closing of the university, Hegel found employment first as a newspaper editor at Bamberg and later as the head master of a *Gymnasium* at Nurnberg. During these years he began work on his *Science of Logic* and was subsequently called to a professorship first at Heidelberg and then at Berlin, where he suc-ceeded Fichte to a chair of philosophy. His major work of political philosophy, the *Philos-ophy of Right,* was published in 1821. He died in 1831 in the midst of a typhus epidemic.

The *Philosophy of Right* excited controversy almost immediately upon publication. In part because of his prefatory statement that "what is rational is actual and what is actual is rational," critics took the book to be a wholesale justification of the political status quo. Later in the century, it came to be regarded as a rearguard defense of the Prussian state, and dur-ing World War I it was thought to provide a defense for German militarism and imperial-ism. During the cold war Hegelianism was associated with both the rise of German national socialism and Soviet communism, although Marxist defenders of Hegel regarded his dialec-tic as inherently progressive and liberating. Recently, the *Philosophy of Right* has been reassessed as a classic work of reformist or gradualist liberalism in keeping with other great nineteenth-century works by liberals like Benjamin Constant, Alexis de Tocqueville, and John Stuart Mill.

Difficulties with the *Philosophy of Right* often begin with the very title of the book. The subject matter of the work is stated in the Introduction as "the idea of right." The German term for right (*Recht*) is ambiguous. It can mean either "law" in the relatively narrow sense of jurisprudence or "right" in the broader sense of the proper ordering of political relationships. The subtitle of the work, *Natural Right and Political Science in Outline,* indicates Hegel's preference for this wider meaning of the term. The idea of right refers to more than the structure of civil rights and liberties, but to the entire normative dimension of a people's way of life, their ethical norms and values, including their system of public morality and religion.

The opening paragraphs of the *Philosophy of Right* provide an account of the source or ground of right in a theory of the human will (pars. 5–7). Like the entire modern tradition of moral and political philosophy as developed by philosophers from Hobbes to Kant, Hegel believes that the will is the ultimate source of political legitimacy. Hegel treats the will as consisting of three aspects or "moments." The first is defined by the will's ability to abstract freely from all content, from everything empirical or merely given in experience. This kind of freedom is associated with the element of pure "indeterminacy," the will's ability to choose anything and everything. This moment of sheer negativity is deeply resistant to any form of limitation. As such it is entirely empty.

The first moment of the will's activity leads dialectically to the second. Freedom of the will does not mean arbitrary choice. To will means to choose something determinate, the decision to be this rather than that. To will is not merely to declare one's independence from all content, it is to become something specific. The need for the will to be something concrete or specific is not a constraint on freedom, but is essential to it. Furthermore, willing is not an arbitrary choice, but an act of rational deliberation. So long as we understand the will to mean arbitrary choice, it is not truly free. The freedom identified with arbitrary choice (*Wilkur*) is associated by Hegel with slavery to natural appetites and passions. The self-determination of the rational will, by contrast, is characterized not just by a capacity for choice, but for reflection and deliberation over the ends we choose. Rational liberty consists in the ability to reflect evaluatively upon the kinds of things we ought to desire, including the kinds of persons we ought to become.

The final aspect of the will's activity consists in determining what kind of content is appropriate to freedom. To what ought the free will to give its consent? Despite his often fierce rejection of social contract theory, there is built into Hegel's theory of the will an idea of rational consent as the only plausible justification for modern political institutions. The person largely credited for recognizing this principle is Rousseau, who is congratulated for "adducing the will as the principle of the state" (par. 258). The aim of making the rational will the ultimate arbiter of the state is to make citizens feel "at home" in their world, to overcome the various forms of division (*Zerrissenheit*) that have previously alienated citizens from their public institutions. The major headings of the *Philosophy of Right* are thus given over to an account of the kinds of public institutions that the free will can ratify or affirm as its own. The whole domain of these institutions and practices constitutes the sphere of right.

Before indicating briefly how these institutions satisfy the conditions of rational freedom, Hegel's views must be distinguished from two positions with which he is frequently identified. The first maintains that Hegel has no independent theory of moral justification because he ultimately subordinates the rights of individual judgment and conscience to the will of the state. To be sure, there are more than enough passages in the work affirming such sentiments as "the state in and by itself is the ethical whole" (par. 260a). He frequently criticizes the standpoint of Kantian *Moralitat* as an "empty formalism" for its attempt to generate a universal principle of right action (par. 135). As he sometimes writes, there is no principle of right over and above the state. He enjoys recalling the ancient story of a man who asked a philosopher the best way of educating his son. The philosopher replied, "Make him a citizen of a state with good laws" (par. 153).

A second criticism turns on Hegel's frequently noted historicism. On this account Hegel subordinates the moral will to the forward or progressive march of history. "Every individual," he notes in the Preface to the *Philosophy of Right,* "is a child of his time." Morality is thus made relative to time, place, and circumstance. History is advanced precisely by great leaders like Caesar and Napoleon who serve the cause of moral progress but at the expense of much misery and human suffering. In the Introduction to the *Philosophy of History* Hegel presents these "World-Historical Individuals" as moral heroes whose greatness consists in embodying the dominant ethos or spirit of their times. "World-historical men," Hegel writes, "the heroes of an epoch, must therefore be recognized as its clear sighted ones: their deeds, their words are the best of that time." However, even the most farsighted of heroes play a limited role as the agents or instruments of a historical process they cannot in principle comprehend. Once they achieve their ends, they are fated to fade from the scene. "When their object is attained," Hegel hints darkly, "they fall off like empty hulls from the kernel."

Hegel's answer to these objections can be found in his concept of *Sittlichkeit* or ethical life that comprises the entire third part of the *Philosophy of Right.* The German word for ethics, *Sitte,* emphasizes the role of practice, custom, and habituation in forming moral judgment and character (pars. 144, 151). In contrast to Kant's view of morality, Hegel stresses that moral reasoning is not something that applies to individuals in the abstract, but takes place within a context or tradition, a community of moral reasoners. Hegel's use of the term is intended to evoke the place of habituation and practice in the moral life. He enjoys tweaking the modern moral standpoint by evoking the largely unreflective and habitual character of ethical life. His conception of fully developed moral virtue takes the form of "rectitude," which involves little more than obeying the laws and fulfilling the duties of one's station (par. 150).

Hegel often and deliberately overstates his case against the Kantian moral standpoint. His point is not to deny the role of individual moral reflection, but to show that morality is a social institution and exists only within a framework of institutions that makes morality itself possible. To be sure, Hegel does not deny the possibility of moral conflict. His favorite examples of moral conflict come from the ancient Greek world, where individual moral reflection was initially introduced as a "destructive" force within Greek ethical life. In a section entitled "The Political Work of Art" from the *Philosophy of History,* he notes:

> To the Greek his country was a necessary of life, without which existence was impossible. It was the Sophists—the "Teachers of Wisdom"—who first introduced subjective reflection, and the new doctrine that each man should act according to his own conviction. . . . Instead of holding by the existing state of things, internal conviction is relied upon; and thus begins a subjective independent freedom, in which the individual finds himself in a position to bring everything to the test of his own conscience, even in defiance of the existing constitution.

Another of Hegel's favored examples of the conflict between an ethic of community and an ethic of individual reflection comes from Sophocles's *Antigone.* The drama turns on a collision between Antigone's obligation to bury her brother who has betrayed the state and Creon's demand that obligation to the state outweighs all other moral commitments (pars. 144, 166). Such examples of moral conflict are genuinely tragic not because they pit right against wrong, but because they pit right against right. Between Antigone and Creon there simply is no higher decision rule to which we can appeal to determine who is in the right. But while such examples may be illuminating, they indicate for Hegel a *Sittlichkeit* in decay. In a healthy, well-developed social order, conflicts of duties will be relatively rare. Virtue will be less heroic than in the past, a more mundane aspect of everyday life.

Many interpreters have seen in Hegel's conception of social ethics an incipient relativism according to which standards of right and wrong can come only from within existing conventions and institutions. His identification of *Sittlichkeit* with "absolutely valid laws and institutions" appears to give it a conservative dimension reminiscent of Burkean traditionalism. But this is to misidentify Hegel's conception of *Sittlichkeit*. Ethical life is not just a descriptive sociological term, but a term of moral classification and evaluation. It is not just a description of what institutions happen to exist; it is a rational account of what institutions must exist if rational freedom is to be possible. Institutions and practices are not called upon to be judges in their own case. Rather they are judged by their capacity to further and sustain the human desire for freedom.

The *Philosophy of Right* is nothing less than an articulation of those institutions of modern ethical life that most completely correspond to the moral imperative of freedom. These institutions—the famous Hegelian triad of family, civil society, and state—are judged by how well they promote mutual recognition or respect between citizens. Hegel's conception of *Sittlichkeit* does not celebrate existing standards whatever they happen to be, but is tied to a distinctive conception of human agency and moral personality. "Be a person and respect others as persons" is his watchword (par. 36). Being a person means having a sense of oneself as an autonomous agent with a will and consciousness of one's own. Hegel reminds us that the attainment of personality is not just an individual but a social and even a historical accomplishment. The institutions of modern *Sittlichkeit,* chiefly a robust market economy and a developed constitutional state, provide the conditions for complete moral satisfaction.

Hegel's defense of the moral legitimacy of social institutions obviously makes sense only against the background of his general conception of philosophy. The aim of philosophy, he remarks in the Preface to the *Philosophy of Right,* is not to construct a Platonic utopia, but to discover the rationality in what exists. Philosophy, he avers, cannot give advice about what ought to be the case, but should seek to "reconcile" citizens to the world they actually inhabit. This is not a counsel of despair. For Hegel, the world we now inhabit is so arranged that we see ourselves perfectly expressed within the institutions of modern *Sittlichkeit*. Freedom need no longer be sought in an ideal world that perpetually eludes our grasp, but in the forms of social and political life now before us. For some, this strategy will seem far too accommodationist to prove satisfactory. However, to reverse Marx's famous dictum, the purpose of philosophy is not to change the world but to interpret it.

There are a number of excellent commentaries and interpretations of the *Philosophy of Right.* Among works that interpret Hegel in a more liberal vein along roughly the lines developed here, see Charles Taylor, *Hegel and Modern Society* (Cambridge: Cambridge University Press, 1979); Manfred Riedel, *Between Tradition and Revolution: The Hegelian*

*Transformation of Political Philosophy* (Cambridge: Cambridge University Press, 1984); Steven B. Smith, *Hegel's Critique of Liberalism: Rights in Context* (Chicago: University of Chicago Press, 1989); Allen Wood, *Hegel's Ethical Thought* (Cambridge: Cambridge University Press, 1990); Michael O. Hardimon, *Hegel's Social Philosophy: The Project of Reconciliation* (Cambridge: Cambridge University Press, 1994); Robert Pippin, "Hegel's Ethical Rationalism," in *Idealism as Modernism: Hegelian Variations* (Cambridge: Cambridge University Press, 1997), pp. 417–450; Paul Franco, *Hegel's Philosophy of Freedom* (New Haven, Conn.: Yale University Press, 1999); John Rawls, "Hegel," in *Lectures on the History of Moral Philosophy,* ed. Barbara Herman (Cambridge: Harvard University Press, 2000), pp. 329–371. For a comprehensive recent biography, see Terry Pinkard, *Hegel* (Cambridge: Cambridge University Press, 2000).

# Philosophy of Right

. . . *What is rational is actual and what is actual is rational.* On this conviction the plain man like the philosopher takes his stand, and from it philosophy starts in its study of the universe of mind as well as the universe of nature. If reflection, feeling, or whatever form subjective consciousness may take, looks upon the present as something vacuous and looks beyond it with the eyes of superior wisdom, it finds itself in a vacuum, and because it is actual only in the present, it is itself mere vacuity. If on the other hand the Idea passes for 'only an Idea', for something represented in an opinion, philosophy rejects such a view and shows that nothing is actual except the Idea. Once that is granted, the great thing is to apprehend in the show of the temporal and transient the substance which is immanent and the eternal which is present. For since rationality (which is synonymous with the Idea) enters upon external existence simultaneously with its actualization, it emerges with an infinite wealth of forms, shapes, and appearances. Around its heart it throws a motley covering with which consciousness is at home to begin with, a covering which the concept has first to penetrate before it can find the inward pulse and feel it still beating in the outward appearances. But the infinite variety of circumstance which is developed in this externality by the light of the essence glinting in it—this endless material and its organization—this is not the subject matter of philosophy. To touch this at all would be to meddle with things to which philosophy is unsuited; on such topics it may save itself the trouble of giving good advice. Plato might have omitted his recommendation to nurses to keep on the move with infants and to rock them continually in their arms. And Fichte too need not have carried what has been called the 'construction' of his passport regulations to such a pitch of perfection as to require suspects not merely to sign their passports but to have their likenesses painted on them. Along such tracks all trace of philosophy is lost, and such super-erudition it can the more readily disclaim since its attitude to this infinite multitude of topics should of course be most liberal. In adopting this attitude, philosophic science shows itself to be poles apart from the hatred with which the folly of superior wisdom regards a vast number of affairs and institutions, a hatred in which pettiness takes the greatest delight because only by venting it does it attain a feeling of its self-hood.

This book, then, containing as it does the science of the state, is to be nothing other than the endeavour to apprehend and portray the state as something inherently rational. As a work of philosophy, it must

Reprinted from *Hegel's Philosophy of Right,* translated by T. M. Knox (1942), by permission of Oxford University Press.

be poles apart from an attempt to construct a state as it ought to be. The instruction which it may contain cannot consist in teaching the state what it ought to be; it can only show how the state, the ethical universe, is to be understood. . . .

*Hic* Rhodus, *hic* saltus.

To comprehend what is, this is the task of philosophy, because what is, is reason. Whatever happens, every individual is a child of his time; so philosophy too is its own time apprehended in thoughts. It is just as absurd to fancy that a philosophy can transcend its contemporary world as it is to fancy that an individual can overleap his own age, jump over Rhodes. If his theory really goes beyond the world as it is and builds an ideal one as it ought to be, that world exists indeed, but only in his opinions, an unsubstantial element where anything you please may, in fancy, be built.

With hardly an alteration, the proverb just quoted would run:

*Here is the rose, dance thou here.*

What lies between reason as self-conscious mind and reason as an actual world before our eyes, what separates the former from the latter and prevents it from finding satisfaction in the latter, is the fetter of some abstraction or other which has not been liberated [and so transformed] into the concept. To recognize reason as the rose in the cross of the present and thereby to enjoy the present, this is the rational insight which reconciles us to the actual, the reconciliation which philosophy affords to those in whom there has once arisen an inner voice bidding them to comprehend, not only to dwell in what is substantive while still retaining subjective freedom, but also to possess subjective freedom while standing not in anything particular and accidental but in what exists absolutely.

It is this too which constitutes the more concrete meaning of what was described above rather abstractly as the unity of form and content; for form in its most concrete signification is reason as specula-

tive knowing, and content is reason as the substantial essence of actuality, whether ethical or natural. The known identity of these two is the philosophical Idea. It is a sheer obstinacy, the obstinacy which does honour to mankind, to refuse to recognize in conviction anything not ratified by thought. This obstinacy is the characteristic of our epoch, besides being the principle peculiar to Protestantism. What Luther initiated as faith in feeling and in the witness of the spirit, is precisely what spirit, since become more mature, has striven to apprehend in the concept in order to free and so to find itself in the world as it exists to-day. The saying has become famous that 'a half-philosophy leads away from God'—and it is the same half-philosophy that locates knowledge in an 'approximation' to truth—'while true philosophy leads to God'; and the same is true of philosophy and the state. Just as reason is not content with an approximation which, as something 'neither cold nor hot', it will 'spue out of its mouth', so it is just as little content with the cold despair which submits to the view that in this earthly life things are truly bad or at best only tolerable, though here they cannot be improved and that this is the only reflection which can keep us at peace with the world. There is less chill in the peace with the world which knowledge supplies.

One word more about giving instruction as to what the world ought to be. Philosophy in any case always comes on the scene too late to give it. As the thought of the world, it appears only when actuality is already there cut and dried after its process of formation has been completed. The teaching of the concept, which is also history's inescapable lesson, is that it is only when actuality is mature that the ideal first appears over against the real and that the ideal apprehends this same real world in its substance and builds it up for itself into the shape of an intellectual realm. When philosophy paints its grey in grey, then has a shape of life grown old. By philosophy's grey in grey it cannot be rejuvenated but only understood. The owl of Minerva spreads its wings only with the falling of the dusk.

But it is time to close this preface. After all, as a preface, its only business has been to make some external and subjective remarks about the standpoint of the book it introduces. If a topic is to be discussed philosophically, it spurns any but a scientific and objective treatment, and so too if criticisms of the author take any form other than a scientific discussion of the thing itself, they can count only as a personal epilogue and as capricious assertion, and he must treat them with indifference.

# SECOND PART

## *Morality*

105. The standpoint of morality is the standpoint of the will which is infinite not merely in itself but for itself. . . . In contrast with the will's implicit being, with its immediacy and the determinate characteristics developed within it at that level, this reflection of the will into itself and its explicit awareness of its identity makes the person into the subject.

106. It is as subjectivity that the concept has now been determined, and since subjectivity is distinct from the concept as such, i.e. from the implicit principle of the will, and since furthermore it is at the same time the will of the subject as a single individual aware of himself (i.e. still has immediacy in him), it constitutes the determinate *existence* of the concept. In this way a higher ground has been assigned to freedom; the Idea's existential aspect, or its moment of reality, is now the subjectivity of the will. Only in the will as subjective can freedom or the implicit principle of the will be actual.

> The second sphere, Morality, therefore throughout portrays the real aspect of the concept of freedom, and the movement of this sphere is as follows: the will, which at the start is aware only of its independence and which before it is mediated is only implicitly identical with the universal will or the principle of the will, is raised beyond its [explicit] difference from the universal will, beyond this situation in which it sinks deeper and deeper into itself, and is established as explicitly identical with the principle of the will. This process is accordingly the cultivation of the ground in which freedom is now

set, i.e. subjectivity. What happens is that subjectivity, which is abstract at the start, i.e. distinct from the concept, becomes likened to it, and thereby the Idea acquires its genuine realization. The result is that the subjective will determines itself as objective too and so as truly concrete.

107. The self-determination of the will is at the same time a moment in the concept of the will, and subjectivity is not merely its existential aspect but its own determinate character. . . . The will aware of its freedom and determined as subjective is at the start concept alone, but itself has determinate existence in order to exist as Idea. The moral standpoint therefore takes shape as the right of the subjective will. In accordance with this right, the will recognizes something and is something, only in so far as the thing is its own and as the will is present to itself there as something subjective.

> The same process through which the moral attitude develops (see the Remark to the preceding Paragraph) has from this point of view the form of being the development of the right of the subjective will, or of the mode of its existence. In this process the subjective will further determines what it recognizes as its own in its object (*Gegenstand*), so that this object becomes the will's own true concept, becomes objective (*objektiv*) as the expression of the will's own universality.

108. The subjective will, directly aware of itself, and distinguished from the principle of the will (see Remark to Paragraph 106), is therefore abstract, restricted, and formal. But not merely is subjectivity itself formal; in addition, as the infinite self-determination of the will, it constitutes the form of all willing. In this, its first appearance in the single will, this form has not yet been established as identical with the concept of the will, and therefore the moral point of view is that of relation, of ought-to-be, or demand. And since the self-difference of subjectivity involves at the same time the character of being opposed to objectivity as external fact, it follows that the point of view of consciousness comes on the scene here too. . . . The general point of view here is that of the will's self-difference, finitude, and appearance.

The moral is not characterized primarily by its having already been opposed to the immoral, nor is right directly characterized by its opposition to wrong. The point is rather that the general characteristics of morality and immorality alike rest on the subjectivity of the will.

109. This form of all willing primarily involves in accordance with its general character (*a*) the opposition of subjectivity and objectivity, and (*b*) the activity . . . related to this opposition. Now existence and specific determinacy are identical in the concept of the will . . . , and the will as subjective is itself this concept. Hence the moments of this activity consist more precisely in (*a*) distinguishing between objectivity and subjectivity and even ascribing independence to them both, and (*b*) establishing them as identical. In the will which is self-determining, (α) its specific determinacy is in the first place established in the will itself by itself as its inner particularization, as a content which it gives to itself. This is the first negation, and the formal limitation (*Grenze*) of this negation is that of being only something posited, something subjective. (β) As infinitely reflected into itself, this limitation exists for the will, and the will is the struggle to transcend this barrier (*Schranke*), i.e. it is the activity of translating this content in some way or other from subjectivity into objectivity, into an immediate existence. (γ) The simple identity of the will with itself in this opposition is the content which remains self-identical in both these opposites and indifferent to this formal distinction of opposition. In short, it is my aim [the purpose willed].

110. But, at the standpoint of morality, where the will is aware of its freedom, of this identity of the will with itself (see Paragraph 105), this identity of content acquires the more particularized character appropriate to itself.

(*a*) The content as 'mine' has for me this character: by virtue of its identity in subject and object it enshrines for me my subjectivity, not merely as my inner purpose, but also inasmuch as it has acquired outward existence.

111. (*b*) Though the content does have in it something particular, whencesoever it may be derived,

still it is the content of the will reflected into itself in its determinacy and thus of the self-identical and universal will; and therefore:

(α) the content is inwardly characterized as adequate to the principle of the will or as possessing the objectivity of the concept;
(β) since the subjective will, as aware of itself, is at the same time still formal (see Paragraph 108), the content's adequacy to the concept is still only something demanded, and hence this entails the possibility that the content may *not* be adequate to the concept.

112. (*c*) Since in carrying out my aims I retain my subjectivity (see Paragraph 110), during this process of objectifying them I simultaneously supersede the immediacy of this subjectivity as well as its character as this my individual subjectivity. But the external subjectivity which is thus identical with me is the will of others. . . . The will's ground of existence is now subjectivity (see Paragraph 106) and the will of others is that existence which I give to my aim and which is at the same time to me an other. The achievement of my aim, therefore, implies this identity of my will with the will of others, it has a positive bearing on the will of others.

The objectivity of the aim achieved thus involves three meanings, or rather it has three moments present within it at once; it is:

(α) something existing externally and immediately (see Paragraph 109);
(β) adequate to the concept (see Paragraph 111);
(γ) *universal* subjectivity.

The subjectivity which maintains itself in this objectivity consists:

(α) in the fact that the objective aim is mine, so that in it I maintain myself as *this* individual (see Paragraph 110);
(β) and (γ), in moments which coincide with the moments (β) and (γ) above.

At the standpoint of morality, subjectivity and objectivity are distinct from one another, or united only by their mutual contradiction; it is this fact more particularly which constitutes the finitude of this sphere or its character as mere appearance (see Paragraph 108), and the development of this standpoint is the development of these contradictions and their resolutions, resolutions, however, which within this field can be no more than relative.

113. The externalization of the subjective or moral will is action. Action implies the determinate characteristics here indicated:

(α) in its externality it must be known to me as *my* action;
(β) it must bear essentially on the concept as an 'ought' [see Paragraph 131];
(γ) it must have an essential bearing on the will of others.

It is not until we come to the externalization of the moral will that we come to action. The existence which the will gives to itself in the sphere of formal rights is existence in an immediate thing and is itself immediate; to start with, it neither has in itself any express bearing on the concept, which is at that point not yet contrasted with the subjective will and so is not distinguished from it, nor has it a positive bearing on the will of others; in the sphere of right, command in its fundamental character is only prohibition. . . . In contract and wrong, there is the beginning of a bearing on the will of others; but the correspondence established in contract between one will and another is grounded in arbitrariness, and the essential bearing which the will has there on the will of the other is, as a matter of rights, something negative, i.e. one party retains his property (the value of it) and allows the other to retain his. On the other hand, crime in its aspect as issuing from the subjective will, and the question of the mode of its existence in that will, come before us now for consideration for the first time.

The content of an action at law (*actio*), as something determined by legal enactment, is not imputable to me. Consequently, such an action contains only some of the moments of a moral action proper, and contains them only incidentally. The aspect of an action in virtue of which it is properly moral is therefore distinct from its aspect as legal.

114. The right of the moral will involves three aspects:

(*a*) The abstract or formal right of action, the right

that the content of the action as carried out in immediate existence, shall be in principle mine, that thus the action shall be the *Purpose* of the subjective will.

(*b*) The particular aspect of the action is its inner content (α) as I am aware of it in its general character; my awareness of this general character constitutes the worth of the action and the reason I think good to do it—in short my *Intention*. (β) Its content is my special aim, the aim of my particular, merely individual, existence, i.e. *Welfare*.

(*c*) This content (as something which is inward and which yet at the same time is raised to its universality as to absolute objectivity) is the absolute end of the will, the *Good*—with the opposition in the sphere of reflection, of *subjective* universality, which is now wickedness and now conscience.

## *Subsection 1*

### PURPOSE AND RESPONSIBILITY

115. The finitude of the subjective will in the immediacy of acting consists directly in this, that its action *presupposes* an external object with a complex environment. The deed sets up an alteration in this state of affairs confronting the will, and my will has responsibility in general for its deed in so far as the abstract predicate 'mine' belongs to the state of affairs so altered.

An event, a situation which has been produced, is a concrete external actuality which because of its concreteness has in it an indeterminable multiplicity of factors. Any and every single element which appears as the condition, ground, or cause of one such factor, and so has contributed its share to the event in question, may be looked upon as responsible for the event, or at least as sharing the responsibility for it. Hence, in the case of a complex event (e.g. the French Revolution) it is open to the abstract Understanding to choose which of an endless number of factors it will maintain to be responsible for it.

116. It is, of course, not my own doing if damage is caused to others by things whose owner I am and which as external objects stand and are effective in manifold connexions with other things (as may also be the case with my self as a bodily mechanism or

as a living thing). This damage, however, is to some extent chargeable to me because the things that cause it are in principle mine, although it is true that they are subject to my control, vigilance, &c., only to an extent varying with their special character.

117. The freely acting will, in directing its aim on the state of affairs confronting it, has an idea of the attendant circumstances. But because the will is finite, since this state of affairs is presupposed, the objective phenomenon is contingent so far as the will is concerned, and may contain something other than what the will's idea of it contains. The will's right, however, is to recognize as its action, and to accept responsibility for, only those presuppositions of the deed of which it was conscious in its aim and those aspects of the deed which were contained in its purpose. The deed can be imputed to me only if my will is responsible for it—this is the right to know.

118. Further, action is translated into external fact, and external fact has connexions in the field of external necessity through which it develops itself in all directions. Hence action has a multitude of consequences. These consequences are the outward form whose inner soul is the aim of the action, and thus they are the consequences *of the action,* they belong to the action. At the same time, however, the action, as the aim posited in the external world, has become the prey of external forces which attach to it something totally different from what it is explicitly and drive it on into alien and distant consequences. Thus the will has the right to repudiate the imputation of all consequences except the first, since it alone was purposed.

> To determine which results are accidental and which necessary is impossible, because the necessity implicit in the finite comes into determinate existence as an external necessity, as a relation of single things to one another, things which as self-subsistent are conjoined in indifference to one another and externally. The maxim: 'Ignore the consequences of actions' and the other: 'Judge actions by their consequences and make these the criterion of right and good' are both alike maxims of the abstract Understanding. The consequences,

as the shape proper to the action and immanent within it, exhibit nothing but its nature and are simply the action itself; therefore the action can neither disavow nor ignore them. On the other hand, however, among the consequences there is also comprised something interposed from without and introduced by chance, and this is quite unrelated to the nature of the action itself.

The development in the external world of the contradiction involved in the *necessity* of the *finite* is just the conversion of necessity into contingency and vice versa. From this point of view, therefore, acting means surrendering oneself to this law. It is because of this that it is to the advantage of the criminal if his action has comparatively few bad consequences (while a good action must be content to have had no consequences or very few), and that the fully developed consequences of a crime are counted as part of the crime.

The self-consciousness of heroes (like that of Oedipus and others in Greek tragedy) had not advanced out of its primitive simplicity either to reflection on the distinction between act and action, between the external event and the purpose and knowledge of the circumstances, or to the subdivision of consequences. On the contrary, they accepted responsibility for the whole compass of the deed.

## *Subsection 2*

### INTENTION AND WELFARE

119. An action as an external event is a complex of connected parts which may be regarded as divided into units *ad infinitum,* and the action may be treated as having touched in the first instance only one of these units. The truth of the single, however, is the universal; and what explicitly gives action its specific character is not an isolated content limited to an external unit, but a universal content, comprising in itself the complex of connected parts. Purpose, as issuing from a thinker, comprises more than the mere unit; essentially it comprises that universal side of the action, i.e. the intention.

> Etymologically, *Absicht* (intention) implies abstraction, either the form of universality or the extraction of a particular aspect of the concrete thing. The endeavour to justify an action by the

intention behind it involves the isolation of one or other of its single aspects which is alleged to be the essence of the action on its subjective side.

To judge an action as an external deed without yet determining its rightness or wrongness is simply to bestow on it a universal predicate, i.e. to describe it as burning, killing, &c.

The discrete character of the external world shows what the nature of that world is, namely a chain of external relations. Actuality is touched in the first instance only at a single point (arson, for instance, *directly* concerns only a tiny section of the firewood, i.e. is describable in a proposition, not a judgement), but the universal nature of this point entails its expansion. In a living thing, the single part is there in its immediacy not as a mere part, but as an organ in which the universal is really present as the universal; hence in murder, it is not a piece of flesh, as something isolated, which is injured, but life itself which is injured in that piece of flesh. It is subjective reflection, ignorant of the logical nature of the single and the universal, which indulges *ad libitum* in the subdivision of single parts and consequences; and yet it is the nature of the finite deed itself to contain such separable contingencies.— The device of *dolus indirectus* has its basis in these considerations.

120. The right of intention is that the universal quality of the action shall not merely be implicit but shall be known by the agent, and so shall have lain from the start in his subjective will. Vice versa, what may be called the right of the objectivity of action is the right of the action to evince itself as known and willed by the subject as a *thinker*.

This right to insight of this kind entails the complete, or almost complete, irresponsibility of children, imbeciles, lunatics, &c., for their actions.— But just as actions on their external side as events include accidental consequences, so there is involved in the subjective agent an indeterminacy whose degree depends on the strength and force of his self-consciousness and circumspection. This indeterminacy, however, may not be taken into account except in connexion with childhood or imbecility, lunacy, &c., since it is only such well marked states of mind that nullify the trait of thought and freedom of will, and permit us to treat

the agent as devoid of the dignity of being a thinker and a will.

121. The universal quality of the action is the manifold content of the action as such, reduced to the simple form of universality. But the subject, an entity reflected into himself and so particular in correlation with the particularity of his object, has in his end his own particular content, and this content is the soul of the action and determines its character. The fact that this moment of the particularity of the agent is contained and realized in the action constitutes subjective freedom in its more concrete sense, the right of the subject to find his satisfaction in the action.

122. It is on the strength of this particular aspect that the action has subjective worth or interest for me. In contrast with this *end*—the content of the intention—the direct character of the action in its further content is reduced to a *means*. In so far as such an end is something finite, it may in its turn be reduced to a means to some further intention and so on *ad infinitum*.

123. For the content of these ends nothing is available at this point except (α) pure activity itself, i.e. the activity present owing to the fact that the subject puts himself into whatever he is to look upon and promote as his end. Men are willing to be *active* in pursuit of what interests them, or should interest them, as something which is their own. (β) A more determinate content, however, the still abstract and formal freedom of subjectivity possesses only in its natural subjective embodiment, i.e. in needs, inclinations, passions, opinions, fancies, &c. The satisfaction of these is welfare or happiness, both in general and in its particular species—the ends of the whole sphere of finitude.

Here—the standpoint of relation (see Paragraph 108), when the subject is characterized by his self-difference and so counts as a particular—is the place where the content of the natural will (see Paragraph 11) comes on the scene. But the will here is not as it is in its immediacy; on the contrary, this content now belongs to a will reflected into itself and so is elevated to become a universal end, the end of welfare or happiness; this happens at the level of the thinking which does not yet apprehend the will in its freedom but reflects on its content as on one natural and given—the level, for example, of the time of Croesus and Solon.

124. Since the subjective satisfaction of the individual himself (including the recognition which he receives by way of honour and fame) is also part and parcel of the achievement of ends of absolute worth, it follows that the demand that such an end alone shall appear as willed and attained, like the view that, in willing, objective and subjective ends are mutually exclusive, is an empty dogmatism of the abstract Understanding. And this dogmatism is more than empty, it is pernicious if it passes into the assertion that because subjective satisfaction is present, as it always is when any task is brought to completion, it is what the agent intended in essence to secure and that the objective end was in his eyes only a means to that.—What the subject is, is the series of his actions. If these are a series of worthless productions, then the subjectivity of his willing is just as worthless. But if the series of his deeds is of a substantive nature, then the same is true also of the individual's inner will.

The right of the subject's particularity, his right to be satisfied, or in other words the right of subjective freedom, is the pivot and centre of the difference between antiquity and modern times. This right in its infinity is given expression in Christianity and it has become the universal effective principle of a new form of civilization. Amongst the primary shapes which this right assumes are love, romanticism, the quest for the eternal salvation of the individual, &c.; next come moral convictions and conscience; and, finally, the other forms, some of which come into prominence in what follows as the principle of civil society and as moments in the constitution of the state, while others appear in the course of history, particularly the history of art, science, and philosophy.

Now this principle of particularity is, to be sure, one moment of the antithesis, and in the first place at least it is just as much identical with the universal as distinct from it. Abstract reflection, however, fixes this moment in its distinction from and opposition to the universal and so produces a view of morality as nothing but a bitter, unending, struggle

against self-satisfaction, as the command: 'Do with abhorrence what duty enjoins.'

It is just this type of ratiocination which adduces that familiar psychological view of history which understands how to belittle and disparage all great deeds and great men by transforming into the main intention and operative motive of actions the inclinations and passions which likewise found their satisfaction from the achievement of something substantive, the fame and honour, &c., consequential on such actions, in a word their particular aspect, the aspect which it has decreed in advance to be something in itself pernicious. Such ratiocination assures us that, while great actions and the efficiency which has subsisted through a series of them have produced greatness in the world and have had as their consequences for the individual agent power, honour, and fame, still what belongs to the individual is not the greatness itself but what has accrued to him from it, this purely particular and external result; because this result is a consequence, it is therefore supposed to have been the agent's end and even his sole end. Reflection of this sort stops short at the subjective side of great men, since it itself stands on purely subjective ground, and consequently it overlooks what is substantive in this emptiness of its own making. This is the view of those valet psychologists 'for whom there are no heroes, not because there are no heroes, but because these psychologists are only valets'.

125. The subjective element of the will, with its particular content—welfare, is reflected into itself and infinite and so stands related to the universal element, to the principle of the will. This moment of universality, posited first of all within this particular content itself, is the welfare of others also, or, specified completely, though quite emptily, the welfare of all. The welfare of many other unspecified particulars is thus also an essential end and right of subjectivity. But since the absolutely universal, in distinction from such a particular content, has not so far been further determined than as 'the right', it follows that these ends of particularity, differing as they do from the universal, may be in conformity with it, but they also may not.

126. My particularity, however, like that of others, is only a right at all in so far as I am a free entity. There-

fore it may not make claims for itself in contradiction to this its substantive basis, and an intention to secure my welfare or that of others (and it is particularly in this latter case that such an intention is called 'moral') cannot justify an action which is wrong.

> It is one of the most prominent of the corrupt maxims of our time to enter a plea for the so-called 'moral' intention behind wrong actions and to imagine bad men with well-meaning hearts, i.e. hearts willing their own welfare and perhaps that of others also. This doctrine is rooted in the 'benevolence' (*guten Herzens*) of the pre-Kantian philosophers and constitutes, e.g., the quintessence of well-known touching dramatic productions; but to-day it has been resuscitated in a more extravagant form, and inner enthusiasm and the heart, i.e. the form of particularity as such, have been made the criterion of right, rationality, and excellence. The result is that crime and the thoughts that lead to it, be they fancies however trite and empty, or opinions however wild, are to be regarded as right, rational, and excellent, simply because they issue from men's hearts and enthusiasms. . . .
>
> Incidentally, however, attention must be paid to the point of view from which right and welfare are being treated here. We are considering right as abstract right and welfare as the particular welfare of the single agent. The so-called 'general good', the welfare of the state, i.e. the right of mind actual and concrete, is quite a different sphere, a sphere in which abstract right is a subordinate moment like particular welfare and the happiness of the individual. As was remarked above, it is one of the commonest blunders of abstract thinking to make private rights and private welfare count as *absolute* in opposition to the universality of the state.

127. The particularity of the interests of the natural will, taken in their entirety as a single whole, is personal existence or life. In extreme danger and in conflict with the rightful property of someone else, this life may claim (as a right, not a mercy) a right of distress, because in such a situation there is on the one hand an infinite injury to a man's existence and the consequent loss of rights altogether, and on the other hand only an injury to a single restricted embodiment of freedom, and this implies a recognition both of right as such and also of the injured

man's capacity for rights, because the injury affects only *this* property of his.

> The right of distress is the basis of *beneficium competentiae* whereby a debtor is allowed to retain of his tools, farming implements, clothes, or, in short, of his resources, i.e. of his creditor's property, so much as is regarded as indispensable if he is to continue to support life—to support it, of course, on his own social level.

128. This distress reveals the finitude and therefore the contingency of both right and welfare, of right as the abstract embodiment of freedom without embodying the particular person, and of welfare as the sphere of the particular will without the universality of right. In this way they are *established* as one-sided and ideal, the character which in *conception* they already possessed. Right has already (see Paragraph 106) determined its embodiment as the particular will; and subjectivity, in its particularity as a comprehensive whole, is itself the *embodiment* of freedom (see Paragraph 127), while as the infinite relation of the will to itself, it is implicitly the *universal* element in freedom. The two moments present in right and subjectivity, thus integrated and attaining their truth, their identity, though in the first instance still remaining *relative* to one another, are (*a*) the good (as the concrete, absolutely determinate, universal), and (*b*) conscience (as infinite subjectivity inwardly conscious and inwardly determining its content).

### *Subsection 3*

#### GOOD AND CONSCIENCE

129. The good is the Idea as the unity of the concept of the will with the particular will. In this unity, abstract right, welfare, the subjectivity of knowing and the contingency of external fact, have their independent self-subsistence superseded, though at the same time they are still contained and retained within it in their essence. The good is thus freedom realized, the absolute end and aim of the world.

130. In this Idea, welfare has no independent validity as the embodiment of a single particular

will but only as universal welfare and essentially as universal in principle, i.e. as according with freedom. Welfare without right is not a good. Similarly, right without welfare is not the good; *fiat justitia* should not be followed by *pereat mundus*. Consequently, since the good must of necessity be actualized through the particular will and is at the same time its substance, it has absolute right in contrast with the abstract right of property and the particular aims of welfare. If either of these moments becomes distinguished from the good, it has validity only in so far as it accords with the good and is subordinated to it.

131. For the subjective will, the good and the good alone is the essential, and the subjective will has value and dignity only in so far as its insight and intention accord with the good. Inasmuch as the good is at this point still only this *abstract* Idea of good, the subjective will has not yet been caught up into it and established as according with it. Consequently, it stands in a *relation* to the good, and the relation is that the good *ought* to be substantive for it, i.e. it ought to make the good its aim and realize it completely, while the good on its side has in the subjective will its only means of stepping into actuality.

132. The right of the subjective will is that whatever it is to recognize as valid shall be seen by it as good, and that an action, as its aim entering upon external objectivity, shall be imputed to it as right or wrong, good or evil, legal or illegal, in accordance with its *knowledge* of the worth which the action has in this objectivity.

The good is in principle the essence of the will in its substantiality and universality, i.e. of the will in its truth, and therefore it exists simply and solely in thinking and by means of thinking. Hence assertions such as 'man cannot know the truth but has to do only with phenomena', or 'thinking injures the good will' are dogmas depriving mind not only of intellectual but also of all ethical worth and dignity.

The right of giving recognition only to what my insight sees as rational is the highest right of the subject, although owing to its subjective character it remains a formal right; against it the right which reason *qua* the objective possesses over the subject remains firmly established.

On account of its formal character, insight is capable equally of being true and of being mere opinion and error. The individual's acquisition of this right of insight is, on the principles of the sphere which is still moral only, part and parcel of his particular subjective education. I may demand from myself, and regard it as one of my subjective rights, that my insight into an obligation shall be based on good reasons, that I shall be convinced of the obligation and even that I shall apprehend it from its concept and fundamental nature. But whatever I may claim for the satisfaction of my conviction about the character of an action as good, permitted, or forbidden, and so about its imputability in respect of this character, this in no way detracts from the right of objectivity.

This right of insight into the good is distinct from the right of insight in respect of action as such (see Paragraph 117); the form of the right of objectivity which corresponds to the latter is this, that since action is an alteration which is to take place in an actual world and so will have recognition in it, it must in general accord with what has validity there. Whoever wills to act in this world of actuality has *eo ipso* submitted himself to its laws and recognized the right of objectivity.

Similarly, in the state as the objectivity of the concept of reason, legal responsibility cannot be tied down to what an individual may hold to be or not to be in accordance with his reason, or to his subjective insight into what is right or wrong, good or evil, or to the demands which he makes for the satisfaction of his conviction. In this objective field, the right of insight is valid as insight into the legal or illegal, *qua* into what is recognized as right, and it is restricted to its elementary meaning, i.e. to knowledge in the sense of acquaintance with what is legal and to that extent obligatory. By means of the publicity of the laws and the universality of manners, the state removes from the right of insight its formal aspect and the contingency which it still retains for the subject at the level of morality. The subject's right to know action in its specific character as good or evil, legal or illegal, has the result of diminishing or cancelling in this respect too the responsibility of children, imbeciles, and lunatics, although it is impossible to delimit precisely either childhood, imbecility, &c., or their degree of irresponsibility. But to turn momentary blindness, the goad of passion, intoxication, or, in a word, what is called the strength of sensual impulse (excluding impulses which are the basis of the right of distress—see Paragraph 127) into *reasons* when the imputation, specific character, and culpability of a crime are in question, and to look upon such circumstances as if they took away the criminal's guilt, again means (compare Paragraph 100 and the Remark to Paragraph 120) failing to treat the criminal in accordance with the right and honour due to him as a man; for the nature of man consists precisely in the fact that he is essentially something universal, not a being whose knowledge is an abstractly momentary and piecemeal affair.

Just as what the incendiary really sets on fire is not the isolated square inch of wooden surface to which he applies his torch, but the universal in that square inch, e.g. the house as a whole, so, as subject, he is neither the single existent of this moment of time nor this isolated hot feeling of revenge. If he were, he would be an animal which would have to be knocked on the head as dangerous and unsafe because of its liability to fits of madness.

The claim is made that the criminal in the moment of his action must have had a 'clear idea' of the wrong and its culpability before it can be imputed to him as a crime. At first sight, this claim seems to preserve the right of his subjectivity, but the truth is that it deprives him of his indwelling nature as intelligent, a nature whose effective presence is not confined to the 'clear ideas' of Wolff's psychology, and only in cases of lunacy is it so deranged as to be divorced from the knowing and doing of isolated things.

The sphere in which these extenuating circumstances come into consideration as grounds for the mitigation of punishment is a sphere other than that of rights, the sphere of pardon.

133. The particular subject is related to the good as to the essence of his will, and hence his will's obligation arises directly in this relation. Since particularity is distinct from the good and falls within the subjective will, the good is characterized to begin with only as the universal abstract essentiality of the will, i.e. as duty. Since duty is thus abstract and universal in character, it should be done for duty's sake.

134. Because every action explicitly calls for a particular content and a specific end, while duty as an abstraction entails nothing of the kind, the question arises: what is my duty? As an answer nothing is so far available except: (*a*) to do the right, and (*b*) to strive after welfare, one's own welfare, and welfare in universal terms, the welfare of others (see Paragraph 119).

135. These specific duties, however, are not contained in the definition of duty itself; but since both of them are conditioned and restricted, they *eo ipso* bring about the transition to the higher sphere of the unconditioned, the sphere of duty. Duty itself in the moral self-consciousness is the essence or the universality of that consciousness, the way in which it is inwardly related to itself alone; all that is left to it, therefore, is abstract universality, and for its determinate character it has identity without content, or the abstractly positive, the indeterminate.

However essential it is to give prominence to the pure unconditioned self-determination of the will as the root of duty, and to the way in which knowledge of the will, thanks to Kant's philosophy, has won its firm foundation and starting-point for the first time owing to the thought of its infinite autonomy, still to adhere to the exclusively moral position, without making the transition to the conception of ethics, is to reduce this gain to an empty formalism, and the science of morals to the preaching of duty for duty's sake. From this point of view, no immanent doctrine of duties is possible; of course, material may be brought in from outside and particular duties may be arrived at accordingly, but if the definition of duty is taken to be the absence of contradiction, formal correspondence with itself—which is nothing but abstract indeterminacy stabilized—then no transition is possible to the specification of particular duties nor, if some such particular content for acting comes under consideration, is there any criterion in that principle for deciding whether it is or is not a duty. On the contrary, by this means any wrong or immoral line of conduct may be justified.

Kant's further formulation, the possibility of visualizing an action as a *universal* maxim, does lead to the more concrete visualization of a situation, but in itself it contains no principle beyond abstract identity and the 'absence of contradiction' already mentioned.

The absence of property contains in itself just as little contradiction as the non-existence of this or that nation, family, &c., or the death of the whole human race. But if it is already established on other grounds and presupposed that property and human life are to exist and be respected, then indeed it is a contradiction to commit theft or murder; a contradiction must be a contradiction of something, i.e. of some content presupposed from the start as a fixed principle. It is to a principle of that kind alone, therefore, that an action can be related either by correspondence or contradiction. But if duty is to be willed simply for duty's sake and not for the sake of some content, it is only a formal identity whose nature it is to exclude all content and specification.

The further antinomies and configurations of this never-ending ought-to-be, in which the exclusively moral way of thinking—thinking in terms of *relation*—just wanders to and fro without being able to resolve them and get beyond the ought-to-be, I have developed in my *Phenomenology of Mind*.

136. Because of the abstract characterization of the good, the other moment of the Idea—particularity in general—falls within subjectivity. Subjectivity in its universality reflected into itself is the subject's absolute inward certainty (*Gewißheit*) of himself, that which establishes the particular and is the determining and decisive element in him, his conscience (*Gewissen*).

137. True conscience is the disposition to will what is absolutely good. It therefore has fixed principles and it is aware of these as its explicitly objective determinants and duties. In distinction from this its content (i.e. truth), conscience is only the formal side of the activity of the will, which as *this* will has no special content of its own. But the objective system of these principles and duties, and the union of subjective knowing with this system, is not present until we come to the standpoint of ethical life. Here at the abstract standpoint of morality, conscience lacks this objective content and so its explicit character is that of infinite abstract self-certainty, which at the same time is for this very reason the self-certainty of *this* subject.

Conscience is the expression of the absolute title of subjective self-consciousness to know in itself and from within itself what is right and obligatory, to give recognition only to what it thus knows as good, and at the same time to maintain that whatever in this way it knows and wills is in truth right and obligatory. Conscience as this unity of subjective knowing with what is absolute is a sanctuary which it would be sacrilege to violate. But whether the conscience of a specific individual corresponds with this Idea of conscience, or whether what it takes or declares to be good is actually so, is ascertainable only from the content of the good it seeks to realize. What is right and obligatory is the absolutely rational element in the will's volitions and therefore it is not in essence the *particular* property of an individual, and its form is not that of feeling or any other private (i.e. sensuous) type of knowing, but essentially that of universals determined by thought, i.e. the form of laws and principles. Conscience is therefore subject to the judgement of its truth or falsity, and when it appeals only to itself for a decision, it is directly at variance with what it wishes to be, namely the rule for a mode of conduct which is rational, absolutely valid, and universal. For this reason, the state cannot give recognition to conscience in its private form as subjective knowing, any more than science can grant validity to subjective opinion, dogmatism, and the appeal to a subjective opinion. In true conscience, its elements are not different, but they may become so, and it is the determining element, the subjectivity of willing and knowing, which can sever itself from the true content of conscience, establish its own independence, and reduce that content to a form and a show. The ambiguity in connexion with conscience lies therefore in this: it is presupposed to mean the *identity* of subjective knowing and willing with the true good, and so is claimed and recognized to be something sacrosanct; and yet at the same time, as the mere subjective reflection of self-consciousness into itself, it still claims for itself the title due, solely on the strength of its absolutely valid rational *content,* to that identity alone.

At the level of morality, distinguished as it is in

this book from the level of ethics, it is only formal conscience that is to be found. True conscience has been mentioned only to indicate its distinction from the other and to obviate the possible misunderstanding that here, where it is only formal conscience that is under consideration, the argument is about true conscience. The latter is part of the ethical disposition which comes before us for the first time in the following section.—The religious conscience, however, does not belong to this sphere at all.

# THIRD PART

## *Ethical Life*

142. Ethical life is the Idea of freedom in that on the one hand it is the good become alive—the good endowed in self-consciousness with knowing and willing and actualized by self-conscious action— while on the other hand self-consciousness has in the ethical realm its absolute foundation and the end which actuates its effort. Thus ethical life is the concept of freedom developed into the existing world and the nature of self-consciousness.

143. Since this unity of the concept of the will with its embodiment—i.e. the particular will—is knowing, consciousness of the distinction between these two moments of the Idea is present, but present in such a way that now each of these moments is in its own eyes the totality of the Idea and has that totality as its foundation and content.

144. (a) The objective ethical order, which comes on the scene in place of good in the abstract, is substance made concrete by subjectivity as infinite form. Hence it posits within itself distinctions whose specific character is thereby determined by the concept, and which endow the ethical order with a stable content independently necessary and subsistent in exaltation above subjective opinion and caprice. These distinctions are absolutely valid laws and institutions.

145. It is the fact that the ethical order is the system of these specific determinations of the Idea which constitutes its rationality. Hence the ethical order is freedom or the absolute will as what is objective, a circle of necessity whose moments are the ethical powers which regulate the life of individuals. To these powers individuals are related as accidents to substance, and it is in individuals that these powers are represented, have the shape of appearance, and become actualized.

146. (b) The substantial order, in the self-consciousness which it has thus actually attained in individuals, knows itself and so is an object of knowledge. This ethical substance and its laws and powers are on the one hand an object over against the subject, and from his point of view they *are*— 'are' in the highest sense of self-subsistent being. This is an absolute authority and power infinitely more firmly established than the being of nature.

> The sun, the moon, mountains, rivers, and the natural objects of all kinds by which we are surrounded, *are*. For consciousness they have the authority not only of mere being but also of possessing a particular nature which it accepts and to which it adjusts itself in dealing with them, using them, or in being otherwise concerned with them. The authority of ethical laws is infinitely higher, because natural objects conceal rationality under the cloak of contingency and exhibit it only in their utterly external and disconnected way.

147. On the other hand, they are not something alien to the subject. On the contrary, his spirit bears witness to them as to its own essence, the essence in which he has a feeling of his selfhood, and in which he lives as in his own element which is not distinguished from himself. The subject is thus directly linked to the ethical order by a relation which is more like an identity than even the relation of faith or trust.

> Faith and trust emerge along with reflection; they presuppose the power of forming ideas and making distinctions. For example, it is one thing to be a pagan, a different thing to believe in a pagan religion. This relation or rather this absence of relation, this identity in which the ethical order is the actual living soul of self-consciousness, can no doubt pass over into a relation of faith and conviction and into a relation produced by means of further reflection, i.e. into an *insight* due to reasoning starting perhaps from some particular purposes interests, and considerations, from fear or hope, or from historical conditions. But adequate *knowl-*

*edge* of this identity depends on thinking in terms of the concept.

148. As substantive in character, these laws and institutions are duties binding on the will of the individual, because as subjective, as inherently undetermined, or determined as particular, he distinguishes himself from them and hence stands related to them as to the substance of his own being.

> The 'doctrine of duties' in moral philosophy (I mean the objective doctrine, not that which is supposed to be contained in the empty principle of moral subjectivity, because that principle determines nothing—see Paragraph 134) is therefore comprised in the systematic development of the circle of ethical necessity which follows in this Third Part. The difference between the exposition in this book and the form of a 'doctrine of duties' lies solely in the fact that, in what follows, the specific types of ethical life turn up as necessary relationships; there the exposition ends, without being supplemented in each case by the addition that 'therefore men have a duty to conform to this institution'.
>
> A 'doctrine of duties' which is other than a philosophical science takes its material from existing relationships and shows its connexion with the moralist's personal notions or with principles and thoughts, purposes, impulses, feelings, &c., that are forthcoming everywhere; and as reasons for accepting each duty in turn, it may tack on its further consequences in their bearing on the other ethical relationships or on welfare and opinion. But an immanent and logical 'doctrine of duties' can be nothing except the serial exposition of the relationships which are necessitated by the Idea of freedom and are therefore actual in their entirety, to wit in the state.

149. The bond of duty can appear as a restriction only on indeterminate subjectivity or abstract freedom, and on the impulses either of the natural will or of the moral will which determines its indeterminate good arbitrarily. The truth is, however, that in duty the individual finds his liberation; first, liberation from dependence on mere natural impulse and from the depression which as a particular subject he cannot escape in his moral reflections on what ought to be and what might be; secondly, liberation from the indeterminate subjectivity which, never reaching reality or the objective determinacy of action, remains self-enclosed and devoid of actuality. In duty the individual acquires his substantive freedom.

150. Virtue is the ethical order reflected in the individual character so far as that character is determined by its natural endowment. When virtue displays itself solely as the individual's simple conformity with the duties of the station to which he belongs, it is rectitude.

> In an *ethical* community, it is easy to say what man must do, what are the duties he has to fulfil in order to be virtuous: he has simply to follow the well-known and explicit rules of his own situation. Rectitude is the general character which may be demanded of him by law or custom. But from the standpoint of *morality,* rectitude often seems to be something comparatively inferior, something beyond which still higher demands must be made on oneself and others, because the craving to be something special is not satisfied with what is absolute and universal; it finds consciousness of peculiarity only in what is exceptional.
>
> The various facets of rectitude may equally well be called virtues, since they are also properties of the individual, although not specially of him in contrast with others. Talk about virtue, however, readily borders on empty rhetoric, because it is only about something abstract and indeterminate; and furthermore, argumentative and expository talk of the sort is addressed to the individual as to a being of caprice and subjective inclination. In an existing ethical order in which a complete system of ethical relations has been developed and actualized, virtue in the strict sense of the word is in place and actually appears only in exceptional circumstances or when one obligation clashes with another. The clash, however, must be a genuine one, because moral reflection can manufacture clashes of all sorts to suit its purpose and give itself a consciousness of being something special and having made sacrifices. It is for this reason that the phenomenon of virtue proper is commoner when societies and communities are uncivilized, since in those circumstances ethical conditions and their actualization are more a matter of private choice or the natural genius of an exceptional individual. For instance, it was especially to Hercules that the ancients ascribed virtue. In the states of antiquity, ethical life had not grown into

this free system of an objective order self-subsistently developed, and consequently it was by the personal genius of individuals that this defect had to be made good. It follows that if a 'doctrine of virtues' is not a mere 'doctrine of duties', and if therefore it embraces the particular facet of character, the facet grounded in natural endowment, it will be a natural history of mind.

Since virtues are ethical principles applied to the particular, and since in this their subjective aspect they are something indeterminate, there turns up here for determining them the quantitative principle of more or less. The result is that consideration of them introduces their corresponding defects or vices, as in Aristotle, who defined each particular virtue as strictly a mean between an excess and a deficiency.

The content which assumes the form of duties and then virtues is the same as that which also has the form of Impulses. . . . Impulses have the same basic content as duties and virtues, but in impulses this content still belongs to the immediate will and to instinctive feeling; it has not been developed to the point of becoming ethical. Consequently, impulses have in common with the content of duties and virtues only the abstract object on which they are directed, an object indeterminate in itself, and so devoid of anything to discriminate them as good or evil. Or in other words, impulses, considered abstractly in their positive aspect alone, are good, while, considered abstractly in their negative aspect alone, they are evil. . . .

151. But when individuals are simply identified with the actual order, ethical life (*das Sittliche*) appears as their general mode of conduct, i.e. as custom (*Sitte*), while the habitual practice of ethical living appears as a second nature which, put in the place of the initial, purely natural will, is the soul of custom permeating it through and through, the significance and the actuality of its existence. It is mind living and present as a world, and the substance of mind thus exists now for the first time as mind.

152. In this way the ethical substantial order has attained its right, and its right its validity. That is to say, the self-will of the individual has vanished together with his private conscience which had claimed independence and opposed itself to the ethical substance. For, when his character is ethical, he recognizes as the end which moves him to act the uni-

versal which is itself unmoved but is disclosed in its specific determinations as rationality actualized. He knows that his own dignity and the whole stability of his particular ends are grounded in this same universal, and it is therein that he actually attains these. Subjectivity is itself the absolute form and existent actuality of the substantial order, and the distinction between subject on the one hand and substance on the other, as the object, end, and controlling power of the subject, is the same as, and has vanished directly along with, the distinction between them in form.

> Subjectivity is the ground wherein the concept of freedom is realized (see Paragraph 106). At the level of morality, subjectivity is still distinct from freedom, the concept of subjectivity; but at the level of ethical life it is the realization of the concept in a way adequate to the concept itself.

153. The right of individuals to be subjectively destined to freedom is fulfilled when they belong to an actual ethical order, because their conviction of their freedom finds its truth in such an objective order, and it is in an ethical order that they are actually in possession of their own essence or their own inner universality (see Paragraph 147).

> When a father inquired about the best method of educating his son in ethical conduct, a Pythagorean replied: 'Make him a citizen of a state with good laws.' (The phrase has also been attributed to others.)

154. The right of individuals to their *particular* satisfaction is also contained in the ethical substantial order, since particularity is the outward appearance of the ethical order—a mode in which that order is existent.

155. Hence in this identity of the universal will with the particular will, right and duty coalesce, and by being in the ethical order a man has rights in so far as he has duties, and duties in so far as he has rights. In the sphere of abstract right, I have the right and another has the corresponding duty. In the moral sphere, the right of my private judgement and will, as well as of my happiness, has not, but only ought to have, coalesced with duties and become objective.

156. The ethical substance, as containing independent self-consciousness united with its concept, is the actual mind of a family and a nation.

157. The concept of this Idea has being only as mind, as something knowing itself and actual, because it is the objectification of itself, the movement running through the form of its moments. It is therefore

(A) ethical mind in its natural or immediate phase—the *Family*. This substantiality loses its unity, passes over into division, and into the phase of relation, i.e. into

(B) *Civil Society*—an association of members as self-subsistent individuals in a universality which, because of their self-subsistence, is only abstract. Their association is brought about by their needs, by the legal system—the means to security of person and property—and by an external organization for attaining their particular and common interests. This external state
(C) is brought back to and welded into unity in the *Constitution of the State* which is the end and actuality of both the substantial universal order and the public life devoted thereto.

# The Philosophy of History

II. The inquiry into the *essential destiny* of Reason—as far as it is considered in reference to the World—is identical with the question, *what is the ultimate design of the World?* And the expression implies that that design is destined to be realized. Two points of consideration suggest themselves; first, the *import* of this design—its abstract definition; and secondly, its *realization.*

It must be observed at the outset, that the phenomenon we investigate—Universal History—belongs to the realm of *Spirit.* The term "*World,*" includes both physical and psychical Nature. Physical Nature also plays its part in the World's History, and attention will have to be paid to the fundamental natural relations thus involved. But Spirit, and the course of its development, is our substantial object. Our task does not require us to contemplate Nature as a Rational System in itself—though in its own proper domain it proves itself such—but simply in its relation to *Spirit.* On the stage on which we are observing it—Universal History—Spirit displays itself in its most concrete reality. Notwithstanding this (or rather for the very purpose of comprehending the *general* principles which this, its form of *concrete reality,*

embodies) we must premise some abstract characteristics of the *nature of Spirit.* Such an explanation, however, cannot be given here under any other form than that of bare assertion. The present is not the occasion for unfolding the idea of Spirit speculatively; for whatever has a place in an Introduction, must, as already observed, be taken as simply historical; something assumed as having been explained and proved elsewhere; or whose demonstration awaits the sequel of the Science of History itself.

We have therefore to mention here:

(1) The abstract characteristics of the nature of Spirit.
(2) What means Spirit uses in order to realize its Idea.
(3) Lastly, we must consider the shape which the perfect embodiment of Spirit assumes—the State.

(1) The nature of Spirit may be understood by a glance at its direct opposite—*Matter.* As the essence of Matter is Gravity, so, on the other hand, we may affirm that the substance, the essence of Spirit is

Freedom. All will readily assent to the doctrine that Spirit, among other properties, is also endowed with Freedom; but philosophy teaches that all the qualities of Spirit exist only through Freedom; that all are but means for attaining Freedom; that all seek and produce this and this alone. It is a result of speculative Philosophy, that Freedom is the sole truth of Spirit. Matter possesses gravity in virtue of its tendency toward a central point. It is essentially composite; consisting of parts that *exclude* each other. It seeks its Unity; and therefore exhibits itself as self-destructive, as verging toward its opposite [an indivisible point]. If it could attain this, it would be Matter no longer, it would have perished. It strives after the realization of its Idea; for in Unity it exists *ideally*. Spirit, on the contrary, may be defined as that which has its centre in itself. It has not a unity outside itself, but has already found it; it exists *in* and *with itself.* Matter has its essence out of itself; Spirit is *self-contained existence* (Bei-sich-selbst-seyn). Now this is Freedom, exactly. For if I am dependent, my being is referred to something else which I am not; I cannot exist independently of something external. I am free, on the contrary, when my existence depends upon myself. This self-contained existence of Spirit is none other than self-consciousness—consciousness of one's own being. Two things must be distinguished in consciousness; first, the fact *that I know;* secondly, *what I know.* In *self* consciousness these are merged in one; for Spirit *knows itself.* It involves an appreciation of its own nature, as also an energy enabling it to realize itself; to make itself *actually* that which it is *potentially.* According to this abstract definition it may be said of Universal History, that it is the exhibition of Spirit in the process of working out the knowledge of that which it is potentially. And as the germ bears in itself the whole nature of the tree, and the taste and form of its fruits, so do the first traces of Spirit virtually contain the whole of that History. The Orientals have not attained the knowledge that Spirit—Man *as such*—is free; and because they do not know this, they are not free. They only know that *one is free.* But on this very account, the freedom of that one is only caprice; ferocity—brutal recklessness of passion, or a mild-

ness and tameness of the desires, which is itself only an accident of Nature—mere caprice like the former.—That *one* is therefore only a Despot; not a *free man.* The consciousness of Freedom first arose among the Greeks, and therefore they were free; but they, and the Romans likewise, knew only that *some* are free—not man as such. Even Plato and Aristotle did not know this. The Greeks, therefore, had slaves; and their whole life and the maintenance of their splendid liberty, was implicated with the institution of slavery: a fact moreover, which made that liberty on the one hand only an accidental, transient and limited growth; on the other hand, it constituted a rigorous thraldom of our common nature—of the Human. The German nations, under the influence of Christianity, were the first to attain the consciousness, that man, as man, is free: that it is the *freedom* of Spirit which constitutes its essence. This consciousness arose first in religion, the in-most region of Spirit; but to introduce the principle into the various relations of the actual world, involves a more extensive problem than its simple implantation; a problem whose solution and application require a severe and lengthened process of culture. In proof of this, we may note that slavery did not cease immediately on the reception of Christianity. Still less did liberty predominate in States; or Governments and Constitutions adopt a rational organization, or recognize freedom as their basis. That application of the principle to political relations; the thorough moulding and interpenetration of the constitution of society by it, is a process identical with history itself. I have already directed attention to the distinction here involved, between a principle as such, and its *application; i.e.,* its introduction and carrying out in the actual phenomena of Spirit and Life. This is a point of fundamental importance in our science, and one which must be constantly respected as essential. And in the same way as this distinction has attracted attention in view of the *Christian* principle of self-consciousness—Freedom; it also shows itself as an essential one, in view of the principle of Freedom *generally.* The History of the world is none other than the progress of the consciousness of Freedom; a progress whose development according to the necessity of its nature, it is our business to investigate.

The general statement given above, of the various grades in the consciousness of Freedom—and which we applied in the first instance to the fact that the Eastern nations knew only that *one* is free; the Greek and Roman world only that *some* are free; while *we* know that all men absolutely (man *as man*) are free—supplies us with the natural division of Universal History, and suggests the mode of its discussion. This is remarked, however, only incidentally and anticipatively; some other ideas must be first explained.

The destiny of the spiritual World, and—since this is the *substantial World,* while the physical remains subordinate to it, or, in the language of speculation, has no truth *as against* the spiritual—*the final cause of the World at large,* we allege to be the *consciousness* of its own freedom on the part of Spirit, and *ipso facto,* the *reality* of that freedom. But that this term "Freedom," without further qualification, is an indefinite, and incalculable ambiguous term; and that while that which it represents is the *ne plus ultra* of attainment, it is liable to an infinity of misunderstandings, confusions and errors, and to become the occasion for all imaginable excesses—has never been more clearly known and felt than in modern times. Yet, for the present, we must content ourselves with the term itself without farther definition. Attention was also directed to the importance of the infinite difference between a principle in the abstract, and its realization in the concrete. In the process before us, the essential nature of freedom—which involves in it absolute necessity—is to be displayed as coming to a consciousness of itself (for it is in its very nature, self-consciousness) and thereby realizing its existence. Itself is its own object of attainment, and the sole aim of Spirit. This result it is, at which the process of the World's History has been continually aiming; and to which the sacrifices that have ever and anon been laid on the vast altar of the earth, through the long lapse of ages, have been offered. This is the only aim that sees itself realized and fulfilled; the only pole of repose amid the ceaseless change of events and conditions, and the sole

efficient principle that pervades them. This final aim is God's purpose with the world; but God is the absolutely perfect Being, and can, therefore, will nothing other than himself—his own Will. The Nature of His Will—that is, His Nature itself—is what we here call the Idea of Freedom; translating the language of Religion into that of Thought. The question, then, which we may next put, is: What means does this principle of Freedom use for its realization? This is the second point we have to consider.

(2) The question of the *means* by which Freedom develops itself to a World, conducts us to the phenomenon of History itself. Although Freedom is, primarily, an undeveloped idea, the means it uses are external and phenomenal; presenting themselves in History to our sensuous vision. The first glance at History convinces us that the actions of men proceed from their needs, their passions, their characters and talents; and impresses us with the belief that such needs, passions and interests are the sole springs of action—the efficient agents in this scene of activity. Among these may, perhaps, be found aims of a liberal or universal kind—benevolence it may be, or noble patriotism; but such virtues and general views are but insignificant as compared with the World and its doings. We may perhaps see the Ideal of Reason actualized in those who adopt such aims, and within the sphere of their influence; but they bear only a trifling proportion to the mass of the human race; and the extent of that influence is limited accordingly. Passions, private aims, and the satisfaction of selfish desires, are on the other hand, most effective springs of action. Their power lies in the fact that they respect none of the limitations which justice and morality would impose on them; and that these natural impulses have a more direct influence over man than the artificial and tedious discipline that tends to order and self-restraint, law and morality. When we look at this display of passions, and the consequences of their violence; the Unreason which is associated not only with them, but even (rather we might say *especially*) with *good* designs and righteous aims; when we see the evil, the vice, the ruin that has befallen the most flourishing kingdoms

which the mind of man ever created; we can scarce avoid being filled with sorrow at this universal taint of corruption: and, since this decay is not the work of mere Nature, but of the Human Will—a moral embitterment—a revolt of the Good Spirit (if it have a place within us) may well be the result of our reflections. Without rhetorical exaggeration, a simply truthful combination of the miseries that have overwhelmed the noblest of nations and polities, and the finest exemplars of private virtue—forms a picture of most fearful aspect, and excites emotions of the profoundest and most hopeless sadness, counterbalanced by no consolatory result. We endure in beholding it a mental torture, allowing no defence or escape but the consideration that what has happened could not be otherwise; that it is a fatality which no intervention could alter. And at last we draw back from the intolerable disgust with which these sorrowful reflections threaten us, into the more agreeable environment of our individual life—the Present formed by our private aims and interests. In short we retreat into the selfishness that stands on the quiet shore, and thence enjoys in safety the distant spectacle of "wrecks confusedly hurled." But even regarding History as the slaughter-bench at which the happiness of peoples, the wisdom of States, and the virtue of individuals have been victimized—the question involuntarily arises—to what principle, to what final aim these enormous sacrifices have been offered. From this point the investigation usually proceeds to that which we have made the general commencement of our inquiry. Starting from this we pointed out those phenomena which made up a picture so suggestive of gloomy emotions and thoughtful reflections— as *the very field* which we, for our part, regard as exhibiting only the means for realizing what we assert to be the essential destiny—the absolute aim, or—which comes to the same thing—the true *result* of the World's History. We have all along purposely eschewed "moral reflections" as a method of rising from the scene of historical specialties to the general principles which they embody. Besides, it is not the interest of such sentimentalities, really to rise above those depressing emotions; and to solve the enigmas of Providence which the con-

siderations that occasioned them, present. It is essential to their character to find a gloomy satisfaction in the empty and fruitless sublimities of that negative result. We return them to the point of view which we have adopted; observing that the successive steps (Momente) of the analysis to which it will lead us, will also evolve the conditions requisite for answering the inquiries suggested by the panorama of sin and suffering that history unfolds.

The *first* remark we have to make, and which—though already presented more than once—cannot be too often repeated when the occasion seems to call for it—is that what we call *principle, aim, destiny,* or the nature and idea of Spirit, is something merely general and abstract. Principle—Plan of Existence—Law—is a hidden, undeveloped essence, which *as such*—however true in itself—is not completely real. Aims, principles, etc., have a place in our thoughts, in our subjective design only; but not yet in the sphere of reality. That which exists for itself only, is a possibility, a potentiality; but has not yet emerged into Existence. A *second* element must be introduced in order to produce actuality—viz., actuation, realization; and whose motive power is the Will—the activity of man in the widest sense. It is only by this activity that that Idea as well as abstract characteristics generally, are realized, actualized; for of themselves they are powerless. The motive power that puts them in operation, and gives them determinate existence, is the need, instinct, inclination, and passion of man. That some conception of mine should be developed into act and existence, is my earnest desire: I wish to assert my personality in connection with it: I wish to be satisfied by its execution. If I am to exert myself for any object, it must in some way or other be *my* object. In the accomplishment of such or such designs I must at the same time find *my* satisfaction; although the purpose for which I exert myself includes a complication of results, many of which have no interest for me. This is the absolute right of personal existence—to find *itself* satisfied in its activity and labor. If men are to interest themselves for anything, they must (so to speak) have part of their existence involved in it; find their individuality gratified by its attainment. Here a mistake must be avoided. We intend blame, and justly impute it as a fault, when we say of an individual, that he is "interested" (in taking part in such or such transactions), that is, seeks only his private advantage. In reprehending this we find fault with him for furthering his personal aims without any regard to a more comprehensive design; of which he takes advantage to promote his own interest, or which he even sacrifices with this view. But he who is active in *promoting an object,* is not simply "interested," but interested in that object itself. Language faithfully expresses this distinction.—Nothing therefore happens, nothing is accomplished, unless the individuals concerned, seek their own satisfaction in the issue. They are particular units of society; *i.e.,* they have special needs, instincts, and interests generally, peculiar to themselves. Among these needs are not only such as we usually call necessities—the stimuli of individual desire and volition—but also those connected with individual views and convictions; or—to use a term expressing less decision—leanings of opinion; supposing the impulses of reflection, understanding, and reason, to have been awakened. In these cases people demand, if they are to exert themselves in any direction, that the object should commend itself to them; that in point of opinion—whether as to its goodness, justice, advantage, profit—they should be able to "enter into it" (dabei seyn). This is a consideration of especial importance in our age, when people are less than formerly influenced by reliance on others, and by authority; when, on the contrary, they devote their activities to a cause on the ground of their own understanding, their independent conviction and opinion.

We assert then that nothing has been accomplished without interest on the part of the actors; and—if interest be called passion, inasmuch as the whole individuality, to the neglect of all other actual or possible interests and claims, is devoted to an object with every fibre of volition, concentrating all its desires and powers upon it—we may affirm absolutely that *nothing great in the World* has been accomplished without *passion.* Two elements, therefore, enter into the object of our investigation; the first the Idea, the second the complex of human passions; the one the warp, the other the woof of the vast arras-web of Universal History. The concrete mean and union of the two is Liberty, under the conditions of morality in a State. We have spoken of the Idea of Freedom as the nature of Spirit, and the absolute goal of History. Passion is regarded as a thing of sinister aspect, as more or less immoral. Man is required to have no passions. Passion, it is true, is not quite the suitable word for what I wish to express. I mean here nothing more than the human activity as resulting from private interests—special, or if you will, self-seeking designs—with this qualification, that the whole energy of will and character is devoted to their attainment; that other interests (which would in themselves constitute attractive aims) or rather all things else, are sacrificed to them. The object in question is so bound up with the man's will, that it entirely and alone determines the "hue of resolution," and is inseparable from it. It has become the very essence of his volition. For a person is a specific existence; not man in general (a term to which no real existence corresponds) but a particular human being. The term "character" likewise expresses this idiosyncrasy of Will and Intelligence. But *Character* comprehends all peculiarities whatever; the way in which a person conducts himself in private relations, etc., and is not limited to his idiosyncrasy in its practical and active phase. I shall, therefore, use the term "passions"; understanding thereby the particular bent of character, as far as the peculiarities of volition are not limited to private interest, but supply the impelling and actuating force for accomplishing deeds shared in by the community at large. Passion is in the first instance the *subjective,* and therefore the *formal* side of energy, will, and activity—leaving the object or aim still undetermined. And there is a similar relation of formality to reality in merely individual conviction, individual views, individual conscience. It is always a question of essential importance, what is the purport of my conviction, what the object of my passion, in deciding whether the one or the other is of a true and substantial nature. Conversely, if it is so, it will inevitably attain actual existence—be realized.

From this comment on the second essential element in the historical embodiment of an aim, we infer—glancing at the institution of the State in passing—that a State is then well constituted and internally powerful, when the private interest of its citizens is one with the common interest of the State; when the one finds its gratification and realization in the other—a proposition in itself very important. But in a State many institutions must be adopted, much political machinery invented, accompanied by appropriate political arrangements—necessitating long struggles of the understanding before what is really appropriate can be discovered—involving, moreover, contentions with private interest and passions, and a tedious discipline of these latter, in order to bring about the desired harmony. The epoch when a State attains this harmonious condition, marks the period of its bloom, its virtue, its vigor, and its prosperity. But the history of mankind does not begin with a *conscious* aim of any kind, as it is the case with the particular circles into which men form themselves of set purpose. The mere social instinct implies a conscious purpose of security for life and property; and when society has been constituted, this purpose becomes more comprehensive. The History of the World begins with *its general* aim—the *realization of the Idea* of Spirit—only in an *implicit* form (*an sich*) that is, as Nature; a hidden, most profoundly hidden, unconscious instinct; and the whole process of History (as already observed), is directed to rendering this unconscious impulse a conscious one. Thus appearing in the form of merely natural existence, natural will—that which has been called the subjective side—physical craving, instinct, passion, private interest, as also opinion and subjective conception—spontaneously present themselves at the very commencement. This vast congeries of volitions, interests and activities, constitute the instruments and means of the World-Spirit for attaining its object; bringing it to consciousness, and realizing it. And this aim is none other than finding itself—coming to itself—and contemplating itself in concrete actuality. But that those manifestations of vitality on the part of individuals and peoples, in which they seek and satisfy their own purposes, are, at the same time, the means and instruments of a higher and broader purpose of which they know nothing—which they realize unconsciously—might be made a

matter of question; rather has been questioned, and in every variety of form negatived, decried and contemned as mere dreaming and "Philosophy." But on this point I announced my view at the very outset, and asserted our hypothesis—which, however, will appear in the sequel, in the form of a legitimate inference—and our belief, that Reason governs the world, and has consequently governed its history. In relation to this independently universal and substantial existence—all else is subordinate, subservient to it, and the means for its development.—The Union of Universal Abstract Existence generally with the Individual—the Subjective—that this alone is Truth, belongs to the department of speculation, and is treated in this general form in Logic.—But in the process of the World's History itself—as still incomplete—the abstract final aim of history is not yet made the distinct object of desire and interest. While these limited sentiments are still unconscious of the purpose they are fulfilling, the universal principle is implicit in them, and is realizing itself through them. The question also assumes the form of the union of *Freedom* and *Necessity;* the latent abstract process of Spirit being regarded as *Necessity,* while that which exhibits itself in the conscious will of men, as their interest, belongs to the domain of *Freedom.* As the metaphysical connection (*i.e.,* the connection in the Idea) of these forms of thought, belongs to Logic, it would be out of place to analyze it here. The chief and cardinal points only shall be mentioned.

Philosophy shows that the Idea advances to an infinite antithesis; that, viz., between the Idea in its free, universal form—in which it exists for itself—and the contrasted form of abstract introversion, reflection on itself, which is formal existence-for-self, personality, formal freedom, such as belongs to Spirit only. The universal Idea exists thus as the substantial totality of things on the one side, and as the abstract essence of free volition on the other side. This reflection of the mind on itself is individual self-consciousness—the polar opposite of the Idea in its general form, and therefore existing in absolute Limitation. This polar opposite is consequently limitation, particularization, for the universal absolute being; it is the side of its *definite exis-*

*tence;* the sphere of its formal reality, the sphere of the reverence paid to God.—To comprehend the absolute connection of this antithesis, is the profound task of metaphysics. This Limitation originates all forms of particularity of whatever kind. The formal volition [of which we have spoken] wills itself; desires to make its own personality valid in all that it purposes and does: even the pious individual wishes to be saved and happy. This pole of the antithesis, existing for itself, is—in contrast with the Absolute Universal Being—a special separate existence, taking cognizance of specialty only, and willing that alone. In short it plays its part in the region of mere phenomena. This is the sphere of particular purposes, in effecting which individuals exert themselves on behalf of their individuality—give it full play and objective realization. This is also the sphere of happiness and its opposite. He is happy who finds his condition suited to his special character, will, and fancy, and so enjoys himself in that condition. The History of the World is not the theatre of happiness. Periods of happiness are blank pages in it, for they are periods of harmony—periods when the antithesis is in abeyance. Reflection on self—the Freedom above described—is abstractly defined as the formal element of the activity of the absolute Idea. The realizing *activity* of which we have spoken is the middle term of the Syllogism, one of whose extremes is the Universal essence, the *Idea,* which reposes in the penetralia of Spirit; and the other, the complex of external things—objective matter. That activity is the medium by which the universal latent principle is translated into the domain of objectivity.

I will endeavor to make what has been said more vivid and clear by examples.

The building of a house is, in the first instance, a subjective aim and design. On the other hand we have, as means, the several substances required for the work—Iron, Wood, Stones. The elements are made use of in working up this material: fire to melt the iron, wind to blow the fire, water to set wheels in motion, in order to cut the wood, etc. The result is, that the wind, which has helped to build the house, is shut out by the house; so also are the violence of rains and floods, and the destructive powers of fire,

so far as the house is made fireproof. The stones and beams obey the law of gravity—press downward—and so high walls are carried up. Thus the elements are made use of in accordance with their nature, and yet to co-operate for a product, by which their operation is limited. Thus the passions of men are gratified; they develop themselves and their aims in accordance with their natural tendencies, and build up the edifice of human society; thus fortifying a position for Right and Order *against themselves.*

The connection of events above indicated, involves also the fact, that in history an additional result is commonly produced by human actions beyond that which they aim at and obtain—that which they immediately recognize and desire. They gratify their own interest; but something further is thereby accomplished, latent in the actions in question, though not present to their consciousness, and not included in their design. An analogous example is offered in the case of a man who, from a feeling of revenge—perhaps not an unjust one, but produced by injury on the other's part—burns that other man's house. A connection is immediately established between the deed itself and a train of circumstances not directly included in it, taken abstractedly. In itself it consisted in merely presenting a small flame to a small portion of a beam. Events not involved in that simple act follow of themselves. The part of the beam which was set fire to is connected with its remote portions; the beam itself is united with the woodwork of the house generally, and this with other houses; so that a wide conflagration ensues, which destroys the goods and chattels of many other persons besides his against whom the act of revenge was first directed; perhaps even costs not a few men their lives. This lay neither in the deed abstractedly, nor in the design of the man who committed it. But the action has a further general bearing. In the design of the doer it was only revenge executed against an individual in the destruction of his property, but it is moreover a crime, and that involves punishment also. This may not have been present to the mind of the perpetrator, still less in his intention; but his deed itself, the general principles it calls into play, its substantial content entails it. By this example I wish only to impress on you the consideration, that in a simple act, something further may be implicated than lies in the intention and consciousness of the agent. The example before us involves, however, this additional consideration, that the substance of the act, consequently we may say the act itself, recoils upon the perpetrator—reacts upon him with destructive tendency. This union of the two extremes—the embodiment of a general idea in the form of direct reality, and the elevation of a speciality into connection with universal truth—is brought to pass, at first sight, under the conditions of an utter diversity of nature between the two, and an indifference of the one extreme towards the other. The aims which the agents set before them are limited and special; but it must be remarked that the agents themselves are intelligent thinking beings. The purport of their desires is interwoven with *general, essential* considerations of justice, good, duty, etc.; for mere desire—volition in its rough and savage forms—falls not within the scene and sphere of Universal History. Those general considerations, which form at the same time a norm for directing aims and actions, have a determinate purport; for such an abstraction as "good for its own sake," has no place in living reality. If men are to act, they must not only intend the Good, but must have decided for themselves whether this or that particular thing is a Good. What special course of action, however, is good or not, is determined, as regards the ordinary contingencies of private life, by the laws and customs of a State; and here no great difficulty is presented. Each individual has his position; he knows on the whole what a just, honorable course of conduct is. As to ordinary, private relations, the assertion that it is difficult to choose the right and good—the regarding it as the mark of an exalted morality to find difficulties and raise scruples on that score—may be set down to an evil or perverse will, which seeks to evade duties not in themselves of a perplexing nature; or, at any rate, to an idly reflective habit of mind—where a feeble will affords no sufficient exercise to the faculties—leaving them therefore to find occupation within themselves, and to expend themselves on moral self-adulation.

It is quite otherwise with the comprehensive relations that History has to do with. In this sphere are presented those momentous collisions between existing, acknowledged duties, laws, and rights, and those contingencies which are adverse to this fixed system; which assail and even destroy its foundations and existence; whose tenor may nevertheless seem good—on the large scale advantageous—yes, even indispensable and necessary. These contingencies realize themselves in History: they involve a general principle of a different order from that on which depends the *permanence* of a people or a State. This principle is an essential phase in the development of the *creating* Idea, of Truth striving and urging towards [consciousness of] itself. Historical men—*World-Historical Individuals*—are those in whose aims such a general principle lies.

Cæsar, in danger of losing a position, not perhaps at that time of superiority, yet at least of equality with the others who were at the head of the State, and of succumbing to those who were just on the point of becoming his enemies—belongs essentially to this category. These enemies—who were at the same time pursuing *their* personal aims—had the form of the constitution, and the power conferred by an appearance of justice, on their side. Cæsar was contending for the maintenance of his position, honor, and safety; and, since the power of his opponents included the sovereignty over the provinces of the Roman Empire, his victory secured for him the conquest of that entire Empire; and he thus became—though leaving the form of the constitution—the Autocrat of the State. That which secured for him the execution of a design, which in the first instance was of negative import—the Autocracy of Rome—was, however, at the same time an independently necessary feature in the history of Rome and of the world. It was not, then, his private gain merely, but an unconscious impulse that occasioned the accomplishment of that for which the time was ripe. Such are all great historical men—whose own particular aims involve those large issues which are the will of the World-Spirit. They may be called Heroes, inasmuch as they have derived their purposes and their vocation, not from the calm, regular course of things, sanctioned by the existing order; but from a concealed fount—one which has not attained to phenomenal, present existence—from that inner Spirit, still hidden beneath the surface, which, impinging on the outer world as on a shell, bursts it in pieces, because it is another kernel than that which belonged to the shell in question. They are men, therefore, who appear to draw the impulse of their life from themselves; and whose deeds have produced a condition of things and a complex of historical relations which appear to be only *their* interest, and *their* work.

Such individuals had no consciousness of the general Idea they were unfolding, while prosecuting those aims of theirs; on the contrary, they were practical, political men. But at the same time they were thinking men, who had an insight into the requirements of the time—*what was ripe for development.* This was the very Truth for their age, for their world; the species next in order, so to speak, and which was already formed in the womb of time. It was theirs to know this nascent principle; the necessary, directly sequent step in progress, which their world was to take; to make this their aim, and to expend their energy in promoting it. World-historical men—the Heroes of an epoch—must, therefore, be recognized as its clear-sighted ones; *their* deeds, *their* words are the best of that time. Great men have formed purposes to satisfy themselves, not others. Whatever prudent designs and counsels they might have learned from others, would be the more limited and inconsistent features in their career; for it was they who best understood affairs; from whom *others* learned, and approved, or at least acquiesced in—their policy. For that Spirit which had taken this fresh step in history is the inmost soul of all individuals; but in a state of unconsciousness which the great men in question aroused. Their fellows, therefore, follow these soul-leaders; for they feel the irresistible power of their own inner Spirit thus embodied. If we go on to cast a look at the fate of these World-Historical persons, whose vocation it was to be the agents of the World-Spirit—we shall find it to have been no happy one. They attained no calm enjoyment; their whole life was labor and trouble;

their whole nature was nought else but their masterpassion. When their object is attained they fall off like empty hulls from the kernel. They die early, like Alexander; they are murdered, like Cæsar; transported to St. Helena, like Napoleon. This fearful consolation—that historical men have not enjoyed what is called happiness, and of which only private life (and this may be passed under very various external circumstances) is capable—this consolation those may draw from history, who stand in need of it; and it is craved by Envy—vexed at what is great and transcendant—striving, therefore, to depreciate it, and to find some flaw in it. Thus in modern times it has been demonstrated *ad nauseam* that princes are generally unhappy on their thrones; in consideration of which the possession of a throne is tolerated, and men acquiesce in the fact that not themselves but the personages in question are its occupants. The Free Man, we may observe, is not envious, but gladly recognizes what is great and exalted, and rejoices that it exists.

It is in the light of those common elements which constitute the interest and therefore the passions of individuals, that these historical men are to be regarded. They are *great* men, because they willed and accomplished something great; not a mere fancy, a mere intention, but that which met the case and fell in with the needs of the age. This mode of considering them also excludes the so-called "psychological" view, which—serving the purpose of envy most effectually—contrives so to refer all actions to the heart—to bring them under such a subjective aspect—as that their authors appear to have done everything under the impulse of some passion, mean or grand—some *morbid craving*—and on account of these passions and cravings to have been not moral men. Alexander of Macedon partly subdued Greece, and then Asia; therefore he was possessed by a *morbid craving* for conquest. He is alleged to have acted from a craving for fame, for conquest; and the proof that these were the impelling motives is that he did that which resulted in fame. What pedagogue has not demonstrated of Alexander the Great—of Julius Cæsar—that they were instigated by such passions, and were consequently immoral men?—whence the conclusion immediately follows that he, the pedagogue, is a better man than they, because he has not such passions; a proof of which lies in the fact that he does not conquer Asia—vanquish Darius and Porus—but while he enjoys life himself, lets others enjoy it too. These psychologists are particularly fond of contemplating those peculiarities of great historical figures which appertain to them as private persons. Man must eat and drink; he sustains relations to friends and acquaintances; he has passing impulses and ebullitions of temper. "No man is a hero to his *valet-de-chambre,*" is a well-known proverb; I have added—and Goethe repeated it ten years later—"but not because the former is no hero, but because the latter is a valet." He takes off the hero's boots, assists him to bed, knows that he prefers champagne, etc. Historical personages waited upon in historical literature by such psychological valets, come poorly off; they are brought down by these their attendants to a level with—or rather a few degrees below the level of—the morality of such exquisite discerners of spirits. The Thersites of Homer who abuses the kings is a standing figure for all times. Blows—that is beating with a solid cudgel—he does not get in every age, as in the Homeric one; but his envy, his egotism, is the thorn which he has to carry in his flesh; and the undying worm that gnaws him is the tormenting consideration that his excellent views and vituperations remain absolutely without result in the world. But our satisfaction at the fate of Thersitism also, may have its sinister side.

A World-historical individual is not so unwise as to indulge a variety of wishes to divide his regards. He is devoted to the One Aim, regardless of all else. It is even possible that such men may treat other great, even sacred interests, inconsiderately; conduct which is indeed obnoxious to moral reprehension. But so mighty a form must trample down many an innocent flower—crush to pieces many an object in its path.

The special interest of passion is thus inseparable from the active development of a general principle: for it is from the special and determinate and from its negation, that the Universal results. Particularity

contends with its like, and some loss is involved in the issue. It is not the general idea that is implicated in opposition and *combat,* and that is exposed to *danger.* It remains in the background, untouched and uninjured. This may be called the *cunning of reason*—that it sets the passions to work for itself, while that which develops its existence through such impulsion pays the penalty, and suffers loss. For it is *phenomenal* being that is so treated, and of this, part is of no value, part is positive and real. The particular is for the most part of too trifling value as compared with the general: individuals are sacrificed and abandoned. The Idea pays the penalty of determinate existence and of corruptibility, not from itself, but from the passions of individuals. . . .

## CHAPTER III

### *The Political Work of Art*

The State unites the two phases just considered, viz., the Subjective and the Objective Work of Art. In the State, Spirit is not a mere Object, like the deities, nor, on the other hand, is it merely subjectively developed to a beautiful physique. It is here a living, universal Spirit, but which is at the same time the self-conscious Spirit of the individuals composing the community.

The *Democratical* Constitution alone was adapted to the Spirit and political condition in question. In the East we recognized Despotism, developed in magnificent proportions, as a form of government strictly appropriate to the Dawn-Land of History. Not less adapted is the democratical form in Greece, to the part assigned to it in the same great drama. In Greece, viz., we have the freedom of the Individual, but it has not yet advanced to such a degree of abstraction, that the subjective unit is conscious of direct dependence on the [general] substantial principle—the State as such. In this grade of Freedom, the individual will is unfettered in the entire range of its vitality, and embodies that substantial principle [the bond of the political union], according to its particular idiosyncrasy. In Rome, on the other hand, we shall observe a harsh sovereignty dominating over the individual members of the State; as also in the German Empire, a monarchy, in which the Individual is connected with and has *devoirs* to perform not only in regard to the monarch, but to the whole monarchical organization.

The Democratical State is not Patriarchal—does not rest on a still unreflecting, undeveloped confidence—but implies laws, with the consciousness of their being founded on an equitable and moral basis, and the recognition of these laws as positive. At the time of the Kings, no political life had as yet made its appearance in Hellas; there are, therefore, only slight traces of Legislation. But in the interval from the Trojan War till near the time of Cyrus, its necessity was felt. The first Lawgivers are known under the name of The Seven Sages—a title which at that time did not imply any such character as that of the Sophists—teachers of wisdom, designedly [and systematically] proclaiming the Right and True—but merely thinking men, whose thinking stopped short of Science, properly so called. They were *practical* politicians; the good counsels which two of them— Thales of Miletus and Bias of Priene—gave to the Ionian cities, have been already mentioned. Thus Solon was commissioned by the Athenians to give them laws, as those then in operation no longer sufficed. Solon gave the Athenians a constitution by which all obtained equal rights, yet not so as to render the Democracy a quite abstract one. The main point in Democracy is moral disposition. *Virtue* is the basis of Democracy, remarks Montesquieu; and this sentiment is as important as it is true in reference to the idea of Democracy commonly entertained. The Substance, [the Principle] of Justice, the common weal, the general interest, is the main consideration; but it is so only as Custom, in the form of Objective Will, so that morality properly so called— subjective conviction and intention—has not yet manifested itself. Law exists, and is in point of substance, the Law of Freedom—rational [in its form and purport,] and valid *because it is Law, i.e.* without ulterior sanction. As in Beauty the Natural element—its sensuous coefficient—remains, so also in this customary morality, laws assume the form of a

necessity of Nature. The Greeks occupy the middle ground of *Beauty* and have not yet attained the higher standpoint of Truth. While Custom and Wont is the form in which the Right is willed and done, that form is a stable one, and has not yet admitted into it the foe of [unreflected] immediacy—reflection and subjectivity of Will. The interests of the community may, therefore, continue to be intrusted to the will and resolve of the citizens—and this must be the basis of the Greek constitution; for no principle has as yet manifested itself, which can contravene such Choice conditioned by Custom, and hinder its realizing itself in action. The Democratic Constitution is here the only possible one: the citizens are still unconscious of particular interests, and therefore of a corrupting element: the Objective Will is in their case not disintegrated. Athene the goddess is Athens itself—*i.e.,* the real and concrete spirit of the citizens. The divinity ceases to inspire their life and conduct, only when the Will has retreated within itself—into the *adytum* of cognition and conscience—and has posited the infinite schism between the Subjective and the Objective. The above is the true position of the Democratic polity; its justification and absolute necessity rest on this still immanent Objective Morality. For the modern conceptions of Democracy this justification cannot be pleaded. These provide that the interests of the community, the affairs of State, shall be discussed and decided by the People; that the individual members of the community shall deliberate, urge their respective opinions, and give their votes; and this on the ground that the interests of the State and its concerns are the interests of such individual members. All this is very well; but the essential condition and distinction in regard to various phases of Democracy is: *What is the character of* these individual members? They are absolutely authorized to assume their position, only in as far as their will is still *Objective Will*—not one that wishes this or that, not mere "good" will. For good will is something particular— rests on the morality of individuals, on their conviction and subjective feeling. That very subjective Freedom which constitutes the principle and determines the peculiar form of Freedom in *our* world—

which forms the absolute basis of our political and religious life, could not manifest itself in Greece otherwise than as a *destructive* element. Subjectivity was a grade not greatly in advance of that occupied by the Greek Spirit; that phase must of necessity soon be attained: but it plunged the Greek world into ruin, for the polity which that world embodied was not calculated for this side of humanity—did not recognize this phase; since it had not made its appearance when that polity began to exist. Of the Greeks in the first and genuine form of their Freedom, we may assert, that they had no conscience; the habit of living for their country without further [analysis or] reflection, was the principle dominant among them. The consideration of the State in the abstract—which to our understanding is the essential point—was alien to them. Their grand object was their country in its living and real aspect;—*this actual* Athens, this Sparta, these Temples, these Altars, this form of social life, this union of fellow-citizens, these manners and customs. To the Greek his country was a necessary of life, without which existence was impossible. It was the Sophists—the "Teachers of Wisdom"—who first introduced subjective reflection, and the new doctrine that each man should act according to his own conviction. When reflection once comes into play, the inquiry is started whether the Principles of Law (*das Recht*) cannot be improved. Instead of holding by the existing state of things, *internal* conviction is relied upon; and thus begins a subjective independent Freedom, in which the individual finds himself in a position to bring everything to the test of his own conscience, even in defiance of the existing constitution. Each one has his "principles," and that view which accords with his private judgment he regards as *practically* the best, and as claiming practical realization. This decay even Thucydides notices, when he speaks of every one's thinking that things are going on badly when he has not a hand in the management.

To this state of things—in which every one presumes to have a judgment of his own—confidence in Great Men is antagonistic. When, in earlier times, the Athenians commission Solon to legislate for them, or when Lycurgus appears at Sparta as law-

giver and regulator of the State, it is evidently not supposed that the people in general think that they know best what is politically right. At a later time also, it was distinguished personages of plastic genius in whom the people placed their confidence: Cleisthenes, *e.g.* who made the constitution still more democratic than it had been—Miltiades, Themistocles, Aristides, and Cimon, who in the Median wars stand at the head of Athenian affairs—and Pericles, in whom Athenian glory centres as in its focus. But as soon as any of these great men had performed what was needed, envy intruded—*i.e.* the recoil of the sentiment of equality against conspicuous talent—and he was either imprisoned or exiled. Finally, the Sycophants arose among the people, aspersing all individual greatness, and reviling those who took the lead in public affairs.

But there are three other points in the condition of the Greek republics that must be particularly observed.

1. With Democracy in that form in which alone it existed in Greece, *Oracles* are intimately connected. To an independent resolve, a consolidated Subjectivity of the Will (in which the latter is determined by preponderating reasons) is absolutely indispensable; but the Greeks had not this element of strength and vigor in their volition. When a colony was to be founded, when it was proposed to adopt the worship of foreign deities, or when a general was about to give battle to the enemy, the oracles were consulted. Before the battle of Platæa, Pausanias took care that an augury should be taken from the animals offered in sacrifice, and was informed by the soothsayer Tisamenus that the sacrifices were favorable to the Greeks provided they remained on the hither side of the Asopus, but the contrary, if they crossed the stream and began the battle. Pausanias, therefore, awaited the attack. In their private affairs, too, the Greeks came to a determination not so much from subjective conviction as from some extraneous suggestion. With the advance of democracy we observe the oracles no longer consulted on the most important matters, but the particular views of popular orators influencing and deciding the policy of the State. As at this time Socrates relied upon

his "Dæmon," so the popular leaders and the people relied on their individual convictions in forming their decisions. But contemporaneously with this were introduced corruption, disorder, and an unintermitted process of change in the constitution.

2. Another circumstance that demands special attention here, is the element of *Slavery*. This was a necessary condition of an æsthetic democracy, where it was the right and duty of every citizen to deliver or to listen to orations respecting the management of the State in the place of public assembly, to take part in the exercise of the Gymnasia, and to join in the celebration of festivals. It was a necessary condition of such occupations, that the citizens should be freed from handicraft occupations; consequently, that what among us is performed by free citizens—the work of daily life—should be done by slaves. Slavery does not cease until the Will has been infinitely self-reflected—until Right is conceived as appertaining to every freeman, and the term freeman is regarded as a synonym for man in his generic nature as endowed with Reason. But here we still occupy the standpoint of Morality as mere Wont and Custom, and therefore known only as a peculiarity attaching to a certain kind of existence [not as absolute and universal Law].

3. It must also be remarked, thirdly, that such democratic constitutions are possible only in small states—states which do not much exceed the compass of cities. The whole Polis of the Athenians is united in the one city of Athens. Tradition tells that Theseus united the scattered Demes into an integral totality. In the time of Pericles, at the beginning of the Peloponnesian War, when the Spartans were marching upon Attica, its entire population took refuge in the city. Only in such cities can the interests of all be similar; in large empires, on the contrary, diverse and conflicting interests are sure to present themselves. The living together in one city, the fact that the inhabitants see each other daily, render a common culture and a *living* democratic polity possible. In Democracy, the main point is that the character of the citizen be plastic, all "of a piece." He must be present at the critical stages of public business; he must take part in decisive crises with his entire personality—not with his vote merely; he must mingle in the heat of action—the passion and interest of the whole man being absorbed in the affair, and the warmth with which a resolve was made being equally ardent during its execution. That unity of opinion to which the whole community must be brought [when any political step is to be taken,] must be produced in the individual members of the state by *oratorical suasion*. If this were attempted by *writing*—in an abstract, lifeless way—no general fervor would be excited among the social units; and the greater the number, the less weight would each individual vote have. In a large empire a general inquiry might be made, votes might be gathered in the several communities, and the results reckoned up—as was done by the French Convention. But a political existence of this kind is destitute of life, and the World is *ipso facto* broken into fragments and dissipated into a mere Paper-world. In the French Revolution, therefore, the republican constitution never actually became a Democracy: Tyranny, Despotism, raised its voice under the mask of Freedom and Equality. . . .

# KARL MARX
# AND FRIEDRICH ENGELS
## ~

### INTRODUCTION

## RICHARD MILLER

Karl Marx (1818–1883) was born in Trier, in a Prussian province along the Rhine. His family was upper middle class, nominally Protestant, and ethnically Jewish. From 1835 to 1841, Marx pursued his university studies, first at Bonn, then at Berlin, Hegel's old university, where his tenuous interest in the law shifted to a commitment to philosophy. Marx became one of the "Young Hegelians" who followed Hegel in viewing history as the rational development of the idea of freedom through the generation and resolution of contradictions, and, much more than Hegel, criticized received traditions and institutions as obstacles to this progress.

Although Marx earned a doctorate in philosophy in 1841, he turned to journalism as his most effective means of social criticism. But Prussian repression intervened. His newspaper was shut down in 1843, largely in response to Marx's investigations of poverty among the Rhenish peasantry.

Marx moved to Paris, where he combined more journalism with intensive study of English economists, French political historians, and "Communists," that is, advocates of communal ownership and the leveling of economic differences who had begun to attract a working-class following in France and Germany. The source of our first selection, a series of rough drafts now known as the "*Economic and Philosophical Manuscripts* of 1844," was the most important product of this diverse ferment. First published in 1927, the *Manuscripts* mark a large step away from the rationalist reformism of the Young Hegelians and have served, since their publication, as an epitome of Marx's abiding spiritual concerns.

Often, Marx's project in these manuscripts is to use his experience and reading concerning economic life to transform certain diagnoses of psychological impoverishment that he had encountered in Hegel and in the atheist, materialist philosopher Ludwig Feuerbach (1804–1872). Both philosophers were concerned with processes of "alienation," in which aspects of human life through which people could potentially express themselves or their common humanity are instead confronted as external phenomena, opposed to self-expression. Marx's predecessors locate the roots of this self-estrangement in confused thinking: the self's overly rigid conceptualization of its relation to objective reality (Hegel), or humans' conversion of "species-being," our appreciation of our common humanity, into awe at an imagined God embodying our common strivings (Feuerbach). Marx accepts the devastating effect of estrangement from oneself and others but traces it to a specific feature of economic life under capitalism: the necessity that wage earners face of selling their life activity as a commodity in order to survive. Unrestrained economic competition leads more and more people to lose control of means of production, forcing them to submit to the labor market. So the cure for alienation is not mere removal of political restrictions but the creation of a new kind of economy, based on common control of production in the interest of reciprocity, expressive work, and the satisfaction of the needs characteristic of cooperating human beings.

In 1845, the French government, under pressure from the Prussian monarchy, expelled Marx, who moved to Brussels. There, Marx began his lifelong collaboration with Friedrich Engels, with whom he had become friends in Paris. One of their first coauthored works, *The German Ideology* (finished in 1846, but unpublished until 1932), is the source of our second reading. As in the 1844 *Manuscripts*, the project is sometimes the economic explanation of spiritual ills, both alienation and the one-sided personal development that Marx and Engels trace to the division of labor. A new theme is the explanation of how social systems develop. In a vague outline that would be filled in and revised in much future work, Marx and Engels propose that the pursuit of enhanced powers of material production has the unintended consequence of creating new social relations of production, which, in turn, mold the political and cultural features of an era.

Along with this theoretical work, Marx and Engels were getting to know working-class radicals, especially members of the League of the Just, a conspiratorial Communist group with branches throughout western Europe. As they moved the League closer to their own views, they joined it. In a congress in London, the League renamed itself "The Communist League" and adopted guiding principles that Marx and Engels were asked to elaborate in a manifesto. The result, *Manifesto of the Communist Party*, our next selection, came off the presses in February 1848, just as a continental wave of revolutions began with the overthrow of the French monarchy.

The *Manifesto*'s astounding mixture of advocacy, theorizing, and historical narration centers on a conception of capitalist society as based on an antagonistic relation that will, inevitably, destroy it, the relation between the proletariat and the bourgeoisie. Broadly speaking, the proletariat are those who control no significant means of production and must make a living by selling the use of their labor power to others who do. The bourgeoisie are these others, people exercising significant control over means of production and mainly deriving their income from the sale of what proletarians working these means produce. The two classes are "two great hostile camps," since the competitive bourgeois drive for profits creates relentless pressure to reduce wages and to eliminate individualized ways of working that conflict with industrial routines. Marx and Engels view political and cultural institutions (including "the modern representative state") as advancing the long-term interests of the bourgeoisie in this conflict. Yet, in the face of this "ruling class" dominance, the bourgeoisie "produces . . . , above all, its own grave-diggers." Economic interdependence, the reduced importance of mastercraftsmen's expertise, mass literacy, and ease of communication are features of modern proletarian life due to the bourgeois drive to expand production. Yet their utterly unintended result is increased unity in resistance to the burdens of capitalist production, ultimately progressing to full-scale revolution and the creation of a proletarian ruling class. Marx and Engels see this as the basis for yet further transformations, ultimately including a stateless society in which work is motivated by a desire for mutual benefit.

Responding to the revolutionary fervor that coincided with the appearance of the *Manifesto*, Marx and Engels returned to Germany—Marx as organizer and main writer of a revolutionary newspaper, Engels both as journalist and officer in a revolutionary army. The failure of the revolutions brought Marx's final exile. He was expelled from Prussia in 1850 on account of the "dangerous tendencies" of his newspaper, soon settling in London, where he spent the rest of his life. The Marx family was desperately poor at the start, and, for the next two decades (after which Engels provided a stipend), Marx's struggle to make ends meet as a freelance journalist never kept them far from poverty.

Most of Marx's theoretical work in this second half of his life was devoted to the description of the economic "laws of motion" of capitalism, which eventually took the form of his multivolume treatise, *Capital*. Only the first volume appeared in Marx's lifetime, in 1867. Marx's most important political activity in London was his leading role in the International Workingmen's Association (1864–1876), an international group of predominantly working-class activists, which led demonstrations of English workers in favor of Irish independence, organized international strike support, and outraged the respectable classes of Europe by supporting the Paris Commune, a revolutionary government, including members of the International, which controlled Paris for two months at the end of the Franco-Prussian War.

What Marx learned in these theoretical and practical activities led to significant departures from the perspective of the *Manifesto*. While the *Manifesto* emphasizes spontaneous tendencies of capitalism to disolve divisions among workers based on ethnicity, religion, or nationality, Marx came to see the ideological maintenance of these divisions as characteristic of mature capitalism. For example, in his later view, the antagonism between ethnically English and ethnically Irish workers was "the secret of the impotence of the English working class," a division maintained by the mass media of the time, calling for organized opposition by groups such as the International.

In addition, while the *Manifesto* describes a downward trend of wages and working conditions to the threshold of bare physical survival, Marx became acutely aware of the sustained upward trend in real wages in Britain and the benefits of the shortened working day. In his later view, workers under capitalism could effect some beneficial changes through trades-union militancy and political activism. But the superior bargaining power of capitalist firms and the bourgeois bias of government and ideological institutions would ensure that workers would do no better, over the long run, than maintain their proportionate share in the total social product by sharing in gains from improved technology. Such long-term growth income would barely keep pace with the growth of needs, since people's needs grow as they perceive growth in what their society can provide. (As Marx puts it in *Wage Labor and Capital,* "Let a palace arise beside the little house and it sinks from a little house to a hut."

Despite these modifications of the specific predictions of the *Manifesto*, Marx always foresaw a long-term trend of increasing proletarian misery. In this trajectory leading to socialist revolution, capitalist firms plan production on an ever-larger scale, mobilize increasingly capital-intensive technology, and find less and less precapitalist territory to exploit, coping with consequent obstacles to successful expansion in the absence of a central plan and in the face of an increasingly knowledgeable and coordinated workers' movement. As a result, Marx expected workers to be victimized by increasing and increasingly violent instability—deepening industrial depressions, wars of mounting severity, and increasingly, the abandonment of parliamentary democracy for unconstrained and brutal repression.

Marx's investigation of capitalist economics and politics was accompanied by much inquiry into the dynamics of past social transformations and the structure of precapitalist socities. Discussions of his general theory of history often center on our next selection, the celebrated Preface to an otherwise little-read work that prefigured parts of *Capital* I—*A*

*Contribution to a Critique of Political Economy* (1859). Its fame rests on part of a paragraph in a brief autobiographical sketch, a few lines that contain Marx's most detailed statement of his general conception of social stability and social change. With the help of other writings by Marx and the many thousands of pages of commentary inspired by these few lines, some features of Marx's meaning here have become fairly well established. As in his analysis of capitalist society in the *Manifesto*, Marx takes relations of control that dominate material production to be the foundation on which political and cultural institutions rest: that is, the most important features of these "superstructural" institutions are as they are because this helps to maintain the "economic structure" consisting of those "relations of production." Despite these stabilizing institutions, Marx thinks that there are processes internal to some social systems that make change inevitable. The ultimate origin of such internal change lies in the mode of production, that is, the ensemble of relations of control, work relations, and technological capacities through which material goods are produced. In particular, people's locations in an initially stable economic structure may lead them to increase the productive capacity of resources they control until further productive improvement is inhibited by the old relations of production. Marx's paradigm is the inhibition of productive capitalist investment by guild rules, traditional overlord-tenant ties, and economically arbitrary grants of royal monopolies in late-feudal England. Eventually, the enhanced productive forces, together with their fettering, provide resources and motivations for an effective social revolution, so that the chains are broken and a new structure is established, facilitating the growth of productive power.

The last selection is our only one solely written by Friedrich Engels. Engels (1820–1895) was born to a wealthy, devoutly Pietist family in Barmen, about 100 miles north of Marx's Trier, also in Prussian territory near the Rhine. The family business was an international textile-manufacturing firm, with a branch in Manchester, England. As he became part of the family business, Engels was increasingly appalled by the conditions he encountered among factory workers. This experience, together with his readings in philosophy and political economy, led him through the same phases as the young Marx had gone through, culminating in his widely read indictment of the most advanced capitalism of the time, *The Condition of the Working Class in England* (1845).

From his joining the Manchester branch of the family firm in 1843 until his death, Engels' home was in England, apart from his fateful travels in continental radical circles in the mid-1840s and his participation in the revolutions of 1848 and 1849. Until 1869, Engels played an active role in the financial (though not the managerial) affairs of his firm, quite painfully aware of the irony, which was made all the more sardonic by his common-law marriage to an Irish immigrant whom he met when she was a factory worker. Having saved enough to retire on (despite giving away much of his income as a one-man foundation helping Marx and other radicals), Engels left the firm at age 48, with vast relief. In many of his later writings, he extends his and Marx's perspective to anthropology, the natural sciences, and the philosophical description of knowledge and reality.

Engels is not as complex and suggestive a writer as Marx, whose rich narratives and flashing metaphors yield fresh insights after many readings. But if what is there in a work of Engels' is largely what first meets the eye, this is a tribute to great expository powers at the service of very wide-ranging thoughts. These skills served Engels well when he distilled parts of a long and frequently abstract work, *Herr Eugen Duehring's Revolution in Science*

(1878), into the widely read popularization that is our last selection, *Socialism: Utopian and Scientific* (1880). Of special interest is Engels' argument that capitalism gives rise to industrial crises of increasing severity: Capitalism has already begun to socialize production, through worldwide interdependence and the concentration of control; but production still depends on the anarchic decisions of profit-seeking firms, whose efforts to expand at one another's expense lead to periodic crises in which swollen inventories trigger a downward spiral of cutbacks in employment and production. As the scope and interdependence of production grows, so too does the severity of the crises. This thesis was one important substitute for the earlier claim that real wages decline to the margin of physical subsistence. In Marx's writings, tendencies toward wars of increasing violence and toward increasingly repressive regimes also play a role in eventually motivating proletarian revolution.

Some of the most important works by Marx and Engels that have not been cited are Marx, *The Eighteenth Brumaire of Louis Bonaparte* (1852), his most detailed political history; Marx, *The Civil War in France* (1871), notable for his response to political innovations of the Paris Commune; Marx, "Critique of the Gotha Program" (1875), which includes his most detailed vision of postcapitalist institutions; and Engels, *The Origin of the Family, Private Property and the State* (1884).

Among the many questions about Marx's and Engels' meanings, some have proved especially apt to shed light on large issues in political and social theory. The Preface to *A Contribution to the Critique of Political Economy* seems to many readers to make technological innovation the ultimate source of social change, but Marx's specific historical explanations, including the economic histories in *Capital*, rarely give technology the leading role. Is there an underlying theory that fits both general statements and concrete practice? In the *Manifesto* and elsewhere, Marx and Engels seem to reject appeals to justice and even to morality as part of their "radical rupture with traditional ideas." Is there any sense in which the rejections are genuine, and, if so, what replaces justice and morality? Marx and Engels treat politics and culture as "superstructural," yet political goals and religious beliefs have obviously motivated conduct of socially important kinds. Can they admit that social processes are based on individual conduct that often has these motives, without watering down their intriguing claims into banalities about the need to eat and the presence of economic and technological processes as some of the many important sources of change? Recent work exploring these questions includes Gerald Cohen, *Karl Marx's Theory of History* (Princeton, N.J.: Princeton University Press, 1978), a defense of a technological determinist interpretation; Jon Elster, *Making Sense of Marx* (Cambridge, Mass.: Cambridge University Press, 1985), which defends a "methodological individualist" view of Marx; Alan Gilbert, *Marx's Politics* (Rutgers: Rutgers University Press, 1981), which questions economic deterministic understandings of Marx; Richard W. Miller, *Analyzing Marx* (Princeton, N.J.: Princeton University Press, 1984), with discussions of morality, the nature of the state, and (from an antitechnological-determinist perspective) history; Allen Wood, *Karl Marx* (London: Routledge & Kegan Paul, 1981), including discussions of morality and alienation.

# Economic and Philosophic Manuscripts of 1844

## ESTRANGED LABOR

We have proceeded from the premises of political economy. We have accepted its language and its laws. We presupposed private property, the separation of labor, capital and land, and of wages, profit of capital and rent of land—likewise division of labor, competition, the concept of exchange-value, etc. On the basis of political economy itself, in its own words, we have shown that the worker sinks to the level of a commodity and becomes indeed the most wretched of commodities; that the wretchedness of the worker is in inverse proportion to the power and magnitude of his production; that the necessary result of competition is the accumulation of capital in a few hands, and thus the restoration of monopoly in a more terrible form; and that finally the distinction between capitalist and land rentier, like that between the tiller of the soil and the factory worker, disappears and that the whole of society must fall apart into the two classes—the property *owners* and the propertyless *workers*.

Political economy starts with the fact of private property, but it does not explain it to us. It expresses in general, abstract formulas the *material* process through which private property actually passes, and these formulas it then takes for *laws*. It does not *comprehend* these laws, i.e., it does not demonstrate how they arise from the very nature of private property. Political economy does not disclose the source of the division between labor and capital, and between capital and land. When, for example, it defines the relationship of wages to profit, it takes the interest of the capitalists to be the ultimate cause, i.e., it takes for granted what it is supposed to explain. Similarly, competition comes in everywhere. It is explained from external circumstances. As to how far these external and apparently accidental circumstances are but the expression of a necessary course of development, political economy teaches us nothing. We have seen how exchange itself appears to it as an accidental fact. The only wheels which political economy sets in motion are *greed* and the war *amongst the greedy—competition.*

Precisely because political economy does not grasp the way the movement is connected, it was possible to oppose, for instance, the doctrine of competition to the doctrine of monopoly, the doctrine of the freedom of the crafts to the doctrine of the guild, the doctrine of the division of landed property to the doctrine of the big estate—for competition, freedom of the crafts and the division of landed property were explained and comprehended only as accidental, premeditated and violent consequences of monopoly, of the guild system, and of feudal property, not as their necessary, inevitable and natural consequences.

Now, therefore, we have to grasp the essential connection between private property; greed, and the separation of labor, capital and landed property; between exchange and competition, value and the devaluation of men, monopoly and competition, etc.—the connection between this whole estrangement and the *money* system.

Do not let us go back to a fictitious primordial condition as the political economist does, when he tries to explain. Such a primordial condition explains nothing; it merely pushes the question away into a gray nebulous distance. It assumes in the form of a fact, of an event, what the economist is supposed to deduce—namely, the necessary relationship between two things—between, for example, division of labor and exchange. Theology in the same way explains the

Translated by Martin Milligan. Reprinted by permission of International Publishers.

origin of evil by the fall of man; that is, it assumes as a fact, in historical form, what has to be explained.

We proceed from an economic fact *of the present.*

The worker becomes all the poorer the more wealth he produces, the more his production increases in power and size. The worker becomes an ever cheaper commodity the more commodities he creates. With the *increasing value* of the world of things proceeds in direct proportion the *devaluation* of the world of men. Labor produces not only commodities: it produces itself and the worker as a *commodity*—and this in the same general proportion in which it produces commodities.

This fact expresses merely that the object which labor produces—labor's product—confronts it as *something alien*, as a *power independent* of the producer. The product of labor is labor which has been embodied in an object, which has become material: it is the objectification of labor. Labor's realization is its objectification. In the sphere of political economy this realization of labor appears as loss of *realization* for the workers; objectification as loss of the *object* and *bondage to it*; appropriation as *estrangement*, as *alienation.*

So much does labor's realization appear as loss of realization that the worker loses realization to the point of starving to death. So much does objectification appear as loss of the object that the worker is robbed of the objects most necessary not only for his life but for his work. Indeed, labor itself becomes an object which he can obtain only with the greatest effort and with the most irregular interruptions. So much does the appropriation of the object appear as estrangement that the more objects the worker produces the less he can possess and the more he falls under the sway of his product, capital.

All these consequences result from the fact that the worker is related to the *product of his labor* as to an *alien* object. For on this premise it is clear that the more the worker spends himself, the more powerful becomes the alien world of objects which he creates over and against himself, the poorer he himself—his inner world—becomes, the less belongs to him as his own. It is the same in religion. The more man puts into God, the less he retains in himself. The worker

puts his life into the object; but now his life no longer belongs to him but to the object. Hence, the greater this activity, the greater is the worker's lack of objects. Whatever the product of his labor is, he is not. Therefore the greater this product, the less is he himself. The *alienation* of the worker in his product means not only that his labor becomes an object, an *external* existence, but that it exists *outside* him, independently, as something alien to him, and that it becomes a power on its own confronting him. It means that the life which he has conferred on the object confronts him as something hostile and alien.

Let us now look more closely at the *objectification,* at the production of the worker; and in it as the *estrangement,* the *loss* of the object, of his product.

The worker can create nothing without *nature,* without the *sensuous external world.* It is the material on which his labor is realized, in which it is active, from which and by means of which it produces.

But just as nature provides labor with the *means of life* in the sense that labor cannot live without objects on which to operate, on the other hand, it also provides the *means of life* in the more restricted sense, i.e., the means for the physical subsistence of the *worker* himself.

Thus the more the worker by his labor *appropriates* the external world, hence sensuous nature, the more he deprives himself of *means of life* in double manner: first, in that the sensuous external world more and more ceases to be an object belonging to his labor—to be his labor's *means of life;* and secondly, in that it more and more ceases to be *means of life* in the immediate sense, means for the physical subsistence of the worker.

In both respects, therefore, the worker becomes a slave of his object, first, in that he receives an *object of labor,* i.e., in that he receives *work;* and secondly, in that he receives *means of subsistence.* Therefore, it enables him to exist, first, as a *worker;* and, second as a *physical subject.* The height of this bondage is that it is only as a *worker* that he continues to maintain himself as a *physical subject,* and that is only as a *physical subject* that he is a *worker.*

(The laws of political economy express the estrangement of the worker in his object thus: the more the worker produces, the less he has to consume; the more values he creates, the more valueless, the more unworthy he becomes; the better formed his product, the more deformed becomes the worker; the more civilized his object, the more barbarous becomes the worker; the more powerful labor becomes, the more powerless becomes the worker; the more ingenious labor becomes, the less ingenious becomes the worker and the more he becomes nature's bondsman.)

*Political economy conceals the estrangement inherent in the nature of labor by not considering the direct relationship between the worker* (labor) *and production.* It is true that labor produces for the rich wonderful things—but for the worker it produces privation. It produces palaces—but for the worker, hovels. It produces beauty—but for the worker, deformity. It replaces labor by machines, but it throws a section of the workers back to a barbarous type of labor, and turns the other workers into machines. It produces intelligence—but for the worker stupidity, cretinism.

*The direct relationship of labor to its products is the relationship of the worker to the objects of his production.* The relationship of the man of means to the objects of productio dn and to production itself is only a *consequence* of this first relationship—and confirms it. We shall consider this other aspect later.

When we ask, then, what is the essential relationship of labor we are asking about the relationship of the *worker* to production.

Till now we have been considering the estrangement, the alienation of the worker only in one of its aspects, i.e., the worker's *relationship to the products of his labor.* But the estrangement is manifested not only in the result but in the *act of production,* within the *producing activity*, itself. How would the worker come to face the product of his activity as a stranger, were it not that in the very act of production he was estranging himself from himself? The product is after all but the summary of the activity, of production. If then the product of labor is alienation, production itself must be active alienation, the alienation of activity, the activity of alienation. In the estrangement of the object of labor is merely sum-

marized the estrangement, the alienation, in the activity of labor itself.

What, then, constitutes the alienation of labor?

First, the fact that labor is *external* to the worker, i.e., it does not belong to his essential being; that in his work, therefore, he does not affirm himself but denies himself, does not feel content but unhappy, does not develop freely his physical and mental energy but mortifies his body and ruins his mind. The worker therefore only feels himself outside his work, and in his work feels outside himself. He is at home when he is not working, and when he is working he is not at home. His labor is therefore not voluntary, but coerced; it is *forced labor*. It is therefore not the satisfaction of a need; it is merely a *means* to satisfy needs external to it. Its alien character emerges clearly in the fact that as soon as no physical or other compulsion exists, labor is shunned like the plague. External labor, labor in which man alienates himself, is a labor of self-sacrifice, of mortification. Lastly, the external character of labor for the worker appears in the fact that it is not his own, but someone else's, that it does not belong to him, that in it he belongs, not to himself, but to another. Just as in religion the spontaneous activity of the human imagination, of the human brain and the human heart, operates independently of the individual—that is, operates on him as an alien, divine or diabolical activity—so is the worker's activity not his spontaneous activity. It belongs to another; it is the loss of his self.

As a result, therefore, man (the worker) only feels himself freely active in his animal functions—eating, drinking, procreating, or at most in his dwelling and in dressing-up, etc.; and in his human functions he no longer feels himself to be anything but an animal. What is animal becomes human and what is human becomes animal.

Certainly eating, drinking, procreating, etc., are also genuinely human functions. But abstractly taken, separated from the sphere of all other human activity and turned into sole and ultimate ends, they are animal functions.

We have considered the act of estranging practical human activity, labor, in two of its aspects. (1) The relation of the worker to the *product of labor* as an alien object exercising power over him. This relation is at the same time the relation to the sensuous external world, to the objects of nature, as an alien world inimically opposed to him. (2) The relation of labor to the *act of production* within the *labor* process. This relation is the relation of the worker to his own activity as an alien activity not belonging to him; it is activity as suffering, strength as weakness, begetting as emasculating, the worker's *own* physical and mental energy, his personal life indeed, what is life but activity?—as an activity which is turned against him, independent of him and not belonging to him. Here we have *self-estrangement,* as previously we had the estrangement of the *thing*.

We have still a third aspect of *estranged labor* to deduce from the two already considered.

Man is a species being, not only because in practice and in theory he adopts the species as his object (his own as well as those of other things), but—and this is only another way of expressing it—also because he treats himself as the actual, living species; because he treats himself as a *universal* and therefore a free being.

The life of the species, both in man and in animals, consists physically in the fact that man (like the animal) lives on inorganic nature; and the more universal man is compared with an animal, the more universal is the sphere of inorganic nature on which he lives. Just as plants, animals, stones, air, light, etc., constitute theoretically a part of human consciousness, partly as objects of natural science, partly as objects of art—his spiritual inorganic nature, spiritual nourishment which he must first prepare to make palatable and digestible—so also in the realm of practice they constitute a part of human life and human activity. Physically man lives only on these products of nature, whether they appear in the form of food, heating, clothes, a dwelling, etc. The universality of man appears in practice precisely in the universality which makes all nature his *inorganic* body—both inasmuch as nature is (1) his direct means of life, and (2) the material, the object, and the instrument of his life activity. Nature is man's *inorganic body*—nature, that is, in so far as it is not itself the human body. Man *lives* on nature—

means that nature is his body, with which he must remain in continuous interchange if he is not to die. That man's physical and spiritual life is linked to nature means simply that nature is linked to itself, for man is a part of nature.

In estranging from man (1) nature, and (2) himself, his own active functions, his life activity, estranged labor estranges the *species* from man. It changes for him the *life of the species* into a means of individual life, and secondly it makes individual life in its abstract form the purpose of the life of the species, likewise in its abstract and estranged form.

Indeed, labor, *life-activity, productive life* itself, appears in the first place merely as a means of satisfying a need—the need to maintain physical existence. Yet the productive life is the life of the species. It is life-engendering life. The whole character of a species—its species character—is contained in the character of its life activity; and free, conscious activity is man's species character. Life itself appears only as a *means to life.*

The animal is immediately one with its life activity. It does not distinguish itself from it. It is *its life activity.* Man makes his life activity itself the object of his will and of his consciousness. He has conscious life activity. It is not a determination with which he directly merges. Conscious life activity distinguishes man immediately from animal life activity. It is just because of this that he is a species being. Or rather, it is only because he is a species being that he is a conscious being, i.e., that his own life is an object for him. Only because of that is his activity free activity. Estranged labor reverses this relationship, so that it is just because man is a conscious being that he makes his life activity, his *essential* being, a mere means to his *existence.*

In creating a *world of objects* by his practical activity, in *his work upon* inorganic nature, man proves himself a conscious species being, i.e., as a being that treats the species as its own essential being, or that treats itself as a species being. Admittedly animals also produce. They build themselves nests, dwellings, like the bees, beavers, ants, etc. But an animal only produces what it immediately needs for itself or its young. It produces one-sidedly, whilst man produces universally. It produces only under the dominion of immediate physical need, whilst man produces even when he is free from physical need and only truly produces in freedom therefrom. An animal produces only itself, whilst man reproduces the whole of nature. An animal's product belongs immediately to its physical body, whilst man freely confronts his product. An animal forms things in accordance with the standard and the need of the species to which it belongs, whilst man knows how to produce in accordance with the standard of every species, and knows how to apply everywhere the inherent standard to the object. Man therefore also forms things in accordance with the laws of beauty.

It is just in his work upon the objective world, therefore, that man first really proves himself to be a *species being.* This production is his active species life. Through and because of this production, nature appears as his work and his reality. The object of labor is, therefore, the *objectification of man's species life:* for he duplicates himself not only, as in consciousness, intellectually, but also actively, in reality, and therefore he contemplates himself in a world that he has created. In tearing away from man the object of his production, therefore, estranged labor tears from him his *species life,* his real objectivity as a member of the species and transforms his advantage over animals into the disadvantage that his inorganic body, nature, is taken away from him.

Similarly, in degrading spontaneous, free, activity, to a means, estranged labor makes man's species life a means to his physical existence.

The consciousness which man has of his species is thus transformed by estrangement in such a way that species life becomes for him a means.

Estranged labor turns thus:

(3) *Man's species being,* both nature and his spiritual species property, into a being *alien* to him, into a *means* to his *individual existence.* It estranges from man his own body, as well as external nature and his spiritual essence, his *human* being.

(4) An immediate consequence of the fact that man is estranged from the product of his labor, from his life activity, from his species being is the *es-*

*trangement of man* from *man.* When man confronts himself, he confronts the *other* man. What applies to a man's relation to his work, to the product of his labor and to himself, also holds of a man's relation to the other man, and to the other man's labor and object of labor.

In fact, the proposition that man's species nature is estranged from him means that one man is estranged from the other, as each of them is from man's essential nature.

The estrangement of man, and in fact every relationship in which man stands to himself, is first realized and expressed in the relationship in which a man stands to other men.

Hence within the relationship of estranged labor each man views the other in accordance with the standard and the relationship in which he finds himself as a worker.

We took our departure from a fact of political economy—the estrangement of the worker and his production. We have formulated this fact in conceptual terms as *estranged, alienated* labor. We have analyzed this concept—hence analyzing merely a fact of political economy.

Let us now see, further, how the concept of estranged, alienated labor must express and present itself in real life.

If the product of labor is alien to me, if it confronts me as an alien power, to whom, then, does it belong?

If my own activity does not belong to me, if it is an alien, a coerced activity, to whom, then, does it belong?

To a being *other* than myself.

Who is this being?

The *gods?* To be sure, in the earliest times the principal production (for example, the building of temples, etc., in Egypt, India and Mexico) appears to be in the service of the gods, and the product belongs to the gods. However, the gods on their own were never the lords of labor. No more was *nature.* And what a contradiction it would be if, the more man subjugated nature by his labor and the more the miracles of the gods were rendered superfluous by the miracles of industry, the more man were to renounce the joy of production and the enjoyment of the product in favor of these powers.

The *alien* being, to whom labor and the product of labor belongs, in whose service labor is done and for whose benefit the product of labor is provided, can only be *man* himself.

If the product of labor does not belong to the worker, if it confronts him as an alien power, then this can only be because it belongs to some *other man than the worker.* If the worker's activity is a torment to him, to another it must be *delight* and his life's joy. Not the gods, not nature, but only man himself can be this alien power over man.

We must bear in mind the previous proposition that man's relation to himself only becomes for him *objective* and *actual* through his relation to the other man. Thus, if the product of his labor, his labor *objectified,* is for him an *alien,* hostile, powerful object independent of him, then his position towards it is such that someone else is master of this object, someone who is alien, hostile, powerful, and independent of him. If his own activity is to him related as an unfree activity, then he is related to it as an activity performed in the service, under the dominion, the coercion, and the yoke of another man.

Every self-estrangement of man, from himself and from nature, appears in the relation in which he places himself and nature to men other than and differentiated from himself. For this reason religious self-estrangement necessarily appears in the relationship of the layman to the priest, or again to a mediator, etc., since we are here dealing with the intellectual world. In the real practical world self-estrangement can only become manifest through the real practical relationship to other men. The medium through which estrangement takes place is itself *practical.* Thus through estranged labor man not only creates his relationship to the object and to the act of production as to men that are alien and hostile to him; he also creates the relationship in which other men stand to his production and to his product, and the relationship in which he stands to these other men. Just as he creates his own production as the loss of his reality, as his

punishment; his own product as a loss, as a product not belonging to him; so he creates the domination of the person who does not produce over production and over the product. Just as he estranges his own activity from himself, so he confers to the stranger an activity which is not his own.

We have until now only considered this relationship from the standpoint of the worker and later we shall be considering it also from the standpoint of the non-worker.

Through *estranged, alienated* labor, then, the worker produces the relationship to this labor of a man alien to labor and standing outside it. The relationship of the worker to labor creates the relation to it of the capitalist (or whatever one chooses to call the master of labor). *Private property* is thus the product, the result, the necessary consequence, of *alienated labor,* of the external relation of the worker to nature and to himself.

*Private property* thus results by analysis from the concept of *alienated labor,* of *alienated man,* of estranged labor, of estranged life, of estranged man.

True, it as a result of the *movement of private property* that we have obtained the concept of *alienated labor (of alienated life)* from political economy. But on analysis of this concept it becomes clear that though private property appears to be the source, the cause of alienated labor, it is rather its consequence, just as the gods are *originally* not the cause but the effect of man's intellectual confusion. Later this relationship becomes reciprocal.

Only at the last culmination of the development of private property does this, its secret, appear again, namely, that on the one hand it is the *product* of alienated labor, and that on the other it is the *means* by which labor alienates itself, the *realization of this alienation.*

This exposition immediately sheds light on various hitherto unsolved conflicts.

(1) Political economy starts from labor as the real soul of production; yet to labor it gives nothing, and to private property everything. Confronting this contradiction, Proudhon has decided in favor of labor it gives nothing, and to private property every-

thing. Confronting this contradiction, Proudhon has decided in favor of labor against private property. We understand, however, that this apparent contradiction is the contradiction of *estranged labor* with itself, and that political economy has merely formulated the laws of estranged labor.

We also understand, therefore, that *wages* and *private property* are identical: since the product, as the object of labor pays for labor itself, therefore the wage is but a necessary consequence of labor's estrangement. After all, in the wage of labor, labor does not appear as an end in itself but as the servant of the wage. We shall develop this point later, and meanwhile will only derive some conclusions.

*An enforced increase of wages* (disregarding all other difficulties, including the fact that it would only be by force, too, that higher wages, being an anomaly, could be maintained) would therefore be nothing but *better payment for the slave,* and would not win either for the worker or for labor their human status and dignity.

Indeed, even the *equality of wages* demanded by Proudhon only transforms the relationship of the present-day worker to his labor into the relationship of all men to labor. Society is then conceived as an abstract capitalist.

Wages are a direct consequence of estranged labor, and estranged labor is the direct cause of private property. The downfall of the one must involve the downfall of the other.

(2) From the relationship of estranged labor to private property it follows further that the emancipation of society from private property, etc., from servitude, is expressed in the *political* form of the *emancipation of the workers;* not that *their* emancipation alone is at stake, but because the emancipation of the workers contains universal human emancipation—and it contains this, because the whole of human servitude is involved in the relation of the worker to production, and every relation of servitude is but a modification and consequence of this relation.

Just as we have derived the concept of *private property* from the concept of *estranged, alienated labor* by *analysis,* so we can develop every *category* of political economy with the help of these two fac-

tors; and we shall find again in each category, e.g., trade, competition, capital, money, only a *definite* and *developed expression* of these first elements.

Before considering this aspect, however, let us try to solve two problems.

(1) To define the general *nature of private property,* as it has arisen as a result of estranged labor, in its relation to *truly human* and *social property.*

(2) We have accepted the estrangement of labor, its alienation, as a fact, and we have analyzed this fact. How, we now ask, does man come to alienate, to estrange, his labor? How is this estrangement rooted in the nature of human development? We have already gone a long way to the solution of this problem by transforming the question of the origin of private property into the question of the relation of alienated labor to the course of humanity's development. For when one speaks of private property, one thinks of dealing with something external to man. When one speaks of labor, one is directly dealing with man himself. This new formulation of the question already contains its solution.

*As to (1): The general nature of private property and its relation to truly human property.*

Alienated labor has resolved itself for us into two elements which mutually condition one another, or which are but different expressions of one and the same relationship. *Appropriation* appears as *estrangement,* as *alienation;* and *alienation* appears as *appropriation, estrangement* as true introduction into society.

We have considered the one side—*alienated* labor in relation to the *worker* himself, i.e., *the relation of alienated labor to itself.* The *property relation of the non-worker to the worker and to labor* we have found as the product, the necessary outcome of this relationship. *Private property,* as the material, summary expression of alienated labor, embraces both relations—*the relation of the worker to work and to the product of his labor and to the non-worker,* and the relation of the *non-worker to the worker and to the product of his labor.*

Having seen that in relation to the worker who

*appropriates* nature by means of his labor, this appropriation appears as estrangement, his own spontaneous activity as activity for another and as activity of another, vitality as a sacrifice of life, production of the object as loss of the object to an alien power, to an *alien* person—we shall now consider the relation to the worker, to labor and its object of this person who is *alien* to labor and the worker.

First it has to be noted that everything which appears in the worker as an *activity of alienation, of estrangement,* appears in the non-worker as a *state of alienation, of estrangement.*

Secondly, that the worker's *real, practical attitude* in production and to the product (as a state of mind) appears in the non-worker confronting him as a *theoretical* attitude.

*Thirdly,* the non-worker does everything against the worker which the worker does against himself; but he does not do against himself what he does against the worker.

Let us look more closely at these three relations.

*[At this point the manuscript breaks off unfinished.]*

# The German Ideology

## PREFACE

Hitherto men have constantly made up for themselves false conceptions about themselves, about what they are and what they ought to be. They have arranged their relationships according to their ideas of God, of normal man, etc. The phantoms of their brains have got out of their hands. They, the creators, have bowed down before their creations. Let us liberate them from the chimeras, the ideas, dogmas, imaginary beings under the yoke of which they are pining away. Let us revolt against the rule of thoughts. Let us teach men, says one, to exchange these imaginations for thoughts which correspond to the essence of man; says the second, to take up a critical attitude to them; says the third, to knock them out of their heads; and—existing reality will collapse.

These innocent and childlike fancies are the kernel of the modern Young-Hegelian philosophy, which not only is received by the German public with horror and awe, but is announced by our philosophic heroes with the solemn consciousness of its cataclysmic dangerousness and criminal ruthlessness. The first volume of the present publication has the aim of uncloaking these sheep, who take themselves and are taken for wolves of showing how their bleating merely imitates in a philosophic form the conceptions of the German middle class; how the boasting of these philosophic commentators only mirrors the wretchedness of the real conditions in Germany. It is its aim to debunk and discredit the philosophic struggle with the shadows of reality, which appeals to the dreamy and muddled German nation.

Once upon a time a valiant fellow had the idea that men were drowned in water only because they were possessed with the idea of gravity. If they were to knock this notion out of their heads, say by stating it to be a superstition, a religious concept, they would be sublimely proof against any danger from water. His whole life long he fought against the illusion of gravity, of whose harmful results all statistics brought him new and manifold evidence. This honest fellow was the type of the new revolutionary philosophers in Germany.

### FEUERBACH

#### A. Idealism and Materialism

##### First Premises of Materialist Method

The premises from which we begin are not arbitrary ones, not dogmas, but real premises from which abstraction can only be made in the imagination.

Edited by C. J. Arthur. Reprinted by permission of International Publishers.

They are the real individuals, their activity and the material conditions under which they live, both those which they find already existing and those produced by their activity. These premises can thus be verified in a purely empirical way.

The first premise of all human history is, of course, the existence of living human individuals. Thus the first fact to be established is the physical organisation of these individuals and their consequent relation to the rest of nature. Of course, we cannot here go either into the actual physical nature of man, or into the natural conditions in which man finds himself—geological, oreohydrographical, climatic and so on. The writing of history must always set out from these natural bases and their modification in the course of history through the action of men.

Men can be distinguished from animals by consciousness, by religion or anything else you like. They themselves begin to distinguish themselves from animals as soon as they begin to *produce* their means of subsistence, a step which is conditioned by their physical organisation. By producing their means of subsistence men are indirectly producing their actual material life.

The way in which men produce their means of subsistence depends first of all on the nature of the actual means of subsistence they find in existence and have to reproduce. This mode of production must not be considered simply as being the production of the physical existence of the individuals. Rather it is a definite form of activity of these individuals, a definite form of expressing their life, a definite *mode of life* on their part. As individuals express their life, so they are. What they are, therefore, coincides with their production, both with *what* they produce and with *how* they produce. The nature of individuals thus depends on the material conditions determining their production.

This production only makes its appearance with the *increase of population*. In its turn this presupposes the *intercourse* [*Verkehr*] of individuals with one another. The form of this intercourse is again determined by production.

The relations of different nations among themselves depend upon the extent to which each has developed its productive forces, the division of labour and internal intercourse. This statement is generally recognised. But not only the relation of one nation to others, but also the whole internal structure of the nation itself depends on the stage of development reached by its production and its internal and external intercourse. How far the productive forces of a nation are developed is shown most manifestly by the degree to which the division of labour has been carried. Each new productive force, insofar as it is not merely a quantitative extension of productive forces already known (for instance the bringing into cultivation of fresh land), causes a further development of the division of labour.

The division of labour inside a nation leads at first to the separation of industrial and commercial from agricultural labour, and hence to the separation of *town* and *country* and to the conflict of their interests. Its further development leads to the separation of commercial from industrial labour. At the same time through the division of labour inside these various branches there develop various divisions among the individuals co-operating in definite kinds of labour. The relative position of these individual groups is determined by the methods employed in agriculture, industry and commerce (patriarchalism, slavery, estates, classes). These same conditions are to be seen (given a more developed intercourse) in the relations of different nations to one another.

The various stages of development in the division of labour are just so many different forms of ownership, i.e. the existing stage in the division of labour determines also the relations of individuals to one another with reference to the material, instrument, and product of labour.

The first form of ownership is tribal [*Stammeigentum*] ownership. It corresponds to the undeveloped stage of production, at which a people lives by hunting and fishing, by the rearing of beasts or, the highest stage, agriculture. In the latter case it presupposes a great mass of uncultivated stretches of land. The division of labour is at this stage still very elementary and is confined to a further extension of the natural division of labour existing in the family. The social structure is, therefore, limited to an extension of the family; patriarchal family chieftains, below them the members of the tribe, finally slaves. The slavery latent in the family only develops gradually with the increase of population, the growth of wants, and with the extension of external relations, both of war and of barter.

The second form is the ancient communal and State ownership which proceeds especially from the union of several tribes into a *city* by agreement or by conquest, and which is still accompanied by slavery. Beside communal ownership we already find movable, and later also immovable, private property developing, but as an abnormal form subordinate to communal ownership. The citizens hold power over their labouring slaves only in their community, and on this account alone, therefore, they are bound to the form of communal ownership. It is the communal private property which compels the active citizens to remain in this spontaneously derived form of association over against their slaves. For this reason the whole structure of society based on this communal ownership, and with it the power of the people, decays in the same measure as, in particular, immovable private property evolves. The division of labour is already more developed. We already find the antagonism of town and country; later the antagonism between those states which represent town interests and those which represent country interests, and inside the towns themselves the antagonism between industry and maritime commerce. The class relation between citizens and slaves is now completely developed.

With the development of private property, we find here for the first time the same conditions which we shall find again, only on a more extensive scale, with modern private property. On the one hand, the concentration of private property, which began very early in Rome (as the Licinian agrarian law proves[1]) and proceeded very rapidly from the time of the civil wars and especially under the Emperors; on the other hand, coupled with this, the transformation of the plebeian small peasantry into a proletariat, which, however, owing to its intermediate position between propertied citizens and slaves, never achieved an independent development.

The third form of ownership is feudal or estate property. If antiquity started out from the *town* and its little territory, the Middle Ages started out from the *country*. This different starting-point was determined by the sparseness of the population at that time, which was scattered over a large area and which received no large increase from the conquerors. In contrast to Greece and Rome, feudal development at the outset, therefore, extends over a much wider territory, prepared by the Roman conquests and the spread of agriculture at first associated with it. The last centuries of the declining Roman Empire and its conquest by the barbarians destroyed a number of productive forces; agriculture had declined, industry had decayed for want of a market, trade had died out or been violently suspended, the rural and urban population had decreased. From these conditions and the mode of organisation of the conquest determined by them, feudal property developed under the influence of the Germanic military constitution. Like tribal and communal ownership, it is based again on a community; but the directly producing class standing over against it is not, as in the case of the ancient community, the slaves, but the enserfed small peasantry. As soon as feudalism is fully developed, there also arises antagonism to the towns. The hierarchical structure of landownership, and the armed bodies of retainers associated with it, gave the nobility power over the serfs. This feudal organisation was, just as much as the ancient communal ownership, an association against a subjected producing class; but the form of association and the relation to the direct producers were different because of the different conditions of production.

This feudal system of landownership had its counterpart in the *towns* in the shape of corporative property, the feudal organisation of trades. Here property consisted chiefly in the labour of each individual person. The necessity for association against the organised robber-nobility, the need for communal covered markets in an age when the industrialist was at the same time a merchant, the growing competition of the escaped serfs swarming into the rising towns, the feudal structure of the whole country: these combined to bring about the *guilds*. The gradually accumulated small capital of individual crafts-men and their stable numbers, as against the growing population, evolved the relation of journeyman and apprentice, which brought into being in the towns a hierarchy similar to that in the country.

Thus the chief form of property during the feudal epoch consisted on the one hand of landed property with serf labour chained to it, and on the other of the labour of the individual with small capital com-manding the labour of journeymen. The organisation of both was determined by the restricted conditions of production—the small-scale and primitive culti-vation of the land, and the craft type of industry. There was little division of labour in the heyday of feudalism. Each country bore in itself the antithesis of town and country; the division into estates was certainly strongly marked; but apart from the differ-entiation of princes, nobility, clergy and peasants in the country, and masters, journeymen, apprentices and soon also the rabble of casual labourers in the towns, no division of importance took place. In agri-culture it was rendered difficult by the strip-system, beside which the cottage industry of the peasants themselves emerged. In industry there was no divi-sion of labour at all in the individual trades them-selves, and very little between them. The separation of industry and commerce was found already in exis-tence in older towns; in the newer it only developed later, when the towns entered into mutual relations.

The grouping of larger territories into feudal king-doms was a necessity for the landed nobility as for the towns. The organisation of the ruling class, the nobil-ity, had, therefore, everywhere a monarch at its head.

The fact is, therefore, that definite individuals who are productively active in a definite way enter into these definite social and political relations. Empirical observation must in each separate instance bring out empirically, and without any mystification and spec-ulation, the connection of the social and political structure with production. The social structure and the State are continually evolving out of the life-process of definite individuals, but of individuals, not as they may appear in their own or other people's imagination, but as they *really* are; i.e. as they oper-ate, produce materially, and hence as they work

under definite material limits, presuppositions and conditions independent of their will.

The production of ideas, of conceptions, of con-sciousness, is at first directly interwoven with the material activity and the material intercourse of men, the language of real life. Conceiving, thinking, the mental intercourse of men, appear at this stage as the direct efflux of their material behavior. The same applies to mental production as expressed in the lan-guage of politics, laws, morality, religion, metaphy-sics, etc. of a people. Men are the producers of their conceptions, ideas, etc.—real, active men, as they are conditioned by a definite development of their pro-ductive forces and of the intercourse corresponding to these, up to its furthest forms. Consciousness can never be anything else than conscious existence, and the existence of men is their actual life-process. If in all ideology men and their circumstances appear upside-down as in a *camera obscura*, this phenome-non arises just as much from their historical life-process as the inversion of objects on the retina does from their physical life-process.

In direct contrast to German philosophy which descends from heaven to earth, here we ascend from earth to heaven. That is to say, we do not set out from what men say, imagine, conceive, nor from men as narrated, thought of, imagined, conceived, in order to arrive at men in the flesh. We set out from real, active men, and on the basis of their real life-process we demonstrate the development of the ideological re-flexes and echoes of this life-process. The phantoms formed in the human brain are also, necessarily, sub-limates of their material life-process, which is empir-ically verifiable and bound to material premises. Morality, religion, metaphysics, all the rest of ideol-ogy and their corresponding forms of consciousness, thus no longer retain the semblance of independence. They have no history, no development; but men, developing their material production and their mate-rial intercourse, alter, along with this their real exis-tence, their thinking and the products of their think-ing. Life is not determined by consciousness, but consciousness by life. In the first method of approach the starting-point is consciousness taken as the living individual; in the second method, which conforms to real life, it is the real living individuals themselves, and consciousness is considered solely as *their* consciousness.

This method of approach is not devoid of premises. It starts out from the real premises and does not abandon them for a moment. Its premises are men, not in any fantastic isolation and rigidity, but in their actual, empirically perceptible process of development under definite conditions. As soon as this active life-process is described, history ceases to be a collection of dead facts as it is with the empiricists (themselves still abstract), or an imagined activity of imagined subjects, as with the idealists.

Where speculation ends—in real life—there real, positive science begins: the representation of the practical activity, of the practical process of development of men. Empty talk about consciousness ceases, and real knowledge has to take its place. When reality is depicted, philosophy as an independent branch of knowledge loses its medium of existence. At the best its place can only be taken by a summing-up of the most general results, abstractions which arise from the observation of the historical development of men. Viewed apart from real history, these abstractions have in themselves no value whatsoever. They can only serve to facilitate the arrangements of historical materials, to indicate the sequence of its separate strata. But they by no means afford a recipe or schema, as does philosophy, for neatly trimming the epochs of history. On the contrary, our difficulties begin only when we set about the observation and the arrangement—the real depiction—of our historical material, whether of a past epoch or of the present. The removal of these difficulties is governed by premises which it is quite impossible to state here, but which only the study of the actual life-process and the activity of the individuals of each epoch will make evident. We shall select here some of these abstractions, which we use in constradistinction to the ideologists, and shall illustrate them by historical examples.

## History: Fundamental Conditions

Since we are dealing with the Germans, who are devoid of premises, we must begin by stating the first premise of all human existence and, therefore, of all history, the premise, namely, that men must be in a position to live in order to be able to "make history". But life involves before everything else eating and drinking, a habitation, clothing and many other things. The first historical act is thus the production of the means to satisfy these needs, the production of material life itself. And indeed this is an historical act, a fundamental condition of all history, which today, as thousands of years ago, must daily and hourly be fulfilled merely in order to sustain human life. Even when the sensuous world is reduced to a minimum, to a stick as with Saint Bruno [Bauer], it presupposes the action of producing the stick. Therefore in any interpretation of history one has first of all to observe this fundamental fact in all its significance and all its implications and to accord it its due importance. It is well known that the Germans have never done this, and they have never, therefore, had an *earthly* basis for history and consequently never an historian. The French and the English, even if they have conceived the relation of this fact with so-called history only in an extremely one-sided fashion, particularly as long as they remained in the toils of political ideology, have nevertheless made the first attempts to give the writing of history a materialistic basis by being the first to write histories of civil society, of commerce and industry.

The second point is that the satisfaction of the first need (the action of satisfying, and the instrument of satisfaction which has been acquired) leads to new needs; and this production of new needs is the first historical act. Here we recognise immediately the spiritual ancestry of the great historical wisdom of the Germans who, when they run out of positive material and when they can serve up neither theological nor political nor literary rubbish, assert that this is not history at all, but the "prehistoric era". They do not, however, enlighten us as to how we proceed from this nonsensical "prehistory" to history proper; although, on the other hand, in their historical speculation they seize upon this "prehistory" with especial eagerness because they imagine themselves safe there from interference on the part of "crude facts", and, at the same time, because there they can give full rein to their speculative impulse and set up and knock down hypotheses by the thousand.

The third circumstance which, from the very outset, enters into historical development, is that men, who daily remake their own life, begin to make other men, to propagate their kind: the relation between man and woman, parents and children, the *family*. The family, which to begin with is the only social relationship, becomes later, when increased needs create new social relations and the increased population new needs, a subordinate one (except in Germany), and must then be treated and analysed according to the existing empirical data, not according to "the concept of the family", as is the custom in Germany. These three aspects of social activity are not of course to be taken as three different stages, but just as three aspects or, to make it clear to the Germans, three "moments", which have existed simultaneously since the dawn of history and the first men, and which still assert themselves in history today.

The production of life, both of one's own labour and of fresh life in procreation, now appears as a double relationship; on the one hand as a natural, on the other as a social relationship. By social we understand the co-operation of several individuals, no matter under what conditions, in what manner and to what end. It follows from this that a certain mode of production, or industrial stage, is always combined with a certain mode of co-operation, or social stage, and this mode of co-operation is itself a "productive force". Further, that the multitude of productive forces accessible to men determines the nature of society, hence, that the "history of humanity" must always be studied and treated in relation to the history of humanity and exchange. But it is also clear how in Germany it is impossible to write this sort of history, because the Germans lack not only the necessary power of comprehension and the material but also the "evidence of their senses", for across the Rhine you cannot have any experience of these things since history has stopped happening. Thus it is quite obvious from the start that there exists a materialistic connection of men with one another, which is determined by their needs and their mode of production, and which is as old as men

themselves. This connection is ever taking on new forms, and thus presents a "history" independently of the existence of any political or religious nonsense which in addition may hold men together.

Only now, after having considered four moments, four aspects of the primary historical relationships, do we find that man also possesses "consciousness", but, even so, not inherent, not "pure" consciousness. From the start the "spirit" is afflicted with the curse of being "burdened" with matter, which here makes its appearance in the form of agitated layers of air, sounds, in short, of language. Language is as old as consciousness, language *is* practical consciousness that exists also for other men, and for that reason alone it really exists for me personally as well; language, like consciousness, only arises from the need, the necessity, of intercourse with other men. Where there exists a relationship, it exists for me: the animal does not enter into *"relations"* with anything, it does not enter into any relation at all. For the animal, its relation to others does not exist as a relation. Consciousness is, therefore, from the very beginning a social product, and remains so as long as men exist at all. Consciousness is at first, of course, merely consciousness concerning the *immediate* sensuous environment and consciousness of the limited connection with other persons and things outside the individual who is growing self-conscious. At the same time it is consciousness of nature, which first appears to men as a completely alien, all-powerful and unassailable force, with which men's relations are purely animal and by which they are overawed like beasts; it is thus a purely animal consciousness of nature (natural religion) just because nature is as yet hardly modified historically. (We see here immediately: this natural religion or this particular relation of men to nature is determined by the form of society and vice versa. Here, as everywhere, the identity of nature and man appears in such a way that the restricted relation of men to nature determines their restricted relation to one another, and their restricted relation to one another determines men's restricted relation to nature.) On the other hand, man's consciousness of the necessity of associating with the individuals around him is the beginning of the consciousness that he is living in society at all. This beginning is as animal as social life itself at this stage. It is mere herd-consciousness, and at this point man is only distinguished from sheep by the fact that with him consciousness takes the place of instinct or that his instinct is a conscious one. This sheep-like or tribal consciousness receives its further development and extension through increased productivity, the increase of needs, and, what is fundamental to both of these, the increase of population. With these there develops the division of labour, which was originally nothing but the division of labour in the sexual act, then that division of labour which develops spontaneously or "naturally" by virtue of natural predisposition (e.g. physical strength), needs, accidents, etc. etc. Division of labour only becomes truly such from the moment when a division of material and mental labour appears. (The first form of ideologists, *priests*, is concurrent.) From this moment onwards consciousness *can* really flatter itself that it is something other than consciousness of existing practice, that it *really* represents something without representing something real; from now on consciousness is in a position to emancipate itself from the world and to proceed to the formation of "pure" theory, theology, philosophy, ethics, etc. But even if this theory, theology, philosophy, ethics, etc. comes into contradiction with the existing relations, this can only occur because existing social relations have come into contradiction with existing forces of production; this, moreover, can also occur in a particular national sphere of relations through the appearance of the contradiction, not within the national orbit, but between this national consciousness and the practice of other nations, i.e. between the national and the general consciousness of a nation (as we see it now in Germany).

Moreover, it is quite immaterial what consciousness starts to do on its own: out of all such muck we get only the one inference that these three moments, the forces of production, the state of society, and consciousness, can and must come into contradiction with one another, because the *division of labour* implies the possibility, nay the fact that intellectual and material activity—enjoyment and labour, production and consumption—devolve on different

individuals, and that the only possibility of their not coming into contradiction lies in the negation in its turn of the division of labour. It is self-evident, moreover, that "spectres", "bonds", "the higher being", "concept", "scruple", are merely the idealistic, spiritual expression, the conception apparently of the isolated individual, the image of very empirical fetters and limitations, within which the mode of production of life and the form of intercourse coupled with it move.

## Private Property and Communism

With the division of labour, in which all these contradictions are implicit, and which in its turn is based on the natural division of labour in the family and the separation of society into individual families opposed to one another, is given simultaneously the *distribution*, and indeed the *unequal* distribution, both quantitative and qualitative, of labour and its products, hence property: the nucleus, the first form, of which lies in the family, where wife and children are the slaves of the husband. This latent slavery in the family, though still very crude, is the first property, but even at this early stage it corresponds perfectly to the definition of modern economists who call it the power of disposing of the labour-power of others. Division of labour and private property are, moreover, identical expressions: in the one the same thing is affirmed with reference to activity as is affirmed in the other with reference to the product of the activity.

Further, the division of labour implies the contradiction between the interest of the separate individual or the individual family and the communal interest of all individuals who have intercourse with one another. And indeed, this communal interest does not exist merely in the imagination, as the "general interest", but first of all in reality, as the mutual interdependence of the individuals among whom the labour is divided. And finally, the division of labour offers us the first example of how, as long as man remains in natural society, that is, as long as a cleavage exists between the particular and the common interest, as long, therefore, as activity is not voluntarily, but naturally, divided, man's own deed becomes an alien power opposed to him, which enslaves him instead of being controlled by him. For as soon as the distribution of labour comes into being, each man has a particular, exclusive sphere of activity, which is forced upon him and from which he cannot escape. He is a hunter, a fisherman, a shepherd, or a critical critic, and must remain so if he does not want to lose his means of livelihood; while in communist society, where nobody has one exclusive sphere of activity but each can become accomplished in any branch he wishes, society regulates the general production and thus makes it possible for me to do one thing today and another tomorrow, to hunt in the morning, fish in the afternoon, rear cattle in the evening, criticise after dinner, just as I have a mind, without ever becoming hunter, fisherman, shepherd or critic. This fixation of a social activity, this consolidation of what we ourselves produce into an objective power above us, growing out of our control, thwarting our expectations, bringing to naught our calculations, is one of the chief factors in historical development up till now.

(And out of this very contradiction between the interest of the individual and that of the community the latter takes an independent form as the *State*, divorced from the real interests of individual and community, and at the same time as an illusory communal life, always based, however, on the real ties existing in every family and tribal conglomeration—such as flesh and blood, language, division of labour on a larger scale, and other interests—and especially, as we shall enlarge upon later, on the classes, already determined by the division of labour, which in every such mass of men separate out, and of which one dominates all the others. It follows from this that all struggles within the State, the struggle between democracy, aristocracy, and monarchy, the struggle for the franchise, etc. etc. are merely the illusory forms in which the real struggles of the different classes are fought out among one another. Of this the German theoreticians have not the faintest inkling, although they have received a sufficient introduction to the subject in the *Deutsch-Französische Jahrbücher* and *Die heilige Familie*. Further, it follows that every class which is struggling for mastery, even

when its domination, as is the case with the proletariat, postulates the abolition of the old form of society in its entirety and of domination itself, must first conquer for itself political power in order to represent its interest in turn as the general interest, which immediately it is forced to do. Just because individuals seek *only* their particular interest, which for them does not coincide with their communal interest, the latter will be imposed on them as an interest "alien" to them, and "independent" of them, as in its turn a particular, peculiar "general" interest; or they themselves must remain within this discord, as in democracy. On the other hand, too, the *practical* struggle of these particular interests, which constantly *really* run counter to the communal and illusory communal interests, makes *practical* intervention and control necessary through the illusory "general" interest in the form of the State.)

The social power, i.e. the multiplied productive force, which arises through the cooperation of different individuals as it is determined by the division of labour, appears to these individuals, since their cooperation is not voluntary but has come about naturally, not as their own united power, but as an alien force existing outside them, of the origin and goal of which they are ignorant, which they thus cannot control, which on the contrary passes through a peculiar series of phases and stages independent of the will and the action of man, nay even being the prime governor of these.

How otherwise could for instance property have had a history at all, have taken on different forms, and landed property, for example, according to the different premises given, have proceeded in France from parcellation to centralisation in the hands of a few, in England from centralisation in the hands of a few to parcellation, as is actually the case today? Or how does it happen that trade, which after all is nothing more than the exchange of products of various individuals and countries, rules the whole world through the relation of supply and demand—a relation which, as an English economist says, hovers over the earth like the fate of the ancients, and with invisible hand allots fortune and misfortune to men, sets up empires and overthrows empires, causes nations to rise and to disappear—while with the abolition of the basis of private property, with the communistic regulation of production (and, implicit in this, the destruction of the alien relation between men and what they themselves produce), the power of the relation of supply and demand is dissolved into nothing, and men get exchange, production, the mode of their mutual relation, under their own control again?

In history up to the present it is certainly an empirical fact that separate individuals have, with the broadening of their activity into world-historical activity, become more and more enslaved under a power alien to them (a pressure which they have conceived of as a dirty trick on the part of the so-called universal spirit, etc.), a power which has become more and more enormous and, in the last instance, turns out to be the *world market*. But it is just as empirically established that, by the overthrow of the existing state of society by the communist revolution (of which more below) and the abolition of private property which is identical with it, this power, which so baffles the German theoreticians, will be dissolved; and that then the liberation of each single individual will be accomplished in the measure in which history becomes transformed into world history. From the above it is clear that the real intellectual wealth of the individual depends entirely on the wealth of his real connections. Only then will the separate individuals be liberated from the various national and local barriers, be brought into practical connection with the material and intellectual production of the whole world and be put in a position to acquire the capacity to enjoy this all-sided production of the whole earth (the creations of man). *All-round* dependence, this natural form of the *world-historical* co-operation of individuals, will be transformed by this communist revolution into the control and conscious mastery of these powers, which, born of the action of men on one another, have till now overawed and governed men as powers completely alien to them. Now this view can be expressed again in speculative-idealistic, i.e. fantastic, terms as "self-generation of the species" ("society as the subject"), and thereby the consecutive series of interrelated individuals connected with each other can be conceived as a single individual, which accomplishes the mystery of generating itself. It is clear here that individuals certainly make *one another*, physically and mentally, but do not make themselves.

This "alienation" (to use a term which will be comprehensible to the philosophers) can, of course, only be abolished given two *practical* premises. For it to become an "intolerable" power, i.e. a power against which men make a revolution, it must necessarily have rendered the great mass of humanity "propertyless", and produced, at the same time, the contradiction of an existing world of wealth and culture, both of which conditions presuppose a great increase in productive power, a high degree of its development. And, on the other hand, this development of productive forces (which itself implies the actual empirical existence of men in their *world-historical*, instead of local, being) is an absolutely necessary practical premise because without it *want* is merely made general, and with *destitution* the struggle for necessities and all the old filthy business would necessarily be produced; and furthermore, because only with this universal development of productive force is a *universal* intercourse between men established, which produces in all nations simultaneously the phenomenon of the "propertyless" mass (universal competition), makes each nation dependent on the revolutions of the others, and finally has put *world-historical*, empirically universal individuals in the place of local ones. Without this, (1) communism could only exist as a local event; (2) the *forces* of intercourse themselves could not have developed as *universal*, hence intolerable powers: they would have remained home-bred conditions surrounded by superstition; and (3) each extension of intercourse would abolish local communism. Empirically, communism is only possible as the act of the dominant peoples "all at once" and simultaneously, which presupposes the universal development of productive forces and the world intercourse bound up with communism. Moreover, the mass of *propertyless* workers—the utterly precarious position of labour-power on a mass scale cut off from capital or from even a limited satisfaction and, therefore, no longer merely temporarily deprived of work itself as a secure source of life—presupposes the *world market* through competition. The proletariat can thus only exist *world-historically*, just as communism, its activity, can only have a "world-historical" existence. World-historical existence of individuals means, existence of individuals which is directly linked up with world history.

Communism is for us not a *state of affairs* which is to be established, an *ideal* to which reality [will] have to adjust itself. We call communism the *real* movement which abolishes the present state of things. The conditions of this movement result from the premises now in existence. . . .

### Note

1. The building of houses. With savages each family has as a matter of course its own cave or hut like the separate family tent of the nomads. This separate domestic economy is made only the more necessary by the further development of private property. With the agricultural peoples a communal domestic economy is just as impossible as a communal cultivation of the soil. A great advance was the building of towns. In all previous periods, however, the abolition of individual economy, which is inseparable from the abolition of private property, was impossible for the simple reason that the material conditions governing it were not present. The setting-up of a communal domestic economy presupposes the development of machinery, of the use of natural forces and of many other productive forces—e.g. of water-supplies, of gas-lighting, steam-heating, etc., the removal [of the antagonism] of town and country. Without these conditions a communal economy would not in itself form a new productive force; lacking any material basis and resting on a purely theoretical foundation, it would be a mere freak and would end in nothing more than a monastic economy—What was possible can be seen in the towns brought about by condensation and the erection of communal buildings for various definite purposes (prisons, barracks, etc.). That the abolition of individual economy is inseparable from the abolition of the family is self-evident.

# Manifesto of the Communist Party

A specter is haunting Europe—the specter of communism. All the powers of old Europe have entered into a holy alliance to exorcise this specter: Pope and Czar, Metternich and Guizot, French radicals and German police spies.

Where is the party in opposition that has not been decried as communistic by its opponents in power? Where the opposition that has not hurled back the branding reproach of communism against the more advanced opposition parties, as well as against its reactionary adversaries?

Two things result from this fact:

I. Communism is already acknowledged by all European powers to be itself a power.

II. It is high time that communists should openly, in the face of the whole world, publish their views, their aims, their tendencies, and meet this nursery tale of the specter of communism with a Manifesto of the party itself.

To this end, communists of various nationalities have assembled in London and sketched the following Manifesto, to be published in the English, French, German, Italian, Flemish, and Danish languages.

## I. BOURGEOIS AND PROLETARIANS[1]

The history of all hitherto existing society[2] is the history of class struggles.

Free man and slave, patrician and plebeian, lord and serf, guild master[3] and journeyman, in a word, oppressor and oppressed, stood in constant opposition to one another, carried on an uninterrupted, now hidden, now open fight, a fight that each time ended either in a revolutionary reconstitution of society at large or in the common ruin of the contending classes.

In the earlier epochs of history we find almost everywhere a complicated arrangement of society into various orders, a manifold gradation of social rank. In ancient Rome we have patricians, knights, plebeians, slaves; in the Middle Ages, feudal lords, vassals, guild masters, journeymen, apprentices, serfs; in almost all of these classes, again, subordinate gradations.

The modern bourgeois society that has sprouted from the ruins of feudal society has not done away with class antagonisms. It has but established new classes, new conditions of oppression, new forms of struggle in place of the old ones.

Our epoch, the epoch of the bourgeoisie, possesses, however, this distinctive feature: it has simplified the class antagonisms. Society as a whole is more and more splitting up into two great hostile camps, into two great classes directly facing each other: bourgeoisie and proletariat.

From the serfs of the Middle Ages sprang the chartered burghers of the earliest towns. From these burgesses the first elements of the bourgeoisie were developed.

The discovery of America, the rounding of the Cape, opened up fresh ground for the rising bourgeoisie. The East Indian and Chinese markets, the colonization of America, trade with the colonies, the increase in the means of exchange and in commodities generally, gave to commerce, to navigation, to industry an impulse never before known, and thereby, to the revolutionary element in the tottering feudal society, a rapid development.

The feudal system of industry, under which industrial production was monopolized by closed guilds, now no longer sufficed for the growing wants of the new markets. The manufacturing system took its place. The guild masters were pushed on one side by the manufacturing middle class; division of labor between the different corporate guilds vanished in the face of division of labor in each single workshop.

Meantime the markets kept ever growing, the demand ever rising. Even manufacture no longer sufficed. Thereupon steam and machinery revolutionized industrial production. The place of manufacture was taken by the giant, modern industry, the place of the industrial middle class by industrial mil-

lionaires, the leaders of whole industrial armies, the modern bourgeois.

Modern industry has established the world market, for which the discovery of America paved the way. This market has given an immense development to commerce, to navigation, to communication by land. This development has, in its turn, reacted on the extension of industry; and in proportion as industry, commerce, navigation, railways extended, in the same proportion the bourgeoisie developed, increased its capital, and pushed into the background every class handed down from the Middle Ages.

We see, therefore, how the modern bourgeoisie is itself the product of a long course of development, of a series of revolutions in the modes of production and of exchange.

Each step in the development of the bourgeoisie was accompanied by a corresponding political advance of that class. An oppressed class under the sway of the feudal nobility, an armed and self-governing association in the medieval commune,[4] here independent urban republic (as in Italy and Germany), there taxable "third estate" of the monarchy (as in France), afterwards, in the period of manufacture proper, serving either the semi-feudal or the absolute monarchy as a counterpoise against the nobility, and, in fact, cornerstone of the great monarchies in general, the bourgeoisie has at last, since the establishment of modern industry and of the world market, conquered for itself, in the modern representative state, exclusive political sway. The executive of the modern state is but a committee for managing the common affairs of the whole bourgeoisie.

The bourgeoisie, historically, has played a most revolutionary part.

The bourgeoisie, wherever it has got the upper hand, has put an end to all feudal, patriarchal, idyllic relations. It has pitilessly torn asunder the motley feudal ties that bound man to his "natural superiors," and has left remaining no other nexus between man and man than naked self-interest, than callous "cash payment." It has drowned the most heavenly ecstasies of religious fervor, of chivalrous enthusiasm, of Philistine sentimentalism in the icy water of egotistical calculation. It has resolved personal worth into exchange value and, in place of the numberless indefeasible chartered free-doms, has set up that single, unconscionable freedom—free trade. In one word, for exploitation, veiled by religious and political illusions, it has substituted naked, shameless, direct, brutal exploitation.

The bourgeoisie has stripped of its halo every occupation hitherto honored and looked up to with reverent awe. It has converted the physician, the lawyer, the priest, the poet, the man of science into its paid wage laborers.

The bourgeoisie has torn away from the family its sentimental veil, and has reduced the family relation to a mere money relation.

The bourgeoisie has disclosed how it came to pass that the brutal display of vigor in the Middle Ages, which reactionists so much admire, found its fitting complement in the most slothful indolence. It has been the first to show what man's activity can bring about. It has accomplished wonders far surpassing Egyptian pyramids, Roman aqueducts, and Gothic cathedrals; it has conducted expeditions that put in the shade all former exoduses of nations and crusades.

The bourgeoisie cannot exist without constantly revolutionizing the instruments of production, and thereby the relations of production, and with them the whole relations of society. Conservation of the old modes of production in unaltered form was, on the contrary, the first condition of existence for all earlier industrial classes. Constant revolutionizing of production, uninterrupted disturbance of all social conditions, everlasting uncertainty and agitation distinguish the bourgeois epoch from all earlier ones. All fixed, fast-frozen relations, with their train of ancient and venerable prejudices and opinions, are swept away, all newformed ones become antiquated before they can ossify. All that is solid melts into air, all that is holy is profaned, and man is at last compelled to face with sober senses his real conditions of life and his relations with his kind.

The need of a constantly expanding market for its products chases the bourgeoisie over the whole surface of the globe. It must nestle everywhere, settle everywhere, establish connections everywhere.

The bourgeoisie has through its exploitation of the world market given a cosmopolitan character to production and consumption in every country. To the great chagrin of reactionists, it has drawn from under the feet of industry the national ground on which it stood. All old-established national industries have been destroyed or are daily being destroyed. They are dislodged by new industries, whose introduction becomes a life and death question for all civilized nations, by industries that no longer work up indigenous raw material, but raw material drawn from the remotest zones; industries whose products are consumed not only at home, but in every quarter of the globe. In place of the old wants, satisfied by the productions of the country, we find new wants, requiring for their satisfaction the products of distant lands and climes. In place of the old local and national seclusion and self-sufficiency we have intercourse in every direction, universal interdependence of nations. And as in material, so also in intellectual production. The intellectual creations of individual nations become common property. National one-sidedness and narrow-mindedness become more and more impossible, and from the numerous national and local literatures there arises a world literature.

The bourgeoisie, by the rapid improvement of all instruments of production, by the immensely facilitated means of communication, draws all, even the most barbarian, nations into civilization. The cheap prices of its commodities are the heavy artillery with which it batters down all Chinese walls, with which it forces the barbarians' intensely obstinate hatred of foreigners to capitulate. It compels all nations, on pain of extinction, to adopt the bourgeois mode of production; it compels them to introduce what it calls civilization into their midst, i.e., to become bourgeois themselves. In one word, it creates a world after its own image.

The bourgeoisie has subjected the country to the rule of the towns. It has created enormous cities, has greatly increased the urban population as compared with the rural, and has thus rescued a considerable part of the population from the idiocy of rural life. Just as it has made the country dependent on the towns, so it has made barbarian and semi-barbarian countries dependent on the civilized ones, nations of peasants on nations of bourgeois, the East on the West.

The bourgeoisie keeps more and more doing

away with the scattered state of the population, of the means of production, and of property. It has agglomerated population, centralized means of production, and has concentrated property in a few hands. The necessary consequence of this was political centralization. Independent, or but loosely connected provinces, with separate interests, laws, governments and systems of taxation, became lumped together into one nation, with one government, one code of laws, one national class interest, one frontier, and one customs tariff.

The bourgeoisie, during its rule of scarce one hundred years, has created more massive and more colossal productive forces than have all preceding generations together. Subjection of nature's forces to man, machinery, application of chemistry to industry and agriculture, steam navigation, railways, electric telegraphs, clearing of whole continents for cultivation, canalization of rivers, whole populations conjured out of the ground—what earlier century had even a presentiment that such productive forces slumbered in the lap of social labor?

We see then: the means of production and of exchange, on whose foundation the bourgeoisie built itself up, were generated in feudal society. At a certain stage in the development of these means of production and of exchange, the conditions under which feudal society produced and exchanged, the feudal organization of agriculture and manufacturing industry, in one word, the feudal relations of property, became no longer compatible with the already developed productive forces; they became so many fetters. They had to be burst asunder; they were burst asunder.

Into their place stepped free competition, accompanied by a social and political constitution adapted to it, and by the economic and political sway of the bourgeois class.

A similar movement is going on before our own eyes. Modern bourgeois society with its relations of production, of exchange, and of property, a society that has conjured up such gigantic means of production and of exchange, is like the sorcerer who is no longer able to control the powers of the nether world whom he has called up by his spells. For many a decade past, the history of industry and commerce is but the history of the revolt of modern productive forces

against modern conditions of production, against the property relations that are the conditions for the existence of the bourgeoisie and of its rule. It is enough to mention the commercial crises that by their periodic return put on its trial, each time more threatening, the existence of the entire bourgeois society. In these crises a great part not only of the existing products but also of the previously created productive forces are periodically destroyed. In these crises there breaks out an epidemic that in all earlier epochs would have seemed an absurdity—the epidemic of overproduction. Society suddenly finds itself put back into a state of momentary barbarism; it appears as if a famine, a universal war of devastation had cut off the supply of every means of subsistence; industry and commerce seem to be destroyed; and why? Because there is too much civilization, too much means of subsistence, too much industry, too much commerce. The productive forces at the disposal of society no longer tend to further the development of the conditions of bourgeois property; on the contrary, they have become too powerful for these conditions, by which they are fettered, and as soon as they overcome these fetters they bring disorder into the whole of bourgeois society, endanger the existence of bourgeois property. The conditions of bourgeois society are too narrow to comprise the wealth created by them. And how does the bourgeoisie get over these crises? On the one hand, by enforced destruction of a mass of productive forces; on the other, by the conquest of new markets, and by the more thorough exploitation of the old ones. That is to say, by paving the way of more extensive and more destructive crises, and by diminishing the means whereby crises are prevented.

The weapons with which the bourgeoisie felled feudalism to the ground are now turned against the bourgeoisie itself.

But not only has the bourgeoisie forged the weapons that bring death to itself; it has also called into existence the men who are to wield those weapons—the modern working class—the proletarians.

In proportion as the bourgeoisie, i.e., capital, is developed, in the same proportion is the proletariat, the modern working class, developed—a class of laborers, who live only so long as they find work, and who find work only so long as their labor increases capital. These laborers, who must sell them-selves piecemeal, are a commodity, like every other article of commerce, and are consequently exposed to all the vicissitudes of competition, to all the fluc-tuations of the market.

Owing to the extensive use of machinery and to division of labor, the work of the proletarians has lost all individual character and, consequently, all charm for the workman. He becomes an appendage of the machine, and it is only the simplest, most monoto-nous, and most easily acquired knack that is required of him. Hence the cost of production of a workman is restricted, almost entirely, to the means of subsis-tence that he requires for his maintenance and for the propagation of his race. But the price of a commodity, and therefore also of labor, is equal to its cost of pro-duction. In proportion, therefore, as the repulsiveness of the work increases, the wage decreases. Nay, more, in proportion as the use of machinery and divi-sion of labor increases, in the same proportion the burden of toil also increases, whether by prolonga-tion of the working hours, by increase of the work exacted in a given time, or by increased speed of the machinery, etc.

Modern industry has converted the little work-shop of the patriarchal master into the great factory of the industrial capitalist. Masses of laborers, crowded into the factory, are organized like soldiers. As pri-vates of the industrial army they are placed under the command of a perfect hierarchy of officers and ser-geants. Not only are they slaves of the bourgeois class, and of the bourgeois state; they are daily and hourly enslaved by the machine, by the overlooker, and, above all, by the individual bourgeois manufac-turer himself. The more openly this despotism pro-claims gain to be its end and aim, the more petty, the more hateful, and the more embittering it is.

The less the skill and exertion of strength implied in manual labor, in other words, the more modern industry becomes developed, the more is the labor of men superseded by that of women. Differences of age and sex have no longer any distinctive social validity for the working class. All are instruments of labor, more or less expensive to use, according to their age and sex.

No sooner is the exploitation of the laborer by the manufacturer over, to the extent that he receives his wages in cash, than he is set upon by the other por-tions of the bourgeoisie, the landlord, the shop-keeper, the pawnbroker, etc.

The lower strata of the middle class—the small tradespeople, shopkeepers, and retired tradesman generally, the handicraftsmen and peasants—all these sink gradually into the proletariat, partly be-cause their diminutive capital does not suffice for the scale on which modern industry is carried on, and is swamped in the competition with the large capitalists, partly because their specialized skill is rendered worthless by new methods of production. Thus the proletariat is recruited from all classes of the population.

The proletariat goes through various stages of development. With its birth begins its struggle with the bourgeoisie. At first the contest is carried on by individual laborers, then by the workpeople of a fac-tory, then by the operatives of one trade, in one local-ity, against the individual bourgeois who directly exploits them. They direct their attacks not against the bourgeois conditions of production, but against the instruments of production themselves; they destroy imported wares that compete with their labor, they smash to pieces machinery, they set factories ablaze, they seek to restore by force the vanished status of the workman of the Middle Ages.

At this stage the laborers still form an incoherent mass scattered over the whole country, and broken up by their mutual competition. If anywhere they unite to form more compact bodies, this is not yet the con-sequence of their own active union, but of the union of the bourgeoise, which class, in order to attain its own political ends, is compelled to set the whole pro-letariat in motion, and is moreover yet, for a time, able to do so. At this stage, therefore, the proletarians do not fight their enemies, but the enemies of their enemies, the remnants of absolute monarchy, the landowners, the non-industrial bourgeois, the petty bourgeoisie. Thus the whole historical movement is concentrated in the hands of the bourgeoisie; every victory so obtained is a victory for the bourgeoisie.

But with the development of industry the proletariat not only increases in number; it becomes concentrated in greater masses, its strength grows, and it feels that strength more. The various interests and conditions of life within the ranks of the proletariat are more and more equalized, in proportion as machinery obliterates all distinctions of labor and nearly everywhere reduces wages to the same low level. The growing competition among the bourgeois and the resulting commercial crises make the wages of the workers ever more fluctuating. The unceasing improvement of machinery, ever more rapidly developing, makes their livelihood more and more precarious; the collisions between individual workmen and individual bourgeois take more and more the character of collisions between two classes. Thereupon the workers begin to form combinations (trade unions) against the bourgeois; they club together in order to keep up the rate of wages; they found permanent associations in order to make provision beforehand for these occasional revolts. Here and there the contest breaks out into riots.

Now and then the workers are victorious, but only for a time. The real fruit of their battles lies not in the immediate result, but in the ever expanding union of the workers. This union is helped on by the improved means of communication that are created by modern industry and that place the workers of different localities in contact with one another. It was just this contact that was needed to centralize the numerous local struggles, all of the same character, into one national struggle between classes. But every class struggle is a political struggle. And that union, to attain which the burghers of the Middle Ages, with their miserable highways, required centuries, the modern proletarians, thanks to railways, achieve in a few years.

This organization of the proletarians into a class, and consequently into a political party, is continually being upset again by the competition between the workers themselves. But it ever rises up again, stronger, firmer, mightier. It compels legislative recognition of particular interests of the workers by taking advantage of the divisions among the bourgeoisie itself. Thus the ten-hour bill in England was carried.

Altogether collisions between the classes of the old society further, in many ways, the course of development of the proletariat. The bourgeoisie finds itself involved in a constant battle. At first with the aristocracy, later on with those portions of the bourgeoisie itself whose interests have become antagonistic to the progress of industry; at all times, with the bourgeoisie of foreign countries. In all these battles it sees itself compelled to appeal to the proletariat, to ask for is help, and thus to drag it into the political arena. The bourgeoisie itself, therefore, supplies the proletariat with its own elements of political and general education: in other words, it furnishes the proletariat with weapons for fighting the bourgeoisie.

Further, as we have already seen, entire sections of the ruling classes are, by the advance of industry, precipitated into the proletariat, or are at least threatened in their conditions of existence. These also supply the proletariat with fresh elements of enlightenment and progress.

Finally, in times when the class struggle nears the decisive hour, the process of dissolution going on within the ruling class, in fact within the whole range of old society, assumes such a violent, glaring character that a small section of the ruling class cuts itself adrift and joins the revolutionary class, the class that holds the future in its hands. Just as, therefore, at an earlier period, a section of the nobility went over to the bourgeoisie, so now a portion of the bourgeoisie goes over to the proletariat, and in particular a portion of the bourgeois ideologists, who have raised themselves to the level of comprehending theoretically the historical movement as a whole.

Of all the classes that stand face to face with the bourgeoisie today, the proletariat alone is a really revolutionary class. The other classes decay and finally disappear in the face of modern industry; the proletariat is its special and essential product.

The lower-middle class, the small manufacturer, the shopkeeper, the artisan, the peasant, all these fight against the bourgeoisie, to save from extinction their existence as fractions of the middle class. They are therefore not revolutionary, but conservative. Nay, more, they are reactionary, for they try to roll back the wheel of history. If by chance they are revolutionary they are so only in view of their impending transfer into the proletariat; they thus defend not their present but their future interests, they desert their own standpoint to place themselves at that of the proletariat.

The "dangerous class," the social scum, that passively rotting mass thrown off by the lowest layers of old society, may, here and there, be swept into the movement by a proletarian revolution; its conditions of life, however, prepare it far more for the part of a bribed tool of reactionary intrigue.

In the conditions of the proletariat those of old society at large are already virtually swamped. The proletarian is without property; his relation to his wife and children has no longer anything in common with the bourgeois family relations; modern industrial labor, modern subjection to capital, the same in England as in France, in America as in Germany, has stripped him of every trace of national character. Law, morality, religion are to him so many bourgeois prejudices, behind which lurk in ambush just as many bourgeois interests.

All the preceding classes that got the upper hand sought to *fortify* their already acquired status by subjecting society at large to their conditions of appropriation. The proletarians cannot become masters of the productive forces of society, except by abolishing their own previous mode of appropriation, and thereby also every other previous mode of appropriation. They have nothing of their own to secure and to fortify; their mission is to destroy all previous securities for, and insurances of, individual property.

All previous historical movements were movements of minorities, or in the interest of minorities. The proletarian movement is the self-conscious, independent movement of the immense majority, in the interests of the immense majority. The proletariat, the lowest stratum of our present society, cannot stir, cannot raise itself up, without the whole superincumbent strata of official society being sprung into the air.

Though not in substance, yet in form, the struggle of the proletariat with the bourgeoisie is at first a national struggle. The proletariat of each country must, of course, first of all settle matters with its own bourgeoisie.

In depicting the most general phases of the development of the proletariat, we traced the more or less veiled civil war, raging within existing society, up to the point where that war breaks out into open revolution, and where the violent overthrow of the bourgeoisie lays the foundation for the sway of the proletariat.

Hitherto every form of society has been based, as we have already seen, on the antagonism of oppressing and oppressed classes. But in order to oppress a class certain conditions must be assured to it under which it can, at least, continue its slavish existence. The serf, in the period of serfdom, raised himself to membership in the commune just as the petty bourgeois, under the yoke of feudal absolutism, managed to develop into a bourgeois. The modern laborer, on the contrary, instead of rising with the progress of industry, sinks deeper and deeper below the conditions of existence of his own class. He becomes a pauper, and pauperism develops more rapidly than population and wealth. And here it becomes evident that the bourgeoisie is unfit any longer to be the ruling class in society, and to impose its conditions of existence upon society as an overriding law. It is unfit to rule because it is incompetent to assure an existence to its slave within his slavery, because it cannot help letting him sink into such a state that it has to feed him instead of being fed by him. Society can no longer live under this bourgeoisie: in other words, its existence is no longer compatible with society.

The essential condition for the existence, and for the sway of the bourgeois class, is the formation and augmentation of capital; the condition for capital is wage labor. Wage labor rests exclusively on competition between the laborers. The advance of industry, whose involuntary promoter is the bourgeoisie, replaces the isolation of the laborers, due to competition, by their revolutionary combination, due to association. The development of modern industry, therefore, cuts from under its feet the very foundation on which the bourgeoisie produces and appropriates products. What the bourgeoisie, therefore, produces, above all, is its own gravediggers. Its fall and the victory of the proletariat are equally inevitable.

## II. PROLETARIANS AND COMMUNISTS

In what relation do the communists stand to the proletarians as a whole?

The communists do not form a separate party opposed to other working-class parties.

They have no interests separate and apart from those of the proletariat as a whole.

They do not set up any sectarian principles of their own, by which to shape and mold the proletarian movement.

The communists are distinguished from the other working-class parties by this only: 1. In the national struggles of the proletarians of the different countries they point out and bring to the front the common interests of the entire proletariat, independent of all nationality. 2. In the various stages of development which the struggle of the working class against the bourgeoisie has to pass through, they always and everywhere represent the interests of the movement as a whole.

The communists, therefore, are on the one hand, practically, the most advanced and resolute section of the working-class parties of every country, that section which pushes forward all others; on the other hand, theoretically, they have over the great mass of the proletariat the advantage of clearly understanding the line of march, the conditions, and the ultimate general results of the proletarian movement.

The immediate aim of the communists is the same as that of all the other proletarian parties: formation of the proletariat into a class, overthrow of the bourgeois supremacy, conquest of political power by the proletariat.

The theoretical conclusions of the communists are in no way based on ideas or principles that have been invented, or discovered, by this or that would-be universal reformer.

They merely express, in general terms, actual relations springing from an existing class struggle, from a historical movement going on under our very eyes. The abolition of existing property relations is not at all a distinctive feature of communism.

All property relations in the past have continually been subject to historical change consequent upon the change in historical conditions.

The French Revolution, for example, abolished feudal property in favor of bourgeois property.

The distinguishing feature of communism is not the abolition of property generally, but the abolition of bourgeois property. But modern bourgeois private property is the final and most complete expression of the system of producing and appropriating products that is based on antagonisms, on the exploitation of the many by the few.

In this sense the theory of the communists may be summed up in the single sentence: Abolition of private property.

We communists have been reproached with the desire of abolishing the right of personally acquiring property as the fruit of a man's own labor, which property is alleged to be the groundwork of all personal freedom, activity, and dependence.

Hard-won, self-acquired, self-earned property! Do you mean the property of the petty artisan and of the small peasant, a form of property that preceded the bourgeois form? There is no need to abolish that; the development of industry has to a great extent already destroyed it and is still destroying it daily.

Or do you mean modern bourgeois private property?

But does wage labor create any property for the laborer? Not a bit. It creates capital, i.e., that kind of property which exploits wage labor, and which cannot increase except upon condition of begetting a new supply of wage labor for fresh exploitation. Property, in its present form, is based on the antagonism of capital and wage labor. Let us examine both sides of this antagonism.

To be a capitalist is to have not only a purely personal but a social *status* in production. Capital is a collective product, and only by the united action of many members, nay, in the last resort only by the united action of all members of society, can it be set in motion.

Capital is, therefore, not a personal, it is a social power.

When, therefore, capital is converted into common property, into the property of all members of society, personal property is not thereby transformed into social property. It is only the social character of the property that is changed. It loses its class character.

Let us now take wage labor.

The average price of wage labor is the minimum wage, i.e., that quantum of the means of subsistence which is absolutely requisite to keep the laborer in bare existence as a laborer. What, therefore, the wage laborer appropriates by means of his labor merely suffices to prolong and reproduce a bare existence. We by no means intend to abolish this personal appropriation of the products of labor, an appropriation that is made for the maintenance and reproduction of human life, and that leaves no surplus wherewith to command the labor of others. All that we want to do away with is the miserable character of this appropriation, under which the laborer lives merely to increase capital, and is allowed to live only in so far as the interest of the ruling class requires it.

In bourgeois society living labor is but a means to increase accumulated labor. In communist society accumulated labor is but a means to widen, to enrich, to promote the existence of the laborer.

In bourgeois society, therefore, the past dominates the present; in communist society the present dominates the past. In bourgeois society capital is independent and has individuality, while the living person is dependent and has no individuality.

And the abolition of this state of things is called by the bourgeois abolition of individuality and freedom! And rightly so. The abolition of bourgeois individuality, bourgeois independence, and bourgeois freedom is undoubtedly aimed at.

By freedom is meant, under the present bourgeois conditions of production, free trade, free selling and buying.

But if selling and buying disappear, free selling and buying disappear also. This talk about free selling and buying, and all the other "brave words" of our bourgeoisie about freedom in general, have a meaning, if any, only in contrast with restricted selling and buying, with the fettered traders of the Middle Ages, but have no meaning when opposed to the communistic abolition of buying and selling, of the bourgeois conditions of production, and of the bourgeoisie itself.

You are horrified at our intending to do away with private property. But in your existing society private property is already done away with for nine tenths of the population; its existence for the few is solely due to its nonexistence in the hands of those nine tenths. You reproach us, therefore, with intending to do away with a form of property the necessary condition for whose existence is the non-existence of any property for the immense majority of society.

In one word, you reproach us with intending to do away with your property. Precisely so; that is just what we intend.

From the moment when labor can no longer be converted into capital, money, or rent, into a social power capable of being monopolized, i.e., from the moment when individual property can no longer be transformed into bourgeois property, into capital, from that moment, you say, individuality vanishes.

You must, therefore, confess that by "individual" you mean no other person than the bourgeois, than the middle-class owner of property. This person must, indeed, be swept out of the way and made impossible.

Communism deprives no man of the power to appropriate the products of society; all that it does is to deprive him of the power to subjugate the labor of others by means of such appropriation.

It has been objected that upon the abolition of private property all work will cease and universal laziness will overtake us.

According to this, bourgeois society ought long ago have gone to the dogs through sheer idleness, for those of its members who work acquire nothing and those who acquire anything do not work. The whole of this objection is but another expression of the tautology that there can no longer be any wage labor when there is no longer any capital.

All objections urged against the communistic mode of producing and appropriating material products have, in the same way, been urged against the communistic modes of producing and appropriating intellectual products. Just as, to the bourgeois, the disappearance of class property is the disappearance of production itself, so the disappearance of class culture is to him identical with the disappearance of all culture.

That culture, the loss of which he laments, is, for the enormous majority, a mere training to act as a machine.

But don't wrangle with us so long as you apply, to our intended abolition of bourgeois property, the standard of your bourgeois notions of freedom, culture, law, etc. Your very ideas are but the outgrowth of the conditions of your bourgeois production and bourgeois property, just as your jurisprudence is but the will of your class made into a law for all, a well whose essential character and direction are determined by the economic conditions of existence of your class.

The selfish misconception that induces you to transform into eternal laws of nature and of reason the social forms springing from your present mode of production and form of property—historical relations that rise and disappear in the progress of production—this misconception you share with every ruling class that has preceded you. What you see clearly in the case of ancient property, what you admit in the case of feudal property you are of course forbidden to admit in the case of your own bourgeois form of property.

Abolition of the family! Even the most radical flare up at this infamous proposal of the communists.

On what foundation is the present family, the bourgeois family, based? On capital, on private gain. In its completely developed form this family exists only among the bourgeoisie. But this state of things finds its complement in the practical absence of the family among the proletarians, and in public prostitution.

The bourgeois family will vanish as a matter of course when its complement vanishes, and both will vanish with the vanishing of capital.

Do you charge us with wanting to stop the exploitation of children by their parents? To this crime we plead guilty.

But, you will say, we destroy the most hallowed of relations when we replace home education by social.

And your education! Is not that also social, and determined by the social conditions under which you educate, by the intervention, direct or indirect, of society, by means of schools, etc.? The communists have not invented the intervention of society in education; they do but seek to alter the character of that intervention, and to rescue education from the influence of the ruling class.

The bourgeois claptrap about the family and education, about the hallowed co-relation of parent and child, becomes all the more disgusting, the more, by the action of modern industry, all family ties among the proletarians are torn asunder and their children transformed into simple articles of commerce and instruments of labor.

"But you communists would introduce community of women," screams the whole bourgeoisie in chorus.

The bourgeois sees in his wife a mere instrument of production. He hears that the instruments of production are to be exploited in common and, naturally, can come to no other conclusion than that the lot of being common to all will likewise fall to the women.

He has not even a suspicion that the real point aimed at is to do away with the status of women as mere instruments of production.

For the rest, nothing is more ridiculous than the virtuous indignation of our bourgeois at the community of women which, they pretend, is to be openly and officially established by the communists. The communists have no need to introduce community of women; it has existed almost from time immemorial.

Our bourgeois, not content with having the wives and daughters of their proletarians at their disposal, not to speak of common prostitutes, take the greatest pleasure in seducing each other's wives.

Bourgeois marriage is in reality a system of wives in common and thus, at the most, what the communists might possibly be reproached with is that they desire to introduce, in substitution for a hypocritically concealed, an openly legalized community of women. For the rest, it is self-evident that the abolition of the present system of production must bring with it the abolition of the community of women springing from that system, i.e., of prostitution, both public and private.

The communists are further reproached with desiring to abolish countries and nationality.

The workingmen have no country. We cannot take from them what they have not got. Since the proletariat must first of all acquire political supremacy, must rise to be the leading class of the nation, must constitute itself *the* nation, it is, so far, itself national, though not in the bourgeois sense of the word.

National differences and antagonisms between peoples are daily more and more vanishing, owing to the development of the bourgeoisie, to freedom of commerce, to the world market, to uniformity in the mode of production and in the conditions of life corresponding thereto.

The supremacy of the proletariat will cause them to vanish still faster. United action, of the leading civilized countries at least, is one of the first conditions for the emancipation of the proletariat.

In proportion as the exploitation of one individual by another is put to an end, the exploitation of one nation by another will also be put to an end. In proportion as the antagonism between classes within the nation vanishes, the hostility of one nation to another will come to an end.

The charges against communism made from a religious, a philosophical, and, generally, from an ideological standpoint are not deserving of serious examination.

Does it require deep intuition to comprehend that man's ideas, views, and conceptions, in one word, man's consciousness, change with every change in the conditions of his material existence, in his social relations, and in his social life?

What else does the history of ideas prove than that intellectual production changes its character in proportion as material production is changed? The ruling ideas of each age have ever been the ideas of its ruling class.

When people speak of ideas that revolutionize society they do but express the fact that within the old society the elements of a new one have been created, and that the dissolution of the old ideas keeps even pace with the dissolution of the old conditions of existence.

When the ancient world was in its last throes, the ancient religions were overcome by Christianity. When Christian ideas succumbed in the eighteenth century to rationalist ideas, feudal society fought its death battle with the then revolutionary bourgeoisie. The ideas of religious liberty and freedom of conscience merely gave expression to the sway of free competition within the domain of knowledge.

"Undoubtedly," it will be said, "religious, moral, philosophical, and juridical ideas have been modified in the course of historical development. But religion, morality, philosophy, political science, and law constantly survived this change.

There are, besides, eternal truths, such as freedom, justice, etc., that are common to all states of society. But communism abolishes eternal truths, it abolishes all religion, and all morality, instead of constituting them on a new basis; it therefore acts in contradiction to all past historical experience."

What does this accusation reduce itself to? The history of all past society has consisted in the development of class antagonisms, antagonisms that assumed different forms at different epochs.

But whatever form they may have taken, one fact is common to all past ages, viz., the exploitation of one part of society by the other. No wonder then that the social consciousness of past ages, despite all the multiplicity and variety it displays, moves within certain common forms, or general ideas, which cannot completely vanish except with the total disappearance of class antagonisms.

The communist revolution is the most radical rupture with traditional property relations; no wonder that its development involves the most radical rupture with traditional ideas.

But let us have done with the bourgeois objections to communism.

We have seen above that the first step in the revolution by the working class to raise the proletariat to the position of ruling class, to win the battle of democracy.

The proletariat will use its political supremacy to

wrest, by degrees, all capital from the bourgeoisie, to centralize all instruments of production in the hands of the state, i.e., of the proletariat organized as the ruling class, and to increase the total of productive forces as rapidly as possible.

Of course, in the beginning this cannot be effected except by means of despotic inroads on the rights of property and on the conditions of bourgeois production; by means of measures, therefore, which appear economically insufficient and untenable, but which, in the course of the movement, outstrip themselves, necessitate further inroads upon the old social order, and are unavoidable as a means of entirely revolutionizing the mode of production.

These measures will of course be different in different countries.

Nevertheless, in the most advanced countries the following will be pretty generally applicable:

1. Abolition of property in land and application of all rents of land to public purposes.
2. A heavy progressive or graduated income tax.
3. Abolition of all right of inheritance.
4. Confiscation of the property of all emigrants and rebels.
5. Centralization of credit in the hands of the state, by means of a national bank with state capital and an exclusive monopoly.
6. Centralization of the means of communication and transport in the hands of the state.
7. Extension of factories and instruments of production owned by the state; the bringing into cultivation of wastelands, and the improvement of the soil generally in accordance with a common plan.
8. Equal liability of all to labor. Establishment of industrial armies, especially for agriculture.
9. Combination of agriculture with manufacturing industries; gradual abolition of the distinction between town and country, by a more equable distribution of the population over the country.
10. Free education for all children in public schools. Abolition of children's factory labor

in its present form. Combination of education with industrial production, etc.

When, in the course of development, class distinctions have disappeared and all production has been concentrated in the hands of a vast association of the whole nation, the public power will lose its political character. Political power, properly so called, is merely the organized power of one class for oppressing another. If the proletariat during its contest with the bourgeoisie is compelled, by the force of circumstances, to organize itself as a class, if by means of a revolution, it makes itself the ruling class and, as such, sweeps away by force the old conditions of production, then it will, along with these conditions, have swept away the conditions for the existence of class antagonisms and of classes generally, and will thereby have abolished its own supremacy as a class.

In place of the old bourgeois society, with its classes and class antagonisms, we shall have an association in which the free development of each is the condition for the free development of all.

# III. SOCIALIST AND COMMUNIST LITERATURE

## 1. Reactionary Socialism

### a. Feudal Socialism

Owing to their historical position, it became the vocation of the aristocracies of France and England to write pamphlets against modern bourgeois society. In the French Revolution of July 1830, and in the English reform agitation, these aristocracies again succumbed to the hateful upstart. Thenceforth a serious political contest was altogether out of the question. A literary battle alone remained possible. But even in the domain of literature the old cries of the Restoration period[5] had become impossible.

In order to arouse sympathy, the aristocracy were obliged to lose sight, apparently, of their own interests, and to formulate their indictment against the bourgeoisie in the interest of the exploited working class alone. Thus the aristocracy took their revenge by singing lampoons on their new master, and whispering in his ears sinister prophecies of coming catastrophe.

In this way arose feudal socialism: half lamentation, half lampoon; half echo of the past, half menace of the future; at times, by its bitter, witty, and incisive criticism, striking the bourgeoisie to the very heart's core, but always ludicrous in its effect, through total incapacity to comprehend the march of modern history.

The aristocracy, in order to rally the people to them, waved the proletarian alms bag in front for a banner. But the people, as often as it joined them, saw on their hindquarters the old feudal coats of arms, and deserted with loud and irreverent laughter.

One section of the French Legitimists and "Young England" exhibited this spectacle.

In pointing out that their mode of exploitation was different from that of the bourgeoisie, the feudalists forget that they exploited under circumstances and conditions that were quite different and that are now antiquated. In showing that, under their rule, the modern proletariat never existed, they forget that the modern bourgeoisie is the necessary offspring of their own form of society.

For the rest, so little do they conceal the reactionary character of their criticism that their chief accusation against the bourgeoisie amounts to this, that under the bourgeois regime a class is being developed which is destined to cut up root and branch the old order of society.

What they upbraid the bourgeoisie with is not so much that it creates a proletariat as that it creates a *revolutionary* proletariat.

In political practice, therefore, they join in all coercive measures against the working class; and in ordinary life, despite their highfalutin phrases, they stoop to pick up the golden apples dropped from the tree of industry, and to barter truth, love, and honor for traffic in wool, beetroot sugar, and potato spirits.[6]

As the parson has ever gone hand in hand with the landlord, so has clerical socialism with feudal socialism.

Nothing is easier than to give Christian asceticism a socialist tinge. Has not Christianity declaimed against private property, against marriage, against the state? Has it not preached, in the place of these, charity and poverty, celibacy and mortification of the flesh, monastic life and Mother Church? Christian socialism is but the holy water with which the priest consecrates the heartburnings of the aristocrat.

### b. Petty-Bourgeois Socialism

The feudal aristocracy was not the only class that was ruined by the bourgeoisie, not the only class whose conditions of existence pined and perished in the atmosphere of modern bourgeoisie society. The medieval burgesses and the small peasant proprietors were the precursors of the modern bourgeoisie. In those countries which are but little developed, industrially and commercially, these two classes still vegetate side by side with the rising bourgeoisie.

In countries where modern civilization has become fully developed, a new class of petty bourgeois has been formed, fluctuating between proletariat and bourgeoisie and ever renewing itself as a supplementary part of bourgeois society. The individual members of this class, however, are being constantly hurled down into the proletariat by the action of competition, and as modern industry develops they even see the moment approaching when they will completely disappear as an independent section of modern society, to be replaced, in manufactures, agriculture, and commerce, by overlookers, bailiffs, and shopmen.

In countries like France, where the peasants constitute far more than half of the population, it was natural that writers who sided with the proletariat against the bourgeoisie should use, in their criticism of the bourgeois regime, the standard of the peasant and petty bourgeois, and from the standpoint of these intermediate classes should take up the cudgels for the working class. Thus arose petty–bourgeois socialism. Sismondi was the head of this school, not only in France but also in England.

This school of socialism dissected with great acuteness the contradictions in the conditions of modern production. It laid bare the hypocritical apologies of economists. It proved, incontrovertibly, the disastrous effects of machinery and division of labor, the concentration of capital and land in a few hands, overproduction and crises; it pointed out the inevitable ruin of the petty bourgeois and peasant, the misery of the proletariat, the anarchy in production, the crying inequalities in the distribution of wealth, the industrial war of extermination between nations, the dissolution of old moral bonds, of the old family relations, of the old nationalities.

In its positive aims, however, this form of socialism aspires either to restoring the old means of production and of exchange, and with them the old property relations and the old society, or to cramping the modern means of production and of exchange within the framework of the old property relations that have been, and were bound to be, exploded by those means. In either case it is both reactionary and utopian.

Its last words are: corporate guilds for manufacture; patriarchal relations in agriculture.

Ultimately, when stubborn historical facts had dispersed all intoxicating effects of self-deception, this form of socialism ended in a miserable fit of the blues.

### c. German, or "True," Socialism

The socialist and communist literature of France, a literature that originated under the pressure of a bourgeoisie in power, and that was the expression of the struggle against this power, was introduced into Germany at a time when the bourgeoisie in that country had just begun its contest with feudal absolutism.

German philosophers, would-be philosophers, and *beaux esprits* eagerly seized on this literature, only forgetting that when these writings immigrated from France into Germany, French social conditions had not immigrated along with them. In contact with German social conditions, this French literature lost all its immediate practiced significance, and assumed a purely literary aspect. Thus, to the German philosophers of the eighteenth century, the demands of the first French Revolution were nothing more than the demands of "practical reason" in general, and the utterance of the will of the revolutionary French bourgeoisie signified in their eyes the laws of pure will, of will as it was bound to be, of true human will generally.

The work of the German *literati* consisted solely in bringing the new French ideas into harmony with their ancient philosophical conscience, or rather, in annexing the French ideas without deserting their own philosophic point of view.

This annexation took place in the same way in which a foreign language is appropriated, namely, by translation.

It is well known how the monks wrote silly lives of Catholic saints *over* the manuscripts on which the classical works of ancient heathendom had been written. The German *literati* reversed this process with the profane French literature. They wrote their philosophical nonsense beneath the French original. For instance, beneath the French criticism of the economic functions of money they wrote *Alienation of Humanity* and beneath the French criticism of the bourgeois state they wrote, *Dethronement of the Category of the General*, and so forth.

The introduction of these philosophical phrases at the back of the French historical criticisms they dubbed, "philosophy of action," "true socialism," "German science of socialism," "philosophical foundation of socialism," and so on.

The French socialist and communist literature was thus completely emasculated. And since it ceased in the hands of the German to express the struggle of one class with the other he felt conscious of having overcome "French one-sidedness" and of representing not true requirements, but the requirements of truth; not the interests of the proletariat, but the interests of human nature, of man in general, who belongs to no class, has no reality, who exists only in the misty realm of philosophical fantasy.

This German socialism, which took its schoolboy task so seriously and solemnly, and extolled its poor stock-in-trade in such mountebank fashion, meanwhile gradually lost its pedantic innocence.

The fight of the German, and especially of the Prussian, bourgeoisie against feudal aristocracy and absolute monarchy, in other words, the liberal movement, became more earnest.

By this, the long-wished-for opportunity was

offered to "true" socialism of confronting the political movement with the socialist demands, of hurling the traditional anathemas against liberalism, against representative government, against bourgeois competition, bourgeois freedom of the press, bourgeois legislation, bourgeois liberty and equality, and of preaching to the masses that they had nothing to gain, and everything to lose, by this bourgeois movement. German socialism forgot, in the nick of time, that the French criticism, whose silly echo it was, presupposed the existence of modern bourgeois society, with its corresponding economic conditions of existence, and the political constitution adapted thereto, the very things whose attainment was the object of the pending struggle in Germany.

To the absolute governments, with their following of parsons, professors, country squires, and officials, it served as a welcome scarecrow against the threatening bourgeoisie.

It was a sweet finish after the bitter pills of floggings and bullets with which these same governments, just at that time, dosed the German working-class risings.

While this "true" socialism thus served the governments as a weapon for fighting the German bourgeoisie, it, at the same time, directly represented a reactionary interest, the interest of the German Philistines. In Germany the *petty-bourgeois* class, a relic of the sixteenth century, and since then constantly cropping up again under various forms, is the real social basis of the existing state of things.

To preserve this class is to preserve the existing state of things in Germany. The industrial and political supremacy of the bourgeoisie threatens it with certain destruction: on the one hand, from the concentration of capital; on the other, from the rise of a revolutionary proletariat. "True" socialism appeared to kill these two birds with one stone. It spread like an epidemic.

The robe of speculative cobwebs, embroidered with flowers of rhetoric, steeped in the dew of sickly sentiment, this transcendental robe in which the German socialists wrapped their sorry "eternal truths," all skin and bone, served to wonderfully increase the sale of their goods among such a public.

And on its part, German socialism recognized more and more its own calling as the bombastic representative of the petty-bourgeois Philistine.

It proclaimed the German nation to be the model nation and the German petty Philistine to be the typical man. To every villainous meanness of this model man it gave a hidden, higher, socialistic interpretation, the exact contrary of its real character. It went to the extreme length of directly opposing the "brutally destructive" tendency of communism, and of proclaiming its supreme and impartial contempt of all class struggles. With very few exceptions, all the so-called socialist and communist publications that now (1847) circulate in Germany belong to the domain of this foul and enervating literature.

## 2. Conservative, or Bourgeois, Socialism

A part of the bourgeoisie is desirous of redressing social grievances, in order to secure the continued existence of bourgeois society.

To this section belong economists, philanthropists, humanitarians, improvers of the condition of the working class, organizers of charity, members of societies for the prevention of cruelty to animals, temperance fanatics, hole-and-corner reformers of every imaginable kind. This form of socialism has, moreover, been worked out into complete systems.

We may cite Proudhon's *Philosophie de la Misère* [*Philosophy of Poverty*] as an example of this form.

The socialistic bourgeois want all the advantages of modern social conditions without the struggles and dangers necessarily resulting therefrom. They desire the existing state of society minus its revolutionary and disintegrating elements. They wish for a bourgeoisie without a proletariat. The bourgeoisie naturally conceives the world in which it is supreme to be the best; and bourgeois socialism develops this comfortable conception into various more or less complete systems. In requiring the proletariat to carry out such a system, and thereby to march straightway into the social New Jerusalem, it but requires in reality that the proletariat should remain within the bounds of existing society, but should cast away all its hateful ideas concerning the bourgeoisie.

A second and more practical, but less systematic,

form of this socialism sought to depreciate every revolutionary movement in the eyes of the working class, by showing that no mere political reform, but only a change in the material conditions of existence, in economic relations, could be of any advantage to them. By changes in the material conditions of existence, this form of socialism, however, by no means understands abolition of the bourgeois relations of production, an abolition that can be effected only by a revolution, but administrative reforms, based on the continued existence of these relations; reforms, therefore, that in no respect affect the relations between capital and labor, but, at the best, lessen the cost and simplify the administrative work of bourgeois government.

Bourgeois socialism attains adequate expression when, and only when, it becomes a mere figure of speech.

Free trade: for the benefit of the working class. Protective duties: for the benefit of the working class. Prison reform: for the benefit of the working class. This is the last word and the only seriously meant word of bourgeois socialism.

The socialism of the bourgeoisie simply consists of the assertion that the bourgeois are bourgeois—for the benefit of the working class.

## 3. Critical Utopian Socialism and Communism

We do not here refer to that literature which, in every great modern revolution, has always given voice to the demands of the proletariat, such as the writings of Babeuf and others.

The first direct attempts of the proletariat to attain its own ends, made in times of universal excitement when feudal society was being overthrown, these attempts necessarily failed, owing to the then undeveloped state of the proletariat, as well as to the absence of the economic conditions for its emancipation, conditions that had yet to be produced, and could be produced by the impending bourgeois epoch alone. The revolutionary literature that accompanied these first movements of the proletariat had necessarily a reactionary character. It inculcated universal asceticism and social leveling in its crudest form.

The socialist and communist systems properly so called, those of St. Simon, Fourier, Owen, and others, spring into existence in the early undeveloped period, described above, of the struggle between proletariat and bourgeoisie (see Section I, Bourgeois and Proletarians).

The founders of these systems see, indeed, the class antagonisms as well as the action of the decomposing elements in the prevailing form of society. But the proletariat, as yet in its infancy, offers to them the spectacle of a class without any historical initiative or any independent political movement.

Since the development of class antagonism keeps even pace with the development of industry, the economic situation, as they find it, does not as yet offer to them the material conditions for the emancipation of the proletariat. They therefore search after a new social science, after new social laws that are to create these conditions.

Historical action is to yield to their personal inventive action, historically created conditions of emancipation to fantastic ones, and the gradual, spontaneous class organization of the proletariat to an organization of society specially contrived by these inventors. Future history resolves itself, in their eyes, into the propaganda and the practical carrying out of their social plans.

In the formation of their plans they are conscious of caring chiefly for the interests of the working class as being the most suffering class. Only from the point of view of being the most suffering class does the proletariat exist for them.

The undeveloped state of the class struggle, as well as their own surroundings, causes socialists of this kind to consider themselves far superior to all class antagonisms. They want to improve the condition of every member of society, even that of the most favored. Hence they habitually appeal to society at large, without distinction of class; nay, by preference, to the ruling class. For how can people, when once they understand their system, fail to see in it the best possible plan of the best possible state of society?

Hence they reject all political, and especially all revolutionary, action; they wish to attain their ends by peaceful means, and endeavor, by small experiments, necessarily doomed to failure, and by the force of example, to pave the way for the new social gospel.

Such fantastic pictures of future society, painted at a time when the proletariat is still in a very undeveloped state and has but a fantastic conception of its own position, correspond with the first instinctive yearnings of that class for a general reconstruction of society.

But these socialist and communist publications contain also a critical element. They attack every principle of existing society. Hence they are full of the most valuable materials for the enlightenment of the working class. The practical measures proposed in them-such as the abolition of the distinction between town and country, of the family, of the carrying on of industries for the account of private individuals, and of the wage system, the proclamation of social harmony, the conversion of the functions of the state into a mere superintendence of production—all these proposals point solely to the disappearance of class antagonisms which were, at that time, only just cropping up, and which, in these publications, are recognized in their earliest, indistinct and undefined forms only. These proposals, therefore, are of a purely utopian character.

The significance of critical utopian socialism and communism bears an inverse relation to historical development. In proportion as the modern class struggle develops and takes definite shape, this fantastic standing apart from the contest, these fantastic attacks on it lose all practical value and all theoretical justification. Therefore, although the originators of these systems were, in many respects, revolutionary, their disciples have, in every case, formed mere reactionary sects. They hold fast by the original views of their masters, in opposition to the progressive historical development of the proletariat. They, therefore, endeavor, and that consistently, to deaden the class struggle and to reconcile the class antagonisms. They still dream of experimental realization of their social utopias, of founding isolated *"phalanstères,"* of establishing "home colonies," of setting up a "Little Icaria"[7] duodecimo editions of the New Jerusalem—and to

realize all these castles in the air they are compelled to appeal to the feelings and purses of the bourgeois. By degrees they sink into the category of the reactionary conservative socialists depicted above, differing from these only by more systematic pedantry, and by their fanatical and superstitious belief in the miraculous effects of their social science.

They, therefore, violently oppose all political action on the part of the working class; such action, according to them, can only result from blind unbelief in the new gospel.

The Owenites in England and the Fourierists in France, respectively, oppose the Chartists and the Réformistes.

## IV. POSITION OF THE COMMUNISTS IN RELATION TO THE VARIOUS EXISTING OPPOSITION PARTIES

Section II has made clear the relations of the communists to the existing working-class parties, such as the Chartists in England and the agrarian reformers in America.

The communists fight for the attainment of the immediate aims, for the enforcement of the momentary interests of the working class, but in the movement of the present they also represent and take care of the future of that movement. In France the communists ally themselves with the social democrats,[8] against the conservative and radical bourgeoisie, reserving, however, the right to take up a critical position in regard to phrases and illusions traditionally handed down from the Great Revolution.

In Switzerland they support the radicals, without losing sight of the fact that this party consists of antagonistic elements, partly of democratic socialists, in the French sense, partly of radical bourgeois.

In Poland they support the party that insists on an agrarian revolution as the prime condition for national emancipation, that party which fomented the insurrection of Cracow in 1846.

In Germany they fight with the bourgeoisie whenever it acts in a revolutionary way, against the absolute monarchy, the feudal squirearchy, and the petty bourgeoisie.

But they never cease, for a single instant, to instill into the working class the clearest possible recognition of the hostile antagonism between bourgeoisie and proletariat, in order that the German workers may straightway use, as so many weapons against the bourgeoisie, the social and political conditions that the bourgeoisie must necessarily introduce along with its supremacy, and in order that, after the fall of the reactionary classes in Germany, the fight against the bourgeoisie itself may immediately begin.

The communists turn their attention chiefly to Germany, because that country is on the eve of a bourgeois revolution that is bound to be carried out under more advanced conditions of European civilization, and with a much more developed proletariat, than that of England was in the seventeenth and of France in the eighteenth century, and because the bourgeois revolution in Germany will be but the prelude to an immediately following proletarian revolution.

In short, the communists everywhere support every revolutionary movement against the existing social and political order of things.

In all these movements they bring to the front, as the leading question in each, the property question, no matter what its degree of development at the time.

Finally, they labor everywhere for the union and agreement of the democratic parties of all countries.

The communists disdain to conceal their views and aims. They openly declare that their ends can be attained only by the forcible overthrow of all existing social conditions. Let the ruling classes tremble at a communistic revolution. The proletarians have nothing to lose but their chains. They have a world to win.

WORKING MEN OF ALL COUNTRIES, UNITE!

## Notes

1. By "bourgeoisie" is meant the class of modern capitalists, owners of the means of social production and employers of wage labor. By proletariat, the class of modern wage laborers who, having no means of production of their own, are reduced to selling their labor power in order to live.

2. That is, all *written* history. In 1847 the pre-history of society, the social organization existing previous to recorded history, was all but unknown. Since then Haxthausen discovered common ownership of land in Russia, Maurer proved it to be the social foundation from which all Teutonic races started in history, and by and by village communities were found to be, or to have been the primitive form of society everywhere from India to Ireland. The inner organization of this primitive communistic society was laid bare, in its typical form, by Morgan's crowning discovery of the true nature of the *gens* and its relation to the *tribe*. With the dissolution of these primeval communities society begins to be differentiated into separate and finally antagonistic classes. I have attempted to retrace this process of dissolution in *Der Ursprung der Familie des Privateigenthums und des Staats* [*The Origin of the Family, Private Property and the State*], second edition, Stuttgart, 1886.

3. Guild master, that is, a full member of a guild, a master within, not a head of a guild.

4. "Commune" was the name taken, in France, by the nascent towns even before they had conquered from their feudal lords and masters local self-government and political rights as the "third estate." Generally speaking, for the economic development of the bourgeoisie, England is here taken as the typical country; for its political development, France.

5. Not the English Restoration, 1660 to 1689, but the French Restoration, 1814 to 1830.

6. This applies chiefly to Germany, where the landed aristocracy and squirearchy have large portions of their estates cultivated for their own account by stewards, and are, moreover extensive beetroot sugar manufacturers and distillers of potato spirits. The wealthier British aristocracy are, as yet, rather above that; but they, too, know how to make up for declining rents by lending their names to floaters of more or less shady joint-stock companies.

7. *Phalanstères* were socialist colonies on the plan of Charles Fourier; "Icaria" was the name given by Cabet to his utopia and, later on, to his American communist colony.

8. The party then represented in Parliament by Ledru-Rollin, in literature by Louis Blanc, in the daily press by the *Réforme*. The name of social democracy signified, with these its inventors, a section of the democratic or republican party more or less tinged with socialism.

# A Contribution to the Critique of Political Economy

## PREFACE

I examine the system of bourgeois economy in the following order: *capital, landed property, wage-labour; the State, foreign trade, world market*. The economic conditions of "existence of the three great classes into which modern bourgeois society is divided are analysed under the first three headings; the interconnection of the other three headings is self-evident. The first part of the first book, dealing with Capital, comprises the following chapters: 1. The commodity; 2. Money or simple circulation; 3. Capital in general. The present part consists of the first two chapters. The entire material lies before me in the form of monographs, which were written not for publication but for self-clarification at widely separated periods; their remoulding into an integrated whole according to the plan I have indicated will depend upon circumstances.

A general introduction, which I had drafted, is omitted, since on further consideration it seems to me confusing to anticipate results which still have to be substantiated, and the reader who really wishes to follow me will have to decide to advance from the particular to the general. A few brief remarks regarding the course of my study of political economy may, however, be appropriate here.

Although I studied jurisprudence, I pursued it as a subject subordinated to philosophy and history. In the year 1842–43, as editor of the *Rheinische Zeitung,* I first found myself in the embarrassing position of having to discuss what is known as material interests. The deliberations of the Rhenish Landtag on forest thefts and the division of landed property; the official polemic started by Herr von Schaper, then Oberpräsi-dent of the Rhine Province, against the *Rheinische Zeitung* about the condition of the Moselle peasantry, and finally the debates on free trade and protective tariffs caused me in the first instance to turn my attention to economic questions. On the other hand, at that time when good intentions "to push forward" often took the place of factual knowledge, an echo of French socialism and communism, slightly tinged by philosophy, was noticeable in the *Rheinische Zeitung*. I objected to this dilettantism, but at the same time frankly admitted in a controversy with the *Allgemeine Augsburger Zeitung* that my previous studies did not allow me to express any opinion on the content of the French theories. When the publishers of the *Rheinische Zeitung* conceived the illusion that by a more compliant policy on the part of the paper it might be possible to secure the abrogation of the death sentence passed upon it, I eagerly grasped the opportunity to withdraw from the public stage to my study.

The first work which I undertook to dispel the doubts assailing me was a critical re-examination of the Hegelian philosophy of law; the introduction to this work being published in the *Deutsch-Französi-sche Jahrbücher* issued in Paris in 1844. My inquiry led me to the conclusion that neither legal relations nor political forms could be comprehended whether by themselves or on the basis of a so-called general development of the human mind, but that on the contrary they originate in the material conditions of life, the totality of which Hegel, following the example of English and French thinkers of the eighteenth century, embraces within the term "civil society"; that the anatomy of this civil society, however, has to be sought in political economy. The study of this, which I began in Paris, I continued in Brussels, where I moved

Translated by S. W. Ryazanskaya. Reprinted with permission of International Publishers.

owing to an expulsion order issued by M. Guizot. The general conclusion at which I arrived and which, once reached, became the guiding principle of my studies can be summarised as follows. In the social production of their existence, men inevitably enter into definite relations, which are independent of their will, namely relations of production appropriate to a given stage in the development of their material forces of production. The totality of these relations of production constitutes the economic structure of society, the real foundation, on which arises a legal and political superstructure and to which correspond definite forms of social consciousness. The mode of production of material life conditions the general process of social, political and intellectual life. It is not the consciousness of men that determines their existence, but their social existence that determines their consciousness. At a certain stage of development, the material productive forces of society come into conflict with the existing relations of production or—this merely expresses the same thing in legal terms—with the property relations within the framework of which they have operated hitherto. From forms of development of the productive forces these relations turn into their fetters. Then begins an era of social revolution. The changes in the economic foundation lead sooner or later to the transformation of the whole immense superstructure. In studying such transformations it is always necessary to distinguish between the material transformation of the economic conditions of production, which can be determined with the precision of natural science, and the legal, political, religious, artistic or philosophic—in short, ideological forms in which men become conscious of this conflict and fight it out. Just as one does not judge an individual by what he thinks about himself, so one cannot judge such a period of transformation by its consciousness, but, on the contrary, this consciousness must be explained from the contradictions of material life, from the conflict existing between the social forces of production and the relations of production. No social order is ever destroyed before all the productive forces for which it is sufficient have been developed, and new superior relations of production never replace older ones before the material conditions for their existence have

matured within the framework of the old society. Mankind thus inevitably sets itself only such tasks as it is able to solve, since closer examination will always show that the problem itself arises only when the material conditions for its solution are already present or at least in the course of formation. In broad outline, the Asiatic, ancient, feudal and modern bourgeois modes of production may be designated as epochs marking progress in the economic development of society. The bourgeois mode of production is the last antagonistic form of the social process of production—antagonistic not in the sense of individual antagonism but of an antagonism that emanates from the individuals' social conditions of existence—but the productive forces developing within bourgeois society create also the material conditions for a solution of this antagonism. The prehistory of human society accordingly closes with this social formation.

Frederick Engels, with whom I maintained a constant exchange of ideas by correspondence since the publication of his brilliant essay on the critique of economic categories (printed in the *Deutsch-Französische Jahrbücher*), arrived by another road (compare his *Lage der arbeitenden Klasse in England*) at the same result as I, and when in the spring of 1845 he too came to live in Brussels, we decided to set forth together our conception as opposed to the ideological one of German philosophy, in fact to settle accounts with our former philosophical conscience. The intention was carried out in the form of a critique of post-Hegelian philosophy. The manuscript, two large octavo volumes, had long ago reached the publishers in Westphalia when we were informed that owing to changed circumstances it could not be printed. We abandoned the manuscript to the gnawing criticism of the mice all the more willingly since we had achieved our main purpose—self-clarification. Of the scattered works in which at that time we presented one or another aspect of our views to the public, I shall mention only the *Manifesto of the Communist Party,* jointly written by Engels and myself, and a *Discours sur le libre échange,* which I myself published. The salient points of our conception were first outlined in an academic, although polemical, form in my *Misère de la philosophie* . . . , this book which was aimed at Proudhon appeared in 1847. The publication of an essay on *Wage-Labour* written in German in which I combined the lectures I had held on this subject at the German Workers' Association in Brussels, was interrupted by the February Revolution and my forcible removal from Belgium in consequence.

The publication of the *Neue Rheinische Zeitung* in 1848 and 1849 and subsequent events cut short my economic studies, which I could only resume in London in 1850. The enormous amount of material relating to the history of political economy assembled in the British Museum, the fact that London is a convenient vantage point for the observation of bourgeois society, and finally the new stage of development which this society seemed to have entered with the discovery of gold in California and Australia, induced me to start again from the very beginning and to work carefully through the new material. These studies led partly of their own accord to apparently quite remote subjects on which I had to spend a certain amount of time. But it was in particular the imperative necessity of earning my living which reduced the time at my disposal. My collaboration, continued now for eight years, with the *New York Tribune,* the leading Anglo-American newspaper, necessitated an excessive fragmentation of my studies, for I wrote only exceptionally newspaper correspondence in the strict sense. Since a considerable part of my contributions consisted of articles dealing with important economic events in Britain and on the Continent, I was compelled to become conversant with practical detail which, strictly speaking, lie outside the sphere of political economy.

This sketch of the course of my studies in the domain of political economy is intended merely to show that my views—no matter how they may be judged and how little they conform to the interested prejudices of the ruling classes—are the outcome of conscientious research carried on over many years. At the entrance to science, as at the entrance to hell, the demand must be made:

> *Qui si convien lasciare ogni sospetto*
> *Ogni viltà convien che qui sia morta.*

# Socialism: Utopian and Scientific

## I

Modern socialism is, in its essence, the direct product of the recognition, on the one hand, of the class antagonisms existing in the society of today between proprietors and non-proprietors, between capitalists and wage workers; on the other hand, of the anarchy existing in production. But in its theoretical form modern socialism originally appears ostensibly as a more logical extension of the principles laid down by the great French philosophers of the eighteenth century. Like every new theory, modern socialism had, at first, to connect itself with the intellectual stock-in-trade ready to its hand, however deeply its roots lay in material economic facts.

The great men, who in France prepared men's minds for the coming revolution, were themselves extreme revolutionists. They recognized no external authority of any kind whatever. Religion, natural science, society, political institutions—everything was subjected to the most unsparing criticism: everything must justify its existence before the judgment seat of reason or give up existence. Reason became the sole measure of everything. It was the time when, as Hegel says, the world stood upon its head[1]; first in the sense that the human head, and the principles arrived at by its thought, claimed to be the basis of all human action and association; but by and by, also, in the wider sense that the reality which was in contradiction to these principles had, in fact, to be turned

Translated by Edward Aveling.

upside down. Every form of society and government then existing, every old traditional notion was flung into the lumber room as irrational; the world had hitherto allowed itself to be led solely by prejudices; everything in the past deserved only pity and contempt. Now, for the first time, appeared the light of day, the kingdom of reason; henceforth superstition, injustice, privilege, oppression were to be superseded by eternal truth, eternal right, equality based on nature and the inalienable rights of man.

We know today that this kingdom of reason was nothing more than the idealized kingdom of the bourgeoisie; that this eternal right found its realization in bourgeois justice; that this equality reduced itself to bourgeois equality before the law; that bourgeois property was proclaimed as one of the essential rights of man; and that the government of reason, the *contrat social* of Rousseau, came into being, and only could come into being, as a democratic bourgeois republic. The great thinkers of the eighteenth century could, no more than their predecessors, go beyond the limits imposed upon them by their epoch.

But, side by side with the antagonism of the feudal nobility and the burghers, who claimed to represent all the rest of society, was the general antagonism of exploiters and exploited, of rich idlers and poor workers. It was this very circumstance that made it possible for the representatives of the bourgeoisie to put themselves forward as representing not one special class, but the whole of suffering humanity. Still further. From its origin the bourgeoisie was saddled with its antithesis: capitalists cannot exist without wage workers, and, in the same proportion as the medieval burgher of the guild developed into the modern bourgeois, the guild journeyman and the day laborer, outside the guilds, developed into the proletarian. And although, upon the whole, the bourgeoisie, in their struggle with the nobility, could claim to represent at the same time the interests of the different working classes of that period, yet in every great bourgeois movement there were independent outbursts of that class which was the forerunner, more or less developed, of the modern proletariat. For example, at the time of the German Reformation and the Peasants' War, the Anabaptists and Thomas

Münzer; in the great English Revolution, the Levelers; in the great French Revolution, Babeuf.

There were theoretical enunciations corresponding with these revolutionary uprisings of a class not yet developed: in the sixteenth and seventeenth centuries, utopian pictures of ideal social conditions; in the eighteenth, actual communistic theories (Morelly and Mably). The demand for equality was no longer limited to political rights; it was extended also to the social conditions of individuals. It was not simply class privileges that were to be abolished, but class distinctions themselves. A communism, ascetic, denouncing all the pleasures of life, Spartan, was the first form of the new teaching. Then came the three great Utopians: St. Simon, to whom the middle-class movement, side by side with the proletarian, still had a certain significance; Fourier; and Owen, who in the country where capitalist production was most developed, and under the influence of the antagonisms begotten of this, worked out his proposals for the removal of class distinction systematically and in direct relation to French materialism.

One thing is common to all three. Not one of them appears as a representative of the interests of that proletariat which historical development had, in the meantime, produced. Like the French philosophers, they to not claim to emancipate a particular class to begin with, but all humanity at once. Like them, they wish to bring in the kingdom of reason and eternal justice, but this kingdom, as they see it, is as far as heaven from earth from that of the French philosophers.

For, to our three social reformers, the bourgeois world, based upon the principles of these philosophers, is quite as irrational and unjust and, therefore, finds its way to the dust hole quite as readily as feudalism and all the earlier stages of society. If pure reason and justice have not hitherto ruled the world, this has been the case only because men have not rightly understood them. What was wanted was the individual man of genius, who has now arisen and who understands the truth. That he has now arisen, that the truth has now been clearly understood, is not an inevitable event, following of necessity in the chain of historical development, but a mere happy accident. He might just as well have been born five hundred years earlier, and might then have spared humanity five hundred years of error, strife, and suffering.

We saw how the French philosophers of the eighteenth century, the forerunners of the Revolution, appealed to reason as the sole judge of all that is. A rational government, rational society were to be founded; everything that ran counter to eternal reason was to be remorselessly done away with. We saw also that this eternal reason was in reality nothing but the idealized understanding of the eighteenth-century citizen, just then evolving into the bourgeois. The French Revolution had realized this rational society and government.

But the new order of things, rational enough as compared with earlier conditions, turned out to be by no means absolutely rational. The state based upon reason completely collapsed. Rousseau's *contrat social* had found its realization in the Reign of Terror, from which the bourgeoisie, who had lost confidence in their own political capacity, had taken refuge first in the corruption of the Directorate, and, finally, under the wing of the Napoleonic despotism. The promised eternal peace was turned into an endless war of conquest. The society based upon reason had fared no better. The antagonism between rich and poor, instead of dissolving into general prosperity, had become intensified by the removal of the guild and other privileges, which had to some extent bridged it, and by the removal of the charitable institutions of the Church. The "freedom of property" from feudal fetters, now veritably accomplished, turned out to be, for the small capitalists and small proprietors, the freedom to sell their small property, crushed under the overmastering competition of the large capitalists and landlords, to these great lords, and thus, as far as the small capitalists and peasant proprietors were concerned, became "freedom *from* property." The development of industry upon a capitalistic basis made poverty and misery of the working masses conditions of existence of society. Cash payment became more and more, in Carlyle's phrase, "the sole nexus between man and man." The number of crimes increased from year to year. Formerly the feudal vices had openly stalked about in broad day-

light; though not eradicated, they were now at any rate thrust into the background. In their stead the bourgeois vices, hitherto practiced in secret, began to blossom all the more luxuriantly. Trade became to a greater and greater extent cheating. The "fraternity" of the revolutionary motto was realized in the chicanery and rivalries of the battle of competition. Oppression by force was replaced by corruption; the sword, as the first social lever, by gold. The right of the first night was transferred from the feudal lords to the bourgeois manufacturers. Prostitution increased to an extent never heard of. Marriage itself remained, as before, the legally recognized form, the official cloak of prostitution, and, moreover, was supplemented by rich crops of adultery.

In a word, compared with the splendid promises of the philosophers, the social and political institutions born of the "triumph of reason" were bitterly disappointing caricatures. All that was wanting was the men to formulate this disappointment, and they came with the turn of the century. In 1802, St. Simon's Geneva letters appeared; in 1808 appeared Fourier's first work, although the ground work of his theory dated from 1799; on January 1, 1800, Robert Owen undertook the direction of New Lanark.

At this time, however, the capitalist mode of production, and with it the antagonism between the bourgeoisie and the proletariat, was still very incompletely developed. Modern industry, which had just arisen in England, was still unknown in France. But modern industry develops, on the one hand, the conflicts which make absolutely necessary a revolution in the mode of production and the doing away with its capitalistic character—conflicts not only between the classes begotten of it, but also between the very productive forces and the forms of exchange created by it. And, on the other hand, it develops, in these very gigantic productive forces, the means of ending these conflicts. If, therefore, about the year 1800 the conflicts arising from the new social order were only just beginning to take shape, this holds still more fully as to the means of ending them. The "have-nothing" masses of Paris, during the Reign of Terror, were able for a moment to gain the mastery, and thus to lead the bourgeois revolution to victory in spite of the bourgeoisie themselves. But in doing so they only proved how impossible it was for their domination to last under the conditions then obtaining. The proletariat, which then for the first time evolved from these "have-nothing" masses as the nucleus of a new class, as yet quite incapable of independent political action, appeared as an oppressed, suffering order, to which, in its incapacity to help itself, help could, at best, be brought in from without or down from above.

This historical situation also dominated the founders of socialism. To the crude conditions of capitalistic production and the crude class conditions corresponded crude theories. The solution of the social problems, which as yet lay hidden in undeveloped economic conditions, the Utopians attempted to evolve out of the human brain. Society presented nothing but wrongs; to remove these was the task of reason. It was necessary, then, to discover a new and more perfect system of social order and to impose this upon society from without by propaganda, wherever it was possible, by the example of model experiments. These new social systems were foredoomed as utopian; the more completely they were worked out in detail, the more they could not avoid drifting off into pure fantasies.

These facts once established, we need not dwell a moment longer upon this side of the question, now wholly belonging to the past. We can leave it to the literary small fry to solemnly quibble over these fantasies, which today only make us smile, and to crow over the superiority of their own bald reasoning as compared with such "insanity." For ourselves, we delight in the stupendously grand thoughts and germs of thought that everywhere break out through their fantastic covering, and to which these Philistines are blind.

St. Simon was a son of the great French Revolution, at the outbreak of which he was not yet thirty. The Revolution was the victory of the third estate, i.e., of the great masses of the nation, *working* in production and in trade, over the privileged *idle* classes, the nobles and the priests. But the victory of the third estate soon revealed itself as exclusively the victory of a small part of this "estate," as the conquest of political power by the socially privileged section of it, i.e., the propertied bourgeoisie. And the bourgeoisie had certainly developed rapidly during the Revolution, partly by speculation in the lands of the nobility and of the Church, confiscated and afterwards put up for sale, and partly by frauds upon the nation by means of army contracts. It was the domination of these swindlers that, under the Directorate, brought France to the verge of ruin, and thus gave Napoleon the pretext for his *coup d'etat*.

Hence to St. Simon the antagonism between the third estate and the privileged classes took the form of an antagonism between "workers" and "idlers." The idlers were not merely the old privileged classes, but also all who, without taking any part in production or distribution, lived on their incomes. And the workers were not only the wage workers, but also the manufacturers, the merchants, the bankers. That the idlers had lost the capacity for intellectual leadership and political supremacy had been proved, and was by the Revolution finally settled. That the non-possessing classes had not this capacity seemed to St. Simon proved by the experiences of the Reign of Terror. Then who was to lead and command? According to St. Simon, science and industry, both united by a new religious bond, destined to restore that unity of religious ideas which had been lost since the time of the Reformation—a necessarily mystic and rigidly hierarchic "new Christianity." But science, that was the scholars; and industry, that was, in the first place, the working bourgeois, manufacturers, merchants, bankers. These bourgeois were certainly intended by St. Simon to transform themselves into a class of public officials, of social trustees; but they were still to hold, vis-a-vis the workers, a commanding and economically privileged position. The bankers especially were to be called upon to direct the whole of social production by the regulation of credit. This conception was in exact keeping with a time in which modern industry in France and, with it, the chasm between bourgeoisie and proletariat was only just coming into existence. But what St. Simon especially lays stress upon is this: what interests him first, and above all other things, is the lot of the class that is the most numerous and the poorest (*"la classe la plus nombreuse et la plus pauvre"*).

Already in his Geneva letters St. Simon lays down the proposition that "all men ought to work." In the same work he recognizes also that the Reign of Terror was the reign of the non-possessing masses. "See," says he to them, "what happened in France at the time when your comrades held sway there; they brought about a famine." But to recognize the French Revolution as a class war, and not simply one between nobility and bourgeoisie, but between nobility, bourgeoisie, and the non-possessors, was, in the year 1802, a most pregnant discovery. In 1816 he declares that politics is the science of production, and foretells the complete absorption of politics by economics. The knowledge that economic conditions are the basis of political institutions appears here only in embryo. Yet what is here already very plainly expressed is the idea of the future conversion of political rule over men into an administration of things and a direction of processes of production—that is to say, the "abolition of the state," about which recently there has been so much noise.

St. Simon shows the same superiority over his contemporaries, when in 1814, immediately after the entry of the allies into Paris, and again in 1815, during the Hundred Days' War, he proclaims the alliance of France with England, and then of both these countries with Germany, as the only guarantee for the prosperous development and peace of Europe. To preach to the French in 1815 an alliance with the victors of Waterloo required as much courage as historical foresight.

If in St. Simon we find a comprehensive breadth of view, by virtue of which almost all the ideas of later socialists that are not strictly economic are found in him in embryo, we find in Fourier a criticism of the existing conditions of society, genuinely French and witty, but not upon that account any the less thorough. Fourier takes the bourgeoisie, their inspired prophets before the Revolution, and their interested eulogists after it at their own word. He remorselessly lays bare the material and moral misery of the bourgeois world. He confronts it with the earlier philosophers' dazzling promises of a society in which reason alone should reign, of a civilization in which happiness should be universal, of an illimitable human perfectibility, and with the rose-colored phraseology of the bourgeois ideologists of his time. He points out how everywhere the most pitiful reality corresponds with the most high-sounding phrases, and he over-

whelms this hopeless fiasco of phrases with his mordant sarcasm.

Fourier is not only a critic; his imperturbably serene nature makes him a satirist, and assuredly one of the greatest satirists of all time. He depicts with equal power and charm the swindling speculations that blossomed out upon the downfall of the Revolution and the shopkeeping spirit prevalent in, and characteristic of, French commerce at that time. Still more masterly is his criticism of the bourgeois form of the relations between the sexes and the position of woman in bourgeois society. He was the first to declare that in any given society the degree of woman's emancipation is the natural measure of the general emancipation.

But Fourier is at his greatest in his conception of the history of society. He divides its whole course, thus far, into four stages of evolution—savagery, barbarism, the patriarchate, civilization. This last is identical with the so-called civil, or bourgeois, society of today—i.e., with the social order that came in with the sixteenth century. He proves "that the civilized stage raises every vice practiced by barbarism in a simple fashion into a form of existence, complex, ambiguous, equivocal, hypocritical"—that civilization moves in "a vicious circle," in contradictions which it constantly reproduces without being able to solve them; hence it constantly arrives at the very opposite to that which it wants to attain, or pretends to want to attain, so that, e.g., "under civilization poverty is born of superabundance itself."

Fourier, as we see, uses the dialectic method in the same masterly way as his contemporary, Hegel. Using these same dialectics, he argues against the talk about illimitable human perfectibility, that every historical phase has its period of ascent and also its period of descent, and he applies this observation to the future of the whole human race. As Kant introduced into natural science the idea of the ultimate destruction of the earth, Fourier introduced into historical science that of the ultimate destruction of the human race.

While in France the hurricane of the Revolution swept over the land, in England a quieter, but not on that account less tremendous, revolution was going on. Steam and the new tool-making machinery were transforming manufacture into modern industry, and thus revolutionizing the whole foundation of bourgeois society. The sluggish march of development of the manufacturing period changed into a veritable storm-and-stress period of production. With constantly increasing swiftness the splitting up of society into large capitalists and non-possessing proletarians went on. Between these, instead of the former stable middle class, an unstable mass of artisans and small shopkeepers, the most fluctuating portion of the population, now led a precarious existence.

The new mode of production was, as yet, only at the beginning of its period of ascent; as yet it was the normal, regular method of production—the only one possible under existing conditions. Nevertheless, even then it was producing crying social abuses— the herding together of a homeless population in the worst quarters of the large towns; the loosening of all traditional moral bonds, of patriarchal subordination, of family relations; overwork, especially of women and children, to a frightful extent; complete demoralization of the working class, suddenly flung into altogether new conditions, from the country into the town, from agriculture into modern industry, from stable conditions of existence into insecure ones that changed from day to day.

At this juncture there came forward as a reformer a manufacturer twenty-nine years old—a man of almost sublime, childlike simplicity of character, and at the same time one of the few born leaders of men. Robert Owen had adopted the teaching of the materialistic philosophers: that man's character is the product, on the one hand, of heredity; on the other, of the environment of the individual during his lifetime, and especially during his period of development. In the industrial revolution most of his class saw only chaos and confusion, and the opportunity of fishing in these troubled waters and making large fortunes quickly. He saw in it the opportunity of putting into practice his favorite theory, and so of bringing order out of chaos. He had already tried it with success, as superintendent of more than five hundred men in a Manchester factory. From 1800 to 1829 he directed the great cotton mill at New Lanark, in Scotland, as managing partner, along the same lines, but with greater freedom of action and with a success

that made him a European reputation. A population, originally consisting of the most diverse and, for the most part, very demoralized elements, a population that gradually grew to twenty-five hundred, he turned into a model colony, in which drunkenness, police, magistrates, lawsuits, poor laws, charity were unknown. And all this simply by placing the people in conditions worthy of human beings, and especially by carefully bringing up the rising generation. He was the founder of infant schools, and introduced them first at New Lanark. At the age of two the children came to school, where they enjoyed themselves so much that they could scarcely be got home again. While his competitors worked their people thirteen or fourteen hours a day, in New Lanark the working day was only ten and a half hours. When a crisis in cotton stopped work for four months, his workers received their full wages all the time. And with all this the business more than doubled in value, and to the last yielded large profits to its proprietors.

In spite of all this Owen was not content. The existence which he secured for his workers was, in his eyes, still far from being worthy of human beings. "The people were slaves at my mercy." The relatively favorable conditions in which he had placed them were still far from allowing a rational development of the character and of the intellect in all directions, much less of the free exercise of all their faculties. "And yet, the working part of this population of twenty-five hundred persons was daily producing as much real wealth for society as, less than half a century before, it would have required the working part of a population of six hundred thousand to create. I asked myself, what became of the difference between the wealth consumed by twenty-five hundred persons and that which would have been consumed by six hundred thousand?"[2]

The answer was clear. It had been used to pay the proprietors of the establishment 5 per cent on the capital they had laid out, in addition to over three hundred thousand pounds' clear profit. And that which held for New Lanark held to a still greater extent for all the factories in England. "If this new wealth had not been created by machinery, imperfectly as it has been applied, the wars of Europe, in opposition to Napoleon, and to support the aristocratic principles of society, could not have been maintained. And yet this new power was the creation of the working class."[3] To them, therefore, the fruits of this new power belonged. The newly created gigantic productive forces, hitherto used only to enrich individuals and to enslave the masses, offered to Owen the foundations for a reconstruction of society; they were destined, as the common property of all, to be worked for the common good of all.

Owen's communism was based upon this purely business foundation, the outcome, so to say, of commercial calculation. Throughout it maintained this practical character. Thus in 1823 Owen proposed the relief of the distress in Ireland by communist colonies, and drew up complete estimates of costs of founding them, yearly expenditure, and probable revenue. And in his definite plan for the future the technical working out of details is managed with such practical knowledge—ground plan, front and side and bird's-eye views all included—that, the Owen method of social reform once accepted, there is from the practical point of view little to be said against the actual arrangement of details.

His advance in the direction of communism was the turning point in Owen's life. As long as he was simply a philanthropist he was rewarded with nothing but wealth, applause, honor, and glory. He was the most popular man in Europe. Not only men of his own class, but statesmen and princes listened to him approvingly. But when he came out with his communist theories, that was quite another thing. Three great obstacles seemed to him especially to block the path to social reform: private property, religion, the present form of marriage. He knew what confronted him if he attacked these—outlawry, excommunication from official society, the loss of his whole social position. But nothing of this prevented him from attacking them without fear of consequences, and what he had foreseen happened. Banished from official society, with a conspiracy of silence against him in the press, ruined by his unsuccessful communist experiments in America, in which he sacrificed all his fortune, he turned directly to the working class and continued working in their midst for thirty years.

Every social movement, every real advance in England on behalf of the workers links itself to the name of Robert Owen. He forced through in 1819, after five years' fighting the first law limiting the hours of labor of women and children in factories. He was president of the first congress at which all the trade unions of England united in a single great trade association. He introduced as transition measures to the complete communistic organization of society, on the one hand, co-operative societies for retail trade and production. These have since that time, at least, given practical proof that the merchant and the manufacturer are socially quite unnecessary. On the other hand, he introduced labor bazaars for the exchange of the products of labor through the medium of labor notes, whose unit was a single hour of work; institutions necessarily doomed to failure, but completely anticipating Proudhon's bank of exchange of a much later period, and differing entirely from this in that it did not claim to be the panacea for all social ills, but only a first step towards a much more radical revolution of society.

The Utopians' mode of thought has for a long time governed the socialist ideas of the nineteenth century, and still governs some of them. Until very recently all French and English socialists did homage to it. The earlier German communism, including that of Weitling, was of the same school. To all these socialism is the expression of absolute truth, reason, and justice, and has only to be discovered to conquer all the world by virtue of its own power. And as absolute truth is independent of time, space, and of the historical development of man, it is a mere accident when and where it is discovered. With all this, absolute truth, reason, and justice are different with the founder of each different school. And as each one's special kind of absolute truth, reason, and justice is again conditioned by his subjective understanding, his conditions of existence, the measure of his knowledge, and his intellectual training, there is no other ending possible in this conflict of absolute truths than that they shall be mutually exclusive one of the other. Hence from this nothing could come but a kind of eclectic, average socialism, which, as a matter of fact, has up to the present time dominated the minds of most of the socialist workers in France and England. Hence a mishmash allowing of the most manifold shades of opinion; a mishmash of such critical statements, economic theories, pictures of future society by the founders of different sects as excite a minimum of opposition; a mishmash which is the more easily brewed the more the definite sharp edges of the individual constituents are rubbed down in the stream of debate, like rounded pebbles in a brook.

To make a science of socialism it had first to be placed upon a real basis.

## II

In the meantime, along with and after the French philosophy of the eighteenth century, had arisen the new German philosophy, culminating in Hegel. Its greatest merit was the taking up again of dialectics as the highest form of reasoning. The old Greek philosophers were all born natural dialecticians, and Aristotle, the most encyclopedic intellect of them, had already analyzed the most essential forms of dialectic thought. The newer philosophy, on the other hand, although in it, also, dialectics had brilliant exponents (e.g., Descartes and Spinoza), had, especially through English influence, become more and more rigidly fixed in the so-called metaphysical mode of reasoning, by which also the French of the eighteenth century were almost wholly dominated, at all events in their special philosophical work. Outside of philosophy in the restricted sense the French, nevertheless, produced masterpieces of dialectics. We need only call to mind Diderot's *Le Neveu de Rameau,* and Rousseau's *Discours sur l'origine et les fondements de l'inegalite parmi les hommes.* We give here, in brief, the essential character of these two modes of thought.

When we consider and reflect upon nature at large or the history of mankind or our own intellectual activity, at first we see the picture of an endless entanglement of relations and reactions, permutations and combinations, in which nothing remains what, where, and as it was, but everything moves, changes, comes into being, and passes away. We see, therefore, at first the picture as a whole, with its

individual parts still more or less kept in the background; we observe the movements, transitions, connections rather than the things that move, combine, and are connected. This primitive, naive but intrinsically correct conception of the world is that of ancient Greek philosophy, and was first clearly formulated by Heraclitus: everything is and is not, for everything is fluid, is constantly changing, constantly coming into being and passing away.

But this conception, correctly as it expresses the general character of the picture of appearances as a whole, does not suffice to explain the details of which this picture is made up, and so long as we do not understand these we have not a clear idea of the whole picture. In order to understand these details we must detach them from their natural or historical connection and examine each one separately, its nature, special causes, effects, etc. This is primarily the task of natural science and historical research: branches of science which the Greeks of classical times, on very good grounds, relegated to a subordinate position, because they had, first of all, to collect materials for these sciences to work upon. A certain amount of natural and historical material must be collected before there can be any critical analysis, comparison, and arrangement in classes, orders, and species. The foundations of the exact natural sciences were, therefore, first worked out by the Greeks of the Alexandrian period, and later on, in the Middle Ages, by the Arabs. Real natural science dates from the second half of the fifteenth century, and thence onward it had advanced with constantly increasing rapidity. The analysis of nature into its individual parts, the grouping of the different natural processes and objects in definite classes, the study of the internal anatomy of organic bodies in their manifold forms—these were the fundamental conditions of the gigantic strides in our knowledge of nature that have been made during the last four hundred years. But this method of work has also left us as legacy the habit of observing natural objects and processes in isolation, apart from their connection with the vast whole; of observing them in repose, not in motion; as constants, not as essentially variables; in their death, not in their life. And when this way of looking at things was transferred by Bacon and Locke from natural science to philosophy, it begot the narrow, metaphysical mode of thought peculiar to the last century.

To the metaphysician things and their mental reflexes, ideas, are isolated, are to be considered one after the other and apart from each other, are objects of investigation fixed, rigid, given once for all. He thinks in absolutely irreconcilable antitheses. "His communication is 'yea, yea; nay, nay'; for whatsoever is more than these cometh of evil." For him a thing either exists or does not exist; a thing cannot at the same time be itself and something else. Positive and negative absolutely exclude one another; cause and effect stand in a rigid antithesis one to the other.

At first sight this mode of thinking seems to us very luminous, because it is that of so-called sound common sense. Only sound common sense, respectable fellow that he is, in the homely realm of his own four walls, has very wonderful adventures, directly he ventures out into the wide world of research. And the metaphysical mode of thought, justifiable and necessary as it is in a number of domains whose extent varies according to the nature of the particular object of investigation, sooner or later reaches a limit beyond which it becomes one-sided, restricted, abstract, lost in insoluble contradictions. In the contemplation of individual things it forgets the connection between them; in the contemplation of their existence it forgets the beginning and end of that existence; of their repose, it forgets their motion. It cannot see the wood for the trees.

For everyday purposes we know and can say, e.g., whether an animal is alive or not. But upon closer inquiry, we find that this is, in many cases, a very complex question, as the jurists know very well. They have cudgeled their brains in vain to discover a rational limit beyond which the killing of the child in its mother's womb is murder. It is just as impossible to determine absolutely the moment of death, for physiology proves that death is not an instantaneous, momentary phenomenon, but a very protracted process.

In like manner every organic being is every moment the same and not the same; every moment it assimilates matter supplied from without and gets rid of other matter; every moment some cells of its body die and others build themselves anew; in a longer or shorter time the matter of its body is completely renewed, and is replaced by other molecules of matter, so that every organic being is always itself and yet something other than itself.

Further, we find upon closer investigation that the two poles of an antithesis, positive and negative, e.g., are as inseparable as they are opposed, and that despite all their opposition they mutually interpenetrate. And we find, in like manner, that cause and effect are conceptions which hold good only in their application to individual cases; but as soon as we consider the individual cases in their general connection with the universe as a whole they run into each other, and they become confounded when we contemplate that universal action and reaction in which causes and effects are eternally changing places, so that what is effect here and now will be cause there and then, and vice versa.

None of these processes and modes of thought enters into the framework of metaphysical reasoning. Dialectics, on the other hand, comprehends things and their representations, ideas, in their essential connection, concatenation, motion, origin, and ending. Such processes as those mentioned above are, therefore, so many corroborations of its own method of procedure.

Nature is the proof of dialectics, and it must be said for modern science that it has furnished this proof with very rich materials, increasing daily, and thus has shown that, in the last resort, nature works dialectically and not metaphysically; that she does not move in the eternal oneness of a perpetually recurring circle, but goes through a real historical evolution. In this connection Darwin must be named before all others. He dealt the metaphysical conception of nature the heaviest blow by his proof that all organic beings, plants, animals, and man himself are the products of a process of evolution going on through millions of years. But the naturalists who have learned to think dialectically are few and far between, and this conflict of the results of discovery with preconceived modes of thinking explains the endless confusion now reigning in theoretical natural science, the despair of teachers as well as learners, of authors and readers alike.

An exact representation of the universe, of its evolution, of the development of mankind, and of the reflection of this evolution in the minds of men can therefore be obtained only by the methods of dialectics, with its constant regard to the innumerable actions and reactions of life and death, of progressive or retrogressive changes. And in this spirit the new German philosophy has worked. Kant began his career by resolving the stable solar system of Newton and its eternal duration, after the famous initial impulse had once been given, into the result of a historic process, the formation of the sun and all the planets out of a rotating nebulous mass. From this he at the same time drew the conclusion that, given this origin of the solar system, its future death followed of necessity. His theory half a century later was established mathematically by Laplace, and half a century after that the spectroscope proved the existence in space of such incandescent masses of gas in various stages of condensation.

This new German philosophy culminated in the Hegelian system. In this system—and herein is its great merit—for the first time the whole world, natural, historical, intellectual, is represented as a process, i.e., as in constant motion, change, transformation, development; and the attempt is made to trace out the internal connection that makes a continuous whole of all this movement and development. From this point of view the history of mankind no longer appeared as a wild whirl of senseless deeds of violence, all equally condemnable at the judgment seat of mature philosophic reason and best forgotten as quickly as possible, but as the process of evolution of man himself. It was now the task of the intellect to follow the gradual march of this process through all its devious ways, and to trace out the inner law running through all its apparently accidental phenomena.

That the Hegelian system did not solve the problem it propounded is here immaterial. Its epoch-making merit was that it propounded the problem. This problem is one that no single individual will ever be able to solve. Although Hegel was—with St. Simon—the most encyclopedic mind of his time, yet he was limited, first, by the necessarily limited extent of his own knowledge and, second, by the

limited extent and depth of the knowledge and conceptions of his age. To these limits a third must be added. Hegel was an idealist. To him the thoughts within his brain were not the more or less abstract pictures of actual things and processes, but, conversely, things and their evolution were only the realized pictures of the "Idea," existing somewhere from eternity before the world was. This way of thinking turned everything upside down, and completely reversed the actual connection of things in the world. Correctly and ingeniously as many individual groups of facts were grasped by Hegel, yet, for the reasons just given, there is much that is botched, artificial, labored—in a word, wrong—in point of detail. The Hegelian system, in itself, was a colossal miscarriage—but it was also the last of its kind. It was suffering, in fact, from an internal and incurable contradiction. Upon the one hand, its essential proposition was the conception that human history is a process of evolution, which, by its very nature, cannot find its intellectual final term in the discovery of any so-called absolute truth. But, on the other hand, it laid claim to being the very essence of this absolute truth. A system of natural and historical knowledge, embracing everything, and final for all time, is a contradiction to the fundamental law of dialectic reasoning. This law, indeed, by no means excludes, but, on the contrary, includes the idea that the systematic knowledge of the external universe can make giant strides from age to age.

The perception of the fundamental contradiction in German idealism led necessarily back to materialism, but, *nota bene,* not to the simply metaphysical, exclusively mechanical materialism of the eighteenth century. Old materialism looked upon all previous history as a crude heap of irrationality and violence; modern materialism sees in it the process of evolution of humanity, and aims at discovering the laws thereof. With the French of the eighteenth century, and even with Hegel, the conception obtained of nature as a whole, moving in narrow circles and forever immutable, with its eternal celestial bodies, as Newton, and unalterable organic species, as Linnaeus, taught. Modern materialism embraces the more recent discoveries of natural science, according to which nature also has its history in

KARL MARX AND FRIEDRICH ENGELS

time, the celestial bodies, like the organic species that under favorable conditions people them, being born and perishing. And even if nature as a whole must still be said to move in recurrent cycles, these cycles assume infinitely larger dimensions. In both aspects modern materialism is essentially dialectic, and no longer requires the assistance of that sort of philosophy which, queenlike, pretended to rule the remaining mob of sciences. As soon as each special science is bound to make clear its position in the great totality of things and of our knowledge of things, a special science dealing with this totality is superfluous or unnecessary. That which still survives of all earlier philosophy is the science of thought and its laws—formal logic and dialectics. Everything else is subsumed in the positive science of nature and history.

While, however, the revolution in the conception of nature could be made only in proportion to the corresponding positive materials furnished by research, already much earlier certain historical facts had occurred which led to a decisive change in the conception of history. In 1831 the first working-class rising took place in Lyons; between 1838 and 1842 the first national working-class movement, that of the English Chartists, reached its height. The class struggle between proletariat and bourgeoisie came to the front in the history of the most advanced countries in Europe, in proportion to the development, upon the one hand, of modern industry; upon the other, of the newly acquired political supremacy of the bourgeoisie. Facts more and more strenuously gave the lie to the teachings of bourgeois economy as to the identity of the interests of capital and labor, as to the universal harmony and universal prosperity that would be the consequence of unbridled competition. All these things could no longer be ignored, any more than the French and English socialism, which was their theoretical, though very imperfect, expression. But the old idealist conception of history, which was not yet dislodged, knew nothing of class struggles based upon economic interests, knew nothing of economic interests; production and all economic relations appeared in it only as incidental, subordinate elements in the "history of civilization."

The new facts made imperative a new examina-

tion of all past history. Then it was seen that *all* past history, with the exception of its primitive stages, was the history of class struggles; that these warring classes of society are always the products of the modes of production and of exchange—in a word, of the *economic* conditions of their time; that the economic structure of society always furnishes the real basis, starting from which we can alone work out the ultimate explanation of the whole superstructure of juridical and political institutions as well as of the religious, philosophical, and other ideas of a given historical period. Hegel had freed history from metaphysics—he had made it dialectic; but his conception of history was essentially idealistic. But now idealism was driven from its last refuge, the philosophy of history, now a materialistic treatment of history was propounded, and a method found of explaining man's "knowing" by his "being" instead of, as heretofore, his "being" by his "knowing."

From that time forward socialism was no longer an accidental discovery of this or that ingenious brain, but the necessary outcome of the struggle between two historically developed classes—the proletariat and the bourgeoisie. Its task was no longer to manufacture a system of society as perfect as possible, but to examine the historico-economic succession of events from which these classes and their antagonism had of necessity sprung, and to discover in the economic conditions thus created the means of ending the conflict. But the socialism of earlier days was as incompatible with this materialistic conception as the conception of nature of the French materialists was with dialectics and modern natural science. The socialism of earlier days certainly criticized the existing capitalistic mode of production and its consequences. But it could not explain them, and, therefore, could not get the mastery of them. It could only simply reject them as bad. The more strongly this earlier socialism denounced the exploitation of the working class, inevitable under capitalism, the less able was it clearly to show in what this exploitation consisted and how it arose. But for this it was necessary (1) to present the capitalistic method of production in its historical connection and its inevitableness during a particular historical period, and therefore, also, to present its inevitable downfall; and (2) to lay bare its essential character, which was still a secret. This was done by the discovery of *surplus value*. It was shown that the appropriation of unpaid labor is the basis of the capitalist mode of production, and of the exploitation of the worker that occurs under it; that even if the capitalist buys the labor power of his laborer at its full value as a commodity on the market he yet extracts more value from it than he paid for, and that in the ultimate analysis this surplus value forms those sums of value from which are heaped up the constantly increasing masses of capital in the hands of the possessing classes. The genesis of capitalist production and the production of capital were both explained.

These two great discoveries, the materialistic conception of history and the revelation of the secret of capitalistic production through surplus value, we owe to Marx. With these discoveries socialism became a science. The next thing was to work out all its details and relations.

# III

The materialist conception of history starts from the proposition that the production of the means to support human life—and, next to production, the exchange of things produced—is the basis of all social structure; that in every society that has appeared in history, the manner in which wealth is distributed and society divided into classes or orders is dependent upon what is produced, how it is produced, and how the products are exchanged. From this point of view the final causes of all social changes and political revolutions are to be sought not in men's brains, not in man's better insight into eternal truth and justice, but in changes in the modes of production and exchange. They are to be sought not in the *philosophy,* but in the *economics* of each particular epoch. The growing perception that existing social institutions are unreasonable and unjust, that reason has become unreason and right wrong, is only proof that in the modes of production and exchange changes have silently taken place with which the social order, adapted to earlier economic conditions, is no longer in keeping. From this it also follows that the means

of getting rid of the incongruities that have been brought to light must also be present, in a more or less developed condition, within the changed modes of production themselves. These means are not to be invented by deduction from fundamental principles, but are to be discovered in the stubborn facts of the existing system of production.

What is, then, the position of modern socialism in this connection?

The present structure of society—this is now pretty generally conceded—is the creation of the ruling class of today, of the bourgeoisie. The mode of production peculiar to the bourgeoisie, known, since Marx, as the capitalist mode of production, was incompatible with the feudal system, with the privileges it conferred upon individuals, entire social ranks, and local corporations, as well as with the hereditary ties of subordination which constituted the framework of its social organization. The bourgeoisie broke up the feudal system and built upon its ruins the capitalist order of society, the kingdom of free competition, of personal liberty, of the equality, before the law, of all commodity owners, of all the rest of the capitalist blessings. Thenceforward the capitalist mode of production could develop in freedom. Since steam, machinery, and the making of machines by machinery transformed the older manufacture into modern industry, the productive forces evolved under the guidance of the bourgeoisie developed with a rapidity and in a degree unheard of before. But just as the older manufacture, in its time, and handicraft, becoming more developed under its influence, had come into collision with the feudal trammels of the guilds, so now modern industry, in its more complete development, comes into collision with the bounds within which the capitalistic mode of production holds it confined. The new productive forces have already outgrown the capitalistic mode of using them. And this conflict between productive forces and modes of production is not a conflict engendered in the mind of man, like that between original sin and divine justice. It exists, in fact, objectively, outside us, independently of the will and actions even of the men who have brought it on. Modern socialism is nothing but the reflex in thought of this conflict in fact;

its ideal reflection in the minds, first, of the class directly suffering under it, the working class.

Now in what does this conflict consist?

Before capitalistic production, i.e., in the Middle Ages, the system of petty industry obtained generally, based upon the private property of the laborers in their means of production; in the country, the agriculture of the small peasant, free man, or serf; in the towns, the handicrafts organized in guilds. The instruments of labor—land, agricultural implements, the workshop, the tool—were the instruments of labor of single individuals, adapted for the use of one worker, and, therefore, of necessity, small, dwarfish, circumscribed. But for this very reason they belonged, as a rule, to the producer himself. To concentrate these scattered, limited means of production, to enlarge them, to turn them into the powerful levers of production of the present day—this was precisely the historic role of capitalist production and of its upholder, the bourgeoisie. In the fourth section of *Capital*, Marx has explained in detail how since the fifteenth century this has been historically worked out through the three phases of simple cooperation, manufacture, and modern industry. But the bourgeoisie, as is also shown there, could not transform these puny means of production into mighty productive forces without transforming them, at the same time, from means of production of the individual into *social* means of production workable only by a collectivity of men. The spinning wheel, the hand loom, the blacksmith's hammer were replaced by the spinning machine, the power loom, the steam hammer; the individual workshop, by the factory, implying the co-operation of hundreds and thousands of workmen. In like manner production itself changed from a series of individual into a series of social acts, and the products from individual to social products. The yarn, the cloth, the metal articles that now came out of the factory were the joint product of many workers, through whose hands they successively had to pass before they were ready. No one person could say of them: "I made that; this is *my* product."

But where, in a given society, the fundamental form of production is that spontaneous division of labor which creeps in gradually and not upon any pre-

conceived plan, there the products take on the form of *commodities,* whose mutual exchange, buying and selling, enable the individual producers to satisfy their manifold wants. And this was the case in the Middle Ages. The peasant, e.g., sold to the artisan agricultural products and bought from him the products of handicraft. Into this society of individual producers, of commodity producers, the new mode of production thrust itself. In the midst of the old division of labor, grown up spontaneously and upon *no definite plan,* which had governed the whole of society, now arose division of labor upon a *definite plan,* as organized in the factory; side by side with *individual* production appeared *social* production. The products of both were sold in the same market, and, therefore, at prices at least approximately equal. But organization upon a definite plan was stronger than spontaneous division of labor. The factories working with the combined social forces of a collectivity of individuals produced their commodities far more cheaply than the individual small producers. Individual production succumbed in one department after another. Socialized production revolutionized all the old methods of production. But its revolutionary character was, at the same time, so little recognized that it was, on the contrary, introduced as a means of increasing and developing the production of commodities. When it arose it found ready-made, and made liberal use of, certain machinery for the production and exchange of commodities: merchants' capital, handicraft, wage labor. Socialized production thus introducing itself as a new form of the production of commodities, it was a matter of course that under it the old forms of appropriation remained in full swing and were applied to its products as well.

In the medieval stage of evolution of the production of commodities the question as to the owner of the product of labor could not arise. The individual producer, as a rule, had, from raw material belonging to himself and generally his own handiwork, produced it with his own tools, by the labor of his own hands or of his family. There was no need for him to appropriate the new product. It belonged wholly to him, as a matter of course. His property in the product was, therefore, based *upon his own labor*. Even where external help was used, this was, as a rule, of little importance, and very generally was compensated by something other than wages. The apprentices and journeymen of the guilds worked less for board and wages than for education, in order that they might become master craftsmen themselves.

Then came the concentration of the means of production and of the producers in large workshops and manufactories, their transformation into actual socialized means of production and socialized producers. But the socialized producers and means of production and their products was still treated, after this change, just as they had been before, i.e., as the means of production and the products of individuals. Hitherto the owner of the instruments of labor had himself appropriated the product because, as a rule, it was his own product and the assistance of others was the exception. Now the owner of the instruments of labor always appropriated to himself the product, although it was no longer his product, but exclusively the product of the *labor of others*. Thus the products now produced socially were not appropriated by those who had actually set in motion the means of production and actually produced the commodities, but by the *capitalists*. The means of production, and production itself, had become in essence socialized. But they were subjected to a form of appropriation which presupposes the private production of individuals, under which, therefore, everyone owns his own product and brings it to market. The mode of production is subjected to this form of appropriation, although it abolishes the conditions upon which the latter rests.[4]

This contradiction, which gives to the new mode of production its capitalistic character, *contains the germ of the whole of the social antagonisms of today*. The greater the mastery obtained by the new mode of production over all important fields of production and in all manufacturing countries, the more it reduced individual production to an insignificant residuum, *the more clearly was brought out the incompatibility of socialized production with capitalistic appropriation*.

The first capitalists found, as we have said, alongside of other forms of labor, wage labor ready-made for them on the market. But it was exceptional, complementary, accessory, transitory wage labor. The

agricultural laborer, though upon occasion he hired himself out by the day, had a few acres of his own land on which he could at all events live in a pinch. The guilds were so organized that the journeyman of today became the master of tomorrow. But all this changed as soon as the means of production became socialized and concentrated in the hands of capitalists. The means of production, as well as the product, of the individual producer became more and more worthless; there is nothing left for him but to turn wage worker under the capitalist. Wage labor, aforetime the exception and accessory, now became the rule and basis of all production; aforetime complementary, it now became the sole remaining function of the worker. The wage worker for a time became a wage worker for life. The number of these permanent wage workers was further enormously increased by the breaking up of the feudal system that occurred at the same time, by the disbanding of the retainers of the feudal lords, the eviction of the peasants from their homesteads, etc. The separation was made complete between the means of production, concentrated in the hands of the capitalists, on the one side, and the producers, possessing nothing but their labor power, on the other. *The contradiction between socialized production and capitalistic appropriation manifested itself as the antagonism of proletariat and bourgeoisie.*

We have seen that the capitalistic mode of production thrust its way into a society of commodity producers, of individual producers, whose social bond was the exchange of their products. But every society based upon the production of commodities has this peculiarity: that the producers have lost control over their own social interrelations. Each man produces for himself with such means of production as he may happen to have, and for such exchange as he may require to satisfy his remaining wants. No one knows how much of his particular article is coming on the market, nor how much of it will be wanted. No one knows whether his individual product will meet an actual demand, whether he will be able to make good his costs of production or even to sell his commodity at all. Anarchy reigns in socialized production.

But the production of commodities, like every

other form of production, has its peculiar, inherent laws inseparable from it; and these laws work, despite anarchy, in and through anarchy. They reveal themselves in the only persistent form of social interrelations, i.e., in exchange, and here they affect the individual producers as compulsory laws of competition. They are, at first, unknown to these producers themselves, and have to be discovered by them gradually and as the result of experience. They work themselves out, therefore, independently of the producers, and in antagonism to them, as inexorable natural laws of their particular form of production. The product governs the producers.

In medieval society, especially in the earlier centuries, production was essentially directed towards satisfying the wants of the individual. It satisfied, in the main, only the wants of the producer and his family. Where relations of personal dependence existed, as in the country, it also helped to satisfy the wants of the feudal lord. In all this there was, therefore, no exchange; the products, consequently, did not assume the character of commodities. The family of the peasant produced almost everything it wanted: clothes and furniture, as well as means of subsistence. Only when it began to produce more than was sufficient to supply its own wants and the payments in kind to the feudal lord, only than did it also produce commodities. This surplus, thrown into socialized exchange and offered for sale, became commodities.

The artisans of the towns, it is true, had from the first to produce for exchange. But they, also, themselves supplied the greatest part of their own individual wants. They had gardens and plots of land. They turned their cattle out into the communal forest, which, also, yielded them timber and firing. The women spun flax, wool, and so forth. Production for the purpose of exchange, production of commodities, was only in its infancy. Hence exchange was restricted, the market narrow, the methods of production stable; there was local exclusiveness without, local unity within; the mark in the country; in the town, the guild.

But with the extension of the production of commodities, and especially with the introduction of the capitalist mode of production, the laws of commodity production, hitherto latent, came into action more openly and with greater force. The old bonds were loosened, the old exclusive limits broken through, the producers were more and more turned into independent, isolated producers of commodities. It became apparent that the production of society at large was ruled by absence of plan, by accident, by anarchy; and this anarchy grew to greater and greater height. But the chief means by aid of which the capitalist mode of production intensified this anarchy of socialized production was the exact opposite of anarchy. It was the increasing organization of production, upon a social basis, in every individual productive establishment. By this the old, peaceful, stable condition of things was ended. Whatever this organization of production was introduced into a branch of industry, it brooked no other method of production by its side. The field of labor became a battleground. The great geographical discoveries, and the colonization following upon them, multiplied markets and quickened the transformation of handicraft into manufacture. The war did not break out simply between the individual producers of particular localities. The local struggles begot in their turn national conflicts, the commercial wars of the seventeenth and the eighteenth centuries.

Finally, modern industry and the opening of the world market made the struggle universal, and at the same time gave it an unheard-of virulence. Advantages in natural or artificial conditions of production now decide the existence or non-existence of individual capitalists, as well as of whole industries and countries. He that falls is remorselessly cast aside. It is the Darwinian struggle of the individual for existence transferred from nature to society with intensified violence. The conditions of existence natural to the animal appear as the final term of human development. The contradiction between socialized production and capitalistic appropriation now presents itself as *an antagonism between the organization of production in the individual workshop and the anarchy of production in society generally.*

The capitalistic mode of production moves in these two forms of the antagonism immanent to it from its very origin. It is never able to get out of that "vicious circle" which Fourier had already discovered. What Fourier could not, indeed, see in his time is that this circle is gradually narrowing; that the movement becomes more and more a spiral, and must come to an end, like the movement of the planets, by collision with the center. It is the compelling force of anarchy in the production of society at large that more and more completely turns the great majority of men into proletarians, and it is the masses of the proletariat again who will finally put an end to anarchy in production. It is the compelling force of anarchy in social production that turns the limitless perfectibility of machinery under modern industry into a compulsory law by which every individual industrial capitalist must perfect his machinery more and more, under penalty of ruin.

But the perfecting of machinery is making human labor superfluous. If the introduction and increase of machinery means the displacement of millions of manual by a few machine workers, improvement in machinery means the displacement of more and more of the machine workers themselves. It means, in the last instance, the production of a number of available wage workers in excess of the average needs of capital, the formation of a complete industrial reserve army, as I called it in 1845,[5] available at the times when industry is working at high pressure, to be cast out upon the street when the inevitable crash comes, a constant dead weight upon the limbs of the working class in its struggle for existence with capital, a regulator for the keeping of wages down to the low level that suits the interests of capital. Thus it comes about, to quote Marx, that machinery becomes the most powerful weapon in the war of capital against the working class; that the instruments of labor constantly tear the means of subsistence out of the hands of the laborer; that the very product of the worker is turned into an instrument for his subjugation. Thus it comes about that the economizing of the instruments of labor becomes at the same time, from the outset, the most reckless waste of labor power, and robbery based upon the normal conditions under which labor functions; that machinery, "the most powerful instrument for shortening labor time, becomes the most unfailing means for placing every moment of the laborer's time and that of his family at the disposal of the capitalist for the purpose of expanding the value of his capital."

(*Capital*, American edition, page 445.) Thus it comes about that the overwork of some becomes the preliminary condition for the idleness of others, and that modern industry, which hunts after new consumers over the whole world, forces the consumption of the masses at home down to a starvation minimum, and in doing thus destroys its own home market. "The law that always equilibrates the relative surplus population, or industrial reserve army, to the extent and energy of accumulation, this law rivets the laborer to capital more firmly than the wedges of Vulcan did Prometheus to the rock. It establishes an accumulation of misery corresponding with accumulation of capital. Accumulation of wealth at one pole is, therefore, at the same time accumulation of misery, agony of toil, slavery, ignorance, brutality, mental degradation at the opposite pole, i.e., on the side of the class that produces *its own product in the form of capital.*" (Marx's *Capital,* American edition, page 661.) And to expect any other division of the products from the capitalistic mode of production is the same as expecting the electrodes of a battery not to decompose acidulated water, not to liberate oxygen at the positive, hydrogen at the negative pole, so long as they are connected with the battery.

We have seen that the ever increasing perfectibility of modern machinery is, by the anarchy of social production, turned into a compulsory law that forces the individual industrial capitalist always to improve his machinery, always to increase its protective force. The bare possibility of extending the field of protection is transformed for him into a similar compulsory law. The enormous expansive force of modern industry, compared with which that of gases is mere child's play, appears to us now as a *necessity* for expansion, both qualitative and quantitative, that laughs at all resistance. Such resistance is offered by consumption, by sales, by the markets for the products of modern industry. But the capacity for expansion, extensive and intensive, of the markets is primarily governed by quite different laws that work much less energetically. The expansion of the markets cannot keep pace with the extension of production. The collision becomes inevitable, and as this cannot produce any real solution so long as it does not break into pieces the cap-italist mode of production, the collisions become periodic. Capitalist production has begotten another "vicious circle."

As a matter of fact, since 1825, when the first general crisis broke out, the whole industrial and commercial world, production and exchange among a civilized peoples and their more or less barbaric hangers-on, are thrown out of joint about once every ten years. Commerce is at a standstill, the markets are glutted, products accumulate, as multitudinous as they are unstable, hard cash disappears, credit vanishes, factories are closed, the mass of the workers are in want of the means of subsistence because they have produced too much of the means of subsistence; bankruptcy follows upon bankruptcy, execution upon execution. The stagnation lasts for years; productive forces and products are wasted and destroyed wholesale, until the accumulated mass of commodities finally filters off, more or less depreciated in value, until production and exchange gradually begin to move again. Little by little the pace quickens. It becomes a trot. The industrial trot breaks into a canter, the canter in turn grows into the headlong gallop of a perfect steeplechase of industry, commercial credit, and speculation, which finally, after breakneck leaps, ends where it began—in the ditch of a crisis. And so over and over again. We have now, since the year 1825, gone through this five times, and at the present moment (1877) we are going through it for the sixth time. And the character of these crises is so clearly defined that Fourier hit all of them off when he described the first as *"crise plethorique,"* a crisis from plethora.

In these crises the contradiction between socialized production and capitalist appropriation ends in a violent explosion. The circulation of commodities is, for the time being, stopped. Money, the means of circulation, becomes a hindrance to circulation. All the laws of production and circulation of commodities are turned upside down. The economic collision has reached its apogee. *The mode of production is in rebellion against the mode of exchange.*

The fact that the socialized organization of production within the factory has developed so far that it has become incompatible with the anarchy of pro-duction in society, which exists side by side with and dominates it, is brought home to the capitalists themselves by the violent concentration of capital that occurs during crises, through the ruin of many large, and a still greater number of small, capitalists. The whole mechanism of the capitalist mode of production breaks down under the pressure of the productive forces, its own creations. It is no longer able to turn all this mass of means of production into capital. They lie fallow, and for that very reason the industrial reserve army must also lie fallow. Means of production, means of subsistence, available laborers, all the elements of production and of general wealth, are present in abundance. But "abundance becomes the source of distress and want" (Fourier), because it is the very thing that prevents the transformation of the means of production and subsistence into capital. For in capitalistic society the means of production can function only when they have undergone a preliminary transformation into capital, into the means of exploiting human labor power. The necessity of this transformation into capital of the means of production and subsistence stands like a ghost between these and the workers. It alone prevents the coming together of the material and personal levers of production; it alone forbids the means of production to function, the workers to work and live. On the one hand, therefore, the capitalistic mode of production stands convicted of its own incapacity to further direct these productive forces. On the other, these productive forces themselves, with increasing energy, press forward to the removal of the existing contradiction, to the abolition of their quality as capital, to the *practical recognition of their character as social productive forces.*

This rebellion of the productive forces, as they grow more and more powerful, against their quality as capital, this stronger and stronger command that their social character shall be recognized, forces the capitalist class itself to treat them more and more as social productive forces, so far as this is possible under capitalist conditions. The period of industrial high pressure, with its unbounded inflation of credit, not less than the crash itself, by the collapse of great capitalist establishments, tends to bring about that form of the socialization of great masses of means of production which we meet with in the different kinds of joint-stock companies. Many of these means of production and of distribution are, from the outset, so colossal that, like the railways, they exclude all other forms of capitalistic exploitation. At a further stage of evolution this form also becomes insufficient. The producers on a large scale in a particular branch of industry in a particular country unite in a "trust," a union for the purpose of regulating production. They determine the total amount to be produced, parcel it out among themselves, and thus enforce the selling price fixed beforehand. But trusts of this kind, as soon as business becomes bad, are generally liable to break up, and on this very account compel a yet greater concentration of association. The whole of the particular industry is turned into one gigantic joint-stock company; internal competition gives place to the internal monopoly of this one company. This has happened in 1890 with the English *alkali* production, which is now, after the fusion of forty-eight large works, in the hands of one company, conducted upon a single plan and with a capital of six million pounds.

In the trusts freedom of competition changes into its very opposite—into monopoly; and the production without any definite plan of capitalistic society capitulates to the production upon a definite plan of the invading socialistic society. Certainly this is so far still to the benefit and advantage of the capitalists. But in this case the exploitation is so palpable that it must break down. No nation will put up with production conducted by trusts, with so barefaced an exploitation of the community by a small band of dividend-mongers.

In any case, with trusts or without, the official representative of capitalist society—the state—will ultimately have to undertake the direction of production.[6] This necessity for conversion into state property is felt first in the great institutions for intercourse and communication—the post office, the telegraphs, the railways.

If the crises demonstrate the incapacity of the bourgeoisie for managing any longer modern productive forces, the transformation of the great establishments for production and distribution into joint-stock companies, trusts, and state property show

how unnecessary the bourgeoisie are for that purpose. All the social functions of the capitalist are now performed by salaried employees. The capitalist has no further social function than that of pocketing dividends, tearing off coupons, and gambling on the stock exchange, where the different capitalists despoil one another of their capital. At first the capitalistic mode of production forces out the workers. Now it forces out the capitalists, and reduces them, just as it reduced the workers, to the ranks of the surplus population, although not immediately into those of the industrial reserve army.

But the transformation either into joint-stock companies and trusts or into state ownership, does not do away with the capitalistic nature of the productive forces. In the joint-stock companies and trusts this is obvious. And the modern state, again, is only the organization that bourgeois society takes on in order to support the external conditions of the capitalist mode of production against the encroachments as well of the workers as of individual capitalists. The modern state, no matter what its form, is essentially a capitalist machine, the state of the capitalists, the ideal personification of the total national capital. The more it proceeds to the taking over of productive forces, the more does it actually become the national capitalist, the more citizens does it exploit. The workers remain wage workers—proletarians. The capitalist relation is not done away with. It is rather brought to a head. But, brought to a head, it topples over. State ownership of the productive forces is not the solution of the conflict, but concealed within it are the technical conditions that form the elements of that solution.

This solution can consist only in the practical recognition of the social nature of the modern forces of production, and therefore in the harmonizing of the modes of production, appropriation, and exchange with the socialized character of the means of production. And this can come about only by society openly and directly taking possession of the productive forces which have outgrown all control except that of society as a whole. The social character of the means of production and of the products today reacts against the producers, periodically disrupts all production and exchange, acts only like a law of nature working blindly, forcibly, destructively. But with the taking over by society of the productive forces, the social character of the means of production and of the products will be utilized by the producers with a perfect understanding of its nature, and instead of being a source of disturbance and periodic collapse will become the most powerful lever of production itself.

Active social forces work exactly like natural forces: blindly, forcibly, destructively, so long as we do not understand, and reckon with, them. But when once we understand them, when once we grasp their action, their direction, their effects, it depends only upon ourselves to subject them more and more to our own will, and by means of them to reach our own ends. And this holds quite especially of the mighty productive forces of today. As long as we obstinately refuse to understand the nature and the character of these social means of action—and this understanding goes against the grain of the capitalist mode of production and its defenders—so long as these forces are at work in spite of us, in opposition to us, so long do they master us, as we have shown above in detail.

But when once their nature is understood, they can, in the hands of the producers working together, be transformed from master demons into willing servants. The difference is as that between the destructive force of electricity in the lightning of the storm and electricity under command in the telegraph and the voltaic arc, the difference between a conflagration and fire working in the service of man. With this recognition, at last, of the real nature of the productive forces of today, the social anarchy of production gives place to a social regulation of production upon a definite plan, according to the needs of the community and of each individual. Then the capitalist mode of appropriation, in which the product enslaves first the producer and then the appropriator, is replaced by the mode of appropriation of the products that is based upon the nature of the modern means of production: upon the one hand, direct social appropriation as means to the maintenance and extension of production; on the other, direct individual appropriation as means of subsistence and of enjoyment.

While the capitalist mode of production more and more completely transforms the great majority of the population into proletarians, it creates the power which, under penalty of its own destruction, is forced to accomplish this revolution. While it forces on more and more the transformation of the vast means of production, already socialized, into state property, it shows itself the way to accomplishing this revolution. *The proletariat seizes political power and turns the means of production into state property.*

But in doing this it abolishes itself as proletariat, abolishes all class distinctions and class antagonisms, abolishes also the state as state. Society thus far, based upon class antagonisms, has had need of the state. That is, of an organization of the particular class which was *pro tempore* the exploiting class, an organization for the purpose of preventing any interference from without with the existing conditions of production, and, therefore, especially for the purpose of forcibly keeping the exploited classes in the condition of oppression corresponding with the given mode of production (slavery, serfdom, wage labor). The state was the official representative of society as a whole; the gathering of it together into a visible embodiment. But it was this only in so far as it was the state of that class which itself represented, for the time being, society as a whole: in ancient times, the state of slave-owning citizens; in the Middle Ages, the feudal lords; in our own time, the bourgeoisie. When at last it becomes the real representative of the whole of society it renders itself unnecessary. As soon as there is no longer any social class to be held in subjection, as soon as class rule and the individual struggle for existence based upon our present anarchy in production, with the collisions and excesses arising from these, are removed, nothing more remains to be repressed, and a special repressive force, a state, is no longer necessary. The first act by virtue of which the state really constitutes itself the representative of the whole of society—the taking possession of the means of production in the name of society—this is, at the same time, its last independent act as a state. State interference in social relations becomes, in one domain after another, superfluous, and then dies out of itself; the government of persons is replaced by the administration of things, and by the conduct of processes of production. The state is not "abolished." *It dies out.* This gives the measure of the value of the phrase *"a free state,"* both as to its justifiable use at times by agitators and as to its ultimate scientific insufficiency, and also of the demands of the so-called anarchists for the abolition of the state out of hand.

Since the historical appearance of the capitalist production, the appropriation by society of all the means of production has often been dreamed of, more or less vaguely, by individuals as well as by sects, as the ideal of the future. But it could become possible, could become a historical necessity, only when the actual conditions for its realization were there. Like every other social advance, it becomes practicable not by men understanding that the existence of classes is in contradiction to justice, equality, etc., not by the mere willingness to abolish these classes, but by virtue of certain new economic conditions. The separation of society into an exploiting and an exploited class, a ruling and an oppressed class, was the necessary consequence of the deficient and restricted development of production in former times. So long as the total social labor yields only a produce which but slightly exceeds that barely necessary for the existence of all; so long, therefore, as labor engages all or almost all the time of the great majority of the members of society—so long, of necessity, this society is divided into classes. Side by side with the great majority, exclusively bond slaves to labor, arises a class freed from directly productive labor, which looks after the general affairs of society: the direction of labor, state business, law, science, art, etc. It is, therefore, the law of division of labor that lies at the basis of the division into classes. But this does not prevent this division into classes from being carried out by means of violence and robbery, trickery and fraud. It does not prevent the ruling class, once having the upper hand, from consolidating its power at the expense of the working class, from turning its social leadership into an intensified exploitation of the masses.

But if, upon this showing, division into classes has a certain historical justification, it has this only for a given period, only under given social conditions. It was based upon the insufficiency of production. It will be swept away by the complete development of modern productive forces. And, in fact, the abolition of classes in society presupposes a degree of historical evolution at which the existence not simply of this—or that particular ruling class, but of any ruling class at all, and, therefore, the existence of class distinction itself, has become an anachronism. It presupposes, therefore, the development of production carried out to a degree at which appropriation of the means of production and of the products, and, with this, of political domination, of the monopoly of culture, and of intellectual leadership by a particular class of society, has become not only superfluous but economically, politically, intellectually a hindrance to development.

This point is now reached. Their political and intellectual bankruptcy is scarcely any longer a secret to the bourgeoisie themselves. Their economic bankruptcy recurs regularly every ten years. In every crisis society is suffocated beneath the weight of its own productive forces and products, which it cannot use, and stands helpless, face to face with the absurd contradiction that the producers have nothing to consume because consumers are wanting. The expansive force of the means of production bursts the bonds that the capitalist mode of production imposed upon them. Their deliverance from these bonds is the one pre-condition for an unbroken, constantly accelerated development of the productive forces, and therewith for a practically unlimited increase of production itself. Nor is this all. The socialized appropriation of the means of production does away not only with the present artificial restrictions upon production, but also with the positive waste and devastation of productive forces and products that are at the present time the inevitable concomitants of production, and that reach their height in the crises. Further, it sets free for the community at large a mass of means of production and of products by doing away with the senseless extravagance of the ruling classes of today and their political representatives. The possibility of securing for every member of society, by means of socialized production, an existence not only fully sufficient materially, and becoming day by day fuller, but an existence guaranteeing to all the free development and exercise of their physical and mental faculties—this possibility is now for the first time here, but *it is here*.[7]

With the seizing of the means of production by society, production of commodities is done away with, and, simultaneously, the mastery of the product over the producer. Anarchy in social production is replaced by systematic, definite organization. The struggle for individual existence disappears. Then for the first time man, in a certain sense, is finally marked off from the rest of the animal kingdom and emerges from mere animal conditions of existence into really human ones. The whole sphere of the conditions of life which environ man, and which have hitherto ruled man, now comes under the dominion and control of man, who for the first time becomes the real, conscious lord of nature because he has now become master of his own social organization. The laws of his own social action, hitherto standing face to face with man as laws of nature foreign to and dominating him, will now be used with full understanding, and so mastered by him. Man's own social organization, hitherto confronting him as a necessity imposed by nature and history, now becomes the result of his own free action. The extraneous objective forces that have hitherto governed history pass under the control of man himself. Only from that time will man himself, more and more consciously, make his own history—only from that time will the social causes set in movement by him have, in the main and in a constantly growing measure, the results intended by him. It is the ascent of man from the kingdom of necessity to the kingdom of freedom.

Let us briefly sum up our sketch of historical evolution.

*I. Medieval Society*—Individual production on a small scale. Means of production adapted for individual use; hence primitive, ungainly, petty, dwarfed in action. Production for immediate consumption, either of the producer himself or of his feudal lord. Only where an excess of production over this consumption occurs is such excess offered for sale, enters into exchange. Production of commodities, therefore, only in its infancy. But already it contains within itself, in embryo, *anarchy in the production of society at large.*

*II. Capitalist Revolution*—Transformation of industry, at first by means of simple co-operation and manufacture. Concentration of the means of production, hitherto scattered, into great workshops. As a consequence their transformation from individual to social means of production—a transformation which does not, on the whole, affect the form of exchange. The old forms of appropriation remain in force. The capitalist appears. In his capacity as owner of the means of production he also appropriates the products and turns them into commodities. Production has become a *social* act. Exchange and appropriation continue to be *individual* acts, the acts of individuals. *The social product is appropriated by the individual capitalist.* Fundamental contradiction, whence arise all the contradictions in which our present-day society moves, and which modern industry brings to light.

A. Severance of the producer from the means of production. Condemnation of the worker to wage labor for life. *Antagonism between the proletariat and the bourgeoisie.*

B. Growing predominance and increasing effectiveness of the laws governing the production of commodities. Unbridled competition. *Contradiction between socialized organization in the individual factory and social anarchy in production as a whole.*

C. On the one hand, perfecting of machinery, made by competition compulsory for each individual manufacturer, and complemented by a constantly growing displacement of laborers. *Industrial reserve army.* On the other hand, unlimited extension of production, also compulsory under competition, for every manufacturer. On both sides, unheard-of development of productive forces, excess of supply and demand, overproduction, glutting of the markets, crises every ten years, the vicious circle: excess here of means of production and products—excess there of laborers, without employment and without means of existence. But these two levers of production and of social well-being are unable to work together because the capitalist form of production prevents the productive forces from working and the products from circulating, unless they are first turned into capital—which their very superabundance prevents. The contradiction has grown into an absurdity. *The mode of production rises in rebellion against the form of exchange.* The bourgeoisie are convicted of incapacity further to manage their own social productive forces.

D. Partial recognition of the social character of the

productive forces forced upon the capitalists themselves. Taking over of the great institutions for production and communication, first by joint-stock companies, later on by trusts, then by the state. The bourgeoisie demonstrated to be a superfluous class. All its social functions are now performed by salaried employees.

*III. Proletarian Revolution*—Solution of the contradictions. The proletariat seizes the public power, and by means of this transforms the socialized means of production, slipping from the hands of the bourgeoisie, into public property. By this act the proletariat frees the means of production from the character of capital they have thus far borne and gives their socialized character complete freedom to work itself out. Socialized production upon a predetermined plan becomes henceforth possible. The development of production makes the existence of different classes of society thenceforth an anachronism. In proportion as anarchy in social production vanishes, the political authority of the state dies out. Man, at last the master of his own form of social organization, becomes at the same time the lord over nature, his own master—free.

To accomplish this act of universal emancipation is the historical mission of the modern proletariat. To thoroughly comprehend the historical conditions and thus the very nature of this act, to impart to the now oppressed proletarian class a full knowledge of the conditions and of the meaning of the momentous act it is called upon to accomplish, this is the task of the theoretical expression of the proletarian movement, scientific socialism.

# Notes

1. This is the passage on the French Revolution: "Thought, the concept of law, all at once made itself felt, and against this the old scaffolding of wrong could make no stand. In this conception of law, therefore, a constitution has now been established, and henceforth everything must be based upon this. Since the sun had been in the firmament, and the planets circled round him, the sight had never been seen of man standing upon his head—i.e., on the Idea—and building reality after this image. Anaxagoras first said that the nous, reason, rules the world; but

now, for the first time, had man come to recognize that the Idea must rule the mental reality. And this was a magnificent sunrise. All thinking beings have participated in celebrating this holy day. A sublime emotion swayed men at that time, an enthusiasm of reason pervaded the world, as if now had come the reconciliation of the Divine Principle with the world." Is it not high time to set the anti-socialist law in action against such teachings, subversive and to the common danger, by the late Professor Hegel?

2. From *The Revolution in Mind and Practice*, p. 21, a memorial addressed to all the "red Republicans, Communists and Socialists of Europe," and sent to the provisional government of France, 1848, and also "to Queen Victoria and her responsible advisers."

3. *Ibid.* p. 22.

4. It is hardly necessary in this connection to point out that, even if the form of appropriation remains the same, the *character* of the appropriation is just as much revolutionized as production is by the changes described above. It is, of course, a very different matter whether I appropriate to myself my own product or that of another. Note in passing that wage labor, which contains the whole capitalistic mode of production in embryo, is very ancient; in a sporadic, scattered form it existed for centuries alongside of slave labor. But the embryo could duly develop into the capitalistic mode of production only when the necessary historical preconditions had been furnished.

5. *The Condition of the Working Class in England.*

6. I say "have to." For only when the means of production and distribution have *actually* outgrown the form of management by joint-stock companies and when, therefore, the taking them over by the state has become *economically* inevitable, only then—even if it is the state of today that effects this—is there an economic advance, the attainment of another step preliminary to the taking over of all productive forces by society itself. But of late, since Bismarck went in for state ownership of industrial establishments, a kind of spurious socialism has arisen, degenerating, now and again, into something of flunkyism, that without more ado declares *all* state ownership, even of the Bismarckian sort, to be socialistic. Certainly if the taking over by the state of the tobacco industry is socialistic, then Napoleon and Metternich must be numbered among the founders of socialism. If the Belgian state, for quite ordinary political and financial reasons, itself constructed its chief railway lines; if Bismarck, not under any economic compulsion, took over for the state the chief Prussian lines, simply to be the better able to have them in hand in case of war, to bring up the railway

employees as voting cattle for the government, and especially to create for himself a new source of income independent of parliamentary votes—this was in no sense a socialistic measure, directly or indirectly, consciously or unconsciously. Otherwise the Royal Maritime Company, the Royal porcelain manufacture, and even the regimental tailor of the army would also be socialistic institutions, or even, as was seriously proposed by a sly dog in Frederick William III's reign, the taking over by the state of the brothels.

7. A few figures may serve to give an approximate idea of the enormous expansive force of the modern means of production, even under the capitalist pressure. According to Mr. Giffen, the total wealth of Great Britain and Ireland amounted, in round numbers, in

1814 to £2,200,000,000
1865 to £6,100,000,000
1875 to £8,500,000,000

As an instance of the squandering of means of production and of products during a crisis the total loss in the German iron industry alone, in the crisis 1873–78, was given at the Second German Industrial Congress (Berlin, February 21, 1878) as £22,750,000.

# JOHN STUART MILL
~

## INTRODUCTION

## JEREMY WALDRON

John Stuart Mill (1806–1873) was born in London and educated privately by his father, James Mill, a utilitarian, a friend and follower of Jeremy Bentham, and a considerable political thinker in his own right.

The story of Mill's peculiar education is notorious, largely through his own account of it in the *Autobiography* published shortly after his death. Under Bentham's guidance and (as the boy grew older) in the company of such distinguished thinkers as the economist David Ricardo and the jurist John Austin, Mill senior set out to cultivate in his son the perfect utilitarian mind—an intellect equipped with the material and analytical skills that would enable it to focus without distraction on the Benthamite political agenda.

"Without distraction" turned out to mean without the benefit of any religion, art, poetry, or philosophy (besides the basic empiricism that Bentham's system required or presupposed), or more generally without any sense of the proper place the emotions should occupy in a healthy view of the world. These deficiencies surfaced in a mental crisis that beset the young man in 1826–1827, and Mill's realization that they *were* deficiencies meant that his own outlook and (because of the eventual importance of his work) utilitarian philosophy were never the same again. The young man who had worked so assiduously for social improvement—who among other things had been arrested in 1823 for distributing leaflets about birth control in London—became convinced that a Benthamite calculus of cost and benefit, pain and pleasure, was too crude to be deployed as a tool of social change. In its place, Mill sought to reconstruct utilitarianism, so that it incorporated elements of Romantic thought and embodied a sense that while happiness in general was good, certain experiences and enjoyments were qualitatively, not just quantitatively, better than others.

The distinction between the "higher" and "lower" pleasures elaborated in Mill's book,

*Utilitarianism* (1861)—"Better to be a human being dissatisfied than a pig satisfied"—can easily be made to sound elitist, or indulgently aestheticist. Three points are worth bearing in mind in assessing its influence in Mill's political theory. First, the higher pleasures were not understood as languid or effete enjoyments. What counted most for Mill was the cultivation and employment of our *active* faculties: our curiosity, our questioning, and our ability to make something of our lives and of the world we experience. Second, Mill was convinced—rightly or wrongly—that true happiness, even on his elevated definition, was not just the birthright of the few. Mill was an optimist: He believed that a life "of few and transitory pains, many and various pleasures, with a decided predominance of the active over the passive," was already the lot of many and that "the present wretched education, and wretched social arrangements, are the only real hindrance to its being available to all."

And so—thirdly—though he repudiated Bentham's psychology and theory of value, Mill never abandoned his commitment to forward-looking social reform in a broadly utilitarian spirit. On the contrary, the works included here represent a sustained effort to alter the "wretched social arrangements"—such as the subordination of women, the tyranny of mass culture, and the exclusion of the great majority of working people from participation in politics—which stood in the way of human happiness.

In each of these instances, a case was made by supporters of the status quo that people were often better off submitting to others' ideas of how to live their lives or letting others look after their interests. In each case, Mill responded: "What sort of human beings can be formed under such a regimen? What development can either their thinking or their active faculties attain under it?" And in each case he did his best, through his writings, to swing the spirit of reform in England away from paternalism and toward the cultivation of freedom and individuality of which he thought all men and women were capable. As he said at the beginning of *On Liberty,* he continued to "regard utility as the ultimate appeal on all ethical questions"—he remained Benthamite enough not to be interested in abstract theories of natural right—but it must, he said, be "utility in the largest sense, grounded on the permanent interests of man as a progressive being."

Thus, after his mental crisis, Mill did not retreat, under the influence of Schiller or Coleridge, into the indulgent life of a Victorian romantic, concerned only to protect beauty and feeling from the ravages of routinized utilitarianism. His whole career was one of public service, whether in the pages of the *London and Westminster Review,* which he founded in 1836 along with other young Benthamite radicals, or in the offices of the East India Company, where he worked from 1823 to 1858, or in Parliament where he served one term as M.P. for Westminster in the mid-1860s.

His political career in and out of Parliament was notable for his principled stands in favor of the rights of workers, the rights of political prisoners, and the rights of colonial peoples to a just and decent administration, stands that made him, in Isaiah Berlin's words, "the most passionate and best-known champion of the insulted and the oppressed" of his day. In 1862, he published an article entitled "The Contest in America" in which he attempted to influence public opinion in Britain against the Southern states and to impress on them that the issue was slavery, not just the right to secession—by no means an easy task even in the liberal circles in which he moved. In the House of Commons, Mill spoke against capital punishment and against the suspension of habeas corpus in Ireland, and in favor of proportional representation, municipal reform, and women's suffrage.

In particular, his position on women's rights is a striking exception to the casual indifference of most liberal philosophers to the issue. It is explained in part by his association from 1830 with Harriet Taylor, a woman he described in the dedication to *On Liberty* as "the inspirer, and in part the author of all that is best in my writings." But though *The Subjection of Women* was written and published after her death in 1858, there is no reason to doubt the assertion in the opening lines of that tract that opposition to "the legal subordination of one sex to the other" was an opinion he had held from the earliest period of his moral and political thinking.

Harriet Taylor's influence is discernible in other areas of Mill's writing. There is no doubt that he was more favorably inclined to socialism than he would have been without her presence (though he believed that in an ideal world, capitalist arrangements were better, provided something could be done to mitigate the sources of inherited inequality). There is no doubt, either, that Mill's experience of an open and committed friendship with a married woman—for the two were wed only after the death of Harriet Taylor's husband in 1849—laid an important experiential foundation for the loathing of the repressive, moralistic, and, as Isaiah Berlin put it, "uniformitarian despotism" of contemporary public opinion expressed in *On Liberty*.

The works represented here—*Utilitarianism, On Liberty,* the *Considerations on Representative Government,* and *The Subjection of Women*—were all composed during a period of Mill's life (1854–1861) in which, as John Gray has pointed out, he thought that his life might be short, following a grave illness, and that he should say what he had to say on the issues he judged central in his time. But Mill's earlier writings are important too. *A System of Logic* (1843) and *Principles of Political Economy* (1848) quickly became standard texts in their respective subjects, and the essays collected in Mill's *Dissertations and Discussions,* including a long review of Alexis de Tocqueville's *Democracy in America,* add a dimension of sociological and cultural insight that often eludes those who confine themselves to his better-known works. In particular, the affinity with de Tocqueville helps us understand that Mill's primary concerns in *On Liberty* are to do with social not just legal repression, and with the threat to individuality from mass society even more than majoritarian legislation.

There is an immense and growing literature on Mill's moral and political theory. Isaiah Berlin's essay, "John Stuart Mill and the Ends of Life," in his collection *Four Essays on Liberty* (Oxford: Oxford University Press, 1969), is an excellent starting point, while Alan Ryan's book, *The Philosophy of John Stuart Mill* (London: Macmillan, 1970), provides an authoritative overview of Mill's arguments. Much of the modern literature focuses on the essay *On Liberty*. Two good book-length studies are C. L. Ten, *Mill on Liberty* (Oxford: Clarendon Press, 1980); and John Gray, *Mill on Liberty—A Defence* (London: Routledge, 1983)—the latter arguing for the consistency of *On Liberty* and *Utilitarianism*. P. Radcliff has put together a useful collection of articles in *Limits of Liberty: Studies of Mill's On Liberty* (Belmont, Calif.: Wadsworth, 1966). D. F. Thompson, *John Stuart Mill and Representative Government* (Princeton, N. J.: Princeton University Press, 1976), is a useful study of Mill's democratic theory, and there is a fine discussion of Mill's feminism in Susan Moller Okin, *Women in Western Political Thought* (Princeton, N.J.: Princeton University Press, 1979).

# Utilitarianism

## CHAPTER I

### *General Remarks*

There are few circumstances among those which make up the present condition of human knowledge more unlike what might have been expected, or more significant of the backward state in which speculation on the most important subjects still lingers, than the little progress which has been made in the decision of the controversy respecting the criterion of right and wrong. From the dawn of philosophy, the question concerning the *summum bonum,* or, what is the same thing, concerning the foundation of morality, has been accounted the main problem in speculative thought, has occupied the most gifted intellects and divided them into sects and schools carrying on a vigorous warfare against one another. And after more than two thousand years the same discussions continue, philosophers are still ranged under the same contending banners, and neither thinkers nor mankind at large seem nearer to being unanimous on the subject than when the youth Socrates listened to the old Protagoras and asserted (if Plato's dialogue be grounded on a real conversation) the theory of utilitarianism against the popular morality of the so-called sophist.

It is true that similar confusion and uncertainty and, in some cases, similar discordance exist respecting the first principles of all the sciences, not excepting that which is deemed the most certain of them—mathematics, without much impairing, generally indeed without impairing at all, the trustworthiness of the conclusions of those sciences. An apparent anomaly, the explanation of which is that the detailed doctrines of a science are not usually deduced from, nor depend for their evidence upon, what are called its first principles. Were it not so, there would be no science more precarious, or whose conclusions were more insufficiently made out, than algebra, which derives none of its certainty from what are commonly taught to learners as its elements, since these, as laid down by some of its most eminent teachers, are as full of fictions as English law, and of mysteries as theology. The truths which are ultimately accepted as the first principles of a science are really the last results of metaphysical analysis practiced on the elementary notions with which the science is conversant; and their relation to the science is not that of foundations to an edifice, but of roots to a tree, which may perform their office equally well though they be never dug down to and exposed to light. But though in science the particular truths precede the general theory, the contrary might be expected to be the case with a practical art, such as morals or legislation. All action is for the sake of some end, and rules of action, it seems natural to suppose, must take their whole character and color from the end to which they are subservient. When we engage in pursuit, a clear and precise conception of what we are pursuing would seem to be the first thing we need, instead of the last we are to look forward to. A test of right and wrong must be the means, one would think, of ascertaining what is right or wrong, and not a consequence of having already ascertained it.

The difficulty is not avoided by having recourse to the popular theory of a natural faculty, a sense of instinct, informing us of right and wrong. For— besides that the existence of such a moral instinct is itself one of the matters in dispute—those believers in it who have any pretensions to philosophy have been obliged to abandon the idea that it discerns what is right or wrong in the particular case in hand, as our other senses discern the sight or sound actually present. Our moral faculty, according to all those of its interpreters who are entitled to the name of thinkers, supplies us only with the general principles of moral judgments; it is a branch of our reason, not of our sensitive faculty, and must be looked to for the abstract doctrines of morality, not for perception of it in the concrete. The intuitive, no less than what may be termed the inductive, school of ethics insists on the necessity of general laws. They both agree that the morality of an individual action is not a question of direct perception, but of the application of a law to an individual case. They recognize also, to a great extent, the same moral laws, but differ as to their evidence and the source from which they derive their authority. According to the one opinion, the principles of morals are evident *a priori,* requiring nothing to command assent except that the meaning of the terms be understood. According to the other doctrine, right and wrong, as well as truth and falsehood, are questions of observation and experience. But both hold equally that morality must be deduced from principles; and the intuitive school affirm as strongly as the inductive that there is a science of morals. Yet they seldom attempt to make out a list of the *a priori* principles which are to serve as the premises of the science; still more rarely do they make any effort to reduce those various principles to one first principle or common ground of obligation. They either assume the ordinary precepts of morals as of *a priori* authority, or they lay down as the common groundwork of those maxims some generality much less obviously authoritative than the maxims themselves, and which has never succeeded in gaining popular acceptance. Yet to support their pretensions there ought either to be some one fundamental principle or law at the root of all morality, or, if there be several, there should be a determinate order of precedence among them; and the one principle, or the rule for deciding between the various principles when they conflict, ought to be self-evident.

To inquire how far the bad effects of this deficiency have been mitigated in practice, or to what extent the moral beliefs of mankind have been vitiated or made uncertain by the absence of any distinct recognition of an ultimate standard, would imply a complete survey and criticism of past and present ethical doctrine. It would, however, be easy to show that whatever steadiness or consistency these moral beliefs have attained has been mainly due to the tacit influence of a standard not recognized. Although the nonexistence of an acknowledged first principle has made ethics not so much a guide as a consecration of men's actual sentiments, still, as men's sentiments, both of favor and of aversion, are greatly influenced by what they suppose to be the effects of things upon their happiness, the principle of utility, or, as Bentham latterly called it, the greatest happiness principle, has had a large share in forming the moral doctrines even of those who most scornfully reject its authority. Nor is there any school of thought which refuses to admit that the influence of actions on happiness is a most material and even predominant consideration in many of the details of morals, however unwilling to acknowledge it as the fundamental principle of morality and the source of moral obligation. I might go much further and say that to all those *a priori* moralists who deem it necessary to argue at all, utilitarian arguments are indispensable. It is not my present purpose to criticize these thinkers; but I cannot help referring, for illustration, to a systematic treatise by one of the most illustrious of them, the *Metaphysics of Ethics* by Kant. This remarkable man, whose system of thought will long remain one of the landmarks in the history of philosophical speculation, does, in the treatise in question, lay down a universal first principle as the origin and ground of moral obligation; it is this: "So act that the rule on which thou actest would admit of being adopted as a law by all rational beings." But when he begins to deduce from this precept any of the actual duties of morality, he fails, almost grotesquely, to show that there would be any contradiction, any logical (not to say physical) impossibility, in the adoption by all rational beings of the most outrageously immoral rules of conduct. All he shows is that the *consequences* of their universal adoption would be such as no one would choose to incur.

On the present occasion, I shall, without further discussion of the other theories, attempt to contribute something toward the understanding and appreciation of the "utilitarian" or "happiness" theory, and toward such proof as it is susceptible of. It is evident that this cannot be proof in the ordinary and popular meaning of the term. Questions of ultimate ends are not amenable to direct proof. Whatever can be proved to be good must be so by being shown to be a means to something admitted to be good without proof. The medical art is proved to be good by its conducing to health; but how is it possible to prove that health is good? The art of music is good, for the reason, among others, that it produces pleasure; but what proof is it possible to give that pleasure is good? If, then, it is asserted that there is a comprehensive formula, including all things which are in themselves good, and that whatever else is good is not so as an end but as a means, the formula may be accepted or rejected, but is not a subject of what is commonly understood by proof. We are not, however, to infer that its acceptance or rejection must depend on blind impulse or arbitrary choice. There is a larger meaning of the word "proof," in which this question is as amenable to it as any other of the disputed questions of philosophy. The subject is within the cognizance of the rational faculty; and neither does that faculty deal with it solely in the way of intuition. Considerations may be presented capable of determining the intellect either to give or withhold its assent to the doctrine; and this is equivalent to proof.

We shall examine presently of what nature are these considerations; in what manner they apply to the case, and what rational grounds, therefore, can be given for accepting or rejecting the utilitarian formula. But it is a preliminary condition of rational acceptance or rejection that the formula should be correctly understood. I believe that the very imperfect notion ordinarily formed of its meaning is the chief obstacle which impedes its reception, and that, could it be cleared even from only the grosser misconceptions, the question would be greatly simplified and a large proportion of its difficulties removed. Before, therefore, I attempt to enter into the philosophical grounds which can be given for assenting to the utilitarian standard, I shall offer some illustrations of the doctrine itself, with the view of showing more clearly what it is, distinguishing it from what it is not, and disposing of such of the practical objections to it as either originate in, or are closely connected with, mistaken interpretations of its meaning. Having thus prepared the ground, I shall afterwards endeavor to throw such light as I can call upon the question considered as one of philosophical theory.

## CHAPTER II

### *What Utilitarianism Is*

A passing remark is all that needs to be given to the ignorant blunder of supposing that those who stand up for utility as the test of right and wrong use the term in that restricted and merely colloquial sense in which utility is opposed to pleasure. An apology is due to the philosophical opponents of utilitarianism for even the momentary appearance of confounding them with anyone capable of so absurd a misconception; which is the more extraordinary, inasmuch as the contrary accusation, of referring everything to pleasure, and that, too, in its grossest form, is another of the common charges against utilitarianism: and, as has been pointedly remarked by an able writer, the same sort of persons, and often the very same persons, denounce the theory "as impracticably dry when the word 'utility' precedes the word 'pleasure,' and as too practically voluptuous when the word 'pleasure' precedes the word 'utility.'" Those who know anything about the matter are aware that every writer, from Epicurus to Bentham, who maintained the theory of utility meant by it, not something to be contradistinguished from pleasure, but pleasure itself, together with exemption from pain; and instead of opposing the useful to the agreeable or the ornamental, have always declared that the useful means these, among other things. Yet the common herd, including the herd of writers, not only in newspapers and periodicals, but in books of weight and pretension, are perpetually falling into this shallow mistake. Having caught up the word "utilitarian," while knowing nothing whatever about it but its sound, they habitually express by it the rejection or the neglect of pleasure in some of its forms: of beauty, of ornament, or of amusement. Nor is the term thus ignorantly misapplied solely in disparagement, but occasionally in compliment, as though it implied superiority to frivolity and the mere pleasures of the moment. And this perverted use is the only one in which the word is popularly known, and the one from which the new generation are acquiring their sole notion of its meaning. Those who introduced the word, but who had for many years discontinued it as a distinctive appellation, may well feel themselves called upon to resume it if by doing so they can hope to contribute anything toward rescuing it from this utter degradation.[1]

The creed which accepts as the foundation of morals "utility" or the "greatest happiness principle" holds that actions are right in proportion as they tend to promote happiness; wrong as they tend to produce the reverse of happiness. By happiness is intended pleasure and the absence of pain; by unhappiness, pain and the privation of pleasure. To give a clear view of the moral standard set up by the theory, much more requires to be said; in particular, what things it includes in the ideas of pain and pleasure, and to what extent this is left an open question. But these supplementary explanations do not affect the theory of life on which this theory of morality is grounded—namely, that pleasure and freedom from pain are the only things desirable as ends; and that all desirable things (which are as numerous in the utilitarian as in any other scheme) are desirable either for pleasure inherent in themselves or as means to the promotion of pleasure and the prevention of pain.

Now such a theory of life excites in many minds, and among them in some of the most estimable in feeling and purpose, inveterate dislike. To suppose that life has (as they express it) no higher end than pleasure—no better and nobler object of desire and pursuit—they designate as utterly mean and groveling, as a doctrine worthy only of swine, to whom the followers of Epicurus were, at a very early period, contemptuously likened; and modern holders of the doctrine are occasionally made the subject of equally polite comparisons by its German, French, and English assailants.

When thus attacked, the Epicureans have always answered that it is not they, but their accusers, who represent human nature in a degrading light, since the accusation supposes human beings to be capable of no pleasures except those of which swine are capable. If this supposition were true, the charge could not be gainsaid, but would then be no longer an imputation; for if the sources of pleasure were precisely the same to human beings and to swine, the rule of life which is good enough for the one would be good enough for the other. The comparison of the Epicurean life to that of beasts is felt as degrading, precisely because a beast's pleasures do not satisfy a human being's conceptions of happiness. Human beings have faculties more elevated than the animal appetites and, when once made conscious of them, do not regard anything as happiness which does not include their gratification. I do not indeed, consider the Epicureans to have been by any means faultless in drawing out their scheme of consequences from the utilitarian principle. To do this in any sufficient manner, many Stoic, as well as Christian, elements require to be included. But there is no known Epicurean theory of life which does not assign to the pleasures of the intellect, of the feelings and imagination, and of the moral sentiments a much higher value as pleasures than to those of mere sensation. It must be admitted, however, that utilitarian writers in general have placed the superiority of mental over bodily pleasures chiefly in the greater permanency, safety, uncostliness, etc., of the former—that is, in their circumstantial advantages rather than in their intrinsic nature. And on all these points utilitarians have fully proved their case; but they might have taken the other and, as it may be called, higher ground with entire consistency. It is quite compatible with the principle of utility to recognize the fact that some kinds of pleasures are more desirable and more valuable than others. It would be absurd that, while in estimating all other things quality is considered as well as quantity, the estimation of pleasure should be supposed to depend on quantity alone.

If I am asked what I mean by difference of quality in pleasures, or what makes one pleasure more valuable than another, merely as a pleasure, except its being greater in amount, there is but one possible answer. Of two pleasures, if there be one to which all or almost all who have experience of both give a decided preference, irrespective of any feeling of moral obligation to prefer it, that is the more desirable pleasure. If one of the two is, by those who are competently acquainted with both, placed so far above the other that they prefer it, even though knowing it to be attended with a greater amount of discontent, and would not resign it for any quantity of the other pleasure which their nature is capable of, we are justified in ascribing to the preferred enjoyment a superiority in quality so far outweighing quantity as to render it, in comparison, of small account.

Now it is an unquestionable fact that those who are equally acquainted with and equally capable of appreciating and enjoying both do give a most marked preference to the manner of existence which employs their higher faculties. Few human creatures would consent to be changed into any of the lower animals for a promise of the fullest allowance of a beast's pleasures; no intelligent human being would consent to be a fool, no instructed person would be an ignoramus, no person of feeling and conscience would be selfish and base, even though they should be persuaded that the fool, the dunce, or the rascal is better satisfied with his lot than they are with theirs. They would not resign what they possess more than he for the most complete satisfaction of all the desires which they have in common with him. If they ever fancy they would, it is only in cases of unhappiness so extreme that to escape from it they would exchange their lot for almost any other, however undesirable in their own eyes. A being of higher faculties requires more to make him happy, is capable probably of more acute suffering, and certainly accessible to it at more points, than one of an inferior type; but in spite of these liabilities, he can never really wish to sink into what he feels to be a lower grade of existence. We may give what explanation we please of this unwillingness; we may attribute it to pride, a name which is given indiscriminately to some of the most and to some of the least estimable feelings of which mankind are capable; we may refer it to the love of liberty and personal independence, an appeal to which was with the Stoics one of the most effective means for the inculcation of it; to the love of power or to the love of excitement, both of which do really enter into and contribute to it; but its most appropriate appellation is a sense of dignity, which all human beings possess in one form or other,

and in some, though by no means in exact, proportion to their higher faculties, and which is so essential a part of the happiness of those in whom it is strong that nothing which conflicts with it could be otherwise than momentarily an object of desire to them. Whoever supposes that this preference takes place at a sacrifice of happiness—that the superior being, in anything like equal circumstances, is not happier than the inferior—confounds the two very different ideas of happiness and content. It is indisputable that the being whose capacities of enjoyment are low has the greatest chance of having them fully satisfied; and a highly endowed being will always feel that any happiness which he can look for, as the world is constituted, is imperfect. But he can learn to bear its imperfections, if they are at all bearable; and they will not make him envy the being who is indeed unconscious of the imperfections, but only because he feels not at all the good which those imperfections qualify. It is better to be a human being dissatisfied than a pig satisfied; better to be Socrates dissatisfied than a fool satisfied. And if the fool, or the pig, are of a different opinion, it is because they only know their own side of the question. The other party to the comparison knows both sides.

It may be objected that many who are capable of the higher pleasures occasionally, under the influence of temptation, postpone them to the lower. But this is quite compatible with a full appreciation of the intrinsic superiority of the higher. Men often, from infirmity of character, make their election for the nearer good, though they know it to be the less valuable; and this no less when the choice is between two bodily pleasures than when it is between bodily and mental. They pursue sensual indulgences to the injury of health, though perfectly aware that health is the greater good. It may be further objected that many who begin with youthful enthusiasm for everything noble, as they advance in years, sink into indolence and selfishness. But I do not believe that those who undergo this very common change voluntarily choose the lower description of pleasures in preference to the higher. I believe that, before they devote themselves exclusively to the one, they have already become incapable of the other. Capacity for the nobler feelings is in most natures a very tender plant, easily killed, not only by hostile influences, but by mere want of sustenance; and in the majority of young persons it speedily dies away if the occupations to which their position in life has devoted them, and the society into which it has thrown them, are not favorable to keeping that higher capacity in exercise. Men lose their high aspirations as they lose their intellectual tastes, because they have not time or opportunity for indulging them; and they addict themselves to inferior pleasures, not because they deliberately prefer them, but because they are either the only ones to which they have access or the only ones which they are any longer capable of enjoying. It may be questioned whether anyone who has remained equally susceptible to both classes of pleasures ever knowingly and calmly preferred the lower, though many, in all ages, have broken down in an ineffectual attempt to combine both.

From this verdict of the only competent judges, I apprehend there can be no appeal. On a question which is the best worth having of two pleasures, or which of two modes of existence is the most grateful to the feelings, apart from its moral attributes and from its consequences, the judgment of those who are qualified by knowledge of both, or, if they differ, that of the majority among them, must be admitted as final. And there needs be the less hesitation to accept this judgment respecting the quality of pleasures, since there is no other tribunal to be referred to even on the question of quantity. What means are there of determining which is the acutest of two pains, or the intensest of two pleasurable sensations, except the general suffrage of those who are familiar with both? Neither pains nor pleasures are homogeneous, and pain is always heterogeneous with pleasure. What is there to decide whether a particular pleasure is worth purchasing at the cost of a particular pain, except the feelings and judgment of the experienced? When, therefore, those feelings and judgment declare the pleasures derived from the higher faculties to be preferable *in kind,* apart from the question of intensity, to those of which the animal nature, disjoined from the higher faculties, is susceptible, they are entitled on this subject to the same regard.

I have dwelt on this point as being a necessary part of a perfectly just conception of utility or happiness considered as the directive rule of human conduct. But it is by no means an indispensable condition to the acceptance of the utilitarian standard; for that standard is not the agent's own greatest happiness, but the greatest amount of happiness altogether; and if it may possibly be doubted whether a noble character is always the happier for its nobleness, there can be no doubt that it makes other people happier, and that the world in general is immensely a gainer by it. Utilitarianism, therefore, could only attain its end by the general cultivation of nobleness of character, even if each individual were only benefited by the nobleness of others, and his own, so far as happiness is concerned, were a sheer deduction from the benefit. But the bare enunciation of such an absurdity as this last renders refutation superfluous.

According to the greatest happiness principle, as above explained, the ultimate end, with reference to and for the sake of which all other things are desirable—whether we are considering our own good or that of other people—is an existence exempt as far as possible from pain, and as rich as possible in enjoyments, both in point of quantity and quality; the test of quality and the rule for measuring it against quantity being the preference felt by those who, in their opportunities of experience, to which must be added their habits of self-consciousness and self-observation, are best furnished with the means of comparison. This, being according to the utilitarian opinion the end of human action, is necessarily also the standard of morality, which may accordingly be defined "the rules and precepts for human conduct," by the observance of which an existence such as has been described might be, to the greatest extent possible, secured to all mankind; and not to them only, but, so far as the nature of things admits to, to the whole sentient creation.

Against this doctrine, however, arises another class of objectors who say that happiness, in any form, cannot be the rational purpose of human life and action; because, in the first place, it is unattainable; and they contemptuously ask, What right hast thou to be happy?—a question which Mr. Carlyle clinches by the addition, What right, a short time ago, hadst thou even *to be?* Next they say that men can do *without* happiness; that all noble human beings have felt this, and could not have become noble but by learning the lesson of *Entsagen,* or renunciation; which lesson, thoroughly learned and submitted to, they affirm to be the beginning and necessary condition of all virtue.

The first of these objections would go to the root of the matter were it well founded; for if no happiness is to be had at all by human beings, the attainment of it cannot be the end of morality or of any rational conduct. Though, even in that case, something might still be said for the utilitarian theory, since utility includes not solely the pursuit of happiness, but the prevention or mitigation of unhappiness; and if the former aim be chimerical, there will be all the greater scope and more imperative need for the latter, so long at least as mankind think fit to live and do not take refuge in the simultaneous act of suicide recommended under certain conditions by Novalis. When, however, it is thus positively asserted to be impossible that human life should be happy, the assertion, if not something like a verbal quibble, is at least an exaggeration. If by happiness be meant a continuity of highly pleasurable excitement, it is evident enough that this is impossible. A state of exalted pleasure lasts only moments or in some cases, and with some intermissions, hours or days, and is the occasional brilliant flash of enjoyment, not its permanent and steady flame. Of this the philosophers who have taught that happiness is the end of life were as fully aware as those who taunt them. The happiness which they meant was not a life of rapture, but moments of such, in an existence made up of few and transitory pains, many and various pleasures, with a decided predominance of the active over the passive, and having as the foundation of the whole not to expect more from life than it is capable of bestowing. A life thus composed, to those who have been fortunate enough to obtain it, has always appeared worthy of the name of happiness. And such an existence is even now the lot of many during some considerable portion of their lives. The present wretched education and wretched social arrangements are the only real hindrance to its being attainable by almost all.

The objectors perhaps may doubt whether human beings, if taught to consider happiness as the end of life, would be satisfied with such a moderate share of it. But great numbers of mankind have been satisfied with much less. The main constituents of a satisfied life appear to be two, either of which by itself is often found sufficient for the purpose: tranquility and excitement. With much tranquility, many find that they can be content with very little pleasure; with much excitement, many can reconcile themselves to a considerable quantity of pain. There is assuredly no inherent impossibility of enabling even the mass of mankind to unite both, since the two are so far from being incompatible that they are in natural alliance, the prolongation of either being a preparation for, and exciting a wish for, the other. It is only those in whom indolence amounts to a vice that do not desire excitement after an interval of respose; it is only those in whom the need of excitement is a disease that feel the tranquillity which follows excitement dull and insipid, instead of pleasurable in direct proportion to the excitement which preceded it. When people who are tolerably fortunate in their outward lot do not find in life sufficient enjoyment to make it valuable to them, the cause generally is caring for nobody but themselves. To those who have neither public nor private affections, the excitements of life are much curtailed, and in any case dwindle in value as the time approaches when all selfish interests must be terminated by death; while those who leave after them objects of personal affection, and especially those who have also cultivated a fellow-feeling with the collective interests of mankind, retain as lively an interest in life on the eve of death as in the vigor of youth and health. Next to selfishness, the principal cause which makes life unsatisfactory is want of mental cultivation. A cultivated mind—I do not mean that of a philosopher, but any mind to which the fountains of knowledge have been opened, and which has been taught, in any tolerable degree, to exercise its faculties—finds sources of inexhaustible interest in all that surrounds it: in the objects of nature, the achievements of art, the imaginations of poetry, the incidents of history, the ways of mankind, past and present, and their prospects in the future. It is possible, indeed, to become indifferent to all this, and that too without having exhausted a thousandth part of it, but only when one has had from the beginning no moral or human interest in these things and has sought in them only the gratification of curiosity.

Now there is absolutely no reason in the nature of things why an amount of mental culture sufficient to give an intelligent interest in these objects of contemplation should not be the inheritance of everyone born in a civilized country. As little is there an inherent necessity that any human being should be a selfish egotist, devoid of every feeling or care but those which center in his own miserable individuality. Something far superior to this is sufficiently common even now, to give ample earnest of what the human species may be made. Genuine private affections and a sincere interest in the public good are possible, though in unequal degrees, to every rightly brought up human being. In a world in which there is so much to interest, so much to enjoy, and so much also to correct and improve, everyone who has this moderate amount of moral and intellectual requisites is capable of an existence which may be called enviable; and unless such a person, through bad laws or subjection to the will of others, is denied the liberty to use the sources of happiness within his reach, he will not fail to find this enviable existence, if he escapes the positive evils of life, the great sources of physical and mental suffering—such as indigence, disease, and the unkindness, worthlessness, or premature loss of objects of affection. The main stress of the problem lies, therefore, in the contest with these calamities from which it is a rare good fortune entirely to escape; which, as things now are, cannot be obviated, and often cannot be in any material degree mitigated. Yet no one whose opinion deserves a moment's consideration can doubt that most of the great positive evils of the world are in themselves removable, and will, if human affairs continue to improve, be in the end reduced within narrow limits. Poverty, in any sense implying suffering, may be completely extinguished by the wisdom of society combined with the good sense and providence of individuals. Even that most intractable of enemies, disease, may be indefinitely reduced in dimensions by good physical and moral education and proper control

of noxious influences, while the progress of science holds out a promise for the future of still more direct conquests over this detestable foe. And every advance in that direction relieves us from some, not only of the chances which cut short our own lives, but, what concerns us still more, which deprive us of those in whom our happiness is wrapt up. As for vicissitudes of fortune and other disappointments connected with wordly circumstances, these are principally the effect either of gross imprudence, of ill-regulated desires, or of bad or imperfect social institutions. All the grand sources, in short, of human suffering are in a great degree, many of them almost entirely, conquerable by human care and effort; and though their removal is grievously slow—though a long succession of generations will perish in the breach before the conquest is completed, and this world becomes all that, if will and knowledge were not wanting, it might easily be made—yet every mind sufficiently intelligent and generous to bear a part, however small and inconspicuous, in the endeavour will draw a noble enjoyment from the contest itself, which he would not for any bribe in the form of selfish indulgence consent to be without.

And this leads to the true estimation of what is said by the objectors concerning the possibility and the obligation of learning to do without happiness. Unquestionably it is possible to do without happiness; it is done involuntarily by nineteen-twentieths of mankind, even in those parts of our present world which are least deep in barbarism; and it often has to be done voluntarily by the hero or the martyr, for the sake of something which he prizes more than his individual happiness. But this something, what is it, unless the happiness of others or some of the requisites of happiness? It is noble to be capable of resigning entirely one's own portion of happiness, or chances of it; but, after all, this self-sacrifice must be for some end, it is not its own end; and if we are told that its end is not happiness but virtue, which is better than happiness, I ask, would the sacrifice be made if the hero or martyr did not believe that it would earn for others immunity from similar sacrifices? Would it be made if he thought that his renunciation of happiness for himself would produce no fruit for any of his fellow creatures, but to make their lot like his and place them also in the condition of persons who have renounced happiness? All honor to those who can abnegate for themselves the personal enjoyment of life when by such renunciation they contribute worthily to increase the amount of happiness in the world; but he who does it or professes to do it for any other purpose is no more deserving of admiration than the ascetic mounted on his pillar. He may be an inspiriting proof of what men *can* do, but assuredly not an example of what they *should.*

Though it is only in a very imperfect state of the world's arrangements that anyone can best serve the happiness of others by the absolute sacrifice of his own, yet, so long as the world is in that imperfect state, I fully acknowledge that the readiness to make such a sacrifice is the highest virtue which can be found in man. I will add that in this condition of the world, paradoxical as the assertion may be, the conscious ability to do without happiness gives the best prospect of realizing such happiness as is attainable. For nothing except that consciousness can raise a person above the chances of life by making him feel that, let fate and fortune do their worst, they have not power to subdue him; which, once felt, frees him from excess of anxiety concerning the evils of life and enables him, like many a Stoic in the worst times of the Roman Empire, to cultivate in tranquillity the sources of satisfaction accessible to him, without concerning himself about the uncertainty of their duration any more than about their inevitable end.

Meanwhile, let utilitarians never cease to claim the morality of self-devotion as a possession which belongs by as good a right to them as either to the Stoic or to the Transcendentalist. The utilitarian morality does recognize in human beings the power of sacrificing their own greatest good for the good of others. It only refuses to admit that the sacrifice is itself a good. A sacrifice which does not increase or tend to increase the sum total of happiness, it considers as wasted. The only self-renunciation which it applauds is devotion to the happiness, or to some of the means of happiness, of others, either of mankind collectively or of individuals within the limits imposed by the collective interests of mankind.

I must again repeat what the assailants of utilitarianism seldom have the justice to acknowledge, that the happiness which forms the utilitarian standard of what is right in conduct is not the agent's own happiness but that of all concerned. As between his own happiness and that of others, utilitarianism requires him to be as strictly impartial as a disinterested and benevolent spectator. In the golden rule of Jesus of Nazareth, we read the complete spirit of the ethics of utility. "To do as you would be done by," and "to love your neighbor as yourself," constitute the ideal perfection of utilitarian morality. As the means of making the nearest approach to this ideal, utility would enjoin, first, that laws and social arrangements should place the happiness or (as, speaking practically, it may be called) the interest of every individual as nearly as possible in harmony with the interest of the whole; and, secondly, that education and opinion, which have so vast a power over human character, should so use that power as to establish in the mind of every individual an indissoluble association between his own happiness and the good of the whole, especially between his own happiness and the practice of such modes of conduct, negative and positive, as regard for the universal happiness prescribes; so that not only he may be unable to conceive the possibility of happiness to himself, consistently with conduct opposed to the general good, but also that a direct impulse to promote the general good may be in every individual one of the habitual motives of action, and the sentiments connected therewith may fill a large and prominent place in every human being's sentient existence. If the impugners of the utilitarian morality represented it to their own minds in this its true character, I know not what recommendation possessed by any other morality they could possibly affirm to be wanting to it; what more beautiful or more exalted developments of human nature any other ethical system can be supposed to foster, or what springs of action, not accessible to the utilitarian, such systems rely on for giving effect to their mandates.

The objectors to utilitarianism cannot always be charged with representing it in a discreditable light. On the contrary, those among them who entertain anything like a just idea of its disinterested character sometimes find fault with its standard as being too high for humanity. They say it is exacting too much to require that people shall always act from the inducement of promoting the general interests of society. But this is to mistake the very meaning of a standard of morals and confound the rule of action with the motive of it. It is the business of ethics to tell us what are our duties, or by what test we may know them; but no system of ethics requires that the sole motive of all we do shall be a feeling of duty; on the contrary, ninety-nine hundredths of all our actions are done from other motives, and rightly so done if the rule of duty does not condemn them. It is the more unjust to utilitarianism that this particular misapprehension should be made a ground of objection to it, inasmuch as utilitarian moralists have gone beyond almost all others in affirming that the motive has nothing to do with the morality of the action, though much with the worth of the agent. He who saves a fellow creature from drowning does what is morally right, whether his motive be duty or the hope of being paid for his trouble; he who betrays the friend that trusts him is guilty of a crime, even if his object be to serve another friend to whom he is under greater obligations.[2] But to speak only of actions done from the motive of duty, and in direct obedience to principle: it is a misapprehension of the utilitarian mode of thought to conceive it as implying that people should fix their minds upon so wide a generality as the world, or society at large. The great majority of good actions are intended not for the benefit of the world, but for that of individuals, of which the good of the world is made up; and the thoughts of the most virtuous man need not on these occasions travel beyond the particular persons concerned, except so far as is necessary to assure himself that in benefiting them he is not violating the rights, that is, the legitimate and authorized expectations, of anyone else. The multiplication of happiness is, according to the utilitarian ethics, the object of virtue: the occasions on which any person (except one in a thousand) has it in his power to do this on an extended scale—in other words, to be a public benefactor—are but exceptional; and on these occasions alone is he called on to consider public utility; in every other case, private utility, the interest or happiness of some few persons, is all he has to attend to. Those alone the influence of whose actions extends to society in general need concern themselves habitually about so large an object. In the case of abstinences indeed—of things which people forbear to do from moral considerations, though the consequences in the particular case might be beneficial—it would be unworthy of an intelligent agent not to be consciously aware that the action is of a class which, if practiced generally, would be generally injurious, and that this is the ground of the obligation to abstain from it. The amount of regard for the public interest implied in this recognition is no greater than is demanded by every system of morals, for they all enjoin to abstain from whatever is manifestly pernicious to society.

The same considerations dispose of another reproach against the doctrine of utility, founded on a still grosser misconception of the purpose of a standard of morality and of the very meaning of the words "right" and "wrong." It is often affirmed that utilitarianism renders men cold and unsympathizing; that it chills their moral feelings toward individuals; that it makes them regard only the dry and hard consideration of the consequences of actions, not taking into their moral estimate the qualities from which those actions emanate. If the assertion means that they do not allow their judgment respecting the rightness or wrongness of an action to be influenced by their opinion of the qualities of the person who does it, this is a complaint not against utilitarianism, but against any standard or morality at all; for certainly no known ethical standard decides an action to be good or bad because it is done by a good or bad man, still less because done by an amiable, a brave, or a benevolent man, or the contrary. These considerations are relevant, not to the estimation of actions, but of persons; and there is nothing in the utilitarian theory inconsistent with the fact that there are other things which interest us in persons besides the rightness and wrongness of their actions. The Stoics, indeed, with the paradoxical misuse of language which was part of their system, and by which they strove to raise themselves above all concern about anything but virtue, were fond of saying that he who has that has everything; that he, and only he, is rich, is beautiful, is a king. But no claim of this description is made for the virtuous man by the utilitarian doctrine. Utilitarians are quite aware that there are other desirable possessions and qualities besides virtue, and are perfectly willing to allow to all of them their full worth. They are also aware that a right action does not necessarily indicate a virtuous character, and that actions which are blamable often proceed from qualities entitled to praise. When this is apparent in any particular case, it modifies their estimation, not certainly of the act, but of the agent. I grant that they are, notwithstanding, of opinion that in the long run the best proof of a good character is good actions; and resolutely refuse to consider any mental disposition as good of which the predominant tendency is to produce bad conduct. This makes them unpopular with many people, but it is an unpopularity which they must share with everyone who regards the distinction between right and wrong in a serious light; and the reproach is not one which a conscientious utilitarian need be anxious to repel.

If no more be meant by the objection than that many utilitarians look on the morality of actions, as measured by the utilitarian standards, with too exclusive a regard, and do not lay sufficient stress upon the other beauties of character which go toward making a human being lovable or admirable, this may be admitted. Utilitarians who have cultivated their moral feelings, but not their sympathies, nor their artistic perceptions, do fall into this mistake; and so do all other moralists under the same conditions. What can be said in excuse for other moralists is equally available for them, namely, that, if there is to be any error, it is better that it should be on that side. As a matter of fact, we may affirm that among utilitarians, as among adherents of other systems, there is every imaginable degree of rigidity and of laxity in the application of their standard; some are even puritanically rigorous, while others are as indulgent as can possibly be desired by sinner or by sentimentalist. But on the whole, a doctrine which brings prominently forward the interest that mankind have in the repression and prevention of conduct which violates the moral law is likely to be inferior to no other in turning the sanctions of opinion against such violations. It is true, the question "What does violate the moral law?" is one on which those who recognize different standards of morality are likely now and then to differ. But difference of opinion on moral questions was not first introduced into the world by utilitarianism, while the doctrine does supply, if not always an easy, at all events a tangible and intelligible, mode of deciding such differences.

It may not be superfluous to notice a few more of the common misapprehensions of utilitarian ethics, even those which are so obvious and gross that it might appear impossible for any person of candor and intelligence to fall into them; since persons, even of considerable mental endowment, often give themselves so little trouble to understand the bearings of any opinion against which they entertain a prejudice, and men are in general so little conscious of this voluntary ignorance as a defect that the vulgarest misunderstandings of ethical doctrines are continually met with in the deliberate writings of persons of the greatest pretensions both to high principle and to philosophy. We not uncommonly hear the doctrine of utility inveighed against a *godless* doctrine. If it be necessary to say anything at all against so mere an assumption, we may say that the question depends upon what idea we have formed of the moral character of the Deity. If it be a true belief that God desires, above all things, the happiness of his creatures, and that this was his purpose in their creation, utility is not only a godless doctrine, but more profoundly religious than any other. If it be meant that utilitarianism does not recognize the revealed will of God as the supreme law of morals, I answer that a utilitarian who believes in the perfect goodness and wisdom of *God* necessarily believes that whatever God has thought fit to reveal on the subject of morals must fulfill the requirements of utility in a supreme degree. But others besides utilitarians have been of opinion that the Christian revelation was intended, and is fitted, to inform the hearts and minds of mankind with a spirit which should enable them to find for themselves what is right, and incline them to do it when found, rather than to tell them, except in a very general way, what it is; and that we need a doctrine of ethics, carefully followed out, to *interpret* to us the will of God. Whether this opinion is correct or not, it is superfluous here to discuss; since whatever aid religion, either natural or revealed, can afford to ethical investigation is as open to the utilitarian moralist as to any other. He can use it as the testimony of God to the usefulness or hurtfulness of any given course of action by as good a right as others can use it for the indication of a transcendental law having no connection with usefulness or with happiness.

Again, utility is often summarily stigmatized as an immoral doctrine by giving it the name of "expediency," and taking advantage of the popular use of that term to contrast it with principle. But the expedient, in the sense in which it is opposed to the right, generally means that which is expedient for the particular interest of the agent himself; as when a minister sacrifices the interests of his country to keep himself in place. When it means anything better than this, it means that which is expedient for some immediate object, some temporary purpose, but which violates a rule whose observance is expedient in a much higher degree. The expedient, in this sense, instead of being the same thing with the useful, is a branch of the hurtful. Thus it would often be expedient, for the purpose of getting over some momentary embarrassment, or attaining some object immediately useful to ourselves or others, to tell a lie. But inasmuch as the cultivation in ourselves of a sensitive feeling on the subject of veracity is one of the most useful, and the enfeeblement of that feeling one of the most hurtful, things to which our conduct can be instrumental; and inasmuch as any, even unintentional, deviation from truth does that much toward weakening the trustworthiness of human assertion, which is not only the principal support of all present social well-being, but the insufficiency of which does more than any one thing that can be named to keep back civilization, virtue, everything on which human happiness on the largest scale depends—we feel that the violation, for a present advantage, of a rule of such transcendent expediency is not expedient, and that he who, for the sake of convenience to himself or to some other individual, does what depends on him to deprive mankind of the good, and inflict upon them the evil,

involved in the greater or less reliance which they can place in each other's word, acts the part of one of their worst enemies. Yet that even this rule, sacred as it is, admits of possible exceptions is acknowledged by all moralists; the chief of which is when the withholding of some fact (as of information from a malefactor, or of bad news from a person dangerously ill) would save an individual (especially an individual other than oneself) from great and unmerited evil, and when the withholding can only be effected by denial. But in order that the exception may not extend itself beyond the need, and may have the least possible effect in weakening reliance on veracity, it ought to be recognized and, if possible, its limits defined; and, if the principle of utility is good for anything, it must be good for weighing these conflicting utilities against one another and marking out the region within which one or the other preponderates.

Again, defenders of utility often find themselves called upon to reply to such objections as this—that there is not time, previous to action, for calculating and weighing the effects of any line of conduct on the general happiness. This is exactly as if anyone were to say that it is impossible to guide our conduct by Christianity because there is not time, on every occasion on which anything has to be done, to read through the Old and New Testaments. The answer to the objection is that there has been ample time, namely, the whole past duration of the human species. During all that time mankind have been learning by experience the tendencies of actions; on which experience all the prudence as well as all the morality of life are dependent. People talk as if the commencement of this course of experience had hitherto been put off, and as if, at the moment when some man feels tempted to meddle with the property or life of another, he had to begin considering for the first time whether murder and theft are injurious to human happiness. Even then I do not think that he would find the question very puzzling; but, at all events, the matter is now done to his hand. It is truly a whimsical supposition that, if mankind were agreed in considering utility to be the test of morality, they would remain without any agreement as to what *is* useful, and would take no measures for having their notions on the subject taught to the young and enforced by law and opinion. There is no difficulty in proving any ethical standard whatever to work ill if we suppose universal idiocy to be conjoined with it; but on any hypothesis short of that, mankind must by this time have acquired positive beliefs as to the effects of some actions on their happiness; and the beliefs which have thus come down are the rules of morality for the multitude, and for the philosopher until he has succeeded in finding better. That philosophers might easily do this, even now, on many subjects; that the received code of ethics is by no means of divine right; and that mankind have still much to learn as to the effects of actions on the general happiness, I admit or rather earnestly maintain. The corollaries from the principle of utility, like the precepts of every practical art, admit of indefinite improvement, and, in a progressive state of the human mind, their improvement is perpetually going on. But to consider the rules of morality as improvable is one thing; to pass over the intermediate generalization entirely and endeavor to test each individual action directly by the first principle is another. It is a strange notion that the acknowledgment of a first principle is inconsistent with the admission of secondary ones. To inform a traveler respecting the place of his ultimate destination is not to forbid the use of landmarks and direction-posts on the way. The proposition that happiness is the end and aim of morality does not mean that no road ought to be laid down to that goal, or that persons going thither should not be advised to take one direction rather than another. Men really ought to leave off talking a kind of nonsense on this subject, which they would neither talk nor listen to on other matters of practical concernment. Nobody argues that the art of navigation is not founded on astronomy because sailors cannot wait to calculate the Nautical Almanac. Being rational creatures, they go to sea with it ready calculated; and all rational creatures go out upon the sea of life with their minds made up on the common questions of right and wrong, as well as on many of the far more difficult questions of wise and foolish. And this, as long as foresight is a human quality, it is to be presumed they will continue to do. Whatever we adopt as the fundamental principle of morality, we require subordinate principles to apply it by; the impossibility of doing without them, being common to all systems, can afford no argument against any one in particular; but gravely to argue as if no such secondary principles could be had, and as if mankind had remained till now, and always must remain, without drawing any general conclusions from the experience of human life is as high a pitch, I think, as absurdity has ever reached in philosophical controversy.

The remainder of the stock arguments against utilitarianism mostly consist in laying to its charge the common infirmities of human nature, and the general difficulties which embarrass conscientious persons in shaping their course through life. We are told that a utilitarian will be apt to make his own particular case an exception to moral rules, and, when under temptation, will see a utility in the breach of a rule, greater than he will see in its observance. But is utility the only creed which is able to furnish us with excuses for evil-doing and means of cheating our own conscience? They are afforded in abundance by all doctrines which recognize as a fact in morals the existence of conflicting considerations, which all doctrines do that have been believed by sane persons. It is not the fault of any creed, but of the complicated nature of human affairs, that rules of conduct cannot be so framed as to require no exceptions, and that hardly any kind of action can safely be laid down as either always obligatory or always condemnable. There is no ethical creed which does not temper the rigidity of its laws by giving a certain latitude, under the moral responsibility of the agent, for accommodation to peculiarities of circumstances; and under every creed, at the opening thus made, self-deception and dishonest casuistry get in. There exists no moral system under which there do not arise unequivocal cases of conflicting obligation. These are the real difficulties, the knotty points both in the theory of ethics and in the conscientious guidance of personal conduct. They are overcome practically, with greater or with less success, according to the intellect and virtue of the individual; but it can hardly be pretended that anyone will be the less qualified for dealing with them,

from possessing an ultimate standard to which conflicting rights and duties can be referred. If utility is
the ultimate source of moral obligations, utility may
be invoked to decide between them when their
demands are incompatible. Though the application
of the standard may be difficult, it is better than none
at all; while in other systems, the moral laws all
claiming independent authority, there is no common
umpire entitled to interfere between them; their
claims to precedence one over another rest on little
better than sophistry, and, unless determined, as they
generally are, by the unacknowledged influence of
consideration of utility, afford a free scope for the
action of personal desires and partialities. We must
remember that only in these cases of conflict
between secondary principles is it requisite that first
principles should be appealed to. There is no case of
moral obligation in which some secondary principle
is not involved; and if only one, there can seldom be
any real doubt which one it is, in the mind of any
person by whom the principle itself is recognized.

## CHAPTER III

### *Of the Ultimate Sanction*
### *of the Principle of Utility*

The question is often asked, and properly so, in
regard to any supposed moral standard—What is its
sanction? what are the motives to obey? or, more
specifically, what is the source of its obligation?
whence does it derive its binding force? It is a necessary part of moral philosophy to provide the answer
to this question, which, though frequently assuming
the shape of an objection to the utilitarian morality, as
if it had some special applicability to that above others, really arises in regard to all standards. It arises, in
fact, whenever a person is called on to *adopt* a standard, or refer morality to any basis on which he has
not been accustomed to rest it. For the customary
morality, that which education and opinion have consecrated, is the only one which presents itself to the
mind with the feeling of being *in itself* obligatory; and
when a person is asked to believe that this morality

*derives* its obligation from some general principle
round which custom has not thrown the same halo,
the assertion is to him a paradox; the supposed corollaries seem to have a more binding force than the
original theorem; the superstructure seems to stand
better without than with what is represented as its
foundation. He says to himself, I feel that I am bound
not to rob or murder, betray or deceive; but why am I
bound to promote the general happiness? If my own
happiness lies in something else, why may I not give
that the preference?

If the view adopted by the utilitarian philosophy
of the nature of the moral sense be correct, this difficulty will always present itself until the influences
which form moral character have taken the same
hold of the principle which they have taken of some
of the consequences—until, by the improvement of
education, the feeling of unity with our fellow creatures shall be (what it cannot be denied that Christ
intended it to be) as deeply rooted in our character,
and to our own consciousness as completely a part of
our nature, as the horror of crime is in an ordinarily
well-brought up young person. In the meantime,
however, the difficulty has no peculiar application to
the doctrine of utility, but is inherent in every
attempt to analyze morality and reduce it to principles; which, unless the principle is already in men's
minds invested with as much sacredness as any of its
applications, always seems to divest them of a part
of their sanctity.

The principle of utility either has, or there is no
reason why it might not have, all the sanctions which
belong to any other system of morals. Those sanctions are either external or internal. Of the external
sanctions it is not necessary to speak at any length.
They are the hope of favor and the fear of displeasure
from our fellow creatures or from the Ruler of the
universe, along with whatever we may have of sympathy or affection for them, or of love and awe of
Him, inclining us to do His will independently of
selfish consequences. There is evidently no reason
why all these motives for observance should not
attach themselves to the utilitarian morality as completely and as powerfully as to any other. Indeed,
those of them which refer to our fellow creatures are

sure to do so, in proportion to the amount of general intelligence; for whether there be any other ground of moral obligation than the general happiness or not, men do desire happiness; and however imperfect may be their own practice, they desire and commend all conduct in others toward themselves by which they think their happiness is promoted. With regard to the religious motive, if men believe, as most profess to do, in the goodness of God, those who think that conduciveness to the general happiness is the essence or even only the criterion of good must necessarily believe that it is also that which God approves. The whole force therefore of external reward and punishment, whether physical or moral, and whether proceeding from God or from our fellow men, together with all that the capacities of human nature admit of disinterested devotion to either, become available to enforce the utilitarian morality, in proportion as that morality is recognized; and the more powerfully, the more the appliances of education and general cultivation are bent to the purpose.

So far as to external sanctions. The internal sanction of duty, whatever our standard of duty may be, is one and the same—a feeling in our own mind; a pain, more or less intense, attendant on violation of duty, which in properly cultivated moral natures rises, in the more serious cases, into shrinking from it as an impossibility. This feeling, when disinterested and connecting itself with the pure idea of duty, and not with some particular form of it, or with any of the merely accessory circumstances, is the essence of conscience; though in that complex phenomenon as it actually exists, the simple fact is in general all encrusted over with collateral associations derived from sympathy, from love, and still more from fear; from all the forms of religious feeling; from the recollections of childhood and of all our past life; from self-esteem, desire of the esteem of others, and occasionally even self-abasement. This extreme complication is, I apprehend, the origin of the sort of mystical character which, by a tendency of the human mind of which there are many other examples, is apt to be attributed to the idea of moral obligation, and which leads people to believe that the idea cannot possibly attach itself to any other objects than those which, by

a supposed mysterious law, are found in our present experience to excite it. Its binding force, however, consists in the existence of a mass of feeling which must be broken through in order to do what violates our standard of right, and which, if we do nevertheless violate that standard, will probably have to be encountered afterwards in the form of remorse. Whatever theory we have of the nature or origin of conscience, this is what essentially constitutes it.

The ultimate sanction, therefore, of all morality (external motives apart) being a subjective feeling in our own minds, I see nothing embarrassing to those whose standard is utility in the question, What is the sanction of that particular standard? We may answer, the same as of all other moral standards—the conscientious feelings of mankind. Undoubtedly this sanction has no binding efficacy on those who do not possess the feelings it appeals to; but neither will these persons be more obedient to any other moral principle than to the utilitarian one. On them morality of any kind has no hold but through the external sanctions. Meanwhile the feelings exist, a fact in human nature, the reality of which, and the great power with which they are capable of acting on those in whom they have been duly cultivated, are proved by experience. No reason has ever been shown why they may not be cultivated to as great intensity in connection with the utilitarian as with any other rule of morals.

There is, I am aware, a disposition to believe that a person who sees in moral obligation a transcendental fact, an objective reality belonging to the province of "things in themselves," is likely to be more obedient to it than one who believes it to be entirely subjective, having its seat in human consciousness only. But whatever a person's opinion may be on this point of ontology, the force he is really urged by is his own subjective feeling, and is exactly measured by its strength. No one's belief that duty is an objective reality is stronger than the belief that God is so; yet the belief in God, apart from the expectation of actual reward and punishment, only operates on conduct through, and in proportion to, the subjective religious feeling. The sanction, so far as it is disinterested, is always in the mind itself; and the motion, therefore, of the transcendental moralists must be that this sanction will not exist *in* the mind unless it is believed to have its root out of the mind; and that if a person is able to say to himself, "That which is restraining me and which is called my conscience is only a feeling in my own mind," he may possibly draw the conclusion that when the feeling ceases the obligation ceases, and that if he find the feeling inconvenient, he may disregard it and endeavor to get rid of it. But is this danger confined to the utilitarian morality? Does the belief that moral obligation has its seat outside the mind make the feeling of it too strong to get rid of? The fact is so far otherwise that all moralists admit and lament the ease with which, in the generality of minds, conscience can be silenced or stifled. The question, "Need I obey my conscience?" is quite as often put to themselves by persons who never heard of the principle of utility as by its adherents. Those whose conscientious feelings are so weak as to allow of their asking this question, if they answer it affirmatively, will not do so because they believe in the transcendental theory, but because of the external sanctions.

It is not necessary, for the present purpose, to decide whether the feeling of duty is innate or implanted. Assuming it to be innate, it is an open question to what objects it naturally attaches itself; for the philosophic supporters of that theory are now agreed that the intuitive perception is of principles of morality and not of the details. If there be anything innate in the matter, I see no reason why the feeling which is innate should not be that of regard to the pleasures and pains of others. If there is any principle of morals which is intuitively obligatory, I should say it must be that. If so, the intuitive ethics would coincide with the utilitarian, and there would be no further quarrel between them. Even as it is, the intuitive moralists, though they believe that there are other intuitive moral obligations, do already believe this to be one; for they unanimously hold that a large *portion* of morality turns upon the consideration due to the interests of our fellow creatures. Therefore, if the belief in the transcendental origin of moral obligation gives any additional efficacy to the internal sanction, it appears to me that the utilitarian principle has already the benefit of it.

On the other hand, if, as is my own belief, the moral feelings are not innate but acquired, they are not for that reason the less natural. It is natural to man to speak, to reason, to build cities, to cultivate the ground, though these are acquired faculties. The moral feelings are not indeed a part of our nature in the sense of being in any perceptible degree present in all of us; but this, unhappily, is a fact admitted by those who believe the most strenuously in their transcendental origin. Like the other acquired capacities above referred to, the moral faculty, if not a part of our nature, is a natural outgrowth from it; capable, like them, in a certain small degree, of springing up spontaneously; and susceptible of being brought by cultivation to a high degree of development. Unhappily it is also susceptible, by a sufficient use of the external sanctions and of the force of early impressions, of being cultivated in almost any direction, so that there is hardly anything so absurd or so mischievous that it may not, by means of these influences, be made to act on the human mind with all the authority of conscience. To doubt that the same potency might be given by the same means to the principle of utility, even if it had no foundation in human nature, would be flying in the face of all experience.

But moral associations which are wholly of artificial creation, when the intellectual culture goes on, yield by degrees to the dissolving force of analysis; and if the feeling of duty, when associated with utility, would appear equally arbitrary; if there were no leading department of our nature, no powerful class of sentiments, with which that association would harmonize, which would make us feel congenial and incline us not only to foster it in ourselves—if there were not, in short, a natural basis of sentiments for utilitarian morality, it might well happen that this association also, even after it had been implanted by education, might be analyzed away.

But there *is* this basis of powerful natural sentiment; and that it is which, when once the general happiness is recognized as the ethical standard, will constitute the strength of the utilitarian morality. This firm foundation is that of the social feelings of mankind—the desire to be in unity with our fellow creatures, which is already a powerful principle in human nature, and happily one of those which tend to become stronger, even without express inculcation, from the influences of advancing civilization. The social state is at once so natural, so necessary, and so habitual to man, that, except in some unusual circumstances or by an effort of voluntary abstraction, he never conceives himself otherwise than as a member of a body; and this association is riveted more and more, as mankind are further removed from the state of savage independence. Any condition, therefore, which is essential to a state of society becomes more and more an inseparable part of every person's conception of the state of things which he is born into, and which is the destiny of a human being. Now society between human beings, except in the relation of master and slave, is manifestly impossible on any other footing than that of the interests of all are to be consulted. Society between equals can only exist on the understanding that the interests of all are to be regarded equally. And since in all states of civilization, every person, except an absolute monarch, has equals, everyone is obliged to live on these terms with somebody; and in every age some advance is made toward a state in which it will be impossible to live permanently on other terms with anybody. In this way people grow up unable to conceive as possible to them a state of total disregard of other people's interests. They are under a necessity of conceiving themselves as at least abstaining from all the grosser injuries, and (if only for their own protection) living in a state of constant protest against them. They are also familiar with the fact of co-operating with others and proposing to themselves a collective, not an individual, interest as the aim (at least for the time being) of their actions. So long as they are co-operating, their ends are identified with those of others; there is at least a temporary feeling that the interests of others are their own interests. Not only does all strengthening of social ties, and all healthy growth of society, give to each individual a stronger personal interest in practically consulting the welfare of others, it also leads him to identify his *feelings* more and more with their good, or at least with an even greater degree of practical consideration for

it. He comes, as though instinctively, to be conscious of himself as a being who *of course* pays regard to others. The good of others becomes to him a thing naturally and necessarily to be attended to, like any of the physical conditions of our existence. Now, whatever amount of this feeling a person has, he is urged by the strongest motives both of interest and of sympathy to demonstrate it, and to the utmost of his power encourage it in others; and even if he has none of it himself, he is as greatly interested as anyone else that others should have it. Consequently, the smaller germs of the feeling are laid hold of and nourished by the contagion of sympathy and the influences of education; and a complete web of corroborative association is woven round it by the powerful agency of the external sanctions. This mode of conceiving ourselves and human life, as civilization goes on, is felt to be more and more natural. Every step in political improvement renders it more so, by removing the sources of opposition of interest and leveling those inequalities of legal privilege between individuals or classes, owing to which there are large portions of mankind whose happiness it is still practicable to disregard. In an improving state of the human mind, the influences are constantly on the increase which tend to generate in each individual a feeling of unity with all the rest; which, if perfect, would make him never think of, or desire, any beneficial condition for himself in the benefits of which they are not included. If we now suppose this feeling of unity to be taught as a religion, and the whole force of education, of institutions, and of opinion directed, as it once was in the case of religion, to make every person grow up from infancy surrounded on all sides both by the profession and the practice of it, I think that no one who can realize this conception will feel any misgiving about the sufficiency of the ultimate sanction for the happiness morality. To any ethical student who finds the realization difficult, I recommend, as a means of facilitating it, the second of M. Comte's two principal works, the *Traité de politique positive*. I entertain the strongest objections to the system of politics and morals set forth in that treatise, but I think it has superabundantly shown the possibility of giving to the service of humanity, even without the aid of belief in a Providence, both the psychological power and the social efficacy of a religion, making it take hold of human life, and color all thought, feeling, and action in a manner of which the greatest ascendancy ever exercised by any religion may be but a type and fore-taste; and of which the danger is, not that it should be insufficient, but that it should be so excessive as to interfere unduly with human freedom and individuality.

Neither is it necessary to the feeling which constitutes the binding force of the utilitarian morality on those who recognize it to wait for those social influences which would make its obligation felt by mankind at large. In the comparatively early state of human advancement in which we now live, a person cannot, indeed, feel that entireness of sympathy with all others which would make any real discordance in the general direction of their conduct in life impossible, but already a person in whom the social feeling is at all developed cannot bring himself to think of the rest of his fellow creatures as struggling rivals with him for the means of happiness, whom he must desire to see defeated in their object in order that he may succeed in his. The deeply rooted conception which every individual even now has of himself as a social being tends to make him feel it one of his natural wants that there should be harmony between his feelings and aims and those of his fellow creatures. If differences of opinion and of mental culture make it impossible for him to share many of their actual feelings—perhaps make him denounce and defy those feelings—he still needs to be conscious that his real aim and theirs do not conflict; that he is not opposing himself to what they really wish for, namely, their own good, but is, on the contrary, promoting it. This feeling in most individuals is much inferior in strength to their selfish feelings, and is often wanting altogether. But to those who have it, it possesses all the characters of a natural feeling. It does not present itself to their minds as a superstition of education or a law despotically imposed by the power of society, but as an attribute which it would not be well for them to be without. This conviction is the ultimate sanction of

the greatest happiness morality. This it is which makes any mind of well-developed feelings work with, and not against, the outward motives to care for others, afforded by what I have called the external sanctions; and, when those sanctions are wanting or act in an opposite direction, constitutes in itself a powerful internal binding force, in proportion to the sensitiveness and thoughtfulness of the character, since few but those whose mind is a moral blank could bear to lay out their course of life on the plan of paying no regard to others except so far as their own private interest compels.

## CHAPTER IV

### *Of What Sort of Proof the Principle of Utility Is Susceptible*

It has already been remarked that questions of ultimate ends do not admit of proof, in the ordinary acceptation of the term. To be incapable of proof by reasoning is common to all first principles, to the first premises of our knowledge, as well as to those of our conduct. But the former, being matters of fact, may be the subject of a direct appeal to the faculties which judge of fact—namely, our senses and our internal consciousness. Can an appeal be made to the same faculties on questions of practical ends? Or by what other faculty is cognizance taken of them?

Questions about ends are, in other words, questions what things are desirable. The utilitarian doctrine is that happiness is desirable, and the only thing desirable, as an end; all other things being only desirable as means to that end. What ought to be required of this doctrine, what conditions is it requisite that the doctrine should fulfill—to make good its claim to be believed?

The only proof capable of being given that an object is visible is that people actually see it. The only proof that a sound is audible is that people hear it; and so of the other sources of our experience. In like manner, I apprehend, the sole evidence it is possible to produce that anything is desirable is that people do actually desire it. If the end which the utilitarian doctrine proposes to itself were not, in theory and in practice, acknowledged to be an end, nothing could ever convince any person that it was so. No reason can be given why the general happiness is desirable, except that each person, so far as he believes it to be attainable, desires his own happiness. This, however, being a fact, we have not only all the proof which the case admits of, but all which it is possible to require, that happiness is a good, that each person's happiness is a good to that person, and the general happiness, therefore, a good to the aggregate of all persons. Happiness has made out its title as *one* of the ends of conduct and, consequently, one of the criteria of morality.

But it has not, by this alone, proved itself to be the sole criterion. To do that, it would seem, by the same rule, necessary to show, not only that people desire happiness, but that they never desire anything else. Now it is palpable that they do desire things which, in common language, are decidedly distinguished from happiness. They desire, for example, virtue and the absence of vice no less really than pleasure and the absence of pain. The desire of virtue is not as universal, but it is as authentic a fact as the desire of happiness. And hence the opponents of the utilitarian standard deem that they have a right to infer that there are other ends of human action besides happiness, and that happiness is not the standard of approbation and disapprobation.

But does the utilitarian doctrine deny that people desire virtue, or maintain that virtue is not a thing to be desired? The very reverse. It maintains not only that virtue is to be desired, but that it is to be desired disinterestedly, for itself. Whatever may be the opinion of utilitarian moralists as to the original conditions by which virtue is made virtue, however they may believe (as they do) that actions and dispositions are only virtuous because they promote another end than virtue, yet this being granted, and it having been decided, from considerations of this description, what *is* virtuous, they not only place virtue at the very head of the things which are good as means to the ultimate end, but they also recognize as a psychological fact the possibility of its being, to the individual, a good in itself, without looking to any end beyond it; and hold that the mind is not in a right state, not in a state conformable to utility, not in the state most con-

ducive to the general happiness, unless it does love virtue in this manner—as a thing desirable in itself, even although, in the individual instance, it should not produce those other desirable consequences which it tends to produce, and on account of which it is held to be virtue. This opinion is not, in the smallest degree, a departure from the happiness principle. The ingredients of happiness are very various, and each of them is desirable in itself, and not merely when considered as swelling an aggregate. The principle of utility does not mean that any given pleasure, as music, for instance, or any given exemption from pain, as for example health, is to be looked upon as means to a collective something termed happiness, and to be desired on that account. They are desired and desirable in and for themselves; besides being means, they are a part of the end. Virtue, according to the utilitarian doctrine, is not naturally and originally part of the end, but it is capable of becoming so; and in those who live it disinterestedly it has become so, and is desired and cherished, not as a means to happiness, but as a part of their happiness.

To illustrate this further, we may remember that virtue is not the only thing originally a means, and which if it were not a means to anything else would be and remain indifferent, but which by association with what it is a means to comes to be desired for itself, and that too with the utmost intensity. What, for example, shall we say of the love of money? There is nothing originally more desirable about money than about any heap of glittering pebbles. Its worth is solely that of the things which it will buy; the desires for other things than itself, which it is a means of gratifying. Yet the love of money is not only one of the strongest moving forces of human life, but money is, in many cases, desired in and for itself; the desire to possess it is often stronger than the desire to use it, and goes on increasing when all the desires which point to ends beyond it, to be compassed by it, are falling off. It may, then, be said truly that money is desired not for the sake of an end, but as part of the end. From being a means to happiness, it has come to be itself a principal ingredient of the individual's conception of happiness. The same may be said of the majority of the great objects of human life:

power, for example, or fame, except that to each of these there is a certain amount of immediate pleasure annexed, which has at least the semblance of being naturally inherent in them—a thing which cannot be said of money. Still, however, the strongest natural attraction, both of power and of fame, is the immense aid they give to the attainment of our other wishes; and it is the strong association thus generated between them and all our objects of desire which gives to the direct desire of them the intensity it often assumes, so as in some characters to surpass in strength all other desires. In these cases the means have become a part of the end, and a more important part of it than any of the things which they are means to. What was once desired as an instrument for the attainment of happiness has come to be desired for its own sake. In being desired for its own sake it is, however, desired as *part* of happiness. The person is made, or thinks he would be made, happy by its mere possession; and is made unhappy by failure to obtain it. The desire of it is not a different thing from the desire of happiness any more than the love of music or the desire of health. They are included in happiness. They are some of the elements of which the desire of happiness is made up. Happiness is not an abstract idea but a concrete whole; and these are some of its parts. And the utilitarian standard sanctions and approves their being so. Life would be a poor thing, very ill provided with sources of happiness, if there were not this provision of nature by which things originally indifferent, but conducive to, or otherwise associated with, the satisfaction of our primitive desires, become in themselves sources of pleasure more valuable than the primitive pleasures, both in permanency, in the space of human existence that they are capable of covering, and even in intensity.

Virtue, according to the utilitarian conception, is a good of this description. There was no original desire of it, or motive to it, save its conduciveness to pleasure, and especially to protection from pain. But through the association thus formed it may be felt a good in itself, and desired as such with as great intensity as any other good; and with this difference between it and the love of money, of power, or of fame—that all of these may, and often do, render

the individual noxious to the other members of the society to which he belongs, whereas there is nothing which makes him so much a blessing to them as the cultivation of the disinterested love of virtue. And consequently, the utilitarian standard, while it tolerates and approves those other acquired desires, up to the point beyond which they would be more injurious to the general happiness than promotive of it, enjoins and requires the cultivation of the love of virtue up to the greatest strength possible, as being above all things important to the general happiness.

It results from the preceding considerations that there is in reality nothing desired except happiness. Whatever is desired otherwise than as a means to some end beyond itself, and ultimately to happiness, is desired as itself a part of happiness, and is not desired for itself until it has become so. Those who desire virtue for its own sake desire it either because the consciousness of it is a pleasure, or because the consciousness of being without it is a pain, or for both reasons united; as in truth the pleasure and pain seldom exist separately, but almost always together—the same person feeling pleasure in the degree of virtue attained, and pain in not having attained more. If one of these gave him no pleasure, and the other no pain, he would not love or desire virtue, or would desire it only for the other benefits which it might produce to himself or to persons whom he cared for.

We have now, then, an answer to the question, of what sort of proof the principle of utility is susceptible. If the opinion which I have now stated is psychologically true—if human nature is so constituted as to desire nothing which is not either a part of happiness or a means of happiness—we can have no other proof, and we require no other, that these are the only things desirable. If so, happiness is the sole end of human action, and the promotion of it the test by which to judge of all human conduct; from whence it necessarily follows that it must be the criterion of morality, since a part is included in the whole.

And now to decide whether this is really so, whether mankind do desire nothing for itself but that which is a pleasure to them, or of which the absence is a pain, we have evidently arrived at a question of fact and experience, dependent, like all similar questions, upon evidence. It can only be determined by practiced self-consciousness and self-observation, assisted by observation of others. I believe that these sources of evidence, impartially consulted, will declare that desiring a thing and finding it pleasant, aversion to it and thinking of it as painful, are phenomena entirely inseparable or, rather, two parts of the same phenomenon—in strictness of language, two different modes of naming the same psychological fact; that to think of an object as desirable (unless for the sake of its consequences) and to think of it as pleasant are one and the same thing; and that to desire anything except in proportion as the idea of it is pleasant is a physical and metaphysical impossibility.

So obvious does this appear to me that I expect it will hardly be disputed; and the objection made will be, not that desire can possibly be directed to anything ultimately except pleasure and exemption from pain, but that the will is a different thing from desire; that a person of confirmed virtue or any other person whose purposes are fixed carries out his purposes without any thought of the pleasure he has in contemplating them or expects to derive from their fulfillment, and persists in acting on them, even though these pleasures are much diminished by changes in his character or decay of his passive sensibilities, or are outweighed by the pains which the pursuit of the purposes may bring upon him. All this I fully admit and have stated it elsewhere as positively and emphatically as anyone. Will, the active phenomenon, is a different thing from desire, the state of passive sensibility, and, though originally an offshoot from it, may in time take root and detach itself from the parent stock, so much so that in the case of a habitual purpose, instead of willing the thing because we desire it, we often desire it only because we will it. This, however, is but an instance of that familiar fact, the power of habit, and is nowise confined to the case of virtuous actions. Many indifferent things which men originally did from a motive of some sort they continue to do from habit. Sometimes this is done unconsciously, the consciousness coming only after the action; at other times with con-

scious volition, but volition which has become habitual and is put in operation by the force of habit, in opposition perhaps to the deliberate preference, as often happens with those who have contracted habits of vicious or hurtful indulgence. Third and last comes the case in which the habitual act of will in the individual instance is not in contradiction to the general intention prevailing at other times, but in fulfillment of it, as in the case of the person of confirmed virtue and of all who pursue deliberately and consistently any determinate end. The distinction between will and desire thus understood is an authentic and highly important psychological fact; but the fact consists solely in this—that will, like all other parts of our constitution, is amenable to habit, and that we may will from habit what we no longer desire for itself, or desire only because we will it. It is not the less true that will, in the beginning, is entirely produced by desire, including in that term the repelling influence of pain as well as the attractive one of pleasure. Let us take into consideration no longer the person who has a confirmed will to do right, but him in whom that virtuous will is still feeble, conquerable by temptation, and not to be fully relied on; by what means can it be strengthened? How can the will to be virtuous, where it does not exist in sufficient force, be implanted or awakened? Only by making the person *desire* virtue—by making him think of it in a pleasurable light, or of its absence in a painful one. It is by associating the doing right with pleasure, or the wrong with pain, or by eliciting and impressing and bringing home to the person's experience the pleasure naturally involved in the one or the pain in the other, that it is possible to call forth that will to be virtuous which, when confirmed, acts without any thought of either pleasure or pain. Will is the child of desire, and passes out of the dominion of its parent only to come under that of habit. That which is the result of habit affords no presumption of being intrinsically good; and there would be no reason for wishing that the purpose of virtue should become independent of pleasure and pain were it not that the influence of the pleasurable and painful associations which prompt to virtue is not sufficiently to be depended on for unerring constancy of action until it has acquired the support of habit. Both in feeling and in conduct, habit is the only thing which imparts certainty; and it is because of the importance to others of being able to rely absolutely on one's feelings and conduct, and to oneself of being able to rely on one's own, that the will to do right ought to be cultivated into this habitual independence. In other words, this state of the will is a means to good, not intrinsically a good; and does not contradict the doctrine that nothing is a good to human beings but in so far as it is either itself pleasurable or a means of attaining pleasure or averting pain.

But if this doctrine be true, the principle of utility is proved. Whether it is so or not must now be left to the consideration of the thoughtful reader.

# CHAPTER V

## *On the Connection Between Justice and Utility*

In all ages of speculation one of the strongest obstacles to the reception of the doctrine that utility or happiness is the criteria of right and wrong has been drawn from the idea of justice. The powerful sentiment and apparently clear perception which that word recalls with a rapidity and certainty resembling an instinct have seemed to the majority of thinkers to point to an inherent quality in things; to show that the just must have an existence in nature as something absolute, generically distinct from every variety of the expedient and, in idea, opposed to it, though (as is commonly acknowledged) never, in the long run, disjoined from it in fact.

In the case of this, as of our other moral sentiments, there is no necessary connection between the question of its origin and that of its binding force. That a feeling is bestowed on us by nature does not necessarily legitimate all its promptings. The feeling of justice might be a peculiar instinct, and might yet require, like our other instincts, to be controlled and enlightened by a higher reason. If we have intellectual instincts leading us to judge in a particular way,

as well as animal instincts that prompt us to act in a particular way, there is no necessity that the former should be more infallible in their sphere than the latter in theirs; it may as well happen that wrong judgments are occasionally suggested by those, as wrong actions by these. But though it is one thing to believe that we have natural feelings of justice, and another to acknowledge them as an ultimate criterion of conduct, these two opinions are very closely connected in point of fact. Mankind are always predisposed to believe that any subjective feeling, not otherwise accounted for, is a revelation of some objective reality. Our present object is to determine whether the reality to which the feeling of justice corresponds is one which needs any such special revelation, whether the justice or injustice of an action is a thing intrinsically peculiar and distinct from all its other qualities or only a combination of certain of those qualities presented under a peculiar aspect. For the purpose of this inquiry it is practically important to consider whether the feeling itself, of justice and injustice, is *sui generis* like our sensations of color and taste or a derivative feeling formed by a combination of others. And this it is the more essential to examine, as people are in general willing enough to allow that objectively the dictates of justice coincide with a part of the field of general expediency; but inasmuch as the subjective mental feeling of justice is different from that which commonly attaches to simple expediency, and, except in the extreme cases of the latter, is far more imperative in its demands, people find it difficult to see in justice only a particular kind or branch of general utility, and think that its superior binding force requires a totally different origin.

To throw light upon this question, it is necessary to attempt to ascertain what is the distinguishing character of justice, or of injustice; what is the quality, or whether there is any quality, attributed in common to all modes of conduct designated as unjust (for justice, like many other moral attributes, is best defined by its opposite), and distinguishing them from such modes of conduct as are disapproved, but without having that particular epithet of disapprobation applied to them. If in everything which men are accustomed to characterize as just or unjust some one common attribute or collection of attributes is always present, we may judge whether this particular attribute or combination of attributes would be capable of gathering round it a sentiment of that peculiar character and intensity by virtue of the general laws of our emotional constitution, or whether the sentiment is inexplicable and requires to be regarded as a special provision of nature. If we find the former to be the case, we shall, in resolving this question, have resolved also the main problem; if the latter, we shall have to seek for some other mode of investigating it.

To find the common attributes of a variety of objects, it is necessary to begin by surveying the objects themselves in the concrete. Let us therefore advert successively to the various modes of action and arrangements of human affairs which are classed, by universal or widely spread opinion, as just or as unjust. The things well known to excite the sentiments associated with those names are of a very multifarious character. I shall pass them rapidly in review, without studying any particular arrangement.

In the first place, it is mostly considered unjust to deprive anyone of his personal liberty, his property, or any other thing which belongs to him by law. Here, therefore, is one instance of the application of the terms "just" and "unjust" in a perfectly definite sense, namely, that it is just to respect, unjust to violate, the *legal rights* of anyone. But this judgment admits of several exceptions, arising from the other forms in which the notions of justice and injustice present themselves. For example, the person who suffers the deprivation may (as the phrase is) have *forfeited* the rights which he is so deprived of—a case to which we shall return presently. But also—

Secondly, the legal rights of which he is deprived may be rights which *ought* not to have belonged to him; in other words, the law which confers on him these rights may be a bad law. When it is so or when (which is the same thing for our purpose) it is supposed to be so, opinions will differ as to the justice or injustice of infringing it. Some maintain that no law, however bad, ought to be disobeyed by an individual citizen; that his opposition to it, if shown at all, should

only be shown in endeavoring to get it altered by competent authority. This opinion (which condemns many of the most illustrious benefactors of mankind, and would often protect pernicious institutions against the only weapons which, in the state of things existing at the time, have any chance of succeeding against them) is defended by those who hold it on grounds of expediency, principally on that of the importance to the common interest of mankind, of maintaining inviolate the sentiment of submission to law. Other persons, again, hold the directly contrary opinion that any law, judged to be bad, may blamelessly be disobeyed, even though it be not judged to be unjust but only inexpedient, while others would confine the license of disobedience to the case of unjust laws; but, again, some say that all laws which are inexpedient are unjust, since every law imposes some restriction on the natural liberty of mankind, which restriction is an injustice unless legitimated by tending to their good. Among these diversities of opinion it seems to be universally admitted that there may be unjust laws, and that law, consequently, is not the ultimate criterion of justice, but may give to one person a benefit, or impose on another an evil, which justice condemns. When, however, a law is thought to be unjust, it seems always to be regarded as being so in the same way in which a breach of law is unjust, namely, by infringing somebody's right, which, as it cannot in this case be a legal right, receives a different appellation and is called a moral right. We may say, therefore, that a second case of injustice consists in taking or withholding from any person that to which he has a *moral right.*

Thirdly, it is universally considered just that each person should obtain that (whether good or evil) which he *deserves,* and unjust that he should obtain a good or be made to undergo an evil which he does not deserve. This is, perhaps, the clearest and most emphatic form in which the idea of justice is conceived by the general mind. As it involves the notion of desert, the question arises what constitutes desert? Speaking in a general way, a person is understood to deserve good if he does right, evil if he does wrong; and in a more particular sense, to deserve good from those to whom he does or has done good, and evil from those to whom he does or has done evil. The precept of returning good for evil has never been regarded as a case of the fulfillment of justice, but as one in which the claims of justice are waived, in obedience to other considerations.

Fourthly, it is confessedly unjust to *break faith* with anyone: to violate an engagement, either express or implied, or disappoint expectations raised by our own conduct, at least if we have raised those expectations knowingly and voluntarily. Like the other obligations of justice already spoken of, this one is not regarded as absolute, but as capable of being overruled by a stronger obligation of justice on the other side, or by such conduct on the part of the person concerned as is deemed to absolve us from our obligation to him and to constitute a *forfeiture* of the benefit which he has been led to expect.

Fifthly, it is, by universal admission, inconsistent with justice to be *partial*—to show favor or preference to one person over another in matters to which favor and preference do not properly apply. Impartiality, however, does not seem to be regarded as a duty in itself, but rather as instrumental to some other duty; for it is admitted that favor and preference are not always censurable, and, indeed, the cases in which they are condemned are rather the exception than the rule. A person would be more likely to be blamed than applauded for giving his family or friends no superiority in good offices over strangers when he could do so without violating any other duty; and no one thinks it unjust to seek one person in preference to another as a friend, connection, or companion. Impartiality where rights are concerned is of course obligatory, but this is involved in the more general obligation of giving to everyone his right. A tribunal, for example, must be impartial because it is bound to award, without regard to any other consideration, a disputed object to the one of two parties who has the right to it. There are other cases in which impartiality means being solely influenced by desert, as with those who, in the capacity of judges, preceptors, or parents, administer reward and punishment as such. There are cases, again, in which it means being solely influenced by consideration for the public interest, as in making a selection among candidates for a government employment. Impartiality, in short, as an obligation of justice, may be said to mean being exclusively influenced by the considerations which it is supposed ought to influence the particular case in hand, and resisting solicitation of any motives which prompt to conduct different from what those considerations would dictate.

Nearly allied to the idea of impartiality is that of *equality,* which often enters as a component part both into the conception of justice and into the practice of it, and, in the eyes of many persons, constitutes its essence. But in this, still more than in any other case, the notion of justice varies in different persons, and always conforms in its variations to their notion of utility. Each person maintains that equality is the dictate of justice, except where he thinks that expediency requires inequality. The justice of giving equal protection to the rights of all is maintained by those who support the most outrageous inequality in the rights themselves. Even in slave countries it is theoretically admitted that the rights of the slave, such as they are, ought to be as sacred as those of the master, and that a tribunal which fails to enforce them with equal strictness is wanting in justice; while, at the same time, institutions which leave to the slave scarcely any rights to enforce are not deemed unjust because they are not deemed inexpedient. Those who think that utility requires distinctions of rank do not consider it unjust that riches and social privileges should be unequally dispensed; but those who think this inequality inexpedient think it unjust also. Whoever thinks that government is necessary sees no injustice in as much inequality as is constituted by giving to the magistrate powers not granted to other people. Even among those who hold leveling doctrines, there are differences of opinion about expediency. Some communists consider it unjust that the produce of the labor of the community should be shared on any other principle than that of exact equality; others think it just that those should receive most whose wants are greatest; while others hold that those who work harder, or who produce more, or whose services are more valuable to the community, may justly claim a larger quota in the division of the produce. And the sense of natural justice may be plausibly appealed to in behalf of every one of these opinions.

Among so many diverse applications of the term "justice," which yet is not regarded as ambiguous, it is a matter of some difficulty to seize the mental link which holds them together, and on which the moral sentiment adhering to the term essentially depends. Perhaps, in this embarrassment, some help may be derived from the history of the word, as indicated by its etymology.

In most if not in all languages, the etymology of the word which corresponds to "just" points distinctly to an origin connected with the ordinances of law. *Justum* is a form of *jussum,* that which has been ordered. *Dikaion* comes directly from *dike,* a suit at law. *Recht,* from which came *right* and *righteous,* is synonymous with law. The courts of justice, the administration of justice, are the courts and the administration of law. *La justice,* in French, is the established term for judicature. I am not committing the fallacy, imputed with some show of truth to Horne Tooke, of assuming that a word must still continue to mean what it originally meant. Etymology is slight evidence of what the idea now signified is, but the very best evidence of how it sprang up. There can, I think, be no doubt that the *idée mère,* the primitive element, in the formation of the notion of justice was conformity to law. It constituted the entire idea among the Hebrews, up to the birth of Christianity; as might be expected in the case of a people whose laws attempted to embrace all subjects on which precepts were required, and who believed those laws to be a direct emanation from the Supreme Being. But other nations, and in particular the Greeks and Romans, who knew that their laws had been made originally, and still continued to be made, by men, were not afraid to admit that those men might make bad laws; might do, by law, the same things, and from the same motives, which if done by individuals without the sanction of law would be called unjust. And hence the sentiment of injustice came to be attached, not to all violations of law, but only to violations of such laws as *ought* to exist, including such as ought to exist but do not, and to laws themselves if supposed to be contrary to what ought to be law. In this manner the idea

of law and of its injunctions was still predominant in the notion of justice, even when the laws actually in force ceased to be accepted as the standard of it.

It is true that mankind consider the idea of justice and its obligations as applicable to many things which neither are, nor is it desired that they should be, regulated by law. Nobody desires that laws should interfere with the whole detail of private life; yet everyone allows that in all daily conduct a person may and does show himself to be either just or unjust. But even here, the idea of the breach of what ought to be law still lingers in a modified shape. It would always give us pleasure, and chime in with our feelings of fitness, that acts which we deem unjust should be punished, though we do not always think it expedient that this should be done by the tribunals. We forego that gratification on account of incidental inconveniences. We should be glad to see just conduct enforced and injustice repressed, even in the minutest details, if we were not, with reason, afraid of trusting the magistrate with so unlimited an amount of power over individuals. When we think that a person is bound in justice to do a thing, it is an ordinary form of language to say that he ought to be compelled to do it. We should be gratified to see the obligation enforced by anybody who had the power. If we see that its enforcement by law would be inexpedient, we lament the impossibility, we consider the impunity given to injustice as an evil, and strive to make amends for it by bringing a strong expression of our own and the public disapprobation to bear upon the offender. Thus the idea of legal constraint is still the generating idea of the notion of justice, though undergoing several transformations before that notion as it exists in an advanced state of society becomes complete.

The above is, I think, a true account, as far as it goes, of the origin and progressive growth of the idea of justice. But we must observe that it contains as yet nothing to distinguish that obligation from moral obligation in general. For the truth is that the idea of penal sanction, which is the essence of law, enters not only into the conception of injustice, but into that of any kind of wrong. We do not call anything wrong unless we mean to imply that a person ought to be punished in some way or other for doing it—if not by law, by the opinion of his fellow creatures; if not by opinion, by the reproaches of his own conscience. This seems the real turning point of the distinction between morality and simple expediency. It is a part of the notion of duty in every one of its forms that a person may rightfully be compelled to fulfill it. Duty is a thing which may be *exacted* from a person, as one exacts a debt. Unless we think that it may be exacted from him, we do not call it his duty. Reasons of prudence, or the interest of other people, may militate against actually exacting it, but the person himself, it is clearly understood, would not be entitled to complain. There are other things, on the contrary, which we wish that people should do, which we like or admire them for doing, perhaps dislike or despise them for not doing, but yet admit that they are not bound to do; it is not a case of moral obligation; we do not blame them, that is, we do not think that they are proper objects of punishment. How we come by these ideas of deserving and not deserving punishment will appear, perhaps, in the sequel; but I think there is no doubt that this distinction lies at the bottom of the notions of right and wrong; that we call any conduct wrong, or employ, instead, some other term of dislike or disparagement, according as we think that the person ought, or ought not, to be punished for it; and we say it would be right to do so and so, or merely that it would be desirable or laudable, according as we would wish to see the person whom it concerns compelled, or only persuaded and exhorted, to act in that manner.[3]

This, therefore, being the characteristic difference which marks off, not justice, but morality in general from the remaining provinces of expediency and worthiness, the character is still to be sought which distinguishes justice from other branches of morality. Now it is known that ethical writers divide moral duties into two classes, denoted by the ill-chosen expressions, duties of perfect and of imperfect obligation; the latter being those in which, though the act is obligatory, the particular occasions of performing it are left to our choice, as in the case of charity or beneficence, which we are indeed bound to practice but not toward any definite person, nor at any pre-

scribed time. In the more precise language of philosophic jurists, duties of perfect obligation are those duties in virtue of which a correlative *right* resides in some person or persons; duties of imperfect obligation are those moral obligations which do not give birth to any right. I think it will be found that this distinction exactly coincides with that which exists between justice and the other obligations of morality. In our survey of the various popular acceptations of justice, the term appeared generally to involve the idea of a personal right—a claim on the part of one or more individuals, like that which the law gives when it confers a proprietary or other legal right. Whether the injustice consists in depriving a person of a possession, or in breaking faith with him, or in treating him worse than he deserves, or worse than other people who have no greater claims—in each case the supposition implies two things: a wrong done, and some assignable person who is wronged. Injustice may also be done by treating a person better than others; but the wrong in this case is to his competitors, who are also assignable persons. It seems to me that this feature in the case—a right in some person, correlative to the moral obligation—constitutes the specific difference between justice and generosity of beneficence. Justice implies something which it is not only right to do, and wrong not to do, but which some individual person can claim from us as his moral right. No one has a moral right to our generosity or beneficence because we are not morally bound to practice those virtues toward any given individual. And it will be found with respect to this as to every correct definition that the instances which seem to conflict with it are those which most confirm it. For if a moralist attempts, as some have done, to make out that mankind generally, though not any given individual, have a right to all the good we can do them, he at once, by that thesis, includes generosity and beneficence within the category of justice. He is obliged to say that our utmost exertions are *due* to our fellow creatures, thus assimilating them to a debt; or that nothing less can be a sufficient *return* for what society does for us, thus classing the case as one of gratitude; both of which are acknowledged cases of justice, and not of the virtue of beneficence; and whoever does not place the distinction between justice and morality in general, where we have now placed it, will be found to make no distinction between them at all, but to merge all morality in justice.

Having thus endeavored to determine the distinctive elements which enter into the composition of the idea of justice, we are ready to enter on the inquiry whether the feeling which accompanies the idea is attached to it by a special dispensation of nature, or whether it could have grown up, by any known laws, out of the idea itself; and, in particular, whether it can have originated in considerations of general expediency.

I conceive that the sentiment itself does not arise from anything which would commonly or correctly be termed an idea of expediency, but that, though the sentiment does not, whatever is moral in it does.

We have seen that the two essential ingredients in the sentiment of justice are the desire to punish a person who has done harm and the knowledge or belief that there is some definite individual or individuals to whom harm has been done.

Now it appears to me that the desire to punish a person who has done harm to some individual is a spontaneous outgrowth from two sentiments, both in the highest degree natural and which either are or resemble instincts: the impulse of self-defense and the feeling of sympathy.

It is natural to resent and to repel or retaliate any harm done or attempted against ourselves or against those with whom we sympathize. The origin of this sentiment it is not necessary here to discuss. Whether it be an instinct or a result of intelligence, it is, we know, common to all animal nature; for every animal tries to hurt those who have hurt, or who it thinks are about to hurt, itself or its young. Human beings, on this point, only differ from other animals in two particulars. First, in being capable of sympathizing, not solely with their offspring, or, like some of the more noble animals, with some superior animal who is kind to them, but with all human, and even with all sentient, beings; secondly, in having a more developed intelligence, which gives a wider range to the whole of their sentiments, whether self-regarding or sympathetic. By virtue of his superior

intelligence, even apart from his superior range of sympathy, a human being is capable of apprehending a community of interest between himself and the human society of which he forms a part, such that any conduct which threatens the security of the society generally is threatening to his own, and calls forth his instinct (if instinct it be) of self-defense. The same superiority of intelligence, joined to the power of sympathizing with human beings generally, enables him to attach himself to the collective idea of his tribe, his country, or mankind in such a manner that any act hurtful to them raises his instinct of sympathy and urges him to resistance.

The sentiment of justice, in that one of its elements which consists of the desire to punish, is thus, I conceive, the natural feeling of retaliation or vengeance, rendered by intellect and sympathy applicable to those injuries, that is, to those hurts, which wound us through, or in common with, society at large. This sentiment, in itself, has nothing moral in it; what is moral is the exclusive subordination of it to the social sympathies, so as to wait on and obey their call. For the natural feeling would make us resent indiscriminately whatever anyone does that is disagreeable to us; but, when moralized by the social feeling, it only acts in the directions conformable to the general good: just persons resenting a hurt to society, though not otherwise a hurt to themselves, and not resenting a hurt to themselves, however painful, unless it be of the kind which society has a common interest with them in the repression of.

It is no objection against this doctrine to say that, when we feel our sentiment of justice outraged, we are not thinking of society at large or of any collective interest, but only of the individual case. It is common enough, certainly, though the reverse of commendable, to feel resentment merely because we have suffered pain; but a person whose resentment is really a moral feeling, that is, who considers whether an act is blamable before he allows himself to resent it—such a person, though he may not say expressly to himself that he is standing up for the interest of society, certainly does feel that he is asserting a rule which is for the benefit of others as well as for his own. If he is not feeling this, if he is regarding the act solely as it affects him individually, he is not consciously just; he is not concerning himself about the justice of his actions. This is admitted even by anti-utilitarian moralists. When Kant (as before remarked) propounds as the fundamental principle of morals, "So act that thy rule of conduct might be adopted as a law by all rational beings," he virtually acknowledges that the interest of mankind collectively, or at least of mankind indiscriminately, must be in the mind of the agent when conscientiously deciding on the morality of the act. Otherwise he uses words without a meaning; for that a rule even of utter selfishness could not *possibly* be adopted by all rational beings—that there is any insuperable obstacle in the nature of things to its adoption—cannot be even plausibly maintained. To give any meaning to Kant's principle, the sense put upon it must be that we ought to shape our conduct by a rule which all rational beings might adopt *with benefit to their collective interest.*

To recapitulate: the idea of justice supposes two things—a rule of conduct and a sentiment which sanctions the rule. The first must be supposed common to all mankind and intended for their good. The other (the sentiment) is a desire that punishment may be suffered by those who infringe the rule. There is involved, in addition, the conception of some definite person who suffers by the infringement, whose rights (to use the expression appropriated to the case) are violated by it. And the sentiment of justice appears to me to be the animal desire to repel or retaliate a hurt or damage to oneself or to those with whom one sympathizes, widened so as to include all persons, by the human capacity of enlarged sympathy and the human conception of intelligent self-interest. From the latter elements the feeling derives its morality; from the former, its peculiar impressiveness and energy of self-assertion.

I have, throughout, treated the idea of a *right* residing in the injured person and violated by the injury, not as a separate element in the composition of the idea and sentiment, but as one of the forms in which the other two elements clothe themselves. These elements are a hurt to some assignable person or persons, on the one hand, and a demand for punishment, on the other. An examination of our own minds, I think, will show that these two things include all that we mean when we speak of violation of a right. When we call anything a person's right, we mean that he has a valid claim on society to protect him in the possession of it, either by the force of law or by that of education and opinion. If he has what we consider a sufficient claim, on whatever account, to have something guaranteed to him by society, we say that he has a right to it. If we desire to prove that anything does not belong to him by right, we think this done as soon as it is admitted that society ought not to take measure for securing it to him, but should leave him to chance or to his own exertions. Thus a person is said to have a right to what he can earn in fair professional competition, because society ought not to allow any other person to hinder him from endeavoring to earn in that manner as much as he can. But he has not a right to three hundred a year, though he may happen to be earning it; because society is not called on to provide that he shall earn that sum. On the contrary, if he owns ten thousand pounds three-per-cent stock, he *has* a right to three hundred a year because society has come under an obligation to provide him with an income of that amount.

To have a right, then, is, I conceive, to have something which society ought to defend me in the possession of. If the objector goes on to ask why it ought, I can give him no other reason than general utility. If that expression does not seem to convey a sufficient feeling of the strength of the obligation, nor to account for the peculiar energy of the feeling, it is because there goes to the composition of the sentiment, not a rational only but also an animal element—the thirst for retaliation; and this thirst derives its intensity, as well as its moral justification, from the extraordinarily important and impressive kind of utility which is concerned. The interest involved is that of security, to everyone's feelings the most vital of all interests. All other earthly benefits are needed by one person, not needed by another; and many of them can, if necessary, be cheerfully foregone or replaced by something else; but security no human being can possibly do without; on it we depend for all our immunity from evil and for the whole value of all and every good, beyond the passing moment, since nothing but the gratification of the instant could be of any worth to us if we could be deprived of everything the next instant by whoever was momentarily stronger than ourselves. Now this most indispensable of all necessaries, after physical nutriment, cannot be had unless the machinery for providing it is kept unintermittedly in active play. Our notion, therefore, of the claim we have on our fellow creatures to join in making safe for us the very groundwork of our existence gathers feelings around it so much more intense than those concerned in any of the more common cases of utility that the difference in degree (as is often the case in psychology) becomes a real difference in kind. The claim assumes that character of absoluteness, that apparent infinity and incommensurability with all other considerations which constitute the distinction between the feeling of right and wrong and that of ordinary expediency and inexpediency. The feelings concerned are so powerful, and we count so positively on finding a responsive feeling in others (all being alike interested) that *ought* and *should* grow into *must*, and recognized indispensability becomes a moral necessity, analogous to physical, and often not inferior to it in binding force.

If the preceding analysis, or something resembling it, be not the correct account of the notion of justice—if justice be totally independent of utility, and be a standard *per se,* which the mind can recognize by simple introspection of itself—it is hard to understand why that internal oracle is so ambiguous, and why so many things appear either just or unjust, according to the light in which they are regarded.

We are continually informed that utility is an uncertain standard, which every different person interprets differently, and that there is no safety but in the immutable, ineffaceable, and unmistakable dictates of justice, which carry their evidence in themselves and are independent of the fluctuations of opinion. One would suppose from this that on questions of justice there could be no controversy; that, if we take that for our rule, its application to any given case could leave us in as little doubt as a mathematical demonstration. So far is this from being the fact that there is as much difference of opinion, and as much discussion, about what is just as about what is useful to society. Not only have different nations and individuals different notions of justice, but in the mind of one and the same individual, justice is not some one rule, principle, or maxim, but many which do not always coincide in their dictates, and, in choosing between which, he is guided either by some extraneous standard or by his own personal predilections.

For instance, there are some who say that it is unjust to punish anyone for the sake of example to others, that punishment is just only when intended for the good of the sufferer himself. Others maintain the extreme reverse, contending that to punish persons who have attained years of discretion, for their own benefit, is despotism and injustice, since, if the matter at issue is solely their own good, no one has a right to control their own judgment of it; but that they may justly be punished to prevent evil to others, this being the exercise of the legitimate right of self-defense. Mr. Owen, again, affirms that it is unjust to punish at all, for the criminal did not make his own character; his education and the circumstances which surrounded him have made him a criminal, and for these he is not responsible. All these opinions are extremely plausible; and so long as the question is argued as one of justice simply, without going down to the principles which lie under justice and are the source of its authority, I am unable to see how any of these reasoners can be refuted. For in truth every one of the three builds upon rules of justice confessedly true. The first appeals to the acknowledged injustice of singling out an individual and making him a sacrifice, without his consent, for other people's benefit. The second relies on the acknowledged justice of self-defense and the admitted injustice of forcing one person to conform to another's notions of what constitutes his good. The Owenite invokes the admitted principle that it is unjust to punish anyone for what he cannot help. Each is triumphant so long as he is not compelled to take into consideration any other maxims of justice than the one he has selected; but as soon as their several maxims are brought face to face, each disputant seems to have exactly as much to say for himself as the others. No one of them can carry out his own notion of justice without trampling upon another equally binding. These are difficulties; they have always been felt to be such; and many devices have been invented to turn rather than to overcome them. As a refuge from the last of the three, men imagined what they called the freedom of the will—fancying that they could not justify punishing a man whose will is in a thoroughly hateful state unless it be supposed to have come into that state through no influence of anterior circumstances. To escape from the other difficulties, a favorite contrivance has been the fiction of a contract whereby at some unknown period all the members of society engaged to obey the laws and consented to be punished for any disobedience to them, thereby giving to their legislators the right, which it is assumed they would not otherwise have had, of punishing them, either for their own good or for that of society. This happy thought was considered to get rid of the whole difficulty and to legitimate the infliction of punishment, in virtue of another received maxim of justice, *volenti non fit injuria*—that is not unjust which is done with the consent of the person who is supposed to be hurt by it. I need hardly remark that, even if the consent were not a mere fiction, this maxim is not superior in authority to the others which it is brought in to supersede. It is, on the contrary, an instructive specimen of the loose and irregular manner in which supposed principles of justice grow up. This particular one evidently came into use as a help to the coarse exigencies of courts of law, which are sometimes obliged to be content with very uncertain presumptions, on account of the greater evils which would often arise from any attempt on their part to cut finer. But even courts of law are not able to adhere consistently to the maxim, for they allow voluntary engagements to be set aside on the ground of fraud, and sometimes on that of mere mistake or misinformation.

Again, when the legitimacy of inflicting punishment is admitted, how many conflicting conceptions of justice come to light in discussing the proper apportionment of punishments to offenses. No rule on the subject recommends itself so strongly to the primitive and spontaneous sentiment of justice as the *lex talionis,* an eye for an eye and a tooth for a tooth. Though this principle of the Jewish and of the Mohammedan law has been generally abandoned in Europe as a practical maxim, there is, I suspect, in most minds, a secret hankering after it; and when retribution accidentally falls on an offender in that precise shape, the general feeling of satisfaction evinced bears witness how natural is the sentiment to which this repayment in kind is acceptable. With many, the test of justice in penal infliction is that the punishment should be proportioned to the offense, meaning that it should be exactly measured by the moral guilt of the culprit (whatever be their standard for measuring moral guilt), the consideration what amount of punishment is necessary to deter from the offense having nothing to do with the question of justice, in their estimation; while there are others to whom that consideration is all in all, who maintain that it is not just, at least for man, to inflict on a fellow creature, whatever may be his offenses, any amount of suffering beyond the least that will suffice to prevent him from repeating, and others from imitating, his misconduct.

To take another example from a subject already once referred to. In co-operative industrial association, is it just or not that talent or skill should give a title to superior remuneration? On the negative side of the question it is argued that whoever does the best he can deserves equally well, and ought not in justice to be put in a position of inferiority for no fault of his own; that superior abilities have already advantages more than enough, in the admiration they excite, the personal influence they command, and the internal sources of satisfaction attending them, without adding to these a superior share of the world's goods; and that society is bound in justice rather to make compensation to the less favored for this unmerited inequality of advantages than to aggravate it. On the contrary side it is contended that society receives more from the more efficient laborer; that, his services being more useful, society owes him a larger return for them; that a greater share of the joint result is actually his work, and not to allow his claim to it is a kind of robbery; that, if he is only to receive as much as others, he can only be justly required to produce as much, and to give a smaller amount of time and exertion, proportioned to his superior efficiency. Who shall decide between these appeals to conflicting principles of justice? Justice has in this case two sides to it, which it is impossible to bring into harmony, and the two disputants have chosen opposite sides; the one looks to what it is just that the individual should receive, the other to what it is just that the community should give. Each, from his own point of view, is unanswerable; and any choice between them, on grounds of justice, must be perfectly arbitrary. Social utility alone can decide the preference.

How many, again, and how irreconcilable are the standards of justice to which reference is made in discussing the repartition of taxation. One opinion is that payment to the state should be in numerical proportion to pecuniary means. Others think that justice dictates what they term graduated taxation—taking a higher percentage from those who have more to spare. In point of natural justice a strong case might be made for disregarding means altogether, and taking the same absolute sum (whenever it could be got) from everyone; as the subscribers to a mess or to a club all pay the same sum for the same privileges, whether they can all equally afford it or not. Since the protection (it might be said) of law and government is afforded to and is equally required by all, there is no injustice in making all buy it at the same price. It is reckoned justice, not injustice, that a dealer should charge to all customers the same price for the same article, not a price varying according to their means of payment. This doctrine, as applied to taxation, finds no advocates because it conflicts so strongly with man's feelings of humanity and of social expediency, but the principle of justice which it invokes is as true and as binding to those which can be appealed to against it. Accordingly it exerts a tacit influence on the line of defense employed for other modes of assessing taxation. People feel obliged to argue that the state does more for the rich man than for the poor, as a justification for its taking more from them, though this is in reality not true, for the rich would be far better able to protect themselves, in the absence of law or government, than the poor, and indeed would probably be successful in converting the poor into their slaves. Others, again, so far defer to the same concep-

tion of justice as to maintain that all should pay an equal capitation tax for the protection of their persons (these being of equal value to all), and an unequal tax for the protection of their property, which is unequal. To this others reply that the all of one man is as valuable to him as the all of another. From these confusions there is no other mode of extrication than the utilitarian.

Is, then, the difference between the just and the expedient a merely imaginary distinction? Have mankind been under a delusion in thinking that justice is a more sacred thing than policy, and that the latter ought only to be listened to after the former has been satisfied? By no means. The exposition we have given of the nature and origin of the sentiment recognizes a real distinction; and no one of those who profess the most sublime contempt for the consequences of actions as an element in their morality attaches more importance to the distinction than I do. While I dispute the pretensions of any theory which sets up an imaginary standard of justice not grounded on utility, I account the justice which is grounded on utility to be the chief part, and incomparably the most sacred and binding part, of all morality. Justice is a name for certain classes of moral rules which concern the essentials of human well-being more nearly, and are therefore of more absolute obligation, than any other rules for the guidance of life; and the notion which we have found to be of the essence of the idea of justice—that of a right residing in an individual—implies and testifies to this more binding obligation.

The moral rules which forbid mankind to hurt one another (in which we must never forget to include a wrongful interference with each other's freedom) are more vital to human well-being than any maxims, however important, which only point out the best mode of managing some department of human affairs. They have also the peculiarity that they are the main element in determining the whole of the social feelings of mankind. It is their observance which alone preserves peace among human beings; if obedience to them were not the rule, and disobedience the exception, everyone would see in everyone else an enemy against whom he must be perpetually guarding himself. What is hardly less important, these are the precepts which mankind have the strongest and the most direct inducements for impressing upon one another. By merely giving to each other prudential instruction or exhortation, they may gain, or think they gain, nothing; in inculcating on each other the duty of positive beneficence, they have an unmistakable interest, but far less in degree; a person may possibly not need the benefits of others, but he always needs that they should not do him hurt. Thus the moralities which protect every individual from being harmed by others, either directly or by being hindered in his freedom of pursuing his own good, are at once those which he himself has most at heart and those which he has the strongest interest in publishing and enforcing by word and deed. It is by a person's observance of these that his fitness to exist as one of the fellowship of human beings is tested and decided; for on that depends his being a nuisance or not to those with whom he is in contact. Now it is these moralities primarily which compose the obligations of justice. The most marked cases of injustice, and those which give the tone to the feeling of repugnance which characterizes the sentiment, are acts of wrongful aggression or wrongful exercise of power over someone; the next are those which consist in wrongfully withholding from him something which is his due—in both cases inflicting on him a positive hurt, either in the form of direct suffering or of the privation of some good which he had reasonable ground, either of a physical or of a social kind, for counting upon.

The same powerful motives which command the observance of these primary moralities enjoin the punishment of those who violate them; and as the impulses of self-defense, of defense of others, and of vengeance are all called forth against such persons, retribution, or evil for evil, becomes closely connected with the sentiment of justice, and is universally included in the idea. Good for good is also one of the dictates of justice; and this, though its social utility is evident, and though it carries with it a natural human feeling, has not at first sight that obvious connection with hurt or injury which, existing in the most elementary cases of just and unjust, is the source of the characteristic intensity of the sentiment. But the con-

nection, though less obvious, is not less real. He who accepts benefits and denies a return of them when needed inflicts a real hurt by disappointing one of the most natural and reasonable of expectations, and one which he must at least tacitly have encouraged, otherwise the benefits would seldom have been conferred. The important rank, among human evils and wrongs, of the disappointment of expectation is shown in the fact that it constitutes the principal criminality of two such highly immoral acts as a breach of friendship and a breach of promise. Few hurts which human beings can sustain are greater, and none wound more, than when that on which they habitually and with full assurance relied fails them in the hour of need; and few wrongs are greater than this mere withholding of good; none excite more resentment, either in the person suffering or in a sympathizing spectator. The principle, therefore, of giving to each what they deserve, that is, good for good as well as evil for evil, is not only included within the idea of justice as we have defined it, but is a proper object of that intensity of sentiment which places the just human estimation above the simply expedient.

Most of the maxims of justice current in the world, and commonly appealed to in its transactions, are simply instrumental to carrying into effect the principles of justice which we have now spoken of. That a person is only responsible for what he has done voluntarily, or could voluntarily have avoided, that it is unjust to condemn any person unheard; that the punishment ought to be proportioned to the offense, and the like, are maxims intended to prevent the just principle of evil for evil from being perverted to the infliction of evil without that justification. The greater part of these common maxims have come into use from the practice of courts of justice, which have been naturally led to a more complete recognition and elaboration than was likely to suggest itself to others, of the rules necessary to enable them to fulfill their double function—of inflicting punishment when due, and of awarding to each person his right.

That first of judicial virtues, impartiality, is an obligation of justice, partly for the reason last mentioned, as being a necessary condition of the fulfillment of other obligations of justice. But this is not the only source of the exalted rank, among human obligations, of those maxims of equality and impartiality, which, both in popular estimation and in that of the most enlightened, are included among the precepts of justice. In one point of view, they may be considered as corollaries from the principles already laid down. If it is a duty to do to each according to his deserts, returning good for good, as well as repressing evil by evil, it necessarily follows that we should treat all equally well (when no higher duty forbids) who have deserved equally well of *us*, and that society should treat all equally well who have deserved equally well of *it,* that is, who have deserved equally well absolutely. This is the highest abstract standard of social and distributive justice, toward which all institutions and the efforts of all virtuous citizens should be made in the utmost possible degree to converge. But this great moral duty rests upon a still deeper foundation, being a direct emanation from the first principle of morals, and not a mere logical corollary from secondary or derivative doctrines. It is involved in the very meaning of utility, or the greatest happiness principle. That principle is a mere form of words without rational signification unless one person's happiness, supposed equal in degree (with the proper allowance made for kind), is counted for exactly as much as another's. Those conditions being supplied, Bentham's dictum "everybody to count for one, nobody for more than one," might be written under the principle of utility as an explanatory commentary.[4] The equal claim of everybody to happiness, in the estimation of the moralist and of the legislator, involves an equal claim to all the means of happiness except in so far as the inevitable conditions of human life and the general interest in which that of every individual is included set limits to the maxim; and those limits ought to be strictly construed. As every other maxim of justice, so this is by no means applied or held applicable universally; on the contrary, as I have already remarked, it bends to every person's ideas of social expediency. But in whatever case it is deemed applicable at all, it is held to be the dictate of justice. All persons are deemed to have a *right* to equality of treatment, except when some recognized social expediency requires the reverse. And hence all social in-

equalities which have ceased to be considered expedient assume the character, not of simple inexpediency, but of injustice, and appear so tyrannical that people are apt to wonder how they ever could have been tolerated—forgetful that they themselves, perhaps, tolerate other inequalities under an equally mistaken notion of expediency, the correction of which would make that which they approve seem quite as monstrous as what they have at last learned to condemn. The entire history of social improvement has been a series of transitions by which one custom or institution after another, from being a supposed primary necessity of social existence, has passed into the rank of a universally stigmatized injustice and tyranny. So it has been with the distinctions of slaves and freemen, nobles and serfs, patricians and plebeians; and so it will be, and in part already is, with the aristocracies of color, race, and sex.

It appears from what has been said that justice is a name for certain moral requirements which, regarded collectively, stand higher in the scale of social utility, and are therefore of more paramount obligation, than any others, though particular cases may occur in which some other social duty is so important as to overrule any one of the general maxims of justice. Thus, to save a life, it may not only be allowable, but a duty, to steal or take by force the necessary food or medicine, or to kidnap and compel to officiate the only qualified medical practitioner. In such cases, as we do not call anything justice which is not a virtue, we usually say, not that justice must give way to some other moral principle, but that what is just in ordinary cases is, by reason of that other principle, not just in the particular case. By this useful accommodation of language, the character of indefeasibility attributed to justice is kept up, and we are saved from the necessity of maintaining that there can be laudable injustice.

The considerations which have not been adduced resolve, I conceive, the only real difficulty in the utilitarian theory of morals. It has always been evident that all cases of justice are also cases of expediency; the difference is in the peculiar sentiment which attaches to the former, as contradistinguished from the latter. If this characteristic sentiment has been suffi-ciently accounted for; if there is no necessity to as-sume for it any peculiarity of origin; if it is simply the natural feeling of resentment, moralized by being made co-extensive with the demands of social good; and if this feeling not only does but ought to exist in all the classes of cases to which the idea of justice cor-responds—that idea no longer presents itself as a stumbling block to the utilitarian ethics. Justice re-mains the appropriate name for certain social utilities which are vastly more important, and therefore more absolute and imperative, than any others are as a class (though not more so than others may be in particular cases); and which, therefore, ought to be, as well as naturally are, guarded by a sentiment, not only differ-ent in degree, but also in kind; distinguished from the milder feeling which attaches to the mere idea of pro-moting human pleasure or convenience at once by the more definite nature of its commands and by the sterner character of its sanctions.

## Notes

1. The author of this essay has reason for believing himself to be the first person who brought the word "utili-tarian" into use. He did not invent it, but adopted it from a passing expression in Mr. Galt's *Annals of the Parish*. After using it as a designation for several years, he and oth-ers abandoned it from a growing dislike to anything resem-bling a badge or watchword of sectarian distinction. But as a name for one single opinion, not a set of opinions—to de-note the recognition of utility as a standard, not any partic-ular way of applying it—the term supplies a want in the lan-guage, and offers, in many cases, a convenient mode of avoiding tiresome circumlocutions.

2. An opponent, whose intellectual and moral fairness it is a pleasure to acknowledge (the Rev. J. Llewellyn Davies), has objected to this passage, saying, "Surely the rightness or wrongness of saving a man from drowning does depend very much upon the motive with which it is done. Suppose that a tyrant, when his enemy jumped into the sea to escape from him, saved him from drowning sim-ply in order that he might inflict upon him more exquisite tortures, would it tend to clearness to speak of that rescue as 'a morally right action'? Or suppose again, according to one of the stock illustrations of ethical inquiries, that a man betrayed a trust received from a friend, because the

discharge of it would fatally injure that friend himself or someone belonging to him, would utilitarianism compel one to call the betrayal 'a crime' as much as if it had been done from the meanest motive?"

I submit that he who saves another from drowning in order to kill him by torture afterwards does not differ only in motive from him who does the same thing from duty or benevolence; the act itself is different. The rescue of the man is, in the case supposed, only the necessary first step of an act far more atrocious than leaving him to drown would have been. Had Mr. Davies said, "The rightness or wrong-ness of saving a man from drowning does depend very much"—not upon the motive, but—"upon the *intention*," no utilitarian would have differed from him. Mr. Davies, by an oversight too common not to be quite venial, has in this case confounded the very different ideas of Motive and In-tention. There is no point which utilitarian thinkers (and Bentham preeminently) have taken more pains to illustrate than this. The morality of the action depends entirely upon the intention—that is, upon what the agent *wills to do*. But the motive, that is, the feeling which makes him will so to do, if it makes no difference in the act, makes none in the morality: though it makes a great difference in our moral estimation of the agent, especially if it indicates a good or a bad habitual *disposition*—a bent of character from which useful, or from which hurtful actions are likely to arise.

3. See this point enforced and illustrated by Professor Bain, in an admirable chapter (entitled "The Ethical Emo-tions, or the Moral Sense"), of the second of the two treatises composing his elaborate and profound work on the Mind.

4. This implication, in the first principle of the utilitari-an scheme, of perfect impartiality between persons is re-garded by Mr. Herbert Spencer (in his *Social Statics*) as a disproof of the pretensions of utility to be a sufficient guide to right; since (he says) the principle of utility presupposes the anterior principle that everybody has an equal right to happiness. It may be more correctly described as sup-posing that equal amounts of happiness are equally desir-able, whether felt by the same or different persons. This, however, is not a *pre*supposition, not a premise needful to support the principle of utility, but the very principle itself; for what is the principle of utility if it be not that "happi-ness" and "desirable" are synonymous terms? If there is any anterior principle implied, it can be no other than this, that the truths of arithmetic are applicable to the valuation of happiness, as of all other measurable quantities.

(Mr. Herbert Spencer, in a private communication on the subject of the preceding note, objects to being consid-ered an opponent of utilitarianism and states that he regards happiness as the ultimate end of morality; but deems that end only partially attainable by empirical generalizations from the observed results of conduct, and completely attainable only by deducing, from the laws of life and the conditions of existence, what kinds of action necessarily tend to produce happiness, and what kinds to produce unhappiness. With the exception of the word "necessarily," I have no dissent to express from this doctrine; and (omitting that word) I am not aware that any modern advocate of utilitarianism is of a different opinion. Bentham, certainly, to whom in the Social Statics Mr. Spencer particularly referred, is, least of all writers, chargeable with unwillingness to deduce the effect of actions on happiness from the laws of human nature and the universal conditions of human life. The common charge against him is of relying too exclusively upon such deductions and declining altogether to be bound by the generalizations from specific experience which Mr. Spencer thinks that utilitarians generally confine themselves to. My own opinion (and, as I collect, Mr. Spencer's) is that in ethics, as in all other branches of scientific study, the consilience of the results of both these processes, each corroborating and verifying the other, is requisite to give to any general proposition the kind and degree of evidence which constitutes scientific proof.)

# On Liberty

The grand, leading principle, towards which every argument unfolded in these pages directly converges, is the absolute and essential importance of human development in its richest diversity.

—Wilhelm von Humboldt:
*Sphere and Duties of Government*

To the beloved and deplored memory of her who was the inspirer, and in part the author, of all that is best in my writings—the friend and wife whose exalted sense of truth and right was my strongest incitement, and whose approbation was my chief reward—I dedicate this volume. Like all that I have written for many years, it belongs as much to her as to me; but the work as it stands has had, in a very insufficient degree, the inestimable advantage of her revision; some of the most important portions having been reserved for a more careful re-examination, which they are now never destined to receive. Were I but capable of interpreting to the world one half the great thoughts and noble feelings which are buried in her grave, I should be the medium of a greater benefit to it, than is ever likely to arise from anything that I can write, unprompted and unassisted by her all but unrivaled wisdom.

## CHAPTER I

### *Introductory*

The subject of this essay is not the so-called "liberty of the will," so unfortunately opposed to the misnamed doctrine of philosophical necessity; but civil, or social liberty: the nature and limits of the power which can be legitimately exercised by society over the individual. A question seldom stated, and hardly ever discussed in general terms, but which profoundly influences the practical controversies of the age by its latent presence, and is likely soon to make itself recognized as the vital question of the future. It is so far from being new that, in a certain sense, it has divided mankind almost from the remotest ages; but in the stage of progress into which the more civilized portions of the species have now entered, it presents itself under new conditions and requires a different and more fundamental treatment.

The struggle between liberty and authority is the most conspicuous feature in the portions of history with which we are earliest familiar, particularly in that of Greece, Rome, and England. But in old times this contest was between subjects, or some classes of subjects, and the government. By liberty was meant protection against the tyranny of the political rulers. The rulers were conceived (except in some of the popular governments of Greece) as in a necessarily antagonistic position to the people whom they ruled. They consisted of a governing One, or a governing tribe or caste, who derived their authority from inheritance or conquest, who, at all events, did not hold it at the pleasure of the governed, and whose supremacy men did not venture, perhaps did not desire, to contest, whatever precautions might be taken against its oppressive exercise. Their power was regarded as necessary, but also as highly dangerous; as a weapon which they would attempt to use against their subjects, no less than against external enemies. To prevent the weaker members of the community from being preyed upon by innumerable vultures, it was needful that there should be an animal of prey stronger than the rest, commissioned to keep them down. But as the king of the vultures would be no less bent upon preying on the flock than any of the minor harpies, it was indispensable to be in a perpetual attitude of defense against his beak and claws. The aim, therefore, of patriots was to set limits to the power which the ruler should be suffered to exercise over the community; and this limitation was what they meant by liberty. It was attempted in two ways. First, by obtaining a recognition of certain immunities, called political liberties or rights, which it was to be regarded as a breach of duty in the ruler to infringe, and which if he did infringe, specific resistance or general rebellion was held to be justifiable. A second, and generally a later, expedient was the establishment of constitutional checks by which the consent of the community, or of a body of some sort, supposed to represent its interests, was made a necessary condition to some of the more important acts of the governing power. To the first of these modes of limitation, the ruling power, in most European countries, was compelled, more or less, to submit. It was not so with the second; and, to attain this, or, when already in some degree possessed, to attain it more completely, became everywhere the principal object of the lovers of liberty. And so long as mankind were content to combat one enemy by another, and to be ruled by a master on condition of being guaranteed more or less efficaciously against his tyranny, they did not carry their aspirations beyond this point.

A time, however, came, in the progress of human affairs, when men ceased to think it a necessity of nature that their governors should be an independent power opposed in interest to themselves. It appeared to them much better that the various magistrates of the state should be their tenants or delegates, revocable at their pleasure. In that way alone, it seemed, could they have complete security that the powers of government would never be abused to their disadvantage. By degrees this new demand for elective and temporary rulers became the prominent object of the exertions of the popular party wherever any such party existed, and superseded, to a considerable extent, the previous efforts to limit the power of rulers. As the struggle proceeded for making the ruling power emanate from the periodical choice of the ruled, some persons began to think that too much importance had been attached to the limitation of the power itself. *That* (it might seem) was a resource against rulers whose interests were habitually opposed to those of the people. What was now wanted was that the rulers should be identified with the people, that their interest and will should be the interest and will of the nation. The nation did not need to be protected against its own will. There was no fear of its tyrannizing over itself. Let the rulers be effectually responsible to it, promptly removable by it, and it could afford to trust them with power of which it could itself dictate the use to be made. Their power was but the nation's own power, concentrated and in a form convenient for exercise. This mode of thought, or rather perhaps of feeling, was common among the last generation of European liberalism, in the Continental section of which it still apparently predominates. Those who admit any limit to what a government may do, except in the case of such governments as they think ought not to exist, stand out as brilliant exceptions among the political thinkers of the Continent. A similar tone of sentiment might by this time have been prevalent in our country if the circumstances which for a time encouraged it had continued unaltered.

But, in political and philosophical theories as well as in persons, success discloses faults and infirmities which failure might have concealed from observation. The notion that the people have no need to limit their power over themselves might seem axiomatic, when popular government was a thing only dreamed about, or read of as having existed at some distant period of the past. Neither was that notion necessarily disturbed by such temporary aberrations as those of the French Revolution, the worst of which were the work of a usurping few, and which, in any case, belonged, not to the permanent working of popular institutions, but to a sudden and convulsive outbreak against monarchical and aristo-cratic despotism. In time, however, a democratic republic came to occupy a large portion of the earth's surface and made itself felt as one of the most powerful members of the community of nations, and elective and responsible government became subject to the observations and criticisms which wait upon a great existing fact. It was now perceived that such phrases as "self-government," and "the power of the people over themselves," do not express the true state of the case. The "people" who exercise the power are not always the same people with those over whom it is exercised; and the "self-government" spoken of is not the government of each by himself, but of each by all the rest. The will of the people, moreover, practically means the will of the most numerous or the most active *part* of the people—the majority, or those who succeed in making themselves accepted as the majority; the people, consequently, *may* desire to oppress a part of their number, and precautions are as much needed against this as against any other abuse of power. The limitation, therefore, of the power of government over individuals loses none of its importance when the holders of power are regu-larly accountable to the community, that is, to the strongest party therein. This view of things, recom-mending itself equally to the intelligence of thinkers and to the inclination of those important classes in European society to whose real or supposed interests democracy is adverse, has had no difficulty in estab-lishing itself; and in political speculations "the tyranny of the majority" is now generally included among the evils against which society requires to be on its guard.

Like other tyrannies, the tyranny of the majority was at first, and is still vulgarly, held in dread, chiefly as operating through the acts of the public authorities. But reflecting persons perceived that when society is itself the tyrant—society collectively over the sepa-rate individuals who compose it—its means of tyran-nizing are not restricted to the acts which it may do by the hands of its political functionaries. Society can and does execute its own mandates; and if it issues wrong mandates instead of right, or any mandates at all in things with which it ought not to meddle, it prac-tices a social tyranny more formidable than many kinds of political oppression, since, though not usu-ally upheld by such extreme penalties, it leaves fewer means of escape, penetrating much more deeply into the details of life, and enslaving the soul itself. Protection, therefore, against the tyranny of the magistrate is not enough; there needs protection also against the tyranny of the prevailing opinion and feeling, against the tendency of society to impose, by other means than civil penalties, its own ideas and practices as rules of conduct on those who dissent from them; to fetter the development and, if possible, prevent the formation of any individuality not in har-mony with its ways, and compel all characters to fashion themselves upon the model of its own. There is a limit to the legitimate interference of collective opinion with individual independence; and to find that limit, and maintain it against encroachment, is as indispensable to a good condition of human affairs as protection against political despotism.

But though this proposition is not likely to be con-tested in general terms, the practical question where to place the limit—how to make the fitting adjust-ment between individual independence and social control—is a subject on which nearly everything remains to be done. All that makes existence valuable to anyone depends on the enforcement of restraints upon the actions of other people. Some rules of con-duct, therefore, must be imposed—by law in the first place, and by opinion on many things which are not fit subjects for the operation of law. What these rules should be is the principal question in human affairs; but if we except a few of the most obvious cases, it is one of those which least progress has been made in resolving. No two ages, and scarcely any two coun-tries, have decided it alike; and the decision of one age or country is a wonder to another. Yet the people of any given age and country no more suspect any dif-ficulty in it than if it were a subject on which mankind had always been agreed. The rules which obtain among themselves appear to them self-evident and self-justifying. This all but universal illusion is one of the examples of the magical influence of custom, which is not only, as the proverb says, a second nature but is continually mistaken for the first. The effect of custom, in preventing any misgiving respecting the rules of conduct which mankind impose on one another, is all the more complete because the subject is one on which it is not generally considered necessary that reasons should be given, either by one person to others or by each to himself. People are accustomed to believe, and have been encouraged in the belief by some who aspire to the character of philosophers, that their feelings on subjects of this nature are better than reasons and render reasons unnecessary. The practical principle which guides them to their opinions on the regulation of human conduct is the feeling in each person's mind that everybody should be required to act as he, and those with whom he sympathizes, would like them to act. No one, indeed, acknowledges to himself that his standard of judgment is his own liking; but an opinion on a point of conduct, not supported by reasons, can only count as one person's preference; and if the reasons, when given, are a mere appeal to a similar preference felt by other people, it is still only many people's liking instead of one. To an ordinary man, however, his own preference, thus supported, is not only a perfectly satisfactory reason but the only one he generally has for any of his notions of morality, taste, or propriety, which are not expressly written in his religious creed, and his chief guide in the interpretation even of that. Men's opinions, accordingly, on what is laudable or blamable are affected by all the multifarious causes which influence their wishes in regard to the conduct of others, and which are as numerous as those which determine their wishes on any other subject. Sometimes their reason; at other times their prejudices or superstitions; often their social affections, not seldom their antisocial ones, their envy or jealousy, their arrogance or contemptuousness; but most commonly their desires or fear for themselves—their legitimate or illegitimate self-interest. Wherever there is an ascendant class, a large portion of the morality of the country emanates from its class interests and its feelings of class superiority. The morality between Spartans and Helots, between planters and Negroes, between princes and subjects, between nobles and roturiers, between men and women has been for the most part the creation of these class interests and feelings; and the sentiments thus generated react in turn upon the moral feelings of the members of the ascendant class, in their relations among themselves. Where, on the other hand, a class, formerly ascendant, has lost its ascendancy, or where its ascendancy is unpopular, the prevailing moral sentiments frequently bear the impress of an impatient dislike of superiority. Another grand determining principle of the rules of conduct, both in act and forbearance, which have been enforced by law or opinion, has been the servility of mankind toward the supposed preferences or aversions of their temporal masters or of their gods. This servility, though essentially selfish, is not hypocrisy; it gives rise to perfectly genuine sentiments of abhorrence; it made men burn magicians and heretics. Among so many baser influences, the general and obvious interests of society have, of course, had a share, and a large one, in the direction of the moral sentiments; less, however, as a matter of reason, and on their own account, than as a consequence of the sympathies and antipathies which grew out of them; and sympathies and antipathies which had little or nothing to do with the interests of society have made themselves felt in the establishment of moralities with quite as great force.

The likings and dislikings of society, or of some powerful portion of it, are thus the main thing which has practically determined the rules laid down for general observance, under the penalties of law or opinion. And in general, those who have been in advance of society in thought and feeling have left this condition of things unassailed in principle, however they may have come into conflict with it in some of its details. They have occupied themselves rather in inquiring what things society ought to like or dislike than in questioning whether its likings or dislikings should be a law to individuals. They preferred endeavoring to alter the feelings of mankind on the particular points on which they were themselves heretical rather than make common cause in defense of freedom with heretics generally. The only case in which the higher ground has been taken on principle and maintained with consistency, by any but an individual here and there, is that of religious belief: a case instructive in many ways, and not least so as forming a most striking instance of the fallibility of what is called the moral sense; for the *odium theologicum,* in a sincere bigot, is one of the most unequivocal cases of moral feeling. Those who first broke the yoke of what called itself the Universal Church were in general as little willing to permit difference of religious opinion as that church itself. But when the heat of the conflict was over, without giving a complete victory to any party, and each church or sect was reduced to limit its hopes to retaining possession of the ground it already occupied, minorities, seeing that they had no chance of becoming majorities, were under the necessity of pleading to those whom they could not convert for permission to differ. It is accordingly on this battlefield, almost solely, that the rights of the individual against society have been asserted on broad grounds of principle, and the claim of society to exercise authority over dissentients openly controverted. The great writers to whom the world owes what religious liberty it possesses have mostly asserted freedom of conscience as an indefeasible right, and denied absolutely that a human being is accountable to others for his religious belief. Yet so natural to mankind is intolerance in whatever they really care about that religious freedom has hardly anywhere been practically realized, except where religious indifference, which dislikes to have its peace disturbed by theological quarrels, has added its weight to the scale. In the minds of almost all religious persons, even in the most tolerant countries, the duty of toleration is admitted with tacit reserves. One person will bear with dissent in matters of church government, but not of dogma; another can tolerate everybody, short of a Papist or a Unitarian; another, everyone who believes in revealed religion; a few extend their charity a little further, but stop at the belief in a God and in a future state. Wherever the sentiment of the majority is still genuine and intense, it is found to have abated little of its claim to be obeyed.

In England, from the peculiar circumstances of our political history, though the yoke of opinion is perhaps heavier, that of law is lighter than in most other countries of Europe; and there is considerable jealousy of direct interference by the legislative or the executive power with private conduct, not so much from any just regard for the independence of the individual as from the still subsisting habit of looking on the government as representing an opposite interest to the public. The majority have not yet learned to feel the power of the government their power, or its opinions their opinions. When they do so, individual liberty will probably be as much exposed to invasion from the government as it already is from public opinion. But, as yet, there is a considerable amount of feeling ready to be called forth against any attempt of the law to control individuals in things in which they have not hitherto been accustomed to be controlled by it; and this with very little discrimination as to whether the matter is, or is not, within the legitimate sphere of legal control; insomuch that the feeling, highly salutary on the whole, is perhaps quite as often misplaced as well grounded in the particular instances of its application. There is, in fact, no recognized principle by which the propriety or impropriety of government interference is customarily tested. People decide according to their personal preferences. Some, whenever they see any good to be done, or evil to be remedied, would willingly instigate the government to undertake the business, while others prefer to bear almost any amount of social evil rather than add one to the departments of human interests amenable to governmental control. And men range themselves on one or the other side in any particular case, according to this general direction of their sentiments, or according to the degree of interest which they feel in the particular thing which it is proposed that the government should do, or according to the belief they entertain that the government would, or would not, do it in the manner they prefer; but very rarely on account of any opinion to which they consistently adhere, as to what things are fit to be done by a government. And it seems to me that in consequence of this absence of rule or principle, one side is at present as often wrong as the other; the interference of government is, with about equal frequency, improperly invoked and improperly condemned.

The object of this essay is to assert one very simple principle, as entitled to govern absolutely the dealings of society with the individual in the way of compulsion and control, whether the means used be physical force in the form of legal penalties or the moral coercion of public opinion. That principle is that the sole end for which mankind are warranted, individually or collectively, in interfering with the liberty of action of any of their number is self-protection. That the only purpose for which power can be rightfully exercised over any member of a civilized community, against his will, is to prevent harm to others. His own good, either physical or moral, is not a sufficient warrant. He cannot rightfully be compelled to do or forbear because it will be better for him to do so, because it will make him happier, because, in the opinions of others, to do so would be wise or even right. These are good reasons for remonstrating with him, or reasoning with him, or persuading him, or entreating him, but not for compelling him or visiting him with any evil in case he do otherwise. To justify that, the conduct from which it is desired to deter him must be calculated to produce evil to someone else. The only part of the conduct of anyone for which he is amenable to society is that which concerns others. In the part which merely concerns himself, his independence is, of right, absolute. Over himself, over his own body and mind, the individual is sovereign.

It is, perhaps, hardly necessary to say that this doctrine is meant to apply only to human beings in the maturity of their faculties. We are not speaking of children or of young persons below the age which the law may fix as that of manhood or womanhood. Those who are still in a state to require being taken care of by others must be protected against their own actions as well as against external injury. For the same reason we may leave out of consideration those backward states of society in which the race itself may be considered as in its nonage. The early difficulties in the way of spontaneous progress are so great that there is seldom any choice of means for overcoming them; and a ruler full of the spirit of improvement is warranted in the use of any expedients that will attain an end perhaps otherwise unattainable. Despotism is a legitimate mode of government in dealing with barbarians, provided the end be their improvement and the means justified by actu-

ally effecting that end. Liberty, as a principle, has no application to any state of things anterior to the time when mankind have become capable of being improved by free and equal discussion. Until then, there is nothing for them but implicit obedience to an Akbar or a Charlemagne if they are so fortunate as to find one. But as soon as mankind have attained the capacity of being guided to their own improvement by conviction or persuasion (a period long since reached in all nations with whom we need here concern ourselves), compulsion, either in the direct form or in that of pains and penalties for noncompliance, is no longer admissible as a means to their own good, and justifiable only for the security of others.

It is proper to state that I forego any advantage which could be derived to my argument from the idea of abstract right as a thing independent of utility. I regard utility as the ultimate appeal on all ethical questions; but it must be utility in the largest sense, grounded on the permanent interests of man as a progressive being. Those interests, I contend, authorize the subjection of individual spontaneity to external control only in respect to those actions of each which concern the interest of other people. If anyone does an act hurtful to others, there is a *prima facie* case for punishing him by law or, where legal penalties are not safely applicable, by general disapprobation. There are also many positive acts for the benefit of others which he may rightfully be compelled to perform, such as to give evidence in a court of justice, to bear his fair share in the common defense or in any other joint work necessary to the interest of the society of which he enjoys the protection, and to perform certain acts of individual beneficence, such as saving a fellow creature's life or interposing to protect the defenseless against ill usage—things which whenever it is obviously a man's duty to do he may rightfully be made responsible to society for not doing. A person may cause evil to others not only by his actions but by his inaction, and in either case he is justly accountable to them for the injury. The latter case, it is true, requires a much more cautious exercise of compulsion than the former. To make anyone answerable for doing evil to others is the rule; to make him answerable for not preventing evil is, comparatively speaking, the exception. Yet there are many cases clear enough and grave enough to justify that exception. In all things which regard the external relations of the individual, he is *de jure* amenable to those whose interests are concerned, and, if need be, to society as their protector. There are often good reasons for not holding him to the responsibility; but these reasons must arise from the special expediencies of the case: either because it is a kind of case in which he is on the whole likely to act better when left to his own discretion than when controlled in any way in which society have it in their power to control him; or because the attempt to exercise control would produce other evils, greater than those which it would prevent. When such reasons as these preclude the enforcement of responsibility, the conscience of the agent himself should step into the vacant judgment seat and protect those interests of others which have no external protection; judging himself all the more rigidly, because the case does not admit of his being made accountable to the judgment of his fellow creatures.

But there is a sphere of action in which society, as distinguished from the individual, has, if any, only an indirect interest: comprehending all that portion of a person's life and conduct which affects only himself or, if it also affects others, only with their free, voluntary, and undeceived consent and participation. When I say only himself, I mean directly and in the first instance; for whatever affects himself may affect others through himself: and the objection which may be grounded on this contingency will receive consideration in the sequel. This, then, is the appropriate region of human liberty. It comprises, first, the inward domain of consciousness, demanding liberty of conscience in the most comprehensive sense, liberty of thought and feeling, absolute freedom of opinion and sentiment on all subjects, practical or speculative, scientific, moral, or theological. The liberty of expressing and publishing opinions may seem to fall under a different principle, since it belongs to that part of the conduct of an individual which concerns other people, but, being almost of as much importance as the liberty of thought itself and resting in great part on the same reasons, is practi-

cally inseparable from it. Secondly, the principle requires liberty of tastes and pursuits, of framing the plan of our life to suit our own character, of doing as we like, subject to such consequences as may follow, without impediment from our fellow creatures, so long as what we do does not harm them, even though they should think our conduct foolish, perverse, or wrong. Thirdly, from this liberty of each individual follows the liberty, within the same limits, of combination among individuals; freedom to unite for any purpose not involving harm to others: the persons combining being supposed to be of full age and not forced or deceived.

No society in which these liberties are not, on the whole, respected is free, whatever may be its form of government; and none is completely free in which they do not exist absolute and unqualified. The only freedom which deserves the name is that of pursuing our own good in our own way, so long as we do not attempt to deprive others of theirs or impede their efforts to obtain it. Each is the proper guardian of his own health, whether bodily *or* mental and spiritual. Mankind are greater gainers by suffering each other to live as seems good to themselves than by compelling each to live as seems good to the rest.

Though this doctrine is anything but new and, to some persons, may have the air of a truism, there is no doctrine which stands more directly opposed to the general tendency of existing opinion and practice. Society has expended fully as much effort in the attempt (according to its lights) to compel people to conform to its notions of personal as of social excellence. The ancient commonwealths thought themselves entitled to practice, and the ancient philosophers countenanced, the regulation of every part of private conduct by public authority, on the ground that the State had a deep interest in the whole bodily and mental discipline of every one of its citizens—a mode of thinking which may have been admissible in small republics surrounded by powerful enemies, in constant peril of being subverted by foreign attack or internal commotion, and to which even a short interval of relaxed energy and self-command might so easily be fatal that they could not afford to wait for the salutary permanent effects of freedom. In the modern world, the greater size of political communities and, above all, the separation between spiritual and temporal authority (which placed the direction of men's consciences in other hands than those which controlled their worldly affairs) prevented so great an interference by law in the details of private life; but the engines of moral repression have been wielded more strenuously against divergence from the reigning opinion in self-regarding than even in social matters; religion, the most powerful of the elements which have entered into the formation of moral feeling, having almost always been governed either by the ambition of a hierarchy seeking control over every department of human conduct, or by the spirit of Puritanism. And some of those modern reformers who have placed themselves in strongest opposition to the religions of the past have been noway behind either churches or sects in their assertion of the right of spiritual domination: M. Comte, in particular, whose social system, as unfolded in his *Système de Politique Positive*, aims at establishing (though by moral more than by legal appliances) a despotism of society over the individual surpassing anything contemplated in the political ideal of the most rigid disciplinarian among the ancient philosophers.

Apart from the peculiar tenets of individual thinkers, there is also in the world at large an increasing inclination to stretch unduly the powers of society over the individual both by force of opinion and even by that of legislation; and as the tendency of all the changes taking place in the world is to strengthen society and diminish the power of the individual, this encroachment is not one of the evils which tend spontaneously to disappear, but, on the contrary, to grow more and more formidable. The disposition of mankind, whether as rulers or as fellow citizens, to impose their own opinions and inclinations as a rule of conduct on others is so energetically supported by some of the best and by some of the worst feelings incident to human nature that it is hardly ever kept under restraint by anything but want of power; and as the power is not declining, but growing, unless a strong barrier of moral conviction can be raised

against the mischief, we must expect, in the present circumstances of the world, to see it increase.

It will be convenient for the argument if, instead of at once entering upon the general thesis, we confine ourselves in the first instance to a single branch of it on which the principle here stated is, if not fully, yet to a certain point, recognized by the current opinions. This one branch is the Liberty of Thought, from which it is impossible to separate the cognate liberty of speaking and of writing. Although these liberties, to some considerable amount, form part of the political morality of all countries which profess religious toleration and free institutions, the grounds, both philosophical and practical, on which they rest are perhaps not so familiar to the general mind, nor so thoroughly appreciated by many, even of the leaders of opinion, as might have been expected. Those grounds, when rightly understood, are of much wider application than to only one division of the subject, and a thorough consideration of this part of the question will be found the best introduction to the remainder. Those to whom nothing which I am about to say will be new may therefore, I hope, excuse me if on a subject which for now three centuries has been so often discussed I venture on one discussion more.

## CHAPTER II

### *Of the Liberty of Thought and Discussion*

The time, it is hoped, is gone by when any defense would be necessary of the "liberty of the press" as one of the securities against corrupt or tyrannical government. No argument, we may suppose, can now be needed against permitting a legislature or an executive, not identified in interest with the people, to prescribe opinions to them and determine what doctrines or what arguments they shall be allowed to hear. This aspect of the question, besides, has been so often and so triumphantly enforced by preceding writers that it needs not be specially insisted on in this place. Though the law of England, on the subject of the press, is as servile to this day as it was in the time of the Tudors, there is little danger of its being actually put in force against political discussion except during some temporary panic when fear of insurrection drives ministers and judges from their propriety[1]; and, speaking generally, it is not, in constitutional countries, to be apprehended that the government, whether completely responsible to the people or not, will often attempt to control the expression of opinion, except when in doing so it makes itself the organ of the general intolerance of the public. Let us suppose, therefore, that the government is entirely at one with the people, and never thinks of exerting any power of coercion unless in agreement with what it conceives to be their voice. But I deny the right of the people to exercise such coercion, either by themselves or by their government. The power itself is illegitimate. The best government has no more title to it than the worst. It is as noxious, or more noxious, when exerted in accordance with public opinion than when in opposition to it. If all mankind minus one were of one opinion, and only one person were of the contrary opinion, mankind would be no more justified in silencing that one person than he, if he had the power, would be justified in silencing mankind. Were an opinion a personal possession of no value except to the owner, if to be obstructed in the enjoyment of it were simply a private injury, it would make some difference whether the injury was inflicted only on a few persons or on many. But the peculiar evil of silencing the expression of an opinion is that it is robbing the human race, posterity as well as the existing generation—those who dissent from the opinion, still more than those who hold it. If the opinion is right, they are deprived of the opportunity of exchanging error for truth; if wrong, they lose, what is almost as great a benefit, the clearer perception and livelier impression of truth produced by its collision with error.

It is necessary to consider separately these two hypotheses, each of which has a distinct branch of the argument corresponding to it. We can never be sure that the opinion we are endeavoring to stifle is a false opinion; and if we were sure, stifling it would be an evil still.

First, the opinion which it is attempted to suppress by authority may possibly be true. Those who

desire to suppress it, of course, deny its truth; but they are not infallible. They have no authority to decide the question for all mankind and exclude every other person from the means of judging. To refuse a hearing to an opinion because they are sure that it is false is to assume that *their* certainty is the same thing as *absolute* certainty. All silencing of discussion is an assumption of infallibility. Its condemnation may be allowed to rest on this common argument, not the worse for being common.

Unfortunately for the good sense of mankind, the fact of their fallibility is far from carrying the weight in their practical judgment which is always allowed to it in theory; for while everyone well knows himself to be fallible, few think it necessary to take any precautions against their own fallibility, or admit the supposition that any opinion of which they feel very certain may be one of the examples of the error to which they acknowledge themselves to be liable. Absolute princes, or others who are accustomed to unlimited deference, usually feel this complete confidence in their own opinions on nearly all subjects. People more happily situated, who sometimes hear their opinions disputed and are not wholly unused to be set right when they are wrong, place the same unbounded reliance only on such of their opinions as are shared by all who surround them, or to whom they habitually defer; for in proportion to a man's want of confidence in his own solitary judgment does he usually repose, with implicit trust, on the infallibility of "the world" in general. And the world, to each individual, means the part of it with which he comes in contact: his party, his sect, his church, his class of society; the man may be called, by comparison, almost liberal and large-minded to whom it means anything so comprehensive as his own country or his own age. Nor is his faith in this collective authority at all shaken by his being aware that other ages, countries, sects, churches, classes, and parties have thought, and even now think, the exact reverse. He devolves upon his own world the responsibility of being in the right against the dissentient worlds of other people; and it never troubles him that mere accident has decided which of these numerous worlds is the object of his reliance, and that the same causes which make him a churchman in London would have made him a Buddhist or a Confucian in Peking. Yet it is as evident in itself, as any amount of argument can make it, that ages are no more infallible than individuals—every age having held many opinions which subsequent ages have deemed not only false but absurd; and it is as certain that many opinions, now general, will be rejected by future ages, as it is that many, once general, are rejected by the present.

The objection likely to be made to this argument would probably take some such form as the following. There is no greater assumption of infallibility in forbidding the propagation of error than in any other thing which is done by public authority on its own judgment and responsibility. Judgment is given to men that they may use it. Because it may be used erroneously, are men to be told that they ought not to use it at all? To prohibit what they think pernicious is not claiming exemption from error, but fulfilling the duty incumbent on them, although fallible, of acting on their conscientious conviction. If we were never to act on our opinions, because those opinions may be wrong, we should leave all our interests uncared for, and all our duties unperformed. An objection which applies to all conduct can be no valid objection to any conduct in particular. It is the duty of governments, and of individuals, to form the truest opinions they can; to form them carefully, and never impose them upon others unless they are quite sure of being right. But when they are sure (such reasoners may say), it is not conscientiousness but cowardice to shrink from acting on their opinions and allow doctrines which they honestly think dangerous to the welfare of mankind, either in this life or in another, to be scattered abroad without restraint, because other people, in less enlightened times, have persecuted opinions now believed to be true. Let us take care, it may be said, not to make the same mistake; but governments and nations have made mistakes in other things which are not denied to be fit subjects for the exercise of authority: they have laid on bad taxes, made unjust wars. Ought we therefore to lay on no taxes and, under whatever provocation, make no wars? Men and governments must act to the best of their ability.

There is no such thing as absolute certainty, but there is assurance sufficient for the purposes of human life. We may, and must, assume our opinion to be true for the guidance of our own conduct; and it is assuming no more when we forbid bad men to pervert society by the propagation of opinions which we regard as false and pernicious.

I answer, that it is assuming very much more. There is the greatest difference between presuming an opinion to be true because, with every opportunity for contesting it, it has not been refuted, and assuming its truth for the purpose of not permitting its refutation. Complete liberty of contradicting and disproving our opinion is the very condition which justifies us in assuming its truth for purposes of action; and on no other terms can a being with human faculties have any rational assurance of being right.

When we consider either the history of opinion or the ordinary conduct of human life, to what is it to be ascribed that the one and the other are no worse than they are? Not certainly to the inherent force of the human understanding, for on any matter not self-evident there are ninety-nine persons totally incapable of judging of it for one who is capable; and the capacity of the hundredth person is only comparative, for the majority of the eminent men of every past generation held many opinions now known to be erroneous, and did or approved numerous things which no one will now justify. Why is it, then, that there is on the whole a preponderance among mankind of rational opinions and rational conduct? If there really is this preponderance—which there must be unless human affairs are, and have always been, in an almost desperate state—it is owing to a quality of the human mind, the source of everything respectable in man either as an intellectual or as a moral being, namely, that his errors are corrigible. He is capable of rectifying his mistakes by discussion and experience. Not by experience alone. There must be discussion to show how experience is to be interpreted. Wrong opinions and practices gradually yield to fact and argument; but facts and arguments, to produce any effect on the mind, must be brought before it. Very few facts are able to tell their own story, without comments to bring out their meaning. The whole strength and value, then, of human judgment depending on the one property, that it can be set right when it is wrong, reliance can be placed on it only when the means of setting it right are kept constantly at hand. In the case of any person whose judgment is really deserving of confidence, how has it become so? Because he has kept his mind open to criticism of his opinions and conduct. Because it has been his practice to listen to all that could be said against him; to profit by as much of it as was just, and to expound to himself, and upon occasion to others, the fallacy of what was fallacious. Because he has felt that the only way in which a human being can make some approach to knowing the whole of a subject is by hearing what can be said about it by persons of every variety of opinion, and studying all modes in which it can be looked at by every character of mind. No wise man ever acquired his wisdom in any mode but this; nor is it in the nature of human intellect to become wise in any other manner. The steady habit of correcting and completing his own opinion by collating it with those of others, so far from causing doubt and hesitation in carrying it into practice, is the only stable foundation for a just reliance on it; for, being cognizant of all that can, at least obviously, be said against him, and having taken up his position against gainsayers—knowing that he has sought for objections and difficulties instead of avoiding them, and has shut out no light which can be thrown upon the subject from any quarter—he has a right to think his judgment better than that of any person, or any multitude, who have not gone through a similar process.

It is not too much to require that what the wisest of mankind, those who are best entitled to trust their own judgment, find necessary to warrant their relying on it, should be submitted to by that miscellaneous collection of a few wise and many foolish individuals called the public. The most intolerant of churches, the Roman Catholic Church, even at the canonization of a saint admits, and listens patiently to, a "devil's advocate." The holiest of men, it appears, cannot be admitted to posthumous honors until all that the devil could say against him is known and weighed. If even the Newtonian philosophy were not permitted to be questioned, mankind could not feel as complete assurance of its truth as they

now do. The beliefs which we have most warrant for have no safeguard to rest on but a standing invitation to the whole world to prove them unfounded. If the challenge is not accepted, or is accepted and the attempt fails, we are far enough from certainty still, but we have done the best that the existing state of human reason admits of: we have neglected nothing that could give the truth a chance of reaching us; if the lists are kept open, we may hope that, if there be a better truth, it will be found when the human mind is capable of receiving it; and in the meantime we may rely on having attained such approach to truth as is possible in our own day. This is the amount of certainty attainable by a fallible being, and this the sole way of attaining it.

Strange it is that men should admit the validity of the arguments for free discussion, but object to their being "pushed to an extreme," not seeing that unless the reasons are good for an extreme case, they are not good for any case. Strange that they should imagine that they are not assuming infallibility when they acknowledge that there should be free discussion on all subjects which can possibly be *doubtful*, but think that some particular principle or doctrine should be forbidden to be questioned because it is so *certain*, that is, because *they are certain* that it is certain. To call any proposition certain, while there is anyone who would deny its certainty if permitted, but who is not permitted, is to assume that we ourselves, and those who agree with us, are the judges of certainty, and judges without hearing the other side.

In the present age—which has been described as "destitute of faith, but terrified at skepticism"— in which people feel sure, not so much that their opinions are true as that they should not know what to do with them—the claims of an opinion to be protected from public attack are rested not so much on its truth as on its importance to society. There are, it is alleged, certain beliefs so useful, not to say indispensable, to well-being that it is as much the duty of governments to uphold those beliefs as to protect any other of the interests of society. In a case of such necessity, and so directly in the line of their duty, something less than infallibility may, it is maintained, warrant, and even bind, governments to act on their own opinion confirmed by the general opinion of mankind. It is also often argued, and still oftener thought, that none but bad men would desire to weaken these salutary beliefs; and there can be nothing wrong, it is thought, in restraining bad men and prohibiting what only such men would wish to practice. This mode of thinking makes the justification of restraints on discussion not a question of the truth of doctrines but of their usefulness, and flatters itself by that means to escape the responsibility of claiming to be an infallible judge of opinions. But those who thus satisfy themselves do not perceive that the assumption of infallibility is merely shifted from one point to another. The usefulness of an opinion is itself matter of opinion—as disputable, as open to discussion, and requiring discussion as much as the opinion itself. There is the same need of an infallible judge of opinions to decide an opinion to be noxious as to decide it to be false, unless the opinion condemned has full opportunity of defending itself. And it will not do to say that the heretic may be allowed to maintain the utility or harmlessness of his opinion, though forbidden to maintain its truth. The truth of an opinion is part of its utility. If we would know whether or not it is desirable that a proposition should be believed, is it possible to exclude the consideration of whether or not it is true? In the opinion, not of bad men, but of the best men, no belief which is contrary to truth can be really useful; and can you prevent such men from urging that plea when they are charged with culpability for denying some doctrine which they are told is useful, but which they believe to be false? Those who are on the side of received opinions never fail to take all possible advantage of this plea; you do not find *them* handling the question of ability as if it could be completely abstracted from that of truth; on the contrary, it is, above all, because their doctrine is "the truth" that the knowledge or the belief of it is held to be so indispensable. There can be no fair discussion of the question of usefulness when an argument so vital may be employed on one side, but not on the other. And in point of fact, when law or public feeling do not permit the truth of an opinion to be disputed, they are just as little tolerant of a denial of its use-

fulness. The utmost they allow is an extenuation of its absolute necessity, or of the positive guilt of rejecting it.

In order more fully to illustrate the mischief of denying a hearing to opinions because we, in our own judgment, have condemned them, it will be desirable to fix down the discussion to a concrete case; and I choose, by preference, the cases which are least favorable to me—in which the argument against freedom of opinion, both on the score of truth and on that of utility, is considered the strongest. Let the opinions impugned be the belief in a God and in a future state, or any of the commonly received doctrines of morality. To fight the battle on such ground gives a great advantage to an unfair antagonist, since he will be sure to say (and many who have no desire to be unfair will say it internally), Are these the doctrines which you do not deem sufficiently certain to be taken under the protection of law? Is the belief in a God one of the opinions to feel sure of which you hold to be assuming infallibility? But I must be permitted to observe that it is not the feeling sure of a doctrine (be it what it may) which I call an assumption of infallibility. It is the undertaking to decide that question *for others*, without allowing them to hear what can be said on the contrary side. And I denounce and reprobate this pretension not the less if put forth on the side of my most solemn convictions. However positive anyone's persuasion may be, not only of the falsity but of the pernicious consequences—not only of the pernicious consequences, but (to adopt expressions which I altogether condemn) the immorality and impiety of an opinion—yet if, in pursuance of that private judgment, though backed by the public judgment of his country or his contemporaries, he prevents the opinion from being heard in its defense, he assumes infallibility. And so far from the assumption being less objectionable or less dangerous because the opinion is called immoral or impious, this is the case of all others in which it is most fatal. These are exactly the occasions on which the men of one generation commit those dreadful mistakes which excite the astonishment and horror of posterity. It is among such that we find the instances memorable in history, when the arm of the law has been employed to root out the best men and the noblest doctrines; with deplorable success as to the men, though some of the doctrines have survived to be (as if in mockery) invoked in defense of similar conduct toward those who dissent from *them*, or from their received interpretation.

Mankind can hardly be too often reminded that there was once a man called Socrates, between whom and the legal authorities and public opinion of his time there took place a memorable collision. Born in an age and country abounding in individual greatness, this man has been handed down to us by those who best knew both him and the age as the most virtuous man in it; while *we* know him as the head and prototype of all subsequent teachers of virtue, the source equally of the lofty inspiration of Plato and the judicious utilitarianism of Aristotle, *"i maestri di color che sanno,"* the two headsprings of ethical as of all other philosophy. This acknowledged master of all the eminent thinkers who have since lived—whose fame, still growing after more than two thousand years, all but outweighs the whole remainder of the names which make his native city illustrious—was put to death by his countrymen, after a judicial conviction, for impiety and immorality. Impiety, in denying the gods recognized by the State; indeed, his accuser asserted (see the *Apologia*) that he believed in no gods at all. Immorality, in being, by his doctrines and instructions, a "corruptor of youth." Of these charges the tribunal, there is every ground for believing, honestly found him guilty, and condemned the man who probably of all then born had deserved best of mankind, to be put to death as a criminal.

To pass from this to the only other instance of judicial iniquity, the mention of which, after the condemnation of Socrates, would not be an anticlimax: the event which took place on Calvary rather more than eighteen hundred years ago. The man who left on the memory of those who witnessed his life and conversation such an impression of his moral grandeur that eighteen subsequent centuries have done homage to him as the Almighty in person, was ignominiously put to death, as what? As a blasphemer. Men did not merely mistake their benefactor, they mistook him for the exact contrary of what he

was and treated him as that prodigy of impiety which they themselves are now held to be for their treatment of him. The feelings with which mankind now regard these lamentable transactions, especially the later of the two, render them extremely unjust in their judgment of the unhappy actors. These were, to all appearance, not bad men—not worse than men commonly are, but rather the contrary; men who possessed in a full, or somewhat more than a full measure, the religious, moral, and patriotic feelings of their time and people: the very kind of men who, in all times, our own included, have every chance of passing through life blameless and respected. The high priest who rent his garments when the words were pronounced, which, according to all the ideas of his country, constituted the blackest guilt, was in all probability quite as sincere in his horror and indignation as the generality of respectable and pious men now are in the religious and moral sentiments they profess; and most of those who now shudder at his conduct, if they had lived in his time, and been born Jews, would have acted precisely as he did. Orthodox Christians who are tempted to think that those who stoned to death the first martyrs must have been worse men than they themselves are, ought to remember that one of those persecutors was Saint Paul.

Let us add one more example, the most striking of all, if the impressiveness of an error is measured by the wisdom and virtue of him who falls into it. If ever anyone possessed of power had grounds for thinking himself the best and most enlightened among his contemporaries, it was the Emperor Marcus Aurelius. Absolute monarch of the whole civilized world, he preserved through life not only the most unblemished justice, but what was less to be expected from his Stoical breeding, the tenderest heart. The few failings which are attributed to him were all on the side of indulgence, while his writings, the highest ethical product of the ancient mind, differ scarcely perceptibly, if they differ at all, from the most characteristic teachings of Christ. This man, a better Christian in all but the dogmatic sense of the word than almost any of the ostensibly Christian sovereigns who have since reigned, persecuted

Christianity. Placed at the summit of all the previous attainments of humanity, with an open, unfettered intellect, and a character which led him of himself to embody in his moral writings the Christian ideal, he yet failed to see that Christianity was to be a good and not an evil to the world, with his duties to which he was so deeply penetrated. Existing society he knew to be in a deplorable state. But such as it was, he saw, or thought he saw, that it was held together, and prevented from being worse, by belief and reverence of the received divinities. As a ruler of mankind, he deemed it his duty not to suffer society to fall in pieces; and saw not how, if its existing ties were removed, any others could be formed which could again knit it together. The new religion openly aimed at dissolving these ties; unless, therefore, it was his duty to adopt that religion, it seemed to be his duty to put it down. Inasmuch then as the theology of Christianity did not appear to him true or of divine origin, inasmuch as this strange history of a crucified God was not credible to him, and a system which purported to rest entirely upon a foundation to him so wholly unbelievable, could not be foreseen by him to be that renovating agency which, after all abatements, it has in fact proved to be; the gentlest and most amiable of philosophers and rulers, under a solemn sense of duty, authorized the persecution of Christianity. To my mind this is one of the most tragical facts in all history. It is a bitter thought how different a thing the Christianity of the world might have been if the Christian faith had been adopted as the religion of the empire under the auspices of Marcus Aurelius instead of those of Constantine. But it would be equally unjust to him and false to truth to deny that no one plea which can be urged for punishing anti-Christian teaching was wanting to Marcus Aurelius for punishing, as he did, the propagation of Christianity. No Christian more firmly believes that atheism is false and tends to the dissolution of society than Marcus Aurelius believed the same things of Christianity; he who, of all men then living, might have been thought the most capable of appreciating it. Unless anyone who approves of punishment for the promulgation of opinions flatters himself that he is a wiser and better man than Mar-

cus Aurelius—more deeply versed in the wisdom of his time, more elevated in his intellect above it, more earnest in his search for truth, or more single-minded in his devotion to it when found—let him abstain from that assumption of the joint infallibility of himself and the multitude which the great Antoninus made with so unfortunate a result.

Aware of the impossibility of defending the use of punishment for restraining irreligious opinions by any argument which will not justify Marcus Antoninus, the enemies of religious freedom, when hard pressed, occasionally accept this consequence and say, with Dr. Johnson, that the persecutors of Christianity were in the right, that persecution is an ordeal through which truth ought to pass, and always passes successfully, legal penalties being, in the end, powerless against truth, though sometimes beneficially effective against mischievous errors. This is a form of the argument for religious intolerance sufficiently remarkable not to be passed without notice.

A theory which maintains that truth may justifiably be persecuted because persecution cannot possibly do it any harm cannot be charged with being intentionally hostile to the reception of new truths; but we cannot commend the generosity of its dealing with the persons to whom mankind are indebted for them. To discover to the world something which deeply concerns it, and of which it was previously ignorant, to prove to it that it had been mistaken on some vital point of temporal or spiritual interest, is as important a service as a human being can render to his follow creatures, and in certain cases, as in those of the early Christians and of the Reformers, those who think with Dr. Johnson believe it to have been the most precious gift which could be bestowed on mankind. That the authors of such splendid benefits should be requited by martyrdom, that their reward should be to be dealt with as the vilest of criminals, is not, upon this theory, a deplorable error and misfortune for which humanity should mourn in sackcloth and ashes, but the normal and justifiable state of things. The propounder of a new truth, according to this doctrine, should stand, as stood, in the legislation of the Locrians, the proposer of a new law, with a halter round his neck, to be instantly tightened if the public assembly did not, on hearing his reasons, then and there adopt his proposition. People who defend this mode of treating benefactors cannot be supposed to set much value on the benefit; and I believe this view of the subject is mostly confined to the sort of persons who think that new truths may have been desirable once, but that we have had enough of them now.

But, indeed, the dictum that truth always triumphs over persecution is one of those pleasant falsehoods which men repeat after one another till they pass into commonplaces, but which all experience refutes. History teems with instances of truth put down by persecution. If not suppressed forever, it may be thrown back for centuries. To speak only of religious opinions: the Reformation broke out at least twenty times before Luther, and was put down. Arnold of Brescia was put down. Fra Dolcino was put down. Savonarola was put down. The Albigeois were put down. The Vaudois were put down. The Lollards were put down. The Hussites were put down. Even after the era of Luther, wherever persecution was persisted in, it was successful. In Spain, Italy, Flanders, the Austrian empire, Protestantism was rooted out; and, most likely, would have been so in England had Queen Mary lived or Queen Elizabeth died. Persecution has always succeeded save where the heretics were too strong a party to be effectually persecuted. No reasonable person can doubt that Christianity might have been extirpated in the Roman Empire. It spread and became predominant because the persecutions were only occasional, lasting but a short time, and separated by long intervals of almost undisturbed propagandism. It is a piece of idle sentimentality that truth, merely as truth, has any inherent power denied to error of prevailing against the dungeon and the stake. Men are not more zealous for truth than they often are for error, and a sufficient application of legal or even of social penalties will generally succeed in stopping the propagation of either. The real advantage which truth has consists in this, that when an opinion is true, it may be extinguished once, twice, or many times, but in the course of ages there will generally be found persons to rediscover it, until some one of its reappearances falls on a time when from favorable circumstances it escapes persecution until it has made such head as to withstand all subsequent attempts to suppress it.

It will be said that we do not now put to death the introducers of new opinions: we are not like our fathers who slew the prophets; we even build sepulchers to them. It is true we no longer put heretics to death; and the amount of penal infliction which modern feeling would probably tolerate, even against the most obnoxious opinions, is not sufficient to extirpate them. But let us not flatter ourselves that we are yet free from the stain even of legal persecution. Penalties for opinion, or at least for its expression, still exist by law; and their enforcement is not, even in these times, so unexampled as to make it at all incredible that they may some day be revived in full force. In the year 1857, at the summer assizes of the county of Cornwall, an unfortunate man,[2] said to be of unexceptionable conduct in all relations of life, was sentenced to twenty-one months' imprisonment for uttering, and writing on a gate, some offensive words concerning Christianity. Within a month of the same time, at the Old Bailey, two persons,[3] on two separate occasions, were rejected as jurymen, and one of them grossly insulted by the judge and by one of the counsel, because they honestly declared that they had no theological belief; and a third, a foreigner,[4] for the same reason, was denied justice against a thief. This refusal of redress took place in virtue of the legal doctrine that no person can be allowed to give evidence in a court of justice who does not profess belief in a God (any god is sufficient) and in a future state, which is equivalent to declaring such persons to be outlaws, excluded from the protection of the tribunals; who may not only be robbed or assaulted with impunity, if no one but themselves, or persons of similar opinions, be present, but anyone else may be robbed or assaulted with impunity, if the proof of the fact depends on their evidence. The assumption on which this is grounded is that the oath is worthless of a person who does not believe in a future state—a proposition which betokens much ignorance of history in those who assent to it (since it is historically true that a large proportion of infidels in all ages have been persons of distinguished integrity and honor), and would be maintained by no one who had the smallest conception how many of the persons in greatest repute with the world, both for virtues and attainments, are well known, at least to their intimates, to be unbelievers. The rule, besides, is suicidal and cuts away its own foundation. Under pretense that atheists must be liars, it admits the testimony of all atheists who are willing to lie, and rejects only those who brave the obloquy of publicly confessing a detested creed rather than affirm a falsehood. A rule thus self-convicted of absurdity so far as regards its professed purpose can be kept in force only as a badge of hatred, a relic of persecution—a persecution, too, having the peculiarity that the qualification for undergoing it is the being clearly proved not to deserve it. The rule and the theory it implies are hardly less insulting to believers than to infidels. For if he who does not believe in a future state necessarily lies, it follows that they who do believe are only prevented from lying, if prevented they are, by the fear of hell. We will not do the authors and abettors of the rule the injury of supposing that the conception which they have formed of Christian virtue is drawn from their own consciousness.

These, indeed, are but rags and remnants of persecution, and may be thought to be not so much an indication of the wish to persecute, as an example of that very frequent infirmity of English minds, which makes them take a preposterous pleasure in the assertion of a bad principle, when they are no longer bad enough to desire to carry it really into practice. But unhappily there is no security in the state of the public mind that the suspension of worse forms of legal persecution, which has lasted for about the space of a generation, will continue. In this age the quiet surface of routine is as often ruffled by attempts to resuscitate past evils as to introduce new benefits. What is boasted of at the present time as the revival of religion is always, in narrow and uncultivated minds, at least as much the revival of bigotry; and where there is the strong permanent leaven of intolerance in the feelings of a people, which at all times abides in the middle classes of this country, it needs but little to provoke them into actively perse-

cuting those whom they have never ceased to think proper objects of persecution.[5] For it is this—it is the opinions men entertain, and the feelings they cherish, respecting those who disown the beliefs they deem important which makes this country not a place of mental freedom. For a long time past, the chief mischief of the legal penalties is that they strengthen the social stigma. It is that stigma which is really effective, and so effective is it that the profession of opinions which are under the ban of society is much less common in England than is, in many other countries, the avowal of those which incur risk of judicial punishment. In respect to all persons but those whose pecuniary circumstances make them independent of the good will of other people, opinion, on this subject, is as efficacious as law; men might as well be imprisoned as excluded from the means of earning their bread. Those whose bread is already secured, and who desire no favors from men in power, or from bodies of men, or from the public, have nothing to fear from the open avowal of any opinions but to be ill-thought of and ill-spoken of, and this it ought not to require a very heroic mold to enable them to bear. There is no room for any appeal *ad misericordiam* in behalf of such persons. But though we do not now inflict so much evil on those who think differently from us as it was formerly our custom to do, it may be that we do ourselves as much evil as ever by our treatment of them. Socrates was put to death, but the Socratic philosophy rose like the sun in heaven and spread its illumination over the whole intellectual firmament. Christians were cast to the lions, but the Christian church grew up a stately and spreading tree, overtopping the older and less vigorous growths, and stifling them by its shade. Our merely social intolerance kills no one, roots out no opinions, but induces men to disguise them or to abstain from any active effort for their diffusion. With us, heretical opinions do not perceptibly gain, or even lose, ground in each decade or generation; they never blaze out far and wide, but continue to smolder in the narrow circles of thinking and studious persons among whom they originate, without ever lighting up the general affairs of mankind with either a true or a deceptive light. And thus is kept up a state of things very satisfactory to some minds, because, without the unpleasant process of fining or imprisoning anybody, it maintains all prevailing opinions outwardly undisturbed, while it does not absolutely interdict the exercise of reason by dissenients afflicted with the malady of thought. A convenient plan for having peace in the intellectual world, and keeping all things going on therein very much as they do already. But the price paid for this sort of intellectual pacification is the sacrifice of the entire moral courage of the human mind. A state of things in which a large portion of the most active and inquiring intellects find it advisable to keep the general principles and grounds of their convictions within their own breasts, and attempt, in what they address to the public, to fit as much as they can of their own conclusions to premises which they have internally renounced, cannot send forth the open, fearless characters and logical, consistent intellects who once adorned the thinking world. The sort of men who can be looked for under it are either mere conformers to commonplace, or timeservers for truth, whose arguments on all great subjects are meant for their hearers, and are not those which have convinced themselves. Those who avoid this alternative do so by narrowing their thoughts and interest to things which can be spoken of without venturing within the region of principles, that is, to small practical matters which would come right of themselves, if but the minds of mankind were strengthened and enlarged, and which will never be made effectually right until then, while that which would strengthen and enlarge men's minds—free and daring speculation on the highest subjects—is abandoned.

Those in whose eyes this reticence on the part of heretics is no evil should consider, in the first place, that in consequence of it there is never any fair and thorough discussion of heretical opinions; and that such of them as could not stand such a discussion, though they may be prevented from spreading, do not disappear. But it is not the minds of heretics that are deteriorated most by the ban placed on all inquiry which does not end in the orthodox conclusions. The greatest harm done is to those who are not heretics, and whose whole mental development is cramped

and their reason cowed by the fear of heresy. Who can compute what the world loses in the multitude of promising intellects combined with timid characters, who dare not follow out any bold, vigorous, independent train of thought, lest it should land them in something which would admit of being considered irreligious or immoral? Among them we may occasionally see some man of deep conscientiousness and subtle and refined understanding, who spends a life in sophisticating with an intellect which he cannot silence, and exhausts the resources of ingenuity in attempting to reconcile the promptings of his conscience and reason with orthodoxy, which yet he does not, perhaps, to the end succeed in doing. No one can be a great thinker who does not recognize that as a thinker it is his first duty to follow his intellect to whatever conclusions it may lead. Truth gains more even by the errors of one who, with due study and preparation, thinks for himself than by the true opinions of those who only hold them because they do not suffer themselves to think. Not that it is solely, or chiefly, to form great thinkers that freedom of thinking is required. On the contrary, it is as much and even more indispensable to enable average human beings to attain the mental stature which they are capable of. There have been, and may again be, great individual thinkers in a general atmosphere of mental slavery. But there never has been, nor ever will be, in that atmosphere an intellectually active people. Where any people has made a temporary approach to such a character, it has been because the dread of heterodox speculation was for a time suspended. Where there is a tacit convention that principles are not to be disputed, where the discussion of the greatest questions which can occupy humanity is considered to be closed, we cannot hope to find that generally high scale of mental activity which has made some periods of history so remarkable. Never when controversy avoided the subjects which are large and important enough to kindle enthusiasm was the mind of a people stirred up from its foundations, and the impulse given which raised even persons of the most ordinary intellect to something of the dignity of thinking beings. Of such we have had an example in the condition of Europe during the times immediately following the Reformation; another, though limited to the Continent and to a more cultivated class, in the speculative movement of the latter half of the eighteenth century; and a third, of still briefer duration, in the intellectual fermentation of Germany during the Goethian and Fichtean period. These periods differed widely in the particular opinions which they developed, but were alike in this, that during all three the yoke of authority was broken. In each, an old mental despotism had been thrown off, and no new one had yet taken its place. The impulse given at these three periods has made Europe what it now is. Every single improvement which has taken place either in the human mind or in institutions may be traced distinctly to one or other of them. Appearances have for some time indicated that all three impulses are well-nigh spent; and we can expect no fresh start until we again assert our mental freedom.

Let us now pass to the second division of the argument, and dismissing the supposition that any of the received opinions may be false, let us assume them to be true and examine into the worth of the manner in which they are likely to be held when their truth is not freely and openly canvassed. However unwillingly a person who has a strong opinion may admit the possibility that his opinion may be false, he ought to be moved by the consideration that, however true it may be, if it is not fully, frequently, and fearlessly discussed, it will be held as a dead dogma, not a living truth.

There is a class of persons (happily not quite so numerous as formerly) who think it enough if a person assents undoubtingly to what they think true, though he has no knowledge whatever of the grounds of the opinion and could not make a tenable defense of it against the most superficial objections. Such persons, if they can once get their creed taught from authority, naturally think that no good, and some harm, comes of its being allowed to be questioned. Where their influence prevails, they make it nearly impossible for the received opinion to be rejected wisely and considerately, though it may still be rejected rashly and ignorantly; for to shut out discussion entirely is seldom possible, and when it once

gets in, beliefs not grounded on conviction are apt to give way before the slightest semblance of an argument. Waiving, however, this possibility—assuming that the true opinion abides in the mind, but abides as a prejudice, a belief independent of, and proof against, argument—this is not the way in which truth ought to be held by a rational being. This is not knowing the truth. Truth, thus held, is but one superstition the more, accidentally clinging to the words which enunciate a truth.

If the intellect and judgment of mankind ought to be cultivated, a thing which Protestants at least do not deny, on what can these faculties be more appropriately exercised by anyone than on the things which concern him so much that is it considered necessary for him to hold opinions on them? If the cultivation of the understanding consists in one thing more than in another, it is surely in learning the grounds of one's own opinions. Whatever people believe, on subjects on which it is of the first importance to believe rightly, they ought to be able to defend against at least the common objections. But, someone may say, "Let them be *taught* the grounds of their opinions. It does not follow that opinions must be merely parroted because they are never heard controverted. Persons who learn geometry do not simply commit the theorems to memory, but understand and learn likewise the demonstrations; and it would be absurd to say that they remain ignorant of the grounds of geometrical truths because they never hear anyone deny and attempt to disprove them." Undoubtedly: and such teaching suffices on a subject like mathematics, where there is nothing at all to be said on the wrong side of the question. The peculiarity of the evidence of mathematical truths is that all the argument is on one side. There are no objections, and no answers to objections. But on every subject on which difference of opinion is possible, the truth depends on a balance to be struck between two sets of conflicting reasons. Even in natural philosophy, there is always some other explanation possible of the same facts; some geocentric theory instead of heliocentric, some phlogiston instead of oxygen; and it has to be shown why that other theory cannot be the true one; and until this is shown, and until we know how it is shown, we do not understand the grounds of our opinion. But when we turn to subjects infinitely more complicated, to morals, religion, politics, social relations, and the business of life, three-fourths of the arguments for every disputed opinion consist in dispelling the appearances which favor some opinion different from it. The greatest orator, save one, of antiquity, has left it on record that he always studied his adversary's case with as great, if not still greater, intensity than even his own. What Cicero practiced as the means of forensic success requires to be imitated by all who study any subject in order to arrive at the truth. He who knows only his own side of the case knows little of that. His reasons may be good, and no one may have been able to refute them. But if he is equally unable to refute the reasons on the opposite side, if he does not so much as know what they are, he has no ground for preferring either opinion. The rational position for him would be suspension of judgment, and unless he contents himself with that, he is either led by authority or adopts, like the generality of the world, the side to which he feels most inclination. Nor is it enough that he should hear the arguments of adversaries from his own teachers, presented as they state them, and accompanied by what they offer as refutations. That is not the way to do justice to the arguments or bring them into real contact with his own mind. He must be able to hear them from persons who actually believe them, who defend them in earnest and do their very utmost for them. He must know them in their most plausible and persuasive form; he must feel the whole force of the difficulty which the true view of the subject has to encounter and dispose of, else he will never really possess himself of the portion of truth which meets and removes that difficulty. Ninety-nine in a hundred of what are called educated men are in this condition, even of those who can argue fluently for their opinions. Their conclusion may be true, but it might be false for anything they know; they have never thrown themselves into the mental position of those who think differently from them, and considered what such persons may have to say; and, consequently, they do not, in any proper sense of the word, know the doctrine which they themselves profess. They do

not know those parts of it which explain and justify the remainder—the considerations which show that a fact which seemingly conflicts with another is reconcilable with it, or that, of two apparently strong reasons, one and not the other ought to be preferred. All that part of the truth which turns the scale and decides the judgment of a completely informed mind, they are strangers to; nor is it ever really known but to those who have attended equally and impartially to both sides and endeavored to see the reasons of both in the strongest light. So essential is this discipline to a real understanding of moral and human subjects that, if opponents of all-important truths do not exist, it is indispensable to imagine them and supply them with the strongest arguments which the most skillful devil's advocate can conjure up.

To abate the force of these considerations, an enemy of free discussion may be supposed to say that there is no necessity for mankind in general to know and understand all that can be said against or for their opinions by philosophers and theologians. That it is not needful for common men to be able to expose all the misstatements or fallacies of an ingenious opponent. That it is enough if there is always somebody capable of answering them, so that nothing likely to mislead uninstructed persons remains unrefuted. That simple minds, having been taught the obvious grounds of the truths inculcated in them, may trust to authority for the rest and, being aware that they have neither knowledge nor talent to resolve every difficulty which can be raised, may repose in the assurance that all those which have been raised have been or can be answered by those who are specially trained to the task.

Conceding to this view of the subject the utmost that can be claimed for it by those most easily satisfied with the amount of understanding of truth which ought to accompany the belief of it, even so, the argument for free discussion is no way weakened. For even this doctrine acknowledges that mankind ought to have a rational assurance that all objections have been satisfactorily answered; and how are they to be answered if that which requires to be answered is not spoken? Or how can the answer be known to be satisfactory if the objectors have no opportunity of showing that it is unsatisfactory? If not the public, at least the philosophers and theologians who are to resolve the difficulties must make themselves familiar with those difficulties in their most puzzling form; and this cannot be accomplished unless they are freely stated and placed in the most advantageous light which they admit of. The Catholic Church has its own way of dealing with this embarrassing problem. It makes a broad separation between those who can be permitted to receive its doctrines on conviction and those who must accept them on trust. Neither, indeed, are allowed any choice as to what they will accept; but the clergy, such at least as can be fully confided in, may admissibly and meritoriously make themselves acquainted with the arguments of opponents, in order to answer them, and may, therefore, read heretical books; the laity, not unless by special permission, hard to be obtained. This discipline recognizes a knowledge of the enemy's case as beneficial to the teachers, but finds means, consistent with this, of denying it to the rest of the world, thus giving to the *élite* more mental culture, though not more mental freedom, than it allows to the mass. By this device it succeeds in obtaining the kind of mental superiority which its purposes require; for though culture without freedom never made a large and liberal mind, it can make a clever *nisi prius* advocate of a cause. But in countries professing Protestantism, this resource is denied, since Protestants hold, at least in theory, that the responsibility for the choice of a religion must be borne by each for himself and cannot be thrown off upon teachers. Besides, in the present state of the world, it is practically impossible that writings which are read by the instructed can be kept from the uninstructed. If the teachers of mankind are to be cognizant of all that they ought to know, everything must be free to be written and published without restraint.

If, however, the mischievous operation of the absence of free discussion, when the received opinions are true, were confined to leaving men ignorant of the grounds of those opinions, it might be thought that this, if an intellectual, is no moral evil and does not affect the worth of the opinions, regarded in their influence on the character. The fact, however, is that not only the grounds of the opinion are forgotten in the absence of discussion, but too often the meaning of the opinion itself. The words which convey it cease to suggest ideas, or suggest only a small portion of those they were originally employed to communicate. Instead of a vivid conception and a living belief, there remain only a few phrases retained by rote; or, if any part, the shell and husk only of the meaning is retained, the finer essence being lost. The great chapter in human history which this fact occupies and fills cannot be too earnestly studied and meditated on.

It is illustrated in the experience of almost all ethical doctrines and religious creeds. They are all full of meaning and vitality to those who originate them, and to the direct disciples of the originators. Their meaning continues to be felt in undiminished strength, and is perhaps brought out into even fuller consciousness, so long as the struggle lasts to give the doctrine or creed an ascendancy over other creeds. At last it either prevails and becomes the general opinion, or its progress stops; it keeps possession of the ground it has gained, but ceases to spread further. When either of these results has become apparent, controversy on the subject flags, and gradually dies away. The doctrine has taken its place, if not as a received opinion, as one of the admitted sects or divisions of opinion; those who hold it have generally inherited, not adopted it; and conversion from one of these doctrines to another, being now an exceptional fact, occupies little place in the thoughts of their professors. Instead of being, as at first, constantly on the alert either to defend themselves against the world or to bring the world over to them, they have subsided into acquiescence and neither listen, when they can help it, to arguments against their creed, nor trouble dissentients (if there be such) with arguments in its favor. From this time may usually be dated the decline in the living power of the doctrine. We often hear the teachers of all creeds lamenting the difficulty of keeping up in the minds of believers a lively apprehension of the truth which they nominally recognize, so that it may penetrate the feelings and acquire a real mastery over the conduct. No such difficulty is complained of while the creed is still fighting for its existence; even the weaker combatants then know and feel what they are fighting for, and the difference between it and other doctrines; and in that period of every creed's existence not a few persons may be found who have realized its fundamental principles in all the forms of thought, have weighed and considered them in all their important bearings, and have experienced the full effect on the character which belief in that creed ought to produce in a mind thoroughly imbued with it. But when it has come to be an hereditary creed, and to be received passively, not actively—when the mind is no longer compelled, in the same degree as at first, to exercise its vital powers on the questions which its belief presents to it, there is a progressive tendency to forget all of the belief except the formularies, or to give it a dull and torpid assent, as if accepting it on trust dispensed with the necessity of realizing it in consciousness, or testing it by personal experience, until it almost ceases to connect itself at all with the inner life of the human being. Then are seen the cases, so frequent in this age of the world as almost to form the majority, in which the creed remains as it were outside the mind, incrusting and petrifying it against all other influences addressed to the higher parts of our nature; manifesting its power by not suffering any fresh and living conviction to get in, but itself doing nothing for the mind or heart except standing sentinel over them to keep them vacant.

To what an extent doctrines intrinsically fitted to make the deepest impression upon the mind may remain in it as dead beliefs, without being ever realized in the imagination, the feelings, or the understanding, is exemplified by the manner in which the majority of believers hold the doctrines of Christianity. By Christianity, I here mean what is accounted such by all churches and sects—the maxims and precepts contained in the New Testament. These are considered sacred, and accepted as laws, by all professing Christians. Yet it is scarcely too much to say that not one Christian in a thousand guides or tests his individual conduct by reference to those laws. The standard to which he does refer it is the custom of his nation, his class, or his religious profession. He has thus, on the one hand, a collection of ethical maxims which he believes to have been vouchsafed to him by infallible wisdom as rules for his government; and, on the other, a set of everyday judgments and practices which go a certain length with some of those maxims, not so great a length with others, stand in direct opposition to some, and are, on the whole, a compromise between the Christian creed and the interests and suggestions of worldly life. To the first of these standards he gives his homage; to the other his real allegiance. All Christians believe that the blessed are the poor and humble, and those who are ill-used by the world; that it is easier for a camel to pass through the eye of a needle than for a rich man to enter the kingdom of heaven; that they should judge not, lest they be judged; that they should swear not at all; that they should love their neighbor as themselves; that if one take their cloak, they should give him their coat also; that they should take no thought for the morrow; that if they would be perfect they should sell all that they have and give it to the poor. They are not insincere when they say that they believe these things. They do believe them, as people believe what they have always heard lauded and never discussed. But in the sense of that living belief which regulates conduct, they believe these doctrines just up to the point to which it is usual to act upon them. The doctrines in their integrity are serviceable to pelt adversaries with; and it is understood that they are to be put forward (when possible) as the reasons for whatever people do that they think laudable. But anyone who reminded them that the maxims require an infinity of things which they never even think of doing would gain nothing but to be classed among those very unpopular characters who affect to be better than other people. The doctrines have no hold on ordinary believers—are not a power in their minds. They have an habitual respect for the sound of them, but no feeling which spreads from the words to the things signified and forces the mind to take *them* in and make them conform to the formula. Whenever conduct is concerned, they look round for Mr. A and B to direct them how far to go in obeying Christ.

Now we may be well assured that the case was not thus, but far otherwise, with the early Christians. Had it been thus, Christianity never would have expanded from an obscure sect of the despised Hebrews into the religion of the Roman empire. When their enemies said, "See how these Christians love one another" (a remark not likely to be made by anybody now), they assuredly had a much livelier feeling of the meaning of their creed than they have ever had since. And to this cause, probably, it is chiefly owing that Christianity now makes so little progress in extending its domain, and after eighteen centuries is still nearly confined to Europeans and the descendants of Europeans. Even with the strictly religious, who are much in earnest about their doctrines and attach a greater amount of meaning to many of them than people in general, it commonly happens that the part which is thus comparatively active in their minds is that which was made by Calvin, or Knox, or some such person much nearer in character to themselves. The sayings of Christ coexist passively in their minds, producing hardly any effect beyond what is caused by mere listening to words so amiable and bland. There are many reasons, doubtless, why doctrines which are the badge of a sect retain more of their vitality than those common to all recognized sects, and why more pains are taken by teachers to keep their meaning alive; but one reason certainly is that the peculiar doctrines are more questioned and have to be oftener defended against open gainsayers. Both teachers and learners go to sleep at their post as soon as there is no enemy in the field.

The same thing holds true, generally speaking, of all traditional doctrines—those of prudence and knowledge of life as well as of morals or religion. All languages and literatures are full of general observations on life, both as to what it is and how to conduct oneself in it—observations which everybody knows, which everybody repeats or hears with acquiescence, which are received as truisms, yet of which most people first truly learn the meaning when experience, generally of a painful kind, has made it a reality to them. How often, when smarting under some unforeseen misfortune or disappoint-

ment, does a person call to mind some proverb or common saying, familiar to him all his life, the meaning of which, if he had ever before felt it as he does now, would have saved him from the calamity. There are indeed reasons for this, other than the absence of discussion; there are many truths of which the full meaning *cannot* be realized until personal experience has brought it home. But much more of the meaning even of these would have been understood, and what was understood would have been far more deeply impressed on the mind, if the man had been accustomed to hear it argued *pro* and *con* by people who did understand it. The fatal tendency of mankind to leave off thinking about a thing when it is no longer doubtful is the cause of half their errors. A contemporary author has well spoken of "the deep slumber of a decided opinion."

But what! (it may be asked) Is the absence of unanimity an indispensable condition of true knowledge? Is it necessary that some part of mankind should persist in error to enable any to realize the truth? Does a belief cease to be real and vital as soon as it is generally received—and is a proposition never thoroughly understood and felt unless some doubt of it remains? As soon as mankind have unanimously accepted a truth, does the truth perish within them? The highest aim and best result of improved intelligence, it has hitherto been thought, is to unite mankind more and more in the acknowledgment of all important truths; and does the intelligence only last as long as it has not achieved its object? Do the fruits of conquest perish by the very completeness of the victory?

I affirm no such thing. As mankind improve, the number of doctrines which are no longer disputed or doubted will be constantly on the increase; and the well-being of mankind may almost be measured by the number and gravity of the truths which have reached the point of being uncontested. The cessation, on one question after another, of serious controversy is one of the necessary incidents of the consolidation of opinion—a consolidation as salutary in the case of true opinions as it is dangerous and noxious when the opinions are erroneous. But though this gradual narrowing of the bounds of diversity of opinion is necessary in both senses of the term, being at once inevitable and indispensable, we are not therefore obliged to conclude that all its consequences must be beneficial. The loss of so important an aid to the intelligent and living apprehension of a truth as is afforded by the necessity of explaining it to, or defending it against, opponents, though not sufficient to outweigh, is no trifling drawback from the benefit of its universal recognition. Where this advantage can no longer be had, I confess I should like to see the teachers of mankind endeavoring to provide a substitute for it—some contrivance for making the difficulties of the question as present to the learner's consciousness as if they were pressed upon him by a dissentient champion, eager for his conversion.

But instead of seeking contrivances for this purpose, they have lost those they formerly had. The Socratic dialectics, so magnificently exemplified in the dialogues of Plato, were a contrivance of this description. They were essentially a negative discussion of the great questions of philosophy and life, directed with consummate skill to the purpose of convincing anyone who had merely adopted the commonplaces of received opinion that he did not understand the subject—that he as yet attached no definite meaning to the doctrines he professed; in order that, becoming aware of his ignorance, he might be put in the way to obtain a stable belief, resting on a clear apprehension both of the meaning of doctrines and of their evidence. The school disputations of the Middle Ages had a somewhat similar object. They were intended to make sure that the pupil understood his own opinion, and (by necessary correlation) the opinion opposed to it, and could enforce the grounds of the one and confute those of the other. These last-mentioned contests had indeed the incurable defect that the premises appealed to were taken from authority, not from reason; and, as a discipline to the mind, they were in every respect inferior to the powerful dialectics which formed the intellects of the *"Socratici viri"*; but the modern mind owes far more to both than it is generally willing to admit, and the present modes of education contain nothing which in the smallest degree sup-

plies the place either of the one or of the other. A person who derives all his instruction from teachers or books, even if he escape the besetting temptation of contenting himself with cram, is under no compulsion to hear both sides; accordingly it is far from a frequent accomplishment, even among thinkers, to know both sides; and the weakest part of what everybody says in defense of his opinion is what he intends as a reply to antagonists. It is the fashion of the present time to disparage negative logic—that which points out weaknesses in theory or errors in practice without establishing positive truths. Such negative criticism would indeed be poor enough as an ultimate result, but as a means to attaining any positive knowledge or conviction worthy the name it cannot be valued too highly; and until people are again systematically trained to it, there will be few great thinkers and a low general average of intellect in any but the mathematical and physical departments of speculation. On any other subject no one's opinions deserve the name of knowledge, except so far as he has either had forced upon him by others or gone through of himself the same mental process which would have been required of him in carrying on an active controversy with opponents. That, therefore, which, when absent, it is so indispensable, but so difficult, to create, how worse than absurd it is to forego when spontaneously offering itself! If there are any persons who contest a received opinion, or who will do so if law or opinion will let them, let us thank them for it, open our minds to listen to them, and rejoice that there is someone to do for us what we otherwise ought, if we have any regard for either the certainty or the vitality of our convictions, to do with much greater labor for ourselves.

It still remains to speak of one of the principal causes which make diversity of opinion advantageous, and will continue to do so until mankind shall have entered a stage of intellectual advancement which at present seems at an incalculable distance. We have hitherto considered only two possibilities: that the received opinion may be false, and some other opinion, consequently, true; or that, the received opinion being true, a conflict with the opposite error is essential to a clear apprehension and deep feeling of its truth. But there is a commoner case than either of these: when the conflicting doctrines, instead of being one true and the other false, share the truth between them, and the nonconforming opinion is needed to supply the remainder of the truth of which the received doctrine embodies only a part. Popular opinions, on subjects not palpable to sense, are often true, but seldom or never the whole truth. They are a part of the truth, sometimes a greater, sometimes a smaller part, but exaggerated, distorted, and disjointed from the truths by which they ought to be accompanied and limited. Heretical opinions, on the other hand, are generally some of these suppressed and neglected truths, bursting the bonds which kept them down, and either seeking reconciliation with the truth contained in the common opinion, or fronting it as enemies, and setting themselves up, with similar exclusiveness, as the whole truth. The latter case is hitherto the most frequent, as, in the human mind, one-sidedness has always been the rule, and many-sidedness the exception. Hence, even in revolutions of opinion, one part of the truth usually sets while another rises. Even progress, which ought to superadd, for the most part only substitutes one partial and incomplete truth for another; improvement consisting chiefly in this, that the new fragment of truth is more wanted, more adapted to the needs of the time than that which it displaces. Such being the partial character of prevailing opinions, even when resting on a true foundation, every opinion which embodies somewhat of the portion of truth which the common opinion omits ought to be considered precious, with whatever amount of error and confusion that truth may be blended. No sober judge of human affairs will feel bound to be indignant because those who force on our notice truths which we should otherwise have overlooked, overlook some of those which we see. Rather, he will think that so long as popular truth is one-sided, it is more desirable than otherwise that unpopular truth should have one-sided assertors, too, such being usually the most energetic and the most likely to compel reluctant attention to the fragment of wisdom which they proclaim as if it were the whole.

Thus, in the eighteenth century, when nearly all the instructed, and all those of the uninstructed who were led by them, were lost in admiration of what is called civilization, and of the marvels of modern science, literature, and philosophy, and while greatly overrating the amount of unlikeness between the men of modern and those of ancient times, indulged the belief that the whole of the difference was in their own favor; with what a salutary shock did the paradoxes of Rousseau explode like bombshells in the midst, dislocating the compact mass of one-sided opinion and forcing its elements to recombine in a better form and with additional ingredients. Not that the current opinions were on the whole farther from the truth than Rousseau's were; on the contrary, they were nearer to it; they contained more of positive truth, and very much less of error. Nevertheless there lay in Rousseau's doctrine, and has floated down the stream of opinion along with it, a considerable amount of exactly those truths which the popular opinion wanted; and these are the deposit which was left behind them when the flood subsided. The superior worth of simplicity of life, the enervating and demoralizing effect of the trammels and hypocrisies of artificial society are ideas which have never been entirely absent from cultivated minds since Rousseau wrote; and they will in time produce their due effect, though at present needing to be asserted as much as ever, and to be asserted by deeds; for words, on this subject, have nearly exhausted their power.

In politics, again, it is almost a commonplace that a party of order or stability and a party of progress or reform are both necessary elements of a healthy state of political life, until the one or the other shall have so enlarged its mental grasp as to be a party equally of order and of progress, knowing and distinguishing what is fit to be preserved from what ought to be swept away. Each of these modes of thinking derives its utility from the deficiencies of the other; but it is in a great measure the opposition of the other that keeps each within the limits of reason and sanity. Unless opinions favorable to democracy and to aristocracy, to property and to equality, to co-operation and to competition, to luxury and to abstinence, to sociality and individuality, to liberty and discipline, and all the other standing antagonisms of practical life, are expressed with equal freedom and enforced and defended with equal talent and energy, there is no chance of both elements obtaining their due; one scale is sure to go up, and the other down. Truth, in the great practical concerns of life, is so much a question of the reconciling and combining of opposites that very few have minds sufficiently capacious and impartial to make the adjustment with an approach to correctness, and it has to be made by the rough process of a struggle between combatants fighting under hostile banners. On any of the great open questions just enumerated, if either of the two opinions has a better claim than the other, not merely to be tolerated, but to be encouraged and countenanced, it is the one which happens at the particular time and place to be in a minority. That is the opinion which, for the time being, represents the neglected interests, the side of human well-being which is in danger of obtaining less than its share. I am aware that there is not, in this country, any intolerance of differences of opinion on most of these topics. They are adduced to show, by admitted and multiplied examples, the universality of the fact that only through diversity of opinion is there, in the existing state of human intellect, a chance of fair play to all sides of the truth. When there are persons to be found who form an exception to the apparent unanimity of the world on any subject, even if the world is in the right, it is always probable that dissentients have something worth hearing to say for themselves, and that truth would lose something by their silence.

It may be objected, "But *some* received principles, especially on the highest and most vital subjects, are more than half-truths. The Christian morality, for instance, is the whole truth on that subject, and if anyone teaches a morality which varies from it, he is wholly in error." As this is of all cases the most important in practice, none can be fitter to test the general maxim. But before pronouncing what Christian morality is or is not, it would be desirable to decide what is meant by Christian morality. If it means the morality of the New Testament, I wonder that any one who derives his knowledge of this from the book itself can suppose that it was announced, or intended, as a complete doctrine of morals. The Gospel always refers to a preexisting morality and confines its precepts to the particulars in which that morality was to be corrected or superseded by a wider and higher, expressing itself, moreover, in terms most general, often impossible to be interpreted literally, and possessing rather the impressiveness of poetry or eloquence than the precision of legislation. To extract from it a body of ethical doctrine has never been possible without eking it out from the Old Testament, that is, from a system elaborate indeed, but in many respects barbarous, and intended only for a barbarous people. St. Paul, a declared enemy to this Judaical mode of interpreting the doctrine and filling up the scheme of his Master, equally assumes a pre-existing morality, namely that of the Greeks and Romans; and his advice to Christians is in a great measure a system of accommodation to that, even to the extent of giving an apparent sanction to slavery. What is called Christian, but should rather be termed theological, morality was not the work of Christ or the Apostles, but is of much later origin, having been gradually built up by the Catholic Church of the first five centuries, and though not implicitly adopted by moderns and Protestants, has been much less modified by them than might have been expected. For the most part, indeed, they have contented themselves with cutting off the additions which had been made to it in the Middle Ages, each sect supplying the place by fresh additions, adapted to its own character and tendencies. That mankind owe a great debt to this morality, and to its early teachers, I should be the last person to deny, but I do not scruple to say of it that it is, in many important points, incomplete and one-sided, and that, unless ideas and feelings not sanctioned by it had contributed to the formation of European life and character, human affairs would have been in a worse condition than they now are. Christian morality (so called) has all the characters of a reaction; it is, in great part, a protest against paganism. Its ideal is negative rather than positive; passive rather than active; innocence rather than nobleness; abstinence from evil rather than energetic pursuit of good; in its precepts (as has been well said) "thou shalt not" predominates unduly over "though shalt." In its horror of sensuality, it made an idol of asceticism which has been gradually compromised away into one of legality. It holds out the hope of heaven and the threat of hell as the appointed and appropriate motives to a virtuous life: in this falling far below the best of the ancients, and doing what lies in it to give to human morality an essentially selfish character, by disconnecting each man's feelings of duty from the interests of his fellow creatures, except so far as a self-interested inducement is offered to him for consulting them. It is essentially a doctrine of passive obedience; it inculcates submission to all authorities found established; who indeed are not to be actively obeyed when they command what religion forbids, but who are not to be resisted, far less rebelled against, for any amount of wrong to ourselves. And while, in the morality of the best pagan nations, duty to the State holds even a disproportionate place, infringing on the just liberty of the individual, in purely Christian ethics that grand department of duty is scarcely noticed or acknowledged. It is in the Koran, not the New Testament, that we read the maxim: "A ruler who appoints any man to an office, when there is in his dominions another man better qualified for it, sins against God and against the State." What little recognition the idea of obligation to the public obtains in modern morality is derived from Greek and Roman sources, not from Christian; as, even in the morality of private life, whatever exists of magnanimity, high-mindedness, personal dignity, even the sense of honor, is derived from the purely human, not the religious part of our education, and never could have grown out of a standard of ethics in which the only worth, professedly recognized, is that of obedience.

I am as far as anyone from pretending that these defects are necessarily inherent in the Christian ethics in every manner in which it can be conceived, or that the many requisites of a complete moral doctrine which it does not contain do not admit of being reconciled with it. Far less would I insinuate this out of the doctrines and precepts of Christ himself. I believe that the sayings of Christ are all that I can see

any evidence of their having been intended to be; that they are irreconcilable with nothing which a comprehensive morality requires; that everything which is excellent in ethics may be brought within them, with no greater violence to their language than has been done to it by all who have attempted to deduce from them any practical system of conduct whatever. But it is quite consistent with this to believe that they contain, and were meant to contain, only a part of the truth; that many essential elements of the highest morality are among the things which are not provided for, nor intended to be provided for, in the recorded deliverances of the Founder of Christianity, and which have been entirely thrown aside in the system of ethics erected on the basis of those deliverances by the Christian Church. And this being so, I think it a great error to persist in attempting to find in the Christian doctrine that complete rule for our guidance which its Author intended it to sanction and enforce, but only partially to provide. I believe, too, that this narrow theory is becoming a grave practical evil, detracting greatly from the moral training and instruction which so many well-meaning persons are now at length exerting themselves to promote. I much fear that by attempting to form the mind and feelings on an exclusively religious type, and discarding those secular standards (as for want of a better name they may be called) which heretofore coexisted with and supplemented the Christian ethics, receiving some of its spirits, and infusing into it some of theirs, there will result, and is even now resulting, a low, abject, servile type of character which, submit itself as it may to what it deems the Supreme Will, is incapable of rising to or sympathizing in the conception of Supreme Goodness. I believe that other ethics than any which can be evolved from exclusively Christian sources must exist side by side with Christian ethics to produce the moral regeneration of mankind; and that the Christian system is no exception to the rule that in an imperfect state of the human mind the interests of truth require a diversity of opinions. It is not necessary that in ceasing to ignore the moral truths not contained in Christianity men should ignore any of those which it does contain. Such prejudice or oversight, when it occurs, is altogether an evil, but it is one from which we cannot hope to be always exempt, and must be regarded as the price paid for an inestimable good. The exclusive pretension made by a part of the truth to be the whole must and ought to be protested against; and if a reactionary impulse should make the protestors unjust in their turn, this one-sidedness, like the other, may be lamented but must be tolerated. If Christians would teach infidels to be just to Christianity, they should themselves be just to infidelity. It can do truth no service to blink the fact, known to all who have the most ordinary acquaintance with literary history, that a large portion of the noblest and most valuable moral teaching has been the work, not only of men who did not know, but of men who knew and rejected, the Christian faith.

I do not pretend that the most unlimited use of the freedom of enunciating all possible opinions would put an end to the evils of religious or philosophical sectarianism. Every truth which men of narrow capacity are in earnest about is sure to be asserted, inculcated, and in many ways even acted on, as if no other truth existed in the world, or at all events none that could limit or qualify the first. I acknowledge that the tendency of all opinions to become sectarian is not cured by the freest discussion, but is often heightened and exacerbated thereby; the truth which ought to have been, but was not, seen, being rejected all the more violently because proclaimed by persons regarded as opponents. But it is not on the impassioned partisan, it is on the calmer and more disinterested bystander, that this collision of opinions works its salutary effect. Not the violent conflict between parts of the truth, but the quiet suppression of half of it, is the formidable evil; there is always hope when people are forced to listen to both sides; it is when they attend only to one that errors harden into prejudices, and truth itself ceases to have the effect of truth by being exaggerated into falsehood. And since there are few mental attributes more rare than that judicial faculty which can sit in intelligent judgment between two sides of a question, of which only one is represented by an advocate before it, truth has no chance but in proportion as every side of

it, every opinion which embodies any fraction of the truth, not only finds advocates, but is so advocated as to be listened to.

We have now recognized the necessity to the mental well-being of mankind (on which all their other well-being depends) of freedom of opinion, and freedom of the expression of opinion, on four distinct grounds, which we will now briefly recapitulate:

First, if any opinion is compelled to silence, that opinion may, for aught we can certainly know, be true. To deny this is to assume our own infallibility.

Secondly, though the silenced opinion be an error, it may, and very commonly does, contain a portion of truth; and since the general or prevailing opinion on any subject is rarely or never the whole truth, it is only by the collision of adverse opinions that the remainder of the truth has any chance of being supplied.

Thirdly, even if the received opinion be not only true, but the whole truth; unless it is suffered to be, and actually is, vigorously and earnestly contested, it will, by most of those who receive it, be held in the manner of a prejudice, with little comprehension or feeling of its rational grounds. And not only this, but, fourthly, the meaning of the doctrine itself will be in danger of being lost or enfeebled, and deprived of its vital effect on the character and conduct: the dogma becoming a mere formal profession, inefficacious for good, but cumbering the ground and preventing the growth of any real and heartfelt conviction from reason or personal experience.

Before quitting the subject of freedom of opinion, it is fit to take some notice of those who say that the free expression of all opinions should be permitted on condition that the manner be temperate, and do not pass the bounds of fair discussion. Much might be said on the impossibility of fixing where these supposed bounds are to be placed; for if the test be offense to those whose opinions are attacked, I think experience testifies that this offense is given whenever the attack is telling and powerful, and that every opponent who pushes them hard, and whom they find it difficult to answer, appears to them, if he shows any strong feeling on the subject, an intemperate opponent. But this, though an important consideration in a practical point of view, merges in a more fundamental objection. Undoubtedly, the manner of asserting an opinion, even though it be a true one, may be very objectionable and may justly incur severe censure. But the principal offenses of the kind are such as it is mostly impossible, unless by accidental self-betrayal, to bring home to conviction. The gravest of them is, to argue sophistically, to suppress facts or arguments, to misstate the elements of the case, or misrepresent the opposite opinion. But all this, even to the most aggravated degree, is so continually done in perfect good faith by persons who are not considered, and in many other respects may not deserve to be considered, ignorant or incompetent, that it is rarely possible, on adequate grounds, conscientiously to stamp the misrepresentation as morally culpable, and still less could law presume to interfere with this kind of controversial misconduct. With regard to what is commonly meant by intemperate discussion, namely invective, sarcasm, personality, and the like, the denunciation of these weapons would deserve more sympathy if it were ever proposed to interdict them equally to both sides; but it is only desired to restrain the employment of them against the prevailing opinion; against the unprevailing they may not only be used without general disapproval, but will be likely to obtain for him who uses them the praise of honest zeal and righteous indignation. Yet whatever mischief arises from their use is greatest when they are employed against the comparatively defenseless; and whatever unfair advantage can be derived by any opinion from this mode of asserting it accrues almost exclusively to received opinions. The worst offense of this kind which can be committed by a polemic is to stigmatize those who hold the contrary opinion as bad and immoral men. To calumny of this sort, those who hold any unpopular opinion are peculiarly exposed, because they are in general few and uninfluential, and nobody but themselves feels much interested in seeing justice done them; but this weapon is, from the nature of the case, denied to those who attack a prevailing opinion: they can neither use it with safety to themselves, nor, if they could, would it do anything but recoil on their own cause. In general,

opinions contrary to those commonly received can only obtain a hearing by studied moderation of language and the most cautious avoidance of unnecessary offense, from which they hardly ever deviate even in a slight degree without losing ground, while unmeasured vituperation employed on the side of the prevailing opinion really does deter people from professing contrary opinions and from listening to those who profess them. For the interest, therefore, of truth and justice it is far more important to restrain this employment of vituperative language than the other; and, for example, if it were necessary to choose, there would be much more need to discourage offensive attacks on infidelity than on religion. It is, however, obvious that law and authority have no business with restraining either, while opinion ought, in every instance, to determine its verdict by the circumstances of the individual case—condemning everyone, on whichever side of the argument he places himself, in whose mode of advocacy either want of candor, or malignity, bigotry, or intolerance of feeling manifest themselves; but not inferring these vices from the side which a person takes, though it be the contrary side of the question to our own; and giving merited honor to everyone, whatever opinion he may hold, who has calmness to see and honesty to state what his opponents and their opinions really are, exaggerating nothing to their discredit, keeping nothing back which tells, or can be supposed to tell, in their favor. This is the real morality of public discussion; and if often violated, I am happy to think that there are many controversialists who to a great extent observe it, and a still greater number who conscientiously strive toward it.

## CHAPTER III

### *Of Individuality, as One of the Elements of Well-Being*

Such being the reasons which make it imperative that human beings should be free to form opinions and to express their opinions without reserve; and such the baneful consequences to the intellectual, and through that to the moral nature of man, unless this liberty is either conceded or asserted in spite of prohibition; let us next examine whether the same reasons do not require that men should be free to act upon their opinions—to carry these out in their lives without hindrance, either physical or moral, from their fellow men, so long as it is at their own risk and peril. This last proviso is of course indispensable. No one pretends that actions should be as free as opinions. On the contrary, even opinions lose their immunity when the circumstances in which they are expressed are such as to constitute their expression a positive instigation to some mischievous act. An opinion that corn dealers are starvers of the poor, or that private property is robbery, ought to be unmolested when simply circulated through the press, but may justly incur punishment when delivered orally to an excited mob assembled before the house of a corn dealer, or when handed about among the same mob in the form of a placard. Acts, of whatever kind, which without justifiable cause do harm to others may be, and in the more important cases absolutely require to be, controlled by the unfavorable sentiments, and, when needful, by the active interference of mankind. The liberty of the individual must be thus far limited; he must not make himself a nuisance to other people. But if he refrains from molesting others in what concerns them, and merely acts according to his own inclination and judgment in things which concern himself, the same reasons which show that opinion should be free prove also that he should be allowed, without molestation, to carry his opinions into practice at his own cost. That mankind are not infallible; that their truths, for the most part, are only half-truths; that unity of opinion, unless resulting from the fullest and freest comparison of opposite opinions, is not desirable, and diversity not an evil, but a good, until mankind are much more capable than at present of recognizing all sides of the truth, are principles applicable to men's modes of action not less than to their opinions. As it is useful that while mankind are imperfect there should be different opinions, so it is that there should be different experiments of living; that free scope should be given to varieties of character, short of injury to

others; and that the worth of different modes of life should be proved practically, when anyone thinks fit to try them. It is desirable, in short, that in things which do not primarily concern others individuality should assert itself. Where not the person's own character but the traditions or customs of other people are the rule of conduct, there is wanting one of the principal ingredients of human happiness, and quite the chief ingredient of individual and social progress.

In maintaining this principle, the greatest difficulty to be encountered does not lie in the appreciation of means toward an acknowledged end, but in the indifference of persons in general to the end itself. If it were felt that the free development of individuality is one of the leading essentials of well-being; that it is not only a co-ordinate element with all that is designated by the terms civilization, instruction, education, culture, but is itself a necessary part and condition of all those things, there would be no danger that liberty should be undervalued, and the adjustment of the boundaries between it and social control would present no extraordinary difficulty. But the evil is that individual spontaneity is hardly recognized by the common modes of thinking as having any intrinsic worth, or deserving any regard on its own account. The majority, being satisfied with the ways of mankind as they now are (for it is they who make them what they are), cannot comprehend why those ways should not be good enough for everybody; and what is more, spontaneity forms no part of the ideal of the majority of moral and social reformers, but is rather looked on with jealousy, as a troublesome and perhaps rebellious obstruction to the general acceptance of what these reformers, in their own judgment, think would be best for mankind. Few persons, out of Germany, even comprehend the meaning of the doctrine which Wilhelm von Humboldt, so eminent both as a *savant* and as a politician, made the text of a treatise—that "the end of man, or that which is prescribed by the eternal or immutable dictates of reason, and not suggested by vague and transient desires, is the highest and most harmonious development of his powers to a complete and consistent whole"; that, therefore, the object "toward which every human being must ceaselessly direct his efforts, and on which especially those who design to influence their fellow men must ever keep their eyes, is the individuality of power and development"; that for this there are two requisites, "freedom, and variety of situations"; and that from the union of these arise "individual vigor and manifold diversity," which combine themselves in "originality."[6]

Little, however, as people are accustomed to a doctrine like that of von Humboldt, and surprising as it may be to them to find so high a value attached to individuality, the question, one must nevertheless think, can only be one of degree. No one's idea of excellence in conduct is that people should do absolutely nothing but copy one another. No one would assert that people ought not to put into their mode of life, and into the conduct of their concerns, any impress whatever of their own judgment or of their own individual character. On the other hand, it would be absurd to pretend that people ought to live as if nothing whatever had been known in the world before they came into it; as if experience had as yet done nothing toward showing that one mode of existence, or of conduct, is preferable to another. Nobody denies that people should be so taught and trained in youth as to know and benefit by the ascertained results of human experience. But it is the privilege and proper condition of a human being, arrived at the maturity of his faculties, to use and interpret experience in his own way. It is for him to find out what part of recorded experience is properly applicable to his own circumstances and character. The traditions and customs of other people are, to a certain extent, evidence of what their experience has taught *them*—presumptive evidence, and as such, have a claim to his deference: but, in the first place, their experience may be too narrow, or they may have not interpreted it rightly. Secondly, their interpretation of experience may be correct, but unsuitable to him. Customs are made for customary circumstances and customary characters; and his circumstances or his character may be uncustomary. Thirdly, though the customs be both good as customs and suitable to him, yet to conform to custom merely as custom does not educate or develop in him any of the qualities which are the distinctive endowment of a human being. The human faculties of perception, judgment, discriminative feeling, mental activity, and even moral preference are exercised only in making a choice. He who does anything because it is the custom makes no choice. He gains no practice either in discerning or in desiring what is best. The mental and moral, like the muscular, powers are improved only by being used. The faculties are called into no exercise by doing a thing merely because others do it, no more than by believing a thing only because others believe it. If the grounds of an opinion are not conclusive to the person's own reason, his reason cannot be strengthened, but is likely to be weakened, by his adopting it: and if the inducements to an act are not such as are consentaneous to his own feelings and character (where affection, or the rights of others, are not concerned), it is so much done toward rendering his feelings and character inert and torpid instead of active and energetic.

He who lets the world, or his own portion of it, choose his plan of life for him has no need of any other faculty than the ape-like one of imitation. He who chooses his plan for himself employs all his faculties. He must use observation to see, reasoning and judgment to foresee, activity to gather materials for decision, discrimination to decide, and when he has decided, firmness and self-control to hold to his deliberate decision. And these qualities he requires and exercises exactly in proportion as the part of his conduct which he determines according to his own judgment and feelings is a large one. It is possible that he might be guided in some good path, and kept out of harm's way, without any of these things. But what will be his comparative worth as a human being? It really is of importance, not only what men do, but also what manner of men they are that do it. Among the works of man which human life is rightly employed in perfecting and beautifying, the first in importance surely is man himself. Supposing it were possible to get houses built, corn grown, battles fought, causes tried, and even churches erected and prayers said by machinery—by automatons in human form—it would be a considerable loss to exchange for these automatons even the men and women who at present inhabit the more civilized parts of the world, and who assuredly are but starved specimens of what nature can and will produce. Human nature is not a machine to be built after a model, and set to do exactly the work prescribed for it, but a tree, which requires to grow and develop itself on all sides, according to the tendency of the inward forces which make it a living thing.

It will probably be conceded that it is desirable people should exercise their understandings, and that an intelligent following of custom, or even occasionally an intelligent deviation from custom, is better than a blind and simply mechanical adhesion to it. To a certain extent it is admitted that our understanding should be our own; but there is not the same willingness to admit that our desires and impulses should be our own likewise, or that to possess impulses of our own, and of any strength, is anything but a peril and a snare. Yet desires and impulses are as much a part of a perfect human being as beliefs and restraints; and strong impulses are only perilous when not properly balanced, when one set of aims and inclinations is developed into strength, while others, which ought to coexist with them, remain weak and inactive. It is not because men's desires are strong that they act ill; it is because their consciences are weak. There is no natural connection between strong impulses and a weak conscience. The natural connection is the other way. To say that one person's desires and feelings are stronger and more various than those of another is merely to say that he has more of the raw material of human nature and is therefore capable, perhaps of more evil, but certainly of more good. Strong impulses are but another name for energy. Energy may be turned to bad uses; but more good may always be made of an energetic nature than of an indolent and impassive one. Those who have most natural feeling are always those whose cultivated feelings may be made the strongest. The same strong susceptibilities which make the personal impulses vivid and powerful are also the source from whence are generated the most passionate love of virtue and the sternest self-control. It is through the cultivation of these that society both does its duty and protects its interests, not by rejecting the stuff of which heroes are made, because it knows not how to make them. A person whose

desires and impulses are his own—are the expression of his own nature, as it has been developed and modified by his own culture—is said to have a character. One whose desires and impulses are not his own has no character, no more than a steam engine has a character. If, in addition to being his own, his impulses are strong and are under the government of a strong will, he has an energetic character. Whoever thinks that individuality of desires and impulses should not be encouraged to unfold itself must maintain that society has no need of strong natures—is not the better for containing many persons who have much character—and that a high general average of energy is not desirable.

In some early states of society, these forces might be, and were, too much ahead of the power which society then possessed of disciplining and controlling them. There has been a time when the element of spontaneity and individuality was in excess, and the social principle had a hard struggle with it. The difficulty then was to induce men of strong bodies or minds to pay obedience to any rules which required them to control their impulses. To overcome this difficulty, law and discipline, like the Popes struggling against the Emperors, asserted a power over the whole man, claiming to control all his life in order to control his character—which society had not found any other sufficient means of binding. But society has now fairly got the better of individuality; and the danger which threatens human nature is not the excess, but the deficiency, of personal impulses and preferences. Things are vastly changed since the passions of those who were strong by station or by personal endowment were in a state of habitual rebellion against laws and ordinances, and required to be rigorously chained up to enable the persons within their reach to enjoy any particle of security. In our times, from the highest class of society down to the lowest, everyone lives as under the eye of a hostile and dreaded censorship. Not only in what concerns others, but in what concerns only themselves, the individual or the family do not ask themselves, what do I prefer? or, what would suit my character and disposition? or, what would allow the best and highest in me to have fair play and enable it to grow and thrive? They ask themselves, what is suitable to my position? What is usually done by persons of my station and pecuniary circumstances? or (worse still) what is usually done by persons of a station and circumstances superior to mine? I do not mean that they choose what is customary in preference to what suits their own inclination. It does not occur to them to have any inclination except for what is customary. Thus the mind itself is bowed to the yoke: even in what people do for pleasure, conformity is the first thing thought of; they like in crowds; they exercise choice only among things commonly done; peculiarity of taste, eccentricity of conduct are shunned equally with crimes, until by dint of not following their own nature they have no nature to follow: their human capacities are withered and starved; they become incapable of any strong wishes or native pleasures, and are generally without either opinions or feelings of home growth, or properly their own. Now is this, or is it not, the desirable condition of human nature?

It is so, on the Calvinistic theory. According to that, the one great offense of man is self-will. All the good of which humanity is capable is comprised in obedience. You have no choice; thus you must do, and no otherwise: "Whatever is not a duty is a sin." Human nature being radically corrupt, there is no redemption for anyone until human nature is killed within him. To one holding this theory of life, crushing out any of the human faculties, capacities, and susceptibilities is no evil: man needs no capacity but that of surrendering himself to the will of God; and if he uses any of his faculties for any other purpose but to do that supposed will more effectually, he is better without them. This is the theory of Calvinism; and it is held, in a mitigated form, by many who do not consider themselves Calvinists; the mitigation consisting in giving a less ascetic interpretation to the alleged will of God, asserting it to be his will that mankind should gratify some of their inclinations, of course not in the manner they themselves prefer, but in the way of obedience, that is, in a way prescribed to them by authority, and, therefore, by the necessary condition of the case, the same for all.

In some such insidious form there is at present a strong tendency to this narrow theory of life, and to the pinched and hidebound type of human character which it patronizes. Many persons, no doubt, sincerely think that human beings thus cramped and dwarfed are as their Maker designed them to be, just as many have thought that trees are a much finer thing when clipped into pollards, or cut out into figures of animals, than as nature made them. But if it be any part of religion to believe that man was made by a good Being, it is more consistent with that faith to believe that this Being gave all human faculties that they might be cultivated and unfolded, not rooted out and consumed, and that he takes delight in every nearer approach made by his creatures to the ideal conception embodied in them, every increase in any of their capabilities of comprehension, of action, or of enjoyment. There is a different type of human excellence from the Calvinistic: a conception of humanity as having its nature bestowed on it for other purposes than merely to be abnegated. "Pagan self-assertion" is one of the elements of human worth, as well as "Christian self-denial."[7] There is a Greek ideal of self-development, which the Platonic and Christian ideal of self-government blends with, but does not supersede. It may be better to be a John Knox than an Alcibiades, but it is better to be a Pericles than either; nor would a Pericles, if we had one in these days, be without anything good which belonged to John Knox.

It is not by wearing down into uniformity all that is individual in themselves, but by cultivating it and calling it forth, within the limits imposed by the rights and interests of others, that human beings become a noble and beautiful object of contemplation; and as the works partake the character of those who do them, by the same process human life also becomes rich, diversified, and animating, furnishing more abundant aliment to high thoughts and elevating feelings, and strengthening the tie which binds every individual to the race, by making the race infinitely better worth belonging to. In proportion to the development of his individuality, each person becomes more valuable to himself, and is, therefore, capable of being more valuable to others. There is a greater fullness of life about his own existence, and when there is more life in the units there is more in the mass which is composed of them. As much compression as is necessary to prevent the stronger specimens of human nature from encroaching on the rights of others cannot be dispensed with; but for this there is ample compensation even in the point of view of human development. The means of development which the individual loses by being prevented from gratifying his inclinations to the injury of others are chiefly obtained at the expense of the development of other people. And even to himself there is a full equivalent in the better development of the social part of his nature, rendered possible by the restraint put upon the selfish part. To be held to rigid rules of justice for the sake of others develops the feelings and capacities which have the good of others for their object. But to be restrained in things not affecting their good, by their mere displeasure, develops nothing valuable except such force of character as may unfold itself in resisting the restraint. If acquiesced in, it dulls and blunts the whole nature. To give any fair play to the nature of each, it is essential that different persons should be allowed to lead different lives. In proportion as this latitude has been exercised in any age has that age been noteworthy to posterity. Even despotism does not produce its worst effects so long as individuality exists under it; and whatever crushes individuality is despotism, by whatever name it may be called and whether it professes to be enforcing the will of God or the injunctions of men.

Having said that the individuality is the same thing with development, and that it is only the cultivation of individuality which produces, or can produce, well-developed human beings, I might here close the argument; for what more or better can be said of any condition of human affairs than that it brings human beings themselves nearer to the best thing they can be? Or what worse can be said of any obstruction to good than that it prevents this? Doubtless, however, these considerations will not suffice to convince those who most need convincing; and it is necessary further to show that these developed human beings are of some use to the undeveloped— to point out to those who do not desire liberty, and

would not avail themselves of it, that they may be in some intelligible manner rewarded for allowing other people to make use of it without hindrance.

In the first place, then, I would suggest that they might possibly learn something from them. It will not be denied by anybody that originality is a valuable element in human affairs. There is always need of persons not only to discover new truths and point out when what were once truths are true no longer, but also to commence new practices and set the example of more enlightened conduct and better taste and sense in human life. This cannot well be gainsaid by anybody who does not believe that the world has already attained perfection in all its ways and practices. It is true that this benefit is not capable of being rendered by everybody alike; there are but few persons, in comparison with the whole of mankind, whose experiments, if adopted by others, would be likely to be any improvement on established practice. But these few are the salt of the earth; without them, human life would become a stagnant pool. Not only is it they who introduce good things which did not before exist; it is they who keep the life in those which already exist. If there were nothing new to be done, would human intellect cease to be necessary? Would it be a reason why those who do the old things should forget why they are done, and do them like cattle, not like human beings? There is only too great a tendency in the best beliefs and practices to degenerate into the mechanical; and unless there were a succession of persons whose ever-recurring originality prevents the grounds of those beliefs and practices from becoming merely traditional, such dead matter would not resist the smallest shock from anything really alive, and there would be no reason why civilization should not die out, as in the Byzantine Empire. Persons of genius, it is true, are, and are always likely to be, a small minority; but in order to have them, it is necessary to preserve the soil in which they grow. Genius can only breathe freely in an *atmosphere* of freedom. Persons of genius are, *ex vi termini*, more individual than any other people— less capable, consequently, of fitting themselves, without hurtful compression, into any of the small number of molds which society provides in order to save its members the trouble of forming their own character. If from timidity they consent to be forced into one of these molds, and to let all that part of themselves which cannot expand under the pressure remain unexpanded, society will be little the better for their genius. If they are of a strong character and break their fetters, they become a mark for the society which has not succeeded in reducing them to commonplace, to point out with solemn warnings as "wild," "erratic," and the like—much as if one should complain of the Niagara river for not flowing smoothly between its banks like a Dutch canal.

I insist thus emphatically on the importance of genius and the necessity of allowing it to unfold itself freely both in thought and in practice, being well aware that no one will deny the position in theory, but knowing also that almost everyone, in reality, is totally indifferent to it. People think a genius a fine thing if it enables a man to write an exciting poem or paint a picture. But in its true sense, that of originality in thought and action, though no one says that it is not a thing to be admired, nearly all, at heart, think that they can do very well without it. Unhappily this is too natural to be wondered at. Originality is the one thing which unoriginal minds cannot feel the use of. They cannot see what it is to do for them: how should they? If they could see what it would do for them, it would not be originality. The first service which originality has to render them is that of opening their eyes: which being once fully done, they would have a chance of being themselves original. Meanwhile, recollecting that nothing was ever done which someone was not the first to do, and that all good things which exist are the fruits of originality, let them be modest enough to believe that there is something still left for it to accomplish, and assure themselves that they are more in need of originality, the less they are conscious of the want.

In sober truth, whatever homage may be professed, or even paid, to real or supposed mental superiority, the general tendency of things throughout the world is to render mediocrity the ascendant power among mankind. In ancient history, in the Middle Ages, and in a diminishing degree through the long transition from feudality to the present time, the individual was a power in himself; and if he had either great talents or a high social position, he was a considerable power. At present individuals are lost in the crowd. In politics it is almost a triviality to say that public opinion now rules the world. The only power deserving the name is that of masses, and of governments while they make themselves the organ of the tendencies and instincts of masses. This is as true in the moral and social relations of private life as in public transactions. Those whose opinions go by the name of public opinion are not always the same sort of public: in America, they are the whole white population; in England, chiefly the middle class. But they are always a mass, that is to say, collective mediocrity. And what is a still greater novelty, the mass do not now take their opinions from dignitaries in Church or State, from ostensible leaders, or from books. Their thinking is done for them by men much like themselves, addressing them or speaking in their name, on the spur of the moment, through the newspapers. I am not complaining of all this. I do not assert that anything better is compatible, as a general rule, with the present low state of the human mind. But that does not hinder the government of mediocrity from being mediocre government. No government by a democracy or a numerous aristocracy, either in its political acts or in the opinions, qualities, and tone of mind which it fosters, ever did or could rise above mediocrity except in so far as the sovereign. Many have let themselves be guided (which in their best times they always have done) by the counsels and influence of a more highly gifted and instructed *one or few*. The initiation of all wise or noble things comes and must come from individuals; generally at first from some one individual. The honor and glory of the average man is that he is capable of following that initiative; that he can respond internally to wise and noble things, and be led to them with his eyes open. I am not countenancing the sort of "hero-worship" which applauds the strong man of genius for forcibly seizing on the government of the world and making it do his bidding in spite of itself. All he can claim is freedom to point out the way. The power of compelling others into it is not only inconsistent with the freedom and development of all the rest, but corrupting to the strong man himself. It does seem, however, that when the opinions of masses of merely average men are everywhere become or becoming the dominant power, the counterpoise and corrective to that tendency would be the more and more pronounced individuality of those who stand on the higher eminences of thought. It is in these circumstances most especially that exceptional individuals, instead of being deterred, should be encouraged in acting differently from the mass. In other times there was no advantage in their doing so, unless they acted not only differently but better. In this age, the mere example of nonconformity, the mere refusal to bend the knee to custom, is itself a service. Precisely because the tyranny of opinion is such as to make eccentricity a reproach, it is desirable, in order to break through that tyranny, that people should be eccentric. Eccentricity has always abounded when and where strength of character has abounded; and the amount of eccentricity in a society has generally been proportional to the amount of genius, mental vigor, and moral courage it contained. That so few now dare to be eccentric marks the chief danger of the time.

I have said that it is important to give the freest scope possible to uncustomary things, in order that it may in time appear which of these are fit to be converted into customs. But independence of action and disregard of custom are not solely deserving of encouragement for the chance they afford that better modes of action, and customs more worthy of general adoption, may be struck out; nor is it only persons of decided mental superiority who have a just claim to carry on their lives in their own way. There is no reason that all human existence should be constructed on some one or some small number of patterns. If a person possesses any tolerable amount of common sense and experience, his own mode of laying out his existence is the best, not because it is the best in itself, but because it is his own mode. Human beings are not like sheep; and even sheep are not undistinguishably

alike. A man cannot get a coat or a pair of boots to fit him unless they are either made to his measure or he has a whole warehouseful to choose from; and is it easier to fit him with a life than with a coat, or are human beings more like one another in their whole physical and spiritual conformation than in the shape of their feet? If it were only that people have diversities of taste, that is reason enough for not attempting to shape them all after one model. But different persons also require different conditions for their spiritual development; and can no more exist healthily in the same moral than all the variety of plants can in the same physical, atmosphere and climate. The same things which are helps to one person toward the cultivation of his higher nature are hindrances to another. The same mode of life is a healthy excitement to one, keeping all his faculties of action and enjoyment in their best order, while to another it is a distracting burden which suspends or crushes all internal life. Such are the differences among human beings in their sources of pleasure, their susceptibilities of pain, and the operation on them of different physical and moral agencies that, unless there is a corresponding diversity in their modes of life, they neither obtain their fair share of happiness, nor grow up to the mental, moral, and aesthetic stature of which their nature is capable. Why then should tolerance, as far as the public sentiment is concerned, extend only to tastes and modes of life which extort acquiescence by the multitude of their adherents? Nowhere (except in some monastic institutions) is diversity of taste entirely unrecognized; a person may, without blame, either like or dislike rowing, or smoking, or music, or athletic exercises, or chess, or cards, or study, because both those who like each of these things and those who dislike them are too numerous to be put down. But the man, and still more the woman, who can be accused either of doing "what nobody does," or of not doing "what everybody does," is the subject of as much depreciatory remark as if he or she had committed some grave moral delinquency. Persons require to possess a title, or some other badge of rank, or of the consideration of people of rank, to be able to indulge somewhat in the luxury of doing as they like without detriment to their estimation. To indulge somewhat, I repeat: for whoever allow themselves much of that indulgence incur the risk of something worse than disparaging speeches—they are in peril of a commission *de lunatico* and of having their property taken from them and given to their relations.[8]

There is one characteristic of the present direction of public opinion peculiarly calculated to make it intolerant of any marked demonstrations of individuality. The general average of mankind are not only moderate in intellect, but also moderate in inclinations; they have no tastes or wishes strong enough to incline them to do anything unusual, and they consequently do not understand those who have, and class all such with the wild and intemperate whom they are accustomed to look down upon. Now, in addition to this fact which is general, we have only to suppose that a strong movement has set in toward the improvement of morals, and it is evident what we have to expect. In these days such a movement has set in; much has actually been effected in the way of increased regularity of conduct and discouragement of excesses; and there is a philanthropic spirit abroad for the exercise of which there is no more inviting field than the moral and prudential improvement of our fellow creatures. These tendencies of the times cause the public to be more disposed than at most former periods to prescribe general rules of conduct and endeavor to make everyone conform to the approved standard. And that standard, express or tacit, is to desire nothing strongly. Its ideal of character is to be without any marked character—to maim by compression, like a Chinese lady's foot, every part of human nature which stands out prominently and tends to make the person markedly dissimilar in outline to commonplace humanity.

As is usually the case with ideals which exclude one-half of what is desirable, the present standard of approbation produces only an inferior imitation of the other half. Instead of great energies guided by vigorous reason and strong feelings strongly controlled by a conscientious will, its result is weak feelings and weak energies, which therefore can be kept in outward conformity to rule without any strength either of will or of reason. Already energetic characters on any large scale are becoming merely traditional. There is now scarcely any outlet for energy in this country except business. The energy expended in this may still be regarded as considerable. What little is left from that employment is expended on some hobby, which may be a useful, even a philanthropic, hobby, but is always some one thing, and generally a thing of small dimensions. The greatness of England is now all collective; individually small, we only appear capable of anything great by our habit of combining; and with this our moral and religious philanthropists are perfectly contented. But it was men of another stamp than this that made England what it has been; and men of another stamp will be needed to prevent its decline.

The despotism of custom is everywhere the standing hindrance to human advancement, being in unceasing antagonism to that disposition to aim at something better than customary, which is called, according to circumstances, the spirit of liberty, or that of progress or improvement. The spirit of improvement is not always a spirit of liberty, for it may aim at forcing improvements on an unwilling people; and the spirit of liberty, in so far as it resists such attempts, may ally itself locally and temporarily with the opponents of improvement; but the only unfailing and permanent source of improvement is liberty, since by it there are as many possible independent centers of improvement as there are individuals. The progressive principle, however, in either shape, whether as the love of liberty or of improvement, is antagonistic to the sway of custom, involving at least emancipation from that yoke; and the contest between the two constitutes the chief interest of the history of mankind. The greater part of the world has, properly speaking, no history, because the despotism of Custom is complete. This is the case over the whole East. Custom is there, in all things, the final appeal; justice and right mean conformity to custom; the argument of custom no one, unless some tyrant intoxicated with power, thinks of resisting. And we see the result. Those nations must once have had originality; they did not start out of the ground populous, lettered, and versed in many of the arts of life; they made themselves all this, and were then the greatest and most powerful nations of the world. What are they now? The subjects or dependents of tribes whose forefathers wandered in the forests when theirs had magnificent palaces and gorgeous temples, but over whom custom exercised only a divided rule with liberty and progress. A people, it appears, may be progressive for a certain length of time, and then stop: when does it stop? When it ceases to possess individuality. If a similar change should befall the nations of Europe, it will not be in exactly the same shape: the despotism of custom with which these nations are threatened is not precisely stationariness. It proscribes singularity, but it does not preclude change, provided all change together. We have discarded the fixed costumes of our forefathers; everyone must still dress like other people, but the fashion may change once or twice a year. We thus take care that when there is a change, it shall be for change's sake, and not from any idea of beauty or convenience; for the same idea of beauty or convenience would not strike all the world at the same moment, and be simultaneously thrown aside by all at another moment. But we are progressive as well as changeable: we continually make new inventions in mechanical things, and keep them until they are again superseded by better; we are eager for improvement in politics, in education, even in morals, though in this last our idea of improvement chiefly consists in persuading or forcing other people to be as good as ourselves. It is not progress that we object to; on the contrary, we flatter ourselves that we are the most progressive people who ever lived. It is individuality that we war against: we should think we had done wonders if we had made ourselves all alike, forgetting that the unlikeness of one person to another is generally the first thing which draws the attention of either to the imperfection of his own type and the superiority of another, or the possibility, by combining the advantages of both, of producing something better than either. We have a warning example in China—a nation of much talent and, in some respects, even wisdom, owing to the rare good fortune of having been provided at an early period with a particularly good set of customs,

the work, in some measure, of men to whom even the most enlightened European must accord, under certain limitations, the title of sages and philosophers. They are remarkable, too, in the excellence of their apparatus for impressing, as far as possible, the best wisdom they possess upon every mind in the community, and securing that those who have appropriated most of it shall occupy the posts of honor and power. Surely the people who did this have discovered the secret of human progressiveness and must have kept themselves steadily at the head of the movement of the world. On the contrary, they have become stationary—have remained so for thousands of years; and if they are ever to be further improved, it must be by foreigners. They have succeeded beyond all hope in what English philanthropists are so industriously working at—in making a people all alike, all governing their thoughts and conduct by the same maxims and rules; and these are the fruits. The modern *régime* of public opinion is, in an unorganized form, what the Chinese educational and political systems are in an organized; and unless individuality shall be able successfully to assert itself against this yoke, Europe, notwithstanding its noble antecedents and its professed Christianity, will tend to become another China.

What is it that has hitherto preserved Europe from this lot? What has made the European family of nations an improving, instead of a stationary, portion of mankind? Not any superior excellence in them, which, when it exists, exists as the effect, not as the cause, but their remarkable diversity of character and culture. Individuals, classes, nations have been extremely unlike one another: they have struck out a great variety of paths, each leading to something valuable; and although at every period those who traveled in different paths have been intolerant of one another, and each would have thought it an excellent thing if all the rest could have been compelled to travel his road, their attempts to thwart each other's development have rarely had any permanent success, and each has in time endured to receive the good which the others have offered. Europe is, in my judgment, wholly indebted to this plurality of paths for its progressive and many-sided development. But it already begins to possess this benefit in a considerably less degree. It is decidedly advancing toward the Chinese idea of making all people alike. M. de Tocqueville, in his last important work, remarks how much more the Frenchmen of the present day resemble one another than did those even of the last generation. The same remark might be made of Englishmen in a far greater degree. In a passage already quoted from Wilhelm von Humboldt, he points out two things as necessary conditions of human development—because necessary to render people unlike one another—namely, freedom and variety of situations. The second of these two conditions is in this country every day diminishing. The circumstances which surround different classes and individuals, and shape their characters, are daily becoming more assimilated. Formerly, different ranks, different neighborhoods, different trades and professions lived in what might be called different worlds; at present, to a great degree in the same. Comparatively speaking, they now read the same things, listen to the same things, see the same things, go to the same places, have their hopes and fears directed to the same objects, have the same rights and liberties, and the same means of asserting them. Great as are the differences of position which remain, they are nothing to those which have ceased. And the assimilation is still proceeding. All the political changes of the age promote it, since they all tend to raise the low and to lower the high. Every extension of education promotes it, because education brings people under common influences and gives them access to the general stock of facts and sentiments. Improvement in the means of communication promotes it, by bringing the inhabitants of distant places into personal contact, and keeping up a rapid flow of changes of residence between one place and another. The increase of commerce and manufactures promotes it, by diffusing more widely the advantages of easy circumstances and opening all objects of ambition, even the highest, to general competition, whereby the desire of rising becomes no longer the character of a particular class, but of all classes. A more powerful agency than even all these, in bringing about a general similarity among mankind, is the complete establishment, in this and other free countries, of the ascendancy of public opinion in the State. As the various social eminences which enabled persons entrenched on them to disregard the opinion of the multitude gradually become leveled; as the very idea of resisting the will of the public, when it is positively known that they have a will, disappears more and more from the minds of practical politicians, there ceases to be any social support for nonconformity—any substantive power in society which, itself opposed to the ascendancy of numbers, is interested in taking under its protection opinions and tendencies at variance with those of the public.

The combination of all these causes forms so great a mass of influences hostile to individuality that it is not easy to see how it can stand its ground. It will do so with increasing difficulty unless the intelligent part of the public can be made to feel its value—to see that it is good there should be differences, even though not for the better, even though, as it may appear to them, some should be for the worse. If the claims of individuality are ever to be asserted, the time is now while much is still wanting to complete the enforced assimilation. It is only in the earlier stages that any stand can be successfully made against the encroachment. The demand that all other people shall resemble ourselves grows by what it feeds on. If resistance waits till life is reduced *nearly* to one uniform type, all deviations from that type will come to be considered impious, immoral, even monstrous and contrary to nature. Mankind speedily become unable to conceive diversity when they have been for some time unaccustomed to see it.

# CHAPTER IV

## *Of the Limits to the Authority of Society over the Individual*

What, then, is the rightful limit to the sovereignty of the individual over himself? Where does the authority of society begin? How much of human life should be assigned to individuality, and how much to society?

Each will receive its proper share if each has that which more particularly concerns it. To individuality should belong the part of life in which it is chiefly the individual that is interested; to society, the part which chiefly interests society.

Though society is not founded on a contract, and though no good purpose is answered by inventing a contract in order to deduce social obligations from it, everyone who receives the protection of society owes a return for the benefit, and the fact of living in society renders it indispensable that each should be bound to observe a certain line of conduct toward the rest. This conduct consists, first, in not injuring the interests of one another, or rather certain interests which, either by express legal provision or by tacit understanding, ought to be considered as rights; and secondly, in each person's bearing his share (to be fixed on some equitable principle) of the labors and sacrifices incurred for defending the society or its members from injury and molestation. These conditions society is justified in enforcing at all costs to those who endeavor to withhold fulfillment. Nor is this all that society may do. The acts of an individual may be hurtful to others or wanting in due consideration for their welfare, without going to the length of violating any of their constituted rights. The offender may then be justly punished by opinion, though not by law. As soon as any part of a person's conduct affects prejudicially the interests of others, society has jurisdiction over it, and the question whether the general welfare will or will not be promoted by interfering with it becomes open to discussion. But there is no room for entertaining any such question when a person's conduct affects the interests of no persons besides himself, or needs not affect them unless they like (all the persons concerned being of full age and the ordinary amount of understanding). In all such cases, there should be perfect freedom, legal and social, to do the action and stand the consequences.

It would be a great misunderstanding of this doctrine to suppose that it is one of selfish indifference which pretends that human beings have no business with each other's conduct in life, and that they should not concern themselves about the well-doing or well-being of one another, unless their own interest is involved. Instead of any diminution, there is need of a great increase of disinterested exertion to promote the good of others. But disinterested benevolence can find other instruments to persuade people to their good than whips and scourges, either of the literal or the metaphorical sort. I am the last person to undervalue the self-regarding virtues; they are only second in importance, if even second, to the social. It is equally the business of education to cultivate both. But even education works by conviction and persuasion as well as by compulsion, and it is by the former only that, when the period of education is passed, the self-regarding virtues should be inculcated. Human beings owe to each other help to distinguish the better from the worse, and encouragement to choose the former and avoid the latter. They should be forever stimulating each other to increased exercise of their higher faculties and increased direction of their feelings and aims toward wise instead of foolish, elevating instead of degrading, objects and contemplations. But neither one person, nor any number of persons, is warranted in saying to another human creature of ripe years that he shall not do with his life for his own benefit what he chooses to do with it. He is the person most interested in his own well-being: the interest which any other person, except in cases of strong personal attachment, can have in it is trifling compared with that which he himself has; the interest which society has in him individually (except as to his conduct to others) is fractional and altogether indirect, while with respect to his own feelings and circumstances the most ordinary man or woman has means of knowledge immeasurably surpassing those that can be possessed by anyone else. The interference of society to overrule his judgment and purposes in what only regards himself must be grounded on general presumptions which may be altogether wrong and, even if right, are as likely as not to be misapplied to individual cases, by persons no better acquainted with the circumstances of such cases than those are who look at them merely from without. In this department, therefore, of human affairs, individuality has its proper field of action. In the conduct of human beings toward one another it is necessary that general rules should for the most part be observed in order that people may know what they have to expect; but in each person's own concerns his individual spontaneity is entitled to free exercise. Considerations to aid his judgment, exhortations to strengthen his will may be offered to him, even obtruded on him, by others; but he himself is the final judge. All errors which he is likely to commit against advice and warning are far outweighed by the evil of allowing others to constrain him to what they deem his good.

I do not mean that the feelings with which a person is regarded by others ought not to be in any way affected by his self-regarding qualities or deficiencies. This is neither possible nor desirable. If he is eminent in any of the qualities which conduce to his own good, he is, so far, a proper object of admiration. He is so much the nearer to the ideal perfection of human nature. If he is grossly deficient in those qualities, a sentiment the opposite of admiration will follow. There is a degree of folly, and a degree of what may be called (though the phrase is not unobjectionable) lowness or depravation of taste, which, though it cannot justify doing harm to the person who manifests it, renders him necessarily and properly a subject of distaste, or, in extreme cases, even of contempt: a person could not have the opposite qualities in due strength without entertaining these feelings. Though doing no wrong to anyone, a person may so act as to compel us to judge him, and feel to him, as a fool or as a being of an inferior order; and since this judgment and feeling are a fact which he would prefer to avoid, it is doing him a service to warn him of it beforehand, as of any other disagreeable consequence to which he exposes himself. It would be well, indeed, if this good office were much more freely rendered than the common notions of politeness at present permit, and if one person could honestly point out to another that he thinks him in fault, without being considered unmannerly or presuming. We have a right, also, in various ways, to act upon our unfavorable opinion of anyone, not to the oppression of his individuality, but in the exercise of ours. We are not bound, for example, to seek his society; we have a right to avoid it (though not to parade the avoidance), for we have a right to choose the society most acceptable to us. We have a right, and it may be our duty, to caution others against him if we think his example or conversation likely to have a pernicious effect on those with whom he associates. We may give others a preference over him in optional good offices, except those which tend to his improvement. In these various modes a person may suffer very severe penalties at the hands of others for faults which directly concern only himself; but he suffers these penalties only in so far as they are the natural and, as it were, the spontaneous consequences of the faults themselves, not because they are purposely inflicted on him for the sake of punishment. A person who shows rashness, obstinacy, self-conceit—who cannot live within moderate means; who cannot restrain himself from hurtful indulgence; who pursues animal pleasures at the expense of those of feeling and intellect—must expect to be lowered in the opinion of others, and to have a less share of their favorable sentiments; but of this he has no right to complain unless he has merited their favor by special excellence in his social relations and has thus established a title to their good offices, which is not affected by his demerits toward himself.

What I contend for is that the inconveniences which are strictly inseparable from the unfavorable judgment of others are the only ones to which a person should ever be subjected for that portion of his conduct and character which concerns his own good, but which does not affect the interest of others in their relations with him. Acts injurious to others require a totally different treatment. Encroachment on their rights; infliction on them of any loss or damage not justified by his own rights; falsehood or duplicity in dealing with them; unfair or ungenerous use of advantages over them; even selfish abstinence from defending them against injury—these are fit objects of moral reprobation and, in grave cases, of moral retribution and punishment. And not only these acts, but the dispositions which lead to them, are properly immoral and fit subjects of disapprobation which may rise to abhorrence. Cruelty of disposition; malice and ill-nature; that most antisocial and odious of all passions, envy; dissimulation and insincerity, irascibility on insufficient cause, and resentment disproportioned to the provocation; the love of domineering over others; the desire to engross more than one's share of advantages (the *pleonexia* of the Greeks); the pride which derives gratification from the abasement of others; the egotism which thinks self and its concerns more important than everything else, and decides all doubtful questions in its own favor—these are moral vices and constitute a bad and odious moral character; unlike the self-regarding faults previously mentioned, which are not properly immoralities and, to whatever pitch they may be carried, do not constitute wickedness. They may be proofs of any amount of folly or want of personal dignity and self-respect, but they are only a subject of moral reprobation when they involve a breach of duty to others, for whose sake the individual is bound to have care for himself. What are called duties to ourselves are not socially obligatory unless circumstances render them at the same time duties to others. The term duty to oneself, when it means anything more than prudence, means self-respect or self-development, and for none of these is anyone accountable to his fellow creatures, because for none of them is it for the good of mankind that he be held accountable to them.

The distinction between the loss of consideration which a person may rightly incur by defect of prudence or of personal dignity, and the reprobation which is due to him for an offense against the rights of others, is not a merely nominal distinction. It makes a vast difference both in our feelings and in our conduct toward him whether he displeases us in things in which we think we have a right to control him or in things in which we know that we have not. If he displeases us, we may express our distaste, and we may stand aloof from a person as well as from a thing that displeases us; but we shall not therefore feel called on to make his life uncomfortable. We shall reflect that he already bears, or will bear, the whole penalty of his error; if he spoils his life by mismanagement, we shall not, for that reason, desire to spoil it still further; instead of wishing to punish him, we shall rather endeavor to alleviate his punishment by showing him how he may avoid or cure

the evils his conduct tends to bring upon him. He may be to us an object of pity, perhaps of dislike, but not of anger or resentment; we shall not treat him like an enemy of society; the worst we shall think ourselves justified in doing is leaving him to himself, if we do not interfere benevolently by showing interest or concern for him. It is far otherwise if he has infringed the rules necessary for the protection of his fellow creatures, individually or collectively. The evil consequences of his acts do not then fall on himself, but on others; and society, as the protector of all its members, must retaliate on him, must inflict pain on him for the express purpose of punishment, and must take care that it be sufficiently severe. In the one case, he is an offender at our bar, and we are called on not only to sit in judgment on him, but, in one shape or another, to execute our own sentence; in the other case, it is not our part to inflict any suffering on him, except what may incidentally follow from our using the same liberty in the regulation of our own affairs which we allow to him in his.

The distinction here pointed out between the part of a person's life which concerns only himself and that which concerns others, many persons will refuse to admit. How (it may be asked) can any part of the conduct of a member of society be a matter of indifference to the other members? No person is an entirely isolated being; it is impossible for a person to do anything seriously or permanently hurtful to himself without mischief reaching at least to his near connections, and often far beyond them. If he injures his property, he does harm to those who directly or indirectly derived support from it, and usually diminishes, by a greater or less amount, the general resources of the community. If he deteriorates his bodily or mental faculties, he not only brings evil upon all who depended upon him for any portion of their happiness, but disqualifies himself for rendering the services which he owes to his fellow creatures generally, perhaps becomes a burden on their affection or benevolence; and if such conduct were very frequent hardly any offense that is committed would detract more from the general sum of good. Finally, if by his vices or follies a person does no direct harm to others, he is nevertheless (it may be said) injurious by his example, and ought to be compelled to control himself for the sake of those whom the sight or knowledge of his conduct might corrupt or mislead.

And even (it will be added) if the consequences of misconduct could be confined to the vicious or thoughtless individual, ought society to abandon to their own guidance those who are manifestly unfit for it? If protection against themselves is confessedly due to children and persons under age, is not society equally bound to afford it to persons of mature years who are equally incapable of self-government? If gambling, or drunkenness, or incontinence, or idleness, or uncleanliness are as injurious to happiness, and as great a hindrance to improvement, as many or most of the acts prohibited by law, why (it may be asked) should not law, so far as is consistent with practicability and social convenience, endeavor to repress these also? And as a supplement to the unavoidable imperfections of law, ought not opinion at least to organize a powerful police against these vices and visit rigidly with social penalties those who are known to practice them? There is no question here (it may be said) about restricting individuality, or impeding the trial of new and original experiments in living. The only things it is sought to prevent are things which have been tried and condemned from the beginning of the world until now—things which experience has shown not to be useful or suitable to any person's individuality. There must be some length of time and amount of experience after which a moral or prudential truth may be regarded as established; and it is merely desired to prevent generation after generation from falling over the same precipice which has been fatal to their predecessors.

I fully admit that the mischief which a person does to himself may seriously affect, both through their sympathies and their interests, those nearly connected with him and, in a minor degree, society at large. When, by conduct of this sort, a person is led to violate a distinct and assignable obligation to any other person or persons, the case is taken out of the self-regarding class and becomes amenable to moral disapprobation in the proper sense of the term.

If, for example, a man, through intemperance or extravagance, becomes unable to pay his debts, or, having undertaken the moral responsibility of a family, becomes from the same cause incapable of supporting or educating them, he is deservedly reprobated and might be justly punished; but it is for the breach of duty to his family or creditors, not for the extravagance. If the resources which ought to have been devoted to them had been diverted from them for the most prudent investment, the moral culpability would have been the same. George Barnwell murdered his uncle to get money for his mistress, but if he had done it to set himself up in business, he would equally have been hanged. Again, in the frequent case of a man who causes grief to his family by addiction to bad habits, he deserves reproach for his unkindness or ingratitude; but so he may for cultivating habits not in themselves vicious, if they are painful to those with whom he passes his life, or who from personal ties are dependent on him for their comfort. Whoever fails in the consideration generally due to the interests and feelings of others, not being compelled by some more imperative duty, or justified by allowable self-preference, is a subject of moral disapprobation for that failure, but not for the cause of it, nor for the errors, merely personal to himself, which may have remotely led to it. In like manner, when a person disables himself by conduct purely self-regarding, from the performance of some definite duty incumbent on him to the public, he is guilty of a social offense. No person ought to be punished simply for being drunk; but a soldier or policeman should be punished for being drunk on duty. Whenever, in short, there is a definite damage, or a definite risk of damage, either to an individual or to the public, the case is taken out of the province of liberty and placed in that of morality or law.

But with regard to the merely contingent or, as it may be called, constructive injury which a person causes to society by conduct which neither violates any specific duty to the public, nor occasions perceptible hurt to any assignable individual except himself, the inconvenience is one which society can afford to bear, for the sake of the greater good of human freedom. If grown persons are to be punished for not taking proper care of themselves, I would rather it were for their own sake than under pretense of preventing them from impairing their capacity or rendering to society benefits which society does not pretend it has a right to exact. But I cannot consent to argue the point as if society had no means of bringing its weaker members up to its ordinary standard of rational conduct, except waiting till they do something irrational, and then punishing them, legally or morally, for it. Society has had absolute power over them during all the early portion of their existence; it has had the whole period of childhood and nonage in which to try whether it could make them capable of rational conduct in life. The existing generation is master both of the training and the entire circumstances of the generation to come; it cannot indeed make them perfectly wise and good, because it is itself so lamentably deficient in goodness and wisdom; and its best efforts are not always, in individual cases, its most successful ones; but it is perfectly well able to make the rising generation, as a whole, as good as, and a little better than, itself. If society lets any considerable number of its members grow up mere children, incapable of being acted on by rational consideration of distant motives, society has itself to blame for the consequences. Armed not only with all the powers of education, but with the ascendency which the authority of a received opinion always exercises over the minds who are least fitted to judge for themselves, and aided by the *natural* penalties which cannot be prevented from falling on those who incur the distaste or the contempt of those who know them—let not society pretend that it needs, besides all this, the power to issue commands and enforce obedience in the personal concerns of individuals in which, on all principles of justice and policy, the decision ought to rest with those who are to abide the consequences. Nor is there anything which tends more to discredit and frustrate the better means of influencing conduct than a resort to the worse. If there be among those whom it is attempted to coerce into prudence or temperance any of the material of which vigorous and independent characters are made, they will infallibly rebel against the yoke. No such person will ever feel that others have a right to control him in his concerns, such as

they have to prevent him from injuring them in theirs; and it easily comes to be considered a mark of spirit and courage to fly in the face of such usurped authority and do with ostentation the exact opposite of what it enjoins, as in the fashion of grossness which succeeded, in the time of Charles II, to the fanatical moral intolerance of the Puritans. With respect to what is said of the necessity of protecting society from the bad example set to others by the vicious or the self-indulgent, it is true that bad example may have a pernicious effect, especially the example of doing wrong to others with impunity to the wrongdoer. But we are now speaking of conduct which, while it does no wrong to others, is supposed to do great harm to the agent himself; and I do not see how those who believe this can think otherwise than that the example, on the whole, must be more salutary than hurtful, since, if it displays the misconduct, it displays also the painful or degrading consequences which, if the conduct is justly censured, must be supposed to be in all or most cases attendant on it.

But the strongest of all the arguments against the interference of the public with purely personal conduct is that, when it does interfere, the odds are that it interferes wrongly and in the wrong place. On questions of social morality, of duty to others, the opinion of the public, that is, of an overruling majority, though often wrong, is likely to be still oftener right, because on such questions they are only required to judge of their own interests, of the manner in which some mode of conduct, if allowed to be practiced, would affect themselves. But the opinion of a similar majority, imposed as a law on the minority, on questions of self-regarding conduct is quite as likely to be wrong as right, for in these cases public opinion means, at the best, some people's opinion of what is good or bad for other people, while very often it does not even mean that—the public, with the most perfect indifference, passing over the pleasure or convenience of those whose conduct they censure and considering only their own preference. There are many who consider as an injury to themselves any conduct which they have a distaste for, and resent it as an outrage to their feelings; as a religious bigot, when charged with disregarding the religious feelings of others, has been known to retort that they disregard his feelings by persisting in their abominable worship or creed. But there is no parity between the feeling of a person for his own opinion and the feeling of another who is offended at his holding it, no more than between the desire of a thief to take a purse and the desire of the right owner to keep it. And a person's taste is as much his own peculiar concern as his opinion or his purse. It is easy for anyone to imagine an ideal public which leaves the freedom and choice of individuals in all uncertain matters undisturbed and only requires them to abstain from modes of conduct which universal experience has condemned. But where has there been seen a public which set any such limit to its censorship? Or when does the public trouble itself about universal experience? In its interferences with personal conduct it is seldom thinking of anything but the enormity of acting or feeling differently from itself; and this standard of judgment, thinly disguised, is held up to mankind as the dictate of religion and philosophy by nine-tenths of all moralists and speculative writers. These teach that things are right because they are right; because we feel them to be so. They tell us to search in our own minds and hearts for laws of conduct binding on ourselves and on all others. What can the poor public do but apply these instructions and make their own personal feelings of good and evil, if they are tolerably unanimous in them, obligatory on all the world?

The evil here pointed out is not one which exists only in theory; and it may perhaps be expected that I should specify the instances in which the public of this age and country improperly invests its own preferences with the character of moral laws. I am not writing an essay on the aberrations of existing moral feeling. That is too weighty a subject to be discussed parenthetically, and by way of illustration. Yet examples are necessary to show that the principle I maintain is of serious and practical moment, and that I am not endeavoring to erect a barrier against imaginary evils. And it is not difficult to show, by abundant instances, that to extend the bounds of what may be called moral police until it encroaches on the most unquestionably legitimate liberty of the individual is one of the most universal of all human propensities.

As a first instance, consider the antipathies which men cherish on no better grounds than that persons whose religious opinions are different from theirs do not practice their religious observances, especially their religious abstinences. To cite a rather trivial example, nothing in the creed or practice of Christians does more to envenom the hatred of Mohammedans against them than the fact of their eating pork. There are few acts which Christians and Europeans regard with more unaffected disgust than Mussulmans regard this particular mode of satisfying hunger. It is in the first place, an offense against their religion; but this circumstance by no means explains either the degree or the kind of their repugnance; for wine also is forbidden by their religion, and to partake of it is by all Mussulmans accounted wrong, but not disgusting. Their aversion to the flesh of the "unclean beast" is, on the contrary, of that peculiar character, resembling an instinctive antipathy, which the idea of uncleanness, when once it thoroughly sinks into the feelings, seems always to excite even in those whose personal habits are anything but scrupulously cleanly, and of which the sentiment of religious impurity, so intense in the Hindus, is a remarkable example. Suppose now that in a people of whom the majority were Mussulmans, that majority should insist upon not permitting pork to be eaten within the limits of the country. This would be nothing new in Mohammedan countries.[9] Would it be a legitimate exercise of the moral authority of public opinion, and if not, why not? The practice is really revolting to such a public. They also sincerely think that it is forbidden and abhorred by the Deity. Neither could the prohibition be censured as religious persecution. It might be religious in its origin, but it would not be persecution for religion, since nobody's religion makes it a duty to eat pork. The only tenable ground of condemnation would be that with the personal tastes and self-regarding concerns of individuals the public has no business to interfere.

To come somewhat nearer home: the majority of Spaniards consider it a gross impiety, offensive in the highest degree to the Supreme Being, to worship him in any other manner than the Roman Catholic; and no other public worship is lawful on Spanish soil. The people of all southern Europe look upon a married clergy as not only irreligious, but unchaste, indecent, gross, disgusting. What do Protestants think of these perfectly sincere feelings, and of the attempt to enforce them against non-Catholics? Yet, if mankind are justified in interfering with each other's liberty in things which do not concern the interests of others, on what principle is it possible consistently to exclude these cases? Or who can blame people for desiring to suppress what they regard as a scandal in the sight of God and man? No stronger case can be shown for prohibiting anything which is regarded as a personal immorality than is made out for suppressing these practices in the eyes of those who regard them as impieties; and unless we are willing to adopt the logic of persecutors, and to say that we may persecute others because we are right, and that they must not persecute us because they are wrong, we must beware of admitting a principle of which we should resent as a gross injustice the application to ourselves.

The preceding instances may be objected to, although unreasonably, as drawn from contingencies impossible among us—opinion, in this country, not being likely to enforce abstinence from meats or to interfere with people for worshipping and for either marrying or not marrying, according to their creed or inclination. The next example, however, shall be taken from an interference with liberty which we have by no means passed all danger of Wherever the Puritans have been sufficiently powerful, as in New England, and in Great Britain at the time of the Commonwealth, they have endeavored, with considerable success, to put down all public, and nearly all private, amusements: especially music, dancing, public games, or other assemblages for purposes of diversion, and the theater. There are still in this country large bodies of persons by whose notions of morality and religion these recreations are condemned; and those persons belonging chiefly to the middle class, who are the ascendant power in the

present social and political condition of the kingdom, it is by no means impossible that persons of these sentiments may at some time or other command a majority in Parliament. How will the remaining portion of the community like to have the amusements that shall be permitted to them regulated by the religious and moral sentiments of the stricter Calvinists and Methodists? Would they not, with considerable peremptoriness, desire these intrusively pious members of society to mind their own business? This is precisely what should be said to every government and every public who have the pretension that no person shall enjoy any pleasure which they think wrong. But if the principle of the pretension be admitted, no one can reasonably object to its being acted on in the sense of the majority, or other preponderating power in the country; and all persons must be ready to conform to the idea of a Christian commonwealth as understood by the early settlers in New England, if a religious profession similar to theirs should ever succeed in regaining its lost ground, as religions supposed to be declining have so often been known to do.

To imagine another contingency, perhaps more likely to be realized than the one last mentioned. There is confessedly a strong tendency in the modern world toward a democratic constitution of society, accompanied or not by popular political institutions. It is affirmed that in the country where this tendency is most completely realized—where both society and the government are most democratic: the United States—the feeling of the majority, to whom any appearance of a more showy or costly style of living than they can hope to rival is disagreeable, operates as a tolerably effectual sumptuary law, and that in many parts of the Union it is really difficult for a person possessing a very large income to find any mode of spending it which will not incur popular disapprobation. Though such statements as these are doubtless much exaggerated as a representation of existing facts, the state of things they describe is not only a conceivable and possible, but a probable result of democratic feeling combined with the notion that the public has a right

972       JOHN STUART MILL

to veto on the manner in which individuals shall spend their incomes. We have only further to suppose a considerable diffusion of Socialist opinions, and it may become infamous in the eyes of the majority to possess more property than some very small amount, or any income not earned by manual labor. Opinions similar in principle to these already prevail widely among the artisan class and weigh oppressively on those who are amenable to the opinion chiefly of that class, namely, its own members. It is known that the bad workmen who form the majority of the operatives in many branches of industry are decidedly of opinion that bad workmen ought to receive the same wages as good, and that no one ought to be allowed, through piecework or otherwise, to earn by superior skill or industry more than others can without it. And they employ a moral police, which occasionally becomes a physical one, to deter skillful workmen from receiving, and employers from giving, a larger remuneration for a more useful service. If the public have any jurisdiction over private concerns, I cannot see that these people are in fault, or that any individual's particular public can be blamed for asserting the same authority over his individual conduct which the general public asserts over people in general.

But, without dwelling upon supposititious cases, there are, in our own day, gross usurpations upon the liberty of private life actually practiced, and still greater ones threatened with some expectation of success, and opinions propounded which assert an unlimited right in the public not only to prohibit by law everything which it thinks wrong, but, in order to get at what it thinks wrong, to prohibit a number of things which it admits to be innocent.

Under the name of preventing intemperance, the people of one English colony, and of nearly half the United States, have been interdicted by law from making any use whatever of fermented drinks, except for medical purposes, for prohibition of their sale is in fact, as it is intended to be, prohibition of their use. And though the impracticability of executing the law has caused its repeal in several of the States which had adopted it, including the one from which it derives its name, an attempt has notwithstanding been commenced, and is prosecuted with considerable zeal by many of the professed philanthropists, to agitate for a similar law in the country. The association, or "Alliance," as it terms itself, which has been formed for this purpose, has acquired some notoriety through the publicity given to a correspondence between its secretary and one of the very few English public men who hold that a politican's opinions ought to be founded on principles. Lord Stanley's share in this correspondence is calculated to strengthen the hopes already built on him by those who know how rare such qualities as are manifested in some of his public appearances unhappily are among those who figure in political life. The organ of the Alliance, who would "deeply deplore the recognition of any principle which could be wrested to justify bigotry and persecution," undertakes to point out the "broad and impassable barrier" which divides such principles from those of the association. "All matters relating to thought, opinion, conscience, appear to me," he says, "to be without the sphere of legislation; all pertaining to social act, habit, relation, subject only to a discretionary power vested in the State itself, and not in the individual, to be within it." No mention is made of a third class, different from either of these, viz., acts and habits which are not social, but individual; although it is to this class, surely that the act of drinking fermented liquors belongs. Selling fermented liquors, however, is trading, and trading is a social act. But the infringement complained of is not on the liberty of the seller, but on that of the buyer and consumer; since the State might just as well forbid him to drink wine as purposely make it impossible for him to obtain it. The secretary, however, says, "I claim, as a citizen, a right to legislate whenever my social rights are invaded by the social act of another." And now for the definition of these "social rights": "If anything invades my social rights, certainly the traffic in strong drink does. It destroys my primary right of security by constantly creating and stimulating social disorder. It invades my right of equality by deriving a profit from the creation of a misery I am taxed to support. It impedes my right to free moral and intellectual development by surrounding my path with dangers and by weakening and demoralizing society, from which

I have a right to claim mutual aid and intercourse." A theory of "social rights" the like of which probably never before found its way into distinct language: being nothing short of this—that it is the absolute social right of every individual that every other individual shall act in every respect exactly as he ought; that whosoever fails thereof in the smallest particular violates my social right and entitles me to demand from the legislature the removal of the grievance. So monstrous a principle is far more dangerous than any single interference with liberty; there is no violation of liberty which it would not justify; it acknowledges no right to any freedom whatever, except perhaps to that of holding opinions in secret, without ever disclosing them; for the moment an opinion which I consider noxious passes anyone's lips, it invades all the "social rights" attributed to me by the Alliance. The doctrine ascribes to all mankind a vested interest in each other's moral, intellectual, and even physical perfection, to be defined by each claimant according to his own standard.

Another important example of illegitimate interference with the rightful liberty of the individual, not simply threatened, but long since carried into triumphant effect, is Sabbatarian legislation. Without doubt, abstinence on one day in the week, so far as the exigencies of life permit, from the usual daily occupation, though in no respect religiously binding on any except Jews, is a highly beneficial custom. And inasmuch as this custom cannot be observed without a general consent to that effect among the industrious classes, therefore, in so far as some persons by working may impose the same necessity on others, it may be allowable and right that the law should guarantee to each the observance by others of the custom, by suspending the greater operations of industry on a particular day. But this justification, grounded on the direct interest which others have in each individual's observance of the practice, does not apply to the self-chosen occupations in which a person may think fit to employ his leisure, nor does it hold good, in the smallest degree, for legal restrictions on amusements. It is true that the amusement of some is the day's work of others; but the pleasure, not to say the useful recreation, of many is worth the

labor of a few, provided the occupation is freely chosen and can be freely resigned. The operatives are perfectly right in thinking that if all worked on Sunday, seven days' work would have to be given for six days' wages; but so long as the great mass of employments are suspended, the small number who for the enjoyment of others must still work obtain a proportional increase of earnings; and they are not obliged to follow those occupations if they prefer leisure to emolument. If a further remedy is sought, it might be found in the establishment by custom of a holiday on some other day of the week for those particular classes of persons. The only ground, therefore, on which restrictions on Sunday amusements can be defended must be that they are religiously wrong—a motive of legislation which can never be too earnestly protested against. "*Deorum injuriae Dus curae.*" It remains to be proved that society or any of its officers holds a commission from on high to avenge any supposed offense to Omnipotence which is not also a wrong to our fellow creatures. The notion that it is one man's duty that another should be religious was the foundation of all the religious persecutions ever perpetrated, and, if admitted, would fully justify them. Though the feeling which breaks out in the repeated attempts to stop railway traveling on Sunday, in the resistance to the opening of museums, and the like, has not the cruelty of the old persecutors, the state of mind indicated by it is fundamentally the same. It is a determination not to tolerate others in doing what is permitted by their religion, because it is not permitted by the persecutor's religion. It is a belief that God not only abominates the act of the misbeliever, but will not hold us guiltless if we leave him unmolested.

I cannot refrain from adding to these examples of the little account commonly made of human liberty the language of downright persecution which breaks out from the press of this country whenever it feels called on to notice the remarkable phenomenon of Mormonism. Much might be said on the unexpected and instructive fact that an alleged new revelation and a religion founded on it—the product of palpable imposture, not even supported by the *prestige* of extraordinary qualities in its founder—is believed by hundreds of thousands, and has been made the foundation of a society in the age of newspapers, railways, and the electric telegraph. What here concerns us is that this religion, like other and better religions, has its martyrs: that its prophet and founder was, for his teaching, put to death by a mob; that others of its adherents lost their lives by the same lawless violence; that they were forcibly expelled, in a body, from the country in which they first grew up, while, now that they have been chased into a solitary recess in the midst of a desert, many in this country openly declare that it would be right (only that it is not convenient) to send an expedition against them and compel them by force to conform to the opinions of other people. The article of the Mormonite doctrine which is the chief provocative to the antipathy which thus breaks through the ordinary restraints of religious tolerance is its sanction of polygamy; which, though permitted to Mohammedans, and Hindus, and Chinese, seems to excite unquenchable animosity when practiced by persons who speak English and profess to be a kind of Christians. No one has a deeper disapprobation than I have of this Mormon institution; both for other reasons and because, far from being in any way countenanced by the principle of liberty, it is a direct infraction of that principle, being a mere riveting of the chains of one half of the community, and an emancipation of the other from reciprocity of obligation toward them. Still, it must be remembered that this relation is as much voluntary on the part of the women concerned in it, and who may be deemed the sufferers by it, as is the case with any other form of the marriage institution; and however surprising this fact may appear, it has its explanation in the common ideas and customs of the world, which, teaching women to think marriage the one thing needful, make it intelligible that many a woman should prefer being one of several wives to not being a wife at all. Other countries are not asked to recognize such unions, or release any portion of their inhabitants from their own laws on the score of Mormonite opinions. But when the dissentients have conceded to the hostile sentiments of others far more than could justly be demanded; when they have left the countries to which their doctrines were unacceptable and established themselves in a remote corner of the earth,

which they have been the first to render habitable to human beings, it is difficult to see on what principles but those of tyranny they can be prevented from living there under what laws they please, provided they commit no aggression on other nations and allow perfect freedom of departure to those who are dissatisfied with their ways. A recent writer, in some respects of considerable merit, proposes (to use his own words) not a crusade, but a *civilizade*, against this polygamous community, to put an end to what seems to him a retrograde step in civilization. It also appears so to me, but I am not aware that any community has a right to force another to be civilized. So long as the sufferers by the bad law do not invoke assistance from other communities, I cannot admit that persons entirely unconnected with them ought to step in and require that a condition of things with which all who are directly interested appear to be satisfied should be put an end to because it is a scandal to persons some thousands of miles distant who have no part or concern in it. Let them send missionaries, if they please, to preach against it; and let them, by any fair means (of which silencing the teachers is not one), oppose the progress of similar doctrines among their own people. If civilization has got the better of barbarism when barbarism had the world to itself, it is too much to profess to be afraid lest barbarism, after having been fairly got under, should revive and conquer civilization. A civilization that can thus succumb to its vanquished enemy must first have become so degenerate that neither its appointed priests and teachers, nor anybody else, has the capacity, or will take the trouble, to stand up for it. If this be so, the sooner such a civilization receives notice to quit, the better. It can only go on from bad to worse until destroyed and regenerated (like the Western Empire) by energetic barbarians.

# CHAPTER V

## *Applications*

The principles asserted in these pages must be more generally admitted as the basis for discussion of details before a consistent application of them to all the various departments of government and morals can be attempted with any prospect of advantage. The few observations I propose to make on questions of detail are designed to illustrate the principles rather than to follow them out to their consequences. I offer not so much applications as specimens of application, which may serve to bring into greater clearness the meaning and limits of the two maxims which together form the entire doctrine of this essay, and to assist the judgment in holding the balance between them in the cases where it appears doubtful which of them is applicable to the case.

The maxims are, first, that the individual is not accountable to society for his actions in so far as these concern the interests of no person but himself. Advice, instruction, persuasion, and avoidance by other people, if thought necessary by them for their own good, are the only measures by which society can justifiably express its dislike or disapprobation of his conduct. Secondly, that for such actions as are prejudicial to the interests of others, the individual is accountable and may be subjected either to social or to legal punishment if society is of opinion that the one or the other is requisite for its protection.

In the first place, it must by no means be supposed, because damage, or probability of damage, to the interests of others can alone justify the interference of society, that therefore it always does justify such interference. In many cases an individual, in pursuing a legitimate object, necessarily and therefore legitimately causes pain or loss to others, or intercepts a good which they had a reasonable hope of obtaining. Such oppositions of interest between individuals often arise from bad social institutions, but are unavoidable while those institutions last; and some would be unavoidable under any institutions. Whoever succeeds in an overcrowded profession or in a competitive examination, whoever is preferred to another in any contest for an object which both desire, reaps benefit from the loss of others, from their wasted exertion and their disappointment. But it is, by common admission, better for the general interest of mankind that persons should pursue their objects undeterred by this sort of consequences. In other words, society admits no right, either legal or moral, in the disappointed competitors to immunity from this kind of suffering, and feels called on to

interfere only when means of success have been employed which it is contrary to the general interest to permit—namely, fraud or treachery, and force.

Again, trade is a social act. Whoever undertakes to sell any description of goods to the public does what affects the interest of other persons, and of society in general; and thus his conduct, in principle, comes within the jurisdiction of society; accordingly, it was once held to be the duty of governments, in all cases which were considered of importance, to fix prices and regulate the process of manufacture. But it is now recognized, though not till after a long struggle, that both the cheapness and the good quality of commodities are most effectually provided for by leaving the producers and sellers perfectly free, under the sole check of equal freedom to the buyers for supplying themselves elsewhere. This is the so-called doctrine of "free trade," which rests on grounds different from, though equally solid with, the principle of individual liberty asserted in this essay. Restrictions on trade, or on production for purposes of trade, are indeed restraints; and all restraint, *qua* restraint, is an evil; but the restraints in question affect only that part of conduct which society is competent to restrain, and are wrong solely because they do not really produce the results which it is desired to produce by them. As the principle of individual liberty is not involved in the doctrine of free trade, so neither is it in most of the questions which arise respecting the limits of that doctrine, as, for example, what amount of public control is admissible for the prevention of fraud by adulteration; how far sanitary precautions, or arrangements to protect workpeople employed in dangerous occupations, should be enforced on employers. Such questions involve considerations of liberty only in so far as leaving people to themselves is always better, *caeteris paribus,* than controlling them; but that they may be legitimately controlled for these ends is in principle undeniable. On the other hand, there are questions relating to interference with trade which are essentially questions of liberty, such as the Maine Law, already touched upon; the prohibition of the importation of opium into China; the restriction of the sale of poisons—all cases, in short, where the object of the interference is to make it impossible or difficult to obtain a particular commodity. These interferences are objectionable, not as infringements on the liberty of the producer or seller, but on that of the buyer.

One of these examples, that of the sale of poisons, opens a new question: the proper limits of what may be called the functions of police; how far liberty may legitimately be invaded for the prevention of crime, or of accident. It is one of the undisputed functions of government to take precautions against crime before it has been committed, as well as to detect and punish it afterwards. The preventive function of government, however, is far more liable to be abused, to the prejudice of liberty, than the punitory function; for there is hardly any part of the legitimate freedom of action of a human being which would not admit of being represented, and fairly, too, as increasing the facilities for some form or other of delinquency. Nevertheless, if a public authority, or even a private person, sees anyone evidently preparing to commit a crime, they are not bound to look on inactive until the crime is committed, but may interfere to prevent it. If poisons were never bought or used for any purpose except the commission of murder, it would be right to prohibit their manufacture and sale. They may, however, be wanted not only for innocent but for useful purposes, and restrictions cannot be imposed in the one case without operating in the other. Again, it is a proper office of public authority to guard against accidents. If either a public officer or anyone else saw a person attempting to cross a bridge which had been ascertained to be unsafe, and there were no time to warn him of his danger, they might seize him and turn him back, without any real infringement of his liberty; for liberty consists in doing what one desires, and he does not desire to fall into the river. Nevertheless, when there is not a certainty, but only a danger of mischief, no one but the person himself can judge of the sufficiency of the motive which may prompt him to incur the risk; in this case, therefore (unless he is a child, or delirious, or in some state of excitement or absorption incompatible with the full use of the reflecting faculty), he ought, I conceive, to be only warned of the danger; not forcibly prevented from exposing himself to it. Similar considerations, applied to such a question as

the sale of poisons, may enable us to decide which among the possible modes of regulation are or are not contrary to principle. Such a precaution, for example, as that of labeling the drug with some word expressive of its dangerous character may be enforced without violation of liberty: the buyer cannot wish not to know that the thing he possesses has poisonous qualities. But to require in all cases the certificate of a medical practitioner would make it sometimes impossible, always expensive, to obtain the article for legitimate uses. The only mode apparent to me, in which difficulties may be thrown in the way of crime committed through this means, without any infringement worth taking into account upon the liberty of those who desire the poisonous substance for other purposes, consists in providing what, in the apt language of Bentham, is called "preappointed evidence." This provision is familiar to everyone in the case of contracts. It is usual and right that the law, when a contract is entered into, should require as the condition of its enforcing performance that certain formalities should be observed, such as signatures, attestation of witnesses, and the like, in order that in case of subsequent dispute there may be evidence to prove that the contract was really entered into, and that there was nothing in the circumstances to render it legally invalid, the effect being to throw great obstacles in the way of fictitious contracts, or contracts made in circumstances which, if known, would destroy their validity. Precautions of a similar nature might be enforced in the sale of articles adapted to be instruments of crime. The seller, for example, might be required to enter in a register the exact time of the transaction, the name and address of the buyer, the precise quality and quantity sold; to ask the purpose for which it was wanted, and record the answer he received. When there was no medical prescription, the presence of some third person might be required to bring home the fact to the purchaser, in case there should afterwards be reason to believe that the article had been applied to criminal purposes. Such regulations would in general be no material impediment to obtaining the article, but a very considerable one to making an improper use of it without detection.

The right inherent in society to ward off crimes

against itself by antecedent precautions suggests the obvious limitations to the maxim that purely self-regarding misconduct cannot properly be meddled with in the way of prevention or punishment. Drunkenness, for example, in ordinary cases, is not a fit subject for legislative interference, but I should deem it perfectly legitimate that a person who had once been convicted of any act of violence to others under the influence of drink should be placed under a special legal restriction, personal to himself; that if he were afterwards found drunk, he should be liable to a penalty, and that if, when in that state, he committed another offense, the punishment to which he would be liable for that other offense should be increased in severity. The making himself drunk, in a person whom drunkenness excites to do harm to others, is a crime against others. So, again, idleness, except in a person receiving support from the public, or except when it constitutes a breach of contract, cannot without tyranny be made a subject of legal punishment; but if, either from idleness or from any other avoidable cause, a man fails to perform his legal duties to others, as for instance to support his children, it is no tyranny to force him to fulfill that obligation by compulsory labor if no other means are available.

Again, there are many acts which, being directly injurious only to the agents themselves, ought not to be legally interdicted, but which, if done publicly, are a violation of good manners and, coming thus within the category of offenses against others, may rightly be prohibited. Of this kind are offenses against decency; on which it is unnecessary to dwell, the rather as they are only connected indirectly with our subject, the objection to publicity being equally strong in the case of many actions not in themselves condemnable, nor supposed to be so.

There is another question to which an answer must be found, consistent with the principles which have been laid down. In cases of personal conduct supposed to be blamable, but which respect for liberty precludes society from preventing or punishing because the evil directly resulting falls wholly on the agent; what the agent is free to do, ought other persons to be equally free to counsel or instigate? This question is not free from difficulty. The case of a person who solicits another to do an act is not strictly a case of self-regarding conduct. To give advice or offer inducements to anyone is a social act and may, therefore, like actions in general which affect others, be supposed amenable to social control. But a little reflection corrects the first impression, by showing that if the case is not strictly within the definition of individual liberty, yet the reasons on which the principle of individual liberty is grounded are applicable to it. If people must be allowed, in whatever concerns only themselves, to act as seems best to themselves, at their own peril, they must equally be free to consult with one another about what is fit to be so done; to exchange opinions, and give and receive suggestions. Whatever it is permitted to do, it must be permitted to advise to do. The question is doubtful only when the instigator derives a personal benefit from his advice, when he makes it his occupation, for subsistence or pecuniary gain, to promote what society and the State consider to be an evil. Then, indeed, a new element of complication is introduced—namely, the existence of classes of persons with an interest opposed to what is considered as the public weal, and whose mode of living is grounded on the counteraction of it. Ought this to be interfered with, or not? Fornication, for example, must be tolerated, and so must gambling; but should a person be free to be a pimp, or to keep a gambling house? The case is one of those which lie on the exact boundary line between two principles, and it is not at once apparent to which of the two it properly belongs. There are arguments on both sides. On the side of toleration it may be said that the fact of following anything as an occupation, and living or profiting by the practice of it, cannot make that criminal which would otherwise be admissible; that the act should either be consistently permitted or consistently prohibited; that if the principles which we have hitherto defended are true, society has no business, *as* society, to decide anything to be wrong which concerns only the individual; that it cannot go beyond dissuasion, and that one person should be as free to persuade as another to dissuade. In opposition to this it may be contended that, although the public, or the State, are not warranted in authoritatively deciding, for purposes of repression or punishment, that such or such conduct affecting only the interests of the individual is good or bad, they are fully justified in assuming, if they regard it as bad, that its being so or not is at least a disputable question: that, this being supposed, they cannot be acting wrongly in endeavoring to exclude the influence of solicitations which are not disinterested, of instigators who cannot possibly be impartial—who have a direct personal interest on one side, and that side the one which the State believes to be wrong, and who confessedly promote it for personal objects only. There can surely, it may be urged, be nothing lost, no sacrifice of good, by so ordering matters that persons shall make their election, either wisely or foolishly, on their own prompting, as free as possible from the arts of persons who stimulate their inclinations for interested purposes of their own. Thus (it may be said), though the statutes respecting unlawful games are utterly indefensible—though all persons should be free to gamble in their own or each other's houses, or in any place of meeting established by their own subscriptions and open only to the members and their visitors—yet public gambling houses should not be permitted. It is true that the prohibition is never effectual, and that, whatever amount of tyrannical power may be given to the police, gambling houses can always be maintained under other pretenses; but they may be compelled to conduct their operations with a certain degree of secrecy and mystery, so that nobody knows anything about them but those who seek them; and more than this society ought not to aim at. There is considerable force in these arguments. I will not venture to decide whether they are sufficient to justify the moral anomaly of punishing the accessory when the principal is (and must be) allowed to go free; of fining or imprisoning the procurer, but not the fornicator—the gambling-house keeper, but not the gambler. Still less ought the common operations of buying and selling to be interfered with on analogous grounds. Almost every article which is bought and sold may be used in excess, and the sellers have a pecuniary interest in encouraging that excess; but no argument can be founded on this in favor, for instance, of the Maine Law; because the class of dealers in strong drinks, though interested in their abuse, are indispensably required for the sake of their legitimate use. The interest, however, of these dealers in promoting intemperance is a real evil and justifies the State in imposing restrictions and requiring guarantees which, but for that justification, would be infringements of legitimate liberty.

A further question is whether the State, while it permits, should nevertheless indirectly discourage conduct which it deems contrary to the best interests of the agent; whether, for example, it should take measures to render the means of drunkenness more costly, or add to the difficulty of procuring them by limiting the number of the places of sale. On this, as on most other practical questions, many distinctions require to be made. To tax stimulants for the sole purpose of making them more difficult to be obtained is a measure differing only in degree from their entire prohibition, and would be justifiable only if that were justifiable. Every increase of cost is a prohibition to those whose means do not come up to the augmented price; and to those who do, it is a penalty laid on them for gratifying a particular taste. Their choice of pleasures and their mode of expending their income, after satisfying their legal and moral obligations to the State and to individuals, are their own concern and must rest with their own judgment. These considerations may seem at first sight to condemn the selection of stimulants as special subjects of taxation for purposes of revenue. But it must be remembered that taxation for fiscal purposes is absolutely inevitable; that in most countries it is necessary that a considerable part of that taxation should be indirect; that the State, therefore, cannot help imposing penalties, which to some persons may be prohibitory, on the use of some articles of consumption. It is hence the duty of the State to consider, in the imposition of taxes, what commodities the consumers can best spare; and *a fortiori*, to select in preference those of which it deems the use, beyond a very moderate quantity, to be positively injurious. Taxation, therefore, of stimulants up to the point which produces the largest amount of revenue (supposing that the State needs all the revenue which it yields) is not only admissible, but to be approved of.

The question of making the sale of these commodities a more or less exclusive privilege must be answered differently, according to the purposes to which the restriction is intended to be subservient. All places of public resort require the restraint of a police, and places of this kind peculiarly, because offenses against society are especially apt to originate there. It is, therefore, fit to confine the power of selling these commodities (at least for consumption on the spot) to persons of known or vouched-for respectability of conduct; to make such regulations respecting hours of opening and closing as may be requisite for public surveillance, and to withdraw the license if breaches of the peace repeatedly take place through the connivance or incapacity of the keeper of the house, or if it becomes a rendezvous for concocting and preparing offenses against the law. Any further restriction I do not conceive to be, in principle, justifiable. The limitation in number, for instance, of beer and spirit houses, for the express purpose of rendering them more difficult of access and diminishing the occasions of temptation, not only exposes all to an inconvenience because there are some by whom the facility would be abused, but is suited only to a state of society in which the laboring classes are avowedly treated as children or savages, and placed under an education of restraint, to fit them for future admission to the privileges of freedom. This is not the principle on which the laboring classes are professedly governed in any free country; and no person who sets due value on freedom will give his adhesion to their being so governed, unless after all efforts have been exhausted to educate them for freedom and govern them as freemen, and it has been definitively proved that they can only be governed as children. The bare statement of the alternative shows the absurdity of supposing that such efforts have been made in any case which needs be considered here. It is only because the institutions of this country are a mass of inconsistencies, that things find admittance into our practice which belong to the system of despotic, or what is called paternal, government, while the general freedom of our institutions precludes the exercise of the amount of control necessary to render the restraint of any real efficacy as a moral education.

It was pointed out in an early part of this essay that the liberty of the individual, in things wherein the individual is alone concerned, implies a corresponding liberty in any number of individuals to regulate by mutual agreement such things as regard them jointly, and regard no persons but themselves. This question presents no difficulty so long as the will of all the persons implicated remains unaltered; but since that will may change it is often necessary, even in things in which they alone are concerned, that they should enter into engagements with one another; and when they do, it is fit, as a general rule, that those engagements should be kept. Yet, in the laws, probably, of every country, this general rule has some exceptions. Not only persons are not held to engagements which violate the rights of third parties, but it is sometimes considered a sufficient reason for releasing them from an engagement that it is injurious to themselves. In this and most other civilized countries, for example, an engagement by which a person should sell himself, or allow himself to be sold, as a slave would be null and void, neither enforced by law nor by opinion. The ground for thus limiting his power of voluntarily disposing of his own lot in life is apparent, and is very clearly seen in this extreme case. The reason for not interfering, unless for the sake of others, with a person's voluntary acts is consideration for his liberty. His voluntary choice is evidence that what he so chooses is desirable, or at least endurable, to him, and his good is on the whole best provided for by allowing him to take his own means of pursuing it. But by selling himself for a slave, he abdicates his liberty; he foregoes any future use of it beyond that single act. He therefore defeats, in his own case, the very purpose which is the justification of allowing him to dispose of himself. He is no longer free, but is thenceforth in a position which has no longer the presumption in its favor that would be afforded by his voluntarily remaining in it. The principle of freedom cannot require that he should be free not to be free. It is not freedom to be allowed to alienate his freedom. These reasons, the force of which is so conspicuous in this peculiar case, are evidently of far wider application, yet a limit is everywhere set to them by the necessities of life, which continually require, not indeed that we should resign our freedom, but that we should consent to this and the other limitation of it. The principle, however, which demands uncontrolled freedom of action in all that concerns only the agents themselves requires that those who have become bound to one another, in things which concern no third party, should be able to release one another from the engagement; and even without such voluntary release there are perhaps no contracts or engagements, except those that relate to money or money's worth, of which one can venture to say that there ought to be no liberty whatever of retraction. Baron Wilhelm von Humboldt, in the excellent essay from which I have already quoted, states it as his conviction that engagements which involve personal relations or services should never be legally binding beyond a limited duration of time; and that the most important of these engagements, marriage, having the peculiarity that its objects are frustrated unless the feelings of both the parties are in harmony with it, should require nothing more than the declared will of either party to dissolve it. This subject is too important and too complicated to be discussed in a parenthesis, and I touch on it only so far as is necessary for purposes of illustration. If the conciseness and generality of Baron Humboldt's dissertation had not obliged him in this instance to content himself with enunciating his conclusion without discussing the premises, he would doubtless have recognized that the question cannot be decided on grounds so simple as those to which he confines himself. When a person, either by express promise or by conduct, has encouraged another to rely upon his continuing to act in a certain way—to build expectations and calculations, and stake any part of his plan of life upon that supposition—a new series of moral obligations arises on his part toward that person, which may possibly be overruled, but cannot be ignored. And again, if the relation between two contracting parties has been followed by consequences to others; if it has placed third parties in any peculiar position, or, as in the case of marriage, has even called third parties into existence, obligations arise on the part of both the contracting parties toward those third persons, the fulfillment of which, or at all events the mode of fulfillment, must be greatly affected by the continuance or disruption of the relation between the original parties to the contract. It does not follow, nor can I admit, that these obligations extend to requiring the fulfillment of the contract at all costs to the happiness of the reluctant party; but they are a necessary element in the question; and, even if, as von Humboldt maintains, they ought to make no difference in the *legal* freedom of the parties to release themselves from the engagement (and I also hold that they ought not to make *much* difference), they necessarily make a great difference in the *moral* freedom. A person is bound to take all these circumstances into account before resolving on a step which may affect such important interests of others; and if he does not allow proper weight to those interests, he is morally responsible for the wrong. I have made these obvious remarks for the better illustration of the general principle of liberty, and not because they are at all needed on the particular question, which, on the contrary, is usually discussed as if the interest of children was everything, and that of grown persons nothing.

I have already observed that, owing to the absence of any recognized general principles, liberty is often granted where it should be withheld, as well as withheld where it should be granted; and one of the cases in which, in the modern European world, the sentiment of liberty is the strongest is a case where, in my view, it is altogether misplaced. A person should be free to do as he likes in his own concerns, but he ought not to be free to do as he likes in acting for another, under the pretext that the affairs of the other are his own affairs. The State, while it respects the liberty of each in what specially regards himself, is bound to maintain a vigilant control over his exercise of any power which it allows him to possess over others. This obligation is almost entirely disregarded in the case of the family relations—a case, in its direct influence on human happiness, more important than all others taken together. The almost despotic power of husbands over wives needs not be enlarged upon here, because nothing more is needed for the complete removal of the evil than that wives should have the same rights and should receive the protection of law in the same manner as all other persons; and because, on this subject, the defenders of established injustice do not avail themselves of the plea of liberty but stand forth openly as the champions of power. It is in the case of children that misapplied notions of liberty are a real obstacle to the fulfillment by the State of its duties. One would almost think that a man's children were supposed to be literally, and not metaphorically, a part of himself, so jealous is opinion of the smallest interference of law with his absolute and exclusive control over them, more jealous than of almost any interference with his own freedom of action: so much less do the generality of mankind value liberty than power. Consider, for example, the case of education. Is it not almost a self-evident axiom that the State should require and compel the education, up to a certain standard, of every human being who is born its citizen? Yet who is there that is not afraid to recognize and assert this truth? Hardly anyone, indeed, will deny that it is one of the most sacred duties of the parents (or, as law and usage now stand, the father), after summoning a human being into the world, to give to that being an education fitting him to perform his part well in life toward others and toward himself. But while this is unanimously declared to be the father's duty, scarcely anybody, in this country, will bear to hear of obliging him to perform it. Instead of his being required to make any exertion or sacrifice for securing education to his child, it is left to his choice to accept it or not when it is provided gratis! It still remains unrecognized that to bring a child into existence without a fair prospect of being able, not only to provide food for its body, but instruction and training for its mind is a moral crime, both against the unfortunate offspring and against society; and that if the parent does not fulfill this obligation, the State ought to see it fulfilled at the charge, as far as possible, of the parent.

Were the duty of enforcing universal education once admitted there would be an end to the difficulties about what the State should teach, and how it should teach, which now convert the subject into a mere battlefield for sects and parties, causing the time and labor which should have been spent in educating to be wasted in quarreling about education. If the government would make up its mind to require for every child a good education, it might save itself the trouble of providing one. It might leave to parents to obtain the education where and how they pleased, and content itself with helping to pay the school fees of the poorer classes of children, and defraying the entire school expenses of those who have no one else to pay for them. The objections which are urged with reason against State education do not apply to the enforcement of education by the State, but to the State's taking upon itself to direct that education; which is a totally different thing. That the whole or any large part of the education of the people should be in State hands, I go as far as anyone in deprecating. All that has been said of the importance of individuality of character, and diversity in opinions and modes of conduct, involves, as of the same unspeakable importance, diversity of education. A general State education is a mere contrivance for molding people to be exactly like one another; and as the mold in which it casts them is that which pleases the predominant power in the government—whether this be a monarch, a priesthood, an aristocracy, or the majority of the existing generation—in proportion as it is efficient and successful, it establishes a despotism over the mind, leading by natural tendency to one over the body. An education established and controlled by the State should only exist, if it exist at all, as one among many competing experiments, carried on for the purpose of example and stimulus to keep the others up to a certain standard of excellence. Unless, indeed, when society in general is in so backward a state that it could not or would not provide for itself any proper institutions of education unless the government undertook the task, then, indeed, the government may, as the less of two great evils, take upon itself the business of schools and universities, as it may that of joint stock companies when private enterprise in a shape fitted for undertaking great works of industry does not exist in the country. But in general, if the country contains a sufficient number of persons qualified to provide education under government auspices, the same persons would be able and willing to give an equally good education on the voluntary principle, under the assurance of remuneration afforded by a law rendering education compulsory, combined with State aid to those unable to defray the expense.

The instrument for enforcing the law could be no other than public examinations, extending to all children and beginning at an early age. An age might be fixed at which every child must be examined, to ascertain if he (or she) is able to read. If a child proves unable, the father, unless he has some sufficient ground of excuse, might be subjected to a moderate fine, to be worked out, if necessary, by his labor, and the child might be put to school at his expense. Once in every year the examination should be renewed, with a gradually extending range of subjects, so as to make the universal acquisition and, what is more, retention of a certain minimum of general knowledge virtually compulsory. Beyond that minimum there should be voluntary examinations on all subjects, at which all who come up to a certain standard of proficiency might claim a certificate. To prevent the State from exercising, through these arrangements, an improper influence over opinion, the knowledge required for passing an examination (beyond the merely instrumental parts of knowledge, such as languages and their use) should, even in the higher classes of examinations, be confined to facts and positive science exclusively. The examinations on religion, politics, or other disputed topics should not turn on the truth or falsehood of opinions, but on the matter of fact that such and such an opinion is held, on such grounds, by such authors, or schools, or churches. Under this system, the rising generation would be no worse off in regard to all disputed truths than they are at present; they would be brought up either churchmen or dissenters as they now are, the State merely taking care that they should be instructed churchmen, or instructed dissenters. There would be nothing to hinder them from being taught religion, if their parents chose, at the same schools where they were taught other things. All attempts by the State to bias the conclusions of its citizens on disputed subjects are evil; but it may very properly offer to ascertain and certify that a person possesses the knowledge requisite to make his conclusions on any given subject worth attending to. A student of philosophy would be the better for being able to stand an examination both in Locke and in Kant, whichever of the two he takes up with, or even if with neither: and there is no reasonable objection to examining an atheist in the evidences of Christianity, provided he is not required to profess a belief in them. The examinations, however, in the higher branches of knowledge should, I conceive, be entirely voluntary. It would be giving too dangerous a power to governments were they allowed to exclude anyone from professions, even from the profession of teacher, for alleged deficiency of qualifications; and I think, with Wilhelm von Humboldt, that degrees or other public certificates of scientific or professional acquirements should be given to all who present themselves for examination and stand the test, but that such certificates should confer no advantage over competitors other than the weight which may be attached to their testimony by public opinion.

It is not in the matter of education only that misplaced notions of liberty prevent moral obligations on the part of parents from being recognized, and legal obligations from being imposed, where there are the strongest grounds for the former always, and in many cases for the latter also. The fact itself, of causing the existence of a human being, is one of the most responsible actions in the range of human life. To undertake this responsibility—to bestow a life which may be either a curse or a blessing—unless the being on whom it is to be bestowed will have at least the ordinary chances of a desirable existence, is a crime against that being. And in a country, either overpeopled or threatened with being so, to produce children, beyond a very small number, with the effect of reducing the reward of labor by their competition is a serious offense against all who live by the remuneration of their labor. The laws which, in many countries on the Continent, forbid marriage unless the parties can show that they have the means of supporting a family do not exceed the legitimate powers of the State; and whether such laws be expedient or not (a question mainly dependent on local circumstances and feelings), they are not objectionable as violations of liberty. Such laws are interferences of the State to prohibit a mischievous act—an act injurious to others, which ought to be a subject of reprobation and social stigma, even when it is not deemed expedient to superadd legal punishment. Yet the current ideas of liberty, which bend so easily to real infringements of the freedom of the individual in things which concern only himself, would repel the attempt to put any restraint upon his inclinations when the consequence of their indulgence is a life or lives of wretchedness and depravity to the offspring, with manifold evils to those sufficiently within reach to be in any way affected by their actions. When we compare the strange respect of mankind for liberty with their strange want of respect for it, we might imagine that a man had an indispensable right to do harm to others, and no right at all to please himself without giving pain to anyone.

I have reserved for the last place a large class of questions respecting the limits of government interference, which, though closely connected with the subject of this essay, do not, in strictness, belong to it. These are cases in which the reasons against interference do not turn upon the principle of liberty: the question is not about restraining the actions of individuals, but about helping them; it is asked whether the government should do, or cause to be done, something for their benefit instead of leaving it to be done by themselves, individually or in voluntary combination.

The objections to government interference, when it is not such as to involve infringement of liberty, may be of three kinds:

The first is when the thing to be done is likely to be better done by individuals than by the government. Speaking generally, there is no one so fit to conduct any business, or to determine how or by whom it shall be conducted, as those who are personally interested in it. This principle condemns the interferences, once so common, of the legislature, or the officers of government, with the ordinary processes of industry. But this part of the subject has been sufficiently enlarged upon by political economists, and is not particularly related to the principles of this essay.

The second objection is more nearly allied to our subject. In many cases, though individuals may not do the particular thing so well, on the average, as the officers of government, it is nevertheless desirable that it should be done by them, rather than by the government, as a means to their own mental education—a mode of strengthening their active faculties, exercising their judgment, and giving them a familiar knowledge of the subjects with which they are thus left to deal. This is a principal, though not the sole, recommendation of jury trial (in cases not political); of free and popular local and municipal institutions; of the conduct of industrial and philanthropic enterprises by voluntary associations. These are not questions of liberty, and are connected with that subject only by remote tendencies, but they are questions of development. It belongs to a different occasion from the present to dwell on these things as parts of national education, as being, in truth, the peculiar training of a citizen, the practical part of the political education of a free people, taking them out of the narrow circle of personal and family selfishness, and accustoming them to the comprehension of joint interests, the management of joint concerns—habituating them to act from public or semi-public motives, and guide their conduct by aims which unite instead of isolating them from one another. Without these habits and powers, a free constitution can neither be worked nor preserved, as is exemplified by the too often transitory nature of political freedom in countries where it does not rest upon a sufficient basis of local liberties. The management of purely local business by the localities, and of the great enterprises of industry by the union of those who voluntarily supply the pecuniary means, is further recommended by all the advantages which have been set forth in this essay as belonging to individuality of development and diversity of modes of action. Government operations tend to be everywhere alike. With individuals and voluntary associations, on the contrary, there are varied experiments and endless diversity of experience. What the State can usefully do is to make itself a central depository, and active circulator and diffuser, of the experience resulting from many trials. Its business is to enable each experimentalist to benefit by the experiments of others, instead of tolerating no experiments but its own.

The third and most cogent reason for restricting

the interference of government is the great evil of adding unnecessarily to its power.

Every function superadded to those already exercised by the government causes its influence over hopes and fears to be more widely diffused, and converts, more and more, the active and ambitious part of the public into hangers-on of the government, or of some party which aims at becoming the government. If the roads, the railways, the banks, the insurance offices, the great joint-stock companies, the universities, and the public charities were all of them branches of the government; if, in addition, the municipal corporations and local boards, with all that now devolves on them, became departments of the central administration; if the employees of all these different enterprises were appointed and paid by the government and looked to the government for every rise in life, not all the freedom of the press and popular constitution of the legislature would make this or any other country free otherwise than in name. And the evil would be greater, the more efficiently and scientifically the administrative machinery was constructed—the more skillful the arrangements for obtaining the best qualified hands and heads with which to work it. In England it has of late been proposed that all the members of the civil service of government should be selected by competitive examination, to obtain for these employments the most intelligent and instructed persons procurable; and much has been said and written for and against this proposal. One of the arguments most insisted on by its opponents is that the occupation of a permanent official servant of the State does not hold out sufficient prospects of emolument and importance to attract the highest talents, which will always be able to find a more inviting career in the professions or in the service of companies and other public bodies. One would not have been surprised if this argument had been used by the friends of the proposition as an answer to its principal difficulty. Coming from the opponents it is strange enough. What is urged as an objection is the safety valve of the proposed system. If, indeed, all the high talent of the country could be drawn into the service of the government, a proposal tending to bring about that result might well inspire uneasiness. If every part of the business of society

which required organized concert, or large and comprehensive views, were in the hands of the government, and if government offices were universally filled by the ablest men, all the enlarged culture and practiced intelligence in the country, except the purely speculative, would be concentrated in a numerous bureaucracy, to whom alone the rest of the community would look for all things—the multitude for direction and dictation in all they had to do; the able and aspiring for personal advancement. To be admitted into the ranks of this bureaucracy, and when admitted, to rise therein, would be the sole objects of ambition. Under this *régime* not only is the outside public ill-qualified, for want of practical experience, to criticize or check the mode of operation of the bureaucracy, but even if the accidents of despotic or the natural working of popular institutions occasionally raise to the summit a ruler or rulers of reforming inclinations, no reform can be effected which is contrary to the interest of the bureaucracy. Such is the melancholy condition of the Russian empire, as shown in the accounts of those who have had sufficient opportunity of observation. The Czar himself is powerless against the bureaucratic body; he can send any one of them to Siberia, but he cannot govern without them, or against their will. On every decree of his they have a tacit veto, by merely refraining from carrying it into effect. In countries of more advanced civilization and of a more insurrectionary spirit, the public, accustomed to expect everything to be done for them by the State, or at least to do nothing for themselves without asking from the State not only leave to do it, but even how it is to be done, naturally hold the State responsible for all evil which befalls them, and when the evil exceeds their amount of patience, they rise against the government and make what is called a revolution; whereupon somebody else, with or without legitimate authority from the nation, vaults into the seat, issues his orders to the bureaucracy, and everything goes on much as it did before; the bureaucracy being unchanged, and nobody else being capable of taking their place.

A very different spectacle is exhibited among a people accustomed to transact their own business. In France, a large part of the people, having been engaged in military service, many of whom have held at least the rank of noncommissioned officers, there are in every popular insurrection several persons competent to take the lead and improvise some tolerable plan of action. What the French are in military affairs, the Americans are in every kind of civil business; let them be left without a government, every body of Americans is able to improvise one and to carry on that or any other public business with a sufficient amount of intelligence, order, and decision. This is what every free people ought to be; and a people capable of this is certain to be free; it will never let itself be enslaved by any man or body of men because these are able to seize and pull the reins of the central administration. No bureaucracy can hope to make such a people as this do or undergo anything that they do not like. But where everything is done through the bureaucracy, nothing to which the bureaucracy is really adverse can be done at all. The constitution of such countries is an organization of the experience and practical ability of the nation into a disciplined body for the purpose of governing the rest; and the more perfect that organization is in itself, the more successful in drawing to itself and educating for itself the persons of greatest capacity from all ranks of the community, the more complete is the bondage of all, the members of the bureaucracy included. For the governors are as much the slaves of their organization and discipline as the governed are of the governors. A Chinese mandarin is as much the tool and creature of a despotism as the humblest cultivator. An individual Jesuit is to the utmost degree of abasement the slave of his order, though the order itself exists for the collective power and importance of its members.

It is not, also, to be forgotten that the absorption of all the principal ability of the country into the governing body is fatal, sooner or later, to the mental activity and progressiveness of the body itself. Banded together as they are—working a system which, like all systems, necessarily proceeds in a great measure by fixed rules—the official body are under the constant temptation of sinking into indolent routine, or, if they now and then desert that mill-horse round, of rushing into some half-examined crudity which has struck the fancy of some leading member of the corps; and the sole check to these closely allied, though seemingly opposite, tendencies, the only stimulus which can keep the ability of the body itself up to a high standard, is liability to the watchful criticism of equal ability outside the body. It is indispensable, therefore, that the means should exist, independently of the government, of forming such ability and furnishing it with the opportunities and experience necessary for a correct judgment of great practical affairs. If we would possess permanently a skillful and efficient body of functionaries—above all a body able to originate and willing to adopt improvements—if we would not have our bureaucracy degenerate into a pedantocracy, this body must not engross all the occupations which form and cultivate the faculties required for the government of mankind.

To determine the point at which evils, so formidable to human freedom and advancement, begin, or rather at which they begin to predominate over the benefits attending the collective application of the force of society, under its recognized chiefs, for the removal of the obstacles which stand in the way of its well-being; to secure as much of the advantages of centralized power and intelligence as can be had without turning into governmental channels too great a proportion of the general activity—is one of the most difficult and complicated questions in the art of government. It is, in a great measure, a question of detail in which many and various considerations must be kept in view, and no absolute rule can be laid down. But I believe that the practical principle in which safety resides, the ideal to be kept in view, the standard by which to test all arrangements intended for overcoming the difficulty, may be conveyed in these words: the greatest dissemination of power consistent with efficiency; but the greatest possible centralization of information and diffusion of it from the center. Thus, in municipal administration, there would be, as in the New England states, a very minute division among separate officers, chosen by the localities, of all business which is not better left to the persons directly interested; but besides this, there would be, in each department of local affairs, a central superintendence, forming a branch of the general government. The organ of this superintendence would concentrate, as in a focus, the variety of information and experience derived from the conduct of that branch of public business in all the localities, from everything analogous which is done in foreign countries, and from the general principles of political science. This central organ should have a right to know all that is done, and its special duty should be that of making the knowledge acquired in one place available for others. Emancipated from the petty prejudices and narrow views of a locality by its elevated position and comprehensive sphere of observation, its advice would naturally carry much authority; but its actual power, as a permanent institution, should, I conceive, be limited to compelling the local officers to obey the laws laid down for their guidance. In all things not provided for by general rules, those officers should be left to their own judgment, under responsibility to their constituents. For the violation of rules, they should be responsible to law, and the rules themselves should be laid down by the legislature; the central administrative authority only watching over their execution and, if they were not properly carried into effect, appealing, according to the nature of the case, to the tribunals to enforce the law, or to the constituencies to dismiss the functionaries who had not executed it according to its spirit. Such, in its general conception, is the central superintendence which the Poor Law Board is intended to exercise over the administrators of the Poor Rate throughout the country. Whatever powers the Board exercises beyond this limit were right and necessary in that peculiar case, for the cure of rooted habits of maladministration in matters deeply affecting not the localities merely, but the whole community; since no locality has a moral right to make itself by mismanagement a nest of pauperism, necessarily overflowing into other localities and impairing the moral and physical condition of the whole laboring community. The powers of administrative coercion and subordinate legislation possessed by the Poor Law Board (but which, owing to the state of opinion on the subject, are very scantily exercised by them), though perfectly justifiable in a case of first-rate national interest, would be wholly out of place in the superintendence of interests purely local. But a central organ of information and instruction for all the localities would be equally valuable in all departments of administration. A government can-

not have too much of the kind of activity which does not impede but aids and stimulates, individual exertion and development. The mischief begins when, instead of calling forth the activity and powers of individuals and bodies, it substitutes its own activity for theirs; when, instead of informing, advising, and, upon occasion, denouncing, it makes them work in fetters, or bids them stand aside and does their work instead of them. The worth of a State, in the long run, is the worth of the individuals composing it; and a State which postpones the interests of their mental expansion and elevation to a little more of administrative skill, or of that semblance of it which practice gives in the details of business; a State which dwarfs its men, in order that they may be more docile instruments in its hands even for beneficial purposes—will find that with small men no great thing can really be accomplished; and that the perfection of machinery to which it has sacrificed everything will in the end avail it nothing, for want of the vital power which, in order that the machine might work more smoothly, it has preferred to banish.

## Notes

1. These words had scarcely been written when, as if to give them an emphatic contradiction, occurred the Government Press Prosecutions of 1858. That ill-judged interference with the liberty of public discussion has not, however, induced me to alter a single word in the text, nor has it at all weakened my conviction that, moments of panic excepted, the era of pains and penalties for political discussion has, in our own country, passed away. For, in the first place, the prosecutions were not persisted in; and, in the second, they were never, properly speaking, political prosecutions. The offense charged was not that of criticizing institutions or the acts or persons of rulers, but of circulating what was deemed an immoral doctrine, the lawfulness of tyrannicide.

If the arguments of the present chapter are of any validity, there ought to exist the fullest liberty of professing and discussing, as a matter of ethical conviction, any doctrine, however immoral it may be considered. It would, therefore, be irrelevant and out of place to examine here whether the doctrine of tyrannicide deserves that title. I shall content myself with saying that the subject has been at all times one of the open questions of morals; that the act of a private citizen in striking down a criminal who, by raising himself above the law, has placed himself beyond the reach of legal punishment or control has been accounted by whole nations, and by some of the best and wisest of men, not a crime but an act of exalted virtue; and that, right or wrong, it is not of the nature of assassination, but of civil war. As such, I hold that the instigation to it, in a specific case, may be a proper subject of punishment, but only if an overt act has followed, and at least a probable connection can be established between the act and the instigation. Even then it is not a foreign government but the very government assailed which alone, in the exercise of self-defense, can legitimately punish attacks directed against its own existence.

2. Thomas Pooley, Bodmin Assizes, July 31, 1857. In December following, he received a free pardon from the Crown.

3. George Jacob Holyoake, August 17, 1857; Edward Truelove, July 1857.

4. Baron de Gleichen, Marlborough-street Police Court, August 4, 1857.

5. Ample warning may be drawn from the large infusion of the passions of a persecutor, which mingled with the general display of the worst parts of our national character on the occasion of the Sepoy insurrection. The ravings of fanatics or charlatans from the pulpit may be unworthy of notice; but the heads of the Evangelical party have announced as their principle for the government of Hindus and Mohammedans that no schools be supported by public money in which the Bible is not taught, and by necessary consequence that no public employment be given to any but real or pretended Christians. An Undersecretary of State, in a speech delivered to his constituents on the 12th of November, 1857, is reported to have said: "Toleration of their faith" (the faith of a hundred millions of British subjects), "the superstition which they called religion, by the British Government, had had the effect of retarding the ascendancy of the British name, and preventing the salutary growth of Christianity. . . . Toleration was the great cornerstone of the religious liberties of this country; but do not let them abuse that precious word 'toleration.' As he understood it, it means the complete liberty to all, freedom of worship, *among Christians, who worshiped upon the same foundation.* It meant toleration of all sects and denominations of *Christians who believed in the one mediation.*" I desire to call attention to the fact that a man who has been deemed fit to fill a high office in the government of this country under a liberal ministry maintains the doctrine that all who do not believe in the divinity of Christ are beyond the pale of tol-

eration. Who, after this imbecile display, can indulge the illusion that religious persecution has passed away, never to return?

6. *The Spheres and Duties of Government,* from the German of Baron Wilhelm von Humboldt, pages 11 to 13.

7. Stirling's *Essays.*

8. There is something both contemptible and frightful in the sort of evidence on which, of late years, any person can be judicially declared unfit for the management of his affairs; and after his death, his disposal of his property can be set aside if there is enough of it to pay the expenses of litigation—which are charged on the property itself. All the minute details of his daily life are pried into, and whatever is found which, seen through the medium of the perceiving and describing faculties of the lowest of the low, bears an appearance unlike absolute commonplace, is laid before the jury as evidence of insanity, and often with success; the jurors being little, if at all, less vulgar and ignorant than the witnesses, while the judges, with that extraordinary want of knowledge of human nature and life which continually astonishes us in English lawyers, often help to mislead them. These trials speak volumes as to the state of feeling and opinion among the vulgar with regard to human liberty. So far from setting any value on individuality—so far from respecting the right of each individual to act, in things indifferent, as seems good to his own judgment and inclinations, judges and juries cannot even conceive that a person in a state of sanity can desire such freedom. In former days, when it was proposed to burn atheists, charitable people used to suggest putting them in a madhouse instead; it would be nothing surprising nowadays were we to see this done, and the doers applauding themselves because, instead of persecuting for religion, they had adopted so humane and Christian a mode of treating these unfortunates, not without a silent satisfaction at their having thereby obtained their deserts.

9. The case of the Bombay Parsees is a curious instance in point. When this industrious and enterprising tribe, the descendants of the Persian fire-worshipers, flying from their native country before the Caliphs, arrived in western India, they were admitted to toleration by the Hindu sovereigns, on condition of not eating beef. When those regions afterward fell under the dominion of Mohammedan conquerors, the Parsees obtained from them a continuance of indulgence, on condition of refraining from pork. What was at first obedience to authority became a second nature, and the Parsees to this day abstain both from beef and pork. Though not required by their religion, the double abstinence has had time to grow into a custom of their tribe; and custom, in the East, is a religion.

# Considerations on Representative Government

## CHAPTER 3

### *That the Ideally Best Form of Government Is Representative Government*

It has long (perhaps throughout the entire duration of British freedom) been a common form of speech, that if a good despot could be insured, despotic monarchy would be the best form of government. I look upon this as a radical and most pernicious misconception of what good government is, which, until it can be got rid of, will fatally vitiate all our speculations on government.

The supposition is, that absolute power, in the hands of an eminent individual, would insure a virtuous and intelligent performance of all the duties of government. Good laws would be established and enforced, bad laws would be reformed; the best men would be placed in all situations of trust; justice would be as well administered, the public burdens would be as light and as judiciously imposed, every branch of administration would be as purely and as intelligently conducted as the circumstances of the country and its degree of intellectual and moral cultivation would admit. I am willing, for the sake of the argument, to concede all this, but I must point out how great the concession is, how much more is needed to produce even an approximation to these results than is conveyed in the simple expression, a good despot. Their realization would in fact imply, not merely a good monarch, but an all-seeing one. He must be at all times informed correctly, in considerable detail, of the conduct and working of every branch of administration, in every district of the country, and must be able, in the twenty-four hours per day, which are all that is granted to a king as to the humblest laborer, to give an effective share of attention and superintendence to all parts of this vast field; or he must at least be capable of discerning and

choosing out, from among the mass of his subjects, not only a large abundance of honest and able men, fit to conduct every branch of public administration under supervision and control, but also the small number of men of eminent virtues and talents who can be trusted not only to do without that supervision, but to exercise it themselves over others. So extraordinary are the faculties and energies required for performing this task in any supportable manner, that the good despot whom we are supposing can hardly be imagined as consenting to undertake it unless as a refuge from intolerable evils, and a transitional preparation for something beyond. But the argument can do without even this immense item in the account. Suppose the difficulty vanished. What should we then have? One man of superhuman mental activity managing the entire affairs of a mentally passive people. Their passivity is implied in the very idea of absolute power. The nation as a whole, and every individual composing it, are without any potential voice in their own destiny. They exercise no will in respect to their collective interests. All is decided for them by a will not their own, which it is legally a crime for them to disobey. What sort of human beings can be formed under such a regimen? What development can either their thinking or their active faculties attain under it? On matters of pure theory they might perhaps be allowed to speculate, so long as their speculations either did not approach politics, or had not the remotest connection with its practice. On practical affairs they could at most be only suffered to suggest; and even under the most moderate of despots, none but persons of already admitted or reputed superiority could hope that their suggestions would be known to, much less regarded by, those who had the management of affairs. A person must have a very unusual taste for intellectual exercise in and for itself who will put himself to the trouble of thought when it is to have no outward effect, or qualify himself for functions which he has no chance of being allowed to exercise. The only sufficient incitement to mental exertion, in any but a few minds in a generation, is the prospect of some practical use to be made of its results. It does not follow that the nation will be wholly destitute of intellectual power. The common business of life, which must necessarily be performed by each individual or family for themselves, will call forth some amount of intelligence and practical ability within a certain narrow range of ideas. There may be a select class of *savants* who cultivate science with a view to its physical uses or for the pleasure of the pursuit. There will be a bureaucracy, and persons in training for the bureaucracy, who will be taught at least some empirical maxims of government and public administration. There may be, and often has been, a systematic organization of the best mental power in the country in some special direction (commonly military) to promote the grandeur of the despot. But the public at large remain without information and without interest on all the greater matters of practice; or, if they have any knowledge of them, it is but a *dilettante* knowledge, like that which people have of the mechanical arts who have never handled a tool. Nor is it only in their intelligence that they suffer. Their moral capacities are equally stunted. Wherever the sphere of action of human beings is artificially circumscribed, their sentiments are narrowed and dwarfed in the same proportion. The food of feeling is action; even domestic affection lives upon voluntary good offices. Let a person have nothing to do for his country, and he will not care for it. It has been said of old that in a despotism there is at most but one patriot, the despot himself; and the saying rests on a just appreciation of the effects of absolute subjection even to a good and wise master. Religion remains; and here, at least, it may be thought, is an agency that may be relied on for lifting men's eyes and minds above the dust at their feet. But religion, even supposing it to escape perversion for the purposes of despotism, ceases in these circumstances to be a social concern, and narrows into a personal affair between an individual and his Maker, in which the issue at stake is but his private salvation. Religion in this shape is quite consistent with the most selfish and contracted egoism, and identifies the votary as little in feeling with the rest of his kind as sensuality itself.

A good despotism means a government in which, so far as depends on the despot, there is no positive oppression by officers of state, but in which all the collective interests of the people are managed for them, all the thinking that has relation to collective interests done for them, and in which their minds are formed by, and consenting to, this abdication of their own energies. Leaving things to the government, like leaving them to Providence, is synonymous with caring nothing about them, and accepting their results, when disagreeable, as visitations of Nature. With the exception, therefore, of a few studious men who take an intellectual interest in speculation for its own sake, the intelligence and sentiments of the whole people are given up to the material interests, and when these are provided for, to the amusement and ornamentation of private life. But to say this is to say, if the whole testimony of history is worth any thing, that the era of national decline has arrived; that is, if the nation had ever attained any thing to decline from. If it has never risen above the condition of an Oriental people, in that condition it continues to stagnate; but if, like Greece or Rome, it had realized any thing higher, through the energy, patriotism, and enlargement of mind, which, as national qualities, are the fruits solely of freedom, it relapses in a few generations into the Oriental state. And that state does not mean stupid tranquillity, with security against change for the worse; it often means being overrun, conquered, and reduced to domestic slavery either by a stronger despot, or by the nearest barbarous people who retain along with their savage rudeness the energies of freedom.

Such are not merely the natural tendencies, but the inherent necessities of despotic government, from which there is no outlet, unless is so far as the despotism consents not to be despotism; in so far as the supposed good despot abstains from exercising his power, and, though holding it in reserve, allows the general business of government to go on as if the people really governed themselves. However little probable it may be, we may imagine a despot observing many of the rules and restraints of constitutional government. He might allow such freedom of the press and of discussion as would enable a public opinion to form and express itself on national affairs. He might suffer local interests to be managed, without the interference of authority, by the people themselves. He might even surround himself with a council or councils of government, freely chosen by the whole or some portion of the nation, retaining in his own hands the power of taxation, and the supreme legislative as well as executive authority. Were he to act thus, and so far abdicate as a despot, he would do away with a considerable part of the evils characteristic of despotism. Political activity and capacity for public affairs would no longer be prevented from growing up in the body of the nation, and a public opinion would form itself, not the mere echo of the government. But such improvement would be the beginning of new difficulties. This public opinion, independent of the monarch's dictation, must be either with him or against him; if not the one, it will be the other. All governments must displease many persons, and these having now regular organs, and being able to express their sentiments, opinions adverse to the measures of government would often be expressed. What is the monarch to do when these unfavorable opinions happen to be in the majority? Is he to alter his course? Is he to defer to the nation? If so, he is no longer a despot, but a constitutional king; an organ or first minister of the people, distinguished only by being irremovable. If not, he must either put down opposition by his despotic power, or there will arise a permanent antagonism between the people and one man, which can have but one possible ending. Not even a religious principle of passive obedience and "right divine" would long ward off the natural consequences of such a position. The monarch would have to succumb, and conform to the conditions of constitutional royalty or give place to some one who would. The despotism, being thus chiefly nominal, would possess few of the advantages supposed to belong to absolute monarchy, while it would realize in a very imperfect degree those of a free government, since, however great an amount of liberty the citizens might practically enjoy, they could never forget that they held it on sufferance, and by a concession which, under the existing constitution of the state, might at any moment be resumed: that they were legally slaves, though of a prudent or indulgent master.

It is not much to be wondered at if impatient or disappointed reformers, groaning under the impediments opposed to the most salutary public improvements by the ignorance, the indifference, the untractableness, the perverse obstinacy of a people, and the corrupt combinations of selfish private interests, armed with the powerful weapons afforded by free institutions, should at times sigh for a strong hand to bear down all these obstacles, and compel a recalcitrant people to be better governed. But (setting aside the fact that for one despot who now and then reforms an abuse, there are ninety-nine who do nothing but create them) those who look in any such direction for the realization of their hopes leave out of the idea of good government its principal element, the improvement of the people themselves. One of the benefits of freedom is that under it the ruler can not pass by the people's minds and amend their affairs for them without amending *them.* If it were possible for a people to be well governed in spite of themselves, their good government would last no longer than the freedom of a people usually lasts who have been liberated by foreign arms without their own co-operation. It is true, a despot may educate the people, and to do so really would be the best apology for his despotism. But any education which aims at making human beings other than machines, in the long run makes them claim to have the control of their own actions. The leaders of French philosophy in the eighteenth century had been educated by the Jesuits. Even Jesuit education, it seems, was sufficiently real to call forth the appetite for freedom. Whatever invigorates the faculties, in however small a measure, creates an increased desire for their more unimpeded exercise; and a popular education is a failure if it educates the people for any state but that which it will certainly induce them to desire, and most probably to demand.

I am far from condemning, in cases of extreme exigency, the assumption of absolute power in the form of temporary dictatorship. Free nations have, in times of old, conferred such power by their own choice, as a necessary medicine for diseases of the body politic which could not be got rid of by less violent means. But its acceptance, even for a time strictly limited, can only be excused, if, like Solon or Pittacus, the dictator employs the whole power he assumes in removing the obstacles which debar the nation from the enjoyment of freedom. A good despotism is an altogether false ideal, which practically (except as a means to some temporary purpose) becomes the most senseless and dangerous of chimeras. Evil for evil, a good despotism, in a country at all advanced in civilization, is more noxious than a bad one, for it is far more relaxing and enervating to the thoughts, feelings, and energies of the people. The despotism of Augustus prepared the Romans for Tiberius. If the whole tone of their character had not first been prostrated by nearly two generations of that mild slavery, they would probably have had spirit enough left to rebel against the more odious one.

There is no difficulty in showing that the ideally best form of government is that in which the sovereignty, or supreme controlling power in the last resort, is vested in the entire aggregate of the community, every citizen not only having a voice in the exercise of that ultimate sovereignty, but being, at least occasionally, called on to take an actual part in the government by the personal discharge of some public function, local or general.

To test this proposition, it has to be examined in reference to the two branches into which, as pointed out in the last chapter, the inquiry into the goodness of a government conveniently divides itself, namely, how far it promotes the good management of the affairs of society by means of the existing faculties, moral, intellectual, and active, of its various members, and what is its effect in improving or deteriorating those faculties.

The ideally best form of government, it is scarcely necessary to say, does not mean one which is practicable or eligible in all states of civilization, but the one which, in the circumstances in which it is practicable and eligible, is attended with the greatest amount of beneficial consequences, immediate and prospective. A completely popular government is the only polity which can make out any claim to this

character. It is pre-eminent in both the departments between which the excellence of a political Constitution is divided. It is both more favorable to present good government, and promotes a better and higher form of national character than any other polity whatsoever.

Its superiority in reference to present well-being rests upon two principles, of as universal truth and applicability as any general propositions which can be laid down respecting human affairs. The first is, that the rights and interests of every or any person are only secure from being disregarded when the person interested is himself able, and habitually disposed to stand up for them. The second is, that the general prosperity attains a greater height, and is more widely diffused, in proportion to the amount and variety of the personal energies enlisted in promoting it.

Putting these two propositions into a shape more special to their present application—human beings are only secure from evil at the hands of others in proportion as they have the power of being, and are *self-protecting;* and they only achieve a high degree of success in their struggle with Nature in proportion as they are *self-dependent,* relying on what they themselves can do, either separately or in concert, rather than on what others can do for them.

The former proposition—that each is the only safe guardian of his own rights and interests—is one of those elementary maxims of prudence which every person capable of conducting his own affairs implicitly acts upon wherever he himself is interested. Many, indeed, have a great dislike to it as a political doctrine, and are fond of holding it up to obloquy as a doctrine of universal selfishness. To which we may answer, that whenever it ceases to be true that mankind, as a rule, prefer themselves to others, and those nearest to them to those more remote, from that moment Communism is not only practicable, but the only defensible form of society, and will, when that time arrives, be assuredly carried into effect. For my own part, not believing in universal selfishness, I have no difficulty in admitting that Communism would even now be practicable among the *élite* of mankind, and may become so among the rest. But as this opinion is any thing but popular with those defenders of existing institutions who find fault with the doctrine of the general predominance of self interest, I am inclined to think they do in reality believe that most men consider themselves before other people. It is not, however, necessary to affirm even thus much in order to support the claim of all to participate in the sovereign power. We need not suppose that when power resides in an exclusive class, that class will knowingly and deliberately sacrifice the other classes to themselves: it suffices that, in the absence of its natural defenders, the interest of the excluded is always in danger of being overlooked; and, when looked at, is seen with very different eyes from those of the persons whom it directly concerns. In this country, for example, what are called the working-classes may be considered as excluded from all direct participation in the government. I do not believe that the classes who do participate in it have in general any intention of sacrificing the working classes to themselves. They once had that intention; witness the persevering attempts so long made to keep down wages by law. But in the present day, their ordinary disposition is the very opposite: they willingly make considerable sacrifices, especially of their pecuniary interest, for the benefit of the working classes, and err rather by too lavish and indiscriminating beneficence; nor do I believe that any rulers in history have been actuated by a more sincere desire to do their duty toward the poorer portion of their countrymen. Yet does Parliament, or almost any of the members composing it, ever for an instant look at any question with the eyes of a working man? When a subject arises in which the laborers as such have an interest, is it regarded from any point of view but that of the employers of labor? I do not say that the working men's view of these questions is in general nearer to truth than the other, but it is sometimes quite as near; and in any case it ought to be respectfully listened to, instead of being, as it is, not merely turned away from, but ignored. On the question of strikes, for instance, it is doubtful if there is so much as one among the leading members of either House who is not firmly convinced that the reason of the matter is unqualifiedly on the side of the masters, and that the men's view of it is simply absurd. Those who have studied the question know well how far this is from being the case, and in how different, and how infinitely less superficial a manner the point would have to be argued if the classes who strike were able to make themselves heard in Parliament.

It is an inherent condition of human affairs that no intention, however sincere, of protecting the interests of others can make it safe or salutary to tie up their own hands. Still more obviously true is it that by their own hands only can any positive and durable improvement of their circumstances in life be worked out. Through the joint influence of these two principles, all free communities have both been more exempt from social injustice and crime, and have attained more brilliant prosperity than any others, or than they themselves after they lost their freedom. Contrast the free states of the world, while their freedom lasted, with the contemporary subjects of monarchical or oligarchical despotism: the Greek cities with the Persian satrapies; the Italian republics, and the free towns of Flanders and Germany, with the feudal monarchies of Europe; Switzerland, Holland, and England with Austria or ante-revolutionary France. Their superior prosperity was too obvious ever to have been gainsaid; while their superiority in good government and social relations is proved by the prosperity, and is manifest besides in every page of history. If we compare, not one age with another, but the different governments which coexisted in the same age, no amount of disorder which exaggeration itself can pretend to have existed amid the publicity of the free states can be compared for a moment with the contemptuous trampling upon the mass of the people which pervaded the whole life of the monarchical countries, or the disgusting individual tyranny which was of more than daily occurrence under the systems of plunder which they called fiscal arrangements, and in the secrecy of their frightful courts of justice.

It must be acknowledged that the benefits of freedom, so far as they have hitherto been enjoyed, were obtained by the extension of its privileges to a part only of the community, and that a government in which they are extended impartially to all is a desideratum still unrealized. But, though every approach to this has an independent value, and in many cases more than an approach could not, in the existing state of general improvement, be made, the participation of all in these benefits is the ideally perfect conception of free government. In proportion as any, no matter who, are excluded from it, the interests of the excluded are left without the guaranty accorded to the rest, and they themselves have less scope and encouragement than they might otherwise have to that exertion of their energies for the good of themselves and of the community to which the general prosperity is always proportioned.

Thus stands the case as regards present well-being—the good management of the affairs of the existing generation. If we now pass to the influence of the form of government upon character, we shall find the superiority of popular government over every other to be, if possible, still more decided and indisputable.

This question really depends upon a still more fundamental one, viz., which of two common types of character, for the general good of humanity, it is most desirable should predominate—the active or the passive type; that which struggles against evils, or that which endures them, that which bends to circumstances, or that which endeavors to bend circumstances to itself.

The commonplaces of moralists and the general sympathies of mankind are in favor of the passive type. Energetic characters may be admired, but the acquiescent and submissive are those which most men personally prefer. The passiveness of our neighbors increases our own sense of security and plays into the hands of our willfulness. Passive characters, if we do not happen to need their activity, seem an obstruction the less in our own path. A contented character is not a dangerous rival. Yet nothing is more certain than that improvement in human affairs is wholly the work of the uncontented characters; and, moreover, that it is much easier for an active mind to acquire the virtues of patience than for a passive one to assume those of energy.

Of the three varieties of mental excellence, intellectual, practical, and moral, there never could be any doubt, in regard to the first two, which side had the advantage. All intellectual superiority is the fruit of active effort. Enterprise, the desire to keep moving, to

be trying and accomplishing new things for our own benefit or that of others, is the parent even of speculative, and much more of practical talent. The intellectual culture compatible with the other type is of that feeble and vague description which belongs to a mind that stops at amusement or at simple contemplation. The test of real and vigorous thinking, the thinking which ascertains truths instead of dreaming dreams, is successful application to practice. Where that purpose does not exist, to give definiteness, precision, and an intelligible meaning to thought, it generates nothing better than the mystical metaphysics of the Pythagoreans or the Veds. With respect to practical improvement, the case is still more evident. The character which improves human life is that which struggles with natural powers and tendencies, not that which gives way to them. The self-benefiting qualities are all on the side of the active and energetic character, and the habits and conduct which promote the advantage of each individual member of the community must be at least a part of those which conduce most in the end to the advancement of the community as a whole.

But, on the point of moral preferability, there seems at first sight to be room for doubt. I am not referring to the religious feeling which has so generally existed in favor of the inactive character, as being more in harmony with the submission due to the divine will. Christianity, as well as other religions, has fostered this sentiment; but it is the prerogative of Christianity, as regards this and many other perversions, that it is able to throw them off. Abstractedly from religious considerations, a passive character, which yields to obstacles instead of striving to overcome them, may not indeed be very useful to others, no more than to itself, but it might be expected to be at least inoffensive. Contentment is always counted among the moral virtues. But it is a complete error to suppose that contentment is necessarily or naturally attendant on passivity of character; and unless it is, the moral consequences are mischievous. Where there exists a desire for advantages not possessed, the mind which does not potentially possess them by means of its own energies is apt to look with hatred and malice on those who do. The person bestirring himself with hopeful prospects to improve his circumstances is the one who feels good-will toward others engaged in, or who have succeeded in the same pursuit. And where the majority are so engaged, those who do not attain the object have had the tone given to their feelings by the general habit of the country, and ascribe their failure to want of effort or opportunity, or to their personal ill luck. But those who, while desiring what others possess, put no energy into striving for it, are either incessantly grumbling that fortune does not do for them what they do not attempt to do for themselves, or overflowing with envy and ill-will toward those who possess what they would like to have.

In proportion as success in life is seen or believed to be the fruit of fatality or accident and not of exertion, in that same ratio does envy develop itself as a point of national character. The most envious of all mankind are the Orientals. In Oriental moralists, in Oriental tales, the envious man is markedly prominent. In real life, he is the terror of all who possess any thing desirable, be it a palace, a handsome child, or even good health and spirits: the supposed effect of his mere look constitutes the all-pervading superstition of the evil eye. Next to Orientals in envy, as in inactivity, are some of the Southern Europeans. The Spaniards pursued all their great men with it, embittered their lives, and generally succeeded in putting an early stop to their successes.[1] With the French, who are essentially a Southern people, the double education of despotism and Catholicism has, in spite of their impulsive temperament, made submission and endurance the common character of the people, and their most received notion of wisdom and excellence; and if envy of one another, and of all superiority, is not more rife among them than it is, the circumstance must be ascribed to the many valuable counteracting elements in the French character, and most of all to the great individual energy which, though less persistent and more intermittent than in the self-helping and struggling Anglo-Saxons, has nevertheless manifested itself among the French in nearly every direction in which the operation of their institutions has been favorable to it.

There are, no doubt, in all countries, really contented characters, who not merely do not seek, but do not desire what they do not already possess, and these

naturally bear no ill-will toward such as have apparently a more favored lot. But the great mass of seeming contentment is real discontent, combined with indolence or self-indulgence, which, taking no legitimate means of raising itself, delights in bringing others down to its own level. And if we look narrowly even at the cases of innocent contentment, we perceive that they only win our admiration when the indifference is solely to improvement in outward circumstances, and there is a striving for perpetual advancement in spiritual worth, or at least a disinterested zeal to benefit others. The contented man, or the contented family, who have no ambition to make any one else happier, to promote the good of their country or their neighborhood, or to improve themselves in moral excellence, excite in us neither admiration nor approval. We rightly ascribe this sort of contentment to mere unmanliness and want of spirit. The content which we approve is an ability to do cheerfully without what can not be had, a just appreciation of the comparative value of different objects of desire, and a willing renunciation of the less when incompatible with the greater. These, however, are excellences more natural to the character, in proportion as it is actively engaged in the attempt to improve its own or some other lot. He who is continually measuring his energy against difficulties, learns what are the difficulties insuperable to him, and what are those which, though he might overcome, the success is not worth the cost. He whose thoughts and activities are all needed for, and habitually employed in, practicable and useful enterprises, is the person of all others least likely to let his mind dwell with brooding discontent upon things either not worth attaining, or which are not so to him. Thus the active, self-helping character is not only intrinsically the best, but is the likeliest to acquire all that is really excellent or desirable in the opposite type.

The striving, go-ahead character of England and the United States is only a fit subject of disapproving criticism on account of the very secondary objects on which it commonly expends its strength. In itself it is the foundation of the best hopes for the general improvement of mankind. It has been acutely remarked, that whenever any thing goes amiss, the habitual impulse of French people is to say, "Il faut de la patience;" and of English people, "What a shame!" The people who think it a shame when anything goes wrong—who rush to the conclusion that the evil could and ought to have been prevented, are those who, in the long run, do most to make the world better. If the desires are low placed, if they extend to little beyond physical comfort and the show of riches, the immediate results of the energy will not be much more than the continual extension of man's power over material objects; but even this makes room, and prepares the mechanical appliances for the greatest intellectual and social achievements; and while the energy is there, some persons will apply it, and it will be applied more and more, to the perfecting, not of outward circumstances alone, but of man's inward nature. Inactivity, unaspiringness, absence of desire, is a more fatal hinderance to improvement than any misdirection of energy, and is that through which alone, when existing in the mass, any very formidable misdirection by an energetic few becomes possible. It is this, mainly which retains in a savage or semi-savage state the great majority of the human race.

Now there can be no kind of doubt that the passive type of character is favored by the government of one or a few, and the active self-helping type by that of the many. Irresponsible rulers need the quiescence of the ruled more than they need any activity but that which they can compel. Submissiveness to the prescriptions of men as necessities of nature is the lesson inculcated by all governments upon those who are wholly without participation in them. The will of superiors, and the law as the will of superiors, must be passively yielded to. But no men are mere instruments or materials in the hands of their rulers who have will, or spirit, or a spring of internal activity in the rest of their proceedings, and any manifestation of these qualities, instead of receiving encouragement from despots, has to get itself forgiven by them. Even when irresponsible rulers are not sufficiently conscious of danger from the mental activity of their subjects to be desirous of repressing it, the position itself is a repression. Endeavor is even more effectually restrained by the certainty of its impotence than by any positive discouragement. Between subjection to the will of others and the virtues of self-help and self-government there

is a natural incompatibility. This is more or less complete according as the bondage is strained or relaxed. Rulers differ very much in the length to which they carry the control of the free agency of their subjects, or the suppression of it by managing their business for them. But the difference is in degree, not in principle; and the best despots often go the greatest lengths in chaining up the free agency of their subjects. A bad despot, when his own personal indulgences have been provided for, may sometimes be willing to let the people alone; but a good despot insists on doing them good by making them do their own business in a better way than they themselves know of. The regulations which restricted to fixed processes all the leading branches of French manufactures were the work of the great Colbert.

Very different is the state of the human faculties where a human being feels himself under no other external restraint than the necessities of nature, or mandates of society which he has his share in imposing, and which it is open to him, if he thinks them wrong, publicly to dissent from, and exert himself actively to get altered. No doubt, under a government partially popular, this freedom may be exercised even by those who are not partakers in the full privileges of citizenship; but it is a great additional stimulus to any one's self-help and self-reliance when he starts from an even ground, and has not to feel that his success depends on the impression he can make upon the sentiments and dispositions of a body of whom he is not one. It is a great discouragement to an individual, and a still greater one to a class, to be left out of the constitution; to be reduced to plead from outside the door to the arbiters of their destiny, not taken into the consultation within. The maximum of the invigorating effect of freedom upon the character is only obtained when the person acted on either is, or is looking forward to become, a citizen as fully privileged as any other. What is still more important than even this matter of feeling is the practical discipline which the character obtains from the occasional demand made upon the citizens to exercise, for a time and in their turn, some social function. It is not sufficiently considered how little there is in most men's ordinary life to give any largeness either to their conceptions or to their sentiments. Their work is a routine; not a labor of love, but of self-interest in the most elementary form, the satisfaction of daily wants; neither the thing done, nor the process of doing it, introduces the mind to thoughts or feelings extending beyond individuals; if instructive books are within their reach, there is no stimulus to read them; and, in most cases, the individual has no access to any person of cultivation much superior to his own. Giving him something to do for the public supplies, in a measure, all these deficiencies. If circumstances allow the amount of public duty assigned him to be considerable, it makes him an educated man. Notwithstanding the defects of the social system and moral ideas of antiquity, the practice of the dicastery and the ecclesia raised the intellectual standard of an average Athenian citizen far beyond any thing of which there is yet an example in any other mass of men, ancient or modern. The proofs of this are apparent in every page of our great historian of Greece; but we need scarcely look farther than to the high quality of the addresses which their great orators deemed best calculated to act with effect on their understanding and will. A benefit of the same kind, though far less in degree, is produced on Englishmen of the lower middle class by their liability to be placed on juries and to serve parish offices, which, though it does not occur to so many, nor is so continuous, nor introduces them to so great a variety of elevated considerations as to admit of comparison with the public education which every citizen of Athens obtained from her democratic institutions, makes them nevertheless very different beings, in range of ideas and development of faculties, from those who have done nothing in their lives but drive a quill, or sell goods over a counter. Still more salutary is the moral part of the instruction afforded by the participation of the private citizen, if even rarely, in public functions. He is called upon, while so engaged, to weigh interests not his own; to be guided, in case of conflicting claims, by another rule than his private partialities; to apply, at every turn, principles and maxims which have for their reason of existence the general good; and he usually finds associated with him in the same work minds more familiarized than his own with these ideas and operations, whose study it will be to supply reasons to his understanding, and stimulation to his feeling for the general good. He is

made to feel himself one of the public, and whatever is their interest to be his interest. Where this school of public spirit does not exist, scarcely any sense is entertained that private persons, in no eminent social situation, owe any duties to society except to obey the laws and submit to the government. There is no unselfish sentiment of identification with the public. Every thought and feeling, either of interest or of duty, is absorbed in the individual and in the family. The man never thinks of any collective interest, of any objects to be pursued jointly with others, but only in competition with them, and in some measure at their expense. A neighbor, not being an ally or an associate, since he is never engaged in any common undertaking for the joint benefit, is therefore only a rival. Thus even private morality suffers, while public is actually extinct. Were this the universal and only possible state of things, the utmost aspirations of the lawgiver or the moralist could only stretch to making the bulk of the community a flock of sheep innocently nibbling the grass side by side.

From these accumulated considerations, it is evident that the only government which can fully satisfy all the exigencies of the social state is one in which the whole people participate; that any participation, even in the smallest public function, is useful; that the participation should every where be as great as the general degree of improvement of the community will allow; and that nothing less can be ultimately desirable than the admission of all to a share in the sovereign power of the state. But since all can not, in a community exceeding a single small town, participate personally in any but some very minor portions of the public business, it follows that the ideal type of a perfect government must be representative.

## Note

1. I limit the expression to past time, because I would say nothing derogatory of a great, and now at last a free people, who are entering into the general movement of European progress with a vigor which bids fair to make up rapidly the ground they have lost. No one can doubt what Spanish intellect and energy are capable of; and their faults as a people are chiefly those for which freedom and industrial ardor are a real specific.

# The Subjection of Women

## I

The object of this Essay is to explain, as clearly as I am able, the grounds of an opinion which I have held from the very earliest period when I had formed any opinions at all on social or political matters, and which, instead of being weakened or modified, has been constantly growing stronger by the progress of reflection and the experience of life: That the principle which regulates the existing social relations between the two sexes—the legal subordination of one sex to the other—is wrong in itself, and now one of the chief hindrances to human improvement; and that it ought to be replaced by a principle of perfect equality, admitting no power or privilege on the one side, nor disability on the other.

The very words necessary to express the task I have undertaken, show how arduous it is. But it would be a mistake to suppose that the difficulty of the case must lie in the insufficiency or obscurity of the grounds of reason on which my conviction rests. The difficulty is that which exists in all cases in which there is a mass of feeling to be contended against. So long as an opinion is strongly rooted in the feelings, it gains rather than loses in stability by having a preponderating weight of argument against it. For if it were accepted as a result of argument, the refutation of the argument might shake the solidity of the conviction; but when it rests solely on feeling, the worse it fares in argumentative contest, the more persuaded its adherents are that their feeling must have some deeper ground, which the arguments do not reach; and while the feeling remains, it is always throwing up fresh entrenchments of argument to repair any breach made in the old. And there are so many causes tending to make the feelings connected with this subject the most intense and most deeply-rooted of all those which gather round and protect old institutions and customs, that we need not won-der to find them as yet less undermined and loosed than any of the rest by the progress of the great modern spiritual and social transition; nor suppose that the barbarisms to which men cling longest must be less barbarisms than those which they earlier shake off.

In every respect the burthen is hard on those who attack an almost universal opinion. They must be very fortunate as well as unusually capable if they obtain a hearing at all. They have more difficulty in obtaining a trial, than any other litigants have in getting a verdict. If they do extort a hearing, they are subjected to a set of logical requirements totally different from those exacted from other people. In all other cases, the burthen of proof is supposed to lie with the affirmative. If a person is charged with a murder, it rests with those who accuse him to give proof of his guilt, not with himself to prove his innocence. If there is a difference of opinion about the reality of any alleged historical event, in which the feelings of men in general are not much interested, as the Siege of Troy for example, those who maintain that the event took place are expected to produce their proofs, before those who take the other side can be required to say anything; and at no time are these required to do more than show that the evidence produced by the others is of no value. Again, in practical matters, the burthen of proof is supposed to be with those who are against liberty; who contend for any restriction or prohibition; either any limitation of the general freedom of human action, or any disqualification or disparity of privilege affecting one person or kind of persons, as compared with others. The *a priori* presumption is in favour of freedom and impartiality. It is held that there should be no restraint not required by the general good, and that the law should be no respecter of persons, but should treat all alike, save where dissimilarity of treatment is required by positive reasons, either of justice or of policy. But of none of these rules of evidence will the benefit be allowed to those who maintain the opinion I profess. It is useless for me to say that those who maintain the doctrine that men have a right to command and women are under an obligation to obey, or that men are fit for government and women unfit, are on the affirmative side of the question, and that they are bound to show positive evidence for the assertions, or submit to their rejection. It is equally unavailing for me to say that those who deny to women any freedom or privilege rightly allowed to men, having the double presumption against them that they are opposing freedom and recommending partiality, must be held to the strictest proof of their case, and unless their success be such as to exclude all doubt, the judgement ought to go against them. These would be thought good pleas in any common case; but will not be thought so in this instance. Before I could hope to make any impression, I should be expected not only to answer all that has ever been said by those who take the other side of the question, but to imagine all that could be said by them—to find them in reasons, as well as answer all I find: and besides refuting all arguments for the affirmative, I shall be called upon for invincible positive arguments to prove a negative. And even if I could do all this, and leave the opposite party with a host of unanswered arguments against them, and not a single unrefuted one on their side, I should be thought to have done little; for a cause supported on the one hand by universal usage, and on the other by so great a preponderance of popular sentiment, is supposed to have a presumption in its favour, superior to any conviction which an appeal to reason has power to produce in any intellects but those of a high class.

I do not mention these difficulties to complain of them; first, because it would be useless; they are inseparable from having to contend through people's understandings against the hostility of their feelings and practical tendencies: and truly the understandings of the majority of mankind would need to be much better cultivated than has ever yet been the case, before they can be asked to place such reliance in their own power of estimating arguments, as to

give up practical principles in which they have been born and bred, and which are the basis of much of the existing order of the world, at the first argumentative attack which they are not capable of logically resisting. I do not therefore quarrel with them for having too little faith in argument, but for having too much faith in custom and the general feeling. It is one of the characteristic prejudices of the reaction of the nineteenth century against the eighteenth, to accord to the unreasoning elements in human nature the infallibility which the eighteenth century is supposed to have ascribed to the reasoning elements. For the apotheosis of Reason we have substituted that of Instinct; and we call everything instinct which we find in ourselves and for which we cannot trace any rational foundation. This idolatry, infinitely more degrading than the other, and the most pernicious of the false worships of the present day, of all of which it is now the main support, will probably hold its ground until it gives way before a sound psychology, laying bare the real root of much that is bowed down to as the intention of Nature and the ordinance of God. As regards the present question, I am willing to accept the unfavourable conditions which the prejudice assigns to me. I consent that established custom, and the general feeling, should be deemed conclusive against me, unless that custom and feeling from age to age can be shown to have owed their existence to other causes than their soundness, and to have derived their power from the worse rather than the better parts of human nature. I am willing that judgement should go against me, unless I can show that my judge has been tampered with. The concession is not so great as it might appear; for to prove this, is by far the easiest portion of my task.

The generality of a practice is in some cases a strong presumption that it is, or at all events once was, conducive to laudable ends. This is the case, when the practice was first adopted, or afterwards kept up, as a means to such ends, and was grounded on experience of the mode in which they could be most effectually attained. If the authority of men over women, when first established, had been the result of a conscientious comparison between dif-

THE SUBJECTION OF WOMEN

ferent modes of constituting the government of society; if, after trying various other modes of social organization—the government of women over men, equality between the two, and such mixed and divided modes of government as might be invented—it had been decided, on the testimony of experience, that the mode in which women are wholly under the rule of men, having no share at all in public concerns, and each in private being under the legal obligation of obedience to the man with whom she has associated her destiny, was the arrangement most conducive to the happiness and well-being of both; its general adoption might then be fairly thought to be some evidence that, at the time when it was adopted, it was the best: though even then the considerations which recommended it may, like so many other primeval social facts of the greatest importance, have subsequently, in the course of ages, ceased to exist. But the state of the case is in every respect the reverse of this. In the first place, the opinion in favour of the present system, which entirely subordinates the weaker sex to the stronger, rests upon theory only; for there never has been trial made of any other: so that experience, in the sense in which it is vulgarly opposed to theory, cannot be pretended to have pronounced any verdict. And in the second place, the adoption of this system of inequality never was the result of deliberation, or forethought, or any social ideas, or any notion whatever of what conduced to the benefit of humanity or the good order of society. It arose simply from the fact that from the very earliest twilight of human society, every woman (owing to the value attached to her by men, combined with her inferiority in muscular strength) was found in a state of bondage to some man. Laws and systems of polity always begin by recognizing the relations they find already existing between individuals. They convert what was a mere physical fact into a legal right, give it the sanction of society, and principally aim at the substitution of public and organized means of asserting and protecting these rights, instead of the irregular and lawless conflict of physical strength. Those who had already been compelled to obedience became in this manner legally

bound to it. Slavery, from being a mere affair of force between the master and the slave, became regularized and a matter of compact among the masters, who, binding themselves to one another for common protection, guaranteed by their collective strength the private possessions of each, including his slaves. In early times, the great majority of the male sex were slaves, as well as the whole of the female. And many ages elapsed, some of them ages of high cultivation, before any thinker was bold enough to question the rightfulness, and the absolute social necessity, either of the one slavery or of the other. By degrees such thinkers did arise: and (the general progress of society assisting) the slavery of the male sex has, in all the countries of Christian Europe at least (though, in one of them, only within the last few years) been at length abolished, and that of the female sex has been gradually changed into a milder form of dependence. But this dependence, as it exists at present, is not an original institution, taking a fresh start from considerations of justice and social expediency—it is the primitive state of slavery lasting on, through successive mitigations and modifications occasioned by the same causes which have softened the general manners, and brought all human relations more under the control of justice and the influence of humanity. It has not lost the taint of its brutal origin. No presumption in its favour, therefore, can be drawn from the fact of its existence. The only such presumption which it could be supposed to have, must be grounded on its having lasted till now, when so many other things which came down from the same odious source have been done away with. And this, indeed, is what makes it strange to ordinary ears, to hear it asserted that the inequality of rights between men and women has no other source than the law of the strongest.

That this statement should have the effect of a paradox, is in some respects creditable to the progress of civilization, and the improvement of the moral sentiments of mankind. We now live—that is to say, one or two of the most advanced nations of the world now live—in a state in which the law of the strongest seems to be entirely abandoned as the regulating principle of the world's affairs: nobody professes it, and, as regards most of the relations between human beings, nobody is permitted to practice it. When any one succeeds in doing so, it is under cover of some pretext which gives him the semblance of having some general social interest on his side. This being the ostensible state of things, people flatter themselves that the rule of mere force is ended; that the law of the strongest cannot be the reason of existence of anything which has remained in full operation down to the present time. However any of our present institutions may have begun, it can only, they think, have been preserved to this period of advanced civilization by a well-grounded feeling of its adaptation to human nature, and conduciveness to the general good. They do not understand the great vitality and durability of institutions which place right on the side of might; how intensely they are clung to; how the good as well as the bad propensities and sentiments of those who have power in their hands, become identified with retaining it; how slowly these bad institutions give way, one at a time, the weakest first, beginning with those which are least interwoven with the daily habits of life; and how very rarely those who have obtained legal power because they first had physical, have ever lost their hold of it until the physical power had passed over to the other side. Such shifting of the physical force not having taken place in the case of women; this fact, combined with all the peculiar and characteristic features of the particular case, made it certain from the first that this branch of the system of right founded on might, though softened in its most atrocious features at an earlier period than several of the others, would be the very last to disappear. It was inevitable that this one case of a social relation grounded on force would survive through generations of institutions grounded on equal justice, an almost solitary exception to the general character of their laws and customs; but which, so long as it does not proclaim its own origin, and as discussion has not brought out its true character, is not felt to jar with modern civilization, any more than domestic slavery among the Greeks jarred with their notion of themselves as a free people.

The truth is, that people of the present and the last two or three generations have lost all practical sense of the primitive condition of humanity; and only the few who have studied history accurately, or have much frequented the parts of the world occupied by the living representatives of ages long past, are able to form any mental picture of what society then was. People are not aware how entirely, in former ages, the law of superior strength was the rule of life; how publicly and openly it was avowed, I do not say cynically or shamelessly—for these words imply a feeling that there was something in it to be ashamed of, and no such notion could find a place in the faculties of any person in those ages, except a philosopher or a saint. History gives a cruel experience of human nature, in showing how exactly the regard due to the life, possessions, and entire earthly happiness of any class of persons was measured by what they had the power of enforcing; how all who made any resistance to authorities that had arms in their hands, however dreadful might be the provocation, had not only the law of force but all other laws, and all the notions of social obligation against them; and, in the eyes of those whom they resisted, were not only guilty of crime, but the worst of all crimes, deserving the most cruel chastisement which human beings could inflict. The first small vestige of a feeling of obligation in a superior to acknowledge any right in inferiors, began when he had been induced, for convenience, to make some promise to them. Though these promises, even when sanctioned by the most solemn oaths, were for many ages revoked or violated on the most trifling provocation or temptation, it is probable that this, except by persons of still worse than the average morality, was seldom done without some twinges of conscience. The ancient republics, being mostly grounded from the first upon some kind of mutual compact, or at any rate formed by an union of persons not very unequal in strength, afforded, in consequence, the first instance of a portion of human relations fenced round, and placed under the dominion of another law than that of force. And though the original law of force remained in full operation between them and their slaves, and also (except so far as limited by express compact) between a commonwealth and its subjects, or other independent commonwealths; the banishment of that primitive law, even from so narrow a field, commenced the regeneration of human nature, by giving birth to sentiments of which experience soon demonstrated the immense value even for material interests, and which thenceforward only required to be enlarged, not created. Though slaves were no part of the commonwealth, it was in the free states that slaves were first felt to have rights as human beings. The Stoics were, I believe, the first (except so far as the Jewish law constitutes an exception) who taught as a part of morality that men were bound by moral obligations to their slaves. No one, after Christianity became ascendant, could ever again have been a stranger to this belief, in theory; nor, after the rise of the Catholic Church, was it ever without persons to stand up for it. Yet to enforce it was the most arduous task which Christianity ever had to perform. For more than a thousand years the Church kept up the contest, with hardly any perceptible success. It was not for want of power over men's minds. Its power was prodigious. It could make kings and nobles resign their most valued possessions to enrich the Church. It could make thousands, in the prime of life and the height of worldly advantages, shut themselves up in convents to work out their salvation by poverty, fasting and prayer. It could send hundreds of thousands across land and sea, Europe and Asia, to give their lives for the deliverance of the Holy Sepulchre. It could make kings relinquish wives who were the objects of their passionate attachment, because the Church declared that they were within the seventh (by our calculation the fourteenth) degree of relationship. All this it did; but it could not make men fight less with one another, nor tyrannize less cruelly over the serfs, and, when they were able, over burgesses. It could not make them renounce either of the applications of force; force militant, or force triumphant. This they could never be induced to do until they were themselves in their turn compelled by superior force. Only by the growing power of kings was an end put to fighting except between kings, or competitors for kingship; only by the growth of a wealthy and warlike bourgeoisie in the

fortified towns, and of a plebeian infantry which proved more powerful in the field than the undisciplined chivalry, was the insolent tyranny of the nobles over the bourgeoisie and peasantry brought within some bounds. It was persisted in not only until, but long after, the oppressed had obtained a power enabling them often to take conspicuous vengeance; and on the Continent much of it continued to the time of the French Revolution, though in England the earlier and better organization of the democratic classes put an end to it sooner, by establishing equal laws and free national institutions.

If people are mostly so little aware how completely, during the greater part of the duration of our species, the law of force was the avowed rule of general conduct, any other being only a special and exceptional consequence of peculiar ties—and from how very recent a date it is that the affairs of society in general have been even pretended to be regulated according to any moral law; as little do people remember or consider, how institutions and customs which never had any ground but the law of force, last on into ages and states of general opinion which never would have permitted their first establishment. Less than forty years ago, Englishmen might still by law hold human beings in bondage as saleable property: within the present century they might kidnap them and carry them off, and work them literally to death. This absolutely extreme case of the law of force, condemned by those who can tolerate almost every other form of arbitrary power, and which, of all others, presents features the most revolting to the feelings of all who look at it from an impartial position, was the law of civilized and Christian England within the memory of persons now living: and in one half of Anglo-Saxon America three or four years ago, not only did slavery exist, but the slave trade, and the breeding of slaves expressly for it, was a general practice between slave states. Yet not only was there a greater strength of sentiment against it, but, in England at least, a less amount either of feeling or of interest in favour of it, than of any other of the customary abuses of force: for its motive was the love of gain, unmixed and undisguised; and those who profited by it were a very small numerical fraction of the country, while the natural feeling of all who were not personally interested in it, was unmitigated abhorrence. So extreme an instance makes it almost superfluous to refer to any other: but consider the long duration of absolute monarchy. In England at present it is the almost universal conviction that military despotism is a case of the law of force, having no other origin or justification. Yet in all the great nations of Europe except England it either still exists, or has only just ceased to exist, and has even now a strong party favourable to it in all ranks of the people, especially among persons of station and consequence. Such is the power of an established system, even when far from universal; when not only in almost every period of history there have been great and well-known examples of the contrary system, but these have almost invariably been afforded by the most illustrious and most prosperous communities. In this case, too, the possessor of the undue power, the person directly interested in it, is only one person, while those who are subject to it and suffer from it are literally all the rest. The yoke is naturally and necessarily humiliating to all persons, except the one who is on the throne, together with, at most, the one who expects to succeed to it. How different are these cases from that of the power of men over women! I am not now prejudging the question of its justifiableness. I am showing how vastly more permanent it could not but be, even if not justifiable, than these other dominations which have nevertheless lasted down to our own time. Whatever gratification of pride there is in the possession of power, and whatever personal interest in its exercise, is in this case not confined to a limited class, but common to the whole male sex. Instead of being, to most of its supporters, a thing desirable chiefly in the abstract, or, like the political ends usually contended for by factions, of little private importance to any but the leaders; it comes home to the person and hearth of every male head of a family, and of every one who looks forward to being so. The clodhopper exercises, or is to exercise, his share of the power equally with the highest nobleman. And the case is that in which the desire of power is the strongest: for every one who desires power, desires it most over those who are nearest to him, with whom

his life is passed, with whom he has most concerns in common, and in whom any independence of his authority is oftenest likely to interfere with his individual preferences. If, in the other cases specified, powers manifestly grounded only on force, and having so much less to support them, are so slowly and with so much difficulty got rid of, much more must it be so with this, even if it rests on no better foundation than those. We must consider, too, that the possessors of the power have facilities in this case, greater than in any other, to prevent any uprising against it. Every one of the subjects lives under the very eye, and almost, it may be said, in the hands, of one of the masters—in closer intimacy with him than with any of her fellow subjects; with no means of combining against him, no power of even locally overmastering him, and, on the other hand, with the strongest motives for seeking his favour and avoiding to give him offence. In struggles for political emancipation, everybody knows how often its champions are bought off by bribes, or daunted by terrors. In the case of women, each individual of the subject-class is in a chronic state of bribery and intimidation combined. In setting up the standard of resistance, a large number of the leaders, and still more of the followers, must make an almost complete sacrifice of the pleasures or the alleviations of their own individual lot. If ever any system of privilege and enforced subjection had its yoke tightly riveted on the necks of those who are kept down by it, this has. I have not yet shown that it is a wrong system: but every one who is capable of thinking on the subject must see that even if it is, it was certain to outlast all other forms of unjust authority. And when some of the grossest of the other forms still exist in many civilized countries, and have only recently been got rid of in others, it would be strange if that which is so much the deepest-rooted had yet been perceptibly shaken anywhere. There is more reason to wonder that the protests and testimonies against it should have been so numerous and so weighty as they are.

Some will object, that a comparison cannot fairly be made between the government of the male sex and the forms of unjust power which I have adduced in illustration of it, since these are arbitrary, and the effect of mere usurpation, while it on the contrary is natural. But was there ever any domination which did not appear natural to those who possessed it? There was a time when the division of mankind into two classes, a small one of masters and a numerous one of slaves, appeared, even to the most cultivated minds, to be a natural, and the only natural, condition of the human race. No less an intellect, and one which contributed no less to the progress of human thought, than Aristotole, held this opinion without doubt or misgiving; and rested it on the same premisses on which the same assertion in regard to the dominion of men over women is usually based, namely that there are different natures among mankind, free natures, and slave natures: that the Greeks were of a free nature, the barbarian races of Thracians and Asiatics of a slave nature. But why need I go back to Aristotle? Did not the slave-owners of the Southern United States maintain the same doctrine, with all the fanaticism with which men cling to the theories that justify their passions and legitimate their personal interests? Did they not call heaven and earth to witness that the dominion of the white man over the black is natural, that the black race is by nature incapable of freedom, and marked out for slavery?—some even going so far as to say that the freedom of manual labourers is an unnatural order of things anywhere. Again, the theorists of absolute monarchy have always affirmed it to be the only natural form of government; issuing from the patriarchal, which was the primitive and spontaneous form of society, framed on the model of the paternal, which is anterior to society itself, and, as they contend, the most natural authority of all. Nay, for that matter, the law of force itself, to those who could not plead any other, has always seemed the most natural of all grounds for the exercise of authority. Conquering races hold it to be Nature's own dictate that the conquered should obey the conquerors, or, as they euphoniously paraphrase it, that the feebler and more unwarlike races should submit to the braver and manlier. The smallest acquaintance with human life in the Middle Ages shows how supremely natural the dominion of the feudal nobility over men of low condition appeared to the nobility themselves,

and how unnatural the conception seemed, of a person of the inferior class claiming equality with them, or exercising authority over them. It hardly seemed less so to the class held in subjection. The emancipated serfs and burgesses, even in their most vigorous struggles, never made any pretension to a share of authority; they only demanded more or less of limitation to the power of tyrannizing over them. So true is it that unnatural generally means only uncustomary, and that everything which is usual appears natural. The subjection of women to men being a universal custom, any departure from it quite naturally appears unnatural. But how entirely, even in this case, the feeling is dependent on custom, appears by ample experience. Nothing so much astonishes the people of distant parts of the world, when they first learn anything about England, as to be told that it is under a queen: the thing seems to them so unnatural as to be almost incredible. To Englishmen this does not seem in the least degree unnatural, because they are used to it; but they do feel it unnatural that women should be soldiers or members of Parliament. In the feudal ages, on the contrary, war and politics were not thought unnatural to women, because not unusual; it seemed natural that women of the privileged classes should be of manly character, inferior in nothing but bodily strength to their husbands and fathers. The independence of women seemed rather less unnatural to the Greeks than to other ancients, on account of the fabulous Amazons (whom they believed to be historical), and the partial example afforded by the Spartan women; who, though no less subordinate by law than in other Greek states, were more free in fact, and being trained to bodily exercises in the same manner with men, gave ample proof that they were not naturally disqualified for them. There can be little doubt that Spartan experience suggested to Plato, among many other of his doctrines, that of the social and political equality of the two sexes.

But, it will be said, the rule of men over women differs from all these others in not being a rule of force: it is accepted voluntarily; women make no complaint, and are consenting parties to it. In the first place, a great number of women do not accept it. Ever since there have been women able to make their sentiments known by their writings (the only mode of publicity which society permits to them), an increasing number of them have recorded protests against their present social condition: and recently many thousands of them, headed by the most eminent women known to the public, have petitioned Parliament for their admission to the Parliamentary Suffrage. The claim of women to be educated as solidly, and in the same branches of knowledge, as men, is urged with growing intensity, and with a great prospect of success; while the demand for their admission into professions and occupations hitherto closed against them, becomes every year more urgent. Though there are not in this country, as there are in the United States, periodical Conventions and an organized party to agitate for the Rights of Women, there is a numerous and active Society organized and managed by women, for the more limited object of obtaining the political franchise. Nor is it only in our own country and in America that women are beginning to protest, more or less collectively, against the disabilities under which they labour. France, and Italy, and Switzerland, and Russia now afford examples of the same thing. How many more women there are who silently cherish similar aspirations, no one can possibly know; but there are abundant tokens how many *would* cherish them, were they not so strenuously taught to repress them as contrary to the proprieties of their sex. It must be remembered, also, that no enslaved class ever asked for complete liberty at once. When Simon de Montfort called the deputies of the commons to sit for the first time in Parliament, did any of them dream of demanding that an assembly, elected by their constituents, should make and destroy ministries, and dictate to the king in affairs of State? No such thought entered into the imagination of the most ambitious of them. The nobility had already these pretensions; the commons pretended to nothing but to be exempt from arbitrary taxation, and from the gross individual oppression of the king's officers. It is a political law of nature that those who are under any power of ancient origin never begin by complaining of the power itself, but only of its

oppressive exercise. There is never any want of women who complain of ill usage by their husbands. There would be infinitely more, if complaint were not the greatest of all provocatives to a repetition and increase of the ill usage. It is this which frustrates all attempts to maintain the power but protect the woman against its abuses. In no other case (except that of a child) is the person who has been proved judicially to have suffered an injury, replaced under the physical power of the culprit who inflicted it. Accordingly wives, even in the most extreme and protracted cases of bodily ill usage, hardly ever dare avail themselves of the laws made for their protection: and if, in a moment of irrepressible indignation, or by the interference of neighbours, they are induced to do so, their whole effort afterwards is to disclose as little as they can, and to beg off their tyrant from his merited chastisement.

All causes, social and natural, combine to make it unlikely that women should be collectively rebellious to the power of men. They are so far in a position different from all other subject classes, that their masters require something more from them than actual service. Men do not want solely the obedience of women, they want their sentiments. All men, except the most brutish, desire to have, in the woman most nearly connected with them, not a forced slave but a willing one; not a slave merely, but a favourite. They have therefore put everything in practice to enslave their minds. The masters of all other slaves rely, for maintaining obedience, on fear; either fear of themselves, or religious fears. The masters of women wanted more than simple obedience, and they turned the whole force of education to effect their purpose. All women are brought up from the very earliest years in the belief that their ideal of character is the very opposite to that of men; not self-will, and government by self-control, but submission, and yielding to the control of others. All the moralities tell them that it is the duty of women, and all the current sentimentalities that it is their nature, to live for others; to make complete abnegation of themselves, and to have no life but in their affections. And by their affections are meant the only ones they are allowed to have—those to the men with whom they are connected, or to the children who constitute an additional and indefeasible tie between them and a man. When we put together three things—first, the natural attraction between opposite sexes; secondly, the wife's entire dependence on the husband, every privilege or pleasure she has being either his gift, or depending entirely on his will; and lastly, that the principal object of human pursuit, consideration, and all objects of social ambition, can in general be sought or obtained by her only through him—it would be a miracle if the object of being attractive to men had not become the polar star of feminine education and formation of character. And, this great means of influence over the minds of women having been acquired, an instinct of selfishness made man avail themselves of it to the utmost as a means of holding women in subjection, by representing to them meekness, submissiveness, and resignation of all individual will into the hands of a man, as an essential part of sexual attractiveness. Can it be doubted that any of the other yokes which mankind have succeeded in breaking, would have subsisted till now if the same means had existed, and had been as sedulously used, to bow down their minds to it? If it had been made the object of the life of every young plebeian to find personal favour in the eyes of some patrician, of every young serf with some seigneur; if domestication with him, and a share of his personal affections, had been held out as the prize which they all should look out for, the most gifted and aspiring being able to reckon on the most desirable prizes; and if, when this prize had been obtained, they had been shut out by a wall of brass from all interests not centring in him, all feelings and desires but those which he shared or inculcated; would not serfs and seigneurs, plebeians and patricians, have been as broadly distinguished at this day as men and women are? and would not all but a thinker here and there have believed the distinction to be a fundamental and unalterable fact in human nature?

The preceding considerations are amply sufficient to show that custom, however universal it may be, affords in this case no presumption, and ought not to create any prejudice, in favour of the arrangements which place women in social and political subjection to men. But I may go farther, and maintain that the course of history, and the tendencies of progressive human society, afford not only no presumption in favour of this system of inequality of rights, but a strong one against it; and that, so far as the whole course of human improvement up to this time, the whole stream of modern tendencies, warrants any inference on the subject, it is, that this relic of the past is discordant with the future, and must necessarily disappear.

For what is the peculiar character of the modern world—the difference which chiefly distinguishes modern institutions, modern social ideas, modern life itself, from those of times long past? It is, that human beings are no longer born to their place in life, and chained down by an inexorable bond to the place they are born to, but are free to employ their faculties, and such favourable chances as offer, to achieve the lot which may appear to them most desirable. Human society of old was constituted on a very different principle. All were born to a fixed social position, and were mostly kept in it by law, or interdicted from any means by which they could emerge from it. As some men are born white and others black, so some were born slaves and others freemen and citizens; some were born patricians, others plebeians; some were born feudal nobles, others commoners and *roturiers*. A slave or serf could never make himself free, nor, except by the will of his master, become so. In most European countries it was not till towards the close of the Middle Ages, and as a consequence of the growth of regal power, that commoners could be enobled. Even among nobles, the eldest son was born the exclusive heir to the paternal possessions, and a long time elapsed before it was fully established that the father could disinherit him. Among the industrious classes, only those who were born members of a guild, or were admitted into it by its members, could lawfully practice their calling within its local limits; and nobody could practice any calling deemed important, in any but the legal manner—by processes authoritatively prescribed. Manufacturers have stood in the pillory for presuming to carry on their business by new and improved methods. In modern Europe, and most in those parts of it which have participated most largely in all other modern improvements, diametrically opposite doctrines now prevail. Law and government do not undertake to prescribe by whom any social or industrial operation shall or shall not be conducted, or what modes of conducting them shall be lawful. These things are left to the unfettered choice of individuals. Even the laws which required that workmen should serve an apprenticeship, have in this country been repealed: there being ample assurance that in all cases in which an apprenticeship is necessary, its necessity will suffice to enforce it. The old theory was, that the least possible should be left to the choice of the individual agent; that all he had to do should, as far as practicable, be laid down for him by superior wisdom. Left to himself he was sure to go wrong. The modern conviction, the fruit of a thousand years of experience, is, that things in which the individual is the person directly interested, never go right but as they are left to his own discretion; and that any regulation of them by authority, except to protect the rights of others, is sure to be mischievous. This conclusion, slowly arrived at, and not adopted until almost every possible application of the contrary theory had been made with disastrous result, now (in the industrial department) prevails universally in the most advanced countries, almost universally in all that have pretensions to any sort of advancement. It is not that all processes are supposed to be equally good, or all persons to be equally qualified for everything; but that freedom of individual choice is now known to be the only thing which procures the adoption of the best processes, and throws each operation into the hands of those who are best qualified for it. Nobody thinks it necessary to make a law that only a strong-armed man shall be a blacksmith. Freedom and competition suffice to make blacksmiths strong-armed men, because the weak-armed can earn more by engaging in occupations for which they are more fit. In consonance with this doctrine, it is felt to be an overstepping of the proper bounds of authority to fix beforehand, on some general presumption, that certain persons are not fit to do certain things. It is now thoroughly known and admitted that if some such

presumptions exist, no such presumption is infallible. Even if it be well grounded in a majority of cases, which it is very likely not to be, there will be a minority of exceptional cases in which it does not hold: and in those it is both an injustice to the individuals, and a detriment to society, to place barriers in the way of their using their faculties for their own benefit and for that of others. In the cases, on the other hand, in which the unfitness is real, the ordinary motives of human conduct will on the whole suffice to prevent the incompetent person from making, or from persisting in, the attempt.

If this general principle of social and economical science is not true; if individuals, with such help as they can derive from the opinion of those who know them, are not better judges that the law and the government, of their own capabilities and vocation; the world cannot too soon abandon this principle, and return to the old system of regulations and disabilities. But if the principle is true, we ought to act as if we believed it, and not to ordain that to be born a girl instead of a boy, any more than to be born black instead of white, or a commoner instead of a nobleman, shall decide the person's position through all life—shall interdict people from all the more elevated social positions, and from all, except a few, respectable occupations. Even were we to admit the utmost that is ever pretended as to the superior fitness of men for all the functions now reserved to them, the same argument applies which forbids a legal qualification for members of Parliament. If only once in a dozen years the conditions of eligibility exclude a fit person, there is a real loss, while the exclusion of thousands of unfit persons is no gain; for if the constitution of the electoral body disposes them to choose unfit persons, there are always plenty of such persons to choose from. In all things of any difficulty and importance, those who can do them well are fewer than the need, even with the most unrestricted latitude of choice: and any limitation of the field of selection deprives society of some chances of being served by the competent, without ever saving it from the incompetent.

At present, in the more improved countries, the disabilities of women are the only case, save one, in which laws and institutions take persons at their birth, and ordain that they shall never in all their lives be allowed to compete for certain things. The one exception is that of royalty. Persons still are born to the throne; no one, not of the reigning family, can ever occupy it, and no one even of that family can, by any means but the course of hereditary succession, attain it. All other dignities and social advantages are open to the whole male sex: many indeed are only attainable by wealth, but wealth may be striven for by any one, and is actually obtained by many men of the very humblest origin. The difficulties, to the majority, are indeed insuperable without the aid of fortunate accidents; but no male human being is under any legal ban: neither law nor opinion superadd artificial obstacles to the natural ones. Royalty, as I have said, is excepted; but in this case every one feels it to be an exception—an anomaly in the modern world, in marked opposition to its customs and principles, and to be justified only by extraordinary special expediencies, which though individuals and nations differ in estimating their weight, unquestionably do in fact exist. But in this exceptional case, in which a high social function is, for important reasons, bestowed on birth instead of being put up to competition, all free nations contrive to adhere in substance to the principle from which they nominally derogate; for they circumscribe this high function by conditions avowedly intended to prevent the person to whom it ostensibly belongs from really performing it; while the person by whom it is performed, the responsible minister, does obtain the post by a competition from which no full-grown citizen of the male sex is legally excluded. The disabilities, therefore, to which women are subject from the mere fact of their birth, are the solitary examples of the kind in modern legislation. In no instance except this, which comprehends half the human race, are the higher social functions closed against any one by a fatality of birth which no exertions, and no change of circumstances, can overcome; for even religious disabilities (besides that in England and in Europe they have practically almost ceased to exist) do not close any career to the disqualified person in case of conversion.

The social subordination of women thus stands out an isolated fact in modern social institutions; a solitary breach of what has become their fundamental law; a single relic of an old world of thought and practice exploded in everything else, but retained in the one thing of most universal interest; as if a gigantic dolmen, or a vast temple of Jupiter Olympus, occupied the site of St. Paul's and received daily worship, while the surrounding Christian churches were only resorted to on fasts and festivals. The entire discrepancy between one social fact and all those which accompany it, and the radical opposition between its nature and the progressive movement which is the boast of the modern world, and which has successively swept away everything else of an analogous character, surely affords, to a conscientious observer of human tendencies, serious matter for reflection. It raises a prima facie presumption on the unfavourable side, far outweighing any which custom and usage could in such circumstances create on the favourable; and should at least suffice to make this, like the choice between republicanism and royalty, a balanced question.

The least that can be demanded is, that the question should not be considered as prejudged by existing fact and existing opinion, but open to discussion on its merits, as a question of justice and expediency: the decision on this, as on any of the other social arrangements of mankind, depending on what an enlightened estimate of tendencies and consequences may show to be most advantageous to humanity in general, without distinction of sex. And the discussion must be a real discussion, descending to foundations, and not resting satisfied with vague and general assertions. It will not do, for instance, to assert in general terms, that the experience of mankind has pronounced in favour of the existing system. Experience cannot possibly have decided between two courses, so long as there has only been experience of one. If it be said that the doctrine of the equality of the sexes rests only on theory, it must be remembered that the contrary doctrine also has only theory to rest upon. All that is proved in its favour by direct experience, is that mankind have been able to exist under it, and to attain the degree of improvement and prosperity which we now see; but whether that prosperity has been attained sooner, or is now greater, than it would have been under the other system, experience does not say. On the other hand, experience does say, that every step in improvement has been so invariably accompanied by a step made in raising the social position of women, that historians and philosophers have been led to adopt their elevation or debasement as on the whole the surest test and most correct measure of the civilization of a people or an age. Through all the progressive period of human history, the condition of women has been approaching nearer to equality with men. This does not of itself prove that the assimilation must go on to complete equality; but it assuredly affords some presumption that such is the case.

Neither does it avail anything to say that the *nature* of the two sexes adapts them to their present functions and position, and renders these appropriate to them. Standing on the ground of common sense and the constitution of the human mind, I deny that any one knows, or can know, the nature of the two sexes, as long as they have only been seen in their present relation to one another. If men had ever been found in society without women, or women without men, or if there had been a society of men and women in which the women were not under the control of the men, something might have been positively known about the mental and moral differences which may be inherent in the nature of each. What is now called the nature of women is an eminently artificial thing—the result of forced repression in some directions, unnatural stimulation in others. It may be asserted without scruple, that no other class of dependents have had their character so entirely distorted from its natural proportions by their relation with their masters; for, if conquered and slave races have been, in some respects, more forcibly repressed, whatever in them has not been crushed down by an iron heel has generally been let alone, and if left with any liberty of development, it has developed itself according to its own laws; but in the case of women, a hothouse and stove cultivation has always been carried on of some of the capabilities of their nature, for the benefit and pleasure of their masters. Then, because certain

products of the general vital force sprout luxuriantly and reach a great development in this heated atmosphere and under this active nurture and watering, while other shoots from the same root, which are left outside in the wintry air, with ice purposely heaped all round them, have a stunted growth, and some are burnt off with fire and disappear; men, with that inability to recognize their own work which distinguishes the unanalytic mind, indolently believe that the tree grows of itself in the way they have made it grow, and that it would die if one half of it were not kept in a vapour bath and the other half in the snow.

Of all difficulties which impede the progress of thought, and the formation of well-grounded opinions on life and social arrangements, the greatest is now the unspeakable ignorance and inattention of mankind in respect to the influences which form human character. Whatever any portion of the human species now are, or seem to be, such, it is supposed, they have a natural tendency to be: even when the most elementary knowledge of the circumstances in which they have been placed, clearly points out the causes that made them what they are. Because a cottier deeply in arrears to his landlord is not industrious, there are people who think that the Irish are naturally idle. Because constitutions can be overthrown when the authorities appointed to execute them turn their arms against them, there are people who think the French incapable of free government. Because the Greeks cheated the Turks, and the Turks only plundered the Greeks, there are persons who think that the Turks are naturally more sincere: and because women, as is often said, care nothing about politics except their personalities, it is supposed that the general good is naturally less interesting to women than to men. History, which is now so much better understood than formerly, teaches another lesson: if only by showing the extraordinary susceptibility of human nature to external influences, and the extreme variableness of those of its manifestations which are supposed to be most universal and uniform. But in history, as in travelling, men usually see only what they already had in their own minds, and few learn much from history, who do not bring much with them to its study.

Hence, in regard to that most difficult question, what are the natural differences between the two sexes—a subject on which it is impossible in the present state of society to obtain complete and correct knowledge—while almost everybody dogmatizes upon it, almost all neglect and make light of the only means by which any partial insight can be obtained into it. This is, an analytic study of the most important department of psychology, the laws of the influence of circumstances on character. For, however great and apparently ineradicable the moral and intellectual differences between men and women might be, the evidence of their being natural differences could only be negative. Those only could be inferred to be natural which could not possibly be artificial—the residuum, after deducting every characteristic of either sex which can admit of being explained from education or external circumstances. The profoundest knowledge of the laws of the formation of character is indispensable to entitle any one to affirm even that there is any difference, much more what the difference is, between the two sexes considered as moral and rational beings; and since no one, as yet, has that knowledge (for there is hardly any subject which, in proportion to its importance, has been so little studied), no one is thus far entitled to any positive opinion on the subject. Conjectures are all that can at present be made; conjectures more or less probable, according as more or less authorized by such knowledge as we yet have of the laws of psychology, as applied to the formation of character.

Even the preliminary knowledge, what the differences between the sexes now are, apart from all question as to how they are made and what they are, is still in the crudest and most incomplete state. Medical practitioners and psychologists have ascertained, to some extent, the differences in bodily constitution; and this is an important element to the psychologist; but hardly any medical practitioner is a psychologist. Respecting the mental characteristics of women; their observations are of no more worth than those of common men. It is a subject on which nothing final can be known, so long as those who alone can really know it, women themselves, have given but little testimony, and that little, mostly suborned. It is easy to know stupid women. Stupidity is much the same all the world over. A stupid person's notions and feelings may confidently be inferred from those which prevail in the circle by which the person is surrounded. Not so with those whose opinions and feelings are an emanation from their own nature and faculties. It is only a man here and there who has any tolerable knowledge of the character even of the women of his own family. I do not mean, of their capabilities; these nobody knows, not even themselves, because most of them have never been called out. I mean their actually existing thoughts and feelings. Many a man thinks he perfectly understands women, because he has had amatory relations with several, perhaps with many of them. If he is a good observer, and his experience extends to quality as well as quantity, he may have learnt something of one narrow department of their nature—an important department, no doubt. But of all the rest of it, few persons are generally more ignorant, because there are few from whom it is so carefully hidden. The most favourable case which a man can generally have for studying the character of a woman, is that of his own wife: for the opportunities are greater, and the cases of complete sympathy not so unspeakably rare. And in fact, this is the source from which any knowledge worth having on the subject has, I believe, generally come. But most men have not had the opportunity of studying in this way more than a single case: accordingly one can, to an almost laughable degree, infer what a man's wife is like, from his opinions about women in general. To make even this one case yield any result, the woman must be worth knowing, and the man not only a competent judge, but of a character so sympathetic in itself, and so well adapted to hers, that he can either read her mind by sympathetic intuition, or has nothing in himself which makes her shy of disclosing it. Hardly anything, I believe, can be more rare, than this conjunction. It often happens that there is the most complete unity of feeling and community of interests as to all external things, yet the one has as little admission into the internal life of the other as if they were common acquaintance. Even with true affection, authority on the one side and subordination on the other prevent perfect confidence. Though nothing may be intentionally withheld, much is not shown. In the analogous relation of parent and child, the corresponding phenomenon must have been in the observation of every one. As between father and son, how many are the cases in which the father, in spite of real affection on both sides, obviously to all the world does not know, nor suspect, parts of the son's character familiar to his companions and equals. The truth is, that the position of looking up to another is extremely unpropitious to complete sincerity and openness with him. The fear of losing ground in his opinion or in his feelings is so strong, that even in an upright character, there is an unconscious tendency to show only the best side, or the side which, though not the best, is that which he most likes to see: and it may be confidently said that thorough knowledge of one another hardly ever exists, but between persons who, besides being intimates, are equals. How much more true, then, must all this be, when the one is not only under the authority of the other, but has it inculcated on her as a duty to reckon everything else subordinate to his comfort and pleasure, and to let him neither see nor feel anything coming from her, except what is agreeable to him. All these difficulties stand in the way of a man's obtaining any thorough knowledge even of the one woman whom alone, in general, he has sufficient opportunity of studying. When we further consider that to understand one woman is not necessarily to understand any other woman; that even if he could study many women of one rank, or of one country, he would not thereby understand women of other ranks or countries; and even if he did, they are still only the women of a single period of history; we may safely assert that the knowledge which men can acquire of women, even as they have been and are, without reference to what they might be, is wretchedly imperfect and superficial, and always will be so, until women themselves have told all that they have to tell.

And this time has not come; nor will it come otherwise than gradually. It is but of yesterday that women have either been qualified by literary accomplishments, or permitted by society, to tell anything to the general public. As yet very few of them dare

tell anything, which men, on whom their literary success depends, are unwilling to hear. Let us remember in what manner, up to a very recent time, the expression, even by a male author, of uncustomary opinions, or what are deemed eccentric feelings, usually was, and in some degree still is, received; and we may form some faint conception under what impediments a woman, who is brought up to think custom and opinion her sovereign rule, attempts to express in books anything drawn from the depths of her own nature. The greatest woman who has left writings behind her sufficient to give her an eminent rank in the literature of her country, thought it necessary to prefix as a motto to her boldest work, 'Un homme peut braver l'opinion; une femme doit s'y soumettre.'[1] The greater part of what women write about women is mere sycophancy to men. In the case of unmarried women, much of it seems only intended to increase their chance of a husband. Many, both married and unmarried, over-step the mark, and inculcate a servility beyond what is desired or relished by any man, except the very vulgarest. But this is not so often the case as, even at quite a late period, it still was. Literary women are becoming more freespoken, and more willing to express their real sentiments. Unfortunately, in this country especially, they are themselves such artificial products, that their sentiments are compounded of a small element of individual observation and consciousness, and a very large one of acquired associations. This will be less and less the case, but it will remain true to a great extent, as long as social institutions do not admit the same free development of originality in women which is possible to men. When that time comes, and not before, we shall see, and not merely hear, as much as it is necessary to know of the nature of women, and the adaptation of other things to it.

I have dwelt so much on the difficulties which at present obstruct any real knowledge by men of the true nature of women, because in this as in so many other things 'opinio copiae inter maximas causas inopiae est'; and there is little chance of reasonable thinking on the matter, while people flatter themselves that they perfectly understand a subject of which most men know absolutely nothing, and of which it is at present impossible that any man, or all men taken together, should have knowledge which can qualify them to lay down the law to women as to what is, or is not, their vocation. Happily, no such knowledge is necessary for any practical purpose connected with the position of women in relation to society and life. For, according to all the principles involved in modern society, the question rests with women themselves—to be decided by their own experience, and by the use of their own faculties. There are no means of finding what either one person or many can do, but by trying—and no means by which any one else can discover for them what it is for their happiness to do or leave undone.

One thing we may be certain of—that what is contrary to women's nature to do, they never will be made to do by simply giving their nature free play. The anxiety of mankind to interfere in behalf of nature, for fear lest nature should not succeed in effecting its purpose, is an altogether unnecessary solicitude. What women by nature cannot do, it is quite superfluous to forbid them from doing. What they can do, but not so well as the men who are their competitors, competition suffices to exclude them from; since nobody asks for protective duties and bounties in favour of women; it is only asked that the present bounties and protective duties in favour of men should be recalled. If women have a greater natural inclination for some things than for others, there is no need of laws or social inculcation to make the majority of them do the former in preference to the latter. Whatever women's services are most wanted for, the free play of competition will hold out the strongest inducements to them to undertake. And, as the words imply, they are most wanted for the things for which they are most fit; by the apportionment of which to them, the collective faculties of the two sexes can be applied on the whole with the greatest sum of valuable result.

The general opinion of men is supposed to be, that the natural vocation of a woman is that of a wife and mother. I say, is supposed to be, because, judging from acts—from the whole of the present constitution of society—one might infer that their opinion

was the direct contrary. They might be supposed to think that the alleged natural vocation of women was of all things the most repugnant to their nature; insomuch that if they are free to do anything else—if any other means of living, or occupation of their time and faculties, is open, which has any chance of appearing desirable to them—there will not be enough of them who will be willing to accept the condition said to be natural to them. If this is the real opinion of men in general, it would be well that it should be spoken out. I should like to hear somebody openly enunciating the doctrine (it is already implied in much that is written on the subject)— 'It is necessary to society that women should marry and produce children. They will not do so unless they are compelled. Therefore it is necessary to compel them.' The merits of the case would then be clearly defined. It would be exactly that of the slaveholders of South Carolina and Louisiana. 'It is necessary that cotton and sugar should be grown. White men cannot produce them. Negroes will not, for any wages which we choose to give. *Ergo* they must be compelled.' An illustration still closer to the point is that of impressment. Sailors must absolutely be had to defend the country. It often happens that they will not voluntarily enlist. Therefore there must be the power of forcing them. How often has this logic been used! and, but for one flaw in it, without doubt it would have been successful up to this day. But it is open to retort—First pay the sailors the honest value of their labour. When you have made it as well worth their while to serve you, as to work for other employers, you will have no more difficulty than others have in obtaining their services. To this there is no logical answer except 'I will not': and as people are now not only ashamed, but are not desirous, to rob the labourer of his hire, impressment is no longer advocated. Those who attempt to force women into marriage by closing all other doors against them, lay themselves open to a similar retort. If they mean what they say, their opinion must evidently be, that men do not render the married condition so desirable to women, as to induce them to accept it for its own recommendations. It is not a sign of one's thinking the boon one offers very attractive, when one allows only Hobson's choice, 'that or none.' And here, I believe, is the clue to the feelings of those men, who have a real antipathy to the equal freedom of women. I believe they are afraid, nor lest women should be unwilling to marry, for I do not think that any one in reality has that apprehension; but lest they should insist that marriage should be on equal conditions; lest all women of spirit and capacity should prefer doing almost anything else, not in their own eyes degrading, rather than marry, when marrying is giving themselves a master, and a master too of all their earthly possessions. And truly, if this consequence were necessarily incident to marriage, I think that the apprehension would be very well founded. I agree in thinking it probable that few women, capable of anything else, would, unless under an irresistible *entraînement,* rendering them for the time insensible to anything but itself, choose such a lot, when any other

means were open to them of filling a conventionally honourable place in life: and if men are determined that the law of marriage shall be a law of despotism, they are quite right, in point of mere policy, in leaving to women only Hobson's choice. But, in that case, all that has been done in the modern world to relax the chain on the minds of women, has been a mistake. They never should have been allowed to receive a literary education. Women who read, much more women who write, are, in the existing constitution of things, a contradiction and a disturbing element: and it was wrong to bring women up with any acquirements but those of an odalisque, or of a domestic servant.

## Note

1. Title page of Mme de Staël's *Delphine*.

# FRIEDRICH NIETZSCHE

## INTRODUCTION

## RICHARD SCHACHT

Friedrich Nietzsche was born on October 15, 1844, in the small town of Röcken in what is now the eastern part of Germany. He was only 4 when his father, the pastor of the local Lutheran church, died; he and his sister were raised by their widowed mother under very modest circumstances in the nearby town of Naumburg. His early loves were literature and music (at which he showed some ability, both as a pianist and as a composer). The brilliance Nietzsche displayed in his university education in the classics led to an astonishingly early appointment (when he was but 24) at the Swiss University of Basel, as professor of classical philology.

After just ten years (in 1879), poor health obliged him to resign. During the decade that followed he lived in boarding houses in Switzerland, Italy, and southern France, seeking a congenial environment and relief from the health problems that plagued him. Most of the writings for which he is best known today derive from that period. In early 1889, at the age of 44, he suffered a complete physical and mental collapse, from which he never recovered. He lived on for another eleven years, under first his mother's and then his sister's care, finally expiring in Weimar (to which his sister had moved him, to link him with Goethe and Schiller) on August 25, 1900; but his productive life had long since come to an end.

Nietzsche migrated intellectually from philology to philosophy on his own during his

Basel years. He in effect invented himself as a philosopher, and found his way to the kind of philosophy he believed to be needed to address the issues with which he believed contemporary humanity to be confronted. He was an astute and severe critic of social, cultural, and political developments in the Europe of his time, as well as of the pretensions of religion, morality, science, and his philosophical predecessors alike. But he also sought new and more adequate ways of comprehending ourselves as human beings and of assessing the kinds of lives human beings have led and might lead.

Proclaiming "the death of God" (by which he meant the collapse of traditional religious and metaphysical ways of thinking, and the untenability of any absolutes beyond this life and this world by reference to which they might be assessed), Nietzsche was deeply concerned about the crisis that might well follow in its wake. He gave the name "nihilism" to this crisis, which he conceived as a paralyzing disillusionment with the very ideas of any sort of truth, value, and meaning by reference to which life might be conceived, assessed, and found endurable and worth living. While commonly considered a nihilist himself, he actually sought to go "beyond" nihilism as well as the addiction to absolutes he believed set the stage for it, to develop a new way of thinking about this life in this world making the affirmation of these absolutes possible.

Nietzsche's new interpretation, which he cast in terms of "will to power," was linked to a project he called the "revaluation of all values." It revolved around the ideas of an "enhancement of life" and an attainable "higher humanity" (symbolized by the image of the *Übermensch* or "overman"), with creativity being the key to value and meaningfulness. He called for a "philosophy of the future" that would be "beyond good and evil" in its reinterpretive and revaluative endeavors. Unlike their European counterparts, academic philosophers in the English-speaking world were slow to take him seriously, but in recent decades they have begun to do so. It is now widely recognized that Nietzsche has much of interest to say about such things as truth and knowledge, human reality and human possibility, and values and morals.

Nietzsche has a good deal to say about politics as well, and its interest is far greater than appearances might seem to suggest. To be sure, he does assert that "what is great culturally has always been unpolitical, even *antipolitical*" (*Twilight of the Idols* VIII:4), and likewise proclaims himself "antipolitical." (*Ecce Homo* I:3) But his profession of "antipoliticism," like his self-proclaimed "immoralism," while an expression of his wish to dissociate himself from the kind of thing that passed for being "political" (and "moral") in the Germany of his day, is not an avowal of disinterest in any and all conceptions and forms of politics (and morals).

It further is undeniable that (thanks in part to the opportunistic promotional efforts of his politically conservative sister, who controlled his literary estate) Nietzsche was appropriated in European politics in the early decades of the twentieth century by the radical right in general, and by the Nazis in particular. But that was an utter travesty. Indeed, Hitler, the Nazis, and their Germany paradigmatically exemplify certain political possibilities and tendencies that Nietzsche contemplated with a mixture of contempt and alarm. Nationalism, statism, and militarism were profoundly alien to him, his occasional rhetoric and remarks seemingly to the contrary notwithstanding.

Thus Nietzsche very differently writes: "Better to perish than to hate and fear, and *twofold better to perish than to make oneself hated and feared*—this must one day become the supreme maxim of every individual state!" (*Human, All Too Human* II:II:284). In *Thus*

*Spoke Zarathustra* (1883), he has Zarathustra excoriate " 'state' " as "the name of the coldest of all cold monsters" (I:11). And he observes in *Twilight of the Idols* (1888): "One pays heavily for coming to power: power *makes stupid*," and laments: "*Deutschland, Deutschland über alles*—I fear that was the end of German philosophy" (VIII:2). Antisemitism likewise became increasingly repugnant to him. Nietzsche's political thinking may be problematic and even flawed in various respects (e.g., in his subscription to Lamarckianism, from which he draws a number of misguided political consequences); but in its many insights and its basic character and direction it needs no apology, and has considerable plausibility and power.

Morals and politics, for Nietzsche, are among the means by which humanity has bootstrapped its way to forms of existence that are no longer merely animal. Morals and politics thus have helped to set the stage for further such developments, through the operation of similar or other educational devices, even if these morals and politics themselves have long tended and commonly continue to be and to employ crude techniques of human engineering, engendered in the service of all-too-human or even pathological social and psychological imperatives, with effects upon those whose lives they touch that are often mixed at best.

Nietzsche's political philosophy, like his moral philosophy, is both interpretive and evaluative. Its basic premise is that politics and morals alike are human phenomena best regarded as *forms of life,* interpreted accordingly, and assessed in terms of whatever sorts of positive, negative, or mixed significance they turn out to have "in the service of life"—which itself can mean quite different things. And much of what he says about various forms of both of them is put forward as a variety of observations of how things tend to go under such differing sorts of arrangements with their associated values, and of what their consequences tend to be for the fostering or hindering of the realization and development of sundry human possibilities.

As a first approximation, politics for Nietzsche might be said to have to do with the mobilization and direction of human resources and associated structurings of human life within and among groups and communities of varying sorts and sizes; with the ways in which such structures are engendered, established, maintained, and modified; and with their impact upon the character and quality of human life. As in the case of his moral philosophy, the analytical and interpretive part of his political philosophy involves an attempt to develop the perspectives and conceptual tools with which to be able to understand its genealogies, motivations, social and psychological functions, and consequences in the lives of those who adopt them, as well as to set the stage for their assessment.

The new "great politics" of which Nietzsche sometimes speaks—in contrast to the "power politics" he derides (e.g., *Twilight of the Idols* VIII:3)—is fundamentally a *politics of culture,* revolving around the shaping and reshaping of institutions and practices affecting the way cultural life develops and proceeds. If Nietzsche approaches politics with an eye to culture (and vice versa), that is because he thinks it a fact of life that political life and cultural life are intimately entangled as well as divergent. Their entanglement is only to be expected, for they both reflect and also redirect the needs, interests, desires, fears, and all else that expresses what he calls the "will to power" of various groups and types of human beings. As a dimension of human social life, politics is an arena of *cultural contest.* Different sets of cultural values and their institutional expressions confront each other in this arena; and that confrontation is commonly conflictual rather than harmonious. That fact of life is not necessarily to be lamented, and indeed may even turn out to result in forms of competition that invigorate both the forms of life involved and their participants.

Indeed, the whole issue of what to make of difference, competition, and conflict in this arena—as elsewhere in human life—is one of Nietzsche's central political-analytical interests. His speculations along these lines are often jarring; but the specific observations he hazards are secondary to his insistence upon the importance of thinking about this whole matter in a manner unblinkered by the moralism that views everything through the lenses of its highly problematic notions of "good and evil." Eschewing political and moral "correctness" by itself may contribute little of a positive nature to its proper comprehension, but it is a necessary condition of getting anywhere in that direction.

Human social life may be thought of along the lines of something like games people have come to play; and politics has to do with the dynamics through which the games are played and how the nature, rules, and manner of playing of the games come to be settled and modified. Human beings are both the games' creators and creatures. They enter into the games as partly formed creatures, with differing constitutions and in differing circumstances; they become fully formed as human beings in the course of playing the games. In doing so, they contribute in some measure to whatever becomes of the games themselves. If it turns out that the games played are geared to the lowest common denominator, or are limited to a cluster of a single type or narrow range, human life will have a character quite different from what it might have had if there were a very different sort of mix of games, calling for diverse and unevenly distributed kinds and levels of play. And in societies of the latter sort it again makes a difference whether the alternatives are many or few, and whether they are static or amenable to change.

These games are not purely individual or simply interpersonal affairs, but rather are socioculturally structured interactions on scales large and small. They may be appealing to some, appalling to others, and indifferent or simply invisible to most; affording opportunities to assert themselves to some, while frustrating or excluding others; competing with each other for allegiance and priority; and waxing and waning in vitality and sway. They may move some to resentment and inspire opposition and reaction, even as they may satisfy and stimulate others. They may also combine with each other in dysfunctional or powerful alliances and chemistries, both in societies and in individuals.

Contemplating this spectacle, Nietzsche deems it foolish to suppose that there is any answer to the question of how it all ought to go. Different forms of life, he observes, do not come about entirely by accident. They answer to something in and about human beings of various sorts and circumstances, all providing in different ways for the channeling and articulation of their affective resources. He may have no enthusiasm for a good many of the games that have fared all too well in the culture wars of the past several millennia; but he is far from thinking that there are any political-theoretical grounds on which they can be faulted.

To be sure, Nietzsche can and does attack certain of these games, as a partisan of what he calls "higher humanity." At the same time, however, he recognizes that there are those for whom such arrangements may be optimal, or at any rate expressive of or ministrative to what they have come to be and to require. And in their preference for such arrangements, he does not suppose people to be making some sort of *theoretical mistake*. The problem he sees is with the spread of the arrangements to others for whom they are far from optimal, and to whose flourishing and development they may indeed be seriously detrimental. And this concerns him because he fears that, if people are induced to buy into and settle for lives lived along the former lines, the possibility of an enhancement of human life rendering human reality worthy of affirmation and a future may be jeopardized. It is from this standpoint that he weighs in polemically against various sorts of cultural, social, and political developments.

It is also with reference to considerations relating to life-enhancement that Nietzsche suggests a reassessment of certain sorts of phenomena that undeniably have had (and could again have) historical and real-world manifestations one might well view with dismay and alarm. They include things he is prepared to call by the harsh names commonly associated with their rudest forms—or at any rate, by names he provocatively uses as a challenge to those who tend to shrink from anything of the kind: for example, domination, exploitation, and even what he is prepared to call "slavery." But it is precisely here, where Nietzsche's language is at its most disturbing, that one must take the greatest care in interpreting as well as assessing him. For much of what he says along these lines at least purports to be genealogically descriptive and tentatively conjectural rather than prescriptive and ideological, and is presented in the spirit of the tough-minded, disillusioned, and intrepid "investigators and microscopists of the soul" he praises in *On the Genealogy of Morals,* who "have trained themselves to sacrifice all desirability to truth, *every* truth, even plain, harsh, ugly, repellent, unchristian, immoral truth. —For such truths do exist.—" (I:1).

Political life, for Nietzsche, may ultimately be an expression of colliding and competing "wills to power" and of the resulting social dynamics; but it is more concretely (if also very broadly) a matter of the *contested mobilization* of human resources, in the service of various human purposes, interests, or goods. And it commonly involves the devising of ways to get people to do things serving purposes they understand poorly if at all. That, for Nietzsche, is just the way it is. It is only to be expected, therefore, that mobilization in support of almost any sort of human endeavor—and quite certainly any that involve the intensive cultivation of human abilities of one sort or another, and the pursuit of ever more creative, refined, and demanding forms of excellence—will typically require manipulation and exploitation. And one must reckon with the idea that strong bonds of some sort or other will be necessary to render most such arrangements durable enough to amount to anything. This is not a happy thought; but if it is right, neither is the alternative.

Politics becomes most interesting, for Nietzsche, when one gets down to cases and begins to consider what sorts of outcomes are worth going for and against; what the conditions of their possibility would seem to be; how they might be furthered in the former case and countered in the latter; and whether the prices to be paid in both instances would appear to be worth it. But at this point political theory gives way to agenda setting; and the issue becomes not how political life is to be understood, but rather what values are to prevail.

The paramount political as well as human questions, for Nietzsche, concern the sorts of humanly possible cultural life that will wind up being fostered and furthered, considered in terms of their significance for the human future and human worth—their "value for life" and its "enhancement." This is what Nietzschean "great politics" is really all about, beyond all Nietzschean political philosophizing. And it is the radical openness of these questions, together with the impossibility of specifying the outcomes that would be most desirable, that accounts for both the trepidation and the fascination that it does and should inspire. But this is neither to its discredit nor to its particular credit; for if Nietzsche is right, what warrants both reactions is not his kind of politics itself, but rather that to which his conception of political life is meant to be true: the open-endedness and uncanniness of human life itself.

Nietzsche discusses things political in many of his writings, from his early unpublished essay "Homer's Contest" and *Human, All Too Human* to *Beyond Good and Evil, On the Genealogy of Morals,* and *Twilight of the Idols,* but nowhere sets forth his political thinking systematically or definitively. Walter Kaufmann's *Nietzsche: Philosopher, Psychologist, Antichrist* (Princeton, N.J.: Princeton University, 1974) remains a useful introduction to Nietzsche. Richard Schacht's *Nietzsche* (London: Routledge, 1983) explores his philosophical thinking more comprehensively and systematically. Mark Warren's *Nietzsche and Political Thought* (Cambridge, Mass.: MIT, 1988), the first substantial book on this subject in English, has been followed by many other studies from differing perspectives, including Bruce Detweiler's *Nietzsche and the Politics of Aristocratic Radicalism* (Chicago: University of Chicago Press, 1990); Lawrence Hatab's *A Nietzschean Defense of Democracy* (Chicago: Open Court, 1995); David Owen's *Nietzsche, Politics and Modernity* (London: Sage, 1995); Daniel Conway's *Nietzsche and the Political* (London and New York: Routledge, 1997); and Fredrick Appel's *Nietzsche Contra Democracy* (Ithaca, N.Y.: Cornell University, 1999).

# Human, All Too Human

## 5

### *Tokens of Higher and Lower Culture*

### 224

*Ennoblement through degeneration.*—History teaches that the branch of a nation that preserves itself best is the one in which most men have, as a consequence of sharing habitual and undiscussable principles, that is to say as a consequence of their common belief, a living sense of community. Here good, sound custom grows strong, here the subordination of the individual is learned and firmness imparted to character as a gift at birth and subsequently augmented. The danger facing these strong communities founded on similarly constituted, firm-charactered individuals is that of the gradually increasing inherited stupidity such as haunts all stability like its shadow. It is the more unfettered, uncertain and morally weaker individuals upon whom *spiritual progress* depends in such communities: it is the men who attempt new things and, in general, many things. Countless numbers of this kind perish on account of their weakness without producing any very visible effect; but in general, and especially when they leave posterity, they effect a loosening up and from time to time inflict an injury on the stable element of a community. It is precisely at this injured and weakened spot that the whole body is as it were *innoculated* with something new; its strength must, however, be as a whole sufficient to receive this new thing into its blood and to assimilate it. Degenerate natures are of the highest significance wherever progress is to be effected. Every progress of the whole has to be preceded by a partial weakening. The strongest natures *preserve* the type, the weaker help it to *evolve*.

Something similar occurs in the case of the individual human being; rarely is a degeneration, a mutilation, even a vice and physical or moral damage in general without an advantage in some other direction. The more sickly man, for example, will if he belongs to a warlike and restless race perhaps have more inducement to stay by himself and thereby acquire more repose and wisdom, the one-eyed will have *one* stronger eye, the blind will see more deeply within themselves and in any event possess sharper hearing. To this extent the celebrated struggle for existence does not seem to me to be the only theory by which the progress or strengthening of a man or a race can be explained. Two things, rather, must come together: firstly the augmentation of the stabilizing force through the union of minds in belief and communal feeling; then the possibility of the attainment of higher goals through the occurrence of degenerate natures and, as a consequence of them, partial weakenings and injurings of the stabilizing force; it is precisely the weaker nature, as the tenderer and more refined, that makes any progress possible at all. A people that becomes somewhere weak and fragile but is as a whole still strong and healthy is capable of absorbing the infection of the new and incorporating it to its own advantage. In the case of the individual human being, the task of education is to imbue him with such firmness and certainty he can no longer as a whole be in any way deflected from his path. Then, however, the educator has to inflict injuries upon him, or employ the injuries inflicted on him by fate, and when he has thus come to experience pain and distress something new and noble can be innoculated into the injured places. It will be taken up into the totality of his nature, and later the traces of its nobility will be perceptible in the fruits of his nature.

So far as the state is concerned, Macchiavelli says that 'the form of government signifies very little, even though semi-educated people think otherwise. The great goal of statecraft should be *duration*, which outweighs everything else, inasmuch as it is much more valuable than freedom.' Only when there is securely founded and guaranteed long duration is a steady evolution and ennobling innoculation at all possible: though the dangerous companion of all duration, established authority, will, to be sure, usually resist it.

### 472

*Religion and Government.*—As long as the state, or, more clearly, the government knows itself appointed as guardian for the benefit of the masses not yet of age, and on their behalf considers the question whether religion is to be preserved or abolished, it is very highly probable that it will always decide for the preservation of religion. . . . After these transitional struggles, which may well last a long time, it will at length be decided whether the religious parties are still strong enough to revive the past and turn back the wheel: in which case the state will unavoidably fall into the hands of enlightened despotism (perhaps less enlightened and more troubled by fear than formerly)—or whether the anti-religious parties will prevail and, perhaps through schooling and education, in the course of generations undermine the propagation of their opponents and finally render it impossible. Then, however, they too will experience a slackening of their enthusiasm for the state: it will grow ever clearer that, together with that religious adoration to which the state is a sacred mystery, a supraterrestrial institution, the attitude of veneration and piety towards it has also been undermined. Henceforth the individual will see only that side of it that promises to be useful or threatens to be harmful to him, and will bend all his efforts to acquiring influence upon it. But this competition will soon become too great, men and parties alternate too quickly, hurl one another too fiercely down from the hill after barely having attained the top. None of the measures effected by a government will be guaranteed continuity; everyone will draw back from undertakings that require quiet tending for decades or centuries if their fruits are to mature. No one will feel towards a law any greater obligation than that of bowing for the moment to the force which backs up the law: one will then at once set to work to subvert it with a new force, the creation of a new majority.

Finally—one can say this with certainty—distrust of all government, insight into the uselessness and destructiveness of these short-winded struggles will impel men to a quite novel resolve: the resolve to do away with the concept of the state, to the abolition of the distinction between private and public. Private companies will step by step absorb the business of the state: even the most resistant remainder of what was formerly the work of government (for example its activities designed to protect the private person from the private person) will in the long run be taken care of by private contractors. Disregard for and the decline and *death of the state,* the liberation of the private person (I take care not to say: of the individual), is the consequence of the democratic conception of the state; it is in this that its mission lies. When it has performed its task—which like everything human bears much rationality and irrationality in its womb—when every relapse into the old sickness has been overcome, a new page will be turned in the storybook of humanity in which there will be many strange tales to read and perhaps some of them good ones.

To repeat in brief what has just been said: the interests of tutelary government and the interests of religion go hand in hand together, so that when the latter begins to die out the foundations of the state too are undermined. The belief in a divine order in the realm of politics, in a sacred mystery in the existence of the state, is of religious origin: if religion disappears the state will unavoidably lose its ancient Isis veil and cease to excite reverence. Viewed from close to, the sovereignty of the people serves then to banish the last remnant of magic and superstition from this realm of feeling; modern democracy is the historical form of the *decay of the state.*

The prospect presented by this certain decay is, however, not in every respect an unhappy one: the prudence and self-interest of men are of all their qualities the best developed; if the state is no longer

equal to the demands of these forces then the last thing that will ensue is chaos: an invention more suited to their purpose than the state was will gain victory over the state. How many an organizing power has mankind not seen die out: for example that of the racial clan, which was for millennia far mightier than that of the family and indeed ruled and regulated long before the family existed. We ourselves have seen the idea of familial rights and power which once ruled as far as the Roman world extended grow ever paler and more impotent. Thus a later generation will see the state too shrink to insignificance in various parts of the earth—a notion many people of the present can hardly contemplate without fear and revulsion. To *work* for the dissemination and realization of this notion is another thing, to be sure: one has to have a very presumptuous idea of one's own intelligence and scarcely half an understanding of history to set one's hand to the plough already—while no one can yet show what seedcorn is afterwards to be scattered on the riven soil. Let us therefore put our trust in 'the prudence and self-interest of men' to preserve the existence of the state for some time yet and to repulse the destructive experiments of the precipitate and the over-zealous!

### 473

*Socialism with regard to its means.*—Socialism is the fanciful younger brother of the almost expired despotism whose heir it wants to be; its endeavours are thus in the profoundest sense reactionary. For it desires an abundance of state power such as only despotism has ever had; indeed it outbids all the despotisms of the past inasmuch as it expressly aspires to the annihilation of the individual, who appears to it like an unauthorized luxury of nature destined to be improved into a useful *organ of the community.* . . . Socialism can serve to teach, in a truly brutal and impressive fashion, what danger there lies in all accumulations of state power, and to that extent to implant mistrust of the state itself. When its harsh voice takes up the watchword 'as *much state as possible*' it thereby at first sounds noisier than ever: but soon the opposite cry comes through with all the greater force: '*as little state as possible*'.

## The Wanderer and His Shadow

### 284

*The means to real peace.*—No government nowadays admits that it maintains an army so as to satisfy occasional thirsts for conquest; the army is supposed to be for defence. That morality which sanctions self-protection is called upon to be its advocate. But that means to reserve morality to oneself and to accuse one's neighbour of immorality, since he has to be thought of as ready for aggression and conquest if our own state is obliged to take thought of means of self-defence; moreover, when our neighbour denies any thirst for aggression just as heatedly as our state does, and protests that he too maintains an army only for reasons of legitimate self-defence, our declaration of why we require an army declares our neighbour a hypocrite and cunning criminal who would be only too happy to *pounce upon* a harmless and unprepared victim and subdue him without a struggle. This is how all states now confront one another: they presuppose an evil disposition in their neighbour and a benevolent disposition in themselves. This presupposition, however, is a piece of *inhumanity* as bad as, if not worse than, a war would be; indeed, fundamentally it already constitutes an invitation to and cause of wars, because, as aforesaid, it imputes immorality to one's neighbour and thereby seems to provoke hostility and hostile acts on his part. The doctrine of the army as a means of self-defence must be renounced just as completely as the thirst for conquest.

And perhaps there will come a great day on which a nation distinguished for wars and victories and for the highest development of military discipline and thinking, and accustomed to making the heaviest sacrifices on behalf of these things, will cry of its own free will: '*we shall shatter the sword*'—and demolish its entire military machine down to its last foundations. *To disarm while being the best armed, out of an *elevation* of sensibility—that is the means to *real* peace, which must always rest on a disposition for peace: whereas the so-called armed peace such as now parades about in every country is a disposition to fractiousness which trusts neither itself nor its neighbour and fails to lay down its arms half out of hatred, half out of fear. Better to perish than to hate and fear, and *twofold better to perish than to make oneself hated and feared*—this must one day become the supreme maxim of every individual state!

As is well known, our liberal representatives of the people lack the time to reflect on the nature of man: otherwise they would know that they labour in vain when they work for a 'gradual reduction of the military burden'. On the contrary, it is only when this kind of distress is at its greatest that the only kind of god that can help here will be closest at hand. The tree of the glory of war can be destroyed only at a single stroke, by a lightning-bolt: lightning, however, as you well know, comes out of a cloud and from on high.

*End and means of democracy.*—Democracy wants to create and guarantee as much *independence* as possible: independence of opinion, of mode of life and of employment. To that end it needs to deprive of the right to vote both those who possess no property and the genuinely rich: for these are the two impermissable classes of men at whose abolition it must work continually, since they continually call its task into question. It must likewise prevent everything that seems to have for its objective the organization of parties. For the three great enemies of independence in the above-named threefold sense are the indigent, the rich and the parties.

I am speaking of democracy as of something yet to come. That which now calls itself democracy differs from older forms of government solely in that it drives with *new horses:* the streets are still the same old streets, and the wheels are likewise the same old wheels.

Have things really got less perilous because the wellbeing of the nations now rides in *this* vehicle?

# Thus Spoke Zarathustra

## FIRST PART

### *On the New Idol*

Somewhere there are still peoples and herds, but not where we live, my brothers: here there are states. State? What is that? Well then, open your ears to me, for now I shall speak to you about the death of peoples.

State is the name of the coldest of all cold monsters. Coldly it tells lies too; and this lie crawls out of its mouth: "I, the state, am the people." That is a lie! It was creators who created peoples and hung a faith and a love over them; thus they served life.

It is annihilators who set traps for the many and call them "state": they hang a sword and a hundred appetites over them.

Where there is still a people, it does not understand the state and hates it as the evil eye and the sin against customs and rights.

This sign I give you: every people speaks its tongue of good and evil, which the neighbor does not understand. It has invented its own language of customs and rights. But the state tells lies in all the tongues of good and evil; and whatever it says it lies—and whatever it has it has stolen. Everything about it is false; it bites with stolen teeth, and bites easily. Even its entrails are false. Confusion of tongues of good and evil: this sign I give you as the sign of the state. Verily, this sign signifies the will to death. Verily, it beckons to the preachers of death.

All-too-many are born: for the superfluous the state was invented.

Behold, how it lures them, the all-too-many—and how it devours them, chews them, and ruminates!

"On earth there is nothing greater than I: the ordering finger of God am I"—thus roars the monster. And it is not only the long-eared and short-sighted who sink to their knees. Alas, to you too, you great souls, it whispers its dark lies. Alas, it detects the rich hearts which like to squander themselves. Indeed, it detects you too, you vanquishers of the old god. You have grown weary with fighting, and now your weariness still serves the new idol. With heroes and honorable men it would surround itself, the new idol! It likes to bask in the sunshine of good consciences—the cold monster!

It will give you everything if you will adore it, this new idol: thus it buys the splendor of your virtues and the look of your proud eyes. It would use you as bait for the all-too-many.

Indeed, a hellish artifice was invented there, a horse of death, clattering in the finery of divine honors. Indeed, a dying for many was invented there, which praises itself as life: verily, a great service to all preachers of death!

State I call it where all drink poison, the good and the wicked; state, where all lose themselves, the good and the wicked; state, where the slow suicide of all is called "life." . . .

Escape from the bad smell! Escape from the steam of these human sacrifices!

The earth is free even now for great souls. There are still many empty seats for the lonesome and the twosome, fanned by the fragrance of silent seas.

A free life is still free for great souls. Verily,

whoever possesses little is possessed that much less: praised be a little poverty!

Only where the state ends, there begins the human being who is not superfluous: there begins the song of necessity, the unique and inimitable tune.

Where the state *ends*—look there, my brothers! Do you not see it, the rainbow and the bridges of the overman?

Thus spoke Zarathustra.

## THIRD PART

### On Old and New Tablets

#### 11

This is my pity for all that is past: I see how all of it is abandoned—abandoned to the pleasure, the spirit, the madness of every generation, which comes along and reinterprets all that has been as a bridge to itself.

A great despot might come along, a shrewd monster who, according to his pleasure and displeasure, might constrain and strain all that is past till it becomes a bridge to him, a harbinger and herald and cockcrow.

This, however, is the other danger and what prompts my further pity: whoever is of the rabble, thinks back as far as the grandfather; with the grandfather, however, time ends.

Thus all that is past is abandoned: for one day the rabble might become master and drown all time in shallow waters.

Therefore, my brothers, a *new nobility* is needed to be the adversary of all rabble and of all that is despotic and to write anew upon new tablets the word "noble."

For many who are noble are needed, and noble men of many kinds, that there may be a nobility. Or as I once said in a parable: "Precisely this is godlike that there are gods, but no God."

#### 12

O my brothers, I dedicate and direct you to a new nobility: you shall become procreators and cultiva-

tors and sowers of the future—verily, not to a nobility that you might buy like shopkeepers and with shopkeepers' gold: for whatever has its price has little value.

Not whence you come shall henceforth constitute your honor, but whither you are going! Your will and your foot which has a will to go over and beyond yourselves—that shall constitute your new honor. . . .

O my brothers, your nobility should not look backward but ahead! Exiles shall you be from all father- and forefather-lands! Your *children's land* shall you love: this love shall be your new nobility—the undiscovered land in the most distant sea. For that I bid your sails search and search.

In your children you shall make up for being the children of your fathers: thus shall you redeem all that is past. This new tablet I place over you.

## FOURTH PART

### On the Higher Man

#### 1

. . . You higher men, learn this from me: in the market place nobody believes in higher men. And if you want to speak there, very well! But the mob blinks: "We are all equal."

"You higher men"—thus blinks the mob—"there are no higher men, we are all equal, man is man; before God we are all equal."

Before God! But now this god has died. And before the mob we do not want to be equal. You higher men, go away from the market place!

#### 2

Before God! But now this god has died. You higher men, this god was your greatest danger. It is only since he lies in his tomb that you have been resurrected. Only now the great noon comes; only now the higher man becomes—lord.

Have you understood this word, O my brothers? You are startled? Do your hearts become giddy? Does the abyss yawn before you? Does the hell-hound howl at you? Well then, you higher men! Only now is the mountain of man's future in labor. God died: now *we* want the overman to live.

# Beyond Good and Evil

## SECTION FIVE

### *Towards a Natural History of Morals*

#### *202*

Let us immediately say once again what we have already said a hundred times, for nowadays ears are reluctant to hear such truths—*our* truths. We know perfectly well how offensive it sounds when someone counts man among the animals plain and simple, without metaphorical intent; but we will almost be accounted a *criminal* for always using expressions such as 'herd', 'herd instincts', and the like when speaking about people of 'modern ideas'. What's the use! We can't do otherwise, for this is just what our new insight is about. We discovered that Europe, and those countries dominated by a European influence, are now of one mind in all their key moral judgements: it is obvious that Europeans nowadays *know* that which Socrates thought he did not know, and what that famous old serpent once promised to teach—people 'know' what is good and evil. It must sound harsh and trouble the ears, then, if we insist over and over that it is the instinct of man the herd animal that thinks it knows, that glorifies itself and calls itself good whenever it allots praise or blame. This instinct has had a breakthrough, has come to predominance, has prevailed over the other instincts and continues to do so as a symptom of the increasing process of physiological approximations and resemblances. *Morality in Europe today is herd animal morality*—and thus, as we understand things, it is only one kind of human morality next to which, before which, after which many others, and especially *higher* moralities, are or should be possible. But this morality defends itself with all its strength against such 'possibilities', against such 'should be's'. Stubbornly and relentlessly it says, 'I am Morality itself, and nothing else is!' Indeed, with the help of a religion that played along with and flattered the most sublime desires of the herd animal, we have reached the point of finding an ever more visible expression of this morality even in political and social structures: the *democratic* movement is Christianity's heir.

#### *203*

We who hold a different belief—we who consider the democratic movement not merely a decadent form of political organization, but a decadent (that is to say, diminished) form of the human being, one that mediocritizes him and debases his value: what can *we* set our hopes on?

On *new philosophers,* we have no other choice; on spirits that are strong and original enough to give impetus to opposing value judgements and to revalue, to reverse 'eternal values'; on forerunners, on men of the future, who in the present will forge the necessary link to force a thousand-year-old will onto *new* tracks. They will teach humans that their future is their *will,* that the future depends on their human will, and they will prepare the way for great risk-taking and joint experiments in discipline and breeding in order to put an end to that terrible reign of nonsense and coincidence that until now has been known as 'history' (the nonsense about the 'greatest number' is only its most recent form). To accomplish this,

Reprinted from *Beyond Good and Evil,* translated by Marion Faber (Oxford University Press, 1998). By permission of the publisher.

new kinds of philosophers and commanders will eventually be necessary, whose image will make all the secretive, frightful, benevolent spirits that have existed in the world look pale and dwarfish. The image of such leaders is what hovers before *our* eyes—may I say it aloud, you free spirits? The circumstances that would have to be in part created, in part exploited to give rise to these leaders; the probable paths and tests by which a soul would grow so great and powerful that it would feel *compelled* to accomplish these projects, a revaluation of values, under whose new hammer and pressure the conscience would be transformed into steel, the heart into bronze, so that they could bear the weight of such responsibility; the indispensability of such leaders; on the other hand, the terrible danger that they might not arrive or might go astray and degenerate—those are really the things that concern and worry *us*—do you know that, you free spirits?—those are the distant oppressive thoughts and thunderstorms that pass across the sky of *our* life. There are few pains so raw as to have once observed, understood, sympathized while an extraordinary man strayed from his path or degenerated: but a person with the rare vision to see the general danger that 'man' himself *is degenerating,* who has recognized as we have the tremendous randomness that thus far has been at play in determining the future of mankind (a play that has been guided by no one's hand, not even by 'God's finger!'), who has guessed the fate that lies hidden in all the stupid innocence and blissful confidence of 'modern ideas', and even more in the entire Christian-European morality: this person suffers from an anxiety that cannot be compared to any other. With one single glance he grasps everything that *mankind could be bred to be* if all its energies and endeavours were gathered together and heightened; with all the knowledge of his conscience, he knows how mankind's greatest possibilities have as yet been untapped, and how many mysterious decisions and new paths the human type has already encountered—he knows better yet, from his most painful memory, what kind of wretched things have usually caused the finest example of an evolving being to shatter, break apart, sink down, become wretched. The *overall degeneration of man,* right down to what socialist fools

and flatheads call their 'man of the future' (their ideal!); this degeneration and diminution of man into a perfect herd animal (or, as they call it, man in a 'free society'); this bestialization of man into a dwarf animal with equal rights and claims is *possible,* no doubt about that! Anyone who has thought this possibility through to its end knows no disgust but other people—and also, perhaps, a new *project!* . . .

## SECTION NINE

### *What Is Noble?*

### *257*

In the past, every elevation of the type 'human being' was achieved by an aristocratic society—and this will always be the case: by a society that believes in a great ladder of hierarchy and value differentiation between people and that requires slavery in one sense or another. Without the *grand feeling of distance* that grows from inveterate class differences, from the ruling caste's constant view downwards onto its underlings and tools, and from its equally constant practice in obeying and commanding, in holding down and holding at arm's length—without this grand attitude, that other, more mysterious attitude could never exist, that longing for ever greater distances within the soul itself, the development of ever higher, rarer, more far-flung, extensive, spacious inner states, in short, the elevation of the type 'human being', the continual 'self-overcoming of the human', to use a moral formula in a supra-moral sense. To be sure, we must not give in to any humanitarian delusions about these aristocratic societies' historical origins (that is, about the preconditions for that elevation of the type 'human'): the truth is harsh. Let us not mince words in describing to ourselves the *beginnings* of every previous higher culture on earth! People who still had a nature that was natural, barbarians in every terrible sense of the word, predatory humans, whose strength of will and desire for power were still unbroken, threw themselves upon the weaker, more well-behaved, peaceable, perhaps trading or stockbreeding races, or upon old, crumbling cultures whose remaining life-force was flickering out in a brilliant fireworks display of wit and depravity. At the beginning, the noble caste was always the barbarian caste: its dominance was not due to its physical strength primarily, but rather to its spiritual—these were the *more complete* human beings (which at every level also means the 'more complete beasts').

## 258

Corruption, as the expression of impending anarchy among the instincts and of the collapse of the emotional foundations called 'life': this corruption will vary fundamentally according to the form of life in which it manifests itself. When for example an aristocracy like pre-Revolutionary France tosses away its privileges with sublime revulsion and sacrifices itself to its excess of moral feeling, this is corruption: it was really only the final act of that centuries-long corruption that caused the aristocracy to abandon its tyrannical authority bit by bit and reduce itself to a *function* of the monarchy (and ultimately in fact to its ornament and showpiece). The crucial thing about a good and healthy aristocracy, however, is that it does *not* feel that it is a function (whether of monarchy or community) but rather its *essence* and highest justification—and that therefore it has no misgivings in condoning the sacrifice of a vast number of people who must *for its sake* be oppressed and diminished into incomplete people, slaves, tools. Its fundamental belief must simply be that society can *not* exist for its own sake, but rather only as a foundation and scaffolding to enable a select kind of creature to ascend to its higher task and in general to its higher *existence*—much like those sun-loving climbing plants on Java (called *sipo matador*) whose tendrils encircle an oak tree so long and so repeatedly that finally, high above it but still supported by it, they are able to unfold their coronas in the free air and make a show of their happiness.

## 259

To refrain from injuring, abusing, or exploiting one another; to equate another person's will with our own: in a certain crude sense this can develop into good manners between individuals, if the precondi-

tions are in place (that is, if the individuals have truly similar strength and standards and if they are united within one single social body). But if we were to try to take this principle further and possibly even make it the *basic principle of society,* it would immediately be revealed for what it is: a will to *deny* life, a principle for dissolution and decline. We must think through the reasons for this and resist all sentimental frailty: life itself *in its essence* means appropriating, injuring, overpowering those who are foreign and weaker; oppression, harshness, forcing one's own forms on others, incorporation, and at the very least, at the very mildest, exploitation—but why should we keep using this kind of language, that has from time immemorial been infused with a slanderous intent? Even that social body whose individuals, as we have just assumed above, treat one another as equals (this happens in every healthy aristocracy) must itself, if the body is vital and not moribund, do to other bodies everything that the individuals within it refrain from doing to one another: it will have to be the will to power incarnate, it will want to grow, to reach out around itself, pull towards itself, gain the upper hand—not out of some morality or immorality, but because it is *alive,* and because life simply *is* the will to power. This, however, more than anything else, is what the common European consciousness resists learning; people everywhere are rhapsodizing, even under the guise of science, about future social conditions that will have lost their 'exploitative character'—to my ear that sounds as if they were promising to invent a life form that would refrain from all organic functions. 'Exploitation'—is not part of a decadent or imperfect, primitive society: it is part of the *fundamental nature* of living things, as its fundamental organic function; it is a consequence of the true will to power, which is simply the will to life.

Assuming that this is innovative as theory—as reality it is the *original fact* of all history: let us at least be this honest with ourselves!

## 260

While perusing the many subtler and cruder moral codes that have prevailed or still prevail on earth thus far, I found that certain traits regularly recurred in combination, linked to one another—until finally two basic types were revealed and a fundamental difference leapt out at me. There are *master moralities* and *slave moralities.* I would add at once that in all higher and more complex cultures, there are also apparent attempts to mediate between the two moralities, and even more often a confusion of the two and a mutual misunderstanding, indeed sometimes even their violent juxtaposition—even in the same person, within one single breast. Moral value distinctions have emerged either from among a masterful kind, pleasantly aware of how it differed from those whom it mastered, or else from among the mastered, those who were to varying degrees slaves or dependants. In the first case, when it is the masters who define the concept 'good', it is the proud, exalted states of soul that are thought to distinguish and define the hierarchy. The noble person keeps away from those beings who express the opposite of these elevated, proud inner states: he despises them. Let us note immediately that in this first kind of morality the opposition 'good' and 'bad' means about the same thing as 'noble' and 'despicable'—the opposition 'good' and 'evil' has a different origin. The person who is cowardly or anxious or petty or concerned with narrow utility is despised; likewise the distrustful person with his constrained gaze, the self-disparager, the craven kind of person who endures maltreatment, the importunate flatterer, and above all the liar: all aristocrats hold the fundamental conviction that the common people are liars. 'We truthful ones'—that is what the ancient Greek nobility called themselves. It is obvious that moral value distinctions everywhere are first attributed to *people* and only later and in a derivative fashion applied to *actions:* for that reason moral historians commit a crass error by starting with questions such as: 'Why do we praise an empathetic action?' The noble type of person feels *himself* as determining value—he does not need approval, he judges that 'what is harmful to me is harmful per se', he knows that he is the one who causes things to be revered in the first place, he *creates values.* Everything that he knows of himself he reveres: this kind of moral code is self-

glorifying. In the foreground is a feeling of fullness, of overflowing power, of happiness in great tension, an awareness of a wealth that would like to bestow and share—the noble person will also help the unfortunate, but not, or not entirely, out of pity, but rather from the urgency created by an excess of power. The noble person reveres the power in himself, and also his power over himself, his ability to speak and to be silent, to enjoy the practice of severity and harshness towards himself and to respect everything that is severe and harsh. 'Wotan placed a harsh heart within my breast,' goes a line in an old Scandinavian saga: that is how it is written from the heart of a proud Viking—and rightly so. For this kind of a person is proud *not* to be made for pity; and so the hero of the saga adds a warning: 'If your heart is not harsh when you are young, it will never become harsh.' The noble and brave people who think like this are the most removed from that other moral code which sees the sign of morality in pity or altruistic behaviour or *désintéressement;* belief in ourselves, pride in ourselves, a fundamental hostility and irony towards 'selflessness'—these are as surely a part of a noble morality as caution and a slight disdain towards empathetic feelings and 'warm hearts'.

It is the powerful who *understand* how to revere, it is their art form, their realm of invention. Great reverence for old age and for origins (all law is based upon this twofold reverence), belief in ancestors and prejudice in their favour and to the disadvantage of the next generation—these are typical in the morality of the powerful; and if, conversely, people of 'modern ideas' believe in progress and 'the future' almost by instinct and show an increasing lack of respect for old age, that alone suffices to reveal the ignoble origin of these 'ideas'. Most of all, however, the master morality is foreign and embarrassing to current taste because of the severity of its fundamental principle: that we have duties only towards our peers, and that we may treat those of lower rank, anything foreign, as we think best or 'as our heart dictates' or in any event 'beyond good and evil'—pity and the like should be thought of in this context. The ability and duty to feel enduring gratitude or vengefulness (both only within a circle of equals), subtlety in the forms of retribution, a refined concept of friendship, a certain need for enemies (as drainage channels for the emotions of envy, combativeness, arrogance—in essence, in order to be a good *friend*): these are the typical signs of a noble morality, which, as we have suggested, is not the morality of 'modern ideas' and is therefore difficult to sympathize with these days, also difficult to dig out and uncover.

It is different with the second type of morality, *slave morality.* Assuming that the raped, the oppressed, the suffering, the shackled, the weary, the insecure engage in moralizing, what will their moral value judgements have in common? They will probably express a pessimistic suspicion about the whole human condition, and they might condemn the human being along with his condition. The slave's eye does not readily apprehend the virtues of the powerful: he is sceptical and distrustful, he is *keenly* distrustful of everything that the powerful revere as 'good'—he would like to convince himself that even their happiness is not genuine. Conversely, those qualities that serve to relieve the sufferers' existence are brought into relief and bathed in light: this is where pity, a kind, helpful hand, a warm heart, patience, diligence, humility, friendliness are revered—for in this context, these qualities are most useful and practically the only means of enduring an oppressive existence. Slave morality is essentially a morality of utility. It is upon this hearth that the famous opposition 'good' and '*evil*' originates— power and dangerousness, a certain fear-inducing, subtle strength that keeps contempt from surfacing, are translated by experience into evil. According to slave morality, then, the 'evil' person evokes fear, according to master morality, it is exactly the 'good' person who evokes fear and wants to evoke it, while the 'bad' person is felt to be despicable. . . .

## 262

A *species* comes into being, a type grows strong and fixed, by struggling for a long time with essentially similar *unfavourable* conditions. Conversely, as we know from the experiences of stock-breeders, a species that is given over-abundant nourishment and

extra protection and care generally shows an immediate and very pronounced tendency to variations in type, and is rich in marvels and monstrosities (and in monstrous vices, too). Now let us consider an aristocratic community, such as the ancient Greek *polis,* say, or Venice, as an organization whose voluntary or involuntary purpose is to *breed:* there are people coexisting in it, relying on one another, who want to further their species, chiefly because they *must* further it or run some sort of terrible risk of extermination. In such a case, good will, excess, and protection, those conditions that favour variation, are missing; the species needs to remain a species, something that by virtue of its very harshness, symmetry, and simplicity of form, can be furthered and in general endure throughout all its continual struggles with its neighbours or with oppressed peoples who threaten rebellion or revolt. From its most diverse experience the species learns which qualities have particularly contributed to its survival, to its continuing victory in defiance of all gods and peoples: these qualities it calls virtues, and these are the only virtues that it cultivates. It is done harshly, indeed it demands harshness; every aristocratic moral code is intolerant, be it in educating its children, in disposing of its women, in its marital customs, in the relations of its old and young, or in its punitive laws (which apply only to the deviant); even intolerance itself is counted as a virtue, going by the name of 'justice'. A type like this, with few but very strong characteristics, a species of severe, warlike, prudently taciturn, closed and uncommunicative people (and as such most subtly attuned to the charms and nuances of society) thus becomes established beyond generational change; as mentioned above, its continual struggle with the same *unfavourable* conditions causes the type to become fixed and harsh. Eventually, however, it arrives at a period of good fortune, the tremendous tension relaxes; perhaps there are no longer any enemies among its neighbours and its means for living, even for enjoying life, are plentiful. At one single stroke the coercing bond of the old discipline is torn apart: it is no longer felt to be essential, critical for existence—if such discipline wished to endure, it could do so only as a kind of *luxury,* as an archaic *taste.* Variation, whether as deviance (into something higher, finer, more rare) or as degeneration and monstrosity is suddenly on the scene in all its greatest fullness and splendour; the individual dares to be an individual and stand out. During these historical turning points, we see splendid, manifold, jungle-like upgrowths and upsurges coexisting and often inextricably tangled up with one another; competition for growth assumes a kind of *tropical* tempo and there is a tremendous perishing and causing-to-perish, owing to the wild egoisms that challenge one another with seeming explosiveness, struggling 'for sun and light', and no longer knowing how to derive any set of limits, any restraint, any forbearance from their earlier moral code. It was this very moral code, in fact, that stored up the energy to such a monstrous extent, that tensed the bow so ominously—and now that code is, or is becoming 'obsolete'. The dangerous and sinister point is reached where the greater, more differentiated, richer life *survives beyond* the old morality; the 'individual' is left standing, forced to be his own lawgiver, to create his own arts and wiles of self-preservation, self-advancement, self-redemption.

# On the Genealogy of Morals

## SECOND ESSAY

### *'Guilt', 'Bad Conscience', and Related Matters*

*1*

The breeding of an animal which is *entitled to make promises*—is this not the paradoxical task which nature has set itself with respect to man? Is this not the real problem which man not only poses but faces also? . . . Even this necessarily forgetful animal—in whom forgetting is a strength, a form of *robust* health—has now bred for himself a counter-faculty, a memory, by means of which forgetfulness is in certain cases suspended—that is, those which involve promising. This development is not merely the result of a passive inability to rid oneself of an impression once etched on the mind, nor of the incapacity to digest a once-given word with which one is never through, but represents rather an active *will* not to let go, an ongoing willing of what was once willed, a real *memory of the will:* so that between the original 'I will', 'I shall do', and the actual realization of the will, its *enactment,* a world of new and strange things, circumstances, even other acts of will may safely intervene, without causing this long chain of the will to break. But how much all this presupposes! In order to dispose of the future in advance in this way, how much man must first have learnt to distinguish necessity from accident! To think in terms of causality, to see and anticipate from afar, to posit ends and means with certainty, to be able above all to reckon and calculate! For that to be the case, how much man himself must have become *calculable, regular, necessary,* even to his own mind, so that finally he would be able to vouch for himself *as future,* in the way that someone making a promise does!

*2*

Such is the long history of the origin of *responsibility.* As we have already grasped, the task of breeding an animal which is entitled to make promises presupposes as its condition a more immediate task, that of first *making* man to a certain extent necessary, uniform, an equal among equals, regular and consequently calculable. The enormous labour of what I have called the 'morality of custom'—the special work of man on himself throughout the longest era of the human race, his whole endeavour *prior to the*

Reprinted from *On the Genealogy of Morals,* translated by Douglas Smith. Oxford University Press, 1996. By permission of the publisher.

*onset of history,* all this finds its meaning, its great justification—regardless of the degree to which harshness, tyranny, apathy, and idiocy are intrinsic to it—in the following fact: it was by means of the morality of custom and the social strait-jacket that man was really *made* calculable. By way of contrast, let us place ourselves at the other end of this enormous process, at the point where the tree finally bears its fruit, where society and its morality of custom finally reveal the *end* to which they were merely a means: there we find as the ripest fruit on their tree the *sovereign individual,* the individual who resembles no one but himself, who has once again broken away from the morality of custom, the autonomous supramoral individual (since 'autonomous' and 'moral' are mutually exclusive)—in short, the man with his own independent, enduring will, the man who is *entitled to make promises.* And in him we find a proud consciousness, tense in every muscle, of *what* has finally been achieved here, of what has become incarnate in him—a special consciousness of power and freedom, a feeling of the ultimate completion of man. This liberated man, who is really *entitled* to make promises, this master of *free* will, this sovereign—how should he not be aware of his superiority over everything which cannot promise and vouch for itself? How should he not be aware of how much trust, how much fear, how much respect he arouses—he '*deserves*' all three—and how much mastery over circumstances, over nature, and over all less reliable creatures with less enduring wills is necessarily given into his hands along with this self-mastery? The 'free' man—the owner of an enduring, indestructible will—possesses also in this property his *measure of value:* looking out at others from his own vantage-point, he bestows respect or contempt. Necessarily, he respects those who are like him—the strong and reliable (those who are *entitled* to make promises), that is, anyone who promises like a sovereign—seriously, seldom, slowly—who is sparing with his trust, who *confers distinction* when he trusts, who gives his word as something which can be relied on, because he knows himself strong enough to uphold it even against accidents, even 'against fate'. Even so, he will have to keep the toe

of his boot poised for the cowering dogs who make promises without entitlement, and hold his stick at the ready for the liar who breaks his word the moment he utters it. The proud knowledge of this extraordinary privilege of *responsibility,* the consciousness of this rare freedom, this power over oneself and over fate has sunk down into his innermost depths and has become an instinct, a dominant instinct—what will he call it, this dominant instinct, assuming that he needs a name for it? About that there can be no doubt: this sovereign man calls it his *conscience.*

### 16

At this point, I can no longer avoid giving my own hypothesis as to the origin of 'bad conscience' its first, provisional expression: it does not make for easy listening and requires a long period of continuous reflection and consideration, filling waking and sleeping hours. I take bad conscience to be the deep sickness to which man was obliged to succumb under the pressure of that most fundamental of all changes—when he found himself definitively locked in the spell of society and peace. These half-animals who were happily adapted to a life of wilderness, war, nomadism, and adventure were affected in a similar way to the creatures of the sea when they were forced either to adapt to life on land or to perish—in a single stroke, all their instincts were devalued and 'suspended'. From that moment on they had to walk on their feet and 'support themselves', where previously they had been supported by water: a horrific weight bore down on them. The simplest tasks made them feel clumsy, they were without their old guides in this new, unknown world, the regulating drives with their instinctive certainty—they were reduced, these unfortunate creatures, to thinking, drawing conclusions, calculating, combining causes and effects, to their 'consciousness', their most meagre and unreliable organ! I believe that never on earth had there been such a feeling of misery, such leaden discomfort. Nor did the old instincts all of a sudden cease making their demands! Only it was difficult and seldom possible to obey them: for the most part, they had to seek new and, at the same time, sub-terranean satisfactions for themselves. Every instinct which does not vent itself externally *turns inwards*—this is what I call the *internalization* of man: it is at this point that what is later called the 'soul' first develops in man. The whole inner world, originally stretched thinly as between two membranes, has been extended and expanded, has acquired depth, breadth, and height in proportion as the external venting of human instinct has been *inhibited*. Those fearful bul-warks by means of which the state organization pro-tected itself against the old instincts of freedom—punishment belongs above all to these bulwarks—, caused all the instincts of the wild, free, nomadic man to turn backwards *against man himself*. Hostility, cruelty, pleasure in persecution, in assault, in change, in destruction,—all that turning against the man who possesses such instincts: *such* is the origin of 'bad conscience'. The man who is forced into an oppres-sively narrow and regular morality, who for want of external enemies and resistance impatiently tears, persecutes, gnaws, disturbs, mistreats himself, this animal which is to be 'tamed', which rubs himself raw on the bars of his cage, this deprived man con-sumed with homesickness for the desert, who had no choice but to transform himself into an adventure, a place of torture, an uncertain and dangerous wilder-ness—this fool, this yearning and desperate prisoner became the inventor of 'bad conscience'. But with him was introduced the greatest and most sinister sickness which still afflicts man even today, man's suffering *from man, from himself:* this as a result of a violent separation from his animal past, of a leap which is also a fall into new situations and conditions of existence, of a declaration of war against the old instincts, which previously constituted the basis of his strength, pleasure, and fearfulness. On the other hand, let us add immediately that with the emergence of an animal soul turned against itself and taking sides against itself, something so new, so deep, so unprecedented, so enigmatic *and pregnant with the future* came into existence that the earth's aspect was essentially altered. In fact, it took divine spectators to appreciate fully the drama which began at that time and whose end is not yet in sight, not by a long way—a drama too fine, too marvellous, too paradoxical to

be allowed to run senselessly unnoticed on just any ridiculous star! Since that time, man *counts* among the most unexpected and exciting lucky throws of the dice played by Heraclitus' 'great child'—whether that be Zeus or chance—he arouses interest, sus-pense, hope, almost certainty, as if in him something were being announced, were being prepared, as if man were not an end in himself, but rather only a pathway, an incident, a bridge, a great promise.

## 17

This hypothesis as to the origin of bad conscience presupposes first that this change was not gradual and voluntary, an organic growth into new condi-tions, but rather a break, a leap, a compulsion, an irrefutable fate, against which there was no struggle nor even any *ressentiment*. And secondly, that the insertion of a previously unrestrained and unshaped population into a fixed form, just as it began with an act of violence, was only brought to completion through simple acts of violence—that the oldest 'state' accordingly emerged and endured as a fearful tyranny, as a crushing and thoughtless machinery, until such a raw material of common people and half-animals was finally not only thoroughly kneaded and malleable but also *formed*. I used the word 'state': it goes without saying what I mean by that—some horde or other of blond predatory ani-mals, a race of conquerors and masters which, itself organized for war and with the strength to organize others, unhesitatingly lays its fearful paws on a pop-ulation which may be hugely superior in numerical terms but remains shapeless and nomadic. Such is the beginning of the 'state' on earth: I think that the sentimental effusion which suggested that it origi-nates in a 'contract' has been done away with. He who is capable of giving commands, who is a 'mas-ter' by nature, who behaves violently in deed and gesture—what are contracts to him! One does not reckon with such beings, they arrive like fate, with-out motive, reason, consideration, pretext, they arrive like lightning, too fearful, too sudden, too con-vincing, too 'different', even to be hated. Their work is an instinctive creation and impression of form, they are the most involuntary, most unconscious artists there are—wherever they appear, something new quickly grows up, a *living* structure of domination, in which parts and functions are demarcated and articulated, where only that which has first been given a 'meaning' with respect to the whole finds a place. The meaning of guilt, responsibility, and consideration is unknown to these born organizers; the fearful egoism of the artist presides in them, with its gaze of bronze and sense of being justified in advance to all eternity in its 'work', like the mother in her child. *They* were not the ones among whom 'bad conscience' grew up, as goes without saying

from the outset—but it would not have grown up *without them,* this ugly weed, it would not exist if, under the force of their hammer-blows, of their artists' violence, a vast quantity of freedom had not been expelled from the world, or at least removed from visibility and, as it were, forcibly made *latent.* This *instinct of freedom* made latent through force—as we have already understood—this instinct of freedom, forced back, trodden down, incarcerated within and ultimately still venting and discharging itself only upon itself: such is *bad conscience* at its origin, that and nothing more.

# Twilight of the Idols

## THE 'IMPROVERS' OF HUMANITY

### 1

People are familiar with my call for the philosopher to place himself *beyond* good and evil—to have the illusion of moral judgement *beneath* him. This call results from an insight which I was the first to formulate: *that there are no moral facts at all.* Moral judgement has this in common with religious judgement, that it believes in realities which do not exist. Morality is merely an interpretation of certain phenomena, more precisely a *mis*interpretation. Moral judgement pertains, like religious judgement, to a level of ignorance on which the very concept of the real, the distinction between the real and the imaginary, is still lacking: so that 'truth', on such a level, designates nothing but what we nowadays call 'illusions'. In this respect moral judgement should never be taken literally: as such it is only ever an absurdity. But as a *semiotics* it remains inestimable: it reveals, at least to anyone who knows, the most valuable realities of cultures and interiorities which did not *know* enough to 'understand' themselves. Morality is merely sign language, merely symptomatology: you must already know *what* is going on in order to profit by it.

### 2

A first, quite provisional example. Throughout the ages people have wanted to 'improve' humanity: this above all is what has been called morality. But under the same word the most extraordinary variety of tendencies is hiding. Both the *taming* of the beast man and the *breeding* of a particular species of man have been called 'improvement': these zoological terms alone express realities—realities, of course, about which the typical 'improver', the priest, knows nothing—*wants* to know nothing . . . To call the taming of an animal its 'improvement' is to our ears almost a joke. Anyone who knows what goes on in menageries will doubt that a beast is 'improved' there. It is weakened, it is made less harmful, it is turned into a *diseased* beast through the depressive emotion of fear, through pain, through wounding, through hunger.—It is no different with the tamed human being whom the priest has 'improved'. In the early Middle Ages, when the church was in fact primarily a menagerie, people on all sides hunted down the finest examples of the 'blond beast'—they 'improved' the noble Teutons, for example. But afterwards what did such an 'improved' Teuton look like, once he had been tempted into the monastery? Like a caricature of a human being, like an abortion:

Reprinted from *Twilight of the Idols,* translated by Duncan Large, Oxford University Press, 1998. By permission of the publisher.

he had become a 'sinner', he was stuck in a cage, he had been locked in between nothing but dreadful concepts. . . . There he now lay, sick, wretched, malevolent towards himself; filled with hatred of the vital drives, filled with suspicion towards all that was still strong and happy. In short, a 'Christian' . . . Physiologically speaking: in the struggle with the beast, making it sick is the only *possible* means of weakening it. The church understood this: it *ruined* man, it weakened him—but it claimed to have 'improved' him.

### 3

Let us take the other case of so-called morality, the case of *breeding* a particular race and kind. The most magnificent example of this is provided by Indian morality, sanctioned as a religion in the *Law of Manu*. Here the task is set of breeding no fewer than four races at once: a priestly one, a warrior one, a commercial and agricultural one, and finally a servant race, the Sudras. Clearly we are no longer among animal-tamers here. . . . But even this organization needed to be *terrible*—this time in struggling not with the beast, but with *its* antithetical concept, the unbred human being, mish-mash man, the Chandala. And again it had no other way of making him harmless and weak than by making him *sick*—it was a struggle with the 'great number'. There is perhaps nothing which contradicts our sensibility more than *these* defensive measures of Indian morality.

### 5

The morality of *breeding* and the morality of *taming* are altogether worthy of each other in the ways they win through: we can set it down as our highest proposition that in order to *make* morality one must have an absolute will to its opposite. This is the great *uncanny* problem which I have been investigating the longest: the psychology of the 'improvers' of humanity. A little and fundamentally modest fact, the so-called *pia fraus,* first gave me access to this problem: the *pia fraus,* the legacy of all the philosophers and priests who have 'improved' humanity. Neither Manu nor Plato nor Confucius, nor the Jewish and Christian

doctors, have ever doubted their *right* to lie. Nor have they doubted *quite different rights.* . . . Expressing it in a formula, one might say: *all* the means by which humanity was meant to have been made moral so far were fundamentally *immoral.*—

## RECONNAISSANCE RAIDS OF AN UNTIMELY MAN

### 37

. . . Periods of strength, *noble* cultures, see something contemptible in sympathy, in 'loving one's neighbour', in a lack of self and self-esteem.—Periods should be measured by their *positive energies*—in which case that Renaissance period, so extravagant and fateful, emerges as the last *great* period, and we, we moderns with our anxious self-welfare and brotherly love, with our virtues of work, unpretentiousness, abiding by the law, scientificity—accumulative, economical, machine-like—emerge as a *weak* period . . . Our virtues are determined, *provoked* by our weakness. . . . 'Equality', a certain actual assimilation, which the theory of 'equal rights' merely expresses, is of the essence of decline: the gulf between man and man, rank and rank; the multiplicity of types; the will to be oneself, to stand out—everything I call *pathos of distance*—is proper to every *strong* period. The tension, the span between extremes is getting smaller and smaller these days—ultimately the extremes themselves are becoming so blurred as to resemble each other . . . All our political theories *and* state constitutions—the 'German Reich' by no means excepted—are derivatives, necessary consequences, of decline; the unconscious effect of *décadence* has mastered even the ideals of specific sciences. . . . *Declining* life, the waning of any organizing energy, i.e., any dividing, gulf-opening, sub- and superordinating energy, is formulated by today's sociology into an *ideal* . . .

### 38

*My Idea of Freedom.*—The value of a thing sometimes depends not on what we manage to do with it, but on what we pay for it—what it *costs* us. Let me give an example. Liberal institutions stop being liberal as soon as they have been set up: afterwards there is no one more inveterate or thorough in damaging freedom than liberal institutions. Now we know *what* they achieve: they undermine the will to power, they are the levelling of mountain and valley elevated to the status of morality, they make things petty, cowardly, and hedonistic—with them the herd animal triumphs every time. Liberalism: in plain words *herd-animalization* . . . While these same institutions are still being fought for, they produce quite different effects: then they are actually powerful promoters of freedom. On closer inspection, it is war that produces these effects, war waged *for* liberal institutions, which as war allows the *illiberal* instincts to persist. And war is an education in freedom. For what is freedom! Having the will to be responsible to oneself. Maintaining the distance which divides us off from each other. Becoming more indifferent towards hardship, harshness, privation, even life itself. Being prepared to sacrifice people to one's cause—oneself included. . . . The nations which were worth something, *became* worth something, never did so under liberal institutions: it was *great danger* that turned them into something worthy of respect, the kind of danger without which we would not know our instruments, our virtues, our defences and weapons, our *spirit*—which *forces* us to be strong . . . *First* principle: you must need to be strong, or else you will never become it.—Those great hothouses for strong, for the strongest kind of people there has yet been—the aristocratic communities such as Rome and Venice—understood freedom in exactly the same sense as I understand the word freedom: as something which one can have and *not* have, which one can *want*, which one can *conquer* . . .

### 48

*Progress in My Sense.*—Even I speak of a 'return to nature', although it is actually not a going back but a *coming up*—up into high, free, even fearful nature and naturalness, the kind which plays—is *entitled* to play—with great tasks . . . To use an *analogy:* Napoleon was a piece of 'return to nature' as I understand it (for example *in rebus tacticis,* and even

more so, as army officers know, in matters strategic).—But Rousseau—where did *he* actually want to go back to? Rousseau, that first modern man, idealist and *canaille* in one person, who needed moral 'dignity' in order to stand the sight of himself; sick with unbridled vanity and unbridled self-contempt. Even this abortion, who lodged himself on the threshold of the new age, wanted a 'return to nature'—where, to repeat my question, did Rousseau want to go back to?—I still hate Rousseau *in* the Revolution: it is the world-historic expression of that duplicity of idealist and *canaille.* The bloody farce with which this Revolution played itself out, its 'immorality', is of little concern to me: what I hate is its Rousseauesque *moral*—the so-called 'truths' of the Revolution, through which it is still having an effect and winning over everything shallow and mediocre. The doctrine of equality! . . . . But there is no more venomous poison in existence: for it *appears* to be preached by justice itself, when it is actually the *end* of justice. . . . 'Equality to the equal; inequality to the unequal'—*that* would be true justice speaking: and its corollary, 'never make the unequal equal'. Because that doctrine of equality was surrounded by so much horror and bloodshed, this 'modern idea' *par excellence* was given a kind of glory and fiery glow, so that the Revolution as *spectacle* seduced even the noblest of minds. Ultimately that is no reason to respect it the more.— I can see only one man who experienced it as it must be experienced, with *revulsion*—Goethe. . . .

### 49

*Goethe*—not a German event but a European one: a magnificent attempt to overcome the eighteenth century by a return to nature, by a coming-*up* to the naturalness of the Renaissance, a kind of self-overcoming on the part of that century.—He bore its strongest instincts in himself: sentimentality, nature-idolatry, the anti-historical, the idealistic, the unreal and revolutionary (—the last being merely a form of the unreal). He made use of history, natural science, antiquity, as well as Spinoza, and of practical activity above all; he surrounded himself with nothing but closed horizons; he did not divorce himself from life but immersed himself in it; he never lost heart, and took as much as possible upon himself, above himself, into himself. What he wanted was *totality;* he fought against the disjunction of reason, sensuality, feeling, will (—preached in the most repulsively scholastic way by *Kant,* Goethe's antipode), he disciplined himself into a whole, he *created* himself. . . . In the midst of an age disposed to unreality, Goethe was a convinced realist: he said yes to all that was related to him in this respect—he had no greater experience than that *ens realissimum* called Napoleon. Goethe conceived of a strong, highly educated man, adept in all things bodily, with a tight rein on himself and a reverence for himself,

who can dare to grant himself the whole range and richness of naturalness, who is strong enough for this freedom; the man of tolerance, not out of weakness, but out of strength, because he knows how to turn to his advantage what would destroy the average type; the man to whom there is no longer anything forbidden except *weakness,* whether it be called vice or virtue. . . . Such a *liberated* spirit stands in the midst of the universe with a joyful and trusting fatalism, with *faith* in the fact that only what is individual is reprehensible, that everything is redeemed and affirmed in the whole—*he no longer denies.* . . . But such a faith is the highest of all possible faiths: I have baptized it with the name of *Dionysus.—*

# JOHN RAWLS
~

## INTRODUCTION

## JOSHUA COHEN

John Rawls was born in Baltimore, Maryland, in 1921. He graduated from Princeton University, and then, after serving in the American army in the Pacific during World War II, returned to Princeton, where he received a Ph.D. in philosophy in 1950. An influential teacher of several generations of moral and political philosophers, Rawls taught at Cornell in the 1950s, moved to The Massachusetts Institute of Technology in 1960, and then to Harvard's Philosophy Department in 1962, where he remained until his retirement in 1991. From the time he received his Ph.D. until 1971, Rawls's principal intellectual project was a book about justice. That book appeared in 1971 under the title *A Theory of Justice,* and provided a comprehensive statement of a theory that Rawls called "justice as fairness." After the book's publication, Rawls spent nearly twenty years rethinking the foundations of justice as fairness, with the aim of making the presentation of his outlook more consistent with the religious and philosophical pluralism characteristic of modern democracies. The fruits of those labors appeared in 1993 in his *Political Liberalism* (New York: Columbia University Press). In 1999, Rawls published *The Law of Peoples* (Cambridge, Mass.: Harvard University Press), which extended his ideas about justice to the international system.

For much of the past century, the idea of an egalitarian-liberal political philosophy seemed to many a contradiction in terms. Egalitarians troubled by vast differences between the lives of rich and poor commonly condemned liberalism for paying excessive attention to legal rights and liberties while exhibiting indifference to the real fate of ordinary people. Equality, they argued, could be found only in the rarified atmosphere of liberal legal and political discourse—with its claims about equality of persons before the law and of citizens in the state—

in disturbing isolation from life on earth. Liberals concerned to ensure individual rights would condemn egalitarianism for being paternalistic and willing to sacrifice human freedom in the name of a bland sameness of circumstance or future utopia. Practically speaking, democratic welfare states tried, with more or less success, to respect liberal and egalitarian values: to ensure basic individual rights to personal and political liberties while protecting individuals from the contingencies of the market. But the philosophical options seemed starkly opposed. In between Friedrich Hayek's classical liberalism and Karl Marx's egalitarianism, everything was an unstable political compromise, or an ad hoc balancing of competing values.

Rawls's *Theory of Justice* reshaped this philosophical terrain. Rawls proposed a conception of justice committed to the individual rights associated with traditional liberalism, to an egalitarian ideal of fair distribution conventionally associated with socialist and radical democratic traditions, and to a reasonable faith in the practical possibility of a form of constitutional democracy ensuring both liberty and equality. In summarizing his view, he said that justice as fairness aims to effect a "reconciliation of liberty and equality."

To appreciate the force of this reconciliation, consider the two principles of justice that Rawls explains and defends in *A Theory of Justice*. Rawls's first principle—a principle of *equal basic liberties*—says that each citizen has an equal right to the most extensive system of equal basic personal and political liberties compatible with a similar system of liberties for others. This principle does not assert a right to "liberty as such," that is, a right that would condemn restrictions on all manner of choices. Instead, the first principle requires stringent protections for certain *specific* liberties: liberty of thought and conscience; political liberty; freedom of association; liberty and integrity of the person; and the rights and liberties associated with the rule of law, and its requirements of generality and predictability. Rawls's first principle also includes a demanding norm of political equality, which holds that political liberty is to be assured a fair value—that the chance to hold office and to exercise influence on the political system ought to be independent of socioeconomic position. So citizens who have the motivation and ability to play an active political role should not be disadvantaged in their efforts by a lack of sufficient private wealth, or advantaged by their greater wealth.

Rawls's second principle of justice expresses egalitarian ideals of distributive justice. The second principle has two components, both of which set limits on acceptable socioeconomic inequalities. The first component states that when inequalities are attached to offices and positions—say, when different jobs are differently rewarded—those offices and positions must be open to everyone under conditions of *fair equality of opportunity*. In particular, people who are equally talented and motivated must have equal chances to attain desirable positions, regardless of their class background. Access to responsible and well-compensated work should not depend on the social circumstances in which people happen to have been born and raised.

But even a society that protects each person's basic personal and political liberties, and ensures fair equality of opportunity, might still have troubling inequalities. Thus, suppose some people, partly because of their native endowments, possess scarce talents that command high returns in the market, while others lack such skills. Assume people in both groups work hard, and contribute according to their abilities. Still, they will reap substantially different rewards, and those differences will have a large impact on their lives. But these inequalities of reward are founded on natural contingencies, bare undeserved luck in life's lottery, and "there is no more reason to permit the distribution of income and wealth to be settled by the distribution of natural assets than by historical and social fortune." So a second part of Rawls's second principle—the difference principle—requires an economic structure that mitigates inequalities in income and wealth owing to differences in natural talent. Instead of permitting differences of reward simply to reflect differences of native endowment, the difference principle requires that we maximize the lifetime expectations of those who are in the least advantaged social position. Thus someone might legitimately be paid more than someone else because the higher income compensates for expensive training and education that enable the person to take on socially desirable tasks; or inequalities might make sense as incentives that encourage people to take on tasks they would otherwise be unable or simply unwilling to take on. According to the difference principle, such inequalities are fully just only if they are to the greatest benefit of those who are least well-off.

While the requirement of fair equality of opportunity, then, condemns a society in which class background is a source of social or economic privilege, the difference principle condemns a society in which, as the sociologist Emile Durkheim put it, "social inequalities exactly express natural inequalities." In effect, then, Rawls urges us to reject the idea that our economic system is a race or talent contest, designed to reward the swift and gifted. Instead, it is one part of a fair scheme of cooperation, designed to ensure a reasonable life for all. "In justice as fairness," Rawls says, "men agree to share one another's fate. In designing institutions they undertake to avail themselves of the accidents of nature and social circumstance *only when* doing so is for the common benefit."

To see how justice as fairness reconciles liberty and equality, then, consider the joint operation of the two principles of justice. Assume that what matters to people is not only to have basic liberties that are legally protected from interferences by others, but that the legally protected liberties provide a meaningful or valuable liberty, that the liberties are worth something to us. Assume, too, that the worth of our liberty to us reflects the resources we have available for using the liberty. In particular, assume that the value of my liberties to me is an increasing function of the resources over which I exercise control: as my command of resources increases, I can do more with my liberties.

Now put the two principles together: the first principle ensures equal basic liberties, and the difference principle guarantees that the minimum level of resources is maximized. If, as I just suggested, the worth of a person's liberty—its value to the person—is an increasing function of the level of that person's resources, then by maximizing the minimum level of resources, we also maximize the minimum worth of liberty. Thus the two principles together require that society "maximize the worth to the least advantaged of the complete scheme of equal liberty shared by all." Maximizing the minimum worth of liberty "defines," Rawls says, "the end of social justice"—what justice aims ultimately to achieve.

The central idea of justice as fairness, then, is that an egalitarian-liberal conception comprising the two principles of justice is the most reasonable conception of justice "for a democratic society." Abraham Lincoln said that the United States was conceived in liberty and dedicated to the proposition that all men are created equal. Justice as fairness argues that the two principles of justice are the most reasonable theory of justice for a society with that conception and dedication—more reasonable than, for example, utilitarianism, or libertarianism, or a less liberal egalitarianism, or a less egalitarian liberalism.

To argue for the two principles of justice over alternatives, Rawls revives the social contract idea associated with Hobbes, Locke Rousseau, and Kant. The social contract idea is that the most reasonable ordering of a society is the ordering that the members themselves would unanimously agree to as the basis for their own association. So Rawls asks us to imagine ourselves in a hypothetical situation—he calls it "the Original Position"—in which we are to choose the principles of justice that will be used in our own society. Whereas the Hobbesian social contract was based on certain fundamental truths about human nature, the construction of the Original Position is designed to reflect the moral idea that we are free and equal moral persons—with a capacity to cooperate with others on fair terms, to choose our ends and devotions, and to pursue the ends we set for ourselves—and that the principles of justice for our society should treat us as such. So certain of our characteristics—those that distinguish among free and equal persons—are irrelevant in deciding what we are entitled to as a matter of justice. Specifically, our social class position, natural talents, sex or race, and conception of the good are irrelevant from the standpoint of justice. When we imagine ourselves making a choice of principles of justice, then, we are to imagine choosing from behind a "veil of ignorance" in which we are assumed to lack knowledge of the irrelevant features. We know that we are free and equal moral persons, but we do not know our class background, native endowments, sex or race, and conception of the good. We do not know, in short, whether the natural and social contingencies have worked in our favor.

When we reason from behind the veil of ignorance, then, we focus only on interests we share as free and equal moral persons, and put aside what distinguishes us from one another. Thus the parties in the original position know only that they represent a person who has some conception of the good (though they do not know what that conception is); an interest in being able to choose and revise their ends; and an interest in forming and acting on a sense of justice. Moreover, advancing those shared interests requires certain goods, called "social primary goods," and so the parties to the social contract know that they need these goods—in particular, the basic liberties; freedom of movement and occupational choice; powers and prerogatives of office and positions of responsibility; income and wealth; and the social bases of self-respect.

Why would parties in the original position choose Rawls's principles? The argument is complicated, but the intuitive idea is reasonably straightforward. You are asked to choose principles for your society under conditions of ignorance about your talents, ideals, and social position, ignorance that models the irrelevance of these properties from the point of view of justice. You do not know which person you will be, but have to live with the principles you choose, so you want to be sure—if this is possible—that your situation is acceptable whatever it turns out to be: you want to be sure that the society is acceptable from the point of view of each person, because you do not know which person you are. In particular, you want to be sure that it will be acceptable even if you land in the lowest social position, where acceptability is least likely. And, according to Rawls, this is precisely the "downside protection," the insurance that the two principles provide. They ensure that social arrangements are acceptable to all members of a society of equals, in particular because they guarantee basic liberties to all, and ensure an acceptable worth of liberty, even at the minimum position.

Starting from the fundamental ideal of fair cooperation among free and equal moral persons, then, we are led to the social contract idea of finding principles that would be the object of an initial agreement. And that initial agreement, made under conditions of ignorance, would endorse an egalitarian-liberal political conception that promises to maximize the minimum worth of liberty and thus to provide terms that are acceptable to all members of a democratic society. It is an inspiring political vision, and in a better world than our own, it would guide the political judgment of democratic citizens.

In addition to Rawls's three main books, his articles are available in John Rawls, *Collected*

*Papers,* edited by Samuel Freeman (Cambridge, Mass.: Harvard University Press, 1999). Some of his lectures, particularly on Kant, have been published in *Lectures on the History of Moral Philosophy,* edited by Barbara Herman (Cambridge, Mass.: Harvard University Press, 2000). And a reformulation of justice as fairness in light of the ideas in *Political Liberalism* is now available in *Justice as Fairness: A Restatement,* edited by Erin Kelly (Cambridge, Mass.: Harvard University Press, 2001). Rawls's work is also the topic of a vast secondary literature. The discussion of Rawls in Brian Barry's *Theories of Justice* (Berkeley and Los Angeles: University of California Press, 1989) is especially illuminating. *Reading Rawls,* edited by Norman Daniels (Stanford, Calif.: Stanford University Press, 1989), contains some of the classic early papers on *Theory of Justice,* including important articles by Thomas Nagel, Ronald Dworkin, and H. L. A. Hart. In chapter 7 of *Anarchy, State, and Utopia* (New York: Basic Books, 1974), Robert Nozick advances a forceful libertarian critique of justice as fairness. Susan Okin's *Justice, Gender, and the Family* (New York: Basic Books, 1989) presents a feminist critique of justice as fairness. In *Liberalism and the Limits of Justice,* 2d ed. (Cambridge: Cambridge University Press, 1998), Michael Sandel argues that there is a fundamental tension between the liberal and egalitarian commitments of justice as fairness—that Rawls's liberalism is founded on an individualistic outlook, whereas his egalitarianism suggests a communitarian philosophy. In a series of papers, G. A. Cohen has argued that Rawls's willingness, under the difference principle, to countenance incentives to people with scarce talents indicates an accommodation to unjust selfishness. See his "Incentives, Inequality, and Community," in Grethe Peterson (ed.), *The Tanner Lectures on Human Values,* vol. 13 (Salt Lake City: University of Utah Press, 1992), pp. 263–329. The articles in a special issue of *Ethics* (October 1989) are helpful in understanding both the substance of justice as fairness and the movement from the presentation of justice as fairness in *Theory of Justice* to its reformulation in *Political Liberalism* as a political conception of justice.

# A Theory of Justice

## 3. THE MAIN IDEA OF THE THEORY OF JUSTICE

My aim is to present a conception of justice which generalizes and carries to a higher level of abstraction the familiar theory of the social contract as found, say, in Locke, Rousseau, and Kant.[1] In order to do this we are not to think of the original contract as one to enter a particular society or to set up a particular form of government. Rather, the guiding idea is that the principles of justice for the basic structure of society are the object of the original agreement. They are the principles that free and rational persons concerned to further their own interests would accept in an initial position of equality as defining the fundamental terms of their association. These principles are to regulate all further agreements; they specify the kinds of social cooperation that can be entered into and the forms of government that can be established. This way of regarding the principles of justice I shall call justice as fairness.

Thus we are to imagine that those who engage in social cooperation choose together, in one joint act, the principles which are to assign basic rights and duties and to determine the division of social benefits. Men are to decide in advance how they are to regulate their claims against one another and what is to be the foundation charter of their society. Just as each person must decide by rational reflection what constitutes his good, that is, the system of ends which it is rational for him to pursue, so a group of persons must decide once and for all what is to count among them as just and unjust. The choice which rational men would make in this hypothetical situation of equal liberty, assuming for the present that this choice problem has a solution, determines the principles of justice.

In justice as fairness the original position of equality corresponds to the state of nature in the traditional theory of the social contract. This original position is not, of course, thought of as an actual historical state of affairs, much less as a primitive condition of culture. It is understood as a purely hypothetical situation characterized so as to lead to a certain conception of justice.[2] Among the essential features of this situation is that no one knows his place in society, his class position or social status, nor does any one know his fortune in the distribution of natural assets and abilities, his intelligence, strength, and the like. I shall even assume that the parties do not know their conceptions of the good or their special psychological propensities. The principles of justice are chosen behind a veil of ignorance. This ensures that no one is advantaged or disadvantaged in the choice of principles by the outcome of natural chance or the contingency of social circumstances. Since all are similarly situated and no one is able to design principles to favor his particular condition, the principles of justice are the result of a fair agreement or bargain. For given the circumstances of the original position, the symmetry of everyone's relations to each other, this initial situation is fair between individuals as moral persons, that is, as rational beings with their own ends and capable, I shall assume, of a sense of justice. The original position is, one might say, the appropriate initial status quo, and thus the fundamental agreements reached in it are fair. This explains the propriety of the name "justice as fairness": it conveys the idea that the principles of justice are agreed to in an initial situation that is fair. The name does not mean that the concepts of justice and fairness are the same, any more than the phrase "poetry as metaphor" means that the concepts of poetry and metaphor are the same.

Justice as fairness begins, as I have said, with one of the most general of all choices which persons might make together, namely, with the choice of the first principles of a conception of justice which is to regulate all subsequent criticism and reform of institutions. Then, having chosen a conception of justice, we can suppose that they are to choose a constitution and a legislature to enact laws, and so on, all in accordance with the principles of justice initially agreed upon. Our social situation is just if it is such that by this sequence of hypothetical agreements we would have contracted into the general system of rules which defines it. Moreover, assuming that the original position does determine a set of principles (that is, that a particular conception of justice would be chosen), it will then be true that whenever social institutions satisfy these principles those engaged in them can say to one another that they are cooperating on terms to which they would agree if they were free and equal persons whose relations with respect to one another were fair. They could all view their arrangements as meeting the stipulations which they would acknowledge in an initial situation that embodies widely accepted and reasonable constraints on the choice of principles. The general recognition of this fact would provide the basis for a public acceptance of the corresponding principles of justice. No society can, of course, be a scheme of cooperation which men enter voluntarily in a literal sense; each person finds himself placed at birth in some particular position in some particular society, and the nature of this position materially affects his life prospects. Yet a society satisfying the principles of justice as fairness comes as close as a society can to being a voluntary scheme, for it meets the principles which free and equal persons would assent to under circumstances that are fair. In this sense its members are autonomous and the obligations they recognize self-imposed.

One feature of justice as fairness is to think of the parties in the initial situation as rational and mutually disinterested. This does not mean that the parties are egoists, that is, individuals with only certain kinds of interests, say in wealth, prestige, and domination. But they are conceived as not taking an interest in one another's interests. They are to presume that even their spiritual aims may be opposed, in the way that the aims of those of different religions may be opposed. Moreover, the concept of rationality must be interpreted as far as possible in the narrow sense, standard in economic theory, of taking the most effective means to given ends. I shall modify this concept to some extent, as explained later, but one must try to avoid introducing into it any controversial ethical elements. The initial situation must be characterized by stipulations that are widely accepted.

In working out the conception of justice as fairness one main task clearly is to determine which principles of justice would be chosen in the original position. To do this we must describe this situation in some detail and formulate with care the problem of choice which it presents. These matters I shall take up in the immediately succeeding chapters. It may be observed, however, that once the principles of justice are thought of as arising from an original agreement in a situation of equality, it is an open question whether the principle of utility would be acknowledged. Off-hand it hardly seems likely that persons who view themselves as equals, entitled to press their claims upon one another, would agree to a principle which may require lesser life prospects for some simply for the sake of a greater sum of advantages enjoyed by others. Since each desires to protect his interests, his capacity to advance his conception of the good, no one has a reason to acquiesce in an enduring loss for himself in order to bring about a greater net balance of satisfaction. In the absence of strong and lasting benevolent impulses, a rational man would not accept a basic structure merely because it maximized the algebraic sum of advantages irrespective of its permanent effects on his own basic rights and interests. Thus it seems that the principle of utility is incompatible with the conception of social cooperation among equals for mutual advantage. It appears to be inconsistent with the idea of reciprocity implicit in the notion of a well-ordered society. Or, at any rate, so I shall argue.

I shall maintain instead that the persons in the initial situation would choose two rather different principles: the first requires equality in the assignment of basic rights and duties, while the second holds that

social and economic inequalities, for example inequalities of wealth and authority, are just only if they result in compensating benefits for everyone, and in particular for the least advantaged members of society. These principles rule out justifying institutions on the grounds that the hardships of some are offset by a greater good in the aggregate. It may be expedient but it is not just that some should have less in order that others may prosper. But there is no injustice in the greater benefits earned by a few provided that the situation of persons not so fortunate is thereby improved. The intuitive idea is that since everyone's well-being depends upon a scheme of cooperation without which no one could have a satisfactory life, the division of advantages should be such as to draw forth the willing cooperation of everyone taking part in it, including those less well situated. The two principles mentioned seem to be a fair basis on which those better endowed, or more fortunate in their social position, neither of which we can be said to deserve, could expect the willing cooperation of others when some workable scheme is a necessary condition of the welfare of all.[3] Once we decide to look for a conception of justice that prevents the use of the accidents of natural endowment and the contingencies of social circumstance as counters in a quest for political and economic advantage, we are led to these principles. They express the result of leaving aside those aspects of the social world that seem arbitrary from a moral point of view.

The problem of the choice of principles, however, is extremely difficult. I do not expect the answer I shall suggest to be convincing to everyone. It is, therefore, worth noting from the outset that justice as fairness, like other contract views, consists of two parts: (1) an interpretation of the initial situation and of the problem of choice posed there, and (2) a set of principles which, it is argued, would be agreed to. One may accept the first part of the theory (or some variant thereof), but not the other, and conversely. The concept of the initial contractual situation may seem reasonable although the particular principles proposed are rejected. To be sure, I want to maintain that the most appropriate conception of this situation does lead to principles of justice contrary to utilitarianism and perfectionism, and therefore that the contract doctrine provides an alternative to these views. Still, one may dispute this contention even though one grants that the contractarian method is a useful way of studying ethical theories and of setting forth their underlying assumptions.

Justice as fairness is an example of what I have called a contract theory. Now there may be an objection to the term "contract" and related expressions, but I think it will serve reasonably well. Many words have misleading connotations which at first are likely to confuse. The terms "utility" and "utilitarianism" are surely no exception. They too have unfortunate suggestions which hostile critics have been willing to exploit; yet they are clear enough for those prepared to study utilitarian doctrine. The same should be true of the term "contract" applied to moral theories. As I have mentioned, to understand it one has to keep in mind that it implies a certain level of abstraction. In particular, the content of the relevant agreement is not to enter a given society or to adopt a given form of government, but to accept certain moral principles. Moreover, the undertakings referred to are purely hypothetical: a contract view holds that certain principles would be accepted in a well-defined initial situation.

The merit of the contract terminology is that it conveys the idea that principles of justice may be conceived as principles that would be chosen by rational persons, and that in this way conceptions of justice may be explained and justified. The theory of justice is a part, perhaps the most significant part, of the theory of rational choice. Furthermore, principles of justice deal with conflicting claims upon the advantages won by social cooperation; they apply to the relations among several persons or groups. The word "contract" suggests this plurality as well as the condition that the appropriate division of advantages must be in accordance with principles acceptable to all parties. The condition of publicity for principles of justice is also connoted by the contract phraseology. Thus, if these principles are the outcome of an agreement, citizens have a knowledge of the principles that others follow. It is characteristic of contract theories to stress the public nature of political principles. Finally there is the long tradition of the contract doctrine. Expressing the tie with this line of thought helps to define ideas and accords with natural piety. There are then several advantages in the use of the term "contract." With due precautions taken, it should not be misleading. . . .

## 4. THE ORIGINAL POSITION AND JUSTIFICATION

I have said that the original position is the appropriate initial status quo which insures that the fundamental agreements reached in it are fair. This fact yields the name "justice as fairness." It is clear, then, that I want to say that one conception of justice is more reasonable than another, or justifiable with respect to it, if rational persons in the initial situation would choose its principles over those of the other for the role of justice. Conceptions of justice are to be ranked by their acceptability to persons so circumstanced. Understood in this way the question of justification is settled by working out a problem of deliberation: we have to ascertain which principles it would be rational to adopt given the contractual situation. This connects the theory of justice with the theory of rational choice.

If this view of the problem of justification is to succeed, we must, of course, describe in some detail the nature of this choice problem. A problem of rational decision has a definite answer only if we know the beliefs and interests of the parties, their relations with respect to one another, the alternatives between which they are to choose, the procedure whereby they make up their minds, and so on. As the circumstances are presented in different ways, correspondingly different principles are accepted. The concept of the original position, as I shall refer to it, is that of the most philosophically favored interpretation of this initial choice situation for the purposes of a theory of justice.

But how are we to decide what is the most favored interpretation? I assume, for one thing, that there is a broad measure of agreement that principles of justice should be chosen under certain conditions. To justify a particular description of the initial situation one shows that it incorporates these commonly shared presumptions. One argues from widely accepted but weak premises to more specific conclusions. Each of the presumptions should be itself be natural and plausible; some of them may seem innocuous or even trivial. The aim of the contract approach is to establish that taken together they impose significant bounds on acceptable principles of justice. The ideal outcome would be that these conditions determine a unique set of principles; but I shall be satisfied if they suffice to rank the main traditional conceptions of social justice.

One should not be misled, then, by the somewhat unusual conditions which characterize the original position. The idea here is simply to make vivid to ourselves the restrictions that it seems reasonable to impose on arguments for principles of justice, and therefore on these principles themselves. Thus it seems reasonable and generally acceptable that no one should be advantaged or disadvantaged by natural fortune or social circumstances in the choice of principles. It also seems widely agreed that it should be impossible to tailor principles to the circumstances of one's own case. We should insure further that particular inclinations and aspirations, and persons' conceptions of their good do not affect the principles adopted. The aim is to rule out those principles that it would be rational to propose for acceptance, however little the chance of success, only if one knew certain things that are irrelevant from the standpoint of justice. For example, if a man knew that he was wealthy, he might find it rational to advance the principle that various taxes for welfare measures be counted unjust; if he knew that he was poor, he would most likely propose the contrary principle. To represent the desired restrictions one imagines a situation in which everyone is deprived of this sort of information. One excludes the knowledge of those contingencies which sets men at odds and allows them to be guided by their prejudices. In this manner the veil of ignorance is arrived at in a natural way. This concept should cause no difficulty if we keep in mind the constraints on arguments that it is meant to express. At any time we can enter the

original position, so to speak, simply by following a certain procedure, namely, by arguing for principles of justice in accordance with these restrictions.

It seems reasonable to suppose that the parties in the original position are equal. That is, all have the same rights in the procedure for choosing principles; each can make proposals, submit reasons for their acceptance, and so on. Obviously the purpose of these conditions is to represent equality between human beings as moral persons, as creatures having a conception of their good and capable of a sense of justice. The basis of equality is taken to be similarity in these two respects. Systems of ends are not ranked in value; and each man is presumed to have the requisite ability to understand and to act upon whatever principles are adopted. Together with the veil of ignorance, these conditions define the principles of justice as those which rational persons concerned to advance their interests would consent to as equals when none are known to be advantaged or disadvantaged by social and natural contingencies.

There is, however, another side to justifying a particular description of the original position. This is to see if the principles which would be chosen match our considered convictions of justice or extend them in an acceptable way. We can note whether applying these principles would lead us to make the same judgments about the basic structure of society which we now make intuitively and in which we have the greatest confidence; or whether, in cases where our present judgments are in doubt and given with hesitation, these principles offer a resolution which we can affirm on reflection. There are questions which we feel sure must be answered in a certain way. For example, we are confident that religious intolerance and racial discrimination are unjust. We think that we have examined these things with care and have reached what we believe is an impartial judgment not likely to be distorted by an excessive attention to our own interests. These convictions are provisional fixed points which we presume any conception of justice must fit. But we have much less assurance as to what is the correct distribution of wealth and authority. Here we may be looking for a way to remove our doubts. We can check an interpretation of the initial situation, then, by the capacity of its principles to accommodate our firmest convictions and to provide guidance where guidance is needed.

In searching for the most favored description of this situation we work from both ends. We begin by describing it so that it represents generally shared and preferably weak conditions. We then see if these conditions are strong enough to yield a significant set of principles. If not, we look for further premises equally reasonable. But if so, and these principles match our considered convictions of justice, then so far well and good. But presumably there will be discrepancies. In this case we have a choice. We can either modify the account of the initial situation or we can revise our existing judgments, for even the judgments we take provisionally as fixed points are liable to revision. By going back and forth, sometimes altering the conditions of the contractual circumstances, at others withdrawing our judgments and conforming them to principle, I assume that eventually we shall find a description of the initial situation that both expresses reasonable conditions and yields principles which match our considered judgments duly pruned and adjusted. This state of affairs I refer to as reflective equilibrium.[4] It is an equilibrium because at last our principles and judgments coincide; and it is reflective since we know to what principles our judgments conform and the premises of their derivation. At the moment everything is in order. But this equilibrium is not necessarily stable. It is liable to be upset by further examination of the conditions which should be imposed on the contractual situation and by particular cases which may lead us to revise our judgments. Yet for the time being we have done what we can to render coherent and to justify our convictions of social justice. We have reached a conception of the original position.

I shall not, of course, actually work through this process. Still, we may think of the interpretation of the original position that I shall present as the result of such a hypothetical course of reflection. It represents the attempt to accommodate within one scheme both reasonable philosophical conditions on principles as well as our considered judgments of justice. In arriving at the favored interpretation of the initial situation

there is no point at which an appeal is made to self-evidence in the traditional sense either of general conceptions or particular convictions. I do not claim for the principles of justice proposed that they are necessary truths or derivable from such truths. A conception of justice cannot be deduced from self-evident premises or conditions on principles; instead, its justification is a matter of the mutual support of many considerations, of everything fitting together into one coherent view.

A final comment. We shall want to say that certain principles of justice are justified because they would be agreed to in an initial situation of equality. I have emphasized that this original position is purely hypothetical. It is natural to ask why, if this agreement is never actually entered into, we should take any interest in these principles, moral or otherwise. The answer is that the conditions embodied in the description of the original position are ones that we do in fact accept. Or if we do not, then perhaps we can be persuaded to do so by philosophical reflection. Each aspect of the contractual situation can be given supporting grounds. Thus what we shall do is to collect together into one conception a number of conditions on principles that we are ready upon due consideration to recognize as reasonable. These constraints express what we are prepared to regard as limits on fair terms of social cooperation. One way to look at the idea of the original position, therefore, is to see it as an expository device which sums up the meaning of these conditions and helps us to extract their consequences. On the other hand, this conception is also an intuitive notion that suggests its own elaboration, so that led on by it we are drawn to define more clearly the standpoint from which we can best interpret moral relationships. We need a conception that enables us to envision our objective from afar: the intuitive notion of the original position is to do this for us.[5]

## 5. CLASSICAL UTILITARIANISM

There are many forms of utilitarianism, and the development of the theory has continued in recent years. I shall not survey these forms here, nor take account of the numerous refinements found in contemporary discussions. My aim is to work out a theory of justice that represents an alternative to utilitarian thought generally and so to all of these different versions of it. I believe that the contrast between the contract view and utilitarianism remains essentially the same in all these cases. Therefore I shall compare justice as fairness with familiar variants of intuitionism, perfectionism, and utilitarianism in order to bring out the underlying differences in the simplest way. With this end in mind, the kind of utilitarianism I shall describe here is the strict classical doctrine which receives perhaps its clearest and most accessible formulation in Sidgwick. The main idea is that society is rightly ordered, and therefore just, when its major institutions are arranged so as to achieve the greatest net balance of satisfaction summed over all the individuals belonging to it.[6]

We may note first that there is, indeed, a way of thinking of society which makes it easy to suppose that the most rational conception of justice is utilitarian. For consider: each man in realizing his own interests is certainly free to balance his own losses against his own gains. We may impose a sacrifice on ourselves now for the sake of a greater advantage later. A person quite properly acts, at least when others are not affected, to achieve his own greatest good, to advance his rational ends as far as possible. Now why should not a society act on precisely the same principle applied to the group and therefore regard that which is rational for one man as right for an association of men? Just as the well-being of a person is constructed from the series of satisfactions that are experienced at different moments in the course of his life, so in very much the same way the well-being of society is to be constructed from the fulfillment of the systems of desires of the many individuals who belong to it. Since the principle for an individual is to advance as far as possible his own welfare, his own system of desires, the principle for society is to advance as far as possible the welfare of the group, to realize to the greatest extent the comprehensive system of desire arrived at from the desires of its members. Just as an individual balances

present and future gains against present and future losses, so a society may balance satisfactions and dissatisfactions between different individuals. And so by these reflections one reaches the principle of utility in a natural way: a society is properly arranged when its institutions maximize the net balance of satisfaction. The principle of choice for an association of men is interpreted as an extension of the principle of choice for one man. Social justice is the principle of rational prudence applied to an aggregative conception of the welfare of the group.[7]

This idea is made all the more attractive by a further consideration. The two main concepts of ethics are those of the right and the good; the concept of a morally worthy person is, I believe, derived from them. The structure of an ethical theory is, then, largely determined by how it defines and connects these two basic notions. Now it seems that the simplest way of relating them is taken by teleological theories: the good is defined independently from the right, and then the right is defined as that which maximizes the good.[8] More precisely, those institutions and acts are right which of the available alternatives produce the most good, or at least as much good as any of the other institutions and acts open as real possibilities (a rider needed when the maximal class is not a singleton). Teleological theories have a deep intuitive appeal since they seem to embody the idea of rationality. It is natural to think that rationality is maximizing something and that in morals it must be maximizing the good. Indeed, it is tempting to suppose that it is self-evident that things should be arranged so as to lead to the most good.

It is essential to keep in mind that in a teleological theory the good is defined independently from the right. This means two things. First, the theory accounts for our considered judgments as to which things are good (our judgments of value) as a separate class of judgments intuitively distinguishable by common sense, and then proposes the hypothesis that the right is maximizing the good as already specified. Second, the theory enables one to judge the goodness of things without referring to what is right. For example, if pleasure is said to be the sole good, then presumably pleasures can be recognized and ranked in value by criteria that do not presuppose any standards of right, or what we would normally think of as such. Whereas if the distribution of goods is also counted as a good, perhaps a higher order one, and the theory directs us to produce the most good (including the good of distribution among others), we no longer have a teleological view in the classical sense. The problem of distribution falls under the concept of right as one intuitively understands it, and so the theory lacks an independent definition of the good. The clarity and simplicity of classical teleological theories derives largely from the fact that they factor our moral judgments into two classes, the one being characterized separately while the other is then connected with it by a maximizing principle.

Teleological doctrines differ, pretty clearly, according to how the conception of the good is specified. If it is taken as the realization of human excellence in the various forms of culture, we have what may be called perfectionism. This notion is found in Aristotle and Nietzsche, among others. If the good is defined as pleasure, we have hedonism; if as happiness, eudaimonism, and so on. I shall understand the principle of utility in its classical form as defining the good as the satisfaction of desire, or perhaps better, as the satisfaction of rational desire. This accords with the view in all essentials and provides, I believe, a fair interpretation of it. The appropriate terms of social cooperation are settled by whatever in the circumstances will achieve the greatest sum of satisfaction of the rational desires of individuals. It is impossible to deny the initial plausibility and attractiveness of this conception.

The striking feature of the utilitarian view of justice is that it does not matter, except indirectly, how this sum of satisfactions is distributed among individuals any more than it matters, except indirectly, how one man distributes his satisfactions over time. The correct distribution in either case is that which yields the maximum fulfillment. Society must allocate its means of satisfaction whatever these are, rights and duties, opportunities and privileges, and various forms of wealth, so as to achieve this maximum if it can. But in itself no distribution of satisfaction is better than another except that the more

equal distribution is to be preferred to break ties.[9] It is true that certain common sense precepts of justice, particularly those which concern the protection of liberties and rights, or which express the claims of desert, seem to contradict this contention. But from a utilitarian standpoint the explanation of these precepts and of their seemingly stringent character is that they are those precepts which experience shows should be strictly respected and departed from only under exceptional circumstances if the sum of advantages is to be maximized.[10] Yet, as with all other precepts, those of justice are derivative from the one end of attaining the greatest balance of satisfaction. Thus there is no reason in principle why the greater gains of some should not compensate for the lesser losses of others; or more importantly, why the violation of the liberty of a few might not be made right by the greater good shared by many. It simply happens that under most conditions, at least in a reasonably advanced stage of civilization, the greatest sum of advantages is not attained in this way. No doubt the strictness of common sense precepts of justice has a certain usefulness in limiting men's propensities to injustice and to socially injurious actions, but the utilitarian believes that to affirm this strictness as a first principle of morals is a mistake. For just as it is rational for one man to maximize the fulfillment of his system of desires, it is right for a society to maximize the net balance of satisfaction taken over all of its members.

The most natural way, then, of arriving at utilitarianism (although not, of course, the only way of doing so) is to adopt for society as a whole the principle of rational choice for one man. Once this is recognized, the place of the impartial spectator and the emphasis on sympathy in the history of utilitarian thought is readily understood. For it is by the conception of the impartial spectator and the use of sympathetic identification in guiding our imagination that the principle for one man is applied to society. It is this spectator who is conceived as carrying out the required organization of the desires of all persons into one coherent system of desire; it is by this construction that many persons are fused into one. Endowed with ideal powers of sympathy and imagination, the impartial spectator is the perfectly rational individual who identifies with and experiences the desires of others as if these desires were his own. In this way he ascertains the intensity of these desires and assigns them their appropriate weight in the one system of desire the satisfaction of which the ideal legislator then tries to maximize by adjusting the rules of the social system. On this conception of society separate individuals are thought of as so many different lines along which rights and duties are to be assigned and scarce means of satisfaction allocated in accordance with rules so as to give the greatest fulfillment of wants. The nature of the decision made by the ideal legislator is not, therefore, materially different from that of an entrepreneur deciding how to maximize his profit by producing this or that commodity, or that of a consumer deciding how to maximize his satisfaction by the purchase of this or that collection of goods. In each case there is a single person whose system of desires determines the best allocation of limited means. The correct decision is essentially a question of efficient administration. This view of social cooperation is the consequence of extending to society the principle of choice for one man, and then, to make this extension work, conflating all persons into one through the imaginative acts of the impartial sympathetic spectator. Utilitarianism does not take seriously the distinction between persons.

## 11. TWO PRINCIPLES OF JUSTICE

I shall now state in a provisional form the two principles of justice that I believe would be agreed to in the original position. The first formulation of these principles is tentative. As we go on I shall consider several formulations and approximate step by step the final statement to be given much later. I believe that doing this allows the exposition to proceed in a natural way.

The first statement of the two principles reads as follows.

First: each person is to have an equal right to the most extensive scheme of equal basic liberties compatible with a similar scheme of liberties for others.

Second: social and economic inequalities are to be arranged so that they are both (a) reasonably expected to be to everyone's advantage, and (b) attached to positions and offices open to all. . . .

These principles primarily apply, as I have said, to the basic structure of society and govern the assignment of rights and duties and regulate the distribution of social and economic advantages. Their formulation presupposes that, for the purposes of a theory of justice, the social structure may be viewed as having two more or less distinct parts, the first principle applying to the one, the second principle to the other. Thus we distinguish between the aspects of the social system that define and secure the equal basic liberties and the aspects that specify and establish social and economic inequalities. Now it is essential to observe that the basic liberties are given by a list of such liberties. Important among these are political liberty (the right to vote and to hold public office) and freedom of speech and assembly; liberty of conscience and freedom of thought; freedom of the person, which includes freedom from psychological oppression and physical assault and dismemberment (integrity of the person); the right to hold personal property and freedom from arbitrary arrest and seizure as defined by the concept of the rule of law. These liberties are to be equal by the first principle.

The second principle applies, in the first approximation, to the distribution of income and wealth and to the design of organizations that make use of differences in authority and responsibility. While the distribution of wealth and income need not be equal, it must be to everyone's advantage, and at the same time, positions of authority and responsibility must be accessiblé to all. One applies the second principle by holding positions open, and then, subject to this constraint, arranges social and economic inequalities so that everyone benefits.

These principles are to be arranged in a serial order with the first principle prior to the second. This ordering means that infringements of the basic equal liberties protected by the first principle cannot be justified, or compensated for, by greater social and economic advantages. These liberties have a central range of application within which they can be limited and compromised only when they conflict with other basic liberties. Since they may be limited when they clash with one another, none of these liberties is absolute; but however they are adjusted to form one system, this system is to be the same for all. It is difficult, and perhaps impossible, to give a complete specification of these liberties independently from the particular circumstances—social, economic, and technological—of a given society. The hypothesis is that the general form of such a list could be devised with sufficient exactness to sustain this conception of justice. Of course, liberties not on the list, for example, the right to own certain kinds of property (e.g., means of production) and freedom of contract as understood by the doctrine of laissez-faire are not basic; and so they are not protected by the priority of the first principle. Finally, in regard to the second principle, the distribution of wealth and income, and positions of authority and responsibility, are to be consistent with both the basic liberties and equality of opportunity.

The two principles are rather specific in their content, and their acceptance rests on certain assumptions that I must eventually try to explain and justify. For the present, it should be observed that these principles are a special case of a more general conception of justice that can be expressed as follows.

> All social values—liberty and opportunity, income and wealth, and the social bases of self-respect—are to be distributed equally unless an unequal distribution of any, or all, of these values is to everyone's advantage.

Injustice, then, is simply inequalities that are not to the benefit of all. Of course, this conception is extremely vague and requires interpretation.

As a first step, suppose that the basic structure of society distributes certain primary goods, that is, things that every rational man is presumed to want. These goods normally have a use whatever a per-

son's rational plan of life. For simplicity, assume that the chief primary goods at the disposition of society are rights, liberties, and opportunities, and income and wealth. (Later on in Part Three the primary good of self-respect has a central place.) These are the social primary goods. Other primary goods such as health and vigor, intelligence and imagination, are natural goods; although their possession is influenced by the basic structure, they are not so directly under its control. Imagine, then, a hypothetical initial arrangement in which all the social primary goods are equally distributed: everyone has similar rights and duties, and income and wealth are evenly shared. This state of affairs provides a benchmark for judging improvements. If certain inequalities of wealth and differences in authority would make everyone better off than in this hypothetical starting situation, then they accord with the general conception.

Now it is possible, at least theoretically, that by giving up some of their fundamental liberties men are sufficiently compensated by the resulting social and economic gains. The general conception of justice imposes no restrictions on what sort of inequalities are permissible; it only requires that everyone's position be improved. We need not suppose anything so drastic as consenting to a condition of slavery. Imagine instead that people seem willing to forego certain political rights when the economic returns are significant. It is this kind of exchange which the two principles rule out; being arranged in serial order they do not permit exchanges between basic liberties and economic and social gains except under extenuating circumstances. . . .

The fact that the two principles apply to institutions has certain consequences. First of all, the rights and basic liberties referred to by these principles are those which are defined by the public rules of the basic structure. Whether men are free is determined by the rights and duties established by the major institutions of society. Liberty is a certain pattern of social forms. The first principle simply requires that certain sorts of rules, those defining basic liberties, apply to everyone equally and that they allow the most extensive liberty compatible with a like liberty for all. The only reason for circumscribing basic liberties and making them less extensive is that otherwise they would interfere with one another.

Further, when principles mention persons, or require that everyone gain from an inequality, the reference is to representative persons holding the various social positions, or offices established by the basic structure. Thus in applying the second principle I assume that it is possible to assign an expectation of well-being to representative individuals holding these positions. This expectation indicates their life prospects as viewed from their social station. In general, the expectations of representative persons depend upon the distribution of rights and duties throughout the basic structure. Expectations are connected: by raising the prospects of the representative man in one position we presumably increase or decrease the prospects of representative men in other positions. Since it applies to institutional forms, the second principle (or rather the first part of it) refers to the expectations of representative individuals. As I shall discuss below, neither principle applies to distributions of particular goods to particular individuals who may be identified by their proper names. The situation where someone is considering how to allocate certain commodities to needy persons who are known to him is not within the scope of the principles. They are meant to regulate basic institutional arrangements. We must not assume that there is much similarity from the standpoint of justice between an administrative allotment of goods to specific persons and the appropriate design of society. Our common sense intuitions for the former may be a poor guide to the latter.

Now the second principle insists that each person benefit from permissible inequalities in the basic structure. This means that it must be reasonable for each relevant representative man defined by this structure, when he views it as a going concern, to prefer his prospects with the inequality to his prospects without it. One is not allowed to justify differences in income or in positions of authority and responsibility on the ground that the disadvantages of those in one position are outweighed by the

greater advantages of those in another. Much less can infringements of liberty be counterbalanced in this way. It is obvious, however, that there are indefinitely many ways in which all may be advantaged when the initial arrangement of equality is taken as a benchmark. How then are we to choose among these possibilities? The principles must be specified so that they yield a determinate conclusion. . . .

## 13. DEMOCRATIC EQUALITY AND THE DIFFERENCE PRINCIPLE

The democratic interpretation . . . is arrived at by combining the principle of fair equality of opportunity with the difference principle. . . . Assuming the framework of institutions required by equal liberty and fair equality of opportunity, the higher expectations of those better situated are just if and only if they work as part of a scheme which improves the expectations of the least advantaged members of society. The intuitive idea is that the social order is not to establish and secure the more attractive prospects of those better off unless doing so is to the advantage of those less fortunate. . . .

To illustrate the difference principle, consider the distribution of income among social classes. Let us suppose that the various income groups correlate with representative individuals by reference to whose expectations we can judge the distribution. Now those starting out as members of the entrepreneurial class in property-owning democracy, say, have a better prospect than those who begin in the class of unskilled laborers. It seems likely that this will be true even when the social injustices which now exist are removed. What, then, can possibly justify this kind of initial inequality in life prospects? According to the difference principle, it is justifiable only if the difference in expectation is to the advantage of the representative man who is worse off, in this case the representative unskilled worker. The inequality in expectation is permissible only if lowering it would make the working class even more worse off. Supposedly, given the rider in the second principle concerning open positions, and the principle of liberty generally, the greater expectations allowed to entrepreneurs encourages them to do things which raise the prospects of laboring class. Their better prospects act as incentives so that the economic process is more efficient, innovation proceeds at a faster pace, and so on. I shall not consider how far these things are true. The point is that something of this kind must be argued if these inequalities are to satisfy by the difference principle. . . .

## 17. THE TENDENCY TO EQUALITY

I wish to conclude this discussion of the two principles by explaining the sense in which they express an egalitarian conception of justice. Also I should like to forestall the objection to the principle of fair opportunity that it leads to a meritocratic society. In order to prepare the way for doing this, I note several aspects of the conception of justice that I have set out.

First we may observe that the difference principle gives some weight to the considerations singled out by the principle of redress. This is the principle that undeserved inequalities call for redress; and since inequalities of birth and natural endowment are undeserved, these inequalities are to be somehow compensated for.[11] Thus the principle holds that in order to treat all persons equally, to provide genuine equality of opportunity, society must give more attention to those with fewer native assets and to those born into the less favorable social positions. The idea is to redress the bias of contingencies in the direction of equality. In pursuit of this principle greater resources might be spent on the education of the less rather than the more intelligent, at least over a certain time of life, say the earlier years of school.

Now the principle of redress has not to my knowledge been proposed as the sole criterion of justice, as the single aim of the social order. It is plausible as most such principles are only as a prima facie principle, one that is to be weighed in the balance with others. For example, we are to weigh it against the principle to improve the average standard of life, or to advance the common good.[12] But whatever other principles we hold, the claims of redress are to be taken into account. It is thought to represent one of the elements in our conception of justice. Now the difference principle is not of course the principle of redress. It does not require society to try to even out handicaps as if all were expected to compete on a fair basis in the same race. But the difference principle would allocate resources in education, say, so as to improve the long-term expectation of the least favored. If this end is attained by giving more attention to the better endowed, it is permissible; otherwise not. And in making this decision, the value of education should not be assessed solely in terms of economic efficiency and social welfare. Equally if not more important is the role of education in enabling a person to enjoy the culture of his society and to take part in its affairs, and in this way to provide for each individual a secure sense of his own worth.

Thus although the difference principle is not the same as that of redress, it does achieve some of the intent of the latter principle. It transforms the aims of the basic structure so that the total scheme of institutions no longer emphasizes social efficiency and technocratic values. The difference principle represents, in effect, an agreement to regard the distribution of natural talents as in some respects a common asset and to share in the greater social and economic benefits made possible by the complementarities of this distribution. Those who have been favored by nature, whoever they are, may gain from their good fortune only on terms that improve the situation of those who have lost out. The naturally advantaged are not to gain merely because they are more gifted, but only to cover the costs of training and education and for using their endowments in ways that help the less fortunate as well. No one deserves his greater natural capacity nor merits a more favorable starting place in society. But, of course, this is no reason to ignore, much less to eliminate these distinctions. Instead, the basic structure can be arranged so that these contingencies work for the good of the least fortunate. Thus we are led to the difference principle if we wish to set up the social system so that no one gains or loses from his arbitrary place in the distribution of natural assets or his initial position in society without giving or receiving compensating advantages in return.

In view of these remarks we may reject the contention that the ordering of institutions is always defective because the distribution of natural talents and the contingencies of social circumstance are unjust, and this injustice must inevitably carry over to human arrangements. Occasionally this reflection is offered as an excuse for ignoring injustice, as if the refusal to acquiesce in injustice is on a par with being unable to accept death. The natural distribution is neither just nor unjust; nor is it unjust that persons are born into society at some particular position. These are simply natural facts. What is just and unjust is the way that institutions deal with these facts. Aristocratic and caste societies are unjust because they make these contingencies the ascriptive basis for belonging to more or less enclosed and privileged social classes. The basic structure of these societies incorporates the arbitrariness found in nature. But there is no necessity for men to resign themselves to these contingencies. The social system is not an unchangeable order beyond human control but a pattern of human action. In justice as fairness men agree to avail themselves of the accidents of nature and social circumstance only when doing so is for the common benefit. The two principles are a fair way of meeting the arbitrariness of fortune; and while no doubt imperfect in other ways, the institutions which satisfy these principles are just.

A further point is that the difference principle expresses a conception of reciprocity. It is a principle of mutual benefit. At first sight, however, it may appear unfairly biased towards the least favored. To consider this question in an intuitive way, suppose for simplicity that there are only two groups in society, one noticeably more fortunate than the other. Subject to the usual constraints (defined by the priority of the first principle and fair equality of opportunity), society could maximize the expectations of either group but not both, since we can maximize with respect to only one aim at a time. It seems clear that society should not do the best it can for those initially more advantaged; so if we reject the difference principle,

we must prefer maximizing some weighted mean of the two expectations. But if we give any weight to the more fortunate, we are valuing for their own sake the gains to those already more favored by natural and social contingencies. No one had an antecedent claim to be benefited in this way, and so to maximize a weighted mean is, so to speak, to favor the more fortunate twice over. Thus the more advantaged, when they view the matter from a general perspective, recognize that the well-being of each depends on a scheme of social cooperation without which no one could have a satisfactory life; they recognize also that they can expect the willing cooperation of all only if the terms of the scheme are reasonable. So they regard themselves as already compensated, as it were, by the advantages to which no one (including themselves) had a prior claim. They forego the idea of maximizing a weighted mean and regard the difference principle as a fair basis for regulating the basic structure.

One may object that those better situated deserve the greater advantages they could acquire for themselves under other schemes of cooperation whether or not these advantages are gained in ways that benefit others. Now it is true that given a just system of cooperation as a framework of public rules, and the expectations set up by it, those who, with the prospect of improving their condition, have done what the system announces it will reward are entitled to have their expectations met. In this sense the more fortunate have title to their better situation; their claims are legitimate expectations established by social institutions and the community is obligated to fulfill them. But this sense of desert is that of entitlement. It presupposes the existence of an ongoing cooperative scheme and is irrelevant to the question whether this scheme itself is to be designed in accordance with the difference principle or some other criterion.

Thus it is incorrect that individuals with greater natural endowments and the superior character that has made their development possible have a right to a cooperative scheme that enables them to obtain even further benefits in ways that do not contribute to the advantages of others. We do not deserve our place in the distribution of native endowments, any more than we deserve our initial starting place in society. That we deserve the superior character that enables us to make the effort to cultivate our abilities is also problematic; for such character depends in good part upon fortunate family and social circumstances in early life for which we can claim no credit. The notion of desert does not apply here. To be sure, the more advantaged have a right to their natural assets, as does everyone else; this right is covered by the first principle under the basic liberty protecting the integrity of the person. And so the more advantaged are entitled to whatever they can acquire in accordance with the rules of a fair system of social cooperation. Our problem is how this scheme, the basic structure of society, is to be designed. From a suitably general standpoint, the difference principle appears acceptable to both the more advantaged and the less advantaged individual. Of course, none of this is strictly speaking an argument for the principle, since in a contract theory arguments are made from the point of view of the original position. But these intuitive considerations help to clarify the principle and the sense in which it is egalitarian. . . .

## 24. THE VEIL OF IGNORANCE

The idea of the original position is to set up a fair procedure so that any principles agreed to will be just. The aim is to use the notion of pure procedural justice as a basis of theory. Somehow we must nullify the effects of specific contingencies which put men at odds and tempt them to exploit social and natural circumstances to their own advantage. Now in order to do this I assume that the parties are situated behind a veil of ignorance. They do not know how the various alternatives will affect their own particular case and they are obliged to evaluate principles solely on the basis of general considerations.[13]

It is assumed, then, that the parties do not know certain kinds of particular facts. First of all, no one knows his place in society, his class position or social status; nor does he know his fortune in the distribution of natural assets and abilities, his intelligence and strength, and the like. Nor, again, does anyone

know his conception of the good, the particulars of his rational plan of life, or even the special features of his psychology such as his aversion to risk or liability to optimism or pessimism. More than this, I assume that the parties do not know the particular circumstances of their own society. That is, they do not know its economic or political situation, or the level of civilization and culture it has been able to achieve. The persons in the original position have no information as to which generation they belong. These broader restrictions on knowledge are appropriate in part because questions of social justice arise between generations as well as within them, for example, the question of the appropriate rate of capital saving and of the conservation of natural resources and the environment of nature. There is also, theoretically anyway, the question of a reasonable genetic policy. In these cases too, in order to carry through the idea of the original position, the parties must not know the contingencies that set them in opposition. They must choose principles the consequences of which they are prepared to live with whatever generation they turn out to belong to.

As far as possible, then, the only particular facts which the parties know is that their society is subject to the circumstances of justice and whatever this implies. It is taken for granted, however, that they know the general facts about human society. They understand political affairs and the principles of economic theory; they know the basis of social organization and the laws of human psychology. Indeed, the parties are presumed to know whatever general facts affect the choice of the principles of justice. There are no limitations on general information, that is, on general laws and theories, since conceptions of justice must be adjusted to the characteristics of the systems of social cooperation which they are to regulate, and there is no reason to rule out these facts. It is, for example, a consideration against a conception of justice that, in view of the laws of moral psychology, men would not acquire a desire to act upon it even when the institutions of their society satisfied it. For in this case there would be difficulty in securing the stability of social cooperation. An important feature of a conception of justice is that it should generate its own support. Its principles should be such that when they are embodied in the basic structure of society men tend to acquire the corresponding sense of justice and develop a desire to act in accordance with its principles. In this case a conception of justice is stable. This kind of general information is admissible in the original position.

The notion of the veil of ignorance raises several difficulties. Some may object that the exclusion of nearly all particular information makes it difficult to grasp what is meant by the original position. Thus it may be helpful to observe that one or more persons can at any time enter this position, or perhaps better, simulate the deliberations of this hypothetical situation, simply by reasoning in accordance with the appropriate restrictions. In arguing for a conception of justice we must be sure that it is among the permitted alternatives and satisfies the stipulated formal constraints. No considerations can be advanced in its favor unless they would be rational ones for us to urge were we to lack the kind of knowledge that is excluded. The evaluation of principles must proceed in terms of the general consequences of their public recognition and universal application, it being assumed that they will be complied with by everyone. To say that a certain conception of justice would be chosen in the original position is equivalent to saying that rational deliberation satisfying certain conditions and restrictions would reach a certain conclusion. If necessary, the argument to this result could be set out more formally. I shall, however, speak throughout in terms of the notion of the original position. It is more economical and suggestive, and brings out certain essential features that otherwise one might easily overlook.

These remarks show that the original position is not to be thought of as a general assembly which includes at one moment everyone who will live at some time or, much less, as an assembly of everyone who could live at some time. It is not a gathering of all actual or possible persons. If we conceived of the original position in either of these ways, the conception would cease to be a natural guide to intuition and would lack a clear sense. In any case, the original position must be interpreted so that one can at

any time adopt its perspective. It must make no difference when one takes up this viewpoint, or who does so: the restrictions must be such that the same principles are always chosen. The veil of ignorance is a key condition in meeting this requirement. It insures not only that the information available is relevant, but that it is at all times the same.

It may be protested that the condition of the veil of ignorance is irrational. Surely, some may object, principles should be chosen in the light of all the knowledge available. There are various replies to this contention. Here I shall sketch those which emphasize the simplifications that need to be made if one is to have any theory at all. (Those based on the Kantian interpretation of the original position are given later, §40.) To begin with, it is clear that since the differences among the parties are unknown to them, and everyone is equally rational and similarly situated, each is convinced by the same arguments. Therefore, we can view the agreement in the original position from the standpoint of one person selected at random. If anyone after due reflection prefers a conception of justice to another, then they all do, and a unanimous agreement can be reached. We can, to make the circumstances more vivid, imagine that the parties are required to communicate with each other through a referee as intermediary, and that he is to announce which alternatives have been suggested and the reasons offered in their support. He forbids the attempt to form coalitions, and he informs the parties when they have come to an understanding. But such a referee is actually superfluous, assuming that the deliberations of the parties must be similar.

Thus there follows the very important consequence that the parties have no basis for bargaining in the usual sense. No one knows his situation in society nor his natural assets, and therefore no one is in a position to tailor principles to his advantage. We might imagine that one of the contractees threatens to hold out unless the others agree to principles favorable to him. But how does he know which principles are especially in his interests? The same holds for the formation of coalitions: if a group were to decide to band together to the disadvantage of the others, they would not know how to favor themselves in the choice of principles. Even if they could get everyone to agree to their proposal, they would have no assurance that it was to their advantage, since they cannot identify themselves either by name or description. The one case where this conclusion fails is that of saving. Since the persons in the original position know that they are contemporaries (taking the present time of entry interpretation), they can favor their generation by refusing to make any sacrifices at all for their successors; they simply acknowledge the principle that no one has a duty to save for posterity. Previous generations have saved or they have not; there is nothing the parties can now do to affect that. So in this instance the veil of ignorance fails to secure the desired result. Therefore, to handle the question of justice between generations, I modify the motivation assumption and add a further constraint. . . . With these adjustments, no generation is able to formulate principles especially designed to advance its own cause and some significant limits on savings principles can be derived. . . . Whatever a person's temporal position, each is forced to choose for all.[14]

The restrictions on particular information in the original position are, then, of fundamental importance. Without them we would not be able to work out any definite theory of justice at all. We would have to be content with a vague formula stating that justice is what would be agreed to without being able to say much, if anything, about the substance of the agreement itself. The formal constraints of the concept of right, those applying to principles directly; are not sufficient for our purpose. The veil of ignorance makes possible a unanimous choice of a particular conception of justice. Without these limitations on knowledge the bargaining problem of the original position would be hopelessly complicated. Even if theoretically a solution were to exist, we would not, at present anyway, be able to determine it. . . .

## 26. THE REASONING LEADING TO THE TWO PRINCIPLES OF JUSTICE

. . . It seems from these remarks that the two principles are at least a plausible conception of justice. The question, though, is how one is to argue for them

more systematically. Now there are several things to do. One can work out their consequences for institutions and note their implications for fundamental social policy. In this way they are tested by a comparison with our considered judgments of justice. . . . But one can also try to find arguments in their favor that are decisive from the standpoint of the original position. In order to see how this might be done, it is useful as a heuristic device to think of the two principles as the maximin solution to the problem of social justice. There is a relation between the two principles and the maximin rule for choice under uncertainty.[15] This is evident from the fact that the two principles are those a person would choose for the design of a society in which his enemy is to assign him his place. The maximin rule tells us to rank alternatives by their worst possible outcomes: we are to adopt the alternative the worst outcome of which is superior to the worst outcomes of the others.[16] The persons in the original position do not, of course, assume that their initial place in society is decided by a malevolent opponent. As I note below, they should not reason from false premises. The veil of ignorance does not violate this idea, since an absence of information is not misinformation. But that the two principles of justice would be chosen if the parties were forced to protect themselves against such a contingency explains the sense in which this conception is the maximin solution. And this analogy suggests that if the original position has been described so that it is rational for the parties to adopt the conservative attitude expressed by this rule, a conclusive argument can indeed be constructed for these principles. Clearly the maximin rule is not, in general, a suitable guide for choices under uncertainty. But it holds only in situations marked by certain special features. My aim, then, is to show that a good case can be made for the two principles based on the fact that the original position has these features to a very high degree.

Now there appear to be three chief features of situations that give plausibility to this unusual rule.[17] First, since the rule takes no account of the likelihoods of the possible circumstances, there must be some reason for sharply discounting estimates of these probabilities. Offhand, the most natural rule of choice would seem to be to compute the expectation of monetary gain for each decision and then to adopt the course of action with the highest prospect. . . . Thus it must be, for example, that the situation is one in which a knowledge of likelihoods is impossible, or at best extremely insecure. In this case it is unreasonable not to be skeptical of probabilistic calculations unless there is no other way out, particularly if the decision is a fundamental one that needs to be justified to others.

The second feature that suggests the maximin rule is the following: the person choosing has a conception of the good such that he cares very little, if anything, for what he might gain above the minimum stipend that he can, in fact, be sure of by following the maximin rule. It is not worthwhile for him to take a chance for the sake of a further advantage, especially when it may turn out that he loses much that is important to him. This last provision brings in the third feature, namely, that the rejected alternatives have outcomes that one can hardly accept. The situation involves grave risks. Of course these features work most effectively in combination. The paradigm situation for following the maximin rule is when all three features are realized to the highest degree.

Let us review briefly the nature of the original position with these three special features in mind. To begin with, the veil of ignorance excludes all knowledge of likelihoods. The parties have no basis for determining the probable nature of their society, or their place in it. Thus they have no basis for probability calculations. They must also take into account the fact that their choice of principles should seem reasonable to others, in particular their descendants, whose rights will be deeply affected by it. These considerations are strengthened by the fact that the parties know very little about the possible states of society. Not only are they unable to conjecture the likelihoods of the various possible circumstances, they cannot say much about what the possible circumstances are, much less enumerate them and foresee the outcome of each alternative available. Those deciding are much more in the dark than illustrations by numerical tables suggest. It is for this reason that I have spoken only of a relation to the maximin rule.

Several kinds of arguments for the two principles of justice illustrate the second feature. Thus, if we can maintain that these principles provide a workable theory of social justice, and that they are compatible with reasonable demands of efficiency, then this conception guarantees a satisfactory minimum. There may be, on reflection, little reason for trying to do better. Thus much of the argument . . . is to show, by their application to some main questions of social justice, that the two principles are a satisfactory conception. These details have a philosophical purpose. Moreover, this line of thought is practically decisive if we can establish the priority of liberty. For this priority implies that the persons in the original position have no desire to try for greater gains at the expense of the basic equal liberties. The minimum assured by the two principles in lexical order is not one that the parties wish to jeopardize for the sake of greater economic and social advantages.

Finally, the third feature holds if we can assume that other conceptions of justice may lead to institutions that the parties would find intolerable. For example, it has sometimes been held that under some conditions the utility principle (in either form) justifies, if not slavery or serfdom, at any rate serious infractions of liberty for the sake of greater social benefits. We need not consider here the truth of this claim. For the moment, this contention is only to illustrate the way in which conceptions of justice may allow for outcomes which the parties may not be able to accept. And having the ready alternative of the two principles of justice which secure a satisfactory minimum, it seems unwise, if not irrational, for them to take a chance that these conditions are not realized. . . .

## 40. THE KANTIAN INTERPRETATION OF JUSTICE AS FAIRNESS

For the most part I have considered the content of the principle of equal liberty and the meaning of the priority of the rights that it defines. It seems appropriate at this point to note that there is a Kantian interpretation of the conception of justice from which this principle derives. This interpretation is based upon Kant's notion of autonomy. It is a mistake, I believe, to emphasize the place of generality and universality in Kant's ethics. That moral principles are general and universal is hardly new with him; and as we have seen these conditions do not in any case take us very far. It is impossible to construct a moral theory on so slender a basis, and therefore to limit the discussion of Kant's doctrine to these notions is to reduce it to triviality. The real force of his view lies elsewhere.[18]

For one thing, he begins with the idea that moral principles are the object of rational choice. They define the moral law that men can rationally will to govern their conduct in an ethical commonwealth. Moral philosophy becomes the study of the conception and outcome of a suitably defined rational decision. This idea has immediate consequences. For once we think of moral principles as legislation for a kingdom of ends, it is clear that these principles must not only be acceptable to all but public as well. Finally Kant supposes that this moral legislation is to be agreed to under conditions that characterize men as free and equal rational beings. The description of the original position is an attempt to interpret this conception. I do not wish to argue here for this interpretation on the basis of Kant's text. Certainly some will want to read him differently. Perhaps the remarks to follow are best taken as suggestions for relating justice as fairness to the high point of the contractarian tradition in Kant and Rousseau.

Kant held, I believe, that a person is acting autonomously when the principles of his action are chosen by him as the most adequate possible expression of his nature as a free and equal rational being. The principles he acts upon are not adopted because of his social position or natural endowments, or in view of the particular kind of society in which he lives or the specific things that he happens to want. To act on such principles is to act heteronomously. Now the veil of ignorance deprives the persons in the original position of the knowledge that would enable them to choose heteronomous principles. The parties arrive at their choice together as free and equal rational persons knowing only that those circumstances obtain which give rise to the need for principles of justice.

To be sure, the argument for these principles does add in various ways to Kant's conception. For example, it adds the feature that the principles chosen are to apply to the basic structure of society; and premises characterizing this structure are used in deriving the principles of justice. But I believe that this and other additions are natural enough and remain fairly close to Kant's doctrine, at least when all of his ethical writings are viewed together. Assuming, then, that the reasoning in favor of the principles of justice is correct, we can say that when persons act on these principles they are acting in accordance with principles that they would choose as rational and independent persons in an original position of equality. The principles of their actions do not depend upon social or natural contingencies, nor do they reflect the bias of the particulars of their plan of life or the aspirations that motivate them. By acting from these principles persons express their nature as free and equal rational beings subject to the general conditions of human life. For to express one's nature as a being of a particular kind is to act on the principles that would be chosen if this nature were the decisive determining element. Of course, the choice of the parties in the original position is subject to the restrictions of that situation. But when we knowingly act on the principles of justice in the ordinary course of events, we deliberately assume the limitations of the original position. One reason for doing this, for persons who can do so and want to, is to give expression to one's nature.

The principles of justice are also analogous to categorical imperatives. For by a categorical imperative Kant understands a principle of conduct that applies to a person in virtue of his nature as a free and equal rational being. The validity of the principle does not presuppose that one has a particular desire or aim. Whereas a hypothetical imperative by contrast does assume this: it directs us to take certain steps as effective means to achieve a specific end. Whether the desire is for a particular thing, or whether it is for something more general, such as certain kinds of agreeable feelings or pleasures, the corresponding imperative is hypothetical. Its applicability depends upon one's having an aim which one need not have as a condition of being a rational human individual. The argument for the two principles of justice does not assume that the parties have particular ends, but only that they desire certain primary goods. These are things that it is rational to want whatever else one wants. Thus given human nature, wanting them is part of being rational; and while each is presumed to have some conception of the good, nothing is known about his final ends. The preference for primary goods is derived, then, from only the most general assumptions about rationality and the conditions of human life. To act from the principles of justice is to act from categorical imperatives in the sense that they apply to us whatever in particular our aims are. This simply reflects the fact that no such contingencies appear as premises in their derivation.

We may note also that the motivational assumption of mutual disinterest parallels Kant's notion of autonomy, and gives another reason for this condition. So far this assumption has been used to characterize the circumstances of justice and to provide a clear conception to guide the reasoning of the parties. We have also seen that the concept of benevolence, being a second-order notion, would not work out well. Now we can add that the assumption of mutual disinterest is to allow for freedom in the choice of a system of final ends.[19] Liberty in adopting a conception of the good is limited only by principles that are deduced from a doctrine which imposes no prior constraints on these conceptions. Presuming mutual disinterest in the original position carries out this idea. We postulate that the parties have opposing claims in a suitably general sense. If their ends were restricted in some specific way, this would appear at the outset as an arbitrary restriction on freedom. Moreover, if the parties were conceived as altruists, or as pursuing certain kinds of pleasures, then the principles chosen would apply, as far as the argument would have shown, only to persons whose freedom was restricted to choices compatible with altruism or hedonism. As the argument now runs, the principles of justice cover all persons with rational plans of life, whatever their content, and these principles represent the appropriate restrictions on free-

dom. Thus it is possible to say that the constraints on conceptions of the good are the result of an interpretation of the contractual situation that puts no prior limitations on what men may desire. There are a variety of reasons, then, for the motivational premise of mutual disinterest. This premise is not only a matter of realism about the circumstances of justice or a way to make the theory manageable. It also connects up with the Kantian idea of autonomy.

There is, however, a difficulty that should be clarified. It is well expressed by Sidgwick.[20] He remarks that nothing in Kant's ethics is more striking than the idea that a man realizes his true self when he acts from the moral law, whereas if he permits his actions to be determined by sensuous desires or contingent aims, he becomes subject to the law of nature. Yet in Sidgwick's opinion this idea comes to naught. It seems to him that on Kant's view the lives of the saint and the scoundrel are equally the outcome of a free choice (on the part of the noumenal self) and equally the subject of causal laws (as a phenomenal self). Kant never explains why the scoundrel does not express in a bad life his characteristic and freely chosen selfhood in the same way that a saint expresses his characteristic and freely chosen selfhood in a good one. Sidgwick's objection is decisive, I think, as long as one assumes, as Kant's exposition may seem to allow, both that the noumenal self can choose any consistent set of principles and that acting from such principles, whatever they are, is sufficient to express one's choice as that of a free and equal rational being. Kant's reply must be that though acting on any consistent set of principles could be the outcome of a decision on the part of the noumenal self, not all such action by the phenomenal self expresses this decision as that of a free and equal rational being. Thus if a person realizes his true self by expressing it in his actions, and if he desires above all else to realize this self, then he will choose to act from principles that manifest his nature as a free and equal rational being. The missing part of the argument concerns the concept of expression. Kant did not show that acting from the moral law expresses our nature in identifiable ways that acting from contrary principles does not.

This defect is made good, I believe, by the conception of the original position. The essential point is that we need an argument showing which principles, if any, free and equal rational persons would choose and these principles must be applicable in practice. A definite answer to this question is required to meet Sidgwick's objection. My suggestion is that we think of the original position as in important ways similar to the point of view from which noumenal selves see the world. The parties qua noumenal selves have complete freedom to choose whatever principles they wish; but they also have a desire to express their nature as rational and equal members of the intelligible realm with precisely this liberty to choose, that is, as beings who can look at the world in this way and express this perspective in their life as members of society. They must decide, then, which principles when consciously followed and acted upon in everyday life will best manifest this freedom in their community, most fully reveal their independence from natural contingencies and social accident. Now if the argument of the contract doctrine is correct, these principles are indeed those defining the moral law, or more exactly, the principles of justice for institutions and individuals. The description of the original position resembles the point of view of noumenal selves, of what it means to be a free and equal rational being. Our nature as such beings is displayed when we act from the principles we would choose when this nature is reflected in the conditions determining the choice. Thus men exhibit their freedom, their independence from the contingencies of nature and society, by acting in ways they would acknowledge in the original position.

Properly understood, then, the desire to act justly derives in part from the desire to express most fully what we are or can be, namely free and equal rational beings with a liberty to choose. It is for this reason, I believe, that Kant speaks of the failure to act on the moral law as giving rise to shame and not to feelings of guilt. And this is appropriate, since for him acting unjustly is acting in a manner that fails to express our nature as a free and equal rational being. Such actions therefore strike at our self-respect, our sense

of our own worth, and the experience of this loss is shame. . . . We have acted as though we belonged to a lower order, as though we were a creature whose first principles are decided by natural contingencies. Those who think of Kant's moral doctrine as one of law and guilt badly misunderstand him. Kant's main aim is to deepen and to justify Rousseau's idea that liberty is acting in accordance with a law that we give to ourselves. And this leads not to a morality of austere command but to an ethic of mutual respect and self-esteem.[21]

The original position may be viewed, then, as a procedural interpretation of Kant's conception of autonomy and the categorical imperative within the framework of an empirical theory. The principles regulative of the kingdom of ends are those that would be chosen in this position, and the description of this situation enables us to explain the sense in which acting from these principles expresses our nature as free and equal rational persons. No longer are these notions purely transcendent and lacking explicable connections with human conduct, for the procedural conception of the original position allows us to make these ties. Of course, I have departed from Kant's views in several respects. I cannot discuss these matters here; but two points should be noted. The person's choice as a noumenal self I have assumed to be a collective one. The force of the self's being equal is that the principles chosen must be acceptable to other selves. Since all are similarly free and rational, each must have an equal say in adopting the public principles of the ethical commonwealth. This means that as noumenal selves, everyone is to consent to these principles. Unless the scoundrel's principles would be agreed to, they cannot express this free choice, however much a single self might be of a mind to adopt them. . . .

Secondly, I have assumed all along that the parties know that they are subject to the conditions of human life. Being in the circumstances of justice, they are situated in the world with other men who likewise face limitations of moderate scarcity and competing claims. Human freedom is to be regulated by principles chosen in the light of these natural restrictions. Thus justice as fairness is a theory of human justice and among its premises are the elementary facts about persons and their place in nature. The freedom of pure intelligences not subject to these constraints (God and the angels) are outside the range of the theory. Kant may have meant his doctrine to apply to all rational beings as such and therefore that men's social situation in the world is to have no role in determining the first principles of justice. If so, this is another difference between justice as fairness and Kant's theory.

But the Kantian interpretation is not intended as an interpretation of Kant's actual doctrine but rather of justice as fairness. Kant's view is marked by a number of deep dualisms, in particular, the dualism between the necessary and the contingent, form and content, reason and desire, and noumena and phenomena. To abandon these dualisms as he understood them is, for many, to abandon what is distinctive in his theory. I believe otherwise. His moral conception has a characteristic structure that is more clearly discernible when these dualisms are not taken in the sense he gave them but recast and their moral force reformulated within the scope of an empirical theory. What I have called the Kantian interpretation indicates how this can be done.

## Notes

1. As the text suggests, I shall regard Locke's *Second Treatise of Government,* Rousseau's *The Social Contract,* and Kant's ethical works beginning with *The Foundations of the Metaphysics of Morals* as definitive of the contract tradition. For all of its greatness, Hobbes's *Leviathan* raises special problems. A general historical survey is provided by J. W. Gough, *The Social Contract,* 2nd ed. (Oxford, The Clarendon Press, 1957), and Otto Gierke, *Natural Law and the Theory of Society,* trans. with an introduction by Ernest Barker (Cambridge, The University Press, 1934). A presentation of the contract view as primarily an ethical theory is to be found in G. R. Grice, *The Grounds of Moral Judgment* (Cambridge, The University Press, 1967). . . .

2. Kant is clear that the original agreement is hypothetical. See *The Metaphysics of Morals,* pt. I (*Rechtslehre*),

especially §§47, 52; and pt. II of the essay "Concerning the Common Saying: This May Be True in Theory but It Does Not Apply in Practice," in *Kant's Political Writings,* ed. Hans Reiss and trans. by H. B. Nisbet (Cambridge, The University Press, 1970), pp. 73–87. See Georges Vlachos, *La Pensée politique de Kant* (Paris, Presses Universitaires de France, 1962), pp. 326–335; and J. G. Murphy, *Kant: The Philosophy of Right* (London, Macmillan. 1970), pp. 109–112, 133–136, for a further discussion.

3. For the formulation of this intuitive idea I am indebted to Allan Gibbard.

4. The process of mutual adjustment of principles and considered judgments is not peculiar to moral philosophy. See Nelson Goodman, *Fact, Fiction, and Forecast* (Cambridge, Mass., Harvard University Press, 1955), pp. 65–68, for parallel remarks concerning the justification of the principles of deductive and inductive inference.

5. Henri Poincaré remarks: "Il nous faut une faculté qui nous fasse voir le but de loin, et, cette faculté, c'est l'intuition." *La Valeur de la science* (Paris, Flammarion, 1909), p. 27.

6. I shall take Henry Sidgwick's *The Methods of Ethics,* 7th ed. (London, 1907), as summarizing the development of utilitarian moral theory. Book III of his *Principles of Political Economy* (London, 1883) applies this doctrine to questions of economic and social justice, and is a precursor of A. C. Pigou, *The Economics of Welfare* (London, Macmillan, 1920). Sidgwick's *Outlines of the History of Ethics,* 5th ed. (London, 1902), contains a brief history of the utilitarian tradition. We may follow him in assuming, somewhat arbitrarily, that it begins with Shaftesbury's *An Inquiry Concerning Virtue and Merit* (1711) and Hutcheson's *An Inquiry Concerning Moral Good and Evil* (1725). Hutcheson seems to have been the first to state clearly the principle of utility. He says in *Inquiry,* sec. 111, §8, that "that action is best, which procures the greatest happiness for the greatest numbers; and that, worst, which, in like manner, occasions misery." Other major eighteenth century works are Hume's *A Treatise of Human Nature* (1739), and *An Enquiry Concerning the Principles of Morals* (1751); Adam Smith's *A Theory of the Moral Sentiments* (1759); and Bentham's *The Principles of Morals and Legislation* (1789). To these we must add the writings of J. S. Mill represented by *Utilitarianism* (1863) and F. Y. Edgeworth's *Mathematical Psychics* (London, 1888).

The discussion of utilitarianism has taken a different turn in recent years by focusing on what we may call the coordination problem and related questions of publicity. This development stems from the essays of R. F. Harrod, "Utilitarianism Revised," *Mind,* vol. 45 (1936); J. D. Mabbott, "Punishment," *Mind,* vol. 48 (1939); Jonathan Harrison, "Utilitarianism, Universalisation, and Our Duty to Be Just," *Proceedings of the Aristotelian Society,* vol. 53 (1952–53): and J. O. Urmson, "The Interpretation of the Philosophy of J. S. Mill," *Philosophical Quarterly,* vol. 3 (1953). See also J. J. C. Smart, "Extreme and Restricted Utilitarianism," *Philosophical Quarterly,* vol. 6 (1956), and his *An Outline of a System of Utilitarian Ethics* (Cambridge, The University Press, 1961). For an account of these matters, see David Lyons, *Forms and Limits of Utilitarianism* (Oxford, The Clarendon Press, 1965); and Allan Gibbard, "Utilitarianisms and Coordination" (dissertation, Harvard University, 1971). The problems raised by these works, as important as they are, I shall leave aside as not bearing directly on the more elementary question of distribution which I wish to discuss.

Finally, we should note here the essays of J. C. Harsanyi, in particular, "Cardinal Utility in Welfare Economics and in the Theory of Risk-Taking," *Journal of Political Economy,* 1953, and "Cardinal Welfare, Individualistic Ethics, and Interpersonal Comparisons of Utility," *Journal of Political Economy,* 1955; and R. B. Brandt, "Some Merits of One Form of Rule-Utilitarianism." *University of Colorado Studies* (Boulder, Colorado, 1967). . . .

7. On this point see also D. P. Gauthier, *Practical Reasoning* (Oxford, Clarendon Press, 1963), pp. 126f. The text elaborates the suggestion found in "Constitutional Liberty and the Concept of Justice," *Nomos VI: Justice,* ed. C. J. Friedrich and J. W. Chapman (New York, Atherton Press, 1963), pp. 124f, which in turn is related to the idea of justice as a higher-order administrative decision. See "Justice as Fairness," *Philosophical Review,* 1958, pp. 185–187. That the principle of social integration is distinct from the principle of personal integration is stated by R. B. Perry, *General Theory of Value* (New York, Longmans, Green, and Company, 1926), pp. 674–677. He attributes the error of overlooking this fact to Emile Durkheim and others with similar views. Perry's conception of social integration is that brought about by a shared and dominant benevolent purpose. . . .

8. Here I adopt W. K. Frankena's definition of teleological theories in *Ethics* (Englewood Cliffs, N. J., Prentice Hall, Inc., 1963), p. 13.

9. On this point see Sidgwick, *The Methods of Ethics,* pp. 416f.

10. See J. S. Mill, *Utilitarianism,* ch. V, last two pars.

11. See Herbert Spiegelberg, "A Defense of Human Equality," *Philosophical Review,* vol. 53 (1944), pp. 101, 113–123; and D. D. Raphael, "Justice and Liberty," *Proceedings of the Aristotelian Society,* vol. 51 (1950–1951), pp. 187f.

12. See, for example, Spiegelberg, pp. 120f.

13. The veil of ignorance is so natural a condition that something like it must have occurred to many. The formulation in the text is implicit, I believe, in Kant's doctrine of the categorical imperative, both in the way this procedural criterion is defined and the use Kant makes of it. Thus when Kant tells us to test our maxim by considering what would be the case were it a universal law of nature, he must suppose that we do not know our place within this imagined system of nature. See, for example, his discussion of the topic of practical judgment in *The Critique of Practical Reason,* Academy Edition, vol. 5, pp. 68–72. A similar restriction on information is found in J. C. Harsanyi, "Cardinal Utility in Welfare Economics and in the Theory of Risk-taking," *Journal of Political Economy,* vol. 61 (1953). However, other aspects of Harsanyi's view are quite different, and he uses the restriction to develop a utilitarian theory. . . .

14. Rousseau, *The Social Contract,* bk. II, ch. IV, par. 5.

15. An accessible discussion of this and other rules of choice under uncertainty can be found in W. J. Baumol, *Economic Theory and Operations Analysis.* 2nd ed. (Englewood Cliffs, N. J., Prentice-Hall Inc., 1965), ch. 24. Baumol gives a geometric interpretation of these rules . . . to illustrate the difference principle. See pp. 558–562. See also R. D. Luce and Howard Raiffa, *Games and Decisions* (New York, John Wiley and Sons, Inc., 1957), ch. XIII, for a fuller account.

16. Consider the gain-and-loss table below. It represents the gains and losses for a situation which is not a game of strategy. There is no one playing against the person making the decision; instead he is faced with several possible circumstances which may or may not obtain. Which circumstances happen to exist does not depend upon what the person choosing decides or whether he announces his moves in advance. The numbers in the table are monetary values (in hundreds of dollars) in comparison with some initial situation. The gain (g) depends upon the individual's decision (d) and the circumstances

(c). Thus g = f (d, c). Assuming that there are three possible decisions and three possible circumstances, we might have this gain-and-loss table.

|  | Circumstances | | |
| Decisions | c1 | c2 | c3 |
| --- | --- | --- | --- |
| $d_1$ | –7 | 8 | 12 |
| $d_2$ | -8 | 7 | 14 |
| $d_3$ | 5 | 6 | 8 |

The maximin rule requires that we make the third decision. For in this case the worst that can happen is that one gains five hundred dollars, which is better than the worst for the other actions. If we adopt one of these we may lose either eight or seven hundred dollars. Thus, the choice of $d_3$ maximizes f (d,c) for that value of c, which for a given d, minimizes f. The term "maximin" means the *maximum minimorum;* and the rule directs our attention to the worst that can happen under any proposed course of action, and to decide in the light of that.

17. Here I borrow from William Fellner, *Probability and Profit* (Homewood, Ill., R. D. Irwin, Inc., 1965), pp. 140–142, where these features are noted.

18. Especially to be avoided is the idea that Kant's doctrine provides at best only the general, or formal, elements for a utilitarian or indeed for any other moral conception. This idea is found in Sidgwick, *The Methods of Ethics,* 7th ed. (London, Macmillan, 1907), pp. xvii and xx of the preface; and in F. H. Bradley, *Ethical Studies,* 2nd ed. (Oxford, Clarendon Press, 1927), Essay IV; and goes back at least to Hegel. One must not lose sight of the full scope of his view and take the later works into consideration. Unfortunately, there is no commentary on Kant's moral theory as a whole; perhaps it would prove impossible to write. But the standard works of H. J. Paton, *The Categorical Imperative* (Chicago, University of Chicago Press, 1948), and L. W. Beck, *A Commentary on Kant's Critique of Practical Reason* (Chicago, University of Chicago Press, 1960), and others need to be further complemented by studies of the other writings. See here M. J. Gregor's *Laws of Freedom* (Oxford, Basil Blackwell, 1963), an account of *The Metaphysics of Morals,* and J. G. Murphy's brief *Kant: The Philosophy of Right* (London, Macmillan, 1970). Beyond this, *The Critique of Judgment, Religion within the Limits of Reason,* and the political writings cannot be neglected without distorting his doctrine. For the last, see *Kant's Political Writings,* ed. Hans Reiss and trans. H. B. Nisbet (Cambridge, The University Press, 1970).

19. For this point I am indebted to Charles Fried.

20. See *The Methods of Ethics,* Appendix, "The Kantian Conception of Free Will" (reprinted from *Mind,* vol. 13, 1888), pp. 511–516, esp. p. 516.

21. See B. A. O. Williams, "The Idea of Equality," in *Philosophy, Politics and Society,* Second Series, ed. Peter Laslett and W. G. Runciman (Oxford, Basil Blackwell, 1962), pp. 115f. For confirmation of this interpretation, see Kant's remarks on moral education in *The Critique of Practical Reason,* pt. II. See also Beck, *A Commentary on Kant's Critique of Practical Reason,* pp. 233–236.

# ROBERT NOZICK

## INTRODUCTION

## THOMAS CHRISTIANO

Robert Nozick, born in 1938 in Brooklyn, New York, was graduated from Columbia College and received his Ph.D. from Princeton University. He is currently Pellegrino University Professor at Harvard University. He is a past president of the American Philosophical Association (Eastern Division), a Fellow of the American Academy of Arts and Sciences, a Corresponding Fellow of the British Academy, and a Senior Fellow in the Society of Fellows at Harvard University.

While Nozick has written path-breaking works in an unusually wide variety of areas in philosophy, his most famous book, winner of the 1975 National Book Award, was *Anarchy, State, and Utopia.* It revived classical liberalism as a serious option in political philosophy, offered the first full-length challenge to John Rawls's *A Theory of Justice,* and defended a version of libertarianism. Nozick's book *Philosophical Explanations* (1981) made lasting contributions to epistemology and our understanding of personal identity, free will, and the foundations of ethics. *The Examined Life* (1989) explored the nature of the good life and the meaning of life. *The Nature of Rationality* (1993) Culminated a lifelong study of theories of rational decision and rational belief. More recently, Nozick published *Socratic Puzzles* (1997), a collection of essays, and *Invariances* (2001), a book on the notion of an objective world and the role that invariance plays in it, including topics in philosophy of science, philosophy of mind, metaphysics, and ethics.

In *Anarchy, State, and Utopia,* published in 1974, Nozick's arguments proceed in the Lockean tradition of natural rights to liberty and property. For Nozick, justice entails absolute constraints on the behavior of people toward others. No one may abridge the liberty of another, harm the other in life or limb, or take property from another, without the other's consent. Persons have the right to act in self-defense, and rectification is appropriate if the rights to property and liberty have been violated. In short, whatever comes about by the voluntary consent of people who do not violate the rights of others is just. Any attempt to interfere with this process is an illegitimate interference with liberty. These theses imply a radical criticism of contemporary welfare states, inasmuch as modern states impose taxes on their citizens and to that extent regulate their behavior in the pursuit of economic and political aims. These views also entail a radical rejection of much contemporary and classical theorizing in political philosophy. Aristotelian, utilitarian, egalitarian, and various forms of contractarian theory, and many contemporary accounts of liberalism, such as that of John Rawls, run afoul of Nozick's stringent restrictions on what persons may do to one another. Much as these theories may celebrate human freedom or dignity, all are committed to ideals of politics that require individuals to relate in ways to which they may not consent.

Nozick's entitlement theory of justice asserts three basic principles. The principle of entitlement in acquisition regulates how each person may acquire holdings in previously unowned things. The principle of entitlement in transfer states that each may legitimately acquire holdings from another if and only if one has the other's voluntary consent and the other has legitimately acquired the holdings. The principle of rectification calls for appropriate rectification for any violation of the two first principles.

A key support for the three principles is the Kantian idea that one must never treat persons as mere means but always as ends in themselves. According to Nozick treating persons as ends requires the persons consent to their treatment. This interpretation of the Kantian principle, however, leaves unanswered questions. Why doesn't it also require that everyone help persons to pursue their reasonable ends even at the expense of those who have more than enough? If I value a person's rational nature, aren't I sometimes under a duty to enhance a person's capacity to exercise that nature? Doesn't treating persons as ends require that one ensure that one's relations and exchanges with them take place under fair conditions, such as an adequate supply of goods that enable those persons to avoid mistreatment?

Nozick argues that persons may act as they wish so long as they do not interfere with others. Hence, individuals may commit suicide or sell themselves into slavery. For Kant, by contrast, a person is not permitted to do these things, because both of these actions amount to treating oneself as a mere means and not as an end.

Another of Nozick's foundational notions is that each person is an owner of himself or herself. This principle is widely accepted but has been interpreted variously. Locke thought that self-ownership did not imply ownership of one's body, which is the property of God; one owns one's self and the activities of the self. For Nozick, a person owns his or her body, and Nozick infers that if I violate another's entitlement to be unmolested, I am acting as if I were part owner of that person. Nozick employs this idea in a defense of property rights; in a striking illustration he argues that if a group taxes a person without the person's consent from the product of that person's labor, then the group is acting as if it were part owner of the person by appropriating a proportion of his or her labor for its own aims. But doing so forces the person to work for the group, which can be permitted only if the group owns the person, at least in part. So, according to Nozick, taxation is a form of forced labor or slavery, which is forbidden without the person's consent.

To the extent that Nozick can found the entitlement theory on the idea that no one may own another without that other's consent, his view has a strong intuitive foundation. The crucial question concerns the relation between self-ownership and the ownership of external things.

But someone's taking something from me does not appear to involve taking any part of me, molesting me, or even exercising control over me. It does involve exercising control over something I own. For instance, if I am taxed, I am still free to do whatever job I please or not do any job at all. Perhaps taxation is theft, but not obviously because taxation is forced labor.

In addition, one can assert some control over another for a just cause, such as self-defense. Or if someone has violated my rights, I may attempt to rectify the situation by taking something back in return. Whether these are cases of asserting part-ownership over another is unclear. If they are not, then the notion of ownership appears to presuppose some principles of justice. If they are, then the notion of self-ownership appears not to be absolute in the face of competing ideas of justice.

Nozick also bases his entitlement theory on a conception of liberty, which plays an intuitive role in his use of the Wilt Chamberlain example: Wilt offers to play basketball for his adoring fans on condition that they pay an extra twenty-five cents, which goes directly to him and not to the team. If a million fans go to see him, he ends up a quarter-million dollars wealthier than anyone else. Nozick asks us to imagine this scenario against the backdrop of some particular conception of distributive justice. For instance, if we suppose that justice requires that each person begins with an equal share of the wealth of the society, then while Wilt and the fans and the players all start out with equal wealth, Wilt ends up a quarter-million dollars wealthier than the others. The egalitarian must now decide whether to redistribute the money Wilt received or allow the inequality that has arisen from the transactions. Nozick believes the egalitarian faces a dilemma. To ban the transactions would be to say that the fans were not legitimately in possession of their holdings. To say that the subsequent unequal distribution accords with equality would surely be puzzling. So, the egalitarian seems committed to say that equality conflicts with liberty, for to maintain any pattern of distribution requires interventions in social life to restore the damage to that pattern done by consenting adults. In other words, patterns of distribution are always under threat, when people are free to do what they want with their goods. By contrast, the entitlement theory, which does not require that any pattern of distribution be maintained, does not conflict with liberty. According to Nozick, the theory is a historical conception of justice, which says that whatever results from persons' just uses of justly held goods is itself just. Since the fans justly hold their money and pay to see Wilt play, the outcome of the exchanges is just.

The Wilt Chamberlain example points to the disturbing prospect of a state, concerned with maintaining patterned distributions, constantly but unpredictably intruding in the lives of its citizens. Nozick challenges pattern theorists to show how one can maintain a pattern while at the same establishing the conditions for autonomous, long-term planning under predictable and secure circumstances.

One may transfer holdings to others only if one has legitimately received the holdings from others or legitimately acquired them from what is unowned. Every exchange is legitimate on condition that the holdings in question were previously legitimately held. With the exception of the parts of one's body, no one is born with legitimate holdings. Thus, a major question for Nozick is how things can be legitimately acquired from unowned things. When one legitimately acquires something previously unowned, one in effect restricts others from using it. Hence, through legitimate acquisition one can limit the liberty of others without their consent. But, isn't this conclusion at odds with one of the founding ideas of the entitlement theory?

Locke argues that one may acquire property from previously unowned things in order to satisfy needs. So the origin of property is linked to the importance of the preservation of oneself and others. And Locke ascribes the same foundation to liberty. He claims that one legitimately acquires property from what is unowned by mixing one's labor with it. Philosophers have interpreted this suggestive idea in a number of ways. Some have said that one makes oneself part of the thing, thus extending the right of self-ownership to it. Others have said that one deserves to own the thing because of one's work put into it. Locke also imposes limits on what can be acquired, arguing that, based on the equal importance of everyone's need, one ought not waste the things one acquires and, secondly, one must leave enough and as good for others.

Nozick accepts Locke's second proviso but rejects his labor-mixing idea on the grounds that it is not clear whether by working one has gained a possession or lost one's labor. Nozick does not offer a complete account of the basis of acquisition or of its justification but tells us that acquisition of unowned things is legitimate as long as the second proviso is satisfied. In other words, what I can acquire is constrained by the needs of others.

However, questions remain. What about future generations that no longer have access to acquisition of unowned external goods? Is the proviso violated in their cases? Or is it sufficient that they have opportunities to live decent lives by virtue of the acquisition and productive efforts of others? What does "as good and enough for others" imply in this circumstance? Nozick responds that the capitalist society justified by his entitlement theory would be so productive that it would obviate any worries about later generations.

For an excellent edition of critical essays on Nozick's book, see Jeffrey Paul (ed.), *Reading Nozick: Essays on Anarchy, State and Utopia* (Totowa, N.J.: Rowman and Littlefield, 1981). A recent critical study devoted largely to a discussion of Nozick's political theory is G. A. Cohen, *Self-Ownership, Freedom and Equality* (Cambridge: Cambridge University

Press, 1995). For a collection of essays by leading contemporary philosophers on different aspects of Nozick's work but devoted in major part to his political philosophy, see David Schmidtz (ed.), *Robert Nozick: Contemporary Philosophers in Focus* (New York: Cambridge University Press, 2001).

# Anarchy, State, and Utopia

## CHAPTER 7

### *Distributive Justice*

The minimal state is the most extensive state that can be justified. Any state more extensive violates people's rights. Yet many persons have put forth reasons purporting to justify a more extensive state. It is impossible within the compass of this book to examine all the reasons that have been put forth. Therefore, I shall focus upon those generally acknowledged to be most weighty and influential, to see precisely wherein they fail. In this chapter we consider the claim that a more extensive state is justified, because necessary (or the best instrument) to achieve distributive justice. . . .

The term "distributive justice" is not a neutral one. Hearing the term "distribution," most people presume that some thing or mechanism uses some principle or criterion to give out a supply of things. Into this process of distributing shares some error may have crept. So it is an open question, at least, whether *re*distribution should take place; whether we should do again what has already been done once, though poorly. However, we are not in the position of children who have been given portions of pie by someone who now makes last minute adjustments to rectify careless cutting. There is no *central* distribution, no person or group entitled to control all the resources, jointly deciding how they are to be doled out. What each person gets, he gets from others who give to him in exchange for something, or as a gift. In a free society, diverse persons control dif-

ferent resources, and new holdings arise out of the voluntary exchanges and actions of persons. There is no more a distributing or distribution of shares than there is a distributing of mates in a society in which persons choose whom they shall marry. The total result is the product of many individual decisions which the different individuals involved are entitled to make. Some uses of the term "distribution," it is true, do not imply a previous distributing appropriately judged by some criterion (for example, "probability distribution"); nevertheless, despite the title of this chapter, it would be best to use a terminology that clearly is neutral. We shall speak of people's holdings; a principle of justice in holdings describes (part of) what justice tells us (requires) about holdings. I shall state first what I take to be the correct view about justice in holdings, and then turn to the discussion of alternate views.

### *Section I*

#### THE ENTITLEMENT THEORY

The subject of justice in holdings consists of three major topics. The first is the *original acquisition of holdings,* the appropriation of unheld things. This includes the issues of how unheld things may come to be held, the process, or processes, by which unheld things may come to be held, the things that may come to be held by these processes, the extent of what comes to be held by a particular process, and so on. We shall refer to the complicated truth about this topic, which we shall not formulate here, as the principle of justice in acquisition. The second topic concerns the *transfer of holdings* from one person to another. By what processes may a person transfer holdings to another? How may a person acquire a holding from another who holds it? Under this topic come general descriptions of voluntary exchange, and gift and (on the other hand) fraud, as well as reference to particular conventional details fixed upon in a given society. The complicated truth about this subject (with placeholders for conventional details) we shall call the principle of justice in transfer. (And we shall suppose it also includes principles governing how a person may divest himself of a holding, passing it into an unheld state.)

If the world were wholly just, the following inductive definition would exhaustively cover the subject of justice in holdings.

1. A person who acquires a holding in accordance with the principle of justice in acquisition is entitled to that holding.
2. A person who acquires a holding in accordance with the principle of justice in transfer, from someone else entitled to the holding, is entitled to the holding.
3. No one is entitled to a holding except by (repeated) applications of 1 and 2.

The complete principle of distributive justice would say simply that a distribution is just if everyone is entitled to the holdings they possess under the distribution.

A distribution is just if it arises from another just distribution by legitimate means. The legitimate means of moving from one distribution to another are specified by the principle of justice in transfer. The legitimate first "moves" are specified by the principle of justice in acquisition.[1] Whatever arises from a just situation by just steps is itself just. The means of change specified by the principle of justice in transfer preserve justice. As correct rules of inference are truth-preserving, and any conclusion deduced via repeated application of such rules from only true premisses is itself true, so the means of transition from one situation to another specified by the principle of justice in transfer are justice-preserving, and any situation actually arising from repeated transitions in accordance with the principle from a just situation is itself just. The parallel between justice-preserving transformations and truth-preserving transformations illuminates where it fails as well as where it holds. That a conclusion could have been deduced by truth-preserving means from premises that are true suffices to show its truth. That from a just situation a situation *could* have arisen via justice-preserving means does *not* suffice to show its justice. The fact that a thief's victims voluntarily *could* have presented him with gifts does not entitle the thief to his ill-gotten gains. Justice in holdings is historical; it depends upon what actually has happened. We shall return to this point later.

Not all actual situations are generated in accordance with the two principles of justice in holdings: the principle of justice in acquisition and the principle of justice in transfer. Some people steal from others, or defraud them, or enslave them, seizing their product and preventing them from living as they choose, or forcibly exclude others from competing in exchanges. None of these are permissible modes of transition from one situation to another. And some persons acquire holdings by means not sanctioned by the principle of justice in acquisition. The existence of past injustice (previous violations of the first two principles of justice in holdings) raises the third major topic under justice in holdings: the rectification of injustice in holdings. If past injustice has shaped present holdings in various ways, some identifiable and some not, what now, if anything, ought to be done to rectify these injustices? What obligations do the performers of injustice have toward those whose position is worse than it would have been had the injustice not been done? Or, than it would have been had compensation been paid promptly? How, if at all, do things change if the beneficiaries and those made worse off are not the direct parties in the act of injustice, but, for example, their descendants? Is an injustice done to someone whose holding was itself based upon an unrectified injustice? How far back must one go in wiping clean the historical slate of injustices? What may victims of injustice permissibly do in order to rectify the injustices being done to them, including the many injustices done by persons acting through their government? I do not know of a thorough or theoretically sophisticated treatment of such issues.[2] Idealizing greatly, let us suppose theoretical investigation will produce a principle of rectification. This principle uses historical information about previous situations and injustices done in them (as defined by the first two principles of justice and rights against interference), and information about the actual course of events that flowed from these injustices, until the present, and it yields a description (or descriptions) of holdings in the society. The principle of rectification presumably will make use of its best estimate of subjunctive information about what would have occurred (or a probability distribution over what might have occurred, using the expected value) if the injustice had not taken place. If the actual description of holdings turns out not to be one of the descriptions yielded by the principle, then one of the descriptions yielded must be realized.[3]

The general outlines of the theory of justice in holdings are that the holdings of a person are just if he is entitled to them by the principles of justice in acquisition and transfer, or by the principle of rectification of injustice (as specified by the first two principles). If each person's holdings are just, then the total set (distribution) of holdings is just. To turn these general outlines into a specific theory we would have to specify the details of each of the three principles of justice in holdings: the principle of acquisition of holdings, the principle of transfer of holdings, and the principle of rectification of violations of the first two principles. I shall not attempt that task here.

## HISTORICAL PRINCIPLES
## AND END-RESULT PRINCIPLES

The general outlines of the entitlement theory illuminate the nature and defects of other conceptions of distributive justice. The entitlement theory of justice in distribution is *historical;* whether a distribution is just depends upon how it came about. In contrast, *current time-slice principles* of justice hold that the

justice of a distribution is determined by how things are distributed (who has what) as judged by some *structural* principle(s) of just distribution. A utilitarian who judges between any two distributions by seeing which has the greater sum of utility and, if the sums tie, applies some fixed equality criterion to choose the more equal distribution, would hold a current time-slice principle of justice. As would someone who had a fixed schedule of trade-offs between the sum of happiness and equality. According to a current time-slice principle, all that needs to be looked at, in judging the justice of a distribution, is who ends up with what; in comparing any two distributions one need look only at the matrix presenting the distributions. No further information need be fed into a principle of justice. It is a consequence of such principles of justice that any two structurally identical distributions are equally just. (Two distributions are structurally identical if they present the same profile, but perhaps have different persons occupying the particular slots. My having ten and your having five, and my having five and your having ten are structurally identical distributions.) Welfare economics is the theory of current time-slice principles of justice. The subject is conceived as operating on matrices representing only current information about distribution. This, as well as some of the usual conditions (for example, the choice of distribution is invariant under relabeling of columns), guarantees that welfare economics will be a current time-slice theory, with all of its inadequacies.

Most persons do not accept current time-slice principles as constituting the whole story about distributive shares. They think it relevant in assessing the justice of a situation to consider not only the distribution it embodies, but also how that distribution came about. If some persons are in prison for murder or war crimes, we do not say that to assess the justice of the distribution in the society we must look only at what this person has, and that person has, and that person has, . . . at the current time. We think it relevant to ask whether someone did something so that he *deserved* to be punished, deserved to have a lower share. Most will agree to the relevance of further information with regard to punishments and penalties. Consider also desired things. One traditional socialist view is that workers are entitled to the product and full fruits of their labor; they have earned it; a distribution is unjust if it does not give the workers what they are entitled to. Such entitlements are based upon some past history. No socialist holding this view would find it comforting to be told that because the actual distribution A happens to coincide structurally with the one he desires D, A therefore is no less just than D; it differs only in that the "parasitic" owners of capital receive under A what the workers are entitled to under D, and the workers receive under A what the owners are entitled to under D, namely very little. This socialist rightly, in my view, holds onto the notions of earning, producing, entitlement, desert, and so forth, and he rejects current time-slice principles that look only to the structure of the resulting set of holdings. (The set of holdings resulting from what? Isn't it implausible that how holdings are produced and come to exist has no effect at all on who should hold what?) His mistake lies in his view of what entitlements arise out of what sorts of productive processes.

We construe the position we discuss too narrowly by speaking of *current* time-slice principles. Nothing is changed if structural principles operate upon a time sequence of current time-slice profiles and, for example, give someone more now to counterbalance the less he has had earlier. A utilitarian or an egalitarian or any mixture of the two over time will inherit the difficulties of his more myopic comrades. He is not helped by the fact that *some* of the information others consider relevant in assessing a distribution is reflected, unrecoverably, in past matrices. Henceforth, we shall refer to such unhistorical principles of distributive justice, including the current time-slice principles, as *end-result principles* or *end-state principles.*

In contrast to end-result principles of justice, *historical principles* of justice hold that past circumstances or actions of people can create differential entitlements or differential deserts to things. An injustice can be worked by moving from one distribution to another structurally identical one, for the second, in profile the same, may violate people's entitlements or deserts; it may not fit the actual history.

## PATTERNING

The entitlement principles of justice in holdings that we have sketched are historical principles of justice. To better understand their precise character, we shall distinguish them from another subclass of the historical principles. Consider, as an example, the principle of distribution according to moral merit. This principle requires that total distributive shares vary directly with moral merit; no person should have a greater share than anyone whose moral merit is greater. (If moral merit could be not merely ordered but measured on an interval or ratio scale, stronger principles could be formulated.) Or consider the principle that results by substituting "usefulness to society" for "moral merit" in the previous principle. Or instead of "distribute according to moral merit," or "distribute according to usefulness to society," we might consider "distribute according to the weighted sum of moral merit, usefulness to society, and need," with the weights of the different dimensions equal. Let us call a principle of distribution *patterned* if it specifies that a distribution is to vary along with some natural dimension, weighted sum of natural dimensions, or lexicographic ordering of natural dimensions. And let us say a distribution is patterned if it accords with some patterned principle. (I speak of natural dimensions, admittedly without a general criterion for them, because for any set of holdings some artificial dimensions can be gimmicked up to vary along with the distribution of the set.) The principle of distribution in accordance with moral merit is a patterned historical principle, which specifies a patterned distribution. "Distribute according to I.Q." is a patterned principle that looks to information not contained in distributional matrices. It is not historical, however, in that it does not look to any past actions creating differential entitlements to evaluate a distribution; it requires only distributional matrices whose columns are labeled by I.Q. scores. The distribution in a society, however, may be composed of such simple patterned distributions, without itself being simply patterned. Different sectors may operate different patterns, or some combination of patterns may operate in different proportions across a society. A distribution composed in this manner, from a small number of patterned distributions, we also shall term "patterned." And we extend the use of "pattern" to include the overall designs put forth by combinations of end-state principles.

Almost every suggested principle of distributive justice is patterned: to each according to his moral merit, or needs, or marginal product, or how hard he tries, or the weighted sum of the foregoing, and so on. The principle of entitlement we have sketched is *not* patterned.[4] There is no one natural dimension or weighted sum or combination of a small number of natural dimensions that yields the distributions generated in accordance with the principle of entitlement. The set of holdings that results when some persons receive their marginal products, others win at gambling, others receive a share of their mate's income, others receive gifts from foundations, others receive interest on loans, others receive gifts from admirers, others receive returns on investment, others make for themselves much of what they have, others find things, and so on, will not be patterned. Heavy strands of patterns will run through it; significant portions of the variance in holdings will be accounted for by pattern-variables. If most people most of the time choose to transfer some of their entitlements to others only in exchange for something from them, then a large part of what many people hold will vary with what they held that others wanted. More details are provided by the theory of marginal productivity. But gifts to relatives, charitable donations, bequests to children, and the like, are not best conceived, in the first instance, in this manner. Ignoring the strands of pattern, let us suppose for the moment that a distribution actually arrived at by the operation of the principle of entitlement is random with respect to any pattern. Though the resulting set of holdings will be unpatterned, it will not be incomprehensible, for it can be seen as arising from the operation of a small number of principles. These principles specify how an initial distribution may arise (the principle of acquisition of holdings)

and how distributions may be transformed into others (the principle of transfer of holdings). The process whereby the set of holdings is generated will be intelligible, though the set of holdings itself that results from this process will be unpatterned.

The writings of F. A. Hayek focus less than is usually done upon what patterning distributive justice requires. Hayek argues that we cannot know enough about each person's situation to distribute to each according to his moral merit (but would justice demand we do so if we did have this knowledge?); and he goes on to say, "our objection is against all attempts to impress upon society a deliberately chosen pattern of distribution, whether it be an order of equality or of inequality."[5] However, Hayek concludes that in a free society there will be distribution in accordance with value rather than moral merit; that is, in accordance with the perceived value of a person's actions and services to others. Despite his rejection of a patterned conception of distributive justice, Hayek himself suggests a pattern he thinks justifiable: distribution in accordance with the perceived benefits given to others, leaving room for the complaint that a free society does not realize exactly this pattern. Stating this patterned strand of a free capitalist society more precisely, we get "To each according to how much he benefits others who have the resources for benefiting those who benefit them." This will seem arbitrary unless some acceptable initial set of holdings is specified, or unless it is held that the operation of the system over time washes out any significant effects from the initial set of holdings. As an example of the latter, if almost anyone would have bought a car from Henry Ford, the supposition that it was an arbitrary matter who held the money then (and so bought) would not place Henry Ford's earnings under a cloud. In any event, *his* coming to hold it is not arbitrary. Distribution according to benefits to others *is* a major patterned strand in a free capitalist society, as Hayek correctly points out, but it is only a strand and does not constitute the whole pattern of a system of entitlements (namely, inheritance, gifts for arbitrary reasons, charity, and so on) or a standard that one should insist a society fit. Will people tolerate for long a system yielding distributions that they believe are unpatterned?[6] No doubt people will not long accept a distribution they believe is *unjust*. People want their society to be and to look just. But must the look of justice reside in a resulting pattern rather than in the underlying generating principles? We are in no position to conclude that the inhabitants of a society embodying an entitlement conception of justice in holdings will find it unacceptable. Still, it must be granted that were people's reasons for transferring some of their holdings to others always irrational or arbitrary, we would find this disturbing. (Suppose people always determined what holdings they would transfer, and to whom, by using a random device.) We feel more comfortable upholding the justice of an entitlement system if most of the transfers under it are done for reasons. This does not mean necessarily that all deserve what holdings they receive. It means only that there is a purpose or point to someone's transferring a holding to one person rather than to another; that usually we can see what the transferrer thinks he's gaining, what cause he thinks he's serving, what goals he thinks he's helping to achieve, and so forth. Since in a capitalist society people often transfer holdings to others in accordance with how much they perceive these others benefiting them, the fabric constituted by the individual transactions and transfers is largely reasonable and intelligible.[7] (Gifts to loved ones, bequests to children, charity to the needy also are nonarbitrary components of the fabric.) In stressing the large strand of distribution in accordance with benefit to others, Hayek shows the point of many transfers, and so shows that the system of transfer of entitlements is not just spinning its gears aimlessly. The system of entitlements is defensible when constituted by the individual aims of individual transactions. No overarching aim is needed, no distributional pattern is required.

To think that the task of a theory of distributive justice is to fill in the blank in "to each according to his _____" is to be predisposed to search for a pattern; and the separate treatment of "from each according to his _____" treats production and distribution as two separate and independent issues. On an entitlement view these are *not* two separate questions. Whoever makes something, having bought or contracted for all other held resources used in the process (transferring some of his holdings for these cooperating factors), is entitled to it. The situation is *not* one of something's getting made, and there being an open question of who is to get it. Things come into the world already attached to people having entitlements over them. From the point of view of the historical entitlement conception of justice in holdings, those who start afresh to complete "to each according to his_____" treat objects as if they appeared from nowhere, out of nothing. A complete theory of justice might cover this limit case as well; perhaps here is a use for the usual conceptions of distributive justice.[8]

So entrenched are maxims of the usual form that perhaps we should present the entitlement conception as a competitor. Ignoring acquisition and rectification, we might say:

> From each according to what he chooses to do, to each according to what he makes for himself (perhaps with the contracted aid of others) and what others choose to do for him and choose to give him of what they've been given previously (under this maxim) and haven't yet expended or transferred.

This, the discerning reader will have noticed, has its defects as a slogan. So as a summary and great simplification (and not as a maxim with any independent meaning) we have:

> *From each as they choose, to each as they are chosen.*

### HOW LIBERTY UPSETS PATTERNS

It is not clear how those holding alternative conceptions of distributive justice can reject the entitlement conception of justice in holdings. For suppose a distribution favored by one of these nonentitlement conceptions is realized. Let us suppose it is your favorite one and let us call this distribution $D_1$; perhaps everyone has an equal share, perhaps shares vary in accordance with some dimension you treasure. Now suppose that Wilt Chamberlain is greatly in demand by basketball teams, being a great gate attraction. (Also suppose contracts run only for a year, with players being free agents.) He signs the following sort of contract with a team: In each home game, twenty-five cents from the price of each ticket of admission goes to him. (We ignore the question of whether he is "gouging" the owners, letting them look out for themselves.) The season starts, and people cheerfully attend his team's games; they buy their tickets, each time dropping a separate twenty-five cents of their admission price into a special box with Chamberlain's name on it. They are excited about seeing him play; it is worth the total admission price to them. Let us suppose that in one season one million persons attend his home games, and Wilt Chamberlain winds up with $250,000, a much larger sum than the average income and larger even than anyone else has. Is he entitled to this income? Is this new distribution $D_2$, unjust? If so, why? There is *no* question about whether each of the people was entitled to the control over the resources they held in $D_1$; because that was the distribution (your favorite) that (for the purposes of argument) we assumed was acceptable. Each of these persons *chose* to give twenty-five cents of their money to Chamberlain. They could have spent it on going to the movies, or on candy bars, or on copies of *Dissent* magazine, or of *Monthly Review*. But they all, at least one million of them, converged on giving it to Wilt Chamberlain in exchange for watching him play basketball. If $D_1$ was a just distribution, and people voluntarily moved from it to $D_2$, transferring parts of their shares they were given under $D_1$ (what was it for if not to do something with?), isn't $D_2$ also just? If the people were entitled to dispose of the resources to which they were entitled (under $D_1$), didn't this include their being entitled to give it to, or exchange it with, Wilt Chamberlain? Can anyone else complain on grounds of justice? Each other person already has his legitimate share under $D_1$. Under $D_1$, there is nothing that anyone has that anyone else has a claim of justice against. After someone transfers something to Wilt Chamberlain, third parties *still* have their legitimate shares; *their* shares are not changed. By what process could such a transfer among two persons give rise to a legitimate

claim of distributive justice on a portion of what was transferred, by a third party who had no claim of justice on any holding of the others *before* the transfer?[9] To cut off objections irrelevant here, we might imagine the exchanges occurring in a socialist society, after hours. After playing whatever basketball he does in his daily work, or doing whatever other daily work he does, Wilt Chamberlain decides to put in *overtime* to earn additional money. (First his work quota is set; he works time over that.) Or imagine it is a skilled juggler people like to see, who puts on shows after hours.

Why might someone work overtime in a society in which it is assumed their needs are satisfied? Perhaps because they care about things other than needs. I like to write in books that I read, and to have easy access to books for browsing at odd hours. It would be very pleasant and convenient to have the resources of Widener Library in my back yard. No society, I assume, will provide such resources close to each person who would like them as part of his regular allotment (under $D_1$). Thus, persons either must do without some extra things that they want, or be allowed to do something extra to get some of these things. On what basis could the inequalities that would eventuate be forbidden? Notice also that small factories would spring up in a socialist society, unless forbidden. I melt down some of my personal possessions (under $D_1$) and build a machine out of the material. I offer you, and others, a philosophy lecture once a week in exchange for your cranking the handle on my machine, whose products I exchange for yet other things, and so on. (The raw materials used by the machine are given to me by others who possess them under $D_1$, in exchange for hearing lectures.) Each person might participate to gain things over and above their allotment under $D_1$. Some persons even might want to leave their job in socialist industry and work full time in this private sector. I shall say something more about these issues in the next chapter. Here I wish merely to note how private property even in means of production would occur in a socialist society that did not forbid people to use as they wished some of the resources they are given under the socialist distribution $D_1$.[10] The socialist society would have to forbid capitalist acts between consenting adults.

The general point illustrated by the Wilt Chamberlain example and the example of the entrepreneur in a socialist society is that no end-state principle or distributional patterned principle of justice can be continuously realized without continuous interference with people's lives. Any favored pattern would be transformed into one unfavored by the principle, by people choosing to act in various ways; for example, by people exchanging goods and services with other people, or giving things to other people, things the transferrers are entitled to under the favored distributional pattern. To maintain a pattern one must either continually interfere to stop people from transferring resources as they wish to, or continually (or periodically) interfere to take from some persons resources that others for some reason chose to transfer to them. (But if some time limit is to be set on how long people may keep resources others voluntarily transfer to them, why let them keep these resources for *any* period of time? Why not have immediate confiscation?) It might be objected that all persons voluntarily will choose to refrain from actions which would upset the pattern. This presupposes unrealistically (1) that all will most want to maintain the pattern (are those who don't, to be "reeducated" or forced to undergo "self-criticism"?), (2) that each can gather enough information about his own actions and the ongoing activities of others to discover which of his actions will upset the pattern, and (3) that diverse and far-flung persons can coordinate their actions to dovetail into the pattern. Compare the manner in which the market is neutral among persons' desires, as it reflects and transmits widely scattered information via prices, and coordinates persons' activities.

It puts things perhaps a bit too strongly to say that every patterned (or end-state) principle is liable to be thwarted by the voluntary actions of the individual parties transferring some of their shares they receive under the principle. For perhaps some *very* weak patterns are not so thwarted.[11] Any distributional pattern with any egalitarian component is overturnable by the voluntary actions of individual persons over time; as is every patterned condition with sufficient content so as actually to have been proposed as presenting the central core of distributive justice. Still, given the possibility that some weak conditions or patterns may not be unstable in this way, it would be better to formulate an explicit description of the kind of interesting and contentful patterns under discussion, and to prove a theorem about their instability. Since the weaker the patterning, the more likely it is that the entitlement system itself satisfies it, a plausible conjecture is that any patterning either is unstable or is satisfied by the entitlement system.

## LOCKE'S THEORY OF ACQUISITION

. . . [W]e must introduce an additional bit of complexity into the structure of the entitlement theory. This is best approached by considering Locke's attempt to specify a principle of justice in acquisition. Locke views property rights in an unowned object as originating through someone's mixing his labor with it. This gives rise to many questions. What are the boundaries of what labor is mixed with? If a private astronaut clears a place on Mars, has he mixed his labor with (so that he comes to own) the whole planet, the whole uninhabited universe, or just a particular plot? Which plot does an act bring under ownership? The minimal (possibly disconnected) area such that an act decreases entropy in that area, and not elsewhere? Can virgin land (for the purposes of ecological investigation by high-flying airplane) come under ownership by a Lockean process? Building a fence around a territory presumably would make one the owner of only the fence (and the land immediately underneath it).

Why does mixing one's labor with something make one the owner of it? Perhaps because one owns one's labor, and so one comes to own a previously unowned thing that becomes permeated with what one owns. Ownership seeps over into the rest. But why isn't mixing what I own with what I don't own a way of losing what I own rather than a way of gaining what I don't? If I own a can of tomato juice and spill it in the sea so that its molecules (made radioactive, so I can check this) mingle evenly throughout the sea, do I thereby come to own the sea, or have I foolishly dissipated my tomato juice? Perhaps the idea, instead, is that laboring on something improves it and makes it more valuable; and anyone is entitled to own a thing whose value he has created. (Reinforcing this, perhaps, is the view that laboring is unpleasant. If some people made things effortlessly, as the cartoon characters in *The Yellow Submarine* trail flowers in their wake, would they have lesser claim to their own products whose making didn't *cost* them anything?) Ignore the fact that laboring on something may make it less valuable (spraying pink enamel paint on a piece of driftwood that you have found). Why should one's entitlement extend to the whole object rather than just to the *added value* one's labor has produced? (Such reference to value might also serve to delimit the extent of ownership; for example, substitute "increases the value of" for "decreases entropy in" in the above entropy criterion.) No workable or coherent value-added property scheme has yet been devised, and any such scheme presumably would fall to objections (similar to those) that fell the theory of Henry George.

It will be implausible to view improving an object as giving full ownership to it, if the stock of unowned objects that might be improved is limited. For an object's coming under one person's ownership changes the situation of all others. Whereas previously they were at liberty (in Hohfeld's sense) to use the object, they now no longer are. This change in the situation of others (by removing their liberty to act on a previously unowned object) need not worsen their situation. If I appropriate a grain of sand from Coney Island, no one else may now do as they will with *that* grain of sand. But there are plenty of other grains of sand left for them to do the same with. Or if not grains of sand, then other things. Alternatively, the things I do with the grain of sand I appropriate might improve the position of others, counterbalancing their loss of the liberty to use that grain. The crucial point is whether appropriation of an unowned object worsens the situation of others.

Locke's proviso that there be "enough and as good left in common for others" (sect. 27) is meant to ensure that the situation of others is not worsened. . . .

Is the situation of persons who are unable to appropriate (there being no more accessible and useful unowned objects) worsened by a system allowing appropriation and permanent property? Here enter the various familiar social considerations favoring private property: it increases the social product by putting means of production in the hands of those who can use them most efficiently (profitably); experimentation is encouraged, because with separate persons controlling resources, there is no one person or small group whom someone with a new idea must convince to try it out; private property enables people to decide on the pattern and types of risks they wish to bear, leading to specialized types of risk bearing; private property protects future persons by leading some to hold back resources from current consumption for future markets; it provides alternate sources of employment for unpopular persons who don't have to convince any one person or small group to hire them, and so on. These considerations enter a Lockean theory to support the claim that appropriation of private property satisfies the intent behind the "enough and as good left over" proviso, *not* as a utilitarian justification of property. They enter to rebut the claim that because the proviso is violated no natural right to private property can arise by a Lockean process. The difficulty in working such an argument to show that the proviso is satisfied is in fixing the appropriate base line for comparison. Lockean appropriation makes people no worse off than they would be *how?*[12] This question of fixing the baseline needs more detailed investigation than we are able to give it here. It would be desirable to have an estimate of the general economic importance of original appropriation in order to see how much leeway there is for differing theories of appropriation and of the location of the baseline. Perhaps this importance can be measured by the percentage of all income that is based upon untransformed raw materials and given resources (rather than upon human actions), mainly rental income representing the unimproved value of land, and the price of raw material *in situ,* and by the percentage of current wealth which represents such income in the past.[13]

We should note that it is not only persons favoring *private* property who need a theory of how property rights legitimately originate. Those believing in collective property, for example those believing that a group of persons living in an area jointly own the territory, or its mineral resources, also must provide a theory of how such property rights arise; they must show why the persons living there have rights to determine what is done with the land and resources there that persons living elsewhere don't have (with regard to the same land and resources).

## THE PROVISO

. . . A theory which includes this proviso in its principle of justice in acquisition must also contain a more complex principle of justice in transfer. Some reflection of the proviso about appropriation constrains later actions. If my appropriating all of a certain substance violates the Lockean proviso, then so does my appropriating some and purchasing all the rest from others who obtained it without otherwise violating the Lockean proviso. If the proviso excludes someone's appropriating all the drinkable water in the world, it also excludes his purchasing it all. (More weakly, and messily, it may exclude his charging certain prices for some of his supply.) This proviso (almost?) never will come into effect; the more someone acquires of a scarce substance which others want, the higher the price of the rest will go, and the more difficult it will become for him to acquire it all. But still, we can imagine, at least, that something like this occurs: someone makes simultaneous secret bids to the separate owners of a substance, each of whom sells assuming he can easily purchase more from the other owners; or some natural catastrophe destroys all of the supply of something except that in one person's possession. The total supply could not be permissibly appropriated by one person at the beginning. His later acquisition of it all does not show that the original appropriation violated the proviso. . . . Rather, it is the combination of the original appropriation *plus* all the later transfers and actions that violates the Lockean proviso.

Each owner's title to his holding includes the historical shadow of the Lockean proviso on appropria-tion. This excludes his transferring it into an agglomeration that does violate the Lockean proviso and excludes his using it in a way, in coordination with others or independently of them, so as to violate the proviso by making the situation of others worse than their baseline situation. Once it is known that someone's ownership runs afoul of the Lockean proviso, there are stringent limits on what he may do with (what it is difficult any longer unreservedly to call) "his property." Thus a person may not appropriate the only water hole in a desert and charge what he will. Nor may he charge what he will if he possesses one, and unfortunately it happens that all the water holes in the desert dry up, except for his. This unfortunate circumstance, admittedly no fault of his, brings into operation the Lockean proviso and limits his property rights.[14] Similarly, an owner's property right in the only island in an area does not allow him to order a castaway from a shipwreck off his island as a trespasser, for this would violate the Lockean proviso. . . .

The fact that someone owns the total supply of something necessary for others to stay alive does *not* entail that his (or anyone's) appropriation of anything left some people (immediately or later) in a situation worse than the baseline one. A medical researcher who synthesizes a new substance that effectively treats a certain disease and who refuses to sell except on his terms does not worsen the situation of others by depriving them of whatever he has appropriated. The others easily can possess the same materials he appropriated; the researcher's appropriation or purchase of chemicals didn't make those chemicals scare in a way so as to violate the Lockean proviso. Nor would someone else's purchasing the total supply of the synthesized substance from the medical researcher. The fact that the medical researcher uses easily available chemicals to synthesize the drug no more violates the Lockean proviso than does the fact that the only surgeon able to perform a particular operation eats easily obtainable food in order to stay alive and to have the energy to work. This shows that the Lockean proviso is not an "end-state principle"; it focuses on a particular way that appropriative actions affect others, and not on the structure of the situation that results.

Intermediate between someone who takes all of the public supply and someone who makes the total supply out of easily obtainable substances is someone who appropriates the total supply of something in a way that does not deprive the others of it. For example, someone finds a new substance in an out-of-the-way place. He discovers that it effectively treats a certain disease and appropriates the total supply. He does not worsen the situation of others; if he did not stumble upon the substance no one else would have, and the others would remain without it. However, as time passes, the likelihood increases that others would have come across the substance; upon this fact might be based a limit to his property right in the substance so that others are not below their baseline position; for example, its bequest might be limited. The theme of someone worsening another's situation by depriving him of something he otherwise would possess may also illuminate the example of patents. An inventor's patent does not deprive others of an object which would not exist if not for the inventor. Yet patents would have this effect on others who independently invent the object. Therefore, these independent inventors, upon whom the burden of proving independent discovery may rest, should not be excluded from utilizing their own invention as they wish (including selling it to others). Furthermore, a known inventor drastically lessens the chances of actual independent invention. For persons who know of an invention usually will not try to reinvent it, and the notion of independent discovery here would be murky at best. Yet we may assume that in the absence of the original invention, sometime later someone else would have come up with it. This suggests placing a time limit on patents, as a rough rule of thumb to approximate how long it would have taken, in the absence of knowledge of the invention, for independent discovery.

I believe that the free operation of a market system will not actually run afoul of the Lockean proviso. . . . If this is correct, the proviso will not play a very important role in the activities of protective agencies and will not provide a significant opportu-

nity for future state action. Indeed, were it not for the effects of previous *illegitimate* state action, people would not think the possibility of the proviso's being violated as of more interest than any other logical possibility. (Here I make an empirical historical claim; as does someone who disagrees with this.) This completes our indication of the complication in the entitlement theory introduced by the Lockean proviso.

## Notes

1. Applications of the principle of justice in acquisition may also occur as part of the move from one distribution to another. You may find an unheld thing now and appropriate it. Acquisitions also are to be understood as included when, to simplify, I speak only of transitions by transfers.

2. See, however, the useful book by Boris Bittker, *The Case for Black Reparations* (New York: Random House, 1973).

3. If the principle of rectification of violations of the first two principles yields more than one description of holdings, then some choice must be made as to which of these is to be realized. Perhaps the sort of considerations about distributive justice and equality that I argue against play a legitimate role in *this* subsidiary choice. Similarly, there may be room for such considerations in deciding which otherwise arbitrary features a statute will embody, when such features are unavoidable because other considerations do not specify a precise line; yet a line must be drawn.

4. One might try to squeeze a patterned conception of distributive justice into the framework of the entitlement conception, by formulating a gimmicky obligatory "principle of transfer" that would lead to the pattern. For example, the principle that if one has more than the mean income one must transfer everything one holds above the mean to persons below the mean so as to bring them up to (but not over) the mean. We can formulate a criterion for a "principle of transfer" to rule out such obligatory transfers, or we can say that no correct principle of transfer, no principle of transfer in a free society will be like this. The former is probably the better course, though the latter also is true.

Alternatively, one might think to make the entitlement conception instantiate a pattern, by using matrix entries that express the relative strength of a person's entitlements as measured by some real-valued function. But even if the limitation to natural dimensions failed to exclude this function, the resulting edifice would *not* capture our system of entitlements to *particular* things.

5. F. A. Hayek, *The Constitution of Liberty* (Chicago: University of Chicago Press, 1960), p. 87.

6. This question does not imply that they will tolerate any and every patterned distribution. In discussing Hayek's views, Irving Kristol has recently speculated that people will not long tolerate a system that yields distributions patterned in accordance with value rather than merit. (" 'When Virtue Loses All Her Loveliness'—Some Reflections on Capitalism and 'The Free Society,' " *The Public Interest,* Fall 1970, pp. 3–15.) Kristol, following some remarks of Hayek's, equates the merit system with justice. Since some case can be made for the external standard of distribution in accordance with benefit to others, we ask about a weaker (and therefore more plausible) hypothesis.

7. We certainly benefit because great economic incentives operate to get others to spend much time and energy to figure out how to serve us by providing things we will want to pay for. It is not mere paradox mongering to wonder whether capitalism should be criticized for most rewarding and hence encouraging, not individualists like Thoreau who go about their own lives, but people who are occupied with serving others and winning them as customers. But to defend capitalism one need not think businessmen are the finest human types. (I do not mean to join here the general maligning of businessmen, either.) Those who think the finest should acquire the most can try to convince their fellows to transfer resources in accordance with *that* principle.

8. Varying situations continuously from that limit situation to our own would force us to make explicit the underlying rationale of entitlements and to consider whether entitlement considerations lexicographically precede the considerations of the usual theories of distributive justice, so that the *slightest* strand of entitlement outweighs the considerations of the usual theories of distributive justice.

9. Might not a transfer have instrumental effects on a third party, changing his feasible options? (But what if the two parties to the transfer independently had used their holdings in this fashion?) I discuss this question below, but note here that this question concedes the point for distributions of ultimate intrinsic noninstrumental goods (pure utility experiences, so to speak) that are transferrable. It also might be objected that the transfer might make a third party more envious because it worsens his position relative to

someone else. I find it incomprehensible how this can be thought to involve a claim of justice. On envy, see Chapter 8.

Here and elsewhere in this chapter, a theory which incorporates elements of pure procedural justice might find what I say acceptable, *if* kept in its proper place; that is, if background institutions exist to ensure the satisfaction of certain conditions on distributive shares. But if these institutions are not themselves the sum or invisible-hand result of people's voluntary (nonaggressive) actions, the constraints they impose require justification. At no point does *our* argument assume any background institutions more extensive than those of the minimal night-watchman state, a state limited to protecting persons against murder, assault, theft, fraud, and so forth.

10. See the selection from John Henry MacKay's novel. *The Anarchists,* reprinted in Leonard Krimmerman and Lewis Perry, eds., *Patterns of Anarchy* (New York: Doubleday Anchor Books, 1966), in which an individualist anarchist presses upon a communist anarchist the following question: "Would you, in the system of society which you call 'free Communism' prevent individuals from exchanging their labor among themselves by means of their own medium of exchange? And further: Would you prevent them from occupying land for the purpose of personal use?" The novel continues: "[the] question was not to be escaped. If he answered 'Yes!' he admitted that society had the right of control over the individual and threw overboard the autonomy of the individual which he had always zealously defended; if on the other hand, he answered 'No!' he admitted the right of private property which he had just denied so emphatically. . . . Then he answered 'In Anarchy any number of men must have the right of forming a voluntary association, and so realizing their ideas in practice. Nor can I understand how any one could justly be driven from the land and house which he uses and occupies . . . every serious man must declare himself: for Socialism, and thereby for force and against liberty, or for Anarchism, and thereby for liberty and against force.' " In contrast, we find Noam Chomsky writing, "Any consistent anarchist must oppose private ownership of the means of production," "the consistent anarchist then . . . will be a socialist . . . of a particular sort." Introduction to Daniel Guerin, *Anarchism: From Theory to Practice* (New York: Monthly Review Press, 1970), pages XIII, XV.

11. Is the patterned principle stable that requires merely that a distribution be Pareto-optimal? One person might give another a gift or bequest that the second could exchange with a third to their mutual benefit. Before

the second makes this exchange, there is not Pareto-optimality. Is a stable pattern presented by a principle choosing that among the Pareto-optimal positions that satisfies some further condition C? It may seem that there cannot be a counterexample, for won't any voluntary exchange made away from a situation show that the first situation wasn't Pareto-optimal? (Ignore the implausibility of this last claim for the case of bequests.) But principles are to be satisfied over time, during which new possibilities arise. A distribution that at one time satisfies the criterion of Pareto-optimality might not do so when some new possibilities arise (Wilt Chamberlain grows up and starts playing basketball); and though people's activities will tend to move then to a new Pareto-optimal position, *this* new one need not satisfy the contentful condition C. Continual interference will be needed to insure the continual satisfaction of C. (The theoretical possibility of a pattern's being maintained by some invisible-hand process that brings it back to an equilibrium that fits the pattern when deviations occur should be investigated.)

12. Compare this with Robert Paul Wolff's "A Refutation of Rawls' Theorem on Justice," *Journal of Philosophy,* March 31, 1966, sect. 2. Wolff's criticism does not apply to Rawls' conception under which the baseline is fixed by the difference principle.

13. I have not seen a precise estimate. David Friedman. *The Machinery of Freedom* (N.Y.: Harper & Row, 1973), pp. XIV, XV, discusses this issue and suggests 5 percent of U.S. national income as an upper limit for the first two factors mentioned. However he does not attempt to estimate the percentage of current wealth which is based upon such income in the past. (The vague notion of "based upon" merely indicates a topic needing investigation.)

14. I discuss overriding and its moral traces in "Moral Complications and Moral Structures," *Natural Law Forum,* 1968, pp. 1–50.

# THOMAS NAGEL

## INTRODUCTION

## JOHN DEIGH

Thomas Nagel (1937–) is among the most distinguished living American philosophers. He is currently Professor of Philosophy and Law at New York University. Previously, he had been Professor of Philosophy at Princeton University and before that he was at the University of California at Berkeley. He grew up in New York City, took an undergraduate degree at Cornell University, and then studied at Oxford University, where he received his B.Phil. in 1960, and at Harvard University, where he received his Ph.D. in 1963. At Harvard, he wrote his doctoral thesis under the supervision of John Rawls, with whom he had also studied at Cornell. His first book, *The Possibility of Altruism,* developed out of this thesis. It was published in 1970 and has since had a substantial impact on contemporary work in Anglo-American moral philosophy. Nagel's other books are *The View from Nowhere (1986), Equality and Partiality (1991), What Does It All Mean? (1987),* and *The Last Word (1997).* He has also published two collections of his essays, *Mortal Questions (1979)* and *Other Minds (1995).* Many of the essays in these collections first appeared as articles in academic journals, at which time they initiated new and fertile lines of thought on the philosophical questions with which they dealt. These articles include "Death," "What Is It Like to Be a Bat?," "The Absurd," "Sexual Perversion," "War and Massacre," "Moral Luck," and "Libertarianism Without Foundations." A good measure of their force and importance is the large number of philosophers who, writing after their appearance and on the same questions, fashioned their views in response to them.

Nagel, in addition to his pathbreaking contributions in moral philosophy, has made significant contributions in metaphysics, epistemology, and political philosophy. His work in all of these areas has been guided by the fundamental belief that the main problems of philosophy are traceable to a tension, which exists within each human being, between a view of things from the standpoint of that person's current local situation, the personal standpoint, and a view of things from the standpoint of complete objectivity with respect to the person's situation and everyone else's, the impersonal standpoint. The idea of a tension within the human mind that is created by the possibility of viewing the world from either a personal or an impersonal standpoint is not original with Nagel. The contemporary English philosopher P. F. Strawson, for one, has also based accounts of philosophical problems on this idea, notably, the problem of free will, and arguably the idea was already at work in Immanuel Kant's use of a distinction between empirical and practical standpoints, in chapter 3 of *The Groundwork of the Metaphysics of Morals,* to explain the possibility of a categorical imperative. Nagel, though, more than any of his contemporaries or predecessors, has expounded and applied the idea across a broad range of philosophical problems. His most systematic treatment of it is found in *The View from Nowhere.*

In moral philosophy, tension between the personal and impersonal standpoints is most apparent in the opposition between egoism and utilitarianism. Egoism is a system of ethics based on the ideal of wisdom in the pursuit of one's own happiness. Utilitarianism is a system of ethics based on the ideal of impartial goodwill toward all. The two systems appeal to different motives within human psychology, self-interest and general benevolence, and the disharmony in these motives reflects the tension between the two standpoints. If there were a way to reconcile egoism and utilitarianism, if one could show, for instance, that they gave the same answer to every question about what the right thing is to do given one's circumstances, then the opposition between them would dissolve. Accordingly, disharmony in the motives to which they appeal would disappear, and this aspect of the tension between the two standpoints would be resolved. In *The Possibility of Altruism,* Nagel advanced a very ambitious argument to show that the motives to which egoism appeals are, if rational, subsumable under those to which utilitarianism appeals. Any personal desire one has that conflicts with desires that express one's impartial benevolence toward all, Nagel argued, must reflect a misunderstanding of oneself and others such that seeking to satisfy it would be unreasonable and therefore inconsistent with the wise pursuit of happiness. Correct understanding of oneself and others, Nagel maintained, removes those personal desires that create disharmony in the motives to which the two systems appeal and thus makes possible their reconciliation. The argument, then, offers an individualist resolution of the tension, for coming to a correct understanding of oneself and others is ultimately a process of individual thought and reflection.

The argument Nagel made in *The Possibility of Altruism* depends on the assumption that every reasonable desire is a desire for something that does not cease to appear desirable when viewed from the impersonal standpoint. This assumption, Nagel subsequently realized, is too strong, and consequently the argument cannot be sustained. Some personal desires and private interests may be reasonable regardless of how their objects appear from the impersonal standpoint and therefore even if they resist subsumption under the motives of impartial benevolence that arise from that standpoint. Hence, a different argument is needed to resolve the tension between the two standpoints that is due to the disharmony between personal desires and benevolent inclinations toward all. In later work, Nagel has tried to find such an argument. In *The View from Nowhere* he broaches the possibility of finding it through a study of political ideals. Having concluded that an individualist resolution could not be sustained, he raises the possibility of a political resolution. He merely touches on this possibility in *The View from Nowhere.* But in his next book, *Equality and Partiality,* he makes the search for such a resolution a full-scale project.

The idea behind this search is that since only saints and obsessives can pursue the good of all to the exclusion of their personal desires and private interests, a resolution of the tension must allow an individual's personal standpoint to be somewhat independent of his or her impersonal standpoint, and such independence, consistent with realizing the latter standpoint's ideal of impartial benevolence, may be possible through collective action. Thus, if one belongs to a society whose governing institutions realize an ideal of social justice, then support for and participation in these institutions might enable one to satisfy the interest in impartial benevolence that springs from the impersonal standpoint while leaving one with sufficient space for satisfying one's personal desires and private interests. That is, if the political institutions of one's society were governed by principles of justice that issued from the impersonal standpoint and required distributions of social wealth for the benefit of all, then one might be able both to satisfy the standpoint's demands for impartiality through support of these institutions and to have a private life. Indeed, the more these institutions advanced the ideal of impartial benevolence, the more supererogatory would individual efforts at achieving it be, and hence the greater the possibility of freedom to pursue private interests. Nagel's idea, in other words, is to make the morality of individual conduct less demanding by having the morality of political institutions do more of the work of resolving the tension between the two standpoints. The central problem of political philosophy, as Nagel conceives it, thus derives from one of the main problems of moral philosophy.

The key to the political resolution that Nagel seeks is to understand the governing institutions of a society as at once expressing impartial benevolence toward all and respecting the individuality of each. Accordingly, these institutions must realize an ideal of social justice that strikes the proper balance between the interest in everyone's having an equal share of the goods on which living a happy life depends and the interest in everyone's having the freedom necessary to live as they choose. The ideal, that is, must lie somewhere between the extremes of utopian socialism and laissez-faire libertarianism, for it can be neither that of maintaining equality in all areas of human life nor that of minimizing the society's regulation of individual conduct. These extremes, in Nagel's view, represent political theorizing from only one of the two standpoints and are, for this reason, untenable. Thus, the former ideal represents the complete subordination of the personal to the impersonal standpoint, and it is simply unrealistic to suppose that people in general, however enthusiastic they may initially be about institutions that eliminate all the inequalities of life, could sustain such subordination beyond the honeymoon that typically follows establishment of a new regime. Similarly, the latter ideal represents complete exclusion of the impersonal standpoint from political theory, and it is equally unrealistic to suppose that the governing institutions of a society could maintain legitimacy without being seen to be impartial in the way they distributed material goods and social positions to individuals. Hence, the political resolution Nagel seeks must somehow split the difference between these extremes. It must find a place in political theory for the impersonal standpoint without letting that standpoint dominate the whole field.

Nagel's search for this resolution focuses on the liberal tradition in modern Western society. Developments in this tradition, he thinks, exhibit increasing concern with the problem of harmonizing the two standpoints, as the tradition's politics and theorizing have paid more and more attention to meeting the requirements of impartial benevolence toward all. The emergence of welfare state liberalism as the prevailing form of liberalism in the twentieth century exemplifies these developments. In political theory they have inspired programs for an egalitarian form of liberalism, of which Rawls's theory is the paradigm. Its ideal of social justice combines an egalitarian distribution of social wealth with protection of individual liberty in the areas of speech, worship, association, and private conduct. In this way it splits the difference between complete subordination of the personal to the impersonal standpoint and complete exclusion of the impersonal standpoint from political theory. On the one hand, institutions designed to promote the egalitarian distribution of social wealth that Rawls's theory favors express an attitude of impartial benevolence that could originate in the impersonal standpoint. On the other, institutions designed to secure the protections of individual liberty that the theory endorses create space for the pursuit of personal desires and private interests that respects the extent to which the personal standpoint is independent of the impersonal. The modern welfare state, then, would seem to consist of the kinds of institution through the support of which a person can satisfy the felt demands of the impersonal standpoint and still enjoy a private life.

Nonetheless, Nagel doubts whether this or any form of liberalism can succeed in resolving the tension between the two standpoints. His doubts arise from his belief that the attitude of impartiality that taking the impersonal standpoint entails is highly egalitarian. Accordingly, as he interprets this attitude, inequalities in wealth that are due to factors about people for which they bear no responsibility cry out for correction when viewed from the impersonal standpoint. These factors include a person's ethnicity, race, sex, and socioeconomic class. They also include a person's natural talents and other innate assets. These latter attributes, above all, define for that person his or her individuality, and as a result any program of correcting inequalities in wealth that are due to them will depend on the willingness of the more talented to suppress their individuality in the interest of seeing the less talented treated as their equals. Specifically, it will depend on the willingness of the more talented to forgo the material rewards that the exercise of their individuality would attract in a free market in the interest of living as equals with those of lesser talent, and this amounts to a willingness to let one's individuality go unrecognized in the interest of egalitarian solidarity. Yet such solidarity is not an integral ideal of the liberal tradition, and one cannot expect the governing institutions of a liberal society to create an environment in which interest in achieving such solidarity is cultured. Indeed, because the protections of individual liberty that are the hallmark of these institutions reflect a strong commitment to the value of individuality, one should expect the opposite. Welfare state liberalism, it seems, as a candidate for resolving the tension between the two standpoints is thus caught in a bind.

The result is that Nagel's search for a political resolution of this tension is inconclusive. By his own admission, it comes up short. He can describe political and economic institutions whose establishment would both satisfy the egalitarian requirements of impartial benevolence he attributes to the impersonal standpoint and respect the extent to which the personal standpoint is independent of the impersonal, but he is at a loss as to how people could acquire the motivations and commitments on which support for these institutions would depend. He sees how the institutions could develop out of those characteristic of welfare state liberalism. But to support them people living in contemporary liberal societies would have to undergo a radical change of motivation, and Nagel sees nothing on the horizon that could conceivably catalyze such a change. Given, then, his understanding of the central problem of political philosophy, the position he holds might best be described as pessimistic liberalism.

Nagel's work on egalitarianism is part of a recent literature on equality in the distribution of wealth and social position that Rawls's *A Theory of Justice* inspired. Other recent books on this topic include Ronald Dworkin's *Sovereign Virtue* (Cambridge, Mass.: Harvard University Press, 2000), Michael Walzer's *Spheres of Justice* (New York: Basic Books, 1983), Amartya Sen's, *Inequality Reexamined* (New York: Russell Sage, 1992), and G. A. Cohen's *If You're an Egalitarian, How Come You're So Rich?* (Cambridge, Mass.: Harvard University Press, 2000). A good general discussion of the topic that predates Rawls's book is Bernard Williams's essay, "The Idea of Equality," which is reprinted in his collection *Problems of the Self* (Cambridge: Cambridge University Press, 1973). An important and influential criticism of the egalitarian position on social justice is Robert Nozick's *Anarchy, State, and Utopia* (New York: Basic Books, 1974), chapters 7 and 8. Two good critical discussions of Nagel's approach to moral and political philosophy are Steven Darwall's *Impartial Reason* (Ithaca, N.Y.: Cornell University Press, 1983), chapters 9 and 10, and Christine Korsgaard's *Creating the Kingdom of Ends* (Cambridge: Cambridge University Press, 1996), chapter 10.

# Equality and Partiality

## 1

### *Introduction*

This essay deals with what I believe to be the central problem of political theory. Rather than proposing a solution to it, I shall try to explain what it is, and why a solution is so difficult to achieve. This result need not be thought of pessimistically, since the recognition of a serious obstacle is always a necessary condition of progress, and I believe there is hope that in the future, political and social institutions may develop which continue our unsteady progress toward moral equality, without ignoring the stubborn realities of human nature.

My belief is not just that all social and political arrangements so far devised are unsatisfactory. That might be due to the failure of all actual systems to realize an ideal that we should all recognize as correct. But there is a deeper problem—not merely practical, but theoretical: We do not yet possess an acceptable political ideal, for reasons which belong to moral and political philosophy. The unsolved problem is the familiar one of reconciling the standpoint of the collectivity with the standpoint of the individual; but I want to approach it not primarily as a question about the relation between the individual and society, but in essence and origin as a question about each individual's relation to himself. This reflects a conviction that ethics, and the ethical basis of political theory, have to be understood as arising from a division in each individual between two standpoints, the personal and the impersonal. The latter represents the claims of the collectivity and gives them their force for each individual. If it did not exist, there would be no morality, only the clash, compromise, and occasional convergence of individual perspectives. It is because a human being does not occupy only his own point of view that each of us is susceptible to the claims of others through private and public morality.

Any social arrangement governing the relations among individuals, or between the individual and the collective, depends on a corresponding balance of forces within the self—its image in microcosm. That image is the relation, for each individual, between the personal and impersonal standpoints, on which the social arrangement depends and which it requires of us. If an arrangement is to claim the support of those living under it—if it is to claim legitimacy, in other words—then it must rely on or call into existence some form of reasonable integration of the elements of their naturally divided selves. The division is rough, and spans a great deal of subordinate complexity, but I believe it is indispensable in thinking about the subject.

The hardest problems of political theory are conflicts within the individual, and no external solution will be adequate which does not deal with them at their source. The impersonal standpoint in each of us produces, I shall claim, a powerful demand for universal impartiality and equality, while the personal standpoint gives rise to individualistic motives and requirements which present obstacles to the pursuit and realization of such ideals. The recognition that this is true of everyone then presents the impersonal standpoint with further questions about what is required to treat such persons with equal regard, and this in turn presents the individual with further conflict.

The same problems arise with respect to the morality of personal conduct, but I shall argue that their treatment must be extended to political theory, where the relations of mutual support or conflict between political institutions and individual motiva-

tion are all-important. It emerges that a harmonious combination of an acceptable political ideal and acceptable standards of personal morality is very hard to come by. Another way of putting the problem, therefore, is this: When we try to discover reasonable moral standards for the conduct of individuals and then try to integrate them with fair standards for the assessment of social and political institutions, there seems no satisfactory way of fitting the two together. They respond to opposing pressures which cause them to break apart.

To a considerable extent, political institutions and their theoretical justifications try to externalize the demands of the impersonal standpoint. But they have to be staffed and supported and brought to life by individuals for whom the impersonal standpoint coexists with the personal, and this has to be reflected in their design. My claim is that the problem of designing institutions that do justice to the equal importance of all persons, without making unacceptable demands on individuals, has not been solved—and that this is so partly because for our world the problem of the right relation between the personal and impersonal standpoints within each individual has not been solved.

Most people feel this on reflection. We live in a world of spiritually sickening economic and social inequality, a world whose progress toward the acknowledgment of common standards of toleration, individual liberty and human development has been depressingly slow and unsteady. There are sometimes dramatic improvements, and recent events in Eastern Europe must give pause to all those, like myself, who in response to the dominant events of this century have cultivated a defensive pessimism about the prospects of humanity. But we really do not know how to live together. The professed willingness of civilized persons to slaughter each other by the millions in a nuclear war now appears to be subsiding, as the conflicts of political conviction which fueled it lose their sharpness. But even in the developed world, and certainly in the world taken as a whole, the problems which generated the great political and moral rift between democratic capitalism and authoritarian communism have not been solved by the utter competitive failure of the latter.

Communism may have been defeated in Europe, and we may live to celebrate its fall in Asia as well, but that does not mean that democratic capitalism is the last word in human social arrangements. At this historical moment it is worth remembering that communism owes its existence in part to an ideal of equality which remains appealing however great the crimes committed and the economic disasters produced in its name. Democratic societies have not found a way to contend with that ideal: it is a problem for the old democracies of the West, and it will be a very serious problem for the emerging democracies which succeed the collapse of communism in Eastern Europe, and perhaps elsewhere. Political philosophy is not going to transform this situation, but it has its role, for some of the apparently practical problems of political life have theoretical and moral sources. Moral convictions drive political choices, and the absence of moral agreement, if severe, can be far more divisive than a mere conflict of interests. Anyone who is inclined to doubt the connection of political theory with reality cannot hold out against the events now unfolding: moral and theoretical battles are being fought across the globe, sometimes with real tanks.

One should think of political theory as an enterprise of discovery—the discovery of human possibilities whose coming to actuality is encouraged and assisted by the discovery itself. That is certainly how most of the traditional figures of political theory have seen it. They were in the business of imagining the moral future, with the hope of contributing to its realization. But this inevitably carries the risk of utopianism, and that problem is an important aspect of our subject.

A theory is utopian in the pejorative sense if it describes a form of collective life that humans, or most humans, could not lead and could not come to be able to lead through any feasible process of social and mental development. It may have value as a possibility for a few people, or as an admirable but unattainable ideal for others. But it cannot be offered as a general solution to the main question of political theory: How should we live together in society?

Worse still, when what is described is not in fact motivationally possible, the illusion of its possibility may motivate people nevertheless to try to institute it, with results that are quite different. Societies are constantly trying to beat people into shape because they stubbornly fail to conform to some preconceived pattern of human possibility. Political theory is in this sense an empirical discipline whose hypotheses give hostages to the future, and whose experiments can be very costly.[1]

But while the avoidance of utopianism is important, it is no more important than the avoidance of hard-nosed realism, its diametrical opposite. To be sure, a theory that offers new possibilities must be aware of the danger that they may be purely imaginary. The real nature of humans and human motivation always has to be an essential part of the subject: Pessimism is always in order, and we have been given ample reason to fear human nature. But we shouldn't be too tied down by limits derived from the baseness of actual motives or by excessive pessimism about the possibility of human improvement. It is important to try to imagine the next step, even before we have come close to implementing the best conceptions already available.

In this enterprise the use of moral intuition is inevitable, and should not be regretted. To trust our intuitions, particularly those that tell us something is wrong even though we don't know exactly what would be right, we need only believe that our moral understanding extends farther than our capacity to spell out the principles which underlie it. Intuition can be corrupted by custom, self-interest, or commitment to a theory, but it need not be, and often a person's intuitions will provide him with evidence that his own moral theory is missing something, or that the arrangements he has been brought up to find natural are really unjust. Intuitive dissatisfaction is an essential resource in political theory. It can tell us that something is wrong, without necessarily telling us how to fix it. It is a reasonable response to even the most ideal versions of current political practice, and I believe it is the correct response also at the level of theory: It tells us, not surprisingly, that we have not yet arrived at the truth. In that way it can help us to cultivate a healthy dissatisfaction with the familiar, without falling into utopianism of the uncritical sort.

I believe that the clash of personal and impersonal standpoints is one of the most pressing problems revealed in this way. If we cannot, through moral theory and institutional design, reconcile an impartial concern for everyone with a view of how each individual can reasonably be expected to live, then we cannot hope to defend the general acceptability of any political order. These problems of integration come with our humanity, and we cannot expect them ever to disappear. But the attempt to deal with them has to be part of any political theory that can claim to be realistic.

What makes this task so difficult is that our ultimate aim in political theory should be to approach as nearly as possible to unanimity, at some level, in support of the basic framework of those political institutions which are maintained by force and into which we are born. . . .

The pure ideal of political legitimacy is that the use of state power should be capable of being *authorized* by each citizen—not in direct detail but through acceptance of the principles, institutions, and procedures which determine how that power will be used. This requires the possibility of unanimous agreement at some sufficiently high level, for if there are citizens who can legitimately object to the way state power is used against them or in their name, the state is not legitimate. To accept such unanimity as an ideal while respecting the complex realities of human motivation and practical reason is inevitably frustrating, but in my conception that is what presents political theory with its task. We must try both to give the condition a morally sensible interpretation and to see how far actual institutions might go toward meeting it.

It is a task which cannot be postponed till the millenium, when conflicts have disappeared and all share a common goal. The secular form of that

seductive and dangerous vision, which condemns the aim of even idealized agreement under existing circumstances, and insists on struggle and the pursuit of victory so long as there are classes whose interests conflict, has been Marx's most conspicuous moral legacy to the world. Harmony is reserved for a future which will be achieved only by eschewing harmony for political war between irreconcilable interests in the present.

This view should be rejected, and the pursuit of human equality decisively separated from it. The aim of idealized agreement has a role at all stages in the pursuit of an improved human condition, even if full justice is far away. Force will always be necessary if that aim is not widely enough shared, but it is a disaster to exclude the aim from political morality until history has proceeded by other means to that mythical terminus at which it will be effortlessly achieved.

# 10

## *Equality and Motivation*

I want to consider what transformations of motive might make possible the realization of a more egalitarian social ideal. Given the inextinguishable appeal of egalitarianism and its enormous failures, together with the political and economic upheavals which they generate, this is an unavoidable question. Such an ideal could be sustained only if it were pervasively internalized. While institutions must play an important role in creating social and economic equality, they cannot sustain it unless they come to express what enough people feel.

Transformations in the tolerance of inequality can occur. In the United States, during my lifetime, and in other Western countries, there has been such a change in attitudes toward overt racial and sexual discrimination. (The change with respect to religious discrimination began a bit earlier.) This change is not limited to greater outspokenness by the victims, but has come to include a broad sense among the potential beneficiaries of discrimination that such benefits are illegitimate. I hope I am not too optimistic in believing that most white males in North America or Western Europe today would feel uncomfortable about being awarded a job or admission to a professional school under a policy that excluded blacks or women, or held them to higher qualifications. Most potential beneficiaries of such discrimination do not want it reinstated and would not, if it occurred, simply count themselves fortunate to be on the winning side of the racial or sexual divide. They would feel that benefits gained in this way were tainted, even dishonorable. Formerly that was not generally true; the legal abolition of overt discrimination—practiced, enforced, or protected by the state—has had a deep mental effect, which gives the legal result stability.

It was not easy to overthrow racial and sexual discrimination, and that is in a way encouraging, for it shows that the strength of resistance to a change does not necessarily forecast the instability of the result. However, societies in which these reforms took place had for some time already had a bad conscience, particularly about racism, and there was a lot of hypocritical rhetoric in the air.

This is not true of social attitudes to economic inequality, except with regard to extreme poverty. Those who win out in the competitive economy or as a result of the inheritance of wealth and social position tend simply to count themselves lucky, or deserving—certainly not, in most cases, as the recipients of ill-gotten gains, or gains whose origins make them disreputable. More people in our culture may feel this queasiness about inherited benefits than about earned benefits resulting from their productivity, but most, I suspect, feel it strongly about neither. The way the chips fall in a competitive economy where equality of opportunity is not blocked by traditional forms of discrimination may seem illegitimate to the losers, but to the winners and potential winners, it generally does not. Those with highly marketable skills rarely feel that their earnings are tainted, or that the difference between their standard of living and that of the average unskilled laborer is dishonorable.

In part this may reflect a belief that there is exter-

nal justification for those inequalities, but it also indicates that for the most part prevailing opinion finds nothing prima facie wrong with them. Their beneficiaries feel on the whole entitled to count themselves fortunate in the natural abilities and social and educational opportunities which, suitably employed, have resulted in competitive advantage, and consequent rewards. Others are less lucky, but that's life. By contrast, the corresponding attitude toward the advantages of membership in a dominant race or sex is no longer respectable.

The creation of stable egalitarian institutions in a developed economy would require a change in these attitudes. Perhaps changed institutions can bring about the change in attitudes or perhaps they cannot; at any rate they will not survive unless they do. Not only the victims but the beneficiaries of socioeconomic inequality would have to come to regard such benefits with suspicion. But what change of this sort is possible? The question cannot really be treated separately from a consideration of the institutions in which equality might be embodied. Still, I should like to address it first as a problem of moral psychology.

It is a question of moral psychology because the problem of integration among different levels of motivation is crucial. The pressure toward change deriving from the claim of impartiality is clearly there, but the task is to imagine a transformed moral sense which responds to this claim better without being impossible to live by. Unlike the case of a theoretical change of world view, any such transformation must keep the personal standpoint constantly in mind.

When a theoretical discovery contradicts the appearances we simply allow it to overrule them with regard to what is true, and there seems to be no difficulty in doing this, even when important practical decisions depend upon it. Deceptive appearances don't continue to demand our belief, unless we are superstitious. Personal desires, on the other hand, remain effective for the most part, and cannot be rendered inactive at will.

If a very well-established principle is invoked, a desire can be decisively sidelined, as when one sees the No Smoking sign and puts out one's cigarette. But this is the manifestation of a requirement that has already been internalized, and I am talking now about the process of expanding, perhaps greatly, the authority of impartial values. Even the authority of No Smoking signs depends on the existence of a convention that most people, smokers and nonsmokers alike, can live with. The construction of an expanded egalitarian sensibility is a much more involved task. I shall try to describe the moral situation as it appears now, and then go on to consider alternatives.

First of all, an egalitarian system would have to completely forget the idea, still popular in certain quarters, that the root of social injustice is exploitation—in the sense of a failure to reward people in accordance with their productive contribution or the true value of their labor. The defense of equality requires that rewards *not* depend on productive contribution, and in particular that some people receive much more of the social product than they contribute.

People's productive contributions are so unequal that the mere avoidance of exploitation would allow great inequalities of economic condition. I assume no one believes in the labor theory of value any more; but just for the record, it is clear that the value of a product is not a function of the amount of labor that went into it. It is the other way around: The value of someone's labor is a function of its contribution to the creation of a product, together with the value of the product. In a factory that manufactures telephones, for example, the subtraction of the designers of the telephones and the production process would cause the productive value of the labor of the factory workers to plummet, roughly, to what they could produce in a pre-industrial economy, whereas the subtraction of an equal number of laborers from the factory would reduce its productivity only slightly by slowing down the rate at which it could produce telephones.

Second, the pursuit of equality requires abandonment of the idea that there is a morally fundamental distinction, in regard to the socioeconomic framework which controls people's life prospects,

between what the state does and what it merely allows. There are other areas of state action, impinging on individual rights, in which this distinction retains its moral significance, and of course it will continue to do so at the level of individual morality. But with regard to income, wealth, social position, health, education, and perhaps other things, it is essential that the society should be regarded by its members as responsible for how things are, if different feasible policies and institutions would result in their being different. And if the society is responsible, they are responsible through it, for it is their agent.

This is an extremely important issue, and one on which current community opinion is unclear. But I believe there is still significant attachment to the idea that certain aspects of the economic system are "natural," and do not have to be justified: Only when government interferes with them is it responsible for the results, and then the question of the justifiability of its policies can be raised. Libertarianism is a radical version of this view, but in less clear form it has considerable influence on more mainstream public opinion. Its decisive abandonment would be a major transformation of the common moral consciousness. . . .

[T]he acceptance of a serious egalitarian ideal would have to appeal to a notion of negative responsibility, on the part of the society, for failing to arrange things differently in ways that it could. If it is possible for people to be economically rewarded more equally under another arrangement, then maintenance of a system which allows rewards to be proportional to productivity would have to be regarded as a social choice to permit rewards to depend substantially on differences in natural talent, education, and background. Noninterference requires justification as much as interference does: *Every* arrangement has to be justified by comparison with every other real possibility, and if egalitarian impartiality has a substantial role in justification of this kind, then significant arguments on the other side will be needed to defend arrangements which permit large inequalities to develop as a consequence of their unimpeded operation.

A laissez-faire system, despite its name, has no special status as a "natural" process for whose results government is not responsible. In deciding to enforce only the rights which make such a system possible, the state makes a choice, and if there is a viable alternative, then it has chosen an arrangement which rewards those with greater productive capacity (and their heirs) at the expense of those with less—not in the sense that the latter are being deprived of some of the value of their labor, but in the sense that they are being deprived of what they could have under an alternative arrangement. The state, and therefore its citizens, are responsible for this result.

The sense that benefits not provided, which could be provided, are being *withheld* from the poor, will seem unnatural only if one rejects the assumption of negative responsibility. Of course if a more equal arrangement is chosen, then it is just as true that benefits are being withheld from the better off, which they would otherwise receive. But in an egalitarian view, this withholding may be justified by the priority of needs of those worse off. Whether it is or not depends on the arguments in the other direction.

In this respect . . . political theory is different from the ethics of individual conduct. There, negative responsibility is much less significant: In a decent society, an individual who devotes most of his energies to the pursuit of his own life is not plausibly accused of withholding from others all the benefits he might provide for them instead. But the society itself must consider all systems of allocation prima facie equally eligible, since it has no "life of its own" to lead, apart from the way it arranges the collective life of its members. In deciding among alternatives, the importance of letting individuals lead their own lives must be weighed along with egalitarian values. But if, even in light of all that, the distribution of rewards is too strongly proportional to the natural or social accidents of birth, then the society must be regarded as having chosen to permit the distribution of benefits on morally irrelevant grounds. There is no default position that doesn't have to be justified because it is not chosen. Any way in which the society arranges things, any system it

enforces, from laissez-faire to socialism, represents a choice which must be justified by comparison with the other viable alternatives.

This contrasts with the Lockean view that government constitutes an interference in the natural moral relations between individuals, which should be allowed to continue unless they threaten to break down without institutional support. In the view I am expressing, the existence of a legal order backed by government coercion is not in question: The only question is what it should do, and preserving the conditions for individual moral relations is only one of the tasks it makes sense to assign to it. It represents the ideal of a collectively held point of view of its members, and this ideal includes an impartial egalitarian element.

So if a society permits some people to become much richer than others and to pass this wealth on to their children, that is what it is doing—in a sense that is what we are all doing—and we have to ask the question whether the alternative arrangements in which these kinds of inequality would be less would be still more objectionable in other ways.

Let me now move to a more detailed discussion of the change in attitudes toward the causes of inequality that would be needed to overcome the resistance to an egalitarian system. We can distinguish three sources of socioeconomic inequality (inequality, from now on), which raise questions of social justice and to which attitudes can easily be different, and a fourth which in itself is relatively unproblematic.

The first is intentional discrimination of the traditional kind: racial, sexual, religious, ethnic. The remedy for this is negative equality of opportunity, or positions open to qualifications (including acquired qualifications such as education).

The second is hereditary advantage both in the possession of resources and in access to the means of obtaining qualifications for open competitive positions. The remedy for this is not so clear, because so long as children grow up in families, they will inevitably benefit or suffer from the advantages or disadvantages of their parents, even if inheritance of property at death is considerably restricted. But some of the effects with respect to access to the kind of background and training which enhance qualifications can be softened by public support for child care, education, and the like. I shall call this *positive* equality of opportunity, to distinguish it from the negative equality of opportunity which results from the mere absence of discrimination. . . .

The third source is the variation in natural abilities themselves. . . .

Let me refer to these three sources of inequality respectively as *Discrimination, Class,* and *Talent.* . . . I am concerned here with the character and legitimacy of differences in our attitudes toward these three sources of inequality. Finally let me add to the catalogue, for completeness and for purposes of contrast, a fourth important source of inequality, somewhat different from the others, which without further explanation I shall call *Effort.*

This fourfold classification omits one important category of causes of inequality, namely those influences on a particular individual's life which do not result from the social structure and which are not the individual's responsibility. These are instances of bad *luck,* in the ordinary sense: such things as being killed or crippled by accident or disease (including genetic disease), becoming unemployed because one's employer goes out of business, losing one's home in a tornado, and so forth. What the state should do about such inequalities is certainly a concern of political theory, but I have not included a separate discussion of it. I believe the main issue from the standpoint of social equality is how to deal with inequalities in the impact of this sort of individual bad luck on persons in different socioeconomic classes.

Whatever the social structure, people's individual luck will differ, often in ways that are not determined at birth. While amelioration of severe disadvantages of this kind should receive social priority directly, through medical benefits, assistance for the handicapped, and unemployment insurance, I believe variation in many of the more occasional forms of bad luck should be incorporated into the definition of the life prospects or expectations of persons born into particular social positions with particular talents. If the resultant risks are much higher for some groups than for others, that is obviously a problem from the standpoint of social equality. But the determination of how much risk of inequality from accidental causes should be allowed *within* any social class seems to me a different kind of problem—a problem of what risks are worth running for what benefits, or what costs are worth paying for the reduction of risk.[2] This is an important question, but quite different from the questions about inequality posed by class and talent—even though they too are in a sense a matter of luck.

I realize that much more needs to be said in elaboration and defense of this claim. It requires an account of when inequality in outcome can be morally dominated by equality in antecedent risk, and when it cannot. But I won't pursue the matter here, and will confine myself to the original list of discrimination, class, talent, and effort, because of their greater importance for political theory.

These four factors can vary independently, though they are often correlated in one way or another, and can also interact causally. Discrimination, class, and talent may influence effort; discrimination, talent, and effort in one generation may influence class in the next. And all of them have their effects on inequality only through the operation of an articulated social system which includes different positions or roles, with different opportunities, advantages, and disadvantages attached to them.

It is clear that effort will always make a difference, but the range of possible outcomes over which effort will determine the result, and the rough functional relation between effort and outcome, is fixed in advance for each person by the combined effects of discrimination pro or con, the class into which he is born, his natural talents, and the existing social structure. Our judgment of the social structure will depend on our attitude toward the way it permits these causes of inequality to operate.

In the order given, the four causes form a natural progression, from external to internal. While all of them affect an individual's sense of who he is, they do not all originate with him.

Deliberate discrimination is a force completely outside the victim, imposed on him by others. Of course it is likely to have internal psychological effects which compound the resulting inequality; but in itself it is not a feature of the victim at all, but a fact about how others treat him.

Class is also environmental but is transmitted to the individual by his family, a kind of native socioeconomic habitat deriving from his most intimate personal relations in virtue of their relation to the rest of society. It is the product not primarily of deliberate imposition by outsiders, but of innumerable personal choices in a competitive economy of families, which constantly generate stratification as a cumulative effect. Class can itself be a target of deliberate discrimination as well, though when this is systematic, with prohibitions on social mobility and intermarriage, it comes closer to a caste system. But even when it is a pure by-product of the operation of an economic system which permits social mobility, the class to which a person is born and bred is entirely the result of causes external to him: He himself contributes nothing to it.

Talent, as I am using the term, is innate, though its development and value depend on the other factors. (I shall usually speak of *ability* when I wish to refer to realized talent.) It is strongly internal to the individual, more an aspect of what he is in himself than either discrimination or class, though of course it generates material advantages only through his interaction with others.

Effort, finally, being a manifestation of the will, is the most personal or internal factor, and uniquely suitable to be regarded as the individual's personal responsibility. . . .

[T]he egalitarian ideal is particularly concerned with equality in advantages and disadvantages for which the recipients are not responsible. . . .

The essence of this moral conception is equality of *treatment* rather than impartial concern for well-being. It applies to inequalities generated by the social system, rather than to inequalities in general. A society that permits significant inequalities among its members, in advantages and disadvantages for which they are not responsible, will be perceived as failing to treat them equally: it distinguishes in its treatment of them along morally arbitrary lines.

The standard of equal treatment is more demanding with respect to equality than mere preference to the worse off . . . , for it finds something unfair even about inequalities that benefit the worst off. That does not mean that the objection to such unfairness cannot be overcome by countervailing factors, including such benefit. But it does mean that the inequality, even if it harms no one, counts as something bad in itself, in a way that cannot be analyzed in terms of the pure priority view.

The pure priority view applies more generally, and it makes no objection to inequality per se: Any advantage to the better off at no cost to the worse off is all to the good, even if it is due to causes for which the recipients are not responsible.[3] This seems to me the only correct view to take of inequalities that arise naturally. For example there can be no possible objection to some people's naturally enjoying immunity to certain diseases or perfect health or sunny dispositions, even though this makes them much better off than those who are constitutionally sickly or depressed. Better is simply better, in such cases, because no inequality of treatment is implied. But once social mechanisms enter into the causation of a benefit, its unequal distribution becomes a form of unequal treatment by the society of its members, and the sense of unfairness makes its appearance. . . .

Let us now consider the four factors listed above from this point of view. By the standard of responsibility it would seem that only the last, effort (to the extent that it is independent of the others), should be immune from suspicion as a legitimate cause of variation in social condition. Yet there is a tendency to treat the other three factors as morally different from one another as well, with discrimination being most objectionable and talent least. Let us consider why this is so.

Discrimination is clearly the worst in one way: It involves deliberate imposition of disadvantages on some by others—unequal treatment in a strong sense—whereas class and talent produce advantages and disadvantages through the normal operation of a competitive economy populated by participants with normal human sentiments. Still, class and talent are not the individual's responsibility, even though they are not other people's responsibility in the way that deliberate discrimination is. This gives us a three-way classification: (1) causes for which others are responsible (discrimination), (2) causes for which no one is specifically responsible, only "the system" (class and talent), and (3) causes for which the individual himself is responsible (effort).

Now it would be possible to take either of two clear-cut positions with respect to this classification: (a) that only the first sort of cause is morally objectionable, or (b) that only the third sort of cause is morally *un*objectionable. But either of these positions would mean taking causes of type (2) as morally similar, either all unobjectionable or all objectionable. Yet many people, rightly or wrongly, perceive a morally significant difference between inequalities in advantages due to class and inequalities in advantages due to talent. While neither is generally condemned, there is more uneasiness about the first than there is about the second. . . .

I think the personal-impersonal conflict can help us to understand the appeal of this contrast, and more generally to understand why the four causes are naturally seen as forming a progression, of increasing moral acceptability. The responsibility of the "victim" is not the only factor determining our response: The entire motivational situation is relevant.

Let me say something about class before going on to talent. Discrimination is the product of a bad motive, prejudice, and there is nothing to be said for it.[4] But class depends on the special interest people take in their relatives, especially their children. There is no possibility of abolishing this interest, and no sane person would wish to do so. The only real possibility, for those of egalitarian sympathies, is to limit its scope of operation and the magnitude of its consequences. So long as people come in families, the approach to fair equality of opportunity can only be partial. The psychological aspect of the problem is the usual one: What division between personal and impersonal motives can be accepted by normal and reasonable human beings, with the support of an appropriate institutional setting?

In civilized societies, the best-entrenched limitation on the exercise of family preference is the rule against nepotism in public and semi-public institutions. This is really part of the principle of negative equality of opportunity, for it prohibits a special form of discrimination in the filling of competitive positions—a form more personal than racial, religious, or sexual discrimination. Given the strength of the preferential motive which it inhibits, the rule against nepotism represents a considerable triumph of the impersonal over the personal where it is in force. And its stability requires a general vigilance and some sense among the possible beneficiaries of nepotism (both those who could get the jobs or benefits and those who could dispense them) that there is something disgraceful about advantages obtained in that way. Even this minimal restriction requires a powerful partition of motives, since the motive behind nepotism remains acceptable in other contexts. Those in positions of influence who refrain from handing out jobs to their relatives or from attempting to bribe others to provide such jobs still spend money on their children's education partly in order to give them a competitive advantage in the open competition for jobs and social position.

If we add to the prohibition of nepotism a public effort to provide fair or positive equality of opportunity, the personal-impersonal division is moved over a few notches, but the division remains. The stability of such a system requires a general sense that large competitive advantages resulting from exclusive access to higher education, for example, due to the accident that one's parents were well-to-do, are somehow tainted. Here again while the resentment of the losers is important, the uneasiness of the winners plays an important role in generating enough support for an egalitarian policy to prevent political revolt against its costs to them.

Yet even if such persons support the public provision of education and health care for all, in order to ensure everyone a fair start in life and a chance to develop those abilities which qualify for access to desirable positions, they will not stop favoring their children in their more personal choices. If they have the resources, they will continue to offer whatever extra advantages they can, by paying for superior education, by direct cultural enrichment, and by various forms of financial support. While these things are good in themselves, they also aim to give the child a competitive edge. This motivational split defines a familiar modern liberal mentality. I realize it attracts a certain amount of scorn, but that is quite unwarranted, for it is simply another example of the partition of motives which pervades morality.

Public institutional support for positive equality of opportunity does not abolish inequalities due to class, because it does not abolish the operation of family preference in the personal sphere, but merely seeks to limit it to that sphere. Operating there, it inevitably continues to have broader social effects because public institutions alone do not determine opportunities. Stratification is enhanced by the tendency of persons to marry within their socioeconomic class, and it is not diminished by social mobility between classes from one generation to the next. Social mobility is compatible with great inequality and it does nothing for those who stay put.

Any attempt to go beyond a certain point in eliminating the effects of class so long as there *are* classes will run up against strong and natural human resistance, which will inevitably invade the political sphere. Attempts to redraw the personal-impersonal boundary through institutional redesign, by making privately purchased education illegal, for example, are likely to generate fierce opposition. This is a controversial issue, but I do not think such resistance can be simply discounted. It would stem not only from concern over the waste of possibilities, but from the feeling that a legitimate expression of familial preference was being blocked—that this was not like the rule against nepotism.

In short, even the standard forms of remedy to class-caused inequalities do not depend on the position that all inequalities due to class are morally unacceptable. A personal core remains protected, and this core has large social consequences, though its scope remains a matter for argument and institutional definition. Only a totalitarian government could even attempt to abolish classes, and even then it would be unlikely to succeed.

It would not be unrealistic to hope for a change in attitude toward the inheritance of wealth, so that the privilege of endowing one's children with independent means was no longer regarded as the kind of expression of family feeling with which the state should not interfere. It might even be possible to design a system of estate and gift taxes without the loopholes that usually plague such efforts. It would be a big change, but not unthinkable, if people ceased to regard it as a reason for someone to be rich that his parents were rich. But this would not make a serious dent in the effects of class, because differences in parental income and personally acquired wealth are enough by themselves to generate large competitive distinctions among children prior to the time that inheritance becomes an issue. So long as there are substantial inequalities in income there will be substantial inequalities due to class, barring some unimaginable evaporation or pathological inhibition of natural family sentiment.

A major cause of inequalities in income is variation in talent, and there we see the problem of how to draw the personal-impersonal division in an even more acute form. For some reason it appears to be harder to internalize the sense that advantages derived from the exercise of talent are in themselves morally suspect, on the ground that the talent itself is a matter of luck. Lucky or not, it seems too intimate an aspect of the individual, too tied up with the pursuit of life itself, for this attitude to sit comfortably. The fact that differences in talent are not themselves socially created may also play a role. This resistance seems to me unreasonable, but it is certainly there. Perhaps because everyone can imagine having been switched in the cradle, it is easy to think, about the members of a deprived class, "There but for the grace of God go I." But one's natural talents are not so easily switched, and that hinders the moral imagination.

It is true, of course, that your talents are an intimate part of you, and that any attempt by the state to prevent you from exercising and developing them would be intolerable. Like beauty, talent and excellence also attract recognition, admiration, and gratitude, and such responses are among the natural rewards of human life. But the economic rewards which some talents are able to command, if properly developed, are another story. They cannot be said to be merited just because the recognition of excellence on which they are based is merited. To try to sever the connection between talent and admiration would be wrong. But to sever the connection between talent and income, if it could be done, would be fine. Those with useful talents do not naturally deserve more material benefits than those who lack them.[5]

The problem would be different if there were an institutional vehicle, as we have seen for other causes of inequality, to limit the effects of talent to a personal domain while blocking its consequences in a more public institutional setting which could then be governed by egalitarian principles. But that is just what is impossible for this case, unlike the case of class. One cannot realistically block the direct employment of talent to gain advantages in the public or semi-public sphere, as one can block nepotism and bribery. To do that one would have to abolish competition. Measures to block the influence of discrimination and class, by contrast, expand competition. In fact the aim of profiting from the exercise of talent is of utmost importance in the public sphere, and needs encouragement, not discouragement.

The advantages due to talent are not handed out as a reward for high scores on tests: They come as the result of demand for scarce resources in a competitive labor market. And the preservation of some forms of labor market, with economic incentives, seems indispensible enough to provide an "external" justification for the differential rewards it generates. But if it is in operation, then people have to work for those rewards, employing their talents where the market reveals they are most in demand, and realizing economic and social gains when they succeed. The lives of people who work are pervaded by attempts to profit from their abilities in this way. I do not mean here to invoke the spectre of that mythical creature, rational economic man.[6] We all know that other motives are essential for the success of cooperative enterprises and that the exercise of a productive skill can itself be a source of real satisfaction. But economic incentives that generate inequalities also play a very significant role.

Any attempt to limit the inequalities due to talent without abolishing the labor market must take the indirect form of progressive and redistributive taxation. But this is quite different from limiting the effects of talent to a special, personal domain. Work is acutely personal, as well as public. So the motives of personal advancement and impersonal egalitarianism come into conflict very directly here. An egalitarian in a competitive economy is expected to strive for precisely those advantages which he simultaneously wants to limit.

If we follow the pattern of discrimination and class, wide support for an egalitarian policy with regard to talent would require that those who can profit from superior talent through the economic system should come to feel that such advantages are tainted, even though it is recognized that they must be allowed for reasons of efficiency. But with what coherent set of attitudes are egalitarians supposed to embrace these motives simultaneously? As acquisitive individuals they must force their socially conscientious selves to permit talent-dependent rewards as the unavoidable price of productivity, efficiency, and growth. As participants in the system they are expected, indeed encouraged, to pursue those advantages, but as citizens they are expected to allow them only reluctantly: They must regard it as legitimate and natural to want them, but in another light not legitimate to have them.

There is an analogy here with the case of nepotism, whose prohibition in the public sphere can coexist with family partiality in the private sphere; but the tensions involved in a partition of motives are in this case much more severe, and present more serious obstacles to equality. With regard to family connections it is possible, in theory at least, to approach a condition in which the institutions of the society are strictly egalitarian—through measures of positive equality of opportunity. But with regard to marketable talent, no such solution is available. The egalitarianism of the institutions is hostage to the anti-egalitarian partiality of the individuals out of which they are constructed.

The personal motives which lead people to develop and exploit their talents will dictate the degrees of inequality in reward that are required to satisfy even a strongly egalitarian standard such as the difference principle. The difference principle permits only those inequalities that benefit the worst off, but it can be applied only against the background of patterns of human interaction and motivation that determine which inequalities pass this test. Social institutions like the tax and transfer system will have to defer to these personal motives at every point, making the public domain an active participant in the generation of inequalities. So long as private motives remain significantly acquisitive and strongly partial, it is impossible to create a strongly egalitarian system without unacceptable invasions of personal freedom and disastrous economic consequences. The personal strictly limits what the impersonal can achieve.

The motivational problem for committed egalitarians in all this is that the egalitarian sense of fairness must make us regard as unfortunate those very inequalities which as economic actors we are bent on getting the benefit of, which our acquisitive demands make necessary, and which therefore are required for the benefit of the worse off. An economically competitive egalitarian with the appropriate partition of motives is supposed to reflect, as he signs the astronomical check for his three-star meal, that although it's a shame that business talent such as his should command such rewards while others are scraping by, there is no help for it, since he and his peers have to be allowed to earn this kind of money if the economy is to function properly. A most unfortunate situation, really, but how lucky for him!

The motivational situation would be less peculiar if an egalitarian system were imposed from outside, and personal acquisitive motives were free to operate within it. But if the maintenance of any such system is a political choice, which the participants are expected to accept, they will have to juggle two conflicting attitudes toward their competitive gains and losses, trying to maximize their take from what they regard as a morally questionable source.

There are really two problems here, one having to do with incentives in the operation of an ostensibly egalitarian system, the other having to do with its sta-

bility and political support. The first problem is that the application of any serious egalitarian standard, such as the difference principle, involves a choice among different *unequal* systems, and the available options will be determined not only by technological and material facts, but by motivational ones. So long as personal motives are permitted to determine individual economic choices, the inequalities that the difference principle must tolerate will be determined by fundamentally anti-egalitarian factors.

The second problem is that it is difficult to combine, in a morally coherent outlook, the attitude toward inequalities due to talent which generates support for an egalitarian system with the attitude toward the employment of their own talents appropriate for individuals operating within it. The first attitude is that such inequalities are unfair and morally suspect, whereas the second attitude is that one is entitled to try to get as much out of the system as one can.

While such a division of motives is not self-contradictory, it is not strictly intelligible. The essential problem is that while we know roughly what is appealing in the way of political and personal ideals, we cannot devise a political morality and a personal morality that fit together satisfactorily. The two pull in opposite directions because they respond to different demands, and the conflicts are too direct to be solved through a division of labor between social institutions and individual conduct. So the combination of egalitarian public values and inegalitarian personal aims to which we are forced by motivational logic simply lacks the character of an integrated moral outlook. The egalitarian sentiment of unfairness will tend to clash with the sense of entitlement to pursue one's own aims, and the acquisitiveness licensed by the latter will tend to erode support for the egalitarian system at the political level among those with higher earning power.[7] It is not like the case of people playing a fiercely competitive sport under strict rules—when support for the rules is guaranteed by the fact that without them winning is meaningless.

The strain of the division between internal and external views in this case is more severe than in the case of class, not because the motives deriving from the internal perspective are stronger, but because they are more pervasive. Life is shaped and controlled every day by the decisions about work and leisure, ambition and competition which drive an efficient system of production. There is no natural domain like that of family relations to which we can limit the operation of these motives, no natural division of the territory.

No such ambivalence surrounds the latitude given to inequalities resulting from differences of effort. They are not really inequalities in the same sense as those resulting from the other factors, since, as Ronald Dworkin has pointed out, decisions about how to allocate one's energies are more accurately regarded as an example of that freedom of choice among alternatives which is an essential element of equality. I believe that, apart from pathological conditions, the level of someone's effort is the result of free choice. Persons with the same resources and the same talents but different preferences will naturally choose to employ their talents differently, some taking their benefits in the form of more leisure, others in the form of this or that kind of commodity or opportunity or security. This enhances rather than disturbs the equality of morally significant advantages.[8]

But the same freedom combined with differences in market value results in genuinely unequal advantages. There is no natural way to divide the causation of those advantages by talent into the legitimate and the illegitimate, along lines that could correspond to a psychologically plausible division between personal and impersonal motivation. All that can be done is to reduce the magnitude of the inequalities in life chances within which effort will determine the result. We cannot, as with class, distinguish those advantages that are inextricable from intimate personal choice and therefore immune from interference from those that are not: There is no analogue here to the distinction between legitimate devotion to one's children and nepotism. When it comes to work (as opposed to the diversions of private life), the use of abilities for our own advantage is both personal and public throughout. This helps, I think, to

explain why inequalities due to ability arouse so much less opposition than inequalities due to class—even though the former inevitably give rise to the latter.

Also, it is impossible in practice to disentangle the effects of talent from the effects of effort, since effort is expended through the exercise of talent, and talent develops into a valuable ability only through effort. I don't mean that we can't distinguish the contributions of the two causes, only that we can't separate them. So if one does not object to inequalities due to effort, reluctance to prevent them will automatically carry over to the effects of talent that go with them.

To be sure, effort also combines inextricably with class in the causation of inequality: Those with privileged background and education, not to mention money, can profit more from a given effort than those with less. But we can at least try to compensate for that through measures of positive equality of opportunity, whereas nothing can be done to equalize natural abilities.

In light of these observations, the prospect of limiting social inequality to the goods for which their possessors are responsible seems remote.

# 11

## *Options*

The general problem that emerges from the discussion of class and talent is this: There is a personal dimension of life in which egalitarian impartiality has no place, but which interacts with the public domain to generate inequalities that raise serious issues of social justice. Individual choices and efforts and personal attachments which are in themselves unexceptionable combine on a large scale and over time to produce effects that are beyond individual control and grossly unequal.

The dual sources of the inequalities compete for dominance in determining the appropriate moral response. On the one hand there is some temptation to say that since family sentiment and inequalities in talent are themselves not objectionable, but simply part of the way the world is, there is nothing either right or wrong about inequalities in benefit that derive from them in a social context. They do not require further positive justification (though it may be justifiable to eliminate or modify them for other reasons). On the other hand there is the sense that once natural differences combine with social institutions to generate inequalities, the results require moral justification in terms of the standards of justice appropriate to public institutions—in the natural-social mixture, the social is morally dominant, as it were.

This is essentially Rawls's view. It is the opposite in spirit to Locke's theory of the generation of property rights by the mixture of personally owned labor with common resources—a mixture in which Locke thought labor was morally dominant, generating ownership in the results. Rawls believes the contribution of the social system to the generation of these results is morally dominant, triggering a presumption against inequalities unless independently justified.

I share Rawls's egalitarian sentiments, and might even defend something more egalitarian than priority to the worse off, given the factor of social causation. The fact that we are not responsible for our talents renders morally questionable all but the most immediate inequalities that derive from them. But this poses the problem, and does not solve it. Individual motives remain, and they work against equality in two ways: by inhibiting support for institutions which attempt to reduce it, and by putting pressure even on institutions that give priority to the interests of the worse off to tolerate substantial inequalities as the price of efficiency. At the same time these motives seem to play an essential role in the successful operation of a modern competitive economy.

Altogether, the possibilities of change seem limited. The psychological difficulties of combining political egalitarianism with personal acquisitiveness are clear. But the substitution of other personal motives will not work either. People can of course be motivated to work hard at something they are interested in for its own sake, and sometimes this will

yield a product which others also want. But it is a romantic fantasy to imagine the world run on such a basis. We cannot all be creative artists, research scientists, or professional athletes. It wouldn't even be enough if everyone was strongly motivated to do his job well. Each of the hundreds or thousands of parts that go into a washing machine or a truck or a ball-bearing factory has to be designed and manufactured by people motivated by economically expressed demand. They are not going to do it as a form of self-expression, and even if they wanted nothing better than to contribute to the well-being of mankind, this would not tell them what exactly to make in their semiconductor plant.

Benevolence is not enough. Even love of semiconductors is not enough. Among those who have to think of new things to do and new and more efficient ways to do them, there seems no substitute for the market as a source of information, and the most effective motive for responding to that information is a strong investment of personal ambition and desire for success in productive activities that will pay off.[9] It is hard to do without people who work hard and exercise their ingenuity for gain and competitive success; yet in a stable egalitarian society they would have to combine this with a desire to live under a system which made it as difficult as possible for them to achieve these goals.

Some restrictions, because of their limited character, combine easily with an ethos of the pursuit of profit. The prevention of negative externalities, through the control of pollution for example, can exclude certain means to economic advantage without requiring a change in the basic motive. Admittedly we find limited enthusiasm for such regulation from those whose profits are reduced by it, but the point is that there is in principle no motivational difficulty about the partition of motives which would permit support for such boundaries around the domain of legitimate acquisitive activity. It is analogous to the rule against nepotism, which limits the ways one can benefit one's relatives, without requiring any basic change in the wish to do so. Another example is anti-trust regulation, which establishes the framework for competition. An impersonal motive in support of the framework can coexist with the personal motives of gain that operate within it, and that would, if left to themselves, lead to violations of the framework. The sense of the participants' common interest in establishing such rules also plays a role in these cases.

Acquisitiveness is motivationally compatible with the desire to provide at public expense a social minimum of some kind, for those who lose out badly in the competitive economy. This might be set at various levels, depending on the wealth of the society. But a decent social minimum is very different from an egalitarian policy. It does not require for its support a general suspicion of inequalities due to class or talent—all it requires is the sense that there are certain things no one should have to suffer through no fault of his own, if they can be prevented without too much cost. Here again the necessary partition of motives is clearly feasible, with acquisitiveness proceeding within a system of moderately redistributive taxation.

The trouble with stronger forms of egalitarianism, from a motivational point of view, is that they require too exclusive a reliance on egalitarian impartiality for support of the economic framework, and too complete an insulation of politics from personal motives. They require some as yet unimagined change either in the motivation of economic actors or in the design of economic systems, or both, which will support the incentives and generate the information needed for productive efficiency without at the same time generating large inequalities. The upshot of the discussion so far is that even if the principle of negative responsibility is widely accepted as regards the society's relation to the life chances conferred by its socioeconomic structure, there are serious obstacles to the additional changes in the pattern of personal and interpersonal motives which would be needed both to generate unanimous support by reasonable persons for a system which tried radically to reduce inequalities due to class and talent—and to make such a system work. If all this is true, then those who are attached to egalitarian ideals seem to be left with two options. Either they can lower their sights and aim for a partial approach to those ideals,

through changes falling within the limits imposed by the present general character of human motives and the consequences of their interaction. Or they can hope for a more radical transformation of attitudes which, together with institutional changes, would lead to a much fuller realization of socioeconomic equality, while nevertheless leaving a personal sphere free for the expression of a reconstituted individuality.

The first option, a plainly nonutopian possibility which has considerable appeal in its own right and which is a natural fall-back position from strong egalitarianism, would be a development of the already existing uneasiness about severe poverty in relatively wealthy societies into a much stronger insistence on a high social minimum, with healthy, comfortable, decent conditions of life and self-respect for everyone. This would be in addition to fair equality of opportunity, so that even those unable to command good incomes in a competitive economy would be guaranteed a decent standard of living.

Such an attitude need not be linked to any discomfort about inequalities above this level. Of course the social minimum would have to be financed by progressive taxation, used to support social services and a negative income tax (which would most effectively express the underlying idea if it were automatically added to wages just as positive income tax is automatically withheld from wages). This would have the effect of reducing the spread of disposable income above the social minimum; but the change of attitude I am imagining would not include a desire for such reduction for its own sake. And it would also, most importantly, not include any uneasiness of conscience on the part of those who are far above the social minimum. Essentially it would abandon the idea of unfairness according to which all socially generated inequalities are suspect unless vindicated by a suitable condition of responsibility. Provided the minimum is set sufficiently high, individuals with competitive advantages would have no reluctance to pursue and enjoy affluence for themselves and their families. Therefore this attitude would do nothing to damp down the acquisitive motives that drive a competitive economy. There would be the task of designing social provision and a negative income tax so as not to destroy incentives among those being subsidized up to the social minimum; but that problem should be soluble. So long as it is possible to maintain a significant positive correlation between work and income, a guaranteed base will not prevent most people from working, since most people want more than they have.

This is essentially the point of view behind contemporary social democracy, which has never been politically significant in the United states, and seems to be in retreat in Europe, but which may have a future. If such an attitude became entrenched in a modern society, it would not support an egalitarian system and would not hinder the formation of classes, nor would it support unqualified application of the difference principle, since the priority of gains to the worse off would cease once they reached the social minimum. But it would mean that the society put every effort into combating the worst aspects of inequality—poverty and severe relative deprivation. While it would imply a rejection of the idea that those with competitive advantages were not entitled thereby to gain economically, it would likewise reject the idea that all anyone was entitled to was what he could command in the labor market. Something like the right of everyone to a decent standard of living, provided this is economically feasible, would be accorded priority in the economic organization of the society.

This is hardly an unworthy goal, and it may be that nothing beyond it can be seriously pursued until this much has been achieved and has become so well entrenched that it is considered the natural order of things: Then it will be time to complain that it is not yet good enough. But those who hope for something more in the long run must consider the second option—a psychological and institutional transformation which would permit innovation and cooperative production without generating substantial inequalities of reward.

In relation to the present state of things this is unavoidably an exercise of utopian imagination; but

the change of attitude that suggests itself, one which would be far more egalitarian and more in line with the traditional ideals of socialism, is the development of a general reluctance on the part of members of the society to be conspicuously better off than others, either in standard of living as measured by consumption or in social advantages—and a corresponding disapproval of those who try to make themselves significantly better off in these ways. The reluctance would have to extend to special advantages for one's family as well.

This would not mean a takeover of all motives by the impersonal standpoint. Impartiality and egalitarianism would apply to the social structure, but not to private life, and individuals would be expected to devote their energies and their personal resources to the pursuit of happiness and the benefit of their families. But they would not be strongly motivated to get ahead of others—in fact the reverse: Their concern would be to reduce gaps between others and themselves, wherever in the socioeconomic spectrum they found themselves. If they were near the bottom, moving ahead would be the goal; if they were near the top, they would want less, and more for others. What I am imagining is not a general outbreak of asceticism. People would still want material comforts, good food, and vacations in Italy; but they would not feel right about having these things if other members of their society could not afford them.

It may be thought that this change is psychologically too bizarre to be worth considering, but I do not think it is out of the question. It might conceivably come about as the result of a long development, in which the attachment to equality extended to wider and wider areas of life, producing an intergenerational shift in people's sense of what they were entitled to, which would reduce resistance. But I grant that such a thing is highly unlikely, even over the very long run.

Apart from the issue of its psychological possibility, however, this change would not be enough by itself to create egalitarian prosperity. Something else would have to happen to fill the gap in incentives to economic activity that would open up if economic competitiveness disappeared from the scene. The desire to have more, but not more than others, seems very difficult to harness as an incentive for productive effort. If the acquisitive impulse disappears among those with the strongest potential competitive advantages, other incentives must replace it or else a market economy will slow down, cease to innovate, and cease to improve its per capita productivity, on which everyone's welfare depends.

Other incentives are possible, at least in some segments of the work force. Peer approval and derision provide very strong competitive incentives in professions in which the "jury" is well defined and the quality of performance is easy to determine. This presents the problem of seeing to it that approval attaches to what really matters. In the academy, the only case with which I am personally acquainted, the "reputation" incentive to engage in research is considerably stronger than the incentive to teach well; still, the appreciation or boredom of students carries weight with some of us. And in uncorrupt countries, civil servants including the military have to be motivated to do their jobs well on noneconomic grounds, more or less.

Perhaps such motives could do much of the work of economic incentives in some professions, and in addition the leveling attitude would prevent the upward pressure on salaries that results from competition for scarce talent. But what about the main productive elements of the economy? It is hard to imagine what could replace economic incentives in the determination of decisions about how to stock a hardware or grocery or clothing store, what colors and kinds of paint to manufacture, or how much to charge for a silicon chip. Success in the economy cannot be identified independently of economic success—at least the economic success of the enterprise in which one is engaged. Profitability is a condition of capital accumulation and increased production, so even if volume and numbers of satisfied customers are the standard of real success, economic gain must be the primary influence on decisions in the business world.

A natural proposal is to try to detach the informational function of markets and profit-maximization from the motive of personal gain—with other, purely moral incentives substituted that follow roughly the same contours of penalty and reward. This would require either a finely graded system of public recognition of economic performance—market socialism with medals and honor rolls—or a change in the basis of most people's self-esteem which made it possible to run the whole system on Monopoly money, which they would be proud to earn even if they couldn't spend it on themselves.

Neither of these scenarios is particularly credible. I think it much more likely that the general settling in of an aversion to consuming more than others would undermine competitiveness generally in most of the economy, and leave it strong only in the arts and sciences, in sports and entertainment, and in those professions which offer the possibility of fame, at least in the eyes of a special audience. Perhaps there is some alternative method of using straightforward economic incentives in such a way that large economic inequalities do not develop from their operation; but no one has yet dreamed up such a system, and it would seem to require an unimaginable level of information and control by the authority that determines what the incentives will be.

My conclusion, as before, is that a strongly egalitarian society populated by reasonably normal people is difficult to imagine and in any case psychologically and politically out of reach, and that a more real possibility lies in the first alternative. Intolerance of severe poverty at least receives lip service in most liberal societies, and it ought to be possible to develop it into insistence on a higher and higher social minimum, until it becomes intolerable in a rich society if anyone does not have a decent standard of living and a fair opportunity to go as far as his natural talents will take him above that.

Even this would be an extraordinary transformation, but it would be compatible with great inequalities and a strong class structure which the absence of obstacles to social mobility would do nothing to destroy. I therefore think it is not a result we can be content with. Rather, it illustrates the difficulty of bringing together personal and impersonal standpoints and encourages the belief that an acceptable combination of individual and political morality remains to be invented.

## Notes

1. As Hannah Arendt once said, "It is true that you can't make an omelet without breaking eggs; but you can break a great many eggs without making an omelet."

2. Thomas Schelling has some interesting things to say about this subject. In particular he points out that against a background of economic inequality, the provision at public expense of specific, untradable benefits like medical care or airport safety may not accurately reflect their value to everyone. Because the rich already have more money, hemodialysis is worth more in money terms to them than to the poor; and given the risks of kidney failure, the public money spent to provide hemodialysis to everyone who needs it, including the poor, might satisfy poor people's preferences better if spent on housing, or dispensed as cash. See *Choice and Consequence,* pp. 9–17 and 141–42.

On the other hand there may be reasons not to allow public provision simply to follow the lead of individual preferences. There are things a society may want to provide for everyone, even if some of the beneficiaries would reasonably prefer to have the money to use for other purposes.

3. For this reason it is not counted by Parfit as a truly egalitarian position. See *On Giving Priority to the Worse Off.*

4. If a group has been systematically discriminated against in the past, it may be necessary in rectifying the situation to exclude other forms of differential treatment of the group as well, even when they are not motivated by prejudice. For example it would be unacceptable on statistical grounds to use membership in such a group as a probabilistic indicator of lower qualification for certain positions—even though other types of statistically based criteria of no greater reliability are admissible in filling those positions. Other criteria with inordinate impact on the group may also be suspect. This is a complication having to do less with the ending of discrimination than with the removal of its effects.

5. Could income be construed as the "natural" reward of certain talents—talents to produce what others are happy to pay for? It is a nice question, but I don't think so.

The concept of a natural reward should be restricted to those advantages that are strictly inseparable from the recognition and appreciation of a quality by others, and I doubt that this is ever true of money. People's willingness to pay for something is a direct manifestation of their valuing it. But it needn't take the form of payment to the producer.

6. See Amartya Sen, "Rational Fools: A Critique of the Behavioral Foundations of Economic Theory."

7. This points is made by Mary Gibson in "Rationality," p. 219.

8. See "What is Equality?" Parts I and II. *Philosophy & Public Affairs* 10 (1981). In Dworkin's theory this is part of a broader claim that the appropriate metric of equality is resources rather than welfare—where resources are measured in terms of their cost to others, and what a person chooses to do with his time is not counted among his resources, even though the leisure of a productive individual may be quite costly to others. So if someone's tastes make it possible for him to be blissfully happy with only moderate resources, that is an inequality of benefit to which there is no objection. I find this plausible: The good fortune of such a person can be regarded as a natural blessing like perfect health, and so not unfair. Giving people the opportunity to determine the allocation of their own efforts, even if some prefer leisure to income and others the reverse, will likewise not of itself result in inequalities which are morally suspect. If the choices are voluntary, the base of equality of resources and options is morally dominant over inequalities in the consequences of such choices.

9. Cf. John Stuart Mill: "The verdict of experience, in the imperfect degree of moral cultivation which mankind have yet reached, is that the motive of conscience and that of credit and reputation, even when they are of some strength, are, in the majority of cases, much stronger as restraining than as impelling forces—are more to be depended on for preventing wrong, than for calling forth the fullest energies in the pursuit of ordinary occupations. In the case of most men the only inducement which has been found sufficiently constant and unflagging to overcome the ever-present influence of indolence and love of ease, and induce men to apply themselves unrelaxingly to work for the most part in itself dull and unexciting, is the prospect of bettering their own economic condition and that of their family; and the closer the connection of every increase of exertion with a corresponding increase of its fruits, the more powerful is this motive." *Chapters on Socialism,* p. 263.

# MICHEL FOUCAULT

~

## INTRODUCTION

## THOMAS A. MCCARTHY

Michel Foucault (1926–1984) was born in Poitiers and studied at the École normale supérieure, where he earned degrees in both philosophy and psychology. After occupying various academic and cultural positions in France, Sweden, Poland, and Germany in the 1950s, he presented his major thesis for the doctorat ès lettres, *Madness and Civilization,* in 1961. Following professorships at the universities of Clermont-Ferrand and Vincennes, separated by a visiting professorship in Tunisia, he was elected in 1969 to the Collège de France, where he designated his chair as being in the "History of the Systems of Thought." In 1971 he helped found an organization for monitoring and improving prison conditions in France, an interest that remained central to his various activities as a public intellectual until he died of an AIDS-related condition in 1984.

Foucault's work can be viewed as falling into several phases. Under the deep and lasting influence of Nietzsche, he adopted early on a critical, historical—"genealogical"—mode of conceptual inquiry that, following the lead of such philosophically oriented French historians of science as his mentor Georges Canguilhcm, he applied to the development of the "sciences of man." Thus his 1961 study of the history of madness and of the circumstances under which the mentally ill began to be confined was at the same time a study of the origins of modern psychiatry in practices of delimiting rationality from irrationality. And the soon-to-follow *Birth of the Clinic* (1963) subjected the development of clinical medicine to the same sort of internal-external analysis. Later in the same decade, in *The Order of Things* (1966), a study of the transmutations in the classical sciences of language, wealth, and living beings from the seventeenth to the nineteenth century, and in *The Archeology of Knowledge* (1969), an extended reflection on method, Foucault elaborated the structural dimension of his approach. Archeology investigates "discursive formations," their rules and regularities, the relations that obtain between discourse and nondiscursive practices and institutions, and the transformations that such formations undergo.

In his publications of the 1970s, particularly in *Discipline and Punish* (1975) and *The History of Sexuality. Volume I: An Introduction* (1976), he amplified the genealogical dimension of his approach in critical social histories of the "will to truth." In these works, as well as in numerous essays, lectures, and interviews of the period, Foucault stressed the internal relationship between knowledge and power, and in particular that the development of the human sciences was closely bound up with the development and deployment of practices, institutions, and techniques for monitoring, controlling, and "normalizing" human beings. Genealogy examines the "lowly origins" of the sciences' central ideas—humankind, reason, normality, criminality, sexuality, and the like—in contingent historical circumstances and traces their functional implications in relations of force. It directs our attention to the rules and prescriptions that are constitutive of epistemic practices in these domains, to the relations of hierarchy these rules and prescriptions encode, to the ways in which they include and exclude, validate and invalidate, dismiss or invest with authority. It also examines the relations of such theoretical discourses to the practical ways in which they are applied by judges, administrators, social workers, therapists, physicians, and others, as well as to the institutional practices with which they are interwoven in courts, prisons, clinics, hospitals, schools, bureaucracies, and the like. In short, what genealogy seeks to demonstrate is that the "politics" of knowledge about the human world does not begin only with the production of ideology but already with the production of truth itself.

In the last phase of his work, roughly the early 1980s, Foucault's attention shifted to ethics. In volumes 2 and 3 of *The History of Sexuality* (1984), *The Use of Pleasure* and *The Care of the Self,* he concerned himself with the ways in which human beings become subjects. In the 1970s he had viewed subjectivity largely as the product of subjugation; that is, different kinds of subjects were analyzed as the effects of different kinds of power. Now, however, he investigated the ways in which individuals could act upon themselves and transform themselves, with reference to the sexual ethics of ancient Greece (vol. 2) and the care of the self in the Roman world of the first two centuries of the common era (vol. 3). This conception of ethics as a form of relation of the self to the self, which Foucault contrasted with the conception of morality as obedience to a code of rules that came to predominate in Christianity, opened up the prospect of attempting to elaborate one's life as a personal work of art.

The selection included here is taken from "Two Lectures" delivered in the mid-1970s, the most influential phase of Foucault's thought. In it we have one of his clearest statements of how the genealogical analysis of "power/knowledge regimes" relates to political theory as traditionally practiced. The classical liberal, or "juridical," conception of power—as something that is possessed by individuals and can be transferred through a social contract that constitutes a legitimate sovereign and relations of "right" or law—is contrasted with the Freudian-Marxist conceptualization of power in terms of conflict, struggle, domination, and repression. Prior to this (1976), Foucault's own treatment of power was clearly close to the latter conception. That is, he analyzed social and political power as "war continued by other means": relations of power legitimized by right rest upon and sanction relations of force that result from conflict and struggle and get inscribed in everything from social institutions and economic inequalities to standard languages and docile bodies. Now he suggests that this "domination-repression" schema itself requires modification if it is to be adequate to the realities of "disciplinary" power. His recent studies of penal reform had shown that truth does not so much limit power as function in its service: the relations of power that permeate modern societies cannot be established and maintained without the production and dissemination of supporting truths. Critical social and political theory has, accordingly, to detect and analyze the multiple forms of domination and subjugation that are transmitted and sanctioned in and through discourses of truth and right. This new mode of analyzing power focuses not on the central power of the sovereign but on "power at the extremities," on the techniques, instruments, practices, and institutions through which it is exercised; not on power at the level of conscious intention but on power as invested in practices, on the "how" of ongoing subjugation; not on the unified will of rational subjects, but on how subjects are formed by subjugation, on how individuals are simultaneously the effects and vehicles of power; not on class domination and ideology, but on the grids and networks of power relations through which power circulates, and on the apparatuses, techniques, and discourses through which it is deployed.

This is Foucault at his Nietzschean best. It is not surprising that the notions of "power/knowledge" regimes, "disciplinary" power, "normalizing" techniques, and the like that he sketches here have exerted a vast influence on critical-theoretical strategies in the humanities and the social sciences. Particularly when combined with his injunction in the first lecture to abjure global, unitary theories as the matrix for critical studies and attempt instead to promote the "insurrection of subjugated knowledges," they have lent themselves to fruitful adaptation in the theory and criticism of gender, race, ethnicity, sexuality, and postcolonialism, among other things.

In addition to the works by Foucault mentioned above, there are a number of valuable collections of his interviews, lectures, essays, and other writings: D. Bouchard (ed.), *Language, Counter-Memory, Practice* (Ithaca, N.Y.: Cornell University Press, 1977); C. Gordon (ed.), *Power/Knowledge* (New York: Pantheon, 1980); P. Rabinow (ed.), *The Foucault Reader* (New York: Pantheon, 1984); L. D. Kritzman (ed.), *Michel Foucault: Politics, Philosophy, Culture* (London: Routledge, 1988); J. Bernauer and D. Rasmussen (eds.), *The Final Foucault* (Cambridge, Mass.: MIT Press, 1988), with a bibliography of Foucault's writings; S. Lotringer (ed.), *Foucault Live* (New York: Semiotext(e), 1989); and G. Burchell, C. Gordon, and P. Miller (eds.), *The Foucault Effect: Studies in Governmentality* (Chicago: University of Chicago Press, 1991). The secondary literature on Foucault is immense. David Macey's *The Lives of Michel Foucault* (New York: Pantheon, 1993) is a good biography. L. McNay, *Foucault: A Critical Introduction* (New York: Continuum, 1994) provides an introductory overview of his thought. General interpretations and discussions can be found in G. Deleuze, *Foucault,* S. Hand (tr.) (Minneapolis: University of Minnesota Press, 1988) and G. Gutting, *Michel Foucault's Archeology of Scientific Reason* (Cambridge: Cambridge University Press, 1989). Studies that focus on aspects of Foucault's social and political thought are Mark Poster, *Foucault, Marxism, and History* (Cambridge: Polity Press, 1984); and Jana Sawicki, *Disciplining Foucault: Feminism, Power, and the Body* (New York: Routledge, 1991). Critical essays with that focus can be found in the following collections: D. Hoy (ed.), *Foucault: A Critical Reader* (Oxford: Blackwell, 1986); I. Diamond and L. Quinby, (eds.), *Feminism and Foucault* (Boston: Northeastern University Press, 1988); M. Kelly (ed.), *Critique and Power: Rethinking the Foucault/Habermas Debate* (Cambridge, Mass.: MIT Press, 1994); and G. Gutting (ed.), *The Cambridge Companion to Foucault* (Cambridge: Cambridge University Press, 1994).

# Power/Knowledge

## LECTURE ONE

. . . [W]hat has emerged in the course of the last ten or fifteen years is a sense of the increasing vulnerability to criticism of things, institutions, practices, discourses. A certain fragility has been discovered in the very bedrock of existence—even, and perhaps above all, in those aspects of it that are most familiar, most solid and most intimately related to our bodies and to our everyday behaviour. But together with this sense of instability and this amazing efficacy of discontinuous, particular and local criticism, one in fact also discovers something that perhaps was not initially foreseen, something one might describe as precisely the inhibiting effect of global, *totalitarian theories*. It is not that these global theories have not provided nor continue to provide in a fairly consistent fashion useful tools for local research: Marxism and psychoanalysis are proofs of this. But I believe these tools have only been provided on the condition that the theoretical unity of these discourses was in some sense put in abeyance, or at least curtailed, divided, overthrown, caricatured, theatricalised, or what you will. In each case, the attempt to think in terms of a totality has in fact proved a hindrance to research.

So, the main point to be gleaned from these events of the last fifteen years, their predominant feature, is the *local* character of criticism. That should not, I believe, be taken to mean that its qualities are those of an obtuse, naive or primitive empiricism; nor is it a soggy eclecticism, an opportunism that laps up any and every kind of theoretical approach; nor does it mean a self-imposed ascetism which taken by itself would reduce to the worst kind of theoretical impoverishment. I believe that what this essentially local character of criticism indicates in reality is an autonomous, non-centralised kind of theoretical production, one that is to say whose validity is not dependent on the approval of the established régimes of thought.

It is here that we touch upon another feature of these events that has been manifest for some time now: it seems to me that this local criticism has proceeded by means of what one might term 'a return of knowledge'. What I mean by that phrase is this: it is a fact that we have repeatedly encountered, at least at a superficial level, in the course of most recent times, an entire thematic to the effect that it is not theory but life that matters, not knowledge but reality, not books but money etc.; but it also seems to me that over and above, and arising out of this thematic, there is something else to which we are witness, and which we might describe as an *insurrection of subjugated knowledges.*

By subjugated knowledges I mean two things: on the one hand, I am referring to the historical contents that have been buried and disguised in a functionalist coherence or formal systemisation. Concretely, it is not a semiology of the life of the asylum, it is not even a sociology of delinquency, that has made it possible to produce an effective criticism of the asylum and likewise of the prison, but rather the immediate emergence of historical contents. And this is simply because only the historical contents allow us to rediscover the ruptural effects of conflict and struggle that the order imposed by functionalist or systematising thought is designed to mask. Subjugated knowledges are thus those blocs of historical knowledge which were present but disguised within

Reprinted from *Power/Knowledge,* translated by Colin Gordon, Leo Marshall, John Mepham, and Kate Soper. New York: Pantheon Books, 1980. Reprinted by permission of Harvester Books, Inc.

POWER/KNOWLEDGE

the body of functionalist and systematising theory and which criticism—which obviously draws upon scholarship—has been able to reveal.

On the other hand, I believe that by subjugated knowledges one should understand something else, something which in a sense is altogether different, namely, a whole set of knowledges that have been disqualified as inadequate to their task or insufficiently elaborated: naive knowledges, located low down on the hierarchy, beneath the required level of cognition or scientificity. I also believe that it is through the re-emergence of these low-ranking knowledges, these unqualified, even directly disqualified knowledges (such as that of the psychiatric patient, of the ill person, of the nurse, of the doctor—parallel and marginal as they are to the knowledge of medicine—that of the delinquent etc.), and which involve what I would call a popular knowledge (*le savoir des gens*) though it is far from being a general commonsense knowledge, but is on the contrary a particular, local, regional knowledge, a differential knowledge incapable of unanimity and which owes its force only to the harshness with which it is opposed by everything surrounding it—that it is through the re-appearance of this knowledge, of these local popular knowledges, these disqualified knowledges, that criticism performs its work.

However, there is a strange kind of paradox in the desire to assign to this same category of subjugated knowledges what are on the one hand the products of meticulous, erudite, exact historical knowledge, and on the other hand local and specific knowledges which have no common meaning and which are in some fashion allowed to fall into disuse whenever they are not effectively and explicitly maintained in themselves. Well, it seems to me that our critical discourses of the last fifteen years have in effect discovered their essential force in this association between the buried knowledges of erudition and those disqualified from the hierarchy of knowledges and sciences.

In the two cases—in the case of the erudite as in that of the disqualified knowledges—with what in fact were these buried, subjugated knowledges really concerned? They were concerned with a *his-torical knowledge of struggles*. In the specialised areas of erudition as in the disqualified, popular knowledge there lay the memory of hostile encounters which even up to this day have been confined to the margins of knowledge.

What emerges out of this is something one might call a genealogy, or rather a multiplicity of genealogical researches, a painstaking rediscovery of struggles together with the rude memory of their conflicts. And these genealogies, that are the combined product of an erudite knowledge and a popular knowledge, were not possible and could not even have been attempted except on one condition, namely that the tyranny of globalising discourses with their hierarchy and all their privileges of a theoretical *avant-garde* was eliminated.

Let us give the term *genealogy* to the union of erudite knowledge and local memories which allows us to establish a historical knowledge of struggles and to make use of this knowledge tactically today. This then will be a provisional definition of the genealogies which I have attempted to compile with you over the last few years.

You are well aware that this research activity, which one can thus call genealogical, has nothing at all to do with an opposition between the abstract unity of theory and the concrete multiplicity of facts. It has nothing at all to do with a disqualification of the speculative dimension which opposes to it, in the name of some kind of scientism, the rigour of well established knowledges. It is not therefore via an empiricism that the genealogical project unfolds, nor even via a positivism in the ordinary sense of that term. What it really does is to entertain the claims to attention of local, discontinuous, disqualified, illegitimate knowledges against the claims of a unitary body of theory which would filter, hierarchise and order them in the name of some true knowledge and some arbitrary idea of what constitutes a science and its objects. Genealogies are therefore not positivistic returns to a more careful or exact form of science. They are precisely anti-sciences. Not that they vindicate a lyrical right to ignorance or non-knowledge: it is not that they are concerned to deny knowledge or that they esteem the virtues of direct cognition and base their practice upon an immediate experience that escapes encapsulation in knowledge. It is not that with which we are concerned. We are concerned, rather, with the insurrection of knowledges that are opposed primarily not to the contents, methods or concepts of a science, but to the effects of the centralising powers which are linked to the institution and functioning of an organised scientific discourse within a society such as ours. Nor does it basically matter all that much that this institutionalisation of scientific discourse is embodied in a university, or, more generally, in an educational apparatus, in a theoretical-commercial institution such as psychoanalysis or within the framework of reference that is provided by a political system such as Marxism; for it is really against the effects of the power of a discourse that is considered to be scientific that the genealogy must wage its struggle. . . .

By comparison, then, and in contrast to the various projects which aim to inscribe knowledges in the hierarchical order of power associated with science, a genealogy should be seen as a kind of attempt to emancipate historical knowledges from that subjection, to render them, that is, capable of opposition and of struggle against the coercion of a theoretical, unitary, formal and scientific discourse. It is based on a reactivation of local knowledges—of minor knowledges, as Deleuze might call them—in opposition to the scientific hierarchisation of knowledges and the effects intrinsic to their power: this, then, is the project of these disordered and fragmentary genealogies. If we were to characterise it in two terms, then 'archaeology' would be the appropriate methodology of this analysis of local discursivities, and 'genealogy' would be the tactics whereby, on the basis of the descriptions of these local discursivities, the subjected knowledges which were thus released would be brought into play. . . .

[I]t will be no part of our concern to provide a solid and homogeneous theoretical terrain for all these dispersed genealogies, nor to descend upon them from on high with some kind of halo of theory that would unite them. Our task, on the contrary, will be to expose and specify the issue at stake in this opposition, this struggle, this insurrection of knowledges against the institutions and against effects of the knowledge and power that invests scientific discourse.

What is at stake in all these genealogies is the nature of this power which has surged into view in all its violence, aggression and absurdity in the course of the last forty years, contemporaneously, that is, with the collapse of Fascism and the decline of Stalinism. What, we must ask, is this power—or rather, since that is to give a formulation to the question that invites the kind of theoretical coronation of the whole which I am so keen to avoid—what are these various contrivances of power, whose operations extend to such differing levels and sectors of society and are possessed of such manifold ramifications? What are their mechanisms, their effects and their relations? The issue here can, I believe, be crystallised essentially in the following question: is the analysis of power or of powers to be deduced in one way or another from the economy? Let me make this question and my reasons for posing it somewhat clearer. It is not at all my intention to abstract from what are innumerable and enormous differences; yet despite, and even because of these differences, I consider there to be a certain point in common between the juridical, and let us call it, liberal, conception of political power (found in the *philosophes* of the eighteenth century) and the Marxist conception, or at any rate a certain conception currently held to be Marxist. I would call this common point an economism in the theory of power. By that I mean that in the case of the classic, juridical theory, power is taken to be a right, which one is able to possess like a commodity, and which one can in consequence transfer or alienate, either wholly or partially, through a legal act or through some act that establishes a right, such as takes place through cession or contract. Power is that concrete power which every individual holds, and whose partial or total cession enables political power or sovereignty to be established. This theoretical construction is essentially based on the idea that the constitution of political power obeys the model of a legal transaction involving a contractual type of exchange (hence the clear analogy that runs through all these theories between power and commodities, power and wealth). In the other case—I am thinking here of the general Marxist conception of power—one finds none of all that. Nonetheless, there is something else inherent in this latter conception, something which one might term an economic functionality of power. This economic functionality is present to the extent that power is conceived primarily in terms of the role it plays in the maintenance simultaneously of the relations of production and of a class domination which the development and specific forms of the forces of production have rendered possible. On this view, then, the historical *raison d'être* of political power is to be found in the economy. Broadly speaking, in the first case we have a political power whose formal model is discoverable in the process of exchange, the economic circulation of commodities; in the second case, the historical *raison d'être* of political power and the principle of its concrete forms and actual functioning, is located in the economy. Well then, the problem involved in the researches to which I refer can, I believe, be broken down in the following manner: in the first place, is power always in a subordinate position relative to the economy? Is it always in the service of, and ultimately answerable to, the economy? Is its essential end and purpose to serve the economy? Is it destined to realise, consolidate, maintain and reproduce the relations appropriate to the economy and essential to its functioning? In the second place, is power modelled upon the commodity? Is it something that one possesses, acquires, cedes through force or contract, that one alienates or recovers, that circulates, that voids this or that region? Or, on the contrary, do we need to employ varying tools in its analysis—even, that is, when we allow that it effectively remains the case that the relations of power do indeed remain profoundly enmeshed in and with economic relations and participate with them in a common circuit? If that is the case, it is not the models of functional subordination or formal isomorphism that will characterise the interconnection between politics and the economy. Their indissolubility will be of a different order, one that it will be our task to determine.

What means are available to us today if we seek to conduct a non-economic analysis of power? Very few, I believe. We have in the first place the assertion that power is neither given, nor exchanged, nor recovered, but rather exercised, and that it only exists in action. Again, we have at our disposal another assertion to the effect that power is not primarily the maintenance and reproduction of economic relations, but is above all a relation of force. The questions to be posed would then be these: if power is exercised, what sort of exercise does it involve? In what does it consist? What is its mechanism? There is an immediate answer that many contemporary analyses would appear to offer: power is essentially that which represses. Power represses nature, the instincts, a class, individuals. Though one finds this definition of power as repression endlessly repeated in present day discourse, it is not that discourse which invented it—Hegel first spoke of it, then Freud and later Reich. In any case, it has become almost automatic in the parlance of the times to define power as an organ of repression. So should not the analysis of power be first and foremost an analysis of the mechanisms of repression?

Then again, there is a second reply we might make: if power is properly speaking the way in which relations of forces are deployed and given concrete expression, rather than analysing it in terms of cession, contract or alienation, or functionally in terms of its maintenance of the relations of production, should we not analyse it primarily in terms of *struggle, conflict* and *war?* One would then confront the original hypothesis, according to which power is essentially repression, with a second hypothesis to the effect that power is war, a war continued by other means. This reversal of Clausewitz's assertion that war is politics continued by other means has a triple significance: in the first place, it implies that the relations of power that function in a society such as ours essentially rest upon a definite relation of forces that is established at a determinate, historically specifiable moment, in war and by war. Furthermore, if it is true that political power puts an end to war, that it installs, or tries to install, the reign of peace in civil society, this by no means implies that it suspends the effects of war or neutralises the disequilibrium revealed in the final battle. The role of political power, on this hypothesis, is perpetually to re-inscribe this relation through a form of unspoken warfare; to re-inscribe it in social institutions, in economic inequalities, in language, in the bodies themselves of each and everyone of us.

So this would be the first meaning to assign to the inversion of Clausewitz's aphorism that war is politics continued by other means. It consists in seeing politics as sanctioning and upholding the disequilibrium of forces that was displayed in war. But there is also something else that the inversion signifies, namely, that none of the political struggles, the conflicts waged over power, with power, for power, the alterations in the relations of forces, the favouring of certain tendencies, the reinforcements etc., etc., that come about within this 'civil peace'—that none of these phenomena in a political system should be interpreted except as the continuation of war. They should, that is to say, be understood as episodes, factions and displacements in that same war. Even when one writes the history of peace and its institutions, it is always the history of this war that one is writing. The third, and final, meaning to be assigned to the inversion of Clausewitz's aphorism, is that the end result can only be the outcome of war, that is, of a contest of strength, to be decided in the last analyses by recourse to arms. The political battle would cease with this final battle. Only a final battle of that kind would put an end, once and for all, to the exercise of power as continual war.

So, no sooner do we attempt to liberate ourselves from economistic analyses of power, than two solid hypotheses offer themselves: the one argues that the mechanisms of power are those of repression. For convenience sake, I shall term this Reich's hypothesis. The other argues that the basis of the relationship of power lies in the hostile engagement of forces. Again for convenience, I shall call this Nietzsche's hypothesis.

These two hypotheses are not irreconcilable; they even seem to be linked in a fairly convincing manner. After all, repression could be seen as the political consequence of war, somewhat as oppression, in

the classic theory of political right, was seen as the abuse of sovereignty in the juridical order.

One might thus contrast two major systems of approach to the analysis of power: in the first place, there is the old system as found in the *philosophes* of the eighteenth century. The conception of power as an original right that is given up in the establishment of sovereignty, and the contract, as matrix of political power, provide its points of articulation. A power so constituted risks becoming oppression when ever it over-extends itself, whenever—that is—it goes beyond the terms of the contract. Thus we have contract-power, with oppression as its limit, or rather as the transgression of this limit. In contrast, the other system of approach no longer tries to analyse political power according to the schema of contract-oppression, but in accordance with that of war-repression, and, at this point, repression no longer occupies the place that oppression occupies in relation to the contract, that is, it is not abuse, but is, on the contrary, the mere effect and continuation of a relation of domination. On this view, repression is none other than the realisation, within the continual warfare of this pseudo-peace, of a perpetual relationship of force.

Thus we have two schemes for the analysis of power. The contract-oppression schema, which is the juridical one, and the domination-repression or war-repression schema for which the pertinent opposition is not between the legitimate and illegitimate, as in the first schema, but between struggle and submission.

It is obvious that all my work in recent years has been couched in the schema of struggle-repression, and it is this—which I have hitherto been attempting to apply—which I have now been forced to reconsider, both because it is still insufficiently elaborated at a whole number of points, and because I believe that these two notions of repression and war must themselves be considerably modified if not ultimately abandoned. In any case, I believe that they must be submitted to closer scrutiny.

I have always been especially diffident of this notion of repression: it is precisely with reference to those genealogies of which I was speaking just now—of the history of penal right, of psychiatric power, of the control of infantile sexuality etc.—that I have tried to demonstrate to you the extent to which the mechanisms that were brought into operation in these power formations were something quite other, or in any case something much more, than repression. The need to investigate this notion of repression more thoroughly springs therefore from the impression I have that it is wholly inadequate to the analysis of the mechanisms and effects of power that it is so pervasively used to characterise today.

## LECTURE TWO

The course of study that I have been following until now—roughly since 1970/71—has been concerned with the *how* of power. I have tried, that is, to relate its mechanisms to two points of reference, two limits: on the one hand, to the rules of right that provide a formal delimitation of power; on the other, to the effects of truth that this power produces and transmits, and which in their turn reproduce this power. Hence we have a triangle: power, right, truth.

Schematically, we can formulate the traditional question of political philosophy in the following terms: how is the discourse of truth, or quite simply, philosophy as that discourse which *par excellence* is concerned with truth, able to fix limits to the rights of power? That is the traditional question. The one I would prefer to pose is rather different. Compared to the traditional, noble and philosophic question it is much more down to earth and concrete. My problem is rather this: what rules of right are implemented by the relations of power in the production of discourses of truth? Or alternatively, what type of power is susceptible of producing discourses of truth that in a society such as ours are endowed with such potent effects? What I mean is this: in a society such as ours, but basically in any society, there are manifold relations of power which permeate, characterise and constitute the social body, and these relations of power cannot themselves be established, consolidated nor implemented without the production, accumulation, circulation and functioning of a dis-

course. There can be no possible exercise of power without a certain economy of discourses of truth which operates through and on the basis of this association. We are subjected to the production of truth through power and we cannot exercise power except through the production of truth. This is the case for every society, but I believe that in ours the relationship between power, right and truth is organised in a highly specific fashion. If I were to characterise, not its mechanism itself, but its intensity and constancy, I would say that we are forced to produce the truth of power that our society demands, of which it has need, in order to function: we *must* speak the truth; we are constrained or condemned to confess or to discover the truth. Power never ceases its interrogation, its inquisition, its registration of truth: it institutionalises, professionalises and rewards its pursuit. In the last analysis, we must produce truth as we must produce wealth, indeed we must produce truth in order to produce wealth in the first place. In another way, we are also subjected to truth in the sense in which it is truth that makes the laws, that produces the true discourse which, at least partially, decides, transmits and itself extends upon the effects of power. In the end, we are judged, condemned, classified, determined in our undertakings, destined to a certain mode of living or dying, as a function of the true discourses which are the bearers of the specific effects of power.

So, it is the rules of right, the mechanisms of power, the effects of truth or if you like, the rules of power and the powers of true discourses, that can be said more or less to have formed the general terrain of my concern, even if, as I know full well, I have traversed it only partially and in a very zig-zag fashion. I should like to speak briefly about this course of research, about what I have considered as being its guiding principle and about the methodological imperatives and precautions which I have sought to adopt. As regards the general principle involved in a study of the relations between right and power, it seems to me that in Western societies since Medieval times it has been royal power that has provided the essential focus around which legal thought has been elaborated. It is in reponse to the demands of royal power, for its profit and to serve as its instrument or justification, that the juridical edifice of our own society has been developed. Right in the West is the King's right. Naturally everyone is familiar with the famous, celebrated, repeatedly emphasised role of the jurists in the organisation of royal power. We must not forget that the re-vitalisation of Roman Law in the twelfth century was the major event around which, and on whose basis, the juridical edifice which had collapsed after the fall of the Roman Empire was reconstructed. This resurrection of Roman Law had in effect a technical and constitutive role to play in the establishment of the authoritarian, administrative, and, in the final analysis, absolute power of the monarchy. And when this legal edifice escapes in later centuries from the control of the monarch, when, more accurately, it is turned against that control, it is always the limits of this sovereign power that are put in question, its prerogatives that are challenged. In other words, I believe that the King remains the central personage in the whole legal edifice of the West. When it comes to the general organisation of the legal system in the West, it is essentially with the King, his rights, his power and its eventual limitations, that one is dealing. Whether the jurists were the King's henchmen or his adversaries, it is of royal power that we are speaking in every case when we speak of these grandiose edifices of legal thought and knowledge.

There are two ways in which we do so speak. Either we do so in order to show the nature of the juridical armoury that invested royal power, to reveal the monarch as the effective embodiment of sovereignty, to demonstrate that his power, for all that it was absolute, was exactly that which befitted his fundamental right. Or, by contrast, we do so in order to show the necessity of imposing limits upon this sovereign power, of submitting it to certain rules of right, within whose confines it had to be exercised in order for it to remain legitimate. The essential role of the theory of right, from medieval times onwards, was to fix the legitimacy of power; that is the major problem around which the whole theory of right and sovereignty is organised.

When we say that sovereignty is the central prob-

lem of right in Western societies, what we mean basically is that the essential function of the discourse and techniques of right has been to efface the domination intrinsic to power in order to present the latter at the level of appearance under two different aspects: on the one hand, as the legitimate rights of sovereignty, and on the other, as the legal obligation to obey it. The system of right is centred entirely upon the King, and it is therefore designed to eliminate the fact of domination and its consequences.

My general project over the past few years has been, in essence, to reverse the mode of analysis followed by the entire discourse of right from the time of the Middle Ages. My aim, therefore, was to invert it, to give due weight, that is, to the fact of domination, to expose both its latent nature and its brutality. I then wanted to show not only how right is, in a general way, the instrument of this domination—which scarcely needs saying—but also to show the extent to which, and the forms in which, right (not simply the laws but the whole complex of apparatuses, institutions and regulations responsible for their application) transmits and puts in motion relations that are not relations of sovereignty, but of domination. Moreover, in speaking of domination I do not have in mind that solid and global kind of domination that one person exercises over others, or one group over another, but the manifold forms of domination that can be exercised within society. Not the domination of the King in his central position, therefore, but that of his subjects in their mutual relations: not the uniform edifice of sovereignty, but the multiple forms of subjugation that have a place and function within the social organism.

The system of right, the domain of the law, are permanent agents of these relations of domination, these polymorphous techniques of subjugation. Right should be viewed, I believe, not in terms of a legitimacy to be established, but in terms of the methods of subjugation that it instigates.

The problem for me is how to avoid this question, central to the theme of right, regarding sovereignty and the obedience of individual subjects in order that I may substitute the problem of domination and subjugation for that of sovereignty and obedience.

Given that this was to be the general line of my analysis, there were a certain number of methodological precautions that seemed requisite to its pursuit. In the very first place, it seemed important to accept that the analysis in question should not concern itself with the regulated and legitimate forms of power in their central locations, with the general mechanisms through which they operate, and the continual effects of these. On the contrary, it should be concerned with power at its extremities, in its ultimate destinations, with those points where it becomes capillary, that is, in its more regional and local forms and institutions. Its paramount concern, in fact, should be with the point where power surmounts the rules of right which organise and delimit it and extends itself beyond them, invests itself in institutions, becomes embodied in techniques, and equips itself with instruments and eventually even violent means of material intervention. To give an example: rather than try to discover where and how the right of punishment is founded on sovereignty, how it is presented in the theory of monarchical right or in that of democratic right, I have tried to see in what ways punishment and the power of punishment are effectively embodied in a certain number of local, regional, material institutions, which are concerned with torture or imprisonment, and to place these in the climate—at once institutional and physical, regulated and violent—of the effective apparatuses of punishment. In other words, one should try to locate power at the extreme points of its exercise, where it is always less legal in character.

A second methodological precaution urged that the analysis should not concern itself with power at the level of conscious intention or decision; that it should not attempt to consider power from its internal point of view and that it should refrain from posing the labyrinthine and unanswerable question: 'Who then has power and what has he in mind? What is the aim of someone who possesses power?' Instead, it is a case of studying power at the point where its intention, if it has one, is completely invested in its real and effective practices. What is needed is a study of power in its external visage, at the point where it is in direct and immediate rela-

tionship with that which we can provisionally call its object, its target, its field of application, there—that is to say—where it installs itself and produces its real effects.

Let us not, therefore, ask why certain people want to dominate, what they seek, what is their overall strategy. Let us ask, instead, how things work at the level of on-going subjugation, at the level of those continuous and uninterrupted processes which subject our bodies, govern our gestures, dictate our behaviours etc. In other words, rather than ask ourselves how the sovereign appears to us in his lofty isolation, we should try to discover how it is that subjects are gradually, progressively, really and materially constituted through a multiplicity of organisms, forces, energies, materials, desires, thoughts etc. We should try to grasp subjection in its material instance as a constitution of subjects. This would be the exact opposite of Hobbes' project in *Leviathan,* and of that, I believe, of all jurists for whom the problem is the distillation of a single will—or rather, the constitution of a unitary, singular body animated by the spirit of sovereignty—from the particular wills of a multiplicity of individuals. Think of the scheme of Leviathan: insofar as he is a fabricated man, Leviathan is no other than the amalgamation of a certain number of separate individualities, who find themselves reunited by the complex of elements that go to compose the State; but at the heart of the State, or rather, at its head, there exists something which constitutes it as such, and this is sovereignty, which Hobbes says is precisely the spirit of Leviathan. Well, rather than worry about the problem of the central spirit, I believe that we must attempt to study the myriad of bodies which are constituted as peripheral *subjects* as a result of the effects of power.

A third methodological precaution relates to the fact that power is not to be taken to be a phenomenon of one individual's consolidated and homogeneous domination over others, or that of one group or class over others. What, by contrast, should always be kept in mind is that power, if we do not take too distant a view of it, is not that which makes the difference between those who exclusively possess and retain it, and those who do not have it and submit to it. Power must by analysed as something which circulates, or rather as something which only functions in the form of a chain. It is never localised here or there, never in anybody's hands, never appropriated as a commodity or piece of wealth. Power is employed and exercised through a net-like organisation. And not only do individuals circulate between its threads; they are always in the position of simultaneously undergoing and exercising this power. They are not only its inert or consenting target; they are always also the elements of its articulation. In other words, individuals are the vehicles of power, not its points of application.

The individual is not to be conceived as a sort of elementary nucleus, a primitive atom, a multiple and inert material on which power comes to fasten or against which it happens to strike, and in so doing subdues or crushes individuals. In fact, it is already one of the prime effects of power that certain bodies, certain gestures, certain discourses, certain desires, come to be identified and constituted as individuals. The individual, that is, is not the *vis-à-vis* of power; it is, I believe, one of its prime effects. The individual is an effect of power, and at the same time, or precisely to the extent to which it is that effect, it is the element of its articulation. The individual which power has constituted is at the same time its vehicle.

There is a fourth methodological precaution that follows from this: when I say that power establishes a network through which it freely circulates, this is true only up to a certain point. In much the same fashion we could say that therefore we all have a fascism in our heads, or, more profoundly, that we all have a power in our bodies. But I do not believe that one should conclude from that that power is the best distributed thing in the world, although in some sense that is indeed so. We are not dealing with a sort of democratic or anarchic distribution of power through bodies. That is to say, it seems to me—and this then would be the fourth methodological precaution—that the important thing is not to attempt some kind of deduction of power starting from its centre and aimed at the discovery of the extent to which it permeates into the base, of the degree to which it reproduces itself down to and including the most molecular elements of society. One must rather conduct an *ascending* analysis of power, starting, that is, from its infinitesimal mechanisms, which each have their own history, their own trajectory, their own techniques and tactics, and then see how these mechanisms of power have been—and continue to be—invested, colonised, utilised, involuted, transformed, displaced, extended etc., by ever more general mechanisms and by forms of global domination. It is not that this global domination extends itself right to the base in a plurality of repercussions: I believe that the manner in which the phenomena, the techniques and the procedures of power enter into play at the most basic levels must be analysed, that the way in which these procedures are displaced, extended and altered must certainly be demonstrated; but above all what must be shown is the manner in which they are invested and annexed by more global phenomena and the subtle fashion in which more general powers or economic interests are able to engage with these technologies that are at once both relatively autonomous of power and act as its infinitesimal elements. In order to make this clearer, one might cite the example of madness. The descending type of analysis, the one of which I believe one ought to be wary, will say that the bourgeoisie has, since the sixteenth or seventeenth century, been the dominant class; from this premise, it will then set out to deduce the internment of the insane. One can always make this deduction, it is always easily done and that is precisely what I would hold against it. It is in fact a simple matter to show that since lunatics are precisely those persons who are useless to industrial production, one is obliged to dispense with them. One could argue similarly in regard to infantile sexuality—and several thinkers, including Wilhelm Reich have indeed sought to do so up to a certain point. Given the domination of the bourgeois class, how can one understand the repression of infantile sexuality? Well, very simply—given that the human body had become essentially a force of production from the time of the seventeenth and eighteenth century, all the forms of its expenditure which did not lend themselves to the constitution of the productive forces—and were therefore exposed as redundant—were banned, excluded and repressed. These kinds of deduction are always possible. They are simultaneously correct and false. Above all they are too glib, because one can always do exactly the opposite and show, precisely by appeal to the principle of the dominance of the bourgeois class, that the forms of control of infantile sexuality could in no way have been predicted. On the contrary, it is equally plausible to suggest that what was needed was sexual training, the encouragement of a sexual precociousness, given that what was fundamentally at stake was the constitution of a labour force whose optimal state, as we well know, at least at the beginning of the nineteenth century, was to be infinite: the greater the labour force, the better able would the system of capitalist production have been to fulfil and improve its functions.

I believe that anything can be deduced from the general phenomenon of the domination of the bourgeois class. What needs to be done is something quite different. One needs to investigate historically, and beginning from the lowest level, how mechanisms of power have been able to function. In regard to the confinement of the insane, for example, or the repression and interdiction of sexuality, we need to see the manner in which, at the effective level of the family, of the immediate environment, of the cells and most basic units of society, these phenomena of repression or exclusion possessed their instruments and their logic, in response to a certain number of needs. We need to identify the agents responsible for them, their real agents (those which constituted the immediate social *entourage,* the family, parents, doctors etc.), and not be content to lump them under the formula of a generalised bourgeoisie. We need to see how these mechanisms of power, at a given moment, in a precise conjuncture and by means of a certain number of transformations, have begun to become economically advantageous and politically useful. I think that in this way one could easily manage to demonstrate that what the bourgeoisie needed, or that in which its system discovered its real interests, was not the exclusion of the mad or the surveillance and prohibition of infantile masturbation (for,

to repeat, such a system can perfectly well tolerate quite opposite practices), but rather, the techniques and procedures themselves of such an exclusion. It is the mechanisms of that exclusion that are necessary, the apparatuses of surveillance, the medicalisation of sexuality, of madness, of delinquency, all the micro-mechanisms of power, that came, from a certain moment in time, to represent the interests of the bourgeoisie. Or even better, we could say that to the extent to which this view of the bourgeoisie and of its interests appears to lack content, at least in regard to the problems with which we are here concerned, it reflects the fact that it was not the bourgeoisie itself which thought that madness had to be excluded or infantile sexuality repressed. What in fact happened instead was that the mechanisms of the exclusion of madness, and of the surveillance of infantile sexuality, began from a particular point in time, and for reasons which need to be studied, to reveal their political usefulness and to lend themselves to economic profit, and that as a natural consequence, all of a sudden, they came to be colonised and maintained by global mechanisms and the entire State system. It is only if we grasp these techniques of power and demonstrate the economic advantages or political utility that derives from them in a given context for specific reasons, that we can understand how these mechanisms come to be effectively incorporated into the social whole.

To put this somewhat differently: the bourgeoisie has never had any use for the insane; but the procedures it has employed to exclude them have revealed and realised—from the nineteenth century onwards, and again on the basis of certain transformations—a political advantage, on occasion even a certain economic utility, which have consolidated the system and contributed to its overall functioning. The bourgeoisie is interested in power, not in madness, in the system of control of infantile sexuality, not in that phenomenon itself. The bourgeoisie could not care less about delinquents, about their punishment and rehabilitation, which economically have little importance, but it is concerned about the complex of mechanisms with which delinquency is controlled, pursued, punished and reformed etc.

As for our fifth methodological precaution: it is quite possible that the major mechanisms of power have been accompanied by ideological productions. There has, for example, probably been an ideology of education, an ideology of the monarchy, an ideology of parliamentary democracy etc.; but basically I do not believe that what has taken place can be said to be ideological. It is both much more and much less than ideology. It is the production of effective instruments for the formation and accumulation of knowledge—methods of observation, techniques of registration, procedures for investigation and research, apparatuses of control. All this means that power, when it is exercised through these subtle mechanisms, cannot but evolve, organise and put into circulation a knowledge, or rather apparatuses of knowledge, which are not ideological constructs.

By way of summarising these five methodological precautions, I would say that we should direct our researches on the nature of power not towards the juridical edifice of sovereignty, the State apparatuses and the ideologies which accompany them, but towards domination and the material operators of power, towards forms of subjection and the inflections and utilisations of their localised systems, and towards strategic apparatuses. We must eschew the model of Leviathan in the study of power. We must escape from the limited field of juridical sovereignty and State institutions, and instead base our analysis of power on the study of the techniques and tactics of domination.

This, in its general outline, is the methodological course that I believe must be followed, and which I have tried to pursue in the various researches that we have conducted over recent years on psychiatric power, on infantile sexuality, on political systems, etc. Now as one explores these fields of investigation, observing the methodological precautions I have mentioned, I believe that what then comes into view is a solid body of historical fact, which will ultimately bring us into confrontation with the problems of which I want to speak this year.

This solid, historical body of fact is the juridical-political theory of sovereignty of which I spoke a moment ago, a theory which has had four roles to play. In the first place, it has been used to refer to a mechanism of power that was effective under the feudal monarchy. In the second place, it has served as instrument and even as justification for the construction of the large scale administrative monarchies. Again, from the time of the sixteenth century and more than ever from the seventeenth century onwards, but already at the time of the wars of religion, the theory of sovereignty has been a weapon which has circulated from one camp to another, which has been utilised in one sense or another, either to limit or else to re-inforce royal power: we find it among Catholic monarchists and Protestant anti-monarchists, among Protestant and more-or-less liberal monarchists, but also among Catholic partisans of regicide or dynastic transformation. It functions both in the hands of aristocrats and in the hands of parliamentarians. It is found among the representatives of royal power and among the last feudatories. In short, it was the major instrument of political and theoretical struggle around systems of power of the sixteenth and seventeenth centuries. Finally, in the eighteenth century, it is again this same theory of sovereignty, re-activated through the doctrine of Roman Law, that we find in its essentials in Rousseau and his contemporaries, but now with a fourth role to play: now it is concerned with the construction, in opposition to the administrative, authoritarian and absolutist monarchies, of an alternative model, that of parliamentary democracy. And it is still this role that it plays at the moment of the Revolution.

Well, it seems to me that if we investigate these four roles there is a definite conclusion to be drawn: as long as a feudal type of society survived, the problems to which the theory of sovereignty was addressed were in effect confined to the general mechanisms of power, to the way in which its forms of existence at the higher level of society influenced its exercise at the lowest levels. In other words, the relationship of sovereignty, whether interpreted in a wider or a narrower sense, encompasses the totality of the social body. In effect, the mode in which power was exercised could be defined in its essentials in terms of the relationship sovereign-subject.

But in the seventeenth and eighteenth centuries, we have the production of the an important phenomenon, the emergence, or rather the invention, of a new mechanism of power possessed of highly specific procedural techniques, completely novel instruments, quite different apparatuses, and which is also, I believe, absolutely incompatible with the relations of sovereignty.

This new mechanism of power is more dependent upon bodies and what they do than upon the Earth and its products. It is a mechanism of power which permits time and labour, rather than wealth and commodities, to be extracted from bodies. It is a type of power which is constantly exercised by means of surveillance rather than in a discontinuous manner by means of a system of levies or obligations distributed over time. It presupposes a tightly knit grid of material coercions rather than the physical existence of a sovereign. It is ultimately dependent upon the principle, which introduces a genuinely new economy of power, that one must be able simultaneously both to increase the subjected forces and to improve the force and efficacy of that which subjects them.

This type of power is in every aspect the antithesis of that mechanism of power which the theory of sovereignty described or sought to transcribe. The latter is linked to a form of power that is exercised over the Earth and its products, much more than over human bodies and their operations. The theory of sovereignty is something which refers to the displacement and appropriation on the part of power, not of time and labour, but of goods and wealth. It allows discontinuous obligations distributed over time to be given legal expression but it does not allow for the codification of a continuous surveillance. It enables power to be founded in the physical existence of the sovereign, but not in continuous and permanent systems of surveillance. The theory of sovereignty permits the foundation of an absolute power in the absolute expenditure of power. It does not allow for a calculation of power in terms of the minimum expenditure for the maximum return.

This new type of power, which can no longer be formulated in terms of sovereignty, is, I believe, one of the great inventions of bourgeois society. It has been a fundamental instrument in the constitution of industrial capitalism and of the type of society that is its accompaniment. This non-sovereign power, which lies outside the form of sovereignty, is disciplinary power. Impossible to describe in the terminology of the theory of sovereignty from which it differs so radically, this disciplinary power ought by rights to have led to the disappearance of the grand juridical edifice created by that theory. But in reality, the theory of sovereignty has continued not only to exist as an ideology of right, but also to provide the organising principle of the legal codes which Europe acquired in the nineteenth century, beginning with the Napoleonic Code.

Why has the theory of sovereignty persisted in this fashion as an ideology and an organising principle of these major legal codes? For two reasons, I believe. On the one hand, it has been, in the eighteenth and again in the nineteenth century, a permanent instrument of criticism of the monarchy and of all the obstacles that can thwart the development of disciplinary society. But at the same time, the theory of sovereignty, and the organisation of a legal code centred upon it, have allowed a system of right to be superimposed upon the mechanisms of discipline in such a way as to conceal its actual procedures, the element of domination inherent in its techniques, and to guarantee to everyone, by virtue of the sovereignty of the State, the exercise of his proper sovereign rights. The juridical systems—and this applies both to their codification and to their theorisation—have enabled sovereignty to be democratised through the constitution of a public right articulated upon collective sovereignty, while at the same time this democratisation of sovereignty was fundamentally determined by and grounded in mechanisms of disciplinary coercion.

To put this in more rigorous terms, one might say that once it became necessary for disciplinary constraints to be exercised through mechanisms of domination and yet at the same time for their effective exercise of power to be disguised, a theory of sovereignty was required to make an appearance at the level of the legal apparatus, and to re-emerge in its codes. Modern society, then, from the nineteenth century up to our own day, has been characterised on the one hand, by a legislation, a discourse, an organisation based on public right, whose principle of articulation is the social body and the delegative status of each citizen; and, on the other hand, by a closely linked grid of disciplinary coercions whose purpose is in fact to assure the cohesion of this same social body. Though a theory of right is a necessary companion to this grid, it cannot in any event provide the terms of its endorsement. Hence these two limits, a right of sovereignty and a mechanism of discipline, which define, I believe, the arena in which power is exercised. But these two limits are so heterogeneous that they cannot possibly be reduced to each other. The powers of modern society are exercised through, on the basis of, and by virtue of, this very heterogeneity between a public right of sovereignty and a polymorphous disciplinary mechanism. This is not to suggest that there is on the one hand an explicit and scholarly system of right which is that of sovereignty, and, on the other hand, obscure and unspoken disciplines which carry out their shadowy operations in the depths, and thus constitute the bedrock of the great mechanism of power. In reality, the disciplines have their own discourse. They engender, for the reasons of which we spoke earlier, apparatuses of knowledge (*savoir*) and a multiplicity of new domains of understanding. They are extraordinarily inventive participants in the order of these knowledge-producing apparatuses. Disciplines are the bearers of a discourse, but this cannot be the discourse of right. The discourse of discipline has nothing in common with that of law, rule, or sovereign will. The disciplines may well be the carriers of a discourse that speaks of a rule, but this is not the juridical rule deriving from sovereignty, but a natural rule, a norm. The code they come to define is not that of law but that of normalisation. Their reference is to a theoretical horizon which of necessity has nothing in common with the edifice of right. It is human science which constitutes their domain, and clinical knowledge their jurisprudence.

In short, what I have wanted to demonstrate in the course of the last few years is not the manner in which at the advance front of the exact sciences the uncertain, recalcitrant, confused dominion of human behaviour has little by little been annexed to science: it is not through some advancement in the rationality of the exact sciences that the human sciences are gradually constituted. I believe that the process which has really rendered the discourse of the human sciences possible is the juxtaposition, the encounter between two lines of approach, two mechanisms, two absolutely heterogeneous types of discourse: on the one hand there is the re-organisation of right that invests sovereignty, and on the other, the mechanics of the coercive forces whose exercise takes a disciplinary form. And I believe that in our own times power is exercised simultaneously through this right and these techniques and that these techniques and these discourses, to which the disciplines give rise invade the area of right so that the procedures of normalisation come to be ever more constantly engaged in the colonisation of those of law. I believe that all this can explain the global functioning of what I would call a *society of normalisation.* I mean, more precisely, that disciplinary normalisations come into ever greater conflict with the juridical systems of sovereignty: their incompatibility with each other is ever more acutely felt and apparent; some kind of arbitrating discourse is made ever more necessary, a type of power and of knowledge that the sanctity of science would render neutral. It is precisely in the extension of medicine that we see, in some sense, not so much the linking as the perpetual exchange or encounter of mechanisms of discipline with the principle of right. The developments of medicine, the general medicalisation of behaviours, conducts, discourses, desires etc., take place at the point of intersection between the two heterogeneous levels of discipline and sovereignty. For this reason, against these usurpations by the disciplinary mechanisms, against this ascent of a power that is tied to scientific knowledge, we find that there is no solid recourse available to us today, such being our situation, except that which lies precisely in the return to a theory of right organised around sovereignty and articulated upon its ancient principle. When today one wants to object in some way to the disciplines and all the effects of power and knowledge that are linked to them, what is it that one does, concretely, in real life, what do the Magistrates Union[1] or other similar institutions do, if not precisely appeal to this canon of right, this famous, formal right, that is said to be bourgeois, and which in reality is the right of sovereignty? But I believe that we find ourselves here in a kind of blind alley: it is not through recourse to sovereignty against discipline that the effects of disciplinary power can be limited, because sovereignty and disciplinary mechanisms are two absolutely integral constituents of the general mechanism of power in our society.

If one wants to look for a non-disciplinary form of power, or rather, to struggle against disciplines and disciplinary power, it is not towards the ancient right of sovereignty that one should turn, but towards the possibility of a new form of right, one which must indeed be anti-disciplinarian, but at the same time liberated from the principle of sovereignty. It is at this point that we once more come up against the notion of repression, whose use in this context I believe to be doubly unfortunate. On the one hand, it contains an obscure reference to a certain theory of sovereignty, the sovereignty of the sovereign rights of the individual, and on the other hand, its usage introduces a system of psychological reference points borrowed from the human sciences, that is to say, from discourses and practices that belong to the disciplinary realm. I believe that the notion of repression remains a juridical-disciplinary notion whatever the critical use one would make of it. To this extent the critical application of the notion of repression is found to be vitiated and nullified from the outset by the two-fold juridical and disciplinary reference it contains to sovereignty on the one hand and to normalisation on the other.

## Note

1. This Union, established after 1968, has adopted a radical line on civil rights, the law and the prisons.

# JÜRGEN HABERMAS
~

## INTRODUCTION

## THOMAS A. MCCARTHY

Jürgen Habermas is the leading contemporary representative of the Frankfurt School of Critical Theory, the first generation of which included thinkers like Max Horkheimer, Theodor Adorno, Herbert Marcuse, and Walter Benjamin. Born in 1929 in Düsseldorf, Germany, he studied at the universities of Göttingen, Zurich, and Bonn after World War II, receiving the doctorate in 1954. From 1956 to 1959 he was Adorno's assistant at the Institute for Social Research in Frankfurt. After habilitating at Marburg University in 1961, he taught philosophy and sociology at the universities of Heidelberg and Frankfurt before becoming codirector-director of the Max Planck Institute in Starnberg in 1971. In 1983 he returned to the University of Frankfurt where he was Professor of Philosophy until his retirement in 1994.

Habermas's life and work have been deeply influenced by the traumatic events of his youth under national socialism. From the time of his involvement with the German student movement in the 1960s, he has been one of Germany's most prominent public intellectuals, speaking out on a wide array of issues, from violations of civil liberties and attempts to "historicize" the Holocaust, to immigration policy and the course of German reunification. These public interventions in the form of essays and lectures have been collected in the many volumes of his *Kleine Politische Schriften.*

Habermas's scholarly work, which aspires to a comprehensive critical theory of modern society, ranges across many of the humanities and social sciences. His earliest and latest writings focused on the normative foundations and empirical preconditions of democratic self-governance. Thus *The Structural Transformation of the Public Sphere* (1962) was a historical, sociological, and philosophical account of the rise of the classical liberal "public sphere" as an arena for critical public discussion of matters of general concern. While the historical features of the bourgeois public sphere reflected the particular constellation of interests that gave rise to it, Habermas argued, the idea it claimed to embody, of legitimating political authority through rational discussion and reasoned agreement, remained central to democratic theory. Thirty years later Habermas returned to these themes in his major political-theoretical work, *Between Facts and Norms* (1992), where he elaborated a "discourse theory" of deliberative democracy around the idea of legitimation by appeal to reasons that are tested in public discourse among free and equal citizens of a constitutional democracy.

One could read Habermas's extensive writings in the intervening years as a protracted examination of the cultural, psychological, and social preconditions for and barriers to the effective realization of this form of deliberative democracy. In the 1960s, in such works as *Theory and Practice* (1963), *On the Logic of the Social Sciences* (1967), and *Knowledge and Human Interests* (1968), he launched a methodological and epistemological critique of positivism to clear the way for critical social theory as a means of enlightening political consciousness and guiding political practice. Over the next two decades, in such works as *Legitimation Crisis* (1973), *Communication and the Evolution of Society* (1976), *Moral Consciousness and Communicative Action* (1983), and *The Philosophical Discourse of Modernity* (1985), he developed the detailed accounts of communication, socialization, sociocultural development, rationality, morality, and legitimacy that were to serve as the underpinnings of his critical theory of modern society. That theory was given its most systematic statement in the two volumes of his monumental *Theory of Communicative Action* (1981), which highlighted the tendencies in contemporary society toward a "colonization of the lifeworld" by forces emerging from the economy and the state, such that markets and bureaucracies have come increasingly to dominate in more and more spheres of modern life. Their relentless attack upon the "communicative infrastructures" of society can be contained, Habermas argued, only by a countervailing expansion of the power of public communication, in particular by subordinating the operations of the economy and the government to informed, critical, public discourse.

In the years since the publication of *Between Facts and Norms,* Habermas has further elaborated his conception of deliberative democracy and demonstrated its relevance to current debates on multiculturalism, nationalism, globalization, and cosmopolitanism in a series of essays collected in such works as *The Inclusion of the Other* (1996) and *The Postnational Constellation* (1998). The two essays included in this volume are taken from the former collection and are concerned more with conceptual and normative issues in the theory of democracy than with empirical and critical questions of its actual practice. A central theme of both essays is what Habermas takes to be the "internal relation" in democratic theory between, on the one hand, the liberal stress on constitutionally guaranteed "negative liberties" that secure individual freedom of choice and, on the other hand, the republican emphasis on the "positive liberties" of political participation that underwrite popular sovereignty. The function of the system of basic citizenship rights, he argues, is simultaneously to secure *both* personal and political autonomy; and the medium in which this is accomplished is modern positive law. Individual rights and liberties are an "enabling condition" of such law, and agreements arrived at through public discourse and negotiation are its only source of legitimation.

Universal morality alone cannot legitimate positive, enacted law. Rather, moral justification is only one element of democratic decision-making processes that also include negotiation and compromise, pragmatic considerations, and "ethical" questions having to do with collective goods, values, and identities central to the self-understandings of particular democratic polities. As a result, constitutional "projects" to articulate and actualize the basic principles of democratic government and the basic rights of citizens ineluctably also express the particular cultural contexts and historical circumstances in which they are founded and developed. They are situated and continuing efforts, in ever changing circumstances, to interpret and embody in practices and institutions the ideal of democratic self-determination by free and equal citizens.

An important implication of Habermas's view of the internal relation between the basic values of liberal individualism and civic republicanism is that equal individual rights can be secured only through democratic public life; for substantive—in contrast to merely formal—equality requires coming to some common understanding about the specific respects in which citizens will be treated equally. As his remarks on the politics of women's equality illustrate, this in turn requires sensitivity to the systematic causes of de facto inequalities in citizens' capacities to exercise de jure equal rights. And that can be fostered and sustained, he argues, only through citizens' participation in public political discourse, for there is no other nonpaternalistic way to determine the concrete meaning and preconditions of equal rights, equal respect, equal consideration, equal treatment, and the like.

In this view, a central feature of democratic society is the political public sphere, about which Habermas wrote at the very beginning of his intellectual career. It is only through the informed, critical, public discussion of the governed that the administrative powers of government can be effectively monitored and channeled by the "communicative power" of citizens. Independent public forums, voluntary associations, social movements, and other networks and processes of unofficial communication in civil society, including the mass media, are the basis of democratic self-governance. And the culturally and politically mobilized publics who make use of them to identify, interpret, and debate social problems are its lifeblood. Not even constitutional principles are exempt from this public use of reason. Because public discourse is inherently open and reflexive, our understanding of the principles of justice must remain so as well. Normative political theory can do no more than spell out the basic conditions and presuppositions of democratic deliberation and leave all substantive matters to the public use of reason by participants themselves. Anything beyond this should be understood as a contribution to public debate and thus susceptible to all its vicissitudes.

There is a vast and growing secondary literature on Habermas in English. A good place to begin might be with his own account of his life and work in the collection of interviews edited by Peter Dews, *Autonomy and Solidarity* (London: Verso, 1992). General discussions of his work in the 1960s and 1970s can be found in Thomas McCarthy, *The Critical Theory of Jürgen Habermas* (Cambridge, Mass. MIT Press, 1978), and of his work into the 1980s in Seyla Benhabib, *Critique Norm and Utopia* (New York: Columbia University Press, 1986) and Stephen White, *The Recent Work of Juergen Habermas* (Cambridge: Cambridge University Press, 1988). Raymond Geuss offers a critical study of Habermas's earlier work in *The Idea of a Critical Theory* (Cambridge: Cambridge University Press, 1982), and J. M. Bernstein of his later work in *Recovering Ethical Life* (London: Routledge, 1995). William Rehg's *Insight and Solidarity* (Berkeley: University of California Press, 1994) offers a systematic treatment of Habermas's "discourse ethics" or moral theory; his political theory is discussed by Kenneth Baynes, *The Normative Grounds of Social Criticism* (Albany: State University of New York Press, 1992); and by Simone Chambers, *Reasonable Democracy* (Ithaca, N.Y.: Cornell University Press, 1996). Some of his interventions in public debates in Germany are reviewed by Robert Holub, *Jürgen Habermas: Critic in the Public Sphere* (London: Routledge, 1991). Among the collections of critical essays on Habermas's work that contain useful treatments of his political thought are C. Calhoun (ed.), *Habermas and the Public Sphere* (Cambridge, Mass.: MIT Press, 1992); S. White (ed.), *The Cambridge Companion to Habermas* (Cambridge: Cambridge University Press, 1995); J. Meehan (ed.), *Feminists Read Habermas* (New York, Routledge, 1995); and M. Rosenfeld and A. Arato (eds.), *Habermas on Law and Democracy* (Berkeley: University of California Press, 1998).

# Three Normative Models of Democracy

In what follows I refer to the idealized distinction between the "liberal" and the "republican" understanding of politics—terms which mark the fronts in the current debate in the United States initiated by the so-called communitarians. Drawing on the work of Frank Michelman, I will begin by describing the two polemically contrasted models of democracy with specific reference to the concept of the citizen, the concept of law, and the nature of processes of political will-formation. In the second part, beginning with a critique of the "ethical overload" of the republican model, I introduce a third, procedural model of democracy for which I propose to reserve the term "deliberative politics."

## I

The crucial difference between liberalism and republicanism consists in how the role of the democratic process is understood. According to the "liberal" view, this process accomplishes the task of programming the state in the interest of society, where the state is conceived as an apparatus of public administration, and society is conceived as a system of market-structured interactions of private persons and their labor. Here politics (in the sense of the citizens' political will-formation) has the function of bundling together and bringing to bear private social interests against a state apparatus that specializes in the administrative employment of political power for collective goals.

On the republican view, politics is not exhausted by this mediating function but is constitutive for the socialization process as a whole. Politics is conceived as the reflexive form of substantial ethical life. It constitutes the medium in which the members of quasi-natural solidary communities become aware of their dependence on one another and, acting with full deliberation as citizens, further shape

From *The Inclusion of the Other: Studies in Political Theory,* Cambridge, Massachusetts: The MIT Press, 1998. Reprinted by permission of The MIT Press.

and develop existing relations of reciprocal recognition into an association of free and equal consociates under law. With this, the liberal architectonic of government and society undergoes an important change. In addition to the hierarchical regulatory apparatus of sovereign state authority and the decentralized regulatory mechanism of the market—that is, besides administrative power and self-interest—*solidarity* appears as a third source of social integration.

This horizontal political will-formation aimed at mutual understanding or communicatively achieved consensus is even supposed to enjoy priority, both in a genetic and a normative sense. An autonomous basis in civil society independent of public administration and market-mediated private commerce is assumed as a precondition for the practice of civic self-determination. This basis prevents political communication from being swallowed up by the government apparatus or assimilated to market structures. Thus, on the republican conception, the political public sphere and its base, civil society, acquire a strategic significance. Together they are supposed to secure the integrative power and autonomy of the communicative practice of the citizens.[1] The uncoupling of political communication from the economy has as its counterpart a coupling of administrative power with the communicative power generated by political opinion- and will-formation.

These two competing conceptions of politics have different consequences.

(a) In the first place, their concepts of the citizen differ. According to the liberal view, the citizen's status is determined primarily by the individual rights he or she has vis-à-vis the state and other citizens. As bearers of individual rights citizens enjoy the protection of the government as long as they pursue their private interests within the boundaries drawn by legal statutes—and this includes protection against state interventions that violate the legal prohibition on government interference. Individual rights are negative rights that guarantee a domain of freedom of choice within which legal persons are freed from external compulsion. Political rights have the same structure: they afford citizens the opportunity to assert their private interests in such a way

that, by means of elections, the composition of parliamentary bodies, and the formation of a government, these interests are finally aggregated into a political will that can affect the administration. In this way the citizens in their political role can determine whether governmental authority is exercised in the interest of the citizens as members of society.[2]

According to the republican view, the status of citizens is not determined by the model of negative liberties to which these citizens can lay claim as private persons. Rather, political rights—preeminently rights of political participation and communication—are positive liberties. They do not guarantee freedom from external compulsion, but guarantee instead the possibility of participating in a common practice, through which the citizens can first make themselves into what they want to be—politically responsible subjects of a community of free and equal citizens.[3] To this extent, the political process does not serve just to keep government activity under the surveillance of citizens who have already acquired a prior social autonomy through the exercise of their private rights and prepolitical liberties. Nor does it act only as a hinge between state and society, for democratic governmental authority is by no means an original authority. Rather, this authority proceeds from the communicative power generated by the citizens' practice of self-legislation, and it is legitimated by the fact that it protects this practice by institutionalizing public freedom.[4] The state's *raison d'être* does not lie primarily in the protection of equal individual rights but in the guarantee of an inclusive process of opinion- and will-formation in which free and equal citizens reach an understanding on which goals and norms lie in the equal interest of all. In this way the republican citizen is credited with more than an exclusive concern with his or her private interests.

(b) The polemic against the classical concept of the legal person as bearer of individual rights reveals a controversy about the concept of law itself. Whereas on the liberal conception the point of a legal order is to make it possible to determine which individuals in each case are entitled to which rights, on the republican conception these "subjective" rights owe their existence to an "objective" legal order that both enables and guarantees the integrity of an autonomous life in common based on equality and mutual respect. On the one view, the legal order is conceived in terms of individual rights; on the other, their objective legal content is given priority.

To be sure, this conceptual dichotomy does not touch on the *intersubjective* content of rights that demand reciprocal respect for rights and duties in symmetrical relations of recognition. But the republican concept at least points in the direction of a concept of law that accords equal weight to both the integrity of the individual and the integrity of the community in which persons as both individuals and members can first accord one another reciprocal recognition. It ties the legitimacy of the laws to the democratic procedure by which they are generated and thereby preserves an internal connection between the citizens' practice of self-legislation and the impersonal sway of the law:

> For republicans, rights ultimately are nothing but determinations of prevailing political will, while for liberals, some rights are always grounded in a "higher law" of transpolitical reason or revelation. . . . In a republican view, a community's objective, common good substantially consists in the success of its political endeavor to define, establish, effectuate, and sustain the set of rights (less tendentiously, laws) best suited to the conditions and *mores* of that community. Whereas in a contrasting liberal view, the higher-law rights provide the transactional structures and the curbs on power required so that pluralistic pursuit of diverse and conflicting interests may proceed as satisfactorily as possible.[5]

The right to vote, interpreted as a positive right, becomes the paradigm of rights as such, not only because it is constitutive for political self-determination, but because it shows how inclusion in a community of equals is connected with the individual right to make autonomous contributions and take personal positions on issues:

> [T]he claim is that we all take an interest in each others' enfranchisement because (i) our choice lies

between hanging together and hanging separately; (ii) hanging together depends on reciprocal assurances to all of having one's vital interests heeded by others; and (iii) in the deeply pluralized conditions of contemporary American society, such assurances are not attainable through virtual representation, but only by maintaining at least the semblance of a politics in which everyone is conceded a voice.[6]

This structure, read off from the political rights of participation and communication, is extended to *all* rights via the legislative process constituted by political rights. Even the authorization guaranteed by private law to pursue private, freely chosen goals simultaneously imposes an obligation to respect the limits of strategic action which are agreed to be in the equal interest of all.

(c) The different ways of conceptualizing the role of citizen and the law express a deeper disagreement about the nature of the political process. On the liberal view, politics is essentially a struggle for positions that grant access to administrative power. The political process of opinion- and will-formation in the public sphere and in parliament is shaped by the competition of strategically acting collectives trying to maintain or acquire positions of power. Success is measured by the citizens' approval of persons and programs, as quantified by votes. In their choices at the polls, voters express their preferences. Their votes have the same structure as the choices of participants in a market, in that their decisions license access to positions of power that political parties fight over with a success-oriented attitude similar to that of players in the market. The input of votes and the output of power conform to the same pattern of strategic action.

According to the republican view, the political opinion- and will-formation in the public sphere and in parliament does not obey the structures of market processes but rather the obstinate structures of a public communication oriented to mutual understanding. For politics as the citizens' practice of self-determination, the paradigm is not the market but dialogue. From this perspective there is a structural difference between communicative power, which proceeds from political communication in the form of discursively generated majority decisions, and the administrative power possessed by the governmental apparatus. Even the parties that struggle over access to positions of governmental power must bend themselves to the deliberative style and the stubborn character of political discourse:

> Deliberation . . . refers to a certain attitude toward social cooperation, namely, that of openness to persuasion by reasons referring to the claims of others as well as one's own. The deliberative medium is a good faith exchange of views—including participants' reports of their own understanding of their respective vital interests— . . . in which a vote, if any vote is taken, represents a pooling of judgments.[7]

Hence the conflict of opinions conducted in the political arena has legitimating force not just in the sense of an authorization to occupy positions of power; on the contrary, the ongoing political discourse also has binding force for the way in which political authority is exercised. Administrative power can only be exercised on the basis of policies and within the limits laid down by laws generated by the democratic process.

## II

So much for the comparison between the two models of democracy that currently dominate the discussion between the so-called communitarians and liberals, above all in the US. The republican model has advantages and disadvantages. In my view it has the advantage that it preserves the radical democratic meaning of a society that organizes itself through the communicatively united citizens and does not trace collective goals back to "deals" made between competing private interests. Its disadvantage, as I see it, is that it is too idealistic in that it makes the democratic process dependent on the virtues of citizens devoted to the public weal. For politics is not concerned in the first place with questions of ethical self-understanding. The mistake of the republican view consists in an ethical foreshortening of political discourse.

To be sure, ethical discourses aimed at achieving a collective self-understanding—discourses in which participants attempt to clarify how they understand themselves as members of a particular nation, as members of a community or a state, as inhabitants of a region, etc., which traditions they wish to cultivate, how they should treat each other, minorities, and marginal groups, in what sort of society they want to live—constitute an important part of politics. But under conditions of cultural and social pluralism, behind politically relevant goals there often lie interests and value-orientations that are by no means constitutive of the identity of the political community as a whole, that is, for the totality of an intersubjectively shared form of life. These interests and value-orientations, which conflict with one another within the same polity without any prospect of consensual resolution, need to be counterbalanced in a way that cannot be effected by ethical discourse, even though the results of this nondiscursive counterbalancing are subject to the proviso that they must not violate the basic values of a culture. The balancing of interests takes the form of reaching a compromise between parties who rely on their power and ability to sanction. Negotiations of this sort certainly presuppose a readiness to cooperate, that is, a willingness to abide by the rules and to arrive at results that are acceptable to all parties, though for different reasons. But compromise-formation is not conducted in the form of a rational discourse that neutralizes power and excludes strategic action. However, the fairness of compromises is measured by presuppositions and procedures which for their part are in need of rational, indeed normative, justification from the standpoint of justice. In contrast with ethical questions, questions of justice are not by their very nature tied to a particular collectivity. Politically enacted law, if it is to be legitimate, must be at least in harmony with moral principles that claim a general validity that extends beyond the limits of any concrete legal community.

The concept of deliberative politics acquires empirical relevance only when we take into account the multiplicity of forms of communication in which a common will is produced, that is, not just ethical self-clarification but also the balancing of interests and compromise, the purposive choice of means, moral justification, and legal consistency-testing. In this process the two types of politics which Michelman distinguishes in an ideal-typical fashion can interweave and complement one another in a rational manner. "Dialogical" and "instrumental" politics can *interpenetrate* in the medium of deliberation if the corresponding forms of communication are sufficiently institutionalized. Everything depends on the conditions of communication and the procedures that lend the institutionalized opinion- and will-formation their legitimating force. The third model of democracy, which I would like to propose, relies precisely on those conditions of communication under which the political process can be presumed to produce rational results because it operates deliberatively at all levels.

Making the proceduralist conception of deliberative politics the cornerstone of the theory of democracy results in differences both from the republican conception of the state as an ethical community and from the liberal conception of the state as the guardian of a market society. In comparing the three models, I take my orientation from that dimension of politics which has been our primary concern, namely, the democratic opinion- and will-formation that issue in popular elections and parliamentary decrees.

According to the liberal view, the democratic process takes place exclusively in the form of compromises between competing interests. Fairness is supposed to be guaranteed by rules of compromise-formation that regulate the general and equal right to vote, the representative composition of parliamentary bodies, their order of business, and so on. Such rules are ultimately justified in terms of liberal basic rights. According to the republican view, by contrast, democratic will-formation is supposed to take the form of an ethical discourse of self-understanding; here deliberation can rely for its content on a culturally established background consensus of the citizens, which is rejuvenated through the ritualistic reenactment of a republican founding act. Discourse

theory takes elements from both sides and integrates them into the concept of an ideal procedure for deliberation and decision making. Weaving together negotiations and discourses of self-understanding and of justice, this democratic procedure grounds the presumption that under such conditions reasonable or fair results are obtained. According to this proceduralist view, practical reason withdraws from universal human rights or from the concrete ethical life of a specific community into the rules of discourse and forms of argumentation that derive their normative content from the validity-basis of action oriented to reaching understanding, and ultimately from the structure of linguistic communication.[8]

These descriptions of the structures of democratic process set the stage for different normative conceptualizations of state and society. The sole presupposition is a public administration of the kind that emerged in the early modern period together with the European state system and in functional interconnection with a capitalist economic system. According to the republican view, the citizens' political opinion- and will-formation forms the medium through which society constitutes itself as a political whole. Society is centered in the state; for in the citizens' practice of political self-determination the polity becomes conscious of itself as a totality and acts on itself via the collective will of the citizens. Democracy is synonymous with the political self-organization of society. This leads to a polemical understanding of politics as directed against the state apparatus. In Hannah Arendt's political writings one can see the thrust of republican arguments: in opposition to the civic privatism of a depoliticized population and in opposition to the acquisition of legitimation through entrenched parties, the political public sphere should be revitalized to the point where a regenerated citizenry can, in the forms of a decentralized self-governance, (once again) appropriate the governmental authority that has been usurped by a self-regulating bureaucracy.

According to the liberal view, this separation of the state apparatus from society cannot be eliminated but only bridged by the democratic process. However, the weak normative connotations of a regulated balancing of power and interests stands in need of constitutional channeling. The democratic will-formation of self-interested citizens, construed in minimalist terms, constitutes just one element within a constitution that disciplines governmental authority through normative constraints (such as basic rights, separation of powers, and legal regulation of the administration) and forces it, through competition between political parties, on the one hand, and between government and opposition, on the other, to take adequate account of competing interests and value orientations. This state-centered understanding of politics does not have to rely on the unrealistic assumption of a citizenry capable of acting collectively. Its focus is not so much the input of a rational political will-formation but the output of successful administrative accomplishments. The thrust of liberal arguments is directed against the disruptive potential of an administrative power that interferes with the independent social interactions of private persons. The liberal model hinges not on the democratic self-determination of deliberating citizens but on the legal institutionalization of an economic society that is supposed to guarantee an essentially non-political common good through the satisfaction of the private aspirations of productive citizens.

Discourse theory invests the democratic process with normative connotations stronger than those of the liberal model but weaker than those of the republican model. Once again, it takes elements from both sides and fits them together in a new way. In agreement with republicanism, it gives center stage to the process of political opinion- and will-formation, but without understanding the constitution as something secondary; on the contrary, it conceives the basic principles of the constitutional state as a consistent answer to the question of how the demanding communicative presuppositions of a democratic opinion- and will-formation can be institutionalized. Discourse theory does not make the success of deliberative politics depend on a collectively acting citizenry but on the institutionalization of corresponding procedures. It no longer operates with the concept of a social whole centered in the state and conceived as a goal-oriented subject writ large. But neither does it

localize the whole in a system of constitutional norms mechanically regulating the interplay of powers and interests in accordance with the market model. Discourse theory altogether jettisons the assumptions of the philosophy of consciousness, which invite us either to ascribe the citizens' practice of self-determination to one encompassing macrosubject or to apply the anonymous rule of law to competing individuals. The former approach represents the citizenry as a collective actor which reflects the whole and acts for its sake; on the latter, individual actors function as dependent variables in systemic processes that unfold blindly because no consciously executed collective decisions are possible over and above individual acts of choice (except in a purely metaphorical sense).

Discourse theory works instead with the *higher-level intersubjectivity* of communication processes that unfold in the institutionalized deliberations in parliamentary bodies, on the one hand, and in the informal networks of the public sphere, on the other. Both within and outside parliamentary bodies geared to decision making, these subjectless modes of communication form arenas in which a more or less rational opinion- and will-formation concerning issues and problems affecting society as a whole can take place. Informal opinion-formation result in institutionalized election decisions and legislative decrees through which communicatively generated power is transformed into administratively utilizable power. As on the liberal model, the boundary between state and society is respected; but here civil society, which provides the social underpinning of autonomous publics, is as distinct from the economic system as it is from the public administration. This understanding of democracy leads to the normative demand for a new balance between the three resources of money, administrative power, and solidarity from which modern societies meet their need for integration and regulation. The normative implications are obvious: the integrative force of solidarity, which can no longer be drawn solely from sources of communicative action, should develop through widely expanded autonomous public spheres as well as through legally institutionalized procedures of democratic deliberation and decision making and gain sufficient strength to hold its own against the other two social forces—money and administrative power.

## III

This view has implications for how one should understand legitimation and popular sovereignty. On the liberal view, democratic will-formation has the exclusive function of *legitimating* the exercise of political power. The outcomes of elections license the assumption of governmental power, though the government must justify the use of power to the public and parliament. On the republican view, democratic will-formation has the significantly stronger function of *constituting* society as a political community and keeping the memory of this founding act alive with each new election. The government is not only empowered by the electorate's choice between teams of leaders to exercise a largely open mandate, but is also bound in a programmatic fashion to carry out certain policies. More a committee than an organ of the state, it is part of a self-governing political community rather than the head of a separate governmental apparatus. Discourse theory, by contrast, brings a thitd idea into play: the procedures and communicative presuppositions of democratic opinion- and will-formation function as the most important sluices for the discursive rationalization of the decisions of a government and an administration bound by law and statute. On this view, *rationalization* signifies more than mere legitimation but less than the constitution of political power. The power available to the administration changes its general character once it is bound to a process of democratic opinion- and will-formation that does not merely retrospectively monitor the exercise of political power but also programs it in a certain way. Notwithstanding this discursive rationalization, only the political system itself can "act." It is a subsystem specialized for collectively binding decisions, whereas the communicative structures of the public sphere comprise a far-flung network of sensors that respond to the pressure of society-wide problems and stimulate influential opinions. The public opinion which is worked up via democratic procedures into communicative power cannot itself "rule" but can only channel the use of administrative power in specific directions.

The concept of *popular sovereignty* stems from the republican appropriation and revaluation of the early modern notion of sovereignty originally associated with absolutist regimes. The state, which monopolizes the means of legitimate violence, is viewed as a concentration of power which can overwhelm all other temporal powers. Rousseau transposed this idea, which goes back to Bodin, to the will of the united people, fused it with the classical idea of the self-rule of free and equal citizens, and sublimated it into the modern concept of autonomy. Despite this normative sublimation, the concept of sovereignty remained bound to the notion of an embodiment in the (at first actually physically assembled) people. According to the republican view, the at least potentially assembled people are the bearers of a sovereignty that cannot in principle be delegated: in their capacity as sovereign, the people cannot let themselves be represented by others. Constitutional power is founded on the citizens' practice of self-determination, not on that of their representatives. Against this, liberalism offers the more realistic view that, in the constitutional state, the authority emanating from the people is exercised only "by means of elections and voting and by specific legislative, executive, and judicial organs."[9]

These two views exhaust the alternatives only on the dubious assumption that state and society must be conceived in terms of a whole and its parts, where the whole is constituted either by a sovereign citizenry or by a constitution. By contrast to the discourse theory of democracy corresponds the image of a *decentered* society, though with the political public sphere it sets apart an arena for the detection, identification, and interpretation of problems affecting society as a whole. If we abandon the conceptual framework of the philosophy of the subject, sovereignty need neither be concentrated in the people in a concretistic manner nor banished into the anonymous agencies established by the constitution. The "self" of the self-organizing legal community disappears in the subjectless forms of communication that regulate the flow of discursive opinion- and will-formation whose fallible results enjoy the presumption of rationality. This is not to repudiate the intuition associated with the idea of popular sovereignty but rather to interpret it in intersubjective terms. Popular sovereignty, even though it has become anonymous, retreats into democratic procedures and the legal implementation of their demanding communicative presuppositions only to be able to make itself felt as communicatively generated power. Strictly speaking, this communicative power springs from the interactions between legally institutionalized will-formation and culturally mobilized publics. The latter for their part find a basis in the associations of a civil society distinct from the state and the economy alike.

The normative self-understanding of deliberative politics does indeed call for a discursive mode of socialization for the *legal community;* but this mode does not extend to the whole of the society in which the constitutionally established political system is *embedded.* Even on its own proceduralist self-understanding, deliberative politics remains a component of a complex society, which as a whole resists the normative approach of legal theory. In this regard, the discourse-theoretic reading of democracy con-

nects with an objectifying sociological approach that regards the political system neither as the peak nor the center, nor even as the structuring model of society, but as just *one* action system among others. Because it provides a kind of surety for the solution of the social problems that threaten integration, politics must indeed be able to communicate, via the medium of law, with all of the other legitimately ordered spheres of action, however these may be structured and steered. But the political system remains dependent on other functional mechanisms, such as the revenue-production of the economic system, in more than just a trivial sense; on the contrary, deliberative politics, whether realized in the formal procedures of institutionalized opinion- and will-formation or only in the informal networks of the political public sphere, stands in an internal relation to the contexts of a rationalized lifeworld that meets it halfway. Deliberatively filtered political communications are especially dependent on the resources of the lifeworld—on a free and open political culture and an enlightened political socialization, and above all on the initiatives of opinion-shaping associations. These resources emerge and regenerate themselves spontaneously for the most part—at any rate, they can only with difficulty be subjected to political control.

# On the Internal Relation Between the Rule of Law and Democracy

In academia we often mention law and politics in the same breath, yet at the same time we are accustomed to consider law, the rule of law, and democracy as subjects of different disciplines: jurisprudence deals with law, political science with democracy, and each deals with the constitutional state in its own way—jurisprudence in normative terms, political science from an empirical standpoint. The scholarly division of labor continues to operate even when legal scholars attend to law and the rule of law, on the one hand, and will-formation in the constitutional state, on the other; or when social scientists, in the role of sociologists of law, examine law and the constitutional state and, in the role of political scientists, examine the democratic process. The constitutional state and

democracy appear to us as entirely separate objects. There are good reasons for this. Because political rule is always exercised in the form of law, legal systems exist where political force has not yet been domesticated by the constitutional state. And constitutional states exist where the power to govern has not yet been democratized. In short, there are legally ordered governments without constitutional institutions and there are constitutional states without democratic constitutions. Of course, these empirical grounds for a division of labor in the academic treatment of the two subjects by no means imply that from a normative standpoint, the constitutional state could exist without democracy.

In this paper I want to treat several aspects of this

internal relation between the rule of law and democracy. This relation results from the concept of modern law itself (section 1) as well as from the fact that positive law can no longer draw its legitimacy from a higher law (section 2). Modern law is legitimated by the autonomy guaranteed equally to each citizen, and in such a way that private and public autonomy reciprocally presuppose each other (section 3). This conceptual interrelation also makes itself felt in the dialectic of legal and factual equality. It was this dialectic that first elicited the social-welfare paradigm of law as a response to the liberal understanding of law, and today this same dialectic necessitates a proceduralist self-understanding of constitutional democracy (section 4). In closing I will elucidate this proceduralist legal paradigm with the example of the feminist politics of equality (section 5).

## 1  FORMAL PROPERTIES OF MODERN LAW

Since Locke, Rousseau, and Kant, a certain concept of law has gradually prevailed not only in philosophical thought but in the constitutional reality of Western societies. This concept is supposed to account simultaneously for both the positivity and the freedom-guaranteeing character of coercible law. The positivity of law—the fact that norms backed by the threat of state sanction stem from the changeable decisions of a political lawgiver—is bound up with the demand for legitimation. According to this demand, positively enacted law should guarantee the autonomy of all legal persons equally; and the democratic procedure of legislation should in turn satisfy this demand. In this way, an internal relation is established between the coercibility and changeability of positive law on the one hand, and a mode of lawmaking that engenders legitimacy on the other. Hence from a normative perspective there is a conceptual or internal relation—and not simply a historically, accidental relation—between law and democracy, between legal theory and democratic theory.

At first glance, the establishment of this internal relation has the look of a philosophical trick. Yet, as a

matter of fact, the relation is deeply rooted in the presuppositions of our everyday practice of law. For in the mode of validity that attaches to law, the facticity of the state's legal enforcement is intermeshed with the legitimating force of a legislative procedure that claims to be rational in that it guarantees freedom. This is shown in the peculiar ambivalence with which the law presents itself to its addressees and expects their obedience: that is, it leaves its addressees free to approach the law in either of two ways. They can either consider norms merely as factual constraints on their freedom and take a strategic approach to the calculable consequences of possible rule-violations, or they can comply with legal statutes in a performative attitude, indeed comply out of respect for results of a common will-formation that claim legitimacy. Kant already expressed this point with his concept of "legality," which highlighted the connection between these two moments without which legal obedience cannot be reasonably expected: legal norms must be fashioned so that they can be viewed simultaneously in two ways, as coercive and as laws of freedom. These two aspects belong to our understanding of modern law: we consider the validity of a legal norm as equivalent to the explanation that the state can simultaneously guarantee factual enforcement and legitimate enactment—thus it can guarantee, on the one hand, the legality of behavior in the sense of average compliance, which can if necessary be compelled by sanctions; and, on the other hand, the legitimacy of the rule itself, which must always make it possible to comply with the norm out of respect for the law.

Of course, this immediately raises the question of how the legitimacy of rules should be grounded when the rules in question can be changed at any time by the political legislator. Constitutional norms too are changeable; and even the basic norms that the constitution itself has declared nonamendable share with all positive law the fate that they can be abrogated, say, after a change of regime. As long as one was able to fall back on a religiously or metaphysically grounded natural law, the whirlpool of temporality enveloping positive law could be held in check by morality. Situated in a hierarchy of law, temporalized positive law was supposed to remain *subordinate* to an eternally valid moral law, from which it was to receive its lasting orientations. But even aside from the fact that in pluralistic societies such integrating worldviews and collectively binding comprehensive doctrines have in any case disintegrated, modern law, simply by virtue of its formal properties, resists the direct control of a posttraditional morality of conscience, which is, so to speak, all we have left.

## 2  THE COMPLEMENTARY RELATION BETWEEN POSITIVE LAW AND AUTONOMOUS MORALITY

Modern legal systems are constructed on the basis of individual rights. Such rights have the character of releasing legal persons from moral obligations in a carefully circumscribed manner. By introducing rights that concede to agents the latitude to act according to personal preferences, modern law as a whole implements the principle that whatever is not explicitly prohibited is permitted. Whereas in morality an inherent symmetry exists between rights and duties, legal duties are a consequence of entitlements, that is, they result only from statutory constraints on individual liberties. This basic conceptual privileging of rights over duties is explained by the modern concepts of the "legal person" and of the "legal community." The moral universe, which is *unlimited* in social space and historical time, includes *all natural persons* with their complex life histories; morality itself extends to the protection of the integrity of fully individuated persons (*Einzelner*). By contrast, the legal community, which is always localized in space and time, protects the integrity of its members precisely insofar as they acquire the artificial status of *rights bearers*. For this reason, the relation between law and morality is more one of complementarity than of subordination.

The same is true if one compares their relative scope. The matters that require legal regulation are at once both narrower and broader in scope than

morally relevant concerns: narrower inasmuch as legal regulation has access only to external, that is, coercible, behavior, and broader inasmuch as law, as an organizational form of politics, pertains not only to the regulations of interpersonal conflicts but also to the pursuit of political goals and the implementation of policies. Hence legal regulations touch not only on moral questions in the narrow sense, but also on pragmatic and ethical questions, and on forming compromises among conflicting interests. Moreover, unlike the clearly delimited normative validity claimed by moral norms, the *legitimacy* claimed by legal norms is based on various sorts of reasons. The legislative practice of justification depends on a complex network of discourses and bargaining, and not just on moral discourse.

The idea from natural law of a hierarchy of laws at different levels of dignity is misleading. Law is better understood as a functional complement to morality. As positively valid, legitimately enacted, and actionable, law can relieve the morally judging and acting person of the considerable cognitive, motivational, and organizational demands of a morality based entirely on individual conscience. Law can compensate for the weaknesses of a highly demanding morality that—if we judge from its empirical results—provides only cognitively indeterminate and motivationally unreliable results. Naturally, this does not absolve legislators and judges from the concern that the law be in harmony with morality. But legal regulations are too concrete to be legitimated solely through their compatibility with moral principles. From what, then, can positive law borrow its legitimacy, if not from a superior moral law?

Like morality, law too is supposed to protect the autonomy of all persons equally. Law too must prove its legitimacy under this aspect of securing freedom. Interestingly enough, though, the positive character of law forces autonomy to split up in a peculiar way, which has no parallel in morality. Moral self-determination in Kant's sense is a unified concept insofar as it demands of each person, *in propria persona,* that she obey just those norms that she herself posits according to her own impartial judgment, or according to a judgment reached in common with all other persons. However, the binding quality of legal norms does not stem solely from processes of opinion- and will-formation, but arises also from the collectively binding decisions of authorities who make and apply law. This circumstance makes it conceptually necessary to distinguish the role of authors who make (and adjudicate) law from that of addressees who are subject to established law. The autonomy that in the moral domain is all of a piece, so to speak, appears in the legal domain only in the dual form of private and public autonomy.

However, these two moments must then be mediated in such a way that the one form of autonomy does not detract from the other. Each form of autonomy, the individual liberties of the subject of private law and the public autonomy of the citizen, makes the other form possible. This reciprocal relation is expressed by the idea that legal persons can be autonomous only insofar as they can understand themselves, in the exercise of their civic rights, as authors of just those rights which they are supposed to obey as addressees.

## 3   THE MEDIATION OF POPULAR SOVEREIGNTY AND HUMAN RIGHTS

It is therefore not surprising that modern natural law theories have answered the legitimation question by referring, on the one hand, to the principle of *popular sovereignty* and, on the other, to the *rule of law* as guaranteed by human rights. The principle of popular sovereignty is expressed in rights of communication and participation that secure the public autonomy of citizens; the rule of law is expressed in those classical basic rights that guarantee the private autonomy of members of society. Thus the law is legitimated as an instrument for the equal protection of private and public autonomy. To be sure, political philosophy has never really been able to strike a balance between popular sovereignty and human rights, or between the "freedom of the ancients" and the "freedom of the moderns." The political autonomy of citizens is supposed to be embodied in the self-organization of a

community that gives itself its laws through the sovereign will of the people. The private autonomy of citizens, on the other hand, is supposed to take the form of basic rights that guarantee the anonymous rule of law. Once the issue is set up in this way, either idea can be upheld only at the expense of the other. The intuitively plausible co-originality of both ideas falls by the wayside.

*Republicanism,* which goes back to Aristotle and the political humanism of the Renaissance, has always given the public autonomy of citizens priority over the prepolitical liberties of private persons. *Liberalism,* which goes back to John Locke, has invoked the danger of tyrannical majorities and postulated the priority of human rights. According to republicanism, human rights owed their legitimacy to the ethical self-understanding and sovereign self-determination achieved by a political community; in liberalism, such rights were supposed to provide, from the very start, legitimate barriers that prevented the sovereign will of the people from encroaching on inviolable spheres of individual freedom. In their concepts of the legal person's autonomy, Rousseau and Kant certainly aimed to conceive of sovereign will and practical reason as unified in such a way that popular sovereignty and human rights would reciprocally interpret one another. But even they failed to do justice to the co-originality of the two ideas; Rousseau suggests more of a republican reading, Kant more of a liberal one. They missed the intuition they wanted to articulate: that the idea of human rights, which is expressed in the right to equal individual liberties, must neither be merely imposed on the sovereign legislator as an external barrier, nor be instrumentalized as a functional requisite for legislative goals.

To express this intuition properly it helps to view the democratic procedure—which alone provides legitimating force to the law-making process in the context of social and ideological pluralism—from a discourse-theoretical standpoint. Here I assume a principle that I cannot discuss in detail, namely, that a regulation may claim legitimacy only if all those possibly affected by it could consent to it after participating in rational discourses. Now, if discourses—and bargaining processes as well, whose fairness is based on discursively grounded procedures—represent the place where a reasonable political will can develop, then the presumption of reasonability, which the democratic procedure is supposed to ground, ultimately rests on an elaborate communicative arrangement: the presumption depends on the conditions under which one can legally institutionalize the forms of communication necessary for legitimate lawmaking. In that case, the desired internal relation between human rights and popular sovereignty consists in this: human rights themselves are what satisfy the requirement that a civic practice of the public use of communicative freedom be legally institutionalized. Human rights, which make the exercise of popular sovereignty legally possible, cannot be imposed on this practice as an external constraint. Enabling conditions must not be confused with such constraints.

Naturally, this analysis is at first plausible only for those political civil rights, specifically the rights of communication and participation, that safeguard the exercise of political autonomy. It is less plausible for the classical human rights that guarantee the citizens' private autonomy. Here we think in the first instance of the fundamental right to the greatest possible degree of equal individual liberties, though also of basic rights that constitute membership status in a state and provide the individual with comprehensive legal protection. These rights, which are meant to guarantee everyone an equal opportunity to pursue his or her private conception of the good, have an intrinsic value, or at least they are not reducible to their instrumental value for democratic will-formation. We will do justice to the intuition that the classical liberties are co-original with political rights only if we state more precisely the thesis that human rights legally enable the citizens' practice of self-determination. I turn now to this more precise statement.

## 4   THE RELATION BETWEEN PRIVATE AND PUBLIC AUTONOMY

However well-grounded human rights are, they may not be paternalistically foisted, as it were, on a sovereign. Indeed, the idea of citizens' legal autonomy demands that the addressees of law be able to understand themselves at the same time as its authors. It would contradict this idea if the democratic legislator were to discover human rights as though they were (preexisting) moral facts that one merely needs to enact as positive law. At the same time, one must also not forget that when citizens occupy the role of co-legislators they are no longer free to choose the medium in which alone they can realize their autonomy. They participate in legislation only as legal subjects; it is no longer in their power to decide which language they will make use of. The democratic idea of self-legislation *must* acquire its validity in the medium of law itself.

However, when citizens judge in the light of the discourse principle whether the law they make is legitimate, they do so under communicative presuppositions that must themselves be legally institutionalized in the form of political civil rights, and for such institutionalization to occur, the legal code as such must be available. But in order to establish this legal code it is necessary to create the status of legal persons who as bearers of individual rights belong to a voluntary association of citizens and when necessary effectively claim their rights. There is no law without the private autonomy of legal persons in general. Consequently, without basic rights that secure the private autonomy of citizens there is also no medium for legally institutionalizing the conditions under which these citizens, as citizens of a state, can make use of their public autonomy. Thus private and public autonomy mutually presuppose each other in such a way that neither human rights nor popular sovereignty can claim primacy over its counterpart.

This mutual presupposition expresses the intuition that, on the one hand, citizens can make adequate use of their public autonomy only if, on the basis of their equally protected private autonomy, they are sufficiently independent; but that, on the other hand, they can arrive at a consensual regulation of their private autonomy only if they make adequate use of their political autonomy as enfranchised citizens.

The internal relation between the rule of law and democracy has been concealed long enough by the competition between the legal paradigms that have been dominant up to the present. The liberal legal paradigm reckons with an economic society that is institutionalized through private law—above all through property rights and contractual freedom—and left to the spontaneous workings of the market. Such a "private law society" is tailored to the autonomy of legal subjects who as market participants more or less rationally pursue their personal life-plans. This model of society is associated with the normative expectation that social justice can be realized by guaranteeing such a negative legal status, and thus solely by delimiting spheres of individual freedom. The well-founded critique of this supposition gave rise to the social welfare model. The objection is obvious: if the free "capacity to have and acquire" is supposed to guarantee social justice, then an equality in "legal capacity" must exist. As a matter of fact, however, the growing inequalities in economic power, assets, and living conditions have increasingly destroyed the factual preconditions for an equal opportunity to make effective use of equally distributed legal powers. If the normative content of legal equality is not to be inverted, then two correctives are necessary. On the one hand, existing norms of private law must be substantively specified, and on the other, basic social rights must be introduced, rights that ground claims to a more just distribution of socially produced wealth and to more effective protection against socially produced dangers.

In the meantime, of course, this *materialization* of law has in turn created the unintended side effects of welfare paternalism. Clearly, efforts to compensate for actual living conditions and power positions must not lead to "normalizing" interventions of a sort that once again restrict the presumptive beneficiaries' pursuit of an autonomous life-project. The further development of the dialectic of legal and factual equality has shown that both legal paradigms are equally committed to the productivist image of an economic society based on industrial capitalism. This society is supposed to function in such a way

that the expectation of social justice can be satisfied by securing each individual's private pursuit of his or her conception of the good life. The only dispute between the two paradigms concerns whether private autonomy can be guaranteed directly by negative liberties (*Freiheitsrechte*), or whether on the contrary the conditions for private autonomy must be secured through the provision of welfare entitlements. In both cases, however, the internal relation between private and public autonomy drops out of the picture.

## 5   AN EXAMPLE: THE FEMINIST POLITICS OF EQUALITY

In closing, I want to examine the feminist politics of equality to show that policies and legal strategies oscillate helplessly between the conventional paradigms as long as they remain limited to securing private autonomy and disregard how the individual rights of private persons are related to the public autonomy of citizens engaged in lawmaking. For, in the final analysis, private legal subjects cannot enjoy even equal individual liberties if they themselves do not jointly exercise their civic autonomy in order to specify clearly which interests and standards are justified, and to agree on the relevant respects that determine when like cases should be treated alike and different cases differently.

Initially, the goal of liberal policies was to uncouple the acquisition of status from gender identity and to guarantee to women equal opportunities in the competition for jobs, social recognition, education, political power, etc., regardless of the outcome. However, the formal equality that was partially achieved merely made more obvious the ways in which women were *in fact* treated unequally. Social welfare politics responded, especially in the areas of social, labor, and family law, by passing special regulations relating, for example, to pregnancy and child care, or to social hardship in the case of divorce. In the meantime feminist critique has targeted not only the unredeemed demands, but also the ambivalent consequences of successfully implemented welfare programs—for example, the higher risk of women losing their jobs as a result of compensatory regulations, the over-representation of women in lower wage brackets, the problematic issue of "what is in the child's best interests," and in general the progressive feminization of poverty. From a legal standpoint, one reason for this reflexively generated discrimination is found in the overgeneralized classifications used to label disadvantaged situations and disadvantaged groups of persons, because these "false" classifications lead to "normalizing" interventions into how people conduct their lives, interventions that transform what was intended as compensation for damages into new forms of discrimination. Thus instead of guaranteeing liberty, such overprotection stifles it. In areas of law that are of concern to feminism, welfare paternalism takes on a literal meaning to the extent that legislation and adjudication are oriented by traditional patterns of interpretation and thus serve to buttress existing stereotypes of sexual identity.

The classification of gender-specific roles and differences touches on fundamental levels of a society's cultural self-understanding. Radical feminism has only now made us aware of the fallible character of this self-understanding, an understanding that is essentially contested and in need of revision. It rightly insists that the appropriate interpretation of needs and criteria be a matter of public debate in the political public sphere. It is here that citizens must clarify the aspects that determine which differences between the experiences and living situations of (specific groups of) men and women are relevant for an equal opportunity to exercise individual liberties. Thus, this struggle for the equal status of women is a particularly good example of the need for a change of the legal paradigm.

The dispute between the two received paradigms—whether the autonomy of legal persons is better secured through individual liberties for private competition or through publicly guaranteed entitlements for clients of welfare bureaucracies—is superseded by a *proceduralist conception of law*. According to this conception, the democratic process must secure private and public autonomy at the same time: the individual rights that are meant to guarantee to women the autonomy to pursue their lives in the private sphere cannot even be adequately formulated unless the affected persons themselves first articulate and justify in public debate those aspects that are relevant to equal or unequal treatment in typical cases. The private autonomy of equally entitled citizens can be secured only insofar as citizens actively exercise their civic autonomy.

## Notes

1. Cf. H. Arendt, *On Revolution* (New York, 1965); *On Violence* (New York, 1970).

2. Cf. F.I. Michelman, "Political Truth and the Rule of Law," *Tel Aviv University Studies in Law* 8 (1988): 283: "The political society envisioned by bumper-sticker republicans is the society of private rights bearers, an association whose first principle is the protection of the lives, liberties, and estates of its individual members. In that society, the state is justified by the protection it gives to those prepolitical interests; the purpose of the constitution is to ensure that the state apparatus, the government, provides such protection for the people at large rather than serves the special interests of the governors or their patrons; the function of citizenship is to operate the constitution and thereby to motivate the governors to act according to that protective purpose; and the value to you of your political franchise—your right to vote and speak, to have your views heard and counted—is the handle it gives you on influencing the system so that it will adequately heed and protect *your* particular, prepolitical rights and other interests."

3. On the distinction between positive and negative freedom see Ch. Taylor, "What is Human Agency?" in *Human Agency and Language: Philosophical Papers 1* (Cambridge, 1985), pp. 15–44

4. Michelman, "Political Truth and the Rule of Law," p. 284: "In [the] civic constitutional vision, political society is primarily the society not of rights bearers, but of citizens, an association whose first principle is the creation and provision of a public realm within which a people, together, argue and reason about the right terms of social coexistence, terms that they will set together and which they understand as comprising their common good. . . . Hence, the state is justified by its purpose of establishing

and ordering the public sphere within which persons can achieve freedom in the sense of self-government by the exercise of reason in public dialogue."

5. Michelman, "Conceptions of Democracy in American Constitutional Argument: Voting Rights," *Florida Law Review* 41 (1989): 446f. (hereafter "Voting Rights").

6. Michelman, "Voting Rights," p. 484.

7. Michelman, "Conceptions of Democracy in Ameri-

can Constitutional Argument: The Case of Pornography Regulation," *Tennessee Law Review* 291 (1989): 293.

8. Cf. J. Habermas, "Popular Sovereignty as Procedure," in *Between Facts and Norms,* trans. W. Rehg (1996), pp. 463–490.

9. Cf. *The Basic Law of the Federal Republic of Germany,* article 20, sec. 2.

# MARTHA C. NUSSBAUM

## INTRODUCTION

## EVA FEDER KITTAY

Martha Craven Nussbaum was born in Bryn Mawr, Pennsylvania, in 1947. She attended Wellesley College and then New York University, from which she was graduated with a degree in classics. She received her advanced degrees in classical philology from Harvard University, becoming the first woman to be accepted into Harvard's Society of Fellows. She subsequently taught at Harvard and at Brown University and is currently Ernst Freund Professor of Law and Ethics at the University of Chicago, where she holds appointments in the Law School, the School of Divinity, and the departments of philosophy and classics. She served as president of the Central Division of the American Philosophical Association. Among her numerous books are *The Fragility of Goodness* (1986), *Love's Knowledge* (1990), *The Therapy of Desire* (1994), *Poetic Justice* (1996), and *Cultivating Humanity* (1997). She has also served as a research advisor at the U.N.-sponsored World Institute for Development Economics Research.

Nussbaum's political philosophy relies on the work of Aristotle, the Stoics, Kant, Mill, and Rawls. From the Stoics and Kant she draws accounts of human dignity and liberty, from Mill the ideals of equality and individualism that support women's aspirations, from Rawls the ideal of political liberalism, and from Aristotle the universal human capabilities implicit in a flourishing life, applicable to all regardless of cultural differences, gender and sexual distinctions, race, age, or ability.

She also acknowledges her admiration for feminist philosophy. She credits it with putting new questions on the moral and political agenda and infusing them with passion and urgency.

Feminist philosophers have subjected nearly every area of philosophy to scrutiny. They have asked: Do political and moral philosophy adequately reflect the concerns of women? Do standard oppositions such as those of reason and emotion, the public and the private, and the good and the right, disadvantage, devalue, or dismiss women and their contributions to moral and political life? Are presuppositions of moral and political philosophy hostile to women's participation in public life? And, conversely, do norms of public life effectively discourage men's full participation in domestic life?

Feminists have also asked: Have claims about nature and the universal features of personhood been constructed from the perspective of men's interests and men's lives? Can gender-specific features of human experience contribute to gender differences in ethical decision-making? Have areas of thought, feeling, or daily life been ignored or devalued in prevailing traditions of philosophy, because they are associated with women? And are any resources in traditional theories useful in overcoming women's subordinate position?

Nussbaum inserts herself into current feminist debates as a defender of liberalism. In fending off feminist criticisms of liberalism, she does not intend to undermine feminist claims as such but to foster a feminism made sturdier and more protective of women's interests (and so more defensible) by limiting its claims to ones that are warranted by a liberal philosophy. At the same time Nussbaum works to refine the meaning and commitments of liberalism by passing its many versions through the flux of feminism.

In the essay that follows she examines three charges feminists have brought against liberalism. The first is that liberalism is too individualistic to speak to the values shared by women. The second is that liberalism is too abstract to address the specific problems of women, in particular the discrepancy in power between men and women. The third is that liberalism relies excessively on reason and does not take seriously enough the role of emotion in our moral lives.

In response, Nussbaum argues in one of two ways. Either she grants that the feminist objection captures an important insight but misrepresents liberalism, or she maintains that the liberal position, properly understood, is preferable to the feminist one.

With regard to the charge of excessive individualism, she replies that liberalism is not an egoist philosophy. Neither Kant's kingdom of ends nor Mill's utilitarianism should be viewed as egoist doctrines, for they presume a sociality essential to our moral nature. Nor is liberalism correctly charged with advocating that we should depend on ourselves alone. We derive pleasure and benefit from the achievements of others, and the liberalism of Mill and Rawls considers these responses integral to a moral life. Liberalism also values family attachments and benevolent actions.

If, however, the charge against liberalism is that it is concerned for the individual as a separate being, having value over and above any social group, be it state, community, or even family, then she believes liberalism is guilty as charged. But she believes feminism would be unwise to forego this sort of individualism. For in pointing to the separateness of individuals, liberalism is acknowledging that we are born and die as separate individuals, that the food we eat does not go into the belly of another, and that pain inflicted on my body is not felt on your flesh. Such individualism was recognized early in the feminist movement, as exemplified in Elizabeth Cady Stanton's "The Solitude of Self," reprinted in the appendix to this volume.

When the well-being of social groups, even intimate groups such as the family, has been valued over that of individuals, women are usually the ones called on to make the greatest sacrifices. Indeed, Nussbaum remarks that, when it comes to the family, liberalism has failed to be individualistic enough, allowing the welfare of women to be submerged in favor of the welfare of the group.

In regard to the feminist's charge that liberalism is too abstract, Nussbaum maintains that the attack involves a mistaken view of liberalism. The liberal can have a robust understanding of the person, while maintaining that only abstract properties need be considered for certain moral purposes. A feminist response is that liberalism's abstractions are, in fact, projections from men's lives onto those of women. Whether by abstracting from concrete differences or elevating the features of men's lives as universal characteristics of all human beings, liberalism is said to encourage laws and policies that are blind to the concrete realities of women's lives. Equality becomes equality to *men*, where men become the norm of humanity. And "neutral" policies at best fail to improve the status of or at worst disadvantage women. For example, pregnancy leave cannot be addressed with sex-blind legislation or legal decisions.

Nussbaum grants that, were such neutrality central to liberalism, it would have been shown to ill serve women's interests. Yet she claims that liberalism, properly understood, has no such implications. She points to affirmative action, a distinctly liberal policy, that calls for different histories and starting positions to be reflected in law in order to treat all persons in the society with equal dignity and respect. Even if some laws and policies enact a neutrality in the name of liberalism that ignores salient differences, other laws and policies recognize these differences and do so claiming justification in liberal values. The latter, according to Nussbaum, is true liberalism, valuing choice in the service of human dignity.

She grants that, by abstracting from religious and cultural differences, liberalism may conflict with illiberal cultures and religions. But she emphasizes the ways in which the antiliberalism in many cultures and religions have frequently ill served women. And if in the context of a liberal society a woman chooses to align herself with a community in which choice is not valued, shouldn't feminists accept her choice?

As to the charge that liberalism values reason (heralded as masculine) over emotion (deemed and demeaned as feminine), she acknowledges that while some strains of liberalism give a preponderance of moral significance to reason—that of Kant comes readily to mind—she points to other liberal thinkers, such as Adam Smith and John Stuart Mill, who give emotion a prominent place in moral evaluation. So emotion is not inherently inimical to liberalism. Furthermore, since emotion and reason are inextricably linked, any account that gives priority to emotion without giving a place to reason would be mistaken. Nussbaum insists that women need rational reflection along with emotion in order to make considered moral judgments, and women are no less capable of reasoning than men. To suggest otherwise is to reinstate the false claim that women are by nature emotional. Nussbaum insists that all emotions are conditioned by social and cognitive features and are subject to rational inspection—an exercise of reason feminists ought to endorse.

If Nussbaum's defense of liberalism succeeds, then she has shown both that liberalism includes feminist insights and that feminist claims incompatible with liberalism harm women. What, then, is feminist theory's distinctive contribution to political philosophy? Does feminism provide, not theoretical tools, but only an arena for the application of political theory? Nussbaum's later work does not support this conclusion.

In "Rawls and Feminism" and "The Future of Feminist Liberalism," Nussbaum considers the further feminist objections that liberalism is inattentive to global structures that might insure women's well-being, that liberalism is silent on matters of justice within the family, and that liberalism aims at a self-sufficiency that ignores dependencies resulting from physical or mental impairment as well as the need to provide caregiving responsibilities for such dependents. These challenges she finds to be more subtle and less tractable. In responding, Nussbaum continues to develop both a feminism that eschews illiberalism and a liberalism shaped by the concerns of feminism.

For feminist discussion of the patriarchal origins of the contractarian tradition and liberal theory, see Carole Pateman, *The Sexual Contract* (Stanford, Calif.: Stanford University Press, 1988), Carole Pateman (ed.), *The Disorder of Women: Democracy, Feminism and Political Theory* (Stanford, Calif.: Stanford University Press, 1989), Jean Bethke Elshtain, *Public Man, Private Woman* (Princeton, N.J.: Princeton University Press, 1981); and Jean Bethke Elshtain (ed.), *The Family in Political Thought* (Amherst: University of Massachusetts Press, 1982).

For essays critical of liberalism from the perspective of care ethics, see Eva Feder Kittay and Diana T. Meyers (eds.), *Women and Moral Theory* (Totowa, N.J.: Rowman & Littlefield, 1987); Marsha Hanen and Kai Nielsen (eds.), *Science, Morality and Feminist Theory* (Calgary: University of Calgary Press, 1987); Eve Browning Cole and Susan Coultrap-McQuin (eds.), *Explorations in Feminist Ethics* (Bloomington: Indiana University Press, 1992); Virginia Held (ed.), *Justice and Care: Essential Readings in Feminist Ethics* (Boulder, Colo.: Westview Press, 1995). Also see Annette Baier, *Moral Prejudices* (Cambridge, Mass.: Harvard University Press, 1994); Virginia Held, *Feminist Morality* (Chicago: University of Chicago Press, 1993); and Eva Feder Kittay, *Love's Labor* (New York and London: Routledge, 1999).

For essays critical of liberalism from additional feminist ethical perspectives, see Seyla Benhabib and Drucilla Cornell (eds.), *Feminism as Critique: On the Politics of Gender* (Minneapolis: University of Minnesota Press, 1987); Claudia Card (ed.), *Feminist Ethics* (Lawrence: University Press of Kansas, 1991). Also see Iris Marion Young, *Intersecting Voices* (Princeton, N.J.: Princeton University Press, 1997); and Nancy Fraser, *Justus Interruptus* (New York and London: Routledge, 1997).

For the limits of liberalism from legal feminist theorists, see Martha Minow, *Making All the Difference* (Ithaca, N.Y.: Cornell University Press, 1990); and Martha Fineman, *The Neutered Mother* (New York and London: Routledge, 1995).

For characteristic examples of feminist political philosophy, see Cass Sunstein (ed.), *Feminism and Political Theory* (Chicago: University of Chicago Press, 1990); Mary Lyndon Shanley and Carole Pateman (eds.), *Feminist Interpretations and Political Theory* (University Park, Pa.: Pennsylvania State University Press, 1991); Judith Butler and Joan Scott (eds.), *Feminists Theorize the Political* (New York and London: Routledge, 1992); Nancy Hirschmann and Christine DiStefano (eds.), *Revisioning the Political* (Boulder, Colo.: Westview Press, 1996); Mary Lyndon Shanley and Uma Narayan (eds.), *Reconstructing Political Theory* (University Park, Pa.: Pennsylvania State University Press, 1997); and Chantal Mouffe (ed.), *The Return of the Political* (London: Verso, 1994).

For discussions of liberal autonomy and individualism, see Seyla Benhabib, *Situating the Self: Gender, Community, and Postmodernism in Contemporary Ethics* (Cambridge: Polity Press, 1992); and Catriona MacKensie and Natalie Stoljar (eds.), *Relational Autonomy* (Oxford: Oxford University Press, 1999).

Nussbaum's political philosophy was the subject of a symposium in *Ethics* 111 (no. 1) (October, 2000).

# The Feminist Critique of Liberalism

Women around the world are using the language of liberalism. Consider some representative examples from recent publications:

1. Roop Rekha Verma, philosopher and grass-roots activist from Lucknow, India, speaks about the many ways in which Indian religious traditions have devalued women. She concludes that the largest problem with these traditions is that they deprive women of "full personhood." "What is personhood?" Verma asks. "To me three things seem essential for [full personhood]: autonomy, self-respect, and a sense of fulfillment and achievement."[1]

2. Nahid Toubia, the first woman surgeon in the Sudan and woman's health activist, writes of the urgent need to mobilize international opposition to the practice of female genital mutilation (FGM), especially when it is performed on young girls without their consent. "International human rights bodies and organizations," she concludes, "must declare FGM to be violence against women and children and a violation of their rights. . . . If women are to be considered as equal and responsible members of society, no aspect of their physical, psychological, or sexual integrity can be compromised."[2]

3. Describing a meeting at the Indian Institute of Management in Bangalore that brought together widows from all over India for a discussion of their living conditions, *The Hindu Magazine* reports as follows:

> Throughout the week they came to realise many things about themselves and their lives—especially how much they had internalised society's perceptions of them as daughters, wives, mothers and widows (their identity invariably defined in terms of

their relationship to men). . . . They were encouraged to see themselves as persons who had a right to exist even if their husbands were dead, and as citizens who had a right to resources—such as land, housing, employment, credit and ration cards—which would enable them to live and bring up their children (if any) with dignity and self-respect.[3]

Personhood, autonomy, rights, dignity, self-respect: These are the terms of the liberal Enlightenment. Women are using them, and teaching other women to use them when they did not use them before. They treat these terms as though they matter, as though they are the best terms in which to conduct a radical critique of society, as though using them is crucial to women's quality of life.

This situation looks in some respects deeply paradoxical, because liberalism has been thought by many feminists to be a political approach that is totally inadequate to the needs and aims of women, and in some ways profoundly subversive of those aims. Over the past twenty years, feminist political thinkers have put forward many reasons to reject liberalism and to define feminism to some extent in opposition to liberalism. In 1983, in *Feminist Politics and Human Nature,* one of the most influential works of feminist political theory, Alison Jaggar concluded that "the liberal conception of human nature and of political philosophy cannot constitute the philosophical foundation for an adequate theory of women's liberation."[4] Many influential feminist thinkers have agreed with Jaggar, treating liberalism as at best negligent of women's concerns and at worst an active enemy of women's progress.

But liberalism has not died in feminist politics; if anything, with the dramatic growth of the movement to recognize various women's rights as central human rights under international law, its radical feminist potential is just beginning to be realized. So it is time to reassess the charges most commonly made in the feminist critique.

Why should this reassessment matter? It is obvious that the activists from whom I have quoted have gone about their business undaunted by the feminist critique, and they will not be daunted now, if feminists once again tell them that autonomy and personhood are bad notions for feminists to use. In that sense a philosophical investigation could be seen as beside the point. But the international political situation is volatile, and the liberal discourse of personhood and rights has come under attack from many directions, some of them practical and influential.[5] Looking at the case for the defense is therefore not simply a scholarly exercise but also a contribution to practical politics.

In general, I shall argue, liberalism of a kind can be defended against the charges that have been made. The deepest and most central ideas of the liberal tradition are ideas of radical force and great theoretical and practical value. These ideas can be formulated in ways that incorporate what is most valuable in the feminist critique—although liberalism needs to learn from feminism if it is to formulate its own central insights in a fully adequate manner. Taking on board the insights of feminism will not leave liberalism unchanged, and liberalism needs to change to respond adequately to those insights: But it will be changed in ways that make it more deeply consistent with its own most foundational ideas. Another way of putting this is to say that there have been many strands within liberalism; thinking about the feminist critique proves important in choosing among these because feminism shows defects in some forms of liberalism that continue to be influential. Some feminist proposals do resist incorporation even into a reformulated liberalism, but I shall argue that these are proposals that should be resisted by anyone who seeks justice for the world's women.

There is danger in speaking so generally about "liberalism," a danger that has often plagued feminist debates. "Liberalism" is not a single position but a family of positions; Kantian liberalism is profoundly different from classical Utilitarian liberalism, and both of these from the Utilitarianism currently dominant in neoclassical economics. Many critiques of liberalism are really critiques of economic Utilitarianism, and would not hold against the views of Kant or Mill. Some feminist attacks oversimplify the tradition, and in responding to them I run a grave risk of oversimplification myself. When I speak of "liberalism," then, I shall have in mind, above all, the tradition of Kantian liberalism represented today in the political thought of John Rawls, and also the classical Utilitarian liberal tradition, especially as exemplified in the work of John Stuart Mill. I shall also refer frequently to some major precursors, namely, Rousseau,[6] Hume, and Adam Smith. It seems reasonable to assess the feminist critique by holding it up against the best examples of liberal political thought; any critique of liberalism that cannot be taken seriously as a criticism of Kant or Mill probably is not worth discussing.

The thinkers I have chosen are not in agreement on many important matters, but a core of common commitments can be scrutinized with the interests of feminism in mind. At the heart of this tradition is a twofold intuition about human beings: namely, that all, just by being human, are of equal dignity and worth, no matter where they are situated in society, and that the primary source of this worth is a power of moral choice within them, a power that consists in the ability to plan a life in accordance with one's own evaluations of ends.[7] To these two intuitions—which link liberalism at its core to the thought of the Greek and Roman Stoics[8]—the liberal tradition adds one more, which the Stoics did not emphasize: that the moral equality of persons gives them a fair claim to certain types of treatment at the hands of society and politics. What this treatment is will be a subject of debate within the tradition, but the shared starting point is that this treatment must do two closely related things. It must respect and promote the liberty of choice, and it must respect and promote the equal worth of persons as choosers.[9]

To what is liberalism, so conceived, opposed? Here again we must begin crudely, with some rough intuitions that we will try to render more precise as we go on. Liberalism is opposed, first of all, to any approach to politics that turns morally irrelevant differences into systematic sources of social hierarchy.[10] It is opposed, then, to the naturalizing of hierarchies—to feudalism and hereditary monarchy, to the caste system characteristics of traditional Indian society, to related caste hierarchies created in many times and places by differences of race and class and power and religion.[11] It is opposed, second, to forms of political organization that are corporatist or organically organized—that seek a good for the group as a whole without focusing above all on the well-being and agency of individual group members.[12] Finally, it is opposed to a politics that is ideologically based, in the sense that it turns one particular conception of value—whether utopian or religious or traditional—into a mandatory standard imposed by authority on all citizens. Religious intolerance, the establishment of a single church, or the establishment of a single utopian political vision of the good—all these strike the liberal as embodying unequal respect for persons, who ought to be free to follow their conscience in the most important matters. Liberalism is thus opposed to Marxism, to theocratic social orders, and to many forms of authoritarian or tradition-based conservatism.[13]

Liberalism so conceived is centrally about the protection of spheres of choice—not, I claim, in a purely negative way, maximizing the sheer number of choices people get to make for themselves but rather in a way closely tied to the norm of equal respect for personhood. The choices that get protection will be those deemed to be of crucial importance to the protection and expression of personhood. Thus, it would be perfectly consistent for a liberal, beginning from these intuitions, to support certain forms of interference with choice if it could be successfully argued that such interference promotes equal respect rather than undermining it, or, even, that the interference makes no difference to personhood one way or another. All liberal views accept some interference with choice, whether to promote more choice, or to constrain force and fraud, or to produce greater overall prosperity or greater fairness. Starting from the

same basic intuitions, then, liberals can end up in very different positions about many matters, such as the justice of various types of economic redistribution or the appropriateness of various types of paternalistic legislation. They will differ about these policies because they differ about what is crucial to respect the equal worth of persons and to give the power of choice the support that is its due. On this account, both John Rawls and Robert Nozick are liberals because both share a central commitment to liberty and equal respect, although they disagree profoundly about the permissibility of economic redistribution—Rawls holding that it is required to show equal respect for persons; Nozick holding that it is incompatible with such equal respect.[14] Many such disagreements arise within liberalism. They involve, often, not only disagreement about means to shared ends but also different concrete specifications of some highly general ends.[15] On the other hand, it would be hard to conceive of a form of liberalism in which religious toleration was not a central tenet, or one that did not protect certain basic freedoms associated with personal choice, such as freedoms of expression, press, and assembly.[16]

Feminists have made three salient charges against this liberal tradition as a philosophy that might be used to promote women's goals. They have charged, first, that it is too "individualistic": that its focus on the dignity and worth of the individual slights and unfairly subordinates the value to be attached to community and to collective social entities such as families, groups, and classes. They have charged, second, that its ideal of equality is too abstract and formal, that it errs through lack of immersion in the concrete realities of power in different social situations. Finally, they have charged that liberalism errs through its focus on reason, unfairly slighting the role we should give to emotion and care in the moral and political life. All these alleged failings in liberalism are linked to specific failings in the tradition's handling of women's issues. It has frequently been claimed that liberalism cannot atone for these defects without changing utterly, and that feminists interested in progress beyond the status quo would be better off choosing a different political philosophy—

whether a form of socialism or Marxism or a form of communitarian or care-based political theory. Let us examine these charges.

## INDIVIDUAL AND COMMUNITY

The most common feminist charge against liberalism is that it is too "individualistic." By taking the individual to be the basic unit for political thought, it treats the individual as prior to society, as capable, in theory if not in fact, of existing outside all social ties. "Logically if not empirically," writes Jaggar of the liberal view, "human individuals could exist outside a social context; their essential characteristics, their needs and interests, their capacities and desires, are given independently of their social context and are not created or even fundamentally altered by that context" (29).[17] Jaggar later restates this liberal "metaphysical assumption" in an even stronger form: "[E]ach human individual has desires, interests, etc. that in principle can be fulfilled quite separately from the desires and interests of other people" (30). Jaggar later describes this as the liberal assumption of "political solipsism, the assumption that human individuals are essentially self-sufficient entities" (40). She holds that this starting point makes liberals characterize "community and cooperation . . . as phenomena whose existence and even possibility is puzzling," if not downright "impossible" (41).

Described this way, liberal individualism lies perilously close to two positions most feminists agree in rejecting: *egoism* and *normative self-sufficiency.* If liberals really did hold, as Jaggar suggests, that the most basic desires of human beings not only are not shaped by society but also are desires that can be satisfied independently of the satisfactions of desires and interests of others, they would indeed be close to endorsing *psychological egoism,* the view that people are all motivated to pursue their own self-interest above all else. And this, of course, is a view that makes cooperation and community at least somewhat puzzling. On the basis of Jaggar's belief that such self-centered desires and interests are given special weight in liberal politics, she apparently

takes the liberal view to lie close to *normative ethical egoism* as well,[18] that is, to a view that it is always best to promote the satisfaction of one's own self-interest—though such a conclusion is rather puzzling given that the political theories she discusses, both Utilitarian and Rawlsian, aim, by Jaggar's own account, at satisfying *everyone's* interests, not just the interests of a single agent. This would seem to make them far from egoistic.[19]

The charge of egoism is unconvincing. Some liberal thinkers do assume a form of psychological egoism, and it is right of both feminists and others to call that assumption into question. Jaggar cites Amartya Sen's article "Rational Fools,"[20] which criticizes economic Utilitarianism for underrating the importance of sympathy and commitment as motives; she is right to find this a powerful objection to some dominant modes of economic modeling. But she herself admits that this view of human motivation is far from universal in the liberal tradition: that John Rawls has a nonegoistic account of human psychology, and that Mill and Kant think of the human being as moved by both egoistic and nonegoistic motives.[21] She does not give us any reason to believe that the egoism she criticizes in economic Utilitarianism is entailed or even encouraged by anything deep in liberalism itself.

Indeed, even Jaggar's weaker psychological claim about the solitary character of basic desires in liberalism appears to be inaccurate. Liberal theorists vary, and no doubt some, in particular Hobbes[22] and Bentham in their different ways, come close to imagining the human individual as having no natural love of others. Kant, because he holds that all sensuous inclinations are accidents of individual endowment, is agnostic on the matter and thinks that we should not rely on such motives too much if we want to promote benevolence. But other liberal thinkers, such as Mill, Hume, Smith, and Rawls, have an evidently social and other-inclusive psychology, building affiliation with and need for others into the very foundations of their accounts of human motivation and denying that individuals can satisfy their basic desires independently of relationship and community. In a very important way Kant himself agrees: For although he holds that with respect to liking and pleasure and other forms of sensuous inclination we are not reliably inclined toward one another, he holds at the same time that the identity of a human being is given in the most fundamental terms by its membership in a certain sort of community, namely, the kingdom of ends, the community of free rational beings who regard one another with respect and awe and who are committed to promote one another's happiness and well-being because of the respect they feel for one another. Rawls, similarly, imagines the agents in the "original position" as held together by a concern for building a community in which they will live together on terms of mutual cooperation.

As for normative ethical egoism, one could not even begin to argue plausibly that either the Utilitarian or the Kantian tradition is guilty. The essential emphasis of liberal individualism is on respect for *others* as individuals; how can this even initially be thought to involve egoism? Both theories are extremely exigent in the demands they make of moral agents in respect of altruism and duties to others. Utilitarianism holds that an action is right only if it maximizes total or average utility—of all the world's people, in its strictest version; some utilitarians would extend the requirement to animals as well. Clearly this is a theory that demands enormous sacrifices of agents and is very far from letting them go about their self-interested business. Kantian duties to others are not quite as severe, because "imperfect duties" of benevolence have much elasticity, and the Kantian agent is allowed to give preference on many occasions to the near and dear. Nonetheless, it would be utterly implausible to call Kant's an egoistic moral theory; duties to promote the happiness of others are at its very core.[23]

More initially plausible is the suggestion that liberalism, by conceiving the human being in a way that imagines her cut off from all others and yet thriving, encourages normative projects of self-sufficiency—urges people, that is, to minimize their needs for one another and to depend on themselves alone. This, I think, is what Jaggar is really worried about when she speaks of "political solipsism." This is certainly one of the charges feminists commonly think true of liberalism, and one of the ways in which feminists have connected liberalism with common male attitudes and concerns. Feminists hold that by encouraging self-sufficiency as a goal, liberalism subverts the values of family and community, ends that feminists rightly prize. What should we say about this charge?

First, we should note that the normative goal of self-sufficiency is not one that feminists should dismiss without argument. The figures in the Western philosophical tradition who have defended some form of detachment and self-sufficiency as goals—in particular, the Stoics and Spinoza—have done so using powerful arguments, in particular arguments that connect the aim of self-sufficiency with the elimination of anger and revenge and the creation of a just and merciful society. Even if feminists want to reject those arguments, they need to grapple with them rather than viewing them as so many signs of heedless maleness.[24] They also need to grapple with the fact that some feminists, especially in the developing world, endorse self-sufficiency as an appropriate goal. To give just one example, the Self-Employed Women's Association in India (SEWA), one of the most successful feminist employment and credit projects worldwide, makes self-sufficiency one of its ten normative points for women, following Gandhi's use of this concept in the struggle against Britain.[25] These feminists do not take self-sufficiency to entail neglect of others, but they do hold that women care for others best when they are economically situated so that they can survive on their own.

Second, we should observe that the ethical aim of self-sufficiency and detachment is not strongly linked to individualism, that is, to the view that the primary focus of ethical and political thought should be the individual, understood as a separate unit. Indeed, in its most influential world form, in the Buddhist and to some extent also Hindu traditions, the normative doctrine of self-sufficiency and detachment presupposes the recognition that individuals as such do not really exist; it is precisely this recognition that grounds indifference to events, such as deaths of loved ones, that might be thought to matter deeply. Individualism, with its focus on what happens here and now in one's very own life, would seem to have an uphill battle in order to cultivate detachment from such external events.[26]

Next, even if the psychology of liberalism were as described, that is, even if liberals did hold that our most basic desires can be satisfied independently of relationships to others, the normative conclusions about self-sufficiency would not follow. For moral theories frequently demand of people things that go against the grain, and we could demand great concern for others from people to whom such concern does not seem to come naturally. Such appears to have been the enterprise of Jeremy Bentham, who combined an extremely self-centered psychology with an exigent normative altruism. Kant, too, was ready to demand of agents that they disregard their most powerful desires; he famously holds that even a man in whose heart nature has placed little sympathy for others can still be expected to be absolutely committed to their good. Kant certainly believes that all altruistic commitment and loving concern in marriage goes against the grain, given the extremely solipsistic tendencies he imputes to sexual desire, but he expected individuals to live up to those commitments, rather than to seek self-sufficiency.[27] Liberals, then, can and do highly value benevolence, family concern, and social/political involvement, even if they should hold that individuals must control strong selfish inclinations. And, as I have argued, liberalism typically endows individuals with powerful other-regarding motives also.

Liberal individualism, then, does not entail either egoism or normative self-sufficiency. What does it really mean, then, to make the individual the basic unit for political thought? It means, first of all, that liberalism responds sharply to the basic fact that each person has a course from birth to death that is not precisely the same as that of any other person; that each person is one and not more than one, that each feels pain in his or her own body, that the food given to A does not arrive in the stomach of B. The separateness of persons is a basic fact of human life; in stressing it, liberalism stresses something experientially true and fundamentally important. In stressing this fact, the liberal takes her stand squarely in the camp of this worldly experience and rejects forms of revisionary metaphysics (e.g., forms of Buddhism or Platonism) that would deny the reality of our separateness and our substantial embodied character.[28] It rejects the Buddhist picture of persons as mere whorls in the ceaseless flux of world energy and the feudal picture of persons as fundamentally characterized by a set of hierarchical relations. It says that the fundamental entity for politics is a living body that goes from here to there, from birth to death, never fused with any other—that we are hungry and joyful and loving and needy one by one, however closely we may embrace one another.[29] In normative terms, this commitment to the recognition of individual separateness means, for the liberal, that the demands of a collectivity or a relation should not as such be made the basic goal of politics: collectivities, such as the state and even the family, are composed of individuals, who never do fuse, who always continue to have their separate brains and voices and stomachs, however much they love one another. Each of these is separate, and each of these is an end. Liberalism holds that the flourishing of human beings taken one by one is both analytically and normatively prior to the flourishing of the state or the nation or the religious group: analytically, because such unities do not really efface the separate reality of individual lives; normatively because the recognition of that separateness is held to be a fundamental fact for ethics, which should recognize each separate entity as an end not as a means to the ends of others. The central question of politics should not be, How is the organic whole doing?, but rather, How are X and Y and Z and Q doing? The central goal for politics will be some sort of amelioration in the lives of X and Y and Z and Q, where a larger amount of happiness for X, where X might be the ruler, does not compensate for a larger amount of misery for Q, where Q might be a poor rural woman.[30]

Putting things this way does not require us to deny that X might love Y intensely and view his life as worthless without Y; it does not require that Z and Q do not plan their lives together and aim at shared ends; it does not require us to hold that all four do not need one another profoundly or vividly hold the pleasure and pain of one another in their imaginations. It just asks us to concern ourselves with the distribution of resources and opportunities in a certain way, namely, with concern to see how well *each and every one of them* is doing, seeing each and every one as an end, worthy of concern.

Put this way, liberal individualism seems to be a good view for feminists to embrace. For it is clear that women have too rarely been treated as ends in themselves, and too frequently treated as means to the ends of others. Women's individual well-being has far too rarely been taken into account in political and economic planning and measurement. Women have very often been treated as parts of a larger unit, especially the family, and valued primarily for their contribution as reproducers and caregivers rather than as sources of agency and worth in their own right. In connection with this nonindividualistic way of valuing women, questions about families have been asked without asking how well each of its individual members are doing. But conflicts for resources and opportunities are ubiquitous in families around the world, and women are often the victims of these conflicts. When food is scarce in families, it is frequently women, and especially girls, who get less, who become malnourished and die. When there is an illness and only some children can be taken to the doctor, it is frequently girls who are neglected. When only some children can go to school, it is frequently the girls who are kept at home.[31]

Again, when there is violence in the family, women and girls are overwhelmingly likely to be its victims. Sexual abuse during childhood and adolescence, forced prostitution (again, often in childhood), domestic violence and marital rape, and genital mutilation all are extremely common parts of women's lives. Many of the world's women do not have the right to consent to a marriage, and few have any recourse from ill treatment within it. Divorce, even if legally available, is commonly not a practical option given women's economic dependency and lack of educational and employment opportunities.[32]

To people who live in the midst of such facts, it is important to say, I am a separate person and an indi-

vidual. I count for something as such, and my pain is not wiped out by someone else's satisfaction. When we reflect that a large number of the world's women inhabit traditions that value women primarily for the care they give to others rather than as ends, we have all the more reason to insist that liberal individualism is good for women.

There is no doubt that liberalism deserves feminist criticism on this point. For, as many feminists have long pointed out, where women and the family are concerned, liberal political thought has not been nearly individualist enough. Liberal thinkers tended to segment the private from the public sphere, considering the public sphere to be the sphere of individual rights and contractual arrangements, the family to be a private sphere of love and comfort into which the state should not meddle. This tendency grew, no doubt, out of a legitimate concern for the protection of choice—but too few questions were asked about whose choices were thereby protected. This meant that liberals often failed to notice the extent to which law and institutions shape the family and determine the privileges and rights of its members. Having failed to notice this, they all too frequently failed to ask whether there were legal deficiencies in this sphere that urgently needed addressing. In 1869, John Stuart Mill already urged British law to address the problem of marital rape, which, he said, made the lot of women lower than that of slaves:

> Hardly any slave . . . is a slave at all hours and all minutes. . . . But it cannot be so with the wife. Above all, a female slave has (in Christian countries) an admitted right, and is considered under a moral obligation, to refuse to her master the last familiarity. Not so the wife: however brutal a tyrant she may unfortunately be chained to—though she may know that he hates her, though it may be his daily pleasure to torture her, and though she may feel it impossible not to loathe him—he can claim from her and enforce the lowest degradation of a human being, that of being made the instrument of an animal function contrary to her inclinations.[33]

Though Mill seems excessively sanguine here about the female slave,[34] he is right on target about the wife, and he sees what a deep violation of basic liberal tenets is involved in the failure to legislate against marital rape. Again, in the same passage, he argues that the laws that deny the wife equal legal rights over children are also a profound violation of personhood and autonomy.[35] In a similar way, he diagnoses other distortions of the family structure caused by male power and the laws that express it, arguing for women's full equality in all that relates to citizenship and therefore for many changes in disabling family laws.

Mill supports his argument in part by appeal to consistency, saying that liberalism cannot plausibly deny women the rights it vindicates for men. But he also argues that *male* citizenship in a liberal regime is ill served by a mode of family organization based on subordination. For such a family order is a vestige of monarchical power and raises up despots who are ill prepared to respect the rights of their fellow citizens.

> Think what it is to a boy, to grow up to manhood in the belief that without any merit or any exertion of his own, though he may be the most frivolous and empty or the most ignorant and stolid of mankind, by the mere fact of being born a male he is by right the superior of all and every one of an entire half of the human race: including probably some whose real superiority to himself he has daily or hourly occasion to feel. . . . Is it imagined that all this does not pervert the whole manner of existence of the man, both as an individual and as a social being? It is an exact parallel to the feeling of a hereditary king that he is excellent above others by being born a king, or a noble by being born a noble. The relation between husband and wife is very like that between lord and vassal, except that the wife is held to more unlimited obedience than the vassal was. However the vassal's character may have been affected, for better or worse, by his subordination, who can help seeing that the lord's was affected greatly for the worse? . . . The self-worship of the monarch, or of the feudal superior, is matched by the self-worship of the male. Human beings do not grow up from childhood in the possession of unearned distinctions, without pluming themselves upon them.

In short, Mill argues, the stability of a liberal regime demands legal reform of the family. All liberals

should and must seek the "advantage of having the most universal and pervading of all human relations regulated by justice instead of injustice."[36]

Mill's arguments in *Subjection* showed that a concern for the individual well-being of family members and a determination to use law to further that concern were in no way alien to liberalism. Indeed, they grew naturally, as he shows, out of liberalism's concern for the fair treatment of each and every individual and its disdain for feudalism and monarchical power, the caste-like ascendancy of morally irrelevant distinctions. But most of the liberal tradition did not follow Mill's lead. Thus, John Rawls, while envisaging a society in which each individual's well-being would be a matter of social concern, still imagined the contracting individuals as heads of households, who would be expected to take thought altruistically for the interests of family members.[37] Here Rawls adopted a strategy similar to that of economist Gary Becker when he assumed that the head of the household is a beneficent altruist who will adequately take thought for the interests of all family members.[38] Liberal reluctance to interfere with the family has run very deep; dispiritingly, many liberal thinkers have failed to notice that the family is not always characterized by a harmony of interests.[39] No model of the family can be adequate to reality if it fails to take into account competition for scarce resources, divergent interests, and differences of power.[40]

Liberalism has much to learn from feminism in this area. It should begin by learning the facts of women's hunger, domestic violence, marital rape, and unequal access to education. It should go on to correct these facts by laws and by moral education. It should also consider the implications of women's individuality for many traditional areas of law and policy, prominently including divorce and taxation.[41] But notice that, as Mill already argued, what we see here is not a failure intrinsic to liberalism itself. It is, in fact, a failure of liberal thinkers to follow their own thought thorough to its socially radical conclusion. What is wrong with the views of the family endorsed by Becker, Rawls, and others is not that they are too individualist but that they are not individualist enough. They assume too much organic unity and harmony. They give people too much credit for altruism and are not worried enough about the damages of competition. For this reason they fail to ask rigorously their own question, namely, How is each and every individual doing? They fail to ask this, perhaps, because they are focused on the autonomy and freedom of males, and they want to give these males plenty of scope for planning their lives in the private sphere. But that is not the liberal tradition, when this freedom is bought at the expense of violence and death to other individuals. To treat males this way is, as Mill said, tantamount to treating them as kings, who have a hereditary title to subordinate others. To treat any group or person this way runs counter to the deepest instincts of the liberal tradition.

For these reasons, theorists eager to remedy the wrongs done to women in the family have been able to propose internal criticisms of liberalism, rather than its wholesale rejection. Susan Moller Okin's *Justice, Gender, and the Family* criticizes liberal theory severely for its failure to consider injustice in the family. But she argues, plausibly, that John Rawls's theory of justice can be reformulated—along lines suggested by Rawls himself when he insisted that the family was one of the institutions that is part of the "basic structure of society," to be ordered in accordance with principles of justice.[42] In this feminist reformulation, parties in the original position would be individuals, rather than representatives of household units;[43] and parties in the original position, in addition to being ignorant of their wealth, class, and conception of the good, would also be ignorant of their sex. Okin argues that this would lead them to design institutions in which the influence of gender (i.e., of the social hierarchies correlated with biological sex) was minimized, and opportunities and resources would be equitably distributed within the family.[44] Rawls has now accepted many parts of this proposal.[45]

In economics, too, approaches to the family have responded to feminist criticism by becoming more rather than less individualistic. Becker himself has now acknowledged that his model assumed too much altruism and that other motives should be ascribed to family members.[46] Although he has not explicitly urged the disaggregation of the family unit into its individual bargaining agents, such a "bargaining model of the family" is by now increasingly dominant in mainstream economics.[47]

In a very similar manner, international women's activists, taking international human rights agencies to task for their neglect of issues such as marital rape, domestic violence, marital consent, and women's hunger, have not moved to jettison the language of human rights. Instead, they have insisted that the major rights already on the agenda be vindicated for women, and also that rights of women to be free from gender-specific abuses be added to the list of human rights. Once again, the defect found in international agencies such as the United Nations is not that they have stressed individualism too much but that, deferring to tradition and male power, they have not done so consistently and deeply enough. Charlotte Bunch, who coordinated the Global Campaign for Women's Human Rights at the United Nations 1993 World Conference on Human Rights, eloquently describes the feminist liberal program: "The concept of human rights, like all vibrant visions, is not static or the property of any one group; rather, its meaning expands as people reconceive of their needs and hopes in relation to it. In this spirit, feminists redefine human rights abuses to include the degradation and violation of women."[48]

This liberal program is already producing transformations in many countries. Some rights language in constitutions and statutes around the world is vague and aspirational, of little practical help. But there is real change. With increasing success in many countries, women are claiming rights of bodily integrity within their marriages;[49] with the help of international agencies and legal reform, they are also achieving a stronger economic bargaining position as family members.[50] In a wide variety of areas, including education, reproduction, and nutrition, they have been winning the right to be recognized as separate beings whose well-being is distinct from that of a husband's. Just so, the widows who gathered in Bangalore were learning to think of themselves not as discarded adjuncts of a family unit, half dead things, but as centers of thought and choice and action, citizens who could make claims against the state for respect and resources. All this is liberal individualism, and liberal individualism, consistently followed through, entails a radical feminist program.

A deep strategic question arises at this point. When liberal people and states prove obtuse, refusing women's legitimate demands to be treated as ends, at what point should women—in pursuit of that liberal end—prefer revolutionary strategies that depart from liberal politics? Many feminists have discovered that Mill is correct: "The generality of the male sex cannot yet tolerate the idea of living with an equal." In consequence, legitimate arguments are met, again and again, not with rational engagement but with a resistance that keeps "throwing up fresh intrenchments of argument to repair any breach made in the old" but is in actuality quite impervious to reason.[51] This sort of thing makes revolutionary collective action deeply attractive to many women. And indeed, in many parts of the world, women have to at least some extent advanced their well-being through alliance with Marxist movements. It is beyond my scope here to give an account of when it is acceptable to use illiberal means for liberal ends, or to give advice to women who are faced with real choices between obtuse liberalism and profeminist collectivism. Even in the United States and Europe, the repeated experience of male irrationality may legitimately cause many feminists to find liberal politics insufficiently radical. In the long run, however, it is unlikely that liberal ends will be effectively served by collectivist means. Any noble ideal, furthermore, can be used as a screen by those who wish to do harm. The right response is to expose the abusers, not to discard the ideal.

## ABSTRACTION AND CONCRETE REALITY

Closely related to the feminist critique of liberal individualism is the criticism that liberalism's vision of persons is too abstract. By thinking of individuals in ways that sever them from their history and their social context, liberal thinkers have deprived themselves of crucial insights. I believe that there are two different criticisms here. The first has great power but can be addressed within liberalism; the second is a genuine attack upon liberalism but does not have great power.

The first attack is pressed by Catharine MacKinnon, Alison Jaggar, and a number of other feminist thinkers.[52] Their claim is that liberalism's disregard of differences between persons that are a product of history and social setting makes it adopt an unacceptably formal conception of equality, one that cannot in the end treat individuals as equals given the reality of social hierarchy and unequal power. Notice that if this were so, it would be an extremely serious *internal* criticism of liberalism, whose central goal is to show equal respect for persons despite actual differences of power. What do these feminist critics have in mind?

It seems plausible that the liberal principle of formally equal treatment, equality under the law, may, if it is applied in an excessively abstract or remote manner, end up failing to show equal respect for persons. For example, one might use basically liberal language to justify schooling children of different races in separate schools: As long as the schools are equal, the children have been treated as equal; and if any disadvantage attaches to the separation, it is an equal disadvantage to them both. This, in fact, was the reasoning of Herbert Wechsler in a famous article critical of the reasoning in *Brown v. Board of Education,* the landmark school-desegregation case.[53] Insisting on abstraction for reasons of liberal equality and neutrality, Wechsler held that the introduction into evidence of the history of racial stigmatization and inequality was illegitimate and could only result in a biased judgment "tailored to the immediate result." Similar reasoning has been used in cases involving gender. In the Indiana sexual harassment case discussed in chapter 1, the lower court judge insisted on abstracting from the asymmetry of power between Mary Carr and her male coworkers, holding that the continual use of obscenities toward Carr by the male workers was exactly the same as the occasional use of a four-letter word by Carr. Judge Posner, overruling the lower court judge on the findings of fact, held that the asymmetry of power—including its social meaning in historical terms—was a crucial part of the facts of the case.[54] Their use of language was harassing and intimidating in a way that hers could not be. If liberal neutrality forbade one to recognize such facts, this would indeed be a difficulty for liberalism.

In general, liberalism has sometimes been taken to require that the law be "sex blind," behaving as if the social reality before us were a neutral starting point and refusing to recognize ways in which the status quo embodies historical asymmetries of power. Feminists have worried, for example, that this sort of neutrality will prevent them from demanding pregnancy and maternity leaves as parts of women's equality of opportunity.[55] Again, if liberal feminism would prevent the government of Bangladesh from investing its money disproportionately in literacy programs aimed at women, this would lose liberalism the regard of most feminists in international politics.[56]

It seems mistaken, however, to think that liberalism has ever been committed to this type of unrealistic and ahistorical abstraction.[57] MacKinnon is correct that some liberal legal thinkers and some important Supreme Court decisions have been guilty of this error; her critique of liberal equality theory is a valuable critique of positions that have been influential in the law. But liberal philosophers have, on the whole, seen more deeply—and, I would say, more consistently—when they have rejected the purely formal notion of equality. Liberals standardly grant that the equality of opportunity that individuals have a right to demand from their governments has material prerequisites, and that these prerequisites may vary depending on one's situation in society. My own preferred way of expressing this (see chapter 1) is to say that liberalism aims at equality of *capabilities:* The aim is not just to distribute some resources around but also to see that they truly go to work in promoting the capacity of people to choose a life in accordance with their own thinking.[58] Even Rawls, with his somewhat greater abstemiousness about the role played by a

view of the good in society's basic structure, nonetheless provides political thought with ample resources to think well about difference and hierarchy. He emphasizes a distinction between merely formal equal liberty and what he calls the "equal worth of liberty" and also between formal equality of opportunity and truly fair equality of opportunity; the latter members of each pair have material prerequisites that are likely to involve redistribution.[59]

One very good example of a liberal appeal to the worth of equality, used to oppose purely formal equality, is in the 1983 Indian case discussed in the Introduction, which declared unconstitutional the portion of the Hindu Marriage Act that mandated the restitution of conjugal rights. Judge Choudary noted that the remedy of restitution is available to both men and women—but, given the asymmetries of power in Indian society, the remedy is likely to be used only by males against females, and the resulting burdens (including nonconsensual pregnancy) borne only by females. He concludes:

> Thus the use of remedy of restitution of conjugal rights in reality becomes partial and one-sided and available only to the husband. The pledge of equal protection of laws is thus inherently incapable of being fulfilled by this matrimonial remedy in our Hindu society. As a result this remedy works in practice only as an oppression, to be operated by the husband for the husband against the wife. By treating the wife and the husband who are inherently unequal as equals, Section 9 of the Act offends the rule of equal protection of laws.[60]

One could not have a better expression of MacKinnon's critique—in the context of a liberal legal conception, in which the right of all citizens to autonomy and privacy is the central issue in question.[61]

Liberals will continue to differ about the topic of differential treatment, especially in the area of affirmative action. Libertarian liberals allow wide latitude for advantages that individuals derive from morally irrelevant attributes of birth and social location but are strict on the rules that should govern benefits, insisting on a type of neutrality in which morally irrelevant characteristics play no role in the design of distributive policies and programs. Rawlsian liberals, noting that individuals arrive in society with many advantages that they have already derived from morally irrelevant characteristics, think it not just reasonable but morally required to readjust things in order that individuals should not be kings and princes; they therefore permit themselves a more extensive scrutiny of the history of group hierarchy and subordination, rejecting abstractness at this point as incompatible with a fully equal treatment. Feminist liberals have typically followed this strand of liberal thinking,[62] and their criticisms of other ideas of neutrality have been very important in generating legal change.

The criticism, then, is a serious criticism of some parts of the liberal political and legal tradition and of the obtusely remote language this tradition has sometimes chosen to characterize human affairs, but it can be and frequently has been accommodated within liberalism. To address it well, however, liberalism needs to pay close attention to history and to the narratives of people who are in situations of inequality. This it will do best if, in the spirit of Rousseau's *Émile,* it allows a generous role for the imagination in the formulation and the writing of liberal theory.

Another criticism of liberal abstractness cuts deeper.[63] Many communitarian thinkers, among them some feminists, have held that liberalism's determination to think of persons in abstraction from allegedly morally irrelevant features, such as birth, class, ethnicity, gender, religion, and race, entails a pernicious form of "essentialism" that disregards the extent to which people are deeply identified with their religious heritage, their ethnicity, and so forth, and the extent to which these social and historical differences shape people. In one sense, we could say again that this is just a mistake: liberalism is very interested in knowing these historical facts of difference in order to ensure fair equality of opportunity.[64] But there is a deep point that is correct: Liberalism does think that the core of rational and moral personhood is something all human beings share, shaped though it may be in different ways by their differing social circumstances. And it does give this core a special salience in political thought, defining

the public realm in terms of it, purposefully refusing the same salience in the public political conception to differences of gender and rank and class and religion.[65] This, of course, does not mean that people may not choose to identify themselves with their religion or ethnicity or gender and to make that identification absolutely central in their lives.[66] But for the liberal, choice is the essential issue; politics can take these features into account only in ways that respect it. This does not mean treating these features of people's lives as unimportant; indeed, in the case of religion it is because they are regarded as so important that any imposition on a person's conscience on these matters is seen as inappropriate in the public political conception.[67]

At this point deep conflicts arise between liberalism and various religious and traditional views of life, insofar as the latter hold that freedom of choice is not a central ethical goal. Even if those views are accommodated respectfully within a liberal polity, their adherents may feel that respectful accommodation within a regime of toleration and free choice is not accommodation enough. Many delicate legal and political issues arise at this point, some of which I pursue in the following chapter.

The more urgent question for our purposes is, What values prized by feminists are likely to be slighted in this liberal emphasis on choice? If women are understood to be, first and foremost, members of families, or members of religious traditions, or even members of ethnic groups—rather than, first and foremost, as human centers of choice and freedom— is this likely to be in any way better for women than is the "abstract individualism" of liberalism? Better in whose terms, we have to ask, and of course we encounter at this point many religious women who sincerely hold that the account of their identity given in the Laws of Manu,[68] or the *Analects,* or the *Koran,* is superior to the account given in Kant and Mill. We cannot follow out all those lines of argument here, except to note that a political type of liberalism such as the type defended in chapter 1 strives to leave space for these other identities.[69]

But we can ask how wise antiliberal feminists are to jettison the liberal account of the human essence in favor of an account that gives more centrality to "accidental" features of religion or class or even gender. These features are especially likely not to have been chosen by the women themselves and to embody views of life that devalue and subordinate them. Even feminists who are themselves communitarians should be skeptical about accepting uncritically this feature of communitarian thought. Communitarianism need not be altogether uncritical of the status quo, as many traditions have an internal critical strand. But feminists who are generally critical of tradition should still be skeptical of communitarian antiessentialism. The idea that all human beings have a core of moral personhood that exerts claims on government no matter what the world has done to it is an idea that the women of the world badly need to vindicate their equality and to argue for change. It is the disparity between humanity and its social deformation that gives rise to claims of justice. And the communitarian vision of persons, in which we are at heart and essentially what our traditions have made us, is a vision that leaves reduced scope for feminist critique.[70]

We can make one further reply to feminists who stress the importance of recognizing differences of race and class. The liberal approach is a principled approach that addresses itself to issues of human dignity in a fully general way. As a liberal feminist, one is also, by the entailment of one's very feminist position, also an antiracist, a defender of religious toleration, and a supporter of fair equality of opportunity across classes. One's feminism is not mere identity politics, putting the interests of women as such above the interests of other marginalized groups. It is part of a systematic and justifiable program that addresses hierarchy across the board in the name of human dignity. To that extent, the liberal feminist is in a better position than are many others to show her fellow women that she has not neglected claims that are peculiar to their own class-, religion-, or race-based identities.

Feminism needs to operate with a general notion of the human core, without forgetting that this core has been differently situated and also shaped in different times and places. We should not overlook the questions raised by these differences, and we cannot formulate a just social policy if we do. But insofar as feminism denies the value of the whole idea of a human core, it gives up something vital to the most powerful feminist arguments.

## REASON AND EMOTION

Liberalism traditionally holds that human beings are above all reasoning beings, and that the dignity of reason is the primary source of human equality. As Jaggar puts it, "Liberal political theory is grounded on the conception of human beings as essentially rational agents."[71] Here liberal thinkers are not alone: They owe much to their forebears in the Western philosophical tradition, in particular the Greek and Roman Stoics, whose conception of the dignity of reason as a source of equal human worth profoundly influenced Kant, Adam Smith, and others. Continuing the Stoic heritage, liberalism typically holds that the relevant type of reason is practical reason, the capacity for understanding moral distinctions, evaluating options, selecting means to ends, and planning a life. Thinkers differ in the relative weight they assign to these different components, but not in their choice of practical over theoretical reasoning power as the essential mark of humanity.

Modern feminist thinkers usually grant that this liberal move has had at least some value for women in seeking to secure their equality. They point out that earlier feminists, from Cartesian philosopher Mary Astell to Mary Wollstonecraft, were able to appeal to women's rational capacity as a ground for claims to full political and moral equality. (They could indeed go much further back in history to support this claim: for Astell's arguments are closely related to the arguments of the Greek and Roman Stoics.[72]) And they could reflect that the decision to base moral and political claims on an innate capacity of persons, rather than on social endowments or relations, is one that opens the door to radical claims of empowerment for the disempowered.

On the other hand, feminists have worried that liberalism is far too rationalist: that by placing all emphasis on reason as a mark of humanity, it has emphasized a trait that males traditionally prize and denigrated traits, such as emotion and imagination, that females traditionally prize. This emphasis has permitted men to denigrate women for their emotional natures and to marginalize them on account of their alleged lack of reason. This would not have been possible, the argument goes, had political philosophy been grounded in a conception that gave, at least, equal weight to reason and to emotion.

Most feminists who make such claims do not argue for innate differences between the sexes, although some do.[73] Their argument is, more frequently, that women, as a result of their experiences of mothering and of family love, have rightly valued some important elements in human life that men often undervalue.[74] Liberal philosophy is accused of making that male error in a way that contributes to the denigration of women.

This is a complicated issue. Grappling with it fully would require us to argue for an account of what emotions are. The objection, as I have stated it, drawing a strong contrast between reason and emotion, suggests that emotions are not forms of thought or reasoning. But is this true? Both the history of philosophy and contemporary psychology debate the issue. On the whole, the dominant view, both in the Western philosophical tradition and in recent cognitive psychology, is that emotions such as fear, anger, compassion, and grief involve evaluative appraisals, in which people (or animals) survey objects in the world with an eye to how important goals and projects are doing. If one holds some such view of what emotions involve, the entire distinction between reason and emotion begins to be called into question, and one can no longer assume that a thinker who focuses on reason is by that move excluding emotion.[75] So we must proceed cautiously, looking both at the view of the emotion-reason contrast a thinker holds and also at the normative judgments the thinker makes about how good or valuable emotions are. This is tricky, because in the liberal tradition these positions cut across one another: Thinkers who hold a strong form of the emotion-reason contrast disagree about the value they attach to emotions, as do thinkers who consider emotions to

involve thought and evaluation. By trying to keep these distinctions straight we can make some progress in understanding the force of the feminist objections.

First, then, we do discover in the liberal tradition some philosophers who conceive of emotions as impulses distinct from reason, unintelligent forces that push the person around. On this basis, they endorse a contrast between reason and emotion. Kant and Hume (to some extent) are very different examples of this tendency. A strong feminist objection to such elements in the liberal tradition is that this is an indefensible picture of what emotions are.[76] To put a complex issue very briefly, it is implausible because it neglects the extent to which perceptions of an object and beliefs about the object are an intrinsic part of the experience of a complex emotion such as grief or fear. Grief, for example, is not simply a tug at the heartstrings: It involves the recognition that an object of great importance has been lost. Emotions involve ways of seeing.[77] This objection has been made by many philosophers and psychologists independently of feminist concerns, but the fact that the oversimple pictures were not criticized sooner may be explained in part by a cultural suspiciousness of emotions as female.[78]

But even Kant and Hume, whatever the deficiencies in their analysis of emotions, are far from dismissing emotions from their normative picture of the moral life. Kant is guarded about the contribution of emotions to moral motivation, but even he sees a necessary role for pity in motivating benevolence. Hume sees the emotions as the source of all the ends that morality pursues. Modern feminist Annette Baier has recently defended Hume's conception of the passions as the one feminists ought to use.[79] Although I am far from agreeing with Baier, because I think Hume's conception indefensible,[80] I think she is right to acknowledge the central place Hume gives to passion in his account of human nature. So even if major liberal thinkers have failed to appreciate sufficiently the amount of intelligence involved in emotion, it has not altogether stopped them from valuing the contribution of emotion to our moral choices.

Let me now turn to the cognitive conceptions of

emotion. Quite a few philosophers who focus on reason, and who make reason a hallmark of the human,
have a strongly cognitive conception of emotion and
see emotions as activities of the rational faculty.
Among these are some ancestors of liberalism, such
as the Stoics and Spinoza. The Stoics and Spinoza
dislike the emotions intensely; they do so, however,
not on the grounds that emotions are not reason
based but because they believe that the emotions
involve confused reasoning, which ascribes to persons and things outside our control more importance
than they actually possess. They hold this because
of their normative views about individual self-
sufficiency; as I have argued, these views are not
widely shared in the liberal tradition.[81]

The position that many feminists would favor as
doing most justice to women's experience of the
value of emotional attachment would be a position
that first analyzes emotions as containing cognition
and then evaluates them positively, as having at least
some value in the ethical life. This position is powerfully represented in the liberal tradition—to some
extent under the influence of Aristotle. Both Jean-
Jacques Rousseau and Adam Smith seem to have
held that emotions involve thought and imagination;
they also hold that the capacity for sympathy is a central mark of both private and public rationality, and
indeed of humanity as such. Rousseau holds that a
person who has no capacity for feeling pain at the distress of others is not fully human, that this capacity
for imaginative response is the essential thing that
draws us together in community and makes political
thought possible in the first place. Smith's entire
account of the "judicious spectator"—his model of
good public judgment—is preoccupied with ascertaining the correct balance in the passions of anger
and sympathy and love that such a public actor will
feel; he explicitly criticizes his Stoic forebears for
their normative doctrine of self-sufficiency and pas-
sionlessness. These thinkers hold conventional and
nonprogressive views of women, but their positions
on emotion offer what feminists have demanded. To
this pair we may add Mill, whose *Autobiography* provides a moving testament to the barrenness of a
rationality starved of emotional attachment and imaginative stimulation.

What, then, is the issue? What does this liberal tradition assert about emotions, that feminist thinkers
might still wish to deny? The liberal tradition holds
that emotions should not be trusted as guides to life
without being subjected to some sort of critical
scrutiny. Emotions are only as reliable as the evaluations they contain, and because such evaluations of
objects are frequently absorbed from society, they
will be only as reliable as those social norms. To naturalize them would be to naturalize the status quo. In
general, emotions, like other forms of thought and
imagination, should be valued as elements in a life
governed by critical reasoning.

Some feminists, however, hold that this entire idea
of subjecting emotion to rational appraisal is mistaken, an imposition of a male norm of cool rationality on the natural vigor of the passions. Unlike other
feminist objections to liberal views of reason and
emotion—which, as I have argued, inaccurately
characterize the strongest liberal positions—this one
directly assails a central tenet of liberalism. In her
influential book *Caring*,[82] Nel Noddings holds that
women's experience of mothering reveals a rich terrain of emotional experience into which judgment
and appraisal do not and should not enter. For example, the primitive bond of joy and love between
mother and child would be sullied by reflection, and
this primitive unscrutinized love should be the model
for our social attachments. From the perspective of a
moral view such as Noddings's, liberalism, by urging
people to ask whether their emotions are appropriate,
robs moral life of a spontaneous movement toward
others that is at the very core of morality.[83] Unless we
give ourselves away to others without asking questions, we have not behaved in a fully moral way. It is
the very unreasoning and unjudicious character of
maternal love and care that make it a fitting paradigm
for social life.

Noddings appeals, here, to images of selfless giving that lie deep in the Jewish and Christian traditions, though her view would certainly be controversial in both.[84] She holds that her maternal paradigm
of care is incompatible with norms of reflective caring that are preferred by liberalism. And she is correct. The liberal tradition is profoundly opposed to
the idea that people should spontaneously give

themselves away without reflection, judgment, or reciprocity. We have finally identified a position about the emotional life that is truly opposed to liberalism; it puts itself forward as a feminist position because it appeals to maternal experience as a paradigm for all human concern. Liberalism says to let them give themselves away to others—provided that they so choose in all freedom. Noddings says that this is one thought too many: love based on reflection lacks some of the spontaneity and moral value of true maternal love.

What should feminists say about this? First of all, we should ask some questions about Noddings's claim that maternal love and joy can and should be innocent of appraisal and judgment. She gives an example that makes at least one mother doubt.

> There is the joy that unaccountably floods over me as I walk into the house and see my daughter asleep on the sofa. She is exhausted from basketball playing, and her hair lies curled on a damp forehead. The joy I feel is immediate. . . . There is a feeling of connectedness in my joy, but no awareness of a particular belief and, certainly, no conscious assessment.[85]

Noddings concludes that such moments in which consciousness is emptied of focus and the personality flows toward another in a condition of fusion lie at the core of morality.

Let us consider this allegedly thoughtless and objectless joy. Noddings thinks nothing; she simply basks in the fused experience of maternal caring.[86] But can it really be the case that she has no thoughts at all? Doesn't Noddings have to have, in fact, the belief that her daughter is alive and asleep on the couch, rather than dead? Change that belief and her emotion would change from joy to devastating grief. She may not have to stop to ponder such a fact, but when her daughter was a baby she probably did.[87] Again, doesn't her joy presuppose the recognition that it is her daughter there on the couch rather than, say, a burglar? Doesn't its intensity also presuppose a recognition of the importance of her daughter in her life? To some extent, then, the view seems just wrong of the case as characterized.

But to the extent to which Noddings does give in

to a joy without thought, how wise is she to do so? It does not occur to her, for example, to ask whether her daughter is sleeping from a drug or alcohol overdose, or following risky sex with a boyfriend, or sexual abuse from a relative. Assuming things are as she thinks, her joy is fine, and her maternal reactions appropriate. But aren't there circumstances in which the erasure of thought (which, as we see, is not complete even in the example) could be pushed too far? If her daughter really is unconscious from an overdose, or from sexual abuse, Nodding's joy would be inappropriate and her maternal responses harmful. Such heedless caring is dangerous in a world where many of the forces affecting children are malign. Noddings may live in a world in which she may safely bracket those concerns, but most mothers do not.

As Nietzsche wrote in a related connection: Blessed are the sleepy ones—for they shall soon nod off.[88]

A child is not an arm or a leg or a wish but a separate person. This person lives in a world full of both delight and danger. Therefore, the mother had better think, and she had better teach her child how to think. And she had better think critically, asking whether the norms and traditions embodied in the emotions of fear and shame and honor in her society—and in her own emotions as well—are reasonable or unreasonable norms. What shall she teach her child to fear, and what not to fear? How shall she urge her child to see the stranger who offers her an ice cream, or the teacher who caresses her, or the friend who says that people with black skin are bad? Unless society is perfect, as it probably is not, critical thought needs to inform emotional development and response. This liberal idea seems a better recipe for maternal care than Nodding's emphasis on thoughtless giving.

Even were symbiotic fused caring a good thing in the mother-child relationship, a very different sort of care seems required in the political life. Here indiscriminate self-giving-away seems a very bad idea, especially for women, who have frequently been brought up to think that they should sacrifice their well-being to others without demanding anything for themselves. This has frequently served male interests and harmed women. A little reflection, far from representing "one thought too many,"[89] might provide the saving distance between social norms and one's own selfhood. Noddings and her allies risk turning some of the pathologies of women's lives into virtues. Even in the family, there is no reason why women should simply give themselves away without demanding a just distribution of resources.

Recall, now, the widows at the conference in Bangalore. Having spent most of their lives thinking of themselves as mere adjuncts of a family, with no rights and no separate identity, they started to learn not to give themselves away without thinking. And this looked like a good thing. The women themselves were delighted with their newfound self-expression and freedom, and the expansion in their set of choices itself seems a definite good. But still, we might ask: Aren't these women being brainwashed by these liberal ideas? The widows in Bangalore gathered under the auspices of regional development workers,[90] who had some goals in mind, liberal goals. The *Hindu* article reports that the women were "urged" to think of themselves in a certain way; Noddings would presumably object that this way of thinking involves giving up a valuable kind of organic unity within the family that women had previously prized. Indian feminist Veena Das develops a similar position, arguing that the notion of personal welfare is alien to Indian women.[91] If a typical Indian rural woman were to be asked about her personal "welfare," Das claims, she would find the question unintelligible, except as a question about how the family is doing. The thinking of these women, Das holds, exemplifies a valuable type of devotion, which would be destroyed by liberal scrutiny.

Here we must distinguish several different aspects of these women's familial devotion. Liberal individualism, I have argued, does not ask a woman to become an egoist, putting her own gratification first and others' second. As far as liberalism is concerned, she may be (and in most versions ought to be) a committed altruist, even to the point of making considerable sacrifices of her own personal welfare for the sake of others. Nor, so far as liberalism is concerned, need she be dedicated to self-sufficiency, to minimiz-

ing her needs from others—although, as I have noted, some Indian feminist programs, following a Gandhian anticolonialist model, do endorse this as a feminist goal. As a liberal, she may continue to place friendship and love squarely at the heart of her plan. What liberalism asks, however, is that the woman *distinguish* her own well-being from the well-being of others, noticing what tensions might exist between the two, even if they are bound up in one another. Liberalism asks, further, that a woman reflect and choose for herself the extent to which she will indeed sacrifice her own well-being for others—that she do so not out of habit or convention but as the result of an individual decision, freely made. It is of course a large matter to spell out the conditions under which such choices would count as freely made, but we can at least agree that many conditions under which women make sacrifices (such as conditions of malnutrition, intimidation, lack of education, and lack of political power) are not such conditions. It is common for people to internalize the roles society gives them and to act unreflectively in accordance with these roles. People also adjust their desires and preferences to what is possible, so that they may even in a limited sense be content with their lot. But in circumstances of traditional hierarchy and limited information, we surely should not assume that the sacrifices of well-being a woman makes are freely chosen, whatever account of free choice and autonomy we ultimately prefer. And this does matter. As Smith and Mill advise: Let her love others and give herself away—provided she does so freely and judiciously, with the proper critical scrutiny of social norms. I believe that this proposal, far from killing love through excessive male rationality, indicates the conditions under which love is a healthy part of a flourishing life.[92]

In fact, the most powerful feminist criticism of liberal views of reason and emotion points in the opposite direction to Noddings's. Made most influentially by Catharine MacKinnon and Andrea Dworkin, and by now commonly accepted in at least some form, the argument is that emotion, desire, and preference are not given or "natural" but shaped by social norms and appraisals—and that many emotions of both men and women are shaped by norms that subordinate women to men.[93] MacKinnon has argued that not only male aggression and female timidity but also the character of both male and female sexual desire are shaped by the social norm that women ought to be the subordinates of men. Men eroticize domination and learn to achieve sexual satisfaction in connection with its assertion. Women eroticize submission and learn to find satisfaction in giving themselves away. This, MacKinnon has argued, harms both individuals and society.

MacKinnon's insistence on criticizing socially deformed preferences goes against one strand in contemporary liberalism, namely, the part of economic utilitarianism that sees preferences as given, a bedrock to which law and politics respond rather than material that is itself shaped by law and politics. Economics is increasingly calling these views into question.[94] They have always been at odds with the Kantian liberal tradition, which insists that individuals' desires are frequently distorted by self-interest. They are even more clearly at odds with Smith and Rousseau, both of whom were highly critical of diseased emotions and desires and blamed bad social arrangements for those diseases. Rousseau vividly shows how differences of rank corrupt human sympathy, preventing nobles from seeing their own pain in the pain they inflict on a peasant.[95] Smith shows how society, attaching importance to money and status, corrupts anger and sympathy, producing bad citizens.[96] Both follow the ancient Stoic tradition, according to which human beings are born good and envy and malice result from social deformation.[97]

Nor are such insights foreign to the utilitarian tradition. Mill recognized that gender hierarchy deformed the desires of both men and women. Women, he held, internalize their inferior status in ways that shape their desires and choice, and many of these ways are very damaging to them and to society. He held that "what is now called the nature of women is an eminently artificial thing—the result of forced repression in some directions, unnatural stimulation in others." It is, he says, as if one had grown a tree half in a vapor bath and half in the snow, and then, noting that one part of it is withered and another part luxuriant, had held that it was the nature of the tree to be that

way.[98] Mill draws special attention to the way in which society eroticizes female "meekness, submissiveness and resignation of all individual will" as "an essential part of sexual attractiveness," whereas strength of will is eroticized in the case of men (16). Given the upbringing of women, it would be "a miracle if the object of being attractive to men had not become the polar star of feminine education and formation of character" (16), and equally miraculous if this object had not been understood to entail subordination. Here again, Mill makes a judicious comparison to feudalism: To both nobles and vassals, domination and subordination seemed natural, and the desires of both were shaped by this sense of the natural. Equality always seems unnatural to the dominator; this is why any departure from women's subjection to men appears unnatural. "But how entirely, even in this case, the feeling is dependent on custom, appears by ample experience" (12–13).

What is new and remarkable in the work of MacKinnon and Dworkin is the insight that even sexual desire—which has often been thought to be natural and presocial, even by thinkers who would not hold this of envy and fear and anger[99]—is socially shaped, and that this shaping is often far from benign. Their central idea is already in Mill, but they have developed it much further, given that they can discuss sexual matters with a candor unavailable to Mill. One may differ with many of their analyses and conclusions, but it seems hard to avoid granting that they have identified a phenomenon of immense human importance, one that lies at the heart of a great deal of human misery. Insofar as liberalism has left the private sphere unexamined, this critique of desire is a critique of liberalism. It challenges liberalism to do for desire what it has often done with greed and anger and envy—that is, to conduct a rigorous examination of its social formation and to think of the moral education of children with these aims in mind. As Mill shows us, such scrutiny of desire is right in line with liberalism's deepest aspirations.

Doesn't this ruin sex? As in the case of maternal caring, so here: Doesn't the liberal ask women to have "one thought too many"? Doesn't sex at its best involve a heedless giving away of oneself to the other, an erasing of conscious reflection? Yes and no. Liberal feminism—and here I believe it is right to treat MacKinnon as a kind of Kantian liberal, inspired by a deep vision of personhood and autonomy[100]—does not ask women not to abandon themselves to and in pleasure, any more than it asks them not to invest themselves deeply in caring for children and loved ones. Once again, however, it says: Fine, so long as you think first. Abandon yourself, as long as you do so within a context of equality and noninstrumental respect.[101] In some areas of life, perhaps, noninstrumental respect can be taken for granted. In this one, because of its history of distortion, it cannot be, and so you must think. If, as Mill plausibly suggests, "the generality of the male sex cannot yet tolerate the idea of living with an equal" (53), this thinking may cause pain. The liberal holds that this pain should be risked rather than endure the hidden pain that arises from subordination.

In short, wherever you most mistrust habit, there you have the most need for reason. Women have lots of grounds to mistrust most habits people have had through the centuries, just as poor people have had reason to mistrust the moral emotions of kings. This means that women have an especially great need for reason. Males can at least take consolation from the thought that the habits they live by have been formed by them, whether for good or for ill. Women should recognize that where the voice of tradition speaks, that voice is most often male, and it has even invented a little squeaky voice for women to speak in, a voice that may be far from being their own true voice, whatever precise content we attach to that idea.

In an age skeptical of reason, as Mill rightly argues, we have a hard time unmasking such deeply habitual fictions. Thus the romantic reaction against reason that he saw in his own time seemed to him profoundly subversive of any critique of established custom. "For the apotheosis of Reason," he concludes, "we have substituted that of Instinct; and we call everything instinct which we find in ourselves and for which we cannot trace any rational foundation." Contemporary feminism should beware of making the same error.

Two things fill the mind with ever-increasing

awe, wrote Kant: "the starry sky above me, and the moral law within me."[102] In that famous statement we see the radical vision of liberalism. Think what real people usually hold in awe: money, power, success, nice clothes, fancy cars, the dignity of kings, the wealth of corporations, the authority of despots of all sorts—and, perhaps most important of all, the authority of custom and tradition. Think what real women frequently hold in awe, or at least in fear: the physical power of men, the authority of men in the workplace, the sexual allure of male power, the alleged maleness of the deity, the control males have over work and shelter and food. The liberal holds none of these things in awe. She feels reverence for the world, its mystery and its wonder. And she reveres the capacity of persons to choose and fashion a life. That capacity has no gender, so the liberal does not revere established distinctions of gender any more than the dazzling equipment of kings. Some liberal thinkers have in fact revered established distinctions of gender. But, insofar as they did, they did not follow the vision of liberalism far enough. It is the vision of a beautiful, rich, and difficult world, in which a community of persons regard one another as free and equal but also as finite and needy—and therefore strive to arrange their relations on terms of justice and liberty. In a world governed by hierarchies of power and fashion, this is still, as it was from the first, a radical vision, a vision that can and should lead to social revolution. It is always radical to make the demand to see and to be seen as human rather than as someone's lord or someone's subject. I believe it is best for women to embrace this vision and make this demand.

## Notes

1. Roop Rekha Verma, "Femininity, Equality, and Personhood," in *Women, Culture, and Development* (hereafter WCD), ed. M. Nussbaum and J. Glover (Oxford: Clarendon Press, 1995), 433–43.

2. Nahid Toubia, "Female Genital Mutilation," in *Women's Rights, Human Rights* (hereafter WRHR), ed. Julie Peters and Andrea Wolper (New York and London: Routledge, 1995), 224–37, at 235, reprinted from Toubia,

*Female Genital Mutilation: A Call for Global Action* (New York: Women, Ink., 1993).

3. *The Hindu,* April 24, 1994.

4. Alison Jaggar, *Feminist Politics and Human Nature* (Totowa, NJ: Rowman and Allanheld, 1983, repr. 1988), 47–8. For related views, see also Carole Pateman, *The Problem of Political Obligation: A Critique of Liberal Theory* (Berkeley: University of California Press, 1979); Nancy C. M. Hartsock, *Money, Sex, and Power* (Boston: Northeastern University Press, 1983). An interesting response to some of the criticisms is found in Marilyn Friedman, "Feminism and Modern Friendship," *Ethics* 99 (1989), 304–19.

5. Among many treatments of these topics, see discussion of the issues in Amartya Sen, "Human Rights and Asian Values," *The New Republic,* July 10/17, 1997, 33–40. See also the exchange between Albie Sachs and Roberto Unger in *Economic and Social Rights and the Right to Health,* Harvard Law School Human Rights Program (Cambridge, MA, 1993), 12–14.

6. Rousseau is, of course, in crucial ways not a liberal, but I shall be referring to those portions of his thought that influenced portions of the liberal tradition.

7. Of course, this power needs development, but the basis for human equality is the possession of the potentiality for that development. Even if individuals possess differing degrees of this basic potentiality, we can say that a sufficient condition for equal moral personality is the possession of a certain basic minimum. See "The Basis of Equality," sec. 77 in John Rawls, *A Theory of Justice* (hereafter TJ) (Cambridge, MA: Harvard University Press, 1970), 504–12; and also the discussion of "basic capabilities," in Martha C. Nussbaum, "Human Capabilities, Female Human Beings," in WCD. This was also the view of the ancient Stoics.

8. See M. Nussbaum, "Kant and Stoic Cosmopolitanism," *The Journal of Political Philosophy* 5 (1997), 1–25. See also Julia Annas, *The Morality of Happiness* (New York: Oxford University Press, 1993).

9. This characterization of the essence of the liberal tradition differs sharply from that given in Ronald Dworkin, "Liberalism," in *A Matter of Principle* (Cambridge, MA: Harvard University Press, 1985), 181–204. Dworkin makes neutrality about conceptions of the good the basic core of liberalism rather than any more positive ideal. I would hold that to the extent that liberals are neutral about the good, this neutrality is explained by the basic intuition about the worth of choice and the respect for the choice-making capacities of the person. Rawls, for example, seems to me to have a far deeper account of the core of liberalism when he begins from an idea of "free and equal moral persons" and derives a measure of neutrality about the good from that idea. See particularly *Kantian Constructivism and Moral Theory: The Dewey Lectures 1980,* Lecture I: "Rational and Full Autonomy," *The Journal of Philosophy* 77 (1980), 515–72, and "The Priority of Right and Ideas of the Good," *Philosophy and Public Affairs* 17 (1988), 251–76.

10. This idea is central in both the Kantian and the Utilitarian traditions. See the extensive discussion in TJ, 11–16, 118–30, etc. For its relation to U.S. constitutional law, see Cass R. Sunstein, *The Partial Constitution* (Cambridge, MA: Harvard University Press, 1993).

11. Some libertarian offshoots of liberalism might be charged with having lost that central idea insofar as they validate existing distributions that have morally irrelevant origins. Some liberals will claim that personal talents and capacities other than the moral faculties ought to be counted as part of the core of the person and, thus, insofar as they confer advantage, as not morally irrelevant; this is one source of the gulf between Nozick and Rawls. But some libertarian arguments also validate existing hierarchies of wealth and class; unless they do so by deriving those advantages from the moral rights of persons (as Nozick tries to do), they are by my account illiberal. For a judicious analysis of Nozick's relationship to two strands of the liberal tradition, see Barbara Fried, "Wilt Chamberlain Revisited: Nozick's 'Justice in Transfer' and the Problem of Market-Based Distribution," *Philosophy and Public Affairs* 24 (1995), 226–45.

12. Thus there is room for doubt whether classical utilitarianism is not, in the end, illiberal in the sense that it treats the desires of all persons as fusable into a single system and ignores the salience of the separateness of persons. This is the primary criticism of utilitarianism developed in the Kantian tradition. See, for example, TJ, 183–92, 554–9.

13. For some of the opponents, see Stephen Holmes, *The Anatomy of Antiliberalism* (Cambridge, MA: Harvard University Press, 1993).

14. TJ; Nozick, *Anarchy, State, and Utopia* (Oxford: Basil Blackwell, 1974). Both understand themselves to be heirs and rival interpreters of the liberal tradition; in characterizing their difference this way I am not saying anything particularly new or surprising. On this point, see the clear account by Ronald Dworkin in *Men of Ideas,* ed. B. Magee (New York, 1978). Nozick is clear that his own validation of existing differences of wealth and class

depends on an argument from basic rights of self-owner-ship and just transfer, and that inequalities that cannot be so justified are unacceptable. His deepest difference from Kantian liberalism is his unargued assumption that features of persons other than the basis of their moral powers have moral weight and relevance: features such as talent in sports, physical strength, cleverness, etc.

15. On this distinction, see Henry S. Richardson, *Practical Reasoning About Final Ends* (New York: Cambridge University Press, 1994), 69–86, 209–27.

16. Even in this area, liberals will differ. Thus, for example, in the area of legal regulation of speech, Cass Sunstein's view holds that political speech is the central type that government needs to protect in protecting respect for persons; Joshua Cohen argues, in contrast, that artistic speech is also worthy of protection as embodying expressive capacities that are central to personhood. See Cass Sunstein, *Democracy and the Problem of Free Speech* (New York: The Free Press, 1993); Joshua Cohen, "Freedom of Expression," *Philosophy and Public Affairs* 22 (1993), pp. 207–63. Once again, we see here differences not only about strategies to achieve equal respect but, as well, about the more concrete specification of the notions involved, such as personhood and autonomy. On specification, with respect to liberal politics, see Richardson, *Practical Reasoning,* 209–27, esp. 218–27.

A note on U.S. politics: In terms of my discussion here, all major positions represented on the U.S. political scene are to at least some degree liberal positions insofar as they defend the Constitution. The strongest inclinations to antiliberalism can be seen in conservative and communitarian politics, though even these forces are held in check by the Bill of Rights. (Thus, in a recent documentary program on Plato's *Republic* made for the Discovery Channel, William Bennett said that Plato had some very good ideas about the promotion of virtue and the control of art—but then immediately said that of course we think that Plato went too far!) Economic libertarians and their opponents (often called "liberals") are, in terms of my argument, rival heirs of the liberal tradition, who differ about how equal respect and liberty should be embodied in laws and institutions. Things are confused by the fact that the Republican Party houses both libertarians and antiliberals. The Democratic Party used to contain many socialist antiliberals and still contains numerous communitarian critics of liberalism.

17. Jaggar, see above n. 4.

18. This would seem to be the meaning of the claim that "the egoistic model of human nature" is unable to admit "the values of community." Ibid., 45.

19. Jaggar appears to grant this in the case of Rawls (31), but she insists, nonetheless, that the psychological egoism inherent in liberal theory has left its deforming marks on Rawls's normative theory.

20. Amartya Sen, "Rational Fools: A Critique of the Behavioural Foundations of Economic Theory," in *Choice, Welfare, and Measurement* (Oxford: Basil Blackwell, 1982), 84–108, discussed in Jaggar, 45.

21. See Jaggar, 31.

22. Although one probably should not count Hobbes as a part of the liberal tradition.

23. Nor is it correct to think that the liberal conception of "happiness" is simply identical to the satisfaction of self-interested desire; there would appear to be no major liberal theorist, with the possible exception of Bentham, of whom that is unqualifiedly true, and in the Kantian tradition there is no tendency at all in this direction.

24. On these arguments, see Martha C. Nussbaum, *The Therapy of Desire: Theory and Practice in Hellenistic Ethics* (Princeton, NJ: Princeton University Press, 1994), especially chaps. 11–13.

25. Personal communication, Ela Bhatt, March 1997 on a visit to SEWA in Ahmedabad. For a history of the SEWA movement, see Kalima Rose, *Where Women Are Leaders: The SEWA Movement in India* (New Delhi: Vistaar, 1992).

26. See Mill, *On Liberty,* arguing that it is crucial to overcome people's lack of interest in the world and get them engaged in life.

27. We may remark that ancient proponents of self-sufficiency favored masturbation as a way of minimizing dependency on others—see Diogenes Laertius's *Life of Diogenes the Cynic.* No modern liberal thinker follows this view.

28. In these remarks about Buddhism I am much indebted to conversation with Paul Griffiths.

29. Thus I find quite puzzling Jaggar's claim that liberalism rejects human embodiment (31, 40–2). One might, of course, have a metaphysic of separate substances without making embodiment central to it, but then it would be difficult to explain why liberalism would devote so much attention to the feeding of those substances.

30. Putting things in terms of happiness and misery should not be taken to suggest either that liberalism is not critical of existing preferences and desires or that the liberal emphasis on separateness requires Pareto optimality for all policies. It might well be that we will allow a larger amount of happiness for Q to compensate for a larger amount of misery for X if we judge that X's self-generated taste for luxury and power is at the root of his misery.

31. For statistics, see chapter 1.

32. See chapters 3, 4, and 5.

33. J. S. Mill, *The Subjection of Women,* ed. S. M. Okin (Indianapolis, IN: Hackett, 1988), 33.

34. Mill's reference to *Uncle Tom's Cabin* in this passage makes it clear that he is thinking about America, yet he appears to be ignorant of the sexual situation of American slaves.

35. Mill, *Subjection,* 33–4. Mill here discusses the Infant Custody Act of 1839, which allowed the Court of Chancery to award mothers custody of children under the age of seven and access to those under the age of sixteen; this small beginning shows graphically how bad the legal situation of mothers was previously.

36. Ibid., 86–8. Compare *Considerations on Republican Government,* where Mill observes that a man who takes no pleasure in his wife's pleasure is "stunted." Similar claims are made by Verma. In the context of contemporary India: Verma argues that in this sense, feminism is "the struggle for the liberation of humanity as a whole" (44).

37. See TJ, 128–29. The focus here is on intergenerational justice, and the issue of distribution to the current members of the household is not raised. Rawls states that in a "broader inquiry" the institution of the family "might be questioned, and other arrangements might indeed prove to be preferable" (463).

38. See chapter 1 [in *Sex and Social Justice*].

39. See Susan Moller Okin, *Women in Western Political Thought* (Princeton, NJ: Princeton University Press, 1979), 282, on the way in which Mill's proposals showed the limitations of previous liberal individualism.

40. See Amartya Sen, "Gender and Cooperative Conflicts," in *Persistent Inequalities,* ed. I. Tinker (New York: Oxford University Press, 1990), 123–49.

41. For one impressive critique of the U.S. tax system's inequities toward women, and a proposal for reform, see Edward McCaffery, *Taxing Women* (Chicago: University of Chicago Press, 1997). McCaffery is a political liberal in the Rawlsian tradition. See, for example, "The Political Liberal Case Against the Estate Tax," *Philosophy and Public Affairs* 23 (1994), 281–312.

42. TJ, 7.

43. Okin, *Justice,* 97. She does not, however, address the issue that is really central to Rawls in the context, namely, the question whether the parties would represent continuing transgenerational lines or simply themselves. See TJ 146, 284–93.

44. Okin, *Justice,* chap. 8. The proposal to make the basic structure of society nongendered does not, of course, imply that gender might not continue to play a role in the private lives of individuals, much in the way that ethnicity or culture could play a role. Among concrete issues, Okin is particularly concerned with the situation of women in the event of divorce; she urges that women who have done housework to facilitate a spouse's career development should be entitled to a substantial share of his income.

45. J. Rawls in "The Idea of Public Reason Revisited," *University of Chicago Law Review* 64 (1997), 765–807. Rawls says that it was always his intention that the parties in the original position do not know the sex of those they represent; he says that distinctions of sex are like distinctions of race and culture: they are based on "fixed natural characteristics" and they often influence people's life chances from the very start (TJ, 99). It should be clear, he says, that the Veil of Ignorance is designed to ensure the parties' ignorance of all features that have this character. Sex (unlike gender, which is a social and institutional category) is a position in the distribution of natural endowments and abilities. See also "Fairness to Goodness," *Philosophical Review* 84 (1975), 537, where Rawls states that the parties do not know their sex. He also states in TJ and reaffirms in "Public Reason" that the family is certainly a part of the basic structure of society, to be constrained by the principles of justice. These will ensure that women who, for religious or other reasons, wish to choose a traditional role are free to do so; nonetheless, political principles impose constraints on the family as an institution to guarantee the basic rights, liberties, and fair opportunities of all its members. There remains a difference between Rawls and Okin, in that Okin holds, it seems, that the internal workings of the family should be governed by principles of justice, whereas Rawls envisages the principles of justice operating as external constraints on what families may choose but not as governing its internal workings. Where adult women are concerned, the difference may not be great. Rawls agrees with Okin, for example, that equal citizenship for women requires compensation, in the event of divorce, for investments a woman has made in the marriage and also public attention to child care ("Public Reason," 793). Differences are likely to be greater in the requirements concerning children, though, because Rawls has not addressed the specifics of this issue, the extent of the difference remains unknown. I discuss Rawls's view of the family at length in *Feminist Internationalism,* the 1998 Seeley Lectures in Political Theory (Cambridge: Cambridge University Press, forthcoming).

46. See chapter 1. [in *Sex and Social Justice*].

47. For some representative examples, see Sen, "Gen-

der and Cooperative Conflicts"; Bina Agarwal, *A Field of One's Own: Gender and Land Rights in South Asia* (hereafter *A Field*) (Cambridge: Cambridge University Press, 1994); "'Bargaining' and Gender Relations: Within and Beyond the Household" (hereafter "Bargaining"), *Feminist Economics* 3 (1997), 1–51, and Shelly Lundberg and Robert A. Pollak, "Bargaining and Distribution in Marriage," *Journal of Economic Perspectives* 10 (1996), 139–58.

48. Charlotte Bunch, "Women's Rights as Human Rights: Toward a Re-Vision of Human Rights," *Human Rights Quarterly* 12, 486–98; see also Bunch, "Transforming Human Rights from a Feminist Perspective," in WRHR, 11–17, and Elisabeth Friedman, "Women's Human Rights: The Emergence of a Movement," in WRHR 18–35.

49. See chapter 3 [in *Sex and Social Justice*], for some examples.

50. See Agarwal, *A Field;* and "Bargaining."

51. Mill notes that when an opinion is grounded in reason, a good counterargument will shake its solidity; when it is grounded in irrational desires and fears, good counterarguments merely intensify the resistance: "The worse it fares in argumentative contest, the more persuaded its adherents are that their feeling must have some deeper ground, which the arguments do not reach; and while the feeling remains, it is always throwing up fresh intrenchments of argument to repair any breach made in the old" (1–2).

52. See Catharine MacKinnon, *Toward a Feminist Theory of the State* (Cambridge, MA: Harvard University Press, 1989), 40–47; "Reflections on Sex Equality Under Law," *Yale Law Journal* 100 (1991), 1281–1328; Jaggar, *Feminist Politics,* 185–85 (noting that liberal feminists have been gradually led to abandon the excessively formal approach).

53. "Toward Neutral Principles of Constitutional Law," *Harvard Law Review* 73 (1959). I discuss Wechsler's argument in detail in *Poetic Justice: The Literary Imagination and Public Life* (hereafter *Poetic Justice*) (Boston: Beacon Press, 1996), chap. 4.

54. See ibid.

55. To some extent, these criticisms are probably inspired by the similar criticism of liberalism made by Marx, for example, in *Critique of the Gotha Program,* where Marx argues that the liberal idea of "equal rights" is "constantly stigmatised by a bourgeois limitation," namely, the neglect of the antecedent role of differences of class and wealth in affecting the productivity of individuals. "It is, therefore, a right of inequality, in its content, like every right. . . . To avoid all these defects, right instead of being equal would have to be unequal." MacKinnon's critique in *Toward a Feminist Theory* is explicitly inspired by the Marxian critique.

56. This would include Gary Becker, who has repeatedly argued for government support for female literacy in connection with global population control.

57. This is not to deny that individual liberal thinkers have made such commitments; and here the libertarian tradition could justly be suspected of having departed from the main line of the liberal tradition, with its strong emphasis on the critique of hierarchies and of the social ascendancy of morally irrelevant distinctions.

58. This is brought out by Amartya Sen, "Freedoms and Needs," *The New Republic,* January 10/17, 1994, and by Martha C. Nussbaum, "The Good as Discipline, the Good as Freedom," in *The Ethics of Consumption and Global Stewardship,* ed. D. Crocker (Lanham, MD: Rowman and Littlefield, 1998), 312–41; also "Capabilities and Human Rights," *Fordham Law Review* 66 (1997), 273–300.

59. See TJ, 83–9, 203–4.

60. *T. Sareetha v. T. Venkata Subbaiah,* AIR 1983 Andhra Pradesh 356.

61. The case was argued primarily as a privacy case, but there was a subsidiary argument that the Hindu Marriage Act violates equal protection.

62. Not all—see the discussion of Sommers in chapter 5 (in this volume).

63. See the discussion of this second criticism in Onora O'Neill, "Justice, Gender, and International Boundaries," in *The Quality of Life,* ed. M. Nussbaum and A. Sen (Oxford: Clarendon Press, 1993), 279–323. The feminists criticized by O'Neill include Carol Gilligan, Eva Kittay, Genevieve Lloyd, Sara Ruddick, and Nel Noddings.

64. This point was well made by Marx in *On the Jewish Question,* where—responding to Bauer's contention that a person could not qua Jew acquire "the rights of man"—he replies that "the incompatibility between religion and the rights of man is so little manifest in the concept of the rights of man that the *right to be religious,* in one's own fashion, and to practise one's own particular religion, is expressly included among the rights of man. The privilege of faith is a *universal right of man.*" Unfortunately, Marx (apparently neglecting this insight) goes on to claim that the "rights of man" treat the individual as purely self-centered, "separated from the community, withdrawn into himself, wholly preoccupied with his private interest and acting in accordance with his private caprice." This mistaken claim has probably influenced some feminist critiques.

65. Or, in the case of Rawls, to talents and propensities not integrally bound up with basic rational humanity.

66. These cases are all different. With gender and frequently with race, it is impossible to disregard the identification altogether, because it is imposed by society; some religious identities (e.g., being Jewish) have this aspect as well as a voluntary aspect. Some (e.g., biological sex and probably sexual orientation) have a biological basis, and some (e.g., race) have none. Nonetheless, in all cases we can say that individuals do have latitude as to how far the identity will be central to their life projects.

67. See, for example, TJ, 207: "To gamble in this way [viz., by allowing the public realm to restrict the liberty of conscience] would show that one did not take one's religious or moral convictions seriously, or highly value the liberty to examine one's beliefs."

68. For a mordant account of those traditions in their relation to feminism, see Verma, in WCD.

69. We should also note that all these traditions view women under some type of universal category and thus cannot attack liberalism simply for its use of an abstract universal. Maistre ridiculed liberalism by saying that "there is no such thing as *man* in the world. I have seen, during my life, Frenchmen, Italians, Russians, etc. . . . But as far as *man* is concerned, I declare that I have never in my life met him; if he exists, he is unknown to me" (cited in Holmes, *The Anatomy of Antiliberalism,* 14). Notice, however, that Maistre is perfectly happy to use high-level abstractions such as "Frenchman," which is, one could argue, far less likely than is "human being" to reveal a set of common features similar across all cases. Compare Catharine MacKinnon, "From Practice to Theory, or What Is a White Woman Anyway?," *Yale Journal of Law and Feminism* 4 (1991), 13–22, who criticizes antiessentialist feminists for using race and class as legitimate categories while refusing the same legitimacy to gender.

MacKinnon's own degree of "essentialism" about the situation of women has come under sharp attack from communitarian and postmodernist feminists. See the discussion in Elizabeth Rappaport, "Generalizing Gender: Reason and Essence in the Legal Thought of Catharine MacKinnon," in *A Mind of One's Own: Feminist Essays on Reason and Objectivity,* ed. L. Antony and C. Witt (Boulder, CO: Westview Press, 1993), 127–44, strongly supporting MacKinnon's type of 'essentialism'; and see MacKinnon, "What Is a White Woman Anyway?," criticizing Elizabeth Spelman's *Inessential Woman.* Charlotte Witt, "Feminist Metaphysics," in *A Mind of One's Own,* 273–88, argues, plausibly, that MacKinnon needs, and

relies on, an idea of the human being, not just an idea of woman. For an excellent discussion of the entire topic, see Charlotte Witt, "Anti-Essentialism in Feminist Theory," *Philosophical Topics* (1996).

70. See Marilyn Friedman in "Feminism and Modern Friendship," in Friedman, *What Are Friends For?* (Ithaca: Cornell University Press, 1993), 231–56.

71. Jaggar, *Feminist Politics,* 28.

72. On Astell, see Margaret Atherton, "Cartesian Reason and Gendered Reason," in *A Mind of One's Own,* 19–34.

73. See Nussbaum, "Emotions and Women's Capabilities," in WCD; also Anne Fausto-Sterling, *Myths of Gender,* 2nd ed. (New York: Basic Books, 1992).

74. Some examples include Carol Gilligan, *In a Different Voice* (Cambridge, MA: Harvard University Press, 1982); Nancy Chodorow, *The Reproduction of Mothering* (Berkeley: University of California Press, 1978); Virginia Held, *Feminist Morality* (Chicago: University of Chicago Press, 1993).

75. For criticisms of the reason-emotion contrast, see Martha Minow and Elizabeth Spelman, "Passions Within Reason," *Cardozo Law Review* 10 (1988), 37–76.

76. See, for example, Catherine Lutz, *Unnatural Emotions: Everyday Sentiments on a Micronesian Atoll and their Challenge to Western Theory* (Chicago: University of Chicago Press, 1988); Helen Longino, "To See Feelingly: Reason, Passion, and Dialogue in Feminist Philosophy," in *Feminisms in the Academy,* ed. D. Stanton and A. Stewart (Ann Arbor: University of Michigan Press, 1995), 19–45.

77. This is the theme of my Gifford Lectures at the University of Edinburgh 1993, now entitled *Upheavals of Thought: A Theory of the Emotions* (Cambridge: Cambridge University Press, forthcoming). See also D. Kahan and M. Nussbaum, "Two Conceptions of Emotions in Criminal Law," *Columbia Law Review* 96 (1996), 270–374.

78. See Genevieve Lloyd, *The Man of Reason* (Minneapolis: University of Minnesota Press, 1984); Lutz, *Unnatural Emotions.*

79. Annette Baier, "Hume: The Reflective Woman's Epistemologist," in *A Mind of One's Own.*

80. For a trenchant critique that has not been displaced, see Anthony Kenny, *Action, Emotion, and Will* (London: MacMillan, 1963).

81. For argument that such views derive from a male desire to be free of all strong attachments, see Longino, "To See Feelingly," summarizing the positions of Lloyd and others. A prominent source of this position within

feminism is the psychoanalytical work of Chodorow, *The Reproduction of Mothering.*

82. Nel Noddings, *Caring: A Feminine Approach to Ethics and Moral Education* (Berkeley: University of California Press, 1984). I do not discuss the even more influential views of Carol Gilligan because it is very unclear what Gilligan's normative view is and also what analysis she gives to emotions of love and care (to what extent she connects them with thought).

83. Noddings's general position is that the notions of "justification, fairness, justice" are "the language of the father," and that the primary defect in contemporary ethical thought is that it focuses on this voice rather than on the "mother's voice" *passim.*

84. A fruitful comparison would be to the more extensive assault on liberal reciprocity in the work of Emmanuel Levinas. Noddings herself does not discuss Levinas, but she does connect her idea to Martin Buber's account of the I-Thou relation (142).

85. Noddings, 137. This forms part of Noddings's argument against Sartre's claim that emotion always has an intentional object.

86. Perhaps I am handicapped by the fact that I simply do not recognize my own experience of motherhood in Noddings's descriptions of fusing and bonding. My first sharp impression of Rachel Nussbaum was as a pair of feet drumming on my diaphragm with a certain distinct separateness, a pair of arms flexing their muscles against my bladder. Before even her hair got into the world a separate voice could be heard inside, proclaiming its individuality or even individualism, and it has not stopped arguing yet, 23 years later. I am sure RN would be quite outraged by the suggestion that her own well-being was at any time merged with that of her mother, and her mother would never dare to make such an overweening suggestion. This liberal experience of maternity as the give and take of argument has equipped me ill to understand the larger mysteries of Nodding's text.

87. See the acute criticism of Noddings in Diana Fritz Cates, *Compassion for Friends in Fellowship with God* (Notre Dame: Notre Dame University Press, 1997).

88. Nietzsche, *Thus Spoke Zarathustra,* Part I, "On the Teachers of Virtue." (Kaufmann translates *einnicken* as "drop off," but I have substituted a more literal rendering.)

89. This is Bernard Williams's phrase ("Persons, Character, and Morality," in *Moral Luck: Philosophical Papers* 1973–80 [Cambridge: Cambridge University Press 1981], 18), used in criticism of impartialist views of

responsibility that would urge us to reflect on whether we may or may not give special privileges to our own family. Williams says that if a man on a raft, knowing that he can save either his wife or a stranger but not both, pauses to deliberate at all, he is having "one thought too many." I am not making any claim here about that particular case (Williams may be correct, though it is not obvious that no thought at all should be given to the choice), but it seems likely that a communitarian might say something similar about cases of female self-sacrifice for family, and there I would wish to insist on the relevance of reason, given the social deformation of the norms in question.

90. Chen is an American citizen but grew up in India and has spent half her life there; the other organizers were all Indian.

91. V. Das and R. Nicholas, "Welfare' and 'Well-Being' in South Asian Societies," ACLS-SSRC Joint Committee on South Asia (New York: Social Science Research Council, 1981); although Das circulated this paper, she has never published it.

92. See also Marcia Homiak, "Feminism and Aristotle's Rational Ideal," in *A Mind of One's Own,* 1–17; Jean Hampton, *"Feminist Contractarianism," ibid.,* 227–55; Susan Moller Okin, "Reason and Feeling in Thinking about Justice," *Ethics* 99 (1989), 229–49.

93. See Catharine MacKinnon, *Feminism Unmodified* (Cambridge, MA: Harvard University Press, 1987); Andrea Dworkin, *Intercourse* (New York: The Free Press, 1988).

94. See chapter 5 [in *Sex and Social Justice*].

95. J.-J. Rousseau, *Emile,* Book IV.

96. Adam Smith, *The Theory of Moral Sentiments* (rep. Liberty Press, 1976), Parts I and III. The remarks especially critical of greed and competition are primarily from the later editions. On Smith's changing attitudes to acquisitiveness, see Ian Simpson Ross, *The Life of Adam Smith* (Oxford: Clarendon Press, 1995).

97. On Rousseau, see Joshua Cohen, "The Natural Goodness of Humanity," in *Reclaiming the History of Ethics,* ed. Christine Korsgaard, Barbara Herman, and Andrews Reath (Cambridge: Cambridge University Press, 1997). Smith is even more profoundly influenced by Stoicism than is Rousseau, and the primary emphasis in his critique of desire and emotion is placed on distorting social forces.

98. The judgment of naturalness is said by Mill to be made "with that inability to recognise their own work which distinguishes the unanalytic mind" (22–3); see also "Was there ever any domination which did not appear nat-

ural to those who possessed it? (12); and "How rarely it is that even men complain of the general order of society; and how much rarer still would such complaint be, if they did not know of any different order existing anywhere else" (84).

99. Both Rousseau and Smith, for example, seem to hold this, although Rousseau's argument about the naturalness of gender distinctions is notoriously difficult to interpret. See Susan Moller Okin, *Women in Western*

*Political Thought* (Princeton, NJ: Princeton University Press, 1979).

100. See chapters 5, 8, and 9.

101. See chapter 8.

102. Kant, *Critique of Practical Reason,* Conclusion. The origin of this passage is probably in Seneca, *Moral Epistle* 40: see Martha C. Nussbaum, "Kant and Stoic Cosmopolitanism," *Journal of Political Philosophy* 5 (1997), 1–25.

# PERICLES

This address was delivered by the Athenian leader Pericles (c. 495–429 BCE) at a funeral ceremony in memory of those soldiers who had died in the Pelponnesian War against Sparta.

## Funeral Oration

Most of those who have stood in this place before me have commended the institution of this closing address. It is good, they have felt, that solemn words should be spoken over our fallen soldiers. I do not share this feeling. Acts deserve acts, not words, in their honour, and to me a burial at the State's charges, such as you see before you, would have appeared sufficient. Our sense of the deserts of a number of our fellow-citizens should not depend upon the felicity of one man's speech. Moreover, it is very hard for a speaker to be appropriate when many of his hearers will scarce believe that he is truthful. For those who have known and loved the dead may think his words scant justice to the memories they would hear honoured: while those who do not know will occasionally, from jealousy, suspect me of overstatement when they hear of any feat beyond their own powers. For it is only human for men not to bear praise of others beyond the point at which they still feel that they can rival their exploits. Transgress that boundary and they are jealous and distrustful. But since the wisdom of our ancestors enacted this law I too must submit and try to suit as best I can the wishes and feelings of every member of this gathering.

My first words shall be for our ancestors; for it is both just to them and seemly that on an occasion such as this our tribute of memory should be paid them. For, dwelling always in this country, generation after generation in unchanging and unbroken succession, they have handed it down to us free by their exertions. So they are worthy of our praises; and still more so are our fathers. For they enlarged the ancestral patrimony by the Empire which we hold to-day and delivered it, not without labour, into the hands of our own generation; while it is we ourselves, those of us who are now in middle life, who consolidated our power throughout the greater part of the Empire and secured the city's complete independence both in war and peace. Of the battles which we and our fathers fought, whether in the winning of our power abroad or in bravely withstanding the warfare of foreigner or Greek at home, I do not wish to say more: they are too familiar to you all. I wish rather to set forth the spirit in which we faced them, and the constitution and manners with which we rose to greatness, and to pass from them to the dead; for I think it not unfitting that these things should be called to mind in to-day's solemnity, and expedient too that the whole gathering of citizens and strangers should listen to them.

For our government is not copied from those of

Reprinted from *Thucydides: The History of the Peloponnesian War,* translated by Sir Richard Livingstone, Oxford University Press, 1943. By permission of the publisher.

our neighbours: we are an example to them rather than they to us. Our constitution is named a democracy, because it is in the hands not of the few but of the many. But our laws secure equal justice for all in their private disputes, and our public opinion welcomes and honours talent in every branch of achievement, not for any sectional reason but on grounds of excellence alone. And as we give free play to all in our public life, so we carry the same spirit into our daily relations with one another. We have no black looks or angry words for our neighbour if he enjoys himself in his own way, and we abstain from the little acts of churlishness which, though they leave no mark, yet cause annoyance to whoso notes them. Open and friendly in our private intercourse, in our public acts we keep strictly within the control of law. We acknowledge the restraint of reverence; we are obedient to whomsoever is set in authority, and to the laws, more especially to those which offer protection to the oppressed and those unwritten ordinances whose transgression brings admitted shame.

Yet ours is no work-a-day city only. No other provides so many recreations for the spirit—contests and sacrifices all the year round, and beauty in our public buildings to cheer the heart and delight the eye day by day. Moreover, the city is so large and powerful that all the wealth of all the world flows in to her, so that our own Attic products seem no more homelike to us than the fruits of the labours of other nations.

Our military training too is different from our opponents'. The gates of our city are flung open to the world. We practise no periodical deportations, nor do we prevent our visitors from observing or discovering what an enemy might usefully apply to his own purposes. For our trust is not in the devices of material equipment, but in our own good spirits for battle.

So too with education. They toil from early boyhood in a laborious pursuit after courage, while we, free to live and wander as we please, march out none the less to face the self-same dangers. Here is the proof of my words. When the Spartans advance into our country, they do not come alone but with all their

allies; but when we invade our neighbours we have little difficulty as a rule, even on foreign soil, in defeating men who are fighting for their own homes. Moreover, no enemy has ever met us in full strength, for we have our navy to attend to, and our soldiers are sent on service to many scattered possessions; but if they chance to encounter some portion of our forces and defeat a few of us, they boast that they have driven back our whole army, or, if they are defeated, that the victors were in full strength. Indeed, if we choose to face danger with an easy mind rather than after a rigorous training, and to trust rather in native manliness than in state-made courage, the advantage lies with us; for we are spared all the weariness of practising for future hardships, and when we find ourselves amongst them we are as brave as our plodding rivals. Here as elsewhere, then, the city sets an example which is deserving of admiration.

We are lovers of beauty without extravagance, and lovers of wisdom without unmanliness. Wealth to us is not mere material for vainglory but an opportunity for achievement; and poverty we think it no disgrace to acknowledge but a real degradation to make no effort to overcome. Our citizens attend both to public and private duties, and do not allow absorption in their own various affairs to interfere with their knowledge of the city's. We differ from other states in regarding the man who holds aloof from public life not as "quiet" but as useless; we decide or debate, carefully and in person, all matters of policy, holding, not that words and deeds go ill together, but that acts are foredoomed to failure when undertaken undiscussed. For we are noted for being at once most adventurous in action and most reflective beforehand. Other men are bold in ignorance, while reflexion will stop their onset. But the bravest are surely those who have the clearest vision of what is before them, glory and danger alike, and yet notwithstanding go out to meet it. In doing good, too, we are the exact opposite of the rest of mankind. We secure our friends not by accepting favours but by doing them. And so we are naturally more firm in our attachments: for we are anxious, as creditors, to cement by kind offices our relation towards our friends. If they do not respond with the same warmness it is because they feel that their services will not be given spontaneously but only as the repayment of a debt. We are alone among mankind in doing men benefits, not on calculations of self-interest, but in the fearless confidence of freedom.

In a word I claim that our city as a whole is an education to Greece, and that her members yield to none, man by man, for independence of spirit, many-sidedness of attainment, and complete self-reliance in limbs and brain.

That this is no vainglorious phrase but actual fact the supremacy which our manners have won us itself bears testimony. No other city of the present day goes out to her ordeal greater than ever men dreamed; no other is so powerful that the invader feels no bitterness when he suffers at her hands, and her subjects no shame at the indignity of their dependence. Great indeed are the symbols and witnesses of our supremacy, at which posterity, as all mankind to-day, will be astonished. We need no Homer or other man of words to praise us; for such give pleasure for a moment, but the truth will put to shame their imaginings of our deeds. For our pioneers have forced a way into every sea and every land, establishing among all mankind, in punishment or beneficence, eternal memorials of their settlement.

Such then is the city for whom, lest they should lose her, the men whom we celebrate died a soldier's death: and it is but natural that all of us, who survive them, should wish to spend ourselves in her service. That, indeed, is why I have spent many words upon the city. I wished to show that we have more at stake than men who have no such inheritance, and to support my praise of the dead by making clear to you what they have done. For if I have chanted the glories of the city it was these men and their like who set hand to array her. With them, as with few among Greeks, words cannot magnify the deeds that they have done. Such an end as we have here seems indeed to show us what a good life is, from its first signs of power to its final consummation. For even where life's previous record showed faults and failures it is just to weigh the last brave hour of devotion against them all. There they wiped out evil with good and did the city more service as soldiers than they did her harm in private life. There no hearts grew faint because they loved riches more than honour; none shirked the issue in the poor man's dreams of wealth. All these they put aside to strike a blow for the city. Counting the quest to avenge her honour as the most glorious of all ventures, and leaving Hope, the uncertain goddess, to send them what she would, they faced the foe as they drew near him in the strength of their own manhood; and when the shock of battle came, they chose rather to suffer the uttermost than to win life by weakness. So their memory has escaped the reproaches of men's lips, but they bore instead on their bodies the marks of men's hands, and in a moment of time, at the climax of their lives, were rapt away from a world filled, for their dying eyes, not with terror but with glory.

Such were the men who lie here and such the city that inspired them. We survivors may pray to be spared their bitter hour, but must disdain to meet the foe with a spirit less triumphant. Fix your eyes on the greatness of Athens as you have it before you day by day, fall in love with her, and when you feel her great, remember that this greatness was won by men with courage, with knowledge of their duty, and with a sense of honour in action, who, if they failed in any ordeal, disdained to deprive the city of their services, but sacrificed their lives as the best offerings on her behalf. So they gave their bodies to the commonwealth and received, each for his own memory, praise that will never die, and with it the grandest of all sepulchres, not that in which their mortal bones are laid, but a home in the minds of men, where their glory remains fresh to stir to speech or action as the occasion comes by. For the whole earth is the sepulchre of famous men; and their story is not graven only on stone over their native earth, but lives on far away, without visible symbol, woven into the stuff of other men's lives. For you now it remains to rival what they have done and, knowing the secret of happiness to be freedom and the secret of freedom a brave heart, not idly to stand aside from the enemy's onset. For it is not the poor and luckless, as having no hope of prosperity, who have most cause to reckon death as little loss, but those for whom fortune may yet keep reversal in store and who would feel the change most if trouble befell them. Moreover, weakly to decline the trial is more painful to a man of spirit than death coming sudden and unperceived in the hour of strength and enthusiasm.

Therefore I do not mourn with the parents of the dead who are here with us. I will rather comfort them. For they know that they have been born into a world of manifold chances and that he is to be accounted happy to whom the best lot falls—the best sorrow, such as is yours to-day, or the best death, such as fell to these, for whom life and happiness were cut to the self-same measure. I know it is not easy to give you comfort. I know how often in the joy of others you will have reminders of what was once your own, and how men feel sorrow, not for the loss of what they have never tasted, but when something that has grown dear to them has been snatched away. But you must keep a brave heart in the hope of other children, those who are still of age to bear them. For the newcomers will help you to forget the gap in your own circle, and will help the city to fill up the ranks of its workers and its soldiers. For no man is fitted to give fair and honest advice in council if he has not, like his fellows, a family at stake in the hour of the city's danger. To you who are past the age of vigour I would say: count the long years of happiness so much gain to set off against the brief space that yet remains, and let your burden be lightened by the glory of the dead.

For the love of honour alone is not staled by age, and it is by honour, not, as some say, by gold, that the helpless end of life is cheered.

I turn to those amongst you who are children or brothers of the fallen, for whom I foresee a mighty contest with the memory of the dead. Their praise is in all men's mouths, and hardly, even for supremest heroism, you will be adjudged to have achieved, not the same but a little less than they. For the living have the jealousy of rivals to contend with, but the dead are honoured with unchallenged admiration.

If I must also speak a word to those who are now in widowhood on the powers and duties of women, I will cast all my advice into one brief sentence. Great will be your glory if you do not lower the nature that is within you—hers greatest of all whose praise or blame is least bruited on the lips of men.

I have spoken such words as I had to say according as the law prescribes, and the graveside offerings to the dead have been duly made. Henceforward the city will take charge of their children till manhood: such is the crown and benefit she holds out to the dead and to their kin for the trials they have undergone for her. For where the prize is highest, there, too, are the best citizens to contend for it.

And now, when you have finished your lamentation, let each of you depart.

# EDMUND BURKE

Edmund Burke (1729–1797), the Irish-born philosopher and politician, delivered this speech on November 3, 1774, in Bristol, England, where he had just been elected a member of Parliament.

## Speech to the Electors of Bristol

. . . I am sorry I cannot conclude without saying a word on a topic touched upon by my worthy colleague. I wish that topic had been passed by at a time when I have so little leisure to discuss it. But since he

has thought proper to throw it out, I owe you a clear explanation of my poor sentiments on that subject.

He tells you that "the topic of instructions has occasioned much altercation and uneasiness in this city"; and he expresses himself (if I understand him rightly) in favor of the coercive authority of such instructions.

Certainly, Gentlemen, it ought to be the happiness and glory of a representative to live in the strictest union, the closest correspondence, and the most unreserved communication with his constituents. Their wishes ought to have great weight with him; their opinions high respect; their business unremitted attention. It is his duty to sacrifice his repose, his pleasure, his satisfactions, to theirs,—and above all, ever, and in all cases, to prefer their interest to his own.

But his unbiased opinion, his mature judgment, his enlightened conscience, he ought not to sacrifice to you, to any man, or to any set of men living. These he does not derive from your pleasure,—no, nor from the law and the Constitution. They are a trust from Providence, for the abuse of which he is deeply answerable. Your representative owes you, not his industry only, but his judgment; and he betrays, instead of serving you, if he sacrifices it to your opinion.

My worthy colleague says, his will ought to be subservient to yours. If that be all, the thing is innocent. If government were a matter of will upon any side, yours, without question, ought to be superior. But government and legislation are matters of reason and judgment, and not of inclination; and what sort of reason is that in which the determination precedes the discussion, in which one set of men deliberate and another decide, and where those who form the conclusion are perhaps three hundred miles distant from those who hear the arguments?

To deliver an opinion is the right of all men; that of constituents is a weighty and respectable opinion, which a representative ought always to rejoice to hear, and which he ought always most seriously to consider. But *authoritative* instructions, *mandates* issued, which the member is bound blindly and implicitly to obey, to vote, and to argue for, though contrary to the clearest conviction of his judgment and conscience,—these are things utterly unknown to the laws of this land, and which arise from a fundamental mistake of the whole order and tenor of our Constitution.

Parliament is not a *congress* of ambassadors from different and hostile interests, which interests each must maintain, as an agent and advocate, against other agents and advocates; but Parliament is a *deliberate* assembly of *one* nation, with *one* interest, that of the whole—where not local purposes, not local prejudices, ought to guide, but the general good, resulting from the general reason of the whole. You choose a member, indeed; but when you have chosen him, he is not a member of Bristol, but he is a member of *Parliament*. If the local constituent should have an interest or should form an hasty opinion evidently opposite to the real good of the rest of the community, the member for that place ought to be as far as any other from any endeavor to give it effect. I beg pardon for saying so much on this subject; I have been unwillingly drawn into it; but I shall ever use a respectful frankness of communication with you. Your faithful friend, your devoted servant, I shall be to the end of my life: a flatterer you do not wish for. On this point of instructions, however, I think it scarcely possible we ever can have any sort of difference. Perhaps I may give you too much, rather than too little, trouble.

From the first hour I was encouraged to court your favor, to this happy day of obtaining it, I have never promised you anything but humble and persevering endeavors to do my duty. The weight of that duty, I confess, makes me tremble; and whoever well considers what it is, of all things in the world, will fly from what has the least likeness to a positive and precipitate engagement. To be a good member of Parliament is, let me tell you, no easy task,—especially at this time, when there is so strong a disposition to run into the perilous extremes of servile compliance or wild popularity. To unite circumspection with vigor is absolutely necessary, but it is extremely difficult. We are now members for a rich commercial *city*; this city, however, is but a part of a rich commercial *nation*, the interests of which are various, multiform, and intricate. We are members for that great nation, which, however, is itself but part of a great *empire*, extended by our virtue and our fortune to the farthest limits of the East and of the West. All these wide-spread interests must be considered,—must be compared,—must be reconciled, if possible. We are members for a *free* country; and surely we all know that the machine of a free constitution is no simple thing, but as intricate and as delicate as it is valuable. We are members in a great and ancient *monarchy*; and we must preserve religiously the true, legal rights of the sovereign, which form the keystone that binds together the noble and well-constructed arch of our empire and our Constitution. A constitution made up of balanced powers must ever be a critical thing. As such I mean to touch that part of it which comes within my reach. I know my inability, and I wish for support from every quarter. In particular I shall aim at the friendship, and shall cultivate the best correspondence, of the worthy colleague you have given me. . . .

# THE DECLARATION
# OF INDEPENDENCE

Thomas Jefferson (1743–1826) was the primary author of this foundational statement of American principles.

*In Congress, July 4th, 1776*
*The Unanimous Declaration Of The Thirteen States of America*

When in the Course of human events, it becomes necessary for one people to dissolve the political bands which have connected them with another, and to assume among the Powers of the earth, the separate and equal station to which the Laws of Nature and of Nature's God entitle them, a decent respect to the opinions of mankind requires that they should declare the causes which impel them to the separation.

We hold these truths to be self-evident, that all men are created equal, that they are endowed by their Creator with certain unalienable Rights, that among these are Life, Liberty and the pursuit of Happiness. That to secure these rights, Governments are instituted among Men, deriving their just powers from the consent of the governed, That whenever any Form of Government becomes destructive of these ends, it is the Right of the People to alter or to abolish it, and to institute new Government, laying its foundation on such principles and organizing its powers in such form, as to them shall seem most likely to effect their Safety and Happiness. Prudence, indeed, will dictate that Governments long established should not be changed for light and transient causes; and accordingly all experience hath shown, that mankind are more disposed to suffer, while evils are sufferable, than to right themselves by abolishing the forms to which they are accustomed. But when a long train of abuses and usurpations, pursuing invariably the same Object evinces a design to reduce them under absolute Despotism, it is their right, it is their duty, to throw off such Government, and to provide new Guards for their future security.—Such has been the patient sufferance of these Colonies; and such is now the necessity which constrains them to alter their former Systems of Government. The history of the present King of Great Britain is a history of repeated injuries and usurpations, all having in direct object the establishment of an absolute Tyranny over these States. To prove this, let Facts be submitted to a candid world.

He has refused his Assent to Laws, the most wholesome and necessary for the public good.

He has forbidden his Governors to pass Laws of immediate and pressing importance, unless suspended in their operation till his Assent should be obtained; and when so suspended, he has utterly neglected to attend to them.

He has refused to pass other Laws for the accommodation of large districts of people, unless those people would relinquish the right of Representation in the Legislature, a right inestimable to them and formidable to tyrants only.

He has called together legislative bodies at places unusual, uncomfortable, and distant from the depository of their Public Records, for the sole purpose of fatiguing them into compliance with his measures.

He has dissolved Representative Houses repeatedly, for opposing with manly firmness his invasions on the rights of the people.

He has refused for a long time, after such dissolutions, to cause others to be elected; whereby the Legislative Powers, incapable of Annihilation, have returned to the People at large for their exercise; the State remaining in the mean time exposed to all the dangers of invasion from without, and convulsions within.

He has endeavoured to prevent the population of these States; for that purpose obstructing the Laws of Naturalization of Foreigners; refusing to pass others to encourage their migration hither, and raising the conditions of new Appropriations of Lands.

He has obstructed the Administration of Justice, by refusing his Assent to Laws for establishing Judiciary Powers.

He has made Judges dependent on his Will alone, for the tenure of their offices, and the amount and payment of their salaries.

He has erected a multitude of New Offices, and sent hither swarms of Officers to harass our People, and eat out their substance.

He has kept among us, in times of peace, Standing Armies without the Consent of our legislature.

He has affected to render the Military independent of and superior to the Civil Power.

He has combined with others to subject us to a jurisdiction foreign to our constitution, and unacknowledged by our laws; giving his Assent to their acts of pretended legislation:

For quartering large bodies of armed troops among us:

For protecting them, by a mock Trial, from Punishment for any Murders which they should commit on the Inhabitants of these States:

For cutting off our Trade with all parts of the world:

For imposing taxes on us without our Consent:

For depriving us in many cases, of the benefits of Trial by Jury:

For transporting us beyond Seas to be tried for pretended offences:

For abolishing the free System of English Laws in a neighbouring Province, establishing therein an Arbitrary government, and enlarging its Boundaries so as to render it at once an example and fit instrument for introducing the same absolute rule into these Colonies:

For taking away our Charters, abolishing our most valuable Laws, and altering fundamentally the Forms of our Governments:

For suspending our own Legislature, and declaring themselves invested with Power to legislate for us in all cases whatsoever.

He has abdicated Government here, by declaring us out of his Protection and waging War against us.

He has plundered our seas, ravaged our Coasts, burnt our towns, and destroyed the lives of our people.

He is at this time transporting large armies of foreign mercenaries to compleat the works of death, desolation and tyranny, already begun with circumstances of Cruelty & perfidy scarcely paralleled in the most barbarous ages, and totally unworthy the Head of a civilized nation.

He has constrained our fellow Citizens taken Captive on the high Seas to bear Arms against their Country, to become the executioners of their friends and Brethren, or to fall themselves by their Hands.

He has excited domestic insurrections amongst us, and has endeavoured to bring on the inhabitants of our frontiers, the merciless Indian Savages, whose known rule of warfare, is an undistinguished destruction of all ages, sexes and conditions.

In every stage of these Oppressions We have Petitioned for Redress in the most humble terms: Our repeated Petitions have been answered only by repeated injury. A Prince, whose character is thus marked by every act which may define a Tyrant, is unfit to be the ruler of a free People.

Nor have We been wanting in attention to our British brethren. We have warned them from time to time of attempts by their legislature to extend an unwarrantable jurisdiction over us. We have reminded them of the circumstances of our emigration and settlement here. We have appealed to their native justice and magnanimity, and we have conjured them by the ties of our common kindred to disavow these usurpations, which, would inevitably interrupt our connections and correspondence. They too have been deaf to the voice of justice and of consanguinity. We must, therefore, acquiesce in the necessity, which denounces our Separation, and hold them, as we hold the rest of mankind, Enemies in War, in Peace Friends.

We, therefore, the Representatives of the united States of America, in General Congress, Assembled, appealing to the Supreme Judge of the world for the rectitude of our intentions, do, in the Name, and by Authority of the good People of these Colonies, solemnly publish and declare, That these United Colonies are, and of Right ought to be Free and Independent States; that they are Absolved from all Allegiance to the British Crown, and that all political connection between them and the State of Great Britain, is and ought to be totally dissolved; and that as Free and Independent States, they have full Power to levy War, conclude Peace, contract Alliances, establish Commerce, and to do all other Acts and Things which Independent States may of right do. And for the support of this Declaration, with a firm reliance on the Protection of Divine Providence, we mutually pledge to each other our Lives, our Fortunes and our sacred Honor.

# THE CONSTITUTION OF THE UNITED STATES

We the people of the United States, in Order to form a more perfect Union, establish justice, insure domestic Tranquillity, provide for the common defence, promote the general Welfare, and secure the Blessings of Liberty to ourselves and our Posterity, do ordain and establish this Constitution of the United States of America.

## ARTICLE I

*Sec. 1.* All legislative Powers herein granted shall be vested in a Congress of the United States, which shall consist of a Senate and House of Representatives.

*Sec. 2.* The House of Representatives shall be composed of Members chosen every second Year by the People of the several States, and the Electors in each State shall have the Qualifications requisite for Electors of the most numerous Branch of the State Legislature.

No Person shall be a Representative who shall not have attained to the Age of twenty five Years, and been seven Years a Citizen of the United States, and who shall not, when elected, be an Inhabitant of that State in which he shall be chosen.

Representatives and direct Taxes shall be apportioned among the several States which may be included within this Union, according to their respective Numbers, which shall be determined by adding to the whole Number of free Persons, including those bound to Service for a Term of Years, and excluding Indians not taxed, three fifths of all other Persons. The actual Enumeration shall be made within three Years after the first Meeting of the Congress of the United States, and within every subsequent Term of ten Years, in such Manner as they shall by Law direct. The Number of Representatives shall not exceed one for every thirty Thousand, but each State shall have at Least one Representative; and until such enumeration shall be made, the State of New Hampshire shall be entitled to chuse three, Massachusetts eight, Rhode-Island and Providence Plantations one, Connecticut five, New-York six, New Jersey four, Pennsylvania eight, Delaware one,

Maryland six, Virginia ten, North Carolina five, South Carolina five, and Georgia three.

When vacancies happen in the Representation from any State, the Executive Authority thereof shall issue Writs of Election to fill such Vacancies.

The House of Representatives shall chuse their Speaker and other Officers; and shall have the sole Power of Impeachment.

*Sec. 3.* The Senate of the United States shall be composed of two Senators from each State, chosen by the Legislature thereof, for six Years; and each Senator shall have one Vote.

Immediately after they shall be assembled in Consequence of the first Election, they shall be divided as equally as may be into three Classes. The Seats of the Senators of the first Class shall be vacated at the Expiration of the second Year, of the second Class at the Expiration of the fourth Year, and of the third Class at the Expiration of the sixth Year, so that one third may be chosen every second Year; and if Vacancies happen by Resignation, or otherwise, during the Recess of the Legislature of any State, the Executive thereof may make temporary Appointments until the next Meeting of the Legislature, which shall then fill such Vacancies.

No Person shall be a Senator who shall not have attained to the Age of thirty Years, and been nine Years a Citizen of the United States, and who shall not, when elected, be an Inhabitant of that State for which he shall be chosen.

The Vice President of the Untied States shall be President of the Senate, but shall have no Vote, unless they be equally divided.

The Senate shall chuse their other, Officers, and also a President pro tempore, in the Absence of the Vice President, or when he shall exercise the Office of President of the United States.

The Senate shall have the sole Power to try all Impeachments. When sitting for that Purpose, they shall be on Oath or Affirmation. When the President of the United States is tried, the Chief justice shall preside: And no Person shall be convicted without the Concurrence of two thirds of the Members present.

Judgment in Cases of Impeachment shall not extend further than to removal from Office, and disqualification to hold and enjoy any Office of honor, Trust or Profit under the United States: but the Party convicted shall nevertheless be liable and subject to Indictment, Trial, Judgment and Punishment, according to Law.

*Sec. 4.* The Times, Places and Manner of holding elections for Senators and Representatives, shall be prescribed in each State by the Legislature thereof; but the Congress may at any time by Law make or alter such Regulations, except as to the Places of Chusing Senators.

The Congress shall assemble at least once in every Year, and such Meeting shall be on the first Monday in December, unless they shall by Law appoint a different Day.

*Sec. 5.* Each House shall be the Judge of the Elections, Returns and Qualifications of its own Members, and a Majority of each shall constitute a Quorum to do business; but a smaller Number may adjourn from day to day, and may be authorized to compel the Attendance of absent Members, in such Manner, and under such Penalties as each House may provide.

Each House may determine the Rules of its Proceedings, punish its Members for disorderly Behaviour, and with the Concurrence of two thirds, expel a Member.

Each House shall keep a Journal of its Proceedings, and from time to time publish the same, excepting such Parts as may in their judgment require Secrecy; and the Yeas and Nays of the Members of either House on any question shall, at the Desire of one fifth of those Present, be entered on the Journal.

Neither House, during the Session of Congress, shall, without the Consent of the other, adjourn for more than three days, nor to any other Place than that in which the two Houses shall be sitting.

*Sec. 6.* The Senators and Representatives shall receive a Compensation for their Services, to be ascertained by Law, and paid out of the Treasury of the United States. They shall in all Cases, except Treason, Felony and Breach of the Peace, be privileged from Arrest during their Attendance at the Session of their respective Houses, and in going to and returning from the same; and for any Speech or Debate in either House, they shall not be questioned in any other Place.

No Senator or Representative shall, during the Time for which he was elected, be appointed to any civil Office under the Authority of the United States which shall have been created, or the Emoluments whereof shall have been encreased during such time; and no Person holding any Office under the United States, shall be a Member of either House during his Continuance in Office.

*Sec. 7.* All Bills for raising Revenue shall originate in the House of Representatives; but the Senate may propose or concur with Amendments as on other Bills.

Every Bill which shall have passed the House of Representatives and the Senate, shall, before it become a Law, be presented to the President of the United States; If he approve he shall sign it, but if not he shall return it, with his Objections to the House in which it shall have originated, who shall enter the Objections at large on their Journal, and proceed to reconsider it. If after such Reconsideration two thirds of that House shall agree to pass the Bill, it shall be sent, together with the Objections, to the other House, by which it shall likewise be reconsidered, and if approved by two thirds of that House, it shall become a Law. But in all such Cases the Votes of both Houses shall be determined by Yeas and Nays, and the Names of the Persons voting for and against the Bill shall be entered on the journal of each House respectively. If any Bill shall not be returned by the President within ten Days (Sundays excepted) after it shall have been presented to him, the Same shall be a Law, in like Manner as if he had signed it, unless the Congress by their Adjournment prevent its Return, in which Case it shall not be a Law.

Every Order, Resolution, or Vote to which the Concurrence of the Senate and House of Representatives may be necessary (except on a question of Ad-

journment) shall be presented to the President of the Untied States; and before the Same shall take Effect, shall be approved by him, or being disapproved by him, shall be repassed by two thirds of the Senate and House of Representatives, according to the Rules and Limitations prescribed in the Case of a Bill.

*Sec. 8.* The Congress shall have Power to lay and collect Taxes, Duties, Imposts and Excises, to pay the Debts and provide for the common Defence and general Welfare of the United States; but all Duties, Imposts and Excises shall be uniform throughout the United States;

To borrow Money on the credit of the United States;

To regulate Commerce with foreign Nations, and among the several States, and with the Indian Tribes;

To establish an uniform Rule of Naturalization, and uniform Laws on the Subject of Bankruptcies throughout the United States;

To coin Money, regulate the Value Thereof, and of foreign Coin, and fix the standard of Weights and Measures;

To provide for the Punishment of counterfeiting the Securities and current Coin of the United States;

To establish Post Offices and post Roads;

To promote the Progress of Science and useful Arts, by securing for limited Times to Authors and Inventors the exclusive Right to their respective Writings and Discoveries;

To constitute Tribunals inferior to the supreme Court;

To define and punish Piracies and Felonies committed on the high Seas, and Offences against the Law of Nations;

To declare War, grant Letters of Marque and Reprisal, and make Rules concerning Captures on Land and Water;

To raise and support Armies, but no Appropriation of Money to that Use shall be for a longer Term than two Years;

To provide and maintain a Navy;

To make Rules for the Government and Regulation of the land and naval Forces;

To provide for calling forth the Militia to execute

the Laws of the Union, suppress Insurrections and repel Invasions;

To provide for organizing, arming, and disciplining the Militia, and for governing such Part of them as may be employed in the Service of the United States, reserving to the States respectively, the Appointment of the Officers, and the Authority of training the Militia according to the discipline prescribed by Congress;

To exercise exclusive Legislation in all Cases whatsoever, over such District (not exceeding ten Miles square) as may, by Cession of particular States, and the Acceptance of Congress, become the Seat of the Government of the United States, and to exercise like Authority over all Places purchased by the Consent of the Legislature of the State in which the Same shall be, for the Erection of Forts, Magazines, Arsenals, dock-Yards, and other needful Buildings;—And

To make all Laws which shall be necessary and proper for carrying into Execution the foregoing Powers, and all other Powers vested by this Constitution in the Government of the United States, or in any Department or Officer thereof.

*Sec. 9.* The Migration or Importation of such Persons as any of the States now existing shall think proper to admit, shall not be prohibited by the Congress prior to the Year one thousand eight hundred and eight, but a Tax or duty may be imposed on such Importation, not exceeding ten dollars for each Person.

The Privilege of the Writ of Habeas Corpus shall not be suspended, unless when in Cases of Rebellion or Invasion the public Safety may require it.

No Bill of Attainder or ex post facto Law shall be passed.

No Capitation, or other direct, Tax shall be laid, unless in Proportion to the Census or Enumeration herein before directed to be taken.

No Tax or Duty shall be laid on Articles exported from any State.

No Preference shall be given by any Regulation of Commerce or Revenue to the Ports of one State over those of another: nor shall Vessels bound to, or from, one State, be obliged to enter, clear, or pay Duties in another.

No Money shall be drawn from the Treasury, but in Consequence of Appropriations made by Law; and a regular Statement and Account of the Receipts and Expenditures of all public Money shall be published from time to time.

No Title of Nobility shall be granted by the United States: And no Person holding any Office of Profit or Trust under them, shall, without the Consent of the Congress, accept of any present, Emolument, Office, or Title, of any kind whatever, from any King, Prince or Foreign State.

*Sec. 10.* No State shall enter into any Treaty, Alliance, or Confederation; grant Letters of Marque and Reprisal; coin Money; emit Bills of Credit; make any Thing but gold and silver Coin a Tender in Payment of Debts; pass any Bill of Attainder, ex post facto Law, or Law impairing the Obligation of Contracts, or grant any Title of Nobility.

No State shall, without the Consent of the Congress, lay any Imposts or Duties on Imports or Exports, except what may be absolutely necessary for executing its inspection Laws: and the net Produce of all Duties and Imposts, laid by any State on Imports or Exports, shall be for the Use of the Treasury of the United States, and all such Laws shall be subject to the Revision and Controul of the Congress.

No State shall, without the Consent of Congress, lay any Duty of Tonnage, keep Troops, or Ships of War in time of Peace, enter in any Agreement or Compact with another State, or with a foreign Power, or engage in War, unless actually invaded, or in such imminent Danger as will not admit of delay.

## ARTICLE II

*Sec. 1.* The executive Power shall be vested in a President of the United States of America. He shall hold his Office during the Term of four Years, and, together with the Vice President, chosen for the same Term, be elected, as follows.

Each State shall appoint, in such Manner as the Legislature thereof may direct, a Number of Electors, equal to the whole Number of Senators and Representatives to which the State may be entitled in the Congress: but no Senator or Representative, or Person holding an Office of Trust or Profit under the United States, shall be appointed an Elector.

The Electors shall meet in their respective States, and vote by Ballot for two Persons, of whom one at least shall not be an Inhabitant of the same State with themselves. And they shall make a List of all the Persons voted for, and of the Number of Votes for each; which List they shall sign and certify, and transmit sealed to the Seat of the Government of the United States, directed to the President of the Senate. The President of the Senate shall, in the Presence of the Senate and House of Representatives, open all the Certificates, and the Votes shall then be counted. The Person having the greatest Number of Votes shall be the President, if such Number be a Majority of the whole Number of Electors appointed; and if there be more than one who have such Majority, and have an equal Number of Votes, then the House of Representatives shall immediately chuse by Ballot one of them for President; and if no person have a Majority, then from the five highest on the List the said House shall in like Manner chuse the President. But in chusing the President, the Votes shall be taken by States, the Representation from each State having one Vote; A quorum for this Purpose shall consist of a Member or Members from two thirds of the States, and a majority of all the States shall be necessary to a Choice. In every Case, after the Choice of the President, the Person having the greatest Number of Votes of the Electors shall be the Vice President. But if there should remain two or more who have equal Votes, the Senate shall chuse from them by Ballot the Vice President.

The Congress may determine the Time of chusing the Electors, and the Day on which they shall give their Votes; which Day shall be the same throughout the United States.

No Person except a natural born Citizen, or a Citizen of the United States, at the time of the Adoption of this Constitution, shall be eligible to the Office of President; neither shall any Person be eligible to that Office who shall not have attained to the Age of thirty five Years, and been fourteen Years a Resident within the United States.

In Case of the Removal of the President from Office, or of his Death, Resignation, or Inability to discharge the Powers and Duties of the said Office, the Same shall devolve on the Vice President, and the Congress may by law provide for the Case of Removal, Death, Resignation or Inability, both of the President and Vice President, declaring what Officer shall then act as President, and such Office shall act accordingly, until the Disability be removed, or a President shall be elected.

The President shall, at stated Times, receive for his Services, a Compensation, which shall neither be encreased nor diminished during the Period for which he shall have been elected, and he shall not receive within that Period any other Emolument from the United States, or any of them.

Before he enter on the Execution of his Office, he shall take the following Oath or Affirmation:—"I do solemnly swear (or affirm) that I will faithfully execute the Office of President of the United States, and will to the best of my Ability, preserve, protect and defend the Constitution of the United States."

*Sec. 2.* The President shall be commander in Chief of the Army and Navy of the United States, and of the Militia of the several States, when called into the actual Service of the United States; he may require the Opinion, in writing, of the principal Officer in each of the executive Departments, upon any Subject relating to the Duties of their respective Officers, and he shall have Power to grant Reprieves and Pardons for Offenses against the United States, except in Cases of Impeachment.

He shall have Power, by and with the Advice and Consent of the Senate, to make Treaties, provided two thirds of the Senators present concur; and he shall nominate, and by and with the Advice and Consent of the Senate, shall appoint Ambassadors, other public Ministers and Consuls, Judges of the supreme Court, and all other Officers of the United States, whose Appointments are not herein otherwise provided for, and which shall be established by Law: but the Congress may by Law vest the Appointment of such inferior Officers, as they think proper, in the President alone, in the Courts of Law, or in the Heads of Departments.

The President shall have Power to fill up all Vacancies that may happen during the Recess of the Senate, by granting Commissions which shall expire at the End of their next Session.

*Sec. 3.* He shall from time to time give to the Congress Information of the State of the Union, and recommend to their consideration such Measures as he shall judge necessary and expedient; he may, on extraordinary Occasion, convene both Houses, or either of them, and in Case of Disagreement between them, with Respect to the Time of Adjournment, he may adjourn them to such Time as he shall think proper; he shall receive Ambassadors and other public Ministers; he shall take Care that the Laws be faithfully executed, and shall Commission all the Officers of the United States.

*Sec. 4.* The President, Vice President and all civil Officers of the United States, shall be removed from Office on Impeachment for, and Conviction of, Treason, Bribery, or other high Crimes and Misdemeanors.

## ARTICLE III

*Sec. 1.* The judicial Power of the United States, shall be vested in one supreme Court, and in such inferior Courts as the Congress may from time to time ordain and establish. The judges, both of the supreme and inferior Courts, shall hold their Offices during good Behaviour, and shall, at stated Times, receive for their Services, a Compensation, which shall not be diminished during their Continuance in Office.

*Sec. 2.* The judicial Power shall extend to all Cases, in Law and Equity, arising under this Constitution, the Laws of the United States, and Treaties made, or

which shall be made, under their Authority;—to all Cases Affecting Ambassadors, other public Ministers and Consuls;—to all Cases of admiralty and maritime jurisdiction;—to Controversies to which the United States shall be a Party;—to Controversies between two or more States;—between a State and Citizens of another State;—between Citizens of different States;—between Citizens of the same State claiming Lands under Grants of different States, and between a State, or the citizens thereof, and foreign States, Citizens or Subjects.

In all Cases affecting Ambassadors, other public Ministers and Consuls, and those in which a State shall be Party, the supreme Court shall have original jurisdiction. In all the other cases before mentioned, the supreme Court shall have appellate jurisdiction, both as to Law and Fact, with such Exceptions, and under such Regulations as the Congress shall make.

The Trial of all Crimes, except in Cases of Impeachment, shall be by jury; and such Trial shall be held in the State where the said Crimes shall have been committed; but when not committed within any State, the Trial shall be at such Place or Places as the Congress may by Law have directed.

*Sec. 3.* Treason against the United States, shall consist only in levying War against them, or in adhering to their Enemies, giving them Aid and Comfort. No Person shall be convicted of Treason unless on the Testimony of two Witnesses to the same overt Act, or on Confession in open Court.

The Congress shall have Power to declare the Punishment of Treason, but no Attainder of Treason shall work Corruption of Blood, or Forfeiture except during the Life of the Person attainted.

## ARTICLE IV

*Sec. 1.* Full Faith and Credit shall be given in each State to the Public Acts, Records, and judicial Proceedings of every other State. And the Congress may by general Laws prescribe the Manner in which such Acts, Records and Proceedings shall be proved, and the Effect thereof.

*Sec. 2.* The Citizens of each State shall be entitled to all Privileges and Immunities of Citizens in the Several States.

A Person charged in any State with Treason, Felony, or other Crime, who shall flee from justice, and be found in another State, shall on Demand of the executive Authority of the State from which he fled, be delivered up, to be removed to the State having jurisdiction of the Crime.

No Person held to Service or Labour in one State, under the Laws thereof, escaping into another, shall, in Consequence of any Law or Regulation therein, be discharged from such Service or Labour, but shall be delivered up on Claim of the Party to whom such Service or Labour may be due.

*Sec. 3.* New States may be admitted by the Congress into this Union; but no new States shall be formed or erected within the jurisdiction of any other State; nor any State be formed by the junction of two or more States, or Parts of States, without Consent of the Legislatures of the States concerned as well as of the Congress.

The Congress shall have Power to dispose of and make all needful Rules and Regulations respecting the Territory or other Property belonging to the United States; and nothing in this Constitution shall be so construed as to Prejudice any Claims of the United States, or of any particular State.

*Sec. 4.* The United States shall guarantee to every State in this Union a Republican Form of Government, and shall protect each of them against Invasion; and on Application of the Legislature, or of the Executive (when the Legislature cannot be convened) against domestic Violence.

## ARTICLE V

The Congress, whenever two thirds of both Houses shall deem it necessary, shall propose Amendments to this Constitution, or, on the Application of the Legislatures of two thirds of the several States, shall call a Convention for proposing Amendments, which, in either Case, shall be valid to all Intents and Purposes, as Part of this Constitution, when ratified by the Legislatures of three fourths of the several States, or by Conventions in three fourths thereof, as the one or the other Mode of Ratification may be proposed by the Congress; Provided that no Amendment which may be made prior to the Year One thousand eight hundred and eight shall in any Manner affect the first and fourth Clauses in the Ninth Section of the first Article; and that no State, without its Consent, shall be deprived of its equal Suffrage in the Senate.

## ARTICLE VI

All Debts contracted and Engagements entered into, before the Adoption of this Constitution, shall be as valid against the United States under this Constitution, as under the Confederation.

This Constitution, and the Laws of the United States which shall be made in Pursuance thereof; and all Treaties made, or which shall be made, under the Authority of the United States, shall be the supreme Law of the Land; and the judges in every State shall be bound thereby, any Thing in the Constitution or Laws of any State to the Contrary notwithstanding.

The Senators and Representatives before mentioned, and the Members of the several State Legislatures, and all executive and judicial Officers, both of the United States and of the several States, shall be bound by Oath or Affirmation, to support this Constitution; but no religious Test shall ever be required as a Qualification to any Office or public Trust under the United States.

## ARTICLE VII

The Ratification of the Conventions of nine States, shall be sufficient for the Establishment of this Constitution between the States so ratifying the Same.

Done in Convention by the Unanimous Consent of the States present the Seventeenth Day of September in the Year of our Lord one thousand seven hundred and Eighty seven and of the Independence of the United States of America the Twelfth. In witness whereof We have hereunto subscribed our Names,

Attest William Jackson Secretary

Geo: Washington—Presidt.
and deputy from Virginia

*Delaware*
Geo: Read
Gunning Bedford junr
John Dickinson
Richard Bassett
Jaco: Broom

*New Hampshire*
John Langdon
Nicholas Gilman

*Maryland*
James McHenry
Dan of St Thos. Jenifer
Danl Carroll

*Massachusetts*
Nathaniel Gorham
Rufus King

*Virginia*
John Blair—
James Madison Jr.

*Connecticut*
Wm: Saml. Johnson
Roger Sherman

*New York*
Alexander Hamilton

*North Carolina*
Wm. Blount
Richd. Dobbs Spaight.
Hu Williamson

*New Jersey*
Wil: Livingston
David Brearley
Wm. Paterson.
Jona: Dayton

*South Carolina*
J. Rutledge
Charles Cotesworth Pinckney
Charles Pinckney
Pierce Butler

*Pennsylvania*
B Franklin
Thomas Mifflin
Robt Morris
Geo. Clymer
Thos. FitzSimons
Jared Ingersoll
James Wilson
Gouv. Morris

*Georgia*
William Few
Abr Baldwin

Articles in Addition to, and Amendment of, the Constitution of the United States of America, proposed by Congress, and ratified by the Legislatures of the several States, pursuant to the fifth Article of the original Constitution.

## ARTICLE I

Congress shall make no law respecting an establishment of religion, or prohibiting the free exercise thereof; or abridging the freedom of speech, or of the press; or the right of the people peacably to assemble, and to petition the government for a redress of grievances.

## ARTICLE II

A well regulated Militia, being necessary to the Security of a free State, the right of the people to keep and bear Arms, shall not be infringed.

## ARTICLE III

No Soldier shall, in time of peace be quartered in any house, without the consent of the Owner, nor in time of war, but in a manner to be prescribed by law.

## ARTICLE IV

The right of the people to be secure in their persons, houses, papers, and effects, against unreasonable searches and seizures, shall not be violated, and no Warrants shall issue, but upon probable cause, supported by Oath or affirmation, and particularly describing the place to be searched, and the persons or things to be seized.

## ARTICLE V

No person shall be held to answer for a capital, or otherwise infamous crime, unless on a presentment or indictment of a Grand Jury, except in cases arising in the land or naval forces, or in the Militia, when in actual service in time of War or public danger; nor shall any person be subject for the same offence to be twice put in jeopardy of life or limb; nor shall be compelled in any criminal case to be a witness against himself, nor be deprived of life, liberty, or property, without due process of law; nor shall private property be taken for public use, without just compensation.

## ARTICLE VI

In all criminal prosecutions, the accused shall enjoy the right to a speedy and public trial, by an impartial jury of the State and district wherein the crime shall have been committed, which district shall have been previously ascertained by law, and to be informed of the nature and cause of the accusation; to be confronted with the witnesses against him; to have compulsory process for obtaining witnesses in his favor, and to have the Assistance of Counsel for his defence.

## ARTICLE VII

In Suits at common law, where the value in controversy shall exceed twenty dollars, the right of trial by jury shall be preserved, and no fact tried by a jury, shall be otherwise re-examined in any Court of the United States, than according to the rules of the common law.

## ARTICLE VIII

Excessive bail shall not be required, nor excessive fines imposed, nor cruel and unusual punishments inflicted.

## ARTICLE IX

The enumeration in the Constitution, of certain rights, shall not be construed to deny or disparage others retained by the people.

# ARTICLE X

The powers not delegated to the United States by the Constitution, nor prohibited by it to the States, are preserved to the States respectively, or to the people.

# ARTICLE XI

The Judicial power of the United States shall not be construed to extend to any suit in law or equity, commenced or prosecuted against one of the United States by Citizens of another State, or by Citizens or Subjects of any Foreign State.

# ARTICLE XII

The Electors shall meet in their respective states, and vote by ballot for President and Vice-President, one of whom, at least, shall not be an inhabitant of the same state with themselves; they shall name in their ballots the person voted for as President, and in distinct ballots the person voted for as Vice-President, and they shall make distinct lists of all persons voted for as President, and of all persons voted for as Vice-President, and of the number of votes for each, which lists they shall sign and certify, and transmit sealed to the seat of the government of the United States, directed to the President of the Senate;—The President of the Senate shall, in the presence of the Senate and House of Representatives, open all the certificates and the votes shall then be counted;—The person having the greatest number of votes for President, shall be the President, if such number be a majority of the whole number of Electors appointed; and if no person have such majority, then from the persons having the highest numbers not exceeding three on the list of those voted for as President, the House of Representatives shall choose immediately, by ballot, the President. But in choosing the President the votes shall be taken by states, the representation from each state having one vote; a quorum for this purpose shall consist of a member or members from two-thirds of the states, and a majority of all the states shall be necessary to a choice. And if the House of Representatives shall not choose a President whenever the right of choice shall devolve upon them, before the fourth day of March next following, then the Vice-President shall act as President, as in the case of the death or other constitutional disability of the President.—The person having the greatest number of votes as Vice-President shall be the Vice-President, if such number be a majority of the whole number of Electors appointed, and if no person have a majority, then from the two highest numbers on the list the Senate shall choose the Vice-President; a quorum for the purpose shall consist of two-thirds of the whole number of Senators, and a majority of the whole number shall be necessary to a choice. But no person constitutionally ineligible to the office of President shall be eligible to that of Vice-President of the United States.

# ARTICLE XIII

*Sec. 1.* Neither slavery nor involuntary servitude, except as a punishment for crime whereof the party shall have been duly convicted, shall exist within the United States, or any place subject to their jurisdiction.

*Sec. 2.* Congress shall have power to enforce this article by appropriate legislation.

# ARTICLE XIV

*Sec. 1.* All persons born or naturalized in the United States, and subject to the jurisdiction thereof, are citizens of the United States and of the State wherein they reside. No State shall make or enforce any law which shall abridge the privileges or immunities of citizens of the United States; nor shall any State deprive any person of life, liberty, or property, without due process of law; nor deny to any person within its jurisdiction the equal protection of the laws.

*Sec. 2.* Representatives shall be apportioned among the several States according to their respective numbers, counting the whole number of persons in each

State, excluding Indians not taxed. But when the right to vote at any election for the choice of electors for President and Vice President of the United States, Representatives in Congress, the Executive and Judicial officers of a State, or the members of the Legislature thereof, is denied to any of the male inhabitants of such State, being twenty-one years of age, and citizens of the United States, or in any way abridged, except for participation in rebellion, or other crime, the basis of representation therein shall be reduced in the proportion which the number of such male citizens shall bear to the whole number of male citizens twenty-one years of age in such State.

*Sec. 3*. No person shall be a Senator or Representative in Congress, or elector of President and Vice President, or hold any office, civil or military, under the United States, or under any State, who, having previously taken an oath, as a member of Congress, or as an officer of the United States, or as a member of any State legislature, or as an executive or judicial officer of any State, to support the Constitution of the United States, shall have engaged in insurrection or rebellion against the same, or given aid or comfort to the enemies thereof. But Congress may by a vote of two-thirds of each House, remove such disability.

*Sec. 4*. The validity of the public debt of the United States, authorized by law, including debts incurred for payment of pensions and bounties for services in suppressing insurrection or rebellion, shall not be questioned. But neither the United States nor any State shall assume or pay any debt or obligation incurred in aid of insurrection or rebellion against the United States, or any claim for the loss or emancipation of any slave; but all such debts, obligations and claims shall be held illegal and void.

*Sec. 5*. The Congress shall have power to enforce, by appropriate the legislation, the provisions of this article.

## ARTICLE XV

*Sec. 1*. The right of citizens of the United States to vote shall not be denied or abridged by the United States or by any State on account of race, color, or previous condition of servitude.

*Sec. 2*. The Congress shall have power to enforce this article by appropriate legislation.

## ARTICLE XVI

The Congress shall have power to lay and collect taxes on incomes, from whatever source derived, without apportionment among the several States, and without regard to any census or enumeration.

## ARTICLE XVII

The Senate of the United States shall be composed of two Senators from each State, elected by the people thereof, for six years; and each Senator shall have one vote. The electors in each State shall have the qualifications requisite for electors of the most numerous branch of the State legislatures.

When vacancies happen in the representation of any State in the Senate, the executive authority of such State shall issue writs of election to fill such vacancies: *Provided*, That the legislature of any State may empower the executive thereof to make temporary appointments until the people fill the vacancies by election as the legislature may direct.

This amendment shall not be so construed as to affect the election or term of any Senator chosen before it becomes valid as part of the Constitution.

## ARTICLE XVIII

*Sec. 1*. After one year from the ratification of this article the manufacture, sale, or transportation of intoxicating liquors within, the importation thereof into, or the exportation thereof from the United States and all territory subject to the jurisdiction thereof for beverage purposes is hereby prohibited.

*Sec. 2*. The Congress and the several States shall have concurrent power to enforce this article by appropriate legislation.

*Sec. 3.* This article shall be inoperative unless it shall have been ratified as an amendment to the Constitution by the legislatures of the several States, as provided in the Constitution, within seven years from the date of the submission hereof to the States by the Congress.

## ARTICLE XIX

The right of citizens of the United States to vote shall not be denied or abridged by the United States or by any State on account of sex.

Congress shall have power to enforce this article by appropriate legislation.

## ARTICLE XX

*Sec. 1.* The terms of the President and Vice President shall end at noon on the 20th day of January, and the terms of Senators and Representatives at noon on the 3d day of January, of the years in which such terms would have ended if this article had not been ratified; and the terms of their successors shall then begin.

*Sec. 2.* The Congress shall assemble at least once in every year, and such meeting shall begin at noon on the 3d day of January, unless they shall by law appoint a different day.

*Sec. 3.* If, at the time fixed for the beginning of the term of the President, the President elect shall have died, the Vice President elect shall become President. If a President shall not have been chosen before the time fixed for the beginning of his term, or if the President elect shall have failed to qualify, then the Vice President elect shall act as President until a President shall have qualified; and the Congress may by law provide for the case wherein neither a President elect nor a Vice President elect shall have qualified, declaring who shall then act as President, or the manner in which one who is to act shall be selected, and such person shall act accordingly until a President or Vice President shall have qualified.

*Sec. 4.* The Congress may by law provide for the case of the death of any of the persons from whom the House of Representatives may choose a President whenever the right of choice shall have devolved upon them, and for the case of the death of any of the persons from whom the Senate may choose a Vice President whenever the right of choice shall have devolved upon them.

*Sec. 5.* Sections 1 and 2 shall take effect on the 15th day of October following the ratification of this article.

*Sec. 6.* This article shall be inoperative unless it shall have been ratified as an amendment to the Constitution by the legislatures of three-fourths of the several States within seven years from the date of its submission.

## ARTICLE XXI

*Sec. 1.* The eighteenth article of amendment to the Constitution of the United States is hereby repealed.

*Sec. 2.* The transportation or importation into any State, Territory, or possession of the United States for delivery or use therein of intoxicating liquors, in violation of the laws thereof, is hereby prohibited.

*Sec. 3.* This article shall be inoperative unless it shall have been ratified as an amendment to the Constitution by conventions in the several States, as provided in the Constitution, within seven years from the date of the submission hereof to the States by the Congress.

## ARTICLE XXII

*Sec. 1.* No person shall be elected to the office of the President more than twice, and no person who has held the office of President, or acted as President, for more than two years of a term to which some other person was elected President shall be elected to the office of the President more than once. But this Article shall not apply to any person holding the office of President when this Article was proposed by the Congress, and shall not prevent any person who may be holding the office of President, or acting as President during the term within which this Article becomes operative from holding the office of President or acting as President during the remainder of such term.

*Sec. 2.* This article shall be inoperative unless it shall have been ratified as an amendment to the Constitution by the legislatures of three-fourths of the several States within seven years from the date of its submission to the States by the Congress.

## ARTICLE XXIII

*Sec. 1.* The District constituting the seat of Government of the United States shall appoint in such manner as the Congress may direct:

A number of electors of President and Vice President equal to the whole number of Senators and Representatives in Congress to which the District would be entitled if it were a State, but in no event more than the least populous State; they shall be in addition to those appointed by the States, but they shall be considered, for the purposes of the election of President and Vice President, to be electors appointed by a State; and they shall meet in the District and perform such duties as provided by the twelfth article of amendment.

*Sec. 2.* The Congress shall have power to enforce this article by appropriate legislation.

## ARTICLE XXIV

The right of citizens of the United States to vote in any primary or other election for President or Vice President, for electors for President or Vice President, or for Senator or Representative in Congress, shall not be denied or abridged by the United States or any State by reason of failure to pay any poll tax or other tax.

*Sec. 2.* The Congress shall have power to enforce this article by appropriate legislation.

## ARTICLE XXV

*Sec. 1.* In case of the removal of the President from office or of his death or resignation, the Vice President shall become President.

*Sec. 2.* Whenever there is a vacancy in the office of the Vice President, the President shall nominate a Vice President who shall take office upon confirmation by a majority vote of both Houses of Congress.

*Sec. 3.* Whenever the President transmits to the President pro tempore of the Senate and the Speaker of the House of Representatives his written declaration that he is unable to discharge the powers and duties of his office, and until he transmits to them a written declaration to the contrary, such powers and duties shall be discharged by the Vice President as Acting President.

*Sec. 4.* Whenever the Vice President and a majority of either the principal officers of the executive departments or of such other body as Congress may by law provide, transmit to the President pro tempore of the Senate and the Speaker of the House of Representatives their written declaration that the President is unable to discharge the powers and duties of his office, the Vice President shall immediately assume the powers and duties of the office as Acting President.

Thereafter, when the President transmits to the President pro tempore of the Senate and the Speaker of the House of Representatives his written declaration that no inability exists, he shall resume the powers and duties of his office unless the Vice President and a majority of either the principal officers of the executive department or of such other body as Congress may by law provide, transmit within four days to the President pro tempore of the Senate and the Speaker of the House of Representatives their written declaration that the President is unable to discharge the powers and duties of his office. Thereupon Congress shall decide the issue, assembling within forty-eight hours for that purpose if not in session. If the Congress, within twenty-one days after receipt of the latter written declaration, or, if Congress is not in session, within twenty-one days after Congress is required to assemble, determines by two-thirds vote of both Houses that the President is unable to discharge the powers and duties of his office, the Vice President shall continue to discharge the same as Acting President; otherwise, the President shall resume the powers and duties of his office.

## ARTICLE XXVI

*Sec. 1.* The right of citizens of the United States, who are eighteen years of age or older, to vote shall not be denied or abridged by the United States or by any State on account of age.

*Sec. 2.* The Congress shall have power to enforce this article by appropriate legislation.

## ARTICLE XXVII

No law, varying the compensation for the services of the Senators and Representatives, shall take effect, until an election of Representatives shall have intervened.

# THE DECLARATION OF THE RIGHTS OF MAN AND OF THE CITIZEN

The Declaration was adopted August 26, 1789, by the French Constituent Assembly and served as a preamble to the French constitution of 1791.

The representatives of the people of France, formed into a National Assembly, considering that ignorance, neglect, or contempt of human rights, are the sole causes of public misfortunes and corruptions of Government, have resolved to set forth in a solemn declaration, these natural, imprescriptible, and inalienable rights: that this declaration being constantly present to the minds of the members of the body social, they may be for ever kept attentive to their rights and their duties; that the acts of the legislative and executive powers of government, being capable of being every moment compared with the end of political institutions, may be respected; and also, that the future claims of the citizens, being directed by simple and incontestable principles, may tend to the maintenance of the Constitution, and the general happiness.

For these reasons, the National Assembly doth recognize and declare, in the presence of the Supreme Being, and with the hope of his blessing and favour, the following *sacred* rights of men and of citizens:

  I.  Men are born, and always continue, free and equal in respect of their rights. Civil distinctions, therefore, can be founded only on public utility.

  II.  The end of all political associations, is the preservation of the natural and impre-

Translated by Thomas Paine.

scriptible rights of man; and these rights are liberty, property, security, and resistance of oppression.

III. The nation is essentially the source of all sovereignty; nor can any individual, or any body of men, be entitled to any authority which is not expressly derived from it.

IV. Political liberty consists in the power of doing whatever does not injure another. The exercise of the natural rights of every man, has no other limits than those which are necessary to secure to every *other* man the free exercise of the same rights; and these limits are determinable only by the law.

V. The law ought to prohibit only actions hurtful to society. What is not prohibited by the law, should not be hindered; nor should any one be compelled to that which the law does not require.

VI. The law is an expression of the will of the community. All citizens have a right to concur, either personally, or by their representatives, in its formation. It should be the same to all, whether it protects or punishes; and all being equal in its sight, are equally eligible to all honours, places, and employments, according to their different abilities, without any other distinction than that created by their virtues and talents.

VII. No man should be accused, arrested, or held in confinement, except in cases determined by the law, and according to the forms which it has prescribed. All who promote, solicit, execute, or cause to be executed, arbitrary orders, ought to be punished, and every citizen called upon, or apprehended by virtue of the law, ought immediately to obey, and renders himself culpable by resistance.

VIII. The law ought to impose no other penalties but such as are absolutely and evidently necessary; and no one ought to be punished, but in virtue of a law promulgated before the offence, and legally applied.

IX. Every man being presumed innocent till he has been convicted, whenever his detention becomes indispensable, all rigour to him, more than is necessary to secure his person, ought to be provided against by the law.

X. No man ought to be molested on account of his opinions, not even on account of his *religious* opinions, provided his avowal of them does not disturb the public order established by law.

XI. The unrestrained communication of thoughts and opinions being one of the most precious rights of man, every citizen may speak, write, and publish freely, provided he is responsible for the abuse of this liberty, in cases determined by law.

XII. A public force being necessary to give security to the rights of men and of citizens, that force is instituted for the benefit of the community and not for the particular benefit of the persons to whom it is intrusted.

XIII. A common contribution being necessary for the support of the public force, and for defraying the other expenses of government, it ought to be divided equally among the members of the community, according to their abilities.

XIV. Every citizen has a right, either by himself or his representative, to a free voice in determining the necessity of public contributions, the appropriation of them, and their account, mode of assessment, and duration.

XV. Every community has had a right to demand of all its agents an account of their conduct.

XVI. Every community in which a separation of powers and a security of rights is not provided for, wants a constitution.

XVII. The right to property being inviolable and sacred, no one ought to be deprived of it, except in cases of evident public necessity, legally ascertained, and on condition of a previous just indemnity.

# ABRAHAM LINCOLN

This address was delivered on March 4, 1861. The following month the Civil War began.

## First Inaugural Address

Fellow citizens of the United States:

In compliance with a custom as old as the government itself, I appear before you to address you briefly, and to take, in your presence, the oath prescribed by the Constitution of the United States, to be taken by the President "before he enters on the execution of his office."

I do not consider it necessary, at present, for me to discuss those matters of administration about which there is no special anxiety, or excitement.

Apprehension seems to exist among the people of the Southern States, that by the accession of a Republican Administration, their property, and their peace, and personal security, are to be endangered. There has never been any reasonable cause for such apprehension. Indeed, the most ample evidence to the contrary has all the while existed, and been open to their inspection. It is found in nearly all the published speeches of him who now addresses you. I do but quote from one of those speeches when I declare that "I have no purpose, directly or indirectly, to interfere with the institution of slavery in the States where it exists. I believe I have no lawful right to do so, and I have no inclination to do so." Those who nominated and elected me did so with full knowledge that I had made this, and many similar declarations, and had never recanted them. And more than this, they placed in the platform, for my acceptance, and as a law to themselves, and to me, the clear and emphatic resolution which I now read:

"*Resolved,* That the maintenance inviolate of the rights of the States, and especially the right of each State to order and control its own domestic institutions according to its own judgment exclusively, is essential to that balance of power on which the perfection and endurance of our political fabric depend; and we denounce the lawless invasion by armed force of the soil of any State or Territory, no matter under what pretext, as among the gravest of crimes."

I now reiterate these sentiments: and in doing so, I only press upon the public attention the most conclusive evidence of which the case is susceptible, that the property, peace and security of no section are to be in anywise endangered by the now incoming Administration. I add too, that all the protection which, consistently with the Constitution and the laws, can be given, will be cheerfully given to all the States when lawfully demanded, for whatever cause—as cheerfully to one section, as to another....

It is seventy-two years since the first inauguration of a President under our national Constitution. During that period fifteen different and greatly distinguished citizens, have, in succession, administered the executive branch of the government. They have conducted it through many perils; and, generally, with great success. Yet, with all this scope for precedent, I now enter upon the same task for the brief constitutional term of four years, under great and peculiar difficulty. A disruption of the Federal Union heretofore only menaced, is now formidably attempted.

I hold, that in contemplation of universal law, and of the Constitution, the Union of these States is perpetual. Perpetuity is implied, if not expressed, in the fundamental law of all national governments. It is safe to assert that no government proper, ever had a provision in its organic law for its own termination. Continue to execute all the express provisions of our national Constitution, and the Union will endure forever—it being impossible to destroy it, except by some action not provided for in the instrument itself.

Again, if the United States be not a government proper, but an association of States in the nature of contract merely, can it, as a contract, be peaceably unmade, by less than all the parties who made it? One party to a contract may violate it—break it, so to speak; but does it not require all to lawfully rescind it?

Descending from these general principles, we find the proposition that, in legal contemplation, the Union is perpetual, confirmed by the history of the Union itself. The Union is much older than the Constitution. It was formed in fact, by the Articles of Association in 1774. It was matured and continued by the Declaration of Independence in 1776. It was further matured and the faith of all the then thirteen States expressly plighted and engaged that it should be perpetual, by the Articles of Confederation in 1778. And finally, in 1787, one of the declared objects for ordaining and establishing the Constitution, was *"to form a more perfect union."*

But if destruction of the Union, by one, or by a part only, of the States, be lawfully possible, the Union is *less* perfect than before the Constitution, having lost the vital element of perpetuity.

It follows from these views that no State, upon its own mere motion, can lawfully get out of the Union,—that *resolves* and *ordinances* to that effect are legally void; and that acts of violence, within any State or States, against the authority of the United States, are insurrectionary or revolutionary, according to circumstances.

I therefore consider that, in view of the Constitution and the laws, the Union is unbroken; and, to the extent of my ability, I shall take care, as the Constitution itself expressly enjoins upon me, that the laws of the Union be faithfully executed in all the States. Doing this I deem to be only a simple duty on my part; and I shall perform it, so far as practicable, unless my rightful masters, the American people, shall withhold

the requisite means, or, in some authoritative manner, direct the contrary. I trust this will not be regarded as a menace, but only as the declared purpose of the Union that it *will* constitutionally defend, and maintain itself.

In doing this there needs to be no bloodshed or violence; and there shall be none, unless it be forced upon the national authority. The power confided to me, will be used to hold, occupy, and possess the property, and places belonging to the government, and to collect the duties and imposts; but beyond what may be necessary for these objects, there will be no invasion—no using of force against, or among the people anywhere. . . .

That there are persons in one section, or another who seek to destroy the Union at all events, and are glad of any pretext to do it, I will neither affirm or deny; but if there be such, I need address no word to them. To those, however, who really love the Union, may I not speak?

Before entering upon so grave a matter as the destruction of our national fabric, with all its benefits, its memories, and its hopes, would it not be wise to ascertain precisely why we do it? Will you hazard so desperate a step, while there is any possibility that any portion of the ills you fly from, have no real existence? Will you, while the certain ills you fly to, are greater than all the real ones you fly from? Will you risk the commission of so fearful a mistake?

All profess to be content in the Union, if all constitutional rights can be maintained. Is it true, then, that any right, plainly written in the Constitution, has been denied? I think not. Happily the human mind is so constituted, that no party can reach to the audacity of doing this. Think, if you can, of a single instance in which a plainly written provision of the Constitution has ever been denied. If, by the mere force of numbers, a majority should deprive a minority of any clearly written constitutional right, it might, in a moral point of view, justify revolution—certainly would, if such right were a vital one. But such is not our case. All the vital rights of minorities, and of individuals, are so plainly assured to them, by affirmations and negations, guaranties and prohibitions, in the Constitution, that controversies never arise concerning them. But no organic law can ever be framed with a provision specifically applicable to every question which may occur in practical administration. No foresight can anticipate, nor any document of reasonable length contain express provisions for all possible questions. Shall fugitives from labor be surrendered by national or by State authority? The Constitution does not expressly say. *May* Congress prohibit slavery in the territories? The Constitution does not expressly say. *Must* Congress protect slavery in the territories? The Constitution does not expressly say.

From questions of this class spring all our constitutional controversies, and we divide upon them into majorities and minorities. If the minority will not acquiesce, the majority must, or the government must cease. There is no other alternative; for continuing the government, is acquiescence on one side or the other. If a minority, in such case, will secede rather than acquiesce, they make a precedent which, in turn, will divide and ruin them; for a minority of their own will secede from them, whenever a majority refuses to be controlled by such minority. For instance, why may not any portion of a new confederacy, a year or two hence, arbitrarily secede again, precisely as portions of the present Union now claim to secede from it. All who cherish disunion sentiments, are now being educated to the exact temper of doing this. Is there such perfect identity of interests among the States to compose a new Union, as to produce harmony only, and prevent renewed secession?

Plainly, the central idea of secession, is the essence of anarchy. A majority, held in restraint by constitutional checks, and limitations, and always changing easily, with deliberate changes of popular opinions and sentiments, is the only true sovereign of a free people. Whoever rejects it, does, of necessity, fly to anarchy or to despotism. Unanimity is impossible; the rule of a minority, as a permanent arrangement, is wholly inadmissible; so that, rejecting the majority principle, anarchy, or despotism in some form, is all that is left. . . .

One section of our country believes slavery is *right,* and ought to be extended, while the other believes it is *wrong,* and ought not to be extended. This is the only substantial dispute. . . .

Physically speaking, we cannot separate. We cannot remove our respective sections from each other, nor build an impassable wall between them. A husband and wife may be divorced, and go out of the presence, and beyond the reach of each other; but the different parts of our country cannot do this. They cannot but remain face to face; and intercourse, either amicable or hostile, must continue between them. Is it possible then to make that intercourse more advantageous, or more satisfactory, *after* separation than *before?* Can aliens make treaties easier than friends can make laws? Can treaties be more faithfully enforced between aliens, than laws can among friends? Suppose you go to war, you cannot fight always; and when, after much loss on both sides, and no gain on either, you cease fighting, the identical old questions, as to terms of intercourse, are again upon you.

This country, with its institutions, belongs to the people who inhabit it. Whenever they shall grow weary of the existing government, they can exercise their *constitutional* right of amending it, or their *revolutionary* right to dismember, or overthrow it. I can not be ignorant of the fact that many worthy, and patriotic citizens are desirous of having the national constitution amended. While I make no recommendation of amendments, I fully recognize the rightful authority of the people over the whole subject, to be exercised in either of the modes prescribed in the instrument itself; and I should, under existing circumstances, favor, rather than oppose, a fair opportunity being afforded the people to act upon it. . . .

Why should there not be a patient confidence in the ultimate justice of the people? Is there any better, or equal hope, in the world? In our present differences, is either party without faith of being in the right? If the Almighty Ruler of nations, with his eternal truth and justice, be on your side of the North, or on yours of the South, that truth, and that justice, will surely prevail, by the judgment of this great tribunal, the American people.

By the frame of the government under which we live, this same people have wisely given their public

ABRAHAM LINCOLN

servants but little power for mischief; and have, with equal wisdom, provided for the return of that little to their own hands at very short intervals.

While the people retain their virtue, and vigilence, no administration, by any extreme of wickedness or folly, can very seriously injure the government, in the short space of four years.

My countrymen, one and all, think calmly and *well,* upon this whole subject. Nothing valuable can be lost by taking time. If there be an object to *hurry* any of you, in hot haste, to a step which you would never take *deliberately,* that object will be frustrated by taking time; but no good object can be frustrated by it. Such of you as are now dissatisfied, still have the old Constitution unimpaired, and, on the sensitive point, the laws of your own framing under it; while the new administration will have no immediate power, if it would, to change either. If it were admitted that you who are dissatisfied, hold the right side in the dispute, there still is no single good reason for pre-

cipitate action. Intelligence, patriotism, Christianity, and a firm reliance on Him, who has never yet forsaken this favored land, are still competent to adjust, in the best way, all our present difficulty.

In *your* hands, my dissatisfied fellow countrymen, and not in *mine,* is the momentous issue of civil war. The government will not assail *you.* You can have no conflict, without being yourselves the aggressors. *You* have no oath registered in Heaven to destroy the government, while *I* shall have the most solemn one to "preserve, protect and defend" it.

I am loth to close. We are not enemies, but friends. We must not be enemies. Though passion may have strained, it must not break our bonds of affection. The mystic chords of memory, stretching from every battlefield, and patriot grave, to every living heart and hearthstone, all over this broad land, will yet swell the chorus of the Union, when again touched, as surely they will be, by the better angels of our nature.

This address was delivered on November 19, 1863, at the dedication of the cemetery at Gettysburg, Pennsylvania.

# Gettysburg Address

Four score and seven years ago our fathers brought forth on this continent, a new nation, conceived in Liberty, and dedicated to the proposition that all men are created equal.

Now we are engaged in a great civil war, testing whether that nation, or any nation so conceived and so dedicated, can long endure. We are met on a great battle-field of that war. We have come to dedicate a portion of that field, as a final resting place for those who here gave their lives that that nation might live. It is altogether fitting and proper that we should do this.

But, in a larger sense, we can not dedicate—we can not consecrate—we can not hallow—this ground. The brave men, living and dead, who struggled here,

have consecrated it, far above our poor power to add or detract. The world will little note, nor long remember what we say here, but it can never forget what they did here. It is for us the living, rather, to be dedicated here to the unfinished work which they who fought here have thus far so nobly advanced. It is rather for us to be here dedicated to the great task remaining before us—that from these honored dead we take increased devotion to that cause for which they gave the last full measure of devotion—that we here highly resolve that these dead shall not have died in vain—that this nation, under God, shall have a new birth of freedom—and that government of the people, by the people, for the people, shall not perish from the earth.

This address was delivered on March 4, 1865. The following month the Civil War ended, and Lincoln was assassinated.

# Second Inaugural Address

Fellow Countrymen:

At this second appearing to take the oath of the presidential office, there is less occasion for an extended address than there was at the first. Then a statement, somewhat in detail, of a course to be pursued, seemed fitting and proper. Now, at the expiration of four years, during which public declarations have been constantly called forth on every point and phase of the great contest which still absorbs the attention, and engrosses the energies of the nation, little that is new could be presented. The progress of our arms, upon which all else chiefly depends, is as well known to the public as to myself; and it is, I trust, reasonably satisfactory and encouraging to all. With high hope for the future, no prediction in regard to it is ventured.

On the occasion corresponding to this four years ago, all thoughts were anxiously directed to an impending civil war. All dreaded it—all sought to avert it. While the inaugural address was being delivered from this place, devoted altogether to *saving* the Union without war, insurgent agents were in the city seeking to *destroy* it without war—seeking to dissolve the Union, and divide effects, by negotiation. Both parties deprecated war; but one of them would *make* war rather than let the nation survive; and the other would *accept* war rather than let it perish. And the war came.

One eighth of the whole population were colored slaves, not distributed generally over the Union, but localized in the Southern part of it. These slaves constituted a peculiar and powerful interest. All knew that this interest was, somehow, the cause of the war. To strengthen, perpetuate, and extend this interest was the object for which the insurgents would rend the Union, even by war; while the government claimed no right to do more than to restrict the territorial enlargement of it. Neither party expected for the war, the magnitude, or the duration, which it has already attained. Neither anticipated that the *cause* of the conflict might cease with, or even before, the conflict itself should cease. Each looked for an easier triumph, and a result less fundamental and astounding. Both read the same Bible, and pray to the same God; and each invokes His aid against the other. It may seem strange that any men should dare to ask a just God's assistance in wringing their bread from the sweat of other men's faces; but let us judge not that we be not judged. The prayers of both could not be answered; that of neither has been answered fully. The Almighty has His own purposes. "Woe unto the world because of offences! for it must needs be that offences come; but woe to that man by whom the offence cometh!" If we shall suppose that American Slavery is one of those offences which, in the providence of God, must needs come, but which, having continued through His appointed time, He now wills to remove, and that He gives to both North and South, this terrible war, as the woe due to those by whom the offence came, shall we discern therein any departure from those divine attributes which the believers in a Living God always ascribe to Him? Fondly do we hope—fervently do we pray—that this mighty scourge of war may speedily pass away. Yet, if God wills that it continue, until all the wealth piled by the bondman's two hundred and fifty years of unrequited toil shall be sunk, and until every drop of blood drawn with the lash, shall be paid by another drawn with the sword, as was said three thousand years ago, so still it must be said "the judgments of the Lord, are true and righteous altogether."

With malice toward none; with charity for all; with firmness in the right, as God gives us to see the right, let us strive on to finish the work we are in; to bind up the nation's wounds; to care for him who shall have borne the battle, and for his widow, and his orphan—to do all which may achieve and cherish a just, and a lasting peace, among ourselves, and with all nations.

# ELIZABETH CADY STANTON

Elizabeth Cady Stanton (1815–1902), leader of the women's rights movement, delivered this address in 1892 before the Judiciary Committee of the U.S. House of Representatives and then before the Committee on Woman Suffrage of the U.S. Senate.

## The Solitude of Self

Mr. Chairman and Gentlemen of the Committee:

We have been speaking before Committees of the Judiciary for the last twenty years, and we have gone over all the arguments in favor of the sixteenth amendment which are familiar to all you gentlemen; therefore, it will not be necessary that I should repeat them again.

The point I wish plainly to bring before you on this occasion is the individuality of each human soul—our Protestant idea, the right of individual conscience and judgment—our republican idea, individual citizenship. In discussing the right of woman, we are to consider, first, what belongs to her as an individual, in a world of her own, the arbiter of her own destiny, an imaginary Robinson Crusoe with her woman Friday on a solitary island. Her rights under such circumstances are to use all her faculties for her own safety and happiness.

Secondly, if we consider her as a citizen, as a member of a great nation, she must have the same rights as all other members, according to the fundamental principles of our government.

Thirdly, viewed as a woman, an equal factor in civilization, her rights and duties are still the same—individual happiness and development.

Fourthly, it is only the incidental relations of life, such as mother, wife, sister, daughter, which may involve some special duties and training. In the usual discussion in regard to woman's sphere, such men as Herbert Spencer, Frederic Harrison, and Grant Allen uniformly subordinate her rights and duties as an individual, as a citizen, as a woman, to the necessities of these incidental relations, some of which a large class of women may never assume. In discussing the sphere of man we do not decide his rights as an individual, as a citizen, as a man, by his duties as a father, a husband, a brother, or a son, relations some of which he may never fill. Moreover, he would be better fitted for these very relations, and whatever special work he might choose to do to earn his bread, by the complete development of all his faculties as an individual.

Just so with woman. The education that will fit her to discharge the duties in the largest sphere of human usefulness, will best fit her for whatever special work she may be compelled to do.

Reprinted from *The Search for Self-Sovereignty: The Oratory of Elizabeth Cady Stanton,* edited by Beth M. Waggonspack, New York, Greenwood Press, 1987. By permission of the publisher.

The isolation of every human soul and the necessity of self-dependence must give each individual the right to choose his own surroundings.

The strongest reason for giving woman all the opportunities for higher education, for the full development of her faculties, her forces of mind and body; for giving her the most enlarged freedom of thought and action; a complete emancipation from all forms of bondage, of custom, dependence, superstition; from all the crippling influences of fear; is the solitude and personal responsibility of her own individual life. The strongest reason why we ask for woman a voice in the government under which she lives; in the religion she is asked to believe; equality in social life, where she is the chief factor; a place in the trades and professions, where she may earn her bread, is because of her birthright to self-sovereignty; because, as an individual, she must rely on herself. No matter how much women prefer to lean, to be protected and supported, nor how much men desire to have them do so, they must make the voyage of life alone, and for safety in an emergency they must know something of the laws of navigation. To guide our own craft, we must be captain, pilot, engineer; with chart and compass to stand at the wheel; to watch the wind and waves and know when to take in the sail, and to read the signs in the firmament over all. It matters not whether the solitary voyager is man or woman.

Nature having endowed them equally, leaves them to their own skill and judgment in the hour of danger, and, if not equal to the occasion, alike they perish.

To appreciate the importance of fitting every human soul for independent action, think for a moment of the immeasurable solitude of self. We come into the world alone, unlike all who have gone before us; we leave it alone under circumstances peculiar to ourselves. No mortal ever has been, no mortal ever will be like the soul just launched on the sea of life. There can never again be just such environments as make up the infancy, youth and manhood of this one. Nature never repeats herself, and the possibilities of one human soul will never be found in another. No one has ever found two blades of ribbon grass alike, and no one will ever find two human

beings alike. Seeing, then, what must be the infinite diversity in human character, we can in a measure appreciate the loss to a nation when any large class of the people is uneducated and unrepresented in the government. We ask for the complete development of every individual, first, for his own benefit and happiness. In fitting out an army we give each soldier his own knapsack, arms, powder, his blanket, cup, knife, fork and spoon. We provide alike for all their individual necessities, then each man bears his own burden.

Again we ask complete individual development for the general good; for the consensus of the competent on the whole round of human interest; on all questions of national life, and here each man must bear his share of the general burden. It is sad to see how soon friendless children are left to bear their own burdens before they can analyze their feelings; before they can even tell their joys and sorrows, they are thrown on their own resources. The great lesson that nature seems to teach us at all ages is self-dependence, self-protection, self-support. What a touching instance of a child's solitude; of that hunger of heart for love and recognition, in the case of a little girl who helped to dress a Christmas tree for the children of the family in which she served. On finding there was no present for herself she slipped away in the darkness and spent the night in an open field sitting on a stone, and when found in the morning was weeping as if her heart would break. No mortal will ever know the thought that passed through the mind of the friendless child in the long hours of that cold night, with only the silent stars to keep her company. The mention of her case in the daily papers moved many generous hearts to send her presents, but in the hours of her keenest sufferings she was thrown wholly on herself for consolation.

In youth our most bitter disappointments, our brightest hopes and ambitions are known only to ourselves; even our friendship and love we never fully share with another; there is something of every passion in every situation we conceal. Even so in our triumphs and our defeats.

The successful candidate for Presidency and his opponent each have a solitude peculiarly his own, and good form forbids either to speak of his pleasure or regret. The solitude of the king on his throne and the prisoner in his cell differs in characters and degree, but it is solitude nevertheless.

We ask no sympathy from others in the anxiety and agony of a broken friendship or shattered love. When death sunders our nearest ties, alone we sit in the shadows of our affliction. Alike mid the greatest triumphs and darkest tragedies of life we walk alone. On the divine heights of human attainments, eulogized and worshipped as a hero or a saint, we stand alone. In ignorance, poverty, and vice, as a pauper or criminal, alone we starve or steal; alone we suffer the sneers and rebuffs of our fellows; alone we are hunted and hounded through dark courts and alleys, in by-ways and highways; alone we stand in the judgment seats; alone in the prison cell we lament our crimes and misfortunes; alone we expiate them on the gallows. In hours like these we realize the awful solitude of individual life, its pains, its penalties, its responsibilities; hours in which the youngest and most helpless are thrown on their own resources for guidance and consolation. Seeing then that life must ever be a march and a battle, that each soldier must be equipped for his own protection, it is the height of cruelty to rob the individual of a single natural right.

To throw obstacles in the way of a complete education, is like putting out the eyes; to deny the rights of property, like cutting off the hands. To deny political equality is to rob the ostracized of all self-respect; of credit in the market place; of recompense in the world of work; of a voice among those who make and administer the law; a choice in the jury before whom they are tried, and in the judge who decides their punishment. Shakespeare's play of Titus and Andronicus [sic] contains a terrible satire on woman's position in the nineteenth century— "Rude men" (the play tells us) seize the king's daughter, cut out her tongue, cut off her hands, and then bade her go call for water and wash her hands." What a picture of woman's position. Robbed of her natural rights, handicapped by law and custom at every turn, yet compelled to fight her own battles, and in the emergencies of life to fall back on herself for protection.

The girl of sixteen, thrown on the world to sup-

port herself, to make her own place in society, to resist the temptations that surround her and maintain a spotless integrity, must do all this by native force or superior education. She does not acquire this power by being trained to trust others and distrust herself. If she wearies of the struggle, finding it hard work to swim upstream, and allows herself to drift with the current, she will find plenty of company, but not one to share her misery in the hour of her deepest humiliation. If she tries to retrieve her position, to conceal the past, her life is hedged about with fears lest willing hands should tear the veil from what she fain would hide. Young and friendless, she knows the bitter solitude of self.

How the little courtesies of life on the surface of society, deemed so important from man towards woman, fade into utter insignificance in view of the deeper tragedies in which she must play her part alone, where no human aid is possible.

The young wife and mother, at the head of some establishment with a kind husband to shield her from the adverse winds of life, with wealth, fortune, and position, has a certain harbor of safety, secure against the ordinary ills of life. But to manage a household, have a desirable influence in society, keep her friends and the affections of her husband, train her children and servants well, she must have a rare common sense, wisdom, diplomacy, and a knowledge of human nature. To do all this she needs the cardinal virtues and the strong points of character that the most successful statesman possesses.

An uneducated woman, trained to dependence, with no resources in herself must make a failure of any position in life. But society says women do not need a knowledge of the world; the liberal training that experience in public life must give, all the advantages of collegiate education; but when for the lack of all this, the woman's happiness is wrecked, alone she bears her humiliation; and the solitude of the weak and the ignorant is indeed pitiful. In the wild chase for the prizes of life they are ground to powder.

In age, when the pleasures of youth are passed, children grown up, married and gone, the hurry and bustle of life in a measure over, when the hands are weary of active service, when the old armchair and the fireside are the chosen resorts, then men and women alike must fall back on their own resources. If they cannot find companionship in books, if they have no interest in the vital questions of the hour, no interest in watching the consummation of reforms, with which they might have been identified, they soon pass into their dotage. The more fully the faculties of the mind are developed and kept in use, the longer the period of vigor and active interest in all around us continues. If from a lifelong participation in public affairs a woman feels responsible for the laws regulating our system of education, the discipline of our jails and prisons, the sanitary conditions of our private homes, public buildings, and thoroughfares, an interest in commerce, finance, our foreign relations, in any or all of these questions, her solitude will at least be respectable, and she will not be driven to gossip or scandal for entertainment.

The chief reason for opening to every soul the doors to the whole round of human duties and pleasures is the individual development thus attained, the resources thus provided under all circumstances to mitigate the solitude that at times must come to everyone. I once asked Prince Krapotkin, the Russian nihilist, how he endured his long years in prison, deprived of books, pen, ink, and paper. "Ah," he said, "I thought out many questions on which I had a deep interest. In the pursuit of an idea I took no note of time. When tired of solving knotty problems I recited all the beautiful passages in prose or verse I had ever learned. I became acquainted with my self and my own resources. I had a world of my own, a vast empire, that no Russian jailor or Czar could invade." Such is the value of liberal thought and broad culture when shut from all human companionship, bringing comfort and sunshine within even the four walls of a prison cell.

As women ofttimes share a similar fate, should they not have all the consolation that the most liberal education can give? Their suffering in the prisons of St. Petersburg; in the long, weary marches to Siberia, and in the mines, working side by side with men, surely call for all the self-support that the most exalted sentiments of heroism can give. When sud-

denly roused at midnight, with the startling cry of "Fire! Fire" to find the house over their heads in flames, do women wait for men to point the way to safety? And are the men, equally bewildered and half suffocated with smoke, in a position to more than save themselves?

At such times the most timid women have shown a courage and heroism in saving their husbands and children that has surprised everybody. Inasmuch, then, as woman shares equally the joys and sorrows of time and eternity, is it not the height of presumption in man to propose to represent her at the ballot box and the throne of grace, do her voting in the state, her praying in the church, and to assume the position of priest at the family altar.

Nothing strengthens the judgment and quickens the conscience like individual responsibility. Nothing adds such dignity to character as the recognition of one's self-sovereignty; the right to an equal place, everywhere conceded; a place earned by personal merit, not an artificial attainment by inheritance, wealth, family, and position. Seeing, then that the responsibilities of life rest equally on man and woman, that their destiny is the same, they need the same preparation for time and eternity. The talk of sheltering woman from the fierce storms of life is the sheerest mockery, for they beat on her from every point of the compass, just as they do on man, and with more fatal results, for he has been trained to protect himself, to resist, to conquer. Such are the facts in human experience, the responsibilities of individual sovereignty. Rich and poor, intelligent and ignorant, wise and foolish, virtuous and vicious, man and woman, it is ever the same, each soul must depend wholly on itself.

Whatever the theories may be of woman's dependence on man, in the supreme moments of her life he can not bear her burdens. Alone she goes to the gates of death to give life to every man that is born into the world. No one can share her fears, no one can mitigate her pangs; and if her sorrow is greater than she can bear, alone she passes beyond the gates into the vast unknown.

From the mountain tops of Judea, long ago, a heavenly voice bade His disciples, "Bear ye one another's burdens," but humanity has not yet risen to that point of self-sacrifice, and if ever so willing, how few the burdens are that one soul can bear for another. In the highways of Palestine; in prayer and fasting on the solitary mountain top; in the Garden of Gethsemane; before the judgment seat of Pilate; betrayed by one of His trusted disciples at His last supper; in His agonies on the cross, even Jesus of Nazareth, in these last sad days on earth, felt the awful solitude of self. Deserted by man, in agony he cries, "My God! My God! Why hast Thou forsaken me." And so it ever must be in the conflicting scenes of life, in the long weary march, each one walks alone. We may have many friends, love, kindness, sympathy and charity to smooth our pathway in everyday life, but in the tragedies and triumphs of human experience each mortal stands alone.

But when all artificial trammels are removed, and women are recognized as individuals, responsible for their own environments, thoroughly educated for all positions in life they may be called to fill; with all the resources in themselves that liberal thought and broad culture can give; guided by their own conscience and judgment; trained to self-protection by a healthy development of the muscular system and skill in the use of weapons of defense, and stimulated to self-support by a knowledge of the business world and the pleasure that pecuniary independence must ever give; when women are trained in this way they will, in a measure, be fitted for those years of solitude that come to all, whether prepared or otherwise. As in our extremity we must depend on ourselves, the dictates of wisdom point to complete individual development.

In talking of education how shallow the argument that each class must be educated for the special work it proposes to do, and all those faculties not needed in this special walk must lie dormant and utterly wither for want of use, when perhaps, these will be the very faculties needed in life's greatest emergencies. Some say, "Where is the use of drilling girls in the languages, the sciences, in law, medicine, theology?"

As wives, mothers, housekeepers, cooks, they need a different curriculum from boys who are to fill all positions. The chief cooks in our great hotels and ocean steamers are men. In large cities men run the bakeries; they make our bread, cake and pies. They manage the laundries; they are now considered our best milliners and dressmakers. Because some men fill these departments of usefulness, shall we regulate the curriculum in Harvard and Yale to their present necessities? If not, why this talk in our best colleges of a curriculum for girls who are crowding into the trades and professions; teachers in all our public schools rapidly filling many lucrative and honorable positions in life? They are showing, too, their calmness and courage in the most trying hours of human experience.

You have probably all read in the daily papers of the terrible storm in the Bay of Biscay when a tidal wave made such havoc on the shore, wrecking vessels, unroofing houses and carrying destruction everywhere. Among other buildings the woman's prison was demolished. Those who escaped saw men struggling to reach the shore. They promptly by clasping hands made a chain of themselves and pushed out into the sea, again and again, at the risk of their lives until they had brought six men to shore, carried them to a shelter, and did all in their power for their comfort and protection.

What special school of training could have prepared these women for this sublime moment of their lives? In times like this humanity rises above all college curriculum and recognizes Nature as the greatest of all teachers in the hour of danger and death. Women are already the equals of men in the whole of realm of thought, in art, science, literature, and government. With telescopic vision they explore the starry firmament, and bring back the history of the planetary world. With chart and compass they pilot ships across the mighty deep, and with skillful finger send electric messages around the globe. In galleries of art the beauties of nature and the virtues of humanity are immortalized by them on their canvas and by their inspired touch dull blocks of marble are transformed into angels of light.

In music they speak again the language of Mendelssohn, Beethoven, Chopin, Schumann, and are worthy interpreters of their great thoughts. The poetry and novels of the century are theirs, and they have touched the keynote of reform in religion, politics, and social life. They fill the editor's and professor's chair, and plead at the bar of justice, walk the wards of the hospital, and speak from the pulpit and the platform; such is the type of womanhood that an enlightened public sentiment welcomes today, and such the triumph of the facts of life over the false theories of the past.

Is it, then, consistent to hold the developed woman of this day within the narrow political limits as the dame with the spinning wheel and knitting needle occupied in the past? No! No! Machinery has taken the labors of woman as well as man on its tireless shoulders; the loom and the spinning wheel are but dreams of the past; the pen, the brush, the easel, the chisel, have taken their places, while the hopes and ambitions of women are essentially changed.

We see reason sufficient in the outer conditions of human beings for individual liberty and development, but when we consider the self-dependence of every human soul we see the need of courage, judgment, and the exercise of every faculty of mind and body, strengthened and developed by use, in woman as well as man.

Whatever may be said of man's protecting power in ordinary conditions, mid all the terrible disasters by land and sea, in the supreme moments of danger, alone, woman must ever meet the horrors of the situation; the Angel of Death even makes no royal pathway for her. Man's love and sympathy enter only into the sunshine of our lives. In that solemn solitude of self, that links us with the immeasurable and the eternal, each soul lives alone forever. A recent writer says:

I remember once, in crossing the Atlantic, to have gone upon the deck of the ship in midnight, when a dense black cloud enveloped the sky, and the great dep was roaring madly under the lashes of demoniac winds. My feelings was not of danger or fear (which is a base surrender of the immortal soul), but of utter desolation and loneliness; a little speck of life shut in by a tremendous darkness. Again I remember to have climbed on the slopes of the Swiss Alps, up beyond the point where vegetation ceases, and the stunted conifers no longer struggle against the unfeeling blasts. Around me lay a huge confusion of rocks, out of which the gigantic ice peaks shot into the measureless blue of the heavens, and again my only feeling was the awful solitude.

And yet, there is a solitude, which each and every one of us has always carried with him, more inaccessible than the ice-cold mountains, more profound than the midnight sea; the solitude of self. Our inner being, which we call ourself, no eye nor touch of man or angel has ever pierced. It is more hidden than the caves of the gnome; the sacred adytum of the oracle; the hidden chamber of eleusinian mystery, for to it only omniscience is permitted to enter.

Such is individual life. Who, I ask you, can take, dare take, on himself the rights, the duties, the responsibilities of another human soul?

# JOHN DEWEY

John Dewey (1859–1952), the foremost American philosopher of the first half of the twentieth century, delivered this talk on February 22, 1937, to the National Education Association, meeting in New Orleans.

# Democracy

[D]emocracy is much broader than a special political form, a method of conducting government, of making laws and carrying on governmental administration by means of popular suffrage and elected officers. It is that of course. But it is something broader and deeper than that.

The political and governmental phase of democracy is a means, the best means so far found, for realizing ends that lie in the wide domain of human relationships and the development of human personality. It is, as we often say, though perhaps without appreciating all that is involved in the saying, a way of life, social and individual. The key-note of democracy as a way of life may be expressed, it seems to me, as the necessity for the participation of every mature human being in formation of the values that regulate the living of men together—which is necessary from the standpoint of both the general social welfare and the full development of human beings as individuals.

Universal suffrage, recurring elections, responsibility of those who are in political power to the voters, and the other factors of democratic government are means that have been found expedient for realizing democracy as the truly human way of living. They are not a final end and a final value. They are to be judged on the basis of their contribution to an end. It is a form of idolatry to erect means into the end which they serve. Democratic political forms are simply the best means that human wit has devised up to a special time in history. But they rest back upon the idea that no man or limited set of men is wise enough or good enough to rule others without their consent; the positive meaning of this statement is that all those who are affected by social institutions must have a share in producing and managing them. The two facts that each one is influenced in what he does and enjoys and in what he becomes by the institutions under which he lives, and that therefore he shall have, in a democracy, a voice in shaping them, are the passive and active sides of the same fact.

The development of political democracy came about through substitution of the method of mutual consultation and voluntary agreement for the method of subordination of the many to the few enforced from above. Social arrangements which involve fixed subordination are maintained by coercion. The coercion need not be physical. There have existed, for short periods, benevolent despotisms. But coercion of some sort there has been; perhaps economic, certainly psychological and moral. The very fact of exclusion from participation is a subtle form of suppression. It gives individuals no opportunity to reflect and decide upon what is good for them. Others who are supposed to be wiser and who in any case have more power decide the question for them and also decide the methods and means by which subjects may arrive at the enjoyment of what is good for them. This form of coercion and suppression is more subtle and more effective than is overt intimidation and restraint. When it is habitual and embodied in social institutions, it seems the normal and natural state of affairs. The mass usually become unaware that they have a claim to a development of their own powers. Their experience is so restricted that they are not conscious of restriction. It is part of the democratic conception that they as individuals are not the only sufferers, but that the whole social body is deprived of the potential resources that should be at its service. The individuals of the submerged mass may not be very wise. But there is one thing they are wiser about than anybody else can be, and that is where the shoe pinches, the troubles they suffer from.

The foundation of democracy is faith in the capacities of human nature; faith in human intelligence, and in the power of pooled and cooperative experience. It is not belief that these things are complete but that if given a show they will grow and be able to generate progressively the knowledge and wisdom needed to guide collective action. Every autocratic and authoritarian scheme of social action rests on a belief that the needed intelligence is confined to a superior few who because of inherent natural gifts are endowed with the ability and the right to control the conduct of others; laying down principles and rules and directing the ways in which they are carried out. It would be foolish to deny that much can be said for this point of view. It is that which controlled human relations in social groups for much the greater part of human history. The democratic faith has emerged very, very recently in the history of mankind. Even where democracies now exist, men's minds and feelings are still permeated with ideas about leadership imposed from above, ideas that developed in the long early history of mankind. After democratic political institutions were nominally established, beliefs and ways of looking at life and of acting that originated when men and women were externally controlled and subjected to arbitrary power, persisted in the family, the church, business and the school, and experience shows that as long as they persist there, political democracy is not secure.

Belief in equality is an element of the democratic credo. It is not, however, belief in equality of natural endowments. Those who proclaimed the idea of equality did not suppose they were enunciating a psychological doctrine, but a legal and political one. All individuals are entitled to equality of treatment by law and in its administration. Each one is affected equally in quality if not in quantity by the institutions under which he lives and has an equal right to express his judgment, although the weight of his judgment may not be equal in amount when it enters into the pooled result to that of others. In short, each one is equally an individual and entitled to equal opportunity of development of his own capacities, be they large or small in range. Moreover, each has needs of his own, as significant to him as those of others are to them. The very fact of natural and psychological inequality is all the more reason for establishment by law of equality of opportunity, since otherwise the former becomes a means of oppression of the less gifted.

While what we call intelligence be distributed in unequal amounts, it is the democratic faith that it is sufficiently general so that each individual has something to contribute whose value can be assessed only as it enters into the final pooled intelligence constituted by the contributions of all. Every authoritarian scheme, on the contrary assumes that its value may be assessed by some *prior* principle, if not of family and birth or race and color or possession of material wealth, then by the position and rank a person occupies in the existing social scheme. The democratic faith in equality is the faith that each individual shall have the chance and opportunity to contribute whatever he is capable of contributing, and that the value of his contribution be decided by its place and function in the organized total of similar contributions—not on the basis of prior status of any kind whatever.

I have emphasized in what precedes the importance of the effective release of intelligence in connection with personal experience in the democratic way of living. I have done so purposely because democracy is so often and so naturally associated in our minds with freedom of *action,* forgetting the importance of freed intelligence which is necessary to direct and to warrant freedom of action. Unless freedom of individual action has intelligence and informed conviction back of it, its manifestation is almost sure to result in confusion and disorder. The democratic idea of freedom is not the right of each individual to *do* as he pleases, even if it be qualified by adding "provided he does not interfere with the same freedom on the part of others." While the idea is not always, not often enough, expressed in words, the basic freedom is that of freedom of *mind* and of whatever degree of freedom of action and experience is necessary to produce freedom of intelligence. The modes of freedom guaranteed in the Bill of Rights are all of this nature: Freedom of belief and conscience, of expression of opinion, of assembly for discussion and conference, of the press as an organ of communication. They are guaranteed because without them individuals are not free to develop and society is deprived of what they might contribute. . . .

There is some kind of government, of control, wherever affairs that concern a number of persons who act together are engaged in. It is a superficial view that holds government is located in Washington and Albany. There is government in the family, in business, in the church, in every social group. There are regulations, due to custom if not to enactment, that settle how individuals in a group act in connection with one another.

It is a disputed question of theory and practice just how far a democratic political government should go in control of the conditions of action within special groups. At the present time, for example, there are those who think the federal and state governments leave too much freedom of independent action to industrial and financial groups and there are others who think the Government is going altogether too far at the present time. I do not need to discuss this phase of the problem much less to try to settle it. But it must be pointed out that if the methods of regulation and administration in vogue in the conduct of secondary social groups are non-democratic, whether directly or indirectly or both, there is bound to be an unfavorable reaction back into the habits of feeling, thought

and action of citizenship in the broadest sense of that word. The way in which any organized social interest is controlled necessarily plays an important part in forming the dispositions and tastes, the attitudes, interests, purposes and desires, of those engaged in carrying on the activities of the group. For illustration, I do not need to do more than point to the moral, emotional, and intellectual effect upon both employers and laborers of the existing industrial system. Just what the effects specifically are is a matter about which we know very little. But I suppose that every one who reflects upon the subject admits that it is impossible that the ways in which activities are carried on for the greater part of the waking hours of the day; and the way in which the shares of individuals are involved in the management of affairs in such a matter as gaining a livelihood and attaining material and social security, can only be a highly important factor in shaping personal dispositions; in short, forming character and intelligence.

In the broad and final sense all institutions are educational in the sense that they operate to form the attitudes, dispositions, abilities, and disabilities that constitute a concrete personality. The principle applies with special force to the school. For it is the main business of the family and the school to influence directly the formation and growth of attitudes and dispositions, emotional, intellectual and moral. Whether this educative process is carried on in a predominantly democratic or non-democratic way becomes therefore a question of transcendent importance not only for education itself but for its final effect upon all the interests and activities of a society that is committed to the democratic way of life. . . .

[T]here are certain corollaries which clarify the meaning of the issue. Absence of participation tends to produce lack of interest and concern on the part of those shut out. The result is a corresponding lack of effective responsibility. Automatically and unconsciously, if not consciously, the feeling develops, "this is none of our affair; it is the business of those at the top; let that particular set of Georges do what needs to be done." The countries in which autocratic government prevails are just those in which there is least public spirit and the greatest indifference to matters of general as distinct from personal concern. . . . Where there is little power, there is correspondingly little sense of positive responsibility—It is enough to do what one is told to do sufficiently well to escape flagrant unfavorable notice. About larger matters a spirit of passivity is engendered. . . .

[I]t still is also true that incapacity to assume the responsibilities involved in having a voice in shaping policies is bred and increased by conditions in which that responsibility is denied. I suppose there has never been an autocrat, big or little, who did not justify his conduct on the ground of the unfitness of his subjects to take part in government. . . . But, as was said earlier, habitual exclusion has the effect of reducing a sense of responsibility for what is done and its consequences. What the argument for democracy implies is that the best way to produce initiative and constructive power is to exercise it. Power, as well as interest, comes by use and practice. . . .

The fundamental beliefs and practices of democracy are now challenged as they never have been before. In some nations they are more than challenged. They are ruthlessly and systematically destroyed. Everywhere there are waves of criticism and doubt as to whether democracy can meet pressing problems of order and security. The causes for the destruction of political democracy in countries where it was nominally established are complex. But of one thing I think we may be sure. Wherever it has fallen it was too exclusively political in nature. It had not become part of the bone and blood of the people in daily conduct of its life. Democratic forms were limited to Parliament, elections, and combats between parties. What is happening proves conclusively, I think, that unless democratic habits of thought and action are part of the fiber of a people, political democracy is insecure. It cannot stand in isolation. It must be buttressed by the presence of democratic methods in all social relationships. The relations that exist in educational institutions are second only in importance in this respect to those which exist in industry and business, perhaps not even to them. . . .

I can think of nothing so important in this country at present as a rethinking of the whole problem of democracy and its implications. Neither the rethinking nor the action it should produce can be brought into being in a day or year. The democratic idea itself demands that the thinking and activity proceed cooperatively.

# MARTIN LUTHER KING, JR.

Martin Luther King, Jr. (1929–1968), a Baptist minister and leader of the civil rights movement, wrote this letter in 1963, while serving a jail sentence for participating in a civil rights demonstration. King was awarded the Nobel Peace Prize in 1964. He was assassinated in 1968.

## Letter from a Birmingham City Jail

My dear Fellow Clergymen,

While confined here in the Birmingham city jail, I came across your recent statement calling our present activities "unwise and untimely." Seldom, if ever, do I pause to answer criticism of my work and ideas. If I sought to answer all of the criticisms that cross my desk, my secretaries would be engaged in little else in the course of the day, and I would have no time for constructive work. But since I feel that you are men of genuine good will and your criticisms are sincerely set forth, I would like to answer your statement in what I hope will be patient and reasonable terms.

I think I should give the reason for my being in Birmingham, since you have been influenced by the argument of "outsiders coming in." I have the honor of serving as president of the Southern Christian Leadership Conference, an organization operating in every southern state, with headquarters in Atlanta, Georgia. We have some eighty-five affiliate organizations all across the South—one being the Alabama Christian Movement for Human Rights. Whenever necessary and possible we share staff, educational and financial resources with our affiliates. Several months ago our local affiliate here in Birmingham invited us to be on call to engage in a nonviolent direct-action program if such were deemed necessary. We readily consented and when the hour came we lived up to our promises. So I am here, along with several members of my staff, because we were invited here. I am here because I have basic organizational ties here.

Beyond this, I am in Birmingham because injustice is here. Just as the eighth century prophets left their little villages and carried their "thus saith the Lord" far beyond the boundaries of their hometowns; and just as the Apostle Paul left his little village of Tarsus and carried the gospel of Jesus Christ to practically every hamlet and city of the Graeco-Roman world, I too am compelled to carry the gospel of freedom beyond my particular hometown. Like Paul, I must constantly respond to the Macedonian call for aid.

Moreover, I am cognizant of the interrelatedness of all communities and states. I cannot sit idly by in Atlanta and not be concerned about what happens in Birmingham. Injustice anywhere is a threat to justice anywhere. We are caught in an inescapable network of mutuality, tied in a single garment of destiny. Whatever affects one directly affects all indirectly. Never again can we afford to live with the narrow, provincial "outside agitator" idea. Anyone who lives in the United States can never be considered an outsider anywhere in this country.

You deplore the demonstrations that are presently taking place in Birmingham. But I am sorry that your statement did not express a similar concern for the conditions that brought the demonstrations into being. I am sure that each of you would want to go beyond the superficial social analyst who looks merely at effects, and does not grapple with underlying causes. I would not hesitate to say that it is unfortunate that so-called demonstrations are taking place in Birmingham at this time, but I would say in more emphatic terms that it is even more unfortunate that the white power structure of this city left the Negro community with no other alternative.

In any nonviolent campaign there are four basic steps: (1) collection of the facts to determine whether injustices are alive, (2) negotiation, (3) self-purification, and (4) direct action. We have gone through all of these steps in Birmingham. There can be no gainsaying of the fact that racial injustice engulfs this community.

Birmingham is probably the most thoroughly segregated city in the United States. Its ugly record of police brutality is known in every section of this country. Its unjust treatment of Negroes in the courts is a notorious reality. There have been more unsolved bombings of Negro homes and churches in Birmingham than any city in this nation. These are the hard, brutal and unbelievable facts. On the basis of these conditions Negro leaders sought to negotiate with the city fathers. But the political leaders consistently refused to engage in good faith negotiation.

Then came the opportunity last September to talk with some of the leaders of the economic community. In these negotiating sessions certain promises were made by the merchants—such as the promise to remove the humiliating racial signs from the stores. On the basis of these promises Rev. Shuttlesworth and the leaders of the Alabama Christian Movement for Human Rights agreed to call a moratorium on any type of demonstrations. As the weeks and months unfolded we realized that we were the victims of a broken promise. The signs remained. Like so many experiences of the past we were confronted with blasted hopes, and the dark shadow of a deep disappointment settled upon us. So we had no alternative except that of preparing for direct action, whereby we would present our very bodies as a means of laying our case before the conscience of the local and national community. We were not unmindful of the difficulties involved. So we decided to go through a process of self-purification. We started having workshops on nonviolence and repeatedly asked ourselves the questions, "Are you able to accept blows without retaliating?" "Are you able to endure the ordeals of jail?" We decided to set our direct-action program around the Easter season, realizing that with the exception of Christmas, this was the largest shopping period of the year. Knowing that a strong economic withdrawal program would be the by-product of direct action, we felt that this was the best time to bring pressure on the merchants for the needed changes. Then it occurred to us that the March election was ahead and so we speedily decided to postpone action until after election day. When we discovered that Mr. Connor was in the run-off, we decided again to postpone action so that the demonstrations could not be used to cloud the issues. At this time we agreed to begin our nonviolent witness the day after the run-off.

This reveals that we did not move irresponsibly into direct action. We too wanted to see Mr. Connor defeated; so we went through postponement after postponement to aid in this community need. After this we felt that direct action could be delayed no longer.

You may well ask, "Why direct action? Why sit-ins, marches, etc.? Isn't negotiation a better path?" You are exactly right in your call for negotiation. Indeed, this is the purpose of direct action. Nonviolent direct action seeks to create such a crisis and establish such creative tension that a community that has constantly refused to negotiate is forced to confront the issue. It seeks so to dramatize the issue that it can no longer be ignored. I just referred to the creation of tension as a part of the work of the nonviolent resister. This may sound rather shocking. But I must confess that I am not afraid of the word tension. I have earnestly worked and preached against violent tension, but there is a type of constructive nonviolent tension that is necessary for growth. Just as

Socrates felt that it was necessary to create a tension in the mind so that individuals could rise from the bondage of myths and half-truths to the unfettered realm of creative analysis and objective appraisal, we must see the need of having nonviolent gadflies to create the kind of tension in society that will help men to rise from the dark depths of prejudice and racism to the majestic heights of understanding and brotherhood. So the purpose of the direct action is to create a situation so crisis-packed that it will inevitably open the door to negotiation. We, therefore, concur with you in your call for negotiation. Too long has our beloved Southland been bogged down in the tragic attempt to live in monologue rather than dialogue.

One of the basic points in your statement is that our acts are untimely. Some have asked, "Why didn't you give the new administration time to act?" The only answer that I can give to this inquiry is that the new administration must be prodded about as much as the outgoing one before it acts. We will be sadly mistaken if we feel that the election of Mr. Boutwell will bring the millennium to Birmingham. While Mr. Boutwell is much more articulate and gentle than Mr. Connor, they are both segregationists, dedicated to the task of maintaining the status quo. The hope I see in Mr. Boutwell is that he will be reasonable enough to see the futility of massive resistance to desegregation. But he will not see this without pressure from the devotees of civil rights. My friends, I must say to you that we have not made a single gain in civil rights without determined legal and nonviolent pressure. History is the long and tragic story of the fact that privileged groups seldom give up their privileges voluntarily. Individuals may see the moral light and voluntarily give up their unjust posture; but as Reinhold Neibuhr has reminded us, groups are more immoral than individuals.

We know through painful experience that freedom is never voluntarily given by the oppressor; it must be demanded by the oppressed. Frankly, I have never yet engaged in a direct action movement that was "well-timed," according to the timetable of those who have not suffered unduly from the disease of segregation. For years now I have heard the words

"Wait!" It rings in the ear of every Negro with a piercing familiarity. This "Wait" has almost always meant "Never." It has been a tranquilizing thalidomide, relieving the emotional stress for a moment, only to give birth to an ill-formed infant of frustration. We must come to see with the distinguished jurist of yesterday that "justice too long delayed is justice denied." We have waited for more than 340 years for our constitutional and God-given rights. The nations of Asia and Africa are moving with jet-like speed toward the goal of political independence, and we still creep at horse and buggy pace toward the gaining of a cup of coffee at the lunch counter. I guess it is easy for those who have never felt the stinging darts of segregation to say, "Wait." But when you have seen vicious mobs lynch your mothers and fathers at will and drown your sisters and brothers at whim; when you have seen hatefilled policemen curse, kick, brutalize and even kill your black brothers and sisters with impunity; when you see the vast majority of your twenty million Negro brothers smothering in an airtight cage of poverty in the midst of an affluent society; when you suddenly find your tongue twisted and your speech stammering as you seek to explain to your six-year-old daughter why she can't go to the public amusement park that has just been advertised on television, and see tears welling up in her little eyes when she is told that Funtown is closed to colored children, and see the depressing clouds of inferiority begin to form in her little mental sky, and see her begin to distort her little personality by unconsciously developing a bitterness toward white people; when you have to concoct an answer for a five-year-old son asking in agonizing pathos: "Daddy, why do white people treat colored people so mean?"; when you take a cross-country drive and find it necessary to sleep night after night in the uncomfortable corners of your automobile because no motel will accept you; when you are humiliated day in and day out by nagging signs reading "white" and "colored"; when your first name becomes "nigger" and your middle name becomes "boy" (however old you are) and your last name becomes "John," and when your wife and mother are never given the respected title "Mrs.";

when you are harried by day and haunted by night by the fact that you are a Negro, living constantly at tip-toe stance never quite knowing what to expect next, and plagued with inner fears and outer resentments; when you are forever fighting a degenerating sense of "nobodiness"; then you will understand why we find it difficult to wait. There comes a time when the cup of endurance runs over, and men are no longer willing to be plunged into an abyss of injustice where they experience the blackness of corroding despair. I hope, sirs, you can understand our legitimate and unavoidable impatience.

You express a great deal of anxiety over our willingness to break laws. This is certainly a legitimate concern. Since we so diligently urge people to obey the Supreme Court's decision of 1954 outlawing segregation in the public schools, it is rather strange and paradoxical to find us consciously breaking laws. One may well ask, "How can you advocate breaking some laws and obeying others?" The answer is found in the fact that there are two types of laws: there are *just* and there are *unjust* laws. I would agree with Saint Augustine that "An unjust law is no law at all."

Now what is the difference between the two? How does one determine when a law is just or unjust? A just law is a man-made code that squares with the moral law or the law of God. An unjust law is a code that is out of harmony with the moral law. To put it in the terms of Saint Thomas Aquinas, an unjust law is a human law that is not rooted in eternal and natural law. Any law that uplifts human personality is just. Any law that degrades human personality is unjust. All segregation statutes are unjust because segregation distorts the soul and damages the personality. It gives the segregator a false sense of superiority, and the segregated a false sense of inferiority. To use the words of Martin Buber, the great Jewish philosopher, segregation substitutes an "I-it" relationship for the "I-thou"relationship, and ends up relegating persons to the status of things. So segregation is not only politically, economically and sociologically unsound, but it is morally wrong and sinful. Paul Tillich has said that sin is separation. Isn't segregation an existential expression of man's

tragic separation, an expression of his awful estrangement, his terrible sinfulness? So I can urge men to disobey segregation ordinances because they are morally wrong.

Let us turn to a more concrete example of just and unjust laws. An unjust law is a code that a majority inflicts on a minority that is not binding on itself. This is difference made legal. On the other hand a just law is a code that a majority compels a minority to follow that it is willing to follow itself. This is sameness made legal.

Let me give another explanation. An unjust law is a code inflicted upon a minority which that minority had no part in enacting or creating because they did not have the unhampered right to vote. Who can say that the legislature of Alabama which set up the segregation laws was democratically elected? Throughout the state of Alabama all types of conniving methods are used to prevent Negroes from becoming registered voters and there are some counties without a single Negro registered to vote despite the fact that the Negro constitutes a majority of the population. Can any law set up in such a state be considered democratically structured?

These are just a few examples of unjust and just laws. There are some instances when a law is just on its face and unjust in its application. For instance, I was arrested Friday on a charge of parading without permit. Now there is nothing wrong with an ordinance which requires a permit for a parade, but when the ordinance is used to preserve segregation and to deny citizens the First Amendment privilege of peaceful assembly and peaceful protest, then it becomes unjust.

I hope you can see the distinction I am trying to point out. In no sense do I advocate evading or defying the law as the rabid segregationist would do. This would lead to anarchy. One who breaks an unjust law must do it *openly, lovingly* (not hatefully as the white mothers did in New Orleans when they were seen on television screaming, "nigger, nigger, nigger"), and with a willingness to accept the penalty. I submit that an individual who breaks law that conscience tells him is unjust, and willingly accepts the penalty by staying in jail to arouse the conscience of the community over its injustice, is in reality expressing the very highest respect for law.

Of course, there is nothing new about this kind of civil disobedience. It was seen sublimely in the refusal of Shadrach, Meshach and Abednego to obey the laws of Nebuchadnezzar because a higher moral law was involved. It was practiced superbly by the early Christians who were willing to face hungry lions and the excruciating pain of chopping blocks, before submitting to certain unjust laws of the Roman Empire. To a degree academic freedom is a reality today because Socrates practiced civil disobedience.

We can never forget that everything Hitler did in Germany was "legal" and everything the Hungarian freedom fighters did in Hungary was "illegal." It was "illegal" to aid and comfort a Jew in Hitler's Germany. But I am sure that if I had lived in Germany during that time I would have aided and comforted my Jewish brothers even though it was illegal. If I lived in a Communist country today where certain principles dear to the Christian faith are suppressed, I believe I would openly advocate disobeying these anti-religious laws. I must make two honest confessions to you, my Christian and Jewish brothers. First, I must confess that over the last few years I have been gravely disappointed with the white moderate. I have almost reached the regrettable conclusion that the Negro's great stumbling block in the stride toward freedom is not the White Citizen's Counciler or the Ku Klux Klanner, but the white moderate who is more devoted to "order" than to justice; who prefers a negative peace which is the absence of tension to a positive peace which is the presence of justice; who constantly says, "I agree with you in the goal you seek, but I can't agree with your methods of direct action"; who paternalistically feels that he can set the timetable for another man's freedom; who lives by the myth of time and who constantly advised the Negro to wait until a "more convenient season." Shallow understanding from people of good will is more frustrating than absolute misunderstanding from people of ill will. Lukewarm acceptance is much more bewildering than outright rejection.

I had hoped that the white moderate would under-stand that law and order exist for the purpose of establishing justice, and that when they fail to do this they become dangerously structured dams that block the flow of social progress. I had hoped that the white moderate would understand that the present tension of the South is merely a necessary phase of the transition from an obnoxious negative peace, where the Negro passively accepted his unjust plight, to a substance-filled positive peace, where all men will respect the dignity and worth of human personality. Actually, we who engage in nonviolent direct action are not the creators of tension. We merely bring to the surface the hidden tension that is already alive. We bring it out in the open where it can be seen and dealt with. Like a boil that can never be cured as long as it is covered up but must be opened with all its pus-flowing ugliness to the natural medicines of air and light, injustice must likewise be exposed, with all of the tension its exposing creates, to the light of human conscience and the air of national opinion before it can be cured.

In your statement you asserted that our actions, even though peaceful, must be condemned because they precipitate violence. But can this assertion be logically made? Isn't this like condemning the robbed man because his possession of money precipitated the evil act of robbery? Isn't this like condemning Socrates because his unswerving commitment to truth and his philosophical delvings precipitated the misguided popular mind to make him drink the hemlock? Isn't this like condemning Jesus because His unique God-consciousness and never-ceasing devotion to his will precipitated the evil act of crucifixion? We must come to see, as federal courts have consistently affirmed, that it is immoral to urge an individual to withdraw his efforts to gain his basic constitutional rights because the quest precipitates violence. Society must protect the robbed and punish the robber.

I had also hoped that the white moderate would reject the myth of time. I received a letter this morning from a white brother in Texas which said: "All Christians know that the colored people will receive equal rights eventually, but it is possible that you are in too great of a religious hurry. It has taken Christianity almost two thousand years to accomplish what it has. The teachings of Christ take time to come to earth." All that is said here grows out of a tragic misconception of time. It is the strangely irrational notion that there is something in the very flow of time that will inevitably cure all ills. Actually time is neutral. It can be used either destructively or constructively. I am coming to feel that the people of ill will have used time much more effectively than the people of good will. We will have to repent in this generation not merely for the vitriolic words and actions of the bad people, but for the appalling silence of the good people. We must come to see that human progress never rolls in on wheels of inevitability. It comes through the tireless efforts and persistent work of men willing to be co-workers with God, and without this hard work time itself becomes an ally of the forces of social stagnation. We must use time creatively, and forever realize that the time is always ripe to do right. Now is the time to make real the promise of democracy, and transform our pending national elegy into a creative psalm of brotherhood. Now is the time to lift our national policy from the quicksand of racial injustice to the solid rock of human dignity.

You spoke of our activity in Birmingham as extreme. At first I was rather disappointed that fellow clergymen would see my nonviolent efforts as those of the extremist. I started thinking about the fact that I stand in the middle of two opposing forces in the Negro community. One is a force of complacency made up of Negroes who, as a result of long years of oppression, have been so completely drained of self-respect and a sense of "somebodiness" that they have adjusted to segregation, and, of a few Negroes in the middle class who, because of a degree of academic and economic security, and because at points they profit by segregation, have unconsciously become insensitive to the problems of the masses. The other force is one of bitterness and hatred, and comes perilously close to advocating violence. It is expressed in the various black nationalist groups that are springing up over the nation, the largest and best known being Elijah Muhammad's Muslim movement. This movement is nourished by the contemporary frustration over the continued existence of racial discrimination. It is made up of people who have lost faith in America, who have absolutely repudiated Christianity, and who have concluded that the white man is an incurable "devil." I have tried to stand between these two forces, saying that we need not follow the "donothingism" of the complacent or the hatred and despair of the black nationalist. There is the more excellent way of love and nonviolent protest. I'm grateful to God that, through the Negro church, the dimension of nonviolence entered our struggle. If this philosophy had not emerged, I am convinced that by now many streets of the South would be flowing with floods of blood. And I am further convinced that if our white brothers dismiss as "rabble-rousers" and "outside agitators" those of us who are working through the channels of nonviolent direct action and refuse to support our nonviolent efforts, millions of Negroes, out of frustration and despair, will seek solace and security in black nationalist ideologies, a development that will lead inevitably to a frightening racial nightmare.

Oppressed people cannot remain oppressed forever. The urge for freedom will eventually come. This is what happened to the American Negro. Something within has reminded him of his birthright of freedom; something without has reminded him that he can gain it. Consciously and unconsciously, he has been swept in by what the Germans call the *Zeitgeist,* and with his black brothers of Africa, and his brown and yellow brothers of Asia, South America and the Caribbean, he is moving with a sense of cosmic urgency toward the promised land of racial justice. Recognizing this vital urge that has engulfed the Negro community, one should readily understand public demonstrations. The Negro has many pent-up resentments and latent frustrations. He has to get them out. So let him march sometime; let him have his prayer pilgrimages to the city hall; understand why he must have sit-ins and freedom rides. If his repressed emotions do not come out in these nonviolent ways, they will come out in ominous expressions of violence. This is not a threat; it is a fact of history. So I have not said to my people "get rid of your discontent." But I have tried to say that this normal and healthy discontent can be channelized through the creative outlet of nonviolent direct action. Now this approach is being dismissed as extremist. I must admit that I was initially disappointed in being so categorized.

But as I continued to think about the matter I gradually gained a bit of satisfaction from being considered an extremist. Was not Jesus an extremist in love—"Love your enemies, bless them that curse you, pray for them that despitefully use you." Was not Amos an extremist for justice—"Let justice roll down like waters and righteousness like a mighty stream." Was not Paul an extremist for the gospel of Jesus Christ—"I bear in my body the marks of the Lord Jesus." Was not Martin Luther an extremist— "Here I stand; I can do none other so help me God." Was not John Bunyan an extremist—"I will stay in jail to the end of my days before I make a butchery of my conscience." Was not Abraham Lincoln an extremist—"This nation cannot survive half slave and half free." Was not Thomas Jefferson an extremist— "We hold these truths to be self-evident, that all men are created equal." So the question is not whether we will be extremist but what kind of extremist will we be. Will we be extremists for hate or will we be extremists for love? Will we be extremists for the preservation of injustice—or will we be extremists for the cause of justice? In that dramatic scene on Calvary's hill, three men were crucified. We must not forget that all three were crucified for the same crime—the crime of extremism. Two were extremists for immorality, and thusly fell below their environment. The other, Jesus Christ, was an extremist for love, truth and goodness, and thereby rose above his environment. So, after all, maybe the South, the nation and the world are in dire need of creative extremists.

I had hoped that the white moderate would see this. Maybe I was too optimistic. Maybe I expected too much. I guess I should have realized that few members of a race that has oppressed another race can understand or appreciate the deep groans and passionate yearnings of those that have been oppressed and still fewer have the vision to see that injustice must be rooted out by strong, persistent and determined action. I am thankful, however, that some of our white brothers have grasped the meaning of this social revolution and committed themselves to it. They are still all too small in quantity, but they are big in quality. Some like Ralph McGill, Lillian Smith, Harry Golden and James Dabbs have written about our struggle in eloquent, prophetic and understanding terms. Others have marched with us down nameless streets of the South. They have languished in filthy roach-infested jails, suffering the abuse and brutality of angry policemen who see them as "dirty nigger-lovers." They, unlike so many of their moderate brothers and sisters, have recognized the urgency of the moment and sensed the need for powerful "action" antidotes to combat the disease of segregation.

Let me rush on to mention my other disappointment. I have been so greatly disappointed with the white church and its leadership. Of course, there are some notable exceptions. I am not unmindful of the fact that each of you has taken some significant stands on this issue. I commend you, Rev. Stallings, for your Christian stance on this past Sunday, in welcoming Negroes to your worship service on a nonsegregated basis. I commend the Catholic leaders of this state for integrating Springhill College several years ago.

But despite these notable exceptions I must honestly reiterate that I have been disappointed with the church. I do not say that as one of the negative critics who can always find something wrong with the church. I say it as a minister of the gospel, who loves the church; who was nurtured in its bosom; who has been sustained by its spiritual blessings and who will remain true to it as long as the cord of life shall lengthen.

I had the strange feeling when I was suddenly catapulted into the leadership of the bus protest in Montgomery several years ago that we would have the support of the white church. I felt that the white ministers, priests and rabbis of the South would be some of our strongest allies. Instead, some have been outright opponents, refusing to understand the freedom movement and misrepresenting its leaders; all too many others have been more cautious than courageous and have remained silent behind the anesthetizing security of the stained-glass windows.

In spite of my shattered dreams of the past, I came to Birmingham with the hope that the white religious leadership of this community would see the justice of our cause, and with deep moral concern, serve as the channel through which our just grievances would get to the power structure. I had hoped that each of you would understand. But again I have been disappointed. I have heard numerous religious leaders of the South call upon their worshippers to comply with a desegregation decision because it is the *law,* but I have longed to hear white ministers say, "Follow this decree because integration is morally *right* and the Negro is your brother." In the midst of blatant injustices inflicted upon the Negro, I have watched white churches stand on the sideline and merely mouth pious irrelevancies and sanctimonious trivialities. In the midst of a mighty struggle to rid our nation of racial and economic injustice, I have heard so many ministers say, "Those are social issues with which the gospel has no real concern," and I have watched so many churches commit themselves to a completely otherworldly religion which made a strange distinction between body and soul, the sacred and the secular.

So here we are moving toward the exit of the twentieth century with a religious community largely adjusted to the status quo, standing as a taillight behind other community agencies rather than a headlight leading men to higher levels of justice.

I have traveled the length and breadth of Alabama, Mississippi and all the other southern states. On sweltering summer days and crisp autumn mornings I have looked at her beautiful churches with their lofty spires pointing heavenward. I have beheld the impressive outlay of her massive religious education buildings. Over and over again I have found myself asking: "What kind of people worship here? Who is their God? Where were their voices when the lips of Governor Barnett dripped with words of interposition and nullification? Where were they when Governor Wallace gave the clarion call for defiance and hatred? Where were their voices of support when tired, bruised and weary Negro men and women

decided to rise from the dark dungeons of complacency to the bright hills of creative protest?"

Yes, these questions are still in my mind. In deep disappointment, I have wept over the laxity of the church. But be assured that my tears have been tears of love. There can be no deep disappointment where there is not deep love. Yes, I love the church; I love her sacred walls. How could I do otherwise? I am in a rather unique position of being the son, the grandson and the great-grandson of preachers. Yes, I see the church as the body of Christ. But, oh! How we have blemished and scarred that body through social neglect and fear of being nonconformists.

There was a time when the church was very powerful. It was during that period when the early Christians rejoiced when they were deemed worthy to suffer for what they believed. In those days the church was not merely a thermometer that recorded the ideas and principles of popular opinion; it was a thermostat that transformed the mores of society. Wherever the early Christians entered a town the power structure got disturbed and immediately sought to convict them for being "disturbers of the peace" and "outside agitators." But they went on with the conviction that they were "a colony of heaven," and had to obey God rather than man. They were small in number but big in commitment. They were too God-intoxicated to be "astronomically intimidated." They brought an end to such ancient evils as infanticide and gladiatorial contest.

Things are different now. The contemporary church is often a weak, ineffectual voice with an uncertain sound. It is so often the arch-supporter of the status quo. Far from being disturbed by the presence of the church, the power structure of the average community is consoled by the church's silent and often vocal sanction of things as they are.

But the judgment of God is upon the church as never before. If the church of today does not recapture the sacrificial spirit of the early church, it will lose its authentic ring, forfeit the loyalty of millions, and be dismissed as an irrelevant social club with no meaning for the twentieth century. I am meeting young people every day whose disappointment with the church has risen to outright disgust.

Maybe again, I have been too optimistic. Is organized religion too inextricably bound to the status quo to save our nation and the world? Maybe I must turn my faith to the inner spiritual church, the church within the church, as the true *ecclesia* and the hope of the world. But again I am thankful to God that some noble souls from the ranks of organized religion have broken loose from the paralyzing chains of conformity and joined us as active partners in the struggle for freedom. They have left their secure congregations and walked the streets of Albany, Georgia, with us. They have gone through the highways of the South on tortuous rides for freedom. Yes, they have gone to jail with us. Some have been kicked out of their churches, and lost support of their bishops and fellow ministers. But they have gone with the faith that right defeated is stronger than evil triumphant. These men have been the leaven in the lump of the race. Their witness has been the spiritual salt that has preserved the true meaning of the gospel in these troubled times. They have carved a tunnel of hope through the dark mountain of disappointment.

I hope the church as a whole will meet the challenge of this decisive hour. But even if the church does not come to the aid of justice, I have no despair about the future. I have no fear about the outcome of our struggle in Birmingham, even if our motives are presently misunderstood. We will reach the goal of freedom in Birmingham and all over the nation, because the goal of America is freedom. Abused and scorned though we may be, our destiny is tied up with the destiny of America. Before the Pilgrims landed at Plymouth we were here. Before the pen of Jefferson etched across the pages of history the majestic words of the Declaration of Independence, we were here. For more than two centuries our foreparents labored in this country without wages; they made cotton king; and they built the homes of their masters in the midst of brutal injustice and shameful humiliation—and yet out of a bottomless vitality they continued to thrive and develop. If the inexpressible cruelities of slavery could not stop us, the opposition we now face will surely fail. We will win our freedom because the sacred heritage of our nation and the eternal will of God are embodied in our echoing demands.

I must close now. But before closing I am impelled to mention one other point in your statement that troubled me profoundly. You warmly commended the Birmingham police force for keeping "order" and "preventing violence." I don't believe you would have so warmly commended the police force if you had seen its angry violent dogs literally biting six unarmed, nonviolent Negroes. I don't believe you would so quickly commend the policemen if you would observe their ugly and inhuman treatment of Negroes here in the city jail; if you would watch them push and curse old Negro women and young Negro girls; if you would see them slap and kick old Negro men and young boys; if you will observe them, as they did on two occasions, refuse to give us food because we wanted to sing our grace together. I'm sorry that I can't join you in your praise for the police department.

It is true that they have been rather disciplined in their public handling of the demonstrators. In this sense they have been rather publicly "nonviolent." But for what purpose? To preserve the evil system of segregation. Over the last few years I have consistently preached that nonviolence demands that the means we use must be as pure as the ends we seek. So I have tried to make it clear that it is wrong to use immoral means to attain moral ends. But now I must affirm that it is just as wrong, or even more so, to use moral means to preserve immoral ends. Maybe Mr. Connor and his policemen have been rather publicly nonviolent, as Chief Pritchett was in Albany, Georgia, but they have used the moral means of nonviolence to maintain the immoral end of flagrant racial injustice. T. S. Eliot has said that there is no greater treason than to do the right deed for the wrong reason.

I wish you had commended the Negro sit-inners and demonstrators of Birmingham for their sublime courage, their willingness to suffer and their amazing discipline in the midst of the most inhuman provocation. One day the South will recognize its real heroes. They will be the James Merediths, courageously and with a majestic sense of purpose facing jeering and hostile mobs and the agonizing loneliness that characterizes the life of the pioneer. They will be old, oppressed, battered Negro women, symbolized in a seventy-two-year-old woman of Montgomery, Alabama, who rose up with a sense of dignity and with her people decided not to ride the segregated buses, and responded to one who inquired about her tiredness with ungrammatical profundity: "My feet is tired, but my soul is rested." They will be the young high school and college students, young ministers of the gospel and a host of their elders courageously and nonviolently sitting-in at lunch counters and willingly going to jail for conscience's sake. One day the South will know that when these disinherited children of God sat down at lunch counters they were in reality standing up for the best in the American dream and the most sacred values in our Judeo-Christian heritage, and thusly, carrying our whole nation back to those great walls of democracy which were dug deep by the Founding Fathers in the formulation of the Constitution and the Declaration of Independence.

Never before have I written a letter this long (or should I say a book?). I'm afraid that it is much too long to take your precious time. I can assure you that it would have been much shorter if I had been writing from a comfortable desk, but what else is there to do when you are alone for days in the dull monotony of a narrow jail cell other than write long letters, think strange thoughts, and pray long prayers?

If I have said anything in this letter that is an overstatement of the truth and is indicative of an unreasonable impatience, I beg you to forgive me. If I have said anything in this letter that is an understatement of the truth and is indicative of my having a patience that makes me patient with anything less than brotherhood, I beg God to forgive me.

I hope this letter finds you strong in the faith. I also hope that circumstances will soon make it possible for me to meet each of you, not as an integrationist or a civil rights leader, but as a fellow clergyman and a Christian brother. Let us all hope that the dark clouds of racial prejudice will soon pass away and the deep fog of misunderstanding will be lifted from our fear-drenched communities and in some not too distant tomorrow the radiant stars of love and brotherhood will shine over our great nation with all of their scintillating beauty.

Yours for the cause of Peace and Brotherhood,
Martin Luther King, Jr.

This speech was delivered before the Lincoln Memorial on August 28, 1963, as the keynote address of the March on Washington, D.C., for Civil Rights.

# The March on Washington Address

I am happy to join with you today in what will go down in history as the greatest demonstration for freedom in the history of our nation.

Fivescore years ago, a great American, in whose symbolic shadow we stand today, signed the Emancipation Proclamation. This momentous decree came as a great beacon light of hope to millions of Negro slaves who had been seared in the flames of withering injustice. It came as a joyous daybreak to end the long night of their captivity.

But one hundred years later, the Negro still is not free; one hundred years later, the life of the Negro is still sadly crippled by the manacles of segregation and the chains of discrimination; one hundred years later, the Negro lives on a lonely island of poverty in the midst of a vast ocean of material prosperity; one hundred years later, the Negro is still languished in the corners of American society and finds himself in exile in his own land.

So we've come here today to dramatize a shameful condition. In a sense we've come to our nation's capital to cash a check. When the architects of our republic wrote the magnificent words of the Constitution and the Declaration of Independence, they were signing a promissory note to which every American was to fall heir. This note was the promise that all men, yes, black men as well as white men, would be guaranteed the unalienable rights of life, liberty, and the pursuit of happiness.

It is obvious today that America has defaulted on this promissory note in so far as her citizens of color are concerned. Instead of honoring this sacred obligation, America has given the Negro people a bad check; a check which has come back marked "insufficient funds." We refuse to believe that there are insufficient funds in the great vaults of opportunity of this nation. And so we've come to cash this check, a check that will give us upon demand the riches of freedom and the security of justice.

We have also come to this hallowed spot to remind America of the fierce urgency of now. This is no time to engage in the luxury of cooling off or to take the tranquilizing drug of gradualism. Now is the time to make real the promises of democracy; now is the time to rise from the dark and desolate valley of segregation to the sunlit path of racial justice; now is the time to lift our nation from the quicksands of racial injustice to the solid rock of brotherhood; now is the time to make justice a reality for all God's children. It would be fatal for the nation to overlook the urgency of the moment. This sweltering summer of the Negro's legitimate discontent will not pass until there is an invigorating autumn of freedom and equality.

Nineteen sixty-three is not an end, but a beginning. And those who hope that the Negro needed to blow off steam and will now be content, will have a rude awakening if the nation returns to business as usual.

There will be neither rest nor tranquility in America until the Negro is granted his citizenship rights. The whirlwinds of revolt will continue to shake the foundations of our nation until the bright day of justice emerges.

But there is something that I must say to my people who stand on the warm threshold which leads into the palace of justice. In the process of gaining our rightful place we must not be guilty of wrongful deeds.

Let us not seek to satisfy our thirst for freedom by drinking from the cup of bitterness and hatred. We must forever conduct our struggle on the high plane of dignity and discipline. We must not allow our creative protest to degenerate into physical violence. Again and again we must rise to the majestic heights of meeting physical force with soul force.

The marvelous new militancy which has engulfed the Negro community must not lead us to a distrust of all white people, for many of our white brothers, as evidenced by their presence here today, have come to realize that their destiny is tied up with our destiny and they have come to realize that their freedom is inextricably bound to our freedom. This offense we share mounted to storm the battlements of injustice must be carried forth by a biracial army. We cannot walk alone.

And as we walk, we must make the pledge that we shall always march ahead. We cannot turn back. There are those who are asking the devotees of civil rights, "When will you be satisfied?" We can never be satisfied as long as the Negro is the victim of the unspeakable horrors of police brutality.

We can never be satisfied as long as our bodies, heavy with fatigue of travel, cannot gain lodging in the motels of the highways and the hotels of the cities. We cannot be satisfied as long as the Negro's basic mobility is from a smaller ghetto to a larger one.

We can never be satisfied as long as our children are stripped of their selfhood and robbed of their dignity by signs stating "for whites only." We cannot be satisfied as long as a Negro in Mississippi cannot vote and a Negro in New York believes he has nothing for which to vote. No, we are not satisfied, and we will not be satisfied until justice rolls down like waters and righteousness like a mighty stream.

I am not unmindful that some of you have come here out of excessive trials and tribulation. Some of you have come fresh from narrow jail cells. Some of you have come from areas where your quest for freedom left you battered by the storms of persecution and staggered by the winds of police brutality. You have been the veterans of creative suffering. Continue to work with the faith that unearned suffering is redemptive.

Go back to Mississippi; go back to Alabama; go back to South Carolina; go back to Georgia; go back to Louisiana; go back to the slums and ghettos of the northern cities, knowing that somehow this situation can, and will be changed. Let us not wallow in the valley of despair.

So I say to you, my friends, that even though we must face the difficulties of today and tomorrow, I still have a dream. It is a dream deeply rooted in the American dream that one day this nation will rise up and live out the true meaning of its creed—we hold these truths to be self-evident, *that all men are created equal.*

I have a dream that one day on the red hills of Georgia, sons of former slaves and sons of former slave-owners will be able to sit down together at the table of brotherhood.

I have a dream that one day, even the state of Mississippi, a state sweltering with the heat of injustice, sweltering with the heat of oppression, will be transformed into an oasis of freedom and justice.

I have a dream that my four little children will one day live in a nation where they will not be judged by the color of their skin but by the content of their character. I have a dream today!

I have a dream that one day, down in Alabama, with its vicious racists, with its governor having his lips dripping with the words of interposition and nullification, that one day, right there in Alabama, little black boys and black girls will be able to join hands with little white boys and white girls as sisters and brothers. I have a dream today!

I have a dream that one day every valley shall be exalted, every hill and mountain shall be made low, the rough places shall be made plain, and the crooked places shall be made straight and the glory of the Lord will be revealed and all flesh shall see it together.

This is our hope. This is the faith that I go back to the South with.

With this faith we will be able to hew out of the mountain of despair a stone of hope. With this faith we will be able to transform the jangling discords of our nation into a beautiful symphony of brotherhood.

With this faith we will be able to work together, to pray together, to struggle together, to go to jail together, to stand up for freedom together, knowing that we will be free one day. This will be the day when all of God's children will be able to sing with new meaning—"my country 'tis of thee: sweet land of liberty; of thee I sing; land where my fathers died, land of the pilgrim's pride; from every mountain side, let freedom ring"—and if America is to be a great nation, this must become true.

So let freedom ring from the prodigious hilltops of New Hampshire.

Let freedom ring from the mighty mountains of New York.

Let freedom ring from the heightening Alleghenies of Pennsylvania.

Let freedom ring from the snow-capped Rockies of Colorado.

Let freedom ring from the curvaceous slopes of California.

But not only that.

Let freedom ring from Stone Mountain of Georgia.

Let freedom ring from Lookout Mountain of Tennessee.

Let freedom ring from every hill and molehill of Mississippi, from every mountainside, let freedom ring.

And when we allow freedom to ring, when we let it ring from every village and hamlet, from every state and city, we will be able to speed up that day when all of God's children—black men and white men, Jews and Gentiles, Catholics and Protestants—will be able to join hands and to sing in the words of the old Negro spiritual, "Free at last, free at last; thank God Almighty, we are free at last."